BRIEF FIFTH EDITION

The Wadsworth Anthology of

drama

W. B. WORTHEN
University of California, Berkeley

THOMSON
———— ✦ ————
WADSWORTH

Australia • Brazil • Canada • Mexico • Singapore • Spain • United Kingdom • United States

THOMSON

™

WADSWORTH

The Wadsworth Anthology of Drama
Brief Fifth Edition
W. B. Worthen

Publisher: *Michael Rosenberg*
Acquisitions Editor: *Aron Keesbury*
Development Editor: *Mary Beth Walden*
Editorial Assistant: *Cheryl Forman*
Technology Project Manager: *Tim Smith*
Managing Marketing Manager: *Mandee Eckersley*
Marketing Assistant: *Dawn Giovanniello*
Associate Marketing Communications Manager: *Patrick Rooney*
Senior Project Manager, Editorial Production: *Samantha Ross*
Senior Art Director: *Bruce Bond*

Senior Print Buyer: *Mary Beth Hennebury*
Senior Permissions Editor: *Isabel Alves*
Permissions Editor: *Marcy Lunetta*
Production Service/Compositor: *Graphic World Inc.*
Photo Manager: *Sheri Blaney*
Photo Researcher: *Lili Weiner*
Cover Designer: *Lucille Tenazas*
Cover Printer: *Phoenix Color*
Printer: *Transcontinental Printing*
Cover Art: © *Randy Faris/Corbis*

Printed in Canada
3 4 5 6 7 09 08 07

Library of Congress Control Number: 2006920437

ISBN-13: 978-1-4130-2918-5
ISBN-10: 1-4130-2918-3

Thomson Higher Education
25 Thomson Place
Boston, MA 02210-1202
USA

For more information about our products, contact us at:
Thomson Learning Academic Resource Center
1-800-423-0563

For permission to use material from this text or product, submit a request online at **http://www.thomsonrights.com** Any additional questions about permissions can be submitted by e-mail to **thomsonrights@thomson.com**

Credits appear on pages 977–980 which constitute a continuation of the copyright page.

Contents

UNIT III

Medieval and Renaissance England 143

UNIT IV

Early Modern Europe 261

UNIT V

Modern Europe 389

UNIT VI

The United States 647

Preface

Studying drama is more than reading plays. It requires us to study the theaters where the plays were produced, the cultures that framed those theaters, and the critical and performance history that has framed the meanings of drama over time. *The Wadsworth Anthology of Drama, Brief Edition* presents drama in these two important contexts: in the play's original theater and the society that sustained it, and in **our** culture, where the play continues to live both as literature and as theatrical performance.

The Wadsworth Anthology of Drama, Brief Fifth Edition offers a comprehensive collection of classic and contemporary plays from Europe, the Americas, Africa, and Asia. Designed to be used in a variety of drama and theater courses, in general surveys of drama and theater, in courses on tragedy and/or comedy, or in classes on modern theater, *The Wadsworth Anthology of Drama, Brief Edition* offers an unusually comprehensive collection of classic theater and an unrivaled selection of contemporary drama drawn from around the world.

The fifth edition of *The Wadsworth Anthology of Drama, Brief Edition* builds on the strengths and success of previous editions. It is divided into seven units, each focused on a significant period in the history of drama and theater: Athens in the fifth century BCE; feudal Japan; England in the late Middle Ages and Renaissance; England, France, Spain, and colonial Mexico in the seventeenth and eighteenth centuries; Europe from 1850 through the twentieth century; the United States; and contemporary stages around the world. Each unit of the text begins with an extensive introduction, placing drama in the context of a specific historical era and using illustrations of theater design to develop a precise sense of stage practice. The Unit introductions include a section, "Reading the Material Theater," which presents original documents from the history of the theater for students' consideration. Each play is accompanied by a brief biography of the playwright and a short introduction to the play. Each unit concludes with a selection of "Critical Contexts" readings. *The Wadsworth Anthology of Drama, Brief Edition* emphasizes the diversity of drama and theater throughout history, both in its selection of plays and essays and in the issues and ideas raised for discussion as well.

The fifth edition of *The Wadsworth Anthology of Drama, Brief Edition* has been extensively revised and while it continues to be a comprehensive text, it has been updated to be the most topical and useful volume for con-temporary students of dramatic literature and of theater history. The brief text features plays by Sophocles, Euripides, Aristophanes, Shakespeare, Calderón, Molière, Ibsen, Chekhov, Shaw, Brecht, Beckett, Churchill, Glaspell, Wilson, Kushner, and Friel. In addition, the text offers several distinctive features:

- A revision of the last unit, "World Stages," focusing on postcolonial drama and theater.
- A streamlined collection of critical essays in each unit.
- A greater emphasis on the history of theatrical production and contemporary production practices.
- A large selection of plays by women.
- A large selection of comedies.
- An example of Britain's "New Brutalism," Sarah Kane's *Blasted*.
- A significant commitment to the unit on American drama, which continues to include Arthur Miller's *Death of a Salesman* and other cornerstones of the American stage.
- Inclusion of Luis Valdez's masterwork, *Zoot Suit*, to accompany plays from Latin America (Gambaro's *Information for Foreigners*), a Spanish Golden Age classic (Calderón's *Life Is a Dream*) and a brilliant play from colonial Mexico, Sor Juana's *loa* to *The Divine Narcissus*.
- A significant focus on "race" in American theater, including plays by Luis Valdez (*Zoot Suit*) and August Wilson (*Fences*).
- An expansion of the unit on modern European theater, to include a greater emphasis on women's playwriting throughout the period, including Caryl Churchill's *Cloud Nine* and Sarah Kane's *Blasted*.
- "Aside" sections in each unit—an opening essay devoted to topics of special importance: Roman drama and theater, Sanskrit drama and theater, the masque, the new Shakespeare's Globe Theatre in London, *commedia dell' arte*, melodrama, the Federal Theater Project, performance art, and intercultural performance.
- Two student essays in the online "Writing about Drama and Theater" section, focusing on different approaches to Caryl Churchill's *Cloud Nine*.

The *Wadsworth Anthology of Drama, Brief Edition*, offers essential critical selections by Aristotle, Zeami, Sir Philip Sidney, John Dryden, Nietzsche, Émile Zola, Bertolt Brecht, Antonin Artaud, Arthur Miller, and Frantz Fanon, adding an important essay from Augusto Boal's

Theatre of the Oppressed. The Wadsworth Anthology of Drama, Brief Edition continues its effort to enable students and teachers to explore the issues of representation in the theater and the ways that culture shapes identity, gender and sexuality, power, and race.

The Wadsworth Anthology of Drama, Brief Edition is designed for both beginning and advanced students. An introduction to writing about drama and theater furnishes beginning students with an outline of the formal and rhetorical practices used in writing about plays; this essay complements the documentary essays on "Reading the Material Theater" in each unit. The book also includes a useful glossary of dramatic, theatrical, and literary terms and an extensive bibliography of drama, of theater history, and of works about plays and playwrights is available online. *The Wadsworth Anthology of Drama, Brief Edition* provides a wide-ranging survey of drama and theater, one that presents both traditional issues and the materials to interrogate those traditions.

Acknowledgments

This edition of *The Wadsworth Anthology of Drama* has faced many unique challenges, and I am grateful to the editorial staff of Wadsworth for bringing this fifth edition to fruition. I'm especially grateful to Michael Rosenberg, Aron Keesbury, and Mary Beth Walden for their involvement in the project, and to Samantha Ross, Lili Weiner, Sheri Blaney, Marcy Lunetta, and Mike Ederer.

I would also like to thank the many instructors and scholars who commented on the fourth edition of the full text, The Wadsworth Anthology of Drama, suggesting ways we might improve this edition:

Gwendolyn Alker, *New York University*
Joe Allen, *Dutchess Community College*
Lisa Bernd, *Case Western Reserve University*
Cynthia Bowers, *Kennesaw State University*
Barry Brunetti, *DePaul University*
Paul Buczkowski, *Eastern Michigan University*
Lon Bumgarner, *University of North Carolina-Charlotte*
Steven Burch, *University of Alabama*
Sydney Chalfa, *Macon State College*
David Charles, *Rollins College*
Una Chaudhuri, *New York University*
Greg A. Chavez, *DePaul University*
Teresa Choate, *Kean University*
Gail Ciociola, *Villanova University*
Michael Cooper, *Texarkana College*
Linda Nell Cooper, *Liberty University*
Mark Gosdon, *Allegheny College*
Sergio Costola, *Southwestern University*
Thomas DeFrantz, *Massachusetts Institute of Technology*

Kathleen Dimmick, *Bennington College*
Bill Dynes, *University of Indianapolis*
Jay Edelnant, *University of Northern Iowa*
D. Layne Ehlers, *Bacone College*
Brenda Eppley, *Harrisburg Area Community College*
David S. Escoffery, *Southwest Missouri State University*
Anne Megan Evans, *Reed College*
Patsy Fowler, *Gonzaga University*
Jeffrey Frame, *Trevecca Nazarene University*
Dave Hartley, *Central Florida Community College*
Anne-Charlotte Harvey, *San Diego State University*
Ann Haugo, *Illinois State University*
Charles L. Hayes, *Radford University*
Graley Herren, *Xavier University*
Robin Huber, *Cerritos College*
Amy Hughes, *Baruch College*
Melissa Hurt, *Dodge City Community College*
David Jortner, *Allegheny College*
Hilary Justice, *Illinois State University*
Jonathan Kalb, *Hunter College, City University of New York*
Douglas Lanier, *University of New Hampshire*
Dawn Larsen, *Volunteer State College*
Ralph Leary, *Clarion University*
David E. Majewski, *Richard Bland College*
Joan McAfee, *Southern Connecticut State University*
Janet E. McLean, *Viterbo University*
Lee E. Neibert, *St. Gregory's University*
Wendy C. Nielsen, *Montclair State University*
Karen O'Brien, *University of California, Irvine*
Keith O'Neill, *Dutchess Community College*
Elinor L. Parker, *Westfield State College*
Jennifer Parker, *Florida State University*
Leslie Pasternack, *Northeastern University*
Katricia G. Pierson, *William Woods University*
Mark Pizzato, *University of North Carolina–Charlotte*
Marthe Reed, *University of Louisiana at Lafayette*
Joan E. Robbins, *Ohio Northern University*
R. Gary Rogers, *Lake-Sumter Community College*
Jeff Skillings, *Dean College*
James Symons, *University of Colorado, Boulder*
C. Patrick Tyndall, *University of Arkansas—Fayetteville*
Jef Vowell, *University of California, Irvine*
Chris Wixson, *Eastern Illinois University*
Boyd H. Wolz, *University of Louisiana at Monroe*
Leigh Woods, *University of Michigan*
Robert L. Yowell, *Northern Arizona University*

I would also like to thank the instructors and scholars who commented on the third edition, suggesting ways we might improve the fourth edition:

Sherri Dienstfrey (Idaho State University), Oliver Gerland (University of Colorado at Boulder), Sue Hagedorn (Virginia Tech), Michael Harrawood (Florida Atlantic University), Gregory Kable (University of North Carolina at Chapel Hill), Margaret Knapp (Arizona State University), Kim Marra (University of Iowa), Jenna Moskowitz (New York University), Scott Phillips (Auburn University), Gary Rogers (Lake Sumter Community College), Susan Speers (University of Akron), Wanda Strukus (Boston College), Stephanie Etheridge Woodson (Arizona State University).

I would also like to thank those who responded to our survey on the second edition, suggesting ways we might improve the third edition:

David Adamson (University of North Carolina at Chapel Hill), Gilbert L. Bloom (Ball State University), Brian Boney (University of Texas), Cynthia Bowers (Loyola University), Karen Buckley (University of Wisconsin, Whitewater), Susan Carlson (Iowa State University), Allen Chesler (Northern Illinois University), Barbara Clayton (University of Wisconsin, Madison), Kathleen Colligan Cleary (Clark State Community College), Jill Dolan (City University of New York), David S. Escoffery (University of Pittsburgh), Anthony Graham-White (University of Illinois at Chicago), John E. Hallwas (Western Illinois University), L.W. Harrison (Santa Rosa Junior College), Anne-Charlotte Harvey (San Diego State University), Gregory Kable (University of North Carolina, Chapel Hill), Lawrence Kinsman (New Hampshire College), Ann Klautsch (Boise State University), Margaret Knapp (Arizona State University), Josephine Lee (University of Minnesota), Michael J. Longrie (University of Wisconsin, Whitewater), Kim Marra (University of Iowa), Carla McDonough (Eastern Illinois University), John F. O'Malley (DePaul University), Michael Peterson (Millikin University), Carol Rocamora (NYU Tisch School of the Arts), Hans Rudnick (Southern Illinois University). Terry Donovan Smith (University of Washington). Tramble Turner (Penn State University). Jon W. Tuttle (Francis Marion University). Timothy Wiles (Indiana University), Barry Yzereef (University of Calgary).

I would also like to thank those who responded to the survey for the third edition:

George Adams (University of Wisconsin, Whitewater), Ruth Anderson (San Diego State University), Cynthia Bowers (Loyola University), Ruth Contrell (New Mexico State University), Kenneth Cox (Oklahoma State University), Mary Emery (University of Wisconsin, Whitewater), Tom Empy (Casper College), Lawrence Fink (Ohio State University), James Fisher (Wabash College), Kay Forston (Phillips University), Melissa Gibson (University of Pittsburgh), Marsha Morrison (Genesee Community College), Chris Mullen (University of North Carolina, Chapel Hill), Lurana O'Malley (University of

Hawai'i), Gwendolyn Orel (University of Pittsburgh), Eva Patton (Fordham University), Richard Schauer (University of Wisconsin, Whitewater), John Terhes (Chemeketa Community College), Charles Trainer (Siena College), Tramble Turner (Penn State University).

I am also indebted to Stanton Garner, Jr (University of Tennessee), Josephine Lee (University of Minnesota), Sarah Bryant-Bertail (University of Washington), Jorge Huerta (University of California, San Diego), Kristin Pauka (Univerrsity of Hawai'i), and Barbara Sellars-Young (University of California, Davis) for their help and advice on the third edition. My special thanks to Lurana Donnels O'Malley, of the University of Hawai'i, for her assistance with Units II and VII; to James Brandon, again of the University of Hawai'i, for graciously providing photographs and other materials related to the University's productions of *Matsukaze* and *Chuushingura;* and to Octavio Rivera, of la Universidad de las Américas, for his help in providing photographs of his excellent production of Sor Juana's *loa* to *The Divine Narcissus.*

I would also like to thank reviewers for the second edition: George R. Adams (University of Wisconsin, Whitewater), Bonnie M. Anderson (San Diego State University), Karen Buckley (University of Wisconsin, Whitewater), Kathleen Colligan Cleary (Clark State Community College), Mary Ann Emery (University of Wisconsin, Whitewater), Lawrence E. Fink (Ohio State University), Melissa Gibson (University of Pittsburgh), Kiki Gounaridou (University of Pittsburgh), Anne-Charlotte Harvey (San Diego State University), Dennis Kennedy (Trinity College, Dublin), Chris Mullen (University of North Carolina, Chapel Hill), Lurana O'Malley (University of Hawai'i), Gwen Orel (University of Pittsburgh), Angela Peckenpaugh (University of Wisconsin, Whitewater), Ruth Schauer (University of Wisconsin, Whitewater). In addition, I am grateful to the following reviewers of the manuscript of the second edition for their valuable revision suggestions: Anne Brannen (Duquesne University), Bradley Boney (University of Texas, Austin), Susan Carlson (Iowa State University), S. Alan Chesler (Northern Illinois University), Jill Dolan (City University of New York), Anthony J. Fichera (University of North Carolina at Chapel Hill), L. W. Harrison (Santa Rosa Junior College), Margaret Knapp (Arizona State University), Josephine Lee (University of Minnesota), Michael Longrie (University of Wisconsin, Whitewater), Michael Peterson (University of Wisconsin, Madison), Eula Thompson (Jefferson State Community College), Jon Tuttle (Francis Marion University).

My thanks to the people who read and commented on the manuscript of the first edition, making it more accurate and useful for instructors: Stanton B. Garner Jr. (University of Tennessee), Josephine Lee (University of

Minnesota), Don Moore (Louisiana State University), Cyndia Susan Clegg (Pepperdine University).

I remain grateful to Sharon Mazer, of the University of Canterbury (New Zealand) for her superb work on the Instructor's Manual to previous editions. I would also like to thank Kathleen M. Gough for her superb work on the new edition of the Instructor's Manual. And my sincere thanks to Stephen T. Jordan for originally proposing this project, to Oscar G. Brockett of the University of Texas at Austin for allowing me to think out loud about what a book like this one might accomplish.

I am grateful to my wife, Hana Worthen, for everything she has done for me, and for her great help with this edition.

Finally, I would like to encourage anyone using this book to feel free to drop me a line with ideas and suggestions for later editions. To the many students and colleagues who have called, sent me a note to correct my oversights and omissions, or have graciously spoken to me about the book at professional meetings and conferences, my sincere thanks for your attention and kindness. The flaws and faults that remain are, of course, entirely my own doing.

—W. B. W.

Introduction: Drama, Theater, and Culture

Of the many kinds of literature, drama is perhaps the most immediately involved in the life of its community. Drama shares with such other literary modes as lyric poetry, the novel, the epic, and romance the ability to represent and challenge social, political, philosophical, and esthetic attitudes. But unlike most literature, drama has generally been composed for performance, confronting the audience in the public, sociable confines of a theater.

To understand **DRAMA,** we need to understand **THEATER,** because the theater forges the active interplay between drama and its community.[1] On a practical level, for instance, the community must determine where drama will take place, and it is in the theater that a space is carved out for dramatic performance. Not surprisingly, the place of the theater in a city's social and physical geography often symbolizes drama's place in the culture at large. In classical Athens, the theater adjoined a sacred precinct, and plays were part of an extensive religious and civic festival. Greek drama accordingly engages questions of moral, political, and religious authority. In seventeenth-century Paris, the close affiliation between the theater and the court of Louis XIV is embodied in drama's concern with power, authority, and the regulation of rebellious passions. In the United States today, most live theater takes place either in the privileged setting of colleges and universities or in the "theater districts" of major cities, competing for an audience alongside movie theaters, nightclubs, and other entertainments. Drama also seems to be struggling to define itself as part of an established cultural tradition reaching back to Aeschylus and as part of the lively diversity of contemporary popular culture. Social attitudes are reflected in the theater in other ways, too; during performance, the theater constructs its own "society" of performers and spectators. Staging a play puts it immediately into a dynamic social exchange: the interaction between dramatic characters, between characters and the actors who play them, between the performers and the audience, between the drama onstage and the drama of life outside the theater.

READING DRAMA AND SEEING THEATER

The Greek word for theater, *THEATRON,* means "seeing place," and plays performed in the theater engage their audiences largely through visual means. Less than a century ago, live plays could be seen only on the stage; today, most of us see drama in a variety of media: on film and television as well as in the theater. Yet for the past 500 years or so we have also had access to plays in another, nontheatrical venue: by reading them in books. To see a play performed and to read it in a book are two very different activities, but these distinct experiences of drama can be made to enrich one another in a number of ways.

In the theater, a dramatic text is fashioned into an event, something existing in space and time. The space of the stage, with whatever setting is devised, becomes the place of the drama. The characters are embodied by specific individuals. How a given actor interprets a role tends to shape the audience's sense of that dramatic character; for the duration of the play, it is difficult to imagine another kind of performance—a different Oedipus, Lear, or Nora Helmer than the one standing before us in the flesh. The drama onstage is also bound by the temporal exigencies of performance. The process of performance is irreversible; for the duration of the performance, each moment becomes significant and yet unrecoverable—we can't flip back a few pages to an earlier scene, or rewind the videotape. When a company puts a play into stage production, it inevitably confronts these material facts of the theater: a specific cast of actors, a given theatrical space, a certain amount of money to spend, and the necessity of transforming the rich possibilities offered by the play into a clear and meaningful performance. To make the drama active and concrete, theatrical production puts a specific interpretation of the play on the stage. Whether or

---

[1] Terms in boldface small capital letters are defined in the Glossary; italicized terms are non-English terms.

not to play Caliban in Shakespeare's *The Tempest* as a native of the West Indies; whether to play Torvald Helmer in Ibsen's *A Doll House* as a patriarchal autocrat or as someone bewildered by a changing world; whether to set *Tartuffe* in a classical, neoclassical, or a modern setting; whether to use cross-gender or intercultural casting in *The Homecoming*—these are some of the kinds of questions that a production must face, and how the production decides such issues inevitably leads the audience toward a particular sense of the play. Everything that happens onstage becomes meaningful for an audience, something to interpret. Even apparently irrelevant facts—a short actor cast to play Hamlet in Shakespeare's play, or a beautiful actress playing Brecht's Mother Courage—become part of the audience's experience of the play, particularizing the play, lending it a definite flavor and meaning.

Reading a play presents us with a different experience of the drama. Reading plays is, first of all, a relatively recent phenomenon. In early theaters, such as those of classical Athens and Rome, medieval Europe, and even Renaissance Europe of the sixteenth century, drama was almost entirely a theatrical mode, rather than a mode of literature. Although the texts of plays were written down, by and large, audiences came into contact with drama primarily through theatrical performance. By the late sixteenth century, though, the status of drama began to change. The recovery and prestige of Greek and Latin literature led to pervasive familiarity with classical texts, including plays. Throughout Europe, schooling was conducted mainly in Latin, and the plays of Roman playwrights such as Plautus, Terence, and Seneca were frequently used to teach Latin grammar and rhetoric. These plays were widely imitated by playwrights writing drama in vernacular languages for emerging secular, commercial theaters. Printing made it possible to disseminate texts more widely, and plays slowly came to be regarded as worthy of publication and preservation in book form. By the late nineteenth century, widespread literacy created a large reading public and a great demand for books; continued improvements in printing technology provided the means to meet the demand. Playwrights often published their plays as books before they could be produced onstage, with some profound effects. The detailed narrative stage directions in plays by Bernard Shaw, Eugene O'Neill, or Henrik Ibsen, for instance, are useful to a stage director and set designer, but they principally fill in a kind of novelistic background for the reading audience who will experience the play only on the page.

Theater audiences are bound to the temporality and specificity of the stage, but readers have the freedom to compose the play in much more varied ways. A reader can pause over a line, teasing out possible meanings, in effect stopping the progress of the play. Readers are not bound by the linear progress of the play's action, in that they can flip back and forth in the play, looking for clues, confirmations, or connections. Nor are readers bound by the stringent physical economy of the stage, the need to embody the characters with individual actors, to specify the dramatic locale as a three-dimensional space. While actors and directors must decide on a specific interpretation of each moment and every character in the play, readers can keep several competing interpretations alive in the imagination at the same time.

Both ways of thinking about drama are demanding, and students of drama should try to develop a sensitivity to both approaches. Treating the play like a novel or poem, decomposing and recomposing it critically, leads to a much fuller sense of the play's potential meanings, its gaps and inconsistencies; it allows us to question the text without the need to come to definite conclusions. Treating the play as a design for the stage forces us to make commitments, to articulate and defend a particular version of the play, and to find ways of making those meanings active onstage, visible in performance. As readers, one way to develop a sense of the reciprocity between stage and page is to think of the play as constructed mainly of actions, not of words. Think of seeing a play in an unknown language: the *action* of the play would still emerge in its larger outlines, carried by the deeds of the characters. Not knowing the words would not prevent the audience from understanding what a character is doing onstage—threatening, lying, persuading, boasting.

When reading a play, it is easy to be seduced by the text, to think of the play's language as mainly narrative, describing the attitudes of the character. For performers onstage, however, speech—language in action—is always a way of doing something. One way for readers to attune themselves to this active quality of dramatic writing is to ask questions of the text from the point of view of performers or characters. What do I—Lysistrata, Everyman, Miranda—want in this speech? How can I use this speech to help me get it? What am I trying to do by speaking in this way? Although questions like these are still removed from the actual practice of performance, they can help readers unfamiliar with drama begin to read plays in theatrical terms.

Another way to enrich the reading experience of drama is to imagine staging the play: how could the design of the set, the movements of the actors, the pacing of the scenes affect the play's meaning, make the play mean something in particular? Questions of this kind can help to make the play seem more concrete, but they have one important limitation. When asking questions like these, it is tempting to imagine the play being performed in today's theaters, according to our conventions of acting and stagecraft, and within the social and cultural context that frames the theater now. To imagine the play on our stage is, of course, to produce it in our contemporary idiom, informed by our notions both of theater and of the world our theater represents. However, while envisioning performance, we should also imagine the play in the circumstances of its original theater, a theater located in a different culture and possibly sharing few practices of stagecraft with the modern theater. How would Hamlet's advice to the players have appeared on the Globe theater's empty platform stage in 1601? Are there ways in which the text capitalizes on this likeness between Shakespeare's company of actors and those Hamlet addresses fictively in the play? In a theater where a complete, "realistic" illusion was not possible (and, possibly, not even desirable), how does Shakespeare's play turn the conditions of theatrical performance to dramatic advantage? Both reading drama and staging drama involve a complex double-consciousness, inviting us to see the plays with contemporary questions in mind, while at the same time imagining them on their original stages. In this doubleness lies an important dramatic principle: plays can speak to us in our theater but perhaps always retain something of their original accents.

DRAMA AND THEATER IN HISTORY

Throughout its development, dramatic art has changed as the theater's place in the surrounding society has changed. The categories that we apply to drama and theater today—art versus entertainment, popular versus classic, literary versus theatrical—are of relatively recent vintage. They imply ways of thinking about drama and theater that are foreign to the function of theater in many other cultures. Much as drama and theater today emerge in relation to other media of dramatic performance like film and television, so in earlier eras the theater defined itself in relation to other artistic, social, and religious institutions. Placed in a different sphere of culture, drama and theater gained a different kind of significance than they have in the United States today.

Drama and theater often arise in relation to religious observance. In ancient Egypt, for instance, religious rituals involved the imitation of events in a god's or goddess's life. In Greece, drama may have had similar origins; by the sixth century BCE, the performance of plays had become part of a massive religious festival celebrating the god Dionysus. The plays performed in this theater—including those of Aeschylus, Sophocles, Euripides, and Aristophanes gathered here—were highly wrought and intellectually, morally, and esthetically complex and demanding works. Aristotle classes drama among other forms of poetry, but in classical Athens these plays occupied a very different position in the spectrum of culture than do drama or "art" today, precisely because of their central role in the City Dionysia. The Roman theater set drama in the context of a much greater variety of performance—chariot racing, juggling, gladiatorial shows—and while plays were performed on religious holidays, drama was more clearly related to secular entertainments than it had been in Athens. Theater waned in Europe with the decline of the Roman Empire and the systematic efforts of the Catholic church to prevent theatrical performance. Yet when theater was revived in the late Middle Ages, it emerged with the support of the church itself. By the year 1000, brief dramatizations illustrated the liturgy of the Catholic Mass; by the fourteenth century, a full range of dramatic forms—plays dramatizing the lives of saints, morality plays, narrative plays on Christian history—was used to illustrate Christian doctrine and to celebrate important days in the Christian year. Like plays in classical Athens, these plays were produced through community effort rather than by specialized "theaters" in the modern sense. Although we now regard medieval drama as extraordinarily rich and complex "literature," in its own era it was part of a different strand of culture, sharing space with other forms of pageantry and religious celebration, rather than being read with the poetry of Chaucer or Dante.

Similarly, in feudal Japan, the Buddhists developed a form of theater to illustrate the central concepts of their faith. Throughout the twelfth and thirteenth centuries, an increasing number of professional players came to imitate these dramatic performances on secular occasions, and for secular audiences. By the fourteenth century, it became conventional for the great samurai lords, or *SHOGUNS,* to patronize a theatrical company, giving rise to the classical era of the Noh theater. The social history of theater in Japan was complicated by other factors as well. The aristocratic **NOH** theater was rivaled by the popular, often quite contemporary, **KABUKI** theater. Government restrictions on the professions (which tended to make acting a family business, passed on through generations), and Japan's militant isolationism (coming to an end only in the mid-nineteenth century), have contributed to making Japan's classical theater survive in many ways unchanged. Moreover, in many parts of Asia, including China and India, theater was understood as a mixed medium, more centrally emphasizing song and dance as a way of developing the narrative, and many forms of performance—the wide variety of Indian folk theater forms, and of Chinese traditional forms, including **BEIJING OPERA**—developed extremely disciplined and highly stylized performance conventions. These traditional theaters, sometimes tied to aristocratic privilege, sometimes to religious ritual, sometimes to civic celebration, were sharply challenged by the influence of Western dramatic and theatrical practices—spoken drama, dramatic realism, and the notion of a secular, profit-making entertainment-theater—beginning in the eighteenth and nineteenth centuries. The rise of *SHINGEKI* or modern theater in the early twentieth century in Japan, of "spoken drama" at the same time in China, and of Western theatrical methods in India are closely tied to the characteristic forms of globalization of that period, economic imperialism and political colonialism; anticolonial, nationalist, and independence movements throughout Asia have tended both to revive classical forms of traditional theater, and to force a rapprochement with the imported forms of Western theater.

Secular performance did, of course, also take place in classical and medieval Europe, including improvised farces on contemporary life, fairground shows, puppetry, mimes, and other quasi-dramatic events. Many plays were performed only on religious occasions, though, and their performers were usually itinerant, lacking the social and institutional support that would provide them with lasting and continuous existence. Only in the Renaissance of the fifteenth and sixteenth centuries did the Western theater begin to assume the function it has today: a fully secular, profit-making, commercial enterprise. Although Renaissance theaters continually vied with religious and state officials for the freedom to practice their trade, by the sixteenth century, the European theater was part of a secular entertainment market, competing with bear-baiting, animal shows, athletic contests, public executions, royal and civic pageants, public preaching, and many other attractions to draw a paying public. The theater emerged in this period as a distinct institution, supported by its own income; the theater became a trade, a profession, a business, rather than a necessary function of the state or of religious worship. Indeed, if drama in classical Athens was conceived more as religious ritual than as "art" in a modern sense, drama in Renaissance London was classed mainly as popular "entertainment." The theater only gradually became recognized as an arena for "literary" accomplishment, for literary status in this period was reserved mainly for skill demonstrated in forms like the sonnet, the prose romance, or the epic—forms that could win the authors a measure of aristocratic prestige and patronage. As part of the motley, vulgar world of the public theater, plays were not considered serious, permanent literature.

However, the desire to transform drama from ephemeral theatrical "entertainment" into permanent literary "art" begins to be registered in the Renaissance. The poet and playwright Ben Jonson included plays in the 1616 edition of his *Works,* insisting on the literary importance of the volume by publishing it in the large, **FOLIO** format generally reserved for classical authors. In 1623, seven years after his death, William Shakespeare's friends and colleagues published a similar, folio-sized collection of his plays, a book that was reprinted several times throughout the seventeenth century. By the 1660s and 1670s, writers at the court of Louis XIV in Paris could achieve both literary and social distinction as dramatists; Jean Racine's reputation as a playwright, in part at least, helped to win his appointment as Louis's royal historiographer. Yet, despite many notable exceptions, the theatrical origins of drama prevented contemporary plays from being regarded as "literature"—although plays from earlier eras were increasingly republished and gradually seen to have "literary" merit. Indeed, by the nineteenth century, contemporary plays often achieved "literary" recognition by avoiding the theater altogether. English poets like Lord Byron and Percy Bysshe Shelley, for instance, wrote plays that were in many ways unstageable, and so preserved them from degrading contact with the tawdry stage. The English critic Charles Lamb remarked in a famous essay that he preferred reading Shakespeare's plays to seeing them in the theater; for Lamb, the practical mechanics of acting and the stage intruded on the experience of the drama's poetic dimension. In fact, the great playwrights of the late nineteenth century— Henrik Ibsen, Anton Chekhov, August Strindberg, and even the young Bernard Shaw—carved a space for themselves as dramatists by writing plays *in opposition* to the values of their contemporary audiences and to the practice of their contemporary theater—a strategy that would have seemed unimaginable to Aeschylus, Shakespeare, or even Molière. To bring their plays successfully to the stage, new theaters and new theater practices had to be devised, and a new audience had to be found, or made.

This split between the "literary drama" and the "popular theater" has become the condition of twentieth-century drama and theater: plays of the artistic **AVANT-GARDE** are more readily absorbed into the **CANON** of literature, while more conventional entertainments—television screenplays, for instance—remain outside it. The major modern playwrights from Ibsen to Luigi Pirandello to Samuel Beckett first wrote for small theaters and were produced by experimental companies playing to coterie audiences on the fringes of the theatrical "mainstream." This sense of modernist "art" as opposed to the values of bourgeois culture was not confined to drama and theater. Modernist fiction and poetry, cubist and abstract painting and sculpture, modern dance, and modern music all developed a new formal complexity, thematic abstraction, and critical self-consciousness in opposition to the sentimental superficiality they found in conventional art forms. This modernist tendency has itself produced a kind of reaction, a desire to bring the devices of popular culture and mass culture into drama, as a way of altering the place of the theater in society and changing the relationship between the spectators and the stage. Bertolt Brecht's **ALIENATION EFFECT,** Samuel Beckett's importation of circus and film clowns to absurdist theater, Heiner Müller's **PASTICHE** of *Hamlet* in his **POSTMODERN** *Hamletmachine,* or Wole Soyinka's interweaving of African ritual and fourth-wall realism in *Death and the King's Horseman* are all examples of this reaction. For the theater has been challenged by film and television to define its space in contemporary culture, and, given the pervasive availability of other media, theater has increasingly seemed to occupy a place akin to that of opera, among the privileged, elite forms of "high culture." As a result, innovation in today's theater often takes place on the margins or fringes of mainstream theater and mainstream culture: in smaller companies experimenting with new performance forms, in subversive theaters confronting political oppression in many parts of the world, and in theaters working to form a new audience and a new sense of theater by conceiving new forms of drama.

DRAMATIC GENRES

Perhaps because its meaning must emerge rapidly and clearly in performance, drama tends to be compressed and condensed; its characters tend toward types, and its action tends toward certain general patterns as well. It is conventional to speak of these kinds of drama as **GENRES,** each with its own identifying formal structure and typical themes. In the Western theater, following Aristotle's *The Poetics,* **TRAGEDY** is usually considered to concern the fate of an individual hero, singled out from the community through circumstances and through his or her own actions. In the course of the drama, the hero's course of action entwines with events and circumstances beyond his or her control. As a result, the hero's final downfall—usually, but not always, involving death—seems at once both chosen and inevitable. **COMEDY** on the other hand, focuses on the fortunes of the community itself. While the hero of tragedy is usually unique, the heroes of comedy often come in pairs—the lovers who triumph over their parents in romantic comedies, the dupe and the trickster at the center of more ironic or satirical comic modes. While tragedy points toward the hero's downfall or death, comedy generally points toward some kind of broader reform or remaking of society, usually signaled by a wedding or other celebration at the end of the play.

To speak of genre in this way, though, is to suggest that these ideal critical abstractions actually exist in some form, exemplified more or less adequately by particular plays. Yet, as the very different genres of Japanese or Indian theater suggest, terms like *tragedy* and *comedy,* or **MELODRAMA, TRAGOCOMEDY, FARCE,** and others, arise from our efforts to find continuities between extraordinarily different kinds of drama: between plays written in different theaters, for different purposes, to please different audiences, under different historical pressures. When we impose these terms in a prescriptive way, we usually find that the drama eludes them or even calls them into question. Aristotle's brilliant sense of Greek tragedy in *The Poetics,* for instance, hardly "applies" with equal force to Greek plays as different as *Agamemnon, Oedipus the King,* and *Medea,* or Kan'ami's elegant Noh drama, *Matsukaze,* let alone later plays like *Hamlet* or *Endgame.* In his essay, "Tragedy and the Common Man," Arthur Miller tries to preserve "tragedy" for modern drama by redefining Aristotle's description of the hero of tragedy. Instead of Aristotle's hero, a man (not a woman) of an elevated social station, Miller argues that the modern hero should be an average, "common" man (not a woman), precisely because the "best families" do not seem normative to us or representative of our basic values, a goal he pursued in his classic American tragedy, *Death of a Salesman.* Our exemplary characters are taken from the middle classes. Yet to redefine the hero in this way calls Aristotle's other qualifications—the idea of the hero's character and actions, the meaning of the tragic "fall"—into question as well, forcing us to redefine Aristotelian tragedy in ways that make it something entirely new, something evocative in modern terms.

In approaching the question of genre, then, it is often useful to avoid asking how a play exemplifies the universal and unchanging features of tragedy or comedy. Instead, one could ask how a play or a theater *invents* tragedy or comedy for its contemporary audience. What terms does the drama present, what formal features does it use, to represent human experience? How do historically "local" genres—Renaissance **REVENGE TRAGEDY,** French **NEOCLASSICAL DRAMA,** modern **THEATER OF THE ABSURD, KABUKI,** or even the **KATHAKALI** of southern India—challenge, preserve, or redefine broader notions of genre?

DRAMATIC FORM

In about 335 BCE, Aristotle's *The Poetics* set down the formal elements of drama, and the influence of Aristotle's description has been massive: today we still speak of dramatic form in terms of its **PLOT, CHARACTERS, LANGUAGE, THEME,** and its performative elements, what Aristotle called **MUSIC** and **SPECTACLE.** Any student of drama can profit by thinking about how these formal elements function in a given play. How are the incidents of the play—its plot—arranged? What effects are achieved by *this* ordering, rather than by another? How does the plot relate to the play's narrative story, which includes events dating from before the play begins? How does the plot, the structure of the events—for instance, Nora Helmer's first act in *A Doll House* is to enter the house, and her last act is to leave it—develop the play's themes? We might then ask how the play defines its characters. What elements of human experience—family history, psychological motivation, public action—seem to be most prominent in a play's conception of "character"? How do the formal conventions of characterization, such as blank verse in Shakespeare's plays and the densely poetic language of Noh theater, affect our reading of the characters and our understanding of them as representations of human beings?

Although Aristotle presents these elements of drama as distinct, in practice they are mutually defining, making it very difficult to speak of them separately. A play's language, for example, can be analyzed purely for its verbal and rhetorical features, but it is more interesting to ask how the language affects our understanding of the characters or invests the play with certain thematic possibilities. Similarly, while we may regard a play's themes as inside the play, they actually arise only in our interpretation of the play. The themes are something we create by asking certain questions about the play's plotting, its characterization, its use of language. The artificiality of separating these features becomes especially clear when we turn to a play's theatrical dimension. Although Aristotle suggests that a play's literary and theatrical dimensions are independent, to get a real sense of drama we must see the play both as literature and as theater. We must assess how an audience's sense of the play's plot, characters, and themes are shaped by the kinds of spectacle demanded by the play and provided by the theater. The "meaning" of Greek drama cannot be separated from its conditions of performance: the religious festival, the huge amphitheater, the masked actors, the singing, dancing chorus. The barren "sterile promontory" of *Hamlet,* cross-dressed performance in Churchill's *Cloud Nine:* these elements of the theatrical spectacle are not outside the meaning of the drama; they are the means, the vehicle for achieving that meaning on the stage.

In a book like this one—indeed, in any book—it is difficult to convey a real sense of the power of theater. It is possible, though, to imagine this experience and to discuss it through the materials collected here: dramatic texts, descriptions of stage practice, illustrations of theaters, photographs, essays. However, an obstacle to understanding arises from a split between the disciplines we use to understand drama and theater. At many colleges and universities, this split is represented in the geography of the campus itself, where the English or Literature departments, which teach dramatic literature, are housed in one building, and the Theater or Drama department, which teaches acting, directing, design, and which actually stages the plays, is housed in another. "Literary" approaches to drama focus our attention initially, sometimes exclusively, on the text of a play and train the complex strategies of poetics and poetic interpretation on it. Such interpretation regards the dramatic text as incomplete and specifies the text's range of possible meanings by placing it in various textual and cultural contexts; in a sense, the negotiation between the text and these contexts determines what we can say the play *means*.

"Theatrical" approaches to drama tend to see a play in terms of stage practice, both in the terms of the play's original production and in the light of performance practice today. This approach interrogates the play's staging: how it can be set, what obstacles it presents to acting and casting, what the dramatic effects of costume and design will be. "Theatrical" interpretation regards the dramatic text as an incomplete design for performance and trains the complex machinery of stage representation—directing, acting, design, costuming on the task of fleshing the script out as performed action. The meaning of the play in this regard emerges from what we can make the play *do*.

The literary and theatrical approaches to drama and theater share the assumption that plays are not fully meaningful in themselves; they share the sense that the meaning of drama emerges from the kinds of questions we ask of it, the contexts—literary, historical, theoretical, theatrical—in which we can make it perform, and make it mean something in particular. Although each approach can seem needlessly mysterious, involving its own specialized language and critical practice, its own set of "right" questions and "right" answers, this book has been assembled with the belief that the literary and the theatrical approaches are necessary complements to each other.

In the units that follow, each introductory essay attempts to provide an overview of the dense implication of drama and theater in its culture, and, often, how dramatic literature and theatrical practices have been revived, engaged, or transformed by succeeding generations. Each essay, in other words, introduces the social, political, and cultural milieu of the theater; the theater's physical and symbolic position in the landscape of its culture; the theater's representation of gendered, sexual, and racial identities; the physical design of theaters, and the practices of acting and staging; and the dynamic impact of dramatic—literary—innovation on the work of performance. Although these issues are treated differently, given different prominence in each essay, this constellation of questions stems from a single conviction: that thinking about drama requires that we think about how plays perform as literature, in culture and history, and on the stage.

One of the greatest challenges, for professional scholars and students alike, to understanding the history of drama and theater has to do with the nature of evidence. As any detective drama illustrates—think of Sherlock Holmes—"facts" only become "evidence" when they are subjected to a coherent interpretation, an explanatory narrative. So, too, understanding the "facts" of the theatrical past means transforming them into "evidence," evidence that materializes a certain understanding, interpretation, or explanation of the meaning of drama and theater in history. The difficulties of historiography—the writing of history—with regard to early drama and theater are self-evident. Most of the plays of classical Athens, for example, have been lost; those that survive represent only a small percentage of the "evidence" for the practice of Greek playwrights. Much of the evidence for theatrical practice—how actors worked, the movements of the chorus, the function of music, the behavior of audiences, even the composition of audiences—has had to be adduced from written documents and visual images often far-removed from the theater itself, for these practices (much like the teaching of acting today) were part of an ongoing tradition that was handed directly from performer to performer, or citizen to citizen. Many theatrical traditions around the world originated in nonliterate oral cultures, which successfully preserved the developing forms and practices of performance over centuries, as long as the communities who sustained them continued to flourish. Often regarded as "primitive," "uncivilized," or simply subversive by invading colonial powers, even traditional practices that survived well into the historical period have sometimes been eradicated (Wole Soyinka's *Death and the King's Horseman* provides a striking image of the ways the English governors of Nigeria regarded several centuries-old traditional performance practices). Nonetheless, some of these traditions survive: though they date from about the sixteenth century, *kathakali* performances in southern India seem to preserve some of the dramatic and performance traditions of ancient Sanskrit performance, as it was described in Bharatamuni's *Natyasastra*. Of course, the rise of print not only forged a fissure between literary drama and theatrical performance: it also provided the means to document a wide variety of theatrical practice and—since the purpose of print is to multiply texts in great numbers—to provide a greater chance that such documents would survive. For this reason, beginning in the sixteenth century, the print-record provides a massive archive of information about the practices of performance: in the publication of plays; in the efflorescence of diaries and memoirs containing information about the stage; in the rise of theatrical journalism in the eighteenth century; in playbills, posters, programs; and in a wide variety of theatrical illustrations—pictures of actors, plays, theaters. In combination with the increasing likelihood that theatrical buildings, sets, costumes, and the records of theater companies have survived, the history of the modern theater is, comparatively speaking, an embarrassment of riches. Needless to say, it has recently become possible even to record performance, on still photographs and film, videotape, and digital media. While it is important to recognize that such recordings are themselves only partial "evidence" for the work of a given production—What is the camera leaving out of the picture? How is close-up distorting what an audience might see? How did the production change in order to be filmed? How did the live production change after it was filmed?—they do provide an invaluable resource for future generations of students.

In each unit, this edition of *The Wadsworth Anthology of Drama* provides a piece of that material past, a document or an image that provides some insight into theatrical practice. Some of these records are visual, and indeed may have had no direct relation to performance in their day: scholars now use them to attempt to reconstruct elements of lost theaters. Several of these records are written documents, often chestnuts in the history of drama and theater. The purpose of including these records here is experimental: how can you use such records to interrogate some aspect of a past performance? What kind of story does the document tell, and what stories does it conceal? What kind of interpretation of theater history does the document enable? What kinds of evidentiary problems does it pose? Reading the documents of the theater's material past is one way to engage in the challenging work of imagining the power of dramatic performance.

Classical Athens

Greek amphitheater at the site of the ancient city of Morgantina, Sicily.

Great drama arises where the theater occupies an important place in the life of the community. In many respects, Western understanding of drama originated in fifth-century (500–400) BCE classical Athens, where the theater played a central role in politics, religion, and society. The Athenians invented forms of **TRAGEDY** and **COMEDY** that persist to the present day. In tragedy, the Greeks dramatized climactic events in the lives of legendary heroes from prehistory and myth, bringing ethical problems of motive and action to the stage. In comedy, the theater staged satiric portraits of the life of the ***POLIS*** (the city-state), vividly depicting the energetic conflicts of contemporary Athens in matters of politics, war, education—even the arts of drama. Playwrights through the long history of the theater have continued to find in Greek drama both a model and a point of resistance against which to practice their own craft (see, for example, Bernard Shaw's *Major Barbara* in this book). And we need only recall Sigmund Freud's understanding of the "Oedipus complex" to sense the influence of models of action derived from the Greek theater on later Western culture.

Athens and Sparta were dominant rival powers in fifth-century Greece, which comprised many small independent city-states, each with its own political and cultural institutions, form of government, and alliances. Dramatic performances took place under a variety of circumstances in all Greek cities, but drama as we know it developed in Athens. Dramatic performance in Athens was part of citywide religious festivals honoring the god Dionysus, the most important being the **CITY DIONYSIA.** Plays were produced for contests in which playwrights, actors, and choruses competed for prizes and for distinction among their fellow citizens. These contests, held in an outdoor amphitheater adjoining the sacred temple of the god, followed several days of religious parades and sacrifices. This connection between early drama and religion suggests that the essential nature of Greek drama lies in its supposed "origins" in religious ritual. But the City Dionysia was also a massive civic spectacle that went far beyond religious worship, emphasizing the theater's implication in other areas of public life. Dramatic performance contributed to this celebration of Athens' economic power, cultural accomplishment, and military might. The City Dionysia united religion and politics, enabling Athenians to celebrate both Dionysus and the achievements of their *polis*.

THE CITY DIONYSIA

The City Dionysia was the most prominent of four religious festivals held in Athens and the surrounding province of Attica between December and April; it took place in the month of Elaphebolion (March–April), one month after the previous festival. Although its purpose was primarily a religious one, the City Dionysia was structured around a series of contests between individual citizens and between major Athenian social groups—the ten (later twelve to fifteen) "tribes" that formed the city's basic political and military units. Dramatic performance was introduced to the City Dionysia during the sixth century BCE and became the centerpiece of the elaborate festival. Each year a city magistrate, or ***ARCHON,*** honored selected wealthy citizens by choosing them to finance one of the three principal tragic dramatists competing for a prize at the festival. Each sponsor, called a ***CHOREGOS,*** was responsible for hiring the **CHORUS** of young men who sang and danced in the plays. The *choregos* hired musicians and provided costumes and other support for the playwright to whom he was assigned. Later in the period, the state assigned the leading actor to the *choregos* as well, and this actor also competed for a prize. The playwright was responsible for training the chorus and the actors, and for some of the acting himself, and he shared his prize with the *choregos.* Serving as a *choregos* was both a civic duty and an important honor, equivalent to other tasks imposed on the wealthy—maintaining a battleship for a year or training athletes for the Olympic games.

Taking place over several days, the City Dionysia opened with a display of actors and choruses to the city; on the next day there was a lavish parade of religious officials through the city, followed by religious observances and sacrifices held in the theater. Athens also received its annual tribute of goods, money, and slaves from subject and allied states at this time, and war orphans raised at state expense were displayed to the audience. After this display of religious worship and civic pride, two days were devoted to contests of **DITHYRAMBS,** hymns sung and danced by a large chorus. Each of Athens' tribes sponsored two choruses: one consisting of fifty men, another consisting of fifty boys. The city's politics revolved around the tribes, and their contribution to the festival was prominent in this contest. The dithyrambic contest involved a thousand Athenian citizens directly in the performance, a significant portion of the adult male citizens. (It is estimated that Athens in the fifth century had a total population of about 300,000: 100,000 slaves, 30,000 noncitizen foreigners, and 30,000 to 40,000 adult male citizens; women and children were not citizens.) Following the dithyrambs, the main dramatic contest began. The competing playwrights each produced a **TRILOGY** of tragedies, staged over three days. A trilogy could take a single theme or series of events as its subject (like the three plays of Aeschylus' *Oresteia,* 458 BCE), or present three distinct, unrelated dramas. A rugged farce called a **SATYR PLAY** followed the performance of each complete trilogy and was considered part of it; these plays parodied a god's activities, with actors dressed as satyrs—half-man, half-goat. After 486 BCE, comedies were also awarded prizes, but it is unclear whether the comedies were performed on a single day or spread over several days. Prominent citizens representing each of the tribes served as judges and awarded prizes to the playwrights, their *choregoi,* and the actors.

THE THEATER OF DIONYSUS

The Greek theater was a public spectacle, a kind of combination of Inauguration Day, the Super Bowl, the Academy Awards, Memorial Day, and a major religious holiday. Plays were first produced in the *AGORA* (marketplace), which often served as a performance place for festivals in Athens and in the surrounding **DEMES** of Attica, which also staged dramatic performances. However, the size and importance of the City Dionysia required a separate site, and a theater was built on the slope of the Acropolis, near the precinct of Dionysus. The original theater, a ring of wooden seats facing a circular floor, was later refined, enlarged, and constructed of stone. By the time of Aeschylus, Euripides, Sophocles, and Aristophanes, the Athenian theater had achieved its basic design: a circular floor for dancing and acting, ringed by a hillside **AMPHITHEATER** and backed by a low, rectangular building.

The focus of the classical amphitheater, which seated about 14,000 people, was the round **ORCHESTRA** ("dancing place") containing the central altar of Dionysus, at which the festival sacrifices were performed. The dithyrambic choruses performed their ecstatic dances in the orchestra, and most of the action of the plays took place there as well. Facing the orchestra, the hillside was divided into wedge-shaped seating areas. The citizens sat on wooden benches with their tribes: leaders and priests in the front of the sections, women perhaps toward the rear or possibly in a separate section. *Metics* (resident aliens) and visitors were probably seated in a separate area. Special front and center seats, called *prohedria,* were reserved for the judges and the priests of Dionysus.

Behind the *orchestra,* a low building called the **SKENE** faced the audience. Although the *skene* became a permanent stone structure in the fourth century BCE, in the fifth century it was a temporary wooden building, used for changing masks and possibly also for changing costumes. Playwrights quickly found the theatrical potential latent in the *skene*'s facade and

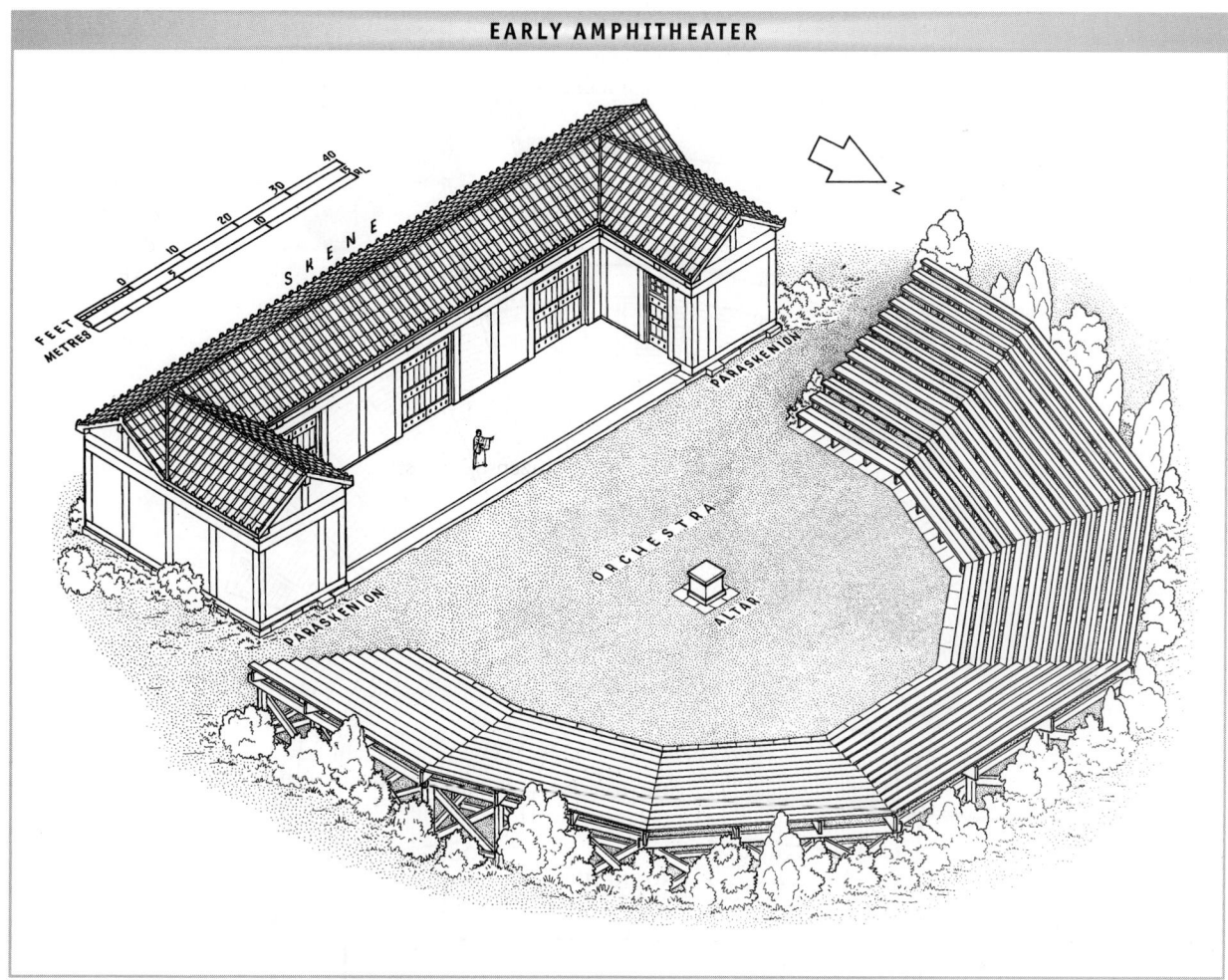

EARLY AMPHITHEATER

This is an artist's reconstruction of an early theater in Eretria, Greece. Notice that the seating is constructed of wooden benches and the *skene* is a temporary structure.

set of doors; through these doors the audience heard Agamemnon being murdered in his bath, or saw eyeless Oedipus return to confront the Chorus and his future in exile. In Aeschylus' *Agamemnon,* the Watchman awaits the signal fires on the palace roof, and in performance he may have waited on the roof of the *skene*. The theater also used some machinery for scenic effects: a rolling platform (the ***EKKYKLEMA***) used to bring objects or bodies from the *skene* into the orchestra; a crane (***MACHINA***) to raise or lower characters— the gods, for instance—from the orchestra over the roof of the *skene;* later, in the fourth century, painted panels were used to indicate the play's setting or location.

THEATER AND SOCIAL LIFE

The experience of theater in classical Athens was in some ways akin to participation in other institutions of civic life. Athens was a participatory democracy for its citizens, although citizenship was restricted to adult male Athenians: women, foreigners, slaves, freed slaves, and children were not citizens. Citizens sat in the assembly to discuss and vote on matters of state policy, and they were eligible to serve in all public and military offices as well. Attendance at the City Dionysia was, then, like other aspects of Athenian public life, a privilege and an

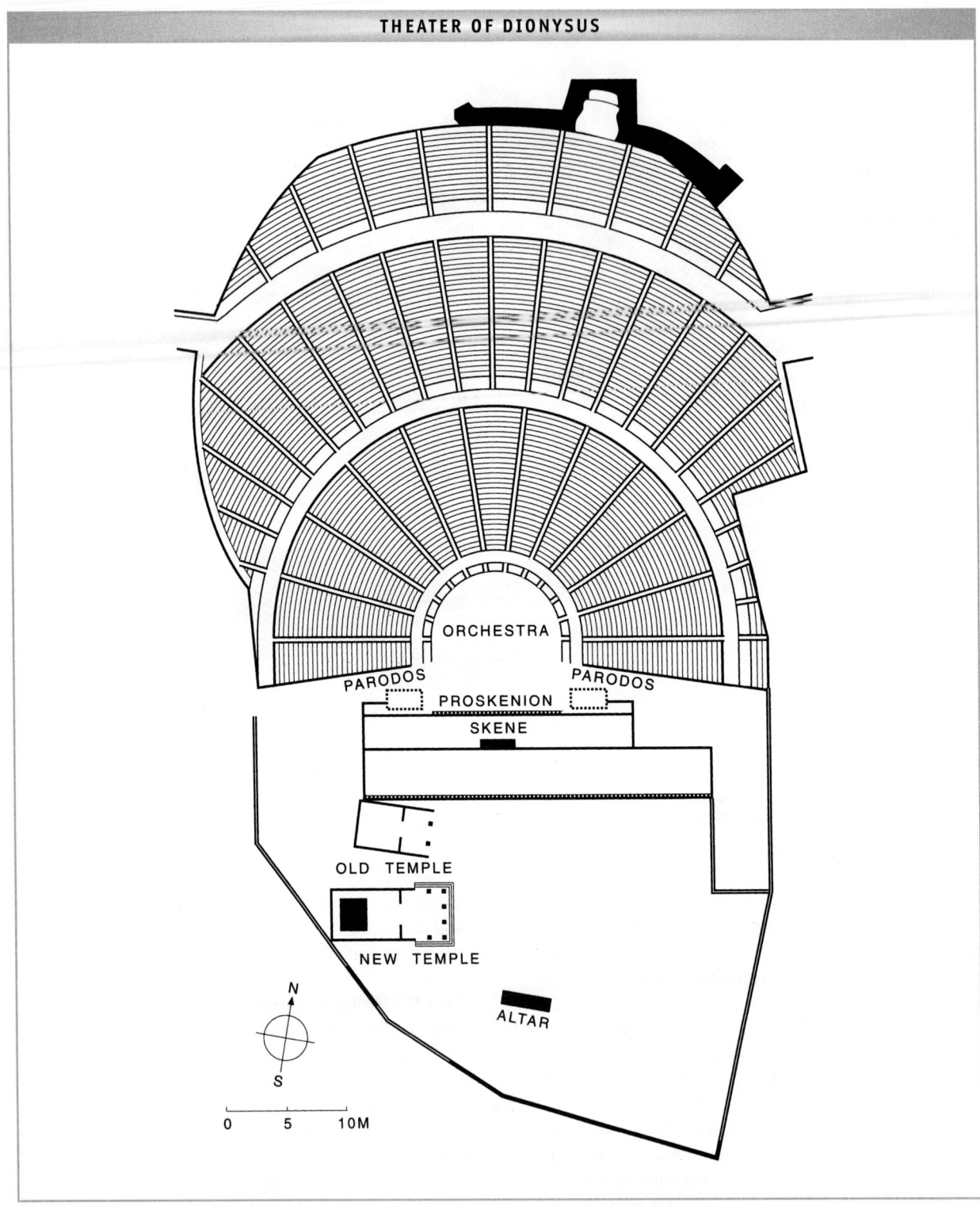

THEATER OF DIONYSUS

This ground plan is of the sacred precinct of Dionysus in Athens, fourth century BCE. Notice that the theater is much larger than the earlier theater at provincial Eretria. The large and permanent skene was constructed after the fifth century BCE.

obligation mainly reserved for citizens. Citizens received tickets to the festival from officials in their neighborhood, or **DEME;** tickets may have been awarded on the basis of participation in other civic obligations—serving in the courts, the assembly, the army. At the theater, citizens sat together with members of their tribe. In a sense, the theater offered a visual map of the organization of Athenian society, for the tribes formed the basis of political participation outside the theater: The Athenian Assembly and the army were similarly arranged by tribe. Organized by tribes, with precedence given to religious officials and with inferior status or nonparticipation accorded to noncitizens such as women, slaves, and foreigners, the theater of Dionysus mirrored the structure of Athenian society.

The fifth century BCE was the era of Athens' greatest political power and cultural vitality and an era of intense reciprocity between Athenian theater and society. Yet the tension manifest in Greek drama perhaps points to the precarious stability of the Athenian *polis.* The Athenian maritime empire, forged after the defeat of massive Persian forces in 479, was resisted by the smaller Greek states and opposed by Athens' chief rival, the military state of Sparta. Following a long period of hostility and skirmishing, Athens and Sparta declared war against each other in 431 BCE, resulting in Athens' utter defeat in 404. Athenian democracy was replaced by an oppressive oligarchy, the Thirty Tyrants. Although the tyrants were rapidly overthrown and democracy restored, Athens never regained the dynamic cultural life and political power it enjoyed during the fifth century. And although dramatic performance continued after the restoration of democracy, the theater's central role in the *polis* seems to have declined after the Spartan victory. Yet, the theater became one of Greece's most widely disseminated cultural products. When Alexander the Great conquered Greece, the Near East, and northern Africa, he took Greek culture—including theater and drama—with him throughout his empire. And when the Roman Empire later absorbed Alexander's former dominions, it also appropriated Greek dramatic traditions, the design of Greek theaters, and the arts and religion of Greece, as well.

DRAMA AND PERFORMANCE

In his *Poetics,* Aristotle suggests that drama originated in the singing of the dithyrambic choruses; a masked actor was first used to respond to the chorus as an individualized "character" in the mid–sixth century BCE, an innovation attributed to the playwright Thespis, about whom little else is known. Aeschylus was the first to use two actors, probably taking one of the parts himself; in the 460s, Sophocles introduced a third actor and was successfully imitated by Aeschylus in his *Oresteia* in 458 BCE. In general, classical tragedy can be performed with three actors and comedy with four, although each actor may play several parts. All of the performers in the Greek theater—the dramatists, actors, musicians, and chorus members—were male citizens of Athens, as was most of the audience. The dramatic choruses were perhaps composed of young men between the ages of seventeen, when military training began, and twenty-one, when Athenian men entered into adulthood.

The chorus of tragedy both sang and danced, and it was expected to perform with grace and precision. Actors and choruses wore full-head masks made of painted linen or lightweight wood. The main characters' masks were individualized, but the members of the chorus all wore identical masks, giving a special force to the conflict between the unique claims of the protagonist and the more diffuse claims of his society. Costuming in comedy was somewhat more complex. Aristophanes' plays suggest that the chorus at times wore animal masks. The comic protagonists' masks, though, were again individualized; since Aristophanes often put his contemporaries in his plays—Socrates in *Clouds,* for instance, or Euripides in *Frogs*—the masks probably resembled these citizens quite closely. Comic actors often sported a leather **PHALLUS,** clearly visible in statues depicting comic actors and of much dramatic use in plays like *Lysistrata.*

In reading Greek drama, we should remember that its leading parts—both the leading character and the chorus—were designed for competition, as instruments for the actor and chorus to win prizes. The literary brilliance of the plays is, in this sense, a means to enable a particular virtuosity in performance.

WOMEN IN THE ATHENIAN THEATER

In Athenian tragedy and comedy, female characters were played by men. Not only did men sponsor and write the plays, but the "women" onstage were literally men in disguise. Yet, many plays throw the theatrical convention of men playing women into relief. In Euripides' play *The Bacchae,* Pentheus is possessed by Dionysus when he dresses up as a woman and Dionysus admires his good looks; in *Lysistrata,* the Spartan woman Lampito is closely and physically examined by Lysistrata and the other women in ways that focus the audience's attention precisely on the fact that the woman is being played by a man. Drama, then, participated fully in Athens' denial of equality to women. Athena says as much in Aeschylus' *The Eumenides* when she judges Orestes' murder of his mother as a lesser crime than Clytaemnestra's murder of her husband. Looking closely at both the drama and its performance can help us to see how justice, power, and gender came to be arranged in Athenian society.

Although the theater—like Athenian society—was a male-dominated institution, Greek drama repeatedly inquires into the nature of gendered behavior and uses female characters to focus some of its most challenging questions. Given the absence of women from the stage and their marginal status in the theater and in the state, it is fascinating to note how many plays turn on the action of female characters. Women were not themselves citizens of Athens, and their prerogatives, which were considerable, in the *polis* were defined only through marriage to a citizen. Yet many of the plays raise critical moral, ethical, and political problems through the actions of women: Clytaemnestra and Cassandra in Aeschylus' *Agamemnon,* Medea in Euripides' *Medea,* and the women of Aristophanes' *Lysistrata* and *Assembly of Women.* Although Aristotle probably voices his contemporaries' views when he remarks in his *Poetics* that "a woman can be good, or a slave, although one of these classes [women] is inferior and the other, as a class, worthless," the theater stages women in ways that implicitly challenge the authority of this "natural" connection between the good, the legitimate, and the masculine. As a category that troubles the "natural" linkage between masculinity and humanity itself, women in Greek drama often appear to stage a crisis in how the state imagines and justifies itself.

FORMS OF GREEK DRAMA

Formally, the organization of Greek tragedy is somewhat different from that of modern plays, because Greek drama is based on the singing and dancing of the chorus, for whom many of the plays were named. Most plays begin with a **PROLOGUE,** such as the Watchman's speech at the opening of *Agamemnon,* followed by the **PARODOS** (entrance) of the singing and dancing chorus. Several **EPISODES** follow, in which the central characters engage one another and the chorus; the chorus itself often sings (and dances) several **ODES,** which are used to enunciate and enlarge on the play's pivotal issues, and the chorus often becomes a decisive character in the play, as it does in Aeschylus' *Agamemnon* or Euripides' *The Bacchae.* The choral odes are written in lyric meters different from the meters used for the characters' speeches. The play's **CATASTROPHE,** literally its "down turn," marks some change in the hero's status and is followed by the departure of the characters from the stage and the **EXODOS,** or final song, dance, and departure of the chorus. Comedy—at least for Aristophanes, whose plays are the only surviving comedies from the period—is structured similarly, although Aristophanes' plays usually include a long **PARABASIS,** a choral ode delivered to the audience discussing political issues, and a final **KOMOS,** a scene of choral dancing and revelry.

This formal description, however, hardly accounts for the real and continued power of Greek drama, which arises from an intense and economical relationship between (1) a situation, usually at the point of climax as the play opens, (2) a complex of characters, each with distinctive goals and motives, (3) a chorus used both as a character and as a commentator on the action, and (4) a series of incidents that precipitates a crisis and brings the meaning of the **PROTAGONIST**'s actions into focus. Aristotle called this crisis the ***PERIPETEIA,*** or "reversal," in the external situation or fortunes of the main character, and he argued that it should be accompanied by an act of ***ANAGNORISIS,*** or "recognition," in which the character responds to this change. Indeed, Aristotle argued that when the pressure of the tragic action produces a close relationship between reversal and recognition, it instills in the audience intense feelings of fear and pity and then effects ***CATHARSIS,*** a purgation of these emotions.

Because the plays were written for a contest, it is not surprising that their language and construction provide opportunity for powerful acting, particularly since the plays were judged only in performance. Yet the stage action of Greek drama is hardly spectacular in the modern sense. Although the visual dimension of Agamemnon's descent from the chariot onto the blood-red tapestry, or Medea's appearance in the dragon-drawn chariot, or even the aching gait of the men in *Lysistrata* is critical to any understanding of these plays, scenes of murder, suicide, or battle usually take place offstage, to be vividly reported by messengers— as in the reports of Jocasta's death and Oedipus' blinding, or of the death of Jason's young bride in *Medea*. Cassandra's graphic prophecy of Agamemnon's murder likewise provides a brutal counterpoint to the slaughter taking place offstage.

The scenic simplicity of the Greek theater enabled playwrights to achieve a special kind of concentration, one that capitalized on the special circumstances of the open-air, festival theater. Greek comedy has come down to us in the work of only two playwrights, Aristophanes and Menander (c. 342–c. 291 BCE). While Aristophanes' plays—usually called **OLD COMEDY**— are energetic and sometimes ribald comedies lampooning the Athenian *polis* and its leading citizens, Menander's comedies—called **NEW COMEDY**—are more generally concerned with mores and manners. Menander wrote more than 100 plays, but only one of his comedies— *The Grouch*—survives in its entirety. Menander's plays were often focused on a comic conflict between parents and children, devising situations and characters that forged an important link between the Greek and Roman theaters, and helped to establish the enduring traditions of stage comedy.

While the comedies center on the life of the community, the stage action of Greek tragedy focuses on the relation between the hero's intention, action, and consequence in ways that typically pit the hero's greatest talents against his unavoidable destiny, his society, his family, and himself. This recipe has provided—in plays from the era of Aeschylus, Sophocles, and Euripides to our own—the substance of tragic drama. The characteristic concerns of Greek drama speak undeniably of classical Athens, but the plays also represent trials of decision, suffering, and desperation with a power and purpose that continue to speak to us in accents very much our own.

GREEK DRAMA IN PERFORMANCE HISTORY

The forms of Greek drama and theater remained in use after the fall of Athens to Sparta; indeed, they were both exported to Rome, Egypt, and the Middle East by Alexander. Yet while tragedy and comedy continued to be written and performed throughout the Greek Mediterranean throughout the Hellenistic period (fourth and third centuries BCE) and beyond, and theater design continued to develop and refine the classical amphitheater, in an important sense the tradition of dramatic writing and performance inaugurated in fifth-century Athens was confined to the Greek provinces. The modes of Greek drama and (to a lesser extent) performance survived somewhat longer in the eastern reaches of the Roman Empire, but in the west they gradually disappeared under the influence of Roman culture. Moreover, although the manuscripts of Greek drama—and of important collateral texts, such as Aristotle's *Poetics*—continued

(ASIDE)
ROMAN DRAMA AND THEATER

Although many of their traditions were absorbed from Greece, the Romans developed a distinctive theater, quite different from the Athenian stage. From its beginnings, Roman theater was more varied than the Greek stage, including acrobatics, juggling, athletic events, gladiatorial combats, and skits. In the sixth and seventh centuries BCE, Rome was a relatively unimportant town, ruled by the Etruscan kingdoms of northern Italy. In 509 the Romans drove out the Etruscans and founded a republic; the republic expanded its influence throughout the fourth century BCE and eventually came to control many territories once governed by the Greeks and by Alexander. Much as the Romans absorbed other Greek cultural institutions, they also absorbed Greek theater and drama, which were first performed in Rome in the mid–third century, in 240 BCE. As Rome's political influence expanded, particularly under the Roman Empire (27 BCE–476 CE), the Romans disseminated their characteristic cultural institutions—including theater and drama—throughout Europe, North Africa, and the Middle East.

Like the Greeks, the Romans associated the drama with festivals, but the Romans not only produced plays on festival occasions throughout the year, they also developed a much wider variety of theatrical entertainments, of which drama was only a small part. Some of the Roman entertainments descended from the sixth-century BCE *ludi Romani,* which included chariot racing, boxing, and other athletic contests, and Greek drama was first performed in Rome at these games. Moreover, Greek drama not only competed with other nondramatic entertainment, it also was rivaled by an indigenous dramatic form known as **ATELLAN FARCE.** Associated with the town of Atella (near present-day Naples), these farces were probably improvised comic skits, involving stock characters and played by masked actors.

After the introduction of tragedy and comedy to the *ludi Romani* in 240 BCE, dramatic performances were introduced to several other festivals, and by 179 BCE, drama was being performed at major religious festivals throughout the year: at the *ludi Romani* honoring Jupiter in September, at a second festival consecrated to Jupiter in November, at festivals honoring Flora and the Great Mother in April, and at a festival honoring Apollo in July. Dramatic performances, though still associated with festivals, were much more common in Rome than in fifth-century Athens, not only because special celebrations sometimes included theatrical performance, but also because any disruption in the rituals connected with the festivals required that the entire festival be repeated, including the dramatic performances.

Given the variety of entertainments offered in Rome—including the chariot races and gladiatorial combats that became increasingly popular in the later Empire, especially after 300 CE—it is not surprising that the Romans built several different kinds of entertainment buildings, stadiums and racecourses as well as theaters. Yet until 55 BCE, theaters in Rome were temporary, built and taken down for each festival. In the first century BCE, the Romans began to build permanent theaters with some regularity. Like their Greek predecessors, the Roman theaters were outdoor amphitheaters, but the Romans built their theaters on level ground, and their superior engineering—particularly the Romans' use of arches in construction—enabled them to build much more massive buildings. Roman theaters were generally three stories in height. A rectangular stage house, or *SCAENA,* stood like the Greek *skene* behind the semicircular orchestra and faced a steeply tiered semicircular auditorium. The facade of the *scaena* was elaborately ornamented with columns and porticos. The Romans built theaters of stone throughout the Empire; many of the Greek theaters that remain today were refurbished and redesigned by the Romans.

Although the Romans continued to perform plays from the Greek theater, they also developed a native strain of drama—represented in the plays of Plautus, Terence, and Seneca. Titus Maccius Plautus (c. 254–c. 184 BCE) is

to be copied for students and readers, they fell out of public circulation. The few texts that have survived of the plays of Aeschylus, Sophocles, Euripides, and Aristophanes are based on copies made for teachers and scholars in Byzantium, dating from the third and fourth centuries CE. Not only have most of their plays been lost (Sophocles is said to have written 123 plays, of which we have seven; Aeschylus is thought to have written more than seventy, of which seven remain; Euripides' nineteen plays are all that remain of more than ninety), but the entire dramatic output of 700 years of theater was lost as well—the names of Agathon, Thespis, Chairemon, Theodektes, Philokles, Ariastas, and others are all that remain of their work. Moreover, since these manuscripts were collected in scholarly or monastic libraries, they have been subject to the destructive forces of history. Many Greek plays were lost in the burning of the library at Alexandria during Caesar's invasion of Egypt; the crusaders sacked Constantinople (previously known as Byzantium) in 1204, and in the process destroyed a city that had joined eastern and western cultures for centuries.

probably the most influential Roman comic playwright. His earliest surviving plays date from 205 BCE, or about thirty-five years after Greek drama was first introduced to Rome; Plautus is thought to have based many of his comedies on Greek New Comedy, but none of these prototypes survives. Plautus is thought to have written more than 100 comedies, many of which—*Amphitryon, The Braggart Warrior, The Rope,* and *The Menaechmus Twins,* for example—established the formal conventions of later comedy. Publius Terentius Afer (c. 195–159 BCE), usually called Terence, was probably born in Carthage and brought to Rome as a slave. Unlike the prolific Plautus, Terence wrote only six comedies, all of which survive, and strove throughout his career to adapt Greek originals to the Roman stage: *The Woman of Andros, Mother-in-Law, Self-Tormentor, Eunuch, Phormio,* and *The Brothers.* The plays of Plautus and Terence have been particularly influential on the form and structure of later European comedy; not only did they establish many of the forms and character types developed by later playwrights, but in the late Middle Ages and Renaissance, their plays were often used to teach Latin in the schools, giving rise to generations of playwrights—including William Shakespeare, Christopher Marlowe, and Molière—who found in Roman drama a form for their own contemporary plays.

The only surviving Roman tragedies were written by Lucius Annaeus

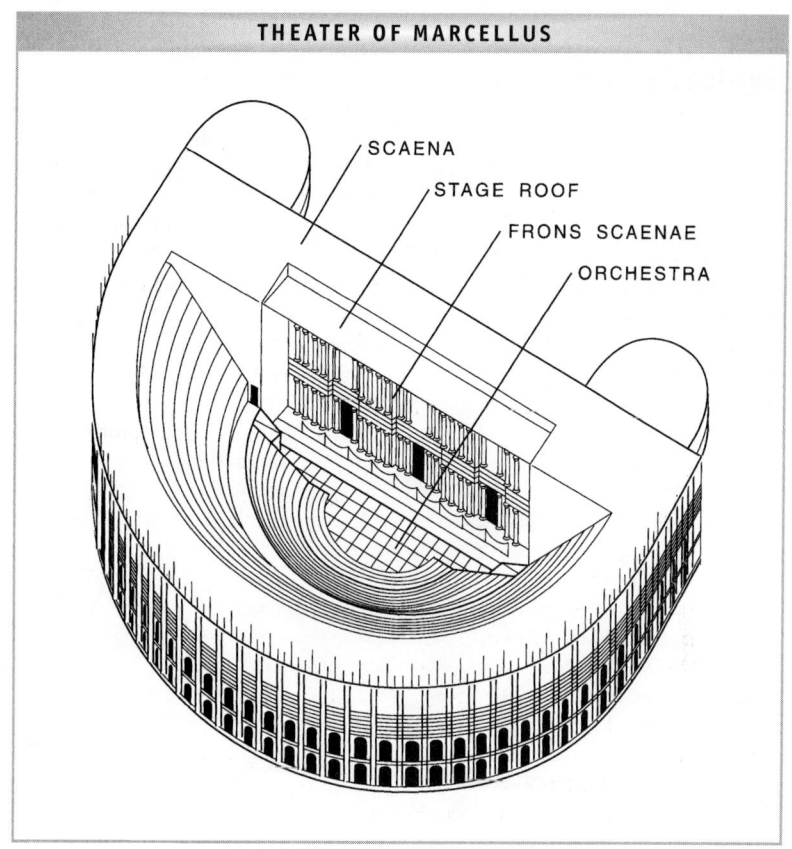

THEATER OF MARCELLUS

SCAENA
STAGE ROOF
FRONS SCAENAE
ORCHESTRA

The Theater of Marcellus was built in Rome, 13–11 BCE.

Seneca (5 BCE–65 CE). Seneca's tragedies were adapted from Greek plays but tend to be more sensational and violent; indeed, it is doubtful that they were performed in the theater. Although only nine of Seneca's plays survive—*The Trojan Women, Medea, Oedipus, Phaedra, Thyestes, Hercules on Oeta, Hercules Mad, The Phoenecian Women, Agamemnon*—Senecan tragedy also exerted an important influence on later drama, especially in the English Renaissance, where Senecan tragedy provided a prototype for the nascent English drama of the sixteenth century.

However, for all their violence, the Crusades also reopened cultural contact with the Islamic Middle East; many of the texts of Greek and Roman culture had been translated into Arabic or had been preserved by Islamic scholars and libraries. With the reopening of European trading and military contacts in the fourteenth, fifteenth, and sixteenth centuries, Europe was able to rediscover the literature of classical Greece, sometimes in Latin translations, sometimes only through commentaries on still-lost texts (such as Aristotle's *Poetics*). In many respects, though, this recovery was principally of Roman theater and drama. The prestige and availability of texts by Latin authors like Plautus, Terence, and Seneca meant that these playwrights were widely taught in schools, convents (such as Gandersheim, where the canoness Hrosvitha [953–973 CE] wrote six comedies modeled on Terence's plays), and universities, where their plays were often performed; the influence of these playwrights can be felt everywhere in European drama of the sixteenth century, most familiarly in Shakespeare's early comedies (like *A Comedy of Errors,* based on Plautus' *The Menaechmus Twins*) and in the

READING THE MATERIAL THEATER

This illustration, taken from an Attic red-figure volute *krater* painted by the "Pronomos painter" c. 450 BCE, is an important document in the history of Greek theater. While it doesn't directly represent the performance of a satyr play onstage, there is much to learn from this vase painting. Look closely at the illustration: What distinctions can you make among the various figures? First, of course, many of the figures seem to be holding their theatrical masks, and several seem to be gazing at them. But among the male figures, several are bearded adult men, while a larger number are beardless, suggesting that they are younger, adolescents. What role do you think they play in the performance? One

THE PRONOMOS *KRATER*

These actors, apparently in a satyr play, appear on a vase painting by the Pronomos painter. Notice that the central seated figure of Dionysus (holding the polelike *thyrsus*) is surrounded by actors holding their masks. The older, bearded actor to the right of Dionysus, wearing the lionskin over his shoulder, is apparently playing Hercules, the

vogue for violent tragedies reminiscent of Seneca's unstaged dramas, plays like Shakespeare's *Titus Andronicus*. The rediscovery of Vitruvius' first-century book on Roman architecture, *De Architectura,* in 1414 (it was printed—a new technology—in 1486) also led a generation of fifteenth- and sixteenth-century architects to design and build theaters on what they took to be a Roman model.

In many respects, though, Greek drama only became widely known in Europe in the later seventeenth and eighteenth centuries, where Greek plays often provided the models for contemporary playwrights, such as Jean Racine, as well as for the first operas. And it was only in the nineteenth and twentieth centuries that the restoration of classical amphitheaters and the historical and archaeological recovery of the theatrical practices of classical Athens began to make possible experiments in staging classical Greek drama in ways that attempted to approximate the circumstances of classical theater or that attempted to translate those circumstances into a more effective modern idiom. Since the late nineteenth century, for example, the amphitheater at Epidaurus has often been used to stage classical Greek plays in ways that attempt to approximate the traditions of fifth-century Athenian performance.

hint here may be the figure dancing in the bottom row of figures: He has put on his mask, is wearing the *phallos,* and seems to have a satyr's tail. The central figure seated on the throne, with the *thyrsus* in his hand and vines growing just to the left, is labeled "Dionysus," as though the god were seated among the players (he shares the seat with his wife, Ariadne), but there are several other characters who seem to be in costume; the most identifiable is looking at his mask, wearing a full-body costume and carrying the lion-skin of Heracles. Although the illustration seems to provide some fascinating clues to the nature of theatrical performance, it is also misleading in some obvious ways: Just to the right of Ariadne is a seated female figure holding a mask.

protagonist of the play. The other, younger and beardless figures may compose the chorus. While Hercules holds an individualized mask, the chorus members all hold masks similar to each other, and they wear costumes suggestive of satyrs.

Clearly, of course, much has changed in the last 2,500 years, and performing classical drama poses a series of challenges to modern performers. First, the chorus—both its singing and dancing performance style and its function in the drama—has posed a critical problem for modern companies and audiences: German director Max Reinhardt staged a production of *The Oresteia* in 1919 that was among the first of his productions to experiment with large crowds onstage; later productions have tended to make the chorus smaller and more energetic in an attempt to recapture the exciting movement of the classical chorus. Beyond that, the use of masks in classical theater is no longer conventional on the modern stage, although many modern playwrights—Eugene O'Neill, for example, in *Strange Interlude* (1928)—have experimented with masks in an attempt to render psychological complexity with what they take to be "classical" decorum. The 1981 National Theatre (London) production of *The Oresteia,* directed by Sir Peter Hall, used an entirely male cast and performed the play in masks; this production was the first English-language production of a Greek tragedy to be performed in the classical theater at Epidaurus. Although this effort to "recover" the initial circumstances and flavor of Greek performance has driven many performances, Greek drama has also provided the framework for a number of important **AVANT-GARDE** theatrical experiments in the modern era. Of course, Racine's adaptation of Euripides in *Phaedra* might be considered an "updating" of this kind, but in the modern era, stage practices have often been used not so much to recover the classical past as to restage the plays in a modern idiom. Josef Svoboda's brilliant 1963 production of *Oedipus the King* in Prague, for example, took place on a thirty-foot-wide staircase that rose from the bottom of the orchestra pit to beyond the top of the proscenium. The French director Ariane Mnouchkine staged a production of Euripides' *Iphigeneia at Aulis* as an introduction to her staging of *The Oresteia* in 1990 (under the overall title *Les Atrides*); this brilliant production used makeup, costume, movement, and dance idioms from classical Indian and Indonesian theater, implying that a contemporary staging of the Greek classics might well turn to another tradition of "classical" performance to find a still-living stage language. Both for directors—Peter Sellars' 1993 staging of Aeschylus' *The Persians* framed the play with allusions to the Gulf War—and for writers, such as Heiner Müller (*Medeamaterial*), Charles Mee, Jr. (*Orestes*), Caryl Churchill (*A Mouthful of Birds,* based on Euripides' *The Bacchae,* and written with David Lan), Timberlake Wertenbaker (who has translated several Greek plays), Wole Soyinka (*The Bacchae of Euripides*), and others, the theater and drama of classical Athens continue to provide a way to see and understand ourselves.

Framed by a masked member of the Chorus and Jocasta, Oedipus—played here by Laurence Olivier in the landmark 1945 production of *Oedipus the King*—seems finally to recognize the "truth" that he has been seeking.

Framed in a doorway and lit in profile, Diana Rigg embodies the isolation and abandonment of Euripides' Medea.

Sophocles

Like Aeschylus, Sophocles (c. 496–406 BCE) had an important career in the civic life of Athens as well as in the theater. He was treasurer for the Athenian imperial league, and served as one of ten generals who led a campaign against Samos, an island threatening to secede from the Athenian alliance. In 411 BCE, he was appointed to a committee called to examine Athens' disastrous military campaign in Sicily. Sophocles' greatest achievements, though, were in the theater. Sophocles was responsible for introducing a third actor into dramatic performance, an innovation rapidly imitated by other playwrights, including Aeschylus and Euripides. He also enlarged the size of the chorus from twelve to fifteen men. Sophocles won his first victory, against Aeschylus, in 468 BCE; he was victorious twenty-four times in his career and never finished lower than second in the dramatic competition. Of the 120 plays attributed to Sophocles, only seven survive: *Ajax, Trachiniae, Antigone, Oedipus the King, Electra, Philoctetes,* and *Oedipus at Colonus.* Fragments of a satyr play, *The Trackers,* also remain. The three "Theban" plays—*Antigone, Oedipus the King,* and *Oedipus at Colonus*—are thematically related, but, unlike *The Oresteia* of Aeschylus, were not composed as a trilogy. *Antigone,* a play about Oedipus' daughters after his banishment from Thebes, was composed about 441 BCE; *Oedipus the King* was first produced sometime shortly after the declaration of war with Sparta in 431 BCE; and *Oedipus at Colonus* was first produced after Sophocles' death and Athens' defeat.

Oedipus the King is framed by two acts of identification, recognition, and acknowledgment. The action of the play is about the deepening and horrible understanding of what it means for the hero to recognize who he is—what it means to *be* Oedipus.

OEDIPUS THE KING

This production of Sophocles' *Oedipus the King* adapts the ritualized elements of Greek theater to a modern African setting.

In *The Poetics,* written nearly a century later (about 335 BCE), Aristotle frequently refers to *Oedipus the King* as a definitive example of the form and purpose of tragedy. Modern audiences, though, sometimes find the play baffling, in part because the prophecy delivered to Oedipus' parents, Laius and Jocasta—that their son will murder his father and marry his mother—seems to rob Oedipus of the ability to act, to decide his fate through his own deeds. The tension between destiny and discovery is central to the play; to understand it, we should pay attention to the function of the oracle at Delphi both in the Greek world and in Oedipus the King. The Greeks consulted the oracle at Delphi on a variety of matters, ranging from personal decisions to problems of state. For example, in the play, Laius and Jocasta have consulted the oracle to learn the future of their child, and Oedipus turns to Delphi to find out whether Polybus is actually his father. At the same time, the oracle also speaks on important public issues—about the cause of the plague afflicting Thebes and about what should be done with Oedipus after his blinding. Sophocles lived in an era of increasing skepticism, when political conflict and the rise of rhetorical training raised questions about the nature and significance of truth—even the truth of oracular revelation. It is not surprising that characters in *Oedipus the King* frequently question such prophecy or have difficulty learning how to accept and interpret it, as when Oedipus flees Corinth to avoid murdering his father.

Critical as the prophecy is to Oedipus' life, Oedipus' deeds are really at issue in *Oedipus the King.* Sophocles chose to begin and end his drama on the day of Oedipus' discovery of his own identity. The play focuses less on the prophecy than on the course and meaning of Oedipus' actions, on *how* he comes to recognize himself as the criminal he seeks. Oedipus arrives at this recognition only through an extraordinary effort of action and decision: Oedipus calls for the exile of Laius' murderer; he insults Tiresias when the prophet tries to evade his questions; he accuses Creon; he threatens the old shepherd with torture in order to learn the truth of his birth. The oracle says that Oedipus will commit his terrible crimes of murder and incest, but Oedipus *chooses* the relentless, brutal pursuit of the truth himself, even to the point of his own incrimination and destruction. The tragedy of *Oedipus the King* lies in the fearsome turn of events caused by Oedipus' inflexible compulsion to discover the truth.

Aristotle considers the hero of tragedy at some length, in terms that are at once compelling and confusing, particularly in the case of Oedipus. Aristotle suggests in *The Poetics* that the hero of tragedy should be "a man who is neither a paragon of virtue and justice nor undergoes the change to misfortune through any real badness or wickedness but because of some mistake," a description that leads some to look for the cause of this error within Oedipus' character, in a so-called tragic flaw. But, in fact, when he says that the character's "mistake"—or HAMARTIA—is not the result of "any real badness or wickedness," Aristotle seems to deny that the hero's downfall is the effect of any moral "flaw" at all. It might help us to remember that to his audience, Oedipus may have seemed to share some typically "Athenian" characteristics. Oedipus' passion for inquiry, his abrupt decisiveness, and his impulsive desire to act were seen as the stereotypical traits of Athenian citizens and of Athens as a city. Far from being "flaws," these are just the qualities that made Oedipus (and Athens) successful. What is "tragic" about Oedipus' fate in *Oedipus the King* is the way that his own surest strengths—the aggressive, pragmatic qualities that enabled him to outwit the Sphinx—lead, on this one occasion, to his destruction. Oedipus' "mistake" is neither a moral failing nor a deed that he might have avoided; it is simply that he is Oedipus and acts like Oedipus—intelligent, masterful, assertive, impatient, impulsive. The tragedy lies in the way that acting like Oedipus leads him, as it has always led him in the past, to the discovery of the truth he seeks, this time with ruinous consequences

OEDIPUS THE KING

Sophocles

TRANSLATED BY ROBERT FAGLES

CHARACTERS

OEDIPUS, *king of Thebes*
A PRIEST *of Zeus*
CREON, *brother of Jocasta*
A CHORUS *of Theban citizens and their* LEADER
TIRESIAS, *a blind prophet*
JOCASTA, *the queen, wife of Oedipus*

A MESSENGER *from Corinth*
A SHEPHERD
A MESSENGER *from inside the palace*
ANTIGONE, ISMENE, *daughters of Oedipus and Jocasta*
GUARDS *and* ATTENDANTS
PRIESTS *of Thebes*

TIME AND SCENE: *The royal house of Thebes. Double doors dominate the façade; a stone altar stands at the center of the stage.*

Many years have passed since OEDIPUS *solved the riddle of the Sphinx and ascended the throne of Thebes, and now a plague has struck the city. A procession of* PRIESTS *enters; suppliants, broken and despondent, they carry branches wound in wool and lay them on the altar.*

The doors open. GUARDS *assemble.* OEDIPUS *comes forward, majestic but for a telltale limp, and slowly views the condition of his people.*

OEDIPUS: Oh my children, the new blood of ancient Thebes,
why are you here? Huddling at my altar,
praying before me, your branches wound in wool.
Our city reeks with the smoke of burning incense,
5 rings with cries for the Healer and wailing for the dead.
I thought it wrong, my children, to hear the truth
from others, messengers. Here I am myself—
you all know me, the world knows my fame:
I am Oedipus.

(Helping a PRIEST *to his feet.)*

　　　　　　　　Speak up, old man. Your years,
10 your dignity—you should speak for the others.
Why here and kneeling, what preys upon you so?
Some sudden fear? some strong desire?
You can trust me. I am ready to help,
I'll do anything. I would be blind to misery
15 not to pity my people kneeling at my feet.
PRIEST: O Oedipus, king of the land, our greatest power!
You see us before you now, men of all ages
clinging to your altars. Here are boys,
still too weak to fly from the nest,
20 and here the old, bowed down with the years,
the holy ones—a priest of Zeus myself—and here
the picked, unmarried men, the young hope of Thebes.
And all the rest, your great family gathers now,
branches wreathed, massing in the squares,
25 kneeling before the two temples of queen Athena
or the river-shrine where the embers glow and die
and Apollo sees the future in the ashes.
　　　　　　　　Our city—
look around you, see with your own eyes
our ship pitches wildly, cannot lift her head
30 from the depths, the red waves of death . . .
Thebes is dying. A blight on the fresh crops
and the rich pastures, cattle sicken and die,

and the women die in labor, children stillborn,
and the plague, the fiery god of fever hurls down
on the city, his lightning slashing through us—　35
raging plague in all its vengeance, devastating
the house of Cadmus! And black Death luxuriates
in the raw, wailing miseries of Thebes.

Now we pray to you. You cannot equal the gods,
your children know that, bending at your altar.　40
But we do rate you first of men,
both in the common crises of our lives
and face-to-face encounters with the gods.
You freed us from the Sphinx, you came to Thebes
and cut us loose from the bloody tribute we had paid　45
that harsh, brutal singer. We taught you nothing,
no skill, no extra knowledge, still you triumphed.
A god was with you, so they say, and we believe it—
you lifted up our lives.
　　　　　　　　So now again,
Oedipus, king, we bend to you, your power—　50
we implore you, all of us on our knees:
find us strength, rescue! Perhaps you've heard
the voice of a god or something from other men,
Oedipus . . . what do you know?
The man of experience—you see it every day—　55
his plans will work in a crisis, his first of all.

Act now—we beg you, best of men, raise up our city!
Act, defend yourself, your former glory!
Your country calls you savior now
for your zeal, your action years ago.　60
Never let us remember of your reign:
you helped us stand, only to fall once more.
Oh raise up our city, set us on our feet.
The omens were good that day you brought us joy—
be the same man today!　65
Rule our land, you know you have the power,
but rule a land of the living, not a wasteland.
Ship and towered city are nothing, stripped of men
alive within it, living all as one.
OEDIPUS:　　　　　　　　My children,
I pity you. I see—how could I fail to see　70
what longings bring you here? Well I know
you are sick to death, all of you,
but sick as you are, not one is sick as I.

Your pain strikes each of you alone, each
75   in the confines of himself, no other. But my spirit
grieves for the city, for myself and all of you.
I wasn't asleep, dreaming. You haven't wakened me—
I have wept through the nights, you must know that,
groping, laboring over many paths of thought.
80   After a painful search I found one cure:
I acted at once. I sent Creon,
my wife's own brother, to Delphi—
Apollo the Prophet's oracle—to learn
what I might do or say to save our city.
85   Today's the day. When I count the days gone by
it torments me . . . what is he doing?
Strange, he's late, he's gone too long.
But once he returns, then, then I'll be a traitor
if I do not do all the god makes clear.
90   PRIEST: Timely words. The men over there
are signaling—Creon's just arriving.
OEDIPUS: (*Sighting* CREON, *then turning to the altar.*) Lord Apollo,
let him come with a lucky word of rescue,
shining like his eyes!
PRIEST: Welcome news, I think—he's crowned, look,
95   and the laurel wreath is bright with berries.
OEDIPUS: We'll soon see. He's close enough to hear

(*Enter* CREON *from the side; his face is shaded with a wreath.*)

Creon, prince, my kinsman, what do you bring us?
What message from the god?
CREON: Good news.
I tell you even the hardest things to bear,
100   if they should turn out well, all would be well.
OEDIPUS: Of course, but what were the god's *words?* There's
no hope
and nothing to fear in what you've said so far.
CREON: If you want my report in the presence of these
people . . .

(*Pointing to the* PRIESTS *while drawing* OEDIPUS *toward the palace.*)

I'm ready now, or we might go inside.
OEDIPUS: Speak out,
105   speak to us all. I grieve for these, my people,
far more than I fear for my own life.
CREON: Very well,
I will tell you what I heard from the god.
Apollo commands us—he was quite clear—
"Drive the corruption from the land,
110   don't harbor it any longer, past all cure,
don't nurse it in your soil—root it out!"
OEDIPUS: How can we cleanse ourselves—what rites?
What's the source of the trouble?
CREON: Banish the man, or pay back blood with blood.
115   Murder sets the plague-storm on the city.
OEDIPUS: Whose murder?
Whose fate does Apollo bring to light?
CREON: Our leader,
my lord, was once a man named Laius,
before you came and put us straight on course.
OEDIPUS: I know—
or so I've heard. I never saw the man myself.

CREON: Well, he was killed, and Apollo commands us now—   120
he could not be more clear,
"Pay the killers back—whoever is responsible."
OEDIPUS: Where on earth are they? Where to find it now,
the trail of the ancient guilt so hard to trace?
CREON: "Here in Thebes," he said.   125
Whatever is sought for can be caught, you know,
whatever is neglected slips away.
OEDIPUS: But where,
in the palace, the fields or foreign soil,
where did Laius meet his bloody death?
CREON: He went to consult an oracle, Apollo said,   130
and he set out and never came home again.
OEDIPUS: No messenger, no fellow-traveler saw what
happened?
Someone to cross-examine?
CREON: No,
they were all killed but one. He escaped,
terrified, he could tell us nothing clearly,   135
nothing of what he saw—just one thing.
OEDIPUS: What's that?
One thing could hold the key to it all,
a small beginning give us grounds for hope.
CREON: He said thieves attacked them—a whole band,
not single-handed, cut King Laius down.   140
OEDIPUS: A thief,
so daring, so wild, he'd kill a king? Impossible,
unless conspirators paid him off in Thebes.
CREON: We suspected as much. But with Laius dead
no leader appeared to help us in our troubles.
OEDIPUS: Trouble? Your *king* was murdered—royal blood!   145
What stopped you from tracking down the killer
then and there?
CREON: The singing, riddling Sphinx.
She . . . persuaded us to let the mystery go
and concentrate on what lay at our feet.
OEDIPUS: No,
I'll start again—I'll bring it all to light myself!   150
Apollo is right, and so are you, Creon,
to turn our attention back to the murdered man.
Now you have *me* to fight for you, you'll see:
I am the land's avenger by all rights,
and Apollo's champion too.   155
But not to assist some distant kinsman, no,
for my own sake I'll rid us of this corruption.
Whoever killed the king may decide to kill me too,
with the same violent hand—by avenging Laius
I defend myself.   160

(*To the* PRIESTS.)

Quickly, my children.
Up from the steps, take up your branches now.

(*To the* GUARDS.)

One of you summon the city here before us,
tell them I'll do everything. God help us,
we will see our triumph—or our fall.

(OEDIPUS *and* CREON *enter the palace, followed by the* GUARDS.)

165 PRIEST: Rise, my sons. The kindness we came for
    Oedipus volunteers himself.
    Apollo has sent his word, his oracle—
    Come down, Apollo, save us, stop the plague.

(*The* PRIESTS *rise, remove their branches, and exit to the side. Enter a* CHORUS, *the citizens of Thebes, who have not heard the news that* CREON *brings. They march around the altar, chanting.*)

CHORUS: Zeus!
    Great welcome voice of Zeus, what do you bring?
170 What word from the gold vaults of Delphi
    comes to brilliant Thebes? Racked with terror—
                    terror shakes my heart
    and I cry your wild cries, Apollo, Healer of Delos
    I worship you in dread . . . what now, what is your price?
175 some new sacrifice? some ancient rite from the past
    come round again each spring?—
           what will you bring to birth?
    Tell me, child of golden Hope
        warm voice that never dies!

180 You are the first I call, daughter of Zeus
    deathless Athena—I call your sister Artemis,
    heart of the market place enthroned in glory,
               guardian of our earth—
    I call Apollo, Archer astride the thunderheads of heaven—
185 O triple shield against death, shine before me now!
    If ever, once in the past, you stopped some ruin
    launched against our walls
        you hurled the flame of pain
    far, far from Thebes—you gods
190 come now, come down once more!
                  No, no
    the miseries numberless, grief on grief, no end—
    too much to bear, we are all dying
    O my people . . .
        Thebes like a great army dying
195 and there is no sword of thought to save us, no
    and the fruits of our famous earth, they will not ripen
    no and the women cannot scream their pangs to birth—
    screams for the Healer, children dead in the womb
        and life on life goes down
200   you can watch them go
    like seabirds winging west, outracing the day's fire
    down the horizon, irresistibly
            streaking on to the shores of Evening
                  Death
    so many deaths, numberless deaths on deaths, no end—
205 Thebes is dying, look, her children
    stripped of pity . . .
        generations strewn on the ground
    unburied, unwept, the dead spreading death
    and the young wives and gray-haired mothers with them
210 cling to the altars, trailing in from all over the city—
    Thebes, city of death, one long cortege
        and the suffering rises
            wails for mercy rise
    and the wild hymn for the Healer blazes out
215 clashing with our sobs our cries of mourning—
        O golden daughter of god, send rescue
    radiant as the kindness in your eyes!

Drive him back!—the fever, the god of death
             that raging god of war
not armored in bronze, not shielded now, he burns me, 220
battle cries in the onslaught burning on—
O rout him from our borders!
Sail him, blast him out to the Sea-queen's chamber
             the black Atlantic gulfs
    or the northern harbor, death to all 225
where the Thracian surf comes crashing.
Now what the night spares he comes by day and kills—
the god of death.
           O lord of the stormcloud,
you who twirl the lightning, Zeus, Father,
thunder Death to nothing! 230

Apollo, lord of the light, I beg you—
    whip your longbow's golden cord
showering arrows on our enemies—shafts of power
champions strong before us rushing on!

Artemis, Huntress, 235
torches flaring over the eastern ridges—
           ride Death down in pain!

God of the headdress gleaming gold, I cry to you—
your name and ours are one, Dionysus—
    come with your face aflame with wine 240
              your raving women's cries
    your army on the march! Come with the lightning
come with torches blazing, eyes ablaze with glory!
Burn that god of death that all gods hate!

(OEDIPUS *enters from the palace to address the* CHORUS, *as if addressing the entire city of Thebes.*)

OEDIPUS: You pray to the gods? Let me grant your prayers. 245
    Come, listen to me—do what the plague demands:
    you'll find relief and lift your head from the depths.

    I will speak out now as a stranger to the story,
    a stranger to the crime. If I'd been present then,
    there would have been no mystery, no long hunt 250
    without a clue in hand. So now, counted
    a native Theban years after the murder,
    to all of Thebes I make this proclamation:
    if any one of you knows who murdered Laius,
    the son of Labdacus, I order him to reveal 255
    the whole truth to me. Nothing to fear,
    even if he must denounce himself,
    let him speak up
    and so escape the brunt of the charge—
    he will suffer no unbearable punishment, 260
    nothing worse than exile, totally unharmed.

(OEDIPUS *pauses, waiting for a reply.*)

                        Next,
    if anyone knows the murderer is a stranger,
    a man from alien soil, come, speak up.
    I will give him a handsome reward, and lay up
    gratitude in my heart for him besides. 265

(*Silence again, no reply.*)

But if you keep silent, if anyone panicking,
trying to shield himself or friend or kin,
rejects my offer, then hear what I will do.
I order you, every citizen of the state
270 where I hold throne and power: banish this man—
whoever he may be—never shelter him, never
speak a word to him, never make him partner
to your prayers, your victims burned to the gods.
Never let the holy water touch his hands.
275 Drive him out, each of you, from every home.
He is the plague, the heart of our corruption,
as Apollo's oracle has just revealed to me.
So I honor my obligations:
I fight for the god and for the murdered man.

280 Now my curse on the murderer. Whoever he is,
a lone man unknown in his crime
or one among many, let that man drag out
his life in agony, step by painful step—
I curse myself as well . . . if by any chance
285 he proves to be an intimate of our house,
here at my hearth, with my full knowledge,
may the curse I just called down on him strike me!

These are your orders: perform them to the last.
I command you, for my sake, for Apollo's, for this
    country
290 blasted root and branch by the angry heavens.
Even if god had never urged you on to act,
how could you leave the crime uncleansed so long?
A man so noble—your king, brought down in blood—
you should have searched. But I am the king now,
295 I hold the throne that he held then, possess his bed
and a wife who shares our seed . . . why, our seed
might be the same, children born of the same mother
might have created blood-bonds between us
if his hope of offspring had not met disaster—
300 but fate swooped at his head and cut him short.
So I will fight for him as if he were my father,
stop at nothing, search the world
to lay my hands on the man who shed his blood,
the son of Labdacus descended of Polydorus,
305 Cadmus of old and Agenor, founder of the line:
their power and mine are one.
              Oh dear gods,
my curse on those who disobey these orders!
Let no crops grow out of the earth for them—
shrivel their women, kill their sons,
310 burn them to nothing in this plague
that hits us now, or something even worse.
But you, loyal men of Thebes who approve my actions,
may our champion, Justice, may all the gods
be with us, fight beside us to the end!
315 LEADER: In the grip of your curse, my king, I swear
I'm not the murderer, I cannot point him out.
As for the search, Apollo pressed it on us—
he should name the killer.
  OEDIPUS: Quite right,
but to force the gods to act against their will
320 no man has the power.
  LEADER: Then if I might mention
the next best thing . . .

OEDIPUS: The third best too—
don't hold back, say it.
LEADER: I still believe . . .
Lord Tiresias sees with the eyes of Lord Apollo.
Anyone searching for the truth, my king,
might learn it from the prophet, clear as day. 325
OEDIPUS: I've not been slow with that. On Creon's cue
I sent the escorts, twice, within the hour.
I'm surprised he isn't here.
LEADER: We need him—
without him we have nothing but old, useless rumors.
OEDIPUS: Which rumors? I'll search out every word. 330
LEADER: Laius was killed, they say, by certain travelers.
OEDIPUS: I know—but no one can find the murderer.
LEADER: If the man has a trace of fear in him
he won't stay silent long,
not with your curses ringing in his ears. 335
OEDIPUS: He didn't flinch at murder,
he'll never flinch at words.

(*Enter* TIRESIAS, *the blind prophet, led by a boy with escorts in attendance. He remains at a distance.*)

LEADER: Here is the one who will convict him, look,
they bring him on at last, the seer, the man of god.
The truth lives inside him, him alone. 340
OEDIPUS: O Tiresias,
master of all the mysteries of our life,
all you teach and all you dare not tell,
signs in the heavens, signs that walk the earth!
Blind as you are, you can feel all the more
what sickness haunts our city. You, my lord, 345
are the one shield, the one savior we can find.

We asked Apollo—perhaps the messengers
haven't told you—he sent his answer back:
"Relief from the plague can only come one way.
Uncover the murderers of Laius, 350
put them to death or drive them into exile."
So I beg you, grudge us nothing now, no voice,
no message plucked from the birds, the embers
or the other mantic ways within your grasp.
Rescue yourself, your city, rescue me— 355
rescue everything infected by the dead.
We are in your hands. For a man to help others
with all his gifts and native strength:
that is the noblest work.
TIRESIAS: How terrible—to see the truth
when the truth is only pain to him who sees! 360
I knew it well, but I put it from my mind,
else I never would have come.
OEDIPUS: What's this? Why so grim, so dire?
TIRESIAS: Just send me home. You bear your burdens,
I'll bear mine. It's better that way, 365
please believe me.
OEDIPUS: Strange response . . . unlawful,
unfriendly too to the state that bred and reared you—
you withhold the word of evil.
TIRESIAS: I fail to see
that your own words are so well-timed.
I'd rather not have the same thing said of me . . . 370

OEDIPUS: For the love of god, don't turn away,
    not if you know something. We beg you,
    all of us on our knees.
TIRESIAS: None of you knows—
    and I will never reveal my dreadful secrets,
375   not to say your own.
OEDIPUS: What? You know and you won't tell?
    You're bent on betraying us, destroying Thebes?
TIRESIAS: I'd rather not cause pain for you or me.
    So why this . . . useless interrogation?
380   You'll get nothing from me.
OEDIPUS: Nothing! You,
    you scum of the earth, you'd enrage a heart of stone!
    You won't talk? Nothing moves you?
    Out with it, once and for all!
TIRESIAS: You criticize my temper . . . unaware
385   of the one *you* live with, you revile me.
OEDIPUS: Who could restrain his anger hearing you?
    What outrage—you spurn the city!
TIRESIAS: What will come will come.
    Even if I shroud it all in silence.
390 OEDIPUS: What will come? You're bound to *tell* me that.
TIRESIAS: I will say no more. Do as you like, build your anger
    to whatever pitch you please, rage your worst—
OEDIPUS: Oh I'll let loose, I have such fury in me—
    now I see it all. You helped hatch the plot,
395   you did the work, yes, short of killing him
    with your own hands—and given eyes I'd say
    you did the killing single-handed!
TIRESIAS: Is that so!
    I charge you, then, submit to that decree
    you just laid down: from this day onward
400   speak to no one, not these citizens, not myself.
    You are the curse, the corruption of the land!
OEDIPUS: You, shameless—
    aren't you appalled to start up such a story?
    You think you can get away with this?
TIRESIAS: I have already.
405   The truth with all its power lives inside me.
OEDIPUS: Who primed you for this? Not your prophet's trade.
TIRESIAS: You did, you forced me, twisted it out of me.
OEDIPUS: What? Say it again—I'll understand it better.
TIRESIAS: Didn't you understand, just now?
410   Or are you tempting me to talk?
OEDIPUS: No, I can't say I grasped your meaning.
    Out with it, again!
TIRESIAS: I say you are the murderer you hunt.
OEDIPUS: That obscenity, twice—by god, you'll pay.
415 TIRESIAS: Shall I say more, so you can really rage?
OEDIPUS: Much as you want. Your words are nothing—
    futile.
TIRESIAS: You cannot imagine . . . I tell you,
    you and your loved ones live together in infamy,
    you cannot see how far you've gone in guilt.
420 OEDIPUS: You think you can keep this up and never suffer?
TIRESIAS: Indeed, if the truth has any power.
OEDIPUS: It does
    but not for you, old man. You've lost your power,
    stone-blind, stone-deaf—senses, eyes blind as stone!
TIRESIAS: I pity you, flinging at me the very insults
425   each man here will fling at you so soon.

OEDIPUS: Blind,
    lost in the night, endless night that nursed you!
    You can't hurt me or anyone else who sees the light—
    you can never touch me.
TIRESIAS: True, it is not your fate
    to fall at my hands. Apollo is quite enough,
    and he will take some pains to work this out.   430
OEDIPUS: Creon! Is this conspiracy his or yours?
TIRESIAS: Creon is not your downfall, no, you are your own.
OEDIPUS: O power—
    wealth and empire, skill outstripping skill
    in the heady rivalries of life,
    what envy lurks inside you! Just for this,   435
    the crown the city gave me—I never sought it,
    they laid it in my hands—for this alone, Creon,
    the soul of trust, my loyal friend from the start
    steals against me . . . so hungry to overthrow me
    he sets this wizard on me, this scheming quack,   440
    this fortune-teller peddling lies, eyes peeled
    for his own profit—seer blind in his craft!

Come here, you pious fraud. Tell me,
    when did you ever prove yourself a prophet?
    When the Sphinx, that chanting Fury kept her   445
        deathwatch here,
    why silent then, not a word to set our people free?
    There was a riddle, not for some passer-by to solve—
    it cried out for a prophet. Where were you?
    Did you rise to the crisis? Not a word,
    you and your birds, your gods—nothing.   450
    No, but I came by, Oedipus the ignorant,
    I stopped the Sphinx! With no help from the birds,
    the flight of my own intelligence hit the mark.

And this is the man you'd try to overthrow?
    You think you'll stand by Creon when he's king?   455
    You and the great mastermind—
    you'll pay in tears, I promise you, for this,
    this witch-hunt. If you didn't look so senile
    the lash would teach you what your scheming means!
LEADER: I would suggest his words were spoken in anger,   460
    Oedipus . . . yours too, and it isn't what we need.
    The best solution to the oracle, the riddle
    posed by god—we should look for that.
TIRESIAS: You are the king no doubt, but in one respect,
    at least, I am your equal: the right to reply.   465
    I claim that privilege too.
    I am not your slave. I serve Apollo.
    I don't need Creon to speak for me in public.
          So,
    you mock my blindness? Let me tell you this.
    You with your precious eyes,   470
    you're blind to the corruption of your life,
    to the house you live in, those you live with—
    who *are* your parents? Do you know? All unknowing
    you are the scourge of your own flesh and blood,
    the dead below the earth and the living here above,   475
    and the double lash of your mother and your father's
        curse
    will whip you from this land one day, their footfall
    treading you down in terror, darkness shrouding
    your eyes that now can see the light!

Soon, soon
480   you'll scream aloud—what haven won't reverberate?
What rock of Cithaeron won't scream back in echo?
That day you learn the truth about your marriage,
the wedding-march that sang you into your halls,
the lusty voyage home to the fatal harbor!
485   And a crowd of other horrors you'd never dream
will level you with yourself and all your children.

There. Now smear us with insults—Creon, myself
and every word I've said. No man will ever
be rooted from the earth as brutally as you.
490 OEDIPUS: Enough! Such filth from him? Insufferable—
what, still alive? Get out—
faster, back where you came from—vanish!
TIRESIAS: I would never have come if you hadn't called me here.
OEDIPUS: If I thought you would blurt out such absurdities,
495   you'd have died waiting before I'd had you summoned.
TIRESIAS: Absurd, am I! To you, not to your parents:
the ones who bore you found me sane enough.
OEDIPUS: Parents—who? Wait . . . who is my father?
TIRESIAS: This day will bring your birth and your destruction.
500 OEDIPUS: Riddles—all you can say are riddles, murk and
darkness.
TIRESIAS: Ah, but aren't you the best man alive at solving
riddles?
OEDIPUS: Mock me for that, go on, and you'll reveal my
greatness.
TIRESIAS: Your great good fortune, true, it was your ruin.
OEDIPUS: Not if I saved the city—what do I care?
505 TIRESIAS: Well then, I'll be going.

(*To his* ATTENDANT.)

Take me home, boy.
OEDIPUS: Yes, take him away. You're a nuisance here.
Out of the way, the irritation's gone.

(*Turning his back on* TIRESIAS, *moving toward the palace.*)

TIRESIAS: I will go,
once I have said what I came here to say.
I will never shrink from the anger in your eyes—
510   you can't destroy me. Listen to me closely:
the man you've sought so long, proclaiming,
cursing up and down, the murderer of Laius—
he is here. A stranger,
you may think, who lives among you,
515   he soon will be revealed a native Theban
but he will take no joy in the revelation.
Blind who now has eyes, beggar who now is rich,
he will grope his way toward a foreign soil,
a stick tapping before him step by step.

(OEDIPUS *enters the palace.*)

520   Revealed at last, brother and father both
to the children he embraces, to his mother
son and husband both—he sowed the loins
his father sowed, he spilled his father's blood!

Go in and reflect on that, solve that.
525   And if you find I've lied
from this day onward call the prophet blind.

(TIRESIAS *and the boy exit to the side.*)

CHORUS: Who—
who is the man the voice of god denounces
resounding out of the rocky gorge of Delphi?
    The horror too dark to tell,
whose ruthless bloody hands have done the work?   530
His time has come to fly
    to outrace the stallions of the storm
                 his feet a streak of speed—
Cased in armor, Apollo son of the Father
lunges on him, lightning-bolts afire!   535
And the grim unerring Furies
             closing for the kill.
                    Look,
the word of god has just come blazing
flashing off Parnassus' snowy heights!
    That man who left no trace—   540
after him, hunt him down with all our strength!
Now under bristling timber
    up through rocks and caves he stalks
             like the wild mountain bull—
cut off from men, each step an agony, frenzied, racing blind   545
but he cannot outrace the dread voices of Delphi
ringing out of the heart of Earth,
    the dark wings beating around him shrieking doom
              the doom that never dies, the terror—
The skilled prophet scans the birds and shatters me with   550
terror!
I can't accept him, can't deny him, don't know what to say,
I'm lost, and the wings of dark foreboding beating—
I cannot see what's present, what's still to come . . .
and what could breed a blood feud between
    Laius' house and the son of Polybus?   555
I know of nothing, not in the past and not now,
no charge to bring against our king, no cause
to attack his fame that rings throughout Thebes—
    not without proof—not for the ghost of Laius,
    not to avenge a murder gone without a trace.   560

Zeus and Apollo know, they know, the great masters
    of all the dark and depth of human life.
But whether a mere man can know the truth,
whether a seer can fathom more than I—
there is no test, no certain proof   565
    though matching skill for skill
a man can outstrip a rival. No, not till I see
these charges proved will I side with his accusers.
We saw him then, when the she-hawk swept against him,
saw with our own eyes his skill, his brilliant triumph—   570
    there was the test—he was the joy of Thebes!
    Never will I convict my king, never in my heart.

(*Enter* CREON *from the side.*)

CREON: My fellow-citizens, I hear King Oedipus
levels terrible charges at me. I had to come.
I resent it deeply. If, in the present crisis,
he thinks he suffers any abuse from me,   575
anything I've done or said that offers him
the slightest injury, why, I've no desire
to linger out this life, my reputation in ruins.

580 The damage I'd face from such an accusation
is nothing simple. No, there's nothing worse:
branded a traitor in the city, a traitor
to all of you and my good friends.
LEADER: True,
but a slur might have been forced out of him,
585 by anger perhaps, not any firm conviction.
CREON: The charge was made in public, wasn't it?
I put the prophet up to spreading lies?
LEADER: Such things were said . . .
I don't know with what intent, if any.
590 CREON: Was his glance steady, his mind right
when the charge was brought against me?
LEADER: I really couldn't say, I never look
to judge the ones in power.

(*The doors open.* OEDIPUS *enters.*)

                                    Wait,
here's Oedipus now.
OEDIPUS: You—here? You have the gall
595 to show your face before the palace gates?
You, plotting to kill me, kill the king—
I see it all, the marauding thief himself
scheming to steal my crown and power!
                                    Tell me,
in god's name, what did you take me for,
600 coward or fool, when you spun out your plot?
Your treachery—you think I'd never detect it
creeping against me in the dark? Or sensing it,
not defend myself? Aren't you the fool,
you and your high adventure. Lacking numbers,
605 powerful friends, out for the big game of empire—
you need riches, armies to bring that quarry down!
CREON: Are you quite finished? It's your turn to listen
for just as long as you've . . . instructed me.
Hear me out, then judge me on the facts.
610 OEDIPUS: You've a wicked way with words, Creon,
but I'll be slow to learn—from you.
I find you a menace, a great burden to me.
CREON: Just one thing, hear me out in this.
OEDIPUS: Just one thing,
don't tell *me* you're not the enemy, the traitor.
615 CREON: Look, if you think crude, mindless stubbornness
such a gift, you've lost your sense of balance.
OEDIPUS: If you think you can abuse a kinsman,
then escape the penalty, you're insane.
CREON: Fair enough, I grant you. But this injury
620 you say I've done you, what is it?
OEDIPUS: Did you induce me, yes or no,
to send for that sanctimonious prophet?
CREON: I did. And I'd do the same again.
OEDIPUS: All right then, tell me, how long is it now
625 since Laius . . .
CREON: Laius—what did *he* do?
OEDIPUS: Vanished,
swept from sight, murdered in his tracks.
CREON: The count of the years would run you far back . . .
OEDIPUS: And that far back, was the prophet at his trade?
CREON: Skilled as he is today, and just as honored.

OEDIPUS: Did he ever refer to me then, at that time? 630
CREON: No,
never, at least, when I was in his presence.
OEDIPUS: But you did investigate the murder, didn't you?
CREON: We did our best, of course, discovered nothing.
OEDIPUS: But the great seer never accused me then—why not?
CREON: I don't know. And when I don't, *I* keep quiet. 635
OEDIPUS: You do know this, you'd tell it too—
if you had a shred of decency.
CREON: What?
If I know, I won't hold back.
OEDIPUS: Simply this:
if the two of you had never put heads together,
we would never have heard about *my* killing Laius. 640
CREON: If that's what he says . . . well, you know best.
But now I have a right to learn from you
as you just learned from me.
OEDIPUS: Learn your fill,
you never will convict me of the murder.
CREON: Tell me, you're married to my sister, aren't you? 645
OEDIPUS: A genuine discovery—there's no denying that.
CREON: And you rule the land with her, with equal power?
OEDIPUS: She receives from me whatever she desires.
CREON: And I am the third, all of us are equals?
OEDIPUS: Yes, and it's there you show your stripes— 650
you betray a kinsman.
CREON: Not at all.
Not if you see things calmly, rationally,
as I do. Look at it this way first:
who in his right mind would rather rule
and live in anxiety than sleep in peace? 655
Particularly if he enjoys the same authority.
Not I, I'm not the man to yearn for kingship,
not with a king's power in my hands. Who would?
No one with any sense of self-control.
Now, as it is, you offer me all I need, 660
not a fear in the world. But if I wore the crown . . .
there'd be many painful duties to perform,
hardly to my taste.
                  How could kingship
please me more than influence, power
without a qualm? I'm not that deluded yet, 665
to reach for anything but privilege outright,
profit free and clear.
Now all men sing my praises, all salute me,
now all who request your favors curry mine.
I am their best hope: success rests in me. 670
Why give up that, I ask you, and borrow trouble?
A man of sense, someone who sees things clearly
would never resort to treason.
No, I have no lust for conspiracy in me,
nor could I ever suffer one who does. 675

Do you want proof? Go to Delphi yourself,
examine the oracle and see if I've reported
the message word-for-word. This too:
if you detect that I and the clairvoyant
have plotted anything in common, arrest me, 680
execute me. Not on the strength of one vote,
two in this case, mine as well as yours.

But don't convict me on sheer unverified surmise.
How wrong it is to take the good for bad,
685   purely at random, or take the bad for good.
But reject a friend, a kinsman? I would as soon
tear out the life within us, priceless life itself.
You'll learn this well, without fail, in time.
Time alone can bring the just man to light—
690   the criminal you can spot in one short day.
LEADER: Good advice,
my lord, for anyone who wants to avoid disaster.
Those who jump to conclusions may go wrong.
OEDIPUS: When my enemy moves against me quickly,
plots in secret, I move quickly too, I must.
695   I plot and pay him back. Relax my guard a moment,
waiting his next move—he wins his objective,
I lose mine.
CREON: What do you want?
You want me banished?
OEDIPUS: No, I want you dead.
CREON: Just to show how ugly a grudge can . . .
OEDIPUS: So,
700   still stubborn? you don't think I'm serious?
CREON: I think you're insane.
OEDIPUS: Quite sane—in my behalf.
CREON: Not just as much in mine?
OEDIPUS: You—my mortal enemy?
CREON: What if you're wholly wrong?
OEDIPUS: No matter—I must rule.
CREON: Not if you rule unjustly.
OEDIPUS: Hear him, Thebes, my city!
705 CREON: My city too, not yours alone!
LEADER: Please, my lords.

(*Enter* JOCASTA *from the palace.*)

                    Look, Jocasta's coming,
and just in time too. With her help
you must put this fighting of yours to rest.
JOCASTA: Have you no sense? Poor misguided men,
710   such shouting—why this public outburst?
Aren't you ashamed, with the land so sick,
to stir up private quarrels?

(*To* OEDIPUS.)

Into the palace now. And Creon, you go home.
Why make such a furor over nothing?
715 CREON: My sister, it's dreadful . . . Oedipus, your husband,
he's bent on a choice of punishments for me,
banishment from the fatherland or death.
OEDIPUS: Precisely. I caught him in the act, Jocasta,
plotting, about to stab me in the back.
720 CREON: Never—curse me, let me die and be damned
if I've done you any wrong you charge me with.
JOCASTA: Oh god, believe it, Oedipus,
honor the solemn oath he swears to heaven.
Do it for me, for the sake of all your people.

(*The* CHORUS *begins to chant.*)

725 CHORUS: Believe it, be sensible
    give way, my king, I beg you!

OEDIPUS: What do you want from me, concessions?
CHORUS: Respect him—he's been no fool in the past
and now he's strong with the oath he swears to god.
OEDIPUS: You know what you're asking?   730
CHORUS: I do.
OEDIPUS: Then out with it!
CHORUS: The man's your friend, your kin, he's under oath—
don't cast him out, disgraced,
branded with guilt on the strength of hearsay only.
OEDIPUS: Know full well, if that is what you want
you want me dead or banished from the land.   735
CHORUS: Never—
no, by the blazing Sun, first god of the heavens!
    Stripped of the gods, stripped of loved ones,
let me die by inches if that ever crossed my mind.
But the heart inside me sickens, dies as the land dies
and now on top of the old griefs you pile this,   740
your fury—both of you!
OEDIPUS: Then let him go,
even if it does lead to my ruin, my death
or my disgrace, driven from Thebes for life.
It's you, not him I pity—your words move me.
He, wherever he goes, my hate goes with him.   745
CREON: Look at you, sullen in yielding, brutal in your rage—
you will go too far. It's perfect justice:
natures like yours are hardest on themselves.
OEDIPUS: Then leave me alone—get out!
CREON: I'm going.
You're wrong, so wrong. These men know I'm right.   750

(*Exit to the side. The* CHORUS *turns to* JOCASTA.)

CHORUS: Why do you hesitate, my lady
    why not help him in?
JOCASTA: Tell me what's happened first.
CHORUS: Loose, ignorant talk started dark suspicions
and a sense of injustice cut deeply too.   755
JOCASTA: On both sides?
CHORUS: Oh yes.
JOCASTA: What did they say?
CHORUS: Enough, please, enough! The land's so racked already
or so it seems to me . . .
End the trouble here, just where they left it.
OEDIPUS: You see what comes of your good intentions now?   760
And all because you tried to blunt my anger.
CHORUS: My king,
I've said it once, I'll say it time and again—
    I'd be insane, you know it,
senseless, ever to turn my back on you.
You who set our beloved land—storm-tossed, shattered—   765
straight on course. Now again, good helmsman,
steer us through the storm!

(*The* CHORUS *draws away, leaving* OEDIPUS *and* JOCASTA *side by side.*)

JOCASTA: For the love of god,
Oedipus, tell me too, what is it?
Why this rage? You're so unbending.
OEDIPUS: I will tell you. I respect you, Jocasta,   770
much more than these men here . . .

(*Glancing at the* CHORUS.)

Creon's to blame, Creon schemes against me.
JOCASTA: Tell me clearly, how did the quarrel start?
OEDIPUS: He says I murdered Laius—I am guilty.
775 JOCASTA: How does he know? Some secret knowledge
or simple hearsay?
OEDIPUS: Oh, he sent his prophet in
to do his dirty work. You know Creon,
Creon keeps his own lips clean.
JOCASTA: A prophet?
Well then, free yourself of every charge!
780 Listen to me and learn some peace of mind:
no skill in the world,
nothing human can penetrate the future.
Here is proof, quick and to the point.

An oracle came to Laius one fine day
785 (I won't say from Apollo himself
but his underlings, his priests) and it declared
that doom would strike him down at the hands of a son,
our son, to be born of our own flesh and blood. But Laius,
so the report goes at least, was killed by strangers,
790 thieves, at a place where three roads meet . . . my son—
he wasn't three days old and the boy's father
fastened his ankles, had a henchman fling him away
on a barren, trackless mountain.
                                There, you see?
Apollo brought neither thing to pass. My baby
795 no more murdered his father than Laius suffered—
his wildest fear—death at his own son's hands.
That's how the seers and all their revelations
mapped out the future. Brush them from your mind.
Whatever the god needs and seeks
800 he'll bring to light himself, with ease.
OEDIPUS: Strange,
hearing you just now . . . my mind wandered,
my thoughts racing back and forth.
JOCASTA: What do you mean? Why so anxious, startled?
OEDIPUS: I thought I heard you say that Laius
805 was cut down at a place where three roads meet.
JOCASTA: That was the story. It hasn't died out yet.
OEDIPUS: Where did this thing happen? Be precise.
JOCASTA: A place called Phocis, where two branching roads,
one from Daulia, one from Delphi,
810 come together—a crossroads.
OEDIPUS: When? How long ago?
JOCASTA: The heralds no sooner reported Laius dead
than you appeared and they hailed you king of Thebes.
OEDIPUS: My god, my god—what have you planned to do to me?
815 JOCASTA: What, Oedipus? What haunts you so?
OEDIPUS: Not yet.
Laius—how did he look? Describe him.
Had he reached his prime?
JOCASTA: He was swarthy,
and the gray had just begun to streak his temples,
and his build . . . wasn't far from yours.
OEDIPUS: Oh no no,
820 I think I've just called down a dreadful curse
upon myself—I simply didn't know!

JOCASTA: What are you saying? I shudder to look at you.
OEDIPUS: I have a terrible fear the blind seer can see.
I'll know in a moment. One thing more—
JOCASTA: Anything,
afraid as I am—ask, I'll answer, all I can.   825
OEDIPUS: Did he go with a light or heavy escort,
several men-at-arms, like a lord, a king?
JOCASTA: There were five in the party, a herald among them,
and a single wagon carrying Laius.
OEDIPUS: Ai—
now I can see it all, clear as day.   830
Who told you all this at the time, Jocasta?
JOCASTA: A servant who reached home, the lone survivor.
OEDIPUS: So, could he still be in the palace—even now?
JOCASTA: No indeed. Soon as he returned from the scene
and saw you on the throne with Laius dead and gone,   835
he knelt and clutched my hand, pleading with me
to send him into the hinterlands, to pasture,
far as possible, out of sight of Thebes.
I sent him away. Slave though he was,
he'd earned that favor—and much more.   840
OEDIPUS: Can we bring him back, quickly?
JOCASTA: Easily. Why do you want him so?
OEDIPUS: I am afraid,
Jocasta, I have said too much already.
That man—I've got to see him.
JOCASTA: Then he'll come.
But even I have a right, I'd like to think,   845
to know what's torturing you, my lord.
OEDIPUS: And so you shall—I can hold nothing back from you,
now I've reached this pitch of dark foreboding.
Who means more to me than you? Tell me,
whom would I turn toward but you   850
as I go through all this?

My father was Polybus, king of Corinth.
My mother, a Dorian, Merope. And I was held
the prince of the realm among the people there,
till something struck me out of nowhere,   855
something strange . . . worth remarking perhaps,
hardly worth the anxiety I gave it.
Some man at a banquet who had drunk too much
shouted out—he was far gone, mind you—
that I am not my father's son. Fighting words!   860
I barely restrained myself that day
but early the next I went to mother and father,
questioned them closely, and they were enraged
at the accusation and the fool who let it fly.
So as for my parents I was satisfied,   865
but still this thing kept gnawing at me,
the slander spread—I had to make my move.
                                        And so,
unknown to mother and father I set out for Delphi,
and the god Apollo spurned me, sent me away
denied the facts I came for,   870
but first he flashed before my eyes a future
great with pain, terror, disaster—I can hear him cry,
"You are fated to couple with your mother, you will bring
a breed of children into the light no man can bear to see—
you will kill your father, the one who gave you life!"   875

I heard all that and ran. I abandoned Corinth,
from that day on I gauged its landfall only
by the stars, running, always running
toward some place where I would never see
880   the shame of all those oracles come true.
And as I fled I reached that very spot
where the great king, you say, met his death.

Now, Jocasta, I will tell you all.
Making my way toward this triple crossroad
885   I began to see a herald, then a brace of colts
drawing a wagon, and mounted on the bench . . . a man,
just as you've described him, coming face-to-face,
and the one in the lead and the old man himself
were about to thrust me off the road—brute force—
890   and the one shouldering me aside, the driver,
I strike him in anger!—and the old man, watching me
coming up along his wheels—he brings down
his prod, two prongs straight at my head!
I paid him back with interest!
895   Short work, by god—with one blow of the staff
in this right hand I knock him out of his high seat,
roll him out of the wagon, sprawling headlong—
I killed them all—every mother's son!

Oh, but if there is any blood-tie
900   between Laius and this stranger . . .
what man alive more miserable than I?
More hated by the gods? *I* am the man
no alien, no citizen welcomes to his house,
law forbids it—not a word to me in public,
905   driven out of every hearth and home.
And all these curses I—no one but I
brought down these piling curses on myself!
And you, his wife, I've touched your body with these,
the hands that killed your husband cover you with blood.

910   Wasn't I born for torment? Look me in the eyes!
I am abomination—heart and soul!
I must be exiled, and even in exile
never see my parents, never set foot
on native ground again. Else I am doomed
915   to couple with my mother and cut my father down . . .
Polybus who reared me, gave me life.
                              But why, why?
Wouldn't a man of judgment say—and wouldn't he be
     right—
some savage power has brought this down upon my head?

Oh no, not that, you pure and awesome gods,
920   never let me see that day! Let me slip
from the world of men, vanish without a trace
before I see myself stained with such corruption,
stained to the heart.
     LEADER: My lord, you fill our hearts with fear.
925   But at least until you question the witness,
     do take hope.
     OEDIPUS: Exactly. He is my last hope—
I am waiting for the shepherd. He is crucial.
JOCASTA: And once he appears, what then? Why so urgent?
OEDIPUS: I will tell you. If it turns out that his story
930   matches yours, I've escaped the worst.

JOCASTA: What did I say? What struck you so?
OEDIPUS: You said
     thieves—
he told you a whole band of them murdered Laius.
So, if he still holds to the same number,
I cannot be the killer. One can't equal many.
But if he refers to one man, one alone,   935
clearly the scales come down on me:
I am guilty.
JOCASTA: Impossible. Trust me,
I told you precisely what he said,
and he can't retract it now;
the whole city heard it, not just I.   940
And even if he should vary his first report
by one man more or less, still, my lord,
he could never make the murder of Laius
truly fit the prophecy. Apollo was explicit:
my son was doomed to kill my husband . . . my son,   945
poor defenseless thing, he never had a chance
to kill his father. They destroyed him first.

So much for prophecy. It's neither here nor there.
From this day on, I wouldn't look right or left.
OEDIPUS: True, true. Still, that shepherd,   950
     someone fetch him—now!
JOCASTA: I'll send at once. But do let's go inside.
     I'd never displease you, least of all in this.

(OEDIPUS *and* JOCASTA *enter the palace.*)

CHORUS: Destiny guide me always
     Destiny find me filled with reverence   955
          pure in word and deed.
     Great laws tower above us, reared on high
     born for the brilliant vault of heaven—
          Olympian Sky their only father,
     nothing mortal, no man gave them birth,   960
     their memory deathless, never lost in sleep:
     within them lives a mighty god, the god does not
          grow old.

     Pride breeds the tyrant
     violent pride, gorging, crammed to bursting
          with all that is overripe and rich with ruin—   965
     clawing up to the heights, headlong pride
     crashes down the abyss—sheer doom!
          No footing helps, all foothold lost and gone.
     But the healthy strife that makes the city strong—
     I pray that god will never end that wrestling: 970
     god, my champion, I will never let you go.

     But if any man comes striding, high and mighty
          in all he says and does,
     no fear of justice, no reverence
     for the temples of the gods—   975
          let a rough doom tear him down,
     repay his pride, breakneck, ruinous pride!
     If he cannot reap his profits fairly
          cannot restrain himself from outrage—
     mad, laying hands on the holy things untouchable!   980

          Can such a man, so desperate, still boast
          he can save his life from the flashing bolts of god?

985

If all such violence goes with honor now
    why join the sacred dance?

Never again will I go reverent to Delphi,
    the inviolate heart of Earth
or Apollo's ancient oracle at Abae
or Olympia of the fires—
    unless these prophecies all come true
990
for all mankind to point toward in wonder.
King of kings, if you deserve your titles
    Zeus, remember, never forget!
You and your deathless, everlasting reign.

995
They are dying, the old oracles sent to Laius,
    now our masters strike them off the rolls.
    Nowhere Apollo's golden glory now—
        the gods, the gods go down.

(*Enter* JOCASTA *from the palace, carrying a suppliant's branch wound in wool.*)

JOCASTA: Lords of the realm, it occurred to me,
    just now, to visit the temples of the gods,
1000
so I have my branch in hand and incense too.

Oedipus is beside himself. Racked with anguish,
    no longer a man of sense, he won't admit
the latest prophecies are hollow as the old—
he's at the mercy of every passing voice
1005
if the voice tells of terror.
I urge him gently, nothing seems to help,
so I turn to you, Apollo, you are nearest.

(*Placing her branch on the altar, while an old herdsman enters from the side, not the one just summoned by the King but an unexpected* MESSENGER *from Corinth.*)

I come with prayers and offerings . . . I beg you,
    cleanse us, set us free of defilement!
1010
Look at us, passengers in the grip of fear,
    watching the pilot of the vessel go to pieces.
MESSENGER: (*Approaching* JOCASTA *and the* CHORUS.) Strangers,
    please, I wonder if you could lead us
to the palace of the king . . . I think it's Oedipus.
Better, the man himself—you know where he is?
1015 LEADER: This is his palace, stranger. He's inside.
    But here is his queen, his wife and mother
    of his children.
MESSENGER: Blessings on you, noble queen,
    queen of Oedipus crowned with all your family—
    blessings on you always!
1020 JOCASTA: And the same to you, stranger, you deserve it . . .
    such a greeting. But what have you come for?
    Have you brought us news?
MESSENGER: Wonderful news—
    for the house, my lady, for your husband too.
JOCASTA: Really, what? Who sent you?
MESSENGER: Corinth.
1025 I'll give you the message in a moment.
    You'll be glad of it—how could you help it?—
    though it costs a little sorrow in the bargain.
JOCASTA: What can it be, with such a double edge?

MESSENGER: The people there, they want to make your Oedipus
    king of Corinth, so they're saying now.   1030
JOCASTA: Why? Isn't old Polybus still in power?
MESSENGER: No more. Death has got him in the tomb.
JOCASTA: What are you saying? Polybus, dead?—dead?
MESSENGER: If not,
    if I'm not telling the truth, strike me dead too.
JOCASTA: (*To a* SERVANT.) Quickly, go to your master, tell him
    this!   1035

You prophecies of the gods, where are you now?
This is the man that Oedipus feared for years,
he fled him, not to kill him—and now he's dead,
quite by chance, a normal, natural death,
not murdered by his son.   1040
OEDIPUS: (*Emerging from the palace.*)
                Dearest,
    what now? Why call me from the palace?
JOCASTA: (*Bringing the* MESSENGER *closer.*) Listen to *him,* see for
    yourself what all
    those awful prophecies of god have come to.
OEDIPUS: And who is he? What can he have for me?
JOCASTA: He's from Corinth, he's come to tell you   1045
    your father is no more—Polybus—he's dead!
OEDIPUS: (*Wheeling on the* MESSENGER.) What? Let me have it
    from your lips.
MESSENGER: Well,
    if that's what you want first, then here it is:
    make no mistake, Polybus is dead and gone.
OEDIPUS: How—murder? sickness?—what? what killed him?   1050
MESSENGER: A light tip of the scales can put old bones to rest.
OEDIPUS: Sickness then—poor man, it wore him down.
MESSENGER: That,
    and the long count of years he'd measured out.
OEDIPUS: So!
    Jocasta, why, why look to the Prophet's hearth,
    the fires of the future? Why scan the birds   1055
    that scream above our heads? They winged me on
    to the murder of my father, did they? That was my doom?
    Well look, he's dead and buried, hidden under the earth,
    and here I am in Thebes, I never put hand to sword—
    unless some longing for me wasted him away,   1060
    then in a sense you'd say I caused his death.
    But now, all those prophecies I feared—Polybus
    packs them off to sleep with him in hell!
    They're nothing, worthless.
JOCASTA: There.
    Didn't I tell you from the start?   1065
OEDIPUS: So you did. I was lost in fear.
JOCASTA: No more, sweep it from your mind forever.
OEDIPUS: But my mother's bed, surely I must fear—
JOCASTA: Fear?
    What should a man fear? It's all chance,
    chance rules our lives. Not a man on earth   1070
    can see a day ahead, groping through the dark.
    Better to live at random, best we can.
    And as for this marriage with your mother—
    have no fear. Many a man before you,
    in his dreams, has shared his mother's bed.   1075
    Take such things for shadows, nothing at all—

Live, Oedipus,
as if there's no tomorrow!

OEDIPUS: Brave words,
and you'd persuade me if mother weren't alive.

1080   But mother lives, so for all your reassurances
I live in fear, I must.

JOCASTA: But your father's death,
that, at least, is a great blessing, joy to the eyes!

OEDIPUS: Great, I know . . . but I fear *her*—she's still alive.

MESSENGER: Wait, who is this woman, makes you so afraid?

1085   OEDIPUS: Merope, old man. The wife of Polybus.

MESSENGER: The queen? What's there to fear in her?

OEDIPUS: A dreadful prophecy, stranger, sent by the gods.

MESSENGER: Tell me, could you? Unless it's forbidden
other ears to hear.

OEDIPUS: Not at all.

1090   Apollo told me once—it is my fate—
I must make love with my own mother,
shed my father's blood with my own hands.
So for years I've given Corinth a wide berth,
and it's been my good fortune too. But still,

1095   to see one's parents and look into their eyes
is the greatest joy I know.

MESSENGER: You're afraid of that?
That kept you out of Corinth?

OEDIPUS: My *father*, old man—
so I wouldn't kill my father.

MESSENGER: So that's it.
Well then, seeing I came with such good will, my king,

1100   why don't I rid you of that old worry now?

OEDIPUS: What a rich reward you'd have for that!

MESSENGER: What do you think I came for, majesty?
So you'd come home and I'd be better off.

OEDIPUS: Never, I will never go near my parents.

1105   MESSENGER: My boy, it's clear, you don't know what you're
doing.

OEDIPUS: What do you mean, old man? For god's sake, explain.

MESSENGER: If you ran from *them,* always dodging home . . .

OEDIPUS: Always, terrified Apollo's oracle might come true—

MESSENGER: And you'd be covered with guilt, from both your
parents.

1110   OEDIPUS: That's right, old man, that fear is always
with me.

MESSENGER: Don't you know? You've really nothing to fear.

OEDIPUS: But why? If I'm their son—Merope, Polybus?

MESSENGER: Polybus was nothing to you, that's why, not in
blood.

OEDIPUS: What are you saying—Polybus was not my father?

1115   MESSENGER: No more than I am. He and I are equals.

OEDIPUS: My father—
how can my father equal nothing? You're nothing to me!

MESSENGER: Neither was he, no more your father than I am.

OEDIPUS: Then why did he call me his son?

MESSENGER: You were a gift,
years ago—know for a fact he took you

1120   from my hands.

OEDIPUS: No, from another's hands?
Then how could he love me so? He loved me, deeply . . .

MESSENGER: True, and his early years without a child
made him love you all the more.

OEDIPUS: And you, did you . . .
buy me? find me by accident?

MESSENGER: I stumbled on you,
down the woody flanks of Mount Cithaeron.   1125

OEDIPUS: So close,
what were you doing here, just passing through?

MESSENGER: Watching over my flocks, grazing them on the
slopes.

OEDIPUS: A herdsman, were you? A vagabond, scraping for
wages?

MESSENGER: Your savior too, my son, in your worst hour.

OEDIPUS: Oh—
when you picked me up, was I in pain? What exactly?   1130

MESSENGER: Your ankles . . . they tell the story. Look at
them.

OEDIPUS: Why remind me of that, that old affliction?

MESSENGER: Your ankles were pinned together. I set you free.

OEDIPUS: That dreadful mark—I've had it from the cradle.

MESSENGER: And you got your name from that misfortune   1135
too,
the name's still with you.

OEDIPUS: Dear god, who did it?—
mother? father? Tell me.

MESSENGER: I don't know.
The one who gave you to me, he'd know more.

OEDIPUS: What? You took me from someone else?
You didn't find me yourself?   1140

MESSENGER: No sir,
another shepherd passed you on to me.

OEDIPUS: Who? Do you know? Describe him.

MESSENGER: He called himself a servant of . . .
if I remember rightly—Laius.

(JOCASTA *turns sharply.*)

OEDIPUS: The king of the land who ruled here long ago?   1145

MESSENGER: That's the one. That herdsman was *his* man.

OEDIPUS: Is he still alive? Can I see him?

MESSENGER: They'd know best, the people of these parts.

(OEDIPUS *and the* MESSENGER *turn to the* CHORUS.)

OEDIPUS: Does anyone know that herdsman,
the one he mentioned? Anyone seen him   1150
in the fields, here in the city? Out with it!
The time has come to reveal this once for all.

LEADER: I think he's the very shepherd you wanted to see,
a moment ago. But the queen, Jocasta,
she's the one to say.   1155

OEDIPUS: Jocasta,
you remember the man we just sent for?
Is *that* the one he means?

JOCASTA: That man . . .
why ask? Old shepherd, talk, empty nonsense,
don't give it another thought, don't even think—

OEDIPUS: What—give up now, with a clue like this?   1160
Fail to solve the mystery of my birth?
Not for all the world!

JOCASTA: Stop—in the name of god,
if you love your own life, call off this search!
My suffering is enough.

OEDIPUS: Courage!
1165   Even if my mother turns out to be a slave,
        and I a slave, three generations back,
        you would not seem common.
JOCASTA: Oh no,
        listen to me, I beg you, don't do this.
OEDIPUS: Listen to you? No more. I must know it all,
1170   must see the truth at last.
JOCASTA: No, please—
        for your sake—I want the best for you!
OEDIPUS: Your best is more than I can bear.
JOCASTA: You're doomed—
        may you never fathom who you are!
OEDIPUS: (*To a servant.*) Hurry, fetch me the herdsman, now!
1175   Leave her to glory in her royal birth.
JOCASTA: Aieeeeee—
                man of agony—
        that is the only name I have for you,
        that, no other—ever, ever, ever!

(*Flinging through the palace doors. A long, tense silence follows.*)

LEADER: Where's she gone, Oedipus?
1180   Rushing off, such wild grief . . .
        I'm afraid that from this silence
        something monstrous may come bursting forth.
OEDIPUS: Let it burst! Whatever will, whatever must!
        I must know my birth, no matter how common
1185   it may be—I must see my origins face-to-face.
        She perhaps, she with her woman's pride
        may well be mortified by my birth,
        but I, I count myself the son of Chance,
        the great goddess, giver of all good things—
1190   I'll never see myself disgraced. She is my mother!
        And the moons have marked me out, my blood-brothers,
        one moon on the wane, the next moon great with power.
        That is my blood, my nature—I will never betray it,
        never fail to search and learn my birth!
1195 CHORUS: Yes—if I am a true prophet
            if I can grasp the truth,
            by the boundless skies of Olympus,
        at the full moon of tomorrow, Mount Cithaeron
        you will know how Oedipus glories in you—
1200   you, his birthplace, nurse, his mountain-mother!
        And we will sing you, dancing out your praise—
        you lift our monarch's heart!
            Apollo, Apollo, god of the wild cry
                may our dancing please you!
                            Oedipus—
1205   son, dear child, who bore you?
        Who of the nymphs who seem to live forever
        mated with Pan, the mountain-striding Father?
        Who was your mother? who, some bride of Apollo
        the god who loves the pastures spreading toward the sun?
1210   Or was it Hermes, king of the lightning ridges?
        Or Dionysus, lord of frenzy, lord of the barren peaks—
        did he seize you in his hands, dearest of all his lucky
            finds?—
            found by the nymphs, their warm eyes dancing, gift
        to the lord who loves them dancing out his joy!

(OEDIPUS *strains to see a figure coming from the distance. Attended by
palace* GUARDS, *an old* SHEPHERD *enters slowly, reluctant to approach
the king.*)

OEDIPUS: I never met the man, my friends . . . still,   1215
        if I had to guess, I'd say that's the shepherd,
        the very one we've looked for all along.
        Brothers in old age, two of a kind,
        he and our guest here. At any rate
        the ones who bring him in are my own men,   1220
        I recognize them.

(*Turning to the* LEADER.)

                    But you know more than I,
        you should, you've seen the man before.
LEADER: I know him, definitely. One of Laius' men,
        a trusty shepherd, if there ever was one.
OEDIPUS: You, I ask you first, stranger,   1225
        you from Corinth—is this the one you mean?
MESSENGER: You're looking at him. He's your man.
OEDIPUS: (*To the* SHEPHERD.) You, old man, come over here—
        look at me. Answer all my questions.
        Did you ever serve King Laius?   1230
SHEPHERD: So I did . . .
        a slave, not bought on the block though,
        born and reared in the palace.
OEDIPUS: Your duties, your kind of work?
SHEPHERD: Herding the flocks, the better part of my life.
OEDIPUS: Where, mostly? Where did you do your grazing?   1235
SHEPHERD: Well,
        Cithaeron sometimes, or the foothills round about.
OEDIPUS: This man—you know him? ever see him there?
SHEPHERD: (*Confused, glancing from the* MESSENGER *to the king.*)
        Doing what? What man do you mean?
OEDIPUS: (*Pointing to the* MESSENGER.) This one here—ever
        have dealings with him?
SHEPHERD: Not so I could say, but give me a chance,   1240
        my memory's bad . . .
MESSENGER: No wonder he doesn't know me, master.
        But let me refresh his memory for him.
        I'm sure he recalls old times we had
        on the slopes of Mount Cithaeron;   1245
        he and I, grazing our flocks, he with two
        and I with one—we both struck up together,
        three whole seasons, six months at a stretch
        from spring to the rising of Arcturus in the fall,
        then with winter coming on I'd drive my herds   1250
        to my own pens, and back he'd go with his
        to Laius' folds.

(*To the* SHEPHERD.)

                Now that's how it was,
        wasn't it—yes or no?
SHEPHERD: Yes, I suppose . . .
        it's all so long ago.
MESSENGER: Come, tell me,
        you gave me a child back then, a boy, remember?   1255
        A little fellow to rear, my very own.
SHEPHERD: What? Why rake up that again?

MESSENGER: Look, here he is, my fine old friend—
 the same man who was just a baby then.
1260 SHEPHERD: Damn you, shut your mouth—quiet!
OEDIPUS: Don't lash out at him, old man—
 you need lashing more than he does.
SHEPHERD: Why,
 master, majesty—what have I done wrong?
OEDIPUS: You won't answer his question about the boy.
1265 SHEPHERD: He's talking nonsense, wasting his breath.
OEDIPUS: So, you won't talk willingly—
 then you'll talk with pain.

(*The* GUARDS *seize the* SHEPHERD.)

SHEPHERD: No, dear god, don't torture an old man!
OEDIPUS: Twist his arms back, quickly!
SHEPHERD: God help us, why?
1270 what more do you need to know?
OEDIPUS: Did you give him that child? He's asking.
SHEPHERD: I did . . . I wish to god I'd died that day.
OEDIPUS: You've got your wish if you don't tell the truth.
SHEPHERD: The more I tell, the worse the death I'll die.
1275 OEDIPUS: Our friend here wants to stretch things out,
 does he?

(*Motioning to his men for torture.*)

SHEPHERD: No, no, I gave it to him—I just said so.
OEDIPUS: Where did you get it? Your house? Someone else's?
SHEPHERD: It wasn't mine, no, I got it from . . . someone.
OEDIPUS: Which one of them?

(*Looking at the citizens.*)

        Whose house?
SHEPHERD: No—
1280 god's sake, master, no more questions!
OEDIPUS: You're a dead man if I have to ask again.
SHEPHERD: Then—the child came from the house . . .
 of Laius.
OEDIPUS: A slave? or born of his own blood?
SHEPHERD: Oh no,
1285 I'm right at the edge, the horrible truth—I've got to say it!
OEDIPUS: And I'm at the edge of hearing horrors, yes, but I
  must hear!
SHEPHERD: All right! His son, they said it was—his son!
 But the one inside, your wife,
 she'd tell it best.
OEDIPUS: My wife—
1290 *she* gave it to you?
SHEPHERD: Yes, yes, my king.
OEDIPUS: Why, what for?
SHEPHERD: To kill it.
OEDIPUS: Her own child,
1295 how could she?
SHEPHERD: She was afraid—
 frightening prophecies.
OEDIPUS: What?
SHEPHERD: They said—
 he'd kill his parents.
1300 OEDIPUS: But you gave him to this old man—why?

SHEPHERD: I pitied the little baby, master,
 hoped he'd take him off to his own country,
 far away, but he saved him for this, this fate.
 If you are the man he says you are, believe me,
 you were born for pain. 1305
OEDIPUS: O god—
 all come true, all burst to light!
 O light—now let me look my last on you!
 I stand revealed at last—
 cursed in my birth, cursed in marriage,
 cursed in the lives I cut down with these hands! 1310

(*Rushing through the doors with a great cry. The Corinthian* MESSENGER, *the* SHEPHERD, *and* ATTENDANTS *exit slowly to the side.*)

CHORUS: O the generations of men
 the dying generations—adding the total
 of all your lives I find they come to nothing . . .
  does there exist, is there a man on earth
 who seizes more joy than just a dream, a vision? 1315
 And the vision no sooner dawns than dies
 blazing into oblivion.

 You are my great example, you, your life
 your destiny, Oedipus, man of misery—
 I count no man blest. 1320

    You outranged all men!
  Bending your bow to the breaking-point
 you captured priceless glory, O dear god,
 and the Sphinx came crashing down,
     the virgin, claws hooked
 like a bird of omen singing, shrieking death— 1325
 like a fortress reared in the face of death
 you rose and saved our land.

 From that day on we called you king
 we crowned you with honors, Oedipus, towering over all—
 mighty king of the seven gates of Thebes. 1330
 But now to hear your story—is there a man more agonized?
 More wed to pain and frenzy? Not a man on earth,
 the joy of your life ground down to nothing
 O Oedipus, name for the ages—
  one and the same wide harbor served you 1335
       son and father both
 son and father came to rest in the same bridal chamber.
 How, how could the furrows your father plowed
 bear you, your agony, harrowing on
 in silence O so long? 1340

      But now for all your power
 Time, all-seeing Time has dragged you to the light,
 judged your marriage monstrous from the start—
 the son and the father tangling, both one—
 O child of Laius, would to god
  I'd never seen you, never never! 1345
   Now I weep like a man who wails the dead
 and the dirge comes pouring forth with all my heart!
 I tell you the truth, you gave me life
 my breath leapt up in you
 and now you bring down night upon my eyes. 1350

(*Enter a* MESSENGER *from the palace.*)

MESSENGER: Men of Thebes, always first in honor,
what horrors you will hear, what you will see,
what a heavy weight of sorrow you will shoulder . . .
if you are true to your birth, if you still have
1355 some feeling for the royal house of Thebes.
I tell you neither the waters of the Danube
nor the Nile can wash this palace clean.
Such things it hides, it soon will bring to light—
terrible things, and none done blindly now,
1360 all done with a will. The pains
we inflict upon ourselves hurt most of all.
LEADER: God knows we have pains enough already.
What can you add to them?
MESSENGER: The queen is dead.
LEADER: Poor lady—how?
1365 MESSENGER: By her own hand. But you are spared the worst,
you never had to watch . . . I saw it all,
and with all the memory that's in me
you will learn what that poor woman suffered.

Once she'd broken in through the gates,
1370 dashing past us, frantic, whipped to fury,
ripping her hair out with both hands—
straight to her rooms she rushed, flinging herself
across the bridal-bed, doors slamming behind her—
once inside, she wailed for Laius, dead so long,
1375 remembering how she bore his child long ago,
the life that rose up to destroy him, leaving
its mother to mother living creatures
with the very son she'd borne.
Oh how she wept, mourning the marriage-bed
1380 where she let loose that double brood—monsters—
husband by her husband, children by her child.
                         And then—
but how she died is more than I can say. Suddenly
Oedipus burst in, screaming, he stunned us so
we couldn't watch her agony to the end,
1385 our eyes were fixed on him. Circling
like a maddened beast, stalking, here, there,
crying out to us—
                    Give him a sword! His wife,
no wife, his mother, where can he find the mother earth
that cropped two crops at once, himself and all his
   children?
1390 He was raging—one of the dark powers pointing the way,
none of us mortals crowding around him, no,
with a great shattering cry—someone, something leading
   him on—
he hurled at the twin doors and bending the bolts back
out of their sockets, crashed through the chamber.
1395 And there we saw the woman hanging by the neck,
cradled high in a woven noose, spinning,
swinging back and forth. And when he saw her,
giving a low, wrenching sob that broke our hearts,
slipping the halter from her throat, he eased her down,
1400 in a slow embrace he laid her down, poor thing . . .
then, what came next, what horror we beheld!

He rips off her brooches, the long gold pins
holding her robes—and lifting them high,
looking straight up into the points,

he digs them down the sockets of his eyes, crying, "You, 1405
you'll see no more the pain I suffered, all the pain I caused!
Too long you looked on the ones you never should have seen,
blind to the ones you longed to see, to know! Blind
from this hour on! Blind in the darkness—blind!"
His voice like a dirge, rising, over and over 1410
raising the pins, raking them down his eyes.
And at each stroke blood spurts from the roots,
splashing his beard, a swirl of it, nerves and clots—
black hail of blood pulsing, gushing down.

These are the griefs that burst upon them both, 1415
coupling man and woman. The joy they had so lately,
the fortune of their old ancestral house
was deep joy indeed. Now, in this one day,
wailing, madness and doom, death, disgrace,
all the griefs in the world that you can name, 1420
all are theirs forever.
LEADER: Oh poor man, the misery—
has he any rest from pain now?

(A voice within, in torment.)

MESSENGER: He's shouting,
"Loose the bolts, someone, show me to all of Thebes!
My father's murderer, my mother's—"
No, I can't repeat it, it's unholy. 1425
Now he'll tear himself from his native earth,
not linger, curse the house with his own curse.
But he needs strength, and a guide to lead him on.
This is sickness more than he can bear.

(The palace doors open.)

                              Look,
he'll show you himself. The great doors are opening— 1430
you are about to see a sight, a horror
even his mortal enemy would pity.

(Enter OEDIPUS, blinded, led by a boy. He stands at the palace steps,
as if surveying his people once again.)

CHORUS: Oh, the terror—
the suffering, for all the world to see,
the worst terror that ever met my eyes.
What madness swept over you? What god, 1435
what dark power leapt beyond all bounds,
beyond belief, to crush your wretched life?—
godforsaken, cursed by the gods!
I pity you but I can't bear to look.
I've much to ask, so much to learn, 1440
so much fascinates my eyes,
but you . . . I shudder at the sight.
OEDIPUS: Oh, Ohh—
the agony! I am agony—
where am I going? where on earth?
      where does all this agony hurl me? 1445
where's my voice?—
            winging, swept away on a dark tide—
   My destiny, my dark power, what a leap you made!
CHORUS: To the depths of terror, too dark to hear, to see.
OEDIPUS: Dark, horror of darkness 1450

my darkness, drowning, swirling around me
crashing wave on wave—unspeakable, irresistible
  headwind, fatal harbor! Oh again,
 the misery, all at once, over and over
1455 the stabbing daggers, stab of memory
 raking me insane.
CHORUS: No wonder you suffer
 twice over, the pain of your wounds,
 the lasting grief of pain.
OEDIPUS: Dear friend, still here?
 Standing by me, still with a care for me,
1460 the blind man? Such compassion,
   loyal to the last. Oh it's you,
 I know you're here, dark as it is
 I'd know you anywhere, your voice—
it's yours, clearly yours.
CHORUS: Dreadful, what you've done . . .
1465 how could you bear it, gouging out your eyes?
 What superhuman power drove you on?
OEDIPUS: Apollo, friends, Apollo—
 he ordained my agonies—these, my pains on pains!
 But the hand that struck my eyes was mine,
1470 mine alone—no one else—
   I did it all myself!
 What good were eyes to me?
 Nothing I could see could bring me joy.
CHORUS: No, no, exactly as you say.
OEDIPUS: What can I ever see?
1475 What love, what call of the heart
 can touch my ears with joy? Nothing, friends.
 Take me away, far, far from Thebes,
 quickly, cast me away, my friends—
 this great murderous ruin, this man cursed to heaven,
1480 the man the deathless gods hate most of all!
CHORUS: Pitiful, you suffer so, you understand so much . . .
 I wish you had never known.
OEDIPUS: Die, die—
 whoever he was that day in the wilds
 who cut my ankles free of the ruthless pins,
1485 he pulled me clear of death, he saved my life
 for this, this kindness—
   Curse him, kill him!
 If I'd died then, I'd never have dragged myself,
 my loved ones through such hell.
CHORUS: Oh if only . . . would to god.
1490 OEDIPUS: I'd never have come to
 this,
   my father's murderer—never been branded
 mother's husband, all men see me now! Now,
 loathed by the gods, son of the mother I defiled
 coupling in my father's bed, spawning lives in the loins
1495 that spawned my wretched life. What grief can crown this
 grief?
   It's mine alone, my destiny—I am Oedipus!
CHORUS: How can I say you've chosen for the best?
 Better to die than be alive and blind.
OEDIPUS: What I did was best—don't lecture me,
1500 no more advice. I, with *my* eyes,
 how could I look my father in the eyes
 when I go down to death? Or mother, so abused . . .

I have done such things to the two of them,
crimes too huge for hanging.
    Worse yet,
the sight of my children, born as they were born, 1505
how could I long to look into their eyes?
No, not with these eyes of mine, never.
Not this city either, her high towers,
the sacred glittering images of her gods—
I am misery! I, her best son, reared 1510
as no other son of Thebes was ever reared,
I've stripped myself, I gave the command myself.
All men must cast away the great blasphemer,
the curse now brought to light by the gods,
the son of Laius—I, my father's son! 1515

Now I've exposed my guilt, horrendous guilt,
could I train a level glance on you, my countrymen?
Impossible! No, if I could just block off my ears,
the springs of hearing, I would stop at nothing—
I'd wall up my loathsome body like a prison, 1520
blind to the sound of life, not just the sight.
Oblivion—what a blessing . . .
for the mind to dwell a world away from pain.

O Cithaeron, why did you give me shelter?
Why didn't you take me, crush my life out on the spot? 1525
I'd never have revealed my birth to all mankind.

O Polybus, Corinth, the old house of my fathers,
so I believed—what a handsome prince you raised—
under the skin, what sickness to the core.
Look at me! Born of outrage, outrage to the core. 1530
O triple roads—it all comes back, the secret,
dark ravine, and the oaks closing in
where the three roads join . . .
You drank my father's blood, my own blood
spilled by my own hands—you still remember me? 1535
What things you saw me do? Then I came here
and did them all once more!
    Marriages! O marriage,
you gave me birth, and once you brought me into the
 world
you brought my sperm rising back, springing to light,
fathers, brothers, sons—one murderous breed— 1540
brides, wives, mothers. The blackest things
a man can do, I have done them all!
    No more—
it's wrong to name what's wrong to do. Quickly,
for the love of god, hide me somewhere,
kill me, hurl me into the sea 1545
where you can never look on me again.

(*Beckoning to the* CHORUS *as they shrink away.*)

    Closer,
it's all right. Touch the man of grief.
Do. Don't be afraid. My troubles are mine
and I am the only man alive who can sustain them.

(*Enter* CREON *from the palace, attended by palace* GUARDS.)

LEADER: Put your requests to Creon. Here he is, 1550
just when we need him. He'll have a plan, he'll act.

Now that he's the sole defense of the country
in your place.
OEDIPUS: Oh no, what can I say to him?
How can I ever hope to win his trust?
1555 I wronged him so, just now, in every way.
You must see that—I was so wrong, so wrong.
CREON: I haven't come to mock you, Oedipus,
or to criticize your former failings.

(*Turning to the* GUARDS.)

                              You there,
have you lost all respect for human feelings?
1560 At least revere the Sun, the holy fire
that keeps us all alive. Never expose a thing
of guilt and holy dread so great it appalls
the earth, the rain from heaven, the light of day!
Get him into the halls—quickly as you can.
1565 Piety demands no less. Kindred alone
should see a kinsman's shame. This is obscene.
OEDIPUS: Please, in god's name . . . you wipe my fears away,
coming so generously to me, the worst of men.
Do one thing more, for your sake, not mine.
1570 CREON: What do you want? Why so insistent?
OEDIPUS: Drive me out of the land at once, far from sight,
where I can never hear a human voice.
CREON: I'd have done that already, I promise you.
First I wanted the god to clarify my duties.
1575 OEDIPUS: The god? His command was clear, every word:
death for the father-killer, the curse—
he said destroy me!
CREON: So he did. Still. In such a crisis
it's better to ask precisely what to do.
OEDIPUS: So miserable—
1580 you would consult the god about a man like me?
CREON: By all means. And this time, I assume,
even you will obey the god's decrees.
OEDIPUS: I will,
I will. And you, I command you—I beg you . . .
the woman inside, bury her as you see fit.
1585 It's the only decent thing,
to give your own the last rites. As for me,
never condemn the city of my fathers
to house my body, not while I'm alive, no,
let me live on the mountains, on Cithaeron,
1590 my favorite haunt, I have made it famous.
Mother and father marked out that rock
to be my everlasting tomb—buried alive.
Let me die there, where they tried to kill me.

Oh but this I know: no sickness can destroy me,
1595 nothing can. I would never have been saved
from death—I have been saved
for something great and terrible, something strange.
Well let my destiny come and take me on its way!
About my children, Creon, the boys at least,
1600 don't burden yourself. They're men,
wherever they go, they'll find the means to live.
But my two daughters, my poor helpless girls,
clustering at our table, never without me
hovering near them . . . whatever I touched,

they always had their share. Take care of them, 1605
I beg you. Wait, better—permit me, would you?
Just to touch them with my hands and take
our fill of tears. Please . . . my king.
Grant it, with all your noble heart.
If I could hold them, just once, I'd think 1610
I had them with me, like the early days
when I could see their eyes.

(ANTIGONE *and* ISMENE, *two small children, are led in from the palace by a nurse.*)

                              What's that?
O god! Do I really hear you sobbing?—
my two children. Creon, you've pitied me?
Sent me my darling girls, my own flesh and blood! 1615
Am I right?
CREON: Yes, it's my doing.
I know the joy they gave you all these years,
the joy you must feel now.
OEDIPUS: Bless you, Creon!
May god watch over you for this kindness,
better than he ever guarded me. 1620
                              Children, where are you?
Here, come quickly—

(*Groping for* ANTIGONE *and* ISMENE, *who approach their father cautiously, then embrace him.*)

                              Come to these hands of mine,
your brother's hands, your own father's hands
that served his once bright eyes so well—
that made them blind. Seeing nothing, children,
knowing nothing, I became your father, 1625
I fathered you in the soil that gave me life.

How I weep for you—I cannot see you now . . .
just thinking of all your days to come, the bitterness,
the life that rough mankind will thrust upon you.
Where are the public gatherings you can join, 1630
the banquets of the clans? Home you'll come,
in tears, cut off from the sight of it all,
the brilliant rites unfinished.
And when you reach perfection, ripe for marriage,
who will he be, my dear ones? Risking all 1635
to shoulder the curse that weighs down my parents,
yes and you too—that wounds us all together.
What more misery could you want?
Your father killed his father, sowed his mother,
one, one and the selfsame womb sprang you— 1640
he cropped the very roots of his existence.

Such disgrace, and you must bear it all!
Who will marry you then? Not a man on earth.
Your doom is clear: you'll wither away to nothing,
single, without a child. 1645

(*Turning to* CREON.)

                              Oh Creon,
you are the only father they have now . . .
we who brought them into the world
are gone, both gone at a stroke—

1650 Don't let them go begging, abandoned,
women without men. Your own flesh and blood!
Never bring them down to the level of my pains.
Pity them. Look at them, so young, so vulnerable,
shorn of everything—you're their only hope.
Promise me, noble Creon, touch my hand!

(*Reaching toward* CREON, *who draws back.*)

1655 You, little ones, if you were old enough
to understand, there is much I'd tell you.
Now, as it is, I'd have you say a prayer.
Pray for life, my children,
live where you are free to grow and season.
1660 Pray god you find a better life than mine,
the father who begot you.
CREON: Enough.
You've wept enough. Into the palace now.
OEDIPUS: I must, but I find it very hard.
CREON: Time is the great healer, you will see.
1665 OEDIPUS: I am going—you know on what condition?
CREON: Tell me. I'm listening.
OEDIPUS: Drive me out of Thebes, in exile.
CREON: Not I. Only the gods can give you that.
OEDIPUS: Surely the gods hate me so much—
1670 CREON: You'll get your wish at once.

OEDIPUS: You consent?
CREON: I try to say what I mean; it's my habit.
OEDIPUS: Then take me away. It's time.
CREON: Come along, let go of the children.
OEDIPUS: No—
don't take them away from me, not now! No no no!

(*Clutching his daughters as the* GUARDS *wrench them loose and take
them through the palace doors.*)

CREON: Still the king, the master of all things?   1675
No more: here your power ends.
None of your power follows you through life.

(*Exit* OEDIPUS *and* CREON *to the palace. The* CHORUS *comes forward
to address the audience directly.*)

CHORUS: People of Thebes, my countrymen, look on Oedipus.
He solved the famous riddle with his brilliance,
he rose to power, a man beyond all power.   1680
Who could behold his greatness without envy?
Now what a black sea of terror has overwhelmed him.
Now as we keep our watch and wait the final day,
count no man happy till he dies, free of pain at last.

(*Exit in procession.*)

Euripides

Euripides (c. 484–406 BCE) was the youngest of the three tragic playwrights whose plays remain today. Although he first competed in the City Dionysia in 455 BCE and won his first victory in 441 BCE, Euripides won only four victories in his lifetime and left Athens about 408 BCE for the court of King Archileus of Macedon, where he died. We do not know why Euripides won so infrequently, but his tragedies are much more bitter and ironic than those of Aeschylus or Sophocles, brilliantly unfolding the selfish capriciousness of gods and heroes alike. Of the roughly ninety plays Euripides is thought to have written, eighteen survive, and most of these were written and produced during the war with Sparta: *Alcestis, Medea, Heracleidae, Hippolytus, Cyclops* (a satyr play), *Heracles, Iphigeneia in Tauris, Helen, Hecuba, Andromache, The Trojan Women, Ion, The Suppliant Women, Orestes, Electra, The Phoenician Women.* Three additional plays—*Iphigeneia at Aulis, The Bacchae,* and *Alcmaeon at Corinth* (now lost)—were written in Macedon and brought to Athens by the playwright's son, Euripides the Younger. This trilogy, produced after Euripides' death, won him his final prize at the City Dionysia.

Although many Greek tragedies center on female characters—think of Clytaemnestra in Aeschylus' *Agamemnon,* for example, or Sophocles' *Antigone*—Euripides was famous in Athens for centering his tragedies so frequently on women. Euripides was hardly a feminist in any modern sense, yet more than his contemporaries, he used his tragic heroines to explore the relationship between gender and the other conceptual, political, social, and esthetic categories organizing Athenian life.

As in all roles in the Athenian theater, the role of Medea was played by a male actor; nonetheless, in many ways *Medea* illustrates Euripides' skeptical and ironic regard for conventional attitudes and his tendency toward a more sensational form of tragic action. Like Shakespeare's *Hamlet, Medea* is a tragedy of revenge, in which Medea poisons her husband Jason's newly married wife and her father, Creon, and in the play's climactic moment executes

In this modernized production of Euripides' *Medea* by the Abbey Theatre of Dublin, Fiona Shaw's Medea enacts the slaughter of the children behind an illuminated Plexiglas screen.

her own children from her marriage with Jason. What sometimes seems most monstrous to modern readers and audiences is that Medea herself—in one of Euripides' most striking uses of the *machina*—flees Corinth alive at the end of the play, rising above the *skene* in a dragon-drawn chariot, draped in the bodies of her dead children, taunting and reviling the impotent Jason. That is, modern audiences sometimes feel that Medea herself should die at the play's close if *Medea* is to be a truly tragic drama, as though by dying Medea would be "punished" for her revenge in some appalling vision of tragic "justice." But Euripides seems uninterested in such a moralized version of tragedy. Indeed, as Aristotle implies in *The Poetics,* tragedy is a deeply dialectical, contradictory way of representing human experience: tragedy arises from the unresolvable tension between pity and fear, from the relationship between the hero's actions (remembering that the tragic hero is neither a paragon of virtue nor inherently wicked) and their terrible, somehow fitting consequences. Although Aristotle praises Sophocles' *Oedipus the King* as the best-constructed tragedy, he also remarks that Euripides "is felt by the audience to be the most tragic, at least, of the poets." To grasp Euripides' sense of tragedy means placing Medea's execution of the children within the context of the action as a whole—an act that brings her history to bear in one exacting deed; an act like Agamemnon's treading on the carpet or Oedipus' blistering interrogation of the ancient shepherd.

At the play's opening, Medea is an outcast, a foreign exile in Corinth, and the play repeatedly stresses Medea's otherness—she is an Eastern exotic, she has little respect for Greek culture and its institutions, and she is a sorceress as well. Medea is consistently shown to be a figure of willful passion, brought into exile through her love for Jason. Falling in love with Jason when he went to Colchis in search of the Golden Fleece, Medea used her sorcery to help Jason gain the Fleece, betraying her father and killing her brother in the bargain. When the play opens, Jason has returned to Greece with Medea and their children; in Corinth, however, Jason decides to marry the daughter of King Creon. Creon, no doubt recognizing that Medea and her children will pose a constant threat to his own line of succession, has ruled that Medea and her children must again be sent into exile.

Yet as Medea suggests to the Chorus, the indignity that Jason has thrust upon her—being doubly exiled, from her country and from her marriage—is in an important sense merely an extension of the state of all women in Greek culture. For once women "Buy a husband and take for our bodies / A master," they are exiled from their own homes, and from the mastery of their own lives. Inasmuch as women are represented as creatures of passion, they are "exiled" as well from the organizing principles of the Greek state: Reason, the law, and legitimate society are identified in the play as the preserve of men. Euripides makes Jason the spokesman for these values. When Jason first confronts Medea, he takes pride in his talents as a speaker, listing his arguments in support of taking a new wife almost as though he were arguing in the courtroom or conducting a philosophical demonstration. But while Oedipus, for instance, uses the strategies of philosophic inquiry to discover the truth, Jason's arguments seem to conceal the truth—he is betraying Medea and their children, after all—behind a smokescreen of sophistic rhetoric. Having brought Medea into exile, Jason argues that she is fortunate merely to "inhabit a Greek land and understand our ways / How to live by law instead of the sweet will of force." Yet the law that Jason praises seems designed to enable him to act out his own "sweet will"—taking a second wife—while it prevents Medea from acting on hers. The more Jason insists that he is acting reasonably, the more unreasonable his arguments become; he grows increasingly irritable, and finally insulting: "You women have got into such a state of mind / That, if your life at night is good, you think you have / Everything." Euripides' treatment of Jason is typical of his tendency to present an ironic view of the heroes of Greek mythology. Here, in making Jason the representative of Greek values—reason, law, justice—Euripides suggests the limits of those values. For the Chorus clearly sees Jason's "reason" as a self-indulgent pretense: "Though you have made this speech of yours look well, / . . . / You have betrayed your wife and are acting badly."

As Medea comes to recognize, both Jason and the masculine laws of Corinth are willing to betray her, to call her fidelity and love merely irrational, to force her again into exile. Having poisoned Creon and his daughter, Medea first claims to kill the children in order that they not be slain "by another hand less kindly to them." But it is also clear that in killing the children, Medea revenges herself on Jason in the only way open to her; he has little regard for her love for him, but the children are his property, an extension of himself, of his identity. What is more important, the children are his successors, representing his continued presence in the world. For as Jason laments, Medea has contrived a punishment for him that no Greek woman would have dared: In leaving him childless, Medea transforms Jason into an exile like herself, prophesying that he will die "without distinction."

Medea's acts epitomize the ethical ambiguity that drives Greek tragedy. Agamemnon strides on the blood-red carpet, magisterially desecrating the honor of his family as he had once done in sacrificing Iphigeneia; Oedipus sentences the hidden criminal to exile, only to discover that he is the criminal he seeks. To force Jason into a childless exile, Medea commits the kind of crime that Jason has repeatedly drawn her to enact: She murders what she loves in order to insist on the priority and power of her love for him. As in other classical tragedies, the hero chooses to act in a way that is not only consistent with her past, but a self-conscious reenactment of it. The *peripeteia,* the reversal that defines the tragic action, seems in many ways to be a kind of restoration as well, revealing destructive consequences that have been latent in the action from the beginning.

It should be clear that while Euripides interrogates the relationship between reason and passion, culture and nature, the rational and the irrational, science and magic, *Medea* does not finally disrupt or overturn this relationship. Nor does the play finally question the way that Greek culture gendered these categories as masculine and feminine, expressing the conceptual and political hierarchies of its own making as the "natural" outgrowth of some essential gender difference. Euripides exposes the destructive tension lurking in Greek conceptions of gender, power, and identity, but the language of tragedy is not the language of revolution, because although tragedy frequently exposes the values of its world as contradictory and destructive, it also accepts those values as somehow inevitable, unavoidable. Medea flees Corinth and the abusive Jason, but only by destroying herself in the same way she destroys Jason; Medea triumphs over Jason, but only by destroying her family and becoming an exile yet again. The only alternative that *Medea* offers to the way that Medea—and, she argues, all women—is positioned as an outsider, an "exile" to the governing categories of Greek life, is a deeper, more permanent isolation.

MEDEA

Euripides

TRANSLATED BY REX WARNER

CHARACTERS

MEDEA, *princess of Colchis*
and wife of
JASON, *son of Aeson,*
king of Iolcus
TWO CHILDREN *of Medea*
and Jason
CREON, *king of Corinth*

AEGEUS, *king of Athens*
NURSE *to Medea*
TUTOR *to Medea's children*
MESSENGER
CHORUS *of Corinthian women*
ATTENDANTS

SCENE: *In front of* MEDEA's *house in Corinth.*

Enter from the house Medea's NURSE.

NURSE: How I wish the Argo never had reached the land
    Of Colchis, skimming through the blue Symplegades,
    Nor ever had fallen in the glades of Pelion
    The smitten fir-tree to furnish oars for the hands
5   Of heroes who in Pelias' name attempted
    The Golden Fleece! For then my mistress Medea
    Would not have sailed for the towers of the land of Iolcus,
    Her heart on fire with passionate love for Jason;
    Nor would she have persuaded the daughters of Pelias
10   To kill their father, and now be living here
    In Corinth with her husband and children. She gave
    Pleasure to the people of her land of exile,
    And she herself helped Jason in every way.
    This is indeed the greatest salvation of all—
15   For the wife not to stand apart from the husband.
    But now there's hatred everywhere, Love is diseased.
    For, deserting his own children and my mistress,
    Jason has taken a royal wife to his bed,
    The daughter of the ruler of this land, Creon.
20   And poor Medea is slighted, and cries aloud on the
    Vows they made to each other, the right hands clasped
    In eternal promise. She calls upon the gods to witness
    What sort of return Jason has made to her love.
    She lies without food and gives herself up to suffering,
25   Wasting away every moment of the day in tears.
    So it has gone since she knew herself slighted by him.
    Not stirring an eye, not moving her face from the ground,
    No more than either a rock or surging sea water
    She listens when she is given friendly advice.
30   Except that sometimes she twists back her white neck and
    Moans to herself, calling out on her father's name,
    And her land, and her home betrayed when she came away
      with
    A man who now is determined to dishonor her.
    Poor creature, she has discovered by her sufferings
35   What it means to one not to have lost one's own country.

---

1 **Argo** Jason's ship on the expedition of the Argonauts, sent by Pelias, king of Iolcus in Thessaly (Jason's uncle, who had usurped the throne), to Colchis on the Black Sea. The Symplegades were clashing rocks, one of the obstacles along the way. Pelion is a mountain in Thessaly. Medea was a princess of Colchis who fell in love with Jason and followed him back to Greece

---

    She has turned from the children and does not like to see
      them.
    I am afraid she may think of some dreadful thing,
    For her heart is violent. She will never put up with
    The treatment she is getting. I know and fear her
    Lest she may sharpen a sword and thrust to the heart,   40
    Stealing into the palace where the bed is made,
    Or even kill the king and the new-wedded groom,
    And thus bring a greater misfortune on herself.
    She's a strange woman. I know it won't be easy
    To make an enemy of her and come off best.   45
    But here the children come. They have finished playing.
    They have no thought at all of their mother's trouble.
    Indeed it is not usual for the young to grieve.

(Enter from the right the slave who is the TUTOR *to Medea's two small children. The* CHILDREN *follow him.)*

TUTOR: You old retainer of my mistress' household,
    Why are you standing here all alone in front of the   50
    Gates and moaning to yourself over your misfortune?
    Medea could not wish you to leave her alone.
NURSE: Old man, and guardian of the children of Jason,
    If one is a good servant, it's a terrible thing
    When one's master's luck is out; it goes to one's heart.   55
    So I myself have got into such a state of grief
    That a longing stole over me to come outside here
    And tell the earth and air of my mistress' sorrows.
TUTOR: Has the poor lady not yet given up her crying?
NURSE: Given up? She's at the start, not halfway through her   60
    tears.
TUTOR: Poor fool—if I may call my mistress such a name—
    How ignorant she is of trouble more to come.
NURSE: What do you mean, old man? You needn't fear to
    speak.
TUTOR: Nothing. I take back the words which I used just now.
NURSE: Don't, by your beard, hide this from me, your   65
    fellow-servant.
    If need be, I'll keep quiet about what you tell me.
TUTOR: I heard a person saying, while I myself seemed
    Not to be paying attention, when I was at the place
    Where the old draught-players sit, by the holy fountain,
    That Creon, ruler of the land, intends to drive   70
    These children and their mother in exile from Corinth.
    But whether what he said is really true or not
    I do not know. I pray that it may not be true.

NURSE: And will Jason put up with it that his children
75   Should suffer so, though he's no friend to their mother?
TUTOR: Old ties give place to new ones. As for Jason, he
    No longer has a feeling for this house of ours.
NURSE: It's black indeed for us, when we add new to old
    Sorrows before even the present sky has cleared.
80 TUTOR: But you be silent, and keep all this to yourself.
    It is not the right time to tell our mistress of it.
NURSE: Do you hear, children, what a father he is to you?
    I wish he were dead—but no, he is still my master.
    Yet certainly he has proved unkind to his dear ones.
85 TUTOR: What's strange in that? Have you only just discovered
    That everyone loves himself more than his neighbor?
    Some have good reason, others get something out of it.
    So Jason neglects his children for the new bride.
NURSE: Go indoors, children. That will be the best thing.
90   And you, keep them to themselves as much as possible.
    Don't bring them near their mother in her angry mood.
    For I've seen her already blazing her eyes at them
    As though she meant some mischief and I am sure that
    She'll not stop raging until she has struck at someone.
95   May it be an enemy and not a friend she hurts!

(MEDEA *is heard inside the house.*)

MEDIA: Ah, wretch! Ah, lost in my sufferings,
    I wish, I wish I might die.
NURSE: What did I say, dear children? Your mother
    Frets her heart and frets it to anger.
100   Run away quickly into the house.
    And keep well out of her sight.
    Don't go anywhere near, but be careful
    Of the wildness and bitter nature
    Of that proud mind.
105   Go now! Run quickly indoors.
    It is clear that she soon will put lightning
    In that cloud of her cries that is rising
    With a passion increasing. O, what will she do,
    Proud-hearted and not to be checked on her course,
110   A soul bitten into with wrong?

(*The* TUTOR *takes the* CHILDREN *into the house.*)

MEDEA: Ah, I have suffered
    What should be wept for bitterly. I hate you,
    Children of a hateful mother. I curse you
    And your father. Let the whole house crash.
115 NURSE: Ah, I pity you, you poor creature.
    How can your children share in their father's
    Wickedness? Why do you hate them? Oh children,
    How much I fear that something may happen!
    Great people's tempers are terrible, always
120   Having their own way, seldom checked.
    Dangerous they shift from mood to mood.
    How much better to have been accustomed
    To live on equal terms with one's neighbors.
    I would like to be safe and grow old in a
125   Humble way. What is moderate sounds best,
    Also in practice is best for everyone.
    Greatness brings no profit to people.
    God indeed, when in anger, brings
    Greater ruin to great men's houses.

(*Enter, on the right, a* CHORUS *of Corinthian women. They have come
to inquire about* MEDEA *and to attempt to console her.*)

CHORUS: I heard the voice, I heard the cry   130
    Of Colchis' wretched daughter.
    Tell me, mother, is she not yet
    At rest? Within the double gates
    Of the court I heard her cry. I am sorry
    For the sorrow of this home. O, say, what has happened?   135
NURSE: There is no home. It's over and done with.
    Her husband holds fast to his royal wedding,
    While she, my mistress, cries out her eyes
    There in her room, and takes no warmth from
    Any word of any friend.   140
MEDEA: O, I wish
    That lightning from heaven would split my head open.
    Oh, what use have I now for life?
    I would find my release in death
    And leave hateful existence behind me.   145
CHORUS: O God and Earth and Heaven!
    Did you hear what a cry was that
    Which the sad wife sings?
    Poor foolish one, why should you long.
    For that appalling rest?   150
    The final end of death comes fast.
    No need to pray for that.
    Suppose your man gives honor
    To another woman's bed.
    It often happens. Don't be hurt.   155
    God will be your friend in this.
    You must not waste away
    Grieving too much for him who shared your bed.
MEDEA: Great Themis, lady Artemis, behold
    The things I suffer, though I made him promise,   160
    My hateful husband. I pray that I may see him,
    Him and his bride and all their palace shattered
    For the wrong they dare to do me without cause.
    Oh, my father! Oh, my country! In what dishonor
    I left you, killing my own brother for it.   165
NURSE: Do you hear what she says, and how she cries
    On Themis, the goddess of Promises, and on Zeus,
    Whom we believe to be the Keeper of Oaths?
    Of this I am sure, that no small thing
    Will appease my mistress' anger.   170
CHORUS: Will she come into our presence?
    Will she listen when we are speaking
    To the words we say?
    I wish she might relax her rage
    And temper of her heart.   175
    My willingness to help will never
    Be wanting to my friends.
    But go inside and bring her
    Out of the house to us,
    And speak kindly to her: hurry,   180
    Before she wrongs her own.
    This passion of hers moves to something great.

---

159 **Themis . . . Artemis** goddesses: Themis was the goddess of
justice; the virgin Artemis would be sensitive to the plight of
women   165 **brother** during the escape from Colchis, to delay
her father's pursuit

NURSE: I will, but I doubt if I'll manage
To win my mistress over.
185 But still I'll attempt it to please you.
Such a look she will flash on her servants
If any comes near with a message.
Like a lioness guarding her cubs,
It is right, I think, to consider
190 Both stupid and lacking in foresight
Those poets of old who wrote songs
For revels and dinners and banquets.
Pleasant sounds for men living at ease;
But none of them all has discovered
195 How to put to an end with their singing
Or musical instruments grief,
Bitter grief, from which death and disaster
Cheat the hopes of a house. Yet how good
If music could cure men of this! But why raise
200 To no purpose the voice at a banquet? For *there* is
Already abundance of pleasure for men
With a joy of its own.

(*The* NURSE *goes into the house.*)

CHORUS: I heard a shriek that is laden with sorrow,
Shrilling out her hard grief she cries out
205 Upon him who betrayed both her bed and her marriage.
Wronged, she calls on the gods,
On the justice of Zeus, the oath sworn,
Which brought her away
To the opposite shore of the Greeks
210 Through the gloomy salt straits to the gateway
Of the salty unlimited sea.

(MEDEA, *attended by servants, comes out of the house.*)

MEDEA: Women of Corinth, I have come outside to you
Lest you should be indignant with me; for I know
That many people are overproud, some when alone,
215 And others when in company. And those who live
Quietly, as I do, get a bad reputation.
For a just judgment is not evident in the eyes
When a man at first sight hates another, before
Learning his character, being in no way injured;
220 And a foreigner especially must adapt himself.
I'd not approve of even a fellow-countryman
Who by pride and want of manners offends his neighbors.
But on me this thing has fallen so unexpectedly.
It has broken my heart. I am finished. I let go
225 All my life's joy. My friends, I only want to die.
It was everything to me to think well of one man,
And he, my own husband, has turned out wholly vile.
Of all things which are living and can form a judgment
We women are the most unfortunate creatures.
230 Firstly, with an excess of wealth it is required
For us to buy a husband and take for our bodies
A master; for not to take one is even worse.
And now the question is serious whether we take
A good or bad one; for there is no easy escape
235 For a woman, nor can she say no to her marriage.
She arrives among new modes of behavior and manners.
And needs prophetic power, unless she has learned at home,
How best to manage him who shares the bed with her.

And if we work out all this well and carefully.
And the husband lives with us and lightly bears his yoke. 240
Then life is enviable. If not, I'd rather die.
A man, when he's tired of the company in his home,
Goes out of the house and puts an end to his boredom
And turns to a friend or companion of his own age.
But we are forced to keep our eyes on one alone. 245
What they say of us is that we have a peaceful time
Living at home, while they do the fighting in war.
How wrong they are! I would very much rather stand
Three times in the front of battle than bear one child.
Yet what applies to me does not apply to you. 250
You have a country. Your family home is here.
You enjoy life and the company of your friends.
But I am deserted, a refugee, thought nothing of
By my husband—something he won in a foreign land.
I have no mother or brother, nor any relation 255
With whom I can take refuge in this sea of woe.
This much then is the service I would beg from you:
If I can find the means or devise any scheme
To pay my husband back for what he has done to me—
Him and his father-in-law and the girl who married him— 260
Just to keep silent. For in other ways a woman
Is full of fear, defenseless, dreads the sight of cold
Steel; but, when once she is wronged in the matter of love,
No other soul can hold so many thoughts of blood.
CHORUS: This I will promise. You are in the right, Medea, 265
In paying your husband back. I am not surprised at you
For being sad.
　　　　　But look! I see our King Creon
Approaching. He will tell us of some new plan.

(*Enter, from the right,* CREON, *with attendants.*)

CREON: You, with that angry look, so set against your husband.
Medea, I order you to leave my territories 270
An exile, and take along with you your two children,
And not to waste time doing it. It is my decree,
And I will see it done. I will not return home
Until you are cast from the boundaries of my land.
MEDEA: Oh, this is the end for me. I am utterly lost. 275
Now I am in the full force of the storm of hate
And have no harbor from ruin to reach easily.
Yet still, in spite of it all, I'll ask the question:
What is your reason, Creon, for banishing me?
CREON: I am afraid of you—why should I dissemble it?— 280
Afraid that you may injure my daughter mortally.
Many things accumulate to support my feeling.
You are a clever woman, versed in evil arts.
And are angry at having lost your husband's love.
I hear that you are threatening, so they tell me, 285
To do something against my daughter and Jason
And me, too. I shall take my precautions first.
I tell you, I prefer to earn your hatred now
Than to be soft-hearted and afterward regret it.
MEDEA: This is not the first time, Creon. Often previously 290
Through being considered clever I have suffered much.
A person of sense ought never to have his children
Brought up to be more clever than the average.
For, apart from cleverness bringing them no profit,
It will make them objects of envy and ill-will. 295
If you put new ideas before the eyes of fools

They'll think you foolish and worthless into the bargain;
And if you are thought superior to those who have
Some reputation for learning, you will become hated.
300 I have some knowledge myself of how this happens;
For being clever, I find that some will envy me,
Others object to me. Yet all my cleverness
Is not so much.
                   Well, then, are you frightened, Creon,
That I should harm you? There is no need. It is not
305 My way to transgress the authority of a king.
How have you injured me? You gave your daughter away
To the man you wanted. Oh, certainly I hate
My husband, but you, I think, have acted wisely;
Nor do I grudge it you that your affairs go well.
310 May the marriage be a lucky one! Only let me
Live in this land. For even though I have been wronged,
I will not raise my voice, but submit to my betters.
CREON: What you say sounds gentle enough. Still in my heart
I greatly dread that you are plotting some evil,
315 And therefore I trust you even less than before.
A sharp-tempered woman, or, for that matter, a man,
Is easier to deal with than the clever type
Who holds her tongue. No. You must go. No need for more
Speeches. The thing is fixed. By no manner of means
320 Shall you, an enemy of mine, stay in my country.
MEDEA: I beg you. By your knees, by your new-wedded girl.
CREON: Your words are wasted. You will never persuade me.
MEDEA: Will you drive me out, and give no heed to my prayers?
CREON: I will, for I love my family more than you.
325 MEDEA: O my country! How bitterly now I remember you!
CREON: I love my country too—next after my children.
MEDEA: O what an evil to men is passionate love!
CREON: That would depend on the luck that goes along with it.
MEDEA: O God, do not forget who is the cause of this!
330 CREON: Go. It is no use. Spare me the pain of forcing you.
MEDEA: I'm spared no pain. I lack no pain to be spared me.
CREON: Then you'll be removed by force by one of my men.
MEDEA: No. Creon, not that! But do listen, I beg you.
CREON: Woman, you seem to want to create a disturbance.
335 MEDEA: I *will* go into exile. *This* is not what I beg for.
CREON: Why then this violence and clinging to my hand?
MEDEA: Allow me to remain here just for this one day,
So I may consider where to live in my exile.
And look for support for my children, since their father
340 Chooses to make no kind of provision for them.
Have pity on them! You have children of your own.
It is natural for you to look kindly on them.
For myself I do not mind if I go into exile.
It is the children being in trouble that I mind.
345 CREON: There is nothing tyrannical about my nature,
And by showing mercy I have often been the loser.
Even now I know that I am making a mistake.
All the same you shall have your will. But this I tell you,
That if the light of heaven tomorrow shall see you,
350 You and your children in the confines of my land,
You die. This word I have spoken is firmly fixed.
But now, if you must stay, stay for this day alone.
For in it you can do none of the things I fear.

(*Exit* CREON, *with his attendants.*)

CHORUS: Oh, unfortunate one! Oh, cruel!
Where will you turn? Who will help you? 355
What house or what land to preserve you
From ill can you find?
Medea, a god has thrown suffering
Upon you in waves of despair.
MEDEA: Things have gone badly every way. No doubt of that 360
But not these things this far, and don't imagine so.
There are still trials to come for the new-wedded pair,
And for their relations pain that will mean something.
Do you think that I would ever have fawned on that man
Unless I had some end to gain or profit in it? 365
I would not even have spoken or touched him with my hands.
But he has got to such a pitch of foolishness
That, though he could have made nothing of all my plans
By exiling me, he has given me this one day
To stay here, and in this I will make dead bodies 370
Of three of my enemies—father, the girl, and my husband.
I have many ways of death which I might suit to them,
And do not know, friends, which one to take in hand;
Whether to set fire underneath their bridal mansion,
Or sharpen a sword and thrust it to the heart. 375
Stealing into the palace where the bed is made.
There is just one obstacle to this. If I am caught
Breaking into the house and scheming against it,
I shall die, and give my enemies cause for laughter.
It is best to go by the straight road, the one in which 380
I am most skilled, and make away with them by poison.
So be it then.
And now suppose them dead. What town will receive me?
What friend will offer me a refuge in his land,
Or the guaranty of his house and save my own life? 385
There is none. So I must wait a little time yet,
And if some sure defense should then appear for me,
In craft and silence I will set about this murder.
But if my fate should drive me on without help,
Even though death is certain, I will take the sword 390
Myself and kill, and steadfastly advance to crime.
It shall not be—I swear it by her, my mistress,
Whom most I honor and have chosen as partner,
Hecate, who dwells in the recesses of my hearth—
That any man shall be glad to have injured me. 395
Bitter I will make their marriage for them and mournful,
Bitter the alliance and the driving me out of the land.
Ah, come, Medea, in your plotting and scheming
Leave nothing untried of all those things which you know.
Go forward to the dreadful act. The test has come 400
For resolution. You see how you are treated. Never
Shall you be mocked by Jason's Corinthian wedding,
Whose father was noble, whose grandfather Helius.
You have the skill. What is more, you were born a woman,
And women, though most helpless in doing good deeds, 405
Are of every evil the cleverest of contrivers.
CHORUS: Flow backward to your sources, sacred rivers,
And let the world's great order be reversed.
It is the thoughts of *men* that are deceitful,
Their pledges that are loose. 410

394 **Hecate** a goddess of the night   403 **Helius** sun god

Story shall now turn my condition to a fair one,
Women are paid their due.
No more shall evil-sounding fame be theirs.

Cease now, you muses of the ancient singers,
415 To tell the tale of my unfaithfulness;
For not on us did Phoebus, lord of music,
Bestow the lyre's divine
Power, for otherwise I should have sung an answer
To the other sex. Long time
420 Has much to tell of us, and much of them.

You sailed away from your father's home,
With a heart on fire you passed
The double rocks of the sea.
And now in a foreign country
425 You have lost your rest in a widowed bed,
And are driven forth, a refugee
In dishonor from the land.

Good faith has gone, and no more remains
In great Greece a sense of shame.
430 It has flown away to the sky.
No father's house for a haven
Is at hand for you now, and another queen
Of your bed has dispossessed you and
Is mistress of your home.

(*Enter* JASON, *with attendants.*)

435 JASON: This is not the first occasion that I have noticed
How hopeless it is to deal with a stubborn temper.
For, with reasonable submission to our ruler's will,
You might have lived in this land and kept your home.
As it is you are going to be exiled for your loose speaking.
440 Not that I mind myself. You are free to continue
Telling everyone that Jason is a worthless man.
But as to your talk about the king, consider
Yourself most lucky that exile is your punishment.
I, for my part, have always tried to calm down
445 The anger of the king, and wished you to remain.
But you will not give up your folly, continually
Speaking ill of him, and so you are going to be banished.
All the same, and in spite of your conduct, I'll not desert
My friends, but have come to make some provision for you,
450 So that you and the children may not be penniless
Or in need of anything in exile. Certainly
Exile brings many troubles with it. And even
If you hate me, I cannot think badly of you.
MEDEA: O coward in every way—that is what I call you,
455 With bitterest reproach for your lack of manliness,
You have come, you, my worst enemy, have come to me!
It is not an example of overconfidence
Or of boldness thus to look your friends in the face,
Friends you have injured—no, it is the worst of all
460 Human diseases, shamelessness. But you did well
To come, for I can speak ill of you and lighten
My heart, and you will suffer while you are listening.
And first I will begin from what happened first.
I saved your life, and every Greek knows I saved it.
465 Who was a shipmate of yours aboard the Argo.

When you were sent to control the bulls that breathed fire
And yoke them, and when you would sow that deadly field.
Also that snake, who encircled with his many folds
The Golden Fleece and guarded it and never slept,
I killed, and so gave you the safety of the light.   470
And I myself betrayed my father and my home,
And came with you to Pelias' land of Iolcus.
And then, showing more willingness to help than wisdom,
I killed him, Pelias, with a most dreadful death
At his own daughters' hands, and took away your fear.   475
This is how I behaved to you, you wretched man,
And you forsook me, took another bride to bed,
Though you had children; for, if that had not been,
You would have had an excuse for another wedding.
Faith in your word has gone. Indeed, I cannot tell   480
Whether you think the gods whose names you swore by then
Have ceased to rule and that new standards are set up,
Since you must know you have broken your word to me.
O my right hand, and the knees which you often clasped
In supplication, how senselessly I am treated   485
By this bad man, and how my hopes have missed their mark!
Come, I will share my thoughts as though you were a
   friend—
You! Can I think that you would ever treat me well?
But I will do it, and these questions will make you
Appear the baser. Where am I to go? To my father's?   490
Him I betrayed and his land when I came with you.
To Pelias' wretched daughters? What a fine welcome
They would prepare for me who murdered their father!
For this is my position—hated by my friends
At home, I have, in kindness to you, made enemies   495
Of others whom there was no need to have injured.
And how happy among Greek women you have made me
On your side for all this! A distinguished husband
I have—for breaking promises. When in misery
I am cast out of the land and go into exile,   500
Quite without friends and all alone with my children,
That will be a fine shame for the new-wedded groom,
For his children to wander as beggars and she who saved
   him.
O God, you have given to mortals a sure method
Of telling the gold that is pure from the counterfeit;   505
Why is there no mark engraved upon men's bodies,
By which we could know the true ones from the false ones?
CHORUS: It is a strange form of anger, difficult to cure,
When two friends turn upon each other in hatred.
JASON: As for me, it seems I must be no bad speaker.   510
But, like a man who has a good grip of the tiller,
Reef up his sail, and so run away from under
This mouthing tempest, woman, of your bitter tongue.
Since you insist on building up your kindness to me.
My view is that Cypris was alone responsible   515
Of men and gods for the preserving of my life.
You are clever enough—but really I need not enter
Into the story of how it was love's inescapable
Power that compelled you to keep my person safe.
On this I will not go into too much detail.   520

416 **Phoebus** Apollo

515 **Cypris** Aphrodite, goddess of love

In so far as you helped me, you did well enough.
But on this question of saving me, I can prove
You have certainly got from me more than you gave.
Firstly, instead of living among barbarians,
525 You inhabit a Greek land and understand our ways,
How to live by law instead of the sweet will of force.
And all the Greeks considered you a clever woman.
You were honored for it; while, if you were living at
The ends of the earth, nobody would have heard of you.
530 For my part, rather than stores of gold in my house
Or power to sing even sweeter songs than Orpheus,
I'd choose the fate that made me a distinguished man.
There is my reply to your story of my labors.
Remember it was you who started the argument.
535 Next for your attack on my wedding with the princess:
Here I will prove that, first, it was a clever move,
Secondly, a wise one, and, finally, that I made it
In your best interests and the children's. Please keep calm.
When I arrived here from the land of Iolcus,
540 Involved, as I was, in every kind of difficulty,
What luckier chance could I have come across than this,
An exile to marry the daughter of the king?
It was not—the point that seems to upset you—that I
Grew tired of your bed and felt the need of a new bride;
545 Nor with any wish to outdo your number of children.
We have enough already. I am quite content.
But—this was the main reason—that we might live well,
And not be short of anything. I know that all
A man's friends leave him stone-cold if he becomes poor.
550 Also that I might bring my children up worthily
Of my position, and, by producing more of them
To be brothers of yours, we would draw the families
Together and all be happy. You need no children.
And it pays me to do good to those I have now
555 By having others. Do you think this a bad plan?
You wouldn't if the love question hadn't upset you.
But you women have got into such a state of mind
That, if your life at night is good, you think you have
Everything; but, if in that quarter things go wrong,
560 You will consider your best and truest interests
Most hateful. It would have been better far for men
To have got their children in some other way, and women
Not to have existed. Then life would have been good.
CHORUS: Jason, though you have made this speech of yours
look well,
565 Still I think, even though others do not agree,
You have betrayed your wife and are acting badly.
MEDEA: Surely in many ways I hold different views
From others, for I think that the plausible speaker
Who is a villain deserves the greatest punishment.
570 Confident in his tongue's power to adorn evil,
He stops at nothing. Yet he is not really wise.
As in your case. There is no need to put on the airs
Of a clever speaker, for one word will lay you flat.
If you were not a coward, you would not have married
575 Behind my back, but discussed it with me first.
JASON: And you, no doubt, would have furthered the proposal,
If I had told you of it, you who even now
Are incapable of controlling your bitter temper.
MEDEA: It was not that. No, you thought it was not respectable
580 As you got on in years to have a foreign wife.

JASON: Make sure of this: it was not because of a woman
I made the royal alliance in which I now live.
But, as I said before, I wished to preserve you
And breed a royal progeny to be brothers
To the children I have now, a sure defense to us.   585
MEDEA: Let me have no happy fortune that brings pain with it,
Or prosperity which is upsetting to the mind!
JASON: Change your ideas of what you want, and show more
sense.
Do not consider painful what is good for you.
Nor, when you are lucky, think yourself unfortunate.   590
MEDEA: You can insult me. You have somewhere to turn to.
But I shall go from this land into exile, friendless.
JASON: It was what you chose yourself. Don't blame others for it.
MEDEA: And how did I choose it? Did I betray my husband?
JASON: You called down wicked curses on the king's family.   595
MEDEA: A curse, that is what I am become to your house too.
JASON: I do not propose to go into all the rest of it;
But, if you wish for the children or for yourself
In exile to have some of my money to help you,
Say so, for I am prepared to give with open hand,   600
Or to provide you with introductions to my friends
Who will treat you well. You are a fool if you do not
Accept this. Cease your anger and you will profit.
MEDEA: I shall never accept the favors of friends of yours,
Nor take a thing from you, so you need not offer it.   605
There is no benefit in the gifts of a bad man.
JASON: Then, in any case, I call the gods to witness that
I wish to help you and the children in every way,
But you refuse what is good for you. Obstinately
You push away your friends. You are sure to suffer for it.   610
MEDEA: Go! No doubt you hanker for your virginal bride,
And are guilty of lingering too long out of her house.
Enjoy your wedding. But perhaps—with the help of God—
You will make the kind of marriage that you will regret.

(JASON *goes out with his attendants.*)

CHORUS: When love is in excess
It brings a man no honor   615
Nor any worthiness.
But if in moderation Cypris comes,
There is no other power at all so gracious.
O goddess, never on me let loose the unerring
Shaft of your bow in the poison of desire.   620

Let my heart be wise.
It is the gods' best gift.
On me let mighty Cypris
Inflict no wordy wars or restless anger
To urge my passion to a different love.   625
But with discernment may she guide women's weddings,
Honoring most what is peaceful in the bed.

O country and home,
Never, never may I be without you,   630
Living the hopeless life,
Hard to pass through and painful,
Most pitiable of all.
Let death first lay me low and death
Free me from this daylight,   635
There is no sorrow above
The loss of a native land.

I have seen it myself,
Do not tell of a secondhand story.
640   Neither city nor friend
Pitied you when you suffered
The worst of sufferings.
O let him die ungraced whose heart
Will not reward his friends,
645   Who cannot open an honest mind
No friend will he be of mine.

(Enter AEGEUS, *king of Athens, an old friend of* MEDEA.)

AEGEUS: Medea, greeting! This is the best introduction
Of which men know for conversation between friends.
MEDEA: Greeting to you too, Aegeus, son of King Pandion.
650   Where have you come from to visit this country's soil?
AEGEUS: I have just left the ancient oracle of Phoebus.
MEDEA: And why did you go to earth's prophetic center?
AEGEUS: I went to inquire how children might be born to me.
MEDEA: Is it so? Your life still up to this point is childless?
655   AEGEUS: Yes. By the fate of some power we have no children.
MEDEA: Have you a wife, or is there none to share your bed?
AEGEUS: There is. Yes, I am joined to my wife in marriage.
MEDEA: And what did Phoebus say to you about children?
AEGEUS: Words too wise for a mere man to guess their
meaning.
660   MEDEA: It is proper for me to be told the god's reply?
AEGEUS: It is. For sure what is needed is cleverness.
MEDEA: Then what was his message? Tell me, if I may hear.
AEGEUS: I am not to loosen the hanging foot of the wineskin …
MEDEA: Until you have done something, or reached some
country?
665   AEGEUS: Until I return again to my hearth and house.
MEDEA: And for what purpose have you journeyed to this
land?
AEGEUS: There is a man called Pittheus, king of Troezen.
MEDEA: A son of Pelops, they say, a most righteous man.
AEGEUS: With him I wish to discuss the reply of the god.
670   MEDEA: Yes. He is wise and experienced in such matters.
AEGEUS: And to me also the dearest of all my spear-friends.
MEDEA: Well, I hope you have good luck, and achieve your
will.
AEGEUS: But why this downcast eye of yours, and this pale
cheek?
MEDEA: O Aegeus, my husband has been the worst of all to me.
675   AEGEUS: What do you mean? Say clearly what has caused this
grief.
MEDEA: Jason wrongs me, though I have never injured him.
AEGEUS: What has he done? Tell me about it in clearer words.
MEDEA: He has taken a wife to his house, supplanting me.
AEGEUS: Surely he would not dare to do a thing like that.
680   MEDEA: Be sure he has. Once dear, I now am slighted by him.
AEGEUS: Did he fall in love? Or is he tired of your love?
MEDEA: He was greatly in love, this traitor to his friends.
AEGEUS: Then let him go, if, as you say, he is so bad.
MEDEA: A passionate love—for an alliance with the king.
685   AEGEUS: And who gave him his wife? Tell me the rest of it.
MEDEA: It was Creon, he who rules this land of Corinth.
AEGEUS: Indeed, Medea, your grief was understandable.
MEDEA: I am ruined. And there is more to come: I am
banished.

AEGEUS: Banished? By whom? Here you tell me of a new
wrong.
MEDEA: Creon drives me an exile from the land of Corinth.   690
AEGEUS: Does Jason consent? I cannot approve of this.
MEDEA: He pretends not to, but he will put up with it.
Ah, Aegeus, I beg and beseech you, by your beard
And by your knees I am making myself your suppliant,
Have pity on me, have pity on your poor friend,   695
And do not let me go into exile desolate,
But receive me in your land and at your very hearth.
So may your love, with God's help, lead to the bearing
Of children, and so may you yourself die happy.
You do not know what a chance you have come on here.   700
I will end your childlessness, and I will make you able
To beget children. The drugs I know can do this.
AEGEUS: For many reasons, woman, I am anxious to do
This favor for you. First, for the sake of the gods,
And then for the birth of children which you promise,   705
For in that respect I am entirely at my wits' end.
But this is my position: if you reach my land,
I, being in my rights, will try to befriend you.
But this much I must warn you of beforehand:
I shall not agree to take you out of this country;   710
But if you by yourself can reach my house, then you
Shall stay there safely. To none will I give you up
But from this land you must make your escape yourself,
For I do not wish to incur blame from my friends.
MEDEA: It shall be so. But, if I might have a pledge from you   715
For this, then I would have from you all I desire.
AEGEUS: Do you not trust me? What is it rankles with you?
MEDEA: I trust you, yes. But the house of Pelias hates me,
And so does Creon. If you are bound by this oath,
When they try to drag me from your land, you will not   720
Abandon me; but if our pact is only words,
With no oath to the gods, you will be lightly armed,
Unable to resist their summons. I am weak,
While they have wealth to help them and a royal house.
AEGEUS: You show much foresight for such negotiations.   725
Well, if you will have it so, I will not refuse.
For, both on my side this will be the safest way
To have some excuse to put forward to your enemies,
And for you it is more certain. You may name the gods.
MEDEA: Swear by the plain of Earth, and Helius, father   730
Of my father, and name together all the gods …
AEGEUS: That I will act or not act in what way? Speak.
MEDEA: That you yourself will never cast me from your land,
Nor, if any of my enemies should demand me,
Will you, in your life, willingly hand me over.   735
AEGEUS: I swear by the Earth, by the holy light of Helius,
By all the gods, I will abide by this you say.
MEDEA: Enough. And, if you fail, what shall happen to you?
AEGEUS: What comes to those who have no regard for heaven.
MEDEA: Go on your way. Farewell. For I am satisfied.   740
And I will reach your city as soon as I can,
Having done the deed I have to do and gained my end.

(AEGEUS *goes out.*)

CHORUS: May Hermes, god of travelers,
Escort you, Aegeus, to your home!
And may you have the things you wish   745
So eagerly; for you

Appear to me to be a generous man.

MEDEA: God, and God's daughter, justice, and light of Helius!
Now, friends, has come the time of my triumph over
750　My enemies, and now my foot is on the road.
Now I am confident they will pay the penalty.
For this man, Aegeus, has been like a harbor to me
In all my plans just where I was most distressed.
To him I can fasten the cable of my safety
755　When I have reached the town and fortress of Pallas.
And now I shall tell to you the whole of my plan.
Listen to these words that are not spoken idly.
I shall send one of my servants to find Jason
And request him to come once more into my sight.
760　And when he comes, the words I'll say will be soft ones.
I'll say that I agree with him, that I approve
The royal wedding he has made, betraying me.
I'll say it was profitable, an excellent idea.
But I shall beg that my children may remain here:
765　Not that I would live in a country that hates me
Children of mine to feel their enemies' insults,
But that by a trick I may kill the king's daughter.
For I will send the children with gifts in their hands
To carry to the bride, so as not to be banished—
770　A finely woven dress and a golden diadem.
And if she takes them and wears them upon her skin
She and all who touch the girl will die in agony;
Such poison will I lay upon the gifts I send.
But there, however, I must leave that account paid.
775　I weep to think of what a deed I have to do
Next after that; for I shall kill my own children.
My children, there is none who can give them safety.
And when I have ruined the whole of Jason's house,
I shall leave the land and flee from the murder of my
780　Dear children, and I shall have done a dreadful deed.
For it is not bearable to be mocked by enemies.
So it must happen. What profit have I in life?
I have no land, no home, no refuge from my pain.
My mistake was made the time I left behind me
785　My father's house, and trusted the words of a Greek,
Who, with heaven's help, will pay me the price for that.
For those children he had from me he will never
See alive again, nor will he on his new bride
Beget another child, for she is to be forced
790　To die a most terrible death by these my poisons.
Let no one think me a weak one, feeble-spirited,
A stay-at-home, but rather just the opposite,
One who can hurt my enemies and help my friends;
For the lives of such persons are most remembered.

795　CHORUS: Since you have shared the knowledge of your plan
　　　with us,
I both wish to help you and support the normal
Ways of mankind, and tell you not to do this thing.

MEDEA: I can do no other thing. It is understandable
For you to speak thus. You have not suffered as I have.

800　CHORUS: But can you have the heart to kill your flesh and
　　　blood?

MEDEA: Yes, for this is the best way to wound my husband.

CHORUS: And you, too. Of women you will be most unhappy.

MEDEA: So it must be. No compromise is possible.

(*She turns to the* NURSE.)

Go, you, at once, and tell Jason to come to me.
You I employ on all affairs of greatest trust.　805
Say nothing of these decisions which I have made.
If you love your mistress, if you were born a woman.

CHORUS: From of old the children of Erechtheus are
Splendid, the sons of blessed gods. They dwell
In Athens' holy and unconquered land,　810
Where famous Wisdom feeds them and they pass gaily
Always through that most brilliant air where once, they say,
That golden Harmony gave birth to the nine
Pure Muses of Pieria.

And beside the sweet flow of Cephisus' stream,　815
Where Cypris sailed, they say, to draw the water,
And mild soft breezes breathed along her path,
And on her hair were flung the sweet-smelling garlands
Of flowers of roses by the Lovers, the companions
Of Wisdom, her escort, the helpers of men　820
In every kind of excellence.

How then can these holy rivers
Or this holy land love you,
Or the city find you a home,
You, who will kill your children,　825
You, not pure with the rest?
O think of the blow at your children
And think of the blood that you shed.
O, over and over I beg you,
By your knees I beg you do not　830
Be the murderess of your babes!

O where will you find the courage
Or the skill of hand and heart,
When you set yourself to attempt
A deed so dreadful to do?　835
How, when you look upon them,
Can you tearlessly hold the decision
For murder? You will not be able,
When your children fall down and implore you,
You will not be able to dip　840
Steadfast your hand in their blood.

(*Enter* JASON, *with attendants.*)

JASON: I have come at your request. Indeed, although you are
Bitter against me, this you shall have: I will listen
To what new thing you want, woman, to get from me.

MEDEA: Jason, I beg you to be forgiving toward me　845
For what I said. It is natural for you to bear with
My temper, since we have had much love together.
I have talked with myself about this and I have
Reproached myself. "Fool" I said, "why am I so mad?
Why am I set against those who have planned wisely?　850
Why make myself an enemy of the authorities
And of my husband, who does the best thing for me
By marrying royalty and having children who
Will be as brothers to my own? What is wrong with me?

---

755 **fortress of Pallas** Athens, the town of Athena

808 **children of Erechtheus** the Athenians　815 **beside . . .
stream** at Athens

855 Let me give up anger, for the gods are kind to me.
Have I not children, and do I not know that we
In exile from our country must be short of friends?"
When I considered this I saw that I had shown
Great lack of sense, and that my anger was foolish.

860 Now I agree with you. I think that you are wise
In having this other wife as well as me, and I
Was mad. I should have helped you in these plans of yours,
Have joined in the wedding, stood by the marriage bed,
Have taken pleasure in attendance on your bride.

865 But we women are what we are—perhaps a little
Worthless; and you men must not be like us in this,
Nor be foolish in return when we are foolish.
Now, I give in, and admit that then I was wrong.
I have come to a better understanding now

(*She turns toward the house.*)

870 Children, come here, my children, come outdoors to us!
Welcome your father with me, and say goodbye to him,
And with your mother, who just now was his enemy,
Join again in making friends with him who loves us.

(*Enter the* CHILDREN, *attended by the* TUTOR.)

We have made peace, and all our anger is over.
875 Take hold of his right hand—O God, I am thinking
Of something which may happen in the secret future.
O children, will you just so, after a long life,
Hold out your loving arms at the grave? O children,
How ready to cry I am, how full of foreboding!
880 I am ending at last this quarrel with your father,
And, look my soft eyes have suddenly filled with tears.
CHORUS: And the pale tears have started also in my eyes.
O may the trouble not grow worse than now it is!
JASON: I approve of what you say. And I cannot blame you
Even for what you said before. It is natural
885 For a woman to be wild with her husband when he
Goes in for secret love. But now your mind has turned
To better reasoning. In the end you have come to
The right decision, like the clever woman you are.
And of you, children, your father is taking care.
890 He has made, with God's help, ample provision for you.
For I think that a time will come when you will be
The leading people in Corinth with your brothers.
You must grow up. As to the future, your father
And those of the gods who love him will deal with that.
895 I want to see you, when you have become young men,
Healthy and strong, better men than my enemies.
Medea, why are your eyes all wet with pale tears?
Why is your cheek so white and turned away from me?
Are not these words of mine pleasing for you to hear?
900 MEDEA: It is nothing. I was thinking about these children.
JASON: You must be cheerful. I shall look after them well.
MEDEA: I will be. It is not that I distrust your words,
But a woman is a frail thing, prone to crying.
JASON: But why then should you grieve so much for these
children?
905 MEDEA: I am their mother. When you prayed that they
might live
I felt unhappy to think that these things will be.
But come, I have said something of the things I meant
To say to you, and now I will tell you the rest.

Since it is the king's will to banish me from here—   910
And for me, too, I know that this is the best thing,
Not to be in your way by living here or in
The king's way, since they think me ill-disposed to them—
I then am going into exile from this land;
But do you, so that you may have the care of them,   915
Beg Creon that the children may not be banished.
JASON: I doubt if I'll succeed, but still I'll attempt it.
MEDEA: Then you must tell your wife to beg from her father
That the children may be reprieved from banishment.
JASON: I will, and with her I shall certainly succeed.   920
MEDEA: If she is like the rest of us women, you will.
And I, too, will take a hand with you in this business,
For I will send her some gifts which are far fairer,
I am sure of it, than those which now are in fashion,
A finely woven dress and a golden diadem,   925
And the children shall present them. Quick, let one of you
Servants bring here to me that beautiful dress.

(*One of her attendants goes into the house.*)

She will be happy not in one way, but in a hundred,
Having so fine a man as you to share her bed,
And with this beautiful dress which Helius of old,   930
My father's father, bestowed on his descendants.

(*Enter attendant carrying the poisoned dress and diadem.*)

There, children, take these wedding presents in your hands.
Take them to the royal princess, the happy bride,
And give them to her. She will not think little of them.
JASON: No, don't be foolish, and empty your hands of these.   935
Do you think the palace is short of dresses to wear?
Do you think there is no gold there? Keep them, don't
give them
Away. If my wife considers me of any value,
She will think more of me than money, I am sure of it.
MEDEA: No, let me have my way. They say the gods themselves   940
Are moved by gifts, and gold does more with men than words.
Hers is the luck, her fortune that which god blesses;
She is young and a princess; but for my children's reprieve
I would give my very life, and not gold only.
Go children, go together to that rich palace,   945
Be suppliants to the new wife of your father,
My lady, beg her not to let you be banished.
And give her the dress—for this is of great importance,
That she should take the gift into her hand from yours.
Go, quick as you can. And bring your mother good news   950
By your success of those things which she longs to gain.

(JASON *goes out with his attendants, followed by the* TUTOR *and
the* CHILDREN *carrying the poisoned gifts.*)

CHORUS: Now there is no hope left for the children's lives.
Now there is none. They are walking already to murder.
The bride, poor bride, will accept the curse of the gold,
Will accept the bright diadem.   955
Around her yellow hair she will set that dress
Of death with her own hands.

The grace and the perfume and glow of the golden robe
Will charm her to put them upon her and wear the wreath,
And now her wedding will be with the dead below,   960
Into such a trap she will fall,

Poor thing, into such a fate of death and never
Escape from under that curse.

You, too, O wretched bridegroom, making your match
       with kings,
965   You do not see that you bring
Destruction on your children and on her,
Your wife, a fearful death.
Poor soul, what a fall is yours!

In your grief, too, I weep, mother of little children,
970   You who will murder your own,
In vengeance for the loss of married love
Which Jason has betrayed
As he lives with another wife.

(*Enter the* TUTOR *with the* CHILDREN.)

TUTOR: Mistress, I tell you that these children are reprieved,
975   And the royal bride has been pleased to take in her hands
Your gifts. In that quarter the children are secure.
But come,
Why do you stand confused when you are fortunate?
Why have you turned round with your cheek away from me?
980   Are not these words of mine pleasing for you to hear?
MEDEA: Oh! I am lost!
TUTOR: That word is not in harmony with my tidings.
MEDEA: I am lost, I am lost!
TUTOR: Am I in ignorance telling you
Of some disaster, and not the good news I thought?
985 MEDEA: You have told what you have told. I do not blame you.
TUTOR: Why then this downcast eye, and this weeping of tears?
MEDEA: Oh, I am forced to weep, old man. The gods and I,
I in a kind of madness, have contrived all this.
TUTOR: Courage! You, too, will be brought home by your
children.
990 MEDEA: Ah, before that happens I shall bring others home.
TUTOR: Others before you have been parted from their
children.
Mortals must bear in resignation their ill luck.
MEDEA: That is what I shall do. But go inside the house,
And do for the children your usual daily work.

(*The* TUTOR *goes into the house.* MEDEA *turns to her* CHILDREN.)

995   O children, O my children, you have a city,
You have a home, and you can leave me behind you,
And without your mother you may live there forever.
But I am going in exile to another land
Before I have seen you happy and taken pleasure in you,
1000   Before I have dressed your brides and made your marriage
beds
And held up the torch at the ceremony of wedding.
Oh, what a wretch I am in this my self-willed thought!
What was the purpose, children, for which I reared you?
For all my travail and wearing myself away?
1005   They were sterile, those pains I had in the bearing of you.
Oh surely once the hopes in you I had, poor me,
Were high ones: you would look after me in old age,
And when I died would deck me well with your own
hands;
A thing which all would have done. Oh but now it is gone,
1010   That lovely thought. For, once I am left without you,

Sad will be the life I'll lead and sorrowful for me.
And you will never see your mother again with
Your dear eyes, gone to another mode of living.
Why, children, do you look upon me with your eyes?
Why do you smile so sweetly that last smile of all?   1015
Oh, Oh, what can I do? My spirit has gone from me,
Friends, when I saw that bright look in the children's eyes.
I cannot bear to do it. I renounce my plans
I had before. I'll take my children away from
This land. Why should I hurt their father with the pain   1020
They feel, and suffer twice as much of pain myself?
No, no, I will not do it. I renounce my plans.
Ah, what is wrong with me? Do I want to let go
My enemies unhurt and be laughed at for it?
I must face this thing. Oh, but what a weak woman   1025
Even to admit to my mind these soft arguments.
Children, go into the house. And he whom law forbids
To stand in attendance at my sacrifices,
Let him see to it. I shall not mar my handiwork.
Oh! Oh!   1030
Do not, O my heart, you must not do these things!
Poor heart, let them go, have pity upon the children.
If they live with you in Athens they will cheer you.
No! By Hell's avenging furies it shall not be—
This shall never be, that I should suffer my children   1035
To be the prey of my enemies' insolence.
Every way is it fixed. The bride will not escape.
No, the diadem is now upon her head, and she,
The royal princess, is dying in the dress, I know it.
But—for it is the most dreadful of roads for me   1040
To tread, and them I shall send on a more dreadful still—
I wish to speak to the children.

(*She calls the* CHILDREN *to her.*)

                              Come, children, give
Me your hands, give your mother your hands to kiss them.
Oh the dear hands, and O how dear are these lips to me,
And the generous eyes and the bearing of my children!   1045
I wish you happiness, but not here in this world.
What is here your father took. Oh how good to hold you!
How delicate the skin, how sweet the breath of children!
Go, go! I am no longer able, no longer
To look upon you. I am overcome by sorrow.   1050

(*The* CHILDREN *go into the house.*)

I know indeed what evil I intend to do,
But stronger than all my afterthoughts is my fury,
Fury that brings upon mortals the greatest evils.

(*She goes out to the right, toward the royal palace.*)

CHORUS: Often before
I have gone through more subtle reasons,   1055
And have come upon questionings greater
Than a woman should strive to search out.
But we too have a goddess to help us
And accompany us into wisdom.
Not all of us. Still you will find   1060
Among many women a few,
And our sex is not without learning.
This I say, that those who have never
Had children, who know nothing of it,

1065   In happiness have the advantage
        Over those who are parents.
        The childless, who never discover
        Whether children turn out as a good thing
        Or as something to cause pain, are spared
1070   Many troubles in lacking this knowledge.
        And those who have in their homes
        The sweet presence of children, I see that their lives
        Are all wasted away by their worries.
        First they must think how to bring them up well and
1075   How to leave them something to live on.
        And then after this whether all their toil
        Is for those who will turn out good or bad,
        Is still an unanswered question.
        And of one more trouble, the last of all,
1080   That is common to mortals I tell.
        For suppose you have found them enough for their living,
        Suppose that the children have grown into youth
        And have turned out good, still, if God so wills it,
        Death will away with your children's bodies,
1085   And carry them off into Hades.
        What is our profit, then, that for the sake of
        Children the gods should pile upon mortals
        After all else
        This most terrible grief of all?

(Enter MEDEA, *from the spectators' right*.)

1090   MEDEA: Friends, I can tell you that for long I have waited
        For the event. I stare toward the place from where
        The news will come. And now, see one of Jason's servants
        Is on his way here, and that labored breath of his
        Shows he has tidings for us, and evil tidings.

(Enter, *also from the right, the* MESSENGER.)

1095   MESSENGER: Medea, you who have done such a dreadful thing,
        So outrageous, run for your life, take what you can,
        A ship to bear you hence or chariot on land.
        MEDEA: And what is the reason deserves such flight as this?
        MESSENGER: She is dead, only just now, the royal princess,
1100   And Creon dead, too, her father, by your poisons.
        MEDEA: The finest words you have spoken. Now and hereafter
        I shall count you among my benefactors and friends.
        MESSENGER: What! Are you right in the mind? Are you not mad,
        Woman? The house of the king is outraged by you.
1105   Do you enjoy it? Not afraid of such doings?
        MEDEA: To what you say I on my side have something too
        To say in answer. Do not be in a hurry, friend,
        But speak. How did they die? You will delight me twice
        As much again if you say they died in agony.
1110   MESSENGER: When those two children, born of you, had
                entered in,
        Their father with them, and passed into the bride's house,
        We were pleased, we slaves who were distressed by your
                wrongs.
        All through the house we were talking of but one thing,
        How you and your husband had made up your quarrel.
1115   Some kissed the children's hands and some their yellow
                hair,
        And I myself was so full of my joy that I
        Followed the children into the women's quarters.

Our mistress, whom we honor now instead of you,
Before she noticed that your two children were there,
Was keeping her eye fixed eagerly on Jason.   1120
Afterwards, however, she covered up her eyes,
Her cheek paled, and she turned herself away from him,
So disgusted was she at the children's coming there.
But your husband tried to end the girl's bad temper,
And said "You must not look unkindly on your friends. 1125
Cease to be angry. Turn your head to me again.
Have as your friends the same ones as your husband has.
And take these gifts, and beg your father to reprieve
These children from their exile. Do it for my sake."
She, when she saw the dress, could not restrain herself. 1130
She agreed with all her husband said, and before
He and the children had gone far from the palace,
She took the gorgeous robe and dressed herself in it,
And put the golden crown around her curly locks,
And arranged the set of the hair in a shining mirror, 1135
And smiled at the lifeless image of herself in it.
Then she rose from her chair and walked about the room,
With her gleaming feet stepping most soft and delicate,
All overjoyed with the present. Often and often
She would stretch her foot out straight and look along it. 1140
But after that it was a fearful thing to see.
The color of her face changed, and she staggered back,
She ran, and her legs trembled, and she only just
Managed to reach a chair without falling flat down.
An aged woman servant who, I take it, thought   1145
This was some seizure of Pan or another god,
Cried out "God bless us," but that was before she saw
The white foam breaking through her lips and her rolling
The pupils of her eyes and her face all bloodless.
Then she raised a different cry from that "God bless us," 1150
A huge shriek, and the women ran, one to the king,
One to the newly wedded husband to tell him
What had happened to his bride; and with frequent sound
The whole of the palace rang as they went running.
One walking quickly round the course of a race-track 1155
Would now have turned the bend and be close to the goal,
When she, poor girl, opened her shut and speechless eye,
And with a terrible groan she came to herself.
For a twofold pain was moving up against her.
The wreath of gold that was resting around her head 1160
Let forth a fearful stream of all-devouring fire,
And the finely woven dress your children gave to her,
Was fastening on the unhappy girl's fine flesh.
She leapt up from the chair, and all on fire she ran,
Shaking her hair now this way and now that, trying   1165
To hurl the diadem away; but fixedly
The gold preserved its grip, and, when she shook her hair,
Then more and twice as fiercely the fire blazed out.
Till, beaten by her fate, she fell down to the ground,
Hard to be recognized except by a parent.   1170
Neither the setting of her eyes was plain to see,
Nor the shapeliness of her face. From the top of
Her head there oozed out blood and fire mixed together.
Like the drops on pine-bark, so the flesh from her bones
Dropped away, torn by the hidden fang of the poison. 1175
It was a fearful sight; and terror held us all
From touching the corpse. We had learned from what had
        happened.
But her wretched father, knowing nothing of the event,

1180 Came suddenly to the house, and fell upon the corpse,
And at once cried out and folded his arms about her,
And kissed her and spoke to her, saying, "O my poor child,
What heavenly power has so shamefully destroyed you?
And who has set me here like an ancient sepulcher,
Deprived of you? O let me die with you, my child!"
1185 And when he had made an end of his wailing and crying,
Then the old man wished to raise himself to his feet;
But, as the ivy clings to the twigs of the laurel,
So he stuck to the fine dress, and he struggled fearfully.
For he was trying to lift himself to his knee,
1190 And she was pulling him down, and when he tugged hard
He would be ripping his aged flesh from his bones.
At last his life was quenched, and the unhappy man
Gave up the ghost, no longer could hold up his head.
There they lie close, the daughter and the old father,
1195 Dead bodies, an event he prayed for in his tears.
As for your interests, I will say nothing of them,
For you will find your own escape from punishment.
Our human life I think and have thought a shadow,
And I do not fear to say that those who are held
1200 Wise among men and who search the reasons of things
Are those who bring the most sorrow on themselves.
For of mortals there is no one who is happy.
If wealth flows in upon one, one may be perhaps
Luckier than one's neighbor, but still not happy.

(*Exit.*)

1205 CHORUS: Heaven, it seems, on this day has fastened many
Evils on Jason, and Jason has deserved them.
Poor girl, the daughter of Creon, how I pity you
And your misfortunes, you who have gone quite away
To the house of Hades because of marrying Jason.
1210 MEDEA: Women, my task is fixed: as quickly as I may
To kill my children, and start away from this land,
And not, by wasting time, to suffer my children
To be slain by another hand less kindly to them.
Force every way will have it they must die, and since
1215 This must be so, then I, their mother, shall kill them.
Oh, arm yourself in steel, my heart! Do not hang back
From doing this fearful and necessary wrong.
Oh, come, my hand, poor wretched hand, and take the
sword.
Take it, step forward to this bitter starting point,
1220 And do not be a coward, do not think of them,
How sweet they are, and how you are their mother. Just for
This one short day be forgetful of your children,
Afterward weep; for even though you will kill them,
They were very dear—Oh, I am an unhappy woman!

(*With a cry she rushes into the house.*)

1225 CHORUS: O Earth, and the far shining
Ray of the Sun, look down, look down upon
This poor lost woman, look, before she raises
The hand of murder against her flesh and blood.
Yours was the golden birth from which
1230 She sprang, and now I fear divine
Blood may be shed by men.
O heavenly light, hold back her hand,
Check her, and drive from out the house
The bloody Fury raised by fiends of Hell.

Vain waste, your care of children; 1235
Was it in vain you bore the babes you loved,
After you passed the inhospitable strait
Between the dark blue rocks, Symplegades?
O wretched one, how has it come,
This heavy anger on your heart, 1240
This cruel bloody mind?
For God from mortals asks a stern
Price for the stain of kindred blood
In like disaster falling on their homes.

(*A cry from* ONE OF THE CHILDREN *is heard.*)

CHORUS: Do you hear the cry, do you hear the children's cry? 1245
O you hard heart, O woman fated for evil!
ONE OF THE CHILDREN: (*From within.*) What can I do and how
escape my mother's hands?
ANOTHER CHILD: (*From within.*) O my dear brother, I cannot tell.
We are lost.
CHORUS: Shall I enter the house? Oh, surely I should
Defend the children from murder. 1250
A CHILD: (*From within.*) O help us, in God's name, for now we
need your help.
Now, now we are close to it. We are trapped by the sword.
CHORUS: O your heart must have been made of rock or steel,
You who can kill
With your own hand the fruit of your own womb. 1255
Of one alone I have heard, one woman alone
Of those of old who laid her hands on her children,
Ino, sent mad by heaven when the wife of Zeus
Drove her out from her home and made her wander;
And because of the wicked shedding of blood 1260
Of her own children she threw
Herself, poor wretch, into the sea and stepped away
Over the sea-cliff to die with her two children.
What horror more can be? O women's love,
So full of trouble, 1265
How many evils have you caused already!

(*Enter* JASON, *with attendants.*)

JASON: You women, standing close in front of this dwelling,
Is she, Medea, she who did this dreadful deed,
Still in the house, or has she run away in flight?
For she will have to hide herself beneath the earth, 1270
Or raise herself on wings into the height of air,
If she wishes to escape the royal vengeance.
Does she imagine that, having killed our rulers,
She will herself escape uninjured from this house?
But I am thinking not so much of her as for 1275
The children—her the king's friends will make to suffer
For what she did. So I have come to save the lives
Of my boys, in case the royal house should harm them
While taking vengeance for their mother's wicked deed.
CHORUS: O Jason, if you but knew how deeply you are 1280
Involved in sorrow, you would not have spoken so.
JASON: What is it? That she is planning to kill me also?
CHORUS: Your children are dead, and by their own mother's
hand.
JASON: What! That is it? O woman, you have destroyed me!
CHORUS: You must make up your mind your children are no 1285
more.
JASON: Where did she kill them? Was it here or in the house?

CHORUS: Open the gates and there you will see them murdered.
JASON: Quick as you can unlock the doors, men, and undo
    The fastenings and let me see this double evil,
1290   My children dead and her—Oh her I will repay.

(His attendants rush to the door. MEDEA *appears above the house in a chariot drawn by dragons. She has the dead bodies of the* CHILDREN *with her.)*

MEDEA: Why do you batter these gates and try to unbar them,
    Seeking the corpses and for me who did the deed?
    You may cease your trouble, and, if you have need of me,
    Speak, if you wish. You will never touch me with your hand,
1295   Such a chariot has Helius, my father's father,
    Given me to defend me from my enemies.
JASON: You hateful thing, you woman most utterly loathed
    By the gods and me and by all the race of mankind,
    You who have had the heart to raise a sword against
1300   Your children, you, their mother, and left me childless—
    You have done this, and do you still look at the sun
    And at the earth, after these most fearful doings?
    I wish you dead. Now I see it plain, though at that time
    I did not, when I took you from your foreign home
1305   And brought you to a Greek house, you, an evil thing,
    A traitress to your father and your native land.
    The gods hurled the avenging curse of yours on me.
    For your own brother you slew at your own hearthside,
    And then came aboard that beautiful ship, the Argo.
1310   And that was your beginning. When you were married
    To me, your husband, and had borne children to me,
    For the sake of pleasure in the bed you killed them.
    There is no Greek woman who would have dared such deeds,
    Out of all those whom I passed over and chose you
1315   To marry instead, a bitter destructive match,
    A monster, not a woman, having a nature
    Wilder than that of Scylla in the Tuscan sea.
    Ah! no, not if I had ten thousand words of shame
    Could I sting you. You are naturally so brazen.
1320   Go, worker in evil, stained with your children's blood.
    For me remains to cry aloud upon my fate,
    Who will get no pleasure from my newly wedded love,
    And the boys whom I begot and brought up, never
    Shall I speak to them alive. Oh, my life is over!
1325 MEDEA: Long would be the answer which I might have made to
    These words of yours, if Zeus the father did not know
    How I have treated you and what you did to me.
    No, it was not to be that you should scorn my love,
    And pleasantly live your life through, laughing at me;
1330   Nor would the princess, nor he who offered the match,
    Creon, drive me away without paying for it.
    So now you may call me a monster, if you wish,
    A Scylla housed in the caves of the Tuscan sea.
    I too, as I had to, have taken hold of your heart.
1335 JASON: You feel the pain yourself. You share in my sorrow.
MEDEA: Yes, and my grief is gain when you cannot mock it.
JASON: O children, what a wicked mother she was to you!
MEDEA: They died from a disease they caught from their father.

———————

1317 **Scylla** a monster in the *Odyssey*

JASON: I tell you it was not my hand that destroyed them.
MEDEA: But it was your insolence, and your virgin wedding. 1340
JASON: And just for the sake of that you chose to kill them.
MEDEA: Is love so small a pain, do you think, for a woman?
JASON: For a wise one, certainly. But you are wholly evil.
MEDEA: The children are dead. I say this to make you suffer.
JASON: The children, I think, will bring down curses on you. 1345
MEDEA: The gods know who was the author of this sorrow.
JASON: Yes, the gods know indeed, they know your loathsome
    heart.
MEDEA: Hate me. But I tire of your barking bitterness.
JASON: And I of yours. It is easier to leave you.
MEDEA: How then? What shall I do? I long to leave you too. 1350
JASON: Give me the bodies to bury and to mourn them.
MEDEA: No, that I will not. I will bury them myself,
    Bearing them to Hera's temple on the promontory;
    So that no enemy may evilly treat them
    By tearing up their grave. In this land of Corinth 1355
    I shall establish a holy feast and sacrifice
    Each year for ever to atone for the blood guilt.
    And I myself go to the land of Erechtheus
    To dwell in Aegeus' house, the son of Pandion.
    While you, as is right, will die without distinction, 1360
    Struck on the head by a piece of the Argo's timber,
    And you will have seen the bitter end of my love.
JASON: May a Fury for the children's sake destroy you,
    And justice, Requitor of blood.
MEDEA: What heavenly power lends an ear 1365
    To a breaker of oaths, a deceiver?
JASON: Oh, I hate you, murderess of children.
MEDEA: Go to your palace. Bury your bride.
JASON: I go, with two children to mourn for.
MEDEA: Not yet do you feel it. Wait for the future. 1370
JASON: Oh, children I loved!
MEDEA: I loved them, you did not.
JASON: You loved them, and killed them.
MEDEA: To make you feel
    pain.
JASON: Oh, wretch that I am, how I long
    To kiss the dear lips of my children!
MEDEA: Now you would speak to them, now you would kiss 1375
    them.
    Then you rejected them.
JASON: Let me, I beg you,
    Touch my boys delicate flesh.
MEDEA: I will not. Your words are all wasted.
JASON: O God, do you hear it, this persecution,
    These my sufferings from this hateful 1380
    Woman, this monster, murderess of children?
    Still what I can do that I will do:
    I will lament and cry upon my fate,
    Calling the gods to bear me witness
    How you have killed my boys and prevent me from 1385
    Touching their bodies or giving them burial.
    I wish I had never begot them to see them
    Afterward slaughtered by you.
CHORUS: Zeus in Olympus is the overseer
    Of many doings. Many things the gods 1390
    Achieve beyond our judgment. What we thought
    Is not confirmed and what we thought not god
    Contrives. And so it happens in this story.

Aristophanes

Aristophanes (c. 450–c. 388 BCE) pursued his career as a playwright throughout the Peloponnesian War. As he observed the decline and defeat of Athens, his comedies relentlessly attacked the war and the individuals and attitudes that supported it. Aristophanes first entered the City Dionysia in 427 BCE and first won in 426 BCE with a now-lost play that satirized the policies and character of the military leader Cleon. Many of Aristophanes' plays—*Birds, Lysistrata, Assembly of Women*—use a utopian premise to criticize the war, but in other plays, Aristophanes lampoons other aspects of city life. In *Frogs,* for instance, a pompous Aeschylus and an embittered Euripides come from Hades to vie with one another once again; in *Clouds,* Aristophanes ridicules the sophists—professional teachers of rhetoric—for their ability to argue any side of an issue, and he particularly singles out Socrates for blame. The impact of Aristophanes' comedy on Athens should not be underestimated. In Plato's *Apology,* Socrates cites Aristophanes' portrayal of him in *Clouds* as one of the factors that turned Athenian sentiment against him, resulting in his trial and sentence of execution. Aristophanes' plays include *Acharnians, Knights, Clouds, Wasps, Peace, Birds, Lysistrata, Women Celebrating the Thesmophoria, Frogs, Assembly of Women,* and *Plutus.*

LYSISTRATA

Lysistrata is one of several plays critical of Athens' war with Sparta. Produced in 411 BCE, the play follows shortly on a disastrous phase of the war for Athens. Two years earlier, the Athenian raid on Sicily had failed, and the navy was decimated, leaving Athens vulnerable to attack by Sparta. Although the navy was rebuilt before Sparta mounted its final assault, Athens fell to Sparta in 404 BCE.

Lysistrata explores the premise that the women of Greece—drawn from all the major city-states and regions—could unite to oppose the war. Led by the Athenian Lysistrata (her name means "disband the army"), the women barricade themselves on the Acropolis, withholding sex from the men until peace can be declared. Aristophanes provides each of his

Displaying an "eclectic" design combining classical and modern costume elements, this production of Aristophanes' *Lysistrata* also displays an updated version of the Greek costume *phallus* as well.

women with the physical attributes and accent typical of her region. The large and powerful Spartan woman Lampito, for example, is both an expert in the Spartan rump-kicking dance and speaks in what was—to an Athenian audience—an outlandish accent (to make this clear for English-speaking readers, this translation gives Lampito an exaggerated Southern drawl).

Lysistrata addresses the politics of its era in a variety of ways. It is, of course, a passionate plea for peace, concluding with a scene of comic feasting and dancing enjoyed by all the characters in the play, Athenians and Spartans, men and women. For modern audiences, though, the play's connection between gender and politics may seem more immediate. On one hand, the play implies an equality between men and women. The women claim that the morality of their domestic sphere is superior to the military morality pursued by the men, and to get the women back, the men are forced to compromise with them. On the other hand, although *Lysistrata* seems to provide women with political power, their power resides wholly in their sexuality; they can interrupt, but not change, the fact that they are the property of men. The Theater of Dionysus could not, of course, put women on the stage, and Lysistrata, Lampito, Kalonike, and the rest—even the naked girl Harmony—were all played by men in padded costumes. In the play and in the *polis,* women were defined principally through their relation to men. The limited influence women could exert was subordinate to the civil power that Aristophanes and his audience took to be the "natural" preserve of the male audience. Despite the play's earthy humor and apparent feminism, *Lysistrata* documents the actual status of women in classical Athens; their power is restricted to the sphere of the *oikos,* or home, and can be practiced only through their subservience to men, who, as citizens, finally can command women's bodies, the home, and the state as well.

LYSISTRATA

Aristophanes

TRANSLATED BY DONALD SUTHERLAND

CHARACTERS

LYSISTRATA
KALONIKE } *Athenian women*
MYRRHINA
LAMPITO, *a Spartan woman*
CHORUS OF OLD MEN
CHORUS OF OLD WOMEN
ATHENIAN COMMISSIONER

OLD MARKET WOMAN
CINESIAS, *an Athenian,*
      husband of Myrrhina
SPARTAN HERALD
SCYTHIAN POLICEMEN
PORTER
ATHENIAN OFFICIAL

ATHENIANS
SPARTAN AMBASSADORS
ATHENIAN AMBASSADORS
HARMONY
LADY COP

A street in Athens before daylight.

LYSISTRATA: If anyone had asked them to a festival
  of Aphrodite or of Bacchus or of Pan,
  you couldn't get through Athens for the tambourines,
  but now there's not one solitary woman here.
5 Except my next-door neighbor. Here she's coming out.
  Hello, Kalonike.
KALONIKE: Hello, Lysistrata.
  What are you so upset about? Don't scowl so, dear.
  You're less attractive when you knit your brows and glare.
LYSISTRATA: I know, Kalonike, but I am smoldering
10 with indignation at the way we women act.
  Men think we are so gifted for all sorts of crime
  that we will stop at nothing—
KALONIKE: Well, we are, by Zeus!
LYSISTRATA: —but when it comes to an appointment here
    with me
  to plot and plan for something really serious
15 they lie in bed and do not come.
KALONIKE: They'll come, my dear.
  You know what trouble women have in going out:
  one of us will be wrapped up in her husband still,
  another waking up the maid, or with a child
  to put to sleep, or give its bath, or feed its pap.
20 LYSISTRATA: But they had other more important things to do
  than those.
KALONIKE: What ever is it, dear Lysistrata?
  What have you called us women all together for?
  How much of a thing is it?
LYSISTRATA: Very big.
KALONIKE: And thick?
LYSISTRATA: Oh very thick indeed.
KALONIKE: Then *how* can we be late?
25 LYSISTRATA: That's not the way it is. Or we would all be here.
  But it is something I have figured out myself
  and turned and tossed upon for many a sleepless night.
KALONIKE: It must be something slick you've turned and
    tossed upon!
30 LYSISTRATA: So slick that the survival of all Greece depends
  upon the women.
KALONIKE: On the women? In that case
  poor Greece has next to nothing to depend upon.
LYSISTRATA: Since now it's we who must decide affairs of state:
  either there is to be no Spartan left alive—
KALONIKE: A very good thing too, if none were left,
  by Zeus!

LYSISTRATA: —and every living soul in Thebes to be destroyed— 35
KALONIKE: Except the eels! Spare the delicious eels of Thebes!
LYSISTRATA: —and as for Athens—I can't bring myself to say
  the like of that for us. But just think what I mean!
  Yet if the women meet here as I told them to
  from Sparta, Thebes, and all of their allies,   40
  and we of Athens, all together we'll save Greece.
KALONIKE: What reasonable thing could women ever do,
  or glorious, we who sit around all prettied up
  in flowers and scandalous saffron-yellow gowns,
  groomed and draped to the ground in oriental stuffs 45
  and fancy pumps?
LYSISTRATA: And those are just the very things
  I count upon to save us—wicked saffron gowns,
  perfumes and pumps and rouge and sheer transparent
  frocks.
KALONIKE: But what use can they be?
LYSISTRATA: So no man in our time
  will raise a spear against another man again— 50
KALONIKE: I'll get a dress dyed saffron-yellow, come what may!
LYSISTRATA: —nor touch a shield—
KALONIKE: I'll slip into the sheerest gown!
LYSISTRATA: —nor so much as a dagger—
KALONIKE: I'll buy a pair of pumps!
LYSISTRATA: So don't you think the women should be here
  by now?
KALONIKE: I don't. They should have *flown* and got here 55
  long ago.
LYSISTRATA: You'll see, my dear. They will, like good Athenians,
  do everything too late. But from the coastal towns
  no woman is here either, nor from Salamis.
KALONIKE: I'm certain those from Salamis have crossed the
    strait:
  they're always straddling *something* at this time of night. 60
LYSISTRATA: Not even those I was expecting would be first
  to get here, from Acharnae, from so close to town,
  not even they are here.
KALONIKE: But one of them, I know,
  is under way, and three sheets to the wind, by now.
  But look—some women are approaching over there. 65
LYSISTRATA: And over here are some, coming this way—
KALONIKE: Phew! Phew!
  Where are they from?
LYSISTRATA: Down by the marshes.
KALONIKE: Yes, by Zeus!
  It smells as if the bottoms had been all churned up!

(*Enter* MYRRHINA, *and others.*)

MYRRHINA: Hello Lysistrata. Are we a little late?
70   What's that? Why don't you speak?
LYSISTRATA: I don't think much of you,
    Myrrhina, coming to this business only now.
MYRRHINA: Well, I could hardly find my girdle in the dark.
    If it's so urgent, tell us what it is. We're here.
KALONIKE: Oh no. Let's wait for just a little while until
75   the delegates from Sparta and from Thebes arrive.
LYSISTRATA: You show much better judgment.

(*Enter* LAMPITO, *and others.*)

                                    Here comes Lampito!
LYSISTRATA: Well, darling Lampito! My dearest Spartan friend!
    How very sweet, how beautiful you look! That fresh
    complexion! How magnificent your figure is!
80   Enough to crush a bull!
LAMPITO: Ah shorely think Ah could.
    Ah take mah exacise. Ah jump and thump mah butt.
KALONIKE: And really, what a handsome set of tits you have!
LAMPITO: You feel me ovah lahk a cow fo sacrafahce!
LYSISTRATA: And this other young thing—where ever is *she* from?
85 LAMPITO: She's prominent, Ah sweah, in Thebes—a delegate
    ample enough.
LYSISTRATA: By Zeus, she represents Thebes well,
    having so trim a ploughland.
KALONIKE: Yes, by Zeus, she does!
    There's not a weed of all her field she hasn't plucked.
LYSISTRATA: And who's the other girl?
LAMPITO: Theah's nothing small, Ah sweah,
90   or tahght about her folks in Corinth.
KALONIKE: No, by Zeus!—
    to judge by this side of her, nothing small or tight.
LAMPITO: But who has called togethah such a regiment
    of all us women?
LYSISTRATA: Here I am. I did.
LAMPITO: Speak up,
    just tell us what you want.
KALONIKE: Oh yes, by Zeus, my dear,
95   do let us know what the important business is!
LYSISTRATA: Let me explain it, then. And yet . . . before I do . . .
    I have one little question.
KALONIKE: Anything you like.
LYSISTRATA: Don't you all miss the fathers of your little ones,
    your husbands who have gone away to war? I'm sure
100   you all have husbands in the armies far from home.
KALONIKE: Mine's been away five months in Thrace—
    a general's guard,
    posted to see his general does not desert.
MYRRHINA: And mine has been away in Pylos seven whole
    months.
LAMPITO: And mahn, though he does get back home on leave
    sometahms,
105   no soonah has he come than he is gone again.
LYSISTRATA: No lovers either. Not a sign of one is left.
    For since our eastern allies have deserted us
    they haven't sent a single six-inch substitute
    to serve as leatherware replacement for our men.
110   Would you be willing, then, if I thought out a scheme,
    to join with me to end the war?

KALONIKE: Indeed I would,
    even if I had to pawn this very wrap-around
    and drink up all the money in one day, I would!
MYRRHINA: And so would I, even if I had to see myself
    split like a flounder, and give half of me away!   115
LAMPITO: And so would Ah! Ah'd climb up Mount
    Taÿgetos
    if Ah just had a chance of seeing peace from theah!
LYSISTRATA: Then I will tell you. I may now divulge my
    plan.
    Women of Greece!—if we intend to force the men
    to make a peace, we must abstain . . .   120
KALONIKE: From what? Speak out!
LYSISTRATA: But will you do it?
KALONIKE: We will, though death should be the price!
LYSISTRATA: Well then, we must abstain utterly from the prick.
    Why do you turn your backs? Where are you off to now?
    And you—why pout and make such faces, shake your heads?
    Why has your color changed? Why do you shed those tears?   125
    Will you do it or will you not? Why hesitate?
KALONIKE: I will not do it. Never. Let the war go on!
MYRRHINA: Neither will I. By Zeus, no! Let the war go on!
LYSISTRATA: How can you say so, Madam Flounder, when just
    now
    you were declaiming you would split yourself in half?   130
KALONIKE: Anything else you like, anything! If I must
    I'll gladly walk through fire. That, rather than the prick!
    Because there's nothing like it, dear Lysistrata.
LYSISTRATA: How about you?
MYRRHINA: I too would gladly walk through fire.
LYSISTRATA: Oh the complete depravity of our whole sex!   135
    It is no wonder tragedies are made of us,
    we have such unrelenting unity of mind!
    But you, my friend from Sparta, dear, if you alone
    stand by me, only you, we still might save the cause.
    Vote on my side!   140
LAMPITO: They'ah hahd conditions, mahty hahd,
    to sleep without so much as the fo'skin of one . . .
    but all the same . . . well . . . yes. We need peace just as
    bad.
LYSISTRATA: Oh dearest friend!—the one real woman of them all!
KALONIKE: And if we really should abstain from what you say—
    which Heaven forbid!—do you suppose on that account   145
    that peace might come to be?
LYSISTRATA: I'm absolutely sure.
    If we should sit around, rouged and with skins well
    creamed,
    with nothing on but a transparent negligé,
    and come up to them with our deltas plucked quite smooth,
    and, once our men get stiff and want to come to grips,   150
    we do not yield to them at all but just hold off,
    they'll make a truce in no time. There's no doubt of that.
LAMPITO: We say in Spahta that when Menelaos saw
    Helen's ba'e apples he just tossed away his swo'd.
KALONIKE: And what, please, if our husbands just toss *us* away?   155
LYSISTRATA: Well, you have heard the good old saying: Know
    Thyself.
KALONIKE: It isn't worth the candle. I hate cheap substitutes.
    But what if they should seize and drag us by brute force
    into the bedroom?
LYSISTRATA!   Hang onto the doors!
KALONIKE: And if—
    they beat us?   160

LYSISTRATA: Then you must give in, but nastily,
and do it badly. There's no fun in it by force.
And then, just keep them straining. They will give it up
in no time—don't you worry. For never will a man
enjoy himself unless the woman coincides.

165 KALONIKE: If both of you are for this plan, then so are we.

LAMPITO: And we of Spahta shall persuade ouah men to keep
the peace sinceahly and with honah in all ways,
but how could anyone pe'suade the vulgah mob
of Athens not to deviate from discipline?

170 LYSISTRATA: Don't worry, we'll persuade our men. They'll keep
the peace.

LAMPITO: They won't, so long as they have battleships afloat
and endless money sto'ed up in the Pahthenon.

LYSISTRATA: But that too has been carefully provided for:
wc shall take over the Acropolis today.

175 The oldest women have their orders to do that:
while *we* meet here, *they* go as if to sacrifice
up there, but really seizing the Acropolis.

LAMPITO: All should go well. What you say theah is very
smaht.

LYSISTRATA: In that case, Lampito, what are we waiting for?

180 Let's take an oath, to bind us indissolubly.

LAMPITO: Well, just you show us what the oath is. Then we'll
sweah.

LYSISTRATA: You're right. Where is that lady cop?

(*To the armed* LADY COP *looking around for a* LADY COP.)

What do you think
you're looking for? Put down your shield in front of us,
there, on its back, and someone get some scraps of gut.

185 KALONIKE: Lysistrata, what in the world do you intend
to make us take an oath on?

LYSISTRATA: What? Why, on a shield,
just as they tell me some insurgents in a play
by Aeschylus once did, with a sheep's blood and guts.

KALONIKE: Oh *don't,* Lysistrata, don't swear upon a *shield,*

190 not if the oath has anything to do with peace!

LYSISTRATA: Well then, what *will* we swear on? Maybe we
should get
a white horse somewhere, like the Amazons, and cut
some bits of gut from it.

KALONIKE: *Where* would we get a horse?

LYSISTRATA: But what kind of an oath *is* suitable for us?

195 KALONIKE: By Zeus, I'll tell you if you like. First we put down
a big black drinking-cup, face up, and then we let
the neck of a good jug of wine bleed into it,
and take a solemn oath to—add no water in.

LAMPITO: Bah Zeus, Ah jest can't tell you how Ah lahk that
oath!

200 LYSISTRATA: Someone go get a cup and winejug from inside.

(KALONIKE *goes and is back in a flash.*)

KALONIKE: My dears, my dearest dears—how's *this* for pottery?
You feel good right away, just laying hold of it.

LYSISTRATA: Well, set it down, and lay your right hand on
this pig.
O goddess of Persuasion, and O Loving-cup,

205 accept this victim's blood! Be gracious unto us.

KALONIKE: It's not anaemic, and flows clear. Those are good signs

LAMPITO: What an aroma, too! Bah Castah it *is* sweet!

KALONIKE: My dears, if you don't mind—I'll be the first to
swear.

LYSISTRATA: By Aphrodite, no! If you had drawn first place
by lot—but now let all lay hands upon the cup.   210
Yes, Lampito—and now, let one of you repeat
for all of you what I shall say. You will be sworn
by every word she says, and bound to keep this oath:
No lover and no husband and no man on earth—

KALONIKE: No lover and no husband and no man on earth—   215

LYSISTRATA: *shall e'er approach me with his penis up.* Repeat.

KALONIKE: shall e'er approach me with his penis up. Oh dear,
my knees are buckling under me, Lysistrata!

LYSISTRATA: *and I shall lead an unlaid life alone at home,*

KALONIKE: and I shall lead an unlaid life alone at home,   220

LYSISTRATA: *wearing a saffron gown and groomed and beautified*

KALONIKE: wearing a saffron gown and groomed and beautified

LYSISTRATA: *so that my husband will be all on fire for me*

KALONIKE: so that my husband will be all on fire for me

LYSISTRATA: *but I will never willingly give in to him*   225

KALONIKE: but I will never willingly give in to him

LYSISTRATA: *and if he tries to force me to against my will*

KALONIKE: and if he tries to force me to against my will

LYSISTRATA: *I'll do it badly and not wiggle in response*

KALONIKE: I'll do it badly and not wiggle in response   230

LYSISTRATA: *nor toward the ceiling will I lift my Persian pumps*

KALONIKE: nor toward the ceiling will I lift my Persian pumps

LYSISTRATA: *nor crouch down as the lions on cheese-graters do*

KALONIKE: nor crouch down as the lions on cheese-graters do

LYSISTRATA: *and if I keep my promise, may I drink of this—*   235

KALONIKE: and if I keep my promise, may I drink of this—

LYSISTRATA: *but if I break it, then may water fill the cup!*

KALONIKE: but if I break it, then may water fill the cup!

LYSISTRATA: Do you all swear to this with her?

ALL: We do, by Zeus!

LYSISTRATA: I'll consecrate our oath now.   240

KALONIKE: Share alike, my dear,
so we'll be friendly to each other from the start.

LAMPITO: What was that screaming?

LYSISTRATA: That's what I was telling you:
the women have already seized the Parthenon
and the Acropolis. But now, dear Lampito,
return to Sparta and set things in order there—   245
but leave these friends of yours as hostages with us—
And let *us* join the others in the citadel
and help them bar the gates.

KALONIKE: But don't you think the men
will rally to the rescue of the citadel,
attacking us at once?   250

LYSISTRATA: They don't worry me much:
they'll never bring against us threats or fire enough
to force open the gates, except upon our terms.

KALONIKE: Never by Aphrodite! Or we'd lose our name
for being battle-axes and unbearable!

(*Exeunt. The scene changes to the Propylaea of the Acropolis. A* CHORUS OF VERY OLD MEN *struggles slowly in, carrying logs and firepots.*)

ONE OLD MAN: Lead on! O Drakës, step by step, although your   255
shoulder's aching
and under this green olive log's great weight
your back be breaking!

ANOTHER: Eh, life is long but always has
260   more surprises for us!
      Now who'd have thought we'd live to hear
          this, O Strymodorus?—

      The wives we fed and looked upon
      as helpless liabilities
265   now dare to occupy the Parthenon,
      our whole Acropolis, for once they seize
      the Propylaea, straightway
      they lock and bar the gateway.

CHORUS: Let's rush to the Acropolis with due precipitation
270   and lay these logs down circlewise, till presently we turn them
      into one mighty pyre to make a general cremation
      of all the women up there—eh! with our own hands we'll
      burn them,
      the leaders and the followers, without discrimination!

AN OLD MAN: They'll never have the laugh on me!
275   Though I may not look it,
      I rescued the Acropolis
          when the Spartans took it
      about a hundred years ago.
      We laid a siege that kept their king
280   six years unwashed, so when I made him throw
      his armor off, for all his blustering,
      in nothing but his shirt he
      looked very very dirty.

CHORUS: How strictly I besieged the man! These gates were
      all invested
285   with seventeen ranks of armored men all equally ferocious!
      Shall women—by Euripides and all the gods detested—
      not be restrained—with me on hand—from something so
      atrocious?
      They shall!—or may our trophies won at Marathon be bested!
          But we must go a long way yet
290   up that steep and winding road
          before we reach the fortress where we want to get.
           How shall we ever drag this load,
           lacking pack-mules, way up there?
      I can tell you that my shoulder has caved in
      beyond repair!
295   Yet we must trudge ever higher,
           ever blowing on the fire,
      so its coals will still be glowing when we get
      where we are going
          Fooh! Fooh!
          Whoo! I choke!
300   What a smoke!

          Lord Heracles! How fierce it flies
          out against me from the pot!
      and like a rabid bitch it bites me in the eyes!
          It's female fire, or it would not
305   scratch my poor old eyes like this.
      Yet undaunted we must onward, up the high
      Acropolis
          where Athena's temple stands
          fallen into hostile hands.
      O my comrades! shall we ever have a greater
      need to save her?
310   Fooh! Fooh!
          Whoo! I choke!
          What a smoke!

FIRST OLD MAN: Well, thank the gods, I see the fire is yet
      alive and waking!

SECOND OLD MAN: Why don't we set our lumber down right
      here in handy batches,
      then stick a branch of grape-vine in the pot until it catches   315

THIRD OLD MAN: and hurl ourselves against the gate with
      battering and shaking?

FIRST OLD MAN: and if the women won't unbar at such an
      ultimatum
      we'll set the gate on fire and then the smoke will suffocate
      'em.

SECOND OLD MAN: Well, let's put down our load. Fooh fooh,
      what smoke! But blow as needed!

THIRD OLD MAN: Your ablest generals *these* days would not carry   320
      wood like *we* did.

SECOND OLD MAN: At last the lumber ceases grinding my poor
      back to pieces!

THIRD OLD MAN: These are your orders, Colonel Pot: wake up
      the coals and bid them
      report here and present to me a torch lit up and flaring.

FIRST OLD MAN: O Victory, be with us! If you quell the
      women's daring
      we'll raise a splendid trophy of how you and we undid   325
      them!

(*A* CHORUS OF MIDDLE-AGED WOMEN *appears in the offing.*)

A WOMAN: I think that I perceive a smoke in which appears a
      flurry
      of sparks as of a lighted fire. Women, we'll have to hurry!

CHORUS OF WOMEN: Oh fleetly fly, oh swiftly flit,
          my dears, e'er Kalykë be lit
          and with Kritylla swallowed up alive   330
            in flames which the gales dreadfully drive
            and deadly old men fiercely inflate!
      Yet one thing I'm afraid of: will I not arrive too late?
      for filling up my water-jug has been no easy matter
      what with the crowd at the spring in the dusk and the   335
          clamor and pottery clatter.
          Pushed as I was, jostled by slave-
          women and sluts marked with a brand
          yet with my jug firmly in hand
          here I have come, hoping to save   340
           my burning friends and brave,

          for certain windy, witless, old,
          and wheezy fools, so I was told,
      with wood some tons in weight crept up this path,
          not having in mind heating a bath   345
          but uttering threats, vowing they will
      consume those nasty women into cinders on grill!
      But O Athena! never may I see my friends igniting!
      Nay!—let them save all the cities of Greece and their
          people from folly and fighting!   350
      Goddess whose crest flashes with gold,
      they were so bold taking your shrine
      only for this—Goddess who holds
      Athens—for *this* noble design,
      braving the flames, calling on you   355
      to carry water too!

(ONE OF THE OLD MEN *urinates noisily.*)

CHORUS OF WOMEN: Be still! What was that noise? Aha! Oh, wicked and degraded!

Would any good religious men have ever done what *they* did?

CHORUS OF MEN: Just look! It's a surprise-attack! Oh, dear, we're being raided

360 by swarms of them below us when we've got a swarm above us!

CHORUS OF WOMEN: Why panic at the sight of us? This is not many of us.

We number tens of thousands but you've hardly seen a fraction.

CHORUS OF MEN: O Phaidrias, shall they talk so big and we not take some action?

Oh, should we not be bashing them and splintering our lumber?

(*The* OLD MEN *begin to strip for combat.*)

365 CHORUS OF WOMEN: Let us, too, set our pitchers down, so they will not encumber

our movements if these gentlemen should care to offer battle.

CHORUS OF MEN: Oh someone should have clipped their jaws— twice, thrice, until they rattle—

(as once the poet put it)—then we wouldn't hear their prating.

CHORUS OF WOMEN: Well, here's your chance. Won't someone hit me? Here I stand, just waiting!

370 No other bitch will ever grab your balls, the way I'll treat you!

CHORUS OF MEN: Shut up—or I will drub you so old age will never reach you!

CHORUS OF WOMEN: Won't anyone step and lay one finger on Stratyllis?

CHORUS OF MEN: And if we pulverize her with our knuckles, will you kill us?

CHORUS OF WOMEN: No, only chew your lungs out and your innards and your eyes, sir.

375 CHORUS OF MEN: How clever is Euripides! There is no poet wiser:

he says indeed that women are the worst of living creatures.

CHORUS OF WOMEN: Now is the time, Rhodippe: let us raise our brimming pitchers.

CHORUS OF MEN: Why come up here with water, you, the gods' abomination?

CHORUS OF WOMEN: And why come here with fire, you tomb? To give yourself cremation?

380 CHORUS OF MEN: To set your friends alight upon a pyre erected for them.

CHORUS OF WOMEN: And so we brought our water-jugs. Upon your pyre we'll pour them.

CHORUS OF MEN: *You'll* put my fire out?

CHORUS OF WOMEN: Any time! You'll see there's nothing to it.

CHORUS OF MEN: I think I'll grill you right away, with just this torch to do it!

CHORUS OF WOMEN: Have you some dusting-powder? Here's your wedding-bath all ready.

385 CHORUS OF MEN: *You'll* bathe me, garbage that you are?

CHORUS OF WOMEN: Yes, bridegroom, just hold steady!

CHORUS OF MEN: Friends, you have heard her insolence—

CHORUS OF WOMEN: I'm free-born, not your slave, sir.

CHORUS OF MEN: I'll have this noise of yours restrained—

CHORUS OF WOMEN: Court's out—so be less grave, sir.

CHORUS OF MEN: Why don't you set her hair on fire?

CHORUS OF WOMEN: Oh, Water, be of service!

CHORUS OF MEN: Oh woe is me!

CHORUS OF WOMEN: Was it too hot?

CHORUS OF MEN: Oh, stop! What *is* this? Hot? Oh no! 390

CHORUS OF WOMEN: I'm watering you to make you grow.

CHORUS OF MEN: I'm withered from this chill I got!

CHORUS OF WOMEN: You've got a fire, so warm yourself. You're trembling: are you nervous?

(*Enter* ATHENIAN COMMISSIONER, *escorted by four* SCYTHIAN POLICEMEN *with bows and quivers slung on their backs.*)

COMMISSIONER: Has the extravagance of women broken out into full fury, with their banging tambourines 395 and constant wailings for their oriental gods, and on the roof-tops their Adonis festival, which I could hear myself from the Assembly once? For while Demostratos—that numbskull—had the floor, urging an expedition against Sicily, 400 his wife was dancing and we heard her crying out "Weep for Adonis!"—so the expedition failed with such an omen. When the same Demostratos was urging that we levy troops from our allies his wife was on the roof again, a little drunk: 405 "Weep for Adonis! Beat your breast!" says she. At that, he gets more bellicose, that god-Damn-ox-tratos. To this has the incontinence of women come!

CHORUS OF MEN: You haven't *yet* heard how outrageous they can be!

With other acts of violence, these women here 410 have showered us from their jugs, so now we are reduced to shaking out our shirts as if we'd pissed in them.

COMMISSIONER: Well, by the God of Waters, what do you expect? When we ourselves conspire with them in waywardness and give them good examples of perversity 415 such wicked notions naturally sprout in them. We go into a shop and say something like this: "Goldsmith, about that necklace you repaired: last night my wife was dancing, when the peg that bolts the catch fell from its hole. I have to sail for Salamis, 420 but if you have the time, by all means try to come towards evening, and put in the peg she needs." Another man says to a cobbler who is young and has no child's-play of a prick, "Cobbler," he says, "her sandal-strap is pinching my wife's little toe, 425 which is quite delicate. So please come by at noon and stretch it for her so it has a wider play." Such things as that result of course in things like this: when I, as a Commissioner, have made a deal to fit the fleet with oars and need the money now, 430 I'm locked out by these women from the very gates. But it's no use just standing here. Bring on the bars, so I can keep these women in their proper place. What are *you* gaping at, you poor unfortunate? Where are *you* looking? Only seeing if a bar 435 is open yet downtown? Come, drive these crowbars in under the gates on that side, pry away, and I will pry away on this.

(LYSISTRATA *comes out.*)

LYSISTRATA: No need to pry at all.
　I'm coming out, of my own will. What use are bars?
440　It isn't bolts and bars we need so much as brains.
COMMISSIONER: Really, you dirty slut? Where is that officer?
　Arrest her, and tie both her hands behind her back.
LYSISTRATA: By Artemis, just let him lift a hand at me
　and, public officer or not, you'll hear him howl.
445 COMMISSIONER: You let her scare you? Grab her round the
　　middle, you.
　Then *you* go help him and between you get her tied.

(KALONIKE *comes out.*)

KALONIKE: By Artemis, if you just lay one hand on her
　I have a mind to trample the shit out of you.
COMMISSIONER: It's out already! Look! Now where's the other
　　one?
450　Tie up *that* woman first. She babbles, with it all.

(MYRRHINA *comes out.*)

MYRRHINA: By Hecatë, if you just lay a hand on her
　you'll soon ask for a cup—to get your swellings down!

(*The* POLICEMAN *dashes behind the* COMMISSIONER *and clings to
him for protection.*)

COMMISSIONER: What happened? Where's that bowman, now?
　Hold onto *her!*

(*He moves quickly away downhill.*)

　I'll see that none of you can get away through here!
455 LYSISTRATA: By Artemis, you come near her and I'll bereave
　your head of every hair! You'll weep for each one, too.
COMMISSIONER: What a calamity! This one has failed me too.
　But never must we let ourselves be overcome
　by women. All together now, O Scythians—
460　let's march against them in formation!
LYSISTRATA: You'll find out
　that inside there we have four companies
　of fighting women perfectly equipped for war.
COMMISSIONER: Charge! Turn their flanks, O Scythians! and tie
　their hands!
LYSISTRATA: O allies—comrades—women! Sally forth and fight!
465　O vegetable vendors, O green-grocery-
　grain-garlic-bread-bean-dealers and inn-keepers all!

(*A group of fierce* OLD MARKET-WOMEN, *carrying baskets of vegetables, spindles, etc., emerges. There is a volley of vegetables. The*
SCYTHIANS *are soon routed.*)

　Come pull them, push them, smite them, smash them
　　into bits!
　Rail and abuse them in the strongest words you know!
　Halt, Halt! Retire in order! We'll forego the spoils!
470 COMMISSIONER: (*Tragically, like say Xerxes.*) Oh what reverses
　have my bowmen undergone!
LYSISTRATA: But what did you imagine? Did you think you came
　against a pack of slaves? Perhaps you didn't know
　that women can be resolute?
COMMISSIONER: I know they can—
　above all when they spot a bar across the way.

CHORUS OF MEN: Commissioner of Athens, you are spending 475
　words unduly,
　to argue with these animals, who only roar the louder,
　or don't you know they showered us so coldly and so
　　cruelly,
　and in our undershirts at that, and furnished us no powder?
CHORUS OF WOMEN: But beating up your neighbor is
　inevitably bringing
　a beating on yourself, sir, with your own eyes black and 480
　　bloody.
　I'd rather sit securely like a little girl demurely
　not stirring up a single straw nor harming anybody,
　So long as no one robs my hive and rouses me to stinging.
CHORUS OF MEN: How shall we ever tame these brutes? We
　　cannot tolerate
　the situation further, so we must investigate 485
　　this occurrence and find
　with what purpose in mind
　they profane the Acropolis, seize it, and lock
　the approach to this huge and prohibited rock,
　　to our holiest ground! 490
　Cross-examine them! Never believe one word
　　they tell you—refute them, confound them!
　We must get to the bottom of things like this
　　and the circumstances around them.
COMMISSIONER: Yes indeed! and I want to know first one 495
　thing:
　just *why* you committed this treason,
　barricading the fortress with locks and bars—
　　I insist on knowing the reason.
LYSISTRATA: To protect all the money up there from you—
　you'll have nothing to fight for without it. 500
COMMISSIONER: You think it is *money* we're fighting for?
LYSISTRATA: All the troubles we have are about it.
　It was so Peisander and those in power
　　of his kind could embezzle the treasure
　that they cooked up emergencies all the time. 505
　　Well, let them, if such is their pleasure,
　but they'll never get into this money again,
　　though you men should elect them to spend it.
COMMISSIONER: And just what will *you* do with it?
LYSISTRATA: Can you ask?
　　Of course we shall superintend it. 510
COMMISSIONER: You will superintend the treasury, *you!?*
LYSISTRATA: And why should it strike you so funny?
　when we manage our houses in everything
　　and it's we who look after your money.
COMMISSIONER: But it's not the same thing! 515
LYSISTRATA: Why not?
COMMISSIONER: It's war,
　　and *this* money must pay the expenses.
LYSISTRATA: To begin with, you needn't be waging war.
COMMISSIONER: To survive, we don't need our defenses?
LYSISTRATA: You'll survive: we shall save you.
COMMISSIONER: Who? You?
LYSISTRATA: Yes, we.
COMMISSIONER: You absolutely disgust me. 520
LYSISTRATA: You may like it or not, but you *shall be saved*
COMMISSIONER: I protest!
LYSISTRATA: If you care to, but, trust me,
　this has got to be done all the same.

COMMISSIONER: It has?
        It's illegal, unjust, and outrageous!
525 LYSISTRATA: We must save you, sir.
     COMMISSIONER: Yes? And if I refuse?
     LYSISTRATA: You will much the more grimly engage us.
     COMMISSIONER: And whence does it happen that war and peace
            are fit matters for women to mention?
     LYSISTRATA: I will gladly explain—
     COMMISSIONER: And be quick, or else
530   you'll be howling!
     LYSISTRATA: Now, just pay attention
       and keep your hands to yourself, if you can!
     COMMISSIONER: But I can't. You can't think how I suffer
       from holding them back in my anger!
     AN OLD WOMAN: Sir—
       if you don't you will have it much rougher.
535 COMMISSIONER: You may croak that remark to yourself, you hag!
          Will *you* do the explaining?
     LYSISTRATA: I'll do it.
       Heretofore we women in time of war
              have endured very patiently through it,
       putting up with whatever you men might do,
540   for never a peep would you let us
       deliver on your unstatesmanly acts
              no matter how much they upset us,
       but we knew very well, while we sat at home,
              when you'd handled a big issue poorly,
545   and we'd ask you then, with a pretty smile
              though our heart would be grieving us sorely,
       "And what were the terms for a truce, my dear,
              you drew up in assembly this morning?"
       "And what's it to you?" says our husband, "Shut up!"
550   —so, as ever, at this gentle warning
       I of course would discreetly shut up.
     KALONIKE: Not me!
          You can bet I would never be quiet!
     COMMISSIONER: I'll bet, if you weren't, you were beaten up.
     LYSISTRATA: *I'd* shut up, and I do not deny it,
555   but when plan after plan was decided on,
              so bad we could scarcely believe it,
       I would say "This last is so mindless, dear,
              I cannot think how you achieve it!"
       And then he would say, with a dirty look,
560   "Just you think what your spindle is for, dear,
       or your head will be spinning for days on end—
          let the *men* attend to the war, dear."
     COMMISSIONER: By Zeus, *he* had the right idea!
     LYSISTRATA: You fool!
          Right ideas were quite out of the question,
565   when your reckless policies failed, and yet
              we never could make a suggestion.
       And lately we heard you say so yourselves:
              in the streets there'd be someone lamenting:
       "There's not one man in the country now!"
570   —and we heard many others assenting.
       After that, we conferred through our deputies
              and agreed, having briefly debated,
       to act in common to save all Greece
              at once—for why should we have waited?
575   So now, when we women are talking sense,
          if you'll only agree to be quiet

and to listen to us as we did to you,
          you'll be very much edified by it.
COMMISSIONER: *You* will edify *us!* I protest!
LYSISTRATA: Shut up!
COMMISSIONER: *I'm* to shut up and listen, you scum, you?!   580
    Sooner death! And a veil on your head at that!
LYSISTRATA: We'll fix that. It may really become you:
    do accept this veil as a present from me.
    Drape it modestly—so—round your head, do you see?
    And now—*not* a word more, sir.   585
KALONIKE: Do accept this dear little wool-basket, too!
    Hitch your girdle and card! Here are beans you may
       chew
    the way all of the nicest Athenians do—
    and the *women* will see to the war, sir!
CHORUS OF WOMEN: Oh women, set your jugs aside and keep 590
       a closer distance:
    our friends may need from us as well some resolute
       assistance.

       Since never shall I weary of the stepping of the dance
    nor will my knees of treading, for these ladies I'll advance
          anywhere they may lead,
          and they're daring indeed,   595
       they have wit, a fine figure, and boldness of heart,
       they are prudent and charming, efficient and smart,
          patriotic and brave!

    But, O manliest grandmothers, onward now!   600
          And you matronly nettles, don't waver!
    but continue to bristle and rage, my dears,
       for you've still got the wind in your favor!

(*The* CHORUS OF WOMEN *and the* OLD MARKET-WOMEN *join.*)

LYSISTRATA: But if only the spirit of tender Love
    and the power of sweet Aphrodite
    were to breathe down over our breasts and thighs   605
       an attraction both melting and mighty,
    and infuse a pleasanter rigor in men,
       raising only their cudgels of passion,
    then I think we'd be known throughout all of Greece
       as makers of peace and good fashion.   610
COMMISSIONER: Having done just what?
LYSISTRATA: Well, first of all
    we shall certainly make it unlawful
    to go madly to market in armor.
AN OLD MARKET-WOMAN: Yes!
    By dear Aphrodite, it's awful!
LYSISTRATA: For now, in the midst of the pottery-stalls   615
    and the greens and the beans and the garlic,
    men go charging all over the market-place
    in full armor and beetling and warlike.
COMMISSIONER: They must do as their valor impels them to!
LYSISTRATA: But it makes a man only look funny   620
    to be wearing a shield with a Gorgon's head
    and be wanting sardines for less money.
OLD MARKET-WOMAN: Well, I saw a huge cavalry-captain once
    on a stallion that scarcely could hold him,
    pouring into his helmet of bronze a pint   625
    of pea-soup an old women had sold him,
    and a Thracian who, brandishing shield and spear
    like some savage Euripides staged once,

when he'd frightened a vendor of figs to death,
630   gobbled up all her ripest and aged ones.
COMMISSIONER: And how, on the international scale,
can you straighten out the enormous
confusion among all the states of Greece?
LYSISTRATA: Very easily.
COMMISSIONER: How? Do inform us.
635   LYSISTRATA: When our skein's in a tangle we take it thus
on our spindles, or haven't you seen us?—
one on this side and one on the other side,
and we work out the tangles between us.
And that is the way we'll undo this war,
640   by exchanging ambassadors, whether
you like it or not, one from either side,
and we'll work out the tangles together.
COMMISSIONER: Do you really think that with wools and skeins
and just being able to spin you
645   can end these momentous affairs, you fools?
LYSISTRATA: With any intelligence in you
you statesmen would govern as we work wool,
and in everything Athens would profit.
COMMISSIONER: How so? Do tell.
LYSISTRATA: First, you take raw fleece
650   and you wash the beshittedness off it:
just so, you should first lay the city out
on a washboard and beat out the rotters
and pluck out the sharpers like burrs, and when
you find tight knots of schemers and plotters
655   who are out for key offices, card them loose,
but best tear off their heads in addition.
Then into one basket together card
all those of a good disposition
be they citizens, resident aliens, friends,
660   an ally or an absolute stranger,
even people in debt to the commonwealth,
you can mix them all in with no danger.
And the cities which Athens has colonized—
by Zeus, you should try to conceive them
665   as so many shreddings and tufts of wool
that are scattered about and not leave them
to lie around loose, but from all of them
draw the threads in here, and collect them
into one big ball and then weave a coat
670   for the people, to warm and protect them.
COMMISSIONER: Now, isn't this awful? They treat the state
like wool to be beaten and carded,
who have nothing at all to do with war!
LYSISTRATA: Yes we do, you damnable hard-head!
675   We have none of your honors but we have more
than double your sufferings by it.
First of all, we bear sons whom you send to war.
COMMISSIONER: Don't bring up our old sorrows! Be quiet!
LYSISTRATA: And now, when we ought to enjoy ourselves,
680   making much of our prime and our beauty,
we are sleeping alone because all the men
are away on their soldierly duty.
But never mind *us*—when young girls grow old
in their bedrooms with no men to share them.
685   COMMISSIONER: You seem to forget that men, too, grow old
LYSISTRATA: By Zeus, but you cannot compare them!

When a man gets back, though he be quite gray,
he can wed a young girl in a minute,
but the season of woman is very short:
she must take what she can while she's in it.   690
And you know she must, for when it's past,
although you're not awfully astute, you're
aware that no man will marry her then
and she sits staring into the future.
COMMISSIONER: But he who can raise an erection still—   695
LYSISTRATA: Is there some good reason you don't drop dead?
We'll sell you a coffin if you but will.
Here's a string of onions to crown your head
and I'll make a honey-cake large and round
you can feed to Cerberus underground!   700
FIRST OLD MARKET-WOMAN: Accept these few fillets of leek
from me!
SECOND OLD MARKET-WOMAN: Let me offer you these for your
garland, sir!
LYSISTRATA: What now? Do you want something else you see?
Listen! Charon's calling his passenger—
will you catch the ferry or still delay   705
when his other dead want to sail away?
COMMISSIONER: Is it not downright monstrous to treat *me* like
this?
By Zeus, I'll go right now to the Commissioners
and show myself in evidence, just as I am!

(*He begins to withdraw with dignity and his four Scythian policemen.*)

LYSISTRATA: Will you accuse us of not giving you a wake?   710
But your departed spirit will receive from us
burnt offerings in due form, two days from now at dawn!

(LYSISTRATA *with the other women goes into the Acropolis. The*
COMMISSIONER, *etc., have left. The* MALE CHORUS *and the mixed*
FEMALE CHORUS *are alone.*)

CHORUS OF MEN: No man now dare fall to drowsing, if he
wishes to stay free!
Men, let's strip and gird ourselves for this eventuality!

To me this all begins to have a smell   715
of bigger things and larger things as well:
most of all I sniff a tyranny afoot. I'm much afraid
certain secret agents of the Spartans may have come,
meeting under cover here, in Cleisthenes' home,
instigating those damned women by deceit to make a raid   720
upon our treasury and that great sum
the city paid my pension from.

Sinister events already!—think of lecturing the state,
women as they are, and prattling on of things like shields
of bronze,
even trying hard to get us reconciled to those we hate—   725
those of Sparta, to be trusted like a lean wolf when it
yawns!
All of this is just a pretext, men, for a dictatorship—
but to me they shall not dictate! Watch and ward! A
sword I'll hide
underneath a branch of myrtle, through the agora I'll slip,
following Aristogeiton, backing the tyrannicide!   730

(The OLD MEN *pair off to imitate the gestures of the famous group statue of the tyrannicides Harmodius and Aristogeiton.)*

Thus I'll take my stand beside him! Now my rage is
    goaded raw
I'm as like as not to clip this damned old woman on the jaw!
CHORUS OF WOMEN: Your own mother will not know you when
    you come home, if you do!
Let us first, though, lay our things down, O my dear old
    friends
and true.

735   For now, O fellow-citizens, we would
    consider what will do our city good.
Well I may, because it bred me up in wealth and elegance:
    letting me at seven help with the embroidering
    of Athena's mantle, and at ten with offering
740   cakes and flowers. When I was grown and beautiful I had
    my chance
    to bear her baskets, at my neck a string
    of figs, and proud as anything.

Must I not, then, give my city any good advice I can?
Need you hold the fact against me that I was not born a man,
745   when I offer better methods than the present ones, and when
I've a share in this economy, for I contribute men?
But, you sad old codgers, *yours* is forfeited on many scores:
you have drawn upon our treasure dating from the Persian
    wars,
what they call grampatrimony, and you've paid no taxes back.
750   Worse, you've run it nearly bankrupt, and the prospect's
    pretty black.
Have you anything to answer? Say you were within the law
and I'll take this rawhide boot and clip you one across the
    jaw!
CHORUS OF MEN: Greater insolence than ever!—
    that's the method that she calls
755   "better"—if you would believe her.
But this threat must be prevented! Every man with both
    his balls
must make ready—take our shirts off, for a man must reek
    of male
outright—not wrapped up in leafage like an omelet for sale!

      Forward and barefoot: we'll do it again
760   to the death, just as when we resisted
      tyranny out at Leipsydrion, when
      we really existed!

      Now or never we must grow
      young again and, sprouting wings
765   over all our bodies, throw
      off this heaviness age brings!

For if any of us give them even just a little hold
nothing will be safe from their tenacious grasp. They are
    so bold
they will soon build ships of war and, with exorbitant intent,
770   send such navies out against us as Queen Artemisia sent.
But if they attack with horse, our knights we might as
    well delete:
nothing rides so well as woman, with so marvelous a seat,
never slipping at the gallop. Just look at those Amazons

in that picture in the Stoa, from their horses bringing bronze
axes down on men. We'd better grab *these* members of the   775
    sex
one and all, arrest them, get some wooden collars on their
    necks!
CHORUS OF WOMEN: By the gods, if you chagrin me
    or annoy me, if you dare,
    I'll turn loose the sow that's in me
till you rouse the town to help you with the way I've done   780
    your hair!
Let us too make ready, women, and our garments quickly
    doff
so we'll smell like women angered fit to bite our fingers off!

      Now I am ready: let one of the men
      come against me, and *he'll* never hanker
      after a black bean or garlic again: 785
      no woman smells ranker!

      Say a single unkind word,
      I'll pursue you till you drop,
      as the beetle did the bird.
      My revenge will never stop!   790

Yet you will not worry me so long as Lampito's alive
and my noble friends in Thebes and other cities still
    survive.
You'll not overpower us, even passing seven decrees or eight,
you, poor brutes, whom everyone and everybody's
    neighbors hate.
Only yesterday I gave a party, honoring Hecatë,   795
but when I invited in the neighbor's child to come and play,
such a pretty thing from Thebes, as nice and quiet as you
    please,
just an eel, they said she couldn't, on account of your
    decrees.
You'll go on forever passing such decrees without a check
till somebody takes you firmly by the leg and breaks your   800
    neck!

*(*LYSISTRATA *comes out. The* CHORUS OF WOMEN *addresses her in the manner of tragedy.)*

Oh Queen of this our enterprise and all our hopes,
    wherefore in baleful brooding hast thou issued forth?
LYSISTRATA: The deeds of wicked women and the female mind
    discourage me and set me pacing up and down.
CHORUS OF WOMEN: What's that? What's that you say?   805
LYSISTRATA: The truth, alas, the truth!
CHORUS OF WOMEN: What is it that's so dreadful? Tell it to
    your friends.
LYSISTRATA: A shameful thing to tell and heavy not to tell.
CHORUS OF WOMEN: Oh, never hide from me misfortune that is
    ours!
LYSISTRATA: To put it briefly as I can, we are in heat.   810
CHORUS OF WOMEN: Oh Zeus!
LYSISTRATA: Why call on Zeus? This is the
    way things are.
At least it seems I am no longer capable
of keeping them from men. They are deserting me.
This morning I caught one of them digging away
to make a tunnel to Pan's grotto down the slope,   815

another letting herself down the parapet
with rope and pulley, and another climbing down
its sheerest face, and yesterday was one I found
sitting upon a sparrow with a mind to fly
820 down to some well-equipped whoremaster's place in town.
Just as she swooped I pulled her backward by the hair.
They think of every far-fetched excuse they can
for going home. And here comes one deserter now.
You there, where are you running?
FIRST WOMAN: I want to go home,
825 because I left some fine Milesian wools at home
that must be riddled now with moths.
LYSISTRATA: Oh, damn your moths!
Go back inside.
FIRST WOMAN: But I shall come back right away,
just time enough to stretch them out upon my bed.
LYSISTRATA: Stretch nothing out, and don't you go away at all.
830 FIRST WOMAN: But shall I let my wools be ruined?
LYSISTRATA: If you must.
SECOND WOMAN: Oh miserable me! I sorrow for the flax
I left at home unbeaten and unstripped!
LYSISTRATA: One more—
wanting to leave for stalks of flax she hasn't stripped.
Come back here!
SECOND WOMAN: But, by Artemis, I only want
835 to strip my flax. Then I'll come right back here again.
LYSISTRATA: Strip me no strippings! If you start this kind of
thing
some other woman soon will want to do the same.
THIRD WOMAN: O lady Artemis, hold back this birth until
I can get safe to some unconsecrated place!
840 LYSISTRATA: What is this raving?
THIRD WOMAN: I'm about to have a child.
LYSISTRATA: But you weren't pregnant yesterday.
THIRD WOMAN: I am today.
Oh, send me home this instant, dear Lysistrata,
so I can find a midwife.
LYSISTRATA: What strange tale is this?
What is this hard thing you have here?
THIRD WOMAN: The child is male.
845 LYSISTRATA: By Aphrodite, no! You obviously have
some hollow thing of bronze. I'll find out what it is.
You silly thing!—you have Athena's helmet here—
and claiming to be pregnant!
THIRD WOMAN: So I am, by Zeus!
LYSISTRATA: In that case, what's the helmet for?
THIRD WOMAN: So if the pains
850 came on me while I'm still up here, I might give birth
inside the helmet, as I've seen the pigeons do.
LYSISTRATA: What an excuse! The case is obvious. Wait here.
I want to show this bouncing baby helmet off.

(*She passes the huge helmet around the* CHORUS OF WOMEN.)

SECOND WOMAN: But I can't even sleep in the Acropolis,
855 not for an instant since I saw the sacred snake!
FOURTH WOMAN: The owls are what are killing *me*. How can I
sleep
with their eternal whit-to-whoo-to-whit-to-whoo?
LYSISTRATA: You're crazy! Will you stop this hocus-pocus now?

No doubt you miss your husbands: don't you think that they
are missing us as much? I'm sure the nights they pass   860
are just as hard. But, gallant comrades, do bear up,
and face these gruelling hardships yet a little while.
There is an oracle that says we'll win, if we
only will stick together. Here's the oracle.
CHORUS OF WOMAN: Oh, read us what it says!   865
LYSISTRATA: Keep silence, then and hear:
"*Now when to one high place are gathered the fluttering
swallows,
Fleeing the Hawk and the Cock however hotly it follows.
Then will their miseries end, and that which is over be under:
Thundering Zeus will decide.*
A WOMAN: Will *we* lie on top now, I wonder?
LYSISTRATA: *But if the Swallows go fighting each other and*   870
springing and winging
Out of the holy and high sanctuary, then people will never
Say there was any more dissolute bitch of a bird whatsoever."
A WOMAN: The oracle is clear, by Zeus!
LYSISTRATA: By *all* the gods!
So let us not renounce the hardships we endure.
But let us go back in. Indeed, my dearest friends,   875
it would be shameful to betray the oracle.

(*Exeunt into the Acropolis.*)

CHORUS OF MEN: Let me tell you a story I heard one day
when I was a child:
There was once a young fellow Melanion by name
who refused to get married and ran away   880
to the wild.
To the mountains he came
and inhabited there
in a grove
and hunted the hare   885
both early and late
with nets that he wove
and also a hound
and he never came home again, such was his hate,
all women he found   890
so nasty, and we
quite wisely agree.

Let us kiss you, dear old dears!
CHORUS OF WOMEN: With no onions, you'll shed tears!
CHORUS OF MEN: I mean, lift my leg and *kick*.   895
CHORUS OF WOMEN: My, you wear your thicket thick!
CHORUS OF MEN: Great Myronides was rough
at the front and black enough
in the ass to scare his foes.
Just ask anyone who knows: 900
it's with hair that wars are won—
take for instance Phormion.
CHORUS OF WOMEN: Let me tell you a story in answer to
Melanion's case.
There is now a man, Timon, who wanders around   905
in the wilderness, hiding his face from view
in a place
where the brambles abound
so he looks like a chip
off a Fury,   910

curling his lip.
Now Timon retired
in hatred and pure
contempt of all men
915   and he cursed them in words that were truly inspired
again and again
but women he found
delightful and sound.

Would you like your jaw repaired?
920   CHORUS OF MEN: Thank you, no. You've got me scared.
CHORUS OF WOMEN: Let me jump and kick it though.
CHORUS OF MEN: You will let your man-sack show.
CHORUS OF WOMEN: All the same you wouldn't see,
old and gray as I may be,
925   any superfluity
of unbarbered hair on me;
it is plucked and more, you scamp,
since I singe it with a lamp!

(*Enter* LYSISTRATA *on the wall.*)

LYSISTRATA: Women, O women, come here quickly, here to me!
930   WOMAN: Whatever is it? Tell me! What's the shouting for?
LYSISTRATA: I see a man approaching, shaken and possessed,
seized and inspired by Aphrodite's power.
O thou, of Cyprus, Paphos, and Cythera, queen!
continue straight along this way you have begun!
935   A WOMAN: Whoever he is, where is he?
LYSISTRATA: Near Demeter's shrine.
A WOMAN: Why yes, by Zeus, he is. Whoever can he be?
LYSISTRATA: Well, look at him. Do any of you know him?
MYRRHINA: Yes.
I do. He's my own husband, too, Cinesias.
LYSISTRATA: Then it's your duty now to turn him on a spit,
940   cajole him and make love to him and not make love,
to offer everything, short of those things of which
the wine-cup knows.
MYRRHINA: I'll do it, don't you fear.
LYSISTRATA: And I
will help you tantalize him. I will stay up here
and help you roast him slowly. But now, disappear!

(*Enter* CINESIAS.)

945   CINESIAS: Oh how unfortunate I am, gripped by what spasms,
stretched tight like being tortured on a wheel!
LYSISTRATA: Who's there? Who has got this far past the
sentries?
CINESIAS: I.
LYSISTRATA: A man?
CINESIAS: A man, for sure.
LYSISTRATA: Then clear away from here.
CINESIAS: Who're you, to throw me out?
LYSISTRATA: The look-out for the day.
950   CINESIAS: Then, for the gods' sake, call Myrrhina out for me.
LYSISTRATA: You don't say! Call Myrrhina out! And who are you?
CINESIAS: Her husband. I'm Cinesias Paionides.
LYSISTRATA: Well, my dear man, hello! Your name is not
unknown
among us here and not without a certain fame,
955   because your wife has it forever on her lips.

She can't pick up an egg or quince but she must say:
Cinesias would enjoy it so!
CINESIAS: How wonderful!
LYSISTRATA: By Aphrodite, yes. And if we chance to talk
of husbands, your wife interrupts and says the rest
are nothing much compared to her Cinesias.   960
CINESIAS: Go call her.
LYSISTRATA: Will you give me something if I do?
CINESIAS: Indeed I will, by Zeus, if it is what you want.
I can but offer what I have, and I have this.
LYSISTRATA: Wait there. I will go down and call her.
CINESIAS: Hurry up!
because I find no charm whatever left in life   965
since she departed from the house. I get depressed
whenever I go into it, and everything
seems lonely to me now, and when I eat my food
I find no taste in it at all because I'm stiff.
MYRRHINA: (*offstage*) I love him, how I love him! But he   970
doesn't want
my love! (*on wall*) So what's the use of calling me to him?
CINESIAS: My sweet little Myrrhina, why do you act like that?
Come down here.
MYRRHINA: There? By Zeus, I certainly will not.
CINESIAS: Won't you come down, Myrrhina, when I'm calling
you?
MYRRHINA: Not when you call me without needing   975
anything.
CINESIAS: Not needing anything? I'm desperate with need.
MYRRHINA: I'm going now.
CINESIAS: Oh no! No, don't go yet! At least
you'll listen to the baby. Call your mammy, you.
BABY: Mammy mammy mammy!
CINESIAS: What's wrong with you? Have you no pity on your   980
child
when it is six days now since he was washed or nursed?
MYRRHINA: Oh, *I* have pity. But his father takes no care of him.
CINESIAS: Come down, you flighty creature, for the child.
MYRRHINA: Oh, what it is to be a mother! I'll come down,
for what else can I do?   985

(MYRRHINA *exits to reenter below.*)

CINESIAS: It seems to me she's grown
much younger, and her eyes have a more tender look.
Even her being angry with me and her scorn
are just the things that pain me with the more desire.
MYRRHINA: Come let me kiss you, dear sweet little baby mine,
with such a horrid father. Mammy loves you, though.   990
CINESIAS: But why are you so mean? Why do you listen to
those other women, giving me such pain?—And you,
you're suffering yourself.
MYRRHINA: Take your hands off of me!
CINESIAS: But everything we have at home, my things and yours,
you're letting go to pieces.   995
MYRRHINA: Little do I care!
CINESIAS: Little you care even if your weaving's pecked apart
and carried off by chickens?
MYRRHINA: (*Bravely.*)   Little I care, by Zeus!
CINESIAS: You have neglected Aphrodite's rituals
for such a long time now. Won't you come back again?

1000   MYRRHINA: Not I, unless you men negotiate a truce
              and make an end of war.
         CINESIAS: Well, if it's so decreed,
              we will do even that.
         MYRRHINA: Well, if it's so decreed,
              I will come home again. Not now. I've sworn I won't.
         CINESIAS: All right, all right. But now lie down with me once
              more.
1005   MYRRHINA: No! No!—yet I don't say I'm not in love with you.
         CINESIAS: You love me? Then why not lie down, Myrrhina dear?
         MYRRHINA: Don't be ridiculous! Not right before the child!
         CINESIAS: By Zeus, of course not. Manes, carry him back home.
              There now. You see the baby isn't in your way.
1010   Won't you lie down?
         MYRRHINA: But *where,* you rogue, just where
              is one to do it?
         CINESIAS: Where? Pan's grotto's a fine place.
         MYRRHINA: But how could I come back to the Acropolis
              in proper purity?
         CINESIAS: Well, there's a spring below
              the grotto—you can very nicely bathe in that.

(Ekkyklema or inset-scene with grotto.)

1015   MYRRHINA: And then I'm under oath. What if I break my vows?
         CINESIAS: Let me bear all the blame. Don't worry about your
              oath.
         MYRRHINA: Wait here, and I'll go get a cot for us.
         CINESIAS: No no,
              the ground will do.
         MYRRHINA: No, by Apollo! Though you *are*
              so horrid, I can't have you lying on the ground.

(Leaves.)

1020   CINESIAS: You know, the woman loves me—*that's* as plain as day.
         MYRRHINA: There. Get yourself in bed and I'll take off my
              clothes.
              Oh, what a nuisance! I must go and get a mat.
         CINESIAS: What for? I don't need one.
         MYRRHINA: Oh yes, by Artemis!
              On the bare cords? How ghastly!
         CINESIAS: Let me kiss you now.
1025   MYRRHINA: Oh, very well.
         CINESIAS: Wow! Hurry, hurry and come back.

(MYRRHINA leaves. A long wait.)

         MYRRHINA: Here is the mat. Lie down now, while I get
              undressed.
              Oh, what a nuisance! You don't have a pillow, dear.
         CINESIAS: But I don't need one, not one bit!
         MYRRHINA: By Zeus, I do!

(Leaves.)

         CINESIAS: Poor prick, the service around here is terrible!
1030   MYRRHINA: Sit up, my dear, jump up! Now I've got
              everything.
         CINESIAS: Indeed you have. And now, my golden girl, come
              here.

MYRRHINA: I'm just untying my brassiere. Now don't forget:
     about that treaty—you won't disappoint me, dear?
CINESIAS: By Zeus, no! On my life!
MYRRHINA: You have no blanket, dear.
CINESIAS: By Zeus, I do not need one. I just want to screw.   1035
MYRRHINA: Don't worry, dear, you will. I'll be back right away.

(Leaves.)

CINESIAS: This number, with her bedding, means to murder me.
MYRRHINA: Now raise yourself upright.
CINESIAS: But *this* is upright now!
MYRRHINA: Wouldn't you like some perfume?
CINESIAS: By Apollo, no!
MYRRHINA: By Aphrodite, yes! You must—like it or not.   1040

(Leaves.)

CINESIAS: Lord Zeus! Just let the perfume spill! That's all I ask!
MYRRHINA: Hold out your hand. Take some of this and rub it on.
CINESIAS: This perfume, by Apollo, isn't sweet at all.
     It smells a bit of stalling—not of wedding nights!
MYRRHINA: I brought the *Rhodian* perfume! How absurd of me!   1045
CINESIAS: It's fine! Let's keep it.
MYRRHINA: You *will* have your little joke.

(Leaves.)

CINESIAS: Just let me at the man who first distilled perfumes!
MYRRHINA: Try this, in the long vial.
CINESIAS: I've got one like it, dear.
     But don't be tedious. Lie down. And please don't bring
     anything more.   1050
MYRRHINA: *(Going.)* That's what I'll do, by Artemis!
     I'm taking off my shoes. But dearest, don't forget
     you're going to vote for peace.
CINESIAS: I will consider it.
     She has destroyed me, murdered me, that woman has!
     On top of which she's got me skinned and gone away!

     What shall I do? Oh, whom shall I screw,   1055
     cheated of dear Myrrhina, the first
     beauty of all, a creature divine?
     How shall I tend this infant of mine?
     Find me a pimp: it has to be nursed!
CHORUS OF MEN: *(In tragic style, as if to Prometheus or
     Andromeda bound.)*
     In what dire woe, how heavy-hearted   1060
     I see thee languishing, outsmarted!
          I pity thee, alas I do.
     What kidney could endure such pain,
     what spirit could, what balls, what back,
     what loins, what sacroiliac,   1065
     if they came under such a strain
     and never had a morning screw?
CINESIAS: O Zeus! the twinges! Oh, the twitches!
CHORUS OF MEN: And this is what she did to you,
     that vilest, hatefullest of bitches!   1070
CINESIAS: Oh nay, by Zeus, she's dear and sweet!
CHORUS OF MEN: How can she be? She's vile, O Zeus, she's vile!
     Oh treat her, Zeus, like so much wheat—
     O God of Weather, hear my prayer—

1075 and raise a whirlwind's mighty blast
to roll her up into a pile
and carry her into the sky
far up and up and then at last
drop her and land her suddenly
1080 astride that pointed penis there!

(*The ekkyklema turns, closing the inset-scene. Enter, from opposite sides, a* SPARTAN HERALD *and an* ATHENIAN OFFICIAL.)

SPARTAN: Wheah is the Senate-house of the Athenians?
Ah wish to see the chaihman. Ah have news fo him.
ATHENIAN: And who are you? Are you a Satyr or a man?
SPARTAN: Ah am a herald, mah young friend, yes, by the gods,
1085 and Ah have come from Sparta to negotiate.
ATHENIAN: And yet you come here with a spear under your arm?
SPARTAN: Not Ah, bah Zeus, not Ah!
ATHENIAN: Why do you turn around?
Why throw your cloak out so in front? Has the long trip given you a swelling?
SPARTAN: Ah do think the man is queah!
1090 ATHENIAN: But you have an erection, oh you reprobate!
SPARTAN: Bah Zeus, Ah've no sech thing! And don't you fool around!
ATHENIAN: And what have you got there?
SPARTAN: A Spahtan scroll-stick, suh.
ATHENIAN: Well, if it is, *this* is a Spartan scroll-stick, too.
But look, I know what's up: you can tell *me* the truth.
1095 Just how are things with you in Sparta: tell me that.
SPARTAN: Theah is uprising in all Spahta. Ouah allies
are all erect as well. We need ouah milkin'-pails.
ATHENIAN: From where has this great scourge of frenzy fallen on you?
From Pan?
SPARTAN: No, Ah think Lampito began it all,
1100 and then, the othah women throughout Spahta joined
togethah, just lahk at a signal fo a race,
and fought theah husbands off and drove them from theah cunts.
ATHENIAN: So, how're you getting on?
SPARTAN: We suffah. Through the town
we walk bent ovah as if we were carrying
1105 lamps in the wind. The women will not let us touch
even theah berries, till we all with one acco'd
have made a peace among the cities of all Greece.
ATHENIAN: This is an international conspiracy
launched by the women! Now I comprehend it all!
1110 Return at once to Sparta. Tell them they must send
ambassadors fully empowered to make peace.
And our Assembly will elect ambassadors
from our side, when I say so, showing them this prick.
SPARTAN: Ah'll run! Ah'll flah! Fo all you say is excellent!
1115 CHORUS OF MEN: No wild beast is more impossible than
woman is to fight,
nor is fire, nor has the panther such unbridled appetite!
CHORUS OF WOMEN: Well you know it, yet you go on warring
with me without end,
when you might, you cross-grained creature, have me as a
trusty friend.

CHORUS OF MEN: Listen: I will never cease from hating women
till I die!
CHORUS OF WOMEN: Any time you like. But meanwhile is   1120
there any reason why
I should let you stand there naked, looking so ridiculous?
I am only coming near you, now, to slip your coat on, thus.
CHORUS OF MEN: That was very civil of you, very kind to treat
me so,
when in such uncivil rage I took it off a while ago.
CHORUS OF WOMEN: Now you're looking like a man again,   1125
and not ridiculous.
If you hadn't hurt my feelings, I would not have made a fuss,
I would even have removed that little beast that's in your eye.
CHORUS OF MEN: *That* is what was hurting me! Well, won't
you take my ring to pry
back my eyelid? Rake the beast out. When you have it, let
me see,
for some time now it's been at my eye and irritating me.   1130
CHORUS OF WOMEN: Very well, I will—though you were *born*
an irritable man.
What a monster of a gnat, by Zeus! Look at it if you can.
Don't you see it? It's a native of great marshes, can't you tell?
CHORUS OF MEN: Much obliged, by Zeus! The brute's been
digging at me like a well!
So that now you have removed it, streams of tears come   1135
welling out.
CHORUS OF WOMEN: I will dry them. You're the meanest man
alive, beyond a doubt,
yet I will, and kiss you, too.
CHORUS OF MEN: Don't kiss me!
CHORUS OF WOMEN: If you will or not!
CHORUS OF MEN: Damn you! Oh, what wheedling flatterers
you all are, born and bred!
That old proverb is quite right and not inelegantly said:
"There's no living *with* the bitches and, without them,   1140
even *less*"—
so I might as well make peace with you, and from now on,
I guess,
I'll do nothing mean to you and, from you, suffer nothing
wrong.
So let's draw our ranks together now and start a little song:

For a change, we're not preparing
any mean remark or daring   1145
aimed at any man in town,
but the very opposite: we plan to do and say
only good to everyone,
when the ills we have already are sufficient anyway.
Any man or woman who   1150
wants a little money, oh
say three minas, maybe two,
kindly let us know.
What we have is right in here.
(Notice we have purses, too!)   1155
And if ever peace appear,
he who takes our loan today
never need repay.

We are having guests for supper,
allies asked in by our upper   1160
classes to improve the town.

There's pea-soup, and I had killed a sucking-pig of mine:
I shall see it is well done,
so you will be tasting something very succulent and fine.

1165 Come to see us, then, tonight
early, just as soon as you
have a bath and dress up right:
bring your children, too.
Enter boldly, never mind
1170 asking anyone in sight.
Go straight in and you will find
you are quite at home there, but
all the doors are shut.

And here come the Spartan ambassadors,
1175 dragging beards that are really the biggest I
have ever beheld, and around their thighs
they are wearing some sort of a pig-sty.

Oh men of Sparta, let me bid you welcome first,
and then you tell us how you are and why you come.
1180 SP. AMB.: What need is theah to speak to you in many words?
Fo you may see youahself in what a fix we come.
CHORUS OF MEN: Too bad! Your situation has become
terribly hard and seems to be at fever-pitch.
SP. AMB.: Unutterably so! And what is theah to say?
1185 Let someone bring us peace on any tuhms he will!
CHORUS OF MEN: And here I see some natives of Athenian soil,
holding their cloaks far off their bellies, like the best
wrestlers, who sicken at the touch of cloth. It seems
that overtraining may bring on this strange disease.
1190 ATH. AMB.: Will someone tell us where to find Lysistrata?
We're men, and here we are, in this capacity.
CHORUS OF MEN: This symptom and that other one sound
much alike.
Toward morning I expect convulsions do occur?
ATH. AMB.: By Zeus, we are exhausted with just doing that,
1195 so, if somebody doesn't reconcile us quick,
there's nothing for it: we'll be screwing Cleisthenes.
CHORUS OF MEN: Be carefulput your cloaks on, or you might
be seen
by some young blade who knocks the phalluses off herms.
ATH. AMB.: By Zeus, an excellent idea!
SP. AMB.: (*Having overheard.*) Yes, bah the gods!
1200 It altogethah is. Quick, let's put on our cloaks.

(*Both groups cover quick and then recognize each other with full
diplomatic pomp.*)

ATH. AMB.: Greetings, O men of Sparta! (*To his group.*) We have
been disgraced!
SP. AMB.: (*To one of his group.*) Mah dearest fellah, what a
dreadful thing fo *us,*
if these Athenians had seen ouah wo'st defeat!
ATH. AMB.: Come now, O Spartans: one must specify each point.
1205 Why have you come here?
SP. AMB.: To negotiate a peace.
We ah ambassadahs.
ATH. AMB.: Well put. And so are we.
Therefore, why do we not call in Lysistrata,
she who alone might get us to agree on terms?
SP. AMB.: Call her or any man, even a Lysistratus!

CHORUS OF MEN: But you will have no need, it seems, to call 1210
her now,
for here she is. She heard you and is coming out.
CHORUS OF MEN *and* CHORUS OF WOMEN: All hail, O manliest
woman of all!
It is time for you now to be turning
into something still better, more dreadful, mean,
unapproachable, charming, discerning, 1215
for here are the foremost nations of Greece,
bewitched by your spells like a lover,
who have come to you, bringing you all their claims,
and to *you* turning everything over.
LYSISTRATA: The work's not difficult, if one can catch them now 1220
while they're excited and not making passes at
each other. I will soon find out. Where's *HARMONY?*

(*A naked maid, perhaps wearing a large ribbon reading* HARMONY,
appears from inside.)

Go take the Spartans first, and lead them over here,
not with a rough hand nor an overbearing one,
nor, as our husbands used to do this, clumsily, 1225
but like a woman, in our most familiar style:
If he won't give his hand, then lead him by the prick.
And now, go bring me those Athenians as well,
leading them by whatever they will offer you.
O men of Sparta, stand right here, close by my side, 1230
and you stand over there, and listen to my words.
I am a woman, yes, but there is mind in me.
In native judgment I am not so badly off,
and, having heard my father and my elders talk
often enough, I have some cultivation, too. 1235
And so, I want to take and scold you, on both sides,
as you deserve, for though you use a lustral urn
in common at the altars, like blood-relatives,
when at Olympia, Delphi, or Thermopylae—
how many others I might name if I took time!— 1240
yet, with barbarian hordes of enemies at hand,
it is Greek men, it is Greek cities, you destroy.
That is one argument so far, and it is done.
ATH. AMB.: My prick is skinned alive—that's what's destroying *me.*
LYSISTRATA: Now, men of Sparta—for I shall address you first— 1245
do you not know that once one of your kings came here
and as a suppliant of the Athenians
sat by our altars, death-pale in his purple robe,
and begged us for an army? For Messenë then
oppressed you, and an earthquake from the gods as well. 1250
Then Cimon went, taking four thousand infantry,
and saved the whole of Lacedaemon for your state.
That is the way Athenians once treated you;
you ravage their land now, which once received you well.
ATH. AMB.: By Zeus, these men are in the wrong, Lysistrata! 1255
SP. AMB.: (*With his eyes on* HARMONY.) We'ah wrong . . .
What an unutterably lovely ass!
LYSISTRATA: Do you suppose I'm letting you Athenians off?
Do you not know that once the Spartans in their turn,
when you were wearing the hide-skirts of slavery,
came with their spears and slew many Thessalians, 1260
many companions and allies of Hippias?

They were the only ones who fought for you that day,
freed you from tyranny and, for the skirt of hide,
gave back your people the wool mantle of free men.

1265 SP. AMB.: Ah nevah saw a woman broadahin her views.
ATH. AMB.: And I have never seen a lovelier little nook.
LYSISTRATA: So why, when you have done each other so much
    good,
    go on fighting with no end of malevolence?
    Why don't you make a peace? Tell me, what's in your way?
1270 SP. AMB.: Whah, *we ah willin'*, if *they* will give up to us
    that very temptin' cuhve. (*Of* HARMONY, *as hereafter.*)
LYSISTRATA: What curve, my friend?
SP. AMB.:   The bay
    of Pylos, which we've wanted and felt out so long.
ATH. AMB.: No, by Poseidon, you will not get into that!
LYSISTRATA: Good friend, do let them have it.
ATH. AMB.:   No! What other town
1275   can we manipulate so well?
LYSISTRATA: Ask them for one.
ATH. AMB.: Damn, let me think! Now first suppose you cede
    to us
    that bristling tip of land, Echinos, behind which
    the gulf of Malia recedes, and those long walls,
    the legs on which Megara reaches to the sea.
1280 SP. AMB.: No, mah deah man, not *everything*, bah Castah, no!
LYSISTRATA: Oh, give them up. Why quarrel for a pair of legs?
ATH. AMB.: I'd like to strip and get to plowing right away.
SP. AMB.: And *Ah* would lahk to push manuah, still earliah.
LYSISTRATA: When you have made a peace, then you will do
    all that.
1285   But if you want to do it, first deliberate,
    go and inform your allies and consult with them.
ATH. AMB.: Oh, damn our allies, my good woman! We are stiff.
    Will all of our allies not stand resolved with us—
    namely, to screw?
SP. AMB.:   And so will ouahs, Ah'll guarantee.
1290 ATH. AMB.: Our mercenaries, even, will agree with us.
LYSISTRATA: Excellent. Now to get you washed and purified
    so you may enter the Acropolis, where we
    women will entertain you out of our supplies.
    You will exchange your pledges there and vows for peace.
1295   And after that each one of you will take his wife,
    departing then for home.
ATH. AMB.:   Let's go in right away.
SP. AMB.: Lead on, ma'am, anywheah you lahk.
ATH. AMB.:   Yes, and be quick.

(*Exeunt into Acropolis.*)

CHORUS OF MEN *and* CHORUS OF WOMEN:
    All the rich embroideries, the
    scarves, the gold accessories, the
1300   trailing gowns, the robes I own
    I begrudge to no man: let him take what things he will
    for his children or a grown
    daughter who must dress for the procession up Athena's
    hill.
    Freely of my present stocks
1305   I invite you all to take.
    There are here no seals nor locks

very hard to break.
Search through every bag and box,
Look—you will find nothing there   1310
if your eyesight isn't fine—
sharper far than mine!

Are there any of you needing
food for all the slaves you're feeding,
all your little children, too?

I have wheat in tiny grains for you, the finest sort,   1315
and I also offer you
plenty of the handsome strapping grains that slaves get by the
    quart.

    So let any of the poor
    visit me with bag or sack
    which my slave will fill with more   1320
    wheat than they can pack,
    giving each his ample share.
    Might I add that at my door
    I have watch-dogs? So beware.
    Come too close by day or night,   1325
    you will find they bite.

(*Voice of drunken* ATHENIANS *from inside.*)

FIRST ATHENIAN: Open the door! (*Shoves the* PORTER *aside.*)
                And will you get out of my way?

(*A second drunken* ATHENIAN *follows. The first sees the* CHORUS.)

    What are you sitting there for? Shall I, with this torch,
    burn you alive? (*Drops character.*)
              How vulgar! Oh, how commonplace!
    I can not do it!   1330

(*Starts back in. The second* ATHENIAN *stops him and remonstrates
with him in a whisper. The first turns and addresses the audience.*)

           Well, if it really must be done
    to please you, we shall face it and go through with it.
CHORUS OF MEN *and* CHORUS OF WOMEN:
    And we shall face it and go through with it with you.
FIRST ATHENIAN: (*In character again, extravagantly.*)
    Clear out of here! Or you'll be wailing for your hair!

(CHORUS OF WOMEN *scours away in mock terror.*)

    Clear out of here! so that the Spartans can come out
    and have no trouble leaving, after they have dined.   1335

(CHORUS OF MEN *scours away in mock terror.*)

SECOND ATHENIAN: I never saw a drinking-party like this
    one:
    even the Spartans were quite charming, and of course
    we make the cleverest company, when in our cups.
FIRST ATHENIAN: You're right, because when sober we are not
    quite sane.
    If I can only talk the Athenians into it,   1340
    we'll always go on any embassy quite drunk,
    for now, going to Sparta sober, we're so quick
    to look around and see what trouble we can make
    that we don't listen to a single word they say—

1345 instead we think we hear them say what they do not—
and none of our reports on anything agree.
But just now everything was pleasant. If a man
got singing words belonging to another song,
we all applauded and swore falsely it was fine!
1350 But here are those same people coming back again
to the same spot! Go and be damned, the pack of you!

(*The* CHORUS OF MEN AND WOMEN, *having thrown off their masks, put on other cloaks, and rushed back on stage, stays put.*)

SECOND ATHENIAN: Yes, damn them, Zeus! Just when the
party's coming out!

(*The party comes rolling out.*)

A SPARTAN: (*To another.*) Mah very chahmin friend, will you
take up youah flutes?
1355 Ah'll dance the dipody and sing a lovely song
of us and the Athenians, of both at once!
FIRST ATHENIAN: (*As pleasantly as he can.*)
Oh yes, take up your little reeds, by all the gods:
I very much enjoy seeing you people dance.

SPARTAN: Memory, come,
1360 come inspiah thah young
votaries to song,
come inspiah theah dance!

(*Other* SPARTANS *join.*)

Bring thah daughtah, bring the sweet
Muse, fo well she knows
1365 us and the Athenians,
how at Ahtemisium
they in godlike onslaught rose
hahd against the Puhsian fleet,
drove it to defeat!
1370 Well she knows the Spartan waws,
how Leonidas
in the deadly pass
led us on lahk baws
whettin' shahp theah tusks, how sweat
1375 on ouah cheeks in thick foam flowahed,
off ouah legs how thick it showahed,
fo the Puhsian men were mo'
than the sands along the sho'.
Goddess, huntress, Ahtemis,
1380 slayeh of the beasts, descend:
vuhgin goddess, come to this
feast of truce to bind us fast
so ouah peace may nevah end.
Now let friendship, love, and wealth
1385 come with ouah acco'd at last.
May we stop ouah villainous
wahly foxy stealth!
Come, O huntress, heah to us,
heah, O vuhgin, neah to us!

LYSISTRATA: Come, now that all the rest has been so well
arranged,
you Spartans take these women home; these others, you. 1390
Let husband stand beside his wife, and let each wife
stand by her husband: then, when we have danced a dance
to thank the gods for our good fortune, let's take care
hereafter not to make the same mistakes again.
ATHENIAN: Bring on the chorus! Invite the three Graces to 1395
follow,
and then call on Artemis, call her twin brother,
the leader of choruses, healer Apollo!
CHORUS OF MEN AND WOMEN: (*Joins.*) Pray for their friendliest
favor, the one and the other.
Call Dionysus, his tender eyes casting
flame in the midst of his Maenads ecstatic with dancing. 1400
Call upon Zeus, the resplendent in fire,
call on his wife, rich in honor and ire,
call on the powers who possess everlasting
memory, call them to aid,
call them to witness the kindly, entrancing 1405
peace Aphrodite has made!
Alalai!
Bound, and leap high! Alalai!
Cry, as for victory, cry
Alalai! 1410
LYSISTRATA: Sing us a new song, Spartans, capping our new song.
SPARTANS: Leave thah favohed mountain's height,
Spahtan Muse, come celebrate
Amyclae's lord with us and great
Athena housed in bronze; 1415
praise Tyndareus' paih of sons,
gods who pass the days in spoht
wheah the cold Eurotas runs.

(*General dancing.*)

Now to tread the dance,
now to tread it light, 1420
praising Spahta, wheah you find
love of singing quickened bah the pounding beat
of dancing feet,
when ouah guhls lahk foals cavoht
wheah the cold Eurotas runs, 1425
when they fleetly bound and prance
till theah haih unfilleted shakes in the wind,
as of Maenads brandishin'
ahvied wands and revelin',
Leda's daughtah, puah and faiah, 1430
leads the holy dances theah.
FULL CHORUS: (*As everyone leaves dancing.*)
So come bind up youah haih with youah hand,
with youah feet make a bound
lahk a deeah; fo the chorus clap out
an encouragin' sound, 1435
singin' praise of the temple of bronze
housin' her we adaw:
sing the praise of Athena: the goddess unvanquished in
waw!

CRITICAL CONTEXTS

ARISTOTLE (384–322 BCE)

from *The Poetics* (c. 335 BCE)

TRANSLATED BY GERALD F. ELSE

Born near Macedonia, Aristotle entered the Academy in Athens at the age of seventeen to study with Plato. After Plato's death, Aristotle conducted research in natural history, mainly botany and zoology, throughout the Aegean region and served as the tutor of the young Alexander the Great in Macedon before returning to Athens to found the Lyceum in 355 BCE.

Aristotle wrote extensively on topics ranging from ethics, rhetoric, and metaphysics to physics and natural history. In The Poetics, *he analyzes the field of poetry into different "species" or genres (epic, tragedy, comedy, dithyramb) and attempts to discover the basic features of each. The Poetics demonstrates Aristotle's extensive knowledge of drama, which he uses to refine a keen sense of the form and purpose of tragedy. We should remember that* The Poetics *was written sometime after 335 BCE, roughly a century after the height of the Athenian theater. And although* The Poetics *is the cornerstone of Western dramatic criticism, the meaning of several of Aristotle's key terms—MIMESIS (imitation), CATHARSIS (purgation), and HAMARTIA (error)—remain controversial.*

Students approaching The Poetics *for the first time often have difficulty with the compressed logic of Aristotle's text, which may have formed something akin to notes for a lecture—a basis for expansion and discussion. Given Aristotle's representation of poetry according to natural "species," one way into his thinking may be to attempt to relate the functions of the various parts of tragedy: What is the relationship between Aristotle's conception of plot and of character? What is the logic that sustains his claim that plot is the principal element of tragedy, more important than character, language, or spectacle? What is the nature of "imitation," as Aristotle expresses it here? Given Aristotle's sense of just and unjust imitation, should we take imitation as a straightforward synonym for realism?*

BASIC CONSIDERATIONS

The art of poetic composition in general and its various species, the function and effect of each of them; how the plots should be constructed if the composition is to be an artistic success; how many other component elements are involved in the process, and of what kind; and similarly all the other questions that fall under this same branch of inquiry—these are the problems we shall discuss; let us begin in the right and natural way, with basic principles.

Epic composition, then; the writing of tragedy, and of comedy also; the composing of dithyrambs; and the greater part of the making of music with flute and lyre: these are all in point of fact, taken collectively, imitative processes. They differ from each other, however, in three ways, namely by virtue of having (1) different means, (2) different objects, and (3) different methods of imitation.

THE DIFFERENTIATION ACCORDING TO MEDIUM

First, in the same way that certain people imitate a variety of things by means of shapes and colors, making visible replicas of them (some doing this on the basis of art, others out of habit), while another group produces its mimicry with the voice, so in the case of the arts we just mentioned: they all carry on their imitation through the media of rhythm, speech, and melody, but with the latter two used separately

or together. Thus the arts of flute and lyre music, and any others of similar nature and effect, such as the art of the pan-pipe, produce their imitation using melody and rhythm alone, while there is another which does so using speeches or verses alone, bare of music, and either mixing the verses with one another or employing just one certain kind—an art which is, as it happens, nameless up to the present time. In fact, we could not even assign a common name to the mimes of Sophron and Xenarchus and the Socratic discourses: nor again if somebody should compose his imitation in trimeters or elegiac couplets or certain other verses of that kind. (Except people do link up poetic composition with verse and speak of "elegiac poets," "epic poets," not treating them as poets by virtue of their imitation, but employing the term as a common appellation going along with the use of verse. And in fact the name is also applied to anyone who treats a medical or scientific topic in verses, yet Homer and Empedocles actually have nothing in common except their verse; hence the proper term for the one is "poet," for the other, "science-writer" rather than "poet.") and likewise if someone should mix all the kinds of verse together in composing his imitation, as Chaeremon composed a *Centaur* using all the verses.

Such is the disjunction we feel is called for in these cases. There are on the other hand certain arts which use all the aforesaid media, I mean such as rhythm, song, and verse. The composition of dithyrambs and of nomes does so, and both tragedy and comedy. But there is a difference in that some of these arts use all the media at once while others use them in different parts of the work.

These then are the differentiations of the poetic arts with respect to the media in which the poets carry on their imitation.

THE OBJECTS OF IMITATION

Since those who imitate men in action, and these must necessarily be either worthwhile or worthless people (for definite characters tend pretty much to develop in men of action), it follows that they imitate men either better or worse than the average, as the painters do—for Polygnotus used to portray superior and Pauson inferior men; and it is evident that each of the forms of imitation aforementioned will include these differentiations, that is, will differ by virtue of imitating objects which are different in this sense. Indeed, it is possible for these dissimilarities to turn up in flute and lyre playing, and also in prose dialogues and bare verses: Thus Homer imitated superior men and Hegemon of Thasos, the inventor of parody, and Nicochares, the author of the *Deiliad,* inferior ones, likewise in connection with dithyrambs and nomes, for one can make the imitation the way Timotheus and Philoxenus did their *Cyclopes.* Finally, the difference between tragedy and comedy coincides exactly with the master-difference: Namely the one tends to imitate people better, the other one people worse, than the average.

THE MODES OF IMITATION

The third way of differentiating these arts is by the mode of imitation. For it is possible to imitate the same objects, and in the same media, (1) by narrating part of the time and dramatizing the rest of the time, which is the way Homer composes (mixed mode), or (2) with the same person continuing without change (straight narrative), or (3) with all the persons who are performing the imitation acting, that is, carrying on for themselves (straight dramatic mode).

JOTTINGS, CHIEFLY ON COMEDY

Poetic imitation, then, shows these three *differentiae,* as we said at the beginning: in the media, objects, and modes of imitation. So in one way Sophocles would be the same (kind of) imitator as Homer, since they both imitate worthwhile people, and in another way the same as Aristophanes, for they both imitate people engaged in action, doing things. In fact some authorities maintain that that is why plays are called dramas, because the imitation is of men acting (*drôn-tas* from *drân,* "do, act"). It is also the reason why both tragedy and comedy are claimed by the Dorians: comedy by

the Megarians, both those from hereabouts, who say that it came into being during the period of their democracy, and those in Sicily, and tragedy by some of those in the Peloponnese. They use the names "comedy" and "drama" as evidence; for *they* say that they call their outlying villages *kômai* while the Athenians call theirs "demes" (*dêmoi*)—the assumption being that the participants in comedy were called *kômôidoi* not from their being revelers but because they wandered from one village to another, being degraded and excluded from the city—and that they call "doing" or "acting" *drân* while the Athenians designate it by *prattein.*

THE ORIGIN AND DEVELOPMENT OF POETRY

So much, then, for the *differentiae* of imitation, their number and identity. As to the origin of the poetic art as a whole, it stands to reason that two operative causes brought it into being, both of them rooted in human nature. Namely (1) the habit of imitating is congenital to human beings from childhood (actually man differs from the other animals in that he is the most imitative and learns his first lessons through imitation), and so is (2) the pleasure that all men take in works of imitation. A proof of this is what happens in our experience. There are things which we see with pain so far as they themselves are concerned but whose images, even when executed in very great detail, we view with pleasure. Such is the case for example with renderings of the least favored animals, or of cadavers. The cause of this also is that learning is eminently pleasurable not only to philosophers but to the rest of mankind in the same way, although their share in the pleasure is restricted. For the reason they take pleasure in seeing the images is that in the process of viewing they find themselves learning, that is, reckoning what kind a given thing belongs to: "This individual is a So-and-so." Because if the viewer happens not to have seen such a thing before, the reproduction will not produce the pleasure *qua* reproduction but through its workmanship or color or something else of that sort.

Since, then, imitation comes naturally to us, and melody and rhythm too (it is obvious that verses are segments of the respective rhythms), in the beginning it was those who were most gifted in these respects who, developing them little by little, brought the making of poetry into being out of improvisations. And the poetic enterprise split into two branches, in accordance with the two kinds of character. Namely, the soberer spirits were imitating noble actions and the actions of noble persons, while the cheaper ones were imitating those of the worthless, producing lampoons and invectives at first just as the other sort were producing hymns and encomia. . . . In them (that is, the invectives), in accordance with what is suitable and fitting, iambic verse also put in its appearance; indeed that is why it is called "iambic" now, because it is the verse in which they used to "iambize," that is, lampoon each other. And so some of the early poets became composers of epic, the others of iambic, verses.

Now it happens that we cannot name anyone before Homer as the author of that kind of poem (that is, an iambic poem), though it stands to reason that there were many who were; but from Homer on we can do so: thus his *Margites* and other poems of that sort. However, just as on the serious side Homer was most truly a poet, since he was the only one who not only composed well but constructed dramatic imitations, so too he was the first to adumbrate the forms of comedy by producing a (1) dramatic presentation, and not of invective but of (2) the ludicrous. For as the *Iliad* stands in relation to our tragedies, so the *Margites* stands in relation to our comedies.

Once tragedy and comedy had been partially brought to light, those who were out in pursuit of the two kinds of poetic activity, in accordance with their own respective natures, became in the one case comic poets instead of iambic poets, in the other case producers of tragedies instead of epics, because these genres were higher and more esteemed than the others. Now to review the question whether even tragedy is adequate to the basic forms or not—a question which is (can be) judged both by itself, in the abstract, and in relationship to our theater audiences—that is another story. However that may be, it did spring from an improvisational beginning (both it and comedy: the one from those who led off the dithyramb, the other from those who did so for the phallic performances [?] which still remain on the program in many of our cities); it did expand gradually, each feature being further developed as it appeared; and after it had gone through a number of phases it stopped upon attaining its full natural growth. Thus Aeschylus was the first to expand the troupe of assisting actors from one to two, shorten the choral parts, and see to it that the dialogue takes first place; (. . .) at the same time the verse became iambic trimeter instead of trochaic tetrameter. For in the beginning they used the tetrameter because the form of composition was "satyr-like," that is, more given over to dancing, but when speech came along the very nature of the case turned up the appropriate verse. For iambic is the most speech-like of verses. An indication of this is that we speak more iambics than any other kind of verse in our conversation with each other, whereas we utter hexameters rarely, and when we do we abandon the characteristic tone-pattern of ordinary speech.

Further, as to plurality of episodes and the other additions which are recorded as having been made to tragedy, let our account stop here; for no doubt it would be burdensome to record them in detail.

COMEDY

Comedy is as we said it was, an imitation of persons who are inferior; not, however, going all the way to full villainy, but imitating the ugly, of which the ludicrous is one part. The ludicrous, that is, is a failing or a piece of ugliness which causes no pain or destruction; thus, to go no farther, the comic mask is something ugly and distorted but painless.

Now the stages of development of tragedy, and the men who were responsible for them, have not escaped notice, but comedy did escape notice in the beginning because it was not taken seriously. (In fact it was late in its history that the presiding magistrate officially "granted a chorus" to the comic poets; until then they were volunteers.) Thus comedy already possessed certain defining characteristics when the first "comic poets," so-called, appear in the record. Who gave it masks, or prologues, or troupes of actors and all that sort of thing, is not known. The composing of plots came originally from Sicily; of the Athenian poets, Crates was the first to abandon the lampooning mode and compose arguments, that is, plots, of a general nature.

EPIC AND TRAGEDY

Well then, epic poetry followed in the wake of tragedy up to the point of being a (1) good-sized (2) imitation (3) in verse (4) of people who are to be taken seriously; but in its having its verse unmixed with any other and being narrative in character, there they differ. Further, so far as its length is concerned tragedy tries as hard as it can to exist during a single daylight period, or to vary but little, while the epic is not limited in its time and so differs in that respect. Yet originally they used to do this in tragedies just as much as they did in epic poems.

The constituent elements are partly identical and partly limited to tragedy. Hence anybody who knows about good and bad tragedy knows about epic also; for the elements that the epic possesses appertain to tragedy as well, but those of tragedy are not all found in the epic.

TRAGEDY AND ITS SIX CONSTITUENT ELEMENTS

Our discussions of imitative poetry in hexameters, and of comedy, will come later; at present let us deal with tragedy, recovering from what has been said so far the definition of its essential nature, as it was in development. Tragedy, then, is a process of imitating an action which has serious implications, is complete, and possesses magnitude; by means of language which has been made sensuously attractive, with each of its varieties found separately in the parts; enacted by the persons themselves and not presented through narrative; through a course of pity and fear completing the purification of tragic acts which have those emotional characteristics. By "language made sensuously attractive" I mean language that has rhythm and melody, and by "its varieties found separately" I mean the fact that certain parts of the play are carried on through spoken verses alone and others the other way round, through song.

Now first of all, since they perform the imitation through action (by acting it), the adornment of their visual appearance will perforce constitute some part of the making of tragedy; and song-composition and verbal expression also, for those are the media in which they perform the imitation. By "verbal expression" I mean the actual composition of the verses, and by "song-composition" something whose meaning is entirely clear.

Next, since it is an imitation of an action and is enacted by certain people who are performing the action, and since those people must necessarily have certain traits both of character and thought (for it is thanks to these two factors that we speak of people's actions also as having a defined character, and it is in accordance with their actions that all either succeed or fail); and since the imitation of the action is the plot, for by "plot" I mean here the structuring of the events, and by the "characters" that in accordance with which we say that the persons who are acting have a defined moral character, and by "thought" all the passages in which they attempt to prove some thesis or set forth an opinion—it follows of necessity, then, that tragedy as a whole has just six constituent elements, in relation to the essence that makes it a distinct species; and they are plot, characters, verbal expression, thought, visual adornment, and song-composition. For the elements by which they imitate are two (i.e., verbal expression and song-composition), the manner in which they imitate is one (visual adornment), the things they imitate are three (plot, characters, thought), and there is nothing more beyond these. These then are the constituent forms they use.

THE RELATIVE IMPORTANCE OF THE SIX ELEMENTS

The greatest of these elements is the structuring of the incidents. For tragedy is an imitation not of men but of a life, an action, and they have moral quality in accordance with their characters but are happy or unhappy in accordance with their actions; hence they are not active in order to imitate their characters, but they include the characters along with the actions for the sake of the latter. Thus the structure of events, the plot, is the goal of tragedy, and the goal is the greatest thing of all.

Again: a tragedy cannot exist without a plot, but it can without characters: thus the tragedies of most of our modern poets are devoid of character, and in general many poets are like that; so also with the relationship between Zeuxis and Polygnotus, among the painters: Polygnotus is a good portrayer of character, while Zeuxis' painting has no dimension of character at all.

Again: if one strings end to end speeches that are expressive of character and carefully worked in thought and expression, he still will not achieve the result which we said was the aim of tragedy; the job will be done much better by a tragedy that is more deficient in these other respects but has a plot, a structure of events. It is much the same case as with painting: the most beautiful pigments smeared on at random will not give as much pleasure as a black-and-white outline picture. Besides, the most powerful means tragedy has for swaying our feelings, namely the peripeties and recognitions, are elements of the plot.

Again: an indicative sign is that those who are beginning a poetic career manage to hit the mark in verbal expression and character portrayal sooner than they do in plot construction; and the same is true of practically all the earliest poets.

So plot is the basic principle, the heart and soul, as it were, of tragedy, and the characters come second: . . . it is the imitation of an action and imitates the persons primarily for the sake of their action.

Third in rank is thought. This is the ability to state the issues and appropriate points pertaining to a given topic, an ability which springs from the arts of politics and rhetoric; in fact the earlier poets made their characters talk "politically," the present-day poets rhetorically. But "character" is that kind of utterance which clearly reveals the bent of a man's moral choice (hence there is no character in that class of utterances in which there is nothing at all that the speaker is choosing or rejecting), while "thought" is the passages in which they try to prove that something is so or not so, or state some general principle.

Fourth is the verbal expression of the speeches. I mean by this the same thing that was said earlier, that the "verbal expression" is the conveyance of thought through language: a statement which has the same meaning whether one says "verses" or "speeches."

The song-composition of the remaining parts is the greatest of the sensuous attractions, and the visual adornment of the dramatic persons can have a strong emotional effect but is the least artistic element, the least connected with the poetic art; in fact the force of tragedy can be felt even without benefit of public performance and actors, while for the production of the visual effect the property man's art is even more decisive than that of the poets.

GENERAL PRINCIPLES OF THE TRAGIC PLOT

With these distinctions out of the way, let us next discuss what the structuring of the events should be like, since this is both the basic and the most important element in the tragic art. We have established, then, that tragedy is an imitation of an action which is complete and whole and has some magnitude (for there is also such a thing as a whole that has no magnitude). "Whole" is that which has beginning, middle, and end. "Beginning" is that which does not necessarily follow on something else, but after it something else naturally is or happens; "end," the other way round, is that which naturally follows on something else, either necessarily or for the most part, but nothing else after it; and "middle" that which naturally follows on something else and something else on it. So, then, well-constructed plots should neither begin nor end at any chance point but follow the guidelines just laid down.

Furthermore, since the beautiful, whether a living creature or anything that is composed of parts, should not only have these in a fixed order to one another but also possess a definite size which does not depend on chance—for beauty depends on size and order; hence neither can a very tiny creature turn out to be beautiful (since our perception of it grows blurred as it approaches the period of imperceptibility) nor an excessively huge one (for then it cannot all be perceived at once and so its unity and wholeness are lost), if for example there were a creature a thousand miles long—so, just as in the case of living creatures they must have some size, but one that can be taken in in a single view, so with plots: they should have length, but such that they are easy to remember. As to a limit of the length, the one is determined by the tragic competitions and the ordinary span of attention. (If they had to compete with a hundred tragedies they would compete by the water clock, as they say used to be done [?].) But the limit fixed by the very nature of the case is: the longer the plot, up to the point of still being perspicuous as a whole, the finer it is so far as size is concerned; or to put it in general terms, the length in which, with things happening in unbroken sequence, a shift takes place either probably or necessarily from bad to good fortune or from good to bad—that is an acceptable norm of length.

But a plot is not unified, as some people think, simply because it has to do with a single person. A large, indeed an indefinite number of things can happen to a given individual, some of which go to constitute no unified event; and in the same way there can be many acts of a given individual from which no single action emerges. Hence it seems clear that those poets are wrong who have composed *Heracleïds, Theseïds,* and the like. They think that since Heracles was a single person it follows that the plot will be single too. But Homer, superior as he is in all other respects, appears to have grasped this point well also, thanks either to art or nature, for in composing an *Odyssey* he did not incorporate into it everything

that happened to the hero, for example how he was wounded on Mt. Parnassus or how he feigned madness at the muster, neither of which events, by happening, made it at all necessary or probable that the other should happen. Instead, he composed the *Odyssey*—and the *Iliad* similarly—around a unified action of the kind we have been talking about.

A poetic imitation, then, ought to be unified in the same way as a single imitation in any other mimetic field, by having a single object: since the plot is an imitation of an action, the latter ought to be both unified and complete, and the component events ought to be so firmly compacted that if any one of them is shifted to another place, or removed, the whole is loosened up and dislocated; for an element whose addition or subtraction makes no perceptible extra difference is not really a part of the whole.

From what has been said it is also clear that the poet's job is not to report what has happened but what is likely to happen: that is, what is capable of happening according to the rule of probability or necessity. Thus the difference between the historian and the poet is not in their utterances being in verse or prose (it would be quite possible for Herodotus' work to be translated into verse, and it would not be any the less a history with verse than it is without it); the difference lies in the fact that the historian speaks of what has happened, the poet of the kind of thing that *can* happen. Hence also poetry is a more philosophical and serious business than history; for poetry speaks more of universals, history of particulars. "Universal" in this case is what kind of person is likely to do or say certain kinds of things, according to probability or necessity; that is what poetry aims at, although it gives its persons particular names afterward; while the "particular" is what Alcibiades did or what happened to him.

In the field of comedy this point has been grasped: our comic poets construct their plots on the basis of general probabilities and then assign names to the persons quite arbitrarily, instead of dealing with individuals as the old iambic poets did. But in tragedy they still cling to the historically given names. The reason is that what is possible is persuasive; so what has not happened we are not yet ready to believe is possible, while what has happened is, we feel, obviously possible: for it would not have happened if it were impossible. Nevertheless, it is a fact that even in our tragedies, in some cases only one or two of the names are traditional, the rest being invented, and in some others none at all. It is so, for example, in Agathon's *Antheus*—the names in it are as fictional as the events—and it gives no less pleasure because of that. Hence the poets ought not to cling at all costs to the traditional plots, around which our tragedies are constructed. And in fact it is absurd to go searching for this kind of authentication, since even the familiar names are familiar to only a few in the audience and yet give the same kind of pleasure to all.

So from these considerations it is evident that the poet should be a maker of his plots more than of his verses, insofar as he is a poet by virtue of his imitations and what he imitates is actions. Hence even if it happens that he puts something that has actually taken place into poetry, he is none the less a poet; for there is nothing to prevent some of the things that have happened from being the kind of things that can happen, and that is the sense in which he is their maker.

SIMPLE AND COMPLEX PLOTS

Among simple plots and actions the episodic are the worst. By "episodic" plot I mean one in which there is no probability or necessity for the order in which the episodes follow one another. Such structures are composed by the bad poets because they are bad poets, but by the good poets because of the actors: in composing contest pieces for them, and stretching out the plot beyond its capacity, they are forced frequently to dislocate the sequence.

Furthermore, since the tragic imitation is not only of a complete action but also of events that are fearful and pathetic, and these come about best when they come about contrary to one's expectation yet logically, one following from the other; that way they will be more productive of wonder than if they happen merely at random, by chance— because even among chance occurrences the ones people consider most marvelous are those that seem to have come about as if on purpose: for example the way the statue of Mitys at Argos killed the man who had been the cause of Mitys' death, by falling on him while he was attending the festival; it stands to reason, people think, that such things don't happen by chance—so plots of that sort cannot fail to be artistically superior.

Some plots are simple, others are complex; indeed the actions of which the plots are imitations already fall into these two categories. By "simple" action I mean one the development of which being continuous and unified in the manner stated above, the reversal comes without peripety or recognition, and by "complex" action one in which the reversal is continuous but with recognition or peripety or both. And these developments must grow out of the very structure of the plot itself, in such a way that on the basis of what has happened previously this particular outcome follows either by necessity or in accordance with probability; for there is a great difference in whether these events happen because of those or merely after them.

"Peripety" is a shift of what is being undertaken to the opposite in the way previously stated, and that in accordance with probability or necessity as we have just been saying; as

for example in the *Oedipus* the man who has come, thinking that he will reassure Oedipus, that is, relieve him of his fear with respect to his mother, by revealing who he once was, brings about the opposite; and in the *Lynceus,* as he (Lynceus) is being led away with every prospect of being executed, and Danaus pursuing him with every prospect of doing the executing, it comes about as a result of the other things that have happened in the play that he is executed and Lynceus is saved. And "recognition" is, as indeed the name indicates, a shift from ignorance to awareness, pointing in the direction either of close blood ties or of hostility, of people who have previously been in a clearly marked state of happiness or unhappiness.

The finest recognition is one that happens at the same time as a peripety, as is the case with the one in the *Oedipus*. Naturally, there are also other kinds of recognition: it is possible for one to take place in the prescribed manner in relation to inanimate objects and chance occurrences, and it is possible to recognize whether a person has acted or not acted. But the form that is most integrally a part of the plot, the action, is the one aforesaid; for that kind of recognition combined with peripety will excite either pity or fear (and these are the kinds of action of which tragedy is an imitation according to our definition), because both good and bad fortune will also be most likely to follow that kind of event. Since, further, the recognition is a recognition of persons, some are of one person by the other one only (when it is already known who the "other one" is), but sometimes it is necessary for both persons to go through a recognition, as for example Iphigenia is recognized by her brother through the sending of the letter, but of him by Iphigenia another recognition is required.

These then are two elements of plot: peripety and recognition; third is the *pathos*. Of these, peripety and recognition have been discussed; a *pathos* is a destructive or painful act, such as deaths on stage, paroxysms of pain, woundings, and all that sort of thing.

THE TRAGIC SIDE OF TRAGEDY: PITY AND FEAR AND THE PATTERNS OF THE COMPLEX PLOT

The "parts" of tragedy which should be used as constituent elements were mentioned earlier; . . . but what one should aim at and what one should avoid in composing one's plots, and whence the effect of tragedy is to come, remains to be discussed now, following immediately upon what has just been said.

Since, then, the construction of the finest tragedy should be not simple but complex and at the same time imitative of fearful and pitiable happenings (that being the special character of this kind of poetry), it is clear first of all that

(1) neither should virtuous men appear undergoing a change from good to bad fortune, for that is not fearful, nor pitiable either, but morally repugnant; nor (2) the wicked from bad fortune to good—that is the most untragic form of all, it has none of the qualities that one wants: it is productive neither of ordinary sympathy nor of pity nor of fear—nor again (3) the really wicked man changing from good fortune to bad, for that kind of structure will excite sympathy but neither pity nor fear, since the one (pity) is directed towards the man who does not deserve his misfortune and the other (fear) towards the one who is like the rest of mankind—what is left is the man who falls between these extremes. Such is a man who is neither a paragon of virtue and justice nor undergoes the change to misfortune through any real badness or wickedness but because of some mistake; one of those who stand in great repute and prosperity, like Oedipus and Thyestes: conspicuous men from families of that kind.

So, then, the artistically made plot must necessarily be single rather than double, as some maintain, and involve a change not from bad fortune to good fortune but the other way round, from good fortune to bad, and not thanks to wickedness but because of some mistake of great weight and consequence, by a man such as we have described or else on the good rather than the bad side. An indication comes from what has been happening in tragedy: at the beginning the poets used to "tick off" whatever plots came their way, but nowadays the finest tragedies are composed about a few houses: they deal with Alcmeon, Oedipus, Orestes, Meleager, Thyestes, Telephus, and whichever others have had the misfortune to do or undergo fearful things.

Thus the technically finest tragedy is based on this structure. Hence those who bring charges against Euripides for doing this in his tragedies are making the same mistake. His practice is correct in the way that has been shown. There is a very significant indication: on our stages and in the competitions, plays of this structure are accepted as the most tragic, *if* they are handled successfully, and Euripides, though he may not make his other arrangements effectively, still is felt by the audience to be the most tragic, at least, of the poets.

Second comes the kind which is rated first by certain people, having its structure double like the *Odyssey* and with opposite endings for the good and bad. Its being put first is due to the weakness of the audiences; for the poets follow along, catering to their wishes. But this particular pleasure is not the one that springs from tragedy but is more characteristic of comedy.

PITY AND FEAR AND THE TRAGIC ACT

Now it is possible for the fearful or pathetic effect to come from the actors' appearance, but it is also possible for it to arise from the very structure of the events, and this is closer to the mark and characteristic of a better poet. Namely, the plot must be so structured, even without benefit of any visual effect, that the one who is hearing the events unroll shudders with fear and feels pity at what happens: which is what one would experience on hearing the plot of the *Oedipus*. To set out to achieve this by means of the masks and costumes is less artistic, and requires technical support in the staging. As for those who do not set out to achieve the fearful through the masks and costumes, but only the monstrous, they have nothing to do with tragedy at all; for one should not seek any and every pleasure from tragedy, but the one that is appropriate to it.

Since it is the pleasure derived from pity and fear by means of imitation that the poet should seek to produce, it is clear that these qualities must be built into the constituent events. Let us determine, then, which kinds of happening are felt by the spectator to be fearful, and which pitiable. Now such acts are necessarily the work of persons who are near and dear (close blood kin) to one another, or enemies, or neither. But when an enemy attacks an enemy there is nothing pathetic about either the intention or the deed, except in the actual pain suffered by the victim; nor when the act is done by "neutrals"; but when the tragic acts come within the limits of close blood relationship, as when brother kills or intends to kill brother or do something else of that kind to him, or son to father or mother to son or son to mother—those are the situations one should look for.

Now although it is not admissible to break up the transmitted stories—I mean for instance that Clytemestra was killed by Orestes, or Eriphyle by Alcmeon—one should be artistic both in inventing stories and in managing the ones that have been handed down. But what we mean by "artistic" requires some explanation.

It is possible, then, (1) for the act to be performed as the older poets presented it, knowingly and wittingly; Euripides did it that way also, in Medea's murder of her children. It is possible (2) to refrain from performing the deed, with knowledge. Or it is possible (3) to perform the fearful act, but unwittingly, then recognize the blood relationship later, as Sophocles' Oedipus does; in that case the act is outside the play, but it can be in the tragedy itself, as with Astydamas' Alcmeon, or Telegonus in the *Wounding of Odysseus*. A further mode, in addition to these, is (4) while intending because of ignorance to perform some black crime, to discover the relationship before one does it. And there is no other mode besides these; for one must necessarily either do the deed or not, and with or without knowledge of what it is.

Of these modes, to know what one is doing but hold off and not perform the act (No. 2) is worst: it has the morally repulsive character and at the same time is not tragic; for there is no tragic act. Hence nobody composes that way, or only rarely, as, for example, Haemon threatens Creon in the *Antigone*. Performing the act (with knowledge) (No. 1) is second (poorest). Better is to perform it in ignorance and recognize what one has done afterward (No. 3); for the repulsive quality does not attach to the act, and the recognition has a shattering emotional effect. But the best is the last (No. 4): I mean a case like the one in the *Cresphontes* where Merope is about to kill her son but does not do so because she recognizes him first; or in *Iphigenia in Tauris* the same happens with sister and brother; or in the *Helle* the son recognizes his mother just as he is about to hand her over to the enemy.

The reason for what was mentioned a while ago, namely that our tragedies have to do with only a few families, is this: It was because the poets, when they discovered how to produce this kind of effect in their plots, were conducting their search on the basis of chance, not art; hence they have been forced to focus upon those families which happen to have suffered tragic happenings of this kind.

THE TRAGIC CHARACTERS

Enough, then, concerning the structure of events and what traits the tragic plots should have. As for the characters, there are four things to be aimed at. First and foremost, that they be good. The persons will have character if in the way previously stated their speech or their action reveals the moral quality of some choice, and good character if a good choice. Good character exists, moreover, in each category of persons; a woman can be good, or a slave, although one of these classes (to wit, women) is inferior and the other, as a class, worthless. Second, that they be appropriate; for it is possible for a character to be brave, but inappropriately to a woman. Third is likeness to human nature in general; for this is different from making the character good and appropriate according to the criteria previously mentioned. And fourth is consistency. For even if the person being imitated is inconsistent, and that kind of character has been taken as the theme, he should be inconsistent in a consistent fashion.

An example of moral depravity that accomplishes no necessary purpose is the Menelaus in Euripides' *Orestes;* of an unsuitable and inappropriate character, the lamentation of Odysseus in the *Scylla* and the speech of Melanippe; and of the inconsistent, *Iphigenia at Aulis,* for the girl who pleads for her life is in no way like the later one.

In character portrayal also, as in plot construction, one should always strive for either the necessary or the probable, so that it is either necessary or probable for that kind of person to do or say that kind of thing, just as it is for one event to follow the other. It is evident, then, that the dénouements of plots also should come out of the character itself, and not from the "machine" as in the *Medea* or with the sailing of the fleet in the *Aulis*. Rather the machine should be used for things that lie outside the drama proper, either previous events that a human being cannot know, or subsequent events which require advance prophecy and exposition; for we grant the gods the ability to foresee everything. But let there be no illogicality in the web of events, or if there is, let it be outside the play like the one in Sophocles' *Oedipus*.

Since tragedy is an imitation of persons who are better than average, one should imitate the good portrait painters, for in fact, while rendering likenesses of their sitters by reproducing their individual appearance, they also make them better-looking; so the poet, in imitating men who are irascible or easygoing or have other traits of that kind, should make them, while still plausibly drawn, morally good, as Homer portrayed Achilles as good yet like other men.

TECHNIQUES OF RECOGNITION

What recognition is generically, was stated earlier; now as to its varieties: First comes the one that is least artistic and is most used, merely out of lack of imagination, that by means of tokens. Of these some are inherited, like "the lance that all the Earth-born wear," or "stars" such as Carcinus employs in his *Thyestes;* some are acquired, and of those some are on the body, such as scars, others are external, like the well-known amulets or the recognition in the *Tyro* by means of the little ark. There are better and poorer ways of using these; for example, Odysseus was recognized in different ways by means of his scar, once by the nurse and again by the swineherds. Those that are deliberately cited for the sake of establishing an identity, and all that kind, are less artistic, while those that develop naturally but unexpectedly, like the one in the foot-washing scene, are better.

Second poorest are those that are contrived by the poet and hence are inartistic; for example the way, in the *Iphigenia,* she recognizes that it is Orestes: *she* was recognized by means of the letter, but *he* goes out of his way to say what the poet, rather than the plot, wants him to say. Thus this mode is close kin to the error mentioned above: he might as well have actually worn some tokens. Similarly, in Sophocles' *Tereus,* the "voice of the shuttle."

Third poorest is that through recollection, by means of a certain awareness that follows on seeing or hearing something, like the one in the *Cypriotes* of Dicaeogenes where the hero bursts into tears on seeing the picture, and the one in Book 8 of the *Odyssey:* Odysseus weeps when he hears the lyre-player and is reminded of the War; in both cases the recognition follows.

Fourth in ascending order is the recognition based on reasoning; for example in the *Libation-Bearers:* "Somebody like me has come; nobody is like me but Orestes; therefore he has come." And the one suggested by the sophist Polyidus in speaking of the *Iphigenia:* it would have been natural, he said, for Orestes to draw the conclusion (aloud): "My sister was executed as a sacrifice, and now it is my turn." Also in the *Tydeus* of Theodectes: "I came expecting to find my son, and instead I am being destroyed myself." Or the one in the *Daughters of Phineus:* when they see the spot they reflect that it was indeed their fate to die here; for they had been exposed here as babies also. There is also one based on mistaken inference on the part of the audience, as in *Odysseus the False Messenger.* In that play, that he and no one else can string the bow is an assumption, a premise invented by the poet, and also his saying that he would recognize the bow when in fact he had not seen it; whereas the notion that he (the poet) has made his invention for the sake of the other person who would make the recognition, that is a mistaken inference.

The best recognition of all is the one that arises from the events themselves; the emotional shock of surprise is then based on probabilities, as in Sophocles' *Oedipus* and in the *Iphigenia;* for it was only natural that she should wish to send a letter. Such recognitions are the only ones that dispense with artificial inventions and visible tokens. And second-best are those based on reasoning. . . .

Classical Japan

Acting in the Noh theater.

The drama and theater of the Asian world has a history as complex and multifaceted as the histories of the many civilizations, peoples, and nations that have been said—by the West—to compose the "Asian world." India, for example, has a literature—in **SANSKRIT**—more than 3,000 years old. Although the golden age of Sanskrit theater took place in the fourth and fifth centuries, theater of various kinds—folk, classical, and modern—thrives in India today. The conventions of Indian theater have pervasively influenced the theater of southeast Asia; the Sanskrit epic poems *Mahabharata* and *Ramayana* provide the characters and settings, for example, for the beautiful shadow-puppet theater of Java in Indonesia—the *WAYANG KULIT*—and related forms of performance using dolls or live actors.

The masked dance drama of Korea—called *KAMYONGUK*—is related both to Chinese and Japanese theater, and Korea, like other Asian countries, has developed an important modern theater as well.

European knowledge of China's theater probably dates from Marco Polo's visits (1254–1324); we know of more than 550 playwrights who wrote after the Mongol invasion during China's Yüan dynasty (1279–1368), part of a theatrical tradition that is recorded as early as 1000 BCE and that developed throughout the Han (206 BCE–221 CE), Hui (589–614), T'ang (618–904), and Sung (960–1279) periods. Several plays from the Yüan theater have been adapted by European playwrights; Voltaire's *The Orphan of China* (1755), an adaptation of Chi Chunhsiang's *The House of Chao,* was the first Chinese play to become widely known in Europe, and Li Hsing's *The Story of the Chalk Circle* has been adapted several times, notably by Bertolt Brecht in *The Caucasian Chalk Circle* (1944). After the Mongols were expelled during the Ming dynasty (1368–1644), the center of theatrical activity shifted from northern China toward southern cities such as Hangchow. It was only during the eighteenth and nineteenth centuries, under the Ch'ing dynasty (1644–1912), that the most characteristic form of modern Chinese theater, the **BEIJING OPERA,** began to take the shape that it has today, sharing the stage with both Western and Western-style plays, and with a vigorous experimental theater working in a more distinctly Chinese dramatic idiom.

Although no one theater can be said to represent these rich and diverse theatrical traditions, the classical theater of Japan shares many features common to other Asian theaters: it blends aristocratic and popular affiliations; it descends from social and religious ritual traditions; it coordinates acting, dance, music, and spectacle; many of its plots and characters are derived from familiar literary and historical narratives and legends; its performance conventions are elaborately stylized and refined; and its performers are often trained with a level of formality not found in Western theater. This is hardly surprising, in that the introduction of Buddhism into Japan during the sixth century coincided with an important period of Japanese cultural and political expansion; for the next two centuries, Japan was actively in contact with the vital cultures of India, China, and Korea. Although the period of "classical" Japanese theater—roughly the twelfth through the eighteenth centuries—coincides with an extended period of cultural isolation, the expansion of Japan's military, political, and economic power in the nineteenth and twentieth centuries has again brought Japanese culture into dialogue with Asia and the West. Indeed, while Japan's imperial ambitions—the invasion of China and much of the Pacific Rim before and during World War II—were extinguished with the atomic bombing of Hiroshima and Nagasaki, Japanese theater and drama have continued to develop both in response to Western culture and through the experimental innovation of its own traditions.

The classical Japanese theater is a product of a distinctive period in the history of Japan, extending from 1192, when the emperor gave all civil and secular power to a **SHOGUN,** a hereditary military leader, to 1868, when the emperor regained state as well as religious authority. For better than 750 years the Japanese emperors lived in Kyoto, engaged in largely ceremonial duties, while the *shoguns,* based in Edo, exercised all political and judicial authority. The Genroku period (1680–1730) saw an extraordinary flowering of Japanese art and culture supported by the shogunate; this was the period of Basho, the famous *haiku* poet; of Ihara Saikaku, the novelist; and of Chikamatsu Monzaemon, Japan's greatest playwright. Although the Noh theater was in decline by the Genroku period, the three principal modes of Japanese classical theater—**NOH, DOLL THEATER,** and **KABUKI**—are in different ways the product of the elaborately hierarchical culture of feudal Japan, and of the increasing tension between the class of warriors who ruled Japan and a class of artisans and merchants—sometimes called simply **CHONIN,** or townsmen—whose economic power was centered in Japan's cities. With the rise of the shogunate, Japanese society assumed a feudal character that represented the interests and values of its ruling class of **SAMURAI** warriors. Owing their allegiance to the *shogun,* the ranks of the *samurai* comprised various warrior lords, or **DAIMYO,** and their attendant warriors. As in other feudal societies, in Japan it was both a right and an obligation to display the signs and behavior of one's caste. The *samurai,* for example, were expected to obey a stringent honor code, one that required their absolute loyalty to the *shogun,* to the *samurai* caste, and to its military ethos. If a *samurai* betrayed his lord, he and his followers risked becoming outcasts, called **RŌNIN** or "men adrift." The most famous Kabuki drama, *Chūshingura* (1748), takes the fortunes of such a *samurai* lord and his forty-seven followers as its subject, and *rōnin* are common figures in the Japanese theater. This organization extended throughout Japanese society; not only was Japanese society divided into major castes, but its professions—including theater and prostitution, often closely associated in the popular imagination—were strictly controlled through an elaborate guild system. In the major cities, theaters were built in specifically licensed quarters, and actors were generally required to live in or near those districts. Much as tradespeople had to make their trade known through conventions of dress (a practice common in Europe at this time as well), so actors were required in 1709 to shave their forelocks as a public sign of their profession.

Under the Ashikaga shogunate, which began in 1338 and ended in a civil war in the late sixteenth century, not only were the values of the *samurai* dominant, but the privileges of the *samurai* relative to other castes—such as the many ranks of merchants, artisans, farmers, and peasants—were rigidly observed. The principal forms of theatrical entertainment, especially Noh (or Nō) theater, were both sponsored by and largely reserved for the elite *samurai* castes and represented the literary and cultural values of their patrons. In 1603, Tokugawa Ieyasu (1542–1616) became the Emperor's *shogun,* and in the Tokugawa period (1603–1867; sometimes called the Edo period, after the city that was his seat, present-day Tokyo), Japan entered a period of extended peace and increasing cultural isolation. In the seventeenth century, the *shoguns* began to expel all foreigners from Japan, reserving specific enclaves in port cities like Nagasaki as protected zones where foreign trade might be undertaken. As cities such as Osaka, Tokyo, and Kyoto became significant urban centers, the merchant classes became wealthier and more powerful. Although their status was lower than that of the *samurai,* many of the merchants amassed huge fortunes that far exceeded the wealth of many *samurai.* The *samurai* still exerted political authority—in 1705 the *samurai* confiscated the fortune of a merchant to whom many of them were indebted—but the merchant classes came to dominate the cultural sphere as they became the principal audience for poetry, fiction, and theater. Although all three forms of classical Japanese theater are preserved and performed today, they first became popular in different eras of Japan's history: The Noh, as it is now known, was developed largely between the fourteenth and early seventeenth centuries; the doll theater's greatest popularity was in the late seventeenth century; Kabuki, which is said to have originated when Okuni, a dancer from the Izumo Shrine in Kyoto, began to perform satirical skits in Kyoto in 1603, developed largely between the late seventeenth and mid-eighteenth centuries.

THE DEVELOPMENT OF NOH THEATER

Although Noh theater achieved its highly literary and ceremonial form in the fourteenth century, it is usually said to have developed from performance modes popular throughout the tenth and eleventh centuries, the *SARUGAKU-NO,* and a related form, *DENGAKU-NO.* "Noh" means "accomplishment" or "performance," and both forms of entertainment contributed elements to the development of Noh theater and drama. *Dengaku-no* may have had more explicit ritual elements, and was initially associated with the native Japanese religion of Shinto, but both forms involved acrobatics, comic role-playing, and dance. *Sarugaku* means "monkey music," which may give some idea of the exuberance of these performances. In the twelfth century, however, *sarugaku-no* was adapted by Buddhist priests to illustrate tenets of Buddhist thought and belief, and performances were given to large audiences at major temples, acted by lower-ranking priests. In time, professional players both imitated these performances outside the temples and were hired to replace the priests in temple performances; by the mid-twelfth century, guilds of performers were attached to major temples. In return for free performances during religious ceremonies and festivals, the professional guilds were given a monopoly on performing in the region of the temple.

Although the *sarugaku-no* and *dengaku-no* seem to have been energetic and spirited forms of entertainment, it was the association with the contemplative and literary elements of Buddhism that were to have the greatest effect on the formation of Noh theater. In 1374, Kan'ami Kiyotsugu (1333–1384)—a leader of one of the four main *sarugaku-no* troupes—performed before the *shogun* Yoshimitsu Ashikaga (1358–1408). Kan'ami was one of the great innovators of his era and is thought to have contributed to giving the Noh its current form. He emphasized the rhythmic nature of the musical accompaniment, developed a greater use of mime in acting, and correlated dance and musical elements more closely with a dramatic plot. These innovations might well have been lost, however, had the *shogun* not been so impressed that he took Kan'ami and his son, Zeami Motokiyo (1363–1444), under his patronage. Kan'ami's troupe became the most influential in Japan, and after his father's death Zeami assumed control of the company, until he was exiled from the court in 1434 by one of Yoshimitsu's sons. Together, Kan'ami and Zeami gave the Noh drama its now-traditional ethos and shape. Kan'ami's innovations were explored and formalized by Zeami, who wrote or revised more than 100 of the 241 plays that make up the Noh repertoire and described the philosophical, esthetic, and practical goals of Noh performance in several theoretical essays. In time, the *daimyo,* emulating the *shogun,* came to sponsor their own Noh performers. Because the performers and performances were so closely bound to the status of the *samurai* caste, however, Noh never became a popular or even very public form of theater. Although *samurai* occasionally sponsored "subscription" performances of Noh for the "townsmen," these highly refined, intensely literary dramas were definitively the entertainment of the elite.

The esthetics of Noh derive from the Buddhist emphasis on **ZEN,** or contemplation, an attitude of repose and withdrawal from worldly desire and distraction. Noh performance aims to induce a similar kind of attentive repose in its audience, to evoke what is called *YUGEN* (often translated as "grace," although for Western readers this may have irrelevant Christian connotations), a mood or state of mind responsive to the mysterious, graceful, and impermanent beauty of the performance. For this reason, perhaps, Noh drama is not really driven by the cause-and-effect narrative logic of Western drama. Noh plays are typically centered on scenes of revelation that climax in the main actor's principal dance. Rather than imitating life, a Noh play should evoke the "flower," as Zeami termed the fusion of esthetic, spiritual, and moral beauty arising from the performance.

Noh Dramatic Form   A "typical" Noh play might begin with the *WAKI,* or secondary actor, meeting the *SHITE,* or principal actor, at a site of historical, legendary, or mythological importance. The *waki* enters first, and in his opening song—sometimes called the **TRAVELING SONG,** because he sings it while making his entrance—announces who he is (often a priest) and where he is going. The *shite* then enters, taking the role of an ordinary person. They discuss the significance of the place, perhaps where a legendary warrior was killed in battle. The characters speak a densely literary language, for part of the Noh dramatist's skill is shown in his cunning ability to borrow allusions and quotations from Japanese literature; the actors repeat and emphasize a network of phrases and images that convey the play's central theme. The chorus—kneeling stage left—also contributes to this "literary" texture, narrating some of the action and singing or reciting some of the dialogue. The *shite* then leaves the stage, and in some Noh productions a *KYŌGEN* (a brief farce also descended from *sarugaku*) is performed. When the *shite* returns, however, he reveals who he really is, usually a god, hero, or demon connected with the place whose destiny is troubled; he might, for example, be the ghost of the legendary warrior. In a manner of speaking, the character continues to haunt this place because he or she is unable to let go of the world, of the "character" and its investment in the world that are the essence of his or her being. The ghost is haunted by the tortuous attitude or emotion that keeps him or her connected to the world. Unlike a Greek or Shakespearean tragedy, a Noh play does not conclude with a speech of recognition or response; instead, Noh drama concludes with an intricate dance, a beautiful interplay of dialogue, dance, narration, and music for the audience's contemplation.

Since the active repertoire of Noh drama has remained more or less the same for over 400 years, it is perhaps not surprising that other elements of Noh theater and performance have become highly systematic and conventionalized. There are five types of Noh drama— plays praising the gods, plays about warriors, plays about women, plays about madness or

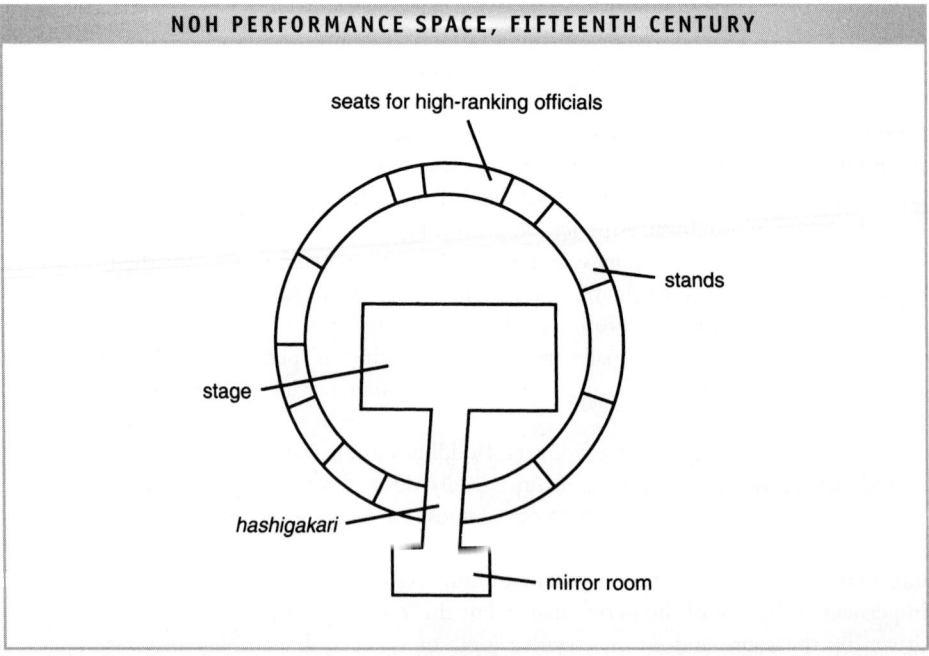

NOH PERFORMANCE SPACE, FIFTEENTH CENTURY

seats for high-ranking officials

stands

stage

hashigakari

mirror room

This is the ground plan of the performance space in the time of Zeami.

spirits, and plays about demons—and in classical Japan, a program of Noh performance included one play from each of these categories, performed in this order, with a *kyōgen* between each Noh play. In modern Japan it has become more common to perform only two or three plays followed by a *kyōgen,* in part because the pace of performance is much slower today. Although women at one time performed in Noh theater, in 1629 women were banned from the Japanese stage; while women do perform in the modern Japanese theater, Noh companies are now traditionally all male. Plays are performed by the *shite* who is masked, an unmasked *waki,* and actors who play the *shite*'s companions (*TSURE*). A chorus of six to ten men both sings and narrates from a position to the side of the stage, and musicians—a flute and two or three drums—are positioned at the rear of the stage. The drums beat rhythmically, punctuating and accentuating the actors' delivery, while the flute plays in a kind of counterpoint to their speech. The *shite*'s mask is drawn from one of five categories—old person, male, female, gods, monsters—and the clothing of the performers is similarly stylized: The actors sometimes wear elaborate headdresses, and sumptuous silk clothing, arranged and layered in particular ways for certain roles. The members of the chorus wear the traditional dress of the *samurai*. Attendants clothed in black are present onstage throughout the performance, helping the actors with costumes and masks and placing and removing properties when needed; they are always senior actors of the company, because they may also need to step in to finish a performance if an actor is unable to continue. The stage is bare of sets, and hand properties are few and conventional; a bundle of firewood might be represented by a few sticks bound with flowers. Similarly, many of the properties are purely symbolic: A twig carried by a grieving woman is the sign of her madness. Throughout the performance, the actors move slowly and ceremonially; indeed, many of their actions must take place at a prescribed area of the stage.

Although the Noh stage was shaped somewhat differently in Kan'ami's and Zeami's era, by 1615 it had assumed the shape it retains to this day. A stage (*BUTAI*), roughly eighteen feet square, extends into the audience area; the stage is roofed like the early shrines from which

The Noh Stage

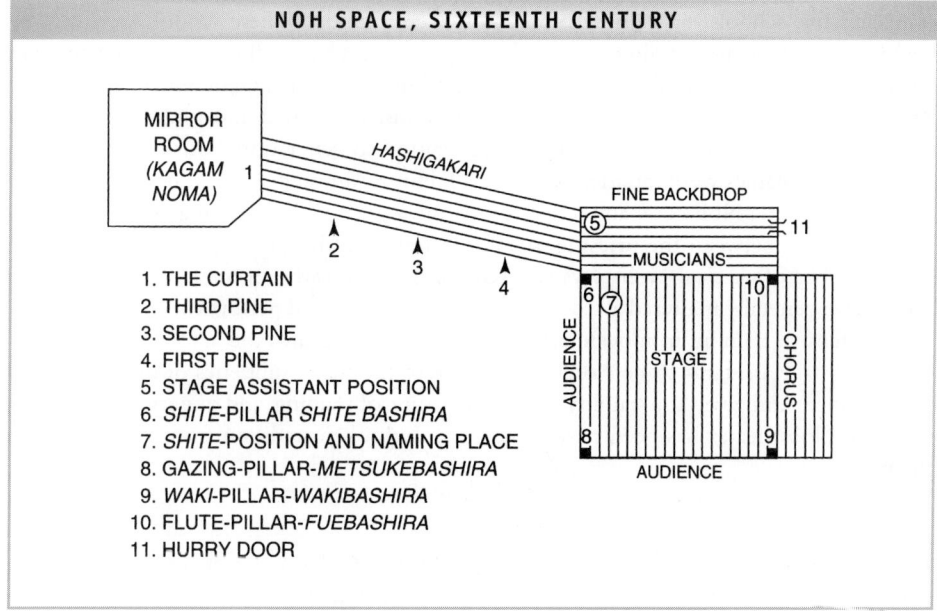

NOH SPACE, SIXTEENTH CENTURY

MIRROR ROOM (*KAGAM NOMA*) 1

HASHIGAKARI

FINE BACKDROP

11

MUSICIANS

2

3

4

5

6 7

10

AUDIENCE

STAGE

CHORUS

8   9

AUDIENCE

1. THE CURTAIN
2. THIRD PINE
3. SECOND PINE
4. FIRST PINE
5. STAGE ASSISTANT POSITION
6. *SHITE*-PILLAR *SHITE BASHIRA*
7. *SHITE*-POSITION AND NAMING PLACE
8. GAZING-PILLAR-*METSUKEBASHIRA*
9. *WAKI*-PILLAR-*WAKIBASHIRA*
10. FLUTE-PILLAR-*FUEBASHIRA*
11. HURRY DOOR

This ground plan shows the stage with the mirror room, the *hashigakari,* the *shitebashira,* the *wakibashira,* the *metsukebashira,* and the *fuebashira,* as well as the locations for the musicians and the chorus.

it derives, and the audience is seated in front and on the stage-right side. A painted backdrop behind the stage always pictures the Yogo Pine at the Kasuga Shrine in Nara. The stage is always of highly polished wood, with sounding jars concealed beneath it to resonate with the emphatic stamping that is part of the actors' performance. The musicians are seated directly behind the main stage area on a second, narrow stage (*ATOZA*); they are in full view of the audience and are able to see the actors and adjust their playing to the actors' performance throughout the play. A small entrance, called the **HURRY DOOR,** leads off the stage-left side of the *atoza,* which is used by the stage assistants, the chorus, and for the exit of dead characters. A second narrow stage runs along the stage-left side of the stage, the **WAKI-ZA,** where the chorus is seated, again in view of the audience and able to adjust their narration and singing to the pace of the actors. Finally, a long bridge, the **HASHIGAKARI,** leads from the upstage right corner of the stage out to the **MIRROR ROOM,** where the costumed actors have been studying themselves to get into the character. The *hashigakari* is six feet wide by thirty-three to fifty-two feet long; it is bordered by a narrow strip of white pebbles, on which stand three pine trees, representing heaven, earth, and man.

The four pillars that support the roof over the stage also have specific functions in the performance and provide a sense of the ceremonial formality of Noh theater. The upstage right pillar closest to the *hashigakari* is called the **SHITEBASHIRA,** or *shite*'s pillar. When the *shite* enters the *hashigakari,* he slides his feet (which are bound in cotton cloth) slowly along the floor; reaching the *shitebashira,* he pauses to announce who he is, where he is coming from, and where he is going (sometimes the *waki* will make this announcement when the *shite* reaches the *shitebashira*). The pillar downstage right is called the **METSUKEBASHIRA,** the gazing or eye-fixing pillar. It is the place where the *shite* looks while delivering his speech and which he watches through the slits in his mask to help orient his performance; given the tiny eye-openings in Noh masks, the *metsukebashira* is nearly all the *shite* can see. Downstage left, diagonally across from the *shitebashira,* is the **WAKIBASHIRA,** where the *waki* is often stationed when the *shite* enters. Upstage left is the **FUEBASHIRA,** the flute-player's pillar, where the flute-player is positioned.

As Zeami suggests in "Teachings on Style and the Flower", the training of a Noh actor in the fourteenth century was presumed to be lifelong, more a vocation than an occupation. Under the shogunate, Noh performers were given the privileges of the *samurai* caste, and five schools for training Noh actors were founded. These schools were run by hereditary masters, and certain families of Noh performers have influenced the theater over several generations; indeed, we owe the preservation of many documents (including Zeami's treatises), properties, and masks to the unusually closed and traditional ways in which Noh training has been passed from generation to generation. Four of the five current Noh companies were founded in Zeami's lifetime. Although Japan is no longer a caste society, acting in a Noh company today still requires years of dedication and intense training, something between the priesthood and the military. Moreover, because the relatively small number of classical Noh plays was stabilized in the early seventeenth century, Noh actors have generally mastered all the roles of the repertoire and perform without rehearsal. Their intensive training in movement, song, and dance prepares the actors, chorus, musicians, and stage assistants to be closely responsive to the many subtleties of their collective performance. And given the stability of the repertoire, of training, and of performance conventions, Noh theater has been performed in an unbroken tradition from Zeami's era to the present day.

THE DEVELOPMENT OF DOLL THEATER

Like the Noh theater, the doll theater owes something to the desire of Buddhist priests to educate a wider Japanese audience in their teachings. Unlike the Noh, however, the doll theater was not supported or protected directly by the shogunate, and it came to enjoy a more popular audience. The doll theater arose from the confluence of two kinds of performance: puppet shows and storytelling to music. Much like the itinerant performers of *sarugaku-no,* wandering puppeteers became associated with shrines and temples in the twelfth century. At the same time, a form of live storytelling also became popular, the singing and recitation of legends and stories to the accompaniment of the *BIWA,* a four-stringed, plucked instrument. One of the most popular of these narratives was *The Tale of Jōruri,* a love story about a wealthy girl named Jōruri; although the story dates from the fifteenth century, it became popular when it was performed to a musical instrument imported from the Ryukyu Islands between 1558 and 1569, the *SAMISEN.* The *samisen,* a three-stringed instrument that is both plucked and struck, has a much wider tonal and dynamic range than the *biwa.* Samisen-accompanied dialogue and narrative became so popular that this kind of performance was termed simply *JŌRURI.* In effect, the doll theater is a form of *jōruri* in which the song and spoken narrative are accompanied by puppet performance.

Although puppets had been used in Japan for several centuries, puppets were first used in conjunction with *jōruri* performances in the sixteenth century; puppet-*jōruri* performances have been recorded in Kyoto as early as 1596, and by the late seventeenth century there were important doll theaters in both Tokyo and Osaka. As in the Noh, the plays performed in the doll theaters used narrative, dialogue, music, and acting to convey the dramatic action, and in the seventeenth century playwrights writing for the doll theaters adapted plots and characters directly from Noh models. In part, however, because of their derivation from the romantic *jōruri* narratives, in part because their audiences were well-to-do merchants and citizens rather than the aristocratic *samurai,* and in part because they were competing with the more salacious Kabuki theaters for that audience, the doll theaters came to dramatize events more closely approaching contemporary life. Although the earliest doll theater plays were on historical and legendary subjects (like the Noh plays), by the late seventeenth and early eighteenth centuries, doll drama concerned stagings of current events, and romanticized portrayals of contemporary life, called "domestic plays" or *SEWAMONO.* Although the shogunate forbade the staging of current events in 1703, the shoguns were more concerned about the satirical portrayals of *samurai* common in Kabuki; playwrights continued to write about contemporary events.

The doll theater played a major role in the development of Japanese theater generally. When Gidayu Takemoto (1651–1714), a famous performer of *jōruri,* opened the Takemoto Theater in Osaka in 1684, he began a collaboration with Chikamatsu Monzaemon (1653–1725), now generally recognized as Japan's greatest dramatist. Chikamatsu wrote an important body of plays for the doll theater, on historical subjects as well as on contemporary life. His play *Love Suicides at Sonezaki* (1703) concerns the double suicide of a young merchant and a prostitute in 1703 and was renowned for the beauty of its language and the power of its performance. The genre became so popular that in 1722 the shogunate banned plays about double suicide, which were common in both the doll theater and the Kabuki theater, perhaps fearing that Chikamatsu's play would be imitated by romantic young Japanese. Not only did Chikamatsu and other playwrights—notably Chikamatsu Hanji (1725–1783) and Uemura Bunrakuken (1737–1810), for whom the current puppet theater of Japan, *BUNRAKU,* is named—produce an extraordinarily rich body of plays, but also these plays were immediately mined by the Kabuki theaters, providing a source of material for living actors as well as the doll theater's elaborate puppets.

The stage of the doll theater is thirty-six feet wide by twenty-six feet deep and is divided into three sections, each separated by a low screen. The three puppeteers who operate each puppet are visible throughout the performance. They are costumed in elegant traditional clothes and are seated behind the screens. The puppeteers and their dolls share the stage with several other performers: the stage assistants, dressed in black as in the Noh theater; the an-

The Doll Theater Stage

nouncer; the narrator; and the *samisen* player. The announcer begins the performance by announcing the title of the play and introducing the narrator and the *samisen* player. The narrator is responsible for the verbal art of the play in a direct development of his role in the *jōruri:* he narrates the story of the play, speaks the dialogue of the characters and expresses their emotions as well, smiling, laughing, weeping, and so on. Later in the eighteenth century several narrators were used, one for each of the major characters in the drama. The *samisen* is played to augment, clarify, and deepen the narrator's performance, lending it a special plangency.

As in the Noh theater, performance in the doll theater is extremely ceremonial and precise, and performers undergo years of training to achieve their craft. Although marionettes were used in the seventeenth century, hand-operated puppets became increasingly popular and by 1736 had supplanted earlier forms. The typical doll is three or four feet tall and is operated by three puppeteers. The most senior operator, dressed in a formal nineteenth-century costume, stands behind the doll and holds it up; he works a system of strings and pulleys within the head that control the doll's head, eyebrows, and eyelids, and he also operates the doll's right arm and right hand by means of hidden strings. His two assistants are clothed in black like the stage assistants, and their faces are covered; one assistant operates the left arm and hand, and the other assistant operates the legs and feet. Much as training in the Noh theater resembles that of a traditional art, so learning to operate the puppets of the doll theater entails a lifetime of commitment. Puppeteers take an apprenticeship of ten years to learn to operate the legs and feet of the dolls with sufficient grace; they then take another ten years to learn the correct operation of the left arm and hand before spending the final ten years on mastering the subtleties of the right arm, right hand, and head.

Doll theater contributed extensively to the dramatic repertoire of the Kabuki theater, and the fixed poses of the puppets are sometimes thought to contribute to the exaggerated expressive stance of the Kabuki actors, the **MIE**. But the doll theater contributed other innovations to Japanese theater and to world theater generally. Much as the dolls increased in complexity throughout the late seventeenth century and early eighteenth century—gaining eye movement in 1730, finger joints and movements in 1733, and so on—so the stage itself became increasingly mechanized. By 1715 the doll theaters were using movable settings, and by 1727 elevator traps were used to raise and lower scenery visibly through the floor of the stage. This machinery not only was put to use in the more spectacular Kabuki theater, but also was adapted and imitated by theaters around the world. Although the doll theater was surpassed in popularity by the Kabuki in the nineteenth century, it continues to be sponsored by the Japanese government and performed regularly in Osaka and Tokyo.

THE DEVELOPMENT OF KABUKI THEATER

Kabuki is in many ways the most energetic and spectacular mode of classical Japanese theater, using live actors to stage intense and passionate dramas whose effect is heightened by a range of powerful performance conventions and by an elaborately mechanized stage. As in the doll theater, Kabuki arose as a popular form of entertainment, supported by audiences outside the aristocratic sphere of Noh performance. Although Kabuki drama, as in the drama of the doll theaters, was initially derived from the plays of the Noh theater, Kabuki theater rapidly developed its own dramatic style and performance esthetics.

Unlike Noh and doll theater, Kabuki did not originate in medieval performance forms like the *sarugaku-no* and the *biwa*-accompanied narratives that became *jōruri*. Instead, Kabuki began in 1603, when Okuni, who claimed to be a priestess from the Izumo Grand Shrine, set up an impromptu stage in the Kyoto riverbed, where she performed dances and satirical skits. Okuni's company was largely composed of women, and within a short time a number of companies—some involving prostitutes, who offered performances as entertainment—were established in Kyoto and elsewhere. Although comic roles—called *SARUWAKA*—were always performed by men, the earliest troupes were composed mainly of women, called either *ONNA KABUKI* (women's Kabuki) or *YŪGO KABUKI* (prostitutes' Kabuki). At the same time, however, other Kabuki companies, composed mainly of adolescent boys, became popular.

Throughout the early period of Kabuki, its performers—both women and boys—were frequently associated with prostitution, which extended in various ways to a variety of leisure activities: to bathhouses, dances, and to the practice of *GEISHA,* which has its origins at this time. All of these activities, however, were distinct from the work of the *YŪGO,* or professional prostitute. As in other respects, the shogunate treated Kabuki like prostitution, beginning in 1624 to license companies and theater districts.

The boundary between theater and prostitution—by men, women, and boys—was difficult to police, though, and in 1652 authorities finally banned the boys' Kabuki—*WAKASHU KABUKI*—outright. Thereafter, the only Kabuki companies that were licensed to perform were the *YARO KABUKI,* or adult male Kabuki companies, which are now traditional.

The repertoire of Kabuki theater contains two kinds of plays, one based on historical or legendary incidents, and *sewamono* or "domestic plays," based on contemporary events. Okuni had once acted the role of a young *samurai* soliciting a prostitute, and plays based on the visit of a wealthy and powerful young man to the "licensed quarter" became a popular Kabuki genre, particularly in Kyoto and Osaka. Many of these plays, including *Love Letter from the Licensed Quarter* (1780), concern the fortunes of Yūgiri, a well-known courtesan of the Osaka Shinmachi quarter who died in 1678. Chikamatsu—whose *Love Suicides at Sonezaki* (1703) adapted the conventions of Kabuki to the doll stage—played a central role in this regard as well: he worked as the house playwright to a famous Kabuki company for more than twenty years. Although plays that dramatize love suicides and plays staging the scandals of the *samurai* caste were banned after 1722, playwrights continued to write about contemporary life under the guise of one of the other major genres of Kabuki theater, the history play. It quickly became apparent that by changing names and setting the drama in the past, playwrights were able to write domestic plays thinly veiled as history. For example, in 1703 the forty-seven retainers of Lord Asano took revenge on their master's disgrace at the hands of a shogunate official by killing the official and then committing *seppuku,* or ritual disembowelment. Within two weeks, a Kabuki play alluding to the incident was staged, and then was rapidly closed by the government. When Chikamatsu turned to these events in 1710, he set the play in the fourteenth century to sidestep the ban, and one of the most famous Kabuki plays—*Chūshingura* (1748)—concerns these events as well.

The Kabuki Stage

Kabuki is very much a performance genre, and its plays were organized around the abilities of its actors rather than around a literary script. For this reason, even the plays written by the most influential Kabuki playwrights—Chikamatsu Monzaemon, Takedo Izumo (1691–1756), and Kawatake Mokuami (1816–1893)—began as outlines of scenes to be elaborated by a cadre of assistant playwrights. A Kabuki company contained forty to sixty actors, each of whom specialized in a certain kind of role and expected the playwright to devise scenes that would allow him to display his talents. Companies generally included a leading-man actor, or *TACHIYAKU,* and specialists in villainous men (*KATAKIYAKU*), in young men and boys (*WAKASHUGATA*), in comic roles (*DOKEKATA*), and in women's roles (*ONNAGATA*), which were also divided according to age and type.

Finally, the unusual duration of a Kabuki performance also demanded the talents of the playwright's staff of assistants. Kabuki performances originally began about three o'clock in the morning and did not conclude until dusk; the fourteen- to fifteen-hour production was composed of a series of scenes arranged around a common theme or mood. The production usually began with a dance play, followed by a familiar play from the company's repertoire. Because the play was familiar to the company, it required little preparation. Then the

KABUKI STAGE, NINETEENTH CENTURY

Notice the screens to the side of the stage, the *hanamichi* (which attaches to the front of the stage in the lower left-center of the picture), and a revolving platform in the center of the stage. (From Brockett, Oscar G. *History of the Theatre,* 7ᵗʰ Edition. Published by Allyn and Bacon, Boston, MA. Copyright © 1995 by Pearson Education. Reprinted by permission of the publisher.)

company would perform one or two short practice plays, written by apprentice playwrights and performed by actors-in-training as part of their education. The main play—the **HON KYŌGEN**—would be performed at about seven o'clock in the morning and lasted until dusk. This play was outlined by the house playwright in collaboration with the company's leading actor and manager, and he would write the most important sections himself; the company's second and third rank playwrights would elaborate dialogue for the rest of the play. The play was customarily divided into four sections: a history section in four to six acts (**JIDAIMONO**) concerning the exploits of the *samurai;* a dance; a *sewamono* (contemporary) section in one to three acts, set in the milieu of artisans, traders, and merchants; and a concluding dance drama. Kabuki performances today are generally given in two programs, lasting from eleven to four o'clock and from four-thirty until nine-thirty in the evening. Although it is rare to see a full-length Kabuki play performed today, the four-part sequence is still followed.

Kabuki is very much an actor's theater. The actors undergo a long period of training, and as in Noh theater, certain families of actors have dominated the history of Kabuki. Indeed, Kabuki actors often wear their family crest in performance, and audiences frequently compare an actor's performance in a given role with his father's or his uncle's. Originating as a form of dance, Kabuki places a premium on choreography, which accompanies gesture and speech as a means of realizing the character's essential tone or feeling in a precise and elegant image. Yet the actors play directly to the audience, and the most striking moments in the performance—the *mie,* a highly conventionalized posed performance of passion—are underscored as performance when the stage assistants clap two pieces of wood loudly and

rhythmically together. The actors play conventional roles, and each role in the Kabuki repertoire has a conventional costume associated with it. The costumes are extremely cumbersome, so the actors are often helped by stage assistants clothed in black who position properties and move pieces of the set. The actors are not masked, but wear an elaborate and
conventionalized makeup, usually of red and black lines and patterns ranged over a white
base; *onnagata* actors generally add only eyebrow lines and rouged cheeks and lips to an otherwise white face. Given its close relationship to *jōruri* and doll theater, it is not surprising
that Kabuki usually requires a narrator onstage as well who not only sets the scene, but comments on the action throughout; he also occasionally speaks dialogue. Kabuki actors never
sing, so their songs are sung by the narrator and by an onstage chorus. Moreover, each play
is accompanied by traditional music, played by musicians wearing the traditional *samurai* costume. The orchestra for Kabuki is considerably larger than that for Noh and makes use of
flutes, bells, drums, cymbals, and gongs, as well as the *samisen*.

Although the first Kabuki companies played on impromptu stages, they soon were allowed to use Noh theaters; given their raffish character, however, Kabuki companies were
not allowed to have roofed theaters until 1724. Like the doll theater, Kabuki theater quickly
made use of scenic technology; the elevator stage was in use by 1736, and by the late eighteenth century it was common for Kabuki theaters to have a revolving stage, sometimes two
independent turntables with one turning inside the other. Kabuki makes extensive use of
scenery, though much of it is of a symbolic or ornamental nature. Like properties in this theater, which tend to be suggestive of the objects they represent, the scenery of a Kabuki performance is openly theatrical in character: the scenery is changed in view of the audience
by visible assistants (who help the actors as well) and aims to suggest the locale of the scene
rather than put it on the stage in a realistic way. It is a measure, though, of the relationship
between the extroverted Kabuki performance and its audience that its most distinguishing
feature involves the audience more directly in the production. In the early eighteenth century, Kabuki theaters added a **HANAMICHI,** or elevated bridge, extending from the rear of
the auditorium to the stage. Actors made their exits and entrances here, and scenes could be
played on the *hanamichi* as well. By the 1770s, a second *hanamichi* was added, and the area
between the two *hanamichi* was divided into floor boxes, while other rows of seating ran
along the sides of the auditorium. Although the second *hanamichi* is still required for some
plays, it is generally no longer in use.

The restoration of the emperor in 1868 not only brought about the collapse of the
shogunate, but also ended Japan's isolation. It also dramatized the economic weakness of the
samurai relative to the merchant class. In many respects, Japan's theater was vulnerable to extinction, especially the Noh and doll theaters, which had no truly popular audience; Kabuki
was the only theater which continued to attract new plays, playwrights, and audiences in the
nineteenth and twentieth centuries. But the Japanese worked to preserve their classical theater, and it is still possible today to see plays from the Noh, doll theater, and Kabuki repertoire in excellent, traditional productions.

CLASSICAL JAPANESE DRAMA IN PERFORMANCE HISTORY

After 1868, Japan became open to cultural influence from the West, and a variety of dramatic and theatrical forms came to rival the traditional genres of Noh, *jōruri,* and Kabuki.
SHIMPA, a theatrical movement originating in Osaka in the 1880s, responded to the Western theater's use of more colloquial language and contemporary dramatic settings. However,
because many of the *shimpa* actors were drawn from Kabuki, *shimpa* gradually came to
resemble Kabuki in performance, even though its dramas were more evidently based on recent news events, crimes, and political controversies. Although *shimpa* and its successor,
SHINGEKI—a "realistic" dramatic movement that both imported and imitated the plays of
Ibsen, Chekhov, Shaw, and others—marked an important move away from the classical genres, they continued to be performed in the twentieth century.

(ASIDE)
SANSKRIT DRAMA AND THEATER

The cultures, languages, and theater of the Indian subcontinent have been transformed by three massive invasions: by the Aryans sometime between 3000 and 2000 BCE; by the Moslems, who brought both the Persian language and the Koran, in the tenth and eleventh centuries; and by the British, beginning in the seventeenth century. The Aryan language—Sanskrit (literally, "the perfected tongue")—became the foundation of ancient Indian culture. Sanskrit was a spoken language until early in the first millennium, when Prakit became the vernacular. Something like Latin in medieval Europe, Sanskrit was reserved for ritual, religious, and academic uses, and for India's rich literature and theater. Sanskrit is the language of the *Rgveda,* a collection of prayers and hymns composed between 1500 and 1000 BCE that is the oldest work in any Indo-European language. The two major epics of Indian culture—the *Mahabharata* and the *Ramayana*—date from around 1000 BCE, but took their current form during India's golden age, which lasted from the second century CE into the ninth century. Although it had long been thought in the West that Sanskrit theater gradually disappeared after the Moslem invasions of the tenth and eleventh centuries, Sanskrit plays were still performed in Kerala—a state in the southwest of India—by performers who were part of a hereditary caste connected to religious temples.

Hindu belief and the caste structure of ancient Indian society inform the esthetics of Sanskrit theater and drama. Ancient India was a rigidly stratified society composed of four hereditary castes, each of which was subdivided: the *Brahmins* (priests and intellectuals), *Kshatriyas* (aristocrats, warriors), *Vaisyas* (craftsmen, farmers), and *Sudras* (unskilled workers, peasants). Although these castes were devised and perpetuated along racial and economic lines, they also translated Hindu religious beliefs into the organizing structure of society. Hindu is based on a belief in Brahman, or "world-soul." Although different aspects of Brahman are often represented as distinct gods—Brahma the creator, Siva the destroyer, Vishnu the preserver, for example—these gods are really aspects of Brahman, the only whole, perfect, and unchanging being. The created universe is arrayed hierarchically, according to the degree that each being is able to contemplate or participate in this sense of wholeness or perfection.

In performance, Sanskrit drama emblematizes this dichotomy between the distracting diversity of lived experience and the contemplation of wholeness and perfection; Sanskrit theater offers its audience a richly varied performance while inducing the audience to adopt a unifying and impersonal, even contemplative mood. Most of our understanding of Sanskrit drama derives from the second-century *Natyasastra,* or *Art of the Theater,* usually attributed to the playwright Bharata, from several other treatises, and from the twenty-five plays that remain. Much as ancient Greek plays were based on myth and legend mainly drawn from the *Iliad* and the *Odyssey,* Sanskrit plays were generally based on heroic stories taken from the *Mahabharata* and the *Ramayana* and were divided into two groups: *RUPAKA* (major drama) and *UPA-RUPAKA* (minor drama). *Rupaka* are of various lengths and include the plays of Bharata; Bhasa's second-century plays *The Vision of Vasavadatta* and *Carudatta;* King Sudraka's *The Clay Cart* (written sometime between the fourth and eighth centuries); Kalidasa's fifth-century *Sakuntala;* and the seventh-century plays of King Harsa and Bhavabhuti. As in the Japanese Noh, the narrative of the play is less critical than the attitude it produces: the impersonal and contemplative mood of wholeness called *RASA.* According to the *Natyasastra,* there are eight basic *rasas* or moods that a play should strive to produce—erotic, comic, pathetic, furious, heroic, terrible, odious, and marvelous—and while a given play may include several *rasas,* it should be designed so that one mood dominates. Moreover, these *rasas* are related to the *BHAVA,* the emotions or feelings displayed in the play by the characters. The eight *bhavas*—desire, comic or sympathetic laughter, sadness, anger, vigor or power, fear, loathing, and wonder—are the organizing, "stable" emotions staged in the play, and are complicated by thirty-three "unsta-

Indeed, the Japanese classical theater was perhaps most keenly threatened by Japan's defeat in World War II and the subsequent occupation. As part of the postwar occupation of Japan, the United States established a Civil Information and Education Section, which had as part of its duties both the protection of traditional Japanese culture and the importation of "progressive," democratic culture, including American literature and drama. This office often came into conflict with the occupation's censorship office, concerned as it was to prevent the spread of imperial Japanese political ideas. Although neither Noh nor *jōruri* seemed to pose much of a political threat, the popular Kabuki theater had long been associated with the feudal ideology of Japanese nationalism, and the censors were much more careful in their approval of Kabuki theater. The first Kabuki play to be produced after the end of occupable" emotions. The subtle balance and interplay of the *bhavas* should evoke a sense of harmony and perfection, the dominant *rasa* of the play.

As in Hindu philosophy, Sanskrit drama aims to produce a sense of oneness from the diversity of experience; *rasa* arises from each play's cunning interplay of the range of *bhavas,* of dialogue written in both verse and prose, of Sanskrit and Prakit, and of character types ranging from gods, kings, and heroes to servants, peasants, and children. Yet despite this diversity, Sanskrit plays have several common characteristics. Each play not only produces its main mood or *rasa,* it also illustrates the workings of *karma* or cosmic justice. For this reason, Sanskrit drama falls outside the Western understanding of tragedy, and Sanskrit playwrights are urged by the *Natyasastra* not to represent death onstage. Sanskrit is spoken by all the male Brahmin and Kshatriya characters in the play, whereas women, peasants, and children speak Prakit, as does the jester character who appears in most plays, often as the hero's sidekick. Although plays vary in length from one act to ten acts, each act generally takes place within a single day; the action usually takes place in several earthly and heavenly locations.

Plays were performed on a variety of occasions in ancient India—at festivals, weddings, coronations, and at other public events—and the play's *rasa* was appropriate to the occasion. The *Natyasastra* describes three kinds of theater structure—square, rectangular, and triangular—each in three different sizes. The rectangular theaters

CLASSICAL SANSKRIT PERFORMANCE

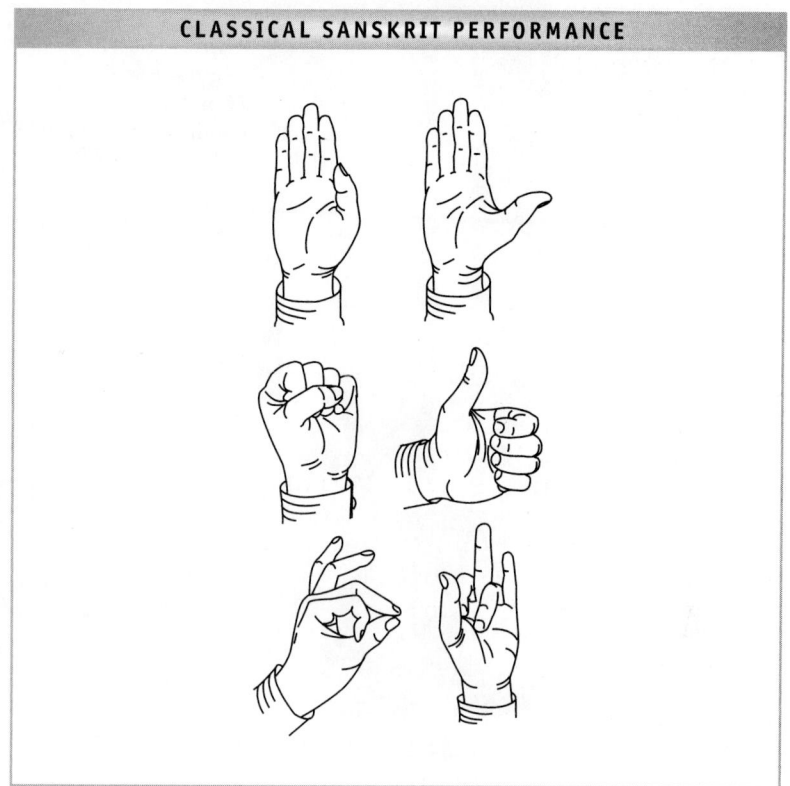

These six hand positions are used in a classical Sanskrit performance.

were divided into two equal areas. The audience area was supported by four pillars, representing both the four compass points and the four principal castes. The stage area was divided into two parts—a relatively shallow performing space divided from a backstage area by a wall.

Performances were accompanied by a variety of musical instruments and were elaborately ceremonial in character; actors used an elaborate system of movement, gesture, and speech. Because the performers were to represent codified *bhavas,* the *Natyasastra* described the gestures appropriate to them: for instance, thirty-two different eye movements, thirty-two positions for the feet, twenty-four gestures for one hand. Both the Sanskrit drama and texts like the *Natyasastra* document the extraordinary theatrical vitality of the golden age of classical Indian culture.

tion censorship in 1948 was, in fact, the great *samurai* revenge play, *Chūshingura,* often known in English as *The Loyal Forty-Seven Samurai.*

Since the war, the traditional modes of Japanese theater have become popular not only in Japan, but throughout the world. Several modern playwrights—notably Mishima Yukio—have either written new Noh or Kabuki plays or have adapted earlier dramas to modern settings. Moreover, the revival of Japanese classical theater has been part of an important resurgence of interest in traditional modes of artistic expression in Japan, which has taken place alongside Japan's emergence as a leading political, economic, and cultural power in the late twentieth century.

In this 1989 English-language production at the University of Hawai'i, *Matsukaze* is played on a traditional Noh stage.

Exemplifying the elegant movement of Kabuki theater, this scene from the University of Hawai'i production of *Chūshingura* shows Kampei protecting Okaru from attackers, who threaten them with cherry-blossom weapons.

This view of the *Matsukaze* shows the musicians and chorus, as well as the *hashigakari*.

In the University of Hawai'i production of *Chūshingura* (1979), Lord Enya Hangan commits *seppuku,* watched by the shogun's messengers.

READING THE MATERIAL THEATER

One of the great traditions of Japan is the art of portraiture, and many of Japan's greatest artists made portraits of celebrated actors. As historical records, however, these portraits are somewhat difficult to use: like Japanese theater, Japanese painting was itself a highly conventionalized activity. Nonetheless, these illustrations provide a striking insight into the power of performance on Japan's classical stage. Here is a portrait of the actor Seki Sanjūrō II (1805–1870) in the role of Kyōgoku Takumi, by the great artist Kunisada (1786–1865). Kunisada lived toward the end of the Edo period; shortly after his death, in 1867, the last of the Tokugawa shoguns resigned, leading to the increasing openness to the West characteristic of the Meiji period. In this sense, Kunisada's printmaking—which covers natural subjects, as well as the circumscribed life of the court, the brothels, and the theaters—documents the final phases of traditional Japanese culture before the massive impact of European and American modernity.

In his long career, Kunisada made a large number of theatrical portraits which were engraved and printed; he also occasionally illustrated scenes of backstage life. (See the excellent overview of Kunisada's work provided by Sebastian Izzard, J. Thomas Rimer, and John T. Carpenter in *Kunisada's World,* a catalogue of the exhibition "Kunisada's World" shown at the Japan Society Gallery in New York in 1993 [New York: Japan Society, 1993] from which this portrait and descriptive information are taken.) This portrait is part of a series of 150 portraits of Kabuki actors that Kunisada planned to print late in his life; he completed seventy-two. The cartouches—the small bars with en-graved Japanese characters—list the actor's name and the role he is playing in the illustration, as well as Kunisada's signature. In many respects these portraits seem heavily conventionalized, even idealized, and we know that Kunisada based many of them on earlier portraits; some portraits—of actors whose careers were over before Kunisada began his work—are based on portraits executed by other artists. Nonetheless, the portraits capture a number of significant features of Kabuki theater. In most of the portraits, Kunisada shows the actor in the *mie*—a moment of intense passion, in which the actor freezes and moves his eyes rapidly, as a way of demonstrating the intensity of his feelings; this action is usually sustained by the musicians' drumming and often prompts shouts of encouragement and applause from the audience.

Beyond that, what features of the portrait seem prominent? What kind of roles do you think were his speciality? Given the conventionality of the portrait, how do you interpret the strong and energetic sense of line in the image, evident especially around his nose and chin?

Seki Sanjūrō II as Kyōgoku Takumi, in a portrait by Kunisada.

Kan'ami Kiyotsugu

Kan'ami Kiyotsugu (1333–1384) was one of the principal performers of *sarugaku-no* and the leader of a prominent company. When he appeared before the *shogun* Yoshimitsu Ashikiga in 1374, the *shogun* was so impressed with the company that he retained them as his players. Kan'ami is generally credited with refining and systematizing the Noh for his aristocratic audience and with writing many of the plays that became part of the standard Noh repertoire. Kan'ami's son, Zeami Motokiyo (1363–1444), succeeded his father as the leader of the company and had a massive influence on the development of the Noh. Zeami both reworked older plays and wrote many new plays of his own; of the 241 plays in the Noh repertoire, more than 100 are connected to Zeami. Zeami influenced the development of Noh in other respects as well, mainly in writing sixteen essays on Noh esthetics. These essays cover a range of topics, including the training of actors, the proper style of dramatic writing, and the goals of performance. Although Zeami enjoyed the favor of Yoshimitsu until the *shogun's* death in 1408, he fared less well under the rule of Yoshimitsu's son, Yoshimochi (1386–1428) and was banished to the remote island of Sado in 1434 when Yoshimochi's younger brother Yoshinori (1394–1441) became *shogun*. The reasons for Yoshinori's hostility to Zeami are not clear but may involve Yoshinori's preference for another playwright, On'ami. Zeami did succeed in passing his essays on to his son-in-law, Komparu Zenchiku (1405–1468), who became an important Noh playwright and theoretician. Not much is known about the end of Zeami's life; legend has it that he was able to return to the mainland after Yoshinori was assassinated in 1441.

MATSUKAZE

Matsukaze was originally written by Kan'ami and extensively reworked by Zeami; it has remained in the Noh repertoire since the fifteenth century and is performed by all Noh companies.

This elegant drama, like most Noh plays, takes place in a setting familiar from the classic literature of Japan, the Bay of Suma. Suma is principally associated with the famous poet, courtier, and scholar Ariwaka no Yukihira (818–893), whose exile at Suma was recounted in his own poetry and formed the basis for many stories and legends. It also inspired the narrative of Genji's exile at Suma in the Japanese epic *Tale of Genji*. The narrative of the play, though, seems to have been invented by Kan'ami. The play opens when the *waki*—playing a priest—enters the stage, singing a traveling song about his arrival at Suma. He asks the *kyōgen* (playing a villager) about the significance of the pine tree, and he is informed that it memorializes two fisher girls, Murasame and Matsukaze, who have long since died. Shortly thereafter, Murasame—played by the *tsure*—enters, followed by the *shite,* Matsukaze. The two girls elaborately mime dipping brine into their cart with their fans, and in speeches that quote from Yukihira and from other poets, they describe their desolation. Their language here is rich with imagery, particularly of the changing sea, the hard lives of the fishermen, and of the moon, a Buddhist symbol of enlightenment. As is typical of the Noh, many of their lines are spoken by the Chorus.

Although the *shite* and his *tsure* do not leave the stage, they retire to the *shitebashira*, where they mime sitting in their small hut. The *waki*—who has observed them throughout the first scene—approaches the hut and asks for shelter, quoting one of Yukihira's poems in passing. The girls then reveal that they are the ghosts of Matsukaze and Murasame, still "steeped in longing" for the exiled poet, even in death. They had fallen in love with Yukihira during his exile at Suma, and he had given them their names, "Wind in the Pines" (*matsukaze*) and "Autumn Rain" (*murasame*), names redolent of the imagery of classical Japanese poetry. The girls were not able to follow Yukihira when he returned to court after his exile;

This production of Kan'ami's *Matsukaze* emphasizes the traditional spatial, costume, and performance elements of Noh theater.

all they have in his memory is his hunting cloak and court hat. Driven nearly to madness with her eternal grief, Matsukaze puts on Yukihira's cloak and hat for her final dance.

Matsukaze is an evocative example of the way Noh theater attempts to capture a particular mood through the collaborative interplay between each of its highly wrought arts. The beauty of the language, the delicacy of characterization, the succinct action, the music of the flute and drums, the chanting of the Chorus, and the refinement of the acting combine to capture the subtle intensity of feeling for which Noh theater is famous.

MATSUKAZE

Kan'ami Kiyotsugu
TRANSLATED BY ROYALL TYLER

CHARACTERS

AN ITINERANT PRIEST (*waki*)   MATSUKAZE (*shite*)
A VILLAGER (*kyōgen*)   MURASAME (*tsure*)

PLACE: *Suma Bay in Settsu Province*
TIME: *Autumn, the Ninth Month*

(*The stage assistant places a stand with a pine sapling set into it at the front of the stage. The* PRIEST *enters and stands at the naming-place. He carries a rosary.*)

PRIEST: I am a priest who travels from province to province. Lately I have been in the Capital. I visited the famous sites and ancient ruins, not missing a one. Now I intend to make a pilgrimage to the western provinces. (*He faces forward.*) I have hurried, and here I am already at the Bay of Suma in Settsu Province. (*His attention is caught by the pine tree.*) How strange! That pine on the beach has a curious look. There must be a story connected with it. I'll ask someone in the neighborhood. (*He faces the bridgeway.*) Do you live in Suma?

(*The* VILLAGER *comes down the bridgeway to the first pine. He wears a short sword.*)

VILLAGER: Perhaps I am from Suma; but first tell me what you want.
PRIEST: I am a priest and I travel through the provinces. Here on the beach I see a solitary pine tree with a wooden tablet fixed to it, and a poem slip hanging from the tablet. Is there a story connected with the tree? Please tell me what you know.
VILLAGER: The pine is linked with the memory of two fisher girls, Matsukaze and Murasame. Please say a prayer for them as you pass.
PRIEST: Thank you. I know nothing about them, but I will stop at the tree and say a prayer for them before I move on.
VILLAGER: If I can be of further service, don't hesitate to ask.
PRIEST: Thank you for your kindness.
VILLAGER: At your command, sir.

(*The* VILLAGER *exits. The* PRIEST *goes to stage center and turns toward the pine tree.*)

PRIEST: So, this pine tree is linked with the memory of two fisher girls, Matsukaze and Murasame. It is sad! Though their bodies are buried in the ground, their names linger on. This lonely pine tree lingers on also, ever green and untouched by autumn, their only memorial. Ah! While I have been chanting sutras and invoking Amida Buddha for their repose, the sun, as always on autumn days, has quickly set. That village at the foot of the mountain is a long way. Perhaps I can spend the night in this fisherman's salt shed.

(*He kneels at the* waki-*position. The stage assistant brings out the prop, a cart for carrying pails of brine, and sets it by the gazing-pillar. He places a pail on the cart.*)

(MURASAME *enters and comes down the bridgeway as far as the first pine. She wears the* tsure *mask.* MATSUKAZE *follows her and stops at the third pine. She wears the* wakaonna *mask. Each carries a water pail. They face each other.*)

MATSUKAZE AND MURUSAME: A brine cart wheeled along the beach
    Provides a meager livelihood:
    The sad world rolls
    Life by quickly and in misery!
MURASAME: Here at Suma Bay
    The waves shatter at our feet,
    And even the moonlight wets our sleeves
    With its tears of loneliness.

(MURASAME *goes to stage center while* MATSUKAZE *moves to the* shite *position.*)

MATSUKAZE: The autumn winds are sad.
    When the Middle Counselor Yukihira
    Lived here back a little from the sea,
    They inspired his poem,
    "Salt winds blowing from the mountain pass. . . ."
    On the beach, night after night,
    Waves thunder at our door;
    And on our long walks to the village
    We've no companion but the moon.
    Our toil, like all of life, is dreary,
    But none could be more bleak than ours.
    A skiff cannot cross the sea,
    Nor we this dream world.
    Do we exist, even?
    Like foam on the salt sea,
    We draw a cart, friendless and alone,
    Poor fisher girls whose sleeves are wet
    With endless spray, and tears
    From our hearts' unanswered longing.
CHORUS: Our life is so hard to bear
    That we envy the pure moon

---

48 **"Salt . . . pass"** from the poem by Yukihira, No. 876 in the *Shinkokinshū*: "The sleeves of the traveler have turned cold; the wind from Suma Bay blows through the pass." 52 **We've . . . moon** a modified quotation from the poem by Hōkyō Chūmei, No. 187 in the *Kin'yōshū*: "Pillow of grass—as I sleep on my journey I realize I have no companion but the moon." 58–59 **salt sea** the words "salt sea," which can also be translated "brine," lead to mention of the brine cart even though the cart does not logically belong in the context 64 **That . . . moon** from the poem by Fujiwara Takamitsu, No. 435 in the *Shūishū*: "In this world which seems difficult to pass through, how I envy the pure moon!"

65   Now rising with the tide.
      But come, let us dip brine,
      Dip brine from the rising tide!
      Our reflections seem to shame us!

(*They look down as if catching a glimpse of their reflections in the
water. The movement of their heads "clouds" the expression on their
masks, making it seem sad.*)

      Yes, they shame us!
70   Here, where we shrink from men's eyes,
      Drawing our timorous cart;
      The withdrawing tide
      Leaves stranded pools behind.
      How long do they remain?
75   If we were the dew on grassy fields,
      We would vanish with the sun.
      But we are sea tangle,
      Washed up on the shore,
      Raked into heaps by the fishermen,
80   Fated to be discarded, useless,
      Withered and rotting,
      Like our trailing sleeves,
      Like our trailing sleeves.

(*They look down again.*)

      Endlessly familiar, still how lovely
85   The twilight at Suma!
      The fishermen call out in muffled voices;
      At sea, the small boats loom dimly.
      Across the faintly glowing face of the moon
      Flights of wild geese streak,
90   And plovers flock below along the shore.
      Fall gales and stiff sea winds:
      These are things, in such a place,
      That truly belong to autumn.
      But oh, the terrible, lonely nights!

(*They hide their faces.*)

95   MATSUKAZE: Come, dip the brine.
      MURASAME: Where the seas flood and fall,
         Let us tie our sleeves back to our shoulders.
      MATSUKAZE: Think only, "Dip the brine."
      MURUSAME: We ready ourselves for the task,
100   MATSUKAZE: But for women, this cart is too hard.
      CHORUS: While the rough breakers surge and fall,

(MURASAME *moves upstage to stand beside* MATSUKAZE.)

      While the rough breakers surge and fall,
      And cranes among the reeds
      Fly up with sharp cries.
105   The four winds add their wailing.
      How shall we pass the cold night?

(*They look up.*)

      The late moon is so brilliant—
      What we dip is its reflection!
      Smoke from the salt fires
110   May cloud the moon—take care!

_____

85 **The twilight** the following description is generally inspired
by the "Exile at Suma" chapter of *The Tale of Genji*

      Are we always to spend only
      The sad autumns of fishermen?
      At Ojima in Matsushima

(MATSUKAZE *half-kneels by the brine cart and mimes dipping with
her fan.*)

      The fisherfolk, like us,
      Delight less in the moon   115
      Than in the dipping of its reflection;
      There they take delight in dipping
      Reflections of the moon.

(MATSUKAZE *returns to the* shite *position.*)

      We haul our brine from afar,
      As in far-famed Michinoku   120
      And at the salt kilns of Chika—
      Chika, whose name means "close by."
      MATSUKAZE: Humble folk hauled wood for salt fires
         At the ebb tide on Akogi Shore.
      CHORUS: On Ise Bay there's Twice-See Beach—   125
         Oh, could I live my life again!

(MATSUKAZE *looks off into the distance.*)

      MATSUKAZE: On days when pine groves stand hazy,
         And the sea lanes draw back
         From the coast at Narumi—
      CHORUS: You speak of Narumi; this is Naruo,   130
         Where pines cut off the moonlight
         From the reed-thatched roofs of Ashinoya.
      MATSUKAZE: Who is to tell of our unhappiness
         Dipping brine at Nada?
         With boxwood combs set in our hair,   135
         From rushing seas we draw the brine,
         Oh look! I have the moon in my pail!

_____

113 **Ojima** is one of the islands at Matsushima, a place renowned
for its scenic beauty. Both names are conventionally associated in
poetry with *ama*, fisherwomen   120 **As in far-famed** the following passage is a *tsukushi*, or "exhaustive enumeration," of place-
names associated with the sea, including allusions and plays on
words. This passage was apparently borrowed from an older work,
a play called *Tōei* that was set by Ashinoya Bay. Michinoku is a
general name for the northern end of the island of Honshu. Chika
was another name for Shiogama ("Salt Kiln"), and sounds like the
word meaning "near"   124 **Akogi** the name of a stretch of
shore on Ise Bay. The pulling in of the nets and the hauling of the
wood for the salt kilns at Akogi were frequently mentioned in poetry   125 **Twice-See Beach** (*Futami-ga-ura*) is a word evocative
of Ise and often used in poetry for the meaning of its name
129 **Narumi** often mentioned in poetry because of its dry flats that
appeared at low tide   132 **Ashinoya** (modern Ashiya) and
Naruo are two places near Suma. Ashinoya means literally "reed
house"   134 **Dipping . . . Nada** derived from the poem in the
eighty-seventh episode of the *Ise Monogatari*: "At Nada by
Ashinoya, I have no respite from boiling brine for salt; I have come
without even putting a boxwood comb in my hair."   135 **With
boxwood** the line recalls the poem quoted in the previous note,
but it is used because of the pivot-word *tsuge no*, "of boxwood," and
tsuge, "to inform." Similarly, *kushi sashi*, "Setting a comb (in the
hair)," leads into *sashi-kuru nami*, "in-rushing waves"

(MURASAME *kneels before the brine cart and places her pail on it.* MATSUKAZE, *still standing, looks into her pail.*)

MATSUKAZE: In my pail too I hold the moon!
CHORUS: How lovely! A moon here too!

(MURASAME *picks up the rope tied to the cart and gives it to* MATSUKAZE, *then moves to the* shite *position.* MATSUKAZE *looks up.*)

140 MATSUKAZE: The moon above is one;
      Below it has two, no, three reflections

(*She looks into both pails.*)

      Which shine in the flood tide tonight,

(*She pulls the cart to a spot before the musicians.*)

      And on our cart we load the moon!
      No, life is not all misery
145   Here by the sea lanes.

(*She drops the rope. The stage assistant removes the cart.* MATSUKAZE *sits on a low stool and* MURASAME *kneels beside her, a sign that the two women are resting inside their hut. The* PRIEST *rises.*)

PRIEST: The owner of the salt shed has returned. I shall ask for a night's lodging. (*To* MATSUKAZE *and* MURASAME.) I beg your pardon. Might I come inside?
MURASAME: (*Standing and coming forward a little.*) Who might
150   you be?
PRIEST: A traveler, overtaken by night on my journey. I should like to ask lodging for the night.
MURASAME: Wait here. I must ask the owner. (*She kneels before* MATSUKAZE.) A traveler outside asks to come in and spend
155   the night.
MATSUKAZE: That is little enough, but our hut is so wretched we cannot ask him in. Please tell him so.
MURASAME: (*Standing, to the* PRIEST.) I have spoken to the owner. She says the house is too wretched to put anyone up.
160   PRIEST: I understand those feelings
      Perfectly, but poverty makes
      No difference at all to me.
      I am only a priest. Please
      Say I beg her to let
165   Me spend the night.
MURASAME: No, we really cannot put you up.
MATSUKAZE: (*To* MURASAME.) Wait!
      I see in the moonlight
      One who has renounced the world.
170   He will not mind a fisherman's hut,
      With its rough pine pillars and bamboo fence;
      I believe it is very cold tonight,
      So let him come in and warm himself
      At our sad fire of rushes.
175   You may tell him that.
MURASAME: Please come in.
PRIEST: Thank you very much. Forgive me for intruding.

(*He takes a few steps forward and kneels.* MURASAME *goes back beside* MATSUKAZE.)

MATSUKAZE: I wished from the beginning to invite you in, but this place is so poor I felt I must refuse.

PRIEST: You are very kind. I am a priest and a traveler, and   180
never stay anywhere very long. Why prefer one lodging to another? In any case, what sensitive person would not prefer to live here at Suma, in the quiet solitude. Yukihira wrote,
      "If ever anyone   185
      Chances to ask for me,
      Say I live alone,
      Soaked by the dripping seaweed
      On the shore of Suma Bay."
(*He looks at the pine tree.*) A while ago I asked someone the   190
meaning of that solitary pine on the beach. I was told it grows there in memory of two fisher girls, Matsukaze and Murasame. There is no connection between them and me, but I went to the pine anyway and said a prayer for them.
(MATSUKAZE *and* MURASAME *weep. The* PRIEST *stares at*   195
them.) This is strange! They seem distressed at the mention of Matsukaze and Murasame. Why?
MATSUKAZE AND MURASAME: Truly, when a grief is hidden,
      Still, signs of it will show.
      His poem, "If ever anyone   200
      Chances to ask for me,"
      Filled us with memories which are far too fond.
      Tears of attachment to the world
      Wet our sleeves once again.
PRIEST: Tears of attachment to the world? You speak as   205
though you are no longer of the world. Yukihira's poem overcame you with memories. More and more bewildering! Please, both of you, tell me who you are.
MATSUKAZE AND MURASAME: We would tell you our names,
      But we are too ashamed!   210
      No one, ever,
      Has chanced to ask for us,
      Long dead as we are,
      And so steeped in longing
      For the world by Suma Bay   215
      That pain has taught us nothing.
      Ah, the sting of regret!
      But having said this,
      Why should we hide our names any longer?
      At twilight you said a prayer   220
      By a mossy grave under the pine
      For two fisher girls,
      Matsukaze and Murasame.
      We are their ghosts, come to you.
      When Yukihira was here he whiled away   225
      Three years of weary exile
      Aboard his pleasure boat,
      His heart refreshed
      By the moon of Suma Bay.
      There were, among the fisher girls   230
      Who hauled brine each evening,
      Two sisters whom he chose for his favors.
      "Names to fit the season!"
      He said, calling us
      Pine Wind and Autumn Rain.   235
      We had been Suma fisher girls,
      Accustomed to the moon,

185–189 "**If ever** ... **Bay**" poem No. 962 in the *Kokinshū*

But he changed our salt makers' clothing
To damask robes,
240 Burnt with the scent of faint perfumes.
MATSUKAZE: Then, three years later, Yukihira
Returned to the Capital.
MURASAME: Soon, we heard he had died, oh so young!
MATSUKAZE: How we both loved him!
245 Now the message we pined for
Would never, never come.
CHORUS: Pine Wind and Autumn Rain
Both drenched their sleeves with the tears
Of hopeless love beyond their station,
250 Fisher girls of Suma.
Our sin is deep, O priest.
Pray for us, we beg of you!

(*They press their palms together in supplication.*)

Our love grew rank as wild grasses;
Tears and love ran wild.
255 It was madness that touched us.
Despite spring purification,
Performed in our old robes,
Despite prayers inscribed on paper streamers,
The gods refused us their help.
260 We were left to melt away
Like foam on the waves,
And, in misery, we died.

(MATSUKAZE *looks down, shading her mask.*)

Alas! How the past evokes our longing!
Yukihira, the Middle Counselor,

(*The stage assistant puts a man's cloak and court hat in* MAT-
SUKAZE'*s left hand.*)

265 Lived three years here by Suma Bay.
Before he returned to the Capital,
He left us these keepsakes of his stay:
A court hat and a hunting cloak.
Each time we see them,

(*She looks at the cloak.*)

270 Our love grows again,
And gathers like dew
On the tip of a leaf
So that there's no forgetting,
Not for an instant.
275 Oh endless misery!

(*She places the cloak in her lap.*)

"This keepsake
Is my enemy now;
For without it

(*She lifts the cloak.*)

I might forget."

(*She stares at the cloak.*)

The poem says that 280
And it's true:
My anguish only deepens.

(*She weeps.*)

MATSUKAZE: "Each night before I go to sleep,
I take off the hunting cloak
CHORUS: And hang it up . . ." 285

(*The keepsakes in her hand, she stands and, as in a trance, takes a
few steps toward the gazing-pillar.*)

I hung all my hopes
On living in the same world with him,
But being here makes no sense at all
And these keepsakes are nothing.

(*She starts to drop the cloak, only to cradle it in her arms and press
it to her.*)

I drop it, but I cannot let it lie; 290
So I take it up again
To see his face before me yet once more.

(*She turns to her right and goes toward the naming-place, then stares
down the bridgeway as though something were coming after her.*)

"Awake or asleep,
From my pillow, from the foot of my bed,
Love rushes in upon me." 295
Helplessly I sink down,
Weeping in agony.

(*She sits at the* shite *position, weeping. The stage assistant helps her
take off her outer robe and replace it with the cloak. He also helps tie
on the court hat.*)

MATSUKAZE: The River of Three Fords
Has gloomy shallows
Of never-ending tears; 300
I found, even there,
An abyss of wildest love.

---

240 **Burnt . . .** derived from a poem by Fujiwara Tameuji, No.
361 in the *Shingo-senshū*: "The fishermen of Suma are accustomed to the moon, spending the autumn in clothes wet with
waves blown by the salt wind." 258 **Despite prayers . . .** literally, "purification on the day of the serpent." The ceremony
was performed on the first day of the serpent in the third month.
Genji had the ceremony performed while he was at Suma. The
streamers were conventional Shinto offerings

276–279 **"This keepsake . . . forget"** a slightly modified quotation of the anonymous poem, No. 746 in the *Kokinshū*. It is also
quoted in *Lady Han* 283–285 **"Each night . . . up"** the first
part of a poem by Ki no Tomomori, No. 593 in the *Kokinshū*. The
last two lines run: "When I wear it there is no instant when I do
not long for him." 293–295 **"Awake . . . me"** the first part of
an anonymous poem, No. 1023 in the *Kokinshū*. The last part
runs: "Helpless, I stay in the middle of the bed." 298 **River of
Three Fords** the river of the afterworld

Oh joy! Look! Over there!
Yukihira has returned!

(*She rises, staring at the pine tree.*)

305 He calls me by my name, Pine Wind!
I am coming!

(*She goes to the tree.* MURASAME *hurriedly rises and follows. She catches* MATSUKAZE's *sleeve.*)

MURASAME: For shame! For such thoughts as these
You are lost in the sin of passion.
All the delusions that held you in life—
310 None forgotten!

(*Both step back from the tree.*)

That is a pine tree.
And Yukihira is not here.
MATSUKAZE: You are talking nonsense!

(*She looks at the pine tree.*)

This pine is Yukihira!
315 "Though we may part for a time,
If I hear you are pining for me,
I'll hurry back."
Have you forgotten those words he wrote?
MURASAME: Yes, I had forgotten!
320 He said, "Though we may part for a time,
If you pine, I will return to you."
MATSUKAZE: I have not forgotten.
And I wait for the pine wind
To whisper word of his coming.
325 MURASAME: If that word should ever come,
My sleeves for a while
Would be wet with autumn rain.
MATSUKAZE: So we await him. He will come,
Constant ever, green as a pine.
330 MURASAME: Yes, we can trust
MATSUKAZE: his poem:
CHORUS: "I have gone away

315–317 **"Though . . . back"** paraphrase of the poem by Yuki-hira, No. 365 in the *Kokinshū*. Another paraphrase is given in the following speech by Murasame, and the poem is given in its correct form below. In Japanese *matsu* means both "pine tree" and "to wait."

(MURASAME, *weeping, kneels before the flute player.* MATSUKAZE *goes to the first pine on the bridgeway, then returns to the stage and dances.*)

MATSUKAZE: Into the mountains of Inaba,
Covered with pines,
But if I hear you pine,   335
I shall come back at once."
Those are the mountain pines
Of distant Inaba,

(*She looks up the bridgeway.*)

And these are the pines
On the curving Suma shore.   340
Here our dear prince once lived.
If Yukihira comes again,
I shall go stand under the tree

(*She approaches the tree.*)

Bent by the sea-wind,
And, tenderly, tell him   345

(*She stands next to the tree.*)

I love him still!

(*She steps back a little and weeps. Then she circles the tree, her dancing suggesting madness.*)

CHORUS: Madly the gale howls through the pines,
And breakers crash in Suma Bay;
Through the frenzied night
We have come to you   350
In a dream of deluded passion.
Pray for us! Pray for our rest!

(*At stage center,* MATSUKAZE *presses her palms together in supplication.*)

Now we take our leave. The retreating waves
Hiss far away, and a wind sweeps down
From the mountain to Suma Bay.   355
The cocks are crowing on the barrier road.
Your dream is over. Day has come.
Last night you heard the autumn rain;
This morning all that is left
Is the wind in the pines,   360
The wind in the pines.

---

336 **"I . . . once"** the poem by Yukihira mentioned in the previous note

Chūshingura: The Forty-Seven Samurai

In 1701, at the court of the *shogun* in Edo, the *daimyo* of *Akō,* Lord Asano, drew his sword and slightly wounded Lord Kira, one of the *shogun's* officials; as a consequence of drawing his sword at the court—a capital crime—Lord Asano was sentenced to *seppuku,* or ritual suicide. In the following months, Asano's *rōnin,* or retainers, felt themselves to have been dishonored and humiliated by the ruling against their lord, and plotted to take revenge. In January of 1703 they made a bold nighttime raid on Lord Kira's mansion. When they found Kira, they beheaded him, and ceremoniously marched with his head to Lord Asano's tomb. The raid on Lord Kira was, not surprisingly, a major scandal, and posed the shogunate with a difficult legal and political problem: on the one hand, Lord Asano's *rōnin* had acted with superb loyalty, risking their lives to avenge the honor of their feudal lord, upholding the values of the *samurai;* on the other hand, they had formed an illegal secret conspiracy and had carried out murder. Two months after taking revenge on Lord Kira, the *rōnin* were ordered by the *shogun* to commit *seppuku* themselves.

These are the historical events standing behind one of the *jōruri* and Kabuki theaters' most famous and enduring narratives, the tale of *The Forty-Seven Samurai.* Within weeks of the verdict, a host of plays were written and performed, mainly in the *jōruri* theaters; in most cases, however, the Tokagawa edict against staging contemporary events forced playwrights to alter the characters' names, and to set the story in an earlier historical period. In 1710, the great playwright Chikamatsu Monzaemon (1623–1725) wrote a play for the puppet theater entitled *Goban Taiheiki,* which relocated the events of contemporary Edo to the four-

This scene from the University of Hawai'i production of *Chūshingura* emphasizes the formal energy of Kabuki theater.

teenth century. Probably the first professional playwright in Japanese history, Chikamatsu (born Sugimori Nobumori) was the second son of the Sugimori *samurai* family. He moved with his family to Kyoto in his teens, and took the stage name Chikamatsu in his thirties, becoming a celebrated playwright for the *jōruri* theater, and collaborating with the most famous Kabuki actor of his era, Tojuro Sakata (1647–1709). A member of the *rōnin* himself, Chikamatsu was sympathetic with the dishonor done to Asano's retainers, and in his staging of their dramatic revenge established many of the dramatic conventions that would become standard in later versions of the story. In the next thirty years, Chikamatsu's play was one of hundreds of plays on the subject performed before the opening of the classic version of the story—*Kanadehon Chūshingura*—at the Takemoto puppet theater in 1748. Within the year, four Kabuki theaters (three in Edo and one in Kyoto) staged versions of *Chūshingura* which rapidly became part of the standard Kabuki repertory. The story of the forty-seven samurai has been one of the most enduring and popular of all Kabuki plays.

Although the Kabuki versions of *Chūshingura* are based on *jōruri* narratives, the genesis of plays in the Kabuki theater was quite different from that in the puppet theater. While the *jōruri* theaters closely followed the elaborately crafted dramatic text supplied by the playwright, in the Kabuki theater, the performers tended to take existing stories and refashion them in order to showcase their talents. While *Chūshingura* is one of the few plays still occasionally performed in the all-day form of *jōruri*, Kabuki performance tends to concentrate on several scenes from the narrative that have now become standard, which enables the play to be performed within the shorter duration of contemporary Kabuki theater. In this sense, the version of *Chūshingura: The Forty-Seven Samurai* printed here follows traditional Kabuki practice: it is a version of *Kanadehon Chūshingura* prepared by the professional Kabuki actor Nakamura Matagorō II, for a three-hour, English-language production at the University of Hawai'i in 1979. Readers who wish to consult the entire *jōruri* text should consult Donald Keene's *Chūshingura: The Treasury of Loyal Retainers*.

CHŪSHINGURA: THE FORTY-SEVEN SAMURAI

Adaptation by Nakamura Matagorō II and James R. Brandon

TRANSLATED BY JAMES R. BRANDON, JUNKO BERBERICH, AND MICHAEL FELDMAN

CHARACTERS

TADAYOSHI, *younger brother of the shogun*

KŌNO MORONAO, *chief councilor of the shogun and governor of Kamakura*

MOMONOI WAKASANOSUKE, *a young samurai*

ENYA HANGAN, *a young provincial lord*

KAOYO, *wife of Enya Hangan*

KAKOGAWA HONZŌ, *chief retainer of Wakasanosuke*

SAGISAKA BANNAI, *retainer of Moronao*

OKARU, *in love with Kampei, and later his wife*

KAMPEI, *retainer of Enya Hangan*

ISHIDŌ, *the shogun's representative at Hangan's death*

YAKUSHIJI, *envoy from the shogun*

GOEMON, *elderly retainer of Enya Hangan*

RIKIYA, *son of Yuranosuke*

ŌBOSHI YURANOSUKE, *chief retainer of Enya Hangan*

KUDAYŪ, *former retainer of Enya Hangan, now Moronao's spy*

HEIEMON, *older brother of Okaru*

SHIMIZU ICHIGAKU, *Moronao's bodyguard*

TAKEMORI KITAHACHI, *retainer to Enya Hangan*

PROVINCIAL LORDS

FOOTMEN

RETAINERS

LADIES–IN–WAITING

MAIDS

MALE GEISHA

FIGHTING CHORUS

SOLDIERS

STAGE ASSISTANTS

SAMISEN PLAYER

NARRATOR

STAGE MANAGER

SECOND STAGE MANAGER

KIYOMOTO SINGER

JESTER

TIME AND PLACE OF ACTION

Act I SCENE 1: Hachiman Shrine in Kamakura, 1338.

SCENE 2: Outside the gate of the shogunal mansion in Kamakura, the next evening.

SCENE 3: The Pine Room of the shogunal mansion in Kamakura, a few minutes later.

Act II SCENE 1: Along the road, near Mt. Fuji, the following morning.

SCENE 2: A reception room in Enya Hangan's mansion, the same day.

SCENE 3: The rear gate of Enya Hangan's mansion, immediately following.

Act III SCENE 1: The Ichiriki Brothel in Kyoto, eighteen months later.

SCENE 2: The garden of Moronao's mansion in Kamakura, several days later.

ACT ONE

SCENE I

Hachiman Shrine

Two sharp clacks of the hardwood ki signal offstage musicians to begin slow and regular drum and flute music, "Kata Shagiri" ("Half-Shagiri"). The deliberate pace of the music gradually accelerates. The lights in the auditorium dim slightly; the audience watches the kabuki curtain of broad rust, black, and green stripes. Very slowly, the curtain is pushed open by a STAGE ASSISTANT *walking from stage right to left. Ki clacks intersperse every eighth, every fourth, then every second drum beat. Drumming and ki intermingle as the tempo rapidly increases during the last few feet of the curtain opening. The scene is a ceremonial audience before Hachiman Shrine in Kamakura. The shogun's brother,* TADAYOSHI, *is seated on the center of a broad stone platform running across the back of the stage. He wears a subdued Chinese-style court robe with bloused trousers and a gold lacquered hat. On his left sits the highest local official of the government,* KŌNO MORONAO. *A voluminous black robe with large sleeves and trailing trousers encase his body and a high black hat increases his height. Six* PROVINCIAL LORDS *kneel behind them on the platform. Kneeling on the ground before them are two samurai officials,* MOMONOI WAKASANOSUKE *and ENYA HANGAN, aroused, respectively, in powder blue and yellow robes of the same exaggerated cut as* MORONAO's, *and* HANGAN's *wife,* KAOYO. *She wears a silk embroidered kimono and outer robe of deep blue. Two* FOOTMEN *sit on the ground cross-legged to the right. The heads of all the charac-*

ters are dropped forward limply on their chests, in imitation of puppets before they have been brought to life. Two ki clacks signal the music to stop and the action of the scene to begin.

STAGE MANAGER: (*Rhythmic, prolonged calls from offstage right.*) Hear ye, hear ye, hear ye, hear ye, hear ye, hear ye . . . hear ye!

(*Deep, thick chords of a jōruri, or puppet-style, samisen are heard from the small room above the set stage left. The team of jōruri* SAMISEN PLAYER *and* NARRATOR *are not seen, but they can see the action on stage through the thin bamboo blind that hangs in front of them. The* NARRATOR *constantly shifts his vocal style between a kind of half-spoken chanting and singing. His tones are rich and full and unabashedly project the extremes of human emotion. Each syllable is precisely uttered. Sharp samisen chords punctuate the end of a chanted phrase; they become melodic under sung passages. A syllable can be clipped or staccato, or it can be prolonged into a lengthy obligato, spread over many samisen chords, so that the narrative line compresses or expands in time in order to best project the theatrical needs of the moment.*)

NARRATOR: (*Chants.*) "A banquet laid out before your eyes! Without eating of its food, never will you be able to know its taste! Likewise, a country in peace . . . its able retainers will hide their gallantry and chivalry. (*Sings.*) Take our story as an example . . . witness here and now . . .

SECOND STAGE MANAGER: (*Calling from offstage left.*) Hear ye, hear ye, hear ye, hear ye . . . hear ye!

5

10 STAGE MANAGER: (*Calling from offstage center.*) Hear ye, hear ye . . . hear ye!

NARRATOR: (*Chants.*) Ashikaga government chief Takauji has Kyoto as the headquarters of his reign, his power expand-ing far. The time is the closing of February, thirteen thirty-

15 eight. The place is Kamakura in the east, at Hachiman Shrine, now completed in its awesome grandeur. (*Sings.*) Gathered here to celebrate a battle fought and won are lords of distinction, in their solemn moments. (*Chants.*) Acting as government proxy, Ashikaga Tadayoshi has just

20 arrived from the capital . . . of Kyoto!

(*At the mention of his name,* TADAYOSHI *raises his head, opens his eyes, and elegantly flicks open his sleeves: puppetlike, he has been "brought to life."*)

Here in Kamakura, he is received by the shogun's official, Kōno Moronao! The officers of the reception are: Momonoi Wakasanosuke Yasuchika, Moronao's target of displeasure for his rough manners, and Hakushu's castle

25 lord, Enya Hangan Takasada. (*Sings.*) Among these men, a single flower, Lady Kaoyo, wife of Hangan.

(*Each character, as named, comes to life, showing his or her person-ality through the simple actions of lifting the head, opening the eyes, and adjusting the trailing kimono sleeves:* MORONAO's *evil nature—seven abrupt head jerks ending in a fierce* mie *pose with eyes crossed, arms extending aggressively forward as two loud beats of the wooden* tsuke *call attention to the pose;* WAKASANOSUKE's *impetuosity—five strong movements of the head, sudden opening of the eyes, each arm flicked out independently;* HANGAN's *composure—three smooth head movements, gentle eye opening, and both sleeves elegantly adjusted;* KAOYO's *modesty—no movement at all except for the slow raising of the head. Narrative shifts to song.*)

Moronao casts amorous eyes at this rare beauty. Loyal men, bowing low. . .

(MORONAO *leers openly at* KAOYO. *Then everyone places their hands on the floor and they make a ceremonious, deep bow to* TADAYOSHI. *Narrative returns to chanting.*)

As Tadayoshi speaks, all listen in reverence!

(*All lift their heads and listen respectfully.*)

30 TADAYOSHI: (*Clear, unaffected voice, looking straight ahead.*) At-tend, Lady Kaoyo!

KAOYO: (*Bowing.*) My lord.

TADAYOSHI: It is the shogun, not I, who has summoned you here. You served the emperor Godaigo when he bestowed

35 upon the warrior Yoshisada the imperial battle crown. Now, with prayers commemorating our victory in battle, my brother the shogun wills that this battle crown be ded-icated to the shrine of Hachiman, god of war. If you can, confirm that this, and no other, is the one! Come, come!

40 Answer me, answer me!

KAOYO: (*Bowing.*) My lord.

NARRATOR: (*Chants.*) Attendants carry forth the precious bat-tle crown, bending down to open up the heavy wooden chest. Lifting up the battle crown . . . is it the one of fame?

45 (*Sings.*) Though gazing closely at the battle crown held high, she will only speak when she is certain . . . and then, floating famous fragrance of the crown well known . . .

(*The two* FOOTMEN *place a large wooden chest center and remove its lid. They bring out a samurai helmet. Its golden fittings gleam in the light.* KAOYO *moves forward the better to observe it, kneels, and noticing its special perfume, nods decisively.*)

KAOYO: This is the very crown Yoshisada wore in battle, I can say with certainty.

NARRATOR: (*Chants.*) Saying these words, Kaoyo bows deep 50 in reverence.

(*She bows. A* FOOTMAN *places the helmet at* TADAYOSHI's *feet. With the second* FOOTMAN, *he carries off the chest.*)

TADAYOSHI: Enya Hangan! Momonoi Wakasanosuke! In con-junction with the dedication, all ceremonies are placed in your care. Consult Lord Moronao. Kaoyo, you may go!

KAOYO: (*Bowing.*) My lord. 55

NARRATOR: (*Chants.*) Kaoyo has now been freed of her de-manding task, waiting as his lordship . . . into the palace goes!

(TADAYOSHI *rises; a* STAGE ASSISTANT *takes off the stool he has been sitting on. Without looking to the right or left, he walks with a dignified gait down the steps. He stops and poses. Drum and flute play stately exit music.* TADAYOSHI *flicks open his sleeves, turns, and moves slowly off left.* PROVINCIAL LORDS *rise and follow, their for-mal court trousers trailing behind them.* FOOTMEN *bring up the rear. They exit. The music continues in the background as* HANGAN, WAKASANOSUKE, *and* KAOYO *play out in silence their petitions to* MORONAO *for permission to depart. To* HANGAN's *polite bow of re-quest* MORONAO *nods condescendingly.* HANGAN *rises, and with unruffled composure, goes off left, carrying the helmet with him, to be deposited in the shrine.* WAKASANOSUKE *bows brusquely, scarcely bothering to conceal his contempt for* MORONAO. *In response,* MORONAO *deliberately and disdainfully averts his gaze. Moving to where he is in* MORONAO's *line of sight again,* WAKASANOSUKE *bows a second time, more brusquely still. Again* MORONAO *ignores him and looks away. Trembling with fury,* WAKASANOSUKE *moves directly in front of* MORONAO *and bows a third time.* MORONAO *looks over his head as if the young samurai were not there.* WAKASANOSUKE *leaps up in rage, strikes back his sleeve, and rushes off left. Music stops.* MORONAO *laughs soundlessly, then looks ex-pectantly to* KAOYO, *who bows politely, rises, and starts to move away.* MORONAO *rises, a* STAGE ASSISTANT *removing the stool on which he has been sitting. He stops* KAOYO *with an unctuous, but clearly threatening, command.*)

MORONAO: One moment, Lady Kaoyo! I wish to have a word with you. I believe that you and I share in common an unspoken passion, for the art of writing poetry. Will 60 you accept from me this poem, composed with loving care, your reply to which I will not be displeased to re-ceive from your own lips, Kaoyo, my lady.

NARRATOR: (*Chants.*) From his sleeve to her sleeve, a love let-ter from Moronao! (*Sings.*) Saying not a single word, she 65 throws it aside.

(*Crossing to her,* MORONAO *looks around to see that no one is watching. He passes a love letter into* KAOYO's *sleeve. She takes it out, and looking at the salutation, knows immediately what it is. Coldly she drops it to the ground.* MORONAO *scoops it up and tucks it away in the breast of his kimono.*)

MORONAO: (*Insinuatingly.*) Casually you cast my letter to the ground, but you will not cast down my intentions that easily. Until you accept my love, I will track you, chase
70   you, wear you down. In the palace your husband is my puppet, to rise or to fall in his duties, solely on Moronao's will. Kaoyo, my lady . . . well? Do you not agree?

(*He glances about again, then moves behind her and enfolds her in a rough embrace. She discreetly tries to free herself: their bodies sway back and forth.*)

NARRATOR: (*Sings.*) In her heart are angry words but Kaoyo refrains. Dear Lady Kaoyo, tears in her eyes.

(*Without warning* WAKASANOSUKE *strides on. Taking in the situation at a glance, he turns his back.*)

75   WAKASANOSUKE: Ahem! Ahem! (*Furious,* MORONAO *breaks away.* WAKASANOSUKE *moves beside* KAOYO.) Lady Kaoyo, Lord Tadayoshi dismissed you long ago. If you linger, you are risking his displeasure. Go! Do not stay a moment longer!
80   KAOYO: Yes, good Lord Wakasanosuke, with your permission, I shall take my leave.
NARRATOR: (*Sings.*) Burdened with care, to her mansion . . . Kaoyo returns.

(KAOYO *bows and moves quickly onto the* hanamichi, *the rampway which extends from the stage, through the audience, to the rear of the auditorium. She stops at the "seven-three" position, that is, the position seven-tenths of the distance from the back of the auditorium and three-tenths from the stage. She poses, puts her hands inside her kimono sleeves, then regally moves down the* hanamichi. *She passes out of sight as the narration ends.*)

MORONAO: (*Snarling.*) No one summoned you! You are inso-
85   lent, Wakasanosuke! Kaoyo was entreating me, in private audience, to guide Hangan in his palace duties. That is how even the mighty must grovel before the shogun's chief councilor. And who are you? A country rustic, a nobody. So low a single word from Moronao would send you tumbling
90   into the streets to beg for your food! And you call yourself a samurai? A samurai? (MORONAO *strikes* WAKASANOSUKE'*s chest with his heavy fan.*) You . . . a sa-mu-rai? (*On the last three syllables,* MORONAO *strikes* WAKASANOSUKE'*s chest, sword hilt, and chest again.* WAKASANOSUKE *falls back.*) B-b-blockhead
95   country bumpkin!
NARRATOR: (*Chants.*) You dare to meddle, little man? Moronao's revenge! Bursting in hot anger, Wakasanosuke . . . here in the sacred shrine before his Majesty, a moment of patience is all I need! One more word decides my life,
100   death may be my fate! Wakasanosuke now holds himself in!

(*To the narration:* WAKASANOSUKE *poses with hand on the hilt of his sword; he notices he is in a sacred shrine and falls back; his hand trembles; he nods with determination, throws his fan into the air, and lunges forward as if to draw his sword.* MORONAO *slaps his fan against* WAKASANOSUKE'*s sword arm and glares at his young opponent in alarm and rage. At that moment a cry is heard from offstage announcing the return of* TADAYOSHI.)

VOICES OFF: (*In unison.*) Bow down!
MORONAO: (*Snarling.*) Bow down, I say!

(MORONAO *strikes* WAKASANOSUKE'*s sword arm viciously with his closed fan.* WAKASANOSUKE *drops to one knee, glares at* MORONAO, *and poses with his hand on his sword.* MORONAO *rushes up the platform steps, suddenly pivots back to face* WAKASANOSUKE, *flips open his sleeves, and poses in a fierce mie.* MORONAO *crosses his eyes and glares to two loud beats of the* tsuke. WAKASANOSUKE *restrains himself; his chest heaves. The curtain is run closed to accelerating ki clacks. A single ki clack marks the end of the scene and signals the offstage drum and flute to play "Sagariha" ["Departure"] as the scene is changed.*)

SCENE II
Bribery and Rendezvous

Two ki clacks: the curtain is run open. Ki clacks accelerate, then fade away. The scene is the rear gate of the shogunal mansion in Kamakura where the state ceremonies are to be held. It is night. Pale blue light floods the stage. One ki clack signals action to begin.

NARRATOR: (*Chants.*) Chief retainer of Wakasanosuke, (*Sings.*) Kakogawa Honzō comes in with a tray full of gifts, a self-assigned task.

(HONZŌ, *carrying a tray of silks as a bribe for* MORONAO, *comes onto the* hanamichi. *He stops at the seven-three position, looks toward the gate, and poses.*)

HONZŌ: Bannai. Master Bannai.

(BANNAI, *a comic villain, enters from inside the gate.* HONZŌ *moves quickly onto the stage, places the gifts on the ground, and kneels respectfully before* BANNAI.)

BANNAI: (*Officiously.*) Someone calls me. Who is it, who is it?   5
(*Notices* HONZŌ. *Starts.*) State your business, I am a busy man!
HONZŌ: (*Bowing obsequiously.*) I am Kakogawa Honzō, chief retainer of Momonoi Wakasanosuke.
BANNAI: (*Chuckles delightedly.*) The bluebird Wakasanosuke   10
and his friend, the yellow canary Enya Hangan, are country chickens. What a cackling they will make in the palace. Oh, my master, Lord Moronao, will pluck them clean!
HONZŌ: (*Carefully watching* BANNAI'*s expression.*) That is the matter on which I have come, good Bannai. My master is   15
young and untutored in the intricacies of palace etiquette. Only with Lord Moronao's generous guidance will he be able to carry out his important duties. Taking this opportunity, I express my gratitude for your master's favor.

(HONZŌ *bows low.* BANNAI *turns front with a self-satisfied smirk on his face.*)

BANNAI: Everyone needs a chief councilor's favors. But your   20
Wakasanosuke was rude to my master. Go back where you came from, go back, go away! (BANNAI *strikes a pose: feet together, head up, right fist extended toward* HONZŌ.)
HONZŌ: What you say is true, still please accept these gifts on behalf of Wakasanosuke and his grateful followers.   25

(HONZŌ *bows toward the gifts of silk. He looks about, to be sure they are unseen, then takes out a wrapped package of gold coins. Moving forward on his knees to* BANNAI'*s side, he drops the package into the open kimono sleeve.*)

Carry my message to Lord Moronao. Do what is necessary, good Bannai. Will you do so, Bannai? Bannai?

(HONZŌ *tugs lightly on* BANNAI's *sleeve.*)

NARRATOR: (*Chants.*) Wondering, Bannai takes it in his hand!

(BANNAI *flicks* HONZŌ's *hand away and in doing so strikes the heavy coins. He clutches his fingers in pain, then wonders what his hand hit. He sneaks a look at the coins. He reacts with delighted surprise.*)

NARRATOR: (*Sings.*) Money talks words of power!
30 BANNAI: (*Effusive, his attitude completely changed.*) Well, well, Kakogawa Honzō, how nice of you to come. (*He squats and bows to* HONZŌ.) You have come at the right moment: the ceremonial rooms are being prepared. Come, come!

(BANNAI *picks up the tray of gifts, rises, and gestures for* HONZŌ *to follow him.*)

HONZŌ: (*Bowing carefully.*) I am a person of no importance, I
35   do not dare enter the palace.
BANNAI: (*Proudly.*) If Lord Moronao is with you, who would dare object? Come, I will show you the rooms.
HONZŌ: I will enter then, most gratefully.
BANNAI: Then come along. Come along!

(BANNAI *poses.* HONZŌ *bows. They cross toward the gate: three times* BANNAI *turns back, chuckling and bowing, to beckon* HONZŌ *forward. At the gate* BANNAI *stops short.*)

40   Master Honzō, the threshold is high.
NARRATOR: (*Sings.*) Moronao is happy. Honzō bought the life of Wakasanosuke. His scheme now is accomplished. Together they go.

(BANNAI *steps carefully over the foot-high threshold of the gate and goes inside, followed by* HONZŌ.)

NARRATOR: (*A* nō *song, as if part of the entertainment inside the mansion.*)
    "At the end of the journey we have reached Takasago Bay;
45   At the end of the journey we have reached Takasago Bay."

(OKARU, *a beautiful young girl in her late teens, enters on the* hanamichi. *She wears a maiden's trailing kimono with long sleeves, in a purple arrow pattern. She holds a lacquered letter box in her right hand. She stops at the seven-three position, looks toward the gate, and poses.*)

OKARU: My Lady Kaoyo urgently sends this letter to her husband, Lord Enya Hangan. How fortunate that I, her favorite, was allowed to bring it. Dearest Kampei, I cannot bear to be apart from you a single moment.

(*Offstage musicians play* nō-*style drum and flute music in the background.* KAMPEI, *a young samurai, enters from the gate followed by a* RETAINER. *They wear black kimono under stiff vests; their divided skirts are folded up to their knees, showing that they are on guard duty.* KAMPEI *is in the service of* HANGAN *and is* OKARU's *lover.* OKARU *sees him and runs to meet him.*)

50 KAMPEI: Okaru, is it you?
OKARU: (*Coquettishly.*) Dearest Kampei, I missed you so.

KAMPEI: (*Flustered and worried about meeting her while he is on duty.*) But why are you here at the palace gate, at night, and all alone?
OKARU: I've come for Lady Kaoyo. "Meet Kampei and tell 55
him he is to ask my husband to deliver this letter to Lord Moronao"—those were her very words.

(OKARU *passes him the letter box.*)

KAMPEI: (*Unsure.*) I am to deliver this directly to Lord Hangan?
HOKARU: Yes, dearest Kampei.

(*She smiles invitingly at him.*)

KAMPEI: Wait for me, Okaru.   60

(*He turns to go.*)

OKARU: (*She holds his sleeve.*) Kampei!
KAMPEI: I should take it to our master myself. I should be with him. It is my duty not to leave his side in the palace. I . . .

(*He is irresolute. He tries to leave; she tugs gently, persuasively at his sleeve. He looks into her pleading eyes. He decides. He turns to the* RETAINER.)

    Take this immediately to Lord Hangan.   65
RETAINER: I will.

(*The* RETAINER *takes the letter box, bows, and crosses into the gate.*)

OKARU: I want to be with you so. Now that we are here, together . . .
KAMPEI: You are flushed with excitement, Okaru!
OKARU: (*Taking his hand in hers.*) Please come. I don't care! 70
NARRATOR: (*Sings.*) Seizing fast her lover's hand . . . she leads him away!

(*She presses against him boldly, folding her arm over his. They pose: a sharp* ki *clack emphasizes the moment. Offstage drum and samisen resume in the background. They look excitedly into each other's eyes and then hurriedly cross into the darkness of the trees beyond the gate. The curtain is run quickly closed to accelerating* ki *clacks. Music ends. Soft, intermittent* ki *clacks mark time while the scene is changed.*)

SCENE III
Pine Room

Two ki *clacks: the curtain opens. The scene is a large reception room of the shogunal mansion called the Pine Room because of the designs painted on the gold sliding doors extending across the full stage. A single* ki *clack: action begins.*

NARRATOR: (*Chants.*) Utter indignation, for Moronao is late! Impatiently waiting in the palace . . . Wakasanosuke!

(WAKASANOSUKE *rushes onto the* hanamichi. *He drops to one knee at the seven-three position, resolutely slaps his thigh, and poses, waiting for the arrival of* MORONAO. *A sliding door left opens. Rapid drum and flute music.* BANNAI *ushers* MORONAO *on stage, bowing obsequiously. He carries a small paper lantern to light the room. Without a word,* WAKASANOSUKE *leaps to his feet, slips his sword arm free of the restricting formal vest, and rushes to attack* MORONAO. BANNAI *momentarily is able to block* WAKASANOSUKE's *path, but then is hurled to the floor as* WAKASANOSUKE *pushes past.* MORONAO *falls to his knees. He clasps his hands together pleadingly.* BANNAI *throws his arms around* WAKASANOSUKE's *lower leg, holding him fast. Music stops.*)

MORONAO: There you are, there you are, Lord Wakasanosuke, good Wakasanosuke. Your early arrival makes me ashamed,
5   ashamed, so very ashamed. I was rude to you at Hachiman Shrine. I was. (WAKASANOSUKE *edges forward as if to draw.*) Now, now, now, you have every right to be angry. But have pity on a foolish old samurai. I throw my sword at your feet. I clasp my hands and apologize. Bannai, Bannai,
10   you too, bow, apologize to Lord Wakasanosuke.
NARRATOR: (*Sings.*) Flattering, and what is more, detestable words so sweet. Taken aback completely, Wakasanosuke wonders what has happened. There is nothing he can do . . .

(MORONAO *bows his head low to the floor.* WAKASANOSUKE *cannot believe his eyes, seeing the proud councilor abasing himself. He kicks* BANNAI *away, slips his sword arm inside his vest, and strides past* MORONAO. MORONAO *circles to avoid him, crawling on his hands and knees indecorously.* WAKASANOSUKE *turns back, spitting out his words.*)

WAKASANOSUKE: Contemptible samurai!

(*He strides off stage left.*)

15   MORONAO: I was wrong, I was wrong, I apologize, I apologize, I . . .

(*Eyes fearfully on the ground,* MORONAO *continues.* BANNAI *registers comic shock, seeing his master bowing and speaking to no one. He scurries forward on his hands and knees. He pulls* MORONAO's *sleeve. Music stops. Their eyes meet.* BANNAI *nods in the direction of* WAKASANOSUKE's *exit.* MORONAO *sees that he is alone and sighs with relief. Recovering his dignity, he sits up.*)

MORONAO: Bannai, that stupid young puppy meant, I think, to kill me. "A sword in a fool's hand makes the wise man cautious."
20   BANNAI: (*Bowing.*) Oh yes, my lord, how true.
NARRATOR: (*Chants "Jo no Mai" ["Slow Dance"] drum and flute music.*) Who has planned this mischievous fate? (*Sings.*) Enya Hangan . . . innocent of this all, proceeds to Moronao. (*Chants.*) Moronao . . . seeing his victim!

(*Simultaneously,* BANNAI *arranges his master's sword and the lantern and exits stage left while* HANGAN *appears on the* hanamichi, *carrying in his left hand the letter box given by* KAMPEI's *retainer. Noh-style "Jo no Mai" drum and flute music continues in the background.*)

MORONAO: (*Ominously.*) Late, late, late! You're late, Hangan!

(HANGAN *bows slightly and hurries on stage. He kneels, bowing again.*)

25   HANGAN: I humbly beg your pardon for being a few moments late. I come ready for your instructions. First, however, I have been asked by my wife to place this letter in your hands.

(*He moves forward on his knees, places the letter box on the floor beside* MORONAO, *moves back, and bows respectfully.*)

MORONAO: (*Feigning ignorance.*) Hmm, hmm. A letter from Lady Kaoyo? To me? (*Opens the box and removes the letter card.*) Ah, I understand. My poetic skill is renowned. No   30 doubt she wishes me to place the touch of my pen upon her heartfelt words, to correct any blemishes. There is time before the ceremonies. Sit and be at ease. (*He reads.*) "A woman's love does, not lie in the hopeful eye, of her beholder; not beholden to lie I, aver never to lie with you."   35 (*Music stops.* MORONAO *again.*) "Not beholden to lie I, aver never to lie . . . with you."
NARRATOR: (*Chanting rapidly.*) After weighing the words . . . Kaoyo has rejected my love and this is the proof! This must mean that Hangan has found out my intention! (*Sings.*)   40 Anger and humiliation . . . but pretending ignorance.

(MORONAO *looks straight forward, his face frozen in humiliated rage, his right hand slowly closing into a rigid fist that crushes his brocade silk robe. Masking his emotions he turns toward* HANGAN. *Drum and flute music resume.*)

MORONAO: Hangan, was this poem shown to you?
HANGAN: (*Bows politely.*) I have not seen it until this moment, your Excellency.

(*Reassured that* HANGAN *is not party to* KAOYO's *insult,* MORONAO *proceeds to deliberately humiliate him.*)

MORONAO: Is that so? Well, the lord of little Hakushu castle   45 has a clever wife. She can dash off a subtle poem like this. A woman so talented and famous for her beauty must be a source of great husbandly pride. Such a superlative creature in fact, that her infatuated husband, not bearing to be separated from her, finds his sacred duties at the palace . . .   50 wearisome!

(MORONAO *casually turns his back to* HANGAN, *idly playing with his fan.*)

NARRATOR: (*Chants.*) Moronao is filled with spiteful words of insinuation. Riding on his frustration . . . any may be his prey. Hangan is perplexed at the burst of displeasure. (*Sings.*) Gushing anger, he holds it down, holds it in!   55

(HANGAN *starts. He almost turns to confront* MORONAO, *but then suppresses his anger. He pretends to smile, as if sharing* MORONAO's *joke. Ominous drum beats continue in the background.*)

HANGAN: Ha, ha, ha, ha. I see my lordship is in a playful mood. He has, perhaps, been drinking and is feeling in good humor. Yes, surely my lord has been drinking. Ha, ha, ha, ha.
MORONAO: (*Dangerously, facing* HANGAN.) What is that? When   60 have you seen me drinking? You, who have never offered me as much as a cup of wine? Whether I, Moronao, choose to drink or not, nothing keeps me from *my* duty! The one who's been drinking is you, Hangan. You've come from a drinking party with your charming wife, she   65 pouring for you, and you pouring for her! Isn't that why you come to the palace late?

(HANGAN's *face tightens.* MORONAO *notices and turns away with a malicious look in his eye.*)

Isn't there a story about a stay-at-home like you, helpless beyond his front door? I seem to recall . . . ah, yes, the
70   "Tadpole in the Puddle." There once was a young tadpole that lived in a tiny puddle. He knew no other place between heaven and earth, and so he thought his puddle the most wonderful home in the world. One day a compassionate person passed by, just like Moronao, who, taking
75   pity, lifted him from his stagnant pool and released him in the waters of a broad river. (*Arms out,* MORONAO *deliberately strikes* HANGAN's *chest with his heavy fan.*) Well, the tadpole was out of his depth, dropped suddenly into the great world from his shallow one. Completely at a loss, willy-
80   nilly he went this way, and willy-nilly he went that way. (*Pointing with fan.*) And in the end he ran headfirst smack into a bridgepost. (*Strikes* HANGAN *full in the chest with his fan.*) And shivering and quivering, and shivering and quivering, the little tadpole expired. (*Twirling his fan in limp fin-*
85   *gers.*) The tadpole is . . . you! (*Looks full into* HANGAN's *straining face.*) Oh? I do believe the young tadpole has lost his tail and is turning into a toad. (HANGAN *turns and glares furiously at* MORONAO.) Yes, with your eyes bulging out, Hangan, you look exactly like a toad. Ha, ha, ha, ha! This
90   Moronao has lived many years, but this is the first time I've seen in the palace a toad wearing clothes. Oh, come here, come here, Bannai, Hangan's turning into a toad. Hangan *is* a toad, a sa-mu-rai toad! (*Drum beats stop. Silence.* MORONAO *deliberately strikes* HANGAN's *chest, sword*
95   *hilt, and chest with his fan.*) Ha, ha, ha, ha, ha!
NARRATOR: (*Chants.*) Toad! Devil talk! Demon words!

(MORONAO *rears back, points contemptuously at* HANGAN *with his fan, rotates his head, and poses in a* mie *to two loud* tsuke *beats. Music stops.*)

Hangan can no more take the vile old man!
HANGAN: (*Slowly, with dangerous, suppressed fury.*) Do you dare compare Enya Hangan Takasada, castle lord of Hakushu . . .
100   to a toad? You cannot possibly mean the words you have said! Have you gone out of your mind . . . Councilor Moronao!

(HANGAN *pivots to face* MORONAO, *slapping his thigh for emphasis.*)

MORONAO: (*Darkly.*) Watch yourself, Hangan! Remember I am councilor of the shogun. No one calls me insane. You
105   are ludicrous!
HANGAN: You have been deliberately insulting me? Do you dare tell me that!
MORONAO: (*Insinuating.*) Indeed, I dare. And if I dare, who are you to complain?
110 HANGAN: (*Drawn out.*) If you dare . . .
MORONAO: (*Leaning in insolently.*) If I dare . . . ?
HANGAN: Hmm!

(HANGAN's *patience snaps. He rises on one knee, his hand on his sword.* MORONAO *instantly parries* HANGAN's *sword arm with his closed fan.*)

MORONAO: (*Commandingly.*) The palace! (MORONAO *slaps* HANGAN's *sword arm away and the two men pull back:* MORONAO *fearfully,* HANGAN *furious.*) The palace! The   115
palace! It is the palace! Don't you know the law? Draw your sword in the palace and your house will be destroyed! Don't you know that! (*Drum beats resume.* MORONAO *slaps his fan commandingly on the floor.* HANGAN, *anguished that he must restrain his rage, folds his arms tightly over the hilts of his*   120
swords and slowly sinks back onto his haunches. MORONAO *notes this and is emboldened to continue his provocation.*) Hm, since you know . . . then go ahead, kill me. Well . . . draw . . . draw . . . draw your sword. Come, kill me! Kill me . . . Hangan!

(MORONAO *forces himself bodily against* HANGAN *and leans against* HANGAN's *swords. They pose. Burning with humiliation,* HANGAN *abases himself in order to fulfill his ceremonial duties. He backs away and bows low.*)

HANGAN: A moment, a moment, Lord Moronao, I beg your   125
indulgence. Without thinking I spoke out of turn. I implore you, instruct me in my duties for the ceremony. I will do as you say. Humbly, I beseech you, your Excellency.

(*Music stops.* HANGAN *looks up from his bow.* MORONAO *smugly turns away, avoiding his gaze.* HANGAN's *patience snaps a second time: his hand leaps for his sword. Instantly* MORONAO *reacts.*)

MORONAO: Your hand!
HANGAN: My hand?   130
MORONAO: (*With all his authority.*) Yes, your hand!
HANGAN: This hand . . .

(*He hesitates, looks at his trembling hand, then drops his hands to the floor and bows in defeat.*)

. . . humbly begs your forgiveness.
MORONAO: (*Savoring his victory.*) So, you apologize, do you? Very well, very well. Soon instructions in great detail for   135
today's ceremony . . .
HANGAN: (*Looks up hopefully.*) . . . will be given to me?
MORONAO: (*Viciously.*) No, not to you! To Wakasanosuke! (HANGAN *is stunned, motionless. In silence* MORONAO *casually rises, tears* KAOYO's *letter card in two, and throws the pieces in*   140
HANGAN's *face.*) There is no educating a provincial barbarian.

(MORONAO *deliberately turns his back and kicks his left and right trailing trouser legs in* HANGAN's *face.* HANGAN *rears back. Chuckling,* MORONAO *starts to leave.*)

HANGAN: Moronao! Wait!

(HANGAN *steps on* MORONAO's *trailing trouser leg.* MORONAO *is brought up short. He tugs at the trouser; it is held fast.*)

MORONAO: (*Deadly calm.*) Be careful. You'll soil my trousers. Hop. Hop, hop, hop. (MORONAO *turns to leave, but cannot*   145
move.) So, you won't hop away, little toad? Can there be something else you want?
HANGAN: What I want is . . .
MORONAO: What you want is . . . ?

(HANGAN *quietly slips his sword arm free of the stiff vest.* MO-
RONAO *turns and thrusts his sneering face toward* HANGAN.)

150 HANGAN: (*A scream.*) You!

(HANGAN's *short sword flashes out of its sheath and gashes* MORONAO's
forehead. Drum and flute play furious "Haya Mai" ("Fast Dance").
MORONAO *staggers and falls.* BANNAI *rushes on to help his master flee.*
HANGAN *leaps to his feet and is about to finish* MORONAO *with a second blow when* HONZŌ, *who has been hiding behind a decorative screen
stage right, rushes out and seizes* HANGAN *from behind.*)

NARRATOR: "Hold me not! My foe is there!"

(*Six* PROVINCIAL LORDS *run on from right.* HANGAN *struggles to
get free, but he is encircled and held fast. In desperation he hurls his
sword after the disappearing enemy. A single sharp clack of the ki. The
sword falls short. He reaches out with both hands after* MORONAO
*and poses: his fingers curl into fists and his chest heaves with sobs of
mortification. But* HONZŌ *and the* PROVINCIAL LORDS *hold him
fast. To gradually accelerating ki clacks the curtain is run closed. Offstage musicians play "Shagiri." A single ki clack concludes the act.*)

ACT TWO

SCENE I
Fugitive Travel

*The large drum beats melancholy "Yama Oto" ("Mountain Pat-
tern"). To accelerating ki clacks the curtain is slowly pushed open. A
sky-blue curtain fills the stage. A single ki clack: the blue curtain
drops and is whisked away by black-robed* STAGE ASSISTANTS *to reveal a colorful springtime scene in the country. Snow-covered Mt.
Fuji is seen in the background, pink cherry blossoms bloom everywhere.* OKARU *and* KAMPEI *stand center, their faces hidden behind a
straw hat. A temple bell tolls in the distance. Kiyomoto music begins
from offstage.* KAMPEI *lowers the hat and we see the lovers dressed
for traveling: kimono skirts raised and a bundle over* KAMPEI's *shoulder. They mime in slow dance movements to the kiyomoto lyrics the
story of their disgrace and flight.*)

KIYOMOTO SINGER: Oh, you who flee, do you not see yon
  green field, a veil of new green?

(*They look at the flowers at their feet, to the left and the right. They
look into each other's eyes, then pose gazing into the distance.
Singing ends; samisen continues in the background. Facing upstage,
they pass their sandals and* KAMPEI's *hat and bundle to two* STAGE
ASSISTANTS. *They turn front and kneel center stage.* KAMPEI *places
his long sword on the ground beside him.*)

KAMPEI: (*Melancholy.*) Giving myself over in love to you, I failed
  our master when he needed me, and now we are fugitives
5 fleeing in the dead of night I know not where. When I
  think of it, I no longer have the heart to live. Say prayers
  over the grave of this dishonored samurai. Okaru . . .
  farewell.

(KAMPEI *takes his short sword from his sash and is about to draw
the blade. Gently she seizes it and prevents him.*)

OKARU: No, I won't have you saying that again. I am to blame
10 that you were not beside Lord Hangan. I cannot live with-

out you. If you die then so must I. But rather than praising your spirit, people will say we died as lovers frequently
do. Please, live, dearest Kampei. Live . . . in love . . . for me.

(KAMPEI *tries to draw the sword again. She pulls one way, he the
other.* KAMPEI, *irresolute, allows her to take the short sword. She
places it beside her, away from his reach.*)

KIYOMOTO SINGER: " 'Twas then my heart went astray. It was
  when you, yes, you made me love, oh, so imprudently.   15
  Blame my imprudent heart that spoke to me thus: 'So easy
  it is to die, but you must live, live on.' "

(KAMPEI *takes up the long sword to kill himself. Again, she gently
holds the scabbard so that he cannot draw. They rise and move left,
then right, in a delicate struggle for the sword. Allowing himself to be
persuaded, they pose with the sword held firmly in her hands. He
looks away, wiping his falling tears. She takes the sword and places
it out of his reach. They kneel side-by-side.*)

KAMPEI: Your tenderness overwhelms me. (*Nods with resolution.*)
  We will flee across the mountains to your father's home.
OKARU: (*Smiling, relieved.*) You make me so happy.   20
KAMPEI: In time I know I can find a way to atone for desert-
  ing my master. Come, let us go.
OKARU: (*Meekly.*) Yes, Kampei.
KIYOMOTO SINGER: Now for travel they prepare, but who
  should confront them!   25

(KAMPEI *rises and poses facing front.*)

BANNAI: (*Off, at the rear of the* hanamichi.) Hey, hey! Here we go!
FIGHTING CHORUS: (*Also off.*) Haaa!

(*Loud beats of the big drum. Strong accelerating* tsuke *pattern as*
BANNAI *runs onto the* hanamichi *followed by eight of his men, the*
FIGHTING CHORUS. BANNAI *has his kimono tucked up to his
knees, and a cord holds back his sleeves. His makeup has become ludicrous: bat-shaped eyebrows, drooping eyes, and a tiny blue-gray
mustache. The* FIGHTING CHORUS *is dressed identically in red leg-
gings and arm coverings and red and white patterned kimono that
stop at their knees. Each carries a branch of cherry blossoms as a
weapon.* BANNAI *stops at the seven-three position.* KAMPEI *escorts*
OKARU *to the left, out of harm's way, and stands calmly.*)

BANNAI: (*A comic challenge.*) Hey, hey! Kampei!

(*He stamps forward with two steps, each accented by two* tsuke *beats.
He and his men march on stage. The men, alert for their master's call,
kneel upstage in two rows.* BANNAI *faces front, with a supercilious
look. He speaks in a special rhythmical pattern,* nori, *in which each
dialogue phrase fits into an eight-beat samisen musical phrase. He
accompanies the tale with comic gestures.*)

Your stupid master, Enya Hangan, Takasada and my honored master, Councilor Moronao, met in the palace while,   30
  chittering chattering, chittering chattering, your master
  Hangan, flew into a snit. Taking a teensy sword he
  whipped it out, he made a slash. He is a traitor, locked up
  in his residence, boxed up like a criminal. Ha ha ha . . . ha
  ha ha . . . haha haha hahaha! Hangan has been hauled   35
  away! I'll catch you like a chick! I'll pluck you like a duck!
  I am claiming Okaru! Well? Well? Well, well? (*Accelerating.*)

Well, well, well, well, well! Kampei! Your goose is cooked! Give her . . . to me!

(BANNAI *stands on tiptoe, holds his sword hilts threateningly, and cocks his head in comic* mie *to two beats of the tsuke.*)

40   KIYOMOTO SINGER: "Give her to me," yells Sagisaka Bannai. Kampei bursts out with mocking laughter.
KAMPEI: (*Laughs, then speaks in rhythmic* nori *phrases.*) You are a funny bird, Sagisaka Bannai, a little chirping sparrow, I could swallow in a bite. (*Rapidly.*) Kampei's fiery gaze
45   could fry you to a crisp! But instead of eating you, I will make you eat crow!

(KAMPEI *slips his fists out of the breast of his kimono, allowing the black outer kimono to drop. An inner kimono of brilliant crimson color is revealed. He stamps aggressively forward, then poses with arms outstretched, head cocked in a* mie *to two* tsuke *beats.* BANNAI *tumbles to the ground terrified.*)

KIYOMOTO SINGER: Glaring and with arms outstretched, Kampei stands before him!
BANNAI: (*Weakly.*) Help!

(KIYOMOTO *samisen and drums play instrumental music as the eight members of the* FIGHTING CHORUS *attack* KAMPEI. KAMPEI *waves half of them past him until he stands center in a* mie *position. Four men face him from either side, holding their cherry branches as if they were swords. They strike at him right, left, right. He forces them back. They fall away. They pose in a* mie *to two* tsuke *beats.* KAMPEI *now fights his opponents in a series of group combats that are executed in delicate, controlled dance patterns. Rhythmic drums and* samisen *support the action.*)

50   KIYOMOTO SINGER: Cherry, cherry blossoms! A name, oh, so beloved.

(*One man on each side strikes at* KAMPEI *with the cherry branch. Three times* KAMPEI *avoids, then seizing the tips of the branches, he whirls them in a circle and presses them to their knees. He poses in a* mie. *Flicking the branches away, the men are hit on the forehead; they retreat.* KAMPEI *nonchalantly dusts off his hands.*)

"No, no, you can't have her," and why should that be?

(*One man on each side seizes* KAMPEI's *arms. They struggle right, left, right.* KAMPEI *flicks them forward onto their knees. They try to seize his feet, he backs up. They rush in to encircle him. He avoids, then casually taps them on the back. They do a cartwheel and fall prostrate on the ground.* KAMPEI *poses in a* mie.)

So tender, so fine, so frail, never to be won by you!

(*Four men form a square around* KAMPEI. *Two-by-two they attack, but he pivots to avoid them. Six men strike with their cherry branches.* KAMPEI *drops to his knees, deftly knocks the wind out of them with an open-hand blow, and, with a sweeping gesture, knocks them off their feet. They fall on their bottoms in unison.*)

Delightful, though she's only to be seen. How can you
55   ever feel true love, if she won't play with you!

(*The* FIGHTING CHORUS *retires upstage.* BANNAI *pulls* OKARU *by the sleeve. Foolishly flirting, he touches his cheek to her hand.* KAMPEI

pushes him away, and when BANNAI *tries to get past to* OKARU, *blocks his way.* BANNAI *slips under* KAMPEI's *sleeve, but is caught and held by the nape of the neck.* BANNAI *struggles free, strikes at* KAMPEI, *is kicked to his knees, and finally is grasped by the ear, lifted, and spun around.* BANNAI *is near tears in frustration and humiliation. Trying once again, he raises his fist, but* KAMPEI *turns and casually pushes* BANNAI *to the ground.* KAMPEI *stamps forward and poses in a strong* mie *to two* tsuke *beats.*)

BANNAI: (*Plaintively.*) Take him!

(*Large drum and* tsuke *beats. The* FIGHTING CHORUS *attacks in unison:* KAMPEI *passes them off right and left as he strides from stage left to right; he turns and passes unharmed between them as they strike at him with their cherry branches. One man, coming from hiding, strikes at* KAMPEI *from behind.* KAMPEI *kicks him to the ground, places his foot on his back, and poses in a strong* mie *to two beats of the tsuke.* KAMPEI *kicks the man away and attacks. Booming drum accelerates. The* FIGHTING CHORUS *retreats. They run pell-mell down the* hanamichi *and out of sight.* KAMPEI *poses in a powerful "stone-throwing"* mie *to two beats of the* tsuke. BANNAI *sneaks up.*)

BANNAI: Kampei, here I come!

(BANNAI *raises his sword to strike.* KAMPEI *catches his wrist, spins him around, forces him to his knees, and raises the sword.*)

KAMPEI: (*Bantering.*) Shall I cut your ears off? (*Terrified,* BANNAI *covers his ears with wildly trembling hands.*) Shall I cut off your nose? (BANNAI *covers his nose.*) Or shall I simply kill you?   60
OKARU: Killing him would bring more trouble. So, please, just let him go.
BANNAI: (*Foolishly, imitating* OKARU's *inflections.*) So, please, just let him go!

(BANNAI *clasps his trembling hands together in prayer.*)

KIYOMOTO SINGER: Oh, how he prattles on, that bird, Sag-   65
isaka! Smoothing his ruffled feathers, slowly, then faster, flirts with death, and yet to live, away he flies!

(KAMPEI *nods agreement. He casually rolls* BANNAI *across the stage away from* OKARU. *He poses facing front.* BANNAI *rubs his throat, then noticing* KAMPEI *is holding his sword, meekly gestures a request that it be returned. Contemptuously,* KAMPEI *tosses the sword on the ground.* BANNAI *leaps back in terror. Gathering his courage, he snares the sword with his foot, then suddenly turns and raises the sword as if to strike. A fierce glance from* KAMPEI *deflates him completely. He turns and escapes off right, lifting his legs high in the air in a "stork walk."*)

KAMPEI: He deserved to die. But his death would be a crime to add to my disloyalty.

(*A cock crows in the distance. They both look up into the sky. They speak in melancholy, poetic tones.*)

Already it is dawning . . .   70
OKARU: . . . on the peaks of the mountains . . .
KAMPEI: . . . the eastern light glows . . .
OKARU and KAMPEI: (*In unison.*) . . . lighting trailing clouds.

(*They pose together center stage, absorbed in their own melancholy.*)

KIYOMOTO SINGER: They fly away at daybreak, like the crows
75 that cry, "caw, caw." So dear to each other, in love, in love.

(*A* STAGE ASSISTANT *passes to* OKARU *the hat, bundle, and swords.
Dutifully,* OKARU *helps* KAMPEI *adjust the bundle and slide the
swords into his sash. They put on their sandals. A temple bell tolls.
They move apart, pose, then move back-to-back.*)

Though they must hasten to depart, their minds are filled
with woe. Who would doubt their loyalty if they proved
the guilt they feel? Away they go.

(*They look into each other's eyes. Restraining tears,* KAMPEI *puts on
a manly bearing, takes* OKARU *by the hand, and turns to begin their
long journey.* BANNAI *sneaks up behind them. He holds* OKARU *by
the waist.*)

BANNAI: Okaru is mine, all mine!

(KAMPEI *moves to block* BANNAI, *passing* OKARU *to safety on the*
hanamichi. *He pushes* BANNAI *away and turns to join* OKARU.)

80 BANNAI: Kampei, wait!
KAMPEI: (*Turning back at the seven-three position.*) Bannai, you
want. . . . ?
BANNAI: (*Posing.*) Kampei, I want . . .
KAMPEI: Hmm?
85 BANNAI: (*Deflated.*) Nothing.
KAMPEI: Simpleton!

(*A loud* ki *clack:* BANNAI *collapses to the ground. Drum booms
loudly.* KAMPEI *takes* OKARU's *hand and slowly they exit down the*
hanamichi. *Kiyomoto samisen plays plaintive chords and* ki *clacks
accelerate as the curtain begins to close.* BANNAI *is in the path of
the curtain. He retreats before it, then, realizing it is hopeless, seizes
the curtain with both hands and, grinning happily, prances across the
stage, closing the curtain and disappearing from sight. A single* ki
clack: drum and flute play lively "Shagiri" to close the scene.)

SCENE II
Hangan's Suicide

Two ki *clacks: the curtain is slowly opened to the rachetlike sound of
an old-fashioned clock. The scene is a large, formal room in* HANGAN's
*mansion. Sliding doors that make up the rear wall are painted powder
blue and covered with silver crests of* HANGAN's *clan. Tatami matting
covers the floor.* HANGAN, *dressed in a simple kimono and vest so pale
a blue-gray that it verges on white, kneels center. He faces two envoys
from the shogun,* ISHIDŌ *and* YAKUSHIJI, *who are sitting stage left on
high stools. They wear dark kimono, vests, and trousers.* ISHIDŌ's *sympathetic manner contrasts sharply with* YAKUSHIJI's *derisive attitude.*
GOEMON, *a senior retainer of* HANGAN, *kneels upstage. Silence.*
ISHIDŌ *rises and faces* HANGAN. *He takes from the breast of his kimono a large folded letter. He holds it reverently to his forehead.*

ISHIDŌ: Hear the shogun's command. (*Removing the letter from
its envelope, he reads.*) "Whereas, Enya Hangan Takasada,
you have willfully committed an act of bloodshed against
our chief councilor, Moronao, and thereby have defiled
5   the palace, know that your estates, large and small, are
hereby confiscated and you are ordered to end your life by
seppuku."

(ISHIDŌ *gravely holds the open letter in front of him, so* HANGAN
can read the order with his own eyes. After glancing at it, HANGAN
bows respectfully.)

HANGAN: (*With perfect control.*) In all respects I accept the
shogun's command.
NARRATOR: (*Chants.*) From the adjoining room, knocking   10
on the door . . .

(*A* RETAINER *knocks on the sliding door. He speaks in a faint, muffled voice, suggesting tears.*)

RETAINER: (*Off.*) Goemon, Goemon. We, Lord Hangan's re-
tainers, beg permission to see our master . . .
RETAINERS: (*Off, quietly in unison.*) . . . one last time.
GOEMON: (*Bowing to* HANGAN.) My lord, your retainers wish   15
to see you.
HANGAN: Tell them not until Chief Retainer Yuranosuke has
arrived from our province.
GOEMON: (*Facing the door.*) You heard our lord. You may enter
when Yuranosuke arrives, not before.   20
RETAINERS: (*Scarcely audible.*) Ahhh.
NARRATOR: (*Sings.*) Their plea, not granted . . . no one dares
utter a single word. In the room, silence prevails.

(HANGAN *rises and retires upstage, where he kneels with his back to
the audience.*)

GOEMON: (*Quietly, facing offstage right.*) Proceed.
RETAINER: (*Faintly, off.*) Yes.   25

(*In complete silence arrangements are made for* HANGAN's *death by
ritual disembowelment.* RETAINERS, *dressed in somber blue and gray
kimono, vests, and split trousers, swiftly and unobtrusively enter. They
place two tatami mats center to make a six-foot square platform. They
cover it with a pure white cloth. Sprigs of green, in small bamboo holders, are placed at the four corners. With downcast eyes, the* RETAINERS
slip quietly away. GOEMON *bows to* HANGAN *indicating that the place
of suicide is ready.* HANGAN *rises, slowly pivots front, and crosses down
to the cloth seat. Unconsciously his gaze drifts to the* hanamichi: *he
is waiting for the arrival of his chief retainer,* YURANOSUKE, *and does
not want to die before passing to him his last instructions. His right foot
touches the cloth. He remembers it is obligatory to step into the place
of suicide with the left foot. He glances at the envoys to see if they have
noticed: they are gazing straight ahead. He deliberately steps onto the
cloth and slowly kneels.*)

NARRATOR: (*Chants.*) Rikiya proceeds with the saddest order. (*Sings.*) The master's suicide blade weighing heavy on
his heart . . .

(YURANOSUKE's *son,* RIKIYA, *enters from up left. He carries a plain
wooden tray bearing the short dagger with which* HANGAN *will kill
himself. The long sleeves of his black kimono and a delicate forelock
of hair indicate he is a youth, not yet grown to manhood. He places
the tray on the floor before the envoys for their verification. He bows.*
ISHIDŌ *and* YAKUSHIJI *look at the blade, then nod to each other that
it is satisfactory.* ISHIDŌ *nods gravely to* RIKIYA.)

NARRATOR: Before Lord Hangan he lays the blade.

(RIKIYA *places the tray on the cloth before* HANGAN, *bows low, and
then looks up for instructions.* HANGAN *looks gently into* RIKIYA's

eyes and with a single head movement indicates that RIKIYA *is to leave: a boy so young should not have to witness* seppuku. RIKIYA *politely shakes his head: until his father arrives, he must fulfill his father's duties.* HANGAN *repeats the order to leave; again* RIKIYA *shakes his head. Impressed by the boy's loyalty,* HANGAN *nods that he may stay.* RIKIYA *bows gratefully, rises, backs away, and takes a place beside* GOEMON.)

30 NARRATOR: (*Sings.*) Taking off, in hushed silence, his outer clothes to expose his death robe . . . securing the seat of death.

(HANGAN *prepares himself for death with calm deliberation. He slips off the vest, letting it drop to his waist. He tucks the ends under his legs so as to hold his body in place after he has died. He drops the outer kimono to his waist and tucks it in as well. Beneath he is wearing a pure white kimono appropriate for death, an indication to the envoys that he was prepared to die even before they brought the shogun's command. He places his hands firmly on his thighs and looks intently down the* hanamichi.)

HANGAN: (*Softly but urgently.*) Rikiya.
RIKIYA: (*Bowing.*) Yes.
35 HANGAN: Yuranosuke . . . ?
RIKIYA: Yuranosuke . . . (*He looks down the* hanamichi *for a sign that his father has arrived.*) . . . has not as yet arrived.
NARRATOR: (*Sings.*) Proper steps for suicide, he lifts the tray and bows. (*Chants.*) Waiting no longer, the blade in his
40 hand.

(HANGAN *prepares the dagger. He lifts the tray to his forehead respectfully. He ceremoniously takes the dagger in his right hand and a sheet of white paper in his left. He wraps the paper around the blade until only its tip is bare. He is now able to grasp the blade low for extra leverage. He holds the blade at ready on his thigh. The tip points to his stomach. Outwardly calm, his voice betrays his anxiety.*)

HANGAN: Rikiya, Rikiya!
RIKIYA: (*Bowing.*) Yes.
HANGAN: Yuranosuke . . . ?
RIKIYA: Yes! (RIKIYA *bows and rushes to the end of the* hanamichi.
45 *He falls to his knees, looks to the right, the left, then straight ahead, searching for sight of his father. His lip trembles, he is close to tears.*) Yuranosuke . . . (*He rushes back and throws himself on the floor before* HANGAN.) . . . has not as yet arrived!
HANGAN: (*Calmly.*) Tell him that I regret . . . not seeing him
50 one last time. (HANGAN *nods that* RIKIYA *may retire and pivots slightly toward* ISHIDŌ.) Lord Ishidō, I ask that you witness and report my death.
NARRATOR: (*Sings.*) Here at last the time has come, the blade is aimed. Hangan . . . thrusts it in . . . thrusts it deep!

(HANGAN *places the tray behind him. He rises slightly on his knees, looking one last time down the* hanamichi *for* YURANOSUKE. *He holds the dagger under the ribs on his left side. With a sudden jerk he thrusts the blade into his stomach. Involuntarily his body drops forward and his head falls. Rapid narrative shifts to chanting.*)

55 Running at a desperate speed, the awaited person comes! Here at last is Ōboshi Yuranosuke! A frantic gaze at his master: "Is he still alive?" Overcome by the sight, he falls on his knees!

(YURANOSUKE *bursts onto the* hanamichi, *running frantically, all decorum cast aside. He wears a formal gray kimono, vest, and trousers pulled up for travel. Reaching the seven-three position, he sees his master in the midst of suicide. He reels, falls back, then slowly sinks to his knees.*)

ISHIDŌ: (*Rising.*) Is it Ōboshi Yuranosuke? 60
YURANOSUKE: It is.
ISHIDŌ: (*Urgently.*) Approach, approach quickly!

(YURANOSUKE *attempts to rise, but his legs will not function. He weeps unashamedly. To gain control of himself, he reaches inside the breast of his kimono to pull tight the inner cloth binding his waist. With great effort he pushes himself up from the floor and moves unsteadily to* HANGAN's *side. He falls to his knees and bows deeply.*)

NARRATOR: (*Chants.*) The men of Hangan, all, till now forbidden . . . but no longer! They come rushing in!

(*Ten* RETAINERS *enter swiftly from up right. They are barefooted and carry no swords. They fall to their knees in a row upstage and, following* YURANOSUKE's *lead, bow deeply to their master* HANGAN. YURANOSUKE's *eyes remain downcast and* HANGAN, *in pain, does not yet look up.*)

YURANOSUKE: Ōboshi Yuranosuke kneels before my lord.
HANGAN: (*Weakly.*) Yuranosuke? 65
YURANOSUKE: I am here.
HANGAN: At last you've come.
YURANOSUKE: All that I could ever ask is to be at your side in these last moments . . .
HANGAN: Ah, it makes me content as well. (*Slowly their gazes* 70 *meet.*) You have heard, have you not . . . everything . . . everything . . . ?

(*His voice trails off in pain.* YURANOSUKE *edges closer, looking meaningfully at* HANGAN.)

YURANOSUKE: Yes!
HANGAN: (*Rousing himself.*) I am humiliated . . . !
YURANOSUKE: (*Interrupting.*) No words can express such feel- 75 ings as I hold. Nothing remains now but for me to assure you a just end.
HANGAN: (*Meaningfully.*) One thing remains.
NARRATOR: (*Chants.*) Gripping tight the blade, cutting straight across in disembowelment. (*Sings.*) Such moments 80 of agony . . . exhaling his breath . . .

(HANGAN *cuts his stomach across from left to right. Although the pain is excruciating and his lips tremble and his breathing grows labored,* HANGAN *maintains the stoic decorum expected of a samurai until the blade reaches its final point just under the right ribs. Then breath seems to leave him. His body sags. He braces his left hand on his thigh.*)

HANGAN: (*Faintly.*) Yuranosuke . . . Yuranosuke . . . come close . . .
YURANOSUKE: Yes.

(HANGAN *is near death.* YURANOSUKE *slides forward urgently. Knowing* HANGAN *cannot speak openly because the shogun's envoys are present, he searches his master's face for some command.*)

85 HANGAN: Take this blade . . . to remind you . . . do not forget. Re-ve-n . . . (*YURANOSUKE starts. HANGAN must not say "revenge" out loud. HANGAN catches himself.*) . . . remember me.

(*Weakly HANGAN looks into YURANOSUKE's face, then down the hanamichi. YURANOSUKE follows HANGAN's gaze. Master and retainer look deeply into each other's eyes. YURANOSUKE understands that in spite of his master's seeming calm acceptance of the death sentence, HANGAN passionately desires vengeance against the enemy outside the mansion, that is, MORONAO.*)

YURANOSUKE: (*Passionately.*) I swear!

(*YURANOSUKE slaps his chest for emphasis and bows deeply. HANGAN knows that YURANOSUKE understands. He is now free to die. He smiles.*)

HANGAN: Ha ha. Ha ha. Ha, ha, ha, ha . . .

(*The laugh fades. With ebbing strength, HANGAN pulls the blade from his stomach. He gasps.*)

90 NARRATOR: (*Chants.*) Aiming the blade at his throat . . . one slash across. Breathing his last breath, lifeless he crumples.

(*Weakened hands, trembling violently, lift the blade upward. He tilts his head. His neck is exposed. A quick slash and the jugular vein is cut. His body rises upward in three spasms of breath. His eyes flutter closed. He falls limply forward, dead. Silently ISHIDŌ rises. A STAGE ASSISTANT whisks his stool offstage. ISHIDŌ places the shogun's letter on his open fan and places them on HANGAN's body. He moves stage right and kneels beside YURANOSUKE.*)

ISHIDŌ: (*Quietly.*) Yuranosuke, Yakushiji now assumes authority over Hangan's estates. Hangan's retainers are hereby denied the rank of samurai and are disbanded. I will report to the shogun that the death of Hangan is accomplished. You have my deepest sympathy, Yuranosuke.

NARRATOR: (*Sings.*) Ishidō, the envoy, expresses sympathy. His sad assignment is over.

(*ISHIDŌ rises facing the line of RETAINERS. He raises his arms in a gesture of condolence. The RETAINERS look up, then bow respectfully. Slowly ISHIDŌ walks to the seven-three position on the hanamichi. At a signal from YURANOSUKE, RIKIYA moves forward to see him out. ISHIDŌ turns back.*)

ISHIDŌ: There is no need. There is no need.

100 NARRATOR: He prays silently.

(*ISHIDŌ folds his hands and, with downcast eyes, walks slowly down the hanamichi and out of sight.*)

NARRATOR: (*Chants.*) Yakushiji holds them in contempt!

(*YAKUSHIJI rises brusquely. The STAGE ASSISTANT takes away his stool.*)

YAKUSHIJI: Now that he's dead, I'm master here! Cart the corpse away, while I settle in. Show me the way! (*He starts to go, then turns back.*) It's a sad time, isn't it! Ha, ha, ha, ha!

(*YAKUSHIJI strides off left, shown out by a RETAINER. Complete silence. YURANOSUKE moves in to attend to his master's body. He straightens the legs and brings kimono and vest up over the torso. He moves closer and tries to take the dagger from HANGAN's hand. In death HANGAN's fingers hold it tightly. YURANOSUKE falls back weeping. He gently massages his master's hand until the fingers are warmed, softened, and the dagger slips from their grasp. YURANOSUKE places the dagger carefully into the breast of his kimono. He backs away. He and the RETAINERS bow expectantly.*)

NARRATOR: (*Singing plaintively.*) Lady Kaoyo enters from an- 105 other room. Her hair so long and black, oh, so beautiful, now pitiful, it is no more. She will pray as a nun, till her end.

(*KAOYO and four LADIES-IN-WAITING enter from the left, walking with downcast eyes. They are dressed in pure white kimono and hold Buddhist rosaries. The last LADY-IN-WAITING carries a small tray on which rests the cloth-wrapped remains of KAOYO's long hair. They kneel left. The MAIDS bow deeply.*)

KAOYO: (*Quietly.*) Yuranosuke. When I think of why my husband had to die, and that I was the cause . . .

YURANOSUKE: (*Firmly.*) My lady, please understand our 110 heartfelt feelings. All of us, each retainer offers his deepest condolence.

(*YURANOSUKE bows to KAOYO, then nods to GOEMON. GOEMON and the RETAINERS rise and move in a circle around their master. Silently, they take up the white cloth, the tatami mats, tray, and sprigs of green. They exit upstage right. HANGAN moves off behind the cloth. In an instant all sign of the suicide is removed.*)

KAOYO: Yuranosuke.

YURANOSUKE: Yes, my lady.

KAOYO: I offer my lock of hair.

(*The LADY-IN-WAITING places the tray with the hair center stage. YURANOSUKE sees it and weeps. KAOYO turns to show her close-cropped head.*)

NARRATOR: (*Prolonged, melancholy singing.*) Kaoyo is left be- 115 hind, her grief is so . . . o . . . o . . . She yearns to go to the temple . . .

(*She rises, as if to follow her husband, but YURANOSUKE stops her with a commanding gesture.*)

YURANOSUKE: My lady!

(*She falls back weakly. A single ki clack. They move into a pose: YURANOSUKE picks up the tray with one hand and forces her back with the other; KAOYO faces front, lifts the rosary to her eyes, and sobs silently. Ki clacks accelerate as the curtain is slowly walked closed.*)

SCENE III
Outer Gate

Two ki clacks signal drum and flute to play "Toki no Taiko" ("Time Drum"). The curtain is pushed quickly open. The scene is outside the massive outer gate of HANGAN's mansion. No one is on stage.

NARRATOR: (*Chanting rapidly.*) Farewell to Hangan. Now his body lies alone. The young retainers run back from the temple! They no longer can hold the shame inside!

(*To loud, accelerating tsuke beats, RIKIYA leads a band of RETAINERS onto the hanamichi. They urge each other on with shouts of "Kill*

them!" "They won't have our lord's mansion!" "We'll fight them!"
"Lord Hangan was unjustly killed!" At the same time YURANOSUKE
and GOEMON come out of a small door in the gate. GOEMON rushes
up to the RETAINERS with outstretched arms, shouting, "Stop, stop!"
YURANOSUKE roughly pushes RIKIYA to the ground.)

YURANOSUKE: (*Furious.*) What, you too, Rikiya? What are
5   you thinking of, trying to attack the mansion? We are no
       longer samurai. We cannot fight Yakushiji's men. (*Drops to
       one knee, hand on the hilt of his short sword.*) If you do not
       stop, I shall commit seppuku on this very spot! Do you
       want to be my seconds, all of you?
10 RETAINERS: No, but master . . .
    YURANOSUKE: (*Implacably.*) Then will you stop when I tell you?
    RETAINERS: Yes, but . . .
    YURANOSUKE: It will achieve nothing to die now!

(*The* RETAINERS *cannot disobey. Grumbling and rebellious, they
begin to fall back.*)

NARRATOR: (*Chants.*) Behind the gate is heard . . . Yakushiji's
15   voice!
YAKUSHIJI: (*Off.*) Hey, men, there's a sight. Newly hatched
       ex-samurai, milling around like chickens with their heads
       cut off! It's enough to make you laugh!
YAKUSHIJI'S MEN: (*Off.*) Ha, ha, ha, ha, ha!
20 FIRST RETAINER: Do you . . .
    RETAINERS: . . . hear that?

(*Furious, they turn to storm the gate, hands on the hilts of their
swords.* YURANOSUKE *springs into their path and blocks the way.*)

YURANOSUKE: Have you forgotten our late lord?
RETAINERS: No, but . . .
YURANOSUKE: Not now! Go back, go back! Go back I tell you!

(YURANOSUKE *draws himself up commandingly. He runs his hand
up the edge of his vest and poses in a furious* mie. *Two* tsuke *beats.*)

25 NARRATOR: (*Sings.*) "Go back," he commands!
    YURANOSUKE: (*Almost in a scolding tone now.*) Back, back, back.

(YURANOSUKE *waves them away. They fall back grudgingly, then
turn and stride off down the* hanamichi. YURANOSUKE *watches
them leave. He is alone. Silence. He sighs with relief. The hand at his
breast slides down until it accidentally touches the dagger. He slowly
drops to his knees and takes it out. He unwraps the covering purple
cloth. The blade tip is red with* HANGAN's *blood.*)

NARRATOR: (*Sings.*) The suicide blade, red with blood, cries
       out for revenge . . . cries out for revenge! Burning tears rake
       his heart, tears . . . falling . . . falling . . . falling . . . falling . . .

(*Gazing at the blade,* YURANOSUKE's *chest heaves. He covers his
eyes to hide the tears.*)

30   Hangan's last words of vengeance imbedded deep in
       Yuranosuke. (*Chanting.*) We know indeed the motive of
       Yuranosuke, his revenge to be noted for many ages . . .
       forty-seven loyal men immortalized!

(*He wipes blood from the blade onto his palm and then deliberately
brings his hand up to his mouth. He licks the blood as an oath of*

vengeance. *Music stops. Silence.* YURANOSUKE *begins his long pantomime of departure. He carefully wraps the dagger in the purple
cloth. He holds it to his forehead respectfully. He places it in the
breast of his kimono. He rises and stands. He slaps the dust from his
knees. He adjusts his trousers. He folds both hands inside his kimono
sleeves. He rests his hands on the hilts of his swords. He half-closes
his eyes, regretting deeply that he must abandon his master's mansion. A temple bell tolls in the distance. Pensively, he begins to walk
away from the gate. The gate recedes, indicating* YURANOSUKE *has
covered a long distance. He turns back. A crow caws in the distance.
He resumes the painful separation. A crow caws a second time. A second bell tolls. He stops, stricken with the finality of parting. Then, he
moves onto the* hanamichi. *Once more he turns back and, as if he
has no heart to continue, slides to his knees. A temple bell tolls.
Plaintive, tentative chords of the* samisen *begin. He rises, begins to
walk away, looks sadly over his shoulder for one last glimpse, then
resolutely turns and strides down the* hanamichi *and out of sight.
Music crescendoes and* ki *clacks accelerate: the curtain is run closed.
Drum and flute play rapid "Shagiri" to end the scene.*)

ACT THREE

SCENE I
Ichiriki Brothel

Two ki *clacks: the curtain is pushed open to offstage singing of
"Hana ni Asobaba" ("If You Play in the Flowers"). The scene is
the Ichiriki Brothel in the Gion licensed quarter in Kyoto. Two pavil-
ions are set in a garden. Lying on his side in the larger room, stage
center, is* YURANOSUKE. *He is feigning sleep, his face covered with
a half-open fan. He wears an elegant purple kimono and matching
cloak. Curtains are at the back and a stone water basin is left. Three
steps lead down into the garden. Paper-covered sliding doors conceal
the interior of the smaller pavilion, stage left. It is several feet higher
off the ground than the center pavilion.*

NARRATOR: (*Singing briskly.*) The mountains and the moon.
       From the eastern mountains, just a few miles, breathless
       from running fast, the young man . . . Rikiya.

(RIKIYA *enters on the* hanamichi. *A purple scarf covers his head and
serves as a partial disguise. His black kimono is hiked up at the
sides, to free his legs for running. He stops at a garden gate set on the*
hanamichi *at the seven-three position. He looks back to see if he is
being observed, then swiftly passes through the gate, closing it.*)

       Entering the brothel garden . . . there lies Yuranosuke, pre-
       tending to be drunk. Taking caution to wake his father in 5
       secrecy, he walks softly in, stepping close to him. The
       sword guard speaks!

(RIKIYA *sees his father. He mounts the steps, kneels, and makes a
ringing sound by striking sword guard against sheath.* YURANOSUKE
gestures RIKIYA *away with a sleepy movement of the fan.* RIKIYA
*crosses swiftly back through the gate, closes it, looks around to be cer-
tain they are not being observed, and kneels to wait for his father.
Offstage* samisen *play tentative chords.* YURANOSUKE *rises. He
staggers as if drunk, ad-libbing, "That was heady wine. I need some
air. Don't go away, girls. I'll be in the garden." He looks through the
curtains to see if anyone is watching. He crosses to the gate, stumbling
several times in order to have the chance to look carefully in all directions. He stands swaying, fan before his face. He speaks guardedly.*)

YURANOSUKE: Rikiya, do I hear the sound of urgency in the echo of your sword?

10 RIKIYA: Yes, Father. I bring a secret message from Lady Kaoyo. (RIKIYA *brings out a letter from his right sleeve and passes it to* YURANOSUKE, *who puts it immediately into the breast of his kimono without examining it.*)

YURANOSUKE: (*Carefully.*) Did she say anything to you?

15 RIKIYA: (*Rising on his knees urgently.*) Soon, soon our enemy . . .

YURANOSUKE: Rikiya! "Soon at night our enemy, flees like plovers o'er the sea. . . ."

(*Music swells. To cover the slip of his son's tongue,* YURANOSUKE *sings a well-known passage from a now play. He staggers in a circle looking to see if anyone has heard* RIKIYA's *remark. Simultaneously,* RIKIYA *pivots in the opposite direction, looking for eavesdroppers.* YURANOSUKE *gestures for* RIKIYA *to come closer;* RIKIYA *whispers* KAOYO's *message in his father's ear. The curtains in the room center part.* KUDAYŪ *peeks out. He is a gray-haired former retainer of* HANGAN, *now secretly working for* MORONAO. *He wears a plain brown kimono and cloak. He watches for a moment, then slips away.*)

YURANOSUKE: Send a palanquin for me tonight. Tell the others to be ready. Go, go!

20 NARRATOR: (*Sings.*) No time left for hesitation . . . to the eastern hills, homeward now . . .

(YURANOSUKE *sharply gestures with the fan.* RIKIYA *bows, rises, and holding firmly onto the hilts of his swords, begins to leave.*)

YURANOSUKE: Rikiya!

RIKIYA: (*Returning and bowing.*) Yes.

YURANOSUKE: Be careful while passing through the quarter.

25 Then hurry! Go now!

RIKIYA: Yes!

NARRATOR: Rikiya returns home.

(RIKIYA *realizes his mistake; he is holding his swords ready to draw, thus calling attention to himself. He hides the hilts with his sleeves. Swiftly, carefully, he hurries down the* hanamichi *out of sight. Offstage* samisen *play "Odoriji Aikata" ("Dance Melody"). Four* MAIDS *and a male* JESTER *enter through the curtain, ad-libbing, "Yura, where are you?" "Come drink with us." "Don't leave us, Yura."* YURANOSUKE *pretends drunkenness again.*)

FIRST MAID: Yura, Yura, are you here?

YURANOSUKE: Hmm. You've come to get me? I'm a lucky

30 man. Come close all of you, let's amuse ourselves. Come, sing and dance for me.

(YURANOSUKE *sits on the steps. The* MAIDS *and the* JESTER *kneel in the garden in a semicircle around him.*)

SECOND MAID: Very well . . .

ALL: . . . let's begin, let's begin!

(*Lilting music of offstage* samisen, *drum, and bell accompanies various dances and songs. These are extemporized by the performers from production to production.* MAIDS *and* JESTER *ad-lib comic banter throughout.*)

MAIDS: (*Clapping as they sing.*) What will it be like, what will

35 it be like? If you don't be careful, we will make you drink. Ah, what will it be like, what will it be like?"

(JESTER *and* THIRD MAID *rise and move center. They do a game of jan-ken-po, "scissors-paper-stone." He loses. She laughingly pushes him. He falls in a heap on the ground. The* MAIDS *rise and form pairs.*)

FOURTH MAID: Come, let's dance!

ALL: "First your left foot, then your right, tap, tap, tap; Around we go, back again; Are you ready, one, two, three!" 40

(*They circle left, then right, touching palms of their outstretched hands. They turn their backs to each other and bump bottoms on the count of three. With peals of laughter they recover their balance. The* JESTER *and* YURANOSUKE *laugh and applaud.*)

YURANOSUKE: Very good, very good!

FIRST MAID: How about a game, Yura dear?

JESTER: Blind man's bluff!

SECOND MAID: You be It!

ALL: Yes, yes! 45

(YURANOSUKE *tries to wave them away, but they playfully surround him and put a cloth over his eyes. They twirl him around in the center of the garden, and move left, laughing and clapping in time to their song.*)

ALL: "Yura, Yura, over here; Listen to our clapping hands."

YURANOSUKE: (*Sings.*) "I'll catch you all, soon enough you'll see."

(*He stumbles in their direction. They easily avoid his outstretched arms and flee to the other side of the garden.*)

ALL: "Yura, Yura over here; Come and catch us if you can." 50

YURANOSUKE: "I'll catch you all, and make you drink with me."

(*They duck under his arms. When he turns back to continue pursuit, they take him by the hands and, still singing and clapping, lead him off to the inner room with his blindfold still in place. They are no sooner off than* KUDAYŪ's *head pops through the curtain on the other side of the stage. Samisen* music *stops.* KUDAYŪ *peers about intently. He slips into the room.*)

KUDAYŪ: That letter Rikiya gave to Yuranosuke . . . the rumor of a vendetta must be true! He has not forgotten; they are plotting, just as I thought. When I tell Moronao, what will be my great reward? If, of course, it's true. I'll spy him out! 55 Here's a perfect place to hide.

(*He sees a hiding place. He removes a board under the veranda, opening a space for him to crawl in. He hides behind the steps.* YURANOSUKE *enters alone from upstage, pretending to be drunk.*)

YURANOSUKE: I'll be back . . . don't wait, girls . . . in a minute, I'll be back.

(Samisen *music resumes. He looks around. Seeing he is alone, he drops his pretense. He rinses his mouth with water from the stone basin. He spits it out. It falls on the unsuspecting* KUDAYŪ. *He takes out the letter from* KAOYO *and holds it respectfully to his forehead. He begins to read, slowly unrolling the letter until it reaches the ground. At the same time the paper doors slide open to reveal* OKARU *in the small room left. She wears the elaborate hairstyle and clinging kimono of a courtesan.)*

NARRATOR: *(Sings.)* Evening breeze, brings a courtesan, Kam-
60   pei's wife Okaru, away from her love. Someone has sent a
      love letter, "I wish it were for me." Okaru from a room
      above, tries to see the words. Too far in the evening dusk, the
      letters are not clear to read. Thinking of a way out, a mirror
      in her hand, she leans back . . . mirror held up high, reflec-
65   tion of the letter. Under the floor a spy, Kudayū waits . . . the
      trailing letter glows in the moonlight. *(Chants.)* Who could
      know someone is reading words of confidence?

(The three form a tableau: YURANOSUKE *is engrossed in reading the secret letter;* OKARU *views the letter backwards in a mirror; and* KU-DAYŪ, *spectacles on his nose, reads the bottom portion, line-by-line, as it comes down to him. Narrative shifts to singing.)*

      Okaru, unaware that her hairpin has loosened! *(Chants.)* It
      drops to the floor! Surprised by the sound above, he
70   quickly hides the letter . . . Yuranosuke! Underneath Ku-
      dayū smirking at his game. *(Sings.)* Okaru pretends noth-
      ing has happened here.

*(*YURANOSUKE *quickly resumes his drunken role. He begins to roll up the letter, but not before* KUDAYŪ *rips off the part he has been reading.* OKARU *puts down the mirror, picks up a fan, and turns to* YURANOSUKE.)*

OKARU: *(Languidly.)* Yura dear, is it you?
YURANOSUKE: Hmm, Okaru? So close at hand, what are you
75   doing?
OKARU: *(In poetic form of seven and five syllables.)* Yura dear, it's
      all your fault, I drank too much wine; my head is whirling
      round and I can scarcely see; I have come to sober up,
      wafted by the evening breeze.

*(*YURANOSUKE *reaches the end of the letter. He feels the ragged edge. Startled, he looks quickly at the letter, then puts it away in the breast of his kimono. He takes out a piece of tissue paper and wads it up, covering his action by improvising conversation with* OKARU.)*

80 YURANOSUKE: Hmm. Wafted by the evening breeze, you say?
      Wafted by the evening breeze? Ah!

(He drops the wad of paper to the ground. KUDAYŪ, *thinking it is part of the letter, snatches it and stuffs it into his kimono breast.* YURANOSUKE *falls back, supposedly in a drunken stupor, but actually wanting to ponder what to do next. He decides. Soft* samisen *plays "Odoriji Aikata" in the background.)*

      Hm. Okaru, there is something I want to talk to you
      about. Come over here.
OKARU: *(Rises as if to leave her room.)* Very well, I'll come
85   around and visit you.
YURANOSUKE: *(Coming down into the garden.)* No, Okaru, if
      you go that way the maids will catch you. They will force
      on you more wine. Ah, a ladder. Fortune smiles. Climb
      down this way and you won't be seen. *(Places a ladder against*
90   OKARU's *pavilion. Bantering.)* Descend for me, Okaru!
OKARU: *(Coquettishly on the ladder.)* I've never climbed a lad-
      der before.
YURANOSUKE: You've climbed other things.

OKARU: I'm not used to this strange position. It frightens me.
YURANOSUKE: You're past the age to be afraid of a new po-   95
      sition. Straddle it, open your legs, it'll all go smoothly.
OKARU: Don't be naughty, Yura. I tell you it frightens me. It's
      swaying like a boat.
YURANOSUKE: Never mind, I'll throw in my anchor. That
      will hold you down. Where shall I put it? *(He tries to lift*   100
      her skirt with his fan. She brushes his hand away.)
OKARU: You mustn't peek, Yura.
YURANOSUKE: *(Singing.)* "I adore your crescent moon, glis-
      tening in its secret grotto." Ha, ha, ha.
OKARU: *(Pouting.)* If you talk that way, I won't come down.   105
YURANOSUKE: Don't prattle like a virgin. You're a courtesan
      in the Gion brothel. I'll take you from behind. *(*YURA-
      NOSUKE *embraces her from behind.)*
OKARU: Oh, stop it.
YURANOSUKE: Then come, come.   110
OKARU: I am, I am!

(Laughing, she slips off the final rung of the ladder and moves away from YURANOSUKE. *She kneels right, fanning herself.* YURA-NOSUKE *glances at her sharply, then resumes the drunken pose. He stoops to retrieve the dropped hairpin and crosses to give it to her.)*

YURANOSUKE: *(Casually.)* Just now, Okaru, did something
      catch your eye?
OKARU: I . . . nothing.
YURANOSUKE: *(Coaxing.)* Come now, didn't you see, didn't   115
      you see . . .
OKARU: . . . your interesting letter . . .
YURANOSUKE: . . . from up above?
OKARU: *(Lightly.)* Hmm, yes.
YURANOSUKE: And you read it all?   120
OKARU: Oh, you do go on.

(Covering his concern, he pretends to stumble. He recovers his bal-ance, singing a now *song which both hides and expresses his feelings.)*

YURANOSUKE: "Fate conspires to bring, my life to this crisis. . . ."
      (Mimes striking a nō *drum.)* Ya, tum, tum, tum! Ha, ha, ha!
OKARU: *(Turns to him, laughing.)* What in the world do you
      mean?   125
YURANOSUKE: It means that of all the women in the world, I
      have become enamored of you. Come live with me, Okaru.
OKARU: Stop it. You're such a tease!
YURANOSUKE: *(Grandiloquently.)* I will redeem your contract
      with the master of the brothel and take you away.   130
OKARU: I don't believe it. You're making fun of me.
YURANOSUKE: I'll prove it's not a lie. Be my mistress for just
      three days, and after that, Okaru, your spirit will be free to
      go where it will.
OKARU: *(Taking him seriously for the first time.)* For three days? 135
YURANOSUKE: On my sacred oath as a samurai. Live with me
      for three days. I'll find the master and buy your contract
      now. Well, is it agreed?

*(*OKARU *looks carefully at him to see if it possibly can be true. They pose. She bows low.)*

OKARU: I am grateful, Yuranosuke.
YURANOSUKE: Can it make you happy to be redeemed . . .   140
      by this Yuranosuke?

OKARU: Oh, yes!

YURANOSUKE: Such radiance shines in that happy face.

(*They pose: she looks at him with gratitude; flicking open his fan, he covers his face to hide his stricken expression.*)

YURANOSUKE: Don't go away now. I'll be right back.

145 OKARU: Three days? Yes, Yuranosuke. I'll be here.

(*Offstage, sad "Yo ni mo Inga" ["Nighttime Fate"] is sung quietly. They lightly ad-lib to cover his exit. Still pretending to be drunk, he staggers up the steps. He turns back several times. He passes through the curtains in search of the master of the house. When he is gone she kneels center stage, trembling with excitement.*)

OKARU: How happy I am! I must write to dearest Kampei that I am coming home! And to Mother and Father, to tell the wonderful news!

(*She hurries up the steps into the center room, brings out a writing box and roll of letter paper, kneels, and begins to write a letter home. Song ends.*)

NARRATOR: (*Chants.*) Now appears . . . Heiemon!

(*Offstage samisen briskly play "Odoriji Aikata." A young samurai strides on from the right into the garden. His hair is severely drawn back and his plain kimono suggests poverty. It is* HEIEMON, OKARU's *older brother, in search of both* YURANOSUKE *and* OKARU. *He looks around, then seeing a woman in the room, enters and sits behind her. He speaks brusquely, almost rudely.*)

150 HEIEMON: Sorry to trouble you, Miss, but I am looking for a young woman, from my hometown of Yamazaki, by the name of Okaru, brought here a year ago . . .

(*Hearing her name* OKARU *turns. They recognize each other.*)

Sister!

OKARU: Heiemon! Oh! I feel ashamed for you to see me here!

(*OKARU's demeanor completely changes: in the presence of a male family member who is her elder, she becomes submissive, gentle, a little girl seeking approbation. She hides her face. She rushes down the steps, and falls to her knees.* HEIEMON, *though stern, acts protectively toward her. He rises and poses on the steps.*)

155 HEIEMON: What is there to feel ashamed of? When I returned home Mother told me you had sold yourself to this brothel, hoping that with your contract price Kampei could contribute to the vendetta against Lord Hangan's enemy. You have willingly sacrificed yourself for your hus-
160 band and for Lord Hangan. I am proud of you, Okaru! (*He poses at the top of the steps: right foot forward, right arm extended protectively in her direction.*)

OKARU: (*Hesitantly, looks up at him.*) Then you're not going to scold me?

165 HEIEMON: Scold you? I am filled with admiration, filled with admiration!

(*He crosses down the steps and kneels. He sits proudly, sword placed on the ground beside him.*)

OKARU: I'm happy that you think kindly of me. (*Becoming excited.*) Oh, there are so many things I want to ask my dear big brother. I don't know where to begin . . . how is Kam . . .

HEIEMON: (*Uneasy.*) Kam . . . ? 170

(OKARU *is embarrassed to have asked about her husband first. She changes the subject.*)

OKARU: Come . . . tell me, how is Mother?

HEIEMON: Set your mind at ease. Mother is well.

OKARU: And Father? Nothing troubles him, I hope?

HEIEMON: (*Uncomfortably.*) Hm . . . Father . . . he is at rest . . . he is at rest. 175

OKARU: (*Modestly.*) And what of Kampei?

HEIEMON: Kampei? Ah . . . well . . . he is as well as can be.

OKARU: You set my heart at ease. (*Bubbling.*) Oh, I forgot. . . be happy for me, Brother. Tonight, without warning, Yuranosuke offered to buy out my contract. 180

HEIEMON: Yuranosuke did that? (*Trying to understand how such a thing could be.*) Ah, then he's become your patron?

OKARU: Nonsense. We have only drunk together two or three times. And Heiemon, it's almost too good to be true. After three days he will let me come home. 185

HEIEMON: Hm? Then you told him you are Kampei's wife?

OKARU: How could I, a prostitute, tell him that and bring disgrace to Kampei and to my parents?

HEIEMON: (*Facing front.*) Hm! Then he is no more than a whoremaster! (*He slaps his thigh in anger.*) He has no in- 190 tention of avenging Hangan, our lord and master!

OKARU: Oh, no, Brother, he has. He has. Listen . . .

NARRATOR: (*Sings.*) In whispers, the content of the letter is revealed.

(OKARU *and* HEIEMON *rise. He leans forward. She whispers in his ear. They pose for a moment, then break apart and kneel.*)

OKARU: . . . so you see? 195

HEIEMON: (*Shocked.*) Then you read it all?

OKARU: Yes, and after reading it, his eye met mine, and flirting, he looked me up and down, up and down, and then began to talk of taking me away.

(OKARU *mimes his flirting by pressing the backs of her index fingers together, right on top of left, then left on top of right.* HEIEMON *is puzzled. He tries to understand her words, miming as she did.*)

HEIEMON: What? After reading it, flirting, he looked you up 200 and down, up and down . . . (*He slaps his thigh for emphasis.*) Ah! Now I understand!

OKARU: (*Laughing.*) You startled me.

HEIEMON: (*Facing the inner room, he bows low.*) Forgive me, Master Yuranosuke, I misjudged you! I was wrong, forgive me! 205

OKARU: Dearest Brother, what in the world are you doing?

HEIEMON: (*Turns and looks into* OKARU's *eyes.*) Dear Sister. There is something I must ask of you. Okaru, do now exactly as I say.

OKARU: You sound so very stiff and formal. What must you 210 ask of me!

HEIEMON: What I must ask of you is . . .

OKARU: What you must ask of me is . . . ?

HEIEMON: Okaru, let your brother take your life!

(He springs to his feet and whips out his long sword. She falls back. Rapid "Odoriji Aikata." To double beats of the tsuke, he slashes at her right, left, right. She avoids. She rises and pushes him away. He turns to strike; she distracts him with a shower of tissue paper drawn from her breast and thrown in the air. She runs to the hanamichi; *he follows. She closes the gate between them. They pose in a mie to two loud* tsuke *beats: on the ground, she holds up her hands imploringly; he stands with legs together, the sword directly overhead as if to strike. Music stops.)*

215 OKARU: *(Appealing to him.)* What am I supposed to have done wrong? You have no right to just do as you please. I have my husband and both my parents to care for. Forgive me if I have spoken out of turn. I clasp my hands and beg you to spare me!
220 NARRATOR: *(Sings.)* Seeing his sister's clasped hands . . . a brother's love overwhelms the dutiful heart. He can only cry.

(He tries to but cannot strike his sister. He falls back distraught, turns upstage to face away from her, holds the sword behind his back, and weeps unashamedly. When the narration is finished, he turns to face OKARU. *He is contrite. Slow offstage "Odoriji Aikata" resumes in the background.)*

HEIEMON: I was wrong, Okaru, not to explain. Come, come over here.

(He waves her to him. She flounces.)

OKARU: No, I will not come near you.
225 HEIEMON: *(Sternly.)* When your elder brother calls, why don't you come?
OKARU: *(Sweetly.)* If you want to know, I'll tell you why: I think you still intend to kill me, and I don't like that at all!

(HEIEMON notices the long sword in his hand. He puts it on the ground and pushes it toward her.)

HEIEMON: Ah, this. There is nothing to stop you now. So
230 come, come!
OKARU: Yes, there is. Something else.

(She points at the short sword in his sash. Annoyed, he pushes it toward her.)

HEIEMON: There, now. Come over here!

(She rises and is about to cross through the gate. She looks at him and stops.)

OKARU: Your face is so frightening.
HEIEMON: I can't help that. This is the face I was born with.
235 OKARU: Well then, please turn around.
HEIEMON: What a nuisance. Like this? Like this?

(Grumbling, he turns his back. He poses with arms stretched out to either side.)

OKARU: Now, don't look. Keep your face turned away. *(She cautiously goes through the gate, picks up the swords, and puts them out of his reach. She kneels behind him, placing her hands
240 on his sash. Music stops. She poses.)* All right, here I am.

Brother dear, what is it you want? *(He turns to face her. He places his hands protectively on her shoulders. They pose.)*
HEIEMON: *(Voice filled with emotion, he speaks in poetic form of seven and five syllables.)* Once you were a samurai, now a courtesan; combing out your silken hair, while the world 245 has changed; precious Sister how pitiful, totally unaware of the life you left behind!

(HEIEMON breaks away and kneels left. OKARU moves close.)

OKARU: Totally unaware . . . of what, Heiemon?
HEIEMON: Soon after you left home last year, one rainy night, Father was . . . 250
OKARU: *(Frightened.)* Father was . . . ?
HEIEMON: *(Choked scream.)* . . . struck down by a robber and slain by his sword!
OKARU: *(Falls back slackly.)* That cannot be true.
HEIEMON: You must be strong, Okaru. You look forward to 255 leaving here and being with your husband . . .
OKARU: Yes . . . Kampei . . . what about Kampei?
HEIEMON: Kampei . . .
OKARU: Kampei . . . ?
HEIEMON: *(A terrible scream.)* Cut open his stomach and is dead! 260

(He mimes the suicide and collapses, weeping. OKARU falls back, shocked, hardly able to breathe.)

OKARU: Kampei . . . oh . . . no. What shall I do? What shall I do?
HEIEMON: I know, I know, I know . . .

(They speak alternately, then faster and faster, until they are speaking at the same time. Then their grief-stricken voices fade away. OKARU *crawls to her older brother and puts her head on his lap. She weeps pitiably. At last* HEIEMON *gains control of himself. He gently disengages himself.)*

HEIEMON: Don't you see? Yuranosuke is not a man to be infatuated, and he did not know you were Kampei's wife. 265 Okaru, you were wrong to have read that secret letter. Yuranosuke's loyalty is clear. He cannot risk letting you live and he intends to buy your contract . . . just to kill you! Rather than dying at someone else's hand, let me be the one to take your life. Let me prove to Yuranosuke and his 270 followers that though I am a mere foot soldier, my spirit is as loyal as theirs. Let me serve our late master. Give me your life, dear Sister!
NARRATOR: *(Sings.)* The tragedy is disclosed! Okaru is prepared!

(HEIEMON is agonized by the conflict between his duty to HANGAN *and his love for* OKARU. *He beseeches her with clasped hands.* OKARU *willingly prepares to sacrifice herself. Gently she opens his hands.)*

OKARU: It is my karma not to meet my beloved husband and 275 father again. There is no reason for me to live.

(She crosses to get the swords, returns, and places them before him.)

Brother dear, please end my life now.

(She turns her back, clasps her hands in prayer, and drops her head forward, exposing her neck to his sword.)

HEIEMON: Admirable resolve. Namu Amida Butsu. Praise Buddha the Merciful.

(*He stands. He unsheaths the sword. He raises it to strike.* YURANOSUKE'*s voice is heard from behind the curtain.*)

280 YURANOSUKE: (*Off.*) Wait, wait! Stop at once! (*He enters.*) Your behavior is admirable, both of you. I acknowledge your loyalty. Heiemon, I hereby permit you to accompany us on our journey to the east.

(HEIEMON *and* OKARU *move right and kneel respectfully.* HEIEMON *is excited by* YURANOSUKE'*s acceptance of him into the vendetta group.*)

HEIEMON: Then you are ready? And I may go with you?
285 Okaru, Sister, do you hear? I am forever grateful.

(HEIEMON *bows to* YURANOSUKE. YURANOSUKE *comes down the steps.*)

YURANOSUKE: Okaru, for your loyalty, your husband, Kampei, will be admitted to our league. And since he was unable during his life to kill even a single enemy, let your action, Okaru, serve as his apology to Lord Hangan in the
290 afterlife . . . here and now . . .

(YURANOSUKE *takes* HEIEMON'*s long sword and places it in* OKARU'*s hands. He guides her to the veranda. They pose.*)

NARRATOR: (*Chants.*) Thrusting deep through the dark of the hiding place. The hateful spy, Kudayū, a fatal blow in his shoulder, rolls and turns in deadly pain!

(*They thrust the sword under the veranda. Double* tsuke *beats.* KUDAYŪ *cries out.* HEIEMON *drags the mortally wounded* KUDAYŪ *into the garden and throws him to the ground.* YURANOSUKE *kneels, and holding* KUDAYŪ *by the scruff of the neck, strikes furiously with closed fan.*)

YURANOSUKE: Kudayū, you wretch! Traitor! More than forty
295 of us day and night have shed tears of agony. We have parted from our children, deserted our parents, and sold our wives into prostitution all in order to avenge our Lord Hangan's death. And you, who enjoyed wealth and honor in his service, have betrayed your master and become Mo-
300 ronao's spy! Fiend! Demon! You are a monster!
NARRATOR: (*Sings.*) As if to grind him into the ground, Yuranosuke . . . his burst of anger cannot be gratified!

(*He strikes him five times to sharp* tsuke *beats. Then contemptuously he pushes him away. Bringing his hand to his eyes,* YURANOSUKE *openly weeps. Just then the* MAIDS *cry out offstage. Rapid "Odoriji Aikata." Instantly* YURANOSUKE *reverts to his pose as a drunken brothel patron. He rises, staggering. The* MAIDS *enter and kneel in a semicircle in the center room.*)

FIRST MAID: Master Yuranosuke, Master Yuranosuke . . .
SECOND MAID: . . . your palanquin has arrived.
305 YURANOSUKE: You've come for me?
ALL: We will see you out.

(YURANOSUKE *crosses up the steps and stands at the top. He gestures for* OKARU *to join him there and for* HEIEMON *to pick up the nearly dead* KUDAYŪ. *Music stops.*)

YURANOSUKE: Heiemon. Take our drunken friend to the Kamo River. Let him drown his sorrows . . . in the waters there!

(YURANOSUKE *flicks open his fan and raises it overhead.* OKARU *kneels beside* YURANOSUKE, *placing her hands on his sash.* HEIEMON *drapes* KUDAYŪ'*s limp body over his shoulder. A single sharp clack of the* ki. *They freeze in a group* mie *pose. Ki clacks accelerate, drum beats speed up, and offstage "Odoriji Aikata" crescendoes as the curtain is slowly pushed closed.*)

SCENE II
Vendetta

Two sharp ki *clacks: large drum softly beats "Yuki Oto" ("Snow Sound"). The* ki *clacks accelerate to accompany the opening of the curtain. The scene is the garden of* MORONAO'*s mansion in Edo. It is night. Snow is falling. Rocks, trees, ground, and small bridge across a pond are covered with a mantle of white. Soft, rapid* tsuke *beats. Several* WOMEN *from* MORONAO'*s household rush on from the left. They are wearing nightclothes. Frightened and confused they urge each other to flee. They disappear. Drum and* tsuke *beats crescendo. Two* RETAINERS *with drawn swords rush on from the right. They pose.*

MORONAO'S RETAINER: I am Riku Handayū, retainer of Moronao. Name yourself!
HANGAN'S RETAINER: Akagaki Genzō, loyal to Enya Hangan. Let me pass!

(*They pose. Another two* RETAINERS *run on from the left.*)

MORONAO'S RETAINER: You will burn in hell before you 5 touch Lord Moronao!
HANGAN'S RETAINER: I, Katayama Genta, will take his head for Lord Hangan! Stand aside!

(*Large drum pattern of triple beats, "Mitsudaiko," and loud continuous* tsuke *beats. The paired opponents fight: they slash and parry with their long swords. In the end* HANGAN'*s men gain the upper hand;* MORONAO'*s men turn and are pursued off stage. Drumming changes to quiet "Snow Sound."* SHIMIZU *enters on the* hanamichi. *He is a famous swordsman hired by* MORONAO *as a bodyguard. A woman's kimono is draped over his head as a disguise, to allow him to reach the side of his master without being detained by* HANGAN'*s men. He stops at the seven-three position.*)

SHIMIZU: The war drum. Yuranosuke has come at last. But he will not succeed. The moon shall see the severed heads of 10 forty-seven rōnin before it witnesses the death of Lord Moronao!

(SHIMIZU *rushes on stage. He meets* TAKEMORI, *one of* HANGAN'*s men. They circle each other warily.* SHIMIZU'*s swords are seen.*)

TAKEMORI: Stop! Who are you?
SHIMIZU: (*Dropping the kimono to his waist.*) I am Shimizu Ichigaku, protector of Lord Moronao. 15
TAKEMORI: And I am Takemori Kitahachi! I've come for Moronao's head!
SHIMIZU: Then you must take mine first.
TAKEMORI: Come, fight! Fight!

(*"Mitsudaiko" drumming, loud* tsuke *beats, and "Chuuya Aikata" samisen music accompany the battle.* TAKEMORI *attacks, rushing past*

SHIMIZU. SHIMIZU *throws tiny daggers at* TAKEMORI, *who falls to the ground to evade. One of* HANGAN's *spearmen rushes on from the right, forcing* SHIMIZU *away from* TAKEMORI. SHIMIZU *is attacked from both sides. He slips free and runs onto the bridge over the pond. He is attacked by spear and sword simultaneously.* TAKEMORI *reaches under his guard and stabs* SHIMIZU *in the chest. A second slash, down his back, sends* SHIMIZU *toppling into the water of the pond and out of sight. Drum crescendoes. A loud whistle is heard off left. It signals* MORONAO's *capture.* MORONAO *is dragged on by several of* HANGAN's *men. He is thrown to the ground. He wears nothing except a white sleeping kimono. He is unarmed.* YURANOSUKE, RIKIYA, GOEMON, HEIEMON, *and other* RETAINERS *enter. They surround* MORONAO, *watching him carefully.* YURANOSUKE *kneels beside* MORONAO *politely.*)

20   YURANOSUKE: We allow you to die, Moronao, by your own hand . . . with this blade.

(*He unwraps* HANGAN's *suicide dagger and respectfully places it before* MORONAO, *offering him the opportunity to die with honor, instead of being killed.* MORONAO *is shaking with fright. He picks up the dagger as if to kill himself, then lunges at* YURANOSUKE. *Seizing* MORONAO's *wrist,* YURANOSUKE *turns the dagger against* MORONAO *and plunges it into his breast.* MORONAO *cries out once, then falls back dead. The* RETAINERS *form a ring around* MORONAO, *hiding him from view.* TAKEMORI *raises his sword and with a single stroke cuts off* MORONAO's *head. Two loud* tsuke *beats. It is wrapped in a white cloth and held high at the end of a spear.* MORONAO *moves offstage unseen behind a black cloth held by a* STAGE ASSISTANT. *The* RETAINERS *rise triumphantly.*)

YURANOSUKE: You have fought bravely, all of you. Your years of hardship, endured without thought of self, have brought success to our cherished plan. What joy Lord Hangan's spirit must feel for your deeds. On his behalf I thank you.   25
GOEMON: And now, let us bring Moronao's head to our master!

(*Spoken lightly, the lines are in poetic phrases of seven and five syllables.*)

YURANOSUKE: Deep concerns like drifted snow, melt in the clear of day . . .
RIKIYA: . . . at last our long awaited, vengeance is achieved . . .   30
GOEMON: . . . together with the clearing, of the morning clouds . . .
AGAKI: . . . at the cock's crow announcing, dawn of a new day . . .
TAKEMORI: . . . our hearts filled to overflowing, rise with the   35
rising sun . . .
GOEMON: . . . as we go together to . . .
ALL: . . . our Lord Hangan's grave.
YURANOSUKE: Shout victory together! Victory!

(*Single* ki *clack: offstage drum and* samisen *play "Taka no Hara" ("Hawk Plain") slowly, gradually accelerating until the scene is over. Each person turns to those next to him, nods, wipes tears of gratitude, grips an elbow, or places a hand on a shoulder. Then their thoughts return to their master,* HANGAN, *and all of them stand silent, posed in mingled happiness and grief. The curtain closes to rapidly accelerating* ki *clacks. The offstage musicians play "Shagiri" indicating the play is over.*)

CRITICAL CONTEXTS

ZEAMI MOTOKIYO (1363–1444)

from "A Mirror Held to the Flower" (1424)

TRANSLATED BY J. THOMAS RIMER AND YAMAZAKI MASAKAZU

Although Zeami's treatises describe the practical and esthetic foundations of the Noh (Nō) theater, they were not well known until the twentieth century. Since the Noh was organized around prominent families of actors, Zeami's texts were passed on in private and shown only to those who had been properly initiated. The first definitive edition of the treatises was published in 1940.

In "A Mirror Held to the Flower," Zeami discusses the training of Noh performers, emphasizing the interplay between physical training, spiritual development, and acting style in the production of the "flower"—beauty—in Noh performance. In this translation, the central term yugen has been translated as "Grace." Although Zeami's language can seem remote to modern students, it is important to pay attention to the ways his understanding of acting relates to the process of Noh drama. How would you relate the kind of skills and attention that Zeami describes here to the demands of Noh drama?

An actor must not only rehearse thoroughly with his teachers but he must learn through practice to imitate their peerless performances. Indeed, it is precisely because the art of these great performers has been brought to the highest levels of training that they can present in their acting an appearance of total mastery and ease, thus fascinating their audiences. If a beginner wishes merely to imitate this level of accomplishment, he may seem to achieve its semblance, yet there will be nothing moving in his performance. A truly great artist has for many years succeeded in training both his body and his spirit; he can hold back much of his potential in reserve and perform in an easy fashion, so that only seven-tenths of his art is visible. If a beginner tries to perform in this fashion, without the proper practice, he will only imitate what he can observe, and so his spirit and his performance can not reach beyond that seven-tenths he can grasp. What is more, his own progress will be blocked.

Therefore, when a student is learning his craft, the teacher should show not his own high level of ability [in which there is a reserve of artistry], but, as he did when he too was a beginner, indicate to his pupils how to use fully both their minds and bodies. After such lessons have been absorbed the students will gradually reach a level of mastery and attain a level of ease in their own performances, understand how to hold in reserve a certain amount of their own physical energy, and grasp of themselves the principle that "what is felt by the heart is ten, what appears in movement seven."

UNDERSTANDING THE PROPER MEANING OF LEARNING OUR ART

In general, a performance of Perfect Fluency cannot be imitated. And if an actor makes an attempt to imitate it, the very effort involved in the attempt will produce a tension that cannot be a part of Perfect Fluency. Only something that is meant to appear difficult can actually be imitated. "The truth and what looks like it are two different things,"[1] it is said. Thus, could there be any way to imitate the truth of the master actor's easy performance? Indeed, ease and difficulty are two aspects of the same thing. There is a separate teaching on this matter. The means by which a student learns from a teacher are well known, and so no special comment is needed here. However, the teacher's official certification of the student must be based on a thorough examination of his capacities and devotion; otherwise, certification should not be given. If the student's basic abilities are insufficient, no certification is possible. Should certification be given when talent is lacking, a level of accomplishment is suggested that cannot actually be matched. The certification will be fraudulent and the results meaningless; therefore, it should not be given. In the *Book of Changes* it is written that "if suitable teachings are given to those who are not suitable, the hatred of Heaven will be aroused."[2] In order that such a suitable person can be created, three conditions must be present. First, he must possess himself the requisite talent. Secondly, he must adore his art and show a total dedication to the path of *Nō*. Thirdly, he must have a teacher capable of showing him the proper way. If these three conditions cannot be met, the candidate will not be suitable. A suitable person is one who has the capacity to achieve the highest reaches of his art, to be recognized himself as a teacher.

---

[1] A popular saying found in many texts circulated in this period.

[2] The quotation as recorded here does not appear in the *Book of Changes* (*I ching*).

When I observe the artistic abilities of young perform-ers now, it appears that "skipping"[3] has become common-place. This situation comes about because they imitate without study. An actor must begin by studying the Two Ba-sic Arts and the Three Role Types, continue to practice all that is appropriate for his age, and carry on his studies in the proper sequence, so that he will reach a stage of mas-tery in all the arts of the *Nō* that can permit him to perform in any artistic style. To learn only by imitation and so only manage a temporary resolution seems indeed to represent a kind of "skipping." For example, when studying the Two Ba-sic Arts, one must not study the Three Role Types. When the time comes to study the Three Role Types, one must put off for a certain time the study of military roles [as they de-mand intense physical effort]. When an actor does come to study the military roles, then the demon roles in both the Delicacy within Strength and Rough styles of movement should be put off for a certain time, since there is an ap-propriate moment to learn them as well. To attempt to learn all these roles at once—what a terribly difficult thing it would be. And the degree of difficulty would be unex-pectedly high. Therefore, even if by "skipping" a young per-former manages to fool the public into thinking that he is a master, he will achieve a momentary Flower. And as such an artist grows older, his art will decline. And even should his art not decline, it would be impossible for him to achieve true renown. This point must be firmly kept in mind.

Concerning "skipping," there is another matter to con-sider. If an actor is inordinately fond of new plays, and should he come step by step to abandon the older repertory he per-formed in the past, he can never master the art of *Nō* and will only be "skipping." Rather, the actor must fix a repertory of standard plays at which he excels and then mix new plays in with them. If he plays only fresh pieces and neglects the plays to which he is accustomed, the results, in terms of the art of the *Nō,* will be a disgraceful "skipping" indeed. Be-sides, if only unusual pieces are performed, then that proce-dure of itself loses its novelty. If a mixture of old and new is achieved, then both the old and the new alike will seem novel. Such becomes the undying flower. As Confucius said, "He who by reanimating the Old can gain knowledge of the New is fit to be a teacher."[4]

HAVING A REAL UNDERSTANDING OF SKILL

If an actor has become fully proficient at music and dance, he may be called skillful. If he has not become fully accom-plished, there will be no denying his shortcomings. On the other hand, there is a kind of real skill based on still different considerations. For example, there are actors whose abilities in dance and chant show no shortcomings, yet who have not achieved a high reputation. Then again, there are actors whose voices are not attractive and whose mastery of danc-ing and singing show defects, yet who are widely thought of as accomplished performers. The reason for this is that both dancing and gesture are external skills. The essentials of our art lie in the spirit. They represent a true enlightenment es-tablished through art. Thus, if an actor knows how to create interest and can perform from an understanding of this spirit, he will gain a reputation as a fine actor even if he has not mastered every aspect of his craft. Such being the case, if an actor really wants to become a master, he cannot simply depend on his skill in dance and gesture. Rather, mas-tery seems to depend on the actor's own state of self-understanding and the sense of style with which he has been blessed. Real discernment of the nature of the differences between external skill and interior understanding forms the basis of true mastery. Thus it is that an actor who has merely perfected his technique will have little of interest to show. Other actors, from the beginning of their careers, can fasci-nate their audiences. So it is that an actor, from the time he is young until he masters seven-tenths, eight-tenths, even all of his technique and reaches the level of a master, will continue to interest others for quite separate considerations.

Still higher than the level of interest, there is a level of skill that will simply make the audience gasp, without reflec-tion, in surprise and pleasure. This level will be termed one of a pure Feeling that Transcends Cognition. The response to such a performance is such that there is no occasion for re-flection, no time for a spectator to realize how well the per-formance is contrived. Such a state might be referred to as "purity unmixed."[5] In the *Book of Changes,* when the Chinese character for "feeling" (*kan*) is written, the element that stands for "mind" (*kokoro*) is eliminated [and the character is written as] in order to illustrate the fact that when true feel-ing is involved, there is no room in the concept for reflection as a function of the mind.[6]

[3]"Skipping" (*tendoku*) was a term originally used to mean "turning the *sutras,*" chanting the first few lines and then skipping the rest to save time, as a kind of devotional exercise. Zeami of course uses the term ironically.

[4]See Arthur Waley, *The Analects of Confucius,* Book II, No. 11, page 90.

[5]A term sometimes used to indicate the high level of excel-lence in *waka* poetry. The term is probably of Zen origin.

[6]For a translation into English of this section of the *I ching,* see Richard Wilhelm, tr., *The I Ching or Book of Changes,* pages 122–125. The interpretation of the passage is evidently Zeami's.

Thus it is that the actor comes to possess various levels of artistic skill. If a beginning actor continues on through all the various stages of his training, he will be called a good actor, but not necessarily anything more. Yet there is still a higher level where real mastery is possible. If the spectators are truly fascinated with an actor's performance, he can be said to have reached the level of a master. If, in addition, he possesses the ability to create for his audience an intensity of pure feeling that goes beyond the workings of the mind, he will have achieved the level of greatest reputation. Thus an actor should pursue his study of *Nō* through these various levels, develop his skills, and through his own spiritual understanding, bring his art to the highest possible level of fulfillment.

SHALLOW AND DEEP

Concerning *Nō* performance, there is one matter that must be given particularly serious consideration. If a performance is given without sufficient attention to detail, it will be without interest. On the other hand, if too much attention is given by the performer to details, the whole performance risks to shrink in scale. Then again, if the actor thinks to play his part as liberally as possible, the opportunities for the audience to witness his skill will be fewer, and there will be a tendency for his performance to become slow and monotonous. An understanding of this distinction is of the greatest importance. An actor might, on first reflection, think that the parts of the play requiring intricate skills should be played in as complex a fashion as possible, while those moments requiring a more general approach should be played as broadly as possible. Yet in fact this kind of distinction cannot be made unless an actor knows the art of *Nō* very well indeed. A student must question his teacher closely on such matters, so that these distinctions become clear. There is, however, one general principle that can be kept in mind. For the chant, the dance, and the various sorts of gestures that will be employed, the actor's spirit should be as delicately attuned as possible, but, at the same time, his physical stance should be as relaxed and broad as possible. An actor must comprehend these principles and stick to them.

In general, it can be said that, in the case of the *Nō*, an art that is based on general and flexible principles can be made subtle and detailed. But a *Nō* that is merely meticulous in conception cannot easily develop on a large and relaxed scale. After all, the small can be contained in the large, but not the large in the small. A great deal of skill needs to be given over to this matter. A *Nō* that possesses both these qualities will truly be full and rich. Indeed, when ice formed during the deep cold melts, the ice formed during a brief chilly spell will melt as well.

ENTERING THE REALM OF GRACE

The aesthetic quality of Grace is considered the highest ideal of perfection in many arts. Particularly in the *Nō,* Grace can be regarded as the highest principle. However, although the quality of Grace is manifested in performance and audiences give it high appreciation, there are very few actors who in fact possess that quality. This is because they have never had a taste of the real Grace themselves. So it is that few actors have entered this world.

What kind of realm is represented by what is termed Grace? For example, if we take the general appearance of the world and observe the various sorts of people who live there, it might be said that Grace is best represented in the character of the nobility, whose deportment is of such a high quality and who receive the affection and respect not given to others in society. If such is the case, then their dignified and mild appearance represents the essence of Grace. Therefore, the stage appearance of Grace is best indicated by their refined and elegant carriage. If an actor examines closely the nobility's beautiful way of speaking and studies the words and habitual means of expression that such elevated persons use, even to observing their tasteful choice of language when saying the smallest things, such can be taken to represent the Grace of speech. In the case of the chant, when the melody flows smoothly and naturally on the ear and sounds suitably mild and calm, this quality can be said to represent the Grace of music. In the case of the dance, if the actor studies until he is truly fluent, so that his appearance on stage will be sympathetic and his carriage both unostentatious and moving to those who observe him, he will surely manifest the Grace of the dance. When he is acting a part, if he makes his appearance beautiful in the Three Role Types, he will have achieved Grace in his performance. Again, when presenting a role of fearsome appearance, a demon's role for example, even should the actor use a rough manner to a certain extent, he must not forget to preserve a graceful appearance, and he must remember the principles of "what is felt in the heart is ten," and "violent body movements, gentle foot movements," so that his stage appearance will remain elegant. Thus he may manifest the Grace of a demon's role.

An actor must come to grasp those various types of Grace and absorb them within himself; for no matter what kind of role he may assume, he must never separate himself from the virtue of Grace. No matter what the role—whether the character be of high or low rank, a man, a woman, a priest or lay person, a farmer or country person, even a beggar or an outcast—it should seem as though each were holding a branch of flowers in his hand. In this one respect they exhibit the same appeal, despite whatever differences they may show in their social positions. This Flower represents the beauty of their stance in the *nō,* and the ability to reveal this kind of stance in performance represents, of course, its spirit. In order to study the Grace of words, the actor must study the art of composing poetry; and to study the Grace of physical appearance, he must study the aesthetic qualities of elegant costume, so that, in every aspect of his art, no matter how the role may change that the actor is playing, he will always maintain one aspect in his performance that shows Grace. Such it is to know the seed of Grace.

However, it may well happen that an actor will put such an importance on his impersonation of the particulars of his role, regarding this aspect of his performance as the highest of his art, that he will neglect to maintain the beauty of the stance he has properly assumed. Thus he will fail to enter the world of Grace. And if he does not enter into the world of Grace, he cannot approach the level of Highest Fruition. And unless he reaches this highest level of accomplishment, he will never be recognized as a great actor. There are indeed few masters who have attained those heights. Thus an actor must rehearse with the utmost diligence on this critical point of the representation of Grace.

This Highest Fruition of an actor represents precisely the appearance of this deeply beautiful posture. I cannot repeat too often that an actor must rehearse with the need for the proper preparation of his body always in mind. Thus it is of crucial importance that, beginning with the Two Basic Arts down to the specifics of any role that may be played, the stance of the actor be attractive so as to represent this Highest Fruition in every circumstance. If the actor's posture is unattractive, his art will invariably appear vulgar. In any case, whatever gestures may be seen or music may be heard, however great the variety, the fact that the actor's stance is beautifully assumed represents the true attainment of Grace. An actor may be said to have entered the world of Grace when he has of his own accord studied these principles and made himself master of them. If an actor does not work to fulfill them and thinks that, without mastering every aspect of his art, he can still try to attain this Grace, he will, in fact, never know it during his entire lifetime.

PAYING HEED TO THE ACCUMULATION OF SKILLS

Studying the art of the *Nō,* having the reputation of a superior actor, and rising in merit as the years pass by depends on a proper accumulation of skills. Yet the nature of such an accumulation will differ depending on where the actor lives and performs. Even if he earns a reputation as a fine actor, if the praise he earns is not from those who live in the capital, it can have little significance for him. Even an actor who has earned genuine praise in the capital, should he return to his native place and continue to perform in the countryside, will merely expend his energies in attempting not to forget those means of expression that he learned in the capital, and because of his false sense that he still remembers how to perform properly, he will little by little slacken in his persistence in maintaining his beauty of performance. The result will be an accumulation of bad experiences. Such a stagnation of experience must be shunned.

In the capital, on the other hand, the actor will be performing before discerning spectators so that, should he become careless concerning any element in his art and so fail to progress, he will soon notice a response from his audience; then too, as criticism and comment come to him, he will eventually disregard the unsatisfactory elements in his art, accumulate only positive artistic experiences, and discover that his art has become polished. Of its own accord his skill will become as burnished as a jewel. There is a saying that "sagebrush, which has the ability to bend, even should it grow up among flax plants, will come out straight, without correction, while white sand, when mixed with earth, will become black like the rest."[7] Thus by living in the capital, an actor is in the proper environment, and the insufficiencies in his art will naturally disappear. This gradual lessening of error is in itself the accumulation of good experience. There is no way that an artist can simply set out to pile up these experiences of his own accord. Rather, let me repeat again and again a warning that, if an actor does not take cognizance of his good experiences, they will stagnate and turn into an accumulation of bad experiences.

So it is that even a skilled performer as he grows older will come to depend on his increasingly old-fashioned art, which has become so through an accumulation caused by his own stagnation. Although audiences may dislike his performances, he thinks only that he has been recognized as an artist of great merit for a long time. Thus he does not recognize the real feelings of his audiences. He therefore loses the chance to make his final appearances on the stage successful—such an important opportunity in an actor's career.

All of this is the result of piling up of such bad experiences. The greatest caution must be taken against this.

CONNECTING ALL THE ARTS THROUGH ONE INTENSITY OF MIND

It is often commented on by audiences that "many times a performance is effective when the actor does nothing." Such an accomplishment results from the actor's greatest, most

---

[7]An expression widely circulated during the medieval period in various forms, probably originating in the writings of Tseng Ts'an, one of the most important disciples of Confucius.

secret skill. From the techniques involved in the Two Basic Arts down to all the gestures and the various kinds of Role Playing, all such skills are based on the abilities found in the actor's body. Thus to speak of an actor "doing nothing" actually signifies that interval which exists between two physical actions. When one examines why this interval "when nothing happens" may seem so fascinating, it is surely because of the fact that, at the bottom, the artist never relaxes his inner tension. At the moment when the dance has stopped, or the chant has ceased, or indeed at any of those intervals that can occur during the performance of a role, or, indeed, during any pause or interval, the actor must never abandon his concentration but must keep his consciousness of that inner tension. It is this sense of inner concentration that manifests itself to the audience and makes the moment enjoyable.

However, it is wrong to allow an audience to observe the actor's inner state of control directly. If the spectators manage to witness this, such concentration will merely become another ordinary skill or action, and the feeling in the audience that "nothing is happening" will disappear.

The actor must rise to a selfless level of art, imbued with a concentration that transcends his own consciousness, so that he can bind together the moments before and after that instant when "nothing happens." Such a process constitutes that inner force that can be termed "connecting all the arts through one intensity of mind."

"Indeed, when we come to face death, our life might be likened to a puppet on a cart (decorated for a great festival). As soon as one string is cut, the creature crumbles and fades."[8] Such is the image given of the existence of man, caught in the perpetual flow of life and death. This constructed puppet, on a cart, shows various aspects of himself but cannot come to life of itself. It represents a deed performed by moving strings. At the moment when the strings are cut, the figure falls and crumbles. *Sarugaku* too is an art that makes use of just such artifice. What supports these illusions and gives them life is the intensity of mind of the actor. Yet the existence of this intensity must not be shown directly to the audience. Should they see it, it would be as though they could see the strings of a puppet. Let me repeat again: the actor must make his spirit the strings, and without letting his audience become aware of them, he will draw together the forces of his art. In that way, true life will reside in his *Nō*.

In general, such attitudes need not be limited to the moments involved in actual performance. Morning and night alike, and in all the activities of daily life, an actor must never abandon his concentration, and he must retain his resolve.

_____
[8]A saying attributed to a priest of the Rinzai sect of Zen Buddhism in Japan, Gettan Sowkow (1316?–1389).

Thus, if without ever slackening, he manages to increase his skills, his art of the *Nō* will grow ever greater. This particular point represents one of the most secret of all the teachings concerning our art. However, in actual rehearsal, there must be within this concentration some variations of tension and relaxation.

THE MOMENT OF PEERLESS CHARM

The character *myō* in the term *myōsho* [Peerless Charm] means "exquisite" or "delicate." But it also has the meaning of an appearance that transcends any specific form. Such a transcendence of form represents an expression of this Peerless Charm.

When one speaks of such moments in terms of the *Nō*, this Charm should exist in every aspect of our art, from the Two Basic Arts to gesture. Yet precisely where can it be located? It seems to be found nowhere. If an actor can possess this arresting power, he must be a performer of surpassing skill. However, if an actor is truly blessed with great talent, he will show from his beginnings some shadow of this Charm. The actor will not himself be conscious of it, but spectators of discernment will always find this quality within him. Ordinary spectators, on the other hand, will merely find that his performances are enjoyable in some mysterious fashion. And indeed even in the case of an actor of the highest skill, he will at best have come only to the realization that he somehow does possess this skill. Still, he will have no consciousness that he is practicing it at any given moment. An actor will possess this quality precisely because he does not recognize it; if such a moment could in any way be put into words, this Charm could no longer exist.

When one ponders carefully the substance of this Peerless Charm, can it not be said that an artist may approach it when he has truly learned his craft and attained Perfect Fluency, when he has transcended all stages of his art to the point where he performs everything with ease and exhibits every skill without care, thus achieving a selfless art that rises above any artifice? When an actor manages to ascend to the aesthetic level of Grace, will he indeed not be somewhat closer to this power of beauty? These matters must be pondered deeply.

JUDGING THE *NŌ*

When it comes to making crucial judgments concerning the *Nō*, people invariably have different ideas. It is difficult indeed for any particular *Nō* to match the tastes of everyone. Thus the basis of judgment should be made on the strength of the performances of accomplished actors who enjoy a wide reputation.

First of all, one should look and listen with great care during actual performances so as to understand why some plays succeed and why others do not. Plays that succeed possess three qualities: Sight, Sound, and Heart.

As for the *Nō* that succeeds through Sight, the stage atmosphere will be colorful from the beginning, the dancing and music will have an attractive air, the spectators, noblemen and commoners alike, will be spontaneous in their praise, the atmosphere brilliant. Such is the *Nō* that is effective to the eye. It goes without saying that such a performance will please the discriminating; even those who know nothing of the *Nō* will find such a performance enjoyable. However, concerning such performances, there is one point that an actor must keep in mind. If the performance passes by altogether too well and with too much appeal, and if every aspect seems enjoyable, then the feelings of the audience will tend to become over-stimulated, and their sensibilities in appreciating the details of the acting will be coarsened. For this part, an actor may be impetuous and, since he wants to exhaust every aspect of his art, will make no allowance for a slackening of pace, either for himself or for the audience. In an attempt to make every aspect of the performance successful, a surface brilliance is achieved, but the end results may be unsatisfactory. This kind of abuse arises when the play goes too well. On such an occasion, the play should be performed in a more restrained manner, all the artistic appearances made more moderate, and the eyes and ears of the spectators given some surcease, so that they can have an occasion to rest and breathe easily and the audience can be given the quiet necessary to observe the really skillful elements in the performance. Then, if the results are successful, the plays that follow will seem stronger, so that, whatever the number of plays that may be staged, their fascination for the audience will never be exhausted. So it is that an effective *Nō* performance can be said to succeed through the art of Sight.

Nō that can be said to succeed through Sound shows from the very beginning a serious atmosphere. The music and text are chosen in accord with the season [and the time of day], thus creating a gentle, relaxed, and enjoyable effect. Above all, it is the chant that should create the main impression. Only a peerless artist of highest experience can achieve this effect during a performance. However, the kind of sober flavor engendered by such a performance cannot be understood by country audiences and the like.

This kind of *Nō,* when performed by a peerless actor, can give rise through his spiritual resources to various aesthetic qualities that make the play become more and more enjoyable as it goes along. In the case of an artist of the second rank, however, whose art has not fully matured, he will cause the day's performance to lag if he decides to follow such a presentation by a famous actor with one of his own in a *Nō* that is also of this particular variety. When such a player follows the kind of performance that has successfully created a cool and quiet atmosphere, as he continues on he will only create a gloomy mood in the succeeding plays. An actor must be aware of this difficulty and put his energies into his performance in order to begin to increase the number of stimulating moments in the play, so as to bring an element of surprise to his audience. Of course, as a truly peerless player has naturally a wide repertory and is highly trained in body and mind, his art will be effectively manifested in his dance and chant, so that his performance will naturally progress in an enjoyable manner. A player of the second rank, however, must take great care so that, as the performance continues, the atmosphere does not go dead. Concerning this point, when thinking to keep up the atmosphere of his performance, the actor must not reveal his methods to the audience. The spectators must merely feel that the performance is enjoyable. Such is the actor's secret, based on long-mastered precedents as to how to perform successfully. All I have written above can explain how a *Nō* can succeed through Sound.

When it comes to the *Nō* that succeeds through the Heart, a truly gifted actor of *sarugaku,* after he has mastered the whole repertory, will have the ability even when performing a play of no particular distinction in terms of chant, dance, gesture, or plot, to create even in the midst of a certain dullness a particular poetic quality that can move the hearts of his audience. This level of attainment is not usually grasped even by connoisseurs; how much more beyond any imaginings of a country audience must be such an art. Indeed, such a quality must seem to represent the propitious manifestation of an actor of the highest abilities. Such a performance can be termed a *Nō* that succeeds through the Heart, a *Nō* that surpasses technique, a *Nō* that transcends outward manifestation.

An actor must learn to discriminate between the kinds of artistic qualities that display those various differences. There are spectators of discernment who do not really understand the art of the *Nō*. On the other hand, there are those spectators who possess a true grasp of the essential nature of the *Nō* but who cannot observe subtle differences. Those who have both a practical and a theoretical understanding of *Nō* represent the highest level of spectator. For example, there are occasions when a fine performance does not meet with success, and times when an unskilled performance pleases, but no one must use these exceptions as a basis for one's general judgments. For example, truly gifted players customarily have success with outdoor and other large-scale performances, while lesser actors perform profitably at smaller playing areas at country fairs or on other such occasions.

An actor who understands how to make his performance attractive to his audience brings good fortune to the *Nō*.

Then too, a spectator who understands the heart of the actor as he watches a performance is a gifted spectator. The following might be said concerning making judgments: forget the specifics of a performance and examine the whole. Then forget the performance and examine the actor. Then forget the actor and examine his inner spirit. Then, forget that spirit, and you will grasp the nature of the *Nō*.

THE MATTER OF MASTERING THE CHANT

There are two aspects to the study of the chant. The person who composes the text should know the principles of music and how to make the words flow together in a euphonious fashion. For his part, the performer who sings must know how to fit the melody to the words and to chant the syllables and words in a clear and correct manner. Since the beauty of the chant derives from the syllables and the words performed, the melodies must be composed in such a way that the pronunciation is always correctly represented, and the linking between the phrases smooth and flexible. When the chant is performed, if the singer has mastered these principles and really knows them well, both the composition and the performance will reinforce each other and produce an enjoyable effect. As this is true, a standard should be established by which the melody is attached to the chant. The flow of the phrases must be attractive, and the sound characteristics of the text must be in harmony with the melody, so that the results will of themselves be musical. That is, the melody provides the basic frame for the musical composition, and the artistic effect derives from the spirit of the performer, who shades the melody in terms of the flow of the phrases. Thus an actor has various elements of music that he must master—the physical problems of using the breath, the development of his own emotional concentration in order to direct it properly, and the understanding of the melody, as well as the music that lies behind the melody. In terms of practicing the musical aspects of *Nō*, the following should be taken to heart: forget the voice and understand the shading of the melody. Forget the melody and understand the pitch. Forget the pitch and understand the rhythm.

In learning the art of musical performance, there is a proper order to be followed: first, the words of the text must be learned thoroughly; then the melody must be mastered; then the actor must learn how to color the melody; finally, he must learn how to apply the proper pitch accent. After all these steps are taken, the actor must concentrate on how to bring his performances to flower. At every stage, an emphasis must be placed on the rhythm. When practicing the voice, miss no occasion to obtain this kind of training, so beneficial to personal development.

Then there is the matter of accent in musical performance. In the case of auxiliary words or particles, the prob-

lem is not a serious one. However, mistaken accents on such substantive words as nouns, verbs, and adjectives[9] are harmful. Understanding the importance of this distinction is crucial. Serious study must be given to this point. When speaking of mistaken accents on these substantive words, I refer to pronunciations with improper pitch accent, which affect the meaning of the words. In the case of particles and auxiliary words, the problem has to do with the voicing of such sounds as *te, ni, ha,* and the like. Concerning correct pronunciation for these sounds, when the flow of words in the course of the singing moves effectively, even if the pronunciation becomes altered to some extent, so long as the rhythm is correct, the problem is not a serious one. It is said that words that make a heavy or a light effect, that are clear or complex in sound, depend on the forward flow of the text. In addition, there are various customs and rules concerning sound changes when words are juxtaposed together. Study the transmitted teachings carefully on this matter. As concerns particles that come at the end of phrases, such as *ha, ni, no, o, ka, te, mo, shi,* and so forth, even if there should be some deviation in their pronunciation, there will be nothing disagreeable in the sound as long as the melody is tasteful. In other words, the movement of the melody should be supported by these various particles. In the chanting, every syllable must not simply be pronounced in a flat manner, with an equal length and emphasis given to all of them. Those sounds which represent substantive words should be pronounced briskly, so that their meaning remains clear, while the sound of the auxiliary syllables can be rather freely regulated—slow or fast—in order to make the melody more colorful.

[Remember that] the principle of using four basic tones is used [in Chinese].[10]

In *The History of the Former Han* by Pan Ku,[11] it is written [concerning the legendary origin of the melody] that "as for the origins of the twelve-pitch gamut, a man [named Ling

---

[9]That is, independent, uninflected words usually written with Chinese characters.

[10]Zeami doubtless wished to stress the importance of proper pitch accent for substantive words in Japanese, usually written in Chinese characters, by this reference to the Chinese language. For a concise description of the function of tones in classical Chinese, see James J.Y. Liu, *The Art of Chinese Poetry*, pages 21–22.

[11]Pan Ku's history was the first of the so-called dynastic histories of China. For a general description of the text and its subject matter, see Burton Watson, *Early Chinese Literature*, pages 103–109. Zeami's quotation contains minor errors. For an explanation of the significance of the passage in the history of Chinese music, see Kenneth J. DeWoskin, *A Song for One or Two*, pages 59–61.

Lun] climbed Mount Kun-lun and, hearing the voice of the male and female phoenix, created the six *ryo* pitches and six *ritsu* pitches of the twelve-pitch gamut." *Ritsu,* since it is derived from the voice of the male phoenix, represents the principle of *yang. Ryo,* which imitates the voice of the female phoenix, represents *yin. Ritsu* represents the kind of sound that goes from high to low, and the breath is inhaled. *Ryo* represents a sound that goes from low to high, and the breath is exhaled. Breathing appropriate to *ritsu* is produced through a state of tension; *ryo* is produced in a state of ease. Then too, *ritsu* can be considered as appropriate to Non-Being, *ryo* appropriate to Being. Thus, a thin, high voice [a "vertical" voice] is appropriate for *ritsu,* while a thick, low voice [a "horizontal" voice] is appropriate for *ryo.*

In the *Analects,*[12] it is written that "the hides of the bear, the tiger, and the panther are used as targets [for the hunter's] arrow. The tiger is the prince's target, the panther the nobleman's target, and the bear the target of the officers of state." If this sequence is followed, it would doubtless be correct to write "tiger, panther, bear." But for the sake of euphony, the order is changed to "bear, tiger, and panther."

THE ULTIMATE KEYS OF OUR ART

The contents of this work have now all been set forth. There is nothing to learn in addition to what has been set down here. Indeed, there is nothing else involved but to "understand the *Nō*" with one's very being. If this fundamental principle is not observed, the various matters discussed here will serve no purpose. If an actor really wishes to master the *Nō,* he must set aside all other pursuits and truly give his whole soul to our art; then, as his learning increases and his experience grows, he will gradually of himself reach a level of awareness and so come to understand the *Nō.*

First of all, an actor must deeply believe what his teacher tells him and take those instructions to heart. The numerous teachings involved are contained in the various points discussed in this book, but the actor must truly master them and engrave them on his heart, so that, when he is actually in a performance, he can try out in practice the various things that he has learned. Then, as a result, he will value those principles, and, as he comes to revere the art of *Nō,* he will as time passes come to understand the real secret of success in our art. In whatever artistic pursuit, one studies and then understands, so that he will know how to carry out his art in ac-

---

[12]No such passage appears in the *Analects,* but a somewhat similar one does appear in the *Chou li* or *Rites of Chou.* Both this passage and the preceding section on *The History of the Former Han* were added to Zeami's text in the form of notes, and may not be by his hand.

tual practice. In *sarugaku* as well, one must study and learn, so that these various principles can be put into practice.

All these secret teachings can be summed up by saying that an actor must continually earn mastery through constant practice, from his apprenticeship through his old age. When I speak of studying through old age, I refer to the fact that from the time of an actor's apprenticeship until the peak of his maturity there are various arts that must be mastered. It is only from the time that an actor passes forty that he can slowly begin to make use of restraint in his physical performance. In other words, he must learn the means of artistic expression appropriate for an actor of his age. When the actor passes fifty, then he can begin to use the technique of "doing nothing." This represents a crucial stage in an actor's career. The first thing to learn at this point is the necessity to limit the kinds of plays in the actor's repertory. His musical performance now becomes the center of his style of performance, his acting style becomes simpler, and his dancing and gestures grow more restrained. He should only give a hint of his former colorful appearance. In fact, the art of music remains the one area in which an actor at this age can excel. This is true because an older voice will have exhausted its natural and untrained qualities, and the voice that remains will be highly polished, in whatever style of vocal production the actor may wish to use; thus whatever music is chanted, the results will always be enjoyable. This is a sure means to achieve a successful performance. Thus an older actor should learn carefully to make his age serve his own artistic purposes and work all the harder to train himself appropriately.

Concerning roles that can be played by older actors, old men and women are doubtless the most appropriate. However, depending on the strong points of a particular actor, he may not necessarily be limited to these two. Still, an actor who wishes to create an atmosphere of serenity in his performance will find the roles of older characters best suited to him. If his special strength lies in roles demanding energetic movement, however, those will not be suitable for the aesthetic qualities appropriate to the art of older actors. In any case, within these limits, he should perform his dances and gestures while limiting himself to six-tenths or seven-tenths of "what is felt by the heart is ten," so as to perform in a manner appropriate to his age. Such is the means to master the art suitable for the older actor.

In our Kanze school, there is one phrase that is of infinite value concerning the fundamentals of any artistic accomplishment: an actor must never forget the experiences he has undergone as a beginning artist. In the transmitted teaching, there are three explanations provided for this. Accordingly:

—He must never forget the fresh experiences he first went through as a young performer.

—At each level of accomplishment, there are new levels of fresh experience that the actor must encounter for the first time, as though he were a beginner, and then never forget.

—After the actor becomes older, there are still new stages of fresh experience that must never be forgotten.

Here are the teachings contained in these maxims in more detail.

Concerning the maxim that "he must never forget the fresh experiences he first went through as a young performer," it can be said that, if the actor retains the feelings he had at that time, he will profit from them in many ways as he grows older. As the expression has it, "an understanding of errors in the past will turn them into advantages in the future." Or, "seeing the cart in front turn over serves as a warning to the cart that follows." Forgetting the arts one has learned as a beginner amounts in fact to forgetting the skills an actor may possess at a later point in his career. The fact that his art has been perfected and his reputation has been made can only be the result of the development of his own skill. But if he does not take cognizance of how his skills have improved, he will unknowingly revert to the level he possessed as a beginner. Such a reversal means that his art is actually degenerating. His ability to maintain a sense of his present level of accomplishment shows that he has not forgotten the skills learned as a young performer. I cannot stress this principle too strongly: if an actor loses his memory of his unmatured skills, he will be forced to revert to them. On the other hand, if he does not forget them, his later accomplishments will be genuine. And, if they are genuine, his abilities, as they increase, will insure that his art can never retrogress. Thus, this truth can serve as a distinction between truth and error.

Young actors must therefore take cognizance of the current level of their accomplishment, realize that they are still only beginners, and understand that they must not lose sight of their own skills that still remain to be developed. In this way, they can truly work to lift the level of their art. To lose consciousness of the level of one's ability is to forget how to advance in the art; under such circumstances, an artist's skill will not increase. Therefore, young artists must never lose their perceptions of their actual level of ability.

Secondly, there is the principle that "at each level of accomplishment, there are new levels of fresh experience that the actor must encounter for the first time, as though he were a beginner, and then never forget." This means that, for the actor, from his beginnings through the height of his career and into his old age, there are always various suitable means of expression he must practice and learn. On all these occasions he can be seen as a beginner. Therefore, if at each stage he abandons and forgets what has come before, he will

only possess the artistic ability that matches what he is doing at that particular moment in his career. If, on the other hand, he has managed to maintain in himself all the skills that he has previously mastered, so that he can still make use of them, then he can perform in an ever-increasing variety of styles. These "new skills" refer to those he has learned for the first time at every successive stage in his career. Maintaining them all and combining them together at one time means that he has forgotten none of them. It is just through such efforts that a *shite* becomes an artist of wide-ranging abilities. Thus one must never forget what he has learned at each stage of his career.

Finally, "after the actor becomes older, there are still new stages of fresh experience that must never be forgotten." Truly, although there are limits on a human life, the *Nō* never comes to an end. If an actor has mastered every technique appropriate to each stage in his career, then when it comes time to learn what is correct for an older actor, he will still be able to enjoy a new experience even at this late stage in his career. If an actor still possesses this attitude when he reaches this high level, his art will still contain everything about the *Nō* that he has managed to learn before. When he passes the age of fifty, as I have said, an actor need have no other plan than to "do nothing special." To face the challenge of having no other technique than to "do nothing special"—is the art of an older actor really so different than that of a beginner?

So it is that if an actor manages to live his whole life without forgetting how and what he has learned at any one time in his career, the level of his art will steadily increase during his last years, and his abilities will never degenerate. To live one's life without ever exhausting the depths of the *Nō* represents the most profound principle of our school, a principle that must be passed on from child to grandchild, generation to generation as a secret teaching of our house. Passing on the importance of these attitudes I have described above will serve as a means to develop the artistry of all generations to come. On the other hand, if an actor forgets this "experience of a beginner," he will surely not be able to pass the conception along to others in later generations. An artist must not forget this "experience of a beginner," but must convey it to those who follow, for countless generations.

In addition to what I have written here, another who studies the *Nō* may, depending on his own abilities and discernment, be able to discover still other truths.

All of the *Teachings on Style and the Flower* (Zeami's treatise on Noh theater), beginning with the chapter called "The Practice of the *Nō* in Relation to the Age of the Actor" down to the "Separate Secret Teaching," is a secret document that makes clear the *Nō* by using the metaphor of the flower. That text represents an account of various elements in the art of my father Kan'ami, set down twenty years after his death, and serves as a record of what I learned from him. The present treatise, on the other hand, represents discoveries that have occurred to me from time to time concerning the *Nō* over a period of forty years, down to the time of my own advanced age. Summing them up, I have written out my observations in six sections and twenty parts,[13] which I leave behind as a memento of my art.

Ōe 31 [1424], 1st day of the 6th month

Zeami

---

[13]The indication of twenty parts suggests that the manuscript was originally arranged in some different fashion.

This teaching was passed on by Zeami himself for the succeeding generations of his house and should not be shown to actors from other troupes. Luckily, thanks to the Will of Heaven, which knows that my heart reveres the art of the *Nō*, this manuscript has come into my hands. This secret teaching forms the very core of the art of our school, and it has been written down to guide the art of our family. It is a text of fearsome power. Thus it must not be shown carelessly to others.

Eikyō 9 [1437], 8th month, 8th day

Komparu Zenchiku[14]

---

[14]Komparu's signature is an attribution; the identity of the writer is not altogether certain.

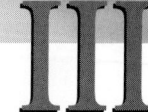

Medieval and Renaissance England

A performance of *The Tempest* at the new Shakespeare's Globe Theatre, on the Bankside in London. The theater is a meticulous reconstruction of the Globe Theatre of 1613.

T he fifteenth, sixteenth, and seventeenth centuries saw Europe transformed by the extraordinary cultural revolution we now call the European Renaissance. Fueled by new technology such as printing and by new scientific, political, and religious ideas, explosive change transformed European culture. The known world expanded beyond the sea to embrace the New World; the recovery of Greek and Latin literature spurred a sweeping intellectual revolution; strong centralized monarchies in Spain, Portugal, France, and England created new empires abroad and fought to control an increasingly restive populace at home; the Protestant Reformation undermined the religious and political authority of the Catholic church, beginning a period of violent religious conflict; and the "new philosophy"—modern science—of Copernicus, Bacon, and Galileo seemed to put even the physical world of heaven and earth in doubt. "'Tis all in pieces, all coherence gone," the poet John Donne wrote in 1611, voicing the profound anxiety and exhilaration of many of his contemporaries: "Prince, subject, father, son are things forgot. / For every man alone thinks that he hath got / To be a Phoenix." The changing tides of thought swept away the crumbling edifice of the medieval world—the feudal state, the universal church, scholastic philosophy, an ordered heaven, and revealed truth—and opened the way for the modern world.

This revolution also infused the theater; the Renaissance, especially in Italy, France, Spain, and England, is one of the great ages of theatrical and dramatic achievement. In England, the professional theater as we know it originated at this time: the history of the secular, profit-making, commercial theater is conventionally dated from the opening of the first theater building, The Theatre, in London in 1576. Licensed and protected as an aristocratic entertainment, the theater was also a popular institution in which commoners such as William Shakespeare, Richard Burbage, Edward Alleyn, Inigo Jones, and others, could indeed rise like the phoenix. However, to understand the revolutionary impact of theater and drama in Shakespeare's era, we need to understand their conservative inheritance, their deep indebtedness to the medieval stage that preceded them.

DRAMA AND THEATER IN MEDIEVAL ENGLAND

Dramatic performance in medieval Europe was thoroughly conditioned by the Catholic church's central role in the life of the community. Having closed the Roman theaters in the sixth century, the church maintained a vigilant opposition to the secular theater and the vices associated with it. Yet the revival of theater in Europe, beginning in the tenth century, was inspired and sponsored by the church itself. The four major dramatic forms in the late Middle Ages were connected with the church, its rituals, and its calendar of religious observances: LITURGICAL DRAMA enacted as part of the liturgy of the Catholic Mass; CYCLE PLAYS, illustrating scriptural history and performed by craft guilds on the feast of Corpus Christi; MORALITY DRAMA, enacting the symbolic structure of Christian life; and plays written and performed in schools and universities, sometimes imitating classical plays. In England, cycle and morality plays particularly influenced the later, secular drama of the sixteenth century.

Liturgical Drama

The earliest dramatic records, dating from the ninth century, are musical TROPES, brief elaborations of the authorized liturgy, written to amplify the scriptural text and enhance its impact and appeal. These compositions were set to music and sung in ANTIPHONAL

PERFORMANCE (back and forth, in dialogue) between monks or boy choristers to accompany the liturgy of the Mass. In England, Ethelwold, Bishop of Winchester, wrote a series of lessons concerning the conduct of the Mass, the *Regularis Concordia* (965–975), including instructions for such performances. What follows are his instructions to the priests for representing the visit of the three Marys to the tomb of Christ after the Crucifixion (translated from Latin). This trope is often called the *Quem Quaeritis,* after the Latin text spoken by the "angel": "Whom seek you?":

> While the third lesson is being chanted, let four brethren vest themselves; of whom, let one, vested in an alb, enter as if to take part in the service, and let him without being observed approach the place of the sepulchre [i.e., near the altar], and there, holding a palm in his hand, let him sit down quietly. While the third responsory is being sung, let the remaining three follow, all of them vested in copes, and carrying in their hands censers filled with incense, and slowly, in the manner of seeking something, let them come before the place of the sepulchre. These things are done in imitation of the angel seated in the monument, and of the women coming with spices to anoint the body of Jesus. When therefore that one seated shall see the three, as if straying about and seeking something, approach him, let him begin in a dulcet voice of medium pitch to sing:

> *Whom seek ye in the sepulchre, O followers of Christ?*

> When he has sung this to the end, let the three respond in unison:

> *Jesus of Nazareth, which was crucified, O celestial one.*

> To whom that one:

> *He is not here; he is risen; just as he foretold.*
> *Go, announce that he is risen from the dead.*

> At the word of this command let those three turn themselves to the choir, saying:

> *Alleluia! The Lord is risen to-day.*
> *The strong lion, the Christ, the Son of God. Give thanks to God.*

> This said, let the former, again seating himself, as if recalling them, sing the anthem:

> *Come, and see the place where the Lord was laid. Alleluia! Alleluia!*

> And saying this, let him rise and let him lift the veil and show them the place bare of the cross, but only the cloths laid there with which the cross was wrapped. Seeing which, let them set down the censers which they carried into the same sepulchre, and let them take up the cloth and spread it out before the eyes of the clergy; and as if making known that the Lord had risen and was not now therein wrapped, let them sing this anthem:

> *The Lord is risen from the sepulchre.*
> *Who for us hung upon the cross.*

> And let them place the cloth upon the altar. The anthem being ended, let the Prior, rejoicing with them at the triumph of our King, in that, having conquered death, he arose, begin the hymn:

> *We praise thee, O God.*

> This begun, all the bells chime out together.[1]

Despite its brevity and the limitations imposed by the liturgy itself, this trope has the elements of drama: a progressive plot, the involvement of specific characters, conflict and resolution. Ethelwold's "stage directions" convey a subtle sense of how character can be created by performance and a fine sense of visual spectacle as well, all within the narrow scope allowed by the Mass.

---

[1] *Regularis Concordia,* in *Chief Pre-Shakespearean Dramas,* ed. Joseph Quincy Adams (Boston: Houghton Mifflin, 1924), 9–10.

Throughout the Middle Ages and beyond, liturgical plays of this kind became increasingly common and complex. Enacted in different locations within the church, called **MANSIONS,** liturgical drama provided a model for the forms of religious drama that came to be performed outside the church and outside the framework of the liturgy. In the tenth and eleventh centuries, the church sponsored dramatized scenes from the life of Christ or the lives of the saints, staged on important Christian holidays. For example, a town might commemorate the entrance of Christ into Jerusalem on Palm Sunday with a procession to the cathedral in which townspeople enacted various roles. In addition, the church oversaw the production of cycles of plays, which became a principal mode of theatrical and dramatic innovation. These cycles were performed sixty days after Easter as part of the feast of Corpus Christi, a holiday inaugurated in the fourteenth century to celebrate the doctrine of the Eucharist. The Corpus Christi festival frequently featured the performance of a series of plays dramatizing scriptural history: the Creation, Old Testament events (Noah and the Flood, Abraham and Isaac), scenes from the New Testament (the Annunciation, Herod and the Slaughter of the Innocents), and prophetic plays concerning the Harrowing of Hell and the Last Judgment. The production of these plays could last several days or weeks and called on the services of the entire town. Each craft guild (or *mystery,* as the guilds were called; the cycles are sometimes called **MYSTERY CYCLES**) financed and produced a different play, often on a subject appropriate to the guild. The shipwrights' guild might undertake the Noah play, the Three Kings play might be assigned to the goldsmiths, and so on. The plays were the property of the guilds and passed through generations of guild members. In major towns with many craft guilds, the cycles often included a large number of plays. Of the English cycles, the York cycle is the longest, containing forty-eight plays; the Wakefield cycle has thirty-two; and the Chester cycle has twenty-four.

Although they were produced for a popular, largely illiterate audience, the cycle dramas are extremely sophisticated and required the talents of trained performers. One of the cycles' most powerful and typical features is their use of **ANACHRONISM**—the blending of the historical past with contemporary events and characters. Many of the characters who appear in the plays are medieval English peasants, who often display an ironic, even theatrical sense of their involvement in the scriptural events of the past. One of the most telling uses of this technique occurs in the York *Crucifixion;* the York playwright conveys the Roman soldiers' hardness to the message of Christ by making them jest with him about the crucifixion they are performing:

> **1 SOLDIER:** (*To* CHRIST.) Say, Sir, how likes you now
> This work that we have wrought?
> **2 SOLDIER:** We pray you say us how
> Ye feel, or faint ye aught.
> **JESUS:** . . . My Father, that all bales [evils] may beet [abate].
> Forgive these men that do me pine [pain].
> What they work wot [know] they nought;
> Therefore, my Father, I crave,
> Let never their sins be sought,
> But see their souls to save.
> **1 SOLDIER:** We! Hark! he jangles like a jay.

By characterizing the jesting Roman soldiers as, in effect, contemporaries of the medieval audience, the play implies that biblical events are part of the audience's contemporary history. Seeing their neighbors enacting the biblical scenes and seeing contemporary characters share the stage with biblical figures must have emphasized the immediacy of the ongoing Christian story.

Cycle Drama

Morality Drama   Like the cycle plays, morality plays dramatized elements of Christian life. Instead of staging events from scriptural history, morality drama stages a symbolic **ALLEGORY** of the Christian's spiritual journey through life. Increasingly popular throughout the fourteenth and fifteenth centuries, plays like *The Castle of Perseverance* (c. 1425), *Mankind* (c. 1470), and *Everyman* (c. 1500) emphasized the individual's struggle with sin, while the cycle plays emphasized the larger patterns of Christian history. Later playwrights, including Shakespeare, found both models useful. The cycles provided a pattern for staging the epic sweep of secular English history, and morality drama provided a supple device for representing psychological and moral conflict. Morality plays often provided the structure for the secular plays written at schools and universities as well, and for the **INTERLUDES** performed at court as a break from holiday feasting. They also provided a staple technique for characterization in the later secular drama. Christopher Marlowe's *Doctor Faustus* (1590) uses the Good and Evil Angels to externalize Faustus's moral conflict, and other playwrights frequently used the devices of morality drama to dramatize the difficulties of political choice. In John Skelton's interlude, *Magnificence* (1516), written for Henry VIII or Thomas Sackville, and Thomas Norton's *Gorboduc* (1561), the monarch is shown to make his decisions framed by a host of allegorized counselors, good and bad advisers who approximate the role played in morality drama by angels and demons.

STAGING MEDIEVAL DRAMA

Medieval plays were often acted on or near **PAGEANT WAGONS.** In some towns the audience seems to have remained stationary at various locations while the wagons and their plays proceeded past them; in other towns, the wagons were drawn in a procession of **TABLEAUX VIVANTS** (posed scenes) through the town and then arranged in an open area for the performance, allowing the audience to move from play to play. In Chester, for example, a list survives of the stations where the plays were performed, and for York it is possible to trace the route of the pageant wagons through the city. Given the size and complexity of these performances, it's not surprising to find that they were not easily performed on one day: the procession took three days at Chester, and began at 4:30 A.M. in York, lasting until past midnight. The plays combined historical and contemporary elements; in performance, the staging produced a close and powerful relationship between the dramatic characters and the audience. In the Coventry play of the Magi, for example, Herod raves when he discovers that the three kings have escaped him:

> I Stamp! I Stare! I look all about!
> Might I them take, I should them burn at a glede [fire]!
> I rant! I run! and now run I wode [mad]
> A! That these villain traitors hath marred this my mood!
> They shall be hanged, if I may come them to!
>
> (*Here Herod rages in the pagond* [pageant wagon] *and in the street also.*)[2]

Herod's rage was certainly one of the highlights of the medieval cycles. Shakespeare, at least, seems to refer to it in *Hamlet* (1600), when he has Hamlet remind his actors that they should be restrained and natural in their performance, because overacting "out-Herods Herod." The stage direction also suggests that Herod's frenzy carried him from the wagon and into the street, into a closer and more effective relationship to his audience. This interaction between actor and audience is characteristic of popular theater and is a feature of medieval performance carried into Renaissance acting. It also suggests that the "place" of

---

[2]The Coventry *Magi, Herod, and the Slaughter of the Innocents,* in *Chief Pre-Shakespearean Dramas,* ed. Joseph Quincy Adams (Boston: Houghton Mifflin, 1924), 163.

medieval drama, the fictitious locale of the play, was not firmly localized onstage; the actors/characters could move easily back and forth between Herod's Jerusalem and the medieval audience, and even onstage places could be rapidly and easily transformed. This flexibility also allowed medieval playwrights to treat stage space symbolically. The ground plot for *The Castle of Perseverance,* for instance—with its scaffolds for various evils, its moat, and its central castle—clearly offers us a symbolic locale rather than an actual geography. The

MEDIEVAL PAGEANT WAGON

One actor is playing in the street in front of the wagon.

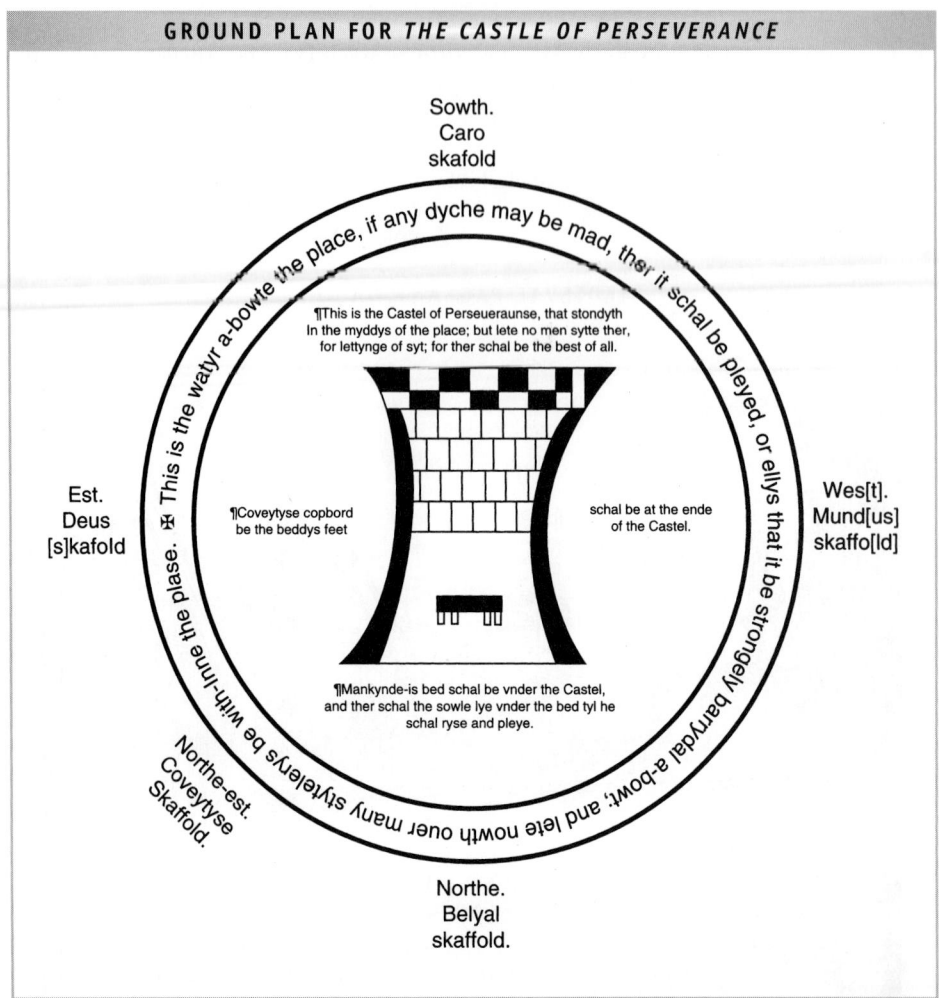

GROUND PLAN FOR *THE CASTLE OF PERSEVERANCE*

Sowth.
Caro
skafold

This is the watyr a-bowte the place, if any dyche may be mad, ther it schal be pleyed, or ellys that it be strongyly barryd al a-bowt; and lete nowth ouer many stytelerys be with-inne the plase. This is the watyr a-bowte the place,

¶This is the Castel of Perseueraunse, that stondyth
In the myddys of the place; but lete no men sytte ther,
for lettynge of syt; for ther schal be the best of all.

Est.
Deus
[s]kafold

¶Coveytyse copbord
be the beddys feet

schal be at the ende
of the Castel.

Wes[t].
Mund[us]
skaffo[ld]

¶Mankynde-is bed schal be vnder the Castel,
and ther schal the sowle lye vnder the bed tyl he
schal ryse and pleye.

Northe-est.
Coveytyse
Skaffold.

Northe.
Belyal
skaffold.

The ground-plot for the medieval morality play shows five scaffolds (North, Northeast, South, East, and West) arranged around a playing area, with a castle in the center. A ditch enclosed the castle to keep spectators at a distance. In the manuscript, a note beneath the drawing describes the costumes and special effects: "He that shall play Belial (a devil), look that he have gunpowder burning in pipes in his hands and in his ears, and in his arse, when he goes to battle. The four daughters should be clad in mantles; Mercy in white, Ruthwiseness in red, all together, Truth in sad green, and Peace all in black; and they shall play in the place all together until they bring up the soul."

various demons on their scaffolds stand at a symbolic distance, not an actual distance, from the central castle.

This complex of dramatic conventions, staging practices, and audience attitudes is a legacy of the medieval theater passed on to later theater. Although the medieval stage was only one of many influences on it, the drama of the sixteenth and seventeenth centuries is reminiscent of medieval drama in many ways. Renaissance drama frequently treats secular history according to a providential design similar to that of the cycles; it often treats its characters in the symbolic terms of the medieval morality dramas; and it uses both acting and stage space to create an immediacy between the fictive play and its audience. These habits take on very different meanings in Renaissance London, in a city and in a state in which the Anglican Protestant church is the state religion and where signs of Catholicism—or, in fact, of any religious subject matter—in the theater could be read as an act of sedition. The medieval theater provided the forms of drama and the practices of theater that were refashioned by the political, social, and theatrical pressures of the new era.

DRAMA AND THEATER IN RENAISSANCE LONDON

The explosion of theatrical and dramatic activity in London can be marked by two dates: 1567, when John Brayne built the Red Lion, London's first purpose-built theater (his brother-in-law, James Burbage, built The Theatre in 1576); and 1642, when plays were suspended and theaters were closed at the outbreak of the Civil War. The theater underwent profound changes from the reign of Elizabeth I (ruled 1558–1603) to the reigns of her successors James I (1603–1625) and Charles I (1625–1642, executed 1649), yet at the same time it endured the intense social and cultural upheavals of the period with remarkable consistency. As an institution, the new professional theater witnessed the emergence of England as a modern state; the rise of England as an important mercantile and naval power, aided by the defeat of the Spanish Armada in 1588; the expansion of English interests in the New World; the growth of the city of London to roughly 250,000 inhabitants; and the ascendance of the Puritan faction that closed the theaters and deposed and executed the king.

The professional theater—a new institution in England, though already established on the continent—necessarily reflected the political and social strains of the time. These strains are most readily visible in the many laws regulating theatrical performance. The location of theater buildings, the structure and organization of theater companies, and the entire scene of theatrical activity in Renaissance London epitomized the fundamental tensions of English society as it moved from the medieval to the modern world.

THE PROFESSIONAL THEATER AND ITS SOCIETY

The sixteenth century witnessed intense religious and civil controversy, dating in part from Henry VIII's divorce from Catherine of Aragon in 1532 and his consequent excommunication from the Catholic church in 1533. Once Henry established the Protestant Church of England as the religion of the realm in 1535, English politics were often dictated by England's vulnerability to the massive, hostile powers of the Catholic church in Rome and Catholic states such as France and Spain. Within England, a variety of Protestant sects competed with each other, with the government, and with the Church of England for power. This was also a period of profound changes in the ordering of society, a period of growing mercantile power, of aristocratic discontent with the power of the monarchy, and of the rise of new merchants and other social groups into prominence and power. As a result, the Crown was eternally on guard to suppress civil unrest or religious nonconformity.

Given this volatile political climate, it is not surprising that the Crown sought to limit and control public assembly, including theatrical performances. Laws were frequently directed against the theater, particularly against productions identified with England's Catholic past. In 1548, for example, the English church cancelled the Feast of Corpus Christi, and the production of the cycle plays was systematically suppressed. In 1569, the York cycle was performed for the last time, and in 1575, the mayor of Chester was arrested for allowing cycle plays to be performed. The last cycle performance took place in Coventry in 1576, and the last record of any Corpus Christi play being performed in England (before the modern era) dates from 1605, in Kendal. Morality plays may have seemed less sectarian in the kind of instruction they offered; features of morality drama were more readily absorbed by the secular theater.

Yet while the Crown limited and censored the stage, it also maintained its traditional patronage of the theater. The population of London nearly tripled in Shakespeare's lifetime, from roughly 80,000 in 1564 to more than 200,000 at his death in 1616. The Elizabethan era was characterized by several large crop failures, a deflation in the value of currency, repeated bouts of the plague, and persistent threats of invasion from without and sedition from within. Not surprisingly, both the queen and her Privy Council, and the local city magistrates throughout England, were fearful both of itinerant travelers and of large—potentially riotous—assemblies. The famous "Act for the punishment of Vagabonds" of 1572 is a case in point. The law prohibited itinerant players and entertainers from wandering throughout the realm, but its ultimate effect was to establish permanent theatrical companies under the protection of noble patrons. The law ordered that "all Fencers, Bearwards, Common Players in Interludes, and Minstrels, not belonging to any Baron of this Realm, or towards any other honorable Personage of greater Degree . . . [who] wander abroad and have not License of two Justices of the Peace at the least . . . shall be taken adjudged and deemed Rogues Vagabonds and Sturdy Beggars." Unless they belonged to the retinue of a nobleman, players were classed with common vagrants and could be arrested and fined. Protected as servants, a company of players could receive a license to perform in public.

The statute points to the strong bond between the theater and the aristocracy, and patents granted by Elizabeth entitled noblemen to retain companies of actors as servants. These patents—granted for the Lord Chamberlain's Men (Shakespeare's company), the Lord Admiral's Men (who produced Marlowe's plays), and others—shaped the professional theater of Renaissance London. Elizabeth authorized such companies to perform "Comedies, Tragedies, Interludes, and stage plays" in public, in London and elsewhere. Yet, in granting these privileges, the Crown made significant qualifications. Elizabeth expanded the powers of her Master of Revels, Edmund Tilney, requiring "all and every plaier or plaiers with their playmakers, either belonging to any noble man or otherwise" to "appear before him with all such plaies, Tragedies, Comedies or showes as they shall in readiness or meane to sett forth," and to receive his approval before their performance. Censorship in the period was extensive, and Elizabeth also stipulated that plays "be not published or shown in the time of common prayer, or in the time of great and common plague in our said City of London." Religious and civic officials exerted considerable authority over when and where plays could actually be performed and where theaters could legally be built, and they often closed theaters for months at a time because of plague or civil strife. In 1594, the Privy Council restricted London to two companies (the Lord Chamberlain's Men and the Lord Admiral's Men) and restricted them to public performance at the Globe and Rose theaters when in London.

Professional Companies

The City of London, as in many towns, had its own ordinances prohibiting plays within the city limits, and for this reason James Burbage—a member of the Earl of Leicester's company—built The Theatre to the north of the city. Within a decade theaters had been built to the north of the city and to the south, across the Thames River.

Although they were technically "servants," the major acting companies—the most famous being the Lord Chamberlain's Men, patented in 1593 and then given royal sponsorship as the King's Men when King James I succeeded Elizabeth in 1603—were organized as stockholding, profit-making corporations; that is, as business enterprises in the modern sense. Their economic survival depended on their public performances, because their patron might command and finance only a few productions per year. Several investors, or **SHARERS,** put up the capital to finance the company and took a percentage of its profits. The sharers were not just investors; they were involved in all aspects of the theater. In 1603, for instance, the sharers of the King's Men included Shakespeare (playwright and actor), Richard Burbage (James Burbage's son and the company's principal actor, who was the first to play Shakespeare's King Lear, Hamlet, and Macbeth), the actors John Heminges and Henry Condell (who later published Shakespeare's plays), and the comic actors William Sly (see *The Taming of the Shrew*) and Robert Armin (who played the Fool in *King Lear*), among others. The sharers were responsible for building or leasing a theater, for purchasing plays, for taking on boy actors as apprentices, and for hiring other actors for each production. They also were liable when legal proceedings were brought against the company.

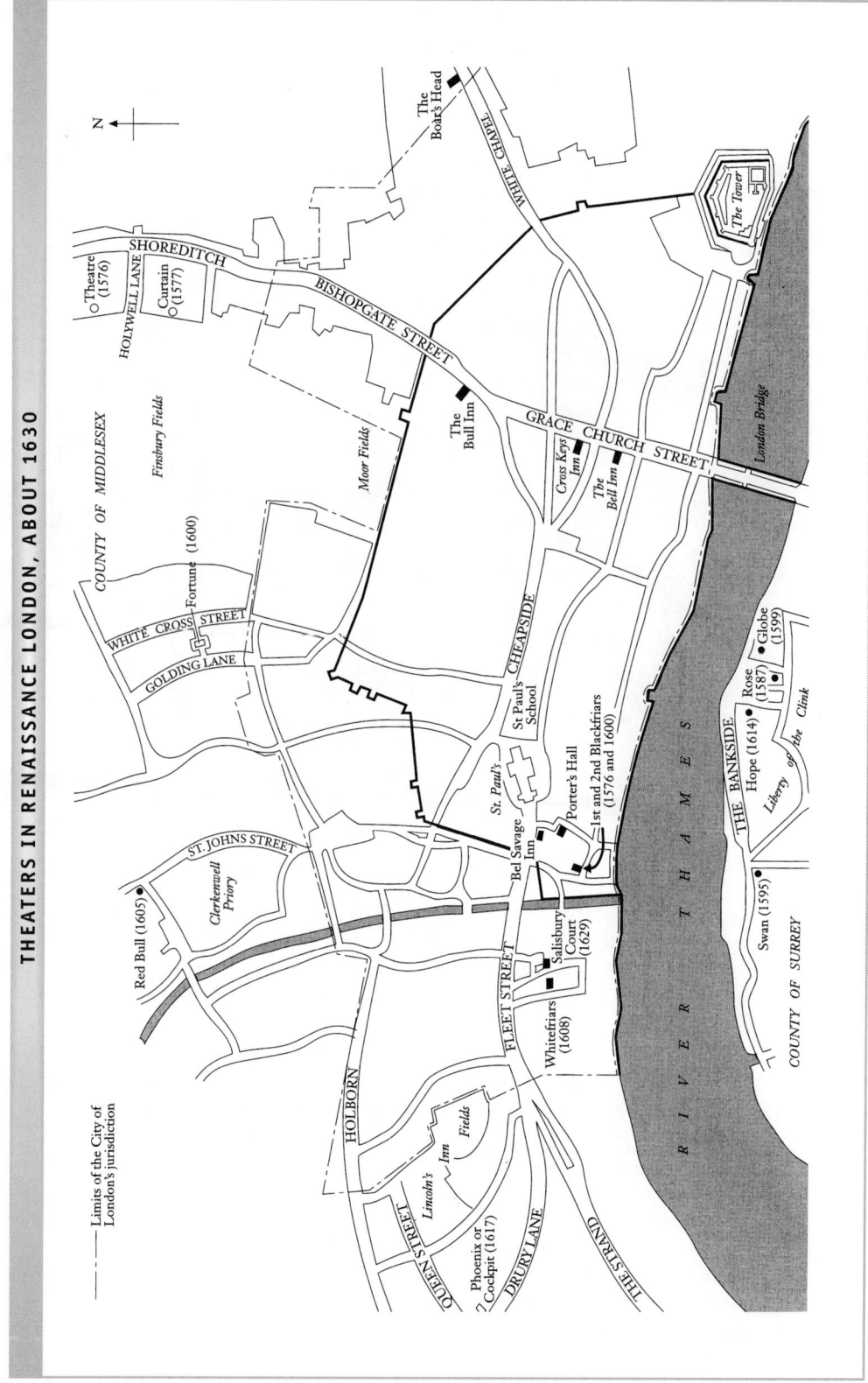

THEATERS IN RENAISSANCE LONDON, ABOUT 1630

A number of theaters were constructed in London after 1574. The dark line extending from The Tower (lower right) to Blackfriars in the west is the old city wall. Note that, with the exception of the first and second Blackfriars theaters, the theaters are either north of the city (the Fortune, The Theatre, the Curtain, the Red Bull) or south of the Thames River (the Swan, the Hope, the Rose, the Globe).

SKETCH OF THE SWAN THEATER, 1596

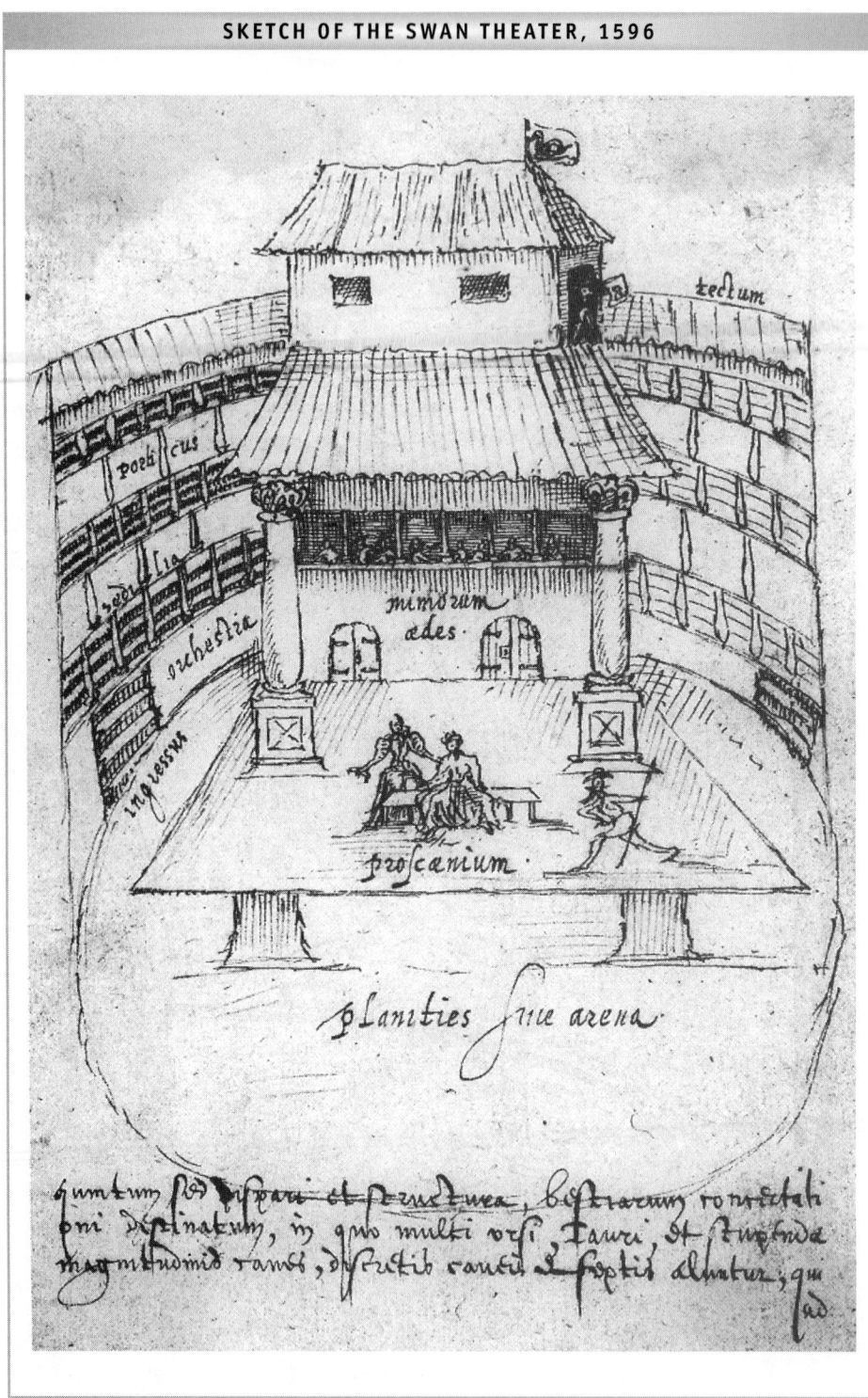

Johannes de Witt, a Dutch visitor to London, drew a sketch of a play in progress at the Swan in 1596. He sent the sketch to a friend, who made this copy. The drawing shows the tiring house with its two stage doors, a three-tiered gallery, the platform stage, and the standing pit.

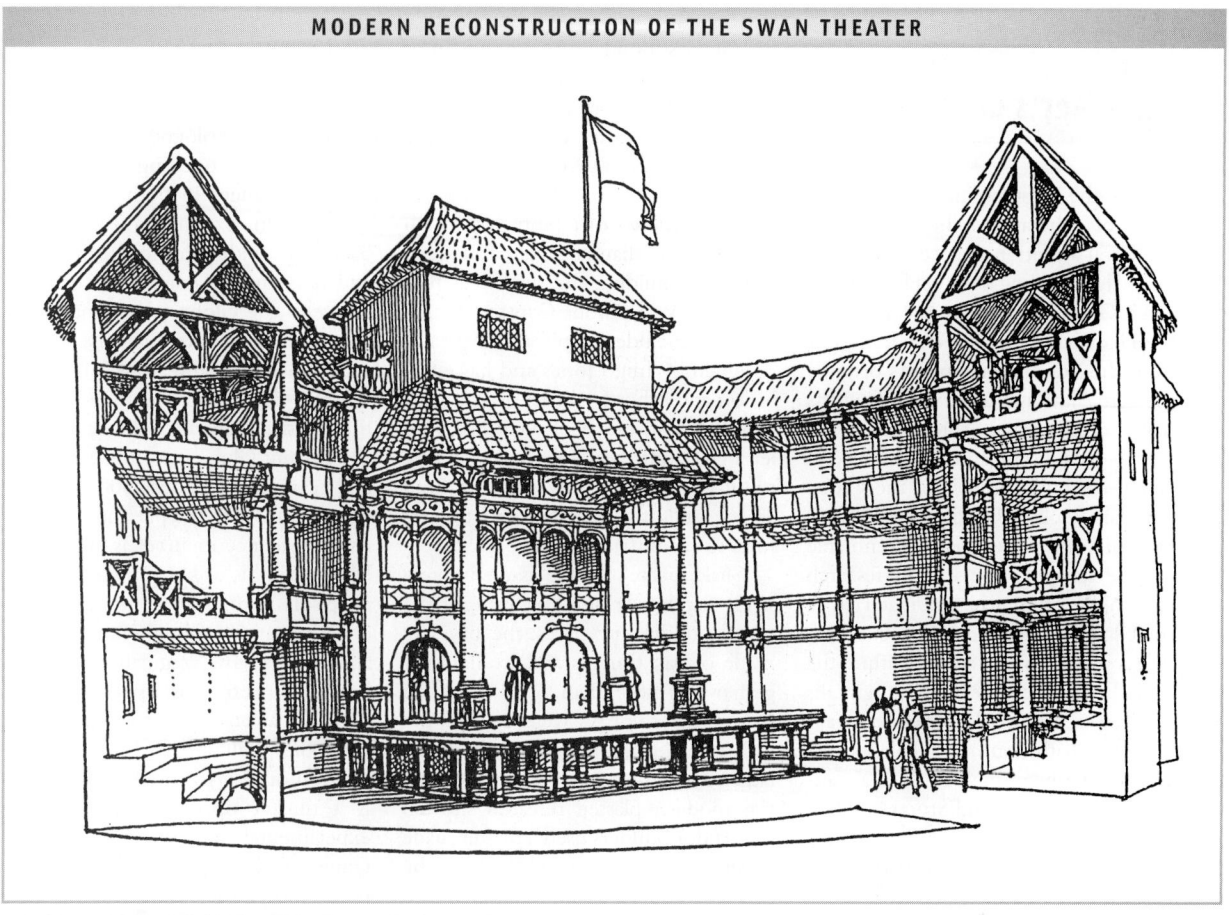

MODERN RECONSTRUCTION OF THE SWAN THEATER

C. Walter Hodges based this reconstruction on the de Witt sketch.

Although several companies flourished during the theater's heyday, life for actors and playwrights was hard. Until 1594, all professional playing companies were forced to perform in a variety of places, in London's various theaters and on tour. Although the scene with the players in *Hamlet* implies that touring was an occasional hardship of the London companies, recent research demonstrates that touring had been commonplace before the building of London's theaters and remained an important aspect of a theater company's vitality throughout the period. Playwrights, who were paid a flat fee by the company for the script of a play, hustled to scrape together a living: Thomas Dekker spent time in debtors' prison, and Ben Jonson died in penury. On the other hand, the theater also provided an opportunity for advancement as well. Several actors, including Richard Burbage and Edward Alleyn, were able to amass considerable fortunes. Shakespeare used the money he received as sharer to invest in property both in London and in his home, Stratford-upon-Avon, where he purchased a large house and land. Such careers were the exception rather than the rule, however, in an era when the theater was widely regarded as illicit and was frequently declared illegal.

The Theaters

English companies performed on three kinds of stage—large, open, outdoor buildings called PUBLIC THEATERS that held as many as 3,000 people; smaller, indoor, more elite PRIVATE THEATERS holding perhaps 700; and private performances at court or at the home of the patron. Public theaters, inspired both by the innyard booths where companies performed on

SHAKESPEARE'S GLOBE

One of the most fascinating constellations of scholarly, architectural, and theatrical ambition in recent years has been the building of a replica of the 1613 Globe theater on the banks of the Thames River, a few hundred yards from the site of Shakespeare's original theater. Although a variety of efforts have been made throughout the world—one is currently under way in Japan—to build models of the Globe or other English Renaissance theaters, the Bankside project has been notable for the scrupulousness of its research into the location, size, and materials of the Globe and for the care with which it has been constructed. Within the limits of modern legal requirements (fire laws) and social conventions (accessible bathrooms), "Shakespeare's Globe" has been built both as an experiment in Tudor and Stuart building practices and to foster an experiential experiment in the performance of Renaissance plays.

The American actor Sam Wanamaker instigated the project and remained its guiding force until his death in 1993. Part of Wanamaker's vision was that the theater should be both a theatrical and a scholarly endeavor, and much of the success of the final project is due to the team he assembled, including the scholar Andrew Gurr, architect Theo Crosby (who died in 1994), and artistic director Mark Rylance. The accuracy of the building was immeasurably helped by the discovery in 1989 of a section of the Globe's foundation beneath a nineteenth-century building adjacent to the Southwark bridge; although Anchor Terrace is protected as a landmark (preventing much excavation of the Globe's foundation), the section of foundation that has been unearthed has enabled scholars, using the familiar seventeenth-century engraving of the London skyline by Wenceslaus Hollar, to deduce that the Globe was a polygon constructed of twenty bays, with an exterior diameter of 100 feet. However, building the theater as part of the Bankside Globe Centre—which will also include a replica of a theater designed by Inigo Jones and has exhibition and other facilities—was not an easy task, and much of what has been learned about the Globe has been the result of scholarly investigation into Tudor building practices and the efforts to reconstruct them.

Shakespeare's Globe is an impressively handmade building, using traditional building practices: the bays are made of oak timbers and are held together by more than 6,000 wooden pegs. Once the bays were erected, the walls were filled in with oak staves, lath, and then plastered: rather than using modern plaster, research showed that Tudor builders used a plaster made of lime and cow's hair. Because the hair of modern English cows is too short, the Globe builders used a lime plaster mixed with goat hair. A fire sheet was put between each wall, and tests on the resulting lath-and-plaster showed that it could resist 1,000 degrees Fahrenheit for three hours—long enough to empty the theater in an emergency (when the Globe burned in 1613, no injuries were reported, either). The building is also the first wood-framed building to be built in London since the great fire of 1666: its thatched roof is applied in the traditional manner and has been treated with a fire-retardant chemical, and a sprinkler system is installed just under the roofline.

By far the most controversial aspect of the building has been the location of the two pillars that hold up the "heavens," and the design of the back wall of the stage, the tiring house wall. Between the Prologue Season (1996) and the Globe's opening in 1997, a variety of changes in both were made, resulting in a sumptuously painted backdrop with additional tapestries, and faux-marble columns. Audiences going to the Globe today find themselves in a theater somewhat less crowded than a full house in Shakespeare's day might have been. Although the original Globe held 3,000, the current Globe seats just over 1,000 and can hold about 500 standing "groundlings" in the pit (today, the average audience member is about 10% larger than his or her Elizabethan predecessor; beyond that, modern audiences are not willing—nor are they allowed by fire regulations—to be jammed together as tightly as Elizabethan patrons probably were). But what they will also find—as the production of *Henry V* in 1997 showed—is a theater operating as a kind of experimental venue, using the container of Shakespeare's drama to explore how the plays might have worked in their original conditions. At the present time, the company intends to do some productions in period dress (the costumes often themselves made with Tudor clothmaking and dye techniques), but to do others in modern dress. The result of a massive and energetic combination of talents, Shakespeare's Globe is finally meant to work as a living theater.[1]

---

[1] The building of the Globe was recorded in a variety of newspaper and scholarly accounts throughout the early 1990s; students interested in learning more about Shakespeare's Globe should consult Shakespeare's Globe Education Centre, Bankside, London SE1 9DT, United Kingdom.

THE GLOBE THEATER FOUNDATION

N

stair - well

foundation of
outer gallery wall

crosswall

area of
gravel
surface

crosswall

area of crushed
hazelnuts

0   3m

inner gallery
wall

In 1989, part of the foundation of the Globe theater was discovered. This portion of the Globe foundation extends from beneath a landmark nineteenth-century building; the remainder of the Globe foundation is beneath the building and therefore cannot be excavated. Nonetheless, this section of the inner and outer wall of the theater, and of the exterior stairwell which led to the galleries, has enabled scholars to gauge with much greater accuracy both the size and configuration of Shakespeare's theater.

DESIGNING SHAKESPEARE'S GLOBE

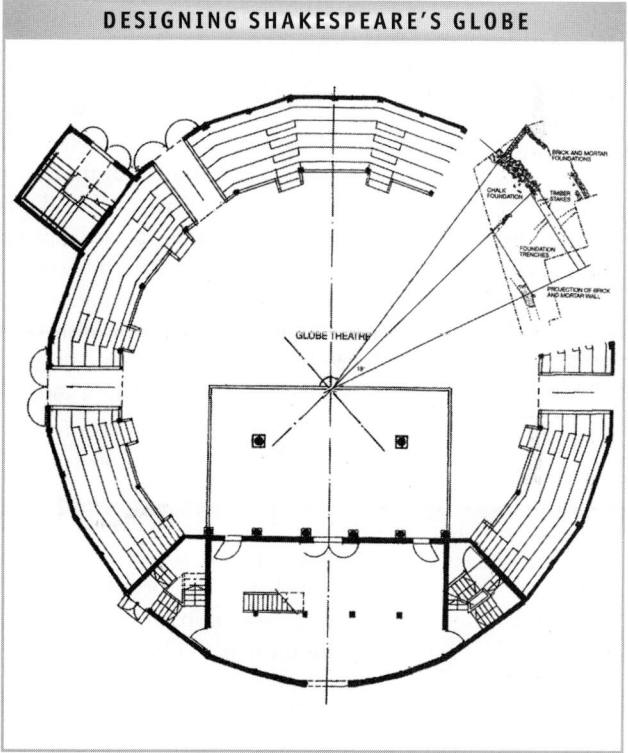

This illustration shows how the archaeological evidence of the Globe theater foundations has been used, along with other evidence, to develop a new understanding of the theater's size and shape. The foundations, which comprise two "bays" or sections of the Globe's exterior structure, enabled Theo Crosby, the architect of the reconstructed Shakespeare's Globe in London, to estimate the overall dimensions of the building (about ninety-nine feet in diameter) and also to determine that the Globe was a twenty-sided polygon.

tour and by the circular arenas used for animal baiting, were outdoor buildings accommodating a large and diverse audience for afternoon performances. Although one theater, the Fortune, was rectangular, most public theaters were polygonal structures. The roughly circular, three-story gallery surrounded an open pit for standing audiences, into which a stage extended at a height of about five feet. The stage was partly roofed, and two doors used for entrances were set into the rear wall, or **TIRING HOUSE.** On the gallery level above the stage, small rooms were used for aristocratic seating, for music, and for scenes requiring action above the stage—as in the balcony scene in *Romeo and Juliet,* or when Prospero appears "aloft" in *The Tempest.* The stage had a central trapdoor (or **GRAVE TRAP**), and its roofed area held a pulley for raising or lowering actors (as in the masque scene in *The Tempest*) or properties. The public theaters catered to a paying audience, charging one penny to enter the pit and an additional penny to enter each of the galleries, where seating was provided on benches. Estimates on the size of the theaters vary, but the largest, such as the Globe or the Fortune, were about 100 feet in external diameter, with a standing yard about 70 feet across, and a stage 45 feet wide and 27 feet deep; they could hold tightly-packed audiences of 2,000 to 3,000 people. Some theaters were considerably smaller. The Rose theater (whose foundation was discovered in 1989) was a twelve-sided building about 70 feet across, with a pit 50 feet in diameter and a stage roughly 25 by 15 feet. Most of the plays we associate with the Renaissance theater—those of Marlowe, Shakespeare, Jonson, John Webster, John Fletcher, and others—were produced in public theaters such as the Globe, the Rose, the Hope, the Swan, and the Fortune.

Although a number of theaters were built in this period, the prestige of the public theaters seems to have declined in the 1620s and 1630s as companies shifted much of their attention to the more lucrative private theaters. These theaters stood within the City of London, on lands called "liberties"; a liberty was a property that had once belonged to monasteries and had remained outside the city's legal jurisdiction, even though it was within the city limit. Best known of these theaters is the Blackfriars playhouse (the property originally belonged to the Dominican friars, who wore black gowns). Blackfriars was used intermittently throughout the 1590s by boys' companies, troupes of boy chapel choristers who were formed into companies for acting plays. Blackfriars was acquired by the King's Men and used by them for performances after 1608. These theaters were modeled along the lines of a great-house banqueting room: long indoor rooms illuminated by candles, with a low stage at one end, faced by benches for seating and flanked by additional seats along side galleries. The private theaters generally charged sixpence or more for basic admission, with additional charges for special seating. Companies performed at private theaters in winter and at public theaters in summer and generally brought the same repertoire to both venues. The private theaters did develop the reputation, however, for originating a more satirical and erudite body of drama.

DRAMA AND PERFORMANCE

Performing plays in **REPERTORY** over perhaps as many as 200 days a year, the London companies competed with each other for their audiences and generated an enormous demand for new plays. The plays that they bought and performed are among the greatest works of English literature. English drama in this period comprises plays on English history (such as Shakespeare's *Henry V* and *Richard III,* or Marlowe's *Edward II*); on classical history (Shakespeare's *Julius Caesar* and *Coriolanus,* Ben Jonson's *Sejanus*); romantic comedies (such as Shakespeare's *A Midsummer Night's Dream*); city comedies (Shakespeare's *Measure for Measure*); heroic tragedies (Shakespeare's *Hamlet* and *King Lear,* John Webster's *The Duchess of Malfi*); and plays of intrigue or satire (John Marston's *The Malcontent,* Thomas Middleton's *The Changeling*). Later in the period, audiences seemed to develop a taste for plays they called **TRAGICOMEDIES,** usually romantic plays that begin in the tragic vein but proceed to a happy resolution. Several of John Fletcher's plays are tragicomedies of this kind, and Shakespeare's *Cymbeline* and *The Tempest* resemble tragicomedy as well.

This list of genres suggests both the fertile range of innovation in the Renaissance theater and the drama's dependence on models drawn from the classical and medieval theaters. Roman drama—the comedies of Plautus and Terence and the tragedies of Seneca—was widely used in schools and universities as part of the teaching of Latin, and university students often staged these plays in Latin. It is not surprising, then, that some features of classical drama made their way into the Renaissance theater. The model of Shakespearean romantic comedy—mistaken identities, separated lovers, an irascible old man or father, a wily servant—derives directly from Plautus's plays; indeed, Shakespeare's *Comedy of Errors* directly adapts Plautus's *The Menaechmus Twins.* In a similar fashion, the violence of Seneca's tragedies makes its way directly into the action of Elizabethan drama. Formally and thematically, however, Renaissance drama also differs sharply from its classical ancestors. Renaissance plays tend to be more diffuse, involving a greater variety of characters and multiple plots; in tragedy, the action is often not quite as closely focused on the fortunes of a single hero as it is in classical tragedy. In these and other ways—in the Christian providence that seems to stand behind the action of many plays, in its variety of contemporary characters, in its use of symbolic anachronism, and in the complex relationship between the dramatic world and the world of the audience—Renaissance drama bears the signs of its medieval inheritance.

Playwrights generally wrote in **BLANK VERSE,** an unrhymed **IAMBIC PENTAMETER** line (ten syllables with alternating stress), and occasionally used other verse forms as well. They often used prose, sometimes for emphasis, sometimes to develop the qualities of a particular character. Although modern editors divided the plays into five acts, in most cases Renaissance playwrights probably did not compose their plays in this form. Performance on the public theater stage was rapid and continuous. The theaters used an open stage, few large properties, and had little or no scenery onstage, so that scenes could follow one another without interruption.

Despite the absence of elaborate stage sets, performance in the Renaissance theater was nonetheless spectacular. Actors used costumes, properties, and language to transform the midafternoon stage into a dramatic locale—Prospero's desert island, Lear's heath, Faustus's study. Some larger properties could be wheeled out from the rear doors, or perhaps raised from the trap: a throne, for instance, or a bed for Desdemona in *Othello,* or the hell-mouth used at the end of *Doctor Faustus.* A cannon fired during a production of Shakespeare's *Henry VIII* in 1613 unfortunately set fire to the Globe and burned it to the ground.

The unlocalized stage of medieval drama can be seen as the forerunner of the Renaissance theater's fluid use of stage space. The open stage made for an almost cinematic flexibility in performance, as the play could range rapidly from scene to scene, place to place. Costuming was eclectic and anachronistic: the actors wore mainly Elizabethan clothing, adding armor, royal finery, motley, or some "classical" style of gowns when needed. The actors—Burbage, Alleyn, Will Kemp, among many others—were widely praised for their power and effectiveness. Their acting style was oratorical in tragedy and extemporaneous in comedy, but there is no doubt that many were consummate performers, in command of dozens of roles that could be put into play at short notice.

Boy actors played a significant part in the experience of English theater, for boy actors played the parts of women and girls onstage, including major roles like Lady Macbeth, Ophelia, and Cleopatra. Much as they did in classical Athens, "women" emerged onstage in Renaissance London only as a side-effect of masculine attitudes and performances. In the English theater, this **CROSS-DRESSING** came into special prominence, though, because the romantic, sexual, and political intrigue so popular in Renaissance plays was often focused on

WOMEN IN DRAMA AND PERFORMANCE

THE JACOBEAN COURT MASQUE

One of the principal obligations of the professional companies was to perform at court or for their patron. Performances at court often took place during holidays and were commanded with increasing frequency by James I and Charles I. The companies performed many of their staple plays at court, but they also performed special entertainments called **MASQUES,** plays written in verse, usually on mythological subjects, that involved dancing, fanciful costumes, music, and special scenic machinery and effects. While the actors spoke the lines in these plays, they shared the stage with members of the court, who performed in the elaborate dances that began, punctuated, and ended the masques. The little play that Prospero puts on for Ferdinand and Miranda in Shakespeare's *The Tempest* resembles court masques in many ways, with its cast of goddesses, its formal singing and dancing, and the ceremonial quality of the occasion it celebrates.

Masques were an elaborate and expensive entertainment; some were performed on special state occasions. Jonson's *Hymenaei* (1605) celebrated the marriage of Lady Essex and *The Masque of Oberon* (1610) was written to celebrate Prince Henry's investiture as Prince of Wales, and all had important implications for the mythology of the Stuart dynasty. Because members of the royal and aristocratic families performed in the masques, the poet was challenged to devise a setting and dramatic narrative that were elevated enough for the courtly audience and to dignify the aristocratic performers. Each masque included several "grand masquing dances," which were performed by members of the court, often costumed as "characters" in the masque.

Jonson was by far the most renowned writer of masques, though the playwrights James Shirley, William Davenant (who became a critically important theater manager after the restoration of the monarchy in 1660), and others also wrote masques. Jonson wrote more than a dozen masques, and in the course of his long career innovated the genre in several ways. While the earlier Stuart masques tend to have a relatively simple narrative, later masques, beginning with *The Masque of Queens* (1609), adopted a more complicated structure. *The Masque of Queens* begins with an **ANTIMASQUE,** a scene involving witches, goblins, or demons who are magically transformed into goddesses or allegorical virtues in the course of the action.

His majesty, then, being set, and the whole company in full expectation, the part of the scene which first presented itself was an ugly hell, which flaming beneath, smoked unto the top of the roof. And in respect all evils are, morally said to come from hell, . . . these witches, with a kind of hollow and infernal music, came forth from thence. First one, then two, and three, and more, till their number increased to eleven, all differently attired: some with rats on their head, some on their shoulders; others with ointment pots at their girdles; all with spindles, timbrels, rattles or other venefical [having to do with witchcraft] instruments, making a confused noise, with strange gestures.

The witches dance and pronounce a series of charms until, suddenly, "with a strange and sudden music,"

they fell into a magical dance full of preposterous change and gesticulation. . . . In the heat of their dance on the sudden was heard a sound of loud music, as if many instruments had made one blast; with which not only the hags themselves but the hell into which they ran quite vanished, and the whole face of the scene altered, scarce suffering the memory of such a thing. But in the place of it appeared a glorious and magnificent building figuring the House of Fame, in the top of which were discovered the twelve masquers sitting upon a throne triumphal erected in form of a pyramid and circled with all store of light. From whom a person, by this time descended, in the furniture of Perseus, and expressing heroic and masculine virtue began to speak.[1]

The antimasque establishes a world of demonic disorder, which suddenly vanishes when the members of the court appear in the House of Fame, among classical heroes and virtues. We can get a sense of the delicacy of Jonson's situation when we recognize that the performers of the masque included the queen herself, as well as the countesses of Arundel, Derby, Huntington, Bedford, Essex, and Montgomery, Viscountess Cranborne, and several ladies in waiting. Members of the court were both performers and the audience of this self-enclosed spectacle, which almost of necessity reflected back on its audience an idealized vision of courtly perfection. Indeed, in the last Stuart masque, *Salmacida Spolia,* written by Davenant, both the king and the queen were among the dancers.

As an ambitious writer, Jonson thought the masques were essentially a vehicle for his splendid poetry. But as even this brief description suggests, the masques were highly dependent on the development of new scenic technology and on the skills of the architect and designer Inigo Jones (1573–1652). The masques were unusually expensive: one of King James's masques cost more than £4,000, and one of King Charles's cost £21,000. Much of

[1] From *Ben Jonson: Selected Masques,* ed. Stephen Orgel (New Haven, CT: Yale University Press, 1970).

this money was spent on the elaborate, changeable scenery that accompanied the masques, the first changeable scenery in the English theater. Inigo Jones designed the theater space where masques were performed, the banqueting hall of Whitehall Palace. Jones had visited Italy in 1600; he may have visited again during 1607–1608, and he is known to have been in Italy from 1613 to 1615. In Italy he came into contact with the theater designs of Andrea Palladio (1518–1580), who adapted the design of classical Roman theaters for indoor stages: Palladio's Teatro Olimpico had a curved amphitheater-like auditorium and a proscenium stage. As court architect and designer, Jones had the opportunity both to import Palladio's understanding of theatrical design, and to develop his own interest in elaborate spectacle. The stage at Whitehall was about forty feet wide by twenty-eight feet deep, and gently raked. Although Jones's theater at Whitehall changed during his long tenure at court, it eventually consisted of staggered wings and a backdrop to convey a sense of perspective. Unlike both the public and private theaters of Renaissance London, Jones's theater was the first to use changeable scenery, and when the theaters reopened in 1660, the English companies brought this aristocratic inheritance with them: Jones's **WINGS-AND-BACKDROP** designs became the basic model for changeable scenery throughout the eighteenth century.

Jones's interest in spectacle was far reaching, and he devised the instruments to execute many of Jonson's most elaborate poetic images: flying machines, a globe that opened to reveal several aristocratic dancers, and brilliant costumes to dress the masques' allegorical characters. But it was Jones's development of a perspective in the theater that was most deeply implicated in the rhetoric of court life. At Whitehall performances, the King sat on a raised, central dais directly in front of the stage; since none of the other courtiers could be seated with their backs to the King,

FIERY SPIRIT

Inigo Jones created this costume for a fiery spirit in 1635.

those closer to the stage were seated along the side walls of the room, while others were seated behind the royal spectator. It has been argued that the king was positioned in a complex relation to the stage and to the rest of the audience: not only was he the only spectator for whom the illusion of perspective was complete (the other spectators could probably see between the wings, for example), but the rest of the audience could *see* that only the king had a perfect vision of the world onstage. The closer one sat to the royal seat, the more one's view of the illusion onstage approximated the king's ideal vantage. Spectators and performers, in other words, engaged in a richly hierarchical sense of illusion in which the King's centrality—and, in a sense, his omniscience—was constantly displayed, and each spectator's distance from that sense of illusion was constantly experienced. Like Jonson, whose texts frequently betray his intense

awareness of his royal audience and aristocratic performers, Jones's perspective theater reflects the increasingly absolutist ideology of the Stuart monarchy.

The banqueting hall at Whitehall played one more ironic role in the history of performance. Charles I became increasingly hostile to Parliament—he refused to call Parliament from 1629 to 1640—and when civil war broke out in 1642, Charles fled London. The Royalist forces were concentrated in Oxford, and in 1647 Charles was defeated and captured by the Parliamentary army. In 1649, he was sentenced to death by Parliament, and he visited the Whitehall banquet hall on his way to his execution. The executioner's block was set on a large public stage outside a window of the banquet hall; Charles was led through the room where the masques' brilliant fantasies had been staged for him to his own last performance—the public stage where he was beheaded.

COSTUMES FOR SHAKESPEARE'S *TITUS ANDRONICUS*

Dating from about 1595, this drawing appears to show a scene from *Titus Andronicus,* by William Shakespeare. Two of the actors wear pseudoclassical Roman costumes; the others are dressed in Elizabethan clothing.

female characters and therefore on the performance of the boy actors. Indeed, the drama frequently uses cross-dressing as a way of interrogating the power and perquisites of gender, in ways that sometimes confirm and sometimes question the role of gender in English society. English society was an overtly hierarchical one, and despite the power of the "Virgin Queen," women had little access to education, most could not hold property, and they were generally subject to discrimination of many kinds. In this social economy and in a theater in which Puritan opposition to the stage frequently criticized the theater's "effeminacy," the absence of women from the stage became a powerful sign of their absence from other scenes of power. Much as sumptuary laws prevented individuals from wearing jewels and clothing above their social station, so too was cross-dressing a legal offense in sixteenth-century England, punishable by whipping and a prison sentence. The license of the theater, the freedom to create magical new worlds on the stage, was, like other forms of power in the period, the prerogative of men, and the images that men created for the stage are in important ways imprinted with the signs of a specifically masculine imagination. As with all stage conventions, cross-dressing was deeply implicated in the values of the culture outside the theater, so much so that when women did perform onstage in England—a French company used actresses at Blackfriars in 1629—they met with hostility, ridicule, and rejection.

Nonetheless, women not only attended the theater, but a few—aristocratic women, who often patronized poets and other artists—also wrote plays, and sometimes performed in them at court. Queen Elizabeth is thought to have translated a passage from Seneca's *Hercules on Mount Oeta,* and other women similarly adapted or wrote plays. Mary Sidney, Countess of Pembroke and sister of Sir Philip Sidney, translated Robert Garnier's play *The Tragedy of Antonie* in the 1590s. Her niece, Lady Mary Wroth (daughter of Mary Sidney's brother, Robert, and a frequent participant in Jacobean court masques), wrote a mythological play,

Love's Victory, probably in the early 1620s. Perhaps the best-known plays today are Elizabeth Cary, Viscountess of Falkland's *Tragedy of Miriam* (published in 1613) and the plays published by Margaret Cavendish, Marchioness of Newcastle, in 1662 and 1668. Although these plays were not staged—aristocratic women did not traffic in theater business—they have since become a critical part of our understanding of English Renaissance drama.

The theater had an extraordinary hold on the English imagination. In their many progresses, pageants, and allegorical entertainments, the English monarchs revealed a keen sense of the power of fictive images to represent reality, or a version of it, and so to shape their subjects' understanding of royal power. Playwrights and audiences also found in the theater a magical image of human possibility. Think of Prospero summoning the storm, Ariel, and other spirits with his stagey magic; or of the playwright John Webster's description of "an excellent actor": "All men have been of his occupation, and indeed what he doth feignedly, that do others essentially: this day one plays a Monarch, the next a private person. Here one acts a Tyrant, on the morrow an Exile; a Parasite [sponger] this man tonight, tomorrow a Precisian [Puritan], and so of divers others." Acting and the theater provided a liberating image of human—or, at least, masculine—power: the power to transform oneself and the world. However, the rich, strange, transforming freedom of the theater could also seem empty and terrifying, even demonic. Rather than an image of human potential, the theater could seem to offer an image of the poverty of human action, the sterile and deceptive emptiness of the world we make and inhabit. As King Lear preaches to blinded Gloucester, "When we are born, we cry that we are come / To this great stage of fools." Puritan critics of the theater insistently reminded audiences that the stage's methods—to seduce with the vain and showy image of a false reality—were also Satan's, and that the theater subversively invited audiences to "unman, unChristian, uncreate themselves." Yet it is precisely this transforming power that lies at the heart of the Renaissance theater's fascination for its audience. Although the theater sometimes seemed to depict a world threatened with constant change and loss, it also presented the power of illusion to recreate the real.

MEDIEVAL AND RENAISSANCE DRAMA IN PERFORMANCE AND HISTORY

Although the banning of the cycle dramas in England in the sixteenth century marked an ending of the traditions of medieval drama and theater there, the same was not true on the continent, where both cycle dramas and morality dramas continued to be performed. In Spain, for example, the **AUTOS SACRAMENTALES**—morality plays on Christian themes—were produced in major cities such as Madrid, and had an important influence on dramatic writing as well (see Unit IV). Similarly, staging short pageants—like the shepherd plays or *pastorelas* performed today throughout Latin America, and in many Latino communities in the United States, before Christmas—has remained a part of religious festivities in many places; perhaps the most striking of these is the processional staging of the Passion held in Oberammergau, Germany.

In many respects, though, the vivid and popular style of the cycle plays had to wait until the late nineteenth and early twentieth centuries to find an audience; when the manuscripts of the four English cycles first began to be studied seriously in the nineteenth century, their plays were seen merely as primitive precursors to the more finished, literary achievement of English Renaissance dramatists. However, this model of the "evolution" of dramatic forms, from "simple" to "complex," is not really borne out by a close examination of the plays themselves, which use a popular literary and theatrical medium to undertake a drama of enormous subtlety, scope, and power. Beginning in the twentieth century, a number of efforts were made to stage medieval drama—both the cycle plays and morality plays, such as *Everyman*—and the force and theatrical vitality of the plays became immediately apparent. In recent years, the cycle plays have been staged frequently, both in their traditional locations (at York, for instance), and elsewhere: the University of Toronto and the Court Theater at the University of Chicago have mounted very well received versions.

Although the English theaters were closed in 1642, interrupting the practices both of playwriting and of theatrical performance, the secular drama of Renaissance England has had in many respects a more sustained tradition. When the theaters reopened in 1660, they reopened in a very different form—indoor theaters, using lights and stage machinery, re-placed the outdoor public theaters of the Jacobean and Caroline periods—and to a much more narrowly circumscribed audience (see Unit IV). And while there was considerable de-mand for new plays, for many years some plays of the Renaissance period held the stage, and indeed provided the dramatic conventions on which new plays were mapped. While today we tend to think of Shakespeare as the preeminent writer of his era, in the Restora-tion period, Shakespeare's plays were revived less frequently than those of other playwrights, notably Ben Jonson, James Shirley, and Francis Beaumont and John Fletcher; it was only in the eighteenth century that Shakespeare's plays began to have something approaching their current popularity.

The history of Shakespeare in the theater, however, is a history of adaptation: the con-cept that Shakespeare's plays have an inner logic and should be performed "as they were written" is a purely modern idea. Shakespeare's plays were, of course, altered in the practice of his own company, and playwrights in the later seventeenth and eighteenth centuries adapted the plays to the taste of their era. John Dryden, for example, transformed Shake-speare's erotically supercharged Antony and Cleopatra into an honorable Roman and his staid matron in his version of *Antony and Cleopatra,* called *All for Love* (1677). Nahum Tate's version of Shakespeare's *King Lear* (1681) concludes with Edgar marrying Cordelia (yes, she lives) and retiring happily offstage with Lear (he lives, too) and Kent; this version of *Lear* held the stage well into the nineteenth century. Rather than regarding these revisions as quaintly misguided, we should recognize that theatrical production always rewrites the drama in the idiom of the day; to their audiences, these productions were fully "Shake-spearean," just as recent films—Kenneth Branagh's setting of *Hamlet* in the nineteenth cen-tury, Baz Luhrmann's framing *Romeo and Juliet* as a gang war in a Latin American Verona, or Michael Almereyda's use of Ethan Hawke as an alienated, technologically adept modern New Yorker in his *Hamlet*—are efforts to make Shakespeare speak in ways that will be pow-erful to audiences today.

Indeed, today we tend to think of Shakespeare across a variety of media: in film and tele-vision and advertising as well as in a range of theatrical venues. But for the seventeenth, eigh-teenth, and nineteenth centuries, Shakespeare was the property of the theater, and many actors and actresses became famous for their portrayals of Shakespearean roles: Thomas Betterton (1635–1710), Charles Macklin (1700–1797), Sarah Siddons (1755–1831), Edmund Kean (1789–1833), Sir Henry Irving (1838–1905), the first English actor to be knighted, and Ellen Terry (1847–1928) are just a few. In many respects, though, David Garrick (1717–1779) had the greatest impact as a Shakespearean actor. In part through his celebrated performances—he was renowned as Hamlet, Macbeth, and Richard III—Garrick helped to create a new interest in Shakespeare in the theater: he had his portrait painted frequently in Shakespearean roles (Hogarth's painting of Garrick as Richard III is a famous example), and he used his popularity to advance Shakespeare's reputation, not least by staging a Shakespeare Jubilee in Stratford. Garrick was a friend of the great literary critic Samuel Johnson, and Garrick's efforts in the the-ater coincided with a series of attempts to produce better, more accurate editions of Shake-speare's plays. But although Garrick had the reputation of restoring "Shakespeare's" original texts to the stage, he could hardly hope to succeed in the face of a century of popular stage adaptations. Although Garrick did introduce some Shakespearean material that had previously been cut from performances, his King Lear survived the play just as Nahum Tate's did, and his Richard III bawled out—as he had ever since Colley Cibber revised the play in 1700—"Off with his head!" (Indeed, Cibber's version of *Richard III* cuts several characters and persisted on-stage well into the twentieth century; it also partly informs Laurence Olivier's film of the play.)

The stage production of Shakespearean drama has always responded to the beliefs and values of its contemporary audiences. Tate's adaptation of *King Lear* was praised by Johnson, for example, for its happy ending seemed to restore justice in the theater; Johnson thought Shakespeare's original ending fine for readers, but too bleak and destructive for the stage. Shakespeare's plays were adapted to the more melodramatic and sentimental tastes of the eighteenth century; in the nineteenth century, a vogue for historical accuracy and stage realism led to a series of splendid efforts to reconstruct the historical setting of the plays: medieval Scotland in Charles Kean's 1853 *Macbeth* or Christian-era England in Henry Irving's *Cymbeline* (1896). These changes in taste are reflected in acting style as well: Betterton's portrayal of Hamlet was renowned in the late seventeenth century for its gravity and grace; Betterton is said never to have raised his arms above his waist, an illustration of neoclassical decorum in performance. By the early decades of the nineteenth century, Samuel Taylor Coleridge remarked that watching Edmund Kean in performance was akin to reading Shakespeare "by flashes of lightning"; Kean's performance impressed his audiences precisely through his well-crafted *lack* of decorum, in accord with Romantic beliefs about emotional expressivity. Irving is in many ways the first modern actor in what we would recognize as a psychological tradition of acting; although his career preceded the Russian director Constantin Stanislavski's pioneering work on the style of realistic performance (see Unit V), Irving's penchant for subtle physical details of characterization—his enemies called them mannerisms—gave his work a psychological concreteness and complexity that was powerful to an audience whose understanding of dramatic character was trained on the novels of Charles Dickens and George Eliot.

The theater also registers its culture's changing social attitudes in its portrayal of Shakespearean roles. Charles Macklin, for example, was probably the first actor to take a more sympathetic portrayal of the Jewish moneylender Shylock in *The Merchant of Venice;* the role had traditionally been performed as a satiric stereotype. Yet even Macklin retained the comic red wig and beard with which Shylock had always been performed; Edmund Kean was the first actor to get rid of them. Henry Irving's production of the play ended after the Act IV trial scene: in his version, *The Merchant of Venice* becomes something more like "The Tragedy of Shylock." In 1994, Peter Sellars set the play in a version of Los Angeles and drew explicit parallels to the police beating of Rodney King and the uprising that followed the acquittal of the officers involved. In Sellars's production the play's Jews were all played as African Americans; the Venetians were all played as Latinos and Latinas; and Portia and her retinue were all played as Asian Americans. Although Sellars's production was deservedly controversial, it illustrates a sense that Shakespeare's drama is capable of entering into new situations unimagined by Shakespeare, and of saying new things as well.

In the twentieth century, the pictorial style favored by Victorian theaters has largely been replaced in an effort to stage the plays in the simpler style of Shakespeare's theater. The first experiments of this kind were undertaken by William Poel (1852–1934), who used his Elizabethan Stage Society to produce versions of *Twelfth Night* and other plays on an open stage, and using a text more closely approximating Shakespeare's. Poel made it possible to see Shakespeare's plays as lively and fast-moving (all those scene changes in Victorian productions had made a Shakespeare play a very long evening, requiring many cuts to compensate for all the time it took to raise and lower sets), and regardless of whether directors (a new role in the theater also dating to this period) have chosen to stage the plays in Elizabethan or other settings, the sense of a rapidly changing series of scenes, localized not by extensive sets onstage but by the language and action, informs most twentieth-century Shakespeare. Indeed, it is often said that filmic techniques—quick cutting between scenes made possible by camera work and editing—provided a means to understand how Shakespearean drama might be played differently onstage.

It is now possible to see a range of Shakespeares on the contemporary stage—not only Shakespeare performed in languages other than English, but through the eclectic range of theatrical styles characteristic of the modern stage. Some productions—the "restored" versions, such as the 1997 *Henry V,* at Shakespeare's Globe in London—work hard to use Elizabethan costumes to produce the flavor of Shakespeare's theater. Other productions set the plays in a different historical era (there have been several recent *Henry V* productions set in the American Civil War, for example) to make the workings of the play's society visible to us in more familiar circumstances. Still others use eclectic staging, combining set and costume elements from a variety of periods to take Shakespeare out of history—in the Royal Shakespeare Company's 1991 *Troilus and Cressida,* for example, Agamemnon appeared in a breastplate and a ratty old cardigan sweater: a kind of timeless image of the doddering old general.

Of course, the ability of the modern stage to bring a great technological flexibility to Shakespeare is matched by the possibilities of film. Shakespeare plays were among the first subjects of silent filmmakers, and many of the most distinguished films of the twentieth century are versions of Shakespearean drama. Indeed, contemporary students of Shakespeare are often much more likely to see a Shakespeare film than a live Shakespeare performance, especially with the number of exciting Shakespeare films produced in the 1990s: Kenneth Branagh in *Henry V, Much Ado About Nothing,* and *Hamlet;* Ian McKellan in *Richard III;* Mel Gibson in *Hamlet;* Leonardo Di Caprio and Claire Danes in *Romeo + Juliet.* As a part of the common cultural inheritance of the West—and indeed, frequently challenged as such by resistant, postcolonial productions in India, Canada, Africa, and elsewhere—Shakespeare is produced today across the spectrum of performance.

Michael Pennington appears as Hamlet in the Royal Shakespeare Company production, 1980.

In this scene from an American Shakespeare Theater production of *The Tempest,* Ariel describes how he has performed Prospero's commands.

As the "cavalier" costumes suggest, John Gielgud's acclaimed 1934 production of *Hamlet* was set in the later seventeenth century, rather than in the Elizabethan era; here, Hamlet and Laertes duel in the play's final scene.

READING THE MATERIAL THEATER

One of the most chastening facts concerning the early modern theater is that most of the drama performed on its stages has been lost: plays were given to the theater companies in handwritten manuscript; they were copied out by hand into parts—scrolls containing each actor's part, with cues for each of his speeches—and the copy of the play maintained by the company was, likewise, a handwritten copy. Needless to say, nearly all such manuscripts have been lost.

Although by the later sixteenth century typesetting was a familiar technology in Renaissance England, the proliferation of printed documents —volumes of classical Latin texts, broadsides, ballads, religious pamphlets, guides to domestic work, conduct books for courtiers—presented Shakespeare's audiences with an information explosion much akin to the one we face in the digital age. At the same time, print was not understood to be an appropriate vehicle for all forms of writing. Poets, for example, saw print—associated with declassé mercantile world—as an inferior mode for circulating their poems: to gain the kind of aristocratic prestige (and patronage) they most desired, poets typically circulated their poems in manuscript among the aristocrats at court.

Beyond that, printing was a relatively expensive endeavor, and theater companies—who owned the text of the play, having purchased it from the playwright—had little incentive to publish a successful play. Yet plays were published, frequently in a small, inexpensive format; because the sheet of paper on which the text is printed is folded twice (into four) before the book is bound, these small books are known bibliographically as **QUARTOS.** Because of their size, the sometimes slipshod character of their presswork, and their association with the theater, quarto volumes of plays were also stigmatized; Sir Thomas Bodley—whose library, the Bodleian, remains the Oxford University library—famously refused to purchase such "idle riffe-raffes" for his collection. Since quarto-sized volumes of individual plays were usually published in very small quantities, they are today quite rare.

Many of Shakespeare's plays were published in quarto form during his lifetime (*Hamlet,* for example, was published in two very different quarto versions), but nearly half of his plays—including *Macbeth, Antony and Cleopatra, The Tempest* and others—would be unknown to us without the efforts of two of his fellow-sharers, John Heminges and Henry Condell, who published a nearly complete collection of Shakespeare's plays (in the large-size **FOLIO** format) in 1623, seven years after the playwright's death. This was a signal event in the history of dramatic publishing—in 1623, only one other English dramatist, Ben Jonson, had published a collected *Works* on this scale.

We can learn a lot about the condition of the theater and about the relationship between theater practice and the emerging norms of print culture by closely examining the printed texts of Shakespeare's plays in both quarto and folio versions. Here, for example, is the title page of *Titus Andronicus,* one of Shakespeare's earliest successes, a play that has been adapted for film by the director and designer Julie Taymor, and a play that testifies to the fascination that Senecan drama held for playwrights and audiences in the 1580s and 1590s. It is a violent, rhetorically rich play. What can we learn about the theater, and about Renaissance attitudes toward theater, drama, and literature, from this title page? Some aspects to consider: How is the page designed? What are its most prominent visual features? How are different typefaces used to highlight different kinds of information? How is the book designed to appeal to a potential purchaser? What elements are visually prominent and which are less prominent? Is there information missing that might seem necessary to a modern purchaser? How can we read the information presented here as an index of the relation between two newly emerging industries—professional theater and literary publishing—in the period?

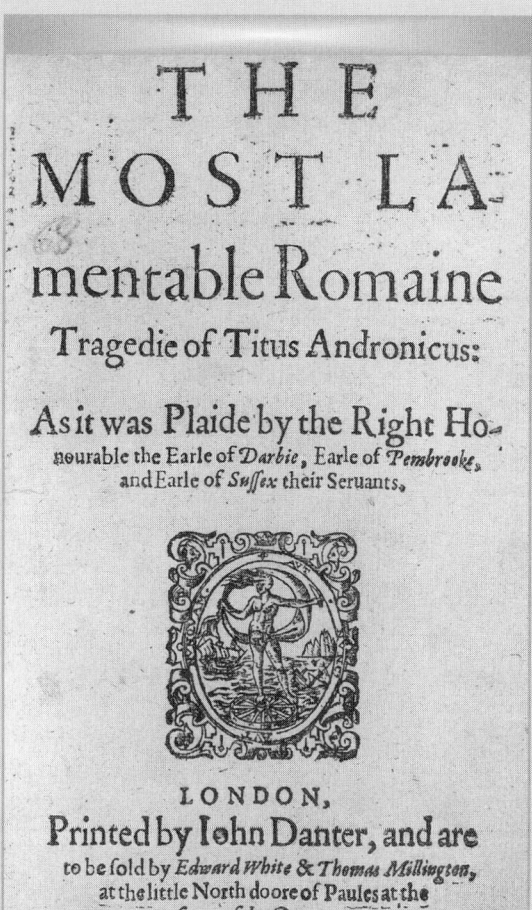

EVERYMAN

Everyman was written late in the fifteenth century and strongly resembles a Flemish play, *Elckerlijc* ("Everyman"), which was printed in 1495. It seems likely that one of the two plays is a translation of the other, but scholars are uncertain about which is the original. Given the play's subtle treatment of the Catholic doctrine of salvation, it has sometimes been argued that *Everyman* was written by a monk or cleric. Yet *Everyman* is hardly a theological treatise; it brims with a vitality that brings the reality of impending death vividly to the stage.

In the play, God orders Death to seek out Everyman and prepare him to die. Like most people, though, Everyman is not ready to meet his end. He first tries to bribe Death and then pleads unsuccessfully for mercy. When Death does not relent, Everyman begins a kind of spiritual journey, confronting several allegorical figures and asking them to accompany him to the grave. Medieval allegory often involved the personification of moral or psychological abstractions, much like the characters that Everyman meets: Fellowship, Kindred, Goods, Good Deeds, Knowledge, and so on. In performance, however, these abstractions become vividly fleshed-out, for the playwright gives these characters traits and behaviors that make them powerfully "real" and recognizable as individuals on the stage rather than as abstract moral emblems. As Everyman proceeds toward death, he is deserted by most of his worldly attributes, but Good Deeds remains faithful to him, especially once he has repented. Although the playwright concludes *Everyman* with a moralizing sermon by the Doctor, we may well feel that the theatrical lesson of the play has at least as much to do with the humanizing of Everyman and his poignant confrontation with our common mortality.

This production of *Everyman* transforms what may at first seem a statically "allegorical" drama into a visceral, choreographed spectacle.

EVERYMAN

Anonymous

TRANSLATED BY A. C. CAWLEY

CHARACTERS

GOD	COUSIN	STRENGTH
MESSENGER	GOODS	DISCRETION
DEATH	GOOD DEEDS	FIVE WITS
EVERYMAN	KNOWLEDGE	ANGEL
FELLOWSHIP	CONFESSION	DOCTOR
KINDRED	BEAUTY	

Here beginneth a treatise how the High Father of Heaven sendeth death to summon every creature to come and give account of their lives in this world, and is in manner of a moral play.

MESSENGER: I pray you all give your audience,
 And hear this matter with reverence,
 By figure a moral play:
 The *Summoning of Everyman* called it is,
5 That of our lives and ending shows
 How transitory we be all day.
 This matter is wondrous precious,
 But the intent of it is more gracious,
 And sweet to bear away.
10 The story saith: Man, in the beginning
 Look well, and take good heed to the ending,
 Be you never so gay!
 Ye think sin in the beginning full sweet,
 Which in the end causeth the soul to weep,
15 When the body lieth in clay.
 Here shall you see how Fellowship and Jollity,
 Both Strength, Pleasure, and Beauty,
 Will fade from thee as flower in May;
 For ye shall hear how our Heaven King
20 Calleth Everyman to a general reckoning:
 Give audience, and hear what he doth say.   (*Exit.*)

(GOD *speaketh:*)

GOD: I perceive, here in my majesty,
 How that all creatures be to me unkind,
 Living without dread in worldly prosperity:
25 Of ghostly sight the people be so blind,
 Drowned in sin, they know me not for their God;
 In worldly riches is all their mind,
 They fear not my righteousness, the sharp rod.
 My law that I showed, when I for them died,
30 They forget clean, and shedding of my blood red;
 I hanged between two, it cannot be denied;
 To get them life I suffered to be dead;
 I healed their feet, with thorns hurt was my head.
 I could do no more than I did, truly;
35 And now I see the people do clean forsake me:
 They use the seven deadly sins damnable,
 As pride, covetise, wrath, and lechery
 Now in the world be made commendable;

 And thus they leave of angels the heavenly company.
 Every man liveth so after his own pleasure, 40
 And yet of their life they be nothing sure:
 I see the more that I them forbear
 The worse they be from year to year.
 All that liveth appaireth fast;
 Therefore I will, in all the haste, 45
 Have a reckoning of every man's person;
 For, and I leave the people thus alone
 In their life and wicked tempests,
 Verily they will become much worse than beasts;
 For now one would by envy another up eat; 50
 Charity they do all clean forget.
 I hoped well that every man
 In my glory should make his mansion,
 And thereto I had them all elect;
 But now I see, like traitors deject, 55
 They thank me not for the pleasure that I to them meant,
 Nor yet for their being that I them have lent,
 I proffered the people great multitude of mercy,
 And few there be that asketh it heartily.
 They be so cumbered with worldly riches 60
 That needs on them I must do justice,
 On every man living without fear.
 Where art thou, Death, thou mighty messenger?

(*Enter* DEATH.)

DEATH: Almighty God, I am here at your will,
 Your commandment to fulfill. 65
GOD: Go thou to Everyman,
 And show him, in my name,
 A pilgrimage he must on him take,
 Which he in no wise may escape;
 And that he bring with him a sure reckoning 70
 Without delay or any tarrying.

(GOD *withdraws.*)

DEATH: Lord, I will in the world go run overall,
 And cruelly outsearch both great and small;
 Every man will I beset that liveth beastly
 Out of God's laws, and dreadeth not folly. 75

---

3 **By figure** in form 6 **all day** always 8 **But . . . gracious** but the purpose of it is more devout 23 **unkind** ungrateful 25 **Of ghostly sight** in spiritual vision 32 **I . . . dead** I consented to die 37 **covetise** covetousness

---

41 **And . . . sure** and yet their lives are by no means obscure 44 **appaireth** degenerates 47 **and** if 48 **tempests** tumults 55 **deject** abject 59 **heartily** earnestly 72 **overall** everywhere

He that loveth riches I will strike with my dart,
His sight to blind, and from heaven to depart—
Except that alms be his good friend—
In hell for to dwell, world without end.
80 Lo, yonder I see Everyman walking.
Full little he thinketh on my coming;
His mind is on fleshly lusts and his treasure,
And great pain it shall cause him to endure
Before the Lord, Heaven King.

(*Enter* EVERYMAN.)

85 Everyman, stand still! Whither art thou going
Thus gaily? Hast thou thy Maker forget?
EVERYMAN: Why askest thou?
Wouldest thou wit?
DEATH: Yea, sir; I will show you:
90 In great haste I am sent to thee
From God out of his majesty.
EVERYMAN: What, sent to me?
DEATH: Yea, certainly.
Though thou have forget him here,
95 He thinketh on thee in the heavenly sphere,
As, ere we depart, thou shalt know.
EVERYMAN: What desireth God of me?
DEATH: That shall I show thee:
A reckoning he will needs have
100 Without any longer respite.
EVERYMAN: To give a reckoning longer leisure I crave;
This blind matter troubleth my wit.
DEATH: On thee thou must take a long journey;
Therefore thy book of count with thee thou bring,
105 For turn again thou cannot by no way.
And look thou be sure of thy reckoning,
For before God thou shalt answer, and show
Thy many bad deeds, and good but a few;
How thou hast spent thy life, and in what wise,
110 Before the chief Lord of paradise.
Have ado that we were in that way,
For, wit thou well, thou shalt make none attorney.
EVERYMAN: Full unready I am such reckoning to give.
I know thee not. What messenger art thou?
115 DEATH: I am Death, that no man dreadeth,
For every man I rest, and no man spareth;
For it is God's commandment
That all to me should be obedient.
EVERYMAN: O Death, thou comest when I had thee least in
mind!
120 In thy power it lieth me to save;
Yet of my good will I give thee, if thou will be kind:
Yea, a thousand pound shalt thou have,
And defer this matter till another day.
DEATH: Everyman, it may not be, by no way.
125 I set not by gold, silver, nor riches,

Ne by pope, emperor, king, duke, ne princes;
For, and I would receive gifts great,
All the world I might get;
But my custom is clean contrary.
I give thee no respite. Come hence, and not tarry. 130
EVERYMAN: Alas, shall I have no longer respite?
I may say Death giveth no warning!
To think on thee, it maketh my heart sick,
For all unready is my book of reckoning.
But twelve year and I might have abiding, 135
My counting-book I would make so clear
That my reckoning I should not need to fear.
Wherefore, Death, I pray thee, for God's mercy,
Spare me till I be provided of remedy.
DEATH: Thee availeth not to cry, weep, and pray; 140
But haste thee lightly that thou were gone that journey,
And prove thy friends if thou can;
For, wit thou well, the tide abideth no man,
And in the world each living creature
For Adam's sin must die of nature. 145
EVERYMAN: Death, if I should this pilgrimage take,
And my reckoning surely make,
Show me, for saint charity,
Should I not come again shortly?
DEATH: No, Everyman; and thou be once there, 150
Thou mayst never more come here,
Trust me verily.
EVERYMAN: O gracious God in the high seat celestial,
Have mercy on me in this most need!
Shall I have no company from this vale terrestrial 155
Of mine acquaintance, that way me to lead?
DEATH: Yea, if any be so hardy
That would go with thee and bear thee company.
Hie thee that thou were gone to God's magnificence,
Thy reckoning to give before his presence. 160
What, weenest thou thy life is given thee,
And thy worldly goods also?
EVERYMAN: I had wend so, verily.
DEATH: Nay, nay; it was but lent thee;
For as soon as thou art go, 165
Another a while shall have it, and then go therefro,
Even as thou hast done.
Everyman, thou art mad! Thou hast thy wits five,
And here on earth will not amend thy life;
For suddenly I do come. 170
EVERYMAN: O wretched caitiff, whither shall I flee,
That I might scape this endless sorrow?
Now, gentle Death, spare me till to-morrow,
That I may amend me
With good advisement. 175
DEATH: Nay, thereto I will not consent,
Nor no man will I respite;
But to the heart suddenly I shall smite
Without any advisement.
And now out of thy sight I will me hie; 180
See thou make thee ready shortly,

---

77 **depart** separate   88 **wit** know   102 **blind** obscure   104
count account   105 **turn again** return   111 **Have . . . way**
i.e., let's see about making that journey   112 **none attorney** no
one [your] advocate   115 **that . . . dreadeth** who fears no man
116 **rest** arrest   121 **good** goods   123 **And defer** if you defer
125 **set not by** care not for

---

143 **tide** time   161 **weenest** suppose   163 **wend** supposed
165 **go** gone   166 **therefro** from it   175 **advisement** reflection

For thou mayst say this is the day
That no man living may scape away.

(*Exit* DEATH.)

EVERYMAN: Alas, I may well weep with sighs deep!
185　Now have I no manner of company
To help me in my journey, and me to keep;
And also my writing is full unready.
How shall I do now for to excuse me?
I would to God I had never be get!
190　To my soul a full great profit it had be;
For now I fear pains huge and great.
The time passeth, Lord, help, that all wrought!
For though I mourn it availeth nought.
The day passeth. and is almost ago;
195　I wot not well what for to do.
To whom were I best my complaint to make?
What and I to Fellowship thereof spake,
And showed him of this sudden chance?
For in him is all mine affiance;
200　We have in the world so many a day
Be good friends in sport and play.
I see him yonder, certainly.
I trust that he will bear me company;
Therefore to him will I speak to ease my sorrow.
205　Well met, good Fellowship, and good morrow!

(FELLOWSHIP *speaketh:*)

FELLOWSHIP: Everyman, good morrow, by this day!
Sir, why lookest thou so piteously?
If any thing be amiss, I pray thee me say,
That I may help to remedy.
210　EVERYMAN: Yea, good Fellowship, yea;
I am in great jeopardy.
FELLOWSHIP: My true friend, show to me your mind;
I will not forsake thee to my life's end,
In the way of good company.
215　EVERYMAN: That was well spoken, and lovingly.
FELLOWSHIP: Sir, I must needs know your heaviness;
I have pity to see you in any distress.
If any have you wronged, ye shall revenged be,
Though I on the ground be slain for thee—
220　Though that I know before that I should die.
EVERYMAN: Verily, Fellowship, gramercy.
FELLOWSHIP: Tush! by thy thanks I set not a straw.
Show me your grief, and say no more.
EVERYMAN: If I my heart should to you break,
225　And then you to turn your mind from me,
And would not me comfort when ye hear me speak,
Then should I ten times sorrier be.
FELLOWSHIP: Sir, I say as I will do indeed.
EVERYMAN: Then be you a good friend at need:
230　I have found you true herebefore.
FELLOWSHIP: And so ye shall evermore;
For, in faith; and thou go to hell,

I will not forsake thee by the way.
EVERYMAN: Ye speak like a good friend; I believe you well.
I shall deserve it, and I may.　235
FELLOWSHIP: I speak of no deserving, by this day!
For he that will say, and nothing do,
Is not worthy with good company to go;
Therefore show me the grief of your mind,
As to your friend most loving and kind.　240
EVERYMAN: I shall show you how it is:
Commanded I am to go a journey,
A long way, hard and dangerous,
And give a strait count, without delay,
Before the high Judge, Adonai.　245
Wherefore, I pray you, bear me company,
As ye have promised, in this journey.
FELLOWSHIP: That is matter indeed. Promise is duty;
But, and I should take such a voyage on me,
I know it well, it should be to my pain;　250
Also it maketh me afeard, certain.
But let us take counsel here as well as we can,
For your words would fear a strong man.
EVERYMAN: Why, ye said if I had need
Ye would me never forsake, quick ne dead,　255
Though it were to hell, truly.
FELLOWSHIP: So I said, certainly,
But such pleasures be set aside, the sooth to say;
And also, if we took such a journey,
When should we come again?　260
EVERYMAN: Nay, never again, till the day of doom.
FELLOWSHIP: In faith, then will not I come there!
Who hath you these tidings brought?
EVERYMAN: Indeed, Death was with me here.
FELLOWSHIP: Now, by God that all hath bought,　265
If Death were the messenger,
For no man that is living to-day
I will not go that loath journey—
Not for the father that begat me!
EVERYMAN: Ye promised, otherwise, pardie.　270
FELLOWSHIP: I wot well I said so, truly;
And yet if thou wilt eat, and drink, and make good cheer,
Or haunt to women the lusty company,
I would not forsake you while the day is clear,
Trust me verily.　275
EVERYMAN: Yea, thereto ye would be ready!
To go to mirth, solace, and play,
Your mind will sooner apply,
Than to bear me company in my long journey.
FELLOWSHIP: Now, in good faith, I will not that way.　280
But and thou will murder, or any man kill,
In that I will help thee with a good will.
EVERYMAN: O, that is a simple advice indeed.
Gentle fellow, help me in my necessity!
We have loved long, and now I need;　285
And now, gentle Fellowship, remember me.

235　**deserve** repay　244　**strait count** strict account
245　**Adonai** a Hebrew name for God　248　**That . . . indeed** that
is a good reason indeed [for asking me]　253　**fear** frighten
265　**bought** redeemed　268　**loath** loathsome　270　**pardie** by
God　273　**Or . . . company** or frequent the pleasant company of
women　274　**while . . . clear** until daybreak　278　**apply** attend

---

186　**keep** guard　187　**writing** the writing of Everyman's accounts　189　**be get** been born　194　**ago** gone　197　**and** if
199　**affiance** trust　206　**by this day** an asseveration　216　**heaviness** sorrow　224　**break** open

FELLOWSHIP: Whether ye have loved me or no,
  By Saint John, I will not with thee go.
EVERYMAN: Yet, I pray thee, take the labour, and do so much
    for me
290 To bring me forward, for saint charity,
  And comfort me till I come without the town.
FELLOWSHIP: Nay, and thou would give me a new gown,
  I will not a foot with thee go;
  But, and thou had tarried, I would not have left thee so.
295 And as now God speed thee in thy journey,
  For from thee I will depart as fast as I may.
EVERYMAN: Whither away, Fellowship? Will thou forsake me?
FELLOWSHIP: Yea, by my fay! To God I betake thee.
EVERYMAN: Farewell, good Fellowship; for thee my heart is
    sore.
300 Adieu for ever! I shall see thee no more
FELLOWSHIP: In faith, Everyman, farewell now at the ending;
  For you I will remember that parting is mourning.

(*Exit* FELLOWSHIP.)

EVERYMAN: Alack! shall we thus depart indeed—
  Ah, Lady, help!—without any more comfort?
305 Lo, Fellowship forsaketh me in my most need.
  For help in this world whither shall I resort?
  Fellowship herebefore with me would merry make,
  And now little sorrow for me doth he take.
  It is said, 'In prosperity men friends may find,
310 Which in adversity be full unkind.'
  Now whither for succour shall I flee,
  Sith that Fellowship hath forsaken me?
  To my kinsmen I will, truly,
  Praying them to help me in my necessity;
315 I believe that they will do so,
  For kind will creep where it may not go.
  I will go say, for yonder I see them.
  Where be ye now, my friends and kinsmen?

(*Enter* KINDRED *and* COUSIN.)

KINDRED: Here be we now at your commandment.
320 Cousin, I pray you show us your intent
  In any wise, and do not spare.
COUSIN: Yea, Everyman, and to us declare
  If ye be disposed to go anywhither;
  For, wit you well, we will live and die together.
325 KINDRED: In wealth and woe we will with you hold,
  For over his kin a man may be bold.
EVERYMAN: Gramercy, my friends and kinsmen kind.
  Now shall I show you the grief of my mind:
  I was commanded by a messenger,
330 That is a high king's chief officer;
  He bade me go a pilgrimage, to my pain,

And I know well I shall never come again;
  Also I must give a reckoning strait,
  For I have a great enemy that hath me in wait,
  Which intendeth me for to hinder.   335
KINDRED: What account is that which ye must render?
  That would I know.
EVERYMAN: Of all my works I must show
  How I have lived and my days spent;
  Also of ill deeds that I have used   340
  In my time, sith life was me lent;
  And of all virtues that I have refused.
  Therefore, I pray you, go thither with me
  To help to make mine account, for saint charity.
COUSIN: What, to go thither? Is that the matter?   345
  Nay, Everyman, I had liefer fast bread and water
  All this five year and more.
EVERYMAN: Alas, that ever I was bore!
  For now shall I never be merry,
  If that you forsake me.   350
KINDRED: Ah, sir, what ye be a merry man!
  Take good heart to you, and make no moan.
  But one thing I warn you, by Saint Anne—
  As for me, ye shall go alone.
EVERYMAN: My Cousin, will you not with me go?   355
COUSIN: No, by our Lady! I have the cramp in my toe.
  Trust not to me, for, so God me speed,
  I will deceive you in your most need.
KINDRED: It availeth not us to tice.
  Ye shall have my maid with all my heart;   360
  She loveth to go to feasts, there to be nice,
  And to dance, and abroad to start:
  I will give her leave to help you in that journey,
  If that you and she may agree.
EVERYMAN: Now show me the very effect of your mind: 365
  Will you go with me, or abide behind?
KINDRED: Abide behind? Yea, that will I, and I may!
  Therefore farewell till another day.

(*Exit* KINDRED.)

EVERYMAN: How should I be merry or glad?
  For fair promises men to me make,   370
  But when I have most need they me forsake.
  I am deceived; that maketh me sad.
COUSIN: Cousin Everyman, farewell now,
  For verily I will not go with you.
  Also of mine own an unready reckoning   375
  I have to account; therefore I make tarrying.
  Now God keep thee, for now I go.

(*Exit* COUSIN.)

---

290 **bring me forward** escort me   298 **fay** faith; **betake** commend   303 **depart** part   312 **Sith** since   316 **For . . . go** For kinship will creep where it cannot walk, that is, blood is thicker than water   317 **go say** essay, try   321 **In . . . spare** without fail, and do not hold back   323 **anywhither** anywhere   325 **hold** with   326 **For . . . bold** for a man may be sure of his kinsfolk

334 **For . . . wait** a great enemy (the devil) who has me under observation   340 **used** practised   346 **I . . . water** I had rather fast on bread and water   348 **bore** born   351 **what . . . man** what a merry man you are   359 **It . . . tice** it is no use trying to entice us   361 **nice** wanton   362 **abroad to start** go out and about   365 **effect** tenor

EVERYMAN: Ah, Jesus, is all come hereto?
    Lo, fair words maketh fools fain;
380   They promise, and nothing will do, certain.
    My kinsmen promised me faithfully
    For to abide with me steadfastly,
    And now fast away do they flee:
    Even so Fellowship promised me.
385   What friend were best me of to provide?
    I lose my time here longer to abide.
    Yet in my mind a thing there is:
    All my life I have loved riches;
    If that my Good now help me might,
390   He would make my heart full light.
    I will speak to him in this distress—
    Where art thou, my Goods and riches?

(GOODS *speaks from a corner.*)

GOODS: Who calleth me? Everyman? What! hast thou haste?
    I lie here in corners, trussed and piled so high,
395   And in chests I am locked so fast,
    Also sacked in bags. Thou mayst see with thine eye
    I cannot stir; in packs low I lie.
    What would ye have? Lightly me say.
    EVERYMAN: Come hither, Goods, in all the haste thou may,
400   For of counsel I must desire thee.
    GOODS: Sir, and ye in the world have sorrow or adversity,
    That can I help you to remedy shortly.
    EVERYMAN: It is another disease that grieveth me;
    In this world it is not, I tell thee so.
405   I am sent for, another way to go,
    To give a strait count general
    Before the highest Jupiter of all;
    And all my life I have had joy and pleasure in thee,
    Therefore, I pray thee, go with me;
410   For, peradventure, thou mayst before God Almighty
    My reckoning help to clean and purify;
    For it is said ever among
    That money maketh all right that is wrong.
    GOODS: Nay, Everyman, I sing another song.
415   I follow no man in such voyages;
    For, and I went with thee,
    Thou shouldst fare much the worse for me;
    For because on me thou did set thy mind,
    Thy reckoning I have made blotted and blind,
420   That thine account thou cannot make truly;
    And that hast thou for the love of me.
    EVERYMAN: That would grieve me full sore,
    When I should come to that fearful answer.
    Up, let us go thither together.
425   GOODS: Nay, not so! I am too brittle, I may not endure;
    I will follow no man one foot, be ye sure.
    EVERYMAN: Alas, I have thee loved, and had great pleasure
    All my life-days on good and treasure.

GOODS: That is to thy damnation, without leasing,
    For my love is contrary to the love everlasting;   430
    But if thou had me loved moderately during,
    As to the poor to give part of me,
    Then shouldst thou not in this dolour be,
    Nor in this great sorrow and care.
EVERYMAN: Lo, now was I deceived ere I was ware,   435
    And all I may wite misspending of time.
GOODS: What, weenest thou that I am thine?
EVERYMAN: I had wend so.
GOODS: Nay, Everyman, I say no.
    As for a while I was lent thee;   440
    A season thou hast had me in prosperity.
    My condition is man's soul to kill;
    If I save one, a thousand I do spill.
    Weenest thou that I will follow thee?
    Nay, not from this world, verily.   445
EVERYMAN: I had wend otherwise.
GOODS: Therefore to thy soul Goods is a thief;
    For when thou art dead, this is my guise—
    Another to deceive in this same wise
    As I have done thee, and all to his soul's reprief.   450
EVERYMAN: O false Goods, cursed may thou be.
    Thou traitor to God, that hast deceived me
    And caught me in thy snare!
GOODS: Marry, thou brought thyself in care,
    Whereof I am glad;   455
    I must needs laugh, I cannot be sad.
EVERYMAN: Ah, Goods, thou hast had long my heartly love;
    I gave thee that which should be the Lord's above.
    But wilt thou not go with me indeed?
    I pray thee truth to say.   460
GOODS: No, so God me speed!
    Therefore farewell, and have good day.

(*Exit* GOODS.)

EVERYMAN: O, to whom shall I make my moan
    For to go with me in that heavy journey?
    First Fellowship said he would with me gone;   465
    His words were very pleasant and gay,
    But afterward he left me alone.
    Then spake I to my kinsmen, all in despair,
    And also they gave me words fair;
    They lacked no fair speaking,   470
    But all forsook me in the ending.
    Then went I to my Goods, that I loved best,
    In hope to have comfort, but there had I least;
    For my Goods sharply did me tell
    That he bringeth many into hell.   475
    Then of myself I was ashamed,

---

385 **me . . . provide** to provide myself with   389 **Good** Goods
398 **Lightly** quickly   400 **For . . . thee** for I must entreat your
advice   403 **disease** trouble   412 **For . . . among** for it is
sometimes said   419 **blind** obscure

---

429 **without leasing** without a lie, that is, truly   431–432 **But
. . . me** but if you had loved me moderately during your lifetime,
so as to give part of me to the poor   433 **dolour** distress
435 **ware** aware   436 **And . . . time** and I may blame it all on
the bad use I have made of time   438 **wend** supposed   442 **condition** nature   443 **spill** ruin   448 **guise** practice   450 **re-
prief** shame   457 **heartly** heartfelt

And so I am worthy to be blamed;
Thus may I well myself hate.
Of whom shall I now counsel take?
480   I think that I shall never speed
Till that I go to my Good Deed.
But, alas, she is so weak
That she can neither go nor speak;
Yet will I venture on her now.
485   My Good Deeds, where be you?

(GOOD DEEDS *speaks from the ground.*)

GOOD DEEDS: Here I lie, cold in the ground;
Thy sins hath me sore bound,
That I cannot stir.
EVERYMAN: O Good Deeds, I stand in fear!
490   I must you pray of counsel,
For help now should come right well.
GOOD DEEDS: Everyman, I have understanding
That ye be summoned account to make
Before Messias, of Jerusalem King;
495   And you do by me, that journey with you will I take.
EVERYMAN: Therefore I come to you, my moan to make;
I pray you that ye will go with me,
GOOD DEEDS: I would full fain, but I cannot stand, verily.
EVERYMAN: Why, is there anything on you fall?
500 GOOD DEEDS: Yea, sir, I may thank you of all;
If ye had perfectly cheered me,
Your book of count full ready had be.
Look, the books of your works and deeds eke!
Behold how they lie under the feet,
505   To your soul's heaviness.
EVERYMAN: Our Lord Jesus help me!
For one letter here I cannot see.
GOOD DEEDS: There is a blind reckoning in time of distress.
EVERYMAN: Good Deeds, I pray you help me in this need,
510   Or else I am for ever damned indeed;
Therefore help me to make reckoning
Before the Redeemer of all thing,
That King is, and was, and ever shall.
GOOD DEEDS: Everyman, I am sorry of your fall,
515   And fain would I help you, and I were able.
EVERYMAN: Good Deeds, your counsel I pray you give me.
GOOD DEEDS: That shall I do verily;
Though that on my feet I may not go,
I have a sister that shall with you also,
520   Called Knowledge, which shall with you abide,
To help you to make that dreadful reckoning.

(*Enter* KNOWLEDGE.)

KNOWLEDGE: Everyman, I will go with thee, and be thy guide,
In thy most need to go by thy side.
EVERYMAN: In good condition I am now in every thing,
And am wholly content with this good thing,   525
Thanked be God my creator.
GOOD DEEDS: And when she hath brought you there
Where thou shalt heal thee of thy smart,
Then go you with your reckoning and your Good Deeds
   together,
For to make you joyful at heart   530
Before the blessed Trinity.
EVERYMAN: My Good Deeds, gramercy!
I am well content, certainly,
With your words sweet.
KNOWLEDGE: Now go we together lovingly   535
To Confession, that cleansing river.
EVERYMAN: For joy I weep; I would we were there!
But, I pray you, give me cognition
Where dwelleth that holy man, Confession.
KNOWLEDGE: In the house of salvation: 540
We shall find him in that place,
That shall us comfort, by God's grace.

(KNOWLEDGE *takes* EVERYMAN *to* CONFESSION.)

Lo, this is Confession. Kneel down and ask mercy,
For he is in good conceit with God Almighty.
EVERYMAN: O glorious fountain, that all uncleanness doth clarify, 545
Wash from me the spots of vice unclean,
That on me no sin may be seen.
I come with Knowledge for my redemption,
Redempt with heart and full contrition;
For I am commanded a pilgrimage to take,   550
And great accounts before God to make.
Now I pray you, Shrift, mother of salvation,
Help my Good Deeds for my piteous exclamation.
CONFESSION: I know your sorrow well, Everyman.
Because with Knowledge ye come to me,   555
I will you comfort as well as I can,
And a precious jewel I will give thee,
Called penance, voider of adversity;
Therewith shall your body chastised be,
With abstinence and perseverance in God's service.   560
Here shall you receive that scourge of me,
Which is penance strong that ye must endure,
To remember thy Saviour was scourged for thee
With sharp scourges, and suffered it patiently;
So must thou, ere thou scape that painful pilgrimage.   565
Knowledge, keep him in this voyage,
And by that time Good Deeds will be with thee.
But in any wise be siker of mercy,
For your time draweth fast; and ye will saved be,
Ask God mercy, and he will grant truly.   570

---

483 **go** walk   484 **venture** gamble   491 **For . . . well** for help
would now be very welcome   495 **And . . . me** if you do as I
advise   499 **fall** befallen   500 **of** for   501 **If . . . me** if you had
encouraged me fully   503 **eke** also   508 **There . . . distress** a
sinful person in this hour of need finds that the account of his
good deeds is dimly written and difficult to read   520 **Knowledge** the meaning of Knowledge here is acknowledgment or
recognition of sins

---

528 **smart** pain   538 **cognition** knowledge   540 **In . . . salvation** in the church   544 **conceit** esteem   549 **Redempt . . .
contrition** redeemed by heartfelt and full contrition   552 **Shrift**
confession   553 **for . . . exclamation** in answer to my piteous
cry   558 **voider** expeller   568 **siker** sure   569 **draweth fast**
draws quickly to an end; **and** if

When with the scourge of penance man doth him bind,
The oil of forgiveness then shall he find.
EVERYMAN: Thanked be God for his gracious work!
For now I will my penance begin;
575 This hath rejoiced and lighted my heart,
Though the knots be painful and hard within.
KNOWLEDGE: Everyman, look your penance that ye fulfil,
What pain that ever it to you be;
And Knowledge shall give you counsel at will
580 How your account ye shall make clearly.
EVERYMAN: O eternal God, O heavenly figure,
O way of righteousness, O goodly vision,
Which descended down in a virgin pure
Because he would every man redeem,
585 Which Adam forfeited by his disobedience:
O blessed Godhead, elect and high divine,
Forgive my grievous offence;
Here I cry thee mercy in this presence.
O ghostly treasure, O ransomer and redeemer,
590 Of all the world hope and conductor,
Mirror of joy, and founder of mercy,
Which enlumineth heaven and earth thereby,
Hear my clamorous complaint, though it late be;
Receive my prayers, of thy benignity;
595 Though I be a sinner most abominable,
Yet let my name be written in Moses' table.
O Mary, pray to the Maker of all thing,
Me for to help at my ending;
And save me from the power of my enemy,
600 For Death assaileth me strongly.
And, Lady, that I may by mean of thy prayer
Of your Son's glory to be partner,
By the means of his passion, I it crave,
I beseech you help my soul to save.
605 Knowledge, give me the scourge of penance;
My flesh therewith shall give acquittance:
I will now begin, if God give me grace.
KNOWLEDGE: Everyman, God give you time and space!
Thus I bequeath you in the hands of our Saviour;
610 Now may you make your reckoning sure.
EVERYMAN: In the name of the Holy Trinity,
My body sore punished shall be:
Take this, body, for the sin of the flesh!

(*Scourges himself.*)

---

571 **him** himself   575 **lighted** lightened   576 **Though . . .
within** though the knots [of the scourge] be painful and hard to
my body   586 **divine** divinity   588 **in this presence** in the
presence of this company   592 **thereby** besides   596 **Yet . . .
table** medieval theologians regarded the two tables given on Sinai
as symbols of baptism and penance, respectively. Thus Everyman
is asking to be numbered among those who have escaped damnation by doing penance for their sins   599 **my enemy** the devil
601–603 **And . . . crave** and, Lady, I beg that through the me-
diation of thy prayer I may share in your Son's glory, in consequence of His passion   606 **acquittance** satisfaction (as a part of
the sacrament of penance)   608 **space** opportunity

Also thou delightest to go gay and fresh,
And in the way of damnation thou did me bring,   615
Therefore suffer now strokes and punishing.
Now of penance I will wade the water clear,
To save me from purgatory, that sharp fire.

(GOOD DEEDS *rises from the ground.*)

GOOD DEEDS: I thank God, now I can walk and go,
And am delivered of my sickness and woe.   620
Therefore with Everyman I will go, and not spare;
His good works I will help him to declare.
KNOWLEDGE: Now, Everyman, be merry and glad!
Your Good Deeds cometh now; ye may not be sad.
Now is your Good Deeds whole and sound,   625
Going upright upon the ground.
EVERYMAN: My heart is light, and shall be evermore;
Now will I smite faster than I did before.
GOOD DEEDS: Everyman, pilgrim, my special friend,
Blessed be thou without end;   630
For thee is preparate the eternal glory.
Ye have me made whole and sound,
Therefore I will bide by thee in every stound.
EVERYMAN: Welcome, my Good Deeds; now I hear thy voice,
I weep for very sweetness of love.   635
KNOWLEDGE: Be no more sad, but ever rejoice;
God seeth thy living in his throne above.
Put on this garment to thy behoof,
Which is wet with your tears,
Or else before God you may it miss,   640
When ye to your journey's end come shall.
EVERYMAN: Gentle Knowledge, what do ye it call?
KNOWLEDGE: It is a garment of sorrow:
From pain it will you borrow;
Contrition it is,   645
That geteth forgiveness;
It pleaseth God passing well.
GOOD DEEDS: Everyman, will you wear it for your heal?
EVERYMAN: Now blessed be Jesu, Mary's Son,
For now have I on true contrition.   650
And let us go now without tarrying;
Good Deeds, have we clear our reckoning?
GOOD DEEDS: Yea, indeed, I have it here.
EVERYMAN: Then I trust we need not fear;
Now, friends, let us not part in twain.   655
KNOWLEDGE: Nay, Everyman, that will we not, certain.
GOOD DEEDS: Yet must thou lead with thee
Three persons of great might.
EVERYMAN: Who should they be?
GOOD DEEDS: Discretion and Strength they hight,   660
And thy Beauty may not abide behind.
KNOWLEDGE: Also ye must call to mind
Your Five Wits as for your counsellors.
GOOD DEEDS: You must have them ready at all hours.
EVERYMAN: How shall I get them hither?   665

---

631 **preparate** prepared   633 **stound** trial   638 **behoof** advantage   644 **borrow** release   647 **passing** exceedingly   648 **heal**
salvation   660 **hight** are called   663 **Wits** senses

KNOWLEDGE: You must call them all together,
  And they will hear you incontinent.
EVERYMAN: My friends, come hither and be present,
  Discretion, Strength, my Five Wits, and Beauty.

(*Enter* BEAUTY, STRENGTH, DISCRETION, *and* FIVE WITS.)

670 BEAUTY: Here at your will we be all ready.
  What will ye that we should do?
  GOOD DEEDS: That ye would with Everyman go,
  And help him in his pilgrimage.
  Advise you, will ye with him or not in that voyage?
675 STRENGTH: We will bring him all thither,
  To his help and comfort, ye may believe me.
  DISCRETION: So will we go with him all together.
  EVERYMAN: Almighty God, lofed may thou be!
  I give thee laud that I have hither brought
680   Strength, Discretion, Beauty, and Five Wits. Lack
      I nought.
  And my Good Deeds, with Knowledge clear,
  All be in my company at my will here;
  I desire no more to my business.
  STRENGTH: And I, Strength, will by you stand in distress,
685   Though thou would be in battle fight on the ground.
  FIVE WITS: And though it were through the world round,
  We will not depart for sweet ne sour.
  BEAUTY: No more will I unto death's hour
  Whatsoever thereof befall.
690 DISCRETION: Everyman, advise you first of all;
  Go with a good advisement and deliberation.
  We all give you virtuous monition
  That all shall be well.
  EVERYMAN: My friends, harken what I will tell:
695   I pray God reward you in his heavenly sphere.
  Now harken, all that be here,
  For I will make my testament
  Here before you all present:
  In alms half my good I will give with my hands twain
700   In the way of charity, with good intent,
  And the other half still shall remain
  In queth, to be returned there it ought to be.
  This I do in despite of the fiend of hell,
  To go quit out of his peril
705   Ever after and this day.
  KNOWLEDGE: Everyman, harken what I say:
  Go to priesthood, I you advise,
  And receive of him in any wise
  The holy sacrament and ointment together.
710   Then shortly see ye turn again hither;
  We will all abide you here.
  FIVE WITS: Yea, Everyman, hie you that ye ready were.

There is no emperor, king, duke, ne baron,
  That of God hath commission
  As hath the least priest in the world being;   715
  For of the blessed sacraments pure and benign
  He beareth the keys, and thereof hath the cure
  For man's redemption—it is ever sure—
  Which God for our soul's medicine
  Gave us out of his heart with great pine.   720
  Here in this transitory life, for thee and me,
  The blessed sacraments seven there be:
  Baptism, confirmation, with priesthood good,
  And the sacrament of God's precious flesh and blood,
  Marriage, the holy extreme unction, and penance;   725
  These seven be good to have in remembrance,
  Gracious sacraments of high divinity.
EVERYMAN: Fain would I receive that holy body,
  And meekly to my ghostly father I will go.
FIVE WITS: Everyman, that is the best that ye can do.   730
  God will you to salvation bring,
  For priesthood exceedeth all other thing:
  To us Holy Scripture they do teach,
  And converteth man from sin heaven to reach;
  God hath to them more power given   735
  Than to any angel that is in heaven.
  With five words he may consecrate,
  God's body in flesh and blood to make,
  And handleth his Maker between his hands.
  The priest bindeth and unbindeth all bands,   740
  Both in earth and in heaven.
  Thou ministers all the sacraments seven;
  Though we kissed thy feet, thou were worthy;
  Thou art surgeon that cureth sin deadly:
  No remedy we find under God   745
  But all only priesthood.
  Everyman, God gave priests that dignity,
  And setteth them in his stead among us to be;
  Thus be they above angels in degree.

(EVERYMAN *goes to the priest to receive the last sacraments.*)

KNOWLEDGE: If priests be good, it is so, surely.   750
  But when Jesus hanged on the cross with great smart,
  There he gave out of his blessed heart
  The same sacrament in great torment:
  He sold them not to us, that Lord omnipotent.
  Therefore Saint Peter the apostle doth say   755
  That Jesu's curse hath all they
  Which God their Saviour do buy or sell,
  Or they for any money do take or tell.
  Sinful priests giveth the sinners example bad;
  Their children sitteth by other men's fires, I have heard;   760

---

667 **incontinent** immediately 674 **Advise** consider 678 **lofed** praised 683 **to** for 687 **for . . . sour** that is, in happiness or adversity 688 **unto** until 691 **advisement** reflection 692 **monition** forewarning 701–702 **And . . . be** the meaning seems to be that Everyman's immovable property (his body) will lie at rest in the earth 704–705 **To . . . day** to go free out of his power today and ever after 708 **in any wise** without fail 712 **hie . . . were** hurry and prepare yourself

714 **commission** authority 715 **being** living 720 **pine** suffering 728 **that holy body** the sacrament 729 **ghostly** spiritual 737 **five words** *Hoc est enim corpus meum* ("This is my body") 742 **ministers** administer 746 **But . . . priesthood** except only from the priesthood 749 **it is so** that they are above the angels 755–757 **Therefore . . . sell** the reference here is to the sin of simony (Acts 8:18 ff.) 760 **Their . . . fires** their children are illegitimate

And some haunteth women's company
With unclean life, as lusts of lechery:
These be with sin made blind.

FIVE WITS: I trust to God no such may we find;
765　Therefore let us priesthood honour,
And follow their doctrine for our souls' succour.
We be their sheep, and they shepherds be
By whom we all be kept in surety.
Peace, for yonder I see Everyman come,
770　Which hath made true satisfaction.

GOOD DEEDS: Methink it is he indeed.

(*Re-enter* EVERYMAN.)

EVERYMAN: Now Jesu be your alder speed!
I have received the sacrament for my redemption,
And then mine extreme unction:
775　Blessed be all they that counselled me to take it!
And now, friends, let us go without longer respite;
I thank God that ye have tarried so long.
Now set each of you on this rood your hand,
And shortly follow me:
780　I go before there I would be; God be our guide!

STRENGTH: Everyman, we will not from you go
Till ye have done this voyage long.

DISCRETION: I, Discretion, will bide by you also.

KNOWLEDGE: And though this pilgrimage be never so strong,
785　I will never part you fro.

STRENGTH: Everyman, I will be as sure by thee
As ever I did by Judas Maccabee.

(EVERYMAN *comes to his grave.*)

EVERYMAN: Alas, I am so faint I may not stand;
My limbs under me doth fold.
790　Friends, let us not turn again to this land,
Not for all the world's gold;
For into this cave must I creep
And turn to earth, and there to sleep.

BEAUTY: What, into this grave? Alas!
795　EVERYMAN: Yea, there shall ye consume, more and less.

BEAUTY: And what, should I smother here?

EVERYMAN: Yea, by my faith, and never more appear.
In this world live no more we shall,
But in heaven before the highest Lord of all.
800　BEAUTY: I cross out all this; adieu, by Saint John!
I take my cap in my lap, and am gone.

EVERYMAN: What, Beauty, whither will ye?

BEAUTY: Peace, I am deaf; I look not behind me,
Not and thou wouldest give me all the gold in thy chest.

(*Exit* BEAUTY.)

EVERYMAN: Alas, whereto may I trust?　805
Beauty goeth fast away from me;
She promised with me to live and die.

STRENGTH: Everyman, I will thee also forsake and deny;
Thy game liketh me not at all.

EVERYMAN: Why, then, ye will forsake me all?　810
Sweet Strength, tarry a little space.

STRENGTH: Nay, sir, by the rood of grace!
I will hie me from thee fast,
Though thou weep till thy heart to-brast.

EVERYMAN: Ye would ever bide by me, ye said.　815

STRENGTH: Yea, I have you far enough conveyed.
Ye be old enough, I understand,
Your pilgrimage to take on hand;
I repent me that I hither came.

EVERYMAN: Strength, you to displease I am to blame;　820
Yet promise is debt, this ye well wot.

STRENGTH: In faith, I care not.
Thou art but a fool to complain;
You spend your speech and waste your brain.
Go thrust thee into the ground!　825

(*Exit* STRENGTH.)

EVERYMAN: I had wend surer I should you have found.
He that trusteth in his Strength
She him deceiveth at the length.
Both Strength and Beauty forsaketh me;
Yet they promised me fair and lovingly.　830

DISCRETION: Everyman, I will after Strength be gone;
As for me, I will leave you alone.

EVERYMAN: Why, Discretion, will you forsake me?

DISCRETION: Yea, in faith, I will go from thee,
For when Strength goeth before　835
I follow after evermore.

EVERYMAN: Yet, I pray thee, for the love of the Trinity,
Look in my grave once piteously.

DISCRETION: Nay, so nigh will I not come;
Farewell, every one!　840

(*Exit* DISCRETION.)

EVERYMAN: O, all thing faileth, save God alone—
Beauty, Strength, and Discretion;
For when Death bloweth his blast,
They all run from me full fast.

FIVE WITS: Everyman, my leave now of thee I take;　845
I will follow the other, for here I thee forsake.

EVERYMAN: Alas, then may I wail and weep,
For I took you for my best friend.

FIVE WITS: I will no longer thee keep;
Now farewell, and there an end.　850

(*Exit* FIVE WITS.)

EVERYMAN: O Jesu, help! All hath forsaken me.

GOOD DEEDS: Nay, Everyman; I will bide with thee.
I will not forsake thee indeed;

---

772 **be . . . speed** be the helper of you all　778 **rood** cross
784 **strong** grievous　785 **you fro** from you　786–787 **Everyman . . . Maccabee** I will stand by you as steadfastly as ever I did by Judas Maccabaeus (I Macc. 3)　795 **consume . . . less** decay, all of you　800 **I . . . this** I cancel all this, that is, my promise to stay with you　801 **I . . . lap** I doff my cap (so low that it comes) into my lap

---

809 **liketh** pleases　811 **space** while　814 **to-brast** break
820 **you . . . blame** I am to blame for displeasing you

Thou shalt find me a good friend at need.
855 EVERYMAN: Gramercy, Good Deeds! Now may I true friends
see.
They have forsaken me, every one;
I loved them better than my Good Deeds alone.
Knowledge, will ye forsake me also?
KNOWLEDGE: Yea, Everyman, when ye to Death shall go;
860 But not yet, for no manner of danger.
EVERYMAN: Gramercy, Knowledge, with all my heart.
KNOWLEDGE: Nay, yet I will not from hence depart
Till I see where ye shall become.
EVERYMAN: Methink, alas, that I must be gone
865 To make my reckoning and my debts pay,
For I see my time is nigh spent away.
Take example, all ye that this do hear or see,
How they that I loved best do forsake me,
Except my Good Deeds that bideth truly.
870 GOOD DEEDS: All earthly things is but vanity:
Beauty, Strength, and Discretion do man forsake,
Foolish friends, and kinsmen, that fair spake—
All fleeth save Good Deeds, and that am I.
EVERYMAN: Have mercy on me, God most mighty;
875 And stand by me, thou mother and maid, holy Mary.
GOOD DEEDS: Fear not; I will speak for thee.
EVERYMAN: Here I cry God mercy.
GOOD DEEDS: Short our end, and minish our pain;
Let us go and never come again.
880 EVERYMAN: Into thy hands, Lord, my soul I commend;
Receive it, Lord, that it be not lost,
As thou me boughtest, so me defend,
And save me from the fiend's boast,
That I may appear with that blessed host
885 That shall be saved at the day of doom.
In manus tuas, of mights most
For ever, *commendo spiritum meum.*

(*He sinks into his grave.*)

KNOWLEDGE: Now hath he suffered that we all shall endure;
The Good Deeds shall make all sure.
Now hath he made ending; 890
Methinketh that I hear angels sing,
And make great joy and melody
Where Everyman's soul received shall be.
ANGEL: Come, excellent elect spouse, to Jesu!
Hereabove thou shalt go 895
Because of thy singular virtue.
Now the soul is taken the body fro,
Thy reckoning is crystal-clear.
Now shalt thou into the heavenly sphere,
Unto the which all ye shall come 900
That liveth well before the day of doom.

(*Enter* DOCTOR..)

DOCTOR: This moral men may have in mind.
Ye hearers, take it of worth, old and young,
And forsake Pride, for he deceiveth you in the end;
And remember Beauty, Five Wits, Strength, and 905
Discretion,
They all at the last do every man forsake,
Save his Good Deeds there doth he take.
But beware, for and they be small
Before God, he hath no help at all;
None excuse may be there for every man. 910
Alas, how shall he do then?
For after death amends may no man make,
For then mercy and pity doth him forsake.
If his reckoning be not clear when he doth come,
God will say: '*Ite, maledicti, in ignem eternum.*' 915
And he that hath his account whole and sound,
High in heaven he shall be crowned;
Unto which place God bring us all thither,
That we may live body and soul together.
Thereto help the Trinity! 920
Amen, say ye, for saint charity.

THUS ENDETH THIS MORAL PLAY OF EVERYMAN

863 **where . . . become** what shall become of you   878 **Short . . . pain** shorten our end, and diminish our pain   886–887 *In . . . meum* Into thy hands, most mighty One for ever, I commend my spirit

894 **spouse** bride of Jesus [a common medieval metaphor to express the idea of the soul's union with God]   903 **take . . . worth** value it   907 **Save** unless   915 *Ite . . . eternum* depart, ye cursed, into everlasting fire (Matthew xxv.41)

William Shakespeare

Given the fact that William Shakespeare (1564–1616) was a commoner and that he worked in the ephemeral trades of the theater, what we know about his life is extraordinarily rich and revealing, especially in comparison to the lives of other playwrights of the period, such as Christopher Marlowe or John Webster. William Shakespeare was born in Stratford-upon-Avon, a town to the northwest of London in Warwickshire. He was baptized on April 26, 1564, and was probably born a few days earlier—his birth date is conventionally given as April 23, the feast day of St. George, the patron saint of England, and the day on which Shakespeare died fifty-two years later in 1616, again at his home in Stratford. One of eight children, Shakespeare was the son of a glover—a tradesman who worked with a variety of leather goods. It is not known whether Shakespeare attended the local school, the King's New School, but like other schools of the period, it would have provided him with an extensive grounding in Latin grammar, rhetoric, and literature. Later in his career, Shakespeare often drew on works he could have read at such a school: plays by Terence and Plautus, the poetry of Virgil and Ovid, the writings of Caesar.

He married Anne Hathaway in November 1582; she was twenty-six and he was eighteen. In May 1583 they had their first daughter, Susannah, followed by twins, Hamnet and Judith, born in 1585. Although his wife and children remained in Stratford throughout his career, Shakespeare went to London sometime in the late 1580s, possibly joining one of the theater companies that passed through Stratford.

In the celebrated 1954 production of Shakespeare's *Hamlet,* Richard Burton takes leave of Claire Bloom as Ophelia.

By the 1590s, Shakespeare was established in London as an up-and-coming playwright; he was associated with the Lord Chamberlain's Men; he had written several plays on English history; and he was at work on several comedies and tragedies. When plague closed the theaters in London from the summer of 1592 through the spring of 1594, Shakespeare wrote two narrative poems, *Venus and Adonis* and *The Rape of Lucrece,* which he dedicated to Henry Wriothesley, the third Earl of Southampton, in a bid for patronage. He later wrote *The Phoenix and the Turtle* and circulated a brilliant and ambitious sequence of sonnets in manuscript before publishing it in 1609. As a shareholder of the Lord Chamberlain's Men, Shakespeare would have had many duties; no doubt he acted many parts, and we know he appeared in two plays by his contemporary, Ben Jonson—*Every Man in His Humour* and *Sejanus.* In 1598, the Lord Chamberlain's men tore down The Theatre, brought the timbers south of the city, and used them to build a new theater, the Globe. The Globe would remain the principal public-theater venue for the rest of Shakespeare's career, complemented by court and private-theater performances.

Shakespeare became the most popular playwright in London. He profited handsomely from his efforts at the Globe and from the patronage of the court, particularly after James I came to the throne in 1603 and took on the Lord Chamberlain's company as his own King's Men. Shakespeare used his income to buy a large house, called New Place, in Stratford, and throughout his career added to his property there; he retired and returned to Stratford in 1613. He drew up a will shortly before he died in 1616, leaving property to his family and mentioning gifts for several of his friends, including members of the King's Men: Richard Burbage, John Heminges, and Henry Condell. Heminges and Condell proved true to Shakespeare, for in 1623 they took Shakespeare's plays and published them in a single large volume. In an era when plays were not regarded as "literature," this was an important event. Although many of Shakespeare's plays had been published individually during his lifetime, roughly half of Shakespeare's plays (*Macbeth, Antony and Cleopatra,* and *The Tempest,* for instance) existed only in manuscript form at Shakespeare's death and certainly would not have survived without the efforts of Heminges and Condell. This complete volume is now usually called the "First Folio," because it is printed in a large, **FOLIO**-sized format (about twice the dimensions of this book). The First Folio contains thirty-six of Shakespeare's plays; two more plays all or partly by Shakespeare and published in his lifetime (*Pericles* and *The Two Noble Kinsmen*) were left out of the Folio, and it is generally thought that Shakespeare contributed to a thirty-ninth play, *Sir Thomas More,* of which only a short manuscript section survives. More recently, several scholars have argued that Shakespeare collaborated on a history play, *Edward III.* Finally, although many people have advanced the thesis that someone else actually wrote the "Shakespeare" plays—Sir Francis Bacon, Francis Walsingham, the Earl of Oxford, among others—these claims belong to the realm of myth, not to the realm of history.

The range of Shakespeare's accomplishment as a playwright is astonishing. Early in his career, Shakespeare wrote two cycles of plays on English history—*Henry VI* (Parts 1, 2, and 3) and *Richard III; and Richard II, Henry IV* (Parts 1 and 2), and *Henry V*—that not only established a vogue for history plays but gave the English audience an epic version of the struggles that founded the Tudor and Stuart dynasties. Shakespeare's early comedies—*The Comedy of Errors, Two Gentlemen of Verona*—are very much in the vein of Plautus. Later comedies—*A Midsummer Night's Dream, As You Like It, Twelfth Night, The Merchant of Venice*—explore a variety of complex relations between love, sexuality, adulthood, ethnic discrimination, power, politics, and money. To many audiences today, Shakespeare is most remembered for *Hamlet* and the magisterial series of tragedies that followed, including *Othello, King Lear,* and *Macbeth.* Shakespeare's achievements often began with experimentation. The major tragedies benefitted from his earlier efforts in the mode of the Roman playwright Seneca in *Titus Andronicus,* in morality drama in *Richard III,* in romantic tragedy in *Romeo and Juliet,* and political intrigue–drama in *Julius Caesar.* In his final years as a playwright, Shakespeare seems to have collaborated with John Fletcher on a few occasions and to have turned his hand to plays in the vein of "tragicomedy," now generally called **ROMANCE:** *Pericles, Cymbeline, The Winter's Tale,* and *The Tempest.*

HAMLET

In his landmark study, *The Idea of a Theater,* actor/scholar Francis Fergusson characterized *Hamlet* as one of the "sphinxes of literature," a play that has repeatedly drawn actors, audiences, and scholars into its labyrinthine mystery. Yet while *Hamlet,* like the brooding young prince of Denmark, may now seem like a difficult and philosophical problem, to its original audiences the play was a version of a popular genre on the Elizabethan stage, the revenge tragedy. As in many of his other plays, Shakespeare adapted his tragedy from a variety of known materials. The story of Amlethus, a disinherited Danish prince who uses feigned madness and cunning to avenge his father's murder and regain the throne from his villainous uncle, dates from the twelfth-century *Historia Danica* of the Danish historian Saxo Grammaticus; it was later adapted as a tragic narrative by François de Belleforest and included in his *Histoires tragiques* in 1576. Although Shakespeare may have known these versions, it is more certain that he knew a now-lost play on the subject of Hamlet's revenge that was staged in the 1580s. This play—usually called the *Ur-Hamlet* by scholars—was possibly written by Thomas Kyd, the author of another popular revenge tragedy, *The Spanish Tragedy*. While little is known about this play, we do know that it had at least one element of Shakespeare's play; in 1596, the playwright and novelist Thomas Lodge remarked on a play in which a pale ghost "cried so miserably at the Theater, like an oyster-wife, '*Hamlet, revenge!*'"

A ghost, a sinister and deceptive family, a court full of busybodies and spies, a broken romance, an elaborate play-within-the-play, a command, sometimes from beyond the grave, to take revenge, an elaborate finale in which the stage is littered with corpses—these devices were common in revenge tragedies preceding Shakespeare's play, such as *The Spanish Tragedy,* and common also in those which capitalized on *Hamlet*'s success in 1601, plays like John Marston's *The Malcontent* and Cyril Tourneur's *The Revenger's Tragedy* (which opens with a man speaking to a skull) and John Webster's *The White Devil. Hamlet* avails itself of all these devices, but it also reflects and refracts them; the play seems to question what it means to take action, simply to act, let alone take revenge, in a world of such complete duplicity that any behavior might seem the treacherous "actions that a man might play." In his famous essay, "The World of *Hamlet,*" Maynard Mack suggests that the play is in the "interrogative mood": not only does Hamlet repeatedly ask questions of himself and others ("To be or not to be . . . ," "Is it not monstrous . . . ," and so on), but much of the action of the play involves, as Polonius suggests, using theatrical "indirections" to "find directions out": Polonius sends Reynaldo to spread dishonorable rumors about Laertes, to see whether Laertes is being virtuous in Paris; Claudius and Polonius "stage" Ophelia for Hamlet, hoping to discover whether he's mad for revenge or madly in love; Hamlet hopes that the players' *The Murder of Gonzago* will reveal Claudius's guilt; Polonius hides fatally behind the arras while Hamlet interrogates Gertrude; Claudius stages a "duel" between Hamlet and Laertes that is really a design for murder.

The world of *Hamlet* is a world in which appearances sometimes deceive and sometimes speak the truth: not being able to read the signs—as Ophelia, Rosencrantz and Guildenstern, and Polonius all discover—can be fatal. Indeed, the play's obsession with seeming ("Seems, madam? Nay, it is. I know not 'seems,'" Hamlet declares in his first scene in the play) perhaps explains its obsession with the arts of seeming, with acting, performance, theater. In *Hamlet,* Shakespeare undertakes an extended meditation on the purpose and limits of theater. Hamlet, of course, is quite familiar with the theater, and Shakespeare clearly characterizes the troupe of players as his audience's contemporaries; not only is the company all male, but they seem to have left the city—as many professional companies did in the late 1590s—as a result of the "war of the theaters," the contemporary vogue for companies of boy-actors performing satirical plays. Moreover, Hamlet's famous advice to the players (3.2) suggests that he has a keen eye for performance. He chastens the actors not to "mouth it, as many of our players do," not to "saw the air too much with your hand," but to "Suit the action to the word, the word to the action." Yet in *Hamlet,* words and actions are more often than not suited to deception, to the extent that to Hamlet "this goodly frame, the earth, seems . . . a sterile promontory." Hamlet's blatant reference to the Globe itself—an actor, surrounded by the circular frame of the Globe, standing on the bare platform of the stage—suggests a skeptical regard for the theater's creation. While plays like *A Midsummer Night's Dream* or perhaps *The Tempest* suggest the theater's ability to present healing fictions, the theater in *Hamlet* is presented from a more ironic, even disaffected perspective: to be trapped in a theatrical world, a world where performance outruns truth, is to be trapped in a world of empty and sterile pretending.

Shakespeare was clearly captivated by the character of Hamlet, which is often described as the richest acting role in the theatrical repertoire. But the theatricality that besets Hamlet in the shady world of Elsinore also poses problems for Hamlet's many interpreters, not only for Polonius and Claudius—who spend much of the play trying to "read" Hamlet, figure him out—but for the generations of actors, audiences, and scholars who have attempted to "pluck out the heart of [his] mystery." The difficulties of sounding Hamlet, however, are also part of the play's elaborate design. From his opening scene in the play, in which Hamlet both wears the conventional black of mourning and chides his mother for presuming that he is seeming to be in mourning, Hamlet's performance challenges his audiences (both onstage and off) to "read" him, to interpret his character through the signs and signals of his behavior. That is, Hamlet presents the audience with the same challenges that any actor does, inviting us to interpret "that within" from the various behaviors that pass "show." And, contrary to Laurence Olivier—whose brilliant film of the play opens with a voice intoning that *Hamlet* is the story "of a man who could not make up his mind"—Hamlet seems to act decisively throughout the play; what's difficult about reading Hamlet is that it's hard to tell when he's *acting* and when he's "acting in earnest." Hamlet feigns madness in some scenes, but seems madly out of control in others, such as the "nunnery" scene with Ophelia or the scene in Gertrude's closet. He asks the player to act the part of vengeful Pyrrhus, then seems to adopt the murderous swagger of the stage revenger, and then to question his performance ("Why, what an ass am I"). He directs the players to insert a scene into *The Murder of Gonzago* to trick Claudius into revealing his guilt, and then can't seem to keep himself off the stage, interrupting and interpreting the play as they play it. He's so offended when Laertes stagily leaps into Ophelia's grave that he outperforms Laertes's overacting: "Nay, an thou'lt mouth, / I'll rant as well as thou." Even Hamlet's soliloquies are problematic in this regard. For although we might think that we hear the "true" Hamlet when he speaks alone onstage, how can we know that Hamlet isn't trying on another role, either for his own benefit or ours—as he seems to do when he plays the revenger in the "O what a rogue and peasant slave am I" speech? And as the play proceeds, Hamlet's soliloquies become less frequent, and less revealing: when he returns from England in Act 5—having sent his friends Rosencrantz and Guildenstern to their death—the play provides him with no more solo speeches; like the court, we have only Hamlet's abrupt and irritable actions to go on.

Hamlet was evidently a success when it was first performed in 1600 or 1601; a pirated version of the play (the so-called bad quarto, Q1) was published in 1603, presumably because the play's popularity suggested that a published text could make some money. A version of the play authorized by the King's Men was published in 1604 (the second quarto, Q2), and the play was later included in the 1623 Folio (F); although Q1 is the most corrupt version of the play, Q2 and F are by no means identical, and most modern texts collate elements of both versions.

From its inception, *Hamlet* has been a popular play with actors and audiences, and from Richard Burbage's creation of the role, Hamlet has been a mark of distinction in the history of English acting: the Restoration actor Thomas Betterton and the great eighteenth-century actor David Garrick were both admired in the part (Henry Fielding's novel *Tom Jones* contains a memorable parody of Garrick's performance). In the late nineteenth century Sir Henry Irving, the first actor to be knighted in England, gave a celebrated performance in which Hamlet never left the stage, but several other characters

(Rosencrantz and Guildenstern, for instance) were cut entirely. In the twentieth century, the play has, if anything, confirmed its reputation as an obligatory test for great actors, who have given a host of brilliant performances: Sir John Gielgud and Sir Laurence Olivier both produced fine stage versions of the play, and Olivier later won a Best Film Academy Award for his film version. Since World War II, Richard Burton, Jonathan Pryce, Derek Jacobi, and Michael Pennington are among the many actors to have given distinguished performances of this demanding play. The complexity of the play is something that faces actors even more immediately than readers of the play, because they will have to find a way to suit their acting to Hamlet's wild and whirling character. As Michael Pennington remarks in an essay on playing Hamlet, "To pull it off will take the actor further down into his psyche, memory and imagination, and further outwards to the limits of his technical knowledge and equipment, than he has probably been before."[1]

---

[1]Philip Brockbank, ed., *Players of Shakespeare: Essays in Shakespearean Performance by Twelve Players with the Royal Shakespeare Company* (Cambridge: Cambridge University Press, 1985), 117.

HAMLET

William Shakespeare

EDITED BY CYRUS HOY

CHARACTERS

CLAUDIUS, *King of Denmark*
HAMLET, *son to the late, and nephew to the present king*
POLONIUS, *Lord Chamberlain*
HORATIO, *friend to Hamlet*
LAERTES, *son to Polonius*
VOLTEMAND
CORNELIUS
ROSENCRANTZ ⎱ *courtiers*
GUILDENSTERN ⎰
OSRIC
A GENTLEMAN
A PRIEST
MARCELLUS ⎱ *officers*
BERNARDO ⎰

FRANCISCO, *a soldier*
REYNALDO, *servant to Polonius*
PLAYERS
TWO CLOWNS, *grave-diggers*
FORTINBRAS, *Prince of Norway*
A NORWEGIAN CAPTAIN
ENGLISH AMBASSADORS
GERTRUDE, *Queen of Denmark, and mother of Hamlet*
OPHELIA, *daughter to Polonius*
GHOST OF HAMLET'S FATHER
LORDS, LADIES, OFFICERS, SOLDIERS, SAILORS, MESSENGERS,
   and ATTENDANTS

SCENE: *Denmark.*

ACT ONE

SCENE I

Enter BERNARDO *and* FRANCISCO, *two sentinels.*

BERNARDO: Who's there?
FRANCISCO: Nay, answer me. Stand, and unfold yourself.
BERNARDO: Long live the king!
FRANCISCO: Bernardo?
5 BERNARDO: He.
FRANCISCO: You come most carefully upon your hour.
BERNARDO: 'Tis now struck twelve. Get thee to bed, Francisco.
FRANCISCO: For this relief much thanks. 'Tis bitter cold,
   And I am sick at heart.
10 BERNARDO: Have you had quiet guard?
FRANCISCO: Not a mouse stirring.
BERNARDO: Well, good night.
   If you do meet Horatio and Marcellus,
   The rivals of my watch, bid them make haste.

(*Enter* HORATIO *and* MARCELLUS.)

FRANCISCO: I think I hear them. Stand, ho! Who is there?
15 HORATIO: Friends to this ground.
MARCELLUS: And liegemen to the Dane.
FRANCISCO: Give you good night.
MARCELLUS: O, farewell, honest soldier!
   Who hath relieved you?
FRANCISCO: Bernardo hath my place.
   Give you good night.

(*Exit* FRANCISCO.)

MARCELLUS: Holla, Bernardo!
BERNARDO: Say—
   What, is Horatio there?

HORATIO: A piece of him.
20 BERNARDO: Welcome, Horatio. Welcome, good Marcellus.
HORATIO: What, has this thing appeared again to-night?
BERNARDO: I have seen nothing.
MARCELLUS: Horatio says 'tis but our fantasy,
   And will not let belief take hold of him
   Touching this dreaded sight twice seen of us.   25
   Therefore I have entreated him along
   With us to watch the minutes of this night,
   That if again this apparition come,
   He may approve our eyes and speak to it.
HORATIO: Tush, tush, 'twill not appear.   30
BERNARDO: Sit down awhile,
   And let us once again assail your ears,
   That are so fortified against our story,
   What we have two nights seen.
HORATIO: Well, sit we down,
   And let us hear Bernardo speak of this.
BERNARDO: Last night of all,   35
   When yond same star that's westward from the pole
   Had made his course t' illume that part of heaven
   Where now it burns, Marcellus and myself,
   The bell then beating one—

(*Enter* GHOST.)

MARCELLUS: Peace, break thee off. Look where it comes again. 40
BERNARDO: In the same figure like the king that's dead.
MARCELLUS: Thou art a scholar; speak to it, Horatio.
BERNARDO: Looks 'a not like the king? Mark it, Horatio.
HORATIO: Most like. It harrows me with fear and wonder.
BERNARDO: It would be spoke to.   45
MARCELLUS: Question it, Horatio.
HORATIO: What art thou that usurp'st this time of night
   Together with that fair and warlike form

---

13 rivals partners   15 **Dane** King of Denmark

29 **approve** confirm   36 **pole** polestar   44 **harrows** afflicts, distresses

In which the majesty of buried Denmark
Did sometimes march? By heaven I charge thee, speak.
50 MARCELLUS: It is offended.
BERNARDO: See, it stalks away.
HORATIO: Stay. Speak, speak. I charge thee, speak.

(*Exit* GHOST.)

MARCELLUS: 'Tis gone and will not answer.
BERNARDO: How now, Horatio! You tremble and look pale.
    Is not this something more than fantasy?
55   What think you on't?
HORATIO: Before my God, I might not this believe
    Without the sensible and true avouch
    Of mine own eyes.
MARCELLUS: Is it not like the king?
HORATIO: As thou art to thyself.
60   Such was the very armour he had on
    When he the ambitious Norway combated.
    So frowned he once when, in an angry parle,
    He smote the sledded Polacks on the ice.
    'Tis strange.
65 MARCELLUS: Thus twice before, and jump at this dead hour,
    With martial stalk hath he gone by our watch.
HORATIO: In what particular thought to work I know not,
    But in the gross and scope of mine opinion,
    This bodes some strange eruption to our state.
70 MARCELLUS: Good now, sit down, and tell me he that knows,
    Why this same strict and most observant watch
    So nightly toils the subject of the land,
    And why such daily cast of brazen cannon
    And foreign mart for implements of war;
75   Why such impress of shipwrights, whose sore task
    Does not divide the Sunday from the week.
    What might be toward that this sweaty haste
    Doth make the night joint-laborer with the day?
    Who is't that can inform me?
HORATIO: That can I.
80   At least, the whisper goes so. Our last king,
    Whose image even but now appeared to us,
    Was as you know by Fortinbras of Norway,
    Thereto pricked on by a most emulate pride,
    Dared to the combat; in which our valiant Hamlet
85   (For so this side of our known world esteemed him)
    Did slay this Fortinbras; who by a sealed compact
    Well ratified by law and heraldry,
    Did forfeit, with his life, all those his lands
    Which he stood seized of, to the conqueror;
90   Against the which a moiety competent

Was gagèd by our king; which had returned
To the inheritance of Fortinbras,
Had he been vanquisher; as, by the same comart
And carriage of the article designed,
His fell to Hamlet. Now, sir, young Fortinbras,   95
Of unimprovèd mettle hot and full,
Hath in the skirts of Norway here and there
Sharked up a list of lawless resolutes
For food and diet to some enterprise
That hath a stomach in't; which is no other,   100
As it doth well appear unto our state,
But to recover of us by strong hand
And terms compulsatory, those foresaid lands
So by his father lost; and this, I take it,
Is the main motive of our preparations,   105
The source of this our watch, and the chief head
Of this post-haste and romage in the land.
BERNARDO: I think it be no other but e'en so.
    Well may it sort that this portentous figure
    Comes armèd through our watch; so like the king   110
    That was and is the question of these wars.
HORATIO: A mote it is to trouble the mind's eye.
    In the most high and palmy state of Rome,
    A little ere the mightiest Julius fell,
    The graves stood tenantless and the sheeted dead 115
    Did squeak and gibber in the Roman streets;
    As stars with trains of fire, and dews of blood,
    Disasters in the sun; and the moist star,
    Upon whose influence Neptune's empire stands,
    Was sick almost to doomsday with eclipse.   120
    And even the like precurse of feared events,
    As harbingers preceding still the fates
    And prologue to the omen coming on,
    Have heaven and earth together demonstrated
    Unto our climatures and countrymen.   125

(*Enter* GHOST.)

    But soft, behold, lo where it comes again!
    I'll cross it though it blast me.—Stay, illusion.

([GHOST] *spreads his arms.*)

    If thou hast any sound or use of voice,
    Speak to me.
    If there be any good thing to be done,   130
    That may to thee do ease, and grace to me,
    Speak to me.
    If thou art privy to thy country's fate,
    Which happily foreknowing may avoid,

---

48 **buried Denmark** the buried King of Denmark   49 **sometimes** formerly   57 **sensible** confirmed by one of the senses   61 **Norway** King of Norway   62 **parle** parley   63 **sledded Polacks** the Poles mounted on sleds or sledges   65 **jump** just, exactly   68 **gross and scope** general drift   72 **toils** causes to toil; **subject** people   74 **mart** traffic, bargaining   75 **impress** conscription   77 **toward** imminent, impending   83 **emulate** ambitious   87 **heraldry** the law of arms, regulating tournaments and state combats   89 **seized** possessed   90 **moiety competent** sufficient portion

91 **gagèd** pledged   93 **comart joint** bargain   94 **carriage** import   96 **unimprovèd** unrestrained   98 **Sharked up** picked up indiscriminately   100 **stomach** spice of adventure   106 **head** fountainhead   107 **romage** turmoil   109 **sort suit**, be in accordance   112 **mote** particle of dust   113 **palmy** flourishing   115 **sheeted** in shrouds   118 **Disasters** ominous signs; **moist star** the moon   121 **precurse** heralding, foreshadowing   122 **harbingers** forerunners; **still** ever   123 **omen** ominous event   125 **climatures** regions   127 **cross it** cross its path   134 **happily** haply, perchance

135   O, speak!
      Or if thou hast uphoarded in thy life
      Extorted treasure in the womb of earth,
      For which, they say, you spirits oft walk in death,

(*The cock crows.*)

      Speak of it. Stay, and speak. Stop it, Marcellus.
140 MARCELLUS: Shall I strike at it with my partisan?
    HORATIO: Do, if it will not stand.
    BERNARDO: 'Tis here.
    HORATIO: 'Tis here!

(*Exit* GHOST.)

    MARCELLUS: 'Tis gone!
      We do it wrong, being so majestical,
      To offer it the show of violence;
145   For it is as the air, invulnerable,
      And our vain blows malicious mockery.
    BERNARDO: It was about to speak when the cock crew.
    HORATIO: And then it started like a guilty thing
      Upon a fearful summons. I have heard
150   The cock, that is the trumpet to the morn,
      Doth with his lofty and shrill-sounding throat
      Awake the god of day and at his warning,
      Whether in sea or fire, in earth or air,
      Th' extravagant and erring spirit hies
155   To his confine; and of the truth herein
      This present object made probation.
    MARCELLUS: It faded on the crowing of the cock.
      Some say that ever 'gainst that season comes
      Wherein our Saviour's birth is celebrated,
160   The bird of dawning singeth all night long,
      And then, they say, no spirit dare stir abroad.
      The nights are wholesome, then no planets strike,
      No fairy takes, nor witch hath power to charm,
      So hallowed and so gracious is that time.
165 HORATIO: So have I heard and do in part believe it.
      But look, the morn in russet mantle clad
      Walks o'er the dew of yon high eastward hill.
      Break we our watch up, and by my advice
      Let us impart what we have seen to-night
170   Unto young Hamlet, for, upon my life
      This spirit, dumb to us, will speak to him.
      Do you consent we shall acquaint him with it,
      As needful in our loves, fitting our duty?
    MARCELLUS: Let's do't, I pray, and I this morning know
175   Where we shall find him most convenient.

(*Exeunt.*)

SCENE II

Flourish. Enter CLAUDIUS, KING OF DENMARK, GERTRUDE THE
QUEEN, COUNCILLORS, [*including*] POLONIUS *and his son* LAERTES,
HAMLET, *cum aliis* [*including* VOLTEMAND *and* CORNELIUS.]

KING: Though yet of Hamlet our dear brother's death
      The memory be green, and that it us befitted
      To bear our hearts in grief, and our whole kingdom
      To be contracted in one brow of woe,
      Yet so far hath discretion fought with nature   5
      That we with wisest sorrow think on him,
      Together with remembrance of ourselves.
      Therefore our sometime sister, now our queen,
      Th' imperial jointress to this warlike state,
      Have we, as 'twere with a defeated joy,   10
      With an auspicious and a dropping eye,
      With mirth in funeral and with dirge in marriage,
      In equal scale weighing delight and dole,
      Taken to wife; nor have we herein barred
      Your better wisdoms, which have freely gone   15
      With this affair along. For all, our thanks.
      Now follows that you know young Fortinbras,
      Holding a weak supposal of our worth,
      Or thinking by our late dear brother's death
      Our state to be disjoint and out of frame,   20
      Colleaguèd with this dream of his advantage,
      He hath not failed to pester us with message
      Importing the surrender of those lands
      Lost by his father, with all bands of law,
      To our most valiant brother. So much for him.   25
      Now for ourself, and for this time of meeting,
      Thus much the business is: we have here writ
      To Norway, uncle of young Fortinbras—
      Who, impotent and bedrid, scarcely hears
      Of this his nephew's purpose—to suppress   30
      His further gait herein, in that the levies,
      The lists, and full proportions are all made
      Out of his subject; and we here dispatch
      You, good Cornelius, and you, Voltemand,
      For bearers of this greeting to old Norway,   35
      Giving to you no further personal power
      To business with the king, more than the scope
      Of these delated articles allow.
      Farewell, and let your haste commend your duty.
    CORNELIUS: ⎫ In that and all things will we show our duty 40
    VOLTEMAND: ⎭
    KING: We doubt it nothing, heartily farewell.

(*Exeunt* VOLTEMAND *and* CORNELIUS.)

      And now, Laertes, what's the news with you?
      You told us of some suit. What is't, Laertes?
      You cannot speak of reason to the Dane
      And lose your voice. What wouldst thou beg, Laertes, 45
      That shall not be my offer, not thy asking?
      The head is not more native to the heart,
      The hand more instrumental to the mouth,
      Than is the throne of Denmark to thy father.
      What wouldst thou have, Laertes?   50

---

140 **partisan** pike   154 **extravagant** straying, vagrant; **erring**
wandering   156 **probation** proof   158 **'gainst** just before
162 **strike** blast, destroy by malign influence   163 **takes** be-
witches

I.ii. s.d. **cum aliis** with others

9 **jointress** a widow who holds a jointure or life interest in an
estate   14 **barred** excluded   21 **Colleaguèd** united   31 **gait**
proceeding   32 **proportions** forces or supplies for war   38
delated expressly stated   44 **Dane** King of Denmark   45 **lose
your voice** speak in vain   47 **native** joined by nature   48 **instrumental** serviceable

LAERTES: My dread lord,
    Your leave and favour to return to France,
    From whence, though willingly, I came to Denmark
    To show my duty in your coronation,
    Yet now I must confess, that duty done,
55   My thoughts and wishes bend again toward France,
    And bow them to your gracious leave and pardon.
KING: Have you your father's leave? What says Polonius?
POLONIUS: He hath, my lord, wrung from me my slow leave
    By laborsome petition, and at last
60   Upon his will I sealed my hard consent.
    I do beseech you give him leave to go.
KING: Take thy fair hour, Laertes. Time be thine,
    And thy best graces spend it at thy will.
    But now, my cousin Hamlet, and my son—
65 HAMLET: (*Aside.*) A little more than kin, and less than kind.
KING: How is it that the clouds still hang on you?
HAMLET: Not so, my lord. I am too much in the sun.
QUEEN: Good Hamlet, cast thy nighted color off,
    And let thine eye look like a friend on Denmark.
70   Do not for ever with thy vailèd lids
    Seek for thy noble father in the dust.
    Thou know'st 'tis common—all that lives must die,
    Passing through nature to eternity.
HAMLET: Ay, madam, it is common.
QUEEN: If it be,
75   Why seems it so particular with thee?
HAMLET: Seems, madam? Nay, it is. I know not 'seems.'
    'Tis not alone my inky cloak, good mother,
    Nor customary suits of solemn black,
    Nor windy suspiration of forced breath,
80   No, nor the fruitful river in the eye,
    Nor the dejected haviour of the visage,
    Together with all forms, moods, shapes of grief,
    That can denote me truly. These indeed seem,
    For they are actions that a man might play,
85   But I have that within which passeth show—
    These but the trappings and the suits of woe.
KING: 'Tis sweet and commendable in your nature, Hamlet,
    To give these mourning duties to your father,
    But you must know your father lost a father,
90   That father lost, lost his, and the survivor bound
    In filial obligation for some term
    To do obsequious sorrow. But to persever
    In obstinate condolement is a course
    Of impious stubbornness. 'Tis unmanly grief.
95   It shows a will most incorrect to heaven,
    A heart unfortified, a mind impatient,
    An understanding simple and unschooled.
    For what we know must be, and is as common
    As any the most vulgar thing to sense,
100   Why should we in our peevish opposition
    Take it to heart? Fie, 'tis a fault to heaven,
    A fault against the dead, a fault to nature,

To reason most absurd, whose common theme
    Is death of fathers, and who still hath cried,
    From the first corse till he that died to-day,   105
    'This must be so.' We pray you throw to earth
    This unprevailing woe, and think of us
    As of a father, for let the world take note
    You are the most immediate to our throne,
    And with no less nobility of love   110
    Than that which dearest father bears his son
    Do I impart toward you. For your intent
    In going back to school in Wittenberg,
    It is most retrograde to our desire,
    And we beseech you, bend you to remain   115
    Here in the cheer and comfort of our eye,
    Our chiefest courtier, cousin, and our son.
QUEEN: Let not thy mother lose her prayers, Hamlet.
    I pray thee stay with us, go not to Wittenberg.
HAMLET: I shall in all my best obey you, madam.   120
KING: Why, 'tis a loving and a fair reply.
    Be as ourself in Denmark. Madam, come.
    This gentle and unforced accord of Hamlet
    Sits smiling to my heart, in grace whereof,
    No jocund health that Denmark drinks to-day   125
    But the great cannon to the clouds shall tell,
    And the king's rouse the heaven shall bruit again,
    Respeaking earthly thunder. Come away.

(*Flourish. Exeunt all but* HAMLET.)

HAMLET: O, that this too too sallied flesh would melt,
    Thaw and resolve itself into a dew,   130
    Or that the Everlasting had not fixed
    His canon 'gainst self-slaughter. O God, God,
    How weary, stale, flat, and unprofitable
    Seem to me all the uses of this world!
    Fie on't, ah, fie, 'tis an unweeded garden   135
    That grows to seed. Things rank and gross in nature
    Possess it merely. That it should come to this,
    But two months dead, nay, not so much, not two.
    So excellent a king, that was to this
    Hyperion to a satyr, so loving to my mother,   140
    That he might not beteem the winds of heaven
    Visit her face too roughly. Heaven and earth,
    Must I remember? Why, she would hang on him
    As if increase of appetite had grown
    By what it fed on, and yet, within a month—   145
    Let me not think on't. Frailty, thy name is woman—
    A little month, or ere those shoes were old
    With which she followed my poor father's body

---

56 **pardon** indulgence   60 **hard** reluctant   64 **cousin** kinsman of any kind except parent, child, brother, or sister   65 **kin** related as nephew; **kind** (1) affectionate (2) natural, lawful   70 **vailèd** lowered   75 **particular** personal, individual   92 **obsequious** dutiful in performing funeral obsequies or manifesting regard for the dead; **persever** persevere

105 **corse** corpse   114 **retrograde** contrary   127 **rouse** full draught of liquor; **bruit** echo   129 **sallied** sullied. "Sallied" is the reading of *Quarto 2* (*Q2*, also *Q1*). *Folio* (*F*) reads "solid." Since Hamlet's primary concern is with the fact of the flesh's impurity, not with its corporeality, the choice as between *Q* and *F* clearly lies with *Q*. "Sally" is a legitimate sixteenth-century form of "sully"; it occurs in Dekker's *Patient Grissil* (1.1.12), printed in 1603, as F.T. Bowers has pointed out (in "Hamlet's 'Sullied' or 'Solid' Flesh. A Bibliographical Case-History," *Shakespeare Survey* 9 [1956]: p. 44); and it occurs as a noun at 2.1.39 of *Hamlet*   132 **canon** law   137 **merely** entirely   140 **Hyperion** the sun god   141 **beteem** allowed

Like Niobe, all tears, why she—
150 O God, a beast that wants discourse of reason
Would have mourned longer—married with my uncle,
My father's brother, but no more like my father
Than I to Hercules. Within a month,
Ere yet the salt of most unrighteous tears
155 Had left the flushing in her gallèd eyes,
She married. O, most wicked speed, to post
With such dexterity to incestuous sheets!
It is not, nor it cannot come to good.
But break my heart, for I must hold my tongue.

(*Enter* HORATIO, MARCELLUS, *and* BERNARDO.)

160 HORATIO: Hail to your lordship!
HAMLET: I am glad to see you well.
Horatio—or I do forget myself.
HORATIO: The same, my lord, and your poor servant ever.
HAMLET: Sir, my good friend, I'll change that name with you.
And what make you from Wittenberg, Horatio?
165 Marcellus?
MARCELLUS: My good lord!
HAMLET: I am very glad to see you. (*To* BERNARDO.) Good
even, sir.—
But what, in faith, make you from Wittenberg?
HORATIO: A truant disposition, good my lord.
170 HAMLET: I would not hear your enemy say so,
Nor shall you do my ear that violence
To make it truster of your own report
Against yourself. I know you are no truant.
But what is your affair in Elsinore?
175 We'll teach you to drink deep ere you depart.
HORATIO: My lord, I came to see your father's funeral.
HAMLET: I prithee, do not mock me, fellow-student,
I think it was to see my mother's wedding.
HORATIO: Indeed, my lord, it followed hard upon.
180 HAMLET: Thrift, thrift, Horatio. The funeral baked meats
Did coldly furnish forth the marriage tables.
Would I had met my dearest foe in heaven
Or ever I had seen that day, Horatio!
My father—methinks I see my father.
185 HORATIO: Where, my lord?
HAMLET: In my mind's eye, Horatio.
HORATIO: I saw him once, 'a was a goodly king.
HAMLET: 'A was a man, take him for all in all,
I shall not look upon his like again.
HORATIO: My lord, I think I saw him yesternight.
190 HAMLET: Saw who?
HORATIO: My lord, the king your father.
HAMLET: The king my father?
HORATIO: Season your admiration for a while
With an attent ear, till I may deliver

Upon the witness of these gentlemen
This marvel to you.   195
HAMLET: For God's love, let me hear!
HORATIO: Two nights together had these gentlemen,
Marcellus and Bernardo, on their watch
In the dead waste and middle of the night
Been thus encountered. A figure like your father,
Armed at point exactly, cap-a-pe,   200
Appears before them, and with solemn march
Goes slow and stately by them. Thrice he walked
By their oppressed and fear-surprisèd eyes
Within his truncheon's length, whilst they, distilled
Almost to jelly with the act of fear,   205
Stand dumb and speak not to him. This to me
In dreadful secrecy impart they did,
And I with them the third night kept the watch,
Where, as they had delivered, both in time,
Form of the thing, each word made true and good,   210
The apparition comes. I knew your father.
These hands are not more like.
HAMLET: But where was this?
MARCELLUS: My lord, upon the platform where we watch.
HAMLET: Did you not speak to it?
HORATIO: My lord, I did,
But answer made it none. Yet once methought   215
It lifted up it head and did address
Itself to motion, like as it would speak;
But even then the morning cock crew loud,
And at the sound it shrunk in haste away
And vanished from our sight.   220
HAMLET: 'Tis very strange.
HORATIO: As I do live, my honoured lord, 'tis true,
And we did think it writ down in our duty
To let you know of it.
HAMLET: Indeed, sirs, but
This troubles me. Hold you the watch to-night?
ALL: We do, my lord.   225
HAMLET: Armed, say you?
ALL: Armed, my lord.
HAMLET: From top to toe?
ALL: My lord, from head to foot.
HAMLET: Then saw you not his face.
HORATIO: O yes, my lord, he wore his beaver up.
HAMLET: What, looked he frowningly?
HORATIO: A countenance more in sorrow than in anger.   230
HAMLET: Pale or red?
HORATIO: Nay, very pale.
HAMLET: And fixed his eyes upon you?
HORATIO: Most constantly.
HAMLET: I would I had been there.
HORATIO: It would have much amazed you.
HAMLET: Very like.
Stayed it long?   235
HORATIO: While one with moderate haste might tell
a hundred.
BOTH: Longer, longer.

---

149 **Niobe** wife of Amphion, King of Thebes, she boasted of having more children than Leto and was punished when her seven sons and seven daughters were slain by Apollo and Artemis, children of Leto; in her grief she was changed by Zeus into a stone, which continually dropped tears 150 **wants** lacks; **discourse of reason** the reasoning faculty 155 **gallèd** sore from rubbing or chafing 163 **change** exchange 164 **make do** 182 **dearest** direst 192 **season** temper, moderate; **admiration** wonder, astonishment

---

200 **at point** exactly in every particular; **cap-a-pe** from head to foot 204 **truncheon** military leader's baton 216 **it** its 228 **beaver** the part of the helmet that was drawn down to cover the face 235 **tell** count

HORATIO: Not when I saw't.
HAMLET: His beard was grizzled, no?
HORATIO: It was as I have seen it in his life,
    A sable silvered.
HAMLET: I will watch to-night.
240   Perchance 'twill walk again.
HORATIO: I warr'nt it will.
HAMLET: If it assume my noble father's person,
    I'll speak to it though hell itself should gape
    And bid me hold my peace. I pray you all,
    If you have hitherto concealed this sight,
245   Let it be tenable in your silence still,
    And whatsomever else shall hap to-night,
    Give it an understanding but no tongue.
    I will requite your loves. So fare you well.
    Upon the platform 'twixt eleven and twelve
250   I'll visit you.
ALL: Our duty to your honor.
HAMLET: Your loves, as mine to you. Farewell.

(*Exeunt* [*all but* HAMLET].)

    My father's spirit in arms? All is not well.
    I doubt some foul play. Would the night were come!
    Till then sit still, my soul. Foul deeds will rise,
255   Though all the earth o'erwhelm them, to men's eyes.

(*Exit.*)

SCENE III

Enter LAERTES *and* OPHELIA *his sister.*

LAERTES: My necessaries are embarked. Farewell.
    And, sister, as the winds give benefit
    And convoy is assistant, do not sleep,
    But let me hear from you.
OPHELIA: Do you doubt that?
5 LAERTES: For Hamlet, and the trifling of his favor,
    Hold it a fashion and a toy in blood,
    A violet in the youth of primy nature,
    Forward, not permanent, sweet, not lasting,
    The perfume and suppliance of a minute,
10   No more.
OPHELIA: No more but so?
LAERTES: Think it no more.
    For nature crescent does not grow alone
    In thews and bulk, but as this temple waxes
    The inward service of the mind and soul
    Grows wide withal. Perhaps he loves you now,
15   And now no soil nor cautel doth besmirch
    The virtue of his will, but you must fear,
    His greatness weighed, his will is not his own,
    For he himself is subject to his birth.

He may not, as unvalued persons do,
Carve for himself, for on his choice depends   20
The safety and health of this whole state,
And therefore must his choice be circumscribed
Unto the voice and yielding of that body
Whereof he is the head. Then if he says he loves you,
It fits your wisdom so far to believe it   25
As he in his particular act and place
May give his saying deed, which is no further
Than the main voice of Denmark goes withal.
Then weigh what loss your honor may sustain
If with too credent ear you list his songs,   30
Or lose your heart, or your chaste treasure open
To his unmastered importunity.
Fear it, Ophelia, fear it, my dear sister,
And keep you in the rear of your affection,
Out of the shot and danger of desire.   35
The chariest maid is prodigal enough
If she unmask her beauty to the moon.
Virtue itself scapes not calumnious strokes.
The canker galls the infants of the spring
Too oft before their buttons be disclosed,   40
And in the morn and liquid dew of youth
Contagious blastments are most imminent.
Be wary then; best safety lies in fear.
Youth to itself rebels, though none else near.
OPHELIA: I shall the effect of this good lesson keep   45
    As watchman to my heart. But, good my brother,
    Do not as some ungracious pastors do,
    Show me the steep and thorny way to heaven,
    Whiles like a puffed and reckless libertine
    Himself the primrose path of dalliance treads   50
    And recks not his own rede.
LAERTES: O, fear me not.

(*Enter* POLONIUS.)

    I stay too long. But here my father comes.
    A double blessing is a double grace;
    Occasion smiles upon a second leave.
POLONIUS: Yet here, Laertes? Aboard, aboard, for shame!   55
    The wind sits in the shoulder of your sail,
    And you are stayed for. There, my blessing with thee,
    And these few precepts in thy memory
    Look thou character. Give thy thoughts no tongue,
    Nor any unproportioned thought his act.   60
    Be thou familiar, but by no means vulgar.
    Those friends thou hast, and their adoption tried,
    Grapple them to thy soul with hoops of steel,
    But do not dull thy palm with entertainment
    Of each new-hatched, unfledged courage. Beware   65
    Of entrance to a quarrel, but being in,

---

237 **grizzled** grayish   239 **sable silvered** black mixed with white   245 **tenable** retained   246 **whatsomever** whatsover   253 **doubt** suspect

I.iii.   6 **fashion** the creation of a season only; **toy in blood** passing fancy   7 **primy** of the springtime   11 **crescent** growing   12 **thews** sinews, strength; **this temple** the body   15 **cautel** deceit   16 **will** desire   17 **greatness weighed** high position considered

---

19 **unvalued persons** persons of no social importance   20 **Carve for himself** act according to his own inclination   23 **yielding** assent   30 **credent** trusting   34 **affection** feeling   39 **canker** canker-worm (which feeds on roses); **galls** injures   40 **buttons** buds   42 **blastments** blights   51 **recks** regards; **rede** counsel   59 **character** engrave   60 **unproportioned** inordinate   61 **vulgar** common   65 **courage** young blood, man of spirit

Bear't that th' opposèd may beware of thee.
Give every man thy ear, but few thy voice;
Take each man's censure, but reserve thy judgement.
70 Costly thy habit as thy purse can buy,
But not expressed in fancy; rich not gaudy,
For the apparel oft proclaims the man,
And they in France of the best rank and station
Are of a most select and generous chief in that.
75 Neither a borrower nor a lender be,
For loan oft loses both itself and friend,
And borrowing dulls th' edge of husbandry.
This above all, to thine own self be true,
And it must follow as the night the day
80 Thou canst not then be false to any man.
Farewell. My blessing season this in thee!
LAERTES: Most humbly do I take my leave, my lord.
POLONIUS: The time invites you. Go, your servants tend
LAERTES: Farewell, Ophelia, and remember well
85 What I have said to you.
OPHELIA: 'Tis in my memory locked,
And you yourself shall keep the key of it.
LAERTES: Farewell.

(*Exit* LAERTES.)

POLONIUS: What is 't, Ophelia, he hath said to you?
OPHELIA: So please you, something touching the Lord
    Hamlet.
90 POLONIUS: Marry, well bethought.
'Tis told me he hath very oft of late
Given private time to you, and you yourself
Have of your audience been most free and bounteous.
If it be so—as so 'tis put on me,
95 And that in way of caution—I must tell you,
You do not understand yourself so clearly
As it behooves my daughter and your honor.
What is between you? Give me up the truth.
OPHELIA: He hath, my lord, of late made many tenders
100 Of his affection to me.
POLONIUS: Affection? Pooh! You speak like a green girl,
Unsifted in such perilous circumstance.
Do you believe his tenders, as you call them?
OPHELIA: I do not know, my lord, what I should think.
105 POLONIUS: Marry, I will teach you. Think yourself a baby
That you have ta'en these tenders for true pay
Which are not sterling. Tender yourself more dearly,
Or (not to crack the wind of the poor phrase,
Running it thus) you'll tender me a fool.
110 OPHELIA: My lord, he hath importuned me with love
In honorable fashion.
POLONIUS: Ay, fashion you may call it. Go to, go to.
OPHELIA: And hath given countenance to his speech, my lord,
With almost all the holy vows of heaven.
115 POLONIUS: Ay, springes to catch woodcocks. I do know,
When the blood burns, how prodigal the soul
Lends the tongue vows. These blazes, daughter,
Giving more light than heat, extinct in both

Even in their promise, as it is a-making,
You must not take for fire. From this time   120
Be something scanter of your maiden presence.
Set your entreatments at a higher rate
Than a command to parle. For Lord Hamlet,
Believe so much in him that he is young,
And with a larger tether may he walk   125
Than may be given you. In few, Ophelia,
Do not believe his vows, for they are brokers,
Not of that dye which their investments show,
But mere implorators of unholy suits,
Breathing like sanctified and pious bawds,   130
The better to beguile. This is for all:
I would not, in plain terms, from this time forth
Have you so slander any moment leisure
As to give words or talk with the Lord Hamlet.
Look to't, I charge you. Come your ways.   135
OPHELIA: I shall obey, my lord.

(*Exeunt.*)

SCENE IV

Enter HAMLET, HORATIO, *and* MARCELLUS.

HAMLET: The air bites shrewdly; it is very cold.
HORATIO: It is a nipping and an eager air.
HAMLET: What hour now?
HORATIO: I think it lacks of twelve.
MARCELLUS: No, it is struck.
HORATIO: Indeed? I heard it not. It then draws near the season 5
Wherein the spirit held his wont to walk.

(*A flourish of trumpets, and two pieces go off.*)

What does this mean, my lord?
HAMLET: The king doth wake to-night and takes his rouse,
Keeps wassail, and the swagg'ring up-spring reels,
And as he drains his draughts of Rhenish down,   10
The kettledrum and trumpet thus bray out
The triumph of his pledge.
HORATIO: Is it a custom?
HAMLET: Ay, marry, is't,
But to my mind, though I am native here
And to the manner born, it is a custom   15
More honored in the breach than the observance.
This heavy-headed revel east and west
Makes us traduced and taxed of other nations.
They clepe us drunkards, and with swinish phrase
Soil our addition, and indeed it takes   20
From our achievements, though performed at height,
The pith and marrow of our attribute.
So oft it chances in particular men,
That for some vicious mole of nature in them,

---

122 **entreatments** military negotiations for surrender   127
brokers go-betweens   128 **investments** clothes   129 **implorators** solicitors

I.iv, 2 **eager** sharp   9 **wassail** carousal; **up-spring** a German dance   18 **taxed of** censured by   19 **clepe** call   20 **addition** title added to a man's name to denote his rank   22 **attribute** reputation

---

74 **chief** eminence   77 **husbandry** thriftiness   81 **season** ripen   83 **tend** attend, wait   90 **Marry** by Mary   99 **tenders** offers   102 **Unsifted** untried   115 **springes** snares

25   As, in their birth, wherein they are not guilty
        (Since nature cannot choose his origin),
        By the o'ergrowth of some complexion,
        Oft breaking down the pales and forts of reason,
        Or by some habit that too much o'er-leavens
30   The form of plausive manners—that these men,
        Carrying, I say, the stamp of one defect,
        Being nature's livery or fortune's star,
        His virtues else, be they as pure as grace,
        As infinite as man may undergo,
35   Shall in the general censure take corruption
        From that particular fault. The dram of evil
        Doth all the noble substance often doubt
        To his own scandal.

(Enter GHOST.)

HORATIO: Look, my lord, it comes.
HAMLET: Angels and ministers of grace defend us!
40   Be thou a spirit of health or goblin damned,
        Bring with thee airs from heaven or blasts from hell,
        Be thy intents wicked or charitable,
        Thou com'st in such a questionable shape
        That I will speak to thee. I'll call thee Hamlet,
45   King, father, royal Dane. O, answer me!
        Let me not burst in ignorance, but tell
        Why thy canonized bones, hearsèd in death,
        Have burst their cerements; why the sepulchre
        Wherein we saw thee quietly interred,
50   Hath oped his ponderous and marble jaws
        To cast thee up again. What may this mean
        That thou, dead corse, again in complete steel
        Revisits thus the glimpses of the moon,
        Making night hideous, and we fools of nature
55   So horridly to shake our disposition
        With thoughts beyond the reaches of our souls?
        Say, why is this? wherefore? What should we do?

*([*GHOST*] beckons.)*

HORATIO: It beckons you to go away with it,
        As if it some impartment did desire
60   To you alone.
MARCELLUS: Look, with what courteous action
        It waves you to a more removèd ground.
        But do not go with it.
HORATIO: No, by no means.
HAMLET: It will not speak; then I will follow it.
HORATIO: Do not, my lord.
HAMLET: Why, what should be the fear?
65   I do not set my life at a pin's fee,
        And for my soul, what can it do to that,
        Being a thing immortal as itself?
        It waves me forth again. I'll follow it.

---

26 **his** its   27 **complexion** one of the four temperaments (sanguine, melancholy, choleric, and phlegmatic)   29 **o'er-leavens** works change throughout   30 **plausive** pleasing   32 **livery** badge; **star** a person's fortune, rank, or destiny, viewed as determined by the stars   37 **doubt** put out, obliterate   38 **his** its   47 **canonized** buried according to the church's rule; **hearsèd** coffined, buried   59 **impartment** communication

HORATIO: What if it tempt you toward the flood, my lord,
        Or to the dreadful summit of the cliff   70
        That beetles o'er his base into the sea,
        And there assume some other horrible form,
        Which might deprive your sovereignty of reason
        And draw you into madness? Think of it.
        The very place puts toys of desperation,   75
        Without more motive, into every brain
        That looks so many fathoms to the sea
        And hears it roar beneath.
HAMLET: It waves me still.
        Go on. I'll follow thee.
MARCELLUS: You shall not go, my lord.   80
HAMLET: Hold off your hands.
HORATIO: Be ruled; You shall not go.
HAMLET: My fate cries out,
        And makes each petty artere in this body
        As hardy as the Nemean lion's nerve.
        Still am I called. Unhand me, gentlemen.
        By heaven, I'll make a ghost of him that lets me.   85
        I say, away—Go on. I'll follow thee.

*([*Exeunt*] GHOST *and* HAMLET.)*

HORATIO: He waxes desperate with imagination.
MARCELLUS: Let's follow. 'Tis not fit thus to obey him.
HORATIO: Have after. To what issue will this come?
MARCELLUS: Something is rotten in the state of Denmark.   90
HORATIO: Heaven will direct it.
MARCELLUS: Nay, let's follow him.

(Exeunt.)

SCENE V

Enter GHOST *and* HAMLET.

HAMLET: Whither wilt thou lead me? Speak. I'll go no further.
GHOST: Mark me.
HAMLET: I will.
GHOST: My hour is almost come
        When I to sulph'rous and tormenting flames
        Must render up myself.
HAMLET: Alas, poor ghost!
GHOST: Pity me not, but lend thy serious hearing   5
        To what I shall unfold.
HAMLET: Speak. I am bound to hear.
GHOST: So art thou to revenge, when thou shalt hear.
HAMLET: What?
GHOST: I am thy father's spirit,
        Doomed for a certain term to walk the night,   10
        And for the day confined to fast in fires,
        Till the foul crimes done in my days of nature
        Are burnt and purged away. But that I am forbid
        To tell the secrets of my prison house,
        I could a tale unfold whose lightest word   15
        Would harrow up thy soul, freeze thy young blood,

---

71 **beetles** juts out   73 **sovereignty of reason** state of being ruled by reason   75 **toys** fancies, impules   82 **artere** artery   83 **Nemean lion** slain by Hercules in the performance of one of his twelve labors   85 **lets** hinders

Make thy two eyes like stars start from their spheres,
Thy knotted and combinèd locks to part,
And each particular hair to stand an end,
20   Like quills upon the fretful porpentine.
But this eternal blazon must not be
To ears of flesh and blood. List, list, O, list!
If thou didst ever thy dear father love—
HAMLET: O God!
25   GHOST: Revenge his foul and most unnatural murder.
HAMLET: Murder!
GHOST: Murder most foul, as in the best it is,
But this most foul, strange, and unnatural.
HAMLET: Haste me to know't, that I, with wings as swift
30   As meditation or the thoughts of love,
May sweep to my revenge.
GHOST: I find thee apt,
And duller shouldst thou be than the fat weed
That roots itself in ease on Lethe wharf,
Wouldst thou not stir in this. Now, Hamlet, hear.
35   'Tis given out that, sleeping in my orchard,
A serpent stung me. So the whole ear of Denmark
Is by a forgèd process of my death
Rankly abused. But know, thou noble youth,
The serpent that did sting thy father's life
40   Now wears his crown.
HAMLET: O my prophetic soul!
My uncle!
GHOST: Ay, that incestuous, that adulterate beast,
With witchcraft of his wits, with traitorous gifts—
O wicked wit and gifts that have the power
45   So to seduce!—won to his shameful lust
The will of my most seeming virtuous queen.
O Hamlet, what a falling off was there,
From me, whose love was of that dignity
That it went hand in hand even with the vow
50   I made to her in marriage, and to decline
Upon a wretch whose natural gifts were poor
To those of mine!
But virtue, as it never will be moved,
Though lewdness court it in a shape of heaven,
55   So lust, though to a radiant angel linked,
Will sate itself in a celestial bed
And prey on garbage.
But soft, methinks I scent the morning air.
Brief let me be. Sleeping within my orchard,
60   My custom always of the afternoon,
Upon my secure hour thy uncle stole,
With juice of cursed hebona in a vial,
And in the porches of my ears did pour
The leperous distilment, whose effect
65   Holds such an enmity with blood of man
That swift as quicksilver it courses through
The natural gates and alleys of the body,
And with a sudden vigor it doth posset
And curd, like eager droppings into milk,

The thin and wholesome blood. So did it mine,   70
And a most instant tetter barked about
Most lazar-like with vile and loathsome crust
All my smooth body.
Thus was I sleeping by a brother's hand
Of life, of crown, of queen, at once dispatched,   75
Cut off even in the blossoms of my sin,
Unhouseled, disappointed, unaneled,
No reck'ning made, but sent to my account
With all my imperfections on my head.
O, horrible! O, horrible! most horrible!   80
If thou hast nature in thee, bear it not,
Let not the royal bed of Denmark be
A couch for luxury and damnèd incest.
But howsomever thou pursues this act,
Taint not thy mind, nor let thy soul contrive   85
Against thy mother aught. Leave her to heaven,
And to those thorns that in her bosom lodge
To prick and sting her. Fare thee well at once.
The glowworm shows the matin to be near,
And gins to pale his uneffectual fire.   90
Adieu, adieu, adieu. Remember me.

(*Exit.*)

HAMLET: O all you host of heaven! O earth! What else?
And shall I couple hell? O, fie! Hold, hold, my heart,
And you, my sinews, grow not instant old,
But bear me stiffly up. Remember thee?   95
Ay, thou poor ghost, whiles memory holds a seat
In this distracted globe. Remember thee?
Yea, from the table of my memory
I'll wipe away all trivial fond records,
All saws of books, all forms, all pressures past   100
That youth and observation copied there,
And thy commandment all alone shall live
Within the book and volume of my brain,
Unmixed with baser matter. Yes, by heaven!
O most pernicious woman!   105
O villain, villain, smiling, damnèd villain!
My tables—meet it is I set it down
That one may smile, and smile, and be a villain
At least I am sure it may be so in Denmark.   (*Writing.*)
So, uncle, there you are. Now to my word: 110
It is 'Adieu, adieu! Remember me,'
I have sworn't.

(*Enter* HORATIO *and* MARCELLUS.)

HORATIO: My lord, my lord!
MARCELLUS: Lord Hamlet!
HORATIO: Heavens secure him!
HAMLET: So be it!

I.v. 19 **an** on   20 **porpentine** porcupine   21 **eternal blazon** proclamation of the secrets of eternity   33 **Lethe** the river in Hades that brings forgetfulness   37 **process** account   61 **secure** free from suspicion   62 **hebona** an imaginary poison, associated with henbane   68 **posset** curdle   69 **eager** acid

71 **tetter** a skin eruption; **barked** covered as with bark   77 **Unhouseled** without having received the sacrament; **disappointed** unprepared; **unaneled** without extreme unction   83 **luxury** lust   89 **matin** morning   97 **globe** head   98 **table** writing tablet, memorandum book (as at line 107, below; here metaphorically of the mind)   99 **fond** foolish   100 **saws** sayings; **forms** concepts; **pressures** impressions

MARCELLUS: Illo, ho, ho, my lord!   115
HAMLET: Hillo, ho, ho, boy! Come, bird, come.
MARCELLUS: How is't, my noble lord?
HORATIO: What news, my lord?
HAMLET: O, wonderful!
HORATIO: Good my lord, tell it.
HAMLET: No, you will reveal it.
HORATIO: Not I, my lord, by heaven.   120
MARCELLUS: Nor I, my lord.
HAMLET: How say you then, would heart of man once think it?
    But you'll be secret?
BOTH: Ay, by heaven, my lord.
HAMLET: There's never a villain dwelling in all Denmark
    But he's an arrant knave.
HORATIO: There needs no ghost, my lord, come from the grave   125
    To tell us this.
HAMLET: Why, right, you are in the right,
    And so without more circumstance at all
    I hold it fit that we shake hands and part,
    You, as your business and desire shall point you,
    For every man has business and desire   130
    Such as it is, and for my own poor part,
    I will go pray.
HORATIO: These are but wild and whirling words, my lord.
HAMLET: I am sorry they offend you, heartily;
    Yes, faith, heartily.   135
HORATIO: There's no offence, my lord.
HAMLET: Yes, by Saint Patrick, but there is, Horatio,
    And much offence too. Touching this vision here,
    It is an honest ghost, that let me tell you
    For your desire to know what is between us,
    O'ermaster't as you may. And now, good friends,   140
    As you are friends, scholars, and soldiers,
    Give me one poor request.
HORATIO: What is't, my lord? We will.
HAMLET: Never make known what you have seen to-night.
BOTH: My lord, we will not.   145
HAMLET: Nay, but swear't.
HORATIO: In faith,
    My lord, not I.
MARCELLUS: Nor I, my lord, in faith.
HAMLET: Upon my sword.
MARCELLUS: We have sworn, my lord, already.
HAMLET: Indeed, upon my sword, indeed.

(GHOST *cries under the stage.*)

GHOST: Swear.
HAMLET: Ha, ha, boy, say'st thou so? Art thou there, truepenny?
    Come on. You hear this fellow in the cellarage.   150
    Consent to swear.
HORATIO: Propose the oath, my lord.
HAMLET: Never to speak of this that you have seen,
    Swear by my sword.
GHOST: (*Beneath.*) Swear.
HAMLET: Hic et ubique? Then we'll shift our ground.   155

Come hither, gentlemen,
And lay your hands again upon my sword.
Swear by my sword
Never to speak of this that you have heard.
GHOST: (*Beneath*.) Swear by his sword.   160
HAMLET: Well said, old mole! Canst work i' th' earth so fast?
    A worthy pioneer! Once more remove, good friends.
HORATIO: O day and night, but this is wondrous strange!
HAMLET: And therefore as a stranger give it welcome.
    There are more things in heaven and earth, Horatio,   165
    Than are dreamt of in your philosophy.
    But come.
    Here as before, never, so help you mercy,
    How strange or odd some'er I bear myself
    (As I perchance hereafter shall think meet   170
    To put an antic disposition on),
    That you, at such times, seeing me, never shall,
    With arms encumbered thus, or this head-shake,
    Or by pronouncing of some doubtful phrase,
    As 'Well, well, we know,' or 'We could, and if we would'   175
    Or 'If we list to speak,' or 'There be, and if they might'
    Or such ambiguous giving out, to note
    That you know aught of me—this do swear,
    So grace and mercy at your most need help you.
GHOST: (*Beneath*.) Swear.   180
HAMLET: Rest, rest, perturbèd spirit! So, gentlemen,
    With all my love I do commend me to you,
    And what so poor a man as Hamlet is
    May do t' express his love and friending to you,
    God willing, shall not lack. Let us go in together,   185
    And still your fingers on your lips, I pray.
    The time is out of joint. O cursèd spite
    That ever I was born to set it right!
    Nay, come, let's go together.

(*Exeunt.*)

ACT TWO

SCENE I

Enter old POLONIUS *with his man* [REYNALDO].

POLONIUS: Give him this money and these notes, Reynaldo.
REYNALDO: I will, my lord.
POLONIUS: You shall do marvellous wisely, good Reynaldo,
    Before you visit him, to make inquire
    Of his behavior.   5
REYNALDO: My lord, I did intend it.
POLONIUS: Marry, well said, very well said. Look you, sir,
    Enquire me first what Danskers are in Paris,
    And how, and who, what means, and where they keep,
    What company, at what expense; and finding
    By this encompassment and drift of question   10
    That they do know my son, come you more nearer
    Than your particular demands will touch it.
    Take you as 'twere some distant knowledge of him,

---

115 **Illo, ho, ho** cry of the falconer to summon his hawk   136
Saint Patrick associated, in the late middle ages, with purgatory,
whence the ghost has presumably come   149 **truepenny** honest fellow   155 **Hic et ubique** here and everywhere

---

162 **pioneer** miner   171 **antic** mad   173 **encumbered** folded
II.i. 7 **Danskers** Danes   8 **means** wealth   10 **encompassment** talking round the matter

As thus, 'I know his father and his friends,
15 And in part him,' do you mark this, Reynaldo?
REYNALDO: Ay, very well, my lord.
POLONIUS: 'And in part him, but,' you may say, 'not well,
But if't be he I mean, he's very wild,
Addicted so and so.' And there put on him
20 What forgeries you please; marry, none so rank
As may dishonour him. Take heed of that.
But, sir, such wanton, wild, and usual slips
As are companions noted and most known
To youth and liberty.
REYNALDO: As gaming, my lord?
25 POLONIUS: Ay, or drinking, fencing, swearing, quarrelling,
Drabbing—you may go so far.
REYNALDO: My lord, that would dishonour him.
POLONIUS: Faith, no, as you may season it in the charge.
You must not put another scandal on him,
30 That he is open to incontinency.
That's not my meaning. But breathe his faults so quaintly
That they may seem the taints of liberty,
The flash and outbreak of a fiery mind,
A savageness in unreclaimèd blood,
35 Of general assault.
REYNALDO: But, my good lord—
POLONIUS: Wherefore should you do this?
REYNALDO: Ay, my lord,
I would know that.
POLONIUS: Marry, sir, here's my drift,
And I believe it is a fetch of warrant.
You laying these slight sullies on my son,
40 As 'twere a thing a little soiled i' th' working,
Mark you,
Your party in converse, him you would sound,
Having ever seen in the prenominate crimes
The youth you breathe of guilty, be assured
45 He closes with you in this consequence,
'Good sir', or so, or 'friend', or 'gentleman',
According to the phrase or the addition
Of man and country.
REYNALDO: Very good, my lord.
POLONIUS: And then, sir, does 'a this—'a does—What was I
about to say?
50 By the mass, I was about to say something.
Where did I leave?
REYNALDO: At 'closes in the consequence.'
POLONIUS: At 'closes in the consequence'—ay, marry,
He closes thus: 'I know the gentleman.
55 I saw him yesterday, or th' other day,
Or then, or then, with such, or such, and as you say,
There was 'a gaming, there o'ertook in 's rouse;
There falling out at tennis', or perchance
'I saw him enter such a house of sale',
60 Videlicet, a brothel, or so forth.

See you, now—
Your bait of falsehood takes this carp of truth,
And thus do we of wisdom and of reach,
With windlasses and with assays of bias,
By indirections find directions out;   65
So by my former lecture and advice
Shall you my son. You have me, have you not?
REYNALDO: My lord, I have.
POLONIUS: God bye ye; fare ye well.
REYNALDO: Good my lord.
POLONIUS: Observe his inclination in yourself.   70
REYNALDO: I shall, my lord.
POLONIUS: And let him ply his music.
REYNALDO: Well, my lord.
POLONIUS: Farewell.

(*Exit* REYNALDO.)

(*Enter* OPHELIA.)

                         How now, Ophelia! what's the matter?
OPHELIA: O my lord, my lord, I have been so affrighted!
POLONIUS: With what, i' th' name of God?   75
OPHELIA: My lord, as I was sewing in my closet,
Lord Hamlet, with his doublet all unbraced,
No hat upon his head, his stockings fouled,
Ungartered, and down-gyvèd to his ankle,
Pale as his shirt, his knees knocking each other,   80
And with a look so piteous in purport
As if he had been loosèd out of hell
To speak of horrors—he comes before me.
POLONIUS: Mad for thy love?
OPHELIA: My lord, I do not know,
But truly I do fear it.   85
POLONIUS: What said he?
OPHELIA: He took me by the wrist, and held me hard,
Then goes he to the length of all his arm,
And with his other hand thus o'er his brow,
He falls to such perusal of my face
As 'a would draw it. Long stayed he so.   90
At last, a little shaking of mine arm
And thrice his head thus waving up and down,
He raised a sigh so piteous and profound
As it did seem to shatter all his bulk
And end his being. That done, he lets me go,   95
And with his head over his shoulder turned,
He seemed to find his way without his eyes,
For out adoors he went without their helps,
And to the last bended their light on me.
POLONIUS: Come, go with me. I will go seek the king.   100
This is the very ecstasy of love,
Whose violent property fordoes itself,
And leads the will to desperate undertakings
As oft as any passion under heaven
That does afflict our natures. I am sorry.   105
What, have you given him any hard words of late?

---

20 **forgeries** invented wrongdoings 24 **liberty** license 26
Drabbing whoring 28 **season** moderate 31 **quaintly** delicately 34 **unreclaimèd** untamed 35 **Of general assault** as-
sailing all 38 **fetch of warrant** allowable device 43
prenominate before-named 45 **closes** agrees; **in this consequence** as follows 47 **addition** title 60 **Videlicet** namely

---

63 **reach** ability 64 **windlasses** roundabout approaches; **assays of bias** indirect attempts 68 **God buy ye** God be with
you 76 **closet** private room 77 **unbraced** unlaced 79
down-gyvèd hanging down, like gyves or fetters on a prisoner's
ankles 101 **ecstasy** madness 102 **fordoes** destroys

OPHELIA: No, my good lord, but as you did command
    I did repel his letters, and denied
    His access to me.
POLONIUS: That hath made him mad.
110   I am sorry that with better heed and judgement
    I had not quoted him. I feared he did but trifle,
    And meant to wrack thee; but beshrew my jealousy.
    By heaven, it is as proper to our age
    To cast beyond ourselves in our opinions
115   As it is common for the younger sort
    To lack discretion. Come, go we to the king.
    This must be known, which being kept close, might move
    More grief to hide than hate to utter love.
    Come.

(*Exeunt.*)

SCENE II

Flourish. Enter KING *and* QUEEN, ROSENCRANTZ, *and*
GUILDENSTERN [*and* ATTENDANTS].

KING: Welcome, dear Rosencrantz and Guildenstern.
    Moreover that we much did long to see you,
    The need we have to use you did provoke
    Our hasty sending. Something have you heard
5   Of Hamlet's transformation—so call it,
    Sith nor th' exterior nor the inward man
    Resembles that it was. What it should be,
    More than his father's death, that thus hath put him
    So much from th' understanding of himself,
10   I cannot dream of. I entreat you both
    That, being of so young days brought up with him,
    And sith so neighboured to his youth and havior,
    That you vouchsafe your rest here in our court
    Some little time, so by your companies
15   To draw him on to pleasures, and to gather
    So much as from occasion you may glean,
    Whether aught to us unknown afflicts him thus,
    That opened, lies within our remedy.
QUEEN: Good gentlemen, he hath much talked of you,
20   And sure I am two men there is not living
    To whom he more adheres. If it will please you
    To show us so much gentry and good will
    As to expend your time with us awhile
    For the supply and profit of our hope,
25   Your visitation shall receive such thanks
    As fits a king's remembrance.
ROSENCRANTZ: Both your majesties
    Might, by the sovereign power you have of us,
    Put your dread pleasures more into command
    Than to entreaty.
GUILDENSTERN: But we both obey,
30   And here give up ourselves in the full bent
    To lay our service freely at your feet,
    To be commanded.
KING: Thanks, Rosencrantz and gentle Guildenstern.

QUEEN: Thanks, Guildenstern and gentle Rosencrantz.
    And I beseech you instantly to visit   35
    My too much changed son. Go, some of you,
    And bring these gentlemen where Hamlet is.
GUILDENSTERN: Heavens make our presence and our practices
    Pleasant and helpful to him!
QUEEN: Ay, amen!

(*Exeunt* ROSENCRANTZ *and* GUILDENSTERN [*with some* AT-
TENDANTS].)

(*Enter* POLONIUS.)

POLONIUS: Th' ambassadors from Norway, my good lord,   40
    Are joyfully returned.
KING: Thou still hast been the father of good news.
POLONIUS: Have I, my lord? I assure my good liege,
    I hold my duty as I hold my soul,
    Both to my God and to my gracious king;   45
    And I do think—or else this brain of mine
    Hunts not the trail of policy so sure
    As it hath used to do—that I have found
    The very cause of Hamlet's lunacy.
KING: O, speak of that, that do I long to hear.   50
POLONIUS: Give first admittance to th' ambassadors.
    My news shall be the fruit to that great feast.
KING: Thyself do grace to them, and bring them in.

(*Exit* POLONIUS.)

    He tells me, my dear Gertrude, he hath found
    The head and source of all your son's distemper.   55
QUEEN: I doubt it is no other but the main,
    His father's death and our o'erhasty marriage.
KING: Well, we shall sift him.

(*Enter* AMBASSADORS [VOLTEMAND *and* CORNELIUS], *with*
POLONIUS.)

                    Welcome, my good friends,
    Say, Voltemand, what from our brother Norway?
VOLTEMAND: Most fair return of greetings and desires.   60
    Upon our first, he sent out to suppress
    His nephew's levies, which to him appeared
    To be a preparation 'gainst the Polack,
    But better looked into, he truly found
    It was against your highness, whereat grieved,   65
    That so his sickness, age, and impotence
    Was falsely borne in hand, sends out arrests
    On Fortinbras, which he in brief obeys,
    Receives rebuke from Norway, and in fine,
    Makes vow before his uncle never more   70
    To give th' assay of arms against your majesty.
    Whereon old Norway, overcome with joy,
    Gives him three score thousand crowns in annual fee,
    And his commission to employ those soldiers,
    So levied as before, against the Polack,   75
    With an entreaty, herein further shown,   (*Gives a paper.*)
    That it might please you to give quiet pass
    Through your dominions for this enterprise,

---

111 **quoted** observed   112 **wrack** ruin   113 **proper to** characteristic of   117 **close** secret; **move** cause

II.ii. 6 Sith **since**   18 **opened** disclosed   22 **gentry** courtesy

---

42 **still** ever   56 **doubt** suspect   63 **the Polack** the Polish
nation   67 **borne in hand** deceived   69 **in fine** in the end
71 **assay** trial

On such regards of safety and allowance
80 As therein are set down.
KING: It likes us well,
And at our more considered time we'll read,
Answer, and think upon this business.
Meantime we thank you for your well-took labor.
Go to your rest; at night we'll feast together.
85 Most welcome home!

(*Exeunt* AMBASSADORS.)

POLONIUS: This business is well ended.
My liege and madam, to expostulate
What majesty should be, what duty is,
Why day is day, night night, and time is time,
Were nothing but to waste night, day and time.
90 Therefore, since brevity is the soul of wit,
And tediousness the limbs and outward flourishes,
I will be brief. Your noble son is mad.
Mad call I it, for to define true madness,
What is't but to be nothing else but mad?
95 But let that go.
QUEEN: More matter with less art.
POLONIUS: Madam, I swear I use no art at all.
That he is mad, 'tis true: 'tis true 'tis pity.
And pity 'tis 'tis true. A foolish figure,
But farewell it, for I will use no art.
100 Mad let us grant him, then, and now remains
That we find out the cause of this effect,
Or rather say the cause of this defect,
For this effect defective comes by cause.
Thus it remains, and the remainder thus.
105 Perpend.
I have a daughter—have while she is mine—
Who in her duty and obedience, mark,
Hath given me this. Now gather, and surmise.   (*Reads.*)
      'To the celestial, and my soul's idol, the most beautified
110 Ophelia'—That's an ill phrase, a vile phrase, 'beautified' is
      a vile phrase. But you shall hear. Thus: (*Reads.*)
         'In her excellent white bosom, these, etc.'
QUEEN: Came this from Hamlet to her?
POLONIUS: Good madam, stay awhile. I will be faithful.
   (*Reads letter.*)

115   'Doubt thou the stars are fire,
            Doubt that the sun doth move;
            Doubt truth to be a liar;
            But never doubt I love.

      'O dear Ophelia, I am ill at these numbers. I have not
120 art to reckon my groans, but that I love thee best, O most
best, believe it. Adieu.
               'Thine evermore, most dear lady, whilst
                  this machine is to him, Hamlet.'
This in obedience hath my daughter shown me,
125 And more above, hath his solicitings,
As they fell out by time, by means and place,
All given to mine ear.

KING: But how hath she
Received his love?
POLONIUS: What do you think of me?
KING: As of a man faithful and honourable.
POLONIUS: I would fain prove so. But what might you think,   130
When I had seen this hot love on the wing,
(As I perceived it, I must tell you that,
Before my daughter told me), what might you,
Or my dear majesty your queen here, think,
If I had played the desk or table-book,   135
Or given my heart a winking, mute and dumb,
Or looked upon this love with idle sight,
What might you think? No, I went round to work,
And my young mistress thus I did bespeak:
'Lord Hamlet is a prince out of thy star.   140
This must not be'. and then I prescripts gave her,
That she should lock herself from his resort,
Admit no messengers, receive no tokens.
Which done, she took the fruits of my advice;
And he repelled, a short tale to make,   145
Fell into a sadness, then into a fast,
Thence to a watch, thence into a weakness,
Thence to a lightness, and, by this declension,
Into the madness wherein now he raves,
And all we mourn for.   150
KING: Do you think 'tis this?
QUEEN: It may be, very like.
POLONIUS: Hath there been such a time—I would fain
      know that—
That I have positively said ''Tis so,'
When it proved otherwise?
KING: Not that I know.
POLONIUS: (*Pointing to his head and shoulder.*) Take this from   155
   this, if this be otherwise:
If circumstances lead me, I will find
Where truth is hid, though it were hid indeed
Within the centre.
KING: How may we try it further?
POLONIUS: You know, sometimes he walks four hours together
Here in the lobby.   160
QUEEN: So he does, indeed.
POLONIUS: At such a time I'll loose my daughter to him.
Be you and I behind an arras then.
Mark the encounter. If he love her not,
And be not from his reason fall'n thereon,
Let me be no assistant for a state,   165
But keep a farm and carters.
KING: We will try it.

(*Enter* HAMLET [*reading on a book*].)

QUEEN: But look where sadly the poor wretch comes reading.
POLONIUS: Away, I do beseech you both away,
   I'll board him presently.

([*Exeunt*] king and queen [*with attendants*].)

                  O, give me leave.

---

79 **regards** considerations   90 **wit** understanding   95 **matter**
meaning, sense   105 **Perpend** consider   119 **numbers** verses
123 **machine** body

135 **played . . . table-book** acted as silent go-between   138
round directly   147 **watch** sleeplessness   148 **lightness** light-
headedness   158 **centre** centre of the earth and of the Ptole-
maic universe   169 **board** accost; **presently** immediately

170   How does my good Lord Hamlet?
HAMLET: Well, God-a-mercy.
POLONIUS: Do you know me, my lord?
HAMLET: Excellent well, you are a fishmonger.
POLONIUS: Not I, my lord.
175 HAMLET: Then I would you were so honest a man.
POLONIUS: Honest, my lord?
HAMLET: Ay, sir, to be honest as this world goes, is to be one
    man picked out of ten thousand.
POLONIUS: That's very true, my lord.
180 HAMLET: For if the sun breed maggots in a dead dog, being a
    good kissing carrion—Have you a daughter?
POLONIUS: I have, my lord.
HAMLET: Let her not walk i' th' sun. Conception is a blessing,
    but as your daughter may conceive—friend, look to 't.
185 POLONIUS: (*Aside.*) How say you by that? Still harping on my
    daughter. Yet he knew me not at first. 'A said I was a fish-
    monger. 'A is far gone. And truly in my youth I suffered
    much extremity for love, very near this. I'll speak to him
    again.—What do you read, my lord?
190 HAMLET: Words, words, words.
POLONIUS: What is the matter, my lord?
HAMLET: Between who?
POLONIUS: I mean the matter that you read, my lord.
HAMLET: Slanders, sir; for the satirical rogue says here that old
195   men have grey beards, that their faces are wrinkled, their
    eyes purging thick amber and plum-tree gum, and that
    they have a plentiful lack of wit, together with most weak
    hams—all which, sir, though I most powerfully and po-
    tently believe, yet I hold it not honesty to have it thus set
200   down, for yourself, sir, shall grow old as I am, if like a crab
    you could go backward.
POLONIUS: (*Aside.*) Though this be madness, yet there is
    method in 't.—Will you walk out of the air, my lord?
HAMLET: Into my grave?
205 POLONIUS: (*Aside.*) Indeed, that's out of the air. How preg-
    nant sometimes his replies are! a happiness that often mad-
    ness hits on, which reason and sanity could not so
    prosperously be delivered of. I will leave him, and sud-
    denly contrive the means of meeting between him and
210   my daughter.—My lord, I will take my leave of you.
HAMLET: You cannot take from me anything that I will not
    more willingly part withal—except my life, except my
    life, except my life.

(*Enter* GUILDENSTERN *and* ROSENCRANTZ.)

POLONIUS: Fare you well, my lord.
215 HAMLET: These tedious old fools!
POLONIUS: You go to seek the Lord Hamlet. There he is.
ROSENCRANTZ: (*To* POLONIUS.) *God save you, sir!*

(*Exit* POLONIUS.)

GUILDENSTERN: My honored lord!
ROSENCRANTZ: My most dear lord!
220 HAMLET: My excellent good friends! How dost thou,
    Guildenstern?
       Ah, Rosencrantz! Good lads, how do ye both?

ROSENCRANTZ: As the indifferent children of the earth.
GUILDENSTERN: Happy in that we are not over-happy;
    On Fortune's cap we are not the very button.   225
HAMLET: Nor the soles of her shoe?
ROSENCRANTZ: Neither, my lord.
HAMLET: Then you live about her waist, or in the middle of
    her favors?
GUILDENSTERN: Faith, her privates we.   230
HAMLET: In the secret parts of Fortune? O, most true, she is a
    strumpet. What news?
ROSENCRANTZ: None, my lord, but that the world's grown
    honest.
HAMLET: Then is doomsday near. But your news is not true. 235
    Let me question more in particular. What have you, my
    good friends, deserved at the hands of Fortune, that she
    sends you to prison hither?
GUILDENSTERN: Prison, my lord!
HAMLET: Denmark's a prison.   240
ROSENCRANTZ: Then is the world one.
HAMLET: A goodly one, in which there are many confines,
    wards, and dungeons, Denmark being one o' th' worst.
ROSENCRANTZ: We think not so, my lord.
HAMLET: Why then 'tis none to you; for there is nothing either 245
    good or bad, but thinking makes it so. To me it is a prison.
ROSENCRANTZ: Why then your ambition makes it one. 'Tis
    too narrow for your mind.
HAMLET: O God, I could be bounded in a nutshell and count
    myself a king of infinite space, were it not that I have bad 250
    dreams.
GUILDENSTERN: Which dreams indeed are ambition; for the
    very substance of the ambitious is merely the shadow of a
    dream.
HAMLET: A dream itself is but a shadow.   255
ROSENCRANTZ: Truly, and I hold ambition of so airy and
    light a quality that it is but a shadow's shadow.
HAMLET: Then are our beggars bodies, and, our monarchs and
    outstretched heroes the beggars' shadows. Shall we to th'
    court? for, by my fay, I cannot reason.   260
BOTH: We'll wait upon you.
HAMLET: No such matter. I will not sort you with the rest of
    my servants; for to speak to you like an honest man, I am
    most dreadfully attended. But in the beaten way of friend-
    ship, what make you at Elsinore?   265
ROSENCRANTZ: To visit you, my lord; no other occasion.
HAMLET: Beggar that I am, I am ever poor in thanks, but I
    thank you; and sure, dear friends, my thanks are too dear
    a halfpenny. Were you not sent for? Is it your own inclin-
    ing? Is it a free visitation? Come, come, deal justly with 270
    me. Come, come, nay speak.
GUILDENSTERN: What should we say, my lord?
HAMLET: Anything but to the purpose. You were sent for, and
    there is a kind of confession in your looks, which your
    modesties have not craft enough to color. I know the 275
    good king and queen have sent for you.
ROSENCRANTZ: To what end, my lord?
HAMLET: That you must teach me. But let me conjure you by
    the rights of our fellowship, by the consonancy of our

---
205 **pregnant** full of meaning   206 **happiness** aptness

223 **indifferent** average   225 **button** knob on the top of the
cap   260 **fay** faith   262 **sort you with** put you in the same
class with

280 youth, by the obligation of our ever-preserved love, and by
what more dear a better proposer can charge you withal be
even and direct with me whether you were sent for or no.
ROSENCRANTZ: (*Aside to* GUILDENSTERN.) What say you?
HAMLET: (*Aside.*) Nay, then, I have an eye of you.—If you
285 love me, hold not off.
GUILDENSTERN: My lord, we were sent for.
HAMLET: I will tell you why; so shall my anticipation prevent
your discovery, and your secrecy to the king and queen
moult no feather. I have of late—but wherefore I know
290 not—lost all my mirth, forgone all custom of exercises; and
indeed it goes so heavily with my disposition, that this
goodly frame the earth seems to me a sterile promontory,
this most excellent canopy the air, look you, this brave
o'er-hanging firmament, this majestical roof fretted with
295 golden fire, why it appeareth nothing to me but a foul and
pestilent congregation of vapors. What a piece of work is a
man, how noble in reason, how infinite in faculties, in form
and moving, how express and admirable in action, how like
an angel in apprehension, how like a god: the beauty of the
300 world, the paragon of animals. And yet to me, what is this
quintessence of dust? Man delights not me, nor woman
neither, though by your smiling you seem to say so.
ROSENCRANTZ: My lord, there was no such stuff in my
thoughts.
305 HAMLET: Why did ye laugh, then, when I said 'Man delights
not me'?
ROSENCRANTZ: To think, my lord, if you delight not in man,
what lenten entertainment the players shall receive from
you. We coted them on the way, and hither are they com-
310 ing to offer you service.
HAMLET: He that plays the king shall be welcome—his
majesty shall have tribute on me; the adventurous knight
shall use his foil and target; the lover shall not sigh gratis;
the humorous man shall end his part in peace; the clown
315 shall make those laugh whose lungs are tickle o' th' sere;
and the lady shall say her mind freely, or the blank verse
shall halt for 't. What players are they?
ROSENCRANTZ: Even those you were wont to take such delight in, the tragedians of the city.
320 HAMLET: How chances it they travel? Their residence, both in
reputation and profit, was better both ways.
ROSENCRANTZ: I think their inhibition comes by the means
of the late innovation.

HAMLET: Do they hold the same estimation they did when I
was in the city? Are they so followed?   325
ROSENCRANTZ: No, indeed, are they not.
HAMLET: How comes it? Do they grow rusty?
ROSENCRANTZ: Nay, their endeavour keeps in the wonted pace;
but there is, sir, an eyrie of children, little eyases, that cry out
on the top of question, and are most tyrannically clapped   330
for 't. These are now the fashion, and so berattle the common
stages (so they call them) that many wearing rapiers are afraid
of goose quills and dare scarce come thither.
HAMLET: What, are they children? Who maintains 'em? How
are they escoted? Will they pursue the quality no longer   335
than they can sing? Will they not say afterwards, if they
should grow themselves to common players (as it is most
like, if their means are no better), their writers do them
wrong to make them exclaim against their own succession?
ROSENCRANTZ: 'Faith, there has been much to do on both   340
sides; and the nation holds it no sin to tarre them to controversy. There was for a while no money bid for argument,
unless the poet and the player went to cuffs in the question.
HAMLET: Is't possible?
GUILDENSTERN: O, there has been much throwing about of 345
brains.
HAMLET: Do the boys carry it away?
ROSENCRANTZ: Ay, that they do, my lord, Hercules and his
load too.
HAMLET: It is not very strange, for my uncle is King of Den- 350
mark, and those that would make mouths at him while
my father lived give twenty, forty, fifty, a hundred ducats
apiece for his picture in little. 'Sblood, there is something
in this more than natural, if philosophy could find it out.

(*A flourish.*)

GUILDENSTERN: There are the players.   355
HAMLET: Gentlemen, you are welcome to Elsinore. Your
hands. Come then th' appurtenance of welcome is fashion
and ceremony. Let me comply with you in this garb, lest
my ex-tent to the players, which I tell you must show
fairly outwards, should more appear like entertainment   360
than yours. You are welcome. But my uncle-father and
aunt-mother are deceived.
GUILDENSTERN: In what, my dear lord?
HAMLET: I am but mad north-north-west; when the wind is
southerly I know a hawk from a handsaw.   365

---

287 **prevent** forestall   288 **discovery** disclosure   294 **fretted**
decorated with fretwork   308 **lenten** scanty   309 **coted** passed
313 **foil and target** spear and shield   313–314 **humorous
man** the actor who plays the eccentric character dominated by
one of the four humors   315 **tickle o' th' sere** easily set off
(**sere** is that part of a gunlock which keeps the hammer at full or
half cock)   316 **halt** limp   322 **inhibition** prohibition of plays
by authority (possibly with reference to decree of the Privy
Council of 22 June 1600, limiting the number of London theater
companies to two, and stipulating that the two were to perform
only twice a week)   323 **innovation** meaning uncertain (sometimes taken to refer to the reintroduction, ca. 1600 on the London theatrical scene of companies of boy actors performing in
private theaters; sometimes interpreted as "political upheaval,"
with special reference to Essex's rebellion, February, 1601)

329 **eyrie** nest; **eyases** nestling hawks (here, the boys in the children's companies training as actors)   330 **on the top of question** louder than all others on matter of dispute   331–332
common stages public theaters of the **common players** (below, line 337), organized in companies composed of adult
actors   333 **goose quills** pens (of the satiric dramatists writing
for the private theaters)   335 **escoted** maintained; **pursue the
quality** continue in the profession of acting   336 **sing** i.e., until their voices change   341 **tarre** incite   342 **argument** plot
of a play   349 **load** i.e., the world (the sign of the Globe theater represented Hercules bearing the world on his shoulders)
351 **mouths** grimaces   353 **in little** in miniature   357 **appurtenance** adjuncts   358–359 **extent** welcome   365 **hawk**
mattock or pickaxe (also called "hack," here used with a play on
hawk as a bird); **handsaw** a saw managed with one hand (here
used with a play on some corrupt form of *hernshaw,* "heron")

(*Enter* POLONIUS.)

POLONIUS: Well be with you, gentlemen.
HAMLET: Hark you, Guildenstern—and you too—at each ear
  a hearer. That great baby you see there is not yet out of
  his swaddling clouts.
370 ROSENCRANTZ: Happily he is the second time come to
  them, for they say an old man is twice a child.
HAMLET: I will prophesy he comes to tell me of the players.
  Mark it.—You say right, sir, a Monday morning, 'twas
  then indeed.
375 POLONIUS: My lord, I have news to tell you.
HAMLET: My lord, I have news to tell you. When Roscius
  was an actor in Rome—
POLONIUS: The actors are come hither, my lord.
HAMLET: Buzz, buzz.
380 POLONIUS: Upon my honor—
HAMLET: Then came each actor on his ass—
POLONIUS: The best actors in the world, either for tragedy,
  comedy, history, pastoral, pastoral-comical, historical-
  pastoral, tragical-historical, tragical-comical-historical-
385 pastoral, scene individable, or poem unlimited. Seneca
  cannot be too heavy nor Plautus too light. For the law of
  writ and the liberty, these are the only men.
HAMLET: O Jephthah, judge of Israel, what a treasure hadst
  thou!
390 POLONIUS: What a treasure had he, my lord?
HAMLET: Why—

    'One fair daughter, and no more,
    The which he loved passing well.'

POLONIUS: (*Aside.*) Still on my daughter.
395 HAMLET: Am I not i' th' right, old Jephthah?
POLONIUS: If you call me Jephthah, my lord, I have a daughter that I love passing well.
HAMLET: Nay, that follows not.
POLONIUS: What follows then, my lord?
400 HAMLET: Why—

    'As by lot, God wot,'

and then, you know,

    'It came to pass, as most like it was.'

  The first row of the pious chanson will show you more,
405 for look where my abridgement comes.

(*Enter the* PLAYERS.)

You are welcome, masters; welcome, all.—I am glad to see
thee well.—Welcome, good friends. O, old friend! Why
thy face is valanced since I saw thee last. Come'st thou to
beard me in Denmark?—What, my young lady and mistress? By'r lady, your ladyship is nearer to heaven than 410
when I saw you last by the altitude of a chopine. Pray
God, your voice, like a piece of uncurrent gold, be not
cracked within the ring.—Masters, you are all welcome.
We'll e'en to't like French falconers, fly at any thing we
see. We'll have a speech straight. Come give us a taste of 415
your quality, come a passionate speech.
1 PLAYER: What speech, my good lord?
HAMLET: I heard thee speak me a speech once, but it was never
acted, or if it was, not above once, for the play, I remember,
pleased not the million; 'twas caviary to the general. But it 420
was—as I received it, and others whose judgements in such
matters cried in the top of mine—an excellent play, well
digested in the scenes, set down with as much modesty as
cunning. I remember one said there were no sallets in the
lines to make the matter savory, nor no matter in the phrase 425
that might indict the author of affectation, but called it an
honest method, as wholesome as sweet, and by very much
more handsome than fine. One speech in't I chiefly loved.
'Twas Æneas' tale to Dido and thereabout of it especially
when he speaks of Priam's slaughter. If it live in your mem- 430
ory, begin at this line—let me see, let me see:

    'The rugged Pyrrhus, like th' Hyrcanian beast'—

'tis not so;—it begins with Pyrrhus—

    'The rugged Pyrrhus, he whose sable arms,
    Black as his purpose, did the night resemble   435
    When he lay couchèd in the ominous horse,
    Hath now this dread and black complexion smeared
    With heraldry more dismal; head to foot
    Now is he total gules, horridly tricked
    With blood of fathers, mothers, daughters, sons,   440
    Baked and impasted with the parching streets,
    That lend a tyrannous and a damnèd light
    To their lord's murder. Roasted in wrath and fire,
    And thus o'er-sizèd with coagulate gore,
    With eyes like carbuncles, the hellish Pyrrhus   445
    Old grandsire Priam seeks.'

So, proceed you.
POLONIUS: Fore God, my lord, well spoken, with good accent
and good discretion.
1 PLAYER: 'Anon he finds him   450
Striking too short at Greeks. His antique sword,
Rebellious to his arm, lies where it falls,

---

370 **Happily** perhaps 376 **Roscius** the greatest of Roman comic actors, though regarded by the Elizabethans as a tragic one 384–385 **scene individable** i.e., a play that observes the unities of time and place 385 **poem unlimited** a play that does not observe the unities; **Seneca** Roman writer of tragedies 386 **Plautus** Roman comic dramatist; **law of writ and the liberty** i.e., plays according to strict classical rules, and those that ignored the unities of time and place 388 **Jephthah** was compelled to sacrifice a beloved daughter (Judges 2). Hamlet quotes from a contemporary ballad titled *Jephthah, Judge of Israel* at lines 392–393, 401, and 403 404 **row** stanza

408 **valanced** bearded 409 **young lady** i.e., the boy who plays female roles 411 **chopine** a shoe with high cork heel and sole 412–413 **cracked within the ring** a coin cracked within the circle surrounding the head of the sovereign was no longer legal tender and so *uncurrent* 415 **straight** immediately 420 **caviary** caviare; **general** multitude 422–423 **digested** arranged 424 **sallets** salads, highly seasoned passages 428 **more handsome than fine** admirable rather than appealing by mere cleverness 432 **Hyrcanian beast** tiger 436 **horse** i.e., the Trojan horse 439 **gules** heraldic term for red; **tricked** delineated 444 **o'er-sizèd** covered as with size; **coagulate** clotted

Repugnant to command. Unequal matched,
Pyrrhus at Priam drives, in rage strikes wide.
455 But with the whiff and wind of his fell sword
Th' unnervèd father falls. Then senseless Ilium,
Seeming to feel this blow, with flaming top
Stoops to his base, and with a hideous crash
Takes prisoner Pyrrhus' ear. For, lo! his sword,
460 Which was declining on the milky head
Of reverend Priam, seemed i' th' air to stick.
So as a painted tyrant Pyrrhus stood,
And like a neutral to his will and matter,
Did nothing.
465 But as we often see, against some storm,
A silence in the heavens, the rack stand still,
The bold winds speechless, and the orb below
As hush as death, anon the dreadful thunder
Doth rend the region; so, after Pyrrhus' pause,
470 A rousèd vengeance sets him new awork,
And never did the Cyclops' hammers fall
On Mars's armor, forged for proof eterne
With less remorse than Pyrrhus' bleeding sword
Now falls on Priam.
475 Out, out, thou strumpet, Fortune! All you gods,
In general synod take away her power,
Break all the spokes and fellies from her wheel,
And bowl the round nave down the hill of heaven
As low as to the fiends.'
480 POLONIUS: This is too long.
HAMLET: It shall to the barber's with your beard.—Prithee,
say on. He's for a jig, or a tale of bawdry, or he sleeps. Say
on, come to Hecuba.
1 PLAYER: 'But who, ah woe! had seen the mobled queen—'
485 HAMLET: 'The mobled queen'?
POLONIUS: That's good.
1 PLAYER: 'Run barefoot up and down, threat'ning the flames
With bisson rheum; a clout upon that head
Where late the diadem stood, and for a robe,
490 About her lank and all o'er-teemèd loins,
A blanket, in the alarm of fear caught up—
Who this had seen, with tongue in venom steeped,
'Gainst Fortune's state would treason have pronounced.
But if the gods themselves did see her then,
495 When she saw Pyrrhus make malicious sport
In mincing with his sword her husband's limbs,
The instant burst of clamor that she made,
Unless things mortal move them not at all,
Would have made milch the burning eyes of heaven,
500 And passion in the gods.'
POLONIUS: Look whe'r he has not turned his color, and has
tears in's eyes. Prithee no more.

HAMLET: 'Tis well. I'll have thee speak out the rest of this
soon.—Good my lord, will you see the players well bestowed? Do you hear, let them be well used, for they are 505
the abstract and brief chronicles of the time; after your
death you were better have a bad epitaph than their ill report while you live.
POLONIUS: My lord, I will use them according to their desert.
HAMLET: God's bodkin, man, much better. Use every man af- 510
ter his desert, and who shall 'scape whipping? Use them
after your own honor and dignity. The less they deserve,
the more merit is in your bounty. Take them in.
POLONIUS: Come, sirs.
HAMLET: Follow him, friends. We'll hear a play tomorrow. 515
(*Aside to* 1 PLAYER.) Dost thou hear me, old friend, can
you play the 'Murder of Gonzago'?
1 PLAYER: Ay, my lord.
HAMLET: We'll ha't tomorrow night. You could for a need
study a speech of some dozen or sixteen lines which I 520
would set down and insert in't, could you not?
1 PLAYER: Ay, my lord.
HAMLET: Very well. Follow that lord, and look you mock him
not.

(*Exeunt* POLONIUS *and* PLAYERS.)

My good friends, I'll leave you till night. You are welcome 525
to Elsinore.
ROSENCRANTZ: Good my lord!

(*Exeunt* [ROSENCRANTZ *and* GUILDENSTERN].)

HAMLET: Ay, so God by to you. Now I am alone.
O, what a rogue and peasant slave am I!
Is it not monstrous that this player here, 530
But in a fiction, in a dream of passion,
Could force his soul so to his own conceit
That from her working all his visage wanned;
Tears in his eyes, distraction in his aspect,
A broken voice, and his whole function suiting 535
With forms to his conceit? And all for nothing,
For Hecuba!
What's Hecuba to him or he to Hecuba,
That he should weep for her? What would he do
Had he the motive and the cue for passion 540
That I have? He would drown the stage with tears,
And cleave the general ear with horrid speech,
Make mad the guilty, and appal the free,
Confound the ignorant, and amaze indeed
The very faculties of eyes and ears. 545
Yet I,
A dull and muddy-mettled rascal, peak
Like John-a-dreams, unpregnant of my cause,
And can say nothing; no, not for a king
Upon whose property and most dear life 550
A damned defeat was made. Am I a coward?
Who calls me villain, breaks my pate across,

---

453 **Repugnant** refractory   455 **fell** fierce, cruel   465 **against**
just before   466 **rack** mass of cloud   469 **region** air   471
Cyclops giant workmen who made armor in the smithy of Vulcan   472 **proof eterne** to be forever impenetrable   477 **fellies**
the curved pieces forming the rim of a wheel   478 **nave** hub of
a wheel   484 **mobled** muffled   488 **bisson rheum** blinding
tears   490 **o'er-teemed** exhausted by many births   493 **state**
government   499 **milch** moist, tearful (lit., milk, giving)

506 **abstract** summary account   510 **God's bodkin** by God's
dear body   532 **conceit** imagination   542 **general** public
547 **muddy-mettled** dull-spirited; **peak** mope   548 **unpregnant** not quickened to action

Plucks off my beard and blows it in my face,
Tweaks me by the nose, gives me the lie i' th' throat
555   As deep as to the lungs? Who does me this?
Ha, 'swounds, I should take it; for it cannot be
But I am pigeon-livered and lack gall
To make oppression bitter, or ere this
I should 'a fatted all the region kites
560   With this slave's offal. Bloody, bawdy villain!
Remorseless, treacherous, lecherous, kindless villain!
Why, what an ass am I! This is most brave,
That I, the son of a dear father murdered,
Prompted to my revenge by heaven and hell,
565   Must like a whore unpack my heart with words,
And fall a-cursing like a very drab,
A scullion! Fie upon 't! foh!
About, my brains! Hum—I have heard
That guilty creatures sitting at a play,
570   Have by the very cunning of the scene
Been struck so to the soul that presently
They have proclaimed their malefactions:
For murder, though it have no tongue, will speak
With most miraculous organ. I'll have these players
575   Play something like the murder of my father
Before mine uncle. I'll observe his looks.
I'll tent him to the quick. If 'a do blench,
I know my course. The spirit that I have seen
May be the devil, and the devil hath power
580   T' assume a pleasing shape, yea, and perhaps
Out of my weakness and my melancholy,
As he is very potent with such spirits,
Abuses me to damn me. I'll have grounds
More relative than this. The play's the thing
585   Wherein I'll catch the conscience of the king.

(*Exit.*)

ACT THREE

SCENE I

Enter KING, QUEEN, POLONIUS, OPHELIA, ROSENCRANTZ,
GUILDENSTERN, LORDS.

KING: And can you by no drift of conference
Get from him why he puts on this confusion,
Grating so harshly all his days of quiet
With turbulent and dangerous lunacy?
5   ROSENCRANTZ: He does confess he feels himself distracted,
But from what cause 'a will by no means speak.

---

559 **region kites** kites of the air   561 **kindless** unnatural. Following this line, *F* adds the words "Oh Vengeance!" Their inappropriateness to the occasion is noted by Professor Harold Jenkins (in his "Playhouse Interpolations in the Folio Text of Hamlet," *Studies in Bibliography* 13 [1960]: 37). Professor Jenkins remarks that the folio text, by introducing Hamlet's "call for vengeance while he is still absorbed in self-reproaches, both anticipates and misconstrues" the crisis of his passion and of the speech, which comes in fact at line 568 ("**About, my brains**"), when "he abandons his self-reproaches and plans action"   567 **scullion** kitchen wench   571 **presently** immediately   577 **tent** probe; **blench** flinch   583 **Abuses** deludes   584 **relative** relevant

GUILDENSTERN: Nor do we find him forward to be sounded,
But with a crafty madness keeps aloof
When we would bring him on to some confession
Of his true state.   10
QUEEN: Did he receive you well?
ROSENCRANTZ: Most like a gentleman.
GUILDENSTERN: But with much forcing of his disposition.
ROSENCRANTZ: Niggard of question, but of our demands
Most free in his reply.
QUEEN: Did you assay him
To any pastime?   15
ROSENCRANTZ: Madam, it so fell out that certain players
We o'er-raught on the way. Of these we told him,
And there did seem in him a kind of joy
To hear of it. They are here about the court,
And as I think, they have already order   20
This night to play before him.
POLONIUS: 'Tis most true,
And he beseeched me to entreat your majesties
To hear and see the matter.
KING: With all my heart, and it doth much content me
To hear him so inclined.   25
Good gentlemen, give him a further edge,
And drive his purpose into these delights.
ROSENCRANTZ: We shall, my lord.

(*Exeunt* ROSENCRANTZ *and* GUILDENSTERN.)

KING: Sweet Gertrude, leave us too;
For we have closely sent for Hamlet hither,
That he, as 'twere by accident, may here   30
Affront Ophelia.
Her father and myself (lawful espials)
We'll so bestow ourselves that, seeing unseen,
We may of their encounter frankly judge,
And gather by him, as he is behaved,   35
If't be th' affliction of his love or no
That thus he suffers for.
QUEEN: I shall obey you.—
And for your part, Ophelia, I do wish
That your good beauties be the happy cause
Of Hamlet's wildness. So shall I hope your virtues   40
Will bring him to his wonted way again,
To both your honors.
OPHELIA: Madam, I wish it may.

(*Exit* QUEEN *with* LORDS.)

POLONIUS: Ophelia, walk you here.—Gracious, so please you,
We will bestow ourselves.—(*To* OPHELIA.) Read on this book,
That show of such an exercise may color   45
Your loneliness.—We are oft to blame in this,
'Tis too much proved, that with devotion's visage
And pious action we do sugar o'er
The devil himself.

III.i. 7 forward willing   **14 assay** try to win   **17 o'er-raught** overtook   **26 give him a further edge** sharpen his inclination   **29 closely** privately   **31 Affront** meet face to face   **32 espials** spies   **45 exercise** act of devotion; **color** give an appearance of naturalness to

KING: (*Aside.*)   O, 'tis too true.
50   How smart a lash that speech doth give my conscience!
      The harlot's cheek, beautied with plast'ring art,
      Is not more ugly to the thing that helps it
      Then is my deed to my most painted word.
      O heavy burden!
55 POLONIUS: I hear him coming. Let's withdraw, my lord.

(*Exeunt* KING *and* POLONIUS.)

(*Enter* HAMLET.)

    HAMLET: To be, or not to be, that is the question:
      Whether 'tis nobler in the mind to suffer
      The slings and arrows of outrageous fortune,
      Or to take arms against a sea of troubles,
60   And by opposing end them. To die, to sleep—
      No more; and by a sleep to say we end
      The heartache, and the thousand natural shocks
      That flesh is heir to: 'tis a consummation
      Devoutly to be wished. To die, to sleep—
65   To sleep, perchance to dream, ay there's the rub;
      For in that sleep of death what dreams may come
      When we have shuffled off this mortal coil
      Must give us pause. There's the respect
      That makes calamity of so long life:
70   For who would bear the whips and scorns of time,
      Th' oppressor's wrong, the proud man's contumely,
      The pangs of despised love, the law's delay,
      The insolence of office, and the spurns
      That patient merit of th' unworthy takes,
75   When he himself might his quietus make
      With a bare bodkin? Who would fardels bear,
      To grunt and sweat under a weary life,
      But that the dread of something after death,
      The undiscovered country, from whose bourn
80   No traveller returns, puzzles the will,
      And makes us rather bear those ills we have
      Than fly to others that we know not of?
      Thus conscience does make cowards of us all,
      And thus the native hue of resolution
85   Is sicklied o'er with the pale cast of thought,
      And enterprises of great pitch and moment
      With this regard their currents turn awry
      And lose the name of action. Soft you now,
      The fair Ophelia.—Nymph, in thy orisons
90   Be all my sins remembered.
    OPHELIA: Good my lord,
      How does your honor for this many a day?
    HAMLET: I humbly thank you, well.
    OPHELIA: My lord, I have remembrances of yours
      That I have longed long to re-deliver.
95   I pray you now receive them.
    HAMLET: No, not I,
      I never gave you aught.

OPHELIA: My honored lord, you know right well you did,
      And with them words of so sweet breath composed
      As made the things more rich. Their perfume lost,
      Take these again, for to the noble mind   100
      Rich gifts wax poor when givers prove unkind.
      There, my lord.
HAMLET: Ha, ha! are you honest?
OPHELIA: My lord?
HAMLET: Are you fair?   105
OPHELIA: What means your lordship?
HAMLET: That if you be honest and fair, your honesty should
      admit no discourse to your beauty.
OPHELIA: Could beauty, my lord, have better commerce than
      with honesty?   110
HAMLET: Ay, truly, for the power of beauty will sooner trans-
      form honesty from what it is to a bawd than the force of
      honesty can translate beauty into his likeness. This was
      sometime a paradox, but now the time gives it proof. I did
      love you once.   115
OPHELIA: Indeed, my lord, you made me believe so.
HAMLET: You should not have believed me, for virtue cannot
      so inoculate our old stock but we shall relish of it. I loved
      you not.
OPHELIA: I was the more deceived.   120
HAMLET: Get thee to a nunnery. Why wouldst thou be a
      breeder of sinners? I am myself indifferent honest, but yet I
      could accuse me of such things that it were better my
      mother had not borne me: I am very proud, revengeful, am-
      bitious, with more offences at my beck than I have thoughts 125
      to put them in, imagination to give them shape, or time to
      act them in. What should such fellows as I do crawling be-
      tween earth and heaven? We are arrant knaves all; believe
      none of us. Go thy ways to a nunnery. Where's your father?
OPHELIA: At home, my lord.   130
HAMLET: Let the doors be shut upon him, that he may play
      the fool nowhere but in's own house. Farewell.
OPHELIA: O, help him, you sweet heavens!
HAMLET: If thou dost marry, I'll give thee this plague for thy
      dowry: be thou as chaste as ice, as pure as snow, thou shalt 135
      not escape calumny. Get thee to a nunnery, farewell. Or if
      thou wilt needs marry, marry a fool, for wise men know
      well enough what monsters you make of them. To a nun-
      nery, go, and quickly too. Farewell.
OPHELIA: Heavenly powers, restore him!   140
HAMLET: I have heard of your paintings well enough. God
      hath given you one face, and you make yourselves another.
      You jig and amble, and you lisp; you nickname God's crea-
      tures, and make your wantonness your ignorance. Go to, I'll
      no more on't, it hath made me mad. I say we will have no   145
      moe marriage. Those that are married already, all but one,
      shall live. The rest shall keep as they are. To a nunnery, go.

(*Exit.*)

OPHELIA: O, what a noble mind is here o'erthrown!
      The courtier's, soldier's, scholar's, eye, tongue, sword,

---

52 **to** compared to   65 **rub** obstacle (lit., obstruction encountered by bowler's ball)   67 **coil** bustle, turmoil   75 **quietus** set
tlement   76 **bodkin** dagger · **fardels** burdens   79 **bourn** realm
86 **pitch** height   87 **regard** consideration   89 **orisons** prayers

---

103 **honest** chaste   118 **inoculate** graft   122 **indifferent
honest** moderately respectable   144 **make your wantonness
your ignorance** excuse your wanton behavior with the plea
that you don't know any better   145 **moe** more

150   Th' expectancy and rose of the fair state,
      The glass of fashion and the mould of form,
      Th' observed of all observers, quite quite down!
      And I of ladies most deject and wretched,
      That sucked the honey of his musiced vows,
155   Now see that noble and most sovereign reason
      Like sweet bells jangled, out of time and harsh;
      That unmatched form and feature of blown youth
      Blasted with ecstasy. O, woe is me
      T' have seen what I have seen, see what I see!

(Enter KING and POLONIUS.)

160   KING: Love? His affections do not that way tend,
      Nor what he spake, though it lacked form a little,
      Was not like madness. There's something in his soul,
      O'er which his melancholy sits on brood,
      And I do doubt the hatch and the disclose
165   Will be some danger; which for to prevent,
      I have in quick determination
      Thus set it down: he shall with speed to England
      For the demand of our neglected tribute.
      Haply the seas and countries different,
170   With variable objects, shall expel
      This something-settled matter in his heart
      Whereon his brains still beating puts him thus
      From fashion of himself. What think you on't?
      POLONIUS: It shall do well. But yet do I believe
175   The origin and commencement of his grief
      Sprung from neglected love.—How now, Ophelia?
      You need not tell us what Lord Hamlet said;
      We heard it all.—My lord, do as you please,
      But if you hold it fit, after the play
180   Let his queen-mother all alone entreat him
      To show his grief. Let her be round with him,
      And I'll be placed, so please you, in the ear
      Of all their conference. If she find him not,
      To England send him; or confine him where
185   Your wisdom best shall think.
      KING: It shall be so.
      Madness in great ones must not unwatched go.

(Exeunt.)

SCENE II

Enter HAMLET and three of the PLAYERS.

   HAMLET: Speak the speech, I pray you, as I pronounced it to
      you, trippingly on the tongue; but if you mouth it as many
      of our players do, I had as lief the town-crier spoke my
      lines. Nor do not saw the air too much with your hand
5   thus, but use all gently, for in the very torrent, tempest, and
      as I may say, whirlwind of your passion, you must acquire
      and beget a temperance that may give it smoothness. O, it
      offends me to the soul to hear a robustious periwig-pated
      fellow tear a passion to tatters, to very rags, to split the ears

of the groundlings, who for the most part are capable of 10
nothing but inexplicable dumb shows and noise. I would
have such a fellow whipped for o'erdoing Termagant. It
out-Herods Herod. Pray you avoid it.
   1 PLAYER: I warrant your honour.
   HAMLET: Be not too tame neither, but let your own discre- 15
      tion be your tutor. Suit the action to the word, the word
      to the action, with this special observance, that you o'er-
      step not the modesty of nature; for any thing so o'erdone
      is from the purpose of playing, whose end both at the first,
      and now, was and is, to hold as 'twere the mirror up to na- 20
      ture, to show virtue her own feature, scorn her own im-
      age, and the very age and body of the time his form and
      pressure. Now this overdone, or come tardy off, though it
      make the unskilful laugh, cannot but make the judicious
      grieve, the censure of the which one must in your al- 25
      lowance o'erweigh a whole theatre of others. O, there be
      players that I have seen play—and heard others praise, and
      that highly—not to speak it profanely, that neither having
      th' accent of Christians, nor the gait of Christian, pagan,
      nor man, have so strutted and bellowed that I have thought 30
      some of nature's journeymen had made men, and not
      made them well, they imitated humanity so abominably.
   1 PLAYER: I hope we have reformed that indifferently with us.
   HAMLET: O, reform it altogether. And let those that play your
      clowns speak no more than is set down for them, for there 35
      be of them that will themselves laugh, to set on some
      quantity of barren spectators to laugh too, though in the
      meantime some necessary question of the play be then to
      be considered. That's villanous, and shows a most pitiful
      ambition in the fool that uses it. Go, make you ready. 40

(Exeunt PLAYERS.)

(Enter POLONIUS, GUILDENSTERN, and ROSENCRANTZ.)

      How now, my lord? Will the king hear this piece of work?
   POLONIUS: And the queen too, and that presently.
   HAMLET: Bid the players make haste. *(Exit POLONIUS.)*
      Will you two help to hasten them?
   ROSENCRANTZ: Ay, my lord. 45

(Exeunt they two.)

   HAMLET: What, ho! Horatio!

(Enter HORATIO.)

   HORATIO: Here, sweet lord, at your service.
   HAMLET: Horatio, thou art e'en as just a man
      As e'er my conversation coped withal.
   HORATIO: O my dear lord! 50
   HAMLET: Nay, do not think I flatter,
      For what advancement may I hope from thee,
      That no revenue hast but thy good spirits

---

150 **expectancy** hope   151 **glass** mirror   157 **blown** bloom-
ing   158 **ecstasy** madness   160 **affections** emotions   164
doubt fear   181 **round** plain-spoken

III.ii. 10 **groundlings** spectators who paid least and stood on
the ground   12 **Termagant** thought to be a Mohammedan deity, and represented in medieval mystery plays as a violent and
ranting personage; **Herod** represented in the mystery plays as a
blustering tyrant   25 **censure** judgment, opinion   33 **indifferently** fairly well   49 **coped** encountered

To feed and clothe thee? Why should the poor be flattered?
No, let the candied tongue lick absurd pomp,
55 And crook the pregnant hinges of the knee
Where thrift may follow fawning. Dost thou hear?
Since my dear soul was mistress of her choice
And could of men distinguish her election,
S'hath sealed thee for herself, for thou hast been
60 As one in suff'ring all that suffers nothing,
A man that Fortune's buffets and rewards
Hast ta'en with equal thanks; and blest are those
Whose blood and judgment are so well comeddled
That they are not a pipe for Fortune's finger
65 To sound what stop she please. Give me that man
That is not passion's slave, and I will wear him
In my heart's core, ay, in my heart of heart,
As I do thee. Something too much of this.
There is a play to-night before the king.
70 One scene of it comes near the circumstance
Which I have told thee of my father's death.
I prithee, when thou seest that act afoot,
Even with the very comment of thy soul
Observe my uncle. If his occulted guilt
75 Do not itself unkennel in one speech,
It is a damnèd ghost that we have seen,
And my imaginations are as foul
As Vulcan's stithy. Give him heedful note,
For I mine eyes will rivet to his face,
80 And after we will both our judgements join
In censure of his seeming.
HORATIO: Well, my lord.
If 'a steal aught the whilst this play is playing,
And 'scape detecting, I will pay the theft.

(*Enter Trumpets and Kettledrums,* KING, QUEEN, POLONIUS,
OPHELIA, [ROSENCRANTZ, GUILDENSTERN, *and other* LORDS
attendant].)

HAMLET: They are coming to the play. I must be idle.
85   Get you a place.
KING: How fares our cousin Hamlet?
HAMLET: Excellent, i' faith, of the chameleon's dish. I eat the
air, promise-crammed. You cannot feed capons so.
KING: I have nothing with this answer, Hamlet. These words
90   are not mine.
HAMLET: No, nor mine now. (*To* POLONIUS.) My lord, you
played once i' th' university, you say?
POLONIUS: That did I, my lord; and was accounted a good
actor.
95 HAMLET: What did you enact?
POLONIUS: I did enact Julius Caesar. I was killed i' th' Capi-
tol; Brutus killed me.
HAMLET: It was a brute part of him to kill so capital a calf
there. Be the players ready?
100 ROSENCRANTZ: Ay, my lord, they stay upon your patience.

---

55 **pregnant** ready   56 **thrift** profit   58 **election** choice   63
co-meddled mingled   73 **the very comment of thy soul**
with a keenness of observation that penetrates to the very being
74 **occulted** hidden   75 **unkennel** reveal   78 **stithy** forge
81 **censure** opinion   84 **idle** crazy   07 **chameleon's dish** the
air, on which the chameleon was supposed to feed

QUEEN: Come hither, my dear Hamlet, sit by me.
HAMLET: No, good mother, here's metal more attractive.
POLONIUS: (*To the* KING.) O, ho! do you mark that?
HAMLET: Lady, shall I lie in your lap?

(*Lying down at* OPHELIA's *feet*.)

OPHELIA: No, my lord.   105
HAMLET: I mean, my head upon your lap?
OPHELIA: Ay, my lord.
HAMLET: Do you think I meant country matters?
OPHELIA: I think nothing, my lord.
HAMLET: That's a fair thought to lie between maids' legs.   110
OPHELIA: What is, my lord?
HAMLET: Nothing.
OPHELIA: You are merry, my lord.
HAMLET: Who, I?
OPHELIA: Ay, my lord.   115
HAMLET: O God, your only jig-maker! What should a man
do but be merry? For look you how cheerfully my
mother looks, and my father died within's two hours.
OPHELIA: Nay, 'tis twice two months, my lord.
HAMLET: So long? Nay then, let the devil wear black, for I'll   120
have a suit of sables. O heavens! die two months ago, and
not forgotten yet? Then there's hope a great man's memory may outlive his life half a year, but, by'r lady 'a must
build churches then, or else shall 'a suffer not thinking on,
with the hobby-horse, whose epitaph is   125

     'For O, for O, the hobby-horse is forgot!'

(*The trumpets sound. Dumb Show follows.*)

(*Enter a* KING *and a* QUEEN [*very lovingly*]; *the* QUEEN *embracing
him and he her.* [*She kneels, and makes show of protestation unto
him.*] *He takes her up, and declines his head upon her neck. He lies
him down upon a bank of flowers; she, seeing him asleep, leaves him.
Anon comes in another man, takes off his crown, kisses it, pours poison in the sleeper's ears, and leaves him. The* QUEEN *returns, finds
the* KING *dead, makes passionate action. The* POISONER *with some
three or four come in again, seem to condole with her. The dead body
is carried away. The* POISONER *woos the* QUEEN *with gifts; she
seems harsh awhile, but in the end accepts love.*)

(*Exeunt.*)

OPHELIA: What means this, my lord?
HAMLET: Marry, this is miching mallecho; it means mischief.
OPHELIA: Belike this show imports the argument of the play.

(*Enter* PROLOGUE.)

HAMLET: We shall know by this fellow. The players cannot   130
keep counsel; they'll tell all.
OPHELIA: Will 'a tell us what this show meant?
HAMLET: Ay, or any show that you will show him. Be not you
ashamed to show, he'll not shame to tell you what it means.

---

125 **hobby-horse** the figure of a horse fastened round the waist
of a morris dancer. Puritan efforts to suppress the country sports
in which the hobby-horse figured led to a popular ballad
lamenting the fact that "the hobby-horse is forgot"   128 **miching mallecho** skulking or crafty crime

135 OPHELIA: You are naught, you are naught. I'll mark the play.
PROLOGUE:

> For us, and for our tragedy,
> Here stooping to your clemency,
> We beg your hearing patiently.

(*Exit.*)

HAMLET: Is this a prologue, or the posy of a ring?
140 OPHELIA: 'Tis brief, my lord.
HAMLET: As woman's love.

(*Enter [the* PLAYER] KING *and* QUEEN.)

PLAYER KING: Full thirty times hath Phoebus' cart gone round
  Neptune's salt wash and Tellus' orbèd ground,
  And thirty dozen moons with borrowed sheen
145 About the world have times twelve thirties been,
  Since love our hearts and Hymen did our hands
  Unite comutual in most sacred bands.
PLAYER QUEEN: So many journeys may the sun and moon
  Make us again count o'er ere love be done!
150 But woe is me, you are so sick of late,
  So far from cheer and from your former state,
  That I distrust you. Yet though I distrust,
  Discomfort you, my lord, it nothing must.
  For women's fear and love hold quantity,
155 In neither aught, or in extremity.
  Now what my love is proof hath made you know,
  And as my love is sized, my fear is so.
  Where love is great, the littlest doubts are fear;
  Where little fears grow great, great love grows there.
160 PLAYER KING: Faith, I must leave thee, love, and shortly too;
  My operant powers their functions leave to do.
  And thou shalt live in this fair world behind,
  Honored, beloved; and haply one as kind
  For husband shalt thou—
PLAYER QUEEN: O, confound the rest!
165 Such love must needs be treason in my breast.
  In second husband let me be accurst!
  None wed the second but who killed the first.
HAMLET: That's wormwood.
PLAYER QUEEN: The instances that second marriage move
170 Are base respects of thrift, but none of love.
  A second time I kill my husband dead,
  When second husband kisses me in bed.
PLAYER KING: I do believe you think what now you speak,
  But what we do determine oft we break.
175 Purpose is but the slave to memory,
  Of violent birth, but poor validity;
  Which now, like fruit unripe, sticks on the tree,
  But fall unshaken when they mellow be.
  Most necessary 'tis that we forget
180 To pay ourselves what to ourselves is debt.

What to ourselves in passion we propose,
The passion ending, doth the purpose lose.
The violence of either grief or joy
Their own enactures with themselves destroy.
Where joy most revels, grief doth most lament;   185
Grief joys, joy grieves, on slender accident.
This world is not for aye, nor 'tis not strange
That even our loves should with our fortunes change;
For 'tis a question left us yet to prove,
Whether love lead fortune, or else fortune love.   190
The great man down, you mark his favorite flies;
The poor advanced makes friends of enemies;
And hitherto doth love on fortune tend,
For who not needs shall never lack a friend,
And who in want a hollow friend doth try,   195
Directly seasons him his enemy.
But orderly to end where I begun,
Our wills and fates do so contrary run
That our devices still are overthrown;
Our thoughts are ours, their ends none of our own.   200
So think thou wilt no second husband wed,
But die thy thoughts when thy first lord is dead.
PLAYER QUEEN: Nor earth to me give food, nor heaven light,
  Sport and repose lock from me day and night.
  To desperation turn my trust and hope,   205
  An anchor's cheer in prison be my scope,
  Each opposite that blanks the face of joy
  Meet what I would have well, and it destroy,
  Both here and hence pursue me lasting strife,
  If once a widow, ever I be wife!   210
HAMLET: If she should break it now!
PLAYER KING: 'Tis deeply sworn. Sweet, leave me here awhile.
  My spirits grow dull, and fain I would beguile
  The tedious day with sleep.

(*Sleeps.*)

PLAYER QUEEN: Sleep rock thy brain.
  And never come mischance between us twain!   215

(*Exit.*)

HAMLET: Madam, how like you this play?
QUEEN: The lady doth protest too much, methinks.
HAMLET: O, but she'll keep her word.
KING: Have you heard the argument? Is there no offence in't?
HAMLET: No, no, they do but jest, poison in jest; no offence 220
  i' th' world.
KING: What do you call the play?
HAMLET: 'The Mouse-trap.' Marry, how? Tropically. This play
  is the image of a murder done in Vienna. Gonzago is the
  duke's name; his wife, Baptista. You shall see anon. 'Tis a 225
  knavish piece of work, but what of that? Your majesty, and
  we that have free souls, it touches us not. Let the galled
  jade winch, our withers are unwrung.

(*Enter* LUCIANUS.)

---

135 **naught** naughty, lewd   139 **posy** brief motto engraved on
a fingerring   142 **Phoebus' cart** the sun's chariot   143 **Tellus'
orbed ground** the earth (Tellus was the Roman goddess of the
earth)   146 **Hymen** god of marriage   152 **distrust** fear for
154 **hold quantity** are proportional, weigh alike   157 **as my
love is sized** according to the greatness of my love   161 **operant** vital   169 **instances** motives   176 **validity** endurance

---

184 **enactures** enactments   187 **aye** ever   196 **seasons him**
ripens him into   206 **anchor's** anchorite's   227 **galled jade**
sorebacked horse

This is one Lucianus, nephew to the king.

230 OPHELIA: You are as good as a chorus, my lord.

HAMLET: I could interpret between you and your love, if I could see the puppets dallying.

OPHELIA: You are keen, my lord, you are keen.

HAMLET: It would cost you a groaning to take off mine edge.

235 OPHELIA: Still better, and worse.

HAMLET: So you mis-take your husbands.—Begin, murderer. Leave thy damnable faces and begin. Come, the croaking raven doth bellow for revenge.

LUCIANUS: Thoughts black, hands apt, drugs fit, and time

240   agreeing,

    Confederate season, else no creature seeing.

    Thou mixture rank, of midnight weeds collected,

    With Hecate's ban thrice blasted, thrice infected,

    Thy natural magic and dire property

    On wholesome life usurp immediately.

(Pours the poison in his ears.)

245 HAMLET: 'A poisons him i' th' garden for his estate. His name's Gonzago. The story is extant, and written in very choice Italian. You shall see anon how the murderer gets the love of Gonzago's wife.

OPHELIA: The king rises.

250 HAMLET: What, frighted with false fire?

QUEEN: How fares my lord?

POLONIUS: Give o'er the play.

KING: Give me some light. Away!

POLONIUS: Lights, lights, lights!

(Exeunt all but HAMLET and HORATIO.)

255 HAMLET: Why, let the strucken deer go weep,

    The hart ungallèd play.

    For some must watch, while some must sleep;

    Thus runs the world away.

    Would not this, sir, and a forest of feathers—if the rest of

260   my fortunes turn Turk with me—with two Provincial roses on my razed shoes, get me a fellowship in a cry of players?

HORATIO: Half a share.

HAMLET: A whole one, I.

    For thou dost know, O Damon dear,

265   This realm dismantled was

    Of Jove himself, and now reigns here

    A very, very—pajock.

HORATIO: You might have rhymed.

HAMLET: O good Horatio, I'll take the ghost's word for a

270   thousand pound. Didst perceive?

HORATIO: Very well, my lord.

HAMLET: Upon the talk of the poisoning.

HORATIO: I did very well note him.

HAMLET: Ah, ha! Come, some music. Come, the recorders.

    For if the king like not the comedy,   275

    Why then, belike, he likes it not, perdy.

Come, some music.

(Enter ROSENCRANTZ and GUILDENSTERN.)

GUILDENSTERN: Good my lord, vouchsafe me a word with you.

HAMLET: Sir, a whole history.

GUILDENSTERN: The king, sir—   280

HAMLET: Ay, sir what of him?

GUILDENSTERN: Is in his retirement marvellous distempered.

HAMLET: With drink, sir?

GUILDENSTERN: No, my lord, with choler.

HAMLET: Your wisdom should show itself more richer to sig-   285 nify this to the doctor, for for me to put him to his purgation would perhaps plunge him into more choler.

GUILDENSTERN: Good my lord, put your discourse into some frame, and start not so wildly from my affair.

HAMLET: I am tame, sir. Pronounce.   290

GUILDENSTERN: The queen, your mother, in most great affliction of spirit, hath sent me to you.

HAMLET: You are welcome.

GUILDENSTERN: Nay, good my lord, this courtesy is not of the right breed. If it shall please you to make me a wholesome   295 answer, I will do your mother's commandment. If not, your pardon and my return shall be the end of my business.

HAMLET: Sir, I cannot.

GUILDENSTERN: What, my lord?

HAMLET: Make you a wholesome answer; my wit's diseased.   300 But, sir, such answer as I can make, you shall command, or rather, as you say, my mother. Therefore no more, but to the matter. My mother, you say—

ROSENCRANTZ: Then thus she says: your behaviour hath struck her into amazement and admiration.   305

HAMLET: O wonderful son, that can so stonish a mother! But is there no sequel at the heels of this mother's admiration? Impart.

ROSENCRANTZ: She desires to speak with you in her closet ere you go to bed.   310

HAMLET: We shall obey, were she ten times our mother. Have you any further trade with us?

ROSENCRANTZ: My lord, you once did love me.

HAMLET: And do still, by these pickers and stealers.

ROSENCRANTZ: Good my lord, what is your cause of distem-   315 per? You do surely bar the door upon your own liberty, if you deny your griefs to your friend.

HAMLET: Sir, I lack advancement.

ROSENCRANTZ: How can that be, when you have the voice of the king himself for your succession in Denmark?   320

HAMLET: Ay, sir, but 'While the grass grows'—the proverb is something musty.

---

242 **Hecate** goddess of witchcraft; **blasted** fallen under a blight 259 **feathers** plumes for actors' costumes   260 **Provincial roses** i.e., Provençal roses. Ribbon rosettes resembling these French roses were used to decorate shoes   261 **razed** with ornamental slashing; **cry** company   267 **pajock** presumably a variant form of "patch-cock," a despicable person. Cf. 3.4.104

275 **For if . . . comedy** a seeming parody of *The Spanish Tragedy*, 4.1.197–98 ("And if the world like not this tragedy, / Hard is the hap of old Hieronimo"), where another revenger's dramatic entertainment is referred to   287 **choler** one of the four bodily humors, an excess of which gave rise to anger   295 **wholesome** reasonable   307 **admiration** wonder   314 **pickers and stealers** hands   321 **'while the grass grows'** a proverb ending 'the horse starves'

(*Enter the* PLAYERS *with recorders.*)

O, the recorders! Let me see one. To withdraw with
you—why do you go about to recover the wind of me, as
325   if you would drive me into a toil?

GUILDENSTERN: O, my lord, if my duty be too bold, my love
is too unmannerly.

HAMLET: I do not well understand that. Will you play upon
this pipe?

330 GUILDENSTERN: My lord, I cannot.

HAMLET: I pray you.

GUILDENSTERN: Believe me, I cannot.

HAMLET: I beseech you.

GUILDENSTERN: I know no touch of it, my lord.

335 HAMLET: It is easy as lying. Govern these ventages with your
fingers and thumb, give it breath with your mouth, and it
will discourse most eloquent music. Look you, these are
the stops.

GUILDENSTERN: But these cannot I command to any ut-
340   t'rance of harmony. I have not the skill.

HAMLET: Why look you now, how unworthy a thing you make
of me! You would play upon me, you would seem to know
my stops, you would pluck out the heart of my mystery, you
would sound me from my lowest note to the top of my com-
345   pass; and there is music, excellent voice, in this little organ,
yet cannot you make it speak. 'Sblood, do you think I am easier to be played on than a pipe? Call me what instrument you
will, though you can fret me, you cannot play upon me.

(*Enter* POLONIUS.)

350 God bless you, sir!

POLONIUS: My lord, the queen would speak with you, and
presently.

HAMLET: Do you see yonder cloud that's almost in shape of a
camel?

355 POLONIUS: By th' mass and 'tis, like a camel indeed.

HAMLET: Methinks it is like a weasel.

POLONIUS: It is backed like a weasel.

HAMLET: Or like a whale.

POLONIUS: Very like a whale.

360 HAMLET: Then I will come to my mother by and by. (*Aside.*)
They fool me to the top of my bent.—I will come by and by.

POLONIUS: I will say so.

(*Exit* POLONIUS.)

HAMLET: 'By and by' is easily said. Leave me, friends.

(*Exeunt all but* HAMLET.)

'Tis now the very witching time of night,
365 When churchyards yawn and hell itself breathes out
Contagion to this world. Now could I drink hot blood,
And do such bitter business as the day
Would quake to look on. Soft, now to my mother.
O heart, lose not thy nature; let not ever
370 The soul of Nero enter this firm bosom.

---

323 **withdraw** step aside for private conversation   325 **toil** net,
snare   335 **ventages** holes or stops in the recorder   348 **fret**
(1) a stop on the fingerboard of a guitar (2) annoy   370 **Nero**
Roman emperor who murdered his mother

Let me be cruel, not unnatural;
I will speak daggers to her, but use none.
My tongue and soul in this be hypocrites:
How in my words somever she be shent,
To give them seals never my soul consent!   375

(*Exit.*)

SCENE III

Enter KING, ROSENCRANTZ, *and* GUILDENSTERN.

KING: I like him not, nor stands it safe with us
To let his madness range. Therefore prepare you.
I your commission will forthwith dispatch,
And he to England shall along with you.
The terms of our estate may not endure   5
Hazard so near's as doth hourly grow
Out of his brows.

GUILDENSTERN: We will ourselves provide,
Most holy and religious fear it is
To keep those many many bodies safe
That live and feed upon your majesty.   10

ROSENCRANTZ: The single and peculiar life is bound
With all the strength and armor of the mind
To keep itself from noyance, but much more
That spirit upon whose weal depends and rests
The lives of many. The cess of majesty   15
Dies not alone, but like a gulf doth draw
What's near it with it. It is a massy wheel
Fixed on the summit of the highest mount,
To whose huge spokes ten thousand lesser things
Are mortised and adjoined, which when it falls,   20
Each small annexment, petty consequence,
Attends the boist'rous ruin. Never alone
Did the king sigh, but with a general groan.

KING: Arm you, I pray you, to this speedy voyage,
For we will fetters put about this fear,   25
Which now goes too free-footed.

ROSENCRANTZ: We will haste us.

(*Exeunt Gentlemen* [ROSENCRANTZ *and* GUILDENSTERN].)

(*Enter* POLONIUS.)

POLONIUS: My lord, he's going to his mother's closet.
Behind the arras I'll convey myself
To hear the process. I'll warrant she'll tax him home,
And as you said, and wisely was it said,   30
'Tis meet that some more audience than a mother,
Since nature makes them partial, should o'erhear
The speech of vantage. Fare you well, my liege.
I'll call upon you ere you go to bed,
And tell you what I know.   35

---

374 **somever,** soever; **shent** reproved, abused

III.iii. 5 **terms of our estate** conditions required for our rule
as king   7 **brows** threatening looks that suggest the dangerous
plots Hamlet's brain is hatching   11 **peculiar** private   13 **noyance** harm   15 **cess** cessation, extinction   20 **mortised**
jointed (as with mortise and tenon)   33 **of vantage** (1) in addition; (2) from a convenient place for listening

KING: Thanks, dear my lord. (*Exit* POLONIUS.)
O, my offence is rank, it smells to heaven;
It hath the primal eldest curse upon't,
A brother's murder. Pray can I not,
Though inclination be as sharp as will.
40 My stronger guilt defeats my strong intent,
And like a man to double business bound,
I stand in pause where I shall first begin,
And both neglect. What if this cursèd hand
Were thicker than itself with brother's blood,
45 Is there not rain enough in the sweet heavens
To wash it white as snow? Whereto serves mercy
But to confront the visage of offence?
And what's in prayer but this twofold force,
To be forestallèd ere we come to fall,
50 Or pardoned being down? Then I'll look up.
My fault is past. But, O, what form of prayer
Can serve my turn? 'Forgive me my foul murder'?
That cannot be, since I am still possessed
Of those effects for which I did the murder—
55 My crown, mine own ambition, and my queen.
May one be pardoned and retain th' offence?
In the corrupted currents of this world
Offence's gilded hand may shove by justice,
And oft 'tis seen the wicked prize itself
60 Buys out the law. But 'tis not so above
There is no shuffling: there the action lies
In his true nature, and we ourselves compelled,
Even to the teeth and forehead of our faults,
To give in evidence. What then? What rests?
65 Try what repentance can. What can it not?
Yet what can it when one can not repent?
O wretched state! O bosom black as death!
O limèd soul, that struggling to be free
Art more engaged! Help, angels! Make assay.
70 Bow, stubborn knees, and heart with strings of steel,
Be soft as sinews of the new-born babe.
All may be well.

(*He kneels.*)

(*Enter* HAMLET.)

HAMLET: Now might I do it pat, now 'a is a-praying,
And now I'll do't—and so 'a goes to heaven,
75 And so am I revenged. That would be scanned.
A villain kills my father, and for that,
I, his sole son, do this same villain send
To heaven.
Why, this is hire and salary, not revenge.
80 'A took my father grossly, full of bread,
With all his crimes broad blown, as flush as May;
And how his audit stands who knows save heaven?
But in our circumstance and course of thought
'Tis heavy with him; and am I then revenged

To take him in the purging of his soul, 85
When he is fit and seasoned for his passage?
No.
Up, sword, and know thou a more horrid hent.
When he is drunk asleep, or in his rage,
Or in th' incestuous pleasure of his bed, 90
At game a-swearing, or about some act
That has no relish of salvation in't—
Then trip him, that his heels may kick at heaven,
And that his soul may be as damned and black
As hell, whereto it goes. My mother stays. 95
This physic but prolongs thy sickly days.

(*Exit.*)

KING: (*Rising.*) My words fly up, my thoughts remain below.
Words without thoughts never to heaven go.

(*Exit.*)

SCENE IV

Enter [QUEEN] GERTRUDE *and* POLONIUS.

POLONIUS: 'A will come straight. Look you lay home to him.
Tell him his pranks have been too broad to bear with,
And that your grace hath screened and stood between
Much heat and him. I'll silence me even here.
Pray you be round. 5
QUEEN: I'll warrant you. Fear me not.
Withdraw, I hear him coming.

(POLONIUS *goes behind the arras.*)

(*Enter* HAMLET.)

HAMLET: Now, mother, what's the matter?
QUEEN: Hamlet, thou hast thy father much offended.
HAMLET: Mother, you have my father much offended.
QUEEN: Come, come, you answer with an idle tongue. 10
HAMLET: Go, go, you question with a wicked tongue.
QUEEN: Why, how, now, Hamlet?
HAMLET: What's the matter now?
QUEEN: Have you forgot me?
HAMLET: No, by the rood, not so:
You are the queen, your husband's brother's wife,
And would it were not so, you are my mother. 15
QUEEN: Nay, then I'll set those to you that can speak.
HAMLET: Come, come, and sit you down. You shall not budge.
You go not till I set you up a glass
Where you may see the inmost part of you.
QUEEN: What will thou do? Thou wilt not murder me? 20
Help, ho!
POLONIUS: (*Behind.*) What, ho! help!
HAMLET: (*Draws.*) How now! a rat?
Dead for a ducat, dead!

(*Thrusts his sword through the arras and kills* POLONIUS.)

---

39 **will** carnal desire   61 **shuffling** doubledealing; **action** legal action   68 **limèd** soul caught by sin as the bird by lime   69 **assay** an effort   80 **grossly** unprepared spiritually   81 **as flush as May** in full flower   83 **in our circumstance** considering all evidence, **course** beaten way, habit

---

88 **hent** occasion, opportunity

III.iv. 5 Following Polonius's "Pray you be round" (which in *F* reads "Pray you be round with him"), *F* adds the line: "*Hamlet within.* Mother, mother, mother"   13 **rood** cross

25 POLONIUS: (*Behind.*) O, I am slain!
   QUEEN: O me, what hast thou done?
   HAMLET: Nay, I know not.
     Is it the king?
   QUEEN: O, what a rash and bloody deed is this!
   HAMLET: A bloody deed? Almost as bad, good mother,
30   As kill a king and marry with his brother.
   QUEEN: As kill a king?
   HAMLET: Ay, lady, it was my word.

(*Lifts up the arras and sees the body of* POLONIUS.)

    Thou wretched, rash, intruding fool, farewell!
    I took thee for thy better. Take thy fortune.
    Thou find'st to be too busy is some danger.—
35   Leave wringing of your hands. Peace, sit you down
    And let me wring your heart, for so I shall
    If it be made of penetrable stuff,
    If damnèd custom have not brazed it so
    That it be proof and bulwark against sense.
40 QUEEN: What have I done that thou dar'st wag thy tongue
    In noise so rude against me?
   HAMLET: Such an act
    That blurs the grace and blush of modesty,
    Calls virtue hypocrite, takes off the rose
    From the fair forehead of an innocent love,
45   And sets a blister there, makes marriage-vows
    As false as dicers' oaths. O, such a deed
    As from the body of contraction plucks
    The very soul, and sweet religion makes
    A rhapsody of words. Heaven's face does glow
50   O'er this solidity and compound mass
    With heated visage, as against the doom—
    Is thought-sick at the act.
   QUEEN: Ay me, what act,
    That roars so loud, and thunders in the index?
   HAMLET: Look here, upon this picture and on this.
55   The counterfeit presentment of two brothers.
    See what a grace was seated on this brow:
    Hyperion's curls, the front of Jove himself,
    An eye like Mars, to threaten and command,
    A station like the herald Mercury
60   New lighted on a heaven-kissing hill—
    A combination and a form indeed
    Where every god did seem to set his seal
    To give the world assurance of a man.
    This was your husband. Look you now what follows.
65   Here is your husband, like a mildewed ear
    Blasting his wholesome brother. Have you eyes?
    Could you on this fair mountain leave to feed,
    And batten on this moor? Ha! have you eyes?
    You cannot call it love, for at your age
70   The heyday in the blood is tame, it's humble,

And waits upon the judgement, and what judgement
Would step from this to this? Sense sure you have,
Else could you not have motion, but sure that sense
Is apoplexed, for madness would not err
Nor sense to ecstasy was ne'er so thralled   75
But it reserved some quantity of choice
To serve in such a difference. What devil was't
That thus hath cozened you at hoodman-blind?
Eyes without feeling, feeling without sight,
Ears without hands or eyes, smelling sans all,   80
Or but a sickly part of one true sense
Could not so mope. O shame! where is thy blush?
Rebellious hell,
If thou canst mutine in a matron's bones,
To flaming youth let virtue be as wax   85
And melt in her own fire. Proclaim no shame
When the compulsive ardor gives the charge,
Since frost itself as actively doth burn,
And reason pandars will.
QUEEN: O Hamlet, speak no more!
    Thou turn'st mine eyes into my very soul,   90
    And there I see such black and grainèd spots
    As will not leave their tinct.
HAMLET: Nay, but to live
    In the rank sweat of an enseamèd bed,
    Stewed in corruption, honeying and making love
    Over the nasty sty—   95
QUEEN: O, speak to me no more!
    These words like daggers enter in mine ears.
    No more, sweet Hamlet.
HAMLET: A murderer and a villain,
    A slave that is not twentieth part the tithe
    Of your precedent lord, a vice of kings,
    A cutpurse of the empire and the rule,   100
    That from a shelf the precious diadem stole
    And put it in his pocket—
QUEEN: No more.

(*Enter* GHOST.)

HAMLET: A king of shreds and patches—
    Save me and hover o'er me with your wings,   105
    You heavenly guards! What would your gracious figure?
QUEEN: Alas, he's mad.
HAMLET: Do you not come your tardy son to chide,
    That lapsed in time and passion lets go by
    Th' important acting of your dread command?   110
    O, say!
GHOST: Do not forget. This visitation
    Is but to whet thy almost blunted purpose.
    But look, amazement on thy mother sits.
    O, step between her and her fighting soul!   115

---

38 **brazed** plated it as with brass   39 **proof** impenetrable, as of armor   47 **contraction** the contract of marriage   50 **this solidity and compound mass** the earth, as compounded of the four elements   51 **doom** Judgment Day   53 **index** table of contents; thus, indication of what is to follow   55 **counterfeit presentment** portrait   57 **front** forehead   59 **station** bearing figure   68 **batten** feed like an animal   70 **heyday** ardor

72 **Sense** the senses collectively, which according to Aristotelian tradition are found in all creatures that have the power of locomotion   75 **ecstasy** madness   78 **hoodman-blind** blindman's bluff   80 **sans** without   82 **mope** act without full use of one's wits   89 **will** desire   91 **grainèd spots** indelible stains   92 **tinct** color   93 **enseamèd** greasy   99 **vice** a character in the morality plays, presented often as a buffoon (here, a caricature)

Conceit in weakest bodies strongest works.
Speak to her, Hamlet.
HAMLET: How is it with you, lady?
QUEEN: Alas, how is't with you,
That you do bend your eye on vacancy,
120   And with th' incorporal air do hold discourse?
Forth at your eyes your spirits wildly peep,
And as the sleeping soldiers in th' alarm,
Your bedded hair like life in excrements
Start up and stand an end. O gentle son,
125   Upon the heat and flame of thy distemper
Sprinkle cool patience. Whereon do you look?
HAMLET: On him, on him! Look you how pale he glares.
His form and cause conjoined, preaching to stones,
Would make them capable.—Do not look upon me,
130   Lest with this piteous action you convert
My stern effects. Then what I have to do
Will want true color—tears perchance for blood.
QUEEN: To whom do you speak this?
HAMLET: Do you see nothing there?
135 QUEEN: Nothing at all, yet all that is I see.
HAMLET: Nor did you nothing hear?
QUEEN: No, nothing but ourselves.
HAMLET: Why, look you there. Look, how it steals away.
My father, in his habit as he lived!
140   Look where he goes even now out at the portal.

(*Exit* GHOST.)

QUEEN: This is the very coinage of your brain.
This bodiless creation ecstasy
Is very cunning in.
HAMLET: My pulse as yours doth temperately keep time,
145   And makes us healthful music. It is not madness
That I have uttered. Bring me to the test,
And I the matter will re-word, which madness
Would gambol from. Mother, for love of grace,
Lay not that flattering unction to your soul,
150   That not your trespass but my madness speaks.
It will but skin and film the ulcerous place
Whiles rank corruption, mining all within,
Infects unseen. Confess yourself to heaven,
Repent what's past, avoid what is to come,
155   And do not spread the compost on the weeds,
To make them ranker. Forgive me this my virtue,
For in the fatness of these pursy times
Virtue itself of vice must pardon beg,
Yea, curb and woo for leave to do him good.
160 QUEEN: O Hamlet, thou hast cleft my heart in twain.
HAMLET: O, throw away the worser part of it,
And live the purer with the other half.
Good night—but go not to my uncle's bed.
Assume a virtue, if you have it not.
165   That monster custom, who all sense doth eat,

Of habits devil, is angel yet in this,
That to the use of actions fair and good
He likewise gives a frock or livery
That aptly is put on. Refrain to-night,
And that shall lend a kind of easiness   170
To the next abstinence; the next more easy;
For use almost can change the stamp of nature,
And either curb the devil, or throw him out
With wondrous potency. Once more, good night,
And when you are desirous to be blest,   175
I'll blessing beg of you. For this same lord,
I do repent; but heaven hath pleased it so,
To punish me with this, and this with me,
That I must be their scourge and minister.
I will bestow him and will answer well   180
The death I gave him. So, again, good night.
I must be cruel only to be kind.
This bad begins and worse remains behind.
One word more, good lady.
QUEEN: What shall I do?
HAMLET: Not this, by no means, that I bid you do: 185
Let the bloat king tempt you again to bed,
Pinch wanton on your cheek, call you his mouse,
And let him, for a pair of reechy kisses,
Or paddling in your neck with his damned fingers,
Make you to ravel all this matter out,   190
That I essentially am not in madness,
But mad in craft. 'Twere good you let him know,
For who that's but a queen, fair, sober, wise,
Would from a paddock, from a bat, a gib,
Such dear concernings hide? Who would so do?   195
No, in despite of sense and secrecy,
Unpeg the basket on the house's top,
Let the birds fly, and like the famous ape,
To try conclusions, in the basket creep
And break your own neck down.   200
QUEEN: Be thou assured, if words be made of breath
And breath of life, I have no life to breathe
What thou hast said to me.
HAMLET: I must to England; you know that?
QUEEN: Alack,
I had forgot. 'Tis so concluded on.   205
HAMLET: There's letters sealed, and my two school-fellows,
Whom I will trust as I will adders fanged,
They bear the mandate; they must sweep my way
And marshal me to knavery. Let it work,

---

116 **Conceit** imagination   123 **excrements** nails, hair (whatever grows out of the body)   124 **an on**   129 **capable** able to respond   132 **want** lack   148 **gambol** leap or start, as a shying horse   149 **unction** ointment; hence, soothing notion   152 **mining** undermining   157 **fatness** grossness, slackness; **pursy** corpulent   165 **who all sense doth eat** who consumes all human sense, both bodily and spiritual

166 **Of habits devil** being a devil in, or in respect of, habits (with a play on "habits," as meaning both settled practices and garments, whereby devilish practices contrast with "actions fair and good," line 167, and devilish garments contrast with the "frock or livery" of line   168, which custom in its angelic aspect provides)   183 **This** i.e., the death of Polonius (cf. line 178); **remains behind** is yet to come   188 **reechy** dirty   191 **essentially** in fact   194 **paddock, gib** toad; **gib** tom-cat   197–200 **Unpeg the basket . . . neck down** the story is lost (in it, apparently, the ape carries a cage of birds to the top of a house, releases them by accident, and, surprised at their flight, imagines he can imitate it by first creeping into the basket and then leaping out. The moral of the story, for the queen, is not to expose herself to destruction by making public what good sense decrees should be kept secret.)

210 For 'tis the sport to have the engineer
Hoist with his own petar; and 't shall go hard
But I will delve one yard below their mines
And blow them at the moon. O, 'tis most sweet
When in one line two crafts directly meet.
215 This man shall set me packing.
I'll lug the guts into the neighbour room.
Mother, good night indeed. This counsellor
Is now most still, most secret and most grave,
Who was in life a foolish prating knave.
220 Come sir, to draw toward an end with you.
Good night, mother.

(*Exit* [HAMLET *tugging in* POLONIUS].)

ACT FOUR

SCENE I

Enter KING [*to the*] QUEEN, *with* ROSENCRANTZ *and* GUILDEN-
STERN.

KING: There's matter in these sighs, these profound heaves,
You must translate, 'tis fit we understand them.
Where is your son?
QUEEN: Bestow this place on us a little while.

(*Exeunt* ROSENCRANTZ *and* GUILDENSTERN.)

5 Ah, mine own lord, what have I seen to-night!
KING: What, Gertrude, how does Hamlet?
QUEEN: Mad as the sea and wind when both contend
Which is the mightier. In his lawless fit,
Behind the arras hearing something stir,
10 Whips out his rapier, cries 'A rat, a rat!'
And in this brainish apprehension kills
The unseen good old man.
KING: O heavy deed!
It had been so with us had we been there.
His liberty is full of threats to all—
15 To you yourself, to us, to every one.
Alas, how shall this bloody deed be answered?
It will be laid to us, whose providence
Should have kept short, restrained, and out of haunt,
This mad young man. But so much was our love,
20 We would not understand what was most fit,
But like the owner of a foul disease,
To keep it from divulging, let it feed
Even on the pith of life. Where is he gone?
QUEEN: To draw apart the body he hath killed,
25 O'er whom his very madness, like some ore
Among a mineral of metals base,
Shows itself pure: 'a weeps for what is done.
KING: O Gertrude, come away!
The sun no sooner shall the mountains touch
30 But we will ship him hence, and this vile deed

We must with all our majesty and skill,
Both countenance and excuse. Ho, Guildenstern!

(*Enter* ROSENCRANTZ *and* GUILDENSTERN.)

Friends both, go join you with some further aid.
Hamlet in madness hath Polonius slain,
And from his mother's closet hath he dragged him. 35
Go seek him out; speak fair, and bring the body
Into the chapel. I pray you haste in this.

(*Exeunt* ROSENCRANTZ *and* GUILDENSTERN.)

Come, Gertrude, we'll call up our wisest friends
And let them know both what we mean to do
And what's untimely done; so haply slander—   40
Whose whisper o'er the world's diameter,
As level as the cannon to his blank,
Transports his poisoned shot—may miss our name,
And hit the woundless air. O, come away!
My soul is full of discord and dismay.   45

(*Exeunt.*)

SCENE II

Enter HAMLET.

HAMLET: Safely stowed.—But soft, what noise? who calls on
Hamlet? O, here they come.

([*Enter*] ROSENCRANTZ, [GUILDENSTERN,] *and* OTHERS.)

ROSENCRANTZ: What have you done, my lord, with the dead
body?
HAMLET: Compounded it with dust, whereto 'tis kin.   5
ROSENCRANTZ: Tell us where 'tis, that we may take it thence
And bear it to the chapel.
HAMLET: Do not believe it.
ROSENCRANTZ: Believe what?
HAMLET: That I can keep your counsel and not mine own. 10
Besides, to be demanded of a sponge—what replication
should be made by the son of a king?
ROSENCRANTZ: Take you me for a sponge, my lord?
HAMLET: Ay, sir, that soaks up the king's countenance, his re-
wards, his authorities. But such officers do the king best 15
service in the end. He keeps them, like an apple in the
corner of his jaw, first mouthed to be last swallowed.
When he needs what you have gleaned, it is but squeez-
ing you and, sponge, you shall be dry again.
ROSENCRANTZ: I understand you not, my lord.   20
HAMLET: I am glad of it. A knavish speech sleeps in a foolish
ear.
ROSENCRANTZ: My lord, you must tell us where the body is,
and go with us to the king.
HAMLET: The body is with the king, but the king is not with 25
the body.
The king is a thing—

---

211 **petar** a bomb or charge for blowing in gates   217 **indeed**
in earnest (cf. lines 163, 174, 181)

IV.i. The action is continuous with that of the preceding scene.
The Queen does not leave the stage.   2 **translate** explain   11
brainish apprehension frenzied delusion   18 **out of haunt**
away from society   26 **mineral** mine

---

42 **As level as** sure of aim; **blank** target

IV.ii. 1 After the words "Safely stowed," *F* adds the line: "*Gentlemen within. Hamlet, Lord Hamlet.*" Here, as at 3.4.5 "when a
character speaks of hearing someone coming, *F* provides, though
Q does not, for the audience to hear it too" (Jenkins, *SB*, 13.35)
11 **replication** reply

GUILDENSTERN: A thing, my lord!

HAMLET: Of nothing. Bring me to him. Hide fox, and all after.

(*Exeunt.*)

SCENE III

Enter KING, *and two or three.*

KING: I have sent to seek him, and to find the body.
How dangerous is it that this man goes loose!
Yet must not we put the strong law on him.
He's loved of the distracted multitude,
5   Who like not in their judgement but their eyes,
And where 'tis so, th' offender's scourge is weighed,
But never the offence. To bear all smooth and even,
This sudden sending him away must seem
Deliberate pause. Diseases desperate grown
10   By desperate appliance are relieved,
Or not at all.

(*Enter* ROSENCRANTZ, [GUILDENSTERN,] *and all the rest.*)

              How now! what hath befall'n?

ROSENCRANTZ: Where the dead body is bestowed, my lord,
We cannot get from him.

KING: But where is he?

ROSENCRANTZ: Without, my lord; guarded, to know your
pleasure.

15 KING: Bring him before us.

ROSENCRANTZ: Ho! bring in the lord.

(*They enter* [*with* HAMLET].)

KING: Now, Hamlet, where's Polonius?

HAMLET: At supper.

KING: At supper? Where?

HAMLET: Not where he eats, but where 'a is eaten. A certain
20   convocation of politic worms are e'en at him. Your worm
is your only emperor for diet. We fat all creatures else to
fat us, and we fat ourselves for maggots. Your fat king and
your lean beggar is but variable service—two dishes, but
to one table. That's the end.

25 KING: Alas, alas!

HAMLET: A man may fish with the worm that hath eat of a
king, and eat of the fish that hath fed of that worm.

KING: What dost thou mean by this?

HAMLET: Nothing but to show you how a king may go a
30   progress through the guts of a beggar.

KING: Where is Polonius?

HAMLET: In heaven. Send thither to see. If your messenger
find him not there, seek him i' th' other place yourself. But
if, indeed, you find him not within this month, you shall
35   nose him as you go up the stairs into the lobby.

KING: (*To* ATTENDANTS.) Go seek him there.

HAMLET: 'A will stay till you come.

---

29 **Hide fox, and all after** presumably a cry in some game such as hide-and-seek. The words, which do not occur in *Q2,* may be an actor's addition

IV.iii. 9 **Deliberate pause** carefully considered 30 **progress** the state journey of a ruler

(*Exeunt* ATTENDANTS.)

KING: Hamlet, this deed, for thine especial safety—
Which we do tender, as we dearly grieve
For that which thou hast done—must send thee hence 40
With fiery quickness. Therefore prepare thyself.
The bark is ready, and the wind at help,
Th' associates tend, and everything is bent
For England.

HAMLET: For England?

KING: Ay, Hamlet.

HAMLET: Good.

KING: So is it, if thou knew'st our purposes. 45

HAMLET: I see a cherub that sees them. But come, for England!
Farewell, dear mother.

KING: Thy loving father, Hamlet.

HAMLET: My mother. Father and mother is man and wife, man
and wife is one flesh. So, my mother. Come, for England. 50

(*Exit.*)

KING: Follow him at foot: tempt him with speed aboard.
Delay it not: I'll have him hence to-night.
Away! for every thing is sealed and done
That else leans on th' affair. Pray you make haste.

(*Exeunt all but the* KING.)

And, England, if my love thou hold'st at aught— 55
As my great power thereof may give thee sense,
Since yet thy cicatrice looks raw and red
After the Danish sword, and thy free awe
Pays homage to us—thou mayst not coldly set
Our sovereign process, which imports at full 60
By letters conguring to that effect
The present death of Hamlet. Do it, England.
For like the hectic in my blood he rages,
And thou must cure me. Till I know 'tis done,
Howe'er my haps, my joys were ne'er begun. 65

(*Exit.*)

SCENE IV

Enter FORTINBRAS *with his* ARMY *over the stage.*

FORTINBRAS: Go, captain, from me greet the Danish king.
Tell him that by his license Fortinbras
Craves the conveyance of a promised march
Over his kingdom. You know the rendezvous.
If that his majesty would aught with us, 5
We shall express our duty in his eye,
And let him know so.

CAPTAIN: I will do't, my lord.

---

39 **tender** value 46 **cherub** one of the cherubim, the watchmen or sentinels of heaven, and thus endowed with the keenest vision 57 **cicatrice** scar, used here of memory of a defeat 59 **coldly set** regard with indifference 60 **process** mandate 61 **conguring to** in accordance with 63 **hectic** consumptive fever 65 **haps** fortunes

IV.iv. 3 **conveyance** conduct 6 **eye** presence

FORTINBRAS: Go softly on.

(*Exeunt all but the* CAPTAIN.)

(*Enter* HAMLET, ROSENCRANTZ, [GUILDENSTERN,] *and* OTHERS.)

HAMLET: Good sir, whose powers are these?
10 CAPTAIN: They are of Norway, sir.
HAMLET: How purposed, sir, I pray you?
CAPTAIN: Against some part of Poland.
HAMLET: Who commands them, sir?
CAPTAIN: The nephew to old Norway, Fortinbras.
15 HAMLET: Goes it against the main of Poland, sir,
    Or for some frontier?
CAPTAIN: Truly to speak, and with no addition,
    We go to gain a little patch of ground
    That hath in it no profit but the name.
20   To pay five ducats, five, I would not farm it;
    Nor will it yield to Norway or the Pole
    A ranker rate should it be sold in fee.
HAMLET: Why, then the Polack never will defend it.
CAPTAIN: Yes, it is already garrisoned.
25 HAMLET: Two thousand souls and twenty thousand ducats
    Will not debate the question of this straw.
    This is th' imposthume of much wealth and peace,
    That inward breaks, and shows no cause without
    Why the man dies. I humbly thank you, sir.
30 CAPTAIN: God buy you, sir.

(*Exit.*)

ROSENCRANTZ: Will 't please you go, my lord?
HAMLET: I'll be with you straight. Go a little before.

(*Exeunt all but* HAMLET.)

    How all occasions do inform against me,
    And spur my dull revenge! What is a man,
    If his chief good and market of his time
35   Be but to sleep and feed? A beast, no more.
    Sure he that made us with such large discourse,
    Looking before and after, gave us not
    That capability and godlike reason
    To fust in us unused. Now, whether it be
40   Bestial oblivion, or some craven scruple
    Of thinking too precisely on th' event—
    A thought which, quartered, hath but one part wisdom
    And ever three parts coward—I do not know
    Why yet I live to say 'This thing's to do',
45   Sith I have cause, and will, and strength, and means,
    To do 't. Examples gross as earth exhort me:
    Witness this army of such mass and charge,
    Led by a delicate and tender prince,
    Whose spirit, with divine ambition puffed,
50   Makes mouths at the invisible event,
    Exposing what is mortal and unsure
    To all that fortune, death, and danger dare,

Even for an eggshell. Rightly to be great
Is not to stir without great argument,
But greatly to find quarrel in a straw   55
When honor's at the stake. How stand I then,
That have a father killed, a mother stained,
Excitements of my reason and my blood,
And let all sleep, while to my shame I see
The imminent death of twenty thousand men   60
That for a fantasy and trick of fame
Go to their graves like beds, fight for a plot
Whereon the numbers cannot try the cause,
Which is not tomb enough and continent
To hide the slain? O, from this time forth,   65
My thoughts be bloody, or be nothing worth!

(*Exit.*)

SCENE V

Enter HORATIO, [QUEEN] GERTRUDE, *and a* GENTLEMAN.

QUEEN: I will not speak with her.
GENTLEMAN: She is importunate, indeed distract.
    Her mood will needs be pitied.
QUEEN: What would she have?
GENTLEMAN: She speaks much of her father, says she hears
    There's tricks i' th' world, and hems, and beats her heart, 5
    Spurns enviously at straws, speaks things in doubt
    That carry but half sense. Her speech is nothing,
    Yet the unshaped use of it doth move
    The hearers to collection; they aim at it,
    And botch the words up fit to their own thoughts,   10
    Which, as her winks and nods and gestures yield them,
    Indeed would make one think there might be thought,
    Though nothing sure, yet much unhappily.
HORATIO: 'Twere good she were spoken with, for she may
        strew
    Dangerous conjectures in ill-breeding minds.   15
QUEEN: Let her come in. (*Exit* GENTLEMAN.)
    (*Aside.*) To my sick soul, as sin's true nature is,
    Each toy seems prologue to some great amiss.
    So full of artless jealousy is guilt,
    It spills itself in fearing to be spilt.   20

(*Enter* OPHELIA [*distracted*].)

OPHELIA: Where is the beauteous majesty of Denmark?
QUEEN: How now, Ophelia!
OPHELIA: (*She sings.*)

53–56 **Rightly to be great . . . honor's at the stake** i.e., to be rightly great is *not* to refuse to act ("stir") in a dispute ("argument") because the grounds are insufficient, but to be moved to action even in trivial circumstances where a question of honor is involved   63 **try the cause** settle by combat   64 **continent** receptacle

IV.v. 6 **Spurns enviously at straws** takes exception, spitefully, to trifles   7 **nothing** nonsense   8 **unshaped use** disordered manner   9 **collection** attempts at shaping meaning, **aim** guess   13 **sure** certain   18 **toy** trifle   19 **artless jealousy** ill-concealed suspicion   20 **spills** destroys

---

15 **main** chief part   17 **addition** exaggeration   20 **To pay** i.e., for a yearly rental   22 **a ranker rate** a greater price; sold in fee sold with absolute and perpetual possession   27 **imposthume** abscess   32 **inform** take shape   34 **market** profit   36 **discourse** power of reasoning   39 **fust** grow musty   50 **Makes mouths at** makes scornful faces at, derides

> How should I your true love know
> From another one?
25   By his cockle hat and staff,
> And his sandal shoon.

QUEEN: Alas, sweet lady, what imports this song?
OPHELIA: Say you? Nay, pray you mark. (*Song.*)

30   He is dead and gone, lady,
> He is dead and gone;
> At his head a grass-green turf,
> At his heels a stone.

> O, ho!
QUEEN: Nay, but Ophelia—
OPHELIA: Pray you mark.

(*Sings.*)

35   White his shroud as the mountain snow—

(*Enter* KING.)

QUEEN: Alas, look here, my lord.
OPHELIA: (*Song.*)

> Larded all with sweet flowers;
> Which bewept to the grave did not go
> With true-love showers.

40 KING: How do you, pretty lady?
OPHELIA: Well, good dild you! They say the owl was a baker's
> daughter. Lord, we know what we are, but know not what
> we may be. God be at your table!
KING: Conceit upon her father.
45 OPHELIA: Pray let's have no words of this, but when they ask
> you what it means, say you this:

(*Song.*)

> To-morrow is Saint Valentine's day,
> All in the morning betime,
> And I a maid at your window,
50   To be your Valentine.
> Then up he rose, and donned his clo'es,
> And dupped the chamber-door,
> Let in the maid, that out a maid
> Never departed more.

55 KING: Pretty Ophelia—
OPHELIA: Indeed, without an oath, I'll make an end on't:

(*Sings.*)

> By Gis and by Saint Charity,
> Alack, and fie for shame!
> Young men will do't, if they come to't;

> By cock, they are to blame.   60
> Quoth she 'Before you tumbled me,
> You promised me to wed.'

He answers:

> 'So would I a' done, by yonder sun,
> An thou hadst not come to my bed.'   65

KING: How long hath she been thus?
OPHELIA: I hope all will be well. We must be patient, but I
> cannot choose but weep, to think they would lay him i' th'
> cold ground. My brother shall know of it, and so I thank
> you for your good counsel. Come, my coach! Good night,   70
> ladies, good night. Sweet ladies, good night, good night.

(*Exit.*)

KING: Follow her close; give her good watch, I pray you.

(*Exeunt* HORATIO *and* GENTLEMEN.)

> O, this is the poison of deep grief; it springs
> All from her father's death, and now behold!
> O Gertrude, Gertrude,   75
> When sorrows come, they come not single spies,
> But in battalions: first, her father slain;
> Next, your son gone, and he most violent author
> Of his own just remove; the people muddied,
> Thick and unwholesome in their thoughts and whispers   80
> For good Polonius' death; and we have done but greenly
> In hugger-mugger to inter him; poor Ophelia
> Divided from herself and her fair judgement,
> Without the which we are pictures, or mere beasts;
> Last, and as much containing as all these,   85
> Her brother is in secret come from France,
> Feeds on his wonder, keeps himself in clouds,
> And wants not buzzers to infect his ear
> With pestilent speeches of his father's death.
> Wherein necessity, of matter beggared,   90
> Will nothing stick our person to arraign
> In ear and ear, O my dear Gertrude, this,
> Like to a murd'ring piece, in many places
> Gives me superfluous death. Attend,   (*A noise within.*)

(*Enter a* MESSENGER.)

> Where are my Switzers? Let them guard the door.   95
> What is the matter?
MESSENGER: Save yourself, my lord.
> The ocean, overpeering of his list,
> Eats not the flats with more impiteous haste
> Then young Laertes, in a riotous head,
> O'erbears your officers. The rabble call him lord,   100
> And as the world were now but to begin,

---

25 **cockle hat** hat bearing a cockle shell, worn by a pilgrim who had been to the shrine of St. James of Compostella, in Spain   26 **shoon** shoes   37 **Larded** garnished, strewn   41 **good dild you** God yield (requite) you   41–42 **They say the owl was a baker's daughter** allusion to a folktale in which a baker's daughter was transformed into an owl because of her ungenerous behavior (giving short measure) when Christ asked for bread in the baker's shop   44 **Conceit upon her father** i.e., obsessed with her father's death   48 **betime** early   52 **dupped** opened   57 **Gis** Jesus

60 **cock** corruption of God   79 **remove** banishment, departure; **muddied** stirred up and confused   81 **greenly** without judgment   82 **hugger-mugger** secrecy and disorder   87 **in clouds** i.e., of suspicion and rumor   88 **wants** lacks   90 **of matter beggared** lacking facts   91 **nothing stick** in no way hesitate   93 **murd'ring piece** cannon loaded with shot meant to scatter   94 *F* omits the King's 'Attend,' but substitutes, by way of drawing attention to the "noise within"   95 **Switzers** Swiss bodyguard   97 **list** boundary   99 **riotous head** turbulent mob

Antiquity forgot, custom not known,
The ratifiers and props of every word,
They cry 'Choose we, Laertes shall be king'.
105 Caps, hands, and tongues, applaud it to the clouds,
'Laertes shall be king, Laertes king!'
QUEEN: How cheerfully on the false trail they cry!

(*A noise within.*)

O, this is counter, you false Danish dogs!
KING: The doors are broke.

(*Enter* LAERTES *with* OTHERS.)

110 LAERTES: Where is this king?—Sirs, stand you all without.
ALL: No, let's come in.
LAERTES: I pray you give me leave.
ALL: We will, we will.

(*Exeunt his followers.*)

LAERTES: I thank you. Keep the door.—O thou vile king,
Give me my father!
QUEEN: Calmly, good Laertes,
115 LAERTES: That drop of blood that's calm proclaims me bastard,
Cries cuckold to my father, brands the harlot
Even here between the chaste unsmirchèd brow
Of my true mother.
KING: What is the cause, Laertes,
That thy rebellion looks so giant-like?
120 Let him go, Gertrude. Do not fear our person.
There's such divinity doth hedge a king
That treason can but peep to what it would,
Acts little of his will. Tell me, Laertes,
Why thou art thus incensed. Let him go, Gertrude.
125 Speak, man.
LAERTES: Where is my father?
KING: Dead.
QUEEN: But not by him.
KING: Let him demand his fill.
LAERTES: How came he dead? I'll not be juggled with.
To hell allegiance, vows to the blackest devil,
130 Conscience and grace to the profoundest pit!
I dare damnation. To this point I stand,
That both the worlds I give to negligence,
Let come what comes, only I'll be revenged
Most throughly for my father.
135 KING: Who shall stay you?
LAERTES: My will, not all the world's.
And for my means, I'll husband them so well
They shall go far with little.
KING: Good Laertes,
If you desire to know the certainty
Of your dear father, is't writ in your revenge
140 That, swoopstake, you will draw both friend and foe,
Winner and loser?
LAERTES: None but his enemies.

KING: Will you know them, then?
LAERTES: To his good friends thus wide I'll ope my arms,
And like the kind life-rend'ring pelican,
Repast them with my blood.   145
KING: Why, now you speak
Like a good child and a true gentleman.
That I am guiltless of your father's death,
And am most sensibly in grief for it,
It shall as level to your judgement 'pear
As day does to your eye.   150

(*A noise within:* 'Let her come in.')

LAERTES: How now! what noise is that?

(*Enter* OPHELIA.)

O heat, dry up my brains! tears seven times salt
Burn out the sense and virtue of mine eye!
By heaven, thy madness shall be paid with weight
Till our scale turn the beam. O rose of May,   155
Dear maid, kind sister, sweet Ophelia!
O heavens! is 't possible a young maid's wits
Should be as mortal as an old man's life?
Nature is fine in love, and where 'tis fine
It sends some precious instance of itself   160
After the thing it loves.
OPHELIA: (*Song.*)

They bore him barefac'd on the bier;
Hey non nonny, nonny, hey nonny;
And in his grave rain'd many a tear—

Fare you well, my dove!   165
LAERTES: Hadst thou thy wits, and didst persuade revenge,
It could not move thus.
OPHELIA: You must sing 'A-down, a-down,' and you 'Call him
a-down-a.' O, how the wheel becomes it! It is the false
stew ard, that stole his master's daughter.   170
LAERTES: This nothing's more than matter.
OPHELIA: There's rosemary, that's for remembrance. Pray you,
love, remember. And there is pansies, that's for thoughts.
LAERTES: A document in madness, thoughts and remem-
brance fitted.   175

---

144 **pelican** supposed to feed her young with her own blood
149 **level** plain   153 **virtue** power   159 **fine** refined to purity
169 **wheel** burden, refrain   172–180 Harold Jenkins, in his Arden edition of *Hamlet* (London and New York, 1982) 536–542, suggests that Ophelia gives rosemary (emblematic of remembrance) and pansies (of thoughts) to Laertes; that she gives fennel and columbines (both signifying marital infidelity) to the queen; she gives rue (for repentance) to the king (keeping some for herself as a sign of her sorrow, but noting that the king is to wear his rue with a **difference,** an heraldic term designating a mark for distinguishing one branch of a family from another in a coat-of-arms). The daisy, an emblem of love's victims, is given to the king as substitute for the absent Hamlet, whose absence he has caused. The king would also be given the violets (emblems of faithfulness, associated both with Ophelia's love for Hamlet, and Polonius's service to the state, both now lost) were these still available. Each gift of flowers represents a symbolic reproach to the recipient

---

108 **counter** hunting backward on the trail   120 **fear** fear for
134 **throughly** thoroughly   140 **swoopstake** sweepstake, taking all the stakes on the gambling table

OPHELIA: There's fennel for you, and columbines. There's rue
for you, and here's some for me. We may call it herb of grace
a Sundays. O, you must wear your rue with a difference.
There's a daisy. I would give you some violets, but they with
180 ered all when my father died. They say 'a made a good end,

    (*Sings.*)   For bonny sweet Robin is all my joy.

LAERTES: Thought and affliction, passion, hell itself,
    She turns to favor and to prettiness.
OPHELIA: (*Song.*)

        And will 'a not come again?
185   And will 'a not come again?
        No, no, he is dead:
        Go to thy death-bed:
        He never will come again.

        His beard was as white as snow,
190   All flaxen was his poll:
        He is gone, he is gone,
        And we cast away moan:
        God ha' mercy on his soul!

And of all Christian souls, I pray God. God buy you. (*Exit.*)
195 LAERTES: Do you see this, O God?
    KING: Laertes, I must commune with your grief,
    Or you deny me right. Go but apart,
    Make choice of whom your wisest friends you will,
    And they shall hear and judge 'twixt you and me.
200   If by direct or by collateral hand
    They find us touched, we will our kingdom give,
    Our crown, our life, and all that we call ours,
    To you in satisfaction; but if not,
    Be you content to lend your patience to us,
205   And we shall jointly labour with your soul
    To give it due content.
    LAERTES: Let this be so.
    His means of death, his obscure funeral—
    No trophy, sword, nor hatchment, o'er his bones,
    No noble rite nor formal ostentation—
210   Cry to be heard, as 'twere from heaven to earth,
    That I must call't in question.
    KING: So you shall;
    And where th' offence is let the great axe fall.
    I pray you go with me.

(*Exeunt.*)

SCENE VI

Enter HORATIO *and* OTHERS.

HORATIO: What are they that would speak with me?
GENTLEMAN: Sea-faring men, sir. They say they have letters
    for you.
HORATIO: Let them come in. (*Exit* GENTLEMAN.)
    I do not know from what part of the world
5   I should be greeted, if not from Lord Hamlet.

(*Enter* SAILOR.)

---

190 **poll** head   208 **hatchment** coat of arms

SAILOR: God bless you, sir.
HORATIO: Let him bless thee too.
SAILOR: 'A shall sir, an't please him. There's a letter for you,
    sir—it comes from th' ambassador that was bound for En-
    gland—if your name be Horatio, as I am let to know it is. 10
HORATIO: (*Reads.*) 'Horatio, when thou shalt have over-
    looked this, give these fellows some means to the king.
    They have letters for him. Ere we were two days old at
    sea, a pirate of very warlike appointment gave us chase.
    Finding ourselves too slow of sail, we put on a compelled 15
    valor, and in the grapple I boarded them. On the instant
    they got clear of our ship, so I alone became their pris-
    oner. They have dealt with me like thieves of mercy, but
    they knew what they did; I am to do a good turn for
    them. Let the king have the letters I have sent, and repair 20
    thou to me with as much speed as thou wouldest fly
    death. I have words to speak in thine ear will make thee
    dumb; yet are they much too light for the bore of the
    matter. These good fellows will bring thee where I am.
    Rosencrantz and Guildenstern hold their course for En- 25
    gland. Of them I have much to tell thee, Farewell.
                    'He that thou knowest thine, Hamlet.'
    Come, I will give you way for these your letters,
    And do't the speedier that you may direct me
    To him from whom you brought them.

(*Exeunt.*)

SCENE VII

Enter KING *and* LAERTES.

KING: Now must your conscience my acquittance seal,
    And you must put me in your heart for friend,
    Sith you have heard, and with a knowing ear,
    That he which hath your noble father slain
    Pursued my life.   5
LAERTES: It well appears. But tell me
    Why you proceeded not against these feats,
    So criminal and so capital in nature,
    As by your safety, wisdom, all things else,
    You mainly were stirred up.
KING: O, for two special reasons,
    Which may to you, perhaps, seem much unsinewed, 10
    But yet to me th' are strong. The queen his mother
    Lives almost by his looks, and for myself—
    My virtue or my plague, be it either which—
    She's so conjunctive to my life and soul
    That, as the star moves not but in his sphere, 15
    I could not but by her. The other motive,
    Why to a public count I might not go,
    Is the great love the general gender bear him,
    Who, dipping all his faults in their affection,
    Work, like the spring that turneth wood to stone, 20
    Convert his gyves to graces; so that my arrows,
    Too slightly timbered for so loud a wind,

IV.vi. 23 **bore** literally, caliber of a gun; hence, size, importance

IV.vii. 7 **capital** punishable by death   10 **unsinewed** weak
14 **conjunctive** closely joined   17 **count** reckoning   18 **general gender** common people   21 **gyves** fetters

Would have reverted to my bow again,
And not where I had aimed them.
25 LAERTES: And so have I a noble father lost,
A sister driven into desp'rate terms,
Whose worth, if praises may go back again,
Stood challenger on mount of all the age
For her perfections. But my revenge will come.
30 KING: Break not your sleeps for that. You must not think
That we are made of stuff so flat and dull
That we can let our beard be shook with danger,
And think it pastime. You shortly shall hear more.
I loved your father, and we love our self,
35   And that, I hope, will teach you to imagine—

(*Enter a* MESSENGER *with letters.*)

MESSENGER: These to your majesty; this to the queen.
KING: From Hamlet! Who brought them?
MESSENGER: Sailors, my lord, they say. I saw them not.
They were given me by Claudio; he received them
40   Of him that brought them.
KING: Laertes, you shall hear them.—
Leave us. (*Exit* MESSENGER.)
(*Reads.*) 'High and mighty, you shall know I am set naked
on your kingdom. To-morrow shall I beg leave to see
your kingly eyes, when I shall, first asking your pardon,
45 thereunto recount the occasion of my sudden and more
strange return.   Hamlet.'
What should this mean? Are all the rest come back?
Or is it some abuse, and no such thing?
LAERTES: Know you the hand?
50 KING: 'Tis Hamlet's character. 'Naked!'
And in a postscript here, he says 'alone.'
Can you devise me?
LAERTES: I am lost in it, my lord. But let him come.
It warms the very sickness in my heart
55   That I shall live and tell him to his teeth
'Thus didst thou.'
KING: If it be so, Laertes—
As how should it be so, how otherwise?—
Will you be ruled by me?
LAERTES: Ay, my lord,
So you will not o'errule me to a peace.
60 KING: To thine own peace. If he be now returned,
As checking at his voyage, and that he means

---

35 Following the entrance of the Messenger, the King says in *F* "How now? What Newes?" and the Messenger replies, "Letters my Lord from *Hamlet*." Jenkins comments (*SB* 13.36): "In Q the King is not told the letters come from Hamlet; he is left to find this out as he reads, and his cry 'From *Hamlet*' betokens his astonishment on doing so. I think Hamlet would not have approved of the *F* messenger who robs his bomb of the full force of its explosion. Shakespeare's messenger did not even know he carried such a bomb, for the letters had reached him via sailors who were ignorant of their sender. They took him for 'th' Embassador that was bound for *England*' (4.4.9). *F*, with its too knowledgeable messenger, by seeking to enhance the effect, destroys it"   52 **devise** explain to   61 **checking at** turning aside from (like a falcon turning from its quarry for other prey)

No more to undertake it, I will work him
To an exploit now ripe in my device,
Under the which he shall not choose but fall;
And for his death no wind of blame shall breathe   65
But even his mother shall uncharge the practice
And call it accident.
LAERTES: My lord, I will be ruled;
The rather if you could devise it so
That I might be the organ.
KING: It falls right.
You have been talked of since your travel much,   70
And that in Hamlet's hearing, for a quality
Wherein they say you shine. Your sum of parts
Did not together pluck such envy from him
As did that one, and that, in my regard,
Of the unworthiest siege.   75
LAERTES: What part is that, my lord?
KING: A very riband in the cap of youth,
Yet needful too, for youth no less becomes
The light and careless livery that it wears
Than settled age his sables and his weeds,
Importing health and graveness. Two months since   80
Here was a gentleman of Normandy.
I have seen myself, and served against, the French,
And they can well on horseback, but this gallant
Had witchcraft in't. He grew unto his seat,
And to such wondrous doing brought his horse,   85
As had he been incorpsed and demi-natured
With the brave beast. So far he topped my thought
That I, in forgery of shapes and tricks,
Come short of what he did.
LAERTES: A Norman was't?
KING: A Norman.   90
LAERTES: Upon my life, Lamord.
KING: The very same.
LAERTES: I know him well. He is the brooch indeed
And gem of all the nation.
KING: He made confession of you,
And gave you such a masterly report   95
For art and exercise in your defence,
And for your rapier most especial,
That he cried out 'twould be a sight indeed
If one could match you. The scrimers of their nation,
He swore had neither motion, guard, nor eye,   100
If you opposed them. Sir, this report of his
Did Hamlet so envenom with his envy
That he could nothing do but wish and beg
Your sudden coming o'er, to play with you.
Now out of this—   105
LAERTES: What out of this, my lord?
KING: Laertes, was your father dear to you?
Or are you like the painting of a sorrow,
A face without a heart?
LAERTES: Why ask you this?

---

66 **uncharge the practice** regard the deed as free from villainy   69 **organ** instrument   75 **siege** rank   79 **weeds** garments   86 **incorpsed** made one body; **demi-natured** like a centaur, half man half horse   87 **topped** excelled   88 **forgery** invention   99 **scrimers** fencers (French *escrimeurs*)

KING: Not that I think you did not love your father,
110   But that I know love is begun by time,
    And that I see, in passages of proof,
    Time qualifies the spark and fire of it.
    There lives within the very flame of love
    A kind of wick or snuff that will abate it,
115   And nothing is at a like goodness still,
    For goodness, growing to a plurisy,
    Dies in his own too much. That we would do,
    We should do when we would; for this 'would' changes,
    And hath abatements and delays as many
120   As there are tongues, are hands, are accidents,
    And then this 'should' is like a spendthrift's sigh,
    That hurts by easing. But to the quick of th' ulcer—
    Hamlet comes back; what would you undertake
    To show yourself in deed your father's son
125   More than in words?
    LAERTES: To cut his throat i' th' church.
    KING: No place, indeed, should murder sanctuarize;
    Revenge should have no bounds. But good Laertes,
    Will you do this, keep close within your chamber;
    Hamlet returned shall know you are come home;
130   We'll put on those shall praise your excellence,
    And set a double varnish on the fame
    The Frenchman gave you, bring you in fine together,
    And wager on your heads. He, being remiss,
    Most generous, and free from all contriving,
135   Will not peruse the foils, so that with ease,
    Or with a little shuffling, you may choose
    A sword unbated, and in a pass of practice
    Requite him for your father.
    LAERTES: I will do't,
    And for that purpose I'll anoint my sword.
140   I bought an unction of a mountebank
    So mortal that but dip a knife in it,
    Where it draws blood no cataplasm so rare,
    Collected from all simples that have virtue
    Under the moon, can save the thing from death
145   That is but scratched withal. I'll touch my point
    With this contagion, that if I gall him slightly,
    It may be death.
    KING: Let's further think of this,
    Weigh what convenience both of time and means
    May fit us to our shape. If this should fail,
150   And that our drift look through our bad performance,
    'Twere better not assayed. Therefore this project
    Should have a back or second that might hold
    If this should blast in proof. Soft! let me see.
    We'll make a solemn wager on your cunnings—
155   I ha't.
    When in your motion you are hot and dry—

As make your bouts more violent to that end—
    And that he calls for drink, I'll have preferred him
    A chalice for the nonce, whereon but sipping,
    If he by chance escape your venomed stuck,   160
    Our purpose may hold there.—But stay, what noise?

(*Enter* QUEEN.)

QUEEN: One woe doth tread upon another's heel,
    So fast they follow. Your sister's drowned, Laertes.
LAERTES: Drowned! O, where?
QUEEN: There is a willow grows askant the brook   165
    That shows his hoar leaves in the glassy stream.
    Therewith fantastic garlands did she make
    Of crowflowers, nettles, daisies, and long purples
    That liberal shepherds give a grosser name,
    But our cold maids do dead men's fingers call them.   170
    There on the pendent boughs her crownet weeds
    Clamb'ring to hang, an envious sliver broke,
    When down her weedy trophies and herself
    Fell in the weeping brook. Her clothes spread wide,
    And mermaid-like awhile they bore her up,   175
    Which time she chanted snatches of old lauds,
    As one incapable of her own distress,
    Or like a creature native and indued
    Unto that element. But long it could not be
    Till that her garments, heavy with their drink,   180
    Pulled the poor wretch from her melodious lay
    To muddy death.
LAERTES: Alas, then, she is drowned?
QUEEN: Drowned, drowned.
LAERTES: Too much of water hast thou, poor Ophelia,
    And therefore I forbid my tears; but yet   185
    It is our trick; nature her custom holds,
    Let shame say what it will. When these are gone,
    The woman will be out. Adieu, my lord.
    I have a speech o' fire that fain would blaze
    But that this folly drowns it.   190

(*Exit.*)

KING: Let's follow, Gertrude.
    How much I had to do to calm his rage!
    Now fear I this will give it start again;
    Therefore let's follow.

(*Exeunt.*)

ACT FIVE

SCENE I

Enter two CLOWNS.

---

111 **passages of proof** incidents of experience   112 **qualifies** weakens   116 **plurisy** excess   122 **quick** sensitive flesh   126 **sanctuarize** give sanctuary to   133 **remiss** careless   135 **peruse** inspect   137 **unbated** not blunted; **pass of practice** treacherous thrust   142 **cataplasm** poultice   143 **simples** medicinal herbs   149 **shape** plan   150 **drift** scheme   152 **back or second** something in support   153 **blast in proof** burst during trial (like a faulty cannon)   156 **motion** exertion

158 **preferred** offered to   159 **nonce** occasion   160 **stuck** thrust   165 **askant** alongside   166 **hoar** gray   169 **liberal** free-spoken, licentious   170 **cold** chaste   171 **crownet** coronet   172 **envious** malicious   176 **lauds** hymns   177 **incapable of** insensible to   178 **indued** endowed   188 **woman** unmanly part of nature

V.i. s.d. **clowns** rustics

CLOWN: Is she to be buried in Christian burial when she wil-
fully seeks her own salvation?

OTHER: I tell thee she is, therefore make her grave straight.
The crowner hath sat on her, and finds it Christian burial.

5 CLOWN: How can that be, unless she drowned herself in her
own defence?

OTHER: Why, 'tis found so.

CLOWN: It must be 'se offendendo', it cannot be else. For here
lies the point: if I drown myself wittingly, it argues an act,
10 and an act hath three branches—it is to act, to do, and to
perform; argal, she drowned herself wittingly.

OTHER: Nay, but hear you, Goodman Delver.

CLOWN: Give me leave. Here lies the water; good. Here
stands the man; good. If the man go to this water and
15 drown himself, it is, will he, nill he, he goes—mark you
that. But if the water come to him and drown him, he
drowns not himself. Argal, he that is not guilty of his own
death shortens not his own life.

OTHER: But is this law?

20 CLOWN: Ay, marry, is't; crowner's quest law.

OTHER: Will you ha' the truth on 't? If this had not been a
gentlewoman, she should have been buried out o' Christian burial.

CLOWN: Why, there thou say'st. And the more pity that great
25 folk should have count'nance in this world to drown or
hang themselves more than their even-Christen. Come, my
spade. There is no ancient gentlemen but gard'ners, ditch-
ers, and grave-makers. They hold up Adam's profession.

OTHER: Was he a gentleman?

30 CLOWN: 'A was the first that ever bore arms.

OTHER: Why, he had none.

CLOWN: What, art a heathen? How dost thou understand the
Scripture? The Scripture says Adam digged. Could he dig
without arms? I'll put another question to thee. If thou
35 answerest me not to the purpose, confess thyself—

OTHER: Go to.

CLOWN: What is he that builds stronger than either the mason, the shipwright, or the carpenter?

OTHER: The gallows-maker for that frame outlives a thousand
40 tenants.

CLOWN: I like thy wit well, in good faith. The gallows does
well. But how does it well? It does well to those that do
ill. Now thou dost ill to say the gallows is built stronger
than the church. Argal, the gallows may do well to thee.
45 To't again, come.

OTHER: 'Who builds stronger than a mason, a shipwright, or
a carpenter?'

CLOWN: Ay tell me that, and unyoke.

OTHER: Marry, now I can tell.

50 CLOWN: To't.

OTHER: Mass, I cannot tell.

(*Enter* HAMLET *and* HORATIO *afar off.*)

CLOWN: Cudgel thy brains no more about it, for your dull ass
will not mend his pace with beating. And when you are
asked this question next, say 'a grave-maker.' The houses
he makes lasts till doomsday. Go, get thee in, and fetch me 55
a stoup of liquor. (*Exit* OTHER CLOWN.)

(HAMLET *and* HORATIO *come forward as* CLOWN *digs and sings.*)

(*Song.*)

> In youth, when I did love, did love,
>   Methought it was very sweet,
> To contract-O-the time, for-a-my behove,
>   O, methought, there-a-was nothing-a-meet. 60

HAMLET: Has this fellow no feeling of his business, that 'a
sings at gravemaking?

HORATIO: Custom hath made it in him a property of easiness.

HAMLET: 'Tis e'en so. The hand of little employment hath
the daintier sense. 65

CLOWN: (*Song.*)

> But age, with his stealing steps,
>   Hath clawed me in his clutch,
> And hath shipped me into the land,
>   As if I had never been such.

(*Throws up a skull.*)

HAMLET: That skull had a tongue in it, and could sing once. 70
How the knave jowls it to the ground, as if 'twere Cain's
jawbone, that did the first murder! This might be the pate
of a politician, which this ass now o'erreaches; one that
would circumvent God, might it not?

HORATIO: It might, my lord. 75

HAMLET: Or of a courtier, which could say 'Good morrow,
sweet lord! How dost thou, sweet lord?' This might be my
Lord Such-a-one, that praised my Lord Such-a-one's
horse, when 'a went to beg it, might it not?

HORANTIO: Ay, my lord. 80

HAMLET: Why, e'en so, and now my Lady Worm's, chopless,
and knock'd about the mazzard with a sexton's spade.
Here's fine revolution, an we had the trick to see't. Did
these bones cost no more the breeding but to play at loggats with them? Mine ache to think on't. 85

CLOWN: (*Song.*)

> A pick-axe and a spade, a spade,
>   For and a shrouding sheet:
> O, a pit of clay for to be made
>   For such a guest is meet.

(*Throws up another skull.*)

HAMLET: There's another. Why may not that be the skull of 90
a lawyer? Where be his quiddities now, his quillets, his

---

4 **crowner** coroner   8 **se offendendo** the Clown's blunder for
se defendendo ("in self-defense")   11 **argal** therefore (corrupt form of *ergo*)   20 **quest** inquest   26 **even-Christen** fellow Christian   48 **tell me that, and unyoke** answer the
question and then you can relax

56 **stoup** tankard   59 **behove** benefit   59–60 The repeated *a*
and *o* may represent the Clown's vocal embellishments, but more
probably they represent his grunting as he takes breath in the
course of his digging   63 **a property of easiness** a habit that
comes easily to him   71 **jowls** hurls   74 **circumvent** cheat
81 **chopless** with lower jaw missing   82 **mazzard** head
84–85 **loggats** small logs of wood for throwing at a mark   91
quiddities subtle distinctions; **quillets** quibbles

cases, his tenures, and his tricks? Why does he suffer this mad knave now to knock him about the sconce with a dirty shovel, and will not tell him of his action of battery?
95 Hum! This fellow might be in's time a great buyer of land, with his statutes, his recognizances, his fines, his double vouchers, his recoveries. Is this the fine of his fines, and the recovery of his recoveries, to have his fine pate full of fine dirt? Will his vouchers vouch him no more of his pur-
100 chases, and double ones too, than the length and breadth of a pair of indentures? The very conveyances of his lands will scarcely lie in this box, and must th' inheritor himself have no more, ha?

HORATIO: Not a jot more, my lord.
105 HAMLET: Is not parchment made of sheepskins?

HORATIO: Ay, my lord, and of calves' skins too.

HAMLET: They are sheep and calves which seek out assurance in that. I will speak to this fellow. Whose grave's this, sirrah?

CLOWN: Mine, sir. (*Sings.*)

110   O, a pit of clay for to be made—

HAMLET: I think it be thine indeed, for thou liest in't.

CLOWN: You lie out on't, sir, and therefore 'tis not yours. For my part, I do not lie in't, yet it is mine.

HAMLET: Thou dost lie in't, to be in't and say it is thine. 'Tis
115 for the dead, not for the quick; therefore thou liest.

CLOWN: 'Tis a quick lie, sir; 'twill away again from me to you.

HAMLET: What man dost thou dig it for?

CLOWN: For no man, sir.

HAMLET: What woman, then?
120 CLOWN: For none neither.

HAMLET: Who is to be buried in't?

CLOWN: One that was a woman, sir; but, rest her soul, she's dead.

HAMLET: How absolute the knave is! We must speak by the
125 card, or equivocation will undo us. By the Lord, Horatio, this three years I have took note of it, the age is grown so picked that the toe of the peasant comes so near the heel of the courtier, he galls his kibe. How long hast thou been a grave-maker?
130 CLOWN: Of all the day i' th' year, I came to't that day that our last King Hamlet overcame Fortinbras.

HAMLET: How long is that since?

CLOWN: Cannot you tell that? Every fool can tell that. It was that very day that young Hamlet was born—he that is
135 mad, and sent into England.

HAMLET: Ay, marry, why was he sent into England?

CLOWN: Why, because 'a was mad. 'A shall recover his wits there; or, if a do not, 'tis no great matter there.

HAMLET: Why?
140 CLOWN: 'Twill not be seen in him there. There the men are as mad as he.

---

96 **recognizances** legal bonds, defining debts; vouchers persons vouched or called on to warrant a title   97 **recoveries** legal processes to break an entail   100–101 **pair of indentures** deed or legal agreement in duplicate   101 **conveyances** deeds by which property is transferred   124 **absolute** positive   125 **card** card on which the points of the mariner's compass are marked (i.e., absolutely to the point)   127 **picked** fastidious   128 **kibe** chilblain

HAMLET: How came he mad?

CLOWN: Very strangely, they say.

HAMLET: How strangely?

CLOWN: Faith, e'en with losing his wits.
145

HAMLET: Upon what ground?

CLOWN: Why, here in Denmark. I have been sexton here, man and boy, thirty years.

HAMLET: How long will a man lie i' th' earth ere he rot?

CLOWN: Faith, if 'a be not rotten before 'a die—as we have
150 many pocky corses now-a-days that will scarce hold the laying in—'a will last you some eight year or nine year. A tanner will last you nine year.

HAMLET: Why he more than another?

CLOWN: Why, sir, his hide is so tanned with his trade that 'a
155 will keep out water a great while and your water is a sore decayer of your whoreson dead body. Here's a skull now hath lain you i' th' earth three and twenty years.

HAMLET: Whose was it?

CLOWN: A whoreson mad fellow's it was. Whose do you
160 think it was?

HAMLET: Nay, I know not.

CLOWN: A pestilence on him for a mad rogue! 'a poured a flagon of Rhenish on my head once. This same skull, sir, was, sir, Yorick's skull, the king's jester.
165

HAMLET: (*Takes the skull.*) This?

CLOWN: E'en That.

HAMLET: Alas, poor Yorick! I knew him, Horatio—a fellow of infinite jest, of most excellent fancy. He hath bore me on his back a thousand times, and now how abhorred in my
170 imagination it is! My gorge rises at it. Here hung those lips that I have kissed I know not how oft. Where be your gibes now, your gambols, your songs, your flashes of merriment that were wont to set the table on a roar? Not one now to mock your own grinning? Quite chop-fall'n?
175 Now get you to my lady's chamber, and tell her, let her paint an inch thick, to this favour she must come. Make her laugh at that. Prithee, Horatio, tell me one thing.

HORATIO: What's that, my lord?

HAMLET: Dost thou think Alexander looked o' this fashion i'
180 th' earth?

HORATIO: E'en so.

HAMLET: And smelt so? Pah!

(*Throws down the skull.*)

HORATIO: E'en so, my lord.

HAMLET: To what base uses we may return, Horatio! Why
185 may not imagination trace the noble dust of Alexander till 'a find it stopping a bung-hole?

HORATIO: 'Twere to consider too curiously to consider so.

HAMLET: No, faith, not a jot, but to follow him thither with modesty enough, and likelihood to lead it. Alexander died,
190 Alexander was buried, Alexander returneth to dust; the dust is earth; of earth we make loam; and why of that loam whereto he was converted might they not stop a beer-barrel?

Imperious Caesar, dead and turned to clay,
Might stop a hole to keep the wind away.
195

---

151 **pocky** infected with pox (syphilis)   164 **Rhenish** Rhine wine   188 **too curiously** over ingeniously

O, that that earth which kept the world in awe
Should patch a wall t'expel the winter's flaw!

But soft, but soft awhile! Here comes the king,
The queen, the courtiers.

(*Enter* KING, QUEEN, LAERTES, *and the Corse* [*with a Doctor of Divinity as* PRIEST *and* LORDS *attendant*].)

200   Who is this they follow?
And with such maimèd rites? This doth betoken
The corse they follow did with desperate hand
Fordo it own life. 'Twas of some estate.
Couch we awhile and mark.

(*Retires with* HORATIO.)

LAERTES: What ceremony else?
205 HAMLET: That is Laertes, a very noble youth. Mark.
LAERTES: What ceremony else?
DOCTOR: Her obsequies have been as far enlarged
  As we have warranty. Her death was doubtful,
  And but that great command o'ersways the order,
210 She should in ground unsanctified been lodged
  Till the last trumpet. For charitable prayers,
  Shards, flints and pebbles should be thrown on her.
  Yet here she is allowed her virgin crants,
  Her maiden strewments and the bringing home
215 Of bell and burial.
LAERTES: Must there no more be done?
DOCTOR: No more be done.
  We should profane the service of the dead
  To sing a requiem and such rest to her
  As to peace-parted souls.
LAERTES: Lay her i' th' earth,
220 And from her fair and unpolluted flesh
  May violets spring! I tell thee, churlish priest,
  A minist'ring angel shall my sister be
  When thou liest howling.
HAMLET: What, the fair Ophelia!
QUEEN: Sweets to the sweet. Farewell!

(*Scatters flowers.*)

225 I hoped thou shouldst have been my Hamlet's wife.
  I thought thy bride-bed to have decked, sweet maid,
  And not have strewed thy grave.
LAERTES: O treble woe
  Fall ten times treble on that cursèd head,
  Whose wicked deed thy most ingenious sense
230 Deprived thee of! Hold off the earth awhile,
  Till I have caught her once more in mine arms.

(*Leaps into the grave.*)

Now pile your dust upon the quick and dead,
Till of this flat a mountain you have made

T' o'er-top old Pelion or the skyish head
Of blue Olympus.   235
HAMLET: (*Coming forward.*) What is he whose grief
  Bears such an emphasis, whose phrase of sorrow
  Conjures the wand'ring stars, and makes them stand
  Like wonder-wounded hearers? This is I,
  Hamlet the Dane.

(LAERTES *climbs out of the grave.*)
240
LAERTES: The devil take thy soul!

(*Grappling with him.*)

HAMLET: Thou pray'st not well.
  I prithee take thy fingers from my throat,
  For though I am not splenitive and rash,
  Yet have I in me something dangerous,
  Which let thy wisdom fear. Hold off thy hand.
KING: Pluck them asunder.   245
QUEEN: Hamlet! Hamlet!
ALL: Gentlemen!
HORATIO: Good my lord, be quiet.

(*The* ATTENDANTS *part them.*)

HAMLET: Why, I will fight with him upon this theme
  Until my eyelids will no longer wag.   250
QUEEN: O my son, what theme?
HAMLET: I loved Ophelia. Forty thousand brothers
  Could not with all their quantity of love
  Make up my sum. What wilt thou do for her?
KING: O, he is mad, Laertes.   255
QUEEN: For love of God, forbear him.
HAMLET: 'Swounds, show me what thou't do.
  Woo't weep, woo't fight, woo't fast, woo't tear thyself,
  Woo't drink up eisel, eat a crocodile?
  I'll do't. Dost come here to whine?   260
  To outface me with leaping in her grave?
  Be buried quick with her, and so will I,
  And if thou prate of mountains, let them throw
  Millions of acres on us, till our ground,
  Singeing his pate against the burning zone,   265
  Make Ossa like a wart! Nay, an thou'lt mouth,
  I'll rant as well as thou.
QUEEN: This is mere madness;
  And thus awhile the fit will work on him.
  Anon, as patient as the female dove
  When that her golden couplets are disclosed,   270
  His silence will sit drooping.
HAMLET: Hear you, sir.
  What is the reason that you use me thus?

---

234 **Pelion** a mountain in Thessaly, like Olympus, line 235, and Ossa, line 266 (the allusion is to the war in which the Titans fought the gods and, in their attempt to scale heaven, heaped Ossa and Olympus on Pelion, or Pelion and Ossa on Olympus)
237 **such an emphasis** so vehement an expression or display
242 **splenitive** fiery-tempered (from the spleen, seat of anger)
258 **Woo't** wilt (thou) 259 **eisel** vinegar 270 **couplets** newly hatched pair

---

197 **flaw** gust   202 **Fordo** destroy; **it** its   212 **Shards** bits of broken pottery   213 **crants** garland   229 **most ingenious** of quickest apprehension

I loved you ever. But it is no matter.
Let Hercules himself do what he may,
275   The cat will mew, and dog will have his day.
KING: I pray thee, good Horatio, wait upon him.

(*Exit* HAMLET *and* HORATIO.)

(*To* LAERTES.) Strengthen your patience in our last night's
speech.
We'll put the matter to the present push.—
Good Gertrude, set some watch over your son.—
280   This grave shall have a living monument.
An hour of quiet shortly shall we see;
Till then in patience our proceeding be.

(*Exeunt.*)

SCENE II

Enter HAMLET *and* HORATIO.

HAMLET: So much for this, sir; now shall you see the other.
You do remember all the circumstance?
HORATIO: Remember it, my lord!
HAMLET: Sir, in my heart there was a kind of fighting
5   That would not let me sleep. Methought I lay
Worse than the mutines in the bilboes. Rashly,
And praised be rashness for it—let us know,
Our indiscretion sometime serves us well,
When our deep plots do pall; and that should learn us
10   There's a divinity that shapes our ends,
Rough-hew them how we will—
HORATIO: That is most certain.
HAMLET: Up from my cabin,
My sea-gown scarfed about me, in the dark
Groped I to find out them, had my desire,
15   Fingered their packet, and in fine withdrew
To mine own room again, making so bold,
My fears forgetting manners, to unseal
Their grand commission; where I found, Horatio—
Ah, royal knavery!—an exact command,
20   Larded with many several sorts of reasons
Importing Denmark's health and England's too,
With, ho! such bugs and goblins in my life,
That on the supervise, no leisure bated,
No, not to stay the grinding of the axe,
25   My head should be struck off.
HORATIO: Is't possible?
HAMLET: Here's the commission; read it at more leisure.
But will thou hear me how I did proceed?
HORATIO: I beseech you.
HAMLET: Being thus benetted round with villainies,
30   Or I could make a prologue to my brains,
They had begun the play. I sat me down,
Devised a new commission, wrote it fair.

I once did hold it, as our statists do,
A baseness to write fair, and laboured much
How to forget that learning; but sir, now   35
It did me yeoman's service. Wilt thou know
Th' effect of what I wrote?
HORATIO: Ay, good my lord.
HAMLET: An earnest conjuration from the king,
As England was his faithful tributary,
As love between them like the palm might flourish,   40
As peace should still her wheaten garland wear
And stand a comma 'tween their amities,
And many such like as's of great charge,
That on the view and knowing of these contents,
Without debatement further more or less,   45
He should the bearers put to sudden death,
Not shriving-time allowed.
HORATIO: How was this sealed?
HAMLET: Why, even in that was heaven ordinant,
I had my father's signet in my purse,
Which was the model of that Danish seal,   50
Folded the writ up the form of th' other,
Subscribed it, gave't th' impression, placed it safely,
The changeling never known. Now the next day
Was our sea-fight, and what to this was sequent
Thou knowest already.   55
HORATIO: So Guildenstern and Rosencrantz go to't.
HAMLET: Why, man, they did make love to this employment.
They are not near my conscience; their defeat
Does by their own insinuation grow.
'Tis dangerous when the baser nature comes   60
Between the pass and fell incensèd points
Of mighty opposites.
HORATIO: Why, what a king is this!
HAMLET: Does it not, think thee, stand me now upon—
He that hath killed my king and whored my mother,
Popped in between th' election and my hopes,   65
Thrown out his angle for my proper life,
And with such coz'nage—is't not perfect conscience,
To quit him with this arm? And is't not to be damned
To let this canker of our nature come
In further evil?   70
HORATIO: It must be shortly known to him from England
What is the issue of the business there.
HAMLET: It will be short; the interim is mine.
And a man's life's no more than to say 'one.'
But I am very sorry, good Horatio,   75
That to Laertes I forgot myself;
For by the image of my cause I see
The portraiture of his. I'll court his favours.

V.ii. 6 **mutines** mutineers; **bilboes** fetters 9 **pall** fail 15
Fingered filched 20 **Larded** garnished 22 **bugs and goblins** imaginary horrors (here, horrendous crimes attributed to
Hamlet, and represented as dangers should he be allowed to live)
23 **supervise** perusal; **bated** deducted, allowed 24 **stay** await
30 **Or** ere

33 **statists** statesmen 42 **comma** a connective that also acknowledges separateness 43 **charge** (1) importance (2) burden
(the double meaning fits the play that makes "as's" into "asses")
48 **ordinant** guiding 52 **Subscribed** signed 59 **insinuation**
intrusion 61 **pass** thrust; **fell** fierce 63 **Does it not . . .
stand me now upon** is it not incumbent upon me 65 **election** i.e., to the kingship. Denmark being an elective monarchy
66 **angle** fishing line; **proper** own 68 **quit** repay

But sure the bravery of his grief did put me
80   Into a tow'ring passion.
HORATIO: Peace; who comes here?

(*Enter* [OSRIC] *a courtier.*)

OSRIC: Your lordship is right welcome back to Denmark.
HAMLET: I humbly thank you, sir. (*Aside to* HORATIO.) Dost
know this water-fly?
HORATIO: (*Aside to* HAMLET.) No, my good lord.
85 HAMLET: (*Aside to* HORATIO.) Thy state is the more gracious,
for 'tis a vice to know him. He hath much land, and fertile. Let a beast be lord of beasts, and his crib shall stand at
the king's mess. 'Tis a chough, but as I say, spacious in the
possession of dirt.
90 OSRIC: Sweet lord, if your lordship were at leisure, I should
impart a thing to you from his majesty.
HAMLET: I will receive it, sir, with all diligence of spirit. Put
your bonnet to his right use. 'Tis for the head.
OSRIC: I thank you lordship, it is very hot.
95 HAMLET: No, believe me, 'tis very cold; the wind is northerly.
OSRIC: It is indifferent cold, my lord, indeed.
HAMLET: But yet methinks it is very sultry and hot for my
complexion.
OSRIC: Exceedingly, my lord; it is very sultry, as 'twere—I can
100 not tell how. My lord, his majesty bade me signify to you
that 'a has laid a great wager on your head. Sir, this is the
matter—
HAMLET: I beseech you, remember.

(HAMLET *moves him to put on his hat.*)

OSRIC: Nay, good my lord; for my ease, in good faith. Sir, here
105 is newly come to court Laertes; believe me, an absolute
gentleman, full of most excellent differences, of very soft
society and great showing. Indeed, to speak feelingly of
him, he is the card or calendar of gentry, for you shall find
in him the continent of what part a gentleman would see.
110 HAMLET: Sir, his definement suffers, no perdition in you,
though I know to divide him inventorially would dozy th'
arithmetic of memory, and yet but yaw neither in respect
of his quick sail. But in the verity of extolment, I take him
to be a soul of great article, and his infusion of such dearth
115 and rareness as, to make true diction of him, his semblable
is his mirror, and who else would trace him, his umbrage,
nothing more.
OSRIC: Your lordship speaks most infallibly of him.
HAMLET: The concernancy, sir? Why do we wrap the gentle-
120 man in our more rawer breath?
OSRIC: Sir?

HORATIO: It's not possible to understand in another tongue?
You will to't, sir, really.
HAMLET: What imports the nomination of this gentleman?
OSRIC: Of Laertes?   125
HORATIO: (*Aside.*) His purse is empty already. All's golden
words are spent.
HAMLET: Of him, sir.
OSRIC: I know you are not ignorant—
HAMLET: I would you did, sir; yet, in faith, if you did, it would 130
not much approve me. Well, sir.
OSRIC: You are not ignorant of what excellence Laertes is—
HAMLET: I dare not confess that, lest I should compare with
him in excellence; but to know a man well were to know
himself.   135
OSRIC: I mean, sir, for his weapon; but in the imputation laid
on him by them in his meed, he's unfellowed.
HAMLET: What's his weapon?
OSRIC: Rapier and dagger.
HAMLET: That's two of his weapons—but well.   140
OSRIC: The king, sir, hath wagered with him six Barbary
horses, against the which he has impawned, as I take it, six
French rapiers and poniards, with their assigns, as girdle,
hangers, and so. Three of the carriages, in faith, are very
dear to fancy, very responsive to the hilts, most delicate 145
carriages, and of very liberal conceit.
HAMLET: What call you the carriages?
HORATIO: (*Aside to* HAMLET.) I knew you must be edified by
the margent ere you had done.
OSRIC: The carriages, sir, are the hangers.   150
HAMLET: The phrase would be more germane to the matter
if we could carry cannon by our sides. I would it might
be hangers till then. But on! Six Barbary horses against six
French swords, their assigns, and three liberal conceited
carriages; that's the French bet against the Danish. Why is 155
this all impawned, as you call it?
OSRIC: The king, sir, hath laid, sir, that in a dozen passes between yourself and him he shall not exceed you three hits;
he hath laid on twelve for nine, and it would come to immediate trial if your lordship would vouchsafe the answer. 160
HAMLET: How if I answer no?
OSRIC: I mean, my lord, the opposition of your person in trial.
HAMLET: Sir, I will walk here in the hall. If it please his
majesty, it is the breathing time of day with me. Let the
foils be brought, the gentleman willing, and the king hold 165
his purpose; I will win for him an I can. If not, I will gain
nothing but my shame and the odd hits.

---

79 **bravery** ostentatious display   88 **mess** table; **chough** jackdaw; thus, a chatterer   96 **indifferent** somewhat   98 **complexion** temperament   106 **differences** distinguishing
qualities   107 **great showing** distinguished appearance   108
card map   109 **continent** all-containing embodiment   110
definement definition   111 **divide him inventorially** classify
him in detail; **dozy** dizzy   112 **yaw** hold to a course unsteadily,
like a ship that steers wild   114 **article** scope, importance; **infusion** essence; **dearth** scarcity   115 **semblable** likeness   116
trace (1) draw, (2) follow; **umbrage** shadow   119 **concernancy** import, relevance

123 **to't** i.e., to get an understanding   124 **nomination** mention
131 **approve** commend   133 **compare** compete   137 **meed**
pay; **unfellowed** unequaled   142 **impawned** staked   143 **assigns** appendages   144 **carriages** an affected word for hangers,
i.e., straps from which the weapon was hung   146 **liberal conceit**
elaborate design   149 **margent** margin (where explanatory notes
were printed)   157–158 **in a dozen passes . . . he shall not exceed you three hits** the odds the King proposes seem to be that in
a match of twelve bouts, Hamlet will win at least five. Laertes would
need to win by at least eight to four   159 **he hath laid on twelve
for nine** "he" apparently is Laertes, who has seemingly raised the
odds against himself by wagering that out of twelve bouts he will win
nine   164 **breathing time** time for taking exercise   166 **an** if

OSRIC: Shall I deliver you so?

HAMLET: To this effect, sir, after what flourish your nature will.

170 OSRIC: I commend my duty to your lordship.

HAMLET: Yours. (*Exit* OSRIC.) He does well to commend it himself; there are no tongues else for's turn.

HORATIO: This lapwing runs away with the shell on his head.

HAMLET: 'A did comply, sir, with his dug, before 'a sucked it.
175 Thus has he, and many more of the same bevy that I know the drossy age dotes on, only got the tune of the time; and out of an habit of encounter, a kind of yesty collection which carries them through and through the most fanned and winnowed opinions; and do but blow them to their
180 trial, the bubbles are out.

(*Enter a* LORD.)

LORD: My lord, his majesty commended him to you by young Osric, who brings back to him that you attend him in the hall. He sends to know if your pleasure hold to play with Laertes, or that you will take longer time.

185 HAMLET: I am constant to my purposes: they follow the king's pleasure. If his fitness speaks, mine is ready; now or whensoever, provided I be so able as now.

LORD: The king and queen and all are coming down.

HAMLET: In happy time.

190 LORD: The queen desires you to use some gentle entertainment to Laertes before you fall to play.

HAMLET: She well instructs me.

(*Exit* LORD.)

HORATIO: You will lose, my lord.

HAMLET: I do not think so. Since he went into France, I have
195 been in continual practice. I shall win at the odds. But thou wouldst not think how ill all's here about my heart. But it is no matter.

HORATIO: Nay, good my lord—

HAMLET: It is but foolery, but it is such a kind of gaingiving
200 as would perhaps trouble a woman.

HORATIO: If your mind dislike any thing, obey it. I will forestall their repair hither, and say you are not fit.

HAMLET: Not a whit, we defy augury. There is a special providence in the fall of a sparrow. If it be now, 'tis not to
205 come; if it be not to come, it will be now; if it be not now, yet it will come. The readiness is all. Since no man of aught he leaves knows, what is't to leave betimes? Let be.

(*A table prepared.* [*Enter*] *trumpets, drums, and* OFFICERS *with cushions;* KING, QUEEN, [OSRIC,] *and all the* STATE, [*with*] *foils, daggers, and* LAERTES.)

KING: Come, Hamlet, come, and take this hand from me.

(*The* KING *puts* LAERTES' *hand into* HAMLET'*s.*)

210 HAMLET: Give me your pardon, sir. I have done you wrong,
But pardon 't as you are a gentleman.
This presence knows, and you must needs have heard,
How I am punished with a sore distraction.
What I have done   215
That might your nature, honour, and exception,
Roughly awake, I here proclaim was madness.
Was 't Hamlet wronged Laertes? Never Hamlet.
If Hamlet from himself be ta'en away,
And when he's not himself does wrong Laertes,   220
Then Hamlet does it not. Hamlet denies it.
Who does it then? His madness. If't be so,
Hamlet is of the faction that is wronged;
His madness is poor Hamlet's enemy.
Sir, in this audience,   225
Let my disclaiming from a purposed evil
Free me so far in your most generous thoughts
That I have shot mine arrow o'er the house,
And hurt my brother.

LAERTES: I am satisfied in nature,
Whose motive in this case should stir me most   230
To my revenge. But in my terms of honor
I stand aloof, and will no reconcilement
Till by some elder masters of known honor,
I have a voice and precedent of peace
To keep my name ungored. But till that time   235
I do receive your offered love like love,
And will not wrong it.

HAMLET: I embrace if freely,
And will this brother's wager frankly play.
Give us the foils.

LAERTES: Come, one for me.

HAMLET: I'll be your foil, Laertes. In mine ignorance   240
Your skill shall, like a star i' th' darkest night,
Stick fiery off indeed.

LAERTES: You mock me, sir.

HAMLET: No, by this hand.

KING: Give them the foils, young Osric. Cousin Hamlet,
You know the wager?

HAMLET: Very well, my lord;   245
Your Grace has laid the odds o'th' weaker side.

KING: I do not fear it, I have seen you both;
But since he is bettered, we have therefore odds.

LAERTES: This is too heavy; let me see another.

HAMLET: This likes me well. These foils have all a length?

(*They prepare to play.*)
                                                                                   250

OSRIC: Ay, my good lord.

KING: Set me the stoups of wine upon that table.
If Hamlet give the first or second hit,

---

173 **lapwing** a bird reputedly so precocious as to run as soon as hatched   174 **comply** observe the formalities of courtesy; **dug** mother's nipple   175 **bevy** a covey of quails or lapwings   176 **drossy** frivolous   177 **encounter** manner of address or accosting; **yesty collection** a frothy and superficial patchwork of terms from the conversation of others   179 **winnowed** tested, freed from inferior elements   186 **fitness** convenience, inclination   199 **gaingiving** misgiving

232 **voice and precedent** authoritative statement justified by precedent   238 **foil** (1) setting for gem (2) weapon   246 **bettered** perfected through training   248 **have all a length** are all of the same length   252 **quit in answer** literally, give as good as he gets (i.e., if the third bout is a draw)

Or quit in answer of the third exchange,
255 Let all the battlements their ordnance fire.
The king shall drink to Hamlet's better breath,
And in the cup an union shall he throw,
Richer than that which four successive kings
In Denmark's crown have worn. Give me the cups,
260 And let the kettle to the trumpet speak,
The trumpet to the cannoneer without,
The cannons to the heavens, the heaven to earth,
'Now the king drinks to Hamlet.' Come begin—

(*Trumpets the while.*)

And you, the judges, bear a wary eye.
HAMLET: Come on, sir.
LAERTES: Come, my lord.

(*They play.*)

HAMLET: One.
LAERTES: No.
HAMLET: Judgment.
OSRIC: A hit, a very palpable hit.

265 (*Drums, trumpets, and shot. Flourish; a piece goes off.*)

LAERTES: Well, again.
KING: Stay, give me drink. Hamlet, this pearl is thine.
Here's to thy health. Give him the cup.
HAMLET: I'll play this bout first; set it by awhile.
Come.

270 (*They play.*)

Another hit; what say you?
LAERTES: I do confess't.
KING: Our son shall win.
QUEEN: He's fat, and scant of breath.
275 Here, Hamlet, take my napkin, rub thy brows.
The queen carouses to thy fortune, Hamlet.
HAMLET: Good madam!
KING: Gertrude, do not drink.
QUEEN: I will, my lord; I pray you pardon me.
280 KING: (*Aside.*) It is the poisoned cup; it is too late.
HAMLET: I dare not drink yet, madam; by and by.
QUEEN: Come, let me wipe thy face.
LAERTES: My lord, I'll hit him now.
KING: I do not think't.
LAERTES: (*Aside.*) And yet it is almost against my conscience.
285 HAMLET: Come, for the third, Laertes. You but dally.
I pray you pass with your best violence;
I am afeard you make a wanton of me.
LAERTES: Say you so? come on.

(*They play.*)

OSRIC: Nothing, neither way.
LAERTES: Have at you now!

(LAERTES *wounds* HAMLET; *then, in scuffling, they change rapiers.*)
290
KING: Part them. They are incensed.
HAMLET: Nay, come again.

(HAMLET *wounds* LAERTES.   *The* QUEEN *falls.*)

OSRIC: Look to the queen there, ho!
HORATIO: They bleed on both sides. How is it, my lord?
OSRIC: How is't Laertes?   295
LAERTES: Why, as a woodcock to mine own springe, Osric.
I am justly killed with mine own treachery.
HAMLET: How does the queen?
KING: She swoons to see them bleed.
QUEEN: No, no, the drink, the drink! O my dear Hamlet!
The drink, the drink! I am poisoned.

(*Dies.*)
300
HAMLET: O villany! Ho! let the door be locked.
Treachery! Seek it out.

(LAERTES *falls. Exit* OSRIC.)

LAERTES: It is here, Hamlet. Hamlet, thou art slain;
No med'cine in the world can do thee good.
In thee there is not half an hour's life.   305
The treacherous instrument is in thy hand,
Unbated and envenomed. The foul practice
Hath turned itself on me. Lo, here I lie,
Never to rise again. Thy mother's poisoned.
I can no more. The king, the king's to blame.   310
HAMLET: The point envenomed too!
Then, venom, to thy work.

(*Wounds the* KING.)

ALL: Treason! treason!
KING: O, yet defend me, friends. I am but hurt.
HAMLET: Here, thou incestuous, murd'rous, damnèd Dane,   315
Drink off this potion. Is thy union here?
Follow my mother.

(KING *dies.*)

LAERTES: He is justly served.
It is a poison tempered by himself.
Exchange forgiveness with me, noble Hamlet.
Mine and my father's death come not upon thee,
Nor thine on me!

(*Dies.*)   320

HAMLET: Heaven make thee free of it! I follow thee.
I am dead, Horatio. Wretched queen, adieu!
You that look pale and tremble at this chance,
That are but mutes or audience to this act,   325
Had I but time, as this fell sergeant Death

---

255 **union** pearl   272 **fat** out of training   285 **make a wan-**
ton of me trifle with me

---

294 **springe** trap   305 **Unbated** unblunted; practice plot   324
fell cruel; **sergeant** an officer whose duty is to summon persons
to appear before a court

Is strict in his arrest, O, I could tell you—
But let it be. Horatio, I am dead:
Thou livest; report me and my cause aright
To the unsatisfied.

330 HORATIO: Never believe it:
I am more an antique Roman than a Dane.
Here's yet some liquor left.

HAMLET: As th'art a man,
Give me the cup. Let go. By heaven, I'll ha't.
O God, Horatio, what a wounded name,
335 Things standing thus unknown, shall live behind me!
If thou didst ever hold me in thy heart,
Absent thee from felicity awhile,
And in this harsh world draw thy breath in pain,
To tell my story.

(A march afar off.)

What warlike noise is this?

(Enter OSRIC.)

340 OSRIC: Young Fortinbras, with conquest come from Poland,
To th' ambassadors of England gives
This warlike volley.

HAMLET: O, I die, Horatio!
The potent poison quite o'er-crows my spirit.
I cannot live to hear the news from England,
345 But I do prophesy th' election lights
On Fortinbras. He has my dying voice.
So tell him, with th' occurrents, more and less,
Which have solicited—the rest is silence.

(Dies.)

HORATIO: Now cracks a noble heart. Good night, sweet
prince, And flights of angels sing thee to thy rest!

(March within.)

Why does the drum come hither?

(Enter FORTINBRAS, with the AMBASSADORS [and with drum, col-
350 *ors, and ATTENDANTS].)*

FORTINBRAS: Where is this sight?
HORATIO: What is it you would see?
If aught of woe or wonder, cease your search.

---

341 **o'er-crows** triumphs over   344 **voice** vote   345 **more and less** great and small   346 **solicited** incited, prompted

FORTINBRAS: This quarry cries on havoc. O proud Death,
What feast is toward in thine eternal cell   355
That thou so many princes at a shot
So bloodily hast struck?

AMBASSADORS: The sight is dismal;
And our affairs from England come too late.
The ears are senseless that should give us hearing
To tell him his commandment is fulfilled,   360
That Rosencrantz and Guildenstern are dead.
Where should we have our thanks?

HORATIO: Not from his mouth,
Had it th' ability of life to thank you.
He never gave commandment for their death.
But since, so jump upon this bloody question,   365
You from the Polack wars, and you from England,
Are here arrived, give order that these bodies
High on a stage be placèd to the view,
And let me speak to th' yet unknowing world
How these things came about. So shall you hear   370
Of carnal, bloody, and unnatural acts;
Of accidental judgements, casual slaughters;
Of deaths put on by cunning and forced cause;
And, in this upshot, purposes mistook
Fall'n on th' inventors' heads. All this can I
Truly deliver.   375

FORTINBRAS: Let us haste to hear it.
And call the noblest to the audience.
For me, with sorrow I embrace my fortune.
I have some rights of memory in this kingdom,
Which now to claim my vantage doth invite me.   380

HORATIO: Of that I shall have also cause to speak,
And from his mouth whose voice will draw on more.
But let this same be presently performed,
Even while men's minds are wild, lest more mischance
On plots and errors happen.

FORTINBRAS: Let four captains   385
Bear Hamlet like a soldier to the stage,
For he was likely, had he been put on,
To have proved most royal; and for his passage
The soldier's music and the rite of war
Speak loudly for him.   390
Take up the bodies. Such a sight as this
Becomes the field, but here shows much amiss.
Go, bid the soldiers shoot.

---

352 **quarry** pile of dead   353 **toward** impending   363 **jump** exactly   371 **put on** instigated; **forced cause** by reason of compulsion   385 **put on** set to perform in office   386 **passage** death

THE TEMPEST

The Tempest was staged at court in 1611. It is probably the last play that Shakespeare wrote without a collaborator, and generations of readers and audiences have taken Prospero as an image of Shakespeare himself: when Prospero puts aside his powerful, theatrical magic, Shakespeare may in a sense be making his farewell to the stage.

Renaissance audiences might have taken *The Tempest* as an example of a new kind of play becoming increasingly popular in the early seventeenth century: tragicomedy. Renaissance tragicomedy generally opens in the severe, disturbing mood of tragedy and builds to a moment of crisis; it then resolves into a comic finale of festivity, marriage, and harmony. That is, this version of "tragicomedy" concerns the play's plot structure, rather than its tone or mood. Shakespeare's company, the King's Men, had staged several plays by John Fletcher, one of the premier writers of tragicomedy, and it is inviting to see Shakespeare trying out his hand at the new genre late in his career in plays such as *Pericles, Cymbeline, The Winter's Tale,* and *The Tempest. The Tempest* begins as something like a revenge tragedy: Prospero plots to revenge himself on his usurping brother Antonio, and Sebastian's plot to murder Alonso also smacks of tragic intrigue. However, *The Tempest*, while raising the problems of tragedy, resolves them in the mode of comedy. Instead of murdering his brother, Prospero marries his daughter, Miranda, to Alonso's son, Ferdinand. The spirit Ariel prompts Prospero to discover that "The rarer action is / In virtue than in vengeance."

In other respects, *The Tempest* shares the forms and moods of Shakespearean comedy. In

Patrick Stewart as Prospero conjures the storm in the Joseph Papp Public Theater production of Shakespeare's *The Tempest*.

a plot reminiscent of many of Shakespeare's earlier comedies, Prospero's daughter, Miranda, falls instantly in love with Alonso's son, Ferdinand, for in *The Tempest,* virtue "naturally" recognizes virtue in others. The marriage also promises to heal the political rifts between Milan and Naples, and Prospero devises an elegant entertainment to lend the engagement an aura of sanctity. In its mythological characters, verse, song, and dance, Prospero's play resembles the masques frequently performed at court on such occasions. The romantic comedy of Ferdinand and Miranda is balanced by the play's more ironic treatment of Caliban, Stephano, and Trinculo. If the magical meeting of the lovers urges us to believe that the virtuous are drawn naturally together, the fact that Caliban takes the boozy Stephano and Trinculo for gods, and that the three of them try to overthrow Prospero from his second kingdom, suggests a parallel recognition—that bad nature also seeks itself out in others.

Although Prospero and Doctor Faustus may practice different kinds of magic, both are figures of the common desire to transcend nature through art. But much as Faustus is finally damned for his bargain with Mephostophilis, so Prospero learns that his own nature, and human nature generally, cannot be overcome. Prospero must learn to forgive to return to the world from his magic island-prison. Indeed, if the power of Prospero's artful magic is symbolized by the capable spirit Ariel, its limitations are suggested by Caliban. In some ways, Caliban represents a European imagination of human nature in its elemental form, an image of human nature that in the sixteenth and seventeenth centuries was often reinforced by European contacts with the indigenous peoples of the Americas and Africa. For although Prospero's island is located in the Mediterranean, many of its features—and the shipwreck motif—seem to be drawn from pamphlets describing the exploration of the New World. In 1609, a fleet of English ships bound for Virginia was wrecked by a storm in the Bermudas; and while many of the ships eventually reached Jamestown, one, the Sea Adventure, remained lost for nearly a year. When the ship finally reached Virginia in May of 1610, the Englishmen's story of survival and their encounters with the natives of the "still-vexed Bermoothes" was widely published in pamphlets that Shakespeare seems to have read while writing the play.

The play's setting and sources have led critics to see *The Tempest* as a play not only about the state of human nature, but also about the conquest and subjection of the native peoples represented by Caliban. Caliban is clearly seen from the point of view of the European settlers: Prospero calls him a devil and a slave and uses him as a beast of burden; his language is simple; and instead of using the arts of romance on Miranda, as Ferdinand does, he tries to rape Miranda in an effort to people the island with Calibans. Caliban was the master of the island's nature, its "fresh springs, brine pits, barren place and fertile," but in attempting to civilize Caliban, Prospero has succeeded only in deforming him. Caliban is now neither "natural" nor civilized, but a parody of European "humanity": "You taught me language, and my profit on't / Is, I know how to curse."

Prospero's stagey magic, his ability to conjure storms and spectacles, is a glorious image of Renaissance "overreaching." As in *A Midsummer Night's Dream* or *Hamlet,* Shakespeare uses *The Tempest* to frame his final, most subtle imaging of the extraordinary powers of art—the arts of magic, of civilization, of the theater. At the same time, *The Tempest* also expresses the limitations of that art: neither Sebastian nor Antonio seems fundamentally changed by Prospero's magic. And much as Caliban has been changed, the play finally can find no voice, no language for Caliban to speak. In recent years, stage productions have sometimes taken the play as an opportunity to investigate the dynamics of colonialism. Lewis Baumander's production (Toronto, 1987) set the play on the Queen Charlotte Islands, off the coast of British Columbia, Canada, during the late eighteenth century, when these islands were being explored and settled by British seamen. Not only have other productions (Jonathan Miller's 1988 *Tempest*) more generally interrogated the questions of cultural and racial domination posed in Shakespeare's play, but many writers—Roberto Fernández Retamar, for example, in *Caliban* (1989)—have seen in Shakespeare's play an allegory of the West's continued representational power over its colonial and postcolonial subjects. Aimé Césaire's play *A Tempest* is perhaps the best-known dramatic response to *The Tempest*.

The Tempest is also the subject of one of the most famous and experimental Shakespeare films of the 1990s, Peter Greenaway's *Prospero's Books* (1991).

THE TEMPEST

William Shakespeare

EDITED BY DAVID BEVINGTON

CHARACTERS

ALONSO, *King of Naples*	MASTER *of a Ship*
SEBASTIAN, *his brother*	BOATSWAIN
PROSPERO, *the right Duke of Milan*	MARINERS
ANTONIO, *his brother, the usurping Duke of Milan*	MIRANDA, *daughter to Prospero*
FERDINAND, *son to the King of Naples*	ARIEL, *an airy Spirit*
GONZALO, *an honest old Counselor*	IRIS
ADRIAN *and* ⎱ *Lords*	CERES
FRANCISCO ⎰	JUNO ⎱ *[presented by]* SPIRITS
CALIBAN, *a savage and deformed Slave*	NYMPHS
TRINCULO, *a Jester*	REAPERS
STEPHANO, *a drunken Butler*	*[Other* SPIRITS *attending on Prospero.]*

ACT ONE

SCENE I

An uninhabited island.

A tempestuous noise of thunder and lightning heard. Enter a SHIP-
MASTER *and a* BOATSWAIN.

MASTER: Boatswain!
BOATSWAIN: Here, master. What cheer?
MASTER: Good speak to th' mariners. Fall to 't, yarely, or we
    run ourselves aground. Bestir, bestir.

(Exit.)

(Enter MARINERS.)

5 BOATSWAIN: Heigh, my hearts! Cheerly, cheerly, my hearts!
    Yare, yare! Take in the topsail. Tend to th' master's whis-
    tle.— Blow till thou burst thy wind, if room enough!

(Enter ALONSO, SEBASTIAN, ANTONIO, FERDINAND, GONZALO,
and others.)

ALONSO: Good boatswain, have care. Where's the master?
    Play the men.
10 BOATSWAIN: I pray now, keep below.
ANTONIO: Where is the master, bos'n?
BOATSWAIN: Do you not hear him? You mar our labor. Keep
    your cabins; you do assist the storm.
GONZALO: Nay, good, be patient.
15 BOATSWAIN: When the sea is. Hence! What cares these roar-
    ers for the name of king? To cabin! Silence! Trouble us not.
GONZALO: Good, yet remember whom thou hast aboard.
BOATSWAIN: None that I more love than myself. You are a
    counselor; if you can command these elements to silence,
20   and work the peace of the present, we will not hand a

rope more. Use your authority. If you cannot, give thanks
you have liv'd so long, and make yourself ready in your
cabin for the mischance of the hour, if it so hap.—
Cheerly, good hearts!—Out of our way, I say.

(Exit.)

GONZALO: I have great comfort from this fellow. Methinks he   25
    hath no drowning mark upon him; his complexion is per-
    fect gallows. Stand fast, good Fate, to his hanging! Make the
    rope of his destiny our cable, for our own doth little advan-
    tage. If he be not born to be hang'd, our case is miserable.

(Exeunt.)

(Enter BOATSWAIN.)

BOATSWAIN: Down with the topmast! Yare! Lower, lower!   30
    Bring her to try with main-course. *(A cry within.)* A
    plague upon this howling! They are louder than the
    weather or our office.

(Enter SEBASTIAN, ANTONIO, *and* GONZALO.)

    Yet again? What do you here? Shall we give o'er and
    drown? Have you a mind to sink?   35
SEBASTIAN: A pox o' your throat, you bawling, blasphemous,
    incharitable dog!
BOATSWAIN: Work you then.
ANTONIO: Hang, cur! Hang, you whoreson, insolent noise-
    maker! We are less afraid to be drown'd than thou art.   40
GONZALO: I'll warrant him for drowning, though the ship
    were no stronger than a nutshell and as leaky as an un-
    stanch'd wench.

I.i. Location: On a ship at sea. 3 Good i.e., it's good you've
come; or, my good fellow; **yarely** nimbly **6 Tend** attend **7 Blow**
(addressed to the wind); **if room enough** as long as we have sea-
room enough **8–9 Play the men** act like men (?) ply, urge the men
to exert themselves (?) **15 roarers** waves or winds, or both; spoken
to as though they were "bullies" or "blusterers" **20 hand** handle

26–27 complexion . . . gallows appearance shows he was born
to be hanged (and therefore, according to the proverb, in no danger of drowning) **28 our . . . advantage** i.e., our own cable is
of little benefit **31 Bring . . . course** sail her close to the wind
by means of the mainsail **32 our office** i.e., the noise we make
at our work **41 warrant him for drowning** guarantee that
he will never be drowned **42 unstanch'd** insatiable, loose, unrestrained

231

BOATSWAIN: Lay her a-hold, a-hold! Set her two courses off
45   to sea again! Lay her off!

(*Enter* MARINERS *wet.*)

MARINERS: All lost! To prayers, to prayers! All lost!

(*Exeunt.*)

BOATSWAIN: What, must our mouths be cold?
GONZALO: The King and Prince at prayers! Let's assist them,
    For our case is as theirs.
SEBASTIAN: I am out of patience.
50 ANTONIO: We are merely cheated of our lives by drunkards.
    This wide-chopp'd rascal! Would thou mightst lie drowning
    The washing of ten tides!
GONZALO: He'll be hang'd yet,
    Though every drop of water swear against it
    And gape at wid'st to glut him.

(*A confused noise within:*)

                "Mercy on us!"—
55   "We split, we split!"—"Farewell my wife and children!"–
    "Farewell, brother!"—"We split, we split, we split!"

(*Exit* BOATSWAIN.)

ANTONIO: Let's all sink wi' th' King.
SEBASTIAN: Let's take leave of him.

(*Exit* [*with* ANTONIO].)

GONZALO: Now would I give a thousand furlongs of sea for an
60   acre of barren ground, long heath, brown furze, anything.
    The wills above be done! But I would fain die a dry death.

(*Exit.*)

SCENE II

Enter PROSPERO [*in his magic robes*] *and* MIRANDA.

MIRANDA: If by your art, my dearest father, you have
    Put the wild waters in this roar, allay them.
    The sky, it seems, would pour down stinking pitch,
    But that the sea, mounting to th' welkin's cheek,
5   Dashes the fire out. O, I have suffered
    With those that I saw suffer! A brave vessel,
    Who had, no doubt, some noble creature in her,
    Dash'd all to pieces. O, the cry did knock
    Against my very heart! Poor souls, they perish'd.

---

44 **a-hold** a-hull, close to the wind; **courses** sails, i.e., foresail as well as mainsail, set in an attempt to get the ship back out into open water   47 **must . . . cold** i.e., let us heat up our mouths with liquor   50 **merely** quite   51 **wide-chopp'd** with mouth wide open   51–52 **lie . . . tides** (Pirates were hanged on the shore and left until three tides had come in.)   54 **glut** swallow   60 **heath** uncultivated ground; heather; **furze** a weed growing on waste land

I.ii. Location: The island. Before Prospero's cell.   4 **welkin's cheek** sky's face   6 **brave** gallant, splendid

---

    Had I been any god of power, I would   10
    Have sunk the sea within the earth or ere
    It should the good ship so have swallow'd and
    The fraughting souls within her.
PROSPERO: Be collected.
    No more amazement. Tell your piteous heart
    There's no harm done.   15
MIRANDA: O, woe the day!
PROSPERO: No harm.
    I have done nothing but in care of thee,
    Of thee, my dear one, thee, my daughter, who
    Art ignorant of what thou art, nought knowing
    Of whence I am, nor that I am more better
    Than Prospero, master of a full poor cell,   20
    And thy no greater father.
MIRANDA: More to know
    Did never meddle with my thoughts.
PROSPERO: 'Tis time
    I should inform thee farther. Lend thy hand,
    And pluck my magic garment from me. So,

(*Lays down his magic robe and staff.*)

    Lie there, my art. Wipe thou thine eyes; have comfort.   25
    The direful spectacle of the wrack, which touch'd
    The very virtue of compassion in thee,
    I have with such provision in mine art
    So safely ordered that there is no soul—
    No, not so much perdition as an hair   30
    Betid to any creature in the vessel
    Which thou heard'st cry, which thou saw'st sink. Sit down;
    For thou must now know farther.
MIRANDA: You have often
    Begun to tell me what I am, but stopp'd
    And left me to a bootless inquisition,   35
    Concluding, "Stay, not yet."
PROSPERO: The hour's now come;
    The very minute bids thee ope thine ear.
    Obey and be attentive. Canst thou remember
    A time before we came unto this cell?
    I do not think thou canst, for then thou wast not   40
    Out three years old.
MIRANDA: Certainly, sir, I can.
PROSPERO: By what? By any other house or person?
    Of anything the image, tell me, that
    Hath kept with thy remembrance.
MIRANDA: 'Tis far off,
    And rather like a dream than an assurance   45
    That my remembrance warrants. Had I not
    Four or five women once that tended me?
PROSPERO: Thou hadst, and more, Miranda. But how is it
    That this lives in thy mind? What seest thou else
    In the dark backward and abysm of time?   50

---

11 **or ere** before   13 **fraughting** forming the cargo; **collected** calm, composed   14 **amazement** consternation   20 **full** very   30 **perdition** loss   31 **Betid** happened   35 **bootless inquisition** profitless inquiry   41 **Out** fully   45–46 **assurance . . . warrants** certainty that my memory guarantees

If thou rememb'rest aught ere thou cam'st here,
How thou cam'st here thou mayst.
MIRANDA: But that I do not.
PROSPERO: Twelve year since, Miranda, twelve year since,
Thy father was the Duke of Milan and
55   A prince of power.
MIRANDA: Sir, are not you my father?
PROSPERO: Thy mother was a piece of virtue, and
She said thou wast my daughter; and thy father
Was Duke of Milan; and thou his only heir
And princess no worse issued.
MIRANDA: O the heavens!
60   What foul play had we, that we came from thence?
Or blessed was 't we did?
PROSPERO: Both, both, my girl.
By foul play, as thou say'st, were we heav'd thence,
But blessedly holp hither.
MIRANDA: O, my heart bleeds
To think o' th' teen that I have turn'd you to,
65   Which is from my remembrance! Please you, farther.
PROSPERO: My brother and thy uncle, call'd Antonio—
I pray thee mark me—that a brother should
Be so perfidious!—he whom next thyself
Of all the world I lov'd, and to him put
70   The manage of my state, as at that time
Through all the signories it was the first
And Prospero the prime duke, being so reputed
In dignity, and for the liberal arts
Without a parallel; those being all my study,
75   The government I cast upon my brother
And to my state grew stranger, being transported
And rapt in secret studies. Thy false uncle—
Dost thou attend me?
MIRANDA: Sir, most heedfully.
PROSPERO: Being once perfected how to grant suits,
80   How to deny them, who t' advance and who
To trash for overtopping, new created
The creatures that were mine, I say, or chang'd 'em,
Or else new form'd 'em; having both the key
Of officer and office, set all hearts i' th' state
85   To what tune pleas'd his ear, that now he was
The ivy which had hid my princely trunk,
And suck'd my verdure out on 't. Thou attend'st not.
MIRANDA: O, good sir, I do.
PROSPERO: I pray thee mark me.
I, thus neglecting worldly ends, all dedicated
90   To closeness and the bettering of my mind
With that which, but by being so retir'd,
O'er-priz'd all popular rate, in my false brother
Awak'd an evil nature; and my trust,

Like a good parent, did beget of him
A falsehood in its contrary as great   95
As my trust was, which had indeed no limit,
A confidence sans bound. He being thus lorded,
Not only with what my revenue yielded,
But what my power might else exact—like one
Who having into truth, by telling of it,   100
Made such a sinner of his memory
To credit his own lie—he did believe
He was indeed the Duke, out o' th' substitution,
And executing th' outward face of royalty,
With all prerogative. Hence his ambition growing—   105
Dost thou hear?
MIRANDA: Your tale, sir, would cure deafness.
PROSPERO: To have no screen between this part he play'd
And him he play'd it for, he needs will be
Absolute Milan. Me, poor man, my library
Was dukedom large enough. Of temporal royalties   110
He thinks me now incapable; confederates—
So dry he was for sway—wi' th' King of Naples
To give him annual tribute, do him homage,
Subject his coronet to his crown, and bend
The dukedom yet unbow'd—alas, poor Milan!—   115
To most ignoble stooping.
MIRANDA: O the heavens!
PROSPERO: Mark his condition and th' event, then tell me
If this might be a brother.
MIRANDA: I should sin
To think but nobly of my grandmother.
Good wombs have borne bad sons   120
PROSPERO: Now the condition.
This King of Naples, being an enemy
To me inveterate, hearkens my brother's suit,
Which was that he, in lieu o' th' premises
Of homage and I know not how much tribute,
Should presently extirpate me and mine   125
Out of the dukedom and confer fair Milan
With all the honors on my brother. Whereon,
A treacherous army levied, one midnight
Fated to th' purpose, did Antonio open
The gates of Milan, and, i' th' dead of darkness,   130
The ministers for th' purpose hurried thence
Me and thy crying self.
MIRANDA: Alack, for pity!
I, not rememb'ring how I cried out then,

---

56 **piece** masterpiece, exemplar 59 **issued** born, descended
63 **holp** helped 64 **teen . . . to** trouble I've caused you to remember, or put you to 65 **from** out of 71 **signories** i.e.,
city-states of northern Italy 79 **perfected** grown skillful 81
trash check a hound by tying a weight to its neck; **overtopping**
running too far ahead of the pack; or, growing too tall 82
creatures dependents; **or** either 83 **key** (1) key for unlocking
(2) tool for tuning stringed instruments 90 **closeness** retirement, seclusion 91–92 **but . . . rate** except that it was done in
retirement, (would have) surpassed in value all popular estimate

94 **good parent** alludes to the proverb that good parents often
bear bad children; see also line 120 97 **sans** without; **lorded**
raised to lordship, with power and wealth 100–102 **Who . . .
lie** i.e., who, by repeatedly telling the lie (that he was indeed
Duke of Milan), made his memory such a confirmed sinner
against truth that he began to believe his own lie 103 **out o'**
as a result of 104 **And . . . royalty** and (as a result) his carrying out all the ceremonial functions of royalty 108 **him** i.e.,
himself 109 **Absolute Milan** unconditional Duke of Milan
110 **temporal royalties** practical prerogatives and responsibilities of a sovereign 111 **confederates** conspires, allies himself
112 **dry** thirsty 113 **him** i.e., the King of Naples 114 **his . . .
his** Antonio's . . . the King of Naples' 117 **condition** pact;
event outcome 123 **in . . . premises** in return for the stipu-
lation 125 **presently extirpate** at once remove

Will cry it o'er again. It is a hint
135 That wrings mine eyes to 't.
PROSPERO: Hear a little further,
And then I'll bring thee to the present business
Which now's upon 's, without the which this story
Were most impertinent.
MIRANDA: Wherefore did they not
That hour destroy us?
PROSPERO: Well demanded, wench.
140 My tale provokes that question. Dear, they durst not,
So dear the love my people bore me, nor set
A mark so bloody on the business, but
With colors fairer painted their foul ends.
In few, they hurried us aboard a bark,
145 Bore us some leagues to sea, where they prepar'd
A rotten carcass of a butt, not rigg'd,
Nor tackle, sail, nor mast; the very rats
Instinctively have quit it. There they hoist us,
To cry to th' sea that roar'd to us, to sigh
150 To th' winds whose pity, sighing back again,
Did us but loving wrong.
MIRANDA: Alack, what trouble
Was I then to you!
PROSPERO: O, a cherubin
Thou wast that did preserve me. Thou didst smile,
Infused with a fortitude from heaven,
155 When I have deck'd the sea with drops full salt,
Under my burden groan'd, which rais'd in me
An undergoing stomach, to bear up
Against what should ensue.
MIRANDA: How came we ashore?
PROSPERO: By Providence divine.
160 Some food we had, and some fresh water, that
A noble Neapolitan, Gonzalo,
Out of his charity, who being then appointed
Master of this design, did give us, with
Rich garments, linens, stuffs, and necessaries,
165 Which since have steaded much. So, of his gentleness,
Knowing I lov'd my books, he furnish'd me
From mine own library with volumes that
I prize above my dukedom.
MIRANDA: Would I might
But ever see that man!
PROSPERO: Now I arise.

(*Resumes his magic robes.*)

170 Sit still, and hear the last of our sea-sorrow.
Here in this island we arriv'd; and here
Have I, thy schoolmaster, made thee more profit
Than other princess' can that have more time
For vainer hours and tutors not so careful.

MIRANDA: Heavens thank you for 't! And now, I pray you, sir, 175
For still 'tis beating in my mind, your reason
For raising this sea-storm?
PROSPERO: Know thus far forth.
By accident most strange, bountiful Fortune,
Now my dear lady, hath mine enemies
Brought to this shore; and by my prescience 180
I find my zenith doth depend upon
A most auspicious star, whose influence
If now I court not but omit, my fortunes
Will ever after droop. Here cease more questions.
Thou art inclin'd to sleep; 'tis a good dullness, 185
And give it way. I know thou canst not choose.

(MIRANDA *sleeps.*)

Come away, servant, come! I am ready now.
Approach, my Ariel, come.

(*Enter* ARIEL.)

ARIEL: All hail, great master! Grave sir, hail! I come
To answer thy best pleasure; be 't to fly, 190
To swim, to dive into the fire, to ride
On the curl'd clouds. To thy strong bidding, task
Ariel and all his quality.
PROSPERO: Hast thou, spirit,
Perform'd to point the tempest that I bade thee?
ARIEL: To every article. 195
I boarded the King's ship; now on the beak,
Now in the waist, the deck, in every cabin,
I flam'd amazement. Sometime I'd divide,
And burn in many places; on the topmast,
The yards, and boresprit, would I flame distinctly, 200
Then meet and join. Jove's lightnings, the precursors
O' th' dreadful thunder-claps, more momentary
And sight-outrunning were not; the fire and cracks
Of sulphurous roaring the most mighty Neptune
Seem to besiege and make his bold waves tremble, 205
Yea, his dread trident shake.
PROSPERO: My brave spirit!
Who was so firm, so constant, that this coil
Would not infect his reason?
ARIEL: Not a soul
But felt a fever of the mad and play'd
Some tricks of desperation. All but mariners 210
Plung'd in the foaming brine and quit the vessel;
Then all afire with me, the King's son, Ferdinand,
With hair up-staring—then like reeds, not hair—
Was the first man that leapt; cried, "Hell is empty,
And all the devils are here." 215

---

134 **hint** occasion   138 **impertinent** irrelevant   144 **few** few words   146 **butt** cask, tub   151 **loving wrong** i.e., the winds pitied Prospero and Miranda though of necessity they blew them from shore   155 **deck'd** covered (with salt tears); adorned   156 **which** i.e., the smile   157 **undergoing stomach** courage to go on   165 **steaded much** been of much use   172 **more profit** profit more   173 **princess'** princesses

---

181 **zenith** height of fortune (astrological term)   182 **influence** astrological power   187 **Come away** come   192 **task** make demands upon   193 **quality** (1) fellow-spirits (2) abilities 194 **to point** to the smallest detail   196 **beak** prow   197 **waist** midships; **deck** poopdeck at the stern   198 **flam'd amazement** struck terror in the guise of fire, i.e., St. Elmo's fire 200 **boresprit** bowsprit; distinctly in different places   207 **coil** tumult   209 **of the mad** i.e., such as madmen feel   213 **up-staring** standing on end

PROSPERO: Why, that's my spirit!
But was not this nigh shore?
ARIEL: Close by, my master.
PROSPERO: But are they, Ariel, safe?
ARIEL: Not a hair perish'd.
On their sustaining garments not a blemish,
But fresher than before; and, as thou bad'st me,
220 In troops I have dispers'd them 'bout the isle.
The King's son have I landed by himself,
Whom I left cooling of the air with sighs
In an odd angle of the isle and sitting,
His arms in this sad knot.

(*Folds his arms.*)

PROSPERO: Of the King's ship,
225 The mariners, say how thou hast dispos'd,
And all the rest o' th' fleet.
ARIEL: Safely in harbor
Is the King's ship; in the deep nook, where once
Thou call'dst me up at midnight to fetch dew
From the still-vex'd Bermoothes, there she's hid;
230 The mariners all under hatches stow'd,
Who, with a charm join'd to their suff'red labor,
I have left asleep; and for the rest o' th' fleet,
Which I dispers'd, they all have met again
And are upon the Mediterranean flote
235 Bound sadly home for Naples,
Supposing that they saw the King's ship wrack'd
And his great person perish.
PROSPERO: Ariel, thy charge
Exactly is perform'd. But there's more work.
What is the time o' th' day?
ARIEL: Past the mid season.
240 PROSPERO: At least two glasses. The time 'twixt six and now
Must by us both be spent most preciously.
ARIEL: Is there more toil? Since thou dost give me pains,
Let me remember thee what thou hast promis'd,
Which is not yet perform'd me.
PROSPERO: How now? Moody?
245 What is 't thou canst demand?
ARIEL: My liberty.
PROSPERO: Before the time be out? No more!
ARIEL: I prithee,
Remember I have done thee worthy service,
Told thee no lies, made thee no mistakings, serv'd
Without or grudge or grumblings. Thou didst promise
250 To bate me a full year.
PROSPERO: Dost thou forget
From what a torment I did free thee?
ARIEL: No.

PROSPERO: Thou dost, and think'st it much to tread the ooze
Of the salt deep,
To run upon the sharp wind of the north,
To do me business in the veins o' th' earth   255
When it is bak'd with frost.
ARIEL: I do not, sir.
PROSPERO: Thou liest, malignant thing! Hast thou forgot
The foul witch Sycorax, who with age and envy
Was grown into a hoop? Hast thou forgot her?
ARIEL: No, sir.   260
PROSPERO: Thou hast. Where was she born? Speak. Tell me.
ARIEL: Sir, in Argier.
PROSPERO: O, was she so? I must
Once in a month recount what thou hast been,
Which thou forget'st. This damn'd witch Sycorax,
For mischiefs manifold and sorceries terrible   265
To enter human hearing, from Argier,
Thou know'st, was banish'd; for one thing she did
They would not take her life. Is not this true?
ARIEL: Ay, sir.
PROSPERO: This blue-ey'd hag was hither brought with child 270
And here was left by th' sailors. Thou, my slave,
As thou report'st thyself, was then her servant;
And, for thou wast a spirit too delicate
To act her earthy and abhorr'd commands,
Refusing her grand hests, she did confine thee,   275
By help of her more potent ministers,
And in her most unmitigable rage,
Into a cloven pine, within which rift
Imprison'd thou didst painfully remain
A dozen years; within which space she died   280
And left thee there, where thou did'st vent thy groans
As fast as mill-wheels strike. Then was this island—
Save for the son that she did litter here,
A freckled whelp hag-born—not honor'd with
A human shape.   285
ARIEL: Yes, Caliban her son.
PROSPERO: Dull thing, I say so; he, that Caliban
Whom now I keep in service. Thou best know'st
What torment I did find thee in; thy groans
Did make wolves howl and penetrate the breasts
Of ever angry bears. It was a torment   290
To lay upon the damn'd, which Sycorax
Could not again undo. It was mine art,
When I arriv'd and heard thee, that made gape
The pine and let thee out.
ARIEL: I thank thee, master.
PROSPERO: If thou more murmur'st, I will rend an oak 295
And peg thee in his knotty entrails till
Thou hast howl'd away twelve winters.
ARIEL: Pardon, master;
I will be correspondent to command
And do my spriting gently.

---

218 **sustaining garments** garments that buoyed them up in the sea   223 **angle** corner   224 **sad knot** folded arms are indicative of melancholy   227 **nook** bay   229 **still-vex'd Bermoothes** ever stormy Bermudas. Perhaps refers to the then-recent Bermuda shipwreck; see Play Introduction   231 **with . . . labor** by means of a spell added to all the labor they have undergone   234 **flote** sea   239 **mid season** noon   240 **glasses** i.e., hourglasses   243 **remember** remind   250 **bate** remit, deduct

258 **envy** malice   262 **Argier** Algiers   267 **one . . . did** perhaps a reference to her pregnancy, for which her life would be spared   270 **blue-ey'd** with dark circles under the eyes   273 **for** because   275 **hests** commands   296 **his** its   298 **correspondent** responsive, submissive

300 PROSPERO: Do so, and after two days
    I will discharge thee.
  ARIEL: That's my noble master!
    What shall I do? Say what? What shall I do?
  PROSPERO: Go make thyself like a nymph o' th' sea.
      Be subject
    To no sight but thine and mine, invisible
305   To every eyeball else. Go take this shape
    And hither come in 't. Go, hence with diligence!

(*Exit* [ARIEL].)

    Awake, dear heart, awake! Thou hast slept well;
    Awake!
  MIRANDA: The strangeness of your story put
310   Heaviness in me.
  PROSPERO: Shake it off. Come on;
    We'll visit Caliban my slave, who never
    Yields us kind answer.
  MIRANDA: 'Tis a villain, sir,
    I do not love to look on.
  PROSPERO: But, as 'tis,
    We cannot miss him. He does make our fire,
315   Fetch in our wood, and serves in offices
    That profit us. What, ho! Slave! Caliban!
    Thou earth, thou! Speak.
  CALIBAN: (*Within.*)   There's wood enough within.
  PROSPERO: Come forth, I say! There's other business for thee.
    Come, thou tortoise! When?

(*Enter* ARIEL *like a water-nymph.*)

320   Fine apparition! My quaint Ariel,
    Hark in thine ear.

(*Whispers.*)

  ARIEL: My lord, it shall be done.

(*Exit.*)

  PROSPERO: Thou poisonous slave, got by the devil himself
    Upon thy wicked dam, come forth!

(*Enter* CALIBAN.)

  CALIBAN: As wicked dew as e'er my mother brush'd
325   With raven's feather from unwholesome fen
    Drop on you both! A south-west blow on ye
    And blister you all o'er!
  PROSPERO: For this, be sure, tonight thou shalt have cramps,
    Side-stitches that shall pen thy breath up; urchins
330   Shall, for that vast of night that they may work,
    All exercise on thee. Thou shalt be pinch'd

As thick as honeycomb, each pinch more stinging
Than bees that made 'em.
  CALIBAN: I must eat my dinner.
    This island's mine, by Sycorax my mother,
    Which thou tak'st from me. When thou cam'st first,   335
    Thou strok'st me and made much of me, wouldst
      give me
    Water with berries in 't, and teach me how
    To name the bigger light, and how the less,
    That burn by day and night; and then I lov'd thee
    And show'd thee all the qualities o' th' isle,   340
    The fresh springs, brine-pits, barren place and fertile.
    Curs'd be I that did so! All the charms
    Of Sycorax, toads, beetles, bats, light on you!
    For I am all the subjects that you have,
    Which first was mine own king; and here you sty me   345
    In this hard rock, whiles you do keep from me
    The rest o' th' island.
  PROSPERO: Thou most lying slave,
    Whom stripes may move, not kindness! I have us'd thee,
    Filth as thou art, with humane care, and lodg'd thee
    In mine own cell, till thou didst seek to violate   350
    The honor of my child.
  CALIBAN: O ho, O ho! Would't had been done!
    Thou didst prevent me; I had peopled else
    This isle with Calibans.
  MIRANDA: Abhorred slave,
    Which any print of goodness wilt not take,   355
    Being capable of all ill! I pitied thee,
    Took pains to make thee speak, taught thee each hour
    One thing or other. When thou didst not, savage,
    Know thine own meaning, but wouldst gabble like
    A thing most brutish, I endow'd thy purposes   360
    With words that made them known. But thy vile race,
    Though thou didst learn, had that in 't which good
      natures
    Could not abide to be with; therefore wast thou
    Deservedly confin'd into this rock,
    Who hadst deserv'd more than a prison.   365
  CALIBAN: You taught me language, and my profit on 't
    Is, I know how to curse. The red plague rid you
    For learning me your language!
  PROSPERO: Hag-seed, hence!
    Fetch us in fuel; and be quick, thou'rt best,
    To answer other business. Shrug'st thou, malice?   370
    If thou neglect'st or dost unwillingly
    What I command, I'll rack thee with old cramps,
    Fill all thy bones with aches, make thee roar
    That beasts shall tremble at thy din.
  CALIBAN: No, pray thee.
    (*Aside.*) I must obey. His art is of such pow'r,   375

---

314 **miss** do without 320 **quaint** ingenious 323 **wicked** mischievous, harmful 326 **south-west** i.e., wind thought to bring disease 329 **urchins** hedgehogs; here, suggesting goblins in the guise of hedgehogs 330 **vast** lengthy, desolate time; **that ... work** malignant spirits were thought to be restricted to the hours of darkness

348 **stripes** lashes 354–365 **Abhorred . . . prison** sometimes assigned by editors to Prospero 360 **purposes** meanings, desires 361 **race** natural disposition; species, nature 367 **red plague** bubonic plague; **rid** destroy 368 **learning** teaching; **Hag-seed** offspring of a female demon 369 **thou'rt best** you'd be well advised 372 **old** such as old people suffer; or, plenty of 373 **aches** pronounced "aitches"

It would control my dam's god, Setebos,
And make a vassal of him.
PROSPERO: So, slave, hence!

(*Exit* CALIBAN.)

(*Enter* FERDINAND; *and* ARIEL, *invisible, playing and singing.*
[FERDINAND *does not see* PROSPERO *and* MIRANDA.])

(ARIEL's *song.*)

   Come unto these yellow sands,
    And then take hands.
380   Curtsied when you have and kiss'd,
    The wild waves whist,
   Foot it featly here and there;
   And, sweet sprites, the burden bear.
    Hark, hark!

(*Burden, dispersedly* [*within*].)

385   Bow-wow.
   The watch-dogs bark.

(*Burden, dispersedly* [*within*].)

   Bow-wow.
   Hark, hark! I hear
   The strain of strutting chanticleer
390   Cry, Cock-a-diddle-dow.

FERDINAND: Where should this music be? I' th' air or th'
  earth?
It sounds no more; and, sure, it waits upon
Some god o' th' island. Sitting on a bank,
Weeping again the King my father's wrack,
395 This music crept by me upon the waters,
Allaying both their fury and my passion
With its sweet air. Thence I have follow'd it,
Or it hath drawn me rather. But 'tis gone.
No, it begins again.

(ARIEL's *song.*)

400   Full fathom five thy father lies;
    Of his bones are coral made;
   Those are pearls that were his eyes.
    Nothing of him that doth fade
   But doth suffer a sea-change
405   Into something rich and strange.
   Sea-nymphs hourly ring his knell:

(*Burden* [*within*].)

   Ding-dong.
   Hark, now I hear them—Ding-dong,
    bell.

410 FERDINAND: The ditty does remember my drown'd father.
This is no mortal business, nor no sound
That the earth owes. I hear it now above me.

PROSPERO: The fringed curtains of thine eye advance
And say what thou seest yond.
MIRANDA: What is 't! A spirit!
Lord, how it looks about! Believe me, sir,
It carries a brave form. But 'tis a spirit.   415
PROSPERO: No, wench, it eats and sleeps and hath such
  senses
As we have, such. This gallant which thou seest
Was in the wrack; and, but he's something stain'd
With grief, that's beauty's canker, thou mightst call him
A goodly person. He hath lost his fellows   420
And strays about to find 'em.
MIRANDA: I might call him
A thing divine, for nothing natural
I ever saw so noble.
PROSPERO: (*Aside.*) It goes on, I see,
As my soul prompts it. Spirit, fine spirit, I'll free thee
Within two days for this.   425
FERDINAND: (*Seeing* MIRANDA.) Most sure, the goddess
On whom these airs attend!—Vouchsafe my pray'r
May know if you remain upon this island,
And that you will some good instruction give
How I may bear me here. My prime request,
Which I do last pronounce, is, O you wonder! 430
If you be maid or no?
MIRANDA: No wonder, sir,
But certainly a maid.
FERDINAND: My language? Heavens!
I am the best of them that speak this speech,
Were I but where 'tis spoken.
PROSPERO: (*Coming forward.*) How? The best?
What wert thou, if the King of Naples heard thee? 435
FERDINAND: A single thing, as I am now, that wonders
To hear thee speak of Naples. He does hear me;
And that he does I weep. Myself am Naples,
Who with mine eyes, never since at ebb, beheld
The King my father wrack'd.   440
MIRANDA: Alack, for mercy!
FERDINAND: Yes, faith, and all his lords, the Duke of Milan
And his brave son being twain.
PROSPERO: (*Aside.*) The Duke of Milan
And his more braver daughter could control thee,
If now 'twere fit to do 't. At the first sight
They have chang'd eyes. Delicate Ariel,   445
I'll set thee free for this. (*To* FERDINAND.) A word, good sir.
I fear you have done yourself some wrong. A word!

---

413 **advance** raise 415 **brave** excellent 418 **but** except that;
something stain'd somewhat disfigured 419 **canker** canker-
worm (feeding on buds and leaves) 423 **It goes on** i.e., my
plan works 427 **remain** dwell 429 **bear me** conduct myself;
prime chief 433 **best** i.e., in birth 436 **single** (1) solitary (2)
feeble 437–438 **He . . . weep** i.e., this man to whom I speak
(Prospero) hears me as I hear him, proving to me I am indeed
alive, not dreaming, and am in the sad plight I imagined (?) 438
Naples the King of Naples (also in line 437) 442 **son** the only
reference in the play to a son of Antonio 443 **control** confute
445 **chang'd eyes** exchanged amorous glances 447 **done . . .
wrong** i.e., spoken falsely

---

381 **whist** being hushed 382 **featly** nimbly 383 **burden** refrain, undersong 384 s.d. **dispersedly** i.e., from all directions
410 **remember** commemorate 412 **owes** owns

MIRANDA: (*Aside.*) Why speaks my father so ungently? This
    Is the third man that e'er I saw, the first
450   That e'er I sigh'd for. Pity move my father
    To be inclin'd my way!
FERDINAND: O, if a virgin,
    And your affection not gone forth, I'll make you
    The Queen of Naples.
PROSPERO: Soft, sir! One word more.
    (*Aside.*) They are both in either's pow'rs; but this swift
      business
455   I must uneasy make, lest too light winning
    Make the prize light. (*To* FERDINAND.) One word more:
      I charge thee
    That thou attend me. Thou dost here usurp
    The name thou ow'st not, and hast put thyself
    Upon this island as a spy, to win it
460   From me, the lord on 't.
FERDINAND: No, as I am a man.
MIRANDA: There's nothing ill can dwell in such a temple.
    If the ill spirit have so fair a house,
    Good things will strive to dwell with 't.
PROSPERO: Follow me.—
    Speak not you for him; he's a traitor.—Come,
465   I'll manacle thy neck and feet together.
    Sea-water shalt thou drink; thy food shall be
    The fresh-brook mussels, wither'd roots, and husks
    Wherein the acorn cradled. Follow.
FERDINAND: No.
    I will resist such entertainment till
470   Mine enemy has more pow'r.

(*He draws, and is charmed from moving.*)

MIRANDA: O dear father,
    Make not too rash a trial of him, for
    He's gentle, and not fearful.
PROSPERO: What, I say,
    My foot my tutor?—Put thy sword up, traitor,
    Who mak'st a show but dar'st not strike, thy conscience
475   Is so possess'd with guilt. Come, from thy ward,
    For I can here disarm thee with this stick
    And make thy weapon drop.

(*Brandishes his staff.*)

MIRANDA: (*Trying to hinder him.*)   Beseech you, father.
PROSPERO: Hence! Hang not on my garments.
MIRANDA: Sir, have pity!
    I'll be his surety.
PROSPERO: Silence! One word more
480   Shall make me chide thee, if not hate thee. What,
    An advocate for an imposter? Hush!
    Thou think'st there is no more such shapes as he,
    Having seen but him and Caliban. Foolish wench,

    To th' most of men this is a Caliban
    And they to him are angels. 485
MIRANDA: My affections
    Are then most humble; I have no ambition
    To see a goodlier man.
PROSPERO: (*To* FERDINAND.) Come on, obey.
    Thy nerves are in their infancy again
    And have no vigor in them.
FERDINAND: So they are.
    My spirits, as in a dream, are all bound up. 490
    My father's loss, the weakness which I feel,
    The wrack of all my friends, nor this man's threats
    To whom I am subdu'd, are but light to me,
    Might I put through my prison once a day
    Behold this maid. All corners else o' th' earth 495
    Let liberty make use of; space enough
    Have I in such a prison.
PROSPERO: (*Aside.*) It works. (*To* FERDINAND.) Come on.—
    Thou hast done well, fine Ariel! (*To* FERDINAND.) Follow
      me.
    (*To* ARIEL.) Hark what thou else shalt do me.
MIRANDA: (*To* FERDINAND.)   Be of comfort.
    My father's of a better nature, sir, 500
    Than he appears by speech. This is unwonted
    Which now came from him.
PROSPERO: (*To* ARIEL.)   Thou shalt be as free
    As mountain winds, but then exactly do
    All points of my command.
ARIEL: To th' syllable.
PROSPERO: (*To* FERDINAND.) Come, follow. (*To* MIRANDA.) 505
    Speak not for him.

(*Exeunt.*)

ACT TWO

SCENE I

Enter ALONSO, SEBASTIAN, ANTONIO, GONZALO, ADRIAN,
FRANCISCO, *and others.*

GONZALO: Beseech you, sir, be merry. You have cause,
    So have we all, of joy, for our escape
    Is much beyond our loss. Our hint of woe
    Is common; every day some sailor's wife,
    The masters of some merchant, and the merchant, 5
    Have just our theme of woe; but for the miracle,
    I mean our preservation, few in millions
    Can speak like us. Then wisely, good sir, weigh
    Our sorrow with our comfort.
ALONSO: Prithee, peace.
SEBASTIAN: (*To* ANTONIO.) He receives comfort like cold 10
    porridge.

---

455 **uneasy** difficult 455–456 **light . . . light** easy . . . cheap
458 **ow'st** ownest 469 **entertainment** treatment 472 **gentle** wellborn; **fearful** cowardly 473 **foot** subordinate (Miranda, the foot, presumes to instruct Prospero, the head) 475 **ward** defensive posture (in fencing)

484 **To** compared to 488 **nerves** sinews 499 **me** for me
II.i. Location: Another part of the island. 3 **hint of** occasion for 5 **masters . . . the merchant** officers of some merchant vessel and the merchant himself, the owner 11 **porridge** with a pun on *peace* and *pease*, a usual ingredient of porridge

ANTONIO: (*To* SEBASTIAN.) The visitor will not give him o'er so.

SEBASTIAN: Look, he's winding up the watch of his wit; by and by it will strike.

GONZALO: Sir—

SEBASTIAN: (*To* ANTONIO.) One. Tell.

GONZALO: When every grief is entertain'd that's offer'd, Comes to th' entertainer—

SEBASTIAN: A dollar.

GONZALO: Dolor comes to him, indeed. You have spoken truer than you purpos'd.

SEBASTIAN: You have taken it wiselier than I meant you should.

GONZALO: Therefore, my lord—

ANTONIO: Fie, what a spendthrift is he of his tongue!

ALONSO: I prithee, spare.

GONZALO: Well, I have done. But yet—

SEBASTIAN: He will be talking.

ANTONIO: Which, of he or Adrian, for a good wager, first begins to crow?

SEBASTIAN: The old cock.

ANTONIO: The cock'rel.

SEBASTIAN: Done. The wager?

ANTONIO: A laughter.

SEBASTIAN: A match!

ADRIAN: Though this island seem to be desert—

SEBASTIAN: Ha, ha, ha!

ANTONIO: So, you're paid.

ADRIAN: Uninhabitable and almost inaccessible—

SEBASTIAN: Yet—

ADRIAN: Yet—

ANTONIO: He could not miss 't.

ADRIAN: It must needs be of subtle, tender, and delicate temperance.

ANTONIO: Temperance was a delicate wench.

SEBASTIAN: Ay, and a subtle, as he most learnedly deliver'd.

ADRIAN: The air breathes upon us here most sweetly.

SEBASTIAN: As if it had lungs, and rotten ones.

ANTONIO: Or as 'twere perfum'd by a fen.

GONZALO: Here is everything advantageous to life.

ANTONIO: True, save means to live.

SEBASTIAN: Of that there's none, or little.

GONZALO: How lush and lusty the grass looks! How green!

ANTONIO: The ground indeed is tawny.

SEBASTIAN: With an eye of green in 't.

ANTONIO: He misses not much.

SEBASTIAN: No; he doth but mistake the truth totally.

GONZALO: But the rarity of it is—which is indeed almost beyond credit—

SEBASTIAN: As many vouch'd rarities are.

GONZALO: That our garments, being, as they were, drench'd in the sea, hold notwithstanding their freshness and glosses, being rather new-dyed than stain'd with salt water.

ANTONIO: If but one of his pockets could speak, would it not say he lies?

SEBASTIAN: Ay, or very falsely pocket up his report.

GONZALO: Methinks our garments are now as fresh as when we put them on first in Afric, at the marriage of the King's fair daughter Claribel to the King of Tunis.

SEBASTIAN: 'Twas a sweet marriage, and we prosper well in our return.

ADRIAN: Tunis was never grac'd before with such a paragon to their queen.

GONZALO: Not since widow Dido's time.

ANTONIO: Widow! A pox o' that! How came that widow in? Widow Dido!

SEBASTIAN: What if he had said "widower Aeneas" too? Good Lord, how you take it!

ADRIAN: "Widow Dido" said you? You make me study of that. She was of Carthage, not of Tunis.

GONZALO: This Tunis, sir, was Carthage.

ADRIAN: Carthage?

GONZALO: I assure you, Carthage.

ANTONIO: His word is more than the miraculous harp.

SEBASTIAN: He hath rais'd the wall and houses too.

ANTONIO: What impossible matter will he make easy next?

SEBASTIAN: I think he will carry this island home in his pocket and give it his son for an apple.

ANTONIO: And, sowing the kernels of it in the sea, bring forth more islands.

GONZALO: Ay.

---

12 **visitor** one taking nourishment and comfort to the sick, i.e., Gonzalo; **give him o'er** abandon him   17 **Tell** keep count   18–19 **When . . . entertainer** when every sorrow that presents itself is accepted without resistance, there comes to the recipient   20 **dollar** widely circulated coin, the German *Thaler* and the Spanish *piece of eight*. Sebastian puns on *entertainer* in the sense of *innkeeper*; to Gonzalo, *dollar* suggests *dolor*, grief.   29–30 **Which . . . crow** which of the two, Gonzalo or Adrian, do you bet will speak (crow) first   31 **old cock** i.e., Gonzalo   32 **cock'rel** i.e., Adrian   34 **laughter** (1) burst of laughter (2) sitting of eggs. When Adrian, the *cock'rel*, begins to speak two lines later, Sebastian loses the bet. Some editors alter the speech prefixes in lines 37–38 so that Antonio enjoys his laugh as the prize for winning, but possibly Sebastian pays for losing with a laugh   35 **A match** a bargain; agreed   42 **miss 't** (1) avoid saying "Yet" (2) miss the island   44 **temperance** climate   45 **Temperance** a girl's name; **delicate** here it means *given to pleasure, voluptuous;* in line 43, *pleasant*. Antonio is evidently suggesting that "tender, and delicate temperance" sounds like a Puritan phrase, which Antonio then mocks by applying the words to a woman rather than an island. He began this bawdy comparison with a double entendre on *inaccessible,* line 39   46 **subtle** here it means *tricky;* in line 43, *delicate;* **deliver'd** uttered. Sebastian joins in the Puritan baiting of Antonio with his use of the pious cant phrase "learnedly deliver'd"

---

53 **lusty** healthy   54 **tawny** dull brown, yellowish   55 **eye** tinge, or spot (perhaps with reference to Gonzalo's eye or judgment)   60 **vouch'd** certified   64 **pockets** i.e., because they are muddy   66 **pocket up** receive unprotestingly, fail to respond to a challenge   72 **to** for   74 **widow Dido** Queen of Carthage, deserted by Aeneas. She was in fact a widow when Aeneas, a widower, met her, but Antonio may be amused at the term "widow" to describe a woman deserted by her lover   84 **miraculous harp** alludes to Amphion's harp with which he raised the walls of Thebes; Gonzalo has exceeded that deed by creating a modern Carthage—walls *and houses*—mistakenly on the site of Tunis   91 **Ay** Gonzalo may be reasserting his point about Carthage, or he may be responding ironically to Antonio who in turn answers sarcastically

ANTONIO: Why, in good time.

GONZALO: (*To* ALONSO.) Sir, we were talking that our garments seem now as fresh as when we were at Tunis at the
95 marriage of your daughter, who is now queen.

ANTONIO: And the rarest that e'er came there.

SEBASTIAN: Bate, I beseech you, widow Dido.

ANTONIO: O, widow Dido? Ay, widow Dido.

GONZALO: Is not, sir, my doublet as fresh as the first day I
100 wore it? I mean, in a sort.

ANTONIO: That "sort" was well fish'd for.

GONZALO: When I wore it at your daughter's marriage?

ALONSO: You cram these words into mine ears against
The stomach of my sense. Would I had never
105 Married my daughter there! For, coming thence,
My son is lost and, in my rate, she too,
Who is so far from Italy removed
I ne'er again shall see her. O thou mine heir
Of Naples and of Milan, what strange fish
110 Hath made his meal on thee?

FRANCISCO: Sir, he may live.
I saw him beat the surges under him,
And ride upon their backs. He trod the water,
Whose enmity he flung aside, and breasted
The surge most swoll'n that met him. His bold head
115 'Bove the contentious waves he kept, and oared
Himself with his good arms in lusty stroke
To th' shore, that o'er his wave-worn basis bowed,
As stooping to relieve him. I not doubt
He came alive to land.

ALONSO: No, no, he's gone.

120 SEBASTIAN: Sir, you may thank yourself for this great loss,
That would not bless our Europe with your daughter,
But rather loose her to an African,
Where she at least is banish'd from your eye,
Who hath cause to wet the grief on 't.

ALONSO: Prithee, peace.

125 SEBASTIAN: You were kneel'd to and importun'd otherwise
By all of us, and the fair soul herself
Weigh'd between loathness and obedience, at
Which end o' th' beam should bow. We have lost your son,
I fear, for ever. Milan and Naples have
130 Moe widows in them of their business' making
Than we bring men to comfort them.
The fault's your own.

ALONSO: So is the dear'st o' th' loss.

GONZALO: My lord Sebastian,
The truth you speak doth lack some gentleness,

And time to speak it in. You rub the sore, 135
When you should bring the plaster.

SEBASTIAN: Very well.

ANTONIO: And most chirurgeonly.

GONZALO: It is foul weather in us all, good sir,
When you are cloudy.

SEBASTIAN: (*To* ANTONIO.) Foul weather?

ANTONIO: (*To* SEBASTIAN.) Very foul.

GONZALO: Had I plantation of this isle, my lord— 140

ANTONIO: He'd sow 't with nettle-seed.

SEBASTIAN: Or docks, or mallows.

GONZALO: And were the king on 't, what would I do?

SEBASTIAN: Scape being drunk for want of wine.

GONZALO: I' th' commonwealth I would by contraries
Execute all things; for no kind of traffic 145
Would I admit; no name of magistrate;
Letters should not be known; riches, poverty,
And use of service, none; contract, succession,
Bourn, bound of land, tilth, vineyard, none;
No use of metal, corn, or wine, or oil; 150
No occupation; all men idle, all,
And women too, but innocent and pure;
No sovereignty—

SEBASTIAN: Yet he would be king on 't.

ANTONIO: The latter end of his commonwealth forgets the
beginning.

GONZALO: All things in common nature should produce 155
Without sweat or endeavor. Treason, felony,
Sword, pike, knife, gun, or need of any engine,
Would I not have; but nature should bring forth,
Of it own kind, all foison, all abundance,
To feed my innocent people. 160

SEBASTIAN: No marrying 'mong his subjects?

ANTONIO: None, man; all idle—whores and knaves.

GONZALO: I would with such perfection govern, sir,
T' excel the golden age.

SEBASTIAN: Save his Majesty!

ANTONIO: Long live Gonzalo! 165

GONZALO: And—do you mark me, sir?

ALONSO: Prithee, no more. Thou dost talk nothing to me.

GONZALO: I do well believe your Highness, and did it to minister occasion to these gentlemen, who are of such sensible
and nimble lungs that they always use to laugh at nothing.

ANTONIO: 'Twas you we laugh'd at. 170

GONZALO: Who in this kind of merry fooling am nothing to
you; so you may continue and laugh at nothing still.

---

92 **in good time** an expression of ironical acquiescence or amazement; i.e., *sure, right away* 96 **rarest** most remarkable, beautiful 97 **Bate** abate, except, leave out (i.e., don't forget Dido; or, let's have no more talk of Dido) 100 **in a sort** in a way 104 **stomach** appetite 105 **Married** given in marriage 106 **rate** estimation, consideration 116 **lusty** vigorous 117 **that . . . bowed** that hung out over its wave-worn foot 118 **As** as if 124 **Who** which, i.e., the eye 126–128 **the fair . . . bow** i.e., Claribel herself was poised uncertain between unwillingness to marry and obedience to her father as to which end of the scale should sink, which should prevail 130 **Moe** more 133 **dear'st** heaviest, most costly

135 **time** appropriate time 137 **chirurgeonly** like a skilled surgeon. Antonio mocks Gonzalo's medical analogy of a *plaster* applied curatively to a wound 140 **plantation** colonization (with subsequent wordplay on the literal meaning) 141 **docks, mallows** various weeds 144 **by contraries** by what is directly opposite to usual custom 145 **traffic** trade 147 **Letters** learning 148 **use of service** custom of employing servants, **succession** holding of property by right of inheritance 149 **Bourn** boundaries; bound of land landmarks; **tilth** tillage of soil 150 **corn** grain 157 **engine** instrument of warfare 159 **it** its; **foison** plenty 164 **Save** God save 167–168 **minister occasion** furnish opportunity 168 **sensible** sensitive

ANTONIO: What a blow was there given!

SEBASTIAN: An it had not fall'n flat-long.

175 GONZALO: You are gentlemen of brave mettle; you would lift the moon out of her sphere, if she would continue in it five weeks without changing.

(Enter ARIEL *[invisible] playing solemn music.)*

SEBASTIAN: We would so, and then go a-batfowling.

ANTONIO: Nay, good my lord, be not angry.

180 GONZALO: No, I warrant, you, I will not adventure my discretion so weakly. Will you laugh me asleep? For I am very heavy.

ANTONIO: Go sleep, and hear us.

(All sleep except ALONSO, SEBASTIAN, *and* ANTONIO.*)*

ALONSO: What, all so soon asleep? I wish mine eyes
185 Would, with themselves, shut up my thoughts. I find
    They are inclin'd to do so.

SEBASTIAN: Please you, sir,
    Do not omit the heavy offer of it.
    It seldom visits sorrow; when it doth,
    It is a comforter.

ANTONIO: We two, my lord,
190 Will guard your person while you take your rest,
    And watch your safety.

ALONSO: Thank you. Wondrous heavy.

*(*ALONSO *sleeps. Exit* ARIEL.*)*

SEBASTIAN: What a strange drowsiness possesses them!

ANTONIO: It is the quality o' th' climate.

SEBASTIAN: Why
    Doth it not then our eyelids sink? I find not
195 Myself dispos'd to sleep.

ANTONIO: Nor I; my spirits are nimble.
    They fell together all, as by consent;
    They dropp'd, as by a thunder-stroke. What might,
    Worthy Sebastian? O, what might—? No more—
    And yet methinks I see it in thy face,
200 What thou shouldst be. Th' occasion speaks thee, and
    My strong imagination sees a crown
    Dropping upon thy head.

SEBASTIAN: What, art thou waking?

ANTONIO: Do you not hear me speak?

SEBASTIAN: I do; and surely
    It is a sleepy language and thou speak'st
205 Out of thy sleep. What is it thou didst say?

This is a strange repose, to be asleep
With eyes wide open—standing, speaking, moving—
And yet so fast asleep.

ANTONIO: Noble Sebastian,
    Thou let'st thy fortune sleep—die, rather; wink'st
    Whiles thou art waking.   210

SEBASTIAN: Thou dost snore distinctly;
    There's meaning in thy snores.

ANTONIO: I am more serious than my custom. You
    Must be so too, if heed me; which to do
    Trebles thee o'er.

SEBASTIAN: Well, I am standing water.

ANTONIO: I'll teach you how to flow.   215

SEBASTIAN: Do so. To ebb
    Hereditary sloth instructs me.

ANTONIO: O,
    If you but knew how you the purpose cherish
    Whiles thus you mock it! How, in stripping it,
    You more invest it! Ebbing men, indeed,
    Most often do so near the bottom run   220
    By their own fear or sloth.

SEBASTIAN: Prithee say on.
    The setting of thine eye and cheek proclaim
    A matter from thee, and a birth indeed
    Which throes thee much to yield.

ANTONIO: Thus, sir:
    Although this lord of weak remembrance, this,   225
    Who shall be of as little memory
    When he is earth'd, hath here almost persuaded—
    For he's a spirit of persuasion, only
    Professes to persuade—the King his son's alive,
    'Tis as impossible that he's undrown'd   230
    As he that sleeps here swims.

SEBASTIAN: I have no hope
    That he's undrown'd.

ANTONIO: O, out of that "no hope"
    What great hope have you! No hope that way is
    Another way so high a hope that even
    Ambition cannot pierce a wink beyond,   235

---

174 **An** if; **flat-long** with the flat of the sword, i.e., ineffectually. (Cf. *fallen flat.*) 178 **a-batfowling** hunting birds at night with lantern and stick; also, gulling a simpleton. Gonzalo is the simpleton, or fowl, and Sebastian will use the moon as his lantern 180–81 **adventure . . . weakly** risk my reputation for discretion for so trivial a cause (by getting angry at these sarcastic fellows) 182 **heavy** sleep 183 **Go . . . us** let our laughing send you to sleep, or, go to sleep and hear us laugh at you 187 **omit** neglect; **heavy** drowsy 200 **speaks** calls upon; or, pronounces, proclaims. Sebastian as usurper of Alonso's crown

209 **wink'st** shut your eyes 214 **Trebles thee o'er** makes you three times as great and rich; **standing water** water which neither ebbs nor flows, at a standstill, indecisive 216 **Hereditary sloth** natural laziness 217 **purpose** i.e., of being king; **cherish** i.e., make dear, enrich 219 **invest** clothe. Antonio's paradox is that by skeptically stripping away illusions Sebastian can see the essence of a situation and the opportunity it presents, or that by disclaiming and deriding his purpose Sebastian shows how he values it 220 **the bottom** i.e., on which unadventurous men may go aground and miss the tide of fortune 222 **setting** set expression (of earnestness) 223 **matter** matter of importance 224 **throes** causes pain, as in giving birth 225 **this lord** i.e., Gonzalo; **remembrance** (1) power of remembering (2) being remembered after his death 227 **earth'd** buried 228–229 **only . . . persuade** i.e., whose whole function (as a privy councilor) is to persuade 233 **that way** i.e., in regard to Ferdinand's being saved 235–236 **Ambition . . . there** ambition itself cannot see any further than that hope (of the crown), but is unsure of itself in seeing even so far, is dazzled by daring to think so high

But doubt discovery there. Will you grant with me
That Ferdinand is drown'd?
SEBASTIAN: He's gone.
ANTONIO: Then, tell me,
Who's the next heir of Naples?
SEBASTIAN: Claribel.
ANTONIO: She that is Queen of Tunis; she that dwells
240   Ten leagues beyond man's life; she that from Naples
Can have no note, unless the sun were post—
The man i' th' moon's too slow—till new-born chins
Be rough and razorable; she that from whom
We all were sea-swallow'd, though some cast again,
245   And by that destiny to perform an act
Whereof what's past is prologue, what to come
In yours and my discharge.
SEBASTIAN: What stuff is this? How say you?
'Tis true, my brother's daughter's Queen of Tunis;
250   So is she heir of Naples; 'twixt which regions
There is some space.
ANTONIO: A space whose ev'ry cubit
Seems to cry out, "How shall that Claribel
Measure us back to Naples? Keep in Tunis,
And let Sebastian wake." Say this were death
255   That now hath seiz'd them; why, they were no worse
Than now they are. There be that can rule Naples
As well as he that sleeps; lords that can prate
As amply and unnecessarily
As this Gonzalo; I myself could make
260   A chough of as deep chat. O, that you bore
The mind that I do! What a sleep were this
For your advancement! Do you understand me?
SEBASTIAN: Methinks I do.
ANTONIO: And how does your content
Tender your own good fortune?
SEBASTIAN: I remember
265   You did supplant your brother Prospero.
ANTONIO: True.
And look how well my garments sit upon me,
Much feater than before. My brother's servants
Were then my fellows; now they are my men.
SEBASTIAN: But, for your conscience?
270   ANTONIO: Ay, sir, where lies that? If 'twere a kibe,
'Twould put me to my slipper; but I feel not
This deity in my bosom. Twenty consciences,
That stand 'twixt me and Milan, candied be they
And melt ere they molest! Here lies your brother,
275   No better than the earth he lies upon,

---

240 **Ten . . . life** i.e., it would take more than a lifetime to get
there   241 **note** news, intimation; **post** messenger   243 **from**
on our voyage from   244 **cast** were disgorged (with a pun on
casting of parts for a play)   247 **discharge** performance   253
Measure us i.e., traverse the cubits, find her way   254 **wake**
i.e., to his good fortune   259–260 **I . . . chat** I could teach a
jackdaw to talk as wisely, or, be such a garrulous talker myself
263 **content** desire, inclination   264 **Tender** regard, look after
267 **feater** more becomingly, fittingly   270 **kibe** chilblain, sore
on the heel   271 **put me to** oblige me to wear   273 **Milan**
the dukedom of Milan; **candied** frozen, congealed in crystalline
form

If he were that which now he's like—that's dead,
Whom I, with this obedient steel, three inches of it,
Can lay to bed forever; whiles you, doing thus,
To the perpetual wink for aye might put
This ancient morsel, this Sir Prudence, who   280
Should not upbraid our course. For all the rest,
They'll take suggestion as a cat laps milk;
They'll tell the clock to any business that
We say befits the hour.
SEBASTIAN: Thy case, dear friend,
Shall be my precedent. As thou got'st Milan,   285
I'll come by Naples. Draw thy sword. One stroke
Shall free thee from the tribute which thou payest,
And I the king shall love thee.
ANTONIO: Draw together;
And when I rear my hand, do you the like,
To fall it on Gonzalo.   290

(*They draw.*)

SEBASTIAN: O, but one word.

(*They talk apart.*)

(*Enter* ARIEL [*invisible*], *with music and song.*)

ARIEL: My master through his art foresees the danger
That you, his friend, are in, and sends me forth—
For else his project dies—to keep them living.

(*Sings in* GONZALO's *ear.*)

While you here do snoring lie,
Open-ey'd conspiracy   295
His time doth take.
If of life you keep a care,
Shake off slumber, and beware.
Awake, awake!

ANTONIO: Then let us both be sudden.   300
GONZALO: (*Waking.*) Now, good angels preserve the King!

(*The others wake.*)

ALONSO: Why, how now, ho, awake? Why are you drawn?
Wherefore this ghastly looking?
GONZALO: What's the matter?
SEBASTIAN: Whiles we stood here securing your repose,
Even now, we heard a hollow burst of bellowing   305
Like bulls, or rather lions. Did 't not wake you?
It struck mine ear most terribly.
ALONSO: I heard nothing.
ANTONIO: O, 'twas a din to fright a monster's ear,
To make an earthquake! Sure it was the roar
Of a whole herd of lions.   310
ALONSO: Heard you this, Gonzalo?
GONZALO: Upon mine honor, sir, I heard a humming,
And that a strange one too, which did awake me.

---

279 **wink** sleep, closing of eyes   283 **tell the clock** i.e., answer
appropriately, chime   287 **tribute** (See 1.2.113–24)   296 **time**
opportunity   304 **securing** standing guard over

315 I shak'd you, sir, and cried. As mine eyes open'd,
     I saw their weapons drawn. There was a noise,
     That's verily. 'Tis best we stand upon our guard,
     Or that we quit this place. Let's draw our weapons.

ALONSO: Lead off this ground, and let's make further search
     For my poor son.

320 GONZALO: Heavens keep him from these beasts!
     For he is, sure, i' th' island.

ALONSO: Lead away.

ARIEL: (*Aside.*) Prospero my lord shall know what I have done.
     So, King, go safely on to seek thy son.

(*Exeunt [severally].*)

SCENE II

Enter CALIBAN *with a burden of wood. A noise of thunder heard.*

CALIBAN: All the infections that the sun sucks up
     From bogs, fens, flats, on Prosper fall and make him
     By inch-meal a disease! His spirits hear me,
     And yet I needs must curse. But they'll nor pinch,
5   Fright me with urchin-shows, pitch me i' th' mire,
     Nor lead me, like a firebrand, in the dark
     Out of my way, unless he bid 'em; but
     For every trifle are they set upon me;
     Sometime like apes that mow and chatter at me
10   And after bite me, then like hedgehogs which
     Lie tumbling in my barefoot way and mount
     Their pricks at my footfall; sometime am I
     All wound with adders who with cloven tongues
     Do hiss me into madness.

(*Enter* TRINCULO.)

                              Lo, now, lo!
15   Here comes a spirit of his, and to torment me
     For bringing wood in slowly. I'll fall flat;
     Perchance he will not mind me.

(*Lies down.*)

TRINCULO: Here's neither bush nor shrub, to bear off any
     weather at all, and another storm brewing; I hear it sing i'
20   th' wind. Yond same black cloud, yond huge one, looks like
     a foul bombard that would shed his liquor. If it should
     thunder as it did before, I know not where to hide my
     head. Yond same cloud cannot choose but fall by pailfuls.
     (*Sees* CALIBAN.) What have we here? A man or a fish? Dead
25   or alive? A fish, he smells like a fish; a very ancient and fish-
     like smell; a kind of not of the newest Poor-John. A strange
     fish! Were I in England now, as once I was, and had but this
     fish painted, not a holiday fool there but would give a piece

of silver. There would this monster make a man; any strange
beast there makes a man. When they will not give a doit to 30
relieve a lame beggar, they will lay out ten to see a dead Indian. Legg'd like a man! And his fins like arms! Warm, o' my
troth! I do now let loose my opinion, hold it no longer: this
is no fish, but an islander, that hath lately suffer'd by a thunderbolt. (*Thunder.*) Alas, the storm is come again! My best 35
way is to creep under his gaberdine; there is no other shelter hereabout. Misery acquaints a man with strange bedfellows. I will here shroud till the dregs of the storm be past.

(*Creeps under* CALIBAN'*s garment.*)

(*Enter* STEPHANO, *singing,* [*a bottle in his hand*].)

STEPHANO: "I shall no more to sea, to sea,   40
               Here shall I die ashore—"

This is a very scurvy tune to sing at a man's funeral.
Well, here's my comfort.

(*Drinks.*)

(*Sings.*)

     "The master, the swabber, the boatswain and I,
       The gunner and his mate
     Lov'd Mall, Meg, and Marian, and Margery,   45
       But none of us car'd for Kate;
       For she had a tongue with a tang,
       Would cry to a sailor, 'Go hang!'
     She lov'd not the savor of tar nor of pitch,
     Yet a tailor might scratch her where'er she did itch. 50
       Then to sea, boys, and let her go hang!"

This is a scurvy tune too; but here's my comfort.

(*Drinks.*)

CALIBAN: Do not torment me! Oh!

STEPHANO: What's the matter? Have we devils here? Do you
     put tricks upon 's with savages and men of Ind, ha? I have 55
     not scap'd drowning to be afeard now of your four legs;
     for it hath been said, "As proper a man as ever went on
     four legs cannot make him give ground"; and it shall be
     said so again while Stephano breathes at' nostrils.

CALIBAN: This spirit torments me! Oh!   60

STEPHANO: This is some monster of the isle with four legs,
     who hath got, as I take it, an ague. Where the devil should
     he learn our language? I will give him some relief, if it be
     but for that. If I can recover him and keep him tame and
     get to Naples with him, he's a present for any emperor 65
     that ever trod on neat's-leather.

CALIBAN: Do not torment me, prithee. I'll bring my wood
     home faster.

II.ii. Location: Another part of the island.   3 **By inch-
meal** inch by inch   4 **nor** neither   5 **urchin-shows** apparitions shaped like hedgehogs   6 **like a firebrand** in the guise of
a will-o'-the-wisp   9 **mow** make faces   17 **mind** notice   18
bear off keep off   21 **foul bombard** dirty leathern bottle; his
its   26 **Poor-John** salted hake, type of poor fare   28 **painted**
i.e., painted on a sign set up outside a booth or tent at a fair

29 **make a man** make one's fortune   30 **doit** small coin   36
gaberdine cloak, loose upper garment   38 **shroud** take shelter;
dregs i.e., last remains   55 **Ind** India   57 **proper** handsome;
four legs the conventional phrase would supply *two legs*   59 **at'**
at the   64 **for that** i.e., for knowing our language; recover restore   66 **neat's-leather** cowhide

STEPHANO: He's in his fit now and does not talk after the wis-
70   est. He shall taste of my bottle; if he have never drunk
wine afore, it will go near to remove his fit. If I can recover
him and keep him tame, I will not take too much for him;
he shall pay for him that hath him, and that soundly.

CALIBAN: Thou dost me yet but little hurt;
75   Thou wilt anon, I know it by thy trembling.
Now Prosper works upon thee.

STEPHANO: Come on your ways; open your mouth; here is
that which will give language to you, cat. Open your
mouth; this will shake your shaking, I can tell you, and
80   that soundly. (*Gives* CALIBAN *drink*.) You cannot tell who's
your friend. Open your chaps again.

TRINCULO: I should know that voice. It should be—but he is
drown'd; and these are devils. O defend me!

STEPHANO: Four legs and two voices; a most delicate mon-
85   ster! His forward voice now is to speak well of his friend;
his backward voice is to utter foul speeches and to detract.
If all the wine in my bottle will recover him, I will help
his ague. Come. (*Gives drink*.) Amen! I will pour some in
thy other mouth.

90   TRINCULO: Stephano!

STEPHANO: Doth thy other mouth call me? Mercy, mercy!
This is a devil, and no monster. I will leave him; I have no
long spoon.

TRINCULO: Stephano! If thou beest Stephano, touch me and
95   speak to me; for I am Trinculo—be not afeard—thy good
friend Trinculo.

STEPHANO: If thou beest Trinculo, come forth. I'll pull thee by
the lesser legs. If any be Trinculo's legs, these are they. (*Pulls
him out*.) Thou art very Trinculo indeed! How cam'st thou
100   to be the siege of this moon-calf? Can he vent Trinculos?

TRINCULO: I took him to be kill'd with a thunder-stroke. But
art thou not drown'd, Stephano? I hope now thou art not
drown'd. Is the storm overblown? I hid me under the dead
moon-calf's gaberdine for fear of the storm. And art thou
105   living, Stephano? O Stephano, two Neapolitans scap'd!

STEPHANO: Prithee, do not turn me about; my stomach is not
constant.

CALIBAN: These be fine things, an if they be not sprites.
That's a brave god and bears celestial liquor.
110   I will kneel to him.

STEPHANO: How didst thou scape? How cam'st thou hither?
Swear by this bottle how thou cam'st hither. I escap'd
upon a butt of sack which the sailors heav'd o'erboard—
by this bottle, which I made of the bark of a tree with
115   mine own hands since I was cast ashore.

CALIBAN: (*Kneeling*.) I'll swear upon that bottle to be thy true
subject, for the liquor is not earthly.

---

72 **I will . . . much** i.e., no sum can be too much   73 **hath**
possesses, receives   78 **cat . . . mouth** allusion to the proverb,
"Good liquor will make a cat speak"   81 **chaps** jaws   92–93
long spoon allusion to the proverb, "He that sups with the devil
has need of a long spoon"   100 **siege** excrement; **moon-calf**
monster, abortion. Supposed to be caused by the influence of the
moon; **vent** emit   106–107 not constant unsteady   108 **an if**
if   109 **brave** fine, magnificent   113 **butt of sack** barrel of
Canary wine

STEPHANO: Here; swear then how thou escap'dst.

TRINCULO: Swum ashore, man, like a duck. I can swim like a
duck, I'll be sworn.   120

STEPHANO: Here, kiss the book. Though thou canst swim like
a duck, thou art made like a goose.

(*Gives drink*.)

TRINCULO: O Stephano, hast any more of this?

STEPHANO: The whole butt, man. My cellar is in a rock by
the sea-side where my wine is hid. How now, moon-calf?   125
How does thine ague?

CALIBAN: Hast thou not dropp'd from heaven?

STEPHANO: Out o' th' moon, I do assure thee. I was the man
i' th' moon when time was.

CALIBAN: I have seen thee in her and I do adore thee.   130
My mistress show'd me thee and thy dog and thy bush.

STEPHANO: Come, swear to that; kiss the book. I will furnish
it anon with new contents. Swear.

(*Gives drink*.)

TRINCULO: By this good light, this is a very shallow monster!
I afeard of him? A very weak monster! The man i' th'   135
moon? A most poor credulous monster! Well drawn, monster, in good sooth!

CALIBAN: I'll show thee every fertile inch o' th' island;
And I will kiss thy foot. I prithee, by my god.

TRINCULO: By this light, a most perfidious and drunken   140
monster! When's god's asleep, he'll rob his bottle.

CALIBAN: I'll kiss thy foot. I'll swear myself thy subject.

STEPHANO: Come on then; down, and swear.

(CALIBAN *swears*.)

TRINCULO: I shall laugh myself to death at this puppy-headed
monster. A most scurvy monster! I could find in my heart   145
to beat him—

STEPHANO: Come, kiss.

TRINCULO: But that the poor monster's in drink. An abominable monster!

CALIBAN: I'll show thee the best springs; I'll pluck thee berries;   150
I'll fish for thee and get thee wood enough.
A plague upon the tyrant that I serve!
I'll bear him no more sticks, but follow thee,
Thou wondrous man.

TRINCULO: A most ridiculous monster, to make a wonder of   155
a poor drunkard!

CALIBAN: I prithee, let me bring thee where crabs grow;
And I with my long nails will dig thee pig-nuts,
Show thee a jay's nest, and instruct thee how
To snare the nimble marmoset. I'll bring thee   160

---

121 **book** i.e., bottle   129 **when time was** once upon a time
131 **dog . . . bush** the man in the moon was popularly imagined to have with him a dog and a bush of thorn   134 **By . . .
light** by God's light, by this good light from heaven   136 **Well
drawn** well pulled (on the bottle)   157 **crabs** crab apples   158
pig-nuts peanuts   160 **marmoset** small monkey

To clust'ring filberts, and sometimes I'll get thee
Young scamels from the rock. Wilt thou go with me?
STEPHANO: I prithee now, lead the way without any more
talking. Trinculo, the King and all our company else being
165   drown'd, we will inherit here. Here! Bear my bottle. Fellow Trinculo, we'll fill him by and by again.
CALIBAN: (*Sings drunkenly.*)

Farewell, master; farewell, farewell!

TRINCULO: A howling monster; a drunken monster!
CALIBAN: No more dams I'll make for fish,
170   Nor fetch in firing
          At requiring,
          Nor scrape trenchering, nor wash dish.
            'Ban, 'Ban, Ca-Caliban
          Has a new master, get a new man.
175   Freedom, high-day! High-day, freedom!
          Freedom, high-day, freedom!

STEPHANO: O brave monster! Lead the way.

(*Exeunt.*)

ACT THREE

SCENE I

Enter FERDINAND, *bearing a log.*

FERDINAND: There be some sports are painful, and their labor
Delight in them sets off; some kinds of baseness
Are nobly undergone; and most poor matters
Point to rich ends. This my mean task
5   Would be as heavy to me as odious, but
The mistress which I serve quickens what's dead
And makes my labors pleasures. O, she is
Ten times more gentle than her father's crabbed,
And he's compos'd of harshness. I must remove
10   Some thousands of these logs and pile them up,
Upon a sore injunction. My sweet mistress
Weeps when she sees me work, and says such baseness
Had never like executor. I forget;
But these sweet thoughts do even refresh my labors,
15   Most busy lest, when I do it.

(*Enter* MIRANDA; *and* PROSPERO [*at a distance, unseen*].)

MIRANDA: Alas, now, pray you,
Work not so hard. I would the lightning had
Burnt up those logs that you are enjoin'd to pile!
Pray, set it down and rest you. When this burns,

---

162 **scamels** possibly "seamews," mentioned in Strachey's letter, or
shellfish; or perhaps from *squamelle,* furnished with little scales.
Contemporary French and Italian travel accounts report that the
natives of Patagonia in South America ate small fish described as
fort scameux and *squame*   165 **inherit** take possession   172
trenchering trenchers, wooden plates   175 **high-day** holiday (?)

III.i. Location: Before Prospero's cell.   2 **sets off** makes seem
greater by contrast   6 **quickens** gives life to   11 **sore injunction**
severe command   15 **Most . . . it** i.e., least troubled by my labor
when I think of her (?) The line may be in need of emendation

'Twill weep for having wearied you. My father
Is hard at study; pray now, rest yourself.   20
He's safe for these three hours.
FERDINAND: O most dear mistress,
The sun will set before I shall discharge
What I must strive to do.
MIRANDA: If you'll sit down,
I'll bear your logs the while. Pray give me that.
I'll carry it to the pile.   25
FERDINAND: No, precious creature,
I had rather crack my sinews, break my back,
Than you should such dishonor undergo
While I sit lazy by.
MIRANDA: It would become me
As well as it does you; and I should do it
With much more ease, for my good will is to it,   30
And yours it is against.
PROSPERO: (*Aside.*)   Poor worm, thou art infected!
This visitation shows it.
MIRANDA: You look wearily.
FERDINAND: No, noble mistress, 'tis fresh morning with me
When you are by at night. I do beseech you—
Chiefly that I might set it in my prayers—   35
What is your name?
MIRANDA: Miranda.—O my father,
I have broke your hest to say so.
FERDINAND: Admir'd Miranda!
Indeed the top of admiration! Worth
What's dearest to the world! Full many a lady
I have ey'd with best regard, and many a time   40
Th' harmony of their tongues hath into bondage
Brought my too diligent ear. For several virtues
Have I lik'd several women, never any
With so full soul but some defect in her
Did quarrel with the noblest grace she ow'd   45
And put it to the foil. But you, O you,
So perfect and so peerless, are created
Of every creature's best!
MIRANDA: I do not know
One of my sex; no woman's face remember,
Save, from my glass, mine own. Nor have I seen   50
More that I may call men than you, good friend,
And my dear father. How features are abroad,
I am skilless of; but, by my modesty,
The jewel in my dower, I would not wish
Any companion in the world but you,   55
Nor can imagination form a shape,
Besides yourself, to like of. But I prattle
Something too wildly, and my father's precepts
I therein do forget.
FERDINAND: I am in my condition
A prince, Miranda; I do think, a king—   60
I would, not so!—and would no more endure
This wooden slavery than to suffer
The flesh-fly blow my mouth. Hear my soul speak:

---

32 **visitation** (1) visit (2) visitation of the plague, i.e., infection
of love   37 **hest** command   45 **ow'd** owned   46 **put . . . foil**
(1) overthrew it (as in wrestling) (2) served as a "foil" or contrast
to set it off   53 **skilless** ignorant   63 **blow** befoul with fly-eggs

The very instant that I saw you, did
65 My heart fly to your service; there resides,
To make me slave to it; and for your sake
Am I this patient log-man.

MIRANDA: Do you love me?

FERDINAND: O heaven, O earth, bear witness to this sound,
And crown what I profess with kind event
70 If I speak true! If hollowly, invert
What best is boded me to mischief! I
Beyond all limit of what else i' th' world
Do love, prize, honor you.

MIRANDA: (*Weeping.*)   I am a fool
To weep at what I am glad of.

PROSPERO: (*Aside.*)   Fair encounter
75 Of two most rare affections! Heavens rain grace
On that which breeds between 'em!

FERDINAND: Wherefore weep you?

MIRANDA: At mine unworthiness, that dare offer
What I desire to give, and much less take
What I shall die to want. But this is trifling,
80 And all the more it seeks to hide itself
The bigger bulk it shows. Hence, bashful cunning,
And prompt me, plain and holy innocence!
I am your wife, if you will marry me;
If not, I'll die your maid. To be your fellow
85 You may deny me, but I'll be your servant,
Whether you will or no.

FERDINAND: My mistress, dearest,
And I thus humble ever.

MIRANDA: My husband, then?

FERDINAND: Ay, with a heart as willing
As bondage e'er of freedom. Here's my hand.
90 MIRANDA: And mine, with my heart in 't. And now farewell
Till half an hour hence.

FERDINAND: A thousand thousand!

(*Exeunt* [FERDINAND *and* MIRANDA *severally*].)

PROSPERO: So glad of this as they I cannot be,
Who are surpris'd with all; but my rejoicing
At nothing can be more. I'll to my book,
95 For yet ere supper-time must I perform
Much business appertaining.

SCENE II

Enter CALIBAN, STEPHANO, *and* TRINCULO.

STEPHANO: Tell not me. When the butt is out, we will drink water, not a drop before. Therefore bear up, and board 'em. Servant-monster, drink to me.

TRINCULO: Servant-monster? The folly of this island! They
5   say there's but five upon this isle; we are three of them. If th' other two be brain'd like us, the state totters.

STEPHANO: Drink, servant-monster, when I bid thee. Thy eyes are almost set in thy head.

(*Gives drink.*)

TRINCULO: Where should they be set else? He were a brave
monster indeed if they were set in his tail.   10

STEPHANO: My man-monster hath drown'd his tongue in sack. For my part, the sea cannot drown me; I swam, ere I could recover the shore, five and thirty leagues off and on. By this light, thou shalt be my lieutenant, monster, or my standard.

TRINCULO: Your lieutenant, if you list; he's no standard.   15

STEPHANO: We'll not run, Monsieur Monster.

TRINCULO: Nor go neither, but you'll lie like dogs and yet say nothing neither.

STEPHANO: Moon-calf, speak once in thy life, if thou beest a
good moon-calf.   20

CALIBAN: How does thy honor? Let me lick thy shoe. I'll not serve him; he is not valiant.

TRINCULO: Thou liest, most ignorant monster, I am in case to justle a constable. Why, thou debosh'd fish thou, was there
ever man a coward that hath drunk so much sack as I to-   25
day? Wilt thou tell a monstrous lie, being but half a fish and half a monster?

CALIBAN: Lo, how he mocks me! Wilt thou let him, my lord?

TRINCULO: "Lord," quoth he? That a monster should be such
a natural!   30

CALIBAN: Lo, lo, again! Bite him to death, I prithee.

STEPHANO: Trinculo, keep a good tongue in your head. If you prove a mutineer—the next tree! The poor monster's my subject and he shall not suffer indignity.

CALIBAN: I thank my noble lord. Wilt thou be pleas'd   35
To hearken once again to the suit I made to thee?

STEPHANO: Marry, will I. Kneel and repeat it; I will stand, and so shall Trinculo.

(CALIBAN *kneels*.)

(*Enter* ARIEL, *invisible*.)

CALIBAN: As I told thee before, I am subject to a tyrant,
A sorcerer, that by his cunning hath   40
Cheated me of the island.

ARIEL: Thou liest.

CALIBAN: Thou liest, thou jesting monkey, thou!
I would my valiant master would destroy thee.
I do not lie.

STEPHANO: Trinculo, if you trouble him any more in 's tale,   45
by this hand, I will supplant some of your teeth.

---

69 **kind event** favorable outcome   70 **hollowly** insincerely, falsely   71 **boded** destined for   79 **want** lack   84 **fellow** mate, equal

III.ii. Location: Another part of the island.   1 **out** empty   2 **bear . . . 'em** Stephano uses the terminology of maneuvering up to and boarding a vessel under attack as a way of urging an assault on the liquor supply

8 **set** fixed in a drunken stare; or sunk, like the sun   9 **brave** fine, splendid   13 **recover** arrive at   14 **standard** standard-bearer, ancient, i.e., ensign (as distinguished from *lieutenant,* line 15)   15 **list** prefer; **no standard** i.e., not able to stand up   16 **run** (1) retreat (2) urinate (taking Trinculo's *standard* line 15, in the old sense of *conduit*)   17 **go** walk; **lie** (1) tell lies (2) lie prostrate (3) excret   23–24 **case . . . constable** i.e., in fit condition, made valiant by drink, to taunt or challenge the police; **debosh'd** i.e., debauched   30 **natural** (1) idiot (2) natural as opposed to unnatural, monster-like   33 **the next tree** i.e., you'll hang   37 **Marry** i.e., indeed (originally an oath by the Virgin Mary)

TRINCULO: Why, I said nothing.

STEPHANO: Mum, then, and no more.—Proceed.

CALIBAN: I say, by sorcery he got this isle;
50   From me he got it. If thy greatness will
      Revenge it on him—for I know thou dar'st,
      But this thing dare not—

STEPHANO: That's most certain.

CALIBAN: Thou shalt be lord of it, and I'll serve thee.

55 STEPHANO: How now shall this be compass'd? Canst thou
      bring me to the party?

CALIBAN: Yea, yea, my lord. I'll yield him thee asleep,
      Where thou mayst knock a nail into his head.

ARIEL: Thou liest; thou canst not.

60 CALIBAN: What a pied ninny's this! Thou scurvy patch!
      I do beseech thy greatness, give him blows
      And take his bottle from him. When that's gone
      He shall drink nought but brine, for I'll now show him
      Where the quick freshes are.

65 STEPHANO: Trinculo, run into no further danger. Interrupt
      the monster one word further, and, by this hand, I'll turn
      my mercy out o' doors and make a stock-fish of thee.

TRINCULO: Why, what did? I did nothing. I'll go farther off.

STEPHANO: Didst thou not say he lied?

70 ARIEL: Thou liest.

STEPHANO: Do I so? Take thou that. (*Beats* TRINCULO.) As
      you like this, give me the lie another time.

TRINCULO: I did not give the lie. Out o' your wits and hearing
      too? A pox o' your bottle! This can sack and drinking do. A
75   murrain on your monster, and the devil take your fingers!

CALIBAN: Ha, ha, ha!

STEPHANO: Now, forward with your tale.

(*To* TRINCULO.)

      Prithee, stand further off.

CALIBAN: Beat him enough. After a little time
80   I'll beat him too.

STEPHANO: Stand farther.—Come, proceed.

CALIBAN: Why, as I told thee, 'tis a custom with him
      I' th' afternoon to sleep. There thou mayst brain him,
      Having first seiz'd his books, or with a log
85   Batter his skull, or paunch him with a stake,
      Or cut his wezand with thy knife. Remember
      First to possess his books; for without them
      He's but a sot, as I am, nor hath not
      One spirit to command. They all do hate him
90   As rootedly as I. Burn but his books.
      He has brave utensils—for so he calls them—
      Which, when he has a house, he'll deck withal.
      And that most deeply to consider is
      The beauty of his daughter. He himself
95   Calls her a nonpareil. I never saw a woman,
      But only Sycorax my dam and she;

      But she as far surpasseth Sycorax
      As great'st does least.

STEPHANO: Is it so brave a lass?

CALIBAN: Ay, lord; she will become thy bed, I warrant,   100
      And bring thee forth brave brood.

STEPHANO: Monster, I will kill this man. His daughter and I will
      be king and queen—save our Graces!—and Trinculo and
      thyself shall be viceroys. Dost thou like the plot, Trinculo?

TRINCULO: Excellent.   105

STEPHANO: Give me thy hand. I am sorry I beat thee; but,
      while thou liv'st, keep a good tongue in thy head.

CALIBAN: Within this half hour will he be asleep.
      Wilt thou destroy him then?

STEPHANO: Ay, on mine honor.   110

ARIEL: (*Aside.*) This will I tell my master.

CALIBAN: Thou mak'st me merry; I am full of pleasure.
      Let us be jocund. Will you troll the catch
      You taught me but while-ere?

STEPHANO: At thy request, monster, I will do reason, any rea-   115
      son. Come on, Trinculo, let us sing.

(*Sings.*)

              "Flout 'em and scout 'em
              And scout 'em and flout 'em!
              Thought is free."

CALIBAN: That's not the tune.   120

(ARIEL *plays the tune on a tabor and pipe.*)

STEPHANO: What is this same?

TRINCULO: This is the tune of our catch, play'd by the pic-
      ture of Nobody.

STEPHANO: If thou beest a man, show thyself in thy likeness.
      If thou beest a devil, take 't as thou list.   125

TRINCULO: O, forgive me my sins!

STEPHANO: He that dies pays all debts. I defy thee. Mercy
      upon us!

CALIBAN: Art thou afeard?

STEPHANO: No, monster, not I.   130

CALIBAN: Be not afeard. This isle is full of noises,
      Sounds and sweet airs, that give delight and hurt not.
      Sometimes a thousand twangling instruments
      Will hum about mine ears, and sometimes voices
      That, if I then had wak'd after long sleep,   135
      Will make me sleep again; and then, in dreaming,
      The clouds methought would open and show riches
      Ready to drop upon me, that, when I wak'd,
      I cried to dream again.

STEPHANO: This will prove a brave kingdom to me, where I   140
      shall have my music for nothing.

CALIBAN: When Prospero is destroy'd.

STEPHANO: That shall be by and by. I remember the story.

---

52 **this thing** i.e., Trinculo   60 **pied ninny** fool in motley;
patch fool   64 **quick freshes** running springs   67 **stock-fish**
dried cod beaten before cooking   72 **give me the lie** call me
a liar to my face   75 **murrain** plague (literally, a cattle disease)
85 **paunch** stab in the belly   86 **wezand** windpipe   88 **sot**
fool   91 **brave utensils** fine furnishings

---

113 **troll the catch** sing the round   114 **while-ere** a short
time ago   118 **scout** deride s.d. **tabor** small drum   122–123
picture of Nobody refers to a familiar figure with head, arms,
and legs, but no trunk   125 **take 't . . . list** i.e., take my defi-
ance as you please, as best you can

TRINCULO: The sound is going away. Let's follow it, and after
145   do our work.
STEPHANO: Lead, monster; we'll follow. I would I could see
    this taborer; he lays it on.
TRINCULO: Wilt come? I'll follow, Stephano.

(*Exeunt [following* ARIEL'*s music].*)

SCENE III

Enter ALONSO, SEBASTIAN, ANTONIO, GONZALO, ADRIAN,
FRANCISCO, *etc.*

GONZALO: By 'r lakin, I can go no further, sir;
    My old bones aches. Here's a maze trod indeed
    Through forth-rights and meanders! By your patience,
    I needs must rest me.
ALONSO: Old lord, I cannot blame thee,
5   Who am myself attach'd with weariness,
    To th' dulling of my spirits. Sit down, and rest.
    Even here I will put off my hope and keep it
    No longer for my flatterer. He is drown'd
    Whom thus we stray to find, and the sea mocks
10 Our frustrate search on land. Well, let him go.

(ALONSO *and* GONZALO *sit.*)

ANTONIO: (*Aside to* SEBASTIAN.) I am right glad that he's so
    out of hope.
    Do not, for one repulse, forego the purpose
    That you resolv'd t' effect.
SEBASTIAN: (*To* ANTONIO.)   The next advantage
    Will we take throughly.
15 ANTONIO: (*To* SEBASTIAN.) Let it be tonight,
    For, now they are oppress'd with travail, they
    Will not, nor cannot, use such vigilance
    As when they are fresh.
SEBASTIAN: (*To* ANTONIO.) I say tonight. No more.

(*Solemn and strange music; and* PROSPERO *on the top, invisible.*)

ALONSO: What harmony is this? My good friends, hark!
GONZALO: Marvelous sweet music!

(*Enter several strange shapes, bringing in a banquet, and dance about
it with gentle actions of salutations; and, inviting* [ALONSO], *etc., to
eat, they depart.*)

20 ALONSO: Give us kind keepers, heavens! What were these?
SEBASTIAN: A living drollery. Now I will believe
    That there are unicorns, that in Arabia
    There is one tree, the phoenix' throne, one phoenix
    At this hour reigning there.

ANTONIO: I'll believe both;
    And what does else want credit, come to me,   25
    And I'll be sworn 'tis true. Travelers ne'er did lie,
    Though fools at home condemn 'em.
GONZALO: If in Naples
    I should report this now, would they believe me
    If I should say I saw such islanders?
    For, certes, these are people of the island,   30
    Who, though they are of monstrous shape, yet, note,
    Their manners are more gentle, kind, than of
    Our human generation you shall find
    Many, nay, almost any.
PROSPERO: (*Aside.*)   Honest lord,
    Thou hast said well; for some of you there present   35
    Are worse than devils.
ALONSO: I cannot too much muse
    Such shapes, such gesture, and such sound, expressing,
    Although they want the use of tongue, a kind
    Of excellent dumb discourse.
PROSPERO: (*Aside.*)   Praise in departing.
FRANCISCO: They vanish'd strangely.   40
SEBASTIAN: No matter, since
    They have left their viands behind; for we have stomachs.
    Will 't please you taste of what is here?
ALONSO: Not I.
GONZALO: Faith, sir, you need not fear. When we were boys,
    Who would believe that there were mountaineers
    Dew-lapp'd like bulls, whose throats had hanging at 'em   45
    Wallets of flesh? Or that there were such men
    Whose heads stood in their breasts? Which now we find
    Each putter-out of five for one will bring us
    Good warrant of.
ALONSO: I will stand to and feed,
    Although my last—no matter, since I feel   50
    The best is past. Brother, my lord the Duke,
    Stand to and do as we.

(*They approach the table.*)

(*Thunder and lightning. Enter* ARIEL, *like a harpy; claps his wings
upon the table; and, with a quaint device, the banquet vanishes.*)

ARIEL: You are three men of sin, whom Destiny,
    That hath to instrument this lower world
    And what is in 't, the never-surfeited sea   55

III.iii. Location: Another part of the island.   1 **By 'r lakin**
by our Ladykin, by our Lady   3 **forth-rights and meanders**
paths straight and crooked   5 **attach'd** seized   12 **for** because
of   14 **throughly** thoroughly   17 s.d. **on the top** at some
high point of the tiring-house or the theatre   20 **kind keepers**
guardian angels   21 **drollery** puppet show

25 **want credit** lack credence   30 **certes** certainly   36 **muse**
wonder at   39 **Praise in departing** i.e., save your praise until
the end of the performance   45 **Dew-lapp'd** having a dewlap,
or fold of skin hanging from the neck, like cattle   47 **in their
breasts** i.e., like the Anthropophagi described in Othello   48
putter-out . . . one one who invests money, or gambles on the
risks of travel on the condition that, if he returns safely, he is to
receive five times the amount deposited; hence, any traveler   49
stand to fall to; take the risk   52 s.d. **harpy** a fabulous monster
with a woman's face and vulture's body, supposed to be a minister of divine vengeance; **quaint device** ingenious stage contrivance; **banquet vanishes** i.e., the food vanishes; the table
remains until line 82   54 **to** i.e., as its

Hath caus'd to belch up you, and on this island
Where man doth not inhabit—you 'mongst men
Being most unfit to live. I have made you mad;
And even with such-like valor men hang and drown
60   Their proper selves.

(ALONSO, SEBASTIAN, *and* ANTONIO *draw their swords.*)

                    You fools! I and my fellows
Are ministers of Fate. The elements,
Of whom your swords are temper'd, may as well
Wound the loud winds, or with bemock'd-at stabs
Kill the still-closing waters, as diminish
65   One dowle that's in my plume. My fellow-ministers
Are like invulnerable. If you could hurt,
Your swords are now too massy for your strengths
And will not be uplifted. But remember—
For that's my business to you—that you three
70   From Milan did supplant good Prospero;
Expos'd unto the sea, which hath requit it,
Him and his innocent child; for which foul deed
The pow'rs, delaying, not forgetting, have
Incens'd the seas and shores, yea, all the creatures,
75   Against your peace. Thee of thy son, Alonso,
They have bereft; and do pronounce by me
Ling'ring perdition, worse than any death
Can be at once, shall step by step attend
You and your ways; whose wraths to guard you from—
80   Which here, in this most desolate isle, else falls
Upon your heads—is nothing but heart's sorrow
And a clear life ensuring.

(*He vanishes in thunder; then, to soft music, enter the shapes again,
and dance, with mocks and mows, and carrying out the table.*)

PROSPERO: Bravely the figure of this harpy hast thou
Perform'd, my Ariel; a grace it had devouring.
85   Of my instruction hast thou nothing bated
In what thou hadst to say. So, with good life
And observation strange, my meaner ministers
Their several kinds have done. My high charms work,
And these mine enemies are all knit up
90   In their distractions. They now are in my pow'r;
And in these fits I leave them, while I visit
Young Ferdinand, whom they suppose is drown'd,
And his and mine lov'd darling.

───────────

59 **such-like valor** i.e., the reckless valor derived from madness
60 **proper** own   62 **whom** which   64 **still-closing** always
closing again when parted   65 **dowle** soft, fine feather   66 **like**
likewise, similarly; **If** even if   71 **requit** requited, avenged   79
whose refers to the heavenly powers s.d. **mocks and mows**
mocking gestures and grimaces   83 **Bravely** finely, dashing
84 **a grace . . . devouring** i.e., you gracefully caused the banquet to disappear as if you had consumed it (with puns on *grace*
meaning "gracefulness" and "a blessing on the meal," and on *devouring* meaning "a literal eating" and "an all-consuming or ravishing grace")   85 **bated** abated, diminished   86 **good life**
faithful reproduction   87 **observation strange** exceptional attention to detail; **meaner** i.e., subordinate to Ariel   88 **several
kinds** individual parts

(*Exit above.*)

GONZALO: I' th' name of something holy, sir, why stand you
In this strange stare?   95
ALONSO: O, it is monstrous, monstrous!
Methought the billows spoke and told me of it;
The winds did sing it to me, and the thunder,
That deep and dreadful organ-pipe, pronounc'd
The name of Prosper; it did bass my trespass.
Therefore my son i' th' ooze is bedded, and   100
I'll seek him deeper than e'er plummet sounded
And with him there lie mudded.

(*Exit.*)

SEBASTIAN: But one fiend at a time,
I'll fight their legions o'er.
ANTONIO: I'll be thy second.

(*Exeunt* [SEBASTIAN *and* ANTONIO].)

GONZALO: All three of them are desperate. Their great guilt,   105
Like poison given to work a great time after,
Now 'gins to bite the spirits. I do beseech you,
That are of suppler joints, follow them swiftly
And hinder them from what this ecstasy
May now provoke them to.   110
ADRIAN: Follow, I pray you.

(*Exeunt omnes.*)

ACT FOUR

SCENE I

Enter PROSPERO, FERDINAND, *and* MIRANDA.

PROSPERO: If I have too austerely punish'd you,
Your compensation makes amends, for I
Have given you here a third of mine own life,
Or that for which I live; who once again
I tender to thy hand. All thy vexations   5
Were but my trials of thy love, and thou
Hast strangely stood the test. Here, afore Heaven,
I ratify this my rich gift. O Ferdinand,
Do not smile at me that I boast her off,
For thou shalt find she will outstrip all praise   10
And make it halt behind her.
FERDINAND: I do believe it
Against an oracle.

───────────

94 **why** Gonzalo was not addressed in Ariel's speech to the
"three men of sin," line 53, and is not as they are in a maddened
state; see lines 105–107   95 **it** i.e., my sin   99 **bass my trespass** proclaim my trespass like a bass note in music   104 **o'er
one** after another

IV.i. Location: Before Prospero's cell.   3 **a third** i.e., Miranda, into whose education Prospero has put a third of his life (?)
or who represents a large part of what he cares about, along with
his dukedom and his learned study (?)   7 **strangely** extraordinarily   9 **boast her off** i.e., praise her so   11 **halt** limp   12
Against an oracle i.e., even if an oracle should declare otherwise

PROSPERO: Then, as my gift and thine own acquisition
Worthily purchas'd, take my daughter. But

15 If thou dost break her virgin-knot before
All sanctimonious ceremonies may
With full and holy rite be minist'red,
No sweet aspersion shall the heavens let fall
To make this contract grow; but barren hate,

20 Sour-ey'd disdain, and discord shall bestrew
The union of your bed with weeds so loathly
That you shall hate it both. Therefore take heed,
As Hymen's lamps shall light you.

FERDINAND: As I hope
For quiet days, fair issue, and long life,

25 With such love as 'tis now, the murkiest den,
The most opportune place, the strong'st suggestion
Our worser genius can, shall never melt
Mine honor into lust, to take away
The edge of that day's celebration

30 When I shall think or Phoebus' steeds are founder'd
Or Night kept chain'd below.

PROSPERO: Fairly spoke.
Sit then and talk with her; she is thine own.

(FERDINAND *and* MIRANDA *sit*.)

What, Ariel! My industrious servant, Ariel!

(*Enter* ARIEL.)

ARIEL: What would my potent master? Here I am.

35 PROSPERO: Thou and thy meaner fellows your last service
Did worthily perform; and I must use you
In such another trick. Go bring the rabble,
O'er whom I give thee pow'r, here to this place.
Incite them to quick motion, for I must

40 Bestow upon the eyes of this young couple
Some vanity of mine art. It is my promise,
And they expect it from me.

ARIEL: Presently?

PROSPERO: Ay, with a twink.

ARIEL: Before you can say "come" and "go,"

45   And breathe twice and cry "so, so,"
Each one, tripping on his toe,
Will be here with mop and mow.
Do you love me, master? No?

PROSPERO: Dearly, my delicate Ariel. Do not approach
50   Till thou dost hear me call.

ARIEL: Well, I conceive.

(*Exit*.)

---

16 **sanctimonious** sacred   18 **aspersion** dew, shower   23 **Hymen's** Hymen was the Greek and Roman god of marriage   27 **worser genius** evil genius, or evil attendant spirit   30 **or** either; **founder'd** broken down, made lame (i.e., Ferdinand will wait impatiently for the bridal night)   37 **rabble** band, i.e., the *meaner* fellows of line 35   41 **vanity** illusion   47 **mop and mow** gestures and grimaces   50 **conceive** understand

PROSPERO: Look thou be true; do not give dalliance
Too much the rein. The strongest oaths are straw
To th' fire i' th' blood. Be more abstemious,
Or else good night your vow!

FERDINAND: I warrant you, sir;
The white cold virgin snow upon my heart   55
Abates the ardor of my liver.

PROSPERO: Well.
Now come, my Ariel! Bring a corollary,
Rather than want a spirit. Appear, and pertly!
No tongue! All eyes! Be silent.

(*Soft music*.)

(*Enter* IRIS.)

IRIS: Ceres, most bounteous lady, thy rich leas   60
Of wheat, rye, barley, vetches, oats, and pease;
Thy turfy mountains, where live nibbling sheep,
And flat meads thatch'd with stover, them to keep;
Thy banks with pioned and twilled brims,
Which spongy April at thy hest betrims,   65
To make cold nymphs chaste crowns; and thy broom-
    groves,
Whose shadow the dismissed bachelor loves,
Being lass-lorn; thy pole-clipt vineyard;
And thy sea-marge, sterile and rocky-hard,
Where thou thyself dost air—the queen o' th' sky,   70
Whose wat'ry arch and messenger am I,
Bids thee leave these, and with her sovereign grace.

(JUNO *descends* [*slowly in her car*].)

Here on this grass-plot, in this very place,
To come and sport. Her peacocks fly amain.
Approach, rich Ceres, her to entertain.   75

(*Enter* CERES.)

CERES: Hail, many-color'd messenger, that ne'er
Dost disobey the wife of Jupiter,
Who with thy saffron wings upon my flow'rs
Diffusest honey-drops, refreshing show'rs,
And with each end of thy blue bow dost crown   80
My bosky acres and my unshrubb'd down,

---

56 **liver** as the presumed seat of the passions   57 **corollary** surplus, extra supply   58 **want** lack; **pertly** briskly s.d. **Iris** goddess of the rainbow, and Juno's messenger   60 **Ceres** goddess of the generative power of nature; **leas** meadows   61 **vetches** plants for forage, fodder   63 **stover** winter fodder for cattle   64 **pioned and twilled** undercut by the swift current and protected by roots and branches woven into a mat (?)   66 **broom-groves** clumps of broom, gorse, yellow-flowered shrub   67 **dismissed bachelor** rejected male lover   68 **pole-clipt** hedged in with poles; or pruned   70 **queen o' th' sky** i.e., Juno   71 **wat'ry arch** rainbow   72 s.d. **Juno descends** i.e., starts her descent from the "heavens" above the stage (?)   74 **peacocks** birds sacred to Juno, and used to pull her chariot; **amain** with full speed   75 **entertain** receive   81 **bosky** wooded; **down** upland

Rich scarf to my proud earth; why hath thy Queen
Summon'd me hither, to this short-grass'd green?
IRIS: A contract of true love to celebrate,
85   And some donation freely to estate
On the bless'd lovers.
CERES: Tell me, heavenly bow,
If Venus or her son, as thou dost know,
Do now attend the Queen? Since they did plot
The means that dusky Dis my daughter got,
90   Her and her blind boy's scandal'd company
I have forsworn.
IRIS: Of her society
Be not afraid. I met her deity
Cutting the clouds towards Paphos, and her son
Dove-drawn with her. Here thought they to have done
95   Some wanton charm upon this man and maid,
Whose vows are, that no bed-right shall be paid
Till Hymen's torch be lighted; but in vain;
Mars's hot minion is return'd again;
Her waspish-headed son has broke his arrows,
100   Swears he will shoot no more, but play with sparrows
And be a boy right out.

(JUNO *alights.*)

CERES: Highest Queen of state,
Great Juno, comes; I know her by her gait.
JUNO: How does my bounteous sister? Go with me
To bless this twain, that they may prosperous be
105   And honor'd in their issue.

(*They sing.*)

JUNO: Honor, riches, marriage-blessing,
Long continuance, and increasing,
Hourly joys be still upon you!
Juno sings her blessings on you.

110 CERES: Earth's increase, foison plenty,
Barns and garners never empty,
Vines with clust'ring bunches growing,
Plants with goodly burden bowing;
Spring come to you at the farthest
115   In the very end of harvest!
Scarcity and want shall shun you;
Ceres' blessing so is on you.

FERDINAND: This is a most majestic vision, and
Harmonious charmingly. May I be bold
120   To think these spirits?
PROSPERO: Spirits, which by mine art
I have from their confines call'd to enact
My present fancies.

FERDINAND: Let me live here ever;
So rare a wond'red father and a wife
Makes this place Paradise.

(JUNO *and* CERES *whisper, and send* IRIS *on employment.*)

PROSPERO: Sweet now, silence!
Juno and Ceres whisper seriously;   125
There's something else to do. Hush and be mute,
Or else our spell is marr'd.
IRIS: You nymphs, call'd Naiads, of the windring brooks,
With your sedg'd crowns and ever-harmless looks,
Leave your crisp channels, and on this green land   130
Answer your summons; Juno does command.
Come, temperate nymphs, and help to celebrate
A contract of true love; be not too late.

(*Enter certain* NYMPHS.)

You sunburnt sicklemen, of August weary,
Come hither from the furrow and be merry.   135
Make holiday; your rye-straw hats put on
And these fresh nymphs encounter every one
In country footing.

(*Enter certain* REAPERS, *properly habited. They join with the* NYMPHS *in a graceful dance, towards the end whereof* PROSPERO *starts suddenly, and speaks; after which, to a strange, hollow, and confused noise, they heavily vanish.*)

PROSPERO: (*Aside.*) I had forgot that foul conspiracy
Of the beast Caliban and his confederates   140
Against my life. The minute of their plot
Is almost come. (*To the* SPIRITS.) Well done! Avoid; no
more!
FERDINAND: This is strange. Your father's in some passion
That works him strongly.
MIRANDA: Never till this day
Saw I him touch'd with anger so distemper'd.   145
PROSPERO: You do look, my son, in a mov'd sort,
As if you were dismay'd. Be cheerful, sir.
Our revels now are ended. These our actors,
As I foretold you, were all spirits and
Are melted into air, into thin air;   150
And, like the baseless fabric of this vision,
The cloud-capp'd tow'rs, the gorgeous palaces,
The solemn temples, the great globe itself,
Yea, all which it inherit, shall dissolve
And, like this insubstantial pageant faded,   155
Leave not a rack behind. We are such stuff
As dreams are made on, and our little life
Is rounded with a sleep. Sir, I am vex'd.
Bear with my weakness; my old brain is troubled.

---

85 **estate** bestow   87 **son** i.e., Cupid   89 **Dis . . . got** Pluto, or Dis, god of the infernal regions, carried off Persephone, daughter of Ceres, to be his bride in Hades   90 **Her** i.e., Venus; **scandal'd** scandalous   92 **her deity** i.e., her highness   93 **Paphos** place on the island of Cyprus, sacred to Venus   98 **Mars' hot minion** i.e., Venus, the beloved of Mars   99 **waspish-headed** fiery, hotheaded, peevish   100 **sparrows** supposed lustful, and sacred to Venus   101 **right out** outright   110 **foison plenty** plentiful harvest   111 **garners** granaries

---

123 **wond'red** wonder-performing, wondrous; **wife** sometimes emended to *wise*   128 **windring** wandering, winding (?)   130 **crisp** curled, rippled   132 **temperate** chaste   138 **country footing** country dancing; s.d. **heavily** slowly, dejectedly   142 **Avoid** depart, withdraw   146 **mov'd sort** troubled state, condition   148 **revels** entertainments, pageants   151 **baseless** without substance   154 **which it inherit** who occupy it   156 **rack** wisp of cloud   157 **on** of

160   Be not disturb'd with my infirmity.
        If you be pleas'd, retire into my cell
        And there repose. A turn or two I'll walk
        To still my beating mind.
    FERDINAND, MIRANDA: We wish your peace.

(*Exeunt.*)

PROSPERO: Come with a thought! I thank thee, Ariel. Come.

(*Enter* ARIEL.)

165 ARIEL: Thy thoughts I cleave to. What's thy pleasure?
    PROSPERO: Spirit,
        We must prepare to meet with Caliban.
    ARIEL: Ay, my commander. When I presented Ceres,
        I thought to have told thee of it, but I fear'd
        Lest I might anger thee.
170 PROSPERO: Say again, where didst thou leave these varlets?
    ARIEL: I told you, sir, they were red-hot with drinking,
        So full of valor that they smote the air
        For breathing in their faces; beat the ground
        For kissing of their feet; yet always bending
175   Towards their project. Then I beat my tabor,
        At which, like unback'd colts, they prick'd their ears,
        Advanc'd their eyelids, lifted up their noses
        As they smelt music. So I charm'd their ears
        That calf-like they my lowing follow'd through
180   Tooth'd briers, sharp furzes, pricking goss, and thorns,
        Which ent'red their frail shins. At last I left them
        I' th' filthy-mantled pool beyond your cell,
        There dancing up to th' chins, that the foul lake
        O'erstunk their feet.
    PROSPERO: This was well done, my bird.
185   Thy shape invisible retain thou still.
        The trumpery in my house, go bring it hither,
        For stale to catch these thieves.
    ARIEL: I go, I go.

(*Exit.*)

PROSPERO: A devil, a born devil, on whose nature
        Nurture can never stick; on whom my pains,
190   Humanely taken, all, all lost, quite lost!
        And as with age his body uglier grows,
        So his mind cankers. I will plague them all,
        Even to roaring.

(*Enter* ARIEL, *loaden with glistering apparel, etc.*)

               Come, hang them on this line.

([ARIEL *hangs up the showy finery;* PROSPERO *and* ARIEL *remain, invisible.*] Enter CALIBAN, STEPHANO, *and* TRINCULO, *all wet.*)

CALIBAN: Pray you, tread softly, that the blind mole may not
    Hear a foot fall. We now are near his cell.   195
STEPHANO: Monster, your fairy, which you say is a harmless
    fairy, has done little better than play'd the Jack with us.
TRINCULO: Monster, I do smell all horse-piss, at which my
    nose is in great indignation.
STEPHANO: So is mine. Do you hear, monster? If I should take 200
    a displeasure against you, look you—
TRINCULO: Thou wert but a lost monster.
CALIBAN: Good my lord, give me thy favor still.
    Be patient, for the prize I'll bring thee to
    Shall hoodwink this mischance. Therefore speak softly.   205
    All's hush'd as midnight yet.
TRINCULO: Ay, but to lose our bottles in the pool—
STEPHANO: There is not only disgrace and dishonor in that,
    monster, but an infinite loss.
TRINCULO: That's more to me than my wetting. Yet this is 210
    your harmless fairy, monster!
STEPHANO: I will fetch off my bottle, though I be o'er ears
    for my labor.
CALIBAN: Prithee, my King, be quiet. See'st thou here,
    This is the mouth o' th' cell. No noise, and enter. 215
    Do that good mischief which may make this island
    Thine own for ever, and I, thy Caliban,
    For aye thy foot-licker.
STEPHANO: Give me thy hand. I do begin to have bloody
    thoughts.   220
TRINCULO: (*Seeing the finery.*) O King Stephano! O peer! O
    worthy Stephano! Look what a wardrobe here is for thee!
CALIBAN: Let it alone, thou fool! It is but trash.
TRINCULO: O, ho, monster! We know what belongs to a frip-
    pery. O King Stephano! (*Takes a gown.*)   225
STEPHANO: Put off that gown, Trinculo. By this hand, I'll have
    that gown.
TRINCULO: Thy Grace shall have it.
CALIBAN: The dropsy drown this fool! What do you mean
    To dote thus on such luggage? Let's alone   230
    And do the murder first. If he awake,
    From toe to crown he'll fill our skins with pinches,
    Make us strange stuff.
STEPHANO: Be you quiet, monster. Mistress line, is not this
    my jerkin? (*Takes it down.*) Now is the jerkin under the 235
    line. Now, jerkin, you are like to lose your hair and prove
    a bald jerkin.
TRINCULO: Do, do! We steal by line and level, an 't like your
    Grace.

---

164 **with a thought** i.e., on the instant, or summoned by my thought, no sooner thought on than here   167 **presented** acted the part of, or introduced   176 **unback'd** unbroken, unridden   177 **Advanc'd** lifted up   180 **goss** gorse, a prickly shrub   182 **filthy-mantled** covered with a slimy coating   186 **trumpery** cheap goods, the *glistering apparel* mentioned in the following stage direction   187 **stale** (1) decoy (2) out of fashion garments (with possible further suggestions of *fit for a stale* or prostitute, *stale* meaning "horse-piss," line 198, and *steal,* pronounced like *stale*)   192 **cankers** festers, grows malignant   193 **line** lime tree or linden

197 **Jack** (1) Knave (2) will-o-the-wisp   205 **hoodwink** cover up, make you not see (a hawking term)   221 **King . . . peer** alludes to the old ballad beginning, "King Stephen was a worthy peer"   224 **frippery** place where cast-off clothes are sold   230 **luggage** cumbersome trash   235 **jerkin** jacket make of leather; **under the line** under the lime tree (with punning sense of being south of the equinoctial line or equator; sailors to the southern regions were popularly supposed to lose their hair from scurvy or other diseases. Stephano also quibbles bawdily on losing hair through syphilis and in *Mistress* and *jerkin*)   238 **by line and level** i.e., by means of plumb-line and carpenter's level, methodically (with pun on *line,* "lime tree," line 235, and *steal* pronounced *stale,* i.e., prostitute, continuing Stephano's bawdy quibble); **an 't like** if it please

240 STEPHANO: I thank thee for that jest. Here's a garment for 't.
      (*Gives a garment.*) Wit shall not go unrewarded while I am
      king of this country. "Steal by line and level" is an excel-
      lent pass of pate. There's another garment for 't.
    TRINCULO: Monster, come, put some lime upon your fingers,
245   and away with the rest.
    CALIBAN: I have none on 't. We shall lose our time,
    And all be turn'd to barnacles, or to apes
      With foreheads villainous low.
    STEPHANO: Monster, lay to your fingers. Help to bear this
250   away where my hogshead of wine is, or I'll turn you out
      of my kingdom. Go to, carry this.
    TRINCULO: And this.
    STEPHANO: Ay, and this.

(*They collect more and more garments.*)

(*A noise of hunters heard. Enter divers* SPIRITS, *in shape of dogs and
hounds, hunting them about,* PROSPERO *and* ARIEL *setting them on.*)

    PROSPERO: Hey, Mountain, hey!
255 ARIEL: Silver! There it goes, Silver!
    PROSPERO: Fury, Fury! There, Tyrant, there! Hark! Hark!

(CALIBAN, STEPHANO, *and* TRINCULO *are driven out.*)

      Go charge my goblins that they grind their joints
      With dry convulsions, shorten up their sinews
      With aged cramps, and more pitch-spotted make them
260   Than pard or cat o' mountain.
    ARIEL: Hark, they roar!
    PROSPERO: Let them be hunted soundly. At this hour
      Lies at my mercy all mine enemies.
      Shortly shall all my labors end, and thou
      Shalt have the air at freedom. For a little
265   Follow, and do me service.

(*Exeunt.*)

ACT FIVE

SCENE I

Enter PROSPERO *in his magic robes,* [*with his staff,*] *and* ARIEL.

    PROSPERO: Now does my project gather to a head.
      My charms crack not, my spirits obey, and Time
      Goes upright with his carriage. How's the day?
    ARIEL: On the sixth hour; at which time, my lord,
5   You said our work should cease.

    PROSPERO: I did say so,
      When first I rais'd the tempest. Say, my spirit,
      How fares the King and 's followers?
    ARIEL: Confin'd together
      In the same fashion as you gave in charge,
      Just as you left them; all prisoners, sir,
      In the line-grove which weather-fends your cell.   10
      They cannot budge till your release. The King,
      His brother, and yours, abide all three distracted,
      And the remainder mourning over them,
      Brimful of sorrow and dismay; but chiefly
      Him that you term'd, sir, "The good old lord, Gonzalo." 15
      His tears runs down his beard like winter's drops
      From eaves of reeds. Your charm so strongly works 'em
      That if you now beheld them, your affections
      Would become tender.
    PROSPERO: Dost thou think so, spirit?
    ARIEL: Mine would, sir, were I human.   20
    PROSPERO: And mine shall.
      Hast thou, which art but air, a touch, a feeling
      Of their afflictions, and shall not myself,
      One of their kind, that relish all as sharply,
      Passion as they, be kindlier mov'd than thou art?
      Though with their high wrongs I am struck to th' quick, 25
      Yet with my nobler reason 'gainst my fury
      Do I take part. The rarer action is
      In virtue than in vengeance. They being penitent,
      The sole drift of my purpose doth extend
      Not a frown further. Go release them, Ariel.   30
      My charms I'll break, their senses I'll restore,
      And they shall be themselves.
    ARIEL: I'll fetch them, sir.

(*Exit.*)

(PROSPERO *traces a charmed circle with his staff.*)

    PROSPERO: Ye elves of hills, brooks, standing lakes, and groves,
      And ye that on the sands with printless foot
      Do chase the ebbing Neptune, and do fly him   35
      When he comes back; you demi-puppets that
      By moonshine do the green sour ringlets make,
      Whereof the ewe not bites; and you whose pastime
      Is to make midnight mushrooms, that rejoice
      To hear the solemn curfew; by whose aid,   40
      Weak masters though ye be, I have bedimm'd
      The noontide sun, call'd forth the mutinous winds,
      And 'twixt the green sea and the azur'd vault
      Set roaring war; to the dread rattling thunder
      Have I given fire, and rifted Jove's stout oak   45

---

243 **pass of pate** sally of wit   244 **lime** birdlime, sticky substance (to give Caliban sticky fingers)   247 **barnacles** barnacle
geese, formerly supposed to be hatched from seashells attached
to trees and to fall thence into the water; here evidently used, like
apes, as types of simpletons   248 **villainous** miserably   258
dry associated with age, arthritic (?); **convulsions** cramps   259
aged characteristic of old age   260 **pard** panther or leopard;
cat o' mountain wildcat

V.i. Location: Before Prospero's cell.   3 **his carriage** its
burden (i.e., Time is unstopped, runs smoothly)

10 **line-grove** grove of lime trees; **weather-fends** protects from
the weather   11 **your release** you release them   17 **eaves of
reeds** thatched roofs   23 **relish all** experience quite   24 **Passion** experience deep feeling   27 **rarer** nobler   33–50 **Ye . . .
art** this famous passage is an embellished paraphrase of Golding's
translation of Ovid's *Metamorphoses,* 7.197–219   36 **demi-
puppets** puppets of half-size, i.e., elves and fairies   37 **green
sour ringlets** fairy rings, circles in grass (actually produced by
mushrooms)   44–45 **to . . . fire** I have discharged the dread rattling thunderbolt   45 **rifted** riven, split

With his own bolt; the strong-bas'd promontory
Have I made shake, and by the spurs pluck'd up
The pine and cedar; graves at my command
Have wak'd their sleepers, op'd, and let 'em forth
50 By my so potent art. But this rough magic
I here abjure, and, when I have requir'd
Some heavenly music, which even now I do,
To work mine end upon their senses that
This airy charm is for, I'll break my staff,
55 Bury it certain fathoms in the earth,
And deeper than did ever plummet sound
I'll drown my book.

(*Solemn music.*)

(*Here enters* ARIEL *before, then* ALONSO, *with a frantic gesture, attended by* GONZALO; SEBASTIAN *and* ANTONIO *in like manner, attended by* ADRIAN *and* FRANCISCO. *They all enter the circle which* PROSPERO *had made, and there stand charm'd; which* PROSPERO *observing, speaks:*)

A solemn air, and the best comforter
To an unsettled fancy, cure thy brains,
60 Now useless, boil'd within thy skull! There stand,
For you are spell-stopp'd.
Holy Gonzalo, honorable man,
Mine eyes, ev'n sociable to the show of thine,
Fall fellowly drops. The charm dissolves apace,
65 And as the morning steals upon the night,
Melting the darkness, so their rising senses
Begin to chase the ignorant fumes that mantle
Their clearer reason. O good Gonzalo,
My true preserver, and a loyal sir
70 To him thou follow'st! I will pay thy graces
Home both in word and deed. Most cruelly
Didst thou, Alonso, use me and my daughter.
Thy brother was a furtherer in the act.
Thou art pinch'd for 't now, Sebastian. Flesh and blood,
75 You, brother mine, that entertain'd ambition,
Expell'd remorse and nature, who, with Sebastian,
Whose inward pinches therefore are most strong,
Would here have kill'd your king, I do forgive thee,
Unnatural though thou art.—Their understanding
80 Begins to swell, and the approaching tide
Will shortly fill the reasonable shore
That now lies foul and muddy. Not one of them
That yet looks on me, or would know me. Ariel,
Fetch me the hat and rapier in my cell.

(ARIEL *goes to the cell and returns immediately.*)

85 I will discase me, and myself present
As I was sometime Milan. Quickly, spirit;
Thou shalt ere long be free.

(ARIEL *sings and helps to attire him.*)

ARIEL: Where the bee sucks, there suck I;
    In a cowslip's bell I lie;
    There I couch when owls do cry.   90
    On the bat's back I do fly
    After summer merrily.
    Merrily, merrily shall I live now
    Under the blossom that hangs on the bough.

PROSPERO: Why, that's my dainty Ariel! I shall miss thee;   95
    But yet thou shalt have freedom. So, so, so.
    To the King's ship, invisible as thou art!
    There shalt thou find the mariners asleep
    Under the hatches. The master and the boatswain
    Being awake, enforce them to this place,   100
    And presently, I prithee.
ARIEL: I drink the air before me, and return
    Or ere your pulse twice beat. (*Exit.*)
GONZALO: All torment, trouble, wonder, and amazement
    Inhabits here. Some heavenly power guide us   105
    Out of this fearful country!
PROSPERO: Behold, sir King,
    The wronged Duke of Milan, Prospero.
    For more assurance that a living prince
    Does now speak to thee, I embrace thy body;
    And to thee and thy company I bid   110
    A hearty welcome.

(*Embraces him.*)

ALONSO: Whe'er thou be'st he or no,
    Or some enchanted trifle to abuse me,
    As late I have been, I not know. Thy pulse
    Beats as of flesh and blood; and, since I saw thee,
    Th' affliction of my mind amends, with which,   115
    I fear, a madness held me. This must crave,
    An if this be at all, a most strange story.
    Thy dukedom I resign, and do entreat
    Thou pardon me my wrongs. But how should Prospero
    Be living and be here?   120
PROSPERO: (*To* GONZALO.)   First, noble friend,
    Let me embrace thine age, whose honor cannot
    Be measur'd or confin'd.

(*Embraces him.*)

GONZALO: Whether this be
    Or be not, I'll not swear.
PROSPERO: Yet do yet taste
    Some subtleties o' th' isle, that will not let you
    Believe things certain. Welcome, my friends all!   125
    (*Aside to* SEBASTIAN *and* ANTONIO.) But you, my brace of
        lords, were I so minded,

---

47 **spurs** roots   51 **requir'd** requested   58 **and** i.e., which is
63 **sociable** sympathetic; **show** appearance   64 **Fall** let fall   70
pay thy graces reward your favors   71 **Home** fully   76 **remorse** pity; **nature** natural feeling   85 **discase** disrobe   86 **As
. . . Milan** in my former appearance as Duke of Milan

96 **So, so, so** expresses approval of Ariel's help as valet   112 **trifle** trick of magic; **abuse** deceive   116 **crave** require   117 **An
. . . all** if this is actually happening   119 **Thy . . . resign** Alonso
made arrangement with Antonio at the time of Prospero's banishment for Milan to pay tribute to Naples; see 1.2.113–127
124 **subtleties** illusions, magical powers

I here could pluck his Highness' frown upon you
And justify you traitors. At this time
I will tell no tales.
SEBASTIAN: The devil speaks in him.
PROSPERO: No.
130 For you, most wicked sir, whom to call brother
Would even infect my mouth, I do forgive
Thy rankest fault—all of them; and require
My dukedom of thee, which perforce I know
Thou must restore.
ALONSO: If thou be'st Prospero,
135 Give us particulars of thy preservation,
How thou hast met us here, who three hours since
Were wrack'd upon this shore; where I have lost—
How sharp the point of this remembrance is!—
My dear son Ferdinand.
PROSPERO: I am woe for 't, sir.
140 ALONSO: Irreparable is the loss, and Patience
Says it is past her cure.
PROSPERO: I rather think
You have not sought her help, of whose soft grace
For the like loss I have her sovereign aid
And rest myself content.
ALONSO: You the like loss?
145 PROSPERO: As great to me as late; and, supportable
To make the dear loss, have I means much weaker
Than you may call to comfort you, for I
Have lost my daughter.
ALONSO: A daughter?
150 O heavens, that they were living both in Naples,
The king and queen there! That they were, I wish
Myself were mudded in that oozy bed
Where my son lies. When did you lose your daughter?
PROSPERO: In this last tempest. I perceive these lords
155 At this encounter do so much admire
That they devour their reason and scarce think
Their eyes do offices of truth, their words
Are natural breath. But, howsoev'r you have
Been justled from your senses, know for certain
160 That I am Prospero and that very duke
Which was thrust forth of Milan, who most strangely
Upon this shore, where you were wrack'd, was landed,
To be the lord on 't. No more yet of this,
For 'tis a chronicle of day by day,
165 Not a relation for a breakfast nor
Befitting this first meeting. Welcome, sir;
This cell's my court. Here have I few attendants
And subjects none abroad. Pray you look in.
My dukedom since you have given me again,
170 I will requite you with as good a thing,
At least bring forth a wonder, to content ye
As much as me my dukedom.

(*Here* PROSPERO *discovers* FERDINAND *and* MIRANDA, *playing at chess.*)

MIRANDA: Sweet lord, you play me false.
FERDINAND: No, my dearest love,
I would not for the world.   175
MIRANDA: Yes, for a score of kingdoms you should wrangle,
And I would call it fair play.
ALONSO: If this prove
A vision of the island, one dear son
Shall I twice lose.
SEBASTIAN: A most high miracle!
FERDINAND: Though the seas threaten, they are merciful; 180
I have curs'd them without cause. (*Kneels.*)
ALONSO: Now all the blessings
Of a glad father compass thee about!
Arise, and say how thou cam'st here.
MIRANDA: O, wonder!
How many goodly creatures are there here!
How beauteous mankind is! O brave new world, 185
That has such people in 't!
PROSPERO: 'Tis new to thee.
ALONSO: What is this maid with whom thou wast at play?
Your eld'st acquaintance cannot be three hours.
Is she the goddess that hath sever'd us,
And brought us thus together?   190
FERDINAND: Sir, she is mortal;
But by immortal Providence she's mine.
I chose her when I could not ask my father
For his advice, nor thought I had one. She
Is daughter to this famous Duke of Milan,
Of whom so often I have heard renown,   195
But never saw before; of whom I have
Receiv'd a second life; and second father
This lady makes him to me.
ALONSO: I am hers.
But, O, how oddly will it sound that I
Must ask my child forgiveness!   200
PROSPERO: There, sir, stop.
Let us not burden our remembrances with
A heaviness that's gone.
GONZALO: I have inly wept
Or should have spoke ere this. Look down, you gods,
And on this couple drop a blessed crown!
For it is you that have chalk'd forth the way 205
Which brought us hither.
ALONSO: I say Amen, Gonzalo!
GONZALO: Was Milan thrust from Milan, that his issue
Should become kings of Naples? O, rejoice
Beyond a common joy, and set it down
With gold on lasting pillars: In one voyage   210
Did Claribel her husband find at Tunis,
And Ferdinand, her brother, found a wife

128 **justify you** prove you to be   139 **woe** sorry   145 **late** recent   155 **admire** wonder   156–158 **scarce . . . breath** scarcely believe that their eyes inform them accurately what they see or that their words are naturally spoken   172 s.d. **discovers** i.e., by opening a curtain, presumably rear-stage

176–177 **Yes . . . play** i.e., yes, even if we were playing for twenty kingdoms, something less than the whole world, you would still contend mightily against me and play me false, and I would let you do it as though it were fair play; or, if you were to play not just for stakes but literally for kingdoms, my accusation of false play would be out of order in that your "wrangling" would be proper   185 **brave** splendid, gorgeously appareled, handsome   188 **eld'st** longest   207 **Was Milan** was the Duke of Milan

Where he himself was lost; Prospero his dukedom
In a poor isle; and all of us ourselves
215　When no man was his own.
ALONSO: (*To* FERDINAND *and* MIRANDA.) Give me your hands.
Let grief and sorrow still embrace his heart
That doth not wish you joy!
GONZALO:　　　　　　　　　Be it so! Amen!

(*Enter* ARIEL, *with the* MASTER *and* BOATSWAIN *amazedly following.*)

O, look, sir, look, sir! Here is more of us.
I prophesied, if a gallows were on land,
220　This fellow could not drown. Now, blasphemy,
That swear'st grace o'erboard, not an oath on shore?
Hast thou no mouth by land? What is the news?
BOATSWAIN: The best news is that we have safely found
Our King and company; the next, our ship—
225　Which, but three glasses since, we gave out split—
Is tight and yare and bravely rigg'd as when
We first put out to sea.
ARIEL: (*Aside to* PROSPERO.) Sir, all this service
Have I done since I went.
PROSPERO: (*Aside to* ARIEL.) My tricksy spirit!
ALONSO: These are not natural events; they strengthen
230　From strange to stranger. Say, how came you hither?
BOATSWAIN: If I did think, sir, I were well awake,
I'd strive to tell you. We were dead of sleep,
And—how we know not—all clapp'd under hatches;
Where but even now with strange and several noises
235　Of roaring, shrieking, howling, jingling chains,
And moe diversity of sounds, all horrible,
We were awak'd; straightway, at liberty;
Where we, in all her trim, freshly beheld
Our royal, good, and gallant ship, our master
240　Cap'ring to eye her. On a trice, so please you,
Even in a dream, were we divided from them
And were brought moping hither.
ARIEL: (*Aside to* PROSPERO.)　　　　Was 't well done?
PROSPERO: (*Aside to* ARIEL.) Bravely, my diligence. Thou
shalt be free.
ALONSO: This is as strange a maze as e'er men trod,
245　And there is in this business more than nature
Was ever conduct of. Some oracle
Must rectify our knowledge.
PROSPERO:　　　　　　　Sir, my liege,
Do not infest your mind with beating on
The strangeness of this business. At pick'd leisure,
250　Which shall be shortly, single I'll resolve you,
Which to you shall seem probable, of every
These happen'd accidents; till when, be cheerful
And think of each thing well. (*Aside to* ARIEL.) Come
hither, spirit.
Set Caliban and his companions free;

Untie the spell. (*Exit* ARIEL.) How fares my gracious sir?　255
There are yet missing of your company
Some few odd lads that you remember not.

(*Enter* ARIEL, *driving in* CALIBAN, STEPHANO, *and* TRINCULO, *in their stol'n apparel.*)

STEPHANO: Every man shift for all the rest, and let no man
take care of himself; for all is but fortune. Coragio, bully-
monster, coragio!　260
TRINCULO: If these be true spies which I wear in my head,
here's a goodly sight.
CALIBAN: O Setebos, these be brave spirits indeed!
How fine my master is! I am afraid
He will chastise me.　265
SEBASTIAN: Ha, ha!
What things are these, my lord, Antonio?
Will money buy 'em?
ANTONIO:　　　　　　Very like. One of them
Is a plain fish, and no doubt marketable.
PROSPERO: Mark but the badges of these men, my lords,　270
Then say if they be true. This misshapen knave,
His mother was a witch, and one so strong
That could control the moon, make flows and ebbs,
And deal in her command without her power.
These three have robb'd me; and this demi-devil—　275
For he's a bastard one—had plotted with them
To take my life. Two of these fellows you
Must know and own; this thing of darkness I
Acknowledge mine.
CALIBAN:　　　　　　I shall be pinch'd to death.
ALONSO: Is not this Stephano, my drunken butler?　280
SEBASTIAN: He is drunk now. Where had he wine?
ALONSO: And Trinculo is reeling ripe. Where should they
Find this grand liquor that hath gilded 'em?
How cam'st thou in this pickle?
TRINCULO: I have been in such a pickle since I saw you last　285
that, I fear me, will never out of my bones. I shall not fear
flyblowing.
SEBASTIAN: Why, how now, Stephano?
STEPHANO: O, touch me not! I am not Stephano, but a cramp.　290
PROSPERO: You'd be king o' the isle, sirrah?
STEPHANO: I should have been a sore one then.
ALONSO: (*Pointing to* CALIBAN.) This is a strange thing as e'er
I look'd on.

---

216 **still** always; **his** that man's　217 **That** who　225 **glasses** i.e., hours; **gave** out reported　226 **yare** ready　240 **Cap'ring to eye** dancing for joy to see　242 **moping** in a daze　246 **conduct** guide, leader　248 **infest** harass, disturb　249 **pick'd** chosen, convenient　250 **single** i.e., by my own human powers　252 **accidents** occurrences

259 **Coragio** courage; bully-monster gallant monster (ironical)　264 **fine** splendidly attired　270 **badges** emblems of cloth or silver worn on the arms of retainers. Prospero refers here to the stolen clothes as emblems of their villainy　271 **true** honest　274 **deal . . . power** wield the moon's power, either without her authority or beyond her influence　278 **own** recognize, admit as belonging to you　283 **gilded** (1) flushed, made drunk (2) covered with gilt (suggesting the horse-urine)　284 **pickle** (1) fix, predicament (2) pickling brine (in this case, horse urine)　286–287 **fly-blowing** i.e., being fouled by fly-eggs (from which he is saved by being pickled)　291 **sirrah** Standard form of address to an inferior　292 **sore** (1) tyrannical (2) wracked by pain

PROSPERO: He is as disproportion'd in his manners
295   As in his shape. Go, sirrah, to my cell;
     Take with you your companions. As you look
     To have my pardon, trim it handsomely.
CALIBAN: Ay, that I will; and I'll be wise hereafter
     And seek for grace. What a thrice-double ass
300   Was I to take this drunkard for a god
     And worship this dull fool!
PROSPERO: Go to; away!
ALONSO: Hence, and bestow your luggage where you found it.
SEBASTIAN: Or stole it, rather.

(*Exeunt* CALIBAN, STEPHANO, *and* TRINCULO.)

PROSPERO: Sir, I invite your Highness and your train
305   To my poor cell, where you shall take your rest
     For this one night; which, part of it, I'll waste
     With such discourse as, I not doubt, shall make it
     Go quick away—the story of my life,
     And the particular accidents gone by
310   Since I came to this isle. And in the morn
     I'll bring you to your ship, and so to Naples,
     Where I have hope to see the nuptial
     Of these our dear-belov'd solemnized;
     And thence retire me to my Milan, where
315   Every third thought shall be my grave.
ALONSO: I long
     To hear the story of your life, which must
     Take the ear strangely.
PROSPERO: I'll deliver all;
     And promise you calm seas, auspicious gales,
     And sail so expeditious that shall catch
320   Your royal fleet far off. (*Aside to* ARIEL.) My Ariel, chick,

---

306 **waste** spend   309 **accidents** occurrences   317 **Take** take
effect upon, enchant; **deliver** declare, relate

     That is thy charge. Then to the elements
     Be free, and fare thou well!—Please you, draw near.

(*Exeunt omnes.*)

EPILOGUE

Spoken by PROSPERO.

     Now my charms are all o'erthrown,
     And what strength I have 's mine own,
     Which is most faint. Now, 'tis true,
     I must be here confin'd by you,
     Or sent to Naples. Let me not,   5
     Since I have my dukedom got
     And pardon'd the deceiver, dwell
     In this bare island by your spell,
     But release me from my bands
     With the help of your good hands.   10
     Gentle breath of yours my sails
     Must fill, or else my project fails,
     Which was to please. Now I want
     Spirits to enforce, art to enchant,
     And my ending is despair,   15
     Unless I be reliev'd by prayer,
     Which pierces so that it assaults
     Mercy itself and frees all faults.
     As you from crimes would pardon'd be,
     Let your indulgence set me free.   20

(*Exit.*)

---

322 **draw near** i.e., enter my cell

Epilogue   9 **bands** bonds   10 **hands** i.e., applause (the noise of which would break the spell of silence)   13 **want** lack   16 **prayer** i.e., Prospero's petition to the audience   17 **assaults** rightfully gains the attention of   18 **frees** obtains forgiveness of   19 **crimes** sins

CRITICAL CONTEXTS

SIR PHILIP SIDNEY (1554–1586)

from *Apology for Poetry* (1598)

EDITED BY FORREST G. ROBINSON

Philip Sidney was one of the preeminent courtiers of his day. He was a familiar figure at the court of Queen Elizabeth I, led an ill-fated military expedition to the Netherlands (where he was fatally wounded), wrote an important sonnet sequence, Astrophil and Stella, *and a prose romance,* Arcadia. *His* Apology for Poetry *develops a defense of poets and poetry based on their ability to offer a fictive "golden world," an idealized image of reality that can edify, entertain, and instruct.*

Reading Sidney's Apology, *it is useful to bear several questions in mind: What is the problem that Sidney is attempting to address here? Is there a moral or ethical problem posed by poetry, particularly by the fact that poetry is a form of fiction, of lying? Why is it important to Sidney to compare the poet with the historian and the philosopher? What are the underlying problems that Sidney is attempting to address in his assessment of contemporary dramatic genres?*

. . . There is no art delivered to mankind that hath not the works of nature for his principal object, without which they could not consist, and on which they so depend, as they become actors and players, as it were, of what nature will have set forth. So doth the astronomer look upon the stars, and by that he seeth, setteth down what order nature hath taken therein. So do the geometrician and arithmetician in their diverse sorts of quantities. So doth the musician in times tell you which by nature agree, which not. The natural philosopher thereon hath his name, and the moral philosopher standeth upon the natural virtues, vices, and passions of man; and follow nature (saith he) therein, and thou shalt not err. The lawyer saith what men have determined; the historian what men have done. The grammarian speaketh only of the rules of speech, and the rhetorician and logician, considering what in nature will soonest prove and persuade, thereon give artificial[1] rules, which still are compassed within the circle of a question, according to the proposed matter. The physician weigheth the nature of a man's body, and the nature of things helpful or hurtful unto it. And the metaphysic, though it be in the second and abstract notions, and therefore be counted supernatural, yet doth he indeed build upon the depth of nature. Only the poet, disdaining to be tied to any such subjection, lifted up with the vigor of his own invention, doth grow in effect another nature, in making things either better than nature bringeth forth, or quite anew, forms such as never were in nature, as the Heroes, Demigods, Cyclops, Chimeras, Furies, and such like; so as he goeth hand in hand with nature, not enclosed within the narrow warrant of her gifts, but freely ranging only within the zodiac of his own wit.

Nature never set forth the earth in so rich tapestry as divers poets have done, neither with pleasant rivers, fruitful trees, sweet smelling flowers, nor whatsoever else may make the too much loved earth more lovely. Her world is brazen, the poets only deliver a golden. . . .

Our tragedies and comedies (not without cause cried out against), observing rules neither of honest civility nor of skillful poetry, excepting *Gorboduc*[2] (again I say, of those that I have seen), which notwithstanding, as it is full of stately speeches and well sounding phrases, climbing to the height of Seneca his[3] style, and as full of notable morality, which it doth most delightfully teach, and so obtain the very end of poesy; yet in troth it is very defectious in the circumstances, which grieveth me, because it might not remain as an exact model of all tragedies. For it is faulty both in place and time, the two necessary companions of all corporal actions. For where the stage should always represent but one place, and the uttermost time presupposed in it should be, both by Aristotle's precept and common reason, but one day, there is both many days and many places inartificially[4] imagined.

But if it be so in *Gorboduc,* how much more in all the rest? where you shall have Asia of the one side, and Afric of the other, and so many other under-kingdoms, that the player, when he cometh in, must ever begin with telling where he is, or else the tale will not be conceived. Now ye shall have three ladies walk to gather flowers, and then we must believe the stage to be a garden. By and by we hear news of shipwreck in

---

[1]**artificial** humanly contrived, rather than natural

[2]**Gorboduc** an early English play (first performed in 1562), modeled on the tragedies of Seneca

[3]**Seneca his** Seneca's

[4]**inartificially** artlessly

the same place, and then we are to blame if we accept it not for a rock. Upon the back of that comes out a hideous monster with fire and smoke, and then the miserable beholders are bound to take it for a cave. While in the meantime two armies fly in, represented with four swords and bucklers, and then what hard heart will not receive it for a pitched field?

Now of time they are much more liberal, for ordinary it is that two young princes fall in love. After many traverses, she is got with child, delivered of a fair boy, he is lost, groweth a man, falls in love, and is ready to get another child, and all this in two hours' space: which, how absurd it is in sense, even sense may imagine, and art hath taught, and all ancient examples justified, and at this day, the ordinary players in Italy will not err in. Yet will some bring in an example of Eunuchus in Terence, that containeth matter of two days, yet far short of twenty years. True it is, and so was it to be played in two days, and so fitted to the time it set forth. And though Plautus hath in one place done amiss, let us hit with him, and not miss with him. But they will say, how then shall we set forth a story which containeth both many places and many times? And do they not know that a tragedy is tied to the laws of poesy, and not of history, not bound to follow the story, but having liberty, either to feign a quite new matter, or to frame the history to the most tragical conveniency? Again, many things may be told which cannot be showed, if they know the difference betwixt reporting and representing. . . .

IV

Early Modern Europe

The 1993 Willamette College production of Aphra Behn's *The Rover*.

I n London, Paris, and Madrid, theater and drama experienced a second "renaissance" in the later seventeenth century. In these cities, the theater came under the influence and protection of the king and his court, and the theaters of both London and Paris adapted Italian staging practices, as did the theaters of the Spanish court. As scenic technology became increasingly complex and spectacular, theater buildings achieved the form they would hold well into the nineteenth century, and the work of new playwrights and new dramatic designs invigorated the dramatic repertoire.

Yet for all their similarities, the theaters of Restoration England, of Louis XIV's France, and of the Spanish "Golden Age" were sustained by very different social and political climates. In France, Louis XIV declared *"L'état, c'est moi"*—"I am the state"—in 1660, confidently drawing all state authority into the person of the king and his magnificent court. The later seventeenth century in France was a period of royal absolutism, as the throne worked to consolidate its power. In England, conditions were very different, for 1660 brought the restoration of the monarchy. The Restoration period saw an ongoing negotiation between newly installed Charles II and Parliament for power, in which Parliament gradually gained control of many royal prerogatives. In both countries, the theater became associated with the throne and reflected the tensions animating social and political life.

In France, a character in Molière's play *Tartuffe* drew the official portrait of the absolute monarch: "A Prince who sees into our inmost hearts, / And can't be fooled by any trickster's arts." Yet the authoritarian policies of the French government, the internecine competition among members of the court, and even the fortunes of the theater suggest that the king's claim of absolute power was challenged in a variety of ways. Under Louis XIII (reigned 1610–1643) and Louis XIV (reigned 1643–1715), the Crown strove to centralize its power by crushing the claims of the landed nobility and by expanding French rule in a series of costly wars. Since Louis XIII came to the throne at the age of nine, when his father—Henry IV—was assassinated, much of this expansion was carried on by his chief minister, Cardinal Richelieu (1585–1642), and Richelieu's successor, Cardinal Mazarin (1602–1661). The suppression of the traditional nobility was achieved largely through Richelieu's formation of a new bureaucracy loyal to the Crown, partly composed of politically active clergy and partly of commoners promoted over the heads of the nobility to critical positions in the government. Allowing these "new men" to buy aristocratic titles, the Crown raised money and further diluted the power of the nobility. The Crown's ravenous appetite for cash to pay for the lavish life of the court and for expensive building projects, such as the palace of Versailles (built by Louis XIV in 1673), further weakened the nobility and alienated the peasantry. Using tax-farmers, who paid a fixed sum to the government in exchange for the authority to collect taxes and pocket the excess as profit, the Crown squeezed the nobles' wealth directly into the royal coffers, impoverishing their lands and making the peasantry increasingly rebellious.

A poor and disaffected peasantry, a jealous aristocracy, an upstart bourgeoisie, and an increasingly authoritarian and isolated monarchy: this became the recipe for revolution. Although the French Revolution did not erupt until 1789, France suffered civil convulsions throughout the seventeenth century that dramatize the tension between Louis' absolutist rhetoric and the political realities of his reign. The nobles led a series of rebellions called

THE POLITICAL CLIMATE

the Fronde throughout the 1640s and 1650s, in an effort to unseat Louis and his powerful ministers. Louis defeated these uprisings and finally sealed the fate of his enemies when he required the nobility to attend him at Versailles, so he could keep his eye on their activities. However, the Fronde was part of a more pervasive unrest. Relentless taxation, economic stagnation, and repeated famines throughout the seventeenth century made the peasants angry as well, and peasant riots and rebellions took place in nearly every province of France in nearly every decade of the century. Finally, Louis XIV also had difficulty with the most volatile issue of seventeenth-century Europe—religious dissent. The close ties between the Crown and the church often resulted in the suppression of Protestant sects, particularly the Calvinist French Huguenots. Protestant rebellion had forced the enactment of the Edict of Nantes in 1598, granting the Huguenots considerable religious freedom. Louis XIV revoked the Edict in 1685, giving the government wider latitude to suppress increasingly energetic religious protest. Louis XIV carefully crafted the image of the "Le Roi Soleil"—the Sun King—whose absolute authority seemed almost a force of nature, not a fact of politics. Throughout his reign, though, Louis had to contend with recalcitrant factions who refused to accept completely his characterization of the king's power.

In England, resistance to royal authority had been much more successful. Between 1603 and 1642, the Stuart kings James I (reigned 1603–1625) and his son, Charles I (reigned 1625–1649), worked to limit the power of Parliament and to enforce increasingly strict religious laws that suppressed the Protestant Puritan sects and demanded conformity with the Church of England. In 1642, Parliament passed legislation limiting the powers of the throne, and Civil War between Parliamentary and Royalist forces erupted. Charles I was executed in 1649; his wife and children (including the future king, Charles II) escaped to France. From 1653 to 1658, Oliver Cromwell served as Lord Protector of the realm, but Royalist sentiments eventually prevailed and established Charles II (reigned 1660–1685) on the throne.

Although the monarchy was restored—the term *Restoration* refers generally to the period of Charles II's reign and the remainder of the seventeenth century—Charles II was in no position to command the nation, and English politics in the later seventeenth century mainly concerned the negotiation of power between the Crown and Parliament. Charles' death in 1685 spurred a crisis in that his son James II (reigned 1685–1688) was Catholic and threatened to compromise English religious and civil autonomy from the Catholic church and the Catholic states of Europe. In 1689, Parliament effectively deposed James, inviting his Protestant daughter Mary (reigned as Mary II, 1689–1694) and her husband, William of Orange (reigned as William III, 1689–1702), to return to England and assume the throne. While Louis XIV increasingly insisted on the autonomous power of the throne in France, the Parliament in England finally achieved a lasting compromise with the Crown in the form of a constitutional monarchy. In bringing William and Mary into power, Parliament gained the authority of consent over royal succession, a power it confirmed in 1702 in naming James II's daughter Anne as successor (reigned as Queen Anne, 1702–1714).

While in an important sense the gulf separating French and English culture has always been narrow and deep, like the English Channel, Spanish culture in the Renaissance arises from a very different history. Spain was occupied by the Moors in 711 and is still marked by its five centuries of Islamic culture. In 1479, Ferdinand of Aragon and Isabella of Castile were married, forming the alliance that gave rise to modern Spain. In 1480 they joined forces with the Catholic Inquisition, expelling Jews from the country. At the Conquest of Granada in 1492, the Moors were finally driven out of Spain.

Having formed a single state, the Spanish monarchy successfully expanded its reach into a global empire during the sixteenth century. Under Charles V, Spain's territory included its many New World colonies as well as the Netherlands and the Holy Roman Empire of central Europe, and the culture of the Spanish court was unrivaled in Europe; this was the era of Velásquez and El Greco. During the reign of Philip II (1556–1598), however, Spain's domination of Europe began to wane. Spain became involved in a brutal and expensive effort to retain control of the Netherlands, a hotbed of Protestant resistance. English soldiers— Sir Philip Sidney and Ben Jonson, among others—fought the Spanish in the Netherlands, and Philip tried in several ways to outmaneuver the English. He proposed marriage to Queen Elizabeth, but as with other suitors, she strung him along for political purposes and finally refused him. He also mounted a massive naval invasion of England, the Spanish Armada of 1588, which was surprisingly defeated. Spain continued to wane in the seventeenth century, eventually losing the Netherlands and losing Portugal in 1657. By 1665, Spain was ruled by the last of the Hapsburg kings, the deformed imbecile Charles II (1665–1700). The death of Charles II drew all of Europe into the Wars of the Spanish Succession.

THEATER IN FRANCE, 1660–1700

Louis XIV's familiar sobriquet, "Le Roi Soleil," derives from a role he played in a court ballet devised for him in 1653. A fine dancer, Louis sponsored and took part in a wide variety of entertainments. Moreover, the centralization of power in the king and the court paralleled the increasing institutionalization of the arts under Louis XIV, as a means of advancing his own prestige and of keeping control over potentially seditious activities. The most famous of these institutions—the **ACADÉMIE FRANÇAISE**—was chartered in 1637 and used by Cardinal Richelieu to evaluate a critical controversy surrounding Pierre Corneille's play *The Cid*. Corneille's detractors had sharply attacked the play, and Richelieu urged the Académie to resolve whether *The Cid* could legitimately be described as effective tragedy in neoclassical terms (on *neoclassicism,* see p. 274). In return, Richelieu promoted the Académie and its aims, the purification of French language and literature, and the advancement of official French culture. Louis XIV assumed the role of official protector of the Académie Française in 1672 and sponsored other institutions as ornaments to his reign: the Académie Royale de Musique (1672), the Académie Royale de Peinture et de Sculpture (1648), the Académie des Inscriptions (1663), the Académie des Sciences (1666), and the Académie de l'Architecture (1671). The institution of the stage was no exception. Theatrical companies had always needed the king's license to play in Paris, and Louis licensed several companies and named Molière's company as the *Troupe du roi.* After Molière's death in 1673, the leading tragic actress in Paris, Mademoiselle Champmeslé, joined with Molière's troupe and gained the king's patronage. The new company—the **COMÉDIE FRANÇAISE**— opened in August of 1680. It held a **MONOPOLY** on the production of all spoken drama in French, and although this monopoly has long since vanished, the Comédie Française remains the principal company performing the French classical repertoire.

In Louis XIV's Paris, the institutions of art—including the theater—were identified with the prerogatives of the king and his court, though the structure of the theater had its roots in practices dating back to the Middle Ages. Throughout the later Middle Ages and into the sixteenth century, stage production in Paris was controlled by the Confrérie de la Passion, a guildlike corporation initially formed to stage religious drama. In 1545 the Confrérie purchased land in Paris from the Duke of Burgundy and erected the Hôtel de Bourgogne, at the time probably the only permanent theater building in Europe (*hôtel* in this case means "hall" or "large building"). Extensively remodeled in 1647, the Hôtel de Bourgogne served as the model for other theaters built in the seventeenth century: the Théâtre du Marais (built in a tennis court in 1629, rebuilt in 1644); the Palais-Cardinal (built by Richelieu in 1640; later renamed the Palais-Royal); the Salle des Machines (1642), and the Comédie Française (1689).

The shape of these theaters owes something to the Hôtel de Bourgogne, and something to tennis courts as well, for tennis courts were often used as theaters. (In the sixteenth and seventeenth centuries, tennis courts were long indoor rooms with side galleries.) These

GROUND PLAN OF THE COMÉDIE FRANÇAISE THEATER

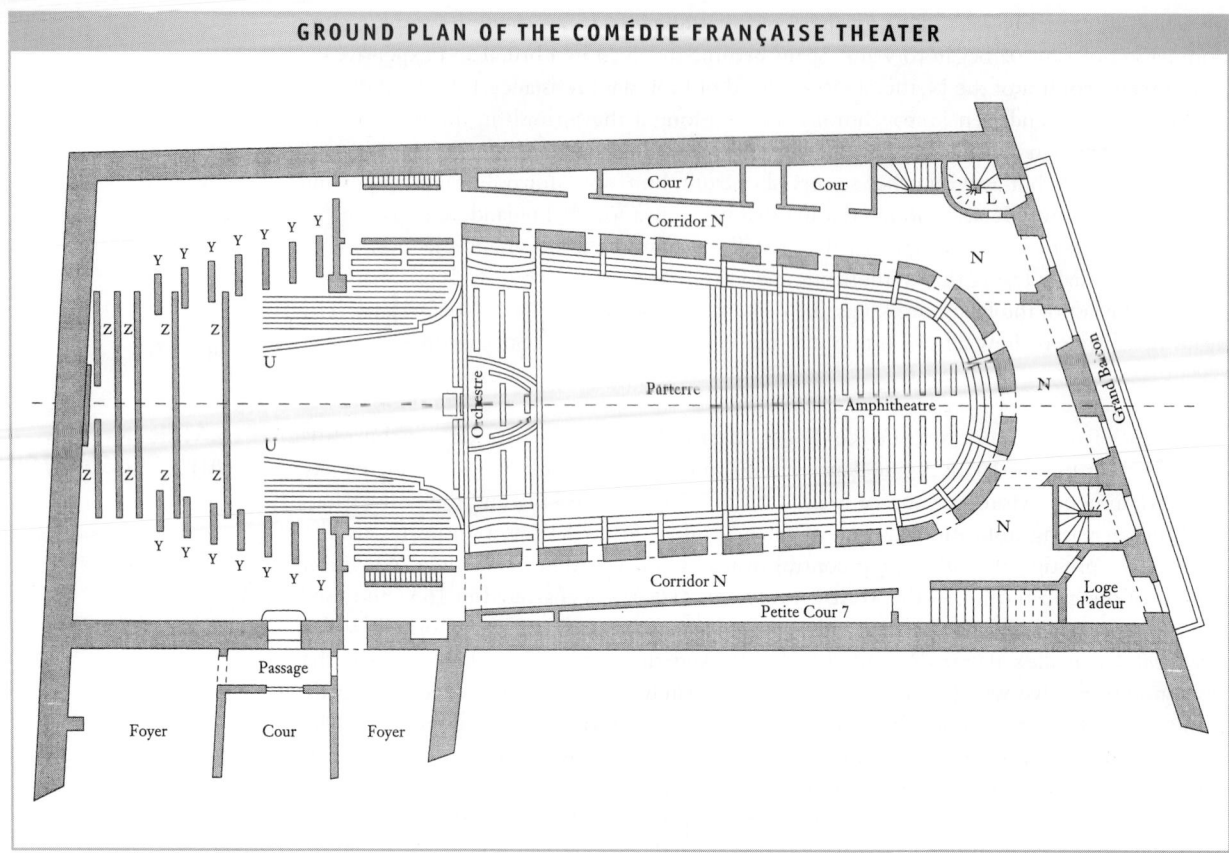

The Comédie Française had this basic design from 1689 to 1770. Note the open *parterre,* the wings (marked Y), and the backdrops (Z). The benches on the stage were added during the eighteenth century.

theaters generally had deep, **RAKED STAGES** (40 feet deep, 45 feet wide at the Hôtel de Bourgogne) that faced an open **PIT** called the **PARTERRE** (literally, "on the ground") which was used for standing spectators. The auditorium had **BOXES** on three sides; **GALLERY** seating rose above the boxes opposite the stage; some patrons were also seated on the stage itself. The theaters were large—the Hôtel de Bourgogne initially held 1,600 spectators, the Comédie Française held 2,000—and many theaters made extensive use of stage scenery, sometimes concocting extraordinary spectacles. In a fantasy celebrating Louis XIV's wedding in 1662, the entire royal family and its entourage were "flown" by machines in the Salle des Machines; in a production in 1671, 300 deities were lifted aloft. The dramatic theaters— the Hôtel de Bourgogne, the Palais-Royal, the Comédie Française—tended to avoid such effects, using instead a single setting for each play, depending on the genre of the play. The theaters generally used a series of staggered **WINGS AND BACKDROP** to create the effect of perspective, adapting both scenic practices and scene-changing technology from Italian theaters.

Acting companies in Paris were organized as investment corporations requiring the patronage of the Crown and had long included women in their ranks. Louis XIV's reign saw a series of great actresses take the stage, Mademoiselle DuParc and Mademoiselle Champmeslé among them. Companies were comprised of twelve members (eight men, four women), who shared the company's profits. The company hired additional actors when necessary. The Comédie Française standardized this practice: its twelve main actors—called

SOCIÉTAIRES—ran the company for twenty years, and new *sociétaires* could be recruited only after the retirement of current members. Actors in the Comédie Française received an annual subsidy from the Crown and a retirement pension if they completed their twenty years with the company. The company purchased plays, which were cast by the author. Throughout the 1650s and 1660s the major companies kept about 70 plays in repertoire and generally played three or four times per week. After the 1680s, the Comédie Française began daily performances, beginning at 5 P.M.

We should recall that life at court was itself a kind of performance, and that attending the theater provided ample opportunity for aristocrats, courtiers, and aspiring courtiers to display and preen themselves. In a milieu so dependent on the king's preference, we can easily imagine how stage seating and side boxes emphasized that the evening's entertainment included the audience's performances as well as the actors'. This sense of the reciprocity between court and stage is signaled more concretely by the fortunes of the Parisian theaters after Louis XIV moved the court to Versailles. Although five companies flourished in Paris while Louis kept court in the city, by 1700 only two remained.

At the outbreak of the English Civil War in 1642, Parliament closed the London theaters, putting a stop to dramatic performance. Some companies managed to mount secret productions between 1642 and 1660, but Parliament and city officials moved quickly to suppress them, sometimes by destroying the theater buildings. In the 1650s, however, William Davenant (1606–1668), a Royalist supporter of Charles I and successor to Ben Jonson as writer of court masques, attempted to mount operas. In 1656 he succeeded in staging a production of *The Siege of Rhodes* at Rutland House, performing it again in 1658 and 1659 at the Cockpit theater and elsewhere in London.

THEATER IN ENGLAND, 1660–1737

The restoration of Charles II to the throne in 1660 inaugurated a period of renewed theatrical vitality. As in France—where Charles developed a taste for theater during his exile—the theater was closely associated with royal prerogatives. Upon his return, Charles rewarded **PATENTS** to William Davenant and Thomas Killegrew (1612–1683) to open theaters under royal authority. These **PATENT THEATERS** (also called "theaters royal")—Davenant's Duke's company, and Killigrew's King's company—thus held a royal monopoly on the production of spoken English drama. Although they underwent huge modifications, the patent theaters dominated the legitimate theater until the mid-nineteenth century, when legislation was passed that finally broke their monopoly. Yet monopoly could not guarantee support. The two companies, unable to turn a profit, were united into a single company from 1682 to 1695.

When the theaters reopened in 1660, theatrical taste had changed significantly. Although a few of the older, pre-1642 theater buildings were still standing, they could not handle the new theater technology. For, as in the French theater, the English theater rapidly encouraged the development of scenic practices already well-known in Italy—a **PROSCENIUM** stage and moveable painted wings and backdrop used to create a visual setting for the play. Onstage, theaters used stock sets—one for classical tragedy, one for romantic comedy, and so on—that conformed to the dramatic genre of the play. In 1661, Davenant converted Lisle's Tennis Court to the Lincoln's Inn Fields Theater, which measured 30 by 70 feet; he replaced this theater with the Dorset Garden Theater in 1671. Killegrew erected his Theatre Royal in Bridges Street in 1663. When it burned in 1672, he built a new Theatre Royal in Drury Lane, which opened in 1674; a theater has occupied this site down to the present time.

The new English theaters were much smaller than the French theaters. The Drury Lane theater, for example, held 650 to 700 people, though it was expanded throughout the late seventeenth and eighteenth centuries and eventually held more than 2,000. Nonetheless,

CHRISTOPHER WREN'S THEATRE ROYAL, DRURY LANE

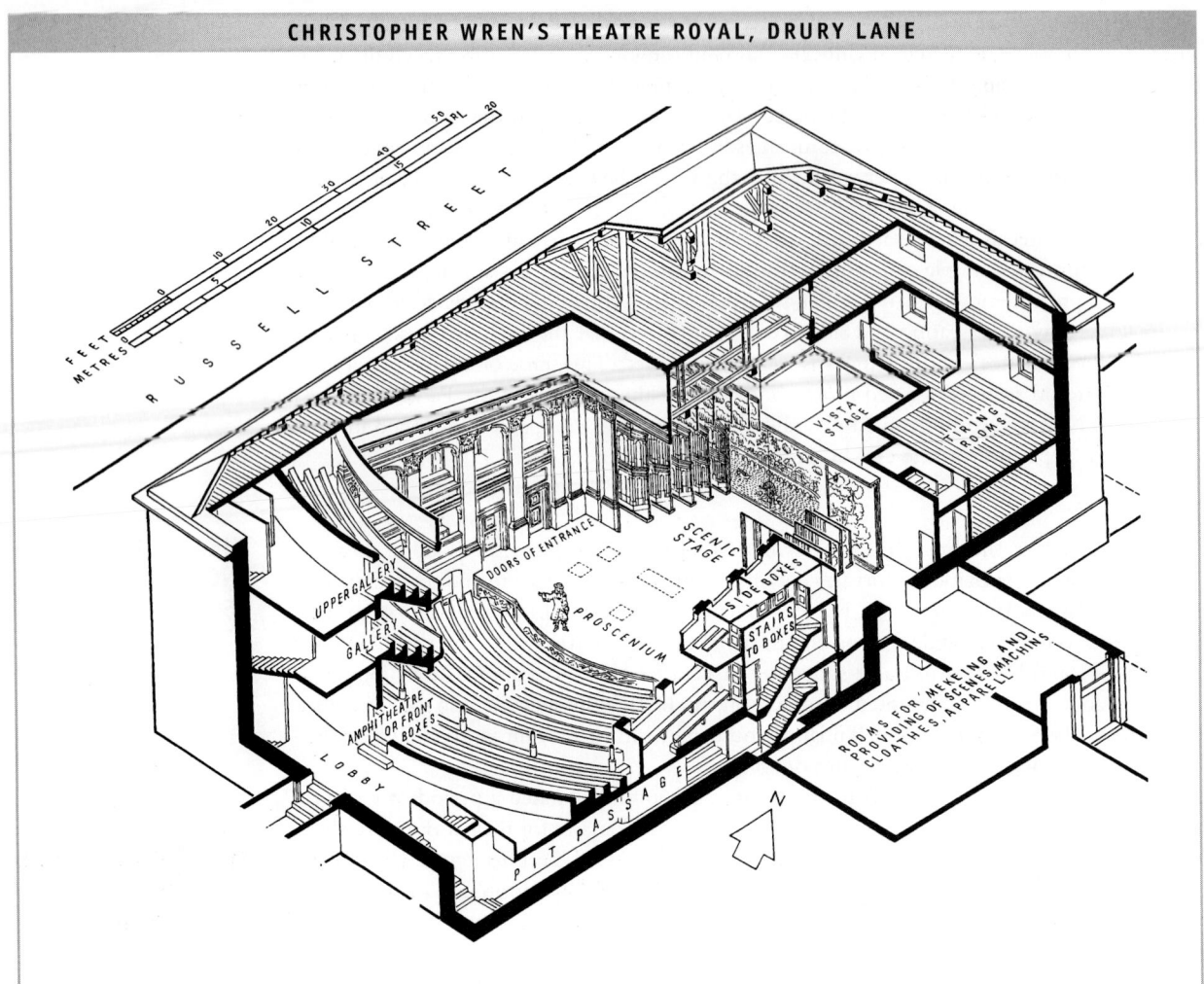

In 1674, Christopher Wren designed a new Theatre Royal, Drury Lane. Note that the acting area extends to the apron, in front of the wing and backdrop stage scenery. Pit seating, side boxes, and two galleries also are visible.

like the French theaters, the English houses also introduced new design and staging practices: a proscenium stage flanked by a large **APRON,** footlights to illuminate the stage, a raked pit with benches (the French *parterre* was flat and had no seats), side and rear box seats, and a rear gallery. This division of the house accorded with social and class distinctions in the audience, which was in any event a narrow selection of the English public, in part because the theater was recognized as the ornament of the privileged, and—not incidentally—because plays were produced in the afternoon, when working people could not easily attend. The entire auditorium was lighted by chandeliers, making the audience itself very much a part of the show: in an important sense the performance did not stop at the edge of the stage. Although the theaters were not at the court itself, they were frequently patronized by courtiers and the nobility, who preened and displayed themselves to the audience—sometimes from seats onstage. Charles II—who numbered the well-known actress Nell Gwynn (1650–1687) among his many mistresses—was also frequently in the audience.

Companies were generally managed by one of the actors, and they avoided the need for lengthy casting and rehearsal by developing **LINES OF BUSINESS,** in which each actor would specialize in a particular type of character: heroic lead, comic lead, male heavy, female heavy, utility player, and so on. Acting style was relatively formal, and actors often played downstage on the apron directly to the audience; a famous speech—one of Hamlet's soliloquies, for example—would be delivered directly to the audience, something like an operatic aria today, a practice called **POINTING.** As the theater developed in the later seventeenth century, sharing companies were replaced by companies financed by outside investors, who paid the actors salaries and took a percentage of the profits. Companies were large and salaries low; actors were compensated by **BENEFIT** performances, in which the actor (on his or her benefit night) received the entire profit from a given evening's performance, minus the operating expenses of the house. The practice of supplementing salaries with benefit performances continued well into the nineteenth century, and although most benefit nights—after the house expenses were deducted—left the actors with little additional pay, benefits provided an excuse to keep actors' salaries low.

By far the greatest innovation in the English theater, though, was the introduction of actresses onstage. English comedies in this period were often frankly concerned with sexual intrigue, and the actresses who played in them—and in the new heroic tragedies, and in the plays by Shakespeare, Jonson, Fletcher, and other Renaissance playwrights who continued to hold the stage—also had a reputation for sexual licentiousness. Yet, while several actresses, like Nell Gwynne, were mistresses of the famous and powerful, the phenomenon of regarding actresses as sexual objects, of classing them with prostitutes, has more to do with the status and vulnerability of working women in a highly stratified and patriarchal society than it does with the immorality of the stage or its performers. Indeed, actresses' ongoing struggle to assert themselves as legitimate performers was born at this time as well, epitomized in the careers of Elizabeth Barry (1658–1713), Anne Bracegirdle (1663–1748), and many others.

THEATER IN SPAIN'S GOLDEN AGE, 1580–1680

As in medieval England and France, medieval Spanish theater was strongly influenced by the church, which saw in the drama a source of instruction and inspiration. Although there is some evidence for liturgical drama as early as the twelfth century, the principal form of medieval theater was the *AUTO SACRAMENTALE,* a form of allegorical religious drama initially devised to celebrate the feast of Corpus Christi. But while the mystery cycles were suppressed in Protestant England, the Spanish *autos* continued to be performed alongside the secular theater until they were banned in 1765. Like the English cycles, the *autos* were in civic hands, and by the late sixteenth century major cities would perform *autos* as many as three times per year, usually in the central city plaza before a gathering of citizens and civic officials. Professional actors were hired for the *autos* and were drawn through the city on wagons (*CARROS*); the *carros* were heavily decorated, and a prize was given for the most spectacular *carro*. Despite their abstract themes, the *autos* remained extremely popular and drew on the talents of the best playwrights of the era—between 1647 and 1681, for instance, all the *autos* performed in Madrid were written by Pedro Calderón de la Barca.

Philip II, Philip III, and Philip IV were all interested in theater and commissioned playwrights to devise entertainments; during the reign of Philip III, Spain developed an impressive court theater. Early in the seventeenth century, this court theater merely occupied a hall at the Alcázar palace, as Ben Jonson and Inigo Jones had done at Whitehall palace in England, and it produced a similar kind of entertainment: mythological dramas that required spectacular scenery, effects, and costumes. But by the 1630s, the center of court theater shifted to the new palace of Buen Retiro. Here, in 1640 Cosme Lotti (d. 1643) was retained to build a permanent theater that could perform the scenic effects of the Italian theater. This theater was roofed, but in its basic design resembled the most influential of Spanish theaters in the Golden Age, the public theater or *CORRAL*.

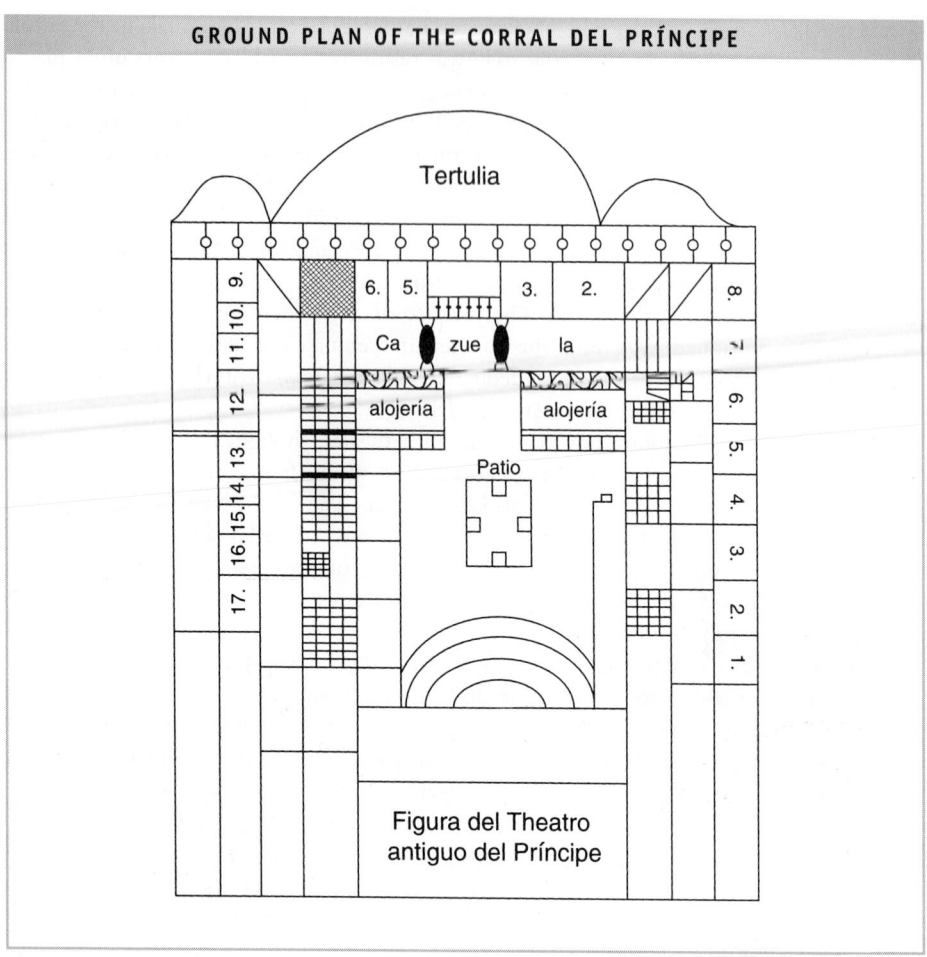

GROUND PLAN OF THE CORRAL DEL PRÍNCIPE

Tertulia

9. 6. 5. 3. 2. 8.

Ca zue la 7.

alojería alojería 6.

Patio 5.

4.

3.

2.

1.

10. 11. 12. 13. 14. 15. 16. 17.

Figura del Theatro
antiguo del Príncipe

Made in 1730, this drawing of the Corral del Príncipe shows the important features of the theater: the *patio,* the *alojería,* the *gradas* (unmarked), and the *cazuela.*

Although the Spanish public theater resembled the public theaters of Elizabethan London, it stood in a much different relationship to city life. While the English theaters were banned from the city proper and were erected across the Thames in Southwark, the Spanish theaters were public institutions. Since the medieval church held the rights to theatrical production, the public theaters were licensed by religious confraternities in the sixteenth century, which used the funds for various charitable purposes, including maintaining the general hospital of Madrid. By the early seventeenth century, these funds were paid directly to the city, and theaters continued to subsidize charities well into the nineteenth century. Companies of actors were licensed to play in the city, and took a lease on a *corral* for a stated period of time. In general, Spanish companies toured major cities and towns, and only Seville and Madrid allowed two companies to perform at the same time. While playwrights were initially associated with individual companies, by the seventeenth century playwrights would sell their plays to the company: they were paid very well for an *auto,* and adequately for a regular play—about 500 reales, or about 10 times the daily wage of a laborer. Although companies were composed of men and boys until 1587, when women were allowed to appear onstage, the church issued a decree banning women from performing onstage in 1596. By 1599, however, a royal council ruled that actresses could be permitted, providing they were married to a member of the company; it also ruled against cross-dressing, so that when

VIEW OF THE CORRAL DEL PRÍNCIPE

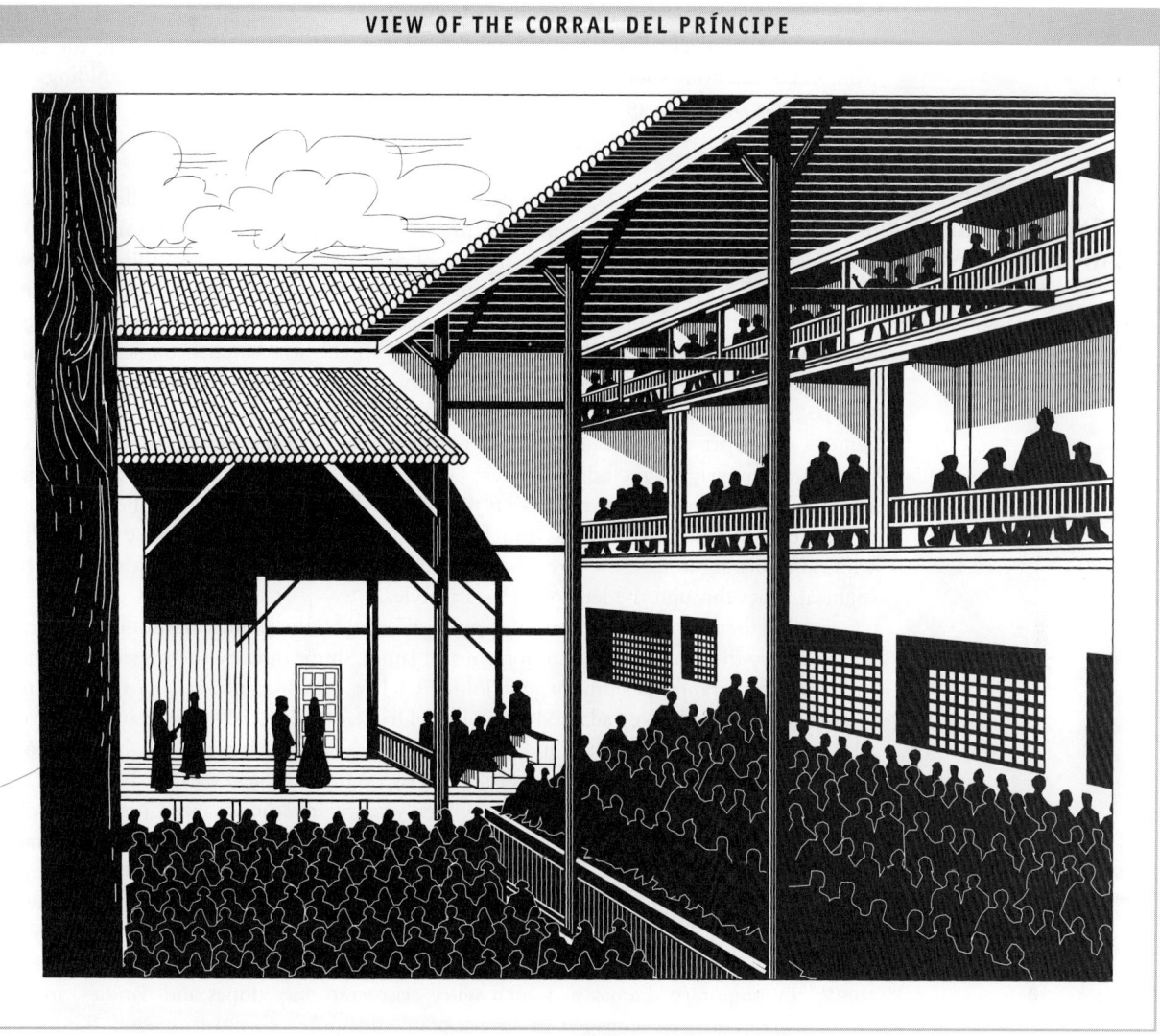

This illustration provides a view of the Corral del Príncipe from the rear of the *patio,* perhaps from the *cazuela.*

Rosaura appeared dressed as a man in Calderón's *Life Is a Dream,* the actress wore a man's costume only down to the waist with a skirt below.

The reciprocity between the city and the theater is also revealed in the design of public theaters of the golden age, particularly the two principal theaters of Madrid, the Corral de la Cruz, opened in 1579 as Spain's first theater, and the Corral del Príncipe, opened in 1583. The theaters were originally merely stages placed in a courtyard enclosed on three or four sides by four-story buildings; over time the theaters gradually acquired possession of these structures, but in the meantime the buildings' galleries and windows could be sold to spectators separately. The central courtyard or **PATIO** was unroofed, and like the pit of English theaters was occupied by standing spectators. In the seventeenth century, a few rows of benches (called **TABURETES**) were erected near the stage, on a raised and fenced dais. Along the sides of the *patio* rose the **GRADAS,** steeply raked rows of seats that rose to the second floor. The **ALOJERÍA,** a tavern, served refreshments, and was located at the rear of the *patio;* above the *alojería* were several stories of galleries: the **CAZUELA,** or women's gallery, on the second floor; above it galleries for the City of Madrid and Council of Castile officials; and a gallery for intellectual and church officials, the *TERTULIA.* Above the *gradas,* the grated windows of the houses served as box seats. The third and fourth floors of the buildings were converted to *DESVANES* or "attics," small open galleries.

DRAMATIC INNOVATION IN FRANCE, ENGLAND, AND SPAIN

Although theatrical production extended into a number of other forms—ballet, opera, royal pageants, and the special-effects extravaganzas called **MACHINE PLAYS**—prevailing attitudes, particularly in France, prohibited the mixing of dramatic genres: Tragedy and comedy were firmly discriminated from one another and from others kinds of entertainment. In France, comedy—and, indeed, the organization of theatrical companies—was particularly influenced by the techniques of the Italian *COMMEDIA DELL'ARTE.* French tragic drama inherited a taste for classical subject matter from the schools and universities, which had led Europe in translating Greek and Roman playwrights into French. Throughout the sixteenth century, the court sponsored a variety of efforts to classicize the theater, supporting several important playwrights, including Robert Garnier and Étienne Jodelle, who created highly wrought and refined tragedies based on the model of classical drama. The heroic tragedies of Pierre Corneille (1606–1684) and Jean Racine (1639–1699) epitomize this tradition while also turning it in a new direction, refracting contemporary moral, political, and philosophical issues through the lens of a classical style.

English drama in the Restoration also was affected by the **HEROIC TRAGEDIES** of France and Spain, by the comedies of Ben Jonson and James Shirley, and by the tragedies of Shakespeare and of Francis Beaumont and John Fletcher, which continued to be performed, though often in revised or adapted form. John Dryden (1631–1700), for example, not only adapted versions of *The Tempest* and *Antony and Cleopatra* (the latter as *All for Love,* 1677), but also wrote plays in the mode of heroic tragedy, such as *Aureng-Zebe* (1675) and *The Conquest of Granada* (1669). Heroic tragedy generally represents the idealized passions of characters forced to choose between love and personal honor. Comic drama took its inspiration both from European models—Molière's plays, for example—and from the earlier plays of Ben Jonson, but in the plays of William Wycherly (1640–1716), Sir George Etherege (1635–1692), and William Congreve (1670–1729), English comedy rapidly developed its own original style. Restoration comedies are most often in the vein of **COMEDY OF MANNERS,** contemporary dramas in which witty aristocrats, city dupes and dandies, and dull country gentlemen are engaged in an elaborate adventure of sexual intrigue. Restoration comedy is often elegant and verbally polished, and obsessed with issues of class, privilege, manners, and sex. In addition, much as the Restoration theater witnessed the rise of actresses onstage, it also saw the first women to achieve success as playwrights: Aphra Behn (1640–1689), Catharine Trotter (1679–1749), and Susanna Centlivre (1670–1723).

After the turn of the century, the risqué character of many plays spurred one of the perennial movements to restrain the theater as an immoral institution. Partly as a result of Jeremy Collier's diatribe *A Short View of the Immorality and Profaneness of the English Stage* (1698), and partly as a result of changing attitudes and social mores, English comedy after 1700—the plays of Sir Richard Steele (1672–1729), Colley Cibber (1671–1757), George Farquhar (1678–1707), Oliver Goldsmith (1728–1774), and Richard Brinsley Sheridan (1751–1816), for instance—became more romantic and sentimental. Moreover, political satire in English theater was also sharply limited with the passing of the Stage Licensing Act of 1737. After 1737, all plays produced for public entertainment had to be submitted for censorship prior to production. The censor could require changes, delete words, passages, or scenes, or refuse to grant permission entirely. Confronting the Act by producing a nonlicensed play was to risk the fining and imprisonment of everyone involved in the production. While theaters found a variety of ways to subvert or sidestep the law, the censorship remained in effect—with some modifications—until 1968, inhibiting the possibility of dramatic innovation.

The term *commedia dell' arte* means the "comedy of the professional players," and *commedia* became popular throughout Europe in the sixteenth century. *Commedia* companies were itinerant (though one was established in Paris for part of Louis XIV's reign), organized around ten or twelve actors, men and women, each of whom played a stock character who could be easily recognized by typical and routine behavior. Although the characters were fixed, the plots that *commedia* companies played were generally improvised; the actor relied on the traits of his or her character and a core of stage business from which to invent action and dialogue. The cast usually included one or two pairs of young lovers (the **INNAMORATO** and **INNAMORATA**), good-looking, aristocratic, or fashionable characters played without masks. The rest of the cast was masked and played more stereotypical roles: the **CAPITANO,** a military braggart and coward, played with sword and cape; the **PANTALONE,** an elderly dupe, often in love, played in stockings, breeches, and slippers; the **DOTTORE,** sometimes actually a doctor, but otherwise a pedantic friend of the Pantalone; and a variety of comic parts called **ZANNI,** usually sly servants. The most familiar of these parts is *Arlecchino,* or **HARLEQUIN,** a cunning character who is usually an acrobat, wearing a patched costume (later refined to a diamond-shaped pattern), a black cap, and carrying his slapstick—the origin of our term "slapstick," which gives some idea of what *commedia* humor was like. *Commedia* was also popular in England, but it had fewer long-term effects on the comic drama than on the rise of English **PANTOMIME.** In England, plays were often followed by a short **AFTERPIECE,** which frequently led Harlequin into adventures with mythological characters. John Rich (1692–1761), taking the name Lun, was the most famous Harlequin of the early eighteenth-century English stage.

PANTALONE AND HARLEQUIN

Note the mask and breeches of the Pantalone (left), and the mask, slapstick, and diamond-shaped patches of the Harlequin (right).

In the early sixteenth century, a Spanish theatrical manager may well have written his own plays and acted in them himself. Lope de Rueda (1510–1565), for example, was a touring performer and the author of both *autos* and secular plays. But by the late sixteenth century, companies would pay a playwright for the play, and the theaters had made several genres popular: the *CAPA Y ESPADA* or heroic/romantic "cape and sword" play was very popular, as was the *RUIDO* or "noise" play. But the forms of Golden Age drama were in many ways determined by the extraordinary and prolific career of Lope Félix de Vega Carpio (1562–1635). Lope de Vega is frequently said to have written more than 1,500 plays—which points to the immense popularity of the theater and its constant need for new material—and more than 450 of his plays have survived. He is particularly associated with *COMEDIA NUEVA,* a genre mixing the tragic and the comic, high and low characters (including the *GRACIOSO,* a comic fool), and usually having a romantic plot. In the intervals between the acts of his plays, short interludes (*ENTREMESES*) were performed, which were coherent plays in themselves. Like other playwrights in this period, Lope de Vega also wrote *autos,* but his best-known work is *Fuente Ovejuna* (1614), a play about a vicious tyrant that critics have seen as an allegory on Portuguese independence.

Lope shared the stage with several equally brilliant playwrights, principally with Pedro Calderón de la Barca (1600–1681), who succeeded Lope de Vega as Spain's most influential dramatist. Miguel de Cervantes (1547–1616), the author of *Don Quixote,* wrote about thirty plays, of which sixteen remain. Tirso de Molina (1584–1648) was a friar who had written more than 400 plays—eighty survive—before he was reprimanded by the Council of Castile; his best-known play, *El Burlador de Seville* (*The Trickster of Seville*) is the earliest play on the subject of Don Juan. The playwright Guillén de Castro (1569–1631) was a friend of Lope de Vega; his influence on the French theater is perhaps as marked as it was in Spain. Guillén de Castro wrote *Las Mocedades del Cid* (*The Youthful Adventures of the Cid*), which was adapted by Corneille as *Le Cid* and ignited a furious controversy about neoclassical esthetics.

NEOCLASSICISM, DRAMA, AND THEATER

In both France and England, the arts in general and drama in particular were closely regulated by the state, a state of affairs sustained by the rise of **NEOCLASSICISM.** Neoclassicism is, in the simplest sense, the revival of what was taken to be a "classical" ordering of the arts. The literature of classical Greece and Rome began to be recovered in the fourteenth and fifteenth centuries, first through the dissemination of texts preserved in monasteries and later through expanded contact with the Islamic world in the sixteenth and seventeenth centuries. Translating, imitating, and adapting classical texts, European writers in the later seventeenth century appeared to "revive" the principles of classical art. In practice, however, neoclassicism offered an *interpretation* of the classics, emphasizing order, control, decorum, reason, and harmony.

In many respects, neoclassicism relied on the authority of Aristotle's *Poetics,* published first in Latin translation in 1498 and then in Italian in 1549, and on the series of critical commentaries written on Aristotle throughout the sixteenth century. Aristotle's *Poetics* is something of a naturalist's description of the several species of poetry and their characteristics, but readers in the sixteenth and seventeenth centuries fell under the influence of Aristotle's enormous authority (as in *Doctor Faustus,* Act 1) and quickly transformed the *Poetics* into a prescription, a series of rules, for producing the most perfect and effective tragedies. Two central precepts of the *Poetics* regard the tragic hero's actions: Those acts must seem both necessary and probable, and they should not entirely violate moral expectations. Neoclassical critics and playwrights schematized Aristotle's descriptions as necessary features of dramatic composition, arguing that a tragedy should be rigorously and causally plotted and should reveal the workings of providential justice through the actions of universalized or typical characters. These goals were transformed into the famous "unities" of neoclassicism: A play should take place within a single day (unity of time), in one location (unity of place), and consist of a single line of action, a single plot (unity of action). The action of neoclassical tragedy, therefore, is concentrated, maintaining a uniformity of tone and style called **DECORUM.** Plays in this mode maintain a single, narrow range of language and behavior; the action is either idealized (rather than realistic) in tragedy, or commonplace in comedy: tragic characters are classic and heroic, while comic characters are contemporary, even bourgeois; tragedy undertakes the conflict between the ideal passions of love and honor, while comedy takes its cue from more earthly desires—lust, greed, hypocrisy, and so on. Following the recovery of Vitruvius' *De Architectura* (15 BCE) in 1414, this neoclassical sensibility urged the modern stage to imitate Vitruvius' distinction between the proper stage settings of tragedy and comedy: classical architecture for tragedy, urban architecture for comedy. Especially in seventeenth-century Paris, theaters adjusted their stagecraft to these ideals of regularity and decorum, assigning a generalized palace setting to the elevated world of tragedy, and the *chambre à quatre portes*—the room with four doors—to the lower, contemporary world of comedy.

Writing later in the eighteenth century, the Englishman Thomas Davies characterized the differences between French and English audiences and suggests that neoclassical ideals did not take root as deeply in the English theater as they did in France:

> The Frenchman, when he goes to a play, seems to make his entertainment a matter of importance. The long speeches in the plays of Corneille, Racine, Crébillon, and Voltaire, which would disgust an English ear, are extremely pleasing to our light neighbours: they sit in silence, and enjoy the beauty of sentiment, and energy of language; and are taught habitually to cry at scenes of distress. The Englishman looks upon the theatre as a place of amusement; he does not expect to be alarmed with terror, or wrought upon by scenes of commiseration; but he is surprised into the feeling of those passions, and sheds tears because he cannot avoid it. The theatre, to most Englishmen, becomes a place of instruction by chance.

Davies, of course, betrays a common chauvinism of the English toward the French: while the French are pedantic and calculating, the English are spontaneous. But this distinction between English and French theaters—one for "art," one for "entertainment"; one tragic, one comic—conceals the fundamental likenesses between the two institutions and the plays they put on the stage. As the plays of Corneille, Racine, and Dryden suggest, neoclassical tragedy imposes severe and artificial forms on the irrepressible forces of the passions, which inevitably break through the formal speech and decorous behavior of the characters to destroy them and sometimes the state as well. Comedy of the period in England and in France reveals a cognate tension, as the formal acting styles and stereotyped characters common in Restoration comedy seem barely able to contain the bottomless appetites of the plays' heroes. To this extent, neoclassical decorum embodies a barely contained anxiety about the power of forms—forms of conduct, forms of art, forms of state—to prevent a revolution of unreason and disorder.

EARLY MODERN DRAMA IN PERFORMANCE AND HISTORY

In many respects, the theater of seventeenth-century Europe is continuous with our own. Given the fact that the European monarchies were rapidly expanding their political and mercantile influence around the globe, it's not surprising to find that their culture became exported as well, often to the cultivated elites of their new colonies. In Mexico, for example, the seventeenth-century nun Sor Juana Inés de la Cruz (1651–1695) composed both *autos* and full-length dramas that echo—and, indeed, rival—the plays of the Spanish playwrights Calderón and Lope de Vega. The English drama of this period was exported as well; Farquhar's *The Recruiting Officer* was the first play to be performed in the penal colony of Australia. Moreover, the seventeenth century saw the institutionalization of theater as a commercial activity: in its architecture (indoor theaters, proscenium stages), in its greater appeal to a bourgeois audience, even in institutions like the Comédie Française (which, of course, continues to produce the plays of Molière and Racine), this theater is the direct forebear of the modern European theater, and in many ways the progenitor of its colonial theaters as well.

While the plays in this unit are all still in the classical repertory of modern theaters, these plays tend to pose particular problems to modern directors and actors. Although many

READING THE MATERIAL THEATER

One of the most challenging elements of theater history is the interpretation of the documentary record. Indeed, with the rise of print, the theater spawned its own information explosion, as newspaper descriptions, reviews, memoirs, and even published letters provide accounts of the practices of the stage. Yet these documents themselves often require a skeptical eye. Anthony Aston's *A Brief Supplement to Colley Cibber, Exq: His Lives of the Late Famous Actors and Actresses* (published in London in 1748) provides what seems to be an eyewitness account of the acting style of Thomas Betterton (1635–1710). What features of Betterton's physique and style emerge most strongly to Aston? Are there class or cultural implications in the various terms Aston uses to praise Betterton? How does Aston distinguish between Betterton's success in comic and tragic roles? How does he distinguish between Betterton's style in comedy and that of Estcourt and Harper?

Mr. Betterton (although a superlative good Actor) labour'd under ill Figure, being clumsily made, having a great Head, a short thick Neck, stoop'd in the Shoulders, and had fat short Arms, which he rarely lifted higher than his Stomach. —His Left Hand frequently lodg'd in his Breast, between his Coat and Waistcoat, while, with his Right, he prepar'd his Speech. —His Actions were few, but just. —He had little Eyes, and a broad Face, a little Pock-fretten, a corpulent Body, and thick Legs, with large Feet. —He was better to meet, than to follow; for his Aspect was serious, venerable, and majestic; in his latter Time a little Paralytic. —His Voice was low and grumbling; yet he could Time it by an artificial *Climax*, which enforc'd universal Attention, even from the *Fops* and *Orange-girls*. —He was incapable of dancing, even in a Country-Dance; as was MRS. BARRY: But their good Qualities were more than equal to their Deficiencies. —While MRS. BRACEGIRDLE sung very agreeably in the LOVES of *Mars and Venus*, and danced in a Country-Dance, as well as MR. WILKS, though not with so much Art and Foppery, but like a well-bred Gentleman. —Mr. BETTER-TON was the most extensive Actor, from *Alexander* to *Sir John Falstaff*; but in that last Character, he wanted the Waggery of EST-COURT, the Drollery of HARPER, and Sallaciousness of JACK EVANS. —But, then *Estcourt* was too trifling; *Harper* had too much of the *Bartholomew-Fair*; and *Evans* misplac'd his Humour. —Thus, you see what *Flaws* are in *bright Diamonds*; —And I have often wish'd that Mr. *Betterton* would have resign'd the Part of HAMLET to some young Actor, (who might have Personated, though not have Acted, it better) for, when he threw himself at *Ophelia's* Feet, he appear'd a little too grave for a young Student, lately come from the University of *Wirtemberg*; and his *Repartees* seem'd rather as *Apophthegms* from a *sage Philosopher*, than the *sporting Flashes* of a young HAMLET; and no one else could have pleas'd the Town, he was so rooted in their Opinion. His younger Contemporary (*Betterton* 63, *Powell* 40 Years old), POWELL attempted several of *Betterton's* Parts, as *Alexander, Jaffeir, &c*, but lost his Credit; as, in *Alexander*, he maintain'd not the Dignity of a King, but Out-Heroded HEROD; and in his poison'd mad Scene, *outrav'd all Probability;* while *Betterton* kept his Passion under, and shew'd it most (as Fame smoaks most, when stifled). *Betterton*, from the Time he was dress'd to the End of the Play, kept his Mind in the same Temperament and Adaptness, as the present Character required.

plays of this period—*Tartuffe* or *The Rover*—are given a contemporary setting, and concern themselves with relatively familiar characters, their language and characterization tends to be quite formal. Molière, for example, writes in a rich and fluid verse, even for the part of Tartuffe; Behn's cavaliers speak in prose, but their language is nonetheless dynamic and rhetorically complex. For modern actors, the elegance of this language often provides a point of entry to these characters, a way of seizing on the carefully discriminated social hierarchies at work in the cultures of these plays. Indeed, this verbal formality often becomes a kind of keynote to other aspects of performance as well, leading to a certain stateliness of physical movement and gesture, and an elegant balance of design elements as well. And yet in part because they are part of a classical repertoire, these plays have also inspired experiment and adaptation, a challenge to directors, designers, and actors to make it new.

PEDRO CALDERÓN DE LA BARCA

Like many of his contemporaries, Pedro Calderón de la Barca (1600–1681) was a prolific playwright; he is thought to have written more than 200 plays, of which about 100 survive. Calderón was born in Madrid on January 17, 1600, the son of a minor court official. He was educated at a Jesuit "college," or preparatory school, before attending the University of Alcalá de Henares and the University of Salamanca. In 1620 he entered and won a poetry competition in honor of St. Isidore, which brought his writing to the attention of Lope de Vega, one of the judges of the contest. His first play, *Love, Honor, and Power,* was performed at court in 1623, but Calderón—who served intermittently in the military in the early 1620s—did not become established as a playwright until some time after 1626, when his plays were popular both at court and in the public theaters. With the death of Lope in 1635, Calderón became the most important playwright in Spain; he was knighted by Philip IV and became the principal court playwright in 1636.

Many of Calderón's plays in this period are either *capa y espada* plays, like *The Phantom Lady* (1629), or "love and honor" plays. *El alcalde de Zalamea* (*The Mayor of Zalamea,* 1642) is typical of the "love and honor" genre. In the play, a peasant's daughter is raped by a soldier; through a series of coincidents, the peasant becomes the mayor just as the soldier is apprehended, and he is torn between his desire for revenge, his obligation to enforce the process of law, and Christian charity. Calderón's most important play, *La vida es sueño* (*Life Is a Dream*) was produced in 1636. Throughout his career, Calderón also wrote *autos sacramentales,* but these became more significant later in his life. Calderón's mistress died in 1648, and Calderón entered the priesthood in 1651, possibly in grief over her loss; he also adopted and raised her child, who may have been his natural son. He was appointed priest of a Toledo parish, but the bishop objected to his playwriting, and Calderón devoted himself to *autos* thereafter; his *autos* were so popular that between 1647 and 1681 the only *autos* performed in Madrid were by Calderón. Calderón was made chaplain to the king in 1663 and died in retirement in 1681.

LIFE IS A DREAM

Life Is a Dream typifies the concerns of Calderón's mature drama: It is a play that tests the relationship between love and honor and conducts a searching meditation on human nature itself. The play is set in a mythological Poland, ruled by King Basil. Several years before the current action, it was predicted that if Basil's son, Segismund, were to succeed to the throne, he "would be the most outrageous / Of all men, the most cruel of all princes, / And impious of all monarchs, by whose acts / The kingdom would be torn up and divided." Basil, not willing to murder his son to save his country, has had Segismund removed from court and imprisoned in a cave, where he is attended only by the old courtier Clotaldo. This is where Rosaura—a well-born woman, also forsaken by her father—finds Segismund at the opening of the play.

Calderón begins his interrogation of human nature in the characterization of Segismund. Raised like a beast, Segismund is impulsive and untamed; though he opens the play complaining about his life of constant punishment, when he sees Rosaura (disguised as a man) watching him, he seizes and threatens to kill her. Yet when Rosaura kneels to him and begs for mercy, Segismund feels a strange sensation:

> Your voice has softened me, your presence halted me,
> And now, confusingly, I feel respect
> For you.

In the opening of Pedro Calderon de la Barca's *Life Is a Dream*, Rosaura defends herself against Segismund, who is clothed in animal hides.

Living in captivity and isolation, Segismund is a "human monster": his behavior is ruled neither by reason nor by the conventions of polite society. Yet Segismund responds to Rosaura's plea for mercy as though some element of human sympathy were native to him. At the outset of the play, Calderón presents two contrasting views of human nature. In one perspective, human beings—like other animals—are ruled by their passions, which can only be governed by the civilizing force of law and reason; since Segismund has been raised without benefit of culture, he represents humanity in this unadorned state. Yet at the same time, Segismund's innate response to Rosaura suggests a second view of human nature, one in which sympathy, kindness, and morality are not imposed on human nature by education and society, but are somehow innate to humanity itself.

Just as Segismund relents toward Rosaura, Clotaldo suddenly bursts in and arrests her; Basil has decreed that even the existence of his son must remain a secret. But in arresting Rosaura, Clotaldo takes her sword, which he immediately recognizes as the sword he had left "fair Violante" years before: Rosaura—who has traveled to Poland disguised as a man for protection—must be Clotaldo's "son." Clotaldo is now caught in the classic "love-and-honor" bind. His duty to his king requires him to arrest and eventually execute anyone who spies Basil's secret son; yet to honor his bond to the king, he must betray the natural love he should show to his own child.

As the play proceeds, Clotaldo's effort to reclaim his son is paralleled by Basil's guilty desire to restore his own son to society. Basil hits on an experiment: He will put Segismund to sleep and awaken him at court; when he awakens, Segismund will be told that he is now the king. If his behavior is civilized and restrained, then Basil will know that the prophecy was wrong and will acknowledge Segismund as his heir; if his behavior is threatening, he will be sent back to prison. But Basil's plan has one flaw: Having been raised in solitude, Segismund has no understanding of the elaborate conventions of courtly behavior. When he awakens as "king," he is rude to Prince Astolfo, offensively forward to Stella, and murderously impulsive to the servants who try to restrain and control his behavior. His behavior is so outrageous that he is again knocked unconscious and sent back to his prison.

Returned to captivity, Segismund can only understand his sojourn at court as a beautiful dream, a dream that becomes an image for the fleeting and illusory joys of life itself. But this recognition reforms Segismund, enables him to recognize that he can only assume his full humanity by governing his passions. In the play's final moments, Segismund is released from prison by a rebellious mob, who have come to release Segismund in order to overthrow Basil. When Segismund and his army confront Basil, the old king not only assumes that he has lost his kingdom, but that Segismund will kill him, in part to repay Basil for stealing the better part of his life. But Segismund now understands that although Basil's treatment has made him "savage" in his passions—an "inhuman monster"—the only way to regain his humanity is to govern his desire for revenge. So Segismund submits himself to Basil, who recognizes that his son has been reformed and gives him the kingdom: in conquering himself, Segismund wins the throne as well.

Calderón's drama is a deeply philosophical play, and the characters meditate extensively on the nature and meaning of their behavior. But *Life Is a Dream* is in some sense also a political play; its rich examination of "human nature" is conducted from a deeply aristocratic perspective. The only way that Segismund can demonstrate his humanity, after all, is to recognize and accept the conventions of courtly behavior as "natural." It is a sign of Segismund's acceptance of those values that his first act as king is to sentence the soldier who liberated him from prison to a life imprisonment of his own.

LIFE IS A DREAM

Pedro Calderón de la Barca

TRANSLATED BY ROY CAMPBELL

CHARACTERS

BASIL, *King of Poland*
SEGISMUND, *Prince*
ASTOLFO, *Duke of Muscovy*
CLOTALDO, *old man*
CLARION, *a comical servant*
ROSAURA, *a lady*

STELLA, *a princess*
SOLDIERS, GUARDS, MUSICIANS, SERVANTS, RETINUES, WOMEN

The scene is laid in the court of Poland, a nearby fortress, and the open country

ACT ONE

On one side a craggy mountain: on the other a rude tower whose base serves as a prison for SEGISMUND. *The door facing the spectators is open. The action begins at nightfall.*

ROSAURA, *dressed as a man, appears on the rocks climbing down to the plain: behind her comes* CLARION.

ROSAURA: You headlong hippogriff who match the gale
  In rushing to and fro, you lightning-flicker
  Who give no light, you scaleless fish, you bird
  Who have no coloured plumes, you animal
5 Who have no natural instinct, tell me whither
  You lead me stumbling through this labyrinth
  Of naked crags! Stay here upon this peak
  And be a Phaëthon to the brute-creation!
  For I, pathless save only for the track
10 The laws of destiny dictate for me,
  Shall, blind and desperate, descend this height
  Whose furrowed brows are frowning at the sun.
  How rudely, Poland, you receive a stranger
  (Hardly arrived, but to be treated hardly)
15 And write her entry down in blood with thorns.
  My plight attests this well, but after all,
  Where did the wretchèd ever pity find?

CLARION: Say *two* so wretchèd. Don't you leave me out
  When you complain! If we two sallied out
20 From our own country, questing high adventure,
  And after so much madness and misfortune
  Are still two here, and were two when we fell
  Down those rough crags—shall I not be offended
  To share the trouble yet forego the credit?

25 ROSAURA: I did not give you shares in my complaint
  So as not to rob you of the right to sorrow
  Upon your own account. There's such relief
  In venting grief that a philosopher
  Once said that sorrows should not be bemoaned
30 But sought for pleasure.

CLARION: Philosopher?
  I call him a long-bearded, drunken sot
  And would they'd cudgelled him a thousand blows
  To give him something worth his while lamenting!
  But, madam, what should we do, by ourselves,
35 On foot and lost at this late hour of day,

Here on this desert mountain far away—
  The sun departing after fresh horizons?

ROSAURA: Clarion, how can I answer, being both
  The partner of your plight and your dilemma?

CLARION: Would anyone believe such strange events?   40

ROSAURA: If there my sight is not deceived by fancy,
  In the last timid light that yet remains
  I seem to see a building.

CLARION: Either my hopes
  Are lying or I see the signs myself.

ROSAURA: Between the towering crags, there stands so small   45
  A royal palace that the lynx-eyed sun
  Could scarce perceive it at midday, so rude
  In architecture that it seems but one
  Rock more down-toppled from the sun-kissed crags
  That form the jaggèd crest.   50

CLARION: Let's go closer,
  For we have stared enough: it would be better
  To let the inmates makes us welcome.

ROSAURA: See:
  The door, or, rather, that funereal gap,
  Is yawning wide—whence night itself seems born,
  Flowing out from its black, rugged centre.   55

(A sound of chains is heard.)

CLARION: Heavens! What's that I hear?

ROSAURA: I have become
  A block immovable of ice and fire.

CLARION: Was that a little chain? Why, I'll be hanged
  If that is not the clanking ghost of some
  Past galley-slave—my terror proves it is!   60

SEGISMUND: Oh, miserable me! Unhappy me!

ROSAURA: How sad a cry that is! I fear new trials
  And torments.

CLARION: It's a fearful sound.

ROSAURA: Oh, come,
  My Clarion, let us fly from suffering!

CLARION: I'm in such sorry trim, I've not the spirit   65
  Even to run away.

ROSAURA: And if you had,
  You'd not have seen that door, not known of it.
  When one's in doubt, the common saying goes
  One walks between two lights.

CLARION: I'm the reverse.

70   It's not that way with me.
        ROSAURA: What then disturbs you?
        CLARION: I walk in doubt between two darknesses.
        ROSAURA: Is not that feeble exhalation there
              A light? That pallid star whose fainting tremors,
              Pulsing a doubtful warmth of glimmering rays,
75   Make even darker with its spectral glow
              That gloomy habitation? Yes! because
              By its reflection (though so far away)
              I recognise a prison, grim and sombre,
              The sepulchre of some poor living carcase.
80   And, more to wonder at, a man lies there
              Clothed in the hides of savage beasts, with limbs
              Loaded with fetters, and a single lamp
              For company. So, since we cannot flee,
              Let us stay here and listen to his plaint
85   And what his sorrows are.
        SEGISMUND: Unhappy me!
              Oh, miserable me! You heavens above,
              I try to think what crime I've done against you
              By being born. Although to have been born,
              I know, is an offence, and with just cause
90   I bear the rigours of your punishment:
              Since to be born is man's worst crime. But yet
              I long to know (to clarify my doubts)
              What greater crime, apart from being born,
              Can thus have earned my greater chastisement.
95   Aren't others born like me? And yet they seem
              To boast a freedom that I've never known.
              The bird is born, and in the hues of beauty
              Clothed with its plumes, yet scarce has it become
              A feathered posy—or a flower with wings—
100   When through ethereal halls it cuts its way,
              Refusing the kind shelter of its nest.
              And I, who have more soul than any bird,
              Must have less liberty?
              The beast is born, and with its hide bright-painted,
105   In lovely tints, has scarce become a spangled
              And starry constellation (thanks to the skilful
              Brush of the Painter) than its earthly needs
              Teach it the cruelty to prowl and kill,
              The monster of its labyrinth of flowers.
110   Yet I, with better instincts than a beast,
              Must have less liberty?
              The fish is born, the birth of spawn and slime,
              That does not even live by breathing air.
              No sooner does it feel itself a skiff
115   Of silver scales upon the wave than swiftly
              It roves about in all directions taking
              The measure of immensity as far
              As its cold blood's capacity allows.
              Yet I, with greater freedom of the will,
120   Must have less liberty?
              The brook is born, and like a snake unwinds
              Among the flowers. No sooner, silver serpent,
              Does it break through the blooms than it regales
              And thanks them with its music for their kindness,
125   Which opens to its course the majesty
              Of the wide plain. Yet I, with far more life,
              Must have less liberty?

              This fills me with such passion, I become
              Like the volcano Etna, and could tear
              Pieces of my own heart out of my breast!   130
              What law, justice, or reason can decree
              That man alone should never know the joys
              And be alone excepted from the rights
              God grants a fish, a bird, a beast, a brook?
        ROSAURA: His words have filled me full of fear and pity. 135
        SEGISMUND: Who is it overheard my speech? Clotaldo?
        CLARION: Say "yes!"
        ROSAURA: It's only a poor wretch, alas,
              Who in these cold ravines has overheard
              Your sorrows.
        SEGISMUND: Then I'll kill you

        (*Seizes her.*)

              So as to leave no witness of my frailty.   140
              I'll tear you into bits with these strong arms!
        CLARION: I'm deaf. I wasn't able to hear that.
        ROSAURA: If you were human born, it is enough
              That I should kneel to you for you to spare me.
        SEGISMUND: Your voice has softened me, your presence   145
              halted me,
              And now, confusingly, I feel respect
              For you. Who are you? Though here I have learned
              So little of the world, since this grim tower
              Has been my cradle and my sepulchre;
              And though since I was born (if you can say   150
              I really have been born) I've only seen
              This rustic desert where in misery
              I dwell alone, a living skeleton,
              An animated corpse; and though till now,
              I never spoke, save to one man who hears   155
              My griefs and through whose converse I have heard
              News of the earth and of the sky; and though,
              To astound you more, and make you call me
              A human monster, I dwell here, and am
              A man of the wild animals, a beast   160
              Among the race of men; and though in such
              Misfortune, I have studied human laws,
              Instructed by the birds, and learned to measure
              The circles of the gentle stars, you only
              Have curbed my furious rage, amazed my vision,   165
              And filled with wonderment my sense of hearing.
              Each time I look at you, I feel new wonder!
              The more I see of you, the more I long
              To go on seeing more of you. I think
              My eyes are dropsical, to go on drinking   170
              What it is death for them to drink, because
              They go on drinking that which I am dying
              To see and that which, seen, will deal me death.
              Yet let me gaze on you and die, since I
              Am so bewitched I can no longer think   175
              What not seeing you would do to me—the sight
              Itself being fatal! that would be more hard
              Than dying, madness, rage, and fiercest grief:
              It would be life—worst fate of all because
              The gift of life to such a wretchèd man   180
              Would be the gift of death to happiness!

ROSAURA: Astonished as I look, amazed to hear,
    I know not what to say nor what to ask.
    All I can say is that heaven guided me
185   Here to be comforted, if it is comfort
    To see another sadder than oneself.
    They say a sage philosopher of old,
    Being so poor and miserable that he
    Lived on the few plain herbs he could collect,
190   One day exclaimed: "Could any man be poorer
    Or sadder than myself?"—when, turning round,
    He saw the very answer to his words.
    For there another sage philosopher
    Was picking up the scraps he'd thrown away.
195   I lived cursing my fortune in this world
    And asked within me: "Is there any other
    Suffers so hard a fate?" Now out of pity
    You've given me the answer. For within me
    I find upon reflection that my griefs
200   Would be as joys to you and you'd receive them
    To give you pleasure. So if they perchance
    In any measure may afford relief,
    Listen attentively to my misfortune
    And take what is left over for yourself.
205   I am . . .
CLOTALDO: (*Within.*) Guards of the tower! You sluggards
    Or cowards, you have let two people pass
    Into the prison bounds . . .
ROSAURA: Here's more confusion!
SEGISMUND: That is Clotaldo, keeper of my prison.
    Are my misfortunes still not at an end?
210 CLOTALDO: Come. Be alert, and either seize or slay them
    Before they can resist!
VOICES: (*Within.*)   Treason! Betrayal!
CLARION: Guards of the tower who let us pass unhindered,
    Since there's a choice, to seize us would be simpler.

(*Enter* CLOTALDO *with* SOLDIERS. *He holds a pistol and they all wear masks.*)

CLOTALDO: (*Aside to the* SOLDIERS.) Cover your faces, all! It's
    a precaution
215   Imperative that nobody should know us
    While we are here.
CLARION: What's this? A masquerade?
CLOTALDO: O you, who ignorantly passed the bounds
    And limits of this region, banned to all—
    Against the king's decree which has forbidden
220   That any should find out the prodigy
    Hidden in these ravines—yield up your weapons
    Or else this pistol, like a snake of metal,
    Will spit the piercing venom of two shots
    With scandalous assault upon the air.
225 SEGISMUND: Tyrannic master, ere you harm these people
    Let my life be the spoil of these sad bonds
    In which (I swear it by Almighty God)
    I'll sooner rend myself with hands and teeth
    Amid these rocks than see them harmed and mourn
230   Their suffering.
CLOTALDO: Since you know, Segismund,
    That your misfortunes are so huge that, even

    Before your birth, you died by heaven's decree,
    And since you know these walls and binding chains
    Are but the brakes and curbs to your proud frenzies,
    What use is it to bluster?   235

(*To the* GUARDS.)

                  Shut the door
    Of this close prison! Hide him in its depths!
SEGISMUND: Ah, heavens, how justly you denied me freedom!
    For like a Titan I would rise against you,
    Pile jasper mountains high on stone foundations
    And climb to burst the windows of the sun!   240
CLOTALDO: Perhaps you suffer so much pain today
    Just to forestall that feat.
ROSAURA: Now that I see
    How angry pride offends you, I'd be foolish
    Not to plead humbly at your feet for life.
    Be moved by me to pity. It would be   245
    Notoriously harsh that neither pride
    Nor humbleness found favour in your eyes!
CLARION: And if neither Humility nor Pride
    Impress you (characters of note who act
    And motivate a thousand mystery plays)   250
    Let me, here, who am neither proud nor humble,
    But merely something halfway in between,
    Plead to you both for shelter and for aid.
CLOTALDO: Ho, there!
SOLDIER: Sir?
CLOTALDO: Take their weapons. Bind their eyes
    So that they cannot see the way they're led.   255
ROSAURA: This is my sword. To nobody but you
    I yield it, since you're, after all, the chief.
    I cannot yield to one of meaner rank.
CLARION: My sword is such that I will freely give it
    To the most mean and wretched.   260

(*To one* SOLDIER.)

                  Take it, you!
ROSAURA: And if I have to die, I'll leave it to you
    In witness of your mercy. It's a pledge
    Of great worth and may justly be esteemed
    For someone's sake who wore it long ago.
CLOTALDO: (*Apart.*) Each moment seems to bring me new   265
    misfortune!
ROSAURA: Because of that, I ask you to preserve
    This sword with care. Since if inconstant Fate
    Consents to the remission of my sentence,
    It has to win me honour. Though I know not
    The secret that it carries, I do know   270
    It has got one—unless I trick myself—
    And prize it just as the sole legacy
    My father left me.
CLOTALDO: Who then was your father?
ROSAURA: I never knew.
CLOTALDO: And why have you come here?
ROSAURA: I came to Poland to avenge a wrong.   275
CLOTALDO: (*Apart.*) Sacred heavens!

(*On taking the sword he becomes very perturbed.*)

What's this? Still worse and worse.
I am perplexed and troubled with more fears.

(*Aloud.*)

Tell me: who gave that sword to you?
ROSAURA: A woman.
CLOTALDO: Her name?
ROSAURA: A secret I am forced to keep.
280 CLOTALDO: What makes you think this sword contains a
        secret?
    ROSAURA: That she who gave it to me said: "Depart
        To Poland. There with subtlety and art
        Display it so that all the leading people
        And noblemen can see you wearing it,
285   And I know well that there's a lord among them
        Who will both shelter you and grant you favour."
        But, lest he should be dead, she did not name him.
    CLOTALDO: (*Aside.*) Protect me, heavens! What is this I hear?
        I cannot say if real or imagined
290   But here's the sword I gave fair Violante
        In token that, whoever in the future
        Should come from her to me wearing this sword,
        Would find in me a tender father's love.
        Alas, what can I do in such a pass,
295   When he who brings the sword to win my favour
        Brings it to find his own red death instead
        Arriving at my feet condemned already?
        What strange perplexity! How hard a fate!
        What an inconstant fortune to be plagued with!
300   This is my son not only by all signs
        But also by the promptings of my heart,
        Since, seeing him, my heart seems to cry out
        To him, and beat its wings, and, though unable
        To break the locks, behaves as one shut in,
305   Who, hearing noises in the street outside,
        Cranes from the window-ledge. Just so, not knowing
        What's really happening, but hearing sounds,
        My heart runs to my eyes which are its windows
        And out of them flows into bitter tears.
310   Protect me, heaven! What am I to do?
        To take him to the king is certain death.
        To hide him is to break my sacred oath
        And the strong law of homage. From one side
        Love of one's own, and from the other loyalty—
315   Call me to yield. Loyalty to my king
        (Why do I doubt?) comes before life and honour.
        Then live my loyalty, and let him die!
        When I remember, furthermore, he came
        To avenge an injury—a man insulted
320   And unavenged is in disgrace. My son
        Therefore he is not, nor of noble blood.
        But if some danger has mischanced, from which
        No one escapes, since honour is so fragile
        That any act can smash it, and it takes
325   A stain from any breath of air, what more
        Could any nobleman have done than he,
        Who, at the cost of so much risk and danger,
        Comes to avenge his honour? Since he's so brave
        He is my son, and my blood's in his veins.

And so betwixt the one doubt and the other,   330
The most important mean between extremes
Is to go to the king and tell the truth—
That he's my son, to kill, if so he wishes.
Perhaps my loyalty thus will move his mercy
And if I thus can merit a live son   335
I'll help him to avenge his injury.
But if the king prove constant in his rigour
And deal him death, he'll die in ignorance
That I'm his father.

(*Aloud to* ROSAURA *and* CLARION.)

                            Come then, strangers, come!
And do not fear that you have no companions   340
In your misfortunes, since, in equal doubt,
Tossed between life and death, I cannot guess
Which is the greater evil or the less.

A hall at the royal palace, in court

Enter ASTOLFO *and* SOLDIERS *at one side: from the other side*
PRINCESS STELLA *and* [WOMEN]. *Military music and salvos.*

ASTOLFO: To greet your excellent bright beams
    As brilliant as a comet's rays,   345
    The drums and brasses mix their praise
    With those of fountains, birds, and streams.
    With sounds alike, in like amaze,
    Your heavenly face each voice salutes,
    Which puts them in such lively fettle,   350
    The trumpets sound like birds of metal,
    The songbirds play like feathered flutes.
    And thus they greet you, fair señora—
    The salvos, as their queen, the brasses,
    As to Minerva when she passes,   355
    The songbirds to the bright Aurora,
    And all the flowers and leaves and grasses
    As doing homage unto Flora,
    Because you come to cheat the day
    Which now the night has covered o'er—   360
    Aurora in your spruce array,
    Flora in peace, Pallas in war,
    But in my heart the queen of May.
STELLA: If human voice could match with acts
    You would have been unwise to say   365
    Hyperboles that a few facts
    May well refute some other day
    Confounding all this martial fuss
    With which I struggle daringly,
    Since flatteries you proffer thus   370
    Do not accord with what I see.
    Take heed that it's an evil thing
    And worthy of a brute accursed,
    Loud praises with your mouth to sing
    When in your heart you wish the worst.   375
ASTOLFO: Stella, you have been badly misinformed
    If you doubt my good faith. Here let me beg you
    To listen to my plea and hear me out.
    The third Eugtorgius died, the King of Poland.

380 Basil, his heir, had two fair sisters who
Bore you, my cousin, and myself. I would not
Tire you with all that happened here. You know
Clorilene was your mother who enjoys,
Under a better reign, her starry throne.
385 She was the elder. Lovely Recisunda
(Whom may God cherish for a thousand years!)
The younger one, my mother and your aunt,
Was wed in Muscovy. Now to return:
Basil has yielded to the feebleness
390 Of age, loves learnèd study more than women,
Has lost his wife, is childless, will not marry.
And so it comes that you and I both claim
The heirdom of the realm. You claim that you
Were daughter to the elder daughter. I
395 Say that my being born a man, although
Son of the younger daughter, gives me title
To be preferred. We've told the king, our uncle,
Of both of our intentions. And he answered
That he would judge between our rival claims,
400 For which the time and place appointed was
Today and here. For the same reason I
Have left my native Muscovy. With that
Intent I come—not seeking to wage war
But so that you might thus wage war on me!
405 May Love, wise god, make true what people say
(Your "people" is a wise astrologer)
By settling this through your being chosen queen—
Queen and my consort, sovereign of my will;
My uncle crowning you, for greater honour;
410 Your courage conquering, as it deserves;
My love applauding you, its emperor!
STELLA: To such chivalrous gallantry, my breast
Cannot hold out. The imperial monarchy
I wish were mine only to make it yours—
415 Although my love is not quite satisfied
That you are to be trusted since your speech
Is somewhat contradicted by that portrait
You carry in the locket round your neck.
ASTOLFO: I'll give you satisfaction as to that.

(*Drums.*)

420 But these loud instruments will not permit it
That sound the arrival of the king and council.

(*Enter* KING BASIL *with his following.*)

STELLA: Wise Thales . . .
ASTOLFO: Learned Euclid . . .
STELLA: Among the signs . . .
ASTOLFO: Among the stars . . .
STELLA: Where you preside in power . . .
ASTOLFO: Where you reside . . .
STELLA: And plot their paths . . .
425 ASTOLFO: And trace their fiery trails . . .
STELLA: Describing . . .
ASTOLFO: . . . Measuring and judging them . . .
STELLA: Please read my stars that I, in humble bonds . . .
ASTOLFO: Please read them, so that I in soft embraces . . .
STELLA: May twine as ivy to this tree!

ASTOLFO: May find
430 Myself upon my knees before these feet!
BASIL: Come and embrace me, niece and nephew. Trust me,
Since you're both loyal to my loving precepts,
And come here so affectionately both—
In nothing shall I leave you cause to cavil,
435 And both of you as equals will be treated.
The gravity of what I have to tell
Oppresses me, and all I ask of you
Is silence: the event itself will claim
Your wonderment. So be attentive now,
440 Belovèd niece and nephew, illustrious courtiers,
Relatives, friends, and subjects! You all know
That for my learning I have merited
The surname of The Learnèd, since the brush
Of great Timanthes, and Lisippus' marbles—
445 Stemming oblivion (consequence of time)—
Proclaimed me to mankind Basil the Great.
You know the science that I most affect
And most esteem is subtle mathematics
(By which I forestall time, cheat fame itself)
450 Whose office is to show things gradually.
For when I look my tables up and see,
Present before me, all the news and actions
Of centuries to come, I gain on Time—
Since Time recounts whatever I have said
455 After I say it. Those snowflaking haloes,
Those canopies of crystal spread on high,
Lit by the sun, cut by the circling moon,
Those diamond orbs, those globes of radiant crystal
Which the bright stars adorn, on which the signs
460 Parade in blazing excellence, have been
My chiefest study all through my long years.
They are the volumes on whose adamantine
Pages, bound up in sapphire, heaven writes,
In lines of burnished gold and vivid letters,
465 All that is due to happen, whether adverse
Or else benign. I read them in a flash,
So quickly that my spirit tracks their movements—
Whatever road they take, whatever goal
They aim at. Would to heaven that before
470 My genius had been the commentary
Writ in their margins, or the index to
Their pages, that my life had been the rubble,
The ruin, and destruction of their wrath,
And that my tragedy in them had ended,
475 Because, to the unlucky, even their merit
Is like a hostile knife, and he whom knowledge
Injures is but a murderer to himself.
And this I say myself, though my misfortunes
Say it far better, which, to marvel at,
480 I beg once more for silence from you all.
With my late wife, the queen, I had a son,
Unhappy son, to greet whose birth the heavens
Wore themselves out in prodigies and portents.
Ere the sun's light brought him live burial
485 Out of the womb (for birth resembles death)
His mother many times, in the delirium
And fancies of her sleep, saw a fierce monster
Bursting her entrails in a human form,

Born spattered with her lifeblood, dealing death,
490 The human viper of this century!
The day came for his birth, and every presage
Was then fulfilled, for tardily or never
Do the more cruel ones prove false. At birth
His horoscope was such that the bright sun,
495 Stained in its blood, entered ferociously
Into a duel with the moon above.
The whole earth seemed a rampart for the strife
Of heaven's two lights, who—though not hand-to-hand—
Fought light-to-light to gain the mastery!
500 The worst eclipse the sun has ever suffered
Since Christ's own death horrified earth and sky.
The whole earth overflowed with conflagrations
So that it seemed the final paroxysm
Of existence. The skies grew dark. Buildings shook.
505 The clouds rained stones. The rivers ran with blood.
In this delirious frenzy of the sun,
Thus, Segismund was born into the world,
Giving a foretaste of his character
By killing his own mother, seeming to speak thus
510 By his ferocity: "I am a man,
Because I have begun now to repay
All kindnesses with evil." To my studies
I went forthwith, and saw in all I studied
That Segismund would be the most outrageous
515 Of all men, the most cruel of all princes,
And impious of all monarchs, by whose acts
The kingdom would be torn up and divided
So as to be a school of treachery
And an academy of vices. He,
520 Risen in fury, amidst crimes and horrors,
Was born to trample me (with shame I say it)
And make of my grey hairs his very carpet.
Who is there but believes an evil Fate?
And more if he discovers it himself,
525 For self-love lends its credit to our studies.
So I, believing in the Fates, and in
The havoc that their prophecies predestined,
Determined to cage up this newborn tiger
To see if on the stars we sages have
530 Some power. I gave out that the prince had died
Stillborn, and, well-forewarned, I built a tower
Amidst the cliffs and boulders of yon mountains
Over whose tops the light scarce finds its way,
So stubbornly their obelisks and crags
535 Defend the entry to them. The strict laws
And edicts that I published then (declaring
That nobody might enter the forbidden
Part of the range) were passed on that account.
There Segismund lives to this day, a captive,
540 Poor and in misery, where, save Clotaldo,
His guardian, none have seen or talked to him.
The latter has instructed him in all
Branches of knowledge and in the Catholic faith,
Alone the witness of his misery.
545 There are three things to be considered now:
Firstly, Poland, that I love you greatly,
So much that I would free you from the oppression
And servitude of such a tyrant king.

He would not be a kindly ruler who
Would put his realm and homeland in such danger. 550
The second fact that I must bear in mind
Is this: that to deny my flesh and blood
The rights which law, both human and divine,
Concedes, would not accord with Christian charity,
For no law says that, to prevent another 555
Being a tyrant, I may be one myself,
And if my son's a tyrant, to prevent him
From doing outrage, I myself should do it.
Now here's the third and last point I would speak of,
Namely, how great an error it has been 560
To give too much belief to things predicted,
Because, even if his inclination should
Dictate some headlong, rash precipitancies,
They may perhaps not conquer him entirely,
For the most accursèd destiny, the most 565
Violent inclination, the most impious
Planet—all can but influence, not force,
The free will which man holds direct from God.
And so, between one motive and another
Vacillating discursively, I hit 570
On a solution that will stun you all.
I shall tomorrow, but without his knowing
He is my son—your king—place Segismund
(For that's the name with which he was baptised)
Here on my throne, beneath my canopy, 575
Yes, in my very place, that he may govern you
And take command. And you must all be here
To swear him fealty as his loyal subjects.
Three things may follow from this test, and these
I'll set against the three which I proposed. 580
The first is that should the prince prove prudent,
Stable, and benign—thus giving the lie
To all that prophecy reports of him—
Then you'll enjoy in him your rightful ruler
Who was so long a courtier of the mountains 585
And neighbour to the beasts. Here is the second:
If he prove proud, rash, cruel, and outrageous,
And with a loosened rein gallop unheeding
Across the plains of vice, I shall have done
My duty, and fulfilled my obligation 590
Of mercy. If I then re-imprison him,
That's incontestably a kingly deed—
Not cruelty but merited chastisement.
The third thing's this: that if the prince should be
As I've described him, then—by the love I feel 595
For you, my vassals—I shall give you worthier
Rulers to wear the sceptre and the crown;
Because your king and queen will be my nephew
And niece, each with an equal right to rule,
Each gaining the inheritance he merits, 600
And joined in faith of holy matrimony.
This I command you as a king, I ask you
As a kind father, as a sage I pray you,
As an experienced old man I tell you,
And (if it's true, as Spanish Seneca 605
Says, that the king is slave unto his nation)
This, as a humble slave, I beg of you.
ASTOLFO: If it behoves me to reply (being

The person most involved in this affair)
610   Then, in the name of all, let Segismund
    Appear! It is enough that he's your son!
ALL: Give us our prince: we want him for our king!
BASIL: Subjects, I thank you for your kindly favour.
    Accompany these, my two Atlases,
615   Back to their rooms. Tomorrow you shall see him.
ALL: Long live the great King Basil! Long live Basil!

(*Exeunt all, accompanying* STELLA *and* ASTOLFO. *The king remains.*)

(*Enter* CLOTALDO *with* ROSAURA *and* CLARION.)

CLOTALDO: May I have leave to speak, sire?
BASIL: Oh, Clotaldo!
    You're very welcome.
CLOTALDO: Thus to kneel before you
    Is always welcome, sire—yet not today
620 When sad and evil Fate destroys the joy
    Your presence normally concedes.
BASIL: What's wrong?
CLOTALDO: A great misfortune, sire, has come upon me
    Just when I should have met it with rejoicing.
BASIL: Continue.
CLOTALDO: Sire, this beautiful young man
625 Who inadvertently and daringly
    Came to the tower, wherein he saw the prince,
    Is my . . .
BASIL: Do not afflict yourself, Clotaldo.
    Had it not been just now, I should have minded,
    I must confess. But I've revealed the secret,
630 And now it does not matter if he knows it.
    Attend me afterwards. I've many things
    To tell you. You in turn have many things
    To do for me. You'll be my minister,
    I warn you, in the most momentous action
635 The world has ever seen. These prisoners, lest you
    Should think I blame your oversight, I'll pardon.

(*Exit.*)

CLOTALDO: Long may you live, great sire! A thousand years!

(*Aside.*)

    Heaven improves our fates. I shall not tell him
    Now that he is my son, since it's not needed
640 Till he's avenged.

(*Aloud.*)

    Strangers, you may go free.
ROSAURA: Humbly I kiss your feet.
CLARION: Whilst I'll just *miss* them—
    Old friends will hardly quibble at one letter.
ROSAURA: You've granted me my life, sir. I remain
645 Your servant and eternally your debtor.
CLOTALDO: No! It was not your life I gave you. No!
    Since any wellborn man who, unavenged,
    Nurses an insult does not live at all.
    And seeing you have told me that you came

For that sole reason, it was not life I spared—   650
Life in disgrace is not a life at all.

(*Aside.*)

I see this spurs him.
ROSAURA: Freely I confess it—
    Although you spared my life, it was no life.
    But I will wipe my honour's stain so spotless
    That after I have vanquished all my dangers   655
    Life well may seem a shining gift from you.
CLOTALDO: Take here your burnished steel: 'twill be enough,
    Bathed in your enemies' red blood, to right you.
    For steel that once was mine (I mean of course
    Just for the time I've had it in my keeping)   660
    Should know how to avenge you
ROSAURA: Now, in your name I gird it on once more
    And on it I will swear to take revenge
    Although my foe were even mightier.
CLOTALDO: Is he so powerful?   665
ROSAURA: So much so that . . .
    Although I have no doubt in your discretion . . .
    I say no more because I'd not estrange
    Your clemency.
CLOTALDO: You would have won me had you told me, since
    That would prevent me helping him.   670

(*Aside.*)

    If only I could discover who he is!
ROSAURA: So that you'll not think that I value lightly
    Such confidence, know that my adversary
    Is no less than Astolfo, Duke of Muscovy.
CLOTALDO: (*Aside.*) (I hardly can withstand the grief it   675
    gives me
    For it is worse than aught I could imagine!
    Let us inquire of him some further facts.)

(*Aloud.*)

    If you were born a Muscovite, your ruler
    Could never have affronted you. Go back
    Home to your country. Leave this headstrong valour.   680
    It will destroy you.
ROSAURA: Though he's been my prince,
    I know that he has done me an affront.
CLOTALDO: Even though he slapped your face, that's no
    affront.

(*Aside.*)

    O heavens!
ROSAURA: My insult was far deeper!
CLOTALDO: Tell it:
    Since nothing I imagine could be deeper.   685
ROSAURA: Yes. I will tell it, yet, I know not why,
    With such respect I look upon your face,
    I venerate you with such true affection,
    With such high estimation do I weigh you,
    That I scarce dare to tell you—these men's clothes   690
    Are an enigma, not what they appear.
    So now you know. Judge if it's no affront

695   That here Astolfo comes to wed with Stella
    Although betrothed to me. I've said enough.

(*Exeunt* ROSAURA *and* CLARION.)

CLOTALDO: Here! Listen! Wait! What mazed confusion!
    It is a labyrinth wherein the reason
    Can find no clue. My family honour's injured.
    The enemy's all powerful. I'm a vassal
    And she's a woman. Heavens! Show a path
700   Although I don't believe there is a way!
    There's nought but evil bodings in the sky.
    The whole world is a prodigy, say I.

ACT TWO

A hall in the royal palace.

Enter BASIL *and* CLOTALDO.

CLOTALDO: All has been done according to your orders.
BASIL: Tell me, Clotaldo, how it went?
CLOTALDO: Why, thus:
    I took to Segismund a calming drug
    Wherein are mixed herbs of especial virtue,
5   Tyrannous in their overpowering strength
    Which seize and steal and alienate man's gift
    Of reasoning, thus making a live corpse
    Of him. His violence evaporated
    With all his faculties and senses too.
10   There is no need to prove it's possible
    Because experience teaches us that medicine
    Is full of natural secrets, that there is no
    Animal, plant, or stone that has not got
    Appointed properties. If human malice
15   Explores a thousand poisons which deal death,
    Who then can doubt, that being so, that other
    Poisons, less violent, cause only sleep?
    But (leaving that doubt aside, as proven false
    By every evidence) hear then the sequel:
20   I went down into Segismund's close prison
    Bearing the drink wherein, with opium,
    Henbane and poppies had been mixed. With him
    I talked a little while of the humanities,
    In which dumb Nature has instructed him,
25   The mountains and the heavens and the stars,
    In whose divine academies he learned
    Rhetoric from the birds and the wild creatures.
    To lift his spirit to the enterprise
    Which you require of him, I chose for subject
30   The swiftness of a stalwart eagle, who,
    Deriding the base region of the wind,
    Rises into the sphere reserved for fire,
    A feathered lightning, an untethered comet.
    Then I extolled such lofty flight and said:
35   "After all, he's the king of birds, and so
    Takes precedence, by right, over the rest."
    No more was needful for, in taking up
    Majesty for his subject, he discoursed
    With pride and high ambition, as his blood

    Naturally moves, incites, and spurs him on   40
    To grand and lofty things, and so he said
    That in the restless kingdom of the birds
    There should be those who swear obedience, too!
    "In this, my miseries console me greatly,
    Because if I'm a vassal here, it's only   45
    By force, and not by choice. Of my own will
    I would not yield in rank to any man."
    Seeing that he grew furious—since this touched
    The theme of his own griefs—I gave the potion
    And scarcely had it passed from cup to breast   50
    Before he yielded all his strength to slumber.
    A chill sweat ran through all his limbs and veins.
    Had I not known that this was mere feigned death
    I would have thought him dead. Then came the men
    To whom you've trusted this experiment,   55
    Who placed him in a coach and brought him here
    To your own rooms, where all things were prepared
    In royalty and grandeur as befitting
    His person. In your own bed they have laid him
    Where, when the torpor wanes, they'll do him service   60
    As if he were Your Majesty himself.
    All has been done as you have ordered it,
    And if I have obeyed you well, my lord,
    I'd beg a favour (pardon me this freedom)—
    To know what your intention is in thus   65
    Transporting Segismund here to the palace.
BASIL: Your curiosity is just, Clotaldo,
    And yours alone I'll satisfy. The star
    Which governs Segismund, my son, in life,
    Threatens a thousand tragedies and woes.   70
    And now I wish to see whether the stars
    (Which never lie—and having shown to us
    So many cruel signs seem yet more certain)
    May yet be brought to moderate their sentence,
    Whether by prudence charmed or valour won,   75
    For man does have the power to rule his stars.
    I would examine this, bringing him here
    Where he may know he is my son, and make
    Trial of his talent. If magnanimously
    He conquers and controls himself, he'll reign,   80
    But if he proves a tyrant and is cruel,
    Back to his chains he'll go. Now, you will ask,
    Why did we bring him sleeping in this manner
    For the experiment? I'll satisfy you,
    Down to the smallest detail, with my answer.   85
    If he knows that he is my son today,
    And if tomorrow he should find himself
    Once more reduced to prison, to misery,
    He would despair entirely, knowing truly
    Who, and whose son, he is. What consolation   90
    Could he derive, then, from his lot? So I
    Contrive to leave an exit for such grief,
    By making him believe it was a dream.
    By these means we may learn two things at once:
    First, his character—for he will really be   95
    Awake in all he thinks and all his actions;
    Second, his consolation—which would be
    (If he should wake in prison on the morrow,
    Although he saw himself obeyed today)
    That he might understand he had been dreaming,   100

And he will not be wrong, for in this world,
Clotaldo, all who live are only dreaming.
CLOTALDO: I've proofs enough to doubt of your success,
But now it is too late to remedy it.
105 From what I can make out, I think he's awakened
And that he's coming this way, by the sound.
BASIL: I shall withdraw. You, as his tutor, go
And guide him through his new bewilderments
By answering his queries with the truth.
110 CLOTALDO: You give me leave to tell the truth of it?
BASIL: Yes, because knowing all things, he may find
Known perils are the easiest to conquer.

(*Exit* BASIL. *Enter* CLARION.)

CLARION: It cost me four whacks to get here so quickly.
I caught them from a red-haired halberdier
115 Sprouting a ginger beard over his livery,
And I've come to see what's going on.
No windows give a better view than those
A man brings with him in his head, not asking
For tickets of admission or paid seats,
120 Since at all functions, festivals, or feasts
He looks out with the same nice self-composure.
CLOTALDO: (*Aside.*) Here's Clarion who's the servant of that
person—
That trader in woes, importer from Poland
Of my disgrace.

(*Aloud.*)

Come, Clarion, what news?
125 CLARION: Item the first: encouraged by the fact
Your clemency's disposed to venge her insult,
Rosaura has resumed her proper clothing.
CLOTALDO: That's right: it's less indecorous and bold.
CLARION: Item: she's changed her name, and given out
130 That she's your niece. And now they've made so much
Of her that she's been raised to maid of honour
To the unique and only princess, Stella.
CLOTALDO: That's right: her honour stands to my account.
CLARION: Indeed she merely bides the time till you
135 Will settle all accounts about her honour.
CLOTALDO: Biding the time is wise, for in the end
It's Time that's going to settle all accounts!
CLARION: Item: that she's attended like a queen,
Because they take her for your niece. Item:
140 That I, who trudged along with her, am dying
Of hunger. Nobody remembers me,
Nor yet remembers that I'm like my name
And (should I sound my Clarion) could tell
All to the king and Stella and Astolfo.
145 For I am both a Clarion and a servant—
Two things which ill-accord with secrecy.
If silence should, by chance, let slip my hand,
Then there's a chorus which would fit me well:
"Dawn-breaking Clarion plays no better tune!"
150 CLOTALDO: You've reason for complaint. I'll satisfy it
If you'll but serve me . . .
CLARION: Hush, here's Segismund!

(*Enter* MUSICIANS, *singing, and* SERVANTS *arraying* SEGISMUND,
who seems amazed.)

SEGISMUND: Heavens above! What's this that I am seeing?
I wonder at it all, with naught of fear!
But with a mighty doubt, I disbelieve it!
I?—in a sumptuous palace? I—encircled   155
With rich brocades and silks? I—overwhelmed
With servants in such brilliant liveries?
I—to awake in such a gorgeous bed?
I—in the middle of so many footmen
Who clothe me in rich garments? I'm awake: 160
It would be false to take this for a dream.
Am I not Segismund? Heavens! disabuse me
If I'm mistaken. Say, what could have happened
In my imagination while I slept—
That I should find myself in such a place?   165
But why should I worry, whatever it was?
I'll let myself be served and entertained—
Befall what may.
FIRST SERVANT: (*Aside to* SECOND SERVANT *and* CLARION.)
                        He's very melancholy!
SECOND SERVANT: Who would not be, considering all that's
happened
To him?   170
CLARION: I would not be!
SECOND SERVANT: You, speak to him.
FIRST SERVANT: Shall they begin to sing again?
SEGISMUND: Why, no,
I would not have them sing.
SECOND SERVANT: You're so distraught,
I wish you entertained.
SEGISMUND: My griefs are such
That no mere voices can amuse me now—
Only the martial music pleased my mind.   175
CLOTALDO: Your Highness, mighty prince, give me your hand
To kiss. I'm glad to be the first to offer
Obedience at your feet.
SEGISMUND: (*Aside.*)   This is Clotaldo.
How is it he, that tyrannised my thralldom,
Should now be treating me with such respect?   180

(*Aloud.*)

Tell me what's happening all round me here.
CLOTALDO: With the perplexities of your new state,
Your reason will encounter many doubts,
But I shall try to free you from them all
(If that may be) because you now must know   185
You are hereditary Prince of Poland.
If you have been withdrawn from public sight
Under restraint, it was in strict obedience
To Fate's inclemency, which will permit
A thousand woes to fall upon this empire   190
The moment that you wear the sovereign's crown.
But trusting that you'll prudently defeat
Your own malignant stars (since they can be
Controlled by magnanimity) you've been
Brought to this palace from the tower you knew   195
Even while your soul was yielded up to sleep.
My lord the king, your father, will be coming
To see you, and from him you'll learn the rest.
SEGISMUND: Then, vile, infamous traitor, what have I
To know more than this fact of who I am,   200
To show my pride and power from this day onward?

How have you played your country such a treason
As to deny me, against law and right,
The rank which is my own?
CLOTALDO: Unhappy me!
205 SEGISMUND: You were a traitor to the law, a flattering liar
To your own king, and cruel to myself.
And so the king, the law, and I condemn you,
After such fierce misfortunes as I've borne,
To die here by my hands.
SECOND SERVANT: My lord!
SEGISMUND: Let none
210 Get in the way. It is in vain. By God!
If you intrude, I'll throw you through the window.
SECOND SERVANT: Clotaldo, fly!
CLOTALDO: Alas, poor Segismund!
That you should show such pride, all unaware
That you are dreaming this.

(*Exit.*)

SECOND SERVANT: Take care! Take care!
215 SEGISMUND: Get out!
SECOND SERVANT: He was obeying the king's orders.
SEGISMUND: In an injustice, no one should obey
The king, and I'm his prince.
SECOND SERVANT: He had no right
To look into the rights and wrongs of it.
SEGISMUND: You must be mad to answer back at me.
220 CLARION: The prince is right. It's you who're in the
wrong!
SECOND SERVANT: Who gave you right to speak?
CLARION: I simply took it.
SEGISMUND: And who are you?
CLARION: I am the go-between,
And in this art I think I am a master—
Since I'm the greatest jackanapes alive.
225 SEGISMUND: (*To* CLARION.) In all this new world, you're the
only one
Of the whole crowd who pleases me.
CLARION: Why, my lord,
I am the best pleaser of Segismunds
That ever was: ask anybody here!

(*Enter* ASTOLFO.)

ASTOLFO: Blessèd the day, a thousand times, my prince,
230 On which you landed here on Polish soil
To fill with so much splendour and delight
Our wide horizons, like the break of day!
For you arise as does the rising sun
Out of the rugged mountains, far away.
235 Shine forth then! And although so tardily
You bind the glittering laurels on your brows,
The longer may they last you still unwithered.
SEGISMUND: God save you.
ASTOLFO: That you do not know me, sir,
Is some excuse for greeting me without
240 The honour due to me. I am Astolfo
The Duke of Muscovy. You are my cousin.
We are of equal rank.
SEGISMUND: Then if I say,
"God save you," do I not display good feeling?

But since you take such note of who you are,
The next time that I see you, I shall say   245
"God save you *not*," if you would like that better.
SECOND SERVANT: (*To* ASTOLFO.) Your Highness, make
allowance for his breeding
Amongst the mountains. So he deals with all.

(*To* SEGISMUND.)

Astolfo does take precedence, Your Highness—
SEGISMUND: I have no patience with the way he came   250
To make his solemn speech, then put his hat on!
SECOND SERVANT: He's a grandee!
SEGISMUND: I'm grander than grandees!
SECOND SERVANT: For all that, there should be respect
between you,
More than among the rest.
SEGISMUND: And who told you
To mix in my affairs?   255

(*Enter* STELLA.)

STELLA: Many times welcome to Your Royal Highness,
Now come to grace the dais that receives him
With gratitude and love. Long may you live
August and eminent, despite all snares,
And count your life by centuries, not years!   260
SEGISMUND: (*Aside to* CLARION.) Now tell me, who's this
sovereign deity
At whose divinest feet Heaven lays down
The fleece of its aurora in the east?
CLARION: Sir, it's your cousin Stella.
SEGISMUND: She were better
Named "sun" than "star"!   265

(*To* STELLA.)

                                Though your speech was fair,
Just to have seen you and been conquered by you
Suffices for a welcome in itself.
To find myself so blessed beyond my merit
What can I do but thank you, lovely Stella,
For you could add more brilliance and delight   270
To the most blazing star? When you get up
What work is left the sun to do? O give me
Your hand to kiss, from out whose cup of snow
The solar horses drink the fires of day!
STELLA: Be a more gentle courtier.   275
ASTOLFO: I am lost.
SECOND SERVANT: I know Astolfo's hurt. I must divert him.

(*To* SEGISMUND.)

Sir, you should know that thus to woo so boldly
Is most improper. And, besides, Astolfo . . .
SEGISMUND: Did I not tell you not to meddle with me?
SECOND SERVANT: I only say what's just.   280
SEGISMUND: All this annoys me.
Nothing seems just to me but what I want.
SECOND SERVANT: Why, sir, I heard you say that no obedience
Or service should be lent to what's unjust.
SEGISMUND: You also heard me say that I would throw
Anyone who annoys me from that balcony.   285

SECOND SERVANT: With men like me you cannot do such
    things.
SEGISMUND: No? Well, by God, I'll have to prove it then!

(*He takes him in his arms and rushes out, followed by many, to return soon after.*)

ASTOLFO: What on earth have I seen? Can it be true?
STELLA: Go, all, and stop him!
SEGISMUND: (*Returning.*)   From the balcony
290   He's fallen in the sea. How strange it seems!
ASTOLFO: Measure your acts of violence, my lord:
    From crags to palaces, the distance is
    As great as that between man and the beasts.
SEGISMUND: Well, since you are for speaking out so boldly,
295   Perhaps one day you'll find that on your shoulders
    You have no head to place your hat upon.

(*Exit* ASTOLFO. *Enter* BASIL.)

BASIL: What's happened here?
SEGISMUND: Nothing at all. A man
    Wearied me, so I threw him in the sea.
CLARION: (*To* SEGISMUND.) Be warned. That is the king.
BASIL: On the first day,
300   So soon, your coming here has cost a life?
SEGISMUND: He said I couldn't: so I won the bet.
BASIL: It grieves me, Prince, that, when I hoped to see you
    Forewarned, and overriding Fate, in triumph
    Over your stars, the first thing I should see
305   Should be such rigour—that your first deed here
    Should be a grievous homicide. Alas!
    With what love, now, can I offer my arms,
    Knowing your own have learned to kill already?
    Who sees a dirk, red from a mortal wound,
310   But does not fear it? Who can see the place
    Soaking in blood, where late a man was murdered,
    But even the strongest must respond to nature?
    So in your arms seeing the instrument
    Of death, and looking on a blood-soaked place,
315   I must withdraw myself from your embrace,
    And though I thought in loving bonds to bind
    Your neck, yet fear withholds me from your arms.
SEGISMUND: Without your loving arms I can sustain
    Myself as usual. That such a loving father
320   Could treat me with such cruelty, could thrust me
    From his side ungratefully, could rear me
    As a wild beast, could hold me for a monster,
    And pray that I were dead, that such a father
    Withholds his arms from winding round my neck,
325   Seems unimportant, seeing that he deprives
    Me of my very being as a man.
BASIL: Would to heaven I had never granted it,
    For then I never would have heard your voice,
    Nor seen your outrages.
SEGISMUND: Had you denied
330   Me being, then I would not have complained,
    But that you took it from me when you gave it—
    That is my quarrel with you. Though to give
    Is the most singular and noble action,
    It is the basest action if one gives

    Only to take away.   335
BASIL: How well you thank me
    For being raised from pauper to a prince!
SEGISMUND: In this what is there I should thank you for?
    You tyrant of my will! If you are old
    And feeble, and you die, what can you give me
    More than what is my own by right of birth?   340
    You are my father and my king, therefore
    This grandeur comes to me by natural law.
    Therefore, despite my present state, I'm not
    Indebted to you, rather can I claim
    Account of all those years in which you robbed me   345
    Of life and being, liberty, and honour.
    You ought to thank me that I press no claim
    Since you're my debtor, even to bankruptcy.
BASIL: Barbarous and outrageous brute! The heavens
    Have now fulfilled their prophecy; I call   350
    Them to bear witness to your pride. Although
    You know now, disillusioned, who you are,
    And see yourself where you take precedence,
    Take heed of this I say: be kind and humble
    Since it may be that you are only dreaming,   355
    Although it seems to you you're wide-awake.

(*Exit* BASIL.)

SEGISMUND: Can I perhaps be dreaming, though I seem
    So wide-awake? No: I am not asleep,
    Since I can touch, and realise what I
    Have been before, and what I am today.   360
    And if you even now relented, Father,
    There'd be no cure since I know who I am
    And you cannot, for all your sighs and groans,
    Cheat me of my hereditary crown.
    And if I was submissive in my chains   365
    Before, then I was ignorant of what I am,
    Which I now know (and likewise know that I
    Am partly man but partly beast as well).

(*Enter* ROSAURA *in woman's clothing.*)

ROSAURA: (*Aside.*) I came in Stella's train. I am afraid
    Of meeting with Astolfo, since Clotaldo   370
    Says he must not know who I am, not see me,
    Because (he says) it touches on my honour.
    And well I trust Clotaldo since I owe him
    The safety of my life and honour both.
CLARION: What pleases you, and what do you admire   375
    Most, of the things you've seen here in the world?
SEGISMUND: Why, nothing that I could not have foreseen—
    Except the loveliness of women! Once,
    I read among the books I had out there
    That who owes God most grateful contemplation   380
    Is Man: who is himself a tiny world.
    But I think who owes God more grateful study
    Is Woman—since she is a tiny heaven,
    Having as much more beauty than a man
    As heaven than earth. And even more, I say,   385
    If she's the one that I am looking at.
ROSAURA: (*Aside.*) That is the prince. I'll go.
SEGISMUND: Stop! Woman! Wait!

Don't join the sunset with the breaking day
By fading out so fast. If east and west
390 Should clash like that, the day would surely suffer
A syncope. But what is this I see?
ROSAURA: What I am looking at I doubt, and yet
Believe.
SEGISMUND: (*Aside.*) This beauty I have seen before.
ROSAURA: (*Aside.*) This pomp and grandeur I have seen before
395 Cooped in a narrow dungeon.
SEGISMUND: (*Aside.*)   I have found
My life at last.

(*Aloud.*)

                    Woman (for that sole word
Outsoars all wooing flattery of speech
From one that is a man), woman, who are you?
If even long before I ever saw you
400 You owed me adoration as your prince,
How much the more should you be conquered by me
Now I recall I've seen you once before!
Who are you, beauteous woman?
ROSAURA: (*Aside.*)   I'll pretend.

(*Aloud.*)

In Stella's train, I am a luckless lady.
405 SEGISMUND: Say no such thing. You are the sun from which
The minor star that's Stella draws its life,
Since she receives the splendour of your rays.
I've seen how in the kingdom of sweet odours,
Commander of the squadrons of the flowers,
410 The rose's deity presides, and is
Their empress by divine right of her beauty.
Among the precious stones which can be listed
In the academy of mines, I've seen
The diamond much preferred above the rest,
415 And crowned their emperor, for shining brightest.
In the revolving empire of the stars
The morning star takes pride among the others.
In their perfected spheres, when the sun calls
The planets to his council, he presides
420 And is the very oracle of day.
Then if among stars, gems, planet, and flowers
The fairest are exalted, why do you
Wait on a lesser beauty than yourself
Who are, in greater excellence and beauty,
425 The sun, the morning star, the diamond, and the rose!

(*Enter* CLOTALDO, *who remains by the stage-curtain.*)

CLOTALDO: (*Aside.*) I wish to curb him, since I brought
him up.
But, what is this?
ROSAURA: I reverence your favour,
And yet reply, rhetorical, with silence,
For when one's mind is clumsy and untaught,
430 He answers best who does not speak at all.
SEGISMUND: Stay! Do not go! How can you wish to go
And leave me darkened by my doubts?
ROSAURA: Your Highness,

I beg your leave to go.
SEGISMUND: To go so rudely
Is not to beg my leave but just to take it.
ROSAURA: But if you will not grant it, I must take it.   435
SEGISMUND: That were to change my courtesy to rudeness.
Resistance is like venom to my patience.
ROSAURA: But even if this deadly, raging venom
Should overcome your patience, yet you dare not
And could not treat me with dishonour, sir.   440
SEGISMUND: Why, just to see then if I can, and dare to—
You'll make me lose the fear I bear your beauty,
Since the impossible is always tempting
To me. Why, only now I threw a man
Over this balcony who said I couldn't: 445
And so to find out if I can or not
I'll throw your honour through the window too.
CLOTALDO: (*Aside.*) He seems determined in this course.
Oh, heavens!
What's to be done that for a second time
My honour's threatened by a mad desire?   450
ROSAURA: Then with good reason it was prophesied
Your tyranny would wreak this kingdom
Outrageous scandals, treasons, crimes, and deaths.
But what can such a creature do as you
Who are not even a man, save in the name—   455
Inhuman, barbarous, cruel, and unbending
As the wild beasts amongst whom you were nursed?
SEGISMUND: That you should not insult me in this way
I spoke to you most courteously, and thought
I'd thereby get my way; but if you curse me thus   460
Even when I am speaking gently, why,
By the living God, I'll really give you cause.
Ho there! Clear out, the lot of you, at once!
Leave her to me! Close all the doors upon us.
Let no one enter!   465

(*Exeunt* CLARION *and other* ATTENDANTS.)

ROSAURA: I am lost . . . I warn you . . .
SEGISMUND: I am a tyrant and you plead in vain.
CLOTALDO: (*Aside.*) Oh, what a monstrous thing! I must
restrain him
Even if I die for it.

(*Aloud.*)

                Sir! Wait! Look here!
SEGISMUND: A second time you have provoked my anger,
You feeble, mad old man! Do you prize lightly   470
My wrath and rigour that you've gone so far?
CLOTALDO: Brought by the accents of her voice, I came
To tell you you must be more peaceful
If still you hope to reign, and warn you that
You should not be so cruel, though you rule—   475
Since this, perhaps, is nothing but a dream.
SEGISMUND: When you refer to disillusionment
You rouse me near to madness. Now you'll see,
Here as I kill you, if it's truth or dreaming!

(*As he tries to pull out his dagger,* CLOTALDO *restrains him and throws himself on his knees before him.*)

480 CLOTALDO: It's thus I'd save my life: and hope to do so—
     SEGISMUND: Take your presumptuous hand from off this steel.
     CLOTALDO: Till people come to hold your rage and fury
        I shall not let you go.
     ROSAURA: O heavens!
     SEGISMUND: Loose it,

(*They struggle.*)

        I say, or else—you interfering fool—
485   I'll crush you to your death in my strong arms!
     ROSAURA: Come quickly! Here's Clotaldo being killed!

(*Exit.*)

(ASTOLFO *appears as* CLOTALDO *falls on the floor, and the former stands between* SEGISMUND *and* CLOTALDO.)

     ASTOLFO: Why, what is this, most valiant prince? What?
        Staining
        Your doughty steel in such old, frozen blood?
        For shame! For shame! Sheathe your illustrious weapon!
490 SEGISMUND: When it is stained in his infamous blood!
     ASTOLFO: At my feet here he has found sanctuary
        And there he's safe, for it will serve him well.
     SEGISMUND: Then serve me well by dying, for like this
        I will avenge myself for your behaviour
495   In trying to annoy me first of all.
     ASTOLFO: To draw in self-defence offends no king,
        Though in his palace.

(ASTOLFO *draws his sword and they fight.*)

     CLOTALDO: (*To* ASTOLFO.) Do not anger him!

(*Enter* BASIL, STELLA, *and* ATTENDANTS.)

     BASIL: Hold! Hold! What's this? Fighting with naked swords?
     STELLA: (*Aside.*) It is Astolfo! How my heart misgives me!
500 BASIL: Why, what has happened here?
     ASTOLFO: Nothing, my Lord,
        Since you've arrived.

(*Both sheathe their swords.*)

     SEGISMUND: Much, though you *have* arrived.
        I tried to kill the old man.
     BASIL: Had you no
        Respect for those white hairs?
     CLOTALDO: Sire, since they're only
        Mine, as you well can see, it does not matter!
505 SEGISMUND: It is in vain you'd have me hold white hairs
        In such respect, since one day you may find
        Your own white locks prostrated at my feet
        For still I have not taken vengeance on you
        For the foul way in which you had me reared.

(*Exit.*)

510 BASIL: Before that happens you will sleep once more
        Where you were reared, and where what's happened may
        Seem just a dream (being mere earthly glory).

(*All save* ASTOLFO *and* STELLA *leave.*)

     ASTOLFO: How seldom does prediction fail, when evil!
        How oft, foretelling good! Exact in harm,
        Doubtful in benefit! Oh, what a great   515
        Astrologer would be one who foretold
        Nothing but harms, since there's no doubt at all
        That they are always due! In Segismund
        And me the case is illustrated clearly.
        In him, crimes, cruelties, deaths, and disasters   520
        Were well predicted, since they all came true.
        But in my own case, to predict for me
        (As I foresaw beholding rays which cast
        The sun into the shade and outface heaven)
        Triumphs and trophies, happiness and praise,   525
        Was false—and yet was true: it's only just
        That when predictions start with promised favours
        They should end in disdain.
     STELLA: I do not doubt
        Your protestations are most heartfelt; only
        They're not for me, but for another lady   530
        Whose portrait you were wearing round your neck
        Slung in a locket when you first arrived.
        Since it is so, she only can deserve
        These wooing flatteries. Let her repay you
        For in affairs of love, flatteries and vows   535
        Made for another are mere forged credentials.

(ROSAURA *enters but waits by the curtain.*)

     ROSAURA: (*Aside.*) Thanks be to God, my troubles are near
           ended!
        To judge from what I see, I've naught to fear.
     ASTOLFO: I will expel that portrait from my breast
        To make room for the image of your beauty   540
        And keep it there. For there where Stella is
        Can be no room for shade, and where the sun is
        No place for any star. I'll fetch the portrait.

(*Aside.*)

        Forgive me, beautiful Rosaura, that,
        When absent, men and women seldom keep   545
        More faith than this.

(*Exit.*)

(ROSAURA *comes forward.*)

     ROSAURA: (*Aside.*)   I could not hear a word. I was afraid
        That they would see me.
     STELLA: Oh, Astrea!
     ROSAURA: My lady!
     STELLA: I am delighted that you came. Because
        To you alone would I confide a secret.
     ROSAURA: Thereby you greatly honour me, your servant. 550
     STELLA: Astrea, in the brief time I have known you
        I've given you the latchkey of my will.
        For that, and being who you are, I'll tell you
        A secret which I've very often hidden
        Even from myself.   555

ROSAURA: I am your slave.
STELLA: Then, briefly:
  Astolfo, who's my cousin (the word cousin
  Suffices, since some things are plainly said
  Even by thinking them), is to wed me
  If Fortune thus can wipe so many cares
560 Away with one great joy. But I am troubled
  In that, the day he first came here, he carried
  A portrait of a lady round his neck.
  I spoke to him about it courteously.
  He was most amiable, he loves me well,
565 And now he's gone for it. I am embarrassed
  That he should give it me himself. Wait here,
  And tell him to deliver it to you.
  Do not say more. Since you're discreet and fair:
  You'll surely know just what love is.

(*Exit.*)

ROSAURA: Great heavens!
570 How I wish that I did not! For who could be
  So prudent or so skilful as would know
  What to advise herself in such a case?
  Lives there a person on this earth today
  Who's more beset by the inclement stars,
575 Who has more cares besieging him, or fights
  So many dire calamities at once?
  What can I do in such bewilderment
  Wherein it seems impossible to find
  Relief or comfort? Since my first misfortune
580 No other thing has chanced or happened to me
  But was a new misfortune. In succession
  Inheritors and heirs of their own selves
  (Just like the Phoenix, his own son and father)
  Misfortunes reproduce themselves, are born,
585 And live by dying. In their sepulchre
  The ashes they consume are hot forever.
  A sage once said misfortunes must be cowards
  Because they never dare to walk alone
  But come in crowds. I say they are most valiant
590 Because they always charge so bravely on
  And never turn their backs. Who charges with them
  May dare all things because there is no fear
  That they'll ever desert him; and I say it
  Because in all my life I never once
595 Knew them to leave me, nor will they grow tired
  Of me till, wounded and shot through and through
  By Fate, I fall into the arms of death.
  Alas, what can I do in this dilemma?
  If I reveal myself, then old Clotaldo,
600 To whom I owe my life, may take offence,
  Because he told me to await the cure
  And mending of my honour in concealment.
  If I don't tell Astolfo who I am
  And he detects me, how can I dissimulate?
605 Since even if I say I am not I,
  The voice, the language, and the eyes will falter,
  Because the soul will tell them that they lie.
  What shall I do? It is in vain to study
  What I should do, when I know very well

  That, whatsoever way I choose to act,   610
  When the time comes I'll do as sorrow bids,
  For no one has control over his sorrows.
  Then since my soul dares not decide its actions
  Let sorrow fill my cup and let my grief
  Reach its extremity and, out of doubts   615
  And vain appearances, once and for all
  Come out into the light—and Heaven shield me!

(*Enter* ASTOLFO.)

ASTOLFO: Here, lady, is the portrait . . . but . . . great God!
ROSAURA: Why does Your Highness halt, and stare
    astonished?
ASTOLFO: Rosaura! Why, to see you here!   620
ROSAURA: Rosaura?
  Sir, you mistake me for some other lady.
  I am Astrea, and my humble station
  Deserves no perturbation such as yours.
ASTOLFO: Enough of this pretence, Rosaura, since
  The soul can never lie. Though as Astrea   625
  I see you now, I love you as Rosaura.
ROSAURA: Not having understood Your Highness' meaning
  I can make no reply except to say
  That Stella (who might be the star of Venus)
  Told me to wait here and to tell you from her   630
  To give to me the portrait you were fetching
  (Which seems a very logical request)
  And I myself will take it to my lady.
  Thus Stella bids: even the slightest things
  Which do me harm are governed by some star.   635
ASTOLFO: Even if you could make a greater effort
  How poorly you dissimulate, Rosaura!
  Tell your poor eyes they do not harmonise
  With your own voice, because they needs must jangle
  When the whole instrument is out of time.   640
  You cannot match the falsehood of your words
  With the sincerity of what you're feeling.
ROSAURA: All I can say is—that I want the portrait.
ASTOLFO: As you require a fiction, with a fiction
  I shall reply. Go and tell Stella this: 645
  That I esteem her so, it seems unworthy
  Only to send the counterfeit to her
  And that I'm sending her the original.
  And you, take the original along with you,
  Taking yourself to her.   650
ROSAURA: When a man starts
  Forth on a definite task, resolved and valiant,
  Though he be offered a far greater prize
  Than what he seeks, yet he returns with failure
  If he returns without his task performed.
  I came to get that portrait. Though I bear   655
  The original with me, of greater value,
  I would return in failure and contempt
  Without the copy. Give it me, Your Highness,
  Since I cannot return without it.
ASTOLFO: But
  If I don't give it you, how can you do so?   660
ROSAURA: Like this, ungrateful man! I'll take it from you.

(*She tries to wrest it from him.*)

ASTOLFO: It is in vain.
ROSAURA: By God, it shall not come
   Into another woman's hands!
ASTOLFO: You're terrifying!
ROSAURA: And you're perfidious!
ASTOLFO: Enough, my dear
665   Rosaura!
ROSAURA: I, your dear? You lie, you villain!

(*They are both clutching the portrait.*)

(*Enter* STELLA.)

STELLA: Astrea and Astolfo, what does this mean?
ASTOLFO: (*Aside.*) Here's Stella.
ROSAURA: (*Aside.*)   Love, grant me the strength to win
   My portrait.

(*To* STELLA.)

            If you want to know, my lady,
   What this is all about, I will explain.
670 ASTOLFO: (*To* ROSAURA, *aside.*) What do you mean?
   ROSAURA: You told me to await
   Astolfo here and ask him for a portrait
   On your behalf. I waited here alone
   And as one thought suggests another thought,
   Thinking of portraits, I recalled my own
675   Was here inside my sleeve. When one's alone,
   One is diverted by a foolish trifle
   And so I took it out to look at it.
   It slipped and fell, just as Astolfo here,
   Bringing the portrait of the other lady,
680   Came to deliver it to you as promised.
   He picked my portrait up, and so unwilling
   Is he to give away the one you asked for,
   Instead of doing so, he seized upon
   The other portrait which is mine alone
685   And will not give it back though I entreated
   And begged him to return it. I was angry
   And tried to snatch it back. That's it he's holding,
   And you can see yourself if it's not mine.
STELLA: Let go the portrait.

(*She snatches it from him.*)

ASTOLFO: Madam!
STELLA: The draughtsman
690   Was not unkind to truth.
ROSAURA: Is it not mine?
STELLA: Why, who could doubt it?
ROSAURA: Ask him for the other.
STELLA: Here, take your own, Astrea. You may leave us.
ROSAURA: (*Aside.*) Now I have got my portrait, come what
   will.

(*Exit.*)

STELLA: Now give me up the portrait that I asked for
695   Although I'll see and speak to you no more.
   I do not wish to leave it in your power
   Having been once so foolish as to beg it.

ASTOLFO: (*Aside.*) Now how can I get out of this foul trap?

(*To* STELLA.)

   Beautiful Stella, though I would obey you,
   And serve you in all ways, I cannot give you   700
   The portrait, since . . .
STELLA: You are a crude, coarse villain
   And ruffian of a wooer. For the portrait—
   I do not want it now, since, if I had it,
   It would remind me I had asked you for it.

(*Exit.*)

ASTOLFO: Listen! Look! Wait! Let me explain!   705

(*Aside.*)

                              Oh, damn
   Rosaura! How the devil did she get
   To Poland for my ruin and her own?

The prison of SEGISMUND *in the tower.*

SEGISMUND *lying on the ground loaded with fetters and clothed in
skins as before.* CLOTALDO, *two* ATTENDANTS, *and* CLARION.

CLOTALDO: Here you must leave him—since his reckless pride
   Ends here today where it began.
ATTENDANT: His chain
   I'll rivet as it used to be before.   710
CLARION: O Prince, you'd better not awake too soon
   To find how lost you are, how changed your fate,
   And that your fancied glory of an hour
   Was but a shade of life, a flame of death!
CLOTALDO: For one who knows so well to wield his tongue   715
   It's fit a worthy place should be provided
   With lots of room and lots of time to argue.
   This is the fellow that you have to seize

(*To the* ATTENDANTS.)

   And that's the room in which you are to lock him.

(*Points to the nearest cell.*)

CLARION: Why me?   720
CLOTALDO: Because a Clarion who knows
   Too many secrets must be kept in gaol—
   A place where even clarions are silent.
CLARION: Have I, by chance, wanted to kill my father
   Or thrown an Icarus from a balcony?
   Am I asleep or dreaming? To what end   725
   Do you imprison me?
CLOTALDO: You're Clarion.
CLARION: Well, say I swear to be a cornet now,
   A silent one, a wretched instrument . . . ?

(*They hustle him off.* CLOTALDO *remains.*)

(*Enter* BASIL, *wearing a mask.*)

BASIL: Clotaldo

CLOTALDO: Sire . . . and is it thus alone
730   Your Majesty has come?
BASIL: Vain curiosity
    To see what happens here to Segismund.
CLOTALDO: See where he lies, reduced to misery!
BASIL: Unhappy prince! Born at a fatal moment!
    Come waken him, now he has lost his strength
735   With all the opium he's drunk.
CLOTALDO: He's stirring
    And talking to himself.
BASIL: What is he dreaming?
    Let's listen now.
SEGISMUND: He who chastises tyrants
    Is a most pious prince . . . Now let Clotaldo
    Die by my hand . . . my father kiss my feet . . .
740   CLOTALDO: He threatens me with death!
BASIL: And me with insult
    And cruelty.
CLOTALDO: He'd take my life away.
BASIL: And he'd humiliate me at his feet.
SEGISMUND: (*Still in a dream.*) Throughout the expanse of
        this world's theatre
    I'll show my peerless valour, let my vengeance
745   Be wreaked, and the Prince Segismund be seen
    To triumph—over his father . . . but, alas!

(*Awakening.*)

    Where am I?
BASIL: (*To* CLOTALDO.) Since he must not see me here,
    I'll listen further off. You know your cue.

(*Retires to one side.*)

SEGISMUND: Can this be I? Am I the same who, chained
750   And long imprisoned, rose to such a state?
    Are you not still my sepulchre and grave,
    You dismal tower? God! What things I have dreamed!
CLOTALDO: (*Aside.*) Now I must go to him to disenchant him.

(*Aloud.*)

    Awake already?
SEGISMUND: Yes: it was high time.
755   CLOTALDO: What? Do you have to spend all day asleep?
    Since I was following the eagle's flight
    With tardy discourse, have you still lain here
    Without awaking?
SEGISMUND: No. Nor even now
    Am I awake. It seems I've always slept,
760   Since, if I've dreamed what I've just seen and heard
    Palpably and for certain, then I am dreaming
    What I see now—nor is it strange I'm tired,
    Since what I, sleeping, see, tells me that I
    Was dreaming when I thought I was awake.
765   CLOTALDO: Tell me your dream.
SEGISMUND: That's if it *was* a dream!
    No, I'll not tell you what I dreamed; but what
    I lived and saw, Clotaldo, I *will* tell you.
    I woke up in a bed that might have been
    The cradle of the flowers, woven by Spring.
770   A thousand nobles, bowing, called me Prince,

Attiring me in jewels, pomp, and splendour.
    My equanimity you turned to rapture
    Telling me that I was the Prince of Poland.
CLOTALDO: I must have got a fine reward!
SEGISMUND: Not so:
    For as a traitor, twice, with rage and fury,   775
    I tried to kill you.
CLOTALDO: Such cruelty to me?
SEGISMUND: I was the lord of all, on all I took revenge,
    Except I loved one woman . . . I believe
    That *that* was true, though all the rest has faded.

(*Exit* BASIL.)

CLOTALDO: (*Aside.*) I see the king was moved, to hear him   780
    speak.

(*Aloud.*)

    Talking of eagles made you dream of empires,
    But even in your dreams it's good to honour
    Those who have cared for you and brought you up.
    For Segismund, even in dreams, I warn you
    Nothing is lost by trying to do good.   785

(*Exit.*)

SEGISMUND: That's true, and therefore let us subjugate
    The bestial side, this fury and ambition,
    Against the time when we may dream once more,
    As certainly we shall, for this strange world
    Is such that but to live here is to dream.   790
    And now experience shows me that each man
    Dreams what he is until he is awakened.
    The king dreams he's a king and in this fiction
    Lives, rules, administers with royal pomp.
    Yet all the borrowed praises that he earns   795
    Are written in the wind, and he is changed
    (How sad a fate!) by death to dust and ashes.
    What man is there alive who'd seek to reign
    Since he must wake into the dream that's death.
    The rich man dreams his wealth which is his care   800
    And woe. The poor man dreams his sufferings.
    He dreams who thrives and prospers in this life.
    He dreams who toils and strives. He dreams who injures,
    Offends, and insults. So that in this world
    Everyone dreams the thing he is, though no one   805
    Can understand it. I dream I am here,
    Chained in these fetters. Yet I dreamed just now
    I was in a more flattering, lofty station.
    What is this life? A frenzy, an illusion,
    A shadow, a delirium, a fiction.   810
    The greatest good's but little, and this life
    Is but a dream, and dreams are only dreams.

ACT THREE

The tower.

Enter CLARION.

CLARION: I'm held in an enchanted tower, because
    Of all I know. What would they do to me
    For all I don't know, since—for all I know—
    They're killing me by starving me to death.

5   O that a man so hungry as myself
      Should live to die of hunger while alive!
      I am so sorry for myself that others
      May well say "I can well believe it," since
      This silence ill accords with my name "Clarion,"
10   And I just can't shut up. My fellows here?
      Spiders and rats—fine feathered songsters those!
      My head's still ringing with a dream of fifes
      And trumpets and a lot of noisy humbug
      And long processions as of penitents
15   With crosses, winding up and down, while some
      Faint at the sight of blood besmirching others.
      But now to tell the truth, I am in prison.
      For knowing secrets, I am kept shut in,
      Strictly observed as if I were a Sunday,
20   And feeling sadder than a Tuesday, where
      I neither eat nor drink. They say a secret
      Is sacred and should be as strictly kept
      As any saint's day on the calendar.
      Saint Secret's Day for me's a working day
25   Because I'm never idle then. The penance
      I suffer here is merited, I say:
      Because being a lackey, I was silent,
      Which, in a servant, is a sacrilege.

(*A noise of drums and trumpets.*)

FIRST SOLDIER: (*Within.*) Here is the tower in which he is
      imprisoned.
30   Smash in the door and enter, everybody!
      CLARION: Great God! They've come to seek me. That is
      certain
      Because they say I'm here. What can they want?

(*Enter several* SOLDIERS.)

FIRST SOLDIER: Go in.
SECOND SOLDIER: He's here!
CLARION: No, he's not here!
ALL THE SOLDIERS: Our lord!
CLARION: What, are they drunk?
FIRST SOLDIER: You are our rightful prince.
35   We do not want and never shall allow
      A stranger to supplant our trueborn prince.
      Give us your feet to kiss!
ALL THE SOLDIERS: Long live the prince!
CLARION: Bless me, if it's not real! In this strange kingdom
      It seems the custom, everyday, to take
40   Some fellow and to make him prince and then
      Shut him back in this tower. That *must* be it!
      So I must play my role.
ALL THE SOLDIERS: Give us your feet.
CLARION: I can't. They're necessary. After all
      What sort of use would be a footless prince?
45 SECOND SOLDIER: All of us told your father, as one man,
      We want no prince of Muscovy but you!
CLARION: You weren't respectful to my father? Shame!
FIRST SOLDIER: It was our loyalty that made us tell him.
CLARION: If it was loyalty, you have my pardon.
50 SECOND SOLDIER: Restore your empire. Long live Segismund!

CLARION: (*Aside.*) That is the name they seem to give to all
      These counterfeited princes.

(*Enter* SEGISMUND.)

SEGISMUND: Who called Segismund?
CLARION: (*Aside.*) I seem to be a hollow sort of prince.
FIRST SOLDIER: Which of you's Segismund?
SEGISMUND: I am.
SECOND SOLDIER: (*To* CLARION.)   Then why,
      Rash fool, did you impersonate the prince   55
      Segismund?
CLARION: What? I, Segismund? Yourselves
      Be-Segismunded me without request.
      All yours was both the rashness and the folly.
FIRST SOLDIER: Prince Segismund, whom we acclaim our lord,
      Your father, great King Basil, in his fear   60
      That heaven would fulfil a prophecy
      That one day he would kneel before your feet
      Wishes now to deprive you of the throne
      And give it to the Duke of Muscovy.
      For this he called a council, but the people   65
      Discovered his design and knowing, now,
      They have a native king, will have no stranger.
      So scorning the fierce threats of destiny,
      We've come to seek you in your very prison,
      That aided by the arms of the whole people,   70
      We may restore you to the crown and sceptre,
      Taking them from the tyrant's grasp. Come, then:
      Assembling here, in this wide desert region,
      Hosts of plebeians, bandits, and freebooters,
      Acclaim you king. Your liberty awaits you!   75
      Hark to its voice!

(*Shouts within.*)

                Long life to Segismund!
SEGISMUND: Once more, you heavens will that I should dream
      Of grandeur, once again, 'twixt doubts and shades,
      Behold the majesty of pomp and power
      Vanish into the wind, once more you wish   80
      That I should taste the disillusion and
      The risk by which all human power is humbled,
      Of which all human power should live aware.
      It must not be. I'll not be once again
      Put through my paces by my fortune's stars.   85
      And since I know this life is all a dream,
      Depart, vain shades, who feign, to my dead senses,
      That you have voice and body, having neither!
      I want no more feigned majesty, fantastic
      Display, nor void illusions, that one gust   90
      Can scatter like the almond tree in flower,
      Whose rosy buds, without advice or warning,
      Dawn in the air too soon and then, as one,
      Are all extinguished, fade, and fall, and wither
      In the first gust of wind that comes along!   95
      I know you well. I know you well by now.
      I know that all that happens in yourselves
      Happens as in a sleeping man. For me
      There are no more delusions and deceptions
      Since I well know this life is all a dream.   100

SECOND SOLDIER: If you think we are cheating, just sweep
    Your gaze along these towering peaks, and see
    The hosts that wait to welcome and obey you.
SEGISMUND: Already once before I've seen such crowds
105   Distinctly, quite as vividly as these:
    And yet it was a dream.
SECOND SOLDIER: No great event
    Can come without forerunners to announce it
    And this is the real meaning of your dream.
SEGISMUND: Yes, you say well. It was the fore-announcement
110   And just in case it was correct, my soul,
    (Since life's so short) let's dream the dream anew!
    But it must be attentively, aware
    That we'll awake from pleasure in the end.
    Forewarned of that, the shock's not so abrupt,
115   The disillusion's less. Evils anticipated
    Lose half their sting. And armed with this precaution—
    That power, even when we're sure of it, is borrowed
    And must be given back to its true owner—
    We can risk anything and dare the worst.
120   Subjects, I thank you for your loyalty.
    In me you have a leader who will free you,
    Bravely and skilfully, from foreign rule.
    Sound now to arms, you'll soon behold my valour.
    Against my father I must march and bring
125   Truth from the stars. Yes: he must kneel to me.

(*Aside.*)

    But yet, since I may wake before he kneels,
    Perhaps I'd better not proclaim what may not happen.
ALL: Long live Segismund!

(*Enter* CLOTALDO.)

CLOTALDO: Gracious heavens! What is
    This riot here?
SEGISMUND: Clotaldo!
CLOTALDO: Sir!

(*Aside.*)

                He'll prove
130   His cruelty on me.
CLARION: I bet he throws him
    Over the mountain.
CLOTALDO: At your royal feet
    I kneel, knowing my penalty is death.
SEGISMUND: Rise, rise, my foster father, from the ground,
    For you must be the compass and the guide
135   In which I trust. You brought me up, and I
    Know what I owe your loyalty. Embrace me!
CLOTALDO: What's that you say?
SEGISMUND: I know I'm in a dream,
    But I would like to act well, since good actions,
    Even in a dream, are not entirely lost.
140 CLOTALDO: Since doing good is now to be your glory,
    You will not be offended that I too
    Should do what's right. You march against your father!
    I cannot give you help against my king.
    Here at your feet, my lord, I plead for death.

SEGISMUND: (*Aloud.*) Villain!   145

(*Aside.*)

              But let us suffer this annoyance.
    Though my rage would slay him, yet he's loyal.
    A man does not deserve to die for that.
    How many angry passions does this leash
    Restrain in me, this curb of knowing well
    That I must wake and find myself alone!   150
SECOND SOLDIER: All this fine talk, Clotaldo, is a cruel
    Spurn of the public welfare. We are loyal
    Who wish our own prince to reign over us.
CLOTALDO: Such loyalty, after the king were dead,
    Would honour you. But while the king is living   155
    He is our absolute, unquestioned lord.
    There's no excuse for subjects who oppose
    His sovereignty in arms.
FIRST SOLDIER: We'll soon see well
    Enough, Clotaldo, what this loyalty
    Is worth.   160
CLOTALDO: You would be better if you had some.
    It is the greatest prize.
SEGISMUND: Peace, peace, I pray you.
CLOTALDO: My lord!
SEGISMUND: Clotaldo, if your feelings
    Are truly thus, go you, and serve the king;
    That's prudence, loyalty, and common sense.
    But do not argue here with anyone   165
    Whether it's right or wrong, for every man
    Has his own honour.

CLOTALDO: Humbly I take my leave.

(*Exit.*)

SEGISMUND: Now sound the drums and march in rank and
    order
    Straight to the palace.
ALL: Long live Segismund!
SEGISMUND: Fortune, we go to reign! Do not awake me   170
    If I am dreaming! Do not let me fall
    Asleep if it is true! To act with virtue
    Is what matters, since if this proves true,
    That truth's sufficient reason in itself;
    If not, we win us friends against the time   175
    When we at last awake.

A room in the royal palace.

Enter BASIL *and* ASTOLFO.

BASIL: Whose prudence can rein in a bolting horse?
    Who can restrain a river's pride, in spate?
    Whose valour can withstand a crag dislodged
    And hurtling downwards from a mountain peak?   180
    All these are easier by far than to hold back
    A crowd's proud fury, once it has been roused.
    It has two voices, both proclaiming war,
    And you can hear them echoing through the mountains,

185   Some shouting "Segismund," others "Astolfo."
      The scene I set for swearing of allegiance
      Lends but an added horror to this strife:
      It has become the back cloth to a stage
      Where Fortune plays out tragedies in blood.

190   ASTOLFO: My lord, forget the happiness and wealth
      You promised me from your most blessèd hand.
      If Poland, which I hope to rule, refuses
      Obedience to my right, grudging me honour,
      It is because I've got to earn it first.

195   Give me a horse, that I with angry pride
      May match the thunder in my voice and ride
      To strike, like lightning, terror far and wide.

      (*Exit* ASTOLFO.)

      BASIL: No remedy for what's infallible!
      What is foreseen is perilous indeed!

200   If something has to be, there's no way out;
      In trying to evade it, you but court it.
      This law is pitiless and horrible.
      Thinking one can evade the risk, one meets it:
      My own precautions have been my undoing,

205   And I myself have quite destroyed my kingdom.

      (*Enter* STELLA.)

      STELLA: If you, my lord, in person do not try
      To curb the vast commotion that has started
      In all the streets between the rival factions,
      You'll see your kingdom, swamped in waves of crimson,

210   Swimming in its own blood, with nothing left
      But havoc, dire calamity, and woe.
      So frightful is the damage to your empire
      That, seen, it strikes amazement; heard, despair.
      The sun's obscured, the very winds are hindered.

215   Each stone is a memorial to the dead.
      Each flower springs from a grave while every building
      Appears a mausoleum, and each soldier
      A premature and walking skeleton.

      (*Enter* CLOTALDO.)

      CLOTALDO: Praise be to God, I reach your feet alive!
220   BASIL: Clotaldo! What's the news of Segismund?
      CLOTALDO: The crowd, a headstrong monster blind with rage,
      Entered his dungeon tower and set him free.
      He, now exalted for the second time,
      Conducts himself with valour, boasting how
225   He will bring down the truth out of the stars.
      BASIL: Give me a horse, that I myself, in person,
      May vanquish such a base, ungrateful son!
      For I, in the defence of my own crown,
      Shall do by steel what science failed to do.

      (*Exit*.)

230   STELLA: I'll be Bellona to your Sun, and try
      To write my name next yours in history.
      I'll ride as though I flew on outstretched wings
      That I may vie with Pallas.

      (*Exit*.)

(*Enter* ROSAURA, *holding back* CLOTALDO.)

      ROSAURA: I know that all is war, Clotaldo, yet
      Although your valour calls you to the front,   235
      First hear me out. You know quite well that I
      Arrived in Poland poor and miserable,
      Where, shielded by your valour, I found mercy.
      You told me to conceal myself, and stay
      Here in the palace, hiding from Astolfo.   240
      He saw me in the end, and so insulted
      My honour that (although he saw me clearly)
      He nightly speaks with Stella in the garden.
      I have the key to it and I will show you
      How you can enter there and end my cares.   245
      Thus bold, resolved, and strong, you can recover
      My honour, since you're ready to avenge me
      By killing him.
      CLOTALDO: It's true that I intended,
      Since first I saw you (having heard your tale)
      With my own life to rectify your wrongs.   250
      The first step that I took was bid you dress
      According to your sex, for fear Astolfo
      Might see you as you were, and deem you wanton.
      I was devising how we could recover
      Your honour (so much did it weigh on me)   255
      Even though we had to kill him. (A wild plan—
      Though since he's not my king, I would not flinch
      From killing him.) But then, when suddenly
      Segismund tried to kill me, it was he
      Who saved my life with his surpassing valour.   260
      Consider: how can I requite Astolfo
      With death for giving me my life so bravely,
      And when my soul is full of gratitude?
      So torn between the two of you I stand—
      Rosaura, whose life I saved, and Astolfo,   265
      Who saved my life. What's to be done? Which side
      To take, and whom to help, I cannot judge.
      What I owe you in that I gave you life
      I owe to him in that he gave me life.
      And so there is no course that I can take   270
      To satisfy my love. I am a person
      Who has to act, yet suffer either way.
      ROSAURA: I should not have to tell so brave a man
      That if it is nobility to give,
      It's baseness to receive. That being so   275
      You owe no gratitude to him, admitting
      That it was he who gave you life, and you
      Who gave me life, since he forced you to take
      A meaner role, and through me you assumed
      A generous role. So you should side with me: 280
      My cause is so far worthier than his own
      As giving is than taking.
      CLOTALDO: Though nobility
      Is with the giver, it is gratitude
      That dwells with the receiver. As a giver
      I have the name of being generous: 285
      Then grant me that of being grateful too
      And let me earn the title and be grateful,
      As I am liberal, giving or receiving.
      ROSAURA: You granted me my life, at the same time
      Telling me it was worthless, since dishonoured,   290

And therefore was no life. Therefore from you
I have received no life at all. And since
You should be liberal first and grateful after
(Since so you said yourself) I now entreat you
295   Give me the life, the life you never gave me!
As giving magnifies the most, give first
And then be grateful after, if you will!
CLOTALDO: Won by your argument, I will be liberal.
Rosaura, I shall give you my estate
300   And you shall seek a convent, there to live.
This measure is a happy thought, for, see,
Fleeing a crime, you find a sanctuary.
For when the empire's threatened with disasters
And is divided thus, I, born a noble,
305   Am not the man who would augment its woes.
So with this remedy which I have chosen
I remain loyal to the kingdom, generous
To you, and also grateful to Astolfo.
And thus I choose the course that suits you best.
310   Were I your father, what could I do more?
ROSAURA: Were you my father, then I would accept
The insult. Since you are not, I refuse.
CLOTALDO: What do you hope to do then?
ROSAURA: Kill the duke!
CLOTALDO: A girl who never even knew her father
315   Armed with such courage?
ROSAURA: Yes.
CLOTALDO: What spurs you on?
ROSAURA: My good name.
CLOTALDO: In Astolfo you will find . . .
ROSAURA: My honour rides on him and strikes him
down!
CLOTALDO: Your king, too, Stella's husband!
ROSAURA: Never, never
Shall that be, by almighty God, I swear!
320   CLOTALDO: Why, this is madness!
ROSAURA: Yes it is!
CLOTALDO: Restrain it.
ROSAURA: That I cannot.
CLOTALDO: Then you are lost forever!
ROSAURA: I know it!
CLOTALDO: Life and honour both together!
ROSAURA: I well believe it!
CLOTALDO: What do you intend?
ROSAURA: My death.
CLOTALDO: This is despair and desperation.
325   ROSAURA: It's honour.
CLOTALDO: It is nonsense.
ROSAURA: It is valour.
CLOTALDO: It's frenzy.
ROSAURA: Yes, it's anger! Yes, it's fury!
CLOTALDO: In short you cannot moderate your passion?
ROSAURA: No.
CLOTALDO: Who is there to help you?
ROSAURA: I, myself.
CLOTALDO: There is no cure?
ROSAURA: There is no cure!
CLOTALDO: Think well
330   If there's not some way out . . .
ROSAURA: Some other way
To do away with me . . .

(*Exit.*)

CLOTALDO: If you are lost,
My daughter, let us both be lost together!

In the country.

Enter SEGISMUND *clothed in skins.* SOLDIERS *marching.* CLARION.
Drums beating.

SEGISMUND: If Rome, today, could see me here, renewing
Her olden triumphs, she might laugh to see
A wild beast in command of mighty armies,   335
A wild beast, to whose fiery aspirations
The firmament were all too slight a conquest!
But stoop your flight, my spirit. Do not thus
Be puffed to pride by these uncertain plaudits
Which, when I wake, will turn to bitterness   340
In that I won them only to be lost.
The less I value them, the less I'll miss them.

(*A trumpet sounds.*)

CLARION: Upon a rapid courser (pray excuse me,
Since if it comes to mind I must describe it)
In which it seems an atlas was designed   345
Since if its body is earth, its soul is fire
Within its breast, its foam appears the sea,
The wind its breath, and chaos its condition,
Since in its soul, its foam, its breath and flesh,
It seems a monster of fire, earth, sea, and wind,   350
Upon the horse, all of a patchwork colour,
Dappled, and rushing forward at the will
Of one who plies the spur, so that it flies
Rather than runs— see how a woman rides
Boldly into your presence.   355
SEGISMUND: Her light blinds me.
CLARION: Good God! Why, here's Rosaura!
SEGISMUND: It is heaven
That has restored her to my sight once more.

(*Enter* ROSAURA *with sword and dagger in riding costume.*)

ROSAURA: Generous Segismund, whose majesty
Heroically rises in the lustre
Of his great deeds out of his night of shadows,   360
And as the greatest planet, in the arms
Of his aurora, lustrously returns
To plants and roses, over hills and seas,
When, crowned with gold, he looks abroad, dispersing
Radiance, flashing his rays, bathing the summits,   365
And broidering the fringes of the foam,
So may you dawn upon the world, bright sun
Of Poland, that a poor unhappy woman
May fall before your feet and beg protection
Both as a woman and unfortunate—   370
Two things that must oblige you, sire, as one
Who prizes yourself as valiant, each of them
More than suffices for your chivalry.

343–355 **Upon a . . . presence** Clarion's speech is a parody of
exaggerated style including Calderón's [R.C.]

Three times you have beheld me now, three times
375 Been ignorant of who I am, because
Three times you saw me in a different clothing.
The first time you mistook me for a man,
Within that rigorous prison, where your hardships
Made mine seem pleasure. Next time, as a woman,
380 You saw me, when your pomp and majesty
Were as a dream, a phantasm, a shade.
The third time is today when, as a monster
Of both the sexes, in a woman's costume
I bear a soldier's arms. But to dispose you
385 The better to compassion, hear my story.
My mother was a noble in the court
Of Moscow, who, since most unfortunate,
Must have been beautiful. Then came a traitor
And cast his eyes on her (I do not name him,
390 Not knowing who he is). Yet I deduce
That he was valiant too from my own valour,
Since he gave form to me—and I could wish
I had been born in pagan times, that I might
Persuade myself he was some god of those
395 Who rain in showers of gold, turn into swans
Or bulls, for Danaës, Ledas, or Europas.
That's strange: I thought I was just rambling on
By telling old perfidious myths, yet find
I've told you how my mother was cajoled.
400 Oh, she was beautiful as no one else
Has been, but was unfortunate like all.
He swore to wed her (that's an old excuse)
And this trick reached so nearly to her heart
That thought must weep, recalling it today.
405 The tyrant left her only with his sword
As Aeneas left Troy. I sheathed its blade here
Upon my thigh, and I will bare it too
Before the ending of this history.
Out of this union, this poor link which neither
410 Could bind the marriage nor handcuff the crime,
Myself was born, her image and her portrait,
Not in her beauty, but in her misfortune,
For mine's the same. That's all I need to say.
The most that I can tell you of myself
415 Is that the man who robbed me of the spoils
And trophies of my honour is Astolfo.
Alas! to name him my heart rages so
(As hearts will do when men name enemies).
Astolfo was my faithless and ungrateful
420 Lord, who (quite forgetful of our happiness,
Since of a past love even the memory fades)
Came here to claim the throne and marry Stella
For she's the star who rises as I set.
It's hard to credit that a star should sunder
425 Lovers the stars had made conformable!
So hurt was I, so villainously cheated,
That I became mad, brokenhearted, sick,
Half wild with grief, and like to die, with all
Hell's own confusion ciphered on my mind
430 Like Babel's incoherence. Mutely I told
My griefs (since woes and griefs declare themselves
Better than can the mouth, by their effects),
When, with my mother (we were by ourselves),

She broke the prison of my pent-up sorrows
And from my breast they all rushed forth in troops. 435
I felt no shyness, for in knowing surely
That one to whom one's errors are recounted
Has also been an ally in her own,
One finds relief and rest, since bad example
Can sometimes serve for a good purpose too. 440
She heard my plaint with pity, and she tried
To palliate my sorrows with her own.
How easily do judges pardon error
When they've offended too! An example,
A warning, in herself, she did not trust 445
To idleness, or to the slow cure of time,
Nor try to find a remedy for her honour
In my misfortunes, but, with better counsel,
She bade me follow him to Poland here
And with prodigious gallantry persuade him 450
To pay the debt to honour that he owes me.
So that it would be easier to travel,
She bade me don male clothing, and took down
This ancient sword which I am wearing now.
Now it is time that I unsheathe the blade 455
As I was bid, for, trusting in its sign,
She said: "Depart to Poland, show this sword
That all the nobles may behold it well,
And it may be that one of them will take
Pity on you, and counsel you, and shield you." 460
I came to Poland and, you will remember,
Entered your cave. You looked at me in wonder.
Clotaldo passionately took my part
To plead for mercy to the king, who spared me,
Then, when he heard my story, bade me change 465
Into my own clothes and attend on Stella,
There to disturb Astolfo's love and stop
Their marriage. Again you saw me in woman's dress
And were confused by the discrepancy.
But let's pass to what's new: Clotaldo, now 470
Persuaded that Astolfo must, with Stella,
Come to the throne, dissuades me from my purpose,
Against the interests of my name and honour.
But seeing you, O valiant Segismund,
Are claiming your revenge, now that the heavens 475
Have burst the prison of your rustic tower,
(Wherein you were the tiger of your sorrows,
The rock of sufferings and direful pains)
And sent you forth against your sire and country,
I come to aid you, mingling Dian's silks 480
With the hard steel of Pallas. Now, strong Captain,
It well behoves us both to stop this marriage—
Me, lest my promised husband should be wed,
You, lest, when their estates are joined, they weigh
More powerfully against your victory. 485
I come, as a mere woman, to persuade you
To right my shame; but, as a man, I come
To help you battle for your crown. As woman,
To melt your heart, here at your feet I fall;
But, as a man, I come to serve you bravely 490
Both with my person and my steel, and thus,
If you today should woo me as a woman,
Then I should have to kill you as a man would

In honourable service of my honour;
495 Since I must be three things today at once—
Passionate, to persuade you: womanly,
To ply you with my woes: manly, to gain
Honour in battle.
SEGISMUND: Heavens! If it is true I'm dreaming,
Suspend my memory, for in a dream
500 So many things could not occur. Great heavens!
If I could only come free of them all!
Or never think of any! Who ever felt
Such grievous doubts? If I but dreamed that triumph
In which I found myself, how can this woman
505 Refer me to such sure and certain facts?
Then all of it was true and not a dream.
But if it be the truth, why does my past life
Call it a dream? This breeds the same confusion.
Are dreams and glories so alike, that fictions
510 Are held for truths, realities for lies?
Is there so little difference in them both
That one should question whether what one sees
And tastes is true or false? What? Is the copy
So near to the original that doubt
515 Exists between them? Then if that is so,
And grandeur, power, majesty, and pomp,
Must all evaporate like shades at morning,
Let's profit by it, this time, to enjoy
That which we only can enjoy in dreams.
520 Rosaura's in my power: my soul adores her beauty.
Let's take the chance. Let love break every law
On which she has relied in coming here
And kneeling, trustful, prostrate at my feet.
This is a dream. If so, dream pleasures now
525 Since they must turn to sorrows in the end!
But with my own opinions, I begin
Once again to convince myself. Let's think.
If it is but vainglory and a dream,
Who for mere human vainglory would lose
530 True glory? What past blessing is not merely
A dream? Who has known heroic glories,
That deep within himself, as he recalls them
Has never doubted that they might be dreams?
But if this all should end in disenchantment,
535 Seeing that pleasure is a lovely flame
That's soon converted into dust and ashes
By any wind that blows, then let us seek
That which endures in thrifty, lasting fame
In which no pleasures sleep, nor grandeurs dream.
540 Rosaura's without honour. In a prince
It's worthier to restore it than to steal it.
I shall restore it, by the living God,
Before I win my throne! Let's shun the danger
And fly from the temptation which is strong!
545 Then sound to arms!

(*To a* SOLDIER.)

Today I must give battle before darkness
Buries the rays of gold in green-black waves!
ROSAURA: My lord! Alas, you stand apart, and offer
No word of pity for my plight. How is it

You neither hear nor see me nor even yet   550
Have turned your face on me?
SEGISMUND: Rosaura, for your honour's sake
I must be cruel to you, to be kind.
My voice must not reply to you because
My honour must reply to you. I am silent
Because my deeds must speak to you alone.   555
I do not look at you since, in such straits,
Having to see your honour is requited,
I must not see your beauty.

(*Exit with* SOLDIERS.)

ROSAURA: What strange enigma's this? After such trouble
Still to be treated with more doubtful riddles!   560

(*Enter* CLARION.)

CLARION: Madam, may you be visited just now?
ROSAURA: Why, Clarion, where have you been all this time?
CLARION: Shut in the tower, consulting cards
About my death: "to be or not to be."
And it was a near thing.   565
ROSAURA: Why?
CLARION: Because I know
The secret who you are: in fact, Clotaldo . . .

(*Drums.*)

But hush what noise is that?
ROSAURA: What can it be?
CLARION: From the beleaguered palace a whole squadron
Is charging forth to harry and defeat
That of fierce Segismund.   570
ROSAURA: Why, what a coward
Am I, not to be at his side, the terror
And scandal of the world, while such fierce strife
Presses all round in lawless anarchy.

(*Exit.*)

VOICES OF SOME: Long live our king!
VOICES OF OTHERS: Long live our liberty!
CLARION: Long live both king and liberty. Yes, live!   575
And welcome to them both! I do not worry.
In all this pother, I behave like Nero
Who never grieved at what was going on.
If I had anything to grieve about
It would be me, myself. Well hidden here   580
Now, I can watch the sport that's going on.
This place is safe and hidden between crags,
And since death cannot find me here, two figs for death!

(*He hides. Drums and the clash of arms are heard.*)

(*Enter* BASIL, CLOTALDO, *and* ASTOLFO, *fleeing.*)

BASIL: Was ever king so hapless as myself
Or father more ill used?   585
CLOTALDO: Your beaten army
Rush down, in all directions, in disorder.
ASTOLFO: The traitors win!

BASIL: In battles such as these
    Those on the winning side are ever "loyal,"
    And traitors the defeated. Come, Clotaldo,
590   Let's flee from the inhuman cruelty
    Of my fierce son!

(Shots are fired within. CLARION *falls wounded.)*

CLARION: Heavens, save me!
ASTOLFO: Who is this
    Unhappy soldier bleeding at our feet?
CLARION: I am a most unlucky man who, wishing
    To guard myself from death, have sought it out
595   By fleeing from it. Shunning it, I found it,
    Because, to death, no hiding-place is secret.
    So you can argue that whoever shuns it
    Most carefully runs into it the quickest.
    Turn, then, once more into the thick of battle:
600   There is more safety there amidst the fire
    And clash of arms than here on this secluded
    Mountain, because no hidden path is safe
    From the inclemency of Fate; and so,
    Although you flee from death, yet you may find it
605   Quicker than you expect, if God so wills.

(He falls dead.)

BASIL: "If God so wills" . . . With what strange eloquence
    This corpse persuades our ignorance and error
    To better knowledge, speaking from the mouth
    Of its fell wound, where the red liquid flowing
610   Seems like a bloody tongue which teaches us
    That the activities of man are vain
    When they are pitted against higher powers.
    For I, who wished to liberate my country
    From murder and sedition, gave it up
615   To the same ills from which I would have saved it.
CLOTALDO: Though Fate, my lord, knows every path, and finds
    Him whom it seeks even in the midst of crags
    And thickets, it is not a Christian judgment
    To say there is no refuge from its fury.
620   A prudent man can conquer Fate itself.
    Though you are not exempted from misfortune,
    Take action to escape it while you can!
ASTOLFO: Clotaldo speaks as one mature in prudence,
    And I as one in valour's youthful prime.
625   Among the thickets of this mount is hidden
    A horse, the very birth of the swift wind.
    Flee on him, and I'll guard you in the rear.
BASIL: If it is God's will I should die, or if
    Death waits here for my coming, I will seek
630   Him out today, and meet him face to face.

(Enter SEGISMUND, STELLA, ROSAURA, SOLDIERS, *and their* TRAIN.)

A SOLDIER: Amongst the thickets of this mountain
635   The king is hiding.
SEGISMUND: Seek him out at once!
    Leave no foot of the summit unexplored
    But search from stem to stem and branch to branch!
CLOTALDO: Fly, sir!

BASIL: What for?
ASTOLFO: What do you mean to do?
BASIL: Astolfo, stand aside!
CLOTALDO: What is your wish?
BASIL: To take a cure I've needed for sometime.

(To SEGISMUND.)

    If you have come to seek me, here I am.

(Kneeling.)

    Your father, prince, kneels humbly at your feet.
    The white snow of my hair is now your carpet.   640
    Tread on my neck and trample on my crown!
    Lay low and drag my dignity in dust!
    Take vengeance on my honour! Make a slave
    Of me and, after all I've done to thwart them,
    Let Fate fulfil its edict and claim homage   645
    And Heaven fulfil its oracles at last!
SEGISMUND: Illustrious court of Poland, who have been
    The witnesses of such unwonted wonders,
    Attend to me, and hear your prince speak out.
    What Heaven decrees and God writes with his finger   650
    (Whose prints and ciphers are the azure leaves
    Adorned with golden lettering of the stars)
    Never deceives nor lies. They only lie
    Who seek to penetrate the mystery
    And, having reached it, use it to ill purpose.   655
    My father, who is here to evade the fury
    Of my proud nature, made me a wild beast:
    So, when I, by my birth of gallant stock,
    My generous blood, and inbred grace and valour,
    Might well have proved both gentle and forbearing,   660
    The very mode of life to which he forced me,
    The sort of bringing up I had to bear
    Sufficed to make me savage in my passions.
    What a strange method of restraining them!
    If one were to tell any man: "One day   665
    You will be killed by an inhuman monster,"
    Would it be the best method he could choose
    To wake that monster when it was asleep?
    Or if they told him: "That sword which you're wearing
    Will be your death," what sort of cure were it   670
    To draw it forth and aim it at his breast?
    Or if they told him: "Deep blue gulfs of water
    Will one day be your sepulchre and grave
    Beneath a silver monument of foam,"
    He would be mad to hurl himself in headlong   675
    When the sea highest heaved its showy mountains
    And crystalline sierras plumed with spray.
    The same has happened to the king as to him
    Who wakes a beast which threatens death, to him
    Who draws a naked sword because he fears it,   680
    To him who dives into the stormy breakers.
    Though my ferocious nature (hear me now)
    Was like a sleeping beast, my inborn rage
    A sheathèd sword, my wrath a quiet ripple,
    Fate should not be coerced by man's injustice—   685
    This rouses more resentment. So it is
    That he who seeks to tame his fortune must

Resort to moderation and to measure.
He who foresees an evil cannot conquer it
690 Thus in advance, for though humility
Can overcome it, this it can do only
When the occasion's there, for there's no way
To dodge one's fate and thus evade the issue.
Let this strange spectacle serve as example—
695 This prodigy, this horror, and this wonder,
Because it is no less than one, to see,
After such measures and precautions taken
To thwart it, that a father thus should kneel
At his son's feet, a kingdom thus be shattered.
700 This was the sentence of the heavens above,
Which he could not evade, much though he tried.
Can I, younger in age, less brave, and less
In science than the king, conquer that fate?

(*To the* KING.)

Sire, rise, give me your hand, now that the heavens
705 Have shown you that you erred as to the method
To vanquish them. Humbly I kneel before you
And offer you my neck to tread upon.
BASIL: Son, such a great and noble act restores you
Straight to my heart. Oh, true and worthy prince!
710 You have won both the laurel and the palm.
Crown yourself with your deeds! For you *have* conquered!
ALL: Long live Segismund! Long live Segismund!
SEGISMUND: Since I have other victories to win,
The greatest of them all awaits me now:
715 To conquer my own self. Astolfo, give
Your hand here to Rosaura, for you know
It is a debt of honour and must be paid.
ASTOLFO: Although, it's true, I owe some obligations—
She does not know her name or who she is,
720 It would be base to wed a woman who . . .
CLOTALDO: Hold! Wait! Rosaura's of as noble stock
As yours, Astolfo. In the open field
I'll prove it with my sword. She is my daughter

And that should be enough.
ASTOLFO: What do you say?
CLOTALDO: Until I saw her married, righted, honoured,   725
I did not wish for it to be discovered.
It's a long story but she is my daughter.
ASTOLFO: That being so, I'm glad to keep my word.
SEGISMUND: And now, so that the princess Stella here
Will not remain disconsolate to lose   730
A prince of so much valour, here I offer
My hand to her, no less in birth and rank.
Give me your hand.
STELLA: I gain by meriting
So great a happiness.
SEGISMUND: And now, Clotaldo,
So long so loyal to my father, come   735
To my arms. Ask me anything you wish.
FIRST SOLDIER: If thus you treat a man who never served you,
What about me who led the revolution
And brought you from your dungeon in the tower?
What will you give me?   740
SEGISMUND: That same tower and dungeon
From which you never shall emerge till death.
No traitor is of use after his treason.
BASIL: All wonder at your wisdom!
ASTOLFO: What a change
Of character!
ROSAURA: How wise and prudent!
SEGISMUND: Why
Do you wonder? Why do you marvel, since   745
It was a dream that taught me and I still
Fear to wake up once more in my close dungeon?
Though that may never happen, it's enough
To dream it might, for thus I came to learn
That all our human happiness must pass   750
Away like any dream, and I would here
Enjoy it fully ere it glide away,
Asking (for noble hearts are prone to pardon)
Pardon for faults in the actors or the play.

Molière

Jean-Baptiste Poquelin (1622–1673) was born into a prosperous mercantile family with connections at court; his father, Jean Poquelin, secured the honor of *tapissier ordinaire du roi,* the upholsterer to the court, which carried an annual pension. Jean Poquelin also educated his son in the traditional disciplines of the humanities, philosophy, and the classics and must have intended a life at court for him. In 1643, Jean-Baptiste joined with the Illustre Théâtre, a theatrical company run by the Béjart family, took the stage name Molière, and after a brief period performing in Parisian tennis courts, left with the company to play in the provinces. In 1658, after several hard and impoverished years of touring, when Molière is thought to have mastered the techniques of *commedia dell' arte,* the company was invited to perform in Paris.

Molière's career was closely tied to the court. When his brother died in 1660, he received the position of court upholsterer and the income it provided. More important, Molière became a significant playwright and both wrote and acted in a splendid series of plays that satirized the manners and morals of elegant society: *Les Précieuses Ridicules* (1659), *Sganarelle* (1660), *School for Husbands* (1661), *School for Wives* (1662), *Dom Juan* (1665), *The Misanthrope* (1666), *The Doctor in Spite of Himself* (1666), *The Miser* (1668), *The Learned Ladies* (1672), and *The Imaginary Invalid* (1673). Molière also prepared other entertainments at court, including many royal pageants, ballets, and machine plays devised by and for Louis XIV. In addition to being a great dramatist, Molière was a fine comic actor as well and performed in his own plays; he died shortly after playing the title role in the fourth performance of *The Imaginary Invalid.*

The fortunes of *Tartuffe* suggest Molière's importance at court. When Molière initially produced the first three acts of the play in 1664, the clergy protested and banned the play from production in Paris. Many of Molière's plays had excited controversy, and in this case Molière appealed to the king and proceeded to revise the play. Louis's attitude is perhaps revealed by the fact that he made Molière's company the *Troupe du roi* ("King's Company") in 1665, but even the throne could not prevent the clergy from censoring Molière's second version of the play in 1667, newly titled *The Impostor.* Molière finally produced the play to acclaim in 1669, and the record of his efforts is preserved in the series of letters and prefaces included here.

Molière's theatrical company was the most influential of its day. After his death, his young wife Amanda Béjart and the actress Mademoiselle Champmeslé—newly defected from the rival company at the Hôtel de Bourgogne—established a new company, the Comédie Française. Yet although Molière achieved extraordinary status at court, because he was an actor he remained stigmatized in ways that playwrights like Racine and Corneille were not. Following its standard practice, and perhaps because of *Tartuffe*'s notoriety, the church refused to bury Molière in sacred ground. Louis XIV intervened, but was only able to persuade the Archbishop of Paris to bury Molière in a parish cemetery. The burial was conducted at night, by two priests, with no funeral ceremony.

TARTUFFE

The Catholic church criticized *Tartuffe* for its portrait of hypocritical piety, but the fact that Molière played the part of Orgon may suggest that the play is as much about Tartuffe's effect on that benighted householder as it is about the title character. For if Tartuffe is hypocritical, Orgon is obsessed, less with piety than with his own desire to achieve a kind of total power and authority in his household, a kind of domestic absolutism; he is, in a sense, a comic, bourgeois Louis XIV in miniature. Moreover, Tartuffe dupes Orgon not by tricking him, but by inviting Orgon to fulfill his own fantasy of autonomy and authority. As he brags

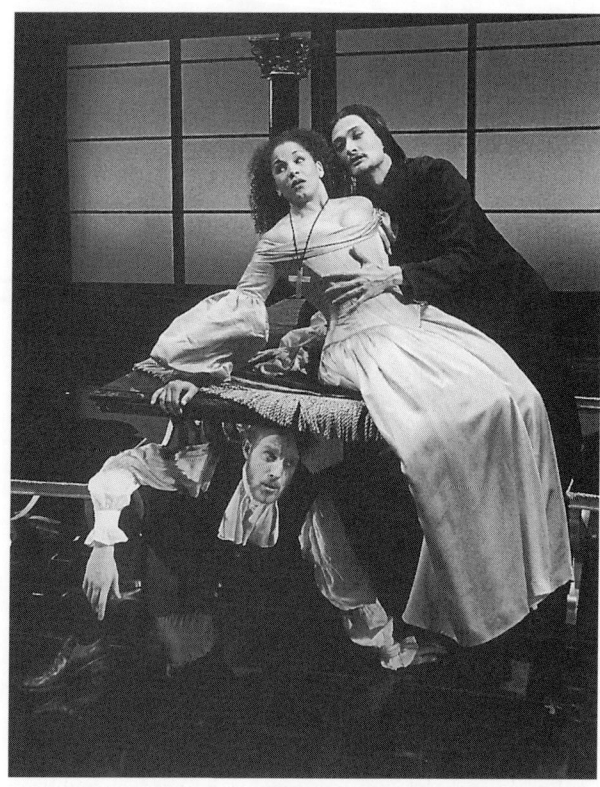

Tartuffe seduces Elmire while Orgon hides beneath the table in Molière's *Tartuffe*.

to the sensible Cléante, under Tartuffe's teaching, "my soul's been freed / From earthly loves, and every human tie: / My mother, children, brother, and wife could die, / And I'd not feel a single moment's pain." Helping Orgon to realize this fantasy, Tartuffe transforms him into a kind of monster: Orgon comes near to selling his daughter, disinheriting his son, allowing his wife to be raped, and losing his family's property and fortune.

Tartuffe is very much a play of the world, a satiric comedy. Set in an urban landscape, the play insistently translates the idealized passions of tragedy and romantic comedy—love, honor, loyalty—into their ironic counterparts—lust, hypocrisy, betrayal. Molière peoples the play with individualized versions of the unchanging types of *commedia dell' arte* and the Roman comedy that inspired it: the reasonable and attractive heroes; an old, pedantic, self-absorbed dupe; a wily and conniving villain; a clever and witty servant. Yet Molière reinvents this range of stock characters, brilliantly turning his play toward an exploration of the folly of self-deception. For while we might take the neoclassical conflict between reason and the passions to be the hallmark of tragedy, it surges through this play as well. Orgon's passionate solipsism is, for all its ridiculousness, no less profound, troubling, or destructive than the obsessed affections of Racine's Phaedra and Hippolytus. Also, Orgon's redemption, by fiat of the king, seems no less arbitrary than the vengeful caprice of Venus or Neptune in Racine's tragedy.

Since the characters cannot change in Molière's comedy, change must happen to them. Molière's most brilliant device here arises in the person of the king's officer, who appears to apprehend Tartuffe and to restore Orgon and his family to their property: property is what establishes the position, the place, the social and individual identity of these characters. Although Molière's DEUS EX MACHINA might be regarded as an elegant (though somewhat clumsy) compliment to the king—and, perhaps, as a sly jab at the clerical critics who attacked *Tartuffe*—this device plays a subtle role in dramatizing the nature of royal authority. For in *Tartuffe,* the king has the power to assign every person to his or her proper place, to see into our inmost hearts, to structure the moral and social order of the world as the reflection of his own will and judgment: *"L'état, c'est moi."* In this sense, even though *Tartuffe* unleashes the uncontrollable power of self-delusion and the power and destructive fantasies of absolute authority, the play concludes by asserting the legitimacy of that absolute power. Molière's *deus ex machina* testifies both to the power and to the arbitrariness of the king's authority.

PREFACE[1]

TRANSLATED BY RICHARD WILBUR

Here is a comedy that has excited a good deal of discussion and that has been under attack for a long time; and the persons who are mocked by it have made it plain that they are more powerful in France than all whom my plays have satirized up to this time. Noblemen, ladies of fashion, cuckolds, and doctors all kindly consented to their presentation, which they themselves seemed to enjoy along with everyone else; but hypocrites do not understand banter: they became angry at once, and found it strange that I was bold enough to represent their actions and to care to describe a profession shared by so many good men. This is a crime for which they cannot forgive me, and they have taken up arms against my comedy in a terrible rage. They were careful not to attack it at the point that had wounded them: they are too crafty for that and too clever to reveal their true character. In keeping with their lofty custom, they have used the cause of God to mask their private interests; and *Tartuffe,* they say, is a play that offends piety: It is filled with abominations from beginning to end, and nowhere is there a line that does not deserve to be burned. Every syllable is wicked, the very gestures are criminal, and the slightest glance, turn of the head, or step from right to left conceals mysteries that they are able to explain to my disadvantage. In vain did I submit the play to the criticism of my friends and the scrutiny of the public: all the corrections I could make, the judgment of the king and queen who saw the play,[2] the approval of great princes and ministers of state who honored it with their presence, the opinion of good men who found it worthwhile; all this did not help. They will not let go of their prey, and every day of the week they have pious zealots abusing me in public and damning me out of charity.

I would care very little about all they might say except that their devices make enemies of men whom I respect and gain the support of genuinely good men, whose faith they know and who, because of the warmth of their piety, readily accept the impressions that others present to them. And it is this which forces me to defend myself. Especially to the truly devout do I wish to vindicate my play, and I beg of them with all my heart not to condemn it before seeing it, to rid themselves of preconceptions, and not aid the cause of men dishonored by their actions.

If one takes the trouble to examine my comedy in good faith, he will surely see that my intentions are innocent throughout, and tend in no way to make fun of what men revere; that I have presented the subject with all the precautions that its delicacy imposes; and that I have used all the art and skill that I could to distinguish clearly the character of the hypocrite from that of the truly devout man. For that purpose I used two whole acts to prepare the appearance of my scoundrel. Never is there a moment's doubt about his character; he is known at once from the qualities I have given him; and from one end of the play to the other, he does not say a word, he does not perform an action which does not depict to

---

[1]Molière added his three petitions to Louis XIV; they follow the preface.

[2]Louis XIV was married to Marie Thérèse of Austria.

the audience the character of a wicked man, and which does not bring out in sharp relief the character of the truly good man which I oppose to it.

I know full well that by way of reply, these gentlemen try to insinuate that it is not the role of the theater to speak of these matters; but with their permission, I ask them on what do they base this fine doctrine. It is a proposition they advance as no more than a supposition, for which they offer not a shred of proof; and surely it would not be difficult to show them that comedy, for the ancients, had its origin in religion and constituted a part of its ceremonies; that our neighbors, the Spaniards, have hardly a single holiday celebration in which a comedy is not a part; and that even here in France, it owes its birth to the efforts of a religious brotherhood who still own the Hôtel de Bourgogne, where the most important mystery plays of our faith were presented[3]; that you can still find comedies printed in gothic letters under the name of a learned doctor of the Sorbonne[4]; and without going so far, in our own day the religious dramas of Pierre Corneille[5] have been performed to the admiration of all France.

If the function of comedy is to correct men's vices, I do not see why any should be exempt. Such a condition in our society would be much more dangerous than the thing itself; and we have seen that the theater is admirably suited to provide correction. The most forceful lines of a serious moral statement are usually less powerful than those of satire; and nothing will reform most men better than the depiction of their faults. It is a vigorous blow to vices to expose them to public laughter. Criticism is taken lightly, but men will not tolerate satire. They are quite willing to be mean, but they never like to be ridiculed.

I have been attacked for having placed words of piety in the mouth of my impostor. Could I avoid doing so in order to represent properly the character of a hypocrite? It seemed to me sufficient to reveal the criminal motives which make him speak as he does, and I have eliminated all ceremonial phrases, which nonetheless he would not have been found using incorrectly. Yet some say that in the fourth act he sets forth a vicious morality; but is not this a morality which everyone has heard again and again? Does my comedy say anything new here? And is there any fear that ideas so thoroughly detested by everyone can make an impression on men's minds; that I make them dangerous by presenting them in the theater; that they acquire authority from the lips of a scoundrel? There is not the slightest suggestion of any of this; and one must either approve the comedy of *Tartuffe* or condemn all comedies in general.

This has indeed been done in a furious way for some time now, and never was the theater so much abused.[6] I cannot deny that there were Church Fathers who condemned comedy; but neither will it be denied me that there were some who looked on it somewhat more favorably. Thus authority, on which censure is supposed to depend, is destroyed by this disagreement; and the only conclusion that can be drawn from this difference of opinion among men enlightened by the same wisdom is that they viewed comedy in different ways, and that some considered it in its purity, while others regarded it in its corruption and confused it with all those wretched performances which have been rightly called performances of filth.

---

[3]A reference to the *Confrérie de la Passion et Résurrection de Notre-Seigneur* (the Fraternity of the Passion and Resurrection of Our Saviour), founded in 1402. The Hôtel de Bourgogne was a rival theater of Molière.

[4]Probably Maitre Jehán Michel, a medical doctor who wrote mystery plays.

[5]Pierre Corneille (1606–1684) and Racine were France's two greatest writers of classic tragedy. The two dramas Molière doubtlessly had in mind were *Polyeucte* (1643) and *Théodore, vierge et martyre* (1645).

[6]Molière had in mind Nicole's two attacks on the theater: *Visionnaries* (1666) and *Traité de Comédie*, and the Prince de Condé's *Traité de Comédie* (1666).

And in fact, since we should talk about things rather than words, and since most misunderstanding comes from including contrary notions in the same word, we need only to remove the veil of ambiguity and look at comedy in itself to see if it warrants condemnation. It will surely be recognized that as it is nothing more than a clever poem which corrects men's faults by means of agreeable lessons, it cannot be condemned without injustice. And if we listened to the voice of ancient times on this matter, it would tell us that its most famous philosophers have praised comedy—they who professed so austere a wisdom and who ceaselessly denounced the vices of their times. It would tell us that Aristotle spent his evenings at the theater[7] and took the trouble to reduce the art of making comedies to rules. It would tell us that some of its greatest and most honored men took pride in writing comedies themselves,[8] and that others did not disdain to recite them in public; that Greece expressed its admiration for this art by means of handsome prizes and magnificent theaters to honor it; and finally, that in Rome this same art also received extraordinary honors; I do not speak of Rome run riot under the license of the emperors, but of disciplined Rome, governed by the wisdom of the consuls, and in the age of the full vigor of Roman dignity.

I admit that there have been times when comedy became corrupt. And what do men not corrupt every day? There is nothing so innocent that men cannot turn it to crime; nothing so beneficial that its values cannot be reversed; nothing so good in itself that it cannot be put to bad uses. Medical knowledge benefits mankind and is revered as one of our most wonderful possessions; and yet there was a time when it fell into discredit, and was often used to poison men. Philosophy is a gift of Heaven; it has been given to us to bring us to the knowledge of a God by contemplating the wonders of nature; and yet we know that often it has been turned away from its function and has been used openly in support of impiety. Even the holiest of things are not immune from human corruption, and every day we see scoundrels who use and abuse piety, and wickedly make it serve the greatest of crimes. But this does not prevent one from making the necessary distinctions. We do not confuse in the same false inference the goodness of things that are corrupted with the wickedness of the corrupt. The function of an art is always distinguished from its misuse; and as medicine is not forbidden because it was banned in Rome,[9] nor philosophy because it was publicly condemned in Athens,[10] we should not suppress comedy simply because it has been condemned at certain times. This censure was justified then for reasons which no longer apply today; it was limited to what was then seen; and we should not seize on these limits, apply them more rigidly than is necessary, and include in our condemnation the innocent along with the guilty. The comedy that this censure attacked is in no way the comedy that we want to defend. We must be careful not to confuse the one with the other. There may be two persons whose morals may be completely different. They may have no resemblance to one another except in their names, and it would be a terrible injustice to want to condemn Olympia, who is a good woman, because there is also an Olympia who is lewd. Such procedures would make for great confusion everywhere. Everything under the sun would be condemned; now since this rigor is not applied to the countless instances of abuse we see every day, the same should hold for comedy, and those plays should be approved in which instruction and virtue reign supreme.

---

[7]A reference to Aristotle's *The Poetics* (composed between 335 and 322 BCE, the year of his death).

[8]The Roman consul and general responsible for the final destruction of Carthage in 146 BCE, Scipio Africanus Minor (c. 185–129 BCE), collaborated with the writer of comedies, Terence (Publius Terentius Afer, c. 195 or 185–c. 159 BCE).

[9]Pliny the Elder says that the Romans expelled their doctors at the same time that the Greeks did theirs.

[10]An allusion to Socrates' condemnation to death.

I know there are some so delicate that they cannot tolerate a comedy, who say that the most decent are the most dangerous, that the passions they present are all the more moving because they are virtuous, and that men's feelings are stirred by these presentations. I do not see what great crime it is to be affected by the sight of a generous passion; and this utter insensitivity to which they would lead us is indeed a high degree of virtue! I wonder if so great a perfection resides within the strength of human nature, and I wonder if it is not better to try to correct and moderate men's passions than to try to suppress them altogether. I grant that there are places better to visit than the theater; and if we want to condemn every single thing that does not bear directly on God and our salvation, it is right that comedy be included, and I should willingly grant that it be condemned along with everything else. But if we admit, as is in fact true, that the exercise of piety will permit interruptions, and that men need amusement, I maintain that there is none more innocent than comedy. I have dwelled too long on this matter. Let me finish with the words of a great prince on the comedy, *Tartuffe*.[11]

Eight days after it had been banned, a play called *Scaramouche the Hermit*[12] was performed before the court; and the king, on his way out, said to this great prince: "I should really like to know why the persons who make so much noise about Molière's comedy do not say a word about *Scaramouche*." To which the prince replied, "It is because the comedy of *Scaramouche* makes fun of Heaven and religion, which these gentlemen do not care about at all, but that of Molière makes fun of *them,* and that is what they cannot bear."

Molière

First Petition[13]
(PRESENTED TO THE KING ON THE COMEDY OF TARTUFFE)

Sire,

As the duty of comedy is to correct men by amusing them, I believed that in my occupation I could do nothing better than attack the vices of my age by making them ridiculous; and as hypocrisy is undoubtedly one of the most common, most improper, and most dangerous, I thought, Sire, that I would perform a service for all good men of your kingdom if I wrote a comedy which denounced hypocrites and placed in proper view all of the contrived poses of these incredibly virtuous men, all of the concealed villainies of these counterfeit believers who would trap others with a fraudulent piety and a pretended virtue.

I have written this comedy, Sire, with all the care and caution that the delicacy of the subject demands; and so as to maintain all the more properly the admiration and respect due to truly devout men, I have delineated my character as sharply as I could; I have left no room for doubt; I have removed all that might confuse good with evil, and have used for this painting only the specific colors and essential lines that make one instantly recognize a true and brazen hypocrite.

Nevertheless, all my precautions have been to no avail. Others have taken advantage of the delicacy of your feelings on religious matters, and they have been able to deceive you

---

[11]One of Molière's benefactors who liked the play was the Prince de Condé; the Prince had *Tartuffe* read to him and also privately performed for him.

[12]A troupe of Italian comedians had just performed the licentious farce, where a hermit dressed as a monk makes love to a married woman, announcing that *questo e per mortificar la carne* ("this is to mortify the flesh").

[13]The first of the three *petitions* or *placets* to Louis XIV concerning the play. On May 12, 1664, *Tartuffe*—or at least the first three acts roughly as they now stand—was performed at Versailles. A cabal unfavorable to Molière, including the Archbishop of Paris, Hardouin de Péréfixe, Queen-Mother Anne of Austria, certain influential courtiers, and the Brotherhood or Company of the Holy Sacrament (formed in 1627 to enforce morality), arranged that the play be banned and Molière censured.

on the only side of your character which lies open to deception: your respect for holy things. By underhanded means, the Tartuffes have skillfully gained Your Majesty's favor, and the models have succeeded in eliminating the copy, no matter how innocent it may have been and no matter what resemblance was found between them.

Although the suppression of this work was a serious blow for me, my misfortune was nonetheless softened by the way in which Your Majesty explained his attitude on the matter; and I believed, Sire, that Your Majesty removed any cause I had for complaint, as you were kind enough to declare that you found nothing in this comedy that you would forbid me to present in public.

Yet, despite this glorious declaration of the greatest and most enlightened king in the world, despite the approval of the Papal Legate[14] and of most of our churchmen, all of whom, at private readings of my work, agreed with the views of Your Majesty, despite all this, a book has appeared by a certain priest[15] which boldly contradicts all of these noble judgments. Your Majesty expressed himself in vain, and the Papal Legate and churchmen gave their opinion to no avail: Sight unseen, my comedy is diabolical, and so is my brain; I am a devil garbed in flesh and disguised as a man,[16] a libertine, a disbeliever who deserves a punishment that will set an example. It is not enough that fire expiate my crime in public, for that would be letting me off too easily: The generous piety of this good man will not stop there; he will not allow me to find any mercy in the sight of God; he demands that I be damned, and that will settle the matter.

This book, Sire, was presented to Your Majesty; and I am sure that you see for yourself how unpleasant it is for me to be exposed daily to the insults of these gentlemen, what harm these abuses will do my reputation if they must be tolerated, and finally, how important it is for me to clear myself of these false charges and let the public know that my comedy is nothing more than what they want it to be. I will not ask, Sire, for what I need for the sake of my reputation and the innocence of my work: enlightened kings such as you do not need to be told what is wished of them; like God, they see what we need and know better than we what they should give us. It is enough for me to place my interests in Your Majesty's hands, and I respectfully await whatever you may care to command.

(August, 1664)

Second Petition[17]

(PRESENTED TO THE KING IN HIS CAMP BEFORE THE CITY OF LILLE, IN FLANDERS)

Sire,

It is bold indeed for me to ask a favor of a great monarch in the midst of his glorious victories; but in my present situation, Sire, where will I find protection anywhere but where I seek it, and to whom can I appeal against the authority of the power that crushes me,[18] if not to the source of power and authority, the just dispenser of absolute law, the sovereign judge and master of all?

---

[14]Cardinal Legate Chigi, nephew to Pope Alexander VII, heard a reading of *Tartuffe* at Fontainebleau on August 4, 1664.

[15]Pierre Roullé, the curate of St. Barthélémy, who wrote a scathing attack on the play and sent his book to the king.

[16]Molière took some of these phrases from Roullé.

[17]On August 5, 1667, *Tartuffe* was performed at the Palais-Royal. The opposition—headed by the First President of Parliament—brought in the police, and the play was stopped. Since Louis was campaigning in Flanders, friends of Molière brought the second *placet* to Lille. Louis had always been favorable toward the playwright; in August 1665, Molière's company, the *Troupe de Monsieur* (nominally sponsored by Louis's brother Philippe, Duc d'Orléans) had become the *Troupe du Roi*.

[18]President de Lanvignon, in charge of the Paris police.

My comedy, Sire, has not enjoyed the kindnesses of Your Majesty. All to no avail, I produced it under the title of *The Hypocrite* and disguised the principal character as a man of the world; in vain I gave him a little hat, long hair, a wide collar, a sword, and lace clothing,[19] softened the action and carefully eliminated all that I thought might provide even the shadow of grounds for discontent on the part of the famous models of the portrait I wished to present; nothing did any good. The conspiracy of opposition revived even at mere conjecture of what the play would be like. They found a way of persuading those who in all other matters plainly insist that they are not to be deceived. No sooner did my comedy appear than it was struck down by the very power which should impose respect; and all that I could do to save myself from the fury of this tempest was to say that Your Majesty had given me permission to present the play and I did not think it was necessary to ask this permission of others, since only Your Majesty could have refused it.

I have no doubt, Sire, that the men whom I depict in my comedy will employ every means possible to influence Your Majesty, and will use, as they have used already, those truly good men who are all the more easily deceived because they judge of others by themselves.[20] They know how to display all of their aims in the most favorable light; yet, no matter how pious they may seem, it is surely not the interests of God which stir them; they have proven this often enough in the comedies they have allowed to be performed hundreds of times without making the least objection. Those plays attacked only piety and religion, for which they care very little; but this play attacks and makes fun of them, and that is what they cannot bear. They will never forgive me for unmasking their hypocrisy in the eyes of everyone. And I am sure that they will not neglect to tell Your Majesty that people are shocked by my comedy. But the simple truth, Sire, is that all Paris is shocked only by its ban, that the most scrupulous persons have found its presentation worthwhile, and men are astounded that individuals of such known integrity should show so great a deference to people whom everyone should abominate and who are so clearly opposed to the true piety which they profess.

I respectfully await the judgment that Your Majesty will deign to pronounce: But it's certain, Sire, that I need not think of writing comedies if the Tartuffes are triumphant, if they thereby seize the right to persecute me more than ever, and find fault with even the most innocent lines that flow from my pen.

Let your goodness, Sire, give me protection against their envenomed rage, and allow me, at your return from so glorious a campaign, to relieve Your Majesty from the fatigue of his conquests, give him innocent pleasures after such noble accomplishments, and make the monarch laugh who makes all Europe tremble!

(August, 1667)

Third Petition
(PRESENTED TO THE KING)

Sire,

A very honest doctor[21] whose patient I have the honor to be, promises and will legally contract to make me live another thirty years if I can obtain a favor for him from Your Majesty. I told him of his promise that I do not deserve so much, and that I should be glad to help him if he will merely agree not to kill me. This favor, Sire, is a post of canon at your royal chapel of Vincennes, made vacant by death.

---

[19]There is evidence that in 1664 Tartuffe played his role dressed in a cassock, thus allying him more directly to the clergy.

[20]Molière apparently did not know that de Lanvignon had been affiliated with the Company of the Holy Sacrament for the previous ten years.

[21]A physician friend, M. de Mauvillain, who helped Molière with some of the medical details of *Le Malade imaginaire*.

May I dare to ask for this favor from Your Majesty on the very day of the glorious resurrection of *Tartuffe,* brought back to life by your goodness? By this first favor I have been reconciled with the devout, and the second will reconcile me with the doctors.[22] Undoubtedly this would be too much grace for me at one time, but perhaps it would not be too much for Your Majesty, and I await your answer to my petition with respectful hope.

(February, 1669)

---

[22]Doctors are ridiculed to varying degrees in earlier plays of Molière: *Dom Juan, L'Amour médecin,* and *Le Médecin malgré lui.*

TARTUFFE

Molière

TRANSLATED BY RICHARD WILBUR

CHARACTERS

MADAME PERNELLE, *Orgon's mother*
ORGON, *Elmire's husband*
ELMIRE, *Orgon's wife*
DAMIS, *Orgon's son, Elmire's stepson*
MARIANE, *Orgon's daughter, Elmire's stepdaughter, in love with Valère*
VALÈRE, *in love with Mariane*
CLÉANTE, *Orgon's brother-in-law*

TARTUFFE, *a hypocrite*
DORINE, *Mariane's lady's-maid*
M. LOYAL, *a bailiff*
A POLICE OFFICER
FLIPOTE, *Madame Pernelle's maid*

The scene throughout: Orgon's house in Paris

ACT ONE

SCENE I

MADAME PERNELLE *and* FLIPOTE, *her maid,* ELMIRE, MARIANE, DORINE, DAMIS, CLÉANTE

MADAME PERNELLE: Come, come, Flipote; it's time I left this
   place.
ELMIRE: I can't keep up, you walk at such a pace.
MADAME PERNELLE: Don't trouble, child; no need to show
   me out.
   It's not your manners I'm concerned about.
5 ELMIRE: We merely pay you the respect we owe.
   But, Mother, why this hurry? Must you go?
MADAME PERNELLE: I must. This house appals me. No one in it
   Will pay attention for a single minute.
   Children, I take my leave much vexed in spirit.
10 I offer good advice, but you won't hear it.
   You all break in and chatter on and on.
   It's like a madhouse with the keeper gone.
DORINE: If . . .
MADAME PERNELLE: Girl, you talk too much, and I'm afraid
   You're far too saucy for a lady's-maid.
15 You push in everywhere and have your say.
DAMIS: But . . .
MADAME PERNELLE: You, boy, grow more foolish every day.
   To think my grandson should be such a dunce!
   I've said a hundred times, if I've said it once,
   That if you keep the course on which you've started,
20 You'll leave your worthy father broken-hearted.
MARIANE: I think . . .
MADAME PERNELLE: And you, his sister, seem so pure,
   So shy, so innocent, and so demure.
   But you know what they say about still waters.
   I pity parents with secretive daughters.
25 ELMIRE: Now, Mother . . .
MADAME PERNELLE: And as for you, child, let me add
   That your behavior is extremely bad,
   And a poor example for these children, too.
   Their dear, dead mother did far better than you.
   You're much too free with money, and I'm distressed
30 To see you so elaborately dressed.
   When it's one's husband that one aims to please,
   One has no need of costly fripperies.

CLÉANTE: Oh, Madam, really . . .
MADAME PERNELLE: You are her brother, Sir,
   And I respect and love you; yet if I were
   My son, this lady's good and pious spouse,   35
   I wouldn't make you welcome in my house.
   You're full of worldly counsels which, I fear,
   Aren't suitable for decent folk to hear.
   I've spoken bluntly, Sir; but it behooves us
   Not to mince words when righteous fervor moves us. 40
DAMIS: Your man Tartuffe is full of holy speeches . . .
MADAME PERNELLE: And practises precisely what he preaches.
   He's a fine man, and should be listened to.
   I will not hear him mocked by fools like you.
DAMIS: Good God! Do you expect me to submit   45
   To the tyranny of that carping hypocrite?
   Must we forgo all joys and satisfactions
   Because that bigot censures all our actions?
DORINE: To hear him talk—and he talks all the time—
   There's nothing one can do that's not a crime.   50
   He rails at everything, your dear Tartuffe.
MADAME PERNELLE: Whatever he reproves deserves reproof.
   He's out to save your souls, and all of you
   Must love him, as my son would have you do.
DAMIS: Ah no, Grandmother, I could never take   55
   To such a rascal, even for my father's sake.
   That's how I feel, and I shall not dissemble.
   His every action makes me seethe and tremble
   With helpless anger, and I have no doubt
   That he and I will shortly have it out.   60
DORINE: Surely it is a shame and a disgrace
   To see this man usurp the master's place—
   To see this beggar who, when first he came,
   Had not a shoe or shoestring to his name
   So far forget himself that he behaves   65
   As if the house were his, and we his slaves.
MADAME PERNELLE: Well, mark my words, your souls would
   fare far better
   If you obeyed his precepts to the letter.
DORINE: You see him as a saint. I'm far less awed;
   In fact, I see right through him. He's a fraud.   70
MADAME PERNELLE: Nonsense!
DORINE: His man Laurent's the same, or worse;
   I'd not trust either with a penny purse.
MADAME PERNELLE: I can't say what his servant's morals may be;

His own great goodness I can guarantee.
75 You all regard him with distaste and fear
Because he tells you what you're loath to hear,
Condemns your sins, points out your moral flaws,
And humbly strives to further Heaven's cause.
DORINE: If sin is all that bothers him, why is it
80 He's so upset when folk drop in to visit?
Is Heaven so outraged by a social call
That he must prophesy against us all?
I'll tell you what I think: if you ask me,
He's jealous of my mistress' company.
85 MADAME PERNELLE: Rubbish! (*To* ELMIRE.) He's not alone,
child, in complaining
Of all of your promiscuous entertaining.
Why, the whole neighborhood's upset, I know,
By all these carriages that come and go,
With crowds of guests parading in and out
90 And noisy servants loitering about.
In all of this, I'm sure there's nothing vicious;
But why give people cause to be suspicious?
CLÉANTE: They need no cause; they'll talk in any case.
Madam, this world would be a joyless place
95 If, fearing what malicious tongues might say,
We locked our doors and turned our friends away.
And even if one did so dreary a thing,
D'you think those tongues would cease their chattering?
One can't fight slander; it's a losing battle;
100 Let us instead ignore their tittle-tattle.
Let's strive to live by conscience' clear decrees,
And let the gossips gossip as they please.
DORINE: If there is talk against us, I know the source:
It's Daphne and her little husband, of course.
105 Those who have greatest cause for guilt and shame
Are quickest to besmirch a neighbor's name.
When there's a chance for libel, they never miss it;
When something can be made to seem illicit
They're off at once to spread the joyous news,
110 Adding to fact what fantasies they choose.
By talking up their neighbor's indiscretions
They seek to camouflage their own transgressions,
Hoping that others' innocent affairs
Will lend a hue of innocence to theirs,
115 Or that their own black guilt will come to seem
Part of a general shady color-scheme.
MADAME PERNELLE: All that is quite irrelevant. I doubt
That anyone's more virtuous and devout
Than dear Orante; and I'm informed that she
120 Condemns your mode of life most vehemently.
DORINE: Oh, yes, she's strict, devout, and has no taint
Of worldliness; in short, she seems a saint.
But it was time which taught her that disguise;
She's thus because she can't be otherwise.
125 So long as her attractions could enthrall,
She flounced and flirted and enjoyed it all,
But now that they're no longer what they were
She quits a world which fast is quitting her,
And wears a veil of virtue to conceal
130 Her bankrupt beauty and her lost appeal.
That's what becomes of old coquettes today:
Distressed when all their lovers fall away,
They see no recourse but to play the prude,

And so confer a style on solitude.
Thereafter, they're severe with everyone,   135
Condemning all our actions, pardoning none,
And claiming to be pure, austere, and zealous
When, if the truth were known, they're merely jealous,
And cannot bear to see another know
The pleasures time has forced them to forgo.   140
MADAME PERNELLE: (*Initially to* ELMIRE.) That sort of talk is
what you like to hear;
Therefore you'd have us all keep still, my dear,
While Madam rattles on the livelong day.
Nevertheless, I mean to have my say.
I tell you that you're blest to have Tartuffe   145
Dwelling, as my son's guest, beneath this roof;
That Heaven has sent him to forestall its wrath
By leading you, once more, to the true path;
That all he reprehends is reprehensible,
And that you'd better heed him, and be sensible.   150
These visits, balls, and parties in which you revel
Are nothing but inventions of the Devil.
One never hears a word that's edifying:
Nothing but chaff and foolishness and lying,
As well as vicious gossip in which one's neighbor   155
Is cut to bits with épée, foil, and saber.
People of sense are driven half-insane
At such affairs, where noise and folly reign
And reputations perish thick and fast.
As a wise preacher said on Sunday last,   160
Parties are Towers of Babylon, because
The guests all babble on with never a pause;
And then he told a story which, I think . . .

(*To* CLÉANTE.)

I heard that laugh, Sir, and I saw that wink!
Go find your silly friends and laugh some more!   165
Enough; I'm going; don't show me to the door.
I leave this household much dismayed and vexed;
I cannot say when I shall see you next.

(*Slapping* FLIPOTE.)

Wake up, don't stand there gaping into space!
I'll slap some sense into that stupid face.   170
Move, move, you slut.

SCENE II

CLÉANTE, DORINE

CLÉANTE: I think I'll stay behind;
I want no further pieces of her mind.
How that old lady . . .
DORINE: Oh, what wouldn't she say
If she could hear you speak of her that way!
She'd thank you for the *lady*, but I'm sure   5
She'd find the *old* a little premature.
CLÉANTE: My, what a scene she made, and what a din!
And how this man Tartuffe has taken her in!
DORINE: Yes, but her son is even worse deceived;
His folly must be seen to be believed.   10

In the late troubles, he played an able part
And served his king with wise and loyal heart,
But he's quite lost his senses since he fell
Beneath Tartuffe's infatuating spell.
15 He calls him brother, and loves him as his life,
Preferring him to mother, child, or wife.
In him and him alone will he confide;
He's made him his confessor and his guide;
He pets and pampers him with love more tender
20 Than any pretty mistress could engender,
Gives him the place of honor when they dine,
Delights to see him gorging like a swine,
Stuffs him with dainties till his guts distend,
And when he belches, cries "God bless you, friend!"
25 In short, he's mad; he worships him; he dotes;
His deeds he marvels at, his words he quotes,
Thinking each act a miracle, each word
Oracular as those that Moses heard.
Tartuffe, much pleased to find so easy a victim,
30 Has in a hundred ways beguiled and tricked him,
Milked him of money, and with his permission
Established here a sort of Inquisition.
Even Laurent, his lackey, dares to give
Us arrogant advice on how to live;
35 He sermonizes us in thundering tones
And confiscates our ribbons and colognes.
Last week he tore a kerchief into pieces
Because he found it pressed in a *Life of Jesus*:
He said it was a sin to juxtapose
40 Unholy vanities and holy prose.

SCENE III

ELMIRE, MARIANE, DAMIS, CLÉANTE, DORINE

ELMIRE: (*To* CLÉANTE.) You did well not to follow; she stood
    in the door
    And said *verbatim* all she'd said before.
    I saw my husband coming. I think I'd best
    Go upstairs now, and take a little rest.
5 CLÉANTE: I'll wait and greet him here; then I must go.
    I've really only time to say hello.
DAMIS: Sound him about my sister's wedding, please.
    I think Tartuffe's against it, and that he's
    Been urging Father to withdraw his blessing.
10 As you well know, I'd find that most distressing.
    Unless my sister and Valère can marry,
    My hopes to wed *his* sister will miscarry,
    And I'm determined . . .
DORINE: He's coming.

SCENE IV

ORGON, CLÉANTE, DORINE

ORGON: Ah, Brother, good-day.
CLÉANTE: Well, welcome back. I'm sorry I can't stay.
    How was the country? Blooming, I trust, and green?
ORGON: Excuse me, Brother; just one moment.

(*To* DORINE.)

                                      Dorine . . .

(*To* CLÉANTE.)

    To put my mind at rest, I always learn   5
    The household news the moment I return.

(*To* DORINE.)

    Has all been well, these two days I've been gone?
    How are the family? What's been going on?
DORINE: Your wife, two days ago, had a bad fever,
    And a fierce headache which refused to leave her.   10
ORGON: Ah. And Tartuffe?
DORINE: Tartuffe? Why, he's round and red,
    Bursting with health, and excellently fed.
ORGON: Poor fellow!
DORINE: That night, the mistress was unable
    To take a single bite at the dinner-table.
    Her headache-pains, she said, were simply hellish.   15
ORGON: Ah. And Tartuffe?
DORINE: He ate his meal with relish,
    And zealously devoured in her presence
    A leg of mutton and a brace of pheasants.
ORGON: Poor fellow!
DORINE: Well, the pains continued strong,
    And so she tossed and tossed the whole night long,   20
    Now icy-cold, now burning like a flame.
    We sat beside her bed till morning came.
ORGON: Ah. And Tartuffe?
DORINE: Why, having eaten, he rose
    And sought his room, already in a doze,
    Got into his warm bed, and snored away   25
    In perfect peace until the break of day.
ORGON: Poor fellow!
DORINE: After much ado, we talked her
    Into dispatching someone for the doctor.
    He bled her, and the fever quickly fell.
ORGON: Ah. And Tartuffe?   30
DORINE: He bore it very well.
    To keep his cheerfulness at any cost,
    And make up for the blood *Madame* had lost,
    He drank, at lunch, four beakers full of port.
ORGON: Poor fellow!
DORINE: Both are doing well, in short.
    I'll go and tell *Madame* that you've expressed   35
    Keen sympathy and anxious interest.

SCENE V

ORGON, CLÉANTE

CLÉANTE: That girl was laughing in your face, and though
    I've no wish to offend you, even so
    I'm bound to say that she had some excuse.
    How can you possibly be such a goose?
    Are you so dazed by this man's hocus-pocus   5
    That all the world, save him, is out of focus?
    You've given him clothing, shelter, food, and care;
    Why must you also . . .
ORGON: Brother, stop right there.
    You do not know the man of whom you speak.
CLÉANTE: I grant you that. But my judgment's not so weak   10
    That I can't tell, by his effect on others . . .

ORGON: Ah, when you meet him, you two will be like brothers!
    There's been no loftier soul since time began.
    He is a man who . . . a man who . . . an excellent man.
15   To keep his precepts is to be reborn,
    And view this dunghill of a world with scorn.
    Yes, thanks to him I'm a changed man indeed.
    Under his tutelage my soul's been freed
    From earthly loves, and every human tie:
20   My mother, children, brother, and wife could die,
    And I'd not feel a single moment's pain.
CLÉANTE: That's a fine sentiment, Brother; most humane.
ORGON: Oh, had you seen Tartuffe as I first knew him,
    Your heart, like mine, would have surrendered to him.
25   He used to come into our church each day
    And humbly kneel nearby, and start to pray.
    He'd draw the eyes of everybody there
    By the deep fervor of his heartfelt prayer;
    He'd sigh and weep, and sometimes with a sound
30   Of rapture he would bend and kiss the ground;
    And when I rose to go, he'd run before
    To offer me holy-water at the door.
    His serving-man, no less devout than he,
    Informed me of his master's poverty;
35   I gave him gifts, but in his humbleness
    He'd beg me every time to give him less.
    "Oh, that's too much," he'd cry, "too much by twice!
    I don't deserve it. The half, Sir, would suffice."
    And when I wouldn't take it back, he'd share
40   Half of it with the poor, right then and there.
    At length, Heaven prompted me to take him in
    To dwell with us, and free our souls from sin.
    He guides our lives, and to protect my honor
    Stays by my wife, and keeps an eye upon her;
45   He tells me whom she sees, and all she does,
    And seems more jealous than I ever was!
    And how austere he is! Why, he can detect
    A mortal sin where you would least suspect;
    In smallest trifles, he's extremely strict.
50   Last week, his conscience was severely pricked
    Because, while praying, he had caught a flea
    And killed it, so he felt, too wrathfully.
CLÉANTE: Good God, man! Have you lost your common sense—
    Or is this all some joke at my expense?
55   How can you stand there and in all sobriety . . .
ORGON: Brother, your language savors of impiety.
    Too much free-thinking's made your faith unsteady,
    And as I've warned you many times already,
    'Twill get you into trouble before you're through.
60 CLÉANTE: So I've been told before by dupes like you:
    Being blind, you'd have all others blind as well;
    The clear-eyed man you call an infidel,
    And he who sees through humbug and pretense
    Is charged, by you, with want of reverence.
65   Spare me your warnings, Brother; I have no fear
    Of speaking out, for you and Heaven to hear,
    Against affected zeal and pious knavery.
    There's true and false in piety, as in bravery,
    And just as those whose courage shines the most
70   In battle, are the least inclined to boast,
    So those whose hearts are truly pure and lowly
    Don't make a flashy show of being holy.
    There's a vast difference, so it seems to me,
    Between true piety and hypocrisy:
    How do you fail to see it, may I ask?   75
    Is not a face quite different from a mask?
    Cannot sincerity and cunning art,
    Reality and semblance, be told apart?
    Are scarecrows just like men, and do you hold
    That a false coin is just as good as gold?   80
    Ah, Brother, man's a strangely fashioned creature
    Who seldom is content to follow Nature,
    But recklessly pursues his inclination
    Beyond the narrow bounds of moderation,
    And often, by transgressing Reason's laws,   85
    Perverts a lofty aim or noble cause.
    A passing observation, but it applies.
ORGON: I see, dear Brother, that you're profoundly wise;
    You harbor all the insight of the age.
    You are our one clear mind, our only sage,   90
    The era's oracle, its Cato too,
    And all mankind are fools compared to you.
CLÉANTE: Brother, I don't pretend to be a sage,
    Nor have I all the wisdom of the age.
    There's just one insight I would dare to claim: 95
    I know that true and false are not the same;
    And just as there is nothing I more revere
    Than a soul whose faith is steadfast and sincere,
    Nothing that I more cherish and admire
    Than honest zeal and true religious fire,   100
    So there is nothing that I find more base
    Than specious piety's dishonest face—
    Than these bold mountebanks, these histrios
    Whose impious mummeries and hollow shows
    Exploit our love of Heaven, and make a jest   105
    Of all that men think holiest and best;
    These calculating souls who offer prayers
    Not to their Maker, but as public wares,
    And seek to buy respect and reputation
    With lifted eyes and sighs of exaltation;   110
    These charlatans, I say, whose pilgrim souls
    Proceed, by way of Heaven, toward earthly goals,
    Who weep and pray and swindle and extort,
    Who preach the monkish life, but haunt the court,
    Who make their zeal the partner of their vice—   115
    Such men are vengeful, sly, and cold as ice,
    And when there is an enemy to defame
    They cloak their spite in fair religion's name,
    Their private spleen and malice being made
    To seem a high and virtuous crusade,   120
    Until, to mankind's reverent applause,
    They crucify their foe in Heaven's cause.
    Such knaves are all too common; yet, for the wise,
    True piety isn't hard to recognize,
    And, happily, these present times provide us   125
    With bright examples to instruct and guide us.
    Consider Ariston and Périandre;
    Look at Oronte, Alcidamas, Clitandre;
    Their virtue is acknowledged; who could doubt it?
    But you won't hear them beat the drum about it.   130
    They're never ostentatious, never vain,
    And their religion's moderate and humane;
    It's not their way to criticize and chide:
    They think censoriousness a mark of pride,
    And therefore, letting others preach and rave,   135

They show, by deeds, how Christians should behave.
They think no evil of their fellow man,
But judge of him as kindly as they can.
They don't intrigue and wangle and conspire;
140   To lead a good life is their one desire;
The sinner wakes no rancorous hate in them;
It is the sin alone which they condemn;
Nor do they try to show a fiercer zeal
For Heaven's cause than Heaven itself could feel.
145   These men I honor, these men I advocate
As models for us all to emulate.
Your man is not their sort at all, I fear:
And, while your praise of him is quite sincere,
I think that you've been dreadfully deluded.
150   ORGON: Now then, dear Brother, is your speech concluded?
CLÉANTE: Why, yes.
ORGON: Your servant, Sir.

(*He turns to go.*)

CLÉANTE: No, Brother; wait.
There's one more matter. You agreed of late
That young Valère might have your daughter's hand.
ORGON: I did.
CLÉANTE: And set the date, I understand.
155   ORGON: Quite so.
CLÉANTE: You've now postponed it; is that true?
ORGON: No doubt.
CLÉANTE: The match no longer pleases you?
ORGON: Who knows?
CLÉANTE: D'you mean to go back on your word?
ORGON: I won't say that.
CLÉANTE: Has anything occurred
Which might entitle you to break your pledge?
160   ORGON: Perhaps.
CLÉANTE: Why must you hem, and haw, and hedge?
The boy asked me to sound you in this affair . . .
ORGON: It's been a pleasure.
CLÉANTE: But what shall I tell Valère?
ORGON: Whatever you like.
CLÉANTE: But what have you decided?
What are your plans?
ORGON: I plan, Sir, to be guided
165   By Heaven's will.
CLÉANTE: Come, Brother, don't talk rot.
You've given Valère your word; will you keep it, or not?
ORGON: Good day.
CLÉANTE: This looks like poor Valère's undoing;
I'll go and warn him that there's trouble brewing.

ACT TWO

SCENE I

ORGON, MARIANE

ORGON: Mariane.
MARIANE: Yes, Father?
ORGON: A word with you; come here.
MARIANE: What are you looking for?
ORGON: (*Peering into a small closet.*)
                                Eavesdroppers, dear.

I'm making sure we shan't be overheard.
Someone in there could catch our every word.
Ah, good, we're safe. Now, Mariane, my child,   5
You're a sweet girl who's tractable and mild,
Whom I hold dear, and think most highly of.
MARIANE: I'm deeply grateful, Father, for your love.
ORGON: That's well said, Daughter; and you can repay me
If, in all things, you'll cheerfully obey me.   10
MARIANE: To please you, Sir, is what delights me best.
ORGON: Good, good. Now, what d'you think of Tartuffe, our
    guest?
MARIANE: I, Sir?
ORGON: Yes. Weigh your answer; think it through.
MARIANE: Oh, dear. I'll say whatever you wish me to.
ORGON: That's wisely said, my Daughter. Say of him, then,   15
That he's the very worthiest of men,
And that you're fond of him, and would rejoice
In being his wife, if that should be my choice.
Well?
MARIANE: What?
ORGON: What's that?
MARIANE: I . . .
ORGON: Well?
MARIANE: Forgive me, pray.
ORGON: Did you not hear me?   20
MARIANE: Of *whom,* Sir, must I say
That I am fond of him, and would rejoice
In being his wife, if that should be your choice?
ORGON: Why, of Tartuffe.
MARIANE: But, Father, that's false, you know.
Why would you have me say what isn't so?
ORGON: Because I am resolved it shall be true.   25
That it's my wish should be enough for you.
MARIANE: You can't mean, Father . . .
ORGON: Yes, Tartuffe shall be
Allied by marriage to this family,
And he's to be your husband, is that clear?
It's a father's privilege . . .   30

SCENE II

DORINE, ORGON, MARIANE

ORGON: (*To* DORINE.)   What are you doing in here?
Is curiosity so fierce a passion
With you, that you must eavesdrop in this fashion?
DORINE: There's lately been a rumor going about—
Based on some hunch or chance remark, no doubt—   5
That you mean Mariane to wed Tartuffe.
I've laughed it off, of course, as just a spoof.
ORGON: You find it so incredible?
DORINE: Yes, I do.
I won't accept that story, even from you.
ORGON: Well, you'll believe it when the thing is done.   10
DORINE: Yes, yes, of course. Go on and have your fun.
ORGON: I've never been more serious in my life.
DORINE: Ha!
ORGON: Daughter, I mean it; you're to be his wife.
DORINE: No, don't believe your father; it's all a hoax.
ORGON: See here, young woman . . .   15
DORINE: Come, Sir, no more jokes;

You can't fool us.

ORGON: How dare you talk that way?

DORINE: All right, then: we believe you, sad to say.
But how a man like you, who looks so wise
And wears a moustache of such splendid size,
20 Can be so foolish as to . . .

ORGON: Silence, please!
My girl, you take too many liberties.
I'm master here, as you must not forget.

DORINE: Do let's discuss this calmly; don't be upset.
You can't be serious, Sir, about this plan.
25 What should that bigot want with Mariane?
Praying and fasting ought to keep him busy.
And then, in terms of wealth and rank, what is he?
Why should a man of property like you
Pick out a beggar son-in-law?

ORGON: That will do.
30 Speak of his poverty with reverence.
His is a pure and saintly indigence
Which far transcends all worldly pride and pelf.
He lost his fortune, as he says himself,
Because he cared for Heaven alone, and so
35 Was careless of his interests here below.
I mean to get him out of his present straits
And help him to recover his estates—
Which, in his part of the world, have no small fame.
Poor though he is, he's a gentleman just the same.

40 DORINE: Yes, so he tells us; and, Sir, it seems to me
Such pride goes very ill with piety.
A man whose spirit spurns this dungy earth
Ought not to brag of lands and noble birth;
Such worldly arrogance will hardly square
45 With meek devotion and the life of prayer.
. . . But this approach, I see, has drawn a blank;
Let's speak, then, of his person, not his rank.
Doesn't it seem to you a trifle grim
To give a girl like her to a man like him?
50 When two are so ill-suited, can't you see
What the sad consequences is bound to be?
A young girl's virtue is imperilled, Sir,
When such a marriage is imposed on her;
For if one's bridegroom isn't to one's taste,
55 It's hardly an inducement to be chaste,
And many a man with horns upon his brow
Has made his wife the thing that she is now.
It's hard to be a faithful wife, in short,
To certain husbands of a certain sort,
60 And he who gives his daughter to a man she hates
Must answer for her sins at Heaven's gates.
Think, Sir, before you play so risky a role.

ORGON: This servant-girl presumes to save my soul!

DORINE: You would do well to ponder what I've said.

65 ORGON: Daughter, we'll disregard this dunderhead.
Just trust your father's judgment. Oh, I'm aware
That I once promised you to young Valère;
But now I hear he gambles, which greatly shocks me;
What's more, I've doubts about his orthodoxy.
70 His visits to church, I note, are very few.

DORINE: Would you have him go at the same hours as you,
And kneel nearby, to be sure of being seen?

ORGON: I can dispense with such remarks, Dorine.

(*To* MARIANE.)

Tartuffe, however, is sure of Heaven's blessing,
And that's the only treasure worth possessing.   75
This match will bring you joys beyond all measure;
Your cup will overflow with every pleasure;
You two will interchange your faithful loves
Like two sweet cherubs, or two turtle-doves.
No harsh word shall be heard, no frown be seen,   80
And he shall make you happy as a queen.

DORINE: And she'll make him a cuckold, just wait and see.

ORGON: What language!

DORINE: Oh, he's a man of destiny;
He's *made* for horns, and what the stars demand
Your daughter's virtue surely can't withstand.   85

ORGON: Don't interrupt me further. Why can't you learn
That certain things are none of your concern?

DORINE: It's for your own sake that I interfere.

(*She repeatedly interrupts* ORGON *just as he is turning to speak to
his daughter.*)

ORGON: Most kind of you. Now, hold your tongue, d'you
hear?

DORINE: If I didn't love you . . .   90

ORGON: Spare me your affection.

DORINE: I'll love you, Sir, in spite of your objection.

ORGON: Blast!

DORINE: I can't bear, Sir, for your honor's sake,
To let you make this ludicrous mistake.

ORGON: You mean to go on talking?

DORINE: If I didn't protest
This sinful marriage, my conscience couldn't rest.   95

ORGON: If you don't hold your tongue, you little shrew . . .

DORINE: What, lost your temper? A pious man like you?

ORGON: Yes! Yes! You talk and talk. I'm maddened by it.
Once and for all, I tell you to be quiet.

DORINE: Well, I'll be quiet. But I'll be thinking hard.   100

ORGON: Think all you like, but you had better guard
That saucy tongue of yours, or I'll . . .

(*Turning back to* MARIANE.)

Now, child,
I've weighed this matter fully.

DORINE: (*Aside.*) It drives me wild
That I can't speak.

(ORGON *turns his head, and she is silent.*)

ORGON: Tartuffe is no young dandy,
But, still, his person . . .   105

DORINE: (*Aside.*) Is as sweet as candy.

ORGON: Is such that, even if you shouldn't care
For his other merits . . .

(*He turns and stands facing* DORINE, *arms crossed.*)

DORINE: (*Aside.*) They'll make a lovely pair.
If I were she, no man would marry me
Against my inclination, and go scot-free.
He'd learn, before the wedding-day was over,   110
How readily a wife can find a lover.

ORGON: (*To* DORINE.) It seems you treat my orders as a joke.
DORINE: Why, what's the matter? 'Twas not to you I spoke.
ORGON: What *were* you doing?
DORINE: Talking to myself, that's all.
115 ORGON: Ah! (*Aside.*) One more bit of impudence and gall,
And I shall give her a good slap in the face.

(*He puts himself in position to slap her;* DORINE, *whenever he glances at her, stands immobile and silent.*)

Daughter, you shall accept, and with good grace,
The husband I've selected . . . Your wedding-day . . .

(*To* DORINE.)

Why don't you talk to yourself?
DORINE: I've nothing to say.
120 ORGON: Come, just one word.
DORINE: No thank you, Sir. I pass.
ORGON: Come, speak; I'm waiting.
DORINE: I'd not be such an ass.
ORGON: (*Turning to* MARIANE.) In short, dear Daughter, I
mean to be obeyed,
And you must bow to the sound choice I've made.
DORINE: (*Moving away.*) I'd not wed such a monster, even in jest.

(ORGON *attempts to slap her, but misses.*)

125 ORGON: Daughter, that maid of yours is a thorough pest;
She makes me sinfully annoyed and nettled.
I can't speak further; my nerves are too unsettled.
She's so upset me by her insolent talk,
I'll calm myself by going for a walk.

SCENE III

DORINE, MARIANE

DORINE: (*Returning.*) Well, have you lost your tongue, girl?
Must I play
Your part, and say the lines you ought to say?
Faced with a fate so hideous and absurd,
Can you not utter one dissenting word?
5 MARIANE: What good would it do? A father's power is great.
DORINE: Resist him now, or it will be too late.
MARIANE: But . . .
DORINE: Tell him one cannot love at a father's whim;
That you shall marry for yourself, not him;
That since it's you who are to be the bride,
10 It's you, not he, who must be satisfied;
And that if his Tartuffe is so sublime,
He's free to marry him at any time.
MARIANE: I've bowed so long to Father's strict control,
I couldn't oppose him now, to save my soul.
15 DORINE: Come, come, Mariane. Do listen to reason, won't you?
Valère has asked your hand. Do you love him, or don't you?
MARIANE: Oh, how unjust of you! What can you mean
By asking such a question, dear Dorine?
You know the depth of my affection for him;
20 I've told you a hundred times how I adore him.
DORINE: I don't believe in everything I hear;
Who knows if your professions were sincere?

MARIANE: They were, Dorine, and you do me wrong to
doubt it;
Heaven knows that I've been all too frank about it.
DORINE: You love him, then?   25
MARIANE: Oh, more than I can express.
DORINE: And he, I take it, cares for you no less?
MARIANE: I think so.
DORINE: And you both, with equal fire,
Burn to be married?
MARIANE: That is our one desire.
DORINE: What of Tartuffe, then? What of your father's plan?
MARIANE: I'll kill myself, if I'm forced to wed that man.   30
DORINE: I hadn't thought of that recourse. How splendid!
Just die, and all your troubles will be ended!
A fine solution. Oh, it maddens me
To hear you talk in that self-pitying key.
MARIANE: Dorine, how harsh you are! It's most unfair.   35
You have no sympathy for my despair.
DORINE: I've none at all for people who talk drivel
And, faced with difficulties, whine and snivel.
MARIANE: No doubt I'm timid, but it would be wrong . . .
DORINE: True love requires a heart that's firm and strong.   40
MARIANE: I'm strong in my affection for Valère,
But coping with my father is his affair.
DORINE: But if your father's brain has grown so cracked
Over his dear Tartuffe that he can retract
His blessing, though your wedding-day was named,   45
It's surely not Valère who's to be blamed.
MARIANE: If I defied my father, as you suggest,
Would it not seem unmaidenly, at best?
Shall I defend my love at the expense
Of brazeness and disobedience?   50
Shall I parade my heart's desires, and flaunt . . .
DORINE: No, I ask nothing of you. Clearly you want
To be Madame Tartuffe, and I feel bound
Not to oppose a wish so very sound.
What right have I to criticize the match?   55
Indeed, my dear, the man's a brilliant catch.
Monsieur Tartuffe! Now, there's a man of weight!
Yes, yes, Monsieur Tartuffe, I'm bound to state,
Is quite a person; that's not to be denied;
'Twill be no little thing to be his bride.   60
The world already rings with his renown;
He's a great noble—in his native town;
His ears are red, he has a pink complexion,
And all in all, he'll suit you to perfection.
MARIANE: Dear God!   65
DORINE: Oh, how triumphant you will feel
At having caught a husband so ideal!
MARIANE: Oh, do stop teasing, and use your cleverness
To get me out of this appalling mess.
Advise me, and I'll do whatever you say.
DORINE: Ah no, a dutiful daughter must obey   70
Her father, even if he weds her to an ape.
You've a bright future; why struggle to escape?
Tartuffe will take you back where his family lives,
To a small town aswarm with relatives—
Uncles and cousins whom you'll be charmed to meet.   75
You'll be received at once by the elite,
Calling upon the bailiff's wife, no less—
Even, perhaps, upon the mayoress,

Who'll sit you down in the *best* kitchen chair.
80   Then, once a year, you'll dance at the village fair
To the drone of bagpipes —two of them, in fact—
And see a puppet-show, or an animal act.
Your husband . . .
MARIANE: Oh, you turn my blood to ice!
Stop torturing me, and give me your advice.
DORINE: (*Threatening to go.*)
85   Your servant, Madam.
MARIANE: Dorine, I beg of you . . .
DORINE: No, you deserve it; this marriage must go through.
MARIANE: Dorine!
DORINE: No.
MARIANE: Not Tartuffe! You know I think him . . .
DORINE: Tartuffe's your cup of tea, and you shall drink him.
MARIANE: I've always told you everything, and relied . . .
90   DORINE: No. You deserve to be tartuffified.
MARIANE: Well, since you mock me and refuse to care,
I'll henceforth seek my solace in despair:
Despair shall be my counsellor and friend,
And help me bring my sorrows to an end.

(*She starts to leave.*)

95   DORINE: There now, come back; my anger has subsided.
You do deserve some pity, I've decided.
MARIANE: Dorine, if Father makes me undergo
This dreadful martyrdom, I'll die, I know.
DORINE: Don't fret; it won't be difficult to discover
100   Some plan of action . . . But here's Valère, your lover.

SCENE IV

VALÈRE, MARIANE, DORINE

VALÈRE: Madam, I've just received some wondrous news
Regarding which I'd like to hear your views.
MARIANE: What news?
VALÈRE: You're marrying Tartuffe.
MARIANE: I find
That Father does have such a match in mind.
5   VALÈRE: Your father, Madam . . .
MARIANE: . . . has just this minute said
That it's Tartuffe he wishes me to wed.
VALÈRE: Can he be serious?
MARIANE: Oh, indeed he can;
He's clearly set his heart upon the plan.
VALÈRE: And what position do you propose to take,
10   Madam?
MARIANE: Why—I don't know.
VALÈRE: For heaven's sake—
You don't know?
MARIANE: No.
VALÈRE: Well, well!
MARIANE: Advise me, do.
VALÈRE: Marry the man. That's my advice to you.
MARIANE: That's your advice?
VALÈRE: Yes.
MARIANE: Truly?
VALÈRE: Oh, absolutely.
You couldn't choose more wisely, more astutely.
15   MARIANE: Thanks for this counsel; I'll follow it, of course.

VALÈRE: Do, do; I'm sure 'twill cost you no remorse.
MARIANE: To give it didn't cause your heart to break.
VALÈRE: I gave it, Madam, only for your sake.
MARIANE: And it's for your sake that I take it, Sir.
DORINE: (*Withdrawing to the rear of the stage.*) Let's see which   20
fool will prove the stubborner.
VALÈRE: So! I am nothing to you, and it was flat
Deception when you . . .
MARIANE: Please, enough of that.
You've told me plainly that I should agree
To wed the man my father's chosen for me,
And since you've deigned to counsel me so wisely,   25
I promise, Sir, to do as you advise me.
VALÈRE: Ah, no, 'twas not by me that you were swayed.
No, your decision was already made;
Though now, to save appearances, you protest
That you're betraying me at my behest.   30
MARIANE: Just as you say.
VALÈRE: Quite so. And I now see
That you were never truly in love with me.
MARIANE: Alas, you're free to think so if you choose.
VALÈRE: I choose to think so, and here's a bit of news:
You've spurned my hand, but I know where to turn   35
For kinder treatment, as you shall quickly learn.
MARIANE: I'm sure you do. Your noble qualities
Inspire affection . . .
VALÈRE: Forget my qualities, please.
They don't inspire you overmuch, I find.
But there's another lady I have in mind   40
Whose sweet and generous nature will not scorn
To compensate me for the loss I've borne.
MARIANE: I'm no great loss, and I'm sure that you'll transfer
Your heart quite painlessly from me to her.
VALÈRE: I'll do my best to take it in my stride.   45
The pain I feel at being cast aside.
Time and forgetfulness may put an end to.
Or if I can't forget, I shall pretend to.
No self-respecting person is expected
To go on loving once he's been rejected.   50
MARIANE: Now, that's a fine, high-minded sentiment.
VALÈRE: One to which any sane man would assent.
Would you prefer it if I pined away
In hopeless passion till my dying day?
Am I to yield you to a rival's arms   55
And not console myself with other charms?
MARIANE: Go then: console yourself; don't hesitate.
I wish you to; indeed, I cannot wait.
VALÈRE: You wish me to?
MARIANE: Yes.
VALÈRE: That's the final straw.
Madam, farewell. Your wish shall be my law.   60

(*He starts to leave, and then returns: this repeatedly.*)

MARIANE: Splendid.
VALÈRE: (*Coming back again.*)
                    This breach, remember, is of your making;
It's you who've driven me to the step I'm taking.
MARIANE: Of course.
VALÈRE: (*Coming back again.*)
                    Remember, too, that I am merely
Following your example.

MARIANE: I see that clearly.
65 VALÈRE: Enough. I'll go and do your bidding, then.
MARIANE: Good.
VALÈRE: (*Coming back again.*)
                    You shall never see my face again.
MARIANE: Excellent.
VALÈRE: (*Walking to the door, then turning about.*)
                    Yes?
MARIANE: What?
VALÈRE: What's that? What did you say?
MARIANE: Nothing. You're dreaming.
VALÈRE: Ah. Well, I'm on my way.
    Farewell, *Madame.*

(*He moves slowly away.*)

MARIANE: Farewell.
DORINE: (*To* MARIANE.)   If you ask me,
70   Both of you are as mad as mad can be.
    Do stop this nonsense, now. I've only let you
    Squabble so long to see where it would get you.
    Whoa there, Monsieure Valère!

(*She goes and seizes* VALÈRE *by the arm; he makes a great show of resistance.*)

VALÈRE: What's this, Dorine?
DORINE: Come here.
VALÈRE: No, no, my heart's too full of spleen.
75   Don't hold me back; her wish must be obeyed.
DORINE: Stop!
VALÈRE: It's too late now; my decision's made.
DORINE: Oh, pooh!
MARIANE: (*Aside.*)
                    He hates the sight of me, that's plain.
    I'll go, and so deliver him from pain.
DORINE: (*Leaving* VALÈRE, *running after* MARIANE.) And now
    you run away! Come back.
MARIANE: No, no.
80   Nothing you say will keep me here. Let go!
VALÈRE: (*Aside.*) She cannot bear my presence, I perceive.
    To spare her further torment, I shall leave.
DORINE: (*Leaving* MARIANE, *running after* VALÈRE.) Again!
    You'll not escape, Sir; don't you try it.
    Come here, you two. Stop fussing, and be quiet.

(*She takes* VALÈRE *by the hand, then* MARIANE, *and draws them together.*)

VALÈRE: (*To* DORINE.)
85   What do you want of me?
MARIANE: (*To* DORINE.)
                    What is the point of this?
DORINE: We're going to have a little armistice.

(*To* VALÈRE.)

    Now, weren't you silly to get so overheated?
VALÈRE: Didn't you see how badly I was treated?
DORINE: (*To* MARIANE.) Aren't you a simpleton, to have lost
    your head?
90 MARIANE: Didn't you hear the hateful things he said?

DORINE: (*To* VALÈRE.) You're both great fools. Her sole
    desire, Valère,
    Is to be yours in marriage. To that I'll swear.

(*To* MARIANE.)

    He loves you only, and he wants no wife
    But you, Mariane. On that I'll stake my life.
MARIANE: (*To* VALÈRE.) Then why you advised me so, I
    cannot see.   95
VALÈRE: (*To* MARIANE.) On such a question, why ask advice
    of *me?*
DORINE: Oh, you're impossible. Give me your hands, you two.

(*To* VALÈRE.)

    Yours first.
VALÈRE: (*Giving* DORINE *his hand.*)
                    But why?
DORINE: (*To* MARIANE.)
                    And now a hand from you.
MARIANE: (*Also giving* DORINE *her hand.*)
    What are you doing?
DORINE: There: a perfect fit.
    You suit each other better than you'll admit.   100

(VALÈRE *and* MARIANE *hold hands for some time without looking at each other.*)

VALÈRE: (*Turning toward* MARIANE.) Ah, come, don't be so
    haughty. Give a man
    A look of kindness, won't you, Mariane?

(MARIANE *turns toward* VALÈRE *and smiles.*)

DORINE: I tell you, lovers are completely mad!
VALÈRE: (*To* MARIANE.) Now come, confess that you were
    very bad
    To hurt my feelings as you did just now.   105
    I have a just complaint, you must allow.
MARIANE: *You* must allow that you were most unpleasant . . .
DORINE: Let's table that discussion for the present;
    Your father has a plan which must be stopped.
MARIANE: Advise us, then; what means must we adopt?   110
DORINE: We'll use all manner of means, and all at once.

(*To* MARIANE.)

    Your father's addled; he's acting like a dunce.
    Therefore you'd better humor the old fossil.
    Pretend to yield to him, be sweet and docile,
    And then postpone, as often as necessary,   115
    The day on which you have agreed to marry.
    You'll thus gain time, and time will turn the trick.
    Sometimes, for instance, you'll be taken sick,
    And that will seem good reason for delay;
    Or some bad omen will make you change the day—   120
    You'll dream of muddy water, or you'll pass
    A dead man's hearse, or break a looking-glass.
    If all else fails, no man can marry you
    Unless you take his ring and say "I do."
    But now, let's separate. If they should find   125
    Us talking here, our plot might be divined.

(*To* VALÈRE.)

Go to your friends, and tell them what's occurred,
And have them urge her father to keep his word.
Meanwhile, we'll stir her brother into action,
130   And get Elmire, as well, to join our faction.
Good-bye.
VALÈRE: (*To* MARIANE.)
                    Though each of us will do his best,
It's your true heart on which my hopes shall rest.
MARIANE: (*To* VALÈRE.) Regardless of what Father may decide,
None but Valère shall claim me as his bride.
135   VALÈRE: Oh, how those words content me! Come what will …
DORINE: Oh, lover, lovers! Their tongues are never still.
Be off, now.
VALÈRE: (*Turning to go, then turning back.*)
                    One last word …
DORINE: No time to chat:
You leave by this door; and *you* leave by that.

(DORINE *pushes them, by the shoulders, toward opposing doors.*)

ACT THREE

SCENE I

DAMIS, DORINE

DAMIS: May lightning strike me even as I speak,
May all men call me cowardly and weak,
If any fear or scruple holds me back
From settling things, at once, with that great quack!
5   DORINE: Now, don't give way to violent emotion.
Your father's merely talked about this notion,
And words and deeds are far from being one.
Much that is talked about is left undone.
DAMIS: No, I must stop that scoundrel's machinations;
10   I'll go and tell him off; I'm out of patience.
DORINE: Do calm down and be practical. I had rather
My mistress dealt with him—and with your father.
She has some influence with Tartuffe, I've noted.
He hangs upon her words, seems most devoted,
15   And may, indeed, be smitten by her charm.
Pray Heaven it's true! 'Twould do our cause no harm.
She sent for him, just now, to sound him out
On this affair you're so incensed about;
She'll find out where he stands, and tell him, too,
20   What dreadful strife and trouble will ensue
If he lends countenance to your father's plan.
I couldn't get in to see him, but his man
Says that he's almost finished with his prayers.
Go, now. I'll catch him when he comes downstairs.
25   DAMIS: I want to hear this conference, and I will.
DORINE: No, they must be alone.
DAMIS: Oh, I'll keep still.
DORINE: Not you. I know your temper. You'd start a brawl,
And shout and stamp your foot and spoil it all.
Go on.
DAMIS: I won't; I have a perfect right …
30   DORINE: Lord, you're a nuisance! He's coming; get out of sight.

(DAMIS *conceals himself in a closet at the rear of the stage.*)

SCENE II

TARTUFFE, DORINE

TARTUFFE: (*Observing* DORINE, *and calling to his manservant offstage.*)
Hang up my hair-shirt, put my scourge in place,
And pray, Laurent, for Heaven's perpetual grace.
I'm going to the prison now, to share
My last few coins with the poor wretches there.
DORINE: (*Aside.*) Dear God, what affectation! What a fake!   5
TARTUFFE: You wished to see me?
DORINE: Yes …
TARTUFFE: (*Taking a handkerchief from his pocket.*)
                          For mercy's sake,
Please take this handkerchief, before you speak.
DORINE: What?
TARTUFFE: Cover that bosom, girl. The flesh is weak,
And unclean thoughts are difficult to control.
Such sights as that can undermine the soul.   10
DORINE: Your soul, it seems, has very poor defenses,
And flesh makes quite an impact on your senses.
It's strange that you're so easily excited;
My own desires are not so soon ignited,
And if I saw you naked as a beast,   15
Not all your hide would tempt me in the least.
TARTUFFE: Girl, speak more modestly; unless you do,
I shall be forced to take my leave of you.
DORINE: Oh, no, it's I who must be on my way;
I've just one little message to convey.   20
Madame is coming down, and begs you, Sir,
To wait and have a word or two with her.
TARTUFFE: Gladly.
DORINE: (*Aside.*) *That* had a softening effect!
I think my guess about him was correct.
TARTUFFE: Will she be long?   25
DORINE: No: that's her step I hear.
Ah, here she is, and I shall disappear.

SCENE III

ELMIRE, TARTUFFE

TARTUFFE: May Heaven, whose infinite goodness we adore,
Preserve your body and soul forevermore,
And bless your days, and answer thus the plea
Of one who is its humblest votary.
ELMIRE: I thank you for that pious wish. But please,   5
Do take a chair and let's be more at ease.

(*They sit down.*)

TARTUFFE: I trust that you are once more well and strong?
ELMIRE: Oh, yes: the fever didn't last for long.
TARTUFFE: My prayers are too unworthy, I am sure,
To have gained from Heaven this most gracious cure;   10
But lately, Madam, my every supplication
Has had for object your recuperation.
ELMIRE: You shouldn't have troubled so. I don't deserve it.

TARTUFFE: Your health is priceless, Madam, and to preserve it
15   I'd gladly give my own, in all sincerity.
ELMIRE: Sir, you outdo us all in Christian charity.
     You've been most kind. I count myself your debtor.
TARTUFFE: 'Twas nothing, Madam. I long to serve you better.
ELMIRE: There's a private matter I'm anxious to discuss.
20   I'm glad there's no one here to hinder us.
TARTUFFE: I too am glad; it floods my heart with bliss
     To find myself alone with you like this.
     For just this chance I've prayed with all my power—
     But prayed in vain, until this happy hour.
25   ELMIRE: This won't take long, Sir, and I hope you'll be
     Entirely frank and unconstrained with me.
TARTUFFE: Indeed, there's nothing I had rather do
     Than bare my inmost heart and soul to you.
     First, let me say that what remarks I've made
30   About the constant visits you are paid
     Were prompted not by any mean emotion,
     But rather by a pure and deep devotion,
     A fervent zeal . . .
ELMIRE: No need for explanation.
     Your sole concern, I'm sure, was my salvation.
TARTUFFE: (*Taking* ELMIRE's *hand and pressing her fingertips.*)
35   Quite so; and such great fervor do I feel . . .
ELMIRE: Ooh! Please! You're pinching!
TARTUFFE: 'Twas from excess of zeal.
     I never meant to cause you pain, I swear.
     I'd rather . . .

(*He places his hand on* ELMIRE's *knee.*)

ELMIRE: What can your hand be doing there?
TARTUFFE: Feeling your gown; what soft, fine-woven stuff!
40   ELMIRE: Please, I'm extremely ticklish. That's enough.

(*She draws her chair away;* TARTUFFE *pulls his after her.*)

TARTUFFE: (*Fondling the lace collar of her gown.*) My, my, what
        lovely lacework on your dress!
     The workmanship's miraculous, no less.
     I've not seen anything to equal it.
ELMIRE: Yes, quite. But let's talk business for a bit.
45   They say my husband means to break his word
     And give his daughter to you, Sir. Had you heard?
TARTUFFE: He did once mention it. But I confess
     I dream of quite a different happiness.
     It's elsewhere, Madam, that my eyes discern
50   The promise of that bliss for which I yearn.
ELMIRE: I see: you care for nothing here below.
TARTUFFE: Ah, well—my heart's not made of stone, you know.
ELMIRE: All your desires mount heavenward, I'm sure,
     In scorn of all that's earthly and impure.
55   TARTUFFE: A love of heavenly beauty does not preclude
     A proper love for earthly pulchritude;
     Our senses are quite rightly captivated
     By perfect works our Maker has created.
     Some glory clings to all that Heaven has made;
60   In you, all Heaven's marvels are displayed.
     On that fair face, such beauties have been lavished,
     The eyes are dazzled and the heart is ravished;
     How could I look on you, O flawless creature,

And not adore the Author of all Nature,
Feeling a love both passionate and pure   65
For you, his triumph of self-portraiture?
At first, I trembled lest that love should be
A subtle snare that Hell had laid for me;
I vowed to flee the sight of you, eschewing
A rapture that might prove my soul's undoing;   70
But soon, fair being, I became aware
That my deep passion could be made to square
With rectitude, and with my bounden duty.
I thereupon surrendered to your beauty.
It is, I know, presumptuous on my part   75
To bring you this poor offering of my heart,
And it is not my merit, Heaven knows,
But your compassion on which my hopes repose.
You are my peace, my solace, my salvation.
On you depends my bliss—or desolation;   80
I bide your judgment and, as you think best,
I shall be either miserable or blest.
ELMIRE: Your declaration is most gallant, Sir,
     But don't you think it's out of character?
     You'd have done better to restrain your passion   85
     And think before you spoke in such a fashion.
     It ill becomes a pious man like you . . .
TARTUFFE: I may be pious, but I'm human too:
     With your celestial charms before his eyes,
     A man has not the power to be wise.   90
     I know such words sound strangely, coming from me,
     But I'm no angel, nor was meant to be,
     And if you blame my passion, you must needs
     Reproach as well the charms on which it feeds.
     Your loveliness I had no sooner seen   95
     Than you became my soul's unrivalled queen;
     Before your seraph glance, divinely sweet,
     My heart's defenses crumbled in defeat,
     And nothing fasting, prayer, or tears might do
     Could stay my spirit from adoring you.   100
     My eyes, my sighs have told you in the past
     What now my lips make bold to say at last,
     And if, in your great goodness, you will deign
     To look upon your slave, and ease his pain,—
     If, in compassion for my soul's distress,   105
     You'll stoop to comfort my unworthiness,
     I'll raise to you, in thanks for that sweet manna,
     An endless hymn, an infinite hosanna.
     With me, of course, there need be no anxiety.
     No fear of scandal or of notoriety.   110
     These young court gallants, whom all the ladies fancy,
     Are vain in speech, in action rash and chancy;
     When they succeed in love, the world soon knows it;
     No favor's granted them but they disclose it
     And by the looseness of their tongues profane   115
     The very altar where their hearts have lain.
     Men of my sort, however, love discreetly,
     And one may trust our reticence completely.
     My keen concern for my good name insures
     The absolute security of yours;   120
     In short, I offer you, my dear Elmire,
     Love without scandal, pleasure without fear.
ELMIRE: I've heard your well-turned speeches to the end,

And what you urge I clearly apprehend.
125 Aren't you afraid that I may take a notion
To tell my husband of your warm devotion,
And that, supposing he were duly told,
His feelings toward you might grow rather cold?
TARTUFFE: I know, dear lady, that your exceeding charity
130 Will lead your heart to pardon my temerity;
That you'll excuse my violent affection
As human weakness, human imperfection;
And that—O fairest!—you will bear in mind
That I'm but flesh and blood, and am not blind.
135 ELMIRE: Some women might do otherwise, perhaps,
But I shall be discreet about your lapse;
I'll tell my husband nothing of what's occurred
If, in return, you'll give your solemn word
To advocate as forcefully as you can
140 The marriage of Valère and Mariane,
Renouncing all desire to dispossess
Another of his rightful happiness,
And . . .

SCENE IV

DAMIS, ELMIRE, TARTUFFE

DAMIS: (*Emerging from the closet where he has been hiding.*)
No! We'll not hush up this vile affair;
I heard it all inside that closet there,
Where Heaven, in order to confound the pride
Of this great rascal, prompted me to hide.
5 Ah, now I have my long-awaited chance
To punish his deceit and arrogance,
And give my father clear and shocking proof
Of the black character of his dear Tartuffe.
ELMIRE: Ah no, Damis; I'll be content if he
10 Will study to deserve my leniency.
I've promised silence—don't make me break my word;
To make a scandal would be too absurd.
Good wives laugh off such trifles, and forget them;
Why should they tell their husbands, and upset them?
15 DAMIS: You have your reasons for taking such a course,
And I have reasons, too, of equal force.
To spare him now would be insanely wrong.
I've swallowed my just wrath for far too long
And watched this insolent bigot bringing strife
20 And bitterness into our family life.
Too long he's meddled in my father's affairs,
Thwarting my marriage-hopes, and poor Valère's.
It's high time that my father was undeceived,
And now I've proof that can't be disbelieved—
25 Proof that was furnished me by Heaven above.
It's too good not to take advantage of.
This is my chance, and I deserve to lose it
If, for one moment, I hesitate to use it.
ELMIRE: Damis . . .
DAMIS: No, I must do what I think right.
30 Madam, my heart is bursting with delight,
And, say whatever you will, I'll not consent
To lose the sweet revenge on which I'm bent.
I'll settle matters without more ado;
And here, most opportunely, is my cue.

SCENE V

ORGON, DAMIS, TARTUFFE, ELMIRE

DAMIS: Father, I'm glad you've joined us. Let us advise you
Of some fresh news which doubtless will surprise you.
You've just now been repaid with interest
For all your loving-kindness to our guest.
He's proved his warm and grateful feelings toward you;   5
It's with a pair of horns he would reward you.
Yes, I surprised him with your wife, and heard
His whole adulterous offer, every word.
She, with her all too gentle disposition,
Would not have told you of his proposition;   10
But I shall not make terms with brazen lechery,
And feel that not to tell you would be treachery.
ELMIRE: And I hold that one's husband's peace of mind
Should not be spoilt by tattle of this kind.
One's honor doesn't require it: to be proficient   15
In keeping men at bay is quite sufficient.
These are my sentiments, and I wish, Damis,
That you had heeded me and held your peace.

SCENE VI

ORGON, DAMIS, TARTUFFE

ORGON: Can it be true, this dreadful thing I hear?
TARTUFFE: Yes, Brother, I'm a wicked man, I fear:
A wretched sinner, all depraved and twisted,
The greatest villain that has ever existed.
My life's one heap of crimes, which grows each minute;   5
There's naught but foulness and corruption in it;
And I perceive that Heaven, outraged by me,
Has chosen this occasion to mortify me.
Charge me with any deed you wish to name;
I'll not defend myself, but take the blame.   10
Believe what you are told, and drive Tartuffe
Like some base criminal from beneath your roof;
Yes, drive me hence, and with a parting curse:
I shan't protest, for I deserve far worse.
ORGON: (*To* DAMIS.) Ah, you deceitful boy, how dare you try   15
To stain his purity with so foul a lie?
DAMIS: What! Are you taken in by such a bluff?
Did you not hear . . . ?
ORGON: Enough, you rogue, enough!
TARTUFFE: Ah, Brother, let him speak: you're being unjust.
Believe his story; the boy deserves your trust.   20
Why, after all, should you have faith in me?
How can you know what I might do, or be?
Is it on my good actions that you base
Your favor? Do you trust my pious face?
Ah, no, don't be deceived by hollow shows;   25
I'm far, alas, from being what men suppose;
Though the world takes me for a man of worth,
I'm truly the most worthless man on earth.

(*To* DAMIS.)

Yes, my dear son, speak out now: call me the chief
Of sinners, a wretch, a murderer, a thief;   30

Load me with all the names men most abhor;
I'll not complain; I've earned them all, and more;
I'll kneel here while you pour them on my head
As a just punishment for the life I've led.
ORGON: (*To* TARTUFFE.)
35   This is too much, dear Brother.

(*To* DAMIS.)

                          Have you no heart?
DAMIS: Are you so hoodwinked by this rascal's art. . . ?
ORGON: Be still, you monster.

(*To* TARTUFFE.)

                       Brother, I pray you, rise.

(*To* DAMIS.)

    Villain!
DAMIS: But . . .
ORGON: Silence!
DAMIS: Can't you realize. . . ?
ORGON: Just one word more, and I'll tear you limb from limb.
40 TARTUFFE: In God's name, Brother, don't be harsh with him.
I'd rather far be tortured at the stake
Than see him bear one scratch for my poor sake.
ORGON: (*To* DAMIS.)
    Ingrate!
TARTUFFE: If I must beg you, on bended knee,
    To pardon him . . .
ORGON: (*Falling to his knees, addressing* TARTUFFE.)
                Such goodness cannot be!

(*To* DAMIS.)

45   Now, *there's* true charity!
DAMIS: What, you. . . ?
ORGON: Villain, be still!
I know your motives; I know you wish him ill:
Yes, all of you—wife, children, servants, all—
Conspire against him and desire his fall,
Employing every shameful trick you can
50   To alienate me from this saintly man.
Ah, but the more you seek to drive him away,
The more I'll do to keep him. Without delay,
I'll spite this household and confound its pride
By giving him my daughter as his bride.
55 DAMIS: You're going to force her to accept his hand?
ORGON: Yes, and this very night, d'you understand?
I shall defy you all, and make it clear
That I'm the one who gives the orders here.
Come, wretch, kneel down and clasp his blessed feet,
60   And ask his pardon for your black deceit.
DAMIS: I ask that swindler's pardon? Why, I'd rather . . .
ORGON: So! You insult him, and defy your father!
A stick! A stick! (*To* TARTUFFE.) No, no—release me, do.

(*To* DAMIS.)

    Out of my house this minute! Be off with you,
65   And never dare set foot in it again.
DAMIS: Well, I shall go, but . . .

ORGON: Well, go quickly, then.
I disinherit you; an empty purse
Is all you'll get from me—except my curse!

SCENE VII

ORGON, TARTUFFE

ORGON: How he blasphemed your goodness! What a son!
TARTUFFE: Forgive him, Lord, as I've already done.

(*To* ORGON.)

    You can't know how it hurts when someone tries
To blacken me in my dear Brother's eyes.
ORGON: Ahh!   5
TARTUFFE: The mere thought of such ingratitude
Plunges my soul into so dark a mood . . .
Such horror grips my heart . . . I gasp for breath,
And cannot speak, and feel myself near death.
ORGON:

(*He runs, in tears, to the door through which he has just driven his son.*)

    You blackguard! Why did I spare you? Why did I not
Break you in little pieces on the spot?   10
Compose yourself, and don't be hurt, dear friend.
TARTUFFE: These scenes, these dreadful quarrels, have got to
    end.
I've much upset your household, and I perceive
That the best thing will be for me to leave.
ORGON: What are you saying!   15
TARTUFFE: They're all against me here;
They'd have you think me false and insincere.
ORGON: Ah, what of that? Have I ceased believing in you?
TARTUFFE: Their adverse talk will certainly continue,
And charges which you now repudiate
You may find credible at a later date.   20
ORGON: No, Brother, never.
TARTUFFE: Brother, a wife can sway
Her husband's mind in many a subtle way.
ORGON: No, no.
TARTUFFE: To leave at once is the solution;
Thus only can I end their persecution.
ORGON: No, no, I'll not allow it; you shall remain.   25
TARTUFFE: Ah, well; 'twill mean much martyrdom and pain,
But if you wish it . . .
ORGON: Ah!
TARTUFFE: Enough; so be it.
But one thing must be settled, as I see it.
For your dear honor, and for our friendship's sake,
There's one precaution I feel bound to take.   30
I shall avoid your wife, and keep away . . .
ORGON: No, you shall not, whatever they may say.
It pleases me to vex them, and for spite
I'd have them see you with her day and night.
What's more, I'm going to drive them to despair   35
By making you my only son and heir;
This very day, I'll give to you alone
Clear deed and title to everything I own.
A dear, good friend and son-in-law-to-be

40   Is more than wife, or child, or kin to me.
     Will you accept my offer, dearest son?
TARTUFFE: In all things, let the will of Heaven be done.
ORGON: Poor fellow! Come, we'll go draw up the deed.
     Then let them burst with disappointed greed!

ACT FOUR

SCENE I

CLÉANTE, TARTUFFE

CLÉANTE: Yes, all the town's discussing it, and truly,
     Their comments do not flatter you unduly.
     I'm glad we've met, Sir, and I'll give my view
     Of this sad matter in a word or two.
5   As for who's guilty, that I shan't discuss;
     Let's say it was Damis who caused the fuss;
     Assuming, then, that you have been ill-used
     By young Damis, and groundlessly accused,
     Ought not a Christian to forgive, and ought
10   He not to stifle every vengeful thought?
     Should you stand by and watch a father make
     His only son an exile for your sake?
     Again I tell you frankly, be advised:
     The whole town, high and low, is scandalized;
15   This quarrel must be mended, and my advice is
     Not to push matters to a further crisis.
     No, sacrifice your wrath to God above,
     And help Damis regain his father's love.
TARTUFFE: Alas, for my part I should take great joy
20   In doing so. I've nothing against the boy.
     I pardon all, I harbor no resentment;
     To serve him would afford me much contentment.
     But Heaven's interest will not have it so:
     If he comes back, then I shall have to go.
25   After his conduct—so extreme, so vicious—
     Our further intercourse would look suspicious.
     God knows what people would think! Why, they'd describe
     My goodness to him as a sort of bribe;
     They'd say that out of guilt I made pretense
30   Of loving-kindness and benevolence—
     That, fearing my accuser's tongue, I strove
     To buy his silence with a show of love.
CLÉANTE: Your reasoning is badly warped and stretched,
     And these excuses, Sir, are most far-fetched.
35   Why put yourself in charge of Heaven's cause?
     Does Heaven need our help to enforce its laws?
     Leave vengeance to the Lord, Sir; while we live,
     Our duty's not to punish, but forgive;
     And what the Lord commands, we should obey
40   Without regard to what the world may say.
     What! Shall the fear of being misunderstood
     Prevent our doing what is right and good?
     No, no; let's simply do what Heaven ordains,
     And let no other thoughts perplex our brains.
45 TARTUFFE: Again, Sir, let me say that I've forgiven
     Damis, and thus obeyed the laws of Heaven;
     But I am not commanded by the Bible
     To live with one who smears my name with libel.
CLÉANTE: Were you commanded, Sir, to indulge the whim

Of poor Orgon, and to encourage him   50
     In suddenly transferring to your name
     A large estate to which you have no claim?
TARTUFFE: 'Twould never occur to those who know me best
     To think I acted from self-interest.
     The treasures of this world I quite despise;   55
     Their specious glitter does not charm my eyes;
     And if I have resigned myself to taking
     The gift which my dear Brother insists on making,
     I do so only, as he well understands,
     Lest so much wealth fall into wicked hands,   60
     Lest those to whom it might descend in time
     Turn it to purposes of sin and crime,
     And not, as I shall do, make use of it,
     For Heaven's glory and mankind's benefit.
CLÉANTE: Forget these trumped-up fears. Your argument   65
     Is one the rightful heir might well resent;
     It is a moral burden to inherit
     Such wealth, but give Damis a chance to bear it.
     And would it not be worse to be accused
     Of swindling, than to see that wealth misused?   70
     I'm shocked that you allowed Orgon to broach
     This matter, and that you feel no self-reproach;
     Does true religion teach that lawful heirs
     May freely be deprived of what is theirs?
     And if the Lord has told you in your heart   75
     That you and young Damis must dwell apart,
     Would it not be the decent thing to beat
     A generous and honorable retreat,
     Rather than let the son of the house be sent,
     For your convenience, into banishment?   80
     Sir, if you wish to prove the honesty
     Of your intentions . . .
TARTUFFE: Sir, it is half-past three.
     I've certain pious duties to attend to,
     And hope my prompt departure won't offend you.
CLÉANTE: (*Alone.*) Damn.   85

SCENE II

ELMIRE, MARIANE, CLÉANTE, DORINE

DORINE: Stay, Sir, and help Mariane, for Heaven's sake!
     She's suffering so, I fear her heart will break.
     Her father's plan to marry her off tonight
     Has put the poor child in a desperate plight.
     I hear him coming. Let's stand together, now,   5
     And see if we can't change his mind, somehow,
     About this match we all deplore and fear.

SCENE III

ORGON, ELMIRE, MARIANE, CLÉANTE, DORINE

ORGON: Hah! Glad to find you all assembled here.

(*To* MARIANE.)

     This contract, child, contains your happiness,
     And what it says I think your heart can guess.
MARIANE: (*Falling to her knees.*) Sir, by that Heaven which
     sees me here distressed,

5   And by whatever else can move your breast,
     Do not employ a father's power, I pray you,
     To crush my heart and force it to obey you,
     Nor by your harsh commands oppress me so
     That I'll begrudge the duty which I owe—
10   And do not so embitter and enslave me
     That I shall hate the very life you gave me.
     If my sweet hopes must perish, if you refuse
     To give me to the one I've dared to choose,
     Spare me at least—I beg you, I implore—
15   The pain of wedding one whom I abhor;
     And do not, by a heartless use of force,
     Drive me to contemplate some desperate course.
     ORGON: (*Feeling himself touched by her.*) Be firm, my soul.
         No human weakness, now.
     MARIANE: I don't resent your love for him. Allow
20   Your heart free rein, Sir; give him your property,
     And if that's not enough, take mine from me;
     He's welcome to my money; take it, do,
     But don't, I pray, include my person too.
     Spare me, I beg you; and let me end the tale
25   Of my sad days behind a convent veil.
     ORGON: A convent! Hah! When crossed in their amours,
     All lovesick girls have the same thought as yours.
     Get up! The more you loathe the man, and dread him,
     The more ennobling it will be to wed him.
30   Marry Tartuffe, and mortify your flesh!
     Enough; don't start that whimpering afresh.
     DORINE: But why. . . ?
     ORGON: Be still, there. Speak when you're
         spoken to.
     Not one more bit of impudence out of you.
     CLÉANTE: If I may offer a word of counsel here . . .
35   ORGON: Brother, in counseling you have no peer;
     All your advice is forceful, sound, and clever;
     I don't propose to follow it, however.
     ELMIRE: (*To* ORGON.) I am amazed, and don't know what
         to say;
     Your blindness simply takes my breath away.
40   You are indeed bewitched, to take no warning
     From our account of what occurred this morning.
     ORGON: Madam, I know a few plain facts, and one
     Is that you're partial to my rascal son;
     Hence, when he sought to make Tartuffe the victim
45   Of a base lie, you dared not contradict him.
     Ah, but you underplayed your part, my pet;
     You should have looked more angry, more upset.
     ELMIRE: When men make overtures, must we reply
     With righteous anger and a battle-cry?
50   Must we turn back their amorous advances
     With sharp reproaches and with fiery glances?
     Myself, I find such offers merely amusing,
     And make no scenes and fusses in refusing;
     My taste is for good-natured rectitude,
55   And I dislike the savage sort of prude
     Who guards her virtue with her teeth and claws,
     And tears men's eyes out for the slightest cause;
     The Lord preserve me from such honor as that,
     Which bites and scratches like an alley-cat!
60   I've found that a polite and cool rebuff
     Discourages a lover quite enough.

ORGON: I know the facts, and I shall not be shaken.
ELMIRE: I marvel at your power to be mistaken.
     Would it, I wonder, carry weight with you
     If I could *show* you that our tale was true?   65
ORGON: Show me?
ELMIRE: Yes.
ORGON: Rot.
ELMIRE: Come, what if I found a way
     To make you see the facts as plain as day?
ORGON: Nonsense.
ELMIRE: Do answer me; don't be absurd.
     I'm not now asking you to trust our word.
     Suppose that from some hiding-place in here   70
     You learned the whole sad truth by eye and ear—
     What would you say of your good friend, after that?
ORGON: Why, I'd say . . . nothing, by Jehoshaphat!
     It can't be true.
ELMIRE: You've been too long deceived,
     And I'm quite tired of being disbelieved.   75
     Come now: let's put my statements to the test,
     And you shall see the truth made manifest.
ORGON: I'll take that challenge. Now do your uttermost.
     We'll see how you make good your empty boast.
ELMIRE: (*To* DORINE.)
     Send him to me.   80
DORINE: He's crafty; it may be hard
     To catch the cunning scoundrel off his guard.
ELMIRE: No, amorous men are gullible. Their conceit
     So blinds them that they're never hard to cheat.
     Have him come down. (*To* CLÉANTE *and* MARIANE.)
         Please leave us, for a bit.

SCENE IV

ELMIRE, ORGON

ELMIRE: Pull up this table, and get under it.
ORGON: What?
ELMIRE: It's essential that you be well-hidden.
ORGON: Why there?
ELMIRE: Oh, Heavens! Just do as you are bidden
     I have my plans; we'll soon see how they fare.
     Under the table, now; and once you're there,   5
     Take care that you are neither seen nor heard.
ORGON: Well, I'll indulge you, since I gave my word
     To see you through this infantile charade.
ELMIRE: Once it is over, you'll be glad we played.

(*To her husband, who is now under the table.*)

     I'm going to act quite strangely, now, and you   10
     Must not be shocked at anything I do.
     Whatever I may say, you must excuse
     As part of that deceit I'm forced to use.
     I shall employ sweet speeches in the task
     Of making that impostor drop his mask;   15
     I'll give encouragement to his bold desires,
     And furnish fuel to his amorous fires.
     Since it's for your sake, and for his destruction,
     That I shall seem to yield to his seduction,
     I'll gladly stop whenever you decide   20

That all your doubts are fully satisfied.
I'll count on you, as soon as you have seen
What sort of man he is, to intervene,
And not expose me to his odious lust
25   One moment longer than you feel you must.
Remember: you're to save me from my plight
Whenever . . . He's coming! Hush! Keep out of sight!

SCENE V

TARTUFFE, ELMIRE, ORGON

TARTUFFE: You wish to have a word with me, I'm told.
ELMIRE: Yes. I've a little secret to unfold
  Before I speak, however, it would be wise
  To close that door, and look about for spies.

(TARTUFFE *goes to the door, closes it, and returns.*)

5   The very last thing that must happen now
Is a repetition of this morning's row.
I've never been so badly caught off guard.
Oh, how I feared for you! You saw how hard
I tried to make that troublesome Damis
10   Control his dreadful temper, and hold his peace.
In my confusion, I didn't have the sense
Simply to contradict his evidence;
But as it happened, that was for the best,
And all has worked out in our interest.
15   This storm has only bettered your position;
My husband doesn't have the least suspicion,
And now, in mockery of those who do,
He bids me be continually with you.
And that is why, quite fearless of reproof,
20   I now can be alone with my Tartuffe,
And why my heart—perhaps too quick to yield—
Feels free to let its passion be revealed.
  TARTUFFE: Madam, your words confuse me. Not long ago,
You spoke in quite a different style, you know.
25 ELMIRE: Ah, Sir, if that refusal made you smart,
It's little that you know of woman's heart,
Or what that heart is trying to convey
When it resists in such a feeble way!
Always, at first, our modesty prevents
30   The frank avowal of tender sentiments;
However high the passion which inflames us,
Still, to confess its power somehow shames us.
Thus we reluct, at first, yet in a tone
Which tells you that our heart is overthrown,
35   That what our lips deny, our pulse confesses,
And that, in time, all noes will turn to yesses.
I fear my words are all too frank and free,
And a poor proof of woman's modesty;
But since I'm started, tell me, if you will—
40   Would I have tried to make Damis be still,
Would I have listened, calm and unoffended,
Until your lengthy offer of love was ended,
And been so very mild in my reaction,
Had your sweet words not given me satisfaction?
45   And when I tried to force you to undo

The marriage-plans my husband has in view,
What did my urgent pleading signify
If not that I admired you, and that I
Deplored the thought that someone else might own
Part of a heart I wished for mine alone?   50
  TARTUFFE: Madam, no happiness is so complete
As when, from lips we love, come words so sweet;
Their nectar floods my every sense, and drains
In honeyed rivulets through all my veins.
To please you is my joy, my only goal;   55
Your love is the restorer of my soul;
And yet I must beg leave, now, to confess
Some lingering doubts as to my happiness
Might this not be a trick? Might not the catch
Be that you wish me to break off the match   60
With Mariane, and so have feigned to love me?
I shan't quite trust your fond opinion of me
Until the feelings you've expressed so sweetly
Are demonstrated somewhat more concretely,
And you have shown, by certain kind concessions,   65
That I may put my faith in your professions.
ELMIRE:

(*She coughs, to warn her husband.*)

  Why be in such a hurry? Must my heart
Exhaust its bounty at the very start?
To make that sweet admission cost me dear,
But you'll not be content, it would appear,   70
Unless my store of favors is disbursed
To the last farthing, and at the very first.
  TARTUFFE: The less we merit, the less we dare to hope,
And with our doubts, mere words can never cope.
We trust no promised bliss till we receive it;   75
Not till a joy is ours can we believe it.
I, who so little merit your esteem,
Can't credit this fulfillment of my dream,
And shan't believe it, Madam, until I savor
Some palpable assurance of your favor.   80
ELMIRE: My, how tyrannical your love can be,
And how it flusters and perplexes me!
How furiously you take one's heart in hand,
And make your every wish a fierce command!
Come, must you hound and harry me to death?   85
Will you not give me time to catch my breath?
Can it be right to press me with such force,
Give me no quarter, show me no remorse,
And take advantage, by your stern insistence,
Of the fond feelings which weaken my resistance?   90
TARTUFFE: Well, if you look with favor upon my love,
Why, then, begrudge me some clear proof thereof?
ELMIRE: But how can I consent without offense
To Heaven, toward which you feel such reverence?
TARTUFFE: If Heaven is all that holds you back, don't worry.   95
I can remove that hindrance in a hurry.
Nothing of that sort need obstruct our path.
ELMIRE: Must one not be afraid of Heaven's wrath?
TARTUFFE: Madam, forget such fears, and be my pupil,
And I shall teach you how to conquer scruple.   100
Some joys, it's true, are wrong in Heaven's eyes;

Yet Heaven is not averse to compromise;
There is a science, lately formulated,
Whereby one's conscience may be liberated,
105 And any wrongful act you care to mention
May be redeemed by purity of intention.
I'll teach you, Madam, the secrets of that science;
Meanwhile, just place on me your full reliance.
Assuage my keen desires, and feel no dread:
110 The sin, if any, shall be on my head.

(ELMIRE *coughs, this time more loudly.*)

You've a bad cough.
ELMIRE: Yes, yes. It's bad indeed.
TARTUFFE: (*Producing a little paper bag.*) A bit of licorice may
    be what you need.
ELMIRE: No, I've a stubborn cold, it seems. I'm sure it
    Will take much more than licorice to cure it.
115 TARTUFFE: How aggravating.
ELMIRE: Oh, more than I can say.
TARTUFFE: If you're still troubled, think of things this way:
    No one shall know our joys, save us alone,
    And there's no evil till the act is known;
    It's scandal, Madam, which makes it an offense,
120 And it's no sin to sin in confidence.
ELMIRE: (*Having coughed once more.*) Well, clearly I must do as
    you require,
    And yield to your importunate desire.
    It is apparent, now, that nothing less
    Will satisfy you, and so I acquiesce.
125 To go so far is much against my will;
    I'm vexed that it should come to this; but still,
    Since you are so determined on it, since you
    Will not allow mere language to convince you,
    And since you ask for concrete evidence, I
130 See nothing for it, now, but to comply.
    If this is sinful, if I'm wrong to do it,
    So much the worse for him who drove me to it.
    The fault can surely not be charged to me.
TARTUFFE: Madam, the fault is mine, if fault there be,
135 And . . .
ELMIRE: Open the door a little, and peek out;
    I wouldn't want my husband poking about.
TARTUFFE: Why worry about the man? Each day he grows
    More gullible; one can lead him by the nose.
    To find us here would fill him with delight,
140 And if he saw the worst, he'd doubt his sight.
ELMIRE: Nevertheless, do step out for a minute
    Into the hall, and see that no one's in it.

SCENE VI

ORGON, ELMIRE

ORGON: (*Coming out from under the table.*) That man's a
    perfect monster, I must admit!
    I'm simply stunned. I can't get over it.
ELMIRE: What, coming out so soon? How premature!
    Get back in hiding, and wait until you're sure.
5 Stay till the end, and be convinced completely;

We mustn't stop till things are proved concretely.
ORGON: Hell never harbored anything so vicious!
ELMIRE: Tut, don't be hasty. Try to be judicious.
    Wait, and be certain that there's no mistake.
    No jumping to conclusions, for Heaven's sake!   10

(*She places* ORGON *behind her, as* TARTUFFE *re-enters.*)

SCENE VII

TARTUFFE, ELMIRE, ORGON

TARTUFFE: (*Not seeing* ORGON.) Madam, all things have
    worked out to perfection;
    I've given the neighboring rooms a full inspection;
    No one's about; and now I may at last . . .
ORGON: (*Intercepting him.*) Hold on, my passionate fellow,
    not so fast!
    I should advise a little more restraint.   5
    Well, so you thought you'd fool me, my dear saint!
    How soon you wearied of the saintly life—
    Wedding my daughter, and coveting my wife!
    I've long suspected you, and had a feeling
    That soon I'd catch you at your double-dealing.   10
    Just now, you've given me evidence galore;
    It's quite enough; I have no wish for more.
ELMIRE: (*To* TARTUFFE.) I'm sorry to have treated you so
    slyly.
    But circumstances forced me to be wily.
TARTUFFE: Brother, you can't think . . .   15
ORGON: No more talk from you;
    Just leave this household, without more ado.
TARTUFFE: What I intended . . .
ORGON: That seems fairly clear.
    Spare me your falsehoods and get out of here.
TARTUFFE: No, I'm the master, and you're the one to go!
    This house belongs to me, I'll have you know,   20
    And I shall show you that you can't hurt *me*
    By this contemptible conspiracy,
    That those who cross me know not what they do,
    And that I've means to expose and punish you,
    Avenge offended Heaven, and make you grieve   25
    That ever you dared order me to leave.

SCENE VIII

ELMIRE, ORGON

ELMIRE: What was the point of all that angry chatter?
ORGON: Dear God, I'm worried. This is no laughing
    matter.
ELMIRE: How so?
ORGON: I fear I understood his drift.
    I'm much disturbed about that deed of gift.
ELMIRE: You gave him . . . ?   5
ORGON: Yes, it's all been drawn and signed.
    But one thing more is weighing on my mind.
ELMIRE: What's that?
ORGON: I'll tell you; but first let's see if there's
    A certain strong-box in his room upstairs.

ACT FIVE

SCENE I

ORGON, CLÉANTE

CLÉANTE: Where are you going so fast?
ORGON: God knows!
CLÉANTE: Then wait;
    Let's have a conference, and deliberate
    On how this situation's to be met.
ORGON: That strong-box has me utterly upset;
5   This is the worst of many, many shocks.
CLÉANTE: Is there some fearful mystery in that box?
ORGON: My poor friend Argas brought that box to me
    With his own hands, in utmost secrecy;
    'Twas on the very morning of his flight.
10   It's full of papers which, if they came to light,
    Would ruin him—or such is my impression.
CLÉANTE: Then why did you let it out of your possession?
ORGON: Those papers vexed my conscience, and it seemed
        best
    To ask the counsel of my pious guest.
15   The cunning scoundrel got me to agree
    To leave the strong-box in his custody,
    So that, in case of an investigation,
    I could employ a slight equivocation
    And swear I didn't have it, and thereby,
20   At no expense to conscience, tell a lie.
CLÉANTE: It looks to me as if you're out on a limb.
    Trusting him with that box, and offering him
    That deed of gift, were actions of a kind
    Which scarcely indicate a prudent mind.
25   With two such weapons, he has the upper hand,
    And since you're vulnerable, as matters stand,
    You erred once more in bringing him to bay.
    You should have acted in some subtler way.
ORGON: Just think of it: behind that fervent face,
30   A heart so wicked, and a soul so base!
    I took him in, a hungry beggar, and then . . .
    Enough, by God! I'm through with pious men:
    Henceforth I'll hate the whole false brotherhood.
    And persecute them worse than Satan could.
35 CLÉANTE: Ah, there you go—extravagant as ever.
    Why can you not be rational? You never
    Manage to take the middle course, it seems,
    But jump, instead, between absurd extremes
    You've recognized your recent grave mistake
40   In falling victim to a pious fake;
    Now, to correct that error, must you embrace
    An even greater error in its place,
    And judge our worthy neighbors as a whole
    By what you've learned of one corrupted soul?
45   Come, just because one rascal made you swallow
    A show of zeal which turned out to be hollow,
    Shall you conclude that all men are deceivers,
    And that, today, there are no true believers?
    Let atheists make that foolish inference;
50   Learn to distinguish virtue from pretense,
    Be cautious in bestowing admiration,
    And cultivate a sober moderation.

    Don't humor fraud, but also don't asperse
    True piety; the latter fault is worse,
    And it is best to err, if err one must,   55
    As you have done, upon the side of trust.

SCENE II

DAMIS, ORGON, CLÉANTE

DAMIS: Father, I hear that scoundrel's uttered threats
    Against you; that he pridefully forgets
    How, in his need, he was befriended by you,
    And means to use your gifts to crucify you
ORGON: It's true, my boy. I'm too distressed for tears.   5
DAMIS: Leave it to me, Sir; let me trim his ears.
    Faced with such insolence, we must not waver.
    I shall rejoice in doing you the favor
    Of cutting short his life, and your distress.
CLÉANTE: What a display of young hotheadedness!   10
    Do learn to moderate your fits of rage.
    In this just kingdom, this enlightened age,
    One does not settle things by violence.

SCENE III

MADAME PERNELLE, MARIANE, ELMIRE, DORINE, DAMIS, OR-
GON, CLÉANTE

MADAME PERNELLE: I hear strange tales of very strange
        events.
ORGON: Yes, strange events which these two eyes beheld.
    The man's ingratitude is unparalleled.
    I save a wretched pauper from starvation.
    House him, and treat him like a blood relation,   5
    Shower him every day with my largesse,
    Give him my daughter, and all that I possess;
    And meanwhile the unconscionable knave
    Tries to induce my wife to misbehave;
    And not content with such extreme rascality,   10
    Now threatens me with my own liberality,
    And aims, by taking base advantage of
    The gifts I gave him out of Christian love,
    To drive me from my house, a ruined man,
    And make me end a pauper, as he began.   15
DORINE: Poor fellow!
MADAME PERNELLE: No, my son, I'll never bring
    Myself to think him guilty of such a thing.
ORGON: How's that?
MADAME PERNELLE: The righteous always were maligned.
ORGON: Speak clearly, Mother. Say what's on your mind.
MADAME PERNELLE: I mean that I can smell a rat, my dear.   20
    You know how everybody hates him, here.
ORGON: That has no bearing on the case at all.
MADAME PERNELLE: I told you a hundred times, when you
        were small,
    That virtue in this world is hated ever;
    Malicious men may die, but malice never.   25
ORGON: No doubt that's true, but how does it apply?
MADAME PERNELLE: They've turned you against him by a
        clever lie.
ORGON: I've told you, I was there and saw it done.

MADAME PERNELLE: Ah, slanderers will stop at nothing, Son.

30 ORGON: Mother, I'll lose my temper . . . For the last time,
    I tell you I was witness to the crime.

MADAME PERNELLE: The tongues of spite are busy night and
        noon
    And to their venom no man is immune.

ORGON: You're talking nonsense. Can't you realize
35   I saw it; saw it; saw it with my eyes?
    Saw, do you understand me? Must I shout it
    Into your ears before you'll cease to doubt it?

MADAME PERNELLE: Appearances can deceive, my son.
        Dear me,
    We cannot always judge by what we see.

40 ORGON: Drat! Drat!

MADAME PERNELLE: One often interprets things awry;
    Good can seem evil to a suspicious eye.

ORGON: Was I to see his pawing at Elmire
    As an act of charity?

MADAME PERNELLE: Till his guilt is clear,
    A man deserves the benefit of the doubt.
45   You should have waited, to see how things turned out.

ORGON: Great God in Heaven, what more proof did I need?
    Was I to sit there, watching, until he'd . . .
    You drive me to the brink of impropriety.

MADAME PERNELLE: No, no, a man of such surpassing piety
50   Could not do such a thing. You cannot shake me.
    I don't believe it, and you shall not make me.

ORGON: You vex me so that, if you weren't my mother,
    I'd say to you . . . some dreadful thing or other.

DORINE: It's your turn now, Sir, not to be listened to;
55   You'd not trust us, and now she won't trust you.

CLÉANTE: My friends, we're wasting time which should be
        spent
    In facing up to our predicament.
    I fear that scoundrel's threats weren't made in sport.

DAMIS: Do you think he'd have the nerve to go to court?

60 ELMIRE: I'm sure he won't: they'd find it all too crude
    A case of swindling and ingratitude.

CLÉANTE: Don't be too sure. He won't be at a loss
    To give his claims a high and righteous gloss;
    And clever rogues with far less valid cause
65   Have trapped their victims in a web of laws.
    I say again that to antagonize
    A man so strongly armed was most unwise.

ORGON: I know it; but the man's appalling cheek
    Outraged me so, I couldn't control my pique.

70 CLÉANTE: I wish to Heaven that we could devise
    Some truce between you, or some compromise.

ELMIRE: If I had known what cards he held, I'd not
    Have roused his anger by my little plot.

ORGON: (*To* DORINE, *as* M. LOYAL *enters.*) What is that fellow
        looking for? Who is he?
75   Go talk to him—and tell him that I'm busy.

SCENE IV

MONSIEUR LOYAL, MADAME PERNELLE, ORGON, DAMIS, MARI-
ANE, DORINE, ELMIRE, CLÉANTE

MONSIEUR LOYAL: Good day, dear sister. Kindly let me see
    Your master.

DORINE: He's involved with company,
    And cannot be disturbed just now, I fear.

MONSIEUR LOYAL: I hate to intrude; but what has brought
        me here
    Will not disturb your master, in any event.   5
    Indeed, my news will make him most content.

DORINE: Your name?

MONSIEUR LOYAL: Just say that I bring greetings from
    Monsieur Tartuffe, on whose behalf I've come.

DORINE: (*To* ORGON.) Sir, he's a very gracious man, and bears
    A message from Tartuffe, which, he declares,   10
    Will make you most content.

CLÉANTE: Upon my word,
    I think this man had best be seen, and heard.

ORGON: Perhaps he has some settlement to suggest.
    How shall I treat him? What manner would be best?

CLÉANTE: Control your anger, and if he should mention   15
    Some fair adjustment, give him your full attention.

MONSIEUR LOYAL: Good health to you, good Sir. May
        Heaven confound
    Your enemies, and may your joys abound.

ORGON: (*Aside, to* CLÉANTE.) A gentle salutation: it confirms
    My guess that he is here to offer terms.   20

MONSIEUR LOYAL: I've always held your family most dear;
    I served your father, Sir, for many a year.

ORGON: Sir, I must ask your pardon; to my shame,
    I cannot now recall your face or name.

MONSIEUR LOYAL: Loyal's my name; I come from   25
        Normandy,
    And I'm a bailiff, in all modesty.
    For forty years, praise God, it's been my boast
    To serve with honor in that vital post,
    And I am here, Sir, if you will permit
    The liberty, to serve you with this writ . . .   30

ORGON: To—*what?*

MONSIEUR LOYAL: Now, please, Sir, let us have no friction:
    It's nothing but an order of eviction.
    You are to move your goods and family out
    And make way for new occupants, without
    Deferment or delay, and give the keys . . .   35

ORGON: I? Leave this house?

MONSIEUR LOYAL: Why yes, Sir, if you please.
    This house, Sir, from the cellar to the roof,
    Belongs now to the good Monsieur Tartuffe,
    And he is lord and master of your estate
    By virtue of a deed of present date,   40
    Drawn in due form, with clearest legal phrasing . . .

DAMIS: Your insolence is utterly amazing!

MONSIEUR LOYAL: Young man, my business here is not with
        you,
    But with your wise and temperate father, who,
    Like every worthy citizen, stands in awe   45
    Of justice, and would never obstruct the law.

ORGON: But . . .

MONSIEUR LOYAL: Not for a million, Sir, would you rebel
    Against authority; I know that well.
    You'll not make trouble, Sir, or interfere
    With the execution of my duties here.   50

DAMIS: Someone may execute a smart tattoo
    On that black jacket of yours, before you're through.

MONSIEUR LOYAL: Sir, bid your son be silent. I'd much regret

Having to mention such a nasty threat
55   Of violence, in writing my report.
DORINE: (*Aside.*) This man Loyal's a most disloyal sort!
MONSIEUR LOYAL: I love all men of upright character,
And when I agreed to serve these papers, Sir,
It was your feelings that I had in mind.
60   I couldn't bear to see the case assigned
To someone else, who might esteem you less
And so subject you to unpleasantness.
ORGON: What's more unpleasant than telling a man to leave
His house and home?
MONSIEUR LOYAL: You'd like a short reprieve?
65   If you desire, Sir, I shall not press you,
But wait until tomorrow to dispossess you.
Splendid. I'll come and spend the night here, then,
Most quietly, with half a score of men.
For form's sake, you might bring me, just before
70   You go to bed, the keys to the front door.
My men, I promise, will be on their best
Behavior, and will not disturb your rest.
But bright and early, Sir, you must be quick
And move out all your furniture, every stick;
75   The men I've chosen are both young and strong,
And with their help it shouldn't take you long.
In short, I'll make things pleasant and convenient,
And since I'm being so extremely lenient,
Please show me, Sir, a like consideration,
80   And give me your entire cooperation.
ORGON: (*Aside.*) I may be all but bankrupt, but I vow
I'd give a hundred louis, here and now,
Just for the pleasure of landing one good clout
Right on the end of that complacent snout.
85 CLÉANTE: Careful; don't make things worse.
DAMIS: My bootsole itches
To give that beggar a good kick in the breeches.
DORINE: Monsieur Loyal, I'd love to hear the whack
Of a stout stick across your fine broad back.
MONSIEUR LOYAL: Take care: a woman too may go to jail if
90   She uses threatening language to a bailiff.
CLÉANTE: Enough, enough, Sir. This must not go on.
Give me that paper, please, and then begone.
MONSIEUR LOYAL: Well, *au revoir.* God give you all good cheer!
ORGON: May God confound you, and him who sent you
here!

SCENE V

ORGON, CLÉANTE, MARIANE, ELMIRE, MADAME PERNELLE,
DORINE, DAMIS

ORGON: Now, Mother, was I right or not? This writ
Should change your notion of Tartuffe a bit.
Do you perceive his villainy at last?
MADAME PERNELLE: I'm thunderstruck. I'm utterly aghast.
5 DORINE: Oh, come, be fair. You mustn't take offense
At this new proof of his benevolence.
He's acting out of selfless love, I know.
Material things enslave the soul, and so
He kindly has arranged your liberation
10   From all that might endanger your salvation.
ORGON: Will you not ever hold your tongue, you dunce?

CLÉANTE: Come, you must take some action, and at once.
ELMIRE: Go tell the world of the low trick he's tried.
The deed of gift is surely nullified
By such behavior, and public rage will not   15
Permit the wretch to carry out his plot.

SCENE VI

VALÈRE, ORGON, CLÉANTE, ELMIRE, MARIANE, MADAME PER-
NELLE, DAMIS, DORINE

VALÈRE: Sir, though I hate to bring you more bad news,
Such is the danger that I cannot choose.
A friend who is extremely close to me
And knows my interest in your family
Has, for my sake, presumed to violate   5
The secrecy that's due to things of state,
And sends me word that you are in a plight
From which your one salvation lies in flight.
That scoundrel who's imposed upon you so
Denounced you to the King an hour ago   10
And, as supporting evidence, displayed
The strong-box of a certain renegade
Whose secret papers, so he testified,
You had disloyally agreed to hide.
I don't know just what charges may be pressed,   15
But there's a warrant out for your arrest;
Tartuffe has been instructed, furthermore,
To guide the arresting officer to your door.
CLÉANTE: He's clearly done this to facilitate
His seizure of your house and your estate.   20
ORGON: That man, I must say, is a vicious beast!
VALÈRE: Quick, Sir; you mustn't tarry in the least.
My carriage is outside, to take you hence;
This thousand louis should cover all expense.
Let's lose no time, or you shall be undone;   25
The sole defense, in this case, is to run.
I shall go with you all the way, and place you
In a safe refuge to which they'll never trace you.
ORGON: Alas, dear boy, I wish that I could show you
My gratitude for everything I owe you.   30
But now is not the time; I pray the Lord
That I may live to give you your reward.
Farewell, my dears; be careful . . .
CLÉANTE: Brother, hurry.
We shall take care of things; you needn't worry.

SCENE VII

The OFFICER, TARTUFFE, VALÈRE, ORGON, ELMIRE, MARIANE,
MADAME PERNELLE, DORINE, CLÉANTE, DAMIS

TARTUFFE: Gently, Sir, gently; stay right where you are.
No need for haste; your lodging isn't far.
You're off to prison, by order of the Prince.
ORGON: This is the crowning blow, you wretch; and since
It means my total ruin and defeat,   5
Your villainy is now at last complete.
TARTUFFE: You needn't try to provoke me; it's no use.
Those who serve Heaven must expect abuse.
CLÉANTE: You are indeed most patient, sweet, and blameless.

10 DORINE: How he exploits the name of Heaven! It's shameless.
TARTUFFE: Your taunts and mockeries are all for naught;
　To do my duty is my only thought.
MARIANE: Your love of duty is more meritorious,
　And what you've done is little short of glorious.
15 TARTUFFE: All deeds are glorious, Madam, which obey
　The sovereign prince who sent me here today.
ORGON: I rescued you when you were destitute,
　Have you forgotten that, you thankless brute?
TARTUFFE: No, no, I well remember everything;
20 　But my first duty is to serve my King.
　That obligation is so paramount
　That other claims, beside it, do not count;
　And for it I would sacrifice my wife,
　My family, my friend, or my own life.
25 ELMIRE: Hypocrite!
DORINE:　　　　　　All that we most revere, he uses
　To cloak his plots and camouflage his ruses.
CLÉANTE: If it is true that you are animated
　By pure and loyal zeal, as you have stated,
　Why was this zeal not roused until you'd sought
30 　To make Orgon a cuckold, and been caught?
　Why weren't you moved to give your evidence
　Until your outraged host had driven you hence?
　I shan't say that the gift of all his treasure
　Ought to have damped your zeal in any measure;
35 　But if he is a traitor, as you declare,
　How could you condescend to be his heir?
TARTUFFE: (*To the* OFFICER.) Sir, spare me all this clamor; it's
　growing shrill.
　Please carry out your orders, if you will.
OFFICER: Yes, I've delayed too long, Sir. Thank you kindly.
40 　You're just the proper person to remind me.
　Come, you are off to join the other boarders
　In the King's prison, according to his orders.
TARTUFFE: Who? I, Sir?
OFFICER:　　　　　Yes.
TARTUFFE:　　　　　　　　To prison? This can't be true!
OFFICER: I owe an explanation, but not to you.

　(*To* ORGON.)

45 　Sir, all is well; rest easy, and be grateful.
　We serve a Prince to whom all sham is hateful,
　A Prince who sees into our inmost hearts,
　And can't be fooled by any trickster's arts.
　His royal soul, though generous and human,
50 　Views all things with discernment and acumen;
　His sovereign reason is not lightly swayed,
　And all his judgments are discreetly weighed.
　He honors righteous men of every kind,
　And yet his zeal for virtue is not blind,

Nor does his love of piety numb his wits   55
And make him tolerant of hypocrites.
'Twas hardly likely that this man could cozen
A King who's foiled such liars by the dozen.
With one keen glance, the King perceived the whole
Perverseness and corruption of his soul,   60
And thus high Heaven's justice was displayed:
Betraying you, the rogue stood self-betrayed.
The King soon recognized Tartuffe as one
Notorious by another name, who'd done
So many vicious crimes that one could fill   65
Ten volumes with them, and be writing still.
But to be brief: our sovereign was appalled
By this man's treachery toward you, which he called
The last, worst villainy of a vile career,
And bade me follow the impostor here   70
To see how gross his impudence could be,
And force him to restore your property.
Your private papers, by the King's command,
I hereby seize and give into your hand.
The King, by royal order, invalidates   75
The deed which gave this rascal your estates,
And pardons, furthermore, your grave offense
In harboring an exile's documents.
By these decrees, our Prince rewards you for
Your loyal deeds in the late civil war,   80
And shows how heartfelt is his satisfaction
In recompensing any worthy action,
How much he prizes merit, and how he makes
More of men's virtues than of their mistakes.
DORINE: Heaven be praised!   85
MADAME PERNELLE:　　　　　I breathe again, at last.
ELMIRE: We're safe.
MARIANE:　　　　I can't believe the danger's past.
ORGON: (*To* TARTUFFE.)
　Well, traitor, now you see . . .
CLÉANTE:　　　　　　　　　Ah, Brother, please,
　Let's not descend to such indignities.
　Leave the poor wretch to his unhappy fate,
　And don't say anything to aggravate   90
　His present woes; but rather hope that he
　Will soon embrace an honest piety,
　And mend his ways, and by a true repentance
　Move our just King to moderate his sentence.
　Meanwhile, go kneel before your sovereign's throne   95
　And thank him for the mercies he has shown.
ORGON: Well said: let's go at once and, gladly kneeling,
　Express the gratitude which all are feeling.
　Then, when that first great duty has been done,
　We'll turn with pleasure to a second one,   100
　And give Valère, whose love has proven so true,
　The wedded happiness which is his due.

Aphra Behn

Little is known about the early life of England's first female professional playwright, Aphra Behn (1640–1689), who may have been born Eaffrey Johnson in Kent. She left England just after the restoration of Charles II for the South American colony of Surinam, where she lived from 1663 to 1664. Again, many of the details about her life there are unknown, though Surinam provided the setting for her great novel, *Oroonoko: or, The Royal Slave,* published in 1688. Returning to England, she appears to have married someone named Behn; in *The Passionate Shepherdess: Aphra Behn 1640–89* (London: Jonathan Cape, 1977; p. 48), Maureen Duffy accounts for several possible candidates, but also suggests that Aphra Behn's marriage may have been a legitimating fiction: "Mr. Behn, her putative husband, has less substance than any character she invented." By the mid-1660s, however, Aphra Behn was serving Charles II as a spy in Antwerp and seems to have been caught up in the politics surrounding the Dutch invasion of Surinam. When she returned to England penniless in 1667, she was sent to debtors' prison and appealed to the government for her wages. Between 1670 and her death in 1689, however, Behn emerged as a famous and influential writer; in addition to her novel *Oroonoko,* Behn had a successful career as a poet and celebrated playwright. She wrote fifteen plays, beginning with *The Forced Marriage: or, The Jealous Bridegroom* (1668), a tragicomedy produced by Thomas Betterton at Lincoln's Inn Fields. Behn's major plays are mainly in the mode of Restoration comedy and were successful both in their day and well into the eighteenth century: her best-known plays today are *The Rover* (1677), *The Feigned Courtesans* (1679), which was dedicated to her friend and supporter (and the King's mistress), the actress Nell Gwynn, *The Second Part of The Rover* (1681), and *The City Heiress* (1682). Her novel *Oroonoko* was dramatized by Thomas Southerne in 1695 and was popular onstage throughout the eighteenth century. Aphra Behn was part of the elite milieu of intellectual culture of her day, the friend of courtiers such as Buckingham and Rochester, and of writers like Otway and Dryden. Although her work was, in a sense, recovered for modern readers by Virginia Woolf's famous essay *A Room of One's Own,* Behn's plays have been increasingly popular and successful in the theater. Aphra Behn is buried in Westminster Abbey.

THE ROVER

The Rover is a comedy of intrigue, set in Naples during the Carnival. The play concerns the sexual adventures of a band of Englishmen—Belvile, Willmore (the Rover), and Blunt—and their efforts to seduce the heroine Florinda and her sister Hellena. As in many Restoration comedies, *The Rover* takes a frank attitude toward sexual and financial negotiations, which are often paired in the play. The play opens with Hellena's rejection of a life in the convent and her decision to "provide my self this Carnival, if there be e'er a handsome proper fellow." In the course of the play, Hellena flirts with Willmore; Willmore wins the services (and, unfortunately, the love) of the courtesan Angelica, who eventually tries to murder him; Willmore and Blunt nearly rape Florinda on several occasions; and Blunt is tricked by a prostitute and turned out into the street in his shirt and underwear, "before consummation."

Yet despite the licentiousness of its action, the play clearly depends on a deeply ingrained sense of propriety, much of which operates through class distinctions. While it "would anger us vilely to be trussed up for a rape upon a maid of quality," one of the gentlemen declares, it seems otherwise acceptable to "ruffle a harlot." Morality, in *The Rover,* is in many ways determined by class and wealth. These distinctions are both troubled and confirmed by the important function of disguise and masking in the play. Since the action of *The Rover* takes place during Carnival, the main characters meet only in disguise. Masking enables the characters both to flirt without dishonoring themselves and to discover the truth

The Williamstown Theatre Festival production of *The Rover,* featuring Edward Hermann, Harry Groener, Christopher Reeve, and Stephen Collins.

about one another. In fact, masking in the play empowers the women, in that the temporary masking of the Carnival allows the women to escape their enforced lives at home and to meet men in public. Florinda and Hellena, for instance, can marry only with their brother Pedro's permission. He wants to marry his sisters to the wealthiest—and oldest—suitors, who will be able to settle large fortunes on them. However, the young Englishmen who attract the two sisters are Royalist supporters of Charles II, currently exiled from Cromwell's Protectorate because they support the Crown. As a result, although they are well-born, they are currently without funds and so are a poor match for Florinda and Hellena, at least in Pedro's eyes.

Masking also enables the women to escape Pedro's control, to act on their own behalf. Indeed, although the women are more modest than the Rover, they are equally devious in their pursuit of a lover—though the women insist on marriage as the price of their virginity. In Behn's brilliant comedy, the women emerge as the agents—as well as the objects—of the play's erotic intrigue.

In recent years, *The Rover* has received a number of excellent stage productions—at Minneapolis's Guthrie Theater, the Royal Shakespeare Company, and on many university campuses.

THE ROVER
OR THE BANISH'D CAVALIERS

Aphra Behn
EDITED BY MONTAGUE SUMMERS

CHARACTERS

Don ANTONIO, *the Vice-Roy's Son*
Don PEDRO, *a Noble Spaniard, his Friend*
BELVILE, *an English Colonel in love with Florinda*
WILLMORE, *the Rover*
FREDERICK, *an English Gentleman, and Friend to Belvile and Blunt*
BLUNT, *an English Country Gentleman*
STEPHANO, *Servant to Don Pedro*
PHILIPPO, *Lucetta's Gallant*
SANCHO, *Pimp to Lucetta*
BISKEY *and* SEBASTIAN, *two Bravoes to Angelica*
DIEGO, *Page to Don Antonio*
PAGE *to Hellena*
BOY, *Page to Belvile*

Blunt's MAN
OFFICERS *and* SOLDIERS
FLORINDA, *Sister to Don Pedro*
HELLENA, *a gay young Woman design'd for a Nun, and Sister to Florinda*
VALERIA, *a Kinswoman to Florinda*
ANGELICA BIANCA, *a famous Curtezan*
MORETTA, *her Woman*
CALLIS, *Governess to Florinda and Hellena*
LUCETTA, *a jilting Wench*
SERVANTS, *other* MASQUERADERS, MEN *and* WOMEN

SCENE: *Naples, in Carnival-time.*

PROLOGUE
Written by a Person of Quality

WITS, like Physicians, never can agree,
When of a different Society;
And Rabel's Drops were never more cry'd down
By all the Learned Doctors of the Town,
5   Than a new Play, whose Author is unknown:
Nor can those Doctors with more Malice sue
(And powerful Purses) the dissenting Few,
Than those with an insulting Pride do rail
At all who are not of their own Cabal.
10   If a Young Poet hit your Humour right,
You judge him then out of Revenge and Spite;
So amongst Men there are ridiculous Elves,
Who Monkeys hate for being too like themselves:
So that the Reason of the Grand Debate,
15   Why Wit so oft is damn'd, when good Plays take,
Is, that you censure as you love or hate.
Thus, like a learned Conclave, Poets sit
Catholick Judges both of Sense and Wit,
And damn or save, as they themselves think fit.
20   Yet those who to others Faults are so severe,
Are not so perfect, but themselves may err.
Some write correct indeed, but then the whole
(Bating their own dull Stuff i'th' Play) is stole:
As Bees do suck from Flowers their Honey-dew,
25   So they rob others, striving to please you.
    Some write their Characters genteel and fine,
But then they do so toil for every Line,
That what to you does easy seem, and plain,
Is the hard issue of their labouring Brain.
30   And some th' Effects of all their Pains we see,
Is but to mimick good Extempore.
Others by long Converse about the Town,
Have Wit enough to write a leud Lampoon,

But their chief Skill lies in a Baudy Song.
In short, the only Wit that's now in Fashion   35
Is but the Gleanings of good Conversation.
As for the Author of this coming Play,
I ask'd him what he thought fit I should say,
In thanks for your good Company to day:
He call'd me Fool, and said it was well known,   40
You came not here for our sakes, but your own.
New Plays are stuff'd with Wits, and with Debauches,
That croud and sweat like Cits in *May*-day Coaches.

ACT ONE

SCENE I

A Chamber.

Enter FLORINDA *and* HELLENA.

FLORINDA: What an impertient thing is a young Girl bred in a Nunnery! How full of Questions! Prithee no more, Hellena; I have told thee more than thou understand'st already.

HELLENA: The more's my Grief; I wou'd fain know as much as you, which makes me so inquisitive; nor is't enough to know   5
you're a Lover, unless you tell me too, who 'tis you sigh for.

FLORINDA: When you are a Lover, I'll think you fit for a Secret of that nature.

HELLENA: 'Tis true, I was never a Lover yet—but I begin to have a shrewd Guess, what 'tis to be so, and fancy it very   10
pretty to sigh, and sing, and blush and wish, and dream and wish, and long and wish to see the Man; and when I do, look pale and tremble; just as you did when my Brother brought home the fine *English* Colonel to see you—what do you call him? Don *Belvile*.   15

FLORINDA: Fie, *Hellena*.

HELLENA: That Blush betrays you—I am sure 'tis so—or is it Don *Antonio* the Vice-Roy's Son?—or perhaps the rich

20 old Don *Vincentio,* whom my father designs for your Husband?—Why do you blush again?

FLORINDA: With Indignation; and how near soever my Father thinks I am to marrying that hated Object, I shall let him see I understand better what's due to my Beauty, Birth and Fortune, and more to my Soul, than to obey those unjust
25 Commands.

HELLENA: Now hang me, if I don't love thee for that dear Disobedience. I love Mischief strangely, as most of our Sex do, who are come to love nothing else—But tell me, dear *Florinda,* don't you love that fine *Anglese?*—for I vow next
30 to loving him my self, 'twill please me most that you do so, for he is so gay and so handsom.

FLORINDA: *Hellena,* a Maid design'd for a Nun ought not to be so curious in a Discourse of Love.

HELLENA: And dost thou think that ever I'll be a Nun? Or at
35 least till I'm so old, I'm fit for nothing else. Faith no, Sister; and that which makes me long to know whether you love *Belvile,* is because I hope he has some mad Companion or other, that will spoil my Devotion; nay I'm resolv'd to provide my self this Carnival, if there be e'er a hand-
40 som Fellow of my Humour above Ground, tho I ask first.

FLORINDA: Prithee be not so wild.

HELLENA: Now you have provided your self with a Man, you take no Care for poor me—Prithee tell me, what dost thou see about me that is unfit for Love—have not I a world of
45 Youth? a Humour gay? a Beauty passable? a Vigour desirable? well shap'd? clean limb'd? sweet breath'd? and Sense enough to know how all these ought to be employ'd to the best Advantage: yes, I do and will. Therefore lay aside your Hopes of my Fortune, by my being a Devotee, and tell me
50 how you came acquainted with this *Belvile;* for I perceive you knew him before he came to *Naples.*

FLORINDA: Yes, I knew him at the Siege of *Pampelona,* he was then a Colonel of *French* Horse, who when the Town was ransack'd, nobly treated my Brother and my self, preserv-
55 ing us from all Insolencies; and I must own, (besides great Obligations) I have I know not what, that pleads kindly for him about my Heart, and will suffer no other to enter—But see my Brother.

(*Enter Don* PEDRO, STEPHANO, *with a Masquing Habit, and* CALLIS.)

PEDRO: Good morrow, Sister. Pray, when saw you your Lover
60 Don *Vincentio?*

FLORINDA: I know not, Sir—*Callis,* when was he here? for I consider it so little, I know not when it was.

PEDRO: I have a Command from my Father here to tell you, you ought not to despise him, a Man of so vast a Fortune,
65 and such a Passion for you—*Stephano,* my things—

(*Puts on his Masquing Habit.*)

FLORINDA: A Passion for me! 'tis more than e'er I saw, or had a desire should be known—I hate *Vincentio,* and I would not have a Man so dear to me as my Brother follow the ill Customs of our Country, and make a Slave of his Sis-
70 ter—And Sir, my Father's Will, I'm sure, you may divert.

---

52 **Siege of *Pampelona*** Pampluna, the strongly fortified capital of Navarra and very frequently a center of military operations

PEDRO: I know not how dear I am to you, but I wish only to be rank'd in your Esteem, equal with the *English* Colonel *Belvile*—Why do you frown and blush? Is there any Guilt belongs to the Name of that Cavalier?

FLORINDA: I'll not deny I value *Belvile:* when I was expos'd to such 75 Dangers as the licens'd Lust of common Soldiers threatened, when Rage and Conquest flew thro the City—then *Belvile,* this Criminal for my sake, threw himself into all Dangers to save my Honour, and will you not allow him my Esteem?

PEDRO: Yes, pay him what you will in Honour—but you must 80 consider Don *Vincentio's* Fortune, and the Jointure he'll make you.

FLORINDA: Let him consider my Youth, Beauty and Fortune; which ought not to be thrown away on his Age and Jointure.

PEDRO: 'Tis true, he's not so young and fine a Gentleman as 85 that *Belvile*—but what Jewels will that Cavalier present you with? those of his Eyes and Heart?

HELLENA: And are not those better than any Don *Vincentio* has brought from the *Indies?*

PEDRO: Why how now! Has your Nunnery-breeding taught 90 you to understand the Value of Hearts and Eyes?

HELLENA: Better than to believe *Vincentio* deserves Value from any woman—He may perhaps encrease her Bags, but not her Family.

PEDRO: This is fine—Go up to your Devotion, you are not 95 design'd for the Conversation of Lovers.

HELLENA: (*Aside.*) Nor Saints yet a while I hope.
Is't not enough you make a Nun of me, but you must cast my Sister away too, exposing her to a worse confinement than a religious Life? 100

PEDRO: The Girl's mad—Is it a Confinement to be carry'd into the Country, to an antient Villa belonging to the Family of the *Vincentio's* these five hundred Years, and have no other Prospect than that pleasing one of seeing all her own that meets her Eyes—a fine Air, large Fields and Gar- 105 dens, where she may walk and gather Flowers?

HELLENA: When? By Moon-Light? For I'm sure she dares not encounter with the heat of the Sun; that were a Task only for Don *Vincentio* and his *Indian* Breeding, who loves it in the Dog-days—And if these be her daily Divertisements, 110 what are those of the Night? to lie in a wide Moth-eaten Bed-Chamber with Furniture in Fashion in the Reign of King *Sancho* the First; the Bed that which his Forefathers liv'd and dy'd in.

PEDRO: Very well. 115

HELLENA: This Apartment (new furbisht and fitted out for the young Wife) he (out of Freedom) makes his Dressingroom; and being a frugal and a jealous Coxcomb, instead of a Valet to uncase his feeble Carcase, he desires you to do that Office—Signs of Favour, I'll assure you, and such as you 120 must not hope for, unless your Woman be out of the way.

PEDRO: Have you done yet?

HELLENA: That Honour being past, the Giant stretches it self, yawns and sighs a Belch or two as loud as a Musket, throws

---

113 **King *Sancho* the First** Sancho I, 'the Fat,' of Castile and Leon, reigned 955–967: Sancho I of Aragon 1067–1094. But the phrase is here only in a vague general sense to denote some musty and immemorial antiquity without any exact reference

125 himself into Bed, and expects you in his foul Sheets, and e'er you can get your self undrest, calls you with a Snore or two—And are not these fine Blessings to a young Lady?

PEDRO: Have you done yet?

HELLENA: And this man you must kiss, nay, you must kiss
130 none but him too—and nuzle thro his Beard to find his Lips—and this you must submit to for threescore Years, and all for a Jointure.

PEDRO: For all your Character of Don *Vincentio,* she is as like to marry him as she was before.

135 HELLENA: Marry Don *Vincentio!* hang me, such a Wedlock would be worse than Adultery with another Man: I had rather see her in the *Hostel de Dieu,* to waste her Youth there in Vows, and be a Handmaid to Lazers and Cripples, than to lose it in such a Marriage.

140 PEDRO: You have consider'd, Sister, that *Belvile* has no Fortune to bring you to, is banisht his Country, despis'd at home, and pity'd abroad.

HELLENA: What then? the Vice-Roy's Son is better than that Old Sir Fisty. Don *Vincentio!* Don *Indian!* he thinks he's
145 trading to *Gambo* still, and wou'd barter himself (that Bell and Bawble) for your Youth and Fortune.

PEDRO: *Callis,* take her hence, and lock her up all this Carnival, and at Lent she shall begin her everlasting Penance in a Monastery.

150 HELLENA: I care not, I had rather be a Nun, than be oblig'd to marry as you wou'd have me, if I were design'd for't.

PEDRO: Do not fear the Blessing of that Choice—you shall be a Nun.

HELLENA: Shall I so? you may chance to be mistaken in my
155 way of Devotion—(*Aside.*) A Nun! yes I am like to make a fine Nun! I have an excellent Humour for a Grate: No, I'll have a Saint of my own to pray to shortly, if I like any that dares venture on me.

PEDRO: *Callis,* make it your Business to watch this wild Cat.
160 As for you, *Florinda,* I've only try'd you all this while, and urg'd my Father's Will; but mine is, that you would love *Antonio,* he is brave and young, and all that can compleat the Happiness of a gallant Maid—This Absence of my Father will give us opportunity to free you from *Vincentio,*
165 by marrying here, which you must do to morrow.

FLORINDA: To morrow!

PEDRO: To morrow, or 'twill be too late—'tis not my Friendship to *Antonio,* which makes me urge this, but Love to thee, and Hatred to *Vincentio*—therefore resolve upon't to morrow.

170 FLORINDA: Sir, I shall strive to do, as shall become your Sister.

PEDRO: I'll both believe and trust you—Adieu.

(*Exeunt* PEDRO *and* STEPHANO.)

HELLENA: As become his Sister!—That is, to be as resolved your way, as he is his—

(HELLENA *goes to* CALLIS.)

FLORINDA: I ne'er till now perceiv'd my Ruin near,
175 I've no Defence against *Antonio's* Love,

For he has all the Advantages of Nature,
The moving Arguments of Youth and Fortune.

HELLENA: But hark you, *Callis,* you will not be so cruel to lock me up indeed: will you?

CALLIS: I must obey the Commands I hate—besides, do you 180 consider what a Life you are going to lead?

HELLENA: Yes, *Callis,* that of a Nun: and till then I'll be indebted a World of Prayers to you, if you let me now see, what I never did, the Divertisements of a Carnival.

CALLIS: What, go in Masquerade? 'twill be a fine farewell to 185 the World I take it—pray what wou'd you do there?

HELLENA: That which all the World does, as I am told, be as mad as the rest, and take all innocent Freedom—Sister, you'll go too, will you not? come prithee be not sad— We'll out-wit twenty Brothers, if you'll be ruled by me— 190 Come put off this dull Humour with your Clothes, and assume one as gay, and as fantastick as the Dress my Cousin *Valeria* and I have provided, and let's ramble.

FLORINDA: *Callis,* will you give us leave to go?

CALLIS: (*Aside.*) I have a youthful Itch of going my self. 195 —Madam, if I thought your Brother might not know it, and I might wait on you, for by my troth I'll not trust young Girls alone.

FLORINDA: Thou see'st my Brother's gone already, and thou shalt attend and watch us. 200

(*Enter* STEPHANO.)

STEPHANO: Madam, the Habits are come, and your Cousin *Valeria* is drest, and stays for you.

FLORINDA: 'Tis well—I'll write a Note, and if I chance to see *Belvile,* and want an opportunity to speak to him, that shall let him know what I've resolv'd in favour of him. 205

HELLENA: Come, let's in and dress us.

(*Exeunt.*)

SCENE II

A Long Street.

Enter BELVILE, MELANCHOLY, BLUNT, *and* FREDERICK.

FREDERICK: Why, what the Devil ails the Colonel, in a time when all the World is gay, to look like mere Lent thus? Hadst thou been long enough in *Naples* to have been in love, I should have sworn some such Judgment had befall'n thee.

BELVILE: No, I have made no new Amours since I came to 5 Naples.

FREDERICK: You have left none behind you in Paris.

BELVILE: Neither.

FREDERICK: I can't divine the Cause then; unless the old Cause, the want of Mony. 10

BLUNT: And another old Cause, the want of a Wench— Wou'd not that revive you?

BELVILE: You're mistaken, *Ned.*

BLUNT: Nay, 'Sheartlikins, then thou art past Cure.

FREDERICK: I have found it out; thou hast renew'd thy Ac- 15 quaintance with the Lady that cost thee so many Sighs at the Siege of *Pampelona*—pox on't, what d'ye call her—her Brother's a noble *Spaniard*—Nephew to the dead General—

---

137 **Hostel de Dieu** the first Spanish hospital was erected at Granada by St. Juan de Dios before 1550   145 **Gambo** the Gambia in West Africa has been a British Colony since 1664, when a fort, now Fort James, was founded at the mouth of the river

---

14 **'Sheartlikins** by God's heart

20   *Florinda*—ay, *Florinda*—And will nothing serve thy turn but that damn'd virtuous Woman, whom on my Conscience thou lov'st in spite too, because thou seest little or no possibility of gaining her?

BELVILE: Thou art mistaken, I have Interest enough in that lovely Virgin's Heart, to make me proud and vain, were it
25   not abated by the Severity of a Brother, who perceiving my Happiness—

FREDERICK: Has civilly forbid thee the House?

BELVILE: 'Tis so, to make way for a powerful Rival, the Vice-Roy's Son, who has the advantage of me, in being a Man of
30   Fortune, a *Spaniard,* and her Brother's Friend; which gives him liberty to make his Court, whilst I have recourse only to Letters, and distant Looks from her Window, which are as soft and kind as those which Heav'n sends down on Penitents.

BLUNT: Hey day! 'Sheartlikins, Simile! by this Light the Man
35   is quite spoil'd—*Frederick,* what the Devil are we made of, that we cannot be thus concern'd for a Wench?—'Sheartlikins, our *Cupids* are like the Cooks of the Camp, they can roast or boil a Woman, but they have none of the fine Tricks to set 'em off, no Hogoes to make the Sauce pleas-
40   ant, and the Stomach sharp.

FREDERICK: I dare swear I have had a hundred as young, kind and handsom as this *Florinda;* and Dogs eat me, if they were not as troublesom to me i'th' Morning as they were welcome o'er night.

45   BLUNT: And yet, I warrant, he wou'd not touch another Woman, if he might have her for nothing.

BELVILE: That's thy Joy, a cheap Whore.

BLUNT: Why, 'dsheartlikins, I Love a frank Soul—When did you ever hear of an honest Woman that took a Man's
50   Mony? I warrant 'em good ones—But, Gentlemen, you may be free, you have been kept so poor with Parliaments and Protectors, that the little Stock you have is not worth preserving—but I thank my Stars, I have more Grace than to forfeit my Estate by Cavaliering.

55   BELVILE: Methinks only following the Court should be sufficient to entitle 'em to that.

BLUNT: 'Sheartlikins, they know I follow it to do it no good, unless they pick a hole in my Coat for lending you Mony now and then; which is a greater Crime to my Con-
60   science, Gentlemen, than to the Common-wealth.

(*Enter* WILLMORE.)

WILLMORE: Ha! dear *Belvile!* noble Colonel!

BELVILE: *Willmore!* welcome ashore, my dear Rover!—what happy Wind blew us this good Fortune?

WILLMORE: Let me salute you my dear *Fred,* and then com-
65   mand me—How is't honest Lad?

FREDERICK: Faith, Sir, the old Complement, infinitely the better to see my dear mad *Willmore* again—Prithee why camest thou ashore? and where's the Prince?

WILLMORE: He's well, and reigns still Lord of the watery El-
70   ement—I must aboard again within a Day or two, and my Business ashore was only to enjoy my self a little this Carnival.

BELVILE: Pray know our new Friend, Sir, he's but bashful, a raw Traveller, but honest, stout, and one of us.

---

39 **Hogoes** Haut-goût, a relish

(*Embraces* BLUNT.)

WILLMORE: That you esteem him, gives him an Interest here.

BLUNT: Your Servant, Sir.   75

WILLMORE: But well—Faith I'm glad to meet you again in a warm Climate, where the kind Sun has its god-like Power still over the Wine and Woman.—Love and Mirth are my Business in *Naples*; and if I mistake not the Place, here's an excellent Market for Chapmen of my Humour.   80

BELVILE: See here be those kind Merchants of Love you look for.

(*Enter several* MEN *in masquing Habits, some playing on Musick, others dancing after;* WOMEN *drest like Curtezans, with Papers pinn'd to their Breasts, and Baskets of Flowers in their Hands.*)

BLUNT: 'Sheartlikins, what have we here!

FREDERICK: Now the Game begins.

WILLMORE: Fine pretty Creatures! may a stranger have leave   85
to look and love?—What's here—(*Reads the Paper.*): *Roses for every Month!*

BLUNT: Roses for every Month! what means that?

BELVILE: They are, or wou'd have you think they're Curtezans, who here in *Naples* are to be hir'd by the Month.   90

WILLMORE: Kind and obliging to inform us—Pray where do these Roses grow? I would fain plant some of 'em in a Bed of mine.

WOMAN: Beware such Roses, Sir.

WILLMORE: A Pox of fear: I'll be bak'd with thee between a   95
pair of Sheets, and that's thy proper Still, so I might but strow such Roses over me and under me—Fair one, wou'd you wou'd give me leave to gather at your Bush this idle Month, I wou'd go near to make some Body smell of it all the Year after.   100

BELVILE: And thou hast need of such a Remedy, for thou stinkest of Tar and Rope-ends, like a Dock or Pesthouse.

(*The* WOMAN *puts her self into the Hands of a* MAN*, and Exit.*)

WILLMORE: Nay, nay, you shall not leave me so.

BELVILE: By all means use no Violence here.

WILLMORE: Death! just as I was going to be damnably in   105
love, to have her led off! I could pluck that Rose out of his Hand, and even kiss the Bed, the Bush it grew in.

FREDERICK: No Friend to Love like a long Voyage at Sea.

BLUNT: Except a Nunnery, *Frederick.*

WILLMORE: Death! but will they not be kind, quickly be   110
kind? Thou know'st I'm no tame Sigher, but a rampant Lion of the Forest.

(*Two* MEN *drest all over with Horns of several sorts, making Grimaces at one another, with Papers pinn'd on their Backs, advance from the farther end of the Scene.*)

BELVILE: Oh the fantastical Rogues, how they are dress'd! 'tis a Satir against the whole Sex.

WILLMORE: Is this a Fruit that grows in this warm Country?   115

BELVILE: Yes: 'Tis pretty to see these *Italian* start, swell, and stab at the Word *Cuckold,* and yet stumble at Horns on every Threshold.

WILLMORE: See what's on their Back—(*Reads.*) *Flowers for every Night.*—Ah Rogue! And more sweet than Roses of   120
ev'ry Month! This is a Gardiner of *Adam's* own breeding.

(*They dance.*)

BELVILE: What think you of those grave People?—is a Wake in *Essex* half so mad or extravagant?

125 WILLMORE: I like their sober grave way, 'tis a kind of legal authoriz'd Fornication, where the Men are not chid for 't, nor the Women despis'd, as amongst our dull *English;* even the Monsieurs want that part of good Manners.

BELVILE: But here in *Italy* a Monsieur is the humblest best-bred Gentleman—Duels are so baffled by Bravos that an 130 age shews not one, but between a *Frenchman* and a Hang-man, who is as much too hard for him on the Piazza, as they are for a *Dutchman* on the new Bridge—But see another Crew.

(*Enter* FLORINDA, HELLENA, *and* VALERIA, *drest like Gipsies;* CALLIS *and* STEPHANO, LUCETTA, PHILIPPO, *and* SANCHO *in Masquerade.*)

HELLENA: Sister, there's your *Englishman,* and with him a 135 handsome proper Fellow—I'll to him, and instead of telling him his Fortune, try my own.

WILLMORE: Gipsies, on my Life—Sure these will prattle if a Man cross their Hands. (*Goes to* HELLENA.)—Dear pretty (and I hope) young Devil, will you tell an amorous 140 Stranger what Luck he's like to have?

HELLENA: Have a care how you venture with me, Sir, lest I pick your Pocket, which will more vex your *English* Humour, than an *Italian* Fortune will please you.

WILLMORE: How the Devil cam'st thou to know my Coun-145 try and Humour?

HELLENA: The first I guess by a certain forward Impudence, which does not displease me at this time; and the Loss of your Money will vex you, because I hope you have but very little to lose.

150 WILLMORE: Egad Child, thou'rt i'th' right; it is so little, I dare not offer it thee for a Kindness—But cannot you divine what other things of more value I have about me, that I would more willingly part with?

HELLENA: Indeed no, that's the Business of a Witch, and I am 155 but a Gipsy yet—Yet, without looking in your Hand, I have a parlous Guess, 'tis some foolish Heart you mean, an inconstant *English* Heart, as little worth stealing as your Purse.

WILLMORE: Nay, then thou dost deal with the Devil, that's 160 certain—Thou hast guess'd as right as if thou hadst been one of that Number it has languist for—I find you'll be better acquainted with it; nor can you take it in a better time, for I am come from Sea, Child; and *Venus* not being propitious to me in her own Element, I have a world of 165 Love in store—Wou'd you would be good-natur'd, and take some on't off my Hands.

HELLENA: Why—I could be inclin'd that way—but for a foolish Vow I am going to make—to die a Maid.

WILLMORE: Then thou art damn'd without Redemption; and 170 as I am a good Christian, I ought to charity to divert so wicked a Design—therefore prithee, dear Creature, let me know quickly when and where I shall begin to set a helping hand to so good a Work.

HELLENA: If you should prevail with my tender Heart (as I 175 begin to fear you will, for you have horrible loving Eyes) there will be difficulty in't that you'll hardly undergo for my sake.

WILLMORE: Faith, Child, I have been bred in Dangers, and wear a Sword that has been employ'd in a worse Cause, than for a handsom kind Woman—Name the Danger—let it be any thing but a long Siege, and I'll undertake it. 180

HELLENA: Can you storm?

WILLMORE: Oh, most furiously.

HELLENA: What think you of a Nunnery-wall? for he that wins me, must gain that first.

WILLMORE: A Nun! Oh how I love thee for't! there's no Sin-185 ner like a young Saint—Nay, now there's no denying me: the old Law had no Curse (to a Woman) like dying a Maid; witness *Jephtha's* Daughter.

HELLENA: A very good Text this, if well handled; and I perceive, Father Captain, you would impose no severe Penance on her 190 who was inclin'd to console her self before she took Orders.

WILLMORE: If she be young and handsom.

HELLENA: Ay, there's it—but if she be not—

WILLMORE: By this Hand, Child, I have an implicit Faith, and dare venture on thee with all Faults—besides, 'tis more 195 meritorious to leave the World when thou hast tasted and prov'd the Pleasure on't; then 'twill be a Virtue in thee, which now will be pure Ignorance.

HELLENA: I perceive, good Father Captain, you design only to make me fit for Heaven—but if on the contrary you 200 should quite divert me from it, and bring me back to the World again, I should have a new Man to seek I find; and what a grief that will be—for when I begin, I fancy I shall love like any thing: I never try'd yet.

WILLMORE: Egad, and that's kind—Prithee, dear Creature, 205 give me Credit for a Heart, for faith, I'm a very honest Fellow—Oh, I long to come first to the Banquet of Love; and such a swinging Appetite I bring—Oh, I'm impatient. Thy Lodging, Sweetheart, thy Lodging, or I'm a dead man.

HELLENA: Why must we be either guilty of Fornication or Mur-210 der, if we converse with you Men?—And is there no difference between leave to love me, and leave to lie with me?

WILLMORE: Faith, Child, they were made to go together.

LUCETTA: (*Pointing to* BLUNT.) Are you sure this is the Man?

SANCHO: When did I mistake your Game? 215

LUCETTA: This is a stranger, I know by his gazing; if he be brisk he'll venture to follow me; and then, if I understand my Trade, he's mine: he's *English* too, and they say that's a sort of good natur'd loving People, and have generally so kind an opinion of themselves, that a Woman with any 220 Wit may flatter 'em into any sort of Fool she pleases.

BLUNT: 'Tis so—she is taken—I have Beauties which my false Glass at home did not discover.

(*She often passes by* BLUNT *and gazes on him; he struts, and cocks, and walks, and gazes on her.*)

FLORINDA: This Woman watches me so, I shall get no Opportunity to discover my self to him, and so miss the in-225 tent of my coming—But as I was saying, Sir—(*Looking in his Hand.*) by this Line you should be a Lover.

BELVILE: I thought how right you guess'd, all Men are in love, or pretend to be so—Come, let me go, I'm weary of this fooling. 230

(*Walks away.*)

FLORINDA: I will not, till you have confess'd whether the Passion that you have vow'd *Florinda* be true or false.

(*She holds him, he strives to get from her.*)

BELVILE: *Florinda!*

(*Turns quick towards her.*)

235 FLORINDA: Softly.
BELVILE: Thou hast nam'd one will fix me here for ever.
FLORINDA: She'll be disappointed then, who expects you this Night at the Garden-gate, and if you'll fail not—as let me see the other Hand—you will go near to do—she vows to
240 die or make you happy.

(*Looks on* CALLIS, *who observes 'em.*)

BELVILE: What canst thou mean?
FLORINDA: That which I say—Farewell.

(*Offers to go.*)

BELVILE: Oh charming Sybil, stay, complete that Joy, which, as it is, will turn into Distraction!—Where must I be? at the
245 Garden-gate? I know it—at night you say—I'll sooner forfeit Heaven than disobey.

(*Enter* DON PEDRO *and other Masquers, and pass over the Stage.*)

CALLIS: Madam, your Brother's here.
FLORINDA: Take this to instruct you farther.

(*Gives him a Letter, and goes off.*)

FREDERICK: Have a care, Sir, what you promise; this may be
250 a Trap laid by her Brother to ruin you.
BELVILE: Do not disturb my Happiness with Doubts.

(*Opens the Letter.*)

WILLMORE: My dear pretty Creature, a Thousand Blessings on thee; still in this Habit, you say, and after Dinner at this Place.
HELLENA: Yes, if you will swear to keep your Heart, and not
255 bestow it between this time and that.
WILLMORE: By all the little Gods of Love I swear, I'll leave it with you; and if you run away with it, those Deities of Justice will revenge me.

(*Exeunt all the* WOMEN *except* LUCETTA.)

FREDERICK: Do you know the Hand?
260 BELVILE: 'Tis *Florinda's.*
All Blessings fall upon the virtuous Maid.
FREDERICK: Nay, no Idolatry, a sober Sacrifice I'll allow you.
BELVILE: Oh Friends! the welcom'st News, the softest Letter!—nay, you shall see it; and could you now be serious,
265 I might be made the happiest Man the Sun shines on.
WILLMORE: The Reason of this mighty Joy.
BELVILE: See how kindly she invites me to deliver her from the threaten'd Violence of her Brother—will you not assist me?
WILLMORE: I know not what thou mean'st, but I'll make one
270 at any Mischief where a Woman's concern'd—but she'll be grateful to us for the Favour, will she not?
BELVILE: How mean you?
WILLMORE: How should I mean? Thou know'st there's but one way for a Woman to oblige me.
275 BELVILE: Don't prophane—the Maid is nicely virtuous.

WILLMORE: Who pox, then she's fit for nothing but a Husband; let her e'en go, Colonel.
FREDERICK: Peace, she's the Colonel's Mistress, Sir.
WILLMORE: Let her be the Devil; if she be thy Mistress, I'll serve her—name the way.   280
BELVILE: Read here this Postscript.

(*Gives him a Letter.*)

WILLMORE: (*Reads.*) *At Ten at night—at the Garden-Gate—of which, if I cannot get the Key, I will contrive a way over the Wall—come attended with a Friend or two.*—Kind heart, if we three cannot weave a String to let her down a Garden-   285
Wall, 'twere pity but the Hangman wove one for us all.
FREDERICK: Let her alone for that: your Woman's Wit, your fair kind Woman, will not out-trick a Brother or a Jew, and contrive like a Jesuit in Chains—but see, *Ned Blunt* is stoln out after the Lure of a Damsel.   290

(*Exit* BLUNT *and* LUCETTA.)

BELVILE: So he'll scarce find his way home again, unless we get him cry'd by the Bell-man in the Market-place, and 'twou'd sound prettily—a lost *English* Boy of Thirty.
FREDERICK: I hope 'tis some common crafty Sinner, one that will fit him; it may be she'll sell him for *Peru,* the Rogue's 295
sturdy and would work well in a Mine; at least I hope she'll dress him for our Mirth; cheat him of all, then have him well-favour'dly bang'd, and turn'd out naked at Midnight.
WILLMORE: Prithee what Humour is he of, that you wish him so well?   300
BELVILE: Why, of an *English* Elder Brother's Humour, educated in a Nursery, with a Maid to tend him till Fifteen, and lies with his Grand-mother till he's of Age; one that knows no Pleasure beyond riding to the next Fair, or going up to *London* with his right Worshipful Father in Par-   305
liament-time; wearing gay Clothes, or making honourable Love to his Lady Mother's Landry-Maid; gets drunk at a Hunting-Match, and ten to one then gives some Proofs of his Prowess—A pox upon him, he's our Banker, and has all our Cash about him, and if he fail we are all broke.   310
FREDERICK: Oh let him alone for that matter, he's of a damn'd stingy Quality, that will secure our Stock. I know not in what Danger it were indeed, if the Jilt should pretend she's in love with him, for 'tis a kind believing Coxcomb; otherwise if he part with more than a Piece of   315
Eight—geld him: for which offer he may chance to be beaten, if she be a Whore of the first Rank.
BELVILE: Nay the Rogue will not be easily beaten, he's stout enough; perhaps if they talk beyond his Capacity, he may chance to exercise his Courage upon some of them; else 320
I'm sure they'll find it as difficult to beat as to please him.
WILLMORE: 'Tis a lucky Devil to light upon so kind a Wench!
FREDERICK: Thou hadst a great deal of talk with thy little Gipsy, coud'st thou do no good upon her? for mine was hard-hearted.   325
WILLMORE: Hang her, she was some damn'd honest Person of Quality, I'm sure, she was so very free and witty. If her Face

---

315 **a Piece of Eight** a piastre, a coin of varying values in different countries

be but answerable to her Wit and Humour, I would be bound to Constancy this Month to gain her. In the mean
330 time, have you made no kind Acquaintance since you came to Town?—You do not use to be honest so long, Gentlemen.

FREDERICK: Faith Love has kept us honest, we have been all fir'd with a Beauty newly come to Town, the famous *Paduana Angelica Bianca.*

335 WILLMORE: What, the Mistress of the dead *Spanish* General?

BELVILE: Yes, she's now the only ador'd Beauty of all the Youth in *Naples,* who put on all their charms to appear lovely in her sight, their Coaches, Liveries, and themselves, all gay,
340 as on a Monarch's Birth-Day, to attract the Eyes of this fair Charmer, while she has the Pleasure to behold all languish for her that see her.

FREDERICK: 'Tis pretty to see with how much Love the Men regard her, and how much Envy the Women.

WILLMORE: What Gallant has she?

345 BELVILE: None, she's exposed to Sale, and four Days in the Week she's yours—for so much a Month.

WILLMORE: The very Thought of it quenches all manner of Fire in me—yet prithee let's see her.

BELVILE: Let's first to Dinner, and after that we'll pass the Day
350 as you please—but at Night ye must all be at my Devotion.

WILLMORE: I will not fail you.

(*Exeunt.*)

ACT TWO

SCENE I

The Long Street.

Enter BELVILE *and* FREDERICK *in Masquing-Habits, and* WILLMORE *in his own Clothes, with a Vizard in his Hand.*

WILLMORE: But why thus disguis'd and muzzl'd?

BELVILE: Because whatever Extravagances we commit in these Faces, our own may not be oblig'd to answer 'em.

WILLMORE: I should have chang'd my Eternal Buff too: but
5 no matter, my little Gipsy wou'd not have found me out then: for if she should change hers, it is impossible I should know her, unless I should hear her prattle—A Pox on't, I cannot get her out of my Head: Pray Heaven, if ever I do see her again, she prove damnable ugly, that I may
10 fortify my self against her Tongue.

BELVILE: Have a care of Love, for o' my conscience she was not of a Quality to give thee any hopes.

WILLMORE: Pox on 'em, why do they draw a Man in then? She has play'd with my Heart so, that 'twill never lie still
15 till I have met with some kind Wench, that will play the Game out with me—Oh for my Arms full of soft, white, kind—Woman! such as I fancy *Angelica.*

BELVILE: This is her House, if you were but in stock to get admittance; they have not din'd yet; I perceive the Picture is
20 not out.

(*Enter* BLUNT.)

WILLMORE: I long to see the Shadow of the fair Substance, a Man may gaze on that for nothing.

BLUNT: Colonel, thy Hand—and thine, *Frederick.* I have been an Ass, a deluded Fool, a very Coxcomb from my Birth till this Hour, and heartily repent my little Faith. 25

BELVILE: What the Devil's the matter with thee *Ned?*

BLUNT: Oh such a Mistress, *Frederick,* such a Girl!

WILLMORE: Ha! where? *Frederick.* Ay where!

BLUNT: So fond, so amorous, so toying and fine! and all for sheer Love, ye Rogue! Oh how she lookt and kiss'd! and 30 sooth'd my Heart from my Bosom. I cannot think I was awake, and yet methinks I see and feel her Charms still— *Frederick.*—Try if she have not left the Taste of her balmy Kisses upon my Lips—

(*Kisses him.*)

BELVILE: Ha, ha, ha! *Willmore.* Death Man, where is she? 35

BLUNT: What a Dog was I to stay in dull *England* so long— How have I laught at the Colonel when he sigh'd for Love! but now the little Archer has reveng'd him, and by his own Dart, I can guess at all his Joys, which then I took for Fancies, mere Dreams and Fables—Well, I'm resolved 40 to sell all in Essex, and plant here for ever.

BELVILE: What a Blessing 'tis, thou hast a Mistress thou dar'st boast of; for I know thy Humour is rather to have a proclaim'd Clap, than a secret Amour.

WILLMORE: Dost know her Name? 45

BLUNT: Her Name? No, 'sheartlikins: what care I for Names?— She's fair, young, brisk and kind, even to ravishment: and what a Pox care I for knowing her by another Title?

WILLMORE: Didst give her anything?

BLUNT: Give her!—Ha, ha, ha! why, she's a Person of Quality 50 —That's a good one, give her! 'sheartlikins dost think such Creatures are to be bought? Or are we provided for such a Purchase? Give her, quoth ye? Why she presented me with this Bracelet, for the Toy of a Diamond I us'd to wear: No, Gentlemen, *Ned Blunt* is not every Body—She 55 expects me again to night.

WILLMORE: Egad that's well; we'll all go.

BLUNT: Not a Soul: No, Gentlemen, you are Wits; I am a dull Country Rogue, I.

FREDERICK: Well, Sir, for all your Person of Quality, I shall be 60 very glad to understand your Purse be secure; 'tis our whole Estate at present, which we are loth to hazard in one Bottom: come, Sir, unload.

BLUNT: Take the necessary Trifle, useless now to me, that am belov'd by such a Gentlewoman—'sheartlikins Money! 65 Here take mine too.

FREDERICK: No, keep that to be cozen'd, that we may laugh.

WILLMORE: Cozen'd!—Death! wou'd I cou'd meet with one, that wou'd cozen me of all the Love I cou'd spare to night.

FREDERICK: Pox 'tis some common Whore upon my Life. 70

BLUNT: A Whore! yes with such Clothes! such Jewels! such a House! such Furniture, and so attended! a Whore!

BELVILE: Why yes, Sir, they are Whores, tho they'll neither entertain you with Drinking, Swearing, or Baudy; are Whores in all those gay Clothes, and right Jewels, are 75 Whores with great Houses richly furnisht with Velvet Beds, Store of Plate, handsome Attendance, and fine Coaches, are Whores and errant ones.

WILLMORE: Pox on't, where do these fine Whores live?

80 BELVILE: Where no Rogue in Office yclep'd Constables dare
      give 'em laws, nor the Wine-inspired Bullies of the Town
      break their Windows; yet they are Whores, tho this *Essex*
      Calf believe them Persons of Quality.

    BLUNT: 'Sheartlikins, y'are all Fools, there are things about
85   this *Essex* Calf, that shall take with the Ladies, beyond all
      your Wits and Parts—This Shape and Size, Gentlemen, are
      not to be despis'd; my Waste tolerably long, with other
      inviting Signs, that shall be nameless.

    WILLMORE: Egad I believe he may have met with some Per-
90   son of Quality that may be kind to him.

    BELVILE: Dost thou perceive any such tempting things about
      him, should make a fine Woman, and of Quality, pick him
      out from all Mankind, to throw away her Youth and
      Beauty upon, nay, and her dear Heart too?—no, no, *An-*
95   *gelica* has rais'd the Price too high.

    WILLMORE: May she languish for Mankind till she die, and be
      damn'd for that one Sin alone.

(Enter two BRAVOES, *and hang up a great Picture of* ANGELICA's
against the Balcony, and two little ones at each side of the Door.)

    BELVILE: See there the fair Sign to the Inn, where a Man may
      lodge that's Fool enough to give her Price.

*(*WILLMORE *gazes on the Picture.)*

100 BLUNT: 'Sheartlikins, Gentlemen, what's this?

    BELVILE: A famous Curtezan that's to be sold.

    BLUNT: How! to be sold! nay then I have nothing to say to
      her—sold! what Impudence is practis'd in this Coun-
      try?—With Order and Decency Whoring's established
105   here by virtue of the Inquisition—Come let's be gone,
      I'm sure we're no Chapmen for this Commodity.

    FREDERICK: Thou art none, I'm sure, unless thou could'st
      have her in thy Bed at the Price of a Coach in the Street.

    WILLMORE: How wondrous fair she is—a Thousand Crowns
110   a Month—by Heaven as many Kingdoms were too little.
      A plague of this Poverty—of which I ne'er complain, but
      when it hinders my Approach to Beauty, which Virtue
      ne'er could purchase.

(Turns from the Picture.)

    BLUNT: What's this?—*(Reads.) A Thousand Crowns a Month!*—
115   'Sheartlikins, here's a Sum! sure 'tis a mistake.—Hark you,
      Friend, does she take or give so much by the Month!

    FREDERICK: A Thousand Crowns! Why, 'tis a Portion for the
      Infanta.

    BLUNT: Hark ye, Friends, won't she trust?
120 BRAVO: This is a Trade, Sir, that cannot live by Credit.

(Enter DON PEDRO *in Masquerade, follow'd by* STEPHANO.)*

    BELVILE: See, here's more Company, let's walk off a while.

*(*PEDRO *reads. Exeunt* ENGLISH. *Enter* ANGELICA *and* MORETTA
in the Balcony, and draw a Silk Curtain.)

    PEDRO: Fetch me a Thousand Crowns, I never wish to buy
      this Beauty at an easier Rate.

(Passes off.)

    ANGELICA: Prithee what said those Fellows to thee?

    BRAVO: Madam, the first were Admirers of Beauty only, but   125
      no purchasers; they were merry with your Price and Pic-
      ture, laught at the Sum, and so past off.

    ANGELICA: No matter, I'm not displeas'd with their rallying;
      their Wonder feeds my Vanity, and he that wishes to buy,
      gives me more Pride, than he that gives my Price can   130
      make me Pleasure.

    BRAVO: Madam, the last I knew thro all his disguises to be
      Don *Pedro,* Nephew to the General, and who was with
      him in *Pampelona.*

    ANGELICA: Don *Pedro!* my old Gallant's Nephew! When his   135
      Uncle dy'd, he left him a vast Sum of Money; it is he who
      was so in love with me at *Padua,* and who us'd to make
      the General so jealous.

    MORETTA: Is this he that us'd to prance before our Window
      and take such care to shew himself an amorous Ass? if I am   140
      not mistaken, he is the likeliest Man to give your Price.

    ANGELICA: The Man is brave and generous, but of an Hu-
      mour so uneasy and inconstant, that the victory over his
      Heart is as soon lost as won; a Slave that can add little to
      the Triumph of the Conqueror; but inconstancy's the Sin   145
      of all Mankind, therefore I'm resolv'd that nothing but
      Gold shall charm my Heart.

    MORETTA: I'm glad on't; 'tis only interest that Women of our
      Profession ought to consider: tho I wonder what has kept
      you from that general Disease of our Sex so long, I mean   150
      that of being in love.

    ANGELICA: A kind, but sullen Star, under which I had the
      Happiness to be born; yet I have had no time for Love; the
      bravest and noblest of Mankind have purchas'd my
      Favours at so dear a Rate, as if no Coin but Gold were   155
      current with our Trade—But here's Don *Pedro* again, fetch
      me my Lute—for 'tis for him or Don *Antonio* the Vice-
      Roy's Son, that I have spread my Nets.

(Enter at one Door Don PEDRO, *and* STEPHANO; *Don* ANTONIO
and DIEGO [*his page*], *at the other Door, with people following him
in Masquerade, antickly attir'd, some with Musick: they both go up
to the Picture.)*

    ANTONIO: A thousand Crowns! had not the Painter flatter'd
      her, I should not think it dear.   160

    PEDRO: Flatter'd her! by Heaven he cannot. I have seen the
      Original, nor is there one Charm here more than adorns
      her Face and Eyes; all this soft and sweet, with a certain
      languishing Air, that no Artist can represent.

    ANTONIO: What I heard of her Beauty before had fir'd my   165
      Soul, but this confirmation of it has blown it into a flame.

    PEDRO: Ha!

    PAGE: Sir, I have known you throw away a Thousand Crowns
      on a worse Face, and tho y' are near your Marriage, you
      may venture a little Love here; *Florinda*—will not miss it.   170

    PEDRO: *(Aside.)* Ha! *Florinda!* Sure 'tis *Antonio.*

    ANTONIO: *Florinda!* name not those distant Joys, there's not
      one thought of her will check my Passion here.

    PEDRO: Florinda scorn'd! and all my Hopes defeated of the
      Possession of Angelica! *(A noise of a Lute above. Antonio*   175
      gazes up.) Her Injuries by Heaven he shall not boast of.

(Song to a Lute above.)

Song

When *Damon* first began to love,
He languisht in a soft Desire,
And knew not how the Gods to move,
180   To lessen or increase his Fire,
For *Caelia* in her charming Eyes
  Wore all Love's Sweet, and all his Cruelties.

II

But as beneath a Shade he lay,
Weaving of Flow'rs for *Caelia*'s Hair,
185   She chanc'd to lead her Flock that way,
And saw the am'rous Shepherd there.
She gaz'd around upon the Place,
And saw the Grove (resembling Night)
To all the Joys of Love invite,
190   Whilst guilty Smiles and Blushes drest her Face.
At this the bashful Youth all Transport grew,
And with kind Force he taught the Virgin how
To yield what all his Sighs cou'd never do.

ANTONIO: By Heav'n she's charming fair!

(ANGELICA throws open the Curtains, and bows to ANTONIO, who pulls off his Vizard, and bows and blows up Kisses. PEDRO unseen looks in his Face.)

195   PEDRO: 'Tis he, the false *Antonio!*
ANTONIO: Friend, where must I pay my offering of Love?

(To the bravo.)

  My Thousand Crowns I mean.
PEDRO: That offering I have design'd to make,
  And yours will come too late.
200   ANTONIO: Prithee be gone, I shall grow angry else,
  And then thou art not safe.
PEDRO: My Anger may be fatal, Sir, as yours;
  And he that enters here may prove this Truth.
ANTONIO: I know not who thou art, but I am sure thou'rt
205   worth my killing, and aiming at *Angelica.*

(They draw and fight.)

(Enter WILLMORE and BLUNT, who draw and part 'em.)

BLUNT: 'Sheartlikins, here's fine doings.
WILLMORE: Tilting for the Wench I'm sure—nay gad, if that
  wou'd win her, I have as good a Sword as the best of ye—
  Put up—put up, and take another time and place, for this
210   is design'd for Lovers only.

(They all put up.)

PEDRO: We are prevented; dare you meet me to morrow on
  the *Molo?*
  For I've a Title to a better quarrel,
  That of *Florinda* in whose credulous Heart
  Thou'st made an Int'rest, and destroy'd my Hopes.
215   ANTONIO: Dare?
  I'll meet thee there as early as the Day.

PEDRO: We will come thus disguis'd, that whosoever chance
  to get the better, he may escape unknown.
ANTONIO: It shall be so.

(Exit PEDRO and STEPHANO.)

  Who shou'd this Rival be? unless the *English* Colonel, of   220
  whom I've often heard Don Pedro speak; it must be he, and
  time he were removed, who lays a Claim to all my Happiness.

(WILLMORE having gaz'd all this while on the Picture, pulls down a little one.)

WILLMORE: This posture's loose and negligent,
  The sight on't wou'd beget a warm desire
  In Souls, whom Impotence and Age had chill'd.   225
  —This must along with me.
BRAVO: What means this rudeness, Sir?—restore the Picture.
ANTONIO: Ha! Rudeness committed to the fair *Angelica!*—
  Restore the Picture, Sir.
WILLMORE: Indeed I will not, Sir.   230
ANTONIO: By Heav'n but you shall.
WILLMORE: Nay, do not shew your Sword; if you do, by this
  dear Beauty—I will shew mine too.
ANTONIO: What right can you pretend to't?
WILLMORE: That of Possession which I will maintain—you   235
  perhaps have 1000 Crowns to give for the Original.
ANTONIO: No matter, Sir, you shall restore the Picture.
ANGELICA: Oh, *Moretta!* what's the matter?

(ANGELICA and MORETTA above.)

ANTONIO: Or leave your Life behind.
WILLMORE: Death! you lye—I will do neither.   240
ANGELICA: Hold, I command you, if for me you fight.

(They fight, the Spaniards join with ANTONIO, BLUNT laying on like mad. They leave off and bow.)

WILLMORE: How heavenly fair she is!—ah Plague of her Price.
ANGELICA: You Sir in Buff, you that appear a Soldier, that first
  began this Insolence.
WILLMORE: 'Tis true, I did so, if you call it Insolence for a   245
  Man to preserve himself; I saw your charming Picture, and
  was wounded: quite thro my Soul each pointed Beauty
  ran; and wanting a Thousand Crowns to procure my
  Remedy, I laid this little Picture to my Bosom—which if
  you cannot allow me, I'll resign.   250
ANGELICA: No, you may keep the Trifle.
ANTONIO: You shall first ask my leave, and this.

(Fight again as before.)

(Enter BELVILE and FREDERICK who join with the English.)

ANGELICA: Hold; will you ruin me?—*Biskey, Sebastian,* part them.

(The SPANIARDS are beaten off.)

MORETTA: Oh Madam, we're undone, a pox upon that rude
  Fellow, he's set on to ruin us: we shall never see good days,   255
  till all these fighting poor Rogues are sent to the Gallies.

(Enter BELVILE, BLUNT and WILLMORE, with his shirt bloody.)

BLUNT: 'Sheartlikins, beat me at this Sport, and I'll ne'er wear Sword more.

BELVILE: The Devil's in thee for a mad Fellow, thou art always
260   one at an unlucky Adventure.—Come, let's be gone whilst we're safe, and remember these are *Spaniards,* a sort of People that know how to revenge an Affront.

FREDERICK: (*To* WILLMORE.) You bleed; I hope you are not wounded.

265 WILLMORE: Not much:—a plague upon your Dons, if they fight no better they'll ne'er recover *Flanders.*—What the Devil was't to them that I took down the Picture?

BLUNT: Took it! 'Sheartlikins, we'll have the great one too; 'tis ours by Conquest.—Prithee, help me up, and I'll pull it
270   down.—

ANGELICA: Stay, Sir, and e'er you affront me further, let me know how you durst commit this Outrage—To you I speak, Sir, for you appear like a Gentleman.

WILLMORE: To me, Madam?—Gentlemen, your Servant.

(BELVILE *stays him.*)

275 BELVILE: Is the Devil in thee? Do'st know the danger of en-tring the house of an incens'd Curtezan?

WILLMORE: I thank you for your care—but there are other matters in hand, there are, tho we have no great Tempta-tion.—Death! let me go.

280 FREDERICK: Yes, to your Lodging, if you will, but not in here.—Damn these gay Harlots—by this Hand I'll have as sound and hansome a Whore for a Patacoone.—Death, Man, she'll murder thee.

WILLMORE: Oh! fear me not, shall I not venture where a
285   Beauty calls? a lovely charming Beauty? for fear of dan-ger! when by Heaven there's none so great as to long for her, whilst I want Money to purchase her.

FREDERICK: Therefore 'tis loss of time, unless you had the thousand Crowns to pay.

290 WILLMORE: It may be she may give a Favour, at least I shall have the pleasure of saluting her when I enter, and when I depart.

BELVILE: Pox, she'll as soon lie with thee, as kiss thee, and sooner stab than do either—you shall not go.

ANGELICA: Fear not, Sir, all I have to wound with, is my Eyes.

295 BLUNT: Let him go, 'Sheartlikins, I believe the Gentlewoman means well.

BELVILE: Well, take thy Fortune, we'll expect you in the next Street.—Farewell Fool,—farewell—

WILLMORE: B'ye Colonel—

(*Goes in.*)

300 FREDERICK: The Rogue's stark mad for a Wench.

(*Exeunt.*)

SCENE II

A Fine Chamber.

Enter WILLMORE, ANGELICA, *and* MORETTA.

ANGELICA: Insolent, Sir, how durst you pull down my Picture?

WILLMORE: Rather, how durst you set it up, to tempt poor

amorous Mortals with so much Excellence? which I find you have but too well consulted by the unmerciful price you set upon't.—Is all this Heaven of Beauty shewn to 5 move Despair in those that cannot buy? and can you think the effects of that Despair shou'd be less extravagant than I have shewn?

ANGELICA: I sent for you to ask my Pardon, Sir, not to aggra-vate your Crime.—I thought I shou'd have seen you at 10 my Feet imploring it.

WILLMORE: You are deceived, I came to rail at you, and talk such Truths, too, as shall let you see the Vanity of that Pride, which taught you how to set such a Price on Sin. For such it is, whilst that which is Love's due is meanly barter'd for. 15

ANGELICA: Ha, ha, ha, alas, good Captain, what pity 'tis your edifying Doctrine will do no good upon me—*Moretta,* fetch the Gentleman a Glass, and let him survey himself, to see what Charms he has,—(*Aside in a soft tone.*) and guess my Business. 20

MORETTA: He knows himself of old, I believe those Breeches and he have been acquainted ever since he was beaten at *Worcester.*

ANGELICA: Nay, do not abuse the poor Creature.—

MORETTA: Good Weather-beaten Corporal, will you march 25 off? we have no need of your Doctrine, tho you have of our Charity; but at present we have no Scraps, we can af-ford no kindness for God's sake; in fine, Sirrah, the Price is too high i'th' Mouth for you, therefore troop, I say.

WILLMORE: Here, good Fore-Woman of the Shop, serve me, 30 and I'll be gone.

MORETTA: Keep it to pay your Landress, your Linen stinks of the Gun-Room; for here's no selling by Retail.

WILLMORE: Thou hast sold plenty of thy stale Ware at a cheap Rate. 35

MORETTA: Ay, the more silly kind Heart I, but this is an Age wherein Beauty is at higher Rates.—In fine, you know the price of this.

WILLMORE: I grant you 'tis here set down a thousand Crowns a Month—Baud, take your black Lead and sum it up, that 40 I may have a Pistole-worth of these vain gay things, and I'll trouble you no more.

MORETTA: Pox on him, he'll fret me to Death:—abominable Fellow, I tell thee, we only sell by the whole Piece.

WILLMORE: 'Tis very hard, the whole Cargo or nothing— 45 Faith, Madam, my Stock will not reach it, I cannot be your Chapman.—Yet I have Countrymen in Town, Mer-chants of Love, like me; I'll see if they'll put for a share, we cannot lose much by it, and what we have no use for, we'll sell upon the *Friday's* Mart, at—*Who gives more?* I am 50 studying, Madam, how to purchase you, tho at present I am unprovided of Money.

ANGELICA: Sure, this from any other Man would anger me— nor shall he know the Conquest he has made—Poor an-gry Man, how I despise this railing. 55

WILLMORE: Yes, I am poor—but I'm a Gentleman,
And one that scorns this Baseness which you practise.
Poor as I am, I would not sell my self,
No, not to gain your charming high-priz'd Person.

---

60   Tho I admire you strangely for your Beauty,
     Yet I contemn your Mind.
        —And yet I wou'd at any rate enjoy you;
     At your own rate—but cannot—See here
     The only Sum I can command on Earth;
65   I know not where to eat when this is gone:
     Yet such a Slave I am to Love and Beauty,
     This last reserve I'll sacrifice to enjoy you.
        —Nay, do not frown, I know you are to be bought,
     And wou'd be bought by me, by me,
70   For a mean trifling Sum, if I could pay it down.
     Which happy knowledge I will still repeat,
     And lay it to my Heart, it has a Virtue in't,
     And soon will cure those Wounds your Eyes have made.
        —And yet—there's something so divinely powerful there—
75   Nay, I will gaze—to let you see my Strength.

(*Holds her, looks on her, and pauses and sighs.*)

     By Heaven, bright Creature—I would not for the World
     Thy Fame were half so fair as thy Face.

(*Turns her away from him.*)

     ANGELICA: (*Aside.*) His words go thro me to the very Soul.
        —If you have nothing else to say to me.
80   WILLMORE: Yes, you shall hear how infamous you are—
     For which I do not hate thee:
     But that secures my Heart, and all the Flames it feels
     Are but so many Lusts,
     I know it by their sudden bold intrusion.
85   The Fire's impatient and betrays, 'tis false—
     For had it been the purer Flame of Love,
     I should have pin'd and languish'd at your Feet,
     E'er found the Impudence to have discover'd it.
     I now dare stand your Scorn, and your Denial.
90   MORETTA: Sure she's bewitcht, that you can stand thus tamely,
     and hear his saucy railing.—Sirrah, will you be gone?
     ANGELICA: How dare you take this liberty?—(*To* MORETTA.)
     Withdraw.—Pray, tell me, Sir, are not you guilty of the
     same mercenary Crime? When a Lady is proposed to you
95   for a Wife, you never ask, how fair, discreet, or virtuous she
     is; but what's her Fortune—which if but small, you cry—
     She will not do my business—and basely leave her, tho she
     languish for you.—Say, is not this as poor?
     WILLMORE: It is a barbarous Custom, which I will scorn to
100   defend in our Sex, and do despise in yours.
     ANGELICA: Thou art a brave Fellow! put up thy Gold, and know
     That were thy Fortune large, as is thy Soul,
     Thou shouldst not buy my Love,
     Couldst thou forget those mean Effects of Vanity,
105   Which set me out to sale; and as a Lover, prize
     My yielding Joys.
     Canst thou believe they'l be entirely thine,
     Without considering they were mercenary?
     WILLMORE: (*Aside.*) I cannot tell, I must bethink me first—
110   ha, Death, I'm going to believe her.
     ANGELICA: Prithee, confirm that Faith—or if thou canst
     not—flatter me a little, 'twill please me from thy Mouth.
     WILLMORE: Curse on thy charming Tongue! dost thou return
     My feign'd Contempt with so much subtilty?

(*Aside.*)

     Thou'st found the easiest way into my Heart,   115
     Tho I yet know that all thou say'st is false.

(*Turning from her in a Rage.*)

     ANGELICA: By all that's good 'tis real,
     I never lov'd before, tho oft a Mistress.
        —Shall my first Vows be slighted?
     WILLMORE: (*Aside.*) What can she mean?   120
     ANGELICA: (*In an angry tone.*) I find you cannot credit me.
     WILLMORE: I know you take me for an errant Ass,
     An Ass that may be sooth'd into Belief,
     And then be us'd at pleasure.
        —But, Madam, I have been so often cheated   125
     By perjur'd, soft, deluding Hypocrites,
     That I've no Faith left for the cozening Sex,
     Especially for Women of your Trade.
     ANGELICA: The low esteem you have of me, perhaps
     May bring my Heart again: 130
     For I have Pride that yet surmounts my Love.

(*She turns with Pride, he holds her.*)

     WILLMORE: Throw off this Pride, this Enemy to Bliss,
     And shew the Power of Love: 'tis with those Arms
     I can be only vanquisht, made a Slave.
     ANGELICA: Is all my mighty Expectation vanisht?   135
        —No, I will not hear thee talk,—thou hast a Charm
     In every word, that draws my Heart away.
     And all the thousand Trophies I design'd,
     Thou hast undone—Why are thou soft?
     Thy Looks are bravely rough, and meant for War.   140
     Could thou not storm on still?
     I then perhaps had been as free as thou.
     WILLMORE: (*Aside.*) Death! how she throws her Fire about
        my Soul!
        —Take heed, fair Creature, how you raise my Hopes,
     Which once assum'd pretend to all Dominion.   145
     There's not a Joy thou hast in store
     I shall not then command:
     For which I'll pay thee back my Soul, my Life.
     Come, let's begin th' account this happy minute.
     ANGELICA: And will you pay me then the Price I ask?   150
     WILLMORE: Oh, why dost thou draw me from an awful
        Worship,
     By shewing thou art no Divinity?
     Conceal the Fiend, and shew me all the Angel;
     Keep me but ignorant, and I'll be devout,
     And pay my Vows for ever at this Shrine.   155

(*Kneels, and kisses her Hand.*)

     ANGELICA: The Pay I mean is but thy Love for mine.—Can
     you give that?
     WILLMORE: Intirely—come, let's withdraw: where I'll renew
     my vows, and breathe 'em with such Ardour, thou shalt
     not doubt my Zeal.   160
     ANGELICA: Thou hast a Power too strong to be resisted.

(*Exit* WILLMORE *and* ANGELICA.)

MORETTA: Now my Curse go with you—Is all our Project
    fallen to this? to love the only Enemy to our Trade? Nay,
    to love such a Shameroon, a very Beggar; nay, a Pirate-
165 Beggar, whose Business is to rifle and be gone, a No-Pur-
    chase, No-Pay Tatterdemalion, an English Piccaroon; a
    Rogue that fights for daily Drink, and takes a Pride in be-
    ing loyally lousy—Oh, I could curse now, if I durst—This
    is the Fate of most Whores.

170 *Trophies, which from believing Fops we win,*
    Are Spoils to those who cozen us again.

ACT THREE

SCENE I

A Street.

Enter FLORINDA, VALERIA, HELLENA, *in Antick different Dresses
from what they were in before,* CALLIS *attending.*

FLORINDA: I wonder what should make my Brother in so ill
    a Humour: I hope he has not found out our Ramble this
    Morning.
HELLENA: No, if he had, we should have heard on't at both
5   Ears, and have been mew'd up this Afternoon; which I
    would not for the World should have happen'd—Hey ho!
    I'm sad as a Lover's Lute.
VALERIA: Well, methinks we have learnt this Trade of Gipsies
    as readily as if we had been bred upon the Road to *Loretto:*
10 and yes I did so fumble, when I told the Stranger his For-
    tune, that I was afraid I should have told my own and
    yours by mistake—But methinks *Hellena* has been very se-
    rious ever since.
FLORINDA: I would give my Garters she were in love, to be
15 reveng'd upon her, for abusing me—How is't, *Hellena?*
HELLENA: Ah!—would I had never seen my mad Monsieur—and
    yet for all your laughing I am not in love—and yet this small
    Acquaintance, o'my Conscience, will never out of my Head.
VALERIA: Ha, ha, ha—I laugh to think how thou art fitted with a
20 Lover, a Fellow that, I warrant, loves every new Face he sees.
HELLENA: Hum—he has not kept his Word with me here—
    and may be taken up—that thought is not very pleasant to
    me—what the Duce should this be now that I feel?
VALERIA: What is't like?
25 HELLENA: Nay, the Lord knows—but if I should be hanged, I
    cannot chuse but be angry and afraid, when I think that mad
    Fellow should be in love with any Body but me—What to
    think of my self I know not—Would I could meet with
    some true damn'd Gipsy, that I might know my Fortune.
30 VALERIA: Know it! why there's nothing so easy; thou wilt love
    this wandering Inconstant till thou find'st thy self hanged
    about his Neck, and then be as mad to get free again.
FLORINDA: Yes, *Valeria;* we shall see her bestride his Baggage-
    horse, and follow him to the Campaign.
35 HELLENA: So, so; now you are provided for, there's no care
    taken of poor me—But since you have set my Heart a
    wishing, I am resolv'd to know for what. I will not die of
    the Pip, so I will not.

---

164 **shameroon** a trickster, a cozening rascal

FLORINDA: Art thou mad to talk so? Who will like thee well
    enough to have thee, that hears what a mad Wench thou art? 40
HELLENA: Like me! I don't intend every he that likes me shall
    have me, but he that I like: I shou'd have staid in the Nun-
    nery still, if I had lik'd my Lady Abbess as well as she lik'd
    me. No, I came thence, not (as my wise Brother imagines)
    to take an eternal Farewel of the World, but to love and to 45
    be belov'd; and I will be belov'd, or I'll get one of your
    Men, so I will.
VALERIA: Am I put into the Number of Lovers?
HELLENA: You! my Couz, I know thou art too good natur'd to
    leave us in any Design: Thou wou't venture a Cast, tho thou 50
    comest off a Loser, especially with such a Gamester—I ob-
    serv'd your Man, and your willing ears incline that way; and
    if you are not a Lover, 'tis an Art soon learnt—that I find.

(Sighs.)

FLORINDA: I wonder how you learnt to love so easily, I had a
    thousand Charms to meet my Eyes and Ears, e'er I cou'd 55
    yield; and 'twas the knowledge of *Belvile's* Merit, not the
    surprising Person, took my Soul—Thou art too rash to
    give a Heart at first sight.
HELLENA: Hang your considering Lover; I ne'er thought be-
    yond the Fancy, that 'twas a very pretty, idle, silly kind of 60
    Pleasure to pass ones time with, to write little, soft, non-
    sensical Billets, and with great difficulty and danger re-
    ceive Answers; in which I shall have my Beauty prais'd, my
    Wit admir'd (tho little or none) and have the Vanity and
    Power to know I am desirable; then I have the more In- 65
    clination that way, because I am to be a Nun, and so shall
    not be suspected to have any such earthly Thoughts about
    me—But when I walk thus—and sigh thus—they'll think
    my Mind's upon my Monastery, and cry, how happy 'tis
    she's so resolv'd!—But not a Word of Man. 70
FLORINDA: What a mad Creature's this!
HELLENA: I'll warrant, if my Brother hears either of you sigh,
    he cries (gravely)—I fear you have the Indiscretion to be in
    love, but take heed of the Honour of our House, and your
    own unspotted Fame; and so he conjures on till he has laid 75
    the soft-wing'd God in your Hearts, or broke the
    Birdsnest—But see here comes your Lover: but where's my
    inconstant? let's stop aside, and we may learn something.

(Go aside.)

(Enter BELVILE, FREDERICK, *and* BLUNT.*)*

BELVILE: What means this? the Picture's taken in.
BLUNT: It may be the Wench is good-natur'd, and will be 80
    kind *gratis.* Your Friend's a proper handsom Fellow.
BELVILE: I rather think she has cut his Throat and is fled: I am
    mad he should throw himself into Dangers—Pox on't, I
    shall want him to night—let's knock and ask for him.
HELLENA: My heart goes a-pit a-pat, for fear 'tis my Man they 85
    talk of.

(Knock, MORETTA *above.)*

MORETTA: What would you have?
BELVILE: Tell the Stranger that enter'd here about two Hours
    ago, that his Friends stay here for him.

90   MORETTA: A Curse upon him for *Moretta,* would he were at the Devil—but he's coming to you.

(*Enter* WILLMORE.)

HELLENA: I, I, 'tis he. Oh how this vexes me.

BELVILE: And how, and how, dear Lad, has Fortune smil'd? Are we to break her Windows, or raise up Altars to her! hah!

95   WILLMORE: Does not my Fortune sit triumphant on my Brow? dost not see the little wanton God there all gay and smiling? have I not an Air about my Face and Eyes, that distinguish me from the Croud of common Lovers? By Heav'n, *Cupid's* Quiver has not half so many Darts as her

100   Eyes—Oh such a Bona Roba, to sleep in her Arms is lying in Fresco, all perfum'd Air about me.

HELLENA: (*Aside.*) Here's fine encouragement for me to fool on.

WILLMORE: Hark ye, where didst thou purchase that rich Canary we drank to-day? Tell me, that I may adore the

105   Spigot, and sacrifice to the Butt: the Juice was divine, into which I must dip my Rosary, and then bless all things that I would have bold or fortunate.

BELVILE: Well, Sir, let's go take a Bottle, and hear the Story of your Success.

110   FREDERICK: Would not *French* Wine do better?

WILLMORE: Damn the hungry Balderdash; cheerful Sack has a generous Virtue in't, inspiring a successful Confidence, gives Eloquence to the Tongue, and Vigour to the Soul; and has in a few Hours compleated all my Hopes and Wishes. There's

115   nothing left to raise a new Desire in me—Come let's be gay and wanton—and, Gentlemen, study, study what you want, for here are Friends,—that will supply, Gentlemen,—hark! what a charming sound they make—'tis he and she Gold whilst here, shall beget new Pleasures every moment.

120   BLUNT: But hark ye, Sir, you are not married, are you?

WILLMORE: All the Honey of Matrimony, but none of the Sting, Friend.

BLUNT: 'Sheartlikins, thou'rt a fortunate Rogue.

WILLMORE: I am so, Sir, let these inform you.—Ha, how

125   sweetly they chime! Pox of Poverty, it makes a Man a Slave, makes Wit and Honour sneak, my Soul grew lean and rusty for want of Credit.

BLUNT: 'Sheartlikins, this I like well, it looks like my lucky Bargain! Oh how I long for the Approach of my Squire,

130   that is to conduct me to her House again. Why! here's two provided for.

FREDERICK: By this light y're happy Men.

BLUNT: Fortune is pleased to smile on us, Gentlemen,—to smile on us.

(*Enter* SANCHO, *and pulls* BLUNT *by the Sleeve. They go aside.*)

135   SANCHO: Sir, my Lady expects you—she has remov'd all that might oppose your Will and Pleasure—and is impatient till you come.

BLUNT: Sir, I'll attend you—Oh the happiest Rogue! I'll take no leave, lest they either dog me, or stay me.

(*Exit with* SANCHO.)

140   BELVILE: But then the little Gipsy is forgot?

WILLMORE: A Mischief on thee for putting her into my thoughts; I had quite forgot her else, and this Night's Debauch had drunk her quite down.

HELLENA: Had it so, good Captain?

(*Claps him on the Back.*)

WILLMORE: Ha! I hope she did not hear.   145

HELLENA: What, afraid of such a Champion!

WILLMORE: Oh! you're a fine Lady of your word, are you not? to make a Man languish a whole day—

HELLENA: In tedious search of me.

WILLMORE: Egad, Child, thou'rt in the right, hadst thou seen   150 what a melancholy Dog I have been ever since I was a Lover, how I have walkt the Streets like a *Capuchin,* with my Hands in my Sleeves—Faith, Sweetheart, thou wouldst pity me.

HELLENA: Now, if I should be hang'd, I can't be angry with him, he dissembles so heartily—Alas, good Captain, what   155 pains you have taken—Now were I ungrateful not to reward so true a Servant.

WILLMORE: Poor Soul! that's kindly said, I see thou bearest a Conscience—come then for a beginning shew me thy dear Face.   160

HELLENA: I'm afraid, my small Acquaintance, you have been staying that swinging stomach you boasted of this morning; I remember then my little Collation would have gone down with you, without the Sauce of a handsom Face— Is your Stomach so quesy now?   165

WILLMORE: Faith long fasting, Child, spoils a Man's Appetite—yet if you durst treat, I could so lay about me still.

HELLENA: And would you fall to, before a Priest says Grace?

WILLMORE: Oh fie, fie, what an old out-of-fashion'd thing hast thou nam'd? Thou could'st not dash me more out of   170 Countenance, shouldst thou shew me an ugly Face.

(*Whilst he is seemingly courting* HELLENA, *enter* ANGELICA, MORETTA, BISKEY, *and* SEBASTIAN, *all in Masquerade:* ANGELICA *sees* WILLMORE *and starts.*)

ANGELICA: Heavens, is't he? and passionately fond to see another Woman?

MORETTA: What cou'd you expect less from such a Swaggerer?

ANGELICA: Expect! as much as I paid him, a Heart intire,   175 Which I had pride enough to think when e'er I gave It would have rais'd the Man above the Vulgar, Made him all Soul, and that all soft and constant.

HELLENA: You see, Captain, how willing I am to be Friends with you, till Time and Ill-luck make us Lovers; and ask   180 you the Question first, rather than put your Modesty to the blush, by asking me: for alas, I know you Captains are such strict Men, severe Observers of your Vows to Chastity, that 'twill be hard to prevail with your tender Conscience to marry a young willing Maid.   185

WILLMORE: Do not abuse me, for fear I should take thee at thy word, and marry thee indeed, which I'm sure will be Revenge sufficient.

HELLENA: O' my Conscience, that will be our Destiny, because we are both of one humour; I am as inconstant as you, for   190 I have considered, Captain, that a handsom Woman has a great deal to do whilst her Face is good, for then is our Harvest-time to gather Friends, and should I in these days of my Youth, catch a fit of foolish Constancy, I were undone; 'tis loitering by day-light in our great Journey: there-   195 fore declare, I'll allow but one year for Love, one year for Indifference, and one year for Hate—and then—go hang

200 your self—for I profess myself the gay, the kind, and the inconstant—the Devil's in't if this won't please you.

WILLMORE: Oh most damnably!—I have a Heart with a hole
quite thro it too, no Prison like mine to keep a Mistress in.

ANGELICA: (*Aside.*) Purjur'd Man! how I believe thee now!

HELLENA: Well, I see our Business as well as Humours are
alike, yours to cozen as many Maids as will trust you, and
205 I as many Men as have Faith—See if I have not as desperate a lying look, as you can have for the heart of you.

(*Pulls off her Vizard; he starts.*)

—How do you like it, Captain?

WILLMORE: Like it! by Heav'n, I never saw so much Beauty.
Oh the Charms of those sprightly black Eyes, that strangely
210 fair Face, full of Smiles and Dimples! those soft round melting cherry Lips! and small even white Teeth! not to be ex-
prest, but silently adored!—Oh one Look more, and strike
me dumb, or I shall repeat nothing else till I am mad.

(*He seems to court her to pull off her Vizard: she refuses.*)

ANGELICA: I can endure no more—nor is it fit to interrupt
215 him; for if I do, my Jealousy has so destroy'd my Reason,—I shall undo him—Therefore I'll retire. And you *Sebastian* (*To one of her bravoes.*) follow that Woman, and learn
who 'tis; (*To the other bravo.*) while you tell the Fugitive, I
would speak to him instantly.

(*Exit.*)

(*This while* FLORINDA *is talking to* BELVILE, *who stands sullenly.*
FREDERICK *courting* VALERIA.)

220 VALERIA: Prithee, dear Stranger, be not so sullen; for tho you
have lost your Love, you see my Friend frankly offers you
hers, to play with in the mean time.

BELVILE: Faith, Madam, I am sorry I can't play at her Game.

FREDERICK: Pray leave your Intercession, and mind your own
225 Affair, they'll better agree apart; he's a model Sigher in
Company, but alone no Woman escapes him.

FLORINDA: Sure he does but rally—yet if it should be true—
I'll tempt him farther—Believe me, noble Stranger, I'm no
common Mistress—and for a little proof on't—wear this
230 Jewel—nay, take it, Sir, 'tis right, and Bills of Exchange
may sometimes miscarry.

BELVILE: Madam, why am I chose out of all Mankind to be
the Object of your Bounty?

VALERIA: There's another civil Question askt.

235 FREDERICK: Pox of's Modesty, it spoils his own Markets, and
hinders mine.

FLORINDA: Sir, from my Window I have often seen you; and
Women of Quality have so few opportunities for Love,
that we ought to lose none.

240 FREDERICK: Ay, this is something! here's a Woman!—When
shall I be blest with so much kindness from your fair
Mouth? (*Aside to* BELVILE.) Take the Jewel, Fool.

BELVILE: You tempt me strangely, Madam, every way.

FLORINDA: (*Aside.*) So, if I find him false, my whole Repose
245 is gone.

BELVILE: And but for a Vow I've made to a very fine Lady, this
Goodness had subdu'd me.

FREDERICK: Pox on't be kind, in pity to me be kind, for I am
to thrive here but as you treat her Friend.

250 HELLENA: Tell me what did you in yonder House, and I'll
unmasque.

WILLMORE: Yonder House—oh—I went to—a—to—why,
there's a Friend of mine lives there.

HELLENA: What a she, or a he Friend?

255 WILLMORE: A Man upon my Honour! a Man—A she Friend!
no, no, Madam, you have done my Business, I thank you.

HELLENA: And was't your Man Friend, that had more Darts
in's Eyes than *Cupid* carries in a whole Budget of Arrows?

WILLMORE: So—

260 HELLENA: Ah such a *Bona Roba:* to be in her Arms is lying in
Fresco, all perfumed Air about me—Was this your Man
Friend too?

WILLMORE: So—

HELLENA: That gave you the He, and the She—Gold, that
265 begets young Pleasures.

WILLMORE: Well, well, Madam, then you see there are Ladies
in the World, that will not be cruel—there are, Madam,
there are—

HELLENA: And there be Men too as fine, wild, inconstant Fel-
270 lows as your self, there be, Captain, there be, if you go to
that now—therefore I'm resolv'd—

WILLMORE: Oh!

HELLENA: To see your Face no more—

WILLMORE: Oh!

275 HELLENA: Till to morrow.

WILLMORE: Egad you frighted me.

HELLENA: Nor then neither, unless you'l swear never to see
that Lady more.

WILLMORE: See her!—why! never to think of Womankind
280 again?

HELLENA: Kneel, and swear.

(*Kneels, she gives him her Hand.*)

WILLMORE: I do, never to think—to see—to love—nor lie
with any but thy self.

HELLENA: Kiss the Book.

WILLMORE: Oh, most religiously.   285

(*Kisses her Hand.*)

HELLENA: Now what a wicked Creature am I, to damn a
proper Fellow.

CALLIS: (*To* FLORINDA.) Madam, I'll stay no longer, 'tis e'en dark.

FLORINDA: However, Sir, I'll leave this with you—that when
I'm gone, you may repent the opportunity you have lost   290
by your modesty.

(*Gives him the Jewel, which is her Picture, and Exits. He gazes after her.*)

WILLMORE: 'Twill be an Age till to morrow,—and till then I
will most impatiently expect you—Adieu, my dear pretty
Angel.

(*Exeunt all the* WOMEN.)

BELVILE: Ha! *Florinda*'s Picture! 'twas she her self—what a dull   295
Dog was I? I would have given the World for one minute's
discourse with her.—

FREDERICK: This comes of your Modesty,—ah pox on your
Vow, 'twas ten to one but we had lost the Jewel by't.

300 BELVILE: *Willmore!* the blessed'st Opportunity lost!—*Florinda,* Friends, *Florinda!*

WILLMORE: Ah Rogue! such black Eyes, such a Face, such a Mouth, such Teeth,—and so much Wit!

BELVILE: All, all, and a thousand Charms besides.

305 WILLMORE: Why, dost thou know her?

BELVILE: Know her! ay, ay, and a Pox take me with all my Heart for being modest.

WILLMORE: But hark ye, Friend of mine, are you my Rival? and have I been only beating the Bush all this while?

310 BELVILE: I understand thee not—I'm mad—see here—

(*Shews the Picture.*)

WILLMORE: Ha! whose Picture is this?—'tis a fine Wench.

FREDERICK: The Colonel's Mistress, Sir.

WILLMORE: Oh, oh, here—I thought it had been another Prize—come, come, a Bottle will set thee right again.

(*Gives the Picture back.*)

315 BELVILE: I am content to try, and by that time 'twill be late enough for our Design.

WILLMORE: Agreed.

> *Love does all day the Soul's great Empire keep,*
> *But Wine at night lulls the soft God asleep.*

(*Exeunt.*)

SCENE II

LUCETTA's *House.*

Enter BLUNT *and* LUCETTA *with a Light.*

LUCETTA: Now we are safe and free, no fears of the coming home of my old jealous Husband, which made me a little thoughtful when you came in first—but now Love is all the business of my Soul.

5 BLUNT: (*Aside.*) I am transported—Pox on't, that I had but some fine things to say to her, such as Lovers use—I was a Fool not to learn of *Frederick* a little by Heart before I came—something I must say.—'Sheartlikins, sweet Soul, I am not us'd to complement, but I'm an honest Gentle-

10 man, and thy humble Servant.

LUCETTA: I have nothing to pay for so great a Favour, but such a Love as cannot but be great, since at first sight of that sweet Face and Shape it made me your absolute Captive.

BLUNT: (*Aside.*) Kind heart, how prettily she talks! Egad I'll

15 show her Husband a *Spanish* Trick; send him out of the World, and marry her: she's damnably in love with me, and will ne'er mind Settlements, and so there's that sav'd.

LUCETTA: Well, Sir, I'll go and undress me, and be with you instantly.

20 BLUNT: Make haste then, for 'dsheartlikins, dear Soul, thou canst not guess at the pain of a longing Lover, when his Joys are drawn within the compass of a few minutes.

LUCETTA: You speak my Sense, and I'll make haste to provide it.

(*Exit.*)

BLUNT: 'Tis a rare Girl, and this one night's enjoyment with 25 her will be worth all the days I ever past in Essex.—Would she'd go with me into *England,* tho to say truth, there's plenty of Whores there already.—But a pox on 'em they are such mercenary prodigal Whores, that they want such a one as this, that's free and generous, to give 'em good Ex- 30 amples:—Why, what a House she has! how rich and fine!

(*Enter* SANCHO.)

SANCHO: Sir, my Lady has sent me to conduct you to her Chamber.

BLUNT: Sir, I shall be proud to follow—Here's one of her Ser- vants too: 'dsheartlikins, by his Garb and Gravity he might 35 be a Justice of Peace in *Essex,* and is but a Pimp here.

(*Exeunt.*)

(*The Scene changes to a Chamber with an Alcove-Bed in it, a Table, &c.* LUCETTA *in Bed. Enter* SANCHO *and* BLUNT, *who takes the Candle of* SANCHO *at the Door.*)

SANCHO: Sir, my Commission reaches no farther.

BLUNT: Sir, I'll excuse your Complement:—what, in Bed, my sweet Mistress?

LUCETTA: You see, I still out-do you in kindness. 40

BLUNT: And thou shalt see what haste I'll make to quit scores—oh the luckiest Rogue!

(*Undresses himself.*)

LUCETTA: Shou'd you be false or cruel now!

BLUNT: False, 'Sheartlikins, what dost thou take me for a *Jew?* an insensible Heathen,—A Pox of thy old jealous Hus- 45 band: and he were dead, egad, sweet Soul, it shou'd be none of my fault, if I did not marry thee.

LUCETTA: It never shou'd be mine.

BLUNT: Good Soul, I'm the fortunatest Dog!

LUCETTA: Are you not undrest yet? 50

BLUNT: As much as my Impatience will permit.

(*Goes towards the Bed in his Shirt and Drawers.*)

LUCETTA: Hold, Sir, put out the Light, it may betray us else.

BLUNT: Any thing, I need no other Light but that of thine Eyes!—(*Aside.*) 'sheartlikins, there I think I had it.

(*Puts out the Candle, the Bed descends, he gropes about to find it.*)

—Why—why—where am I got? what, not yet?—where 55 are your sweetest?—ah, the Rogue's silent now—a pretty Love-trick this—how she'll laugh at me anon!—you need not, my dear Rogue! you need not! I'm all on a fire al- ready—come, come, now call me in for pity—Sure I'm enchanted! I have been round the Chamber, and can find 60 neither Woman, nor Bed—I lockt the Door, I'm sure she cannot go that way; or if she cou'd, the Bed cou'd not— Enough, enough, my pretty Wanton, do not carry the Jest too far—Ha, betray'd! Dogs! Rogues! Pimps! help! help!

(*Lights on a Trap, and is let down. Enter* LUCETTA, PHILIPPO, *and* SANCHO *with a Light.*)

65 PHILIPPO: Ha, ha, ha, he's dispatcht finely.

LUCETTA: Now, Sir, had I been coy, we had mist of this Booty.

PHILIPPO: Nay when I saw 'twas a substantial Fool, I was mollified; but when you doat upon a Serenading Coxcomb, upon a Face, fine Clothes, and a Lute, it makes me rage.

70 LUCETTA: You know I never was guilty of that Folly, my dear *Philippo*, but with your self—But come let's see what we have got by this.

PHILIPPO: A rich Coat!—Sword and Hat!—these Breeches too—are well lin'd!—see here a Gold Watch!—a Purse—

75 ha! Gold!—at least two hundred Pistoles! a bunch of Diamond Rings; and one with the Family Arms!—a Gold Box!—with a Medal of his King! and his Lady Mother's Picture!—these were sacred Reliques, believe me!—see, the Wasteband of his Breeches have a Mine of Gold!—

80 Old Queen *Bess's*. We have a Quarrel to her ever since Eighty Eight, and may therefore justify the Theft, the Inquisition might have committed it.

LUCETTA: See, a Bracelet of bow'd Gold, these his Sister ty'd about his Arm at parting—but well—for all this, I fear his

85 being a Stranger may make a noise, and hinder our Trade with them hereafter.

PHILIPPO: That's our security; he is not only a Stranger to us, but to the Country too—the Common-Shore into which he is descended, thou know'st, conducts him into another

90 Street, which this Light will hinder him from ever finding again—he knows neither your Name, nor the Street where your House is, nay, nor the way to his own Lodgings.

LUCETTA: And art not thou an unmerciful Rogue, not to afford him one Night for all this?—I should not have been

95 such a *Jew*.

PHILIPPO: Blame me not, *Lucetta*, to keep as much of thee as I can to my self—come, that thought makes me wanton,—let's to Bed,—*Sancho*, lock up these.

This is the Fleece which Fools do bear,
100 *Design'd for witty Men to sheer.*

(*Exeunt.*)

(*The Scene changes, and discovers* BLUNT, *creeping out of a Common Shore, his Face, &c., all dirty.*)

BLUNT: Oh Lord!

(*Climbing up.*)

I am got out at last, and (which is a Miracle) without a Clue—and now to Damning and Cursing—but if that would ease me, where shall I begin? with my Fortune, my

105 self, or the Quean that cozen'd me—What a dog was I to believe in Women! Oh Coxcomb—ignorant conceited Coxcomb! to fancy she cou'd be enamour'd with my Person, at the first sight enamour'd—Oh, I'm a cursed Puppy, 'tis plain, Fool was writ upon my Forehead, she perceiv'd it,—saw the

110 *Essex* Calf there—for what Allurements could there be in this Countenance? which I can indure, because I'm acquainted with it—Oh, dull silly Dog! to be thus sooth'd into a Cozening! Had I been drunk, I might fondly have credited

the young Quean! but as I was in my right Wits, to be thus cheated, confirms I am a dull believing *English* Country 115 Fop.—But my Comrades! Death and the Devil, there's the worst of all—then a Ballad will be sung to Morrow on the *Prado,* to a lousy Tune of the enchanted Squire, and the annihilated Damsel—But *Frederick* that Rogue, and the Colonel, will abuse me beyond all Christian patience—had she left 120 me my Clothes, I have a Bill of Exchange at home wou'd have sav'd my Credit—but now all hope is taken from me— Well, I'll home (if I can find the way) with this Consolation, that I am not the first kind believing Coxcomb; but there are, Gallants, many such good Natures amongst ye. 125

And tho you've better Arts to hide your Follies,
Adsheartlikins y'are all as errant Cullies.

SCENE III

The Garden, in the Night.

Enter FLORINDA, *undress'd, with a Key, and a little Box.*

FLORINDA: Well, thus far I'm in my way to Happiness; I have got my self free from *Callis*; my Brother too, I find by yonder light, is gone into his Cabinet, and thinks not of me: I have by good Fortune got the Key of the Garden Back-door,— I'll open it, to prevent *Belvile*'s knocking,—a little noise will 5 now alarm my Brother. Now am I as fearful as a young Thief. (*Unlocks the Door.*)—Hark,—what noise is that?— Oh, 'twas the Wind that plaid amongst the Boughs.—*Belvile* stays long, methinks—it's time—stay—for fear of a surprize, I'll hide these Jewels in yonder Jessamin. 10

(*She goes to lay down the Box.*)

(*Enter* WILLMORE *drunk.*)

WILLMORE: What the Devil is become of these Fellows, *Belvile* and *Frederick?* They promis'd to stay at the next corner for me, but who the Devil knows the corner of a full Moon?— Now—whereabouts am I?—hah—what have we here? a Garden!—a very convenient place to sleep in—hah—what 15 has God sent us here?—a Female—by this light, a Woman; I'm a Dog if it be not a very Wench.—

FLORINDA: He's come!—hah—who's there?

WILLMORE: Sweet Soul, let me salute thy Shoe-string.

FLORINDA: 'Tis not my *Belvile*—good Heavens, I know him 20 not.—Who are you, and from whence come you!

WILLMORE: Prithee—prithee, Child—not so many hard Questions—let it suffice I am here, Child—Come, come kiss me.

FLORINDA: Good Gods! what luck is mine?

WILLMORE: Only good luck, Child, parlous good luck.—Come 25 hither,—'tis a delicate shining Wench,—by this Hand she's perfum'd, and smells like any Nosegay.—Prithee, dear Soul, let's not play the Fool, and lose time,—precious time—for as Gad shall save me, I'm as honest a Fellow as breathes, tho I am a little disguis'd at present.—Come, I say,—why, thou may'st 30 be free with me, I'll be very secret. I'll not boast who 'twas oblig'd me, not I—for hang me if I know thy Name.

---

83 **bow'd Gold** *bowed* is still used in the North of England for bent: 'a bowed pin'

30 **disguis'd** a common phrase for drunk

FLORINDA: Heavens! what a filthy beast is this!

WILLMORE: I am so, and thou oughtst the sooner to lie with
35   me for that reason,—for look you, Child, there will be no
Sin in't, because 'twas neither design'd nor premeditated;
'tis pure Accident on both sides—that's a certain thing
now—Indeed should I make love to you, and you vow Fidelity—and swear and lye till you believ'd and yielded—
40   Thou art therefore (as thou art a good Christian) oblig'd
in Conscience to deny me nothing. Now—come, be
kind, without any more idle prating.

FLORINDA: Oh, I am ruin'd—wicked Man, unhand me.

WILLMORE: Wicked! Egad, Child, a Judge, were he young and
45   vigorous, and saw those Eyes of thine, would know 'twas
they gave the first blow—the first provocation,—Come,
prithee let's lose no time, I say—this is a fine convenient
place.

FLORINDA: Sir, let me go, I conjure you, or I'll call out.

50 WILLMORE: Ay, ay, you were best to call Witness to see how
finely you treat me—do.—

FLORINDA: I'll cry Murder, Rape, or any thing, if you do not
instantly let me go.

WILLMORE: A Rape! Come, come, you lye, you Baggage, you
55   lye: What, I'll warrant you would fain have the World believe now that you are not so forward as I. No, not you,—
why at this time of Night was your Cobweb-door set
open, dear Spider—but to catch Flies?—Hah come—or I
shall be damnably angry.—Why what a Coil is here.—

60 FLORINDA: Sir, can you think—

WILLMORE: That you'd do it for nothing? oh, oh, I find what
you'd be at—look here, here's a Pistole for you—here's a
work indeed—here—take it, I say.—

FLORINDA: For Heaven's sake, Sir, as you're a Gentleman—

65 WILLMORE: So—now—she would be wheedling me for
more—what, you will not take it then—you're resolv'd
you will not.—Come, come, take it, or I'll put it up again;
for, look ye, I never give more.—Why, how now, Mistress,
are you so high i'th' Mouth, a Pistole won't down with
70   you?—hah—why, what a work's here—in good time—
come, no struggling, be gone—But an y'are good at a
dumb Wrestle, I'm for ye,—look ye,—I'm for ye.—

(*She struggles with him.*)

(*Enter* BELVILE *and* FREDERICK.)

BELVILE: The Door is open, a Pox of this mad Fellow, I'm angry
that we've lost him, I durst have sworn he had follow'd us.

75 FREDERICK: But you were so hasty, Colonel, to be gone.

FLORINDA: Help, help,—Murder!—help—oh, I'm ruin'd.

BELVILE: Ha, sure that's *Florinda*'s Voice.

(*Comes up to them.*)

—A Man! Villain, let go that Lady.

(*A noise.*)

(WILLMORE *turns and draws*, FREDERICK *interposes*.)

FLORINDA: *Belvile*! Heavens! my Brother too is coming, and
80   'twill be impossible to escape.—*Belvile*, I conjure you to
walk under my Chamber-window, from whence I'll give

you some instructions what to do—This rude Man has
undone us.

(*Exit.*)

WILLMORE: *Belvile!*

(*Enter* PEDRO, STEPHANO, *and other Servants with Lights.*)

PEDRO: I'm betray'd; run, *Stephano*, and see if *Florinda* be safe. 85

(*Exit* STEPHANO.)

So who'er they be, all is not well, I'll to *Florinda*'s Chamber.

(*They fight, and* PEDRO'S *Party beats 'em out; going out, meets*
STEPHANO.)

STEPHANO: You need not, Sir, the poor Lady's fast asleep, and
thinks no harm: I wou'd not wake her, Sir, for fear of
frightning her with your danger.

PEDRO: I'm glad she's there—Rascals, how came the Garden- 90
Door open?

STEPHANO: That Question comes too late, Sir: some of my
Fellow-Servants Masquerading I'll warrant.

PEDRO: Masquerading! a leud Custom to debauch our
Youth—there's something more in this than I imagine. 95

(*Exeunt.*)

SCENE IV

Changes to the Street.

Enter BELVILE *in Rage*, FREDERICK *holding him, and* WILLMORE
melancholy.

WILLMORE: Why, how the Devil shou'd I know *Florinda*?

BELVILE: Ah plague of your ignorance! if it had not been
Florinda, must you be a Beast?—a Brute, a senseless
Swine?

WILLMORE: Well, Sir, you see I am endu'd with Patience—I 5
can bear—tho egad y're very free with me methinks,—I
was in good hopes the Quarrel wou'd have been on my
side, for so uncivilly interrupting me.

BELVILE: Peace, Brute, whilst thou'rt safe—oh, I'm distracted.

WILLMORE: Nay, nay, I'm an unlucky Dog, that's certain. 10

BELVILE: Ah curse upon the Star that rul'd my Birth! or whatsoever other Influence that makes me still so wretched.

WILLMORE: Thou break'st my Heart with these Complaints;
there is no Star in fault, no Influence but Sack, the cursed
Sack I drank. 15

FREDERICK: Why, how the Devil came you so drunk?

WILLMORE: Why, how the Devil came you so sober?

BELVILE: A curse upon his thin Skull, he was always beforehand that way.

FREDERICK: Prithee, dear Colonel, forgive him, he's sorry for 20
his fault.

BELVILE: He's always so after he has done a mischief—a
plague on all such Brutes.

WILLMORE: By this Light I took her for an errant Harlot.

BELVILE: Damn your debaucht Opinion: tell me, Sot, hadst thou 25
so much sense and light about thee to distinguish her to be

a Woman, and could'st not see something about her Face
and Person, to strike an awful Reverence into thy Soul?

30 WILLMORE: Faith no, I consider'd her as mere a Woman as I
could wish.

BELVILE: 'Sdeath I have no patience—draw, or I'll kill you.

WILLMORE: Let that alone till to morrow, and if I set not all
right again, use your Pleasure.

BELVILE: To morrow, damn it.

35 The spiteful Light will lead me to no happiness.
To morrow is *Antonio*'s, and perhaps
Guides him to my undoing;—oh that I could meet
This Rival, this powerful Fortunate.

WILLMORE: What then?

40 BELVILE: Let thy own Reason, or my Rage instruct thee.

WILLMORE: I shall be finely inform'd then, no doubt; hear
me, Colonel—hear me—shew me the Man and I'll do his
Business.

BELVILE: I know him no more than thou, or if I did, I should

45 not need thy aid.

WILLMORE: This you say is *Angelica*'s House, I promis'd the
kind Baggage to lie with her to Night.

(*Offers to go in.*)

(*Enter* ANTONIO *and his Page.* ANTONIO *knocks on the Hilt of his
Sword.*)

ANTONIO: You paid the thousand Crowns I directed?

PAGE: To the Lady's old Woman, Sir, I did.

50 WILLMORE: Who the Devil have we here?

BELVILE: I'll now plant my self under *Florinda*'s Window, and
if I find no comfort there, I'll die.

(*Exit* BELVILE *and* FREDERICK. *Enter* MORETTA.)

MORETTA: Page!

PAGE: Here's my Lord.

55 WILLMORE: How is this, a Piccaroon going to board my
Frigate! here's one Chase-Gun for you.

(*Drawing his Sword, justles* ANTONIO *who turns and draws. They
fight,* ANTONIO *falls.*)

MORETTA: Oh, bless us, we are all undone!

(*Runs in, and shuts the Door.*)

PAGE: Help, Murder!

(BELVILE *returns at the noise of fighting.*)

BELVILE: Ha, the mad Rogue's engag'd in some unlucky Ad-

60 venture again.

(*Enter two or three* MASQUERADERS.)

MASQUERADER: Ha, a Man kill'd!

WILLMORE: How! a Man kill'd! then I'll go home to sleep.

(*Puts up, and reels out. Exeunt* MASQUERADERS *another way.*)

BELVILE: Who shou'd it be! pray Heaven the Rogue is safe, for
all my Quarrel to him.

(*As* BELVILE *is groping about, enter an* OFFICER *and six* SOL-
DIERS.)

SOLDIER: Who's there?   65

OFFICER: So, here's one dispatcht—secure the Murderer.

BELVILE: Do not mistake my Charity for Murder: I came to
his Assistance.

(SOLDIERS *sieze on* BELVILE.)

OFFICER: That shall be tried, Sir.—St. *Jago,* Swords drawn in
the Carnival time!   70

(*Goes to* ANTONIO.)

ANTONIO: Thy Hand prithee.

OFFICER: Ha, Don *Antonio*! look well to the Villain there.—
How is't, Sir?

ANTONIO: I'm hurt.

BELVILE: Has my Humanity made me a Criminal?   75

OFFICER: Away with him.

BELVILE: What a curst Chance is this!

(*Exeunt* SOLDIERS *with* BELVILE.)

ANTONIO: (*To the* OFFICER.) This is the Man that has set upon
me twice—carry him to my Apartment till you have fur-
ther Orders from me.   80

(*Exit.* ANTONIO *led.*)

ACT FOUR

SCENE I

A fine Room.

Discovers BELVILE, *as by Dark alone.*

BELVILE: When shall I be weary of railing on Fortune, who is
resolv'd never to turn with Smiles upon me?—Two such
Defeats in one Night—none but the Devil and that mad
Rogue could have contriv'd to have plagued me with—I
am here a Prisoner—but where?—Heaven knows—and if   5
there be Murder done, I can soon decide the Fate of a
Stranger in a Nation without Mercy—Yet this is nothing
to the Torture my Soul bows with, when I think of losing
my fair, my dear *Florinda*.—Hark—my Door opens—a
Light—a Man—and seems of Quality—arm'd too.—   10
Now shall I die like a Dog without defence.

(*Enter* ANTONIO *in a Night-Gown, with a Light; his Arm in a
Scarf, and a Sword under his Arm: He sets the Candle on the Table.*)

ANTONIO: Sir, I come to know what Injuries I have done
you, that could provoke you to so mean an Action, as to
attack me basely, without allowing time for my Defence.

BELVILE: Sir, for a Man in my Circumstances to plead Inno-   15
cence, would look like Fear—but view me well, and you
will find no marks of a Coward on me, nor any thing that
betrays that Brutality you accuse me of.

ANTONIO: In vain, Sir, you impose upon my Sense,
You are not only he who drew on me last Night,   20

But yesterday before the same House, that of *Angelica*.
Yet there is something in your Face and Mein—

BELVILE: I own I fought to day in the defence of a Friend of
mine, with whom you (if you're the same) and your
25   Party were first engag'd.
Perhaps you think this Crime enough to kill me,
But if you do, I cannot fear you'll do it basely.

ANTONIO: No, Sir, I'll make you fit for a Defence with this.

(*Gives him the Sword.*)

BELVILE: This Gallantry surprizes me—nor know I how to
30   use this Present, Sir, against a Man so brave.

ANTONIO: You shall not need;
For know, I come to snatch you from a Danger
That is decreed against you;
Perhaps your Life, or long Imprisonment:
35   And 'twas with so much Courage you offended,
I cannot see you punisht.

BELVILE: How shall I pay this Generosity?

ANTONIO: It had been safer to have kill'd another,
Than have attempted me:
40   To shew your Danger, Sir, I'll let you know my Quality;
And 'tis the Vice-Roy's Son whom you have wounded.

BELVILE: (*Aside.*) The Vice-Roy's Son!
Death and Confusion! was this Plague reserved
To compleat all the rest?—oblig'd by him!
45   The Man of all the World I would destroy.

ANTONIO: You seem disorder'd, Sir.

BELVILE: Yes, trust me, Sir, I am, and 'tis with pain
That Man receives such Bounties,
Who wants the pow'r to pay 'em back again.

50 ANTONIO: To gallant Spirits 'tis indeed uneasy;
—But you may quickly over-pay me, Sir.

BELVILE: Then I am well—(*Aside.*) kind Heaven! but set us
even,
That I may fight with him, and keep my Honour safe.
—Oh, I'm impatient, Sir, to be discounting
55   The mighty Debt I owe you; command me quickly—

ANTONIO: I have a Quarrel with a Rival, Sir,
About the Maid we love.

BELVILE: (*Aside.*) Death, 'tis *Florinda* he means—
That Thought destroys my Reason, and I shall kill him—

60 ANTONIO: My Rival, Sir,
Is one has all the Virtues Man can boast of.

BELVILE: Death! who shou'd this be?

ANTONIO: He challeng'd me to meet him on the *Molo*,
As soon as Day appear'd; but last Night's quarrel
65   Has made my Arm unfit to guide a Sword.

BELVILE: I apprehend you, Sir, you'd have me kill the Man
That lays a claim to the Maid you speak of.
—I'll do't—I'll fly to do it.

ANTONIO: Sir, do you know her?

70 BELVILE: —No, Sir, but 'tis enough she is admired by you.

ANTONIO: Sir, I shall rob you of the Glory on't,
For you must fight under my Name and Dress.

BELVILE: That Opinion must be strangely obliging that makes
You think I can personate the brave *Antonio*,
75   Whom I can but strive to imitate.

ANTONIO: You say too much to my Advantage.

Come, Sir, the Day appears that calls you forth.
Within, Sir, is the Habit.

(*Exit* ANTONIO.)

BELVILE: Fantastick Fortune, thou deceitful Light,
That cheats the wearied Traveller by Night,   80
Tho on a Precipice each step you tread,
I am resolv'd to follow where you lead.

(*Exit.*)

SCENE II

The Molo.

Enter FLORINDA *and* CALLIS *in Masques, with* STEPHANO.

FLORINDA: (*Aside.*) I'm dying with my fears; *Belvile*'s not coming,
As I expected, underneath my Window,
Makes me believe that all those Fears are true.
—Canst thou not tell with whom my Brother fights?

STEPHANO: No, Madam, they were both in Masquerade, I was   5
by when they challeng'd one another, and they had decided the Quarrel then, but were prevented by some Cavaliers; which made 'em put it off till now—but I am sure
'tis about you they fight.

FLORINDA: (*Aside.*) Nay then 'tis with *Belvile*, for what other   10
Lover have I that dares fight for me, except *Antonio*? and
he is too much in favour with my Brother—If it be he, for
whom shall I direct my Prayers to Heaven?

STEPHANO: Madam, I must leave you; for if my Master see me,
I shall be hang'd for being your Conductor.—I escap'd nar-   15
rowly for the Excuse I made for you last night i'th' Garden.

FLORINDA: And I'll reward thee for't—prithee no more.

(*Exit* STEPHANO.)

(*Enter Don* PEDRO *in his Masquing Habit.*)

PEDRO: *Antonio*'s late to day, the place will fill, and we may be
prevented.

(*Walks about.*)

FLORINDA: (*Aside.*) Antonio! sure I heard amiss.   20

PEDRO: But who would not excuse a happy Lover.
When soft fair Arms comfine the yielding Neck;
And the kind Whisper languishingly breathes,
Must you be gone so soon?
Sure I had dwelt for ever on her Bosom.   25
—But stay, he's here.

(*Enter* BELVILE *drest in* ANTONIO's *Clothes.*)

FLORINDA: 'Tis not *Belvile,* half my Fears are vanisht.

PEDRO: *Antonio*!—

BELVILE: (*Aside.*) This must be he.
You're early, Sir,—I do not use to be out-done this way.   30

PEDRO: The Wretched, Sir, are watchful, and 'tis enough
You have the advantage of me in *Angelica*.

BELVILE: (*Aside.*) Angelica!
Or I've mistook my Man! Or else *Antonio,*

35   Can he forget his Interest in *Florinda*,
    And fight for common Prize?
PEDRO: Come, Sir, you know our terms—
BELVILE: (*Aside.*) Be Heaven, not I.
    —No talking, I am ready, Sir.

(*Offers to fight.* FLORINDA *runs in.*)

40   FLORINDA: (*To* BELVILE.) Oh, hold! who'er you be, I do con-
    jure you hold. If you strike here—I die—
PEDRO: *Florinda!*
BELVILE: *Florinda* imploring for my Rival!
PEDRO: Away, this Kindness is unseasonable.

(*Puts her by, they fight; she runs in just as* BELVILE *disarms* PEDRO.)

45   FLORINDA: Who are you, Sir, that dare deny my Prayers?
BELVILE: Thy Prayers destroy him; if thou wouldst preserve him.
    Do that thou'rt unacquainted with, and curse him.

(*She holds him.*)

FLORINDA: By all you hold most dear, by her you love,
    I do conjure you, touch him not.
50   BELVILE: By her I love!
    See—I obey—and at your Feet resign
    The useless Trophy of my Victory.

(*Lays his sword at her Feet.*)

PEDRO: *Antonio,* you've done enough to prove you love *Florinda.*
BELVILE: Love *Florinda!*
55   Does Heaven love Adoration, Pray'r, or Penitence?
    Love her! here Sir,—your Sword again.

(*Snatches up the Sword, and gives it him.*)

    Upon this Truth I'll fight my Life away.
PEDRO: No, you've redeem'd my Sister, and my Friendship.
BELVILE: Don *Pedro!*

(*He gives him* FLORINDA *and pulls off his Vizard to shew his Face,
and puts it on again.*)

60   PEDRO: Can you resign your Claims to other Women,
    And give your Heart intirely to *Florinda?*
BELVILE: Intire, as dying Saints Confessions are.
    I can delay my happiness no longer.
    This minute let me make *Florinda* mine:
65   PEDRO: This minute let it be—no time so proper,
    This Night my Father will arrive from *Rome,*
    And possibly may hinder what we propose.
FLORINDA: Oh Heavens! this Minute!

(*Enter* MASQUERADERS, *and pass over.*)

BELVILE: Oh, do not ruin me!
70   PEDRO: The place begins to fill; and that we may not be ob-
    serv'd, do you walk off to St. *Peter's* Church, where I will
    meet you, and conclude your Happiness.
BELVILE: I'll meet you there—(*Aside.*) if there be no more
    Saints Churches in *Naples.*

FLORINDA: Oh stay, Sir, and recall your hasty Doom: 75
    Alas I have not yet prepar'd my Heart
    To entertain so strange a Guest.
PEDRO: Away, this silly Modesty is assum'd too late.
BELVILE: Heaven, Madam! what do you do?
FLORINDA: Do! despise the Man that lays a Tyrant's Claim   80
    To what he ought to conquer by Submission.
BELVILE: You do not know me—move a little this way.

(*Draws her aside.*)

FLORINDA: Yes, you may even force me to the Altar,
    But not the holy Man that offers there
    Shall force me to be thine.   85

(PEDRO *talks to* CALLIS *this while.*)

BELVILE: Oh do not lose so blest an opportunity!
    See—'tis your *Belvile*—not *Antonio,*
    Whom your mistaken Scorn and Anger ruins.

(*Pulls off his Vizard.*)

FLORINDA: *Belvile!*
    Where was my Soul it cou'd not meet thy Voice,   90
    And take this knowledge in?

(*As they are talking, enter* WILLMORE *finely drest, and* FREDERICK.)

WILLMORE: No Intelligence! no News of *Belvile* yet—well I am
    the most unlucky Rascal in Nature—ha!—am I deceiv'd
    or is it he—look, *Frederick*—'tis he—my dear *Belvile.*

(*Runs and embraces him.* BELVILE'S *Vizard falls out on's Hand.*)

BELVILE: Hell and Confusion seize thee!   95
PEDRO: Ha! *Belvile!* I beg your Pardon, Sir.

(*Takes* FLORINDA *from him.*)

BELVILE: Nay, touch her not, she's mine by Conquest, Sir.
    I won her by my Sword.
WILLMORE: Did'st thou so—and egad, Child, we'll keep her
    by the Sword.   100

(*Draws on* PEDRO, BELVILE *goes between.*)

BELVILE: Stand off.
    Thou'rt so profanely leud, so curst by Heaven,
    All Quarrels thou espousest must be fatal.
WILLMORE: Nay, an you be so hot, my Valour's coy,
    And shall be courted when you want it next.   105

(*Puts up his Sword.*)

BELVILE: You know I ought to claim a Victor's Right,

(*To* PEDRO.)

    But you're the Brother to divine *Florinda,*
    To whom I'm such a Slave—to purchase her,
    I durst not hurt the Man she holds so dear.
PEDRO: 'Twas by *Antonio's,* not by *Belvile's* Sword,   110
    This Question should have been decided, Sir:

I must confess much to your Bravery's due,
Both now, and when I met you last in Arms.
But I am nicely punctual in my word,
115   As Men of Honour ought, and beg your Pardon.

(*Aside to* FLORINDA *as they are going out.*)

—For this Mistake another Time shall clear.
—This was some Plot between you and *Belvile*:
But I'll prevent you.

(BELVILE *looks after her, and begins to walk up and down in a Rage.*)

WILLMORE: Do not be modest now, and lose the Woman; but
120   if we shall fetch her back, so—
BELVILE: Do not speak to me.
WILLMORE: Not speak to you!—Egad, I'll speak to you, and
will be answered too.
BELVILE: Will you, Sir?
125 WILLMORE: I know I've done some mischief, but I'm so dull
a Puppy, that I am the Son of a Whore, if I know how, or
where—prithee inform my Understanding.—
BELVILE: Leave me I say, and leave me instantly.
WILLMORE: I will not leave you in this humour, nor till I
130   know my Crime.
BELVILE: Death, I'll tell you, Sir—

(*Draws and runs at* WILLMORE; *he runs out;* BELVILE *after him,* FREDERICK *interposes.*)

(*Enter* ANGELICA, MORETTA, *and* SEBASTIAN.)

ANGELICA: Ha—*Sebastian*—Is not that *Willmore?* haste, haste,
and bring him back.
FREDERICK: The Colonel's mad—I never saw him thus be-
135   fore; I'll after 'em, lest he do some mischief, for I am sure
Willmore will not draw on him.

(*Exit.*)

ANGELICA: I am all Rage! my first desires defeated
For one, for ought he knows, that has no
Other Merit than her Quality,—
140   Her being Don *Pedro's* Sister—He loves her:
I know 'tis so—dull, dull, insensible—
He will not see me now tho oft invited;
And broke his Word last night—false perjur'd Man!
—He that but yesterday fought for my Favours,
145   And would have made his Life a Sacrifice
To've gain'd one Night with me,
Must now be hired and courted to my Arms.
MORETTA: I told you what wou'd come on't, but *Moretta's* an
old doating Fool—Why did you give him five hundred
150   Crowns, but to set himself out for other Lovers? You
shou'd have kept him poor, if you had meant to have had
any good from him.
ANGELICA: Oh, name not such mean Trifles.—Had I given him all
My Youth has earn'd from Sin,
155   I had not lost a Thought nor Sigh upon't.
But I have given him my eternal Rest,
My whole Repose, my future Joys, my Heart;
My Virgin Heart. *Moretta!* oh 'tis gone!

MORETTA: Curse on him, here he comes;
How fine she has made him too!   160

(*Enter* WILLMORE *and* SEBASTIAN. ANGELICA *turns and walks away.*)

WILLMORE: How now, turn'd Shadow?
Fly when I pursue, and follow when I fly!

(*Sings.*)

Stay gentle Shadow of my Dove,
And tell me e'er I go,
Whether the Substance may not prove   165
A fleeting Thing like you.

There's a soft kind Look remaining yet.

(*As she turns she looks on him.*)

ANGELICA: Well, Sir, you may be gay; all Happiness, all Joys
pursue you still, Fortune's your Slave, and gives you every
hour choice of new Hearts and Beauties, till you are cloy'd 170
with the repeated Bliss, which others vainly languish
for—But know, false Man, that I shall be reveng'd.

(*Turns away in a Rage.*)

WILLMORE: So, 'gad, there are of those faint-hearted Lovers,
whom such a sharp Lesson next their Hearts would make
as impotent as Fourscore—pox o' this whining—my   175
Bus'ness is to laugh and love—a pox on't; I hate your
sullen Lover, a Man shall lose as much time to put you in
Humour now, as would serve to gain a new Woman.
ANGELICA: I scorn to cool that Fire I cannot raise,
Or do the Drudgery of your virtuous Mistress.   180
WILLMORE: A virtuous Mistress! Death, what a thing thou
hast found out for me! why what the Devil should I do
with a virtuous Woman?—a fort of ill'natur'd Creatures,
that take a Pride to torment a Lover. Virtue is but an In-
firmity in Women, a Disease that renders even the hand- 185
som ungrateful; whilst the ill-favour'd, for want of
Sollicitations and Address, only fancy themselves so.—I
have lain with a Woman of Quality, who has all the while
been railing at Whores.
ANGELICA: I will not answer for your Mistress's Virtue,   190
Tho she be young enough to know no Guilt:
And I could wish you would persuade my Heart,
'Twas the two hundred thousand Crowns you courted.
WILLMORE: Two hundred thousand Crowns! what Story's
this?—what Trick?—what Woman?—ha.   195
ANGELICA: How strange you make it! have you forgot the
Creature you entertain'd on the Piazza last night?
WILLMORE: Ha, my Gipsy worth two hundred thousand
Crowns!—oh how I long to be with her—pox, I knew
she was of Quality.   200
ANGELICA: False Man, I see my Ruin in thy Face.
How many vows you breath'd upon my Bosom,
Never to be unjust—have you forgot so soon?
WILLMORE: Faith no, I was just coming to repeat 'em—but
here's a Humour indeed would make a Man a Saint— 205
(*Aside.*) Wou'd she'd be angry enough to leave me, and
command me not to wait on her.

(*Enter* HELLENA, *drest in Man's Clothes.*)

HELLENA: This must be *Angelica,* I know it by her mumping
    Matron here—Ay, ay, 'tis she: my mad Captain's with her
210   too, for all his swearing—how this unconstant Humour
    makes me love him:—pray, good grave Gentlewoman, is
    not this *Angelica?*
MORETTA: My too young Sir, it is—I hope 'tis one from Don
    Antonio.

(*Goes to* ANGELICA.)

215 HELLENA: (*Aside.*) Well, something I'll do to vex him for this.
ANGELICA: I will not speak with him; am I in humour to re-
    ceive a Lover?
WILLMORE: Not speak with him! why I'll be gone—and wait
    your idler minutes—Can I shew less Obedience to the
220   thing I love so fondly?

(*Offers to go.*)

ANGELICA: A fine Excuse this—stay—
WILLMORE: And hinder your Advantage: should I repay your
    Bounties so ungratefully?
ANGELICA: Come, hither, Boy,—that I may let you see
225   How much above the Advantages you name
    I prize one Minute's Joy with you.
WILLMORE: Oh, you destroy me with this Endearment.

(*Impatient to be gone.*)

    —Death, how shall I get away!—Madam, 'twill not be fit
    I should be seen with you—besides, it will not be conve-
230   nient—and I've a Friend—that's dangerously sick.
ANGELICA: I see you're impatient—yet you shall stay.
WILLMORE: And miss my Assignation with my Gipsy.

(*Aside, and walks about impatiently.* MORETTA *brings* HELLENA,
who addresses her self to ANGELICA.)

HELLENA: Madam, You'l hardly pardon my Intrusion,
    When you shall know my Business;
235   And I'm too young to tell my Tale with Art:
    But there must be a wondrous store of Goodness
    Where so much Beauty dwells.
ANGELICA: A pretty Advocate, whoever sent thee,
    —Prithee proceed—Nay, Sir, you shall not go.

(*To* WILLMORE, *who is stealing off.*)

240 WILLMORE: Then shall I lose my dear Gipsy for ever.
    (*Aside.*)—Pox on't, she stays me out of spite.
HELLENA: I am related to a Lady, Madam,
    Young, rich, and nobly born, but has the fate
    To be in love with a young *English* Gentleman.
245   Strangely she loves him, at first sight she lov'd him,
    But did adore him when she heard him speak;
    For he, she said, had Charms in every word,
    That fail'd not to surprize, to wound, and conquer—
WILLMORE: (*Aside.*) Ha, Egad I hope this concerns me.
250 ANGELICA: 'Tis my false Man, he means—wou'd he were gone.
    This Praise will raise his Pride and ruin me—(*To*
    WILLMORE.) Well,

Since you are so impatient to be gone.
    I will release you, Sir.
WILLMORE: (*Aside.*) Nay, then I'm sure 'twas me he spoke of,
    this cannot be the Effects of Kindness in her.   255
    —No, Madam, I've consider'd better on't,
    And will not give you cause of Jealousy.
ANGELICA: But, Sir, I've—business, that—
WILLMORE: This shall not do, I know 'tis but to try me.
ANGELICA: (*Aside.*) Well, to your Story, Boy,—tho 'twill undo me. 260
HELLENA: With this Addition to his other Beauties,
    He won her unresisting tender Heart,
    He vow'd and sigh'd, and swore he lov'd her dearly;
    And she believ'd the cunning Flatterer,
    And thought her self the happiest Maid alive: 265
    To day was the appointed time by both,
    To consummate their Bliss;
    The Virgin, Altar, and the Priest were drest,
    And whilst she languisht for the expected Bridegroom,
    She heard, he paid his broken Vows to you.   270
WILLMORE: (*Aside.*) So, this is some dear Rogue that's in love
    with me, and this way lets me know it; or if it be not me,
    she means some one whose place I may supply.
ANGELICA: Now I perceive
    The cause of thy Impatience to be gone,   275
    And all the business of this glorious Dress.
WILLMORE: Damn the young Prater, I know not what he means.
HELLENA: Madam,
    In your fair Eyes I read too much concern
    To tell my farther Business.   280
ANGELICA: Prithee, sweet Youth, talk on, thou may'st perhaps
    Raise here a Storm that may undo my Passion,
    And then I'll grant thee any thing.
HELLENA: Madam, 'tis to intreat you, (oh unreasonable!)
    You wou'd not see this Stranger;   285
    For if you do, she vows you are undone,
    Tho Nature never made a Man so excellent;
    And sure he'ad been a God, but for Inconstancy.
WILLMORE: (*Aside.*) Ah, Rogue, how finely he's instructed!
    —'Tis plain some Woman that has seen me *en passant.*   290
ANGELICA: Oh, I shall burst with Jealousy! do you know the
    Man you speak of?—
HELLENA: Yes, Madam, he us'd to be in Buff and Scarlet.
ANGELICA: (*To* WILLMORE.) Thou, false as Hell, what canst
    thou say to this?   295
WILLMORE: By Heaven—
ANGELICA: Hold, do not damn thy self—
HELLENA: Nor hope to be believ'd.

(*He walks about, they follow.*)

ANGELICA: Oh, perjur'd Man!
    Is't thus you pay my generous Passion back?   300
HELLENA: Why wou'd you, Sir, abuse my Lady's Faith?
ANGELICA: And use me so unhumanly?
HELLENA: A Maid so young, so innocent—
WILLMORE: Ah, young Devil!
ANGELICA: Dost thou not know thy Life is in my Power?   305
HELLENA: Or think my Lady cannot be reveng'd?
WILLMORE: (*Aside.*) So, so, the Storm comes finely on.
ANGELICA: Now thou art silent, Guilt has struck thee dumb.

Oh, hadst thou still been so, I'd liv'd in safety.

(*She turns away and weeps.*)

310 WILLMORE: (*Aside to* HELLENA, *looks towards* ANGELICA *to watch her turning; and as she comes towards them, he meets her.*) Sweetheart, the Lady's Name and House—quickly: I'm impatient to be with her.—

HELLENA: (*Aside.*) So now is he for another Woman.

315 WILLMORE: The impudent'st young thing in Nature! I cannot persuade him out of his Error, Madam.

ANGELICA: I know he's in the right,—yet thou'st a Tongue That wou'd persuade him to deny his Faith.

(*In Rage walks away.*)

WILLMORE: (*Said softly to* HELLENA.) Her Name, her Name, dear Boy—

320 HELLENA: Have you forgot it, Sir?

WILLMORE: (*Aside.*) Oh, I perceive he's not to know I am a Stranger to his Lady.
—Yes, yes, I do know—but—I have forgot the—

(ANGELICA *turns.*)

—By Heaven, such early confidence I never saw.

ANGELICA: Did I not charge you with this Mistress, Sir?

325   Which you denied, tho I beheld your Perjury. This little Generosity of thine has render'd back my Heart.

(*Walks away.*)

WILLMORE: So, you have made sweet work here, my little mischief; Look your Lady be kind and good-natur'd now, or I shall have but a cursed Bargain on't.

(ANGELICA *turns towards them.*)

330   —The Rogue's bred up to Mischief, Art thou so great a Fool to credit him?

ANGELICA: Yes, I do; and you in vain impose upon me. —Come hither, Boy—Is not this he you speak of?

HELLENA: (HELLENA *looks in his Face, he gazes on her.*) I think—

335   it is; I cannot swear, but I vow he has just such another lying Lover's look.

WILLMORE: (*Aside.*) Hah! do not I know that Face?— By Heaven, my little Gipsy! what a dull Dog was I? Had I but lookt that way, I'd known her.

340   Are all my hopes of a new Woman banisht? —Egad, if I don't fit thee for this, hang me. —Madam, I have found out the Plot.

HELLENA: Oh Lord, what does he say? am I discover'd now?

WILLMORE: Do you see this young Spark here?

345 HELLENA: He'll tell her who I am.

WILLMORE: Who do you think this is?

HELLENA: Ay, ay, he does know me.—Nay, dear Captain, I'm undone if you discover me.

WILLMORE: Nay, nay, no cogging; she shall know what a pre-

350   cious Mistress I have

---

349 **cogging** to cog = to trick, wheedle, or cajole

HELLENA: Will you be such a Devil?

WILLMORE: Nay, nay, I'll teach you to spoil sport you will not make.—This small Ambassador comes not from a Person of Quality, as you imagine, and he says; but from a very errant Gipsy, the talkingst, pratingst, cantingst little Animal 355 thou ever saw'st.

ANGELICA: What news you tell me! that's the thing I mean.

HELLENA: (*Aside.*) Wou'd I were well off the place.—If ever I go a Captain-hunting again.—

WILLMORE: Mean that thing? that Gipsy thing? thou may'st 360 as well be jealous of thy Monkey, or Parrot as her: a *German* Motion were worth a dozen of her, and a Dream were a better Enjoyment, a Creature of Constitution fitter for Heaven than Man.

HELLENA: (*Aside.*) Tho I'm sure he lyes, yet this vexes me. 365

ANGELICA: You are mistaken, she's a *Spanish* Woman Made up of no such dull Materials.

WILLMORE: Materials! Egad, and she be made of any that will either dispense, or admit of Love, I'll be bound to continence. 370

HELLENA: (*Aside to him.*) Unreasonable Man, do you think so?

WILLMORE: You may Return, my little Brazen Head, and tell your Lady, that till she be handsom enough to be belov'd, or I dull enough to be religious, there will be small hopes of me.

ANGELICA: Did you not promise then to marry her? 375

WILLMORE: Not I, by Heaven.

ANGELICA: You cannot undeceive my fears and torments, till you have vow'd you will not marry her.

HELLENA: If he swears that, he'll be reveng'd on me indeed for all my Rogueries. 380

ANGELICA: I know what Arguments you'll bring against me, Fortune and Honour.

WILLMORE: Honour! I tell you, I hate it in your Sex; and those that fancy themselves possest of that Foppery, are the most impertinently troublesom of all Woman-kind, and 385 will transgress nine Commandments to keep one: and to satisfy your Jealousy I swear—

HELLENA: (*Aside to him.*) Oh, no swearing, dear Captain—

WILLMORE: If it were possible I should ever be inclin'd to marry, it should be some kind young Sinner, one that has 390 Generosity enough to give a favour handsomely to one that can ask it discreetly, one that has Wit enough to manage an Intrigue of Love—oh, how civil such a Wench is, to a Man than does her the Honour to marry her.

ANGELICA: By Heaven, there's no Faith in any thing he says. 395

(*Enter* SEBASTIAN.)

SEBASTIAN: Madam, *Don Antonio*—

ANGELICA: Come hither.

HELLENA: Ha, *Antonio!* he may be coming hither, and he'll certainly discover me, I'll therefore retire without a Ceremony.

(*Exit* HELLENA.)

ANGELICA: I'll see him, get my Coach ready. 400

SEBASTIAN: It waits you, Madam.

WILLMORE: This is lucky: what, Madam, now I may be gone and leave you to the enjoyment of my Rival?

ANGELICA: Dull Man, that canst not see how ill, how poor That false dissimulation looks—Be gone, 405 And never let me see thy cozening Face again,

Lest I relapse and kill thee.

WILLMORE: Yes, you can spare me now,—farewell till you are
in a better Humour—I'm glad of this release—
410   Now for my Gipsy:
For tho to worse we change, yet still we find
New Joys, New Charms, in a new Miss that's kind.

(*Exit* WILLMORE.)

ANGELICA: He's gone, and in this Ague of My Soul
415   The shivering Fit returns;
Oh with what willing haste he took his leave,
As if the long'd for Minute were arriv'd,
Of some blest Assignation.
In vain I have consulted all my Charms,
420   In vain this Beauty priz'd, in vain believ'd
My eyes cou'd kindle any lasting Fires.
I had forgot my Name, my Infamy,
And the Reproach that Honour lays on those
That dare pretend a sober passion here.
425   Nice Reputation, tho it leave behind
More Virtues than inhabit where that dwells,
Yet that once gone, those virtues shine no more.
—Then since I am not fit to belov'd,
I am resolv'd to think on a Revenge
On him that sooth'd me thus to my undoing.

(*Exeunt.*)

SCENE III

A Street.

Enter FLORINDA *and* VALERIA *in Habits different from what they have been seen in.*

FLORINDA: We're happily escap'd, yet I tremble still.
VALERIA: A Lover and fear! why, I am but half a one, and yet
I have Courage for any Attempt. Would *Hellena* were here.
I wou'd fain have had her as deep in this Mischief as we,
5   she'll fare but ill else I doubt.
FLORINDA: She pretended a Visit to the *Augustine* Nuns, but
I believe some other design carried her out, pray Heavens
we light on her.
VALERIA: When I saw no reason wou'd go good on her, I fol-
10   low'd her into the Wardrobe, and as she was looking for
something in a great Chest, I tumbled her in by the Heels,
snatch the Key of the Apartment where you were confin'd, lockt her in, and left her bauling for help.
FLORINDA: 'Tis well you resolve to follow my Fortunes, for
15   thou darest never appear at home again after such an Action.
VALERIA: That's according as the young Stranger and I shall
agree—But to our business—I deliver'd your Letter, your
Note to *Belvile,* when I got out under pretence of going
to Mass, I found him at his Lodging, and believe me it
20   came seasonably; for never was Man in so desperate a
Condition. I told him of your Resolution of making your
escape to day, if your Brother would be absent long
enough to permit you; if not, die rather than be *Antonio's.*
FLORINDA: Thou shou'dst have told him I was confin'd to my
25   Chamber upon my Brother's suspicion, that the Business
on the *Molo* was a Plot laid between him and I.

VALERIA: I said all this, and told him your Brother was now
gone to his Devotion, and he resolves to visit every
Church till he find him; and not only undeceive him in
that, but caress him so as shall delay his return home.   30
FLORINDA: Oh Heavens! he's here, and *Belvile* with him too.

(*They put on their Vizards.*)

(*Enter Don* PEDRO, BELVILE, WILLMORE; BELVILE, *and Don* PE-
DRO *seeming in serious Discourse.*)

VALERIA: Walk boldly by them, I'll come at a distance, lest he
suspect us.

(*She walks by them, and looks back on them.*)

WILLMORE: Ha! A Woman! and of an excellent Micn!
PEDRO: She throws a kind look back on you.   35
WILLMORE: Death, tis a likely Wench, and that kind look shall
not be cast away—I'll follow her.
BELVILE: Prithee do not.
WILLMORE: Do not! By Heavens to the Antipodes, with such
an Invitation.   40

(*She goes out, and* WILLMORE *follows her.*)

BELVILE: 'Tis a mad Fellow for a Wench.

(*Enter* FREDERICK.)

FREDERICK: Oh Colonel, such News.
BELVILE: Prithee what?
FREDERICK: News that will make you laugh in spite of Fortune.
BELVILE: What, *Blunt* has had some damn'd Trick put upon   45
him, cheated, bang'd, or clapt?
FREDERICK: Cheated, Sir, rarely cheated of all but his Shirt
and Drawers; the unconscionable Whore too turn'd him
out before Consummation, so that traversing the Streets at
Midnight, the Watch found him in this *Fresco,* and con-   50
ducted him home: By Heaven 'tis such a slight, and yet I
durst as well have been hang'd as laugh at him, or pity
him; he beats all that do but ask him a Question, and is in
such an Humour—
PEDRO: Who is't has met with this ill usage, Sir?   55
BELVILE: (*Aside.*) A Friend of ours, whom you must see for
Mirth's sake. I'll imploy him to give *Florinda* time for an
escape.
PEDRO: Who is he?
BELVILE: A young Countryman of ours, one that has been ed-   60
ucated at so plentiful a rate, he yet ne'er knew the want of
Money, and 'twill be a great Jest to see how simply he'll
look without it. For my part I'll lend him none, and the
Rogue knows not how to put on a borrowing Face, and
ask first. I'll let him see how good 'tis to play our parts   65
whilst I play his—Prithee, *Frederick* do go home and keep
him in that posture till we come.

(*Exeunt.*)

(*Enter* FLORINDA *from the farther end of the Scene, looking behind her.*)

FLORINDA: I am follow'd still—hah—my Brother too advancing this way, good Heavens defend me from being
seen by him.   70

(*She goes off.*)

(*Enter* WILLMORE, *and after him* VALERIA, *at a little distance.*)

WILLMORE: Ah! There she sails, she looks back as she were willing to be boarded, I'll warrant her Prize.

(*He goes out,* VALERIA *following.*)

(*Enter* HELLENA, *just as he goes out, with a* PAGE.)

HELLENA: Hah, is not that my Captain that has a Woman in chase?—'tis not *Angelica.* Boy, follow those People at a dis-
75 tance, and bring me an Account where they go in.—I'll find his Haunts, and plague him every where.—ha—my Brother!

(*Exit* PAGE. BELVILE, WILLMORE, *and* PEDRO *cross the Stage:* HEL-LENA *runs off.*)

(*Scene changes to another Street. Enter* FLORINDA.)

FLORINDA: What shall I do, my Brother now pursues me. Will no kind Power protect me from his Tyranny?—Hah, here's
80 a Door open, I'll venture in, since nothing can be worse than to fall into his Hands, my Life and Honour are at stake, and my Necessity has no choice.

(*She goes in. Enter* VALERIA, *and* HELLENA's PAGE *peeping after* FLORINDA.)

PAGE: Here she went in, I shall remember this House.

(*Exit* PAGE.)

VALERIA: This is *Belvile's* Lodgings; she's gone in as readily as
85 if she knew it—hah—here's that mad Fellow again, I dare not venture in—I'll watch my Opportunity.

(*Goes aside. Enter* WILLMORE, *gazing about him.*)

WILLMORE: I have lost her hereabouts—Pox on't she must not scape me so.

(*Goes out.*)

(*Scene changes to* BLUNT's *chamber, discovers him sitting on a couch in his shirt and drawers, reading.*)

BLUNT: So, now my Mind's a little at Peace, since I have re-
90 solv'd Revenge—A Pox on this Taylor tho, for not bring-ing home the Clothes I bespoke; and a Pox of all poor Cavaliers, a Man can never keep a spare Suit for 'em; and I shall have these Rogues come in and find me naked; and then I'm undone; but I'm resolv'd to arm my self—the
95 Rascals shall not insult over me too much.

(*Puts on an old rusty Sword and Buff-Belt.*)

—Now, how like a Morrice-Dancer I am equipt—a fine Lady-like Whore to cheat me thus, without affording me a Kindness for my Money, a Pox light on her, I shall never be reconciled to the Sex more, she has made me as faithless as
100 a Physician, as uncharitable as a Churchman, and as ill-natur'd as a Poet. O how I'll use all Womenkind hereafter! what wou'd I give to have one of 'em within my reach now!

any Mortal thing in Petticoats, kind Fortune, send me; and I'll forgive thy last Night's Malice—Here's a cursed Book too, (a Warning to all young Travellers) that can instruct me 105 how to prevent such Mischiefs now 'tis too late. Well 'tis a rare convenient thing to read a little now and then, as well as hawk and hunt.

(*Sits down again and reads.*)

(*Enter to him* FLORINDA.)

FLORINDA: This House is haunted sure, 'tis well furnisht and no living thing inhabits it—hah—a Man! Heavens how 110 he's attir'd! sure 'tis some Rope-dancer, or Fencing-Master; I tremble now for fear, and yet I must venture now to speak to him—Sir, if I may not interrupt your Meditations—

(*He starts up and gazes.*)

BLUNT: Hah—what's here? Are my wishes granted? and is not that a she Creature? Adsheartlikins 'tis! what wretched 115 thing art thou—hah!

FLORINDA: Charitable Sir, you've told your self already what I am; a very wretched Maid, forc'd by a strange unlucky Accident, to seek a safety here, and must be ruin'd, if you do not grant it. 120

BLUNT: Ruin'd! Is there any Ruin so inevitable as that which now threatens thee? Dost thou know, miserable Woman, into what Den of Mischiefs thou art fall'n? what a Bliss of Confusion?—hah—dost not see something in my looks that frights thy guilty Soul, and makes thee wish to change 125 that Shape of Woman for any humble Animal, or Devil? for those were safer for thee, and less mischievous.

FLORINDA: Alas, what mean you, Sir? I must confess your Looks have something in 'em makes me fear; but I be-seech you, as you seem a Gentleman, pity a harmless Vir- 130 gin, that takes your House for Sanctuary.

BLUNT: Talk on, talk on, and weep too, till my faith return. Do, flatter me out of my Senses again—a harmless Virgin with a Pox, as much one as t'other, adsheartlikins. Why, what the Devil can I not be safe in my House for you? not 135 in my Chamber? nay, even being naked too cannot secure me. This is an Impudence greater than has invaded me yet.—Come, no Resistance.

(*Pulls her rudely.*)

FLORINDA: Dare you be so cruel?

BLUNT: Cruel, adsheartlikins as a Gally-slave, or a *Spanish* 140 Whore: Cruel, yes, I will kiss and beat thee all over; kiss, and see thee all over; thou shalt lie with me too, not that I care for the Injoyment, but to let you see I have ta'en de-liberated Malice to thee, and will be revenged on one Whore for the Sins of another; I will smile and deceive 145 thee, flatter thee, and beat thee, kiss and swear, and lye to thee, imbrace thee and rob thee, as she did me, fawn on thee, and strip thee stark naked, then hang thee out at my Window by the Heels with a Paper of scurvy Verses fas-ten'd to thy Breast, in praise of damnable Women—Come, 150 come along.

FLORINDA: Alas, Sir, must I be sacrific'd for the Crimes of the most infamous of my Sex? I never understood the Sins you name.

BLUNT: Do, persuade the Fool you love him, or that one of you
155   can be just or honest; tell me I was not an easy Coxcomb, or
any strange impossible Tale: it will be believ'd sooner than
thy false Showers or Protestations. A Generation of damn'd
Hypocrites, to flatter my very Clothes from my back! dis-
sembling Witches! are these the Returns you make an hon-
160   est Gentleman that trusts, believes, and loves you?—But if I
be not even with you—Come along, or I shall—

(Pulls her again.)

(Enter FREDERICK.)

FREDERICK: Hah, what's here to do?
BLUNT: Adsheartlikins, *Frederick* I am glad thou art come, to
be a Witness of my dire Revenge.
165 FREDERICK: What's this, a Person of Quality too, who is upon
the Ramble to supply the Defects of some grave impotent
Husband?
BLUNT: No, this has another Pretence, some very unfortunate
Accident brought her hither, to save a Life pursued by I
170   know not who, or why, and forc'd to take Sanctuary here
at Fools Haven. Adsheartlikins to me of all Mankind for
Protection? Is the Ass to be cajol'd again, think ye? No,
young one, no Prayers or Tears shall mitigate my Rage;
therefore prepare for both my Pleasure of Enjoyment and
175   Revenge, for I am resolved to make up my Loss here on
thy Body, I'll take it out in kindness and in beating.
FREDERICK: Now, Mistress of mine, what do you think of this?
FLORINDA: I think he will not—dares not be so barbarous.
FREDERICK: Have a care, *Blunt,* she fetch'd a deep Sigh, she is
180   inamour'd with thy Shirt and Drawers, she'll strip thee
even of that. There are of her Calling such unconscionable
Baggages, and such dexterous Thieves, they'll flea a Man,
and he shall ne'er miss his Skin, till he feels the Cold.
There was a Country-man of ours robb'd of a Row of
185   Teeth whilst he was sleeping, which the Jilt made him buy
again when he wak'd—You see, Lady, how little Reason
we have to trust you.
BLUNT: 'Dsheartlikins, why, this is most abominable.
FLORINDA: Some such Devils there may be, but by all that's
190   holy I am none such, I entered here to save a Life in danger.
BLUNT: For no goodness I'll warrant her.
FREDERICK: Faith, Damsel, you had e'en confess the plain
Truth, for we are Fellows not to be caught twice in the
same Trap: Look on that Wreck, a tight Vessel when he set
195   out of Haven, well trim'd and laden, and see how a Female
Piccaroon of this Island of Rogues has shatter'd him, and
canst thou hope for any Mercy?
BLUNT: No, no, Gentlewoman, come along, adsheartlikins we
must be better acquainted—we'll both lie with her, and
200   then let me alone to bang her.
FREDERICK: I am ready to serve you in matters of Revenge,
that has a double Pleasure in't.
BLUNT: Well said. You hear, little one, how you are condem-
n'd by publick Vote to the Bed within, there's no resisting
205   your Destiny, Sweetheart.

(Pulls her.)

FLORINDA: Stay, Sir, I have seen you with *Belvile,* an *English*
Cavalier, for his sake use me kindly; you know how, Sir.

BLUNT: *Belvile!* why, yes, Sweeting, we do know *Belvile,* and
wish he were with us now, he's a Cormorant at Whore and
Bacon, he'd have a Limb or two of thee, my Virgin Pullet: 210
but 'tis no matter, we'll leave him the Bones to pick.
FLORINDA: Sir, if you have any Esteem for that *Belvile,* I conjure you to treat me with more Gentleness; he'll thank
you for the Justice.
FREDERICK: Hark ye, *Blunt,* I doubt we are mistaken in this 215
matter.
FLORINDA: Sir, If you find me not worth *Belvile's* Care, use
me as you please; and that you may think I merit better
treatment than you threaten—pray take this Present—

(Gives him a Ring: He looks on it.)

BLUNT: Hum—A Diamond! why, 'tis a wonderful Virtue now 220
that lies in this Ring, a mollifying Virtue; adsheartlikins
there's more persuasive Rhetorick in't, than all her Sex
can utter.
FREDERICK: I begin to suspect something; and 'twou'd anger
us vilely to be truss'd up for a Rape upon a Maid of Qual- 225
ity, when we only believe we ruffle a Harlot.
BLUNT: Thou art a credulous Fellow, but adsheartlikins I have
no Faith yet; why, my Saint prattled as parlously as this
does, she gave me a Bracelet too, a Devil on her: but I sent
my Man to sell it to day for Necessaries, and it prov'd as 230
counterfeit as her Vows of Love.
FREDERICK: However let it reprieve her till we see *Belvile.*
BLUNT: That's hard, yet I will grant it.

(Enter a SERVANT.)

SERVANT: Oh, Sir, the Colonel is just come with his new
Friend and a *Spaniard* of Quality, and talks of having you 235
to Dinner with 'em.
BLUNT: 'Dsheartlikins, I'm undone—I would not see 'em for
the World: Harkye, *Frederick* lock up the Wench in your
Chamber.
FREDERICK: Fear nothing, Madam, whate'er he threatens, 240
you're safe whilst in my Hands.

(Exit FREDERICK *and* FLORINDA.)

BLUNT: And, Sirrah—upon your Life, say—I am not at
home—or that I am asleep—or—or any thing—away—
I'll prevent them coming this way.

(Locks the Door and Exeunt.)

ACT FIVE

SCENE I

BLUNT'*s Chamber.*

After a great knocking as at his Chamber-door, enter BLUNT *softly,
crossing the Stage in his Shirt and Drawers, as before.*

(Call within.) Ned, Ned Blunt, Ned Blunt.

BLUNT: The Rogues are up in Arms, 'dsheartlikins, this villainous *Frederick* has betray'd me, they have heard of my
blessed Fortune.

(And knocking within.) Ned Blunt, Ned, Ned—   5

BELVILE: Why, he's dead, sir, without dispute dead, he has not been seen to day; let's break open the Door—here—Boy—

BLUNT: Ha, break open the Door! 'dsheartlikins that mad Fellow will be as good as his word.

10 BELVILE: Boy, bring something to force the Door.

(*A great noise within at the Door again.*)

BLUNT: So, now must I speak in my own Defence, I'll try what Rhetorick will do—hold—hold, what do you mean, Gentlemen, what do you mean?

BELVILE: Oh Rogue, art alive? prithee open the Door, and
15   convince us.

BLUNT: Yes, I am alive, Gentlemen—but at present a little busy.

BELVILE: (*Within.*) How! *Blunt* grown a man of Business! come, come, open, and let's see this Miracle.

BLUNT: No, no, no, no, Gentlemen, 'tis no great Business—
20   but—I am—at—my Devotion,—'dsheartlikins, will you not allow a man time to pray?

BELVILE: (*Within.*) Turn'd religious! a greater Wonder than the first, therefore open quickly, or we shall unhinge, we shall.

BLUNT: This won't do—Why, hark ye, Colonel; to tell you
25   the plain Truth, I am about a necessary Affair of Life.—I have a Wench with me—you apprehend me? the Devil's in't if they be so uncivil as to disturb me now.

WILLMORE: How, a Wench! Nay, then we must enter and partake; no Resistance,—unless it be your Lady of Quality,
30   and then we'll keep our distance.

BLUNT: So, the Business is out.

WILLMORE: Come, come, lend more hands to the Door,—now heave altogether—so, well done, my Boys—

(*Breaks open the Door. Enter* BELVILE, WILLMORE, FREDERICK, PEDRO, *and* BELVILE's *page:* BLUNT *looks simply, they all laugh at him, he lays his hand on his Sword, and comes up to* WILLMORE.)

BLUNT: Hark ye, Sir, laugh out your laugh quickly, d'ye hear,
35   and be gone, I shall spoil your sport else; 'dsheartlikins, Sir, I shall—the Jest has been carried on too long,—(*Aside.*) a Plague upon my Taylor—

WILLMORE: 'Sdeath, how the Whore has drest him! Faith, Sir, I'm sorry.

40 BLUNT: Are you so, Sir? keep't to your self then, Sir, I advise you, d'ye hear? for I can as little endure your Pity as his Mirth.

(*Lays his Hand on's Sword.*)

BELVILE: Indeed, *Willmore,* thou wert a little too rough with *Ned Blunt's* Mistress; call a Person of Quality Whore, and one so young, so handsome, and so eloquent!—ha, ha, ha.

45 BLUNT: Hark ye, Sir, you know me, and know I can be angry; have a care—for 'dsheartlikins I can fight too—I can, Sir,—do you mark me—no more.

BELVILE: Why so peevish, good *Ned?* some Disappointments, I'll warrant—What! did the jealous Count her Husband
50   return just in the nick?

(*They laugh.*)

BLUNT: Or the Devil, Sir,—d'ye laugh?
    Look ye, settle me a good sober Countenance, and that quickly too, or you shall know *Ned Blunt* is not—

BELVILE: Not every Body, we know that.

BLUNT: Not an Ass, to be laught at, Sir.   55

WILLMORE: Unconscionable Sinner, to bring a Lover so near his Happiness, a vigorous passionate Lover, and then not only cheat him of his Moveables, but his Desires too.

BELVILE: Ah, Sir, a Mistress is a Trifle with *Blunt,* he'll have a dozen the next time he looks abroad; his Eyes have   60 Charms not to be resisted: There needs no more than to expose that taking Person to the view of the Fair, and he leads 'em all in Triumph.

PEDRO: Sir, tho I'm a stranger to you, I'm ashamed at the rudeness of my Nation; and could you learn who did it,   65 would assist you to make an Example of 'em.

BLUNT: Why, ay, there's one speaks sense now, and handsomly; and let me tell you Gentlemen, I should not have shew'd my self like a Jack-Pudding, thus to have made you Mirth, but that I have revenge within my power; for know, I have got into my   70 possession a Female, who had better have fallen under any Curse, than the Ruin I design her: 'dsheartlikins, she assaulted me here in my own Lodgings, and had doubtless committed a Rape upon me, had not this Sword defended me.

FREDERICK: I knew not that, but o' my Conscience thou   75 hadst ravisht her, had she not redeem'd her self with a Ring—let's see't, *Blunt.*

(BLUNT *shews the Ring.*)

BELVILE: (*Goes to whisper to him.*) Hah!—the Ring I gave *Florinda* when we exchang'd our Vows!—hark ye, *Blunt*—

WILLMORE: No whispering, good Colonel, there's a Woman   80 in the case, no whispering.

BELVILE: Hark ye, Fool, be advis'd, and conceal both the Ring and the Story, for your Reputation's sake; don't let People know what despis'd Cullies we *English* are: to be cheated and abus'd by one Whore, and another rather bribe thee   85 than be kind to thee, is an Infamy to our Nation.

WILLMORE: Come, come, where's the Wench! we'll see her, let her be what she will, we'll see her.

PEDRO: Ay, ay, let us see her, I can soon discover whether she be of Quality, or for your Diversion.   90

BLUNT: She's in *Frederick's* Custody.

WILLMORE: Come, come, the Key.

(*To* FREDERICK *who gives him the Key, they are going.*)

BELVILE: Death! what shall I do?—stay, Gentlemen—yet if I hinder 'em, I shall discover all—hold, let's go one at once—give me the Key.   95

WILLMORE: Nay, hold there, Colonel, I'll go first.

FREDERICK: Nay, no Dispute, *Ned* and I have the property of her.

WILLMORE: Damn Property—then we'll draw Cuts.

(BELVILE *goes to whisper* WILLMORE.)

Nay, no Corruption, good Colonel: come, the longest Sword carries her.—   100

(*They all draw, forgetting Don* PEDRO, *being a Spaniard, had the longest.*)

BLUNT: I yield up my Interest to you Gentlemen, and that will be Revenge sufficient.

WILLMORE: The Wench is yours—(*To* PEDRO.) Pox of his
    Toledo, I had forgot that.
105 FREDERICK: Come, Sir, I'll conduct you to the Lady.

(*Exit* FREDERICK *and* PEDRO.)

BELVILE: (*Aside.*) To hinder him will certainly discover—
    Dost know, dull Beast, what Mischief thou hast done?

(WILLMORE *walking up and down out of Humour.*)

WILLMORE: Ay, ay, to trust our Fortune to Lots, a Devil on't,
    'twas madness, that's the Truth on't.
110 BELVILE: Oh intolerable Sot!

(*Enter* FLORINDA, *running masqu'd,* PEDRO *after her,* WILLMORE
gazing round her.)

FLORINDA: (*Aside.*) Good Heaven, defend me from discovery.
PEDRO: 'Tis but in vain to fly me, you are fallen to my Lot.
BELVILE: Sure she is undiscover'd yet, but now I fear there is
    no way to bring her off.
115 WILLMORE: Why, what a Pox is not this my Woman, the same
    I follow'd but now?

(PEDRO *talking to* FLORINDA, *who walks up and down.*)

PEDRO: As if I did not know ye, and your Business here.
FLORINDA: (*Aside.*) Good Heaven! I fear he does indeed—
PEDRO: Come, pray be kind, I know you meant to be so
120   when you enter'd here, for these are proper Gentlemen.
WILLMORE: But, Sir—perhaps the Lady will not be impos'd
    upon, she'll chuse her Man.
PEDRO: I am better bred, than not to leave her Choice free.

(*Enter* VALERIA, *and is surpriz'd at the Sight of Don* PEDRO.)

VALERIA: (*Aside.*) Don *Pedro* here! there's no avoiding him.
125 FLORINDA: (*Aside.*) *Valeria!* then I'm undone—
VALERIA: (*To* PEDRO, *running to him.*) Oh! have I found you,
    Sir—
    —The strangest Accident—if I had breath—to tell it.
PEDRO: Speak—is *Florinda* safe? *Hellena* well?
130 VALERIA: Ay, ay, Sir—*Florinda*—is safe—from any fears of you.
PEDRO: Why, where's *Florinda*?—speak.
VALERIA: Ay, where indeed, Sir? I wish I could inform you,—
    But to hold you no longer in doubt—
FLORINDA: (*Aside.*) Oh, what will she say!
135 VALERIA: She's fled away in the Habit of one of her Pages,
    Sir—but *Callis* thinks you may retrieve her yet, if you
    make haste away; she'll tell you, Sir, the rest—(*Aside.*) if
    you can find her out.
PEDRO: Dishonourable Girl, she has undone my Aim—Sir—
140   you see my necessity of leaving you, and I hope you'll par-
    don it: my Sister, I know, will make her flight to you; and
    if she do, I shall expect she should be render'd back.
BELVILE: I shall consult my Love and Honour, Sir.

(*Exit* PEDRO.)

FLORINDA: (*To* VALERIA.) My dear Preserver, let me imbrace
145   thee.
WILLMORE: What the Devil's all this?

BLUNT: Mystery by this Light.
VALERIA: Come, come, make haste and get your selves mar-
    ried quickly, for your Brother will return again.
BELVILE: I am so surpriz'd with Fears and Joys, so amaz'd to 150
    find you here in safety, I can scarce persuade my Heart
    into a Faith of what I see—
WILLMORE: Harkye, Colonel, is this that Mistress who has cost
    you so many Sighs, and me so many Quarrels with you?
BELVILE: It is—(*To* FLORINDA.) Pray give him the Honour of 155
    your Hand.
WILLMORE: Thus it must be receiv'd then.

(*Kneels and kisses her Hand.*)

    And with it give your Pardon too.
FLORINDA: The Friend to *Belvile* may command me anything.
WILLMORE: (*Aside.*) Death, wou'd I might, 'tis a surprizing 160
    Beauty.
BELVILE: Boy, run and fetch a Father instantly.

(*Exit* PAGE.)

FREDERICK: So, now do I stand like a Dog, and have not a
    Syllable to plead my own Cause with: by this Hand,
    Madam, I was never thorowly confounded before, nor 165
    shall I ever more dare look up with Confidence, till you
    are pleased to pardon me.
FLORINDA: Sir, I'll be reconcil'd to you on one Condition,
    that you'll follow the Example of your Friend, in marry-
    ing a Maid that does not hate you, and whose Fortune (I 170
    believe) will not be unwelcome to you.
FREDERICK: Madam, had I no Inclinations that way, I shou'd
    obey your kind Commands.
BELVILE: Who, *Frederick* marry; he has so few Inclinations for
    Womankind, that had he been possest of Paradise, he 175
    might have continu'd there to this Day, if no Crime but
    Love cou'd have disinherited him.
FREDERICK: Oh, I do not use to boast of my Intrigues.
BELVILE: Boast! why thou do'st nothing but boast; and I dare
    swear, wer't thou as innocent from the Sin of the Grape, as 180
    thou art from the Apple, thou might'st yet claim that right
    in *Eden* which our first Parents lost by too much loving.
FREDERICK: I wish this Lady would think me so modest a Man.
VALERIA: She shou'd be sorry then, and not like you half so
    well, and I shou'd be loth to break my Word with you; 185
    which was, That if your Friend and mine are agreed, it
    shou'd be a Match between you and I.

(*She gives him her Hand.*)

FREDERICK: Bear witness, Colonel, 'tis a Bargain.

(*Kisses her Hand.*)

BLUNT: (*To* FLORINDA.) I have a Pardon to beg too; but ads-
    heartlikins I am so out of Countenance, that I am a Dog 190
    if I can say any thing to purpose.
FLORINDA: Sir, I heartily forgive you all.
BLUNT: That's nobly said, sweet Lady—*Belvile*, prithee pre-
    sent her her Ring again, for I find I have not Courage to
    approach her my self. 195

(*Gives him the Ring, he gives it to* FLORINDA. *Enter* BOY.)

BOY: Sir, I have brought the Father that you sent for.

BELVILE: 'Tis well, and now my dear *Florinda,* let's fly to compleat that mighty Joy we have so long wish'd and sigh'd for. Come, *Frederick* you'll follow?

200 FREDERICK: Your Example, Sir, 'twas ever my Ambition in War, and must be so in Love.

WILLMORE: And must not I see this juggling Knot ty'd?

BELVILE: No, thou shalt do us better Service, and be our Guard, lest Don *Pedro's* sudden Return interrupt the Ceremony.

205 WILLMORE: Content; I'll secure this Pass.

(*Exit* BELVILE, FLORINDA, FREDERICK, *and* VALERIA. *Enter page.*)

BOY: (*To* WILLMORE.) Sir, there's a Lady without wou'd speak to you.

WILLMORE: Conduct her in, I dare not quit my Post.

BOY: And, Sir, your Taylor waits you in your Chamber.

210 BLUNT: Some comfort yet, I shall not dance naked at the Wedding.

(*Exit* BLUNT *and* BOY.)

(*Enter again the* BOY, *conducting in* ANGELICA *in a masquing Habit and a Vizard,* WILLMORE *runs to her.*)

WILLMORE: This can be none but my pretty Gipsy—Oh, I see you can follow as well as fly—Come, confess thy self the most malicious Devil in Nature, you think you have done

215 my Bus'ness with *Angelica*—

ANGELICA: Stand off, base Villain—

(*She draws a Pistol and holds to his Breast.*)

WILLMORE: Hah, 'tis not she: who art thou? and what's thy Business?

ANGELICA: One thou hast injur'd, and who comes to kill thee

220 for't.

WILLMORE: What the Devil canst thou mean?

ANGELICA: By all my Hopes to kill thee—

(*Holds still the Pistol to his Breast, he going back, she following still.*)

WILLMORE: Prithee on what Acquaintance? for I know thee not.

ANGELICA: Behold this Face!—so lost to thy Remembrance!

225 And then call all thy Sins about thy Soul,

(*Pulls off her Vizard.*)

And let them die with thee.

WILLMORE: *Angelica*!

ANGELICA: Yes, Traitor.

Does not thy guilty Blood run shivering thro thy Veins?

230 Hast thou no Horrour at this Sight, that tells thee,

Thou hast not long to boast thy shameful Conquest?

WILLMORE: Faith, no Child, my Blood keeps its old Ebbs and Flows still, and that usual Heat too, that cou'd oblige thee with a Kindness, had I but opportunity.

235 ANGELICA: Devil! dost wanton with my Pain—have at thy Heart.

WILLMORE: Hold, dear Virago! hold thy Hand a little, I am not now at leisure to be kill'd—hold and hear me—(*Aside.*) Death, I think she's in earnest.

ANGELICA: (*Aside, turning from him.*) Oh if I take not heed, My coward Heart will leave me to his Mercy. 240
—What have you, Sir, to say?—but should I hear thee, Thoud'st talk away all that is brave about me:

(*Follows him with the Pistol to his Breast.*)

And I have vow'd thy Death, by all that's sacred.

WILLMORE: Why, then, there's an end of a proper handsom Fellow, that might have liv'd to have done good Service 245 yet:—That's all I can say to't.

ANGELICA: (*Pausingly.*) Yet—I wou'd give thee—time for Penitence.

WILLMORE: Faith, Child, I thank God, I have ever took care to lead a good, sober, hopeful Life, and am of a Religion that teaches me to believe, I shall depart in Peace. 250

ANGELICA: So will the Devil: tell me How many poor believing Fools thou hast undone; How many Hearts thou hast betray'd to ruin! —Yet, these are little Mischiefs to the Ills Thou'st taught mine to commit: thou'st taught it Love. 255

WILLMORE: Egad, 'twas shrewdly hurt the while.

ANGELICA: —Love, that has robb'd it of its Unconcern, Of all that Pride that taught me how to value it, And in its room a mean submissive Passion was convey'd, That made me humbly bow, which I ne'er did 260 To any thing but Heaven. —Thou, perjur'd Man, didst this, and with thy Oaths, Which on thy Knees thou didst devoutly make, Soften'd my yielding Heart—And then, I was a Slave— Yet still had been content to've worn my Chains, 265 Worn 'em with Vanity and Joy for ever, Hadst thou not broke those Vows that put them on. —'Twas then I was undone.

(*All this while follows him with a Pistol to his Breast.*)

WILLMORE: Broke my Vows! why, where hast thou lived? Amongst the Gods! For I never heard of mortal Man, 270 That has not broke a thousand Vows.

ANGELICA: Oh, Impudence!

WILLMORE: *Angelica*! that Beauty has been too long tempting, Not to have made a thousand Lovers languish, Who in the amorous Favour, no doubt have sworn 275 Like me; did they all die in that Faith? still adoring? I do not think they did.

ANGELICA: No, faithless Man: had I repaid their Vows, as I did thine, I wou'd have kill'd the ungrateful that had abandon'd me. 280

WILLMORE: This old General has quite spoil'd thee, nothing makes a Woman so vain, as being flatter'd; your old Lover ever supplies the Defects of Age, with intolerable Dotage, vast Charge, and that which you call Constancy; and attributing all this to your own Merits, you domineer, and 285 throw your Favours in's Teeth, upbraiding him still with the Defects of Age, and cuckold him as often as he deceives your Expectations. But the gay, young, brisk Lover, that brings his equal Fires, and can give you Dart for Dart, he'll be as nice as you sometimes. 290

ANGELICA: All this thou'st made me know, for which I hate thee.

Had I remain'd in innocent Security,
I shou'd have thought all Men were born my Slaves;
And worn my Pow'r like Lightning in my Eyes,
295   To have destroy'd at Pleasure when offended.
    —But when Love held the Mirror, the undeceiving Glass
    Reflected all the Weakness of my Soul, and made me
        know,
    My richest Treasure being lost, my Honour,
    All the remaining Spoil cou'd not be worth
300   The Conqueror's Care or Value.
    —Oh how I fell like a long worship'd Idol,
    Discovering all the Cheat!
    Wou'd not the Incense and rich Sacrifice,
    Which blind Devotion offer'd at my Altars,
305   Have fall'n to thee?
    Why woud'st thou then destroy my fancy'd Power?
WILLMORE: By Heaven thou art brave, and I admire thee
        strangely.
    I wish I were that dull, that constant thing,
    Which thou woud'st have, and Nature never meant me:
310   I must, like chearful Birds, sing in all Groves,
    And perch on every Bough,
    Billing the next kind She that flies to meet me;
    Yet after all cou'd build my Nest with thee,
    Thither repairing when I'd lov'd my round,
315   And still reserve a tributary Flame.

(Offers her a Purse of Gold.)

    —To gain your Credit, I'll pay you back your Charity,
    And be oblig'd for nothing but for Love.
ANGELICA: Oh that thou wert in earnest!
    So mean a Thought of me,
320   Wou'd turn my Rage to Scorn, and I shou'd pity thee,
    And give thee leave to live;
    Which for the publick Safety of our Sex,
    And my own private Injuries, I dare not do.
    Prepare—

(Follows still, as before.)

325   —I will no more be tempted with Replies.
WILLMORE: Sure—
ANGELICA: Another Word will damn thee! I've heard thee talk
        too long.

(She follows him with a Pistol ready to shoot: he retires still amaz'd.)

(Enter Don ANTONIO, *his Arm in a Scarf, and lays hold on the Pistol.)*

ANTONIO: Hah! *Angelica!*
ANGELICA: *Antonio!* What Devil brought thee hither?
330 ANTONIO: Love and Curiosity, seeing your Coach at Door.
    Let me disarm you of this unbecoming Instrument of
    Death.—

(Takes away the Pistol.)

    Amongst the Number of your Slaves, was there not one
        worthy the Honour to have fought your Quarrel?
335   —Who are you, Sir, that are so very wretched

To merit Death from her?
WILLMORE: One, sir, that cou'd have made a better End of an
    amorous Quarrel without you, than with you.
ANTONIO: Sure 'tis some Rival—hah—the very Man took
    down her Picture yesterday—the very same that set on me   340
    last night—Blest opportunity—

(Offers to shoot him.)

ANGELICA: Hold, you're mistaken, Sir.
ANTONIO: By Heaven the very same!
    —Sir, what pretensions have you to this Lady?
WILLMORE: Sir, I don't use to be examin'd, and am ill at all   345
    Disputes but this—

(Draws, ANTONIO *offers to shoot.)*

ANGELICA: *(To* WILLMORE.) Oh, hold! you see he's arm'd
    with certain Death:
    —And you, *Antonio,* I command you hold,
    By all the Passion you've so lately vow'd me.

(Enter Don PEDRO, *sees* ANTONIO, *and stays.)*

PEDRO: *(Aside.)* Hah, *Antonio!* and *Angelica!*   350
ANTONIO: When I refuse Obedience to your Will,
    May you destroy me with your mortal Hate.
    By all that's Holy I adore you so,
    That even my Rival, who has Charms enough
    To make him fall a Victim to my Jealousy,   355
    Shall live, nay, and have leave to love on still.
PEDRO: *(Aside.)* What's this I hear?
ANGELICA: *(Pointing to* WILLMORE.) Ah thus, 'twas thus he
    talk'd, and I believ'd.
    —*Antonio,* yesterday,
    I'd not have sold my Interest in his Heart,   360
    For all the Sword has won and lost in Battle.
    —But now to show my utmost of Contempt,
    I give thee Life—which if thou would'st preserve,
    Live where my Eyes may never see thee more,
    Live to undo some one, whose Soul may prove   365
    So bravely constant to revenge my Love.

(Goes out, ANTONIO *follows, but* PEDRO *pulls him back.)*

PEDRO: *Antonio*—stay.
ANTONIO: Don *Pedro*—
PEDRO: What Coward Fear was that prevented thee
    From meeting me this Morning on the *Molo?*   370
ANTONIO: Meet thee?
PEDRO: Yes me; I was the Man that dar'd thee to't.
ANTONIO: Hast thou so often seen me fight in War,
    To find no better Cause to excuse my Absence?
    —I sent my Sword and one to do thee Right,   375
    Finding my self uncapable to use a Sword.
PEDRO: But 'twas *Florinda's* Quarrel that we fought,
    And you to shew how little you esteem'd her,
    Sent me your Rival, giving him your Interest.
    —But I have found the Cause of this Affront,   380
    But when I meet you fit for the Dispute,
    —I'll tell you my Resentment.

ANTONIO: I shall be ready, Sir, e'er long to do your Reason.

(*Exit* ANTONIO.)

385 PEDRO: If I cou'd find *Florinda,* now whilst my Anger's high, I think I shou'd be kind, and give her to *Belvile* in Revenge.

WILLMORE: Faith, Sir, I know not what you wou'd do, but I be-lieve the Priest within has been so kind.

PEDRO: How! my Sister married?

WILLMORE: I hope by this time she is, and bedded too, or he 390 has not my longings about him.

PEDRO: Dares he do thus? Does he not fear my Pow'r?

WILLMORE: Faith not at all. If you will go in, and thank him for the Favour he has done your Sister, so; if not, Sir, my Power's greater in this House than yours; I have a damn'd 395 surly Crew here, that will keep you till the next Tide, and then clap you an board my Prize; my Ship lies but a League off the *Molo,* and we shall show your Donship a damn'd *Tramontana* Rover's Trick.

(*Enter* BELVILE.)

BELVILE: This Rogue's in some new Mischief—hah, *Pedro* re-400 turn'd!

PEDRO: Colonel *Belvile,* I hear you have married my Sister.

BELVILE: You have heard truth then, Sir.

PEDRO: Have I so? then, Sir, I wish you Joy.

BELVILE: How!

405 PEDRO: By this Embrace I do, and I glad on't.

BELVILE: Are you in earnest?

PEDRO: By our long Friendship and my Obligations to thee, I am. The sudden Change I'll give you Reasons for anon. Come lead me into my Sister, that she may know I now 410 approve her Choice.

(*Exit* BELVILE *with* PEDRO. WILLMORE *goes to follow them. Enter* HELLENA *as before in Boy's Clothes, and pulls him back.*)

WILLMORE: Ha! my Gipsy—Now a thousand Blessings on thee for this Kindness. Egad, Child, I was e'en in despair of ever seeing thee again; my Friends are all provided for within, each Man his kind Woman.

415 HELLENA: Hah! I thought they had serv'd me some such Trick.

WILLMORE: And I was e'en resolv'd to go aboard, condemn my self to my lone Cabin, and the Thoughts of thee.

HELLENA: And cou'd you have left me behind? wou'd you have been so ill-natur'd?

420 WILLMORE: Why, 'twou'd have broke my Heart, Child—but since we are met again, I defy foul Weather to part us.

HELLENA: And wou'd you be a faithful Friend now, if a Maid shou'd trust you?

WILLMORE: For a Friend I cannot promise, thou art of a 425 Form so excellent, a Face and Humour too good for cold dull Friendship; I am parlously afraid of being in love, Child, and you have not forgot how severely you have us'd me.

HELLENA: That's all one, such Usage you must still look for, to find out all your Haunts, to rail at you to all that love

you, till I have made you love only me in your own De-430 fence, because no body else will love.

WILLMORE: But hast thou no better Quality to recommend thy self by?

HELLENA: Faith none, Captain—Why, 'twill be the greater Charity to take me for thy Mistress, I am a lone Child, a 435 kind of Orphan Lover; and why I shou'd die a Maid, and in a Captain's Hands too, I do not understand.

WILLMORE: Egad, I was never claw'd away with Broad-Sides from any Female before, thou hast one Virtue I adore, good-Nature; I hate a coy demure Mistress, she's as trou-440 blesom as a Colt, I'll break none; no, give me a mad Mis-tress when mew'd, and in flying on[e] I dare trust upon the Wing, that whilst she's kind will come to the Lure.

HELLENA: Nay, as kind as you will, good Captain, whilst it lasts, but let's lose no time. 445

WILLMORE: My time's as precious to me, as thine can be; therefore, dear Creature, since we are so well agreed, let's retire to my Chamber, and if ever thou were treated with such savory Love—Come—My Bed's prepar'd for such a Guest, all clean and sweet as thy fair self; I love to steal a 450 Dish and a Bottle with a Friend, and hate long Graces—Come, let's re-tire and fall to.

HELLENA: 'Tis but getting my Consent, and the Business is soon done; let but old Gaffer *Hymen* and his Priest say Amen to't, and I dare lay my Mother's Daughter by as proper a Fel-455 low as your Father's Son, without fear or blushing.

WILLMORE: Hold, hold, no Bugg Words, Child, Priest and *Hymen*: prithee add Hangman to 'em to make up the Consort—No, no, we'll have no Vows but Love, Child, nor Witness but the Lover; the kind Diety injoins naught but 460 love and enjoy. *Hymen* and Priest wait still upon Portion, and Joynture; Love and Beauty have their own Cere-monies. Marriage is as certain a Bane to Love, as lending Money is to Friendship: I'll neither ask nor give a Vow, tho I could be content to turn Gipsy, and become a Left-hand 465 Bridegroom, to have the Pleasure of working that great Miracle of making a Maid a Mother, if you durst venture; 'tis upse Gipsy that, and if I miss, I'll lose my Labour.

HELLENA: And if you do not lose, what shall I get? A Cradle full of Noise and Mischief, with a Pack of Repentance at 470 my Back? Can you teach me to weave Incle to pass my time with? 'Tis upse Gipsy that too.

WILLMORE: I can teach thee to weave a true Love's Knot better.

HELLENA: So can my Dog.

WILLMORE: Well, I see we are both upon our Guard, and I see 475 there's no way to conquer good Nature, but by yielding—here—give me thy Hand—one Kiss and I am thine—

HELLENA: One Kiss! How like my Page he speaks; I am resolv'd you shall have none, for asking such a sneaking Sum—He that will be satisfied with one Kiss, will never die of that 480 Longing; good Friend single-Kiss, is all your talking come to this? A Kiss, a Caudle! farewel, Captain single-Kiss.

(*Going out he stays her.*)

---

398 *Tramontana* Italian and Spanish *tramontano* = from beyond the mountains

468 **upse** *Op zijn* (Dutch) = in the fashion or manner of, *Upse Gipsy* = like a gipsy   471 **Incle** linen thread or yarn which was woven into a tape once very much in use

WILLMORE: Nay, if we part so, let me die like a Bird upon a
Bough, at the Sheriff's Charge. By Heaven, both the *Indies*
485 shall not buy thee from me. I adore thy Humour and will
marry thee, and we are so of one Humour, it must be a
Bargain—give me thy Hand—

(*Kisses her hand.*)

And now let the blind ones (Love and Fortune) do their worst.
HELLENA: Why, God-a-mercy, Captain!
490 WILLMORE: But harkye—The Bargain is now made; but is it
not fit we should know each other's Names? That when
we have Reason to curse one another hereafter, and People ask me who 'tis I give to the Devil, I may at least be
able to tell what Family you came of.
495 HELLENA: Good reason, Captain; and where I have cause, (as I
doubt not but I shall have plentiful) that I may know at
whom to throw my—Blessings—I beseech ye your Name.
WILLMORE: I am call'd *Robert the Constant*.
HELLENA: A very fine Name! pray was it your Faulkner or
500 Butler that christen'd you? Do they not use to whistle
when then call you?
WILLMORE: I hope you have a better, that a Man may name
without crossing himself, you are so merry with mine.
HELLENA: I am call'd *Hellena the Inconstant*.

(*Enter* PEDRO, BELVILE, FLORINDA, FREDERICK, *and* VALERIA.)

505 PEDRO: Hah! *Hellena!*
FLORINDA: *Hellena!*
HELLENA: The very same—hah my Brother! now, Captain,
shew your Love and Courage; stand to your Arms, and defend me bravely, or I am lost for ever.
510 PEDRO: What's this I hear? false Girl, how came you hither,
and what's your Business? Speak.

(*Goes roughly to her.*)

WILLMORE: Hold off, Sir, you have leave to parly only.

(*Puts himself between.*)

HELLENA: I had e'en as good tell it, as you guess it. Faith,
Brother, my Business is the same with all living Creatures
515 of my Age, to love, and be loved, and here's the Man.
PEDRO: Perfidious Maid, hast thou deceiv'd me too, deceiv'd
thy self and Heaven?
HELLENA: 'Tis time enough to make my Peace with that: Be
you but kind, let me alone with Heaven.
520 PEDRO: *Belvile*, I did not expect this false Play from you; was't
not enough you'd gain *Florinda* (which I pardon'd) but
your leud Friends too must be inrich'd with the Spoils of
a noble Family?
BELVILE: Faith, Sir, I am as much surpriz'd at this as you can be:
525 Yet, Sir, my Friends are Gentlemen, and ought to be esteem'd for their Misfortunes, since they have the Glory to
suffer with the best of Men and Kings; 'tis true, he's a Rover
of Fortune, yet a Prince aboard his little wooden World.
PEDRO: What's this to the maintenance of a Woman or her
530 Birth and Quality?
WILLMORE: Faith, Sir, I can boast of nothing but a Sword
which does me Right where-e'er I come, and has de-

fended a worse Cause than a Woman's: and since I lov'd
her before I either knew her Birth or Name, I must pursue my Resolution, and marry her.   535
PEDRO: And is all your holy Intent of becoming a Nun debauch'd into a Desire of Man?
HELLENA: Why—I have consider'd the matter, Brother, and
find the Three hundred thousand Crowns my Uncle left
me (and you cannot keep from me) will be better laid out 540
in Love than in Religion, and turn to as good an Account—let most Voices carry it, for Heaven or the Captain?
ALL CRY: Captain, a Captain.
HELLENA: Look ye, Sir, 'tis a clear Case.
PEDRO: (*Aside.*) Oh I am mad—if I refuse, my Life's in Dan- 545
ger—Come—There's one motive induces me—take
her—I shall now be free from the fear of her Honour;
guard it you now, if you can, I have been a Slave to't long
enough.

(*Gives her to him.*)

WILLMORE: Faith, Sir, I am of a Nation, that are of opinion a
Woman's Honour is not worth guarding when she has a 550
mind to part with it.
HELLENA: Well said, Captain.
PEDRO: (*To* VALERIA.) This was your Plot, Mistress, but I hope
you have married one that will revenge my Quarrel to
you—   555
VALERIA: There's no altering Destiny, Sir.
PEDRO: Sooner than a Woman's Will, therefore I forgive you
all—and wish you may get my Father's Pardon as easily;
which I fear.

(*Enter* BLUNT *drest in a Spanish Habit, looking very ridiculously;
his* MAN *adjusting his Band.*)

MAN: 'Tis very well, Sir.   560
BLUNT: Well, Sir, 'dsheartlikins I tell you 'tis damnable ill,
Sir—a Spanish Habit, good Lord! cou'd the Devil and my
Taylor devise no other Punishment for me, but the Mode
of a Nation I abominate?
BELVILE: What's the matter, *Ned?*   565
BLUNT: Pray view me round, and judge—

(*Turns round.*)

BELVILE: I must confess thou art a kind of an odd Figure.
BLUNT: In a Spanish Habit with a Vengeance! I had rather be
in the Inquisition for Judaism, than in this Doublet and
Breeches; a Pillory were an easy Collar to this, three 570
Hand-fuls high; and these Shoes too are worse than the
Stocks, with the Sole an Inch shorter than my Foot: In
fine, Gentlemen, methinks I look altogether like a Bag of
Bays stuff'd full of Fools Flesh.
BELVILE: Methinks 'tis well, and makes the look *en Cavalier:* 575
Come, Sir, settle your Face, and salute our Friends, Lady—
BLUNT: Hah! Say'st thou so, my little Rover?

(*To* HELLENA.)

Lady—(if you be one) give me leave to kiss your Hand,
and tell you, adshcartlikins, for all I look so, I am your
humble Servant—A Pox of my *Spanish* Habit.   580

WILLMORE: Hark—what's this?

(*Musick is heard to Play. Enter* BOY.)

BOY: Sir, as the Custom is, the gay People in Masquerade, who make every Man's House their own, are coming up.

(*Enter several* MEN *and* WOMEN *in masquing Habits, with Musick, they put themselves in order and dance.*)

BLUNT: Adsheartlikins, wou'd 'twere lawful to pull off their
585   false Faces, that I might see if my Doxy were not amongst 'em.

BELVILE: Ladies and Gentlemen, since you are come so *a propos*, you must take a small Collation with us.

(*To the* MASQUERADERS.)

WILLMORE: Whilst we'll to the Good Man within, who stays
590   to give us a Cast of his Office.

(*To* HELLENA.)

—Have you no trembling at the near approach?

HELLENA: No more than you have in an Engagement or a Tempest.

595   WILLMORE: Egad, thou'rt a brave Girl, and I admire thy
Love and Courage.
Lead on, no other Dangers they can dread,
Who venture in the Storms o'th' Marriage-Bed.

(*Exeunt.*)

EPILOGUE

THE banisht Cavaliers! a Roving Blade!
A popish Carnival! a Masquerade!
The Devil's in't if this will please the Nation,
In these our blessed Times of Reformation,
5   When Conventicling is so much in Fashion.
And yet—
That mutinous Tribe less Factions do beget,
Than your continual differing in Wit;

Your Judgment's (as your Passions) a Disease:
Nor Muse nor Miss your Appetite can please;   10
You're grown as nice as queasy Consciences,
Whose each Convulsion, when the Spirit moves,
Damns every thing that Maggot disapproves.
    With canting Rule you wou'd the Stage refine,
And to dull Method all our Sense confine.   15
With th' Insolence of Common-wealths you rule,
Where each gay Fop, and politick brave Fool
On Monarch Wit impose without controul.
As for the last who seldom sees a Play,
Unless it be the old Black-Fryers way,   20
Shaking his empty Noodle o'er *Bamboo*,
He crys —Good Faith, these Plays will never do.
—Ah, Sir, in my young days, what lofty Wit,
What high-strain'd Scenes of Fighting there were writ:
These are slight airy Toys. But tell me, pray,   25
What has the *House of Commons* done to day?
Then shews his Politicks, to let you see
Of State Affairs he'll judge as notably,
As he can do of Wit and Poetry.
The younger Sparks, who hither do resort,   30
Cry—
Pox o' your gentle things, give us more Sport;
—Damn me, I'm sure 'twill never please the Court.
    Such Fops are never pleas'd, unless the Play
Be stuff'd with Fools, as brisk and dull as they: 35
Such might the Half-Crown spare, and in a Glass
At home behold a more accomplisht Ass,
Where they may set their Cravats, Wigs and Faces,
And practice all their Buffoonry Grimaces;
See how this—Huff becomes—this Dammy—flare—   40
Which they at home may act, because they dare,
But—must with prudent Caution do elsewhere.
Oh that our *Nokes,* or *Tony Lee* could show
A Fop but half so much to th' Life as you.

---

43 *Nokes,* **or** *Tony Lee* James Nokes and Antony Leigh, the two famous actors, were the leading low comedians of the day

Sor Juana Inés de la Cruz

Juana Inés de Asbaje y Ramírez de Santillana (1648/1651–1695) was probably born in late November or early December of 1648 to the daughter of a wealthy landowner (Isabel Ramírez de Santillana) and an army officer (Pedro Manuel de Asbaje y Vargas Manchucha) serving in the Spanish New World colony of New Spain—present-day Mexico. Although her parents had two other children (Isabel Ramírez had three additional children with another officer), they were not married, and Juana Inés was born an illegitimate "daughter of the church." Raised in the provincial town of Panoyan, Juana had access to her grandfather's library and, by her own account, was a voracious reader, as she later wrote in her *Answer to Sor Filotea* (written 1691):

> When I was six or seven years old and already knew how to read and write, along with all the other skills like embroidery and sewing that women learn, I heard that in Mexico City there were a University and Schools where they studied sciences. As soon as I heard this I began to slay my poor mother with insistent and annoying pleas, begging her to dress me in men's clothes and send me to the capital, to the home of some relatives she had there, so that I could enter the University and study. She refused, and was right in doing so; but I quenched my desire by reading a great variety of books that belonged to my grandfather, and neither punishments nor scoldings could prevent me. And so when I did go to Mexico City, people marveled not so much at my intelligence as at my memory and the facts I knew at an age when it seemed I had scarcely had time to speak.[1]

Juana was sent to live with her mother's relatives in Mexico City in 1659. She lived with them for five years until she moved into the home of the viceroy, where she served in the court of the vicereine, Doña Leonor Carreto, Marquisa de Mancera.

Although she began to write on both religious and secular subjects while at court, Juana's career was closely tied to the church. In 1666, she joined the Carmelite convent of San José, but the penitential strictness of the order seems to have caused her health to suffer, and she left the convent after three months. Still eager to join a convent, she agreed to sit for an examination by the viceroy and forty scholars assembled to test the range of her knowledge, as a means to confirm her suitability for religious life. According to Diego Callega, a priest who wrote the first biography of Sor Juana, she performed like a "royal galleon attacked by canoes," and was admitted to the convent of Santa Paula in 1669, where she took the name Sor Juana Inés de la Cruz. (Illegitimate children were not admissible to convent life; at this time, Juana claimed that her parents had been married, and that her birth date was November 12, 1651; a baptismal record for 1648—listing Juana's aunt and uncle as godparents of an infant "Inés"—is now usually taken as evidence for her birth in that year.)

Although the convent was cloistered, Sor Juana received money to support her servants and was able to receive guests, to study, and to write; she was also closely connected to the social life of New Spain's capital city. The Aztec city of Tenochtitlán had supported some 250,000 inhabitants before the conquest in 1520, but Mexico City was a much smaller city in the seventeenth century. While war, disease, and enslavement drastically reduced the native population, the general population was augmented not only by the annual arrival of *peninsulares* (new inhabitants from Spain), but by an increasing population of *criollos* (people of European descent born in Mexico, like Sor Juana) and *mestizos,* as well as by a growing number of African slaves and immigrants from other Spanish colonies. In the 1800 census, for example, the population of Mexico City was 137,000, making it the largest city in the Americas. The church wielded extensive political power in Mexico (there were sixteen convents in Mexico City alone), and—as in Europe—the leaders of the church and of the state were often drawn from the same aristocratic families. In this sense, it's not surprising that

[1]See *The Answer/La Respuesta, Including a Selection of Poems,* ed. and trans. Electa Arenal and Amanda Powell (New York: Feminist Press, 1994).

Religion, costumed as a Spanish nobleman, surveys the fallen Aztec men and women after the battle between Zeal and Occident, in the 1997 Universidad de las Americas production of the *loa* to *The Divine Narcissus* by Sor Juana Inés de la Cruz.

throughout her life, Sor Juana was an intimate acquaintance of aristocratic circles in Mexico City, particularly of the viceroys and vicereines.

One vicereine, Maria Luisa Manrique de Lara y Gonzaga (whose husband was viceroy 1680–1686), was the inspiration of several of Sor Juana's poems and had her first volume, *Inundación Castálida,* published in Madrid in 1689 (the title refers to the nymph Castálida, who drowned herself rather than be seduced by Apollo); the title-page described Sor Juana as "the Tenth Muse." By 1690, Sor Juana was arguably the most accomplished secular and philosophical writer in the Americas: She mastered the baroque forms of secular Spanish poetry, writing not only sixty-five sonnets and many ballads and occasional poems, but two well-known comedies (including *Los empeños de una casa*) that were staged. She also wrote sixteen sets of **VILLANCICOS,** carols performed at the Mass; these often incorporate her understanding both of African dialects and of the indigenous Nahua language and were performed at cathedrals throughout Mexico during her lifetime. She wrote three *auto sacramentales,* two of which were performed; thirty-two **LOAS;** a brilliant philosophical treatise *The First Dream* (1685); and a defense of women's claim to an intellectual and spiritual life, *Answer to Sor Filotea.*

Yet despite her fame, Sor Juana was under continual pressure from the church to conform to the more "feminine" role of quiet devotion and service. Early in her career she struggled with her confessor, Antonio Núñez de Miranda, who regarded writing as improper for women, especially for women of the church. Although Sor Juana succeeded in dismissing him as her confessor, he continued to agitate for her silence with higher church officials, including the misogynist archbishop Francisco Aguian y Seijas. In 1690—shortly after her second volume of poetry had been published in Madrid, and her brilliant *auto The Divine Narcissus,* had been published in Mexico—the church's opposition came to a head. During that year, Sor Juana wrote a theological critique of a sermon written forty years earlier, an essay clearly not intended for publication; her friend, the bishop of Puebla, Manuel

Fernández de Santa Cruz, asked her to send it to him. Without her permission, he published Sor Juana's essay under the title *Carta atenagórica*—"Letter Worthy of Athena." Despite the praise implied in the title, the bishop was in fact eager to expose Sor Juana to censure and appended his own corrective letter to her treatise—from "Sor Filotea," "lover of God." This public rebuke spurred Sor Juana's brilliant *Answer to Sor Filotea de la Cruz,* a passionate defense of both her intellectual life and its contribution to her faith, written in 1691 but published only after her death in 1700. Despite her defense, however, Sor Juana acceded to the will of the church in 1692. Her last set of *villancicos* was performed at the cathedral in Oaxaca; she sold both her musical instruments and her extensive library (among the largest private libraries in the Americas at the time), and in 1694 she signed—in blood—a new declaration of faith, vowing to give up secular studies as well. She died during an epidemic that swept Mexico City in April 1695.

Sor Juana's poetry, plays, and philosophical writings are well known in Spanish, and many have been published in English translations; the Mexican poet Octavio Paz has written a celebrated biography of Sor Juana: *Sor Juana, or, The Traps of Faith,* trans. Margaret Sayers Peden (Cambridge: Harvard University Press, 1988).

LOA TO THE DIVINE NARCISSUS

The Divine Narcissus is a full-length *auto sacramental,* an allegorical drama on the subject of the Eucharist that Sor Juana wrote in 1687. She intended to submit it to be performed in Madrid as part of a competition for new *autos* following the death of Calderón, who had been the sole author of *autos* performed in the Spanish capital before his death in 1681. Although the death of the queen in 1689 forced the cancellation of the festival, Sor Juana's *The Divine Narcissus* and its introductory *loa* remain among the most accomplished examples of this important genre of Spanish-language drama.

Although the *loa* can be used for either secular or sacred purposes, Sor Juana uses it here specifically to introduce the themes of the *auto,* which uses the Greek story of Echo and Narcissus to allegorize the theological doctrine of the Eucharist. However, to modern readers and audiences, the *loa* is perhaps more interesting for its staging of colonial conflict; through an allegorical conversation between Zeal (a *conquistador*), Religion (a Spanish lady), and the Aztec rulers (Occident and America), the short play also stages an allegory of the conquest of Mexico and its consequences. Although there is no record of the play being performed in Sor Juana's lifetime, it clearly records aspects of Aztec life—the opening dance and ritual worship of the God of the Seeds—that were legally prohibited in seventeenth-century New Spain, while staging a debate between the Aztec leaders and the Spanish invaders who insist on replacing the native religion with the practice of Christianity. While the bullheaded *conquistador,* Zeal, is on the point of murdering the defeated Aztecs, they are spared by Religion, who hears in their account of their religious rituals a profane version of the miracle of the Eucharist:

> What images,
> what dark designs, what shadowings
> of truths most sacred to our Faith
> do these lies seek to imitate?

Religion works to bring Christian salvation to Occident and America by pointing out the similarities between their religion and the mysteries of the Eucharist:

> a God composed
> of human blood, an offering
> of sacrifice, and in himself
> does He combine with bloody death
> the life-sustaining seeds of earth?

To instruct Occident and America, Religion decides to

> make for you a metaphor
> a concept clothed in rhetoric
> so colorful that what I show
> to you, your eyes will clearly see.

The *auto* that follows, *The Divine Narcissus,* is Religion's illustrative "metaphor," her way of explaining the Eucharist to the inhabitants of the New World.

Written by a *criolla,* as part of a competition to take place in Madrid, Sor Juana's play is in many ways a barometer of the situation of colonial writing; the final dialogue between Zeal and Religion considers whether such a play, written in the colony about colonial subjects, will be received in "the crown city of Madrid, / which is the center of the Faith, / the seat of Catholic majesty" as an act of "impropriety." Although written at the height of Spain's imperial expansion, and indeed in many ways written to celebrate that expansion, Sor Juana's *loa* to *The Divine Narcissus* deftly registers many of the tensions that typically inform colonial writing: between the colony and the capital, between the native population and their invaders, for instance. But particularly in the brittle relationship between Zeal and Religion and the more charitable relationship between Religion and America, Sor Juana seems to open another kind of critique as well; Religion refuses, for example, to sanction the extermination, or even the subjugation, of Occident and America. While the *loa* testifies unambigiously to Sor Juana's confidence in the universality of her faith, it also seems to question some of the ways religion is used to advance Spain's political and economic mission in this new and distinct society.

LOA TO THE DIVINE NARCISSUS

Sor Juana Inés de la Cruz

TRANSLATED BY PATRICIA A. PETERS AND RENÉE DOMEIER, O.S.B.

CHARACTERS

OCCIDENT	RELIGION	AZTECS
AMERICA	MUSIC	DANCERS
ZEAL	SOLDIERS	

SCENE ONE

Enter OCCIDENT, *a gallant-looking Aztec, wearing a crown. By his side is* AMERICA, *an Aztec woman of poised self-possession. They are dressed in the mantas and huipiles worn for singing a tocotín. They seat themselves on two chairs. On each side, Aztec men and women dance with feathers and rattles in their hands, as is customary for those doing this dance. While they dance,* MUSIC *sings.*

MUSIC: O, Noble Mexicans,
    whose ancient ancestry
    comes forth from the clear light
    and brilliance of the Sun,
5   since this, of all the year,
    is your most happy feast
    in which you venerate
    your greatest deity,
    come and adorn yourselves
10   with vestments of your rank;
    let your holy fervor be
    made one with jubilation;
    and celebrate in festive pomp
    the great God of the Seeds!

15 MUSIC: Since the abundance of
    our native fields and farms
    is owed to him alone
    who gives fertility,
    then offer him your thanks,
20   for it is right and just
    to give from what has grown,
    the first of the new fruits.
    From your own veins, draw out
    and give, without reserve,
25   the best blood, mixed with seed,
    so that his cult be served,
    and celebrate in festive pomp,
    the great God of the Seeds!

(OCCIDENT *and* AMERICA *sit, and* MUSIC *ceases.*)

OCCIDENT: Of all the deities to whom
30   our rites demand I bend my knee—
    among two thousand gods or more
    who dwell within this royal city
    and who require the sacrifice
    of human victims still entreating
35   for life until their blood is drawn
    and gushes forth from hearts still beating
    and bowels still pulsing—I declare,
    among all these, (it bears repeating),

whose ceremonies we observe,
the greatest is, surpassing all   40
this pantheon's immensity
the great God of the Seeds.
AMERICA: And you are right, since he alone
  daily sustains our monarchy
  because our lives depend on his   45
  providing crops abundantly;
  and since he gives us graciously
  the gift from which all gifts proceed,
  our fields rich with golden maize,
  the source of life through daily bread, 50
  we render him our highest praise.
  Then how will it improve our lives
  if rich America abounds
  in gold from mines whose smoke deprives
  the fields of their fertility   55
  and with their clouds of filthy soot
  will not allow the crops to grow
  which blossom now so fruitfully
  from seeded earth? Moreover, his
  protection of our people far   60
  exceeds our daily food and drink,
  the body's sustenance. Indeed,
  he feeds us with his very flesh
  (first purified of every stain).
  We eat his body, drink his blood, 65
  and by this sacred meal are freed
  and cleansed from all that is profane,
  and thus, he purifies our soul.
  And now, attentive to his rites,
  together let us all proclaim: 70
OCCIDENT, AMERICA, DANCERS and MUSIC: We celebrate in
   festive pomp,
  the great God of the Seeds!

SCENE TWO

They exit dancing. Enter Christian RELIGION *as a Spanish lady,* ZEAL *as a Captain General in armor, and Spanish* SOLDIERS.

RELIGION: How, being Zeal, can you suppress
  the flames of righteous Christian wrath
  when here before your very eyes
  idolatry, so blind with pride,   5
  adores, with superstitious rites
  an idol, leaving your own bride,
  the holy faith of Christ disgraced?
ZEAL: Religion, trouble not your mind
  or grieve my failure to attack,

10   complaining that my love is slack,
for now the sword I wear is bared,
its hilt in hand, clasped ready and
my arm raised high to take revenge.
Please stand aside and deign to wait
15   till I requite your grievances.

(*Enter* OCCIDENT *and* AMERICA *dancing, and accompanied by*
MUSIC, *who enters from the other side.*)

MUSIC: And celebrate in festive pomp,
the great God of the Seeds!
ZEAL: Here they come! I will confront them.
RELIGION: And I, in peace, will also go
20   (before your fury lays them low)
for justice must with mercy kiss;
I shall invite them to arise
from superstitious depths to faith.
ZEAL: Let us approach while they are still
25   absorbed in their lewd rituals.
MUSIC: And celebrate in festive pomp,
the great God of the Seeds!

(ZEAL *and* RELIGION *cross the stage.*)

RELIGION: Great Occident, most powerful;
America, so beautiful
30   and rich; you live in poverty
amid the treasures of your land.
Abandon this irreverent cult
with which the demon has waylaid you.
Open your eyes! Follow the path
35   that leads straightforwardly to truth,
to which my love yearns to persuade you.
OCCIDENT: Who are these unknown people, so
intrusive in my sight, who dare
to stop us in our ecstasy?
40   Heaven forbid such infamy!
AMERICA: Who are these nations, never seen,
that wish, by force, to pit themselves
against my ancient power supreme?
OCCIDENT: Oh, you alien beauty fair;
45   oh, pilgrim woman from afar,
who comes to interrupt my prayer,
please speak and tell me who you are.
RELIGION: Christian Religion is my name,
and I intend that all this realm
50   will make obeisance unto me.
OCCIDENT: An impossible concession!
AMERICA: Yours is but a mad obsession!
OCCIDENT: You will meet with swift repression.
AMERICA: Pay no attention; she is mad!
55   Let us go on with our procession.
MUSIC and AZTECS: And celebrate in festive pomp,
the great God of the Seeds!
ZEAL: How is this, barbarous Occident?
Can it be, sightless Idolatry,
60   that you insult Religion,
the spouse I cherish tenderly?
Abomination fills your cup
and overruns the brim, but see
that God will not permit you to

continue drinking down delight,   65
and I am sent to deal your doom.
OCCIDENT: And who are you who frightens all
who only look upon your face?
ZEAL: I am Zeal. Does that surprise you?
Take heed! for when your excesses   70
bring disgrace to fair Religion,
then will Zeal arise to vengeance;
for insolence I will chastise you.
I am the minister of God,
Who growing weary with the sight   75
of overreaching tyrannies
so sinful that they reach the height
of error, practiced many years,
has sent me forth to penalize you.
And thus, these military hosts   80
with flashing thunderbolts of steel,
the ministers of His great wrath
are sent, His anger to reveal.
OCCIDENT: What god? What sin? What tyranny?
What punishment do you foresee?   85
Your reasons make no sense to me,
nor can I make the slightest guess
who you might be with your insistence
on tolerating no resistance,
impeding us with rash persistence   90
from lawful worship as we sing.
MUSIC: And celebrate with festive pomp,
the great God of the Seeds!
AMERICA: Madman, blind, and barbarous,
with mystifying messages   95
you try to mar our calm and peace,
destroying the tranquility
that we enjoy. Your plots must cease,
unless, of course, you wish to be
reduced to ashes, whose existence   100
even the winds will never sense.
(*To* OCCIDENT.) And you, my spouse, and your cohort,
close off your hearing and your sight
to all their words; refuse to heed
their fantasies of zealous might;   105
proceed to carry out your rite.
Do not concede to insolence
from foreigners intent to dull
our ritual's magnificence.
MUSIC: And celebrate with festive pomp,   110
the great God of the Seeds!
ZEAL: Since our initial offering
of peaceful terms, you held so cheap,
the dire alternative of war,
I guarantee you'll count more dear.   115
Take up your arms! To war! To war!

(*Drums and trumpets sound.*)

OCCIDENT: What miscarriages of justice
has heaven sent against me?
What are these weapons, blazing fire,
before my unbelieving eyes?   120
Get ready, guards! Aim well, my troops,
Your arrows at this enemy!

AMERICA: What lightening bolts does heaven send
    to lay me low? What molten balls
125   of burning lead so fiercely rain?
    What centaurs crush with monstrous force
    and cause my people such great pain?
    (*Within.*) To arms! To arms! War! War!

([*Drums and trumpets*] *sound.*)

(*Within.*) Long life to Spain! Long live her king!

(*The battle begins. Indians enter through one door and flee through another with the Spanish pursuing at their heels. From back stage,* OCCIDENT *backs away from* RELIGION *and* AMERICA *retreats before* ZEAL's *onslaught.*)

SCENE THREE

RELIGION: Give up, arrogant Occident!
OCCIDENT: I must bow to your aggression,
    but not before your arguments.
ZEAL: Die, impudent America!
5 RELIGION: Desist! Do not give her to Death;
    her life is of some worth to us.
ZEAL: How can you now defend this maid
    who has so much offended you?
RELIGION: America has been subdued
10   because your valor won the strife,
    but now my mercy intervenes
    in order to preserve her life.
    It was your part to conquer her
    by force with military might;
15   mine is to gently make her yield,
    persuading her by reason's light.
ZEAL: But you have seen the stubbornness
    with which these blind ones still abhor
    your creed; is it not better far
20   that they all die?
RELIGION: Good Zeal, restrain
    your justice, and do not kill them.
    My gentle disposition deigns
    to forbear vengeance and forgive.
    I want them to convert and live.
25 AMERICA: If your petition for my life
    and show of Christian charity
    are motivated by the hope
    that you, at last, will conquer me,
    defeating my integrity
30   with verbal steel where bullets failed,
    then you are sadly self-deceived.
    A weeping captive, I may mourn
    for liberty, yet my will grows
    beyond these bonds; my heart is free,
35   and I will worship my own gods!
OCCIDENT: Forced to surrender to your power,
    I have admitted my defeat,
    but still it must be clearly said
    that violence cannot devour
40   my will, nor force constrain its right.
    Although in grief, I now lament,
    a prisoner, your cruel might

has limits. You cannot prevent
my saying here within my heart
I worship the great God of Seeds!   45

SCENE FOUR

RELIGION: Wait! What you perceive as force
    is not coercion, but affection.
    What god is this that you adore?
OCCIDENT: The great God of the Seeds
    who causes fields to bring forth fruit.   5
    To him the lofty heavens bow;
    to him the rains obedience give;
    and when, at last, he cleanses us
    from stains of sin, then he invites
    us to the meal that he prepares.   10
    Consider whether you could find
    a god more generous and good
    who blesses more abundantly
    than he whom I describe to you.
RELIGION: (*Aside.*) O God, help me! What images,   15
    what dark designs, what shadowings
    of truths most sacred to our Faith
    do these lies seek to imitate?
    O false, sly, and deceitful snake!
    O asp, with sting so venomous!   20
    O hydra, that from seven mouths
    pours noxious poisons, every one
    a passage to oblivion!
    To what extent, with this facade
    do you intend maliciously   25
    to mock the mysteries of God?
    Mock on! for with your own deceit,
    if God empowers my mind and tongue,
    I'll argue and impose defeat.
AMERICA: Why do you find yourself perplexed?   30
    Do you not see there is no god
    other than ours who verifies
    with countless blessings his great works?
RELIGION: In doctrinal disputes, I hold
    with the apostle Paul, for when   35
    he preached to the Athenians
    and found they had a harsh decree
    imposing death on anyone
    who tried to introduce new gods,
    since he had noticed they were free   40
    to worship at a certain shrine,
    an altar to "the Unknown God,"
    he said to them, "This Lord of mine
    is no new god, but one unknown
    that you have worshipped in this place,   45
    and it is He, my voice proclaims."
    And thus I—

(OCCIDENT *and* AMERICA *whisper to each other.*)

        Listen, Occident!
and hear me, blind Idolatry!
for all your happiness depends
on listening attentively.   50
These miracles that you recount,

these prodigies that you suggest,
these apparitions and these rays
of light in superstition dressed
55 are glimpsed but darkly through a veil.
These portents you exaggerate,
attributing to your false gods
effects that you insinuate,
but wrongly so, for all these works
60 proceed from our true God alone,
and of His Wisdom come to birth.
Then if the soil richly yields,
and if the fields bud and bloom,
if fruits increase and multiply,
65 if seeds mature in earth's dark womb,
if rains pour forth from leaden sky,
all is the work of His right hand;
for neither the arm that tills the soil
nor rains that fertilize the land
70 nor warmth that calls life from the tomb
of winter's death can make plants grow;
for they lack reproductive power
if Providence does not concur,
by breathing into each of them
75 a vegetative soul.

AMERICA: That might be so;
then tell me, is this God so kind—
this deity whom you describe—
that I might touch Him with my hands,
these very hands that carefully
80 create the idol, here before you,
an image made from seeds of earth
and innocent, pure human blood
shed only for this sacred rite?

RELIGION: Although the Essence of Divinity
85 is boundless and invisible,
because already It has been
eternally united with
our nature, He resembles us
so much in our humanity
90 that He permits unworthy priests
to take Him in their humble hands.

AMERICA: In this, at least, we are agreed,
for to my god no human hands
are so unstained that they deserve
95 to touch him; nonetheless, he gives
this honor graciously to those
who serve him with their priestly lives.
No others dare to touch the god,
nor in the sanctuary stand.

100 ZEAL: A reverence most worthily
directed to the one true God!

OCCIDENT: Whatever else you claim, now tell
me this: Is yours a God composed
of human blood, an offering
105 of sacrifice, and in Himself
does He combine with bloody death
the life-sustaining seeds of earth?

RELIGION: As I have said, His boundless
Majesty is insubstantial,
110 but in the Holy Sacrifice

of Mass, His blessed humanity
is placed unbloody under the
appearances of bread, which comes
from seeds of wheat and is transformed
into His Body and His Blood;   115
and this most holy Blood of Christ,
contained within a sacred cup,
is verily the offering
most innocent, unstained, and pure
that on the altar of the cross   120
was the redemption of the world.

AMERICA: Such miracles, unknown to us,
make me desire to believe;
but would the God that you reveal
offer Himself so lovingly   125
transformed for me into a meal
as does the god that I adore?

RELIGION: In truth, He does. For this alone
His Wisdom came upon the earth
to dwell among all humankind.   130

AMERICA: And so that I can be convinced,
may I not see this Deity?

OCCIDENT: And so that I can be made free
of old beliefs that shackle me?

RELIGION: Yes, you will see when you are bathed   135
in crystal waters from the font
of baptism.

OCCIDENT: And well I know,
in preparation to attend
a banquet, I must bathe, or else
our ancient custom I offend.   140

ZEAL: Your vain ablutions will not do
the cleansing that your stains require.

OCCIDENT: Then what?

RELIGION: There is a sacrament
of living waters, which can cleanse
and purify you of your sins.   145

AMERICA: Because you deluge my poor mind
with concepts of theology,
I've just begun to understand;
there is much more I want to see,
and my desire to know is now   150
by holy inspiration led.

OCCIDENT: And I desire more keenly still
to know about the life and death
of the God you say is in the bread.

RELIGION: Then come along with me, and I   155
shall make for you a metaphor,
a concept clothed in rhetoric
so colorful that what I show
to you, your eyes will clearly see;
for now I know that you require   160
objects of sight instead of words,
by which faith whispers in your ears
too deaf to hear; I understand,
for you necessity demands
that through the eyes, faith find her way   165
in her reception in your hearts.

OCCIDENT: Exactly so. I do prefer
to see the things you would impart.

SCENE FIVE

RELIGION: Then come.

ZEAL: Religion, answer me:
what metaphor will you employ
to represent these mysteries?

RELIGION: An *auto* will make visible
5   through allegory images
of what America must learn
and Occident implores to know
about the questions that now burn
within him so.

ZEAL: What will you call
10   this play in allegory cast?

RELIGION: *Divine Narcissus*, let it be,
because if that unhappy maid
adored an idol which disguised
in such strange symbols the attempt
15   the demon made to counterfeit
the great and lofty mystery
of the most Blessed Eucharist,
then there were also, I surmise,
among more ancient pagans hints
20   of such high marvels symbolized.

ZEAL: Where will your drama be performed?

RELIGION: In the crown city of Madrid,
which is the center of the Faith,
the seat of Catholic majesty,
25   to whom the Indies owe their best
beneficence, the blessed gift
of Holy Writ, the Gospel light
illuminating all the West.

ZEAL: That you should write in Mexico
30   for royal patrons don't you see
to be an impropriety?

RELIGION: Is it beyond imagination
that something made in one location
can in another be of use?
35   Furthermore, my writing it
comes, not of whimsical caprice,
but from my vowed obedience
to do what seems beyond my reach.
Well, then, this work, however rough
40   and little polished it might be,
results from my obedience,
and not from any arrogance.

ZEAL: Then answer me, Religion, how
(before you leave the matter now),
45   will you respond when you are chid
for loading the whole Indies on

a stage to transport to Madrid?

RELIGION: The purpose of my play can be
none other than to glorify
the Eucharistic Mystery;   50
and since the cast of characters
are no more than abstractions which
depict the theme with clarity,
then surely no one should object
if they are taken to Madrid;   55
distance can never hinder thought
with persons of intelligence,
nor seas impede exchange of sense.

ZEAL: Then, prostrate at his royal feet,
beneath whose strength two worlds are joined   60
we beg for pardon of the King;

RELIGION: and from her eminence, the Queen;

AMERICA: whose sovereign and anointed feet
the humble Indies bow to kiss;

ZEAL: and from the Royal High Council;   65

RELIGION: and from the ladies, who bring light
into their hemisphere;

AMERICA: and from
their poets, I most humbly beg
forgiveness for my crude attempt,
desiring with these awkward lines   70
to represent the Mystery.

OCCIDENT: Let's go, for anxiously I long to see
exactly how this God of yours
will give Himself as food to me.

(AMERICA, OCCIDENT, *and* ZEAL *sing:*)

The Indies know   75
and do concede
who is the true
God of the Seeds.
In loving tears
which joy prolongs   80
we gladly sing
our happy songs.

ALL: Blest be the day
when I could see
and worship the   85
great God of Seeds.

(*They all exit, dancing and singing.*)

CRITICAL CONTEXTS

JOHN DRYDEN (1631–1700)

"Preface to *Troilus and Cressida,* Containing the Grounds of Criticism in Tragedy" (1679)
EDITED BY ARTHUR C. KIRSCH

John Dryden is the most important English critic and poet of the late seventeenth century; he was appointed poet laureate and royal historiographer in 1668 and was also the author of many plays, both comedies and heroic tragedies. In 1679, he wrote an adaptation of Shakespeare's Troilus and Cressida, *and in his "Preface" to the play Dryden argues for neoclassical principles of unity and decorum.*

In the "Preface," Dryden frames a specifically neoclassical sense of the purpose and function of tragedy. One way into this essay is through a comparison with Aristotle, and indeed, with Greek tragedy. How do Dryden's criteria at once invoke and revise the sense of tragic construction in Aristotle's The Poetics? *Beyond that, what are the features of Shakespearean drama that seem to require Dryden's attention as a reviser? What is the sense of decorum that Dryden wishes to urge, and that Shakespeare's original play seems to violate?*

The poet Aeschylus was held in the same veneration by the Athenians of after ages as Shakespeare is by us; and Longinus has judged, in favor of him, that he had a noble boldness of expression, and that his imaginations were lofty and heroic; but, on the other side, Quintilian affirms that he was daring to extravagance. 'Tis certain that he affected pompous words, and that his sense too often was obscured by figures. Notwithstanding these imperfections, the value of his writings after his decease was such that his countrymen ordained an equal reward to those poets who could alter his plays to be acted on the theater, with those whose productions were wholly new, and of their own. The case is not the same in England; though the difficulties of altering are greater, and our reverence for Shakespeare much more just, than that of the Grecians for Aeschylus. In the age of that poet, the Greek tongue was arrived to its full perfection; they had then amongst them an exact standard of writing and of speaking. The English language is not capable of such a certainty; and we are at present so far from it that we are wanting in the very foundation of it, a perfect grammar. Yet it must be allowed to the present age that the tongue in general is so much refined since Shakespeare's time that many of his words, and more of his phrases, are scarce intelligible. And of those which we understand, some are ungrammatical, others coarse; and his whole style is so pestered with figurative expressions, that it is as affected as it is obscure. 'Tis true, that in his later plays he had worn off somewhat of the rust; but the tragedy which I have undertaken to correct was, in all probability, one of his first endeavors on the stage.[1]

---

[1]Actually, *Troilus and Cressida,* which was probably written around 1602, came at the midpoint of Shakespeare's career.

The original story was written by one Lollius, a Lombard, in Latin verse, and translated by Chaucer into English; intended, I suppose, a satire on the inconstancy of women: I find nothing of it among the Ancients; not so much as the name Cressida once mentioned. Shakespeare (as I hinted), in the apprenticeship of his writing, modeled it into that play which is now called by the name of *Troilus and Cressida*; but so lamely is it left to us, that it is not divided into acts; which fault I ascribe to the actors who printed it after Shakespeare's death; and that too so carelessly, that a more uncorrect copy I never saw. For the play itself, the author seems to have begun it with some fire; the characters of Pandarus and Thersites are promising enough; but as if he grew weary of his task, after an entrance or two, he lets 'em fall: and the later part of the tragedy is nothing but a confusion of drums and trumpets, excursions and alarms. The chief persons, who give name to the tragedy, are left alive; Cressida is false, and is not punished. Yet after all, because the play was Shakespeare's, and that there appeared in some places of it the admirable genius of the author, I undertook to remove that heap of rubbish under which many excellent thoughts lay wholly buried. Accordingly, I new modeled the plot; threw out many unnecessary persons; improved those characters which were begun and left unfinished: as Hector, Troilus, Pandarus, and Thersites; and added that of Andromache. After this I made, with no small trouble, an order and connection of all the scenes; removing them from the places where they were inartificially set; and though it was impossible to keep 'em all unbroken, because the scene must be sometimes in the city and sometimes in the camp, yet I have so ordered them that there is a coherence of 'em with one another, and a dependence on the main design: no leaping from Troy to the Grecian tents, and thence back again in the same act; but a due proportion of time allowed for every motion. I need not say that I have refined his language, which before was obsolete; but I am willing to acknowledge that as I have often drawn his English nearer to our times, so I have sometimes conformed my own to his; and consequently, the language is not altogether so pure as it is significant. The scenes of Pandarus and Cressida, of Troilus and Pandarus, of Andromache with Hector and the Trojans, in the second act, are wholly new; together with that of Nestor and Ulysses with Thersites, and that of Thersites with Ajax and Achilles. I will not weary my reader with the scenes which are added of Pandarus and the lovers, in the third; and those of Thersites, which are wholly altered; but I cannot omit the last scene in it, which is almost half the act, betwixt Troilus and Hector. The occasion of raising it was hinted to me by Mr. Betterton: the contrivance and working of it was my own. They who think to do me an injury by saying that it is an imitation of the scene betwixt Brutus and Cassius, do me an honor by supposing I could imitate the incomparable Shakespeare; but let me add that if Shakespeare's scene, or that faulty copy of it in *Amintor and Melantius*, had never been, yet Euripides had furnished me with an excellent example in his *Iphigenia*, between Agamemnon and Menelaus; and from thence, indeed, the last turn of it is borrowed.[2] The occasion which Shakespeare, Euripides, and Fletcher have all taken is the same; grounded upon friendship: and the quarrel of two virtuous men, raised by natural degrees to the extremity of passion, is conducted in all three to the declination of the same passion, and concludes with a warm renewing of their friendship. But the particular groundwork which Shakespeare has taken is incomparably the best; because he has not only chosen two of the greatest heroes of their age, but has likewise interested the liberty of Rome, and their own honors who were the redeemers of it, in this debate. And if he has made Brutus, who was naturally a patient man, to fly into excess at first, let it be remembered in his defense that, just before, he has received the news of Portia's death; whom the poet, on purpose neglecting a little chronology, supposes to have died before Brutus, only to give him an occasion of being more easily exasperated. Add to this that the injury he had received from Cassius had long been brooding in his mind; and that a melancholy man, upon consideration of an affront, es-

pecially from a friend, would be more eager in his passion than he who had given it, though naturally more choleric.

Euripides, whom I have followed, has raised the quarrel betwixt two brothers who were friends. The foundation of the scene was this: the Grecians were windbound at the port of Aulis, and the oracle had said that they could not sail, unless Agamemnon delivered up his daughter to be sacrificed: he refuses; his brother Menelaus urges the public safety; the father defends himself by arguments of natural affection, and hereupon they quarrel. Agamemnon is at last convinced, and promises to deliver up Iphigenia, but so passionately laments his loss that Menelaus is grieved to have been the occasion of it and, by a return of kindness, offers to intercede for him with the Grecians, that his daughter might not be sacrificed. But my friend Mr. Rymer has so largely, and with so much judgment, described this scene, in comparing it with that of Melantius and Amintor, that it is superfluous to say more of it; I only named the heads of it, that any reasonable man might judge it was from thence I modeled my scene betwixt Troilus and Hector. I will conclude my reflections on it with a passage of Longinus, concerning Plato's imitation of Homer: "We ought not to regard a good imitation as a theft, but as a beautiful idea of him who undertakes to imitate, by forming himself on the invention and the work of another man; for he enters into the lists like a new wrestler, to dispute the prize with the former champion. This sort of emulation, says Hesiod, is honorable, 'this strife is wholesome to man,'[3] when we combat for victory with a hero, and are not without glory even in our overthrow. Those great men whom we propose to ourselves as patterns of our imitation serve us as a torch, which is lifted up before us to enlighten our passage; and often elevate our thoughts as high as the conception we have of our author's genius."[4]

I have been so tedious in three acts that I shall contract myself in the two last. The beginning scenes of the fourth act are either added or changed wholly by me; the middle of it is Shakespeare altered, and mingled with my own; three or four of the last scenes are altogether new. And the whole fifth act, both the plot and the writing, are my own additions.

But having written so much for imitation of what is excellent, in that part of the preface which related only to myself, methinks it would neither be unprofitable nor unpleasant to inquire how far we ought to imitate our own poets, Shakespeare and Fletcher, in their tragedies: and this will occasion another inquiry, how those two writers differ between themselves. But since neither of these questions

---

[2]The comparison of the quarrels between Amintor and Melantius in Beaumont and Fletcher's *Maid's Tragedy* and Agamemnon and Menelaus in Euripides's *Iphigenia in Aulis* had already been made by Rymer in his *Tragedies of the Last Age* (1678), as Dryden acknowledges in the following paragraph.

---

[3]ἀγαθὴ δ᾽ ἔρις ἐστὶ βροτοῖσιν (*Works and Days*, 1.24).
[4]*On the Sublime*, 13.4.

can be solved unless some measures be first taken by which we may be enabled to judge truly of their writings, I shall endeavor, as briefly as I can, to discover the grounds and reason of all criticism, applying them in this place only to tragedy. Aristotle with his interpreters, and Horace, and Longinus, are the authors to whom I owe my lights; and what part soever of my own plans, or of this, which no mending could make regular, shall fall under the condemnation of such judges, it would be impudence in me to defend. . . .

THE GROUNDS OF CRITICISM IN TRAGEDY

Tragedy is thus defined by Aristotle (omitting what I thought unnecessary in his definition). 'Tis an imitation of one entire, great, and probable action; not told, but represented; which, by moving in us fear and pity, is conducive to the purging of those two passions in our minds. More largely thus, tragedy describes or paints an action, which action must have all the proprieties above named. First, it must be one or single, that is, it must not be a history of one man's life; suppose of Alexander the Great, or Julius Caesar, but one single action of theirs. This condemns all Shakespeare's historical plays, which are rather chronicles represented than tragedies, and all double action of plays. As to avoid a satire upon others, I will make bold with my own *Marriage à-la-Mode,* where there are manifestly two actions, not depending on one another: but in *Oedipus* there cannot properly be said to be two actions, because the love of Adrastus and Eurydice has a necessary dependence on the principal design, into which it is woven. The natural reason of rule is plain; for two different independent actions distract the attention and concernment of the audience, and consequently destroy the intention of the poet: if his business be to move terror and pity, and one of his actions be comical, the other tragical, the former will divert the people, and utterly make void his greater purpose. Therefore, as in perspective, so in tragedy, there must be a point of sight in which all the lines terminate; otherwise the eye wanders, and the work is false. This was the practice of the Grecian stage. But Terence made an innovation in the Roman: all his plays have double actions; for it was his custom to translate two Greek comedies, and to weave them into one of his, yet so that both the actions were comical, and one was principal, the other but secondary or subservient. And this has obtained on the English stage, to give us the pleasure of variety.

As the action ought to be one, it ought, as such, to have order in it, that is, to have a natural beginning, a middle, and an end. A natural beginning, says Aristotle, is that which could not necessarily have been placed after another thing, and so of the rest. This consideration will arraign all plays after the new model of Spanish plots, where accident is heaped upon accident, and that which is first might as reasonably be

last: an inconvenience not to be remedied but by making one accident naturally produce another, otherwise 'tis a farce and not a play. Of this nature is the *Slighted Maid,*[5] where there is no scene in the first act which might not by as good reason be in the fifth. And if the action ought to be one, the tragedy ought likewise to conclude with the action of it. Thus in *Mustapha,*[6] the play should naturally have ended with the death of Zanger, and not have given us the grace cup after dinner of Solyman's divorce from Roxolana.

The following properties of the action are so easy that they need not my explaining. It ought to be great, and to consist of great persons, to distinguish it from comedy, where the action is trivial, and the persons of inferior rank. The last quality of the action is that it ought to be *probable,* as well as admirable and great. 'Tis not necessary that there should be historical truth in it; but always necessary that there should be a likeness of truth, something that is more than barely possible, *probable* being that which succeeds or happens oftener than it misses. To invent therefore a probability, and to make it wonderful, is the most difficult undertaking in the art of poetry; for that which is not wonderful is not great; and that which is not probable will not delight a reasonable audience. This action, thus described, must be represented and not told, to distinguish dramatic poetry from epic: but I hasten to the end or scope of tragedy, which is to rectify or purge our passions, fear and pity.

To instruct delightfully is the general end of all poetry. Philosophy instructs, but it performs its work by precept: which is not delightful, or not so delightful as example. To purge the passions by example is therefore the particular instruction which belongs to tragedy. Rapin, a judicious critic, has observed from Aristotle that pride and want of commiseration are the most predominant vices in mankind: therefore, to cure us of these two, the inventors of tragedy have chosen to work upon two other passions, which are fear and pity. We are wrought to fear by their setting before our eyes some terrible example of misfortune, which happened to persons of the highest quality; for such an action demonstrates to us that no condition is privileged from the turns of fortune; this must of necessity cause terror in us, and consequently abate our pride. But when we see that the most virtuous, as well as the greatest, are not exempt from such misfortunes, that consideration moves pity in us, and insensibly works us to be helpful to, and tender over, the distressed, which is the noblest and most god-like of moral virtues. Here 'tis observable that it is absolutely necessary to make a man virtuous, if we desire he should be pitied; we

---

[5]By Sir Robert Stapylton (1663).

[6]By Roger Boyle, Earl of Orrery (first performed in 1665).

lament not, but detest, a wicked man; we are glad when we behold his crimes are punished, and that poetical justice[7] is done upon him. Euripides was censured by the critics of his time for making his chief characters too wicked: for example, Phaedra, though she loved her son-in-law with reluctancy, and that it was a curse upon her family for offending Venus, yet was thought too ill a pattern for the stage. Shall we therefore banish all characters of villainy? I confess I am not of that opinion; but it is necessary that the hero of the play be not a villain; that is, the characters which should move our pity ought to have virtuous inclinations, and degrees of moral goodness in them. As for a perfect character of virtue, it never was in nature, and therefore there can be no imitation of it; but there are allays of frailty to be allowed for the chief persons, yet so that the good which is in them shall outweigh the bad, and consequently leave room for punishment on the one side, and pity on the other.

After all, if anyone will ask me whether a tragedy cannot be made upon any other grounds than those of exciting pity and terror in us, Bossu,[8] the best of modern critics, answers thus in general: that all excellent arts, and particularly that of poetry, have been invented and brought to perfection by men of a transcendent genius; and that therefore they who practice afterwards the same arts are obliged to tread in their footsteps, and to search in their writings the foundation of them; for it is not just that new rules should destroy the authority of the old. But Rapin writes more particularly thus[9]: that no passions in a story are so proper to move our concernment as fear and pity; and that it is from our concernment we receive our pleasure, is undoubted; when the soul becomes agitated with fear for one character, or hope for another, then it is that we are pleased in tragedy by the interest which we take in their adventures.

Here, therefore, the general answer may be given to the first question, how far we ought to imitate Shakespeare and Fletcher in their plots: namely, that we ought to follow them so far only as they have copied the excellencies of those who invented and brought to perfection dramatic poetry: those things only excepted which religion, customs of countries, idioms of languages, etc., have altered in the superstructures, but not in the foundation of the design.

How defective Shakespeare and Fletcher have been in all their plots, Mr. Rymer has discovered in his criticisms: neither can we who follow them be excused from the same or greater errors; which are the more unpardonable in us, be-

cause we want their beauties to countervail our faults. The best of their designs, the most approaching to antiquity, and the most conducing to move pity, is the *King and No King;* which, if the farce of Bessus were thrown away, is of that inferior sort of tragedies which end with a prosperous event. 'Tis probably derived from the story of Oedipus, with the character of Alexander the Great, in his extravagancies, given to Arbaces. The taking of this play, amongst many others, I cannot wholly ascribe to the excellency of the action; for I find it moving when it is read: 'tis true, the faults of the plot are so evidently proved that they can no longer be denied. The beauties of it must therefore lie either in the lively touches of the passion: or we must conclude, as I think we may, that even in imperfect plots there are less degrees of nature, by which some faint emotions of pity and terror are raised in us: as a less engine will raise a less proportion of weight, though not so much as one of Archimedes' making; for nothing can move our nature, but by some natural reason, which works upon passions. And since we acknowledge the effect, there must be something in the cause.

The difference between Shakespeare and Fletcher in their plotting seems to be this: that Shakespeare generally moves more terror, and Fletcher more compassion. For the first had a more masculine, a bolder and more fiery genius; the second, a more soft and womanish. In the mechanic beauties of the plot, which are the observation of the three unities, time, place, and action, they are both deficient; but Shakespeare most. Ben Jonson reformed those errors in his comedies, yet one of Shakespeare's was regular before him; which is, *The Merry Wives of Windsor.* For what remains concerning the design, you are to be referred to our English critic. That method which he has prescribed to raise it from mistake, or ignorance of the crime, is certainly the best, though 'tis not the only: for amongst all the tragedies of Sophocles, there is but one, *Oedipus,* which is wholly built after that model.

After the plot, which is the foundation of the play, the next thing to which we ought to apply our judgment is the manners, for now the poet comes to work above ground: the ground-work indeed is that which is most necessary, as that upon which depends the firmness of the whole fabric; yet it strikes not the eye so much as the beauties or imperfections of the manners, the thoughts, and the expressions.

The first rule which Bossu prescribes to the writer of an heroic poem, and which holds too by the same reason in all dramatic poetry, is to make the moral of the work, that is, to lay down to yourself what that precept of morality shall be, which you would insinuate into the people; as namely, Homer's (which I have copied in my *Conquest of Granada*) was, that union preserves a commonwealth, and discord

---

[7]A phrase first coined by Rymer in *The Tragedies of the Last Age.*

[8]Le Bossu, author of *Traité du poème épique* (1675).

[9]In *Réflexions sur la poétique d'Aristote* (1674).

destroys it; Sophocles, in his *Oedipus,* that no man is to be accounted happy before his death. 'Tis the moral that directs the whole action of the play to one center; and that action or fable is the example built upon the moral, which confirms the truth of it to our experience: when the fable is designed, then and not before, the persons are to be introduced with their manners, characters, and passions.

The manners in a poem are understood to be those inclinations, whether natural or acquired, which move and carry us to actions, good, bad, or indifferent, in a play; or which incline the persons to such or such actions. I have anticipated part of this discourse already, in declaring that a poet ought not to make the manners perfectly good in his best persons; but neither are they to be more wicked in any of his characters than necessity requires. To produce a villain, without other reason than a natural inclination to villainy is, in poetry, to produce an effect without a cause; and to make him more a villain than he has just reason to be, is to make an effect which is stronger than the cause.

The manners arise from many causes; and are either distinguished by complexion, as choleric and phlegmatic, or by the differences of age or sex, of climates, or quality of the persons, or their present condition. They are likewise to be gathered from the several virtues, vices, or passions, and many other commonplaces which a poet must be supposed to have learned from natural philosophy, ethics, and history; of all which whosoever is ignorant, does not deserve the name of poet.

But as the manners are useful in this art, they may be all comprised under these general heads: first, they must be apparent; that is, in every character of the play, some inclinations of the person must appear: and these are shown in the actions and discourse. Secondly, the manners must be suitable, or agreeing to the persons; that is, to the age, sex, dignity, and the other general heads of manners: thus, when a poet has given the dignity of a king to one of his persons, in all his actions and speeches, that person must discover majesty, magnanimity, and jealousy of power, because these are suitable to the general manners of a king. The third property of manners is resemblance; and this is founded upon the particular characters of men, as we have them delivered to us by relation or history; that is, when a poet has the known character of this or that man before him, he is bound to represent him such, at least not contrary to that which fame has reported him to have been. Thus, it is not a poet's choice to make Ulysses choleric, or Achilles patient, because Homer has described 'em quite otherwise. Yet this is a rock on which ignorant writers daily split; and the absurdity is as monstrous as if a painter should draw a coward running from a battle, and tell us it was the picture of Alexander the Great.

The last property of manners is that they be constant and equal, that is, maintained the same through the whole design: thus, when Virgil had once given the name of *pious* to Aeneas, he was bound to show him such, in all his words and actions through the whole poem. All these properties Horace has hinted to a judicious observer: "1. you must mark the manners of each age; 2. or follow tradition; 3. or create your own convention; 4. let each character remain constant and consistent with itself."[10]

From the manners, the characters of persons are derived; for indeed the characters are no other than the inclinations, as they appear in the several persons of the poem; a character being thus defined, that which distinguishes one man from another. Not to repeat the same things over again which have been said of the manners, I will only add what is necessary here. A character, or that which distinguishes one man from all others, cannot be supposed to consist of one particular virtue, or vice, or passion only; but 'tis a composition of qualities which are not contrary to one another in the same person; thus the same man may be liberal and valiant, but not liberal and covetous; so in a comical character, or humour (which is an inclination to this or that particular folly), Falstaff is a liar, and a coward, a glutton, and a buffoon, because all these qualities may agree in the same man; yet it is still to be observed that one virtue, vice, and passion ought to be shown in every man, as predominant over all the rest; as covetousness in Crassus, love of his country in Brutus; and the same in characters which are feigned.

The chief character or hero in a tragedy, as I have already shown, ought in prudence to be such a man who has so much more in him of virtue than of vice, that he may be left amiable to the audience, which otherwise cannot have any concernment for his sufferings; and 'tis on this one character that the pity and terror must be principally, if not wholly, founded—a rule which is extremely necessary, and which none of the critics that I know have fully enough discovered to us. For terror and compassion work but weakly when they are divided into many persons. If Creon had been the chief character in *Oedipus,* there had neither been terror nor compassion moved; but only detestation of the man and joy for his punishment; if Adrastus and Eurydice had been made more appealing characters, then the pity had been divided, and lessened on the part of Oedipus: but making Oedipus the best and bravest person, and even Jocasta but an underpart to him, his virtues and the punishment of his fatal crime drew both the pity and the terror to himself.

---

[10]1. *notandi sunt tibi mores;* 2. *aut famam sequere;* 3. *aut sibi convenientia finge;* 4. *servetur ad imum, qualis ab incepto processerit, et sibi constet* (*Ars poetica,* 11.156, 119, 126–127).

By what had been said of the manners, it will be easy for a reasonable man to judge whether the characters be truly or falsely drawn in a tragedy; for if there be no manners appearing in the characters, no concernment for the persons can be raised; no pity or horror can be moved, but by vice or virtue; therefore, without them, no person can have any business in the play. If the inclinations be obscure, 'tis a sign the poet is in the dark, and knows not what manner of man he presents to you; and consequently you can have no idea, or very imperfect, of that man; nor can judge what resolutions he ought to take; or what words or actions are proper for him. Most comedies made up of accidents or adventures are liable to fall into this error; and tragedies with many turns are subject to it; for the manners never can be evident where the surprises of fortune take up all the business of the stage; and where the poet is more in pain to tell you what happened to such a man than what he was. 'Tis one of the excellencies of Shakespeare that the manners of his persons are generally apparent, and you see their bent and inclinations. Fletcher comes far short of him in this, as indeed he does almost in everything: there are but glimmerings of manners in most of his comedies, which run upon adventures: and in his tragedies, *Rollo, Otto, A King and No King,* Melantius,[11] and many others of his best, are but pictures shown you in the twilight; you know not whether they resemble vice or virtue, and they are either good, bad, or indifferent, as the present scene requires it. But of all poets, this commendation is to be given to Ben Jonson, that the manners even of the most inconsiderable persons in his plays are everywhere apparent.

By considering the second quality of manners, which is that they be suitable to the age, quality, country, dignity, etc., of the character, we may likewise judge whether a poet has followed nature. In this kind, Sophocles and Euripides have more excelled among the Greeks than Aeschylus; and Terence more than Plautus among the Romans. Thus Sophocles gives to Oedipus the true qualities of a king, in both those plays which bear his name; but in the latter, which is the *Oedipus Colonœus,* he lets fall on purpose his tragic style; his hero speaks not in the arbitrary tone, but remembers, in the softness of his complaints, that he is an unfortunate blind old man, that he is banished from his country, and persecuted by his next relations. The present French poets are generally accused that wheresoever they lay the scene, or in whatsoever age, the manners of their heroes are wholly French. Racine's Bajazet is bred at Constantinople, but his civilities are conveyed to him, by some secret passage, from Versailles into the Seraglio. But our Shakespeare, having as-

cribed to Henry the Fourth the character of a king and of a father, gives him the perfect manners of each relation, when either he transacts with his son or with his subjects. Fletcher, on the other side, gives neither to Arbaces, nor to his King in the *Maid's Tragedy,* the qualities which are suitable to a monarch; though he may be excused a little in the latter, for the King there is not uppermost in the character; 'tis the lover of Evadne, who is King only in a second consideration; and though he be unjust, and has other faults which shall be nameless, yet he is not the hero of the play. 'Tis true, we find him a lawful prince (though I never heard of any King that was in Rhodes), and therefore Mr. Rymer's criticism stands good; that he should not be shown in so vicious a character. Sophocles has been more judicious in his *Antigone;* for though he represents in Creon a bloody prince, yet he makes him not a lawful king, but an usurper, and Antigona herself is the heroine of the tragedy. But when Philaster wounds Arethusa and the boy; and Perigot his mistress, in the *Faithful Shepherdess,* both these are contrary to the character of manhood. Nor is Valentinian managed much better, for though Fletcher has taken his picture truly, and shown him as he was, an effeminate, voluptuous man, yet he has forgotten that he was an Emperor, and has given him none of those royal marks which ought to appear in a lawful successor of the throne. If it be inquired what Fletcher should have done on this occasion: ought he not to have represented Valentinian as he was? Bossu shall answer this question for me, by an instance of the like nature: Mauritius, the Greek Emperor, was a prince far surpassing Valentinian, for he was endued with many kingly virtues; he was religious, merciful, and valiant, but withal he was noted of extreme covetousness, a vice which is contrary to the character of a hero, or a prince: therefore, says the critic, that emperor was no fit person to be represented in a tragedy, unless his good qualities were only to be shown, and his covetousness (which sullied them all) were slurred over by the artifice of the poet.[12] To return once more to Shakespeare: no man ever drew so many characters, or generally distinguished 'em better from one another, excepting only Jonson. I will instance but in one, to show the copiousness of his invention: 'tis that of Caliban, or the Monster in the *Tempest.* He seems there to have created a person which was not in nature, a boldness which at first sight would appear intolerable; for he makes him a species of himself, begotten by an incubus on a witch; but this, as I have elsewhere proved, is not wholly beyond the bounds of credibility, at least the vulgar still believe it. We have the separated notions of a spirit, and of a witch (and spirits,

---

[11]Otto is Rollo's brother; Melantius is a character in *The Maid's Tragedy.*

[12]*Traité du poème épique,* 4.7.

according to Plato, are vested with a subtle body; according to some of his followers, have different sexes); therefore, as from the distinct apprehensions of a horse, and of a man, imagination has formed a centaur; so from those of an incubus and a sorceress, Shakespeare has produced his monster. Whether or no his generation can be defended, I leave to philosophy; but of this I am certain, that the poet has most judiciously furnished him with a person, a language, and a character, which will suit him, both by father's and mother's side: he has all the discontents and malice of a witch, and of a devil, besides a convenient proportion of the deadly sins; gluttony, sloth, and lust are manifest; the dejectedness of a slave is likewise given him, and the ignorance of one bred up in a desert island. His person is monstrous, as he is the product of unnatural lust; and his language is as hobgoblin as his person; in all things he is distinguished from other mortals. The characters of Fletcher are poor and narrow, in comparison of Shakespeare's; I remember not one which is not borrowed from him; unless you will except that strange mixture of a man in the *King and No King;* so that in this part Shakespeare is generally worth our imitation; and to imitate Fletcher is but to copy after him who was a copier.

Under this general head of manners, the passions are naturally included, as belonging to the characters. I speak not of pity and of terror, which are to be moved in the audience by the plot; but of anger, hatred, love, ambition, jealousy, revenge, etc., as they are shown in this or that person of the play. To describe these naturally, and to move them artfully, is one of the greatest commendations which can be given to a poet: to write pathetically, says Longinus, cannot proceed but from a lofty genius. A poet must be born with this quality; yet, unless he help himself by an acquired knowledge of the passions, what they are in their own nature, and by what springs they are to be moved, he will be subject either to raise them where they ought not to be raised, or not to raise them by the just degrees of nature, or to amplify them beyond the natural bounds, or not to observe the crisis and turns of them, in their cooling and decay: all which errors proceed from want of judgment in the poet, and from being unskilled in the principles of moral philosophy. Nothing is more frequent in a fanciful writer than to foil himself by not managing his strength; therefore, as in a wrestler, there is first required some measure of force, a well-knit body, and active limbs, without which all instruction would be vain; yet, these being granted, if he want the skill which is necessary to a wrestler, he shall make but small advantage of his natural robustuousness: so, in a poet, his inborn vehemence and force of spirit will only run him out of breath the sooner, if it be not supported by the help of art. The roar of passion indeed may please an audience, three parts of which are igno-

rant enough to think all is moving which is noise, and it may stretch the lungs of an ambitious actor, who will die upon the spot for a thundering clap; but it will move no other passion than indignation and contempt from judicious men. Longinus, whom I have hitherto followed, continues thus: *If the passions be artfully employed, the discourse becomes vehement and lofty: if otherwise, there is nothing more ridiculous than a great passion out of season:* and to this purpose he animadverts severely upon Aeschylus, who writ nothing in cold blood, but was always in a rapture, and in fury with his audience;[13] the inspiration was still upon him, he was ever tearing it upon the tripos[14]; or (to run off as madly as he does, from one similitude to another) he was always at high flood of passion, even in the dead ebb and lowest water-mark of the scene. He who would raise the passion of a judicious audience, says a learned critic, must be sure to take his hearers along with him; if they be in a calm, 'tis in vain for him to be in a huff: he must move them by degrees, and kindle with 'em; otherwise he will be in danger of setting his own heap of stubble on a fire, and of burning out by himself without warming the company that stand about him. They who would justify the madness of poetry from the authority of Aristotle have mistaken the text, and consequently the interpretation: I imagine it to be false read, where he says of poetry that it is εὐφυοῦς ἤ μανικοῦ, that it had always somewhat in it either of a genius, or of a madman. 'Tis more probable that the original ran thus, that poetry was εὐφυοῦς οὐ μανικοῦ, that it belongs to a witty man, but not to a madman.[15] Thus then the passions, as they are considered simply and in themselves, suffer violence when they are perpetually maintained at the same height; for what melody can be made on that instrument, all whose strings are screwed up at first to their utmost stretch, and to the same sound? But this is not the worst: for the characters likewise bear a part in the general calamity, if you consider the passions embodied in them; for it follows of necessity that no man can be distinguished from another by his discourse, when every man is ranting, swaggering, and exclaiming with the same excess: as if it were the only business of all the characters to contend with each other for the prize at Billingsgate; or that the scene of the tragedy lay in Bet'lem.[16] Suppose the poet should intend this man to be choleric, and that man to be patient; yet when they are confounded in the writing, you cannot distinguish

---

[13] *On the Sublime,* 3.

[14] A reference to the tripod at Delphi on which the priestess of Apollo delivered her raving oracles.

[15] Aristotle, *The Poetics,* 17.

[16] Bedlam, a London hospital for the insane.

them from one another: for the man who was called patient and tame is only so before he speaks; but let his clack be set a-going, and he shall tongue it as impetuously, and as loudly, as the errantest hero in the play. By this means, the characters are only distinct in name; but, in reality, all the men and women in the play are the same person. No man should pretend to write who cannot temper his fancy with his judgment: nothing is more dangerous to a raw horseman than a hot-mouthed jade without a curb.

'Tis necessary therefore for a poet who would concern an audience by describing of a passion, first to prepare it, and not to rush upon it all at once. Ovid has judiciously shown the difference of these two ways, in the speeches of Ajax and Ulysses: Ajax, from the very beginning, breaks out into his exclamations, and is swearing by his Maker, "'By Jupiter,' he cried."[17] Ulysses, on the contrary, prepares his audience with all the submissiveness he can practice, and all the calmness of a reasonable man; he found his judges in a tranquillity of spirit, and therefore set out leisurely and softly with 'em, till he had warmed 'em by degrees; and then he began to mend his pace, and to draw them along with his own impetuousness: yet so managing his breath, that it might not fail him at his need, and reserving his utmost proofs of ability even to the last. The success, you see, was answerable; for the crowd only applauded the speech of Ajax:

and the applause of the crowd followed his closing words.[18]

But the judges awarded the prize for which they contended to Ulysses:

the assembly was very moved; and the power of eloquence was revealed, and the skillful orator carried off the hero's arms.[19]

The next necessary rule is to put nothing into the discourse which may hinder your moving of the passions. Too many accidents, as I have said, encumber the poet, as much as the arms of Saul did David; for the variety of passions which they produce are ever crossing and jostling each other out of the way. He who treats of joy and grief together is in a fair way of causing neither of those effects. There is yet another obstacle to be removed, which is pointed wit, and sentences affected out of season; these are nothing of kin to the violence of passion: no man is at leisure to make sentences

and similes when his soul is in an agony. I the rather name this fault that it may serve to mind me of my former errors; neither will I spare myself, but give an example of this kind from my *Indian Emperor.* Montezuma, pursued by his enemies, and seeking sanctuary, stands parleying without the fort, and describing his danger to Cydaria, in a simile of six lines:

As on the sands the frighted traveller
Sees the high seas come rolling from afar, etc.[20]

My Indian potentate was well skilled in the sea for an inland prince, and well improved since the first act, when he sent his son to discover it. The image had not been amiss from another man, at another time: "but not now, in this place"[21]; he destroyed the concernment which the audience might otherwise have had for him; for they could not think the danger near when he had the leisure to invent a simile.

If Shakespeare be allowed, as I think he must, to have made his characters distinct, it will easily be inferred that he understood the nature of the passions: because it has been proved already that confused passions make undistinguishable characters. Yet I cannot deny that he has his failings; but they are not so much in the passions themselves as in his manner of expression: he often obscures his meaning by his words, and sometimes makes it unintelligible. I will not say of so great a poet that he distinguished not the blown puffy style from true sublimity; but I may venture to maintain that the fury of his fancy often transported him beyond the bounds of judgment, either in coining of new words and phrases or racking words which were in use into the violence of a catachresis.[22] 'Tis not that I would explode[23] the use of metaphors from passions, for Longinus thinks 'em necessary to raise it: but to use 'em at every word, to say nothing without a metaphor, a simile, an image, or description, is I doubt to smell a little too strongly of the buskin. I must be forced to give an example of expressing passion figuratively; but that I may do it with respect to Shakespeare, it shall not be taken from anything of his: 'tis an exclamation against Fortune, quoted in his *Hamlet,* but written by some other poet:

Out, out, thou strumpet Fortune! all you gods,
In general synod, take away her power;
Break all the spokes and felleys from her wheel,
And bowl the round nave down the hill of Heav'n,
As low as to the fiends.

---

[17] *agimus, pro Jupiter, inquit* (*Metamorphoses,* 13.5).

[18]   *vulgique secutum*
ultima mumur erat.
       Ibid., 123.

[19] *mota manus procerum est; et quid facundia posset*
tum patuit, fortisque viri tulit arma disertus
       Ibid., 282–83.

---

[20] Act 5.

[21] *sed nunc non erat hisce locus* (*Ars poetica,* 1.19).

[22] A misuse of terms.

[23] Banish, reject.

And immediately after, speaking of Hecuba, when Priam was killed before her eyes:

> The mobled queen ran up and down,
> Threatening the flame with bisson rheum; a clout about that head
> Where late the diadem stood; and for a robe,
> About her lank and all o'er-teemed loins,
> A blanket in th' alarm of fear caught up.
> Who this had seen, with tongue in venom steep'd
> 'Gainst Fortune's state would treason have pronounced;
> But if the gods themselves did see her then,
> When she saw Pyrrhus make malicious sport
> In mincing with his sword her husband's limbs,
> The instant burst of clamour that she made
> (Unless things mortal move them not at all)
> Would have made milch the burning eyes of Heaven,
> And passion in the gods.[24]

What a pudder is here kept in raising the expression of trifling thoughts! Would not a man have thought that the poet had been bound prentice to a wheelwright, for his first rant? and had followed a ragman for the clout and blanket, in the second? Fortune is painted on a wheel, and therefore the writer, in a rage, will have poetical justice down upon every member of that engine: after this execution, he bowls the nave down hill, from Heaven to the fiends (an unreasonable long mark, a man would think); 'tis well there are no solid orbs to stop it in the way, or no element of fire to consume it: but when it came to the earth, it must be monstrous heavy, to break ground as low as to the center. His making milch the burning eyes of Heaven was a pretty tolerable flight too: and I think no man ever drew milk out of eyes before him: yet to make the wonder greater, these eyes were burning. Such a sight indeed were enough to have raised passion in the gods; but to excuse the effects of it, he tells you perhaps they did not see it. Wise men would be glad to find a little sense couched under all those pompous words; for bombast is commonly the delight of that audience which loves poetry, but understands it not: and as commonly has been the practice of those writers who, not being able to infuse a natural passion into the mind, have made it their business to ply the ears and to stun their judges by the noise. But Shakespeare does not often thus; for the passions in his scene between Brutus and Cassius are extremely natural, the thoughts are such as arise from the matter, and the expression of 'em not viciously figurative. I cannot leave this subject before I do justice to that divine poet by giving you one of his passionate descriptions:

'tis of Richard the Second when he was deposed, and led in triumph through the streets of London by Henry of Bolingbroke: the painting of it is so lively, and the words so moving, that I have scarce read anything comparable to it in any other language. Suppose you have seen already the fortunate usurper passing through the crowd, and followed by the shouts and acclamations of the people; and now behold King Richard entering upon the scene: consider the wretchedness of his condition, and his carriage in it; and refrain from pity if you can:

> As in a theater, the eyes of men,
> After a well-graced actor leaves the stage,
> Are idly bent on him that enters next,
> Thinking his prattle to be tedious:
> Even so, or with much more contempt, men's eyes
> Did scowl on Richard: no man cried, God save him:
> No joyful tongue gave him his welcome home,
> But dust was thrown upon his sacred head,
> Which with such gentle sorrow he shook off,
> His face still combating with tears and smiles
> (The badges of his grief and patience),
> That had not God (for some strong purpose) steel'd
> The hearts of men, they must perforce have melted,
> And barbarism itself have pitied him.[25]

To speak justly of this whole matter: 'tis neither height of thought that is discommended, nor pathetic vehemence, nor any nobleness of expression in its proper place; but 'tis a false measure of all these, something which is like 'em, and is not them; 'tis the Bristol-stone,[26] which appears like a diamond; 'tis an extravagant thought, instead of a sublime one; 'tis roaring madness, instead of vehemence; and a sound of words, instead of sense. If Shakespeare were stripped of all the bombast in his passions, and dressed in the most vulgar words, we should find the beauties of his thoughts remaining; if his embroideries were burnt down, there would still be silver at the bottom of the melting-pot: but I fear (at least let me fear it for myself) that we who ape his sounding words have nothing of his thought, but are all outside; there is not so much as a dwarf within our giant's clothes. Therefore, let not Shakespeare suffer for our sakes; 'tis our fault, who succeed him in an age which is more refined, if we imitate him so ill that we copy his failings only, and make a virtue of that in our writings which in his was an imperfection.

For what remains, the excellency of that poet was, as I have said, in the more manly passions; Fletcher's in the softer: Shakespeare writ better betwixt man and man; Fletcher, betwixt man and woman: consequently, the one described friendship better; the other love: yet Shakespeare

---

[24] *Hamlet*, 2.2.475–79, 487–500. [Line numbers cited here are those in this anthology; the lines that Dryden quotes differ slightly from this anthology because of his use of another version of Shakespeare's play.—Editor]

[25] *Richard II*, 5.2.23–36.

[26] A rock crystal.

taught Fletcher to write love: and Juliet, and Desdemona, are originals. 'Tis true, the scholar had the softer soul; but the master had the kinder. Friendship is both a virtue and a passion essentially; love is a passion only in its nature, and is not a virtue but by accident: good nature makes friendship, but effeminacy love. Shakespeare had an universal mind, which comprehended all characters and passions; Fletcher a more confined and limited: for though he treated love in perfection, yet honor, ambition, revenge, and generally all the stronger passions, he either touched not, or not masterly. To conclude all, he was a limb of Shakespeare.

I had intended to have proceeded to the last property of manners, which is that they must be constant, and the characters maintained the same from the beginning to the end; and from thence to have proceeded to the thoughts and expressions suitable to a tragedy: but I will first see how this will relish with the age. 'Tis, I confess, but cursorily written; yet the judgment which is given here is generally founded upon experience: but because many men are shocked at the name of rules, as if they were a kind of magisterial prescription upon poets, I will conclude with the words of Rapin, in his reflections on Aristotle's work of poetry: "If the rules be well considered, we shall find them to be made only to reduce nature into method, to trace her step by step, and not to suffer the least mark of her to escape us: 'tis only by these that probability in fiction is maintained, which is the soul of poetry. They are founded upon good sense, and sound reason, rather than on authority; for though Aristotle and Horace are produced, yet no man must argue that what they write is true because they writ it; but 'tis evident, by the ridiculous mistakes and gross absurdities which have been made by those poets who have taken their fancy only for their guide, that if this fancy be not regulated, 'tis a mere caprice, and utterly incapable to produce a reasonable and judicious poem."[27]

---

[27] *Réflexions*, 12.

V

Modern Europe

Hamm in one of the definitive spaces of modern drama, the empty room of Samuel Beckett's *Endgame,* in the 2000 Rude Mechanicals Theater Company production.

In many ways the world we live in today was forged between 1850 and 1950. Since the mid-nineteenth century, enormous political changes have redrawn the map of the planet: two world wars; the rise of the United States and the rise and fall of the Union of Soviet Socialist Republics as world superpowers; revolutions in Russia and China; worldwide liberation from European colonial rule in Mexico, the Philippines, Latin America, Africa, India, and Southeast Asia. Political change was spurred by a series of industrial and technological revolutions. This century saw the introduction of the telephone, radio, film, and television; of the automobile and the highway; of the airplane and the rocket; of penicillin, anesthetics, vaccinations, and artificial organs; of the assembly line and mass production; of multinational corporations extending their markets and influence around the globe. The acceleration of technological change altered the fabric of daily life, creating new forms of living, working, and relating to one another, and new ways of measuring our lives: suburbs and housing developments, trade unions and public corporations, the time clock and the wristwatch, public education and compulsory retirement. It witnessed huge changes in the landscape of life: the growth of the modern cityscape, of modern slums, skyscrapers, subways, and even city streets; of massive public projects like the Panama and Suez canals, the Empire State Building, the Eiffel Tower, and their grim cousins—the gas chambers of Auschwitz and the nuclear bombing of Hiroshima and Nagasaki.

Political and social changes were rivaled by the intellectual and cultural revolutions that gave—or attempted to give—meaning to modern experience. This was the century of Darwin and the theory of evolution; of Marx and Lenin; of Gandhi's nonviolent resistance; of Einstein, Oppenheimer, and Teller, and a revolution in our understanding of the physical cosmos; of Freud's discovery of the unconscious; of Proust, Joyce, Stein, Eliot, and Woolf; of the Impressionist painters, and of Picasso, and Pollock; of Diaghilev and Nijinsky, of Fred Astaire and Ginger Rogers, of Isadora Duncan and Martha Graham; of Wagner, of Stravinsky and Schoenberg, of ragtime and jazz.

This complex of revolutions extends to the modern theater. Technological innovation, political developments, and two major wars encouraged an increasing internationalism across the arts of Europe, evident in the "international" style of architecture popularized by Le Corbusier, the Bauhaus, and their followers; in Cubist painting and sculpture; and in modernist writing and music. This internationalism, however, hardly fostered a single, monolithic sense of "modernism" in the arts. Instead, it gave rise to a series of fragmentary **AVANT-GARDE** movements—imagism, cubism, vorticism, futurism, symbolism, surrealism, Dada, and so on—each with its own ideals, esthetics, and audience, and usually with its own resistant posture toward society as well. The fragment—the poetic image, Joyce's "epiphanies," Schoenberg's twelve-tone row, montage in film—came to be valued as a means of expression in itself. Since the 1950s, a variety of social, political, and esthetic challenges have been made to modernism—usually under the general rubric of **POSTMODERNISM.** These challenges are discussed later in this essay.

Modernist art also developed a distinction between "high art" and the esthetics of mass culture that parallels the modern division of labor and implies a division between highbrow and lowbrow, the elite and the popular. In many respects, the modernist theater became definitive of "high art" as it was edged from the center of cultural life by other performance media—film, radio, and later, television—which claimed greater immediacy and wider distribution. After the turn of the twentieth century, the modern theater and drama were increasingly pressed to define what is germane, special, essential to live dramatic performance.

Units V, VI, and VII survey the theater more widely than previous units, focusing not on a single city or site of performance, but instead on the broader developments of national and international movements. For although the theaters of Chekhov's Moscow, Shaw's London, and Brecht's Berlin reflected very different social dynamics, they were engaged in a common, distinctly modernist project: bringing the stage into a critical relation to the forms of modern life by taking an experimental attitude toward theatrical production. And many of these projects have a visible legacy in the work of their successors: in Beckett's sterile chambers and in Churchill's parallel between sexual and colonial politics.

The Modern Theater

Theatrical innovation always takes place on three fronts: as technology, as esthetics, and as ideology. The history of the modern theater is in one sense a history of new strategies and techniques for stage production: electric lighting, revolving stages, increasingly spectacular and illusionistic stage machinery, and new techniques of stage design, acting, and direction. What makes these changes meaningful is how they are used to represent and explain the world around us.

Reviewing the history of nineteenth-century drama, Brander Matthews, the first professor of dramatic literature in the United States, remarked in 1910 that modern drama owed its innovation more to Edison than to Ibsen, that the new drama was "the inevitable consequence of the incandescent bulb." The technological revolutions that brought engines and electricity to the public transformed theater throughout Europe and America: the replacement of candle lighting and gas lighting with more flexible electric lighting; the installation of the **PROSCENIUM** frame, emphasizing the pictorial coherence of the stage; the gradual disappearance of galleries and boxes in favor of seating the audience in darkened, fan-shaped theaters, emphasizing a perspective view of the proscenium; elevators to raise and lower sets; revolving stages on which several settings could be placed at one time. This technology could be put to a variety of uses, and the nineteenth-century theaters of Europe and America had an extraordinarily spectacular dimension, fostering a taste for **EXTRAVAGANZAS, MELODRAMAS, NAUTICAL SHOWS, PANTOMIMES,** and **TABLEAUX.** However, the apparatus of the modern theater came increasingly to be dominated by the notion of **SCENIC UNITY,** the idea that the stage set, the costumes, the behavior of the actors, and the dramatic action all should correspond to a single historical era and social milieu. Shakespeare's actors had mixed contemporary Elizabethan dress with "antique" costumes in the production of plays with classical settings. Throughout the eighteenth century, actors wore contemporary clothing regardless of the historical era of the play. By the late nineteenth century, however—following the example of Charles Kean and Henry Irving in England, the company of George II, the Duke of Saxe-Meiningen in Germany, and others—productions increasingly strove to establish a unified style on the stage, in which the dialogue, acting style, costumes, setting, and dramatic action all conformed to a single point of view.

The use of a unified theatrical style to assert a thorough **VERISIMILITUDE,** a photographic "slice of life" onstage, became the cornerstone of modern **REALISM** in drama and theater and of the movement called **NATURALISM** in which it began. In a series of essays calling for a "naturalism in the theater," published in the 1870s, the French novelist and playwright Émile Zola argued that the technology of the late nineteenth-century theater could be used to represent a more clinical or scientific attitude toward the world. He urged the stage to adopt a more lifelike and "naturalistic" style by adopting the "objective" methods and perspective of the natural sciences. By filling the stage with objects—real doors, real walls, pictures, furniture, fireplaces—the theater could place men and women in their "environment" rather than in the idealized "setting" of the classical theater, and the characters could then be

A PROSCENIUM STAGE: SHAKESPEARE MEMORIAL THEATRE

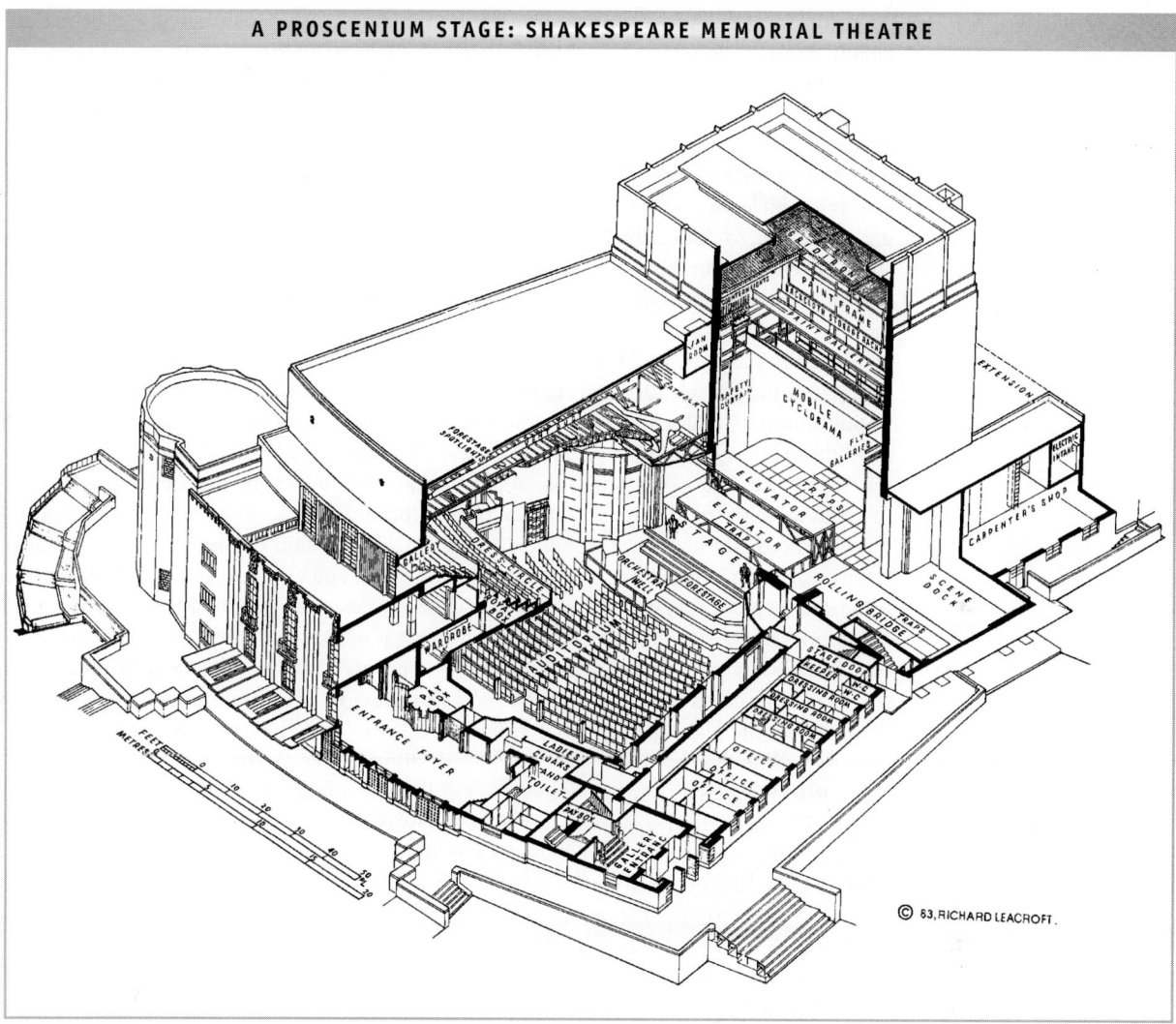

The Shakespeare Memorial Theatre, Stratford-upon-Avon, 1932, displays an extensive backstage area used for scenic machinery.

seen as influenced by that material environment. In contrast to the ideal heroes of earlier drama, the characters of modern plays would become part of that stage milieu, influenced by the forces of history, society, economy, and psychology. Naturalism uses the technology of the stage to claim a "scientific" attitude toward social problems, usually emphasizing the determining role that the social environment plays in the characters' actions. It organized the theater's new technology and the idea of scenic unity it made possible, and provided modern theater with a characteristic kind of meaning: the achievement of verisimilitude.

Naturalism and realism are notoriously difficult to distinguish; here we can describe them as two phases in the history of modern theater and drama. In this sense, naturalism provides the thematic inspiration and many of the dramatic techniques we now associate with modern realistic drama. Realism in the theater is also committed to verisimilitude, but usually develops a wider range of style and a more problematic sense of the relationship of character and environment. While naturalistic plays tend to be preoccupied with the duplication of material reality onstage, realistic plays sometimes distort the verisimilitude of the stage picture in order to dramatize an inner, psychological truth. The domestic space of Sam

Shepard's *True West*, for example, at first seems to frame a reunion between two brothers but rapidly transforms itself into the landscape of fantasy. Realism extends and refines the techniques first explored by Zola's generation of playwrights, directors, and actors: a simple and direct speaking style that usually masks a **SUBTEXT** of subtle, unspoken motives; middle- or lower-class characters; action that revolves around the discovery of some past crime or indiscretion; a three-dimensional stage set, usually a domestic interior. Rather than using the play as a vehicle for a single "star" actor, realistic performance emphasizes the ensemble playing of the cast, so that each character becomes important in the overall action. Onstage, realism often treats the boundary of the proscenium as an invisible fourth wall dividing the environment onstage from the audience. The **FOURTH WALL** prevents the actors from playing to the audience and so from destroying the unity of illusion onstage.

Realism has become the dominant mode of dramatic performance today, so pervasive that it may be difficult for us to recapture its special excitement and danger when first introduced in the 1880s and 1890s. In the first blush of the modern era, the ability to picture an untheatrical, apparently "real" world on the stage was in itself a kind of spectacle, akin to the magic of the new, competing art of photography. Moreover, the first generation of realistic playwrights often adopted a critical posture toward the pieties of the middle-class audience whose attitudes were embodied in the "realistic" vision of the world. Plays such as Ibsen's *Ghosts* and *A Doll House*, Strindberg's *Miss Julie,* and even Glaspell's *Trifles* raised the scandalous topics of sexual betrayal, marital discord, class conflict, sexual freedom, and gender politics in ways that challenged the conventional morality of the bourgeois audience.

The realistic theater developed many of the practices we are familiar with today: new sets for each production, rather than the same furniture recycled from show to show, in order to create the play's specific environment; the fourth wall; the darkened auditorium. Although realistic drama became pervasive, it first flourished in the small avant-garde theaters of the **INDEPENDENT THEATER MOVEMENT** at the turn of the century. Throughout Europe and the United States, playwrights and directors worked to carve a place for themselves outside the commercial mainstream, which often resisted and sometimes censored the controversial plays of the new realism. André Antoine founded the Théâtre Libre ("Free Theater") in Paris as a subscription theater in 1887; since the shows were open only to subscribers and not to the general public, he was able to avoid censorship and to produce plays like Ibsen's *Ghosts* and Strindberg's *The Father*. Antoine's work was paralleled by the German Freie Bühne ("Free Stage") in 1889. In England, the actress Janet Achurch mounted a production of Ibsen's *A Doll House* in 1889; J.T. Grein's Independent Theater opened in 1891 with a production of *Ghosts* and went on to produce plays by Ibsen, Shaw, and other contemporary playwrights. In Russia, Constantin Stanislavski and Vladimir Nemirovich-Danchenko founded the Moscow Art Theater in 1898, launching one of the most influential of modern theaters with their production of Chekhov's *The Seagull*. Independent theaters were often part of nationalist movements as well, especially in Norway, Sweden, Finland, Italy, and Ireland. In Ireland, W. B. Yeats, Lady Augusta Gregory, John Millington Synge, and a solid cast of amateur actors established a nationalist theater company in 1902 and opened The Abbey Theater in 1904. Here, the artistic resistance of the independent theater was allied to political resistance and national self-definition. The influence of these theaters was felt in the United States throughout the first decades of the twentieth century. David Belasco's minute fidelity to detail had firmly established a realistic idiom in the American theater, but it took the **LITTLE THEATER MOVEMENT,** inaugurated by Eugene O'Neill, Susan Glaspell, and the Provincetown Playhouse in 1915, to establish a repertoire of modern drama in the United States, and they were soon followed by other companies.

Forms of Modern Drama

The rise of the independent theaters also points to the theater's fragmentation and its marginalization in modern society. The theater no longer commands the cultural centrality that it had in classical Athens or in London and Paris in the sixteenth and seventeenth centuries.

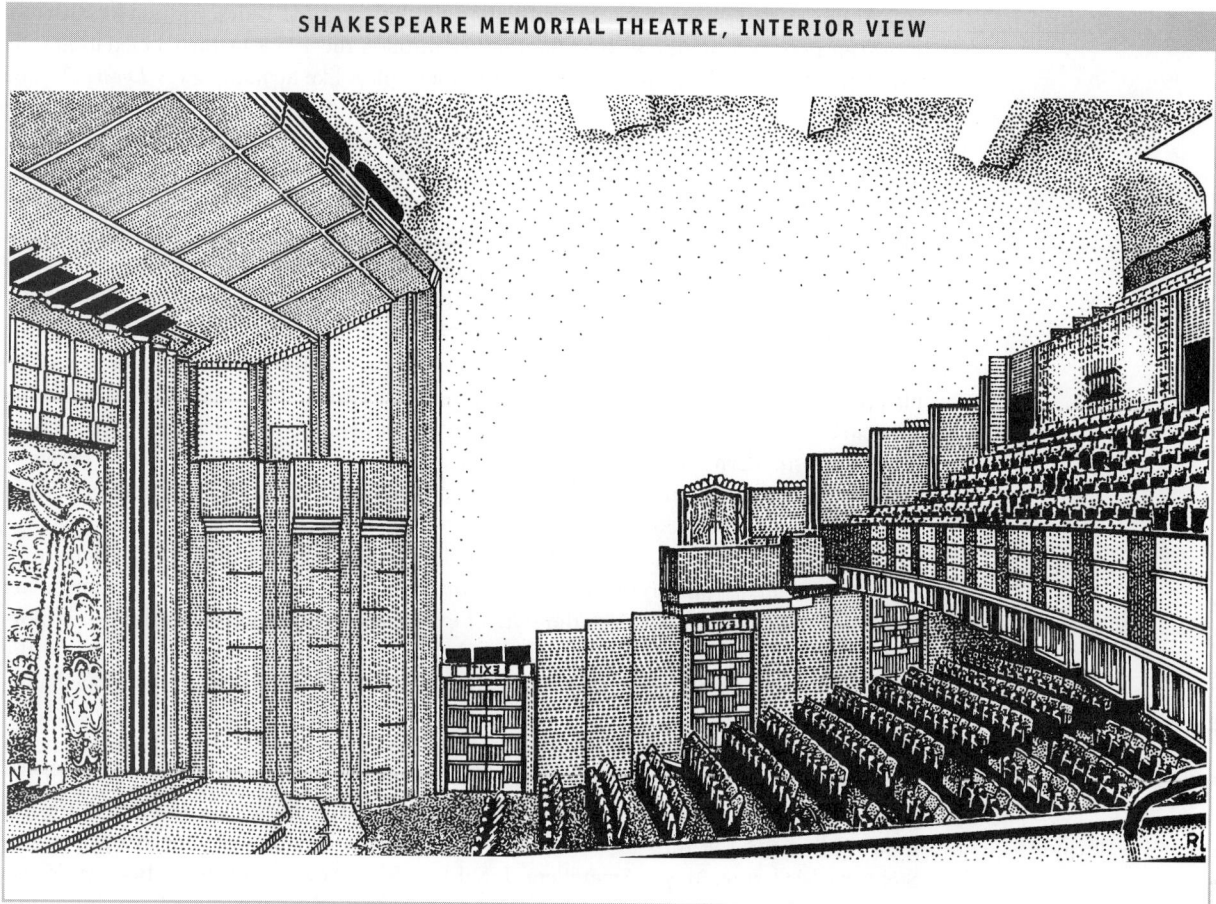

SHAKESPEARE MEMORIAL THEATRE, INTERIOR VIEW

Although the Shakespeare Memorial Theatre has a forestage apron extending toward the audience, it is in many respects typical of the proscenium theaters of the early twentieth century. The audience is seated in a fan-shaped auditorium, in fixed seats, facing the illuminated stage.

Instead, it has become the site for a diverse, sometimes confusing array of artistic experiments. Naturalism and realism were the first dramatic modes to consider themselves not as expressing the dominant political and ideological order, but as criticizing the values and institutions of middle-class society. The major plays of the realistic canon often tend to criticize modern life, particularly its dehumanizing, exploitative routine. The major heroes of the realistic mode—Nora Helmer, Major Barbara, Laura Wingfield—are all characters whose desire for freedom, vitality, and life is threatened by the deadening, deceptive world in which they live. Because realistic drama usually sees that world as an all-embracing "environment," though, its social themes don't finally lead to a call for social change. Modern society may be a prison, but the liberation urged by realistic drama is imagined on the individual level; the characters' search for freedom, value, and meaning leaves the world unchanged. Despite its critical stance toward modern society, realistic drama tacitly accepts the world and its values as an unchanging, and unchangeable, environment in which the characters live out their lives.

For this reason, realistic drama has often seemed an inadequate vehicle for a sustained critique of the forces of modern life, and almost from the moment of its inception in the 1880s and 1890s, realism inspired antagonistic forms of drama and theater. The history of modern drama is a series of reactions against bourgeois society and its values, and against the realistic drama that seemed to represent it and its vision of the world.

Although it was finally concerned with many of the same issues, the **EXPRESSIONIST THEATER** popular from the turn of the century through the 1930s marked an exciting stylistic departure from the realistic mode. Expressionist plays like Strindberg's *A Dream Play,* or American plays like Elmer Rice's *The Adding Machine,* Sophie Treadwell's *Machinal,* or Eugene O'Neill's *The Hairy Ape*, transformed the terms of realistic theater and drama. Rather than showing a character whose inner vitality is crushed by the bourgeois environment, expressionist plays try to show the mind and heart of the character visually, to express it directly in the objects and actions of the stage. The stage set becomes distorted, nearly dreamlike, and it is often peopled by characters who are exaggerated, mechanized, or fantastic, as a way of conveying the emotional coloring of the central character's experience. In O'Neill's *The Emperor Jones,* for instance, Jones is haunted by his "Little Formless Fears" when he flees into the forest; his flight is accompanied by the sound of a drum, which beats faster and louder as the play proceeds. More often, characters in expressionist drama are unnamed, like the Young Woman of *Machinal* or Mr. Zero of *The Adding Machine,* emphasizing that they have become cogs in the modern social and industrial machine. The action of expressionist drama is episodic and much like morality drama. Ernst Toller even named the scenes of his play *Transfiguration* "stations" to stress the play's likeness to a Christian passion play.

Thematically, expressionist theater resembles realism in its attention to character psychology and in its portrayal—however distorted or exaggerated—of the dehumanizing process of modern life. However, the style of expressionism also subverts realism in important ways, challenging both the logical, causal ordering of realistic dramatic action and the visual verisimilitude of the realistic theater. The **SYMBOLIST THEATER** also developed antirealistic attitudes toward drama and staging and extended the expressionist theater's repudiation of the drama of modern life. Written in prose or in verse, symbolic drama created a dim and mysterious other world, sometimes drawn from mythology or simply from the poet's imagination. The Belgian playwright Maurice Maeterlinck created a vogue for this kind of drama at the turn of the century, a drama which finds analogies in the work of Stéphane Mallarmé, August Strindberg, T. S. Eliot, W. B. Yeats, and Samuel Beckett. Yeats's mythological plays—such as *On Baile's Strand*—are typical of this special and influential mode. Relatively static in action, the plays rely on a densely figurative language to enlarge and energize the "poetic" meaning of events onstage.

Finally, an explicitly Marxist theory of the ideologically coercive dimension of realism—the sense that realism claims that its special perspective of the world is *natural;* that is, unavoidable and *real*—stands at the center of modern **EPIC THEATER.** Though usually associated with Bertolt Brecht, many of the techniques of epic theater were developed by Erwin Piscator in Berlin during the 1920s and early 1930s and by Vsevolod Meyerhold in his brilliant experiments with **CONSTRUCTIVIST THEATER** after the Russian Revolution of 1917. Brecht assimilated these techniques to a political purpose that he called epic theater. Rather than claiming to represent reality directly onstage by concealing the workings of the theater, epic theater alerts the audience to the ideological dimension of theater practice by constantly keeping the stage's "means of production" in view. Brecht developed the **ALIENATION EFFECT** as a way of alerting the audience to the constructed nature of stage events. While the realistic theater claims that the theater and drama, actor and character, stage and dramatic locale are the same, epic theater shows how they are different. In so doing, Brecht argued, the epic theater enables the audience to ask how—with what purpose, to what effect—stage practice is making this dramatic effect come about, and so leads the audience to take a more critical view of the process of the theater. Epic acting, then, comments on itself as "acting." The stage is not unified as a single dramatic locale, but always remains visibly a stage. Brecht also argued that epic drama should be structured differently than realistic plays. Instead of the apparently organic, "causal" action of realistic drama, Brecht's plays are written in a series of episodes. This technique, Brecht argued, allows the actors and the audience to reconsider the character's possibilities for action and change afresh in each scene. By calling the audience's attention to how the play comes into being onstage, epic theater encourages the audience to develop a dialectical sense of how social reality—in the theater and in the world at large—comes into being, how it is made through the interaction of individual and social forces and the interaction of material reality and **IDEOLOGY.** Epic theater has had an enormous influence on drama and theater around the world.

Stage practice has developed its own rich history, too—again often in reaction to realistic verisimilitude. Throughout the twentieth century, for instance, designers and architects have experimented with different ways of orienting the audience to the stage, in **THEATER IN THE ROUND** and in **ENVIRONMENTAL THEATER,** for instance. To see the dramatic action surrounded by spectators or to have the play take place among the audience members alters the audience's relationship to both the drama and its performance and changes how they can read the production. The Constructivist experiments of Vsevolod Meyerhold following the Russian Revolution placed a nonrepresentational "construction" onstage, a structure that the actors used as a "machine for acting" rather than as a realistic set. Similarly, experimental performance altered notions of what dramatic and theatrical representation could be like. Following World War I, writers such as Tristan Tzara called for an art that was formless and irrational, a process rather than a product; such "Dada"—a nonsense term—poems, plays, and monologues were often given **CABARET PERFORMANCE** in Zurich, Berlin, and Paris. **DADA** and **SURREALIST THEATER** developed a kind of hallucinatory intimacy between stage and audience, laying the foundations for Artaud's **THEATER OF CRUELTY.** In all of these experiments, the theater worked to disperse the visual unity characteristic of the realistic stage in ways that led to new configurations of the relationship between the audience and the performers and to new interpretive perspectives on drama and the possibilities of theater.

Realism, expressionism, symbolist theater, and *epic theater*—these useful labels necessarily limit and categorize the rich variety of the stage in ways that are artificial and untrue to the dynamics of change in the modern theater, for new innovations tend to draw their techniques from several of these modes. Modern plays, for instance, often blend representational techniques as a way of challenging the audience's understanding of the drama and its implication in the world. Despite their "realistic" anchoring in a material, lifelike setting, for example, Chekhov's plays sometimes disturb the stability of that illusion with odd, almost "symbolic" effects—the breaking string in *The Cherry Orchard,* for instance. The action of Strindberg's *Miss Julie,* too, for all the play's emphasis on domestic and social environment, seems to lurch and accelerate in ways more characteristic of an "expressionist" linking of the dramatic form to the characters' psychological experience. In Pirandello's *Six Characters in Search of an Author*—a play indebted in many ways to the "symbolist" theater—the Characters want the Actors to produce a play much in the manner of Ibsen's drama, a realistic drama of hidden crime and its discovery. These labels are useful in helping us to describe some of the outlines of a given play, but we should remember that many modern playwrights wrote in a variety of modes, and that each play is itself a kind of experiment.

The modern theater's radical redefinitions of the style and purpose of drama required similar redefinitions of acting and performance. At the turn of the century, a theatrical company would have been organized according to each actor's typical **LINE OF BUSINESS.** Something like the company in Pirandello's *Six Characters,* companies had a leading comic actor, a villain or "heavy," a leading man, a leading lady, a comic old man, a comic woman, and a variety of other parts. Unlike *commedia dell' arte,* actors each played a variety of different characters; nonetheless, each actor would have elaborated some relatively conventional "business" for acting the kind of character he or she usually played. The unity of illusion demanded by the realistic theater, however, required each character to be more finely individualized. Much as the stage designer provided a new set for each production and the

**Acting And
Performance**

Although most of the plays included in *The Wadsworth Anthology of Drama* have been popular in the theater, they are all to some extent plays that have been canonized for their qualities as dramatic "literature": rich language and characterization, complex engagement with social and moral issues, deft and original use of dramatic convention, and so on. However, theater and drama pose special problems to the idea of a single literary canon. As popular entertainments, plays have not always been regarded as having "literary" merit. Plays were published only irregularly in Shakespeare's era partly for this reason, and even today few publishers have much commitment to keeping contemporary plays in print—which makes it particularly difficult for contemporary drama to become part of *any* literary canon. More important, plays are produced under very different conditions than novels and poems. Plays are made to be meaningful in a specific theater; their "literary" impact on readers is often secondary to their original purpose, which is to make a theatrical impact on a given body of spectators.

In late-eighteenth and nineteenth-century Europe—in part as a result of the relaxing of restrictions on theatrical performance, and in part as a reflection of a sense of "literature" as part of a circumscribed sphere of "high culture"—a variety of new dramatic genres became popular, of which the most important is **MELODRAMA.** The term was initially used to indicate plays in which music was used to accentuate the emotional coloring of the action; the term became more generally applied to plays with a conventionalized set of characters, a clear narrative structure, and a distinct moral cosmos. In the nineteenth-century theater, melodrama was an extremely popular genre, fusing the theater's increasing capacity for visual spectacle with a strongly colored and direct dramatic action. The world of melodrama is a world of clear-cut moral absolutes: the hero and heroine are thoroughly virtuous and are threatened by villains who are proportionately unscrupulous. The action is organized in a series of episodes, in each of which the hero/heroine's happiness, virtue, fortune, or life is threatened with destruction; each act of a melodrama usually ends with some striking crisis, often calling for an elaborate stage effect—an explosion, train wreck, or storm. The action of melodrama is often highly involved and coincidental, yet usually works eventually toward a happy—or at least sentimental—ending. If the hero must die, he usually dies in the heroine's arms; more often, the couple are restored to one another and live happily ever after.

Melodrama is usually dated from the popularity of plays like Johann Christoph Friedrich von Schiller's (1759–1805) *The Robbers* (1782), August Friedrich Ferdinand von Kotzebue's (1761–1819) *Menschenhass und Reue* (1789), and René Charles Guilbert de Pixérécourt's (1773–1844) *Coelina* (1800); although Kotzebue and Pixérécourt are now rarely read, their plays were widely adapted throughout Europe. Thirty-six of Kotzebue's plays were translated into English, and several remained popular throughout the nineteenth century. Richard Brinsley Sheridan (1751–1816) adapted Kotzebue's *Der Spanier in Peru* as *Pizarro* in 1799, which became a brilliant success for the actor John Philip Kembel; Thomas Holcroft (1744–1809) adapted Pixérécourt's *Coelina* as *A Tale of Mystery* in 1802. While early nineteenth-century melodrama tended toward Gothic settings—mysterious castles, ghostly visitors, and the like—by later in the century melodrama's typical formal and moral patterns were applied to plays with local and contemporary settings. Pierce Egan's novel *Life in London* was adapted as *Tom and Jerry; or, Life in London* in 1821; Edward George Bulwer-Lytton's (1803–1873) *Money* (1840) was one of several plays that held

costume designer provided clothing appropriate to the character and his or her setting, so the actors were forced to particularize their performances in new ways.

A second stimulus for this innovation was the drama itself. Playwrights like Ibsen and Chekhov typically created characters against the grain of theatrical stereotypes. Nora Helmer, for example, seems like a typical **SOUBRETTE** at the opening of *A Doll House,* the pert and clever young woman of light comedy. However, as the play develops, Ibsen challenges this convention and forces the actress to discover new ways of producing the character. Realistic plays frequently ask actors to work against the apparent "type" of the role, to discover the psychological subtext of will and desire beneath the spoken words that motivates the character's actions. Actors and actresses at the turn of the century frequently had difficulty reading the new realistic plays, precisely because they could not see how to represent the more indirect action and individualized characters through the kinds of stage behavior they had been trained to use.

the stage through the end of the century.

Since melodrama drew a wide audience, and often centered on poor-but-virtuous heroes and heroines, it has sometimes been thought to articulate social resistance. For while early versions like Douglas Jerrold's (1803–1857) hugely popular nautical melodrama *Black Ey'd Susan* (1829) emphasized the undying loyalty and patriotism of British navy sailors (or "tars"), the polarized moral ethos of melodrama could be turned into a vehicle for social critique. In the United States, melodrama became one vehicle for dramatizing ethnic and racial conflict. John Augustus Stone's (1800–1834) *Metamora; or, The Last of the Wampanoags* (1829), dramatized a heroic Indian chief's losing battle to save the land of his ancestors from his rapacious white enemies. In *The Octoroon* (1859), Dion Boucicault (1820–1890) staged the fatal love story between the octoroon Zoe, the virtuous plantation owner who loves her, and the wicked Yankee overseer, McCloskey, who threatens to buy her when it emerges that Zoe was never actually freed from slavery. Although these plays end with "tragic" consequences for their heroes and heroines, melodrama tends to locate its evils in the character of its villains, rather than in the structure of society itself: for this reason, melodrama is usually unable to

MELODRAMA: THE BELLS

Sir Henry Irving's (1838–1905) performance in Leopold Lewis's melodrama *The Bells* was one of his greatest roles. The illustration presents both the emotionally exaggerated quality of melodramatic acting and melodrama's use of special effects. In the play, Mathias (Irving's role) has murdered and concealed the body of a Polish Jew. Although many years have passed since the murder, Mathias is haunted by the sound of his victim's sleigh bells. In this scene, he staggers before a vision of the crime itself.

develop a deeper analysis of the social institutions—racism, for example—that afflict its characters' lives. When Bernard Shaw turned to melodrama as a vehicle for his own drama of social critique, he strategically inverted its patterns of characterization as a way of opening its social order to criticism: one way *Major Barbara,* for example, attempts to jolt the audience into examining its attitudes about society at large is by casting Andrew Undershaft—so similar to the scheming and all-powerful industrialist villain of countless popular melodramas—as the moral "hero" of the play.

A new kind of drama requires a new kind of acting, and companies throughout Europe developed ways of acting more behavioristically onstage. The most systematic approach to acting was undertaken by the actor and director Constantin Stanislavski at the Moscow Art Theater around the turn of the twentieth century. Although Stanislavski thought that his techniques could be applied to any play, he discovered the need for such acting largely in his work on Chekhov's plays. Chekhov's plays were frustrating to actors of the old school, because the characters did not conform to traditional types and the action seemed so indirect and inconsequential, lacking familiar dramatic rhythms and climaxes. Stanislavski developed techniques for approaching each character as an individual, techniques that were later systematized as a "method" of actor-training. Stanislavski trained the actor to associate his or her personal history with the invented actions of the dramatic character so that the actor could tap that emotional spontaneity, a "life in art," as part of the performance. By using the **MAGIC IF**—imagining themselves *as* the character, rather than applying a stock line of business—and using their own **EMOTION MEMORY** to vivify the character's inner life, Stanislavski's actors were taught to bring authentic emotional experience into their performances. Of course, Stanislavski also emphasized the many other abilities that an actor must develop—physical training, vocal control, grace, concentration—but his real contribution to the modern stage is the emphasis on the actor's emotional reality in performance. The realistic theater uses real objects to create a persuasive material environment, and its characters come alive through the actor's real feeling. Stanislavski's work has been extremely influential, particularly in the United States, where it was adapted as the school of **METHOD ACTING** in the 1930s, and it remains—in very different and modified forms—at the center of much actor-training today.

Antirealistic drama also called for the development of new styles of performance. Meyerhold developed **BIOMECHANICS** as a way to make the actor's performance more physical, less directly concerned with the behavioral and psychological verisimilitude typical of Stanislavskian realistic acting. His work has analogies in the use of dance and ritualized performance in symbolist theater and in the nonrepresentational physicality of Antonin Artaud's Theater of Cruelty. Symbolist theater also repudiated the lifelike quality of realistic acting. It required a highly artificial and statuesque stillness from performers, allowing the actors to strike powerful but ethereal poses in order to deliver the densely poetic language of the play without interference. Yeats—whose antipathy to realism was profound—thought of training his actors in barrels, to keep them from moving and gesturing as they would do in everyday life: the art of the symbolist theater should be emphatically artificial, thoroughly apart from the conduct of life beyond the stage.

Brecht, again, voiced the most thorough critique of realistic acting. To Brecht, the problem of realistic acting was that it showed the "character" as a finished product, a commodity, rather than revealing *how* the character had come into being, both through the social forces described in the drama and through the decisions taken by the actor as part of the performance. Brecht argued that the actor should acknowledge that he or she both empathizes with the character and demonstrates the character to the audience, that acting is both feeling and showing at the same time. This dialectical approach invites the audience to see how the actor is making the "character" and allows the public to interpret both the process and the product of theater art, the dramatic "character" and the actor's labor.

Women in Modern Drama and Theater

Most readers of modern drama immediately note the prominence of women characters in the plays—Nora Helmer in *A Doll House,* Anna-Liisa in *Anna-Liisa,* Barbara in *Major Barbara,* Courage in *Mother Courage.* Playwrights frequently associated the political and social limitations of middle-class life with male characters and used female characters to pose subversive questions about that social order. However, in the drama, as in society, this subversive freedom sometimes emerges as illusory or problematic. Ibsen, for instance, enables Nora to recognize how she has been defined by the men in her life, but the world outside her home hardly seems inviting; is there really anywhere for her to go? Many of the women—the Stepdaughter of Pirandello's *Six Characters,* Major Barbara—are also assigned an erotic power opposed to the "reason" of their male antagonists. While this power, too, can be disruptive, it sometimes also reinforces traditional gender stereotypes. Feminine erotic power in the drama carries with it other ascribed values, defining women as more emotional, as more subject to the influence of the body, as closer to "nature." Men retain a pragmatic, "rational" authority that places them at the center of society, and that defines the arena of culture and civilization as an implicitly male domain. The apparent freedom of these stage women, that is, often signals their deeper captivity to the gendered economy of modern society, a captivity shared by actresses in the period as well. Although this is also a period in which actresses—Sarah Bernhardt, Eleonora Duse, Elizabeth Robins, or Ellen Terry, for example—could earn an international reputation, they worked in a theater in which men greatly outnumbered women in the audience and in which nearly all of the managers and producers were men. Women were also important playwrights throughout Europe in the first decades of the twentieth century: Elizabeth Robins's *Votes for Women!* brought the "woman question" to the English stage in 1907; Minna Canth was the leading playwright of the Finnish Theater (her portrait graces the proscenium of the National Theater today); Marieluise Fleisser's *Pioneers in Ingolstadt* (1924) in many ways rivaled Brecht's early vision of epic theater. In a male-dominated industry like the modern theater, it is not surprising that women onstage—both dramatic characters and performers—should reflect fundamentally masculine attitudes about the place of women in society.

To think of the history of theater and drama since Ibsen is to think of an increasingly large and problematic array of dramatic styles, modes of theatrical production, and conceptions of the audience and its world. Many of these innovations were local at first, responding to the social and theatrical conditions of a specific time and place: Brecht's Marxist theater arose in the cabaret culture of Berlin in the late 1920s; Pirandello's **METATHEATER** was part of the lively Italian avant-garde following World War I; Shaw's drama was informed by the progressive politics of the British Fabian Society and by dramatic conventions drawn from the popular plays of the late Victorian stage. The drama of modern Europe develops a posture of resistant inquiry toward the pieties of contemporary social life. It works both to represent that world and to change it, to affect our ideas about character and personality, about the political realities of our world, and even about the metaphysical certainties we have come to believe. But it is the impact of global political and cultural change that marks the theater of the second half of the twentieth century.

The impact of film and television has forced the theater to work to define what kinds of performance are specific to the stage, how live dramatic performances can offer something unique, something not already available in other performance media. For this reason, perhaps, theater and drama since 1950 have necessarily been "experimental," working to develop new kinds of plays, new practices of stage production, and new kinds of theatrical experience for their audiences. Much as the proscenium theaters of the early twentieth century have given way to other, more flexible kinds of theater spaces, so dramatic writing has become much more varied and experimental. Even stage realism—the mode of Ibsen and Chekhov, Miller and Williams—has undergone an important reworking in the plays of Sam Shepard, Harold Pinter, Heiner Müller, and others.

Here, we can identify three patterns of innovation as a way of organizing our thinking about the diversity of the contemporary stage. One strategy—inspired most directly by Antonin Artaud's **THEATER OF CRUELTY**—attacks the notion that the theater is essentially a *representational* medium, emphasizing instead the *experiential* aspect of theater. Rather than staging images of some fictive world to an audience of passive spectators, this kind of theater works to structure the *present experience* of the audience in new ways, as in the participatory and ritualistic theater experiments of the 1960s and 1970s. The influence of Artaud's assault on representation is evident in the contemporary theater in several ways: in absurdist drama, in the focus on the body in Griselda Gambaro's *Information for Foreigners,* in the dreamlike density of Müller's *Hamletmachine,* or in the imagistic violence of Sarah Kane's *Blasted.*

The second mode of innovation, **THEATER OF THE ABSURD,** originated as a new form of playwriting rather than as theatrical experimentation. The plays of Samuel Beckett, Slawomir Mrozek, Eugène Ionesco, Boris Vian, Edward Albee, Harold Pinter, Václav Havel, and others create a strangely dislocated dramatic world, in which arbitrary or "absurd" events both confront and mystify the characters.

While Artaud inspired an existential or experiential theater, Bertolt Brecht—whose work became widely known and imitated only after World War II—inspired a different kind

THEATER AND CULTURE SINCE 1950

THEATER IN THE ROUND

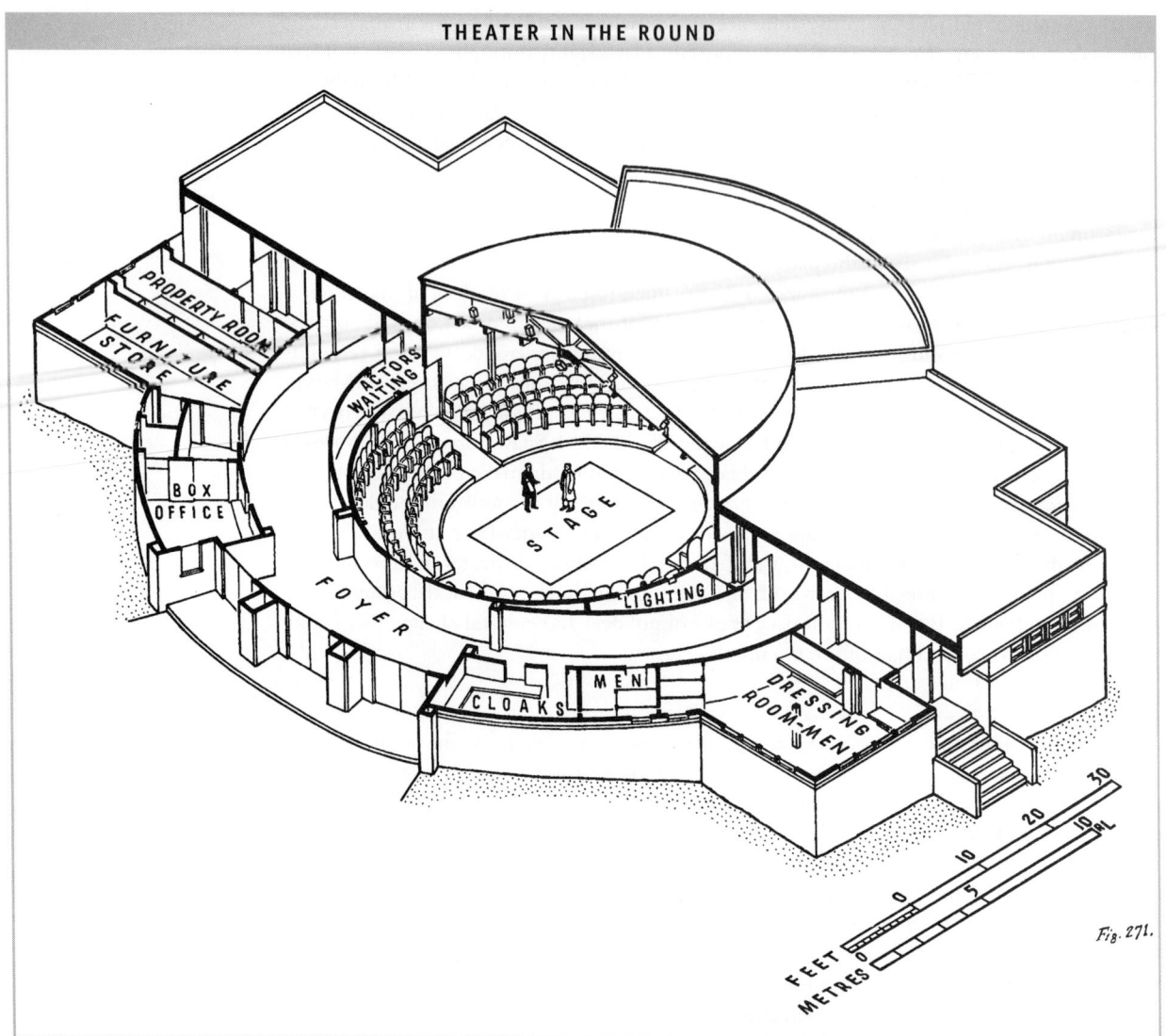

Fig. 271.

In a theater in the round, the audience surrounds the action, rather than facing the stage as in a proscenium theater. Theater space of this kind lends itself to greater immediacy and contact between the performers and the audience.

of assault on the conventions of realistic theater. Contemporary **POLITICAL THEATER** also criticizes the notion of "representation," but in different terms than Artaud or theater of the absurd, *representation* is a word with two senses: in "representing" a picture of the world, the arts necessarily claim that their images are "representative" in some way. Political theater frequently shows how a social or political order uses its power to "represent" others coercively—for example, by depicting those others through demeaning or limiting stereotypes. For this reason, political theater today is intent on using live performance to change the prejudicial attitudes concealed in conventional ideas of representation.

Of course, no plays fit easily or fully into these three categories, but to think of the drama of the postwar period as raising questions of our existential or our political relation to the theater—and so to the world—provides a useful and powerful way of opening that drama to our understanding. Each of these modes of theater creates a different relationship between the stage and its audience, and we should examine each of them in some detail.

The writings of Antonin Artaud, particularly the essays collected in the volume *The Theater and Its Double* (written in the late 1920s and 1930s, published in France in 1938, translated to English in 1958), have had an extraordinary impact on our sense of theater. Like many innovators of his generation—think of Brecht or Pirandello—Artaud worked to undermine the notion that the theater can only show its audiences realistic vignettes of daily life. Instead, Artaud argued that the theater should alter the balance between presentation—the actual, immediate activities of actors and audiences, their *presence* in the theater—and representation, the fictive "drama" that had seemed to define the purpose and scope of theater. Artaud—who used the term *theater of cruelty* for this project—advocated transforming the theater into an all-consuming spectacle, akin both to rituals like the Catholic Mass and to public festivals, in which the boundaries between acting and observing, actor and spectator, fiction and reality, conscious and unconscious would be broken or transgressed. The idea that the theater would "communicate," but not through rational means, is captured in one of Artaud's most powerful metaphors for this nearly unimaginable theater: the plague. Artaud envisioned a theater that would transmit its experiences corporeally, through the body, like disease, like mystical wisdom, alchemically transforming all of its participants. To avoid staging conventional dramas, Artaud called for a theater of "no more masterpieces," one that would use the dramatic text to transform the relations between stage and spectator by making the production a total experience—visual, auditory, gustatory, olfactory, tactile, physical—for the audience.

Stage director Peter Brook once remarked that "Artaud applied is Artaud betrayed," and it is true that Artaud's sense of theater is deeply metaphorical, a kind of theater experience that is almost unimaginable to us, and certainly not imaginable to us as theater. Artaud rarely offers a practical description of how this theater could come into being. Instead, the value and influence of Artaud's writing has been indirect and inspirational, bearing in a variety of tangential ways on kinds of theater that are not in any literal sense "Artaudian." In that Artaud imagines a theater of *presence*—not of representation—involving the audience in an experience rather than showing them a picture, his theater comes into contact with several very different kinds of innovation. Although the American experimental theater of the 1960s and 1970s is the most direct application—and betrayal—of Artaud, Artaud's conception of theater stands distantly behind a variety of more formally constructed plays: the dislocating imagery of Beckett and Müller; the ritualized, hallucinatory violence of Pinter's plays; the elaborate physical rituals of Gao Xingjian's *The Other Shore*. Of course, as *written* plays, "masterpieces," these plays are specifically opposed to the ideals of Artaud's unrealizable theater, while at the same time they explore part of the terrain opened by Artaud's vision.

Coined by the theater critic Martin Esslin in 1961, the phrase *theater of the absurd* tries to capture the special irrationality and unpredictability of a certain wave of dramatic writing of the late 1950s and 1960s, including the plays of Samuel Beckett and Harold Pinter, for example. Taking as his keynote Beckett's famous play *Waiting for Godot* (1953)—a play in which two Chaplinesque tramps wait for a mysterious man named Godot, who never arrives—Esslin finds the theater of the absurd to have certain stylistic and thematic characteristics. It rejects the sense of causality found in realistic plays, the sense that it is possible to find the causes for events either in the environment or in the psychological motives of the characters themselves. Instead, theater of the absurd tends to be about a world in which inexplicable, arbitrary, or irrational events happen. Although the events usually seem to be part of some kind of order or scheme, it is an order that the characters and their audience cannot quite grasp. As Hamm says in Beckett's play *Endgame*, "Something is taking its course," but neither the characters nor the audience are ever sure what that "something" is. In Eugène Ionesco's play *Rhinoceros* (1960), the inhabitants of a small French village begin to turn inexplicably into rhinoceroses. In each act of Boris Vian's *The Empire Builders* (1959), a family moves to a smaller room in an apartment building, always accompanied by a mysterious, bandaged figure. In Slawomir Mrozek's

Artaud and the Theater of Cruelty

Theater of the Absurd

Striptease (1961), two men are commanded by a huge, silent finger to remove their clothes and don huge conical hats that conceal and blind them. As Esslin suggests, this drama insists that the fictions we use to make sense of our world—ideas of order, causality, rationality—are just that: fictions imposed on an arbitrary and mysterious reality, whose meanings remain fugitive and elusive.

Absurdist drama treats its audience somewhat differently than realistic plays do, rejecting the "dramatic irony" of the traditional theater, in which the audience understands more than the characters onstage. Instead, the theater of the absurd refuses to provide this privilege to its spectators. We are as baffled and frustrated by our attempts to make the events mean something as the characters are; "Mean something!" a character remarks in *Endgame,* "You and I, mean something! *(Brief laugh)*." Our *present* experience as an audience is structured and made significant by absurdist theatrical production. In the theater, we don't just observe the "absurd" drama onstage, we are forced to undergo it, to live it through. For this reason, both the drama onstage and the audience's experience in the theater are sometimes described as *existential.* We have to *decide* the meaning of our being in the theater, without the comfort, solace, or guidance of some transcendent, predetermined world view.

Political Theater   Much as theater of the absurd works to make the spectators' situation in the theater an extension of the characters' situation on the stage, political theater since Brecht has worked to make the audience's performance in the theater a recognizably political one. By fragmenting the stage space, by showing how the illusion is made rather than concealing its means of production, and by involving the audience more overtly in deciding the meaning of the play's events, the theater is shown to be a political instrument. Like television, newspapers, universities, the courts, and so on, the theater is an institution that produces the ideas and images with which we govern our lives. Both the example of Brecht's plays and his challenging theory of performance have been absorbed and redefined by the world theater. In common with theater of the absurd, political theater works to resist and complicate realistic representation, the "slice of life" of Ibsen, Chekhov, and Miller. Instead of staging an arbitrarily unreal and absurd world, political theater examines "representative" images of reality. Who makes those images? Who benefits from them? Who is injured, governed, or oppressed by them? How do they help to maintain the social *status quo?*

For this reason, much political theater connects representation onstage with representation in society, showing how various social groups—women, gay men, lesbians, ethnic and racial groups, the poor—have been staged in society and in the theater. A fundamental assumption of political theater is that these stereotypes are part of the larger system of discrimination that operates in society, and that they reveal the dominant attitudes of those who govern, control, or influence society from positions of power. In plays like Amiri Baraka's *Dutchman,* Caryl Churchill's *Cloud Nine,* and Wole Soyinka's *Death and the King's Horseman,* the racial conflicts informing contemporary society and culture are explored in very different ways: in relation to colonialism, to the mythologies of imperial history, to women's experience. These plays are very different in style, ranging from a kind of realism in *Death and the King's Horseman* to the testifying monologues of Anna Deavere Smith. It is not a single point of view or a single dramatic style that defines political theater, but the use of theatrical representation itself as a way to analyze representation in society at large.

A similar approach to theater informs many of the modern plays gathered in this anthology, for many of them explore the issue of representation: how Asia is represented in the minds of the West in David Henry Hwang's *M. Butterfly,* how the English remapped and so represented the Irish in their own language and political system in Brian Friel's *Translations,* how African tribal traditions are tragically misunderstood by British imperialists in Wole Soyinka's *Death and the King's Horseman,* how the Chicano and Anglo cultures interact in Luis Valdez's *Zoot Suit,* how torture and tourism are connected in Griselda Gambaro's *Infor-*

mation for Foreigners, or the literal consumption of the Third World by the First in Manjula Padmanabhan's *Harvest.* Political theater sometimes seems highly message oriented, overtly didactic to readers and audiences used to the more subtle instruction offered by realistic plays. Yet the messages of contemporary political theater tend to be fused into the process of theater, so that the politics of the play come into being not in the prepared script of the play but in our experience as an audience. All of these plays disrupt the expectations, attitudes, and preconceptions of the empowered audience and invite the audience to develop different ways of reading their society as part of their involvement in the play.

On the contemporary stage, though, these modes of theater do not work in isolation from one another, but interact with one another, as part of the dynamic means the theater uses to engage its audiences in an understanding of the world. Indeed, to describe the contemporary theater in terms of its historical inheritance from the modernist theater of Brecht, Artaud, and the absurdists is in an important sense to overlook what is most significant about the stage today: its break from the traditions of modernism. If we look at the range of contemporary performance activity, much of it has little to do with traditional drama. Think of the performance-art monologues of Spalding Gray (one of his best-known, *Swimming to Cambodia,* was made into a film by Jonathan Demme) or Karen Finley (whose work was at the center of the 1990 censorship controversy at the National Endowment for the Arts); of the music of Laurie Anderson; of video art and film; of music television and advertising; of the disorienting stage spectacles of Robert Wilson; even of "plays" like Peter Handke's *Offending the Audience* and *The Ride Across Lake Constance,* or Heiner Müller's *Hamletmachine,* or Samuel Beckett's later work for the theater, *Not I, Footfalls,* and *Ohio Impromptu.*

Theorists of culture and the arts have related these developments to innovations in the visual arts, in architecture, and in writing, characterizing their common features as **POSTMODERN.** The term itself is a difficult one, suggesting that these works often share some of the features of earlier, "modernist" art; the literary and cultural theorist Fredric Jameson suggests that the distinguishing feature of postmodern art is its attitude toward history. Jameson points out that postmodern works frequently invoke or appropriate the style of earlier historical periods, as in the use of neoclassical ornamentation in recent architecture, or the recollection of earlier film styles in more recent movies (**FILM NOIR** in *Chinatown* or *L.A. Confidential*). Jameson labels this technique **PASTICHE.** What is striking about these postmodern quotations of style, though, is not any systematic reinterpretation of tradition or any statement of value, but their tonelessness, their neutrality, the absence of the kind of moral and historical sense we might expect from the act of confronting history. In postmodern pastiche, the recollection of an earlier style does not provide a new understanding of the past, nor does it illuminate our contemporary historical situation. Instead, pastiche denatures that style by removing it from history, and history from it. Style becomes exactly that: simply another option. Hamm's many quotations from English literature in *Endgame* or the pastiche of Gilbert and Sullivan operetta in Churchill's *Cloud Nine* are perhaps part of this complex problem, for in each case the "past" is presented to the audience in terms of an artistic style that is largely emptied of its force as history.

Moreover, Jameson's discussion of pastiche also emphasizes the importance of the esthetic *surface* in postmodern art. Music video and advertising are sometimes taken as the paradigmatic postmodern forms, forms whose "message" lies almost exclusively in a rapidly changing, brilliantly seductive, series of images. Although this technique relates to the modernist use of **MONTAGE** in film and theater, it is different in several important ways. Modernist montage uses a series of images narratively, to tell a story. Although the camera cuts quickly from image to image, the audience assembles the images in a single complete narrative. Both the narrative and the interpreting spectator achieve a sense of wholeness. In contrast, postmodern images are juxtaposed in striking, sometimes contradictory combinations that resist

Drama, Theater, and the "Postmodern"

our ability to impose a single narrative explanation, a single story line. Postmodern performance—on film or video or in the theater—is insistently fragmentary; it asserts the incompletion of the artistic object and the incomplete quality of the spectator's experience as well. Postmodern arts resist imposing a single explanatory interpretation that would both complete the narrative and confirm the audience's sense of wholeness, of self-integration. In this sense, postmodern arts are sometimes described as concerned with the "death of the subject." They question the possibility both of a comprehensible world and of a comprehending individual. By disorienting language, fragmenting narrative, and dispensing with such organizing principles as "plot" and "character," postmodern art claims that we have entered a new age in which the complex disconnections of modern culture have made obsolete many of our beliefs about the world and our ways of representing the world and ourselves.

MODERN EUROPEAN DRAMA IN PERFORMANCE AND HISTORY

The understanding of theater that was inaugurated in the mid-nineteenth century is in many respects continuous with our own today: although various experiments—environmental theater, theater of cruelty, performance art—have contributed to a rich sense of the diversity of theatrical performance forms today, to many people "going to the theater" means going to a specially designated building, sitting in a darkened auditorium, and watching the events that take place on the stage. Of course, this activity is shaped today by social and economic forces still just emerging in the early-modern period: whereas earlier audiences usually had a small number of theaters to turn to for performance, performances are available today in a wide range of spaces—subsidized state and municipal theaters throughout Europe, commercial theaters like those in London's West End and New York's Broadway, college and university playhouses, festival theaters like the annual festival at Grahamstown in South Africa or the Shaw Festival in Stratford, Ontario, and many more. Theater in the twentieth century is characterized by its "optional" character: we choose theater from among a range of other forms of dramatic performance, like film and television; the theaters we attend are positioned in their ambient cultures in a much wider variety of ways; and the performances we see tend to value their "uniqueness" rather than their conventionality in typically modern ways.

Moreover, while the performance practices of earlier European theaters were highly conventionalized—masks and *cothurni* for tragedy in Athens, the phallus for comedy; a standard comic or tragic stage set in the neoclassical theaters of France and Italy—in the modern period, the style of dramatic production has become much more varied, not only as a sign of the director's and designer's artistic signature in the production, but also as part of what the play has to sell to its audiences. Indeed, the invention of the stage director in the late nineteenth century is symptomatic of a trend in modernist esthetics more generally, a trend from the polished deployment of convention to an emphasis on the artwork's originality—an originality that signals the individual creative presence of an author or *auteur*. In earlier theaters, of course, someone usually had the responsibility of organizing and rehearsing the actors: this was sometimes the playwright in classical Athenian theater, or the company's leading actor, like David Garrick, in the later eighteenth century. But in these theaters, performance practice was extremely conventionalized: actors, like Shakespeare's, who have a solid line of business, don't really need much rehearsal—an actor whose typical line of business is comic old men will more or less have an approach ready for characters like Polonius. In the modern theater, however, the director has the responsibility for shaping the diverse talents of the company—set, costume, and lighting designs; acting; music—into a single whole, one that seems to deploy the performance in a unique way. Much as we think of a film as embodying the director's vision, so too in the theater the performance is often understood as an expression of the director's ability to shape the play, the players, and the physical milieu of the stage into a uniquely expressive whole.

For this reason, the modern theater is often called the "director's theater," and in many respects the history of modern stage practice is the history of the innovations of brilliant directors. Although naturalistic or realistic drama—the plays of Ibsen and Chekhov and O'Neill—are duly appreciated for their striking departures from the standard practices of nineteenth-century playwriting, transforming these innovations from the page to the stage required a generation of brilliant directors: Antoine, Stanislavski, Meyerhold, Max Reinhardt. Indeed, throughout the history of the modern theater, actors and directors have sometimes been baffled by the new demands of these scripts; Stanislavski, for example, can be understood to have devised his famous Method in response to the obliquity of Chekhov's plays. Similarly, when one thinks of the landmark theatrical productions of the twentieth-century European theater, they are always associated with the director: Stanislavski's productions of Chekhov at the turn of the century; Meyerhold's brilliant *Hedda Gabler,* with its white set and Hedda's brilliant, snakelike green dress; Piscator's work with Brecht in the 1920s, and Brecht's direction of the Berliner Ensemble in his own and others' plays after World War II; Peter Brook's use of the circus to realize the "magic" of Shakespeare's *A Midsummer Night's Dream* in 1970; Robert Wilson's visualization of Heiner Müller's *Hamletmachine* in the 1980s. As a consequence, one of the most energetic kinds of experiment in the later part of the century has been in the area of a more collaborative theater practice. Like Complicite, many contemporary theater companies are organized as collectives, in which responsibility for the "artistic" decisions is shared, rather than given over to a single person. But even in more conventional circumstances, companies often work to make the playwright's, actors', and designers' work have a more direct impact on the final stage of theater work. Caryl Churchill's play *Cloud Nine,* for example, arose from a series of workshops undertaken by members of the Joint Stock Company, in which the actors experimented by playing different gender, sexual, or racial roles in a variety of situations: Churchill wrote the text of the play out of the workshops, and director Max Stafford-Clark used the results of the workshops as a foundation for the play's theatrical performance. Given the increasing complexity of theatrical production—the use not only of complex technology backstage, but the inclusion of multimedia production as part of the performance itself—we can expect that this struggle to shape the authority of the stage will continue well into the future.

READING THE MATERIAL THEATER

Compared with the documentary record of earlier theaters, the modern theater offers an embarrassment of riches: not only is the print tradition rich in reviews, memoirs, and other accounts of the production and reception of plays in the theater, but also playwrights themselves have often left working drafts of their plays. Henrik Ibsen is particularly notable in this regard: an extremely disciplined and methodical writer, Ibsen not only began most of his plays with a detailed scenario; he retained many of the successive drafts of his plays. These materials provide a unique insight into the process of Ibsen's imagination, and indeed into his practice as a writer as well.

What follows are Ibsen's "Notes for the Modern Tragedy," dated 19 October 1878, and his original scenario for *A Doll House.* Not surprisingly, perhaps, many of the elements of the finished play remain in this outline. At the same time, this document differs from the final drama in a number of respects (including some of the characters' names). Granted that a scenario necessarily tends to streamline the action and emphasize the plot of the play, do you find this scenario surprising in any way? Does it seem to present the same kinds of moral or ethical emphases you find in the play? Are there elements of the finished play that seem larger or more powerful than you might have expected from this scenario alone? Are there elements of the scenario that are less prominent in the final draft? The final lines of the scenario are particularly chilling: "Five: —seven hours till midnight. Twenty-four hours till the next midnight. Twenty-four and seven—thirty-one. Thirty-one hours to live. . . ." How do these lines figure in Ibsen's final imagining of the action of the finale of *A Doll House?*

Notes for the Modern Tragedy

Rome, 19. 10, 78.

There are two kinds of spiritual law, two kinds of conscience, one in man and another, altogether different, in woman. They do not understand each other; but in practical life the woman is judged by man's law, as though she were not a woman but a man.

The wife in the play ends by having no idea of what is right or wrong; natural feeling on the one hand and belief in authority on the other have altogether bewildered her.

A woman cannot be herself in the society of the present day, which is an exclusively masculine society, with laws framed by men and with a judicial system that judges feminine conduct from a masculine point of view.

She has committed forgery, and she is proud of it; for she did it out of love for her husband, to save his life. But this husband with his commonplace principles of honour is on the side of the law and regards the question with masculine eyes.

Spiritual conflicts. Oppressed and bewildered by the belief in authority, she loses faith in her moral right and ability to bring up her children. Bitterness. A mother in modern society, like certain insects who go away and die when she has done her duty in the propagation of the race.[1] Love of life, of home, of husband and children and family. Here and there a womanly shaking-off of her thoughts. Sudden return of anxiety and terror. She must bear it all alone. The catastrophe approaches, inexorably, inevitably. Despair, conflict and destruction.

(Krogstad has acted dishonourably and thereby become well-to-do; now his prosperity does not help him, he cannot recover his honour.)

PERSONS

STENBORG, a Government clerk.

NORA, his wife.

MISS (MRS.) LIND (, a widow).

ATTORNEY KROGSTAD.

KAREN, nurse at the Stenborgs'.

A PARLOUR-MAID at the Stenborgs'.

A PORTER.

THE STENBORGS' THREE LITTLE CHILDREN.

DOCTOR HANK.

SCENARIO

FIRST ACT

A room comfortably, but not showily, furnished. In the back, on the right, a door leads to the hall; on the left another door leads to the room or office of the master of the house, which can be seen when the door is opened. A fire in the stove. Winter day.

She enters from the back, humming gaily; she is in outdoor dress and carries several parcels, has been shopping. As she opens the door, a Porter is seen in the hall, carrying a Christmas-tree. She: Put it down there for the present. (Taking out her purse) How much? Porter: Fifty öre. She: Here is a crown. No, keep the change. The Porter thanks her and goes. She continues humming and smiling with quiet glee as she opens several of the parcels she has brought. Calls off, is he at home? Yes! At first, conversation through the closed door; then he opens it and goes on talking to her while continuing to work most of the time, standing at his desk. There is a ring at the hall-door; he does not want to be disturbed; shuts himself in. The maid opens the door to her mistress's friend, just arrived in town. Happy surprise. Mutual explanation of the position of affairs. He has received the post of manager in the new joint-stock bank and is to enter on his duties at the New Year; all financial worries are at an end. The friend has come to town to look for some small employment in an office or whatever may present itself. Mrs. Stenborg gives her

---

[1] The sentence is elliptical in the original.

good hopes, is certain that all will turn out well. The maid opens the front-door to the debt-collector. Mrs. Stenborg terrified; they exchange a few words; he is shown into the office. Mrs. Stenborg and her friend; the circumstances of the debt-collector are touched upon. Stenborg enters in his overcoat; has sent the collector out the other way. Conversation about the friend's affairs; hesitation on his part. He and the friend go out; his wife follows them into the hall; the Nurse enters with the children. Mother and children play. The collector enters. Mrs. Stenborg sends the children out to the left. Great scene between her and him. He goes. Stenborg enters; has met him on the stairs; displeased; wants to know what he came back for? Her support? No intrigues. His wife cautiously tries to pump him. Strict legal answers. Exit to his room. She (repeating her words when the collector went out) But that's impossible. Why, I did it from love!

SCENARIO

SECOND ACT

The last day of the year. Midday. Nora and the old Nurse. Nora, impelled by uneasiness, is putting on her things to go out. Anxious random questions of one kind and another give a hint that thoughts of death are in her mind. Tries to banish these thoughts, to turn it off, hopes that something or other may intervene. But what? The Nurse goes off to the left.—Stenborg enters from his room. Short dialogue between him and Nora.—The Nurse re-enters, looking for Nora; the youngest child is crying. Annoyance and questioning on Stenborg's part; exit the Nurse; Stenborg is going in to the children.—Doctor Hank enters. Scene between him and Stenborg.—Nora soon re-enters; she has turned back; anxiety has driven her home again. Scene between her, the Doctor and Stenborg. Stenborg goes into his room.—Scene between Nora and the Doctor. The Doctor goes out.—Nora alone.—Mrs. Linde enters. Scene between her and Nora.—Krogstad enters. Short scene between him, Mrs. Linde and Nora. Mrs. Linde goes in to the children.—Scene between Krogstad and Nora.—she entreats and implores him for the sake of her little children; in vain. Krogstad goes out. The letter is seen to fall from outside into the letter-box.—Mrs. Linde re-enters after a short pause. Scene between her and Nora. Half confession. Mrs. Linde goes out.—Nora alone.—Stenborg enters. Scene between him and Nora. He wants to empty the letter-box. Entreaties, jests, half playful persuasion. He promises to let business wait till after New Year's Day; but at 12 o'clock midnight—! Exit. Nora alone. Nora (looking at the clock:) It is five o'clock. Five;—seven hours till midnight. Twenty-four hours till the next midnight. Twenty-four and seven—thirty-one. Thirty-one hours to live.—

THIRD ACT

A muffled sound of dance music is heard from the floor above. A lighted lamp on the table. Mrs. Linde sits in an armchair and absently turns the pages of a book, tries to read, but seems unable to fix her attention; once or twice she looks at her watch. Nora comes down from the dance; uneasiness has driven her; surprise at finding Mrs. Linde, who pretends that she wanted to see Nora in her costume. Helmer, displeased at her going away, comes to fetch her back. The Doctor also enters, but to say good-bye. Meanwhile Mrs. Linde has gone into the side room on the right. Scene between the Doctor, Helmer and Nora. He is going to bed, he says, never to get up again; they are not to come and see him; there is ugliness about a death-bed. He goes out. Helmer goes upstairs again with Nora, after the latter has exchanged a few words of farewell with Mrs. Linde. Mrs. Linde alone. Then Krogstad. Scene and explanation between them. Both go out. Nora and the children. Then she alone. Then Helmer. He takes the letters out of the letter-box. Short scene; good-night; he goes into his room. Nora in despair prepares for the final step; is ready at the door when Helmer enters with the open letter in his hand. Great scene. A ring. Letter to Nora from Krogstad. Final scene. Divorce. Nora leaves the house.—

The photograph of the Moscow Art Theater's original production of Anton Chekhov's *The Cherry Orchard* shows the naturalistic detail for which Constantin Stanislavski's company was famous; Stanislavski is at the left in the role of Gaev, gesturing to the bookcase.

In this scene from Henrik Ibsen's *A Doll House*, Doctor Rank, Helmer, and Nora have just returned from the party; Nora wears her tarantella costume, and Helmer has been given a "mask" of middle-class respectability.

Henrik Ibsen

At the turn of the century, Henrik Ibsen's name was synonymous with modernity in the European theater; much of the territory of modern drama was first explored in Ibsen's work. Born into a mercantile family in provincial Norway, Ibsen (1828–1906) had planned to study medicine; however, after failing to matriculate at the university, he turned to a career as a writer. From 1850 through 1864, Ibsen worked for the nationalist Norwegian Theater in Bergen and then for the Mollergate Theater in Christiania (now Oslo). As literary manager, stage manager, and assistant to the director, Ibsen learned the craft of practical theater firsthand. He also wrote a series of romantic history plays, some in prose and some in verse. Although his fame now rests on the realistic plays he wrote later in his career, in his own lifetime these history plays—such as *The Vikings at Helgeland* (1858)—were quite popular, especially in Norway.

In 1864, Ibsen left Norway and settled in Rome, where he wrote two pivotal plays, *Brand* (1866) and *Peer Gynt* (1867). The story of an idealistic minister, *Brand* established Ibsen as an important European writer and announced one of his central themes: the cost of moral idealism in the modern world. *Peer Gynt* is often taken as a companion-piece to *Brand,* for Peer's picaresque journey throughout Europe is undertaken simply for the purpose of his own self-satisfaction: while Brand's motto is "Be wholly what you are," Peer Gynt's is "To thine own self be . . . enough." In 1877, after extensive work on the Hegelian history drama *Emperor and Galilean,* Ibsen wrote *Pillars of Society,* a prose drama of modern life, inaugurating the stunning series of plays that made him famous and established the contours of modern realistic drama. In *A Doll House* (1879), *Ghosts* (1881), and *An Enemy of the People* (1882), Ibsen explored the conflict between the social and moral restrictions of bourgeois society and the psychological, often unconscious, demands of individual freedom. Ibsen adapted the suspenseful, rigorously plotted form of the **WELL-MADE PLAY** (or *pièce bien faite*) popularized throughout Europe by French playwrights Eugène Scribe and Victorien Sardou and used it in plays of modern life critical of bourgeois morality and society. The well-made play is notoriously difficult to define, even though its features are familiar: a rigorously "causal" plot, a secret gradually revealed to the audience, a "necessary scene" (the *scène-à-faire*) in which the secret is revealed to the characters, a character (the *raisonneur*) who explains and moralizes the action to the others, and a predominance of coincidental events. In his earlier plays, Ibsen takes these formal conventions and makes them function as forces in the dramatic world. The world of the play comes to seem mechanistic, determined by a secret that will out, full of busybodies explaining and interpreting the action. The mechanics of the well-made play, that is, are identified with the deadening force of social convention, which painfully threatens to extinguish the vitality of the central characters. This conflict between deadening social convention and a mysterious inner vitality pervades Ibsen's mature plays as well, which increasingly moved away from the "well-made" form: *The Wild Duck* (1885), *Rosmersholm* (1887), *The Lady from the Sea* (1888), and *Hedda Gabler* (1890). Ibsen's last plays seem more poetic or symbolic, though they take place in the familiar milieu of the realistic stage: *The Master Builder* (1892), *Little Eyolf* (1894), *John Gabriel Borkman* (1896), and the unfinished *When We Dead Awaken* (1900). Ibsen suffered a paralyzing series of strokes in 1900 that left him unable to write. He died in 1906.

Ibsen's effect on his contemporaries and his influence on the course of modern drama were immediate and profound. His plays were rapidly translated into the major European languages, and stage productions—which often inaugurated the new "independent" theaters—frequently became the subject of sensation and controversy. Indeed, "Ibsenism" came to be a catchword for a variety of social causes, though Ibsen himself generally avoided politics. Although Ibsen's plays brought new issues to the stage, it was his practice as a playwright that proved truly revolutionary. Many playwrights had adopted the realistic theater's use of a material stage environment, its emphasis on the burden of the past, and its sense of a mechanized and constricting society. Ibsen not only used this material with powerful subtlety and resonance, he gave the stage its first distinctively modern characters: complex, contradictory individuals driven by a desire for something—the "joy of life," a sense of themselves—that they can barely recognize or name.

A DOLL HOUSE

A Doll House was inspired by a series of incidents that came to Ibsen's attention in 1878 when a woman named Laura Kieler contacted him. Kieler had signed a secret—and illegal—loan to raise money for a cure for her tubercular husband. She wrote to Ibsen asking him to recommend the novel she had written to his publisher, in hopes that the profits from its sale would allow her to repay the loan. Ibsen refused. Kieler forged a check and was caught. Her husband committed her to an asylum, had her charged as an unfit mother, and demanded a legal separation. When she was released from the asylum, however, the family remained together.

We can see the shaping power of Ibsen's imagination in his transformation of Laura Kieler's tragedy into the ironic masterpiece, *A Doll House.* The play, which by the turn of the century was a rallying point for international feminist demands for the vote and for other legal rights and protections for women, organizes the conflict between Nora and Helmer around a subtle set of contrasts: the childlike and protected Nora and the world-weary Mrs. Linde; the upright and protective Helmer and the shady—yet finally generous—Krogstad; the privations of the past and the financial freedom Nora sees on the horizon. However, as the play proceeds, the stable, bourgeois world that Helmer represents is revealed as a tissue of deception; the institutions of marriage, respectability, and social justice turn out to be fictions that the privileged use to manipulate their world. Nora comes to seem effective, efficient, worldly wise, and finally independent, while Helmer readily compromises his principles to save his reputation. The world of financial freedom Nora glimpses at the play's outset turns out to be a kind of prison and is replaced by another kind of freedom at the end of the play: the frightening freedom to cut herself loose from the bonds of marriage, family, and society.

Helmer had more authority with audiences in the 1880s and 1890s than he does today, and Nora was conventionally criticized as an "unwomanly woman" for taking the loan, deceiving her husband, and leaving her family. Indeed, the first English actress to be offered

Owen Teale and Janet McTeer in Henrik Ibsen's *A Doll House,* in the 1997 production using a new translation by Frank McGuinness.

the part turned it down, because she didn't want audiences to think of her as the kind of woman who would desert her children. Yet the play tends to validate Nora's personal growth and her final decision to leave her family and cannily uses the material environment of the stage setting to convey the suffocating situation in which Nora finds herself.

The play takes place in one room: the drawing room where the upwardly mobile Helmers (deluxe books on the shelf, piano against the wall, framed art prints) receive their guests and conduct their lives. The room itself represents the Helmers' concern for social status and assumes a symbolic importance as well: it stands between the unseen privacy of the kitchen and bedroom—the domestic world of marriage and children—and the threatening public world beyond the front door, the world of Krogstad, of the dark and icy river, of Nora's final escape. The room becomes a kind of prison, a room in which Rank's declaration of love for Nora seems inappropriate, in which Helmer criticizes her dizzying tarantella—a Sicilian dance thought to imitate the death throes of someone bitten by a tarantula—as too abandoned, and in which Nora's final discussion with Helmer makes her submission to him impossible. That is, the room makes concrete the play's concern for the social constraints on a woman's life, becoming a visual image of how Helmer's masculine, bourgeois moral authority imprisons Nora. It is not entirely clear that Nora can survive in the harsh social and economic climate outside the comfortable parlor, but it is clear that escape from the parlor is her final alternative.

A Doll House was a successful—and a scandalous—play throughout Europe in the last decades of the nineteenth century, and it has remained in the repertoire ever since. Nora has always been associated with feminist politics, and several productions in the 1960s and 1970s saw in *A Doll House* an anticipatory allegory of the women's movement. Indeed, whereas Helmer appeared to 1880s audiences as a romantic leading man, the challenge for contemporary productions is to make him appear sympathetic, someone worth Nora's years of sacrifice, and someone she will have to struggle to leave.

A DOLL HOUSE

Henrik Ibsen

TRANSLATED BY ROLF FJELDE

CHARACTERS

TORVALD HELMER, *a lawyer*
NORA, *his wife*
DR. RANK
MRS. LINDE
NILS KROGSTAD, *a bank clerk*
THE HELMERS' THREE SMALL CHILDREN

ANNE-MARIE, *their nurse*
A MAID, *Helene*
A DELIVERY BOY

The action takes place in Helmer's residence.

ACT ONE

A comfortable room, tastefully but not expensively furnished. A door to the right in the back wall leads to the entryway; another to the left leads to HELMER's *study. Between these doors, a piano. Midway in the left-hand wall a door, and further back a window. Near the window a round table with an armchair and a small sofa. In the right-hand wall, toward the rear, a door, and nearer the foreground a porcelain stove with two armchairs and a rocking chair beside it. Between the stove and the side door, a small table. Engravings on the walls. An etagère with china figures and other small art objects; a small bookcase with richly bound books; the floor carpeted; a fire burning in the stove. It is a winter day.*

A bell rings in the entryway; shortly after we hear the door being unlocked. NORA *comes into the room, humming happily to herself; she is wearing street clothes and carries an armload of packages, which she puts down on the table to the right. She has left the hall door open; and through it a* DELIVERY BOY *is seen, holding a Christmas tree and a basket, which he gives to the* MAID *who let them in.*

NORA: Hide the tree well, Helene. The children mustn't get a glimpse of it till this evening, after it's trimmed. (*To the* DELIVERY BOY, *taking out her purse.*) How much?

DELIVERY BOY: Fifty, ma'am.

5 NORA: There's a crown. No, keep the change. (*The* BOY *thanks her and leaves.* NORA *shuts the door. She laughs softly to herself while taking off her street things. Drawing a bag of macaroons from her pocket, she eats a couple, then steals over and listens at her husband's study door.*) Yes, he's home. (*Hums again as she*
10 *moves to the table right.*)

HELMER: (*From the study.*) Is that my little lark twittering out there?

NORA: (*Busy opening some packages.*) Yes, it is.

HELMER: Is that my squirrel rummaging around?

15 NORA: Yes!

HELMER: When did my squirrel get in?

NORA: Just now. (*Putting the macaroon bag in her pocket and wiping her mouth.*) Do come in, Torvald, and see what I've bought.

20 HELMER: Can't be disturbed. (*After a moment he opens the door and peers in, pen in hand.*) Bought, you say? All that there? Has the little spendthrift been out throwing money around again?

NORA: Oh, but Torvald, this year we really should let ourselves
25 go a bit. It's the first Christmas we haven't had to economize.

HELMER: But you know we can't go squandering.

NORA: Oh yes, Torvald, we can squander a little now. Can't we? Just a tiny, wee bit. Now that you've got a big salary and are going to make piles and piles of money.

HELMER: Yes—starting New Year's. But then it's a full three 30 months till the raise comes through.

NORA: Pooh! We can borrow that long.

HELMER: Nora! (*Goes over and playfully takes her by the ear.*) Are your scatterbrains off again? What if today I borrowed a thousand crowns, and you squandered them over Christ- 35 mas week, and then on New Year's Eve a roof tile fell on my head, and I lay there—

NORA: (*Putting her hand on his mouth.*) Oh! Don't say such things!

HELMER: Yes, but what if it happened—then what? 40

NORA: If anything so awful happened, then it just wouldn't matter if I had debts or not.

HELMER: Well, but the people I'd borrowed from?

NORA: Them? Who cares about them! They're strangers.

HELMER: Nora, Nora, how like a woman! No, but seriously, 45 Nora, you know what I think about that. No debts! Never borrow! Something of freedom's lost—and something of beauty, too—from a home that's founded on borrowing and debt. We've made a brave stand up to now, the two of us; and we'll go right on like that the little while we have to. 50

NORA: (*Going toward the stove.*) Yes, whatever you say, Torvald.

HELMER: (*Following her.*) Now, now, the little lark's wings mustn't droop. Come on, don't be a sulky squirrel. (*Taking out his wallet.*) Nora, guess what I have here.

NORA: (*Turning quickly.*) Money! 55

HELMER: There, see. (*Hands her some notes.*) Good grief, I know how costs go up in a house at Christmastime.

NORA: Ten—twenty—thirty—forty. Oh, thank you, Torvald; I can manage no end on this.

HELMER: You really will have to. 60

NORA: Oh yes, I promise I will! But come here so I can show you everything I bought. And so cheap! Look, new clothes for Ivar—and a sword. Here a horse and a trumpet for Bob. And a doll and a doll's bed here for Emmy; they're nothing much, but she'll tear them to bits in no time any 65 way. And here I have dress material and handkerchiefs for the maids. Old Anne-Marie really deserves something more.

HELMER: And what's in that package there?

NORA: (*With a cry.*) Torvald, no! You can't see that till tonight!

HELMER: I see. But tell me now, you little prodigal, what have 70 you thought of for yourself?

NORA: For myself? Oh, I don't want anything at all.

HELMER: Of course you do. Tell me just what—within reason—you'd most like to have.

75 NORA: I honestly don't know. Oh, listen, Torvald—

HELMER: Well?

NORA: (*Fumbling at his coat buttons, without looking at him.*) If you want to give me something, then maybe you could— you could—

80 HELMER: Come on, out with it.

NORA: (*Hurriedly.*) You could give me money, Torvald. No more than you think you can spare; then one of these days I'll buy something with it.

HELMER: But Nora—

85 NORA: Oh, please, Torvald darling, do that! I beg you, please. Then I could hang the bills in pretty gilt paper on the Christmas tree. Wouldn't that be fun?

HELMER: What are those little birds called that always fly through their fortunes?

90 NORA: Oh yes, spendthrifts; I know all that. But let's do as I say, Torvald; then I'll have time to decide what I really need most. That's very sensible, isn't it?

HELMER: (*Smiling.*) Yes, very—that is, if you actually hung onto the money I give you, and you actually used it to buy yourself something. But it goes for the house and for all sorts of
95 foolish things, and then I only have to lay out some more.

NORA: Oh, but Torvald—

HELMER: Don't deny it, my dear little Nora. (*Putting his arm around her waist.*) Spendthrifts are sweet, but they use up a
100 frightful amount of money. It's incredible what it costs a man to feed such birds.

NORA: Oh, how can you say that! Really, I save everything I can.

HELMER: (*Laughing.*) Yes, that's the truth. Everything you can.
105 But that's nothing at all.

NORA: (*Humming, with a smile of quiet satisfaction.*) Hm, if you only knew what expenses we larks and squirrels have, Torvald.

HELMER: You're an odd little one. Exactly the way your father
110 was. You're never at a loss for scaring up money; but the moment you have it, it runs right out through your fingers; you never know what you've done with it. Well, one takes you as you are. It's deep in your blood. Yes, these things are hereditary, Nora.

115 NORA: Ah, I could wish I'd inherited many of Papa's qualities.

HELMER: And I couldn't wish you anything but just what you are, my sweet little lark. But wait; it seems to me you have a very—what should I call it?—a very suspicious look today—

120 NORA: I do?

HELMER: You certainly do. Look me straight in the eye.

NORA: (*Looking at him.*) Well?

HELMER: (*Shaking an admonitory finger.*) Surely my sweet tooth hasn't been running riot in town today, has she?

125 NORA: No. Why do you imagine that?

HELMER: My sweet tooth really didn't make a little detour through the confectioner's?

NORA: No, I assure you, Torvald—

HELMER: Hasn't nibbled some pastry?

130 NORA: No, not at all.

HELMER: Not even munched a macaroon or two?

NORA: No, Torvald, I assure you, really—

HELMER: There, there now. Of course I'm only joking.

NORA: (*Going to the table, right.*) You know I could never think
135 of going against you.

HELMER: No, I understand that; and you *have* given me your word. (*Going over to her.*) Well, you keep your little Christmas secrets to yourself, Nora darling. I expect they'll come to light this evening, when the tree is lit.

140 NORA: Did you remember to ask Dr. Rank?

HELMER: No. But there's no need for that; it's assumed he'll be dining with us. All the same, I'll ask him when he stops by here this morning. I've ordered some fine wine. Nora, you can't imagine how I'm looking forward to this evening.

145 NORA: So am I. And what fun for the children, Torvald!

HELMER: Ah, it's so gratifying to know that one's gotten a safe, secure job, and with a comfortable salary. It's a great satisfaction, isn't it?

NORA: Oh, it's wonderful!

150 HELMER: Remember last Christmas? Three whole weeks before, you shut yourself in every evening till long after midnight, making flowers for the Christmas tree, and all the other decorations to surprise us. Ugh, that was the dullest time I've ever lived through.

155 NORA: It wasn't at all dull for me.

HELMER: (*Smiling.*) But the outcome *was* pretty sorry, Nora.

NORA: Oh, don't tease me with that again. How could I help it that the cat came in and tore everything to shreds.

HELMER: No, poor thing, you certainly couldn't. You wanted
160 so much to please us all, and that's what counts. But it's just as well that the hard times are past.

NORA: Yes, it's really wonderful.

HELMER: Now I don't have to sit here alone, boring myself, and you don't have to tire your precious eyes and your fair
165 little delicate hands—

NORA: (*Clapping her hands.*) No, is it really true, Torvald, I don't have to? Oh, how wonderfully lovely to hear! (*Taking his arm.*) Now I'll tell you just how I've thought we should plan things. Right after Christmas—(*The doorbell
170 rings.*) Oh, the bell. (*Straightening the room up a bit.*) Somebody would have to come. What a bore!

HELMER: I'm not at home to visitors, don't forget.

MAID: (*From the hall doorway.*) Ma'am, a lady to see you—

NORA: All right, let her come in.

175 MAID: (*To* HELMER.) And the doctor's just come too.

HELMER: Did he go right to my study?

MAID: Yes, he did.

(HELMER *goes into his room. The* MAID *shows in* MRS. LINDE, *dressed in traveling clothes, and shuts the door after her.*)

MRS. LINDE: (*In a dispirited and somewhat hesitant voice.*) Hello, Nora.

180 NORA: (*Uncertain.*) Hello—

MRS. LINDE: You don't recognize me.

NORA: No, I don't know—but wait, I think—(*Exclaiming.*) What! Kristine! Is it really you?

MRS. LINDE: Yes, it's me.

185 NORA: Kristine! To think I didn't recognize you. But then, how could I? (*More quietly.*) How you've changed, Kristine!

MRS. LINDE: Yes, no doubt I have. In nine—ten long years.

NORA: Is it so long since we met! Yes, it's all of that. Oh, these last eight years have been a happy time, believe me. And

190 so now you've come in to town, too. Made the long trip in the winter. That took courage.

MRS. LINDE: I just got here by ship this morning.

NORA: To enjoy yourself over Christmas, of course. Oh, how lovely! Yes, enjoy ourselves, we'll do that. But take your

195 coat off. You're not still cold? (*Helping her.*) There now, let's get cozy here by the stove. No, the easy chair there! I'll take the rocker here. (*Seizing her hands.*) Yes, now you have your old look again; it was only in that first moment. You're a bit more pale, Kristine—and maybe a bit thinner.

200 MRS. LINDE: And much, much older, Nora.

NORA: Yes, perhaps a bit older; a tiny, tiny bit; not much at all. (*Stopping short; suddenly serious.*) Oh, but thoughtless me, to sit here, chattering away. Sweet, good Kristine, can you forgive me?

205 MRS. LINDE: What do you mean, Nora?

NORA: (*Softly.*) Poor Kristine, you've become a widow.

MRS. LINDE: Yes, three years ago.

NORA: Oh, I knew it, of course; I read it in the papers. Oh, Kristine, you must believe me; I often thought of writing

210 you then, but I kept postponing it, and something always interfered.

MRS. LINDE: Nora dear, I understand completely.

NORA: No, it was awful of me, Kristine. You poor thing, how much you must have gone through. And he left you noth-

215 ing?

MRS. LINDE: No.

NORA: And no children?

MRS. LINDE: No.

NORA: Nothing at all, then?

220 MRS. LINDE: Not even a sense of loss to feed on.

NORA: (*Looking incredulously at her.*) But Kristine, how could that be?

MRS. LINDE: (*Smiling wearily and smoothing her hair.*) Oh, sometimes it happens, Nora.

225 NORA: So completely alone. How terribly hard that must be for you. I have three lovely children. You can't see them now; they're out with the maid. But now you must tell me everything—

MRS. LINDE: No, no, no, tell me about yourself.

230 NORA: No, you begin. Today I don't want to be selfish. I want to think only of you today. But there *is* something I must tell you. Did you hear of the wonderful luck we had recently?

MRS. LINDE: No, what's that?

235 NORA: My husband's been made manager in the bank, just think!

MRS. LINDE: Your husband? How marvelous!

NORA: Isn't it? Being a lawyer is such an uncertain living, you know, especially if one won't touch any cases that aren't

240 clean and decent. And of course Torvald would never do that, and I'm with him completely there. Oh, we're simply delighted, believe me! He'll join the bank right after New Year's and start getting a huge salary and lots of commissions. From now on we can live quite differently—just

245 as we want. Oh, Kristine, I feel so light and happy! Won't it be lovely to have stacks of money and not a care in the world?

MRS. LINDE: Well, anyway, it would be lovely to have enough for necessities.

250 NORA: No, not just for necessities, but stacks and stacks of money!

MRS. LINDE: (*Smiling.*) Nora, Nora, aren't you sensible yet? Back in school you were such a free spender.

NORA: (*With a quiet laugh.*) Yes, that's what Torvald still says.
255 (*Shaking her finger.*) But "Nora, Nora" isn't as silly as you all think. Really, we've been in no position for me to go squandering. We've had to work, both of us.

MRS. LINDE: You too?

NORA: Yes, at odd jobs—needlework, crocheting, embroidery,
260 and such—(*Casually.*) and other things too. You remember that Torvald left the department when we were married? There was no chance of promotion in his office, and of course he needed to earn more money. But that first year he drove himself terribly. He took on all kinds of ex-
265 tra work that kept him going morning and night. It wore him down, and then he fell deathly ill. The doctors said it was essential for him to travel south.

MRS. LINDE: Yes, didn't you spend a whole year in Italy?

NORA: That's right. It wasn't easy to get away, you know. Ivar
270 had just been born. But of course we had to go. Oh, that was a beautiful trip, and it saved Torvald's life. But it cost a frightful sum, Kristine.

MRS. LINDE: I can well imagine.

NORA: Four thousand, eight hundred crowns it cost. That's
275 really a lot of money.

MRS. LINDE: But it's lucky you had it when you needed it.

NORA: Well, as it was, we got it from Papa.

MRS. LINDE: I see. It was just about the time your father died.

NORA: Yes, just about then. And, you know, I couldn't make
280 that trip out to nurse him. I had to stay here, expecting Ivar any moment, and with my poor sick Torvald to care for. Dearest Papa, I never saw him again, Kristine. Oh, that was the worst time I've known in all my marriage.

MRS. LINDE: I know how you loved him. And then you went
285 off to Italy?

NORA: Yes. We had the means now, and the doctors urged us. So we left a month after.

MRS. LINDE: And your husband came back completely cured?

NORA: Sound as a drum!

290 MRS. LINDE: But—the doctor?

NORA: Who?

MRS. LINDE: I thought the maid said he was a doctor, the man who came in with me.

NORA: Yes, that was Dr. Rank—but he's not making a sick call.
295 He's our closest friend, and he stops by at least once a day. No, Torvald hasn't had a sick moment since, and the children are fit and strong, and I am, too. (*Jumping up and clapping her hands.*) Oh, dear God, Kristine, what a lovely thing to live and be happy! But how disgusting of me—I'm talk-
300 ing of nothing but my own affairs. (*Sits on a stool close by* KRISTINE, *arms resting across her knees.*) Oh, don't be angry with me! Tell me, is it really true that you weren't in love with your husband? Why did you marry him, then?

MRS. LINDE: My mother was still alive, but bedridden and
305 helpless—and I had my two younger brothers to look after. In all conscience, I didn't think I could turn him down.

NORA: No, you were right there. But was he rich at the time?

MRS. LINDE: He was very well off, I'd say. But the business was shaky, Nora. When he died, it all fell apart, and nothing
310 was left.

NORA: And then—?

MRS. LINDE: Yes, so I had to scrape up a living with a little shop and a little teaching and whatever else I could find. The last

three years have been like one endless workday without a
315   rest for me. Now it's over, Nora. My poor mother doesn't
need me, for she's passed on. Nor the boys, either; they're
working now and can take care of themselves.

NORA: How free you must feel—

MRS. LINDE: No—only unspeakably empty. Nothing to live
320   for now. (*Standing up anxiously.*) That's why I couldn't take
it any longer out in that desolate hole. Maybe here it'll be
easier to find something to do and keep my mind occupied. If I could only be lucky enough to get a steady job,
some office work—

325 NORA: Oh, but Kristine, that's so dreadfully tiring, and you
already look so tired. It would be much better for you if
you could go off to a bathing resort.

MRS. LINDE: (*Going toward the window.*) I have no father to
give me travel money, Nora.

330 NORA: (*Rising.*) Oh, don't be angry with me.

MRS. LINDE: (*Going to her.*) Nora dear, don't you be angry
with me. The worst of my kind of situation is all the bitterness that's stored away. No one to work for, and yet
you're always having to snap up your opportunities. You
335   have to live; and so you grow selfish. When you told me
the happy change in your lot, do you know I was delighted less for your sakes than for mine?

NORA: How so? Oh, I see. You think maybe Torvald could
do something for you.

340 MRS. LINDE: Yes, that's what I thought.

NORA: And he will, Kristine! Just leave it to me; I'll bring it
up so delicately—find something attractive to humor him
with. Oh, I'm so eager to help you.

MRS. LINDE: How very kind of you, Nora, to be so concerned
345   over me—doubly kind, considering you really know so
little of life's burdens yourself.

NORA: I—? I know so little—?

MRS. LINDE: (*Smiling.*) Well, my heavens—a little needlework
and such—Nora, you're just a child.

350 NORA: (*Tossing her head and pacing the floor.*) You don't have to
act so superior.

MRS. LINDE: Oh?

NORA: You're just like the others. You all think I'm incapable
of anything serious—

355 MRS. LINDE: Come now—

NORA: That I've never had to face the raw world.

MRS. LINDE: Nora dear, you've just been telling me all your
troubles.

NORA: Hm! Trivia! (*Quietly.*) I haven't told you the big thing.

360 MRS. LINDE: Big thing? What do you mean?

NORA: You look down on me so, Kristine, but you shouldn't.
You're proud that you worked so long and hard for your
mother.

MRS. LINDE: I don't look down on a soul. But it is true: I'm
365   proud—and happy, too—to think it was given to me to
make my mother's last days almost free of care.

NORA: And you're also proud thinking of what you've done
for your brothers.

MRS. LINDE: I feel I've a right to be.

370 NORA: I agree. But listen to this, Kristine—I've also got
something to be proud and happy for.

MRS. LINDE: I don't doubt it. But whatever do you mean?

NORA: Not so loud. What if Torvald heard! He mustn't, not
for anything in the world. Nobody must know, Kristine.
375   No one but you.

MRS. LINDE: But what is it, then?

NORA: Come here. (*Drawing her down beside her on the sofa.*)
It's true—I've also got something to be proud and happy
for. I'm the one who saved Torvald's life.

MRS. LINDE: Saved—? Saved how?   380

NORA: I told you about the trip to Italy. Torvald never would
have lived if he hadn't gone south—

MRS. LINDE: Of course; your father gave you the means—

NORA: (*Smiling.*) That's what Torvald and all the rest think,
but—   385

MRS. LINDE: But—?

NORA: Papa didn't give us a pin. I was the one who raised the
money.

MRS. LINDE: You? That whole amount?

NORA: Four thousand, eight hundred crowns. What do you   390
say to that?

MRS. LINDE: But Nora, how was it possible? Did you win the
lottery?

NORA: (*Disdainfully.*) The lottery? Pooh! No art to that.

MRS. LINDE: But where did you get it from then?   395

NORA: (*Humming, with a mysterious smile.*) Hmm, tra-la-la-la.

MRS. LINDE: Because you couldn't have borrowed it.

NORA: No? Why not?

MRS. LINDE: A wife can't borrow without her husband's consent.

NORA: (*Tossing her head.*) Oh, but a wife with a little business 400
sense, a wife who knows how to manage—

MRS. LINDE: Nora, I simply don't understand—

NORA: You don't have to. Whoever said I borrowed the
money? I could have gotten it other ways. (*Throwing herself back on the sofa.*) I could have gotten it from some ad-   405
mirer or other. After all, a girl with my ravishing appeal—

MRS. LINDE: You lunatic.

NORA: I'll bet you're eaten up with curiosity, Kristine.

MRS. LINDE: Now listen here, Nora—you haven't done
something indiscreet?   410

NORA: (*Sitting up again.*) Is it indiscreet to save your husband's
life?

MRS. LINDE: I think it's indiscreet that without his knowledge
you—

NORA: But that's the point: he mustn't know! My Lord, can't 415
you understand? He mustn't ever know the close call he
had. It was to *me* the doctors came to say his life was in
danger—that nothing could save him but a stay in the
south. Didn't I try strategy then! I began talking about
how lovely it would be for me to travel abroad like other 420
young wives; I begged and I cried; I told him please to remember my condition, to be kind and indulge me; and
then I dropped a hint that he could easily take out a loan.
But at that, Kristine, he nearly exploded. He said I was
frivolous, and it was his duty as man of the house not to 425
indulge me in whims and fancies—as I think he called
them. Aha, I thought, now you'll just have to be saved—
and that's when I saw my chance.

MRS. LINDE: And your father never told Torvald the money
wasn't from him?   430

NORA: No, never. Papa died right about then. I'd considered
bringing him into my secret and begging him never to
tell. But he was too sick at the time—and then, sadly, it
didn't matter.

MRS. LINDE: And you've never confided in your husband since? 435

NORA: For heaven's sake, no! Are you serious? He's so strict on
that subject. Besides—Torvald, with all his masculine

pride—how painfully humiliating for him if he ever found out he was in debt to me. That would just ruin our relation-
440 ship. Our beautiful, happy home would never be the same.

MRS. LINDE: Won't you ever tell him?

NORA: (*Thoughtfully, half smiling.*) Yes—maybe sometime, years from now, when I'm no longer so attractive. Don't laugh! I only mean when Torvald loves me less than now,
445 when he stops enjoying my dancing and dressing up and reciting for him. Then it might be wise to have something in reserve—(*Breaking off.*) How ridiculous! That'll never happen—Well, Kristine, what do you think of my big secret? I'm capable of something too, hm? You can imagine,
450 of course, how this thing hangs over me. It really hasn't been easy meeting the payments on time. In the business world there's what they call quarterly interest and what they call amortization, and these are always so terribly hard to manage. I've had to skimp a little here and there,
455 wherever I could, you know. I could hardly spare anything from my house allowance, because Torvald has to live well. I couldn't let the children go poorly dressed; whatever I got for them, I felt I had to use up completely—the darlings!

460 MRS. LINDE: Poor Nora, so it had to come out of your own budget, then?

NORA: Yes, of course. But I was the one most responsible, too. Every time Torvald gave me money for new clothes and such, I never used more than half; always bought the sim-
465 plest, cheapest outfits. It was a godsend that everything looks so well on me that Torvald never noticed. But it did weigh me down at times, Kristine. It *is* such a joy to wear fine things. You understand.

MRS. LINDE: Oh, of course.

470 NORA: And then I found other ways of making money. Last winter I was lucky enough to get a lot of copying to do. I locked myself in and sat writing every evening till late in the night. Ah, I was tired so often, dead tired. But still it was wonderful fun, sitting and working like that, earning
475 money. It was almost like being a man.

MRS. LINDE: But how much have you paid off this way so far?

NORA: That's hard to say, exactly. These accounts, you know, aren't easy to figure. I only know that I've paid out all I could scrape together. Time and again I haven't known
480 where to turn. (*Smiling.*) Then I'd sit here dreaming of a rich old gentleman who had fallen in love with me—

MRS. LINDE: What! Who is he?

NORA: Oh, really! And that he'd died, and when his will was opened, there in big letters it said, "All my fortune shall be
485 paid over in cash, immediately, to that enchanting Mrs. Nora Helmer."

MRS. LINDE: But Nora dear—who was this gentleman?

NORA: Good grief, can't you understand? The old man never existed; that was only something I'd dream up time and
490 again whenever I was at my wits' end for money. But it makes no difference now; the old fossil can go where he pleases for all I care; I don't need him or his will—because now I'm free. (*Jumping up.*) Oh, how lovely to think of that, Kristine! Carefree! To know you're carefree, utterly
495 carefree; to be able to romp and play with the children, and to keep up a beautiful, charming home—everything just the way Torvald likes it! And think, spring is coming, with big blue skies. Maybe we can travel a little then.

Maybe I'll see the ocean again. Oh yes, it is so marvelous to live and be happy!   500

(*The front doorbell rings.*)

MRS. LINDE: (*Rising.*) There's the bell. It's probably best that I go.

NORA: No, stay. No one's expected. It must be for Torvald.

MAID: (*From the hall doorway.*) Excuse me, ma'am—there's a gentleman here to see Mr. Helmer, but I didn't know—   505 since the doctor's with him—

NORA: Who is the gentleman?

KROGSTAD: (*From the doorway.*) It's me, Mrs. Helmer.

(MRS. LINDE *starts and turns away toward the window.*)

NORA: (*Stepping toward him, tense, her voice a whisper.*) You? What is it? Why do you want to speak to my husband?   510

KROGSTAD: Bank business—after a fashion. I have a small job in the investment bank, and I hear now your husband is going to be our chief—

NORA: In other words, it's—

KROGSTAD: Just dry business, Mrs. Helmer. Nothing but that.   515

NORA: Yes, then please be good enough to step into the study. (*She nods indifferently as she sees him out by the hall door, then returns and begins stirring up the stove.*)

MRS. LINDE: Nora—who was that man?

NORA: That was a Mr. Krogstad—a lawyer.   520

MRS. LINDE: Then it really was him.

NORA: Do you know that person?

MRS. LINDE: I did once—many years ago. For a time he was a law clerk in our town.

NORA: Yes, he's been that.   525

MRS. LINDE: How he's changed.

NORA: I understand he had a very unhappy marriage.

MRS. LINDE: He's a widower now.

NORA: With a number of children. There now, it's burning. (*She closes the stove door and moves the rocker a bit to one side.*)   530

MRS. LINDE: They say he has a hand in all kinds of business.

NORA: Oh? That may be true; I wouldn't know. But let's not think about business. It's so dull.

(DR. RANK *enters from* HELMER'*s study.*)

RANK: (*Still in the doorway.*) No, no, really—I don't want to intrude, I'd just as soon talk a little while with your wife.   535 (*Shuts the door, then notices* MRS. LINDE.) Oh, beg pardon. I'm intruding here too.

NORA: No, not at all. (*Introducing him.*) Dr. Rank, Mrs. Linde.

RANK: Well now, that's a name much heard in this house. I believe I passed the lady on the stairs as I came.   540

MRS. LINDE: Yes, I take the stairs very slowly. They're rather hard on me.

RANK: Uh-hm, some touch of internal weakness?

MRS. LINDE: More overexertion, I'd say.

RANK: Nothing else? Then you're probably here in town to   545 rest up in a round of parties?

MRS. LINDE: I'm here to look for work.

RANK: Is that the best cure for overexertion?

MRS. LINDE: One has to live, Doctor.

RANK: Yes, there's a common prejudice to that effect.   550

NORA: Oh, come on, Dr. Rank—you really do want to live yourself.

RANK: Yes, I really do. Wretched as I am, I'll gladly prolong my torment indefinitely. All my patients feel like that.
555   And it's quite the same, too, with the morally sick. Right at this moment there's one of those moral invalids in there with Helmer—

MRS. LINDE: (*Softly.*) Ah!

NORA: Who do you mean?

560   RANK: Oh, it's a lawyer, Krogstad, a type you wouldn't know. His character is rotten to the root—but even he began chattering all-importantly about how he had to *live*.

NORA: Oh? What did he want to talk to Torvald about?

RANK: I really don't know. I only heard something about the
565   bank.

NORA: I didn't know that Krog—that this man Krogstad had anything to do with the bank.

RANK: Yes, he's gotten some kind of berth down there. (*To MRS. LINDE.*) I don't know if you also have, in your neck
570   of the woods, a type of person who scuttles about breathlessly, sniffing out hints of moral corruption, and then maneuvers his victim into some sort of key position where he can keep an eye on him. It's the healthy these days that are out in the cold.

575   MRS. LINDE: All the same, it's the sick who most need to be taken in.

RANK: (*With a shrug.*) Yes, there we have it. That's the concept that's turning society into a sanatorium.

(NORA, *lost in her thoughts, breaks out into quiet laughter and claps her hands.*)

RANK: Why do you laugh at that? Do you have any real idea
580   of what society is?

NORA: What do I care about dreary old society? I was laughing at something quite different—something terribly funny. Tell me, Doctor—is everyone who works in the bank dependent now on Torvald?

585   RANK: Is that what you find so terribly funny?

NORA: (*Smiling and humming.*) Never mind, never mind! (*Pacing the floor.*) Yes, that's really immensely amusing: that we—that Torvald has so much power now over all those people. (*Taking the bag out of her pocket.*) Dr. Rank, a little
590   macaroon on that?

RANK: See here, macaroons! I thought they were contraband here.

NORA: Yes, but these are some that Kristine gave me.

MRS. LINDE: What? I—?

595   NORA: Now, now, don't be afraid. You couldn't possibly know that Torvald had forbidden them. You see, he's worried they'll ruin my teeth. But hmp! Just this once! Isn't that so, Dr. Rank? Help yourself! (*Puts a macaroon in his mouth.*) And you too, Kristine. And I'll also have one, only a little
600   one—or two, at the most. (*Walking about again.*) Now I'm really tremendously happy. Now there's just one last thing in the world that I have an enormous desire to do.

RANK: Well! And what's that?

NORA: It's something I have such a consuming desire to say
605   so Torvald could hear.

RANK: And why can't you say it?

NORA: I don't dare. It's quite shocking.

MRS. LINDE: Shocking?

RANK: Well, then it isn't advisable. But in front of us you certainly can. What do you have such a desire to say so Tor-   610
vald could hear?

NORA: I have such a huge desire to say—to hell and be damned!

RANK: Are you crazy?

MRS. LINDE: My goodness, Nora!

RANK: Go on, say it. Here he is.   615

NORA: (*Hiding the macaroon bag.*) Shh, shh, shh!

(HELMER *comes in from his study, hat in hand, overcoat over his arm.*)

NORA: (*Going toward him.*) Well, Torvald dear, are you through with him?

HELMER: Yes, he just left.

NORA: Let me introduce you—this is Kristine, who's arrived   620
here in town.

HELMER: Kristine—? I'm sorry, but I don't know—

NORA: Mrs. Linde, Torvald dear. Mrs. Kristine Linde.

HELMER: Of course. A childhood friend of my wife's, no doubt?

MRS. LINDE: Yes, we knew each other in those days.   625

NORA: And just think, she made the long trip down here in order to talk with you.

HELMER: What's this?

MRS. LINDE: Well, not exactly—

NORA: You see, Kristine is remarkably clever in office work,   630
and so she's terribly eager to come under a capable man's supervision and add more to what she already knows—

HELMER: Very wise, Mrs. Linde.

NORA: And then when she heard that you'd become a bank manager—the story was wired out to the papers—then she   635
came in as fast as she could and—Really, Torvald, for my sake you can do a little something for Kristine, can't you?

HELMER: Yes, it's not at all impossible. Mrs. Linde, I suppose you're a widow.

MRS. LINDE: Yes.   640

HELMER: Any experience in office work?

MRS. LINDE: Yes, a good deal.

HELMER: Well, it's quite likely that I can make an opening for you—

NORA: (*Clapping her hands.*) You see, you see!   645

HELMER: You've come at a lucky moment, Mrs. Linde.

MRS. LINDE: Oh, how can I thank you?

HELMER: Not necessary. (*Putting his overcoat on.*) But today you'll have to excuse me—

RANK: Wait, I'll go with you. (*He fetches his coat from the hall   650
and warms it at the stove.*)

NORA: Don't stay out long, dear.

HELMER: An hour; no more.

NORA: Are you going too, Kristine?

MRS. LINDE: (*Putting on her winter garments.*) Yes, I have to see   655
about a room now.

HELMER: Then perhaps we can all walk together.

NORA: (*Helping her.*) What a shame we're so cramped here, but it's quite impossible for us to—

MRS. LINDE: Oh, don't even think of it! Good-bye, Nora   660
dear, and thanks for everything.

NORA: Good-bye for now. Of course you'll be back this evening. And you too, Dr. Rank. What? If you're well enough? Oh, you've got to be! Wrap up tight now.

(In a ripple of small talk the company moves out into the hall; children's voices are heard outside on the steps.)

665   NORA: There they are! There they are! *(She runs to open the door. The* CHILDREN *come in with their nurse,* ANNE-MARIE.*)* Come in, come in! *(Bends down and kisses them.)* Oh, you darlings—! Look at them, Kristine. Aren't they lovely!

RANK: No loitering in the draft here.

670   HELMER: Come, Mrs. Linde—this place is unbearable now for anyone but mothers.

(DR. RANK, HELMER, *and* MRS. LINDE *go down the stairs.* ANNE-MARIE *goes into the living room with the* CHILDREN. NORA *follows, after closing the hall door.)*

NORA: How fresh and strong you look. Oh, such red cheeks you have! Like apples and roses. *(The* CHILDREN *interrupt her throughout the following.)* And it was so much fun? That's 675 wonderful. Really? You pulled both Emmy and Bob on the sled? Imagine, all together! Yes, you're a clever boy, Ivar. Oh, let me hold her a bit, Anne-Marie. My sweet little doll baby! *(Takes the smallest from* ANNE-MARIE *and dances with her.)* Yes, yes, Mama will dance with Bob as well. What? Did you 680 throw snowballs? Oh, if I'd only been there! No, don't bother, Anne-Marie—I'll undress them myself. Oh yes, let me. It's such fun. Go in and rest; you look half frozen. There's hot coffee waiting for you on the stove. *(ANNE-MARIE goes into the room to the left.* NORA *takes the* CHILDREN's 685 *winter things off, throwing them about, while the children talk to her all at once.)* Is that so? A big dog chased you? But it didn't bite? No, dogs never bite little, lovely doll babies. Don't peek in the packages, Ivar! What is it? Yes, wouldn't you like to know. No, no, it's an ugly something. Well? Shall we play? 690 What shall we play? Hide-and-seek? Yes, let's play hide-and-seek. Bob must hide first. I must? Yes, let me hide first. *(Laughing and shouting, she and the* CHILDREN *play in and out of the living room and the adjoining room to the right. At last* NORA *hides under the table. The* CHILDREN *come storming in, search,* 695 *but cannot find her, then hear her muffled laughter, dash over to the table, lift the cloth up and find her. Wild shouting. She creeps forward as if to scare them. More shouts. Meanwhile, a knock at the hall door; no one has noticed it. Now the door half opens, and* KROGSTAD *appears. He waits a moment; the game goes on.)*

700   KROGSTAD: Beg pardon, Mrs. Helmer—

NORA: *(With a strangled cry, turning and scrambling to her knees.)* Oh! What do you want?

KROGSTAD: Excuse me. The outer door was ajar; it must be someone forgot to shut it—

705   NORA: *(Rising.)* My husband isn't home, Mr. Krogstad.

KROGSTAD: I know that.

NORA: Yes—then what do you want here?

KROGSTAD: A word with you.

NORA: With—? *(To the* CHILDREN, *quietly.)* Go in to Anne-710   Marie. What? No, the strange man won't hurt Mama. When he's gone, we'll play some more. *(She leads the* CHILDREN *into the room to the left and shuts the door after them. Then, tense and nervous:)* You want to speak to me?

KROGSTAD: Yes, I want to.

715   NORA: Today? But it's not yet the first of the month—

KROGSTAD: No, it's Christmas Eve. It's going to be up to you how merry a Christmas you have.

NORA: What is it you want? Today I absolutely can't—

KROGSTAD: We won't talk about that till later. This is something else. You do have a moment to spare, I suppose? 720

NORA: Oh yes, of course—I do, except—

KROGSTAD: Good. I was sitting over at Olsen's Restaurant when I saw your husband go down the street—

NORA: Yes?

KROGSTAD: With a lady. 725

NORA: Yes. So?

KROGSTAD: If you'll pardon my asking: wasn't that lady a Mrs. Linde?

NORA: Yes.

KROGSTAD: Just now come into town? 730

NORA: Yes, today.

KROGSTAD: She's a good friend of yours?

NORA: Yes, she is. But I don't see—

KROGSTAD: I also knew her once.

NORA: I'm aware of that. 735

KROGSTAD: Oh? You know all about it. I thought so. Well, then let me ask you short and sweet: is Mrs. Linde getting a job in the bank?

NORA: What makes you think you can cross-examine me, Mr. Krogstad—you, one of my husband's employees? But 740 since you ask, you might as well know—yes, Mrs. Linde's going to be taken on at the bank. And I'm the one who spoke for her, Mr. Krogstad. Now you know.

KROGSTAD: So I guessed right.

NORA: *(Pacing up and down.)* Oh, one does have a tiny bit of 745 influence, I should hope. Just because I am a woman, don't think it means that—When one has a subordinate position, Mr. Krogstad, one really ought to be careful about pushing somebody who—hm—

KROGSTAD: Who has influence? 750

NORA: That's right.

KROGSTAD: *(In a different tone.)* Mrs. Helmer, would you be good enough to use your influence on my behalf?

NORA: What? What do you mean?

KROGSTAD: Would you please make sure that I keep my sub-755 ordinate position in the bank?

NORA: What does that mean? Who's thinking of taking away your position?

KROGSTAD: Oh, don't play the innocent with me. I'm quite aware that your friend would hardly relish the chance of 760 running into me again; and I'm also aware now whom I can thank for being turned out.

NORA: But I promise you—

KROGSTAD: Yes, yes, yes, to the point: there's still time, and I'm advising you to use your influence to prevent it. 765

NORA: But Mr. Krogstad, I have absolutely no influence.

KROGSTAD: You haven't? I thought you were just saying—

NORA: You shouldn't take me so literally. I! How can you believe that I have any such influence over my husband?

KROGSTAD: Oh, I've known your husband from our student 770 days. I don't think the great bank manager's more steadfast than any other married man.

NORA: You speak insolently about my husband, and I'll show you the door.

KROGSTAD: The lady has spirit. 775

NORA: I'm not afraid of you any longer. After New Year's, I'll soon be done with the whole business.

KROGSTAD: (*Restraining himself.*) Now listen to me, Mrs. Helmer. If necessary, I'll fight for my little job in the bank as if it were life itself.

NORA: Yes, so it seems.

KROGSTAD: It's not just a matter of income; that's the least of it. It's something else—All right, out with it! Look, this is the thing. You know, just like all the others, of course, that once, a good many years ago, I did something rather rash.

NORA: I've heard rumors to that effect.

KROGSTAD: The case never got into court; but all the same, every door was closed in my face from then on. So I took up those various activities you know about. I had to grab hold somewhere; and I dare say I haven't been among the worst. But now I want to drop all that. My boys are growing up. For their sakes, I'll have to win back as much respect as possible here in town. That job in the bank was like the first rung in my ladder. And now your husband wants to kick me right back down in the mud again.

NORA: But for heaven's sake, Mr. Krogstad, it's simply not in my power to help you.

KROGSTAD: That's because you haven't the will to—but I have the means to make you.

NORA: You certainly won't tell my husband that I owe you money?

KROGSTAD: Hm—what if I told him that?

NORA: That would be shameful of you. (*Nearly in tears.*) This secret—my joy and my pride—that he should learn it in such a crude and disgusting way—learn it from you. You'd expose me to the most horrible unpleasantness—

KROGSTAD: Only unpleasantness?

NORA: (*Vehemently.*) But go on and try. It'll turn out the worse for you, because then my husband will really see what a crook you are, and then you'll *never* be able to hold your job.

KROGSTAD: I asked if it was just domestic unpleasantness you were afraid of?

NORA: If my husband finds out, then of course he'll pay what I owe at once, and then we'd be through with you for good.

KROGSTAD: (*A step closer.*) Listen, Mrs. Helmer—you've either got a very bad memory, or else no head at all for business. I'd better put you a little more in touch with the facts.

NORA: What do you mean?

KROGSTAD: When your husband was sick, you came to me for a loan of four thousand, eight hundred crowns.

NORA: Where else could I go?

KROGSTAD: I promised to get you that sum—

NORA: And you got it.

KROGSTAD: I promised to get you that sum, on certain conditions. You were so involved in your husband's illness, and so eager to finance your trip, that I guess you didn't think out all the details. It might just be a good idea to remind you. I promised you the money on the strength of a note I drew up.

NORA: Yes, and that I signed.

KROGSTAD: Right. But at the bottom I added some lines for your father to guarantee the loan. He was supposed to sign down there.

NORA: Supposed to? He did sign.

KROGSTAD: I left the date blank. In other words, your father would have dated his signature himself. Do you remember that?

NORA: Yes, I think—

KROGSTAD: Then I gave you the note for you to mail to your father. Isn't that so?

NORA: Yes.

KROGSTAD: And naturally you sent it at once—because only some five, six days later you brought me the note, properly signed. And with that, the money was yours.

NORA: Well, then; I've made my payments regularly, haven't I?

KROGSTAD: More or less. But—getting back to the point—those were hard times for you then, Mrs. Helmer.

NORA: Yes, they were.

KROGSTAD: Your father was very ill, I believe.

NORA: He was near the end.

KROGSTAD: He died soon after?

NORA: Yes.

KROGSTAD: Tell me, Mrs. Helmer, do you happen to recall the date of your father's death? The day of the month, I mean.

NORA: Papa died the twenty-ninth of September.

KROGSTAD: That's quite correct; I've already looked into that. And now we come to a curious thing—(*Taking out a paper.*) which I simply cannot comprehend.

NORA: Curious thing? I don't know—

KROGSTAD: This is the curious thing: that your father cosigned the note for your loan three days after his death.

NORA: How—? I don't understand.

KROGSTAD: Your father died the twenty-ninth of September. But look. Here your father dated his signature October second. Isn't that curious, Mrs. Helmer? (NORA *is silent.*) Can you explain it to me? (NORA *remains silent.*) It's also remarkable that the words "October second" and the year aren't written in your father's hand, but rather in one that I think I know. Well, it's easy to understand. Your father forgot perhaps to date his signature, and then someone or other added it, a bit sloppily, before anyone knew of his death. There's nothing wrong in that. It all comes down to the signature. And there's no question about *that,* Mrs. Helmer. It really *was* your father who signed his own name here, wasn't it?

NORA: (*After a short silence, throwing her head back and looking squarely at him.*) No, it wasn't. *I* signed Papa's name.

KROGSTAD: Wait, now—are you fully aware that this is a dangerous confession?

NORA: Why? You'll soon get your money.

KROGSTAD: Let me ask you a question—why didn't you send the paper to your father?

NORA: That was impossible. Papa was so sick. If I'd asked him for his signature, I also would have had to tell him what the money was for. But I couldn't tell him, sick as he was, that my husband's life was in danger. That was just impossible.

KROGSTAD: Then it would have been better if you'd given up the trip abroad.

NORA: I couldn't possibly. The trip was to save my husband's life. I couldn't give that up.

KROGSTAD: But didn't you ever consider that this was a fraud against me?

NORA: I couldn't let myself be bothered by that. You weren't any concern of mine. I couldn't stand you, with all those cold complications you made, even though you knew how badly off my husband was.

KROGSTAD: Mrs. Helmer, obviously you haven't the vaguest idea of what you've involved yourself in. But I can tell you this: it was nothing more and nothing worse that I once did—and it wrecked my whole reputation.

900 NORA: You? Do you expect me to believe that you ever acted bravely to save your wife's life?

KROGSTAD: Laws don't inquire into motives.

NORA: Then they must be very poor laws.

KROGSTAD: Poor or not—if I introduce this paper in court,
905 you'll be judged according to law.

NORA: This I refuse to believe. A daughter hasn't a right to protect her dying father from anxiety and care? A wife hasn't a right to save her husband's life? I don't know much about laws, but I'm sure that somewhere in the
910 books these things are allowed. And you don't know anything about it—you who practice the law? You must be an awful lawyer, Mr. Krogstad.

KROGSTAD: Could be. But business—the kind of business we two are mixed up in—don't you think I know about that?
915 All right. Do what you want now. But I'm telling you *this*: if I get shoved down a second time, you're going to keep me company. (*He bows and goes out through the hall.*)

NORA: (*Pensive for a moment, then tossing her head.*) Oh, really! Trying to frighten me! I'm not so silly as all that. (*Begins*
920 *gathering up the* CHILDREN's *clothes, but soon stops.*) But—? No, but that's impossible! I did it out of love.

THE CHILDREN: (*In the doorway, left.*) Mama, that strange man's gone out the door.

NORA: Yes, yes, I know it. But don't tell anyone about the
925 strange man. Do you hear? Not even Papa!

THE CHILDREN: No, Mama. But now will you play again?

NORA: No, not now.

THE CHILDREN: Oh, but Mama, you promised.

NORA: Yes, but I can't now. Go inside; I have too much to do.
930 Go in, go in, my sweet darlings. (*She herds them gently back in the room and shuts the door after them. Settling on the sofa, she takes up a piece of embroidery and makes some stitches, but soon stops abruptly.*) No! (*Throws the work aside, rises, goes to the hall door and calls out.*) Helene! Let me have the tree in
935 here. (*Goes to the table, left, opens the table drawer, and stops again.*) No, but that's utterly impossible!

MAID: (*With the Christmas tree.*) Where should I put it, ma'am?

NORA: There. The middle of the floor.

MAID: Should I bring anything else?

940 NORA: No, thanks. I have what I need.

(*The* MAID, *who has set the tree down, goes out.*)

NORA: (*Absorbed in trimming the tree.*) Candles here—and flowers here. That terrible creature! Talk, talk, talk! There's nothing to it at all. The tree's going to be lovely. I'll do anything to please you, Torvald. I'll sing for you, dance for you—
945

(HELMER *comes in from the hall, with a sheaf of papers under his arm.*)

NORA: Oh! You're back so soon?

HELMER: Yes. Has anyone been here?

NORA: Here? No.

HELMER: That's odd. I saw Krogstad leaving the front door.

950 NORA: So? Oh yes, that's true. Krogstad was here a moment.

HELMER: Nora, I can see by your face that he's been here, begging you to put in a good word for him.

NORA: Yes.

HELMER: And it was supposed to seem like your own idea? You were to hide it from me that he'd been here. He asked 955 you that, too, didn't he?

NORA: Yes, Torvald, but—

HELMER: Nora, Nora, and you could fall for that? Talk with that sort of person and promise him anything? And then in the bargain, tell me an untruth. 960

NORA: An untruth—?

HELMER: Didn't you say that no one had been here? (*Wagging his finger.*) My little songbird must never do that again. A songbird needs a clean beak to warble with. No false notes. (*Putting his arm about her waist.*) That's the way it 965 should be, isn't it? Yes, I'm sure of it. (*Releasing her.*) And so, enough of that. (*Sitting by the stove.*) Ah, how snug and cozy it is here. (*Leafing among his papers.*)

NORA: (*Busy with the tree, after a short pause.*) Torvald!

HELMER: Yes. 970

NORA: I'm so much looking forward to the Stenborgs' costume party, day after tomorrow.

HELMER: And I can't wait to see what you'll surprise me with.

NORA: Oh, that stupid business!

HELMER: What? 975

NORA: I can't find anything that's right. Everything seems so ridiculous, so inane.

HELMER: So my little Nora's come to *that* recognition?

NORA: (*Going behind his chair, her arms resting on its back.*) Are you very busy, Torvald? 980

HELMER: Oh—

NORA: What papers are those?

HELMER: Bank matters.

NORA: Already?

HELMER: I've gotten full authority from the retiring manage- 985 ment to make all necessary changes in personnel and procedure. I'll need Christmas week for that. I want to have everything in order by New Year's.

NORA: So that was the reason this poor Krogstad—

HELMER: Hm. 990

NORA: (*Still leaning on the chair and slowly stroking the nape of his neck.*) If you weren't so very busy, I would have asked you an enormous favor, Torvald.

HELMER: Let's hear. What is it?

NORA: You know, there isn't anyone who has your good 995 taste—and I want so much to look well at the costume party. Torvald, couldn't you take over and decide what I should be and plan my costume?

HELMER: Ah, is my stubborn little creature calling for a lifeguard? 1000

NORA: Yes, Torvald, I can't get anywhere without your help.

HELMER: All right—I'll think it over. We'll hit on something.

NORA: Oh, how sweet of you. (*Goes to the tree again. Pause.*) Aren't the red flowers pretty—? But tell me, was it really such a crime that this Krogstad committed? 1005

HELMER: Forgery. Do you have any idea what that means?

NORA: Couldn't he have done it out of need?

HELMER: Yes, or thoughtlessness, like so many others. I'm not so heartless that I'd condemn a man categorically for just one mistake. 1010

NORA: No, of course not, Torvald!

HELMER: Plenty of men have redeemed themselves by openly confessing their crimes and taking their punishment.

NORA: Punishment—?

1015 HELMER: But now Krogstad didn't go that way. He got himself out by sharp practices, and that's the real cause of his moral breakdown.

NORA: Do you really think that would—?

HELMER: Just imagine how a man with that sort of guilt in 1020 him has to lie and cheat and deceive on all sides, has to wear a mask even with the nearest and dearest he has, even with his own wife and children. And with the children, Nora—that's where it's most horrible.

NORA: Why?

1025 HELMER: Because that kind of atmosphere of lies infects the whole life of a home. Every breath the children take in is filled with the germs of something degenerate.

NORA: (*Coming closer behind him.*) Are you sure of that?

HELMER: Oh, I've seen it often enough as a lawyer. Almost 1030 everyone who goes bad early in life has a mother who's a chronic liar.

NORA: Why just—the mother?

HELMER: It's usually the mother's influence that's dominant, but the father's works in the same way, of course. Every 1035 lawyer is quite familiar with it. And still this Krogstad's been going home year in, year out, poisoning his own children with lies and pretense; that's why I call him morally lost. (*Reaching his hands out toward her.*) So my sweet little Nora must promise me never to plead his cause. Your hand 1040 on it. Come, come, what's this? Give me your hand. There, now. All settled. I can tell you it'd be impossible for me to work alongside of him. I literally feel physically revolted when I'm anywhere near such a person.

NORA: (*Withdraws her hand and goes to the other side of the Christ-* 1045 *mas tree.*) How hot it is here! And I've got so much to do.

HELMER: (*Getting up and gathering his papers.*) Yes, and I have to think about getting some of these read through before dinner. I'll think about your costume, too. And something to hang on the tree in gilt paper, I may even see about that. 1050 (*Putting his hand on her head.*) Oh you, my darling little songbird. (*He goes into his study and closes the door after him.*)

NORA: (*Softly, after a silence.*) Oh, really! it isn't so. It's impossible. It must be impossible.

ANNE-MARIE: (*In the doorway, left.*) The children are begging 1055 so hard to come in to Mama.

NORA: No, no, no, don't let them in to me! You stay with them, Anne-Marie.

ANNE-MARIE: Of course, ma'am. (*Closes the door.*)

NORA: (*Pale with terror.*) Hurt my children—! Poison my 1060 home? (*A moment's pause; then she tosses her head.*) That's not true. Never. Never in all the world.

ACT TWO

Same room. Beside the piano the Christmas tree now stands stripped of ornament, burned-down candle stubs on its ragged branches. NORA's *street clothes lie on the sofa.* NORA, *alone in the room, moves restlessly about; at last she stops at the sofa and picks up her coat.*

NORA: (*Dropping the coat again.*) Someone's coming! (*Goes toward the door, listens.*) No—there's no one. Of course—nobody's coming today, Christmas Day—or tomorrow, either. But maybe—(*Opens the door and looks out.*) No, nothing in the mailbox. Quite empty. (*Coming forward.*) What nonsense! 5 He won't do anything serious. Nothing terrible could happen. It's impossible. Why, I have three small children.

(ANNE-MARIE, *with a large carton, comes in from the room to the left.*)

ANNE-MARIE: Well, at last I found the box with the masquerade clothes.

NORA: Thanks. Put it on the table. 10

ANNE-MARIE: (*Does so.*) But they're all pretty much of a mess.

NORA: Ahh! I'd love to rip them in a million pieces!

ANNE-MARIE: Oh, mercy, they can be fixed right up. Just a little patience.

NORA: Yes, I'll go get Mrs. Linde to help me. 15

ANNE-MARIE: Out again now? In this nasty weather? Miss Nora will catch cold—get sick.

NORA: Oh, worse things could happen—How are the children?

ANNE-MARIE: The poor mites are playing with their Christmas presents, but— 20

NORA: Do they ask for me much?

ANNE-MARIE: They're so used to having Mama around, you know.

NORA: Yes, but Anne-Marie, I *can't* be together with them as much as I was. 25

ANNE-MARIE: Well, small children get used to anything.

NORA: You think so? Do you think they'd forget their mother if she was gone for good?

ANNE-MARIE: Oh, mercy—gone for good!

NORA: Wait, tell me, Anne-Marie—I've wondered so often— 30 how could you ever have the heart to give your child over to strangers?

ANNE-MARIE: But I had to, you know, to become little Nora's nurse.

NORA: Yes, but how could you *do* it? 35

ANNE-MARIE: When I could get such a good place? A girl who's poor and who's gotten in trouble is glad enough for that. Because that slippery fish, he didn't do a thing for me, you know.

NORA: But your daughter's surely forgotten you. 40

ANNE-MARIE: Oh, she certainly has not. She's written to me, both when she was confirmed and when she was married.

NORA: (*Clasping her about the neck.*) You old Anne-Marie, you were a good mother for me when I was little.

ANNE-MARIE: Poor little Nora, with no other mother but me. 45

NORA: And if the babies didn't have one, then I know that you'd—What silly talk! (*Opening the carton.*) Go in to them. Now I'll have to—Tomorrow you can see how lovely I'll look.

ANNE-MARIE: Oh, there won't be anyone at the party as 50 lovely as Miss Nora. (*She goes off into the room, left.*)

NORA: (*Begins unpacking the box, but soon throws it aside.*) Oh, if I dared to go out. If only nobody would come. If only nothing would happen here while I'm out. What craziness—nobody's coming. Just don't think. This muff— 55 needs a brushing. Beautiful gloves, beautiful gloves. Let it go. Let it go! One, two, three, four, five, six—(*With a cry.*)

Oh, there they are! (*Poises to move toward the door, but remains irresolutely standing.* MRS. LINDE *enters from the hall, where she has removed her street clothes.*)

60 NORA: Oh, it's you, Kristine. There's no one else out there? How good that you've come.

MRS. LINDE: I hear you were up asking for me.

NORA: Yes, I just stopped by. There's something you really

65 can help me with. Let's get settled on the sofa. Look, there's going to be a costume party tomorrow evening at the Stenborgs' right above us, and now Torvald wants me to go as a Neapolitan peasant girl and dance the tarantella that I learned in Capri.

70 MRS. LINDE: Really, are you giving a whole performance?

NORA: Torvald says yes, I should. See, here's the dress. Torvald had it made for me down there; but now it's all so tattered that I just don't know—

MRS. LINDE: Oh, we'll fix that up in no time. It's nothing more

75 than the trimmings—they're a bit loose here and there. Needle and thread? Good, now we have what we need.

NORA: Oh, how sweet of you!

MRS. LINDE: (*Sewing.*) So you'll be in disguise tomorrow, Nora. You know what? I'll stop by then for a moment and

80 have a look at you all dressed up. But listen, I've absolutely forgotten to thank you for that pleasant evening yesterday.

NORA: (*Getting up and walking about.*) I don't think it was as pleasant as usual yesterday. You should have come to town a bit sooner, Kristine—Yes, Torvald really knows how to

85 give a home elegance and charm.

MRS. LINDE: And you do, too, if you ask me. You're not your father's daughter for nothing. But tell me, is Dr. Rank always so down in the mouth as yesterday?

NORA: No, that was quite an exception. But he goes around

90 critically ill all the time—tuberculosis of the spine, poor man. You know, his father was a disgusting thing who kept mistresses and so on—and that's why the son's been sickly from birth.

MRS. LINDE: (*Lets her sewing fall to her lap.*) But my dearest

95 Nora, how do you know about such things?

NORA: (*Walking more jauntily.*) Hmp! When you've had three children, then you've had a few visits from—from women who know something of medicine, and they tell you this and that.

100 MRS. LINDE: (*Resumes sewing; a short pause.*) Does Dr. Rank come here every day?

NORA: Every blessed day. He's Torvald's best friend from childhood, and *my* good friend, too. Dr. Rank almost belongs to this house.

105 MRS. LINDE: But tell me—is he quite sincere? I mean, doesn't he rather enjoy flattering people?

NORA: Just the opposite. Why do you think that?

MRS. LINDE: When you introduced us yesterday, he was proclaiming that he'd often heard my name in this house; but

110 later I noticed that your husband hadn't the slightest idea who I really was. So how could Dr. Rank—?

NORA: But it's all true, Kristine. You see, Torvald loves me beyond words, and, as he puts it, he'd like to keep me all to himself. For a long time he'd almost be jealous if I even

115 mentioned any of my old friends back home. So of course I dropped that. But with Dr. Rank I talk a lot about such things, because he likes hearing about them.

MRS. LINDE: Now listen, Nora; in many ways you're still like a child. I'm a good deal older than you, with a little more

experience. I'll tell you something: you ought to put an 120 end to all this with Dr. Rank.

NORA: What should I put an end to?

MRS. LINDE: Both parts of it, I think. Yesterday you said something about a rich admirer who'd provide you with money— 125

NORA: Yes, one who doesn't exist—worse luck. So?

MRS. LINDE: Is Dr. Rank well off?

NORA: Yes, he is.

MRS. LINDE: With no dependents?

NORA: No, no one. But— 130

MRS. LINDE: And he's over here every day?

NORA: Yes, I told you that.

MRS. LINDE: How can a man of such refinement be so grasping?

NORA: I don't follow you at all.

MRS. LINDE: Now don't try to hide it, Nora. You think I can't 135 guess who loaned you the forty-eight hundred crowns?

NORA: Are you out of your mind? How could you think such a thing! A friend of ours, who comes here every single day. What an intolerable situation that would have been!

MRS. LINDE: Then it really wasn't him. 140

NORA: No, absolutely not. It never even crossed my mind for a moment—And he had nothing to lend in those days; his inheritance came later.

MRS. LINDE: Well, I think that was a stroke of luck for you, Nora dear. 145

NORA: No, it never would have occurred to me to ask Dr. Rank—Still, I'm quite sure that if I had asked him—

MRS. LINDE: Which you won't, of course.

NORA: No, of course not. I can't see that I'd ever need to. But I'm quite positive that if I talked to Dr. Rank— 150

MRS. LINDE: Behind your husband's back?

NORA: I've got to clear up this other thing; *that's* also behind his back. I've *got* to clear it all up.

MRS. LINDE: Yes, I was saying that yesterday, but—

NORA: (*Pacing up and down.*) A man handles these problems 155 so much better than a woman—

MRS. LINDE: One's husband does, yes.

NORA: Nonsense. (*Stopping.*) When you pay everything you owe, then you get your note back, right?

MRS. LINDE: Yes, naturally. 160

NORA: And can rip it into a million pieces and burn it up— that filthy scrap of paper!

MRS. LINDE: (*Looking hard at her, laying her sewing aside, and rising slowly.*) Nora, you're hiding something from me.

NORA: You can see it in my face? 165

MRS. LINDE: Something's happened to you since yesterday morning. Nora, what is it?

NORA: (*Hurrying toward her.*) Kristine! (*Listening.*) Shh! Torvald's home. Look, go in with the children a while. Torvald can't bear all this snipping and stitching. Let 170 Anne-Marie help you.

MRS. LINDE: (*Gathering up some of the things.*) All right, but I'm not leaving here until we've talked this out. (*She disappears into the room, left, as* TORVALD [HELMER] *enters from the hall.*)

NORA: Oh, how I've been waiting for you, Torvald dear. 175

HELMER: Was that the dressmaker?

NORA: No, that was Kristine. She's helping me fix up my costume. You know, it's going to be quite attractive.

HELMER: Yes, wasn't that a bright idea I had?

NORA: Brilliant! But then wasn't I good as well to give in to 180 you?

HELMER: Good—because you give in to your husband's judgment? All right, you little goose, I know you didn't mean it like that. But I won't disturb you. You'll want to have a fitting, I suppose.

NORA: And you'll be working?

HELMER: Yes. (*Indicating a bundle of papers.*) See, I've been down to the bank. (*Starts toward his study.*)

NORA: Torvald.

HELMER: (*Stops.*) Yes.

NORA: If your little squirrel begged you, with all her heart and soul, for something—?

HELMER: What's that?

NORA: Then would you do it?

HELMER: First, naturally, I'd have to know what it was.

NORA: Your squirrel would scamper about and do tricks, if you'd only be sweet and give in.

HELMER: Out with it.

NORA: Your lark would be singing high and low in every room—

HELMER: Come on, she does that anyway.

NORA: I'd be a wood nymph and dance for you in the moonlight.

HELMER: Nora—don't tell me it's that same business from this morning?

NORA: (*Coming closer.*) Yes, Torvald, I beg you, please!

HELMER: And you actually have the nerve to drag that up again?

NORA: Yes, yes, you've got to give in to me; you *have* to let Krogstad keep his job in the bank.

HELMER: My dear Nora, I've slated his job for Mrs. Linde.

NORA: That's awfully kind of you. But you could just fire another clerk instead of Krogstad.

HELMER: This is the most incredible stubbornness! Because you go and give an impulsive promise to speak up for him, I'm expected to—

NORA: That's not the reason, Torvald. It's for your own sake. That man does writing for the worst papers; you said it yourself. He could do you any amount of harm. I'm scared to death of him—

HELMER: Ah, I understand. It's the old memories haunting you.

NORA: What do you mean by that?

HELMER: Of course, you're thinking about your father.

NORA: Yes, all right. Just remember how those nasty gossips wrote in the papers about Papa and slandered him so cruelly. I think they'd have had him dismissed if the department hadn't sent you up to investigate, and if you hadn't been so kind and open-minded toward him.

HELMER: My dear Nora, there's a notable difference between your father and me. Your father's official career was hardly above reproach. But mine is; and I hope it'll stay that way as long as I hold my position.

NORA: Oh, who can ever tell what vicious minds can invent? We could be so snug and happy now in our quiet, carefree home—you and I and the children, Torvald! That's why I'm pleading with you so—

HELMER: And just by pleading for him you make it impossible for me to keep him on. It's already known at the bank that I'm firing Krogstad. What if it's rumored around now that the new bank manager was vetoed by his wife—

NORA: Yes, what then—?

HELMER: Oh yes—as long as our little bundle of stubbornness gets her way—! I should go and make myself ridiculous in front of the whole office—give people the idea I can be swayed by all kinds of outside pressure. Oh, you can bet I'd feel the effects of that soon enough! Besides—there's something that rules Krogstad right out at the bank as long as I'm the manager.

NORA: What's that?

HELMER: His moral failings I could maybe overlook if I had to—

NORA: Yes, Torvald, why not?

HELMER: And I hear he's quite efficient on the job. But he was a crony of mine back in my teens—one of those rash friendships that crop up again and again to embarrass you later in life. Well, I might as well say it straight out: we're on a firstname basis. And that tactless fool makes no effort at all to hide it in front of others. Quite the contrary—he thinks that entitles him to take a familiar air around me, and so every other second he comes booming out with his "Yes, Torvald!" and "Sure thing, Torvald!" I tell you, it's been excruciating for me. He's out to make my place in the bank unbearable.

NORA: Torvald, you can't be serious about all this.

HELMER: Oh no? Why not?

NORA: Because these are such petty considerations.

HELMER: What are you saying? Petty? You think I'm petty!

NORA: No, just the opposite, Torvald dear. That's exactly why—

HELMER: Never mind. You call my motives petty; then I might as well be just that. Petty! All right! We'll put a stop to this for good. (*Goes to the hall door and calls.*) Helene!

NORA: What do you want?

HELMER: (*Searching among his papers.*) A decision. (*The* MAID *comes in.*) Look here; take this letter; go out with it at once. Get hold of a messenger and have him deliver it. Quick now. It's already addressed. Wait, here's some money.

MAID: Yes, sir. (*She leaves with the letter.*)

HELMER: (*Straightening his papers.*) There, now, little Miss Willful.

NORA: (*Breathlessly.*) Torvald, what was that letter?

HELMER: Krogstad's notice.

NORA: Call it back, Torvald! There's still time. Oh, Torvald, call it back! Do it for my sake—for your sake, for the children's sake! Do you hear, Torvald; do it! You don't know how this can harm us.

HELMER: Too late.

NORA: Yes, too late.

HELMER: Nora dear, I can forgive you this panic, even though basically you're insulting me. Yes, you are! Or isn't it an insult to think that I should be afraid of a courtroom hack's revenge? But I forgive you anyway, because this shows so beautifully how much you love me. (*Takes her in his arms.*) This is the way it should be, my darling Nora. Whatever comes, you'll see: when it really counts, I have strength and courage enough as a man to take on the whole weight myself.

NORA: (*Terrified.*) What do you mean by that?

HELMER: The whole weight, I said.

NORA: (*Resolutely.*) No, never in all the world.

HELMER: Good. So we'll share it, Nora, as man and wife. That's as it should be. (*Fondling her.*) Are you happy now? There, there, there—not these frightened dove's eyes. It's nothing at all but empty fantasies—Now you should run through your tarantella and practice your tambourine. I'll go to the inner office and shut both doors, so I won't hear a thing; you can make all the noise you like. (*Turning in the doorway.*) And when Rank comes, just tell him where he can find me. (*He nods to her and goes with his papers into the study, closing the door.*)

310 NORA: (*Standing as though rooted, dazed with fright, in a whisper.*) He really could do it. He will do it. He'll do it in spite of everything. No, not that, never, never! Anything but that! Escape! A way out—(*The doorbell rings.*) Dr. Rank! Any-
315 thing but that! Anything, whatever it is! (*Her hands pass over her face, smoothing it; she pulls herself together, goes over and opens the hall door.* DR. RANK *stands outside, hanging his fur coat up. During the following scene, it begins getting dark.*)

NORA: Hello, Dr. Rank. I recognized your ring. But you
320 mustn't go in to Torvald yet; I believe he's working.

RANK: And you?

NORA: For you, I always have an hour to spare—you know that. (*He has entered, and she shuts the door after him.*)

RANK: Many thanks. I'll make use of these hours while I can.

325 NORA: What do you mean by that? While you can?

RANK: Does that disturb you?

NORA: Well, it's such an odd phrase. Is anything going to happen?

RANK: What's going to happen is what I've been expecting so
330 long—but I honestly didn't think it would come so soon.

NORA: (*Gripping his arm.*) What is it you've found out? Dr. Rank, you have to tell me!

RANK: (*Sitting by the stove.*) It's all over with me. There's nothing to be done about it.

335 NORA: (*Breathing easier.*) Is it you—then—?

RANK: Who else? There's no point in lying to one's self. I'm the most miserable of all my patients, Mrs. Helmer. These past few days I've been auditing my internal accounts. Bankrupt! Within a month I'll probably be laid out and
340 rotting in the churchyard.

NORA: Oh, what a horrible thing to say.

RANK: The thing itself is horrible. But the worst of it is all the other horror before it's over. There's only one final exami-nation left; when I'm finished with that, I'll know about
345 when my disintegration will begin. There's something I want to say. Helmer with his sensitivity has such a sharp dis-taste for anything ugly. I don't want him near my sickroom.

NORA: Oh, but Dr. Rank—

RANK: I won't have him in there. Under no condition. I'll
350 lock my door to him—As soon as I'm completely sure of the worst, I'll send you my calling card marked with a black cross, and you'll know then the wreck has started to come apart.

NORA: No, today you're completely unreasonable. And I
355 wanted you so much to be in a really good humor.

RANK: With death up my sleeve? And then to suffer this way for somebody else's sins. Is there any justice in that? And in every single family, in some way or another, this in-evitable retribution of nature goes on—

360 NORA: (*Her hands pressed over her ears.*) Oh, stuff! Cheer up! Please—be gay!

RANK: Yes, I'd just as soon laugh at it all. My poor, innocent spine, serving time for my father's gay army days.

NORA: (*By the table, left.*) He was so infatuated with asparagus
365 tips and *pâté de foie gras,* wasn't that it?

RANK: Yes—and with truffles.

NORA: Truffles, yes. And then with oysters, I suppose?

RANK: Yes, tons of oysters, naturally.

NORA: And then the port and champagne to go with it. It's so
370 sad that all these delectable things have to strike at our bones.

RANK: Especially when they strike at the unhappy bones that never shared in the fun.

NORA: Ah, that's the saddest of all.

RANK: (*Looks searchingly at her.*) Hm.

375 NORA: (*After a moment.*) Why did you smile?

RANK: No, it was you who laughed.

NORA: No, it was you who smiled, Dr. Rank!

RANK: (*Getting up.*) You're even a bigger tease than I'd thought.

NORA: I'm full of wild ideas today.

380 RANK: That's obvious.

NORA: (*Putting both hands on his shoulders.*) Dear, dear Dr. Rank, you'll never die for Torvald and me.

RANK: Oh, that loss you'll easily get over. Those who go away are soon forgotten.

385 NORA: (*Looks fearfully at him.*) You believe that?

RANK: One makes new connections, and then—

NORA: Who makes new connections?

RANK: Both you and Torvald will when I'm gone. I'd say you're well under way already. What was that Mrs. Linde
390 doing here last evening?

NORA: Oh, come—you can't be jealous of poor Kristine?

RANK: Oh yes, I am. She'll be my successor here in the house. When I'm down under, that woman will probably—

NORA: Shh! Not so loud. She's right in there.

395 RANK: Today as well. So you see.

NORA: Only to sew on my dress. Good gracious, how unrea-sonable you are. (*Sitting on the sofa.*) Be nice now, Dr. Rank. Tomorrow you'll see how beautifully I'll dance; and you can imagine then that I'm dancing only for you—yes, and of course for Torvald, too—that's under-
400 stood. (*Takes various items out of the carton.*) Dr. Rank, sit over here and I'll show you something.

RANK: (*Sitting.*) What's that?

NORA: Look here. Look.

RANK: Silk stockings.

405 NORA: Flesh-colored. Aren't they lovely? Now it's so dark here, but tomorrow—No, no, no, just look at the feet. Oh well, you might as well look at the rest.

RANK: Hm—

NORA: Why do you look so critical? Don't you believe they'll
410 fit?

RANK: I've never had any chance to form an opinion on that.

NORA: (*Glancing at him a moment.*) Shame on you. (*Hits him lightly on the ear with the stockings.*) That's for you. (*Puts them away again.*)

415 RANK: And what other splendors am I going to see now?

NORA: Not the least bit more, because you've been naughty. (*She hums a little and rummages among her things.*)

RANK: (*After a short silence.*) When I sit here together with you like this, completely easy and open, then I don't know—
420 I simply can't imagine—whatever would have become of me if I'd never come into this house.

NORA: (*Smiling.*) Yes, I really think you feel completely at ease with us.

RANK: (*More quietly, staring straight ahead.*) And then to have to
425 go away from it all—

NORA: Nonsense, you're not going away.

RANK: (*His voice unchanged.*)—and not even be able to leave some poor show of gratitude behind, scarcely a fleeting
430   regret—no more than a vacant place that anyone can fill.
NORA: And if I asked you now for—? No—
RANK: For what?
NORA: For a great proof of your friendship—
RANK: Yes, yes?
435   NORA: No, I mean—for an exceptionally big favor—
RANK: Would you really, for once, make me so happy?
NORA: Oh, you haven't the vaguest idea what it is.
RANK: All right, then tell me.
NORA: No, but I can't, Dr. Rank—it's all out of reason. It's
440   advice and help, too—and a favor—
RANK: So much the better. I can't fathom what you're hinting at. Just speak out. Don't you trust me?
NORA: Of course. More than anyone else. You're my best and truest friend, I'm sure. That's why I want to talk to you.
445   All right, then, Dr. Rank: there's something you can help me prevent. You know how deeply, how inexpressibly dearly Torvald loves me; he'd never hesitate a second to give up his life for me.
RANK: (*Leaning close to her.*) Nora—do you think he's the only
450   one—
NORA: (*With a slight start.*) Who—?
RANK: Who'd gladly give up his life for you.
NORA: (*Heavily.*) I see.
RANK: I swore to myself you should know this before I'm
455   gone. I'll never find a better chance. Yes, Nora, now you know. And also you know now that you can trust me beyond anyone else.
NORA: (*Rising, natural and calm.*) Let me by.
RANK: (*Making room for her, but still sitting.*) Nora—
460   NORA: (*In the hall doorway.*) Helene, bring the lamp in. (*Goes over to the stove.*) Ah, dear Dr. Rank, that was really mean of you.
RANK: (*Getting up.*) That I've loved you just as deeply as somebody else? Was *that* mean?
NORA: No, but that you came out and told me. That was
465   quite unnecessary—
RANK: What do you mean? Have you known—?

(*The* MAID *comes in with the lamp, sets it on the table, and goes out again.*)

RANK: Nora—Mrs. Helmer—I'm asking you: have you known about it?
NORA: Oh, how can I tell what I know or don't know?
470   Really, I don't know what to say—Why did you have to be so clumsy, Dr. Rank! Everything was so good.
RANK: Well, in any case, you now have the knowledge that my body and soul are at your command. So won't you speak out?
475   NORA: (*Looking at him.*) After that?
RANK: Please, just let me know what it is.
NORA: You can't know anything now.
RANK: I have to. You mustn't punish me like this. Give me the chance to do whatever is humanly possible for you.
480   NORA: Now there's nothing you can do for me. Besides, actually, I don't need any help. You'll see—it's only my fantasies. That's what it is. Of course! (*Sits in the rocker, looks at him, and smiles.*) What a nice one you are, Dr. Rank. Aren't you a little bit ashamed, now that the lamp is here?

RANK: No, not exactly. But perhaps I'd better go—for good? 485
NORA: No, you certainly can't do that. You must come here just as you always have. You know Torvald can't do without you.
RANK: Yes, but *you?*
NORA: You know how much I enjoy it when you're here.
RANK: That's precisely what threw me off. You're a mystery 490
to me. So many times I've felt you'd almost rather be with me than with Helmer.
NORA: Yes—you see, there are some people that one loves most and other people that one would almost prefer being with.
RANK: Yes, there's something to that. 495
NORA: When I was back home, of course I loved Papa most. But I always thought it was so much fun when I could sneak down to the maids' quarters, because they never tried to improve me, and it was always so amusing, the way they talked to each other. 500
RANK: Aha, so it's *their* place that I've filled.
NORA: (*Jumping up and going to him.*) Oh, dear, sweet Dr. Rank, that's not what I meant at all. But you can understand that with Torvald it's just the same as with Papa—

(*The* MAID *enters from the hall.*)

MAID: Ma'am—please! (*She whispers to* NORA *and hands her a* 505
calling card.)
NORA: (*Glancing at the card.*) Ah! (*Slips it into her pocket.*)
RANK: Anything wrong?
NORA: No, no, not at all. It's only some—it's my new dress—
RANK: Really? But—there's your dress. 510
NORA: Oh, that. But this is another one—I ordered it—Torvald mustn't know—
RANK: Ah, now we have the big secret.
NORA: That's right. Just go in with him—he's back in the inner study. Keep him there as long as— 515
RANK: Don't worry. He won't get away. (*Goes into the study.*)
NORA: (*To the* MAID.) And he's standing waiting in the kitchen?
MAID: Yes, he came up by the back stairs.
NORA: But didn't you tell him somebody was here?
MAID: Yes, but that didn't do any good. 520
NORA: He won't leave?
MAID: No, he won't go till he's talked with you, ma'am.
NORA: Let him come in, then—but quietly. Helene, don't breathe a word about this. It's a surprise for my husband.
MAID: Yes, yes, I understand—(*Goes out.*) 525
NORA: This horror—it's going to happen. No, no, no, it can't happen, it mustn't. (*She goes and bolts* HELMER'*s door. The* MAID *opens the hall door for* KROGSTAD *and shuts it behind him. He is dressed for travel in a fur coat, boots, and a fur cap.*)
NORA: (*Going toward him.*) Talk softly. My husband's home. 530
KROGSTAD: Well, good for him.
NORA: What do you want?
KROGSTAD: Some information.
NORA: Hurry up, then. What is it?
KROGSTAD: You know, of course, that I got my notice. 535
NORA: I couldn't prevent it, Mr. Krogstad. I fought for you to the bitter end, but nothing worked.
KROGSTAD: Does your husband's love for you run so thin? He knows everything I can expose you to, and all the same he dares to— 540
NORA: How can you imagine he knows anything about this?
KROGSTAD: Ah, no—I can't imagine it either, now. It's not at all like my fine Torvald Helmer to have so much guts—

NORA: Mr. Krogstad, I demand respect for my husband!

545 KROGSTAD: Why, of course—all due respect. But since the lady's keeping it so carefully hidden, may I presume to ask if you're also a bit better informed than yesterday about what you've actually done?

NORA: More than you ever could teach me.

550 KROGSTAD: Yes, I *am* such an awful lawyer.

NORA: What is it you want from me?

KROGSTAD: Just a glimpse of how you are, Mrs. Helmer. I've been thinking about you all day long. A cashier, a night—court scribbler, a—well, a type like me also has a little of what they call a heart, you know.

555 NORA: Then show it. Think of my children.

KROGSTAD: Did you or your husband ever think of mine? But never mind. I simply wanted to tell you that you don't need to take this thing too seriously. For the present, I'm not proceeding with any action.

560 NORA: Oh no, really! Well—I knew that.

KROGSTAD: Everything can be settled in a friendly spirit. It doesn't have to get around town at all; it can stay just among us three.

565 NORA: My husband must never know anything of this.

KROGSTAD: How can you manage that? Perhaps you can pay me the balance?

NORA: No, not right now.

KROGSTAD: Or you know some way of raising the money in a day or two?

570 NORA: No way that I'm willing to use.

KROGSTAD: Well, it wouldn't have done you any good, anyway. If you stood in front of me with a fistful of bills, you still couldn't buy your signature back.

575 NORA: Then tell me what you're going to do with it.

KROGSTAD: I'll just hold onto it—keep it on file. There's no outsider who'll even get wind of it. So if you've been thinking of taking some desperate step—

NORA: I have.

580 KROGSTAD: Been thinking of running away from home—

NORA: I have!

KROGSTAD: Or even of something worse—

NORA: How could you guess that?

KROGSTAD: You can drop those thoughts.

585 NORA: How could you guess I was thinking of *that?*

KROGSTAD: Most of us think about *that* at first. I thought about it too, but I discovered I hadn't the courage—

NORA: (*Lifelessly.*) I don't either.

KROGSTAD: (*Relieved.*) That's true, you haven't the courage?

590 You too?

NORA: I don't have it—I don't have it.

KROGSTAD: It would be terribly stupid, anyway. After that first storm at home blows out, why, then—I have here in my pocket a letter for your husband—

595 NORA: Telling everything?

KROGSTAD: As charitably as possible.

NORA: (*Quickly.*) He mustn't ever get that letter. Tear it up. I'll find some way to get money.

KROGSTAD: Beg pardon, Mrs. Helmer, but I think I just told

600 you—

NORA: Oh, I don't mean the money I owe you. Let me know how much you want from my husband, and I'll manage it.

KROGSTAD: I don't want any money from your husband.

NORA: What do you want, then? 605

KROGSTAD: I'll tell you what. I want to recoup, Mrs. Helmer; I want to get on in the world—and there's where your husband can help me. For a year and a half I've kept myself clean of anything disreputable—all that time struggling with the worst conditions; but I was satisfied, 610 working my way up step by step. Now I've been written right off, and I'm just not in the mood to come crawling back. I tell you, I want to move on. I want to get back in the bank—in a better position. Your husband can set up a job for me— 615

NORA: He'll never do that!

KROGSTAD: He'll do it. I know him. He won't dare breathe a word of protest. And once I'm in there together with him, you just wait and see! Inside of a year, I'll be the manager's righthand man. It'll be Nils Krogstad, not Tor- 620 vald Helmer, who runs the bank.

NORA: You'll never see the day!

KROGSTAD: Maybe you think you can—

NORA: I have the courage now—for *that.*

KROGSTAD: Oh, you don't scare me. A smart, spoiled lady like 625 you—

NORA: You'll see; you'll see!

KROGSTAD: Under the ice, maybe? Down in the freezing, coal-black water? There, till you float up in the spring, ugly, unrecognizable, with your hair falling out— 630

NORA: You don't frighten me.

KROGSTAD: Nor do you frighten me. One doesn't do these things, Mrs. Helmer. Besides, what good would it be? I'd still have him safe in my pocket.

NORA: Afterwards? When I'm no longer—? 635

KROGSTAD: Are you forgetting that *I'll* be in control then over your final reputation? (NORA *stands speechless, staring at him.*) Good; now I've warned you. Don't do anything stupid. When Helmer's read my letter, I'll be waiting for his reply. And bear in mind that it's your husband himself who's 640 forced me back to my old ways. I'll never forgive him for that. Good-bye, Mrs. Helmer. (*He goes out through the hall.*)

NORA: (*Goes to the hall door, opens it a crack, and listens.*) He's gone. Didn't leave the letter. Oh no, no, that's impossible too! (*Opening the door more and more.*) What's that? He's 645 standing outside—not going downstairs. He's thinking it over? Maybe he'll—? (*A letter falls in the mailbox; then* KROGSTAD's *footsteps are heard, dying away down a flight of stairs.* NORA *gives a muffled cry and runs over toward the sofa table. A short pause.*) In the mailbox. (*Slips warily over to the* 650 *hall door.*) It's lying there. Torvald, Torvald—now we're lost!

MRS. LINDE: (*Entering with the costume from the room, left.*) There now, I can't see anything else to mend. Perhaps you'd like to try—

NORA: (*In a hoarse whisper.*) Kristine, come here. 655

MRS. LINDE: (*Tossing the dress on the sofa.*) What's wrong? You look upset.

NORA: Come here. See that letter? *There!* Look—through the glass in the mailbox.

MRS. LINDE: Yes, yes, I see it. 660

NORA: That letter's from Krogstad—

MRS. LINDE: Nora—it's Krogstad who loaned you the money!

NORA: Yes, and now Torvald will find out everything.

MRS. LINDE: Believe me, Nora, it's best for both of you.

665 NORA: There's more you don't know. I forged a name.

MRS. LINDE: But for heaven's sake—?

NORA: I only want to tell you that, Kristine, so that you can be my witness.

MRS. LINDE: Witness? Why should I—?

670 NORA: If I should go out of my mind—it could easily happen—

MRS. LINDE: Nora!

NORA: Or anything else occurred—so I couldn't be present here—

MRS. LINDE: Nora, Nora, you aren't yourself at all!

675 NORA: And someone should try to take on the whole weight, all of the guilt, you follow me—?

MRS. LINDE: Yes, of course, but why do you think—?

NORA: Then you're the witness that it isn't true, Kristine. I'm very much myself; my mind right now is perfectly clear;

680 and I'm telling you: nobody else has known about this; I alone did everything. Remember that.

MRS. LINDE: I will. But I don't understand all this.

NORA: Oh, how could you ever understand it? It's the miracle now that's going to take place.

685 MRS. LINDE: The miracle?

NORA: Yes, the miracle. But it's so awful, Kristine. It mustn't take place, not for anything in the world.

MRS. LINDE: I'm going right over and talk with Krogstad.

NORA: Don't go near him; he'll do you some terrible harm!

690 MRS. LINDE: There was a time once when he'd gladly have done anything for me.

NORA: He?

MRS. LINDE: Where does he live?

NORA: Oh, how do I know? Yes. (*Searches in her pocket.*) Here's

695 his card. But the letter, the letter—!

HELMER: (*From the study, knocking on the door.*) Nora!

NORA: (*With a cry of fear.*) Oh! What is it? What do you want?

HELMER: Now, now, don't be so frightened. We're not coming in. You locked the door—are you trying on the dress?

700 NORA: Yes, I'm trying it. I'll look just beautiful, Torvald.

MRS. LINDE: (*Who has read the card.*) He's living right around the corner.

NORA: Yes, but what's the use? We're lost. The letter's in the box.

705 MRS. LINDE: And your husband has the key?

NORA: Yes, always.

MRS. LINDE: Krogstad can ask for his letter back unread; he can find some excuse—

NORA: But it's just this time that Torvald usually—

710 MRS. LINDE: Stall him. Keep him in there. I'll be back as quick as I can. (*She hurries out through the hall entrance.*)

NORA: (*Goes to* HELMER's *door, opens it, and peers in.*) Torvald!

HELMER: (*From the inner study.*) Well—does one dare set foot in one's own living room at last? Come on, Rank, now

715 we'll get a look—(*In the doorway.*) But what's this?

NORA: What, Torvald dear?

HELMER: Rank had me expecting some grand masquerade.

RANK: (*In the doorway.*) That was my impression, but I must have been wrong.

720 NORA: No one can admire me in my splendor—not till tomorrow.

HELMER: But Nora dear, you look so exhausted. Have you practiced too hard?

NORA: No, I haven't practiced at all yet.

HELMER: You know, it's necessary—   725

NORA: Oh, it's absolutely necessary, Torvald. But I can't get anywhere without your help. I've forgotten the whole thing completely.

HELMER: Ah, we'll soon take care of that.

NORA: Yes, take care of me, Torvald, please! Promise me that?   730 Oh, I'm so nervous. That big party—You must give up everything this evening for me. No business—don't even touch your pen. Yes? Dear Torvald, promise?

HELMER: It's a promise. Tonight I'm totally at your service— you little helpless thing. Hm—but first there's one thing I   735 want to—(*Goes toward the hall door.*)

NORA: What are you looking for?

HELMER: Just to see if there's any mail.

NORA: No, no, don't do that, Torvald!

HELMER: Now what?   740

NORA: Torvald, please. There isn't any.

HELMER: Let me look, though. (*Starts out.* NORA, *at the piano, strikes the first notes of the tarantella.* HELMER, *at the door, stops.*) Aha!

NORA: I can't dance tomorrow if I don't practice with you.   745

HELMER: (*Going over to her.*) Nora dear, are you really so frightened?

NORA: Yes, so terribly frightened. Let me practice right now; there's still time before dinner. Oh, sit down and play for me, Torvald. Direct me. Teach me, the way you always   750 have.

HELMER: Gladly, if it's what you want. (*Sits at the piano.*)

NORA: (*Snatches the tambourine up from the box, then a long, vari-colored shawl, which she throws around herself, whereupon she springs forward and cries out:*) Play for me now! Now I'll   755 dance!

(HELMER *plays and* NORA *dances.* RANK *stands behind* HELMER *at the piano and looks on.*)

HELMER: (*As he plays.*) Slower. Slow down.

NORA: Can't change it.

HELMER: Not so violent, Nora!

NORA: Has to be just like this.   760

HELMER: (*Stopping.*) No, no, that won't do at all.

NORA: (*Laughing and swinging her tambourine.*) Isn't that what I told you?

RANK: Let me play for her.

HELMER: (*Getting up.*) Yes, go on. I can teach her more easily   765 then.

(RANK *sits at the piano and plays;* NORA *dances more and more wildly.* HELMER *has stationed himself by the stove and repeatedly gives her directions; she seems not to hear them; her hair loosens and falls over her shoulders; she does not notice, but goes on dancing.* MRS. LINDE *enters.*)

MRS. LINDE: (*Standing dumbfounded at the door.*) Ah—!

NORA: (*Still dancing.*) See what fun, Kristine!

HELMER: But Nora darling, you dance as if your life were at stake.   770

NORA: And it is.

HELMER: Rank, stop! This is pure madness. Stop it, I say!

(RANK *breaks off playing, and* NORA *halts abruptly*).

HELMER: (*Going over to her.*) I never would have believed it. You've forgotten everything I taught you.

775 NORA: (*Throwing away the tambourine.*) You see for yourself.

HELMER: Well, there's certainly room for instruction here.

NORA: Yes, you see how important it is. You've got to teach me to the very last minute. Promise me that, Torvald?

HELMER: You can bet on it.

780 NORA: You mustn't, either today or tomorrow, think about anything else but me; you mustn't open any letters—or the mailbox—

HELMER: Ah, it's still the fear of that man—

NORA: Oh yes, yes, that too.

785 HELMER: Nora, it's written all over you—there's already a letter from him out there.

NORA: I don't know. I guess so. But you mustn't read such things now; there mustn't be anything ugly between us before it's all over.

790 RANK: (*Quietly to* HELMER.) You shouldn't deny her.

HELMER: (*Putting his arm around her.*) The child can have her way. But tomorrow night, after you've danced—

NORA: Then you'll be free.

MAID: (*In the doorway, right.*) Ma'am, dinner is served.

795 NORA: We'll be wanting champagne, Helene.

MAID: Very good, ma'am. (*Goes out.*)

HELMER: So—a regular banquet, hm?

NORA: Yes, a banquet—champagne till daybreak! (*Calling out.*) And some macaroons, Helene. Heaps of them—just

800 this once.

HELMER: (*Taking her hands.*) Now, now, now—no hysterics. Be my own little lark again.

NORA: Oh, I will soon enough. But go on in—and you, Dr. Rank. Kristine, help me put up my hair.

805 RANK: (*Whispering, as they go.*) There's nothing wrong—really wrong, is there?

HELMER: Oh, of course not. It's nothing more than this childish anxiety I was telling you about. (*They go out, right.*)

NORA: Well?

810 MRS. LINDE: Left town.

NORA: I could see by your face.

MRS. LINDE: He'll be home tomorrow evening. I wrote him a note.

NORA: You shouldn't have. Don't try to stop anything now. Af-

815 ter all, it's a wonderful joy, this waiting here for the miracle.

MRS. LINDE: What is it you're waiting for?

NORA: Oh, you can't understand that. Go in to them; I'll be along in a moment.

(MRS. LINDE *goes into the dining room.* NORA *stands a short while as if composing herself; then she looks at her watch.*)

NORA: Five. Seven hours to midnight. Twenty-four hours to

820 the midnight after, and then the tarantella's done. Seven and twenty-four? Thirty-one hours to live.

HELMER: (*In the doorway, right.*) What's become of the little lark?

NORA: (*Going toward him with open arms.*) Here's your lark!

ACT THREE

Same scene. The table, with chairs around it, has been moved to the center of the room. A lamp on the table is lit. The hall door stands open. Dance music drifts down from the floor above. MRS. LINDE *sits at the table, absently paging through a book, trying to read, but apparently unable to focus her thoughts. Once or twice she pauses, tensely listening for a sound at the outer entrance.*

MRS. LINDE: (*Glancing at her watch.*) Not yet—and there's hardly any time left. If only he's not—(*Listening again.*) Ah, there he is. (*She goes out in the hall and cautiously opens the outer door. Quiet footsteps are heard on the stairs. She whispers:*) Come in. Nobody's here. 5

KROGSTAD: (*In the doorway.*) I found a note from you at home. What's back of all this?

MRS. LINDE: I just *had* to talk to you.

KROGSTAD: Oh? And it just *had* to be here in this house?

MRS. LINDE: At my place it was impossible; my room hasn't a 10 private entrance. Come in; we're all alone. The maid's asleep, and the Helmers are at the dance upstairs.

KROGSTAD: (*Entering the room.*) Well, well, the Helmers are dancing tonight? Really?

MRS. LINDE: Yes, why not? 15

KROGSTAD: How true—why not?

MRS. LINDE: All right, Krogstad, let's talk.

KROGSTAD: Do we two have anything more to talk about?

MRS. LINDE: We have a great deal to talk about.

KROGSTAD: I wouldn't have thought so. 20

MRS. LINDE: No, because you've never understood me, really.

KROGSTAD: Was there anything more to understand—except what's all too common in life? A calculating woman throws over a man the moment a better catch comes by.

MRS. LINDE: You think I'm so thoroughly calculating? You 25 think I broke it off lightly?

KROGSTAD: Didn't you?

MRS. LINDE: Nils—is that what you really thought?

KROGSTAD: If you cared, then why did you write me the way you did? 30

MRS. LINDE: What else could I do? If I had to break off with you, then it was my job as well to root out everything you felt for me.

KROGSTAD: (*Wringing his hands.*) So that was it. And this—all this, simply for money! 35

MRS. LINDE: Don't forget I had a helpless mother and two small brothers. We couldn't wait for you, Nils; you had such a long road ahead of you then.

KROGSTAD: That may be; but you still hadn't the right to abandon me for somebody else's sake. 40

MRS. LINDE: Yes—I don't know. So many, many times I've asked myself if I did have that right.

KROGSTAD: (*More softly.*) When I lost you, it was as if all the solid ground dissolved from under my feet. Look at me; I'm a half-drowned man now, hanging onto a wreck. 45

MRS. LINDE: Help may be near.

KROGSTAD: It was near—but then you came and blocked it off.

MRS. LINDE: Without my knowing it, Nils. Today for the first time I learned that it's you I'm replacing at the bank.

KROGSTAD: All right—I believe you. But now that you know, 50 will you step aside?

MRS. LINDE: No, because that wouldn't benefit you in the slightest.

KROGSTAD: Not "benefit" me, hm! I'd step aside anyway.

MRS. LINDE: I've learned to be realistic. Life and hard, bitter 55 necessity have taught me that.

KROGSTAD: And life's taught me never to trust fine phrases.

MRS. LINDE: Then life's taught you a very sound thing. But you do have to trust in actions, don't you?

60 KROGSTAD: What does that mean?

MRS. LINDE: You said you were hanging on like a half-drowned man to a wreck.

KROGSTAD: I've good reason to say that.

MRS. LINDE: I'm also like a half-drowned woman on a wreck.
65   No one to suffer with; no one to care for.

KROGSTAD: You made your choice.

MRS. LINDE: There wasn't any choice then.

KROGSTAD: So—what of it?

MRS. LINDE: Nils, if only we two shipwrecked people could
70   reach across to each other.

KROGSTAD: What are you saying?

MRS. LINDE: Two on one wreck are at least better off than each on his own.

KROGSTAD: Kristine!

75 MRS. LINDE: Why do you think I came into town?

KROGSTAD: Did you really have some thought of me?

MRS. LINDE: I have to work to go on living. All my born days, as long as I can remember, I've worked, and it's been my best and my only joy. But now I'm completely alone
80   in the world; it frightens me to be so empty and lost. To work for yourself—there's no joy in that. Nils, give me something—someone to work for.

KROGSTAD: I don't believe all this. It's just some hysterical feminine urge to go out and make a noble sacrifice.

85 MRS. LINDE: Have you ever found me to be hysterical?

KROGSTAD: Can you honestly mean this? Tell me—do you know everything about my past?

MRS. LINDE: Yes.

KROGSTAD: And you know what they think I'm worth
90   around here.

MRS. LINDE: From what you were saying before, it would seem that with me you could have been another person.

KROGSTAD: I'm positive of that.

MRS. LINDE: Couldn't it happen still?

95 KROGSTAD: Kristine—you're saying this in all seriousness? Yes, you are! I can see it in you. And do you really have the courage, then——?

MRS. LINDE: I need to have someone to care for; and your children need a mother. We both need each other. Nils, I
100   have faith that you're good at heart—I'll risk everything together with you.

KROGSTAD: (*Gripping her hands.*) Kristine, thank you, thank you—Now I know I can win back a place in their eyes. Yes—but I forgot—

105 MRS. LINDE: (*Listening.*) Shh! The tarantella. Go now! Go on!

KROGSTAD: Why? What is it?

MRS. LINDE: Hear the dance up there? When that's over, they'll be coming down.

KROGSTAD: Oh, then I'll go. But—it's all pointless. Of course,
110   you don't know the move I made against the Helmers.

MRS. LINDE: Yes, Nils, I know.

KROGSTAD: And all the same, you have the courage to—?

MRS. LINDE: I know how far despair can drive a man like you.

KROGSTAD: Oh, if I only could take it all back.

115 MRS. LINDE: You easily could—your letter's still lying in the mailbox.

KROGSTAD: Are you sure of that?

MRS. LINDE: Positive. But—

KROGSTAD: (*Looks at her searchingly.*) Is that the meaning of it, then? You'll save your friend at any price. Tell me straight 120 out. Is that it?

MRS. LINDE: Nils—anyone who's sold herself for somebody else once isn't going to do it again.

KROGSTAD: I'll demand my letter back.

MRS. LINDE: No, no.   125

KROGSTAD: Yes, of course. I'll stay here till Helmer comes down; I'll tell him to give me my letter again—that it only involves my dismissal—that he shouldn't read it—

MRS. LINDE: No, Nils, don't call the letter back.

KROGSTAD: But wasn't that exactly why you wrote me to 130 come here?

MRS. LINDE: Yes, in that first panic. But it's been a whole day and night since then, and in that time I've seen such incredible things in this house. Helmer's got to learn everything; this dreadful secret has to be aired; those two have to come to a 135 full understanding; all these lies and evasions can't go on.

KROGSTAD: Well, then, if you want to chance it. But at least there's one thing I can do, and do right away—

MRS. LINDE: (*Listening.*) Go now, go, quick! The dance is over. We're not safe another second.   140

KROGSTAD: I'll wait for you downstairs.

MRS. LINDE: Yes, please do; take me home.

KROGSTAD: I can't believe it; I've never been so happy. (*He leaves by way of the outer door; the door between the room and the hall stays open.*)   145

MRS. LINDE: (*Straightening up a bit and getting together her street clothes.*) How diffc'rent now! How different! Someone to work for, to live for—a home to build. Well, it is worth the try! Oh, if they'd only come! (*Listening.*) Ah, there they are. Bundle up. (*She picks up her hat and coat. NORA's and* 150 *HELMER's voices can be heard outside; a key turns in the lock, and* HELMER *brings* NORA *into the hall almost by force. She is wearing the Italian costume with a large black shawl about her; he has on evening dress, with a black domino open over it.*)

NORA: (*Struggling in the doorway.*) No, no, no, not inside! I'm 155 going up again. I don't want to leave so soon.

HELMER: But Nora dear—

NORA: Oh, I beg you, please, Torvald. From the bottom of my heart, *please*—only an hour more!

HELMER: Not a single minute, Nora darling. You know our 160 agreement. Come on, in we go; you'll catch cold out here. (*In spite of her resistance, he gently draws her into the room.*)

MRS. LINDE: Good evening.

NORA: Kristine!

HELMER: Why, Mrs. Linde—are you here so late?   165

MRS. LINDE: Yes, I'm sorry, but I did want to see Nora in costume.

NORA: Have you been sitting here, waiting for me?

MRS. LINDE: Yes. I didn't come early enough; you were all up-stairs; and then I thought I really couldn't leave without 170 seeing you.

HELMER: (*Removing* NORA's *shawl.*) Yes, take a good look. She's worth looking at, I can tell you that, Mrs. Linde. Is-n't she lovely?

MRS. LINDE: Yes, I should say—   175

HELMER: A dream of loveliness, isn't she? That's what every-one thought at the party, too. But she's horribly stub-born—this sweet little thing. What's to be done with her?

Can you imagine, I almost had to use force to pry her away.

180 NORA: Oh, Torvald, you're going to regret you didn't indulge me, even for just a half hour more.

HELMER: There, you see. She danced her tarantella and got a tumultuous hand—which was well earned, although the performance may have been a bit too naturalistic—I mean

185 it rather overstepped the proprieties of art. But never mind—what's important is, she made a success, an overwhelming success. You think I could let her stay on after that and spoil the effect? Oh no; I took my lovely little Capri girl—my capricious little Capri girl, I should say—

190 took her under my arm; one quick tour of the ballroom, a curtsy to every side, and then—as they say in novels—the beautiful vision disappeared. An exit should always be effective, Mrs. Linde, but that's what I can't get Nora to grasp. Phew, it's hot in here. (*Flings the domino on a chair and opens*

195 *the door to his room.*) Why's it dark in here? Oh yes, of course. Excuse me. (*He goes in and lights a couple of candles.*)

NORA: (*In a sharp, breathless whisper.*) So?

MRS. LINDE: (*Quietly.*) I talked with him.

NORA: And—?

200 MRS. LINDE: Nora—you must tell your husband everything.

NORA: (*Dully.*) I knew it.

MRS. LINDE: You've got nothing to fear from Krogstad, but you have to speak out.

NORA: I won't tell.

205 MRS. LINDE: Then the letter will.

NORA: Thanks, Kristine. I know now what's to be done. Shh!

HELMER: (*Reentering.*) Well, then, Mrs. Linde—have you admired her?

MRS. LINDE: Yes, and now I'll say good night.

210 HELMER: Oh, come, so soon? Is this yours, this knitting?

MRS. LINDE: Yes, thanks. I nearly forgot it.

HELMER: Do you knit, then?

MRS. LINDE: Oh yes.

HELMER: You know what? You should embroider instead.

215 MRS. LINDE: Really? Why?

HELMER: Yes, because it's a lot prettier. See here, one holds the embroidery so, in the left hand, and then one guides the needle with the right—so—in an easy, sweeping curve—right?

MRS. LINDE: Yes, I guess that's—

220 HELMER: But, on the other hand, knitting—it can never be anything but ugly. Look, see here, the arms tucked in, the knitting needles going up and down—there's something Chinese about it. Ah, that was really a glorious champagne they served.

225 MRS. LINDE: Yes, good night, Nora, and don't be stubborn anymore.

HELMER: Well put, Mrs. Linde!

MRS. LINDE: Good night, Mr. Helmer.

HELMER: (*Accompanying her to the door.*) Good night, good

230 night. I hope you get home all right. I'd be very happy to—but you don't have far to go. Good night, good night. (*She leaves. He shuts the door after her and returns.*) There, now, at last we got her out the door. She's a deadly bore, that creature.

235 NORA: Aren't you pretty tired, Torvald?

HELMER: No, not a bit.

NORA: You're not sleepy?

HELMER: Not at all. On the contrary, I'm feeling quite exhilarated. But you? Yes, you really look tired and sleepy.

NORA: Yes, I'm very tired. Soon now I'll sleep. 240

HELMER: See! You see! I was right all along that we shouldn't stay longer.

NORA: Whatever you do is always right.

HELMER: (*Kissing her brow.*) Now my little lark talks sense. Say, did you notice what a time Rank was having tonight? 245

NORA: Oh, was he? I didn't get to speak with him.

HELMER: I scarcely did either, but it's a long time since I've seen him in such high spirits. (*Gazes at her a moment, then comes nearer her.*) Hm—it's marvelous, though, to be back home again—to be completely alone with you. Oh, you 250 bewitchingly lovely young woman!

NORA: Torvald, don't look at me like that!

HELMER: Can't I look at my richest treasure? At all that beauty that's mine, mine alone—completely and utterly.

NORA: (*Moving around to the other side of the table.*) You mustn't 255 talk to me that way tonight.

HELMER: (*Following her.*) The tarantella is still in your blood, I can see—and it makes you even more enticing. Listen. The guests are beginning to go. (*Dropping his voice.*) Nora—it'll soon be quiet through this whole house. 260

NORA: Yes, I hope so.

HELMER: You do, don't you, my love? Do you realize—when I'm out at a party like this with you—do you know why I talk to you so little, and keep such a distance away; just send you a stolen look now and then—you know why I 265 do it? It's because I'm imagining then that you're my secret darling, my secret young bride-to-be, and that no one suspects there's anything between us.

NORA: Yes, yes; oh, yes, I know you're always thinking of me.

HELMER: And then when we leave and I place the shawl over 270 those fine young rounded shoulders—over that wonderful curving neck—then I pretend that you're my young bride, that we're just coming from the wedding, that for the first time I'm bringing you into my house—that for the first time I'm alone with you—completely alone with you, 275 your trembling young beauty! All this evening I've longed for nothing but you. When I saw you turn and sway in the tarantella—my blood was pounding till I couldn't stand it—that's why I brought you down here so early—

NORA: Go away, Torvald! Leave me alone. I don't want all this. 280

HELMER: What do you mean? Nora, you're teasing me. You will, won't you? Aren't I your husband—?

(*A knock at the outside door.*)

NORA: (*Startled.*) What's that?

HELMER: (*Going toward the hall.*) Who is it?

RANK: (*Outside.*) It's me. May I come in a moment? 285

HELMER: (*With quiet irritation.*) Oh, what does he want now? (*Aloud.*) Hold on. (*Goes and opens the door.*) Oh, how nice that you didn't just pass us by!

RANK: I thought I heard your voice, and then I wanted so badly to have a look in. (*Lightly glancing about.*) Ah, me, these old 290 familiar haunts. You have it snug and cozy in here, you two.

HELMER: You seemed to be having it pretty cozy upstairs, too.

RANK: Absolutely. Why shouldn't I? Why not take in everything in life? As much as you can, anyway, and as long as you can. The wine was superb— 295

HELMER: The champagne especially.

RANK: You noticed that too? It's amazing how much I could guzzle down.

NORA: Torvald also drank a lot of champagne this evening.

300 RANK: Oh?

NORA: Yes, and that always makes him so entertaining.

RANK: Well, why shouldn't one have a pleasant evening after a well-spent day?

HELMER: Well spent? I'm afraid I can't claim that.

305 RANK: (*Slapping him on the back.*) But I can, you see!

NORA: Dr. Rank, you must have done some scientific research today.

RANK: Quite so.

HELMER: Come now—little Nora talking about scientific re-
310 search!

RANK: Indeed you may.

NORA: Then they were good?

RANK: The best possible for both doctor and patient—certainty.

315 NORA: (*Quickly and searchingly.*) Certainty?

RANK: Complete certainty. So don't I owe myself a gay evening afterwards?

NORA: Yes, you're right, Dr. Rank.

HELMER: I'm with you—just so long as you don't have to suf-
320 fer for it in the morning.

RANK: Well, one never gets something for nothing in life.

NORA: Dr. Rank—are you very fond of masquerade parties?

RANK: Yes, if there's a good array of odd disguises—

NORA: Tell me, what should we two go as at the next mas-
325 querade?

HELMER: You little featherhead—already thinking of the next!

RANK: We two? I'll tell you what: you must go as Charmed Life—

HELMER: Yes, but find a costume for *that!*

330 RANK: Your wife can appear just as she looks every day.

HELMER: That was nicely put. But don't you know what you're going to be?

RANK: Yes, Helmer, I've made up my mind.

HELMER: Well?

335 RANK: At the next masquerade I'm going to be invisible.

HELMER: That's a funny idea.

RANK: They say there's a hat—black, huge—have you never heard of the hat that makes you invisible? You put it on, and then no one on earth can see you.

340 HELMER: (*Suppressing a smile.*) Ah, of course.

RANK: But I'm quite forgetting what I came for. Helmer, give me a cigar, one of the dark Havanas.

HELMER: With the greatest pleasure. (*Holds out his case.*)

RANK: Thanks. (*Takes one and cuts off the tip.*)

345 NORA: (*Striking a match.*) Let me give you a light.

RANK: Thank you. (*She holds the match for him; he lights the cigar.*) And now good-bye.

HELMER: Good-bye, good-bye, old friend.

NORA: Sleep well, Doctor.

350 RANK: Thanks for that wish.

NORA: Wish me the same.

RANK: You? All right, if you like—Sleep well. And thanks for the light. (*He nods to them both and leaves.*)

HELMER: (*His voice subdued.*) He's been drinking heavily.

355 NORA: (*Absently.*) Could be. (HELMER *takes his keys from his pocket and goes out in the hall.*) Torvald—what are you after?

HELMER: Got to empty the mailbox; it's nearly full. There won't be room for the morning papers.

NORA: Are you working tonight?

360 HELMER: You know I'm not. Why—what's this? Someone's been at the lock.

NORA: At the lock—?

HELMER: Yes, I'm positive. What do you suppose—? I can't imagine one of the maids—? Here's a broken hairpin.
Nora, it's yours—   365

NORA: (*Quickly.*) Then it must be the children—

HELMER: You'd better break them of that. Hm, hm—well, opened it after all. (*Takes the contents out and calls into the kitchen.*) Helene! Helene, would you put out the lamp in the hall. (*He returns to the room, shutting the hall door, then* 370 *displays the handful of mail.*) Look how it's piled up. (*Sort-ing through them.*) Now what's this?

NORA: (*At the window.*) The letter! Oh, Torvald, no!

HELMER: Two calling cards—from Rank.

NORA: From Dr. Rank?   375

HELMER: (*Examining them.*) "Dr. Rank, Consulting Physician." They were on top. He must have dropped them in as he left.

NORA: Is there anything on them?

HELMER: There's a black cross over the name. See? That's a gruesome notion. He could almost be announcing his 380 own death.

NORA: That's just what he's doing.

HELMER: What! You've heard something? Something he's told you?

NORA: Yes. That when those cards came, he'd be taking his 385 leave of us. He'll shut himself in now and die.

HELMER: Ah, my poor friend! Of course I knew he wouldn't be here much longer. But so soon—And then to hide himself away like a wounded animal.

NORA: If it has to happen, then it's best it happens in si- 390 lence—don't you think so, Torvald?

HELMER: (*Pacing up and down.*) He'd grown right into our lives. I simply can't imagine him gone. He with his suffer-ing and loneliness—like a dark cloud setting off our sun-lit happiness. Well, maybe it's best this way. For him, at 395 least. (*Standing still.*) And maybe for us too, Nora. Now we're thrown back on each other, completely. (*Embracing her.*) Oh you, my darling wife, how can I hold you close enough? You know what, Nora—time and again I've wished you were in some terrible danger, just so I could 400 stake my life and soul and everything, for your sake.

NORA: (*Tearing herself away, her voice firm and decisive.*) Now you must read your mail, Torvald.

HELMER: No, no, not tonight. I want to stay with you, dearest.

NORA: With a dying friend on your mind?   405

HELMER: You're right. We've both had a shock. There's ugliness between us—these thoughts of death and corruption. We'll have to get free of them first. Until then—we'll stay apart.

NORA: (*Clinging about his neck.*) Torvald—good night! Good night!   410

HELMER: (*Kissing her on the cheek.*) Good night, little songbird. Sleep well, Nora. I'll be reading my mail now. (*He takes the letters into his room and shuts the door after him.*)

NORA: (*With bewildered glances, groping about, seizing* HELMER'S *domino, throwing it around her, and speaking in short, hoarse,* 415 *broken whispers.*) Never see him again. Never, never. (*Putting her shawl over her head.*) Never see the children either—them, too. Never, never. Oh, the freezing black water! The depths—down—Oh, I wish it were over—He has it now; he's reading it—now. Oh no, no, not yet. Tor- 420 vald, good-bye, you and the children—(*She starts for the hall; as she does,* HELMER *throws open his door and stands with an open letter in his hand.*)

HELMER: Nora!

425 NORA: (*Screams.*) Oh—!

HELMER: What is this? You know what's in this letter?

NORA: Yes, I know. Let me go! Let me out!

HELMER: (*Holding her back.*) Where are you going?

NORA: (*Struggling to break loose.*) You can't save me, Torvald!

430 HELMER: (*Slumping back.*) True! Then it's true what he writes? How horrible! No, no, it's impossible—it can't be true.

NORA: It is true. I've loved you more than all this world.

HELMER: Ah, none of your slippery tricks.

NORA: (*Taking one step toward him.*) Torvald—!

435 HELMER: What *is* this you've blundered into!

NORA: Just let me loose. You're not going to suffer for my sake. You're not going to take on my guilt.

HELMER: No more playacting. (*Locks the hall door.*) You stay right here and give me a reckoning. You understand what
440 you've done? Answer! You understand?

NORA: (*Looking squarely at him, her face hardening.*) Yes. I'm beginning to understand everything now.

HELMER: (*Striding about.*) Oh, what an awful awakening! In all these eight years—she who was my pride and joy—a hyp-
445 ocrite, a liar—worse, worse—a criminal! How infinitely disgusting it all is! The shame! (*NORA says nothing and goes on looking straight at him. He stops in front of her.*) I should have suspected something of the kind. I should have known. All your father's flimsy values—Be still! All your father's flimsy
450 values have come out in you. No religion, no morals, no sense of duty—Oh, how I'm punished for letting him off! I did it for your sake, and you repay me like this.

NORA: Yes, like this.

HELMER: Now you've wrecked all my happiness—ruined my
455 whole future. Oh, it's awful to think of. I'm in a cheap little grafter's hands; he can do anything he wants with me, ask for anything, play with me like a puppet—and I can't breathe a word. I'll be swept down miserably into the depths on account of a featherbrained woman.

460 NORA: When I'm gone from this world, you'll be free.

HELMER: Oh, quit posing. Your father had a mess of those speeches too. What good would that ever do me if you were gone from this world, as you say? Not the slightest. He can still make the whole thing known; and if he does, I could be
465 falsely suspected as your accomplice. They might even think that I was behind it—that I put you up to it. And all that I can thank you for—you that I've coddled the whole of our marriage. Can you see now what you've done to me?

NORA: (*Icily calm.*) Yes.

470 HELMER: It's so incredible, I just can't grasp it. But we'll have to patch up whatever we can. Take off the shawl. I said, take it off! I've got to appease him somehow or other. The thing has to be hushed up at any cost. And as for you and me, it's got to seem like everything between us is just
475 as it was—to the outside world, that is. You'll go right on living in this house, of course. But you can't be allowed to bring up the children; I don't dare trust you with them— Oh, to have to say this to someone I've loved so much, and that I still—! Well, that's done with. From now on
480 happiness doesn't matter; all that matters is saving the bits and pieces, the appearance—(*The doorbell rings. HELMER starts.*) What's that? And so late. Maybe the worst—? You think he'd—? Hide, Nora! Say you're sick. (*NORA remains standing motionless. HELMER goes and opens the door.*)

485 MAID: (*Half dressed, in the hall.*) A letter for Mrs. Helmer.

HELMER: I'll take it. (*Snatches the letter and shuts the door.*) Yes, it's from him. You don't get it; I'm reading it myself.

NORA: Then read it.

HELMER: (*By the lamp.*) I hardly dare. We may be ruined, you and I. But—I've got to know. (*Rips open the letter, skims
490 through a few lines, glances at an enclosure, then cries out joyfully.*) Nora! (*NORA looks inquiringly at him.*) Nora! Wait— better check it again—Yes, yes, it's true. I'm saved. Nora, I'm saved!

495 NORA: And I?

HELMER: You too, of course. We're both saved, both of us. Look. He's sent back your note. He says he's sorry and ashamed—that a happy development in his life—oh, who cares what he says! Nora, we're saved! No one can hurt
500 you. Oh, Nora, Nora—but first, this ugliness all has to go. Let me see—(*Takes a look at the note.*) No, I don't want to see it; I want the whole thing to fade like a dream. (*Tears the note and both letters to pieces, throws them into the stove and watches them burn.*) There—now there's nothing left—He wrote that since Christmas Eve you—Oh, they must have
505 been three terrible days for you, Nora.

NORA: I fought a hard fight.

HELMER: And suffered pain and saw no escape but—No, we're not going to dwell on anything unpleasant. We'll just be grateful and keep on repeating: it's over now, it's
510 over! You hear me, Nora? You don't seem to realize—it's over. What's it mean—that frozen look? Oh, poor little Nora, I understand. You can't believe I've forgiven you. But I have, Nora; I swear I have. I know that what you did, you did out of love for me.
515

NORA: That's true.

HELMER: You loved me the way a wife ought to love her husband. It's simply the means that you couldn't judge. But you think I love you any the less for not knowing how to handle your affairs? No, no—just lean on me; I'll guide
520 you and teach you. I wouldn't be a man if this feminine helplessness didn't make you twice as attractive to me. You mustn't mind those sharp words I said—that was all in the first confusion of thinking my world had collapsed. I've forgiven you, Nora; I swear I've forgiven you.
525

NORA: My thanks for your forgiveness. (*She goes out through the door, right.*)

HELMER: No, wait—(*Peers in.*) What are you doing in there?

NORA: (*Inside.*) Getting out of my costume.

HELMER: (*By the open door.*) Yes, do that. Try to calm yourself
530 and collect your thoughts again, my frightened little songbird. You can rest easy now; I've got wide wings to shelter you with. (*Walking about close by the door.*) How snug and nice our home is, Nora. You're safe here; I'll keep you like a hunted dove I've rescued out of a hawk's claws. I'll
535 bring peace to your poor, shuddering heart. Gradually it'll happen, Nora; you'll see. Tomorrow all this will look different to you; then everything will be as it was. I won't have to go on repeating I forgive you; you'll feel it for yourself. How can you imagine I'd ever conceivably want
540 to disown you—or even blame you in any way? Ah, you don't know a man's heart, Nora. For a man there's something indescribably sweet and satisfying in knowing he's forgiven his wife—and forgiven her out of a full and open heart. It's as if she belongs to him in two ways now: in a
545

sense he's given her fresh into the world again, and she's become his wife and his child as well. From now on that's what you'll be to me—you little, bewildered, helpless thing. Don't be afraid of anything, Nora; just open your heart to me, and I'll be conscience and will to you both—
550 (NORA *enters in her regular clothes.*) What's this? Not in bed? You've changed your dress?

NORA: Yes, Torvald, I've changed my dress.

HELMER: But why now, so late?

555 NORA: Tonight I'm not sleeping.

HELMER: But Nora dear—

NORA: (*Looking at her watch.*) It's still not so very late. Sit down, Torvald; we have a lot to talk over. (*She sits at one side of the table.*)

560 HELMER: Nora—what is this? That hard expression—

NORA: Sit down. This'll take some time. I have a lot to say.

HELMER: (*Sitting at the table directly opposite her.*) You worry me, Nora. And I don't understand you.

NORA: No, that's exactly it. You don't understand me. And
565 I've never understood you either—until tonight. No, don't interrupt. You can just listen to what I say. We're closing out accounts, Torvald.

HELMER: How do you mean that?

NORA: (*After a short pause.*) Doesn't anything strike you about
570 our sitting here like this?

HELMER: What's that?

NORA: We've been married now eight years. Doesn't it occur to you that this is the first time we two, you and I, man and wife, have ever talked seriously together?

575 HELMER: What do you mean—seriously?

NORA: In eight whole years—longer even—right from our first acquaintance, we've never exchanged a serious word on any serious thing.

HELMER: You mean I should constantly go and involve you in
580 problems you couldn't possibly help me with?

NORA: I'm not talking of problems. I'm saying that we've never sat down seriously together and tried to get to the bottom of anything.

HELMER: But dearest, what good would that ever do you?

585 NORA: That's the point right there: you've never understood me. I've been wronged greatly, Torvald—first by Papa, and then by you.

HELMER: What! By us—the two people who've loved you more than anyone else?

590 NORA: (*Shaking her head.*) You never loved me. You've thought it fun to be in love with me, that's all.

HELMER: Nora, what a thing to say!

NORA: Yes, it's true now, Torvald. When I lived at home with Papa, he told me all his opinions, so I had the same ones
595 too; or if they were different I hid them, since he wouldn't have cared for that. He used to call me his doll-child, and he played with me the way I played with my dolls. Then I came into your house—

HELMER: How can you speak of our marriage like that?

600 NORA: (*Unperturbed.*) I mean, then I went from Papa's hands into yours. You arranged everything to your own taste, and so I got the same taste as you—or I pretended to; I can't remember. I guess a little of both, first one, then the other. Now when I look back, it seems as if I'd lived here
605 like a beggar—just from hand to mouth. I've lived by doing tricks for you, Torvald. But that's the way you wanted

it. It's a great sin what you and Papa did to me. You're to blame that nothing's become of me.

HELMER: Nora, how unfair and ungrateful you are! Haven't
610 you been happy here?

NORA: No, never. I thought so—but I never have.

HELMER: Not—not happy!

NORA: No, only lighthearted. And you've always been so kind to me. But our home's been nothing but a playpen.
615 I've been your doll-wife here, just as at home I was Papa's doll-child. And in turn the children have been my dolls. I thought it was fun when you played with me, just as they thought it fun when I played with them. That's been our marriage, Torvald.

620 HELMER: There's some truth in what you're saying—under all the raving exaggeration. But it'll all be different after this. Playtime's over; now for the schooling.

NORA: Whose schooling—mine or the children's?

HELMER: Both yours and the children's, dearest.

625 NORA: Oh, Torvald, you're not the man to teach me to be a good wife to you.

HELMER: And you can say that?

NORA: And I—how am I equipped to bring up children?

HELMER: Nora!

630 NORA: Didn't you say a moment ago that that was no job to trust me with?

HELMER: In a flare of temper! Why fasten on that?

NORA: Yes, but you were so very right. I'm not up to the job. There's another job I have to do first. I have to try to ed-
635 ucate myself. You can't help me with that. I've got to do it alone. And that's why I'm leaving you now.

HELMER: (*Jumping up.*) What's that?

NORA: I have to stand completely alone, if I'm ever going to discover myself and the world out there. So I can't go on
640 living with you.

HELMER: Nora, Nora!

NORA: I want to leave right away. Kristine should put me up for the night—

HELMER: You're insane! You've no right! I forbid you!

645 NORA: From here on, there's no use forbidding me anything. I'll take with me whatever is mine. I don't want a thing from you, either now or later.

HELMER: What kind of madness is this!

NORA: Tomorrow I'm going home—I mean, home where I
650 came from. It'll be easier up there to find something to do.

HELMER: Oh, you blind, incompetent child!

NORA: I must learn to be competent, Torvald.

HELMER: Abandon your home, your husband, your children! And you're not even thinking what people will say.

655 NORA: I can't be concerned about that. I only know how essential this is.

HELMER: Oh, it's outrageous. So you'll run out like this on your most sacred vows?

NORA: What do you think are my most sacred vows?

660 HELMER: And I have to tell you that! Aren't they your duties to your husband and children?

NORA: I have other duties equally sacred.

HELMER: That isn't true. What duties are they?

NORA: Duties to myself.

665 HELMER: Before all else, you're a wife and a mother.

NORA: I don't believe in that anymore. I believe that, before all else, I'm a human being, no less than you—or anyway,

I ought to try to become one. I know the majority thinks you're right, Torvald, and plenty of books agree with you, too. But I can't go on believing what the majority says, or what's written in books. I have to think over these things myself and try to understand them.

HELMER: Why can't you understand your place in your own home? On a point like that, isn't there one everlasting guide you can turn to? Where's your religion?

NORA: Oh, Torvald, I'm really not sure what religion is.

HELMER: What—?

NORA: I only know what the minister said when I was confirmed. He told me religion was this thing and that. When I get clear and away by myself, I'll go into that problem too. I'll see if what the minister said was right, or, in any case, if it's right for me.

HELMER: A young woman your age shouldn't talk like that. If religion can't move you, I can try to rouse your conscience. You do have some moral feeling? Or, tell me— has that gone too?

NORA: It's not easy to answer that, Torvald. I simply don't know. I'm all confused about these things. I just know I see them so differently from you. I find out, for one thing, that the law's not at all what I'd thought—but I can't get it through my head that the law is fair. A woman hasn't a right to protect her dying father or save her husband's life! I can't believe that.

HELMER: You talk like a child. You don't know anything of the world you live in.

NORA: No, I don't. But now I'll begin to learn for myself. I'll try to discover who's right, the world or I.

HELMER: Nora, you're sick; you've got a fever. I almost think you're out of your head.

NORA: I've never felt more clearheaded and sure in my life.

HELMER: And—clearheaded and sure—you're leaving your husband and children?

NORA: Yes.

HELMER: Then there's only one possible reason.

NORA: What?

HELMER: You no longer love me.

NORA: No. That's exactly it.

HELMER: Nora! You can't be serious!

NORA: Oh, this is so hard, Torvald—you've been so kind to me always. But I can't help it. I don't love you anymore.

HELMER: (*Struggling for composure.*) Are you also clearheaded and sure about that?

NORA: Yes, completely. That's why I can't go on staying here.

HELMER: Can you tell me what I did to lose your love?

NORA: Yes, I can tell you. It was this evening when the miraculous thing didn't come—then I knew you weren't the man I'd imagined.

HELMER: Be more explicit; I don't follow you.

NORA: I've waited now so patiently eight long years—for, my Lord, I know miracles don't come every day. Then this crisis broke over me, and such a certainty filled me: *now* the miraculous event would occur. While Krogstad's letter was lying out there, I never for an instant dreamed that you could give in to his terms. I was so utterly sure you'd say to him: go on, tell your tale to the whole wide world. And when he'd done that—

HELMER: Yes, what then? When I'd delivered my own wife into shame and disgrace—!

NORA: When he'd done that, I was so utterly sure that you'd step forward, take the blame on yourself and say: I am the guilty one.

HELMER: Nora—!

NORA: You're thinking I'd never accept such a sacrifice from you? No, of course not. But what good would my protests be against you? That was the miracle I was waiting for, in terror and hope. And to stave that off, I would have taken my life.

HELMER: I'd gladly work for you day and night, Nora—and take on pain and deprivation. But there's no one who gives up honor for love.

NORA: Millions of women have done just that.

HELMER: Oh, you think and talk like a silly child.

NORA: Perhaps. But you neither think nor talk like the man I could join myself to. When your big fright was over— and it wasn't from any threat against me, only for what might damage you—when all the danger was past, for you it was just as if nothing had happened. I was exactly the same, your little lark, your doll, that you'd have to handle with double care now that I'd turned out so brittle and frail. (*Gets up.*) Torvald—in that instant it dawned on me that for eight years I've been living here with a stranger, and that I'd even conceived three children—oh, I can't stand the thought of it! I could tear myself to bits.

HELMER: (*Heavily.*) I see. There's a gulf that's opened between us—that's clear. Oh, but Nora, can't we bridge it somehow?

NORA: The way I am now, I'm no wife for you.

HELMER: I have the strength to make myself over.

NORA: Maybe—if your doll gets taken away.

HELMER: But to part! To part from you! No, Nora, no—I can't imagine it.

NORA: (*Going out, right.*) All the more reason why it has to be. (*She reenters with her coat and a small overnight bag, which she puts on a chair by the table.*)

HELMER: Nora, Nora, not now! Wait till tomorrow.

NORA: I can't spend the night in a strange man's room.

HELMER: But couldn't we live here like brother and sister—

NORA: You know very well how long that would last. (*Throws her shawl about her.*) Good-bye, Torvald. I won't look in on the children. I know they're in better hands than mine. The way I am now, I'm no use to them.

HELMER: But someday, Nora—someday—?

NORA: How can I tell? I haven't the least idea what'll become of me.

HELMER: But you're my wife, now and wherever you go.

NORA: Listen, Torvald—I've heard that when a wife deserts her husband's house just as I'm doing, then the law frees him from all responsibility. In any case, I'm freeing you from being responsible. Don't feel yourself bound, any more than I will. There has to be absolute freedom for us both. Here, take your ring back. Give me mine.

HELMER: That too?

NORA: That too.

HELMER: There it is.

NORA: Good. Well, now it's all over. I'm putting the keys here. The maids know all about keeping up the house— better than I do. Tomorrow, after I've left town, Kristine will stop by to pack up everything that's mine from home. I'd like those things shipped up to me.

HELMER: Over! All over! Nora, won't you ever think about me?

790 NORA: I'm sure I'll think of you often, and about the children and the house here.

HELMER: May I write you?

NORA: No—never. You're not to do that.

HELMER: Oh, but let me send you—

795 NORA: Nothing. Nothing.

HELMER: Or help you if you need it.

NORA: No. I accept nothing from strangers.

HELMER: Nora—can I never be more than a stranger to you?

NORA: (*Picking up the overnight bag.*) Ah, Torvald—it would

800 take the greatest miracle of all—

HELMER: Tell me the greatest miracle!

NORA: You and I both would have to transform ourselves to the point that—Oh, Torvald, I've stopped believing in miracles.

HELMER: But I'll believe. Tell me! Transform ourselves to the

805 point that—?

NORA: That our living together could be a true marriage. (*She goes out down the hall.*)

HELMER: (*Sinks down on a chair by the door, face buried in his hands.*) Nora! Nora! (*Looking about and rising.*) Empty. She's gone. (*A sudden hope leaps in him.*) The greatest miracle—? 810

(*From below, the sound of a door slamming shut.*)

Oscar Wilde

Oscar Fingal O'Flahertie Willis Wilde (1854–1900) is best known as the aesthete's aesthete of 1880s and 1890s London, famous for his epigrammatic wit, for his novel *The Picture of Dorian Gray* (1890) and the moody symbolist drama *Salomé* (1892), for the highly polished dramas he produced in the 1890s—*Lady Windermere's Fan* (1892), *A Woman of No Importance* (1893), *An Ideal Husband* (1895)—capped by his transcendent "trivial comedy for serious people," *The Importance of Being Earnest* (1895). However, Wilde is also remembered for the tragedy of his life, the terrible trial in which he was convicted of homosexual practices and sentenced to two years' hard labor, and for the poverty, isolation, and rejection that ensued.

Wilde was born in Dublin, the second son of Sir William Wilde—an author, oculist, and surgeon—and Jane Francesca Elgee, a poet and translator. He was educated at the Portora Royal School, read classics at Trinity College, Dublin, and then matriculated at Magdalen College, Oxford, where he continued to study classics. Leaving Oxford in 1876, Wilde began a career as a poet—his poem "Ravenna" won the Newdigate prize in 1878—and occasional critic on artistic subjects. By 1881, his wit, his pose, his green carnation (already part of the vestimentary code of Victorian gay culture) were so well known that he could be satirized as Bunthorne in Gilbert and Sullivan's operetta *Patience*. In the early 1880s he perfected his lecture performance on tour throughout the United States and Canada, but once he was married to Constance Lloyd in 1884—his two sons, Cyril and Vyvyan, were born in 1885 and 1886—Wilde had need of an income as a regular reviewer and essayist. Through the late 1880s, Wilde gained additional fame as the paradoxical spokesman of aestheticism, writing a brilliant series of articles for the *Pall Mall Gazette,* the *Dramatic Review, Nineteenth Century,* and other magazines, notably "The Decay of Lying" (1889), "The Artist as Critic" (1890), and "The Truth of Masks" (1885).

The posed, paradoxical, masked quality of Wilde's public persona had another dimension, for Wilde's homosexuality forced him to lead an elaborate double life. The passage of the Criminal Law Amendment Act in 1885 made homosexual activity illegal, and Wilde risked—and eventually suffered—both social rejection and legal punishment. As his career and public visibility began to crest in the early 1890s, with the publication of *The Picture of Dorian Gray* and the success of his first plays, Wilde became involved with a young man, Lord Alfred Douglas. In 1895 Douglas's father, the Marquess of Queensberry, left a card at Wilde's club addressed to "Mr. Oscar Wilde, posing as a somdomite [*sic*]." Against the advice of his friends, Wilde sued the Marquess for criminal libel. When Queensberry was acquitted, Wilde was arrested for "acts of gross indecency with other male persons" and subjected to two jury trials, in which a series of young men were put on the stand, testifying to their sexual relations with Wilde. In the first trial, the jury was unable to reach a verdict; in the second, Wilde was found guilty and given the maximum sentence of two years' hard labor. Although he was eventually moved from hard labor in Pentonville to Wandsworth Prison, and then finally to Reading Gaol, prison broke Wilde's health. Constance changed the last names of Cyril and Vyvyan to avoid association with Wilde, and when he was released in 1897 he was bankrupt and alone. Although Wilde's sexual orientation had long been known or suspected by many of his friends, most were unwilling to associate with Wilde after such public scandal. When Wilde returned to society, he was cruelly and systematically shunned. He settled first in France, then joined Alfred Douglas briefly in Italy; in 1898 he published *The Ballad of Reading Gaol* and settled in Paris, where he died two years later.

Despite its energetic "triviality," *The Importance of Being Earnest* is deeply, symbolically involved in the contours of Wilde's life. The opening of *Earnest* in February of 1895 at George Alexander's fashionable St. James's Theatre was something of a society event; fearing the publicity of Wilde's trial, Alexander closed the hugely successful play only weeks later. But *The Importance of Being Earnest* seems to resonate with Wilde's life in other ways as well. In an important sense, *The Importance of Being Earnest* is a play about masking. Much as Wilde's sexual identity had constantly to be negotiated behind the fictive "conventions" of polite society—his sexuality could be tolerated only as long as it was kept discreetly offstage, disacknowledged, unspoken—so in *Earnest* the process of social life in general seems to depend on a tissue of acceptable lies, which occasionally verge on truth: Algernon Moncrieff invents "an invaluable permanent invalid called Bunbury" so that he will have an excuse to escape London; Jack Worthing invents a wastrel younger brother named Ernest as an excuse to escape the country; Cecily invents scenes for her diary and Gwendolen keeps hers handy to "have something sensational to read on the train"; Jack and Algy, both vying to be baptized "Ernest," turn out to be brothers; and Jack, a foundling, turns out to be named Ernest after all.

As Algy remarks in Act One, "The truth is rarely pure and never simple. Modern life would be very tedious if it were either, and modern literature a complete impossibility!" In *Earnest,* Wilde carefully constructs a comedy in which the deceptive surfaces of experience, the manifest fictions and deceptions of "modern life," turn out to provide the only vehicle for truth the play has to offer. Because beneath the constricted, yet infinitely manipulable conventions of polite society surges the powerful force of desire. It is manifest in the elaborate verbal sparring between Jack, Algy, Gwendolen, and Cecily; in the manic, adolescent energy that drives Jack and Algy to the brink of baptism; even in the appetitive fury of the muffin scene. One final way in which these social conventions are marked is through their connection to the conventions of comedy itself—conventions that are forced to the forefront of the audience's attention throughout the play. *Earnest* comes to a climax in a paroxysm of artificiality: making a mockery of the recognition scene between long-lost siblings of romantic comedy, Wilde's Jack Worthing turns out to *be* his fictitious brother Ernest after all. In *The Importance of Being Earnest,* all convention—both social and comic—is shown to be a kind of mask, a fiction that sometimes enables the expression of truth.

Jack and Algernon confront recalcitrant Gwendolyn and Cecily in the McCarter Theatre production of *The Importance of Being Earnest.*

THE IMPORTANCE OF BEING EARNEST

Oscar Wilde

CHARACTERS

JOHN WORTHING, J.P.
ALGERNON MONCRIEFF
REV. CANON CHASUBLE, D.D.
MERRIMAN (*Butler*)
LANE (*Manservant*)

LADY BRACKNELL
HON. GWENDOLEN FAIRFAX
CECILY CARDEW
MISS PRISM (*Governess*)

THE SCENES OF THE PLAY

ACT I. Algernon Moncrieff's Flat in Half-Moon Street, W.
ACT II. The Garden at the Manor House, Woolton.
ACT III. Drawing-Room of the Manor House, Woolton.

TIME.—*The Present*.   PLACE.—*London*.

ACT ONE

Morning-room in ALGERNON's *flat in Half-Moon Street. The room is luxuriously and artistically furnished. The sound of a piano is heard in the adjoining room.*

(LANE *is arranging afternoon tea on the table, and after the music has ceased,* ALGERNON *enters.*)

ALGERNON: Did you hear what I was playing, Lane?

LANE: I didn't think it polite to listen, sir.

ALGERNON: I'm sorry for that, for your sake. I don't play accurately—anyone can play accurately—but I play with
5 wonderful expression. As far as the piano is concerned,
sentiment is my forte. I keep science for Life.

LANE: Yes, sir.

ALGERNON: And, speaking of the science of Life, have you
got the cucumber sandwiches cut for Lady Bracknell?

10 LANE: Yes, sir. (*Hands them on a salver.*)

ALGERNON: (*Inspects them, takes two, and sits down on the sofa.*)
Oh! . . . by the way, Lane, I see from your book that on
Thursday night, when Lord Shoreman and Mr. Worthing
were dining with me, eight bottles of champagne are en-
15 tered as having been consumed.

LANE: Yes, sir; eight bottles and a pint.

ALGERNON: Why is it that at a bachelor's establishment the
servants invariably drink the champagne? I ask merely for
information.

20 LANE: I attribute it to the superior quality of the wine, sir. I
have often observed that in married households the
champagne is rarely of a first-rate brand.

ALGERNON: Good Heavens! Is marriage so demoralizing as
that?

25 LANE: I believe it *is* a very pleasant state, sir. I have had very
little experience of it myself up to the present. I have only
been married once. That was in consequence of a misunderstanding between myself and a young woman.

ALGERNON: (*Languidly.*) I don't know that I am much inter-
30 ested in your family life, Lane.

LANE: No, sir; it is not a very interesting subject. I never think
of it myself.

ALGERNON: Very natural, I am sure. That will do, Lane, thank
you.

35 LANE: Thank you, sir. (LANE *goes out.*)

ALGERNON: Lane's views on marriage seem somewhat lax.
Really, if the lower orders don't set us a good example,
what on earth is the use of them? They seem, as a class, to
have absolutely no sense of moral responsibility.

(*Enter* LANE.)

LANE: Mr. Ernest Worthing.   40

(*Enter* JACK. LANE *goes out.*)

ALGERNON: How are you, my dear Ernest? What brings you
up to town?

JACK: Oh, pleasure, pleasure! What else should bring one anywhere? Eating as usual, I see, Algy!

ALGERNON: (*Stiffly.*) I believe it is customary in good society   45
to take some slight refreshment at five o'clock. Where
have you been since last Thursday?

JACK: (*Sitting down on the sofa.*) In the country.

ALGERNON: What on earth do you do there?

JACK: (*Pulling off his gloves.*) When one is in town one amuses   50
oneself. When one is in the country one amuses other
people. It is excessively boring.

ALGERNON: And who are the people you amuse?

JACK: (*Airily.*) Oh, neighbours, neighbours.

ALGERNON: Got nice neighbours in your part of Shropshire?   55

JACK: Perfectly horrid! Never speak to one of them.

ALGERNON: How immensely you must amuse them! (*Goes
over and takes sandwich.*) By the way, Shropshire is your
county, is it not?

JACK: Eh? Shropshire? Yes, of course. Hallo! Why all these   60
cups? Why cucumber sandwiches? Why such reckless extravagance in one so young? Who is coming to tea?

ALGERNON: Oh! merely Aunt Augusta and Gwendolen.

JACK: How perfectly delightful!

ALGERNON: Yes, that is all very well; but I am afraid Aunt Au-   65
gusta won't quite approve of your being here.

JACK: May I ask why?

ALGERNON: My dear fellow, the way you flirt with Gwendolen is perfectly disgraceful. It is almost as bad as the way
Gwendolen flirts with you.   70

JACK: I am in love with Gwendolen. I have come up to town
expressly to propose to her.

ALGERNON: I thought you had come up for pleasure? . . . I
call that business.

JACK: How utterly unromantic you are!   75

ALGERNON: I really don't see anything romantic in proposing. It is very romantic to be in love. But there is nothing
romantic about a definite proposal. Why, one may be accepted. One usually is, I believe. Then the excitement is all
over. The very essence of romance is uncertainty. If ever I   80
get married, I'll certainly try to forget the fact.

JACK: I have no doubt about that dear Algy. The Divorce Court was specially invented for people whose memories are so curiously constituted.

85 ALGERNON: Oh! there is no use speculating on that subject. Divorces are made in Heaven—(JACK *puts out his hand to take a sandwich.* ALGERNON *at once interferes.*) Please don't touch the cucumber sandwiches. They are ordered specially for Aunt Augusta. (*Takes one and eats it.*)

90 JACK: Well, you have been eating them all the time.

ALGERNON: That is quite a different matter. She is my aunt. (*Takes plate from below.*) Have some bread and butter. The bread and butter is for Gwendolen. Gwendolen is devoted to bread and butter.

95 JACK: (*Advancing to table and helping himself.*) And very good bread and butter it is, too.

ALGERNON: Well, my dear fellow, you need not eat as if you were going to eat it all. You behave as if you were married to her already. You are not married to her already, and I 100 don't think you ever will be.

JACK: Why on earth do you say that?

ALGERNON: Well, in the first place girls never marry the men they flirt with. Girls don't think it right.

JACK: Oh, that is nonsense!

105 ALGERNON: It isn't. It is a great truth. It accounts for the extraordinary number of bachelors that one sees all over the place. In the second place, I don't give my consent.

JACK: Your consent!

ALGERNON: My dear fellow, Gwendolen is my first cousin. 110 And before I allow you to marry her, you will have to clear up the whole question of Cecily. (*Rings bell.*)

JACK: Cecily! What on earth do you mean? What do you mean, Algy, by Cecily? I don't know anyone of the name of Cecily.

(*Enter* LANE.)

115 ALGERNON: Bring me that cigarette case Mr. Worthing left in the smoking-room the last time he dined here.

LANE: Yes, sir. (LANE *goes out.*)

JACK: Do you mean to say you have had my cigarette case all this time? I wish to goodness you had let me know. I have 120 been writing frantic letters to Scotland Yard about it. I was very nearly offering a large reward.

ALGERNON: Well, I wish you would offer one. I happen to be more than usually hard up.

JACK: There is no good offering a large reward now that the 125 thing is found.

(*Enter* LANE *with the cigarette case on a salver.* ALGERNON *takes it at once.* LANE *goes out.*)

ALGERNON: I think that is rather mean of you, Ernest, I must say. (*Opens case and examines it.*) However, it makes no matter, for, now that I look at the inscription, I find that the thing isn't yours after all.

130 JACK: Of course it's mine. (*Moving to him.*) You have seen me with it a hundred times, and you have no right whatsoever to read what is written inside. It is a very ungentlemanly thing to read a private cigarette case.

ALGERNON: Oh! it is absurd to have a hard-and-fast rule about 135 what one should read and what one shouldn't. More than half of modern culture depends on what one shouldn't read.

JACK: I am quite aware of the fact, and I don't propose to discuss modern culture. It isn't the sort of thing one should talk of in private. I simply want my cigarette case back.

ALGERNON: Yes; but this isn't your cigarette case. This ciga- 140 rette case is a present from someone of the name of Cecily, and you said you didn't know anyone of that name.

JACK: Well, if you want to know, Cecily happens to be my aunt.

ALGERNON: Your aunt!   145

JACK: Yes. Charming old lady she is, too. Lives at Tunbridge Wells. Just give it back to me, Algy.

ALGERNON: (*Retreating to back of sofa.*) But why does she call herself little Cecily if she is your aunt and lives at Tunbridge Wells? (*Reading.*) "From little Cecily with her fondest love." 150

JACK: (*Moving to sofa and kneeling upon it.*) My dear fellow, what on earth is there in that? Some aunts are tall, some aunts are not tall. That is a matter that surely an aunt may be allowed to decide for herself. You seem to think that every aunt should be exactly like your aunt! That is ab- 155 surd! For Heaven's sake give me back my cigarette case. (*Follows* ALGERNON *round the room.*)

ALGERNON: Yes. But why does your aunt call you her uncle? "From little Cecily, with her fondest love to her dear Uncle Jack." There is no objection, I admit, to an aunt being a small 160 aunt, but why an aunt, no matter what her size may be, should call her own nephew her uncle, I can't quite make out. Besides, your name isn't Jack at all; it is Ernest.

JACK: It isn't Ernest; it's Jack.

ALGERNON: You have always told me it was Ernest. I have in- 165 troduced you to everyone as Ernest. You answer to the name of Ernest. You look as if your name was Ernest. You are the most earnest looking person I ever saw in my life. It is perfectly absurd your saying that your name isn't Ernest. It's on your cards. Here is one of them. (*Taking it* 170 *from case.*) "Mr. Ernest Worthing, B 4, The Albany." I'll keep this as a proof your name is Ernest if ever you attempt to deny it to me, or to Gwendolen, or to anyone else. (*Puts the card in his pocket.*)

JACK: Well, my name is Ernest in town and Jack in the coun- 175 try, and the cigarette case was given to me in the country.

ALGERNON: Yes, but that does not account for the fact that your small Aunt Cecily, who lives at Tunbridge Wells, calls you her dear uncle. Come, old boy, you had much better have the thing out at once.   180

JACK: My dear Algy, you talk exactly as if you were a dentist. It is very vulgar to talk like a dentist when one isn't a dentist. It produces a false impression.

ALGERNON: Well, that is exactly what dentists always do. Now, go on! Tell me the whole thing. I may mention that 185 I have always suspected you of being a confirmed and secret Bunburyist; and I am quite sure of it now.

JACK: Bunburyist? What on earth do you mean by a Bunburyist?

ALGERNON: I'll reveal to you the meaning of that incomparable expression as soon as you are kind enough to inform me 190 why you are Ernest in town and Jack in the country.

JACK: Well, produce my cigarette case first.

ALGERNON: Here it is. (*Hands cigarette case.*) Now produce your explanation, and pray make it improbable. (*Sits on sofa.*)   195

JACK: My dear fellow, there is nothing improbable about my explanation at all. In fact it's perfectly ordinary. Old Mr.

Thomas Cardew, who adopted me when I was a little boy, made me in his will guardian to his grand-daughter, Miss Cecily Cardew. Cecily, who addresses me as her uncle from motives of respect that you could not possibly appreciate, lives at my place in the country under the charge of her admirable governess, Miss Prism.

ALGERNON: Where is that place in the country, by the way?

JACK: That is nothing to you, dear boy. You are not going to be invited. . . . I may tell you candidly that the place is not in Shropshire.

ALGERNON: I suspected that, my dear fellow! I have Bunburyed all over Shropshire on two separate occasions. Now, go on. Why are you Ernest in town and Jack in the country?

JACK: My dear Algy, I don't know whether you will be able to understand my real motives. You are hardly serious enough. When one is placed in the position of guardian, one has to adopt a very high moral tone on all subjects. It's one's duty to do so. And as a high moral tone can hardly be said to conduce very much to either one's health or one's happiness, in order to get up to town I have always pretended to have a younger brother of the name of Ernest, who lives in the Albany, and gets into the most dreadful scrapes. That, my dear Algy, is the whole truth pure and simple.

ALGERNON: The truth is rarely pure and never simple. Modern life would be very tedious if it were either, and modern literature a complete impossibility!

JACK: That wouldn't be at all a bad thing.

ALGERNON: Literary criticism is not your forte, my dear fellow. Don't try it. You should leave that to people who haven't been at a University. They do it so well in the daily papers. What you really are is a Bunburyist. I was quite right in saying you were a Bunburyist. You are one of the most advanced Bunburyists I know.

JACK: What on earth do you mean?

ALGERNON: You have invented a very useful younger brother called Ernest, in order that you may be able to come up to town as often as you like. I have invented an invaluable permanent invalid called Bunbury, in order that I may be able to go down into the country whenever I choose. Bunbury is perfectly invaluable. If it wasn't for Bunbury's extraordinary bad health, for instance, I wouldn't be able to dine with you at Willis's to-night, for I have been really engaged to Aunt Augusta for more than a week.

JACK: I haven't asked you to dine with me anywhere to-night.

ALGERNON: I know. You are absolutely careless about sending out invitations. It is very foolish of you. Nothing annoys people so much as not receiving invitations.

JACK: You had much better dine with your Aunt Augusta.

ALGERNON: I haven't the smallest intention of doing anything of the kind. To begin with, I dined there on Monday, and once a week is quite enough to dine with one's own relatives. In the second place, whenever I do dine there I am always treated as a member of the family, and sent down with either no woman at all, or two. In the third place, I know perfectly well whom she will place me next to, to-night. She will place me next Mary Farquhar, who always flirts with her own husband across the dinner-table. That is not very pleasant. Indeed, it is not even decent . . . and that sort of thing is enormously on the increase. The amount of women in London who flirt with their own husbands is perfectly scandalous. It looks so bad. It is simply washing one's clean linen in public. Besides, now that I know you to be a confirmed Bunburyist I naturally want to talk to you about Bunburying. I want to tell you the rules.

JACK: I'm not a Bunburyist at all. If Gwendolen accepts me, I am going to kill my brother, indeed I think I'll kill him in any case. Cecily is a little too much interested in him. It is rather a bore. So I am going to get rid of Ernest. And I strongly advise you to do the same with Mr. . . . with your invalid friend who has the absurd name.

ALGERNON: Nothing will induce me to part with Bunbury, and if you ever get married, which seems to be extremely problematic, you will be very glad to know Bunbury. A man who marries without knowing Bunbury has a very tedious time of it.

JACK: That is nonsense. If I marry a charming girl like Gwendolen, and she is the only girl I ever saw in my life that I would marry, I certainly won't want to know Bunbury.

ALGERNON: Then your wife will. You don't seem to realize, that in married life three is company and two is none.

JACK: (*Sententiously.*) That, my dear young friend, is the theory that the corrupt French Drama has been propounding for the last fifty years.

ALGERNON: Yes; and that the happy English home has proved in half the time.

JACK: For heaven's sake, don't try to be cynical. It's perfectly easy to be cynical.

ALGERNON: My dear fellow, it isn't easy to be anything now-a-days. There's such a lot of beastly competition about. (*The sound of an electric bell is heard.*) Ah! that must be Aunt Augusta. Only relatives, or creditors, ever ring in that Wagnerian manner. Now, if I get her out of the way for ten minutes, so that you can have an opportunity for proposing to Gwendolen, may I dine with you to-night at Willis's?

JACK: I suppose so if you want to.

ALGERNON: Yes, but you must be serious about it. I hate people who are not serious about meals. It is so shallow of them.

(*Enter* LANE.)

LANE: Lady Bracknell and Miss Fairfax. (ALGERNON *goes forward to meet them. Enter* LADY BRACKNELL *and* GWENDOLEN.)

LADY BRACKNELL: Good afternoon, dear Algernon, I hope you are behaving very well.

ALGERNON: I'm feeling very well, Aunt Augusta.

LADY BRACKNELL: That's not quite the same thing. In fact the two things rarely go together. (*Sees* JACK *and bows to him with icy coldness.*)

ALGERNON: (*To* GWENDOLEN.) Dear me, you are smart!

GWENDOLEN: I am always smart! Aren't I, Mr. Worthing?

JACK: You're quite perfect, Miss Fairfax.

GWENDOLEN: Oh! I hope I am not that. It would leave no room for developments, and I intend to develop in *many directions*. (GWENDOLEN *and* JACK *sit down together in the corner.*)

LADY BRACKNELL: I'm sorry if we are a little late, Algernon, but I was obliged to call on dear Lady Harbury. I hadn't been there since her poor husband's death. I never saw a woman so altered; she looks quite twenty years younger. And now I'll have a cup of tea, and one of those nice cucumber sandwiches you promised me.

ALGERNON: Certainly, Aunt Augusta. (*Goes over to tea-table.*)

LADY BRACKNELL: Won't you come and sit here, Gwendolen?

GWENDOLEN: Thanks, mamma, I'm quite comfortable where
320   I am.

ALGERNON: (*Picking up empty plate in horror.*) Good heavens!
Lane! Why are there no cucumber sandwiches? I ordered
them specially.

LANE: (*Gravely.*) There were no cucumbers in the market this
325   morning, sir. I went down twice.

ALGERNON: No cucumbers!

LANE: No, sir. Not even for ready money.

ALGERNON: That will do, Lane, thank you.

LANE: Thank you sir. (*Goes out.*)

330 ALGERNON: I am greatly distressed, Aunt Augusta, about there
being no cucumbers, not even for ready money.

LADY BRACKNELL: It really makes no matter, Algernon. I had
some crumpets with Lady Harbury, who seems to me to
be living entirely for pleasure now.

335 ALGERNON: I hear her hair has turned quite gold from grief.

LADY BRACKNELL: It certainly has changed its colour. From
what cause I, of course, cannot say. (ALGERNON *crosses and
hands tea.*) Thank you. I've quite a treat for you to-night,
Algernon. I am going to send you down with Mary Far-
340   quhar. She is such a nice woman, and so attentive to her
husband. It's delightful to watch them.

ALGERNON: I am afraid, Aunt Augusta, I shall have to give up
the pleasure of dining with you to-night after all.

LADY BRACKNELL: (*Frowning.*) I hope not, Algernon. It would
345   put my table completely out. Your uncle would have to dine
upstairs. Fortunately he is accustomed to that.

ALGERNON: It is a great bore, and, I need hardly say, a terrible disappointment to me, but the fact is I have just had a
telegram to say that my poor friend Bunbury is very ill
350   again. (*Exchanges glances with* JACK.) They seem to think I
should be with him.

LADY BRACKNELL: It is very strange. This Mr. Bunbury seems
to suffer from curiously bad health.

ALGERNON: Yes; poor Bunbury is a dreadful invalid.

355 LADY BRACKNELL: Well, I must say, Algernon, that I think it
is high time that Mr. Bunbury made up his mind whether
he was going to live or to die. This shilly-shallying with
the question is absurd. Nor do I in any way approve of the
modern sympathy with invalids. I consider it morbid. Ill-
360   ness of any kind is hardly a thing to be encouraged in others. Health is the primary duty of life. I am always telling
that to your poor uncle, but he never seems to take much
notice . . . as far as any improvement in his ailments goes.
I should be much obliged if you would ask Mr. Bunbury,
365   from me, to be kind enough not to have a relapse on Saturday, for I rely on you to arrange my music for me. It is
my last reception and one wants something that will encourage conversation, particularly at the end of the season
when everyone has practically said whatever they had to
370   say, which, in most cases, was probably not much.

ALGERNON: I'll speak to Bunbury, Aunt Augusta, if he is still
conscious, and I think I can promise you he'll be all right
by Saturday. You see, if one plays good music, people don't
listen, and if one plays bad music people don't talk. But I'll
375   run over the programme I've drawn out, if you will kindly
come into the next room for a moment.

LADY BRACKNELL: Thank you, Algernon. It is very thoughtful of you. (*Rising, and following* ALGERNON.) I'm sure the
programme will be delightful, after a few expurgations.
380 French songs I cannot possibly allow. People always seem

to think that they are improper, and either look shocked,
which is vulgar, or laugh, which is worse. But German
sounds a thoroughly respectable language, and indeed, I
believe is so. Gwendolen, you will accompany me.

GWENDOLEN: Certainly, mamma. (LADY BRACKNELL *and* 385
ALGERNON *go into the music-room,* GWENDOLEN *remains
behind.*)

JACK: Charming day it has been, Miss Fairfax.

GWENDOLEN: Pray don't talk to me about the weather, Mr.
Worthing. Whenever people talk to me about the 390
weather, I always feel quite certain that they mean something else. And that makes me so nervous.

JACK: I do mean something else.

GWENDOLEN: I thought so. In fact, I am never wrong.

JACK: And I would like to be allowed to take advantage of 395
Lady Bracknell's temporary absence . . .

GWENDOLEN: I would certainly advise you to do so. Mamma
has a way of coming back suddenly into a room that I
have often had to speak to her about.

JACK: (*Nervously.*) Miss Fairfax, ever since I met you I have ad- 400
mired you more than any girl . . . I have ever met since . . .
I met you.

GWENDOLEN: Yes, I am quite aware of the fact. And I often wish
that in public, at any rate, you had been more demonstrative.
For me you have always had an irresistible fascination. Even 405
before I met you I was far from indifferent to you. (JACK *looks
at her in amazement.*) We live, as I hope you know, Mr. Worthing, in an age of ideals. The fact is constantly mentioned in
the more expensive monthly magazines, and has reached the
provincial pulpits I am told: and my ideal has always been to 410
love some one of the name of Ernest. There is something in
that name that inspires absolute confidence. The moment
Algernon first mentioned to me that he had a friend called
Ernest, I knew I was destined to love you.

JACK: You really love me, Gwendolen? 415

GWENDOLEN: Passionately!

JACK: Darling! You don't know how happy you've made me.

GWENDOLEN: My own Ernest!

JACK: But you don't really mean to say that you couldn't love
me if my name wasn't Ernest? 420

GWENDOLEN: But your name is Ernest.

JACK: Yes, I know it is. But supposing it was something else?
Do you mean to say you couldn't love me then?

GWENDOLEN: (*Glibly.*) Ah! that is clearly a metaphysical spec-
ulation, and like most metaphysical speculations has very 425
little reference at all to the actual facts of real life, as we
know them.

JACK: Personally, darling, to speak quite candidly, I don't
much care about the name of Ernest . . . I don't think that
name suits me at all. 430

GWENDOLEN: It suits you perfectly. It is a divine name. It has
a music of its own. It produces vibrations.

JACK: Well, really, Gwendolen, I must say that I think there are
lots of other much nicer names. I think Jack, for instance,
a charming name. 435

GWENDOLEN: Jack? . . . No, there is very little music in the
name Jack, if any at all, indeed. It does not thrill. It produces absolutely no vibration. . . . I have known several
Jacks, and they all, without exception, were more than
usually plain. Besides, Jack is a notorious domesticity for 440
John! And I pity any woman who is married to a man
called John. She would probably never be allowed to

know the entrancing pleasure of a single moment's solitude. The only really safe name is Ernest.

445 JACK: Gwendolen, I must get christened at once—I mean we must get married at once. There is no time to be lost.

GWENDOLEN: Married, Mr. Worthing?

JACK: (*Astounded.*) Well . . . surely. You know that I love you, and you led me to believe, Miss Fairfax, that you were not
450 absolutely indifferent to me.

GWENDOLEN: I adore you. But you haven't proposed to me yet. Nothing has been said at all about marriage. The subject has not even been touched on.

JACK: Well . . . may I propose to you now?

455 GWENDOLEN: I think it would be an admirable opportunity. And to spare you any possible disappointment, Mr. Worthing, I think it only fair to tell you quite frankly beforehand that I am fully determined to accept you.

JACK: Gwendolen!

460 GWENDOLEN: Yes, Mr. Worthing, what have you got to say to me?

JACK: You know what I have got to say to you.

GWENDOLEN: Yes, but you don't say it.

JACK: Gwendolen, will you marry me? (*Goes on his knees.*)

465 GWENDOLEN: Of course I will, darling. How long you have been about it! I am afraid you have had very little experience in how to propose.

JACK: My own one, I have never loved anyone in the world but you.

470 GWENDOLEN: Yes, but men often propose for practice. I know my brother Gerald does. All my girl-friends tell me so. What wonderfully blue eyes you have, Ernest! They are quite, quite blue. I hope you will always look at me just like that, especially when there are other people present.

(*Enter* LADY BRACKNELL.)

475 LADY BRACKNELL: Mr. Worthing! Rise, sir, from this semirecumbent posture. It is most indecorous.

GWENDOLEN: Mamma! (*He tries to rise; she restrains him.*) I must beg you to retire. This is no place for you. Besides, Mr. Worthing has not quite finished yet.

480 LADY BRACKNELL: Finished what, may I ask?

GWENDOLEN: I am engaged to Mr. Worthing, mamma.

(*They rise together.*)

LADY BRACKNELL: Pardon me, you are not engaged to anyone. When you do become engaged to some one, I, or your father, should his health permit him, will inform you
485 of the fact. An engagement should come on a young girl as a surprise, pleasant or unpleasant, as the case may be. It is hardly a matter that she could be allowed to arrange for herself. . . . And now I have a few questions to put to you, Mr. Worthing. While I am making these inquiries, you,
490 Gwendolen, will wait for me below in the carriage.

GWENDOLEN: (*Reproachfully.*) Mamma!

LADY BRACKNELL: In the carriage, Gwendolen! (GWENDOLEN *goes to the door. She and* JACK *blow kisses to each other behind* LADY BRACKNELL's *back.* LADY BRACKNELL *looks vaguely*
495 *about as if she could not understand what the noise was. Finally turns round.*) Gwendolen, the carriage!

GWENDOLEN: Yes, mamma. (*Goes out, looking back at* JACK.)

LADY BRACKNELL: (*Sitting down.*) You can take a seat, Mr. Worthing. (*Looks in her pocket for note-book and pencil.*)

JACK: Thank you, Lady Bracknell, I prefer standing. 500

LADY BRACKNELL: (*Pencil and note-book in hand.*) I feel bound to tell you that you are not down on my list of eligible young men, although I have the same list as the dear Duchess of Bolton has. We work together, in fact. However, I am quite ready to enter your name, should your answers be what a re- 505 ally affectionate mother requires. Do you smoke?

JACK: Well, yes, I must admit I smoke.

LADY BRACKNELL: I am glad to hear it. A man should always have an occupation of some kind. There are far too many idle men in London as it is. How old are you? 510

JACK: Twenty-nine.

LADY BRACKNELL: A very good age to be married at. I have always been of opinion that a man who desires to get married should know either everything or nothing. Which do you know? 515

JACK: (*After some hesitation.*) I know nothing, Lady Bracknell.

LADY BRACKNELL: I am pleased to hear it. I do not approve of anything that tampers with natural ignorance. Ignorance is like a delicate exotic fruit; touch it and the bloom is gone. The whole theory of modern education is radically un- 520 sound. Fortunately in England, at any rate, education produces no effect whatsoever. If it did, it would prove a serious danger to the upper classes, and probably lead to acts of violence in Grosvenor Square. What is your income?

JACK: Between seven and eight thousand a year. 525

LADY BRACKNELL: (*Makes a note in her book.*) In land, or in investments?

JACK: In investments, chiefly.

LADY BRACKNELL: That is satisfactory. What between the duties expected of one during one's life-time, and the duties exacted 530 from one after one's death, land has ceased to be either a profit or a pleasure. It gives one position, and prevents one from keeping it up. That's all that can be said about land.

JACK: I have a country house with some land, of course, attached to it, about fifteen hundred acres, I believe; but I 535 don't depend on that for my real income. In fact, as far as I can make out, the poachers are the only people who make anything out of it.

LADY BRACKNELL: A country house! How many bedrooms? Well, that point can be cleared up afterwards. You have a 540 town house, I hope? A girl with a simple, unspoiled nature, like Gwendolen, could hardly be expected to reside in the country.

JACK: Well, I own a house in Belgrave Square, but it is let by the year to Lady Bloxham. Of course, I can get it back 545 whenever I like, at six months' notice.

LADY BRACKNELL: Lady Bloxham? I don't know her.

JACK: Oh, she goes about very little. She is a lady considerably advanced in years.

LADY BRACKNELL: Ah, now-a-days that is no guarantee of re- 550 spectability of character. What number in Belgrave Square?

JACK: 149.

LADY BRACKNELL: (*Shaking her head.*) The unfashionable side. I thought there was something. However, that could easily be altered. 555

JACK: Do you mean the fashion, or the side?

LADY BRACKNELL: (*Sternly.*) Both, if necessary, I presume. What are your politics?

JACK: Well, I am afraid I really have none. I am a Liberal
560 Unionist.

LADY BRACKNELL: Oh, they count as Tories. They dine with
us. Or comes in the evening, at any rate. Now to minor
matters. Are your parents living?

JACK: I have lost both my parents.

565 LADY BRACKNELL: Both? . . . That seems like carelessness.
Who was your father? He was evidently a man of some
wealth. Was he born in what the Radical papers call the
purple of commerce, or did he rise from the ranks of the
aristocracy?

570 JACK: I am afraid I really don't know. The fact is, Lady Bracknell, I
said I had lost my parents. It would be nearer the truth to say
that my parents seem to have lost me . . . I don't actually know
who I am by birth. I was . . . well, I was found.

LADY BRACKNELL: Found!

575 JACK: The late Mr. Thomas Cardew, an old gentleman of a
very charitable and kindly disposition, found me, and gave
me the name of Worthing, because he happened to have a
first-class ticket for Worthing in his pocket at the time.
Worthing is a place in Sussex. It is a seaside resort.

580 LADY BRACKNELL: Where did the charitable gentleman who
had a first-class ticket for this seaside resort find you?

JACK: (*Gravely.*) In a hand-bag.

LADY BRACKNELL: A hand-bag?

JACK: (*Very seriously.*) Yes, Lady Bracknell. I was in a hand-
585 bag—a somewhat large, black leather hand-bag, with handles to it—an ordinary hand-bag in fact.

LADY BRACKNELL: In what locality did Mr. James, or Thomas,
Cardew come across this ordinary hand-bag?

JACK: In the cloak-room at Victoria Station. It was given to
590 him in mistake for his own.

LADY BRACKNELL: The cloak-room at Victoria Station?

JACK: Yes. The Brighton line.

LADY BRACKNELL: The line is immaterial. Mr. Worthing, I confess I feel somewhat bewildered by what you have just told
595 me. To be born, or at any rate bred, in a hand-bag, whether
it had handles or not, seems to me to display a contempt for
the ordinary decencies of family life that remind one of the
worst excesses of the French Revolution. And I presume
you know what that unfortunate movement led to? As for
600 the particular locality in which the hand-bag was found, a
cloak-room at a railway station might serve to conceal a social indiscretion—has probably, indeed, been used for the
purpose before now—but it could hardly be regarded as an
assured basis for a recognized position in good society.

605 JACK: May I ask you then what you would advise me to do?
I need hardly say I would do anything in the world to ensure Gwendolen's happiness.

LADY BRACKNELL: I would strongly advise you, Mr. Worthing, to
try and acquire some relations as soon as possible, and to
610 make a definite effort to produce at any rate one parent, of
either sex, before the season is quite over.

JACK: Well, I don't see how I could possibly manage to do
that. I can produce the hand-bag at any moment. It is in
my dressing-room at home. I really think that should sat-
615 isfy you, Lady Bracknell.

LADY BRACKNELL: Me, sir! What has it to do with me? You can
hardly imagine that I and Lord Bracknell would dream of
allowing our only daughter—a girl brought up with the utmost care—to marry into a cloak-room, and form an alliance with a parcel? Good morning, Mr. Worthing! (LADY 620
BRACKNELL *sweeps out in majestic indignation.*)

JACK: Good morning! (ALGERNON, *from the other room, strikes
up the Wedding March.* JACK *looks perfectly furious, and goes to
the door.*) For goodness' sake don't play that ghastly tune,
Algy! How idiotic you are! (*The music stops, and* ALGERNON 625
enters cheerily.)

ALGERNON: Didn't it go off all right, old boy? You don't mean
to say Gwendolen refused you? I know it is a way she has.
She is always refusing people. I think it is most ill-natured
of her.   630

JACK: Oh, Gwendolen is as right as a trivet. As far as she is concerned, we are engaged. Her mother is perfectly unbearable.
Never met such a Gorgon . . . I don't really know what a
Gorgon is like, but I am quite sure that Lady Bracknell is
one. In any case, she is a monster, without being a myth, 635
which is rather unfair. . . . I beg your pardon, Algy, I suppose
I shouldn't talk about your own aunt in that way before you.

ALGERNON: My dear boy, I love hearing my relations abused.
It is the only thing that makes me put up with them at all.
Relations are simply a tedious pack of people, who 640
haven't got the remotest knowledge of how to live, nor
the smallest instinct about when to die.

JACK: Oh, that is nonsense!

ALGERNON: It isn't!

JACK: Well, I won't argue about the matter. You always want 645
to argue about things.

ALGERNON: That is exactly what things were originally made
for.

JACK: Upon my word, if I thought that, I'd shoot myself . . .
(*A pause.*) You don't think there is any chance of Gwen- 650
dolen becoming like her mother in about a hundred and
fifty years, do you, Algy?

ALGERNON: All women become like their mothers. That is
their tragedy. No man does. That's his.

JACK: Is that clever?   655

ALGERNON: It is perfectly phrased! and quite as true as any
observation in civilized life should be.

JACK: I am sick to death of cleverness. Everybody is clever
now-a-days. You can't go anywhere without meeting
clever people. The thing has become an absolute public 660
nuisance. I wish to goodness we had a few fools left.

ALGERNON: We have.

JACK: I should extremely like to meet them. What do they
talk about?

ALGERNON: The fools? Oh! about the clever people, of course. 665

JACK: What fools!

ALGERNON: By the way, did you tell Gwendolen the truth
about your being Ernest in town, and Jack in the country?

JACK: (*In a very patronising manner.*) My dear fellow, the truth
isn't quite the sort of thing one tells to a nice, sweet, re- 670
fined girl. What extraordinary ideas you have about the
way to behave to a woman!

ALGERNON: The only way to behave to a woman is to make
love to her, if she is pretty, and to someone else if she is plain.

JACK: Oh, that is nonsense.   675

ALGERNON: What about your brother? What about the prof-
ligate Ernest?

JACK: Oh, before the end of the week I shall have got rid of
him. I'll say he died in Paris of apoplexy. Lots of people
die of apoplexy, quite suddenly, don't they?   680

ALGERNON: Yes, but it's hereditary, my dear fellow. It's a sort of thing that runs in families. You had much better say a severe chill.

685 JACK: You are sure a severe chill isn't hereditary, or anything of that kind?

ALGERNON: Of course it isn't!

JACK: Very well, then. My poor brother Ernest is carried off suddenly in Paris, by a sever chill. That gets rid of him.

ALGERNON: But I thought you said that . . . Miss Cardew was
690 a little too interested in your poor brother Ernest? Won't she feel his loss a good deal?

JACK: Oh, that is all right. Cecily is not a silly, romantic girl, I am glad to say. She has got a capital appetite, goes for long walks, and pays no attention at all to her lessons.

695 ALGERNON: I would rather like to see Cecily.

JACK: I will take very good care you never do. She is excessively pretty, and she is only just eighteen.

ALGERNON: Have you told Gwendolen yet that you have an excessively pretty ward who is only just eighteen?

700 JACK: Oh! one doesn't blurt these things out to people. Cecily and Gwendolen are perfectly certain to be extremely great friends. I'll bet you anything you like that half an hour after they have met, they will be calling each other sister.

ALGERNON: Women only do that when they have called each
705 other a lot of other thing first. Now, my dear boy, if we want to get a good table at Willis's, we really must go and dress. Do you know it is nearly seven?

JACK: (*Irritably.*) Oh! it always is nearly seven.

ALGERNON: Well, I'm hungry.

710 JACK: I never knew you when you weren't. . . .

ALGERNON: What shall we do after dinner? Go to a theatre?

JACK: Oh, no! I loathe listening.

ALGERNON: Well, let us go to the Club?

JACK: Oh, no! I hate talking.

715 ALGERNON: Well, we might trot round to the Empire at ten?

JACK: Oh, no! can't bear looking at things. It is so silly.

ALGERNON: Well, what shall we do?

JACK: Nothing!

ALGERNON: It is awfully hard work doing nothing. However,
720 I don't mind hard work where there is no definite object of any kind.

(*Enter* LANE.)

LANE: Miss Fairfax.

(*Enter* GWENDOLEN. LANE *goes out.*)

ALGERNON: Gwendolen, upon my word!

GWENDOLEN: Algy, kindly turn your back. I have something
725 very particular to say to Mr. Worthing.

ALGERNON: Really, Gwendolen, I don't think I can allow this at all.

GWENDOLEN: Algy, you always adopt a strictly immoral attitude towards life. You are not quite old enough to do that.
730 (ALGERNON *retires to the fireplace.*)

JACK: My own darling!

GWENDOLEN: Ernest, we may never be married. From the expression on mamma's face I fear we never shall. Few parents nowadays pay any regard to what their children
735 say to them. The old-fashioned respect for the young is fast dying out. Whatever influence I ever had over

mamma, I lost at the age of three. But although she may prevent us from becoming man and wife, and I may marry someone else, and marry often, nothing that she can possibly do can alter my eternal devotion to you. 740

JACK: Dear Gwendolen.

GWENDOLEN: The story of your romantic origin, as related to me by mamma, with unpleasing comments, has naturally stirred the deeper fibers of my nature. Your Christian name has an irresistible fascination. The simplicity of your 745 character make you exquisitely incomprehensible to me. Your town address at the Albany I have. What is your address in the country?

JACK: The Manor House, Woolton, Hertfordshire. (ALGERNON, *who has been carefully listening, smiles to himself, and* 750 *writes the address on his shirt-cuff. Then picks up the Railway Guide.*)

GWENDOLEN: There is a good postal service, I suppose? It may be necessary to do something desperate. That, of course, will require serious consideration. I will commu- 755 nicate with you daily.

JACK: My own one!

GWENDOLEN: How long do you remain in town?

JACK: Till Monday.

GWENDOLEN: Good! Algy, you may turn round now. 760

ALGERNON: Thanks, I've turned round already.

GWENDOLEN: You may also ring the bell.

JACK: You will let me see you to your carriage, my own darling?

GWENDOLEN: Certainly. 765

JACK: (*To* LANE, *who now enters.*) I will see Miss Fairfax out.

LANE: Yes, sir. (JACK *and* GWENDOLEN *go off.* LANE *presents several letters on a salver to* ALGERNON. *It is to be surmised that they are bills, as* ALGERNON, *after looking at the envelopes, tears them up.*) 770

ALGERNON: A glass of sherry, Lane.

LANE: Yes, sir.

ALGERNON: To-morrow, Lane, I'm going Bunburying.

LANE: Yes, sir.

ALGERNON: I shall probably not be back till Monday. You can 775 put up my dress clothes, my smoking jacket, and all the Bunbury suits . . .

LANE: Yes, sir. (*Handing sherry.*)

ALGERNON: I hope to-morrow will be a fine day, Lane.

LANE: It never is, sir. 780

ALGERNON: Lane, you're a perfect pessimist.

LANE: I do my best to give satisfaction, sir.

(*Enter* JACK. LANE *goes off.*)

JACK: There's a sensible, intellectual girl! the only girl I ever cared for in my life. (ALGERNON *is laughing immoderately.*) What on earth are you so amused at? 785

ALGERNON: Oh, I'm a little anxious about poor Bunbury, that's all.

JACK: If you don't take care, your friend Bunbury will get you into a serious scrape some day.

ALGERNON: I love scrapes. They are the only things that are 790 never serious.

JACK: Oh, that's nonsense, Algy. You never talk anything but nonsense.

ALGERNON: Nobody ever does. (JACK *looks indignantly at him,*

795   *and leaves the room.* ALGERNON *lights a cigarette, reads his*
        shirt-cuff and smiles.)

ACT TWO

Garden at the Manor House. A flight of gray stone steps leads up to
the house. The garden, an old-fashioned one, full of roses. Time of
year, July. Basket chairs, and a table covered with books, are set un-
der a large yew tree.

(MISS PRISM *discovered seated at the table.* CECILY *is at the back wa-*
tering flowers.)

MISS PRISM: (*Calling.*) Cecily, Cecily! Surely such a utilitarian
    occupation as the watering of flowers is rather Moulton's
    duty than yours? Especially at a moment when intellectual
    pleasures await you. Your German grammar is on the table.
5   Pray open it at page fifteen. We will repeat yesterday's lesson.
CECILY: (*Coming over very slowly.*) But I don't like German. It
    isn't at all a becoming language. I know perfectly well that
    I look quite plain after my German lesson.
MISS PRISM: Child, you know how anxious your guardian is
10 that you should improve yourself in every way. He laid
    particular stress on your German, as he was leaving for
    town yesterday. Indeed, he always lays stress on your Ger-
    man when he is leaving for town.
CECILY: Dear Uncle Jack is so very serious! Sometimes he is
15 so serious that I think he cannot be quite well.
MISS PRISM: (*Drawing herself up.*) Your guardian enjoys the best
    of health, and his gravity of demeanour is especially to be
    commended in one so comparatively young as he is. I know
    no one who has a higher sense of duty and responsibility.
20 CECILY: I suppose that is why he often looks a little bored
    when we three are together.
MISS PRISM: Cecily! I am surprised at you. Mr. Worthing has
    many troubles in his life. Idle merriment and triviality
    would be out of place in his conversation. You must re-
25 member his constant anxiety about that unfortunate
    young man, his brother.
CECILY: I wish Uncle Jack would allow that unfortunate
    young man, his brother, to come down here sometimes.
    We might have a good influence over him, Miss Prism. I
30 am sure you certainly would. You know German, and ge-
    ology, and things of that kind influence a man very much.
    (CECILY *begins to write in her diary.*)
MISS PRISM: (*Shaking her head.*) I do not think that even I could
    produce any effect on a character that, according to his own
35 brother's admission, is irretrievably weak and vacillating. In-
    deed, I am not sure that I would desire to reclaim him. I am
    not in favour of this modern mania for turning bad people
    into good people at a moment's notice. As a man sows so
    let him reap. You must put away your diary, Cecily. I really
40 don't see why you should keep a diary at all.
CECILY: I keep a diary in order to enter the wonderful secrets
    of my life. If I didn't write them down I should probably
    forget all about them.
MISS PRISM: Memory, my dear Cecily, is the diary that we all
45 carry about with us.
CECILY: Yes, but it usually chronicles the things that have
    never happened, and couldn't possibly have happened. I
    believe that Memory is responsible for nearly all the
    three-volume novels that Mudie sends us.

MISS PRISM: Do not speak slightingly of the three-volume   50
    novel, Cecily. I wrote one myself in earlier days.
CECILY: Did you really, Miss Prism? How wonderfully clever
    you are! I hope it did not end happily? I don't like novels
    that end happily. They depress me so much.
MISS PRISM: The good ended happily, and the bad unhappily.   55
    That is what Fiction means.
CECILY: I suppose so. But it seems very unfair. And was your
    novel ever published?
MISS PRISM: Alas! no. The manuscript unfortunately was
    abandoned. I use the word in the sense of lost or mislaid.   60
    To your work, child, these speculations are profitless.
CECILY: (*Smiling.*) But I see dear Dr. Chasuble coming up
    through the garden.
MISS PRISM: (*Rising and advancing.*) Dr. Chasuble! This is in-
    deed a pleasure.   65

(*Enter* CANON CHASUBLE.)

CHASUBLE: And how are we this morning? Miss Prism, you
    are, I trust, well?
CECILY: Miss Prism has just been complaining of a slight
    headache. I think it would do her so much good to have
    a short stroll with you in the park, Dr. Chasuble.   70
MISS PRISM: Cecily, I have not mentioned anything about a
    headache.
CECILY: No, dear Miss Prism, I know that, but I felt instinc-
    tively that you had a headache. Indeed I was thinking
    about that, and not about my German lesson, when the   75
    Rector came in.
CHASUBLE: I hope, Cecily, you are not inattentive.
CECILY: Oh, I am afraid I am.
CHASUBLE: That is strange. Were I fortunate enough to be
    Miss Prism's pupil, I would hang upon her lips. (MISS   80
    PRISM *glares.*) I spoke metaphorically.—My metaphor was
    drawn from bees. Ahem! Mr. Worthing, I suppose, has not
    returned from town yet?
MISS PRISM: We do not expect him till Monday afternoon.
CHASUBLE: Ah yes, he usually likes to spend his Sunday in   85
    London. He is not one of those whose sole aim is enjoy-
    ment, as, by all accounts, that unfortunate young man, his
    brother, seems to be. But I must not disturb Egeria and her
    pupil any longer.
MISS PRISM: Egeria? My name is Lætitia, Doctor.   90
CHASUBLE: (*Bowing.*) A classical allusion merely, drawn from the
    Pagan authors. I shall see you both no doubt at Evensong.
MISS PRISM: I think, dear Doctor, I will have a stroll with you.
    I find I have a headache after all, and a walk might do it
    good.   95
CHASUBLE: With pleasure, Miss Prism, with pleasure. We
    might go as far as the schools and back.
MISS PRISM: That would be delightful. Cecily, you will read
    your Political Economy in my absence. The chapter on
    the Fall of the Rupee you may omit. It is somewhat too   100
    sensational. Even these metallic problems have their melo-
    dramatic side.

(*Goes down the garden with* DR. CHASUBLE.)

CECILY: (*Picks up books and throws them back on table.*) Horrid
    Political Economy! Horrid Geography! Horrid, horrid
    German!   105

(*Enter* MERRIMAN *with a card on a salver.*)

MERRIMAN: Mr. Ernest Worthing has just driven over from the station. He has brought his luggage with him.

CECILY: (*Takes the card and reads it.*) "Mr. Ernest Worthing, B 4 The Albany, W." Uncle Jack's brother! Did you tell him
110   Mr. Worthing was in town?

MERRIMAN: Yes, Miss. He seemed very much disappointed. I mentioned that you and Miss Prism were in the garden. He said he was anxious to speak to you privately for a moment.

CECILY: Ask Mr. Ernest Worthing to come here. I suppose you
115   had better talk to the housekeeper about a room for him.

MERRIMAN: Yes, Miss.

(MERRIMAN *goes off.*)

CECILY: I have never met any really wicked person before. I feel rather frightened. I am so afraid he will look just like everyone else.

(*Enter* ALGERNON, *very gay and debonair.*)

120   He does!

ALGERNON: (*Raising his hat.*) You are my little cousin Cecily, I'm sure.

CECILY: You are under some strange mistake. I am not little. In fact, I am more than usually tall for my age. (ALGERNON
125   *is rather taken aback.*) But I am your cousin Cecily. You, I see from your card, are Uncle Jack's brother, my cousin Ernest, my wicked cousin Ernest.

ALGERNON: Oh! I am not really wicked at all, cousin Cecily. You mustn't think that I am wicked.

130   CECILY: If you are not, then you have certainly been deceiving us all in a very inexcusable manner. I hope you have not been leading a double life, pretending to be wicked and being really good all the time. That would be hypocrisy.

ALGERNON: (*Looks at her in amazement.*) Oh! of course I have
135   been rather reckless.

CECILY: I am glad to hear it.

ALGERNON: In fact, now you mention the subject, I have been very bad in my own small way.

CECILY: I don't think you should be so proud of that, though
140   I am sure it must have been very pleasant.

ALGERNON: It is much pleasanter being here with you.

CECILY: I can't understand how you are here at all. Uncle Jack won't be back till Monday afternoon.

ALGERNON: That is a great disappointment. I am obliged to
145   go up by the first train on Monday morning. I have a business appointment that I am anxious . . . to miss.

CECILY: Couldn't you miss it anywhere but in London?

ALGERNON: No; the appointment is in London.

CECILY: Well, I know, of course, how important it is not to
150   keep a business engagement, if one wants to retain any sense of the beauty of life, but still I think you had better wait till Uncle Jack arrives. I know he wants to speak to you about your emigrating.

ALGERNON: About my what?

155   CECILY: Your emigrating. He has gone up to buy your outfit.

ALGERNON: I certainly wouldn't let Jack buy my outfit. He has no taste in neckties at all.

CECILY: I don't think you will require neckties. Uncle Jack is sending you to Australia.

ALGERNON: Australia! I'd sooner die.   160

CECILY: Well, he said at dinner on Wednesday night, that you would have to choose between this world, the next world, and Australia.

ALGERNON: Oh, well! The accounts I have received of Australia and the next world, are not particularly encourag-   165
ing. This world is good enough for me, cousin Cecily.

CECILY: Yes, but are you good enough for it?

ALGERNON: I'm afraid I'm not that. That is why I want you to reform me. You might make that your mission, if you don't mind, cousin Cecily.   170

CECILY: I'm afraid I've not time, this afternoon.

ALGERNON: Well, would you mind my reforming myself this afternoon?

CECILY: That is rather Quixotic of you. But I think you should try.   175

ALGERNON: I will. I feel better already.

CECILY: You are looking a little worse.

ALGERNON: That is because I am hungry.

CECILY: How thoughtless of me. I should have remembered that when one is going to lead an entirely new life, one requires   180
regular and wholesome meals. Won't you come in?

ALGERNON: Thank you. Might I have a button-hole first? I never have any appetite unless I have a button-hole first.

CECILY: A Maréchal Niel? (*Picks up scissors.*)

ALGERNON: No, I'd sooner have a pink rose.   185

CECILY: Why? (*Cuts a flower.*)

ALGERNON: Because you are like a pink rose, cousin Cecily.

CECILY: I don't think it can be right for you to talk to me like that. Miss Prism never says such things to me.

ALGERNON: Then Miss Prism is a short-sighted old lady.   190
(CECILY *puts the rose in his button-hole.*) You are the prettiest girl I ever saw.

CECILY: Miss Prism says that all good looks are a snare.

ALGERNON: They are a snare that every sensible man would like to be caught in.   195

CECILY: Oh! I don't think I would care to catch a sensible man. I shouldn't know what to talk to him about.

(*They pass into the house.* MISS PRISM *and* DR. CHASUBLE *return.*)

MISS PRISM: You are too much alone, dear Dr. Chasuble. You should get married. A misanthrope I can understand—a womanthrope, never!   200

CHASUBLE: (*With a scholar's shudder.*) Believe me, I do not deserve so neologistic a phrase. The precept as well as the practice of the Primitive Church was distinctly against matrimony.

MISS PRISM: (*Sententiously.*) That is obviously the reason why the Primitive Church has not lasted up to the   205
present day. And you do not seem to realize, dear Doctor, that by persistently remaining single, a man converts himself into a permanent public temptation. Men should be careful; this very celibacy leads weaker vessels astray.   210

CHASUBLE: But is a man not equally attractive when married?

MISS PRISM: No married man is ever attractive except to his wife.

CHASUBLE: And often, I've been told, not even to her.

MISS PRISM: That depends on the intellectual sympathies of   215
the woman. Maturity can always be depended on. Ripeness can be trusted. Young women are green. (DR.

CHASUBLE *starts.*) I spoke horticulturally. My metaphor was drawn from fruits. But where is Cecily?

220 CHASUBLE: Perhaps she followed us to the schools.

(*Enter* JACK *slowly from the back of the garden. He is dressed in the deepest mourning, with crepe hatband and black gloves.*)

MISS PRISM: Mr. Worthing!

CHASUBLE: Mr. Worthing?

MISS PRISM: This is indeed a surprise. We did not look for you till Monday afternoon.

225 JACK: (*Shakes* MISS PRISM's *hand in a tragic manner.*) I have returned sooner than I expected. Dr. Chasuble, I hope you are well?

CHASUBLE: Dear Mr. Worthing, I trust this garb of woe does not betoken some terrible calamity?

230 JACK: My brother.

MISS PRISM: More shameful debts and extravagance?

CHASUBLE: Still leading his life of pleasure?

JACK: (*Shaking his head.*) Dead!

CHASUBLE: Your brother Ernest dead?

235 JACK: Quite dead.

MISS PRISM: What a lesson for him! I trust he will profit by it.

CHASUBLE: Mr. Worthing, I offer you my sincere condolence. You have at least the consolation of knowing that you were always the most generous and forgiving of brothers.

240 JACK: Poor Ernest! He had many faults, but it is a sad, sad blow.

CHASUBLE: Very sad indeed. Were you with him at the end?

JACK: No. He died abroad; in Paris, in fact. I had a telegram last night from the manager of the Grand Hotel.

245 CHASUBLE: Was the cause of death mentioned?

JACK: A severe chill, it seems.

MISS PRISM: As a man sows, so shall he reap.

CHASUBLE: (*Raising his hand.*) Charity, dear Miss Prism, charity! None of us are perfect. I myself am peculiarly suscepti-

250 ble to draughts. Will the interment take place here?

JACK: No. He seems to have expressed a desire to be buried in Paris.

CHASUBLE: In Paris! (*Shakes his head.*) I fear that hardly points to any very serious state of mind at the last. You would no

255 doubt wish me to make some slight allusion to this tragic domestic affliction next Sunday. (JACK *presses his hand convulsively.*) My sermon on the meaning of the manna in the wilderness can be adapted to almost any occasion, joyful, or, as in the present case, distressing. (*All sigh.*) I have

260 preached it at harvest celebrations, christenings, confirmations, on days of humiliation and festal days. The last time I delivered it was in the Cathedral, as a charity sermon on behalf of the Society for the Prevention of Discontentment among the Upper Orders. The Bishop, who was

265 present, was much struck by some of the analogies I drew.

JACK: Ah, that reminds me, you mentioned christenings I think, Dr. Chasuble? I suppose you know how to christen all right? (DR. CHASUBLE *looks astounded.*) I mean, of course, you are continually christening, aren't you?

270 MISS PRISM: It is, I regret to say, one of the Rector's most constant duties in this parish. I have often spoken to the poorer classes on the subject. But they don't seem to know what thrift is.

CHASUBLE: But is there any particular infant in whom you are

interested, Mr. Worthing? Your brother was, I believe, un- 275 married, was he not?

JACK: Oh, yes.

MISS PRISM: (*Bitterly.*) People who live entirely for pleasure usually are.

JACK: But it is not for any child, dear Doctor. I am very fond 280 of children. No! the fact is, I would like to be christened myself, this afternoon, if you have nothing better to do.

CHASUBLE: But surely, Mr. Worthing, you have been christened already?

JACK: I don't remember anything about it. 285

CHASUBLE: But have you any grave doubts on the subject?

JACK: I certainly intend to have. Of course, I don't know if the thing would bother you in any way, or if you think I am a little too old now.

CHASUBLE: Not at all. The sprinkling, and, indeed, the im- 290 mersion of adults is a perfectly canonical practice.

JACK: Immersion!

CHASUBLE: You need have no apprehensions. Sprinkling is all that is necessary, or indeed I think advisable. Our weather is so changeable. At what hour would you wish the cere- 295 mony performed?

JACK: Oh, I might trot around about five if that would suit you.

CHASUBLE: Perfectly, perfectly! In fact I have two similar ceremonies to perform at that time. A case of twins that oc- 300 curred recently in one of the outlying cottages on your own estate. Poor Jenkins the carter, a most hard-working man.

JACK: Oh! I don't see much fun in being christened along with other babies. It would be childish. Would half-past 305 five do?

CHASUBLE: Admirably! Admirably! (*Takes out watch.*) And now, dear Mr. Worthing, I will not intrude any longer into a house of sorrow. I would merely beg you not to be too much bowed down by grief. What seem to us bitter trials at the moment are often blessings in disguise.

MISS PRISM: This seems to me a blessing of an extremely obvious kind. 310

(*Enter* CECILY *from the house.*)

CECILY: Uncle Jack! Oh, I am pleased to see you back. But what horrid clothes you have on! Do go and change them.

MISS PRISM: Cecily!

CHASUBLE: My child! my child! (CECILY *goes towards* JACK; *he kisses her brow in a melancholy manner.*) 315

CECILY: What is the matter, Uncle Jack? Do look happy! You look as if you had a toothache and I have such a surprise for you. Who do you think is in the dining-room? Your brother!

JACK: Who?

CECILY: Your brother Ernest. He arrived about half an hour 320 ago.

JACK: What nonsense! I haven't got a brother.

CECILY: Oh, don't say that. However badly he may have behaved to you in the past he is still your brother. You couldn't be so heartless as to disown him. I'll tell him to 325 come out. And you will shake hands with him, won't you, Uncle Jack. (*Runs back into the house.*)

CHASUBLE: These are very joyful tidings.

MISS PRISM: After we had all been resigned to his loss, his sudden return seems to me peculiarly distressing. 330

JACK: My brother is in the dining-room? I don't know what it all means. I think it is perfectly absurd.

(*Enter* ALGERNON *and* CECILY *hand in hand. They come slowly up to* JACK.)

JACK: Good heavens! (*Motions* ALGERNON *away.*)
ALGERNON: Brother John, I have come down from town to
335   tell you that I am very sorry for all the trouble I have given you, and that I intend to lead a better life in the future. (JACK *glares at him and does not take his hand.*)
CECILY: Uncle Jack, you are not going to refuse your own brother's hand?
340 JACK: Nothing will induce me to take his hand. I think his coming down here disgraceful. He knows perfectly well why.
CECILY: Uncle Jack, do be nice. There is some good in everyone. Ernest has just been telling me about his poor invalid friend, Mr. Bunbury, whom he goes to visit so often. And
345   surely there must be much good in one who is kind to an invalid, and leaves the pleasures of London to sit by a bed of pain.
JACK: Oh, he has been talking about Bunbury, has he?
CECILY: Yes, he has told me all about poor Mr. Bunbury, and
350   his terrible state of health.
JACK: Bunbury! Well, I won't have him talk to you about Bunbury or about anything else. It is enough to drive one perfectly frantic.
ALGERNON: Of course I admit that the faults were all on my
355   side. But I must say that I think that Brother John's coldness to me is peculiarly painful. I expected a more enthusiastic welcome, especially considering it is the first time I have come here.
CECILY: Uncle Jack, if you don't shake hands with Ernest I
360   will never forgive you.
JACK: Never forgive me?
CECILY: Never, never, never!
JACK: Well, this is the last time I shall ever do it. (*Shakes hands with* ALGERNON *and glares.*)
365 CHASUBLE: It's pleasant, is it not, to see so perfect a reconciliation? I think we might leave the two brothers together.
MISS PRISM: Cecily, you will come with us.
CECILY: Certainly, Miss Prism. My little task of reconciliation is over.
370 CHASUBLE: You have done a beautiful action to-day, dear child.
MISS PRISM: We must not be premature in our judgments.
CECILY: I feel very happy. (*They all go off.*)
JACK: You young scoundrel, Algy, you must get out of this place as soon as possible. I don't allow any Bunburying here.

(*Enter* MERRIMAN.)

375 MERRIMAN: I have put Mr. Ernest's things in the room next to yours, sir. I suppose that is all right?
JACK: What?
MERRIMAN: Mr. Ernest's luggage, sir. I have unpacked it and put it in the room next to your own.
380 JACK: His luggage?
MERRIMAN: Yes, sir. Three portmanteaus, a dressing-case, two hat-boxes, and a large luncheon-basket.
ALGERNON: I am afraid I can't stay more than a week this time.

JACK: Merriman, order the dog-cart at once. Mr. Ernest has 385
been suddenly called back to town.
MERRIMAN: Yes, sir. (*Goes back into the house.*)
ALGERNON: What a fearful liar you are, Jack. I have not been called back to town at all.
JACK: Yes, you have. 390
ALGERNON: I haven't heard anyone call me.
JACK: Your duty as a gentleman calls you back.
ALGERNON: My duty as a gentleman has never interfered with my pleasures in the smallest degree.
JACK: I can quite understand that. 395
ALGERNON: Well, Cecily is a darling.
JACK: You are not to talk of Miss Cardew like that. I don't like it.
ALGERNON: Well, I don't like your clothes. You look perfectly ridiculous in them. Why on earth don't you go up and change? It is perfectly childish to be in deep mourning for 400
a man who is actually staying for a whole week with you in your house as a guest. I call it grotesque.
JACK: You are certainly not staying with me for a whole week as a guest or anything else. You have got to leave . . . by the four-five train. 405
ALGERNON: I certainly won't leave you so long as you are in mourning. It would be most unfriendly. If I were in mourning you would stay with me, I suppose. I should think it very unkind if you didn't.
JACK: Well, will you go if I change my clothes? 410
ALGERNON: Yes, if you are not too long. I never saw anybody take so long to dress, and with such little result.
JACK: Well, at any rate, that is better than being always over-dressed as you are.
ALGERNON: If I am occasionally a little over-dressed, I make 415
up for it by being always immensely over-educated.
JACK: Your vanity is ridiculous, your conduct an outrage, and your presence in my garden utterly absurd. However, you have got to catch the four-five, and I hope you will have a pleasant journey back to town. This Bunburying, as you call 420
it, has not been a great success for you. (*Goes into the house.*)
ALGERNON: I think it has been a great success. I'm in love with Cecily, and that is everything. (*Enter* CECILY *at the back of the garden. She picks up the can and begins to water the flowers.*) But I must see her before I go, and make arrange- 425
ments for another Bunbury. Ah, there she is.
CECILY: Oh, I merely came back to water the roses. I thought you were with Uncle Jack.
ALGERNON: He's gone to order the dog-cart for me.
CECILY: Oh, is he going to take you for a nice drive? 430
ALGERNON: He's going to send me away.
CECILY: Then have we got to part?
ALGERNON: I am afraid so. It's a very painful parting.
CECILY: It is always painful to part from people whom one has known for a very brief space of time. The absence of old 435
friends one can endure with equanimity. But even a momentary separation from anyone to whom one has just been introduced is almost unbearable.
ALGERNON: Thank you.

(*Enter* MERRIMAN.)

MERRIMAN: The dog-cart is at the door, sir. (ALGERNON *looks* 440
appealingly at CECILY.)
CECILY: It can wait, Merriman . . . for . . . five minutes.

MERRIMAN: Yes, miss.

(*Exit* MERRIMAN.)

ALGERNON: I hope, Cecily, I shall not offend you if I state quite
445 frankly and openly that you seem to me to be in every way
the visible personification of absolute perfection.

CECILY: I think your frankness does you great credit, Ernest.
If you will allow me I will copy your remarks into my diary. (*Goes over to table and begins writing in diary.*)

450 ALGERNON: Do you really keep a diary? I'd give any thing to
look at it. May I?

CECILY: Oh, no. (*Puts her hand over it.*) You see, it is simply a
very young girl's record of her own thoughts and impressions, and consequently meant for publication. When it
455 appears in volume form I hope you will order a copy. But
pray, Ernest, don't stop. I delight in taking down from dictation. I have reached "absolute perfection." You can go
on. I am quite ready for more.

ALGERNON: (*Somewhat taken aback.*) Ahem! Ahem!

460 CECILY: Oh, don't cough, Ernest. When one is dictating one
should speak fluently and not cough. Besides, I don't
know how to spell a cough. (*Writes as* ALGERNON *speaks.*)

ALGERNON: (*Speaking very rapidly.*) Cecily, ever since I first
looked upon your wonderful and incomparable beauty, I
465 have dared to love you wildly, passionately, devotedly,
hopelessly.

CECILY: I don't think that you should tell me that you love
me wildly, passionately, devotedly, hopelessly. Hopelessly
doesn't seem to make much sense, does it?

470 ALGERNON: Cecily!

(*Enter* MERRIMAN.)

MERRIMAN: The dog-cart is waiting, sir.

ALGERNON: Tell it to come round next week, at the same hour.

MERRIMAN: (*Looks at* CECILY, *who makes no sign.*) Yes, sir.

(MERRIMAN *retires.*)

CECILY: Uncle Jack would be very much annoyed if he knew
475 you were staying on till next week, at the same hour.

ALGERNON: Oh, I don't care about Jack. I don't care for anybody in the whole world but you. I love you, Cecily. You
will marry me, won't you?

CECILY: You silly you! Of course. Why, we have been engaged
480 for the last three months.

ALGERNON: For the last three months?

CECILY: Yes, it will be exactly three months on Thursday.

ALGERNON: But how did we become engaged?

CECILY: Well, ever since dear Uncle Jack first confessed to us
485 that he had a younger brother who was very wicked and
bad, you of course have formed the chief topic of conversation between myself and Miss Prism. And of course a
man who is much talked about is always very attractive.
One feels there must be something in him after all. I dare-
490 say it was foolish of me, but I fell in love with you, Ernest.

ALGERNON: Darling! And when was the engagement actually
settled?

CECILY: On the 14th of February last. Worn out by your entire
ignorance of my existence, I determined to end the matter

one way or the other, and after a long struggle with myself 495
I accepted you under this dear old tree here. The next day I
bought this little ring in your name, and this is the little ban-
gle with the true lovers' knot I promised you always to wear.

ALGERNON: Did I give you this? It's very pretty, isn't it?

CECILY: Yes, you've wonderfully good taste, Ernest. It's the 500
excuse I've always given for your leading such a bad life.
And this is the box in which I keep all your dear letters.
(*Kneels at table, opens box, and produces letters tied up with
blue ribbon.*)

ALGERNON: My letters! But my own sweet Cecily, I have 505
never written you any letters.

CECILY: You need hardly remind me of that, Ernest. I remember only too well that I was forced to write your letters for you. I wrote always three times a week, and
sometimes oftener. 510

ALGERNON: Oh, do let me read them, Cecily?

CECILY: Oh, I couldn't possibly. They would make you far too
conceited. (*Replaces box.*) The three you wrote me after I
had broken off the engagement are so beautiful, and so
badly spelled, that even now I can hardly read them with- 515
out crying a little.

ALGERNON: But was our engagement ever broken off?

CECILY: Of course it was. On the 22nd of last March. You can
see the entry if you like. (*Shows diary.*) "Today I broke off 520
my engagement with Ernest. I feel it is better to do so. The
weather still continues charming."

ALGERNON: But why on earth did you break it off? What had
I done? I had done nothing at all. Cecily, I am very much
hurt indeed to hear you broke it off. Particularly when the 525
weather was so charming.

CECILY: It would hardly have been a really serious engagement if it hadn't been broken off at least once. But I for-
gave you before the week was out.

ALGERNON: (*Crossing to her, and kneeling.*) What a perfect an- 530
gel you are, Cecily.

CECILY: You dear romantic boy. (*He kisses her, she puts her fingers through his hair.*) I hope your hair curls naturally, does
it?

ALGERNON: Yes, darling, with a little help from others. 535

CECILY: I am so glad.

ALGERNON: You'll never break off our engagement again,
Cecily?

CECILY: I don't think I could break it off now that I have actually met you. Besides, of course, that is the question of 540
your name.

ALGERNON: Yes, of course. (*Nervously.*)

CECILY: You must not laugh at me, darling, but it had always
been a girlish dream of mine to love some one whose
name was Ernest. (ALGERNON *rises,* CECILY *also.*) There is 545
something in that name that seems to inspire absolute
confidence. I pity any poor married woman whose husband is not called Ernest.

ALGERNON: But, my dear child, do you mean to say you
could not love me if I had some other name? 550

CECILY: But what name?

ALGERNON: Oh, any name you like—Algernon, for instance.
. . .

CECILY: But I don't like the name of Algernon.

ALGERNON: Well, my own dear, sweet, loving little darling, I re- 555
ally can't see why you should object to the name of Alger-

non. It is not at all a bad name. In fact, it is rather an aristocratic name. Half of the chaps who get into the Bankruptcy
Court are called Algernon. But seriously, Cecily . . . (*Moving
560   *to her.*) . . . if my name was Algy, couldn't you love me?

CECILY: I might respect you, Ernest, I might admire your
character, but I fear that I should not be able to give you
my undivided attention.

ALGERNON: Ahem! Cecily! (*Picking up hat.*) Your Rector here
565   is, I suppose, thoroughly experienced in the practice of all
the rites and ceremonials of the church?

CECILY: Oh, yes. Dr. Chasuble is a most learned man. He has
never written a single book, so you can imagine how
much he knows.

570 ALGERNON: I must see him at once on a most important
christening—I mean on most important business.

CECILY: Oh!

ALGERNON: I sha'n't be away more than half an hour.

CECILY: Considering that we have been engaged since Feb-
575   ruary the 14th, and that I only met you to-day for the first
time, I think it is rather hard that you should leave me for
so long a period as half an hour. Couldn't you make it
twenty minutes?

ALGERNON: I'll be back in no time. (*Kisses her and rushes down
580   the garden.*)

CECILY: What an impetuous boy he is. I like his hair so much.
I must enter his proposal in my diary.

(*Enter* MERRIMAN.)

MERRIMAN: A Miss Fairfax has just called to see Mr. Worthing.
On very important business, Miss Fairfax states.
585 CECILY: Isn't Mr. Worthing in his library?

MERRIMAN: Mr. Worthing went over in the direction of the
Rectory some time ago.

CECILY: Pray ask the lady to come out here; Mr. Worthing is
sure to be back soon. And you can bring tea.
590 MERRIMAN: Yes, miss.

(*Goes out.*)

CECILY: Miss Fairfax! I suppose one of the many good elderly
women who are associated with Uncle Jack in some of his
philanthropic work in London. I don't quite like women
who are interested in philanthropic work. I think it is so
595   forward of them.

(*Enter* MERRIMAN.)

MERRIMAN: Miss Fairfax.

(*Enter* GWENDOLEN. *Exit* MERRIMAN.)

CECILY: (*Advancing to meet her.*) Pray let me introduce myself
to you. My name is Cecily Cardew.

GWENDOLEN: Cecily Cardew? (*Moving to her and shaking hands.*)
600   What a very sweet name! Something tells me that we are
going to be great friends. I like you already more than I can
say. My first impressions of people are never wrong.

CECILY: How nice of you to like me so much after we have
known each other such a comparatively short time. Pray
605   sit down.

GWENDOLEN: (*Still standing up.*) I may call you Cecily, may I
not?

CECILY: With pleasure!

GWENDOLEN: And you will always call me Gwendolen, won't
you?   610

CECILY: If you wish.

GWENDOLEN: Then that is all quite settled, is it not?

CECILY: I hope so. (*A pause. They both sit down together.*)

GWENDOLEN: Perhaps this might be a favorable opportunity
for my mentioning who I am. My father is Lord Brack- 615
nell. You have never heard of papa, I suppose?

CECILY: I don't think so.

GWENDOLEN: Outside the family circle, papa, I am glad to say,
is entirely unknown. I think that is quite as it should be.
The home seems to me to be the proper sphere for the 620
man. And certainly once a man begins to neglect his domestic duties he becomes painfully effeminate, does he
not? And I don't like that. It makes men so very attractive.
Cecily, mamma, whose views on education are remarkably
strict, has brought me up to be extremely short-sighted; it 625
is part of her system; so do you mind my looking at you
through my glasses?

CECILY: Oh, not at all, Gwendolen. I am very fond of being
looked at.

GWENDOLEN: (*After examining* CECILY *carefully through a* 630
lorgnette.) You are here on a short visit, I suppose.

CECILY: Oh, no, I live here.

GWENDOLEN: (*Severely.*) Really? Your mother, no doubt, or
some female relative of advanced years, resides here also?

CECILY: Oh, no. I have no mother, nor, in fact, any relations. 635

GWENDOLEN: Indeed?

CECILY: My dear guardian, with the assistance of Miss Prism,
has the arduous task of looking after me.

GWENDOLEN: Your guardian?

CECILY: Yes, I am Mr. Worthing's ward. 640

GWENDOLEN: Oh! It is strange he never mentioned to me
that he had a ward. How secretive of him! He grows more
interesting hourly. I am not sure, however, that the news
inspires me with feelings of unmixed delight. (*Rising and
going to her.*) I am very fond of you, Cecily; I have liked 645
you ever since I met you. But I am bound to state that
now that I know that you are Mr. Worthing's ward, I cannot help expressing a wish you were—well, just a little
older than you seem to be—and not quite so very allur-
ing in appearance. In fact, if I may speak candidly— 650

CECILY: Pray do! I think that whenever one has anything unpleasant to say, one should always be quite candid.

GWENDOLEN: Well, to speak with perfect candour, Cecily, I
wish that you were fully forty-two, and more than usually
plain for your age. Ernest has a strong upright nature. He 655
is the very soul of truth and honour. Disloyalty would be
as impossible to him as deception. But even men of the
noblest possible moral character are extremely susceptible
to the influence of the physical charms of others. Modern,
no less than Ancient History, supplies us with many most 660
painful examples of what I refer to. If it were not so, indeed, History would be quite unreadable.

CECILY: I beg your pardon, Gwendolen, did you say Ernest?

GWENDOLEN: Yes.

CECILY: Oh, but it is not Mr. Ernest Worthing who is my 665
guardian. It is his brother—his elder brother.

GWENDOLEN: (*Sitting down again.*) Ernest never mentioned to me that he had a brother.

670 CECILY: I am sorry to say they have not been on good terms for a long time.

GWENDOLEN: Ah! that accounts for it. And now that I think of it I have never heard any man mention his brother. The subject seems distasteful to most men. Cecily, you have lifted a
675 load from my mind. I was growing almost anxious. It would have been terrible if any cloud had come across a friendship like ours, would it not? Of course you are quite, quite sure that it is not Mr. Ernest Worthing who is your guardian?

CECILY: Quite sure. (*A pause.*) In fact, I am going to be his.

GWENDOLEN: (*Enquiringly.*) I beg your pardon?

680 CECILY: (*Rather shy and confidingly.*) Dearest Gwendolen, there is no reason why I should make a secret of it to you. Our little county newspaper is sure to chronicle the fact next week. Mr. Ernest Worthing and I are engaged to be married.

GWENDOLEN: (*Quite politely, rising.*) My darling Cecily, I think
685 there must be some slight error. Mr. Ernest Worthing is engaged to me. The announcement will appear in the *Morning Post* on Saturday at the latest.

CECILY: (*Very politely, rising.*) I am afraid you must be under some misconception. Ernest proposed to me exactly ten
690 minutes ago. (*Shows diary.*)

GWENDOLEN: (*Examines diary through her lorgnette carefully.*) It is certainly very curious, for he asked me to be his wife yesterday afternoon at 5:30. If you would care to verify the incident, pray do so. (*Produces diary of her own.*) I never
695 travel without my diary. One should always have something sensational to read in the train. I am so sorry, dear Cecily, if it is any disappointment to you, but I am afraid I have the prior claim.

CECILY: It would distress me more than I can tell you, dear
700 Gwendolen, if it caused you any mental or physical anguish, but I feel bound to point out that since Ernest proposed to you he clearly has changed his mind.

GWENDOLEN: (*Meditatively.*) If the poor fellow has been entrapped into any foolish promise I shall consider it my
705 duty to rescue him at once, and with a firm hand.

CECILY: (*Thoughtfully and sadly.*) Whatever unfortunate entanglement my dear boy may have got into, I will never reproach him with it after we are married.

GWENDOLEN: Do you allude to me, Miss Cardew, as an en-
710 tanglement? You are presumptuous. On an occasion of this kind it becomes more than a moral duty to speak one's mind. It becomes a pleasure.

CECILY: Do you suggest, Miss Fairfax, that I entrapped Ernest into an engagement? How dare you? This is no time for
715 wearing the shallow mask of manners. When I see a spade I call it a spade.

GWENDOLEN: (*Satirically.*) I am glad to say that I have never seen a spade. It is obvious that our social spheres have been widely different.

(*Enter* MERRIMAN, *followed by the footman. He carries a salver, tablecloth, and plate-stand.* CECILY *is about to retort. The presence of the servants exercises a restraining influence, under which both girls chafe.*)

720 MERRIMAN: Shall I lay tea here as usual, miss?

CECILY: (*Sternly, in a calm voice.*) Yes, as usual. (MERRIMAN *begins to clear and lay cloth. A long pause.* CECILY *and* GWENDOLEN *glare at each other.*)

GWENDOLEN: Are there many interesting walks in the vicinity, Miss Cardew? 725

CECILY: Oh, yes, a great many. From the top of one of the hills quite close one can see five counties.

GWENDOLEN: Five counties! I don't think I should like that. I hate crowds.

CECILY: (*Sweetly.*) I suppose that is why you live in town? 730 (GWENDOLEN *bites her lip, and beats her foot nervously with her parasol.*)

GWENDOLEN: (*Looking around.*) Quite a well-kept garden this is, Miss Cardew.

CECILY: So glad you like it, Miss Fairfax. 735

GWENDOLEN: I had no idea there were any flowers in the country.

CECILY: Oh, flowers are as common here, Miss Fairfax, as people are in London.

GWENDOLEN: Personally I cannot understand how anybody 740 manages to exist in the country, if anybody who is anybody does. The country always bores me to death.

CECILY: Ah! This is what the newspapers call agricultural depression, is it not? I believe the aristocracy are suffering very much from it just at present. It is almost an epidemic 745 amongst them, I have been told. May I offer you some tea, Miss Fairfax?

GWENDOLEN: (*With elaborate politeness.*) Thank you. (*Aside.*) Detestable girl! But I require tea!

CECILY: (*Sweetly.*) Sugar? 750

GWENDOLEN: (*Superciliously.*) No, thank you. Sugar is not fashionable any more. (CECILY *looks angrily at her, takes up the tongs and puts four lumps of sugar into the cup.*)

CECILY: (*Severely.*) Cake or bread and butter?

GWENDOLEN: (*In a bored manner.*) Bread and butter, please. 755 Cake is rarely seen at the best houses nowadays.

CECILY: (*Cuts a very large slice of cake, and puts it on the tray.*) Hand that to Miss Fairfax. (MERRIMAN *does so, and goes out with footman.* GWENDOLEN *drinks the tea and makes a grimace. Puts down cup at once, reaches out her hand to the* 760 *bread and butter, looks at it, and finds it is cake. Rises in indignation.*)

GWENDOLEN: You have filled my tea with lumps of sugar, and though I asked most distinctly for bread and butter, you have given me cake. I am known for the gentleness of my 765 disposition, and the extraordinary sweetness of my nature, but I warn you, Miss Cardew, you may go too far.

CECILY: (*Rising.*) To save my poor, innocent, trusting boy from the machinations of any other girl there are no lengths to which I would not go. 770

GWENDOLEN: From the moment I saw you I distrusted you. I felt that you were false and deceitful. I am never deceived in such matters. My first impressions of people are invariably right.

CECILY: It seems to me, Miss Fairfax, that I am trespassing on 775 your valuable time. No doubt you have many other calls of a similar character to make in the neighbourhood.

(*Enter* JACK.)

GWENDOLEN: (*Catching sight of him.*) Ernest! My own Ernest!

JACK: Gwendolen! Darling! (*Offers to kiss her.*)

GWENDOLEN: (*Drawing back.*) A moment! May I ask if you are 780 engaged to be married to this young lady? (*Points to* CECILY.)

JACK: (*Laughing.*) To dear little Cecily! Of course not! What could have put such an idea into your pretty little head?

785 GWENDOLEN: Thank you. You may. (*Offers her cheek.*)

CECILY: (*Very sweetly.*) I knew there must be some misunderstanding, Miss Fairfax. The gentleman whose arm is at present around your waist is my dear guardian, Mr. John Worthing.

790 GWENDOLEN: I beg your pardon?

CECILY: This is Uncle Jack.

GWENDOLEN: (*Receding.*) Jack! Oh!

(*Enter* ALGERNON.)

CECILY: Here is Ernest.

ALGERNON: (*Goes straight over to* CECILY *without noticing anyone*
795 *else.*) My own love! (*Offers to kiss her.*)

CECILY: (*Drawing back.*) A moment, Ernest! May I ask you— are you engaged to be married to this young lady?

ALGERNON: (*Looking round.*) To what young lady? Good heavens! Gwendolen!

800 CECILY: Yes, to good heavens, Gwendolen, I mean to Gwendolen.

ALGERNON: (*Laughing.*) Of course not! What could have put such an idea into your pretty little head?

CECILY: Thank you. (*Presenting her cheek to be kissed.*) You may.
805 (ALGERNON *kisses her.*)

GWENDOLEN: I felt there was some slight error, Miss Cardew. The gentleman who is now embracing you is my cousin, Mr. Algernon Moncrieff.

CECILY: (*Breaking away from* ALGERNON.) Algernon Moncrieff!
810 Oh! (*The two girls move towards each other and put their arms round each other's waists as if for protection.*)

CECILY: Are you called Algernon?

ALGERNON: I cannot deny it.

CECILY: Oh!

815 GWENDOLEN: Is your name really John?

JACK: (*Standing rather proudly.*) I could deny it if I liked. I could deny anything if I liked. But my name certainly is John. It has been John for years.

CECILY: (*To* GWENDOLEN.) A gross deception has been prac-
820 ticed on both of us.

GWENDOLEN: My poor wounded Cecily!

CECILY: My sweet, wronged Gwendolen!

GWENDOLEN: (*Slowing and seriously.*) You will call me sister, will you not? (*They embrace.* JACK *and* ALGERNON *groan and*
825 *walk up and down.*)

CECILY: (*Rather brightly.*) There is just one question I would like to be allowed to ask my guardian.

GWENDOLEN: An admirable idea! Mr. Worthing, there is just one question I would like to be permitted to put to you.
830 Where is your brother Ernest? We are both engaged to be married to your brother Ernest, so it is a matter of some importance to us to know where your brother Ernest is at present.

JACK: (*Slowly and hesitatingly.*) Gwendolen—Cecily—it is very
835 painful for me to be forced to speak the truth. It is the first time in my life that I have ever been reduced to such a painful position, and I am really quite inexperienced in doing anything of the kind. However I will tell you quite frankly that I have no brother Ernest. I have no brother at
840 all. I never had a brother in my life, and I certainly have not the smallest intention of ever having one in the future.

CECILY: (*Surprised.*) No brother at all?

JACK: (*Cheerily.*) None!

GWENDOLEN: (*Severely.*) Had you never a brother of any kind?

JACK: (*Pleasantly.*) Never. Not even of any kind.   845

GWENDOLEN: I am afraid it is quite clear, Cecily, that neither of us is engaged to be married to anyone.

CECILY: It is not a very pleasant position for a young girl suddenly to find herself in. Is it?

GWENDOLEN: Let us go into the house. They will hardly ven-   850
ture to come after us there.

CECILY: No, men are so cowardly, aren't they? (*They retire into the house with scornful looks.*)

JACK: This ghastly state of things is what you call Bunburying, I suppose?   855

ALGERNON: Yes, and a perfectly wonderful Bunbury it is. The most wonderful Bunbury I have ever had in my life.

JACK: Well, you've no right whatsoever to Bunbury here.

ALGERNON: That is absurd. One has a right to Bunbury anywhere one chooses. Every serious Bunburyist knows that.   860

JACK: Serious Bunburyist! Good heavens!

ALGERNON: Well, one must be serious about something, if one wants to have any amusement in life. I happen to be serious about Bunburying. What on earth you are serious about I haven't got the remotest idea. About everything, I   865
should fancy. You have such an absolutely trivial nature.

JACK: Well, the only small satisfaction I have in the whole of this wretched business is that your friend Bunbury is quite exploded. You won't be able to run down to the country quite so often as you used to do, dear Algy. And a very   870
good thing, too.

ALGERNON: Your brother is a little off colour, isn't he, dear Jack? You won't be able to disappear to London quite so frequently as your wicked custom was. And not a bad thing, either.   875

JACK: As for your conduct towards Miss Cardew, I must say that your taking in a sweet, simple, innocent girl like that is quite inexcusable. To say nothing of the fact that she is my ward.

ALGERNON: I can see no possible defence at all for your de-   880
ceiving a brilliant, clever, thoroughly experienced young lady like Miss Fairfax. To say nothing of the fact that she is my cousin.

JACK: I wanted to be engaged to Gwendolen, that is all. I love her.   885

ALGERNON: Well, I simply wanted to be engaged to Cecily. I adore her.

JACK: There is certainly no chance of your marrying Miss Cardew.

ALGERNON: I don't think there is much likelihood, Jack, of   890
you and Miss Fairfax being united.

JACK: Well, that is no business of yours.

ALGERNON: If it was my business, I wouldn't talk about it. (*Begins to eat muffins.*) It is very vulgar to talk about one's business. Only people like stock-brokers do that, and then   895
merely at dinner parties.

JACK: How you can sit there, calmly eating muffins, when we are in this horrible trouble, I can't make out. You seem to me to be perfectly heartless.

ALGERNON: Well, I can't eat muffins in an agitated manner. The   900
butter would probably get on my cuffs. One should always eat muffins quite calmly. It is the only way to eat them.

JACK: I say it's perfectly heartless your eating muffins at all, under the circumstances.

905 ALGERNON: When I am in trouble, eating is the only thing that consoles me. Indeed, when I am in really great trouble, as anyone who knows me intimately will tell you, I refuse everything except food and drink. At the present moment I am eating muffins because I am unhappy. Be-
910 sides, I am particularly fond of muffins. (*Rising.*)

JACK: (*Rising.*) Well, that is no reason why you should eat them all in that greedy way. (*Takes muffin from* ALGERNON.)

ALGERNON: (*Offering tea-cake.*) I wish you would have tea-cake instead. I don't like tea-cake.

915 JACK: Good heavens! I suppose a man may eat his own muffins in his own garden.

ALGERNON: But you have just said it was perfectly heartless to eat muffins.

JACK: I said it was perfectly heartless of you, under the cir-
920 cumstances. That is a very different thing.

ALGERNON: That may be. But the muffins are the same. (*He seizes the muffin dish from* JACK.)

JACK: Algy, I wish to goodness you would go.

ALGERNON: You can't possibly ask me to go without having
925 some dinner. It's absurd. I never go without my dinner. No one ever does, except vegetarians and people like that. Besides I have just made arrangements with Dr. Chasuble to be christened at a quarter to six under the name of Ernest.

JACK: My dear fellow, the sooner you give up that nonsense
930 the better. I made arrangements this morning with Dr. Chasuble to be christened myself at 5:30, and I naturally will take the name of Ernest. Gwendolen would wish it. We can't both be christened Ernest. It's absurd. Besides, I have a perfect right to be christened if I like. There is no
935 evidence at all that I ever have been christened by anybody. I should think it extremely probable I never was, and so does Dr. Chasuble. It is entirely different in your case. You have been christened already.

ALGERNON: Yes, but I have not been christened for years.

940 JACK: Yes, but you have been christened. That is the important thing.

ALGERNON: Quite so. So I know my constitution can stand it. If you are not quite sure about your ever having been christened, I must say I think it rather dangerous your
945 venturing on it now. It might make you very unwell. You can hardly have forgotten that someone very closely connected with you was very nearly carried off this week in Paris by a severe chill.

JACK: Yes, but you said yourself that a severe chill was not
950 hereditary.

ALGERNON: It usedn't to be, I know—but I daresay it is now. Science is always making wonderful improvements in things.

JACK: (*Picking up the muffin-dish.*) Oh, that is nonsense; you are
955 always talking nonsense.

ALGERNON: Jack, you are at the muffins again! I wish you wouldn't. There are only two left. (*Takes them.*) I told you I was particularly fond of muffins.

JACK: But I hate tea-cake.

960 ALGERNON: Why on earth then do you allow tea-cake to be served up for your guests? What ideas you have of hospitality!

JACK: Algernon! I have already told you to go. I don't want you here. Why don't you go?

ALGERNON: I haven't quite finished my tea yet, and there is 965 still one muffin left. (JACK *groans, and sinks into a chair.* ALGERNON *still continues eating.*)

ACT THREE

Morning-room at the Manor House. GWENDOLEN *and* CECILY *are at the window, looking out into the garden.*

GWENDOLEN: The fact that they did not follow us at once into the house, as anyone else would have done, seems to me to show that they have some sense of shame left.

CECILY: They have been eating muffins. That looks like repentance. 5

GWENDOLEN: (*After a pause.*) They don't seem to notice us at all. Couldn't you cough?

GWENDOLEN: They're looking at us. What effrontery!

CECILY: They're approaching. That's very forward of them.

GWENDOLEN: Let us preserve a dignified silence. 10

CECILY: Certainly. It's the only thing to do now.

(*Enter* JACK, *followed by* ALGERNON. *They whistle some dreadful popular air from a British opera.*)

GWENDOLEN: This dignified silence seems to produce an unpleasant effect.

CECILY: A most distasteful one.

GWENDOLEN: But we will not be the first to speak. 15

CECILY: Certainly not.

GWENDOLEN: Mr. Worthing, I have something very particular to ask you. Much depends on your reply.

CECILY: Gwendolen, your common sense is invaluable. Mr. Moncrieff, kindly answer me the following question. Why 20 did you pretend to be my guardian's brother?

ALGERNON: In order that I might have an opportunity of meeting you.

CECILY: (*To* GWENDOLEN.) That certainly seems a satisfactory explanation, does it not? 25

GWENDOLEN: Yes, dear, if you can believe him.

CECILY: I don't. But that does not affect the wonderful beauty of his answer.

GWENDOLEN: True. In matters of grave importance, style, not sincerity, is the vital thing. Mr. Worthing, what explanation 30 can you offer to me for pretending to have a brother? Was it in order that you might have an opportunity of coming up to town to see me as often as possible?

JACK: Can you doubt it, Miss Fairfax?

GWENDOLEN: I have the gravest doubts upon the subject. But 35 I intend to crush them. This is not the moment for German skepticism. (*Moving to* CECILY.) Their explanations appear to be quite satisfactory, especially Mr. Worthing's. That seems to me to have the stamp of truth upon it.

CECILY: I am more than content with what Mr. Moncrieff 40 said. His voice alone inspires one with absolute credulity.

GWENDOLEN: Then you think we should forgive them?

CECILY: Yes. I mean no.

GWENDOLEN: True! I had forgotten. There are principles at stake that one cannot surrender. Which of us should tell 45 them? The task is not a pleasant one.

CECILY: Could we not both speak at the same time?

GWENDOLEN: An excellent idea! I nearly always speak at the same time as other people. Will you take the time from me?

50 CECILY: Certainly. (GWENDOLEN *beats time with uplifted finger.*)

GWENDOLEN *and* CECILY: (*Speaking together.*) Your Christian names are still an insuperable barrier. That is all!

JACK *and* ALGERNON: (*Speaking together.*) Our Christian
55 names! Is that all? But we are going to be christened this afternoon.

GWENDOLEN: (*To* JACK.) For my sake you are prepared to do this terrible thing?

JACK: I am.

60 CECILY: (*To* ALGERNON.) To please me you are ready to face this fearful ordeal?

ALGERNON: I am!

GWENDOLEN: How absurd to talk of the equality of the sexes! Where questions of self-sacrifice are concerned, men are
65 infinitely beyond us.

JACK: We are. (*Clasps hands with* ALGERNON.)

CECILY: They have moments of physical courage of which we women know absolutely nothing.

GWENDOLEN: (*To* JACK.) Darling!

70 ALGERNON: (*To* CECILY.) Darling! (*They fall into each other's arms.*)

(*Enter* MERRIMAN. *When he enters he coughs loudly, seeing the situation.*)

MERRIMAN: Ahem! Ahem! Lady Bracknell!

JACK: Good heavens!

(*Enter* LADY BRACKNELL. *The couples separate in alarm. Exit* MERRIMAN.)

LADY BRACKNELL: Gwendolen! What does this mean?

75 GWENDOLEN: Merely that I am engaged to be married to Mr. Worthing, Mamma.

LADY BRACKNELL: Come here. Sit down. Sit down immediately. Hesitation of any kind is a sign of mental decay in the young, of physical weakness in the old. (*Turns to* JACK.) Ap-
80 prised, sir, of my daughter's sudden flight by her trusty maid, whose confidence I purchased by means of a small coin, I followed her at once by a luggage train. Her unhappy father is, I am glad to say, under the impression that she is attending a more than usually lengthy lecture by the
85 University Extension Scheme on the Influence of a Permanent Income on Thought. I do not propose to undeceive him. Indeed I have never undeceived him on any question. I would consider it wrong. But of course, you will clearly understand that all communication between yourself and
90 my daughter must cease immediately from this moment. On this point, as indeed on all points, I am firm.

JACK: I am engaged to be married to Gwendolen, Lady Bracknell!

LADY BRACKNELL: You are nothing of the kind, sir. And now,
95 as regards Algernon! . . . Algernon!

ALGERNON: Yes, Aunt Augusta.

LADY BRACKNELL: May I ask if it is in this house that your invalid friend Mr. Bunbury resides?

ALGERNON: (*Stammering.*) Oh, no! Bunbury doesn't live here.
100 Bunbury is somewhere else at present. In fact, Bunbury is dead.

LADY BRACKNELL: Dead! When did Mr. Bunbury die? His death must have been extremely sudden.

ALGERNON: (*Airily.*) Oh, I killed Bunbury this afternoon. I mean poor Bunbury died this afternoon. 105

LADY BRACKNELL: What did he die of?

ALGERNON: Bunbury? Oh, he was quite exploded.

LADY BRACKNELL: Exploded! Was he the victim of a revolutionary outrage? I was not aware that Mr. Bunbury was interested in social legislation. If so, he is well punished for 110 his morbidity.

ALGERNON: My dear Aunt Augusta, I mean he was found out! The doctors found out that Bunbury could not live, that is what I mean—so Bunbury died.

LADY BRACKNELL: He seems to have had great confidence in 115 the opinion of his physicians. I am glad, however, that he made up his mind at the last to some definite course of action, and acted under proper medical advice. And now that we have finally got rid of this Mr. Bunbury, may I ask, Mr. Worthing, who is that young person whose hand my 120 nephew Algernon is now holding in what seems to me a peculiarly unnecessary manner?

JACK: That lady is Miss Cecily Cardew, my ward. (LADY BRACKNELL *bows coldly to* CECILY.)

ALGERNON: I am engaged to be married to Cecily, Aunt Au- 125 gusta.

LADY BRACKNELL: I beg your pardon?

CECILY: Mr. Moncrieff and I are engaged to be married, lady Bracknell.

LADY BRACKNELL: (*With a shiver, crossing to the sofa and sitting* 130 *down.*) I do not know whether there is anything peculiarly exciting in the air of this particular part of Hertfordshire, but the number of engagements that go on seems to me considerably above the proper average that statistics have laid down for our guidance. I think some preliminary en- 135 quiry on my part would not be out of place. Mr. Worthing, is Miss Cardew at all connected with any of the larger railway stations in London? I merely desire information. Until yesterday I had no idea that there were any families or persons whose origin was a Terminus. (JACK 140 *looks perfectly furious, but restrains himself.*)

JACK: (*In a clear, cold voice.*) Miss Cardew is the granddaughter of the late Mr. Thomas Cardew of 149, Belgrave Square, S.W.; Gervase Park, Dorking, Surrey; and the Sporran, Fifeshire, N.B. 145

LADY BRACKNELL: That sounds not unsatisfactory. Three addresses always inspire confidence, even in tradesmen. But what proof have I of their authenticity?

JACK: I have carefully preserved the Court Guide of the period. They are open to your inspection, Lady Bracknell. 150

LADY BRACKNELL: (*Grimly.*) I have known strange errors in that publication.

JACK: Miss Cardew's family solicitors are Messrs. Markby, Markby, and Markby.

LADY BRACKNELL: Markby, Markby, and Markby? A firm of 155 the very highest position in their profession. Indeed I am told that one of the Mr. Markbys is occasionally to be seen at dinner parties. So far I am satisfied.

JACK: (*Very irritably.*) How extremely kind of you, Lady Bracknell! I have also in my possession, you will be pleased to hear, 160 certificates of Miss Cardew's birth, baptism, whooping cough, registration, vaccination, confirmation, and the measles; both the German and the English variety.

LADY BRACKNELL: Ah! A life crowded with incident, I see; though perhaps somewhat too exciting for a young girl. I 165

am not myself in favour of premature experiences. (*Rises, looks at her watch.*) Gwendolen! the time approaches for our departure. We have not a moment to lose. As a matter of form, Mr. Worthing, I had better ask you if Miss
170 Cardew has any little fortune?

JACK: Oh, about a hundred and thirty thousand pounds in the Funds. That is all. Good-bye, Lady Bracknell. So pleased to have seen you.

LADY BRACKNELL: (*Sitting down again.*) A moment, Mr. Wor-
175 thing. A hundred and thirty thousand pounds! And in the Funds! Miss Cardew seems to me a most attractive young lady, now that I look at her. Few girls of the present day have any really solid qualities, any of the qualities that last, and improve with time. We live, I regret to say, in an age of
180 surfaces. (*To* CECILY.) Come over here, dear. (CECILY *goes across.*) Pretty child! your dress is sadly simple, and your hair seems almost as Nature might have left it. But we can soon alter all that. A thoroughly experienced French maid produces a really marvelous result in a very brief space of time.
185 I remember recommending one to young Lady Lancing, and after three months her own husband did not know her.

JACK: (*Aside.*) And after six months nobody knew her.

LADY BRACKNELL: (*Glares at* JACK *for a few moments. Then bends, with a practised smile, to* CECILY.) Kindly turn round, sweet
190 child. (CECILY *turns completely round.*) No, the side view is what I want. (CECILY *presents her profile.*) Yes, quite as I expected. There are distinct social possibilities in your profile. The two weak points in our age are its want of principle and its want of profile. The chin a little higher, dear. Style
195 largely depends on the way the chin is worn. They are worn very high, just at present. Algernon!

ALGERNON: Yes, Aunt Augusta!

LADY BRACKNELL: There are distinct social possibilities in Miss Cardew's profile.
200 ALGERNON: Cecily is the sweetest, dearest, prettiest girl in the whole world. And I don't care twopence about social possibilities.

LADY BRACKNELL: Never speak disrespectfully of society, Algernon. Only people who can't get into it do that. (*To* CE-
205 CILY.) Dear child, of course you know that Algernon has nothing but his debts to depend upon. But I do not approve of mercenary marriages. When I married Lord Bracknell I had no fortune of any kind. But I never dreamed for a moment of allowing that to stand in my
210 way. Well, I suppose I must give my consent.

ALGERNON: Thank you, Aunt Augusta.

LADY BRACKNELL: Cecily, you may kiss me!

CECILY: (*Kisses her.*) Thank you, Lady Bracknell.

LADY BRACKNELL: You may also address me as Aunt Augusta
215 for the future.

CECILY: Thank you, Aunt Augusta.

LADY BRACKNELL: The marriage, I think, had better take place quite soon.

ALGERNON: Thank you, Aunt Augusta.
220 CECILY: Thank you, Aunt Augusta.

LADY BRACKNELL: To speak frankly, I am not in favour of long engagements. They give people the opportunity of finding out each other's character before marriage, which I think is never advisable.
225 JACK: I beg your pardon for interrupting you, Lady Bracknell, but this engagement is quite out of the question. I am Miss Cardew's guardian, and she cannot marry without

my consent until she comes of age. That consent I absolutely decline to give.

LADY BRACKNELL: Upon what grounds, may I ask? Algernon 230
is an extremely, I may almost say an ostentatiously, eligible young man. He has nothing, but he looks everything. What more can one desire?

JACK: It pains me very much to have to speak frankly to you, Lady Bracknell, about your nephew, but the fact is that I 235
do not approve at all of his moral character. I suspect him of being untruthful. (ALGERNON *and* CECILY *look at him in indignant amazement.*)

LADY BRACKNELL: Untruthful! My nephew Algernon? Impossible! He is an Oxonian. 240

JACK: I fear there can be no possible doubt about the matter. This afternoon, during my temporary absence in London on an important question of romance, he obtained admission to my house by means of the false pretence of being my brother. Under an assumed name he drank, I've just 245
been informed by my butler, an entire pint bottle of my Perrier-Jouet, Brut, '89; a wine I was specially reserving for myself. Continuing his disgraceful deception, he succeeded in the course of the afternoon in alienating the affections of my only ward. He subsequently stayed to tea, and devoured 250
every single muffin. And what makes his conduct all the more heartless is, that he was perfectly well aware from the first that I have no brother, that I never had a brother, and that I don't intend to have a brother, not even of any kind. I distinctly told him so myself yesterday afternoon. 255

LADY BRACKNELL: Ahem! Mr. Worthing, after careful consideration I have decided entirely to overlook my nephew's conduct to you.

JACK: That is very generous of you, Lady Bracknell. My own decision, however, is unalterable. I decline to give my con- 260
sent.

LADY BRACKNELL: (*To* CECILY.) Come here, sweet child. (CE-CILY *goes over.*) How old are you, dear?

CECILY: Well, I am really only eighteen, but I always admit to twenty when I go to evening parties. 265

LADY BRACKNELL: You are perfectly right in making some slight alteration. Indeed, no woman should ever be quite accurate about her age. It looks so calculating . . . (*In meditative manner.*) Eighteen, but admitting to twenty at evening parties. Well, it will not be very long before you are of age 270
and free from the restraints of tutelage. So I don't think your guardian's consent is, after all, a matter of any importance.

JACK: Pray excuse me, Lady Bracknell, for interrupting you again, but it is only fair to tell you that according to the terms of her grandfather's will Miss Cardew does not 275
come legally of age till she is thirty-five.

LADY BRACKNELL: That does not seem to me to be a grave objection. Thirty-five is a very attractive age. London society is full of women of the very highest birth who have, of their own free choice, remained thirty-five for years. Lady Dum- 280
bleton is an instance in point. To my own knowledge she has been thirty-five ever since she arrived at the age of forty, which was many years ago now. I see no reason why our dear Cecily should not be even still more attractive at the age you mention than she is at present. There will be a 285
large accumulation of property.

CECILY: Algy, could you wait for me till I was thirty-five?

ALGERNON: Of course I could, Cecily. You know I could.

CECILY: Yes, I felt it instinctively, but I couldn't wait all that time. I hate waiting even five minutes for anybody. It al- 290 ways makes me rather cross. I am not punctual myself, I know, but I do like punctuality in others, and waiting, even to be married, is quite out of the question.

ALGERNON: Then what is to be done, Cecily?

295 CECILY: I don't know, Mr. Moncrieff.

LADY BRACKNELL: My dear Mr. Worthing, as Miss Cardew states positively that she cannot wait till she is thirty-five—a remark which I am bound to say seems to me to show a somewhat impatient nature—I would beg of you

300 to reconsider your decision.

JACK: But my dear Lady Bracknell, the matter is entirely in your own hands. The moment you consent to my marriage with Gwendolen, I will most gladly allow your nephew to form an alliance with my ward.

305 LADY BRACKNELL: (*Rising and drawing herself up.*) You must be quite aware that what you propose is out of the question.

JACK: Then a passionate celibacy is all that any of us can look forward to.

LADY BRACKNELL: That is not the destiny I propose for

310 Gwendolen. Algernon, of course, can choose for himself. (*Pulls out her watch.*) Come, dear, (GWENDOLEN *rises.*) we have already missed five, if not six, trains. To miss any more might expose us to comment on the platform.

(*Enter* DR. CHASUBLE.)

CHASUBLE: Everything is quite ready for the christenings.

315 LADY BRACKNELL: The christenings, sir! Is not that somewhat premature?

CHASUBLE: (*Looking rather puzzled, and pointing to* JACK *and* AL-GERNON.) Both these gentlemen have expressed a desire for immediate baptism.

320 LADY BRACKNELL: At their age? The idea is grotesque and irreligious! Algernon, I forbid you to be baptized. I will not hear of such excesses. Lord Bracknell would be highly displeased if he learned that that was the way in which you wasted your time and money.

325 CHASUBLE: Am I to understand then that there are to be no christenings at all this afternoon?

JACK: I don't think that, as things are now, it would be of much practical value to either of us, Dr. Chasuble.

CHASUBLE: I am grieved to hear such sentiments from you,

330 Mr. Worthing. They savour of the heretical views of the Anabaptists, views that I have completely refuted in four of my unpublished sermons. However, as your present mood seems to be one peculiarly secular, I will return to the church at once. Indeed, I have just been informed by

335 the pewopener that for the last hour and a half Miss Prism has been waiting for me in the vestry.

LADY BRACKNELL: (*Starting.*) Miss Prism! Did I hear you mention a Miss Prism?

CHASUBLE: Yes, Lady Bracknell. I am on my way to join her.

340 LADY BRACKNELL: Pray allow me to detain you for a moment. This matter may prove to be one of vital importance to Lord Bracknell and myself. Is this Miss Prism a female of repellent aspect, remotely connected with education?

CHASUBLE: (*Somewhat indignantly.*) She is the most cultivated

345 of ladies, and the very picture of respectability.

LADY BRACKNELL: It is obviously the same person. May I ask what position she holds in your household?

CHASUBLE: (*Severely.*) I am a celibate, madam.

JACK: (*Interposing.*) Miss Prism, Lady Bracknell, has been for the last three years Miss Cardew's esteemed governess and 350 valued companion.

LADY BRACKNELL: In spite of what I hear of her, I must see her at once. Let her be sent for.

CHASUBLE: (*Looking off.*) She approaches; she is nigh.

(*Enter* MISS PRISM *hurriedly.*)

MISS PRISM: I was told you expected me in the vestry, dear 355 Canon. I have been waiting for you there for an hour and three-quarters. (*Catches sight of* LADY BRACKNELL, *who has fixed her with a stony glare.* MISS PRISM *grows pale and quails. She looks anxiously round as if desirous to escape.*)

LADY BRACKNELL: (*In a severe, judicial voice.*) Prism! (MISS 360 PRISM *bows her head in shame.*) Come here, Prism! (MISS PRISM *approaches in a humble manner.*) Prism! Where is that baby? (*General consternation. The Canon starts back in horror.* ALGERNON *and* JACK *pretend to be anxious to shield* CECILY *and* GWENDOLEN *from hearing the details of a terrible public* 365 *scandal.*) Twenty-eight years ago, Prism, you left Lord Bracknell's house, Number 104, Upper Grosvenor Street, in charge of a perambulator that contained a baby, of the male sex. You never returned. A few weeks later, through the elaborate investigations of the Metropolitan police, the 370 perambulator was discovered at midnight, standing by itself in a remote corner of Bayswater. It contained the manuscript of a three-volume novel of more than usually revolting sentimentality. (MISS PRISM *starts in involuntary indignation.*) But the baby was not there! (*Everyone looks at* 375 MISS PRISM.) Prism, where is that baby? (*A pause.*)

MISS PRISM: Lady Bracknell, I admit with shame that I do not know. I only wish I did. The plain facts of the case are these. On the morning of the day you mention, a day that is forever branded on my memory, I prepared as usual to take the baby 380 out in its perambulator. I had also with me a somewhat old but capacious hand-bag in which I had intended to place the manuscript of a work of fiction that I had written during my few unoccupied hours. In a moment of mental abstraction, for which I never can forgive myself, I deposited the manuscript 385 in the bassinette, and placed the baby in the hand-bag.

JACK: (*Who has been listening attentively.*) But where did you deposit the hand-bag?

MISS PRISM: Do not ask me, Mr. Worthing.

JACK: Miss Prism, this is a matter of no small importance to 390 me. I insist on knowing where you deposited the hand-bag that contained that infant.

MISS PRISM: I left it in the cloak-room of one of the larger railway stations in London.

JACK: What railway station? 395

MISS PRISM: (*Quite crushed.*) Victoria. The Brighton line. (*Sinks into a chair.*)

JACK: I must retire to my room for a moment. Gwendolen, wait here for me.

GWENDOLEN: If you are not too long, I will wait here for you 400 all my life.

(*Exit* JACK *in great excitement.*)

CHASUBLE: What do you think this means, Lady Bracknell?

LADY BRACKNELL: I dare not even suspect, Dr. Chasuble. I need hardly tell you that in families of high position

405 strange coincidences are not supposed to occur. They are
hardly considered the thing. (*Noises heard overhead as if
someone was throwing trunks about. Everybody looks up.*)

CECILY: Uncle Jack seems strangely agitated.

CHASUBLE: Your guardian has a very emotional nature.

410 LADY BRACKNELL: This noise is extremely unpleasant. It
sounds as if he was having an argument. I dislike arguments
of any kind. They are always vulgar, and often convincing.

CHASUBLE: (*Looking up.*) It has stopped now. (*The noise is redoubled.*)

415 LADY BRACKNELL: I wish he would arrive at some conclusion.

GWENDOLEN: The suspense is terrible. I hope it will last.

(*Enter* JACK *with a hand-bag of black leather in his hand.*)

JACK: (*Rushing over to* MISS PRISM.) Is this the hand-bag, Miss
Prism? Examine it carefully before you speak. The happiness of more than one life depends on your answer.

420 MISS PRISM: (*Calmly.*) It seems to be mine. Yes, here is the injury it received through the upsetting of a Gower Street
omnibus in younger and happier days. Here is the stain on
the lining caused by the explosion of a temperance bev-
erage, an incident that occurred at Leamington. And here,

425 on the lock, are my initials. I had forgotten that in an extravagant mood I had had them placed there. The bag is
undoubtedly mine. I am delighted to have it so unexpectedly restored to me. It has been a great inconvenience being without it all these years.

430 JACK: (*In a pathetic voice.*) Miss Prism, more is restored to you
than this hand-bag. I was the baby you placed in it.

MISS PRISM: (*Amazed.*) You?

JACK: (*Embracing her.*) Yes . . . mother!

MISS PRISM: (*Recoiling in indignant astonishment.*) Mr. Wor-
435 thing! I am unmarried!

JACK: Unmarried! I do not deny that is a serious blow. But after all, who has the right to cast a stone against one who has
suffered? Cannot repentance wipe out an act of folly? Why
should there be one law for men and another for women?
440 Mother, I forgive you. (*Tries to embrace her again.*)

MISS PRISM: (*Still more indignant.*) Mr. Worthing, there is some
error. (*Pointing to* LADY BRACKNELL.) There is the lady who
can tell you who you really are.

JACK: (*After a pause.*) Lady Bracknell, I hate to seem inquisi-
445 tive, but would you kindly inform me who I am?

LADY BRACKNELL: I am afraid that the news I have to give
you will not altogether please you. You are the son of my
poor sister, Mrs. Moncrieff, and consequently Algernon's
elder brother.

450 JACK: Algy's elder brother! Then I have a brother after all. I
knew I had a brother! I always said I had a brother! Cecily,—
how could you have ever doubted that I had a brother?
(*Seizes hold of* ALGERNON.) Dr. Chasuble, my unfortunate
brother. Miss Prism, my unfortunate brother. Gwendolen,
455 my unfortunate brother. Algy, you young scoundrel, you will
have to treat me with more respect in the future. You have
never behaved to me like a brother in all your life.

ALGERNON: Well, not till to-day, old boy, I admit. I did my best,
however, though I was out of practice. (*Shakes hands.*)

460 GWENDOLEN: (*To* JACK.) My own! But what own are you?
What is your Christian name, now that you have become
someone else?

JACK: Good heavens! . . . I had quite forgotten that point. Your
decision on the subject of my name is irrevocable, I suppose?

GWENDOLEN: I never change, except in my affections.   465

CECILY: What a noble nature you have, Gwendolen!

JACK: Then the question had better be cleared up at once.
Aunt Augusta, a moment. At the time when Miss Prism
left me in the hand-bag, had I been christened already?

LADY BRACKNELL: Every luxury that money could buy, in-   470
cluding christening, had been lavished on you by your
fond and doting parents.

JACK: Then I was christened! That is settled. Now, what name
was I given? Let me know the worst.

LADY BRACKNELL: Being the eldest son you were naturally   475
christened after your father.

JACK: (*Irritably.*) Yes, but what was my father's Christian
name?

LADY BRACKNELL: (*Meditatively.*) I cannot at the present moment recall what the General's Christian name was. But I   480
have no doubt he had one. He was eccentric, I admit. But
only in later years. And that was the result of the Indian
climate, and marriage, and indigestion, and other things of
that kind.

JACK: Algy! Can't you recollect what our father's Christian   485
name was?

ALGERNON: My dear boy, we were never even on speaking
terms. He died before I was a year old.

JACK: His name would appear in the Army Lists of the period, I suppose, Aunt Augusta?   490

LADY BRACKNELL: The General was essentially a man of
peace, except in his domestic life. But I have no doubt his
name would appear in any military directory.

JACK: The Army Lists of the last forty years are here. These
delightful records should have been my constant study.   495
(*Rushes to bookcase and tears the books out.*) M. Generals . . .
Mallam, Maxbohm, Magley, what ghastly names they
have—Markby, Migsby, Mobbs, Moncrieff! Lieutenant
1840, Captain, Lieutenant-Colonel, Colonel, General
1869, Christian names, Ernest John. (*Puts book very quietly*   500
down and speaks quite calmly.) I always told you, Gwendolen, my name was Ernest didn't I? Well, it is Ernest after all, I mean it naturally is Ernest.

LADY BRACKNELL: Yes, I remember the General was called
Ernest. I knew I had some particular reason for disliking   505
the name.

GWENDOLEN: Ernest! My own Ernest! I felt from the first
that you could have no other name!

JACK: Gwendolen, it is a terrible thing for a man to find out
suddenly that all his life he has been speaking nothing but   510
the truth. Can you forgive me?

GWENDOLEN: I can. For I feel sure that you are sure to
change.

JACK: My own one!

CHASUBLE: (*To* MISS PRISM.) Lætitia! (*Embraces her.*)   515

MISS PRISM: (*Enthusiastically.*) Frederick! At last!

ALGERNON: Cecily! (*Embraces her.*) At last!

JACK: Gwendolen! (*Embraces her.*) At last!

LADY BRACKNELL: My nephew, you seem to be displaying
signs of triviality.   520

JACK: On the contrary, Aunt Augusta, I've now realized for
the first time in my life the vital Importance of Being
Earnest.

Anton Chekhov

The work of Anton Chekhov (1860–1904) is noted for its objectivity, its sympathetic yet almost clinical examination of turn-of-the-century Russian life. Born in the provincial town of Taganrog, Chekhov trained for a career in medicine and began practicing as a physician in the mid-1880s. At that time he also began to write his first short stories. In his fiction, as in his later plays, Chekhov adopted a mildly ironic attitude toward his subjects, one that resisted sensation and melodrama in favor of a more neutral stance; as he wrote in a letter, "It is necessary that on stage everything should be as complex and as simple as in life. People are having dinner, and while they're having it, their future happiness may be decided or their lives may be about to be shattered." Chekhov's life was shattered in just this way, simply, suddenly, and casually. In 1884 he coughed up blood, the sure sign that he had contracted tuberculosis. The disease could not be cured and required repeated periods of convalescence; an early death was a certainty.

Chekhov began writing plays in the 1880s as well, mainly short comic sketches he called "vaudevilles," among them *The Bear* (1888), *The Proposal* (1889), and *The Wedding* (1890). In 1896, the Alexandrinsky Theater in St. Petersburg performed his full-length drama, *The Seagull*. The play's indirect plotting and its avoidance of the conventional climaxes of melodrama confused actors and audiences alike, and it failed. Chekhov was persuaded by Constantin Stanislavski and Vladimir Nemirovich-Danchenko to mount the play in their newly founded Moscow Art Theater (MAT) in 1898. Stanislavski's commitment to a restrained style of performance, emphasizing psychological complexity and balanced playing by the entire ensemble is generally credited with making the MAT production a success; a seagull became the company's signature. Chekhov produced three more major plays with the MAT. He revised *The Wood Demon* (1889) as *Uncle Vanya* in 1899 and then produced *Three Sisters* (1901) and *The Cherry Orchard* (1904). Chekhov married the actress Olga Knipper, who played leading roles in his plays, including Madame Ranevskaya in *The Cherry Orchard* in 1901, and spent the final years of his life convalescing in Yalta.

THE CHERRY ORCHARD

The action of Chekhov's plays is usually indirect, not progressive and consequential, in the manner of Ibsen's work. Instead, a Chekhov play generally opens with the arrival of some well-to-do characters in the provincial scene of the play and closes with their departure: Yelena and Serbryakov in *Uncle Vanya,* the regiment and its romantic Lieutenant Colonel Vershinin in *Three Sisters,* Madame Ranevskaya and her entourage in *The Cherry Orchard*. In between, we see how the lives of the characters are changed and yet somehow remain the same, as though their interaction worked to reveal the fundamentally static condition of their lives.

More than Chekhov's earlier plays, perhaps, *The Cherry Orchard* also seems to prefigure the fall of a class: the leisured, ineffectual, yet attractive Madame Ranevskaya and her brother, who own the estate but are incapable of bringing it into the twentieth century. We are left with the final vision of the ancient servant Firs, himself a relic of the emancipation of the serfs half a century before, locked in the house while the orchard falls to the axes. The future seems to promise a brutal and sudden change, which the main characters of the play are unable to face. The play takes, at best, an ironic attitude toward the fortunes of Lyubov and Gaev. Tragedies in Chekhov's plays occur in the momentary actions of daily life; they are casual and haphazard, almost accidental, and yet alter the course of life irrevocably. Varya and Lopakhin, for example, bumble their way through the long-expected scene of their engagement, but the scene doesn't come off, Lopakhin remains uncommitted and Varya remains a poor relation dependent on the charity of her family, soon to be sent away to work as a governess. For Varya, the misplayed scene has a bitter and tragic finality.

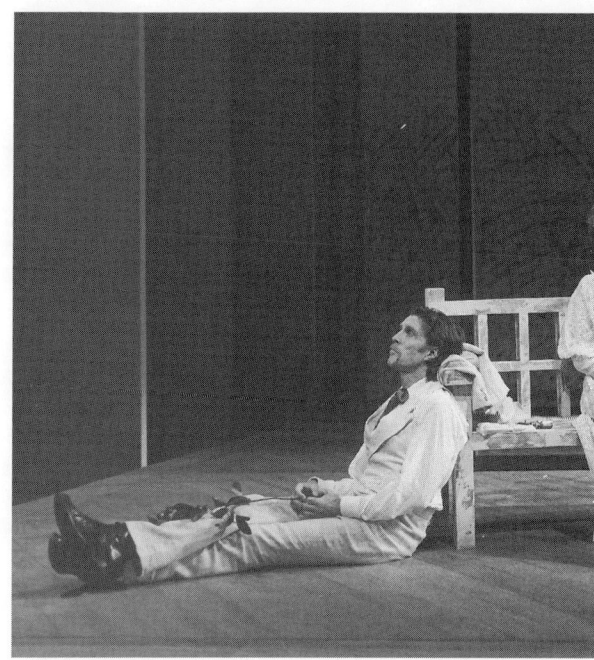

A scene from Anton Chekhov's *The Cherry Orchard*.

Chekhov calls the play a "comedy," and despite its mournful tone we might consider what he might have had in mind. Chekhov seems sympathetic to the tragedies of daily life, but often trains a skeptical eye on characters who assume the self-regarding accents of high tragedy, or whose sense of themselves verges on self-delusion, the solipsistic inability to see the world around them. Throughout *The Cherry Orchard,* some characters seem lost in a world of dreams: think of Gaev and his sister arriving in their childhood nursery, of Trofimov's vague and clumsy plans for the future, of kindly old Firs. Chekhov forces us to regard his characters with a certain distance, largely by weaving a texture of comedy into the fabric of the play. Everyone ridicules Gaev's sentimental apostrophe to the bookcase in act 1, and Chekhov adds a list of vaudeville tricks to his characters' performances: Lopakhin's "Ba-a-a" at the opening of the play, Yepikhodov crushing the hatbox with the suitcase in act 4, Trofimov tumbling down the stairs, Charlotta's music-hall turns, Firs's feeble efforts to keep everyone warm. The famous, inexplicable sound effect of act 2—the breaking string—may work in this way as well. It both underscores the mournful tone of the scene and interrupts the illusionistic surface of the action, forcing the audience out of a fully sympathetic engagement with Chekhov's sentimental characters. The play, in this light, seems "tragic" only if we accept the main characters' view of their predicament and accept their idle, self-absorbed fantasies as the stuff of tragedy.

Chekhov went to some lengths to keep the play's tone unsettled, in part because he knew that Stanislavski tended to regard his work as high tragedy. Chekhov suggested to Stanislavski that he play the part of Lopakhin: "When I was writing Lopakhin," he wrote in a letter to the actor, "I thought of it as a part for you. . . . Lopakhin is a merchant, of course, but he is a very decent person in every sense. He must behave with perfect decorum, like an educated man, with no petty ways or tricks of any sort, and it seemed to me that this part, the central one of the play, would come out brilliantly in your hands. . . . you must remember that Varya, a serious and religious girl, is in love with Lopakhin; she wouldn't be in love with a mere money-grubber." Describing Lopakhin in terms of Varya is typical of

Chekhov's tendency to think of the ensemble as a whole, rather than in terms of individual characters; but we might also think that Chekhov has strategic designs on Stanislavski as well. Fearing that Stanislavski would want to play the part of Gaev, and would play the part too sympathetically, Chekhov tried to persuade him to train his talents on the comic part of Lopakhin. Imagining Stanislavski as Lopakhin, we begin to see the kind of drama Chekhov had imagined: had he taken the part (Stanislavski played Gaev after all), Stanislavski would have played against the grain of broad humor that underlies Lopakhin, humanizing the role, creating neither a fully sympathetic character nor a vulgar comedian, but something in between. Similarly, *The Cherry Orchard* as a whole strikes a balance somewhere between comedy and tragedy, in which comic and tragic possibilities strain against one another as ways of interpreting the play and the experience of our lives.

As it turned out, Stanislavski's direction emphasized the play's sombre tone, the sense of a generation falling before modern progress as the orchard falls to the axes. After the Russian Revolution in 1917, *The Cherry Orchard* came to be regarded as nearly a prophetic allegory of the progress of history, the displacing of the feudal past by the modern, industrial present.

A pronunciation guide for Russian names appears on pp. 482–483.

THE CHERRY ORCHARD

Anton Chekhov
TRANSLATED BY CAROL ROCAMORA

CHARACTERS

RANEVSKAYA, LYUBOV ANDREEVNA, *a landowner*
ANYA, *her daughter, age seventeen*
VARYA, *her adopted daughter, age twenty-four*
GAEV, *Leonid Andreevich, Ranevskaya's brother*
LOPAKHIN, *Yermolai Alekseevich, a merchant*
TROFIMOV, *Pyotr Sergeevich, a student*
SIMEONOV-PISHCHIK, *Boris Borisovich, a landowner*
CHARLOTTA IVANOVNA, *a governess*
YEPIKHODOV, *Semyon Panteleevich, a clerk*
DUNYASHA, *a maid*

FIRS, *a servant, an old man of eighty-seven*
YASHA, *a young servant*
A PASSERBY
A STATIONMASTER
A POST OFFICE CLERK
GUESTS, SERVANTS, CARRIAGE DRIVERS

The action takes place on the estate of Lyubov Andreevna Ranevskaya

ACT ONE

A room, which is still called the nursery. One of the doors leads to ANYA's *room. It is dawn, just before sunrise. It is already May, the cherry trees are all in bloom, but outside it is still cold; there is an early morning frost in the orchard. The windows in the room are closed.*

Enter DUNYASHA *with a candle, and* LOPAKHIN *with a book in his hand.*

LOPAKHIN: The train's arrived, thank God. What time is it?
DUNYASHA: Almost two. (*Puts out the candle.*) It's already getting light out.
LOPAKHIN: So how late is the train, then? A couple of hours,
5 at least. (*Yawns and stretches.*) Well, I've made a fool of myself, then, haven't I! Hm? Came all the way out here, just to meet the train, and fell fast asleep . . . Sat here waiting and dozed right off. Annoying, isn't it . . . You should have woken me up.
10 DUNYASHA: I thought you'd already gone. (*Listens.*) Listen, I think they're here.
LOPAKHIN: (*Listens.*) No . . . They've got to get their baggage first, you know, that sort of thing . . .

(*Pause.*)

Lyubov Andreevna, she's been living abroad for five years,
15 I don't know, I can't even imagine what's become of her now . . . She's a fine person, you know . . . a warm, kind person. I remember, once, when I was a boy, oh, about fifteen years old, say, and my father—he had a shop here in the village then—my father, he hit me in the face with his
20 fist, blood was pouring from my nose . . . We'd come out into the courtyard together, somehow, and he was drunk. And there was Lyubov Andreevna, I remember her so vividly, so young then, so graceful, so slender, she took me by the hand, brought me over to the washstand, right into
25 this very room, into the nursery. "Don't cry, little peasant," she said, "it will heal before your wedding day . . ."

(*Pause.*)

Little peasant . . . Yes, my father was a peasant, it's true enough, and here I am in a three-piece suit and fancy shoes. A silk purse from a sow's ear, or something like that, isn't that how the expression goes . . . Yes . . . The only dif- 30 ference is, now I'm rich, I've got a lot of money, but don't look too closely, once a peasant . . . (*Leafs through the book.*) Look at me, I read through this entire book and didn't understand a word of it. Read it and dozed right off.

(*Pause.*)

DUNYASHA: The dogs didn't sleep at all last night, they can 35 sense their masters are coming home.
LOPAKHIN: What's wrong with you, Dunyasha . . .
DUNYASHA: My hands are trembling. I'm going to faint, I know I am.
LOPAKHIN: You're much too high-strung, Dunyasha. And 40 look at you, all dressed up like a young lady, hair done up, too. You mustn't do that. Remember who you are.

(*Enter* YEPIKHODOV *with a bouquet; he is wearing a jacket and highly polished boots, which squeak loudly; upon entering, he drops the bouquet.*)

YEPIKHODOV: (*Picks up the bouquet.*) Look what the gardener sent. Put them on the dining room table. That's what he said. (*Gives the bouquet to* DUNYASHA.) 45
LOPAKHIN: And bring me some kvass, will you?
DUNYASHA: Yes, sir. (*Leaves.*)
YEPIKHODOV: We have an early morning frost, we have three degrees below zero, and we have the cherry blossoms all in bloom. I don't approve of our climate. (*Sighs.*) Really, I 50 don't. Our climate doesn't work, it just doesn't work. It's not conducive. And would you like to hear more, Yermolai Alekseich, well, then you will, because the day before yesterday, I bought these boots, and, trust me, they squeak so much, that they are beyond hope. Now how can I oil 55 them? Tell me? How?
LOPAKHIN: Enough. You're getting on my nerves.
YEPIKHODOV: Every day some new disaster befalls me. A new day, a new disaster. But do I grumble, do I complain, no, I don't, I accept it, look, I'm smiling, even. 60

(DUNYASHA *enters, gives* LOPAKHIN *some kvass.*)

I'm going now. (*Stumbles against a chair, which falls down.*) There . . . (*As if vindicated.*) You see? I mean, that's the situation, and excuse me for saying so . . . Remarkable, even . . . isn't it! (*Exits.*)

65 DUNYASHA: Yermolai Alekseich, I have something to tell you . . . Yepikhodov has proposed to me.

LOPAKHIN: Ah!

DUNYASHA: But I don't know, really . . . He's a nice enough fellow, you know, quiet and all, it's just that whenever he
70 starts to talk, I can't understand a word he's saying. I mean, it all sounds so sweet and sincere, only it just doesn't make any sense. I like him, I mean, I think I like him. And he? He adores me. But he's such an unfortunate fellow, you know, really, every day it's something else. They even have
75 a name for him, do you know what they call him: "Mister Disaster" . . .

LOPAKHIN: (*Listens.*) I think they're coming . . .

DUNYASHA: They're coming! What's happening to me . . . I'm freezing, look, I'm shivering all over.

80 LOPAKHIN: They're really coming! Let's go meet them. Will she recognize me? We haven't seen each other in five years.

DUNYASHA: (*Agitated.*) I'm going to faint, I know I am . . . Look, I'm fainting!

(*Two carriages are heard pulling up to the house.* LOPAKHIN *and* DUNYASHA *exit quickly. The stage is empty. Then there is noise in the adjacent rooms.* FIRS *hurries across the stage to meet* LYUBOV ANDREEVNA; *he is leaning on a cane, and is dressed in old-fashioned livery and a high hat; he mutters something to himself, but it is impossible to make out a single word. The offstage noise crescendos. A voice calls out; "Let's go this way through here . . ." Enter* LYUBOV ANDREEVNA, ANYA, *and* CHARLOTTA IVANOVNA *with a little dog on a leash; they are all dressed in traveling clothes. Enter* VARYA, *wearing a coat and a shawl,* GAEV, SIMEONOV-PISHCHIK, LOPAKHIN, DUNYASHA *carrying a bundle and an umbrella,* SERVANTS *carrying luggage—they all come through the room.*)

ANYA: This way! Mama, do you remember what room this is?
85 LYUBOV ANDREEVNA: (*Ecstatic, in tears.*) The nursery!

VARYA: How cold it is, my hands are numb. (*To* LYUBOV ANDREEVNA.) Look, Mamochka, your rooms, violet and white, just as you left them.

LYUBOV ANDREEVNA: My nursery, my darling nursery, my
90 beautiful room . . . I slept here, when I was a child . . . (*Weeps.*) And now, I'm a child again . . . (*Kisses her brother,* VARYA, *and her brother again.*) And Varya looks the same as ever, just like a little nun. And Dunyasha I recognize, of course . . . (*Kisses* DUNYASHA.)

95 GAEV: The train was two hours late. How do you like that? How's that for efficiency!

CHARLOTTA: (*To* PISHCHIK.) My dog eats walnuts, too.

PISHCHIK: (*Amazed.*) Imagine that!

(*They all exit, except for* ANYA *and* DUNYASHA.)

DUNYASHA: We've been waiting forever . . . (*Takes* ANYA's *coat*
100 *and hat.*)

ANYA: I didn't sleep one moment the whole journey long, four whole nights . . . and now I'm absolutely frozen!

DUNYASHA: You left during Lent, we had snow then, and frost, and now! My darling! (*Bursts out laughing, kisses her.*) I've waited forever for you, my precious, my joy . . . And I've got 105
something to tell you, I can't wait one minute longer. . . .

ANYA: (*Listlessly.*) Now what . . .

DUNYASHA: Yepikhodov, the clerk, proposed to me just after Easter.

ANYA: Not again . . . (*Adjusts her hair.*) I've lost all my hair- 110
pins . . . (*She is exhausted; she almost sways on her feet.*)

DUNYASHA: No, really, I don't know what to think, any more. He adores me, God, how he adores me!

ANYA: (*Gazes at the door to her room, tenderly.*) My very own room, my windows, it's as if I never left. I'm home! And to- 115
morrow I'll wake up, and I'll run out into the orchard . . . Oh, if only I could rest! I'm so exhausted—I didn't sleep one moment the whole way, I was so worried.

DUNYASHA: Pyotr Sergeich arrived the day before yesterday.

ANYA: (*Overjoyed.*) Petya! 120

DUNYASHA: He's out in the bathhouse, asleep, that's where he's staying. "I'm afraid of being in the way," he said. (*Glances at her pocket watch.*) We ought to wake him up, but Varvara Mikhailovna gave us strict orders not to. "Don't you dare wake him up," she said. 125

(*Enter* VARYA, *a bunch of keys hanging from her belt.*)

VARYA: Dunyasha, go, quickly, bring the coffee . . . Mamochka wants coffee.

DUNYASHA: Right away. (*Exits.*)

VARYA: So, thank God, you're here. You're home at last! (*Embracing her.*) My darling's home! My angel is home! 130

ANYA: I've been through so much.

VARYA: I can imagine.

ANYA: I left during Holy Week, it was so cold then, remember? And Charlotta Ivanovna talked the whole way, talked and played card tricks. How could you have stuck me 135
with Charlotta! . . .

VARYA: You can't travel alone, darling. At seventeen!

ANYA: When we arrived in Paris, it was cold there, too, and snowing. My French is terrible. Mama lived on the fifth floor, and when I finally got there, the flat was filled with 140
all sorts of French people, ladies, an old Catholic priest with a little book, and, oh, it was so uncomfortable there, so stuffy, the room was filled with smoke. And suddenly I felt sorry for Mama, so very sorry, I threw my arms around her neck, I held her so tight, I couldn't let go. And Mama 145
kept clinging to me, and weeping . . .

VARYA: (*In tears.*) Enough, enough . . .

ANYA: She had already sold the dacha near Menton, she had nothing left, nothing at all. And neither did I, not a single kopek, we hardly had enough money to get home. And 150
Mama just doesn't understand it, still! There we are, sitting in the station restaurant, and she orders the most expensive thing on the menu, she gives the waiter a ruble tip for tea. Charlotta, too. And Yasha orders a complete dinner, it's simply terrible. Yasha is Mama's butler, you know. We 155
brought him with us . . .

VARYA: I've seen him, the devil

ANYA: So, tell me! Have we paid the interest yet?

VARYA: With what?

ANYA: Dear God, dear God . . . 160

VARYA: And in August, the estate will be sold . . .

ANYA: Dear God . . .

LOPAKHIN: (*Peeks through the door and makes a 'bleating' sound.*) Ba-a-a . . . (*Exits.*)

165 VARYA: (*In tears.*) I'd like to give him such a . . . (*Makes a threatening gesture with her fist.*)

ANYA: (*Embraces* VARYA, *softly.*) Varya, has he proposed yet? (VARYA *shakes her head "no."*) But he loves you, he does . . . Why don't you talk about it, what are you two waiting

170 for?

VARYA: I know nothing will ever come of it, nothing. He's so busy, he has no time for me, really . . . he pays no attention to me at all. Well, God bless him, but it's too painful for me even to look at him . . . Everyone talks about our wed-

175 ding, everyone congratulates us, but the fact is, there's absolutely nothing to it, it's all a dream . . . (*Changes tone.*) Your brooch looks just like a little bee.

ANYA: (*Sadly.*) Mama bought it. (*She goes to her room, speaking in a gay, child-like voice.*) And in Paris, I went up in a hot air

180 balloon!

VARYA: My darling's home! My angel is home!

(DUNYASHA *has already returned with the coffee pot and prepares the coffee.*)

(*Stands by the doorway.*) All day long, darling, I go about my business, I run the household, I do my chores, but all the time I'm thinking, dreaming. If only we could marry you

185 off to a rich man, then I'd find peace, I'd go to a cloister, and then on a pilgrimage to Kiev, to Moscow, and on and on, from one holy place to the next . . . on and on. A blessing!

ANYA: The birds are singing in the orchard. What time is it?

VARYA: After two, it must be . . . Time for you to sleep, dar-

190 ling. (*Goes into* ANYA's *room.*) Yes, a blessing!

(YASHA *enters with a rug, and a traveling bag.*)

YASHA: (*Crosses the stage, discreetly.*) May I?

DUNYASHA: I wouldn't have recognized you, Yasha. How you've changed, since you've been abroad.

YASHA: Hm . . . And who are you?

195 DUNYASHA: When you left, I was about 'so' high . . . (*Indicates.*) Dunyasha, Fyodor Kozoedov's daughter. Don't you remember!

YASHA: Hm . . . Ripe as a cucumber! (*Glances around, and then grabs her and embraces her; she screams and drops a saucer.*

200 YASHA *exits quickly.*)

VARYA: (*In the doorway, displeased.*) What's going on here?

DUNYASHA: (*In tears.*) I broke a saucer . . .

VARYA: That means good luck.

ANYA: (*Coming out of her room.*) We'd better warn Mama:

205 Petya's here . . .

VARYA: I gave strict orders not to wake him up.

ANYA: (*Deep in thought.*) Father died six years ago, and one month later my little brother Grisha drowned in the river, a lovely little seven-year-old boy. Mama couldn't endure it,

210 she ran away, she ran away without once looking back . . . (*Shudders.*) How well I understand her, if only she knew!

(*Pause.*)

And Petya Trofimov was Grisha's tutor, he might remind her of it all . . .

(*Enter* FIRS, *in a jacket and white waistcoat.*)

FIRS: (*Goes to the coffee pot, anxiously.*) The mistress will take her coffee here . . . (*Puts on white gloves.*) Is the coffee 215 ready? (*Sternly, to* DUNYASHA.) You! Where is the cream?

DUNYASHA: Oh, my God . . . (*Rushes out.*)

FIRS: (*Fusses with the coffee pot.*) Pathetic fool . . . (*Mutters to himself under his breath.*) They've just returned from Paris . . . Now in the old days, the master used to go to Paris, too . . . 220 by horse and carriage . . . (*Bursts out laughing.*)

VARYA: What is it, Firs?

FIRS: Yes, and what may I do for you? (*Overjoyed.*) My mistress has come home! I've waited for so long! Now I can die . . . (*Weeps with joy.*) 225

(*Enter* LYUBOV ANDREEVNA, GAEV, LOPAKHIN, *and* SIMEONOV-PISHCHIK; SIMEONOV-PISHCHIK *wears a lightweight coat, fitted at the waist, and wide trousers. As he walks,* GAEV *gestures, as if he were playing a game of billiards.*)

LYUBOV ANDREEVNA: How does it go? Wait—don't tell me, let me think . . . "Yellow into the corner pocket! Double into the middle!"

GAEV: "Cut shot into the corner!" Once upon a time, sister dearest, we slept in this very room, you and I, and now I'm 230 fifty-one years old, strange, isn't? . . .

LOPAKHIN: Yes, time flies.

GAEV: Beg pardon?

LOPAKHIN: As I was saying, time flies.

GAEV: It smells of patchouli in here. 235

ANYA: I'm going to bed. Good night, Mama. (*Kisses her mother.*)

LYUBOV ANDREEVNA: My beloved child. (*Kisses her hands.*) Are you glad you're home? I simply can't get hold of myself.

ANYA: Good night, Uncle.

GAEV: (*Kisses her face, hands.*) God bless you. You are the im- 240 age of your mother! (*To his sister.*) Lyuba, you looked exactly like this at her age.

(ANYA *gives her hand to* LOPAKHIN *and* PISHCHIK; *she exits, and closes the door behind her.*)

LYUBOV ANDREEVNA: She's exhausted, really.

PISHCHIK: A tiring journey, no doubt.

VARYA: (*To* LOPAKHIN *and* PISHCHIK.) So, gentlemen? It's almost 245 three o'clock in the morning, let's not overstay our welcome.

LYUBOV ANDREEVNA: (*Laughs.*) You're the same as ever, Varya. (*Draws her close and kisses her.*) First I'll have my coffee, then we'll all go, yes?

(FIRS *places a cushion under her feet.*)

Thank you, dearest. I've gotten so used to coffee. I drink 250 it day and night. Thank you, my darling old man. (*Kisses* FIRS.)

VARYA: I'll go see if they've brought everything in . . . (*Exits.*)

LYUBOV ANDREEVNA: Am I really sitting here? (*Bursts out laughing.*) I feel like jumping up and down, and waving my 255 arms in the air! (*Covers her face with her hands.*) No, really, I must be dreaming! God knows, I love my country, I love it passionately, I couldn't even see out of the train window, I wept the whole way. (*In tears.*) Never mind, we must have our coffee. Thank you, Firs, thank you, my darling 260 old man. I'm so glad you're still alive.

FIRS: The day before yesterday.

GAEV: He's hard of hearing.

LOPAKHIN: I'd better be going; I leave for Kharkov at five this
morning. What a nuisance! I only wanted to see you, that's
all, to talk to you a little . . . You're as lovely as ever . . . 265

PISHCHIK: (*Sighs heavily.*) Even lovelier . . . All dressed up,
Parisian style . . . I'm head-over-heels, as they say!

LOPAKHIN: People like Leonid Andreich here, they say all
sorts of things about me, call me a boor, a kulak, but re- 270
ally, it doesn't matter, I couldn't care less. Let them say
whatever they like. I only want you to believe in me, as
you always did, to look at me with those beautiful, soulful
eyes, as you used to, once. Merciful God! My father was a
serf, he belonged to your grandfather and then to your fa- 275
ther, but it was you, yes, you, who did so much for me
once, so much, and I've forgotten everything now, I love
you like my own flesh and blood . . . more, even, than my
own flesh and blood.

LYUBOV ANDREEVNA: I can't sit still, I'm in such a state . . . 280
(*Jumps up and walks around the room, agitated.*) I simply can't
bear all this joy . . . Go ahead, laugh at me, I'm being foolish, I know it . . . My dear little bookcase . . . (*Kisses the
bookcase.*) My own little table.

GAEV: Nanny died while you were gone. 285

LYUBOV ANDREEVNA: (*Sits and drinks coffee.*) Yes, God rest her
soul. They wrote me.

GAEV: Anastasy died, too. And cross-eyed Petrushka—you remember him—he ran away, he lives in town now, at the
district superintendent's. (*Takes a box of fruit drops out of his* 290
pocket, pops one into his mouth.)

PISHCHIK: My daughter, Dashenka . . . she sends her regards . . .

LOPAKHIN: I'd like to tell you some good news, if I may, some
cheerful news, all right? (*Looks at his watch.*) I've got to go,
there's no time to talk . . . so, very briefly, then. As you al- 295
ready know, your cherry orchard is being sold to pay off the
debts, the auction date has been set for the twenty-second
of August, but don't you worry, my dear, you don't have to
lose any sleep over this, rest assured, there is a way out . . .
Here's my plan. Your attention, please! Your estate is located 300
only thirteen miles from town, roughly, a railroad runs
nearby, so if the cherry orchard and the land along the river
are divided up into plots and then leased for summer homes,
why then you'll receive at least 25,000 in yearly income.

GAEV: Forgive me, but what nonsense! 305

LYUBOV ANDREEVNA: I don't quite understand you, Yermolai
Alekseich.

LOPAKHIN: You'll receive at least twenty-five rubles a year per
three acre plot from the summer tenants, and if you ad-
vertise right away, I'll guarantee you, by autumn, there 310
won't be a single plot left, they'll all be bought up. In a
word, congratulations, you're saved. The site is marvelous,
the river is deep. Only, of course, you'll have to clear it
out, get rid of some things . . . for example, let us say, tear
down all the old buildings, and this house, too, which isn't 315
much good for anything any more, cut down the old
cherry orchard . . .

LYUBOV ANDREEVNA: Cut it down? Forgive me, my darling,
but you have no idea what you're talking about. If there is
one thing in the entire province that's of interest, that's re- 320
markable, even, why it's our own cherry orchard.

LOPAKHIN: The only thing remarkable about this orchard is
that it's so big. There's a cherry crop once every two

years, and yes, there are a lot of them, but what good are
they, nobody buys them. 325

GAEV: There is a reference to this cherry orchard in the
Encyclopaedia.

LOPAKHIN: (*Looks at his watch.*) Unless we come up with a plan,
unless we reach a decision, then on the twenty-second of
August the cherry orchard and the entire estate will be auc- 330
tioned off. Make up your minds, will you, please! There is
no other way, I swear to you. None. Absolutely none.

FIRS: Once upon a time, forty—fifty years ago, they used to
dry the cherries, soak them, marinate them, preserve
them, and often . . . 335

GAEV: Hush, Firs.

FIRS: And often, they would send cart loads of dried cherries
to Moscow and Kharkov. Brought in heaps of money!
And those dried cherries, oh, how soft they were, soft,
sweet, plump, juicy, fragrant . . . They knew the recipe in 340
those days . . .

LYUBOV ANDREEVNA: Yes, where is that recipe now?

FIRS: Forgotten. No one remembers it any more.

PISHCHIK: (*To* LYUBOV ANDREEVNA.) Tell us! What is it like in
Paris? Did you eat frogs' legs? 345

LYUBOV ANDREEVNA: I ate crocodile.

PISHCHIK: Imagine that . . .

LOPAKHIN: Up until now, we've only had landowners and
peasants living in our countryside, but now, the summer
people are starting to appear among us. All the towns, 350
even the smallest ones, are surrounded by summer homes
now. And, it's possible to predict that, in twenty years or
so, the summer population will multiply beyond our
wildest dreams. Now they're just sitting out on their bal-
conies, drinking their tea, but just wait, soon it will come 355
to pass, you'll see, they'll start cultivating their little plots
of land, and your cherry orchard will bloom again with
wealth, prosperity, happiness . . .

GAEV: (*Indignant.*) What nonsense!

(*Enter* VARYA *and* YASHA.)

VARYA: Two telegrams came for you, Mamochka. (*Takes keys* 360
and unlocks the antique bookcase; the keys make a clinking
sound.) Here they are.

LYUBOV ANDREEVNA: From Paris. (*Rips them up, without read-*
ing them.) I'm through with Paris.

GAEV: And do you know, Lyuba, how old this bookcase is? 365
Only one week ago, I pull out the bottom drawer, I look,
and what do I see—a mark burned into it, a number. This
bookcase was built exactly one hundred years ago. How
do you like that? Eh? We may now celebrate the jubilee
anniversary of this bookcase, ladies and gentlemen. Yes, it's 370
an inanimate object, of course, but nevertheless, it is still a
book case.

PISHCHIK: (*Amazed.*) One hundred years old. Imagine that! . . .

GAEV: Yes . . . a work of art . . . (*Touching the bookcase.*) O venerable bookcase! I salute thy existence. For over a century, 375
thou hast sought the pure ideals of truth and justice; thy
silent exhortation for fruitful labor has not yet faltered
these one hundred years, inspiring courage and hope for
the brightest future (*In tears.*) in generation after generation of our kin, and fostering in us the noble ideals of 380
charity and good.

(*Pause.*)

LOPAKHIN: Yes . . .

LYUBOV ANDREEVNA: You haven't changed a bit, Lyonya.

GAEV: (*A bit embarrassed.*) "Off the ball . . . right-hand corner!
385   Cut shot into the middle."

LOPAKHIN: (*Glances at his watch.*) Time for me to go.

YASHA: (*Gives* LYUBOV ANDREEVNA *medicine.*) Perhaps you'll
        take your pills now . . .

PISHCHIK: Why bother taking medicine, lovely lady . . .
390   doesn't do any harm, doesn't do any good either . . . Do
        let me have them . . . dearest lady. (*Takes the pills, pours them
        into the palm of his hand, blows on them, puts them in his
        mouth, and washes them down with kvass.*) There!

LYUBOV ANDREEVNA: (*Frightened.*) You've gone mad!

395 PISHCHIK: Took them all.

LOPAKHIN: There's an appetite.

(*Everyone laughs.*)

FIRS: When he was here during Holy Week, he ate half a
        bucket of cucumbers . . . (*Mutters to himself.*)

LYUBOV ANDREEVNA: What is he saying?

400 VARYA: He's been muttering like that for three years now.
        We're used to it.

YASHA: Old age.

(*Enter* CHARLOTTA IVANOVNA *wearing a white dress; she is very
thin and tightly laced, with a lorgnette on her belt; she crosses the
stage.*)

LOPAKHIN: Forgive me, Charlotta Ivanovna, I didn't have the
        chance to greet you. (*Goes to kiss her hand.*)

405 CHARLOTTA IVANOVNA: (*Takes her hand away.*) If I let you kiss
        my hand, next you'll want to kiss my elbow, then my
        shoulder . . .

LOPAKHIN: Not my lucky day.

(*Everyone laughs.*)

So, Charlotta Ivanovna, show us a trick!

410 LYUBOV ANDREEVNA: Yes, Charlotta, show us a trick!

CHARLOTTA: I don't want to. I wish to sleep. (*Exits.*)

LOPAKHIN: We'll see each other again in three weeks. (*Kisses
        LYUBOV ANDREEVNA's hand.*) Farewell for now. Time to
        go. (*To* GAEV.) A very good-bye to you. (*Kisses* PISHCHIK.)
415   And to you. (*Shakes hands with* VARYA, *then with* FIRS *and*
        YASHA.) I don't feel like going. (*To* LYUBOV ANDREEVNA.)
        If you make up your mind about the summer homes, if
        you decide to proceed, just let me know, I'll lend you
        50,000. Think about it, seriously.

420 VARYA: (*Angrily.*) So go, then!

LOPAKHIN: I'm going, I'm going. . . . (*Exits.*)

GAEV: What a boor. Oh, wait, "pardon" . . . Our Varya's going
        to marry him. That's our Varya's fiancé.

VARYA: Don't talk so much, Uncle.

425 LYUBOV ANDREEVNA: Why not, Varya, I'd be so pleased. He's
        a good man.

PISHCHIK: And a most worthy man, as they say, truth be
        told . . . Now my Dashenka . . . she also says, that . . . well,
        she says a variety of things. (*Snores, then suddenly awakes
        with a start.*) Nevertheless, dearest lady, oblige me, would

you, please . . . lend me two hundred and forty rubles . . .
tomorrow I must pay off the interest on my mortgage.

VARYA: (*Startled.*) We have no money! None!

LYUBOV ANDREEVNA: As a matter of fact, I don't, I have noth-
        ing, really.   435

PISHCHIK: Some will turn up, you'll see! (*Bursts out laughing.*)
        I never lose hope. There, I say to myself, all is lost, all is
        ruined, and then suddenly, what do you know—they
        build a railroad right through my land, and . . . they pay
        me for it! So just wait and see, something will happen, if   440
        not today, then tomorrow. My Dashenka is going to win
        200,000 . . . she has a lottery ticket.

LYUBOV ANDREEVNA: The coffee's finished, now we can go
        to bed.

FIRS: (*Brushes* GAEV's *clothes, scolding him.*) And you've gone   445
        and put on the wrong trousers again. What I am going to
        do with you?

VARYA: (*Softly.*) Anya's sleeping. (*Quietly opens the window.*)
        The sun is up now, it isn't cold any more. Look,
        Mamochka: what glorious trees! My God, the air! And the   450
        starlings are singing!

GAEV: (*Opens another window.*) The orchard is all in white. You
        haven't forgotten, Lyuba, have you? Look—that long row
        of trees stretching on and on, like a silver cord, on and on,
        do you remember, how it gleams on moonlit nights? You   455
        haven't forgotten, have you?

LYUBOV ANDREEVNA: (*Looks out the window onto the orchard.*)
        O, my childhood, my innocence! Once I slept in this very
        nursery, I'd look out on the orchard, right from here, and
        happiness would awaken with me, every morning, every   460
        morning, and look, it's all the same, nothing has changed.
        (*Laughs with joy.*) White, all white! O, my orchard! After
        the dark, dreary autumn, the cold winter, you're young
        again, blooming with joy, the heavenly angels have not
        forsaken you . . . If only this terrible weight could be lifted   465
        from my soul, if only I could forget my past!

GAEV: Yes, and the orchard will be sold to pay off our debts,
        strange, isn't it . . .

LYUBOV ANDREEVNA: Look, there's my mother, walking
        through the orchard . . . all in white! (*Laughs with joy.*)   470
        There she is.

GAEV: Where?

VARYA: God bless you, Mamochka.

LYUBOV ANDREEVNA: There's no one there, I only dreamed
        it . . . Look, to the right, on the way to the summer-house,   475
        a white sapling, bowing low, I thought it was a woman . . .

(TROFIMOV *enters, wearing a shabby, threadbare student's uniform,
and spectacles.*)

What an astonishing orchard! Masses of white blossoms,
radiant blue sky . . .

TROFIMOV: Lyubov Andreevna!

(*She turns and looks at him.*)

I only came to pay my respects, I'll go, right away. (*Kisses   480
her hand passionately.*) They told me I had to wait till morning, but I couldn't bear it any longer . . .

(LYUBOV ANDREEVNA *looks at him with bewilderment.*)

VARYA: (*In tears.*) It's Petya Trofimov . . .

TROFIMOV: Petya Trofimov, former tutor to your Grisha . . .
485   Have I really changed that much?

(LYUBOV ANDREEVNA *embraces him and weeps softly.*)

GAEV: (*Embarrassed.*) Now, now, Lyuba.

VARYA: (*Weeps.*) You see, Petya, didn't I tell you to wait till
tomorrow.

LYUBOV ANDREEVNA: My Grisha . . . my little boy . . .
490   Grisha . . . son . . .

VARYA: But what can we do, Mamochka. It's God's will.

TROFIMOV: (*Gently, in tears.*) There, there . . .

LYUBOV ANDREEVNA: (*Weeps softly.*) My little boy . . . lost . . .
drowned . . . Why? Why, my friend? (*Softer.*) Anya's sleep-
495   ing, and here I am, raising my voice . . . carrying on . . . So,
now, Petya, tell me! Why have you grown so ugly? And so
old, too!

TROFIMOV: There was an old peasant woman on the train
once, she called me "a shabby-looking gentleman."

500 LYUBOV ANDREEVNA: You were just a boy then, a sweet,
young student, and now look at you, you're hair's gotten
thin, you wear glasses . . . Don't tell me you're still a student? (*Goes to the door.*)

TROFIMOV: And I shall be an eternal student, so it seems.

505 LYUBOV ANDREEVNA: (*Kisses her brother, then* VARYA.) Better
go to bed now . . . You've gotten old, too, Leonid.

PISHCHIK: (*Follows her.*) Yes, time for bed . . . Ach, this gout of
mine . . . I'll stay the night with you . . . Lyubov Andreevna, lovely lady, tomorrow morning, if only you
510   would . . . two hundred and forty rubles . . .

GAEV: He never gives up.

PISHCHIK: Two hundred and forty rubles . . . to pay the interest on the mortgage.

LYUBOV ANDREEVNA: But I don't have any money, really, my
515   sweet, I don't.

PISHCHIK: I'll pay you back, charming lady . . . Such a small
amount . . .

LYUBOV ANDREEVNA: Oh, all right, Leonid will give it to
you . . . Give it to him, Leonid.

520 GAEV: I should give it to him? Don't hold your pockets open.

LYUBOV ANDREEVNA: Give it to him, what else can we do . . .
He needs it . . . He'll pay it back.

(*Exeunt* LYUBOV ANDREEVNA, TROFIMOV, PISHCHIK, *and* FIRS,
GAEV, VARYA, *and* YASHA *remain.*)

GAEV: My sister just can't seem to hold on to her money. (*To*
YASHA.) Move away, good fellow, you smell like a chicken
525   coop.

YASHA: (*With a grin.*) And you, Leonid Andreich, you haven't
changed a bit.

GAEV: Beg pardon? (*To* VARYA.) What did he say?

VARYA: (*To* YASHA.) Your mother's come from the village to
530   see you, she's been waiting since yesterday in the servants'
quarters . . .

YASHA: Good for her!

VARYA: Shame on you!

YASHA: Who needs her? She could have waited till tomorrow
535   to come. (*Exits.*)

VARYA: Mamochka's the same as she's always been, she hasn't
changed at all. If she could, she'd give away everything.

GAEV: Yes . . .

(*Pause.*)

If there are many remedies offered for a disease, then that
means the disease is incurable. Now, I've been thinking, 540
wracking my brain, and I've got lots of remedies, oh yes,
lots and lots of remedies, and you know what that means,
don't you, in essence, that means I don't have any. Wouldn't
it be nice, for example, if we received a large inheritance
from somebody or other, wouldn't it be nice to marry our 545
Anya off to a very rich fellow, wouldn't it be nice to go to
Yaroslavl and try and get some money from our aunt, the
countess. Our aunty's very very rich, you know.

VARYA: (*Weeps.*) If only God would help us.

GAEV: Stop weeping. The old lady's very rich, it's true, but 550
the fact is, she doesn't like us. For one thing, my dear sister went off and married a lawyer, and not a gentleman . . .

(ANYA *appears in the doorway.*)

She didn't marry a gentleman, and you can't really say
she's led a particularly conventional life. I mean, she's a
good, kind person, a splendid person, and I love her very 555
very much, of course, but, whatever the extenuating circumstances may have been, let's face it, she hasn't exactly
been the model of virtue. Why, you can sense it in everything about her, her slightest gesture, her movements.

VARYA: (*In a whisper.*) Anya's standing in the doorway. 560

GAEV: Beg pardon?

(*Pause.*)

Amazing, there's something in my right eye . . . I can't see a
thing. And on Thursday, when I was at the circuit court . . .

(ANYA *enters.*)

VARYA: Why aren't you in bed, Anya?

ANYA: I can't fall asleep. I just can't. 565

GAEV: My little one. (*Kisses* ANYA's *face, hands.*) My child . . .
(*In tears.*) You're not my niece, you're my angel, you're
everything to me. Believe me, believe me . . .

ANYA: I believe you, Uncle, I do. Everyone loves you, everyone reveres you . . . but, darling Uncle, you must try to be 570
quiet, really, just be quiet. What were you saying just now
about my Mama, about your own sister? Why would you
say such a thing?

GAEV: Yes, yes . . . (*Covers his face with her hand.*) As a matter of
fact, it's terrible! My God! My God, save me! And today, I 575
made a speech before a bookcase . . . how foolish of me!
And it was only after I'd finished, that I realized how foolish it was.

VARYA: It's true, Uncle dear, you should try to be quiet. Just
be very quiet, that's all. 580

ANYA: And if you're quiet, you'll feel much better, really.

GAEV: I'll be quiet. (*Kisses* ANYA's *and* VARYA's *hands.*) I'll be
quiet. Just one small matter. On Thursday I was at the circuit court, and, well, some people got together and started
talking, you know, about this, that, the other thing, and so 585
on and so on, and one thing led to another, and so it seems
that a loan might be arranged, to pay off the interest to the
bank.

VARYA: God willing!

590 GAEV: And, on Tuesday, I'm going to have another little talk with them again. (*To* VARYA.) Stop weeping. (*To* ANYA.) Your mama will have a word with Lopakhin; he won't refuse her, of course . . . As for you, as soon as you've had your rest, off you'll go to Yaroslavl to see the countess,
595 your great-aunt. So that way, we'll mount a three-pronged attack—and presto! it's in the bag. We'll pay off that interest, I'm sure of it . . . (*Pops a fruit drop into his mouth.*) On my honor, I swear to you, if you like, this estate will not be sold! (*Excited.*) I swear on my happiness! I give you my
600 hand, call me a worthless good-for-nothing, a dishonorable fellow, if I allow it to go up for auction! I swear on my entire being!

ANYA: (*She regains her composure: she is happy.*) How good you are, Uncle, how wise! (*Embraces her uncle.*) Now I'm con-
605 tent! I'm content! I'm happy, now!

(*Enter* FIRS.)

FIRS: (*Reproachfully.*) Leonid Andreich, have you no fear of God in you? When are you going to bed?

GAEV: In a minute, in a minute. Go on, Firs. Yes, it's all right, I'm quite capable of undressing myself. So, children dear,
610 night-night . . . Details tomorrow, but now, it's time for bed. (*Kisses* ANYA *and* VARYA.) I am a man of the eighties . . . These are not laudable times, but nevertheless, I can say that I've suffered greatly for my convictions in this life. It's not without reason that the peasants love me. One must
615 give the peasant his due! Give him his due, for . . .

ANYA: You're off again, Uncle!

VARYA: Uncle, be quiet!

FIRS: (*Angrily.*) Leonid Andreich!

GAEV: I'm coming, I'm coming . . . And so, to bed. "Off two
620 cushions into the middle. Pocket the white . . . clean shot." (*Exits, with* FIRS *shuffling behind him.*)

ANYA: Now, I'm content. I don't want to go to Yaroslavl, not really, I don't like my great-aunt that much, but, all the same, I'm content. Thanks to Uncle. (*Sits.*)

625 VARYA: We must get to bed. I know I'm going to . . . Oh, an awful thing happened here while you were gone. You remember the old servants' quarters, well, only the old ones live there now: you know, Yefimyushka, Polya, Yevstigney, oh, and don't forget Karp . . . Anyway, they started letting
630 some homeless folks stay the night with them—I didn't say anything at first. But then, I hear, they're spreading this rumor, that I'd been giving orders to feed them nothing but dried peas. Because I was being stingy, you see . . . And all this coming from Yevstigney . . . So I say to myself, fine.
635 If that's the way you want it, I say, just you wait and see. So I call for Yevstigney . . . (*Yawns.*) And he comes in . . . And I say to him, how dare you, Yevstigney . . . you're such a fool . . . (*Looks at* ANYA.) Anechka!

(*Pause.*)

She's asleep! (*Takes* ANYA *by the arm.*) Come to bed . . .
640 Come ! . . . (*Leads her.*) My darling's sleeping! Come . . .

(*They go.*)

(*Far beyond the orchard, a shepherd plays on a pipe.* TROFIMOV *enters, crosses the stage, and, seeing* VARYA *and* ANYA, *stops.*)

VARYA: Shh . . . She's asleep . . . fast asleep . . . Come, my precious.

ANYA: (*Softly, half-asleep.*) I'm so tired . . . do you hear the bells . . . Dearest Uncle . . . Mama and Uncle . . .

VARYA: Come, my precious, come . . . (*Exits into* ANYA*'s room.*) 645

TROFIMOV: (*Tenderly.*) My sunlight! My springtime!

ACT TWO

A field. There is a small, dilapidated old chapel, long deserted, and beside it, a well, an old bench, and several large stones, once apparently gravestones. The road to GAEV*'s country estate is visible. To the side, towering poplar trees loom darkly, where the cherry orchard begins. In the distance, there is a row of telegraph poles, and far beyond that, on the horizon, is the indistinct outline of a large town, visible only in very clear, fine weather. Soon, it will be sunset.* CHARLOTTA, YASHA, *and* DUNYASHA *sit on the bench;* YEPIKHODOV *stands nearby and plays the guitar; all are lost in thought.* CHARLOTTA *is wearing an old, peaked military cap; she removes the rifle from her shoulder and adjusts the buckle on the rifle sling.*

CHARLOTTA: (*Deep in thought.*) I have no passport, no real one . . . no one ever told me how old I was, not really . . . but I always have this feeling that I'm still very young. When I was a little girl, Papa and Mama traveled in a circus, they were acrobats, good ones. And I performed the 5 "salto-mortale," the dive of death, and all kinds of tricks. And when Papa and Mama died, a German lady took me in, she raised me, gave me lessons. "Gut." I grew up, I became a governess. But where I am from, and who I am— I don't know . . . Who were my parents, were they ever 10 married . . . I don't know. (*Takes a cucumber out of her pocket and eats it.*) I don't know anything.

(*Pause.*)

So now I feel like talking, but to whom . . . I have no one to talk to.

YEPIKHODOV: (*Plays guitar and sings.*) "What care I for worldly 15 woe, / What care I for friend and foe . . ." How pleasant it is to play upon the mandolin!

DUNYASHA: That's a guitar, not a mandolin. (*Looks in a little mirror and powders her nose.*)

YEPIKHODOV: For the man, who is mad with love, it's a man- 20 dolin. (*Sings.*) "If my true love were requited, / It would set my heart aglow . . ."

(YASHA *joins in, harmonizing.*)

CHARLOTTA: These people sing terribly . . . Phooey! Like jackals.

DUNYASHA: (*To* YASHA.) How blissful, to have been abroad. 25

YASHA: Well, of course. I'm not going to disagree with you on that one. (*Yawns, then lights a cigar.*)

YEPIKHODOV: But we know that already. Everything abroad is very well organized, and has been so for a long long time.

YASHA: Right. 30

YEPIKHODOV: I am a man of the world. I am. I read many many remarkable books. But, speaking for myself, personally, I have no clue, no clue as to what direction I, personally, want my life to take, I mean: Do I want to live, or do I want to shoot myself, in the head . . . So just in case, I 35 always carry a revolver around with me. Here it is . . . (*Shows them a revolver.*)

CHARLOTTA: I'm finished. And now, I'm leaving. (*Puts on the rifle.*) You, Yepikhodov, you are a very intelligent man and
40   also a very dangerous one; women must be mad for you. Brrr! (*Starts to leave.*) These clever people, they're all such fools, no one for me to talk to . . . Alone, all alone, I have no one . . . and who I am, why I am on this earth, no one knows . . . (*Exits, without hurrying.*)

45   YEPIKHODOV: Now. Speaking for myself, personally, again, putting all else aside, that is, if I may, when it comes to me, I mean, personally, again, I ask myself: Does fate care? No, fate doesn't care, very much as a terrible storm doesn't care about a tiny boat upon the sea. Now. Let us assume I am
50   wrong in this regard, so then, tell me, would you, please, why is it that this morning, yes, this morning, I wake up, just to give you an example, I look up, and there, sitting right on my chest, is this huge and terrifying spider . . . About 'so' big. (*Indicates with both hands.*) And then, to give
55   you yet another example, I go to pick up a glass of kvass, you know, to drink it, I look inside it, and what do I see? Possibly the most offensive species on the face of this earth—like a cockroach.

(*Pause.*)

Have you ever read Buckle?

(*Pause.*)

60   May I trouble you, Avdotya Fyodorovna, for a word or two.

DUNYASHA: Speak.

YEPIKHODOV: It would be far more desirable to speak to you in private . . . (*Sighs.*)

DUNYASHA: (*Embarrassed.*) Oh, all right . . . only first, bring
65   me my cloak . . . I left it near the cupboard . . . it's a bit chilly out . . .

YEPIKHODOV: Of course . . . Right away . . . Of course. Now I know what to do with my revolver . . . (*Takes the guitar and exits, strumming.*)

70   YASHA: Mister Disaster! He's hopeless, just between you and me. (*Yawns.*)

DUNYASHA: God forbid he should shoot himself.

(*Pause.*)

I'm so nervous, I worry all the time. I was just a girl when they took me in, you know, I'm not used to the simple life
75   any more, look at my hands, how lily-white they are, like a young lady's. Can't you see, I've become so delicate, so fragile, so . . . so sensitive, every little thing upsets me . . . It's just awful. And if you deceive me, Yasha, I just don't know what will happen to my nerves.

80   YASHA: (*Kisses her.*) My little cucumber! Of course, a girl should know how to behave, I can't stand a girl who doesn't know how to behave.

DUNYASHA: I've fallen madly in love with you, you are so refined, you can talk about anything.

(*Pause.*)

85   YASHA: (*Yawns.*) Right! . . . Now, in my opinion, if a girl falls in love, that means she's immoral.

(*Pause.*)

Nice, isn't it, to smoke a cigar in the fresh, open air . . . (*Listens.*) Someone's coming . . . It's the ladies and gentlemen . . .

(DUNYASHA *embraces him impetuously.*)

Go home, pretend you've gone for a swim in the river,   90
take that path there, or else they'll run into you and think I arranged this little rendezvous. I can't have that.

DUNYASHA: (*Coughs quietly.*) I've got a headache from all this cigar smoke . . . (*Exits.*)

(YASHA *remains; he sits by the chapel. Enter* LYUBOV ANDREEVNA, GAEV, *and* LOPAKHIN.)

LOPAKHIN: You must decide, once and for all—time waits for   95
no one. The question's quite simple, you know. Will you or won't you agree to lease your land for conversion into summer homes? Answer in one word: yes or no? One word, that's all!

LYUBOV ANDREEVNA: Who has been smoking those disgust-   100
ing cigars here . . . (*Sits.*)

GAEV: Since they've built the railroad, it's all become so convenient. (*Sits down.*) We took a little ride into town, we had our lunch . . . "yellow into the middle pocket!" Now, if only I'd gone home first, and played one little game . . .   105

LYUBOV ANDREEVNA: You'll have plenty of time.

LOPAKHIN: One word, that's all! (*Entreating.*) Give me your answer!

GAEV: (*Yawns.*) Beg pardon?

LYUBOV ANDREEVNA: (*Looks in her purse.*) Yesterday I had so   110
much money, and today I have hardly any at all. My poor, thrifty Varya feeds everyone milk soup, the old folks in the kitchen get nothing but dried peas to eat, and I manage to let money slip right through my fingers. (*Drops her purse, gold coins scatter.*) There, you see, now I've gone and spilled   115
it . . . (*She is annoyed.*)

YASHA: I'll get them, allow me. (*Collects the coins.*)

LYUBOV ANDREEVNA: Please do, Yasha. And why on earth did I go out to lunch . . . That ridiculous restaurant of yours with the music, and the tablecloths that smell of soap . . . And why   120
drink so much, Lyonya? Why eat so much? Why talk so much? Today in the restaurant you went on and on again, on and on . . . About the seventies, about the decadents. And to whom? Talking to the waiters about the decadents!

LOPAKHIN: Yes.   125

GAEV: (*Waves his hand.*) I'm incorrigible, it's obvious . . . (*Irritably, to* YASHA.) What is it with you, you're always disturbing my line of vision . . .

YASHA: (*Laughs.*) I can't hear the sound of your voice without laughing.   130

GAEV: (*To his sister.*) It's either him or me . . .

LYUBOV ANDREEVNA: Go away, Yasha, go on . . .

YASHA: (*Gives* LYUBOV ANDREEVNA *her purse.*) Right away. (*Barely contains his laughter.*) At once . . . (*Exits.*)

LOPAKHIN: Your estate is going to be bought by that million-   135
aire, Deriganov. He's coming to the auction himself, they say, in person.

LYUBOV ANDREEVNA: And where did you hear that?

LOPAKHIN: They were talking about it in town.

140 GAEV: Our aunty from Yaroslavl promised to send us something, but when and how much she will send, who knows . . .

LOPAKHIN: How much is she sending? One hundred thousand? Two hundred thousand?

LYUBOV ANDREEVNA: Oh, well, . . . ten–fifteen thousand, at
145   most, and that much we can be thankful for . . .

LOPAKHIN: Forgive me, but such frivolous people as you, my friends, such strange, impractical people, I have never before met in my entire life. I'm speaking to you in the Russian language, I'm telling you that your estate is about
150   to be sold, and you simply don't understand.

LYUBOV ANDREEVNA: But what on earth are we to do? Tell us, what?

LOPAKHIN: Every day I've been telling you. Every day I've been repeating the same thing, over and over again. The
155   cherry orchard and the land must be leased for summer homes, it must be done immediately, as soon as possible—the auction is imminent! Do you understand! As soon as you decide, once and for all, about the summer homes, you'll have as much money as you'll ever want, and then
160   you will be saved.

LYUBOV ANDREEVNA: Summer homes, summer people—forgive me, please, it all sounds so vulgar.

GAEV: I agree with you, absolutely.

LOPAKHIN: Either I'm going to burst out sobbing, or scream-
165   ing, or else I'm going to fall on the ground, right here in front of you. I can't stand it any more! You're driving me mad! (*To* GAEV.) And you, you act like an old woman!

GAEV: Beg pardon?

LOPAKHIN: An old woman! (*Wants to leave.*)
170 LYUBOV ANDREEVNA: (*Frightened.*) No, don't go, please, stay, dearest. I beg of you. Who knows, perhaps we'll think of something!

LOPAKHIN: What's there to think of!

LYUBOV ANDREEVNA: Don't go, I beg of you. It's so much
175   more cheerful when you're here . . .

(*Pause.*)

I keep waiting for something to happen, as if the house were going to tumble down on top of us.

GAEV: (*Deep in thought.*) "Double into the corner pocket . . . Croisé into the middle . . ."
180 LYUBOV ANDREEVNA: How we have sinned . . .

LOPAKHIN: What are you talking about, what sins . . .

GAEV: (*Pops a fruit drop in his mouth.*) They say I've squandered a entire fortune on fruit drops . . . (*Laughs.*)

LYUBOV ANDREEVNA: O my sins, my sins . . . I've always
185   thrown money around, uncontrollably, like a madwoman, and I married a man, who did nothing but keep us in debt. My husband died from too much champagne—he drank himself to death,—then, for my next misfortune, I fell in love with another man, I began living with him . . . and just
190   at that time, there came my first great punishment, and what a blow it dealt me—right here in this river. . . my little boy drowned, and so I fled, abroad, I simply fled, never to return, never to see this river again . . . I closed my eyes and I ran, not knowing where I was going, what I was do-
195   ing, and *he* following after . . . ruthlessly, relentlessly. I bought a dacha near Menton, *he* had fallen ill there, and for three years I knew no rest, neither day nor night; his illness

exhausted me, wasted me, my soul withered away. And then last year, when the dacha was sold to pay off the debts, I fled again, to Paris, and there he robbed me, he left me for 200 another woman, I tried to poison myself . . . How stupid, how shameful . . . And suddenly I felt drawn again to Russia, to my homeland, to my daughter . . . (*Wipes away her tears.*) Dear God, dear God, be merciful, forgive me my sins! Don't punish me any longer! (*Pulls a telegram from her* 205 *pocket.*) Today, I received this from Paris . . . He begs my forgiveness, beseeches me to return . . . (*Rips up the telegram.*) There's music playing, somewhere. (*Listens.*)

GAEV: It's our celebrated Jewish orchestra. Don't you remember, four violins, flute, and contrabass. 210

LYUBOV ANDREEVNA: Does it still exist? We ought to invite them sometime, plan a little soirée.

LOPAKHIN: (*Listens.*) I don't hear anything. (*Hums softly.*)

An enterprising man, the Prussian,
He'll make a Frenchman from a Russian! 215

(*Laughs.*) What a play I saw at the theatre last night, it was very funny, really.

LYUBOV ANDREEVNA: There probably wasn't anything funny about it. Why go to the theatre to see a play! Better to see yourselves more often. How grey your lives are, how end- 220 lessly you talk.

LOPAKHIN: It's the truth. And the truth must be told, our lives are foolish . . .

(*Pause.*)

My papa was a peasant, an ignorant fool, he understood nothing, taught me nothing, he only beat me when he was 225 drunk, and always with a stick. And the fact of the matter is, I'm the same kind of ignorant fool that he was. I never learned anything, I'm ashamed of my own handwriting, it's not even human, it's more like a hoof-mark than a signature.

LYUBOV ANDREEVNA: You ought to get married, my friend. 230

LOPAKHIN: Yes . . . It's the truth.

LYUBOV ANDREEVNA: Why not to our Varya? She's a good girl.

LOPAKHIN: Yes.

LYUBOV ANDREEVNA: She's of simple origin, she works all day long, but the important thing is, she loves you. And 235 you've been fond of her for a long time now.

LOPAKHIN: Well . . . I have nothing against it . . . She's a good girl.

(*Pause.*)

GAEV: They've offered me a job at the bank. 6,000 a year . . . Have you heard? 240

LYUBOV ANDREEVNA: You, in a bank! Stay where you are . . .

(FIRS *enters; he is carrying a coat.*)

FIRS: (*To* GAEV.) Please, sir, better put this on . . . it's chilly out.

GAEV: (*Puts on the coat.*) You get on my nerves, old man.

FIRS: Now, there's no need for that . . . You went out this morning, without telling anyone. (*Looks him over.*) 245

LYUBOV ANDREEVNA: How old you've grown, Firs!

FIRS: Yes, what may I do for you?

LOPAKHIN: She said: How old you've grown!

FIRS: Well, I've lived a long time. They were marrying me off, and your papa wasn't even in this world yet . . . 250

(*Laughs.*) Then, when the emancipation came, I was already head valet . . . I didn't want my freedom, so I stayed with my masters . . .

(*Pause.*)

255 I remember how glad everyone was, but what they were glad about, they didn't even know themselves.

LOPAKHIN: Ah yes, the good old days. At least there was flogging.

FIRS: (*Not hearing.*) I'll say. The servants belonged to the masters, the masters belonged to the servants, but now everything's all mixed up, you can't tell one from the other.

260 GAEV: Hush, Firs. Tomorrow I've got to go to town. They've promised to introduce me to some general, he might give us a loan on a promissory note.

LOPAKHIN: Nothing will come of it. And you won't pay off the interest, rest assured.

265 LYUBOV ANDREEVNA: He's delirious. There are no generals, they don't exist.

(*Enter* TROFIMOV, ANYA, *and* VARYA.)

GAEV: Ah, here they come.

ANYA: Here's Mama.

270 LYUBOV ANDREEVNA: (*Tenderly.*) Come, come . . . My darling children . . . (*Embraces* ANYA *and* VARYA.) If only you knew how much I love you both. Sit here, right next to me.

(*They all get settled.*)

LOPAKHIN: Our eternal student is always in the company of the young ladies.

275 TROFIMOV: Mind your own business.

LOPAKHIN: And when he's fifty, he'll still be a student.

TROFIMOV: Stop your foolish joking.

LOPAKHIN: You're such a peculiar fellow! Why are you so angry with me, anyway?

280 TROFIMOV: Because you won't stop bothering me.

LOPAKHIN: (*Laughs.*) Permit me to ask you, if I may, what do you think of me?

TROFIMOV: Here is what I think of you, Yermolai Alekseich: You are a rich man, soon you'll be a millionaire. So, in the

285 general scheme of things, that is, according to the laws of nature, we need you, we need predatory beasts, who devour everything which stands in their path, so in that sense you are a necessary evil.

(*All laugh.*)

VARYA: Petya, you do better when you talk about astronomy.

290 LYUBOV ANDREEVNA: No, let's continue yesterday's conversation.

TROFIMOV: What about?

GAEV: About pride. Pride in man.

TROFIMOV: That. We talked about that forever, but we did not come to any conclusion. According to your way of

295 thinking, there is something mystical about the proud man, an aura, almost. Perhaps you are correct in your beliefs, but if you analyze the issue clearly, without complicating things, then why does this pride even exist, what reason can there be for pride, if a man is not physically distinguished, if the vast majority of mankind is coarse, stu-

300 pid, or profoundly miserable. There is no time for the admiration of self. There is only time for work.

GAEV: We're all going to die, anyway, so what difference does it make?

305 TROFIMOV: Who knows? And what does it really mean—to die? For all we know, man is endowed with a hundred sensibilities, and when he dies, only the five known to us perish along with him, while the other ninety-five remain alive.

310 LYUBOV ANDREEVNA: How intelligent you are, Petya! . . .

LOPAKHIN: (*Ironically.*) Yes, terribly!

TROFIMOV: Mankind marches onward, ever onward, strengthening his skills, his capacities. All that has up until now been beyond his reach may one day be attainable, only he must

315 work, indeed, he must do everything in his power to help those who seek the truth. In Russia, however, very few people actually do work. The vast majority of the intelligentsia, as I know them, do nothing, pursue nothing, and, meanwhile, have no predisposition whatsoever to work, they're

320 completely incapable of it. They call themselves 'the intelligentsia,' and yet they address their servants with disrespect, they treat the peasants as if they were animals, they're dismal students, they're poorly educated, they never read serious literature, they're absolutely idle, they don't do a thing ex-

325 cept sit around talking about science and art, about which they know nothing at all. And they're all so grim looking, they have tense, taut faces, they only talk about 'important things,' they spend all their time philosophizing, and meanwhile, right before their very eyes, the workers live atro-

330 ciously, eat abominably, sleep without bedding, thirty-forty to a room, together with bedbugs, stench, dankness, depravity . . . And so it seems that all this lofty talk is simply meant to conceal the truth from themselves and others. Show me, please, where are the day nurseries, about which they speak

335 so much and so often, where are the public reading rooms? They only write about them in novels, they never become a reality, never. There is only filth, vulgarity, barbarism . . . I dread their serious countenances, their serious conversations, I despise them. Better to be silent!

340 LOPAKHIN: You know, I get up before five every morning, I work from dawn until night, I deal with money, constantly, mine and others, and yes, I see how people really are. You only have to try to get something done to realize how few honest, decent people there are in this world.

345 Sometimes, when I can't fall asleep, I lie there thinking: "Dear Lord, you have given us the vast forests, the boundless plains, the endless horizons, and we who live here on this earth, we should be true giants . . ."

LYUBOV ANDREEVNA: What good are giants . . . They're very

350 nice in fairy tales, you know, but in true life, they're terrifying.

(YEPIKHODOV *crosses upstage, playing the guitar.*)

(*Pensively.*) There goes Yepikhodov.

ANYA: (*Pensively.*) There goes Yepikhodov.

GAEV: The sun has set, ladies and gentlemen.

355 TROFIMOV: Yes.

GAEV: (*Softly, as if reciting.*) O nature, wondrous nature, you shine on, radiant and eternal, beauteous and indifferent,

you whom we call mother, you embody birth and death, you create and you destroy, you . . .

360 VARYA: (*Imploring.*) Uncle, dear!

ANYA: Not again, Uncle!

TROFIMOV: You're better off "pocketing the yellow . . ."

GAEV: I'll be quiet, I'll be quiet.

(*All sit, deep in thought. Silence. Only* FIRS's *muttering can be heard. Suddenly from far, far away, a sound is heard, as if coming from the sky, the sound of a breaking string, dying away in the distance, a mournful sound.*)

LYUBOV ANDREEVNA: What was that?

365 LOPAKHIN: Don't know. Somewhere far away, deep in the mines, a bucket broke loose and fell . . . But somewhere very far away.

GAEV: Or a bird of some kind . . . a heron, perhaps.

TROFIMOV: Or an owl . . .

370 LYUBOV ANDREEVNA: (*Shudders.*) Disturbing, somehow.

(*Pause.*)

FIRS: Right before the time of trouble, it was the same thing: The owl screeched, and the samovar hissed, it never stopped.

GAEV: What time of trouble?

FIRS: Why, before the emancipation of the serfs.

(*Pause.*)

375 LYUBOV ANDREEVNA: Let's go, dear friends, shall we, it's getting dark. (*To* ANYA.) You've got tears in your eyes . . . What is it, my pet? (*Embraces her.*)

ANYA: I'm fine, Mama. It's nothing.

TROFIMOV: Someone's coming.

(*A* PASSERBY *appears in a shabby, white cap and a coat; he is slightly drunk.*)

380 PASSERBY: Permit me to inquire, may I pass through here to get to the train station?

GAEV: You may. Go down that road.

PASSERBY: I'm deeply grateful. (*Coughs.*) What superb weather we're having . . . (*Recites.*) "My brother, my suffering

385 brother . . . Come down to the Volga, whose moan . . ." (*To* VARYA.) Mademoiselle, please, give a poor starving Russian thirty kopeks. . .

(VARYA *cries out in fear.*)

LOPAKHIN: (*Angrily.*) This has gone too far!

LYUBOV ANDREEVNA: (*Stunned.*) Here . . . take this . . .

390 (*Searches in her purse.*) I have no silver . . . Never mind, here's a gold piece . . .

PASSERBY: I'm deeply grateful! (*Exits.*)

(*Laughter.*)

VARYA: (*Frightened.*) I'm leaving . . . I'm leaving . . . Oh, Mamochka, the servants at home have nothing to eat, and

395 you gave him a gold piece.

LYUBOV ANDREEVNA: What are you going to do with me, I'm such a silly fool! I'll give you everything I have. Yermolai Alekseich, please, lend me some more money! . . .

LOPAKHIN: Yes, madam.

400 LYUBOV ANDREEVNA: Come, ladies and gentlemen, time to go. Oh, yes, Varya, we've just made a match for you. Congratulations.

VARYA: (*In tears.*) Mama, you musn't joke about that.

LOPAKHIN: "Oh-phel-i-a, get thee to a nunnery . . ."

405 GAEV: It's been so long since I've played a game of billiards, my hands are shaking.

LOPAKHIN: "Oh-phel-i-a, o nymph, remember me in thy prayers!"

LYUBOV ANDREEVNA: Come, ladies and gentlemen. It's al-

410 most suppertime.

VARYA: How he frightened me. My heart is pounding.

LOPAKHIN: May I remind you, ladies and gentlemen: On the twenty-second of August, the cherry orchard will be sold. Think about it! Think! . . .

(*They all leave, except* TROFIMOV *and* ANYA.)

415 ANYA: (*Laughing.*) The stranger frightened Varya off, thank goodness, now we're alone.

TROFIMOV: Varya's afraid we'll fall madly in love, she hasn't let us out of her sight for days. She's so narrow-minded, she can't understand we're above love. To overcome all obsta-

420 cles, real and imagined, which stand in the path of freedom and happiness,—that is our quest in life. Onward! We set forth, undaunted, toward that star, burning bright in the distance! Onward! Don't fall behind, my friends!

ANYA: (*Clasps her hands.*) How beautifully you talk!

(*Pause.*)

425 It's glorious here today!

TROFIMOV: Yes, the weather is amazing.

ANYA: What have you done to me, Petya, why don't I love the cherry orchard, as I did, once? I loved it so tenderly, I couldn't imagine any other place on earth more lovely

430 than our orchard.

TROFIMOV: All Russia is our orchard. The land is vast and beautiful, there are many marvelous places in it.

(*Pause.*)

Just think, Anya: Your grandfather, your great-grandfather, and his forefathers before him, all were serf-owners, they all

435 owned living souls, so isn't it possible, then, that in every blossom, every leaf, every tree trunk in the orchard, a human soul now gazes down upon us, can't you hear their voices . . . To own human souls—can't you see how this has transformed each and every one of us, those who have lived

440 before and those who live today, so that you, your mother, your uncle, all of you, are no longer aware that you are alive at the expense of others, at the expense of those whom you would not even permit beyond your front hall . . . We have fallen behind, by two hundred years or so, at least, we have

445 nothing left, absolutely nothing, no clear understanding of the past, we only philosophize, complain about our boredom, or drink vodka. And it's all so clear, can't you see, that to begin a new life, to live in the present, we must first redeem our past, put an end to it, and redeem it we shall, but

450 only with suffering, only with extraordinary, everlasting toil and suffering. You must understand this, Anya.

ANYA: The house, in which we live, is no longer our house, and I shall leave it, I give you my word.

TROFIMOV: If you have the key, throw it in the well and run, run far, far away. Be free, like the wind.

455

ANYA: (*Ecstatic.*) How wonderfully you say it!

TROFIMOV: Believe me, Anya, believe me! I'm not even thirty yet, I'm young, I'm still a student, and yet, I've endured so much! Come winter, I'm hungry, sick, anxiety-ridden,

460 poverty-stricken, like a beggar, and wherever fate carries me, there I shall be! And yet, all the while, every waking moment, day and night, my soul is filled with an indescribable premonition, a vision. A vision of happiness, Anya, I can see it now . . .

465 ANYA: (*Pensively.*) The moon is rising.

(YEPIKHODOV *is heard playing the guitar, the same melancholy song as before. The moon is rising. Somewhere near the poplars,* VARYA *is looking for* ANYA *and calling: "Anya! Where are you?"*)

TROFIMOV: Yes, the moon is rising.

(*Pause.*)

Here comes happiness, here it comes, closer and closer, I can already hear its footsteps. And if we don't see it, if we don't recognize it, then what does it matter? Others will!

(VARYA's *voice: "Anya! Where are you?"*)

470 Varya, again! (*Angrily.*) It's disgraceful!

ANYA: I know! Let's go down to the river. It's lovely there.

TROFIMOV: Let's go.

(*They go.*)

(VARYA's *voice: "Anya! Anya!"*)

ACT THREE

The drawing room, separated from the ballroom by an archway. A chandelier burns brightly. A Jewish orchestra, the same one referred to in Act Two, is heard playing in the entrance hall. It is evening. In the ballroom, the crowd is dancing the 'grand-rond.' The voice of SIMEONOV-PISHCHIK *is heard: "Promenade à une paire!" The couples dance through the drawing room, as follows: first* PISHCHIK *and* CHARLOTTA IVANOVNA; *then* TROFIMOV *and* LYUBOV ANDREEVNA; *then* ANYA *and the* POST OFFICE CLERK; *then* VARYA *and the* STATIONMASTER, *and so on.* VARYA *is weeping quietly and wipes away her tears as she dances.* DUNYASHA *is in the last couple. They dance around the drawing room.* PISHCHIK *calls out: "Grand-rond, balancez!" and "Les cavaliers à genoux et remerciez vos dames!"*

FIRS, *wearing a tailcoat, carries a tray with seltzer water.* PISHCHIK *and* TROFIMOV *enter the drawing room.*

PISHCHIK: I have high blood pressure, I've had two strokes already, it's difficult for me to dance, but, you know what they say: "If you run in a pack, whether you bark or not, you'd better wag your tail." Never you mind, I'm as

5 healthy as a horse. My dear departed father, joker that he was, God rest his soul, always used to say, on the subject of our ancestry, that the Simeonov-Pishchiks are descended from the same horse that Caligula appointed to the Senate . . . (*Sits.*) The only trouble is: We don't have any

money! And you know what they say: "A hungry dog believes only in meat . . ." (*Snores and suddenly wakes up.*) And that's my problem . . . all I ever dream about is money . . .

10

TROFIMOV: As a matter of fact, you do bear some resemblance to a horse.

PISHCHIK: And why not . . . a horse is a good animal . . . you can get a very good price for a horse, you know . . .

15

(*In the next room, the sound of a billiard game is heard.* VARYA *appears in the archway to the ballroom.*)

TROFIMOV: (*Teasing.*) Madame Lopakhina! Madame Lopakhina! . . .

VARYA: (*Angrily.*) The shabby-looking gentleman!

TROFIMOV: Yes, I'm a shabby-looking gentleman, and proud of it!

20

VARYA: (*Bitterly.*) We've gone and hired the musicians, now how are we going to pay for them? (*Exits.*)

TROFIMOV: (*To* PISHCHIK.) Think about it: The energy you've wasted your whole life through in search of money to pay off the interest on your debts, if only you'd spent that energy elsewhere, then, no doubt, you could have changed the world.

25

PISHCHIK: Nietzsche . . . the philosopher . . . the supreme, the exalted . . . a man of the greatest genius, this man once said, in his own writings, that it's all right to forge banknotes.

30

TROFIMOV: Have you ever read Nietzsche?

PISHCHIK: Well . . . Dashenka told me that one. And anyway, given my situation, even if I could forge banknotes . . . Day after tomorrow, I owe a payment of three hundred and ten rubles . . . I've already scraped up one hundred and thirty so far . . . (*Searches in his pockets, anxiously.*) My money's gone! I've lost my money! (*In tears.*) Where is my money! (*Overjoyed.*) Here it is, in the lining . . . Look, I even broke into a sweat . . .

35

40

(*Enter* LYUBOV ANDREEVNA *and* CHARLOTTA IVANOVNA.)

LYUBOV ANDREEVNA: (*Humming the 'lezginka.'*) Why has Leonid been gone so long? What is he doing in town? (*To* DUNYASHA.) Dunyasha, offer the musicians some tea . . .

TROFIMOV: The auction didn't take place, in all probability.

LYUBOV ANDREEVNA: And of all times to invite the musicians and give a ball . . . Oh well, never mind . . . (*Sits and hums softly.*)

45

CHARLOTTA: (*Gives* PISHCHIK *a deck of cards.*) Here is a deck of cards, think of a card, any card.

PISHCHIK: I've got one.

50

CHARLOTTA: Now shuffle the deck. Very good. Give it to me, oh my dear Mr. Pishchik, Eins, zwei, drei! Now go look, it's in your side pocket . . .

PISHCHIK: (*Takes a card from his side pocket.*) The eight of spades, you're absolutely right! (*Amazed.*) Imagine that!

55

CHARLOTTA: (*Holds out the deck of cards in her palm to* TROFIMOV.) Tell me, quickly, which card is the top card?

TROFIMOV: What? Oh, the queen of spades.

CHARLOTTA: Right! (*To* PISHCHIK.) So? Which card is the top card?

60

PISHCHIK: The ace of hearts.

CHARLOTTA: Right! (*Claps her hands, and the deck of cards disappears.*) My, what lovely weather we're having today!

(*A mysterious female voice answers her as if coming from underneath the floor: "Oh yes, the weather is splendid, dear lady."*)

You are the image of perfection . . .

(*Voice: "And you I like very much too, dear lady."*)

65 STATIONMASTER: (*Applauds.*) Madame Ventriloquist, bravo!

PISHCHIK: (*Amazed.*) Imagine that! Most enchanting Charlotta Ivanovna . . . I'm head-over-heels in love . . .

CHARLOTTA: In love? (*Shrugs her shoulders.*) How could you possibly be in love? "Guter Mensch, aber schlechter Musikant."

70 TROFIMOV: (*Claps* PISHCHIK *on the shoulder.*) Well done, old horse . . .

CHARLOTTA: Your attention please, for one more trick. (*Gets a lap robe from a chair.*) Here is a very lovely lap robe, I wish to sell it . . . (*Shakes it.*) Doesn't anyone wish to buy it?

75 PISHCHIK: (*Amazed.*) Imagine that!

CHARLOTTA: Eins, zwei, drei! (*Quickly lifts the lap robe.*)

(ANYA *appears behind the lap robe; she curtsies, runs to her mother, embraces her, and runs out into the ballroom, amidst general delight.*)

LYUBOV ANDREEVNA: (*Applauds.*) Bravo, bravo! . . .

CHARLOTTA: Once more! Eins, zwei, drei! (*Lifts the lap robe.*)

(VARYA *appears behind the lap robe; she bows.*)

PISHCHIK: (*Amazed.*) Imagine that!

80 CHARLOTTA: The end! (*Throws the lap robe over* PISHCHIK, *curtsies, and runs out into the ballroom.*)

PISHCHIK: (*Hurries after her.*) Sorceress . . . how did you do it? How? (*Exits.*)

LYUBOV ANDREEVNA: And Leonid is still not back. What can

85 he be doing in town this long, I don't understand it! Surely everything is over by now, either the estate has been sold or else the auction never took place, one or the other, so why must we be kept in the dark forever!

VARYA: (*Attempting to console her.*) Uncle has bought it, I'm

90 sure of it.

TROFIMOV: (*Sarcastically.*) Yes.

VARYA: Great-aunt sent him power of attorney to buy the estate in her name and transfer the mortgage to her. She did it for Anya. And Uncle will buy it, with God's help, I'm sure of it.

95 LYUBOV ANDREEVNA: Great-aunt in Yaroslavl sent 50,000 to buy the estate in her name because she doesn't trust us— and that wasn't even enough to pay the interest. (*Covers her face with her hands.*) Today my destiny will be decided, my destiny . . .

100 TROFIMOV: (*Teasing* VARYA.) Madame Lopakhina!

VARYA: (*Angrily.*) The eternal student! Twice you've been expelled from the university.

LYUBOV ANDREEVNA: Why are you so angry, Varya? He's teasing you about Lopakhin, but what does it matter? If you

105 want to—marry Lopakhin, he's a fine man, a fascinating man. And if you don't want to—don't; no one is forcing you to, darling . . .

VARYA: I take this matter very seriously, Mamochka, I must tell you. He is a good man, I like him, I do.

110 LYUBOV ANDREEVNA: Then marry him. What are you waiting for, I don't understand!

VARYA: But Mamochka, I can't propose to him myself. For two years now everyone's been talking to me about him, every-

one, and either he says nothing, or else he jokes about it. I understand. He's busy getting rich, he's preoccupied with 115 his affairs, he has no time for me. Oh, if only I had money, only a little, a hundred rubles even, I'd give up everything, I'd run away as far as I could. I'd enter a convent.

TROFIMOV: Blessings on you!

VARYA: (*To* TROFIMOV.) A student's supposed to be intelli- 120 gent! (*Gently, in tears.*) How ugly you've grown, Petya, and how old, too! (*To* LYUBOV ANDREEVNA, *no longer crying.*) I simply can't live without work, Mamochka. I must be doing something, every minute.

(*Enter* YASHA.)

YASHA: (*Hardly able to contain his laughter.*) Yepikhodov has 125 broken a billiard cue! . . . (*Exits.*)

VARYA: Why is Yepikhodov here? Who allowed him to play billiards? I don't understand these people . . . (*Exits.*)

LYUBOV ANDREEVNA: Don't tease her, Petya, can't you see how miserable she is. 130

TROFIMOV: She's overbearing, that's what she is . . . always poking her nose into other people's business. She hasn't given Anya and me a moment's peace all summer, she's afraid we might fall in love. What business is it of hers, anyway? And how could she even think that of me, I'm far 135 beyond such vulgarity. We are above love!

LYUBOV ANDREEVNA: And I suppose that means I must be beneath love. (*Tremendously agitated.*) Why isn't Leonid back yet? I only want to know: Is the estate sold or isn't it? This terrible business has gone too far, I don't know 140 what to think any more, I'm at my wits' end . . . I might scream any minute . . . I might do something foolish. Save me, Petya. Say something, anything . . .

TROFIMOV: Whether the estate is sold today or not—does it really matter? It's over, it's been so for a long time, there's no 145 turning back again, that path is long overgrown. Face it, dear friend. You mustn't delude yourself any longer, for once in your life you must look the truth straight in the eye.

LYUBOV ANDREEVNA: What truth? Oh, yes, of course, you see what is true and what is not true, while I have lost my vi- 150 sion, I see nothing. You boldly solve all the problems of the world, don't you, but tell me, my darling, isn't that because you're still so young, because you haven't even suffered through one of life's problems yet, not even one? You boldly look to the future, but isn't that because you see 155 nothing so terrible lying ahead, because life is still safely hidden from your young eyes? You have more courage, more character, more honesty than any of us, so then why not have compassion, find it, somewhere in a corner of your heart, have mercy on me. I was born here, my mother 160 and father lived here, my grandfather, too, I love this house, I can't comprehend a life without the cherry orchard, and if it must be sold, then sell me with it . . . (*Embraces* TROFIMOV, *kisses him on the forehead.*) My son drowned here . . . (*Weeps.*) Have pity on me, my good, kind fellow. 165

TROFIMOV: You know I do, with all my heart.

LYUBOV ANDREEVNA: Yes, but there must be another way to say it, another way . . . (*Takes out a handkerchief, a telegram falls on the floor.*) My soul is so heavy today, you can't possibly imagine. There is such a din here, I'm trembling 170 with each and every sound, trembling all over, but I can't be alone, the silence would be terrifying. Don't judge me, Petya . . . I love you, as if you were my own child. And I'd gladly let you marry Anya, I would, I swear to you, only first you must finish your education, darling, get your degree. You don't do a thing, you just let fate carry you from place to place, and that's such a strange way to live . . . Isn't it? Well? And you simply must do something about that beard, to make it grow, somehow . . . (*Bursts out laughing.*) How funny-looking you are!

TROFIMOV: (*Picks up the telegram.*) I don't wish to be handsome.

LYUBOV ANDREEVNA: It's a telegram from Paris. Every day I receive one. Yesterday, and today, too. That terrible man is ill again, he's in trouble again . . . He begs my forgiveness, he beseeches me to return to him, I really ought to be going to Paris, to be near him. You should see your face now, Petya, so severe, so judgmental, but, really, what am I to do, darling, tell me, what can I do, he's ill, he's alone, unhappy, and who will take care of him, who will keep him from harm, who will nurse him through his illness? Oh, why hide it, why keep silent, I love him, it's the truth. I love him, I love him . . . He is the stone around my neck, and I shall sink with him to the bottom, and how I love this stone, I can't live without it! (*Presses* TROFIMOV's *hand.*) Don't think ill of me, Petya, and don't speak, please, not a word . . .

TROFIMOV: (*In tears.*) Forgive me for saying it, but for God's sake: This man robbed you, he cleaned you out!

LYUBOV ANDREEVNA: No, no, no, you mustn't talk like that . . . (*Covers her ears.*)

TROFIMOV: He's an absolute scoundrel, and you're the only one who doesn't know it! A petty thief, a good-for-nothing . . .

LYUBOV ANDREEVNA: (*With controlled anger.*) And you're twenty-six or twenty-seven years old, and still a schoolboy!

TROFIMOV: So be it!

LYUBOV ANDREEVNA: You're supposed to be a man, at your age you're supposed to understand how lovers behave. Why don't you know this by now . . . why haven't you fallen in love yourself? (*Angrily.*) Yes, yes! You and all your talk about purity . . . why, you're nothing but a prude, that's what you are, an eccentric, a freak . . .

TROFIMOV: (*Horrified.*) What is she saying!

LYUBOV ANDREEVNA: "I am above love." You're not above love, no, as Firs says, you're pathetic! At your age, not to have a lover! . . .

TROFIMOV: (*Horrified.*) This is terrible! What is she saying?! (*Rushes out into the ballroom, holding his head.*) This is terrible . . . I can't bear it, I'm leaving . . . (*Exits, but returns again immediately.*) It's all over between us! (*Exits into the front hall.*)

LYUBOV ANDREEVNA: (*Calls after him.*) Petya, wait! Don't be silly, I was only joking! Petya!

(*In the front hall, someone is heard dashing down the stairs, and suddenly falling the rest of the way with a crash.* ANYA *and* VARYA *cry out, but then, almost immediately, laughter is heard.*)

What happened?

(ANYA *runs in.*)

ANYA: (*Laughing.*) Petya fell down the stairs! (*Runs out.*)

LYUBOV ANDREEVNA: What a peculiar fellow that Petya is . . .

(*The* STATIONMASTER *stands in the middle of the ballroom, and starts to recite a poem: 'The Fallen Woman' by Alexey Konstantinovich Tolstoy. Everyone stops to listen, but after a few lines, the strains of a waltz are heard coming from the front hall, and the recitation is interrupted. Everyone dances.* TROFIMOV, ANYA, VARYA, *and* LYUBOV ANDREEVNA *pass through from the entrance hall.*)

Petya . . . my pure Petya . . . I beg your forgiveness . . . Come, dance with me . . . (*Dances with him.*)

(ANYA *and* VARYA *dance together.* FIRS *enters, and places his cane near the side door.* YASHA *also enters, and watches the dancing.*)

YASHA: So, what's new, grandpa?

FIRS: I don't feel very well. In the old days, we used to have generals, barons, admirals dancing at our balls; nowadays we have to send for the postal clerk and the stationmaster, and even they come reluctantly. And I'm getting weaker, somehow. In the old days, when anyone of us fell ill, my old master—that would be their grandfather—he would treat us all with sealing wax. I've taken a dose of sealing wax every day for twenty years now, even more, who knows; perhaps that's why I'm still alive.

YASHA: You get on my nerves, grandpa. (*Yawns.*) Maybe it's time for you to kick the bucket.

FIRS: And you're a pathetic fool, that's what you are. (*Mumbles.*)

(TROFIMOV *and* LYUBOV ANDREEVNA *dance in the ballroom, and then in the drawing room.*)

LYUBOV ANDREEVNA: "Merci." Let me sit down . . . (*Sits.*) I'm exhausted.

(*Enter* ANYA.)

ANYA: (*Agitated.*) There's a man out in the kitchen, he was just saying that the cherry orchard was sold today.

LYUBOV ANDREEVNA: To whom?

ANYA: He didn't say. He left. (*Dances with* TROFIMOV.)

(*Both exit into the ballroom.*)

YASHA: Some old fellow jabbering, that's all. A stranger.

FIRS: And Leonid Andreich is still not here, he's still not back yet. All he has on is a lightweight overcoat, one for in-between seasons, he's bound to catch cold. Oh, these young people nowadays!

LYUBOV ANDREEVNA: I think I'm going to die. Go, Yasha, hurry, find out to whom it was sold.

YASHA: Oh, he left a long time ago, that old fellow. (*Laughs.*)

LYUBOV ANDREEVNA: (*Slightly annoyed.*) And what are you laughing about? What's so funny?

YASHA: That Yepikhodov, he's a clown. The man is pitiful. "Mister Disaster."

LYUBOV ANDREEVNA: Firs, if the estate is sold, where will you go?

FIRS: Wherever you tell me, that's where I'll go.

LYUBOV ANDREEVNA: Why do you look like that? Are you ill? You should be in bed, you know . . .

FIRS: Yes . . . (*With a grin.*) I'll go to bed, and who will serve, who will manage everything? Hm? One servant for the whole household.

YASHA: (*To* LYUBOV ANDREEVNA.) Lyubov Andreevna! One small request, allow me, please! If you go to Paris again, take

270 me with you, I beg of you. I can't stay here any more, it's absolutely impossible. (*Looks around, in a low voice.*) What can I say, you see for yourself, this is an ignorant country, the people are immoral, and anyway, life here is boring, the food they give you in the kitchen is disgusting, and you 275 have Firs wandering around everywhere, muttering all kinds of nonsense. Take me with you, I beg of you!

(*Enter* PISHCHIK.)

PISHCHIK: May I have the pleasure . . . a little waltz, most charming lady . . .

(LYUBOV ANDREEVNA *joins him.*)

280 But, don't forget, one hundred eighty rubles, enchanting lady . . . That, I'll take . . . (*They dance.*) One hundred and eighty sweet little rubles . . .

(*They cross into the ballroom.*)

YASHA: (*Sings softly.*) "O, do you know how my heart is yearning . . ."

(*In the ballroom, a figure in a grey top hat and checkered trousers waves her hands and jumps up and down; there are cries of: "Bravo, Charlotta Ivanovna!"*)

DUNYASHA: (*Stops to powder her face.*) The mistress told me to dance—too many gentlemen, too few ladies,—but now my 285 head is spinning from too much waltzing, my heart is pounding, and, do you know what else, Firs Nikolaevich, the postmaster just told me something that took my breath away.

(*The music dies down.*)

FIRS: What did he say?
DUNYASHA: "You," he said, "are like a little flower."
290 YASHA: (*Yawns.*) What ignorance . . . (*Exits.*)
DUNYASHA: "A little flower" . . . I'm such a sensitive young woman, you know, I adore a few tender words.
FIRS: You'll get yourself into a lot of trouble.

(*Enter* YEPIKHODOV.)

YEPIKHODOV: Avdotya Fyodorovna, you keep avoiding me . . .
295 what am I, some sort of insect? (*Sighs.*) Ach, life!
DUNYASHA: Yes, what may I do for you?
YEPIKHODOV: And no doubt, probably, you're right. Of course. (*Sighs.*) Who can blame you. And yet, look at it from my point, of view, I mean, if I may say so myself, and 300 I shall, so excuse me, but you have reduced me to a complete state of mind. Now I know my destiny in life, every day some new disaster befalls me, and have I accepted this?—yes, I have, I look upon my fate with a smile. You have given me your word, and though . . .
305 DUNYASHA: Can we have our little talk later, please? Leave me alone now. I'm in a fantasy. (*Plays with her fan.*)
YEPIKHODOV: A new day, a new disaster, and excuse me, I just keep smiling, I even laugh, sometimes.

(*Enter* VARYA *from the ballroom.*)

VARYA: You still haven't left yet, Semyon? Who do you think 310 you are, really. (*To* DUNYASHA.) Get out of here, Dunyasha.

(*To* YEPIKHODOV.) First you play billiards and you break a cue, then you parade around the drawing room like a guest.
YEPIKHIDOV: You should not reprimand me. Excuse me.
VARYA: I'm not reprimanding you, I'm telling you. All you do is float from one place to the next, you don't do a blessed 315 bit of work. Why we keep you as clerk, God only knows.
YEPIKHODOV: (*Offended.*) Whether I work, or float, or eat, or play billiards, for that matter, excuse me, but that's a subject of discussion only for our elders.
VARYA: How dare you speak to me like that! (*Enraged.*) How 320 dare you? Do you mean to tell me I don't know what I'm doing? Get out of here! This minute!
YEPIKHODOV: (*Cowering.*) Excuse me, may I ask that you express yourself in a more delicate fashion?
VARYA: (*Beside herself.*) Get out, this minute! Out! 325

(*He goes to the door, she follows him.*)

"Mister Disaster!" Never set foot in here again, do you hear! I never want to lay eyes on you!

(YEPIKHODOV *has exited; from behind the door, his voice is heard: "I am going to file a complaint against you."*)

So, you're think you're coming back, eh? (*Grabs the cane, which* FIRS *has left by the door.*) Come on . . . come on . . . come on, I'll show you . . . So, are you coming back? Are 330 you? This is for you, then . . . (*Swings the cane.*)

(*Just at this moment* LOPAKHIN *enters.*)

LOPAKHIN: I humbly thank you.
VARYA: (*Angrily and sarcastically.*) Sorry!
LOPAKHIN: Please, it's nothing. I'm most grateful for the warm reception. 335
VARYA: Don't mention it. (*She turns to go, then looks around and asks, meekly.*) I didn't hurt you, did I?
LOPAKHIN: No, of course not, it's nothing. Just a bump, an enormous one, that's all.

(*Voices in the ballroom: "Lopakhin has returned! Yermolai Alekseich!"*)

PISHCHIK: Well, well, well, and speaking of the devil! . . . 340 (*Kisses* LOPAKHIN.) I smell a touch of brandy, my dear, good fellow, yes, I do! And we've been celebrating here, too!

(*Enter* LYUBOV ANDREEVNA.)

LYUBOV ANDREEVNA: Yermolai Alekseich, you're back. Why did it take you so long? Where is Leonid? 345
LOPAKHIN: Leonid Andreich returned with me, he's coming . . .
LYUBOV ANDREEVNA: (*Upset.*) So? Was there an auction? Tell me!
LOPAKHIN: (*Disconcerted, afraid to reveal his excitement.*) The auction was over at four o'clock . . . We missed the train, we had to wait till nine-thirty. (*Sighs heavily.*) Oh! My 350 head is spinning . . .

(*Enter* GAEV. *In his right hand he carries some packages; he wipes away the tears with his left hand.*)

LYUBOV ANDREEVNA: Lyonya, what is it? Lyonya? (*Impatiently, in tears.*) Tell me, quickly, for God's sake . . .

355 GAEV: (*Doesn't answer her, simply waves his hands; weeping, to* FIRS.) Here, take it ... anchovies, and some kerch herring ... I haven't had a thing to eat all day . . . What I have lived through!

(*The door to the billiard room is open; the clicking of billiard balls is heard, and* YASHA's *voice: "Seven and eighteen!"* GAEV's *expression changes; he is no longer crying.*)

I'm terribly tired. Help me change my clothes, Firs. (*Exits through the ballroom to his room,* FIRS *follows behind.*)

360 PISHCHIK: What happened at the auction? Tell us! Please!

LYUBOV ANDREEVNA: Is the cherry orchard sold?

LOPAKHIN: It is sold.

LYUBOV ANDREEVNA: Who bought it?

LOPAKHIN: I bought it.

(*Pause.* LYUBOV ANDREEVNA *is stunned; she might have fallen, were she not standing near an armchair and table.* VARYA *takes the keys off her belt, throws them on the floor in the middle of the drawing room, and exits.*)

365 I bought it! Wait, ladies and gentlemen, bear with me, please, my head is spinning, I can't speak . . . (*Laughs.*) We arrived at the auction, and Deriganov was already there. Leonid Andreich only had 15,000, so right away Deriganov bid 30,000 over and above the debt on the mortgage.

370 I saw how it was going, so I decided to take him on, I bid forty. And he bid forty-five. Then I bid fifty-five. You see—he'd raise it by five, I'd raise it by ten . . . And then, it was all over. I bid ninety over and above the debt, and that was it, it went to me. And now, the cherry orchard is mine!

375 Mine! (*Roars with laughter.*) My God, ladies and gentlemen, the cherry orchard is mine! Tell me that I'm drunk, that I'm out of my mind, that I've made it all up . . . (*Stamps his feet.*) Don't you laugh at me! If only my father and my grandfather could get up from their graves and witness all these

380 events, how their Yermolai, their ignorant little Yermolai, the one who was beaten, the one who ran barefoot in the bitter winter, how this same little Yermolai bought the estate, the most beautiful estate in the world. I bought the estate, where my grandfather and my father were slaves,

385 where they were forbidden to set foot in the kitchen. No, I'm dreaming, I'm hallucinating, it's only an illusion . . . a figment of the imagination, shrouded in a cloak of mystery . . . (*Picks up the keys, smiles tenderly.*) She threw down the keys, she's saying she's not the mistress of the house any

390 more . . . (*Jingles the keys.*) Ah, well, what does it matter.

(*The orchestra can be heard tuning up.*)

Eh, musicians, play, I want to hear you play! Everyone, come and see, how Yermolai Lopakhin will take an axe out into the cherry orchard, and all the trees will come crashing to the ground! And we'll build summer homes,

395 and our grandchildren and great grandchildren will see a new life . . . Let's have music, play!

(*The music plays.* LYUBOV ANDREEVNA *lowers herself into a chair and weeps bitterly.*)

(*Reproachfully.*) Why, why didn't you listen to me? My, poor, dear friend, you'll never get it back now, never. (*In tears.*) Oh, the sooner all this is behind us, the sooner we can change our chaotic lives, our absurd, unhappy lives.   400

PISHCHIK: (*Takes him by the hand, in a low voice.*) She is weeping. Come into the ballroom, let's leave her alone ... Come ... (*Takes him by the hand and leads him into the ballroom.*)

LOPAKHIN: What's going on here? Let there be music! Loud, the way I want it! Let everything be the way I want it!   405 (*With irony.*) Here comes the new master, the owner of the cherry orchard! (*Accidentally shoves against a table, almost turning over a candelabrum.*) I can pay for it all, for everything! (*Exits with* PISHCHIK.)

(*There is no one left in the ballroom or the drawing room, except* LYUBOV ANDREEVNA, *who is sitting, huddled over weeping bitterly. The music plays softly.* ANYA *and* TROFIMOV *rush in.* ANYA *goes to her mother and kneels before her.* TROFIMOV *stays at the entrance to the ballroom.*)

ANYA: Mama! ... Mama, are you crying? My dear, good, kind   410 Mama, my beautiful Mama, I love you ... I bless you. The cherry orchard is sold, it's gone, it's true, it's true, but don't cry, Mama, you still have your whole life before you to live, and your pure and beautiful soul ... Come with me, come, my darling, away from here, come! ... We'll plant   415 a new orchard, more glorious than this one, you'll see, you'll understand, and joy, a deep, peaceful, gentle joy will settle into your soul, like the warm, evening sun, and you will smile, Mama! Come, darling! Come! ...

ACT FOUR

The same setting as Act One. There are no curtains on the windows, no pictures on the walls; only a few pieces of furniture remain, stacked in a corner, as if for sale. There is a feeling of emptiness. There are suitcases, travel bags, etc. piled high upstage by the door leading to the outside. The door to stage left is open, from which the voices of VARYA *and* ANYA *can be heard.* LOPAKHIN *stands there, waiting.* YASHA *holds a tray of glasses, filled with champagne. In the entrance hall,* YEPIKHODOV *is packing a case. Offstage, voices are heard—the peasants have come to say good-bye.* GAEV's *voice is heard: "Thank you, my friends, I thank you."*

YASHA: The peasants have come to say good-bye. Now here's my opinion on that subject, Yermolai Alekseich: The people are good, but what do *they* know.

(*The noise dies down.* LYUBOV ANDREEVNA *and* GAEV *enter through the entrance hall; she is no longer crying, but she is very pale: she is trembling, and it is difficult for her to speak.*)

GAEV: You gave them everything in your purse, Lyuba. No! You mustn't do that!   5

LYUBOV ANDREEVNA: I couldn't help it! I couldn't help it!

(*Both exit.*)

LOPAKHIN: (*At the door, following after them.*) Please, I humbly beg you! A farewell toast! I didn't think to bring any from town . . . and I could only find one bottle at the station. Please!   10

(*Pause.*)

So, my friends! You don't want any? (*Steps away from the door.*) If I'd known, I wouldn't have bought it. Never mind, I won't have any, either.

(YASHA *carefully places the tray on the table.*)

Drink up, Yasha, why don't you.

15   YASHA: To those who are leaving! And to those who are staying behind! (*Drinks.*) This isn't real champagne, that much I can tell you.

LOPAKHIN: Eight rubles a bottle.

(*Pause.*)

Wickedly cold in here, isn't it.

20   YASHA: They didn't stoke up the stoves today, what's the point, everybody's leaving. (*Laughs.*)

LOPAKHIN: What are you laughing about?

YASHA: I'm happy.

LOPAKHIN: It's October, but outside it's sunny and mild, like
25   summertime. Good weather for construction. (*Looks at his watch, at the door.*) Ladies and gentlemen, bear in mind, only forty-six minutes left until the train departs! That means we have to leave for the station in twenty minutes. Hurry, everyone!

(TROFIMOV *enters from the outside, wearing a coat.*)

30   TROFIMOV: I think it's time to go now. They've already brought the horses around. Where are my galoshes, damn it! They've disappeared. (*At the door.*) Anya, my galoshes aren't here! I can't find them!

LOPAKHIN: And I've got to get to Kharkov. I'll go with you as
35   far as the station. I'm going to spend the winter in Kharkov. Yes. Here I am, standing around, talking to you, I'm lost when I'm not working. I can't live without work, I don't know what to do with my hands; isn't it strange, look, they're hanging there, as if they belonged to someone else.

40   TROFIMOV: We'll be leaving momentarily, and you'll return to all your worthy enterprises.

LOPAKHIN: Have a glass with me.

TROFIMOV: I can't.

LOPAKHIN: So, it's off to Moscow, then?

45   TROFIMOV: Yes, that's right, I'll go with them into town, and tomorrow, it's off to Moscow.

LOPAKHIN: Yes . . . Well, the professors haven't started their lectures yet, no doubt they're all waiting for you!

TROFIMOV: That's none of your business.

50   LOPAKHIN: How many years is it, then, since you've been at the university?

TROFIMOV: Think up something new, why don't you? That's a stale and feeble joke, it's not funny any more. (*Searches for his galoshes.*) It's very likely we may never see each other again,
55   you know, so allow me, please, to give you some parting advice: Don't wave your arms around so much! Try to get out of the habit of waving your arms when you talk, if you can. All this planning of yours, you know, building summer houses, creating a new generation of independent landown-
60   ers, and so on and so forth,—why, that's just another form of waving your arms . . . Oh, well, never mind, all things considered, I like you . . . I do. You have delicate, sensitive fingers, the fingers of an artist . . . you have a delicate, sensitive soul . . .

LOPAKHIN: (*Embraces him.*) Good-bye, my friend. Thanks for everything. Just in case, here, take some money for the   65
journey.

TROFIMOV: Why should I? I don't need it.

LOPAKHIN: But you don't have any!

TROFIMOV: Yes, I do, thank you very much. I've just received some money for a translation. Here it is, right here, in my   70
pocket. (*Anxiously.*) Now where are my galoshes!

VARYA: (*From the other room.*) Here, take the filthy things! (*Tosses a pair of rubber galoshes on the stage.*)

TROFIMOV: Why are you so angry, Varya? Hm . . . These are not my galoshes!   75

LOPAKHIN: This spring I planted almost 3,000 acres of poppies, and made a clean profit of 40,000. And when my poppies bloomed, now what a sight that was! So, here's what I'm saying, I've just made 40,000 rubles, and I'm offering you a loan because I can afford to. Why do you look down your   80
nose at me? I'm a peasant . . . what do you expect?

TROFIMOV: Your father was a peasant, mine was a chemist, none of it means a thing.

(LOPAKHIN *takes out his wallet.*)

Stop that, stop . . . Even if you were to give me 200,000, I wouldn't take it. I am a free man. And everything that is   85
so sacred and dear to all of you, rich and poor alike, hasn't the slightest significance to me, it's all dust, adrift in the wind. I can survive without you, I can even surpass you, I am proud and strong. Mankind is on a quest to seek the highest truth, the greatest happiness possible on this earth,   90
and I am in the front ranks!

LOPAKHIN: And will you reach your destination?

TROFIMOV: Yes, I shall.

(*Pause.*)

I shall, or else I'll show others the way.

(*In the distance, the sound is heard of an axe falling on a tree.*)

LOPAKHIN: So, good-bye, my friend. Time to go. Here we are,   95
looking down our noses at one another, and all the while, life goes on, in spite of any of us. When I work, for days on end, without any rest, that's when my thoughts come most clearly, that's when I know why I am on this earth, why I exist. And how many of us are there in Russia, my friend,   100
who still don't know why they exist. Ah well, what does it matter, that's not the point, is it. They say that Leonid Andreich has taken a position at a bank, 6,000 a year . . . He won't be able to keep it, though, he's too lazy . . .

ANYA: (*At the door.*) Mama asks you not to cut down the or-   105
chard till after she's gone.

TROFIMOV: Isn't it possible to show some tact . . . (*Exits through the entrance hall.*)

LOPAKHIN: Yes, yes, right away . . . Really.

ANYA: Have they sent Firs to the hospital yet?   110

YASHA: I told them about it this morning. I'm sure they did.

ANYA: (*To* YEPIKHODOV, *who is walking through the hall.*) Semyon Panteleich, please, go find out, would you, if they've taken Firs to the hospital yet.

YASHA: (*Offended.*) I told Yegor this morning. Why ask the   115
same question over and over!

YEPIKHODOV: The ancient Firs, in my final opinion, is beyond repair; he should return to his forefathers. And I can only envy him. (*Places the suitcase on a hat box, and crushes it.*)
120 Oh, well, of course. I knew it. (*Exits.*)

YASHA: (*Mocking.*) "Mister Disaster" . . .

VARYA: (*From behind the door.*) Have they taken Firs to the hospital?

ANYA: Yes, they have.

125 VARYA: Why didn't they bring the letter to the doctor?

ANYA: We'll just have to send it along . . . (*Exits.*)

VARYA: (*From the adjacent room.*) Where's Yasha? Tell him his mother's here, she wants to say good-bye to him.

YASHA: (*Waves his hand.*) I'm losing my patience.

(*During this,* DUNYASHA *has been busying herself with the luggage; now that* YASHA *is alone, she goes up to him.*)

130 DUNYASHA: Just one last look, Yasha. You're leaving . . . you're abandoning me . . . (*Weeps and throws her arms around his neck.*)

YASHA: What's there to cry about? (*Drinks champagne.*) In six days, I'll be in Paris again. Tomorrow we'll board an ex-
135 press train, and off we'll go, that's the last you'll ever see of us. I just can't believe it. "Vive la France!" . . . This place is not for me, I can't live here . . . and that's all there is to it. I've seen a lot of ignorance—and I've had enough. (*Drinks champagne.*) What's there to cry about? Behave
140 yourself properly, then you won't cry so much.

DUNYASHA: (*Powders her face, looks at herself in the mirror.*) Send me a letter from Paris. You know much I have loved you, Yasha, I have loved you very, very much! I'm a sensitive creature, Yasha!

145 YASHA: They're coming. (*Busies himself with the luggage, hums softly.*)

(*Enter* LYUBOV ANDREEVNA, GAEV, ANYA, *and* CHARLOTTA IVANOVNA.)

GAEV: We really ought to be going. There's hardly any time left. (*Looks at* YASHA.) Who smells of herring in here?

LYUBOV ANDREEVNA: In ten minutes time we'll be getting
150 into the carriages . . . (*Glances around the room.*) Good-bye, beloved home, home of my forefathers. Winter will pass, spring will come, and you'll no longer be here, they will have destroyed you. How much these walls have seen! (*Kisses her daughter passionately.*) My treasure, you're radi-
155 ant, your eyes are sparkling, like two diamonds. Are you happy? Very happy?

ANYA: Very! We're starting a new life, Mama!

GAEV: (*Cheerfully.*) Everything's turned out quite well, as a mat-ter of fact, yes, indeed. Before the cherry orchard was sold,
160 we were all upset, we suffered a great deal, but then, when everything was settled, once and for all, finally and irrevoca-bly, we all calmed down, we were even glad . . . And now I'm a bank official, a financier . . . "yellow into the middle pocket," and you, Lyuba, for all that we've been through,
165 you're looking better than ever, no doubt about it.

LYUBOV ANDREEVNA: Yes, I'm calmer, it's true.

(*She is given her hat and coat.*)

I can sleep better now. Take my things out, Yasha. It's time. (*To* ANYA.) My darling child, we shall see each other again,

soon . . . I am going to Paris, I shall live there on the money your great-aunt from Yaroslavl sent to buy the estate—God 170 bless great-aunt!—but that money won't last very long.

ANYA: You'll come home soon, Mama, soon . . . won't you? And I'll study, take my examinations, and then I'll work, I'll take care of you. And we'll read all sorts of marvelous books together, Mama . . . Won't we? (*Kisses her mother's* 175 *hands.*) We'll read through the long autumn evenings, we'll read so many books, and a wonderful new world will open before us . . . (*Dreaming.*) Come home, Mama . . .

LYUBOV ANDREEVNA: I'll come, my jewel. (*Embraces her daughter.*)

(*Enter* LOPAKHIN, *and* CHARLOTTA, *who is softly humming a tune.*)

GAEV: Charlotta is happy: she's singing! 180

CHARLOTTA: (*Picks up a bundle, resembling an infant in swaddling clothes.*) "My sweet little baby, 'bye, 'bye . . ."

(*The child's cry: "Wa, wa! . . ." can be heard.*)

"Hushabye, baby, my sweet little boy."

(*The child's cry: "Wa! . . . wa! . . ."*)

Poor baby! I feel so sorry for you! (*Throws the bundle down.*) Now, please, find me another job. I can't go on like this. 185

LOPAKHIN: We shall, Charlotta Ivanovna, don't worry.

GAEV: We're all being cast out, Varya's going away . . . suddenly no one needs us any more.

CHARLOTTA: There's nowhere for me to live in town. I must go away . . . (*Hums.*) It doesn't matter . . . 190

(*Enter* PISHCHIK.)

LOPAKHIN: One of nature's wonders! . . .

PISHCHIK: (*Out of breath.*) Oy, let me catch my breath . . . I'm all worn out . . . Most honorable friends . . . Give me some water . . .

GAEV: Looking for money, by any chance? I remain your 195 humble servant, but, forgive me, I really must avoid the temptation . . . (*Exits.*)

PISHCHIK: I haven't been here in such a long, long, time . . . loveliest lady . . . (*To* LOPAKHIN.) And you are here, too . . . so good to see you . . . a man of the highest intelligence . . . 200 here, take it . . . it's yours . . . (*Gives* LOPAKHIN *some money.*) Four hundred rubles . . . I still owe you eight hundred and forty . . .

LOPAKHIN: (*Shrugs his shoulders in amazement.*) I must be dreaming . . . Where on earth did you get this? 205

PISHCHIK: Wait . . . So hot . . . Most extraordinary circum-stances. Some Englishmen came to visit my estate, and what do you know, they found white clay in the earth . . . whatever that is . . . (*To* LYUBOV ANDREEVNA.) And here's four hundred for you . . . elegant, exquisite lady . . . (*Gives* 210 *her some money.*) The rest will come later. (*Drinks the water.*) Just now, a young man on the train was telling us about this great philosopher . . . how he's advising everyone to jump off the roof . . . "Jump!" he says, and that will solve everything. (*Amazed.*) Imagine that! Water! . . . 215

LOPAKHIN: What Englishmen are you talking about?

PISHCHIK: I leased them a plot of the land with the white clay for twenty-four years . . . But now, forgive me, please, I've run out of time . . . a long ride ahead . . . I'm going to the

220 Znoykovs . . . to the Kardamonovs . . . I owe everybody . . . (*Drinks.*) Good day to you all . . . I'll drop by again on Thursday . . .

LYUBOV ANDREEVNA: We're just moving into town now, and tomorrow I'm going abroad . . .

225 PISHCHIK: What? (*Anxiously.*) Why to town? What's this I see . . . furniture . . . suitcases . . . Well, never mind . . . (*In tears.*) Never mind . . . Very very smart people, these Englishmen . . . people of the highest intelligence . . . Never mind . . . I wish you happiness . . . God will watch over you . . .
230 Never mind . . . Everything on this earth must come to an end . . . (*Kisses* LYUBOV ANDREEVNA*s hand.*) And when you hear the news that my own end has come, remember this good old horse, won't you, and say: "Once upon a time there lived an old so-and-so . . . Simeonov-Pishchik . . .
235 God rest his soul" . . . Magnificent weather we're having . . . Yes . . . (*Exits in great confusion, and immediately returns and speaks from the doorway.*) Dashenka sends her regards! (*Exits.*)

LYUBOV ANDREEVNA: And now we can go. But I'm leaving
240 with two worries. The first is Firs—he's ill. (*Looks at her watch.*) We still have five minutes . . .

ANYA: Mama, they've already sent Firs to the hospital. Yasha sent him this morning.

LYUBOV ANDREEVNA: My second sorrow is Varya. She's used
245 to getting up early and working, and now, without work, she's like a fish out of water. She's grown thin and pale, she weeps all the time, poor thing . . .

(*Pause.*)

You know very well, Yermolai Alekseich, I have dreamed . . . that one day she would marry you, in fact, it was ob-
250 vious to everyone that you would be married. (*She whispers to* ANYA, *who motions to* CHARLOTTA, *and both exit.*) She loves you, you seem to be fond of her, and I don't know why, I simply don't know why it is that you go out of your way to avoid one other. I don't understand it!

255 LOPAKHIN: I don't understand it myself, to tell the truth. It's all so strange, somehow . . . If there's still time, then I'm ready to do it now . . . Basta! Let's settle it once and for all; without you here, I don't think I could possibly propose to her.

LYUBOV ANDREEVNA: Excellent. It only takes a minute, you
260 know. I'll call her in right away . . .

LOPAKHIN: Oh yes, and there's champagne, too. (*Looks at glasses.*) It's empty, someone drank it all up.

(YASHA *coughs.*)

Or, should I say, lapped it all up . . .

LYUBOV ANDREEVNA: (*Excited.*) Splendid. We're leaving . . .
265 Yasha, "allez"! I'll call her . . . (*At the door.*) Varya, stop what you're doing, and come here. Come! (*Exits with* YASHA.)

LOPAKHIN: (*Looks at his watch.*) Yes . . .

(*Pause.*)

(*Muffled laughter and whispering is heard from behind the door; finally,* VARYA *enters.*)

VARYA: (*In a lengthy search for something.*) That's strange, I can't find it anywhere . . .

270 LOPAKHIN: What are you looking for?

VARYA: I put it away myself, I can't remember where.

(*Pause.*)

LOPAKHIN: So where will you go now, Varvara Mikhailovna?

VARYA: Me? To the Ragulins' . . . I've agreed to work for them . . . you know . . . as a housekeeper.

LOPAKHIN: Aren't they in Yashnevo? That's about forty-five 275 miles from here.

(*Pause.*)

And so, life has come to an end in this house . . .

VARYA: (*Searching among the things.*) Where can it be . . . Perhaps I put it in the trunk . . . Yes, life has come to an end in this house . . . and will be no more . . . 280

LOPAKHIN: And I'm off to Kharkov now . . . on the same train. I've got a lot of business there. But I'm leaving Yepikhodov here to look after things . . . I've hired him, you know.

VARYA: Really!

LOPAKHIN: Last year at this time it was already snowing, if you 285 remember, and now it's so sunny and calm. Only it's quite cold . . . Three degrees of frost, almost.

VARYA: I hadn't noticed.

(*Pause.*)

Anyway, our thermometer's broken . . .

(*Pause.*)

(*A voice is heard calling from outside: "Yermolai Alekseich! . . ."*)

LOPAKHIN: (*As if he'd long been waiting for this call.*) Coming! 290 (*He hurries out.*)

(VARYA *sits on the floor, puts her head on a bundle of clothing, and sobs quietly. The door opens, and* LYUBOV ANDREEVNA *enters cautiously.*)

LYUBOV ANDREEVNA: So?

(*Pause.*)

We'd better go.

VARYA: (*No longer weeping, wipes her eyes.*) Yes, Mamochka, it's time. If I don't miss the train, I might even get to the Rag- 295 ulins' today . . .

LYUBOV ANDREEVNA: (*At the door.*) Anya, put your coat on!

(*Enter* ANYA, *then* GAEV, CHARLOTTA IVANOVNA. GAEV *is wearing a warm coat with a hood. The* SERVANTS *and* CARRIAGE DRIVERS *assemble.* YEPIKHODOV *is busy with the luggage.*)

Now, we can be on our way.

ANYA: (*Overjoyed.*) We're on our way!

GAEV: My friends, my dear, kind friends! Upon leaving this 300 house forever, how can I be silent, how can I refrain, upon this our departure, from expressing those feelings, which now fill my very being . . .

ANYA: (*Imploring.*) Uncle!

VARYA: Uncle, must you! 305

GAEV: (*Dejected.*) "Double the yellow into the middle . . ." I'll be quiet . . .

(*Enter* TROFIMOV, *then* LOPAKHIN.)

TROFIMOV: All right, ladies and gentlemen, time to depart!

LOPAKHIN: Yepikhodov, my coat!

310 LYUBOV ANDREEVNA: I want to sit for just one minute longer. I never really noticed before, what walls this house has, what ceilings, and now I look at them with such longing, with such tender love . . .

GAEV: I remember, when I was six, on Trinity Sunday, I sat at
315 this window and watched my father walking to church . . .

LYUBOV ANDREEVNA: Have they taken everything out?

LOPAKHIN: I think so. (*To* YEPIKHODOV, *who is putting on his coat.*) Yepikhodov, see to it that everything's been taken care of.

YEPIKHODOV: (*Speaking in a hoarse voice.*) Don't you worry,
320 Yermolai Alekseich.

LOPAKHIN: What's the matter with your voice?

YEPIKHODOV: I just drank some water, and I must have swallowed something.

YASHA: (*Contemptuously.*) What ignorance . . .

325 LYUBOV ANDREEVNA: We're leaving—and not a soul will be left here . . .

LOPAKHIN: Until springtime.

VARYA: (*Pulls an umbrella out of a bundle—it appears as if she were about to strike someone;* LOPAKHIN *pretends to be frightened.*)
330 What's wrong with you? . . . I wouldn't think of it . . .

TROFIMOV: Ladies and gentlemen, please, let's get into the carriages now . . . It's time to go! The train will arrive any minute!

VARYA: Petya, here they are, your galoshes, beside the suitcase.
335 (*In tears.*) Look how old and muddy they are . . .

TROFIMOV: (*Putting on the galoshes.*) We're off, ladies and gentlemen!

GAEV: (*Very confused, afraid of bursting into tears.*) Train . . . station . . . "Croisé into the middle pocket, Double the white
340 into the corner . . ."

LYUBOV ANDREEVNA: We're off!

LOPAKHIN: Is everyone here? No one left behind? (*Locks the side door stage left.*) There are some things stored in here, better lock up. We're off!

345 ANYA: Good-bye, house! Good-bye, old life!

TROFIMOV: Hello, new life . . . (*Exits with* ANYA.)

(VARYA *glances around the room and exits without hurrying. Exit* YASHA, *and* CHARLOTTA, *with the little dog.*)

LOPAKHIN: And so, until springtime. Come now, ladies and gentlemen, we'd better be going . . . Once more, a very good-bye!! . . . (*Exits.*)

(LYUBOV ANDREEVNA *and* GAEV *are left alone together. It is as if they have been waiting for this moment; they throw themselves into each others' arms and sob quietly, with restraint, fearing they might be heard.*)

GAEV: (*In despair.*) My sister, my sister . . .   350

LYUBOV ANDREEVNA: O my precious orchard, my sweet, lovely orchard! . . . My life, my youth, my happiness, farewell! . . . Farewell! . . .

(ANYA's *voice calls out, merrily:* "Mama! . . .")

(TROFIMOV's *voice calls out, gaily, excitedly:* "A-oo! . . .")

LYUBOV ANDREEVNA: For the last time, let me look at these walls, these windows . . . how my mother loved to walk 355 about this room . . .

GAEV: My sister, my sister! . . .

(ANYA's *voice:* "Mama! . . .")

(TROFIMOV's *voice:* "A-oo . . .")

LYUBOV ANDREEVNA: We're off! . . .

(*They exit.*)

(*The stage is empty. There is the sound of all the doors being locked, and then of the carriages pulling away. It grows very still. Through the stillness comes the remote sound of the axe falling on a tree, a lonely, melancholy sound. Footsteps are heard.* FIRS *appears at the door, stage right. He is dressed, as always, in a jacket and a white waistcoat, with slippers on his feet. He is ill.*)

FIRS: (*Goes to the door, tries the handle.*) Locked. They've gone . . . (*Sits on the sofa.*) They've forgotten about me . . . Never 360 mind . . . I'll sit here for a just a bit . . . And Leonid Andreich, most likely, didn't put his fur coat on, went off wearing his light one . . . (*Sighs, anxiously.*) Just slipped my notice . . . These young people nowadays! (*Mutters something incomprehensible.*) And life has passed by, somehow, as 365 if I never lived it at all. (*Lies down.*) I'll lie down for just a bit . . . Don't have too much strength left, now, do you, no, not much, not much at all . . . You pathetic old fool, you! . . . (*Lies there, immobile.*)

(*A distant sound is heard, as if coming from the sky, the sound of a breaking string, dying away, a mournful sound. Silence falls, and all that is heard, far off in the orchard, is the sound of the axe falling on a tree.*)

PRONUNCIATION GUIDE TO RUSSIAN NAMES

Cast of Characters

Lyubov (Lyuba) Andreevna Ranevskaya, Lyoo-bof´ (Lyoo´-ba) An-drey´-ev-na Ra-nyef´-ska-ya
("drey" rhymes with the English word "grey")

Anya (Anechka), An´-ya (An´-yech-ka)

Varya (Varvara Mikhailovna), Va´-rya (Var-var´-a Mee-khai´-lov-na)
("khai" rhymes with the word "why")

Leonid (Lyonya) Andreevich (Andreich) Gaev, Le-o-need´ (Lyon´-ya) Andrey´-e-veech (An-drey´-eech) Ga´-yef

Yermolai Alekseevich (Alekseich) Lopakhin, Yer-mo-lai´ A-lek-syey´-e-veech (A-lek-sey´-eech) Lo-pa´-kheen
("lai" in "Yermolai" rhymes with the word "why")
("syey" rhymes with the word "grey")

Pyotr (Petya) Sergeevich (Sergeich) Trofimov, Pyo´-tr (Pye´-tya) Syer-gey´-e-veech (Syer-gey´-eech) Tro-fee´-mof

Boris Borisovich Simeonov-Pishchik, Bo-rees´ Bo-rees´-o-veech See-myon´-of-Peesh´-cheek

Charlotta Ivanovna, Shar-lo´-ta Ee-van´-ov-na
Semyon Panteleevich (Panteleich) Yepikhodov, Se-myon´ Pan-te-lyey´-e-veech (Pan-te-lyey´-eech) Ye-pee-khod´-of ("lyey" rhymes with the word "grey")

Dunyasha (Avdotya Fyodorovna), Doon-ya´-sha (Av-do´-tya Fyo´-do-rov-na)
Firs Nikolaevich, Feers Nee-ko-la´-ye-veech
Yasha, Ya´-sha

Other Russian Names Appearing in the Text

Anastasy, A-na-sta´-see
Dashenka, Da´-shen-ka
Deriganov, Dye-ree-ga´-nof
Grisha, Gree´-sha
Kardamonov, Kar-da-mo´-nof
Karp, Karp
Kharkov, Khar´-kof
Kozoedov (Fyodor), Ko-zo-ye´-dof (Fyo´-dor)
Lopakhina, Lo-pa´-khee-na
Mama (Mamochka), Ma´-ma (Ma´-moch-ka)
Papa, Pa´-pa

Petrushka, Pye-troosh´-ka
Polya, Po´-lya
Ragulin, Ra-goo´-leen
Yaroslavl, Ya-ro-slavl´
Yashnevo, Yash´-nye-vo
Yefimyushka, Ye-fee´-myoosh-ka
Yegor, Ye-gor´
Yevstigney, Yev-steeg-nyey´ ("nyey" rhymes with the word "grey")
Znoykov, Znoy´-kof

Bernard Shaw

George Bernard Shaw (1856–1950) was a man of wide-ranging passions and huge abilities (Shaw disliked the name "George" and never used it, preferring "Bernard" or simply "G.B.S."). By his fortieth birthday he had written five novels, three volumes of classic music criticism, and three volumes of incendiary theater reviews; he had become visible in the influential socialist political organization, the **FABIAN SOCIETY;** he had written the first books in English on Wagner's operas and on Ibsen's plays; and he had just started his career as a dramatist, a career that would eventually include more than fifty plays.

Shaw was born in Dublin. Like Jonathan Swift and Richard Brinsley Sheridan before him, Shaw retained the satiric perspective of the Irish outsider in England. His mother was a music teacher and his sister was a promising singer when they left for London while Shaw was in his teens. He followed them to London in 1876. A shy and self-effacing young man, Shaw took a variety of jobs that brought him into contact with the public, and he used the opportunity of lecturing for the Fabian Society to develop the brilliantly articulate persona we recognize today as "G.B.S." Throughout the 1880s, Shaw worked with the Fabians, adopting their plan of gradual social reform in place of a more rigorously Marxist call for social revolution. The Fabians strove to change society through a strategy of permeation, working to get their members elected into prominent offices, where their educational and social reforms might be put into effect. Shaw was deeply influenced by the Fabians' gradualist scheme for social improvement—a scheme that underlies the utopian project of his greatest plays—for Fabian gradualism synchronized with Shaw's other passion, Creative Evolution. Appalled by what he regarded as the mindless mechanism of Darwinian natural selection, Shaw resisted the notion that human evolution followed a random and inevitable process. He urged instead that humanity take command of its future by willing itself to evolve in certain humane directions, and he advocated eugenics, capital punishment, and other ideas in the interest of the development of the species. Shaw attempted an uneasy synthesis of the Fabian socialist project of gradual social evolution with the individualist metaphysics of Creative Evolution: the improvement of society through the improvement of each of its members.

Shaw's friend William Archer once described seeing Shaw in the British Museum reading room simultaneously reading Marx's *Das Kapital* and the score of Wagner's *Ring of the Niebelung* cycle. The blending of political substance with a rich and deeply harmonized verbal music became a constant feature of Shaw's drama. Writing as a theater critic in the 1890s, Shaw became the champion of Ibsen in England. Vowing to lay siege to the conventions of the nineteenth-century theater, he touted Ibsen's plays and lambasted the corny tearjerkers, simplistic melodramas, and overstuffed Shakespearean productions that were the theater's common fare. Not incidentally, he worked to create a taste for his own plays, an operatic drama of the intellectual passions.

Shaw's career as a playwright falls into three main phases. Shaw's earliest plays—*Widowers' Houses* (1892) and *Mrs. Warren's Profession* (1893)—attacked specific social problems, like slum landlords and international prostitution. But Shaw more often linked social ills to the smug pieties of conventional morality. His plays generally work to disillusion his main characters—and his audience—from the ready acceptance of bourgeois ideology as a natural "reality." This process of disillusion informs Shaw's lighter comedies of the 1890s, plays like *Arms and the Man* (1894), *Candida* (1894), and *Caesar and Cleopatra* (1898). After the turn of the century, however, Shaw entered on his maturity as a playwright, undertaking a series of major comedies that place this process of disillusion directly in conflict with society's most important institutions: marriage and sexuality in *Man and Superman* (1903); British imperialism in Ireland in *John Bull's Other Island* (1904); salvation, damnation, and raw power in *Major Barbara* (1905); medicine in *The Doctor's Dilemma* (1906); language and class in *Pygmalion* (1912). Several of these plays were first produced at the Court Theater, under the management of Shaw's close friend Harley Granville Barker, who originated the part of Cusins in *Major Barbara* and other Shavian roles. Under Barker and his partner J.E. Vedrenne, the Court Theater in 1904–1907 became the most influential theater in London before World War I. Through its efforts, and Shaw's own energy as playwright, director, and advisor, the Court made Shaw's reputation as a major dramatist. With the coming of World War I, and the violent waste of civilization it brought with it, Shaw's confidence in the eventual perfection of humanity was deeply shaken, and the plays of his final half-century are much bleaker, more uncertain in tone: his magnificent "fantasia in the Russian manner on English themes," *Heartbreak House* (1919), modeled on Chekhov's *The Cherry Orchard; Saint Joan* (1923), perhaps his best-loved play; his five-play quintet on the origin and future of the species, *Back to Methuselah* (1921); and many others. In contrast to the confidence of Shaw's earlier plays, the later dramas generally seem to ask the question that Shaw gave to his Saint Joan: "O God that madest this beautiful earth, when will it be ready to receive Thy saints? How long, O Lord, how long?"

MAJOR BARBARA

Shaw was born before the publication of Darwin's *Origin of Species* in 1859, and he died after the dropping of the atomic bomb on Hiroshima. His major plays, like *Major Barbara,* treat the problems of the twentieth century in the dramatic vocabulary of Edwardian **COMEDY OF MANNERS.** *Major Barbara* is typical of the dialectical process of Shaw's plays. From the

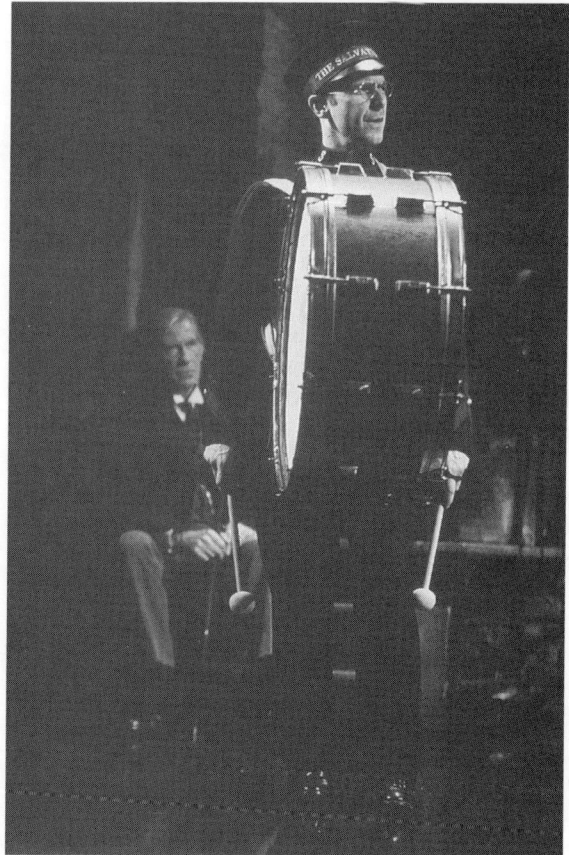

Adolphus Cusins beats the big drum in the finale of act 2 of Bernard Shaw's *Major Barbara.*

outset—when Stephen learns that his income is derived from his father's munitions empire—Shaw forces the audience and his characters to question the nature of their values, particularly the sense that good and evil, morality and economics, the power to save and the power to destroy can be easily or conveniently distinguished from one another. As a result, the play forces a deeply ironic experience on its characters and on the audience. For Shaw is interested in salvation, not simply the moralizing salvation promised by the Salvation Army, but a Nietzschean transvaluation of values, a salvation beyond the conventional abstractions of good and evil that he regards as necessary to the transformation of English society.

The play is structured dialectically, progressing from thesis, to antithesis, to a problematic synthesis. The "thesis" of act 1 concerns the values of Wilton Crescent: the comfortable morality of the English upper classes. As the scene proceeds, though, Shaw suggests that conventional morality, the innate knowledge of right and wrong, is in fact supported by Undershaft's money and gunpowder. The "antithesis" of act 2 offers the unconventional morality of the Salvation Army; Barbara's shelter in West Ham claims to provide true salvation by requiring a more sincere form of religious conviction. However, as it turns out, both Wilton Crescent and West Ham are equally in the grip of Bodger and Undershaft. The distiller and the munitions-maker determine the material realities on which society erects its illusory social "ideals" and calls them "reality." The Dionysian sacrifice of Barbara at the end of act 2— with its echoes of Christ's crucifixion as well—prepares us for her resurrection in the "synthesis" offered by act 3; in Perivale St Andrews, the spiritual Barbara and the intellectual Cusins are married with the blessing of the explosive Undershaft. We might be troubled, though, by the "synthesis" offered by the utopian factory town, for Undershaft's utopia hardly seems revolutionary. In many ways, Perivale St Andrews largely duplicates turn-of-the-century English class society and industrial capitalism, with the poverty and dirt cleaned up. The play's last act is often said to be unconvincing, and we might wonder whether that is in fact part of Shaw's purpose in *Major Barbara*. Once Shaw instructs us in the process of dialectical criticism, perhaps he invites us to scrutinize even Undershaft's bourgeois utopia, to see Perivale St Andrews as itself in need of further (r)evolution.

Shaw made Andrew Undershaft a magnificently melodramatic, attractive, amoral munitions-maker, whose creative ability is harnessed to the power to destroy. Moreover, Shaw drew a parallel between Undershaft and a crucial dramatic precursor, the Dionysus of Euripides' *The Bacchae*. The character of Cusins was modeled on Shaw's friend, the well-known classical scholar Gilbert Murray, and in the original production, Cusins was even played to resemble Murray. In act 2, Cusins quotes a brief passage adapted from Murray's translation of *The Bacchae,* part of the choral speech delivered just before Pentheus is led out to spy on the Bacchae and be killed. We might take this invocation of Dionysus as a final clue to the play's attitude. Much like Euripides, Shaw prevents his audience from sympathizing entirely with his hero, from readily accepting the terrible power necessary to change the world. Although the play ends with a ceremonial marriage characteristic of **ROMANTIC COMEDY**—symbolizing the union of intellect, spirit, and power—the fact that Dionysus Undershaft presides over this union should give us pause. Can the power he wields really be harnessed for our salvation?

Shaw, not surprisingly, had a systematic but unconventional approach to English spelling and punctuation, and insisted that publisher's observe it when printing his plays; this edition of *Major Barbara* accordingly preserves Shaw's style.

MAJOR BARBARA

Bernard Shaw

CHARACTERS

STEPHEN UNDERSHAFT	CHARLES LOMAX
LADY BRITOMART	RUMMY MITCHENS
BARBARA UNDERSHAFT	SNOBBY PRICE
SARAH UNDERSHAFT	PETER SHIRLEY
ANDREW UNDERSHAFT	BILTON
JENNY HILL	MRS BAINES
BILL WALKER	ADOLPHUS CUSINS
MORRISON	

ACT ONE

It is after dinner in January 1906, in the library in LADY BRITO-MART UNDERSHAFT'*s house in Wilton Crescent. A large and comfortable settee is in the middle of the room, upholstered in dark leather. A person sitting on it (it is vacant at present) would have, on his right,* LADY BRITOMART'*s writing table, with the lady herself busy at it; a smaller writing table behind him on his left; the door behind him on* LADY BRITOMART'*s side; and a window with a window seat directly on his left. Near the window is an armchair.*

LADY BRITOMART *is a woman of fifty or thereabouts, well dressed and yet careless of her dress, well bred and quite reckless of her breeding, well mannered and yet appallingly outspoken and indifferent to the opinion of her interlocutors, amiable and yet peremptory, arbitrary, and high-tempered to the last bearable degree, and withal a very typical managing matron of the upper class, treated as a naughty child until she grew into a scolding mother, and finally settling down with plenty of practical ability and worldly experience, limited in the oddest way with domestic and class limitations, conceiving the universe exactly as if it were a large house in Wilton Crescent, though handling her corner of it very effectively on that assumption, and being quite enlightened and liberal as to the books in the library, the pictures on the walls, the music in the portfolios, and the articles in the papers.*

Her son, STEPHEN, *comes in. He is a gravely correct young man under 25, taking himself very seriously, but still in some awe of his mother, from childish habit and bachelor shyness rather than from any weakness of character.*

STEPHEN: Whats the matter?

LADY BRITOMART: Presently, Stephen.

(STEPHEN *submissively walks to the settee and sits down. He takes up a Liberal weekly called* The Speaker.)

LADY BRITOMART: Dont begin to read, Stephen. I shall require all your attention.

5 STEPHEN: It was only while I was waiting—

LADY BRITOMART: Dont make excuses, Stephen. (*He puts down* The Speaker.) Now! (*She finishes her writing; rises; and comes to the settee.*) I have not kept you waiting very long, I think.

STEPHEN: Not at all, mother.

10 LADY BRITOMART: Bring me my cushion. (*He takes the cushion from the chair at the desk and arranges it for her as she sits down on the settee.*) Sit down. (*He sits down and fingers his tie nervously.*) Dont fiddle with your tie, Stephen: there is nothing the matter with it.

STEPHEN: I beg your pardon. (*He fiddles with his watch chain instead.*) 15

LADY BRITOMART: Now are you attending to me, Stephen?

STEPHEN: Of course, mother.

LADY BRITOMART: No: it's not of course. I want something much more than your everyday matter-of-course attention. I am going to speak to you very seriously, Stephen. I 20 wish you would let that chain alone.

STEPHEN: (*Hastily relinquishing the chain.*) Have I done anything to annoy you, mother? If so, it was quite unintentional.

LADY BRITOMART: (*Astonished.*) Nonsense! (*With some remorse.*) My poor boy, did you think I was angry with you? 25

STEPHEN: What is it, then, mother? You are making me very uneasy.

LADY BRITOMART: (*Squaring herself at him rather aggressively.*) Stephen: may I ask how soon you intend to realize that 30 you are a grown-up man, and that I am only a woman?

STEPHEN: (*Amazed.*) Only a—

LADY BRITOMART: Dont repeat my words, please: it is a most aggravating habit. You must learn to face life seriously, Stephen. I really cannot bear the whole burden of our 35 family affairs any longer. You must advise me: you must assume the responsibility.

STEPHEN: I!

LADY BRITOMART: Yes, you, of course. You were 24 last June. Youve been at Harrow and Cambridge. Youve been to India and Japan. You must know a lot of things, now; unless you 40 have wasted your time most scandalously. Well, advise me.

STEPHEN: (*Much perplexed.*) You know I have never interfered in the household—

LADY BRITOMART: No: I should think not. I dont want you 45 to order the dinner.

STEPHEN: I mean in our family affairs.

LADY BRITOMART: Well, you must interfere now; for they are getting quite beyond me.

STEPHEN: (*Troubled.*) I have thought sometimes that perhaps I 50 ought; but really, mother, I know so little about them; and what I do know is so painful! it is so impossible to mention some things to you—(*He stops, ashamed.*)

LADY BRITOMART: I suppose you mean your father.

STEPHEN: (*Almost inaudibly.*) Yes. 55

LADY BRITOMART: My dear: we cant go on all our lives not mentioning him. Of course you were quite right not to

open the subject until I asked you to; but you are old enough now to be taken into my confidence, and to help
60 me to deal with him about the girls.

STEPHEN: But the girls are all right. They are engaged.

LADY BRITOMART: (*Complacently.*) Yes: I have made a very good match for Sarah. Charles Lomax will be a million-aire at 35. But that is ten years ahead; and in the meantime
65 his trustees cannot under the terms of his father's will allow him more than £800 a year.

STEPHEN: But the will says also that if he increases his income by his own exertions, they may double the increase.

LADY BRITOMART: Charles Lomax's exertions are much more
70 likely to decrease his income than to increase it. Sarah will have to find at least another £800 a year for the next ten years; and even then they will be as poor as church mice. And what about Barbara? I thought Barbara was going to make the most brilliant career of all of you. And what
75 does she do? Joins the Salvation Army; discharges her maid; lives on a pound a week and walks in one evening with a professor of Greek whom she has picked up in the street, and who pretends to be a Salvationist, and actually plays the big drum for her in public because he has fallen
80 head over ears in love with her.

STEPHEN: I was certainly rather taken aback when I heard they were engaged. Cusins is a very nice fellow, certainly: nobody would ever guess that he was born in Australia; but—

LADY BRITOMART: Oh, Adolphus Cusins will make a very
85 good husband. After all, nobody can say a word against Greek: it stamps a man at once as an educated gentleman. And my family, thank Heaven, is not a pig-headed Tory one. We are Whigs, and believe in liberty. Let snobbish people say what they please: Barbara shall marry, not the
90 man they like, but the man *I* like.

STEPHEN: Of course I was thinking only of his income. However, he is not likely to be extravagant.

LADY BRITOMART: Dont be too sure of that, Stephen. I know your quiet, simple, refined, poetic people like Adolphus:
95 quite content with the best of everything! They cost more than your extravagant people, who are always as mean as they are second rate. No: Barbara will need at least £2000 a year. You see it means two additional households. Besides, my dear, you must marry soon. I dont approve of the
100 present fashion of philandering bachelors and late marriages; and I am trying to arrange something for you.

STEPHEN: It's very good of you, mother; but perhaps I had better arrange that for myself.

LADY BRITOMART: Nonsense! you are much too young to be-
105 gin matchmaking: you would be taken in by some pretty little nobody. Of course I dont mean that you are not to be consulted: you know that as well as I do. (STEPHEN *closes his lips and is silent.*) Now dont sulk, Stephen.

STEPHEN: I am not sulking, mother. What has all this got to
110 do with—with—with my father?

LADY BRITOMART: My dear Stephen: where is the money to come from? It is easy enough for you and the other children to live on my income as long as we are in the same house; but I cant keep four families in four separate
115 houses. You know how poor my father is: he has barely seven thousand a year now; and really, if he were not the Earl of Stevenage, he would have to give up society. He can do nothing for us. He says, naturally enough, that it is absurd that he should be asked to provide for the children

of a man who is rolling in money. You see, Stephen, your 120
father must be fabulously wealthy, because there is always a war going on somewhere.

STEPHEN: You need not remind me of that, mother. I have hardly ever opened a newspaper in my life without seeing our name in it. The Undershaft torpedo! The Undershaft 125
quick firers! The Undershaft ten inch! the Undershaft disappearing rampart gun! the Undershaft submarine! and now the Undershaft aerial battleship! At Harrow they called me the Woolwich Infant. At Cambridge it was the same. A little brute at King's who was always trying to get 130
up revivals, spoilt my Bible—your first birthday present to me—by writing under my name, "Son and heir to Undershaft and Lazarus, Death and Destruction Dealers: address Christendom and Judea." But that was not so bad as the way I was kowtowed to everywhere because my father 135
was making millions by selling cannons.

LADY BRITOMART: It is not only the cannons, but the war loans that Lazarus arranges under cover of giving credit for the cannons. You know, Stephen, it's perfectly scandalous. Those two men, Andrew Undershaft and Lazarus, positively 140
have Europe under their thumbs. That is why your father is able to behave as he does. He is above the law. Do you think Bismarck or Gladstone or Disraeli could have openly defied every social and moral obligation all their lives as your father has? They simply wouldnt have dared. I asked Glad- 145
stone to take it up. I asked The Times to take it up. I asked the Lord Chamberlain to take it up. But it was just like asking them to declare war on the Sultan. They wouldnt. They said they couldnt touch him. I believe they were afraid.

STEPHEN: What could they do? He does not actually break 150
the law.

LADY BRITOMART: Not break the law! He is always breaking the law. He broke the law when he was born: his parents were not married.

STEPHEN: Mother! Is that true? 155

LADY BRITOMART: Of course it's true: that was why we separated.

STEPHEN: He married without letting you know that!

LADY BRITOMART: (*Rather taken aback by this inference.*) Oh no. To do Andrew justice, that was not the sort of thing he did. Besides, you know the Undershaft motto: Unashamed. 160
Everybody knew.

STEPHEN: But you said that was why you separated.

LADY BRITOMART: Yes, because he was not content with being a foundling himself: he wanted to disinherit you for another foundling. That was what I couldnt stand. 165

STEPHEN: (*Ashamed.*) Do you mean for—for—for—

LADY BRITOMART: Dont stammer, Stephen. Speak distinctly.

STEPHEN: But this is so frightful to me, mother. To have to speak to you about such things!

LADY BRITOMART: It's not pleasant for me, either, especially 170
if you are still so childish that you must make it worse by a display of embarrassment. It is only in the middle classes, Stephen, that people get into a state of dumb helpless horror when they find that there are wicked people in the world. In our class, we have to decide what is to be done 175
with wicked people; and nothing should disturb our self-possession. Now ask your question properly.

STEPHEN: Mother: have you no consideration for me? For Heaven's sake either treat me as a child, as you always do, and tell me nothing at all or tell me everything and let me 180
take it as best I can.

LADY BRITOMART: Treat you as a child! What do you mean? It is most unkind and ungrateful of you to say such a thing. You know I have never treated any of you as chil-
185 dren. I have always made you my companions and friends, and allowed you perfect freedom to do and say whatever you like, so long as you liked what I could approve of.

STEPHEN: (*Desperately.*) I daresay we have been the very imperfect children of a very perfect mother; but I do beg you to
190 let me alone for once, and tell me about this horrible business of my father wanting to set me aside for another son.

LADY BRITOMART: (*Amazed.*) Another son! I never said anything of the kind. I never dreamt of such a thing. This is what comes of interrupting me.

195 STEPHEN: But you said—

LADY BRITOMART: (*Cutting him short.*) Now be a good boy, Stephen, and listen to me patiently. The Undershafts are descended from a foundling in the parish of St Andrew Undershaft in the city. That was long ago, in the reign of
200 James the First. Well, this foundling was adopted by an armorer and gun-maker. In the course of time the foundling succeeded to the business; and from some notion of gratitude, or some vow or something, he adopted another foundling, and left the business to him. And that
205 foundling did the same. Ever since that, the cannon business has always been left to an adopted foundling named Andrew Undershaft.

STEPHEN: But did they never marry? Were there no legitimate sons?

210 LADY BRITOMART: Oh yes: they married just as your father did; and they were rich enough to buy land for their own children and leave them well provided for. But they always adopted and trained some foundling to succeed them in the business; and of course they always quarrelled with
215 their wives furiously over it. Your father was adopted in that way; and he pretends to consider himself bound to keep up the tradition and adopt somebody to leave the business to. Of course I was not going to stand that. There may have been some reason for it when the Undershafts
220 could only marry women in their own class, whose sons were not fit to govern great estates. But there could be no excuse for passing over my son.

STEPHEN: (*Dubiously.*) I am afraid I should make a poor hand of managing a cannon foundry.

225 LADY BRITOMART: Nonsense! you could easily get a manager and pay him a salary.

STEPHEN: My father evidently had no great opinion of my capacity.

LADY BRITOMART: Stuff, child! you were only a baby: it had
230 nothing to do with your capacity. Andrew did it on principle, just as he did every perverse and wicked thing on principle. When my father remonstrated, Andrew actually told him to his face that history tells us of only two successful institutions: one the Undershaft firm, and the other the Ro-
235 man Empire under the Antonines. That was because the Antonine emperors all adopted their successors. Such rubbish! The Stevenages are as good as the Antonines, I hope; and you are a Stevenage. But that was Andrew all over. There you have the man! Always clever and unanswerable when he
240 was defending nonsense and wickedness: always awkward and sullen when he had to behave sensibly and decently!

STEPHEN: Then it was on my account that your home life was broken up, mother. I am sorry.

LADY BRITOMART: Well, dear, there were other differences. I really cannot bear an immoral man. I am not a Pharisee, I 245
hope; and I should not have minded his merely doing wrong things: we are none of us perfect. But your father didnt exactly do wrong things: he said them and thought them: that was what was so dreadful. He really had a sort of religion of wrongness. Just as one doesnt mind men 250
practising immorality so long as they own that they are in the wrong by preaching morality; so I couldnt forgive Andrew for preaching immorality while he practised morality. You would all have grown up without principles, without any knowledge of right and wrong, if he had 255
been in the house. You know, my dear, your father was a very attractive man in some ways. Children did not dislike him; and he took advantage of it to put the wickedest ideas into their heads, and make them quite unmanageable. I did not dislike him myself: very far from it; but 260
nothing can bridge over moral disagreement.

STEPHEN: All this simply bewilders me, mother. People may differ about matters of opinion, or even about religion; but how can they differ about right and wrong? Right is right; and wrong is wrong; and if a man cannot distinguish 265
them properly, he is either a fool or a rascal: thats all.

LADY BRITOMART: (*Touched.*) Thats my own boy! (*She pats his cheek.*) Your father never could answer that: he used to laugh and get out of it under cover of some affectionate nonsense. And now that you understand the situation, 270
what do you advise me to do?

STEPHEN: Well, what can you do?

LADY BRITOMART: I must get the money somehow.

STEPHEN: We cannot take money from him. I had rather go and live in some cheap place like Bedford Square or even 275
Hampstead than take a farthing of his money.

LADY BRITOMART: But after all, Stephen, our present income comes from Andrew.

STEPHEN: (*Shocked.*) I never knew that.

LADY BRITOMART: Well, you surely didnt suppose your 280
grandfather had anything to give me. The Stevenages could not do everything for you. We gave you social position. Andrew had to contribute something. He had a very good bargain, I think.

STEPHEN: (*Bitterly.*) We are utterly dependent on him and his 285
cannons, then?

LADY BRITOMART: Certainly not: the money is settled. But he provided it. So you see it is not a question of taking money from him or not: it is simply a question of how much. I dont want any more for myself. 290

STEPHEN: Nor do I.

LADY BRITOMART: But Sarah does; and Barbara does. That is, Charles Lomax and Adolphus Cusins will cost them more. So I must put my pride in my pocket and ask for it, I suppose. That is your advice, Stephen, is it not? 295

STEPHEN: No.

LADY BRITOMART: (*Sharply.*) Stephen!

STEPHEN: Of course if you are determined—

LADY BRITOMART: I am not determined: I ask your advice; and I am waiting for it. I will not have all the responsibil- 300
ity thrown on my shoulders.

STEPHEN: (*Obstinately.*) I would die sooner than ask him for another penny.

LADY BRITOMART. (*Resignedly.*) You mean that I must ask him. Very well, Stephen: it shall be as you wish. You will be glad 305 to know that your grandfather concurs. But he thinks I ought to ask Andrew to come here and see the girls. After all, he must have some natural affection for them.

STEPHEN: Ask him here!!!

310 LADY BRITOMART: Do not repeat my words, Stephen. Where else can I ask him?

STEPHEN: I never expected you to ask him at all.

LADY BRITOMART: Now dont tease, Stephen. Come! you see that it is necessary that he should pay us a visit, dont you?

315 STEPHEN: (*Reluctantly.*) I suppose so, if the girls cannot do without his money.

LADY BRITOMART: Thank you, Stephen: I knew you would give me the right advice when it was properly explained to you. I have asked your father to come this evening. (STEPHEN

320 *bounds from his seat.*) Dont jump, Stephen: it fidgets me.

STEPHEN: (*In utter consternation.*) Do you mean to say that my father is coming here tonight—that he may be here at any moment?

LADY BRITOMART: (*Looking at her watch.*) I said nine. (*He gasps.*

325 *She rises.*) Ring the bell, please. (STEPHEN *goes to the smaller writing table; presses a button on it; and sits at it with his elbows on the table and his head in his hands, outwitted and overwhelmed.*) It is ten minutes to nine yet; and I have to prepare the girls. I asked Charles Lomax and Adolphus to dinner on purpose

330 that they might be here. Andrew had better see them in case he should cherish any delusions as to their being capable of supporting their wives. (*The butler enters:* LADY BRITOMART *goes behind the settee to speak to him.*) Morrison: go up to the drawing room and tell everybody to come down here at

335 once. (MORRISON *withdraws.* LADY BRITOMART *turns to* STEPHEN.) Now remember, Stephen: I shall need all your countenance and authority. (*He rises and tries to recover some vestige of these attributes.*) Give me a chair, dear. (*He pushes a chair forward from the wall to where she stands, near the smaller*

340 *writing table. She sits down; and he goes to the armchair, into which he throws himself.*) I dont know how Barbara will take it. Ever since they made her a major in the Salvation Army she has developed a propensity to have her own way and order people about which quite cows me sometimes. It's not ladylike:

345 I'm sure I dont know where she picked it up. Anyhow, Barbara shant bully me; but still it's just as well that your father should be here before she has time to refuse to meet him or make a fuss. Dont look nervous, Stephen: it will only encourage Barbara to make difficulties. I am nervous enough,

350 goodness knows; but I dont shew it.

(SARAH *and* BARBARA *come in with their respective young men,* CHARLES LOMAX *and* ADOLPHUS CUSINS. SARAH *is slender, bored, and mundane.* BARBARA *is robuster, jollier, much more energetic.* SARAH *is fashionably dressed:* BARBARA *is in Salvation Army uniform.* LOMAX, *a young man about town, is like many other young men about town. He is afflicted with a frivolous sense of humor which plunges him at the most inopportune moments into paroxysms of imperfectly suppressed laughter.* CUSINS *is a spectacled student, slight, thin haired, and sweet voiced, with a more complex form of* LOMAX's *complaint. His sense of humor is intellectual and subtle, and is complicated by an appalling temper. The lifelong struggle of a benevolent temperament and a high conscience against impulses of inhuman ridicule and fierce impatience has set up a chronic strain which has visibly wrecked his constitution. He is a most implacable, determined, tenacious, intolerant person who by mere force of character presents*

himself as—and indeed actually is—considerate, gentle, explanatory, even mild and apologetic, capable possibly of murder, but not of cruelty or coarseness. By the operation of some instinct which is not merciful enough to blind him with the illusions of love, he is obstinately bent on marrying* BARBARA. LOMAX *likes* SARAH *and thinks it will be rather a lark to marry her. Consequently he has not attempted to resist* LADY BRITOMART's *arrangements to that end.*)

(*All four look as if they had been having a good deal of fun in the drawing room. The girls enter first, leaving the swains outside.* SARAH *comes to the settee.* BARBARA *comes in after her and stops at the door.*)

BARBARA: Are Cholly and Dolly to come in?

LADY BRITOMART: (*Forcibly.*) Barbara: I will not have Charles called Cholly: the vulgarity of it positively makes me ill.

BARBARA: It's all right, mother: Cholly is quite correct nowadays. Are they to come in?   355

LADY BRITOMART: Yes, if they will behave themselves.

BARBARA: (*Through the door.*) Come in, Dolly; and behave yourself.

(BARBARA *comes to her mother's writing table.* CUSINS *enters smiling, and wanders towards* LADY BRITOMART.)

SARAH: (*Calling.*) Come in, Cholly. (LOMAX *enters, controlling his features very imperfectly, and places himself vaguely between* 360 SARAH *and* BARBARA.)

LADY BRITOMART: (*Peremptorily.*) Sit down, all of you. (*They sit.* CUSINS *crosses to the window and seats himself there.* LOMAX *takes a chair.* BARBARA *sits at the writing table and* SARAH *on the settee.*) I dont in the least know what you are 365 laughing at, Adolphus. I am surprised at you, though I expected nothing better from Charles Lomax.

CUSINS: (*In a remarkably gentle voice.*) Barbara has been trying to teach me the West Ham Salvation March.

LADY BRITOMART: I see nothing to laugh at in that; nor 370 should you if you are really converted.

CUSINS: (*Sweetly.*) You were not present. It was really funny, I believe.

LOMAX: Ripping.

LADY BRITOMART: Be quiet, Charles. Now listen to me, chil- 375 dren. Your father is coming here this evening.

(*General stupefaction.* LOMAX, SARAH, *and* BARBARA *rise:* SARAH *scared, and* BARBARA *amused and expectant.*)

LOMAX: (*Remonstrating.*) Oh I say!

LADY BRITOMART: You are not called on to say anything, Charles.

SARAH: Are you serious, mother?   380

LADY BRITOMART: Of course I am serious. It is on your account, Sarah, and also on Charles's. (*Silence.* SARAH *sits, with a shrug.* CHARLES *looks painfully unworthy.*) I hope you are not going to object, Barbara.

BARBARA: I! why should I? My father has a soul to be saved 385 like anybody else. He's quite welcome as far as I am concerned. (*She sits on the table, and softly whistles 'Onward, Christian Soldiers.'*)

LOMAX: (*Still remonstrant.*) But really, dont you know! Oh I say!

LADY BRITOMART: (*Frigidly.*) What do you wish to convey, 390 Charles?

LOMAX: Well, you must admit that this is a bit thick.

LADY BRITOMART: (*Turning with ominous suavity to* CUSINS.)
395   Adolphus: you are a professor of Greek. Can you translate
       Charles Lomax's remarks into reputable English for us?

CUSINS: (*Cautiously.*) If I may say so, Lady Brit, I think
       Charles has rather happily expressed what we all feel.
       Homer, speaking of Autolycus, uses the same phrase.
       πυκινὸν δόμον ελθεῖν means a bit thick.

400   LOMAX: (*Handsomely.*) Not that I mind, you know, if Sarah
       dont. (*He sits.*)

LADY BRITOMART: (*Crushingly.*) Thank you. Have I your per-
       mission, Adolphus, to invite my own husband to my own
       house?

405   CUSINS: (*Gallantly.*) You have my unhesitating support in
       everything you do.

LADY BRITOMART: Tush! Sarah: have you nothing to say?

SARAH: Do you mean that he is coming regularly to live here?

LADY BRITOMART: Certainly not. The spare room is ready
410   for him if he likes to stay for a day or two and see a little
       more of you; but there are limits.

SARAH: Well, he cant eat us, I suppose. *I* dont mind.

LOMAX: (*Chuckling.*) I wonder how the old man will take it.

LADY BRITOMART: Much as the old woman will, no doubt,
415   Charles.

LOMAX: (*Abashed.*) I didnt mean—at least—

LADY BRITOMART: You didnt think, Charles. You never do;
       and the result is, you never mean anything. And now
       please attend to me, children. Your father will be quite a
420   stranger to us.

LOMAX: I suppose he hasnt seen Sarah since she was a little kid.

LADY BRITOMART: Not since she was a little kid, Charles, as
       you express it with that elegance of diction and refinement
       of thought that seem never to desert you. Accordingly—
425   er—(*Impatiently.*) Now I have forgotten what I was going
       to say. That comes of your provoking me to be sarcastic,
       Charles. Adolphus: will you kindly tell me where I was.

CUSINS: (*Sweetly.*) You were saying that as Mr Undershaft has
       not seen his children since they were babies, he will form
430   his opinion of the way you have brought them up from
       their behavior tonight, and that therefore you wish us all
       to be particularly careful to conduct ourselves well, espe-
       cially Charles.

LADY BRITOMART: (*With emphatic approval.*) Precisely.

435   LOMAX: Look here, Dolly: Lady Brit didnt say that.

LADY BRITOMART: (*Vehemently.*) I did, Charles. Adolphus's
       recollection is perfectly correct. It is most important that
       you should be good; and I do beg you for once not to pair
       off into opposite corners and giggle and whisper while I
440   am speaking to your father.

BARBARA: All right, mother. We'll do you credit. (*She comes
       off the table, and sits in her chair with ladylike elegance.*)

LADY BRITOMART: Remember, Charles, that Sarah will want
       to feel proud of you instead of ashamed of you.

445   LOMAX: Oh I say! theres nothing to be exactly proud of, dont
       you know.

LADY BRITOMART: Well, try and look as if there was.

(MORRISON, *pale and dismayed, breaks into the room in uncon-
cealed disorder.*)

MORRISON: Might I speak a word to you, my lady?

LADY BRITOMART: Nonsense! Shew him up.

MORRISON: Yes, my lady. (*He goes.*)

LOMAX: Does Morrison know who it is?   450

LADY BRITOMART: Of course. Morrison has always been with us.

LOMAX: It must be a regular corker for him, dont you know.

LADY BRITOMART: Is this a moment to get on my nerves,
       Charles, with your outrageous expressions?

LOMAX: But this is something out of the ordinary, really—   455

MORRISON: (*At the door.*) The—er—Mr Undershaft. (*He re-
       treats in confusion.*)

(ANDREW UNDERSHAFT *comes in. All rise.* LADY BRITOMART
meets him in the middle of the room behind the settee.)

(ANDREW *is, on the surface, a stoutish, easygoing elderly man, with
kindly patient manners, and an engaging simplicity of character. But
he has a watchful, deliberate, waiting, listening face, and formidable reserves of power, both bodily and mental, in his capacious chest and long
head. His gentleness is partly that of a strong man who has learnt by
experience that his natural grip hurts ordinary people unless he handles them very carefully, and partly the mellowness of age and success.
He is also a little shy in his present very delicate situation.*)

LADY BRITOMART: Good evening, Andrew.

UNDERSHAFT: How d'ye do, my dear.   460

LADY BRITOMART: You look a good deal older.

UNDERSHAFT: (*Apologetically.*) I am somewhat older. (*Taking her
       hand with a touch of courtship.*) Time has stood still with you.

LADY BRITOMART: (*Throwing away his hand.*) Rubbish! This is
       your family.   465

UNDERSHAFT: (*Surprised.*) Is it so large? I am sorry to say my
       memory is failing very badly in some things. (*He offers his
       hand with paternal kindness to* LOMAX.)

LOMAX: (*Jerkily shaking his hand.*) Ahdedoo.

UNDERSHAFT: I can see you are my eldest. I am very glad to   470
       meet you again, my boy.

LOMAX: (*Remonstrating.*) No, but look here dont you know—
       (*Overcome.*) Oh I say!

LADY BRITOMART: (*Recovering from momentary speechlessness.*)
       Andrew: do you mean to say that you dont remember   475
       how many children you have?

UNDERSHAFT: Well, I am afraid I—. They have grown so
       much—er. Am I making any ridiculous mistake? I may as
       well confess: I recollect only one son. But so many things
       have happened since, of course—er—   480

LADY BRITOMART: (*Decisively.*) Andrew: you are talking non-
       sense. Of course you have only one son.

UNDERSHAFT: Perhaps you will be good enough to introduce
       me, my dear.

LADY BRITOMART: That is Charles Lomax, who is engaged to   485
       Sarah.

UNDERSHAFT: My dear sir, I beg your pardon.

LOMAX: Notatall. Delighted, I assure you.

LADY BRITOMART: This is Stephen.

UNDERSHAFT: (*Bowing.*) Happy to make your acquaintance,   490
       Mr Stephen. Then (*Going to* CUSINS.) you must be my son.
       (*Taking* CUSINS' *hands in his.*) How are you, my young
       friend? (*To* LADY BRITOMART.) He is very like you, my love.

CUSINS: You flatter me, Mr Undershaft. My name is Cusins:
       engaged to Barbara. (*Very explicitly.*) That is Major Barbara   495
       Undershaft, of the Salvation Army. That is Sarah, your
       second daughter. This is Stephen Undershaft, your son.

UNDERSHAFT: My dear Stephen, I beg your pardon.

STEPHEN: Not at all.

500 UNDERSHAFT: Mr Cusins: I am much indebted to you for explaining so precisely. (*Turning to* SARAH.) Barbara, my dear—

SARAH: (*Prompting him.*) Sarah.

UNDERSHAFT: Sarah, of course. (*They shake hands. He goes over* 505 *to* BARBARA.) Barbara—I am right this time, I hope?

BARBARA: Quite right. (*They shake hands.*)

LADY BRITOMART: (*Resuming command.*) Sit down, all of you. Sit down, Andrew. (*She comes forward and sits on the settee.* CUSINS *also brings his chair forward on her left.* BARBARA *and* 510 STEPHEN *resume their seats.* LOMAX *gives his chair to* SARAH *and goes for another.*)

UNDERSHAFT: Thank you, my love.

LOMAX: (*Conversationally, as he brings a chair forward between the writing table and the settee, and offers it to* UNDERSHAFT.) Takes 515 you some time to find out exactly where you are, dont it?

UNDERSHAFT: (*Accepting the chair, but remaining standing.*) That is not what embarrasses me, Mr Lomax. My difficulty is that if I play the part of a father, I shall produce the effect of an intrusive stranger; and if I play the part of a discreet 520 stranger, I may appear a callous father.

LADY BRITOMART: There is no need for you to play any part at all, Andrew. You had much better be sincere and natural.

UNDERSHAFT: (*Submissively.*) Yes, my dear: I daresay that will be best. (*He sits down comfortably.*) Well, here I am. Now 525 what can I do for you all?

LADY BRITOMART: You need not do anything, Andrew. You are one of the family. You can sit with us and enjoy yourself.

(*A painfully conscious pause.* BARBARA *makes a face at* LOMAX, *whose too long suppressed mirth immediately explodes in agonized neighings.*)

LADY BRITOMART: (*Outraged.*) Charles Lomax: if you can behave yourself, behave yourself. If not, leave the room.

530 LOMAX: I'm awfully sorry, Lady Brit; but really you know, upon my soul! (*He sits on the settee between* LADY BRITOMART *and* UNDERSHAFT, *quite overcome.*)

BARBARA: Why dont you laugh if you want to, Cholly? It's good for your inside.

535 LADY BRITOMART: Barbara: you have had the education of a lady. Please let your father see that; and dont talk like a street girl.

UNDERSHAFT: Never mind me, my dear. As you know, I am not a gentleman; and I was never educated.

540 LOMAX: (*Encouragingly.*) Nobody'd know it, I assure you. You look all right, you know.

CUSINS: Let me advise you to study Greek, Mr Undershaft. Greek scholars are privileged men. Few of them know Greek; and none of them know anything else; but their 545 position is unchallengeable. Other languages are the qualifications of waiters and commercial travellers: Greek is to a man of position what the hallmark is to silver.

BARBARA: Dolly: dont be insincere. Cholly: fetch your concertina and play something for us.

550 LOMAX: (*Jumps up eagerly, but checks himself to remark doubtfully to* UNDERSHAFT.) Perhaps that sort of thing isnt in your line, eh?

UNDERSHAFT: I am particularly fond of music.

LOMAX: (*Delighted.*) Are you? Then I'll get it. (*He goes upstairs for the instrument.*)

UNDERSHAFT: Do you play, Barbara? 555

BARBARA: Only the tambourine. But Cholly's teaching me the concertina.

UNDERSHAFT: Is Cholly also a member of the Salvation Army?

BARBARA: No: he says it's bad form to be a dissenter. But I dont despair of Cholly. I made him come yesterday to a meeting 560 at the dock gates, and take the collection in his hat.

UNDERSHAFT: (*Looks whimsically at his wife.*)!!

LADY BRITOMART: It is not my doing, Andrew. Barbara is old enough to take her own way. She has no father to advise her.

BARBARA: Oh yes she has. There are no orphans in the Sal- 565 vation Army.

UNDERSHAFT: Your father there has a great many children and plenty of experience, eh?

BARBARA: (*Looking at him with quick interest and nodding.*) Just so. How did you come to understand that? (LOMAX *is* 570 *heard at the door trying the concertina.*)

LADY BRITOMART: Come in, Charles. Play us something at once.

LOMAX: Righto! (*He sits down in his former place, and preludes.*)

UNDERSHAFT: One moment, Mr Lomax. I am rather interested in the Salvation Army. Its motto might be my own: 575 Blood and Fire.

LOMAX: (*Shocked.*) But not your sort of blood and fire, you know.

UNDERSHAFT: My sort of blood cleanses: my sort of fire purifies.

BARBARA: So do ours. Come down tomorrow to my shel- 580 ter—the West Ham shelter—and see what we're doing. We're going to march to a great meeting in the Assembly Hall at Mile End. Come and see the shelter and then march with us: it will do you a lot of good. Can you play anything?

UNDERSHAFT: In my youth I earned pennies, and even 585 shillings occasionally, in the streets and in public house parlors by my natural talent for stepdancing. Later on, I became a member of the Undershaft orchestral society, and performed passably on the tenor trombone.

LOMAX: (*Scandalized—putting down the concertina.*) Oh I say! 590

BARBARA: Many a sinner has played himself into heaven on the trombone, thanks to the Army.

LOMAX: (*To* BARBARA, *still rather shocked.*) Yes; but what about the cannon business, dont you know? (*To* UNDERSHAFT.) Getting into heaven is not exactly in your line, is it? 595

LADY BRITOMART: Charles!!!

LOMAX: Well; but it stands to reason, dont it? The cannon business may be necessary and all that: we cant get on without cannons; but it isnt right, you know. On the other hand, there may be a certain amount of tosh about the 600 Salvation Army—I belong to the Established Church myself—but still you cant deny that it's religion; and you cant go against religion, can you? At least unless youre downright immoral, dont you know.

UNDERSHAFT: You hardly appreciate my position, Mr Lomax— 605

LOMAX: (*Hastily.*) I'm not saying anything against you personally—

UNDERSHAFT: Quite so, quite so. But consider for a moment. Here I am, a profiteer in mutilation and murder. I find myself in a specially amiable humor just now because, this 610 morning, down at the foundry, we blew twenty-seven dummy soldiers into fragments with a gun which formerly destroyed only thirteen.

LOMAX: (*Leniently.*) Well, the more destructive war becomes, the sooner it will be abolished, eh? 615

UNDERSHAFT: Not at all. The more destructive war becomes the more fascinating we find it. No, Mr Lomax: I am obliged to you for making the usual excuse for my trade; but I am not ashamed of it. I am not one of those men
620 who keep their morals and their business in watertight compartments. All the spare money my trade rivals spend on hospitals, cathedrals, and other receptacles for conscience money, I devote to experiments and researches in improved methods of destroying life and property. I have
625 always done so; and I always shall. Therefore your Christmas card moralities of peace on earth and goodwill among men are of no use to me. Your Christianity, which enjoins you to resist not evil, and to turn the other cheek, would make me a bankrupt. My morality—my religion—must
630 have a place for cannons and torpedoes in it.

STEPHEN: (*Coldly—almost sullenly.*) You speak as if there were half a dozen moralities and religions to choose from, instead of one true morality and one true religion.

UNDERSHAFT: For me there is only one true morality; but it
635 might not fit you, as you do not manufacture aerial battleships. There is only one true morality for every man; but every man has not the same true morality.

LOMAX: (*Overtaxed.*) Would you mind saying that again? I didnt quite follow it.

640 CUSINS: It's quite simple. As Euripides says, one man's meat is another man's poison morally as well as physically.

UNDERSHAFT: Precisely.

LOMAX: Oh, that! Yes, yes, yes. True. True.

STEPHEN: In other words, some men are honest and some are
645 scoundrels.

BARBARA: Bosh! There are no scoundrels.

UNDERSHAFT: Indeed? Are there any good men?

BARBARA: No. Not one. There are neither good men nor scoundrels: there are just children of one Father; and the
650 sooner they stop calling one another names the better. You neednt talk to me: I know them. I've had scores of them through my hands: scoundrels, criminals, infidels, philanthropists, missionaries, county councillors, all sorts. Theyre all just the same sort of sinner; and theres the same
655 salvation ready for them all.

UNDERSHAFT: May I ask have you ever saved a maker of cannons?

BARBARA: No. Will you let me try?

UNDERSHAFT: Well, I will make a bargain with you. If I go to see you tomorrow in your Salvation Shelter, will you
660 come the day after to see me in my cannon works?

BARBARA: Take care. It may end in your giving up the cannons for the sake of the Salvation Army.

UNDERSHAFT: Are you sure it will not end in your giving up the Salvation Army for the sake of the cannons?

665 BARBARA: I will take my chance of that.

UNDERSHAFT: And I will take my chance of the other. (*They shake hands on it.*) Where is your shelter?

BARBARA: In West Ham. At the sign of the cross. Ask anybody in Canning Town. Where are your works?

670 UNDERSHAFT: In Perivale St Andrews. At the sign of the sword. Ask anybody in Europe.

LOMAX: Hadnt I better play something?

BARBARA: Yes. Give us 'Onward, Christian Soldiers.'

LOMAX: Well, thats rather a strong order to begin with, dont
675 you know. Suppose I sing 'Thou't passing hence, my brother.' It's much the same tune.

BARBARA: It's too melancholy. You get saved, Cholly; and youll pass hence, my brother, without making such a fuss about it.

LADY BRITOMART: Really, Barbara, you go on as if religion were a pleasant subject. Do have some sense of propriety. 680

UNDERSHAFT: I do not find it an unpleasant subject, my dear. It is the only one that capable people really care for.

LADY BRITOMART: (*Looking at her watch.*) Well, if you are determined to have it, I insist on having it in a proper and respectable way. Charles: ring for prayers. 685

(*General amazement.* STEPHEN *rises in dismay.*)

LOMAX: (*Rising.*) Oh I say!

UNDERSHAFT: (*Rising.*) I am afraid I must be going.

LADY BRITOMART: You cannot go now, Andrew: it would be most improper. Sit down. What will the servants think?

UNDERSHAFT: My dear: I have conscientious scruples. May I 690 suggest a compromise? If Barbara will conduct a little service in the drawing room, with Mr Lomax as organist, I will attend it willingly. I will even take part, if a trombone can be procured.

LADY BRITOMART: Dont mock, Andrew. 695

UNDERSHAFT: (*Shocked—to* BARBARA.) You dont think I am mocking, my love, I hope.

BARBARA: No, of course not; and it wouldnt matter if you were: half the Army came to their first meeting for a lark. (*Rising.*) Come along. (*She throws her arm round her father* 700 *and sweeps him out, calling to the others from the threshold.*) Come, Dolly. Come, Cholly.

(CUSINS *rises.*)

LADY BRITOMART: I will not be disobeyed by everybody. Adolphus: sit down. (*He does not.*) Charles: you may go. You are not fit for prayers: you cannot keep your countenance. 705

LOMAX: Oh I say! (*He goes out.*)

LADY BRITOMART: (*Continuing.*) But you, Adolphus, can behave yourself if you choose to. I insist on your staying.

CUSINS: My dear Lady Brit: there are things in the family prayer book that I couldnt bear to hear you say. 710

LADY BRITOMART: What things, pray?

CUSINS: Well, you would have to say before all the servants that we have done things we ought not to have done, and left undone things we ought to have done, and that there is no health in us. I cannot bear to hear you doing your- 715 self such an injustice, and Barbara such an injustice. As for myself, I flatly deny it: I have done my best. I shouldnt dare to marry Barbara—I couldnt look you in the face— if it were true. So I must go to the drawing room.

LADY BRITOMART: (*Offended.*) Well, go. (*He starts for the door.*) 720 And remember this, Adolphus (*He turns to listen.*): I have a very strong suspicion that you went to the Salvation Army to worship Barbara and nothing else. And I quite appreciate the very clever way in which you systematically humbug me. I have found you out. Take care Barbara 725 doesnt. Thats all.

CUSINS: (*With unruffled sweetness.*) Dont tell on me. (*He steals out.*)

LADY BRITOMART: Sarah: if you want to go, go. Anything's better than to sit there as if you wished you were a thousand miles away. 730

SARAH: (*Languidly.*) Very well, mamma. (*She goes.*)

735 (LADY BRITOMART, *with a sudden flounce, gives way to a little gust of tears.*)

STEPHEN: (*Going to her.*) Mother: whats the matter?

LADY BRITOMART: (*Swishing away her tears with her handker-*
740 *chief.*) Nothing. Foolishness. You can go with him, too, if you like, and leave me with the servants.

STEPHEN: Oh, you mustnt think that, mother. I—I dont like him.

LADY BRITOMART: The others do. That is the injustice of a
745 woman's lot. A woman has to bring up her children; and that means to restrain them, to deny them things they want, to set them tasks, to punish them when they do wrong, to do all the unpleasant things. And then the father, who has nothing to do but pet them and spoil them, comes in when
750 all her work is done and steals their affection from her.

STEPHEN: He has not stolen our affection from you. It is only curiosity.

LADY BRITOMART: (*Violently.*) I wont be consoled, Stephen. There is nothing the matter with me. (*She rises and goes to-*
755 *wards the door.*)

STEPHEN: Where are you going, mother?

LADY BRITOMART: To the drawing room, of course. (*She goes out. 'Onward, Christian Soldiers,' on the concertina, with tambourine accompaniment, is heard when the door opens.*) Are you coming, Stephen?

STEPHEN: No. Certainly not. (*She goes. He sits down on the settee, with compressed lips and an expression of strong dislike.*)

ACT TWO

The yard of the West Ham shelter of the Salvation Army is a cold place on a January morning. The building itself, an old warehouse, is newly whitewashed. Its gabled end projects into the yard in the middle, with a door on the ground floor, and another in the loft above it without any balcony or ladder, but with a pulley rigged over it for hoisting sacks. Those who come from this central gable end into the yard have the gateway leading to the street on their left, with a stone horse-trough just beyond it, and, on the right, a penthouse shielding a table from the weather. There are forms at the table; and on them are seated a man and a woman, both much down on their luck, finishing a meal of bread (one thick slice each, with margarine and golden syrup) and diluted milk.

The man, a workman out of employment, is young, agile, a talker, a poser, sharp enough to be capable of anything in reason except honesty or altruistic considerations of any kind. The woman is a commonplace old bundle of poverty and hard-worn humanity. She looks sixty and probably is forty-five. If they were rich people, gloved and muffed and well wrapped up in furs and overcoats, they would be numbed and miserable; for it is a grindingly cold raw January day; and a glance at the background of grimy warehouses and leaden sky visible over the whitewashed walls of the yard would drive any idle rich person straight to the Mediterranean. But these two, being no more troubled with visions of the Mediterranean than of the moon, and being compelled to keep more of their clothes in the pawnshop, and less on their persons, in winter than in summer, are not depressed by the cold: rather are they stung into vivacity, to which their meal has just now given an almost jolly turn. The man takes a pull at his mug, and then gets up and moves about the yard with his hands deep in his pockets, occasionally breaking into a stepdance.

THE WOMAN: Feel better arter your meal, sir?

THE MAN: No. Call that a meal! Good enough for you, praps; but wot is it to me, an intelligent workin man.

THE WOMAN: Workin man! Wot are you?

THE MAN: Painter. 5

THE WOMAN: (*Sceptically.*) Yus, I dessay.

THE MAN: Yus, you dessay! I know. Every loafer that cant do nothink calls isself a painter. Well, I'm a real painter: grainer, finisher, thirty-eight bob a week when I can get it.

THE WOMAN: Then why dont you go and get it? 10

THE MAN: I'll tell you why. Fust: I'm intelligent—fffff! it's rotten cold here (*He dances a step or two.*)—yes: intelligent beyond the station o life into which it has pleased the capitalists to call me; and they dont like a man that sees through em. Second, an intelligent bein needs a doo share 15 of appiness; so I drink somethink cruel when I get the chawnce. Third, I stand by my class and do as little as I can so's to leave arf the job for me fellow workers. Fourth, I'm fly enough to know wots inside the law and wots outside it; and inside it I do as the capitalists do: pinch wot I can 20 lay me ands on. In a proper state of society I am sober, industrious and honest: in Rome, so to speak, I do as the Romans do. Wots the consequence? When trade is bad—and it's rotten bad just now—and the employers az to sack arf their men, they generally start on me. 25

THE WOMAN: Whats your name?

THE MAN: Price. Bronterre O'Brien Price. Usually called Snobby Price, for short.

THE WOMAN: Snobby's a carpenter, aint it? You said you was a painter. 30

PRICE: Not that kind of snob, but the genteel sort. I'm too uppish, owing to my intelligence, and my father being a Chartist and a reading, thinking man: a stationer, too. I'm none of your common hewers of wood and drawers of water; and dont you forget it. (*He returns to his seat at the* 35 *table, and takes up his mug.*) Wots your name?

THE WOMAN: Rummy Mitchens, sir.

PRICE: (*Quaffing the remains of his milk to her.*) Your elth, Miss Mitchens.

RUMMY: (*Correcting him.*) Missis Mitchens. 40

PRICE: Wot! Oh Rummy, Rummy! Respectable married woman, Rummy, gittin rescued by the Salvation Army by pretendin to be a bad un. Same old game!

RUMMY: What am I to do? I cant starve. Them Salvation lasses is dear good girls; but the better you are, the worse they 45 likes to think you were before they rescued you. Why shouldnt they av a bit o credit, poor loves? theyre worn to rags by their work. And where would they get the money to rescue us if we was to let on we're no worse than other people? You know what ladies and gentlemen are. 50

PRICE: Thievin swine! Wish I ad their job, Rummy, all the same. Wot does Rummy stand for? Pet name praps?

RUMMY: Short for Romola.

PRICE: For wot!?

RUMMY: Romola. It was out of a new book. Somebody me 55 mother wanted me to grow up like.

PRICE: We're companions in misfortune, Rummy. Both on us got names that nobody cawnt pronounce. Consequently I'm Snobby and youre Rummy because Bill and Sally wasnt good enough for our parents. Such is life! 60

RUMMY: Who saved you, Mr Price? Was it Major Barbara?

PRICE: No: I come here on my own. I'm going to be Bronterre O'Brien Price, the converted painter. I know wot
they like. I'll tell em how I blasphemed and gambled and

65   wopped my poor old mother—
RUMMY: (*Shocked.*) Used you to beat your mother?
PRICE: Not likely. She used to beat me. No matter: you come
and listen to the converted painter, and youll hear how she
was a pious woman that taught me me prayers at er knee,

70   an how I used to come home drunk and drag her out o
bed be er snow white airs, an lam into er with the poker.
RUMMY: Thats whats so unfair to us women. Your confessions is just as big lies as ours: you dont tell what you really done no more than us; but you men can tell your lies

75   right out at the meetins be made much of for it; while
the sort o confessions we az to make az to be wispered to
one lady at a time. It aint right, spite of all their piety.
PRICE: Right! Do you spose the Army'd be allowed if it went
and did right? Not much. It combs our air and makes us

80   good little blokes to be robbed and put upon. But I'll play
the game as good as any of em. I'll see somebody struck
by lightnin, or hear a voice sayin 'Snobby Price: where
will you spend eternity?' I'll av a time of it, I tell you.
RUMMY: You wont be let drink, though.

85   PRICE: I'll take it out in gorspellin, then. I dont want to drink
if I can get fun enough any other way.

(JENNY HILL, *a pale, overwrought, pretty Salvation lass of 18, comes
in through the yard gate, leading* PETER SHIRLEY, *a half hardened,
half worn-out elderly man, weak with hunger.*)

JENNY: (*Supporting him.*) Come! pluck up. I'll get you something to eat. Youll be all right then.
PRICE: (*Rising and hurrying officiously to take the old man off*

90   JENNY's *hands.*) Poor old man! Cheer up, brother: youll find
rest and peace and appiness ere. Hurry up with the food,
miss: e's fair done. (JENNY *hurries into the shelter.*) Ere, buck
up, daddy! she's fetchin y'a thick slice o breadn treacle, an a
mug o skyblue. (*He seats him at the corner of the table.*)

95   RUMMY: (*Gaily.*) Keep up your old art! Never say die!
SHIRLEY: I'm not an old man. I'm only 46. I'm as good as ever I
was. The grey patch come in my hair before I was thirty. All
it wants is three pennorth o hair dye: am I to be turned on
the streets to starve for it? Holy God! I've worked ten to

100   twelve hours a day since I was thirteen, and paid my way all
through; and now am I to be thrown into the gutter and my
job given to a young man that can do it no better than me
because Ive black hair that goes white at the first change?
PRICE: (*Cheerfully.*) No good jawrin about it. Youre only a

105   jumped-up, jerked-off, orspittle-turned-out incurable of
an ole workin man: who cares about you? Eh? Make the
thievin swine give you a meal: theyve stole many a one
from you. Get a bit o your own back. (JENNY *returns with
the usual meal.*) There you are, brother. Awsk a blessin an

110   tuck that into you.
SHIRLEY: (*Looking at it ravenously but not touching it, and crying
like a child.*) I never took anything before.
JENNY: (*Petting him.*) Come, come! the Lord sends it to you:
he wasnt above taking bread from his friends; and why

115   should you be? Besides, when we find you a job you can
pay us for it if you like.

SHIRLEY: (*Eagerly.*) Yes, yes: thats true. I can pay you back: it's
only a loan. (*Shivering.*) O Lord! oh Lord! (*He turns to the
table and attacks the meal ravenously.*)
JENNY: Well, Rummy, are you more comfortable now?   120
RUMMY: God bless you, lovey! youve fed my body and saved
my soul, havnt you? (JENNY, *touched, kisses her.*) Sit down
and rest a bit: you must be ready to drop.
JENNY: Ive been going hard since morning. But theres more
work than we can do. I mustnt stop.   125
RUMMY: Try a prayer for just two minutes. Youll work all the
better after.
JENNY: (*Her eyes lighting up.*) Oh isnt it wonderful how a few
minutes prayer revives you! I was quite lightheaded at
twelve o'clock, I was so tired; but Major Barbara just sent 130
me to pray for five minutes; and I was able to go on as if
I had only just begun. (*To* PRICE.) Did you have a piece of
bread?
PRICE: (*With unction.*) Yes, miss; but Ive got the piece that I
value more; and thats the peace that passeth hall hanner-   135
stennin.
RUMMY: (*Fervently.*) Glory Hallelujah!

(BILL WALKER, *a rough customer of about 25, appears at the yard
gate and looks malevolently at* JENNY.)

JENNY: That makes me so happy. When you say that, I feel
wicked for loitering here. I must get to work again.

(*She is hurrying to the shelter, when the new-comer moves quickly
up to the door and intercepts her. His manner is so threatening that
she retreats as he comes at her truculently, driving her down the yard.*)

BILL: Aw knaow you. Youre the one that took awy maw girl.   140
Youre the one that set er agen me. Well, I'm gowin to ev
er aht. Not that Aw care a carse for er or you: see? Bat
Aw'll let er knaow; and Aw'll let you knaow. Aw'm gowing to give her a doin thatll teach er to cat awy from me.
Nah in wiv you and tell er to cam aht afore Aw cam in   145
and kick er aht. Tell er Bill Walker wants er. She'll knaow
wot thet means; and if she keeps me witin itll be worse.
You stop to jawr beck at me; and Aw'll stawt on you: d'ye
eah? Theres your wy. In you gow. (*He takes her by the arm
and slings her towards the door of the shelter. She falls on her*   150
hand and knee. RUMMY *helps her up again.*)
PRICE: (*Rising, and venturing irresolutely towards* BILL.) Easy
there, mate. She aint doin you no arm.
BILL: Oo are you callin mite? (*Standing over him threateningly.*)
Youre gowin to stend ap for er, aw yer? Put ap your ends.   155
RUMMY: (*Running indignantly to him to scold him.*) Oh, you
great brute—(*He instantly swings his left hand back against
her face. She screams and reels back to the trough, where she sits
down, covering her bruised face with her hands and rocking herself and moaning with pain.*)   160
JENNY: (*Going to her.*) Oh, God forgive you! How could you
strike an old woman like that?
BILL: (*Seizing her by the hair so violently that she also screams, and
tearing her away from the old woman.*) You Gawd forgimme
again an Aw'll Gawd forgive you one on the jawr thetll   165
stop you pryin for a week. (*Holding her and turning fiercely
on* PRICE.) Ev you ennything to sy agen it?
PRICE: (*Intimidated.*) No, matey: she aint anything to do with
me.

170 BILL: Good job for you! Aw'd pat two meals into you and fawt you with one finger arter, you stawved cur. (*To* JENNY.) Nah are you gowin to fetch aht Mog Ebbijem; or em Aw to knock your fice off you and fetch her meself?

JENNY: (*Writhing in his grasp.*) Oh please someone go in and

175 tell Major Barbara—(*She screams again as he wrenches her head down; and* PRICE *and* RUMMY *flee into the shelter.*)

BILL: You want to gow in and tell your Mijor of me, do you?

JENNY: Oh please dont drag my hair. Let me go.

BILL: Do you or downt you? (*She stifles a scream.*) Yus or nao?

180 JENNY: God give me strength—

BILL: (*Striking her with his fist in the face.*) Gow an shaow her thet, and tell her if she wants one lawk it to cam and interfere with me. (JENNY, *crying with pain, goes into the shed. He goes to the form and addresses the old man.*) Eah: finish

185 your mess; an git aht o maw wy.

SHIRLEY: (*Springing up and facing him fiercely, with the mug in his hand.*) You take a liberty with me, and I'll smash you over the face with the mug and cut your eye out. Aint you satisfied—young whelps like you—with takin the bread out

190 o the mouths of your elders that have brought you up and slaved for you, but you must come shovin and cheekin and bullyin in here, where the bread o charity is sickenin in our stummicks?

BILL: (*Contemptuously, but backing a little.*) Wot good are you,

195 you aold palsy mag? Wot good are you?

SHIRLEY: As good as you and better. I'll do a day's work agen you or any fat young soaker of your age. Go and take my job at Horrockses, where I worked for ten year. They want young men there: they cant afford to keep men over

200 forty-five. Theyre very sorry—give you a character and happy to help you to get anything suited to your years— sure a steady man wont be long out of a job. Well, let em try you. Theyll find the differ. What do you know? Not as much as how to beeyave yourself—layin your dirty fist

205 across the mouth of a respectable woman!

BILL: Downt provowk me to ly it acrost yours: d'ye eah?

SHIRLEY: (*With blighting contempt.*) Yes: you like an old man to hit, dont you, when youve finished with the women. I aint seen you hit a young one yet.

210 BILL: (*Stung.*) You loy, you aold soupkitchener, you. There was a yang menn eah. Did Aw offer to itt him or did Aw not?

SHIRLEY: Was he starvin or was he not? Was he a man or only a crosseyed thief an a loafer? Would you hit my son-in-law's brother?

215 BILL: Oo's ee?

SHIRLEY: Todger Fairmile o Balls Pond. Him that won £20 off the Japanese wrastler at the music hall by standin out 17 minutes 4 seconds agen him.

BILL: (*Sullenly.*) Aw'm nao music awl wrastler. Ken he box?

220 SHIRLEY: Yes: an you cant.

BILL: Wot! Aw cawnt, cawnt Aw? Wots thet you sy (*Threatening him.*)?

SHIRLEY: (*Not budging an inch.*) Will you box Todger Fairmile if I put him on to you? Say the word.

225 BILL: (*Subsiding with a slouch.*) Aw'll stend ap to enny menn alawv, if he was ten Todger Fairmawls. But Aw dont set ap to be a perfeshnal.

SHIRLEY: (*Looking down on him with unfathomable disdain.*) You borr! Slap an old woman with the back o your hand! You hadnt even the sense to hit her where a magistrate couldnt

230 see the mark of it, you silly young lump of conceit and ig-

norance. Hit a girl in the jaw and ony make her cry! If Todger Fairmile'd done it, she wouldnt a got up inside o ten minutes, no more than you would if he got on to you. Yah! I'd set about you myself if I had a week's feedin in

235 me instead o two months' starvation. (*He turns his back on him and sits down moodily at the table.*)

BILL: (*Following him and stooping over him to drive the taunt in.*) You loy! youve the bread and treacle in you that you cam

240 eah to beg.

SHIRLEY: (*Bursting into tears.*) Oh God! it's true: I'm only an old pauper on the scrap heap. (*Furiously.*) But youll come to it yourself; and then youll know. Youll come to it sooner than a teetotaller like me, fillin yourself with gin

245 at this hour o the mornin!

BILL: Aw'm nao gin drinker, you oald lawr; bat wen Aw want to give my girl a bloomin good awdin Aw lawk to ev a bit o devil in me: see? An eah Aw emm, talkin to a rotten aold blawter like you sted o givin her wot for. (*Working himself*

250 *into a rage.*) Aw'm gowin in there to fetch her aht. (*He makes vengefully for the shelter door.*)

SHIRLEY: Youre going to the station on a stretcher, more likely; and theyll take the gin and the devil out of you there when they get you inside. You mind what youre about: the ma-

255 jor here is the Earl o Stevenage's granddaughter.

BILL: (*Checked.*) Garn!

SHIRLEY: Youll see.

BILL: (*His resolution oozing.*) Well, Aw aint dan nathin to er.

SHIRLEY: Spose she said you did! who'd believe you?

260 BILL: (*Very uneasy, skulking back to the corner of the penthouse.*) Gawd! theres no jastice in this cantry. To think wot them people can do! Aw'm as good as er.

SHIRLEY: Tell her so. It's just what a fool like you would do.

(BARBARA, *brisk and businesslike, comes from the shelter with a note book, and addresses herself to* SHIRLEY. BILL, *cowed, sits down in the corner on a form, and turns his back on them.*)

BARBARA: Good morning.

265 SHIRLEY: (*Standing up and taking off his hat.*) Good morning, miss.

BARBARA: Sit down: make yourself at home. (*He hesitates; but she puts a friendly hand on his shoulder and makes him obey.*) Now then! since youve made friends with us, we want to

270 know all about you. Names and addresses and trades.

SHIRLEY: Peter Shirley. Fitter. Chucked out two months ago because I was too old.

BARBARA: (*Not at all surprised.*) Youd pass still. Why didnt you dye your hair?

275 SHIRLEY: I did. Me age come out at a coroner's inquest on me daughter.

BARBARA: Steady?

SHIRLEY: Teetotaller. Never out of a job before. Good worker. And sent to the knackers like an old horse!

280 BARBARA: No matter: if you did your part God will do his.

SHIRLEY: (*Suddenly stubborn.*) My religion's no concern of anybody but myself.

BARBARA: (*Guessing.*) I know. Secularist?

SHIRLEY: (*Hotly.*) Did I offer to deny it?

285 BARBARA: Why should you? My own father's a Secularist, I think. Our Father—yours and mine—fulfils himself in many ways; and I daresay he knew what he was about when he made a Secularist of you. So buck up, Peter! we

can always find a job for a steady man like you. (SHIRLEY,
290   *disarmed and a little bewildered, touches his hat. She turns from*
him to BILL.) Whats your name?

BILL: (*Insolently.*) Wots thet to you?

BARBARA: (*Calmly making a note.*) Afraid to give his name.
Any trade?

295 BILL: Oo's afride to give is nime? (*Doggedly, with a sense of hero-*
ically defying the House of Lords in the person of Lord Steve-
nage.) If you want to bring a chawge agen me, bring it.
(*She waits, unruffled.*) Moy nime's Bill Walker.

BARBARA: (*As if the name were familiar: trying to remember how.*)
300   Bill Walker? (*Recollecting.*) Oh, I know: you're the man that
Jenny Hill was praying for inside just now. (*She enters his*
name in her note book.)

BILL: Oo's Jenny Ill? And wot call as she to pry for me?

BARBARA: I dont know. Perhaps it was you that cut her lip.

305 BILL: (*Defiantly.*) Yus, it was me that cat her lip. Aw aint afride
o you.

BARBARA: How could you be, since youre not afraid of God?
Youre a brave man, Mr Walker. It takes some pluck to do
our work here; but none of us dare lift our hand against a
310   girl like that, for fear of her father in heaven.

BILL: (*Sullenly.*) I want nan o your kentin jawr. I spowse you think
Aw cam eah to beg from you, like this demmiged lot eah. Not
me. Aw downt want your bread and scripe and ketlep. Aw
dont blieve in your Gawd, no more than you do yourself.

315 BARBARA: (*Sunnily apologetic and ladylike, as on a new footing*
with him.) Oh, I beg your pardon for putting your name
down, Mr Walker. I didnt understand. I'll strike it out.

BILL: (*Taking this as a slight, and deeply wounded by it.*) Eah! you
let maw nime alown. Aint it good enaff to be in your book?

320 BARBARA: (*Considering.*) Well, you see, theres no use putting
down your name unless I can do something for you, is
there? Whats your trade?

BILL: (*Still smarting.*) Thets nao concern o yours.

BARBARA: Just so. (*Very businesslike.*) I'll put you down as
325   (*Writing.*) the man who—struck—poor little Jenny Hill—
in the mouth.

BILL: (*Rising threateningly.*) See eah. Awve ed enaff o this.

BARBARA: (*Quite sunny and fearless.*) What did you come to us
for?

330 BILL: Aw cam for maw gel, see? Aw cam to tike her aht o this
and to brike er jawr for er.

BARBARA: (*Complacently.*) You see I was right about your
trade. (BILL, *on the point of retorting furiously, finds himself, to*
his great shame and terror, in danger of crying instead. He sits
335   *down again suddenly.*) Whats her name?

BILL: (*Dogged.*) Er nime's Mog Ebbijem: thets wot her nime is.

BARBARA: Mog Habbijam! Oh, she's gone to Canning Town,
to our barracks there.

BILL: (*Fortified by his resentment of Mog's perfidy.*) Is she? (*Vin-*
340   *dictively.*) Then Aw'm gowin to Kennintahn arter her. (*He*
crosses to the gate; hesitates; finally comes back at BARBARA.)
Are you loyin to me to git shat o me?

BARBARA: I dont want to get shut of you. I want to keep you
here and save your soul. Youd better stay: youre going to
345   have a bad time today, Bill.

BILL: Oo's gowin to give it to me? You, preps?

BARBARA: Someone you dont believe in. But youll be glad
afterwards.

BILL: (*Slinking off.*) Aw'll gow to Kennintahn to be aht o reach
350   o your tangue. (*Suddenly turning on her with intense malice.*)

And if Aw downt fawnd Mog there, Aw'll cam beck and
do two years for you, selp me Gawd if Aw downt!

BARBARA: (*A shade kindlier, if possible.*) It's no use, Bill. She's
got another bloke.

BILL: Wot!   355

BARBARA: One of her own converts. He fell in love with her
when he saw her with her soul saved, and her face clean,
and her hair washed.

BILL: (*Surprised.*) Wottud she wash it for, the carroty slat? It's
red.   360

BARBARA: It's quite lovely now, because she wears a new look
in her eyes with it. It's a pity youre too late. The new
bloke has put your nose out of joint, Bill.

BILL: Aw'll put his nowse aht o joint for him. Not that Aw
care a carse for er, mawnd thet. But Aw'll teach her to 365
drop me as if Aw was dirt. And Aw'll teach him to meddle with maw judy. Wots iz bleedin nime?

BARBARA: Sergeant Todger Fairmile.

SHIRLEY: (*Rising with grim joy.*) I'll go with him, miss. I want
to see them two meet. I'll take him to the infirmary when 370
it's over.

BILL: (*To* SHIRLEY, *with undissembled misgiving.*) Is thet im you
was speakin on?

SHIRLEY: Thats him.

BILL: Im that wrastled in the music awl?   375

SHIRLEY: The competitions at the National Sportin Club was
worth nigh a hundred a year to him. He's gev em up now
for religion; so he's a bit fresh for want of the exercise he
was accustomed to. He'll be glad to see you. Come along.

BILL: Wots is wight?   380

SHIRLEY: Thirteen four. (BILL's *last hope expires.*)

BARBARA: Go and talk to him, Bill. He'll convert you.

SHIRLEY: He'll convert your head into a mashed potato.

BILL: (*Sullenly.*) Aw aint afride of im. Aw aint afride of ennybody. Bat e can lick me. She's dan me. (*He sits down mood-* 385
ily on the edge of the horse trough.)

SHIRLEY: You aint going. I thought not. (*He resumes his seat.*)

BARBARA: (*Calling.*) Jenny!

JENNY: (*Appearing at the shelter door with a plaster on the corner*
of her mouth.) Yes, Major.   390

BARBARA: Send Rummy Mitchens out to clear away here.

JENNY: I think she's afraid.

BARBARA: (*Her resemblance to her mother flashing out for a mo-*
ment.) Nonsense! she must do as she's told.

JENNY: (*Calling into the shelter.*) Rummy: the Major says you 395
must come.

(JENNY *comes to* BARBARA, *purposely keeping on the side next to*
BILL, *lest he should suppose that she shrank from him or bore malice.*)

BARBARA: Poor little Jenny! Are you tired? (*Looking at the*
wounded cheek.) Does it hurt?

JENNY: No: it's all right now. It was nothing.

BARBARA: (*Critically.*) It was as hard as he could hit, I expect. 400
Poor Bill! You dont feel angry with him, do you?

JENNY: Oh no, no, no: indeed I dont, Major, bless his poor
heart! (BARBARA *kisses her; and she runs away merrily into the*
shelter. BILL *writhes with an agonizing return of his new and*
alarming symptoms, but says nothing. RUMMY MITCHENS *comes* 405
from the shelter.)

BARBARA: (*Going to meet* RUMMY.) Now Rummy, bustle.
Take in those mugs and plates to be washed; and throw
the crumbs about for the birds.

(RUMMY *takes the three plates and mugs; but* SHIRLEY *takes back his mug from her, as there is still some milk left in it.*)

410 RUMMY: There aint any crumbs. This aint a time to waste good bread on birds.

PRICE: (*Appearing at the shelter door.*) Gentleman come to see the shelter, Major. Says he's your father.

BARBARA: All right. Coming. (SNOBBY [PRICE] *goes back into*
415 *the shelter, followed by* BARBARA.)

RUMMY: (*Stealing across to* BILL *and addressing him in a subdued voice, but with intense conviction.*) I'd av the lor of you, you flat eared pignosed potwalloper, if she'd let me. Youre no gentleman, to hit a lady in the face. (BILL, *with greater things*
420 *moving in him, takes no notice.*)

SHIRLEY: (*Following her.*) Here! in with you and dont get yourself into more trouble by talking.

RUMMY: (*With hauteur.*) I aint ad the pleasure o being hintroduced to you, as I can remember. (*She goes into the shelter*
425 *with the plates.*)

SHIRLEY: Thats the—

BILL: (*Savagely.*) Downt you talk to me, d'ye eah? You lea me alown, or Aw'll do you a mischief. Aw'm not dirt under your feet, ennywy.

430 SHIRLEY: (*Calmly.*) Dont you be afeerd. You aint such prime company that you need expect to be sought after. (*He is about to go into the shelter when* BARBARA *comes out, with* UNDERSHAFT *on her right.*)

BARBARA: Oh, there you are, Mr Shirley! (*Between them.*) This
435 is my father: I told you he was a Secularist, didnt I? Perhaps youll be able to comfort one another.

UNDERSHAFT: (*Startled.*) A Secularist! Not the least in the world: on the contrary, a confirmed mystic.

BARBARA: Sorry, I'm sure. By the way, papa, what is your re-
440 ligion? in case I have to introduce you again.

UNDERSHAFT: My religion? Well, my dear, I am a Millionaire. That is my religion.

BARBARA: Then I'm afraid you and Mr Shirley wont be able to comfort one another after all. Youre not a Millionaire,
445 are you, Peter?

SHIRLEY: No; and proud of it.

UNDERSHAFT: (*Gravely.*) Poverty, my friend, is not a thing to be proud of.

SHIRLEY: (*Angrily.*) Who made your millions for you? Me and
450 my like. Whats kep us poor? Keepin you rich. I wouldnt have your conscience, not for all your income.

UNDERSHAFT: I wouldnt have your income, not for all your conscience, Mr Shirley. (*He goes to the penthouse and sits down on a form.*)

455 BARBARA: (*Stopping* SHIRLEY *adroitly as he is about to retort.*) You wouldnt think he was my father, would you, Peter? Will you go into the shelter and lend the lasses a hand for a while: we're worked off our feet.

SHIRLEY: (*Bitterly.*) Yes: I'm in their debt for a meal, aint I?

460 BARBARA: Oh, not because youre in their debt, but for love of them, Peter, for love of them. (*He cannot understand, and is rather scandalized.*) There! dont stare at me. In with you; and give that conscience of yours a holiday (*Bustling him into the shelter.*)

465 SHIRLEY: (*As he goes in.*) Ah! it's a pity you never was trained to use your reason, miss. You'd have been a very taking lecturer on Secularism.

(BARBARA *turns to her father.*)

UNDERSHAFT: Never mind me, my dear. Go about your work; and let me watch it for a while.

BARBARA: All right.   470

UNDERSHAFT: For instance, whats the matter with that outpatient over there?

BARBARA: (*Looking at* BILL, *whose attitude has never changed, and whose expression of brooding wrath has deepened.*) Oh, we shall cure him in no time. Just watch. (*She goes over to* BILL *and* 475
waits. He glances up at her and casts his eyes down again, uneasy, but grimmer than ever.) It would be nice to just stamp on Mog Habbijam's face, wouldnt it, Bill?

BILL: (*Starting up from the trough in consternation.*) It's a loy: Aw never said so. (*She shakes her head.*) Oo taold you wot was 480
in moy mawnd?

BARBARA: Only your new friend.

BILL: Wot new friend?

BARBARA: The devil, Bill. When he gets round people they get miserable, just like you.   485

BILL: (*With a heartbreaking attempt at devil-may-care cheerfulness.*) Aw aint miserable. (*He sits down again, and stretches his legs in an attempt to seem indifferent.*)

BARBARA: Well, if youre happy, why dont you look happy, as we do?   490

BILL: (*His legs curling back in spite of him.*) Aw'm eppy enaff, Aw tell you. Woy cawnt you lea me alown? Wot ev I dan to you? Aw aint smashed your fice, ev Aw?

BARBARA: (*Softly: wooing his soul.*) It's not me thats getting at you, Bill.   495

BILL: Oo else is it?

BARBARA: Somebody that doesnt intend you to smash women's faces, I suppose. Somebody or something that wants to make a man of you.

BILL: (*Blustering.*) Mike a menn o me! Aint Aw a menn? eh? 500
Oo sez Aw'm not a menn?

BARBARA: Theres a man in you somewhere, I suppose. But why did he let you hit poor little Jenny Hill? That wasnt very manly of him, was it?

BILL: (*Tormented.*) Ev dan wiv it, Aw tell you. Chack it. Aw'm 505
sick o your Jenny Ill and er silly little fice.

BARBARA: Then why do you keep thinking about it? Why does it keep coming up against you in your mind? Youre not getting converted, are you?

BILL: (*With conviction.*) Not ME. Not lawkly.   510

BARBARA: Thats right, Bill. Hold out against it. Put out your strength. Dont lets get you cheap. Todger Fairmile said he wrestled for three nights against his salvation harder than he ever wrestled with the Jap at the music hall. He gave in to the Jap when his arm was going to break. But he didnt 515
give in to his salvation until his heart was going to break. Perhaps youll escape that. You havnt any heart, have you?

BILL: Wot d'ye mean? Woy aint Aw got a awt the sime as ennybody else?

BARBARA: A man with a heart wouldnt have bashed poor lit- 520
tle Jenny's face, would he?

BILL: (*Almost crying.*) Ow, will you lea me alown? Ev Aw ever offered to meddle with you, that you cam neggin and provowkin me lawk this? (*He writhes convulsively from his eyes to his toes.*)   525

BARBARA: (*With a steady soothing hand on his arm and a gentle voice that never lets him go.*) It's your soul thats hurting you, Bill, and not me. Weve been through it all ourselves. Come with us, Bill. (*He looks wildly round.*) To brave man-

530 hood on earth and eternal glory in heaven. (*He is on the point of breaking down.*) Come. (*A drum is heard in the shelter; and* BILL, *with a gasp, escapes from the spell as* BARBARA *turns quickly.* ADOLPHUS [CUSINS] *enters from the shelter with a big drum.*) Oh! there you are, Dolly. Let me introduce a
535 new friend of mine, Mr Bill Walker. This is my bloke, Bill: Mr Cusins. (CUSINS *salutes with his drumstick.*)

BILL: Gowin to merry im?

BARBARA: Yes.

BILL: (*Fervently.*) Gawd elp im! Gaw-aw-aw-awd elp im!

540 BARBARA: Why? Do you think he wont be happy with me?

BILL: Awve aony ed to stend it for a mawnin: e'll ev to stend it for a lawftawm.

CUSINS: That is a frightful reflection, Mr Walker. But I cant tear myself away from her.

545 BILL: Well, Aw ken. (*To* BARBARA.) Eah! do you knaow where Aw'm gowin to, and wot Aw'm gowin to do?

BARBARA: Yes: youre going to heaven; and youre coming back here before the week's out to tell me so.

BILL: You loy. Aw'm gowin to Kennintahn, to spit in Todger
550 Fairmawl's eye. Aw beshed Jenny Ill's fice; an nar Aw'll git me aown fice beshed and cam beck and shaow it to er. Ee'll itt me ardern Aw itt her. Thatll mike us square. (*To* ADOLPHUS [CUSINS].) Is thet fair or is it not? Youre a genlmn: you oughter knaow.

555 BARBARA: Two black eyes wont make one white one, Bill.

BILL: Aw didnt awst you. Cawnt you never keep your mahth shat? Oy awst the genlmn.

CUSINS: (*Reflectively.*) Yes: I think youre right, Mr Walker. Yes: I should do it. It's curious: it's exactly what an ancient
560 Greek would have done.

BARBARA: But what good will it do?

CUSINS: Well, it will give Mr Fairmile some exercise; and it will satisfy Mr Walker's soul.

BILL: Rot! there aint nao such a thing as a saoul. Ah kin you
565 tell wevver Awve a saoul or not? You never seen it.

BARBARA: Ive seen it hurting you when you went against it.

BILL: (*With compressed aggravation.*) If you was maw gel and took the word aht o me mahth lawk thet, Aw'd give you sathink youd feel urtin, Aw would. (*To* CUSINS.) You tike
570 maw tip, mite. Stop er jawr; or youll doy afoah your tawm (*With intense expression.*) Wore aht: thets wot youll be: wore aht. (*He goes away through the gate.*)

CUSINS: (*Looking after him.*) I wonder!

BARBARA: Dolly! (*Indignant, in her mother's manner.*)

575 CUSINS: Yes, my dear, it's very wearing to be in love with you. If it lasts, I quite think I shall die young.

BARBARA: Should you mind?

CUSINS: Not at all. (*He is suddenly softened, and kisses her over the drum, evidently not for the first time, as people cannot kiss
580 over a big drum without practice.* UNDERSHAFT *coughs.*)

BARBARA: It's all right, papa, weve not forgotten you. Dolly: explain the place to papa: I havnt time. (*She goes busily into the shelter.*)

(UNDERSHAFT *and* ADOLPHUS [CUSINS] *now have the yard to themselves.* UNDERSHAFT, *seated on a form, and still keenly attentive, looks hard at* ADOLPHUS [CUSINS]. ADOLPHUS [CUSINS] *looks hard at him.*)

UNDERSHAFT: I fancy you guess something of what is in my
585 mind, Mr Cusins. (CUSINS *flourishes his drumsticks as if in the*

act of beating a lively rataplan, but makes no sound.) Exactly so. But suppose Barbara finds you out!

CUSINS: You know, I do not admit that I am imposing on Barbara. I am quite genuinely interested in the views of the Salvation Army. The fact is, I am a sort of collector of 590 religions; and the curious thing is that I find I can believe them all. By the way, have you any religion?

UNDERSHAFT: Yes.

CUSINS: Anything out of the common?

UNDERSHAFT: Only that there are two things necessary to 595 Salvation.

CUSINS: (*Disappointed, but polite.*) Ah, the Church Catechism. Charles Lomax also belongs to the Established Church.

UNDERSHAFT: The two things are—

CUSINS: Baptism and— 600

UNDERSHAFT: No. Money and gunpowder.

CUSINS: (*Surprised, but interested.*) That is the general opinion of our governing classes. The novelty is in hearing any man confess it.

UNDERSHAFT: Just so. 605

CUSINS: Excuse me: is there any place in your religion for honor, justice, truth, love, mercy and so forth?

UNDERSHAFT: Yes: they are the graces and luxuries of a rich, strong, and safe life.

CUSINS: Suppose one is forced to choose between them and 610 money or gunpowder?

UNDERSHAFT: Choose money and gunpowder; for without enough of both you cannot afford the others.

CUSINS: That is your religion?

UNDERSHAFT: Yes. 615

(*The cadence of this reply makes a full close in the conversation,* CUSINS *twists his face dubiously and contemplates* UNDERSHAFT. UNDERSHAFT *contemplates him.*)

CUSINS: Barbara wont stand that. You will have to choose between your religion and Barbara.

UNDERSHAFT: So will you, my friend. She will find out that that drum of yours is hollow.

CUSINS: Father Undershaft: you are mistaken: I am a sincere 620 Salvationist. You do not understand the Salvation Army. It is the army of joy, of love, of courage: it has banished the fear and remorse and despair of the old hell-ridden evangelical sects: it marches to fight the devil with trumpet and drum, with music and dancing, with banner and palm, as 625 becomes a sally from heaven by its happy garrison. It picks the waster out of the public house and makes a man of him: it finds a worm wriggling in a back kitchen, and lo! a woman! Men and women of rank too, sons and daughters of the Highest. It takes the poor professor of Greek, 630 the most artificial and self-suppressed of human creatures, from his meal of roots, and lets loose the rhapsodist in him; reveals the true worship of Dionysos to him; sends him down the public street drumming dithyrambs (*He plays a thundering flourish on the drum.*) 635

UNDERSHAFT: You will alarm the shelter.

CUSINS: Oh, they are accustomed to these sudden ecstasies. However, if the drum worries you—(*He pockets the drumsticks; unhooks the drum; and stands it on the ground opposite the gateway.*) 640

UNDERSHAFT: Thank you.

CUSINS: You remember what Euripides says about your money and gunpowder?

UNDERSHAFT: No.

645 CUSINS: (*Declaiming.*)

> One and another
> In money and guns may outpass his brother;
> And men in their millions float and flow
> And seethe with a million hopes as leaven;
650 > And they win their will; or they miss their will;
> And their hopes are dead or are pined for still;
> But who'er can know
> As the long days go
> That to live is happy, has found his heaven.

655 My translation: what do you think of it?

UNDERSHAFT: I think, my friend, that if you wish to know, as the long days go, that to live is happy, you must first acquire money enough for a decent life, and power enough to be your own master.

660 CUSINS: You are damnably discouraging. (*He resumes his declamation.*)

> Is it so hard a thing to see
> That the spirit of God—whate'er it be—
> The law that abides and changes not, ages long,
665 > The Eternal and Nature-born: these things be strong?
> What else is Wisdom? What of Man's endeavor,
> Or God's high grace so lovely and so great?
> To stand from fear set free? to breathe and wait?
> To hold a hand uplifted over Fate?
670 > And shall not Barbara be loved for ever?

UNDERSHAFT: Euripides mentions Barbara, does he?

CUSINS: It is a fair translation. The word means Loveliness.

UNDERSHAFT: May I ask—as Barbara's father—how much a year she is to be loved for ever on?

675 CUSINS: As for Barbara's father, that is more your affair than mine. I can feed her by teaching Greek: that is about all.

UNDERSHAFT: Do you consider it a good match for her?

CUSINS: (*With polite obstinacy.*) Mr Undershaft: I am in many ways a weak, timid, ineffectual person; and my health is far
680 from satisfactory. But whenever I feel that I must have anything, I get it, sooner or later. I feel that way about Barbara. I dont like marriage: I feel intensely afraid of it; and I dont know what I shall do with Barbara or what she will do with me. But I feel that I and nobody else must marry
685 her. Please regard that as settled.—Not that I wish to be arbitrary; but why should I waste your time in discussing what is inevitable?

UNDERSHAFT: You mean that you will stick at nothing: not even the conversion of the Salvation Army to the worship
690 of Dionysos.

CUSINS: The business of the Salvation Army is to save, not to wrangle about the name of the pathfinder. Dionysos or another: what does it matter?

UNDERSHAFT: (*Rising and approaching him.*) Professor Cusins:
695 you are a young man after my own heart.

CUSINS: Mr Undershaft: you are, as far as I am able to gather, a most infernal old rascal; but you appeal very strongly to my sense of ironic humor.

(UNDERSHAFT *mutely offers his hand. They shake.*)

UNDERSHAFT: (*Suddenly concentrating himself.*) And now to business. 700

CUSINS: Pardon me. We are discussing religion. Why go back to such an uninteresting and unimportant subject as business?

UNDERSHAFT: Religion is our business at present, because it is through religion alone that we can win Barbara.

CUSINS: Have you, too, fallen in love with Barbara? 705

UNDERSHAFT: Yes, with a father's love.

CUSINS: A father's love for a grown-up daughter is the most dangerous of all infatuations. I apologize for mentioning my own pale, coy, mistrustful fancy in the same breath with it.

UNDERSHAFT: Keep to the point. We have to win her; and 710
we are neither of us Methodists.

CUSINS: That doesnt matter. The power Barbara wields here—the power that wields Barbara herself—is not Calvinism, not Presbyterianism, not Methodism—

UNDERSHAFT: Not Greek Paganism either, eh? 715

CUSINS: I admit that. Barbara is quite original in her religion.

UNDERSHAFT: (*Triumphantly.*) Aha! Barbara Undershaft would be. Her inspiration comes from within herself.

CUSINS: How do you suppose it got there?

UNDERSHAFT: (*In towering excitement.*) It is the Undershaft in- 720
heritance. I shall hand on my torch to my daughter. She shall make my converts and preach my gospel—

CUSINS: What! Money and gunpowder!

UNDERSHAFT: Yes, money and gunpowder. Freedom and power. Command of life and command of death. 725

CUSINS: (*Urbanely: trying to bring him down to earth.*) This is extremely interesting, Mr Undershaft. Of course you know that you are mad.

UNDERSHAFT: (*With redoubled force.*) And you?

CUSINS: Oh, mad as a hatter. You are welcome to my secret 730
since I have discovered yours. But I am astonished. Can a madman make cannons?

UNDERSHAFT: Would anyone else than a madman make them? And now (*With surging energy.*) question for question. Can a sane man translate Euripides? 735

CUSINS: No.

UNDERSHAFT: (*Seizing him by the shoulder.*) Can a sane woman make a man of a waster or a woman of a worm?

CUSINS: (*Reeling before the storm.*) Father Colossus—Mammoth Millionaire— 740

UNDERSHAFT: (*Pressing him.*) Are there two mad people or three in this Salvation shelter today?

CUSINS: You mean Barbara is as mad as we are?

UNDERSHAFT: (*Pushing him lightly off and resuming his equanimity suddenly and completely.*) Pooh, Professor! let us call 745
things by their proper names. I am a millionaire; you are a poet; Barbara is a savior of souls. What have we three to do with the common mob of slaves and idolators? (*He sits down again with a shrug of contempt for the mob.*)

CUSINS: Take care! Barbara is in love with the common peo- 750
ple. So am I. Have you never felt the romance of that love?

UNDERSHAFT: (*Cold and sardonic.*) Have you ever been in love with Poverty, like St Francis? Have you ever been in love with Dirt, like St Simeon? Have you ever been in love with disease and suffering, like our nurses and philanthropists? 755
Such passions are not virtues, but the most unnatural of all the vices. This love of the common people may please an earl's granddaughter and a university professor; but I have been a common man and a poor man; and it has no ro-

760 mance for me. Leave it to the poor to pretend that poverty is a blessing: leave it to the coward to make a religion of his cowardice by preaching humility: we know better than that. We three must stand together above the common people: how else can we help their children to climb up beside

765 us? Barbara must belong to us, not to the Salvation Army.

CUSINS: Well, I can only say that if you think you will get her away from the Salvation Army by talking to her as you have been talking to me, you dont know Barbara.

UNDERSHAFT: My friend: I never ask for what I can buy.

770 CUSINS: (*In a white fury.*) Do I understand you to imply that you can buy Barbara?

UNDERSHAFT: No; but I can buy the Salvation Army.

CUSINS: Quite impossible.

UNDERSHAFT: You shall see. All religious organizations exist

775 by selling themselves to the rich.

CUSINS: Not the Army. That is the Church of the poor.

UNDERSHAFT: All the more reason for buying it.

CUSINS: I dont think you quite know what the Army does for the poor.

780 UNDERSHAFT: Oh yes I do. It draws their teeth: that is enough for me as a man of business.

CUSINS: Nonsense! It makes them sober—

UNDERSHAFT: I prefer sober workmen. The profits are larger.

CUSINS: —honest—

785 UNDERSHAFT: Honest workmen are the most economical.

CUSINS: —attached to their homes—

UNDERSHAFT: So much the better: they will put up with anything sooner than change their shop.

CUSINS: —happy—

790 UNDERSHAFT: An invaluable safeguard against revolution.

CUSINS: —unselfish—

UNDERSHAFT: Indifferent to their own interests, which suits me exactly.

CUSINS: —with their thoughts on heavenly things—

795 UNDERSHAFT: (*Rising.*) And not on Trade Unionism nor Socialism. Excellent.

CUSINS: (*Revolted.*) You really are an infernal old rascal.

UNDERSHAFT: (*Indicating* PETER SHIRLEY, *who has just come from the shelter and strolled dejectedly down the yard between*

800 *them.*) And this is an honest man!

SHIRLEY: Yes; and what av I got by it? (*He passes on bitterly and sits on the form, in the corner of the penthouse.*)

(SNOBBY PRICE, *beaming sanctimoniously, and* JENNY HILL, *with a tambourine full of coppers, come from the shelter and go to the drum, on which* JENNY *begins to count the money.*)

UNDERSHAFT: (*Replying to* SHIRLEY.) Oh, your employers

805 must have got a good deal by it from first to last. (*He sits on the table, with one foot on the side form,* CUSINS, *overwhelmed, sits down on the same form nearer the shelter.* BARBARA *comes from the shelter to the middle of the yard. She is excited and a little overwrought.*)

BARBARA: Weve just had a splendid experience meeting at the

810 other gate in Cripps's lane. Ive hardly ever seen them so much moved as they were by your confession, Mr Price.

PRICE: I could almost be glad of my past wickedness if I could believe that it would elp to keep hathers stright.

BARBARA: So it will, Snobby. How much, Jenny?

JENNY: Four and tenpence, Major.   815

BARBARA: Oh Snobby, if you had given your poor mother just one more kick, we should have got the whole five shillings!

PRICE: If she heard you say that, miss, she'd be sorry I didnt. But I'm glad. Oh what a joy it will be to her when she hears I'm saved!   820

UNDERSHAFT: Shall I contribute the odd twopence, Barbara? The millionaire's mite, eh? (*He takes a couple of pennies from his pocket.*)

BARBARA: How did you make that twopence?

UNDERSHAFT: As usual. By selling cannons, torpedoes, sub-   825 marines, and my new patent Grand Duke hand grenade.

BARBARA: Put it back in your pocket. You cant buy your salvation here for twopence: you must work it out.

UNDERSHAFT: Is twopence not enough? I can afford a little more, if you press me.   830

BARBARA: Two million millions would not be enough. There is bad blood on your hands; and nothing but good blood can cleanse them. Money is no use. Take it away. (*She turns to* CUSINS.) Dolly: you must write another letter for me to the papers. (*He makes a wry face.*) Yes: I know you dont like 835 it; but it must be done. The starvation this winter is beating us: everybody is unemployed. The General says we must close this shelter if we cant get more money. I force the collections at the meetings until I am ashamed: dont I, Snobby?   840

PRICE: It's a fair treat to see you work it, miss. The way you got them up from three-and-six to four-and-ten with that hymn, penny by penny and verse by verse, was a caution. Not a Cheap Jack on Mile End Waste could touch you at it.

BARBARA: Yes, but I wish we could do without it. I am getting 845 at last to think more of the collection than of the people's souls. And what are those hatfuls of pence and halfpence? We want thousands! tens of thousands! hundreds of thousands! I want to convert people, not to be always begging for the Army in a way I'd die sooner than beg for myself.   850

UNDERSHAFT: (*In profound irony.*) Genuine unselfishness is capable of anything, my dear.

BARBARA: (*Unsuspectingly, as she turns away to take the money from the drum and put it in a cash bag she carries.*) Yes, isnt it? (UNDERSHAFT *looks sardonically at* CUSINS.)   855

CUSINS: (*Aside to* UNDERSHAFT.) Mephistopheles! Machiavelli!

BARBARA: (*Tears coming into her eyes as she ties the bag and pockets it.*) How are we to feed them? I cant talk religion to a man with bodily hunger in his eyes. (*Almost breaking down.*) It's frightful.   860

JENNY: (*Running to her.*) Major, dear—

BARBARA: (*Rebounding.*) No: dont comfort me. It will be all right. We shall get the money.

UNDERSHAFT: How?

JENNY: By praying for it, of course. Mrs Baines says she prayed 865 for it last night; and she has never prayed for it in vain: never once. (*She goes to the gate and looks out into the street.*)

BARBARA: (*Who has dried her eyes and regained her composure.*) By the way, dad, Mrs Baines has come to march with us to our big meeting this afternoon; and she is very anxious to meet 870 you, for some reason or other. Perhaps she'll convert you.

UNDERSHAFT: I shall be delighted, my dear.

JENNY: (*At the gate: excitedly.*) Major! Major! heres that man back again.

BARBARA: What man?   875

JENNY: The man that hit me. Oh, I hope he's coming back to join us.

(BILL WALKER, *with frost on his jacket, comes through the gate, his hands deep in his pockets and his chin sunk between his shoulders, like a cleaned-out gambler. He halts between* BARBARA *and the drum.*)

BARBARA: Hullo, Bill! Back already!

BILL: (*Nagging at her.*) Bin talkin ever sence, ev you?

880 BARBARA: Pretty nearly. Well, has Todger paid you out for poor Jenny's jaw?

BILL: Nao e aint.

BARBARA: I thought your jacket looked a bit snowy.

BILL: Sao it is snaowy. You want to knaow where the snaow
885 cam from, downt you?

BARBARA: Yes.

BILL: Well, it cam from orf the grahnd in Pawkinses Corner in Kennintahn. It got rabbed orf be maw shaoulders: see?

BARBARA: Pity you didnt rub some off with your knees, Bill!
890 That would have done you a lot of good.

BILL: (*With sour mirthless humor.*) Aw was sivin another menn's knees at the tawm. E was kneelin on moy ed, e was.

JENNY: Who was kneeling on your head?

BILL: Todger was. E was pryin for me: pryin camfortable wiv
895 me as a cawpet. Sow was Mog. Sao was the aol bloomin meetin. Mog she sez 'Ow Lawd brike is stabborn sperrit; bat downt urt is dear art.' Thet was wot she said. 'Downt urt is dear art'! An er blowk—thirteen stun four!— kneelin wiv all is wight on me. Fanny, aint it?

900 JENNY: Oh no. We're so sorry, Mr Walker.

BARBARA: (*Enjoying it frankly.*) Nonsense! of course it's funny. Served you right, Bill! You must have done something to him first.

BILL: (*Doggedly.*) Aw did wot Aw said Aw'd do. Aw spit in is eye.
905 E looks ap at the skoy and sez, 'Ow that Aw should be fahnd worthy to be spit upon for the gospel's sike!' e sez; an Mog sez 'Glaory Allelloolier!'; an then e called me Braddher, an dahned me as if Aw was a kid and e was me mather worshin me a Setterda nawt. Aw ednt jast nao shaow wiv im at all.
910 Arf the street pryed; an the tather arf larfed fit to split theirselves. (*To* BARBARA.) There! are you settisfawd nah?

BARBARA: (*Her eyes dancing.*) Wish I'd been there, Bill.

BILL: Yus: youd a got in a hextra bit o talk on me, wouldnt you?

JENNY: I'm so sorry, Mr Walker.

915 BILL: (*Fiercely.*) Downt you gow being sorry for me: youve no call. Listen eah. Aw browk your jawr.

JENNY: No, it didn't hurt me: indeed it didnt, except for a moment. It was only that I was frightened.

BILL: Aw downt want to be forgive be you, or be ennybody.
920 Wot Aw did Aw'll py for. Aw trawd to gat me aown jawr browk to settisfaw you—

JENNY: (*Distressed.*) Oh no—

BILL: (*Impatiently.*) Tell y' Aw did: cawnt you listen to wots bein taold you? All Aw got be it was bein mide a sawt of
925 in the pablic street for me pines. Well, if Aw cawnt settisfaw you one wy, Aw ken anather. Listen eah! Aw ed two quid sived agen the frost; an Awve a pahnd of it left. A mite o mawn last week ed words with the judy e's gowing to merry. E give er wot-for; an e's bin tawnd fifteen
930 bob. E ed a rawt to itt er cause they was gowin to be mer-

rid; but Aw ednt nao rawt to itt you; sao put anather fawv bob on an call it a pahnd's worth. (*He produces a sovereign.*) Eahs the manney. Tike it; and lets ev no more o your forgivin an prying and your Mijor jawrin me. Let wot Aw dan be dan an pide for; and let there be a end of it. 935

JENNY: Oh, I couldnt take it, Mr Walker. But if you would give a shilling or two to poor Rummy Mitchens! you really did hurt her; and she's old.

BILL: (*Contemptuously.*) Not lawkly. Aw'd give her anather as soon as look at er. Let her ev the lawr o me as she threat- 940 ened! She aint forgiven me: not mach. Wot Aw dan to er is not on me mawnd—wot she (*Indicating* BARBARA.) mawt call on me conscience—no more than stickin a pig. It's this Christian gime o yours that Aw wownt ev plyed agen me: this bloomin forgivin an neggin an jawrin that 945 mikes a menn thet sore that iz lawf's a burdn to im. Aw wownt ev it, Aw tell you; sao tike your manney and stop thraowin your silly beshed fice hap agen me.

JENNY: Major: may I take a little of it for the Army?

BARBARA: No: the Army is not to be bought. We want your 950 soul, Bill; and we'll take nothing less.

BILL: (*Bitterly.*) Aw knaow. Me an maw few shillins is not good enaff for you. Youre a earl's grendorter, you are. Nathink less than a andered pahnd for you.

UNDERSHAFT: Come, Barbara! you could do a great deal of 955 good with a hundred pounds. If you will set this gentleman's mind at ease by taking his pound, I will give the other ninety-nine.

(BILL, *dazed by such opulence, instinctively touches his cap.*)

BARBARA: Oh, youre too extravagant, papa. Bill offers twenty pieces of silver. All you need offer is the other ten. That 960 will make the standard price to buy anybody who's for sale. I'm not; and the Army's not. (*To* BILL.) Youll never have another quiet moment, Bill, until you come round to us. You cant stand out against your salvation.

BILL: (*Sullenly.*) Aw cawnt stend aht agen music awl wrastlers 965 and awtful tangued women. Awve offered to py. Aw can do no more. Tike it or leave it. There it is. (*He throws the sovereign on the drum, and sits down on the horse-trough. The coin fascinates* SNOBBY PRICE, *who takes an early opportunity of dropping his cap on it.*) 970

(MRS BAINES *comes from the shelter. She is dressed as a Salvation Army Commissioner. She is an earnest looking woman of about 40, with a caressing, urgent voice, and an appealing manner.*)

BARBARA: This is my father, Mrs Baines. (UNDERSHAFT *comes from the table, taking his hat off with marked civility.*) Try what you can do with him. He wont listen to me, because he remembers what a fool I was when I was a baby. (*She leaves them together and chats with* JENNY.) 975

MRS BAINES: Have you been shewn over the shelter, Mr Undershaft? You know the work we're doing, of course.

UNDERSHAFT: (*Very civilly.*) The whole nation knows it, Mrs Baines.

MRS BAINES: No, sir: the whole nation does not know it, or 980 we should not be crippled as we are for want of money to carry our work through the length and breadth of the land. Let me tell you that there would have been rioting this winter in London but for us.

985 UNDERSHAFT: You really think so?

MRS BAINES: I know it. I remember 1886, when you rich gentlemen hardened your hearts against the cry of the poor. They broke the windows of your clubs in Pall Mall.

UNDERSHAFT: (*Gleaming with approval of their method.*) And
990 the Mansion House Fund went up next day from thirty thousand pounds to seventy-nine thousand! I remember quite well.

MRS BAINES: Well, wont you help me to get at the people? They wont break windows then. Come here, Price. Let
995 me shew you to this gentleman (PRICE *comes to be inspected.*) Do you remember the window breaking?

PRICE: My ole father thought it was the revolution, maam.

MRS BAINES: Would you break windows now?

PRICE: Oh no, maam. The windows of eaven av bin opened to
1000 me. I know now that the rich man is a sinner like myself.

RUMMY: (*Appearing above at the loft door.*) Snobby Price!

SNOBBY: Wot is it?

RUMMY: Your mother's askin for you at the other gate in Cripps's Lane. She's heard about your confession (PRICE *turns pale.*)

1005 MRS BAINES: Go, Mr Price; and pray with her.

JENNY: You can go through the shelter, Snobby.

PRICE: (*To* MRS BAINES.) I couldnt face her now, maam, with all the weight of my sins fresh on me. Tell her she'll find her son at ome, waitin for her in prayer. (*He skulks off*
1010 *through the gate, incidentally stealing the sovereign on his way out by picking up his cap from the drum.*)

MRS BAINES: (*With swimming eyes.*) You see how we take the anger and the bitterness against you out of their hearts, Mr Undershaft.

1015 UNDERSHAFT: It is certainly most convenient and gratifying to all large employers of labor, Mrs Baines.

MRS BAINES: Barbara: Jenny: I have good news: most wonderful news. (JENNY *runs to her.*) My prayers have been answered. I told you they would, Jenny, didnt I?

1020 JENNY: Yes, yes.

BARBARA: (*Moving nearer to the drum.*) Have we got money enough to keep the shelter open?

MRS BAINES: I hope we shall have enough to keep all the shelters open. Lord Saxmundham has promised us five
1025 thousand pounds—

BARBARA: Hooray!

JENNY: Glory!

MRS BAINES: —if—

BARBARA: 'If!' If what?

1030 MRS BAINES: —if five other gentlemen will give a thousand each to make it up to ten thousand.

BARBARA: Who is Lord Saxmundham? I never heard of him.

UNDERSHAFT: (*Who has pricked up his ears at the peer's name, and is now watching* BARBARA *curiously.*) A new creation, my
1035 dear. You have heard of Sir Horace Bodger?

BARBARA: Bodger! Do you mean the distiller? Bodger's whisky!

UNDERSHAFT: That is the man. He is one of the greatest of our public benefactors. He restored the cathedral at Hakington. They made him a baronet for that. He gave half a million to
1040 the funds of his party: they made him a baron for that.

SHIRLEY: What will they give him for the five thousand?

UNDERSHAFT: There is nothing left to give him. So the five thousand, I should think, is to save his soul.

MRS BAINES: Heaven grant it may! Oh Mr Undershaft, you
1045 have some very rich friends. Cant you help us towards the other five thousand? We are going to hold a great meeting this afternoon at the Assembly Hall in the Mile End Road. If I could only announce that one gentleman had come forward to support Lord Saxmundham, others would follow. Dont you know somebody? couldnt you?
1050 wouldnt you? (*Her eyes fill with tears.*) oh, think of those poor people, Mr Undershaft: think of how much it means to them, and how little to a great man like you.

UNDERSHAFT: (*Sardonically gallant.*) Mrs Baines: you are irresistible. I cant disappoint you; and I cant deny myself the
1055 satisfaction of making Bodger pay up. You shall have your five thousand pounds.

MRS BAINES: Thank God!

UNDERSHAFT: You dont thank me?

MRS BAINES: Oh sir, dont try to be cynical: dont be ashamed
1060 of being a good man. The Lord will bless you abundantly; and our prayers will be like a strong fortification round you all the days of your life. (*With a touch of caution.*) You will let me have the cheque to shew at the meeting, wont you? Jenny: go in and fetch a pen and ink. (JENNY *runs to*
1065 *the shelter door.*)

UNDERSHAFT: Do not disturb Miss Hill: I have a fountain pen. (JENNY *halts. He sits at the table and writes the cheque.* CUSINS *rises to make room for him. They all watch him silently.*)

BILL: (*Cynically, aside to* BARBARA, *his voice and accent horribly*
1070 *debased.*) Wot prawce selvytion nah?

BARBARA: Stop. (UNDERSHAFT *stops writing: they all turn to her in surprise.*) Mrs Baines: are you really going to take this money?

MRS BAINES: (*Astonished.*) Why not, dear?
1075

BARBARA: Why not! Do you know what my father is? Have you forgotten that Lord Saxmundham is Bodger the whisky man? Do you remember how we implored the County Council to stop him from writing Bodger's Whisky in letters of fire against the sky; so that the poor drink-
1080 ruined creatures on the Embankment could not wake up from their snatches of sleep without being reminded of their deadly thirst by that wicked sky sign? Do you know that the worst thing I have had to fight here is not the devil, but Bodger, Bodger, Bodger, with his whisky, his distilleries,
1085 and his tied houses? Are you going to make our shelter another tied house for him, and ask me to keep it?

BILL: Rotten dranken whisky it is too.

MRS BAINES: Dear Barbara: Lord Saxmundham has a soul to be saved like any of us. If heaven has found the way to
1090 make a good use of his money, are we to set ourselves up against the answer to our prayers?

BARBARA: I know he has a soul to be saved. Let him come down here; and I'll do my best to help him to his salvation. But he wants to send his cheque down to buy us, and
1095 go on being as wicked as ever.

UNDERSHAFT: (*With a reasonableness which* CUSINS *alone perceives to be ironical.*) My dear Barbara: alcohol is a very necessary article. It heals the sick—

BARBARA: It does nothing of the sort.
1100

UNDERSHAFT: Well, it assists the doctor: that is perhaps a less questionable way of putting it. It makes life bearable to millions of people who could not endure their existence if they were quite sober. It enables Parliament to do things at eleven at night that no sane person would do at eleven in
1105 the morning. Is it Bodger's fault that this inestimable gift is

deplorably abused by less than one per cent of the poor? (*He turns again to the table; signs the cheque; and crosses it.*)

1110 MRS BAINES: Barbara: will there be less drinking or more if all those poor souls we are saving come tomorrow and find the doors of our shelters shut in their faces? Lord Saxmundham gives us the money to stop drinking—to take his own business from him.

1115 CUSINS: (*Impishly.*) Pure self-sacrifice on Bodger's part, clearly! Bless dear Bodger! (BARBARA *almost breaks down as* ADOLPHUS, *too, fails her.*)

UNDERSHAFT: (*Tearing out the cheque and pocketing the book as he rises and goes past* CUSINS *to* MRS BAINES.) I also, Mrs Baines, may claim a little disinterestedness. Think of my business!

1120 think of the widows and orphans! the men and lads torn to pieces with shrapnel and poisoned with lyddite! (MRS BAINES *shrinks; but he goes on remorselessly*) the oceans of blood, not one drop of which is shed in a really just cause! the ravaged crops! the peaceful peasants forced, women and

1125 men, to till their fields under the fire of opposing armies on pain of starvation! the bad blood of the fierce little cowards at home who egg on others to fight for the gratification of their national vanity! All this makes money for me: I am never richer, never busier than when the papers are full of

1130 it. Well, it is your work to preach peace on earth and good will to men. (MRS BAINES's *face lights up again.*) Every convert you make is a vote against war. (*Her lips move in prayer.*) Yet I give you this money to help you to hasten my own commercial ruin. (*He gives her the cheque.*)

1135 CUSINS: (*Mounting the form in an ecstasy of mischief.*) The millennium will be inaugurated by the unselfishness of Undershaft and Bodger. Oh be joyful! (*He takes the drum-sticks from his pocket and flourishes them.*)

MRS BAINES: (*Taking the cheque.*) The longer I live the more
1140 proof I see that there is an Infinite Goodness that turns everything to the work of salvation sooner or later. Who would have thought that any good could have come out of war and drink? And yet their profits are brought today to the feet of salvation to do its blessed work. (*She is af-*
1145 *fected to tears.*)

JENNY: (*Running to* MRS BAINES *and throwing her arms round her.*) Oh dear! how blessed, how glorious it all is!

CUSINS: (*In a convulsion of irony.*) Let us seize this unspeakable moment. Let us march to the great meeting at once. Ex-
1150 cuse me just an instant. (*He rushes into the shelter.* JENNY *takes her tambourine from the drum head.*)

MRS BAINES: Mr Undershaft: have you ever seen a thousand people fall on their knees with one impulse and pray? Come with us to the meeting. Barbara shall tell them that
1155 the Army is saved, and saved through you.

CUSINS: (*Returning impetuously from the shelter with a flag and a trombone, and coming between* MRS BAINES *and* UNDERSHAFT.) You shall carry the flag down the first street, Mrs Baines. (*He gives her the flag.*) Mr Undershaft is a gifted
1160 trombonist: he shall intone an Olympian diapason to the West Ham Salvation March. (*Aside to* UNDERSHAFT, *as he forces the trombone on him.*) Blow, Machiavelli, blow.

UNDERSHAFT: (*Aside to him, as he takes the trombone.*) The trumpet in Zion! (CUSINS *rushes to the drum, which he takes*
1165 *up and puts on.* UNDERSHAFT *continues, aloud.*) I will do my best. I could vamp a bass if I knew the tune.

CUSINS: It is a wedding chorus from one of Donizetti's operas; but we have converted it. We convert everything to good here, including Bodger. You remember the chorus. 'For
1170 thee immense rejoicing—immenso giubilo—immenso giubilo.' (*With drum obbligato.*) Rum tum ti tum tum, tum tum ti ta—

BARBARA: Dolly: you are breaking my heart.

CUSINS: What is a broken heart more or less here? Dionysos
1175 Undershaft has descended. I am possessed.

MRS BAINES: Come, Barbara: I must have my dear Major to carry the flag with me.

JENNY: Yes, yes, Major darling.

(CUSINS *snatches the tambourine out of* JENNY's *hand and mutely offers it to* BARBARA.)

BARBARA: (*Coming forward a little as she puts the offer behind her
1180 with a shudder, whilst* CUSINS *recklessly tosses the tambourine back to* JENNY *and goes to the gate.*) I cant come.

JENNY: Not come!

MRS BAINES: (*With tears in her eyes.*) Barbara: do you think I am wrong to take the money?

BARBARA: (*Impulsively going to her and kissing her.*) No, no: God
1185 help you, dear, you must: you are saving the Army. Go; and may you have a great meeting!

JENNY: But arnt you coming?

BARBARA: No. (*She begins taking off the silver S brooch from her collar.*)
1190

MRS BAINES: Barbara: what are you doing?

JENNY: Why are you taking your badge off? You cant be going to leave us, Major.

BARBARA: (*Quietly.*) Father: come here.

UNDERSHAFT: (*Coming to her.*) My dear! (*Seeing that she is go-*
1195 *ing to pin the badge on his collar, he retreats to the penthouse in some alarm.*)

BARBARA: (*Following him.*) Dont be frightened. (*She pins the badge on and steps back towards the table, shewing him to the others.*) There! It's not much for £5000, is it?
1200

MRS BAINES: Barbara: if you wont come and pray with us, promise me you will pray for us.

BARBARA: I cant pray now. Perhaps I shall never pray again.

MRS BAINES: Barbara!

JENNY: Major!
1205

BARBARA: (*Almost delirious.*) I cant bear any more. Quick march!

CUSINS: (*Calling to the procession in the street outside.*) Off we go. Play up, there! Immenso giubilo. (*He gives the time with his drum; and the band strikes up the march, which rapidly be-*
1210 *comes more distant as the procession moves briskly away.*)

MRS BAINES: I must go, dear. Youre overworked: you will be all right tomorrow. We'll never lose you. Now Jenny: step out with the old flag. Blood and Fire! (*She marches out through the gate with her flag.*)
1215

JENNY: Glory Hallelujah! (*Flourishing her tambourine and marching.*)

UNDERSHAFT: (*To* CUSINS, *as he marches out past him easing the slide of his trombone.*) 'My ducats and my daughter'!

CUSINS: (*Following him out.*) Money and gunpowder!
1220

BARBARA: Drunkenness and Murder! My God: why hast thou forsaken me?

(She sinks on the form with her face buried in her hands. The march passes away into silence. BILL WALKER *steals across to her.)*

BILL: *(Taunting.)* Wot prawce selvytion nah?

SHIRLEY: Dont you hit her when she's down.

1225 BILL: She itt me wen aw wiz dahn. Waw shouldnt Aw git a bit o me aown beck?

BARBARA: *(Raising her head.)* I didnt take your money, Bill. *(She crosses the yard to the gate and turns her back on the two men to hide her face from them.)*

1230 BILL: *(Sneering after her.)* Naow, it warnt enaff for you. *(Turning to the drum, he misses the money.)* Ellow! If you aint took it sammun else ez. Weres it gorn? Bly me if Jenny Ill didnt tike it after all!

RUMMY: *(Screaming at him from the loft.)* You lie, you dirty black-
1235 guard! Snobby Price pinched it off the drum when he took up his cap. I was up here all the time an see im do it.

BILL: Wot! Stowl maw manney! Waw didnt you call thief on him, you silly aold macker you?

RUMMY: To serve you aht for ittin me across the fice. It's cost
1240 y'pahnd, that az. *(Raising a pæan of squalid triumph.)* I done you. I'm even with you. Uve ad it aht o y—(BILL *snatches up* SHIRLEY's *mug and hurls it at her. She slams the loft door and vanishes. The mug smashes against the door and falls in fragments.)*

1245 BILL: *(Beginning to chuckle.)* Tell us, aol menn, wot o'clock this mawnin was it wen im as they call Snobby Prawce was sived?

BARBARA: *(Turning to him more composedly, and with unspoiled sweetness.)* About half past twelve, Bill. And he pinched
1250 your pound at a quarter to two. *I* know. Well, you cant afford to lose it. I'll send it to you.

BILL: *(His voice and accent suddenly improving.)* Not if Aw wiz to stawve for it. Aw aint to be bought.

SHIRLEY: Aint you? Youd sell yourself to the devil for a pint
1255 o beer; only there aint no devil to make the offer.

BILL: *(Unashamed.)* Sao Aw would, mite, and often ev, cheerful. But she cawnt baw me. *(Approaching* BARBARA.*)* You wanted maw saoul, did you? Well, you aint got it.

BARBARA: I nearly got it, Bill. But weve sold it back to you
1260 for ten thousand pounds.

SHIRLEY: And dear at the money!

BARBARA: No, Peter: it was worth more than money.

BILL: *(Salvationproof.)* It's nao good: you cawnt get rahnd me nah. Aw downt blieve in it; and Awve seen tody that Aw
1265 was rawt. *(Going.)* Sao long, aol soupkitchener! Ta, ta, Major Earl's Grendorter! *(Turning at the gate.)* Wot prawce selvytion nah? Snobby Prawce! Ha! ha!

BARBARA: *(Offering her hand.)* Goodbye, Bill.

BILL: *(Taken aback, half plucks his cap off; then shoves it on again
1270 defiantly.)* Git aht. *(*BARBARA *drops her hand, discouraged. He has a twinge of remorse.)* But thets aw rawt, you knaow. Nathink pasnl. Naow mellice. Sao long, Judy. *(He goes.)*

BARBARA: No malice. So long, Bill.

SHIRLEY: *(Shaking his head.)* You make too much of him, miss,
1275 in your innocence.

BARBARA: *(Going to him.)* Peter: I'm like you now. Cleaned out, and lost my job.

SHIRLEY: Youve youth an hope. Thats two better than me.

BARBARA: I'll get you a job, Peter. Thats hope for you: the youth will have to be enough for me. *(She counts her money.)*   1280 I have just enough left for two teas at Lockharts, a Rowton doss for you, and my tram and bus home. *(He frowns and rises with offended pride. She takes his arm.)* Dont be proud, Peter: it's sharing between friends. And promise me youll talk to me and not let me cry. *(She draws him towards the gate.)*   1285

SHIRLEY: Well, I'm not accustomed to talk to the like of you—

BARBARA: *(Urgently.)* Yes, yes: you must talk to me. Tell me about Tom Paine's books and Bradlaugh's lectures. Come along.

SHIRLEY: Ah, if you would only read Tom Paine in the proper   1290 spirit, miss! *(They go out through the gate together.)*

ACT THREE

Next day after lunch LADY BRITOMART *is writing in the library in Wilton Crescent.* SARAH *is reading in the armchair near the window.* BARBARA, *in ordinary fashionable dress, pale and brooding, is on the settee.* CHARLES LOMAX *enters. He starts on seeing* BARBARA *fashionably attired and in low spirits.*

LOMAX: Youve left off your uniform!

*(*BARBARA *says nothing; but an expression of pain passes over her face.)*

LADY BRITOMART: *(Warning him in low tones to be careful.)* Charles!

LOMAX: *(Much concerned, coming behind the settee and bending sympathetically over* BARBARA.*)* I'm awfully sorry, Barbara.   5 You know I helped you all I could with the concertina and so forth. *(Momentously.)* Still, I have never shut my eyes to the fact that there is a certain amount of tosh about the Salvation Army. Now the claims of the Church of England—

LADY BRITOMART: Thats enough, Charles. Speak of some-   10 thing suited to your mental capacity.

LOMAX: But surely the Church of England is suited to all our capacities.

BARBARA: *(Pressing his hand.)* Thank you for your sympathy, Cholly. Now go and spoon with Sarah.   15

LOMAX: *(Dragging a chair from the writing table and seating himself affectionately by* SARAH's *side.)* How is my ownest today?

SARAH: I wish you wouldnt tell Cholly to do things, Barbara. He always comes straight and does them. Cholly: we're going to the works this afternoon.   20

LOMAX: What works?

SARAH: The cannon works.

LOMAX: What? your governor's shop!

SARAH: Yes.

LOMAX: Oh I say!   25

*(*CUSINS *enters in poor condition. He also starts visibly when he sees* BARBARA *without her uniform.)*

BARBARA: I expected you this morning, Dolly. Didnt you guess that?

CUSINS: *(Sitting down beside her.)* I'm sorry. I have only just breakfasted.

SARAH: But weve just finished lunch.   30

BARBARA: Have you had one of your bad nights?

CUSINS: No: I had rather a good night: in fact, one of the most remarkable nights I have ever passed.

BARBARA: The meeting?

35 CUSINS: No: after the meeting.

LADY BRITOMART: You should have gone to bed after the meeting. What were you doing?

CUSINS: Drinking.

LADY BRITOMART: } { Adolphus!
40 SARAH: } { Dolly!
BARBARA: } { Dolly!
LOMAX: } { Oh I say!

LADY BRITOMART: What were you drinking, may I ask?

CUSINS: A most devilish kind of Spanish burgundy, warranted
45 free from added alcohol: a Temperance burgundy in fact. Its richness in natural alcohol made any addition superfluous.

BARBARA: Are you joking, Dolly?

CUSINS: (*Patiently.*) No. I have been making a night of it with the nominal head of this household: that is all.

50 LADY BRITOMART: Andrew made you drunk!

CUSINS: No: he only provided the wine. I think it was Dionysos who made me drunk. (*To* BARBARA.) I told you I was possessed.

LADY BRITOMART: Youre not sober yet. Go home to bed at
55 once.

CUSINS: I have never before ventured to reproach you, Lady Brit; but how could you marry the Prince of Darkness?

LADY BRITOMART: It was much more excusable to marry him than to get drunk with him. That is a new accom-
60 plishment of Andrew's, by the way. He usent to drink.

CUSINS: He doesnt now. He only sat there and completed the wreck of my moral basis, the rout of my convictions, the purchase of my soul. He cares for you, Barbara. That is what makes him so dangerous to me.

65 BARBARA: That has nothing to do with it, Dolly. There are larger loves and diviner dreams than the fireside ones. You know that, dont you?

CUSINS: Yes: that is our understanding. I know it. I hold to it. Unless he can win me on that holier ground he may amuse me
70 for a while; but he can get no deeper hold, strong as he is.

BARBARA: Keep to that; and the end will be right. Now tell me what happened at the meeting?

CUSINS: It was an amazing meeting. Mrs Baines almost died of emotion. Jenny Hill simply gibbered with hysteria. The
75 Prince of Darkness played his trombone like a madman: its brazen roarings were like the laughter of the damned. 117 conversions took place then and there. They prayed with the most touching sincerity and gratitude for Bodger, and for the anonymous donor of the £5000. Your
80 father would not let his name be given.

LOMAX: That was rather fine of the old man, you know. Most chaps would have wanted the advertisement.

CUSINS: He said all the charitable institutions would be down on him like kites on a battle-field if he gave his name.

85 LADY BRITOMART: Thats Andrew all over. He never does a proper thing without giving an improper reason for it.

CUSINS: He convinced me that I have all my life been doing improper things for proper reasons.

LADY BRITOMART: Adolphus: now that Barbara has left the
90 Salvation Army, you had better leave it too. I will not have you playing that drum in the streets.

CUSINS: Your orders are already obeyed, Lady Brit.

BARBARA: Dolly: were you ever really in earnest about it? Would you have joined if you had never seen me?

CUSINS: (*Disingenuously.*) Well—er—well, possibly, as a collec- 95 tor of religions—

LOMAX: (*Cunningly.*) Not as a drummer, though, you know. You are a very clearheaded brainy chap, Dolly; and it must have been apparent to you that there is a certain amount of tosh about— 100

LADY BRITOMART: Charles: if you must drivel, drivel like a grown-up man and not like a schoolboy.

LOMAX: (*Out of countenance.*) Well, drivel is drivel, dont you know, whatever a man's age.

LADY BRITOMART: In good society in England, Charles, men 105 drivel at all ages by repeating silly formulas with an air of wisdom. Schoolboys make their own formulas out of slang, like you. When they reach your age, and get political private secretaryships and things of that sort, they drop slang and get their formulas out of the *Spectator* or *The* 110 *Times.* You had better confine yourself to *The Times.* You will find that there is a certain amount of tosh about *The Times;* but at least its language is reputable.

LOMAX: (*Overwhelmed.*) You are so awfully strong-minded, Lady Brit— 115

LADY BRITOMART: Rubbish! (MORRISON *comes in.*) What is it?

MORRISON: If you please, my lady, Mr Undershaft has just drove up to the door.

LADY BRITOMART: Well, let him in. (MORRISON *hesitates.*) Whats the matter with you? 120

MORRISON: Shall I announce him, my lady; or is he at home here, so to speak, my lady?

LADY BRITOMART: Announce him.

MORRISON: Thank you, my lady. You wont mind my asking, I hope. The occasion is in a manner of speaking new to me. 125

LADY BRITOMART: Quite right. Go and let him in.

MORRISON: Thank you, my lady. (*He withdraws.*)

LADY BRITOMART: Children: go and get ready. (SARAH *and* BARBARA *go upstairs for their out-of-door wraps.*) Charles: go and tell Stephen to come down here in five minutes: you 130 will find him in the drawing room. (CHARLES *goes.*) Adolphus: tell them to send round the carriage in about fifteen minutes. (ADOLPHUS [CUSINS] *goes.*)

MORRISON: (*At the door.*) Mr Undershaft.

(UNDERSHAFT *comes in.* MORRISON *goes out.*)

UNDERSHAFT: Alone! How fortunate! 135

LADY BRITOMART: (*Rising.*) Dont be sentimental, Andrew. Sit down. (*She sits on the settee: he sits beside her, on her left. She comes to the point before he has time to breathe.*) Sarah must have £800 a year until Charles Lomax comes into his property. Barbara will need more, and need it perma- 140 nently, because Adolphus hasnt any property.

UNDERSHAFT: (*Resignedly.*) Yes, my dear: I will see to it. Anything else? for yourself, for instance?

LADY BRITOMART: I want to talk to you about Stephen.

UNDERSHAFT: (*Rather wearily.*) Dont, my dear. Stephen doesnt 145 interest me.

LADY BRITOMART: He does interest me. He is our son.

UNDERSHAFT: Do you really think so? He has induced us to bring him into the world; but he chose his parents very incongruously, I think. I see nothing of myself in him, and 150 less of you.

LADY BRITOMART: Andrew: Stephen is an excellent son, and a most steady, capable, highminded young man. You are simply trying to find an excuse for disinheriting him.

155 UNDERSHAFT: My dear Biddy: the Undershaft tradition disinherits him. It would be dishonest of me to leave the cannon foundry to my son.

LADY BRITOMART: It would be most unnatural and improper of you to leave it to anyone else, Andrew. Do you suppose
160 this wicked and immoral tradition can be kept up for ever? Do you pretend that Stephen could not carry on the foundry just as well as all the other sons of the big business houses?

UNDERSHAFT: Yes: he could learn the office routine without
165 understanding the business, like all the other sons; and the firm would go on by its own momentum until the real Undershaft—probably an Italian or a German—would invent a new method and cut him out.

LADY BRITOMART: There is nothing that any Italian or Ger-
170 man could do that Stephen could not do. And Stephen at least has breeding.

UNDERSHAFT: The son of a foundling! Nonsense!

LADY BRITOMART: My son, Andrew! And even you may have good blood in your veins for all you know.

175 UNDERSHAFT: True. Probably I have. That is another argument in favour of a foundling.

LADY BRITOMART: Andrew: dont be aggravating. And dont be wicked. At present you are both.

UNDERSHAFT: This conversation is part of the Undershaft tra-
180 dition, Biddy. Every Undershaft's wife has treated him to it ever since the house was founded. It is mere waste of breath. If the tradition be ever broken it will be for an abler man than Stephen.

LADY BRITOMART: (*Pouting.*) Then go away.

185 UNDERSHAFT: (*Deprecatory.*) Go away!

LADY BRITOMART: Yes: go away. If you will do nothing for Stephen, you are not wanted here. Go to your foundling, whoever he is; and look after him.

UNDERSHAFT: The fact is, Biddy—

190 LADY BRITOMART: Dont call me Biddy. I dont call you Andy.

UNDERSHAFT: I will not call my wife Britomart: it is not good sense. Seriously, my love, the Undershaft tradition has landed me in a difficulty. I am getting on in years; and my partner Lazarus has at last made a stand and insisted that the succes-
195 sion must be settled one way or the other; and of course he is quite right. You see, I havent found a fit successor yet.

LADY BRITOMART: (*Obstinately.*) There is Stephen.

UNDERSHAFT: Thats just it: all the foundlings I can find are exactly like Stephen.

200 LADY BRITOMART: Andrew!!

UNDERSHAFT: I want a man with no relations and no schooling: that is, a man who would be out of the running altogether if he were not a strong man. And I cant find him. Every blessed foundling nowadays is snapped up in his in-
205 fancy by Barnardo homes, or School Board officers, or Boards of Guardians; and if he shews the least ability he is fastened on by schoolmasters; trained to win scholarships like a racehorse; crammed with secondhand ideas; drilled and disciplined in docility and what they call good taste;
210 and lamed for life so that he is fit for nothing but teaching. If you want to keep the foundry in the family, you had better find an eligible foundling and marry him to Barbara.

LADY BRITOMART: Ah! Barbara! Your pet! You would sacrifice Stephen to Barbara.

215 UNDERSHAFT: Cheerfully. And you, my dear, would boil Barbara to make soup for Stephen.

LADY BRITOMART: Andrew: this is not a question of our likings and dislikings: it is a question of duty. It is your duty to make Stephen your successor.

220 UNDERSHAFT: Just as much as it is your duty to submit to your husband. Come, Biddy! these tricks of the governing class are of no use with me. I am one of the governing class myself; and it is waste of time giving tracts to a missionary. I have the power in this matter; and I am not to
225 be hum-bugged into using it for your purposes.

LADY BRITOMART: Andrew: you can talk my head off; but you cant change wrong into right. And your tie is all on one side. Put it straight.

UNDERSHAFT: (*Disconcerted.*) It wont stay unless it's pinned
230 (*He fumbles at it with childish grimaces.*)—

(STEPHEN *comes in.*)

STEPHEN: (*At the door.*) I beg your pardon. (*About to retire.*)

LADY BRITOMART: No: come in, Stephen. (STEPHEN *comes forward to his mother's writing table.*)

UNDERSHAFT: (*Not very cordially.*) Good afternoon.

235 STEPHEN: (*Coldly.*) Good afternoon.

UNDERSHAFT: (*To* LADY BRITOMART.) He knows all about the tradition, I suppose?

LADY BRITOMART: Yes. (*To* STEPHEN.) It is what I told you last night, Stephen.

240 UNDERSHAFT: (*Sulkily.*) I understand you want to come into the cannon business.

STEPHEN: *I* go into trade! Certainly not.

UNDERSHAFT: (*Opening his eyes, greatly eased in mind and manner.*) Oh! in that case—

245 LADY BRITOMART: Cannons are not trade, Stephen. They are enterprise.

STEPHEN: I have no intention of becoming a man of business in any sense. I have no capacity for business and no taste for it. I intend to devote myself to politics.

250 UNDERSHAFT: (*Rising.*) My dear boy: this is an immense relief to me. And I trust it may prove an equally good thing for the country. I was afraid you would consider yourself disparaged and slighted. (*He moves towards* STEPHEN *as if to shake hands with him.*)

255 LADY BRITOMART: (*Rising and interposing.*) Stephen: I cannot allow you to throw away an enormous property like this.

STEPHEN: (*Stiffly.*) Mother: there must be an end of treating me as a child, if you please. (LADY BRITOMART *recoils, deeply wounded by his tone.*) Until last night I did not take your
260 attitude seriously, because I did not think you meant it seriously. But I find now that you left me in the dark as to matters which you should have explained to me years ago. I am extremely hurt and offended. Any further discussion of my intentions had better take place with my father, as
265 between one man and another.

LADY BRITOMART: Stephen! (*She sits down again, her eyes filling with tears.*)

UNDERSHAFT: (*With grave compassion.*) You see, my dear, it is only the big men who can be treated as children.

270 STEPHEN: I am sorry, mother, that you have forced me—

UNDERSHAFT: (*Stopping him.*) Yes, yes, yes, yes: thats all right, Stephen. She wont interfere with you any more: your independence is achieved: you have won your latchkey. Dont rub it in; and above all, dont apologize. (*He resumes*
275 *his seat.*) Now what about your future, as between one man and another—I beg your pardon, Biddy: as between two men and a woman.

LADY BRITOMART: (*Who has pulled herself together strongly.*) I quite understand, Stephen. By all means go your own way if
280 you feel strong enough. (STEPHEN *sits down magisterially in the chair at the writing table with an air of affirming his majority.*)

UNDERSHAFT: It is settled that you do not ask for the succession to the cannon business.

STEPHEN: I hope it is settled that I repudiate the cannon business.

285 UNDERSHAFT: Come, come! dont be so devilishly sulky: it's boyish. Freedom should be generous. Besides, I owe you a fair start in life in exchange for disinheriting you. You cant become prime minister all at once. Havnt you a turn for something? What about literature, art, and so forth?

290 STEPHEN: I have nothing of the artist about me, either in faculty or character, thank Heaven!

UNDERSHAFT: A philosopher, perhaps? Eh?

STEPHEN: I make no such ridiculous pretension.

UNDERSHAFT: Just so. Well, there is the army, the navy, the
295 Church, the Bar. The Bar requires some ability. What about the Bar?

STEPHEN: I have not studied law. And I am afraid I have not the necessary push—I believe that is the name barristers give to their vulgarity—for success in pleading.

300 UNDERSHAFT: Rather a difficult case, Stephen. Hardly anything left but the stage, is there? (STEPHEN *makes an impatient movement.*) Well, come! is there anything you know or care for?

STEPHEN: (*Rising and looking at him steadily.*) I know the difference between right and wrong.

305 UNDERSHAFT: (*Hugely tickled.*) You dont say so! What! no capacity for business, no knowledge of law, no sympathy with art, no pretension to philosophy; only a simple knowledge of the secret that has puzzled all the philosophers, baffled all the lawyers, muddled all the men of busi-
310 ness, and ruined most of the artists: the secret of right and wrong. Why, man, youre a genius, a master of masters, a god! At twentyfour, too!

STEPHEN: (*Keeping his temper with difficulty.*) You are pleased to be facetious. I pretend to nothing more than any honor-
315 able English gentleman claims as his birthright (*He sits down angrily.*)

UNDERSHAFT: Oh, thats everybody's birthright. Look at poor little Jenny Hill, the Salvation lassie! she would think you were laughing at her if you asked her to stand up in the
320 street and teach grammar or geography or mathematics or even drawing room dancing; but it never occurs to her to doubt that she can teach morals and religion. You are all alike, you respectable people. You cant tell me the bursting strain of a ten-inch gun, which is a very simple mat-
325 ter; but you all think you can tell me the bursting strain of a man under temptation. You darent handle high explosives; but youre all ready to handle honesty and truth and justice and the whole duty of man, and kill one another at that game. What a country! What a world!

330 LADY BRITOMART: (*Uneasily.*) What do you think he had better do, Andrew?

UNDERSHAFT: Oh, just what he wants to do. He knows nothing and he thinks he knows everything. That points clearly to a political career. Get him a private secretaryship to someone who can get him an Under Secretaryship; and 335 then leave him alone. He will find his natural and proper place in the end on the Treasury Bench.

STEPHEN: (*Springing up again.*) I am sorry, sir, that you force me to forget the respect due to you as my father. I am an Englishman and I will not hear the Government of my 340 country insulted. (*He thrusts his hands in his pockets, and walks angrily across to the window.*)

UNDERSHAFT: (*With a touch of brutality.*) The government of your country! I am the government of your country: I, and Lazarus. Do you suppose that you and half a dozen ama- 345 teurs like you, sitting in a row in that foolish gabble shop, can govern Undershaft and Lazarus? No, my friend: you will do what pays us. You will make war when it suits us, and keep peace when it doesnt. You will find out that trade requires certain measures when we have decided on those 350 measures. When I want anything to keep my dividends up, you will discover that my want is a national need. When other people want something to keep my dividends down, you will call out the police and military. And in return you shall have the support and applause of my newspapers, and 355 the delight of imagining that you are a great statesman. Government of your country! Be off with you, my boy, and play with your caucuses and leading articles and historic parties and great leaders and burning questions and the rest of your toys. *I* am going back to my counting- 360 house to pay the piper and call the tune.

STEPHEN: (*Actually smiling, and putting his hand on his father's shoulder with indulgent patronage.*) Really, my dear father, it is impossible to be angry with you. You dont know how absurd all this sounds to me. You are very properly proud 365 of having been industrious enough to make money; and it is greatly to your credit that you have made so much of it. But it has kept you in circles where you are valued for your money and deferred to for it, instead of in the doubt- less very old-fashioned and behind-the-times public 370 school and university where I formed my habits of mind. It is natural for you to think that money governs England; but you must allow me to think I know better.

UNDERSHAFT: And what does govern England, pray?

STEPHEN: Character, father, character. 375

UNDERSHAFT: Whose character? Yours or mine?

STEPHEN: Neither yours nor mine, father, but the best elements in the English national character.

UNDERSHAFT: Stephen: Ive found your profession for you. Youre a born journalist. I'll start you with a high-toned 380 weekly review. There!

(*Before* STEPHEN *can reply,* SARAH, BARBARA, LOMAX, *and* CUSINS *come in ready for walking.* BARBARA *crosses the room to the window and looks out.* CUSINS *drifts amiably to the armchair.* LOMAX *remains near the door, whilst* SARAH *comes to her mother.*)

(STEPHEN *goes to the smaller writing table and busies himself with his letters.*)

SARAH: Go and get ready, mamma: the carriage is waiting. (LADY BRITOMART *leaves the room.*)

UNDERSHAFT: (*To* SARAH.) Good day, my dear. Good afternoon, Mr Lomax. 385

LOMAX: (*Vaguely.*) Ahdedoo.

UNDERSHAFT: (*To* CUSINS.) Quite well after last night, Euripides, eh?

CUSINS: As well as can be expected.

390 UNDERSHAFT: Thats right. (*To* BARBARA.) So you are coming to see my death and devastation factory, Barbara?

BARBARA: (*At the window.*) You came yesterday to see my salvation factory. I promised you a return visit.

LOMAX: (*Coming forward between* SARAH *and* UNDERSHAFT.)
395 Youll find it awfully interesting. Ive been through the Woolwich Arsenal; and it gives you a ripping feeling of security, you know, to think of the lot of beggars we could kill if it came to fighting. (*To* UNDERSHAFT, *with sudden solemnity.*) Still, it must be rather an awful reflection for
400 you, from the religious point of view as it were. Youre getting on, you know, and all that.

SARAH: You dont mind Cholly's imbecility, papa, do you?

LOMAX: (*Much taken aback.*) Oh I say!

UNDERSHAFT: Mr Lomax looks at the matter in a very proper
405 spirit, my dear.

LOMAX: Just so. Thats all I meant, I assure you.

SARAH: Are you coming, Stephen?

STEPHEN: Well, I am rather busy—er—(*Magnanimously.*) Oh well, yes: I'll come. That is, if there is room for me.

410 UNDERSHAFT: I can take two with me in a little motor I am experimenting with for field use. You wont mind its being rather unfashionable. It's not painted yet; but it's bullet proof.

LOMAX: (*Appalled at the prospect of confronting Wilton Crescent in*
415 *an unpainted motor.*) Oh I say!

SARAH: The carriage for me, thank you. Barbara doesnt mind what she's seen in.

LOMAX: I say, Dolly, old chap: do you really mind the car being a guy? Because of course if you do I'll go in it. Still—

420 CUSINS: I prefer it.

LOMAX: Thanks awfully, old man. Come, my ownest. (*He hurries out to secure his seat in the carriage.* SARAH *follows him.*)

CUSINS: (*Moodily walking across to* LADY BRITOMART's *writing table.*) Why are we two coming to this Works Department
425 of Hell? that is what I ask myself.

BARBARA: I have always thought of it as a sort of pit where lost creatures with blackened faces stirred up smoky fires and were driven and tormented by my father? Is it like that, dad?

UNDERSHAFT: (*Scandalized.*) My dear! It is a spotlessly clean
430 and beautiful hillside town.

CUSINS: With a Methodist chapel? Oh do say theres a Methodist chapel.

UNDERSHAFT: There are two: a Primitive one and a sophisticated one. There is even an Ethical Society; but it is not
435 much patronized, as my men are all strongly religious. In the High Explosives Sheds they object to the presence of Agnostics as unsafe.

CUSINS: And yet they dont object to you!

BARBARA: Do they obey all your orders?

440 UNDERSHAFT: I never give them any orders. When I speak to one of them it is 'Well, Jones, is the baby doing well? and has Mrs Jones made a good recovery?' 'Nicely, thank you, sir.' And thats all.

CUSINS: But Jones has to be kept in order. How do you maintain
445 tain discipline among your men?

UNDERSHAFT: I dont. They do. You see, the one thing Jones wont stand is any rebellion from the man under him, or any

assertion of social equality between the wife of the man with 4 shillings a week less than himself, and Mrs Jones! Of course they all rebel against me, theoretically. Practically, 450 every man of them keeps the man just below him in his place. I never meddle with them. I never bully them. I dont even bully Lazarus. I say that certain things are to be done; but I dont order anybody to do them. I dont say, mind you, that there is no ordering about and snubbing and even bul- 455 lying. The men snub the boys and order them about; the carmen snub the sweepers; the artisans snub the unskilled laborers; the foremen drive and bully both the laborers and artisans; the assistant engineers find fault with the foremen; the chief engineers drop on the assistants; the departmen- 460 tal managers worry the chiefs; and the clerks have tall hats and hymnbooks and keep up the social tone by refusing to associate on equal terms with anybody. The result is a colossal profit, which comes to me.

CUSINS: (*Revolted.*) You really are a—well, what I was saying 465 yesterday.

BARBARA: What was he saying yesterday?

UNDERSHAFT: Never mind, my dear. He thinks I have made you unhappy. Have I?

BARBARA: Do you think I can be happy in this vulgar silly 470 dress? I! who have worn the uniform. Do you understand what you have done to me? Yesterday I had a man's soul in my hand. I set him in the way of life with his face to salvation. But when we took your money he turned back to drunkenness and derision. (*With intense conviction.*) I 475 will never forgive you that. If I had a child, and you destroyed its body with your explosives—if you murdered Dolly with your horrible guns—I could forgive you if my forgiveness would open the gates of heaven to you. But to take a human soul from me, and turn it into the soul of a 480 wolf! that is worse than any murder.

UNDERSHAFT: Does my daughter despair so easily? Can you strike a man to the heart and leave no mark on him?

BARBARA: (*Her face lighting up.*) Oh, you are right: he can never be lost now: where was my faith? 485

CUSINS: Oh, clever clever devil!

BARBARA: You may be a devil; but God speaks through you sometimes. (*She takes her father's hands and kisses them.*) You have given me back my happiness: I feel it deep down now, though my spirit is troubled. 490

UNDERSHAFT: You have learnt something. That always feels at first as if you had lost something.

BARBARA: Well, take me to the factory of death; and let me learn something more. There must be some truth or other behind all this frightful irony. Come, Dolly. (*She goes out.*) 495

CUSINS: My guardian angel! (*To* UNDERSHAFT.) Avaunt! (*He follows* BARBARA.)

STEPHEN: (*Quietly, at the writing table.*) You must not mind Cusins, father. He is a very amiable good fellow; but he is a Greek scholar and naturally a little eccentric. 500

UNDERSHAFT: Ah, quite so. Thank you, Stephen. Thank you. (*He goes out.*)

(STEPHEN *smiles patronizingly; buttons his coat responsibly; and crosses the room to the door.* LADY BRITOMART, *dressed for out-of-doors, opens it before he reaches it. She looks round for others; looks at* STEPHEN; *and turns to go without a word.*)

STEPHEN: (*Embarrassed.*) Mother—

505   LADY BRITOMART: Dont be apologetic, Stephen. And dont forget that you have outgrown your mother. (*She goes out.*)

(*Perivale St Andrews lies between two Middlesex hills, half climbing the northern one. It is an almost smokeless town of white walls, roofs of narrow green slates or red tiles, tall trees, domes, campaniles, and slender chimney shafts, beautifully situated and beautiful in itself. The best view of it is obtained from the crest of a slope about half a mile to the east, where the high explosives are dealt with. The foundry lies hidden in the depths between, the tops of its chimneys sprouting like huge skittles into the middle distance. Across the crest runs an emplacement of concrete, with a firestep, and a parapet which suggests a fortification, because there is a huge cannon of the obsolete Woolwich Infant pattern peering across it at the town. The cannon is mounted on an experimental gun carriage: possibly the original model of the Undershaft disappearing rampart gun alluded to by* STEPHEN. *The firestep, being a convenient place to sit, is furnished here and there with straw disc cushions; and at one place there is the additional luxury of a fur rug.*)

(BARBARA *is standing on the firestep, looking over the parapet towards the town. On her right is the cannon; on her left the end of a shed raised on piles, with a ladder of three or four steps up to the door, which opens outwards and has a little wooden landing at the threshold, with a fire bucket in the corner of the landing. Several dummy soldiers more or less mutilated, with straw protruding from their gashes, have been shoved out of the way under the landing. A few others are nearly upright against the shed; and one has fallen forward and lies, like a grotesque corpse, on the emplacement. The parapet stops short of the shed, leaving a gap which is the beginning of the path down the hill through the foundry to the town. The rug is on the firestep near this gap. Down on the emplacement behind the cannon is a trolley carrying a huge conical bombshell with a red band painted on it. Further to the right is the door of an office, which, like the sheds, is of the lightest possible construction.*)

(CUSINS *arrives by the path from the town.*)

BARBARA: Well?

CUSINS: Not a ray of hope. Everything perfect! wonderful! real! It only needs a cathedral to be a heavenly city instead of a hellish one.

510   BARBARA: Have you found out whether they have done anything for old Peter Shirley?

CUSINS: They have found him a job as gatekeeper and timekeeper. He's frightfully miserable. He calls the timekeeping brainwork, and says he isnt used to it; and his gate

515   lodge is so splendid that he's ashamed to use the rooms, and skulks in the scullery.

BARBARA: Poor Peter!

(STEPHEN *arrives from the town. He carries a fieldglass.*)

STEPHEN: (*Enthusiastically.*) Have you two seen the place? Why did you leave us?

520   CUSINS: I wanted to see everything I was not intended to see; and Barbara wanted to make the men talk.

STEPHEN: Have you found anything discreditable?

CUSINS: No. They call him Dandy Andy and are proud of his being a cunning old rascal; but it's all horribly, frightfully,

525   immorally, unanswerably perfect.

(SARAH *arrives.*)

SARAH: Heavens! what a place! (*She crosses to the trolley.*) Did you see the nursing home!? (*She sits down on the shell.*)

STEPHEN: Did you see the libraries and schools!?

SARAH: Did you see the ball room and the banqueting chamber in the Town Hall!?   530

STEPHEN: Have you gone into the insurance fund, the pension fund, the building society, the various applications of cooperation!?

(UNDERSHAFT *comes from the office, with a sheaf of telegrams in his hand.*)

UNDERSHAFT: Well, have you seen everything? I'm sorry I was called away. (*Indicating the telegrams.*) Good news from   535 Manchuria.

STEPHEN: Another Japanese victory?

UNDERSHAFT: Oh, I dont know. Which side wins does not concern us here. No: the good news is that the aerial battleship is a tremendous success. At the first trial it has   540 wiped out a fort with three hundred soldiers in it.

CUSINS: (*From the platform.*) Dummy soldiers?

UNDERSHAFT: (*Striding across to* STEPHEN *and kicking the prostrate dummy brutally out of his way.*) No: the real thing.

(CUSINS *and* BARBARA *exchange glances. Then* CUSINS *sits on the step and buries his face in his hands.* BARBARA *gravely lays her hand on his shoulder. He looks up at her in whimsical desperation.*)

UNDERSHAFT: Well, Stephen, what do you think of the place?   545

STEPHEN: Oh, magnificent. A perfect triumph of modern industry. Frankly, my dear father, I have been a fool: I had no idea of what it all meant: of the wonderful forethought, the power of organization, the administrative capacity, the financial genius, the colossal capital it represents. I have   550 been repeating to myself as I came through your streets 'Peace hath her victories no less renowned than War.' I have only one misgiving about it all.

UNDERSHAFT: Out with it.

STEPHEN: Well, I cannot help thinking that all this provision   555 for every want of your workmen may sap their independence and weaken their sense of responsibility. And greatly as we enjoyed our tea at that splendid restaurant— how they gave us all that luxury and cake and jam and cream for threepence I really cannot imagine!—still you   560 must remember that restaurants break up home life. Look at the continent, for instance! Are you sure so much pampering is really good for the men's characters?

UNDERSHAFT: Well you see, my dear boy, when you are organizing civilization you have to make up your mind   565 whether trouble and anxiety are good things or not. If you decide that they are, then, I take it, you simply dont organize civilization; and there you are, with trouble and anxiety enough to make us all angels! But if you decide the other way, you may as well go through with it. However,   570 Stephen, our characters are safe here. A sufficient dose of anxiety is always provided by the fact that we may be blown to smithereens at any moment.

SARAH: By the way, papa, where do you make the explosives?

575 UNDERSHAFT: In separate little sheds, like that one. When one of them blows up, it costs very little; and only the people quite close to it are killed.

(STEPHEN, *who is quite close to it, looks at it rather scaredly, and moves away quickly to the cannon. At the same moment the door of the shed is thrown abruptly open; and a foreman in overalls and list slippers comes out on the little landing and holds the door for* LOMAX, *who appears in the doorway.*)

LOMAX: (*With studied coolness.*) My good fellow: you neednt get into a state of nerves. Nothing's going to happen to
580 you; and I suppose it wouldnt be the end of the world if anything did. A little bit of British pluck is what you want, old chap. (*He descends and strolls across to* SARAH.)
UNDERSHAFT: (*To the foreman.*) Anything wrong, Bilton?
BILTON: (*With ironic calm.*) Gentleman walked into the high
585 explosives shed and lit a cigaret, sir: thats all.
UNDERSHAFT: Ah, quite so. (*Going over to* LOMAX.) Do you happen to remember what you did with the match?
LOMAX: Oh come! I'm not a fool. I took jolly good care to blow it out before I chucked it away.
590 BILTON: The top of it was red hot inside, sir.
LOMAX: Well, suppose it was! I didnt chuck it into any of your messes.
UNDERSHAFT: Think no more of it, Mr Lomax. By the way, would you mind lending me your matches.
595 LOMAX: (*Offering his box.*) Certainly.
UNDERSHAFT: Thanks. (*He pockets the matches.*)
LOMAX: (*Lecturing to the company generally.*) You know, these high explosives dont go off like gunpowder, except when theyre in a gun. When theyre spread loose, you can put a
600 match to them without the least risk: they just burn quietly like a bit of paper. (*Warming to the scientific interest of the subject.*) Did you know that, Undershaft? Have you ever tried?
UNDERSHAFT: Not on a large scale, Mr Lomax. Bilton will
605 give you a sample of gun cotton when you are leaving if you ask him. You can experiment with it at home. (BILTON *looks puzzled.*)
SARAH: Bilton will do nothing of the sort, papa. I suppose it's your business to blow up the Russians and Japs; but you
610 might really stop short of blowing up poor Cholly. (BILTON *gives it up and retires into the shed.*)
LOMAX: My ownest, there is no danger. (*He sits beside her on the shell.*)

(LADY BRITOMART *arrives from the town with a bouquet.*)

LADY BRITOMART: (*Impetuously.*) Andrew: you shouldnt have
615 let me see this place.
UNDERSHAFT: Why, my dear?
LADY BRITOMART: Never mind why: you shouldnt have: thats all. To think of all that (*Indicating the town.*) being yours! and that you have kept it to yourself all these years!
620 UNDERSHAFT: It does not belong to me. I belong to it. It is the Undershaft inheritance.
LADY BRITOMART: It is not. Your ridiculous cannons and that noisy banging foundry may be the Undershaft inheritance; but all that plate and linen, all that furniture and those
625 houses and orchards and gardens belong to us. They be-

long to me: they are not a man's business. I wont give them up. You must be out of your senses to throw them all away; and if you persist in such folly, I will call in a doctor.
UNDERSHAFT: (*Stooping to smell the bouquet.*) Where did you get the flowers, my dear? 630
LADY BRITOMART: Your men presented them to me in your William Morris Labor Church.
CUSINS: Oh! It needed only that. A Labor Church! (*He mounts the firestep distractedly, and leans with his elbows on the parapet, turning his back to them.*) 635
LADY BRITOMART: Yes, with Morris's words in mosaic letters ten feet high round the dome. NO MAN IS GOOD ENOUGH TO BE ANOTHER MAN'S MASTER. The cynicism of it!
UNDERSHAFT: It shocked the men at first, I am afraid. But now they take no more notice of it than of the ten com- 640 mandments in church.
LADY BRITOMART: Andrew: you are trying to put me off the subject of the inheritance by profane jokes. Well, you shant. I dont ask it any longer for Stephen: he has inherited far too much of your perversity to be fit for it. But Barbara has rights 645 as well as Stephen. Why should not Adolphus succeed to the inheritance? I could manage the town for him; and he can look after the cannons, if they are really necessary.
UNDERSHAFT: I should ask nothing better if Adolphus were a foundling. He is exactly the sort of new blood that is 650 wanted in English business. But he's not a foundling; and theres an end of it. (*He makes for the office door.*)
CUSINS: (*Turning to them.*) Not quite. (*They all turn and stare at him.*) I think—Mind! I am not committing myself in any way as to my future course—but I think the foundling dif- 655 ficulty can be got over. (*He jumps down to the emplacement.*)
UNDERSHAFT: (*Coming back to him.*) What do you mean?
CUSINS: Well, I have something to say which is in the nature of a confession.
SARAH: 660
LADY BRITOMART:
BARBARA: } Confession!
STEPHEN:
LOMAX: Oh I say!
CUSINS: Yes, a confession. Listen, all. Until I met Barbara I 665 thought myself in the main an honorable, truthful man, because I wanted the approval of my conscience more than I wanted anything else. But the moment I saw Barbara, I wanted her far more than the approval of my con- science. 670
LADY BRITOMART: Adolphus!
CUSINS: It is true. You accused me yourself, Lady Brit, of joining the Army to worship Barbara; and so I did. She bought my soul like a flower at a street corner; but she bought it for herself. 675
UNDERSHAFT: What! Not for Dionysos or another?
CUSINS: Dionysos and all the others are in herself. I adored what was divine in her, and was therefore a true worshipper. But I was romantic about her too. I thought she was a woman of the people, and that a marriage with a professor of Greek 680 would be far beyond the wildest social ambitions of her rank.
LADY BRITOMART: Adolphus!!
LOMAX: Oh I say!!!
CUSINS: When I learnt the horrible truth—
LADY BRITOMART: What do you mean by the horrible truth, 685 pray?

CUSINS: That she was enormously rich; that her grandfather was an earl; that her father was the Prince of Darkness—

UNDERSHAFT: Chut!

690 CUSINS: —and that I was only an adventurer trying to catch a rich wife, then I stooped to deceive her about my birth.

BARBARA: (*Rising.*) Dolly!

LADY BRITOMART: Your birth! Now Adolphus, dont dare to make up a wicked story for the sake of these wretched
695 cannons. Remember: I have seen photographs of your parents; and the Agent General for South Western Australia knows them personally and has assured me that they are most respectable married people.

CUSINS: So they are in Australia; but here they are outcasts.
700 Their marriage is legal in Australia, but not in England. My mother is my father's deceased wife's sister; and in this island I am consequently a foundling. (*Sensation.*)

BARBARA: Silly! (*She climbs to the cannon, and leans, listening, in the angle it makes with the parapet.*)

705 CUSINS: Is the subterfuge good enough, Machiavelli?

UNDERSHAFT: (*Thoughtfully.*) Biddy: this may be a way out of the difficulty.

LADY BRITOMART: Stuff! A man cant make cannons any the better for being his own cousin instead of his proper self
710 (*She sits down on the rug with a bounce that expresses her down-right contempt for their casuistry.*)

UNDERSHAFT: (*To* CUSINS.) You are an educated man. That is against the tradition.

CUSINS: Once in ten thousand times it happens that the
715 schoolboy is a born master of what they try to teach him. Greek has not destroyed my mind: it has nourished it. Besides, I did not learn it at an English public school.

UNDERSHAFT: Hm! Well, I cannot afford to be too particular: you have cornered the foundling market. Let it pass. You
720 are eligible, Euripides: you are eligible.

BARBARA: Dolly: yesterday morning, when Stephen told us all about the tradition, you became very silent; and you have been strange and excited ever since. Were you thinking of your birth then?

725 CUSINS: When the finger of Destiny suddenly points at a man in the middle of his breakfast, it makes him thoughtful.

UNDERSHAFT: Aha! You have had your eye on the business, my young friend, have you?

CUSINS: Take care! There is an abyss of moral horror between
730 me and your accursed aerial battleships.

UNDERSHAFT: Never mind the abyss for the present. Let us settle the practical details and leave your final decision open. You know that you will have to change your name. Do you object to that?

735 CUSINS: Would any man named Adolphus—any man called Dolly!—object to be called something else?

UNDERSHAFT: Good. Now, as to money! I propose to treat you handsomely from the beginning. You shall start at a thousand a year.

740 CUSINS: (*With sudden heat, his spectacles twinkling with mischief.*) A thousand! You dare offer a miserable thousand to the son-in-law of a millionaire! No, by Heavens, Machiavelli! you shall not cheat me. You cannot do without me; and I can do without you. I must have two thousand five hun-
745 dred a year for two years. At the end of that time, if I am a failure, I go. But if I am a success, and stay on, you must give me the other five thousand.

UNDERSHAFT: What other five thousand?

CUSINS: To make the two years up to five thousand a year. The two thousand five hundred is only half pay in case I
750 should turn out a failure. The third year I must have ten per cent on the profits.

UNDERSHAFT: (*Taken aback.*) Ten per cent! Why, man, do you know what my profits are?

CUSINS: Enormous, I hope: otherwise I shall require twenty-
755 five per cent.

UNDERSHAFT: But, Mr Cusins, this is a serious matter of business. You are not bringing any capital into the concern.

CUSINS: What! no capital! Is my mastery of Greek no capital? Is my access to the subtlest thought, the loftiest poetry yet
760 attained by humanity, no capital? My character! my intellect! my life! my career! what Barbara calls my soul! are these no capital? Say another word; and I double my salary.

UNDERSHAFT: Be reasonable—

CUSINS: (*Peremptorily.*) Mr Undershaft: you have my terms.
765 Take them or leave them.

UNDERSHAFT: (*Recovering himself.*) Very well. I note your terms; and I offer you half.

CUSINS: (*Disgusted.*) Half!

UNDERSHAFT: (*Firmly.*) Half.
770

CUSINS: You call yourself a gentleman; and you offer me half!!

UNDERSHAFT: I do not call myself a gentleman; but I offer you half.

CUSINS: This to your future partner! your successor! your son-in-law!
775

BARBARA: You are selling your own soul, Dolly, not mine. Leave me out of the bargain, please.

UNDERSHAFT: Come! I will go a step further for Barbara's sake. I will give you three fifths; but that is my last word.

CUSINS: Done!
780

LOMAX: Done in the eye! Why, *I* get only eight hundred, you know.

CUSINS: By the way, Mac, I am a classical scholar, not an arithmetical one. Is three fifths more than half or less?

UNDERSHAFT: More, of course.
785

CUSINS: I would have taken two hundred and fifty. How you can succeed in business when you are willing to pay all that money to a University don who is obviously not worth a junior clerk's wages!—well! What will Lazarus say?

UNDERSHAFT: Lazarus is a gentle romantic Jew who cares for
790 nothing but string quartets and stalls at fashionable theatres. He will be blamed for your rapacity in money matters, poor fellow! as he has hitherto been blamed for mine. You are a shark of the first order, Euripides. So much the better for the firm!
795

BARBARA: Is the bargain closed, Dolly? Does your soul belong to him now?

CUSINS: No: the price is settled: that is all. The real tug of war is still to come. What about the moral question?

LADY BRITOMART: There is no moral question in the matter
800 at all, Adolphus. You must simply sell cannons and weapons to people whose cause is right and just, and refuse them to foreigners and criminals.

UNDERSHAFT: (*Determinedly.*) No: none of that. You must keep the true faith of an Armorer, or you dont come in here.
805

CUSINS: What on earth is the true faith of an Armorer?

UNDERSHAFT: To give arms to all men who offer an honest price for them, without respect of persons or principles: to aristocrat and republican, to Nihilist and Tsar, to Capitalist and Socialist, to Protestant and Catholic, to burglar and policeman, to black man, white man and yellow man, to all sorts and conditions, all nationalities, all faiths, all follies, all causes and all crimes. The first Undershaft wrote up in his shop IF GOD GAVE THE HAND, LET NOT MAN WITHHOLD THE SWORD. The second wrote up ALL HAVE THE RIGHT TO FIGHT: NONE HAVE THE RIGHT TO JUDGE. The third wrote up TO MAN THE WEAPON: TO HEAVEN THE VICTORY. The fourth had no literary turn; so he did not write up anything; but he sold cannons to Napoleon under the nose of George the Third. The fifth wrote up PEACE SHALL NOT PREVAIL SAVE WITH A SWORD IN HER HAND. The sixth, my master, was the best of all. He wrote up NOTHING IS EVER DONE IN THIS WORLD UNTIL MEN ARE PREPARED TO KILL ONE ANOTHER IF IT IS NOT DONE. After that, there was nothing left for the seventh to say. So he wrote up, simply, UNASHAMED.

CUSINS: My good Machiavelli, I shall certainly write something up on the wall; only, as I shall write it in Greek, you wont be able to read it. But as to your Armorer's faith, if I take my neck out of the noose of my own morality I am not going to put it into the noose of yours. I shall sell cannons to whom I please and refuse them to whom I please. So there!

UNDERSHAFT: From the moment when you become Andrew Undershaft, you will never do as you please again. Dont come here lusting for power, young man.

CUSINS: If power were my aim I should not come here for it. You have no power.

UNDERSHAFT: None of my own, certainly.

CUSINS: I have more power than you, more will. You do not drive this place: it drives you. And what drives the place?

UNDERSHAFT: (*Enigmatically.*) A will of which I am a part.

BARBARA: (*Startled.*) Father! Do you know what you are saying; or are you laying a snare for my soul?

CUSINS: Dont listen to his metaphysics, Barbara. The place is driven by the most rascally part of society, the money hunters, the pleasure hunters, the military promotion hunters; and he is their slave.

UNDERSHAFT: Not necessarily. Remember the Armorer's Faith. I will take an order from a good man as cheerfully as from a bad one. If you good people prefer preaching and shirking to buying my weapons and fighting the rascals, dont blame me. I can make cannons: I cannot make courage and conviction. Bah! you tire me, Euripides, with your morality mongering. Ask Barbara: she understands. (*He suddenly reaches up and takes* BARBARA's *hands, looking powerfully into her eyes.*) Tell him, my love, what power really means.

BARBARA: (*Hypnotized.*) Before I joined the Salvation Army, I was in my own power; and the consequence was that I never knew what to do with myself. When I joined it, I had not time enough for all the things I had to do.

UNDERSHAFT: (*Approvingly.*) Just so. And why was that, do you suppose?

BARBARA: Yesterday I should have said, because I was in the power of God. (*She resumes her self-possession, withdrawing her hands from his with a power equal to his own.*) But you came and shewed me that I was in the power of Bodger and Undershaft. Today I feel—oh! how can I put it into words? Sarah: do you remember the earthquake at Cannes, when we were little children?—how little the surprise of the first shock mattered compared to the dread and horror of waiting for the second? That is how I feel in this place today. I stood on the rock I thought eternal; and without a word of warning it reeled and crumbled under me. I was safe with an infinite wisdom watching me, an army marching to Salvation with me; and in a moment, at a stroke of your pen in a cheque book, I stood alone; and the heavens were empty. That was the first shock of the earthquake: I am waiting for the second.

UNDERSHAFT: Come, come, my daughter! dont make too much of your little tinpot tragedy. What do we do here when we spend years of work and thought and thousands of pounds of solid cash on a new gun or an aerial battleship that turns out just a hairsbreadth wrong after all? Scrap it. Scrap it without wasting another hour or another pound on it. Well, you have made for yourself something that you call a morality or a religion or what not. It doesnt fit the facts. Well, scrap it. Scrap it and get one that does fit. That is what is wrong with the world at present. It scraps its obsolete steam engines and dynamos; but it wont scrap its old prejudices and its old moralities and its old religions and its old political constitutions. Whats the result? In machinery it does very well; but in morals and religion and politics it is working at a loss that brings it nearer bankruptcy every year. Dont persist in that folly. If your old religion broke down yesterday, get a newer and a better one for tomorrow.

BARBARA: Oh how gladly I would take a better one to my soul! But you offer me a worse one. (*Turning on him with sudden vehemence.*) Justify yourself: shew me some light through the darkness of this dreadful place, with its beautifully clean workshops, and respectable workmen, and model homes.

UNDERSHAFT: Cleanliness and respectability do not need justification, Barbara: they justify themselves. I see no darkness here, no dreadfulness. In your Salvation shelter I saw poverty, misery, cold and hunger. You gave them bread and treacle and dreams of heaven. I give from thirty shillings a week to twelve thousand a year. They find their own dreams; but I look after the drainage.

BARBARA: And their souls?

UNDERSHAFT: I save their souls just as I saved yours.

BARBARA: (*Revolted.*) You saved my soul! What do you mean?

UNDERSHAFT: I fed you and clothed you and housed you. I took care that you should have money enough to live handsomely—more than enough; so that you could be wasteful, careless, generous. That saved your soul from the seven deadly sins.

BARBARA: (*Bewildered.*) The seven deadly sins!

UNDERSHAFT: Yes, the deadly seven. (*Counting on his fingers.*) Food, clothing, firing, rent, taxes, respectability and children. Nothing can lift those seven millstones from Man's neck but money; and the spirit cannot soar until the millstones are lifted. I lifted them from your spirit. I enabled Barbara to become Major Barbara; and I saved her from the crime of poverty.

CUSINS: Do you call poverty a crime?

UNDERSHAFT: The worst of crimes. All the other crimes are virtues beside it: all the other dishonors are chivalry itself by comparison. Poverty blights whole cities; spreads horrible pestilences; strikes dead the very souls of all who come within sight, sound, or smell of it. What you call crime is nothing: a murder here and a theft there, a blow now and a curse then: what do they matter? they are only the accidents

and illnesses of life: there are not fifty genuine professional criminals in London. But there are millions of poor people, abject people, dirty people, ill fed, ill clothed people. They poison us morally and physically: they kill the happiness of
935   society: they force us to do away with our own liberties and to organize unnatural cruelties for fear they should rise against us and drag us down into their abyss. Only fools fear crime: we all fear poverty. Pah! (*Turning on* BARBARA.) you talk of your halfsaved ruffian in West Ham: you accuse me of
940   dragging his soul back to perdition. Well, bring him to me here; and I will drag his soul back again to salvation for you. Not by words and dreams; but by thirty-eight shillings a week, a sound house in a handsome street, and a permanent job. In three weeks he will have a fancy waistcoat; in three
945   months a tall hat and a chapel sitting; before the end of the year he will shake hands with a duchess at a Primrose League meeting, and join the Conservative Party.

BARBARA: And will he be the better for that?

UNDERSHAFT: You know he will. Dont be a hypocrite, Barbara.
950   He will be better fed, better housed, better clothed, better behaved; and his children will be pounds heavier and bigger. That will be better than an American cloth mattress in a shelter, chopping firewood, eating bread and treacle, and being forced to kneel down from time to time to thank heaven
955   for it: knee drill, I think you call it. It is cheap work converting starving men with a Bible in one hand and a slice of bread in the other. I will undertake to convert West Ham to Mahometanism on the same terms. Try your hand on my men: their souls are hungry because their bodies are full.

960   BARBARA: And leave the east end to starve?

UNDERSHAFT: (*His energetic tone dropping into one of bitter and brooding remembrance.*) I was an east ender. I moralized and starved until one day I swore that I would be a full-fed free man at all costs; that nothing should stop me except
965   a bullet, neither reason nor morals nor the lives of other men. I said 'Thou shalt starve ere I starve'; and with that word I became free and great. I was a dangerous man until I had my will: now I am a useful, beneficent, kindly person. That is the history of most self-made millionaires,
970   I fancy. When it is the history of every Englishman we shall have an England worth living in.

LADY BRITOMART: Stop making speeches, Andrew. This is not the place for them.

UNDERSHAFT: (*Punctured.*) My dear: I have no other means of
975   conveying my ideas.

LADY BRITOMART: Your ideas are nonsense. You got on because you were selfish and unscrupulous.

UNDERSHAFT: Not at all. I had the strongest scruples about poverty and starvation. Your moralists are quite unscrupu-
980   lous about both: they make virtues of them. I had rather be a thief than a pauper. I had rather be a murderer than a slave. I dont want to be either; but if you force the alternative on me, then, by Heaven, I'll choose the braver and more moral one. I hate poverty and slavery worse than any other crimes
985   whatsoever. And let me tell you this. Poverty and slavery have stood up for centuries to your sermons and leading articles: they will not stand up to my machine guns, Dont preach at them: dont reason with them. Kill them.

BARBARA: Killing. Is that your remedy for everything?

990   UNDERSHAFT: It is the final test of conviction, the only lever strong enough to overturn a social system, the only way of saying Must. Let six hundred and seventy fools loose in the streets; and three policemen can scatter them. But huddle them together in a certain house in Westminster; and let them go through certain ceremonies and call themselves 995 certain names until at last they get the courage to kill; and your six hundred and seventy fools become a government. Your pious mob fills up ballot papers and imagines it is governing its masters; but the ballot paper that really governs is the paper that has a bullet wrapped up in it. 1000

CUSINS: That is perhaps why, like most intelligent people, I never vote.

UNDERSHAFT: Vote! Bah! When you vote, you only change the names of the cabinet. When you shoot, you pull down governments, inaugurate new epochs, abolish old orders 1005 and set up new. Is that historically true, Mr Learned Man, or is it not?

CUSINS: It is historically true. I loathe having to admit it. I repudiate your sentiments. I abhor your nature. I defy you in every possible way. Still, it is true. But it ought not to be true. 1010

UNDERSHAFT: Ought! ought! ought! ought! ought! Are you going to spend your life saying ought, like the rest of our moralists? Turn your oughts into shalls, man. Come and make explosives with me. Whatever can blow men up can blow society up. The history of the world is the history of 1015 those who had courage enough to embrace this truth. Have you the courage to embrace it, Barbara?

LADY BRITOMART: Barbara: I positively forbid you to listen to your father's abominable wickedness. And you, Adolphus, ought to know better than to go about saying that wrong 1020 things are true. What does it matter whether they are true if they are wrong?

UNDERSHAFT: What does it matter whether they are wrong if they are true?

LADY BRITOMART: (*Rising.*) Children: come home instantly. 1025 Andrew: I am exceedingly sorry I allowed you to call on us. You are wickeder than ever. Come at once.

BARBARA: (*Shaking her head.*) It's no use running away from wicked people, mamma.

LADY BRITOMART: It is every use. It shews your disapproba- 1030 tion of them.

BARBARA: It does not save them.

LADY BRITOMART: I can see that you are going to disobey me. Sarah: are you coming home or are you not?

SARAH: I daresay it's very wicked of papa to make cannons; 1035 but I dont think I shall cut him on that account.

LOMAX: (*Pouring oil on the troubled waters.*) The fact is, you know, there is a certain amount of tosh about this notion of wickedness. It doesnt work. You must look at facts. Not that I would say a word in favor of anything wrong; 1040 but then, you see, all sorts of chaps are always doing all sorts of things; and we have to fit them in somehow, dont you know. What I mean is that you cant go cutting everybody; and thats about what it comes to. (*Their rapt attention to his eloquence makes him nervous.*) Perhaps I dont make 1045 myself clear.

LADY BRITOMART: You are lucidity itself, Charles. Because Andrew is successful and has plenty of money to give to Sarah, you will flatter him and encourage him in his wickedness.

LOMAX: (*Unruffled.*) Well, where the carcase is, there will the 1050 eagles be gathered, dont you know. (*To* UNDERSHAFT.) Eh? What?

UNDERSHAFT: Precisely. By the way, may I call you Charles?

LOMAX: Delighted. Cholly is the usual ticket.

1055 UNDERSHAFT: (*To* LADY BRITOMART.) Biddy—

LADY BRITOMART: (*Violently.*) Dont dare call me Biddy. Charles Lomax: you are a fool. Adolphus Cusins: you are a Jesuit. Stephen: you are a prig. Barbara: you are a lunatic. Andrew: you are a vulgar tradesman. Now you all know 1060 my opinion; and my conscience is clear, at all events. (*She sits down with a vehemence that the rug fortunately softens.*)

UNDERSHAFT: My dear: you are the incarnation of morality. (*She snorts.*) Your conscience is clear and your duty done when you have called everybody names. Come, Euripides! it is getting 1065 late; and we all want to go home. Make up your mind.

CUSINS: Understand this, you old demon—

LADY BRITOMART: Adolphus!

UNDERSHAFT: Let him alone, Biddy. Proceed, Euripides.

CUSINS: You have me in a horrible dilemma. I want Barbara.

1070 UNDERSHAFT: Like all young men, you greatly exaggerate the difference between one young woman and another.

BARBARA: Quite true, Dolly.

CUSINS: I also want to avoid being a rascal.

UNDERSHAFT: (*With biting contempt.*) You lust for personal 1075 righteousness, for self-approval, for what you call a good conscience, for what Barbara calls salvation, for what I call patronizing people who are not so lucky as yourself.

CUSINS: I do not: all the poet in me recoils from being a good man. But there are things in me that I must reckon with. Pity—

1080 UNDERSHAFT: Pity! The scavenger of misery.

CUSINS: Well, love.

UNDERSHAFT: I know. You love the needy and the outcast: you love the oppressed races, the negro, the Indian ryot, the underdog everywhere. Do you love the Japanese? Do 1085 you love the French? Do you love the English?

CUSINS: No. Every true Englishman detests the English. We are the wickedest nation on earth; and our success is a moral horror.

UNDERSHAFT: That is what comes of your gospel of love, is it?

1090 CUSINS: May I not love even my father-in-law?

UNDERSHAFT: Who wants your love, man? By what right do you take the liberty of offering it to me? I will have your due heed and respect, or I will kill you. But your love! Damn your impertinence!

1095 CUSINS: (*Grinning.*) I may not be able to control my affections, Mac.

UNDERSHAFT: You are fencing, Euripides. You are weakening: your grip is slipping. Come! try your last weapon. Pity and love have broken in your hand: forgiveness is still left.

1100 CUSINS: No: forgiveness is a beggar's refuge. I am with you there: we must pay our debts.

UNDERSHAFT: Well said. Come! you will suit me. Remember the words of Plato.

CUSINS: (*Starting.*) Plato! You dare quote Plato to me!

1105 UNDERSHAFT: Plato says, my friend, that society cannot be saved until either the Professors of Greek take to making gunpowder, or else the makers of gunpowder become Professors of Greek.

CUSINS: Oh, tempter, cunning tempter!

1110 UNDERSHAFT: Come! choose, man, choose.

CUSINS: But perhaps Barbara will not marry me if I make the wrong choice.

BARBARA: Perhaps not.

CUSINS: (*Desperately perplexed.*) You hear!

BARBARA: Father: do you love nobody? 1115

UNDERSHAFT: I love my best friend.

LADY BRITOMART: And who is that, pray?

UNDERSHAFT: My bravest enemy. That is the man who keeps me up to the mark.

CUSINS: You know, the creature is really a sort of poet in his 1120 way. Suppose he is a great man, after all!

UNDERSHAFT: Suppose you stop talking and make up your mind, my young friend.

CUSINS: But you are driving me against my nature. I hate war.

UNDERSHAFT: Hatred is the coward's revenge for being in- 1125 timidated. Dare you make war on war? Here are the means: my friend Mr Lomax is sitting on them.

LOMAX: (*Springing up.*) Oh I say! You dont mean that this thing is loaded, do you? My ownest: come off it.

SARAH: (*Sitting placidly on the shell.*) If I am to be blown up, the 1130 more thoroughly it is done the better. Dont fuss, Cholly.

LOMAX: (*To* UNDERSHAFT, *strongly remonstrant.*) Your own daughter, you know!

UNDERSHAFT: So I see! (*To* CUSINS.) Well, my friend, may we expect you here at six tomorrow morning? 1135

CUSINS: (*Firmly.*) Not on any account. I will see the whole establishment blown up with its own dynamite before I will get up at five. My hours are healthy, rational hours: eleven to five.

UNDERSHAFT: Come when you please: before a week you will 1140 come at six and stay until I turn you out for the sake of your health. (*Calling.*) Bilton! (*He turns to* LADY BRITO-MART, *who rises.*) My dear: let us leave these two young people to themselves for a moment. (BILTON *comes from the shed.*) I am going to take you through the gun cotton shed. 1145

BILTON: (*Barring the way.*) You cant take anything explosive in here, sir.

LADY BRITOMART: What do you mean? Are you alluding to me?

BILTON: (*Unmoved.*) No, maam. Mr Undershaft has the other gentleman's matches in his pocket. 1150

LADY BRITOMART: (*Abruptly.*) Oh! I beg your pardon. (*She goes into the shed.*)

UNDERSHAFT: Quite right, Bilton, quite right: here you are. (*He gives* BILTON *the box of matches.*) Come, Stephen. Come, Charles. Bring Sarah. (*He passes into the shed.*) 1155

(BILTON *opens the box and deliberately drops the matches into the fire-bucket.*)

LOMAX: Oh! I say (BILTON *stolidly hands him the empty box.*) Infernal nonsense! Pure scientific ignorance! (*He goes in.*)

SARAH: Am I all right, Bilton?

BILTON: Youll have to put on list slippers, miss: thats all. Weve got em inside. (*She goes in.*) 1160

STEPHEN: (*Very seriously to* CUSINS.) Dolly, old fellow, think. Think before you decide. Do you feel that you are a sufficiently practical man? It is a huge undertaking, an enormous responsibility. All this mass of business will be Greek to you. 1165

CUSINS: Oh, I think it will be much less difficult than Greek.

STEPHEN: Well, I just want to say this before I leave you to yourselves. Dont let anything I have said about right and wrong prejudice you against this great chance in life. I have satisfied myself that the business is one of the highest character and a 1170 credit to our country. (*Emotionally.*) I am very proud of my father. I—(*Unable to proceed, he presses* CUSINS' *hand and goes hastily into the shed, followed by* BILTON.)

(BARBARA *and* CUSINS, *left alone together, look at one another silently.*)

CUSINS: Barbara: I am going to accept this offer.

1175 BARBARA: I thought you would.

CUSINS: You understand, dont you, that I had to decide without consulting you. If I had thrown the burden of the choice on you, you would sooner or later have despised me for it.

BARBARA: Yes: I did not want you to sell your soul for me any

1180 more than for this inheritance.

CUSINS: It is not the sale of my soul that troubles me: I have sold it too often to care about that. I have sold it for a professorship. I have sold it for an income. I have sold it to escape being imprisoned for refusing to pay taxes for

1185 hangmen's ropes and unjust wars and things that I abhor. What is all human conduct but the daily and hourly sale of our souls for trifles? What I am now selling it for is neither money nor position nor comfort, but for reality and for power.

1190 BARBARA: You know that you will have no power, and that he has none.

CUSINS: I know. It is not for myself alone. I want to make power for the world.

BARBARA: I want to make power for the world too; but it

1195 must be spiritual power.

CUSINS: I think all power is spiritual: these cannons will not go off by themselves. I have tried to make spiritual power by teaching Greek. But the world can never be really touched by a dead language and a dead civilization. The people

1200 must have power; and the people cannot have Greek. Now the power that is made here can be wielded by all men.

BARBARA: Power to burn women's houses down and kill their sons and tear their husbands to pieces.

CUSINS: You cannot have power for good without having

1205 power for evil too. Even mother's milk nourishes murderers as well as heroes. This power which only tears men's bodies to pieces has never been so horribly abused as the intellectual power, the imaginative power, the poetic, religious power that can enslave men's souls. As a teacher of

1210 Greek I gave the intellectual man weapons against the common man. I now want to give the common man weapons against the intellectual man. I love the common people. I want to arm them against the lawyers, the doctors, the priests, the literary men, the professors, the artists,

1215 and the politicians, who, once in authority, are more disastrous and tyrannical than all the fools, rascals, and impostors. I want a power simple enough for common men to use, yet strong enough to force the intellectual oligarchy to use its genius for the general good.

1220 BARBARA: Is there no higher power than that? (*Pointing to the shell.*)

CUSINS: Yes; but that power can destroy the higher powers just as a tiger can destroy a man: therefore Man must master that power first. I admitted this when the Turks and

1225 Greeks were last at war. My best pupil went out to fight for Hellas. My parting gift to him was not a copy of Plato's

Republic, but a revolver and a hundred Undershaft cartridges. The blood of every Turk he shot—if he shot any—is on my head as well as on Undershaft's. That act committed me to this place for ever. Your father's chal- 1230 lenge has beaten me. Dare I make war on war? I must. I will. And now, is it all over between us?

BARBARA: (*Touched by his evident dread of her answer.*) Silly baby Dolly! How could it be!

CUSINS: (*Overjoyed.*) Then you—you—you—Oh for my 1235 drum! (*He flourishes imaginary drumsticks.*)

BARBARA: (*Angered by his levity.*) Take care, Dolly, take care. Oh, if only I could get away from you and from father and from it all! if I could have the wings of a dove and fly away to heaven! 1240

CUSINS: And leave me!

BARBARA: Yes, you, and all the other naughty mischievous children of men. But I cant. I was happy in the Salvation Army for a moment. I escaped from the world into a paradise of enthusiasm and prayer and soul saving; but the 1245 moment our money ran short, it all came back to Bodger: it was he who saved our people: he, and the Prince of Darkness, my papa. Undershaft and Bodger: their hands stretch everywhere: when we feed a starving fellow creature, it is with their bread, because there is no other bread; 1250 when we tend the sick, it is in the hospitals they endow; if we turn from the churches they build, we must kneel on the stones of the streets they pave. As long as that lasts, there is no getting away from them. Turning our backs on Bodger and Undershaft is turning our backs on life. 1255

CUSINS: I thought you were determined to turn your back on the wicked side of life.

BARBARA: There is no wicked side: life is all one. And I never wanted to shirk my share in whatever evil must be endured, whether it be sin or suffering. I wish I could cure 1260 you of middle-class ideas, Dolly.

CUSINS: (*Gasping.*) Middle cl——! A snub! A social snub to me! from the daughter of a foundling!

BARBARA: That is why I have no class, Dolly: I come straight out of the heart of the whole people. If I were middle- 1265 class I should turn my back on my father's business; and we should both live in an artistic drawing room, with you reading the reviews in one corner, and I in the other at the piano, playing Schumann: both very superior persons, and neither of us a bit of use. Sooner than that, I would 1270 sweep out the guncotton shed, or be one of Bodger's barmaids. Do you know what would have happened if you had refused papa's offer?

CUSINS: I wonder!

BARBARA: I should have given you up and married the man 1275 who accepted it. After all, my dear old mother has more sense than any of you. I felt like her when I saw this place—felt that I must have it—that never, never, never could I let it go; only she thought it was the houses and the kitchen ranges and the linen and china, when it was really all the 1280 human souls to be saved: not weak souls in starved bodies, sobbing with gratitude for a scrap of bread and treacle, but fullfed, quarrelsome, snobbish, uppish creatures, all standing on their little rights and dignities, and thinking that my father ought to be greatly obliged to them for making so 1285 much money for him—and so he ought. That is where salvation is really wanted. My father shall never throw it in my teeth again that my converts were bribed with bread. (*She is transfigured.*) I have got rid of the bribe of bread. I have got rid of the bribe of heaven. Let God's work be done for its own sake: the work he had to create us to do because it cannot be done except by living men and women. When I die, let him be in my debt, not I in his; and let me forgive him as becomes a woman of my rank.

CUSINS: Then the way of life lies through the factory of death?

BARBARA: Yes, through the raising of hell to heaven and of man to God, through the unveiling of an eternal light in the Valley of The Shadow. (*Seizing him with both hands.*) Oh, did you think my courage would never come back? did you believe that I was a deserter? that I, who have stood in the streets, and taken my people to my heart, and talked of the holiest and greatest things with them, could ever turn back and chatter foolishly to fashionable people about nothing in a drawing room? Never, never, never, never: Major Barbara will die with the colors. Oh! and I have my dear little Dolly boy still; and he has found me my place and my work. Glory Hallelujah! (*She kisses him.*)

CUSINS: My dearest: consider my delicate health. I cannot stand as much happiness as you can.

BARBARA: Yes: it is not easy work being in love with me, is it? But it's good for you. (*She runs to the shed, and calls, childlike.*) Mamma! Mamma! (BILTON *comes out of the shed, followed by* UNDERSHAFT.) I want Mamma.

UNDERSHAFT: She is taking off her list slippers, dear. (*He passes on to* CUSINS.) Well? What does she say?

CUSINS: She has gone right up into the skies.

LADY BRITOMART: (*Coming from the shed and stopping on the steps, obstructing* SARAH, *who follows with* LOMAX. BARBARA *clutches like a baby at her mother's skirt.*) Barbara: when will you learn to be independent and to act and think for yourself? I know as well as possible what that cry of 'Mamma, Mamma,' means. Always running to me!

SARAH: (*Touching* LADY BRITOMART'*s ribs with her finger tips and imitating a bicycle horn.*) Pip! pip!

LADY BRITOMART: (*Highly indignant.*) How dare you say Pip! pip! to me, Sarah? You are both very naughty children. What do you want, Barbara?

BARBARA: I want a house in the village to live in with Dolly. (*Dragging at the skirt.*) Come and tell me which one to take.

UNDERSHAFT: (*To* CUSINS.) Six o'clock tomorrow morning, Euripides.

Bertolt Brecht

Bertolt Brecht (1898–1956) changed the course of the modern European theater—and theater around the world—more than any playwright since Ibsen. However, Brecht's sphere of influence extends beyond his career as a playwright. As a dramatist, he wrote an unsurpassed body of plays; as a theoretician, Brecht's conception of "alienation" in the epic theater opened the way for sweeping innovation in our understanding of the possibilities of the stage; as a director, Brecht's work with his company, the Berliner Ensemble, made it the most influential and important theater in postwar Europe. The challenge of understanding Brecht is to understand the dialectical interplay between theory and practice that informs his assault on stage realism, and on the bourgeois theater itself.

Eugen Berthold Brecht (he later changed his name to Bertolt) was born in Augsburg, Bavaria, in 1898 to a prosperous family. In 1917, he enrolled at Munich University in the natural sciences and worked as a drama critic on the side. He also began work on several plays, including *Baal* (1917). In 1918 he was conscripted into military service for the remainder of World War I and worked in a military hospital. He returned briefly to the university after the war, but soon turned his attention full time to the theater. He moved to Berlin—Germany's theatrical capital at the time—and had the good fortune to work with two influential directors, Max Reinhardt and Erwin Piscator. Piscator advocated the use of new technologies in the theater, as a way of developing a kind of performance more responsive to the mechanized and accelerated routines of modern life. Brecht acknowledged that many of his own staging techniques were derived from his work with Piscator in the 1920s. Throughout the 1920s and early 1930s, Brecht wrote a series of plays that brought him notoriety, largely for their satire of the bourgeois establishment: *Drums in the Night* (1919), *In the Jungle of Cities* (1921), *Man Is Man* (1926), and the musical plays he wrote in collaboration with the composer Kurt Weill, *The Threepenny Opera* (1928) and *The Rise and Fall of the City of Mahagonny* (1930). In the 1920s, Brecht also began to collaborate with Margarete Steffin, one of several women—including Elisabeth Hauptmann, Hella Wuoli-joki, and Ruth Berlau—with whom he collaborated as playwright.

Brecht also began his serious reading of Marx in the 1920s, and it was his application of Marxist dialectic to the process of theater that gave rise to his most powerful and original ideas for the stage. From Marx, Brecht adopted a revolutionary posture, not only toward the class struggle, but toward the stage of bourgeois "realism." To Brecht, the realistic theater was not an unbiased window on social reality. Instead, Brecht argued that realistic theater presented a particular political vision, a view of society as inevitably determined by history and evolution, and therefore not susceptible to change. In order to displace "realism," and to demonstrate these hidden politics, Brecht redefined Marx's conception of "alienation" as a theatrical practice. In *Das Kapital*, Marx argues that the division of labor in modern industrial production has altered the relationship between mankind and the world. In modern industry, workers sell their labor in order to produce commodities. These commodities, Marx contends, then seem "alien" in that they appear to have arisen magically. Capitalist production conceals the signs of how they were produced, so that commodities come to have a "natural" life of their own. Yet, even as commodities seem to come alive, the workers become dehumanized, incorporated into the machinery of production. In the world of capital, where everything is for sale, all human relations, lives, and desires become commodified. The prevailing view of the world—in which commodities confront workers as something natural and entirely separate from their makers—is, to Marx, a *false* view, perpetuated within the bourgeois social order to the political advantage of the ruling classes.

Brecht's theater works to provide its audience with ways of regarding bourgeois reality—including realistic theater and drama—as "unnatural," as a political vision, as an ideological view of the world produced in the interest of profit. Brecht's theater, that is, works to "alienate" or "estrange" the audience from the commonplace "realities" of daily life—which we have unreflectively come to regard as "natural" and "inevitable"—in order to train us to question the world made by modern capitalism and the society it sustains. As he wrote in "The Modern Theater Is the Epic Theater," his theater is based on a "radical separation of the elements" of production, rather than on the scenic unity typical of realism. The seamless illusion of the realistic stage is that theater's most seductive commodity: it constantly and subliminally urges the audience to accept its "picture" of reality as a natural, apolitical image of the world as it is. Brecht's theater, in contrast, always shows both the dramatic illusion (the character, the setting, the action) and the process of its making (the work of the actor, the machinery of the theater, the activities of the stage). Brecht works to show the "means of production" in his theater, as a way of suggesting that stage realism, like social reality outside the theater, is *made*, not given.

Brecht called this theater by a variety of names, including **EPIC THEATER,** the term now generally used for Brecht's body of theory and technique. Brecht's plays tend to be episodic, a disconnected, open-ended **MONTAGE** of scenes: The audience must arrive at its own understanding of how the events are linked together, rather than being given an apparently inevitable narrative. Brecht generally left the stage bare in his productions, as a way of preventing the audience from seeing a complete illusion of some fictional dramatic locale. He exposed the lights above the stage, so the audience could see how lights influence the mood of the scene and so influence the audience's judgment. Brecht fragmented the "realistic" unity of the setting in other ways, too. Films could be projected on screens above the stage, forcing the audience to hold the drama in counterpoint to more recent events; placards onstage described the action to take place before the scene began. Finally, Brecht also urged his actors not to empathize entirely with the characters they played, but to strike a balance between a Stanislavskian identification with the character (being "in character," acting the character entirely from his or her point of view) and a more demonstrative attitude, one that enables the actor to represent the character from a variety of perspectives. Through these means, Brecht worked to involve the audience in the process of the play's production. Rather than being seduced by a commodified illusion of reality, the audience of epic theater is invited to consider, and enjoy, how the theater makes its fictions—as a way of teaching the audience to adopt a more critical, "alienated" way of seeing life outside the theater.

Brecht used many of these devices in *The Threepenny Opera* and in the series of plays he wrote in exile. Forced to flee Germany by Nazi purges of left-wing writers in 1933, Brecht spent the greater part of his creative life on the run, living briefly in Sweden, in Finland, and finally in Santa Monica, California, from 1941 to 1947. Although he had drafted *Life of Galileo* in 1938, Brecht continued to work on the play in California, collaborating on an English version with the actor Charles Laughton. He was also questioned by the House Un-American Activities Committee in 1947, as part of its infamous investigation of communism in the entertainment industry. Brecht was not charged and left the United States the following day to return to Europe and Germany. Living in exile, with no theater and little support, Brecht wrote his major plays: *Life of Galileo* (1938), *The Good Person of Szechwan* (1939), *Mother Courage and Her Children* (1939), and *The Caucasian Chalk Circle* (1944). He also wrote his most important theoretical essays, including *A Short Organum for the Theater,* written in Zurich, Switzerland in 1947, but published in 1948 after Brecht returned to Germany.

Brecht returned to East Berlin in 1947 and established his company, the Berliner Ensemble. Brecht's antirealist plays had long been the source of conflict with the **SOCIAL REALISM** advocated by the Communist Party, and even after the war Brecht had to work with a wary eye on the East German authorities. Nonetheless, the Berliner Ensemble—under Brecht's guidance and with the talents of his wife, Helene Weigel—became the leading European production company of the 1950s, sowing the seeds of innovation in every country they visited. Brecht died in August of 1956, just before the Berliner Ensemble's stunning visit to London, but the influence of his conception of theater has become worldwide, visible in plays from Luis Valdez's *Los Vendidos* to Caryl Churchill's *Cloud Nine* to Tony Kushner's *Angels in America* to Maishe Maponya's *Gangsters.*

MOTHER COURAGE AND HER CHILDREN

Mother Courage and Her Children is typical of Brecht's innovative approach to theater and to "political theater" as well. Rather than presenting a thesis, the play works to question the audience's attitudes about a variety of social institutions: warfare, business, motherhood, morality. In a parable-like series of scenes reminiscent both of expressionist theater and of morality drama, *Mother Courage and Her Children* invites the audience to estrange, and so reconsider, its ways of mapping the world.

In his model-book of the play, Brecht wrote that he wanted to show that "war, which is a continuation of business by other means, makes the human virtues fatal to their possessors." The play considers this problem in a variety of challenging ways. Although it is perhaps tempting to see Courage—Why is she called Courage? Was she courageous?—as a tragic heroine, the play relentlessly questions her "heroic" survival, and our own attitudes about the distinctions between war, business, and morality. As Scene I demonstrates, war and business create an all-embracing market in which everything is commodified, that is, for sale. Mother Courage sells a belt buckle and loses a son as part of the same transaction.

Much of the play's power onstage arises through its use of physical space and a few significant properties. The wagon—Courage's home, her means of survival, her mode of production—becomes in a sense the play's central "character." Placing it on a turntable, most productions convey the sense that the wagon is almost always in motion, yet never actually getting anywhere, much as Courage herself enters the play and leaves it singing the same song. Courage's fortunes are emblematized by the wagon as well. Loaded with goods and pulled by her two strong sons in the first scene, it is battered, barren, and empty in the last,

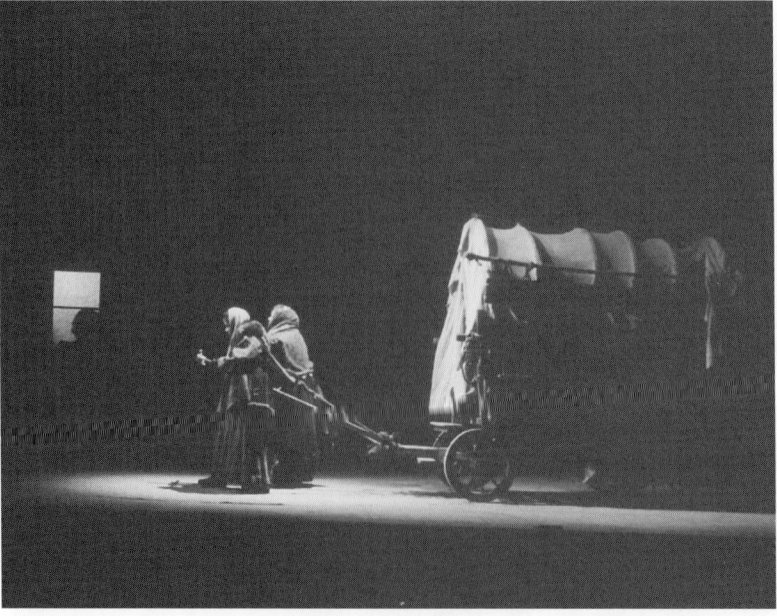

Mother Courage and Kattrin harness themselves to the wagon in Bertolt Brecht's *Mother Courage and Her Children*.

pulled by Mother Courage herself as she struggles to catch up with the army. Brecht was attracted to the idea of using the wagon, the play's economic and material "base," so to speak, to elucidate some of the play's symbolic or moral themes. He used Courage's wash-line to link the wagon to the cannon at the opening of scene 3, tying warfare, the economy, and the domestic sphere together. He raised the harness-poles to form a kind of crucifix after the death of her son Swiss Cheese. Many of the most ironic moments of the Berliner Ensemble production of the play were Weigel's invention: as Mother Courage, she bit the coin in Scene I and slowly measured her pennies out of her purse when she paid the peasants to bury Kattrin at the end of the play. This is the kind of moment that Brecht worked—in theory, as a playwright, in directing productions—to make happen in the theater, a moment when a single gesture forces the audience to consider the scene in a new light, to question the relationship between its ideas of identity and morality and the society that gives them shape and meaning.

MOTHER COURAGE AND HER CHILDREN
A CHRONICLE OF THE THIRTY YEARS' WAR

Bertolt Brecht

TRANSLATED BY JOHN WILLETT

CHARACTERS

MOTHER COURAGE	A CLERK
KATTRIN, *her dumb daughter*	A YOUNG SOLDIER
EILIF, *the elder son*	AN OLDER SOLDIER
SWISS CHEESE, *the younger son*	A PEASANT
THE RECRUITER	THE PEASANT'S WIFE
THE SERGEANT	THE YOUNG MAN
THE COOK	THE OLD WOMAN
THE GENERAL	ANOTHER PEASANT
THE CHAPLAIN	HIS WIFE
THE ARMOURER	THE YOUNG PEASANT
YVETTE POTTIER	THE ENSIGN
THE MAN WITH THE PATCH	SOLDIERS
ANOTHER SERGEANT	A VOICE
THE ANCIENT COLONEL	

SCENE ONE

Spring 1624. The Swedish Commander-in-Chief Count Oxenstierna is raising troops in Dalecarlia for the Polish campaign. The canteen woman Anna Fierling, known under the name of Mother Courage, loses one son.

Country road near a town.

A SERGEANT *and a* RECRUITER *stand shivering.*

RECRUITER: How can you muster a unit in a place like this? I've been thinking about suicide, sergeant. Here am I, got to find our commander four companies before the twelfth of the month, and people round here are so nasty I can't
5 sleep nights. S'pose I get hold of some bloke and shut my eye to his pigeon chest and varicose veins, I get him proper drunk, he signs on the line, I'm just settling up, he goes for a piss, I follow him to the door because I smell a rat; bob's your uncle, he's off like a flea with the itch. No notion of
10 word of honour, loyalty, faith, sense of duty. This place has shattered my confidence in the human race, sergeant.

SERGEANT: It's too long since they had a war here; stands to reason. Where's their sense of morality to come from? Peace—that's just a mess; takes a war to restore order.
15 Peacetime, the human race runs wild. People and cattle get buggered about, who cares? Everyone eats just as he feels inclined, a hunk of cheese on top of his nice white bread, and a slice of fat on top of the cheese. How many young blokes and good horses in that town there, nobody knows;
20 they never thought of counting. I been in places ain't seen a war for nigh seventy years: folks hadn't got names to them, couldn't tell one another apart. Takes a war to get proper nominal rolls and inventories—shoes in bundles and corn in bags, and man and beast properly numbered
25 and carted off, cause it stands to reason: no order, no war.

RECRUITER: Too true.

SERGEANT: Same with all good things, it's a job to get a war going. But once it's blossomed out there's no holding it; folk start fighting shy of peace like punters what can't stop for fear of having to tot up what they lost. Before that it's 30 war they're fighting shy of. It's something new to them.

RECRUITER: Hey, here's a cart coming. Two tarts with two young fellows. Stop her, sergeant. If this one's a flop I'm not standing around in your spring winds any longer, I can tell you. 35

(*Sound of a jew's-harp. Drawn by two young fellows, a covered cart rolls in. On it sit* MOTHER COURAGE *and her dumb daughter* KATTRIN.)

MOTHER COURAGE: Morning, sergeant.

SERGEANT: (*Blocking the way.*) Morning, all. And who are you?

MOTHER COURAGE: Business folk. (*Sings.*)

> You captains, tell the drums to slacken
> And give your infanteers a break: 40
> It's Mother Courage with her waggon
> Full of the finest boots they make.
> With crawling lice and looted cattle
> With lumbering guns and straggling kit—
> How can you flog them into battle 45
> Unless you get them boots that fit?
>   The new year's come. The watchmen shout.
>   The thaw sets in. The dead remain.
>   Whatever life has not died out
>   It staggers to its feet again. 50
>
> Captains, how can you make them face it—
> Marching to death without a brew?
> Courage has rum with which to lace it
> And boil their souls and bodies through.
> Their musket primed, their stomach hollow— 55
> Captains, your men don't look so well.
> So feed them up and let them follow

While you command them into hell.
60   The new year's come. The watchmen shout.
      The thaw sets in. The dead remain.
      Wherever life has not died out
      It staggers to its feet again.

SERGEANT: Halt! Who are you with, you trash?
THE ELDER SON: Second Finnish Regiment.
65   SERGEANT: Where's your papers?
MOTHER COURAGE: Papers?
THE YOUNGER SON: What, mean to say you don't know Mother Courage?
SERGEANT: Never heard of her. What's she called Courage for?
70   MOTHER COURAGE: Courage is the name they gave me because I was scared of going broke, sergeant, so I drove me cart right through the bombardment of Riga with fifty loaves of bread aboard. They were going mouldy, it was high time, hadn't any choice really.
75   SERGEANT: Don't be funny with me. Your papers.
MOTHER COURAGE: (*Pulling a bundle of papers from a tin box and climbing down off the cart.*) That's all my papers, sergeant. You'll find a whole big missal from Altötting in Bavaria for wrapping gherkins in, and a road map of Moravia, the Lord
80   knows when I'll ever get there, might as well chuck it away, and here's a stamped certificate that my horse hasn't got foot-and-mouth, only he's dead worse luck, cost fifteen florins he did—not me luckily. That enough paper for you?
SERGEANT: You pulling my leg? I'll knock that sauce out of
85   you. S'pose you know you got to have a licence.
MOTHER COURAGE: Talk proper to me, do you mind, and don't you dare say I'm pulling your leg in front of my unsullied children, 'tain't decent, I got no time for you. My honest face, that's me licence with the Second Regiment,
90   and if it's too difficult for you to read there's nowt I can do about it. Nobody's putting a stamp on that.
RECRUITER: Sergeant, methinks I smell insubordination in this individual. What's needed in our camp is obedience.
MOTHER COURAGE: Sausage, if you ask me.
95   SERGEANT: Name.
MOTHER COURAGE: Anna Fierling.
SERGEANT: You all called Fierling then?
MOTHER COURAGE: What d'you mean? It's me's called Fierling, not them.
100 SERGEANT: Aren't all this lot your children?
MOTHER COURAGE: You bet they are, but why should they all have to be called the same, eh? (*Pointing to her elder son.*) For instance, that one's called Eilif Nojocki—Why? his father always claimed he was called Kojocki or Mojocki or some-
105 thing. The boy remembers him clearly, except that the one he remembers was someone else, a Frenchie with a little beard. Aside from that he's got his father's wits; that man knew how to snitch a peasant's pants off his bum without him noticing. This way each of us has his own name, see.
110 SERGEANT: What, each one different?
MOTHER COURAGE: Don't tell me you ain't never come across that.
SERGEANT: So I s'pose he's a Chinaman? (*Pointing to the younger son.*)
115 MOTHER COURAGE: Wrong. Swiss.
SERGEANT: After the Frenchman?

MOTHER COURAGE: What Frenchman? I never heard tell of no Frenchman. You keep muddling things up, we'll be hanging around here till dark. A Swiss, but called Fejos, and the name has nowt to do with his father. He was
120 called something quite different and was a fortifications engineer, only drunk all the time.

(SWISS CHEESE *beams and nods; dumb* KATTRIN *too is amused.*)

SERGEANT: How in hell can he be called Fejos?
MOTHER COURAGE: I don't like to be rude, sergeant, but you ain't got much imagination, have you? Course he's called
125 Fejos, because when he arrived I was with a Hungarian, very decent fellow, had terrible kidney trouble though he never touched a drop. The boy takes after him.
SERGEANT: But he wasn't his father . . .
MOTHER COURAGE: Took after him just the same. I call him
130 Swiss Cheese. (*Pointing to her daughter.*) And that's Kattrin Haupt, she's half German.
SERGEANT: Nice family, I must say.
MOTHER COURAGE: Aye, me cart and me have seen the world.
SERGEANT: I'm writing all this down. (*He writes.*) And you're
135 from Bamberg in Bavaria; how d'you come to be here?
MOTHER COURAGE: Can't wait till war chooses to visit Bamberg, can I?
RECRUITER: (*To* EILIF.) You two should be called Jacob Ox and Esau Ox, pulling the cart like that. I s'pose you never
140 get out of harness?
EILIF: Ma, can I clobber him one? I wouldn't half like to.
MOTHER COURAGE: And I says you can't; just you stop where you are. And now two fine officers like you, I bet you could use a good pistol, or a belt buckle, yours is on its last
145 legs, sergeant.
SERGEANT: I could use something else. Those boys are healthy as young birch trees, I observe: chests like barrels, solid leg muscles. So why are they dodging their military service, may I ask?
150 MOTHER COURAGE: (*Quickly.*) Nowt doing, sergeant. Yours is no trade for my kids.
RECRUITER: But why not? There's good money in it, glory too. Flogging boots is women's work. (*To* EILIF.) Come here, let's see if you've muscles in you or if you're a chicken.
155 MOTHER COURAGE: He's a chicken. Give him a fierce look, he'll fall over.
RECRUITER: Killing a young bull that happens to be in his way. (*Wants to lead him off.*)
MOTHER COURAGE: Let him alone, will you? He's nowt for
160 you folk.
RECRUITER: He was crudely offensive and talked about clobbering me. The two of us are going to step into that field and settle it man to man.
EILIF: Don't you worry, mum, I'll fix him.
165 MOTHER COURAGE: Stop there! You varmint! I know you, nowt but fights. There's a knife down his boot. A slasher, that's what he is.
RECRUITER: I'll draw it out of him like a milk-tooth. Come along, sonny.
170 MOTHER COURAGE: Sergeant, I'll tell the colonel. He'll have you both in irons. The lieutenant's going out with my daughter.

SERGEANT: No rough stuff, chum. (*To* MOTHER COURAGE.)
175   What you got against military service? Wasn't his own fa-
    ther a soldier? Died a soldier's death, too? Said it yourself.

MOTHER COURAGE: He's nowt but a child. You want to take
    him off to slaughterhouse, I know you lot. They'll give
    you five florins for him.

180 RECRUITER: First he's going to get a smart cap and boots, eh?

EILIF: Not from you.

MOTHER COURAGE: Let's both go fishing, said angler to
    worm. (*To* SWISS CHEESE.) Run off, call out they're trying
    to kidnap your brother. (*She pulls a knife.*) Go on, you kid-
185   nap him, just try. I'll slit you open, trash. I'll teach you to
    make war with him. We're doing an honest trade in ham
    and linen, and we're peaceable folk.

SERGEANT: Peaceable I don't think; look at your knife. You
    should be ashamed of yourself; put that knife away, you
190   old harridan. A minute back you were admitting you live
    off the war, how else should you live, what from? But
    how's anyone to have war without soldiers?

MOTHER COURAGE: No need for it to be my kids.

SERGEANT: Oh, you'd like war to eat the pips but spit out the
195   apple? It's to fatten up your kids, but you won't invest in
    it. Got to look after itself, eh? And you called Courage,
    fancy that. Scared of the war that keeps you going? Your
    sons aren't scared of it, I can see that.

EILIF: Take more than a war to scare me.

200 SERGEANT: And why? Look at me: has army life done all that
    badly by me? Joined up at seventeen.

MOTHER COURAGE: Still got to reach seventy.

SERGEANT: I don't mind waiting.

MOTHER COURAGE: Under the sod, eh?

205 SERGEANT: You trying to insult me, saying I'll die?

MOTHER COURAGE: S'pose it's true? S'pose I can see the mark's
    on you? S'pose you look like a corpse on leave to me? Eh?

SWISS CHEESE: She's got second sight, Mother has.

RECRUITER: Go ahead, tell the sergeant's fortune, might
210   amuse him.

MOTHER COURAGE: Gimme helmet. (*He gives it to her.*)

SERGEANT: It don't mean a bloody sausage. Anything for a
    laugh though.

MOTHER COURAGE: (*Taking out a sheet of parchment and tearing it*
215   *up.*) Eilif, Swiss Cheese and Kattrin, may all of us be torn apart
    like this if we lets ourselves get too mixed up in the war. (*To*
    the SERGEANT.) Just for you I'm doing it for free. Black's for
    death. I'm putting a big black cross on this slip of paper.

SWISS CHEESE: Leaving the other one blank, see?

220 MOTHER COURAGE: Then I fold them across and shake them.
    All of us is jumbled together like this from our mother's
    womb, and now draw a slip and you'll know. (*The*
    SERGEANT *hesitates.*)

RECRUITER: (*To* EILIF.) I don't take just anybody, they all know
225   I'm choosey, but you got the kind of fire I like to see.

SERGEANT: (*Fishing in the helmet.*) Too silly. Load of eyewash.

SWISS CHEESE: Drawn a black cross, he has. Write him off.

RECRUITER: They're having you on; not everybody's name's
    on a bullet.

230 SERGEANT: (*Hoarsely.*) You've put me in the shit.

MOTHER COURAGE: Did that yourself the day you became a
    soldier. Come along, let's move on now. 'Tain't every day
    we have a war, I got to get stirring.

SERGEANT: God damn it, you can't kid me. We're taking that
    bastard of yours for a soldier.   235

EILIF: Swiss Cheese'd like to be a soldier too.

MOTHER COURAGE: First I've heard of that. You'll have to
    draw too, all three of you. (*She goes to the rear to mark crosses*
    on further slips.)

RECRUITER: (*To* EILIF.) One of the things they say against us is   240
    that it's all holy-holy in the Swedish camp; but that's a mali-
    cious rumour to do us down. There's no hymn singing but
    Sundays, just a single verse, and then only for those got voices.

MOTHER COURAGE: (*Coming back with the slips, which she drops*
    into the SERGEANT'*s helmet.*) Trying to get away from their   245
    ma, the devils, off to war like calves to salt-lick. But I'm
    making you draw lots, and that'll show you the world is no
    vale of joys with 'Come along, son, we need a few more
    generals'. Sergeant, I'm so scared they won't get through
    the war. Such dreadful characters, all three of them. (*She*   250
    hands the helmet to EILIF.) Hey, come on, fish out your slip.
    (*He fishes one out, unfolds it. She snatches it from him.*) There
    you are, it's a cross. Oh, wretched mother that I am, o pain-
    racked giver of birth! Shall he die? Aye, in the springtime
    of life he is doomed. If he becomes a soldier he shall bite   255
    the dust, it's plain to see. He is too foolhardy, like his dad
    was. And if he ain't sensible he'll go the way of all flesh, his
    slip proves it. (*Shouts at him.*) You going to be sensible?

EILIF: Why not?

MOTHER COURAGE: Sensible thing is stay with your mother,   260
    never mind if they poke fun at you and call you chicken,
    just you laugh.

RECRUITER: If you're pissing in your pants I'll make do with
    your brother.

MOTHER COURAGE: I told you laugh. Go on, laugh. Now you   265
    draw, Swiss Cheese. I'm not so scared on your account,
    you're honest. (*He fishes in the helmet.*) Oh, why look at
    your slip in that strange way? It's got to be a blank. There
    can't be any cross on it. Surely I'm not going to lose *you*.
    (*She takes the slip.*) A cross? What, you too? Is that because   270
    you're so simple, perhaps? O Swiss Cheese, you too will
    be sunk if you don't stay utterly honest all the while, like
    I taught you from childhood when you brought the
    change back from the baker's. Else you can't save yourself.
    Look, sergeant, that's a black cross, ain't it?   275

SERGEANT: A cross, that's right. Can't think how I come to
    get one. I always stay in the rear. (*To the* RECRUITER.)
    There's no catch. Her own family get it too.

SWISS CHEESE: I get it too. But I listen to what I'm told.

MOTHER COURAGE: (*To* KATTRIN.) And now you're the only   280
    one I know's all right, you're a cross yourself; got a kind
    heart you have. (*Holds the helmet up to her on the cart, but*
    takes the slip out herself.) No, that's too much. That can't be
    right; must have made a mistake shuffling. Don't be too
    kindhearted, Kattrin, you'll have to give it up, there's a   285
    cross above your path too. Lie doggo, girl, it can't be that
    hard once you're born dumb. Right, all of you know now.
    Look out for yourselves, you'll need to. And now up we
    get and on we go. (*She climbs on to the cart.*)

RECRUITER: (*To the* SERGEANT.) Do something.   290

SERGEANT: I don't feel very well.

RECRUITER: Must of caught a chill taking your helmet off in
    that wind. Involve her in a deal. (*Aloud.*) Might as well

have a look at that belt-buckle, sergeant. After all, our
295   friends here have to live by their business. Hey, you people, the sergeant wants to buy that belt-buckle.
MOTHER COURAGE: Half a florin. Two florins is what a belt
like that's worth. (*Climbs down again.*)
SERGEANT: 'Tain't new. Let me get out of this damned wind and
300   have a proper look at it. (*Goes behind the cart with the buckle.*)
MOTHER COURAGE: Ain't what I call windy.
SERGEANT: I s'pose it might be worth half a florin, it's silver.
MOTHER COURAGE: (*Joining him behind the cart.*) It's six solid
ounces.
305 RECRUITER: (*To* EILIF.) And then we men'll have one together. Got your bounty money here, come along. (EILIF
stands undecided.)
MOTHER COURAGE: Half a florin it is.
SERGEANT: It beats me. I'm always at the rear. Sergeant's the
310   safest job there is. You can send the others up front, cover
themselves with glory. Me dinner hour's properly spoiled.
Shan't be able to hold nowt down, I know.
MOTHER COURAGE: Mustn't let it prey on you so's you can't
eat. Just stay at the rear. Here, take a swig of brandy, man.
315   (*Gives him a drink.*)
RECRUITER: (*Has taken* EILIF *by the arm and is leading him away
up stage.*) Ten florins bounty money, then you're a gallant
fellow fighting for the king and women'll be after you like
flies. And you can clobber me for free for insulting you.

(*Exeunt both.*)

(*Dumb* KATTRIN *leans down from the cart and makes hoarse noises.*)

320 MOTHER COURAGE: All right, Kattrin, all right. Sergeant's just
paying. (*Bites the half-florin.*) I got no faith in any kind of
money. Burnt child, that's me, sergeant. This coin's good,
though. And now let's get moving. Where's Eilif?
SWISS CHEESE: Went off with the recruiter.
325 MOTHER COURAGE: (*Stands quite still, then.*) You simpleton.
(*To* KATTRIN.) 'Tain't your fault, you can't speak, I know.
SERGEANT: Could do with a swig yourself, ma. That's life.
Plenty worse things than being a soldier. Want to live off
war, but keep yourself and family out of it, eh?
330 MOTHER COURAGE: You'll have to help your brother pull
now, Kattrin.

(*Brother and sister hitch themselves to the cart and start pulling.*
MOTHER COURAGE *walks alongside. The cart rolls on.*)

SERGEANT: (*Looking after them.*)
Like the war to nourish you?
Have to feed it something too.

SCENE TWO

In the years 1625 and 1626 Mother Courage crosses
Poland in the train of the Swedish armies. Before the
fortress of Wallhof she meets her son again. Successful
sale of a capon and heyday of her dashing son.

The GENERAL's *tent.*

Beside it, his kitchen. Thunder of cannon. The COOK *is arguing
with* MOTHER COURAGE, *who wants to sell him a capon.*

THE COOK: Sixty hellers for a miserable bird like that?
MOTHER COURAGE: Miserable bird? This fat brute? Mean to
say some greedy old general—and watch your step if you
got nowt for his dinner—can't afford sixty hellers for him?
THE COOK: I can get a dozen like that for ten hellers just   5
down the road.
MOTHER COURAGE: What, a capon like this you can get just
down the road? In time of siege, which means hunger that
tears your guts. A rat you might get: 'might' I say because
they're all being gobbled up, five men spending best part   10
of day chasing one hungry rat. Fifty hellers for a giant
capon in time of siege!
THE COOK: But it ain't us having the siege, it's t'other side.
We're conducting the siege, can't you get that in your head?
MOTHER COURAGE: But we got nowt to eat too, even worse   15
than them in the town. Took it with them, didn't they?
They're having a high old time, everyone says. And look
at us! I been to the peasants, there's nowt there.
THE COOK: There's plenty. They're sitting on it.
MOTHER COURAGE: (*Triumphantly.*) They ain't. They're bust,   20
that's what they are. Just about starving. I saw some, were
grubbing up roots from sheer hunger, licking their fingers
after they boiled some old leather strap. That's way it is.
And me got a capon here and supposed to take forty
hellers for it.   25
THE COOK: Thirty, not forty. I said thirty.
MOTHER COURAGE: Here, this ain't just any old capon. It was
such a gifted beast, I been told, it could only eat to music,
had a military march of its own. It could count, it was that
intelligent. And you say forty hellers is too much? General   30
will make mincemeat of you if there's nowt on his table.
THE COOK: See what I'm doing? (*He takes a piece of beef and
puts his knife to it.*) Here I got a bit of beef, I'm going to
roast it. Make up your mind quick.
MOTHER COURAGE: Go on, roast it. It's last year's.   35
THE COOK: Last night's. That animal was still alive and kicking, I saw him myself.
MOTHER COURAGE: Alive and stinking, you mean.
THE COOK: I'll cook him five hours if need be. I'll just see if
he's still tough. (*He cuts into it.*)   40
MOTHER COURAGE: Put plenty of pepper on it so his lordship the general don't smell the pong.

(*The* GENERAL, *a* CHAPLAIN *and* EILIF *enter the tent.*)

THE GENERAL: (*Slapping* EILIF *on the shoulder.*) Now then, Eilif
my son, into your general's tent with you and sit thou at
my right hand. For you accomplished a deed of heroism,   45
like a pious cavalier; and doing what you did for God, and
in a war of religion at that, is something I commend in
you most highly, you shall have a gold bracelet as soon as
we've taken this town. Here we are, come to save their
souls for them, and what do those insolent dung-   50
encrusted yokels go and do? Drive their beef away from
us. They stuff it into those priests of theirs all right, back
and front, but you taught 'em manners, ha! So here's a pot
of red wine for you, the two of us'll knock it back at one
gulp. (*They do so.*) Piss all for the chaplain, the old bigot.   55
And now, what would you like for dinner, my darling?
EILIF: A bit of meat, why not?
THE GENERAL: Cook! Meat!

THE COOK: And then he goes and brings guests when there's nowt there.

(MOTHER COURAGE *silences him so she can listen.*)

EILIF: Hungry job cutting down peasants.

MOTHER COURAGE: Jesus Christ, it's my Eilif.

THE COOK: Your what?

MOTHER COURAGE: My eldest boy. It's two years since I lost sight of him, they pinched him from me on the road, must think well of him if the general's asking him to dinner, and what kind of a dinner can you offer? Nowt. You heard what the visitor wishes to eat: meat. Take my tip, you settle for the capon, it'll be a florin.

THE GENERAL: (*Has sat down with* EILIF, *and bellows.*) Food, Lamb, you foul cook, or I'll have your hide.

THE COOK: Give it over, dammit, this is blackmail.

MOTHER COURAGE: Didn't someone say it was a miserable bird?

THE COOK: Miserable; give it over, and a criminal price, fifty hellers.

MOTHER COURAGE: A florin, I said. For my eldest boy, the general's guest, no expense is too great for me.

THE COOK: (*Gives her the money.*) You might at least pluck it while I see to the fire.

MOTHER COURAGE: (*Sits down to pluck the fowl.*) He won't half be surprised to see me. He's my dashing clever son. Then I got a stupid one too, he's honest though. The girl's nowt. One good thing, she don't talk.

THE GENERAL: Drink up, my son, this is my best Falernian; only got a barrel or two left, but that's nothing to pay for a sign that's there's still true faith to be found in my army. As for that shepherd of souls he can just look on, because all he does is preach, without the least idea how it's to be carried out. And now, my son Eilif, tell us more about the neat way you smashed those yokels and captured the twenty oxen. Let's hope they get here soon.

EILIF: A day or two at most.

MOTHER COURAGE: Thoughtful of our Eilif not to bring the oxen in till tomorrow, else you lot wouldn't have looked twice at my capon.

EILIF: Well, it was like this, see. I'd heard peasants had been driving the oxen they'd hidden, out of the forest into one particular wood, on the sly and mostly by night. That's where people from the town were s'posed to come and pick them up. So I holds off and lets them drive their oxen together, reckoning they'd be better than me at finding 'em. I had my blokes slavering after the meat, cut their emergency rations even further for a couple of days till their mouths was watering at the least sound of any word beginning with 'me-', like 'measles' say.

THE GENERAL: Very clever of you.

EILIF: Possibly. The rest was a piece of cake. Except that the peasants had cudgels and outnumbered us three to one and made a murderous attack on us. Four of 'em shoved me into a thicket, knocked my sword from my hand and bawled out 'Surrender!' What's the answer, I wondered; they're going to make mincemeat of me.

THE GENERAL: What did you do?

EILIF: I laughed.

THE GENERAL: You did what?

EILIF: Laughed. So we got talking. I put it on a business footing from the start, told them 'Twenty florins a head's too much. I'll give you fifteen'. As if I was meaning to pay. That threw them, and they began scratching their heads. In a flash I'd picked up my sword and was hacking 'em to pieces. Necessity's the mother of invention, eh, sir?

THE GENERAL: What is your view, pastor of souls?

THE CHAPLAIN: That phrase is not strictly speaking in the Bible, but when Our Lord turned the five loaves into five hundred there was no war on and he could tell people to love their neighbours as they'd had enough to eat. Today it's another story.

THE GENERAL: (*Laughs.*) Quite another story. You can have a swig after all for that, you old Pharisee. (*To* EILIF.) Hacked 'em to pieces, did you, so my gallant lads can get a proper bite to eat? What do the Scriptures say? 'Whatsoever thou doest for the least of my brethren, thou doest for me'. And what did you do for them? Got them a good square meal of beef, because they're not accustomed to mouldy bread, the old way was to fix a cold meal of rolls and wine in your helmet before you went out to fight for God.

EILIF: Aye, in a flash I'd picked up my sword and was hacking them to pieces.

THE GENERAL: You've the makings of a young Caesar. You ought to see the King.

EILIF: I have from a distance. He kind of glows. I'd like to model myself on him.

THE GENERAL: You've got something in common already. I appreciate soldiers like you, Eilif, men of courage. Somebody like that I treat as I would my own son. (*He leads him over to the map.*) Have a look at the situation, Eilif; it's a long haul still.

MOTHER COURAGE: (*Who has been listening and now angrily plucks the fowl.*) That must be a rotten general.

THE COOK: He's ravenous all right, but why rotten?

MOTHER COURAGE: Because he's got to have men of courage, that's why. If he knew how to plan a proper campaign what would he be needing men of courage for? Ordinary ones would do. It's always the same; whenever there's a load of special virtues around it means something stinks.

THE COOK: I thought it meant things is all right.

MOTHER COURAGE: No, that they stink. Look, s'pose some general or king is bone stupid and leads his men up shit creek, then those men've got to be fearless, there's another virtue for you. S'pose he's stingy and hires too few soldiers, then they got to be a crowd of Hercules's. And s'pose he's slapdash and don't give a bugger, then they got to be clever as monkeys else their number's up. Same way they got to show exceptional loyalty each time he gives them impossible jobs. Nowt but virtues no proper country and no decent king or general would ever need. In decent countries folk don't have to have virtues, the whole lot can be perfectly ordinary, average intelligence, and for all I know cowards.

THE GENERAL: I'll wager your father was a soldier.

EILIF: A great soldier, I been told. My mother warned me about it. There's a song I know.

THE GENERAL: Sing it to us. (*Roars.*) When's that dinner coming?

EILIF: It's called The Song of the Girl and the Soldier. (*He sings it, dancing a war dance with his sabre.*)

The guns blaze away, and the bay'nit'll slay
And the water can't hardly be colder.
What's the answer to ice? Keep off's my advice!

That's what the girl told the soldier.
Next thing the soldier, wiv' a round up the spout
180 Hears the band playing and gives a great shout:
Why, it's marching what makes you a soldier!
So it's down to the south and then northwards once more:
See him catching that bay'nit in his naked paw!
That's what his comrades done told her.

185 Oh, do not despise the advice of the wise
Learn wisdom from those that are older
And don't try for things that are out of your reach—
That's what the girl told the soldier.
Next thing the soldier, his bay'nit in place
190 Wades into the river and laughs in her face
Though the water comes up to his shoulder.
When the shingle roof glints in the light o' the moon
We'll be wiv' you again, not a moment too soon!
That's what his comrades done told her.

195 MOTHER COURAGE: (*Takes up the song in the kitchen, beating on a pot with her spoon.*)

You'll go out like a light! And the sun'll take flight
For your courage just makes us feel colder.
Oh, that vanishing light! May God see that it's right!—
200 That's what the girl told the soldier.

EILIF: What's that?
MOTHER COURAGE: (*Continues singing.*)

Next thing the soldier, his bay'nit in place
Was caught by the current and went down without trace
205 And the water couldn't hardly be colder.
Then the shingle roof froze in the light o' the moon
As both soldier and ice drifted down to their doom—
And d'you know what his comrades done told her?

He went out like a light. And the sunshine took flight
210 For his courage just made 'em feel colder.
Oh, do not despise the advice of the wise!
That's what the girl told the soldier.

THE GENERAL: The things they get up to in my kitchen these days.
215 EILIF: (*Has gone into the kitchen. He flings his arms round his mother.*) Fancy seeing you again, ma! Where's the others?
MOTHER COURAGE: (*In his arms.*) Snug as a bug in a rug. They made Swiss Cheese paymaster of the Second Finnish; any road he'll stay out of fighting that way, I 220 couldn't keep him out altogether.
EILIF: How's the old feet?
MOTHER COURAGE: Bit tricky getting me shoes on of a morning.
THE GENERAL: (*Has joined them.*) So you're his mother, I hope you've got plenty more sons for me like this one.
225 EILIF: Ain't it my lucky day? You sitting out there in the kitchen, ma, hearing your son commended . . .
MOTHER COURAGE: You bet I heard. (*Slaps his face.*)
EILIF: (*Holding his cheek.*) What's that for? Taking the oxen?
MOTHER COURAGE: No. Not surrendering when those four 230 went for you and wanted to make mincemeat of you. Didn't I say you should look after yourself? You Finnish devil!

(*The GENERAL and the CHAPLAIN stand in the doorway laughing.*)

SCENE THREE

Three years later Mother Courage is taken prisoner along with elements of a Finnish regiment. She manages to save her daughter, likewise her covered cart, but her honest son is killed.

Military camp.

Afternoon. A flagpole with the regimental flag. From her cart, festooned now with all kinds of goods, MOTHER COURAGE *has stretched a washing line to a large cannon, across which she and* KATTRIN *are folding the washing. She is bargaining at the same time with an* ARMOURER *over a sack of shot.* SWISS CHEESE, *now wearing a paymaster's uniform, is looking on.*

A comely person, YVETTE POTTIER, *is sewing a gaily coloured hat, a glass of brandy before her. She is in her stockinged feet, having laid aside her red high-heeled boots.*

THE ARMOURER: I'll let you have that shot for a couple of florins. It's cheap at the price, I got to have the money because the colonel's been boozing with his officers since two days back, and the drink's run out.
MOTHER COURAGE: That's troops' munitions. They catch me 5 with that, I'm for court-martial. You crooks flog the shot, and troops got nowt to fire at enemy.
THE ARMOURER: Have a heart, can't you; you scratch my back and I'll scratch yours.
MOTHER COURAGE: I'm not taking army property. Not at 10 that price.
THE ARMOURER: You can sell it on the q.t. tonight to the Fourth Regiment's armourer for five florins, eight even, if you let him have a receipt for twelve. He's right out of ammunition. 15
MOTHER COURAGE: Why not you do it?
THE ARMOURER: I don't trust him, he's a pal of mine.
MOTHER COURAGE: (*Takes the sack.*) Gimme. (*To* KATTRIN.) Take it away and pay him a florin and a half. (*The* ARMOURER *protests.*) I said a florin and a half. (KATTRIN *drags* 20 *the sack upstage, the* ARMOURER *following her.* MOTHER COURAGE *addresses* SWISS CHEESE.) Here's your woollies, now look after them, it's October and autumn may set in any time. I ain't saying it's got to, cause I've learned nowt's got to come when you think it will, not even seasons of 25 the year. But your regimental accounts got to add up right, come what may. Do they add up right?
SWISS CHEESE: Yes, mother.
MOTHER COURAGE: Don't you forget they made you paymaster cause you was honest, not dashing like your 30 brother, and above all so stupid I bet you ain't even thought of clearing off with it, no not you. That's a big consolation to me. And don't lose those woollies.
SWISS CHEESE: No, mother, I'll put them under my mattress. (*Begins to go.*) 35
THE ARMOURER: I'll go along with you, paymaster.
MOTHER COURAGE: And don't you start learning him none of your tricks.

(*The* ARMOURER *leaves with* SWISS CHEESE *without any farewell gesture.*)

YVETTE: (*Waving to him.*) No reason not to say goodbye, armourer.

MOTHER COURAGE: (*To* YVETTE.) I don't like to see them together. He's wrong company for our Swiss Cheese. Oh well, war's off to a good start. Easily take four, five years before all countries are in. A bit of foresight, don't do nothing silly, and business'll flourish. Don't you know you ain't s'posed to drink before midday with your complaint?

YVETTE: Complaint, who says so, it's a libel.

MOTHER COURAGE: They all say so.

YVETTE: Because they're all telling lies, Mother Courage, and me at my wits' end cause they're all avoiding me like something the cat brought in thanks to those lies, what the hell am I remodelling my hat for? (*She throws it away.*) That's why I drink before midday. Never used to, gives you crows' feet, but now what the hell! All the Second Finnish know me. Ought to have stayed at home when my first fellow did me wrong. No good our sort being proud. Eat shit, that's what you got to do, or down you go.

MOTHER COURAGE: Now don't you start up again about that Pieter of yours and how it all happened, in front of my innocent daughter too.

YVETTE: She's the one should hear it, put her off love.

MOTHER COURAGE: Nobody can put 'em off that.

YVETTE: Then I'll go on, get it off my chest. It all starts with yours truly growing up in lovely Flanders, else I'd never of seen him and wouldn't be stuck here now in Poland, cause he was an army cook, fair-haired, a Dutchman but thin for once. Kattrin, watch out for the thin ones, only in those days I didn't know that, or that he'd got a girl already, or that they all called him Puffing Piet cause he never took his pipe out of his mouth when he was on the job, it meant that little to him. (*She sings the Song of Fraternisation.*)

When I was only sixteen
The foe came into our land.
He laid aside his sabre
And with a smile he took my hand.
After the May parade
The May light starts to fade.
The regiment dressed by the right
The drums were beaten, that's the drill.
The foe took us behind the hill
And fraternised all night.

There were so many foes then
But mine worked in the mess.
I loathed him in the daytime.
At night I loved him none the less.
After the May parade
The May light starts to fade.
The regiment dressed by the right
The drums were beaten, that's the drill.
The foe took us behind the hill
And fraternised all night.

The love which came upon me
Was wished on me by fate.
My friends could never grasp why
I found it hard to share their hate.
The fields were wet with dew
When sorrow first I knew.

The regiment dressed by the right
The drums were beaten, that's the drill.
And then the foe, my lover still
Went marching out of sight.

I followed him, fool that I was, but I never found him, and that was five years back. (*She walks unsteadily behind the cart.*)

MOTHER COURAGE: You left your hat here.

YVETTE: Anyone wants it can have it.

MOTHER COURAGE: Let that be a lesson, Kattrin. Don't you start anything with them soldiers. Love makes the world go round, I'm warning you. Even with fellows not in the army it's no bed of roses. He says he'd like to kiss the ground your feet walk on—reminds me, did you wash them yesterday?—and after that you're his skivvy. Be thankful you're dumb, then you can't contradict yourself and won't be wanting to bite your tongue off for speaking the truth; it's a godsend, being dumb is. And here comes the general's cook, now what's he after?

(*Enter the* COOK *and the* CHAPLAIN.)

THE CHAPLAIN: I have a message for you from your son Eilif, and the cook has come along because you made such a profound impression on him.

THE COOK: I just came along to get a bit of air.

MOTHER COURAGE: That you can always do here if you behave yourself, and if you don't I can deal with you. What does he want? I got no spare cash.

THE CHAPLAIN: Actually I had a message for his brother the paymaster.

MOTHER COURAGE: He ain't here now nor anywhere else neither. He ain't his brother's paymaster. He's not to lead him into temptation nor be clever at his expense. (*Giving him money from the purse slung round her.*) Give him this, it's a sin, he's banking on mother's love and ought to be ashamed of himself.

THE COOK: Not for long, he'll have to be moving off with the regiment, might be to his death. Give him a bit extra, you'll be sorry later. You women are tough, then later on you're sorry. A little glass of brandy wouldn't have been a problem, but it wasn't offered and, who knows, a bloke may lie beneath the green sod and none of you people will ever be able to dig him up again.

THE CHAPLAIN: Don't give way to your feelings, cook. To fall in battle is a blessing, not an inconvenience, and why? It is a war of faith. None of your common wars but a special one, fought for the faith and therefore pleasing to God.

THE COOK: Very true. It's a war all right in one sense, what with requisitioning, murder and looting and the odd bit of rape thrown in, but different from all the other wars because it's a war of faith; stands to reason. But it's thirsty work at that, you must admit.

THE CHAPLAIN: (*To* MOTHER COURAGE, *indicating the* COOK.) I tried to stop him, but he says he's taken a shine to you, you figure in his dreams.

THE COOK: (*Lighting a stumpy pipe.*) Just want a glass of brandy from a fair hand, what harm in that? Only I'm groggy already cause the chaplain here's been telling such jokes all the way along you bet I'm still blushing.

MOTHER COURAGE: Him a clergyman too. I'd best give the
155   pair of you a drink or you'll start making me immoral
      suggestions cause you've nowt else to do.

THE CHAPLAIN: Behold a temptation, said the court preacher,
      and fell. (*Turning back to look at* KATTRIN *as he leaves.*) And
      who is this entrancing young person?

160 MOTHER COURAGE: That ain't an entrancing but a decent
      young person. (*The* CHAPLAIN *and the* COOK *go behind the
      cart with* MOTHER COURAGE. KATTRIN *looks after them, then
      walks away from her washing towards the hat. She picks it up
      and sits down, pulling the red boots towards her.* MOTHER
165   COURAGE *can be heard in the background talking politics with
      the* CHAPLAIN *and the* COOK.)

MOTHER COURAGE: Those Poles here in Poland had no busi-
      ness sticking their noses in. Right, our king moved in on
      them, horse and foot, but did they keep the peace? no, went
170   and stuck their noses into their own affairs, they did, and fell
      on king just as he was quietly clearing off. They committed
      a breach of peace, that's what, so blood's on their own head.

THE CHAPLAIN: All our king minded about was freedom. The
      emperor had made slaves of them all, Poles and Germans
175   alike, and the king had to liberate them.

THE COOK: Just what I say, your brandy's first rate, I weren't
      mistaken in your face, but talk of the king, it cost the king
      dear trying to give freedom to Germany, what with giv-
      ing Sweden the salt tax, what cost the poor folk a bit, so
180   I've heard, on top of which he had to have the Germans
      locked up and drawn and quartered cause they wanted to
      carry on slaving for the emperor. Course the king took a
      serious view when anybody didn't want to be free. He set
      out by just trying to protect Poland against bad people,
185   particularly the emperor, then it started to become a habit
      till he ended up protecting the whole of Germany. They
      didn't half kick. So the poor old king's had nowt but trou-
      ble for all his kindness and expenses, and that's something
      he had to make up for by taxes of course, which caused
190   bad blood, not that he'd let a little matter like that depress
      him. One thing he had on his side, God's word, that was a
      help. Because otherwise folk would of been saying he
      done it all for himself and to make a bit on the side. So
      he's always had a good conscience, which was the main
195   point.

MOTHER COURAGE: Anyone can see you're no Swede or you
      wouldn't be talking that way about the Hero King.

THE CHAPLAIN: After all he provides the bread you eat.

THE COOK: I don't eat it, I bake it.

200 MOTHER COURAGE: They'll never beat him, and why, his men
      got faith in him. (*Seriously.*) To go by what the big shots
      say, they're waging war for almighty God and in the name
      of everything that's good and lovely. But look closer, they
      ain't so silly, they're waging it for what they can get. Else
205   little folk like me wouldn't be in it at all.

THE COOK: That's the way it is.

THE CHAPLAIN: As a Dutchman you'd do better to glance at
      the flag above your head before venting your opinions
      here in Poland.

210 MOTHER COURAGE: All good Lutherans here. Prosit!

(KATTRIN *has put on* YVETTE's *hat and begun strutting around in
imitation of her way of walking.*)

(*Suddenly there is a noise of cannon fire and shooting. Drums.*
MOTHER COURAGE, *the* COOK *and the* CHAPLAIN *rush out from
behind the cart, the two last-named still carrying their glasses. The*
ARMOURER *and another* SOLDIER *run up to the cannon and try to
push it away.*)

MOTHER COURAGE: What's happening? Wait till I've taken my
      washing down, you louts! (*She tries to rescue her washing.*)

THE ARMOURER: The Catholics! Broken through. Don't
      know if we'll get out of here. (*To the* SOLDIER.) Get that
      gun shifted! (*Runs on.*)   215

THE COOK: God, I must find the general. Courage, I'll drop
      by in a day or two for another talk.

MOTHER COURAGE: Wait, you forgot your pipe.

THE COOK: (*In the distance.*) Keep it for me. I'll be needing it.

MOTHER COURAGE: Would happen just as we're making a bit   220
      of money.

THE CHAPLAIN: Ah well, I'll be going too. Indeed, if the en-
      emy is so close as that it might be dangerous. Blessèd are
      the peacemakers is the motto in wartime. If only I had a
      cloak to cover me.   225

MOTHER COURAGE: I ain't lending no cloaks, not on your
      life. I been had too often.

THE CHAPLAIN: But my faith makes it particularly dangerous
      for me.

MOTHER COURAGE: (*Gets him a cloak.*) Goes against my con-   230
      science, this does. Now you run along.

THE CHAPLAIN: Thank you, dear lady, that's very generous of
      you, but I think it might be wiser for me to remain seated
      here; it could arouse suspicion and bring the enemy down
      on me if I were seen to run.   235

MOTHER COURAGE: (*To the* SOLDIER.) Leave it, you fool,
      who's going to pay you for that? I'll look after it for you,
      you're risking your neck.

THE SOLDIER: (*Running away.*) You can tell 'em I tried.

MOTHER COURAGE: Cross my heart. (*Sees her daughter with the*   240
      hat.) What you doing with that strumpet's hat? Take that
      lid off, you gone crazy? And the enemy arriving any
      minute! (*Pulls the hat off* KATTRIN's *head.*) Want 'em to pick
      you up and make a prostitute of you? And she's gone and
      put those boots on, whore of Babylon! Off with those   245
      boots! (*Tries to tug them off her.*) Jesus Christ, chaplain,
      gimme a hand, get those boots off her, I'll be right back.
      (*Runs to the cart.*)

YVETTE: (*Arrives, powdering her face.*) Fancy that, the Catholics
      are coming. Where's my hat? Who's been kicking it   250
      around? I can't go about looking like this if the Catholics
      are coming. What'll they think of me? No mirror either.
      (*To the* CHAPLAIN.) How do I look? Too much powder?

THE CHAPLAIN: Exactly right.

YVETTE: And where are them red boots? (*Fails to find them as*   255
      KATTRIN *hides her feet under her skirt.*) I left them here all
      right. Now I'll have to get to me tent barefoot. It's an out-
      rage.

(*Exit.*)

(SWISS CHEESE *runs in carrying in a small box.*)

MOTHER COURAGE: (*Arrives with her hands full of ashes. To*
      KATTRIN.) Here some ashes. (*To* SWISS CHEESE.) What's   260
      that you're carrying?

SWISS CHEESE: Regimental cash box.

MOTHER COURAGE: Chuck it away. No more paymastering for you.

265 SWISS CHEESE: I'm responsible. (*He goes to the rear.*)

MOTHER COURAGE: (*To the* CHAPLAIN.) Take your clerical togs off, padre, or they'll spot you under that cloak. (*She rubs* KATTRIN's *face with ash.*) Keep still, will you? There you are, a bit of muck and you'll be safe. What a disaster.

270 Sentries were drunk. Hide your light under a bushel, it says. Take a soldier, specially a Catholic one, add a clean face, and there's your instant whore. For weeks they get nowt to eat, then soon as they manage to get it by looting they're falling on anything in skirts. That ought to do.

275 Let's have a look. Not bad. Looks like you been grubbing in muckheap. Stop trembling. Nothing'll happen to you like that. (*To* SWISS CHEESE.) Where d'you leave cash box?

SWISS CHEESE: Thought I'd put it in cart.

MOTHER COURAGE: (*Horrified.*) What, my cart? Sheer crimi-
280 nal idiocy. Only take me eyes off you one instant. Hang us all three, they will.

SWISS CHEESE: I'll put it somewhere else then, or clear out with it.

MOTHER COURAGE: You sit on it, it's too late now.

285 THE CHAPLAIN: (*Who is changing his clothes downstage.*) For heaven's sake, the flag!

MOTHER COURAGE: (*Hauls down the regimental flag.*) Bozhe moi! I'd given up noticing it were there. Twenty-five years I've had it.

(*The thunder of cannon intensifies.*)

(*A morning three days later. The cannon has gone.* MOTHER COURAGE, KATTRIN, *the* CHAPLAIN *and* SWISS CHEESE *are sitting gloomily over a meal.*)

290 SWISS CHEESE: That's three days I been sitting around with nowt to do, and sergeant's always been kind to me but any moment now he'll start asking where's Swiss Cheese with the pay box?

MOTHER COURAGE: You thank your stars they ain't after you.

295 THE CHAPLAIN: What can I say? I can't even hold a service here, it might make trouble for me. Whosoever hath a full heart, his tongue runneth over, it says, but heaven help me if mine starts running over.

MOTHER COURAGE: That's how it goes. Here they sit, one
300 with his faith and the other with his cash box. Dunno which is more dangerous.

THE CHAPLAIN: We are all of us in God's hands.

MOTHER COURAGE: Oh, I don't think it's as bad as that yet, though I must say I can't sleep nights. If it weren't for you,
305 Swiss Cheese, things'd be easier. I think I got meself cleared. I told 'em I didn't hold with Antichrist, the Swedish one with horns on, and I'd observed left horn was a bit unserviceable. Half way through their interrogation I asked where I could get church candles not too dear. I knows the
310 lingo cause Swiss Cheese's dad were Catholic, often used to make jokes about it, he did. They didn't believe me all that much, but they ain't got no regimental canteen lady. So they're winking an eye. Could turn out for the best, you know. We're prisoners, but same like fleas on dog.

THE CHAPLAIN: That's good milk. But we'll need to cut down 315 our Swedish appetites a bit. After all, we've been defeated.

MOTHER COURAGE: Who's been defeated? Look, victory and defeat ain't bound to be same for the big shots up top as for them below, not by no means. Can be times the bottom lot find a defeat really pays them. Honour's lost, nowt else. I re- 320 member once up in Livonia our general took such a beating from enemy I got a horse off our baggage train in the confusion, pulled me cart seven months, he did, before we won and they checked up. As a rule you can say victory and defeat both come expensive to us ordinary folk. Best thing for us is when 325 politics get bogged down solid. (*To* SWISS CHEESE.) Eat up.

SWISS CHEESE: Got no appetite for it. What's sergeant to do when pay day comes round?

MOTHER COURAGE: They don't have pay days on a retreat.

SWISS CHEESE: It's their right, though. They needn't retreat if 330 they don't get paid. Needn't stir a foot.

MOTHER COURAGE: Swiss Cheese, you're that conscientious it makes me quite nervous. I brought you up to be honest, you not being clever, but you got to know where to stop. Chaplain and me, we're off now to buy Catholic flag 335 and some meat. Dunno anyone so good at sniffing meat, like sleepwalking it is, straight to target. I'd say he can pick out a good piece by the way his mouth starts watering. Well, thank goodness they're letting me go on trading. You don't ask tradespeople their faith but their prices. 340 And Lutheran trousers keep cold out too.

THE CHAPLAIN: What did the mendicant say when he heard the Lutherans were going to turn everything in town and country topsy-turvy? 'They'll always need beggars'. (MOTHER COURAGE *disappears into the cart.*) So she's still 345 worried about the cash box. So far they've taken us all for granted as part of the cart, but how long for?

SWISS CHEESE: I can get rid of it.

THE CHAPLAIN: That's almost more dangerous. Suppose you're seen. They have spies. Yesterday a fellow popped 350 up out of the ditch in front of me just as I was relieving myself first thing. I was so scared I only just suppressed an ejaculatory prayer. That would have given me away all right. I think what they'd like best is to go sniffing people's excrement to see if they're Protestants. The spy was 355 a little runt with a patch over one eye.

MOTHER COURAGE: (*Clambering out of the cart with a basket.*) What have I found, you shameless creature? (*She holds up the red boots in triumph.*) Yvette's red high-heeled boots! Coolly went and pinched them, she did. Cause you put it in her 360 head she was an enchanting young person. (*She lays them in the basket.*) I'm giving them back. Stealing Yvette's boots! She's wrecking herself for money. That's understandable. But you'd do it for nothing, for pleasure. What did I tell you: you're to wait till it's peace. No soldiers for you. You're 365 not to start exhibiting yourself till it's peacetime.

THE CHAPLAIN: I don't find she exhibits herself.

MOTHER COURAGE: Too much for my liking. Let her be like a stone in Dalecarlia, where there's nowt else, so folk say 'Can't see that cripple', that's how I'd lief have her. Then 370 nowt'll happen to her. (*To* SWISS CHEESE.) You leave that box where it is, d'you hear? And keep an eye on your sister, she needs it. The pair of you'll have me in grave yet. Sooner be minding a bagful of fleas.

(*She leaves with the* CHAPLAIN. KATTRIN *clears away the dishes.*)

375 SWISS CHEESE: Won't be able to sit out in the sun in shirt-
      sleeves much longer. (KATTRIN *points at a tree.*) Aye, leaves
      turning yellow. (KATTRIN *asks by gestures if he wants a
      drink.*) Don't want no drink. I'm thinking. (*Pause.*) Said
      she can't sleep. Best if I got rid of that box, found a good
380 place for it. All right, let's have a glass. (KATTRIN *goes be-
      hind the cart.*) I'll stuff it down the rat-hole by the river for
      the time being. Probably pick it up tonight before first
      light and take it to Regiment. How far can they have re-
      treated in three days? Bet sergeant's surprised. I'm agree-
385 ably disappointed in you, Swiss Cheese, he'll say. I make
      you responsible for the cash, and you go and bring it back.

(*As* KATTRIN *emerges from behind the cart with a full glass in her
hand, two men confront her. One is a* SERGEANT, *the other doffs his
hat to her. He has a patch over one eye.*)

THE MAN WITH THE PATCH: God be with you, mistress. Have
      you seen anyone round here from Second Finnish Regi-
      mental Headquarters?

(KATTRIN, *badly frightened, runs downstage, spilling the brandy.
The two men look at one another, then withdraw on seeing* SWISS
CHEESE *sitting there.*)

390 SWISS CHEESE: (*Interrupted in his thoughts.*) You spilt half of it.
      What are those faces for? Jabbed yourself in eye? I don't
      get it. And I'll have to be off, I've thought it over, it's the
      only way. (*He gets up. She does everything possible to make him
      realise the danger. He only shrugs her off.*) Wish I knew what
395 you're trying to say. Sure you mean well, poor creature,
      just can't get words out. What's it matter your spilling my
      brandy, I'll drink plenty more glasses yet, what's one more
      or less? (*He gets the box from the cart and takes it under his tu-
      nic.*) Be back in a moment. Don't hold me up now, or I'll
400 be angry. I know you mean well. Too bad you can't speak.

(*As she tries to hold him back he kisses her and tears himself away.
Exit. She is desperate, running hither and thither uttering little
noises. The* CHAPLAIN *and* MOTHER COURAGE *return.* KATTRIN
rushes to her mother.)

MOTHER COURAGE: What's all this? Pull yourself together,
      love. They done something to you? Where's Swiss
      Cheese? Tell it me step by step, Kattrin. Mother under-
      stands you. What, so that bastard did take the box? I'll
405 wrap it round his ears, the little hypocrite. Take your time
      and don't gabble, use your hands, I don't like it when you
      howl like a dog, what'll his reverence say? Makes him un-
      comfortable. What, a one-eyed man came along?
THE CHAPLAIN: That one-eyed man is a spy. Have they ar-
410 rested Swiss Cheese? (KATTRIN *shakes her head, shrugs her
      shoulders.*) We're done for.
MOTHER COURAGE: (*Fishes in her basket and brings out a
      Catholic flag, which the* CHAPLAIN *fixes to the mast.*) Better
      hoist new flag.
415 THE CHAPLAIN: (*Bitterly.*) All good Catholics here.

(*Voices are heard from the rear. The two men bring in* SWISS
CHEESE.)

SWISS CHEESE: Let me go, I got nowt. Don't twist my shoul-
      der, I'm innocent.
SERGEANT: Here's where he came from. You know each other.
MOTHER COURAGE: Us? How?
SWISS CHEESE: I don't know her. Got no idea who she is, had   420
      nowt to do with them. I bought me dinner here, ten
      hellers it cost. You might have seen me sitting here, it was
      too salty.
SERGEANT: Who are you people, eh?
MOTHER COURAGE: We're law-abiding folk. That's right, he   425
      bought a dinner. Said it was too salty.
SERGEANT: Trying to pretend you don't know each other,
      that it?
MOTHER COURAGE: Why should I know him? Can't know
      everyone. I don't go asking 'em what they're called and are   430
      they a heretic; if he pays he ain't a heretic. You a heretic?
SWISS CHEESE: Go on.
THE CHAPLAIN: He sat there very properly, never opening his
      mouth except when eating. Then he had to.
SERGEANT: And who are you?   435
MOTHER COURAGE: He's just my potboy. Now I expect you
      gentlemen are thirsty, I'll get you a glass of brandy, you
      must be hot and tired with running.
SERGEANT: No brandy on duty. (*To* SWISS CHEESE.) You were
      carrying something. Must have hidden it by the river. Was   440
      a bulge in your tunic when you left here.
MOTHER COURAGE: You sure it was him?
SWISS CHEESE: You must be thinking of someone else. I saw
      someone bounding off with a bulge in his tunic. I'm the
      wrong man.   445
MOTHER COURAGE: I'd say it was a misunderstanding too,
      such things happen. I'm a good judge of people, I'm
      Courage, you heard of me, everyone knows me, and I tell
      you that's an honest face he has.
SERGEANT: We're on the track of the Second Finnish Regi-   450
      ment's cash box. We got the description of the fellow re-
      sponsible for it. Been trailing him two days. It's you.
SWISS CHEESE: It's not me.
SERGEANT: And you better cough it up, or you're a goner, you
      know. Where is it?   455
MOTHER COURAGE: (*Urgently.*) Of course he'd give it over
      rather than be a goner. Right out he'd say: I got it, here it
      is, you're too strong. He ain't all that stupid. Speak up, stu-
      pid idiot, here's the sergeant giving you a chance.
SWISS CHEESE: S'pose I ain't got it.   460
SERGEANT: Then come along. We'll get it out of you. (*They
      lead him off.*)
MOTHER COURAGE: (*Calls after them.*) He'd tell you. He's not
      that stupid. And don't you twist his shoulder! (*Runs after
      them.*)   465

(*Evening of the same day. The* CHAPLAIN *and dumb* KATTRIN *are
cleaning glasses and polishing knives.*)

THE CHAPLAIN: Cases like that, where somebody gets caught,
      are not unknown in religious history. It reminds me of the
      Passion of Our Lord and Saviour. There's an old song
      about that. (*He sings the Song of the Hours.*)

----

469 **Song of the Hours** translated by Ralph Manheim

470 In the first hour Jesus mild
Who had prayed since even
Was betrayed and led before
Pontius the heathen.

475 Pilate found him innocent
Free from fault and error
Therefore, having washed his hands
Sent him to King Herod.

In the third hour he was scourged
Stripped and clad in scarlet
480 And a plaited crown of thorns
Set upon his forehead.

On the Son of Man they spat
Mocked him and made merry.
Then the cross of death was brought
485 Given him to carry.

At the sixth hour with two thieves
To the cross they nailed him
And the people and the thieves
Mocked him and reviled him.

490 This is Jesus King of Jews
Cried they in derision
Till the sun withdrew its light
From that awful vision.

At the ninth hour Jesus wailed
495 Why hast thou me forsaken?
Soldiers brought him vinegar
Which he left untaken.

Then he yielded up the ghost
And the earth was shaken.
500 Rended was the temple's veil
And the saints were wakened.

Soldiers broke the two thieves' legs
As the night descended.
Thrust a spear in Jesus' side
505 When his life had ended.

Still they mocked, as from his wound
Flowed the blood and water
And blasphemed the Son of Man
With their cruel laughter.

510 MOTHER COURAGE: (*Entering excitedly.*) It's touch and go. They
say sergeant's open to reason though. Only we mustn't let on
it's Swiss Cheese else they'll say we helped him. It's a matter
of money, that's all. But where's money to come from? Hasn't
Yvette been round? I ran into her, she's got her hooks on
515 some colonel, maybe he'd buy her a canteen business.
THE CHAPLAIN: Do you really wish to sell?
MOTHER COURAGE: Where's money for sergeant to come from?
THE CHAPLAIN: What'll you live on, then?
MOTHER COURAGE: That's just it.

(YVETTE POTTIER *arrives with an extremely ancient* COLONEL.)

520 YVETTE: (*Embracing* MOTHER COURAGE.) My dear Courage,
fancy seeing you so soon. (*Whispers.*) He's not unwilling.
(*Aloud.*) This is my good friend who advises me in business matters. I happened to hear you wanted to sell your
cart on account of circumstances. I'll think it over.
525 MOTHER COURAGE: Pledge it, not sell, just not too much
hurry, 'tain't every day you find a cart like this in wartime.
YVETTE: (*Disappointed.*) Oh, pledge. I thought it was for sale.
I'm not so sure I'm interested. (*To the* COLONEL.) How do
you feel about it?
530 THE COLONEL: Just as you feel, pet.
MOTHER COURAGE: I'm only pledging it.
YVETTE: I thought you'd got to have the money.
MOTHER COURAGE: (*Firmly*) I got to have it, but sooner run
myself ragged looking for a bidder than sell outright. And
535 why? The cart's our livelihood. It's a chance for you,
Yvette; who knows when you'll get another like it and
have a special friend to advise you, am I right?
YVETTE: Yes, my friend thinks I should clinch it, but I'm not
sure. If it's only a pledge . . . so you agree we ought to buy
540 outright?
THE COLONEL: I agree, pet.
MOTHER COURAGE: Best look and see if you can find anything for sale then; maybe you will if you don't rush it,
take your friend along with you, say a week or fortnight,
545 might find something suits you.
YVETTE: Then let's go looking. I adore going around looking
for things, I adore going around with you, Poldi, it's such
fun, isn't it? No matter if it takes a fortnight. How soon
would you pay the money back if you got it?
550 MOTHER COURAGE: I'd pay back in two weeks, maybe one.
YVETTE: I can't make up my mind, Poldi chéri, you advise
me. (*Takes the* COLONEL *aside.*) She's got to sell, I know, no
problem there. And there's that ensign, you know, the fair-
haired one, he'd be glad to lend me the money. He's crazy
555 about me, says there's someone I remind him of. What do
you advise?
THE COLONEL: You steer clear of him. He's no good. He's
only making use of you. I said I'd buy you something,
didn't I, pussykins?
560 YVETTE: I oughtn't to let you. Of course if you think the ensign
might try to take advantage . . . Poldi, I'll accept it from you.
THE COLONEL: That's how I feel too.
YVETTE: Is that your advice?
THE COLONEL: That is my advice.
565 YVETTE: (*To* COURAGE *once more.*) My friend's advice would
be to accept. Make me out a receipt saying the cart's mine
once two weeks are up, with all its contents, we'll check
it now, I'll bring the two hundred florins later. (*To the*
COLONEL.) You go back to the camp, I'll follow, I got to
570 check it all and see there's nothing missing from my cart.
(*She kisses him. He leaves. She climbs up on the cart.*) Not all
that many boots, are there?
MOTHER COURAGE: Yvette, it's no time for checking your
cart, s'posing it is yours. You promised you'd talk to
575 sergeant about Swiss Cheese, there ain't a minute to lose,
they say in an hour he'll be courtmartialled.
YVETTE: Just let me count the shirts.
MOTHER COURAGE: (*Pulling her down by the skirt.*) You bloody
vampire. Swiss Cheese's life's at stake. And not a word about
580 who's making the offer, for God's sake, pretend it's your
friend, else we're all done for cause we looked after him.
YVETTE: I fixed to meet that one-eyed fellow in the copse, he
should be there by now.

THE CHAPLAIN: It doesn't have to be the whole two hundred
585   either, I'd go up to a hundred and fifty, that may be enough.
MOTHER COURAGE: Since when has it been your money?
You kindly keep out of this. You'll get your hotpot all
right, don't worry. Hurry up and don't haggle, it's life or
death. (*Pushes* YVETTE *off.*)
590   THE CHAPLAIN: Far be it from me to interfere, but what are
we going to live on? You're saddled with a daughter who
can't earn her keep.
MOTHER COURAGE: I'm counting on regimental cash box,
Mr. Clever. They'll allow it as his expenses.
595   THE CHAPLAIN: But will she get the message right?
MOTHER COURAGE: It's her interest I should spend her two
hundred so she gets the cart. She's set on that, God knows
how long that colonel of hers'll last. Kattrin, polish the
knives, there's the pumice. And you, stop hanging round
600   like Jesus on Mount of Olives, get moving, wash them
glasses, we'll have fifty or more of cavalry in tonight and I
don't want to hear a lot of 'I'm not accustomed to having
to run about, oh my poor feet, we never ran in church'.
Thank the Lord they're corruptible. After all, they ain't
605   wolves, just humans out for money. Corruption in humans
is same as compassion in God. Corruption's our only hope.
Long as we have it there'll be lenient sentences and even an
innocent man'll have a chance of being let off.
YVETTE: (*Comes in panting.*) They'll do it for two hundred.
610   But it's got to be quick. Soon be out of their hands. Best
thing is I go right away to my colonel with the one-eyed
man. He's admitted he had the box, they put the thumb-
screws on him. But he chucked it in the river soon as he
saw they were on his track. The box is a write-off. I'll go
615   and get the money from my colonel, shall I?
MOTHER COURAGE: Box is a write-off? How'm I to pay back
two hundred then?
YVETTE: Oh, you thought you'd get it from the box, did you?
And I was to be Joe Soap I suppose? Better not count on
620   that. You'll have to pay up if you want Swiss Cheese back,
or would you sooner I dropped the whole thing so's you
can keep your cart?
MOTHER COURAGE: That's something I didn't allow for. Don't
worry, you'll get your cart, I've said goodbye to it, had it
625   seventeen years, I have. I just need a moment to think, it's
bit sudden, what'm I to do, two hundred's too much for
me, pity you didn't beat 'em down. Must keep a bit back,
else any Tom, Dick and Harry'll be able to shove me in
ditch. Go and tell them I'll pay hundred and twenty florins,
630   else it's all off, either way I'm losing me cart.
YVETTE: They won't do it. That one-eyed man's impatient already, keeps looking over his shoulder, he's so worked up.
Hadn't I best pay them the whole two hundred?
MOTHER COURAGE: (*In despair.*) I can't pay that. Thirty years
635   I been working. She's twenty-five already, and no husband. I got her to think of too. Don't push me, I know
what I'm doing. Say a hundred and twenty, or it's off.
YVETTE: It's up to you. (*Rushes off.*)

(*Without looking at either the* CHAPLAIN *or her daughter,* MOTHER
COURAGE *sits down to help* KATTRIN *polish knives.*)

MOTHER COURAGE: Don't smash them glasses, they ain't ours
640   now. Watch what you're doing, you'll cut yourself. Swiss
Cheese'll be back, I'll pay two hundred if it comes to the

pinch. You'll get your brother, love. For eighty florins we
could fill a pack with goods and start again. Plenty of folk
has to make do.
THE CHAPLAIN: The Lord will provide, it says.   645
MOTHER COURAGE: See they're properly dry. (*She cleans knives
in silence.* KATTRIN *suddenly runs behind the cart, sobbing.*)
YVETTE: (*Comes running in.*) They won't do it. I told you so.
The one-eyed man wanted to leave right away, said there
was no point. He says he's just waiting for the drum-roll;   650
that means sentence has been pronounced. I offered a
hundred and fifty. He didn't even blink. I had to convince
him to stay there so's I could have another word with you.
MOTHER COURAGE: Tell him I'll pay the two hundred. Hurry!
(YVETTE *runs off. They sit in silence. The* CHAPLAIN *has stopped*   655
polishing the glasses.) I reckon I bargained too long.

(*In the distance drumming is heard. The* CHAPLAIN *gets up and
goes to the rear.* MOTHER COURAGE *remains seated. It grows dark.
The drumming stops. It grows light once more.* MOTHER COURAGE
is sitting exactly as before.)

YVETTE: (*Arrives, very pale.*) Well, you got what you asked for,
with your haggling and trying to keep your cart. Eleven
bullets they gave him, that's all. You don't deserve I should
bother any more about you. But I did hear they don't be-   660
lieve the box really is in the river. They've an idea it's here
and anyhow that you're connected with him. They're going to bring him here, see if you gives yourself away when
you sees him. Thought I'd better warn you so's you don't
recognise him, else you'll all be for it. They're right on my   665
heels, best tell you quick. Shall I keep Kattrin away?
(MOTHER COURAGE *shakes her head.*) Does she know? She
mayn't have heard the drumming or know what it meant.
MOTHER COURAGE: She knows. Get her.

(YVETTE *fetches* KATTRIN, *who goes to her mother and stands beside
her.* MOTHER COURAGE *takes her hand. Two lansequenets come carrying a stretcher with something lying on it covered by a sheet. The
SERGEANT marches beside them. They set down the stretcher.*)

SERGEANT: Here's somebody we dunno the name of. It's got to   670
be listed, though, so everything's shipshape. He had a meal
here. Have a look, see if you know him. (*He removes the sheet.*)
Know him? (MOTHER COURAGE *shakes her head.*) What,
never see him before he had that meal here? (MOTHER
COURAGE *shakes her head.*) Pick him up. Chuck him in the   675
pit. He's got nobody knows him. (*They carry him away.*)

SCENE FOUR

Mother Courage sings the Song of the Grand Capitulation.

Outside an officer's tent.

MOTHER COURAGE *is waiting. A* CLERK *looks out of the tent.*

THE CLERK: I know you. You had a paymaster from the
Lutherans with you, what was in hiding. I'd not complain
if I were you.
MOTHER COURAGE: But I got a complaint to make. I'm innocent, would look as how I'd a bad conscience if I let this   5

pass. Slashed everything in me cart to pieces with their sabres, they did, then wanted I should pay five taler fine for nowt, I tell you, nowt.

THE CLERK: Take my tip, better shut up. We're short of can-
10   teens, so we let you go on trading, specially if you got a bad conscience and pay a fine now and then.

MOTHER COURAGE: I got a complaint.

THE CLERK: Have it your own way. Then you must wait till the captain's free. (*Withdraws inside the tent.*)

15   YOUNG SOLDIER: (*Enters aggressively.*) Bouque la Madonne! Where's that bleeding pig of a captain what's took my reward money to swig with his tarts? I'll do him.

OLDER SOLDIER: (*Running after him.*) Shut up. They'll put you in irons.

20   YOUNG SOLDIER: Out of there, you thief! I'll slice you into pork chops, I will. Pocketing my prize money after I'd swum the river, only one in the whole squadron, and now I can't even buy meself a beer. I'm not standing for that. Come on out there so I can cut you up!

25   OLDER SOLDIER: Blessed Mother of God, he's asking for trouble.

MOTHER COURAGE: Is it some reward he weren't paid?

YOUNG SOLDIER: Lemme go, I'll slash you too while I'm at it.

OLDER SOLDIER: He rescued the colonel's horse and got no
30   reward for it. He's young yet, still wet behind the ears.

MOTHER COURAGE: Let him go, he ain't a dog you got to chain up. Wanting your reward is good sound sense. Why be a hero otherwise?

YOUNG SOLDIER: So's he can sit in there and booze. You're
35   shit-scared, the lot of you. I done something special and I want my reward.

MOTHER COURAGE: Don't you shout at me, young fellow. Got me own worries, I have; any road you should spare your voice, be needing it when captain comes, else there he'll be
40   and you too hoarse to make a sound, which'll make it hard for him to clap you in irons till you turn blue. People what shouts like that can't keep it up ever; half an hour, and they have to be rocked to sleep, they're so tired.

YOUNG SOLDIER: I ain't tired and to hell with sleep. I'm hun-
45   gry. They make our bread from acorns and hemp-seed, and they even skimp on that. He's whoring away my reward and I'm hungry. I'll do him.

MOTHER COURAGE: Oh I see, you're hungry. Last year that general of yours ordered you all off roads and across fields
50   so corn should be trampled flat; I could've got ten florins for a pair of boots s'pose I'd had boots and s'pose anyone'd been able to pay ten florins. Thought he'd be well away from that area this year, he did, but here he is, still there, and hunger is great. I see what you're angry about.

55   YOUNG SOLDIER: I won't have it, don't talk to me, it ain't fair and I'm not standing for that.

MOTHER COURAGE: And you're right; but how long? How long you not standing for unfairness? One hour, two hours? Didn't ask yourself that, did you, but it's the whole
60   point and why, once you're in irons it's too bad if you suddenly finds you can put up with unfairness after all.

YOUNG SOLDIER: What am I listening to you for, I'd like to know? Bouque la Madonne, where's that captain?

MOTHER COURAGE: You been listening to me because you
65   knows it's like what I say, your anger has gone up in smoke already, it was just a short one and you needed a long one, but where you going to get it from?

YOUNG SOLDIER: Are you trying to tell me asking for my reward is wrong?

MOTHER COURAGE: Not a bit. I'm just telling you your anger   70
ain't long enough, it's good for nowt, pity. If you'd a long one I'd be trying to prod you on. Cut him up, the swine, would be my advice to you in that case; but how about if you don't cut him up cause you feels your tail going between your legs? Then I'd look silly and captain'd take it   75
out on me.

OLDER SOLDIER: You're perfectly right, he's just a bit crazy.

YOUNG SOLDIER: Very well, let's see if I don't cut him up. (*Draws his sword.*) When he arrives I'm going to cut him up.

THE CLERK: (*Looks out.*) The captain'll be here in one minute.   80
Sit down.

(*The* YOUNG SOLDIER *sits down.*)

MOTHER COURAGE: He's sitting now. See, what did I say? You're sitting now. Ah, how well they know us, no one need tell 'em how to go about it. Sit down! and, bingo, we're sitting. And sitting and sedition don't mix. Don't try   85
to stand up, you won't stand the way you was standing before. I shouldn't worry about what I think; I'm no better, not one moment. Bought up all our fighting spirit, they have. Eh? S'pose I kick back, might be bad for business. Let me tell you a thing or two about the Grand Capitu-   90
lation. (*She sings the Song of the Grand Capitulation.*)

Back when I was young, I was brought to realise
What a very special person I must be
(Not just any old cottager's daughter, what with my looks
    and my talents and my urge towards Higher Things)
And insisted that my soup should have no hairs in it.   95
No one makes a sucker out of me!
(All or nothing, only the best is good enough, each man
    for himself, nobody's telling *me* what to do.)
Then I heard a tit
Chirp: Wait a bit!
    And you'll be marching with the band   100
    In step, responding to command
    And striking up your little dance:
    Now we advance.
    And now: parade, form square!
    Then men swear God's there—   105
    Not the faintest chance!

In no time at all anyone who looked could see
That I'd learned to take my medicine with good grace.
(Two kids on my hands and look at the price of bread,
    and things they expect of you!)
When they finally came to feel that they were through   110
    with me
They'd got me grovelling on my face.
(Takes all sorts to make a world, you scratch my back
    and I'll scratch yours, no good banging your head
    against a brick wall.)
Then I heard that tit
Chirp: Wait a bit!
    And you'll be marching with the band   115
    In step, responding to command
    And striking up your little dance:
    Now they advance.
    And now: parade, form square!

120 Then men swear God's there—
     Not the faintest chance!

     I've known people tried to storm the summits:
     There's no star too bright or seems too far away.
     (Dogged does it, where there's a will there's a way, by
        hook or by crook.)
125 As each peak disclosed fresh peaks to come, it's
     Strange how much a plain straw hat could weigh.
     (You have to cut your coat according to your cloth.)
     Then I hear the tit
     Chirp: Wait a bit!
130   And they'll be marching with the band
          In step, responding to command
          And striking up their little dance:
          Now they advance
          And now: parade, form square!
135 Then men swear God's there—
     Not the faintest chance!

MOTHER COURAGE: (*To the* YOUNG SOLDIER.) That's why I
     reckon you should stay there with your sword drawn if
     you're truly set on it and your anger's big enough, because
140 you got grounds, I agree, but if your anger's a short one
     best leave right away.
YOUNG SOLDIER: Oh stuff it. (*He staggers off with the* OLDER
     SOLDIER *following.*)
THE CLERK: (*Sticks his head out.*) Captain's here now. You can
145 make your complaint.
MOTHER COURAGE: I changed me mind. I ain't complaining.
     (*Exit.*)

SCENE FIVE

Two years have gone by. The war is spreading to new
areas. Ceaselessly on the move, Courage's little cart
crosses Poland, Moravia, Bavaria, Italy, then Bavaria
again. 1631. Tilly's victory at Magdeburg costs Mother
Courage four officers' shirts.

MOTHER COURAGE'S *cart has stopped in a badly shot-up village.
Thin military music in the distance. Two* SOLDIERS *at the bar being served by* KATTRIN *and* MOTHER COURAGE. *One of them has
a lady's fur coat over his shoulders.*

MOTHER COURAGE: Can't pay, that it? No money, no
     schnapps. They give us victory parades, but catch them
     giving men their pay.
FIRST SOLDIER: I want my schnapps. I missed the looting.
5   That double-crossing general only allowed an hour's loot-
     ing in the town. He ain't an inhuman monster, he said.
     Town must of paid him.
THE CHAPLAIN: (*Stumbles in.*) There are people still lying in
     that yard. The peasant's family. Somebody give me a hand.
10   I need linen.

(*The* SECOND SOLDIER *goes off with him.* KATTRIN *becomes very
excited and tries to make her mother produce linen.*)

MOTHER COURAGE: I got none. All my bandages was sold to
     regiment. I ain't tearing up my officer's shirts for that lot.
THE CHAPLAIN: (*Calling back.*) I need linen, I tell you.
MOTHER COURAGE: (*Blocking* KATTRIN'S *way into the cart by
     sitting on the step.*) I'm giving nowt. They'll never pay, and 15
     why, nowt to pay with.
THE CHAPLAIN: (*Bending over a woman he has carried in.*) Why
     d'you stay around during the gunfire?
PEASANT WOMAN: (*Feebly.*) Farm.
MOTHER COURAGE: Catch them abandoning anything. But 20
     now I'm s'posed to foot the bill. I won't do it.
FIRST SOLDIER: Those are Protestants. What they have to be
     Protestants for?
MOTHER COURAGE: They ain't bothering about faith. They
     lost their farm.   25
SECOND SOLDIER: They're no Protestants. They're Catholics
     like us.
FIRST SOLDIER: No way of sorting 'em out in a bombardment.
A PEASANT: (*Brought in by the* CHAPLAIN.) My arm's gone.
THE CHAPLAIN: Where's that linen?   30
MOTHER COURAGE: I can't give nowt. What with expenses,
     taxes, loan interest and bribes. (*Making guttural noises,* KAT-
     TRIN *raises a plank and threatens her mother with it.*) You
     gone plain crazy? Put that plank away or I'll paste you
     one, you cow. I'm giving nowt, don't want to, got to think 35
     of meself. (*The* CHAPLAIN *lifts her off the steps and sets her on
     the ground, then starts pulling out shirts and tearing them into
     strips.*) My officers' shirts! Half a florin apiece! I'm ruined.
     (*From the house comes the cry of a child in pain.*)
THE PEASANT: The baby's in there still. (KATTRIN *dashes in.*)   40
THE CHAPLAIN: (*To the woman.*) Don't move. They'll get it out.
MOTHER COURAGE: Stop her, roof may fall in.
THE CHAPLAIN: I'm not going back in there.
MOTHER COURAGE: (*Torn both ways.*) Don't waste my pre-
     cious linen.   45

(KATTRIN *brings a baby out of the ruins.*)

MOTHER COURAGE: How nice, found another baby to cart
     around? Give it to its ma this instant, unless you'd have me
     fighting for hours to get it off you, like last time, d'you
     hear? (*To the* SECOND SOLDIER.) Don't stand there gaw-
     ping, you go back and tell them cut out that music, we can 50
     see it's a victory with our own eyes. All your victories
     mean to me is losses.
THE CHAPLAIN: (*Tying a bandage.*) Blood's coming through.

(KATTRIN *is rocking the baby and making lullaby noises.*)

MOTHER COURAGE: Look at her, happy as a queen in all this
     misery; give it back at once, its mother's coming round. (*She* 55
     catches the FIRST SOLDIER, *who has been attacking the drinks and
     is trying to make off with one of the bottles.*) Psia krew! Thought
     you'd score another victory, you animal? Now pay.
FIRST SOLDIER: I got nowt.
MOTHER COURAGE: (*Pulling the fur coat off his back.*) Then 60
     leave that coat, it's stolen any road.
THE CHAPLAIN: There's still someone under there.

SCENE SIX

Outside the Bavarian town of Ingolstadt Courage participates in the funeral of the late Imperial commander Tilly. Discussions are held about war heroes and the war's duration. The Chaplain complains that his talents are lying fallow, and dumb Kattrin gets the red boots. The year is 1632.

Inside a canteen tent.

It has a bar towards the rear. Rain. Sound of drums and Funeral music. The CHAPLAIN *and the regimental* CLERK *are playing a board game.* MOTHER COURAGE *and her daughter are stocktaking.*

THE CHAPLAIN: Now the funeral procession will be moving off.

MOTHER COURAGE: Too bad about commander in chief—twenty-two pairs those socks—he fell by accident, they say. Mist over fields, that was the trouble. General had just
5 been haranguing a regiment saying they must fight to last man and last round, he was riding back when mist made him lose direction so he was up front and a bullet got him in midst of battle—only four hurricane lamps left. (*A whistle from the rear. She goes to the bar.*) You scrimshankers,
10 dodging your commander in chief's funeral, scandal I call it. (*Pours drinks.*)

THE CLERK: They should never of paid troops out before the funeral. Instead of going now they're all getting pissed.

THE CHAPLAIN: (*To the* CLERK.) Aren't you supposed to go to
15 the funeral?

THE CLERK: Dodged it cause of the rain.

MOTHER COURAGE: It's different with you, your uniform might get wet. I heard they wanted to toll bells for funeral as usual, except it turned out all churches had been blown
20 to smithereens by his orders, so poor old commander in chief won't be hearing no bells as they let the coffin down. They're going to let off three salvoes instead to cheer things up—seventeen belts.

SHOUTS: (*From the bar.*) Hey, Missis, a brandy!

25 MOTHER COURAGE: Let's see your money. No, I ain't having you in my tent with your disgusting boots. You can drink outside, rain or no rain. (*To the* CLERK.) I'm only letting in sergeants and up. Commander in chief had been having his worries, they say. S'posed to have been trouble with
30 Second Regiment cause he stopped their pay, said it was a war of faith and they should do it for free. (*Funeral march. All look to the rear.*)

THE CHAPLAIN: Now they'll be filing past the noble corpse.

MOTHER COURAGE: Can't help feeling sorry for those gener-
35 als and emperors, there they are maybe thinking they're doing something extra special what folk'll talk about in years to come, and earning a public monument, like conquering the world for instance, that's a fine ambition for a general, how's he to know any better? I mean, he plagues
40 hisself to death, then it all breaks down on account of ordinary folk what just wants their beer and bit of a chat, nowt higher. Finest plans get bolloxed up by the pettiness of them as should be carrying them out, because emperors can't do nowt themselves, they just counts on soldiers
45 and people to back 'em up whatever happens, am I right?

THE CHAPLAIN: (*Laughs.*) Courage, you're right, aside from the soldiers. They do their best. Give me that lot outside there, for instance, drinking their brandy in the rain, and I'd guarantee to make you one war after another for a hundred years if need be, and I'm no trained general. 50

MOTHER COURAGE: You don't think war might end, then?

THE CHAPLAIN: What, because the commander in chief's gone? Don't be childish. They're two a penny, no shortage of heroes.

MOTHER COURAGE: Ee, I'm not asking for fun of it, but because I'm thinking whether to stock up, prices are low 55 now, but if war's going to end it's money down the drain.

THE CHAPLAIN: I realise it's a serious question. There've always been people going round saying 'the war can't go on for ever'. I tell you there's nothing to stop it going on for ever. Of course there can be a bit of a breathing space. The war 60 may need to get its second wind, it may even have an accident so to speak. There's no guarantee against that; nothing's perfect on this earth of ours. A perfect war, the sort you might say couldn't be improved on, that's something we shall probably never see. It can suddenly come to a 65 standstill for some quite unforeseen reason, you can't allow for everything. A slight case of negligence, and it's bogged down up to the axles. And then it's a matter of hauling the war out of the mud again. But emperor and kings and popes will come to its rescue. So on the whole it has noth- 70 ing serious to worry about, and will live to a ripe old age.

A SOLDIER: (*Sings at the bar.*)

> A schnapps, landlord, you're late!
> A soldier cannot wait
> To do his emperor's orders. 75

Make it a double, this is a holiday.

MOTHER COURAGE: S'pose I went by what you say . . .

THE CHAPLAIN: Think it out for yourself. What's to compete with the war?

THE SOLDIER: (*At the rear.*) 80

> Your breast, my girl, you're late!
> A soldier cannot wait
> To ride across the borders.

THE CLERK: (*Unexpectedly.*) And what about peace? I'm from Bohemia and I'd like to go home some day. 85

THE CHAPLAIN: Would you indeed? Ah, peace. Where is the hole once the cheese has been eaten?

THE SOLDIER: (*At the rear.*)

> Lead trumps, my friend, you're late!
> A soldier cannot wait. 90
> His emperor needs him badly.

> Your blessing, priest, you're late!
> A soldier cannot wait.
> Must lay his life down gladly.

THE CLERK: In the long run life's impossible if there's no peace. 95

THE CHAPLAIN: I'd say there's peace in war too; it has its peaceful moments. Because war satisfies all requirements, peaceable ones included, they're catered for, and it would simply fizzle out if they weren't. In war you can do a crap like in the depths of peacetime, then between one battle 100 and the next you can have a beer, then even when you're moving up you can lay your head on your arms and have a bit of shuteye in the ditch, it's entirely possible. During a charge you can't play cards maybe, but nor can you in the

105 depths of peacetime when you're ploughing, and after a
victory there are various openings. You may get a leg
blown off, then you start by making a lot of fuss as though
it were serious, but afterwards you calm down or get given
a schnapps, and you end up hopping around and the war's
110 no worse off than before. And what's to stop you being
fruitful and multiplying in the middle of all the butchery,
behind a barn or something, in the long run you can't be
held back from it, and then the war will have your progeny
and can use them to carry on with. No, the war will always
115 find an outlet, mark my words. Why should it ever stop?

(KATTRIN *has ceased working and is staring at the* CHAPLAIN.)

MOTHER COURAGE: I'll buy fresh stock then. If you say so.
(KATTRIN *suddenly flings a basket full of bottles to the ground
and runs off.*) Kattrin! (*Laughs.*) Damn me if she weren't
waiting for peace. I promised her she'd get a husband soon
120 as peace came. (*Hurries after her.*)
THE CLERK: (*Standing up.*) I won. You been talking too
much. Pay up.
MOTHER COURAGE: (*Returning with* KATTRIN.) Don't be silly,
war'll go on a bit longer, and we'll make a bit more
125 money, and peacetime'll be all the nicer for it. Now you
go into town, that's ten minutes' walk at most, fetch things
from Golden Lion, the expensive ones, we can fetch rest
in cart later, it's all arranged, regimental clerk here will go
with you. Nearly everybody's attending commander in
130 chief's funeral, nowt can happen to you. Careful now,
don't let them steal nowt, think of your dowry.

(KATTRIN *puts a cloth over her head and leaves with the* CLERK.)

THE CHAPLAIN: Is that all right to let her go with the clerk?
MOTHER COURAGE: She's not that pretty they'd want to ruin her.
THE CHAPLAIN: I admire the way you run your business and
135 always win through. I see why they called you Courage.
MOTHER COURAGE: Poor folk got to have courage. Why,
they're lost. Simply getting up in morning takes some doing
in their situation. Or ploughing a field, and in a war at that.
Mere fact they bring kids into world shows they got
140 courage, cause there's no hope for them. They have to hang
one another and slaughter one another, so just looking each
other in face must call for courage. Being able to put up with
emperor and pope shows supernatural courage, cause those
two cost 'em their lives. (*She sits down, takes a little pipe from
145 her purse and smokes.*) You might chop us a bit of kindling.
THE CHAPLAIN: (*Reluctantly removing his coat and preparing to chop
up sticks.*) I happen to be a pastor of souls, not a woodcutter.
MOTHER COURAGE: I got no soul, you see. Need firewood,
though.
150 THE CHAPLAIN: Where's that stumpy pipe from?
MOTHER COURAGE: Just a pipe.
THE CHAPLAIN: What d'you mean, 'just', it's a quite particu-
lar pipe, that.
MOTHER COURAGE: Aha?
155 THE CHAPLAIN: That stumpy pipe belongs to the Oxenstierna
Regiment's cook.
MOTHER COURAGE: If you know that already why ask, Mr
Clever?
THE CHAPLAIN: Because I didn't know if you were aware
160 what you're smoking. You might just have been rummag-

ing around in your things, come across some old pipe or
other, and used it out of sheer absence of mind.
MOTHER COURAGE: And why not?
THE CHAPLAIN: Because you didn't. You're smoking that de-
liberately.   165
MOTHER COURAGE: And why shouldn't I?
THE CHAPLAIN: Courage, I'm warning you. It's my duty.
Probably you'll never clap eyes on the gentleman again,
and that's no loss but your good fortune. He didn't make
at all a reliable impression on me. Quite the opposite.   170
MOTHER COURAGE: Really? Nice fellow that.
THE CHAPLAIN: So he's what you would call a nice fellow? I
wouldn't. Far be it from me to bear him the least ill-will,
but nice is not what I would call him. More like one of
those Don Juans, a slippery one. Have a look at that pipe   175
if you don't believe me. You must admit it tells you a good
deal about his character.
MOTHER COURAGE: Nowt that I can see. Worn out, I'd call it.
THE CHAPLAIN: Practically bitten through, you mean. A man
of wrath. That is the pipe of an unscrupulous man of   180
wrath; you must see that if you have any discrimination left.
MOTHER COURAGE: Don't chop my chopping block in two.
THE CHAPLAIN: I told you I'm not a woodcutter by trade. I
studied to be a pastor of souls. My talent and abilities are
being abused in this place, by manual labour. My God-   185
given endowments are denied expression. It's a sin. You
have never heard me preach. One sermon of mine can put
a regiment in such a frame of mind it'll treat the enemy
like a flock of sheep. Life to them is a smelly old foot-
cloth which they fling away in a vision of final victory.   190
God has given me the gift of speech. I can preach so you'll
lose all sense of sight and hearing.
MOTHER COURAGE: I don't wish to lose my sense of sight
and hearing. Where'd that leave me?
THE CHAPLAIN: Courage, I have often thought that your dry   195
way of talking conceals more than just a warm heart. You
too are human and need warmth.
MOTHER COURAGE: Best way for us to get this tent warm is
have plenty of firewood.
THE CHAPLAIN: Don't change the subject. Seriously, Courage, I   200
sometimes ask myself what it would be like if our relationship were to become somewhat closer. I mean, given that
the whirlwind of war has so strangely whirled us together.
MOTHER COURAGE: I'd say it was close enough. I cook meals
for you and you run around and chop firewood for instance.   205
THE CHAPLAIN: (*Coming closer.*) You know what I mean by
closer; it's not a relationship founded on meals and wood-
chopping and other such base necessities. Let your head
speak, harden thyself not.
MOTHER COURAGE: Don't you come at me with that axe.   210
That'd be too close a relationship.
THE CHAPLAIN: You shouldn't make a joke of it. I'm a serious
person and I've thought about what I'm saying.
MOTHER COURAGE: Be sensible, padre. I like you. I don't want
to row you. All I'm after is get myself and children through   215
all this with my cart. I don't see it as mine, and I ain't in the
mood for private affairs. Right now I'm taking a gamble,
buying stores just when commander in chief's fallen and all
the talk's of peace. Where d'you reckon you'd turn if I'm
ruined? Don't know, do you? You chop us some kindling   220
wood, then we can keep warm at night, that's quite some-

thing these times. What's this? (*She gets up. Enter* KATTRIN, *out of breath, with a wound above her eye. She is carrying a variety of stuff: parcels, leather goods, a drum and so on.*)

225 MOTHER COURAGE: What happened, someone assault you? On way back? She was assaulted on her way back. Bet it was that trooper was getting drunk here. I shouldn't have let you go, love. Drop that stuff. Not too bad, just a flesh wound you got. I'll bandage it and in a week it'll be all right. Worse than 230 wild beasts, they are. (*She ties up the wound.*)

THE CHAPLAIN: It's not them I blame. They never went raping back home. The fault lies with those that start wars, it brings humanity's lowest instincts to the surface.

MOTHER COURAGE: Calm down. Didn't clerk come back 235 with you? That's because you're respectable, they don't bother. Wound ain't a deep one, won't leave no mark. There you are, all bandaged up. You'll get something, love, keep calm. Something I put aside for you, wait till you see. (*She delves into a sack and brings out* YVETTE's *red high-heeled* 240 *boots.*) Made you open your eyes, eh? Something you always wanted. They're yours. Put 'em on quick, before I change me mind. Won't leave no mark, and what if it does? Ones I'm really sorry for's the ones they fancy. Drag them around till they're worn out, they do. Those they 245 don't care for they leaves alive. I seen girls before now had pretty faces, then in no time looking fit to frighten a hyaena. Can't even go behind a bush without risking trouble, horrible life they lead. Same like with trees, straight well-shaped ones get chopped down to make beams for 250 houses and crooked ones live happily ever after. So it's a stroke of luck for you really. Them boots'll be all right, I greased them before putting them away.

(KATTRIN *leaves the boots where they are and crawls into the cart.*)

THE CHAPLAIN: Let's hope she's not disfigured.

MOTHER COURAGE: She'll have a scar. No use her waiting for 255 peacetime now.

THE CHAPLAIN: She didn't let them steal the things.

MOTHER COURAGE: Maybe I shouldn't have dinned that into her so. Wish I knew what went on in that head of hers. Just once she stayed out all night, once in all those years. 260 Afterwards she went around like before, except she worked harder. Couldn't get her to tell what had happened. Worried me quite a while, that did. (*She collects the articles brought by* KATTRIN, *and sorts them angrily.*) That's war for you. Nice way to get a living!

(*Sound of cannon fire.*)

265 THE CHAPLAIN: Now they'll be burying the commander in chief. This is a historic moment.

MOTHER COURAGE: What I call a historic moment is them bashing my daughter over the eye. She's half wrecked already, won't get no husband now, and her so crazy about 270 kids; any road she's only dumb from war, soldier stuffed something in her mouth when she was little. As for Swiss Cheese I'll never see him again, and where Eilif is God alone knows. War be damned.

SCENE SEVEN

| Mother Courage at the peak of her business career. |

High road.

The CHAPLAIN, MOTHER COURAGE *and* KATTRIN *are pulling the cart, which is hung with new wares.* MOTHER COURAGE *is wearing a necklace of silver coins.*

MOTHER COURAGE: I won't have you folk spoiling my war for me, I'm told it kills off the weak, but they're write-off in peacetime too. And war gives its people a better deal. (*She sings.*)

> And if you feel your forces fading 5
> You won't be there to share the fruits.
> But what is war but private trading
> That deals in blood instead of boots?

And what's the use of settling down? Them as does are first to go. (*Sings.*) 10

> Some people think to live by looting
> The goods some others haven't got.
> You think it's just a line they're shooting
> Until you hear they have been shot.

> And some I saw dig six feet under 15
> In haste to lie down and pass out.
> Now they're at rest perhaps they wonder
> Just what was all their haste about.

(*They pull it further.*)

SCENE EIGHT

| The same year sees the death of the Swedish king Gustavus Adolphus at the battle of Lützen. Peace threatens to ruin Mother Courage's business. Courage's dashing son performs one heroic deed too many and comes to a sticky end. |

Camp.

A summer morning. In front of the cart stand an OLD WOMAN *and her son. The son* [YOUNG MAN] *carries a large sack of bedding.*

MOTHER COURAGE'S VOICE: (*From inside the cart.*) Does it need to be this ungodly hour?

THE YOUNG MAN: We walked twenty miles in the night and got to be back today.

MOTHER COURAGE'S VOICE: What am I to do with bedding? 5 Folk've got no houses.

THE YOUNG MAN: Best have a look first.

THE OLD WOMAN: This place is no good either. Come on.

THE YOUNG MAN: What, and have them sell the roof over our head for taxes? She might pay three florins if you throw 10 in the bracelet. (*Bells start ringing.*) Listen, mother.

VOICES: (*From the rear.*) Peace! Swedish king's been killed.

MOTHER COURAGE: (*Sticks her head out of the cart. She has not yet done her hair.*) What's that bell-ringing about in mid-week?

THE CHAPLAIN: (*Crawling out from under the cart.*) What are 15 they shouting? Peace?

MOTHER COURAGE: Don't tell me peace has broken out just after I laid in new stock.

THE CHAPLAIN: (*Calling to the rear.*) That true? Peace?

20 VOICES: Three weeks ago, they say, only no one told us.

THE CHAPLAIN: (*To* COURAGE.) What else would they be ringing the bells for?

VOICES: A whole lot of Lutherans have driven into town, they brought the news.

25 THE YOUNG MAN: Mother, it's peace. What's the matter?

(*The* OLD WOMAN *has collapsed.*)

MOTHER COURAGE: (*Speaking into the cart.*) Holy cow! Kattrin, peace! Put your black dress on, we're going to church. Least we can do for Swiss Cheese. Is it true, though?

THE YOUNG MAN: The people here say so. They've made
30 peace. Can you get up? (*The* OLD WOMAN *stands up dumbfounded.*) I'll get the saddlery going again, I promise. It'll all work out. Father will get his bedding back. Can you walk? (*To the* CHAPLAIN.) She came over queer. It's the news. She never thought there'd be peace again. Father al-
35 ways said so. We're going straight home. (*They go off.*)

MOTHER COURAGE'S VOICE: Give her a schnapps.

THE CHAPLAIN: They've already gone.

MOTHER COURAGE'S VOICE: What's up in camp?

THE CHAPLAIN: They're assembling. I'll go on over. Shouldn't
40 I put on my clerical garb?

MOTHER COURAGE'S VOICE: Best check up before parading yourself as heretic. I'm glad about peace, never mind if I'm ruined. Any road I'll have got two of me children through the war. Be seeing Eilif again now.

45 THE CHAPLAIN: And who's that walking down the lines? Bless me, the army commander's cook.

THE COOK: (*Somewhat bedraggled and carrying a bundle.*) What do I behold? The padre!

THE CHAPLAIN: Courage, we've got company.

(MOTHER COURAGE *clambers out.*)

50 THE COOK: I promised I'd drop over for a little talk soon as I had the time. I've not forgotten your brandy, Mrs Fierling.

MOTHER COURAGE: Good grief, the general's cook! After all these years! Where's my eldest boy Eilif?

THE COOK: Hasn't he got here? He left before me, he was on
55 his way to see you too.

THE CHAPLAIN: I shall don my clerical garb, just a moment.

(*Goes off behind the cart.*)

MOTHER COURAGE: Then he may be here any minute. (*Calls into the cart.*) Kattrin, Eilif's on his way. Get cook a glass of brandy, Kattrin! (KATTRIN *does not appear.*) Drag your hair
60 down over it, that's all right. Mr Lamb's no stranger. (*Fetches the brandy herself.*) She don't like to come out, peace means nowt to her. Took too long coming, it did. They gave her a crack over one eye, you barely notice it now but she thinks folks are staring at her.

65 THE COOK: Ah yes. War. (*He and* MOTHER COURAGE *sit down.*)

MOTHER COURAGE: Cooky, you caught me at bad moment. I'm ruined.

THE COOK: What? That's hard.

MOTHER COURAGE: Peace'll wring my neck. I went and took Chaplain's advice, laid in fresh stocks only t'other day. And
70 now they're going to demobilise and I'll be left sitting on me wares.

THE COOK: What d'you want to go and listen to padre for? If I hadn't been in such a hurry that time, the Catholics arriving so quickly and all, I'd warned you against that man. All piss
75 and wind, he is. So he's the authority around here, eh?

MOTHER COURAGE: He's been doing washing-up for me and helping pull.

THE COOK: Him pull! I bet he told you some of those jokes of his too, I know him, got a very unhealthy view of
80 women, he has, all my good influence on him went for nowt. He ain't steady.

MOTHER COURAGE: You steady then?

THE COOK: Whatever else I ain't, I'm steady. Mud in your eye!

MOTHER COURAGE: Steady, that's nowt. I only had one steady
85 fellow, thank God. Hardest I ever had to work in me life; he flogged the kids' blankets soon as autumn came, and he called me mouth-organ an unchristian instrument. Ask me, you ain't saying much for yourself admitting you're steady.

THE COOK: Still tough as nails, I see; but that's what I like
90 about you.

MOTHER COURAGE: Now don't tell me you been dreaming of me nails.

THE COOK: Well, well, here we are, along with armistice bells and your brandy like what nobody else ever serves, it's fa-
95 mous, that is.

MOTHER COURAGE: I don't give two pins for your armistice bells just now. Can't see 'em handing out all the back pay what's owing, so where does that leave me with my famous brandy? Had your pay yet?
100 THE COOK: (*Hesitantly.*) Not exactly. That's why we all shoved off. If that's how it is, I thought, I'll go and visit friends. So here I am sitting with you.

MOTHER COURAGE: Other words you got nowt.

THE COOK: High time they stopped that bloody clanging.
105 Wouldn't mind getting into some sort of trade. I'm fed up being cook to that lot. I'm s'posed to rustle them up meals out of tree roots and old bootsoles, then they fling the hot soup in my face. Cook these days is a dog's life. Sooner do war service, only of course it's peacetime now. (*He sees the*
110 CHAPLAIN *reappearing in his old garments.*) More about that later.

THE CHAPLAIN: It's still all right, only had a few moths in it.

THE COOK: Can't see why you bother. You won't get your old job back, who are you to inspire now to earn his pay hon-
115 ourably and lay down his life? What's more I got a bone to pick with you, cause you advised this lady to buy a lot of unnecessary goods saying war would go on for ever.

THE CHAPLAIN: (*Heatedly.*) I'd like to know what concern that is of yours.
120 THE COOK: Because it's unscrupulous, that sort of thing is. How dare you meddle in other folks' business arrangements with your unwanted advice?

THE CHAPLAIN: Who's meddling? (*To* COURAGE.) I never knew this gentleman was such an intimate you had to ac-
125 count to him for everything.

MOTHER COURAGE: Keep your hair on, cook's only giving his personal opinion and you can't deny your war was a flop.

THE CHAPLAIN: You should not blaspheme against peace,
130   Courage. You are a hyaena of the battlefield.
MOTHER COURAGE: I'm what?
THE COOK: If you're going to insult this lady you'll have to
   settle with me.
THE CHAPLAIN: It's not you I'm talking to. Your intentions
135   are only too transparent. (*To* COURAGE.) But when I see
   you picking up peace betwixt your finger and your thumb
   like some dirty old snot-rag, then my humanity feels outraged; for then I see that you don't want peace but war,
   because you profit from it; in which case you shouldn't
140   forget the ancient saying that whosoever sups with the
   devil needs a long spoon.
MOTHER COURAGE: I got no use for war, and war ain't got
   much use for me. But I'm not being called no hyaena, you
   and me's through.
145 THE CHAPLAIN: Then why grumble about peace when everybody's breathing sighs of relief? Because of some old junk
   in your cart?
MOTHER COURAGE: My goods ain't old junk but what I lives
   by, and you too up to now.
150 THE CHAPLAIN: Off war, in other words. Aha.
THE COOK: (*To the* CHAPLAIN.) You're old enough to know
   it's always a mistake offering advice. (*To* COURAGE.) Way
   things are, your best bet's to get rid of certain goods quick
   as you can before prices hit rock-bottom. Dress yourself
155   and get moving, not a moment to lose.
MOTHER COURAGE: That ain't bad advice. I'll do that, I guess.
THE CHAPLAIN: Because cooky says it.
MOTHER COURAGE: Why couldn't you say it? He's right, I'd
   best go off to market. (*Goes inside the cart.*)
160 THE COOK: That's one to me, padre. You got no presence of
   mind. What you should of said was: what, me offer advice,
   all I done was discuss politics. Better not take me on.
   Cock-fighting don't suit that get-up.
THE CHAPLAIN: If you don't stop your gob I'll murder you,
165   get-up or no get-up.
THE COOK: (*Pulling off his boots and unwrapping his foot-cloths.*)
   Pity the war made such a godless shit of you, else you'd
   easily get another parsonage now it's peacetime. Cooks
   won't be needed, there's nowt to cook, but faith goes on
170   just the same, nowt changed in that direction.
THE CHAPLAIN: Mr Lamb, I'm asking you not to elbow me
   out. Since I came down in the world I've become a better person. I couldn't preach to anyone now.

(*Enter* YVETTE POTTIER *in black, dressed up to the nines, carrying
a cane. She is much older and fatter, and heavily powdered. She is
followed by a manservant.*)

YVETTE: Hullo there, everybody. Is this Mother Courage's es-
175   tablishment?
THE CHAPLAIN: It is. And with whom have we the honour …?
YVETTE: With the Countess Starhemberg, my good man
   Where's Courage?
THE CHAPLAIN: (*Calls into the cart.*) The Countess Starhem-
180   berg wishes to speak to you.
MOTHER COURAGE'S VOICE: Just coming.
YVETTE: It's Yvette.
MOTHER COURAGE'S VOICE: Oh, Yvette!

YVETTE: Come to see how you are. (*Sees the* COOK *turn round
   aghast.*) Pieter!   185
THE COOK: Yvette!
YVETTE: Well I never! How d'you come to be here?
THE COOK: Got a lift.
THE CHAPLAIN: You know each other then? Intimately?
YVETTE: I should think so. (*She looks the* COOK *over.*) Fat.   190
THE COOK: Not all that skinny yourself.
YVETTE: All the same I'm glad to see you, you shit. Gives me
   a chance to say what I think of you.
THE CHAPLAIN: You say it, in full; but don't start till Courage
   is out here.   195
MOTHER COURAGE: (*Coming out with all kinds of goods.*)
   Yvette! (*They embrace.*) But what are you in mourning for?
YVETTE: Suits me, don't it? My husband the colonel died a
   few years back.
MOTHER COURAGE: That old fellow what nearly bought the cart? 200
YVETTE: His elder brother.
MOTHER COURAGE: Then you're sitting pretty. Nice to find
   somebody what's made it in this war.
YVETTE: Up and down and up again, that's the way it went.
MOTHER COURAGE: I'm not hearing a word against colonels,   205
   they make a mint of money.
THE CHAPLAIN: I would put my boots back on if I were you.
   (*To* YVETTE.) You promised you would say what you think
   of the gentleman.
THE COOK: Don't kick up a stink here, Yvette.   210
MOTHER COURAGE: Yvette, this is a friend of mine.
YVETTE: That's old Puffing Piet.
THE COOK: Let's drop the nicknames. I'm called Lamb.
MOTHER COURAGE: (*Laughs.*) Puffing Piet! Him as made all the
   women crazy! Here, I been looking after your pipe for you. 215
THE CHAPLAIN: Smoking it, too.
YVETTE: What luck I can warn you against him. Worst of the
   lot, he was, rampaging along the whole Flanders coastline.
   Got more girls in trouble than he has fingers.
THE COOK: That's all a long while ago. 'Tain't true anyhow.   220
YVETTE: Stand up when a lady brings you into the conversa-
   tion! How I loved this man! All the time he had a little
   dark girl with bandy legs, got her in trouble too of course.
THE COOK: Got you into high society more like, far as I can see.
YVETTE: Shut your trap, you pathetic remnant! Better watch 225
   out for him, though; fellows like that are still dangerous
   even when on their last legs.
MOTHER COURAGE: (*To* YVETTE.) Come along, got to get rid
   of my stuff afore prices start dropping. You might be able
   to put a word in for me at regiment, with your connec-   230
   tions. (*Calls into the cart.*) Kattrin, church is off, I'm going
   to market instead. When Eilif turns up, one of you give
   him a drink. (*Exit with* YVETTE.)
YVETTE: (*As she leaves.*) Fancy a creature like that ever making me leave the straight and narrow path. Thank my   235
   lucky stars I managed to reach the top all the same. But
   I've cooked your goose, Puffing Piet, and that's something
   that'll be credited to me one day in the world to come.
THE CHAPLAIN: I would like to take as a text for our little talk
   'The mills of God grind slowly'. Weren't you complain-   240
   ing about my jokes?
THE COOK: Dead out of luck, I am. It's like this, you see: I
   thought I might get a hot meal. Here am I starving, and

now they'll be talking about me and she'll get quite a
245 wrong picture. I think I'll clear out before she's back.
THE CHAPLAIN: I think so too.
THE COOK: Padre, I'm fed up already with this bloody peace.
  Human race has to go through fire and sword cause it's
  sinful from the cradle up. I wish I could be roasting a fat
250 capon once again for the general, wherever he's got to, in
  mustard sauce with a carrot or two.
THE CHAPLAIN: Red cabbage. Red cabbage for a capon.
THE COOK: You're right, but carrots was what he had to have.
THE CHAPLAIN: No sense of what's fitting.
255 THE COOK: Not that it stopped you guzzling your share.
THE CHAPLAIN: With misgivings.
THE COOK: Anyway you must admit those were the days.
THE CHAPLAIN: I might admit it if pressed.
THE COOK: Now you've called her a hyaena your days here
260 are finished. What you staring at?
THE CHAPLAIN: Eilif! (EILIF *arrives, followed by* SOLDIERS *with
  pikes. His hands are fettered. His face is chalky-white.*) What's
  wrong?
EILIF: Where's mother?
265 THE CHAPLAIN: Gone into town.
EILIF: I heard she was around. They've allowed me to come
  and see her.
THE COOK: (*To the* SOLDIERS.) What you doing with him?
A SOLDIER: Something not nice.
270 THE CHAPLAIN: What's he been up to?
THE SOLDIER: Broke into a peasant's place. The wife's dead.
THE CHAPLAIN: How could you do a thing like that?
EILIF: It's what I did last time, ain't it?
THE COOK: Aye, but it's peace now.
275 EILIF: Shut up. All right if I sit down till she comes?
THE SOLDIER: We've no time.
THE CHAPLAIN: In wartime they recommended him for that,
  sat him at the general's right hand. Dashing, it was, in those
  days. Any chance of a word with the provost-marshal?
280 THE SOLDIER: Wouldn't do no good. Taking some peasant's
  cattle, what's dashing about that?
THE COOK: Dumb, I call it.
EILIF: If I'd been dumb you'd of starved, clever bugger.
THE COOK: But as you were clever you're going to be shot.
285 THE CHAPLAIN: We'd better fetch Kattrin out anyhow.
EILIF: Sooner have a glass of schnapps, could do with that.
THE SOLDIER: No time, come along.
THE CHAPLAIN: And what shall we tell your mother?
EILIF: Tell her it wasn't any different, tell her it was the same
290 thing. Or tell her nowt. (*The* SOLDIERS *propel him away.*)
THE CHAPLAIN: I'll accompany you on your grievous journey.
EILIF: Don't need any bloody parsons.
THE CHAPLAIN: Wait and see. (*Follows him.*)
THE COOK: (*Calls after them.*) I'll have to tell her, she'll want
295 to see him.
THE CHAPLAIN: I wouldn't tell her anything. At most that he
  was here and will come again, maybe tomorrow. By then
  I'll be back and can break it to her. (*Hurries off.*)

(*The* COOK *looks after him, shaking his head, then walks restlessly
around. Finally he comes up to the cart.*)

THE COOK: Hoy! Don't you want to come out? I can under-
300 stand you hiding away from peace. Like to do the same

myself. Remember me, I'm general's cook? I was wondering if you'd a bit of something to eat while I wait for
  your mum. I don't half feel like a bit of pork, or bread
  even, just to fill the time. (*Peers inside.*) Head under blanket. (*Sound of gunfire off.*)   305
MOTHER COURAGE: (*Runs in, out of breath and with all her goods
  still.*) Cooky, peacetime's over. War's been on again three
  days now. Heard news before selling me stuff, thank God.
  They're having a shooting match with Lutherans in town.
  We must get cart away at once. Kattrin, pack up! What   310
  you in the dumps for? What's wrong?
THE COOK: Nowt.
MOTHER COURAGE: Something is. I see it way you look.
THE COOK: Cause war's starting up again, I s'pose. Looks as if
  it'll be tomorrow night before I get next hot food inside me.   315
MOTHER COURAGE: You're lying, cooky.
THE COOK: Eilif was here. Had to leave almost at once, though.
MOTHER COURAGE: Was he now? Then we'll be seeing him
  on march. I'm joining our side this time. How's he look?
THE COOK: Same as usual.   320
MOTHER COURAGE: Oh, he'll never change. Take more than
  war to steal him from me. Clever, he is. You going to help
  me get packed? (*Begins to pack up.*) What's his news? Still
  in general's good books? Say anything about his deeds of
  valour?   325
THE COOK: (*Glumly.*) Repeated one of them, I'm told.
MOTHER COURAGE: Tell it me later, we got to move off. (KAT-
  TRIN *appears.*) Kattrin, peacetime's finished now. We're
  moving on. (*To the* COOK.) How about you?
THE COOK: Have to join up again.   330
MOTHER COURAGE: Why don't you . . . Where's padre?
THE COOK: Went into town with Eilif.
MOTHER COURAGE: Then you come along with us a way.
  Need somebody to help me.
THE COOK: That business with Yvette, you know . . .   335
MOTHER COURAGE: Done you no harm in my eyes. Oppo-
  site. Where there's smoke there's fire, they say. You com-
  ing along?
THE COOK: I won't say no.
MOTHER COURAGE: The Twelfth moved off already. Take the   340
  shaft. Here's a bit of bread. We must get round behind to
  Lutherans. Might even be seeing Eilif tonight. He's my
  favourite one. Short peace, wasn't it? Now we're off again.
  (*She sings as the* COOK *and* KATTRIN *harness themselves up.*)

  From Ulm to Metz, from Metz to Munich   345
  Courage will see the war gets fed.
  The war will show a well-filled tunic
  Given its daily shot of lead.
  But lead alone can hardly nourish
  It must have soldiers to subsist.   350
  It's you it needs to make it flourish.
  The war's still hungry. So enlist!

SCENE NINE

It is the seventeenth year of the great war of faith. Germany has lost more than half her inhabitants. Those
who survive the bloodbath are killed off by terrible
epidemics. Once fertile areas are ravaged by famine,
wolves roam the burnt-out towns. In autumn 1634 we

find Courage in the Fichtelgebirge, off the main axis of the Swedish armies. The winter this year is early and harsh. Business is bad, so that there is nothing to do but beg. The cook gets a letter from Utrecht and is sent packing.

Outside a semi-dilapidated parsonage.

Grey morning in early winter. Gusts of wind. MOTHER COURAGE *and the* COOK *in shabby sheepskins, drawing the cart.*

THE COOK: It's all dark, nobody up yet.

MOTHER COURAGE: Except it's parson's house. Have to crawl out of bed to ring bells. Then he'll have hot soup.

THE COOK: What from when whole village is burnt, we
5   seen it.

MOTHER COURAGE: It's lived in, though, dog was barking.

THE COOK: S'pose parson's got, he'll give nowt.

MOTHER COURAGE: Maybe if we sing. . . .

THE COOK: I've had enough. (*Abruptly.*) Got a letter from
10   Utrecht saying mother died of cholera and inn's mine. Here's letter if you don't believe me. No business of yours the way aunty goes on about my mode of existence, but have a look.

MOTHER COURAGE: (*Reads the letter.*) Lamb, I'm tired too of
15   always being on the go. I feel like butcher's dog, dragging meat round customers and getting nowt off it. I got nowt left to sell, and folk got nowt left to buy nowt with. Saxony a fellow in rags tried landing me a stack of old books for two eggs, Württemberg they wanted to swap their
20   plough for a titchy bag of salt. What's to plough for? Nowt growing no more, just brambles. In Pomerania villages are s'posed to have started in eating the younger kids, and nuns have been caught sticking folk up.

THE COOK: World's dying out.
25   MOTHER COURAGE: Sometimes I sees meself driving through hell with me cart selling brimstone, or across heaven with packed lunches for hungry souls. Give me my kids what's left, let's find some place they ain't shooting, and I'd like a few more years undisturbed.
30   THE COOK: You and me could get that inn going, Courage, think it over. Made up me mind in the night, I did: back to Utrecht with or without you, and starting today.

MOTHER COURAGE: Have to talk to Kattrin. That's a bit quick for me; I'm against making decisions all freezing cold and
35   nowt inside you. Kattrin! (KATTRIN *climbs out of the cart.*) Kattrin, got something to tell you. Cook and I want to go to Utrecht. He's been left an inn there. That'd be a settled place for you, let you meet a few people. Lots of 'em respect somebody mature, looks ain't everything. I'd like it
40   too. I get on with cook. Say one thing for him, got a head for business. We'd have our meals for sure, not bad, eh? And your own bed too; like that, wouldn't you? Road's no life really. God knows how you might finish up. Lousy already, you are. Have to make up our minds, see, we could move
45   with the Swedes, up north, they're somewhere up that way. (*She points to the left.*) Reckon that's fixed, Kattrin.

THE COOK: Anna, I got something private to say to you.

MOTHER COURAGE: Get back in cart, Kattrin.

(KATTRIN *climbs back.*)

THE COOK: I had to interrupt, cause you don't understand,
50   far as I can see. I didn't think there was need to say it, sticks out a mile. But if it don't, then let me tell you straight, no question of taking her along, not on your life. You get me, eh.

(KATTRIN *sticks her head out of the cart behind them and listens.*)

MOTHER COURAGE: You mean I'm to leave Kattrin back here?

THE COOK: Use your imagination. Inn's got no room. It ain't
55   one of the sort got three bar parlours. Put our backs in it we two'll get a living, but not three, no chance of that. She can keep cart.

MOTHER COURAGE: Thought she might find husband in
60   Utrecht.

THE COOK: Go on, make me laugh. Find a husband, how? Dumb and that scar on top of it. And at her age?

MOTHER COURAGE: Don't talk so loud.

THE COOK: Loud or soft, no getting over facts. And that's another reason why I can't have her in the inn. Customers
65   don't want to be looking at that all the time. Can't blame them.

MOTHER COURAGE: Shut your big mouth. I said not so loud.

THE COOK: Light's on in parson's house. We can try singing.

MOTHER COURAGE: Cooky, how's she to pull the cart on her
70   own? War scares her. She'll never stand it. The dreams she must have . . . I hear her nights groaning. Mostly after a battle. What's she seeing in those dreams, I'd like to know. She's got a soft heart. Lately I found she'd got another hedgehog tucked away what we'd run over.
75
THE COOK: Inn's too small. (*Calls out.*) Ladies and gentlemen, domestic staff and other residents! We are now going to give you a song concerning Solomon, Julius Caesar and other famous personages what had bad luck. So's you can see we're respectable folk, which makes it difficult to carry
80   on, particularly in winter. (*They sing.*)

You saw sagacious Solomon
You know what came of him.
To him complexities seemed plain.
He cursed the hour that gave birth to him
85
And saw that everything was vain.
How great and wise was Solomon!
The world however didn't wait
But soon observed what followed on.
It's wisdom that had brought him to this state—
90
How fortunate the man with none!

Yes, the virtues are dangerous stuff in this world, as this fine song proves, better not to have them and have a pleasant life and breakfast instead, hot soup for instance. Look at me: I haven't any but I'd like some. I'm a serving soldier
95   but what good did my courage do me in all them battles, nowt, here I am starving and better have been shit-scared and stayed at home. For why?

You saw courageous Caesar next
You know what he became.
100
They deified him in his life
Then had him murdered just the same.
And as they raised the fatal knife
How loud he cried: You too, my son!

105   The world however didn't wait
    But soon observed what followed on.
    It's courage that had brought him to that state.
    How fortunate the man with none!

(*Sotto voce.*) Don't even look out. (*Aloud.*) Ladies and gen-
110 tlemen, domestic staff and other inmates! All right, you
may say, gallantry never cooked a man's dinner, what
about trying honesty? You can eat all you want then, or
anyhow not stay sober. How about it?

    You heard of honest Socrates
115   The man who never lied:
    They weren't so grateful as you'd think
    Instead the rulers fixed to have him tried
    And handed him the poisoned drink.
    How honest was the people's noble son!
120   The world however didn't wait
    But soon observed what followed on.
    It's honesty that brought him to that state.
    How fortunate the man with none!

Ah yes, they say, be unselfish and share what you've got,
125 but how about if you got nowt? It's all very well to say the
dogooders have a hard time, but you still got to have
something. Aye, unselfishness is a rare virtue, cause it just
don't pay.

    Saint Martin couldn't bear to see
130   His fellows in distress.
    He met a poor man in the snow
    And shared his cloak with him, we know.
    Both of them therefore froze to death.
    His place in Heaven was surely won!
135   The world however didn't wait
    But soon observed what followed on.
    Unselfishness had brought him to that state.
    How fortunate the man with none!

That's how it is with us. We're respectable folk, stick to-
140 gether, don't steal, don't murder, don't burn places down.
And all the time you might say we're sinking lower and
lower, and it's true what the song says, and soup is few and
far between, and if we weren't like this but thieves and
murderers I dare say we'd be eating our fill. For virtues
145 aren't their own reward, only wickednesses are, that's how
the world goes and it didn't ought to.

    Here you can see respectable folk
    Keeping to God's own laws.
    So far he hasn't taken heed.
150   You who sit safe and warm indoors
    Help to relieve our bitter need!
    How virtuously we had begun!
    The world however didn't wait
    But soon observed what followed on.
155   It's fear of God that brought us to that state.
    How fortunate the man with none!

VOICE: (*From above.*) Hey, you there! Come on up! There's
hot soup if you want.
160 MOTHER COURAGE: Lamb, me stomach won't stand nowt.
'Tain't that it ain't sensible, what you say, but is that your
last word? We got on all right.

THE COOK: Last word. Think it over.
MOTHER COURAGE: I've nowt to think. I'm not leaving her here.
THE COOK: That's proper senseless, nothing I can do about it
though. I'm not a brute, just the inn's a small one. So now 165
we better get on up, or there'll be nowt here either and
wasted time singing in the cold.
MOTHER COURAGE: I'll get Kattrin.
THE COOK: Better bring a bit back for her. Scare them if they
sees three of us coming. (*Exeunt both.*) 170

(KATTRIN *climbs out of the cart with a bundle. She looks around to
see if the other two have gone. Then she takes an old pair of trousers
of the* COOK's *and a skirt of her mother's, and lays them side by side
on one of the wheels, so that they are easily seen. She has finished
and is picking up her bundle to go, when* MOTHER COURAGE *comes
back from the house.*)

MOTHER COURAGE: (*With a plate of soup.*) Kattrin! Will you
stop there? Kattrin! Where you off to with that bundle? Has
devil himself taken you over? (*She examines the bundle.*) She's
packed her things. You been listening? I told him nowt doing, Utrecht, his rotten inn, what'd we be up to there? You 175
and me, inn's no place for us. Still plenty to be got out of
war. (*She sees the trousers and the skirt.*) You're plain stupid.
S'pose I'd seen that, and you gone away? (*She holds* KATTRIN
back as she tries to break away.) Don't you start thinking it's on
your account I given him the push. It was cart, that's it. 180
Catch me leaving my cart I'm used to, it ain't you, it's for
cart. We'll go off in t'other direction, and we'll throw cook's
stuff out so he finds it, silly man. (*She climbs in and throws out
a few other articles in the direction of the trousers.*) There, he's out
of our business now, and I ain't having nobody else in, ever. 185
You and me'll carry on now. This winter will pass, same as
all the others. Get hitched up, it looks like snow.

(*They both harness themselves to the cart, then wheel it round and
drag it off. When the* COOK *arrives he looks blankly at his kit.*)

SCENE TEN

| During the whole of 1635 Mother Courage and her daughter Kattrin travel over the highroads of central Germany, in the wake of the increasingly bedraggled armies. |

High road.

MOTHER COURAGE *and* KATTRIN *are pulling the cart. They pass
a* PEASANT's *house inside which there is a voice singing.*

THE VOICE: The roses in our arbour
    Delight us with their show:
    They have such lovely flowers
    Repaying all our labour
    After the summer showers.
    Happy are those with gardens now: 5
    They have such lovely flowers.

    When winter winds are freezing
    As through the woods they blow
    Our home is warm and pleasing. 10
    We fixed the thatch above it

With straw and moss we wove it.
Happy are those with shelter now
When winter winds are freezing.

(MOTHER COURAGE *and* KATTRIN *pause to listen, then continue pulling.*)

SCENE ELEVEN

January 1636. The emperor's troops are threatening the Protestant town of Halle. The stone begins to speak. Mother Courage loses her daughter and trudges on alone. The war is a long way from being over.

The cart is standing, much the worse for wear, alongside a PEASANT's *house with a huge thatched roof, backing on a wall of rock. It is night.*

An ENSIGN *and* THREE SOLDIERS *in heavy armour step out of the wood.*

THE ENSIGN: I want no noise now. Anyone shouts, shove your pike into him.
FIRST SOLDIER: Have to knock them up, though, if we're to find a guide.
5 THE ENSIGN: Knocking sounds natural. Could be a cow bumping the stable wall.

(*The* SOLDIERS *knock on the door of the house. The* PEASANT's *wife opens it. They stop her mouth.* TWO SOLDIERS *go in.*)

MAN'S VOICE: (*Within.*) What is it?

(*The* SOLDIERS *bring out the* PEASANT *and his son* [THE YOUNG PEASANT].)

THE ENSIGN: (*Pointing at the cart, where* KATTRIN's *head has appeared.*) There's another one. (*A* SOLDIER *drags her out.*)
10   Anyone else live here beside you lot?
THE PEASANTS: This is our son. And she's dumb. Her mother's gone into town to buy stuff. For their business, cause so many people's getting out and selling things cheap. They're just passing through. Canteen folk.
15 THE ENSIGN: I'm warning you, keep quiet, or if there's the least noise you get a pike across your nut. Now I want someone to come with us and show us the path to the town. (*Points to the* YOUNG PEASANT.) Here, you.
THE YOUNG PEASANT: I don't know no path.
20 SECOND SOLDIER: (*Grinning.*) He don't know no path.
THE YOUNG PEASANT: I ain't helping Catholics.
THE ENSIGN: (*To the* SECOND SOLDIER.) Stick your pike in his ribs.
THE YOUNG PEASANT: (*Forced to his knees, with the pike threatening him.*) I won't do it, not to save my life.
25
FIRST SOLDIER: I know what'll change his mind. (*Goes towards the stable.*) Two cows and an ox. Listen, you: if you're not reasonable I'll chop up your cattle.
THE YOUNG PEASANT: No, not that!
30 THE PEASANT'S WIFE: (*Weeps.*) Please spare our cattle, captain, it'd be starving us to death.
THE ENSIGN: They're dead if he goes on being obstinate.
FIRST SOLDIER: I'm taking the ox first.

THE YOUNG PEASANT: (*To his father.*) Have I got to? (*The* WIFE *nods.*) Right.   35
THE PEASANT'S WIFE: And thank you kindly, captain, for sparing us, for ever and ever, Amen.

(*The* PEASANT *stops his* WIFE *from further expressions of gratitude.*)

FIRST SOLDIER: I knew the ox was what they minded about most, was I right?

(*Guided by the* YOUNG PEASANT, *the* ENSIGN *and his* SOLDIERS *continue on their way.*)

THE PEASANT: What are they up to, I'd like to know. Nowt good. 40
THE PEASANT'S WIFE: Perhaps they're just scouting. What you doing?
THE PEASANT: (*Putting a ladder against the roof and climbing up it.*) Seeing if they're on their own. (*From the top.*) Something moving in the wood. Can see something down by 45
the quarry. And there are men in armour in the clearing. And a gun. That's at least a regiment. God's mercy on the town and everyone in it!
THE PEASANT'S WIFE: Any lights in the town?
THE PEASANT: No. They'll all be asleep. (*Climbs down.*) If 50
those people get in they'll butcher the lot.
THE PEASANT'S WIFE: Sentries're bound to spot them first.
THE PEASANT: Sentry in the tower up the hill must have been killed, or he'd have blown his bugle.
THE PEASANT'S WIFE: If only there were more of us.   55
THE PEASANT: Just you and me and that cripple.
THE PEASANT'S WIFE: Nowt we can do, you'd say. . . .
THE PEASANT: Nowt.
THE PEASANT'S WIFE: Can't possibly run down there in the blackness.   60
THE PEASANT: Whole hillside's crawling with 'em. We could give a signal.
THE PEASANT'S WIFE: What, and have them butcher us too?
THE PEASANT: You're right, nowt we can do.
THE PEASANT'S WIFE: (*To* KATTRIN.) Pray, poor creature, pray! 65
Nowt we can do to stop bloodshed. You can't talk, maybe, but at least you can pray. He'll hear you if no one else can. I'll help you. (*All kneel,* KATTRIN *behind the two* PEASANTS.) Our Father, which art in Heaven, hear Thou our prayer, let not the town be destroyed with all what's in it sound 70
asleep and suspecting nowt. Arouse Thou them that they may get up and go to the walls and see how the enemy approacheth with picks and guns in the blackness across fields below the slope. (*Turning to* KATTRIN.) Guard Thou our mother and ensure that the watchman sleepeth not 75
but wakes up, or it will be too late. Succour our brother-in-law also, he is inside there with his four children, spare Thou them, they are innocent and know nowt. (*To* KATTRIN, *who gives a groan.*) One of them's not two yet, the eldest's seven. (KATTRIN *stands up distractedly.*) Our Father, 80
hear us, for only Thou canst help; we look to be doomed, for why, we are weak and have no pike and nowt and can risk nowt and are in Thy hand along with our cattle and all the farm, and same with the town, it too is in Thy hand and the enemy is before the walls in great strength.   85

(*Unobserved,* KATTRIN *has slipped away to the cart and taken from it something which she hides beneath her apron; then she climbs up the ladder on to the stable roof.*)

THE PEASANT'S WIFE: Forget not the children, what are in danger, the littlest ones especially, the old folk what can't move, and every living creature.

90 THE PEASANT: And forgive us our trespasses as we forgive them that trespass against us. Amen.

(*Sitting on the roof,* KATTRIN *begins to beat the drum which she has pulled out from under her apron.*)

THE PEASANT'S WIFE: Jesus Christ, what's she doing?
THE PEASANT: She's out of her mind.
THE PEASANT'S WIFE: Quick, get her down.

(*The* PEASANT *hurries to the ladder, but* KATTRIN *pulls it up on to the roof.*)

THE PEASANT'S WIFE: She'll do us in.
95 THE PEASANT: Stop drumming at once, you cripple!
THE PEASANT'S WIFE: Bringing the Catholics down on us!
THE PEASANT: (*Looking for stones to throw.*) I'll stone you.
THE PEASANT'S WIFE: Where's your feelings? Where's your heart? We're done for if they come down on us. Slit our
100 throats, they will.

(KATTRIN *stares into the distance towards the town and carries on drumming.*)

THE PEASANT'S WIFE: (*To her husband.*) I told you we shouldn't have allowed those vagabonds on to farm. What do they care if our last cows are taken?
THE ENSIGN: (*Runs in with his* SOLDIERS *and the* YOUNG PEAS-
105 ANT.) I'll cut you to ribbons, all of you!
THE PEASANT'S WIFE: Please, sir, it's not our fault, we couldn't help it. It was her sneaked up there. A foreigner.
THE ENSIGN: Where's the ladder?
THE PEASANT: There.
110 THE ENSIGN: (*Calls up.*) I order you, throw that drum down.

(KATTRIN *goes on drumming.*)

THE ENSIGN: You're all in this together. It'll be the end of you.
THE PEASANT: They been cutting pine trees in that wood. How about if we got one of the trunks and poked her off....
FIRST SOLDIER: (*To the* ENSIGN.) Permission to make a sug-
115 gestion, sir! (*He whispers something in the* ENSIGN'*s ear.*) Listen, we got a suggestion could help you. Get down off there and come into town with us right away. Show us which your mother is and we'll see she ain't harmed.

(KATTRIN *goes on drumming.*)

THE ENSIGN: (*Pushes him roughly aside.*) She doesn't trust you;
120 with a mug like yours it's not surprising. (*Calls up.*) Suppose I gave you my word? I can give my word of honour as an officer.

(KATTRIN *drums harder.*)

THE ENSIGN: Is nothing sacred to her?
THE YOUNG PEASANT: There's more than her mother involved, sir.
125 FIRST SOLDIER: This can't go on much longer. They're bound to hear in the town.
THE ENSIGN: We'll have somehow to make a noise that's louder than her drumming. What can we make a noise with?

FIRST SOLDIER: Thought we weren't s'posed to make no noise.
THE ENSIGN: A harmless one, you fool. A peaceful one.   130
THE PEASANT: I could chop wood with my axe.
THE ENSIGN: Good: you chop. (*The* PEASANT *fetches his axe and attacks a tree-trunk.*) Chop harder! Harder! You're chopping for your life.

(KATTRIN *has been listening, drumming less loudly the while. She now looks wildly round, and goes on drumming.*)

THE ENSIGN: Not loud enough. (*To the* FIRST SOLDIER.) You   135
chop too.
THE PEASANT: Only got the one axe. (*Stops chopping.*)
THE ENSIGN: We'll have to set the farm on fire. Smoke her out, that's it.
THE PEASANT: It wouldn't help, captain. If the townspeople   140
see a fire here they'll know what's up.

(KATTRIN *has again been listening as she drums. At this point she laughs.*)

THE ENSIGN: Look at her laughing at us. I'm not having that. I'll shoot her down, and damn the consequences. Fetch the harquebus.

(THREE SOLDIERS *hurry off.* KATTRIN *goes on drumming.*)

THE PEASANT'S WIFE: I got it, captain. That's their cart. If we   145
smash it up she'll stop. Cart's all they got.
THE ENSIGN: (*To the* YOUNG PEASANT.) Smash it up. (*Calls up.*) We're going to smash up your cart if you don't stop drumming. (*The* YOUNG PEASANT *gives the cart a few feeble blows.*)
THE PEASANT'S WIFE: Stop it, you animal!   150

(*Desperately looking towards the cart,* KATTRIN *emits pitiful noises. But she goes on drumming.*)

THE ENSIGN: Where are those clodhoppers with the harquebus?
FIRST SOLDIER: Can't have heard nowt in town yet, else we'd be hearing their guns.
THE ENSIGN: (*Calls up.*) They can't hear you at all. And now we're going to shoot you down. For the last time: throw   155
down that drum!
THE YOUNG PEASANT: (*Suddenly flings away his plank.*) Go on drumming! Or they'll all be killed! Go on, go on....

(*The* FIRST SOLDIER *knocks him down and beats him with his pike.* KATTRIN *starts to cry, but she goes on drumming.*)

THE PEASANT'S WIFE: Don't strike his back! For God's sake, you're beating him to death!   160

(*The* SOLDIERS *hurry in with the arquebus.*)

SECOND SOLDIER: Colonel's frothing at the mouth, sir. We're all for court-martial.
THE ENSIGN: Set it up! Set it up! (*Calls up while the gun is being erected.*) For the very last time: stop drumming! (KATTRIN, *in tears, drums as loud as she can.*) Fire! (*The* SOLDIERS *fire.* KAT-   165
TRIN *is hit, gives a few more drumbeats and then slowly crumples.*)
THE ENSIGN: That's the end of that.

(*But* KATTRIN's *last drumbeats are taken up by the town's cannon. In the distance can be heard a confused noise of tocsins and gunfire.*)

FIRST SOLDIER: She's made it.

SCENE TWELVE

Before first light. Sound of the fifes and drums of troops marching off into the distance.

In front of the cart MOTHER COURAGE *is squatting by her daughter. The peasant family are standing near her.*

THE PEASANTS: (*With hostility.*) You must go, missis. There's only one more regiment behind that one. You can't go on your own.

MOTHER COURAGE: I think she's going to sleep. (*She sings.*)

5   Lullaby baby
           What's that in the hay?
           Neighbours' kids grizzle
           But my kids are gay.
           Neighbours' are in tatters
10   And you're dressed in lawn
           Cut down from the raiment an
           Angel has worn.
           Neighbours' kids go hungry
           And you shall eat cake
15   Suppose it's too crumbly
           You've only to speak.
           Lullaby baby
           What's that in the hay?
           The one lies in Poland
20   The other—who can say?

     Better if you'd not told her nowt about your brother-in-law's kids.

THE PEASANT: If you'd not gone into town to get your cut it might never of happened.

25 MOTHER COURAGE: Now she's asleep.

THE PEASANT'S WIFE: She ain't asleep. Can't you see she's passed over?

THE PEASANT: And it's high time you got away yourself. There are wolves around and, what's worse, marauders.

MOTHER COURAGE: Aye.   30

(*She goes and gets a tarpaulin to cover the dead girl with.*)

THE PEASANT'S WIFE: Ain't you got nobody else? What you could go to?

MOTHER COURAGE: Aye, one left. Eilif.

THE PEASANT: (*As* MOTHER COURAGE *covers the dead girl.*) Best look for him, then. We'll mind her, see she gets   35 proper burial. Don't you worry about that.

MOTHER COURAGE: Here's money for expenses.

(*She counts out coins into the* PEASANT's *hands. The* PEASANT *and his* SON *shake hands with her and carry* KATTRIN *away.*)

THE PEASANT'S WIFE: (*As she leaves.*) I'd hurry.

MOTHER COURAGE: (*Harnessing herself to the cart.*) Hope I can pull cart all right by meself. Be all right, nowt much in-   40 side it. Got to get back in business again.

(*Another regiment with its fifes and drums marches past in the background.*)

MOTHER COURAGE: (*Tugging the cart.*) Take me along!

(*Singing is heard from offstage.*)

           With all its luck and all its danger
           The war is dragging on a bit
           Another hundred years or longer   45
           The common man won't benefit.
           Filthy his food, no soap to shave him
           The regiment steals half his pay.
           But still a miracle may save him:
           Tomorrow is another day!   50
               The new year's come. The watchmen shout.
               The thaw sets in. The dead remain.
               Wherever life has not died out
               It staggers to its feet again.

Samuel Beckett

Samuel Beckett (1906–1989) is the most influential European dramatist of the postwar period. Born near Dublin, Ireland, Beckett was educated at Trinity College, Dublin, where he studied modern languages. Taking his B.A. in 1928, Beckett received an appointment as *lecteur* at l'École Normale Supérieure in Paris. While in Paris, Beckett met the Irish novelist James Joyce. Beckett assisted Joyce (who was nearly blind) in a variety of ways and became a close friend. Joyce also exerted a profound influence on Beckett's writing. In 1929, Beckett contributed an essay entitled "Dante . . . Bruno . Vico . . Joyce" to a volume on Joyce's *Finnegans Wake*. Throughout the 1930s, Beckett was associated with Joyce and with a variety of avant-garde movements in Paris. He wrote a series of poems—including the prize-winning "Whoroscope"—as well as a study of Proust (1931), the volume of short stories *More Pricks than Kicks* (1934), and the novel *Murphy* (1938). Although Beckett returned briefly to Ireland on a few occasions, he had settled permanently in Paris. During World War II, Beckett served in the French Resistance. He was discovered by the Nazis and forced to flee Paris in 1942. He worked in the unoccupied zone of southern France for the remainder of the war, where he wrote the novel *Watt* (1953). After the war, Beckett received the Croix de Guerre and the Médaille de la Résistance for his services. He began to write exclusively in French, starting work on a major trilogy of novels—*Molloy* (1951), *Malone Dies* (1951), and *The Unnameable* (1953).

Beckett had experimented with drama during the 1930s and 1940s, but his first staged play, *Waiting for Godot* (first written in French, as *En attendant Godot*), produced at the tiny Théâtre de Babylone in January of 1953, impelled him in a new direction. Although Beckett continued to write fiction—including *From an Abandoned Work* (1956), *How It Is* (1964), *Imagination Dead Imagine* (1965), and *Company* (1979)—his major writing of the 1960s, 1970s, and 1980s was for the theater. His second play, *Endgame*, also written in French, was produced in 1957 and was followed by a series of challenging works for the stage: *Krapp's Last Tape* (1958), *Happy Days* (1962), *Play* (1963), *Not I* (1972), *Footfalls* (1975), *Rockaby* (1981), and *Catastrophe* (1982). For his extraordinarily diverse and influential body of work, Beckett won the Nobel Prize for Literature in 1970. Beckett also wrote several plays for radio and television, as well as a film starring Buster Keaton, *Film* (1965). Beginning in the mid-1960s, Beckett directed productions of his plays, and several productions he directed in France and in Germany now have the status of classics—something like Elia Kazan's productions of Tennessee Williams's plays, or Stanislavski's productions of Chekhov.

Beckett's impact on the contemporary theater can hardly be overestimated and can be seen in the work of Sam Shepard, Harold Pinter, and many others. *Waiting for Godot* signaled new possibilities for stage action—or inaction—and developed the implications of Chekhov's static stage in a more symbolic direction. Each of Beckett's plays explores the nature and limitations of its medium in new and challenging ways. *Endgame* refigures the claustral box of realistic drama, for its characters are trapped in a room of endless—or possibly ending—routine. In *Play,* Beckett puts three urns onstage, from which three heads emerge to deliver, more or less simultaneously, a jarring, repetitive monologue of seduction and betrayal. Once the play has finished, Beckett directs his performers—and his audience—to "Repeat play," and so calls the relationship between actors and spectators, theater and reality into question: If we cannot leave the theater when the play is over, is it possible that there is no way out of the purgatory on the stage and in the auditorium? This sense that the self is always in flight is the theme of several of Beckett's later plays. In *Not I,* for instance, all that the audience sees is a Mouth eight feet above the stage, reciting an endless narrative in which she avoids claiming the speech as her own. In *Ohio Impromptu* (1981), an identical reader and listener relate a painful narrative of loss, in which it is unclear whether they are two individuals or parts of a single person. The power of Beckett's spare, minimalist theater, the beauty of his sculptural use of actors and stage space, and the harsh exigency of the action of his plays have transformed the stage of our time.

ENDGAME

Endgame is Beckett's second full-length play to reach the stage; although its simplicity and repetitiveness are in some ways reminiscent of *Waiting for Godot,* the tone of *Endgame* is bleaker, harsher. As Beckett wrote to Alan Schneider, the play's first American director, *Endgame*'s power is "the power of the text to claw."

The "endgame" of a chess match is the final portion of the game, at which either a checkmate or a stalemate has become inevitable. In *Endgame,* Beckett literalizes the uncertainty of the endgame—will the tortuous nothingness of the characters' lives continue indefinitely, move after move, or will it somehow end? Although some critics have taken the "shelter" and the empty landscape outside as an indication that the play takes place in a bomb shelter after a nuclear bombing, *Endgame* seems to present a microcosm of postmodern life, in which the futile search for fugitive "meanings" raises the despairing feeling that our lives are meaningless, "absurd" after all. Hamm is a kind of ham actor and recalls Shakespeare's Richard III ("My kingdom for a nightman") and Prospero ("Our revels now are ended"), as well as perhaps King Lear and Hamlet in his performance. Hamm is perhaps the first **POSTMODERN** dramatic hero, less a full "character" than a *pastiche* of dramatic roles and possibilities, which exist now only in bits and pieces, recollected fragments. Hamm's blindness also recalls both Oedipus—who also struggled with his father—and Ham the son of Noah, who was blinded when he saw his father naked. Hamm continually reminds us that his performance—it's full of asides, a "last soliloquy," and many self-regarding comments on Hamm's success or failure—is an attempt to impose meaning on the process of the play's action. This recollection of the dramatic and literary tradition also points to the problematic place—or absence—of history in *Endgame.* If there is a kind of past ("Once!") in *Endgame,* it is recalled most clearly by Hamm's parents: Nagg and Nell, legless in their garbage cans, describe an earlier, more sentimental or romantic era, when couples rode tandems in the Ar-

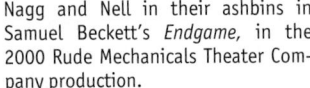
Nagg and Nell in their ashbins in Samuel Beckett's *Endgame,* in the 2000 Rude Mechanicals Theater Company production.

dennes and rowed on Lake Como. Overall, though, time seems to be an endless present moment in *Endgame,* a moment disconnected from the past that once gave it meaning, and from the future which gave it closure. It may be that the play is postnuclear (although Beckett's draft manuscripts suggest that the inspiration was really a war hospital), but this setting is less important than the sense of time that this tiny world contains. For *Endgame* is finally about time and its passing, the painfully slow passage of moment to moment, and its finality once it is past.

Endgame was originally written in French as *Fin de partie* and was rewritten into English by Beckett himself; there are several small differences in dialogue and action between the two versions.

ENDGAME

Samuel Beckett

CHARACTERS

NAGG HAMM
NELL CLOV

Bare interior.

Grey light.

Left and right back, high up, two small windows, curtains drawn.

Front right, a door. Hanging near door, its face to wall, a picture.

Front left, touching each other, covered with an old sheet, two ashbins.

Center, in an armchair on castors, covered with an old sheet, HAMM.

Motionless by the door, his eyes fixed on HAMM, CLOV. *Very red face.*

Brief tableau.

CLOV *goes and stands under window left. Stiff, staggering walk. He looks up at window left. He turns and looks at window right. He goes and stands under window right. He looks up at window right. He turns and looks at window left. He goes out, comes back immediately with a small step-ladder, carries it over and sets it down under window left, gets up on it, draws back curtain. He gets down, takes six steps (for example) towards window right, goes back for ladder, carries it over and sets it down under window right, gets up on it, draws back curtain. He gets down, takes three steps towards window left, goes back for ladder, carries it over and sets it down under window left, gets up on it, looks out of window. Brief laugh. He gets down, takes one step towards window right, goes back for ladder, carries it over and sets it down under window right, gets up on it, looks out of window. Brief laugh. He gets down, goes with ladder towards ashbins, halts, turns, carries back ladder and sets it down under window right, goes to ashbins, removes sheet covering them, folds it over his arm. He raises one lid, stoops and looks into bin. Brief laugh. He closes lid. Same with other bin. He goes to* HAMM, *removes sheet covering him, folds it over his arm. In a dressing-gown, a stiff toque on his head, a large blood-stained handkerchief over his face, a whistle hanging from his neck, a rug over his knees, thick socks on his feet,* HAMM *seems to be asleep.* CLOV *looks him over. Brief laugh. He goes to door, halts, turns towards auditorium.*

CLOV: (*Fixed gaze, tonelessly.*) Finished, it's finished, nearly finished, it must be nearly finished.

(*Pause.*)

Grain upon grain, one by one, and one day, suddenly, there's a heap, a little heap, the impossible heap.

(*Pause.*)

5 I can't be punished any more.

(*Pause.*)

I'll go now to my kitchen, ten feet by ten feet by ten feet, and wait for him to whistle me.

(*Pause.*)

Nice dimensions, nice proportions, I'll lean on the table, and look at the wall, and wait for him to whistle me.

(*He remains a moment motionless, then goes out. He comes back immediately, goes to window right, takes up the ladder and carries it out. Pause.* HAMM *stirs. He yawns under the handkerchief. He removes the handkerchief from his face. Very red face. Black glasses.*)

HAMM: Me— 10

(*He yawns.*)

—to play.

(*He holds the handkerchief spread out before him.*)

Old stancher!

(*He takes off his glasses, wipes his eyes, his face, the glasses, puts them on again, folds the handkerchief and puts it back neatly in the breast-pocket of his dressing-gown. He clears his throat, joins the tips of his fingers.*)

Can there be misery—

(*He yawns.*)

—loftier than mine? No doubt. Formerly. But now?

(*Pause.*)

My father? 15

(*Pause.*)

My mother?

(*Pause.*)

My . . . dog?

(*Pause.*)

Oh I am willing to believe they suffer as much as such creatures can suffer. But does that mean their sufferings equal mine? No doubt. 20

(*Pause.*)

No, all is a—

(*He yawns.*)

—bsolute,

(*Proudly.*)

the bigger a man is the fuller he is.

(*Pause. Gloomily.*)

And the emptier.

(*He sniffs.*)

Clov! 25

(*Pause.*)

No, alone.

(*Pause.*)

What dreams! Those forests!

(*Pause.*)

Enough, it's time it ended, in the shelter too.

(*Pause.*)

And yet I hesitate, I hesitate to . . . to end. Yes, there it is, it's time it ended and yet I hesitate to— 30

(*He yawns.*)

—to end.

(*Yawns.*)

God, I'm tired, I'd be better off in bed.

(*He whistles. Enter* CLOV *immediately. He halts beside the chair.*)

You pollute the air!
(*Pause.*)
   Get me ready, I'm going to bed.
35 CLOV: I've just got you up.
HAMM: And what of it?
CLOV: I can't be getting you up and putting you to bed every
   five minutes, I have things to do.

(*Pause.*)

HAMM: Did you ever see my eyes?
40 CLOV: No.
HAMM: Did you never have the curiosity, while I was sleep-
   ing, to take off my glasses and look at my eyes?
CLOV: Pulling back the lids?
(*Pause.*)
   No.
45 HAMM: One of these days I'll show them to you.
(*Pause.*)
   It seems they've gone all white.
(*Pause.*)
   What time is it?
CLOV: The same as usual.
HAMM: (*Gesture towards window right.*) Have you looked?
50 CLOV: Yes.
HAMM: Well?
CLOV: Zero.
HAMM: It'd need to rain.
CLOV: It won't rain.

(*Pause.*)

55 HAMM: Apart from that, how do you feel?
CLOV: I don't complain.
HAMM: You feel normal?
CLOV: (*Irritably.*) I tell you I don't complain.
HAMM: I feel a little queer.
(*Pause.*)
60   Clov!
CLOV: Yes.
HAMM: Have you not had enough?
CLOV: Yes!
(*Pause.*)
   Of what?
65 HAMM: Of this . . . this . . . thing.
CLOV: I always had.
(*Pause.*)
   Not you?
HAMM: (*Gloomily.*) Then there's no reason for it to change.
CLOV: It may end.
(*Pause.*)
70   All life long the same questions, the same answers.
HAMM: Get me ready.
(CLOV *does not move.*)
   Go and get the sheet.
(CLOV *does not move.*)
   Clov!
CLOV: Yes.
75 HAMM: I'll give you nothing more to eat.
CLOV: Then we'll die.
HAMM: I'll give you just enough to keep you from dying.
   You'll be hungry all the time.

CLOV: Then we won't die.
(*Pause.*)
   I'll go and get the sheet.   80

(*He goes towards the door.*)

HAMM: No!
(CLOV *halts.*)
   I'll give you one biscuit per day.
(*Pause.*)
   One and a half.
(*Pause.*)
   Why do you stay with me?
CLOV: Why do you keep me?   85
HAMM: There's no one else.
CLOV: There's nowhere else.

(*Pause.*)

HAMM: You're leaving me all the same.
CLOV: I'm trying.
HAMM: You don't love me.   90
CLOV: No.
HAMM: You loved me once.
CLOV: Once!
HAMM: I've made you suffer too much.
(*Pause.*)
   Haven't I?   95
CLOV: It's not that.
HAMM: (*Shocked.*) I haven't made you suffer too much?
CLOV: Yes!
HAMM: (*Relieved.*) Ah you gave me a fright!
(*Pause. Coldly.*)
   Forgive me.   100
(*Pause. Louder.*)
   I said, Forgive me.
CLOV: I heard you.
(*Pause.*)
   Have you bled?
HAMM: Less.
(*Pause.*)
   Is it not time for my pain-killer?   105
CLOV: No.

(*Pause.*)

HAMM: How are your eyes?
CLOV: Bad.
HAMM: How are your legs?
CLOV: Bad.   110
HAMM: But you can move.
CLOV: Yes.
HAMM: (*Violently.*) Then move!
(CLOV *goes to back wall, leans against it with his forehead and
hands.*)
   Where are you?
CLOV: Here.   115
HAMM: Come back!
(CLOV *returns to his place beside the chair.*)
   Where are you?
CLOV: Here.
HAMM: Why don't you kill me?

120   CLOV: I don't know the combination of the cupboard.

(*Pause.*)

HAMM: Go and get two bicycle-wheels.
CLOV: There are no more bicycle-wheels.
HAMM: What have you done with your bicycle?
CLOV: I never had a bicycle.
125   HAMM: The thing is impossible.
CLOV: When there were still bicycles I wept to have one. I
      crawled at your feet. You told me to go to hell. Now there
      are none.
HAMM: And your rounds? When you inspected my paupers.
130   Always on foot?
CLOV: Sometimes on horse.
(*The lid of one of the bins lifts and the hands of* NAGG *appear, grip-
ping the rim. Then his head emerges. Nightcap. Very white face.*
NAGG *yawns, then listens.*)
      I'll leave you, I have things to do.
HAMM: In your kitchen?
CLOV: Yes.
135   HAMM: Outside of here it's death.
(*Pause.*)
      All right, be off.
(*Exit* CLOV. *Pause.*)
      We're getting on.
NAGG: Me pap!
HAMM: Accursed progenitor!
140   NAGG: Me pap!
HAMM: The old folks at home! No decency left! Guzzle, guz-
      zle, that's all they think of.
(*He whistles. Enter* CLOV. *He halts beside the chair.*)
      Well! I thought you were leaving me.
CLOV: Oh not just yet, not just yet.
145   NAGG: Me pap!
HAMM: Give him his pap.
CLOV: There's no more pap.
HAMM: (*To* NAGG.) Do you hear that? There's no more pap.
      You'll never get any more pap.
150   NAGG: I want me pap!
HAMM: Give him a biscuit.
(*Exit* CLOV.)
      Accursed fornicator! How are your stumps?
NAGG: Never mind me stumps.

(*Enter* CLOV *with biscuit.*)

CLOV: I'm back again, with the biscuit.

(*He gives biscuit to* NAGG *who fingers it, sniffs it.*)

155   NAGG: (*Plaintively.*) What is it?
CLOV: Spratt's medium.
NAGG: (*As before.*) It's hard! I can't!
HAMM: Bottle him!

(CLOV *pushes* NAGG *back into the bin, closes the lid.*)

CLOV: (*Returning to his place beside the chair.*) If age but knew!
160   HAMM: Sit on him!
CLOV: I can't sit.
HAMM: True. And I can't stand.
CLOV: So it is.

HAMM: Every man his speciality.
(*Pause.*)
      No phone calls?   165
(*Pause.*)
      Don't we laugh?
CLOV: (*After reflection.*) I don't feel like it.
HAMM: (*After reflection.*) Nor I.
(*Pause.*)
      Clov!
CLOV: Yes.   170
HAMM: Nature has forgotten us.
CLOV: There's no more nature.
HAMM: No more nature! You exaggerate.
CLOV: In the vicinity.
HAMM: But we breathe, we change! We lose our hair, our   175
      teeth! Our bloom! Our ideals!
CLOV: Then she hasn't forgotten us.
HAMM: But you say there is none.
CLOV: (*Sadly.*) No one that ever lived ever thought so
      crooked as we.   180
HAMM: We do what we can.
CLOV: We shouldn't.

(*Pause.*)

HAMM: You're a bit of all right, aren't you?
CLOV: A smithereen.

(*Pause.*)

HAMM: This is slow work.   185
(*Pause.*)
      Is it not time for my pain-killer?
CLOV: No.
(*Pause.*)
      I'll leave you, I have things to do.
HAMM: In your kitchen?
CLOV: Yes.   190
HAMM: What, I'd like to know.
CLOV: I look at the wall.
HAMM: The wall! And what do you see on your wall? Mene,
      mene? Naked bodies?
CLOV: I see my light dying.   195
HAMM: Your light dying! Listen to that! Well, it can die just as
      well here, *your* light. Take a look at me and then come
      back and tell me what you think of *your* light.

(*Pause.*)

CLOV: You shouldn't speak to me like that.

(*Pause.*)

HAMM: (*Coldly.*) Forgive me.   200
(*Pause. Louder.*)
      I said, Forgive me.
CLOV: I heard you.

(*The lid of* NAGG's *bin lifts. His hands appear, gripping the rim.
Then his head emerges. In his mouth the biscuit. He listens.*)

HAMM: Did your seeds come up?
CLOV: No.

205   HAMM: Did you scratch round them to see if they had sprouted?
CLOV: They haven't sprouted.
HAMM: Perhaps it's still too early.
CLOV: If they were going to sprout they would have sprouted.
(*Violently.*)
    They'll never sprout!

(*Pause.* NAGG *takes biscuit in his hand.*)

210   HAMM: This is not much fun.
(*Pause.*)
    But that's always the way at the end of the day, isn't it, Clov?
CLOV: Always.
HAMM: It's the end of the day like any other day, isn't it, Clov?
215   CLOV: Looks like it.

(*Pause.*)

HAMM: (*Anguished.*) What's happening, what's happening?
CLOV: Something is taking its course.

(*Pause.*)

HAMM: All right, be off.
(*He leans back in his chair, remains motionless.* CLOV *does not move, heaves a great groaning sigh.* HAMM *sits up.*)
    I thought I told you to be off.
220   CLOV: I'm trying.
(*He goes to door, halts.*)
    Ever since I was whelped.

(*Exit* CLOV.)

HAMM: We're getting on.

(*He leans back in his chair, remains motionless.* NAGG *knocks on the lid of the other bin. Pause. He knocks harder. The lid lifts and the hands of* NELL *appear, gripping the rim. Then her head emerges. Lace cap. Very white face.*)

NELL: What is it, my pet?
(*Pause.*)
    Time for love?
225   NAGG: Were you asleep?
NELL: Oh no!
NAGG: Kiss me.
NELL: We can't.
NAGG: Try.

(*Their heads strain towards each other, fail to meet, fall apart again.*)

230   NELL: Why this farce, day after day?

(*Pause.*)

NAGG: I've lost me tooth.
NELL: When?
NAGG: I had it yesterday.
NELL: (*Elegiac.*) Ah yesterday!

(*They turn painfully towards each other.*)

235   NAGG: Can you see me?
NELL: Hardly. And you?

NAGG: What?
NELL: Can you see me?
NAGG: Hardly.
NELL: So much the better, so much the better.   240
NAGG: Don't say that.
(*Pause.*)
    Our sight has failed.
NELL: Yes.

(*Pause. They turn away from each other.*)

NAGG: Can you hear me?
NELL: Yes. And you?   245
NAGG: Yes.
(*Pause.*)
    Our hearing hasn't failed.
NELL: Our what?
NAGG: Our hearing.
NELL: No.   250
(*Pause.*)
    Have you anything else to say to me?
NAGG: Do you remember—
NELL: No.
NAGG: When we crashed on our tandem and lost our shanks.

(*They laugh heartily.*)

NELL: It was in the Ardennes.   255

(*They laugh less heartily.*)

NAGG: On the road to Sedan.
(*They laugh still less heartily.*)
    Are you cold?
NELL: Yes, perished. And you?
NAGG: (*Pause.*) I'm freezing.
(*Pause.*)
    Do you want to go in?   260
NELL: Yes.
NAGG: Then go in.
(NELL *does not move.*)
    Why don't you go in?
NELL: I don't know.

(*Pause.*)

NAGG: Has he changed your sawdust?   265
NELL: It isn't sawdust.
(*Pause. Wearily.*)
    Can you not be a little accurate, Nagg?
NAGG: Your sand then. It's not important.
NELL: It is important.

(*Pause.*)

NAGG: It was sawdust once.   270
NELL: Once!
NAGG: And now it's sand.
(*Pause.*)
    From the shore.
(*Pause. Impatiently.*)
    Now it's sand he fetches from the shore.
NELL: Now it's sand.   275

NAGG: Has he changed yours?

NELL: No.

NAGG: Nor mine.

(*Pause.*)

I won't have it!

(*Pause. Holding up the biscuit.*)

280   Do you want a bit?

NELL: No.

(*Pause.*)

Of what?

NAGG: Biscuit. I've kept you half.

(*He looks at the biscuit. Proudly.*)

Three quarters. For you. Here.

(*He proffers the biscuit.*)

285   No?

(*Pause.*)

Do you not feel well?

HAMM: (*Wearily.*) Quiet, quiet, you're keeping me awake.

(*Pause.*)

Talk softer.

(*Pause.*)

If I could sleep I might make love. I'd go into the woods.

290   My eyes would see . . . the sky, the earth. I'd run, run, they
wouldn't catch me.

(*Pause.*)

Nature!

(*Pause.*)

There's something dripping in my head.

(*Pause.*)

A heart, a heart in my head.

(*Pause.*)

295   NAGG: (*Soft.*) Do you hear him? A heart in his head!

(*He chuckles cautiously.*)

NELL: One mustn't laugh at those things, Nagg. Why must
you always laugh at them?

NAGG: Not so loud!

NELL: (*Without lowering her voice.*) Nothing is funnier than
300   unhappiness, I grant you that. But—

NAGG: (*Shocked.*) Oh!

NELL: Yes, yes, it's the most comical thing in the world. And
we laugh, we laugh, with a will, in the beginning. But it's
always the same thing. Yes, it's like the funny story we
305   have heard too often, we still find it funny, but we don't
laugh any more.

(*Pause.*)

Have you anything else to say to me?

NAGG: No.

NELL: Are you quite sure?

(*Pause.*)

310   Then I'll leave you.

NAGG: Do you not want your biscuit?

(*Pause.*)

I'll keep it for you.

(*Pause.*)

I thought you were going to leave me.

NELL: I am going to leave you.

315 NAGG: Could you give me a scratch before you go?

NELL: No.

(*Pause.*)

Where?

NAGG: In the back.

NELL: No.

(*Pause.*)

Rub yourself against the rim.   320

NAGG: It's lower down. In the hollow.

NELL: What hollow?

NAGG: The hollow!

(*Pause.*)

Could you not?

(*Pause.*)

Yesterday you scratched me there.   325

NELL: (*Elegiac.*) Ah yesterday!

NAGG: Could you not?

(*Pause.*)

Would you like me to scratch you?

(*Pause.*)

Are you crying again?

NELL: I was trying.   330

(*Pause.*)

HAMM: Perhaps it's a little vein.

(*Pause.*)

NAGG: What was that he said?

NELL: Perhaps it's a little vein.

NAGG: What does that mean?

(*Pause.*)

That means nothing.   335

(*Pause.*)

Will I tell you the story of the tailor?

NELL: No.

(*Pause.*)

What for?

NAGG: To cheer you up.

NELL: It's not funny.   340

NAGG: It always made you laugh.

(*Pause.*)

The first time I thought you'd die.

NELL: It was on Lake Como.

(*Pause.*)

One April afternoon.

(*Pause.*)

Can you believe it?   345

NAGG: What?

NELL: That we once went out rowing on Lake Como.

(*Pause.*)

One April afternoon.

NAGG: We had got engaged the day before.

NELL: Engaged!   350

NAGG: You were in such fits that we capsized. By rights we
should have been drowned.

NELL: It was because I felt happy.

NAGG: (*Indignant.*) It was not, it was not it was my story and
nothing else. Happy! Don't you laugh at it still? Every   355
time I tell it. Happy!

NELL: It was deep, deep. And you could see down to the bottom. So white. So clean.

NAGG: Let me tell it again.

(Raconteur's voice.)

360   An Englishman, needing a pair of striped trousers in a hurry for the New Year festivities, goes to his tailor who takes his measurements.
(Tailor's voice.)
    "That's the lot, come back in four days, I'll have it ready." Good. Four days later.
(Tailor's voice.)
365   "So sorry, come back in a week, I've made a mess of the seat." Good, that's all right, a neat seat can be very ticklish. A week later.
(Tailor's voice.)
    "Frightfully sorry, come back in ten days, I've made a hash of the crotch." Good, can't be helped, a snug crotch is al-
370   ways a teaser. Ten days later.
(Tailor's voice.)
    "Dreadfully sorry, come back in a fortnight, I've made a balls of the fly." Good, at a pinch, a smart fly is a stiff proposition.
(Pause. Normal voice.)
    I never told it worse.
(Pause. Gloomy.)
    I tell this story worse and worse.
(Pause. Raconteur's voice.)
375   Well, to make it short, the bluebells are blowing and he ballockses the buttonholes.
(Customer's voice.)
    "God damn you to hell, Sir, no, it's indecent, there are lim-its! In six days, do you hear me, six days, God made the world. Yes Sir, no less Sir, the WORLD! And you are not
380   bloody well capable of making me a pair of trousers in three months!"
(Tailor's voice, scandalized.)
    "But my dear Sir, my dear Sir, look—
(Disdainful gesture, disgustedly.)
    —at the world—
(Pause.)
    and look—
(Loving gesture, proudly.)
385   —at my TROUSERS!"

(Pause. He looks at NELL who has remained impassive, her eyes un-seeing, breaks into a high forced laugh, cuts it short, pokes his head towards NELL, launches his laugh again.)

HAMM: Silence!

(NAGG starts, cuts short his laugh.)

NELL: You could see down to the bottom.
HAMM: *(Exasperated.)* Have you not finished? Will you never finish?
(With sudden fury.)
390   Will this never finish?
(NAGG disappears into his bin, closes the lid behind him. NELL does not move. Frenziedly.)
    My kingdom for a nightman!
(He whistles. Enter CLOV.)
    Clear away this muck! Chuck it in the sea!

(CLOV goes to bins, halts.)

NELL: So white.

HAMM: What? What's she blathering about?

(CLOV stoops, takes NELL's hand, feels her pulse.)

NELL: *(To CLOV.)* Desert!   395

(CLOV lets go her hand, pushes her back in the bin, closes the lid.)

CLOV: *(Returning to his place beside the chair.)* She has no pulse.
HAMM: What was she drivelling about?
CLOV: She told me to go away, into the desert.
HAMM: Damn busybody! Is that all?
CLOV: No.   400
HAMM: What else?
CLOV: I didn't understand.
HAMM: Have you bottled her?
CLOV: Yes.
HAMM: Are they both bottled?   405
CLOV: Yes.
HAMM: Screw down the lids.
(CLOV goes towards door.)
    Time enough.
(CLOV halts.)
    My anger subsides, I'd like to pee.
CLOV: *(With alacrity.)* I'll go and get the catheter.   410

(He goes towards door.)

HAMM: Time enough.
(CLOV halts.)
    Give me my pain-killer.
CLOV: It's too soon.
(Pause.)
    It's too soon on top of your tonic, it wouldn't act.
HAMM: In the morning they brace you up and in the evening   415
    they calm you down. Unless it's the other way round.
(Pause.)
    That old doctor, he's dead naturally?
CLOV: He wasn't old.
HAMM: But he's dead?
CLOV: Naturally.   420
(Pause.)
    You ask *me* that?

(Pause.)

HAMM: Take me for a little turn.
(CLOV goes behind the chair and pushes it forward.)
    Not too fast!
(CLOV pushes chair.)
    Right round the world!
(CLOV pushes chair.)
    Hug the walls, then back to the center again.   425
(CLOV pushes chair.)
    I was right in the center, wasn't I?
CLOV: *(Pushing.)* Yes.
HAMM: We'd need a proper wheel-chair. With big wheels. Bicycle wheels!
(Pause.)
    Are you hugging?   430
CLOV: *(Pushing.)* Yes.
HAMM: *(Groping for wall.)* It's a lie! Why do you lie to me?
CLOV: *(Bearing closer to wall.)* There! There!

HAMM: Stop!

(CLOV *stops chair close to back wall.* HAMM *lays his hand against wall.*)

435   Old wall!

(*Pause.*)

    Beyond is the . . . other hell.

(*Pause. Violently.*)

    Closer! Closer! Up against!

CLOV: Take away your hand.

(HAMM *withdraws his hand.* CLOV *rams chair against wall.*)

    There!

(HAMM *leans towards wall, applies his ear to it.*)

440 HAMM: Do you hear?

(*He strikes the wall with his knuckles.*)

    Do you hear? Hollow bricks!

(*He strikes again.*)

    All that's hollow!

(*Pause. He straightens up. Violently.*)

    That's enough. Back!

CLOV: We haven't done the round.

445 HAMM: Back to my place!

(CLOV *pushes chair back to center.*)

    Is that my place?

CLOV: Yes, that's your place.

HAMM: Am I right in the center?

CLOV: I'll measure it.

450 HAMM: More or less! More or less!

CLOV: (*Moving chair slightly.*) There!

HAMM: I'm more or less in the center?

CLOV: I'd say so.

HAMM: You'd say so! Put me right in the center!

455 CLOV: I'll go and get the tape.

HAMM: Roughly! Roughly!

(CLOV *moves chair slightly.*)

    Bang in the center!

CLOV: There!

(*Pause.*)

HAMM: I feel a little too far to the left.

(CLOV *moves chair slightly.*)

460   Now I feel a little too far to the right.

(CLOV *moves chair slightly.*)

    I feel a little too far forward.

(CLOV *moves chair slightly.*)

    Now I feel a little too far back.

(CLOV *moves chair slightly.*)

    Don't stay there,

(*i.e., Behind the chair.*)

    you give me the shivers.

(CLOV *returns to his place beside the chair.*)

465 CLOV: If I could kill him I'd die happy.

(*Pause.*)

HAMM: What's the weather like?

CLOV: As usual.

HAMM: Look at the earth.

CLOV: I've looked.

HAMM: With the glass?   470

CLOV: No need of the glass.

HAMM: Look at it with the glass.

CLOV: I'll go and get the glass.

(*Exit* CLOV.)

HAMM: No need of the glass!

(*Enter* CLOV *with telescope.*)

CLOV: I'm back again, with the glass.   475

(*He goes to window right, looks up at it.*)

    I need the steps.

HAMM: Why? Have you shrunk?

(*Exit* CLOV *with telescope.*)

    I don't like that, I don't like that.

(*Enter* CLOV *with ladder, but without telescope.*)

CLOV: I'm back again, with the steps.

(*He sets down ladder under window right, gets up on it, realizes he has not the telescope, gets down.*)

    I need the glass.   480

(*He goes towards door.*)

HAMM: (*Violently.*) But you have the glass!

CLOV: (*Halting, violently.*) No, I haven't the glass!

(*Exit* CLOV.)

HAMM: This is deadly.

(*Enter* CLOV *with telescope. He goes towards ladder.*)

CLOV: Things are livening up.

(*He gets up on ladder, raises the telescope, lets it fall.*)

    I did it on purpose.   485

(*He gets down, picks up the telescope, turns it on auditorium.*)

    I see . . . a multitude . . . in transports . . . of joy.

(*Pause.*)

    That's what I call a magnifier.

(*He lowers the telescope, turns towards* HAMM.)

    Well? Don't we laugh?

HAMM: (*After reflection.*) I don't.

CLOV: (*After reflection.*) Nor I.   490

(*He gets up on ladder, turns the telescope on the without.*)

    Let's see.

(*He looks, moving the telescope.*)

    Zero . . .

(*He looks.*)

    . . . zero . . .

(*He looks.*)

    . . . and zero.

HAMM: Nothing stirs. All is—   495

CLOV: Zer—

HAMM: (*Violently.*) Wait till you're spoken to!

(*Normal voice.*)

    All is . . . all is . . . all is what?

(*Violently.*)

    All is what?

CLOV: What all is? In a word? Is that what you want to know?   500

    Just a moment.

(*He turns the telescope on the without, looks, lowers the telescope, turns towards* HAMM.)

    Corpsed.

(*Pause.*)

    Well? Content?

HAMM: Look at the sea.

505 CLOV: It's the same.

HAMM: Look at the ocean!

(CLOV *gets down, takes a few steps towards window left, goes back for ladder, carries it over and sets it down under window left, gets up on it, turns the telescope on the without, looks at length. He starts, lowers the telescope, examines it, turns it again on the without.*)

CLOV: Never seen anything like that!

HAMM: (*Anxious.*) What? A sail? A fin? Smoke?

CLOV: (*Looking.*) The light is sunk.

510 HAMM: (*Relieved.*) Pah! We all knew that.

CLOV: (*Looking.*) There was a bit left.

HAMM: The base.

CLOV: (*Looking.*) Yes.

HAMM: And now?

515 CLOV: (*Looking.*) All gone.

HAMM: No gulls?

CLOV: (*Looking.*) Gulls!

HAMM: And the horizon? Nothing on the horizon?

CLOV: (*Lowering the telescope, turning towards* HAMM, *exasperated.*) What in God's name could there be on the horizon?

(*Pause.*)

520 HAMM: The waves, how are the waves?

CLOV: The waves?

(*He turns the telescope on the waves.*)

    Lead.

HAMM: And the sun?

CLOV: (*Looking.*) Zero.

525 HAMM: But it should be sinking. Look again.

CLOV: (*Looking.*) Damn the sun.

HAMM: Is it night already then?

CLOV: (*Looking.*) No.

HAMM: Then what is it?

530 CLOV: (*Looking.*) Gray.

(*Lowering the telescope, turning towards* HAMM, *louder.*)

    Gray!

(*Pause. Still louder.*)

    GRRAY!

(*Pause. He gets down, approaches* HAMM *from behind, whispers in his ear.*)

HAMM: (*Starting.*) Gray! Did I hear you say gray?

CLOV: Light black. From pole to pole.

535 HAMM: You exaggerate.

(*Pause.*)

    Don't stay there, you give me the shivers.

(CLOV *returns to his place beside the chair.*)

CLOV: Why this farce, day after day?

HAMM: Routine. One never knows.

(*Pause.*)

    Last night I saw inside my breast. There was a big sore.

CLOV: Pah! You saw your heart. 540

HAMM: No, it was living.

(*Pause. Anguished.*)

    Clov!

CLOV: Yes.

HAMM: What's happening?

CLOV: Something is taking its course. 545

(*Pause.*)

HAMM: Clov!

CLOV: (*Impatiently.*) What is it?

HAMM: We're not beginning to . . . to . . . mean something?

CLOV: Mean something! You and I, mean something!

(*Brief laugh.*)

    Ah that's a good one! 550

HAMM: I wonder.

(*Pause.*)

    Imagine if a rational being came back to earth, wouldn't he be liable to get ideas into his head if he observed us long enough.

(*Voice of rational being.*)

    Ah, good, now I see what it is, yes, now I understand what 555 they're at!

(CLOV *starts, drops the telescope and begins to scratch his belly with both hands. Normal voice.*)

    And without going so far as that, we ourselves . . .

(*With emotion.*)

    . . . we ourselves . . . at certain moments . . .

(*Vehemently.*)

    To think perhaps it won't all have been for nothing!

CLOV: (*Anguished, scratching himself.*) I have a flea! 560

HAMM: A flea! Are there still fleas?

CLOV: On me there's one.

(*Scratching.*)

    Unless it's a crablouse.

HAMM: (*Very perturbed.*) But humanity might start from there all over again! Catch him, for the love of God! 565

CLOV: I'll go and get the powder.

(*Exit* CLOV.)

HAMM: A flea! This is awful! What a day!

(*Enter* CLOV *with a sprinkling-tin.*)

CLOV: I'm back again, with the insecticide.

HAMM: Let him have it!

(CLOV *loosens the top of his trousers, pulls it forward and shakes powder into the aperture. He stoops, looks, waits, starts, frenziedly shakes more powder, stoops, looks, waits.*)

CLOV: The bastard! 570

HAMM: Did you get him?

CLOV: Looks like it.

(*He drops the tin and adjusts his trousers.*)

    Unless he's laying doggo.

HAMM: Laying! Lying you mean. Unless he's *lying* doggo.

CLOV: Ah? One says lying? One doesn't say laying? 575

HAMM: Use your head, can't you. If he was laying we'd be bitched.

CLOV: Ah.

(*Pause.*)

What about that pee?

580 HAMM: I'm having it.

CLOV: Ah that's the spirit, that's the spirit!

(*Pause.*)

HAMM: (*With ardour.*) Let's go from here, the two of us! South! You can make a raft and the currents will carry us away, far away, to other . . . mammals!

585 CLOV: God forbid!

HAMM: Alone, I'll embark alone! Get working on that raft immediately. Tomorrow I'll be gone for ever.

CLOV: (*Hastening towards door*) I'll start straight away.

HAMM: Wait!

(CLOV *halts.*)

590 Will there be sharks, do you think?

CLOV: Sharks? I don't know. If there are there will be.

(*He goes towards door.*)

HAMM: Wait!

(CLOV *halts.*)

Is it not yet time for my pain-killer?

CLOV: (*Violently.*) No!

(*He goes towards door.*)

595 HAMM: Wait!

(CLOV *halts.*)

How are your eyes?

CLOV: Bad.

HAMM: But you can see.

CLOV: All I want.

600 HAMM: How are your legs?

CLOV: Bad.

HAMM: But you can walk.

CLOV: I come . . . and go.

HAMM: In my house.

(*Pause. With prophetic relish.*)

605 One day you'll be blind, like me. You'll be sitting there, a speck in the void, in the dark, for ever, like me.

(*Pause.*)

One day you'll say to yourself, I'm tired, I'll sit down, and you'll go and sit down. Then you'll say, I'm hungry, I'll get up and get something to eat. But you won't get up. You'll

610 say, I shouldn't have sat down, but since I have I'll sit on a little longer, then I'll get up and get something to eat. But you won't get up and you won't get anything to eat.

(*Pause.*)

You'll look at the wall a while, then you'll say, I'll close my eyes, perhaps have a little sleep, after that I'll feel better,

615 and you'll close them. And when you open them again there'll be no wall any more.

(*Pause.*)

Infinite emptiness will be all around you, all the resurrected dead of all the ages wouldn't fill it, and there you'll be like a little bit of grit in the middle of the steppe.

(*Pause.*)

620 Yes, one day you'll know what it is, you'll be like me, except that you won't have anyone with you, because you

won't have had pity on anyone and because there won't be anyone left to have pity on.

(*Pause.*)

CLOV: It's not certain.

(*Pause.*)

And there's one thing you forget. 625

HAMM: Ah?

CLOV: I can't sit down.

HAMM: (*Impatiently.*) Well you'll lie down then, what the hell! Or you'll come to a standstill, simply stop and stand still, the way you are now. One day you'll say, I'm tired, I'll 630 stop. What does the attitude matter?

(*Pause.*)

CLOV: So you all want me to leave you.

HAMM: Naturally.

CLOV: Then I'll leave you.

HAMM: You can't leave us. 635

CLOV: Then I won't leave you.

(*Pause.*)

HAMM: Why don't you finish us?

(*Pause.*)

I'll tell you the combination of the cupboard if you promise to finish me.

CLOV: I couldn't finish you. 640

HAMM: Then you won't finish me.

(*Pause.*)

CLOV: I'll leave you, I have things to do.

HAMM: Do you remember when you came here?

CLOV: No. Too small, you told me.

HAMM: Do you remember your father. 645

CLOV: (*Wearily.*) Same answer.

(*Pause.*)

You've asked me these questions millions of times.

HAMM: I love the old questions.

(*With fervour.*)

Ah the old questions, the old answers, there's nothing like them! 650

(*Pause.*)

It was I was a father to you.

CLOV: Yes.

(*He looks at* HAMM *fixedly.*)

You were that to me.

HAMM: My house a home for you.

CLOV: Yes. 655

(*He looks about him.*)

This was that for me.

HAMM: (*Proudly.*) But for me,

(*Gesture towards himself.*)

no father. But for Hamm,

(*Gesture towards surroundings.*)

no home.

(*Pause.*)

CLOV: I'll leave you. 660

HAMM: Did you ever think of one thing?
CLOV: Never.
HAMM: That here we're down in a hole.
(*Pause.*)
But beyond the hills? Eh? Perhaps it's still green. Eh?
(*Pause.*)
665 Flora! Pomona!
(*Ecstatically.*)
Ceres!
(*Pause.*)
Perhaps you won't need to go very far.
CLOV: I can't go very far.
(*Pause.*)
I'll leave you.
670 HAMM: Is my dog ready?
CLOV: He lacks a leg.
HAMM: Is he silky?
CLOV: He's a kind of Pomeranian.
HAMM: Go and get him.
675 CLOV: He lacks a leg.
HAMM: Go and get him!
(*Exit* CLOV.)
We're getting on.

(*Enter* CLOV *holding by one of its three legs a black toy dog.*)

CLOV: Your dogs are here.

(*He hands the dog to* HAMM *who feels it, fondles it.*)

HAMM: He's white, isn't he?
680 CLOV: Nearly.
HAMM: What do you mean, nearly? Is he white or isn't he?
CLOV: He isn't.

(*Pause.*)

HAMM: You've forgotten the sex.
CLOV: (*Vexed.*) But he isn't finished. The sex goes on at the end.

(*Pause.*)

685 HAMM: You haven't put on his ribbon.
CLOV: (*Angrily.*) But he isn't finished, I tell you! First you finish your dog and then you put on his ribbon!

(*Pause.*)

HAMM: Can he stand?
CLOV: I don't know.
690 HAMM: Try.
(*He hands the dog to* CLOV *who places it on the ground.*)
Well?
CLOV: Wait!

(*He squats down and tries to get the dog to stand on its three legs, fails, lets it go. The dog falls on its side.*)

HAMM: (*Impatiently.*) Well?
CLOV: He's standing.
695 HAMM: (*Groping for the dog.*) Where? Where is he?

(CLOV *holds up the dog in a standing position.*)

CLOV: There.

(*He takes* HAMM's *hand and guides it towards the dog's head.*)

HAMM: (*His hand on the dog's head.*) Is he gazing at me?
CLOV: Yes.
HAMM: (*Proudly.*) As if he were asking me to take him for a walk? 700
CLOV: If you like.
HAMM: (*As before.*) Or as if he were begging me for a bone.
(*He withdraws his hand.*)
Leave him like that, standing there imploring me.

(CLOV *straightens up. The dog falls on its side.*)

CLOV: I'll leave you.
HAMM: Have you had your visions? 705
CLOV: Less.
HAMM: Is Mother Pegg's light on?
CLOV: Light! How could anyone's light be on?
HAMM: Extinguished!
CLOV: Naturally it's extinguished. If it's not on it's extin- 710 guished.
HAMM: No, I mean Mother Pegg.
CLOV: But naturally she's extinguished!
(*Pause.*)
What's the matter with you today?
HAMM: I'm taking my course. 715
(*Pause.*)
Is she buried?
CLOV: Buried! Who would have buried her?
HAMM: You.
CLOV: Me! Haven't I enough to do without burying people?
HAMM: But you'll bury me. 720
CLOV: No I won't bury you.

(*Pause.*)

HAMM: She was bonny once, like a flower of the field.
(*With reminiscent leer.*)
And a great one for the men!
CLOV: We too were bonny—once. It's a rare thing not to have been bonny—once. 725

(*Pause.*)

HAMM: Go and get the gaff.

(CLOV *goes to door, halts.*)

CLOV: Do this, do that, and I do it. I never refuse. Why?
HAMM: You're not able to.
CLOV: Soon I won't do it any more.
HAMM: You won't be able to any more. 730
(*Exit* CLOV.)
Ah the creatures, the creatures, everything has to be explained to them.

(*Enter* CLOV *with gaff.*)

CLOV: Here's your gaff. Stick it up.

(*He gives the gaff to* HAMM *who, wielding it like a puntpole, tries to move his chair.*)

HAMM: Did I move?

735   CLOV: No.

(HAMM *throws down the gaff.*)

HAMM: Go and get the oilcan.
CLOV: What for?
HAMM: To oil the castors.
CLOV: I oiled them yesterday.
740   HAMM: Yesterday! What does that mean? Yesterday!
CLOV: (*Violently.*) That means that bloody awful day, long ago, before this bloody awful day. I use the words you taught me. If they don't mean anything any more, teach me others. Or let me be silent.

(*Pause.*)

745   HAMM: I once knew a madman who thought the end of the world had come. He was a painter—and engraver. I had a great fondness for him. I used to go and see him, in the asylum. I'd take him by the hand and drag him to the window. Look! There! All that rising corn! And there!
750   Look! The sails of the herring fleet! All that loveliness!
(*Pause.*)
He'd snatch away his hand and go back into his corner. Appalled. All he had seen was ashes.
(*Pause.*)
He alone had been spared.
(*Pause.*)
Forgotten.
(*Pause.*)
755   It appears the case is . . . was not so . . . so unusual.
CLOV: A madman? When was that?
HAMM: Oh way back, way back, you weren't in the land of the living.
CLOV: God be with the days!

(*Pause.* HAMM *raises his toque.*)

760   HAMM: I had a great fondness for him.
(*Pause. He puts on his toque again.*)
He was a painter—and engraver.
CLOV: There are so many terrible things.
HAMM: No, no, there are not so many now.
(*Pause.*)
Clov!
765   CLOV: Yes.
HAMM: Do you not think this has gone on long enough?
CLOV: Yes!
(*Pause.*)
What?
HAMM: This . . . this . . . thing.
770   CLOV: I've always thought so.
(*Pause.*)
You not?
HAMM: (*Gloomily.*) Then it's a day like any other day.
CLOV: As long as it lasts.
(*Pause.*)

All life long the same inanities.
HAMM: I can't leave you.   775
CLOV: I know. And you can't follow me.

(*Pause.*)

HAMM: If you leave me how shall I know?
CLOV: (*Briskly.*) Well you simply whistle me and if I don't come running it means I've left you.

(*Pause.*)

HAMM: You won't come and kiss me goodbye?   780
CLOV: Oh I shouldn't think so.

(*Pause.*)

HAMM: But you might be merely dead in your kitchen.
CLOV: The result would be the same.
HAMM: Yes, but how would I know, if you were merely dead in your kitchen?   785
CLOV: Well . . . sooner or later I'd start to stink.
HAMM: You stink already. The whole place stinks of corpses.
CLOV: The whole universe.
HAMM: (*Angrily.*) To hell with the universe.
(*Pause.*)
Think of something.   790
CLOV: What?
HAMM: An idea, have an idea.
(*Angrily.*)
A bright idea!
CLOV: Ah good.
(*He starts pacing to and fro, his eyes fixed on the ground, his hands behind his back. He halts.*)
The pains in my legs! It's unbelievable! Soon I won't be   795
able to think any more.
HAMM: You won't be able to leave me.
(CLOV *resumes his pacing.*)
What are you doing?
CLOV: Having an idea.
(*He paces.*)
Ah!   800

(*He halts.*)

HAMM: What a brain!
(*Pause.*)
Well?
CLOV: Wait!
(*He meditates. Not very convinced.*)
Yes . . .
(*Pause. More convinced.*)
Yes!   805
(*He raises his head.*)
I have it! I set the alarm.

(*Pause.*)

HAMM: This is perhaps not one of my bright days, but frankly—
CLOV: You whistle me. I don't come. The alarm rings. I'm gone. It doesn't ring. I'm dead.   810

(*Pause.*)

HAMM: Is it working?
(*Pause. Impatiently.*)
    The alarm, is it working?
CLOV: Why wouldn't it be working?
HAMM: Because it's worked too much.
815 CLOV: But it's hardly worked at all.
HAMM: (*Angrily.*) Then because it's worked too little!
CLOV: I'll go and see.
(*Exit* CLOV. *Brief ring of alarm off. Enter* CLOV *with alarm-clock. He holds it against* HAMM's *ear and releases alarm. They listen to it ringing to the end. Pause.*)
    Fit to wake the dead! Did you hear it?
HAMM: Vaguely.
820 CLOV: The end is terrific!
HAMM: I prefer the middle.
(*Pause.*)
    Is it not time for my pain-killer?
CLOV: No!
(*He goes to door, turns.*)
    I'll leave you.
825 HAMM: It's time for my story. Do you want to listen to my story.
CLOV: No.
HAMM: Ask my father if he wants to listen to my story.

(CLOV *goes to bins, raises the lid of* NAGG's, *stoops, looks into it. Pause. He straightens up.*)

CLOV: He's asleep.
830 HAMM: Wake him.

(CLOV *stoops, wakes* NAGG *with the alarm. Unintelligible words.* CLOV *straightens up.*)

CLOV: He doesn't want to listen to your story.
HAMM: I'll give him a bon-bon.

(CLOV *stoops. As before.*)

CLOV: He wants a sugar-plum.
HAMM: He'll get a sugar-plum.

(CLOV *stoops. As before.*)

835 CLOV: It's a deal.
(*He goes towards door.* NAGG's *hands appear, gripping the rim. Then the head emerges.* CLOV *reaches door, turns.*)
    Do you believe in the life to come?
HAMM: Mine was always that.
(*Exit* CLOV.)
    Got him that time!
NAGG: I'm listening.
840 HAMM: Scoundrel! Why did you engender me?
NAGG: I didn't know.
HAMM: What? What didn't you know?
NAGG: That it'd be you.
(*Pause.*)
    You'll give me a sugar-plum?
845 HAMM: After the audition.

NAGG: You swear?
HAMM: Yes.
NAGG: On what?
HAMM: My honor.

(*Pause. They laugh heartily.*)

NAGG: Two.   850
HAMM: One.
NAGG: One for me and one for—
HAMM: One! Silence!
(*Pause.*)
    Where was I?
(*Pause. Gloomily.*)
    It's finished, we're finished.   855
(*Pause.*)
    Nearly finished.
(*Pause.*)
    There'll be no more speech.
(*Pause.*)
    Something dripping in my head, ever since the fontanelles.
(*Stifled hilarity of* NAGG.)
    Splash, splash, always on the same spot.
(*Pause.*)
    Perhaps it's a little vein.   860
(*Pause.*)
    A little artery.
(*Pause. More animated.*)
    Enough of that, it's story time, where was I?
(*Pause. Narrative tone.*)
    The man came crawling towards me, on his belly. Pale, wonderfully pale and thin, he seemed on the point of—
(*Pause. Normal tone.*)
    No, I've done that bit.   865
(*Pause. Narrative tone.*)
    I calmly filled my pipe—the meerschaum, lit it with . . . let us say a vesta, drew a few puffs. Aah!
(*Pause.*)
    Well, what is it *you* want?
(*Pause.*)
    It was an extra-ordinarily bitter day, I remember, zero by the thermometer. But considering it was Christmas Eve 870 there was nothing . . . extra-ordinary about that. Seasonable weather, for once in a way.
(*Pause.*)
    Well, what ill wind blows you my way? He raised his face to me, black with mingled dirt and tears.
(*Pause. Normal tone.*)
    That should do it.   875
(*Narrative tone.*)
    No no, don't look at me, don't look at me. He dropped his eyes and mumbled something, apologies I presume.
(*Pause.*)
    I'm a busy man, you know, the final touches, before the festivities, you know what it is.
(*Pause. Forcibly.*)
    Come on now, what is the object of this invasion? 880
(*Pause.*)
    It was a glorious bright day, I remember, fifty by the heliometer, but already the sun was sinking down into the . . . down among the dead.

(*Normal tone.*)
    Nicely put, that.
(*Narrative tone.*)
885   Come on now, come on, present your petition and let me
    resume my labors.
(*Pause. Normal tone.*)
    There's English for you. Ah well . . .
(*Narrative tone.*)
    It was then he took the plunge. It's my little one, he said.
    Tsstss, a little one, that's bad. My little boy, he said, as if the
890   sex mattered. Where did he come from? He named the
    hole. A good half-day, on horse. What are you insinuat-
    ing? That the place is still inhabited? No no, not a soul, ex-
    cept himself and the child—assuming he existed. Good. I
    enquired about the situation at Kov, beyond the gulf. Not
895   a sinner. Good. And you expect me to believe you have
    left your little one back there, all alone, and alive into the
    bargain? Come now!
(*Pause.*)
    It was a howling wild day, I remember, a hundred by the
    anenometer. The wind was tearing up the dead pines and
900   sweeping them . . . away.
(*Pause. Normal tone.*)
    A bit feeble, that.
(*Narrative tone.*)
    Come on, man, speak up, what is it you want from me, I
    have to put up my holly.
(*Pause.*)
    Well to make it short it finally transpired that what he wanted
905   from me was . . . bread for his brat? Bread? But I have no bread,
    it doesn't agree with me. Good. Then perhaps a little corn?
(*Pause. Normal tone.*)
    That should do it.
(*Narrative tone.*)
    Corn, yes, I have corn, it's true, in my granaries. But use
    your head. I give you some corn, a pound, a pound and a
910   half, you bring it back to your child and you make him—
    if he's still alive—a nice pot of porridge,
(NAGG *reacts.*)
    a nice pot and a half of porridge, full of nourishment.
    Good. The colors come back into his little cheeks—per-
    haps. And then?
(*Pause.*)
915   I lost patience.
(*Violently.*)
    Use your head, can't you, use your head, you're on earth,
    there's no cure for that!
(*Pause.*)
    It was an exceedingly dry day, I remember, zero by the hy-
    grometer. Ideal weather, for my lumbago.
(*Pause. Violently.*)
920   But what in God's name do you imagine? That the earth
    will awake in spring? That the rivers and seas will run with
    fish again? That there's manna in heaven still for imbeciles
    like you?
(*Pause.*)
    Gradually I cooled down, sufficiently at least to ask him how
925   long he had taken on the way. Three whole days. Good. In
    what condition he had left the child. Deep in sleep.
(*Forcibly.*)
    But deep in what sleep, deep in what sleep already?

(*Pause.*)
    Well to make it short I finally offered to take him into my
    service. He had touched a chord. And then I imagined al-
    ready that I wasn't much longer for this world.   930
(*He laughs. Pause.*)
    Well?
(*Pause.*)
    Well? Here if you were careful you might die a nice nat-
    ural death, in peace and comfort.
(*Pause.*)
    Well?
(*Pause.*)
    In the end he asked me would I consent to take in the 935
    child as well—if he were still alive.
(*Pause.*)
    It was the moment I was waiting for.
(*Pause.*)
    Would I consent to take in the child . . .
(*Pause.*)
    I can see him still, down on his knees, his hands flat on the
    ground, glaring at me with his mad eyes, in defiance of my 940
    wishes.
(*Pause. Normal tone.*)
    I'll soon have finished with this story.
(*Pause.*)
    Unless I bring in other characters.
(*Pause.*)
    But where would I find them?
(*Pause.*)
    Where would I look for them?   945
(*Pause. He whistles. Enter* CLOV.)
    Let us pray to God.
NAGG: Me sugar-plum!
CLOV: There's a rat in the kitchen!
HAMM: A rat! Are there still rats?
CLOV: In the kitchen there's one.   950
HAMM: And you haven't exterminated him?
CLOV: Half. You disturbed us.
HAMM: He can't get away?
CLOV: No.
HAMM: You'll finish him later. Let us pray to God.   955
CLOV: Again!
NAGG: Me sugar-plum!
HAMM: God first!
(*Pause.*)
    Are you right?
CLOV: (*Resigned.*) Off we go.   960
HAMM: (*To* NAGG.) And you?
NAGG: (*Clasping his hands, closing his eyes, in a gabble.*) Our Fa-
    ther which art—
HAMM: Silence! In silence! Where are your manners?
(*Pause.*)
    Off we go.   965
(*Attitudes of prayer. Silence. Abandoning his attitude, discouraged.*)
    Well?
CLOV: (*Abandoning his attitude.*) What a hope! And you?
HAMM: Sweet damn all!
(*To* NAGG.)
    And you?
NAGG: Wait!   970
(*Pause. Abandoning his attitude.*)

Nothing doing!
HAMM: The bastard! He doesn't exist!
CLOV: Not yet.
NAGG: Me sugar-plum!
975 HAMM: There are no more sugar-plums!

(*Pause.*)

NAGG: It's natural. After all I'm your father. It's true if it hadn't been me it would have been someone else. But that's no excuse.
(*Pause.*)
Turkish Delight, for example, which no longer exists, we
980 all know that, there is nothing in the world I love more. And one day I'll ask you for some, in return for a kindness, and you'll promise it to me. One must live with the times.
(*Pause.*)
Whom did you call when you were a tiny boy, and were frightened, in the dark? Your mother? No. Me. We let you
985 cry. Then we moved you out of earshot, so that we might sleep in peace.
(*Pause.*)
I was asleep, as happy as a king, and you woke me up to have me listen to you. It wasn't indispensable, you didn't really need to have me listen to you.
(*Pause.*)
990 I hope the day will come when you'll really need to have me listen to you, and need to hear my voice, any voice.
(*Pause.*)
Yes, I hope I'll live till then, to hear you calling me like when you were a tiny boy, and were frightened, in the dark, and I was your only hope.
(*Pause.* NAGG *knocks on lid of* NELL's *bin. Pause.*)
995 Nell!
(*Pause. He knocks louder. Pause. Louder.*)
Nell!

(*Pause.* NAGG *sinks back into his bin, closes the lid behind him. Pause.*)

HAMM: Our revels now are ended.
(*He gropes for the dog.*)
The dog's gone.
CLOV: He's not a real dog, he can't go.
1000 HAMM: (*Groping.*) He's not there.
CLOV: He's lain down.
HAMM: Give him up to me.
(CLOV *picks up the dog and gives it to* HAMM. HAMM *holds it in his arms. Pause.* HAMM *throws away the dog.*)
Dirty brute!
(CLOV *begins to pick up the objects lying on the ground.*)
What are you doing?
1005 CLOV: Putting things in order.
(*He straightens up. Fervently.*)
I'm going to clear everything away!

(*He starts picking up again.*)

HAMM: Order!
CLOV: (*Straightening up.*) I love order. It's my dream. A world where all would be silent and still and each thing in its last
1010 place, under the last dust.

(*He starts picking up again.*)

HAMM: (*Exasperated.*) What in God's name do you think you are doing?
CLOV: (*Straightening up.*) I'm doing my best to create a little order.
HAMM: Drop it! 1015

(CLOV *drops the objects he has picked up.*)

CLOV: After all, there or elsewhere.

(*He goes towards door.*)

HAMM: (*Irritably.*) What's wrong with your feet?
CLOV: My feet?
HAMM: Tramp! Tramp!
CLOV: I must have put on my boots. 1020
HAMM: Your slippers were hurting you?

(*Pause.*)

CLOV: I'll leave you.
HAMM: No!
CLOV: What is there to keep me here?
HAMM: The dialogue. 1025
(*Pause.*)
I've got on with my story.
(*Pause.*)
I've got on with it well.
(*Pause. Irritably.*)
Ask me where I've got to.
CLOV: Oh, by the way, your story?
HAMM: (*Surprised.*) What story? 1030
CLOV: The one you've been telling yourself all your days.
HAMM: Ah you mean my chronicle?
CLOV: That's the one.

(*Pause.*)

HAMM: (*Angrily.*) Keep going, can't you, keep going!
CLOV: You've got on with it, I hope. 1035
HAMM: (*Modestly.*) Oh not very far, not very far.
(*He sighs.*)
There are days like that, one isn't inspired.
(*Pause.*)
Nothing you can do about it, just wait for it to come.
(*Pause.*)
No forcing, no forcing, it's fatal.
(*Pause.*)
I've got on with it a little all the same. 1040
(*Pause.*)
Technique, you know.
(*Pause. Irritably.*)
I say I've got on with it a little all the same.
CLOV: (*Admiringly.*) Well I never! In spite of everything you were able to get on with it!
HAMM: (*Modestly.*) Oh not very far, you know, not very far, 1045 but nevertheless, better than nothing.
CLOV: Better than nothing! Is it possible?
HAMM: I'll tell you how it goes. He comes crawling on his belly—

1050   CLOV: Who?
HAMM: What?
CLOV: Who do you mean, he?
HAMM: Who do I mean! Yet another.
CLOV: Ah him! I wasn't sure.
1055   HAMM: Crawling on his belly, whining for bread for his brat.
    He's offered a job as gardener. Before—
(CLOV *bursts out laughing.*)
    What is there so funny about that?
CLOV: A job as gardener!
HAMM: Is that what tickles you?
1060   CLOV: It must be that.
HAMM: It wouldn't be the bread?
CLOV: Or the brat.

(*Pause.*)

HAMM: The whole thing is comical, I grant you that. What
    about having a good guffaw the two of us together?
1065   CLOV: (*After reflection.*) I couldn't guffaw again today.
HAMM: (*After reflection.*) Nor I.
(*Pause.*)
    I continue then. Before accepting with gratitude he asks if
    he may have his little boy with him.
CLOV: What age?
1070   HAMM: Oh tiny.
CLOV: He would have climbed the trees.
HAMM: All the little odd jobs.
CLOV: And then he would have grown up.
HAMM: Very likely.

(*Pause.*)

1075   CLOV: Keep going, can't you, keep going!
HAMM: That's all. I stopped there.

(*Pause.*)

CLOV: Do you see how it goes on.
HAMM: More or less.
CLOV: Will it not soon be the end?
1080   HAMM: I'm afraid it will.
CLOV: Pah! You'll make up another.
HAMM: I don't know.
(*Pause.*)
    I feel rather drained.
(*Pause.*)
    The prolonged creative effort.
(*Pause.*)
1085   If I could drag myself down to the sea! I'd make a pillow
    of sand for my head and the tide would come.
CLOV: There's no more tide.

(*Pause.*)

HAMM: Go and see is she dead.

(CLOV *goes to bins, raises the lid of* NELL's, *stoops, looks into it.
Pause.*)

CLOV: Looks like it.

(*He closes the lid, straightens up.* HAMM *raises his toque. Pause. He
puts it on again.*)

HAMM: (*With his hand to his toque.*) And Nagg?   1090

(CLOV *raises lid of* NAGG's *bin, stoops, looks into it. Pause.*)

CLOV: Doesn't look like it.

(*He closes the lid, straightens up.*)

HAMM: (*Letting go his toque.*) What's he doing?

(CLOV *raises lid of* NAGG's *bin, stoops, looks into it. Pause.*)

CLOV: He's crying.

(*He closes lid, straightens up.*)

HAMM: Then he's living.
(*Pause.*)
    Did you ever have an instant of happiness?   1095
CLOV: Not to my knowledge.

(*Pause.*)

HAMM: Bring me under the window.
(CLOV *goes towards chair.*)
    I want to feel the light on my face.
(CLOV *pushes chair.*)
    Do you remember, in the beginning, when you took me
    for a turn? You used to hold the chair too high. At every   1100
    step you nearly tipped me out.
(*With senile quaver.*)
    Ah great fun, we had, the two of us, great fun.
(*Gloomily.*)
    And then we got into the way of it.
(CLOV *stops the chair under window right.*)
    There already?
(*Pause. He tilts back his head.*)
    Is it light?   1105
CLOV: It isn't dark.
HAMM: (*Angrily.*) I'm asking you is it light.
CLOV: Yes.

(*Pause.*)

HAMM: The curtain isn't closed?
CLOV: No.   1110
HAMM: What window is it?
CLOV: The earth.
HAMM: I knew it!
(*Angrily.*)
    But there's no light there! The other!
(CLOV *pushes chair towards window left.*)
    The earth!   1115
(CLOV *stops the chair under window left.* HAMM *tilts back his head.*)
    That's what I call light!
(*Pause.*)
    Feels like a ray of sunshine.
(*Pause.*)

No?
CLOV: No.
1120 HAMM: It isn't a ray of sunshine I feel on my face?
CLOV: No.

(*Pause.*)

HAMM: Am I very white?
(*Pause. Angrily.*)
   I'm asking you am I very white!
CLOV: Not more so than usual.

(*Pause.*)

1125 HAMM: Open the window.
CLOV: What for?
HAMM: I want to hear the sea.
CLOV: You wouldn't hear it.
HAMM: Even if you opened the window?
1130 CLOV: No.
HAMM: Then it's not worth while opening it?
CLOV: No.
HAMM: (*Violently.*) Then open it!
(CLOV *gets up on the ladder, opens the window. Pause.*)
   Have you opened it?
1135 CLOV: Yes.

(*Pause.*)

HAMM: You swear you've opened it?
CLOV: Yes.

(*Pause.*)

HAMM: Well . . . !
(*Pause.*)
   It must be very calm.
(*Pause. Violently.*)
1140   I'm asking you is it very calm!
CLOV: Yes.
HAMM: It's because there are no more navigators.
(*Pause.*)
   You haven't much conversation all of a sudden. Do you
not feel well?
1145 CLOV: I'm cold.
HAMM: What month are we?
(*Pause.*)
   Close the window, we're going back.
(CLOV *closes the window, gets down, pushes the chair back to its
place, remains standing behind it, head bowed.*)
   Don't stay there, you give me the shivers!
(CLOV *returns to his place beside the chair.*)
   Father!
(*Pause. Louder.*)
1150   Father!
(*Pause.*)
   Go and see did he hear me.

(CLOV *goes to* NAGG's *bin, raises the lid, stoops. Unintelligible words.*
CLOV *straightens up.*)

CLOV: Yes.
HAMM: Both times?

(CLOV *stoops. As before.*)

CLOV: Once only.
HAMM: The first time or the second? 1155

(CLOV *stoops. As before.*)

CLOV: He doesn't know.
HAMM: It must have been the second.
CLOV: We'll never know.

(*He closes lid.*)

HAMM: Is he still crying?
CLOV: No. 1160
HAMM: The dead go fast.
(*Pause.*)
   What's he doing?
CLOV: Sucking his biscuit.
HAMM: Life goes on.
(CLOV *returns to his place beside the chair.*)
   Give me a rug, I'm freezing. 1165
CLOV: There are no more rugs.

(*Pause.*)

HAMM: Kiss me.
(*Pause.*)
   Will you not kiss me?
CLOV: No.
HAMM: On the forehead. 1170
CLOV: I won't kiss you anywhere.

(*Pause.*)

HAMM: (*Holding out his hand.*) Give me your hand at least.
(*Pause.*)
   Will you not give me your hand?
CLOV: I won't touch you.

(*Pause.*)

HAMM: Give me the dog. 1175
(CLOV *looks round for the dog.*)
   No!
CLOV: Do you not want your dog?
HAMM: No.
CLOV: Then I'll leave you.
HAMM: (*Head bowed, absently.*) That's right. 1180

(CLOV *goes to door, turns.*)

CLOV: If I don't kill that rat he'll die.
HAMM: (*As before.*) That's right.
(*Exit* CLOV. *Pause.*)
   Me to play.
(*He takes out his handkerchief, unfolds it, holds it spread out before
him.*)
   We're getting on.
(*Pause.*)
   You weep, and weep, for nothing, so as not to laugh, and 1185
little by little . . . you begin to grieve.
(*He folds the handkerchief, puts it back in his pocket, raises his
head.*)
   All those I might have helped.

(*Pause.*)
Helped!
(*Pause.*)
Saved.
(*Pause.*)
1190   Saved!
(*Pause.*)
The place was crawling with them!
(*Pause. Violently.*)
Use your head, can't you, use your head, you're on earth,
there's no cure for that!
(*Pause.*)
Get out of here and love one another! Lick your neigh-
1195   bor as yourself!
(*Pause. Calmer.*)
When it wasn't bread they wanted it was crumpets.
(*Pause. Violently.*)
Out of my sight and back to your petting parties!
(*Pause.*)
All that, all that!
(*Pause.*)
Not even a real dog!
(*Calmer.*)
1200   The end is in the beginning and yet you go on.
(*Pause.*)
Perhaps I could go on with my story, end it and begin an-
other.
(*Pause.*)
Perhaps I could throw myself out on the floor.
(*He pushes himself painfully off his seat, falls back again.*)
Dig my nails into the cracks and drag myself forward with
1205   my fingers.
(*Pause.*)
It will be the end and there I'll be, wondering what can
have brought it on and wondering what can have . . .
(*He hesitates.*)
. . . why it was so long coming.
(*Pause.*)
There I'll be, in the old shelter, alone against the silence
1210   and . . .
(*He hesitates.*)
. . . the stillness. If I can hold my peace, and sit quiet, it will
be all over with sound, and motion, all over and done with.
(*Pause.*)
I'll have called my father and I'll have called my . . .
(*He hesitates.*)
. . . my son. And even twice, or three times, in case they
1215   shouldn't have heard me, the first time, or the second.
(*Pause.*)
I'll say to myself, He'll come back.
(*Pause.*)
And then?
(*Pause.*)
And then?
(*Pause.*)
He couldn't, he has gone too far.
(*Pause.*)
1220   And then?
(*Pause. Very agitated.*)
All kinds of fantasies! That I'm being watched! A rat!
Steps! Breath held and then . . .

(*He breathes out.*)
Then babble, babble, words, like the solitary child who
turns himself into children, two, three, so as to be together,
and whisper together, in the dark.   1225
(*Pause.*)
Moment upon moment, pattering down, like the millet
grains of . . .
(*He hesitates.*)
. . . that old Greek, and all life long you wait for that to
mount up to a life.
(*Pause. He opens his mouth to continue, renounces.*)
Ah let's get it over!   1230
(*He whistles. Enter* CLOV *with alarm-clock. He halts beside the
chair.*)
What? Neither gone nor dead?
CLOV: In spirit only.
HAMM: Which?
CLOV: Both.
HAMM: Gone from me you'd be dead.   1235
CLOV: And vice versa.
HAMM: Outside of here it's death!
(*Pause.*)
And the rat?
CLOV: He's got away.
HAMM: He can't go far.   1240
(*Pause. Anxious.*)
Eh?
CLOV: He doesn't need to go far.

(*Pause.*)

HAMM: Is it not time for my pain-killer?
CLOV: Yes.
HAMM: Ah! At last! Give it to me! Quick!   1245

(*Pause.*)

CLOV: There's no more pain-killer.

(*Pause.*)

HAMM: (*Appalled.*) Good . . . !
(*Pause.*)
No more pain-killer!
CLOV: No more pain-killer. You'll never get any more pain-
killer.   1250

(*Pause.*)

HAMM: But the little round box. It was full!
CLOV: Yes. But now it's empty.

(*Pause.* CLOV *starts to move about the room. He is looking for a
place to put down the alarm-clock.*)

HAMM: (*Soft.*) What'll I do?
(*Pause. In a scream.*)
What'll I do?
(CLOV *sees the picture, takes it down, stands it on the floor with its
face to the wall, hangs up the alarm-clock in its place.*)
What are you doing?   1255
CLOV: Winding up.
HAMM: Look at the earth.

CLOV: Again!

HAMM: Since it's calling to you.

1260 CLOV: Is your throat sore?

(*Pause.*)

    Would you like a lozenge?

(*Pause.*)

    No.

(*Pause.*)

    Pity.

(CLOV *goes, humming, towards window right, halts before it, looks up at it.*)

HAMM: Don't sing.

1265 CLOV: (*Turning towards* HAMM.) One hasn't the right to sing any more?

HAMM: No.

CLOV: Then how can it end?

HAMM: You want it to end?

1270 CLOV: I want to sing.

HAMM: I can't prevent you.

(*Pause.* CLOV *turns towards window right.*)

CLOV: What did I do with that steps?

(*He looks around for ladder.*)

    You didn't see that steps?

(*He sees it.*)

    Ah, about time.

(*He goes towards window left.*)

1275   Sometimes I wonder if I'm in my right mind. Then it passes over and I'm as lucid as before.

(*He gets up on ladder, looks out of window.*)

    Christ, she's under water!

(*He looks.*)

    How can that be?

(*He pokes forward his head, his hand above his eyes.*)

    It hasn't rained.

(*He wipes the pane, looks. Pause.*)

1280   Ah what a fool I am! I'm on the wrong side!

(*He gets down, takes a few steps towards window right.*)

    Under water!

(*He goes back for ladder.*)

    What a fool I am!

(*He carries ladder towards window right.*)

    Sometimes I wonder if I'm in my right senses. Then it passes off and I'm as intelligent as ever.

(*He sets down ladder under window right, gets up on it, looks out of window. He turns towards* HAMM.)

1285   Any particular sector you fancy? Or merely the whole thing?

HAMM: Whole thing.

CLOV: The general effect? Just a moment.

(*He looks out of window. Pause.*)

HAMM: Clov.

1290 CLOV: (*Absorbed.*) Mmm.

HAMM: Do you know what it is?

CLOV: (*As before.*) Mmm.

HAMM: I was never there.

(*Pause.*)

Clov!

CLOV: (*Turning towards* HAMM, *exasperated.*) What is it? 1295

HAMM: I was never there.

CLOV: Lucky for you.

(*He looks out of window.*)

HAMM: Absent, always. It all happened without me. I don't know what's happened.

(*Pause.*)

    Do you know what's happened? 1300

(*Pause.*)

    Clov!

CLOV: (*Turning towards* HAMM, *exasperated.*) Do you want me to look at this muckheap, yes or no?

HAMM: Answer me first.

CLOV: What? 1305

HAMM: Do you know what's happened?

CLOV: When? Where?

HAMM: (*Violently.*) When! What's happened? Use your head, can't you! What has happened?

CLOV: What for Christ's sake does it matter? 1310

(*He looks out of window.*)

HAMM: I don't know.

(*Pause.* CLOV *turns towards* HAMM.)

CLOV: (*Harshly.*) When old Mother Pegg asked you for oil for her lamp and you told her to get out to hell, you knew what was happening then, no?

(*Pause.*)

    You know what she died of, Mother Pegg? Of darkness. 1315

HAMM: (*Feebly.*) I hadn't any.

CLOV: (*As before.*) Yes, you had.

(*Pause.*)

HAMM: Have you the glass?

CLOV: No, it's clear enough as it is.

HAMM: Go and get it. 1320

(*Pause.* CLOV *casts up his eyes, brandishes his fists. He loses balance, clutches on to the ladder. He starts to get down, halts.*)

CLOV: There's one thing I'll never understand.

(*He gets down.*)

    Why I always obey you. Can you explain that to me?

HAMM: No. . . . Perhaps it's compassion.

(*Pause.*)

    A kind of great compassion.

(*Pause.*)

    Oh you won't find it easy, you won't find it easy. 1325

(*Pause.* CLOV *begins to move about the room in search of the telescope.*)

CLOV: I'm tired of our goings on, very tired.

(*He searches.*)

    You're not sitting on it?

(*He moves the chair, looks at the place where it stood, resumes his search.*)

HAMM: (*Anguished.*) Don't leave me there!
(*Angrily* CLOV *restores the chair to its place.*)
    Am I right in the center?
1330 CLOV: You'd need a microscope to find this—
(*He sees the telescope.*)
    Ah, about time.

(*He picks up the telescope, gets up on the ladder, turns the telescope on the without.*)

HAMM: Give me the dog.
CLOV: (*Looking.*) Quiet!
HAMM: (*Angrily.*) Give me the dog!

(CLOV *drops the telescope, clasps his hands to his head. Pause. He gets down precipitately, looks for the dog, sees it, picks it up, hastens towards* HAMM *and strikes him violently on the head with the dog.*)

1335 CLOV: There's your dog for you!

(*The dog falls to the ground. Pause.*)

HAMM: He hit me!
CLOV: You drive me mad, I'm mad!
HAMM: If you must hit me, hit me with the axe.
(*Pause.*)
    Or with the gaff, hit me with the gaff. Not with the dog.
1340   With the gaff. Or with the axe.

(CLOV *picks up the dog and gives it to* HAMM *who takes it in his arms.*)

CLOV: (*Imploringly.*) Let's stop playing!
HAMM: Never!
(*Pause.*)
    Put me in my coffin.
CLOV: There are no more coffins.
1345 HAMM: Then let it end!
(CLOV *goes towards ladder.*)
    With a bang!
(CLOV *gets up on ladder, gets down again, looks for telescope, sees it, picks it up, gets up ladder, raises telescope.*)
    Of darkness! And me? Did anyone ever have pity on me?
CLOV: (*Lowering the telescope, turning towards* HAMM.) What?
(*Pause.*)
    Is it me you're referring to?
1350 HAMM: (*Angrily.*) An aside, ape! Did you never hear an aside before?
(*Pause.*)
    I'm warming up for my last soliloquy.
CLOV: I warn you. I'm going to look at this filth since it's an order. But it's the last time.
(*He turns the telescope on the without.*)
1355   Let's see.
(*He moves the telescope.*)
    Nothing . . . nothing . . . good . . . good . . . nothing . . . goo—
(*He starts, lowers the telescope, examines it, turns it again on the without. Pause.*)
    Bad luck to it!
HAMM: More complications!
(CLOV *gets down.*)
    Not an underplot, I trust.

(CLOV *moves ladder nearer window, gets up on it, turns telescope on the without.*)

CLOV: (*Dismayed.*) Looks like a small boy! 1360
HAMM: (*Sarcastic.*) A small . . . boy!
CLOV: I'll go and see.
(*He gets down, drops the telescope, goes towards door, turns.*)
    I'll take the gaff.

(*He looks for the gaff, sees it, picks it up, hastens towards door.*)

HAMM: No!

(CLOV *halts.*)

CLOV: No? A potential procreator? 1365
HAMM: If he exists he'll die there or he'll come here. And if he doesn't . . .

(*Pause.*)

CLOV: You don't believe me? You think I'm inventing?

(*Pause.*)

HAMM: It's the end, Clov, we've come to the end. I don't need you any more. 1370

(*Pause.*)

CLOV: Lucky for you.

(*He goes towards door.*)

HAMM: Leave me the gaff.

(CLOV *gives him the gaff, goes towards door, halts, looks at alarm-clock, takes it down, looks round for a better place to put it, goes to bins, puts it on lid of* NAGG's *bin. Pause.*)

CLOV: I'll leave you.

(*He goes towards door.*)

HAMM: Before you go . . .
(CLOV *halts near door.*)
    . . . say something. 1375
CLOV: There is nothing to say.
HAMM: A few words . . . to ponder . . . in my heart.
CLOV: Your heart!
HAMM: Yes.
(*Pause. Forcibly.*)
    Yes! 1380
(*Pause.*)
    With the rest, in the end, the shadows, the murmurs, all the trouble, to end up with.
(*Pause.*)
    Clov. . . . He never spoke to me. Then, in the end, before he went, without my having asked him, he spoke to me. He said . . . 1385
CLOV: (*Despairingly.*) Ah . . . !
HAMM: Something . . . from your heart.
CLOV: My heart!
HAMM: A few words . . . from your heart.

(*Pause.*)

1390 CLOV: (*Fixed gaze, tonelessly, towards auditorium.*) They said to me, That's love, yes, yes, not a doubt, now you see how—

HAMM: Articulate!

CLOV: (*As before.*) How easy it is. They said to me, That's friendship, yes, yes, no question, you've found it. They said

1395 to me, Here's the place, stop, raise your head and look at all that beauty. That order! They said to me, Come now, you're not a brute beast, think upon these things and you'll see how all becomes clear. And simple! They said to me, What skilled attention they get, all these dying of their wounds.

1400 HAMM: Enough!

CLOV: (*As before.*) I say to myself—sometimes, Clov, you must learn to suffer better than that if you want them to weary of punishing you—one day. I say to myself—sometimes, Clov, you must be there better than that if you want them

1405 to let you go—one day. But I feel too old, and too far, to form new habits. Good, it'll never end, I'll never go.

(*Pause.*)

Then one day, suddenly, it ends, it changes, I don't understand, it dies, or it's me, I don't understand, that either. I ask the words that remain—sleeping, waking, morning,

1410 evening. They have nothing to say.

(*Pause.*)

I open the door of the cell and go. I am so bowed I only see my feet, if I open my eyes, and between my legs a little trail of black dust. I say to myself that the earth is extinguished, though I never saw it lit.

(*Pause.*)

1415 It's easy going.

(*Pause.*)

When I fall I'll weep for happiness.

(*Pause. He goes towards door.*)

HAMM: Clov!

(CLOV *halts, without turning.*)

Nothing.

(CLOV *moves on.*)

Clov!

(CLOV *halts, without turning.*)

1420 CLOV: This is what we call making an exit.

HAMM: I'm obliged to you, Clov. For your services.

CLOV: (*Turning, sharply.*) Ah pardon, it's I am obliged to you.

HAMM: It's we are obliged to each other.

(*Pause.* CLOV *goes towards door.*)

One thing more.

(CLOV *halts.*)

1425 A last favor.

(*Exit* CLOV.)

Cover me with the sheet.

(*Long pause.*)

No? Good.

(*Pause.*)

Me to play.

(*Pause. Wearily.*)

Old endgame lost of old, play and lose and have done

1430 with losing.

(*Pause. More animated.*)

Let me see.

(*Pause.*)

Ah yes!

(*He tries to move the chair, using the gaff as before. Enter* CLOV, *dressed for the road. Panama hat, tweed coat, raincoat over his arm, umbrella, bag. He halts by the door and stands there, impassive and motionless, his eyes fixed on* HAMM, *till the end.* HAMM *gives up.*)

Good.

(*Pause.*)

Discard.

(*He throws away the gaff, makes to throw away the dog, thinks better of it.*)

Take it easy. 1435

(*Pause.*)

And now?

(*Pause.*)

Raise hat.

(*He raises his toque.*)

Peace to our . . . arses.

(*Pause.*)

And put on again.

(*He puts on his toque.*)

Deuce. 1440

(*Pause. He takes off his glasses.*)

Wipe.

(*He takes out his handkerchief and, without unfolding it, wipes his glasses.*)

And put on again.

(*He puts on his glasses, puts back the handkerchief in his pocket.*)

We're coming. A few more squirms like that and I'll call.

(*Pause.*)

A little poetry.

(*Pause.*)

You prayed— 1445

(*Pause. He corrects himself.*)

You CRIED for night; it comes—

(*Pause. He corrects himself.*)

It FALLS: now cry in darkness.

(*He repeats, chanting.*)

You cried for night; it falls: now cry in darkness.

(*Pause.*)

Nicely put, that.

(*Pause.*)

And now? 1450

(*Pause.*)

Moments for nothing, now as always, time was never and time is over, reckoning closed and story ended.

(*Pause. Narrative tone.*)

If he could have his child with him. . . .

(*Pause.*)

It was the moment I was waiting for.

(*Pause.*)

You don't want to abandon him? You want him to bloom 1455 while you are withering? Be there to solace your last million last moments?

(*Pause.*)

He doesn't realize, all he knows is hunger, and cold, and death to crown it all. But you! You ought to know what the earth is like, nowadays. Oh I put him before his re- 1460 sponsibilities!

(*Pause. Normal tone.*)

Well, there we are, there I am, that's enough.

(*He raises the whistle to his lips, hesitates, drops it. Pause.*)

Yes, truly!

(*He whistles. Pause. Louder. Pause.*)

Good.

(*Pause.*)

1465   Father!

(*Pause. Louder.*)

Father!

(*Pause.*)

Good.

(*Pause.*)

We're coming.

(*Pause.*)

And to end up with?

(*Pause.*)

1470   Discard.

(*He throws away the dog. He tears the whistle from his neck.*)

With my compliments.

(*He throws whistle towards auditorium. Pause. He sniffs. Soft.*)

Clov!

(*Long pause.*)

No? Good.

(*He takes out the handkerchief.*)

Since that's the way we're playing it . . .

(*He unfolds handkerchief.*)

. . . let's play it that way . . .   1475

(*He unfolds.*)

. . . and speak no more about it . . .

(*He finishes unfolding.*)

. . . speak no more.

(*He holds handkerchief spread out before him.*)

Old stancher!

(*Pause.*)

You . . . remain.

(*Pause. He covers his face with handkerchief, lowers his arms to arm-rests, remains motionless.*)

(*Brief tableau.*)

Caryl Churchill

Caryl Churchill (b. 1938) was born in England and began her education in Canada during World War II; she returned to study at Oxford University, taking her B.A. in 1960. At Oxford, Churchill began her career as a playwright, producing several plays: *Downstairs* (1958), *Having a Wonderful Time* (1960), and *Early Death* (1962). During the 1960s, she wrote a series of brilliant radio plays. She also studied radical politics and returned to the theater in the 1970s with a series of striking political dramas: *Owners* (1972), *Objections to Sex and Violence* (1975), and *A Light Shining in Buckinghamshire* (1976). In the mid-1970s, Churchill began to work more closely with experimental theater companies, collaborating with actors and directors in the writing of her plays. Working with the feminist theater company Monstrous Regiment (the name alludes to the Calvinist preacher John Knox's 1558 diatribe against Queen Mary of England, "The First Blast of the Trumpet against the Monstrous Regiment of Women"), she wrote *Vinegar Tom* (1976), a play about witchcraft and sexual politics in seventeenth-century England. With the Joint Stock company, she investigated the politics of sexuality more extensively in *Cloud Nine* (1979), a pastiche of melodrama, Gilbert and Sullivan operetta, and modern realistic theater that uses CROSS-DRESSING and ROLE-DOUBLING to explore the relationship between colonial and sexual oppression in the nineteenth century and today. The history of gender oppression and the options for contemporary women are the subject of *Top Girls* (1982), and Churchill has continued to write challenging plays on the relationship between class, race, and gender in British social life, including *Fen* (1983), *Serious Money* (1987), and *Three More Sleepless Nights* (1995). *Mad Forest* (1990) concerns the revolution in Rumania and *Skryker* (1994) was developed from Lancashire folktales; *Blue Heart* (1997) was written after Churchill collaborated on several music-theater pieces, including *Lives of the Great Poisoners* (1993) and *Hotel* (1997). Her most recent plays have been short, nearly allegorical dramas: *Far Away* (2001) concerns the problems of political resistance and represents yet another new departure for Churchill, political allegory in the mode of magical realism; *A Number* (2003) takes on the subject of human cloning through the relationship between a father and several identical "sons."

CLOUD NINE

Onstage, the most exciting and interesting device in *Cloud Nine* is its use of CROSS-DRESSING and ROLE-DOUBLING. In the first act, for instance, Betty must be played by a man, Joshua by a white man, and Edward by a woman. By "alienating" actors from the characters they play, Churchill clearly intends to raise the questions of gender, sexual orientation, and race as ideological issues, for in each of these cases the difference between the performer and the role marks what Clive wants to see as real. Betty is played by a man because Clive—and his patriarchal society—cannot envision women's identity; women are constructed on the model of male attitudes. Joshua is played by a white man because imperial and racist culture reduces African identity to the construction of white, European attitudes. Edward is played by a woman to express the impossibility of Edward's conforming to Clive's heterosexual standards. In all three cases, the "identity" of the character is compromised or even erased, to be filled in and embodied by the attitudes that Clive and his society want them to hold. This performative dimension of the play's politics is echoed by the play's doubling of parts—each of the actors in act 1 takes a part in act 2, inviting the audience to draw comparisons between the two characters. Although other doubling patterns are possible, Churchill has suggested doubling Harry Bagley, the explorer, with Martin, the superficially liberated man; Clive, the father, with Cathy, the child; Betty with Edward; and so on. Doubling and cross-dressing are familiar conventions in the theater, but in *Cloud Nine* they have a specific dramatic purpose in developing the themes of the play. By denaturalizing the categories of gender, race, and sexuality, *Cloud*

Danny Scheie as Betty, waving to Harry Bagley in Caryl Churchill's *Cloud Nine*, produced by the Trinity Repertory Theatre.

Nine undertakes a typically postmodern inquiry into the construction of social reality, asking what meanings are created by these categories, and how they work to structure the relationship between self and society.

Author's Note

Cloud Nine was written for Joint Stock Theatre Group in 1978–1979. The company's usual work method is to set up a workshop in which the writer, director and actors research a particular subject. The writer then goes away to write the play, before returning to the company for a rehearsal and rewrite period. In the case of *Cloud Nine* the workshop lasted for three weeks, the writing period for twelve, and the rehearsal for six.

The workshop for *Cloud Nine* was about sexual politics. This meant that the starting point for our research was to talk about ourselves and share our very different attitudes and experiences. We also explored stereotypes and role reversals in games and improvisations, read books and talked to other people. Though the play's situations and characters were not developed in the workshop, it draws deeply on this material, and I wouldn't have written the same play without it.

When I came to write the play, I returned to an idea that had been touched on briefly in the workshop—the parallel between colonial and sexual oppression, which Genet calls "the colonial or feminine mentality of interiorised repression." So the first act of *Cloud Nine* takes place in Victorian Africa, where Clive, the white man, imposes his ideals on his family and the natives. Betty, Clive's wife, is played by a man because she wants to be what men want her to be, and, in the same way, Joshua, the black servant, is played by a white man because he wants to be what whites want him to be. Betty does not value herself as a woman, nor does Joshua value himself as a black. Edward, Clive's son, is played by a woman for a different reason—partly to do with the stage convention of having boys played by women (Peter Pan, radio plays, etc.) and partly with highlighting the way Clive tries to impose traditional male behaviour on him. Clive struggles throughout the act to maintain the world he wants to see—a faithful wife, a manly son. Harry's homosexuality is reviled, Ellen's is invisible. Rehearsing the play for the first time, we were initially taken by how funny the first act was and then by the painfulness of the relationships—which then became more funny than when they had seemed purely farcical.

The second act is set in London in 1979—this is where I wanted the play to end up, in the changing sexuality of our own time. Betty is middle-aged, Edward and Victoria have grown up. A hundred years have passed, but for the characters only twenty-five years. There were two reasons for this. I felt the first act would be stronger set in Victorian times, at the height of colonialism, rather than in Africa during the 1950s. And when the company talked about their childhoods and the attitudes to sex and marriage that they had been given when they were young, everyone felt that they had received very conventional, almost Victorian expectations and that they had made great changes and discoveries in their lifetimes.

The first act, like the society it shows, is male dominated and firmly structured. In the second act, more energy comes from the women and the gays. The uncertainties and changes of society, and a more feminine and less authoritarian feeling, are reflected in the looser structure of the act. Betty, Edward and Victoria all change from the rigid positions they had been left in by the first act, partly because of their encounters with Gerry and Lin.

In fact, all the characters in this act change a little for the better. If men are finding it hard to keep control in the first act, they are finding it hard to let go in the second: Martin dominates Victoria, despite his declarations of sympathy for feminism, and the bitter end of colonialism is apparent in Lin's soldier brother, who dies in Northern Ireland. Betty is now played by a woman, as she gradually becomes real to herself. Cathy is played by a man, partly as a simple reversal of Edward being played by a woman, partly because the size and presence of a man on stage seemed appropriate to the emotional force of young children, and partly, as with Edward, to show more clearly the issues involved in learning what is considered correct behaviour for a girl.

It is essential for Joshua to be played by a white, Betty (I) by a man, Edward (I) by a woman, and Cathy by a man. The soldier should be played by the actor who plays Cathy. The doubling of Mrs Saunders and Ellen is not intended to make a point so much as for sheer fun—and of course to keep the company to seven in each act. The doubling can be done in any way that seems right for any particular production. The first production went Clive-Cathy, Betty-Edward, Edward-Betty, Maud-Victoria, Mrs Saunders/Ellen-Lin, Joshua-Gerry, Harry-Martin. When we did the play again, at the Royal Court in 1980, we decided to try a different doubling: Clive-Edward, Betty-Gerry, Edward-Victoria, Maud-Lin, Mrs Saunders/Ellen-Betty, Joshua-Cathy, Harry-Martin. I've a slight preference for the first way because I like seeing Clive become Cathy, and enjoy the Edward-Betty connections. Some doublings aren't practicable, but any way of doing the doubling seems to set up some interesting resonances between the two acts.

C.C. 1983

THE TEXT

The first edition of *Cloud Nine* (Pluto/Joint Stock 1979) went to press before the end of rehearsal. Further changes were made within the first week or two of production, and these were incorporated in the Pluto/Joint Stock/Royal Court edition (1980). This edition also went to press during rehearsal, so although it may include some small changes made for that production, others don't turn up till the Pluto Plays edition (1983), which also includes a few changes from the American production, a few lines cut here or reinstated there. Other changes for the American production can be found in French's American acting edition—

the main ones are the position of Betty's monologue and some lines of the 'ghosts'. For the Fireside Bookclub and Methuen Inc. (1984) in America I did another brushing up, not very different from Pluto '83, and I have kept almost the same text for this edition. The scenes I tinker with most are the flogging scene and Edward's and Gerry's last scene—I no longer know what's the final version except by looking at the text.

There's a problem with the Maud and Ellen reappearances in Act Two. If Ellen is doubled with Betty, obviously only Maud can appear. Equally Maud–Betty would mean only Ellen could, though that seems a dull doubling. This text gives both Maud and Ellen. In the production at the Court in 1981 only Maud appeared and she has some extra lines so she can talk about sex as well as work; they can be found in Pluto (1983).

C.C. 1984

CLOUD NINE

Caryl Churchill

CHARACTERS

ACT ONE

CLIVE, *a colonial administrator*
BETTY, *his wife, played by a man*
JOSHUA, *his black servant, played by a white*
EDWARD, *his son, played by a woman*
VICTORIA, *his daughter, a dummy*
MAUD, *his mother-in-law*
ELLEN, *Edward's governess*
HARRY BAGLEY, *an explorer*
MRS SAUNDERS, *a widow*

ACT TWO

BETTY
EDWARD, *her son*

VICTORIA, *her daughter*
MARTIN, *Victoria's husband*
LIN
CATHY, *Lin's daughter, age 5, played by a man*
GERRY, *Edward's lover*

Except for CATHY, characters in Act Two are played by actors of their own sex.

Act One takes place in a British colony in Africa in Victorian times.

Act Two takes place in London in 1979. But for the characters it is twenty-five years later.

ACT ONE

SCENE I

Low bright sun. Verandah. Flagpole with union jack. The Family—
CLIVE, BETTY, EDWARD, VICTORIA, MAUD, ELLEN, JOSHUA.

ALL: (*Sing.*)

> Come gather, sons of England, come gather in your pride.
> Now meet the world united, now face it side by side;
> Ye who the earth's wide corners, from veldt to prairie, roam.
> From bush and jungle muster all who call old England "home."
> 5 Then gather round for England,
> Rally to the flag,
> From North and South and East and West
> Come one and all for England!

CLIVE: This is my family. Though far from home
10 We serve the Queen wherever we may roam
I am a father to the natives here,
And father to my family so dear.

(*He presents* BETTY. *She is played by a man.*)

> My wife is all I dreamt a wife should be,
> And everything she is she owes to me.
15 BETTY: I live for Clive. The whole aim of my life
> Is to be what he looks for in a wife.
> I am a man's creation as you see,
> And what men want is what I want to be.

(CLIVE *presents* JOSHUA. *He is played by a white.*)

CLIVE: My boy's a jewel. Really has the knack.
20 You'd hardly notice that the fellow's black.
JOSHUA: My skin is black but oh my soul is white.
I hate my tribe. My master is my light.
I only live for him. As you can see,
What white men want is what I want to be.

(CLIVE *presents* EDWARD. *He is played by a woman.*)

CLIVE: My son is young. I'm doing all I can   25
To teach him to grow up to be a man.
EDWARD: What father wants I'd dearly like to be.
I find it rather hard as you can see.

(CLIVE *presents* VICTORIA, *who is a dummy,* MAUD, *and* ELLEN.)

CLIVE: No need for any speeches by the rest.
My daughter, mother-in-law, and governess.   30
ALL: (*Sing.*)

> O'er countless numbers she, our Queen,
> Victoria reigns supreme;
> O'er Africa's sunny plains, and o'er
> Canadian frozen stream;
> The forge of war shall weld the chains of brotherhood   35
> secure;
> So to all time in ev'ry clime our Empire shall endure.
> Then gather round for England,
> Rally to the flag,
> From North and South and East and West
> Come one and all for England!   40

(*All go except* BETTY. CLIVE *comes.*)

BETTY: Clive?
CLIVE: Betty. Joshua!

(JOSHUA *comes with a drink for* CLIVE.)

BETTY: I thought you would never come. The day's so long
without you.
CLIVE: Long ride in the bush.   45
BETTY: Is anything wrong? I heard drums.
CLIVE: Nothing serious. Beauty is a damned good mare. I
must get some new boots sent from home. These ones
have never been right. I have a blister.
BETTY: My poor dear foot.   50
CLIVE: It's nothing.
BETTY: Oh but it's sore.

575

CLIVE: We are not in this country to enjoy ourselves. Must have ridden fifty miles. Spoke to three different headmen
55 who would all gladly chop off each other's heads and wear them round their waists.

BETTY: Clive!

CLIVE: Don't be squeamish, Betty, let me have my joke. And what has my little dove done today?

60 BETTY: I've read a little.

CLIVE: Good. Is it good?

BETTY: It's poetry.

CLIVE: You're so delicate and sensitive.

BETTY: And I played the piano. Shall I send for the children?

65 CLIVE: Yes, in a minute. I've a piece of news for you.

BETTY: Good news?

CLIVE: You'll certainly think it's good. A visitor.

BETTY: From home?

CLIVE: No. Well of course originally from home.

70 BETTY: Man or woman?

CLIVE: Man.

BETTY: I can't imagine.

CLIVE: Something of an explorer. Bit of a poet. Odd chap but brave as a lion. And a great admirer of yours.

75 BETTY: What do you mean? Whoever can it be?

CLIVE: With an H and a B. And does conjuring tricks for little Edward.

BETTY: That sounds like Mr Bagley.

CLIVE: Harry Bagley.

80 BETTY: He certainly doesn't admire me, Clive, what a thing to say. How could I possibly guess from that. He's hardly explored anything at all, he's just been up a river, he's done nothing at all compared to what you do. You should have said a heavy drinker and a bit of a bore.

85 CLIVE: But you like him well enough. You don't mind him coming?

BETTY: Anyone at all to break the monotony.

CLIVE: But you have your mother. You have Ellen.

BETTY: Ellen is a governess. My mother is my mother.

90 CLIVE: I hoped when she came to visit she would be company for you.

BETTY: I don't think mother is on a visit. I think she lives with us.

CLIVE: I think she does.

95 BETTY: Clive you are so good.

CLIVE: But are you bored my love?

BETTY: It's just that I miss you when you're away. We're not in this country to enjoy ourselves. If I lack society that is my form of service.

100 CLIVE: That's a brave girl. So today has been all right? No fainting? No hysteria?

BETTY: I have been very tranquil.

CLIVE: Ah what a haven of peace to come home to. The coolth, the calm, the beauty.

105 BETTY: There is one thing, Clive, if you don't mind.

CLIVE: What can I do for you, my dear?

BETTY: It's about Joshua.

CLIVE: I wouldn't leave you alone here with a quiet mind if it weren't for Joshua.

110 BETTY: Joshua doesn't like me.

CLIVE: Joshua has been my boy for eight years. He has saved my life. I have saved his life. He is devoted to me and to mine. I have said this before.

BETTY: He is rude to me. He doesn't do what I say. Speak to him.

CLIVE: Tell me what happened.   115

BETTY: He said something improper.

CLIVE: Well, what?

BETTY: I don't like to repeat it.

CLIVE: I must insist.

BETTY: I had left my book inside on the piano. I was in the   120
hammock. I asked him to fetch it.

CLIVE: And did he not fetch it?

BETTY: Yes, he did eventually.

CLIVE: And what did he say?

BETTY: Clive—   125

CLIVE: Betty,

BETTY: He said Fetch it yourself. You've got legs under that dress.

CLIVE: Joshua!

(JOSHUA comes.)

Joshua, madam says you spoke impolitely to her this afternoon.   130

JOSHUA: Sir?

CLIVE: When she asked you to pass her book from the piano.

JOSHUA: She has the book, sir.

BETTY: I have the book now, but when I told you—

CLIVE: Betty, please, let me handle this. You didn't pass it at   135
once?

JOSHUA: No sir, I made a joke first.

CLIVE: What was that?

JOSHUA: I said my legs were tired, sir. That was funny because the book was very near, it would not make my legs tired   140
to get it.

BETTY: That's not true.

JOSHUA: Did madam hear me wrong?

CLIVE: She heard something else.

JOSHUA: What was that, madam?   145

BETTY: Never mind.

CLIVE: Now Joshua, it won't do you know. Madam doesn't like that kind of joke. You must do what madam says, just do what she says and don't answer back. You know your place, Joshua. I don't have to say any more.   150

JOSHUA: No sir.

BETTY: I expect an apology.

JOSHUA: I apologise, madam.

CLIVE: There now. It won't happen again, my dear. I'm very shocked Joshua, very shocked.   155

(CLIVE winks at JOSHUA, unseen by BETTY. JOSHUA goes.)

CLIVE: I think another drink, and send for the children, and isn't that Harry riding down the hill? Wave, wave. Just in time before dark. Cuts it fine, the blighter. Always a hothead, Harry.

BETTY: Can he see us?   160

CLIVE: Stand further forward. He'll see your white dress. There, he waved back.

BETTY: Do you think so? I wonder what he saw. Sometimes sunset is so terrifying I can't bear to look.

CLIVE: It makes me proud. Elsewhere in the empire the sun   165
is rising.

BETTY: Harry looks so small on the hillside.

(ELLEN comes.)

ELLEN: Shall I bring the children?

BETTY: Shall Ellen bring the children?

170 CLIVE: Delightful.

BETTY: Yes, Ellen, make sure they're warm. The night air is deceptive. Victoria was looking pale yesterday.

CLIVE: My love.

(MAUD *comes from inside the house.*)

MAUD: Are you warm enough Betty?

175 BETTY: Perfectly.

MAUD: The night air is deceptive.

BETTY: I'm quite warm. I'm too warm.

MAUD: You're not getting a fever, I hope? She's not strong, you know, Clive. I don't know how long you'll keep her

180   in this climate.

CLIVE: I look after Her Majesty's domains. I think you can trust me to look after my wife.

(ELLEN *comes carrying* VICTORIA, *age 2.* EDWARD, *age 9, lags behind.*)

BETTY: Victoria, my pet, say good evening to papa.

(CLIVE *takes* VICTORIA *on his knee.*)

CLIVE: There's my sweet little Vicky. What have we done today?

185 BETTY: She wore Ellen's hat.

CLIVE: Did she wear Ellen's big hat like a lady? What a pretty.

BETTY: And Joshua gave her a piggy back. Tell papa. Horsy with Joshy?

ELLEN: She's tired.

190 CLIVE: Nice Joshy played horsy. What a big strong Joshy. Did you have a gallop? Did you make him stop and go? Not very chatty tonight are we?

BETTY: Edward, say good evening to papa.

CLIVE: Edward my boy. Have you done your lessons well?

195 EDWARD: Yes papa.

CLIVE: Did you go riding?

EDWARD: Yes papa.

CLIVE: What's that you're holding?

BETTY: It's Victoria's doll. What are you doing with it, Edward?

200 EDWARD: Minding her.

BETTY: Well I should give it to Ellen quickly. You don't want papa to see you with a doll.

CLIVE: No, we had you with Victoria's doll once before, Edward.

ELLEN: He's minding it for Vicky. He's not playing with it.

205 BETTY: He's not playing with it, Clive. He's minding it for Vicky.

CLIVE: Ellen minds Victoria, let Ellen mind the doll.

ELLEN: Come, give it to me.

(ELLEN *takes the doll.*)

EDWARD: Don't pull her about. Vicky's very fond of her. She

210   likes me to have her.

BETTY: He's a very good brother.

CLIVE: Yes, it's manly of you Edward, to take care of your little sister. We'll say no more about it. Tomorrow I'll take you riding with me and Harry Bagley. Would you like that?

215 EDWARD: Is he here?

CLIVE: He's just arrived. There Betty, take Victoria now. I must go and welcome Harry.

(CLIVE *tosses* VICTORIA *to* BETTY, *who gives her to* ELLEN.)

EDWARD: Can I come, papa?

BETTY: Is he warm enough?

EDWARD: Am I warm enough?   220

CLIVE: Never mind the women, Ned. Come and meet Harry.

(*They go. The women are left. There is a silence.*)

MAUD: I daresay Mr Bagley will be out all day and we'll see nothing of him.

BETTY: He plays the piano. Surely he will sometimes stay at home with us.   225

MAUD: We can't expect it. The men have their duties and we have ours.

BETTY: He won't have seen a piano for a year. He lives a very rough life.

ELLEN: Will it be exciting for you, Betty?   230

MAUD: Whatever do you mean, Ellen?

ELLEN: We don't have very much society.

BETTY: Clive is my society.

MAUD: It's time Victoria went to bed.

ELLEN: She'd like to stay up and see Mr Bagley.   235

MAUD: Mr Bagley can see her tomorrow.

(ELLEN *goes.*)

MAUD: You let that girl forget her place, Betty.

BETTY: Mother, she is governess to my son. I know what her place is. I think my friendship does her good. She is not very happy.   240

MAUD: Young women are never happy.

BETTY: Mother, what a thing to say.

MAUD: Then when they're older they look back and see that comparatively speaking they were ecstatic.

BETTY: I'm perfectly happy.   245

MAUD: You are looking very pretty tonight. You were such a success as a young girl. You have made a most fortunate marriage. I'm sure you will be an excellent hostess to Mr Bagley.

BETTY: I feel quite nervous at the thought of entertaining.   250

MAUD: I can always advise you if I'm asked.

BETTY: What a long time they're taking. I always seem to be waiting for the men.

MAUD: Betty you have to learn to be patient. I am patient. My mama was very patient.   255

(CLIVE *approaches, supporting* CAROLINE SAUNDERS.)

CLIVE: It is a pleasure. It is an honour. It is positively your duty to seek my help. I would be hurt, I would be insulted by any show of independence. Your husband would have been one of my dearest friends if he had lived. Betty, look who has come, Mrs Saunders. She has ridden here all 260 alone, amazing spirit. What will you have? Tea or something stronger? Let her lie down, she is overcome. Betty, you will know what to do.

(MRS SAUNDERS *lies down.*)

MAUD: I knew it. I heard drums. We'll be killed in our beds.

CLIVE: Now, please, calm yourself.   265

MAUD: I am perfectly calm. I am just outspoken. If it comes to being killed I shall take it as calmly as anyone.

CLIVE: There is no cause for alarm. Mrs Saunders has been alone since her husband died last year, amazing spirit. Not
270 surprisingly, the strain has told. She has come to us as her nearest neighbours.

MAUD: What happened to make her come?

CLIVE: This is not an easy country for a woman.

MAUD: Clive, I heard drums. We are not children.

275 CLIVE: Of course you heard drums. The tribes are constantly at war, if the term is not too grand to grace their squabbles. Not unnaturally Mrs Saunders would like the company of white women. The piano. Poetry.

BETTY: We are not her nearest neighbours.

280 CLIVE: We are among her nearest neighbours and I was a dear friend of her late husband. She knows that she will find a welcome here. She will not be disappointed. She will be cared for.

MAUD: Of course we will care for her.

285 BETTY: Victoria is in bed. I must go and say goodnight. Mother, please, you look after Mrs Saunders.

CLIVE: Harry will be here at once.

(BETTY goes.)

MAUD: How rash to go out after dark without a shawl.

CLIVE: Amazing spirit. Drink this.

290 MRS SAUNDERS: Where am I?

MAUD: You are quite safe.

MRS SAUNDERS: Clive? Clive? Thank God. This is very kind. How do you do? I am sorry to be a nuisance. Charmed. Have you a gun? I have a gun.

295 CLIVE: There is no need for guns I hope. We are all friends here.

MRS SAUNDERS: I think I will lie down again.

(HARRY BAGLEY and EDWARD have approached.)

MAUD: Ah, here is Mr Bagley.

EDWARD: I gave his horse some water.

CLIVE: You don't know Mrs Saunders, do you Harry? She has at
300 present collapsed, but she is recovering thanks to the good offices of my wife's mother who I think you've met before. Betty will be along in a minute. Edward will go home to school shortly. He is quite a young man since you saw him.

HARRY: I hardly knew him.

305 MAUD: What news have you for us, Mr Bagley?

CLIVE: Do you know Mrs Saunders, Harry? Amazing spirit.

EDWARD: Did you hardly know me?

HARRY: Of course I knew you. I mean you have grown.

EDWARD: What do you expect?

310 HARRY: That's quite right, people don't get smaller.

MAUD: Edward. You should be in bed.

EDWARD: No, I'm not tired, I'm not tired am I Uncle Harry?

HARRY: I don't think he's tired.

CLIVE: He is overtired. It is past his bedtime. Say goodnight.

315 EDWARD: Goodnight, sir.

CLIVE: And to your grandmother.

EDWARD: Goodnight, grandmother.

(EDWARD goes.)

MAUD: Shall I help Mrs Saunders indoors? I'm afraid she may get a chill.

CLIVE: Shall I give her an arm? 320

MAUD: How kind of you, Clive. I think I am strong enough.

(MAUD helps MRS SAUNDERS into the house.)

CLIVE: Not a word to alarm the women.

HARRY: Absolutely.

CLIVE: I did some good today I think. Kept up some alliances. There's a lot of affection there. 325

HARRY: They're affectionate people. They can be very cruel of course.

CLIVE: Well they are savages.

HARRY: Very beautiful people many of them.

CLIVE: Joshua! (To HARRY.) I think we should sleep with guns. 330

HARRY: I haven't slept in a house for six months. It seems extremely safe.

(JOSHUA comes.)

CLIVE: Joshua, you will have gathered there's a spot of bother. Rumours of this and that. You should be armed I think.

JOSHUA: There are many bad men, sir. I pray about it. Jesus 335 will protect us.

CLIVE: He will indeed and I'll also get you a weapon. Betty, come and keep Harry company. Look in the barn, Joshua, every night.

(CLIVE and JOSHUA go. BETTY comes.)

HARRY: I wondered where you were. 340

BETTY: I was singing lullabies.

HARRY: When I think of you I always think of you with Edward in your lap.

BETTY: Do you think of me sometimes then?

HARRY: You have been thought of where no white woman 345 has ever been thought of before.

BETTY: It's one way of having adventures. I suppose I will never go in person.

HARRY: That's up to you.

BETTY: Of course it's not. I have duties. 350

HARRY: Are you happy, Betty?

BETTY: Where have you been?

HARRY: Built a raft and went up the river. Stayed with some people. The king is always very good to me. They have a lot of skulls around the place but not white men's I think. 355 I made up a poem one night. If I should die in this forsaken spot, There is a loving heart without a blot, Where I will live—and so on.

BETTY: When I'm near you it's like going out into the jungle. It's like going up the river on a raft. It's like going out 360 in the dark.

HARRY: And you are safety and light and peace and home.

BETTY: But I want to be dangerous.

HARRY: Clive is my friend.

BETTY: I am your friend. 365

HARRY: I don't like dangerous women.

BETTY: Is Mrs Saunders dangerous?

HARRY: Not to me. She's a bit of an old boot.

(JOSHUA comes, unobserved.)

BETTY: Am I dangerous?

370 HARRY: You are rather.
BETTY: Please like me.
HARRY: I worship you.
BETTY: Please want me.
HARRY: I don't want to want you. Of course I want you.
375 BETTY: What are we going to do?
HARRY: I should have stayed on the river. The hell with it.

(*He goes to take her in his arms, she runs away into the house.* HARRY *stays where he is. He becomes aware of* JOSHUA.)

HARRY: Who's there?
JOSHUA: Only me sir.
HARRY: Got a gun now have you?
380 JOSHUA: Yes sir.
HARRY: Where's Clive?
JOSHUA: Going round the boundaries sir.
HARRY: Have you checked there's nobody in the barns?
JOSHUA: Yes sir.
385 HARRY: Shall we go in a barn and fuck? It's not an order.
JOSHUA: That's all right, yes.

(*They go off.*)

SCENE II

An open space some distance from the house. MRS SAUNDERS *alone, breathless. She is carrying a riding crop.* CLIVE *arrives.*

CLIVE: Why? Why?
MRS SAUNDERS: Don't fuss, Clive, it makes you sweat.
CLIVE: Why ride off now? Sweat, you would sweat if you
5   were in love with somebody as disgustingly capricious as you are. You will be shot with poisoned arrows. You will miss the picnic. Somebody will notice I came after you.
MRS SAUNDERS: I didn't want you to come after me. I wanted to be alone.
CLIVE: You will be raped by cannibals.
10 MRS SAUNDERS: I just wanted to get out of your house.
CLIVE: My God, what women put us through. Cruel, cruel. I think you are the sort of woman who would enjoy whipping somebody. I've never met one before.
MRS SAUNDERS: Can I tell you something, Clive?
15 CLIVE: Let me tell you something first. Since you came to the house I have had an erection twenty-four hours a day except for ten minutes after the time we had intercourse.
MRS SAUNDERS: I don't think that's physically possible.
CLIVE: You are causing me appalling physical suffering. Is this
20   the way to treat a benefactor?
MRS SAUNDERS: Clive, when I came to your house the other night I came because I was afraid. The cook was going to let his whole tribe in through the window.
CLIVE: I know that, my poor sweet. Amazing—
25 MRS SAUNDERS: I came to you although you are not my nearest neighbour—
CLIVE: Rather than to the old major of seventy-two.
MRS SAUNDERS: Because the last time he came to visit me I had to defend myself with a shotgun and I thought you
30   would take no for an answer.
CLIVE: But you've already answered yes.
MRS SAUNDERS: I answered yes once. Sometimes I want to say no.

CLIVE: Women, my God. Look the picnic will start, I have to
35   go to the picnic. Please Caroline—
MRS SAUNDERS: I think I will have to go back to my own house.
CLIVE: Caroline, if you were shot with poisoned arrows do you know what I'd do? I'd fuck your dead body and poison myself. Caroline, you smell amazing. You terrify me.
40   You are dark like this continent. Mysterious. Treacherous. When you rode to me through the night. When you fainted in my arms. When I came to you in your bed, when I lifted the mosquito netting, when I said let me in, let me in. Oh don't shut me out, Caroline, let me in.

(*He has been caressing her feet and legs. He disappears completely under her skirt.*)

MRS SAUNDERS: Please stop. I can't concentrate. I want to go
45   home. I wish I didn't enjoy the sensation because I don't like you, Clive. I do like living in your house where there's plenty of guns. But I don't like you at all. But I do like the sensation. Well I'll have it then. I'll have it, I'll have it—

(*Voices are heard singing The First Noël.*)

Don't stop. Don't stop.   50

(CLIVE *comes out from under her skirt.*)

CLIVE: The Christmas picnic. I came.
MRS SAUNDERS: I didn't.
CLIVE: I'm all sticky.
MRS SAUNDERS: What about me? Wait.
CLIVE: All right, are you? Come on. We mustn't be found.   55
MRS SAUNDERS: Don't go now.
CLIVE: Caroline, you are so voracious. Do let go. Tidy yourself up. There's a hair in my mouth.

(CLIVE *and* MRS SAUNDERS *go off.* BETTY *and* MAUD *come, with* JOSHUA *carrying hamper.*)

MAUD: I never would have thought a guinea fowl could taste so like a turkey.   60
BETTY: I had to explain to the cook three times.
MAUD: You did very well dear.

(JOSHUA *sits apart with gun.* EDWARD *and* HARRY *with* VICTORIA *on his shoulder, singing The First Noël.* MAUD *and* BETTY *are unpacking the hamper.* CLIVE *arrives separately.*)

MAUD: This tablecloth was one of my mama's.
BETTY: Uncle Harry playing horsy.
EDWARD: Crackers crackers.   65
BETTY: Not yet, Edward.
CLIVE: And now the moment we have all been waiting for.

(CLIVE *opens champagne. General acclaim.*)

CLIVE: Oh dear, stained my trousers, never mind.
EDWARD: Can I have some?
MAUD: Oh no Edward, not for you.   70
CLIVE: Give him half a glass.
MAUD: If your father says so.
CLIVE: All rise please. To Her Majesty Queen Victoria, God bless her, and her husband and all her dear children.

75 ALL: The Queen.
EDWARD: Crackers crackers.

(*General cracker pulling, hats.* CLIVE *and* HARRY *discuss champagne.*)

HARRY: Excellent, Clive, wherever did you get it?
CLIVE: I know a chap in French Equatorial Africa.
EDWARD: I won, I won mama.

(ELLEN *arrives.*)

80 BETTY: Give a hat to Joshua, he'd like it.

(EDWARD *takes hat to* JOSHUA. BETTY *takes a ball from the hamper and plays catch with* ELLEN. *Murmurs of surprise and congratulations from the men whenever they catch the ball.*)

EDWARD: Mama, don't play. You know you can't catch a ball.
BETTY: He's perfectly right. I can't throw either.

(BETTY *sits down.* ELLEN *has the ball.*)

EDWARD: Ellen, don't you play either. You're no good. You spoil it.

(EDWARD *takes* VICTORIA *from* HARRY *and gives her to* ELLEN. *He takes the ball and throws it to* HARRY. HARRY, CLIVE *and* EDWARD *play ball.*)

85 BETTY: Ellen come and sit with me. We'll be spectators and clap.

(EDWARD *misses the ball.*)

CLIVE: Butterfingers.
EDWARD: I'm not.
HARRY: Throw straight now.
90 EDWARD: I did, I did.
CLIVE: Keep your eye on the ball.
EDWARD: You can't throw.
CLIVE: Don't be a baby.
EDWARD: I'm not, throw a hard one, throw a hard one—
95 CLIVE: Butterfingers. What will Uncle Harry think of you?
EDWARD: It's your fault. You can't throw. I hate you.

(*He throws the ball wildly in the direction of* JOSHUA.)

CLIVE: Now you've lost the ball. He's lost the ball.
EDWARD: It's Joshua's fault. Joshua's butterfingers.
CLIVE: I don't think I want to play any more. Joshua, find the
100 ball will you?
EDWARD: Yes, please play. I'll find the ball. Please play.
CLIVE: You're so silly and you can't catch. You'll be no good at cricket.
MAUD: Why don't we play hide and seek?
105 EDWARD: Because it's a baby game.
BETTY: You've hurt Edward's feelings.
CLIVE: A boy has no business having feelings.
HARRY: Hide and seek. I'll be it. Everybody must hide. This is the base, you have to get home to base.
110 EDWARD: Hide and seek, hide and seek.
HARRY: Can we persuade the ladies to join us?
MAUD: I'm playing. I love games.

BETTY: I always get found straight away.
ELLEN: Come on, Betty, do. Vicky wants to play.
EDWARD: You won't find me ever.   115

(*They all go except* CLIVE, HARRY, JOSHUA.)

HARRY: It is safe, I suppose?
CLIVE: They won't go far. This is very much my territory and it's broad daylight. Joshua will keep an open eye.
HARRY: Well I must give them a hundred. You don't know   120
what this means to me, Clive. A chap can only go on so
long alone. I can climb mountains and go down rivers, but
what's it for? For Christmas and England and games and
women singing. This is the empire, Clive. It's not me
putting a flag in new lands. It's you. The empire is one big
family. I'm one of its black sheep, Clive. And I know you   125
think my life is rather dashing. But I want you to know I
admire you. This is the empire, Clive, and I serve it. With
all my heart.
CLIVE: I think that's about a hundred.
HARRY: Ready or not, here I come!   130

(*He goes.*)

CLIVE: Harry Bagley is a fine man, Joshua. You should be
proud to know him. He will be in history books.
JOSHUA: Sir, while we are alone.
CLIVE: Joshua of course, what is it? You always have my ear.
Any time.   135
JOSHUA: Sir, I have some information. The stable boys are not
to be trusted. They whisper. They go out at night. They
visit their people. Their people are not my people. I do
not visit my people.
CLIVE: Thank you, Joshua. They certainly look after Beauty.   140
I'll be sorry to have to replace them.
JOSHUA: They carry knives.
CLIVE: Thank you, Joshua.
JOSHUA: And, sir.
CLIVE: I appreciate this, Joshua, very much.   145
JOSHUA: Your wife.
CLIVE: Ah, yes?
JOSHUA: She also thinks Harry Bagley is a fine man.
CLIVE: Thank you, Joshua.
JOSHUA: Are you going to hide?   150
CLIVE: Yes, yes I am. Thank you. Keep your eyes open Joshua.
JOSHUA: I do, sir.

(CLIVE *goes.* JOSHUA *goes.* HARRY *and* BETTY *race back to base.*)

BETTY: I can't run, I can't run at all.
HARRY: There, I've caught you.
BETTY: Harry, what are we going to do?   155
HARRY: It's impossible, Betty.
BETTY: Shall we run away together?

(MAUD *comes.*)

MAUD: I give up. Don't catch me. I have been stung.
HARRY: Nothing serious I hope.
MAUD: I have ointment in my bag. I always carry ointment. I   160
shall just sit down and rest. I am too old for all this fun.
Hadn't you better be seeking, Harry?

(HARRY *goes.* MAUD *and* BETTY *are alone for some time. They don't speak.* HARRY *and* EDWARD *race back.*)

EDWARD: I won, I won, you didn't catch me.
HARRY: Yes I did.
165 EDWARD: Mama, who was first?
BETTY: I wasn't watching. I think it was Harry.
EDWARD: It wasn't Harry. You're no good at judging. I won, didn't I grandma?
MAUD: I expect so, since it's Christmas.
170 EDWARD: I won, Uncle Harry. I'm better than you.
BETTY: Why don't you help Uncle Harry look for the others?
EDWARD: Shall I?
HARRY: Yes, of course.
BETTY: Run along then. He's just coming.

(EDWARD *goes.*)

175   Harry, I shall scream.
HARRY: Ready or not, here I come.

(HARRY *runs off.*)

BETTY: Why don't you go back to the house, mother, and rest your insect-bite?
MAUD: Betty, my duty is here. I don't like what I see. Clive
180   wouldn't like it, Betty. I am your mother.
BETTY: Clive gives you a home because you are my mother.

(HARRY *comes back.*)

HARRY: I can't find anyone else. I'm getting quite hot.
BETTY: Sit down a minute.
HARRY: I can't do that. I'm he. How's your sting?
185 MAUD: It seems to be swelling up.
BETTY: Why don't you go home and rest? Joshua will go with you. Joshua!
HARRY: I could take you back.
MAUD: That would be charming.
190 BETTY: You can't go. You're he.

(JOSHUA *comes.*)

   Joshua, my mother wants to go back to the house. Will you go with her please.
JOSHUA: Sir told me I have to keep an eye.
BETTY: I am telling you to go back to the house. Then you
195   can come back here and keep an eye.
MAUD: Thank you Betty. I know we have our little differences, but I always want what is best for you.

(JOSHUA *and* MAUD *go.*)

HARRY: Don't give way. Keep calm.
BETTY: I shall kill myself.
200 HARRY: Betty, you are a star in my sky. Without you I would have no sense of direction. I need you, and I need you where you are, I need you to be Clive's wife. I need to go up rivers and know you are sitting here thinking of me.
BETTY: I want more than that. Is that wicked of me?
205 HARRY: Not wicked, Betty. Silly.

(EDWARD *calls in the distance.*)

EDWARD: Uncle Harry, where are you?
BETTY: Can't we ever be alone?
HARRY: You are a mother. And a daughter. And a wife.
BETTY: I think I shall go and hide again.

(BETTY *goes.* HARRY *goes.* CLIVE *chases* MRS SAUNDERS *across the stage.* EDWARD *and* HARRY *call in the distance.*)

EDWARD: Uncle Harry!   210
HARRY: Edward!

(EDWARD *comes.*)

EDWARD: Uncle Harry!

(HARRY *comes.*)

   There you are. I haven't found anyone have you?
HARRY: I wonder where they all are.
EDWARD: Perhaps they're lost forever. Perhaps they're dead. 215
   There's trouble going on isn't there, and nobody says because of not frightening the women and children.
HARRY: Yes, that's right.
EDWARD: Do you think we'll be killed in our beds?
HARRY: Not very likely.   220
EDWARD: I can't sleep at night. Can you?
HARRY: I'm not used to sleeping in a house.
EDWARD: If I'm awake at night can I come and see you? I won't wake you up. I'll only come in if you're awake.
HARRY: You should try to sleep.   225
EDWARD: I don't mind being awake because I make up adventures. Once we were on a raft going down to the rapids. We've lost the paddles because we used them to fight off the crocodiles. A crocodile comes at me and I stab it again and again and the blood is everywhere and it tips up the raft and 230 it has you by the leg and it's biting your leg right off and I take my knife and stab it in the throat and rip open its stomach and it lets go of you but it bites my hand but it's dead. And I drag you onto the river bank and I'm almost fainting with pain and we lie there in each other's arms.   235
HARRY: Have I lost my leg?
EDWARD: I forgot about the leg by then.
HARRY: Hadn't we better look for the others?
EDWARD: Wait. I've got something for you. It was in mama's box but she never wears it.   240

(EDWARD *gives* HARRY *a necklace.*)

   You don't have to wear it either but you might like it to look at.
HARRY: It's beautiful. But you'll have to put it back.
EDWARD: I wanted to give it to you.
HARRY: You did. It can go back in the box. You still gave it 245 to me. Come on now, we have to find the others.
EDWARD: Harry, I love you.
HARRY: Yes I know. I love you too.
EDWARD: You know what we did when you were here before. I want to do it again. I think about it all the time. I try to do it 250 to myself but it's not as good. Don't you want to any more?
HARRY: I do, but it's a sin and a crime and it's also wrong.
EDWARD: But we'll do it anyway won't we?
HARRY: Yes of course.

EDWARD: I wish the others would all be killed. Take it out 255
now and let me see it.
HARRY: No.
EDWARD: Is it big now?
HARRY: Yes.
EDWARD: Let me touch it. 260
HARRY: No.
EDWARD: Just hold me.
HARRY: When you can't sleep.
EDWARD: We'd better find the others then. Come on.
HARRY: Ready or not, here we come. 265

(*They go out with whoops and shouts.* BETTY *and* ELLEN *come.*)

BETTY: Ellen, I don't want to play any more.
ELLEN: Nor do I, Betty.
BETTY: Come and sit here with me. Oh Ellen, what will be-
come of me?
ELLEN: Betty, are you crying? Are you laughing? 270
BETTY: Tell me what you think of Harry Bagley.
ELLEN: He's a very fine man.
BETTY: No, Ellen, what you really think.
ELLEN: I think you think he's very handsome.
BETTY: And don't you think he is? Oh Ellen, you're so good 275
and I'm so wicked.
ELLEN: I'm not so good as you think.

(EDWARD *comes.*)

EDWARD: I've found you.
ELLEN: We're not hiding Edward.
EDWARD: But I found you. 280
ELLEN: We're not playing, Edward, now run along.
EDWARD: Come on, Ellen, do play. Come on, mama.
ELLEN: Edward, don't pull your mama like that.
BETTY: Edward, you must do what your governess says. Go
and play with Uncle Harry. 285
EDWARD: Uncle Harry!

(EDWARD *goes.*)

BETTY: Ellen, can you keep a secret?
ELLEN: Oh yes, yes please.
BETTY: I love Harry Bagley. I want to go away with him.
There, I've said it, it's true. 290
ELLEN: How do you know you love him?
BETTY: I kissed him.
ELLEN: Betty.
BETTY: He held my hand like this. Oh I want him to do it
again. I want him to stroke my hair. 295
ELLEN: Your lovely hair. Like this, Betty?
BETTY: I want him to put his arm around my waist.
ELLEN: Like this, Betty?
BETTY: Yes, oh I want him to kiss me again.
ELLEN: Like this Betty? 300

(ELLEN *kisses* BETTY.)

BETTY: Ellen, whatever are you doing? It's not a joke.
ELLEN: I'm sorry, Betty. You're so pretty. Harry Bagley doesn't
deserve you. You wouldn't really go away with him?
BETTY: Oh Ellen, you don't know what I suffer. You don't
know what love is. Everyone will hate me, but it's worth 305
it for Harry's love.

ELLEN: I don't hate you, Betty, I love you.
BETTY: Harry says we shouldn't go away. But he says he wor-
ships me.
ELLEN: I worship you Betty. 310
BETTY: Oh Ellen, you are my only friend.

(*They embrace. The others have all gathered together.* MAUD *has re-
joined the party, and* JOSHUA.)

CLIVE: Come along everyone, you mustn't miss Harry's conjuring trick.

(BETTY *and* ELLEN *go to join the others.*)

MAUD: I didn't want to spoil the fun by not being here.
HARRY: What is it that flies all over the world and is up my 315
sleeve?

(HARRY *produces a union jack from up his sleeve. General acclaim.*)

CLIVE: I think we should have some singing now. Ladies, I
rely on you to lead the way.
ELLEN: We have a surprise for you. I have taught Joshua a
Christmas carol. He has been singing it at the piano but 320
I'm sure he can sing it unaccompanied, can't you, Joshua?
JOSHUA: In the deep midwinter
             Frosty wind made moan,
             Earth stood hard as iron,
             Water like a stone. 325
             Snow had fallen snow on snow
             Snow on snow,
             In the deep midwinter
             Long long ago.

             What can I give him 330
             Poor as I am?
             If I were a shepherd
             I would bring a lamb.
             If I were a wise man
             I would do my part 335
             What can I give him,
             Give my heart.

SCENE III

Inside the house. BETTY, MRS SAUNDERS, MAUD *with* VICTORIA.
*The blinds are down so the light isn't bright though it is day out-
side.* CLIVE *looks in.*

CLIVE: Everything all right? Nothing to be frightened of.

(CLIVE *goes. Silence.*)

MAUD: Clap hands, daddy comes, with his pockets full of
plums. All for Vicky.

(*Silence.*)

MRS SAUNDERS: Who actually does the flogging?
MAUD: I don't think we want to imagine. 5
MRS SAUNDERS: I imagine Joshua.
BETTY: Yes I think it would be Joshua. Or would Clive do it
himself?
MRS SAUNDERS: Well we can ask them afterwards.

10 MAUD: I don't like the way you speak of it, Mrs Saunders.

MRS SAUNDERS: How should I speak of it?

MAUD: The men will do it in the proper way, whatever it is. We have our own part to play.

MRS SAUNDERS: Harry Bagley says they should just be sent
15 away. I don't think he likes to see them beaten.

BETTY: Harry is so tender hearted. Perhaps he is right.

MAUD: Harry Bagley is not altogether—He has lived in this country a long time without any responsibilities. It is part of his charm but it hasn't improved his judgment. If the
20 boys were just sent away they would go back to the village and make more trouble.

MRS SAUNDERS: And what will they say about us in the village if they've been flogged?

BETTY: Perhaps Clive should keep them here.

25 MRS SAUNDERS: That is never wise.

BETTY: Whatever shall we do?

MAUD: I don't think it is up to us to wonder. The men don't tell us what is going on among the tribes, so how can we possibly make a judgment?

30 MRS SAUNDERS: I know a little of what is going on.

BETTY: Tell me what you know. Clive tells me nothing.

MAUD: You would not want to be told about it, Betty. It is enough for you that Clive knows what is happening. Clive will know what to do. Your father always knew what to do.

35 BETTY: Are you saying you would do something different, Caroline?

MRS SAUNDERS: I would do what I did at my own home. I left. I can't see any way out except to leave. I will leave here. I will keep leaving everywhere I suppose.

40 MAUD: Luckily this household has a head. I am squeamish myself. But luckily Clive is not.

BETTY: You are leaving here then, Caroline?

MRS SAUNDERS: Not immediately. I'm sorry.

(*Silence.*)

MRS SAUNDERS: I wonder if it's over.

(EDWARD *comes in.*)

45 BETTY: Shouldn't you be with the men, Edward?

EDWARD: I didn't want to see any more. They got what they deserved. Uncle Harry said I could come in.

MRS SAUNDERS: I never allowed the servants to be beaten in my own house. I'm going to find out what's happening.

(MRS SAUNDERS *goes out.*)

50 BETTY: Will she go and look?

MAUD: Let Mrs Saunders be a warning to you, Betty. She is alone in the world. You are not, thank God. Since your father died, I know what it is to be unprotected. Vicky is such a pretty little girl. Clap hands, daddy comes, with his
55 pockets full of plums. All for Vicky.

(EDWARD, *meanwhile, has found the doll and is playing clap hands with her.*)

BETTY: Edward, what have you got there?

EDWARD: I'm minding her.

BETTY: Edward, I've told you before, dolls are for girls.

MAUD: Where is Ellen? She should be looking after Edward. (*She goes to the door.*) Ellen! Betty, why do you let that girl 60 mope about in her own room? That's not what she's come to Africa for.

BETTY: You must never let the boys at school know you like dolls. Never, never. No one will talk to you, you won't be on the cricket team, you won't grow up to be a man like 65 your papa.

EDWARD: I don't want to be like papa. I hate papa.

MAUD: Edward! Edward!

BETTY: You're a horrid wicked boy and papa will beat you. Of course you don't hate him, you love him. Now give 70 Victoria her doll at once.

EDWARD: She's not Victoria's doll, she's my doll. She doesn't love Victoria and Victoria doesn't love her. Victoria never even plays with her.

MAUD: Victoria will learn to play with her. 75

EDWARD: She's mine and she loves me and she won't be happy if you take her away, she'll cry, she'll cry, she'll cry.

(BETTY *takes the doll away, slaps him, bursts into tears.* ELLEN *comes in.*)

BETTY: Ellen, look what you've done. Edward's got the doll again. Now, Ellen, will you please do your job.

ELLEN: Edward, you are a wicked boy. I am going to lock you 80 in the nursery until supper time. Now go upstairs this minute.

(*She slaps* EDWARD, *who bursts into tears and goes out.*)

I do try to do what you want. I'm so sorry.

(ELLEN *bursts into tears and goes out.*)

MAUD: There now, Vicky's got her baby back. Where did Vicky's naughty baby go? Shall we smack her? Just a little 85 smack. (MAUD *smacks the doll hard.*) There, now she's a good baby. Clap hands, daddy comes, with his pockets full of plums. All for Vicky's baby. When I was a child we honoured our parents. My mama was an angel.

(JOSHUA *comes in. He stands without speaking.*)

BETTY: Joshua? 90

JOSHUA: Madam?

BETTY: Did you want something?

JOSHUA: Sent to see the ladies are all right, madam.

(MRS SAUNDERS *comes in.*)

MRS SAUNDERS: We're very well thank you, Joshua, and how are you? 95

JOSHUA: Very well thank you, Mrs Saunders.

MRS SAUNDERS: And the stable boys?

JOSHUA: They have had justice, madam.

MRS SAUNDERS: So I saw. And does your arm ache?

MAUD: This is not a proper conversation, Mrs Saunders. 100

MRS SAUNDERS: You don't mind beating your own people?

JOSHUA: Not my people, madam.

MRS SAUNDERS: A different tribe?

JOSHUA: Bad people.

(HARRY *and* CLIVE *come in.*)

105   CLIVE: Well this is all very gloomy and solemn. Can we have the shutters open? The heat of the day has gone, we could have some light, I think. And cool drinks on the verandah, Joshua. Have some lemonade yourself. It is most refreshing.

(*Sunlight floods in as the shutters are opened.* EDWARD *comes.*)

EDWARD: Papa, papa, Ellen tried to lock me in the nursery.
110   Mama is going to tell you of me. I'd rather tell you myself. I was playing with Vicky's doll again and I know it's very bad of me. And I said I didn't want to be like you and I said I hated you. And it's not true and I'm sorry, I'm sorry and please beat me and forgive me.

115   CLIVE: Well there's a brave boy to own up. You should always respect and love me, Edward, not for myself, I may not deserve it, but as I respected and loved my own father, because he was my father. Through our father we love our Queen and our God, Edward. Do you understand? It is
120   something men understand.

EDWARD: Yes papa.

CLIVE: Then I forgive you and shake you by the hand. You spend too much time with the women. You may spend more time with me and Uncle Harry, little man.

125   EDWARD: I don't like women. I don't like dolls. I love you, papa, and I love you, Uncle Harry.

CLIVE: There's a fine fellow. Let us go out onto the verandah.

(*They all start to go.* EDWARD *takes* HARRY's *hand and goes with him.* CLIVE *draws* BETTY *back. They embrace.*)

BETTY: Poor Clive.

CLIVE: It was my duty to have them flogged. For you and Ed-
130   ward and Victoria, to keep you safe.

BETTY: It is terrible to feel betrayed.

CLIVE: You can tame a wild animal only so far. They revert to their true nature and savage your hand. Sometimes I feel the natives are the enemy. I know that is wrong. I know I
135   have a responsibility towards them, to care for them and bring them all to be like Joshua. But there is something dangerous. Implacable. This whole continent is my enemy. I am pitching my whole mind and will and reason and spirit against it to tame it, and I sometimes feel it will
140   break over me and swallow me up.

BETTY: Clive, Clive, I am here. I have faith in you.

CLIVE: Yes, I can show you my moments of weakness, Betty, because you are my wife and because I trust you. I trust you, Betty, and it would break my heart if you did not de-
145   serve that trust. Harry Bagley is my friend. It would break my heart if he did not deserve my trust.

BETTY: I'm sorry, I'm sorry. Forgive me. It is not Harry's fault, it is all mine. Harry is noble. He has rejected me. It is my wickedness, I get bored, I get restless, I imagine things.
150   There is something so wicked in me, Clive.

CLIVE: I have never thought of you having the weakness of your sex, only the good qualities.

BETTY: I am bad, bad, bad—

CLIVE: You are thoughtless, Betty, that's all. Women can be
155   treacherous and evil. They are darker and more dangerous than men. The family protects us from that, you protect me

from that. You are not that sort of woman. You are not unfaithful to me, Betty. I can't believe you are. It would hurt me so much to cast you off. That would be my duty.

BETTY: No, no, no.   160

CLIVE: Joshua has seen you kissing.

BETTY: Forgive me.

CLIVE: But I don't want to know about it. I don't want to know. I wonder of course, I wonder constantly. If Harry Bagley was not my friend I would shoot him. If I shot you   165
every British man and woman would applaud me. But no. It was a moment of passion such as women are too weak to resist. But you must resist it, Betty, or it will destroy us. We must fight against it. We must resist this dark female lust, Betty, or it will swallow us up.   170

BETTY: I do, I do resist. Help me. Forgive me.

CLIVE: Yes I do forgive you. But I can't feel the same about you as I did. You are still my wife and we still have duties to the household.

(*They go out arm in arm. As soon as they have gone* EDWARD *sneaks back to get the doll, which has been dropped on the floor. He picks it up and comforts it.* JOSHUA *comes through with a tray of drinks.*)

JOSHUA: Baby. Sissy. Girly.   175

(JOSHUA *goes.* BETTY *calls from off.*)

BETTY: Edward?

(BETTY *comes in.*)

BETTY: There you are, my darling. Come, papa wants us all to be together. Uncle Harry is going to tell how he caught a crocodile. Mama's sorry she smacked you.

(*They embrace.* JOSHUA *comes in again, passing through.*)

BETTY: Joshua, fetch me some blue thread from my sewing   180
box. It is on the piano.

JOSHUA: You've got legs under that skirt.

BETTY: Joshua.

JOSHUA: And more than legs.

BETTY: Edward, are you going to stand there and let a servant   185
insult your mother?

EDWARD: Joshua, get my mother's thread.

JOSHUA: Oh little Eddy, playing at master. It's only a joke.

EDWARD: Don't speak to my mother like that again.

JOSHUA: Ladies have no sense of humour. You like a joke   190
with Joshua.

EDWARD: You fetch her sewing at once, do you hear me? You move when I speak to you, boy.

JOSHUA: Yes sir, master Edward sir.

(JOSHUA *goes.*)

BETTY: Edward, you were wonderful.   195

(*She goes to embrace him but he moves away.*)

EDWARD: Don't touch me.

Song
A BOY'S BEST FRIEND

ALL: While plodding on our way, the toilsome road of life,
How few the friends that daily there we meet.
Not many will stand in trouble and in strife,
200   With counsel and affection ever sweet.
But there is one whose smile will ever on us beam,
Whose love is dearer far than any other;
And wherever we may turn
This lesson we will learn
205   A boy's best friend is his mother.

Then cherish her with care
And smooth her silv'ry hair,
When gone you will never get another.
And wherever we may turn
210   This lesson we shall learn,
A boy's best friend is his mother.

SCENE IV

The verandah as in Scene One. Early morning. Nobody there.
JOSHUA *comes out of the house slowly and stands for some time do-*
ing nothing. EDWARD *comes out.*

EDWARD: Tell me another bad story, Joshua. Nobody else is
even awake yet.
JOSHUA: First there was nothing and then there was the great
goddess. She was very large and she had golden eyes and
5   she made the stars and the sun and the earth. But soon she
was miserable and lonely and she cried like a great water-
fall and her tears made all the rivers in the world. So the
great spirit sent a terrible monster, a tree with hundreds of
eyes and a long green tongue, and it came chasing after
10   her and she jumped into a lake and the tree jumped in after her, and she jumped right up into the sky. And the tree
couldn't follow, he was stuck in the mud. So he picked up
a big handful of mud and he threw it at her, up among the
stars, and it hit her on the head. And she fell down onto
15   the earth into his arms and the ball of mud is the moon
in the sky. And then they had children which is all of us.
EDWARD: It's not true, though.
JOSHUA: Of course it's not true. It's a bad story. Adam and Eve is
true. God made man white like him and gave him the bad
20   woman who liked the snake and gave us all this trouble.

(CLIVE *and* HARRY *come out.*)

CLIVE: Run along now, Edward. No, you may stay. You
mustn't repeat anything you hear to your mother or your
grandmother or Ellen.
EDWARD: Or Mrs Saunders?
25   CLIVE: Mrs Saunders is an unusual woman and does not require protection in the same way. Harry, there was trouble
last night where we expected it. But it's all over now.
Everything is under control but nobody should leave the
house today I think.
30   HARRY: Casualties?
CLIVE: No, none of the soldiers hurt thank God. We did a certain amount of damage, set a village on fire and so forth.
HARRY: Was that necessary?

CLIVE: Obviously, it was necessary, Harry, or it wouldn't have
happened. The army will come and visit, no doubt. You'll   35
like that, eh, Joshua, to see the British army? And a treat
for you, Edward, to see the soldiers. Would you like to be
a soldier?
EDWARD: I'd rather be an explorer.
CLIVE: Ah, Harry, like you, you see. I didn't know an explorer   40
at his age. Breakfast, I think, Joshua.

(CLIVE *and* JOSHUA *go in.* HARRY *is following.*)

EDWARD: Uncle.

(HARRY *stops.*)

EDWARD: Harry, why won't you talk to me?
HARRY: Of course I'll talk to you.
EDWARD: If you won't be nice to me I'll tell father.   45
HARRY: Edward, no, not a word, never, not to your mother,
nobody, please. Edward, do you understand? Please.
EDWARD: I won't tell. I promise I'll never tell. I've cut my fin-
ger and sworn.
HARRY: There's no need to get so excited Edward. We can't   50
be together all the time. I will have to leave soon anyway,
and go back to the river.
EDWARD: You can't, you can't go. Take me with you.
ELLEN: Edward!
HARRY: I have my duty to the Empire.   55

(HARRY *goes in.* ELLEN *comes out.*)

ELLEN: Edward, breakfast time. Edward.
EDWARD: I'm not hungry.
ELLEN: Betty, please come and speak to Edward.

(BETTY *comes.*)

BETTY: Why what's the matter?
ELLEN: He won't come in for breakfast.   60
BETTY: Edward, I shall call your father.
EDWARD: You can't make me eat.

(*He goes in.* BETTY *is about to follow.*)

ELLEN: Betty.

(BETTY *stops.*)

ELLEN: Betty, when Edward goes to school will I have to leave?
BETTY: Never mind, Ellen dear, you'll get another place. I'll   65
give you an excellent reference.
ELLEN: I don't want another place, Betty. I want to stay with
you forever.
BETTY: If you go back to England you might get married,
Ellen. You're quite pretty, you shouldn't despair of getting   70
a husband.
ELLEN: I don't want a husband. I want you.
BETTY: Children of your own, Ellen, think.
ELLEN: I don't want children, I don't like children. I just want
to be alone with you, Betty, and sing for you and kiss you   75
because I love you, Betty.
BETTY: I love you too, Ellen. But women have their duty as
soldiers have. You must be a mother if you can.

ELLEN: Betty, Betty, I love you so much. I want to stay with
80   you forever, my love for you is eternal, stronger than
   death. I'd rather die than leave you, Betty.

BETTY: No you wouldn't, Ellen, don't be silly. Come, don't
   cry. You don't feel what you think you do. It's the loneliness here and the climate is very confusing. Come and
85   have breakfast, Ellen dear, and I'll forget all about it.

(ELLEN *goes,* CLIVE *comes.*)

BETTY: Clive, please forgive me.
CLIVE: Will you leave me alone?

(BETTY *goes back into the house.* HARRY *comes.*)

CLIVE: Women, Harry. I envy you going into the jungle, a
   man's life.
90 HARRY: I envy you.
CLIVE: Harry, I know you do. I have spoken to Betty.
HARRY: I assure you, Clive—
CLIVE: Please say nothing about it.
HARRY: My friendship for you—
95 CLIVE: Absolutely. I know the friendship between us, Harry,
   is not something that could be spoiled by the weaker sex.
   Friendship between men is a fine thing. It is the noblest
   form of relationship.
HARRY: I agree with you.
100 CLIVE: There is the necessity of reproduction. The family is
   all important. And there is the pleasure. But what we put
   ourselves through to get that pleasure, Harry. When I
   heard about our fine fellows last night fighting those savages to protect us I thought yes, that is what I aspire to. I
105   tell you Harry, in confidence, I suddenly got out of Mrs
   Saunders' bed and came out here on the verandah and
   looked at the stars.
HARRY: I couldn't sleep last night either.
CLIVE: There is something dark about women, that threatens
110   what is best in us. Between men that light burns brightly.
HARRY: I didn't know you felt like that.
CLIVE: Women are irrational, demanding, inconsistent,
   treacherous, lustful, and they smell different from us.
HARRY: Clive—
115 CLIVE: Think of the comradeship of men, Harry, sharing ad-
   ventures, sharing danger, risking their lives together.

(HARRY *takes hold of* CLIVE.)

CLIVE: What are you doing?
HARRY: Well, you said—
CLIVE: I said what?
120 HARRY: Between men.

(CLIVE *is speechless.*)

   I'm sorry, I misunderstood, I would never have dreamt, I
   thought—
CLIVE: My God, Harry, how disgusting.
HARRY: You will not betray my confidence.
125 CLIVE: I feel contaminated.
HARRY: I struggle against it. You cannot imagine the shame.
   I have tried everything to save myself.
CLIVE: The most revolting perversion. Rome fell, Harry, and
   this sin can destroy an empire.

HARRY: It is not a sin, it is a disease.   130
CLIVE: A disease more dangerous than diphtheria. Effeminacy
   is contagious. How I have been deceived. Your face does
   not look degenerate. Oh Harry, how did you sink to this?
HARRY: Clive, help me, what am I to do?
CLIVE: You have been away from England too long.   135
HARRY: Where can I go except into the jungle to hide?
CLIVE: You don't do it with the natives, Harry? My God, what
   a betrayal of the Queen.
HARRY: Clive, I am like a man born crippled. Please help me.
CLIVE: You must repent.   140
HARRY: I have thought of killing myself.
CLIVE: That is a sin too.
HARRY: There is no way out, Clive, I beg of you, do not be
   tray my confidence.
CLIVE: I cannot keep a secret like this. Rivers will be named after   145
   you, it's unthinkable. You must save yourself from depravity.
   You must get married. You are not unattractive to women.
   What a relief that you and Betty were not after all—good
   God, how disgusting. Now Mrs Saunders. She's a woman of
   spirit, she could go with you on your expeditions.   150
HARRY: I suppose getting married wouldn't be any worse
   than killing myself.
CLIVE: Mrs Saunders! Mrs Saunders! Ask her now, Harry.
   Think of England.

(MRS SAUNDERS *comes.* CLIVE *withdraws.* HARRY *goes up to* MRS
SAUNDERS.)

HARRY: Mrs Saunders, will you marry me?   155
MRS SAUNDERS: Why?
HARRY: We are both alone.
MRS SAUNDERS: I choose to be alone, Mr Bagley. If I can look
   after myself, I'm sure you can. Clive, I have something im-
   portant to tell you. I've just found Joshua putting earth on   160
   his head. He tells me his parents were killed last night by
   the British soldiers. I think you owe him an apology on
   behalf of the Queen.
CLIVE: Joshua! Joshua!
MRS SAUNDERS: Mr Bagley, I could never be a wife again.   165
   There is only one thing about marriage that I like.

(JOSHUA *comes.*)

CLIVE: Joshua, I am horrified to hear what has happened.
   Good God!
MRS SAUNDERS: His father was shot. His mother died in the
   blaze.   170

(MRS SAUNDERS *goes.*)

CLIVE: Joshua, do you want a day off? Do you want to go to
   your people?
JOSHUA: Not my people, sir.
CLIVE: But you want to go to your parents' funeral?
JOSHUA: No sir.   175
CLIVE: Yes, Joshua, yes, your father and mother. I'm sure they
   were loyal to the crown. I'm sure it was all a terrible mistake.
JOSHUA: My mother and father were bad people.
CLIVE: Joshua, no.
JOSHUA: You are my father and mother.   180

CLIVE: Well really. I don't know what to say. That's very decent of you. Are you sure there's nothing I can do? You can have the day off you know.

(BETTY *comes out followed by* EDWARD.)

BETTY: What's the matter? What's happening?
185 CLIVE: Something terrible has happened. No, I mean some relatives of Joshua's met with an accident.
JOSHUA: May I go sir?
CLIVE: Yes, yes of course. Good God, what a terrible thing. Bring us a drink will you Joshua?

(JOSHUA *goes*.)

190 EDWARD: What? What?
BETTY: Edward, go and do your lessons.
EDWARD: What is it, Uncle Harry?
HARRY: Go and do your lessons.
ELLEN: Edward, come in here at once.
195 EDWARD: What's happened, Uncle Harry?

(HARRY *has moved aside,* EDWARD *follows him*. ELLEN *comes out*.)

HARRY: Go away. Go inside. Ellen!
ELLEN: Go inside, Edward. I shall tell your mother.
BETTY: Go inside, Edward at once. I shall tell your father.
CLIVE: Go inside, Edward. And Betty you go inside too.

(BETTY, EDWARD *and* ELLEN *go*. MAUD *comes out*.)

200 CLIVE: Go inside. And Ellen, you come outside.

(ELLEN *comes out*.)

    Mr Bagley has something to say to you.
HARRY: Ellen. I don't suppose you would marry me?
ELLEN: What if I said yes?
CLIVE: Run along now, you two want to be alone.

(HARRY *and* ELLEN *go out*. JOSHUA *brings* CLIVE *a drink*.)

205 JOSHUA: The governess and your wife, sir.
CLIVE: What's that, Joshua?
JOSHUA: She talks of love to your wife, sir. I have seen them. Bad women.
CLIVE: Joshua, you go too far. Get out of my sight.

SCENE V

The verandah. A table with a white cloth. A wedding cake and a large knife. Bottles and glasses. JOSHUA *is putting things on the table.* EDWARD *has the doll.* JOSHUA *sees him with it. He holds out his hand.* EDWARD *gives him the doll.* JOSHUA *takes the knife and cuts the doll open and shakes the sawdust out of it.* JOSHUA *throws the doll under the table.*

MAUD: Come along Edward, this is such fun.

(*Everyone enters, triumphal arch for* HARRY *and* ELLEN.)

MAUD: Your mama's wedding was a splendid occasion, Edward. I cried and cried.

(*Ellen and* BETTY *go aside*.)

ELLEN: Betty, what happens with a man? I don't know what to do.   5
BETTY: You just keep still.
ELLEN: And what does he do?
BETTY: Harry will know what to do.
ELLEN: And is it enjoyable?
BETTY: Ellen, you're not getting married to enjoy yourself.   10
ELLEN: Don't forget me, Betty.

(ELLEN *goes*.)

BETTY: I think my necklace has been stolen Clive. I did so want to wear it at the wedding.
EDWARD: It was Joshua. Joshua took it.
CLIVE: Joshua?   15
EDWARD: He did, he did, I saw him with it.
HARRY: Edward, that's not true.
EDWARD: It is, it is.
HARRY: Edward, I'm afraid you took it yourself.
EDWARD: I did not.   20
HARRY: I have seen him with it.
CLIVE: Edward, is that true? Where is it? Did you take your mother's necklace? And to try and blame Joshua, good God.

(EDWARD *runs off*.)

BETTY: Edward, come back. Have you got my necklace?
HARRY: I should leave him alone. He'll bring it back.   25
BETTY: I wanted to wear it. I wanted to look my best at your wedding.
HARRY: You always look your best to me.
BETTY: I shall get drunk.

(MRS SAUNDERS *comes*.)

MRS SAUNDERS: The sale of my property is completed. I shall   30
leave tomorrow.
CLIVE: That's just as well. Whose protection will you seek this time?
MRS SAUNDERS: I shall go to England and buy a farm there. I shall introduce threshing machines.   35
CLIVE: Amazing spirit.

(*He kisses her.* BETTY *launches herself on* MRS SAUNDERS. *They fall to the ground*.)

CLIVE: Betty—Caroline—I don't deserve this—Harry, Harry.

(HARRY *and* CLIVE *separate them*. HARRY *holding* MRS SAUNDERS, CLIVE, BETTY.)

CLIVE: Mrs Saunders, how can you abuse my hospitality? How dare you touch my wife? You must leave here at once.
BETTY: Go away, go away. You are a wicked woman.   40
MAUD: Mrs Saunders, I am shocked. This is your hostess.
CLIVE: Pack your bags and leave the house this instant.
MRS SAUNDERS: I was leaving anyway. There's no place for me here. I have made arrangements to leave tomorrow, and tomorrow is when I will leave. I wish you joy, Mr Bagley.   45

(MRS SAUNDERS *goes*.)

CLIVE: No place for her anywhere I should think. Shocking behaviour.

BETTY: Oh Clive, forgive me, and love me like you used to.

CLIVE: Were you jealous my dove? My own dear wife!

50 MAUD: Ah, Mr Bagley, one flesh, you see.

(EDWARD *comes back with the necklace.*)

CLIVE: Good God, Edward, it's true.

EDWARD: I was minding it for mama because of the troubles.

CLIVE: Well done, Edward, that was very manly of you. See
       Betty? Edward was protecting his mama's jewels from the
55   rebels. What a hysterical fuss over nothing. Well done, lit-
       tle man. It is quite safe now. The bad men are dead.
       Edward, you may do up the necklace for mama.

(EDWARD *does up* BETTY's *necklace, supervised by* CLIVE, JOSHUA
is drinking steadily. ELLEN *comes back.*)

MAUD: Ah, here's the bride. Come along, Ellen, you don't cry
      at your own wedding, only at other people's.

60 CLIVE: Now, speeches, speeches. Who is going to make a
       speech? Harry, make a speech.

HARRY: I'm no speaker. You're the one for that.

ALL: Speech, speech.

HARRY: My dear friends—what can I say—the empire—the
65   family—the married state to which I have always
       aspired—your shining example of domestic bliss—my
       great good fortune in winning Ellen's love—happiest day
       of my life.

(*Applause.*)

CLIVE: Cut the cake, cut the cake.

(HARRY *and* ELLEN *take the knife to cut the cake.* HARRY *steps on
the doll under the table.*)

70 HARRY: What's this?

ELLEN: Oh look.

BETTY: Edward.

EDWARD: It was Joshua. It was Joshua. I saw him.

CLIVE: Don't tell lies again.

(*He hits* EDWARD *across the side of the head.*)

75   Unaccustomed as I am to public speaking—

(*Cheers.*)

        Harry, my friend. So brave and strong and supple.
        Ellen, from neath her veil so shyly peeking.
        I wish you joy. A toast—the happy couple.
        Dangers are past. Our enemies are killed.
80   —Put your arm round her, Harry, have a kiss—
        All murmuring of discontent is stilled.
        Long may you live in peace and joy and bliss.

(*While he is speaking* JOSHUA *raises his gun to shoot* CLIVE. *Only*
EDWARD *sees. He does nothing to warn the others. He puts his
hands over his ears.*)

(*Black.*)

ACT TWO

SCENE I

*Winter afternoon. Inside the hut of a one o'clock club, a children's
playcentre in a park,* VICTORIA *and* LIN, *mothers.* CATHY, LIN's
daughter, age 5, played by a man, clinging to LIN. VICTORIA *reading a book.*

CATHY: Yum yum bubblegum.
       Stick it up your mother's bum.
       When it's brown
       Pull it down
       Yum yum bubblegum.   5

LIN: Like your shoes, Victoria.

CATHY: Jack be nimble, Jack be quick,
       Jack jump over the candlestick.
       Silly Jack, he should jump higher,
       Goodness gracious, great balls of fire.   10

LIN: Cathy, do stop. Do a painting.

CATHY: You do a painting.

LIN: You do a painting.

CATHY: What shall I paint?

LIN: Paint a house.   15

CATHY: No.

LIN: Princess.

CATHY: No.

LIN: Pirates.

CATHY: Already done that.   20

LIN: Spacemen.

CATHY: I never paint spacemen. You know I never.

LIN: Paint a car crash and blood everywhere.

CATHY: No, don't tell me. I know what to paint.

LIN: Go on then. You need an apron, where's an apron. Here. 25

CATHY: Don't want an apron.

LIN: Lift up your arms. There's a good girl.

CATHY: I don't want to paint.

LIN: Don't paint. Don't paint.

CATHY: What shall I do? You paint. What shall I do mum?   30

VICTORIA: There's nobody on the big bike, Cathy, quick.

(CATHY *goes out.* VICTORIA *is watching the children playing outside.*)

VICTORIA: Tommy, it's Jimmy's gun. Let him have it. What
          the hell.

(*She goes on reading. She reads while she talks.*)

LIN: I don't know how you can concentrate.

VICTORIA: You have to or you never do anything.   35

LIN: Yeh, well. It's really warm in here, that's one thing. It's
     better than standing out there. I got chilblains last winter.

VICTORIA: It is warm.

LIN: I suppose Tommy doesn't let you read much. I expect he
     talks to you while you're reading.   40

VICTORIA: Yes, he does.

LIN: I didn't get very far with that book you lent me.

VICTORIA: That's all right.

LIN: I was glad to have it, though. I sit with it on my lap while
     I'm watching telly. Well, Cathy's off. She's frightened I'm 45
     going to leave her. It's the babyminder didn't work out
     when she was two, she still remembers. You can't get

them used to other people if you're by yourself. It's no
good blaming me. She clings round my knees every
50   morning up the nursery and they don't say anything but
they make you feel you're making her do it. But I'm desperate for her to go to school. I did cry when I left her
the first day. You wouldn't, you're too fucking sensible.
You'll call the teacher by her first name. I really fancy you.
55 VICTORIA: What?
LIN: Put your book down will you for five minutes. You
didn't hear a word I said.
VICTORIA: I don't get much time to myself.
LIN: Do you ever go to the movies?
60 VICTORIA: Tommy's very funny who he's left with. My
mother babysits sometimes.
LIN: Your husband could babysit.
VICTORIA: But then we couldn't go to the movies.
LIN: You could go to the movies with me.
65 VICTORIA: Oh I see.
LIN: Couldn't you?
VICTORIA: Well yes, I could.
LIN: Friday night?
VICTORIA: What film are we talking about?
70 LIN: Does it matter what film?
VICTORIA: Of course it does.
LIN: You choose then. Friday night.

(CATHY *comes in with gun, shoots them saying Kiou kiou kiou, and*
runs off again.)

Not in a foreign language, ok. You don't go in the movies
to read.

(LIN *watches the children playing outside.*)

75   Don't hit him, Cathy, kill him. Point the gun, kiou, kiou,
kiou. That's the way.
VICTORIA: They've just banned war toys in Sweden.
LIN: The kids'll just hit each other more.
VICTORIA: Well, psychologists do differ in their opinions as to
80   whether or not aggression is innate.
LIN: Yeh?
VICTORIA: I'm afraid I do let Tommy play with guns and just
hope he'll get it out of his system and not end up in the army.
LIN: I've got a brother in the army.
85 VICTORIA: Oh I'm sorry. Whereabouts is he stationed?
LIN: Belfast.
VICTORIA: Oh dear.
LIN: I've got a friend who's Irish and we went on a Troops
Out march. Now my dad won't speak to me.
90 VICTORIA: I don't get on too well with my father either.
LIN: And your husband? How do you get on with him?
VICTORIA: Oh, fine. Up and down. You know. Very well. He
helps with the washing up and everything.
LIN: I left mine two years ago. He let me keep Cathy and I'm
95   grateful for that.
VICTORIA: You shouldn't be grateful.
LIN: I'm a lesbian.
VICTORIA: You still shouldn't be grateful.
LIN: I'm grateful he didn't hit me harder than he did.
100 VICTORIA: I suppose I'm very lucky with Martin.
LIN: Don't get at me about how I bring up Cathy, ok?
VICTORIA: I didn't.

LIN: Yes you did. War toys. I'll give her a rifle for Christmas
and blast Tommy's pretty head off for a start.

(VICTORIA *goes back to her book.*)

LIN: I hate men.   105
VICTORIA: You have to look at it in a historical perspective in
terms of learnt behaviour since the industrial revolution.
LIN: I just hate the bastards.
VICTORIA: Well it's a point of view.

(*By now* CATHY *has come back in and started painting in many*
colours, without an apron. EDWARD *comes in.*)

EDWARD: Victoria, mother's in the park. She's walking round   110
all the paths very fast.
VICTORIA: By herself?
EDWARD: I told her you were here.
VICTORIA: Thanks.
EDWARD: Come on.   115
VICTORIA: Ten minutes talking to my mother and I have to
spend two hours in a hot bath.

(VICTORIA *goes out.*)

LIN: Shit, Cathy, what about an apron. I don't mind you hav-
ing paint on your frock but if it doesn't wash off just don't
tell me you can't wear your frock with paint on, ok?   120
CATHY: Ok.
LIN: You're gay, aren't you?
EDWARD: I beg your pardon?
LIN: I really fancy your sister. I thought you'd understand.
You do but you can go on pretending you don't, I don't   125
mind. That's lovely Cathy, I like the green bit.
EDWARD: Don't go around saying that. I might lose my job.
LIN: The last gardener was ever so straight. He used to flash
at all the little girls.
EDWARD: I wish you hadn't said that about me. It's not true.   130
LIN: It's not true and I never said it and I never thought it and
I never will think it again.
EDWARD: Someone might have heard you.
LIN: Shut up about it then.

(BETTY *and* VICTORIA *come up.*)

BETTY: It's quite a nasty bump.   135
VICTORIA: He's not even crying.
BETTY: I think that's very worrying. You and Edward always
cried. Perhaps he's got concussion.
VICTORIA: Of course he hasn't mummy.
BETTY: That other little boy was very rough. Should you   140
speak to somebody about him?
VICTORIA: Tommy was hitting him with a spade.
BETTY: Well he's a real little boy. And so brave not to cry. You
must watch him for signs of drowsiness. And nausea. If
he's sick in the night, phone an ambulance. Well, you're   145
looking very well darling, a bit tired, a bit peaky. I think
the fresh air agrees with Edward. He likes the open air life
because of growing up in Africa. He misses the sunshine,
don't you, darling? We'll soon have Edward back on his
feet. What fun it is here.   150
VICTORIA: This is Lin. And Cathy.

BETTY: Oh Cathy what a lovely painting. What is it? Well I think it's a house on fire. I think all that red is a fire. Is that right? Or do I see legs, is it a horse? Can I have the lovely painting or is it for mummy? Children have such imagination, it makes them so exhausting. (*To* LIN.) I'm sure you're wonderful, just like Victoria. I had help with my children. One does need help. That was in Africa of course so there wasn't the servant problem. This is my son Edward. This is—

EDWARD: Lin.

BETTY: Lin, this is Lin. Edward is doing something such fun, he's working in the park as a gardener. He does look exactly like a gardener.

EDWARD: I am a gardener.

BETTY: He's certainly making a stab at it. Well it will be a story to tell. I expect he will write a novel about it, or perhaps a television series. Well what a pretty child Cathy is. Victoria was a pretty child just like a little doll—you can't be certain how they'll grow up. I think Victoria's very pretty but she doesn't make the most of herself, do you darling, it's not the fashion I'm told but there are still women who dress out of *Vogue,* well we hope that's not what Martin looks for, though in many ways I wish it was, I don't know what it is Martin looks for and nor does he I'm afraid poor Martin. Well I am rattling on. I like your skirt dear but your shoes won't do at all. Well do they have lady gardeners, Edward, because I'm going to leave your father and I think I might need to get a job, not a gardener really of course. I haven't got green fingers I'm afraid, everything I touch shrivels straight up. Vicky gave me a poinsettia last Christmas and the leaves all fell off on Boxing Day. Well good heavens, look what's happened to that lovely painting.

(CATHY *has slowly and carefully been going over the whole sheet with black paint. She has almost finished.*)

LIN: What you do that for silly? It was nice.

CATHY: I like your earrings.

VICTORIA: Did you say you're leaving Daddy?

BETTY: Do you darling? Shall I put them on you? My ears aren't pierced, I never wanted that, they just clip on the lobe.

LIN: She'll get paint on you, mind.

BETTY: There's a pretty girl. It doesn't hurt does it. Well you'll grow up to know you have to suffer a little bit for beauty.

CATHY: Look mum I'm pretty, I'm pretty, I'm pretty.

LIN: Stop showing off Cathy.

VICTORIA: It's time we went home. Tommy, time to go home. Last go then, all right.

EDWARD: Mum did I hear you right just now?

CATHY: I want my ears pierced.

BETTY: Ooh, not till you're big.

CATHY: I know a girl got her ears pierced and she's three. She's got real gold.

BETTY: I don't expect she's English, darling. Can I give her a sweety? I know they're not very good for the teeth, Vicky gets terribly cross with me. What does mummy say?

LIN: Just one thank you very much.

CATHY: I like your beads.

BETTY: Yes they are pretty. Here you are.

(*It is the necklace from Act One.*)

CATHY: Look at me, look at me. Vicky, Vicky, Vicky look at me.

LIN: You look lovely, come on now.

CATHY: And your hat, and your hat.

LIN: No, that's enough.

BETTY: Of course she can have my hat.

CATHY: Yes, yes, hat, hat. Look look look.

LIN: That's enough, please, stop it now. Hat off, bye bye hat.

CATHY: Give me my hat.

LIN: Bye bye beads.

BETTY: It's just fun.

LIN: It's very nice of you.

CATHY: I want my beads.

LIN: Where's the other earring?

CATHY: I want my beads.

(CATHY *has the other earring in her hand. Meanwhile* VICTORIA *and* EDWARD *look for it.*)

EDWARD: Is it on the floor?

VICTORIA: Don't step on it.

EDWARD: Where?

CATHY: I want my beads. I want my beads.

LIN: You'll have a smack.

(LIN *gets the earring from* CATHY.)

CATHY: I want my beads.

BETTY: Oh dear oh dear. Have you got the earring? Thank you darling.

CATHY: I want my beads, you're horrid, I hate you, mum, you smell.

BETTY: This is the point you see where one had help. Well it's been lovely seeing you dears and I'll be off again on my little walk.

VICTORIA: You're leaving him? Really?

BETTY: Yes you hear alright, Vicky, yes. I'm finding a little flat, that will be fun.

(BETTY *goes.*)

Bye bye Tommy, granny's going now. Tommy don't hit that little girl, say goodbye to granny.

VICTORIA: Fucking hell.

EDWARD: Puking Jesus.

LIN: That was news was it, leaving your father?

EDWARD: They're going to want so much attention.

VICTORIA: Does everybody hate their mothers?

EDWARD: Mind you, I wouldn't live with him.

LIN: Stop snivelling, pigface. Where's your coat? Be quiet now and we'll have doughnuts for tea and if you keep on we'll have dogshit on toast.

(CATHY *laughs so much she lies on the floor.*)

VICTORIA: Tommy, you've had two last goes. Last last last last go.

LIN: Not that funny, come on, coat on.

EDWARD: Can I have your painting?

CATHY: What for?

EDWARD: For a friend of mine.

CATHY: What's his name?

EDWARD: Gerry.

CATHY: How old is he?

EDWARD: Thirty-two.

CATHY: You can if you like. I don't care. Kiou kiou kiou kiou.

(CATHY *goes out.* EDWARD *takes the painting and goes out.*)

LIN: Will you have sex with me?
VICTORIA: I don't know what Martin would say. Does it
260   count as adultery with a woman?
LIN: You'd enjoy it.

SCENE II

Spring. Swing, bench, pond nearby. EDWARD *is gardening.* GERRY
sitting on a bench.

EDWARD: I sometimes pretend we don't know each other.
     And you've come to the park to eat your sandwiches and
     look at me.
GERRY: That would be more interesting, yes. Come and sit
5   down.
EDWARD: If the superintendent comes I'll be in trouble. It's
     not my dinner time yet. Where were you last night? I
     think you owe me an explanation. We always do tell each
     other everything.
10 GERRY: Is that a rule?
EDWARD: It's what we agreed.
GERRY: It's a habit we've got into. Look, I was drunk. I woke
     up at 4 o'clock on somebody's floor. I was sick. I hadn't
     any money for a cab. I went back to sleep.
15 EDWARD: You could have phoned.
GERRY: There wasn't a phone.
EDWARD: Sorry.
GERRY: There was a phone and I didn't phone you. Leave it
     alone, Eddy, I'm warning you.
20 EDWARD: What are you going to do to me, then?
GERRY: I'm going to the pub.
EDWARD: I'll join you in ten minutes.
GERRY: I didn't ask you to come. (EDWARD *goes.*) Two years I've
     been with Edward. You have to get away sometimes or you
25   lose sight of yourself. The train from Victoria to Clapham
     still has those compartments without a corridor. As soon
     as I got on the platform I saw who I wanted. Slim hips,
     tense shoulders, trying not to look at anyone. I put my hand
     on my packet just long enough so that he couldn't miss it.
30   The train came in. You don't want to get in too fast or
     some straight dumbo might get in with you. I sat by the
     window. I couldn't see where the fuck he'd got to. Then
     just as the whistle went he got in. Great. It's a six-minute
     journey so you can't start anything you can't finish. I stared
35   at him and he unzipped his flies. Then he stopped. So I
     stood up and took my cock out. He took me in his mouth
     and shut his eyes tight. He was sort of mumbling it about
     as if he wasn't sure what to do, so I said, 'A bit tighter son'
     and he said 'Sorry' and then got on with it. He was jerking
40   off with his left hand, and I could see he'd got a fairsized
     one. I wished he'd keep still so I could see his watch. I was
     getting really turned on. What if we pulled into Clapham
     Junction now. Of course by the time we sat down again the
     train was just slowing up. I felt wonderful. Then he started
45   talking. It's better if nothing is said. Once you find he's a li-
     brarian in Walthamstow with a special interest in science
     fiction and lives with his aunt, then forget it. He said I hope
     you don't think I do this all the time. I said I hope you will

from now on. He said he would if I was on the train, but
why don't we go out for a meal? I opened the door before 50
the train stopped. I told him I live with somebody, I don't
want to know. He was jogging sideways to keep up. He said
'What's your phone number, you're my ideal physical type,
what sign of the zodiac are you? Where do you live? Where
are you going now?' It's not fair, I saw him at Victoria a 55
couple of months later and I went straight down to the end
of the platform and I picked up somebody really great who
never said a word, just smiled.

(CATHY *is on the swing.*)

CATHY: Batman and Robin
     Had a batmobile.   60
     Robin done a fart
     And paralysed the wheel.
     The wheel couldn't take it,
     The engine fell apart,
     All because of Robin   65
     And his supersonic fart.

(CATHY *goes.* MARTIN, VICTORIA *and* BETTY *walking slowly.*)

MARTIN: Tom!
BETTY: He'll fall in.
VICTORIA: No he won't.
MARTIN: Don't go too near the edge Tom. Throw the bread 70
     from there. The ducks can get it.
BETTY: I'll never be able to manage. If I can't even walk down
     the street by myself. Everything looks so fierce.
VICTORIA: Just watch Tommy feeding the ducks.
BETTY: He's going to fall in. Make Martin make him move back. 75
VICTORIA: He's not going to fall in.
BETTY: It's since I left your father.
VICTORIA: Mummy, it really was the right decision.
BETTY: Everything comes at me from all directions. Martin
     despises me.   80
VICTORIA: Of course he doesn't, mummy.
BETTY: Of course he does.
MARTIN: Throw the bread. That's the way. The duck can get
     it. Quack quack quack quack quack.
BETTY: I don't want to take pills. Lin says you can't trust doctors. 85
VICTORIA: You're not taking pills. You're doing very well.
BETTY: But I'm so frightened.
VICTORIA: What are you frightened of?
BETTY: Victoria, you always ask that as if there was suddenly
     going to be an answer.   90
VICTORIA: Are you all right sitting there?
BETTY: Yes, yes. Go and be with Martin.

(VICTORIA *joins* MARTIN, BETTY *stays sitting on the bench.*)

MARTIN: You take the job, you go to Manchester. You turn it
     down, you stay in London. People are making decisions
     like this every day of the week. It needn't be for more than 95
     a year. You get long vacations. Our relationship might
     well stand the strain of that, and if it doesn't we're better
     out of it. I don't want to put any pressure on you. I'd just
     like to know so we can sell the house. I think we're mov-
     ing into an entirely different way of life if you go to Man- 100
     chester because it won't end there. We could keep the

house as security for Tommy but he might as well get used
to the fact that life nowadays is insecure. You should ask
your mother what she thinks and then do the opposite. I
105   could just take that room in Barbara's house, and then we
could babysit for each other. You think that means I want
to fuck Barbara. I don't. Well, I do, but I won't. And even
if I did, what's a fuck between friends? What are we meant
to do it with, strangers? Whatever you want to do, I'll be
110   delighted. If you could just let me know what it is I'm to
be delighted about. Don't cry again, Vicky, I'm not the
sort of man who makes women cry.

(LIN *has come in and sat down with* BETTY, CATHY *joins them. She
is wearing a pink dress and carrying a rifle.*)

LIN: I've bought her three new frocks. She won't wear jeans to
school any more because Tracy and Mandy called her a boy.
115   CATHY: Tracy's got a perm.
LIN: You should have shot them.
CATHY: They're coming to tea and we've got to have trifle.
Not trifle you make, trifle out of a packet. And you've got
to wear a skirt. And tights.
120   LIN: Tracy's mum wears jeans.
CATHY: She does not. She wears velvet.
BETTY: Well I think you look very pretty. And if that gun has
caps in it please take it a long way away.
CATHY: It's got red caps. They're louder.
125   MARTIN: Do you think you're well enough to do this job? You
don't have to do it. No one's going to think any the less of
you if you stay here with me. There's no point being so liberated you make yourself cry all the time. You stay and
we'll get everything sorted out. What it is about sex, when
130   we talk while it's happening I get to feel it's like a driving
lesson. Left, right, a little faster, carry on, slow down—

(CATHY *shoots* VICTORIA.)

CATHY: You're dead Vicky.
VICTORIA: Aaaargh.
CATHY: Fall over.
135   VICTORIA: I'm not falling over, the ground's wet.
CATHY: You're dead.
VICTORIA: Yes, I'm dead.
CATHY: The Dead Hand Gang fall over. They said I had to fall
over in the mud or I can't play. That duck's a mandarin.
140   MARTIN: Which one? Look, Tommy.
CATHY: That's a diver. It's got a yellow eye and it dives. That's
a goose. Tommy doesn't know it's a goose, he thinks it's a
duck. The babies get eaten by weasels. Kiou kiou.

(CATHY *goes.*)

MARTIN: So I lost my erection last night not because I'm not
145   prepared to talk, it's just that taking in technical information is a different part of the brain and also I don't like to
feel that you do it better to yourself. I have read the Hite
report. I do know that women have to learn to get their
pleasure despite our clumsy attempts at expressing undying
150   devotion and ecstasy, and that what we spent our adolescence thinking was an animal urge we had to suppress is in
fact a fine art we have to acquire. I'm not like whatever
percentage of American men have become impotent as a

direct result of women's liberation, which I am totally in
favour of, more I sometimes think than you are yourself.   155
Nor am I one of your villains who sticks it in, bangs away,
and falls asleep. My one aim is to give you pleasure. My one
aim is to give you rolling orgasms like I do other women.
So why the hell don't you have them? My analysis for what
it's worth is that despite all my efforts you still feel domi-   160
nated by me. I in fact think it's very sad that you don't feel
able to take that job. It makes me feel very guilty. I don't
want you to do it just because I encourage you to do it. But
don't you think you'd feel better if you did take the job?
You're the one who's talked about freedom. You're the one   165
who's experimenting with bisexuality, and I don't stop you,
I think women have something to give each other. You
seem to need the mutual support. You find me too overwhelming. So follow it through, go away, leave me and
Tommy alone for a bit, we can manage perfectly well with-   170
out you. I'm not putting any pressure on you but I don't
think you're being a whole person. God knows I do everything I can to make you stand on your own two feet. Just
be yourself. You don't seem to realise how insulting it is to
me that you can't get yourself together.   175

(MARTIN *and* VICTORIA *go.*)

BETTY: You must be very lonely yourself with no husband.
You don't miss him?
LIN: Not really, no.
BETTY: Maybe you like being on your own.
LIN: I'm seeing quite a lot of Vicky. I don't live alone. I live   180
with Cathy.
BETTY: I would have been frightened when I was your age. I
thought, the poor children, their mother all alone.
LIN: I've a lot of friends.
BETTY: I find when I'm making tea I put out two cups. It's   185
strange not having a man in the house. You don't know
who to do things for.
LIN: Yourself.
BETTY: Oh, that's very selfish.
LIN: Have you any women friends?   190
BETTY: I've never been so short of men's company that I've
had to bother with women.
LIN: Don't you like women?
BETTY: They don't have such interesting conversations as
men. There has never been a woman composer of genius.   195
They don't have a sense of humour. They spoil things for
themselves with their emotions. I can't say I do like
women very much, no.
LIN: But you're a woman.
BETTY: There's nothing says you have to like yourself.   200
LIN: Do you like me?
BETTY: There's no need to take it personally, Lin.

(MARTIN *and* VICTORIA *come back.*)

MARTIN: Did you know if you put cocaine on your prick you
can keep it up all night? The only thing is of course it goes
numb so you don't feel anything. But you would, that's   205
the main thing. I just want to make you happy.
BETTY: Vicky, I'd like to go home.
VICTORIA: Yes, mummy, of course.
BETTY: I'm sorry, dear.

210 VICTORIA: I think Tommy would like to stay out a bit longer.
    LIN: Hello, Martin. We do keep out of each other's way.
    MARTIN: I think that's the best thing to do.
    BETTY: Perhaps you'd walk home with me, Martin. I do feel
    safer with a man. The park is so large the grass seems to tilt.
215 MARTIN: Yes, I'd like to go home and do some work. I'm writ-
    ing a novel about women from the women's point of view.

(MARTIN *and* BETTY *go.* LIN *and* VICTORIA *are alone. They*
embrace.)

VICTORIA: Why the hell can't he just be a wife and come
    with me? Why does Martin make me tie myself in knots?
    No wonder we can't just have a simple fuck. No, not Mar-
220 tin, why do I make myself tie myself in knots. It's got to
    stop, Lin. I'm not like that with you. Would you love me
    if I went to Manchester?
    LIN: Yes.
VICTORIA: Would you love me if I went on a climbing expe-
225 dition in the Andes mountains?
    LIN: Yes.
VICTORIA: Would you love me if my teeth fell out?
    LIN: Yes.
VICTORIA: Would you love me if I loved ten other people?
230 LIN: And me?
VICTORIA: Yes.
    LIN: Yes.
VICTORIA: And I feel apologetic for not being quite so subordi-
    nate as I was. I am more intelligent than him. I am brilliant.
235 LIN: Leave him Vic. Come and live with me.
VICTORIA: Don't be silly.
    LIN: Silly, Christ, don't then. I'm not asking because I need to
    live with someone. I'd enjoy it, that's all, we'd both enjoy
    it. Fuck you. Cathy, for fuck's sake stop throwing stones at
240 the ducks. The man's going to get you.
VICTORIA: What man? Do you need a man to frighten your
    child with?
    LIN: My mother said it.
VICTORIA: You're so inconsistent, Lin.
245 LIN: I've changed who I sleep with, I can't change everything.
VICTORIA: Like when I had to stop you getting a job in a
    boutique and collaborating with sexist consumerism.
    LIN: I should have got that job, Cathy would have liked it. Why
    shouldn't I have some decent clothes? I'm sick of dressing
250 like a boy, why can't I look sexy, wouldn't you love me?
VICTORIA: Lin, you've no analysis.
    LIN: No but I'm good at kissing aren't I? I give Cathy guns,
    my mum didn't give me guns. I dress her in jeans, she
    wants to wear dresses. I don't know. I can't work it out, I
255 don't want to. You read too many books, you get at me all
    the time, you're worse to me than Martin is to you, you
    piss me off, my brother's been killed. I'm sorry to win the
    argument that way but there it is.
VICTORIA: What do you mean win the argument?
260 LIN: I mean be nice to me.
VICTORIA: In Belfast?
    LIN: I heard this morning. Don't don't start. I've hardly seen
    him for two years. I rung my father. You'd think I'd shot
    myself. He doesn't want me to go to the funeral.

(CATHY *approaches.*)

VICTORIA: What will you do?   265
    LIN: Go of course.
CATHY: What is it? Who's killed? What?
    LIN: It's Bill. Your uncle. In the army. Bill that gave you the
    blue teddy.
CATHY: Can I have his gun?   270
    LIN: It's time we went home. Time you went to bed.
CATHY: No it's not.
    LIN: We go home and you have tea and you have a bath and
    you go to bed.
CATHY: Fuck off.   275
    LIN: Cathy, shut up.
VICTORIA: It's only half past five, why don't we—
    LIN: I'll tell you why she has to go to bed—
VICTORIA: She can come home with me.
    LIN: Because I want her out of the fucking way.   280
VICTORIA: She can come home with me.
CATHY: I'm not going to bed.
    LIN: I want her home with me not home with you, I want
    her in bed, I want today over.
CATHY: I'm not going to bed.   285

(LIN *hits* CATHY, CATHY *cries.*)

LIN: And shut up or I'll give you something to cry for.
CATHY: I'm not going to bed.
VICTORIA: Cathy—
    LIN: You keep out of it.
VICTORIA: Lin for God's sake.   290

(*They are all shouting.* CATHY *runs off.* LIN *and* VICTORIA *are*
silent. Then they laugh and embrace.)

LIN: Where's Tommy?
VICTORIA: What? Didn't he go with Martin?
    LIN: Did he?
VICTORIA: God oh God.
    LIN: Cathy! Cathy!   295
VICTORIA: I haven't thought about him. How could I not
    think about him? Tommy!
    LIN: Cathy! Come on, quick, I want some help.
VICTORIA: Tommy! Tommy!

(CATHY *comes back.*)

LIN: Where's Tommy? Have you seen him? Did he go with   300
    Martin? Do you know where he is?
CATHY: I showed him the goose. We went in the bushes.
    LIN: Then what?
CATHY: I came back on the swing.
VICTORIA: And Tommy? Where was Tommy?   305
CATHY: He fed the ducks.
    LIN: No that was before.
CATHY: He did a pee in the bushes. I helped him with his
    trousers.
VICTORIA: And after that?   310
CATHY: He fed the ducks.
VICTORIA: No no.
CATHY: He liked the ducks. I expect he fell in.
    LIN: Did you see him fall in?
VICTORIA: Tommy! Tommy!   315
    LIN: What's the last time you saw him?

CATHY: He did a pee.
VICTORIA: Mummy said he would fall in. Oh God, Tommy!
LIN: We'll go round the pond. We'll go opposite ways round
320   the pond.
ALL: (*Shout.*) Tommy!

(VICTORIA *and* LIN *go off opposite sides.* CATHY *climbs the bench.*)

CATHY: Georgie Best, superstar
   Walks like a woman and wears a bra.
     There he is! I see him! Mum! Vicky! There he is! He's
325   in the bushes.

(LIN *comes back.*)

LIN: Come on Cathy love, let's go home.
CATHY: Vicky's got him.
LIN: Come on.
CATHY: Is she cross?
330 LIN: No. Come on.
CATHY: I found him.
LIN: Yes. Come on.

(CATHY *gets off the bench.* CATHY *and* LIN *hug.*)

CATHY: I'm watching telly.
LIN: Ok.
335 CATHY: After the news.
LIN: Ok.
CATHY: I'm not going to bed.
LIN: Yes you are.
CATHY: I'm not going to bed now.
340 LIN: Not now but early.
CATHY: How early?
LIN: Not late.
CATHY: How not late?
LIN: Early.
345 CATHY: How early?
LIN: Not late.

(*They go off together.* GERRY *comes on. He waits.* EDWARD *comes.*)

EDWARD: I've got some fish for dinner. I thought I'd make a
   cheese sauce.
GERRY: I won't be in.
350 EDWARD: Where are you going?
GERRY: For a start I'm going to a sauna. Then I'll see.
EDWARD: All right. What time will you be back? We'll eat
   then.
GERRY: You're getting like a wife.
355 EDWARD: I don't mind that.
GERRY: Why don't I do the cooking sometime?
EDWARD: You can if you like. You're just not so good at it
   that's all. Do it tonight.
GERRY: I won't be in tonight.
360 EDWARD: Do it tomorrow. If we can't eat it we can always
   go to a restaurant.
GERRY: Stop it.
EDWARD: Stop what?
GERRY: Just be yourself.
365 EDWARD: I don't know what you mean. Everyone's always
   tried to stop me being feminine and now you are too.
GERRY: You're putting it on.

EDWARD: I like doing the cooking. I like being fucked. You
   do like me like this really.
370 GERRY: I'm bored, Eddy.
EDWARD: Go to the sauna.
GERRY: And you'll stay home and wait up for me.
EDWARD: No, I'll go to bed and read a book.
GERRY: Or knit. You could knit me a pair of socks.
375 EDWARD: I might knit. I like knitting.
GERRY: I don't mind if you knit. I don't want to be married.
EDWARD: I do.
GERRY: Well I'm divorcing you.
EDWARD: I wouldn't want to keep a man who wants his
380   freedom.
GERRY: Eddy, do stop playing the injured wife, it's not funny.
EDWARD: I'm not playing. It's true.
GERRY: I'm not the husband so you can't be the wife.
EDWARD: I'll always be here, Gerry, if you want to come
385   back. I know you men like to go off by yourselves. I don't
   think I could love deeply more than once. But I don't
   think I can face life on my own so don't leave it too long
   or it may be too late.
GERRY: What are you trying to turn me into?
390 EDWARD: A monster, darling, which is what you are.
GERRY: I'll collect my stuff from the flat in the morning.

(GERRY *goes.* EDWARD *sits on the bench. It gets darker.* VICTORIA
comes.)

VICTORIA: Tommy dropped a toy car somewhere, you haven't
   seen it? It's red. He says it's his best one. Oh the hell with
   it. Martin's reading him a story. There, isn't it quiet?

(*They sit on the bench, holding hands.*)

EDWARD: I like women.
395 VICTORIA: That should please mother.
EDWARD: No listen Vicky. I'd rather be a woman. I wish I had
   breasts like that, I think they're beautiful. Can I touch
   them?
400 VICTORIA: What, pretending they're yours?
EDWARD: No, I know it's you.
VICTORIA: I think I should warn you I'm enjoying this.
EDWARD: I'm sick of men.
VICTORIA: I'm sick of men.
405 EDWARD: I think I'm a lesbian.

SCENE III

The park. Summer night. VICTORIA, LIN *and* EDWARD *drunk.*

LIN: Where are you?
VICTORIA: Come on.
EDWARD: Do we sit in a circle?
VICTORIA: Sit in a triangle.
5 EDWARD: You're good at mathematics. She's good at mathe-
   matics.
VICTORIA: Give me your hand. We all hold hands.
EDWARD: Do you know what to do?
LIN: She's making it up.
10 VICTORIA: We start off by being quiet.
EDWARD: What?
LIN: Hush.

EDWARD: Will something appear?

VICTORIA: It was your idea.

15 EDWARD: It wasn't my idea. It was your book.

LIN: You said call up the goddess.

EDWARD: I don't remember saying that.

LIN: We could have called her on the telephone.

EDWARD: Don't be so silly, this is meant to be frightening.

20 LIN: Kiss me.

VICTORIA: Are we going to do it?

LIN: We're doing it.

VICTORIA: A ceremony.

LIN: It's very sexy, you said it is. You said the women were
25   priests in the temples and fucked all the time. I'm just
    helping.

VICTORIA: As long as it's sacred.

LIN: It's very sacred.

VICTORIA: Innin, Innana, Nana, Nut, Anat, Anahita, Istar, Isis.

30 LIN: I can't remember all that.

VICTORIA: Lin! Innin, Innana, Nana, Nut, Anat, Anahita, Istar,
    Isis.

(LIN *and* EDWARD *join in and continue the chant under* VICTORIA'S
speech.)

    Goddess of many names, oldest of the old, who walked in
    chaos and created life, hear us calling you back through
35   time, before Jehovah, before Christ, before men drove you
    out and burnt your temples, hear us, Lady, give us back
    what we were, give us the history we haven't had, make us
    the women we can't be.

ALL: Innin, Innana, Nana, Nut, Anat, Anahita, Istar, Isis.

(*Chant continues under other speeches.*)

40 LIN: Come back, goddess.

VICTORIA: Goddess of the sun and the moon her brother, lit-
    tle goddess of Crete with snakes in your hands.

LIN: Goddess of breasts.

VICTORIA: Goddess of cunts.

45 LIN: Goddess of fat bellies and babies. And blood blood blood.

(*Chant continues.*)

    I see her.

EDWARD: What?

(*They stop chanting.*)

LIN: I see her. Very tall. Snakes in her hands. Light light
    light—look out! Did I give you a fright?

50 EDWARD: I was terrified.

VICTORIA: Don't spoil it Lin.

LIN: It's all out of a book.

VICTORIA: Innin Innana—I can't do it now. I was really en-
    joying myself.

55 LIN: She won't appear with a man here.

VICTORIA: They had men, they had sons and lovers.

EDWARD: They had eunuchs.

LIN: Don't give us ideas.

VICTORIA: There's Attis and Tammuz, they're torn to pieces.

60 EDWARD: Tear me to pieces, Lin.

VICTORIA: The priestess chose a lover for a year and he was
    king because she chose him and then he was killed at the
    end of the year.

EDWARD: Hurray.

VICTORIA: And the women had the children and nobody 65
    knew it was done by fucking so they didn't know about
    fathers and nobody cared who the father was and the
    property was passed down through the maternal line—

LIN: Don't turn it into a lecture, Vicky, it's meant to be an orgy.

VICTORIA: It never hurts to understand the theoretical back- 70
    ground. You can't separate fucking and economics.

LIN: Give us a kiss.

EDWARD: Shut up, listen.

LIN: What?

EDWARD: There's somebody there. 75

LIN: Where?

EDWARD: There.

VICTORIA: The priestesses used to make love to total strangers.

LIN: Go on then, I dare you.

EDWARD: Go on, Vicky. 80

VICTORIA: He won't know it's a sacred rite in honour of the
    goddess.

EDWARD: We'll know.

LIN: We can tell him.

EDWARD: It's not what he thinks, it's what we think. 85

LIN: Don't tell him till after, he'll run a mile.

VICTORIA: Hello. We're having an orgy. Do you want me to
    suck your cock?

(*The stranger approaches. It is* MARTIN.)

MARTIN: There you are. I've been looking everywhere. What
    the hell are you doing? Do you know what the time is? 90
    You're all pissed out of your minds.

(*They leap on* MARTIN, *pull him down and start to make love to
him.*)

MARTIN: Well that's all right. If all we're talking about is hav-
    ing a lot of sex there's no problem. I was all for the sixties
    when liberation just meant fucking.

(*Another stranger approaches.*)

LIN: Hey you, come here. Come and have sex with us. 95

VICTORIA: Who is it?

(*The stranger is a soldier.*)

LIN: It's my brother.

EDWARD: Lin, don't.

LIN: It's my brother.

VICTORIA: It's her sense of humour, you get used to it. 100

LIN: Shut up Vicky, it's my brother. Isn't it? Bill?

SOLDIER: Yes it's me.

LIN: And you are dead.

SOLDIER: Fucking dead all right yeh.

LIN: Have you come back to tell us something? 105

SOLDIER: No I've come for a fuck. That was the worst thing in
    the fucking army. Never fucking let out. Can't fucking talk
    to Irish girls. Fucking bored out of my fucking head. That
    or shit scared. For five minutes I'd be glad I wasn't bored,
    then I was fucking scared. Then we'd come in and I'd be 110

glad I wasn't scared and then I was fucking bored. Spent the day reading fucking porn and the fucking night wanking. Man's fucking life in the fucking army? No fun when the fucking kids hate you. I got so I fucking wanted to kill
115   someone and I got fucking killed myself and I want a fuck.
LIN: I miss you. Bill. Bill.

(LIN *collapses.* SOLDIER *goes.* VICTORIA *comforts* LIN.)

EDWARD: Let's go home.
LIN: Victoria, come home with us. Victoria's coming to live with me and Edward.
120 MARTIN: Tell me about it in the morning.
LIN: It's true.
VICTORIA: It is true.
MARTIN: Tell me when you're sober.

(EDWARD, LIN, VICTORIA *go off together.* MARTIN *goes off alone.* GERRY *comes on.*)

GERRY: I come here sometimes at night and pick somebody up.
125   Sometimes I come here at night and don't pick anybody up. I do also enjoy walking about at night. There's never any trouble finding someone. I can have sex any time. You might not find the type you most fancy every day of the week, but there's plenty of people about who just enjoy having a good
130   time. I quite like living alone. If I live with someone I get annoyed with them. Edward always put on Capital radio when he got up. The silence gets wasted. I wake up at four o'clock sometimes. Birds. Silence. If I bring somebody home I never let them stay the night. Edward! Edward!

(EDWARD *from Act One comes on.*)

135 EDWARD: Gerry I love you.
GERRY: Yes, I know. I love you, too.
EDWARD: You know what we did? I want to do it again. I think about it all the time. Don't you want to any more?
GERRY: Yes, of course.

Song

CLOUD NINE

140 ALL: It'll be fine when you reach Cloud Nine.

Mist was rising and the night was dark.
Me and my baby took a walk in the park.
He said Be mine and you're on Cloud Nine.

Better watch out when you're on Cloud Nine.

145   Smoked some dope on the playground swings
Higher and higher on true love's wings
He said Be mine and you're on Cloud Nine.

Twenty-five years on the same Cloud Nine.

Who did she meet on her first blind date?
150   The guys were no surprise but the lady was great
They were women in love, they were on Cloud Nine.

Two the same, they were on Cloud Nine.

The bride was sixty-five, the groom was seventeen,
They fucked in the back of the black limousine.
155   It was divine in their silver Cloud Nine.

Simply divine in their silver Cloud Nine.

The wife's lover's children and my lover's wife,
Cooking in my kitchen, confusing my life.
And it's upside down when you reach Cloud Nine.

Upside down when you reach Cloud Nine.   160

SCENE IV

The park. Afternoon in late summer. MARTIN, CATHY, EDWARD.

CATHY: Under the bramble bushes,
Under the sea boom boom boom,
True love for you my darling,
True love for me my darling,
When we are married,   5
We'll raise a family.
Boy for you, girl for me,
Boom tiddley oom boom
SEXY.
EDWARD: You'll have Tommy and Cathy tonight then ok?   10
Tommy's still on antibiotics, do make him finish the bottle, he takes it in Ribena. It's no good in orange, he spits it out. Remind me to give you Cathy's swimming things.
CATHY: I did six strokes, didn't I Martin? Did I do a width? How many strokes is a length? How many miles is a   15
swimming pool? I'm going to take my bronze and silver and gold and diamond.
MARTIN: Is Tommy still wetting the bed?
EDWARD: Don't get angry with him about it.
MARTIN: I just need to go to the launderette so I've got a   20
spare sheet. Of course I don't get fucking angry, Eddy, for God's sake. I don't like to say he is my son but he is my son. I'm surprised I'm not wetting the bed myself.
CATHY: I don't wet the bed ever. Do you wet the bed Martin?
MARTIN: No.   25
CATHY: You said you did.

(BETTY *comes.*)

BETTY: I do miss the sun living in England but today couldn't be more beautiful. You appreciate the weekend when you're working. Betty's been at work this week, Cathy. It's terrible tiring, Martin, I don't know how you've done it   30
all these years. And the money, I feel like a child with the money, Clive always paid everything but I do understand it perfectly well. Look Cathy let me show you my money.
CATHY: I'll count it. Let me count it. What's that?
BETTY: Five pounds, Five and five is—   35
CATHY: One two three—
BETTY: Five and five is ten, and five—
CATHY: If I get it right can I have one?
EDWARD: No you can't.

(CATHY *goes on counting the money.*)

BETTY: I never like to say anything, Martin, or you'll think   40
I'm being a mother-in-law.
EDWARD: Which you are.
BETTY: Thank you, Edward, I'm not talking to you. Martin, I think you're being wonderful. Vicky will come back. Just let her stay with Lin till she sorts herself out. It's very nice   45

for a girl to have a friend; I had friends at school, that was
very nice. But I'm sure Lin and Edward don't want her
with them all the time. I'm not at all shocked that Lin and
Edward aren't married and she already has a child, we all
50 know first marriages don't always work out. But really
Vicky must be in the way. And poor little Tommy. I hear
he doesn't sleep properly and he's had a cough.

MARTIN: No, he's fine, Betty, thank you.

CATHY: My bed's horrible. I want to sleep in the big bed with
55 Lin and Vicky and Eddy and I do get in if I've got a bad
dream, and my bed's got a bump right in my back. I want
to sleep in a tent.

BETTY: Well Tommy has got a nasty cough, Martin, whatever
you say.

60 EDWARD: He's over that. He's got some medicine.

MARTIN: He takes it in Ribena.

BETTY: Well I'm glad to hear it. Look what a lot of money,
Cathy, and I sit behind a desk of my own and I answer the
telephone and keep the doctor's appointment book and it
65 really is great fun.

CATHY: Can we go camping, Martin, in a tent? We could take
the Dead Hand Gang.

BETTY: Not those big boys, Cathy? They're far too big and
rough for you. They climb back into the park after dark.
70 I'm sure mummy doesn't let you play with them, does she
Edward? Well I don't know.

(*Ice cream bells.*)

CATHY: Ice cream. Martin you promised. I'll have a double
ninety-nine. No I'll have a shandy lolly. Betty, you have a
shandy lolly and I'll have a lick. No, you have a double
75 ninety-nine and I'll have the chocolate.

(MARTIN, CATHY *and* BETTY *go, leaving* EDWARD. GERRY *comes.*)

GERRY: Hello, Eddy. Thought I might find you here.

EDWARD: Gerry.

GERRY: Not working today then?

EDWARD: I don't work here any more.

80 GERRY: Your mum got you into a dark suit?

EDWARD: No of course not. I'm on the dole. I am working,
though, I do housework.

GERRY: Whose wife are you now then?

EDWARD: Nobody's. I don't think like that any more. I'm liv-
85 ing with some women.

GERRY: What women?

EDWARD: It's my sister, Vic, and her lover. They go out to
work and I look after the kids.

GERRY: I thought for a moment you said you were living
90 with women.

EDWARD: We do sleep together, yes.

GERRY: I was passing the park anyway so I thought I'd look in.
I was in the sauna the other night and I saw someone who
looked like you but it wasn't. I had sex with him anyway.

95 EDWARD: I do go to the sauna sometimes.

(CATHY *comes, gives* EDWARD *an ice cream, goes.*)

GERRY: I don't think I'd like living with children. They make
a lot of noise don't they?

EDWARD: I tell them to shut up and they shut up. I wouldn't
want to leave them at the moment.

GERRY: Look why don't we go for a meal sometime?   100

EDWARD: Yes I'd like that. Where are you living now?

GERRY: Same place.

EDWARD: I'll come round for you tomorrow night about 7:30.

GERRY: Great.

(EDWARD *goes.* HARRY *comes.* HARRY *and* GERRY *pick each other
up. They go off.* BETTY *comes back.*)

BETTY: No, the ice cream was my treat, Martin. Off you go.   105
I'm going to have a quiet sit in the sun.

(MAUD *comes.*)

MAUD: Let Mrs Saunders be a warning to you, Betty. I know
what it is to be unprotected.

BETTY: But mother, I have a job. I earn money.

MAUD: I know we have our little differences but I always   110
want what is best for you.

(ELLEN *comes.*)

ELLEN: Betty, what happens with a man?

BETTY: You just keep still.

ELLEN: And is it enjoyable? Don't forget me, Betty.

(MAUD *and* ELLEN *go.*)

BETTY: I used to think Clive was the one who liked sex. But   115
then I found I missed it. I used to touch myself when I was
very little, I thought I'd invented something wonderful. I
used to do it to go to sleep with or to cheer myself up, and
one day it was raining and I was under the kitchen table,
and my mother saw me with my hand under my dress rub-   120
bing away, and she dragged me out so quickly I hit my head
and it bled and I was sick, and nothing was said, and I never
did it again till this year. I thought if Clive wasn't looking
at me there wasn't a person there. And one night in bed in
my flat I was so frightened I started touching myself. I   125
thought my hand might go through space. I touched my
face, it was there, my arm, my breast, and my hand went
down where I thought it shouldn't, and I thought well
there is somebody there. It felt very sweet, it was a feeling
from very long ago, it was very soft, just barely touching,   130
and I felt myself gathering together more and more and I
felt angry with Clive and angry with my mother and I
went on and on defying them, and there was this vast feeling growing in me and all round me and they couldn't stop
me and no one could stop me and I was there and coming   135
and coming. Afterwards I thought I'd betrayed Clive. My
mother would kill me. But I felt triumphant because I was
a separate person from them. And I cried because I didn't
want to be. But I don't cry about it any more. Sometimes I
do it three times in one night and it really is great fun.   140

(VICTORIA *and* LIN *come in.*)

VICTORIA: So I said to the professor, I don't think this is an occasion for invoking the concept of structural causality—oh
hello mummy.

BETTY: I'm going to ask you a question, both of you. I have
a little money from your grandmother. And the three of   145
you are living in that tiny flat with two children. I won-

der if we could get a house and all live in it together? It would give you more room.

VICTORIA: But I'm going to Manchester anyway.

150 LIN: We'd have a garden, Vicky.

BETTY: You do seem to have such fun all of you.

VICTORIA: I don't want to.

BETTY: I didn't think you would.

LIN: Come on, Vicky, she knows we sleep together, and Eddy.

155 BETTY: I think I've known for quite a while but I'm not sure. I don't usually think about it, so I don't know if I know about it or not.

VICTORIA: I don't want to live with my mother.

LIN: Don't think of her as your mother, think of her as Betty.

160 VICTORIA: But she thinks of herself as my mother.

BETTY: I am your mother.

VICTORIA: But mummy we don't even like each other.

BETTY: We might begin to.

(CATHY comes on howling with a nosebleed.)

LIN: Oh Cathy what happened?

165 BETTY: She's been assaulted.

VICTORIA: It's a nosebleed.

CATHY: Took my ice cream.

LIN: Who did?

CATHY: Took my money.

(MARTIN comes.)

170 MARTIN: Is everything all right?

LIN: I thought you were looking after her.

CATHY: They hit me. I can't play. They said I'm a girl.

BETTY: Those dreadful boys, the gang, the Dead Hand.

MARTIN: What do you mean you thought I was looking after her?

175 LIN: Last I saw her she was with you getting an ice cream. It's your afternoon.

MARTIN: Then she went off to play. She goes off to play. You don't keep an eye on her every minute.

LIN: She doesn't get beaten up when I'm looking after her.

180 CATHY: Took my money.

MARTIN: Why the hell should I look after your child anyway? I just want Tommy. Why should he live with you and Vicky all week?

LIN: I don't mind if you don't want to look after her but don't

185 say you will and then this happens.

VICTORIA: When I get to Manchester everything's going to be different anyway, Lin's staying here, and you're staying here, we're all going to have to sit down and talk it through.

MARTIN: I'd really enjoy that.

190 CATHY: Hit me on the face.

LIN: You were the one looking after her and look at her now, that's all.

MARTIN: I've had enough of you telling me.

LIN: Yes you know it all.

195 MARTIN: Now stop it. I work very hard at not being like this, I could do with some credit.

LIN: Ok you're quite nice, try and enjoy it. Don't make me sorry for you, Martin, it's hard for me too. We've better

things to do than quarrel. I've got to go and sort those little bastards out for a start. Where are they, Cathy? 200

CATHY: Don't kill them, mum, hit them. Give them a nosebleed, mum.

(LIN goes.)

VICTORIA: Tommy's asleep in the pushchair. We'd better wake him up or he won't sleep tonight.

MARTIN: Sometimes I keep him up watching television till he 205 falls asleep on the sofa so I can hold him. Come on, Cathy, we'll get another ice cream.

CATHY: Chocolate sauce and nuts.

VICTORIA: Betty, would you like an ice cream?

BETTY: No thank you, the cold hurts my teeth, but what a 210 nice thought, Vicky, thank you.

(VICTORIA goes. BETTY alone. GERRY comes.)

BETTY: I think you used to be Edward's flatmate.

GERRY: You're his mother. He's talked about you.

BETTY: Well never mind. Children are always wrong about their parents. It's a great problem knowing where to live 215 and who to share with. I live by myself just now.

GERRY: Good, So do I. You can do what you like.

BETTY: I don't really know what I like.

GERRY: You'll soon find out.

BETTY: What do you like? 220

GERRY: Waking up at four in the morning.

BETTY: I like listening to music in bed and sometimes for supper I just have a big piece of bread and dip it in very hot lime pickle. So you don't get lonely by yourself? Perhaps you have a lot of visitors. I've been thinking I should have 225 some visitors, I could give a little dinner party. Would you come? There wouldn't just be bread and lime pickle.

GERRY: Thank you very much.

BETTY: Or don't wait to be asked to dinner. Just drop in informally. I'll give you the address shall I? I don't usually 230 give strange men my address but then you're not a strange man, you're a friend of Edward's. I suppose I seem a different generation to you but you are older than Edward. I was married for so many years it's quite hard to know how to get acquainted. But if there isn't a right way to do 235 things you have to invent one. I always thought my mother was far too old to be attractive but when you get to an age yourself it feels quite different.

GERRY: I think you could be quite attractive.

BETTY: If what? 240

GERRY: If you stop worrying.

BETTY: I think when I do more about things I worry about them less. So perhaps you could help me do more.

GERRY: I might be going to live with Edward again.

BETTY: That's nice, but I'm rather surprised if he wants to 245 share a flat. He's rather involved with a young woman he lives with, or two young women, I don't understand Edward but never mind.

GERRY: I'm very involved with him.

BETTY: I think Edward did try to tell me once but I didn't lis- 250 ten. So what I'm being told now is that Edward is gay is

that right? And you are too. And I've been making rather a fool of myself. But Edward does also sleep with women.
GERRY: He does, yes, I don't.
255 BETTY: Well people always say it's the mother's fault but I don't intend to start blaming myself. He seems perfectly happy.
GERRY: I could still come and see you.
BETTY: So you could, yes. I'd like that. I've never tried to pick up a man before.
260 GERRY: Not everyone's gay.
BETTY: No, that's lucky isn't it.

(GERRY *goes.* CLIVE *comes.*)

CLIVE: You are not that sort of woman, Betty. I can't believe you are. I can't feel the same about you as I did. And Africa is to be communist I suppose. I used to be proud to be British. There was a high ideal. I came out onto the 265 verandah and looked at the stars.

(CLIVE *goes.* BETTY *from Act One comes.* BETTY *and* BETTY *embrace.*)

SARAH KANE

A brilliant young playwright, Sarah Kane (1971–1999) changed the landscape of British theater in the 1990s with her series of brilliant, violent parables. The daughter of British journalists, Kane was raised in an environment of religious evangelism; she studied playwriting and acting at the University of Bristol, and then enrolled in the playwriting course founded by the playwright David Edgar at the University of Birmingham. Her first play, *Blasted* (1995), was denounced by the press with a ferocity reminiscent of the reception of earlier landmarks in the British stage—Edward Bond's *Saved* in 1965, John Osborne's *Look Back in Anger* in 1956, or even the first production of Ibsen's *Ghosts* in 1891, when Clement Scott famously called the play "An open drain; a loathsome sore unbandaged; a dirty act done publicly." At the same time, though, Kane's mastery both of an intensity of dramatic action and visual imagery immediately drew defenders as well, among them Edward Bond and Caryl Churchill. In the course of the late 1990s, Kane continued to explore the intersection between language and image in an increasingly experimental series of plays—*Phaedra's Love* (1996), *Skin* (a television play, 1997), *Cleansed* (1998), and *Crave* (1998). Kane suffered from severe depression, and she wrote her final play, *4.48 Psychosis*—a play in free verse without given speakers—about the moment at which she would awaken each morning, clinging to a moment of mental clarity and conviction. Written in the autumn of 1998, the play presaged Kane's suicide on February 20, 1999. *4.48 Psychosis* was produced by the Royal Court Theatre in 2000 as part of a retrospective season that brought earlier work, including *Blasted,* back to the London stage.

BLASTED

By any measure, *Blasted* is an elegant, horrific play. Taking place in the claustrophobic environment of "*a very expensive hotel room in Leeds*," Kane's nearly surreal violence is perhaps implied in the phrase she uses to qualify that setting: "*the kind that is so expensive it could be anywhere in the world.*" For while the action of the play seems initially confined to the domestic naturalism characteristic of much British drama—the naturalism typical of socially critical drama from Shaw and Barker and Galsworthy to Osborne to Kane's contemporaries Mark Ravenhill and Patrick Marber—it immediately swerves into another register, as the brutal relationship between Ian and Cate explodes into a new level of violence with the arrival of the Soldier, the apparent bombing of the hotel, and the transformation of the English landscape to a setting that could indeed be "anywhere in the world." Kane's drama proves challenging precisely because the characters' relationships—Ian's brutal rape of Cate, the Soldier's equally brutal rape of Ian—are set against a shifting social and political backdrop. Ian's irritated muttering in Scene Two—"Speak the Queen's English fucking nigger"—alerts us to a resonant class and racial oppression, a political violence that Kane locates at the core of English culture. With the arrival of the Soldier and the bombing of the hotel, the landscape seems to shift to a different kind of battlefield, reminiscent of the ethnic and political strife of Bosnia in the late 1990s. With a kind of surreal dream logic, Ian's petty prejudice is translated into the Soldier's militarized violence, evoked both in his hardened accounts of mutilation—"Insides of people's heads came out of their eyes. Saw a child most of his face blown off, young girl I fucked hand up inside her trying to claw my liquid out, starving man eating his dead wife's leg"—and in the actions he performs, raping Ian, sucking out his eyes, and then committing suicide. In Kane's world, the cycle of inhuman violence is unalterable; yet while individuals brutalize each other, Kane seems to hold out the hope for tiny acts of community, as when Cate returns to Ian at the end of the play. In its evocative imagery and language, and in the way it enfolds a political critique into a series of brilliant, brutal images, Kane's *Blasted* was the signal work of British theater in the 1990s.

The soldier stands over Ian in the Rude Gorilla Theatre production of Sarah Kane's *Blasted*.

BLASTED

Sarah Kane

FOR VINCENT O'CONNELL, WITH THANKS.

CHARACTERS

IAN
CATE
SOLDIER

AUTHOR'S NOTE

Punctuation is used to indicate delivery, not to conform to the rules of grammar.

A stroke (/) marks the point of interruption in overlapping dialogue.

Words in square brackets [ ] are not spoken, but have been included in the text to clarify meaning

Stage directions in brackets ( ) function as lines.

SCENE ONE

A very expensive hotel room in Leeds—the kind that is so expensive it could be anywhere in the world.

There is a large double bed.
A mini-bar and champagne on ice.
A telephone.
A large bouquet of flowers.
Two doors—one is the entrance from the corridor, the other leads off to the bathroom.

*Two people enter—*IAN *and* CATE.

IAN *is 45, Welsh born but lived in Leeds much of his life and picked up the accent.*

CATE *is 21, a lower-middle-class Southerner with a south London accent and a stutter when under stress.*

They enter.

CATE *stops at the door, amazed at the classiness of the room.* IAN *comes in, throws a small pile of newspapers on the bed, goes straight to the mini-bar and pours himself a large gin. He looks briefly out of the window at the street, then turns back to the room.*

IAN: I've shat in better places than this.

(He gulps down the gin.)

> I stink.
> You want a bath?

CATE: *(Shakes her head.)*

IAN *goes into the bathroom and we hear him run the water. He comes back in with only a towel around his waist and a revolver in his hand. He checks it is loaded and puts it under his pillow.*

5 IAN: Tip that wog when he brings up the sandwiches.

He leaves fifty pence and goes into the bathroom.
CATE *comes further into the room.*
She puts her bag down and bounces on the bed.
She goes around the room, looking in every drawer, touching everything.
She smells the flowers and smiles.

CATE: Lovely.

IAN *comes back in, hair wet, towel around his waist, drying himself off.*
He stops and looks at CATE *who is sucking her thumb.*
He goes back in the bathroom where he dresses.
We hear him coughing terribly in the bathroom.
He spits in the sink and re-enters.

CATE: You all right?
IAN: It's nothing.

He pours himself another gin, this time with ice and tonic, and sips it at a more normal pace.
He collects his gun and puts it in his under-arm holster.
He smiles at CATE.

IAN: I'm glad you've come. Didn't think you would.

(He offers her champagne.)

CATE: *(Shakes her head.)*   10
> I was worried.
IAN: This? *(He indicates his chest.)* Don't matter.
CATE: I didn't mean that. You sounded unhappy.
IAN: *(Pops the champagne. He pours them both a glass.)*
CATE: What we celebrating?   15
IAN: *(Doesn't answer. He goes to the window and looks out.)*
> Hate this city. Stinks. Wogs and Pakis taking over.
CATE: You shouldn't call them that.
IAN: Why not?
CATE: It's not very nice.   20
IAN: You a nigger-lover?
CATE: Ian, don't.
IAN: You like our coloured brethren?
CATE: Don't mind them.
IAN: Grow up.   25
CATE: There's Indians at the day centre where my brother goes. They're really polite.
IAN: So they should be.
CATE: He's friends with some of them.
IAN: Retard, isn't he?   30
CATE: No, he's got learning difficulties.
IAN: Aye. Spaz.
CATE: No he's not.
IAN: Glad my son's not a Joey.
CATE: Don't c- call him that.   35

IAN: Your mother I feel sorry for. Two of you like it.
CATE: Like wh- what?
IAN: (*Looks at her, deciding whether or not to continue. He decides against it.*)
40   You know I love you.
CATE: (*Smiles a big smile, friendly and non-sexual.*)
IAN: Don't want you ever to leave.
CATE: I'm here for the night.
IAN: (*Drinks.*)
45   Sweating again. Stink. You ever thought of getting married?
CATE: Who'd marry me?
IAN: I would.
CATE: I couldn't.
IAN: You don't love me. I don't blame you, I wouldn't.
50 CATE: I couldn't leave Mum.
IAN: Have to one day.
CATE: Why?
IAN: (*Opens his mouth to answer but can't think of one.*)

There is a knock at the door.
IAN starts, and CATE goes to answer it.

IAN: Don't.
55 CATE: Why not?
IAN: I said.

He takes his gun from the holster and goes to the door.
He listens.
Nothing.

CATE: (*Giggles.*)
IAN: Shh.

He listens.
Still nothing.

IAN: Probably the wog with the sarnies. Open it.

CATE opens the door.
There's no one there, just a tray of sandwiches on the floor.
She brings them in and examines them.

60 CATE: Ham. Don't believe it.
IAN: (*Takes a sandwich and eats it.*)

Champagne?

CATE: (*Shakes her head.*)
IAN: Got something against ham?
65 CATE: Dead meat. Blood. Can't eat an animal.
IAN: No one would know.
CATE: No, I can't, I actually can't, I'd puke all over the place.
IAN: It's only a pig.
CATE: I'm hungry.
70 IAN: Have one of these.
CATE: I CAN'T.
IAN: I'll take you out for an Indian.
      Jesus, what's this? Cheese.

CATE beams.
She separates the cheese sandwiches from the ham ones, and eats.
IAN watches her.

IAN: Don't like your clothes.
CATE: (*Looks down at her clothes.*)   75
IAN: You look like a lesbos.
CATE: What's that?
IAN: Don't look very sexy, that's all.
CATE: Oh.

(*She continues to eat.*)

      Don't like your clothes either.   80
IAN: (*Looks down at his clothes.*
      Then gets up, takes them all off and stands in front of her, naked.)
      Put your mouth on me.
CATE: (*Stares. Then bursts out laughing.*)
IAN: No?   85
      Fine.
      Because I stink?
CATE: (*Laughs even more.*)

IAN attempts to dress, but fumbles with embarrassment.
He gathers his clothes and goes into the bathroom where he dresses.
CATE eats, and giggles over the sandwiches.
IAN returns, fully dressed.
He picks up his gun, unloads and reloads it.

IAN: You got a job yet?
CATE: No.   90
IAN: Still screwing the taxpayer.
CATE: Mum gives me money.
IAN: When are you going to stand on your own feet?
CATE: I've applied for a job at an advertising agency.
IAN: (*Laughs genuinely.*)   95
      No chance.
CATE: Why not?
IAN: (*Stops laughing and looks at her.*)
      Cate. You're stupid. You're never going to get a job.
CATE: I am. I am not.   100
IAN: See.
CATE: St- Stop it. You're doing it deliberately.
IAN: Doing what?
CATE: C- Confusing me.
IAN: No, I'm talking, you're just too thick to understand.   105
CATE: I am not, I am not.

CATE begins to tremble. IAN is laughing.
CATE faints.
IAN stops laughing and stares at her motionless body.

IAN: Cate?

(*He turns her over and lifts up her eyelids.*
He doesn't know what to do.
He gets a glass of gin and dabs some on her face.)

CATE: (*Sits bolt upright, eyes open but still unconscious.*)
IAN: Fucking Jesus.
CATE: (*Bursts out laughing, unnaturally, hysterically, uncontrollably.*) 110
IAN: Stop fucking about.
CATE: (*Collapses again and lies still.*)

IAN stands by helplessly.
After a few moments, CATE comes round as if waking up in the morning.

IAN: What the Christ was that?

CATE: Have to tell her.

115 IAN: Cate?

CATE: She's in danger.

*(She closes her eyes and slowly comes back to normal.
She looks at IAN and smiles.)*

IAN: What now?

CATE: Did I faint?

IAN: That was real?

120 CATE: Happens all the time.

IAN: What, fits?

CATE: Since Dad came back.

IAN: Does it hurt?

CATE: I'll grow out of it the doctor says.

125 IAN: How do you feel?

CATE: *(Smiles.)*

IAN: Thought you were dead.

CATE: [I] Suppose that's what it's like.

IAN: Don't do it again, fucking scared me.

130 CATE: Don't know much about it, I just go. Feels like I'm away for minutes or months sometimes, then I come back just where I was.

IAN: It's terrible.

CATE: I didn't go far.

135 IAN: What if you didn't come round?

CATE: Wouldn't know. I'd stay there.

IAN: Can't stand it.

(He goes to the mini-bar and pours himself another large gin and lights a cigarette.)

CATE: What?

IAN: Death. Not being.

140 CATE: You fall asleep and then you wake up.

IAN: How do you know?

CATE: Why don't you give up smoking?

IAN: *(Laughs.)*

CATE: You should. They'll make you ill.

145 IAN: Too late for that.

CATE: Whenever I think of you it's with a cigarette and a gin.

IAN: Good.

CATE: They make your clothes smell.

IAN: Don't forget my breath.

150 CATE: Imagine what your lungs must look like.

IAN: Don't need to imagine. I've seen.

CATE: When?

IAN: Last year. When I came round, surgeon brought in this lump of rotting pork, stank. My lung.

155 CATE: He took it out?

IAN: Other one's the same now.

CATE: But you'll die.

IAN: Aye.

CATE: Please stop smoking.

160 IAN: Won't make any difference.

CATE: Can't they do something?

IAN: No. It's not like your brother, look after him he'll be all right.

CATE: They die young.

165 IAN: I'm fucked.

CATE: Can't you get a transplant?

IAN: Don't be stupid. They give them to people with a life. Kids.

CATE: People die in accidents all the time, they must have some spare.

IAN: Why? What for? Keep me alive to die of cirrhosis in 170 three months' time.

CATE: You're making it worse, speeding it up.

IAN: Enjoy myself while I'm here.

(He inhales deeply on his cigarette and swallows the last of the gin neat.)

[I'll] Call that coon, get some more sent up.

CATE: *(Shakes.)* 175

IAN: Wonder if the conker understands English.

*He notices CATE's distress and cuddles her.
He kisses her.
She pulls away and wipes her mouth.*

CATE: Don't put your tongue in, I don't like it.

IAN: Sorry.

The telephone rings loudly. IAN starts, then answers it.

IAN: Hello?

CATE: Who is it? 180

IAN: *(Covers the mouthpiece.)* Shh.
(Into the mouthpiece.) Got it here.

(He takes a notebook from the pile of newspapers and dictates down the phone.)

A serial killer slaughtered British tourist Samantha Scrace, S - C - R - A - C - E, in a sick murder ritual comma, police revealed yesterday point new par. The bubbly nine- 185 teen year old from Leeds was among seven victims found buried in identical triangular tombs in an isolated New Zealand forest point new par. Each had been stabbed more than twenty times and placed face down comma, hands bound behind their backs point new par. Caps up, 190 ashes at the site showed the maniac had stayed to cook a meal, caps down point new par. Samantha comma, a beautiful redhead with dreams of becoming a model comma, was on the trip of a lifetime after finishing her A levels last year point. Samantha's heartbroken mum said 195 yesterday colon quoting, we pray the police will come up with something dash, anything comma, soon point still quoting. The sooner this lunatic is brought to justice the better point end quote new par. The Foreign Office warned tourists Down Under to take extra care point. A 200 spokesman said colon quoting, common sense is the best rule point end quote, copy ends.

(He listens. Then he laughs.)

Exactly.

(He listens.)

That one again, I went to see her. Scouse tart, spread her legs. No. Forget it. Tears and lies, not worth the space. 205

(He presses a button on the phone to connect him to room service.)

Tosser.

CATE: How do they know you're here?

IAN: Told them.

CATE: Why?

210 IAN: In case they needed me.

CATE: Silly. We came here to be away from them.

IAN: Thought you'd like this. Nice hotel.

(Into the mouthpiece.)

Bring a bottle of gin up, son.

(He puts the phone down.)

CATE: We always used to go to yours.

215 IAN: That was years ago. You've grown up.

CATE: *(Smiles.)*

IAN: I'm not well any more.

CATE: *(Stops smiling.)*

IAN *kisses her.*
She responds.
He puts his hand under her top and moves it towards her breast.
With the other hand he undoes his trousers and starts masturbating.
He begins to undo her top.
She pushes him away.

CATE: Ian, d- don't.

220 IAN: What?

CATE: I don't w- want to do this.

IAN: Yes you do.

CATE: I don't.

IAN: Why not? You're nervous, that's all.

(He starts to kiss her again.)

225 CATE: I t- t- t- t- t- t- t- told you. I really like you but I c- c- c- c- can't do this.

IAN: *(Kissing her.)* Shhh.

(He starts to undo her trousers.)
CATE *panics.*
She starts to tremble and make inarticulate crying sounds.
IAN *stops, frightened of bringing another 'fit' on.*

IAN: All right, Cate, it's all right. We don't have to do anything.

He strokes her face until she has calmed down.
She sucks her thumb.
Then.

IAN: That wasn't very fair.

230 CATE: What?

IAN: Leaving me hanging, making a prick of myself.

CATE: I f- f- felt—

IAN: Don't pity me, Cate. You don't have to fuck me 'cause I'm dying, but don't push your cunt in my face then take

235 it away 'cause I stick my tongue out.

CATE: I- I- Ian.

IAN: What's the m- m- matter?

CATE: I k- k- kissed you, that's all. I l- l- like you.

IAN: Don't give me a hard-on if you're not going to finish me

240 off. It hurts.

CATE: I'm sorry.

IAN: Can't switch it on and off like that. If I don't come my cock aches.

CATE: I didn't mean it.

IAN: Shit. *(He appears to be in considerable pain.)*   245

CATE: I'm sorry. I am. I won't do it again.

IAN, *apparently still in pain, takes her hand and grasps it around his penis, keeping his own hand over the top.*
Like this, he masturbates until the comes with some genuine pain.
He releases CATE'*s hand and she withdraws it.*

CATE: Is it better?

IAN: *(Nods.)*

CATE: I'm sorry.

IAN: Don't worry. Can we make love tonight?   250

CATE: No.

IAN: Why not?

CATE: I'm not your girlfriend any more.

IAN: Will you be my girlfriend again?

CATE: I can't.   255

IAN: Why not?

CATE: I told Shaun I'd be his.

IAN: Have you slept with him?

CATE: No.

IAN: Slept with me before. You're more mine than his.   260

CATE: I'm not.

IAN: What was that about then, wanking me off?

CATE: I d- d- d- d-

IAN: Sorry. Pressure, pressure. I love you, that's all.

CATE: You were horrible to me.   265

IAN: I wasn't.

CATE: Stopped phoning me, never said why.

IAN: It was difficult, Cate.

CATE: Because I haven't got a job?

IAN: No, pet, not that.   270

CATE: Because of my brother?

IAN: No, no, Cate. Leave it now.

CATE: That's not fair.

IAN: I said leave it.

(He reaches for his gun.)
There is a knock at the door.
IAN *starts, then goes to answer it.*

IAN: I'm not going to hurt you, just leave it. And keep quiet. 275 It'll only be Sooty after something.

CATE: Andrew.

IAN: What do you want to know a conker's name for?

CATE: I thought he was nice.

IAN: After a bit of black meat, eh? Won't do it with me but 280 you'll go with a whodat.

CATE: You're horrible.

IAN: Cate, love, I'm trying to look after you. Stop you getting hurt.

CATE: You hurt me.   285

IAN: No, I love you.

CATE: Stopped loving me.

IAN: I've told you to leave that. Now.

He kisses her passionately, then goes to the door.

When his back is turned, CATE *wipes her mouth.*
IAN *opens the door. There is a bottle of gin outside on a tray.*
IAN *brings it in and stands, unable to decide between gin and champagne.*

CATE: Have champagne, better for you.
290 IAN: Don't want it better for me.

(He pours himself a gin.)

CATE: You'll die quicker.
IAN: Thanks. Don't it scare you?
CATE: What?
IAN: Death.
295 CATE: Whose?
IAN: Yours.
CATE: Only for Mum. She'd be unhappy if I died. And my brother.
IAN: You're young.
300 When I was your age—
Now.
CATE: Will you have to go to hospital?
IAN: Nothing they can do.
CATE: Does Stella know?
305 IAN: What would I want to tell her for?
CATE: You were married.
IAN: So?
CATE: She'd want to know.
IAN: So she can throw a party at the coven.
310 CATE: She wouldn't do that. What about Matthew?
IAN: What about Matthew?
CATE: Have you told him?
IAN: I'll send him an invite for the funeral.
CATE: He'll be upset.
315 IAN: He hates me.
CATE: He doesn't.
IAN: He fucking does.
CATE: Are you upset?
IAN: Yes. His mother's a lesbos. Am I not preferable to that?
320 CATE: Perhaps she's a nice person.
IAN: She don't carry a gun.
CATE: I expect that's it.
IAN: I loved Stella till she became a witch and fucked off with a dyke, and I love you, though you've got the potential.
325 CATE: For what?
IAN: Sucking gash.
CATE: *(Utters an inarticulate sound.)*
IAN: You ever had a fuck with a woman?
CATE: No.
330 IAN: You want to?
CATE: Don't think so. Have you? With a man.
IAN: You think I'm a cocksucker? You've seen me. *(He vaguely indicates his groin.)* How can you think that?
CATE: I don't. I asked. You asked me.
335 IAN: You dress like a lesbos. I don't dress like a cocksucker.
CATE: What do they dress like?
IAN: Hitler was wrong about the Jews who have they hurt the queers he should have gone for scum them and the wogs and fucking football fans send a bomber over Elland Road
340 finish them off.

(He pours champagne and toasts the idea.)

CATE: I like football.
IAN: Why?
CATE: It's good.
IAN: And when was the last time you went to a football match? 345
CATE: Saturday. United beat Liverpool 2–0.
IAN: Didn't you get stabbed?
CATE: Why should I?
IAN: That's what football's about. It's not fancy footwork and scoring goals. It's tribalism. 350
CATE: I like it.
IAN: You would. About your level.
CATE: I go to Elland Road sometimes. Would you bomb me?
IAN: What do you want to ask a question like that for?
CATE: Would you though? 355
IAN: Don't be thick.
CATE: But would you?
IAN: Haven't got a bomber.
CATE: Shoot me, then. Could you do that?
IAN: Cate. 360
CATE: Do you think it's hard to shoot someone?
IAN: Easy as shitting blood.
CATE: Could you shoot me?
IAN: Could you shoot me stop asking that could you shoot me you could shoot me. 365
CATE: I don't think so.
IAN: If I hurt you.
CATE: Don't think you would.
IAN: But if.
CATE: No, you're soft. 370
IAN: With people I love.

(He stares at her, considering making a pass.)

CATE: *(Smiles at him, friendly.)*
IAN: What's this job, then?
CATE: Personal Assistant.
IAN: Who to? 375
CATE: Don't know.
IAN: Who did you write the letter to?
CATE: Sir or madam.
IAN: You have to know who you're writing to.
CATE: It didn't say. 380
IAN: How much?
CATE: What?
IAN: Money. How much do you get paid.
CATE: Mum said it was a lot. I don't mind about that as long as I can go out sometimes. 385
IAN: Don't despise money. You got it easy.
CATE: I haven't got any money.
IAN: No and you haven't got kids to bring up neither.
CATE: Not yet.
IAN: Don't even think about it. Who would have children. 390 You have kids, they grow up, they hate you and you die.
CATE: I don't hate Mum.
IAN: You still need her.
CATE: You think I'm stupid. I'm not stupid.
IAN: I worry. 395
CATE: Can look after myself.
IAN: Like me.
CATE: No.

IAN: You hate me, don't you.
400   CATE: You shouldn't have that gun.
IAN: May need it.
CATE: What for?
IAN: (*Drinks.*)
CATE: Can't imagine it.
405   IAN: What?
CATE: You. Shooting someone. You wouldn't kill anything.
IAN: (*Drinks.*)
CATE: Have you ever shot anyone?
IAN: Your mind.
410   CATE: Have you though?
IAN: Leave it now, Cate.

She takes the warning.
IAN *kisses her and lights a cigarette.*

IAN: When I'm with you I can't think about anything else.
      You take me to another place.
CATE: It's like that when I have a fit.
415   IAN: Just you.
CATE: The world don't exist, not like this.
      Looks the same but—
      Time slows down.
      A dream I get stuck in, can't do nothing about it.
420   One time—
IAN: Make love to me.
CATE: Blocks out everything else.
          Once—
IAN: [I'll] Make love to you.
425   CATE: It's like that when I touch myself.

IAN *is embarrassed.*

CATE: Just before I'm wondering what it'll be like, and just af-
      ter I'm thinking about the next one, but just as it happens
      it's lovely, I don't think of nothing else.
IAN: Like the first cigarette of the day.
430   CATE: That's bad for you though.
IAN: Stop talking now, you don't know anything about it.
CATE: Don't need to.
IAN: Don't know nothing. That's why I love you, want to
      make love to you.
435   CATE: But you can't.
IAN: Why not?
CATE: I don't want to.
IAN: Why did you come here?
CATE: You sounded unhappy.
440   IAN: Make me happy.
CATE: I can't.
IAN: Please.
CATE: No.
IAN: Why not?
445   CATE: Can't.
IAN: Can.
CATE: How?
IAN: You know.
CATE: Don't.
450   IAN: Please.
CATE: No.
IAN: I love you.

CATE: I don't love you.
IAN: (*Turns away. He sees the bouquet of flowers and picks it up.*)
      These are for you.   455

Blackout.
The sound of spring rain.

SCENE TWO

The same.
Very early the following morning.
Bright and sunny—it's going to be a very hot day.
*The bouquet of flowers is now ripped apart and scattered around the
room.*

CATE *is still asleep.*
IAN *is awake, glancing through the newspapers.*
IAN *goes to the mini-bar. It is empty.*
*He finds the bottle of gin under the bed and pours half of what is
left into a glass.*
He stands looking out of the window at the street.
He takes the first sip and is overcome with pain.
He waits for it to pass, but it doesn't. It gets worse.
IAN *clutches his side—it becomes extreme.*
*He begins to cough and experiences intense pain in his chest, each
cough tearing at his lung.*
CATE *wakes and watches* IAN.
IAN *drops to his knees, puts the glass down carefully, and gives in to
the pain.*
It looks very much as if he is dying.
*His heart, lung, liver and kidneys are all under attack and he is mak-
ing involuntary crying sounds.*
*Just at the moment when it seems he cannot survive this, it begins to
ease.*
Very slowly, the pain decreases until it has all gone.
IAN *is a crumpled heap on the floor.*
He looks up and sees CATE *watching him.*

CATE: Cunt.
IAN: (*Gets up slowly, picks up the glass and drinks.*
      He lights his first cigarette of the day.)
      I'm having a shower.
CATE: It's only six o'clock.   5
IAN: Want one?
CATE: Not with you.
IAN: Suit yourself. Cigarette?
CATE: (*Makes a noise of disgust.*)

They are silent.
IAN *stands, smoking and drinking neat gin.*
*When he's sufficiently numbed, he comes and goes between the bed-
room and bathroom, undressing and collecting discarded towels.*
He stops, towel around his waist, gun in hand, and looks at CATE.
She is staring at him with hate.

IAN: Don't worry, I'll be dead soon.   10

(*He tosses the gun onto the bed.*)

      Have a pop.

CATE *doesn't move.*

IAN *waits, then chuckles and goes into the bathroom.*
We hear the shower running.
CATE *stares at the gun.*
She gets up very slowly and dresses.
She packs her bag.
She picks up IAN*'s leather jacket and smells it.*
She rips the arms off at the seams.
She picks up his gun and examines it.
We hear IAN *coughing up in the bathroom.*
CATE *puts the gun down and he comes in.*
He dresses.
He looks at the gun.

IAN: No?

(*He chuckles, unloads and reloads the gun and tucks it in his holster.*)

　　We're one, yes?
CATE: (*Sneers.*)
15　IAN: We're one.
　　Coming down for breakfast? It's paid for.
CATE: Choke on it.
IAN: Sarky little tart this morning, aren't we?

He picks up his jacket and puts one arm through a hole.
He stares at the damage, then looks at CATE.
A beat, then she goes for him, slapping him around the head hard and fast.
He wrestles her onto the bed, her still kicking, punching and biting.
She takes the gun from his holster and points it at his groin.
He backs off rapidly.

IAN: Easy, easy, that's a loaded gun.
20　CATE: I d- d- d- d- d- d- d- d- d-
IAN: Catie, come on.
CATE: d- d- d- d- d- d- d- d- d-
IAN: You don't want an accident. Think about your mum. And your brother. What would they think?
25　CATE: I d- d- d- d- d- d- d- d- d- d- d- d-

CATE *trembles and starts gasping for air.*
She faints.
IAN *goes to her, takes the gun and puts it back in the holster.*
Then lies her on the bed on her back.
He puts the gun to her head, lies between her legs, and simulates sex.
As he comes, CATE *sits bolt upright with a shout.*
IAN *moves away, unsure what to do, pointing the gun at her from behind.*
She laughs hysterically, as before, but doesn't stop.
She laughs and laughs and laughs until she isn't laughing any more, she's crying her heart out.
She collapses again and lies still.

IAN: Cate? Catie?

IAN *puts the gun away.*
He kisses her and she comes round.
She stares at him.

IAN: You back?
CATE: Liar.

IAN *doesn't know if this means yes or no, so he just waits.*
CATE *closes her eyes for a few seconds, then opens them.*

IAN: Cate?
CATE: Want to go home now.　　　　　　　　　　　30
IAN: It's not even seven. There won't be a train.
CATE: I'll wait at the station.
IAN: It's raining.
CATE: It's not.
IAN: Want you to stay here. Till after breakfast at least.　35
CATE: No.
IAN: Cate. After breakfast.
CATE: No.
IAN: (*Locks the door and pockets the key.*)
　　I love you.　　　　　　　　　　　　　　　40
CATE: I don't want to stay.
IAN: Please.
CATE: Don't want to.
IAN: You make me feel safe.
CATE: Nothing to be scared of.　　　　　　　　45
IAN: I'll order breakfast.
CATE: Not hungry.
IAN: (*Lights a cigarette.*)
CATE: How can you smoke on an empty stomach?
IAN: It's not empty. There's gin in it.　　　　　50
CATE: Why can't I go home?
IAN: (*Thinks.*)
　　It's too dangerous.

Outside, a car backfires-there is an enormous bang.
IAN *throws himself flat on the floor.*

CATE: (*Laughs.*)
　　It's only a car.　　　　　　　　　　　　55
IAN: You. You're fucking thick.
CATE: I'm not. You're scared of things when there's nothing to be scared of. What's thick about not being scared of cars?
IAN: I'm not scared of cars. I'm scared of dying.　60
CATE: A car won't kill you. Not from out there.
　　Not unless you ran out in front of it.
　　(*She kisses him.*)
　　What's scaring you?
IAN: Thought it was a gun.　　　　　　　　65
CATE: (*Kisses his neck.*)
　　Who'd have a gun?
IAN: Me.
CATE: (*Undoes his shirt.*)
　　You're in here.　　　　　　　　　　　70
IAN: Someone like me.
CATE: (*Kisses his chest.*)
　　Why would they shoot at you?
IAN: Revenge.
CATE: (*Runs her hands down his back.*)　　　75
IAN: For things I've done.
CATE: (*Massages his neck.*)
　　Tell me.
IAN: Tapped my phone.
CATE: (*Kisses the back of his neck.*)　　　　80
IAN: Talk to people and I know I'm being listened to. I'm sorry I stopped calling you but—

CATE: (*Strokes his stomach and kisses between his shoulder blades.*)
IAN: Got angry when you said you loved me, talking soft on
85   the phone, people listening to that.
CATE: (*Kisses his back.*)
    Tell me.
IAN: In before you know it.
CATE: (*Licks his back.*)
90 IAN: Signed the Official Secrets Act, shouldn't be telling you
    this.
CATE: (*Claws and scratches his back.*)
IAN: Don't want to get you into trouble.
CATE: (*Bites his back.*)
95 IAN: Think they're trying to kill me. Served my purpose.
CATE: (*Pushes him onto his back.*)
IAN: Done the jobs they asked. Because I love this land.
CATE: (*Sucks his nipples.*)
IAN: Stood at stations, listened to conversations and given the
100   nod.
CATE: (*Undoes his trousers.*)
IAN: Driving jobs. Picking people up, disposing of bodies, the
    lot.
CATE: (*Begins to perform oral sex on* IAN.)
105 IAN: Said you were dangerous.
    So I stopped.
    Didn't want you in any danger.
    But
    Had to call you again
110 Missed
    This
    Now
    I do
    The real job
115 I
    Am
    A
    Killer

On the word 'killer' he comes.
As soon as CATE *hears the word she bites his penis as hard as she
can.*
IAN's *cry of pleasure turns into a scream of pain.*
He tries to pull away but CATE *holds on with her teeth.*
He hits her and she lets go.
IAN *lies in pain, unable to speak.*
CATE *spits frantically, trying to get every trace of him out of her
mouth.*
She goes to the bathroom and we hear her cleaning her teeth.
IAN *examines himself. He is still in one piece.*
CATE *returns.*

CATE: You should resign.
120 IAN: Don't work like that.
CATE: Will they come here?
IAN: I don't know.
CATE: (*begins to panic.*)
IAN: Don't start that again.
125 CATE: I c- c- c- c- c-
IAN: Cate, I'll shoot you myself you don't stop.
    I told you because I love you, not to scare you.
CATE: You don't.
IAN: Don't argue I do. And you love me.

CATE: No more.   130
IAN: Loved me last night.
CATE: I didn't want to do it.
IAN: Thought you liked that.
CATE: No.
IAN: Made enough noise.   135
CATE: It was hurting.
IAN: Went down on Stella all the time, didn't hurt her.
CATE: You bit me. It's still bleeding.
IAN: Is that what this is all about?
CATE: You're cruel.   140
IAN: Don't be stupid.
CATE: Stop calling me that.
IAN: You sleep with someone holding hands and kissing you
    wank me off then say we can't fuck get into bed but don't
    want me to touch you what's wrong with you Joey?   145
CATE: I'm not. You're cruel. I wouldn't shoot someone.
IAN: Pointed it at me.
CATE: Wouldn't shoot.
IAN: It's my job. I love this country. I won't see it destroyed
    by slag.   150
CATE: It's wrong to kill.
IAN: Planting bombs and killing little kiddies, that's wrong.
    That's what they do. Kids like your brother.
CATE: It's wrong.
IAN: Yes, it is.   155
CATE: No. You. Doing that.
IAN: When are you going to grow up?
CATE: I don't believe in killing.
IAN: You'll learn.
CATE: No I won't.   160
IAN: Can't always be taking it backing down letting them
    think they've got a right turn the other cheek SHIT some
    things are worth more than that have to be protected from
    shite.
CATE: I used to love you.   165
IAN: What's changed?
CATE: You.
IAN: No. Now you see me. That's all.
CATE: You're a nightmare.

She shakes.
IAN *watches a while, then hugs her.*
She is still shaking so he hugs tightly to stop her.

CATE: That hurts.   170
IAN: Sorry.

He hugs her less tightly.
He has a coughing fit.
He spits into his handkerchief and waits for the pain to subside.
Then he lights a cigarette.

IAN: How you feeling?
CATE: I ache.
IAN: (*Nods.*)
CATE: Everywhere.   175
    I stink of you.
IAN: You want a bath?

CATE *begins to cough and retch.*
She puts her fingers down her throat and produces a hair.

She holds it up and looks at IAN *in disgust. She spits.*
IAN *goes into the bathroom and turns on one of the bath taps.*
CATE *stares out of the window.*
IAN *returns.*

CATE: Looks like there's a war on.
IAN: (*Doesn't look.*)
180   Turning into Wogland.
         You coming to Leeds again?
CATE: Twenty-sixth.
IAN: Will you come and see me?
CATE: I'm going to the football.

She goes to the bathroom.
IAN *picks up the phone.*

185   IAN: Two English breakfasts, son.

He finishes the remainder of the gin.
CATE *returns.*

CATE: I can't piss. It's just blood.
IAN: Drink lots of water.
CATE: Or shit. It hurts.
IAN: It'll heal.

There is a knock at the door. They both jump.

190   CATE: DON'T ANSWER IT DON'T ANSWER IT
         DON'T ANSWER IT

She dives on the bed and puts her head under the pillow.

IAN: Cate, shut up.

He pulls the pillow off and puts the gun to her head.

CATE: Do it. Go on, shoot me. Can't be no worse than what
         you've done already. Shoot me if you want, then turn it on
195   yourself and do the world a favour.
IAN: (*Stares at her.*)
CATE: I'm not scared of you, Ian. Go on.
IAN: (*Gets off her.*)
CATE: (*Laughs.*)
200   IAN: Answer the door and suck the cunt's cock.

CATE *tries to open the door. It is locked.*
IAN *throws the key at her.*
She opens the door.
The breakfasts are outside on a tray. She brings them in.
IAN *locks the door.*
CATE *stares at the food.*

CATE: Sausages. Bacon.
IAN: Sorry. Forgot. Swap your meat for my tomatoes and
         mushrooms. And toast.
CATE: (*Begins to retch.*)
205   The smell.

IAN *takes a sausage off the plate and stuffs it in his mouth and keeps
a rasher of bacon in his hand.*
He puts the tray of food under the bed with a towel over it.

IAN: Will you stay another day?

CATE: I'm having a bath and going home.

She picks up her bag and goes into the bathroom, closing the door.
We hear the other bath tap being turned on.
There are two loud knocks at the outer door.
IAN *draws his gun, goes to the door and listens.*
The door is tried from outside. It is locked.
There are two more loud knocks.

IAN: Who's there?

Silence.
Then two more loud knocks.

IAN: Who's there?

Silence.
Then two more knocks.
IAN *looks at the door.*
Then he knocks twice.
Silence.
Then two more knocks from outside.
IAN *thinks.*
Then he knocks three times.
Silence.
Three knocks from outside.
IAN *knocks once.*
One knock from outside.
IAN *knocks twice.*
Two knocks.
IAN *puts his gun back in the holster and unlocks the door.*

IAN: (*Under his breath.*) Speak the Queen's English fucking   210
         nigger.

He opens the door.
Outside is a SOLDIER *with a sniper's rifle.*
IAN *tries to push the door shut and draw his revolver.*
The SOLDIER *pushes the door open and takes* IAN'S *gun easily.*
The two stand, both surprised, staring at each other.
Eventually.

SOLDIER: What's that?

IAN *looks down and realizes he is still holding a rasher of bacon.*

IAN: Pig.

The SOLDIER *holds out his hand.*
IAN *gives him the bacon and he eats it quickly, rind and all.*
The SOLDIER *wipes his mouth.*

SOLDIER: Got any more?
IAN: No.   215
SOLDIER: Got any more?
IAN: I-
      No.
SOLDIER: Got any more?
IAN: (*Points to the tray under the bed.*)   220

The SOLDIER *bends down carefully, never taking his eyes or rifle off*
IAN, *and takes the tray from under the bed.*
He straightens up and glances down at the food.

SOLDIER: Two.
IAN: I was hungry.
SOLDIER: I bet.

The SOLDIER *sits on the edge of the bed and very quickly devours both breakfasts.*
He sighs with relief and burps.
He nods towards the bathroom.

SOLDIER: She in there?
225 IAN: Who?
SOLDIER: I can smell the sex.

(*He begins to search the room.*)

You a journalist?
IAN: I—
SOLDIER: Passport.
230 IAN: What for?
SOLDIER: (*Looks at him.*)
IAN: In the jacket.

The SOLDIER *is searching a chest of drawers.*
He finds a pair of CATE*'s knickers and holds them up.*

SOLDIER: Hers?
IAN: (*Doesn't answer.*)
235 SOLDIER: Or yours.

(*He closes his eyes and rubs them gently over his face, smelling with pleasure.*)

What's she like?
IAN: (*Doesn't answer.*)
SOLDIER: Is she soft?
Is she—?
240 IAN: (*Doesn't answer.*)

The SOLDIER *puts* CATE*'s knickers in his pocket and goes to the bathroom.*
He knocks on the door. No answer.
He tries the door. It is locked.
He forces it and goes in.
IAN *waits, in a panic.*
We hear the bath taps being turned off.
IAN *looks out of the window.*

IAN: Jesus Lord.

The SOLDIER *returns.*

SOLDIER: Gone. Taking a risk. Lot of bastard soldiers out
there.

IAN *looks in the bathroom.* CATE *isn't there.*
The SOLDIER *looks in* IAN*'s jacket pockets and takes his keys, wallet and passport.*

SOLDIER: (*Looks at* IAN*'s press card.*)
245   Ian Jones.
         Journalist.
IAN: Oi.
SOLDIER: Oi.

They stare at each other.

IAN: If you've come to shoot me—
SOLDIER: (*reaches out to touch* IAN*'s face but stops short of physi- 250
cal contact.*)
IAN: You taking the piss?
SOLDIER: Me?

(*He smiles.*)

Our town now.

(*He stands on the bed and urinates over the pillows.*)
IAN *is disgusted.*
There is a blinding light, then a huge explosion.
Blackout.
The sound of summer rain.

SCENE THREE
The hotel has been blasted by a mortar bomb.
There is a large hole in one of the walls, and everything is covered in dust which is still falling.
The SOLDIER *is unconscious, rifle still in hand.*
He has dropped IAN*'s gun which lies between them.*
IAN *lies very still, eyes open.*

IAN: Mum?

Silence.
The SOLDIER *wakes and turns his eyes and rifle on* IAN *with the minimum possible movement.*
He instinctively runs his free hand over his limbs and body to check that he is still in one piece. He is.

SOLDIER: The drink.

IAN *looks around. There is a bottle of gin lying next to him with the lid off.*
He holds it up to the light.

IAN: Empty.
SOLDIER: (*Takes the bottle and drinks the last mouthful.*)
IAN: (*Chuckles.*)   5
Worse than me.

The SOLDIER *holds the bottle up and shakes it over his mouth, catching any remaining drops.*
IAN *finds his cigarettes in his shirt pocket and lights up.*

SOLDIER: Give us a cig.
IAN: Why?
SOLDIER: 'Cause I've got a gun and you haven't.

IAN *considers the logic.*
Then takes a single cigarette out of the packet and tosses it at the SOLDIER.
The SOLDIER *picks up the cigarette and puts it in his mouth.*
He looks at IAN*, waiting for a light.*
IAN *holds out his cigarette.*
The SOLDIER *leans forward, touching the tip of his cigarette against the lit one, eyes always on* IAN.
He smokes.

SOLDIER: Never met an Englishman with a gun before, most 10
of them don't know what a gun is. You a soldier?
IAN: Of sorts.

SOLDIER: Which side, if you can remember.

IAN: Don't know what the sides are here.

15   Don't know where . . .

(*He trails off confused, and looks at the* SOLDIER.)

      Think I might be drunk.

SOLDIER: No, It's real.

(*He picks up the revolver and examines it.*)

      Come to fight for us?

IAN: No, I—

20 SOLDIER: No, course not. English.

IAN: I'm Welsh.

SOLDIER: Sound English, fucking accent.

IAN: I live there.

SOLDIER: Foreigner?

25 IAN: English and Welsh is the same. British. I'm not an import.

SOLDIER: What's fucking Welsh, never heard of it.

IAN: Come over from God knows where have their kids and call them English they're not English born in England don't make you English.

30 SOLDIER: Welsh as in Wales?

IAN: It's attitude.

(*He turns away.*)

      Look at the state of my fucking jacket. The bitch.

SOLDIER: Your girlfriend did that, angry was she?

IAN: She's not my girlfriend.

35 SOLDIER: What, then?

IAN: Mind your fucking own.

SOLDIER: Haven't been here long have you.

IAN: So?

SOLDIER: Learn some manners, Ian.

40 IAN: Don't call me that.

SOLDIER: What shall I call you?

IAN: Nothing.

Silence.
The SOLDIER *looks at* IAN *for a very long time, saying nothing.*
IAN *is uncomfortable.*
Eventually.

IAN: What?

SOLDIER: Nothing.

Silence.
IAN *is uneasy again.*

45 IAN: My name's Ian.

SOLDIER: I
              Am
              Dying to make love
              Ian

50 IAN: (*Looks at him.*)

SOLDIER: You got a girlfriend?

IAN: (*Doesn't answer.*)

SOLDIER: I have,
      Col.

55   Fucking beautiful.

IAN: Cate-

SOLDIER: Close my eyes and think about her.
      She's—
      She's—
      She's—   60
      She's—
      She's—
      She's—
      She's—
      When was the last time you—?   65

IAN: (*Looks at him.*)

SOLDIER: When? I know it was recent, smell it, remember.

IAN: Last night. I think.

SOLDIER: Good?

IAN: Don't know. I was pissed. Probably not.   70

SOLDIER: Three of us—

IAN: Don't tell me.

SOLDIER: Went to a house just outside town. All gone. Apart from a small boy hiding in the corner. One of the others took him outside. Lay him on the ground and 75 shot him through the legs. Heard crying in the basement. Went down. Three men and four women. Called the others. They held the men while I fucked the women. Youngest was twelve. Didn't cry, just lay there. Turned her over and—Then she cried. Made her lick 80 me clean. Closed my eyes and thought of—
      Shot her father in the mouth. Brothers shouted. Hung them from the ceiling by their testicles.

IAN: Charming.

SOLDIER: Never done that?   85

IAN: No.

SOLDIER: Sure?

IAN: I wouldn't forget.

SOLDIER: You would.

IAN: Couldn't sleep with myself.   90

SOLDIER: What about your wife?

IAN: I'm divorced.

SOLDIER: Didn't you ever—

IAN: No.

SOLDIER: What about that girl locked herself in the bathroom.   95

IAN: (*Doesn't answer.*)

SOLDIER: Ah.

IAN: You did four in one go, I've only ever done one.

SOLDIER: You killed her?

IAN: (*Makes a move for his gun.*)   100

SOLDIER: Don't I'll have to shoot you. Then I'd be lonely.

IAN: Course I haven't.

SOLDIER: Why not, don't seem to like her very much.

IAN: I do.
      She's . . . a woman.   105

SOLDIER: So?

IAN: I've never—
      It's not—

SOLDIER: What?

IAN: (*Doesn't answer.*)   110

SOLDIER: Thought you were a soldier.

IAN: Not like that.

SOLDIER: Not like that, do y're all like that.

IAN: My job-

SOLDIER: Even me. Have to be.   115
      My girl—

Not going back to her. When I go back.
She's dead, see. Fucking bastard soldier, he—

He stops.
Silence.

IAN: I'm sorry.
120 SOLDIER: Why?
IAN: It's terrible.
SOLDIER: What is?
IAN: Losing someone, a woman, like that.
SOLDIER: You know, do you?
125 IAN: I—
SOLDIER: Like what?
IAN: Like—
     you said—
     A soldier—
130 SOLDIER: You're a soldier.
IAN: I haven't—
SOLDIER: What if you were ordered to?
IAN: Can't imagine it.
SOLDIER: Imagine it.
135 IAN: (*Imagines it.*)
SOLDIER: In the line of duty. For your country. Wales.
IAN: (*Imagines harder.*)
SOLDIER: Foreign slag.
IAN: (*Imagines harder. Looks sick.*)
140 SOLDIER: Would you?
IAN: (*Nods.*)
SOLDIER: How.
IAN: Quickly. Back of the head. Bam.
SOLDIER: That's all.
145 IAN: It's enough.
SOLDIER: You think?
IAN: Yes.
SOLDIER: You never killed anyone.
IAN: Fucking have.
150 SOLDIER: No.
IAN: Don't you fucking—
SOLDIER: Couldn't talk like this. You'd know.
IAN: Know what?
SOLDIER: Exactly. You don't know.
155 IAN: Know fucking what?
SOLDIER: Stay in the dark.
IAN: What? Fucking what? What don't I know?
SOLDIER: You think—

(*He stops and smiles.*)

     I broke a woman's neck. Stabbed up between her legs,
160   on the fifth stab snapped her spine.
IAN: (*Looks sick.*)
SOLDIER: You couldn't do that.
IAN: No.
SOLDIER: You never killed.
165 IAN: Not like that.
SOLDIER: Not
     Like
     That
IAN: I'm not a torturer.
170 SOLDIER: You're close to them, gun to head. Tie them up, tell
     them what you're going to do to them, make them wait

for it, then . . . what?
IAN: Shoot them.
SOLDIER: You haven't got a clue.
IAN: What then?   175
SOLDIER: You never fucked a man before you killed him?
IAN: No.
SOLDIER: Or after?
IAN: Course not.
SOLDIER: Why not?   180
IAN: What for, I'm not queer.
SOLDIER: Col, they buggered her. Cut her throat. Hacked her
     ears and nose off, nailed them to the front door.
IAN: Enough.
SOLDIER: Ever seen anything like that?   185
IAN: Stop.
SOLDIER: Not in photos?
IAN: Never.
SOLDIER: Some journalist, that's your job.
IAN: What?   190
SOLDIER: Proving it happened. I'm here, got no choice. But
     you. You should be telling people.
IAN: No one's interested.
SOLDIER: You can do something, for me—
IAN: No.   195
SOLDIER: Course you can.
IAN: I can't do anything.
SOLDIER: Try.
IAN: I write . . . stories. That's all. Stories. This isn't a story
     anyone wants to hear.   200
SOLDIER: Why not?
IAN: (*Takes one of the newspapers from the bed and reads.*)
     'Kinky car dealer Richard Morris drove two teenage
     prostitutes into the country, tied them naked to fences
     and whipped them with a belt before having sex.   205
     Morris, from Sheffield, was jailed for three years for un-
     lawful sexual intercourse with one of the girls, aged
     thirteen.'

(*He tosses the paper away.*)

     Stories.
SOLDIER: Doing to them what they done to us, what good is   210
     that? At home I'm clean. Like it never happened.
     Tell them you saw me.
     Tell them . . . you saw me.
IAN: It's not my job.
SOLDIER: Whose is it?   215
IAN: I'm a home journalist, for Yorkshire. I don't cover for-
     eign affairs.
SOLDIER: Foreign affairs, what you doing here?
IAN: I do other stuff. Shootings and rapes and kids getting
     fiddled by queer priests and schoolteachers. Not soldiers 220
     screwing each other for a patch of land. It has to be . . .
     personal. Your girlfriend, she's a story. Soft and clean. Not
     you. Filthy, like the wogs. No joy in a story about blacks
     who gives a shit? Why bring you to light?
SOLDIER: You don't know fuck all about me.   225
     I went to school.
     I made love with Col.
     Bastards killed her, now I'm here.
     Now I'm here.

(*He pushes the rifle in* IAN's *face.*)

230   Turn over, Ian.

IAN: Why?

SOLDIER: Going to fuck you.

IAN: No.

SOLDIER: Kill you then.

235   IAN: Fine.

SOLDIER: See. Rather be shot than fucked and shot.

IAN: Yes.

SOLDIER: And now you agree with anything I say.

He kisses IAN *very tenderly on the lips.*
They stare at each other.

SOLDIER: You smell like her. Same cigarettes.

The SOLDIER *turns* IAN *over with one hand.*
He holds the revolver to IAN's *head with the other.*
He pulls down IAN's *trousers, undoes his own and rapes him—eyes*
closed and smelling IAN's *hair.*
The SOLDIER *is crying his heart out.*
IAN's *face registers pain but he is silent.*
When the SOLDIER *has finished he pulls up his trousers and pushes*
the revolver up IAN's *anus.*

240   SOLDIER: Bastard pulled the trigger on Col.
      What's it like?

IAN: (*Tries to answer. He can't.*)

SOLDIER: (*Withdraws the gun and sits next to* IAN.)
      You never fucked by a man before?

245   IAN: (*Doesn't answer.*)

SOLDIER: Didn't think so. It's nothing. Saw thousands of
      people packing into trucks like pigs trying to leave
      town. Women threw their babies on board hoping
      someone would look after them. Crushing each other to
250   death. Insides of people's heads came out of their eyes.
      Saw a child most of his face blown off, young girl I
      fucked hand up inside her trying to claw my liquid out,
      starving man eating his dead wife's leg. Gun was born
      here and won't die. Can't get tragic about your arse.
255   Don't think your Welsh arse is different to any other arse
      I fucked. Sure you haven't got any more food, I'm
      fucking starving.

IAN: Are you going to kill me?

SOLDIER: Always covering your own arse.

The SOLDIER *grips* IAN's *head in his hands.*
He puts his mouth over one of IAN's *eyes, sucks it out, bites it off*
and eats it.
He does the same to the other eye.

260   SOLDIER: He ate her eyes.
      Poor bastard.
      Poor love.
      Poor fucking bastard.

Blackout.
The sound of autumn rain.

SCENE FOUR

The ruin.
The SOLDIER *lies close to* IAN, *the revolver in his hand.*
He has blown his own brain out.

CATE *enters through the bathroom door, soaking wet and carrying a baby.*
She steps over the SOLDIER *with a glance.*
Then she sees IAN.

CATE: You're a nightmare.

IAN: Cate?

CATE: It won't stop.

IAN: Catie? You here?

CATE: Everyone in town is crying.   5

IAN: Touch me.

CATE: Soldiers have taken over.

IAN: They've won?

CATE: Most people gave up.

IAN: You seen Matthew?   10

CATE: No.

IAN: Will you tell him for me?

CATE: He isn't here.

IAN: Tell him—
      Tell him—   15

CATE: No.

IAN: Don't know what to tell him.
      I'm cold.
      Tell him—
      You here?   20

CATE: A woman gave me her baby.

IAN: You come for me, Catie? Punish me or rescue me makes
      no difference I love you Cate tell him for me do it for me
      touch me Cate.

CATE: Don't know what to do with it.   25

IAN: I'm cold.

CATE: Keeps crying.

IAN: Tell him—

CATE: I CAN'T.

IAN: Will you stay with me, Cate?   30

CATE: No.

IAN: Why not?

CATE: I have to go back soon.

IAN: Shaun know what we did?

CATE: No.   35

IAN: Better tell him.

CATE: No.

IAN: He'll know. Even if you don't.

CATE: How?

IAN: Smell it. Soiled goods. Don't want it, not when you can   40
      have someone clean.

CATE: What's happened to your eyes?

IAN: I need you to stay, Cate. Won't be for long.

CATE: Do you know about babies?

IAN: No.   45

CATE: What about Matthew?

IAN: He's twenty-four.

CATE: When he was born.

IAN: They shit and cry. Hopeless.

CATE: Bleeding.   50

IAN: Will you touch me?

CATE: No.

IAN: So I know you're here.

CATE: You can hear me.

IAN: Won't hurt you, I promise.   55

CATE: (*Goes to him slowly and touches the top of his head.*)

IAN: Help me.

CATE: (*Strokes his hair.*)

IAN: Be dead soon anyway, Cate.
60   And it hurts.
       Help me to—
       Help me—
       Finish
       It
65 CATE: (*Withdraws her hand.*)
    IAN: Catie?
    CATE: Got to get something for Baby to eat.
    IAN: Won't find anything.
    CATE: May as well look.
70 IAN: Fucking bastards ate it all.
    CATE: It'll die.
    IAN: Needs its mother's milk.
    CATE: Ian.
    IAN: Stay.
75   Nowhere to go, where are you going to go?
       Bloody dangerous on your own, look at me.
       Safer here with me.

    CATE *considers.*
    Then sits down with the baby some distance from IAN.
    He relaxes when he hears her sit.
    CATE *rocks the baby.*

    IAN: Not as bad as all that, am I?
    CATE: (*Looks at him.*)
80 IAN: Will you help me, Catie?
    CATE: How.
    IAN: Find my gun?

    CATE *thinks.*
    Then gets up and searches around, baby in arms.
    She sees the revolver in the SOLDIER's *hand and stares at it for some time.*

    IAN: Found it?
    CATE: No.

    She takes the revolver from the SOLDIER *and fiddles with it.*
    It springs open and she stares in at the bullets.
    She removes them and closes the gun.

85 IAN: That it?
    CATE: Yes.
    IAN: Can I have it?
    CATE: I don't think so.
    IAN: Catie.
90 CATE: What?
    IAN: Come on.
    CATE: Don't tell me what to do.
    IAN: I'm not, love. Can you keep that baby quiet.
    CATE: It's not doing anything. It's hungry.
95 IAN: We're all bloody hungry, don't shoot myself I'll starve to death.
    CATE: It's wrong to kill yourself.
    IAN: No it's not.
    CATE: God wouldn't like it.
100 IAN: There isn't one.
    CATE: How do you know?
    IAN: No God. No Father Christmas. No fairies. No Narnia. No fucking nothing.
    CATE: Got to be something.
105 IAN: Why?

CATE: Doesn't make sense otherwise.
IAN: Don't be fucking stupid, doesn't make sense anyway. No reason for there to be a God just because it would be better if there was.
CATE: Thought you didn't want to die.   110
IAN: I can't see.
CATE: My brother's got blind friends. You can't give up.
IAN: Why not?
CATE: It's weak.
IAN: I know you want to punish me, trying to make me live.   115
CATE: I don't.
IAN: Course you fucking do, I would. There's people I'd love to suffer but they don't, they die and that's it.
CATE: What if you're wrong?
IAN: I'm not.   120
CATE: But if.
IAN: I've seen dead people. They're dead. They're not somewhere else, they're dead.
CATE: What about people who've seen ghosts?
IAN: What about them? Imagining it. Or making it up or   125
    wishing the person was still alive.
CATE: People who've died and come back say they've seen tunnels and lights—
IAN: Can't die and come back. That's not dying, it's fainting.
    When you die, it's the end.   130
CATE: I believe in God.
IAN: Everything's got a scientific explanation.
CATE: No.
IAN: Give me my gun.
CATE: What are you going to do?   135
IAN: I won't hurt you.
CATE: I know.
IAN: End it.
    Got to, Cate, I'm ill.
    Just speeding it up a bit.   140
CATE: (*Thinks hard.*)
IAN: Please.
CATE: (*Gives him the gun.*)
IAN: (*Takes the gun and puts it in his mouth.*
    He takes it out again.)   145
    Don't stand behind me.

He puts the gun back in his mouth.
He pulls the trigger. The gun clicks, empty.
He shoots again. And again and again and again.
He takes the gun out of his mouth.

IAN: Fuck.
CATE: Fate, see. You're not meant to do it. God—
IAN: The cunt.

(*He throws the gun away in despair.*)

CATE: (*Rocks the baby and looks down at it.*)   150
    Oh no.
IAN: What.
CATE: It's dead.
IAN: Lucky bastard.
CATE: (*Bursts out laughing, unnaturally, hysterically, uncontrollably.*   155
    She laughs and laughs and laughs and laughs and laughs.)
Blackout.
The sound of heavy winter rain.

SCENE FIVE

The same.
CATE *is burying the baby under the floor.*
She looks around and finds two pieces of wood.
She rips the lining out of IAN'*s jacket and binds the wood together in a cross which she sticks into the floor.*
She collects a few of the scattered flowers and places them under the cross.

CATE: I don't know her name.
IAN: Don't matter. No one's going to visit.
CATE: I was supposed to look after her.
IAN: Can bury me next to her soon. Dance on my grave.
5 CATE: Don't feel no pain or know nothing you shouldn't know—
IAN: Cate?
CATE: Shh.
IAN: What you dong?
10 CATE: Praying. Just in case.
IAN: Will you pray for me?
CATE: No.
IAN: When I'm dead, not now.
CATE: No point when you're dead.
15 IAN: You're praying for her.
CATE: She's baby.
IAN: So?
CATE: Innocent.
IAN: Can't you forgive me?
20 CATE: Don't see bad things or go bad places—
IAN: She's dead, Cate.
CATE: Or meet anyone who'll do bad things.
IAN: She won't, Cate, she's dead.
CATE: Amen.

(*She starts to leave.*)

25 IAN: Where you going?
CATE: I'm hungry.
IAN: Cate, it's dangerous. There's no food.
CATE: Can get some off a soldier.
IAN: How?
30 CATE: (*Doesn't answer.*)
IAN: Don't do that.
CATE: Why not?
IAN: That's not you.
CATE: I'm hungry.
35 IAN: I know so am I.
But.
I'd rather—
It's not—
Please, Cate.
40 I'm blind.
CATE: I'm hungry.

(*She goes.*)

IAN: Cate? Catie?
If you get some food—
Fuck.

Darkness.
Light.
IAN *masturbating.*

IAN: cunt cunt cunt cunt cunt cunt cunt cunt cunt cunt 45 cunt

Darkness.
Light.
IAN *strangling himself with his bare hands.*
Darkness.
Light.
IAN *shitting.*
And then trying to clean it up with newspaper.
Darkness.
Light.
IAN *laughing hysterically.*
Darkness
Light.
IAN *having a nightmare.*
Darkness.
Light.
IAN *crying, huge bloody tears.*
He is hugging the SOLDIER'*s body for comfort.*
Darkness.
Light.
IAN *lying very still, weak with hunger.*
Darkness.
Light.
IAN *tears the cross out of the ground, rips up the floor and lifts the baby's body out.*
He eats the baby.
He puts the remains back in the baby's blanket and puts the bundle back in the hole.
A beat, then he climbs in after it and lies down, head poking out of the floor.
He dies with relief.
It starts to rain on him, coming through the roof.
Eventually.

IAN: Shit.

CATE *enters carrying some bread, a large sausage and a bottle of gin.*
There is blood seeping from between her legs.

CATE: You're sitting under a hole.
IAN: I know.
CATE: Get wet. 50
IAN: Aye.
CATE: Stupid bastard.

She pulls a sheet off the bed and wraps it around her.
She sits next to IAN'*s head.*
She eats her fill of the sausage and bread, then washes it down with gin.
IAN *listens.*
She feeds IAN *with the remaining food.*
She pours gin in IAN'*s mouth.*
She finishes feeding IAN *and sits apart from him huddled for warmth.*
She drinks the gin.
She sucks her thumb.
Silence.
It rains.

IAN: Thank you.

Blackout.

CRITICAL CONTEXTS

FRIEDRICH NIETZSCHE (1844–1900)

from *The Birth of Tragedy* (1872)

TRANSLATED BY WALTER KAUFMANN

*Throughout his career, the German philosopher and poet Friedrich Nietzsche criticized the limitations of modern conceptual and moral categories. This revolutionary subversion of the premises of philosophy forms the core of his most famous works—*The Gay Science *(1882),* Thus Spoke Zarathustra *(1883–92), and* Beyond Good and Evil *(1886). In* The Birth of Tragedy *(1872), Nietzsche argues that Greek tragedy arose from the collision between Athenian rationalism—symbolized by Apollo, Socrates, and Euripides—and an earlier, irrational mysticism, symbolized by Dionysus. Although Nietzsche's reading of Greek history has been generally discredited, the essay offers a powerful and influential reading of the tension between the rational and irrational informing Greek drama. Nietzsche was admired by several modern playwrights represented in this volume, including Bernard Shaw.*

Despite its symbolic contours, Nietzsche's representation of tragedy shares in the dialectical imagination that also drives other major theorists of tragic drama, including Aristotle. In what ways are the Apollinian and the Dionysian complicit in one another? What are the aspects of tragic experience that Nietzsche means to capture in these two images? Why do you think the full title of the essay is The Birth of Tragedy from the Spirit of Music?

SECTION 1

We shall have gained much for the science of aesthetics, once we perceive not merely by logical inference, but with the immediate certainty of vision, that the continuous development of art is bound up with the *Apollinian* and *Dionysian* duality—just as procreation depends on the duality of the sexes, involving perpetual strife with only periodically intervening reconciliations. The terms Dionysian and Apollinian we borrow from the Greeks, who disclose to the discerning mind the profound mysteries of their view of art, not, to be sure, in concepts, but in the intensely clear figures of their gods. Through Apollo and Dionysus, the two art deities of the Greeks, we come to recognize that in the Greek world there existed a tremendous opposition, in origin and aims, between the Apollinian art of sculpture, and the nonimagistic, Dionysian art of music. These two different tendencies run parallel to each other, for the most part openly at variance; and they continually incite each other to new and more powerful births, which perpetuate an antagonism, only superficially reconciled by the common term "art"; till eventually, by a metaphysical miracle of the Hellenic "will," they appear coupled with each other and through this coupling ultimately generate an equally Dionysian and Apollinian form of art—Attic tragedy.

In order to grasp these two tendencies, let us first conceive of them as the separate art worlds of *dreams* and *intoxication*. These physiological phenomena present a contrast analogous to that existing between the Apollinian and the Dionysian. It was in dreams, says Lucretius, that the glorious

divine figures first appeared to the souls of men; in dreams the great shaper beheld the splendid bodies of superhuman beings; and the Hellenic poet, if questioned about the mysteries of poetic inspiration, would likewise have suggested dreams and he might have given an explanation like that of Hans Sachs in the *Meistersinger:*

> The poet's task is this, my friend,
> to read his dreams and comprehend.
> The truest human fancy seems
> to be revealed to us in dreams:
> all poems and versification
> are but true dreams' interpretation.

The beautiful illusion of the dream worlds, in the creation of which every man is truly an artist, is the prerequisite of all plastic art, and, as we shall see, of an important part of poetry also. In our dreams we delight in the immediate understanding of figures; all forms speak to us; there is nothing unimportant or superfluous. But even when this dream reality is most intense, we still have, glimmering through it, the sensation that it is *mere appearance:* at least this is my experience, and for its frequency—indeed, normality—I could adduce many proofs, including the sayings of the poets.

Philosophical men even have a presentiment that the reality in which we live and have our being is also mere appearance, and that another, quite different reality lies beneath it. Schopenhauer actually indicates as the criterion of philosophical ability the occasional ability to view men and things as mere phantoms or dream images. Thus the aesthetically sensitive man stands in the same relation to the reality of dreams as the philosopher does to the reality of existence; he is a close and willing observer, for these images afford him an interpretation of life, and by reflecting on these processes he trains himself for life.

It is not only the agreeable and friendly images that he experiences as something universally intelligible: the serious, the troubled, the sad, the gloomy, the sudden restraints, the tricks of accident, anxious expectations, in short, the whole divine comedy of life, including the inferno, also pass before him, not like mere shadows on a wall—for he lives and suffers with these scenes—and yet not without that fleeting sensation of illusion. And perhaps many will, like myself, recall how amid the dangers and terrors of dreams they have occasionally said to themselves in self-encouragement, and not without success: "It is a dream! I will dream on!" I have likewise heard of people who were able to continue one and the same dream for three and even more successive nights—facts which indicate clearly how our innermost being, our common ground, experiences dreams with profound delight and a joyous necessity.

This joyous necessity of the dream experience has been embodied by the Greeks in their Apollo: Apollo, the god of all plastic energies, is at the same time the soothsaying god. He, who (as the etymology of the name indicates) is the "shining one," the deity of light, is also ruler over the beautiful illusion of the inner world of fantasy. The higher truth, the perfection of these states in contrast to the incompletely intelligible everyday world, this deep consciousness of nature, healing and helping in sleep and dreams, is at the same time the symbolical analogue of the soothsaying faculty and of the arts generally, which make life possible and worth living. But we must also include in our image of Apollo that delicate boundary which the dream image must not overstep lest it have a pathological effect (in which case mere appearance would deceive us as if it were crude reality). We must keep in mind that measured restraint, that freedom from the wilder emotions, that calm of the sculptor god. His eye must be "sunlike," as befits his origin; even when it is angry and distempered it is still hallowed by beautiful illusion. And so, in one sense, we might apply to Apollo the words of Schopenhauer when he speaks of the man wrapped in the veil of *māyā* [illusion]: "Just as in a stormy sea that, unbounded in all directions, raises and drops mountainous waves, howling, a sailor sits in a boat and trusts in his frail bark: so in the midst of a world of torments the individual human being sits quietly, supported by and trusting in the *principium individuationis*." In fact, we might say of Apollo that in him the unshaken faith in this *principium* and the calm repose of the man wrapped up in it receive their most sublime expression; and we might call Apollo himself the glorious divine image of

the *principium individuationis,* through whose gestures and eyes all the joy and wisdom of "illusion," together with its beauty, speak to us.

In the same work Schopenhauer has depicted for us the tremendous terror which seizes man when he is suddenly dumbfounded by the cognitive form of phenomena because the principle of sufficient reason, in some one of its manifestations, seems to suffer an exception. If we add to this terror the blissful ecstasy that wells from the innermost depths of man, indeed of nature, at this collapse of the *principium individuationis,* we steal a glimpse into the nature of the *Dionysian,* which is brought home to us most intimately by the analogy of intoxication.

Either under the influence of the narcotic draught, of which the songs of all primitive men and peoples speak, or with the potent coming of spring that penetrates all nature with joy, these Dionysian emotions awake, and as they grow in intensity everything subjective vanishes into complete self-forgetfulness. In the German Middle Ages, too, singing and dancing crowds, ever increasing in number, whirled themselves from place to place under this same Dionysian impulse. In these dancers of St. John and St. Vitus, we rediscover the Bacchic choruses of the Greeks, with their prehistory in Asia Minor, as far back as Babylon and the orgiastic Sacaea. There are some who, from obtuseness or lack of experience, turn away from such phenomena as from "folk-diseases," with contempt or pity born of the consciousness of their own "healthy-mindedness." But of course such poor wretches have no idea how corpselike and ghostly their so-called "healthy-mindedness" looks when the glowing life of the Dionysian revelers roars past them.

Under the charm of the Dionysian not only is the union between man and man reaffirmed, but nature which has become alienated, hostile, or subjugated, celebrates once more her reconciliation with her lost son, man. Freely, earth proffers her gifts, and peacefully the beasts of prey of the rocks and desert approach. The chariot of Dionysus is covered with flowers and garlands; panthers and tigers walk under its yoke. Transform Beethoven's "Hymn to Joy" into a painting; let your imagination conceive the multitudes bowing to the dust, awestruck—then you will approach the Dionysian. Now the slave is a free man; now all the rigid, hostile barriers that necessity, caprice, or "impudent convention" have fixed between man and man are broken. Now, the gospel of universal harmony, each one feels himself not only united, reconciled, and fused with his neighbor, but as one with him, as if the veil of *māyā* had been torn aside and were now merely fluttering in tatters before the mysterious primordial unity.

In song and in dance man expresses himself as a member of a higher community; he has forgotten how to walk and speak and is on the way toward flying into the air, dancing. His very gestures express enchantment. Just as the animals now talk, and the earth yields milk and honey, supernatural sounds emanate from him, too: he feels himself a god, he himself now walks about enchanted, in ecstasy, like the gods he saw walking in his dreams. He is no longer an artist, he has become a work of art: in these paroxysms of intoxication the artistic power of all nature reveals itself to the highest gratification of the primordial unity. The noblest clay, the most costly marble, man, is here kneaded and cut, and to the sound of the chisel stokes of the Dionysian world-artist rings out the cry of the Eleusinian mysteries: "Do you prostrate yourselves, millions? Do you sense your Maker, world?" . . .

SECTION 10

The tradition is undisputed that Greek tragedy in its earliest form had for its sole theme the sufferings of Dionysus and that for a long time the only stage hero was Dionysus himself. But it may be claimed with equal confidence that until Euripides, Dionysus never ceased to be the tragic hero; that all the celebrated figures of the Greek stage—Prometheus, Oedipus, etc.—are mere masks of this original hero, Dionysus. That behind all these masks there is a deity, that is one essential reason for the typical "ideality" of these famous figures which has caused so much astonishment. Somebody, I do not know who, has claimed that all individuals, taken as individuals, are comic and hence untragic—from which it would follow that the Greeks simply *could* not suffer individuals on the tragic stage. In fact, this is what they seem to have felt; and the Platonic distinction and evaluation of the "idea" and the "idol," the mere image, is very deeply rooted in the Hellenic character.

Using Plato's terms we should have to speak of the tragic figures of the Hellenic stage somewhat as follows: the one truly real Dionysus appears in a variety of forms, in the mask of a fighting hero, and entangled, as it were, in the net of the individual will. The god who appears talks and acts so as to resemble an erring, striving, suffering individual. That he *appears* at all with such epic precision and clarity is the work of the dream-interpreter, Apollo, who through this symbolic appearance interprets to the chorus its Dionysian state. In truth, however, the hero is the suffering Dionysus of the Mysteries, the god experiencing in himself the agonies of individuation, of whom wonderful myths tell that as a boy he was torn to pieces by the Titans and now is worshiped in this state as Zagreus. Thus it is intimated that this dismemberment, the properly Dionysian *suffering,* is like a transformation into air, water, earth, and fire, that we are therefore to regard the state of individuation as the origin and primal cause of all suffering, as something objectionable in itself. From the

smile of this Dionysus sprang the Olympian gods, from his tears sprang man. In this existence as a dismembered god, Dionysus possesses the dual nature of a cruel, barbarized demon and a mild, gentle ruler. But the hope of the epopts [initiates] looked toward a rebirth of Dionysus, which we must now dimly conceive as the end of individuation. It was for this coming third Dionysus that the epopts' roaring hymns of joy resounded. And it is this hope alone that casts a gleam of joy upon the features of a world torn asunder and shattered into individuals; this is symbolized in the myth of Demeter, sunk in eternal sorrow, who *rejoices* again for the first time when told that she may *once more* give birth to Dionysus. This view of things already provides us with all the elements of a profound and pessimistic view of the world, together with the *mystery doctrine of tragedy:* the fundamental knowledge of the oneness of everything existent, the conception of individuation as the primal cause of evil, and of art as the joyous hope that the spell of individuation may be broken in augury of a restored oneness.

We have already suggested that the Homeric epos is the poem of Olympian culture, in which this culture has sung its own song of victory over the terrors of the war of the Titans. Under the predominating influence of tragic poetry, these Homeric myths are now born anew; and this metempsychosis reveals that in the meantime the Olympian culture also has been conquered by a still more profound view of the world. The defiant Titan Prometheus has announced to his Olympian tormentor that some day the greatest danger will menace his rule, unless Zeus should enter into an alliance with him in time. In Aeschylus we recognize how the terrified Zeus, fearful of his end, allies himself with the Titan. Thus the former age of the Titans is once more recovered from Tartarus and brought to the light.

The philosophy of wild and naked nature beholds with the frank, undissembling gaze of truth the myths of the Homeric world as they dance past: they turn pale, they tremble under the piercing glance of this goddess—till the powerful fist of the Dionysian artist forces them into the service of the new deity. Dionysian truth takes over the entire domain of myth as the symbolism of *its* knowledge which it makes known partly in the public cult of tragedy and partly in the secret celebrations of dramatic mysteries, but always in the old mythical garb.

What power was it that freed Prometheus from his vultures and transformed the myth into a vehicle of Dionysian wisdom? It is the Heracleian power of music: having reached its highest manifestation in tragedy, it can invest myths with a new and most profound significance. This we have already characterized as the most powerful function of music. For it is the fate of every myth to creep by degrees into the narrow limits of some alleged historical reality, and to be treated by some later generation as a unique fact with historical claims: and the Greeks were already fairly on the way toward re-stamping the whole of their mythical juvenile dream saga-ciously and arbitrarily into a historico-pragmatical *juvenile history*. For this is the way in which religions are wont to die out: under the stern, intelligent eyes of an orthodox dogma-tism, the mythical premises of a religion are systematized as a sum total of historical events; one begins apprehensively to defend the credibility of the myths, while at the same time one opposes any continuation of their natural vitality and growth; the feeling for myth perishes, and its place is taken by the claim of religion to historical foundations. This dying myth was now seized by the new-born genius of Dionysian music; and in these hands it flourished once more with colors such as it had never yet displayed, with a fragrance that awak-ened a longing anticipation of a metaphysical world. After this final effulgence it collapses, its leaves wither, and soon the mocking Lucians of antiquity catch at the discolored and

faded flowers carried away by the four winds. Through tragedy the myth attains its most profound content, its most expres-sive form; it rises once more like a wounded hero, and its whole excess of strength, together with the philosophic calm of the dying, burns in its eyes with a last powerful gleam.

What did you want, sacrilegious Euripides, when you sought to compel this dying myth to serve you once more? It died under your violent hands—and then you needed a copied, masked myth that, like the ape of Heracles, merely knew how to deck itself out in the ancient pomp. And just as the myth died on you, the genius of music died on you, too. Though with greedy hands you plundered all the gardens of music, you still managed only copied, masked music. And be-cause you had abandoned Dionysus, Apollo abandoned you: rouse all the passions from their resting places and conjure them into your circle, sharpen and whet a sophistical dialec-tic for the speeches of your heroes—your heroes, too, have only copied, masked passions and speak only copied, masked speeches. . . .

ÉMILE ZOLA (1840–1902)

from *Naturalism in the Theatre* (1878)

TRANSLATED BY ALBERT BERMEL

An influential novelist, playwright, and literary theorist, Zola became the spokesman for naturalism in the theater in a series of articles he wrote in the 1870s, collected as Naturalism in the Theatre *in 1878. In these essays, Zola urged the theater to adopt an attitude of scientific objectivity, an attitude reflected in the development of a new dramatic style. The naturalistic theater asserted such objectivity through its choice of subject matter (middle-class life), its treatment of characters (driven by "physiological" motives, not by "metaphysical" passions), its use of a prosaic, antiliterary language, and by the importance attached to the material environment. Zola's energy in summoning a new form of theatrical representation is evident here: what will be the signs of that new theatre onstage? What is the value that Zola ascribes to life-like representation, and how will it become visible onstage? How will this new theater be distinguished from the classical and romantic past?*

It seems impossible that the movement of inquiry and analy-sis, which is precisely the movement of the nineteenth cen-tury, can have revolutionized all the sciences and arts and left dramatic art to one side, as if isolated. The natural sci-ences date from the end of the last century; chemistry and physics are less than a hundred years old; history and criti-cism have been renovated, virtually re-created since the Rev-olution; an entire world has arisen; it has sent us back to the study of documents, to experience, made us realize that to start afresh we must first take things back to the beginning, become familiar with man and nature, verify what is. Thence-forward, the great naturalistic school, which has spread se-cretly, irrevocably, often making its way in darkness but always advancing, can finally come out triumphantly into the light of day. To trace the history of this movement, with the

misunderstandings that might have impeded it and the mul-tiple causes that have thrust it forward or slowed it down, would be to trace the history of the century itself. An irre-sistible current carries our society towards the study of real-ity. In the novel Balzac has been the bold and mighty innovator who has replaced the observation of the scholar with the imagination of the poet. But in the theatre the evo-lution seems slower. No eminent writer has yet formulated the new idea with any clarity.

I certainly do not say that some excellent works have not been produced, with characters in them who are ingeniously examined and bold truths taken right on to the stage. Let me, for instance, cite certain plays by M. Dumas *fils*, whose talent I scarcely admire, and M. Émile Augier, the most hu-mane and powerful of all. Still, they are midgets beside

Balzac; they lack the genius to lay down the formula. It must be said that one can never tell quite when a movement is getting under way; generally its source is remote and lost in the earlier movement from which it emerged. In a manner of speaking, the naturalistic current has always existed. It brings with it nothing absolutely novel. But it has finally flowed into a period favourable to it; it is succeeding and expanding because the human mind has attained the necessary maturity. I do not, therefore, deny the past; I affirm the present. The strength of naturalism is precisely that it has deep roots in our national literature which contains plenty of wisdom. It comes from the very entrails of humanity; it is that much the stronger because it has taken longer to grow and is found in a greater number of our masterpieces.

Certain things have come to pass and I point them out. Can we believe that *L'Ami Fritz* would have been applauded at the Comédie-Française twenty years ago? Definitely not! This play, in which people eat all the time and the lover talks in such homely language, would have disgusted both the classicists and the romantics. To explain its success we must concede that as the years have gone by a secret fermentation has been at work. Lifelike paintings, which used to repel the public, today attract them. The majority has been won over and the stage is open to every experiment. This is the only conclusion to draw.

So that is where we stand. To explain my point better—am not afraid of repeating myself—I will sum up what I have said. Looking closely at the history of our dramatic literature, one can detect several clearly separated periods. First, there was the infancy of the art, farces and the mystery plays of the Middle Ages, the reciting of simple dialogues which developed as part of a naïve convention, with primitive staging and sets. Gradually, the plays became more complex but in a crude fashion. When Corneille appeared he was acclaimed most of all for his status as an innovator, for refining the dramatic formula of the time, and for hallowing it by means of his genius. It would be very interesting to study the pertinent documents and discover how our classical formula came to be created. It corresponded to the social spirit of the period. Nothing is solid that is not built on necessity. Tragedy reigned for two centuries because it satisfied the exact requirements of those centuries. Geniuses of differing temperaments had buttressed it with their masterpieces. And it continued to impose itself long afterwards, even when second-rate talents were producing inferior work. It acquired a momentum. It persisted also as the literary expression of that society, and nothing would have overthrown it if the society, had not itself disappeared. After the Revolution, after that profound disturbance that was meant to transform everything and give birth to a new world, tragedy struggled

to stay alive for a few more years. Then the formula cracked and romanticism broke through. A new formula asserted itself. We must look back at the first half of the century to understand the meaning of this cry for liberty. The young society was in the tremor of its infancy. The excited, bewildered, violently unleashed people were still racked by a dangerous fever; and in the first flush of their new liberty they yearned for prodigious adventures and superhuman love affairs. They gaped at the stars; some committed suicide, a very curious reaction to the social enfranchisement which had just been declared at the cost of so much blood. Turning specifically to dramatic literature, I maintain that romanticism in the theatre was an uncomplicated revolt, the invasion by a victorious group who took over the stage violently with drums beating and flags flying. In these early moments the combatants dreamed of making their imprint with a new form; to one rhetoric they opposed another: the Middle Ages to Antiquity, the exalting of passion to the exalting of duty. And that was all, for only the scenic conventions were altered. The characters remained marionettes in new clothing. Only the exterior aspect and the language were modified. But for the period that was enough. Romanticism had taken possession of the theatre in the name of literary freedom and it carried out its revolutionary task with incomparable bravura. But who does not see today that its role could extend no farther than that? Does romanticism have anything whatever to say about our present society? Does it meet one of our requirements? Obviously not. It is as outmoded as a jargon we no longer follow. It confidently expected to replace classical literature which had lasted for two centuries because it was based on social conditions. But romanticism was based on nothing but the fantasy of a few poets or, if you will, on the passing malady of minds overwhelmed by historical events; it was bound to disappear with the malady. It provided the occasion for a magnificent flowering of lyricism; that will be its eternal glory. Today, however, with the evolution accomplished, it is plain that romanticism was no more than the necessary link between classicism and naturalism. The struggle is over; now we must found a secure state. Naturalism flows out of classical art, just as our present society has arisen from the wreckage of the old society. Naturalism alone corresponds to our social needs; it alone has deep roots in the spirit of our times; and it alone can provide a living, durable formula for our art, because this formula will express the nature of our contemporary intelligence. There may be fashions and passing fantasies that exist outside naturalism but they will not survive for long. I say again, naturalism is the expression of our century and it will not die until a new upheaval transforms our democratic world.

Only one thing is needed now: men of genius who can fix the naturalistic formula. Balzac has done it for the novel and the novel is established. When will our Corneilles, Molières and Racines appear to establish our new theatre? We must hope and wait.

• • •

The period when romantic drama ruled now seems distant. In Paris five or six of its playhouses prospered. The demolition of the old theatres along the Boulevard du Temple was a catastrophe of the first order. The theatres became separated from one another, the public changed, different fashions arose. But the discredit into which the drama has fallen proceeds mostly from the exhaustion of the genre—ridiculous, boring plays have gradually taken over from the potent works of 1830.

To this enfeeblement we must add the absolute lack of new actors who understand and can interpret these kinds of plays, for every dramatic formula that vanishes carries away its interpreters with it. Today the drama, hunted from stage to stage, has only two houses that really belong to it, the Ambigu and the Théâtre-Historique. Even at the Saint-Martin the drama is lucky to win a brief showing for itself, between one great spectacle and the next.

An occasional success may renew its courage. But its decline is inevitable; romantic drama is sliding into oblivion, and if it seems sometimes to check its descent, it does so only to roll even lower afterwards. Naturally, there are loud complaints. The tail-end romanticists are desperately unhappy. They swear that except in the drama—meaning their kind of drama—there is no salvation for dramatic literature. I believe, on the contrary, that we must find a new formula that will transform the drama, just as the writers in the first half of the century transformed tragedy. That is the essence of the matter. Today the battle is between romantic drama and naturalistic drama. By romantic drama I mean every play that mocks truthfulness in its incidents and characterization, that struts about in its puppet-box, stuffed to the belly with noises that flounder, for some idealistic reason or other, in pastiches of Shakespeare and Hugo. Every period has its formula; ours is certainly not that of 1830. We are an age of method, of experimental science; our primary need is for precise analysis. We hardly understand the liberty we have won if we use it only to imprison ourselves in a new tradition. The way is open: we can now return to man and nature.

Finally, there have been great efforts to revive the historical drama. Nothing could be better. A critic cannot roundly condemn the choice of historical subjects, even if his own preferences are entirely for subjects that are modern. It is simply that I am full of distrust. The manager one gives this sort of play to frightens me in advance. It is a question of how history is treated, what unusual characters are presented bearing the names of kings, great captains or great artists, and what awful sauce they are served up in to make the history palatable. As soon as the authors of these concoctions move into the past they think everything is permitted: improbabilities, cardboard dolls, monumental idiocies, the hysterical scribblings that falsely represent local colour. And what strange dialogue—François I talking like a haberdasher straight out of the Rue Saint-Denis, Richelieu using the words of a criminal from the Boulevard du Crime, Charlotte Corday with the weeping sentimentalities of a factory girl.

What astounds me is that our playwrights do not seem to suspect for a moment that the historical genre is unavoidably the least rewarding, the one that calls most strongly for research, integrity, a consummate gift of intuition, a talent for reconstruction. I am all for historical drama when it is in the hands of poets of genius or men of exceptional knowledge who are capable of making the public see an epoch come alive with its special quality, its manners, its civilization. In that case we have a work of prophecy or of profoundly interesting criticism.

But unfortunately I know what it is these partisans of historical drama want to revive: the swaggering and swordplay, the big spectacle with big words, the play of lies that shows off in front of the crowd, the gross exhibition that saddens honest minds. Hence my distrust. I think that all this antiquated business is better left in our museum of dramatic history under a pious layer of dust.

There are, undeniably, great obstacles to original experiments: we run up against the hypocrisies of criticism and the long education in idiocies that has been foisted on the public. This public, which titters at every childishness in melodramas, nevertheless lets itself be carried away by outbursts of fine sentiment. But the public is changing. Shakespeare's public and Molière's are no longer ours. We must reckon with shifts in outlook, with the need for reality which is everywhere getting more insistent. The last few romantics vainly repeat that the public wants this and the public wants that; the day is coming when the public will want the truth.

• • •

The old formulas, classical and romantic, were based on the rearrangement and systematic amputation of the truth. They determined on principle that the truth is not good enough; they tried to draw out of it an essence, a 'poetry', on the pretext that nature must be expurgated and magnified. Up to the present the different literary schools disputed only over the question of the best way to disguise the truth so that it might not look too brazen to the public. The classicists adopted the toga; the romantics fought a revolution to impose the coat of mail and the doublet. Essentially the change of dress made little difference; the counterfeiting of nature went on. But today the naturalistic thinkers are telling us that the truth does not need clothing; it can walk naked. That, I repeat, is the quarrel.

Writers with any sense understand perfectly that tragedy and romantic drama are dead. The majority, though, are badly troubled when they turn their minds to the as-yet-unclear formula of tomorrow. Does the truth seriously ask them to give up the grandeur, the poetry, the traditional epic effects that their ambition tells them to put into their plays? Does naturalism demand that they shrink their horizons and risk not one flight into fantasy?

I will try to reply. But first we must determine the methods used by the idealists to lift their works into poetry. They begin by placing their chosen subject in a distant time. That provides them with costumes and makes the framework of the story vague enough to give them full scope for lying. Next, they generalize instead of particularizing; their characters are no longer living people but sentiments, arguments, passions that have been induced by reasoning. This false framework calls for heroes of marble or cardboard. A man of flesh and bone with his own originality would jar in such a legendary setting. Moreover, when we see the characters in romantic drama or tragedy walking about they are stiffened into an attitude, one representing duty, another patriotism, a third superstition, a fourth maternal love; thus, all the abstract ideas file by. Never the thorough analysis of an organism, never a character whose muscles and brain function as in nature.

These, then, are the mannerisms that writers with epic inclinations do not want to give up. For them poetry resides in the past and in abstraction, in the idealizing of facts and characters. As soon as one confronts them with daily life, with the people who fill our streets, they blink, they stammer, they are afraid; they no longer see clearly; they find everything ugly and not good enough for art. According to them, a subject must enter the lies of legend, men must harden and turn to stone like statues before the artist can accept them and make them fit the disguises he has prepared.

Now, it is at this point that the naturalistic movement comes along and says squarely that poetry is everywhere, in everything, even more in the present and the real than in the past and the abstract. Each event at each moment has its poetic, superb aspect. We brush up against heroes who are great and powerful in different respects from the puppets of the epic-makers. Not one playwright in this century has

brought to life figures as lofty as Baron Hulot, Old Grandet, César Birotteau, and all the other characters of Balzac, who are so individual and so alive. Beside these real, giant creations Greek and Roman heroes quake; the heroes of the Middle Ages fall flat on their faces like lead soldiers.

With the superior works being produced in these times by the naturalistic school—works of high endeavour, pulsing with life—it is ridiculous and false to park our poetry in some antiquated temple and bury it in cobwebs. Poetry flows at its full force through everything that exists; the truer to life, the greater it becomes. And I mean to give the word poetry its widest definition, not to pin it down exclusively to the cadence of two rhymes, nor to burn it in a narrow coterie of dreamers, but to restore its real human significance which concerns the expansion and encouragement of every kind of truth.

Take our present environment, then, and try to make men live in it: you will write great works. It will undoubtedly call for some effort; it means sifting out of the confusion of life the simple formula of naturalism. Therein lies the difficulty: to do great things with the subjects and characters that our eyes, accustomed to the spectacle of the daily round, have come to see as small. I am aware that it is more convenient to present a marionette to the public and name it Charlemagne and puff it up with such tirades that the public believes it is watching a colossus; it is more convenient than taking a bourgeois of our time, a grotesque, unsightly man, and drawing sublime poetry out of him, making him, for example, Père Goriot, the father who gives his guts for his daughters, a figure so gigantic with truth and love that no other literature can offer his equal.

Nothing is as easy as persuading the managers with known formulas; and heroes in the classical or romantic taste cost so little labour that they are manufactured by the dozen, and have become standardized articles that clutter up our literature. But it takes hard work to create a real hero, intelligently analysed, alive and performing. That is probably why naturalism terrifies those authors who are used to fishing up great men from the troubled waters of history. They would have to burrow too deeply into humanity, learn about life, go straight for the greatness of reality and make it function with all their power. And let nobody gainsay this true poetry of humanity; it has been sifted out in the novel and can be in the theatre; only the method of adaptation remains to be found.

I am troubled by a comparison; it has been haunting me and I will now free myself of it. For two long months a play called *Les Danicheff* has been running at the Odéon. It takes place in Russia. It has been very successful here, but is apparently so dishonest, so packed with gross improbabilities, that the author, a Russian, has not even dared to show it in his country. What can you think of this work which is applauded in Paris and would be booed in St Petersburg? Well, imagine for a moment that the Romans could come back to life and see a performance of *Rome vaincue*. Can you hear their roars of laughter? Do you think the play would complete one performance? It would strike them as a parody; it would sink under the weight of mockery. And is there one historical play that could be performed before the society it claims to portray? A strange theatre, this, which is plausible only among foreigners, is based on the disappearance of the generations it deals with, and is made up of so much misinformation that it is good only for the ignorant!

The future is with naturalism. The formula will be found; it will be proved that there is more poetry in the little apartment of a bourgeois than in all the empty, worm-eaten palaces of history; in the end we will see that everything meets in the real: lovely fantasies that are free of capriciousness and whimsy, and idylls, and comedies, and dramas. Once the soil has been turned over, the task that seems alarming and unfeasible today will become easy.

I am not qualified to pronounce on the form that tomorrow's drama will take; that must be left to the voice of some genius to come. But I will allow myself to indicate the path I consider our theatre will follow.

First, the romantic drama must be abandoned. It would be disastrous for us to take over its outrageous acting, its rhetoric, its inherent thesis of action at the expense of character analysis. The finest models of the genre are, as has been said, mere operas with big effects. I believe, then, that we must go back to tragedy—not, heaven forbid, to borrow more of its rhetoric, its system of confidants, its declaiming, its endless speeches, but to return to its simplicity of action and its unique psychological and physiological study of the characters. Thus understood, the tragic framework is excellent; one deed unwinds in all its reality, and moves the characters to passions and feelings, the exact analysis of which constitutes the sole interest of the play—and in a contemporary environment, with the people who surround us.

My constant concern, my anxious vigil, has made me wonder which of us will have the strength to raise himself to the pitch of genius. If the naturalistic drama must come into being, only a genius can give birth to it. Corneille and Racine made tragedy. Victor Hugo made romantic drama. Where is the as-yet-unknown author who must make the naturalistic drama? In recent years experiments have not been wanting. But either because the public was not ready or because none of the beginners had the necessary staying-power, not one of these attempts has had decisive results.

In battles of this kind, small victories mean nothing; we need triumphs that overwhelm the adversary and win the public to the cause. Audiences would give way before the onslaught of a really strong man. This man would come with the expected word, the solution to the problem, the formula for a real life on stage, combining it with the illusions necessary in the theatre. He would have what the newcomers have as yet lacked: the cleverness or the might to impose himself and to remain so close to truth that his cleverness could not lead him into lies.

And what an immense place this innovator would occupy in our dramatic literature! He would be at the peak. He would build his monument in the middle of the desert of mediocrity that we are crossing, among the jerry-built houses strewn about our most illustrious stages. He would put everything in question and remake everything, scour the boards, create a world whose elements he would lift from life, from outside our traditions. Surely there is no more ambitious dream that a writer of our time could fulfil. The domain of the novel is crowded; the domain of the theatre is free. At this time in France an imperishable glory awaits the man of genius who takes up the work of Molière and finds in the reality of living comedy the full, true drama of modern society.

• • •

PHYSIOLOGICAL MAN

. . . In effect, the great naturalistic evolution, which comes down directly from the fifteenth century to ours has everything to do with the gradual substitution of physiological man for metaphysical man. In tragedy metaphysical man, man according to dogma and logic, reigned absolutely. The body did not count; the soul was regarded as the only interesting piece of human machinery; drama took place in the air, in pure mind. Consequently, what use was the tangible world? Why worry about the place where the action was located? Why be surprised at a baroque costume or false declaiming? Why notice that Queen Dido was a boy whose budding beard forced him to wear a mask? None of that mattered; these trifles were not worth stooping to; the play was heard out as if it were a school essay or a law case; it was on a higher plane than man, in the world of ideas, so far away from real man that any intrusion of reality would have spoiled the show.

Such is the point of departure—in Mystery plays, the religious point; the philosophical point in tragedy. And from that beginning natural man, stifling under the rhetoric and dogma, struggled secretly, tried to break free, made lengthy, futile efforts, and in the end asserted himself, limb by limb. The whole history of our theatre is in this conquest by the physiological man, who emerged more clearly in each period from behind the dummy of religious and philosophical idealism. Corneille, Molière, Racine, Voltaire, Beaumarchais and, in our day, Victor Hugo, Émile Augier, Alexandre Dumas *fils*, even Sardou, have had only one task, even when they were not completely aware of it: to increase the reality of our corpus of drama, to progress towards truth, to sift out more and more of the natural man and impose him on the public. And inevitably, the evolution will not end with them. It continues; it will continue forever. Mankind is very young. . . .

COSTUME, STAGE DESIGN, SPEECH

Modern clothes make a poor spectacle. If we depart from bourgeois tragedy, shut in between its four walls, and wish to use the breadth of larger stages for crowd scenes we are embarrassed and constrained by the monotony and the uniformly funereal look of the extras. In this case, I think, we should take advantage of the variety of garb offered by the different classes and occupations. To elaborate: I can imagine an author setting one act in the main marketplace of les Halles in Paris. The setting would be superb, with its bustling life and bold possibilities. In this immense setting we could have a very picturesque ensemble by displaying the porters wearing their large hats, the saleswomen with their white aprons and vividly-coloured scarves, the customers dressed in silk or wool or cotton prints, from the ladies accompanied by their maids to the female beggars on the prowl for anything they can pick up off the street. For inspiration it would be enough to go to les Halles and look about. Nothing is gaudier or more interesting. All of Paris would enjoy seeing this set if it were realized with the necessary accuracy and amplitude.

And how many other settings for popular drama there are for the taking! Inside a factory, the interior of a mine, the gingerbread market, a railway station, flower stalls, a racetrack, and so on. All the activities of modern life can take place in them. It will be said that such sets have already been tried. Unquestionably we have seen factories and railway stations in fantasy plays; but these were fantasy stations and factories. I mean, these sets were thrown together to create an illusion that was at best incomplete. What we need is detailed reproduction: costumes supplied by tradespeople, not sumptuous but adequate for the purposes of truth and for the interest of the scenes. Since everybody mourns the death of the drama our playwrights certainly ought to make a try at this type of popular, contemporary drama. At one stroke they could satisfy the public hunger for spectacle and the need for exact studies which grows more pressing every day. Let us hope, though, that the playwrights will show us real people and not those whining members of the working class who play such strange roles in boulevard melodrama.

As M. Adolphe Jullien has said—and I will never be tired of repeating it—everything is interdependent in the theatre. Lifelike costumes look wrong if the sets, the diction, the plays

themselves are not lifelike. They must all march in step along the naturalistic road. When costume becomes more accurate, so do sets; actors free themselves from bombastic declaiming; plays study reality more closely and their characters are more true to life. I could make the same observations about sets I have just made about costume. With them too, we may seem to have reached the highest possible degree of truth, but we still have long strides to take. Most of all we would need to intensify the illusion in reconstructing the environments, less for their picturesque quality than for dramatic utility. The environment must determine the character. When a set is planned so as to give the lively impression of a description by Balzac; when, as the curtain rises, one catches the first glimpse of the characters, their personalities and behaviour, if only to see the actual locale in which they move, the importance of exact reproduction in the decor will be appreciated. Obviously, that is the way we are going. Environment, the study of which has transformed science and literature, will have to take a large role in the theatre. And here I may mention again the question of metaphysical man, the abstraction who had to be satisfied with his three walls in tragedy—whereas the physiological man in our modern works is asking more and more compellingly to be determined by his setting, by the environment that produced him. We see then that the road to progress is still long, for sets as well as costume. We are coming upon the truth but we can hardly stammer it out.

Another very serious matter is diction. True, we have got away from the chanting, the plainsong, of the seventeenth century. But we now have a "theatre voice," a false recitation that is very obtrusive and very annoying. Everything that is wrong with it comes from the fixed traditional code set up by the majority of critics. They found the theatre in a certain state and, instead of looking to the future, and judging the progress we are making and the progress we shall make by the progress we have already made, they stubbornly defend the relics of the old conventions, swearing that these relics must be preserved. Ask them why, make them see how far we have travelled; they will give you no logical reason. They will reply with assertions based on a set of conditions that are disappearing.

In diction the errors come from what the critics call "theatre language." Their theory is that on stage you must not speak as you do in everyday life. To support this viewpoint they pick examples from traditional practices, from what was happening yesterday—and is happening still—without taking account of the naturalistic movement, the phases of which have been established for us by M. Jullien's book.[1] Let us realize that there is no such thing as "theatre language." There

[1] Adolphe Jullien 1845–1932, writer on music and the theatre. The book Zola cites is *Histoire du costume au théâtre*, 1880.

has been a rhetoric which grew more and more feeble and is now dying out. Those are the facts. If you compare the declaiming of actors under Louis XIV with that of Lekain, and if you compare Lekain's with that of our own artists today, you will clearly distinguish the phases from tragic chanting down to our search for the natural, precise tone, the cry of truth. It follows that "theatre language," that language of booming sonority, is vanishing. We are moving towards simplicity, the exact word spoken without emphasis, quite naturally. How many examples I could give if I had unlimited space! Consider the powerful effect that Geoffroy has on the public; all his talent comes from his natural personality. He holds the public because he speaks on stage as he does at home. When a sentence sounds outlandish he cannot pronounce it; the author has to find another one. That is the fundamental criticism of so-called "theatre language." Again, follow the diction of a talented actor and at the same time watch the public; the cheers go up, the house is in raptures when a truthful accent gives the words the exact value they must have. All the great successes of the stage are triumphs over convention.

Alas, yes, there is a "theatre language." It is the clichés, the resounding platitudes, the hollow words that roll about like empty barrels, all that intolerable rhetoric of our vaudevilles and dramas, which is beginning to make us smile. It would be very interesting to study the style of such talented authors as MM. Augier, Dumas and Sardou. I could find much to criticize, especially in the last two with their conventional language, a language of their own that they put into the mouths of all their characters, men, women, children, old folk, both sexes and all ages. This irritates me, for each character has his own language, and to create living people you must give them to the public not merely in accurate dress and in the environments that have made them what they are, but with their individual ways of thinking and expressing themselves. I repeat that that is the obvious aim of our theatre. There is no theatre language regulated by such a code as "cadenced sentences" or sonority. There is simply a kind of dialogue that is growing more precise and is following—or rather, leading—sets and costumes towards naturalistic progress. When plays are more truthful, the actors' diction will gain enormously in simplicity and naturalness.

To conclude, I will repeat that the battle of the conventions is far from being finished, and that it will no doubt last forever. Today we are beginning to see clearly where we are going, but our steps are still impeded by the melting slush of rhetoric and metaphysics.

CONSTANTIN STANISLAVSKI (1863–1938)
"Direction and Acting" (1929)

One of the founders of the Moscow Art Theater, Stanislavski developed a systematic approach to acting that involved working both on the actor's psychological and on his or her physical portrayal of character. In this article, originally written for the Encyclopedia Britannica, *Stanislavski outlines some of the central features of his "system": public solitude, concentration, internal technique.*

Theatrical art has always been collective, arising only where poetical-dramatic talent was actively combined with the actor's. The basis of a play is always a dramatic conception; a general artistic sense is imparted to the theatrical action by the unifying, creative genius of the actor. Thus the actor's dramatic activity begins at the foundation of the play. In the first place, each actor, either independently or through the theatre manager, must probe for the fundamental motive in the finished play—the creative idea that is characteristic of the author and that reveals itself as the germ from which his work grows organically. The motive of the play always keeps the character developing before the spectator; each personality in the work takes a part conforming to his own character; the work, then developing in the appointed direction, flows on to the final point conceived by the author. The first stage in the work of the actor and theatre manager is to probe for the germ of the play, investigating the fundamental line of action that traverses all of its episodes and is therefore called by the writer its transparent effect or action. In contrast to some theatrical directors, who consider every play only as material for theatrical repetition, the writer believes that in the production of every important drama the director and actor must go straight for the most exact and profound conception of the mind and ideal of the dramatist, and must not change that ideal for their own. The interpretation of the play and the character of its artistic incarnation inevitably appear in a certain measure subjective, and bear the mark of the individual peculiarities of the manager and actors; but only by profound attention to the artistic individuality of the author and to his ideal and mentality, which have been disclosed as the creative germ of the play, can the theatre realize all its artistic depth and transmit, as in a poetical production, completeness and harmony of composition. Every part of the future spectacle is then unified in it by its own artistic work; each part, in the measure of its own genius, will flow on to the artistic realization aimed at by the dramatist.

The actor's task, then, begins with the search for the play's artistic seed. All artistic action—organic action, as in every constructive operation of nature—starts from this seed at the moment when it is conveyed to the mind. On reaching the actor's mind, the seed must wander around, germinate, put out roots, drinking in the juices of the soil in which it is planted, grow and eventually bring forth a lively flowering plant. Artistic process must in all cases flow very rapidly, but usually, in order that it may preserve the character of the true organic action and may lead to the creation of life, of a clear truly artistic theatrical image, and not of a trade substitute, it demands much more time than is allotted to it in the best European theatres. That is why in the writer's theatre every dramatization passes through eight to ten revisions, as is also done in Germany by the famous theatre manager and theorist, K. Hagemann. Sometimes even more than ten revisions are needed, occasionally extending over several months. But even under these conditions, the creative genius of the actor does not appear so freely as does, for instance, the creative genius of the dramatist. Bound by the strict obligations of his *collectif,* the actor must not postpone his work to the moment when his physical and psychic condition appears propitious for creative genius. Meanwhile, his exacting and capricious artistic nature is prompted by aspirations of his artistic intuition, and in the absence of creative genius is not reached by any effort of his will. He is not aided in that respect by outward technique—his skill in making use of his body, his vocal equipment and his powers of speech.

THE ARTISTIC CONDITION

But is it really impossible? Are there no means, no processes that sensibly would help us, and spontaneously lead to that artistic condition which is born of genius without any effort on its part? If that capacity is unattainable all at once, by some process or other, it may, perhaps, be acquired in parts, and through progressive stages may perfect those elements out of which the artistic condition is composed, and which are subject to our will. Of course the general run of acting does not come into being from this genius, but cannot such acting, in some measure, be brought by it near to what is evidence of genius? These are the problems which presented themselves to the writer about 20 years ago, when reflecting on the external obstacles that hamper actors' artistic genius, and partly compel substitution of the crude outward marks of the actor's profession for its results. They drove

him to the rediscovery of processes of external technique, i.e., methods proceeding form consciousness to sub-consciousness, in which domain flow nine-tenths of all real artistic processes. Observations both upon himself and other actors with whom he happened to rehearse, but chiefly upon growing theatrical skill in Russia and abroad, allowed him to do some generalizing, which thereupon he verified in practice.

The first is that, in an artistic condition, full freedom of body plays a principal rôle; i.e., the freedom from that muscular strain which, without our knowing it, fetters us not only on the stage but also in ordinary life, hindering us from being obedient conductors of our psychic action. This muscular strain, reaching its maximum at those times when the actor is called upon to perform something especially difficult in his theatrical work, swallows up the bulk of this external energy, diverting him from activity of the higher centres. This teaches us the possibility of availing ourselves of the muscular energy of our limbs only as necessity demands, and in exact conformity with our creative efforts.

PUBLIC SOLITUDE

The second observation is that the flow of the actor's artistic force is considerably retarded by the visual auditorium and the public, whose presence may hamper his outward freedom of movement, and powerfully hinder his concentration on his own artistic taste. It is almost unnecessary to remark that the artistic achievement of great actors is always bound by the concentration of attention to the action of their own performance, and that when in that condition, i.e., just when the actor's attention is taken away from the spectator, he gains a particular power over the audience, grips it, and compels it to take an active share in his artistic existence. This does not mean, of course, that the actor must altogether cease to feel the public; but the public is concerned only in so far as it neither exerts pressure on him nor diverts him unnecessarily from the artistic demands of the moment, which last might happen to him even while knowing how to regulate his attention. The actor suitably disciplined must automatically restrict the sphere of his attention, concentrating on what comes within this sphere, and only half consciously seizing on what comes within its aura. If need be, he must restrict that sphere to such an extent that it reaches a condition that may be called *public solitude.* But as a rule this sphere of attention is elastic, it expands or contracts for the actor, with regard to the course of his theatrical actions. Within the boundary of this sphere, as one of the actual aspects of the play, there is also the actor's immediate central *object of attention,* the object on which, somehow or other, his will is concentrated at the moment with which, in the course of the play, he is in inward communication. This theatrical sympathy with the object can only be complete when the actor has trained himself by long practice to surrender himself in his own impressions, and also in his reactions to those impressions, with maximum intensity: only so does theatrical action attain the necessary force, only so is created between the actual aspects of the play, i.e., between the actors, that link, that living bond, which is essential for the carrying through of the play to its goal, with the general maintenance of the rhythm and time of each performance.

CONCENTRATION

But whatever may be the sphere of the actor's attention, whether it confines him at some moments to public solitude, or whether it grips the faces of all those before the stage, dramatic artistic genius, as in the preparation of the part so in its repeated performance, requires a full concentration of all the mental and physical talents of the actor, and the participation of the whole of his physical and psychic capacity. It takes hold of his sight and hearing, all his external senses; it draws out not only the periphery but also the essential depth of his existence, and it evokes to activity his memory, imagination, emotions, intelligence and will. The whole mental and physical being of the actor must be directed to that which is derived from his facial expression. At the moment of inspiration, of the involuntary use of all the actor's qualities, at that moment he actually exists. On the other hand, in the absence of this employment of his qualities, the actor is gradually led astray along the road leading to time-honored theatrical traditions; he begins to "produce" wherever he sees them, or, glancing at his own image, imitates the inward manifestations of his emotions, or tries to draw from himself the emotions of the perfected part, to "inspire" them within himself. But when forcing such an image by his own psychic equipment, with its unchanging organic laws, he by no means attains that desired result of artistic genius; he must present only the rough counterfeit of emotion, because emotions do not come to order. By no effort of conscious will can one awake them in oneself at a moment, nor can they ever be of use for creative genius striving to bring this about by searching the depths of its mind. A fundamental axiom, therefore, for the actor who wishes to be a real artist on the stage, may be stated thus: he must not play to produce emotions, and he must not involuntarily evoke them in himself.

ACTIVITY OF IMAGINATION

Considerations on the nature of artistically gifted people, however, inevitably open up the road to the possession of the emotion of the part. This road traverses activity of imagina-

tion, which in most of its stages is subject to the action of consciousness. One must not suddenly begin to operate on emotion; one must put oneself in motion in the direction of artistic imagination, but imagination—as is also shown by observations of scientific psychology—disturbs our aberrant memory, and, luring from the hidden recesses beyond the boundaries of its sense of harmony whatever elements there may be of proved emotions, organizes them afresh in sympathy with those that have arisen in our imagery. So surrounded within our figures of imagination, without effort on our part, the answer to our aberrant memory is found and the sounds of sympathetic emotion are called out from us. This is why the creative imagination presents itself afresh, the indispensable gift of the actor. Without a well developed, mobile imagination, creative faculty is by no means possible, not by instinct nor intuition nor the aid of external technique. In the acquiring of it, that which has lain dormant in the mind of the artist is, when immersed in his sphere of unconscious imagery and emotion, completely harmonized within him.

This practical method for the artistic education of the actor, directed by means of his imagination to the storing up of affective memory, is sufficiently enlarged upon; his individual emotional experience, by its limits, actually leads to the restriction of the sphere of his creative genius, and does not allow him to play parts dissimilar to those of his psychic harmony. This opinion is fundamental for the clearing away of misunderstandings of those elements of reality from which are produced fictitious creations of imagination; these are also derived from organic experience, but a wealth and variety of these creations are only obtained by combinations drawn from a trial of elements. The musical scale has only its basic notes, the solar spectrum its radical colors, but the combination of sounds in music and of colors in painting are infinite. One can in the same way speak of radical emotions preserved in imaginative memory, just as the reception in imagination of outward harmony remains in the intellectual memory; the sum of these radical emotions in the inner experience of each person is limited, but the shades and combinations are as infinite as the combinations that create activity of imagination out of the elements of inward experience.

Certainly, but the actor's outward experience—i.e., his sphere of vital sensations and reflections—must always be elastic, for only in that condition can the actor enlarge the sphere of his creative faculty. On the other hand, he must judiciously develop his imagination, harnessing it again and again to new propositions. But, in order that that imaginary union which is the actor's very foundation, produced by the creative genius of the dramatist, should take hold of him emotionally and lead him on to theatrical action, it is necessary that the actor should "swing toward" that union, as toward something as real as the union of reality surrounding him.

THE EMOTION OF TRUTH

This does not mean that the actor must surrender himself on the stage to some such hallucination as that when playing he should lose the sense of reality around him, to take scenery for real trees, etc. On the contrary, some part of his senses must remain free from the grip of the play to control everything that he attempts and achieves as the performer of his part. He does not forget that surrounding him on the stage are decorations, scenery, etc., but they have no meaning for him. He says to himself, as it were: "I know that all around me on the stage is a rough counterfeit of reality. It is false. But if all should be real, see how I might be carried away to some such scene; then I would act." And at that instant, when there arises in his mind that artistic "suppose," encircling his real life, he loses interest in it, and is transported to another plane, created for him, of imaginary life. Restored to real life again, the actor must perforce modify the truth, as in the actual construction of his invention, so also in the survivals connected to it. His invention can be shown to be illogical, wide of the truth—and then he ceases to believe it. Emotion rises in him with invention; i.e., his outward regard for imagined circumstances may be shown as "determined" without relation to the individual nature of a given emotion. Finally, in the expression of the outward life of his part, the actor, as a living complex emotion, never making use of sufficient perfection of all his bodily equipment, may give an untrue intonation, may not keep the artistic mean in gesticulation and may through the temptation of cheap effect drift into mannerism or awkwardness.

Only by a strongly developed sense of truth may he achieve a single inward beauty in which, unlike the conventional theatrical gestures and poses, the true condition of the character is expressed in every one of his attitudes and outward gestures.

INTERNAL TECHNIQUE

The combination of all the above-named procedure and habits also composes the actor's external technique. Parallel with its development must go also the development of internal technique—the perfecting of that bodily equipment which serves for the incarnation of the theatrical image created by the actor, and the exact, clear expression of his external consciousness. With this aim in view the actor must work out within himself not only the ordinary flexibility and mobility of action, but also the particular consciousness that directs all his groups of muscles, and the ability to feel the energy transfused within him, which, arising from his highest creative centres, forms in a definite manner his mimicry and gestures, and, radiating from him, brings into the circle of its influence his partners on the stage and in the auditorium. The same growth of consciousness and fineness of internal feelings must be worked out by the actor in relation to his vocal equipment. Ordinary speech—as in life, so on the stage—is prosaic and monotonous; in it words sound disjointed, without any harmonious stringing together in a vocal melody as continuous as that of a violin, which by the hand of a master violinist can become fuller, deeper, finer and more transparent, and can without difficulty run from the higher to the lower notes and vice versa, and can alternate from pianissimo to forte. To counteract the wearisome monotony of reading, actors often elaborate, especially when declaiming poetry, with those artificial vocal *fioritures,* cadences and sudden raising and lowering of the voice, which are so characteristic of the conventional, pompous declamation, and which are not influenced by the corresponding emotion of the part, and therefore impress the more sensitive auditors with a feeling of unreality.

But there exists another natural musical sonorousness of speech, which we may see in great actors at the moment of their own true artistic elation, and which is closely knit to the internal sonorousness of their rôle. The actor must develop within himself this natural musical speech by practising his voice with due regard to his sense of reality, almost as much as a singer. At the same time he must perfect his elocution. It is possible to have a strong, flexible, impressive voice, and still distort speech, on the one hand by incorrect pronunciation, on the other by neglect of those almost imperceptible pauses and emphasis through which are attained the exact transmission of the sense of the sentence, and also its particular emotional coloring. In the perfect production of the dramatist, every word, every letter, every punctuation mark has its part in transmitting his inward reality; the actor in his interpretation of the play, according to his intelligence, introduces into each sentence his individual nuances, which must be transmitted not only by the motions of his body, but also by artistically developed speech. He must bear this in mind, that every sound which goes to make a word appears as a separate note, which has its part in the harmonious sound of the word, and which is the expression of one or other particle of the soul drawn out through the word. The perfecting, therefore, of the phonetics of speech cannot be limited to mechanical exercise of the vocal equipment, but must also be directed in such a way that the actor learns to feel each separate sound in a word as an instrument of artistic expression. But in regard to the musical tone of the voice, freedom, elasticity, rhythm of movement and generally all external technique of dramatic art, to say nothing of internal technique, the present day actor is still on a low rung of the ladder of artistic culture, still far behind in this respect, from many causes, the masters of music, poetry and painting, with an almost infinite road of development to travel.

It is evident that under these conditions, the staging of a play, which will satisfy highly artistic demands, cannot be achieved at the speed that economic factors unfortunately make necessary in most theatres. This creative process, which every actor must go through, from his conception of the part to its artistic incarnation, is essentially very complicated, and is hampered by lack of perfection of outward and inward technique. It is also much hindered by the necessity of fitting in the actors one with another—the adjustment of their artistic individualities into an artistic whole.

PRODUCTION

Responsibility for bringing about this accord, and the artistic integrity and expression of the performance rests with the theatre manager. During the period when the manager exercised a despotic rule in the theatre, a period starting with the Meiningen players and still in force even in many of the foremost theatres, the manager worked out in advance all the plans for staging a play, and, while certainly having regard to the existing cast, indicated to the actors the general outlines of the scenic effects, and the mise-en-scène. The writer also adhered to this system, but now he has come to the conclusion that the creative work of the manager must be done in collaboration with the actor's work, neither ignoring nor confirming it. To encourage the actor's creative genius, to control and adjust it, ensuring that this creative genius grows out of the unique artistic germ of the drama, as much as the external building up of the performance—that in the opinion of the writer is the problem of the theatre director to-day.

The joint work of the director and actor begins with the analysis of the drama and the discovery of its artistic germ, and with the investigation of its transparent effect. The next step is the discovery of the transparent effect of individual parts—of that fundamental will direction of each individual actor, which, organically derived from his character, determines his place in the general action of the play. If the actor cannot at once secure this transparent effect, then it must be traced bit by bit with the manager's aid—by dividing the part into sections corresponding to the separate stages of the life of the particular actor—from the separate problems developing before him in his struggle for the attainment of his goal. Each such section of a part of each problem, can, if necessary, be subjected to further psychological analysis, and sub-divided into problems even more detailed, corresponding to those separate mind actions of the performer out of which stage life is summed up. The actor must catch the mind axes of the emotions and temperaments, but not the emotions and temperaments that give color to these sections of the part. In other

words, when studying each portion of his part, he must ask himself what he wants, what he requires as a performer of the play and which definite partial problem he is putting before himself at a given moment. The answer to this question should not be in the form of a noun, but rather of a verb: "I wish to obtain possession of the heart of this lady"—"I wish to enter her house"—"I wish to push aside the servants who are protecting her," etc. Formulated in this manner, the mind problem, of which the object and setting, thanks to the working of his creative imagination, are forming a brighter and clearer picture for the actor, begins to grip him and to excite him, extracting from the recesses of his working memory the combinations of emotions necessary to the part, of emotions that have an active character and mould themselves into dramatic action. In this way the different sections of the actor's part grow more lively and richer by degrees, owing to the involuntary play of the complicated organic survivals. By joining together and grafting these sections, the score of the part is formed; the scores of the separate parts, after the continual joint work of the actors during rehearsals and by the necessary adjustment of them one with another, are summed up in a single score of the performance.

THE SCORE CONDENSED

Nevertheless, the work of the actors and manager is still unfinished. The actor is studying and living in the part and the play deeper and deeper still, finding their deeper artistic motives; so he lives in the score of his part still more profoundly. But the score of the part itself and of the play are actually subject by degrees during the work to further alterations. As in a perfect poetical production there are no superfluous words but only those necessary to the poet's artistic scheme, so in a score of the part there must not be a single superfluous emotion but only emotions necessary for the transparent effect. The score of each part must be condensed, as also the form of its transmitting, and bright, simple and compelling forms of its incarnation must be found. Only then, when in each actor every part not only organically ripens and comes to life but also all emotions are stripped of the superfluous, when they all crystallize and sum up into a live contact, when they harmonize amongst themselves in the general tune, rhythm and time of the performance, then the play may be presented to the public.

During repeated presentations the theatrical score of the play and each part remains in general unaltered. But that does not mean that from the moment the performance is shown to the public the actor's creative process is to be considered ended, and that there remains for him only the mechanical repetition of his achievement at the first presentation. On the contrary, every performance imposes on him creative conditions; all his psychical forces must take part in it, because only in these conditions can they creatively adapt the score of the part to those capricious changes which may develop in them from hour to hour, as in all living nervous creatures influencing one another by their emotions, and only then can they transmit to the spectator that invisible something, inexpressible in words, which forms the spiritual content of the play. And that is the whole origin of the substance of dramatic art.

As regards the outward arrangements of the play—scenery, theatrical properties, etc.—all are of value in so far as they correspond to the expression of dramatic action, i.e., to the actors' talents; in no case may they claim to have an independent artistic importance in the theatre, although up to now they have been so considered by many great scene painters. The art of scene painting, as well as the music included in the play, is on the stage only an auxiliary art, and the manager's duty is to get from each what is necessary for the illumination of the play performed before an audience, while subordinating each to the problems of the actors.

BERTOLT BRECHT (1898–1956)
"Theatre for Pleasure or Theatre for Instruction" (1935–1936)
TRANSLATED BY JOHN WILLETT

In this essay, Brecht attacks the bourgeois notion that the theater can be divided into two kinds of art, as though drama were either instructive or entertaining. As he does in his plays, Brecht dialecticizes these categories, showing that they define one another and therefore exist within one another. Realistic plays, after all, not only entertain their audiences, but also offer an image of the world, a kind of instruction. On the other hand, intellectual or critical activity is not only pleasurable in itself, but it also can lead to a lively kind of theater as well, as Brecht's plays illustrate. This essay was unpublished in Brecht's lifetime: John Willett dates it from 1935 or 1936. He notes that Brecht uses the word Entfremdung *here for "alienation," the same word used by Marx and Hegel. Brecht later coined his own word* Verfremdungseffekt *for "alienation effect."*

A few years back, anybody talking about the modern theatre meant the theatre in Moscow, New York and Berlin. He might have thrown in a mention of one of Jouvet's productions in Paris or Cochran's in London, or *The Dybbuk* as given by the Habima (which is to all intents and purposes part of the Russian theatre, since Vakhtangov was its director). But broadly speaking there were only three capitals so far as modern theatre was concerned.

Russian, American and German theatres differed widely from one another, but were alike in being modern, that is to say in introducing technical and artistic innovations. In a sense they even achieved a certain stylistic resemblance, probably because technology is international (not just that part which is directly applied to the stage but also that which influences it, the film for instance), and because large progressive cities in large industrial countries are involved. Among the older capitalist countries it is the Berlin theatre that seemed of late to be in the lead. For a period all that is common to the modern theatre received its strongest and (so far) maturest expression there.

The Berlin theatre's last phase was the so-called epic theatre, and it showed the modern theatre's trend of development in its purest form. Whatever was labelled '*Zeitstück*' or '*Piscatorbühne*' or '*Lehrstück*' belongs to the epic theatre.

THE EPIC THEATRE

Many people imagine that the term 'epic theatre' is self-contradictory, as the epic and dramatic ways of narrating a story are held, following Aristotle, to be basically distinct. The difference between the two forms was never thought simply to lie in the fact that the one is performed by living beings while the other operates via the written word; epic works such as those of Homer and the medieval singers were at the same time theatrical performances, while dramas like Goethe's *Faust* and Byron's *Manfred* are agreed to have been more effective as books. Thus even by Aristotle's definition the difference between the dramatic and epic forms was attributed to their different methods of construction, whose laws were dealt with by two different branches of aesthetics. The method of construction depended on the different way of presenting the work to the public, sometimes via the stage, sometimes through a book; and independently of that there was the 'dramatic element' in epic works and the 'epic element' in dramatic. The bourgeois novel in the last century developed much that was 'dramatic,' by which was meant the strong centralization of the story, a momentum that drew the separate parts into a common relationship. A particular passion of utterance, a certain emphasis on the clash of forces are hallmarks of the 'dramatic'. The epic writer Döblin provided an excellent criterion when he said that with an epic work, as opposed to a dramatic, one can as it were take a pair of scissors and cut it into individual pieces, which remain fully capable of life.

This is no place to explain how the opposition of epic and dramatic lost its rigidity after having long been held to be irreconcilable. Let us just point out that the technical advances alone were enough to permit the stage to incorporate an element of narrative in its dramatic productions. The possibility of projections, the greater adaptability of the stage due to mechanization, the film, all completed the theatre's equipment, and did so at a point where the most important transactions between people could no longer be shown simply by personifying the motive forces or subjecting the characters to invisible metaphysical powers.

To make these transactions intelligible the environment in which the people lived had to be brought to bear in a big and 'significant' way.

This environment had of course been shown in the existing drama, but only as seen from the central figure's point of view, and not as an independent element. It was defined by the hero's reactions to it. It was seen as a storm can be seen when one sees the ships on a sheet of water unfolding their sails, and the sails filling out. In the epic theatre it was to appear standing on its own.

The stage began to tell a story. The narrator was no longer missing, along with the fourth wall. Not only did the background adopt an attitude to the events on the stage—by big screens recalling other simultaneous events elsewhere, by projecting documents which confirmed or contradicted what the characters said, by concrete and intelligible figures to accompany abstract conversations, by figures and sentences to support mimed transactions whose sense was unclear—but the actors too refrained from going over wholly into their role, remaining detached from the character they were playing and clearly inviting criticism of him.

The spectator was no longer in any way allowed to submit to an experience uncritically (and without practical consequences) by means of simple empathy with the characters in a play. The production took the subject-matter and the incidents shown and put them through a process of alienation: the alienation that is necessary to all understanding. When something seems 'the most obvious thing in the world' it means that any attempt to understand the world has been given up.

What is 'natural' must have the force of what is startling. This is the only way to expose the laws of cause and effect. People's activity must simultaneously be so and be capable of being different.

It was all a great change.

The dramatic theatre's spectator says: Yes, I have felt like that too—Just like me—It's only natural—It'll never change—The sufferings of this man appal me, because they are inescapable—That's great art; it all seems the most obvious thing in the world—I weep when they weep, I laugh when they laugh.

The epic theatre's spectator says: I'd never have thought it—That's not the way—That's extraordinary, hardly believable—It's got to stop—The sufferings of this man appal me, because they are unnecessary—That's great art: nothing obvious in it—I laugh when they weep, I weep when they laugh.

THE INSTRUCTIVE THEATRE

The stage began to be instructive.

Oil, inflation, war, social struggles, the family, religion, wheat, the meat market, all became subjects for theatrical representation. Choruses enlightened the spectator about facts unknown to him. Films showed a montage of events from all over the world. Projections added statistical material. And as the 'background' came to the front of the stage so people's activity was subjected to criticism. Right and wrong courses of action were shown. People were shown who knew what they were doing, and others who did not. The theatre became an affair for philosophers, but only for such philosophers as wished not just to explain the world but also to change it. So we had philosophy, and we had instruction. And where was the amusement in all that? Were they sending us back to school, teaching us to read and write? Were we supposed to pass exams, work for diplomas?

Generally there is felt to be a very sharp distinction between learning and amusing oneself. The first may be useful, but only the second is pleasant. So we have to defend the epic theatre against the suspicion that it is a highly disagreeable, humourless, indeed strenuous affair.

Well: all that can be said is that the contrast between learning and amusing oneself is not laid down by divine rule; it is not one that has always been and must continue to be.

Undoubtedly there is much that is tedious about the kind of learning familiar to us from school, from our professional training, etc. But it must be remembered under what conditions and to what end that takes place.

It is really a commercial transaction. Knowledge is just a commodity. It is acquired in order to be resold. All those who have grown out of going to school have to do their learning virtually in secret, for anyone who admits that he still has something to learn devalues himself as a man whose knowledge is inadequate. Moreover the usefulness of learning is very much limited by factors outside the learner's control. There is unemployment, for instance, against which no knowledge can protect one. There is the division of labour, which makes generalized knowledge unnecessary and impossible. Learning is often among the concerns of those whom no amount of concern will get any forwarder. There is not much knowledge that leads to power, but plenty of knowledge to which only power can lead.

Learning has a very different function for different social strata. There are strata who cannot imagine any improvement in conditions: they find the conditions good enough for them. Whatever happens to oil they will benefit from it. And: they feel the years beginning to tell. There can't be all that many years more. What is the point of learning a lot now? They have said their final word: a grunt. But there are also strata 'waiting their turn' who are discontented with conditions, have a vast interest in the practical side of learning, want at all costs to find out where they stand, and know that they are lost without learning; these are the best and keenest learners. Similar differences apply to countries and peoples. Thus the pleasure of learning depends on all sorts of things; but none the less there is such a thing as pleasurable learning, cheerful and militant learning.

If there were not such amusement to be had from learning the theatre's whole structure would unfit it for teaching.

Theatre remains theatre even when it is instructive theatre, and in so far as it is good theatre it will amuse.

THEATRE AND KNOWLEDGE

But what has knowledge got to do with art? We know that knowledge can be amusing, but not everything that is amusing belongs in the theatre.

I have often been told, when pointing out the invaluable services that modern knowledge and science, if properly applied, can perform for art and specially for the theatre, that art and knowledge are two estimable but wholly distinct fields of human activity. This is a fearful truism, of course, and it is as well to agree quickly that, like most truisms, it is perfectly true. Art and science work in quite different ways: agreed. But, bad as it may sound, I have to admit that I cannot get along as an artist without the use of one or two sciences. This may well arouse serious doubts as to my artistic capacities. People are used to seeing poets as unique and slightly unnatural beings who reveal with a truly godlike assurance things that other people can only recognize after much sweat and toil. It is naturally distasteful to have to admit that one does not belong to this select band. All the same, it must be admitted. It must at the same time be made clear that the scientific occupations just confessed to are not pardonable side interests, pursued on days off after a good week's work. We all know how Goethe was interested in natural history, Schiller in history: as a kind of hobby, it is charitable to assume. I have no wish promptly to accuse these two of having needed these sciences for their poetic activity; I am not trying to shelter behind them; but I must say that I do need the sciences. I have to admit, however, that I look askance at all sorts of people who I know do not operate on the level of scientific understanding: that is to say, who sing as the birds sing, or as people imagine the birds to sing. I don't mean by that that I would reject a charming poem about the taste of fried fish or the delights of a boating party just because the writer had not studied gastronomy or navigation. But in my view the great and complicated things that go on in the world cannot be adequately recognized by people who do not use every possible aid to understanding.

Let us suppose that great passions or great events have to be shown which influence the fate of nations. The lust for power is nowadays held to be such a passion. Given that a poet 'feels' this lust and wants to have someone strive for power, how is he to show the exceedingly complicated machinery within which the struggle for power nowadays takes place? If his hero is a politician, how do politics work? If he is a business man, how does business work? And yet there are writers who find business and politics nothing like so passionately interesting as the individual's lust for power. How are they to acquire the necessary knowledge? They are scarcely likely to learn enough by going round and keeping their eyes open, though even then it is more than they would get by just rolling their eyes in an exalted frenzy. The foundation of a paper like the *Völkischer Beobachter* or a business like Standard Oil is a pretty complicated affair, and such things cannot be conveyed just like that. One important field for the playwright is psychology. It is taken for granted that a poet, if not an ordinary man, must be able without further instruction to discover the motives that lead a man to commit murder; he must be able to give a picture of a murderer's mental state 'from within himself.' It is taken for granted that one only has to look inside oneself in such a case; and then there's always one's imagination. . . . There are various reasons why I can no longer surrender to this agreeable hope of getting a result quite so simply. I can no longer find in myself all those motives which the press or scientific reports show to have been observed in people. Like the average judge when pronouncing sentence, I cannot without further ado conjure up an adequate picture of a murderer's mental state. Modern psychology, from psychoanalysis to behaviourism, acquaints me with facts that lead me to judge the case quite differently, especially if I bear in mind the findings of sociology and do not overlook economics and history. You will say: but that's getting complicated. I have to answer that it *is* complicated. Even if you let yourself be convinced, and agree with me that a large slice of literature is exceedingly primitive, you may still ask with profound concern: won't an evening in such a theatre be a most alarming affair? The answer to that is: no.

Whatever knowledge is embodied in a piece of poetic writing has to be wholly transmuted into poetry. Its utilization fulfils the very pleasure that the poetic element provokes. If it does not at the same time fulfil that which is fulfilled by the scientific element, none the less in an age of great discoveries and inventions one must have a certain inclination to penetrate deeper into things—a desire to make the world controllable—if one is to be sure of enjoying its poetry.

IS THE EPIC THEATRE SOME KIND OF 'MORAL INSTITUTION'?

According to Friedrich Schiller the theatre is supposed to be a moral institution. In making this demand it hardly occurred to Schiller that by moralizing from the stage he might drive the audience out of the theatre. Audiences had no objection to moralizing in his day. It was only later that Friedrich Nietzsche attacked him for blowing a moral trumpet. To Nietzsche any concern with morality was a depressing affair; to Schiller it seemed thoroughly enjoyable. He knew of nothing that could give greater amusement and satisfaction than the propagation of ideas. The bourgeoisie was setting about forming the ideas of the nation.

Putting one's house in order, patting oneself on the back, submitting one's account, is something highly agreeable. But describing the collapse of one's house, having pains in the back, paying one's account, is indeed a depressing affair, and that was how Friedrich Nietzsche saw things a century later. He was poorly disposed towards morality, and thus towards the previous Friedrich too.

The epic theatre was likewise often objected to as moralizing too much. Yet in the epic theatre moral arguments only took second place. Its aim was less to moralize than to observe. That is to say it observed, and then the thick end of the wedge followed: the story's moral. Of course we cannot pretend that we started our observations out of a pure passion for observing and without any more practical motive, only to be completely staggered by their results. Undoubtedly there were some painful discrepancies in our environment, circumstances that were barely tolerable, and this not merely on account of moral considerations. It is not only moral considerations that make hunger, cold and oppression hard to bear. Similarly, the object of our inquiries was not just to arouse moral objections to such circumstances (even though they could easily be felt—though not by all the audience alike; such objections were seldom for instance felt by those who profited by the circumstances in question) but to discover means for their

elimination. We were not in fact speaking in the name of morality but in that of the victims. These truly are two distinct matters, for the victims are often told that they ought to be contented with their lot, for moral reasons. Moralists of this sort see man as existing for morality, not morality for man. At least it should be possible to gather from the above to what degree and in what sense the epic theatre is a moral institution.

CAN EPIC THEATRE BE PLAYED ANYWHERE?

Stylistically speaking, there is nothing all that new about the epic theatre. Its expository character and its emphasis on virtuosity bring it close to the old Asiatic theatre. Didactic tendencies are to be found in the medieval mystery plays and the classical Spanish theatre, and also in the theatre of the Jesuits.

These theatrical forms corresponded to particular trends of their time, and vanished with them. Similarly the modern epic theatre is linked with certain trends. It cannot by any means be practised universally. Most of the great nations today are not disposed to use the theatre for ventilating their problems. London, Paris, Tokyo and Rome maintain their theatres for quite different purposes. Up to now favourable circumstances for an epic and didactic theatre have only been found in a few places and for a short period of time. In Berlin Fascism put a very definite stop to the development of such a theatre.

It demands not only a certain technological level but a powerful movement in society which is interested to see vital questions freely aired with a view to their solution, and can defend this interest against every contrary trend.

The epic theatre is the broadest and most far-reaching attempt at large-scale modern theatre, and it has all those immense difficulties to overcome that always confront the vital forces in the sphere of politics, philosophy, science and art.

ANTONIN ARTAUD (1896–1948)

from *The Theater and Its Double* (1938)
TRANSLATED BY MARY CAROLINE RICHARDS

An early member of the surrealist movement in Paris, Antonin Artaud was well-known between the wars as an actor, playwright, and essayist of the avant-garde theater, and he is one of the formative influences on the modern European theater. Artaud is most often associated with the "theater of cruelty," his label for a theater that would assault the representational dynamics of traditional theater and break the boundaries between actor and audience, stage and spectacle. Artaud was declared insane and committed to a mental hospital in 1939. He remained institutionalized for most of the remainder of his life.

THE THEATER AND CULTURE

Never before, when it is life itself that is in question, has there been so much talk of civilization and culture. And there is a curious parallel between this generalized collapse of life at the root of our present demoralization and our concern for a culture which has never been coincident with life, which in fact has been devised to tyrannize over life.

Before speaking further about culture, I must remark that the world is hungry and not concerned with culture, and that the attempt to orient toward culture thoughts turned only toward hunger is a purely artificial expedient.

What is most important, it seems to me, is not so much to defend a culture whose existence has never kept a man from going hungry, as to extract, from what is called culture, ideas whose compelling force is identical with that of hunger.

We need to live first of all; to believe in what makes us live and that something *makes* us live—to believe that whatever is produced from the mysterious depths of ourselves need not forever haunt us as an exclusively digestive concern.

I mean that if it is important for us to eat first of all, it is even more important for us not to waste in the sole concern for eating our simple power of being hungry.

If confusion is the sign of the times, I see at the root of this confusion a rupture between things and words, between things and the ideas and signs that are their representation.

Not, of course, for lack of philosophical systems; their number and contradictions characterize our old French and European culture: but where can it be shown that life, our life, has ever been affected by these systems? I will not say that philosophical systems must be applied directly and immediately: but of the following alternatives, one must be true:

Either these systems are within us and permeate our being to the point of supporting life itself (and if this is the case, what use are books?), or they do *not* permeate us and therefore do not have the capacity to support life (and in this case what does their disappearance matter?).

We must insist upon the idea of culture-in-action, of culture growing within us like a new organ, a sort of second breath; and on civilization as an applied culture controlling even our subtlest actions, a *presence of mind*; the distinction between culture and civilization is an artificial one, providing two words to signify an identical function.

A civilized man judges and is judged according to his behavior, but even the term "civilized" leads to confusion: a cultivated "civilized" man is regarded as a person instructed in systems, a person who thinks in forms, signs, representations—a monster whose faculty of deriving thoughts from acts, instead of identifying acts with thoughts, is developed to an absurdity.

If our life lacks brimstone, i.e., a constant magic, it is because we choose to observe our acts and lose ourselves in considerations of their imagined form instead of being impelled by their force.

And this faculty is an exclusively human one. I would even say that it is this infection of the human which contaminates ideas that should have remained divine; for far from believing that man invented the supernatural and the divine, I think it is man's age-old intervention which has ultimately corrupted the divine within him.

All our ideas about life must be revised in a period when nothing any longer adheres to life; it is this painful cleavage which is responsible for the revenge of *things*; the poetry which is no longer within us and which we no longer succeed in finding in things suddenly appears on their wrong side: consider the unprecedented number of crimes whose perverse gratuitousness is explained only by our powerlessness to take complete possession of life.

If the theater has been created as an outlet for our repressions, the agonized poetry expressed in its bizarre corruptions of the facts of life demonstrates that life's intensity is still intact and asks only to be better directed.

But no matter how loudly we clamor for magic in our lives, we are really afraid of pursuing an existence entirely under its influence and sign.

Hence our confirmed lack of culture is astonished by certain grandiose anomalies; for example, on an island without any contact with modern civilization, the mere passage of a ship carrying only healthy passengers may provoke the sudden outbreak of diseases unknown on that island but a specialty of nations like our own: shingles, influenza, grippe, rheumatism, sinusitis, polyneuritis, etc.

Similarly, if we think Negroes smell bad, we are ignorant of the fact that anywhere but in Europe it is we whites who "smell bad." And I would even say that we give off an odor as white as the gathering of pus in an infected wound.

As iron can be heated until it turns white, so it can be said that everything excessive is white; for Asiatics white has become the mark of extreme decomposition.

This said, we can begin to form an idea of culture, an idea which is first of all a protest.

A protest against the senseless constraint imposed upon the idea of culture by reducing it to a sort of inconceivable Pantheon, producing an idolatry no different from the image-worship of those religions which relegate their gods to Pantheons.

A protest against the idea of culture as distinct from life—as if there were culture on one side and life on the other, as if true culture were not a refined means of understanding and *exercising* life.

The library at Alexandria can be burnt down. There are forces above and beyond papyrus: we may temporarily be deprived of our ability to discover these forces, but their energy will not be suppressed. It is good that our excessive facilities are no longer available, that forms fall into oblivion: a culture without space or time, restrained only by the capacity of our own nerves, will reappear with all the more energy. It is right that from time to time cataclysms occur which compel us to return to nature, i.e., to rediscover life. The old totemism of animals, stones, objects capable of discharging thunderbolts, costumes impregnated with bestial essences—everything, in short, that might determine, disclose, and direct the secret forces of the universe—is for us a dead thing, from which we derive nothing but static and aesthetic profit, the profit of an audience, not of an actor.

Yet totemism is an actor, for it moves, and has been created in behalf of actors; all true culture relies upon the barbaric and primitive means of totemism whose savage, i.e., entirely spontaneous, life I wish to worship.

What has lost us culture is our Occidental idea of art and the profits we seek to derive from it. Art and culture cannot be considered together, contrary to the treatment universally accorded them!

True culture operates by exaltation and force, while the European ideal of art attempts to cast the mind into an attitude distinct from force but addicted to exaltation. It is a lazy, unserviceable notion which engenders an imminent death. If the Serpent Quetzalcoatl's multiple twists and turns are harmonious, it is because they express the equilibrium and fluctuations of a sleeping force; the intensity of the forms is there only to seduce and direct a force which, in music, would produce an insupportable range of sound.

The gods that sleep in museums: the god of fire with his incense burner that resembles an Inquisition tripod; Tlaloc, one of the manifold Gods of the Waters, on his wall of green granite; the Mother Goddess of Waters, the Mother Goddess of Flowers; the immutable expression, echoing from beneath many layers of water, of the Goddess robed in green jade; the enraptured, blissful expression, features crackling with incense, where atoms of sunlight circle—the countenance of the Mother Goddess of Flowers; this world of obligatory servitude in which a stone comes alive when it has been properly carved, the world of organically civilized men whose vital organs too awaken from their slumber, this human world enters into us, participating in the dance of the gods without turning round or looking back, on pain of becoming, like ourselves, crumbled pillars of salt.

In Mexico, since we are talking about Mexico, there is no art: things are made for use. And the world is in perpetual exaltation.

To our disinterested and inert idea of art an authentic culture opposes a violently egoistic and magical, i.e., *interested* idea. For the Mexicans seek contact with the *Manas,* forces latent in every form, unreleased by contemplation of the forms for themselves, but springing to life by magic identification with these forms. And the old Totems are there to hasten the communication.

How hard it is, when everything encourages us to sleep, though we may look about us with conscious, clinging eyes, to wake and yet look about us as in a dream, with eyes that no longer know their function and whose gaze is turned inward.

This is how our strange idea of disinterested action originated, though it is action nonetheless, and all the more violent for skirting the temptation of repose.

Every real effigy has a shadow which is its double; and art must falter and fail from the moment the sculptor believes he has liberated the kind of shadow whose very existence will destroy his repose.

Like all magic cultures expressed by appropriate hieroglyphs, the true theater has its shadows too, and, of all languages and all arts, the theater is the only one left whose shadows have shattered their limitations. From the beginning, one might say its shadows did not tolerate limitations.

Our petrified idea of the theater is connected with our petrified idea of a culture without shadows, where, no matter which way it turns, our mind *(esprit)* encounters only emptiness, though space is full.

But the true theater, because it moves and makes use of living instruments, continues to stir up shadows where life has never ceased to grope its way. The actor does not make the same gestures twice, but he makes gestures, he moves; and although he brutalizes forms, nevertheless behind them and through their destruction he rejoins that which outlives forms and produces their continuation.

The theater, which is in *no thing,* but makes use of everything—gestures, sounds, words, screams, light, darkness—rediscovers itself at precisely the point where the mind requires a language to express its manifestations.

And the fixation of the theater in one language—written words, music, lights, noises—betokens its imminent ruin, the choice of any one language betraying a taste for the special effects of that language; and the dessication of the language accompanies its limitation.

For the theater as for culture, it remains a question of naming and directing shadows: and the theater, not confined to a fixed language and form, not only destroys false shadows but prepares the way for a new generation of shadows, around which assembles the true spectacle of life.

To break through language in order to touch life is to create or recreate the theater; the essential thing is not to believe that this act must remain sacred, i.e., set apart—the essential thing is to believe that not just anyone can create it, and that there must be a preparation.

This leads to the rejection of the usual limitations of man and man's powers, and infinitely extends the frontiers of what is called reality.

We must believe in a sense of life renewed by the theater, a sense of life in which man fearlessly makes himself master of what does not yet exist, and brings it into being. And everything that has not been born can still be brought to life if we are not satisfied to remain mere recording organisms.

Furthermore, when we speak the word "life," it must be understood we are not referring to life as we know it from its surface of fact, but to that fragile, fluctuating center which forms never reach. And if there is still one hellish, truly accursed thing in our time, it is our artistic dallying with forms, instead of being like victims burnt at the stake, signaling through the flames.

• • •

NO MORE MASTERPIECES

One of the reasons for the asphyxiating atmosphere in which we live without possible escape or remedy—and in which we all share, even the most revolutionary among us—is our respect for what has been written, formulated, or painted, what has been given form, as if all expression were not at last exhausted, were not at a point where things must break apart if they are to start anew and begin fresh.

We must have done with this idea of masterpieces reserved for a self-styled elite and not understood by the general public; the mind has no such restricted districts as those so often used for clandestine sexual encounters.

Masterpieces of the past are good for the past: they are not good for us. We have the right to say what has been said and even what has not been said in a way that belongs to us, a way that is immediate and direct, corresponding to present modes of feeling, and understandable to everyone.

It is idiotic to reproach the masses for having no sense of the sublime, when the sublime is confused with one or another of its formal manifestations, which are moreover always defunct manifestations. And if for example a contemporary public does not understand *Oedipus Rex,* I shall make bold to say that it is the fault of *Oedipus Rex* and not of the public.

In *Oedipus Rex* there is the theme of incest and the idea that nature mocks at morality and that there are certain unspecified powers at large which we would do well to beware of, call them *destiny* or anything you choose.

There is in addition the presence of a plague epidemic which is a physical incarnation of these powers. But the whole in a manner and language that have lost all touch with the rude and epileptic rhythm of our time. Sophocles speaks grandly perhaps, but in a style that is no longer timely. His language is too refined for this age. It is as if he were speaking beside the point.

However, a public that shudders at train wrecks, that is familiar with earthquakes, plagues, revolutions, wars; that is sensitive to the disordered anguish of love, can be affected by all these grand notions and asks only to become aware of them, but on condition that it is addressed in its own language, and that its knowledge of these things does not come to it through adulterated trappings and speech that belong to extinct eras which will never live again.

Today as yesterday, the public is greedy for mystery: it asks only to become aware of the laws according to which destiny manifests itself, and to divine perhaps the secret of its apparitions.

Let us leave textual criticism to graduate students, formal criticism to esthetes, and recognize that what has been said is not still to be said; that an expression does not have the same value twice, does not live two lives; that all words, once spoken, are dead and function only at the moment when they are uttered, that a form, once it has served, cannot be used again and asks only to be replaced by another, and that the theater is the only place in the world where a gesture, once made, can never be made the same way twice.

If the public does not frequent our literary masterpieces, it is because those masterpieces are literary, that is to say, fixed; and fixed in forms that no longer respond to the needs of the time.

Far from blaming the public, we ought to blame the formal screen we interpose between ourselves and the public, and this new form of idolatry, the idolatry of fixed masterpieces which is one of the aspects of bourgeois conformism.

This conformism makes us confuse sublimity, ideas, and things with the forms they have taken in time and in our minds—in our snobbish, precious, aesthetic mentalities which the public does not understand.

How pointless in such matters to accuse the public of bad taste because it relishes insanities, so long as the public is not shown a valid spectacle; and I defy anyone to show me *here* a spectacle valid—valid in the supreme sense of the theater—since the last great romantic melodramas, i.e., since a hundred years ago.

The public, which takes the false for the true, has the sense of the true and always responds to it when it is manifested. However it is not upon the stage that the true is to be sought nowadays, but in the street; and if the crowd in the street is offered an occasion to show its human dignity, it will always do so.

If people are out of the habit of going to the theater, if we have all finally come to think of theater as an inferior art, a means of popular distraction, and to use it as an outlet for our worst instincts, it is because we have learned too well what the theater has been, namely, falsehood and illusion. It is because we have been accustomed for four hundred years, that is since the Renaissance, to a purely descriptive and narrative theater—storytelling psychology; it is because every possible ingenuity has been exerted in bringing to life on the stage plausible but detached beings, with the spectacle on one side, the public on the other—and because the public is no longer shown anything but the mirror of itself.

Shakespeare himself is responsible for this aberration and decline, this disinterested idea of the theater which wishes a theatrical performance to leave the public intact, without setting off one image that will shake the organism to its foundations and leave an ineffaceable scar.

If, in Shakespeare, a man is sometimes preoccupied with what transcends him, it is always in order to determine the ultimate consequences of this preoccupation within him, i.e., psychology.

Psychology, which works relentlessly to reduce the unknown to the known, to the quotidian and the ordinary, is the cause of the theater's abasement and its fearful loss of energy, which seems to me to have reached its lowest point. And I think both the theater and we ourselves have had enough of psychology.

I believe furthermore that we can all agree on this matter sufficiently so that there is no need to descend to the repugnant level of the modern and French theater to condemn the theater of psychology.

Stories about money, worry over money, social careerism, the pangs of love unspoiled by altruism, sexuality sugar-coated with an eroticism that has lost its mystery have nothing to do with the theater, even if they do belong to psychology. These torments, seductions, and lusts before which we are nothing but Peeping Toms gratifying our cravings, tend to go bad, and their rot turns to revolution: we must take this into account.

But this is not our most serious concern.

If Shakespeare and his imitators have gradually insinuated the idea of art for art's sake, with art on one side and life on the other, we can rest on this feeble and lazy idea only as long as the life outside endures. But there are too many signs that everything that used to sustain our lives no longer does so, that we are all mad, desperate, and sick. And I call for us to react.

This idea of a detached art, of poetry as a charm which exists only to distract our leisure, is a decadent idea and an unmistakable symptom of our power to castrate.

Our literary admiration for Rimbaud, Jarry, Lautréamont, and a few others, which has driven two men to suicide, but turned into café gossip for the rest, belongs to this idea of literary poetry, of detached art, of neutral spiritual activity which creates nothing and produces nothing; and I can bear witness that at the very moment when that kind of personal poetry which involves only the man who creates it and only at the moment he creates it broke out in its most abusive fashion, the theater was scorned more than ever before by poets who have never had the sense of direct and concerted action, nor of efficacity, nor of danger.

We must get rid of our superstitious valuation of texts and *written* poetry. Written poetry is worth reading once, and then should be destroyed. Let the dead poets make way for others. Then we might even come to see that it is our veneration for what has already been created, however beautiful and valid it may be, that petrifies us, deadens our responses, and prevents us from making contact with that underlying power, call it thought-energy, the life force, the determinism of change, lunar menses, or anything you like. Beneath the poetry of the texts, there is the actual poetry, without form and without text. And just as the efficacity of masks in the magic practices of certain tribes is exhausted—and these masks are no longer good for anything except museums—so the poetic efficacity of a text is exhausted; yet the poetry and the efficacity of the theater are exhausted least quickly of all, since they permit the *action* of what is gesticulated and pronounced, and which is never made the same way twice.

It is a question of knowing what we want. If we are prepared for war, plague, famine, and slaughter we do not even need to say so, we have only to continue as we are; continue behaving like snobs, rushing en masse to hear such and such a singer, to see such and such an admirable performance which never transcends the realm of art (and even the Russian ballet at the height of its splendor never transcended the realm of art), to marvel at such and such an exhibition of painting in which exciting shapes explode here and there but at random and without any genuine consciousness of the forces they could rouse.

This empiricism, randomness, individualism, and anarchy must cease.

Enough of personal poems, benefitting those who create them much more than those who read them.

Once and for all, enough of this closed, egoistic, and personal art.

Our spiritual anarchy and intellectual disorder is a function of the anarchy of everything else—or rather, everything else is a function of this anarchy.

I am not one of those who believe that civilization has to change in order for the theater to change; but I do believe that the theater, utilized in the highest and most difficult sense possible, has the power to influence the aspect and formation of things: and the encounter upon the stage of two passionate manifestations, two living centers, two nervous magnetisms is something as entire, true, even decisive, as, in life, the encounter of one epidermis with another in a timeless debauchery.

That is why I propose a theater of cruelty.—With this mania we all have for depreciating everything, as soon as I have said "cruelty," everybody will at once take it to mean "blood." But *theater of cruelty* means a theater difficult and cruel for my-self first of all. And, on the level of performance, it is not the cru-elty we can exercise upon each other by hacking at each other's bodies, carving up our personal anatomies, or, like Assyrian emperors, sending parcels of human ears, noses, or neatly de-tached nostrils through the mail, but the much more terrible and necessary cruelty which things can exercise against us. We are not free. And the sky can still fall on our heads. And the the-ater has been created to teach us that first of all.

Either we will be capable of returning by present-day means to this superior idea of poetry and poetry-through-theater which underlies the Myths told by the great ancient tragedians, capable once more of entertaining a religious idea of the theater (without meditation, useless contempla-tion, and vague dreams), capable of attaining awareness and a possession of certain dominant forces, of certain notions that control all others, and (since ideas, when they are effec-tive, carry their energy with them) capable of recovering within ourselves those energies which ultimately create order and increase the value of life, or else we might as well aban-don ourselves now, without protest, and recognize that we are no longer good for anything but disorder, famine, blood, war, and epidemics.

Either we restore all the arts to a central attitude and ne-cessity, finding an analogy between a gesture made in paint-ing or the theater, and a gesture made by lava in a volcanic explosion, or we must stop painting, babbling, writing, or doing whatever it is we do.

I propose to bring back into the theater this elementary magical idea, taken up by modern psychoanalysis, which con-sists in effecting a patient's cure by making him assume the apparent and exterior attitudes of the desired condition.

I propose to renounce our empiricism of imagery, in which the unconscious furnishes images at random, and which the poet arranges at random too, calling them poetic and hence hermetic images, as if the kind of trance that po-etry provides did not have its reverberations throughout the whole sensibility, in every nerve, and as if poetry were some vague force whose movements were invariable.

I propose to return through the theater to an idea of the physical knowledge of images and the means of inducing trances, as in Chinese medicine which knows, over the entire extent of the human anatomy, at what points to puncture in order to regulate the subtlest functions.

Those who have forgotten the communicative power and magical mimesis of a gesture, the theater can reinstruct, be-cause a gesture carries its energy with it, and there are still human beings in the theater to manifest the force of the ges-ture made.

To create art is to deprive a gesture of its reverberation in the organism, whereas this reverberation, if the gesture is made in the conditions and with the force required, incites the organism and, through it, the entire individuality, to take attitudes in harmony with the gesture.

The theater is the only place in the world, the last gen-eral means we still possess of directly affecting the organism and, in periods of neurosis and petty sensuality like the one in which we are immersed, of attacking this sensuality by physical means it cannot withstand.

If music affects snakes, it is not on account of the spiri-tual notions it offers them, but because snakes are long and coil their length upon the earth, because their bodies touch the earth at almost every point; and because the musical vi-brations which are communicated to the earth affect them like a very subtle, very long massage; and I propose to treat the spectators like the snakecharmer's subjects and conduct them *by means of their organisms* to an apprehension of the subtlest notions.

At first by crude means, which will gradually be refined. These immediate crude means will hold their attention at the start.

That is why in the "theater of cruelty" the spectator is in the center and the spectacle surrounds him.

In this spectacle the sonorisation is constant: sounds, noises, cries are chosen first for their vibratory quality, then for what they represent.

Among these gradually refined means light is interposed in its turn. Light which is not created merely to add color or to brighten, and which brings its power, influence, sugges-tions with it. And the light of a green cavern does not sensu-ally dispose the organism like the light of a windy day.

After sound and light there is action, and the dynamism of action: here the theater, far from copying life, puts itself whenever possible in communication with pure forces. And whether you accept or deny them, there is nevertheless a way of speaking which gives the name of "forces" to whatever brings to birth images of energy in the unconscious, and gra-tuitous crime on the surface.

A violent and concentrated action is a kind of lyricism: it summons up supernatural images, a bloodstream of images, a bleeding spurt of images in the poet's head and in the spec-tator's as well.

Whatever the conflicts that haunt the mind of a given pe-riod, I defy any spectator to whom such violent scenes will have transferred their blood, who will have felt in himself the transit of a superior action, who will have seen the extraordi-nary and essential movements of his thought illuminated in extraordinary deeds—the violence and blood having been placed at the service of the violence of the thought—I defy that spectator to give himself up, once outside the theater, to ideas of war, riot, and blatant murder.

So expressed, this idea seems dangerous and sopho-moric. It will be claimed that example breeds example, that if the attitude of cure induces cure, the attitude of murder will induce murder. Everything depends upon the manner and the purity with which the thing is done. There is a risk. But let it not be forgotten that though a theatrical gesture is violent, it is disinterested; and that the theater teaches precisely the uselessness of the action which, once done, is not to be done, and the superior use of the state unused by the action and which, *restored,* produces a purification.

I propose then a theater in which violent physical images crush and hypnotize the sensibility of the spectator seized by the theater as by a whirlwind of higher forces.

A theater which, abandoning psychology, recounts the extraordinary, stages natural conflicts, natural and subtle forces, and presents itself first of all as an exceptional power of redirection. A theater that induces trance, as the dances of Dervishes induce trance, and that addresses itself to the or-ganism by precise instruments, by the same means as those of certain tribal music cures which we admire on records but are incapable of originating among ourselves.

There is a risk involved, but in the present circumstances I believe it is a risk worth running. I do not believe we have managed to revitalize the world we live in, and I do not be-lieve it is worth the trouble of clinging to; but I do propose something to get us out of our marasmus, instead of contin-uing to complain about it, and about the boredom, inertia, and stupidity of everything.

AUGUSTO BOAL

from *Theatre of the Oppressed* (1974)
TRANSLATED BY CHARLES A. MCBRIDE AND MARIA-ODILIA LEAL McBRIDE

One of contemporary world theater's most influential figures, Augusto Boal (b. 1931) pioneered the use of theatrical performance as a means of direct social change. Closely associated with the liberationist educational philosophy of his Brazilian countryman Paolo Friere, Boal's work explores the ways theater games and street theater can be used as pedagogy—instructing even illiterate audiences to become agents of social change, what Boal calls "spect-actors"—and so as direct social practice. In 1971, Boal was apprehended and tortured by Brazilian authorities, and then exiled; he returned to Brazil in 1986, founding the Center for the Theater of the Oppressed in Rio de Janeiro, and continuing to develop the practice of Forum Theater. Boal has published several books on liberationist theater, including Games for Actors and Non-Actors *(1992),* The Rainbow of Desire *(1995), and* Legislative Theater *(1998).*

In this selection from Theater of the Oppressed, *"Poetics of the Oppressed," Boal describes some of the techniques he used with peasants and workers in the cities of Lima and Chiclayo, Peru, in 1973, particularly focusing on the development of the "spect-actor."*

EXPERIMENTS WITH THE PEOPLE'S THEATER IN PERU

These experiments were carried out in August of 1973, in the cities of Lima and Chiclayo, with the invaluable collaboration of Alicia Saco, within the program of the Integral Literacy Op-eration (*Operación Alfabetización Integral* [ALFIN]), directed by Alfonso Lizarzaburu and with the participation, in the vari-ous sectors, of Estela Liñares, Luis Garrido Lecca, Ramón Vilcha, and Jesús Ruiz Durand. The method used by ALFIN in the literacy program was, of course, derived from Paulo Freire.

In 1973, the revolutionary government of Peru began a national literacy campaign called *Operación Alfabetización Integral* with the objective of eradicating illiteracy within the span of four years. It is estimated that in Peru's population of 14 million people, between three and four million are illiter-ate or semi-illiterate.

In any country the task of teaching an adult to read and write poses a difficult and delicate problem. In Peru the prob-lem is magnified because of the vast number of languages and dialects spoken by its people. Recent studies point to the existence of at least 41 dialects of the two principal lan-guages, besides Spanish, which are the Quechua and the Ay-mara. Research carried out in the province of Loreto in the north of the country, verified the existence of 45 different languages in that region. Forty-five *languages,* not mere di-alects! And this is what is perhaps the least populated province in the country.

This great variety of languages has perhaps contributed to an understanding on the part of the organizers of ALFIN, that the illiterate are not people who are unable to express them-selves: they are simply people unable to express themselves in a particular language, which in this case is Spanish. All idioms are "languages," but there is an infinite number of languages that are not idiomatic. There are many languages besides those that are written or spoken. By learning a new language, a person acquires a new way of knowing reality and of passing that knowledge on to others. Each language is absolutely irreplaceable. All languages complement each other in achieving the widest, most complete knowledge of what is real.

Assuming this to be true, the ALFIN project formulated two principal aims:

1) to teach literacy in both the first language and in Spanish without forcing the abandonment of the former in favor of the latter;

2) to teach literacy in all possible languages, especially the artistic ones, such as theater, photography, puppetry, films, journalism, etc.

The training of the educators, chosen from the same regions where literacy was to be taught, was developed in four stages according to the special characteristics of each social group:

1) *barrios* (neighborhoods) or new villages, corresponding to our slums *(cantegril, favela, . . .);*

2) rural areas;

3) mining areas;

4) areas where Spanish is not the first language, which embrace 40 percent of the population. Of this 40 percent, half is made up of bilingual citizens who learned Spanish after acquiring fluency in their own indigenous language. The other half speaks no Spanish.

It is too early to evaluate the results of the ALFIN plan since it is still in its early stages. What I propose to do here is to relate my personal experience as a participant in the theatrical sector and to outline the various experiments we made in considering the theater as language, capable of being utilized by any person, with or without artistic talent. We tried to show in practice how the theater can be placed at the service of the oppressed, so that they can express themselves and so that, by using this new language, they can also discover new concepts.

In order to understand this *poetics of the oppressed* one must keep in mind its main objective: to change the people—"spectators," passive beings in the theatrical phenomenon—into subjects, into actors, transformers of the dramatic action. I hope that the differences remain clear. Aristotle proposes a poetics in which the spectator delegates power to the dramatic character so that the latter may act and think for him. Brecht proposes a poetics in which the spectator delegates power to the character who thus acts in his place but the spectator reserves the right to think for himself, often in opposition to the character. In the first case, a "catharsis" occurs; in the second, an awakening of critical conscious-

ness. But the *poetics of the oppressed* focuses on the action itself: the spectator delegates no power to the character (or actor) either to act or to think in his place; on the contrary, he himself assumes the protagonic role, changes the dramatic action, tries out solutions, discusses plans for change—in short, trains himself for real action. In this case, perhaps the theater is not revolutionary in itself, but it is surely a rehearsal for the revolution. The liberated spectator, as a whole person, launches into action. No matter that the action is fictional; what matters is that it is action!

I believe that all the truly revolutionary theatrical groups should transfer to the people the means of production in the theater so that the people themselves may utilize them. The theater is a weapon, and it is the people who should wield it.

But how is this transference to be achieved? As an example I cite what was done by Estela Liñares, who was in charge of the photography section of the ALFIN Plan.

What would be the old way to utilize photography in a literacy project? Without doubt, it would be to photograph things, streets, people, landscapes, stores, etc., then show the pictures and discuss them. But who would take these pictures? The instructors, group leaders, or coordinators. On the other hand, if we are going to give the people the means of production, it is necessary to hand over to them, in this case, the camera. This is what was done in ALFIN. The educators would give a camera to members of the study group, would teach them how to use it, and propose to them the following:

We are going to ask you some questions. For this purpose we will speak in Spanish. And you must answer us. But you can not speak in Spanish: you must speak in "photography." We ask you things in Spanish, which is a language. You answer us in photography, which is also a language.

The questions asked were very simple, and the answers—that is, the photos—were discussed later by the group. For example, when people were asked, where do you live?, they responded with the following types of photo-answers:

1) A picture showing the interior of a shack. In Lima it rarely rains and for this reason the shacks are made of straw mats, instead of with more permanent walls and roofs. In general they have only one room that serves as kitchen, living room, and bedroom; the families live in great promiscuity and very often young children watch their parents engage in sexual intercourse, which commonly leads to sexual acts between brothers and sisters as young as ten or eleven years old, simply as an imitation of their parents. A photo showing the interior of a shack fully answers the question, where do you live? Every element of each photo has a special meaning, which must be discussed by the group: the objects focused on, the angle from which the picture is taken, the presence or absence of people in it, etc.

2) To answer the same question, a man took a picture of the bank of a river. The discussion clarified its meaning. The river Rímac,

which passes through Lima, overflows at certain times of the year. This makes life on its banks extremely dangerous, since shacks are often swept away, with a consequent loss of human lives. It is also very common for children to fall into the river while playing and the rising waters make rescue difficult. When a man answers the question with that picture, he is fundamentally expressing anguish: how can he work with peace of mind knowing that his child may be drowning in the river?

3) Another man photographed a part of the river where pelicans come to eat garbage in times of great hunger; the people, equally hungry, capture, kill and eat the pelicans. Showing this photo, the man communicated his awareness of living in a place where ironically the people welcomed hunger, because it attracted the pelicans which then served to satisfy their hunger.

4) A woman who had recently emigrated from a small village in the interior answered with a picture of the main street in her *barrio*: the old natives of Lima lived on one side of the street, while those from the interior lived on the other. On one side were those who saw their jobs threatened by the newcomers; on the other, the poor who had left everything behind in search of work. The street was a dividing line between brothers equally exploited, who found themselves facing each other as if they were enemies. The picture helped to reveal their common condition: poverty on both sides—while pictures of the wealthier neighborhoods showed who were their true enemies. The picture of the divided street showed the need to redirect their violent resentment. . . . Studying the picture of her street helped the woman to understand her own reality.

5) One day a man, in answer to the same question, took a picture of a child's face. Of course everyone thought that the man had made a mistake and repeated the question to him:

"You didn't understand; what we want is that you show us where you live. Take a picture and show us where you live. Any picture; the street, the house, the town, the river . . ."

"Here is my answer. Here is where I live."

"But it's a child. . . ."

"Look at his face: there is blood on it. This child, as all the others who live here, have their lives threatened by the rats that infest the whole bank of the river Rímac. They are protected by dogs that attack the rats and scare them away. But there was a mange epidemic and the city dog-catcher came around here catching lots of dogs and taking them away. This child had a dog who protected him. During the day his parents used to go to work and he was left with his dog. But now he doesn't have it any more. A few days ago, when you asked me where I lived, the rats had come while the child was sleeping and had eaten part of his nose. This is why there's so much blood on his face. Look at the picture; it is my answer. I live in a place where things like this still happen."

I could write a novel about the children of the *barrios* along the river Rímac; but only photography, and no other language, could express the pain of that child's eyes, of those tears mixed with blood. And, as if the irony and outrage were not enough, the photograph was in Kodachrome, "Made in U.S.A."

The use of photography may help also to discover valid symbols for a whole community or social group. It happens many times that well intentioned theatrical groups are unable to communicate with a mass audience because they use symbols that are meaningless for that audience. A royal crown may symbolize power, but a symbol only functions as such if its meaning is shared. For some a royal crown may produce a strong impact and yet be meaningless for others.

What is exploitation? The traditional figure of Uncle Sam is, for many social groups throughout the world, the ultimate symbol of exploitation. It expresses to perfection the rapacity of "Yankee" imperialism.

In Lima the people were also asked, what is exploitation? Many photographs showed the grocer; others the landlord; still others, some government office. On the other hand, a child answered with the picture of a nail on a wall. For him that was the perfect symbol of exploitation. Few adults understood it, but all the other children were in complete agreement that the picture expressed their feelings in relation to exploitation. The discussion explained why. The simplest work boys engage in at the age of five or six is shining shoes. Obviously, in the *barrios* where they live there are no shoes to shine and, for this reason, they must go to downtown Lima in order to find work. Their shine-boxes and other tools of the trade are of course an absolute necessity, and yet these boys cannot be carrying their equipment back and forth every day between work and home. So they must rent a nail on the wall of some place of business, whose owner charges them two or three *soles* per night and per nail. Looking at a nail, those children are reminded of oppression and their hatred of it; the sight of a crown, Uncle Sam, or Nixon, however, probably means nothing to them.

It is easy enough to give a camera to someone who has never taken a picture before, tell him how to focus it and which button to press. With this alone the means of photographic production are in the hands of that person. But what is to be done in the case of the theater?

The means for producing a photograph are embodied in the camera, which is relatively easy to handle, but the means of producing theater are made up of man himself, obviously more difficult to manage.

We can begin by stating that the first word of the theatrical vocabulary is the human body, the main source of sound and movement. Therefore, to control the means of theatrical production, man must, first of all, control his own body, know his own body, in order to be capable of making it more expressive. Then he will be able to practice theatrical forms in which by stages he frees himself from his condition of spectator and takes on that of actor, in which he ceases to be an object and becomes a subject, is changed from witness into protagonist.

The plan for transforming the spectator into actor can be systematized in the following general outline of four stages:

First stage: *Knowing the body:* a series of exercises by which one gets to know one's body, its limitations and possibilities, its social distortions and possibilities of rehabilitation.

Second stage: *Making the body expressive:* a series of games by which one begins to express one's self through the body, abandoning other, more common and habitual forms of expression.

Third stage: *The theater as language:* one begins to practice theater as a language that is living and *present,* not as a finished product displaying images form the past:

First degree: *Simultaneous dramaturgy:* the spectators "write" simultaneously with the acting of the actors;

Second degree: *Image theater:* the spectators intervene directly, "speaking" through images made with the actors' bodies;

Third degree: *forum theater:* the spectators intervene directly in the dramatic action and act.

Fourth stage: *The theater as discourse:* simple forms in which the spectator-actor creates "spectacles" according to his need to discuss certain themes or rehearse certain actions.

Examples:

1) *Newspaper theater*

2) *Invisible theater*

3) *Photo-romance theater*

4) *Breaking of repression*

5) *Myth theater*

6) *Trial theater*

7) *Masks and Rituals*

First Stage: Knowing the Body.

The initial contact with a group of peasants, workers, or villagers—if they are confronted with the proposal to put on a theatrical performance—can be extremely difficult. They have quite likely never heard of theater and if they have heard of it, their conception of it will probably have been distorted by television, with its emphasis on sentimentality, or by some traveling circus group. It is also very common for those people to associate theater with leisure or frivolity. Thus caution is required even when the contact takes place through an educator who belongs to the same class as the illiterates or semi-illiterates, even if he lives among them in a shack and shares their comfortless life. The very fact that the educator comes with the mission of eradicating illiteracy (which presupposes a coercive, forceful action) is in itself an alienating factor between the agent and the local people. For this reason the theatrical experience should begin not with something alien to the people (theatrical techniques that are taught or imposed) but with the *bodies* of those who agree to participate in the experiment.

There is a great number of exercises designed with the objective of making each person aware of his own body, of his bodily possibilities, and of deformations suffered because of the type of work he performs. That is, it is necessary for each one to feel the "muscular alienation" imposed on his body by work.

A simple example will serve to clarify this point: compare the muscular structure of a typist with that of the night watchman of a factory. The first performs his or her work seated in a chair: from the waist down the body becomes, during working hours, a kind of pedestal, while arms and fingers are active. The watchman, on the other hand, must walk continually during his eight-hour shift and consequently will develop muscular structures that facilitate walking. The bodies of both become alienated in accordance with their respective types of work.

The same is true of any person whatever the work or social status. The combination of roles that a person must perform imposes on him a "mask" of behavior. This is why those who perform the same roles end up resembling each other: artists, soldiers, clergymen, teachers, workers, peasants, landlords, decadent noblemen, etc.

Compare the angelical placidity of a cardinal walking in heavenly bliss through the Vatican Gardens with, on the other hand, an aggressive general giving orders to his inferiors. The former walks softly, listening to celestial music, sensitive to colors of the purest impressionistic delicacy: if by chance a small bird crosses the cardinal's path, one easily imagines him talking to the bird and addressing it with some amiable word of Christian inspiration. By contrast, it does not befit the general to talk with little birds, whether he cares to or not. No soldier would respect a general who talks to the birds. A general must talk as someone who gives orders, even if it is to tell his wife that he loves her. Likewise, a military man is expected to use spurs, whether he be a brigadier or an admiral. Thus all military officers resemble each other, just as do all cardinals; but vast differences separate generals from cardinals.

The exercises of this first stage are designed to "undo" the muscular structure of the participants. That is, to take them apart, to study and analyze them. Not to weaken or destroy them, but to raise them to the level of consciousness. So that each worker, each peasant understands, sees, and feels to what point his body is governed by his work.

If one is able, in this way, to disjoint one's own muscular structures, one will surely be able to assemble structures characteristic of other professions and social classes; that is, one will be able to physically "interpret" characters different from oneself.

All the exercises of this series are in fact designed to disjoint. Acrobatic and athletic exercises that serve to create muscular structures characteristic of athletes or acrobats are irrelevant here. I offer the following as examples of disjunctive exercises:

1) *Slow motion race*. The participants are invited to run a race with the aim of losing: the last one is the winner. Moving in slow motion, the body will find its center of gravity dislocated at each successive moment and so must find again a new muscular structure which will maintain its balance. The participants must never interrupt the motion or stand still; also they must take the longest step they can and their feet must rise above knee level. In this exercise, a 10-meter run can be more tiring than a conventional 500-meter run, for the effort needed to keep one's balance in each new position is intense.

2) *Cross-legged race*. The participants form pairs, embrace each other and intertwine their legs (the left of one with the right of the other, and vice versa). In the race, each pair acts as if it were a single person and each person acts as if his mate were his leg. The "leg" doesn't move alone: it must be put in motion by its mate!

3) *Monster race*. "Monsters" of four legs are formed: each person embraces the thorax of his mate but in reverse position; so that the legs of one fit around the neck of the other, forming a headless monster with four legs. The monsters then run a race.

4) *Wheel race*. The pairs form wheels, each one grabbing the ankles of the other, and run a race of human wheels.

5) *Hypnosis*. The pairs face each other and one puts his hand a few centimeters from the nose of his partner, who must keep this distance: the first one starts to move his hand in all directions, up and down, from left to right, slowly or faster, while the other moves his body in order to maintain the same distance between his nose and his partner's hand. During these movements he is forced to assume bodily positions that he never takes in his daily life, thus reforming permanently his muscular structures.

Later, groups of three are formed: one leads and the other two follow, one at each hand of the leader. The latter can do anything—cross his arms, separate his hands, etc., while the other two must try to maintain the distance. Afterward, groups of five are formed, one as leader and the other four keeping the distance in relation to the two hands and feet of the leader, while the latter can do what he pleases, even dance, etc.

6) *Boxing match*. The participants are invited to box, but they cannot touch each other under any circumstances; each one must fight as if he were really fighting but without touching his partner, who nevertheless must react as if he had received each blow.

7) *Out West*. A variation of the preceding exercises. The participants improvise a scene typical of bad western movies, with the pianist, the swaggering young cowboy, the dancers, the drunks, the villains who come in kicking the saloon doors, etc. The whole scene is performed in silence; the participants are not allowed to touch each other, but must react to every gesture or action. For example, an *imaginary* chair is thrown against a row of bottles (also imaginary), the pieces of which fly in all directions, and the participants react to the chair, the falling bottles, etc. At the end of the scene all must engage in a free-for-all fight.

All these exercises are included in my book *200 Exercises and Games for the Actor and for the Non-Actor Who Wants to Say Something Through Theater*. There are many more exercises that can be used in the same manner. In proposing exercises it's always advisable to ask the participants to describe or invent others: in this stage, the type that would serve to analyze the muscular structures of each participant. At every stage, however, the maintenance of a creative atmosphere is extremely important.

Second Stage: Making the Body Expressive.

In the second stage the intention is to develop the expressive ability of the body. In our culture we are used to expressing everything through words, leaving the enormous expressive capabilities of the body in an underdeveloped state. A series of "games" can help the participants to begin to use their bodily resources for self-expression. I am talking about parlor games and not necessarily those of a theatrical laboratory. The participants are invited to "play," not to "interpret," characters but they will "play" better to the extent that they "interpret" better.

For example: In one game pieces of paper containing names of animals, male and female, are distributed, one to each participant. For ten minutes, each person tries to give a physical, bodily impression of the animal named on his piece of paper. Talking or making noises that would suggest the animal is forbidden. The communication must be effected entirely through the body. After the first ten minutes, each participant must find his mate among the others who are imitating the animals, since there will always be a male and a female for each one. When two participants are convinced that they constitute a pair, they leave the stage, and the game is over when all participants find their mates through a purely physical communication, without the utilization of words or recognizable sounds.

What is important in games of this type is not to guess right but rather that all the participants try to express themselves through their bodies, something they are not used to doing. Without realizing it they will in fact be giving a "dramatical performance."

I remember one of these games played in a slum area, when a man drew the name *hummingbird*. Not knowing how to express it physically, he remembered nevertheless that this bird flies very rapidly from one flower to another, stops and sucks on a flower while producing a peculiar sound. So with his hands the man imitated the frenetic wings of the hummingbird and, "flying" from participant to participant, halted before each one of them making that sound. After ten minutes, when it was time for him to look for his mate, this man looked all around him and found no one who seemed to be enough of a hummingbird to attract him. Finally he saw a tall, fat man who was making a pendular movement with his hands and, setting aside his doubts, decided that there was his beloved mate; he went straight to "her," making turns around "her" and throwing little kisses to the air while singing joyfully. The fat man, upset, tried to escape, but the other fellow went after him, more and more in love with his hummingbird mate and singing with ever more amorous glee. Finally, though convinced that the other man was not his mate, the fat one—while the others roared with laughter—decided to follow his persistent suitor off stage simply to end the ordeal. Then (for only then were they allowed to talk) the first man, full of joy, cried out:

"I am the male hummingbird, and you are the female? Isn't that right?"

The fat one, very discouraged, looked at him and said: "No, dummy, I'm the bull. . . ."

How the fat man could give an impression of a delicate hummingbird while trying to portray a bull, we will never know. But, no matter: what does matter is that for 15 or 20 minutes all those people tried to "speak" with their bodies.

This type of game can be varied *ad infinitum;* the slips of paper can bear, for example, the names of occupations or professions. If the participants depict an animal, it will perhaps have little to do with their ideology. But if a peasant is called upon to act as a landlord; a worker, the owner of a factory; or if a woman must portray a policeman, all their ideology counts and finds physical expression through the game. The names of the participants themselves may be written on slips of paper, requiring them to convey impressions of each other and thus revealing, physically, their opinions and mutual criticisms.

In this stage, as in the first, regardless of how many games one proposes to the participants, the latter should always be encouraged to invent other games and not to be passive recipients of an entertainment that comes from the outside.

Third Stage: The Theater as Language.
This stage is divided into three parts, each one representing a different degree of direct participation of the spectator in the performance. The spectator is encouraged to intervene in the action, abandoning his condition of object and assuming fully the role of subject. The two preceding stages are preparatory, centering around the work of the participants with their own bodies. Now this stage focuses on the theme to be discussed and furthers the transition from passivity to action.

A performance of Tony Kushner's play *Angels in America, Part I: Millennium Approaches.*

Social and technological change transformed the world in the late nineteenth and early twentieth centuries. Between 1860 and today, the United States emerged from a crippling civil war, two world wars, and the anxieties of the Cold War to become a dominant global power. However, despite the nation's emergence as a major player on the world stage, the arts in the United States were shaped by divided and contradictory impulses. The desire to imitate European models competed with a desire to bring distinctively American arts into being. Even as the Civil War threatened to destroy the nation itself, writers such as Walt Whitman, Ralph Waldo Emerson, Henry David Thoreau, and others gave voice to a national literature that both incorporated and redefined European traditions. With the global expansion of U.S. influence, especially after World War I, the question of an "American culture" became a pressing one; after World War II, certain forms of culture became one of the United States' most significant exports, exports at once assimilated, resisted, and redefined in the contemporary era of globalized culture.

In the theater, the modern era has brought with it the search for a quintessentially "American" drama in which theme, setting, and characterization explore American experience, often by invoking and then discarding styles and attitudes derived from the European stage. In a sense, American drama in the twentieth century translated the idea of American political freedom into more abstract, metaphorical, even Romantic terms, as a conflict between individual freedom and the pressures of confining social realities, such as economic hardship, social class, gender, and race. The search for an American idiom in the theater absorbs the stylistic experiments of European modernism and reshapes them, bending the formal innovation of the European theater to American issues and concerns.

"THE" AMERICAN THEATER?

The democratic experience and populist rhetoric of American public life has generally resisted the idea of a national culture emanating from a single center like New York City or Washington, D.C. For this reason, perhaps, the dream of a national theater has repeatedly failed. In the nineteenth century, westward expansion brought theater from New York, Philadelphia, and Boston to the Midwestern cities of Chicago, St. Louis, and Kansas City, and then to Los Angeles and San Francisco, and to scores of smaller towns between the Mississippi River and the Pacific Ocean. The theater was a widely dispersed local affair. Towns often boasted theaters that could be used for opera, drama, or vaudeville and that supported local companies while also catering to touring shows with stars drawn from New York and Europe. Although a lively local theater thrived throughout the country, offering melodrama, classical plays, comedies, and other entertainments, the appetite for touring shows created a demand for organizations capable of handling scheduling problems for local theaters and regional booking agencies.

In 1896 a group of theatrical entrepreneurs headed by Charles Frohman formed a nationwide organization of booking agents called the **SYNDICATE**. In a sense, they created the first model of how a national theater might work in the United States. The Syndicate offered theater managers a full season of touring shows—provided that the manager contracted to deal only with the Syndicate. By gaining exclusive control over theaters on key travel routes, the Syndicate thwarted competition from other touring producers and often even denied local companies the use of local theaters. At its height, the Syndicate had exclusive rights to more than 700 theaters. It could blackball non-Syndicate performers from working by threatening producers who hired them, and it could withdraw Syndicate support from any manager who booked non-Syndicate shows or performers.

649

The effects of the Syndicate were profound and shaped the American theater for the next half-century. The Syndicate's grip on the theater effectively extinguished major professional theater outside New York as a source of new plays and productions; it also influenced playwriting, since the Syndicate developed plays only as commercial properties that could be successfully marketed to a general audience coast-to-coast. Although the Syndicate's power was resisted by a few famous actors and powerful producers, its approach was imitated by other groups. The parochial interests of the New York stage—where the shows of such organizations originated—became in practice the interests of the American theater, and New York became the center of theatrical production and theatrical investment. The revival of significant, professional "regional" theaters as centers of new productions—Margo Jones's Theater 47 in Dallas, the Alley Theater of Houston, the Arena Stage in Washington, D.C., the Actors Workshop of San Francisco, the Guthrie Theater in Minneapolis—had to wait until the 1940s and 1950s. The Syndicate's fortunes also point out the fallacy inherent in the notion of *an* American theater. Throughout its history, the American theater has embraced a range of dynamic and contradictory attitudes toward the stage and its place in society: New York versus the "provinces," mainstream versus elite, conventional versus experimental, commercial versus artistic. Theatrical innovation has been spurred primarily by theaters outside the commercial mainstream, especially by small, amateur "little theaters," by university and college theaters, by community theaters, and by ethnic theaters.

EUROPEAN INFLUENCE AND AMERICAN INNOVATION

The growth of American drama and theater was decisively shaped by the commercial climate of the stage and also by the United States' isolation from the energetic traditions of European theater. While there had long been a homegrown playwriting tradition, many of the most successful plays in nineteenth-century America were—in an era before copyright protection was extended to dramatic authors—productions, adaptations, or piracies of European novels and plays, as well as of American classics like Harriet Beecher Stowe's *Uncle Tom's Cabin*. Moreover, given the lucrative opportunities of touring, British and European actor/managers frequently brought shows to the United States, and some—notably the prolific playwright and actor Dion Boucicault, whose plays *The Poor of New York* (1857) and *The Octoroon* (1859) were written and successfully staged in the United States—developed plays on American themes. Although turn-of-the-century Broadway developed a homegrown version of theatrical realism—epitomized by writer/producer David Belasco's *The Governor's Lady* (1912), which reproduced the interior of a familiar theater district restaurant onstage—European experimentation made its impact on America in more indirect ways, usually only after those experiments had crystallized into a body of theatrical practices and conventions. Many major companies toured the United States. The Abbey Theater came with John Millington Synge's *The Playboy of the Western World* in 1911–1912, and the German producer Max Reinhardt brought his spectacular productions to the United States in 1912, 1914, 1924, and 1927–1928. The British director Harley Granville Barker, who sponsored Shaw's plays and had gained fame as an innovative director of Shakespeare, directed in New York in 1915; the Ballets Russes toured in 1916; and the Moscow Art Theater, whose disciples Richard Boleslavsky and Maria Ouspenskaya founded the American Laboratory Theater in 1923, performed in 1923–1924.

Many of these companies, the Abbey and the Moscow Art Theater in particular, had begun as small, independent, amateur theaters, and their work was most directly implemented in the United States by similar groups. Some innovation came from the new college and university programs in drama: George Pierce Baker's famous playwriting course at Harvard University in the first decades of the century (taken by Eugene O'Neill, among many others) and Montgomery T. Gregory's program for black writers and performers at Howard University in the 1920s were only the beginning of a concerted effort to bring theater and drama into the university curriculum and to develop a greater awareness of progressive theater. However, it largely fell to the **LITTLE THEATER MOVEMENT** to assimilate this new work and redirect it toward particularly American concerns. Innovation in the American theater came largely from these small companies, committed to mounting new and uncommercial work. The Chicago Little Theater, the Toy Theater of Boston, the Neighborhood Playhouse and the Washington Square Playhouse of New York, and Detroit's Arts and Crafts Theater were all in operation by 1917, and the Little Negro Theater Movement was producing plays in Harlem and Washington, D.C., as well.

The Provincetown Playhouse provides a model of the "little theaters" and their fortunes in the early twentieth century. Founded in 1915 in Provincetown, Massachusetts—an artists' retreat at the tip of Cape Cod—the company was initially a group of young amateurs intent on theater, including the playwright Susan Glaspell; her husband, George Cram Cook; and, later, Eugene O'Neill. In the first year, the players produced plays in their summer homes. In 1916 they converted an old wharf building into a small theater and produced, among other plays, O'Neill's *Bound East for Cardiff.* In the autumn, the players returned to New York and opened a small theater in Greenwich Village. The company could hardly afford complex and expensive sets and turned its efforts instead toward a simple and realistic kind of performance. Eugene O'Neill's early plays were produced by the Provincetown company, and after he became a successful Broadway playwright, he continued to open many of his plays there. Like all of the "little theaters," the Provincetown had difficulty managing the transition from a small amateur company to the larger demands of a self-sustaining professional company. It went through a series of transformations before closing in 1929, having introduced O'Neill to the stage and having staged plays by John Reed, Edna St. Vincent Millay, Susan Glaspell, Djuna Barnes, Edmund Wilson, Paul Green, Wallace Stevens, Theodore Dreiser, August Strindberg, and many others.

In the United States, the freedom to make theater has always been qualified by the need to make it pay. The trials of sustaining artistic ambition in the commercial environment of the theater is the central narrative of the most innovative theatrical companies of the modern era. The ideal of an American theater remained tantalizing yet elusive and was often pursued in several ways, usually by developing a distinctive repertoire of plays, or by trying to define a typically American performance idiom. "Little theaters" like the Provincetown emphasized the production of American drama. Other theaters tried to produce American drama, the new European drama, and the classics for a larger audience than the "little theaters" could reach. The Theater Guild, for example, was organized in 1919 in New York as a subscription company specifically for the purpose of producing noncommercial plays. In the course of the next decade, the Guild staged plays by Shaw, Pirandello, Ibsen, and Strindberg, as well as plays by Americans like O'Neill and Elmer Rice. The Guild succeeded in incorporating American plays like O'Neill's *Strange Interlude* (1928) and Rice's *The Adding Machine* (1923) into the repertoire of serious modern drama and in bringing it to a significant public. However, following the stock market crash of 1929 and the economic depression that ensued, the Guild invested in a less adventuresome repertoire in the hopes of drawing a larger audience and so lost its original mission.

Although it sponsored an innovative selection of plays, the Theater Guild did not develop an original style of production. In 1931, several Guild members began a spin-off company—called simply the Group—for the purpose of investigating different kinds of drama and different approaches to performance. Eventually including Harold Clurman, Cheryl Crawford, Lee Strasberg, Elia Kazan, Sanford Meisner, and many others, the Group at first worked on plays examining the social ferment of the 1930s and the hardship of the Great Depression. Much as Chekhov became the centerpiece of Stanislavski's Moscow Art Theater, so the plays of Clifford Odets became the Group's standards: *Awake and Sing!, Waiting for Lefty,* and *Golden Boy.* However, the Group's most extensive contribution to the American theater was its systematic importation of Stanislavskian acting techniques. In the Group, and later in the Actors Studio, actors were trained in Stanislavski's approach to **EMOTION MEMORY** and **GIVEN CIRCUMSTANCES,** laying the groundwork for what became a distinctly "American" style of acting, acting that was emotionally spontaneous, grounded in subtext, psychologically realistic and nuanced. Nonetheless, the Group, the Studio, and the training they devised produced a generation of actors ready to meet the challenges of the burgeoning American drama of the 1940s and 1950s: Marlon Brando, Ben Gazzara, Karl Malden, Geraldine Page, Kim Stanley, Maureen Stapleton, and many others.

The impact of this acting can be seen in the great stage productions of the post-war period. The 1940s and early 1950s saw the development of a distinctively American approach to stage realism, balancing nuanced characterization with a concern for the social environment. Arthur Miller's *Death of a Salesman* and *The Crucible,* Tennessee Williams's *A Streetcar Named Desire* and *The Glass Menagerie,* and Eugene O'Neill's *The Iceman Cometh* and *Long Day's Journey into Night* demanded the subtle realism that became the hallmark of American acting and of American drama in the world repertoire. These plays—and their descendants, like the plays of Beth Henley, David Mamet, Maria Irene Fornes, August Wilson, or Sam Shepard—succeeded by criticizing American ideals and institutions while at the same time exploring the psyche of the American character. Indeed, in these plays the American character often seems to be thwarted precisely by the process of American society. The fragile beauty of Tennessee Williams's Southern belles is usually crushed by the sordid realities of modern urban life; in Shepard's *True West,* the American West becomes a mythic battleground, where a yuppie and a drifter shoot it out for control of the image.

POSTWAR EXPERIMENTS

After World War II, the most significant innovations in American theater have come from small "experimental" theater companies. In part through the influence of Antonin Artaud's conception of a **THEATER OF CRUELTY** (see Unit V), and the several tours of Jerzy Grotowski's Lab Theater of Poland, experimental theater in the 1960s and 1970s tended to reject the esthetic of stage realism in favor of producing an immediate, quintessentially *theatrical* experience for its audiences. As a result, many productions in the 1960s and 1970s—the Living Theater's *Paradise Now,* the Performance Group's *Dionysus in 69,* the Open Theater's *The Serpent,* the work of the Bread and Puppet Theater, of the San Francisco Mime Troup, of Mabou Mines, and many others—incorporated the audience as participants in the action. Many of these experiments also led to new forms of playwriting, in which classical notions of representation also were broken down. Moreover, these experiments not only led to the incorporation of a more immediate, physical esthetic into American drama (visible, too, in performance art), but also to the exploration of Brechtian epic theater: experiments with narrative (Fornes's *Fefu and Her Friends*), with an episodic epic form (Kushner's *Angels in America*), or with a more politicized performance of "character" (Anna Deavere Smith's monologues).

Indeed, American drama continued to strike a compromise with the innovations of the European theater after World War II. Eric Bentley—a brilliant scholar, director, playwright, and translator—worked indefatigably to bring Bertolt Brecht to the attention of the American theater. Brecht became particularly important in the United States as the Vietnam War and widespread civil and social discontent spurred the theater in more agitational, political directions. Feminist theater, ethnic theater, and gay and lesbian theater have all at times availed themselves of Brecht's theater theory and practice. The work of Luis Valdez and El Teatro Campesino in California in the 1960s and 1970s is a direct extension of Brecht's sense of theater. Bringing a flatbed truck to farmworkers' strikes, Teatro Campesino produced its short, political dramas to an active, involved audience and became part of the process of social change. "Absurdist" playwrights like Samuel Beckett, Harold Pinter, and Eugène Ionesco were also both produced and imitated in the United States, influencing the work of American playwrights like Edward Albee, Maria Irene Fornes, Jack Gelber, Adrienne Kennedy, David Mamet, and Sam Shepard. Indeed, in plays like Amiri Baraka's *Dutch-*

man or Sam Shepard's *True West,* we can see the inflections of **THEATER OF THE ABSURD** in plays that are recognizably "American" in style and subject matter.

In 1935, an act of Congress established the Federal Theater Project, as a way to employ workers left unemployed by the Depression (see Aside box). The Federal Theater Project also sponsored a Negro Unit, directed by John Houseman and Orson Welles, which operated in ten cities around the United States; two of its productions, an all-black *Macbeth* and *The Swing Mikado,* were among the Federal Theater's most successful productions. The fact of a separate Negro Unit points to a different crisis in the idea of an American theater. How could a theater largely in the hands of the white, Anglo, male, middle class adequately represent the diversity of the nation's experience, particularly the experience of the oppressed? As the poet and playwright Langston Hughes observed in "Notes on Commercial Theater," published in 1940, the stage had in many ways appropriated African-American culture, systematically absorbing it into its own dominant values:

> *Yep, you done taken my blues and gone.*
> *You also took my spirituals and gone.*
> *You put me in Macbeth and Carmen Jones*
> *And all kinds of Swing Mikados*
> *And in everything but what's about me—*
> *But someday somebody'll*
> *Stand up and talk about me,*
> *And write about me—*
> *Black and beautiful—*

Far from representing authentic black experience in America, such theater more often confirmed the discriminatory fantasies already prominent on the stage and in society. Such stereotypes as the boozy Irishman, the dull Swede, the sunny and/or murderous Italian, and the greedy Jew—appearing even in "realistic" plays like Rice's *Street Scene* (1929), and dating back through the stereotyped slaves and Indians of Boucicault's *Octoroon*—work to reinforce the "normative" perspective of dominant culture, reflecting the attitudes, behavior, and social practices that oppress such groups in the world outside the theater. It is not surprising, then, that throughout the history of the United States, ethnic theaters have played a prominent part in maintaining the cultural identity of America's minority populations: the Yiddish theater of New York, Polish theaters in Chicago, Scandinavian theaters throughout the Midwest, a thriving circuit of Spanish-language theaters shared by Mexico and Southwestern states from Texas to California, Cuban-influenced theater in Florida, and Puerto Rican theater in New York. Some of these theaters produced versions of classic European plays in their own accents, but most developed their own dramatic forms, as ways of maintaining themselves in the face of a brutally exclusive "American" culture.

The experience of slavery places African Americans in a different position vis-à-vis the culture of the United States, and the black theater has had a profound impact on the course of the American stage. Although an African Theater Company was founded in New York in 1821—sponsoring, among others, the brilliant Shakespearean actor Ira Aldridge (1807–1867) who left the United States for a distinguished career in Europe—in the main, African Americans had little direct access to the theater before the twentieth century. Black characters had long figured as stage villains and comic buffoons in American drama. Played by white actors in blackface makeup, these abusive types literally enacted white attitudes toward racial difference. "Jim Crow" was first popularized by the white song-and-dance man T. D. Rice in the 1830s, and more "sympathetic" characters, like Tom in the hugely popular stage adaptations of Harriet Beecher Stowe's *Uncle Tom's Cabin* (1832), were devised by white authors and played by white actors. The minstrel troupes that became popular after the Civil

THE FEDERAL THEATER PROJECT

If the Group Theater and the Actors Studio created an identifiably "American" approach to acting, the Federal Theater Project succeeded—briefly—in creating a truly national theater. An act of Congress established the Federal Theater Project in 1935 under the Works Projects Administration, with Hallie Flanagan Davis (1890–1969) as director. Like other WPA projects, the Federal Theater was designed both to employ workers idled by the Depression and to provide service to the community. It was an enormous undertaking; in New York City alone, half the theaters were closed by 1933 and half its population of actors unemployed. Given the mission of providing employment by hiring large casts and supporting personnel, and a commitment to dramatizing contemporary social issues, the Federal Theater developed its most notable genre, the Living Newspaper. Living Newspapers incorporated dialogue taken from newspapers and other public media into a series of vignettes, readings, films, and other techniques to a problem in current national and world affairs: the farm crisis in *Triple A Plowed Under* (1936), housing in *One-Third of a Nation* (1938), rural electrification in *Power* (1937). At its height, the Federal Theater had branches in forty states; these branches staged productions devised by the project's directors, using their own local resources, and often developed their own material. In 1936, for instance, a stage adaptation of Sinclair Lewis's *It Can't Happen Here* opened simultaneously in twenty-one theaters around the country, including black-cast and Yiddish productions. The Federal Theater ran for four full seasons before being terminated by Congress in 1939: it financed 1,200 productions of 830 major works, at times employing more than ten thousand people, most of whom had been unemployed. Admission to its shows was inexpensive, and in an average week 500,000 people saw its productions; over its four years of production, its audiences numbered more than 30 million people. In New York alone, more than 12 million people saw its productions. However, in an era of labor unrest and the pervasive fear of outside agitation, the Newspapers were seen by the Project's enemies in government—many of whom opposed the WPA altogether—as too left-wing for government support.

Despite its demise, the United State's' only truly national theater had significant influence on the course of American theater and drama. Not only did the Federal Theater have huge audiences, but it brought new audiences into the theater: 65 percent of its audiences were seeing a stage play for the first time. The Living Newspapers developed a home-grown adaptation of the techniques of European experimental theater (including Brechtian epic theater) in the United States. In this sense, the Federal Theater inspired the work of several distinguished theater companies that survived its demise, notably John Houseman's (1915–1985) Mercury Theater, which produced Mark Blitzstein's *The Cradle Will Rock,* and a distinguished series of productions of modern and classic plays—by Shaw, Büchner, Shakespeare, and others. In addition, the Negro Units of the Federal Theater operated in Seattle, Hartford, Philadelphia, Newark, Los Angeles, Boston, Birmingham, Raleigh, San Francisco, and Chicago, employing more than 800 people and staging seventy-five productions in the project's four years of operation. Most importantly, the Federal Theater enabled a generation of actors, designers, directors, and playwrights to survive the Depression, and it brought the theater powerfully into the national scene.

LIVING NEWSPAPER

The Federal Theater Project dramatizes news events in the New York production of 1935.

War for depicting romanticized vignettes of plantation life were also first performed by white actors. Later, black performers—in minstrel troupes, or in the newly popular "Negro musicals"—often had little choice other than to enact these stereotypes themselves, for such roles were the only openings available on the stage (even black theaters were usually financed and operated by white entrepreneurs). Despite small inroads like the Lafayette Theater (founded in Harlem in 1915), representing black experience to America at large was almost exclusively the prerogative of white actors, producers, playwrights, and performers. In this regard, the theater—like the institutions of literature, the press, the legal system, and state and federal government—denied African Americans their own voice.

Spurred in part by successful plays by white dramatists that self-consciously attempted to "humanize" black characters for white audiences—O'Neill's *The Emperor Jones* (1920) and *All God's Chillun Got Wings* (1924), Marc Connelly's *The Green Pastures* (1930), Paul Green's *In Abraham's Bosom* (1926), and Dubose and Dorothy Heyward's *Porgy* (1920; transformed into the Gershwin musical *Porgy and Bess* in 1935)—black actors and writers became galvanized to "stand up and talk" about themselves. Throughout the 1920s the LITTLE NEGRO THEATER MOVEMENT sponsored plays of black life largely for black audiences. The Lafayette Theater, for example, opened Willis Richardson's *The Chipwoman's Fortune* in 1923; it later became the first play by a black playwright to reach Broadway. In the 1920s and 1930s, black drama increasingly addressed the politics of racism in the United States, while also depicting the effect of racism in daily life. Several organizations worked to sponsor African-American drama and theater. W.E.B. DuBois, a founder of the National Association for the Advancement of Colored People (NAACP), used his *Crisis* magazine—in collaboration with the National Urban League's *Opportunity*—to give a series of prizes to promising African American playwrights; winners included Eulalie Spence's *Foreign Mail* (1926), Zora Neale Hurston's *Colorstruck* and *Spears* (1925), and Georgia Douglas Johnson's *Blue Blood* (1926). The NAACP also sponsored the production of plays, including Angelina Weld Grimké's influential drama of a young woman's reaction to the lynching of her father and brother, *Rachel* (1916). *Rachel* was one of the first of a series of plays about lynching. How this important genre of black theater—and a crucial element of black experience in the United States—was both overlooked and distorted by white theater is the subject of Alice Childress's brilliant play *Trouble in Mind,* which opened off-Broadway in 1955. Finally, black colleges, universities, and even high schools also became centers for a new dramatic repertoire. In 1921, Montgomery T. Gregory formed a department of Dramatic Arts at Howard University in Washington, D.C., and with Alain Locke developed an influential program in acting, playwriting, and theatrical production, offering the first institutionalized training for black writers and performers in the United States.

In a 1926 playbill for Harlem's Krigwa Players, W. E. B. DuBois described the goals of a black theater:

> The plays of a real Negro theater must be: *One: About us.* That is, they must have plots which reveal Negro life as it is. *Two: By us.* That is, they must be written by Negro authors who understand from birth and continual association just what it means to be a Negro today. *Three: For us.* That is, the theater must cater primarily to Negro audiences and be supported and sustained by their entertainment and approval. *Fourth: Near us.* The theater must be in a Negro neighborhood near the mass of ordinary Negro people.

Throughout the 1930s and 1940s, African American playwrights and actors came into increasing national prominence, both by developing DuBois's agenda and by working to bring an authentic black drama to a wider audience. Langston Hughes wrote a number of plays in the 1930s, including the well-known *Mulatto* (1935); the Federal Theater Project produced W. E. B. DuBois's *Haiti* at the Lafayette Theater; and playwrights trained at Howard were produced in New York and elsewhere. The founding of the companies like the American Negro Theater in 1939, the Negro Playwrights Company in 1940, and the Negro Ensemble Company in 1957 began to meet DuBois's charge, developing the actors, the production experience, and the financing that would sustain the explosive growth of black American drama after World War II. When Lorraine Hansberry's *A Raisin in the Sun* opened in 1959, it was the first play written by a black woman to reach Broadway, the first directed by a black director (Lloyd Richards), and the first financed predominantly by African Americans. The success of *Raisin* foretold the success of black theater in the coming decades, as black playwrights—Amiri Baraka, Adrienne Kennedy, Charles Gordone, Ed Bullins, Charles Fuller, Ntozake Shange, August Wilson, Anna Deavere Smith, Suzan-Lori Parks, and many others—came to shape the American theater.

POPULAR THEATER AND MASS CULTURE

The tension between commercial viability and dramatic achievement is perhaps best symbolized by Broadway itself, the American theater's "magnificent invalid," where even the greatest American plays can hardly compare in terms of commercial and popular success with Broadway's most uniquely American genre: the musical. Musical theater has a long history in the United States, and in many respects its fortunes parallel those of the dramatic theater. Musical theater also witnessed the tyranny of national producing syndicates, the impact of European innovation, and the powerful contributions of black and ethnic cultures. However, the integration of song and dance, orchestral music, and (usually) a romantic plot characteristic of the Broadway musical really dates to the period of World War II, probably to Richard Rodgers and Oscar Hammerstein's *Oklahoma!* (1943), which ran for 2,248 performances (*Death of a Salesman,* in contrast, ran for 742). *Oklahoma!* provided the model not only for other Rodgers and Hammerstein hits—*Carousel* (1945), *South Pacific* (1949), *The King and I* (1951)—but for other musicals as well: Alan Jay Lerner and Frederick Loewe's updating of Shaw's *Pygmalion* in *My Fair Lady* (1956), Frank Loesser's *Guys and Dolls* (1950), and Leonard Bernstein, Stephen Sondheim, and Arthur Laurents's *West Side Story* (1957). Although the form of the Broadway musical underwent significant changes in the 1970s and 1980s, its popularity points to one of the ways that the theater has sought to recapture an audience from film and television: by emphasizing the unique excitement of a dazzling live spectacle. This is as true of Broadway hits like *High Society* (1997), which used the Cole Porter music from the 1956 film of the same name, as it is of several musicals adapted from animated films—notably *The Lion King* (1997). The musical theater also points to the fundamental conditions of the Broadway theatrical economy as well. Musicals remain popular with producers because the huge financial investment required to mount a musical can repay much larger returns for investors than any "straight" play.

Throughout the history of the stage in the West, important theaters have succeeded both in creating innovative drama and in creating a public. However, the American theater—if there is *an* American theater—is a different entity altogether from the citizens' theater of classical Athens, the courtly theater of Racine and Molière, or even the educated circle of subscribers to Shaw's Court Theater. In a sense, this difference can be traced to the fact that the American theater first came into force only in the twentieth century, at just the moment when other dramatic media—film and television—began to compete with it. The American theater has had to define itself in the environment of modern mass culture. Not only are film and television more accessible to most people, but the technology and distribution of such mass media have fundamentally altered our understanding both of drama and performance, and of what an audience *is.* "The American theater" has always been a critical fiction, homogenizing the diversity of stage activity in the United States, writing some forms of drama—chiefly American realistic plays—into history, and writing others out of it. Today, it may be equally artificial to separate live theater from other forms of dramatic production, forms that have massively changed the terrain where dramatic performance takes place.

With the global expansion of the United States in the first two thirds of the twentieth century, the development of new modes of commerce and trade in the 1960s and 1970s (notably the multinational corporation), and especially with the breakup of the Soviet Union and its satellite states symbolized by the fall of the Berlin Wall in 1989, "American" culture has become a widely exported commodity. Much as American culture has absorbed both immigrant and conquered cultures as part of the development of the United States, so now the image of "America" is projected around the world, on T-shirts, in cartoons, in the imagery of Mickey Mouse and Michael Jordan, in television programs, in films.

Drama and theater are also part of that projected image, and American drama has rapidly become part of a global canon of modern theater: plays such as *Death of a Salesman* and *Fences* have been performed in the People's Republic of China; *Angels in America* was produced in London before it opened in New York, and has since been produced around the world. One of the most challenging aspects of American theater, however, is what might be called its *diversity,* the way different playwrights have worked to challenge a monolithic notion of "American" culture, and the values—white, masculinist, heterosexual, middle-class, English-speaking—it asserts as definitive. This diversity emerges in several ways, not only through a writer's or a company's decision to make their own alternative perspective *count*—as Luis Valdez and El Teatro Campesino do in *Zoot Suit*—but to use theatrical production to mark, make visible, "alienate" in Brecht's sense the ways the normative values of "American" culture are produced, and the kinds of work those values do.

For this reason, while there remains a large "mainstream" of stage style, much of the most adventurous work in the American theater has experimented with new, alternative ways of representing drama on the stage, and new ways of engaging its audience. The "rep and rev" of Suzan-Lori Parks's plays, the ways they "repeat and revise" a single gesture in order to highlight the *constructedness* of the body and the ways it represents itself culturally is one of these techniques; Anna Deavere Smith's effort to imitate the gestural conventions of her interview subjects does a similar kind of work, implying that those gestures are part of a common cultural repertoire, an individual act of expression that uses social means. This "alienating" of the ways "identity" is produced onstage extends to a wide range of contemporary performance. In 1983, for example, the Wooster Group's *L.S.D.—Just the High Points* set portions of Arthur Miller's *The Crucible* as a trial, literalizing the parallel with the McCarthy hearings that the play was widely thought to allegorize; in *Routes 1 & 9,* the company integrated scenes from Thornton Wilder's *Our Town* into a blackface minstrel show, in effect staging the racist attitudes that "our town"—white America in this case—has both produced and disowned.

This use of the stage to expose dominant or oppressive attitudes that are concealed within the monuments of American culture is also characteristic of performance works like Coco Fusco and Guillermo Gómez-Peña's *Two Undiscovered Amerindians Visit . . . ,* (which has been filmed as *The Couple in the Cage*). In the early 1990s, Gómez-Peña (a performance artist born in Mexico) and Fusco (a Cuban-American) devised a performance in which they portrayed "native" or "indigenous" inhabitants of the (fictitious) Carribean island of Guatinaui. Wearing deeply layered costumes—basketball sneakers, feathered headdresses, sunglasses, bottle-cap–studded vests—Fusco and Gómez-Peña were displayed in a cage, as anthropological "discoveries." During the course of the performance, which was produced in several art museums around the United States, as well as in the Field Museum of Natural History in Chicago, and on a plaza in Madrid, Gómez-Peña and Fusco exhibited behavior: they watched TV, they ate, for a fee they had their photo taken with spectators, or danced, and so on. The purpose of the production, however, was less to portray an exoticized native "other," than it was to *stage* the attitudes of their audiences to the spectacle of these imprisoned, displayed people. Although we might think this an extreme or at least a special case, it might be said that what Gómez-Peña and Fusco did here—stage the audience—is a task that stretches back to Valdez's work in the 1960s, and has become one of the principal innovations of contemporary American performance.

Since the mid-1960s, a variety of non-dramatic performance modes have developed in Western theater that are commonly known by the generic label of "performance art." Although it is difficult to generalize about this wide range of performances, most performance-art works share certain features: many (though certainly not all) are solo works, in which a performer (or performers) relates directly to an audience; the performer(s) may be working from a plan or script, but the performance is not a traditional "drama," enacting a fictitious narrative of the deeds of a fictitious "character" through "acting." Instead, in performance art, the performer uses a variety of means—monologue, physical performance, music, dance—to produce a spectacle that is "really happening" between himself or herself and the spectators.

Many performance-art works of the 1970s and 1980s used the performers' bodies to explore the limits of "theater." Chris Burden, for example, staged several events in which he wounded himself before an audience: in one 1970 work, he shot himself in the arm with a pistol; in another, he was crucified on top of a Volkswagen. In one of Carolee Schneeman's works, she unwinds a long scroll from her vagina, reading it to the audience. Annie Sprinkle, once a pornographic film star, openly objectifies her body onstage for a visible audience of men (and women), as she had once done in the more covert and coercive scene of pornography; in one performance, she invites the audience onstage while she conducts her own cervical examination. Many performance art works take place outside theatrical venues, so that the performance becomes part of the everyday "performance" of street life. Linda Montano spent one year connected by a short rope to Teching

Tsieh; the artists' lack of privacy was constantly on display in the streets of New York. In one of her early performances, Laurie Anderson stood on a large block of ice on a New York City street, playing her violin until the ice melted.

Several performance artists have become well-known for their monologue-performances, which range widely in technique and strategy. Anna Deavere Smith's works—such as *Fires in the Mirror: Crown Heights, Brooklyn and Other Identities* and *Twilight—Los Angeles, 1992*—differ from many performance art monologues in that Smith impersonates and represents a range of speakers; yet both in the brilliance of her individual performance and in her effort to perform the speakers faithfully (rather than "act" them in a theatrical sense), Smith's work touches on the "authentic" aspect of performance art. This emphasis on the "authentic," the "real," enables several performance artists to explore the relationship between identity politics and performance. In *Memory Tricks,* Marga Gomez, daughter of a Cuban theater impresario and a Puerto Rican "exotic dancer," recalls her family and childhood to interrogate the formation of Latina identity in the United States. David Drake's *The Night Larry Kramer Kissed Me* dramatizes the performer's understanding and exploration of his gay sexuality from the time of his sixth birthday, on the night of the 1969 Stonewall Riots in New York's Greenwich Village—in which gay men and lesbians protested abusive treatment by the police—through the AIDS crisis of the 1980s and 1990s.

Many artists use performance to foreground and criticize the everyday racist, sexist, and/or homophobic "performance" commonly accepted as "normal behavior" in U.S. society, and to bring into view other ways of performing identity. Adrian Piper, a light-skinned African American woman, sometimes hands out business cards to people who "ignore" her race:

I am black. I am sure that you did not realize this when you made / laughed at / agreed with that racist remark. In the past, I have attempted to alert white people to my racial identity in advance. Unfortunately, this invariably causes them to react to me as pushy, manipulative, or socially inappropriate. Therefore, my policy is to assume that white people do not make these remarks, even when they believe there are no black people present, and to distribute this card when they do. I regret any discomfort my presence is causing you, just as I am sure you regret the discomfort your racism is causing me.

Lesbian playwright Holly Hughes had written several plays—notably *The Well of Horniness, The Lady Dick,* and *Dress Suits for Hire,* which was performed by Peggy Shaw and Lois Weaver at the WOW Cafe—before developing her well-known performance piece *World Without End* in 1989. In *My Queer Body,* Tim Miller narrates the history of his sexual experience and the formation of his identity as a gay man; he undresses during the performance and performs part of *My Queer Body* in the nude, sometimes moving about the audience. Karen Finley's performances often express her outrage at the implicit and explicit violence against women in American culture; in monologues like *Constant State of Desire* and *We Keep Our Victims Ready,* she uses her body to enact and physicalize the "obscenity" of such violence. In a section of *We Keep Our Victims Ready* entitled "St. Valentine's Massacre," Finley examines the way patriarchal culture encodes a subtle hatred of women, one that women can self-destructively internalize. In performance, while Finley monologues, "My life is worth nothing but shit," she smears her naked body with chocolate pudding and studs it with spermlike bean sprouts, a stunning and physical image of the sexualization of violence.

As the performance continues, though, she layers herself with tinsel and red candies, transforming her abjection into a strange beauty. Such performances purposefully transgress the boundaries of decorous social behavior, in part to dramatize the kind of oppression that lurks in "everyday" performance. By all accounts, audiences who have seen Finley's or Miller's performances have found them powerful and moving; but to some critics (who often proudly claim that they have not seen the performance), such performance verges on "obscenity." In 1990, conservative politicians led by then Senator Jesse Helms (R–North Carolina) pressured the National Endowment for the Arts to withdraw funding from four performance artists who had been recommended by the peer-review process for support. Not only were Tim Miller, Karen Finley, Holly Hughes, and John Fleck denied funding, but the Endowment's head, John Frohnmayer, subsequently resigned, and a "general standards of decency" restriction of dubious constitutionality was required of subsequent recipients of NEA support.

Perhaps the best-known autobiographical performer, however, is Spalding Gray. Gray began his career with The Performance Group, an avant-garde company working with **ENVIRONMENTAL THEATER** in the late 1960s and 1970s. With Elizabeth LeCompte and other members of the group, Gray collaborated on a series of performances, collectively called *The Rhode Island Trilogy*—*Sakonnet Point* (1975), *Rumstick Road* (1977), and *Nyatt School* (1978), followed by an epilogue, *Point Judith* (1979). The Performance Group was committed to authentic "performance" (in which the actors behave as themselves, rather than "acting" in a theatrical sense), and Gray found a sequence of *Rumstick Road*—in which he narrated events of his life to the audience—to be a particularly fertile ground for continued exploration. In the course of the next several years, Gray developed a se-

PERFORMANCE ART

Anna Deavere Smith portrays Angela King at the world premier of Smith's *Twilight—Los Angeles, 1992*.

ries of autobiographical performances. In some of these works, Gray structures a certain degree of randomness in the performance: in *India and After (America)* (1979), for example, he randomly chooses words from a dictionary to key part of his monologue; in *A Personal History of the American Theatre* (1980), he shuffles a collection of index cards with play titles on them and uses the series to direct his performance. Gray's more recent work has been made into films, and so has become known to a wider audience. The film versions of *Swimming to Cambodia* (1984) and *Monster in a Box* (1990) preserve much of the ambience of Gray's performance. In the opening sequence of *Swimming to Cambodia,* for example, we see Gray walking through the streets of the Village, entering the Performance Garage, seating himself onstage at a long table, and opening the notebook that seems to provide the score for his performance. Gray addresses the camera and, as in his stage performances, seems to occupy a startling and fascinating middle ground between acting and being: he is clearly shaping the story, representing and constructing the narrative of his life as a kind of fiction, while at the same time claiming that quasi-fictive narrative as his own, as himself. Like other postmodern art forms, performance art evocatively explores the edge between representation and "reality," refusing to demarcate a fixed difference between them.

READING THE MATERIAL THEATER

As writing, drama is part of the wide horizon of literature, and throughout its history, the stage has been the site of adaptation; the Greek playwrights adapted their dramas from familiar myths, the medieval craft guilds developed original dramas from Biblical narratives, and Shakespeare famously adapted existing narratives—from clas-sical and contemporary literature, as well as from English history—and plays. With the rise of print, however, a different kind of "adaptation" began to take place, as playwrights and theater managers could turn a quick profit by bringing a famous novel to the stage, typically in a pirated version. In the nineteenth century, for instance, Charles Dickens's novels were frequently pirated for the stage; in versions that not only outraged Dickens, but that paid him no fees or royalties. Susan Glaspell's *Trifles,* however, represents an alternative phenome-non: the translation to the page of a work that had first found success on the stage. In 1917, Glaspell adapted her short story "A Jury of Her Peers" from her play *Trifles.* While the story has been, perhaps, even more widely celebrated than the play, it also raises some impor-tant questions about the place of dra-matic writing in the age of print. Although both works tell the same "story," they do so through very different means: how do the resources of the stage and the resources of the page contribute to the creation of a *different* work of art?

SUSAN GLASPELL
"A Jury of Her Peers" (1917)

After the success of Trifles, *Glaspell wrote a short, narrative version of the play, which has been justly celebrated for the ways it deploys a woman's narrative "point of view." Moreover, the short story also dramatizes the different resources that the theater and narrative fiction have available in order to tell the "same" story.*

When Martha Hale opened the storm-door and got the north wind, she ran back for her big woolen scarf. As she hurriedly wound that round her head her eye made a scandalized sweep of her kitchen. It was no ordinary thing that called her away—it was probably farther from ordinary than anything that had ever happened in Dickson County. But her kitchen was in no shape for leaving: bread ready for mixing, half the flour sifted and half unsifted.

She hated to see things half done; but she had been at that when they stopped to get Mr. Hale, and the sher-iff came in to say his wife wished Mrs. Hale would come too—adding, with a grin, that he guessed she was getting scarey and wanted another woman along. So she had dropped everything right were it was.

"Martha!" now came her husband's impatient voice. "Don't keep folks waiting out here in the cold."

She joined the three men and the one woman waiting for her in the sheriff's car.

After she had the robes tucked in she took another look at the woman beside her. She had met Mrs. Peters the year before, at the county fair, and the thing she remembered about her was that she didn't seem like a sheriff's wife. She was small and thin and didn't have a strong voice. Mrs. Gorman, sheriff's wife before Gorman went out and Peters came in, had a voice that seemed to be backing up the law with every word. But if Mrs. Peters didn't look like a sheriff's wife, Peters made it up in looking like a sheriff—a heavy man with a big voice, who was partic-ularly genial with the law-abiding, as if to make it plain that he knew the dif-ference between criminals and non-criminals. And right there it came into Mrs. Hale's mind that this man who was so lively with all of them was go-ing to the Wrights' now as a sheriff.

"The country's not very pleasant this time of year," Mrs. Peters at last ventured.

Mrs. Hale scarcely finished her re-ply, for they had gone up a little hill and could see the Wright place, and seeing it did not make her feel like talking. It looked very lonely this cold March morning. It had always been a lonesome-looking place. It was down in a hollow, and the poplar trees around it were lonely-looking trees. The men were looking at it and talk-ing about what had happened. The county attorney was bending to one side, scrutinizing the place as they drew up to it.

"I'm glad you came with me," Mrs. Peters said nervously, as the two women were about to follow the men in through the kitchen door.

Even after she had her foot on the doorstep, Martha Hale had a moment of feeling she could not cross this threshold. And the reason it seemed she couldn't cross it now was because she hadn't crossed it before. Time and time again it had been in her mind, "I ought to go over and see Minnie Foster"—she still thought of her as Minnie Foster, though for twenty years she had been Mrs. Wright. And then there was always something to do and Minnie Foster would go from her mind. But *now* she could come.

The men went over to the stove. The women stood close together by the door. Young Henderson, the county attorney, turned around and said, "Come up to the fire, ladies."

Mrs. Peters took a step forward, then stopped. "I'm not—cold," she said.

And so the two women stood by

the door, at first not even so much as looking around the kitchen.

The men talked about what a good thing it was the sheriff had sent his deputy out that morning to make a fire for them, and then Sheriff Peters stepped back from the stove, unbuttoned his outer coat, and leaned his hands on the kitchen table in a way that seemed to mark the beginning of official business. "Now, Mr. Hale," he said in a sort of semi-official voice, "before we move things about, you tell Mr. Henderson just what it was you saw when you came here yesterday morning."

The county attorney was looking around the kitchen.

"By the way," he asked, "has anything been moved?" He turned to the sheriff. "Are things just as you left them yesterday?"

Peters looked from cupboard to sink; to a small worn rocker a little to one side of the kitchen table.

"It's just the same."

"Well, Mr. Hale," said the county attorney, "tell just what happened when you came here yesterday morning."

Mrs. Hale, still leaning against the door, had that sinking feeling of the mother whose child is about to speak a piece. Lewis often wandered along and got things mixed up in a story. She hoped he would tell this straight and plain, and not say unnecessary things that would make it harder for Minnie Foster. He didn't begin at once, and she noticed that he looked queer, as if thinking of what he had seen here yesterday.

"Yes, Mr. Hale?" the county attorney reminded.

"Harry and I had started to town with a load of wood," Mrs. Hale's husband began.

Harry was Mrs. Hale's oldest boy. He wasn't with them now, for the wood never got to town yesterday and he was taking it this morning, so he hadn't been home when the sheriff stopped to say he wanted Mr. Hale to come over to the Wright place and tell the county attorney his story there, where he could point it all out. With all Mrs. Hale's other emotions came the fear Harry wasn't dressed warm enough—they hadn't any of them realized how that north wind did bite.

"We come along this road," Hale was going on, "and as we got in sight of the house I says to Harry, 'I'm goin' to see if I can't get John Wright to take a telephone.' You see," he explained to Henderson, "unless I can get somebody to go in with me they won't come out this branch road except for a price I can't pay. I'd spoke to Wright about it before; but he put me off, saying folks talked too much anyway, and all he asked was peace and quiet—guess you know about how much he talked himself. But I thought maybe if I went to the house and talked about it before his wife, and said all the women—folks liked the telephones, and that in this lonesome stretch of road it would be a good thing—well, I said to Harry that that was what I was going to say—though I said at the same time that I didn't know as what his wife wanted made much difference to John—"

Now, there he was!—saying things he didn't need to say. Mrs. Hale tried to catch her husband's eye, but fortunately the county attorney interrupted with:

"Let's talk about that a little later, Mr. Hale. I do want to talk about that, but I'm anxious now to know just what happened when you got here."

When he began this time, it was deliberately, as if he knew it were important.

"I didn't see or hear anything. I knocked at the door. And still it was all quiet inside. I knew they must be up—it was past eight o'clock. So I knocked again, louder, and I thought I heard somebody say, 'Come in.' I wasn't sure—I'm not sure yet. But I opened the door—this door," jerking a hand toward the door by which the two women stood, "and there, in that rocker"—pointing to it—"sat Mrs. Wright."

Everyone in the kitchen looked at the rocker. It came into Mrs. Hale's mind that this chair didn't look in the least like Minnie Foster—the Minnie Foster of twenty years before. It was a dingy red, with wooden rungs up the back, and the middle rung gone; the chair sagged to one side.

"How did she—look?" the county attorney was inquiring.

"Well," said Hale, "she looked—queer?"

"How do you mean—queer?"

He took out note-book and pencil. Mrs. Hale did not like the sight of that pencil. She kept her eye on her husband, as if to keep him from saying unnecessary things that would go into the book and make trouble.

Hale spoke guardedly: "Well, as if she didn't know what she was going to do next. And kind of—done up."

"How did the seem to feel about your coming?"

"Why, I don't think she minded—one way or other. She didn't pay much attention. I said, 'Ho' do, Mrs. Wright. It's cold, ain't it?' And she said, 'Is it?'—and went on pleatin' of her apron.

"Well, I was surprised. She didn't ask me to come up to the stove, but just set there, not even lookin' at me. And so I said, 'I want to see John.'

"And then she—laughed. I guess you would call it a laugh.

"I thought of Harry and the team outside, so I said, a little sharp, 'Can I see John?' 'No,' says she—kind of dull like. 'Ain't he home?' says I. Then she looked at me. 'Yes,' says she, 'he's home.' 'Then why can't I see him?' I asked her, out of patience with her now. ''Cause he's dead,' says she, just as quiet and dull—and fell to pleatin' her apron. 'Dead?' says I, like you do when you can't take in what you've heard.

"She just nodded her head, not getting a bit excited, but rockin' back and forth.

"'Why—where is he?'" says I, not knowing *what* to say.

"She just pointed upstairs—like this"—pointing to the room above.

**READING THE
MATERIAL THEATER (CONTINUED)**

"I got up, with the idea of going up there myself. By this time I—didn't know what to do. I walked from there to here, then I says "'Why, what did he die of?'"

"'He died of a rope round his neck,' says she; and just went on pleatin' at her apron."

Hale stopped speaking, staring at the rocker. Nobody spoke; it was as if all were seeing the woman who had sat there the morning before.

"And what did you do then?" the attorney asked.

"I went out and called Harry, I though I might—need help. I got Harry in, and we went upstairs." His voice fell almost to a whisper. "There he was—lying over the—"

"I think I'd rather have you go into that upstairs," the county attorney interrupted, "where you can point it all out. Just go on now with the rest of the story."

"Well, my first thought was to get that rope off. It looked—"

He stopped; he did not say how it looked.

"But Harry, he went up to him and he said, 'No, he's dead all right, and we'd better not touch anythin'.' So we went downstairs.

"She was still sitting that same way. 'Has anybody been notified?' I asked. 'No,' says she, unconcerned.

"'Who did this, Mrs. Wright?' said Harry. He said it business-like, and she stopped pleatin' at her apron. 'I don't know,' she says. 'You don't *know?*' says Harry. 'Weren't you sleepin' in the bed with him?' 'Yes,' says she, 'but I was on the inside.' 'Somebody slipped a rope round his neck and strangled him, and you didn't wake up?' says Harry. 'I didn't wake up,' she said after him.

"We may have looked as if we didn't see how that could be, for after a minute she said, 'I sleep sound.'

"Harry was going to ask her more questions, but I said maybe that weren't our business; maybe we ought to let her tell her story first to the coroner or the sheriff. So Harry went fast as he could over to High Road—the Rivers' place, where there's a telephone."

"And what did she do when she knew you had gone for the coroner?"

"She moved from that chair to this one over here, and just sat there with her hands held together and looking down. I got a feeling that I ought to make some conversation, so I said I had come in to see if John wanted to put in a telephone; and at that she started to laugh, and then she stopped and looked at me—scared."

At sound of a moving pencil the man who was telling the story looked up.

"I dunno—maybe it wasn't scared; I wouldn't like to say it was. Soon Harry got back, and then Dr. Lloyd came, and you, Mr. Peters, and so I guess that's all I know that you don't."

He said this with relief, moved as if relaxing. The county attorney walked to the stair door.

"I guess we'll go upstairs first—then out to the barn and around there."

He paused and looked around the kitchen.

"You're convinced there was nothing important here?" he asked the sheriff. "Nothing that would—point to any motive?"

The sheriff too looked all around. "Nothing here but kitchen things," he said, with a little laugh for the insignificance of kitchen things.

The county attorney was looking at the cupboard. He opened the upper part and looked in. After a moment he drew his hand away sticky.

"Here's a nice mess," he said resentfully.

The two women had drawn nearer, and now the sheriff's wife spoke.

"Oh—her fruit," she said, looking to Mrs. Hale for understanding. "She worried about that when it turned so cold last night. She said the fire would go out and her jars might burst."

Mrs. Peters' husband broke into a laugh.

"Well, can you beat the women! Held for murder, and worrying about her preserves!"

The young attorney set his lips.

"I guess before we're through with her she may have something more serious than preserves to worry about."

"Oh, well," said Mrs. Hale's husband, with good-natured superiority, "women are used to worrying over trifles."

The two women moved a little closer together. Neither of them spoke. The county attorney seemed to remember his manners—and think of his future.

"And yet," said he, with the gallantry of a young politician, "for all their worries, what would we do without the ladies?"

The women did not speak. He went to the sink to wash his hands, turned to wipe them on the roller towel, pulled it for a cleaner place.

"Dirty towels! Not much of a housekeeper, would you say, ladies?" He kicked his foot against some dirty pans under the sink.

"There's a great deal of work to be done on a farm," said Mrs. Hale stiffly.

"To be sure. And yet"—with a little bow to her—"I know there are some Dickson County farm-houses that do not have such roller towels."

"Those towels get dirty awful quick. Men's hands aren't always as clean as they might be."

"Ah, loyal to your sex, I see," he laughed. He gave her a keen look. "But you and Mrs. Wright were neighbours. I suppose you were friends too."

Martha Hale shook her head.

"I've seen little enough of her of late years. I've not been in this house—it's more than a year."

"And why was that? You didn't like her?"

"I liked her well enough," she replied with spirit. "Farmers' wives have their hands full, Mr. Henderson. And then—" She looked around the kitchen.

"Yes?" he encouraged.

"It never seemed a very cheerful place," said she, more to herself than to him.

"No," he agreed; "I don't think anyone would call it cheerful. I shouldn't say she had the home-making instinct."

"Well, I don't know as Wright had either," she muttered.

"You mean they didn't get on very well?"

"No; I don't mean anything," she answered, with decision. "But I don't think a place would be any the cheer-fuler for John Wright's bein' in it."

"I'd like to talk to you about that a little later, Mrs. Hale." He moved towards the stair door, followed by the two men.

"I suppose anything Mrs. Peters does'll be all right?" the sheriff inquired. "She was to take in some clothes for her, you know—and a few little things. We left in such a hurry yesterday."

The county attorney looked at the two women they were leaving alone among the kitchen things.

"Yes—Mrs. Peters," he said, his glance resting on the woman who was not Mrs. Peters, the big farmer woman who stood behind the sheriff's wife. "Of course Mrs. Peters is one of us," he added in a manner of entrusting responsibility. "And keep your eye out, Mrs. Peters, for anything that might be of use. No telling; you women might come upon a clue to the motive—and that's the thing we need."

Mr. Hale rubbed his face in the fashion of a slow man getting ready for a pleasantry. "But would the women know a clue if they did come

upon it?" he said. Having delivered himself of this, he followed the others through the stair door.

The women stood motionless, listening to the footsteps, first upon the stairs, then in the room above them.

Then, as if releasing herself from something too strange, Mrs. Hale began to arrange the dirty pans under the sink, which the county attorney's disdainful push of the foot had upset.

"I'd hate to have men coming into my kitchen, snoopin' round and criticizing."

"Of course it's no more than their duty," said the sheriff's wife, in her timid manner.

"Duty's all right, but I guess that deputy sheriff that come out to make the fire might have got a little of this on." She gave the roller towel a pull. "Wish I'd thought of that sooner! Seems mean to talk about her for not having things slicked up, when she had to come away in such a hurry."

She looked around the kitchen. Certainly it was not "slicked up." Her eye was held by a bucket of sugar on a low shelf. The cover was off the wooden bucket, and beside it was a paper bag—half full.

Mrs. Hale moved towards it.

"She was putting this in there," she said to herself—slowly.

She thought of the flour in her kitchen at home—half sifted, half not sifted. She had been interrupted, and had left things half done. What had interrupted Minnie Foster? Why had that work been left half done? She made a move as if to finish it—unfinished things always bothered her, and then she saw that Mrs. Peters was watching her, and she didn't want Mrs. Peters to get that feeling she had of work begun and then—for some reason—not finished.

"It's a shame about her fruit," she said, going to the cupboard. "I wonder if it's all gone.

"Here's one that's all right," she said at last. She held it towards the light. "This is cherries, too," She

looked again. "I declare I believe that's the only one.

"She'll feel awful bad, after all her hard work in the hot weather. I remember the afternoon I put up my cherries last summer."

She put the bottle on the table, and was about to sit down in the rocker. But something kept her from sitting in that chair. She stood looking at it, seeing the woman who had sat there "pleatin' at her apron."

The thin voice of the sheriff's wife broke in upon her: "I must be getting those things from the front room closet." She opened the door into the other room, started in, stepped back. "You coming with me, Mrs. Hale?" she asked nervously. "You—you could help me get them."

They were soon back. "My!" said Mrs. Peters, dropping the things on the table and hurrying to the stove.

Mrs. Hale stood examining the clothes the woman who was being detained in town had said she wanted.

"Wright was close!" she exclaimed, holding up a shabby black skirt that bore the marks of much making over. "I think maybe that's why she kept so much to herself. I s'pose she felt she couldn't do her part; and then, you don't enjoy things when you feel shabby. She used to wear pretty clothes and be lively—when she was Minnie Foster, one of the town girls, singing in the choir. But that—oh, that was twenty years ago."

With a carefulness in which there was something tender, she folded the shabby clothes and piled them at one corner of the table. She looked up at Mrs. Peters, and there was something in the other woman's look that irritated her.

"She don't care," she said to herself. "Much difference it makes to her whether Minnie Foster had pretty clothes when she was a girl."

Then she looked again, and she wasn't so sure; in fact, she hadn't at any time been sure about Mrs. Peters.

She had that shrinking manner, and yet her eyes looked as if they could see a long way into things.

"This all you was to take in?" asked Mrs. Hale.

"No," said the sheriff's wife; "she said she wanted an apron. Funny thing to want," she ventured in her nervous way, "for there's not much to get you dirty in jail, goodness knows. But I suppose just to make her feel more natural. She said they were in the bottom drawer of this cupboard. Yes—here they are. And then her little shawl that always hung on the stair door."

She took the small grey shawl from behind the door leading upstairs.

Suddenly Mrs. Hale took a quick step towards the other woman.

"Mrs. Peters!"

"Yes, Mrs. Hale?"

"Do you think she—did it?"

Mrs. Peters looked frightened. "Oh, I don't know," she said, in a voice that seemed to shrink from the subject.

"Well, I don't think she did," affirmed Mrs. Hale. "Asking for an apron, and her little shawl. Worryin' about her fruit."

"Mr. Peters says—" Footsteps were heard in the room above; she stopped, looked up, then went on in a lowered voice: "Mr. Peters says—it looks bad for her. Mr. Henderson is awful sarcastic in a speech, and he's going to make fun of her saying she didn't wake up."

For a moment Mrs. Hale had no answer. Then, "Well, I guess John Wright didn't wake up—when they was slippin' that rope under his neck," she muttered.

"No, it's strange," breathed Mrs. Peters. "They think it was such a— funny way to kill a man."

"That's just what Mr. Hale said," said Mrs. Hale, in a resolutely natural

voice. "There was a gun in the house. He says that's what he can't understand."

"Mr. Henderson said, coming out, that what was needed for the case was a motive. Something to show anger—or sudden feeling."

"Well, I don't see any signs of anger around here," said Mrs. Hale. "I don't—"

She stopped. Her eye was caught by a dishtowel in the middle of the kitchen table. Slowly she moved towards the table. One half of it was wiped clean, the other half untidy. Her eyes made a slow, almost unwilling turn to the bucket of sugar and the half-empty bag beside it. Things begun—and not finished.

She stepped back. "Wonder how they're finding things upstairs? I hope she had it in better shape up there. Seems kind of sneaking, locking her up in town and coming out here to get her own house to turn against her!"

"But, Mrs. Hale," said the sheriff's wife, "the law is the law."

"I s'pose it is," answered Mrs. Hale shortly.

She turned to the stove, saying something about that fire not being much to brag of.

"The law is the law—and a bad stove is a bad stove. How'd you like to cook on this?" with the poker pointing to the broken lining. She opened the oven door. The thought of Minnie Foster trying to bake in that oven—and the thought of her never going over to see Minnie Foster—

She was startled by hearing Mrs. Peters say, "A person gets discouraged—and loses heart."

The sheriff's wife had looked from the stove to the sink—the pail of water which has been carried in from outside. The two women stood there silent, above them the footsteps of the men who were looking for evidence against the woman who had worked in that kitchen. That look of seeing into things, of seeing

through a thing to something else, was in the eyes of the sheriff's wife now. When Mrs. Hale next spoke to her, it was gently.

"Better loosen up your things, Mrs. Peters. We'll not feel them when we go out."

Mrs. Peters went to the back of the room to hang up the fur tippet she was wearing. "Why, she was piecing a quilt," she exclaimed, and held up a large sewing basket piled high with quilt pieces.

Mrs. Hale spread some of the blocks on the table.

"It's log-cabin pattern," she said, putting several of them together. "Pretty, isn't it?"

They were so engaged with the quilt that they did not hear the footsteps on the stairs. As the stair door opened Mrs. Hale was saying, "Do you suppose she was going to quilt it, or just knot it?"

The sheriff threw up his hands.

"They wonder whether she was going to quilt it, or just knot it!"

There was a laugh for the ways of women, a warming of hands over the stove, and then the county attorney said briskly, "Well, let's go right out to the barn and get that cleared up."

"I don't see as there's anything so strange," Mrs. Hale said resentfully, after the outside door had closed on the three men—"our taking up our time with little things while we're waiting for them to get the evidence. I don't see as it's anything to laugh about."

"Of course they've got awful important things on their minds," said the sheriff's wife apologetically.

They returned to an inspection of the blocks for the quilt. Mrs. Hale was looking at the fine, even sewing, preoccupied with thoughts of the woman who had done that sewing, when she heard the sheriff's wife say, in a startled tone, "Why, look at this one."

"The sewing," said Mrs. Peters, in a troubled way. "All the rest of them have been so nice and even—but—

this one. Why, it looks as if she didn't know what she was about!"

Their eyes met—something flashed to life, passed between them; then, as if with an effort, they seemed to pull away from each other. A moment Mrs. Hale sat there, her fingers upon those stitches so unlike the rest of the sewing. Then she had pulled a knot and drawn the threads.

"Oh, what are you doing. Mrs. Hale?" asked the sheriff's wife.

"Just pulling out a stitch or two that's not sewed very good," said Mrs. Hale mildly.

"I don't think we ought to touch things," Mrs. Peters said.

"I'll just finish up this end," answered Mrs. Hale.

She threaded a needle and started to replace bad sewing with good. Then in that thin, timid voice, she heard: "Mrs. Hale!"

"Yes, Mrs. Peters?"

"What do you suppose she was so—nervous about?"

"Oh, *I* don't know," said Mrs. Hale, as if dismissing a thing not important enough to spend much time on. "I don't know as she was—nervous. I sew awful queer sometimes when I'm just tired."

"Well, I must get these clothes wrapped. They may be through sooner than we think. I wonder where I could find a piece of paper—and string."

"In that cupboard, maybe," suggested Mrs. Hale.

One piece of the crazy sewing remained unripped. Mrs. Peters' back turned. Martha Hale scrutinized that piece, compared it with the dainty, accurate stitches of the other blocks. The difference was startling. Holding this block it was hard to remain quiet, as if the distracted thoughts of the woman who had perhaps turned to it to try and quiet herself were communicating themselves to her.

"Here's a bird-cage," Mrs. Peters said. "Did she have a bird, Mrs. Hale?"

"Why, I don't know whether she did or not." She turned to look at the cage Mrs. Peters was holding up. "I've

not been here in so long." She sighed. "There was a man round last year selling canaries cheap—but I don't know as she took one. Maybe she did. She used to sing real pretty herself."

"Seems kind of funny to think of a bird here. But she must have had one—or why would she have a cage? I wonder what happened to it."

"I suppose maybe the cat got it," suggested Mrs. Hale, resuming her sewing.

"No; she didn't have a cat. She's got that feeling some people have about cats—being afraid of them. When they brought her to our house yesterday, my cat got in the room, and she was real upset and asked me to take it out."

"My sister Bessie was like that," laughed Mrs. Hale.

The sheriff's wife did not reply. The silence made Mrs. Hale turn. Mrs. Peters was examining the bird-cage.

"Look at this door," she said slowly. "It's broke. One hinge has been pulled apart."

Mrs. Hale came nearer.

"Looks as if someone must have been—rough with it."

Again their eyes met—startled, questioning, apprehensive. For a moment neither spoke nor stirred. Then Mrs. Hale, turning away, said brusquely. "If they're going to find any evidence, I wish they'd be about it. I don't like this place."

"But I'm awful glad you came with me, Mrs. Hale." Mrs. Peters put the bird-cage on the table and sat down. "It would be lonesome for me—sitting here alone."

"Yes, it would, wouldn't it?" agreed Mrs. Hale. She had picked up the sewing, but now it dropped to her lap, and she murmured: "But I tell you what I *do* wish, Mrs. Peters. I wish I had come over sometimes when she was here. I wish—I had."

"But of course you were awful busy, Mrs. Hale. Your house—and your children."

"I could've come. I stayed away because it weren't cheerful—and that's why I ought to have come. I"—she

looked around—"I've never liked this place. Maybe because it's down in a hollow and you don't see the road. I don't know what it is, but it's a lonesome place, and always was. I wish I had come over to see Minnie Foster sometimes. I can see now—"

"Well, you mustn't reproach yourself. Somehow we just don't see how it is with other folks till—something comes up."

"Not having children makes less work," mused Mrs. Hale, "but it makes a quiet house. And Wright out to work all day—and no company when he did come in. Did you know John Wright, Mrs. Peters?"

"Not to know him. I've seen him in town. They say he was a good man."

"Yes—good," conceded John Wright's neighbour grimly. "He didn't drink, and kept his word as well as most, I guess, and paid his debts. But he was a hard man, Mrs. Peters. Just to pass the time of day with him—" She shivered. "Like a raw wind that gets to the bone." Her eye fell upon the cage on the table before her, and she added, "I should think she would've wanted a bird!"

Suddenly she leaned forward, looking intently at the cage. "But what do you s'pose went wrong with it?"

"I don't know," returned Mrs. Peters; "unless it got sick and died."

But after she said this she reached over and swung the broken door. Both women watched it.

"You didn't know—her?" Mrs. Hale asked.

"Not till they brought her yesterday," said the sheriff's wife.

"She—come to think of it, she was kind of like a bird herself. Real sweet and pretty, but kind of timid and—fluttery. How—she—did—change."

Finally, as if struck with a happy thought and relieved to get back to every-day things: "Tell you what, Mrs. Peters, why don't you take the quilt in with you? It might take up her mind."

"Why, I think that's a real nice idea, Mrs. Hale. There couldn't possibly be any objection to that, could there?

Now, just what will I take? I wonder if her patches are in here?" They turned to the sewing basket.

"Here's some red," said Mrs. Hale, bringing out a roll of cloth. Underneath this was a box. "Here, maybe her scissors are in here—and her things." She held it up. "What a pretty box! I'll warrant that was something she had a long time ago—when she was a girl."

She held it in her hand a moment; then, with a little sigh, opened it.

Instantly her hand went to her nose. "Why!"

Mrs. Peters drew nearer—then turned away.

"There's something wrapped up in this piece of silk," faltered Mrs. Hale.

"This isn't her scissors," said Mrs. Peters, in a shrinking voice.

Mrs. Hale raised the piece of silk. "Oh, Mrs. Peters!" she cried. "It's—"

Mrs. Peters bent closer.

"It's the bird," she whispered.

"But, Mrs. Peters!" cried Mrs. Hale. "*Look* at it! Its *neck*—look at its neck! It's all—other side *to*."

The sheriff's wife again bent closer.

"Somebody wrung its neck," said she, in a voice that was slow and deep.

The eyes of the two women met—this time clung together in a look of dawning comprehension, of growing horror. Mrs. Peters looked from the dead bird to the broken door of the cage. Again their eyes met. And just then there was a sound at the outside door.

Mrs. Hale slipped the box under the quilt pieces in the basket. The county attorney and sheriff came in.

"Well, ladies," said the attorney, as one turning from serious things to little pleasantries, "have you decided whether she was going to quilt it or knot it?"

"We think," said the sheriff's wife hastily, "that she was going to knot it."

"Well, that's very interesting, I'm sure." He caught sight of the cage. "Has the bird flown?"

"We think the cat got it," said Mrs. Hale in a prosaic voice.

He was walking up and down, as if thinking something out.

"Is there a cat?" he asked absently.

Mrs. Hale shot a look up at the sheriff's wife.

"Well, not *now*," said Mrs. Peters. "They're superstitious, you know; they leave."

The county attorney did not heed her. "No sign at all of anyone having come in from the outside," he said to Peters, continuing an interrupted conversation. "Their own rope. Now let's go upstairs again and go over it, piece by piece. It would have to have been someone who knew just the—"

The stair door closed behind them and their voices were lost.

The two women sat motionless, not looking at each other, but as if peering into something and at the same time holding back. When they spoke now it was as if they were afraid of what they were saying, but could not help saying it.

"She liked the bird," said Martha Hale. "She was going to bury it in that pretty box."

"When I was a girl," said Mrs. Peters, under her breath, "my kitten—there was a boy took a hatchet, and before my eyes—before I could get there—" She covered her face an instant. "If they hadn't held me back I would have"—she caught herself, and finished weakly—"hurt him."

Then they sat without speaking or moving.

"I wonder how it would seem," Mrs. Hale began, as if feeling her way over strange ground—"never to have had any children around." Her eyes made a sweep of the kitchen. "No, Wright wouldn't like the bird—a thing that sang. She used to sing. He killed that too."

Mrs. Peters moved. "Of course we don't know who killed the bird."

"I knew John Wright," was the answer.

"It was an awful thing was done in this house that night, Mrs. Hale," said the sheriff's wife. "Killing a man while he slept—slipping a thing round his neck that choked the life out of him."

Mrs. Hale's hand went to the bird-cage. "His neck. Choked the life out of him."

"We don't *know* who killed him," whispered Mrs. Peters wildly. "We don't *know*."

Mrs. Hale had not moved. "If there had been years and years of nothing, then a bird to sing to you, it would be awful—still, after the bird was still."

"I know what stillness is," whispered Mrs. Peters. "When we homesteaded in Dakota, and my first baby died—after he was two years old—and me with no other then—"

Mrs. Hale stirred. "How soon do you suppose they'll be through looking for the evidence?"

"I know what stillness is," repeated Mrs. Peters. Then she too pulled back. "The law has got to punish crime, Mrs. Hale."

"I wish you'd seen Minnie Foster when she wore a white dress with blue ribbons, and stood up there in the choir and sang."

The picture of that girl, the thought that she had lived neighbour to her for twenty years, and had let her die for lack of life, was suddenly more than the woman could bear.

"Oh, I *wish* I'd come over here once in a while!" she cried. "That was a crime! That was a crime! Who's going to punish *that*?"

"We mustn't—take on," said Mrs. Peters, with a frightened look towards the stairs.

"I might 'a' *known* she needed help! I tell you, it's *queer,* Mrs. Peters. We live close together, and we live far apart. We all go through the same things—it's all just a different kind of the same thing! If it weren't—why do you and I *know*—what we know this minute?"

Seeing the jar of fruit on the table, she reached for it. "If I was you I wouldn't *tell* her her fruit was gone! Tell her it *ain't.* Tell her it's all right—all of it. Here—take this in to prove it to her! She—she may never know whether it was broke or not."

Mrs. Peters took the bottle of fruit as if glad to take it—as if touching a familiar thing, having something to do, could keep her from something else. She looked about for something to wrap the fruit in, took a petticoat from the pile of clothes she had brought from the front room, nervously started winding that round the bottle.

"My!" she began, in a high voice, "it's a good thing the men couldn't hear us! Getting all stirred up over a little thing like a—dead canary. As if that could have anything to do with—with—My, wouldn't they *laugh?*"

There were footsteps on the stairs.

"Maybe they would," muttered Mrs. Hale—"maybe they wouldn't."

"No, Peters," said the county attorney, "it's all perfectly clear, except the reason for doing it. But you know juries when it comes to women. If there was some definite thing—something to *show.* Something to make a story about. A thing that would connect up with this clumsy way of doing it."

Mrs. Hale looked at Mrs. Peters. Mrs. Peters was looking at her. Quickly they looked away from one another. The outer door opened and Mr. Hale came in.

"I've nailed back that board we ripped off," he said.

"Much obliged, Mr. Hale," said the sheriff. "We'll be getting along now."

"I'm going to stay here awhile by myself," the county attorney suddenly announced. "You can send Frank out for me, can't you?" he asked the sheriff. "I want to go over everything. I'm not satisfied we can't do better."

Again, for one brief moment, the women's eyes met.

The sheriff came up to the table.

"Did you want to see what Mrs. Peters was going to take in?"

The county attorney picked up the apron. He laughed.

"Oh, I guess they're not very dangerous things the ladies have picked out."

Mrs. Hale's hand was on the sewing basket in which the box was concealed. She felt that she ought to take her hand off the basket. She did not seem able to. She picked up one of the quilt blocks she had piled on to cover the box. She had a fear that if he took up the basket she would snatch it from him.

But he did not take it. With another laugh he turned away, saying, "No, Mrs. Peters doesn't need supervising. For that matter, a sheriff's wife is married to the law. Ever think of it that way, Mrs. Peters?"

Mrs. Peters had turned her face away. "Not—just that way," she said.

"Married to the law!" chuckled Mrs. Peters' husband. He moved towards the door into the front room, and said to the county attorney, "I just want you to come here a minute, George. We ought to take a look at these windows."

"Oh—windows!" scoffed the county attorney.

"We'll be leaving in a second, Mr. Hale," Mr. Peters told the farmer, as he followed the county attorney into the other room.

"Can't be leavin' too soon to suit me," muttered Hale, and went out.

Again, for one final moment, the two women were alone in that kitchen.

Martha Hale sprang up, her hands tight together, looking at that other woman, with whom it rested. At first she could not see her eyes, for the sheriff's wife had not turned back since she turned away at that suggestion of being married to the law. Slowly, unwillingly, Mrs. Peters turned her head until her eyes met the eyes of the other woman. There was a moment when they held each other in a steady, burning look in which there was no evasion nor flinching. Then Martha Hale's eyes pointed the way to the basket in which was hidden the thing that would convict the third woman—that woman who was not there, and yet who had been there with them through that hour.

For a moment Mrs. Peters did not move. And then she did it. Threw back the quilt pieces, got the box, tried to put it in her hand-bag. It was too big. Desperately she opened it, started to take the bird out. But there she broke—she could not touch the bird. She stood there helpless, foolish.

There was a sound at the door. Martha Hale snatched the box from the sheriff's wife and got it in the pocket of her big coat just as the sheriff and the county attorney came back into the kitchen.

"Well, Henry," said the county attorney, facetiously, "at least we found out that she was not going to quilt it. She was going to—what is it you call it, ladies?"

Mrs. Hale's hand was against the pocket of her coat.

"We call it—knot it," was her answer.

THE END

This scene from August Wilson's *Fences* shows how Wilson's attention to the play's social environment has been translated into a detailed mise-en-scène; here, James Earl Jones plays the role of Troy Maxon.

The Angel appears above Prior Walter in Tony Kushner's *Angels in America, Part I: Millennium Approaches*.

Susan Glaspell

Susan Glaspell (1882–1948) was born in Iowa, studied at Drake University in Des Moines and at the University of Chicago, and then briefly pursued a career as a journalist. With her husband, George Cram Cook, she founded the Provincetown Playhouse and wrote many of the plays it produced: *Suppressed Desires* (1914, written with Cook), a spoof of the vogue for psychoanalysis among New York's intellectual elite; *Trifles* (1916); *Close the Book* (1917); *A Woman's Honor* (1918); and *Tickless Time* (1918, again written with Cook). After the reorganization of the Provincetown in 1921, Glaspell wrote a series of full-length, often experimental, plays: *Inheritors* (1920), *The Verge* (1921), and *Alison's House* (1930). *Alison's House,* based loosely on the life of Emily Dickinson and her family, won Glaspell the Pulitzer Prize in 1930. Glaspell then retired from playwriting and largely from the theater as well, returning briefly to serve as the director of the Mid-West Play Bureau for the Federal Theater Project.

TRIFLES

Trifles is an important play in the development of American realism. It poses a distinct contrast to Eugene O'Neill's early plays, with which it shared the Provincetown stage. O'Neill's realistic plays attempt to filter an abstract, metaphysical longing into the drab world of his down-and-out drifters and sailors. Glaspell's drama more directly examines the values and behavior of the society she brings to the stage. In *Trifles*—and in the short story "A Jury of Her Peers," which she adapted from the play the following year—Glaspell considers the relationship between truth, power, and gender. The play is a murder mystery. A local man, John Wright, has been found dead, and his wife, Minnie, is suspected of killing him. Called to investigate, County Attorney George Henderson, Sheriff Henry Peters, and neighbor Lewis Hale readily assume a masculine prerogative to discover the truth of John Wright's murder, telling their wives to remain in the kitchen out of the way. How-

The Provincetown Players' 1917 production of Susan Glaspell's *Trifles*.

ever, the truth of the crime is in fact concealed *in* the kitchen, and only the women are able to discover it. Glaspell shows the audience that the "trifles" of the women's world are the signs of a reality wholly unreadable to the men, precisely because it is a world they regard as feminine, and therefore unimportant and uninteresting. *Trifles,* that is, works to subvert our notions of reality and truth by suggesting how such ideas are constructed within a specific social order—the masculine order of modern society.

TRIFLES

A PLAY IN ONE ACT

Susan Glaspell

CHARACTERS

COUNTY ATTORNEY, *George Henderson*
SHERIFF, *Henry Peters*
LEWIS HALE, *a neighboring farmer*
MRS. PETERS

MRS. HALE

THE SETTING: *The kitchen in the now abandoned farmhouse of John Wright*

SCENE: *The kitchen in the now abandoned farmhouse of John Wright, a gloomy kitchen, and left without having been put in order—unwashed pans under the sink, a loaf of bread outside the breadbox, a dish towel on the table—other signs of incompleted work. At the rear the outer door opens and the* SHERIFF *comes in followed by the* COUNTY ATTORNEY *and* HALE. *The* SHERIFF *and* HALE *are men in middle life, the* COUNTY ATTORNEY *is a young man; all are much bundled up and go at once to the stove. They are followed by the two women—the* SHERIFF's *wife first; she is a slight wiry woman, a thin nervous face.* MRS. HALE *is larger and would ordinarily be called more comfortable looking, but she is disturbed now and looks fearfully about as she enters. The women have come in slowly, and stand close together near the door.*

COUNTY ATTORNEY: (*Rubbing his hands.*) This feels good. Come up to the fire, ladies.

MRS. PETERS: (*After taking a step forward.*) I'm not—cold.

5 SHERIFF: (*Unbuttoning his overcoat and stepping away from the stove as if to mark the beginning of official business.*) Now, Mr. Hale, before we move things about, you explain to Mr. Henderson just what you saw when you came here yesterday morning.

COUNTY ATTORNEY: By the way, has anything been moved?
10 Are things just as you left them yesterday?

SHERIFF: (*Looking about.*) It's just the same. When it dropped below zero last night I thought I'd better send Frank out this morning to make a fire for us—no use getting pneu-monia with a big case on, but I told him not to touch any-
15 thing except the stove—and you know Frank.

COUNTY ATTORNEY: Somebody should have been left here yesterday.

SHERIFF: Oh—yesterday. When I had to send Frank to Mor-ris Center for that man who went crazy—I want you to
20 know I had my hands full yesterday, I knew you could get back from Omaha by today and as long as I went over everything here myself—

COUNTY ATTORNEY: Well, Mr. Hale, tell just what happened when you came here yesterday morning.

25 HALE: Harry and I had started to town with a load of potatoes. We came along the road from my place and as I got here I said, "I'm going to see if I can't get John Wright to go in with me on a party telephone." I spoke to Wright about it once before and he put me off, saying folks talked too
30 much anyway, and all he asked was peace and quiet—I guess you know about how much he talked himself; but I thought maybe if I went to the house and talked about it before his wife, though I said to Harry that I didn't know as what his wife wanted made much difference to John—

COUNTY ATTORNEY: Let's talk about that later, Mr. Hale. I do 35
want to talk about that, but tell now just what happened when you got to the house.

HALE: I didn't hear or see anything; I knocked at the door, and still it was all quiet inside. I knew they must be up, it was past eight o'clock. So I knocked again, and I thought 40
I heard somebody say, "Come in." I wasn't sure, I'm not sure yet, but I opened the door—this door (*Indicating the door by which the two women are still standing.*) and there in that rocker—(*Pointing to it.*) sat Mrs. Wright.

(*They all look at the rocker.*)

COUNTY ATTORNEY: What—was she doing? 45

HALE: She was rockin' back and forth. She had her apron in her hand and was kind of—pleating it.

COUNTY ATTORNEY: And how did she—look?

HALE: Well, she looked queer.

COUNTY ATTORNEY: How do you mean—queer? 50

HALE: Well, as if she didn't know what she was going to do next. And kind of done up.

COUNTY ATTORNEY: How did she seem to feel about your coming?

HALE: Why, I don't think she minded—one way or other. She didn't pay much attention. I said, "How do, Mrs. Wright, 55
it's cold, ain't it?" And she said, "Is it?"—and went on kind of pleating at her apron. Well, I was surprised; she didn't ask me to come up to the stove, or to set down, but just sat there, not even looking at me, so I said, "I want to see John." And then she—laughed. I guess you would call it a 60
laugh. I thought of Harry and the team outside, so I said a little sharp: "Can't I see John?" "No," she says, kind o' dull like. "Ain't he home?" says I. "Yes," says she, "he's home." "Then why can't I see him?" I asked her, out of pa-tience. "'Cause he's dead," says she. "*Dead?*" says I. She just 65
nodded her head, not getting a bit excited, but rockin' back and forth. "Why—where is he?" says I, not knowing what to say. She just pointed upstairs—like that (*Himself pointing to the room above.*) I got up, with the idea of going up there. I walked from there to here—then I says, "Why, 70
what did he die of?" "He died of a rope round his neck," says she, and just went on pleatin' at her apron. Well, I went out and called Harry. I thought I might—need help. We went upstairs and there he was lyin'—

COUNTY ATTORNEY: I think I'd rather have you go into that 75
upstairs, where you can point it all out. Just go on now with the rest of the story.

HALE: Well, my first thought was to get that rope off. It looked . . . (*Stops, his face twitches.*) . . . but Harry, he went up to him,

80 and he said, "No, he's dead all right, and we'd better not touch anything." So we went back down stairs. She was still sitting that same way. "Has anybody been notified?" I asked. "No," says she, unconcerned. "Who did this, Mrs. Wright?" said Harry. He said it businesslike—and she

85 stopped pleatin' of her apron. "I don't know," she says. "You don't *know?*" says Harry. "No," says she. "Weren't you sleepin' in the bed with him?" says Harry. "Yes," says she, "but I was on the inside." "Somebody slipped a rope round his neck and strangled him and you didn't wake up?" says

90 Harry. "I didn't wake up," she said after him. We must 'a looked as if we didn't see how that could be, for after a minute she said, "I sleep sound." Harry was going to ask her more questions but I said maybe we ought to let her tell her story first to the coroner, or the sheriff, so Harry went fast as

95 he could to Rivers' place, where there's a telephone.

COUNTY ATTORNEY: And what did Mrs. Wright do when she knew that you had gone for the coroner?

HALE: She moved from that chair to this one over here (*Pointing to a small chair in the corner.*) and just sat there with her

100 hands held together and looking down. I got a feeling that I ought to make some conversation, so I said I had come in to see if John wanted to put in a telephone, and at that she started to laugh, and then she stopped and looked at me—scared. (*The* COUNTY ATTORNEY, *who has had his*

105 *notebook out, makes a note.*) I dunno, maybe it wasn't scared. I wouldn't like to say it was. Soon Harry got back, and then Dr. Lloyd came, and you, Mr. Peters, and so I guess that's all I know that you don't.

COUNTY ATTORNEY: (*Looking around.*) I guess we'll go up-

110 stairs first—and then out to the barn and around there. (*To the* SHERIFF.) You're convinced that there was nothing important here—nothing that would point to any motive.

SHERIFF: Nothing here but kitchen things.

(*The* COUNTY ATTORNEY *after again looking around the kitchen, opens the door of a cupboard closet. He gets up on a chair and looks on a shelf. Pulls his hand away, sticky.*)

COUNTY ATTORNEY: Here's a nice mess.

(*The women draw nearer.*)

115 MRS. PETERS: (*To the other woman.*) Oh, her fruit; it did freeze. (*To the* COUNTY ATTORNEY.) She worried about that when it turned so cold. She said the fire'd go out and her jars would break.

SHERIFF: Well, can you beat the women! Held for murder and

120 worryin' about her preserves.

COUNTY ATTORNEY: I guess before we're through she may have something more serious than preserves to worry about.

HALE: Well, women are used to worrying over trifles.

(*The two women move a little closer together.*)

COUNTY ATTORNEY: (*With the gallantry of a young politician.*)

125 And yet, for all their worries, what would we do without the ladies? (*The women do not unbend. He goes to the sink, takes a dipperful of water from the pail and pouring it into a basin, washes his hands. Starts to wipe them on the roller towel, turns it for a cleaner place.*) Dirty towels! (*Kicks his foot against*

130 *the pans under the sink.*) Not much of a housekeeper, would you say, ladies?

MRS. HALE: (*Stiffly.*) There's a great deal of work to be done on a farm.

COUNTY ATTORNEY: To be sure. And yet (*With a little bow to her.*) I know there are some Dickson county farmhouses

135 which do not have such roller towels.

(*He gives it a pull to expose its full length again.*)

MRS. HALE: Those towels get dirty awful quick. Men's hands aren't always as clean as they might be.

COUNTY ATTORNEY: Ah, loyal to your sex, I see. But you and Mrs. Wright were neighbors. I suppose you were friends,

140 too.

MRS. HALE: (*Shaking her head.*) I've not seen much of her of late years. I've not been in this house—it's more than a year.

COUNTY ATTORNEY: And why was that? You didn't like her?

MRS. HALE: I liked her all well enough. Farmers' wives have

145 their hands full, Mr. Henderson. And then—

COUNTY ATTORNEY: Yes—?

MRS. HALE: (*Looking about.*) It never seemed a very cheerful place.

COUNTY ATTORNEY: No—it's not cheerful. I shouldn't say she had the homemaking instinct.

150

MRS. HALE: Well, I don't know as Wright had, either.

COUNTY ATTORNEY: You mean that they didn't get on very well?

MRS. HALE: No, I don't mean anything. But I don't think a place'd be any cheerfuller for John Wright's being in it.

COUNTY ATTORNEY: I'd like to talk more of that a little later.

155 I want to get the lay of things upstairs now.

(*He goes to the left, where three steps lead to a stair door.*)

SHERIFF: I suppose anything Mrs. Peters does'll be all right. She was to take in some clothes for her, you know, and a few little things. We left in such a hurry yesterday.

COUNTY ATTORNEY: Yes, but I would like to see what you

160 take, Mrs. Peters, and keep an eye out for anything that might be of use to us.

MRS. PETERS: Yes, Mr. Henderson.

(*The women listen to the men's steps on the stairs, then look about the kitchen.*)

MRS. HALE: I'd hate to have men coming into my kitchen, snooping around and criticising.

165

(*She arranges the pans under sink which the* COUNTY ATTORNEY *had shoved out of place.*)

MRS. PETERS: Of course it's no more than their duty.

MRS. HALE: Duty's all right, but I guess that deputy sheriff that came out to make the fire might have got a little of this on. (*Gives the roller towel a pull.*) Wish I'd thought of that sooner. Seems mean to talk about her for not having things slicked

170 up when she had to come away in such a hurry.

MRS. PETERS: (*Who has gone to a small table in the left rear corner of the room, and lifted one end of a towel that covers a pan.*) She had bread set.

(*Stands still.*)

175 MRS. HALE: (*Eyes fixed on a loaf of bread beside the breadbox, which is on a low shelf at the other side of the room. Moves slowly toward it.*) She was going to put this in there. (*Picks up loaf, then abruptly drops it. In a manner of returning to familiar things.*) It's a shame about her fruit. I wonder if it's all gone. (*Gets
180 up on the chair and looks.*) I think there's some here that's all right, Mrs. Peters. Yes—here; (*Holding it toward the window.*) this is cherries, too. (*Looking again.*) I declare I believe that's the only one. (*Gets down, bottle in her hand. Goes to the sink and wipes it off on the outside.*) She'll feel awful bad after all
185 her hard work in the hot weather. I remember the afternoon I put up my cherries last summer.

(*She puts the bottle on the big kitchen table, center of the room. With a sigh, is about to sit down in the rocking-chair. Before she is seated realizes what chair it is; with a slow look at it, steps back. The chair which she has touched rocks back and forth.*)

MRS. PETERS: Well, I must get those things from the front room closet. (*She goes to the door at the right, but after looking into the other room, steps back.*) You coming with me,
190 Mrs. Hale? You could help me carry them.

(*They go in the other room; reappear,* MRS. PETERS *carrying a dress and skirt,* MRS. HALE *following with a pair of shoes.*)

MRS. PETERS: My, it's cold in there.

(*She puts the clothes on the big table, and hurries to the stove.*)

MRS. HALE: (*Examining the skirt.*) Wright was close. I think maybe that's why she kept so much to herself. She didn't even belong to the Ladies Aid. I suppose she felt she
195 couldn't do her part, and then you don't enjoy things when you feel shabby. She used to wear pretty clothes and be lively, when she was Minnie Foster, one of the town girls singing in the choir. But that—oh, that was thirty years ago. This all you was to take in?
200 MRS. PETERS: She said she wanted an apron. Funny thing to want, for there isn't much to get you dirty in jail, goodness knows. But I suppose just to make her feel more natural. She said they was in the top drawer in this cupboard. Yes, here. And then her little shawl that always hung be-
205 hind the door. (*Opens stair door and looks.*) Yes, here it is.

(*Quickly shuts door leading upstairs.*)

MRS. HALE: (*Abruptly moving toward her.*) Mrs. Peters?
MRS. PETERS: Yes, Mrs. Hale?
MRS. HALE: Do you think she did it?
MRS. PETERS: (*In a frightened voice.*) Oh, I don't know.
210 MRS. HALE: Well, I don't think she did. Asking for an apron and her little shawl. Worrying about her fruit.
MRS. PETERS: (*Starts to speak, glances up, where footsteps are heard in the room above. In a low voice.*) Mr. Peters says it looks bad for her. Mr. Henderson is awful sarcastic in a speech and
215 he'll make fun of her sayin' she didn't wake up.
MRS. HALE: Well, I guess John Wright didn't wake when they was slipping that rope under his neck.
MRS. PETERS: No, it's strange. It must have been done awful crafty and still. They say it was such a—funny way to kill
220 a man, rigging it all up like that.

MRS. HALE: That's just what Mr. Hale said. There was a gun in the house. He says that's what he can't understand.
MRS. PETERS: Mr. Henderson said coming out that what was needed for the case was a motive; something to show anger, or—sudden feeling. 225
MRS. HALE: (*Who is standing by the table.*) Well, I don't see any signs of anger around here. (*She puts her hand on the dish towel which lies on the table, stands looking down at table, one half of which is clean, the other half messy.*) It's wiped to here. (*Makes a move as if to finish work, then turns and looks at loaf 230 of bread outside the breadbox. Drops towel. In that voice of coming back to familiar things.*) Wonder how they are finding things upstairs. I hope she had it a little more red-up up there. You know, it seems kind of *sneaking*. Locking her up in town and then coming out here and trying to get her 235 own house to turn against her!
MRS. PETERS: But Mrs. Hale, the law is the law.
MRS. HALE: I s'pose 'tis. (*Unbuttoning her coat.*) Better loosen up your things, Mrs. Peters. You won't feel them when you go out. 240

(MRS. PETERS *takes off her fur tippet, goes to hang it on hook at back of room, stands looking at the under part of the small corner table.*)

MRS. PETERS: She was piecing a quilt.

(*She brings the large sewing basket and they look at the bright pieces.*)

MRS. HALE: It's log cabin pattern. Pretty, isn't it? I wonder if she was goin' to quilt it or just knot it?

(*Footsteps have been heard coming down the stairs. The* SHERIFF *enters followed by* HALE *and the* COUNTY ATTORNEY.)

SHERIFF: They wonder if she was going to quilt it or just knot it!

(*The men laugh; the women look abashed.*)

COUNTY ATTORNEY: (*Rubbing his hands over the stove.*) Frank's 245 fire didn't do much up there, did it? Well, let's go out to the barn and get that cleared up.

(*The men go outside.*)

MRS. HALE: (*Resentfully.*) I don't know as there's anything so strange, our takin' up our time with little things while we're waiting for them to get the evidence. (*She sits down 250 at the big table smoothing out a block with decision.*) I don't see as it's anything to laugh about.
MRS. PETERS: (*Apologetically.*) Of course they've got awful important things on their minds.

(*Pulls up a chair and joins* MRS. HALE *at the table.*)

MRS. HALE: (*Examining another block.*) Mrs. Peters, look at this 255 one. Here, this is the one she was working on, and look at that sewing! All the rest of it has been so nice and even. And look at this! It's all over the place! Why, it looks as if she didn't know what she was about!

(*After she has said this they look at each other, then start to glance back at the door. After an instant* MRS. HALE *has pulled at a knot and ripped the sewing.*)

260 MRS. PETERS: Oh, what are you doing, Mrs. Hale?

MRS. HALE: (*Mildly.*) Just pulling out a stitch or two that's not sewed very good. (*Threading a needle.*) Bad sewing always made me fidgety.

MRS. PETERS: (*Nervously.*) I don't think we ought to touch things.

265 MRS. HALE: I'll just finish up this end. (*Suddenly stopping and leaning forward.*) Mrs. Peters?

MRS. PETERS: Yes, Mrs. Hale?

MRS. HALE: What do you suppose she was so nervous about?

MRS. PETERS: Oh—I don't know. I don't know as she was

270 nervous. I sometimes sew awful queer when I'm just tired. (MRS. HALE *starts to say something, looks at* MRS. PETERS, *then goes on sewing.*) Well, I must get these things wrapped up. They may be through sooner than we think. (*Putting apron and other things together.*) I wonder where I can find a piece

275 of paper, and string.

MRS. HALE: In that cupboard, maybe.

MRS. PETERS: (*Looking in cupboard.*) Why, here's a birdcage. (*Holds it up.*) Did she have a bird, Mrs. Hale?

MRS. HALE: Why, I don't know whether she did or not—I've

280 not been here for so long. There was a man around last year selling canaries cheap, but I don't know as she took one; maybe she did. She used to sing real pretty herself.

MRS. PETERS: (*Glancing around.*) Seems funny to think of a bird here. But she must have had one, or why would she

285 have a cage? I wonder what happened to it.

MRS. HALE: I s'pose maybe the cat got it.

MRS. PETERS: No, she didn't have a cat. She's got that feeling some people have about cats—being afraid of them. My cat got in her room and she was real upset and asked me to take it out.

290 MRS. HALE: My sister Bessie was like that. Queer, ain't it?

MRS. PETERS: (*Examining the cage.*) Why, look at this door. It's broke. One hinge is pulled apart.

MRS. HALE: (*Looking too.*) Looks as if someone must have been rough with it.

295 MRS. PETERS: Why, yes.

(*She brings the cage forward and puts it on the table.*)

MRS. HALE: I wish if they're going to find any evidence they'd be about it. I don't like this place.

MRS. PETERS: But I'm awful glad you came with me, Mrs. Hale. It would be lonesome for me sitting here alone.

300 MRS. HALE: It would, wouldn't it? (*Dropping her sewing.*) But I tell you what I do wish, Mrs. Peters. I wish I had come over sometimes when *she* was here. I—(*Looking around the room.*)— wish I had.

MRS. PETERS: But of course you were awful busy, Mrs.

305 Hale— your house and your children.

MRS. HALE: I could've come. I stayed away because it weren't cheerful—and that's why I ought to have come. I—I've never liked this place. Maybe because it's down in a hollow and you don't see the road. I dunno what it is, but it's

310 a lonesome place and always was. I wish I had come over to see Minnie Foster sometimes. I can see now—

(*Shakes her head.*)

MRS. PETERS: Well you mustn't reproach yourself, Mrs. Hale. Somehow we just don't see how it is with other folks until—something comes up.

315 MRS. HALE: Not having children makes less work—but it makes a quiet house, and Wright out to work all day, and no company when he did come in. Did you know John Wright, Mrs. Peters?

MRS. PETERS: Not to know him; I've seen him in town. They

320 say he was a good man.

MRS. HALE: Yes—good; he didn't drink, and kept his word as well as most, I guess, and paid his debts. But he was a hard man, Mrs. Peters. Just to pass the time of day with him—(*Shivers.*) Like a raw wind that gets to the bone. (*Pauses, her*

325 *eye falling on the cage.*) I should think she would 'a wanted a bird. But what do you suppose went with it?

MRS. PETERS: I don't know, unless it got sick and died.

(*She reaches over and swings the broken door, swings it again. Both women watch it.*)

MRS. HALE: You weren't raised round here, were you? (MRS. PETERS *shakes her head.*) You didn't know—her?

330 MRS. PETERS: Not till they brought her yesterday.

MRS. HALE: She—come to think of it, she was kind of like a bird herself—real sweet and pretty, but kind of timid and— fluttery. How—she—did—change. (*Silence; then as if struck by a happy thought and relieved to get back to every day things.*) Tell you what, Mrs. Peters, why don't you take the

335 quilt in with you? It might take up her mind.

MRS. PETERS: Why, I think that's a real nice idea, Mrs. Hale. There couldn't possibly be any objection to it, could there? Now, just what would I take? I wonder if her patches are in here—and her things.

340

(*They look in the sewing basket.*)

MRS. HALE: Here's some red. I expect this has got sewing things in it. (*Brings out a fancy box.*) What a pretty box. Looks like something somebody would give you. Maybe her scissors are in here. (*Opens box. Suddenly puts her hand to her nose.*) Why—(MRS. PETERS *bends nearer, then turns her face*

345 *away.*) There's something wrapped up in this piece of silk.

MRS. PETERS: Why, this isn't her scissors.

MRS. HALE: (*Lifting the silk.*) Oh, Mrs. Peters—its—

(MRS. PETERS *bends closer.*)

MRS. PETERS: It's the bird.

MRS. HALE: (*Jumping up.*) But, Mrs. Peters—look at it! Its

350 neck! Look at its neck! It's all—other side *to.*

MRS. PETERS: Somebody—wrung—its—neck.

(*Their eyes meet. A look of growing comprehension, of horror. Steps are heard outside.* MRS. HALE *slips box under quilt pieces, and sinks into her chair. Enter* SHERIFF *and* COUNTY ATTORNEY. MRS. PETERS *rises.*)

COUNTY ATTORNEY: (*As one turning from serious things to little pleasantries.*) Well, ladies, have you decided whether she was going to quilt it or knot it?

355 MRS. PETERS: We think she was going to—knot it.

COUNTY ATTORNEY: Well, that's interesting, I'm sure. (*Seeing the birdcage.*) Has the bird flown?

MRS. HALE: (*Putting more quilt pieces over the box.*) We think the—cat got it.

360

COUNTY ATTORNEY: (*Preoccupied.*) Is there a cat?

(MRS. HALE *glances in a quick covert way at* MRS. PETERS.)

MRS. PETERS: Well, not now. They're superstitious, you know. They leave.

COUNTY ATTORNEY: (*To* SHERIFF PETERS, *continuing an inter-*
365 *rupted conversation.*) No sign at all of anyone having come from the outside. Their own rope. Now let's go up again and go over it piece by piece. (*They start upstairs.*) It would have to have been someone who knew just the—

(MRS. PETERS *sits down. The two women sit there not looking at one another, but as if peering into something and at the same time holding back. When they talk now it is in the manner of feeling their way over strange ground, as if afraid of what they are saying, but as if they cannot help saying it.*)

MRS. HALE: She liked the bird. She was going to bury it in
370 that pretty box.

MRS. PETERS: (*In a whisper.*) When I was a girl—my kitten—there was a boy took a hatchet, and before my eyes—and before I could get there—(*Covers her face an instant.*) If they hadn't held me back I would have—(*Catches herself,*
375 *looks upstairs where steps are heard, falters weakly.*)—hurt him.

MRS. HALE: (*With a slow look around her.*) I wonder how it would seem never to have had any children around. (*Pause.*) No, Wright wouldn't like the bird—a thing that sang. She used to sing. He killed that, too.

380 MRS. PETERS: (*Moving uneasily.*) We don't know who killed the bird.

MRS. HALE: I knew John Wright.

MRS. PETERS: It was an awful thing was done in this house that night, Mrs. Hale. Killing a man while he slept, slipping a
385 rope around his neck that choked the life out of him.

MRS. HALE: His neck. Choked the life out of him.

(*Her hand goes out and rests on the birdcage.*)

MRS. PETERS: (*With rising voice.*) We don't know who killed him. We don't know.

MRS. HALE: (*Her own feeling not interrupted.*) If there'd been
390 years and years of nothing, then a bird to sing to you, it would be awful—still, after the bird was still.

MRS. PETERS: (*Something within her speaking.*) I know what stillness is. When we homesteaded in Dakota, and my first baby died—after he was two years old, and me with no
395 other then—

MRS. HALE: (*Moving.*) How soon do you suppose they'll be through, looking for the evidence?

MRS. PETERS: I know what stillness is. (*Pulling herself back.*) The law has got to punish crime, Mrs. Hale.

400 MRS. HALE: (*Not as if answering that.*) I wish you'd seen Minnie Foster when she wore a white dress with blue ribbons and stood up there in the choir and sang. (*A look around the room.*) Oh, I *wish* I'd come over here once in a while! That was a crime! That was a crime! Who's going to punish that?

405 MRS. PETERS: (*Looking upstairs.*) We mustn't—take on.

MRS. HALE: I might have known she needed help! I know how things can be—for women. I tell you, it's queer, Mrs. Peters. We live close together and we live far apart. We all go through the same things—it's all just a different kind of the same thing. (*Brushes her eyes; noticing the bottle of fruit, reaches* 410
out for it.) If I was you I wouldn't tell her her fruit was gone. Tell her it *ain't*. Tell her it's all right. Take this in to prove it to her. She—she may never know whether it was broke or not.

MRS. PETERS: (*Takes the bottle, looks about for something to wrap it in, takes petticoat from the clothes brought from the other room,* 415
very nervously begins winding this around the bottle. In a false voice.) My, it's a good thing the men couldn't hear us. Wouldn't they just laugh! Getting all stirred up over a lit-tle thing like a—dead canary. As if that could have any-thing to do with—with—wouldn't they *laugh*! 420

(*The men are heard coming down stairs.*)

MRS. HALE: (*Under her breath.*) Maybe they would—maybe they wouldn't.

COUNTY ATTORNEY: No, Peters, it's all perfectly clear except a reason for doing it. But you know juries when it comes to women. If there was some definite thing. Something to 425
show—something to make a story about—a thing that would connect up with this strange way of doing it—

(*The women's eyes meet for an instant. Enter* HALE *from outer door.*)

HALE: Well, I've got the team around. Pretty cold out there.

COUNTY ATTORNEY: I'm going to stay here a while by myself. (*To the* SHERIFF.) You can send Frank out for me, can't you? I want 430
to go over everything. I'm not satisfied that we can't do better.

SHERIFF: Do you want to see what Mrs. Peters is going to take in?

(*The* COUNTY ATTORNEY *goes to the table, picks up the apron, laughs.*)

COUNTY ATTORNEY: Oh, I guess they're not very dangerous things the ladies have picked out. (*Moves a few things about, disturbing the quilt pieces which cover the box. Steps back.*) No, 435
Mrs. Peters doesn't need supervising. For that matter, a sheriff's wife is married to the law. Ever think of it that way, Mrs. Peters?

MRS. PETERS: Not—just that way.

SHERIFF: (*Chuckling.*) Married to the law. (*Moves toward the* 440
other room.) I just want you to come in here a minute, George. We ought to take a look at these windows.

COUNTY ATTORNEY: (*Scoffingly.*) Oh, windows!

SHERIFF: We'll be right out, Mr. Hale.

(HALE *goes outside. The* SHERIFF *follows the* COUNTY ATTORNEY *into the other room. Then* MRS. HALE *rises, hands tight together, look-ing intensely at* MRS. PETERS, *whose eyes make a slow turn, finally meeting* MRS. HALE's. *A moment* MRS. HALE *holds her, then her own eyes point the way to where the box is concealed. Suddenly* MRS. PETERS *throws back quilt pieces and tries to put the box in the bag she is wearing. It is too big. She opens box, starts to take bird out, can-not touch it, goes to pieces, stands there helpless. Sound of a knob turn-ing in the other room.* MRS. HALE *snatches the box and puts it in the pocket of her big coat. Enter* COUNTY ATTORNEY *and* SHERIFF.)

COUNTY ATTORNEY: (*Facetiously.*) Well, Henry, at least we 445
found out that she was not going to quilt it. She was go-ing to—what is it you call it, ladies?

MRS. HALE: (*Her hand against her pocket.*) We call it—knot it, Mr. Henderson.

Tennessee Williams

Like Amanda Wingfield in *The Glass Menagerie,* Tennessee Williams (1911–1983) regarded himself as a product of the Old South and its genteel, rural, and—finally—obsolete traditions. Born Thomas Lanier Williams to a traveling shoe salesman and his wife, Williams was raised in Mississippi before moving to the tenements of St. Louis. As a child, Williams contracted diphtheria, which briefly paralyzed his legs and left him frail and homebound for some time. During his convalescence, Williams read and wrote avidly and published his first story at the age of sixteen. After high school, he briefly attended the University of Missouri, but withdrew when his poor health prevented him from passing the ROTC course. He then worked for three years in a shoe factory, then tried Washington University in St. Louis, but again dropped out. He finally took his degree in playwriting from the University of Iowa in 1938, when he changed his name to "Tennessee." In the 1930s, Williams's embattled relation to the world was deepened by the "loss" of his beloved sister Rose. Rose became chronically depressed, and Williams's mother, unable to cope with her erratic and wild behavior, consented to having a lobotomy performed. Rose was left docile but inert and became the prototype of several of Williams's most memorable dramatic characters, women whose inner beauty is too delicate to be disclosed to the world. At this time Williams also recognized his own homosexuality, a recognition that deepened his sense of the threatening conformity imposed by mainstream American society.

Coming of age in the Great Depression was formative for Williams's drama, particularly the range of themes associated with his mature work: a sexual tension surging beneath the surface of the characters' lives, the collapse of a sustaining family and social order, the attraction of misfits destroyed by a world that will not accept them. Williams wrote several now-lost plays in the late 1930s, and *Battle of Angels* (1940; later revised as *Orpheus Descending* in 1957) was produced by the Theater Guild in Boston, where it failed. Williams scored a major success with his next play, *The Glass Menagerie* (1944). He continued his success with a series of important dramas: *Summer and Smoke* (1947), *A Streetcar Named Desire* (1947), *The Rose Tattoo* (1951), *Camino Real* (1953), *Cat on a Hot Tin Roof* (1955), *Sweet Bird of Youth* (1959), and *Night of the Iguana* (1961). In his later years, Williams's drama became increasingly gothic and sensational, and his personal life suffered as well; Williams became an alcoholic and was institutionalized on several occasions. He continued to write plays to the end of his life, developing his characteristic strengths: a feel for the nuances of character, and a flair for dramatizing the victims of an unfeeling world.

THE GLASS MENAGERIE

First performed in 1944, *The Glass Menagerie* looks back to the 1930s. Its characters are reminiscent of Williams and his family, and their grinding poverty recalls the depression-era plays of Elmer Rice and Clifford Odets. In many ways, *The Glass Menagerie* is a play in the realistic tradition. Laura's menagerie recalls how Ibsen and Chekhov used stage objects (Nora's Christmas tree in *A Doll House,* the cherry orchard in Chekhov's play) to evoke and symbolize the characters' motives and sensibilities. However, Williams also uses the device of the "memory play" to disrupt the linearity of realistic drama. Tom constructs the scene and the characters for the audience, and slide projections of phrases and images often illustrate the action as it takes place. These devices lend *The Glass Menagerie* the flavor of symbolist theater. Moreover, Tom's anticipation of the Spanish Civil War and World War II sets the play in a larger social and political context that looms forebodingly over the fragile and self-absorbed characters. Amanda and Laura seem doomed never to escape the drab apartment, and even Tom, wandering the world, finally cannot escape it either. Deeply personal (Williams's given name was Tom), *The Glass Menagerie* also provides a kind of study for

Tom, Laura, Jim, and Amanda in Tennessee Williams's *The Glass Menagerie* at the Williamstown Theatre Festival.

Williams's later plays, for it includes a typical panoply of Williams's characters: the blunt, sexually aggressive, emotionally stunted Jim; Amanda, the faded Southern belle; Laura, more crippled emotionally than physically; and Tom, who falls in love with long distance yet never succeeds in escaping his past or in finding his future.

Production Notes

Being a "memory play," *The Glass Menagerie* can be presented with unusual freedom of convention. Because of its considerably delicate or tenuous material, atmospheric touches and subtleties of direction play a particularly important part. Expressionism and all other unconventional techniques in drama have only one valid aim, and that is a closer approach to truth. When a play employs unconventional techniques, it is not, or certainly shouldn't be, trying to escape its responsibility of dealing with reality, or interpreting experience, but is actually or should be attempting to find a closer approach, a more penetrating and vivid expression of things as they are. The straight realistic play with its genuine Frigidaire and authentic ice-cubes, its characters who speak exactly as its audience speaks, corresponds to the academic landscape and has the same virtue of a photographic likeness. Everyone should know nowadays the unimportance of the photographic in art: that truth, life, or reality is an organic thing which the poetic imagination can represent or suggest, in essence, only through transformation, through changing into other forms than those which were merely present in appearance.

These remarks are not meant as a preface only to this particular play. They have to do with a conception of a new, plastic theatre which must take the place of the exhausted theatre of realistic conventions if the theatre is to resume vitality as a part of our culture.

THE SCREEN DEVICE

There is *only one important difference between the original and the acting version of the play* and that is the *omission* in the latter of the device that I tentatively included in my *original* script. This device was the use of a screen on which were projected magic-lantern slides bearing images or titles. I do not regret the omission of this device from the original Broadway production. The extraordinary power of Miss Taylor's performance made it suitable to have the utmost simplicity in the physical production. But I think it may be interesting to some readers to see how this device was conceived. So I am putting it into the published manuscript. These images and legends, projected from behind, were cast on a section of wall between the front-room and dining-room areas, which should be indistinguishable from the rest when not in use.

The purpose of this will probably be apparent. It is to give accent to certain values in each scene. Each scene contains a particular point (or several) which is structurally the most important. In an episodic play, such as this, the basic structure or narrative line may be obscured from the audience; the effect may seem fragmentary rather than architectural. This may not be the fault of the play so much as a lack of attention in the audience. The legend or image upon the screen will strengthen the effect of what is merely allusion in the writing and allow the primary point to be made more simply and lightly than if the entire responsibility were on the spoken lines. Aside from this structural value, I think the screen will have a definite emotional appeal, less definable but just as important. An imaginative producer or director may invent many other uses for this device than those indicated in the present script. In fact the possibilities of the device seem much larger to me than the instance of this play can possibly utilize.

THE MUSIC

Another extra-literary accent in this play is provided by the use of music. A single recurring tune, "The Glass Menagerie," is used to give emotional emphasis to suitable passages. This tune is like circus music, not when you are on the grounds or in the immediate vicinity of the parade, but when you are at some distance and very likely thinking of something else. It seems under those circumstances to continue almost interminably and it weaves in and out of your preoccupied consciousness; then it is the lightest, most delicate music in the world and perhaps the saddest. It expresses the surface vivacity of life with the underlying strain of immutable and inexpressible sorrow. When you look at a piece of delicately spun glass you think of two things: how beautiful it is and how easily it can be broken. Both of those ideas should be woven into the recurring tune, which dips in and out of the play as if it were carried on a wind that changes. It serves as a thread of connection and allusion between the narrator with his separate point in time and space and the subject of his story. Between each episode it returns as reference to the emotion, nostalgia, which is the first condition of the play. It is primarily Laura's music and therefore comes out most clearly when the play focuses upon her and the lovely fragility of glass which is her image.

THE LIGHTING

The lighting in the play is not realistic. In keeping with the atmosphere of memory, the stage is dim. Shafts of light are focused on selected areas or actors, sometimes in contradistinction to what is the apparent center. For instance, in the quarrel scene between Tom and Amanda, in which Laura has no active part, the clearest pool of light is on her figure. This is also true of the supper scene, when her silent figure on the sofa should remain the visual center. The light upon Laura should be distinct from the others, having a peculiar pristine clarity such as light used in early religious portraits of female saints or madonnas. A certain correspondence to light in religious paintings, such as El Greco's, where the figures are radiant in atmosphere that is relatively dusky, could be effectively used throughout the play. (It will also permit a more effective use of the screen.) A free, imaginative use of light can be of enormous value in giving a mobile, plastic quality to plays of a more or less static nature.

Tennessee Williams

THE GLASS MENAGERIE

Tennessee Williams

CHARACTERS

AMANDA WINGFIELD (*the mother*), *a little woman of great but confused vitality clinging frantically to another time and place. Her characterization must be carefully created, not copied from type. She is not paranoiac, but her life is paranoia. There is much to admire in Amanda, and as much to love and pity as there is to laugh at. Certainly she has endurance and a kind of heroism, and though her foolishness makes her unwittingly cruel at times, there is tenderness in her slight person.*

LAURA WINGFIELD (*her daughter*), *Amanda, having failed to establish contact with reality, continues to live vitally in her illusions, but Laura's situation is even graver. A childhood illness has left her crippled, one leg slightly shorter than the other, and held in a brace. This defect need not be more than suggested on the stage. Stemming from this, Laura's separation increases till she is like a piece of her own glass collection, too exquisitely fragile to move from the shelf.*

TOM WINGFIELD (*her son*), *and the narrator of the play. A poet with a job in a warehouse. His nature is not remorseless, but to escape from a trap he has to act without pity.*

JIM O'CONNOR (*the gentleman caller*), *a nice, ordinary, young man.*

SCENE: *An Alley in St. Louis*

Part I   Preparation for a Gentleman Caller.

Part II The Gentlemen calls.

TIME: *Now and the Past*

SCENE ONE

The Wingfield apartment is in the rear of the building, one of those vast hive-like conglomerations of the cellular living-units that flower as warty growths in overcrowded urban centers of lower middle-class population and are symptomatic of the impulse of this largest and fundamentally enslaved section of American society to avoid fluidity and differentiation and to exist and function as one interfused mass of automatism.

The apartment faces an alley and is entered by a fire escape, a structure whose name is a touch of accidental poetic truth, for all of these huge buildings are always burning with the slow and implacable fires of human desperation. The fire escape is part of what we see—that is, the landing of it and steps descending from it.

The scene is memory and is therefore nonrealistic. Memory takes a lot of poetic license. It omits some details; others are exaggerated, according to the emotional value of the articles it touches, for memory is seated predominantly in the heart. The interior is therefore rather dim and poetic.

At the rise of the curtain, the audience is faced with the dark, grim rear wall of the Wingfield tenement. This building is flanked on both sides by dark, narrow alleys which run into murky canyons of tangled clotheslines, garbage cans, and the sinister latticework of neighboring fire escapes. It is up and down these side alleys that exterior entrances and exits are made during the play. At the end of TOM's opening commentary, the dark tenement wall slowly becomes transparent and reveals the interior of the ground-floor Wingfield apartment.

Nearest the audience is the living room, which also serves as a sleeping room for LAURA, the sofa unfolding to make her bed. Just beyond, separated from the living room by a wide arch or second proscenium with transparent faded portieres (or second curtain), is the dining room. In an old-fashioned whatnot in the living room are seen scores of transparent glass animals. A blown-up photograph of the father hangs on the wall of the living room, to the left of the archway. It is the face of a very handsome young man in a doughboy's First World War cap. He is gallantly smiling, ineluctably smiling, as if to say "I will be smiling forever."

Also hanging on the wall, near the photograph, are a typewriter keyboard chart and a Gregg shorthand diagram. An upright typewriter on a small table stands beneath the charts.

The audience hears and sees the opening scene in the dining room through both the transparent fourth wall of the building and the transparent gauze portieres of the dining-room arch. It is during this revealing scene that the fourth wall slowly ascends, out of sight. This transparent exterior wall is not brought down again until the very end of the play, during TOM's final speech.

The narrator is an undisguised convention of the play. He takes whatever license with dramatic convention is convenient to his purposes.

TOM *enters, dressed as a merchant sailor, and strolls across to the fire escape. There he stops and lights a cigarette. He addresses the audience.*

TOM: Yes, I have tricks in my pocket, I have things up my sleeve. But I am the opposite of a stage magician. He gives you illusion that has the appearance of truth. I give you truth in the pleasant disguise of illusion.

To begin with, I turn back time. I reverse it to that 5 quaint period, the thirties, when the huge middle class of America was matriculating in a school for the blind. Their eyes had failed them, or they had failed their eyes, and so they were having their fingers pressed forcibly down on the fiery Braille alphabet of a dissolving economy. 10

In Spain there was revolution. Here there was only shouting and confusion. In Spain there was Guernica. Here there were disturbances of labor, sometimes pretty violent, in otherwise peaceful cities such as Chicago, Cleveland, Saint Louis . . . This is the social background of the play. 15

(*Music begins to play.*)

The play is memory. Being a memory play, it is dimly lighted, it is sentimental, it is not realistic. In memory everything seems to happen to music. That explains the fiddle in the wings.

I am the narrator of the play, and also a character in it. 20 The other characters are my mother, Amanda, my sister, Laura, and a gentleman caller who appears in the final

scenes. He is the most realistic character in the play, being an
emissary from a world of reality that we were somehow set
25 apart from. But since I have a poet's weakness for symbols, I
am using this character also as a symbol; he is the long-
delayed but always expected something that we live for.

There is a fifth character in the play who doesn't appear except in this larger-than-life-size photograph over
30 the mantel. This is our father who left us a long time ago.
He was a telephone man who fell in love with long dis-
tances; he gave up his job with the telephone company
and skipped the light fantastic out of town . . .

The last we heard of him was a picture postcard from
35 Mazatlan, on the Pacific coast of Mexico, containing a
message of two words: "Hello—Goodbye!" and no address.

I think the rest of the play will explain itself. . . .

(AMANDA's voice becomes audible through the portieres.)

(Legend on screen: "Ou sont les neiges.")

(TOM divides the portieres and enters the dining room. AMANDA and
LAURA are seated at a drop-leaf table. Eating is indicated by gestures
without food or utensils. AMANDA faces the audience. TOM and
LAURA are seated in profile. The interior has lit up softly and
through the scrim we see AMANDA and LAURA seated at the table.)

AMANDA: (Calling.) Tom?
TOM: Yes, Mother.
40 AMANDA: We can't say grace until you come to the table!
TOM: Coming, Mother. (He bows slightly and withdraws, reappearing a few moments later in his place at the table.)
AMANDA: (To her son.) Honey, don't push with your fingers. If
you have to push with something, the thing to push with
45 is a crust of bread. And chew—chew! Animals have se-
cretions in their stomachs which enable them to digest
food without mastication, but human beings are supposed
to chew their food before they swallow it down. Eat food
leisurely, son, and really enjoy it. A well-cooked meal has
50 lots of delicate flavors that have to be held in the mouth
for appreciation. So chew your food and give your salivary
glands a chance to function!

(TOM deliberately lays his imaginary fork down and pushes his chair
back from the table.)

TOM: I haven't enjoyed one bite of this dinner because of your
constant directions on how to eat it. It's you that make me
55 rush through meals with your hawklike attention to every
bite I take. Sickening—spoils my appetite—all this discussion of—animals' secretion—salivary glands—mastication!
AMANDA: (Lightly.) Temperament like a Metropolitan star!

(TOM rises and walks toward the living room.)

You're not excused from the table.
60 TOM: I'm getting a cigarette.
AMANDA: You smoke too much.

(LAURA rises.)

LAURA: I'll bring in the blanc mange.

(TOM remains standing with his cigarette by the portieres.)

AMANDA: (Rising.) No, sister, no, sister—you be the lady this
time and I'll be the darky.
LAURA: I'm already up. 65
AMANDA: Resume your seat, little sister—I want you to stay
fresh and pretty—for gentlemen callers!
LAURA: (Sitting down.) I'm not expecting any gentlemen callers.
AMANDA: (Crossing out to the kitchenette, airily.) Sometimes
they come when they are least expected! Why, I remem- 70
ber one Sunday afternoon in Blue Mountain—

(She enters the kitchenette.)

TOM: I know what's coming!
LAURA: Yes. But let her tell it.
TOM: Again?
LAURA: She loves to tell it. 75

(AMANDA returns with a bowl of dessert.)

AMANDA: One Sunday afternoon in Blue Mountain—your
mother received—seventeen!—gentlemen callers! Why,
sometimes there weren't chairs enough to accommodate
them all. We had to send the nigger over to bring in folding chairs from the parish house. 80
TOM: (Remaining at the portieres.) How did you entertain those
gentlemen callers?
AMANDA: I understood the art of conversation!
TOM: I bet you could talk.
AMANDA: Girls in those days knew how to talk, I can tell you. 85
TOM: Yes?

(Image on screen: AMANDA as a girl on a porch, greeting callers.)

AMANDA: They knew how to entertain their gentlemen
callers. It wasn't enough for a girl to be possessed of a
pretty face and a graceful figure—although I wasn't
slighted in either respect. She also needed to have a nim- 90
ble wit and a tongue to meet all occasions.
TOM: What did you talk about?
AMANDA: Things of importance going on in the world!
Never anything coarse or common or vulgar.

(She addresses TOM as though he were seated in the vacant chair at
the table though he remains by the portieres. He plays this scene as
though reading from a script.)

My callers were gentlemen—all! Among my callers were 95
some of the most prominent young planters of the Mississippi Delta—planters and sons of planters!

(TOM motions for music and a spot of light on AMANDA. Her eyes
lift, her face glows, her voice becomes rich and elegiac.)

(Screen legend: "Ou sont les neiges d'antan?")

There was young Champ Laughlin who later became
vice president of the Delta Planters Bank. Hadley Steven-
son who was drowned in Moon Lake and left his widow 100
one hundred and fifty thousand in Government bonds.
There were the Cutrere brothers, Wesley and Bates. Bates
was one of my bright particular beaux! He got in a quarrel with that wild Wainwright boy. They shot it out on the
floor of Moon Lake Casino. Bates was shot through the 105

stomach. Died in the ambulance on his way to Memphis. His widow was also well provided-for, came into eight or ten thousand acres, that's all. She married him on the rebound—never loved her—carried my picture on him
110 the night he died! And there was that boy that every girl in the Delta had set her cap for! That beautiful, brilliant young Fitzhugh boy from Greene County!

TOM: What did he leave his widow?

AMANDA: He never married! Gracious, you talk as though all
115 of my old admirers had turned up their toes to the daisies!

TOM: Isn't this the first you've mentioned that still survives?

AMANDA: That Fitzhugh boy went North and made a fortune—came to be known as the Wolf of Wall Street!
He had the Midas touch, whatever he touched turned to
120 gold! And I could have been Mrs. Duncan J. Fitzhugh, mind you! But—I picked your *father!*

LAURA: (*Rising.*) Mother, let me clear the table.

AMANDA: No, dear, you go in front and study your typewriter chart. Or practice your shorthand a little. Stay fresh and
125 pretty!—It's almost time for our gentlemen callers to start arriving. (*She flounces girlishly toward the kitchenette.*) How many do you suppose we're going to entertain this afternoon?

(TOM *throws down the paper and jumps up with a groan.*)

LAURA: (*Alone in the dining room.*) I don't believe we're going to receive any, Mother.

130 AMANDA: (*Reappearing, airily.*) What? No one—not one? You must be joking!

(LAURA *nervously echoes her laugh. She slips in a fugitive manner through the half-open portieres and draws them gently behind her. A shaft of very clear light is thrown on her face against the faded tapestry of the curtains. Faintly the music of "The Glass Menagerie" is heard as she continues, lightly.*)

Not one gentleman caller? It can't be true! There must be a flood, there must have been a tornado!

LAURA: It isn't a flood, it's not a tornado, Mother. I'm just not
135 popular like you were in Blue Mountain. . . .

(TOM *utters another groan.* LAURA *glances at him with a faint, apologetic smile. Her voice catches a little.*)

Mother's afraid I'm going to be an old maid.

(*The scene dims out with the "Glass Menagerie" music.*)

SCENE TWO

On the dark stage the screen is lighted with the image of blue roses. Gradually LAURA's *figure becomes apparent and the screen goes out. The music subsides.*

LAURA *is seated in the delicate ivory chair at the small claw-foot table. She wears a dress of soft violet material for a kimono—her hair is tied back from her forehead with a ribbon. She is washing and polishing her collection of glass.* AMANDA *appears on the fire escape steps. At the sound of her ascent,* LAURA *catches her breath, thrusts the bowl of ornaments away, and seats herself stiffly before the diagram of the typewriter keyboard as though it held her spellbound. Something has happened to* AMANDA. *It is written in her face as she climbs to the landing: a look that is grim and hopeless and a little*

absurd. She has on one of those cheap or imitation velvety-looking cloth coats with imitation fur collar. Her hat is five or six years old, one of those dreadful cloche hats that were worn in the late Twenties, and she is clutching an enormous black patent-leather pocketbook with nickel clasps and initials. This is her full-dress outfit, the one she usually wears to the D.A.R. Before entering she looks through the door. She purses her lips, opens her eyes very wide, rolls them upward and shakes her head. Then she slowly lets herself in the door. Seeing her mother's expression LAURA *touches her lips with a nervous gesture.*

LAURA: Hello, Mother, I was—(*She makes a nervous gesture toward the chart on the wall.* AMANDA *leans against the shut door and stares at* LAURA *with a martyred look.*)

AMANDA: Deception? Deception? (*She slowly removes her hat and gloves, continuing the sweet suffering stare. She lets the hat* 5 *and gloves fall on the floor—a bit of acting.*)

LAURA: (*Shakily.*) How was the D.A.R. meeting?

(AMANDA *slowly opens her purse and removes a dainty white handkerchief which she shakes out delicately and delicately touches to her lips and nostrils.*)

Didn't you go to the D.A.R. meeting, Mother?

AMANDA: (*Faintly, almost inaudibly.*) —No.—No. (*Then more forcibly.*) I did not have the strength—to go to the D.A.R. 10 In fact, I did not have the courage! I wanted to find a hole in the ground and hide myself in it forever! (*She crosses slowly to the wall and removes the diagram of the typewriter keyboard. She holds it in front of her for a second, staring at it sweetly and sorrowfully—then bites her lips and tears it into two pieces.*) 15

LAURA: (*Faintly.*) Why did you do that, Mother?

(AMANDA *repeats the same procedure with the chart of the Gregg Alphabet.*)

Why are you—

AMANDA: Why? Why? How old are you, Laura?

LAURA: Mother, you know my age.

AMANDA: I thought that you were an adult; it seems that I was 20 mistaken. (*She crosses slowly to the sofa and sinks down and stares at* LAURA.)

LAURA: Please don't stare at me, Mother.

(AMANDA *closes her eyes and lowers her head. There is a ten-second pause.*)

AMANDA: What are we going to do, what is going to become of us, what is the future? 25

(*There is another pause.*)

LAURA: Has something happened, Mother?

(AMANDA *draws a long breath, takes out the handkerchief again, goes through the dabbing process.*)

Mother, has—something happened?

AMANDA: I'll be all right in a minute, I'm just bewildered— (*She hesitates.*)—by life. . . .

LAURA: Mother, I wish that you would tell me what's happened! 30

AMANDA: As you know, I was supposed to be inducted into my office at the D.A.R. this afternoon.

(*Screen image:* A swarm of typewriters.)

But I stopped off at Rubicam's Business College to speak to your teachers about your having a cold and ask them what progress they thought you were making down there.
35 LAURA: Oh . . . .
AMANDA: I went to the typing instructor and introduced myself as your mother. She didn't know who you were. "Wingfield," she said, "We don't have any such student
40 enrolled at the school!"
I assured her she did, that you had been going to classes since early in January.
"I wonder," she said, "If you could be talking about that terribly shy little girl who dropped out of school af-
45 ter only a few days' attendance?"
"No," I said, "Laura, my daughter, has been going to school every day for the past six weeks!"
"Excuse me," she said. She took the attendance book out and there was your name, unmistakably printed, and
50 all the dates you were absent until they decided that you had dropped out of school.
I still said, "No, there must have been some mistake! There must have been some mix-up in the records!"
And she said, "No—I remember her perfectly now.
55 Her hands shook so that she couldn't hit the right keys! The first time we gave a speed test, she broke down completely—was sick at the stomach and almost had to be carried into the wash room! After that morning she never showed up any more. We phoned the house but never got
60 any answer"—While I was working at Famous-Barr, I suppose, demonstrating those—

(*She indicates a brassiere with her hands.*)

Oh! I felt so weak I could barely keep on my feet! I had to sit down while they got me a glass of water! Fifty dollars' tuition, all of our plans—my hopes and ambitions for you—
65 just gone up the spout, just gone up the spout like that.

(LAURA *draws a long breath and gets awkwardly to her feet. She crosses to the Victrola and winds it up.*)

What are you doing?
LAURA: Oh! (*She releases the handle and returns to her seat.*)
AMANDA: Laura, where have you been going when you've gone out pretending that you were going to business college?
70 LAURA: I've just been going out walking.
AMANDA: That's not true.
LAURA: It is. I just went walking.
AMANDA: Walking? Walking? In winter? Deliberately courting pneumonia in that light coat? Where did you walk to, Laura?
75 LAURA: All sorts of places—mostly in the park.
AMANDA: Even after you'd started catching that cold?
LAURA: It was the lesser of two evils, Mother.

(*Screen image:* Winter scene in a park.)

I couldn't go back there. I—threw up—on the floor!
AMANDA: From half past seven till after five every day you
80 mean to tell me you walked around in the park, because you wanted to make me think that you were still going to Rubicam's Business College?

LAURA: It wasn't as bad as it sounds. I went inside places to get warmed up.
AMANDA: Inside where?   85
LAURA: I went in the art museum and the bird houses at the Zoo. I visited the penguins every day! Sometimes I did without lunch and went to the movies. Lately I've been spending most of my afternoons in the Jewel Box, that big glass house where they raise the tropical flowers.   90
AMANDA: You did all this to deceive me, just for deception? (LAURA *looks down.*) Why?
LAURA: Mother, when you're disappointed, you get that awful suffering look on your face, like the picture of Jesus' mother in the museum!   95
AMANDA: Hush!
LAURA: I couldn't face it.

(*There is a pause. A whisper of strings is heard. Legend on screen:* "The Crust of Humility.")

AMANDA: (*Hopelessly fingering the huge pocketbook.*) So what are we going to do the rest of our lives? Stay home and watch the parades go by? Amuse ourselves with the glass   100
menagerie, darling? Eternally play those worn-out phonograph records your father left as a painful reminder of him? We won't have a business career—we've given that up because it gave us nervous indigestion! (*She laughs wearily.*) What is there left but dependency all our lives? I know so 105
well what becomes of unmarried women who aren't prepared to occupy a position. I've seen such pitiful cases in the South—barely tolerated spinsters living upon the grudging patronage of sister's husband or brother's wife!—stuck away in some little mousetrap of a room—encour- 110
aged by one in-law to visit another—little birdlike women without any nest—eating the crust of humility all their life!
Is that the future that we've mapped out for ourselves? I swear it's the only alternative I can think of! (*She pauses.*) It isn't a very pleasant alternative, is it? (*She pauses again.*) 115
Of course—some girls *do marry.*

(LAURA *twists her hands nervously.*)

Haven't you ever liked some boy?
LAURA: Yes. I liked one once. (*She rises.*) I came across his picture a while ago.
AMANDA: (*With some interest.*) He gave you his picture?   120
LAURA: No, it's in the yearbook.
AMANDA: (*Disappointed.*) Oh—a high school boy.

(*Screen image:* JIM as the high school hero bearing a silver cup.)

LAURA: Yes. His name was Jim. (*She lifts the heavy annual from the claw-foot table.*) Here he is in *The Pirates of Penzance.*
AMANDA: (*Absently.*) The what?   125
LAURA: The operetta the senior class put on. He had a wonderful voice and we sat across the aisle from each other Mondays, Wednesdays and Fridays in the Aud. Here he is with the silver cup for debating! See his grin?
AMANDA: (*Absently.*) He must have had a jolly disposition.   130
LAURA: He used to call me—Blue Roses.

(*Screen image:* Blue roses.)

AMANDA: Why did he call you such a name as that?

LAURA: When I had that attack of pleurosis—he asked me
what was the matter when I came back. I said pleurosis—
135 he thought that I said Blue Roses! So that's what he always
called me after that. Whenever he saw me, he'd holler,
"Hello, Blue Roses!" I didn't care for the girl that he went
out with. Emily Meisenbach. Emily was the best-dressed
girl at Soldan. She never struck me, though, as being sin-
140 cere . . . It says in the Personal Section—they're engaged.
That's—six years ago! They must be married by now.

AMANDA: Girls that aren't cut out for business careers usually
wind up married to some nice man. (*She gets up with a
spark of revival.*) Sister, that's what you'll do!

(*LAURA utters a startled, doubtful laugh. She reaches quickly for a
piece of glass.*)

145 LAURA: But, Mother—

AMANDA: Yes? (*She goes over to the photograph.*)

LAURA: (*In a tone of frightened apology.*) I'm—crippled!

AMANDA: Nonsense! Laura, I've told you never, never to use
that word. Why, you're not crippled, you just have a little
150 defect—hardly noticeable, even! When people have some
slight disadvantage like that, they cultivate other things to
make up for it—develop charm—and vivacity—and—
charm! That's all you have to do! (*She turns again to the photograph.*) One thing your father had *plenty of—was charm!*

(*The scene fades out with music.*)

SCENE THREE

Legend on screen: "After the fiasco—"

TOM *speaks from the fire escape landing.*

TOM: After the fiasco at Rubicam's Business College, the idea
of getting a gentleman caller for Laura began to play a
more and more important part in Mother's calculations. It
became an obsession. Like some archetype of the univer-
5 sal unconscious, the image of the gentleman caller
haunted our small apartment. . . .

(*Screen image:* A young man at the door of a house with flowers.)

An evening at home rarely passed without some allusion to this image, this specter, this hope . . . Even when he
wasn't mentioned, his presence hung in Mother's preoccu-
10 pied look and in my sister's frightened, apologetic manner—hung like a sentence passed upon the Wingfields!
Mother was a woman of action as well as words. She
began to take logical steps in the planned direction. Late
that winter and in the early spring—realizing that extra
15 money would be needed to properly feather the nest and
plume the bird—she conducted a vigorous campaign on
the telephone, roping in subscribers to one of those magazines for matrons called *The Homemaker's Companion,* the
type of journal that features the serialized sublimations of
20 ladies of letters who think in terms of delicate cuplike
breasts, slim, tapering waists, rich, creamy thighs, eyes like
wood smoke in autumn, fingers that soothe and caress like
strains of music, bodies as powerful as Etruscan sculpture.

(*Screen image:* The cover of a glamor magazine.)

(AMANDA *enters with the telephone on a long extension cord. She is
spotlighted in the dim stage.*)

AMANDA: Ida Scott? This is Amanda Wingfield! We missed
you at the D.A.R. last Monday! I said to myself: She's 25
probably suffering with that sinus condition! How is that
sinus condition?
      Horrors! Heaven have mercy!—You're a Christian
martyr, yes, that's what you are, a Christian martyr!
      Well, I just now happened to notice that your subscrip- 30
tion to the *Companion's* about to expire! Yes, it expires with
the next issue, honey!—just when that wonderful new serial
by Bessie Mae Hopper is getting off to such an exciting start.
Oh, honey, it's something that you can't miss! You remember
how *Gone with the Wind* took everybody by storm? You sim- 35
ply couldn't go out if you hadn't read it. All everybody *talked*
was Scarlett O'Hara. Well, this is a book that critics already
compare to *Gone with the Wind.* It's the *Gone with the Wind* of
the post–World War generation!—What?—Burning?—
Oh, honey, don't let them burn, go take a look in the oven 40
and I'll hold the wire! Heavens—I think she's hung up!

(*The scene dims out.*)

(*Legend on screen:* "You think I'm in love with Continental
Shoemakers?")

(*Before the lights come up again, the violent voices of* TOM *and*
AMANDA *are heard. They are quarreling behind the portieres. In
front of them stands* LAURA *with clenched hands and panicky expression. A clear pool of light is on her figure throughout this scene.*)

TOM: What in Christ's name am I—

AMANDA: (*Shrilly.*) Don't you use that—

TOM: —supposed to do!

AMANDA: —expression! Not in my—   45

TOM: Ohhh!

AMANDA: —presence! Have you gone out of your senses?

TOM: I have, that's true, *driven* out!

AMANDA: What is the matter with you, you—big—big—
IDIOT!   50

TOM: Look!—I've got *no thing,* no single thing—

AMANDA: Lower your voice!

TOM: —in my life here that I can call my OWN! Everything is—

AMANDA: Stop that shouting!

TOM: Yesterday you confiscated my books! You had the nerve 55
to—

AMANDA: I took that horrible novel back to the library—yes!
That hideous book by that insane Mr. Lawrence.

(TOM *laughs wildly.*)

I cannot control the output of diseased minds or people
who cater to them—   60

(TOM *laughs still more wildly.*)

BUT I WON'T ALLOW SUCH FILTH BROUGHT INTO MY
HOUSE! No, no, no, no, no!

TOM: House, house! Who pays rent on it, who makes a slave
of himself to—

65 AMANDA: (*Fairly screeching.*) Don't you DARE to—
TOM: No, no, I mustn't say things! *I've* got to just—
AMANDA: Let me tell you—
TOM: I don't want to hear any more!

(*He tears the portieres open. The dining-room area is lit with a turgid smoky red glow. Now we see* AMANDA; *her hair is in metal curlers and she is wearing a very old bathrobe, much too large for her slight figure, a relic of the faithless Mr. Wingfield. The upright typewriter now stands on the drop-leaf table, along with a wild disarray of manuscripts. The quarrel was probably precipitated by* AMANDA's *interruption of* TOM's *creative labor. A chair lies overthrown on the floor. Their gesticulating shadows are cast on the ceiling by the fiery glow.*)

AMANDA: You *will* hear more, you—
70 TOM: No, I won't hear more, I'm going out!
AMANDA: You come right back in—
TOM: Out, out, out! Because I'm—
AMANDA: Come back here, Tom Wingfield! I'm not through talking to you!
75 TOM: Oh, go—
LAURA: (*Desperately.*)—Tom!
AMANDA: You're going to listen, and no more insolence from you! I'm at the end of my patience!

(*He comes back toward her.*)

TOM: What do you think I'm at? Aren't I supposed to have
80 any patience to reach the end of, Mother? I know, I know. It seems unimportant to you, what I'm *doing*—what I *want* to do—having a little *difference* between them! You don't think that—
AMANDA: I think you've been doing things that you're
85 ashamed of. That's why you act like this. I don't believe that you go every night to the movies. Nobody goes to the movies night after night. Nobody in their right minds goes to the movies as often as you pretend to. People don't go to the movies at nearly midnight, and movies don't let
90 out at two A.M. Come in stumbling. Muttering to yourself like a maniac! You get three hours' sleep and then go to work. Oh, I can picture the way you're doing down there. Moping, doping, because you're in no condition.
TOM: (*Wildly.*) No, I'm in no condition!
95 AMANDA: What right have you got to jeopardize your job? Jeopardize the security of us all? How do you think we'd manage if you were—
TOM: Listen! You think I'm crazy about the *warehouse?* (*He bends fiercely toward her slight figure.*) You think I'm in love
100 with the Continental Shoemakers? You think I want to spend fifty-five years down there in that—*celotex interior!* with—*fluorescent—tubes!* Look! I'd rather somebody picked up a crowbar and battered out my brains—than go back mornings! I *go!* Every time you come in yelling that
105 Goddamn "*Rise and Shine!*" "*Rise and Shine!*" I say to myself, "How *lucky dead* people are!" But I get up. I *go!* For sixty-five dollars a month I give up all that I dream of doing and being *ever!* And you say self—*self's* all I ever think of. Why, listen, if self is what I thought of, Mother, I'd
110 be where he is—GONE! (*He points to his father's picture.*) As far as the system of transportation reaches! (*He starts past her. She grabs his arm.*) Don't grab at me, Mother!
AMANDA: Where are you going?

TOM: I'm going to the *movies!*
AMANDA: I don't believe that lie! 115

(TOM *crouches toward her, overtowering her tiny figure. She backs away, gasping.*)

TOM: I'm going to opium dens! Yes, opium dens, dens of vice and criminals' hangouts, Mother. I've joined the Hogan Gang, I'm a hired assassin, I carry a tommy gun in a violin case! I run a string of cat houses in the Valley! They call me 120 Killer, Killer Wingfield, I'm leading a double-life, a simple, honest warehouse worker by day, by night a dynamic *czar* of the *underworld, Mother.* I go to gambling casinos, I spin away fortunes on the roulette table! I wear a patch over one eye and a false mustache, sometimes I put on green whiskers. 125 On those occasions they call me—*El Diablo!* Oh, I could tell you many things to make you sleepless! My enemies plan to dynamite this place. They're going to blow us all sky-high some night! I'll be glad, very happy, and so will you! You'll go up, up on a broomstick, over Blue Mountain 130 with seventeen gentlemen callers! You ugly—babbling old—*witch* . . . (*He goes through a series of violent, clumsy movements, seizing his overcoat, lunging to the door, pulling it fiercely open. The women watch him, aghast. His arm catches in the sleeve of the coat as he struggles to pull it on. For a moment he is pinioned by the bulky garment. With an outraged groan he tears the coat off 135 again, splitting the shoulder of it, and hurls it across the room. It strikes against the shelf of* LAURA's *glass collection, and there is a tinkle of shattering glass.* LAURA *cries out as if wounded.*)

(*Music.*)

(*Screen legend:* "The Glass Menagerie.")

LAURA: (*Shrilly.*) My glass!—menagerie . . . (*She covers her face and turns away.*) 140

(*But* AMANDA *is still stunned and stupefied by the "ugly witch" so that she barely notices this occurrence. Now she recovers her speech.*)

AMANDA: (*In an awful voice.*) I won't speak to you—until you apologize!

(*She crosses through the portieres and draws them together behind her.* TOM *is left with* LAURA. LAURA *clings weakly to the mantel with her face averted.* TOM *stares at her stupidly for a moment. Then he crosses to the shelf. He drops awkwardly on his knees to collect the fallen glass, glancing at* LAURA *as if he would speak but couldn't.*)

(*"The Glass Menagerie" music steals in as the scene dims out.*)

SCENE FOUR

The interior of the apartment is dark. There is a faint light in the alley. A deep-voiced bell in a church is tolling the hour of five.

TOM *appears at the top of the alley. After each solemn boom of the bell in the tower, he shakes a little noisemaker or rattle as if to express the tiny spasm of man in contrast to the sustained power and dignity of the Almighty. This and the unsteadiness of his advance make it evident that he has been drinking. As he climbs the few steps to the fire escape landing light steals up inside.* LAURA *appears in the front room in a nightdress. She notices that* TOM's *bed is empty.* TOM *fishes in his pockets for his door key, removing a motley assortment of articles in the search, including a shower of movie ticket stubs and an empty bottle. At last he finds the key, but just as he is about to insert it, it slips from his fingers. He strikes a match and crouches below the door.*

TOM: (*Bitterly.*) One crack—and it falls through!

(LAURA *opens the door.*)

LAURA: Tom! Tom, what are you doing?
TOM: Looking for a door key.
LAURA: Where have you been all this time?
5 TOM: I have been to the movies.
LAURA: All this time at the movies?
TOM: There was a very long program. There was a Garbo picture and a Mickey Mouse and a travelogue and a news-reel and a preview of coming attractions. And there was
10 an organ solo and a collection for the Milk Fund—simultaneously—which ended up in a terrible fight be-tween a fat lady and an usher!
LAURA: (*Innocently.*) Did you have to stay through everything?
TOM: Of course! And, oh, I forgot! There was a big stage
15 show! The headliner on this stage show was Malvolio the Magician. He performed wonderful tricks, many of them, such as pouring water back and forth between pitchers. First it turned to wine and then it turned to beer and then it turned to whisky. I know it was whisky it finally turned
20 into because he needed somebody to come up out of the audience to help him, and I came up—both shows! It was Kentucky Straight Bourbon. A very generous fellow, he gave souvenirs. (*He pulls from his back pocket a shimmering rainbow-colored scarf.*) He gave me this. This is his magic
25 scarf. You can have it, Laura. You wave it over a canary cage and you get a bowl of goldfish. You wave it over the goldfish bowl and they fly away canaries . . . But the won-derfullest trick of all was the coffin trick. We nailed him into a coffin and he got out of the coffin without remov-
30 ing one nail. (*He has come inside.*) There is a trick that would come in handy for me—get me out of this two-by-four situation! (*He flops onto the bed and starts removing his shoes.*)
LAURA: Tom—shhh!
35 TOM: What're you shushing me for?
LAURA: You'll wake up Mother.
TOM: Goody, goody! Pay 'er back for all those "Rise an' Shines." (*He lies down, groaning.*) You know it don't take much intelligence to get yourself into a nailed-up coffin,
40 Laura. But who in hell ever got himself out of one with-out removing one nail?

(*As if in answer, the father's grinning photograph lights up. The scene dims out.*)

(*Immediately following, the church bell is heard striking six. At the sixth stroke the alarm clock goes off in* AMANDA's *room, and after a few moments we hear her calling: "Rise and Shine! Rise and Shine!* LAURA, *go tell your brother to rise and shine!"*)

TOM: (*Sitting up slowly.*) I'll rise—but I won't shine.

(*The light increases.*)

AMANDA: Laura, tell your brother his coffee is ready.

(LAURA *slips into the front room.*)

LAURA: Tom!—It's nearly seven. Don't make Mother nervous.

(*He stares at her stupidly.*)

(*Beseechingly.*) Tom, speak to Mother this morning. Make 45
up with her, apologize, speak to her!
TOM: She won't to me. It's her that started not speaking.
LAURA: If you just say you're sorry she'll start speaking.
TOM: Her not speaking—is that such a tragedy?
LAURA: Please—please!   50
AMANDA: (*Calling from the kitchenette.*) Laura, are you going to do what I asked you to do, or do I have to get dressed and go out myself?
LAURA: Going, going—soon as I get on my coat!

(*She pulls on a shapeless felt hat with a nervous, jerky movement, pleadingly glancing at* TOM. *She rushes awkwardly for her coat. The coat is one of* AMANDA's, *inaccurately made-over, the sleeves too short for* LAURA.)

Butter and what else?   55
AMANDA: (*Entering from the kitchenette.*) Just butter. Tell them to charge it.
LAURA: Mother, they make such faces when I do that.
AMANDA: Sticks and stones can break our bones, but the ex-pression on Mr. Garfinkel's face won't harm us! Tell your 60
brother his coffee is getting cold.
LAURA: (*At the door.*) Do what I asked you, will you, will you, Tom?

(*He looks sullenly away.*)

AMANDA: Laura, go now or just don't go at all!
LAURA: (*Rushing out.*) Going—going!   65

(*A second later she cries out.* TOM *springs up and crosses to the door.* TOM *opens the door.*)

TOM: Laura?
LAURA: I'm all right. I slipped, but I'm all right.
AMANDA: (*Peering anxiously after her.*) If anyone breaks a leg on those fire-escape steps, the landlord ought to be sued for every cent he possesses! (*She shuts the door. Now she remem-* 70
bers she isn't speaking to TOM *and returns to the other room.*)

(*As* TOM *comes listlessly for his coffee, she turns her back to him and stands rigidly facing the window on the gloomy gray vault of the areaway. Its light on her face with its aged but childish features is cru-elly sharp, satirical as a Daumier print.*)

(*The music of "Ave Maria" is heard softly.*)

(TOM *glances sheepishly but sullenly at her averted figure and slumps at the table. The coffee is scalding hot; he sips it and gasps and spits it back in the cup. At his gasp,* AMANDA *catches her breath and half turns. Then she catches herself and turns back to the win-dow.* TOM *blows on his coffee, glancing sidewise at his mother. She clears her throat.* TOM *clears his. He starts to rise, sinks back down again, scratches his head, clears his throat again.* AMANDA *coughs.* TOM *raises his cup in both hands to blow on it, his eyes staring over the rim of it at his mother for several moments. Then he slowly sets the cup down and awkwardly and hesitantly rises from the chair.*)

TOM: (*Hoarsely.*) Mother. I—I apologize, Mother.

(AMANDA *draws a quick, shuddering breath. Her face works grotesquely. She breaks into childlike tears.*)

I'm sorry for what I said, for everything that I said, I didn't mean it.

75 AMANDA: (*Sobbingly.*) My devotion has made me a witch and so I make myself hateful to my children!

TOM: *No, you don't.*

AMANDA: I worry so much, don't sleep, it makes me nervous!

TOM: (*Gently.*) I understand that.

80 AMANDA: I've had to put up a solitary battle all these years. But you're my right-hand bower! Don't fall down, don't fail!

TOM: (*Gently.*) I try, Mother.

AMANDA: (*With great enthusiasm.*) Try and you will *succeed!* (*The notion makes her breathless.*) Why, you—you're just *full*

85 of natural endowments! Both of my children—they're *unusual* children! Don't you think I know it? I'm so—*proud!* Happy and—feel I've—so much to be thankful for but—promise me one thing, son!

TOM: What, Mother?

90 AMANDA: Promise, son, you'll—never be a drunkard!

TOM: (*Turns to her grinning.*) I will never be a drunkard, Mother.

AMANDA: That's what frightened me so, that you'd be drinking! Eat a bowl of Purina!

TOM: Just coffee, Mother.

95 AMANDA: Shredded wheat biscuit?

TOM: No. No, Mother, just coffee.

AMANDA: You can't put in a day's work on an empty stomach. You've got ten minutes—don't gulp! Drinking too-hot liquids makes cancer of the stomach . . . Put cream in.

100 TOM: No, thank you.

AMANDA: To cool it.

TOM: No! No, thank you, I want it black.

AMANDA: I know, but it's not good for you. We have to do all that we can to build ourselves up. In these trying times

105 we live in, all that we have to cling to is—each other . . . That's why it's so important to—Tom, I—sent out your sister so I could discuss something with you. If you hadn't spoken I would have spoken to you. (*She sits down.*)

TOM: (*Gently.*) What is it, Mother, that you want to discuss?

110 AMANDA: *Laura!*

(TOM *puts his cup down slowly.*)

(*Legend on screen:* "Laura." *Music:* "The Glass Menagerie.")

TOM: —Oh.—Laura . . .

AMANDA: (*Touching his sleeve.*) You know how Laura is. So quiet but—still water runs deep! She notices things and I think she—broods about them.

(TOM *looks up.*)

115 A few days ago I came in and she was crying.

TOM: What about?

AMANDA: You.

TOM: Me?

AMANDA: She has an idea that you're not happy here.

120 TOM: What gave her that idea?

AMANDA: What gives her any idea? However, you do act strangely. I—I'm not criticizing, understand *that!* I know

your ambitions do not lie in the warehouse, that like everybody in the whole wide world—you've had to— make sacrifices, but—Tom—Tom—life's not easy, it calls 125 for—Spartan endurance! There's so many things in my heart that I cannot describe to you! I've never told you but I—*loved* your father. . . .

TOM: (*Gently.*) I know that, Mother.

AMANDA: And you—when I see you taking after his ways! 130 Staying out late—and—well, you *had* been drinking the night you were in that—terrifying condition! Laura says that you hate the apartment and that you go out nights to get away from it! Is that true, Tom?

TOM: No. You say there's so much in your heart that you 135 can't describe to me. That's true of me, too. There's so much in my heart that I can't describe to *you!* So let's respect each other's—

AMANDA: But, why—*why,* Tom—are you always so *restless?* Where do you *go* to, nights? 140

TOM: I—go to the movies.

AMANDA: Why do you go to the movies so much, Tom?

TOM: I go to the movies because—I like adventure. Adventure is something I don't have much of at work, so I go to the movies. 145

AMANDA: But, Tom, you go to the movies *entirely* too *much!*

TOM: I like a lot of adventure.

(AMANDA *looks baffled, then hurt. As the familiar inquisition resumes,* TOM *becomes hard and impatient again.* AMANDA *slips back into her querulous attitude toward him.*)

(*Image on screen:* A sailing vessel with Jolly Roger.)

AMANDA: Most young men find adventure in their careers.

TOM: Then most young men are not employed in a warehouse.

AMANDA: The world is full of young men employed in ware- 150 houses and offices and factories.

TOM: Do all of them find adventure in their careers?

AMANDA: They do or they do without it! Not everybody has a craze for adventure.

TOM: Man is by instinct a lover, a hunter, a fighter, and none 155 of those instincts are given much play at the warehouse!

AMANDA: Man is by instinct! Don't quote instinct to me! Instinct is something that people have got away from! It belongs to animals! Christian adults don't want it!

TOM: What do Christian adults want, then, Mother? 160

AMANDA: Superior things! Things of the mind and the spirit! Only animals have to satisfy instincts! Surely your aims are somewhat higher than theirs! Than monkeys—pigs—

TOM: I reckon they're not.

AMANDA: You're joking. However, that isn't what I wanted to 165 discuss.

TOM: (*Rising.*) I haven't much time.

AMANDA: (*Pushing his shoulders.*) Sit down.

TOM: You want me to punch in red at the warehouse, Mother?

AMANDA: You have five minutes. I want to talk about Laura. 170

(*Screen legend:* "Plans and Provisions.")

TOM: All right! What about Laura?

AMANDA: We have to be making some plans and provisions for her. She's older than you, two years, and nothing has

happened. She just drifts along doing nothing. It frightens
175   me terribly how she just drifts along.
TOM: I guess she's the type that people call home girls.
AMANDA: There's no such type, and if there is, it's a pity! That
is unless the home is hers, with a husband!
TOM: What?
180   AMANDA: Oh, I can see the handwriting on the wall as plain as I
see the nose in front of my face! It's terrifying! More and
more you remind me of your father! He was out all hours
without explanation!—Then *left! Goodbye!* And me with
the bag to hold. I saw that letter you got from the Merchant
185   Marine. I know what you're dreaming of. I'm not standing
here blindfolded. (*She pauses.*) Very well, then. Then do it!
But not till there's somebody to take your place.
TOM: What do you mean?
AMANDA: I mean that as soon as Laura has got somebody to
190   take care of her, married, a home of her own, independent—why, then you'll be free to go wherever you please,
on land, on sea, whichever way the wind blows you! But
until that time you've got to look out for your sister. I
don't say me because I'm old and don't matter! I say for
195   your sister because she's young and dependent.
    I put her in business college—a dismal failure! Fright-
ened her so it made her sick at the stomach. I took her over
to the Young People's League at the church. Another fiasco.
She spoke to nobody, nobody spoke to her. Now all she
200   does is fool with those pieces of glass and play those worn-
out records. What kind of a life is that for a girl to lead?
TOM: What can I do about it?
AMANDA: Overcome selfishness! Self, self, self is all that you
ever think of!

(TOM *springs up and crosses to get his coat. It is ugly and bulky. He
pulls on a cap with earmuffs.*)

205   Where is your muffler? Put your wool muffler on!

(*He snatches it angrily from the closet, tosses it around his neck and
pulls both ends tight.*)

Tom! I haven't said what I had in mind to ask you.
TOM: I'm too late to—
AMANDA: (*Catching his arm—very importunately; then shyly.*)
Down at the warehouse, aren't there some—nice young
210   men?
TOM: No!
AMANDA: There *must* be—*some.* . . .
TOM: Mother—(*He gestures.*)
AMANDA: Find out one that's clean-living—doesn't drink and
215   ask him out for sister!
TOM: What?
AMANDA: For *sister!* To *meet! Get acquainted!*
TOM: (*Stamping to the door.*) Oh, my *go-osh!*
AMANDA: Will you?

(*He opens the door. She says, imploringly:*)

220   Will you?

(*He starts down the fire escape.*)

Will you? *Will* you, dear?
TOM: (*Calling back.*) Yes!

(AMANDA *closes the door hesitantly and with a troubled but faintly
hopeful expression.*)

(*Screen image:* The cover of a glamor magazine.)

(*The spotlight picks up* AMANDA *at the phone.*)

AMANDA: Ella Cartwright? This is Amanda Wingfield!
How are you, honey?
How is that kidney condition?   225

(*There is a five-second pause.*)

Horrors!

(*There is another pause.*)

You're a Christian martyr, yes, honey, that's what you are, a
Christian martyr! Well, I just now happened to notice in my
little red book that your subscription to the *Companion* has
just run out! I knew that you wouldn't want to miss out on   230
the wonderful serial starting in this new issue. It's by Bessie
Mae Hopper, the first thing she's written since *Honeymoon
for Three.* Wasn't that a strange and interesting story? Well,
this one is even lovelier, I believe. It has a sophisticated, society background. It's all about the horsey set on Long Island!   235

(*The light fades out.*)

SCENE FIVE

Legend on the screen: "Annunciation."

Music is heard as the light slowly comes on.

*It is early dusk of a spring evening. Supper has just been finished in
the Wingfield apartment.* AMANDA *and* LAURA, *in light-colored
dresses, are removing dishes from the table in the dining room, which
is shadowy, their movements formalized almost as a dance or ritual,
their moving forms as pale and silent as moths.* TOM, *in white shirt
and trousers, rises from the table and crosses toward the fire escape.*

AMANDA: (*As he passes her.*) Son, will you do me a favor?
TOM: What?
AMANDA: Comb your hair! You look so pretty when your
hair is combed!

(TOM *slouches on the sofa with the evening paper. Its enormous
headline reads:* "Franco Triumphs.")

There is only one respect in which I would like you to   5
emulate your father.
TOM: What respect is that?
AMANDA: The care he always took of his appearance. He
never allowed himself to look untidy.

(*He throws down the paper and crosses to the fire escape.*)

Where are you going?   10
TOM: I'm going out to smoke.
AMANDA: You smoke too much. A pack a day at fifteen cents a
pack. How much would that amount to in a month? Thirty
times fifteen is how much, Tom? Figure it out and you will
be astounded at what you could save. Enough to give you a   15

night-school course in accounting at Washington U! Just think what a wonderful thing that would be for you, son!

(TOM *is unmoved by the thought.*)

TOM: I'd rather smoke. (*He steps out on the landing, letting the screen door slam.*)
20 AMANDA: (*Sharply.*) I know! That's the tragedy of it.... (*Alone, she turns to look at her husband's picture.*)

(*Dance music:* "The World Is Waiting for the Sunrise!")

TOM: (*To the audience.*) Across the alley from us was the Paradise Dance-hall. On evenings in spring the windows and doors were open and the music came outdoors. Sometimes the
25 lights were turned out except for a large glass sphere that hung from the ceiling. It would turn slowly about and filter the dusk with delicate rainbow colors. Then the orchestra played a waltz or a tango, something that had a slow and sensuous rhythm. Couples would come outside, to the rela-
30 tive privacy of the alley. You could see them kissing behind ash pits and telephone poles. This was the compensation for lives that passed like mine, without any change or adventure. Adventure and change were imminent in this year. They were waiting around the corner for all these kids. Sus-
35 pended in the mist over Berchtesgaden, caught in the folds of Chamberlain's umbrella. In Spain there was Guernica! But here there was only hot swing music and liquor, dance-halls, bars, and movies, and sex that hung in the gloom like a chandelier and flooded the world with brief, deceptive
40 rainbows.... All the world was waiting for bombardments!

(AMANDA *turns from the picture and comes outside.*)

AMANDA: (*Sighing.*) A fire escape landing's a poor excuse for a porch. (*She spreads a newspaper on a step and sits down, gracefully and demurely as if she were settling into a swing on a Mississippi veranda.*) What are you looking at?
45 TOM: The moon.
AMANDA: Is there a moon this evening?
TOM: It's rising over Garfinkel's Delicatessen.
AMANDA: So it is! A little silver slipper of a moon. Have you made a wish on it yet?
50 TOM: Um-hum.
AMANDA: What did you wish for?
TOM: That's a secret.
AMANDA: A secret, huh? Well, I won't tell mine either. I will be just as mysterious as you.
55 TOM: I bet I can guess what yours is.
AMANDA: Is my head so transparent?
TOM: You're not a sphinx.
AMANDA: No, I don't have secrets. I'll tell you what I wished for on the moon. Success and happiness for my precious
60 children! I wish for that whenever there's a moon, and when there isn't a moon, I wish for it, too.
TOM: I thought perhaps you wished for a gentleman caller.
AMANDA: Why do you say that?
TOM: Don't you remember asking me to fetch one?
65 AMANDA: I remember suggesting that it would be nice for your sister if you brought home some nice young man from the warehouse. I think that I've made that suggestion more than once.

TOM: Yes, you have made it repeatedly.
AMANDA: Well? 70
TOM: We are going to have one.
AMANDA: *What?*
TOM: A gentleman caller!

(*The annunciation is celebrated with music.*)

(AMANDA *rises.*)

(*Image on screen:* A caller with a bouquet.)

AMANDA: You mean you have asked some nice young man to come over? 75
TOM: Yep. I've asked him to dinner.
AMANDA: You really did?
TOM: I did!
AMANDA: You did, and did he—*accept?*
TOM: He did! 80
AMANDA: Well, well—well, well! That's—lovely!
TOM: I thought that you would be pleased.
AMANDA: It's definite then?
TOM: Very definite.
AMANDA: Soon? 85
TOM: Very soon.
AMANDA: For heaven's sake, stop putting on and tell me some things, will you?
TOM: What things do you want me to tell you?
AMANDA: *Naturally* I would like to know when he's coming! 90
TOM: He's coming tomorrow.
AMANDA: *Tomorrow?*
TOM: Yep. Tomorrow.
AMANDA: But, Tom!
TOM: Yes, Mother? 95
AMANDA: Tomorrow gives me no time!
TOM: Time for what?
AMANDA: Preparations! Why didn't you phone me at once, as soon as you asked him, the minute that he accepted? Then don't you see, I could have been getting ready! 100
TOM: You don't have to make any fuss.
AMANDA: Oh, Tom, Tom, Tom, of course I have to make a fuss! I want things nice, not sloppy! Not thrown together. I'll certainly have to do some fast thinking, won't I?
TOM: I don't see why you have to think at all. 105
AMANDA: You just don't know. We can't have a gentleman caller in a pigsty! All my wedding silver has to be polished, the monogrammed table linen ought to be laundered! The windows have to be washed and fresh curtains put up. And how about clothes? We have to *wear* something, don't we? 110
TOM: Mother, this boy is no one to make a fuss over!
AMANDA: Do you realize he's the first young man we've introduced to your sister? It's terrible, dreadful, disgraceful that poor little sister has never received a single gentleman caller! Tom, come inside! (*She opens the screen door.*) 115
TOM: What for?
AMANDA: I want to ask you some things.
TOM: If you're going to make such a fuss, I'll call it off, I'll tell him not to come!
AMANDA: You certainly won't do anything of the kind. Noth- 120
ing offends people worse than broken engagements. It simply means I'll have to work like a Turk! We won't be brilliant, but we will pass inspection. Come on inside.

(TOM *follows her inside, groaning.*)

Sit down.

125 TOM: Any particular place you would like me to sit?

AMANDA: Thank heavens I've got that new sofa! I'm also making payments on a floor lamp I'll have sent out! And put the chintz covers on, they'll brighten things up! Of course I'd hoped to have these walls re-papered. . . . What

130 is the young man's name?

TOM: His name is O'Connor.

AMANDA: That, of course, means fish—tomorrow is Friday! I'll have that salmon loaf—with Durkee's dressing! What does he do? He works at the warehouse?

135 TOM: Of course! How else would I—

AMANDA: Tom, he—doesn't drink?

TOM: Why do you ask me that?

AMANDA: Your father *did!*

TOM: Don't get started on that!

140 AMANDA: He *does* drink, then?

TOM: Not that I know of!

AMANDA: Make sure, be certain! The last thing I want for my daughter's a boy who drinks!

TOM: Aren't you being a little bit premature? Mr. O'Connor

145 has not yet appeared on the scene!

AMANDA: But will tomorrow. To meet your sister, and what do I know about his character? Nothing! Old maids are better off than wives of drunkards!

TOM: Oh, my God!

150 AMANDA: Be still!

TOM: (*Leaning forward to whisper.*) Lots of fellows meet girls whom they don't marry!

AMANDA: Oh, talk sensibly, Tom—and don't be sarcastic! (*She has gotten a hairbrush.*)

155 TOM: What are you doing?

AMANDA: I'm brushing that cowlick down! (*She attacks his hair with the brush.*) What is this young man's position at the warehouse?

TOM: (*Submitting grimly to the brush and the interrogation.*) This

160 young man's position is that of a shipping clerk, Mother.

AMANDA: Sounds to me like a fairly responsible job, the sort of a job *you* would be in if you just had more *get-up.* What is his salary? Have you any idea?

TOM: I would judge it to be approximately eighty-five dol-

165 lars a month.

AMANDA: Well—not princely, but—

TOM: Twenty more than I make.

AMANDA: Yes, how well I know! But for a family man, eighty-five dollars a month is not much more than you can just

170 get by on. . . .

TOM: Yes, but Mr. O'Connor is not a family man.

AMANDA: He might be, mightn't he? Some time in the future?

TOM: I see. Plans and provisions.

AMANDA: You are the only young man that I know of who

175 ignores the fact that the future becomes the present, the present the past, and the past turns into everlasting regret if you don't plan for it!

TOM: I will think that over and see what I can make of it.

AMANDA: Don't be supercilious with your mother! Tell me

180 some more about this—what do you call him?

TOM: James D. O'Connor. The D. is for Delaney.

AMANDA: Irish on *both* sides! *Gracious!* And doesn't drink?

TOM: Shall I call him up and ask him right this minute?

AMANDA: The only way to find out about those things is to make discreet inquiries at the proper moment. When I was 185 a girl in Blue Mountain and it was suspected that a young man drank, the girl whose attentions he had been receiving, if any girl *was,* would sometimes speak to the minister of his church, or rather her father would if her father was living, and sort of feel him out on the young man's charac- 190 ter. That is the way such things are discreetly handled to keep a young woman from making a tragic mistake!

TOM: Then how did you happen to make a tragic mistake?

AMANDA: That innocent look of your father's had everyone fooled! He *smiled*—the world was *enchanted!* No girl can do 195 worse than put herself at the mercy of a handsome appearance! I hope that Mr. O'Connor is not too good-looking.

TOM: No, he's not too good-looking. He's covered with freckles and hasn't too much of a nose.

AMANDA: He's not right-down homely, though? 200

TOM: Not right-down homely. Just medium homely, I'd say.

AMANDA: Character's what to look for in a man.

TOM: That's what I've always said, Mother.

AMANDA: You've never said anything of the kind and I suspect you would never give it a thought. 205

TOM: Don't be so suspicious of me.

AMANDA: At least I hope he's the type that's up and coming.

TOM: I think he really goes in for self-improvement.

AMANDA: What reason have you to think so?

TOM: He goes to night school. 210

AMANDA: (*Beaming.*) Splendid! What does he do, I mean study?

TOM: Radio engineering and public speaking!

AMANDA: Then he has visions of being advanced in the world! Any young man who studies public speaking is aiming to have an executive job some day! And radio en- 215 gineering? A thing for the future! Both of these facts are very illuminating. Those are the sort of things that a mother should know concerning any young man who comes to call on her daughter. Seriously or—not.

TOM: One little warning. He doesn't know about Laura. I 220 didn't let on that we had dark ulterior motives. I just said, why don't you come and have dinner with us? He said okay and that was the whole conversation.

AMANDA: I bet it was! You're eloquent as an oyster. However, he'll know about Laura when he gets here. When he sees 225 how lovely and sweet and pretty she is, he'll thank his lucky stars he was asked to dinner.

TOM: Mother, you mustn't expect too much of Laura.

AMANDA: What do you mean?

TOM: Laura seems all those things to you and me because 230 she's ours and we love her. We don't even notice she's crippled any more.

AMANDA: Don't say crippled! You know that I never allow that word to be used!

TOM: But face facts, Mother. She is and—that's not all— 235

AMANDA: What do you mean "not all"?

TOM: Laura is very different from other girls.

AMANDA: I think the difference is all to her advantage.

TOM: Not quite all—in the eyes of others—strangers—she's terribly shy and lives in a world of her own and those things 240 make her seem a little peculiar to people outside the house.

AMANDA: Don't say peculiar.

TOM: Face the facts. She is.

(*The dance-hall music changes to a tango that has a minor and somewhat ominous tone.*)

AMANDA: In what way is she peculiar—may I ask?

245 TOM: (*Gently.*) She lives in a world of her own—a world of little glass ornaments, Mother. . . .

(*He gets up.* AMANDA *remains holding the brush, looking at him, troubled.*)

She plays old phonograph records and—that's about all— (*He glances at himself in the mirror and crosses to the door.*)

AMANDA: (*Sharply.*) Where are you going?

250 TOM: I'm going to the movies. (*He goes out the screen door.*)

AMANDA: Not to the movies, every night to the movies! (*She follows quickly to the screen door.*) I don't believe you always go to the movies!

(*He is gone.* AMANDA *looks worriedly after him for a moment. Then vitality and optimism return and she turns from the door, crossing to the portieres.*)

Laura! Laura!

(LAURA *answers from the kitchenette.*)

255 LAURA: Yes, Mother.

AMANDA: Let those dishes go and come in front!

(LAURA *appears with a dish towel.* AMANDA *speaks to her gaily.*)

Laura, come here and make a wish on the moon!

(*Screen image:* The Moon.)

LAURA: (*Entering.*) Moon—moon?

AMANDA: A little silver slipper of a moon. Look over your left

260 shoulder, Laura, and make a wish!

(LAURA *looks faintly puzzled as if called out of sleep.* AMANDA *seizes her shoulders and turns her at an angle by the door.*)

Now! Now, darling, *wish!*

LAURA: What shall I wish for, Mother?

AMANDA: (*Her voice trembling and her eyes suddenly filling with tears.*) Happiness! Good fortune!

(*The sound of the violin rises and the stage dims out.*)

SCENE SIX

The light comes up on the fire escape landing. TOM *is leaning against the grill, smoking.*

Screen image: The high school hero.

TOM: And so the following evening I brought Jim home to dinner. I had known Jim slightly in high school. In high school Jim was a hero. He had tremendous Irish good nature and vitality with the scrubbed and polished look of

5 white chinaware. He seemed to move in a continual spotlight. He was a star in basketball, captain of the debating club, president of the senior class and the glee club and he sang the male lead in the annual light operas. He was al-

ways running or bounding, never just walking. He seemed always at the point of defeating the law of gravity. He was 10 shooting with such velocity through his adolescence that you would logically expect him to arrive at nothing short of the White House by the time he was thirty. But Jim apparently ran into more interference after his graduation from Soldan. His speed had definitely slowed. Six years af- 15 ter he left high school he was holding a job that wasn't much better than mine.

(*Screen image.* The Clerk.)

He was the only one at the warehouse with whom I was on friendly terms. I was valuable to him as someone who could remember his former glory, who had seen him win 20 basketball games and the silver cup in debating. He knew of my secret practice of retiring to a cabinet of the washroom to work on poems when business was slack in the warehouse. He called me Shakespeare. And while the other boys in the warehouse regarded me with suspicious hostil- 25 ity, Jim took a humorous attitude toward me. Gradually his attitude affected the others, their hostility wore off and they also began to smile at me as people smile at an oddly fashioned dog who trots across their path at some distance.

I knew that Jim and Laura had known each other at Sol- 30 dan, and I had heard Laura speak admiringly of his voice. I didn't know if Jim remembered her or not. In high school Laura had been as unobtrusive as Jim had been astonishing. If he did remember Laura, it was not as my sister, for when I asked him to dinner, he grinned and said, "You know, 35 Shakespeare, I never thought of you as having folks!"

He was about to discover that I did. . . .

(*Legend on screen:* "The accent of a coming foot.")

(*The light dims out on* TOM *and comes up in the Wingfield living room—a delicate lemony light. It is about five on a Friday evening of late spring which comes "scattering poems in the sky."*)

(AMANDA *has worked like a Turk in preparation for the gentleman caller. The results are astonishing. The new floor lamp with its rose silk shade is in place, a colored paper lantern conceals the broken light fixture in the ceiling, new billowing white curtains are at the windows, chintz covers are on the chairs and sofa, a pair of new sofa pillows make their initial appearance. Open boxes and tissue paper are scattered on the floor.*)

(LAURA *stands in the middle of the room with lifted arms while* AMANDA *crouches before her, adjusting the hem of a new dress, devout and ritualistic. The dress is colored and designed by memory. The arrangement of* LAURA's *hair is changed; it is softer and more becoming. A fragile, unearthly prettiness has come out in* LAURA: *she is like a piece of translucent glass touched by light, given a momentary radiance, not actual, not lasting.*)

AMANDA: (*Impatiently.*) Why are you trembling?

LAURA: Mother, you've made me so nervous!

AMANDA: How have I made you nervous? 40

LAURA: By all this fuss! You make it seem so important!

AMANDA: I don't understand you, Laura. You couldn't be satisfied with just sitting home, and yet whenever I try to arrange something for you, you seem to resist it. (*She gets*

45   *up.*) Now take a look at yourself. No, wait! Wait just a mo-
      ment—I have an idea!
      LAURA: What is it now?

(AMANDA *produces two powder puffs which she wraps in handkerchiefs and stuffs in* LAURA'*s bosom.*)

      LAURA: Mother, what are you doing?
      AMANDA: They call them "Gay Deceivers"!
50   LAURA: I won't wear them!
      AMANDA: You will!
      LAURA: Why should I?
      AMANDA: Because, to be painfully honest, your chest is flat.
      LAURA: You make it seem like we were setting a trap.
55   AMANDA: All pretty girls are a trap, a pretty trap, and men ex-
      pect them to be.

(*Legend on screen:* "A pretty trap.")

      Now look at yourself, young lady. This is the prettiest you
      will ever be! (*She stands back to admire* LAURA.) I've got to
      fix myself now! You're going to be surprised by your
60   mother's appearance!

(AMANDA *crosses through the portieres, humming gaily.* LAURA
*moves slowly to the long mirror and stares solemnly at herself. A
wind blows the white curtains inward in a slow, graceful motion and
with a faint, sorrowful sighing.*)

      AMANDA: (*From somewhere behind the portieres.*) It isn't dark
      enough yet.

(LAURA *turns slowly before the mirror with a troubled look.*)

(*Legend on screen:* "This is my sister: Celebrate her with
strings!" *Music plays.*)

      AMANDA: (*Laughing, still not visible.*) I'm going to show you
      something. I'm going to make a spectacular appearance!
65   LAURA: What is it, Mother?
      AMANDA: Possess your soul in patience—you will see! Some-
      thing I've resurrected from that old trunk! Styles haven't
      changed so terribly much after all.... (*She parts the portieres.*)
      Now just look at your mother! (*She wears a girlish frock of
70   yellowed voile with a blue silk sash. She carries a bunch of jon-
      quils—the legend of her youth is nearly revived. Now she speaks
      feverishly.*) This is the dress in which I led the cotillion. Won
      the cakewalk twice at Sunset Hill, wore one Spring to the
      Governor's Ball in Jackson! See how I sashayed around the
75   ballroom, Laura? (*She raises her skirt and does a mincing step
      around the room.*) I wore it on Sundays for my gentlemen
      callers! I had it on the day I met your father.... I had
      malaria fever all that Spring. The change of climate from
      East Tennessee to the Delta—weakened resistance. I had a
80   little temperature all the time—not enough to be seri-
      ous—just enough to make me restless and giddy! Invita-
      tions poured in—parties all over the Delta! "Stay in bed,"
      said Mother, "you have a fever!"—but I just wouldn't. I
      took quinine but kept on going, going! Evenings, dances!
85   Afternoons, long, long rides! Picnics—lovely! So lovely,
      that country in May—all lacy with dogwood, literally
      flooded with jonquils! That was the spring I had the craze
      for jonquils. Jonquils became an absolute obsession.

Mother said, "Honey, there's no more room for jonquils."
And still I kept on bringing in more jonquils. Whenever,   90
wherever I saw them, I'd say "Stop! Stop! I see jonquils!" I
made the young men help me gather the jonquils! It was a
joke, Amanda and her jonquils. Finally there were no more
vases to hold them, every available space was filled with
jonquils. No vases to hold them? All right, I'll hold them   95
myself! And then I—(*She stops in front of the picture. Music
plays.*) met your father! Malaria fever and jonquils and
then—this—boy.... (*She switches on the rose-colored lamp.*) I
hope they get here before it starts to rain. (*She crosses the
room and places the jonquils in a bowl on the table.*) I gave your   100
brother a little extra change so he and Mr. O'Connor could
take the service car home.
LAURA: (*With an altered look.*) What did you say his name was?
AMANDA: O'Connor.
LAURA: What is his first name?   105
AMANDA: I don't remember. Oh, yes, I do. It was—Jim!

(LAURA *sways slightly and catches hold of a chair.*)

(*Legend on screen:* "Not Jim!")

LAURA: (*Faintly.*) Not—Jim!
AMANDA: Yes, that was it, it was Jim! I've never known a Jim
that wasn't nice!

(*The music becomes ominous.*)

LAURA: Are you sure his name is Jim O'Connor?   110
AMANDA: Yes. Why?
LAURA: Is he the one that Tom used to know in high school?
AMANDA: He didn't say so. I think he just got to know him
at the warehouse.
LAURA: There was a Jim O'Connor we both knew in high   115
school—(*Then, with effort.*) If that is the one that Tom is
bringing to dinner—you'll have to excuse me, I won't
come to the table.
AMANDA: What sort of nonsense is this?
LAURA: You asked me once if I'd ever liked a boy. Don't you   120
remember I showed you this boy's picture?
AMANDA: You mean the boy you showed me in the yearbook?
LAURA: Yes, that boy.
AMANDA: Laura, Laura, were you in love with that boy?
LAURA: I don't know, Mother. All I know is I couldn't sit at   125
the table if it was him!
AMANDA: It won't be him! It isn't the least bit likely. But
whether it is or not, you will come to the table. You will
not be excused.
LAURA: I'll have to be, Mother.   130
AMANDA: I don't intend to humor your silliness, Laura. I've had
too much from you and your brother, both! So just sit down
and compose yourself till they come. Tom has forgotten his
key so you'll have to let them in, when they arrive.
LAURA: (*Panicky.*) Oh, Mother—*you* answer the door!   135
AMANDA: (*Lightly.*) I'll be in the kitchen—busy!
LAURA: Oh, Mother, please answer the door, don't make me
do it!
AMANDA: (*Crossing into the kitchenette.*) I've got to fix the dressing for the salmon. Fuss, fuss—silliness!—over a gentle-   140
man caller!

(*The door swings shut.* LAURA *is left alone.*)

(*Legend on screen:* "Terror!")

(*She utters a low moan and turns off the lamp—sits stiffly on the edge of the sofa, knotting her fingers together.*)

(*Legend on screen:* "The Opening of a Door!")

(TOM *and* JIM *appear on the fire escape steps and climb to the landing. Hearing their approach, laura rises with a panicky gesture. She retreats to the portieres. The doorbell rings.* LAURA *catches her breath and touches her throat. Low drums sound.*)

AMANDA: (*Calling.*) Laura, sweetheart! The door!

(LAURA *stares at it without moving.*)

JIM: I think we just beat the rain.
TOM: Uh-huh. (*He rings again, nervously.* JIM *whistles and fishes*
145   *for a cigarette.*)
AMANDA: (*Very, very gaily.*) Laura, that is your brother and Mr. O'Connor! Will you let them in, darling?

(LAURA *crosses toward the kitchenette door.*)

LAURA: (*Breathlessly.*) Mother—you go to the door!

(AMANDA *steps out of the kitchenette and stares furiously at* LAURA. *She points imperiously at the door.*)

LAURA: Please, please!
150 AMANDA: (*In a fierce whisper.*) What is the matter with you, you silly thing?
LAURA: (*Desperately.*) Please, you answer it, *please!*
AMANDA: I told you I wasn't going to humor you, Laura. Why have you chosen this moment to lose your mind?
155 LAURA: Please, please, please, you go!
AMANDA: You'll have to go to the door because I can't!
LAURA: (*Despairingly.*) I can't either!
AMANDA: *Why?*
LAURA: I'm *sick!*
160 AMANDA: I'm sick, too—of your nonsense! Why can't you and your brother be normal people? Fantastic whims and behavior!

(TOM *gives a long ring.*)

Preposterous goings on! Can you give me one reason— (*She calls out lyrically.*) Coming! Just one second!—why you
165   should be afraid to open a door? Now you answer it, Laura!
LAURA: Oh, oh, oh . . . (*She returns through the portieres, darts to the Victrola, winds it frantically and turns it on.*)
AMANDA: Laura Wingfield, you march right to that door!
LAURA: *Yes—yes, Mother!*

(*A faraway, scratchy rendition of "Dardanella" softens the air and gives her strength to move through it. She slips to the door and draws it cautiously open.* TOM *enters with the caller,* JIM O'CONNOR.)

170 TOM: Laura, this is Jim. Jim, this is my sister, Laura.
JIM: (*Stepping inside.*) I didn't know that Shakespeare had a sister!

LAURA: (*Retreating, stiff and trembling, from the door.*) How— how do you do?
JIM: (*Heartily, extending his hand.*) Okay!

(LAURA *touches it hesitantly with hers.*)

JIM: Your hand's *cold,* Laura!   175
LAURA: Yes, well—I've been playing the Victrola. . . .
JIM: Must have been playing classical music on it! You ought to play a little hot swing music to warm you up!
LAURA: Excuse me—I haven't finished playing the Victrola . . . (*She turns awkwardly and hurries into the front room. She* 180
pauses a second by the Victrola. Then she catches her breath and darts through the portieres like a frightened deer.)
JIM: (*Grinning.*) What was the matter?
TOM: Oh—with Laura? Laura is—terribly shy.
JIM: Shy, huh? It's unusual to meet a shy girl nowadays. I don't 185
believe you ever mentioned you had a sister.
TOM: Well, now you know. I have one. Here is the *Post Dispatch.* You want a piece of it?
JIM: Uh-huh.
TOM: What piece? The comics?   190
JIM: Sports! (*He glances at it.*) Ole Dizzy Dean is on his bad behavior.
TOM: (*Uninterested.*) Yeah? (*He lights a cigarette and goes over to the fire-escape door.*)
JIM: Where are *you* going?   195
TOM: I'm going out on the terrace.
JIM: (*Going after him.*) You know, Shakespeare—I'm going to sell you a bill of goods!
TOM: What goods?
JIM: A course I'm taking.   200
TOM: Huh?
JIM: In public speaking! You and me, we're not the warehouse type.
TOM: Thanks—that's good news. But what has public speaking got to do with it?   205
JIM: It fits you for—executive positions!
TOM: Awww.
JIM: I tell you it's done a helluva lot for me.

(*Image on screen:* Executive at his desk.)

TOM: In what respect?
JIM: In every! Ask yourself what is the difference between 210
you an' me and men in the office down front? Brains?— No!— Ability?—No! Then what? Just one little thing—
TOM: What is that one little thing?
JIM: Primarily it amounts to—social poise! Being able to square up to people and hold your own on any social level! 215
AMANDA: (*From the kitchenette.*) Tom?
TOM: Yes, Mother?
AMANDA: Is that you and Mr. O'Connor?
TOM: Yes, Mother.
AMANDA: Well, you just make yourselves comfortable in there. 220
TOM: Yes, Mother.
AMANDA: Ask Mr. O'Connor if he would like to wash his hands.
JIM: Aw, no—no—thank you—I took care of that at the warehouse. Tom—   225
TOM: Yes?
JIM: Mr. Mendoza was speaking to me about you.

TOM: Favorably?

JIM: What do you think?

230 TOM: Well—

JIM: You're going to be out of a job if you don't wake up.

TOM: I am waking up—

JIM: You show no signs.

TOM: The signs are interior.

(Image on screen: The sailing vessel with the Jolly Roger again.)

235 TOM: I'm planning to change. (*He leans over the fire-escape rail, speaking with quiet exhilaration. The incandescent marquees and signs of the first-run movie houses light his face from across the alley. He looks like a voyager.*) I'm right at the point of committing myself to a future that doesn't include the ware-
240 house or Mr. Mendoza or even a night-school course in public speaking.

JIM: What are you gassing about?

TOM: I'm tired of the movies.

JIM: Movies!

245 TOM: Yes, movies! Look at them—(*A wave toward the marvels of Grand Avenue.*) All of those glamorous people—having adventures—hogging it all, gobbling the whole thing up! You know what happens? People go to the *movies* instead of *moving!* Hollywood characters are supposed to have all
250 the adventures for everybody in America, while everybody in America sits in a dark room and watches them have them! Yes, until there's a war. That's when adventure becomes available to the masses! *Everyone's* dish, not only Gable's! Then the people in the dark room come out of
255 the dark room to have some adventures themselves—goody, goody! It's our turn now, to go to the South Sea Island—to make a safari—to be exotic, far-off! But I'm not patient. I don't want to wait till then. I'm tired of the *movies* and I am *about* to *move!*

260 JIM: (*Incredulously.*) Move?

TOM: Yes.

JIM: When?

TOM: Soon!

JIM: Where? Where?

(The music seems to answer the question, while TOM *thinks it over. He searches in his pockets.)*

265 TOM: I'm starting to boil inside. I know I seem dreamy, but inside—well, I'm boiling! Whenever I pick up a shoe, I shudder a little thinking how short life is and what I am doing! Whatever that means, I know it doesn't mean shoes—except as something to wear on a traveler's feet!
270 (*He finds what he has been searching for in his pockets and holds out a paper to Jim.*) Look—

JIM: What?

TOM: I'm a member.

JIM: (*Reading.*) The Union of Merchant Seamen.

275 TOM: I paid my dues this month, instead of the light bill.

JIM: You will regret it when they turn the lights off.

TOM: I won't be here.

JIM: How about your mother?

TOM: I'm like my father. The bastard son of a bastard! Did
280 you notice how he's grinning in his picture in there? And he's been absent going on sixteen years!

JIM: You're just talking, you drip. How does your mother feel about it?

TOM: Shhh! Here comes Mother! Mother is not acquainted with my plans!   285

AMANDA: (*Coming through the portieres.*) Where are you all?

TOM: On the terrace, Mother.

(They start inside. She advances to them. TOM *is distinctly shocked at her appearance. Even* JIM *blinks a little. He is making his first contact with girlish Southern vivacity and in spite of the night-school course in public speaking is somewhat thrown off the beam by the unexpected outlay of social charm. Certain responses are attempted by* JIM *but are swept aside by* AMANDA's *gay laughter and chatter.* TOM *is embarrassed but after the first shock* JIM *reacts very warmly. He grins and chuckles, is altogether won over.)*

(Image on screen: AMANDA *as a girl.)*

AMANDA: (*Coyly smiling, shaking her girlish ringlets.*) Well, well, well, so this is Mr. O'Connor. Introductions entirely unnecessary. I've heard so much about you from my boy. I fi-   290
nally said to him, Tom—good gracious!—why don't you bring this paragon to supper? I'd like to meet this nice young man at the warehouse!—instead of just hearing him sing your praises so much! I don't know why my son is so stand-offish—that's not Southern behavior!   295
    Let's sit down and—I think we could stand a little more air in here! Tom, leave the door open. I felt a nice fresh breeze a moment ago. Where has it gone to? Mmm, so warm already! And not quite summer, even. We're going to burn up when summer really gets started. However,   300
we're having—we're having a very light supper. I think light things are better fo' this time of year. The same as light clothes are. Light clothes an' light food are what warm weather calls fo'. You know our blood gets so thick during th' winter—it takes a while fo' us to *adjust*   305
ou'selves!—when the season changes . . . It's come so quick this year. I wasn't prepared. All of a sudden—heavens! Already summer! I ran to the trunk an' pulled out this light dress—terribly old! Historical almost! But feels so good—so good an' co-ol, y' know. . . .   310

TOM: Mother—

AMANDA: Yes, honey?

TOM: How about—supper?

AMANDA: Honey, you go ask Sister if supper is ready! You know that Sister is in full charge of supper! Tell her you hungry   315
boys are waiting for it. (*To* JIM.) Have you met Laura?

JIM: She—

AMANDA: Let you in? Oh, good, you've met already! It's rare for a girl as sweet an' pretty as Laura to be domestic! But Laura is, thank heavens, not only pretty but also very domestic. I'm   320
not at all. I never was a bit. I never could make a thing but angel-food cake. Well, in the South we had so many servants. Gone, gone, gone. All vestige of gracious living! Gone completely! I wasn't prepared for what the future brought me. All of my gentlemen callers were sons of   325
planters and so of course I assumed that I would be married to one and raise my family on a large piece of land with plenty of servants. But man proposes—and woman accepts the proposal! To vary that old, old saying a little bit—I married no planter! I married a man who worked for the   330

telephone company! That gallantly smiling gentleman over there! (*She points to the picture.*) A telephone man who—fell in love with long-distance! Now he travels and I don't even know where! But what am I going on for about my—tribu-
335 lations? Tell me yours—I hope you don't have any! Tom?

TOM: (*Returning.*) Yes, Mother?

AMANDA: Is supper nearly ready?

TOM: It looks to me like supper is on the table.

AMANDA: Let me look—(*She rises prettily and looks through the
340 portieres.*) Oh, lovely! But where is Sister?

TOM: Laura is not feeling well and she says that she thinks she'd better not come to the table.

AMANDA: What? Nonsense! Laura? Oh, Laura!

LAURA: (*From the kitchenette, faintly.*) Yes, Mother.

345 AMANDA: You really must come to the table. We won't be seated until you come to the table! Come in, Mr. O'Connor. You sit over there, and I'll . . . . Laura? Laura Wingfield! You're keeping us waiting, honey! We can't say grace until you come to the table!

(*The kitchenette door is pushed weakly open and* LAURA *comes in. She is obviously quite faint, her lips trembling, her eyes wide and staring. She moves unsteadily toward the table.*)

(*Screen legend:* "Terror!")

(*Outside a summer storm is coming on abruptly. The white curtains billow inward at the windows and there is a sorrowful murmur from the deep blue dusk.*)

(LAURA *suddenly stumbles; she catches at a chair with a faint moan.*)

350 TOM: Laura!

AMANDA: Laura!

(*There is a clap of thunder.*)

(*Screen legend:* "Ah!")

(*Despairingly.*) Why, Laura, you *are* ill, darling! Tom, help your sister into the living room, dear! Sit in the living room, Laura—rest on the sofa. Well! (*To* JIM *as* TOM *helps
355 his sister to the sofa in the living room.*) Standing over the hot stove made her ill! I told her that it was just too warm this evening, but—

(TOM *comes back to the table.*)

Is Laura all right now?

TOM: Yes.

360 AMANDA: What *is* that? Rain? A nice cool rain has come up! (*She gives* JIM *a frightened look.*) I think we may—have grace—now . . . (TOM *looks at her stupidly.*) Tom, honey— you say grace!

TOM: Oh . . . "For these and all thy mercies—"

(*They bow their heads,* AMANDA *stealing a nervous glance at* JIM. *In the living room* LAURA, *stretched on the sofa, clenches her hand to her lips, to hold back a shuddering sob.*)

365 God's Holy Name be praised—

(*The scene dims out.*)

SCENE SEVEN

It is half an hour later. Dinner is just being finished in the dining room, LAURA *is still huddled upon the sofa, her feet drawn under her, her head resting on a pale blue pillow, her eyes wide and mysteriously watchful. The new floor lamp with its shade of rose-colored silk gives a soft, be-coming light to her face, bringing out the fragile, unearthly prettiness which usually escapes attention. From outside there is a steady murmur of rain, but it is slackening and soon stops; the air outside becomes pale and luminous as the moon breaks through the clouds. A moment after the curtain rises, the lights in both rooms flicker and go out.*

JIM: Hey, there, Mr. Light Bulb!

(AMANDA *laughs nervously.*)

(*Legend on screen:* "Suspension of a public service.")

AMANDA: Where was Moses when the lights went out? Ha-ha. Do you know the answer to that one, Mr. O'Connor?

JIM: No, Ma'am, what's the answer?

AMANDA: In the dark! 5

(JIM *laughs appreciatively.*)

Everybody sit still. I'll light the candles. Isn't it lucky we have them on the table? Where's a match? Which of you gentlemen can provide a match?

JIM: Here.

AMANDA: Thank you, Sir. 10

JIM: Not at all, Ma'am!

AMANDA: (*As she lights the candles.*) I guess the fuse has burnt out. Mr. O'Connor, can you tell a burnt-out fuse? I know I can't and Tom is a total loss when it comes to mechanics.

(*They rise from the table and go into the kitchenette, from where their voices are heard.*)

Oh, be careful you don't bump into something. We don't 15 want our gentleman caller to break his neck. Now wouldn't that be a fine howdy-do?

JIM: Ha-ha! Where is the fuse-box?

AMANDA: Right here next to the stove. Can you see anything?

JIM: Just a minute. 20

AMANDA: Isn't electricity a mysterious thing? Wasn't it Ben-jamin Franklin who tied a key to a kite? We live in such a mysterious universe, don't we? Some people say that sci-ence clears up all the mysteries for us. In my opinion it only creates more! Have you found it yet? 25

JIM: No, Ma'am. All these fuses look okay to me.

AMANDA: Tom!

TOM: Yes, Mother?

AMANDA: That light bill I gave you several days ago. The one I told you we got the notices about? 30

(*Legend on screen:* "Ha!")

TOM: Oh—yeah.

AMANDA: You didn't neglect to pay it by any chance?

TOM: Why, I—

AMANDA: Didn't! I might have known it!

JIM: Shakespeare probably wrote a poem on that light bill, 35 Mrs. Wingfield.

AMANDA: I might have known better than to trust him with
   it! There's such a high price for negligence in this world!

JIM: Maybe the poem will win a ten-dollar prize.

40 AMANDA: We'll just have to spend the remainder of the
   evening in the nineteenth century, before Mr. Edison
   made the Mazda lamp!

JIM: Candlelight is my favorite kind of light.

AMANDA: That shows you're romantic! But that's no excuse
45   for Tom. Well, we got through dinner. Very considerate of
   them to let us get through dinner before they plunged us
   into everlasting darkness, wasn't it, Mr. O'Connor?

JIM: Ha-ha!

AMANDA: Tom, as a penalty for your carelessness you can help
50   me with the dishes.

JIM: Let me give you a hand.

AMANDA: Indeed you will not!

JIM: I ought to be good for something.

AMANDA: Good for something? (*Her tone is rhapsodic.*) *You?*
55   Why, Mr. O'Connor, nobody, *nobody's* given me this much
   entertainment in years—as you have!

JIM: Aw, now, Mrs. Wingfield!

AMANDA: I'm not exaggerating, not one bit! But Sister is all
   by her lonesome. You go keep her company in the par-
60   lor! I'll give you this lovely old candelabrum that used to
   be on the altar at the Church of the Heavenly Rest. It was
   melted a little out of shape when the church burnt down.
   Lightning struck it one spring. Gypsy Jones was holding a
   revival at the time and he intimated that the church was
65   destroyed because the Episcopalians gave card parties.

JIM: Ha-ha.

AMANDA: And how about you coaxing Sister to drink a little
   wine? I think it would be good for her! Can you carry
   both at once?

70 JIM: Sure. I'm Superman!

AMANDA: Now, Thomas, get into this apron!

(JIM *comes into the dining room, carrying the candelabrum, its candles lighted, in one hand and a glass of wine in the other. The door
of the kitchenette swings closed on* AMANDA's *gay laughter; the flick-
ering light approaches the portieres.* LAURA *sits up nervously as* JIM
*enters. She can hardly speak from the almost intolerable strain of be-
ing alone with a stranger.*)

(*Screen legend:* "I don't suppose you remember me at all!")

(*At first, before* JIM's *warmth overcomes her paralyzing shyness,*
LAURA's *voice is thin and breathless, as though she had just run up
a steep flight of stairs.* JIM's *attitude is gently humorous. While the
incident is apparently unimportant, it is to* LAURA *the climax of her
secret life.*)

JIM: Hello there, Laura.

LAURA: (*Faintly.*) Hello.

(*She clears her throat.*)

JIM: How are you feeling now? Better?

75 LAURA: Yes. Yes, thank you.

JIM: This is for you. A little dandelion wine. (*He extends the
   glass toward her with extravagant gallantry.*)

LAURA: Thank you.

JIM: Drink it—but don't get drunk!

(*He laughs heartily.* LAURA *takes the glass uncertainly; she laughs
shyly.*)

   Where shall I set the candles?   80

LAURA: Oh—oh, anywhere. . . .

JIM: How about here on the floor? Any objections?

LAURA: No.

JIM: I'll spread a newspaper under to catch the drippings. I
   like to sit on the floor. Mind if I do?   85

LAURA: Oh, no.

JIM: Give me a pillow?

LAURA: What?

JIM: A pillow!

LAURA: Oh . . . (*She hands him one quickly.*)   90

JIM: How about you? Don't you like to sit on the floor?

LAURA: Oh—yes.

JIM: Why don't you, then?

LAURA: I—will.

JIM: Take a pillow!   95
   (LAURA *does. She sits on the floor on the other side of the candelabrum.* JIM *crosses his legs and smiles engagingly at her.*) I
   can't hardly see you sitting way over there.

LAURA: I can—see you.

JIM: I know, but that's not fair, I'm in the limelight.   100

(LAURA *moves her pillow closer.*)

   Good! Now I can see you! Comfortable?

LAURA: Yes.

JIM: So am I. Comfortable as a cow! Will you have some gum?

LAURA: No, thank you.

JIM: I think that I will indulge, with your permission. (*He*   105
   musingly unwraps a stick of gum and holds it up.) Think of the
   fortune made by the guy that invented the first piece of
   chewing gum. Amazing, huh? The Wrigley Building is
   one of the sights of Chicago—I saw it when I went up to
   the Century of Progress. Did you take in the Century of   110
   Progress?

LAURA: No, I didn't.

JIM: Well, it was quite a wonderful exposition. What impressed
   me most was the Hall of Science. Gives you an idea of
   what the future will be in America, even more wonderful   115
   than the present time is! (*There is a pause.* JIM *smiles at her.*)
   Your brother tells me you're shy. Is that right, Laura?

LAURA: I—don't know.

JIM: I judge you to be an old-fashioned type of girl. Well, I
   think that's a pretty good type to be. Hope you don't   120
   think I'm being too personal—do you?

LAURA: (*Hastily, out of embarrassment.*) I believe I *will* take a
   piece of gum, if you—don't mind. (*Clearing her throat.*)
   Mr. O'Connor, have you—kept up with your singing?

JIM: Singing? Me?   125

LAURA: Yes. I remember what a beautiful voice you had.

JIM: When did you hear me sing?

(LAURA *does not answer, and in the long pause which follows a
man's voice is heard singing offstage.*)

VOICE: O blow, ye winds, heigh-ho,
                       A-roving I will go!
                          I'm off to my love   130
                             With a boxing glove—
                       Ten thousand miles away!

JIM: You say you've heard me sing?

LAURA: Oh, yes! Yes, very often . . . I—don't suppose—you
135 remember me—at all?

JIM: (*Smiling doubtfully.*) You know I have an idea I've seen
you before. I had that idea soon as you opened the door.
It seemed almost like I was about to remember your
name. But the name that I started to call you—wasn't a
140 name! And so I stopped myself before I said it.

LAURA: Wasn't it—Blue Roses?

JIM: (*Springing up, grinning.*) Blue Roses! My gosh, yes—Blue
Roses! That's what I had on my tongue when you opened
the door! Isn't it funny what tricks your memory plays? I
145 didn't connect you with high school somehow or other.
But that's where it was; it was high school. I didn't even
know you were Shakespeare's sister! Gosh, I'm sorry.

LAURA: I didn't expect you to. You—barely knew me!

JIM: But we did have a speaking acquaintance, huh?

150 LAURA: Yes, we—spoke to each other.

JIM: When did you recognize me?

LAURA: Oh, right away!

JIM: Soon as I came in the door?

LAURA: When I heard your name I thought it was probably you.
155 I knew that Tom used to know you a little in high school. So
when you came in the door—well, then I was—sure.

JIM: Why didn't you *say* something, then?

LAURA: (*Breathlessly.*) I didn't know what to say, I was—too
surprised!

160 JIM: For goodness' sakes! You know, this sure is funny!

LAURA: Yes! Yes, isn't it, though. . . .

JIM: Didn't we have a class in something together?

LAURA: Yes, we did.

JIM: What class was that?

165 LAURA: It was—singing—chorus!

JIM: Aw!

LAURA: I sat across the aisle from you in the Aud.

JIM: Aw.

LAURA: Mondays, Wednesdays, and Fridays.

170 JIM: Now I remember—you always came in late.

LAURA: Yes, it was so hard for me, getting upstairs. I had that
brace on my leg—it clumped so loud!

JIM: I never heard any clumping.

LAURA: (*Wincing at the recollection.*) To me it sounded like—
175 thunder!

JIM: Well, well, well, I never even noticed.

LAURA: And everybody was seated before I came in. I had to
walk in front of all those people. My seat was in the back
row. I had to go clumping all the way up the aisle with
180 everyone watching!

JIM: You shouldn't have been self-conscious.

LAURA: I know, but I was. It was always such a relief when
the singing started.

JIM: Aw, yes, I've placed you now! I used to call you Blue
185 Roses. How was it that I got started calling you that?

LAURA: I was out of school a little while with pleurosis.
When I came back you asked me what was the matter. I
said I had pleurosis—you thought I said *Blue Roses.* That's
what you always called me after that!

190 JIM: I hope you didn't mind.

LAURA: Oh, no—I liked it. You see, I wasn't acquainted with
many—people. . . .

JIM: As I remember you sort of stuck by yourself.

LAURA: I—I—never have had much luck at—making friends.

JIM: I don't see why you wouldn't.   195

LAURA: Well, I—started out badly.

JIM: You mean being—

LAURA: Yes, it sort of—stood between me—

JIM: You shouldn't have let it!

LAURA: I know, but it did, and—   200

JIM: You were shy with people!

LAURA: I tried not to be but never could—

JIM: Overcome it?

LAURA: No, I—I never could!

JIM: I guess being shy is something you have to work out of 205
kind of gradually.

LAURA: (*Sorrowfully.*) Yes—I guess it—

JIM: Takes time!

LAURA: Yes—

JIM: People are not so dreadful when you know them. That's 210
what you have to remember! And everybody has problems, not just you, but practically everybody has got some
problems. You think of yourself as having the only problems, as being the only one who is disappointed. But just
look around you and you will see lots of people as disap- 215
pointed as you are. For instance, I hoped when I was going to high school that I would be further along at this
time, six years later, than I am now. You remember that
wonderful write-up I had in *The Torch?*

LAURA: Yes! (*She rises and crosses to the table.*)   220

JIM: It said I was bound to succeed in anything I went into!

(LAURA *returns with the high school yearbook.*)

Holy Jeez! *The Torch!*

(*He accepts it reverently. They smile across the book with mutual
wonder.* LAURA *crouches beside him and they begin to turn the pages.*
LAURA's *shyness is dissolving in his warmth.*)

LAURA: Here you are in *The Pirates of Penzance!*

JIM: (*Wistfully.*) I sang the baritone lead in that operetta.

LAURA: (*Raptly.*) So—*beautifully!*   225

JIM: (*Protesting.*) Aw—

LAURA: Yes, yes—beautifully—beautifully!

JIM: You heard me?

LAURA: All three times!

JIM: No!   230

LAURA: Yes!

JIM: All three performances?

LAURA: (*Looking down.*) Yes.

JIM: Why?

LAURA: I—wanted to ask you to—autograph my program. (*She* 235
takes the program from the back of the yearbook and shows it to him.)

JIM: Why didn't you ask me to?

LAURA: You were always surrounded by your own friends so
much that I never had a chance to.

JIM: You should have just—   240

LAURA: Well, I—thought you might think I was—

JIM: Thought I might think you was—what?

LAURA: Oh—

JIM: (*With reflective relish.*) I was beleaguered by females in
those days.   245

LAURA: You were terribly popular!

JIM: Yeah—

LAURA: You had such a—friendly way—

JIM: I was spoiled in high school.

250 LAURA: Everybody—liked you!

JIM: Including you?

LAURA: I—yes, I—did, too—(*She gently closes the book in her lap.*)

JIM: Well, well, well! Give me that program, Laura.

(*She hands it to him. He signs it with a flourish.*)

There you are—better late than never!

255 LAURA: Oh, I—what a—surprise!

JIM: My signature isn't worth very much right now. But some day—maybe—it will increase in value! Being disappointed is one thing and being discouraged is something else. I am disappointed but I am not discouraged. I'm twenty-three years old. How old are you?

260

LAURA: I'll be twenty-four in June.

JIM: That's not old age!

LAURA: No, but—

JIM: You finished high school?

265 LAURA: (*With difficulty.*) I didn't go back.

JIM: You mean you dropped out?

LAURA: I made bad grades in my final examinations. (*She rises and replaces the book and the program on the table. Her voice is strained.*) How is—Emily Meisenbach getting along?

270 JIM: Oh, that kraut-head!

LAURA: Why do you call her that?

JIM: That's what she was.

LAURA: You're not still—going with her?

JIM: I never see her.

275 LAURA: It said in the "Personal" section that you were—engaged!

JIM: I know, but I wasn't impressed by that—propaganda!

LAURA: It wasn't—the truth?

JIM: Only in Emily's optimistic opinion!

280 LAURA: Oh—

(*Legend:* "What have you done since high school?")

(JIM *lights a cigarette and leans indolently back on his elbows smiling at* LAURA *with a warmth and charm which lights her inwardly with altar candles. She remains by the table, picks up a piece from the glass menagerie collection, and turns it in her hands to cover her tumult.*)

JIM: (*After several reflective puffs on his cigarette.*) What have you done since high school?

(*She seems not to hear him.*)

Huh?

(LAURA *looks up.*)

I said what have you done since high school, Laura?

285 LAURA: Nothing much.

JIM: You must have been doing something these six long years.

LAURA: Yes.

JIM: Well, then, such as what?

LAURA: I took a business course at business college—

JIM: How did that work out?   290

LAURA: Well, not very—well—I had to drop out, it gave me—indigestion—

(JIM *laughs gently.*)

JIM: What are you doing now?

LAURA: I don't do anything—much. Oh, please don't think I sit around doing nothing! My glass collection takes up a   295 good deal of time. Glass is something you have to take good care of.

JIM: What did you say—about glass?

LAURA: Collection I said—I have one—(*She clears her throat and turns away again, acutely shy.*)   300

JIM: (*Abruptly.*) You know what I judge to be the trouble with you? Inferiority complex! Know what that is? That's what they call it when someone low-rates himself! I understand it because I had it, too. Although my case was not so aggravated as yours seems to be. I had it until I took up pub- 305 lic speaking, developed my voice, and learned that I had an aptitude for science. Before that time I never thought of myself as being outstanding in any way whatsoever! Now I've never made a regular study of it, but I have a friend who says I can analyze people better than doctors that   310 make a profession of it. I don't claim that to be necessarily true, but I can sure guess a person's psychology, Laura! (*He takes out his gum.*) Excuse me, Laura. I always take it out when the flavor is gone. I'll use this scrap of paper to wrap it in. I know how it is to get it stuck on a shoe. (*He wraps* 315 *the gum in paper and puts it in his pocket.*) Yep—that's what I judge to be your principal trouble. A lack of confidence in yourself as a person. You don't have the proper amount of faith in yourself. I'm basing that fact on a number of your remarks and also on certain observations I've made. For in- 320 stance that clumping you thought was so awful in high school. You say that you even dreaded to walk into class. You see what you did? You dropped out of school, you gave up an education because of a clump, which as far as I know was practically non-existent! A little physical defect is what   325 you have. Hardly noticeable even! Magnified thousands of times by imagination! You know what my strong advice to you is? Think of yourself as *superior* in some way!

LAURA: In what way would I think?

JIM: Why, man alive, Laura! Just look about you a little. What   330 do you see? A world full of common people! All of 'em born and all of 'em going to die! Which of them has one-tenth of your good points! Or mine! Or anyone else's, as far as that goes—gosh! Everybody excels in some one thing. Some in many! (*He unconsciously glances at himself in* 335 *the mirror.*) All you've got to do is discover in *what!* Take me, for instance. (*He adjusts his tie at the mirror.*) My interest happens to lie in electro-dynamics. I'm taking a course in radio engineering at night school, Laura, on top of a fairly responsible job at the warehouse. I'm taking that   340 course and studying public speaking.

LAURA: Ohhhh.

JIM: Because I believe in the future of television! (*Turning his back to her.*) I wish to be ready to go up right along with it. Therefore I'm planning to get in on the ground floor.   345 In fact I've already made the right connections and all that remains is for the industry itself to get under way! Full steam—(*His eyes are starry.*) *Knowledge*—Zzzzzp! *Money*—Zzzzzp!—*Power!* That's the cycle democracy is built on!

(*His attitude is convincingly dynamic.* LAURA *stares at him, even her shyness eclipsed in her absolute wonder. He suddenly grins.*)

350   I guess you think I think a lot of myself!

LAURA: No—o-o-o, I—

JIM: Now how about you? Isn't there something you take more interest in than anything else?

LAURA: Well, I do—as I said—have my—glass collection—

(*A peal of girlish laughter rings from the kitchenette.*)

355   JIM: I'm not right sure I know what you're talking about. What kind of glass is it?

LAURA: Little articles of it, they're ornaments mostly! Most of them are little animals made out of glass, the tiniest little animals in the world. Mother calls them a glass menagerie!

360   Here's an example of one, if you'd like to see it! This one is one of the oldest. It's nearly thirteen.

(*Music:* "The Glass Menagerie.")

(*He stretches out his hand.*)

Oh, be careful—if you breathe, it breaks!

JIM: I'd better not take it. I'm pretty clumsy with things.

LAURA: Go on, I trust you with him! (*She places the piece in his*
365   *palm.*) There now—you're holding him gently! Hold him over the light, he loves the light! You see how the light shines through him?

JIM: It sure does shine!

LAURA: I shouldn't be partial, but he is my favorite one.

370   JIM: What kind of a thing is this one supposed to be?

LAURA: Haven't you noticed the single horn on his forehead?

JIM: A unicorn, huh?

LAURA: Mmmm-hmmm!

JIM: Unicorns—aren't they extinct in the modern world?

375   LAURA: I know!

JIM: Poor little fellow, he must feel sort of lonesome.

LAURA: (*Smiling.*) Well, if he does, he doesn't complain about it. He stays on a shelf with some horses that don't have horns and all of them seem to get along nicely together.

380   JIM: How do you know?

LAURA: (*Lightly.*) I haven't heard any arguments among them!

JIM: (*Grinning.*) No arguments, huh? Well, that's a pretty good sign! Where shall I set him?

LAURA: Put him on the table. They all like a change of
385   scenery once in a while!

JIM: Well, well, well, well—(*He places the glass piece on the table, then raises his arms and stretches.*) Look how big my shadow is when I stretch!

LAURA: Oh, oh, yes—it stretches across the ceiling!

390   JIM: (*Crossing to the door.*) I think it's stopped raining. (*He opens the fire-escape door and the background music changes to a dance tune.*) Where does the music come from?

LAURA: From the Paradise Dance-hall across the alley.

JIM: How about cutting the rug a little, Miss Wingfield?

395   LAURA: Oh, I—

JIM: Or is your program filled up? Let me have a look at it. (*He grasps an imaginary card.*) Why, every dance is taken! I'll just have to scratch some out.

(*Waltz music:* "La Golondrina.")

Ahhh, a waltz! (*He executes some sweeping turns by himself, then
400   holds his arms toward* LAURA.)

LAURA: (*Breathlessly.*) I—can't dance!

JIM: There you go, that inferiority stuff!

LAURA: I've never danced in my life!

JIM: Come on, try!

405   LAURA: Oh, but I'd step on you!

JIM: I'm not made out of glass.

LAURA: How—how—how do we start?

JIM: Just leave it to me. You hold your arms out a little.

LAURA: Like this?

410   JIM: (*Taking her in his arms.*) A little bit higher. Right. Now don't tighten up, that's the main thing about it—relax.

LAURA: (*Laughing breathlessly.*) It's hard not to.

JIM: Okay.

LAURA: I'm afraid you can't budge me.

415   JIM: What do you bet I can't? (*He swings her into motion.*)

LAURA: Goodness, yes, you can!

JIM: Let yourself go, now, Laura, just let yourself go.

LAURA: I'm—

JIM: Come on!

420   LAURA: —trying!

JIM: Not so stiff—easy does it!

LAURA: I know but I'm—

JIM: Loosen th' backbone! There now, that's a lot better.

LAURA: Am I?

425   JIM: Lots, lots better! (*He moves her about the room in a clumsy waltz.*)

LAURA: Oh, my!

JIM: Ha-ha!

LAURA: Oh, my goodness!

430   JIM: Ha-ha-ha!

(*They suddenly bump into the table, and the glass piece on it falls to the floor.* JIM *stops the dance.*)

What did we hit on?

LAURA: Table.

JIM: Did something fall off it? I think—

LAURA: Yes.

435   JIM: I hope that it wasn't the little glass horse with the horn!

LAURA: Yes. (*She stoops to pick it up.*)

JIM: Aw, aw, aw. Is it broken?

LAURA: Now it is just like all the other horses.

JIM: It's lost its—

440   LAURA: Horn! It doesn't matter. Maybe it's a blessing in disguise.

JIM: You'll never forgive me. I bet that that was your favorite piece of glass.

LAURA: I don't have favorites much. It's no tragedy, Freckles.
445   Glass breaks so easily. No matter how careful you are. The traffic jars the shelves and things fall off them.

JIM: Still I'm awfully sorry that I was the cause.

LAURA: (*Smiling.*) I'll just imagine he had an operation. The horn was removed to make him feel less—freakish!

(*They both laugh.*)

450   Now he will feel more at home with the other horses, the
      ones that don't have horns. . . .
      JIM: Ha-ha, that's very funny! (*Suddenly he is serious.*) I'm glad
      to see that you have a sense of humor. You know—
      you're—well—very different! Surprisingly different from
455   anyone else I know! (*His voice becomes soft and hesitant with
      a genuine feeling.*) Do you mind me telling you that?

(LAURA *is abashed beyond speech.*)

      I mean it in a nice way—

(LAURA *nods shyly, looking away.*)

      You make me feel sort of—I don't know how to put it!
      I'm usually pretty good at expressing things, but—this is
460   something that I don't know how to say!

(LAURA *touches her throat and clears it—turns the broken unicorn
in her hands. His voice becomes softer.*)

      Has anyone ever told you that you were pretty?

(*There is a pause, and the music rises slightly.* LAURA *looks up
slowly, with wonder, and shakes her head.*)

      Well, you are! In a very different way from anyone else.
      And all the nicer because of the difference, too.

(*His voice becomes low and husky.* LAURA *turns away, nearly faint
with the novelty of her emotions.*)

      I wish that you were my sister. I'd teach you to have some
465   confidence in yourself. The different people are not like
      other people, but being different is nothing to be ashamed
      of. Because other people are not such wonderful people.
      They're one hundred times one thousand. You're one
      times one! They walk all over the earth. You just stay here.
470   They're common as—weeds, but—you—well, you're—
      Blue Roses!

(*Image on screen:* Blue Roses.)

(*The music changes.*)

      LAURA: But blue is wrong for—roses. . . .
      JIM: It's right for you! You're—pretty!
      LAURA: In what respect am I pretty?
475   JIM: In all respects—believe me! Your eyes—your hair—are
      pretty! Your hands are pretty! (*He catches hold of her hand.*)
      You think I'm making this up because I'm invited to din-
      ner and have to be nice. Oh, I could do that! I could put
      on an act for you, Laura, and say lots of things without be-
480   ing very sincere. But this time I am. I'm talking to you
      sincerely. I happened to notice you had this inferiority
      complex that keeps you from feeling comfortable with
      people. Somebody needs to build your confidence up and
      make you proud instead of shy and turning away and—
485   blushing. Somebody—ought to—*kiss* you, Laura!

(*His hand slips slowly up her arm to her shoulder as the music swells
tumultuously. He suddenly turns her about and kisses her on the lips.
When he releases her,* LAURA *sinks on the sofa with a bright, dazed
look.* JIM *backs away and fishes in his pocket for a cigarette.*)

(*Legend on screen:* "A souvenir.")

      Stumblejohn!

(*He lights the cigarette, avoiding her look. There is a peal of girlish
laughter from* AMANDA *in the kitchenette.* LAURA *slowly raises and
opens her hand. It still contains the little broken glass animal. She
looks at it with a tender, bewildered expression.*)

      Stumblejohn! I shouldn't have done that—that was way
      off the beam. You don't smoke, do you?

(*She looks up, smiling, not hearing the question. He sits beside her
rather gingerly. She looks at him speechlessly—waiting. He coughs
decorously and moves a little farther aside as he considers the situation
and senses her feelings, dimly, with perturbation. He speaks gently.*)

      Would you—care for a—mint?

(*She doesn't seem to hear him but her look grows brighter even.*)

      Peppermint? Life Saver? My pocket's a regular drug-   490
      store—wherever I go . . . (*He pops a mint in his mouth. Then
      he gulps and decides to make a clean breast of it. He speaks
      slowly and gingerly.*) Laura, you know, if I had a sister like
      you, I'd do the same thing as Tom. I'd bring out fellows
      and—introduce her to them. The right type of boys—of   495
      a type to—appreciate her. Only—well—he made a mis-
      take about me. Maybe I've got no call to be saying this.
      That may not have been the idea in having me over. But
      what if it was? There's nothing wrong about that. The
      only trouble is that in my case—I'm not in a situation   500
      to—do the right thing. I can't take down your number
      and say I'll phone. I can't call up next week and—ask for
      a date. I thought I had better explain the situation in case
      you—misunderstood it and—I hurt your feelings. . . .

(*There is a pause. Slowly, very slowly,* LAURA'S *look changes, her eyes
returning slowly from his to the glass figure in her palm.* AMANDA
utters another gay laugh in the kitchenette.)

      LAURA: (*Faintly.*) You—won't—call again?   505
      JIM: No, Laura. I can't. (*He rises from the sofa.*) As I was just ex-
      plaining, I've—got strings on me. Laura, I've—been going
      steady! I go out all the time with a girl named Betty. She's
      a home-girl like you, and Catholic, and Irish, and in a
      great many ways we—get along fine. I met her last sum-   510
      mer on a moonlight boat trip up the river to Alton, on the
      Majestic. Well—right away from the start it was—love!

(*Legend:* "Love!")

(LAURA *sways slightly forward and grips the arm of the sofa. He fails
to notice, now enrapt in his own comfortable being.*)

      Being in love has made a new man of me!

(*Leaning stiffly forward, clutching the arm of the sofa,* LAURA *struggles visibly with her storm. But* JIM *is oblivious; she is a long way off.*)

      The power of love is really pretty tremendous! Love is
      something that—changes the whole world, Laura!   515

(*The storm abates a little and* LAURA *leans back. He notices her
again.*)

It happened that Betty's aunt took sick, she got a wire and had to go to Centralia. So Tom—when he asked me to dinner—I naturally just accepted the invitation, not knowing that you—that he—that I—(*He stops awkwardly.*)

520   Huh—I'm a stumblejohn!

(*He flops back on the sofa. The holy candles on the altar of* LAURA's *face have been snuffed out. There is a look of almost infinite desolation.* JIM *glances at her uneasily.*)

I wish that you would—say something.

(*She bites her lip which was trembling and then bravely smiles. She opens her hand again on the broken glass figure. Then she gently takes his hand and raises it level with her own. She carefully places the unicorn in the palm of his hand, then pushes his fingers closed upon it.*)

What are you—doing that for? You want me to have him? Laura?

(*She nods.*)

What for?

525   LAURA: A—souvenir. . . .

(*She rises unsteadily and crouches beside the Victrola to wind it up.*)

(*Legend on screen:* "Things have a way of turning out so badly!" *Or image:* Gentleman caller waving goodbye—gaily.)

(*At this moment* AMANDA *rushes brightly back into the living room. She bears a pitcher of fruit punch in an old-fashioned cut-glass pitcher, and a plate of macaroons. The plate has a gold border and poppies painted on it.*)

AMANDA: Well, well, well! Isn't the air delightful after the shower? I've made you children a little liquid refreshment. (*She turns gaily to* JIM.) Jim, do you know that song about lemonade?

530   "Lemonade, lemonade
Made in the shade and stirred with a spade—
Good enough for any old maid!"

JIM: (*Uneasily.*) Ha-ha! No—I never heard it.
AMANDA: Why, Laura! You look so serious!
535   JIM: We were having a serious conversation.
AMANDA: Good! Now you're better acquainted!
JIM: (*Uncertainly.*) Ha-ha! Yes.
AMANDA: You modern young people are much more seri-ousminded than my generation. I was so gay as a girl!
540   JIM: You haven't changed, Mrs. Wingfield.
AMANDA: Tonight I'm rejuvenated! The gaiety of the occasion, Mr. O'Connor! (*She tosses her head with a peal of laughter, spilling some lemonade.*) Oooo! I'm baptizing myself!
JIM: Here—let me—
545   AMANDA: (*Setting the pitcher down.*) There now. I discovered we had some maraschino cherries. I dumped them in, juice and all!
JIM: You shouldn't have gone to that trouble, Mrs. Wingfield.
AMANDA: Trouble, trouble? Why, it was loads of fun! Didn't
550   you hear me cutting up in the kitchen? I bet your ears were burning! I told Tom how outdone with him I was

for keeping you to himself so long a time! He should have brought you over much, much sooner! Well, now that you've found your way, I want you to be a very frequent caller! Not just occasional but all the time. Oh, we're go- 555 ing to have a lot of gay times together! I see them coming! Mmm, just breathe that air! So fresh, and the moon's so pretty! I'll skip back out—I know where my place is when young folks are having a—serious conversation!
JIM: Oh, don't go out, Mrs. Wingfield. The fact of the mat- 560 ter is I've got to be going.
AMANDA: Going, now? You're joking! Why, it's only the shank of the evening, Mr. O'Connor!
JIM: Well, you know how it is.
AMANDA: You mean you're a young workingman and have to 565 keep workingmen's hours. We'll let you off early tonight. But only on the condition that next time you stay later. What's the best night for you? Isn't Saturday night the best night for you workingmen?
JIM: I have a couple of time-clocks to punch, Mrs. Wingfield. 570 One at morning, another one at night!
AMANDA: My, but you are ambitious! You work at night, too?
JIM: No, Ma'am, not work but—Betty!

(*He crosses deliberately to pick up his hat. The band at the Paradise Dance-hall goes into a tender waltz.*)

AMANDA: Betty? Betty? Who's—Betty!

(*There is an ominous cracking sound in the sky.*)

JIM: Oh, just a girl. The girl I go steady with!   575

(*He smiles charmingly. The sky falls.*)

(*Legend:* "The Sky Falls.")

AMANDA: (*A long-drawn exhalation.*) Ohhhh . . . Is it a serious romance, Mr. O'Connor?
JIM: We're going to be married the second Sunday in June.
AMANDA: Ohhhh—how nice! Tom didn't mention that you were engaged to be married.   580
JIM: The cat's not out of the bag at the warehouse yet. You know how they are. They call you Romeo and stuff like that. (*He stops at the oval mirror to put on his hat. He carefully shapes the brim and the crown to give a discreetly dashing effect.*) It's been a wonderful evening, Mrs. Wingfield. I guess this 585 is what they mean by Southern hospitality.
AMANDA: It really wasn't anything at all.
JIM: I hope it don't seem like I'm rushing off. But I promised Betty I'd pick her up at the Wabash depot, an' by the time I get my jalopy down there her train'll be in. Some 590 women are pretty upset if you keep 'em waiting.
AMANDA: Yes, I know—the tyranny of women! (*She extends her hand.*) Goodbye, Mr. O'Connor. I wish you luck—and happiness—and success! All three of them, and so does Laura! Don't you, Laura?   595
LAURA: Yes!
JIM: (*Taking* LAURA's *hand.*) Goodbye, Laura. I'm certainly go-ing to treasure that souvenir. And don't you forget the good advice I gave you. (*He raises his voice to a cheery shout.*) So long, Shakespeare! Thanks again, ladies. Good night!   600

(*He grins and ducks jauntily out. Still bravely grimacing,* AMANDA *closes the door on the gentleman caller. Then she turns back to the room with a puzzled expression. She and* LAURA *don't dare to face each other.* LAURA *crouches beside the Victrola to wind it.*)

AMANDA: (*Faintly.*) Things have a way of turning out so badly. I don't believe that I would play the Victrola. Well, well—well! Our gentleman caller was engaged to be married! (*She raises her voice.*) Tom!

605 TOM: (*From the kitchenette.*) Yes, Mother?

AMANDA: Come in here a minute. I want to tell you something awfully funny.

TOM: (*Entering with a macaroon and a glass of the lemonade.*) Has the gentleman caller gotten away already?

610 AMANDA: The gentleman caller has made an early departure. What a wonderful joke you played on us!

TOM: How do you mean?

AMANDA: You didn't mention that he was engaged to be married.

615 TOM: Jim? Engaged?

AMANDA: That's what he just informed us.

TOM: I'll be jiggered! I didn't know about that.

AMANDA: That seems very peculiar.

TOM: What's peculiar about it?

620 AMANDA: Didn't you call him your best friend down at the warehouse?

TOM: He is, but how did I know?

AMANDA: It seems extremely peculiar that you wouldn't know your best friend was going to be married!

625 TOM: The warehouse is where I work, not where I know things about people!

AMANDA: You don't know things anywhere! You live in a dream; you manufacture illusions!

(*He crosses to the door.*)

Where are you going?

630 TOM: I'm going to the movies.

AMANDA: That's right, now that you've had us make such fools of ourselves. The effort, the preparations, all the expense! The new floor lamp, the rug, the clothes for Laura! All for what? To entertain some other girl's fiancé! Go to

635 the movies, go! Don't think about us, a mother deserted, an unmarried sister who's crippled and has no job! Don't let anything interfere with your selfish pleasure! Just go, go, go—to the movies!

TOM: All right, I will! The more you shout about my selfish-

640 ness to me the quicker I'll go, and I won't go to the movies!

AMANDA: Go, then! Go to the moon—you selfish dreamer!

(TOM *smashes his glass on the floor. He plunges out on the fire escape, slamming the door.* LAURA *screams in fright. The dance-hall music becomes louder.* TOM *stands on the fire escape, gripping the rail. The moon breaks through the storm clouds, illuminating his face.*)

(*Legend on screen:* "And so goodbye . . .")

(TOM*'s closing speech is timed with what is happening inside the house. We see, as though through soundproof glass, that* AMANDA *appears to be making a comforting speech to* LAURA, *who is huddled upon the sofa. Now that we cannot hear the mother's speech, her silliness is gone and she has dignity and tragic beauty.* LAURA*'s hair hides her face until, at the end of the speech, she lifts her head to smile at her mother.* AMANDA*'s gestures are slow and graceful, almost dancelike, as she comforts her daughter. At the end of her speech she glances a moment at the father's picture—then withdraws through the portieres. At the close of* TOM*'s speech,* LAURA *blows out the candles, ending the play.*)

TOM: I didn't go to the moon, I went much further—for time is the longest distance between two places. Not long after that I was fired for writing a poem on the lid of a shoe-box. I left Saint Louis. I descended the steps of this fire escape 645 for a last time and followed, from then on, in my father's footsteps, attempting to find in motion what was lost in space. I traveled around a great deal. The cities swept about me like dead leaves, leaves that were brightly colored but torn away from the branches. I would have stopped, but I 650 was pursued by something. It always came upon me unawares, taking me altogether by surprise. Perhaps it was a familiar bit of music. Perhaps it was only a piece of transparent glass. Perhaps I am walking along a street at night, in some strange city, before I have found companions. I pass 655 the lighted window of a shop where perfume is sold. The window is filled with pieces of colored glass, tiny transparent bottles in delicate colors, like bits of a shattered rainbow. Then all at once my sister touches my shoulder. I turn around and look into her eyes. Oh, Laura, Laura, I tried to 660 leave you behind me, but I am more faithful than I intended to be! I reach for a cigarette, I cross the street, I run into the movies or a bar, I buy a drink, I speak to the nearest stranger—anything that can blow your candles out!

(LAURA *bends over the candles.*)

For nowadays the world is lit by lightning! Blow out your 665 candles, Laura—and so goodbye. . . .

(*She blows the candles out.*)

Arthur Miller

Arthur Miller (1915–2005) was born in Harlem and raised in Brooklyn. The son of Jewish immigrants, Miller often takes the milieu of urban New York as the substance of his drama. Like Tennessee Williams, Miller was formed by the Depression. He worked a variety of jobs to help his family make ends meet, and eventually gained provisional admission to the University of Michigan, where he studied playwriting and graduated in 1938. He worked briefly for the Federal Theater Project. Although his first play—*The Man Who Had All the Luck* (1944)—failed, Miller went on to write a series of gritty and powerful plays: *All My Sons* (1947), *Death of a Salesman* (1949), an adaptation of Ibsen's *An Enemy of the People* (1950), and *The Crucible* (1953). In 1955, Miller wrote *A View from the Bridge,* a story of honor and betrayal among New York's Italian immigrants. He also married Marilyn Monroe in that year, and his next play, *After the Fall* (1964), is a lightly disguised account of their stormy marriage and its break-up. In 1964 he also produced *Incident at Vichy,* a play concerning the Nazi persecution of the Jews during World War II, and he returned to the subject in his 1981 screenplay, *Playing for Time.* Until his death Miller continued to write and have his plays produced worldwide—including *The Price* (1968), *The Creation of the World and Other Business* (1972—revised as *Up from Paradise* 1974), *The Archbishop's Calling* (1977), *The American Clock* (1980), *Danger: Memory* (1987), *The Ride Down Mount Morgan* (1991), *The Last Yankee* (1993); and *Resurrection Blues* (2002). He also published a memoir (*Timebends*), a series of collected essays, and an account of the production of *Salesman* in the People's Republic of China during the 1980s. He wrote and lectured frequently about his career and about American theater.

DEATH OF A SALESMAN

Something like *Oedipus the King* for the classical theater, or *Hamlet* for the English Renaissance stage, *Death of a Salesman* has become an icon of the American theater: Miller's central characters—Willy Loman, the worn-out, dreaming salesman; his two sons, Biff, the All-American star, who can never quite fit into American society, and Happy, the unhappy younger brother—have entered into the popular lexicon of cultural stereotypes, landmarks for later playwrights. (Think of Troy Maxson in August Wilson's *Fences,* or Lee and Austin in Sam Shepard's *True West,* or even Lincoln and Booth in Suzan-Lori Parks's *Topdog/ Underdog.*) And, again like *Hamlet,* the play provides a dominant central role that has tested generations of actors from Lee J. Cobb, who created Willy Loman onstage, to Dustin Hoffman and Brian Dennehy.

As in classical tragedy (see Miller's essay, "Tragedy and the Common Man," later in this unit), the action of *Death of a Salesman* is impelled by a single, climactic event: Willy is approaching the end of his career, his glad-handing sales contacts are all dead or retired, and he's no longer pulling in business for the company—he's about to be fired. While this is perhaps less sensational than the crimes that prompt Oedipus or Hamlet to tragic action, Miller uses the fluidity of his stage and his remarkable ear for the prosaic poetry of everyday speech to give this event an extraordinary resonance. Blending scenes from Willy's past (the affecting scenes of Willy as a young father; the Woman in Boston and Biff's discovery of Willy's hypocrisy) with the Loman family's present straits, *Death of a Salesman* claims Willy as a representative figure, embodying the contradictions of the American dream. As Linda puts it, "Willy Loman never made alot of money. His name was never in the paper. He's not the finest character that ever lived. But he's a human being, and a terrible thing is happening to him. So attention must be paid." Miller deftly focuses a conflict between the material circumstances of Willy's life, his hard work, his exploitation by the company that finally sends him "to his grave like an old dog," and Willy's nonetheless eager belief in the system, in the salesman's ethic that has sustained and destroyed him. *Death of a Salesman* stages a double perspective on deadly mythology of America: Willy at once believes, and teaches his two sons to believe, that to be "well liked" is more important, more critical than ability or achievement; at the same time, he turns aside from the life represented by his uncle Ben, remaining with his good job and steady income instead of pursuing the intangible fortunes of Alaska like his pioneering father. Although the play stages many of the turning points in Willy's life, the opportunities missed to take a new direction, the central "cause" of the play's action took place years earlier, when Willy met an aging salesman and decided to pursue his career rather than light out for the frontier. What most impressed Willy about *that* salesman was his funeral: he died the "death of a salesman, in his green velvet slippers in the smoker of the New York, New Haven and Hartford, going into Boston—when he died, hundreds of salesmen and buyers were at his funeral." Part of Miller's genius in *Death of a Salesman* lies in the reach he gives to this figure and in the central conflict between the city and the frontier still embodied by the career of the salesman, represented in the play as a kind of Kit Carson or Daniel Boone, a rootless wanderer domesticated and destroyed by his willing acceptance of the demands of business and the society it sustains. As Charlie puts it in the "Requiem" ending the play: "Willy was a salesman. And for a salesman, there is no rock bottom to the life. He don't put a bolt to a nut, he don't tell you the law or give you medicine. He's a man way out there in the blue, riding on a smile and a shoeshine. . . . A salesman is got to dream, boy. It comes with the territory."

Jo Mielziner's celebrated set for the premiere production of Arthur Miller's *Death of a Salesman*, showing the cutaway house and the downstage playing area.

DEATH OF A SALESMAN

Arthur Miller

CHARACTERS

WILLY LOMAN

LINDA

BIFF

HAPPY

BERNARD

THE WOMAN

CHARLEY

UNCLE BEN

HOWARD WAGNER

JENNY

STANLEY

MISS FORSYTHE

LETTA

The action takes place in Willy Loman's house and yard and in various places he visits in the New York and Boston of today.

Throughout the play, in the stage directions, left and right mean stage left and stage right.

ACT ONE

A melody is heard, played upon a flute. It is small and fine, telling of grass and trees and the horizon. The curtain rises.

Before us is the Salesman's house. We are aware of towering, angular shapes behind it, surrounding it on all sides. Only the blue light of the sky falls upon the house and forestage; the surrounding area shows an angry glow of orange. As more light appears, we see a solid vault of apartment houses around the small, fragile-seeming home. An air of the dream clings to the place, a dream rising out of reality. The kitchen at center seems actual enough, for there is a kitchen table with three chairs, and a refrigerator. But no other fixtures are seen. At the back of the kitchen there is a draped entrance, which leads to the living-room. To the right of the kitchen, on a level raised two feet, is a bedroom furnished only with a brass bedstead and a straight chair. On a shelf over the bed a silver athletic trophy stands. A window opens onto the apartment house at the side.

Behind the kitchen, on a level raised six and a half feet, is the boys' bedroom, at present barely visible. Two beds are dimly seen, and at the back of the room a dormer window. (This bedroom is above the unseen living-room.) At the left a stairway curves up to it from the kitchen.

The entire setting is wholly, or, in some places, partially transparent. The roof-line of the house is one-dimensional; under and over it we see the apartment buildings. Before the house lies an apron, curving beyond the forestage into the orchestra. This forward area serves as the back yard as well as the locale of all Willy's imaginings and of his city scenes. Whenever the action is in the present the actors observe the imaginary wall-lines, entering the house only through its door at the left. But in the scenes of the past these boundaries are broken, and characters enter or leave a room by stepping "through" a wall onto the forestage.

From the right, Willy Loman, the Salesman, enters, carrying two large sample cases. The flute plays on. He hears but is not aware of it. He is past sixty years of age, dressed quietly. Even as he crosses the stage to the doorway of the house, his exhaustion is apparent. He unlocks the door, comes into the kitchen, and thankfully lets his burden down, feeling the soreness of his palms. A word-sigh escapes his lips—it might be "Oh, boy, oh, boy." He closes the door, then carries his cases out into the living-room, through the draped kitchen doorway.

Linda, his wife, has stirred in her bed at the right. She gets out and puts on a robe, listening. Most often jovial, she has developed an iron repression of her exceptions to Willy's behavior—she more than loves him, she admires him, as though his mercurial nature, his temper, his massive dreams and little cruelties, served her only as sharp reminders of the turbulent longings within him, longings which she shares but lacks the temperament to utter and follow to their end.

LINDA: (*Hearing* WILLY *outside the bedroom, calls with some trepidation.*) Willy!

WILLY: It's all right. I came back.

LINDA: Why? What happened? (*Slight pause.*) Did something happen, Willy? 5

WILLY: No, nothing happened.

LINDA: You didn't smash the car, did you?

WILLY: (*With casual irritation.*) I said nothing happened. Didn't you hear me?

LINDA: Don't you feel well? 10

WILLY: I'm tired to the death. (*The flute has faded away. He sits on the bed beside her, a little numb.*) I couldn't make it. I just couldn't make it, Linda.

LINDA: (*Very carefully, delicately.*) Where were you all day? You look terrible. 15

WILLY: I got as far as a little above Yonkers. I stopped for a cup of coffee. Maybe it was the coffee.

LINDA: What?

WILLY: (*After a pause.*) I suddenly couldn't drive any more. The car kept going off onto the shoulder, y'know? 20

LINDA: (*Helpfully.*) Oh. Maybe it was the steering again. I don't think Angelo knows the Studebaker.

WILLY: No, it's me, it's me. Suddenly I realize I'm goin' sixty miles an hour and I don't remember the last five minutes. I'm—I can't seem to—keep my mind to it. 25

LINDA: Maybe it's your glasses. You never went for your new glasses.

WILLY: No, I see everything. I came back ten miles an hour. It took me nearly four hours from Yonkers.

LINDA: (*Resigned.*) Well, you'll just have to take a rest, Willy, you can't continue this way. 30

WILLY: I just got back from Florida.

LINDA: But you didn't rest your mind. Your mind is overactive, and the mind is what counts, dear.

35 WILLY: I'll start out in the morning. Maybe I'll feel better in the morning. (*She is taking off his shoes.*) These goddam arch supports are killing me.

LINDA: Take an aspirin. Should I get you an aspirin? It'll soothe you.

40 WILLY: (*With wonder.*) I was driving along, you understand? And I was fine. I was even observing the scenery. You can imagine, me looking at scenery, on the road every week of my life. But it's so beautiful up there, Linda, the trees are so thick, and the sun is warm. I opened the windshield

45 and just let the warm air bathe over me. And then all of a sudden I'm goin' off the road! I'm tellin' ya, I absolutely forgot I was driving. If I'd've gone the other way over the white line I might've killed somebody. So I went on again—and five minutes later I'm dreamin' again, and I

50 nearly— (*He presses two fingers against his eyes.*) I have such thoughts, I have such strange thoughts.

LINDA: Willy, dear. Talk to them again. There's no reason why you can't work in New York.

WILLY: They don't need me in New York. I'm the New En-
55 gland man. I'm vital in New England.

LINDA: But you're sixty years old. They can't expect you to keep traveling every week.

WILLY: I'll have to send a wire to Portland. I'm supposed to see Brown and Morrison tomorrow morning at ten
60 o'clock to show the line. Goddammit, I could sell them! (*He starts putting on his jacket.*)

LINDA: (*Taking the jacket from him.*) Why don't you go down to the place tomorrow and tell Howard you've simply got to work in New York? You're too accommodating,
65 dear.

WILLY: If old man Wagner was alive I'd a been in charge of New York now! That man was a prince, he was a masterful man. But that boy of his, that Howard, he don't appreciate. When I went north the first time, the Wagner
70 Company didn't know where New England was!

LINDA: Why don't you tell those things to Howard, dear?

WILLY: (*Encouraged.*) I will, I definitely will. Is there any cheese?

LINDA: I'll make you a sandwich.

75 WILLY: No, go to sleep. I'll take some milk. I'll be up right away. The boys in?

LINDA: They're sleeping. Happy took Biff on a date tonight.

WILLY: (*Interested.*) That so?

LINDA: It was so nice to see them shaving together, one be-
80 hind the other, in the bathroom. And going out together. You notice? The whole house smells of shaving lotion.

WILLY: Figure it out. Work a lifetime to pay off a house. You finally own it, and there's nobody to live in it.

85 LINDA: Well, dear, life is a casting off. It's always that way.

WILLY: No, no, some people—some people accomplish something. Did Biff say anything after I went this morning?

LINDA: You shouldn't have criticized him, Willy, especially after he just got off the train. You mustn't lose your temper
90 with him.

WILLY: When the hell did I lose my temper? I simply asked him if he was making any money. Is that a criticism?

LINDA: But, dear, how could he make any money?

WILLY: (*Worried and angered.*) There's such an undercurrent in him. He became a moody man. Did he apologize when I 95 left this morning?

LINDA: He was crestfallen, Willy. You know how he admires you. I think if he finds himself, then you'll both be happier and not fight any more.

WILLY: How can he find himself on a farm? Is that a life? A 100 farmhand? In the beginning, when he was young, I thought, well, a young man, it's good for him to tramp around, take a lot of different jobs. But it's more than ten years now and he has yet to make thirty-five dollars a week! 105

LINDA: He's finding himself, Willy.

WILLY: Not finding yourself at the age of thirty-four is a disgrace!

LINDA: Shh!

WILLY: The trouble is he's lazy, goddammit! 110

LINDA: Willy, please!

WILLY: Biff is a lazy bum!

LINDA: They're sleeping. Get something to eat. Go on down.

WILLY: Why did he come home? I would like to know what brought him home. 115

LINDA: I don't know. I think he's still lost, Willy. I think he's very lost.

WILLY: Biff Loman is lost. In the greatest country in the world a young man with such—personal attractiveness, gets lost. And such a hard worker. There's one thing about 120 Biff—he's not lazy.

LINDA: Never.

WILLY: (*With pity and resolve.*) I'll see him in the morning; I'll have a nice talk with him. I'll get him a job selling. He could be big in no time. My God! Remember how they 125 used to follow him around in high school? When he smiled at one of them their faces lit up. When he walked down the street. . . (*He loses himself in reminiscences.*)

LINDA: (*Trying to bring him out of it.*) Willy, dear, I got a new kind of American-type cheese today. It's whipped. 130

WILLY: Why do you get American when I like Swiss?

LINDA: I just thought you'd like a change—

WILLY: I don't want a change! I want Swiss cheese. Why am I always being contradicted?

LINDA: (*With a covering laugh.*) I thought it would be a surprise. 135

WILLY: Why don't you open a window in here, for God's sake?

LINDA: (*With infinite patience.*) They're all open, dear.

WILLY: The way they boxed us in here. Bricks and windows, windows and bricks.

LINDA: We should've bought the land next door. 140

WILLY: The street is lined with cars. There's not a breath of fresh air in the neighborhood. The grass don't grow any more, you can't raise a carrot in the back yard. They should've had a law against apartment houses. Remember those two beautiful elm trees out there? When I and Biff 145 hung the swing between them?

LINDA: Yeah, like being a million miles from the city.

WILLY: They should've arrested the builder for cutting those down. They massacred the neighborhood (*Lost.*) More and more I think of those days, Linda. This time of year 150 it was lilac and wisteria. And then the peonies would come out, and the daffodils. What fragrance in this room!

LINDA: Well, after all, people had to move somewhere.

WILLY: No, there's more people, now.

155 LINDA: I don't think there's more people I think—

WILLY: There's more people! That's what's ruining this country! Population is getting out of control. The competition is maddening! Smell the stink from that apartment house! And another one on the other side . . . How can they whip

160 cheese?

(On WILLY's last line, BIFF and HAPPY raise themselves up in their beds, listening.)

LINDA: Go down, try it. And be quiet.

WILLY: (*Turning to LINDA, guiltily.*) You're not worried about me, are you, sweetheart?

BIFF: What's the matter?

165 HAPPY: Listen!

LINDA: You've got too much on the ball to worry about.

WILLY: You're my foundation and my support, Linda.

LINDA: Just try to relax, dear. You make mountains out of molehills.

170 WILLY: I won't fight with him any more. If he wants to go back to Texas, let him go.

LINDA: He'll find his way.

WILLY: Sure. Certain men just don't get started till later in life. Like Thomas Edison, I think. Or B. F. Goodrich. One

175 of them was deaf. (*He starts for the bedroom doorway.*) I'll put my money on Biff.

LINDA: And Willy—if it's warm Sunday we'll drive in the country. And we'll open the windshield, and take lunch.

WILLY: No, the windshields don't open on the new cars.

180 LINDA: But you opened it today.

WILLY: Me? I didn't. (*He stops.*) Now isn't that peculiar! Isn't that a remarkable—(*He breaks off in amazement and fright as the flute is heard distantly.*)

LINDA: What, darling?

185 WILLY: That is the most remarkable thing.

LINDA: What, dear?

WILLY: I was thinking of the Chevvy. (*Slight pause.*) Nineteen twenty-eight . . . when I had that red Chevvy—(*Breaks off.*) That funny? I coulda sworn I was driving that Chevvy

190 today.

LINDA: Well, that's nothing. Something must've reminded you.

WILLY: Remarkable. Ts. Remember those days? The way Biff used to simonize that car? The dealer refused to believe

195 there was eighty thousand miles on it. (*He shakes his head.*) Heh! (*To LINDA.*) Close your eyes, I'll be right up. (*He walks out of the bedroom.*)

HAPPY *to* BIFF: Jesus, maybe he smashed up the car again!

LINDA: (*Calling after WILLY.*) Be careful on the stairs, dear! The

200 cheese is on the middle shelf! (*She turns, goes over to the bed, takes his jacket, and goes out of the bedroom.*)

(Light has risen on the boys' room. Unseen, WILLY is heard talking to himself, "Eighty thousand miles," and a little laugh. BIFF gets out of bed, comes downstage a bit, and stands attentively. BIFF is two years older than his brother HAPPY, well built, but in these days bears a worn air and seems less self-assured. He has succeeded less, and his dreams are stronger and less acceptable than HAPPY's. HAPPY is tall, powerfully made. Sexuality is like a visible color on him, or a scent that many women have discovered. He, like his brother, is lost, but in

a different way, for he has never allowed himself to turn his face toward defeat and is thus more confused and hard-skinned, although seemingly more content.

HAPPY: (*Getting out of bed.*) He's going to get his license taken away if he keeps that up. I'm getting nervous about him, y'know, Biff?

BIFF: His eyes are going. 205

HAPPY: No, I've driven with him. He sees all right. He just doesn't keep his mind on it. I drove into the city with him last week. He stops at a green light and then it turns red and he goes. (*He laughs.*)

BIFF: Maybe he's color-blind. 210

HAPPY: Pop? Why he's got the finest eye for color in the business. You know that.

BIFF: (*Sitting down on his bed.*) I'm going to sleep.

HAPPY: You're not still sour on Dad, are you, Biff?

BIFF: He's all right, I guess. 215

WILLY: (*Underneath them, in the living-room.*) Yes, sir, eighty thousand miles—eighty-two thousand!

BIFF: You smoking?

HAPPY: (*Holding out a pack of cigarettes.*) Want one?

BIFF: (*Taking a cigarette.*) I can never sleep when I smell it. 220

WILLY: What a simonizing job, heh!

HAPPY: (*With deep sentiment.*) Funny, Biff, y'know? Us sleeping in here again? The old beds. (*He pats his bed affectionately.*) All the talk that went across those two beds, huh? Our whole lives. 225

BIFF: Yeah. Lotta dreams and plans.

HAPPY: (*With a deep and masculine laugh.*) About five hundred women would like to know what was said in this room.

(They share a soft laugh.)

BIFF: Remember that big Betsy something—what the hell was her name—over on Bushwick Avenue? 230

HAPPY: (*Combing his hair.*) With the collie dog!

BIFF: That's the one. I got you in there, remember?

HAPPY: Yeah, that was my first time—I think. Boy, there was a pig! (*They laugh, almost crudely.*) You taught me everything I know about women. Don't forget that. 235

BIFF: I bet you forgot how bashful you used to be. Especially with girls.

HAPPY: Oh, I still am, Biff.

BIFF: Oh, go on.

HAPPY: I just control it, that's all. I think I got less bashful and 240 you got more so. What happened, Biff? Where's the old humor, the old confidence? (*He shakes BIFF's knee. BIFF gets up and moves restlessly about the room.*) What's the matter?

BIFF: Why does Dad mock me all the time?

HAPPY: He's not mocking you, he— 245

BIFF: Everything I say there's a twist of mockery on his face. I can't get near him,

HAPPY: He just wants you to make good, that's all. I wanted to talk to you about Dad for a long time, Biff. Something's—happening to him. He—talks to himself. 250

BIFF: I noticed that this morning. But he always mumbled.

HAPPY: But not so noticeable. It got so embarrassing I sent him to Florida. And you know something? Most of the time he's talking to you.

BIFF: What's he say about me? 255

HAPPY: I can't make it out.

BIFF: What's he say about me?

HAPPY: I think the fact that you're not settled, that you're still kind of up in the air . . .

260 BIFF: There's one or two other things depressing him, Happy.

HAPPY: What do you mean?

BIFF: Never mind. Just don't lay it all to me.

HAPPY: But I think if you just got started—I mean—is there any future for you out there?

265 BIFF: I tell ya, Hap, I don't know what the future is. I don't know—what I'm supposed to want.

HAPPY: What do you mean?

BIFF: Well, I spent six or seven years after high school trying to work myself up. Shipping clerk, salesman, business of
270 one kind or another. And it's a measly manner of existence. To get on that subway on the hot mornings in summer. To devote your whole life to keeping stock, or making phone calls, or selling or buying. To suffer fifty weeks of the year for the sake of a two-week vacation,
275 when all you really desire is to be outdoors, with your shirt off. And always to have to get ahead of the next fella. And still—that's how you build a future.

HAPPY: Well, you really enjoy it on a farm? Are you content out there?

280 BIFF: (*With rising agitation.*) Hap, I've had twenty or thirty different kinds of jobs since I left home before the war, and it always turns out the same. I just realized it lately. In Nebraska when I herded cattle, and the Dakotas, and Arizona, and now in Texas. It's why I came home now, I
285 guess, because I realized it. This farm I work on, it's spring there now, see? And they've got about fifteen new colts. There's nothing more inspiring or—beautiful than the sight of a mare and a new colt. And it's cool there now, see? Texas is cool now, and it's spring. And whenever
290 spring comes to where I am, I suddenly get the feeling, my God, I'm not gettin' anywhere! What the hell am I doing, playing around with horses, twenty-eight dollars a week! I'm thirty-four years old, I oughta be makin' my future. That's when I come running home. And now, I get
295 here, and I don't know what to do with myself. (*After a pause.*) I've always made a point of not wasting my life, and everytime I come back here I know that all I've done is to waste my life.

HAPPY: You're a poet, you know that, Biff? You're a—you're
300 an idealist!

BIFF: No, I'm mixed up very bad. Maybe I oughta get married. Maybe I oughta get stuck into something. Maybe that's my trouble. I'm like a boy. I'm not married, I'm not in business, I just—I'm like a boy. Are you content, Hap?
305 You're a success, aren't you? Are you content?

HAPPY: Hell, no!

BIFF: Why? You're making money, aren't you?

HAPPY: (*Moving about with energy, expressiveness.*) All I can do now is wait for the merchandise manager to die. And sup-
310 pose I get to be merchandise manager? He's a good friend of mine, and he just built a terrific estate on Long Island. And he lived there about two months and sold it, and now he's building another one. He can't enjoy it once it's finished. And I know that's just what I would do. I don't
315 know what the hell I'm workin' for. Sometimes I sit in my apartment—all alone. And I think of the rent I'm paying. And it's crazy. But then, it's what I always wanted. My own

apartment, a car, and plenty of women. And still, goddammit, I'm lonely.

BIFF: (*With enthusiasm.*) Listen, why don't you come out West 320 with me?

HAPPY: You and I, heh?

BIFF: Sure, maybe we could buy a ranch. Raise cattle, use our muscles. Men built like we are should be working out in the open. 325

HAPPY: (*Avidly.*) The Loman Brothers, heh?

BIFF: (*With vast affection.*) Sure, we'd be known all over the counties!

HAPPY: (*Enthralled.*) That's what I dream about, Biff. Sometimes I want to just rip my clothes off in the middle of the 330 store and outbox that goddam merchandise manager. I mean I can outbox, outrun, and outlift anybody in that store, and I have to take orders from those common, petty sons-of-bitches till I can't stand it any more.

BIFF: I'm tellin' you, kid, if you were with me I'd be happy 335 out there.

HAPPY: (*Enthused.*) See, Biff, everybody around me is so false that I'm constantly lowering my ideals . . .

BIFF: Baby, together we'd stand up for one another, we'd have someone to trust. 340

HAPPY: If I were around you—

BIFF: Hap, the trouble is we weren't brought up to grub for money. I don't know how to do it.

HAPPY: Neither can I!

BIFF: Then let's go! 345

HAPPY: The only thing is—what can you make out there?

BIFF: But look at your friend. Builds an estate and then hasn't the peace of mind to live in it.

HAPPY: Yeah, but when he walks into the store the waves part in front of him. That's fifty-two thousand dollars a year 350 coming through the revolving door, and I got more in my pinky finger than he's got in his head.

BIFF: Yeah, but you just said—

HAPPY: I gotta show some of those pompous, self-important executives over there that Hap Loman can make the 355 grade. I want to walk into the store the way he walks in. Then I'll go with you, Biff. We'll be together yet, I swear. But take those two we had tonight. Now weren't they gorgeous creatures?

BIFF: Yeah, yeah, most gorgeous I've had in years. 360

HAPPY: I get that any time I want, Biff. Whenever I feel disgusted. The only trouble is, it gets like bowling or something. I just keep knockin' them over and it doesn't mean anything. You still run around a lot?

BIFF: Naa. I'd like to find a girl—steady, somebody with sub- 365 stance.

HAPPY: That's what I long for.

BIFF: Go on! You'd never come home.

HAPPY: I would! Somebody with character, with resistance! Like Mom, y'know? You're gonna call me a bastard when I 370 tell you this. That girl Charlotte I was with tonight is engaged to be married in five weeks. (*He tries on his new hat.*)

BIFF: No kiddin'!

HAPPY: Sure, the guy's in line for the vice-presidency of the store. I don't know what gets into me, maybe I just have 375 an overdeveloped sense of competition or something, but I went and ruined her, and furthermore I can't get rid of her. And he's the third executive I've done that

to. Isn't that a crummy characteristic? And to top it all,
380 I go to their weddings! (*Indignantly, but laughing.*) Like
I'm not supposed to take bribes. Manufacturers offer me
a hundred-dollar bill now and then to throw an order
their way. You know how honest I am, but it's like this
girl, see. I hate myself for it. Because I don't want the
385 girl, and, still, I take it and—I love it!
BIFF: Let's go to sleep.
HAPPY: I guess we didn't settle anything, heh?
BIFF: I just got one idea that I think I'm going to try.
HAPPY: What's that?
390 BIFF: Remember Bill Oliver?
HAPPY: Sure, Oliver is very big now. You want to work for
him again?
BIFF: No, but when I quit he said something to me. He put
his arm on my shoulder, and he said, "Biff, if you ever
395 need anything, come to me."
HAPPY: I remember that. That sounds good.
BIFF: I think I'll go to see him. If I could get ten thousand or
even seven or eight thousand dollars I could buy a beau-
tiful ranch.
400 HAPPY: I bet he'd back you. 'Cause he thought highly of you,
Biff. I mean, they all do. You're well liked, Biff. That's why
I say to come back here, and we both have the apartment.
And I'm tellin' you, Biff, any babe you want . . .
BIFF: No, with a ranch I could do the work I like and still be
405 something. I just wonder though. I wonder if Oliver still
thinks I stole that carton of basketballs.
HAPPY: Oh, he probably forgot that long ago. It's almost ten
years. You're too sensitive. Anyway, he didn't really fire
you.
410 BIFF: Well, I think he was going to. I think that's why I quit.
I was never sure whether he knew or not. I know he
thought the world of me, though. I was the only one he'd
let lock up the place.
WILLY: (*Below.*) You gonna wash the engine, Biff?
415 HAPPY: Shh!

(BIFF *looks at* HAPPY, *who is gazing down, listening.* WILLY *is mumbling in the parlor.*)

HAPPY: You hear that?

(*They listen.* WILLY *laughs warmly.*)

BIFF: (*Growing angry.*) Doesn't he know Mom can hear that?
WILLY: Don't get your sweater dirty, Biff!

(*A look of pain crosses* BIFF's *face.*)

HAPPY: Isn't that terrible? Don't leave again, will you? You'll
420 find a job here. You gotta stick around. I don't know what
to do about him, it's getting embarrassing.
WILLY: What a simonizing job!
BIFF: Mom's hearing that!
WILLY: No kiddin', Biff, you got a date? Wonderful!
425 HAPPY: Go on to sleep. But talk to him in the morning, will
you?
BIFF: (*Reluctantly getting into bed.*) With her in the house.
Brother!
HAPPY: (*Getting into bed.*) I wish you'd have a good talk with
430 him.

(*The light on their room begins to fade.*)

BIFF: (*To himself in bed.*) That selfish, stupid . . .
HAPPY: Sh . . . Sleep, Biff.

(*Their light is out. Well before they have finished speaking,* WILLY's *form is dimly seen below in the darkened kitchen. He opens the refrigerator, searches in there, and takes out a bottle of milk. The apartment houses are fading out, and the entire house and surroundings become covered with leaves. Music insinuates itself as the leaves appear.*)

WILLY: Just wanna be careful with those girls, Biff, that's all.
Don't make any promises. No promises of any kind. Because a girl, y'know, they always believe what you tell 'em, 435
and you're very young, Biff, you're too young to be talking seriously to girls.

(*Light rises on the kitchen.* WILLY, *talking, shuts the refrigerator door and comes downstage to the kitchen table. He pours milk into a glass. He is totally immersed in himself, smiling faintly.*)

WILLY: Too young entirely, Biff. You want to watch your
schooling first. Then when you're all set, there'll be plenty
of girls for a boy like you. (*He smiles broadly at a kitchen* 440
chair.) That so? The girls pay for you? (*He laughs.*) Boy, you
must really be makin' a hit.

(WILLY *is gradually addressing—physically—a point offstage, speaking through the wall of the kitchen, and his voice has been rising in volume to that of a normal conversation.*)

WILLY: I been wondering why you polish the car so careful.
Ha! Don't leave the hubcaps, boys. Get the chamois to the
hubcaps. Happy, use newspaper on the windows, it's the 445
easiest thing. Show him how to do it, Biff! You see,
Happy? Pad it up, use it like a pad. That's it, that's it, good
work. You're doin' all right, Hap. (*He pauses, then nods in
approbation for a few seconds, then looks upward.*) Biff, first
thing we gotta do when we get time is clip that big 450
branch over the house. Afraid it's gonna fall in a storm and
hit the roof. Tell you what. We get a rope and sling her
around, and then we climb up there with a couple of saws
and take her down. Soon as you finish the car, boys, I
wanna see ya. I got a surprise for you, boys. 455
BIFF: (*Offstage.*) Whatta ya got, Dad?
WILLY: No, you finish first. Never leave a job till you're finished—remember that. (*Looking toward the "big trees".*)
Biff, up in Albany I saw a beautiful hammock. I think I'll
buy it next trip, and we'll hang it right between those two 460
elms. Wouldn't that be something? Just swingin' there under those branches. Boy, that would be . . .

(*Young* BIFF *and* YOUNG HAPPY *appear from the direction* WILLY *was addressing.* HAPPY *carries rags and a pail of water.* BIFF, *wearing a sweater with a block "S," carries a football.*)

BIFF: (*Pointing in the direction of the car offstage.*) How's that,
Pop, professional?
WILLY: Terrific. Terrific job, boys. Good work, Biff. 465
HAPPY: Where's the surprise, Pop?
WILLY: In the back seat of the car.
HAPPY: Boy! (*He runs off.*)
BIFF: What is it, Dad? Tell me, what'd you buy?

470 WILLY: (*Laughing, cuffs him.*) Never mind, something I want
you to have.
BIFF: (*Turns and starts off.*) What is it, Hap?
HAPPY: (*Offstage.*) It's a punching bag!
BIFF: Oh, Pop!
475 WILLY: It's got Gene Tunney's signature on it!

(HAPPY *runs onstage with a punching bag.*)

BIFF: Gee, how'd you know we wanted a punching bag?
WILLY: Well, it's the finest thing for the timing.
HAPPY: (*Lies down on his back and pedals with his feet.*) I'm los-
ing weight, you notice, Pop?
480 WILLY: (*To* HAPPY.) Jumping rope is good too.
BIFF: Did you see the new football I got?
WILLY: (*Examining the ball.*) Where'd you get a new ball?
BIFF: The coach told me to practice my passing.
WILLY: That so? And he gave you the ball, heh?
485 BIFF: Well, I borrowed it from the locker room. (*He laughs con-
fidentially.*)
WILLY: (*Laughing with him at the theft.*) I want you to return
that.
HAPPY: I told you he wouldn't like it!
490 BIFF: (*Angrily.*) Well, I'm bringing it back!
WILLY: (*Stopping the incipient argument, to* HAPPY.) Sure, he's
gotta practice with a regulation ball, doesn't he? (*To* BIFF.)
Coach'll probably congratulate you on your initiative!
BIFF: Oh, he keeps congratulating my initiative all the time,
495 Pop.
WILLY: That's because he likes you. If somebody else took that
ball there'd be an uproar. So what's the report, boys, what's
the report?
BIFF: Where'd you go this time, Dad? Gee we were lonesome
500 for you.
WILLY: (*Pleased, puts an arm around each boy and they come down
to the apron.*) Lonesome, heh?
BIFF: Missed you every minute.
WILLY: Don't say? Tell you a secret, boys. Don't breathe it to
505 a soul. Someday I'll have my own business, and I'll never
have to leave home any more.
HAPPY: Like Uncle Charley, heh?
WILLY: Bigger than Uncle Charley! Because Charley is not—
liked. He's liked, but he's not—well liked.
510 BIFF: Where'd you go this time, Dad?
WILLY: Well, I got on the road, and I went north to Providence. Met the Mayor.
BIFF: The Mayor of Providence!
WILLY: He was sitting in the hotel lobby.
515 BIFF: What'd he say?
WILLY: He said, "Morning!" And I said, "You got a fine city
here, Mayor." And then he had coffee with me. And then
I went to Waterbury. Waterbury is a fine city. Big clock
city, the famous Waterbury clock. Sold a nice bill there.
520 And then Boston—Boston is the cradle of the Revolu-
tion. A fine city. And a couple of other towns in Mass.,
and on to Portland and Bangor and straight home!
BIFF: Gee, I'd love to go with you sometime, Dad.
WILLY: Soon as summer comes.
525 HAPPY: Promise?
WILLY: You and Hap and I, and I'll show you all the towns.
America is full of beautiful towns and fine, upstanding

people. And they know me, boys, they know me up and
down New England. The finest people. And when I
bring you fellas up, there'll be open sesame for all of us, 530
'cause one thing, boys: I have friends. I can park my car in
any street in New England, and the cops protect it like
their own. This summer, heh?
BIFF *and* HAPPY: (*Together.*) Yeah! You bet!
WILLY: We'll take our bathing suits. 535
HAPPY: We'll carry your bags, Pop!
WILLY: Oh, won't that be something! Me comin' into the
Boston stores with you boys carryin' my bags. What a
sensation!

(BIFF *is prancing around, practicing passing the ball.*)

WILLY: You nervous, Biff, about the game? 540
BIFF: Not if you're gonna be there.
WILLY: What do they say about you in school, now that they
made you captain?
HAPPY: There's a crowd of girls behind him everytime the
classes change. 545
BIFF: (*Taking* WILLY's *hand.*) This Saturday, Pop, this Satur-
day—just for you, I'm going to break through for a
touchdown.
HAPPY: You're supposed to pass.
BIFF: I'm takin' one play for Pop. You watch me, Pop, and 550
when I take off my helmet, that means I'm breakin' out.
Then you watch me crash through that line!
WILLY: (*Kisses* BIFF.) Oh, wait'll I tell this in Boston!

(BERNARD *enters in knickers. He is younger than* BIFF, *earnest and
loyal, a worried boy.*)

BERNARD: Biff, where are you? You're supposed to study with
me today. 555
WILLY: Hey, looka Bernard. What're you lookin' so anemic
about, Bernard?
BERNARD: He's gotta study, Uncle Willy. He's got Regents
next week.
HAPPY: (*Tauntingly, spinning* BERNARD *around.*) Let's box, 560
Bernard!
BERNARD: Biff! (*He gets away from* HAPPY.) Listen, Biff, I heard
Mr. Birnbaum say that if you don't start studyin' math he's
gonna flunk you, and you won't graduate. I heard him!
WILLY: You better study with him, Biff. Go ahead now. 565
BERNARD: I heard him!
BIFF: Oh, Pop, you didn't see my sneakers! (*He holds up a foot
for* WILLY *to look at.*)
WILLY: Hey, that's a beautiful job of printing!
BERNARD: (*Wiping his glasses.*) Just because he printed Uni- 570
versity of Virginia on his sneakers doesn't mean they've
got to graduate him, Uncle Willy!
WILLY: (*Angrily.*) What're you talking about? With scholar-
ships to three universities they're gonna flunk him?
BERNARD: But I heard Mr. Birnbaum say— 575
WILLY: Don't be a pest, Bernard! (*To his boys.*) What an anemic!
BERNARD: Okay, I'm waiting for you in my house, Biff.

(BERNARD *goes off. The* LOMANS *laugh.*)

WILLY: Bernard is not well liked, is he?
BIFF: He's liked, but he's not well liked.

580 HAPPY: That's right, Pop.

WILLY: That's just what I mean. Bernard can get the best marks in school, y'understand, but when he gets out in the business world, y'understand, you are going to be five times ahead of him. That's why I thank Almighty God you're

585 both built like Adonises. Because the man who makes an appearance in the business world, the man who creates personal interest, is the man who gets ahead. Be liked and you will never want. You take me, for instance, I never have to wait in line to see a buyer. "Willy Loman is here!" That's all

590 they have to know, and I go right through.

BIFF: Did you knock them dead, Pop?

WILLY: Knocked 'em cold in Providence, slaughtered 'em in Boston.

HAPPY: (On his back, pedaling again.) I'm losing weight, you

595 notice, Pop?

(LINDA enters, as of old, a ribbon in her hair, carrying a basket of washing.)

LINDA: (With youthful energy.) Hello, dear!

WILLY: Sweetheart!

LINDA: How'd the Chevvy run?

WILLY: Chevrolet, Linda, is the greatest car ever built. (To the

600 boys.) Since when do you let your mother carry wash up the stairs?

BIFF: Grab hold there, boy!

HAPPY: Where to, Mom?

LINDA: Hang them up on the line. And you better go down

605 to your friends, Biff. The cellar is full of boys. They don't know what to do with themselves.

BIFF: Ah, when Pop comes home they can wait!

WILLY: (Laughs appreciatively.) You better go down and tell them what to do, Biff.

610 BIFF: I think I'll have them sweep out the furnace room.

WILLY: Good work, Biff.

BIFF: (Goes through wall-line of kitchen to doorway at back and calls down.) Fellas! Everybody sweep out the furnace room! I'll be right down!

615 VOICES: All right! Okay, Biff.

BIFF: George and Sam and Frank, come out back! We're hangin' up the wash! Come on, Hap, on the double! (He and HAPPY carry out the basket.)

LINDA: The way they obey him!

620 WILLY: Well, that's training, the training. I'm tellin' you, I was sellin' thousands and thousands, but I had to come home.

LINDA: Oh, the whole block'll be at that game. Did you sell anything?

WILLY: I did five hundred gross in Providence and seven

625 hundred gross in Boston.

LINDA: No! Wait a minute, I've got a pencil. (She pulls pencil and paper out of her apron pocket.) That makes your commission . . . Two hundred—my God! Two hundred, and twelve dollars!

630 WILLY: Well, I didn't figure it yet, but . . .

LINDA: How much did you do?

WILLY: Well, I—I did—about a hundred and eighty gross in Providence. Well, no—it came to—roughly two hundred gross on the whole trip.

635 LINDA: (Without hesitation.) Two hundred gross. That's . . . (She figures.)

WILLY: The trouble was that three of the stores were half closed for inventory in Boston. Otherwise I woulda broke records.

LINDA: Well, it makes seventy dollars and some pennies. 640
That's very good.

WILLY: What do we owe?

LINDA: Well, on the first there's sixteen dollars on the refrigerator—

WILLY: Why sixteen? 645

LINDA: Well, the fan belt broke, so it was a dollar eighty.

WILLY: But it's brand new.

LINDA: Well, the man said that's the way it is. Till they work themselves in, y'know.

(They move through the wall-line into the kitchen.)

WILLY: I hope we didn't get stuck on that machine. 650

LINDA: They got the biggest ads of any of them!

WILLY: I know, it's a fine machine. What else?

LINDA: Well, there's nine-sixty for the washing machine. And for the vacuum cleaner there's three and a half due on the fifteenth. Then the roof, you got twenty-one dollars re- 655
maining.

WILLY: It don't leak, does it?

LINDA: No, they did a wonderful job. Then you owe Frank for the carburetor.

WILLY: I'm not going to pay that man! That goddam Chevro- 660
let, they ought to prohibit the manufacture of that car!

LINDA: Well, you owe him three and a half. And odds and ends, comes to around a hundred and twenty dollars by the fifteenth.

WILLY: A hundred and twenty dollars! My God, if business 665
don't pick up I don't know what I'm gonna do!

LINDA: Well, next week you'll do better.

WILLY: Oh, I'll knock 'em dead next week. I'll go to Hartford. I'm very well liked in Hartford. You know, the trouble is, Linda, people don't seem to take to me. 670

(They move onto the forestage.)

LINDA: Oh, don't be foolish.

WILLY: I know it when I walk in. They seem to laugh at me.

LINDA: Why? Why would they laugh at you? Don't talk that way, Willy.

(WILLY moves to the edge of the stage. LINDA goes into the kitchen and starts to darn stockings.)

WILLY: I don't know the reason for it, but they just pass me 675
by. I'm not noticed.

LINDA: But you're doing wonderful, dear. You're making seventy to a hundred dollars a week.

WILLY: But I gotta be at it ten, twelve hours a day. Other men—I don't know—they do it easier. I don't know 680
why—I can't stop myself—I talk too much. A man oughta come in with a few words. One thing about Charley. He's a man of few words, and they respect him.

LINDA: You don't talk too much, you're just lively.

WILLY: (Smiling.) Well, I figure, what the hell, life is short, a 685
couple of jokes (To himself.) I joke too much! (The smile goes.)

LINDA: Why? You're—

WILLY: I'm fat. I'm very—foolish to look at, Linda. I didn't tell
690 you, but Christmas time I happened to be calling on F. H.
     Stewarts, and a salesman I know, as I was going in to see the
     buyer I heard him say something about—walrus. And I—
     I cracked him right across the face. I won't take that. I sim-
     ply will not take that. But they do laugh at me. I know that.
695 LINDA: Darling . . .
     WILLY: I gotta overcome it. I know I gotta overcome it. I'm
     not dressing to advantage, maybe.
     LINDA: Willy, darling, you're the handsomest man in the
     world—
700 WILLY: Oh, no, Linda.
     LINDA: To me you are. (*Slight pause.*) The handsomest.

(*From the darkness is heard the laughter of a woman.* WILLY *doesn't
turn to it, but it continues through* LINDA'*s lines.*)

     LINDA: And the boys, Willy. Few men are idolized by their
     children the way you are.

(*Music is heard as behind a scrim, to the left of the house,* THE
WOMAN, *dimly seen, is dressing.*)

     WILLY: (*With great feeling.*) You're the best there is, Linda,
705 you're a pal, you know that? On the road—on the road I
     want to grab you sometimes and just kiss the life outa you.

(*The laughter is loud now, and he moves into a brightening area at
the left, where* THE WOMAN *has come from behind the scrim and is
standing, putting on her hat, looking into a "mirror" and laughing.*)

     WILLY: 'Cause I get so lonely—especially when business is
     bad and there's nobody to talk to. I get the feeling that I'll
     never sell anything again, that I won't making a living for
710 you, or a business, a business for the boys. (*He talks through*
     THE WOMAN'*s subsiding laughter;* THE WOMAN *primps at the
     "mirror."*) There's so much I want to make for—
     THE WOMAN: Me? You didn't make me, Willy. I picked you.
     WILLY: (*Pleased.*) You picked me?
715 THE WOMAN: (*Who is quite proper-looking,* WILLY'*s age.*) I did.
     I've been sitting at that desk watching all the salesmen go
     by, day in, day out. But you've got such a sense of humor,
     and we do have such a good time together, don't we?
     WILLY: Sure, sure. (*He takes her in his arms.*) Why do you have
720 to go now?
     THE WOMAN: It's two o'clock . . .
     WILLY: No, come on in! (*He pulls her.*)
     THE WOMAN: . . . my sisters'll be scandalized. When'll you be
     back?
725 WILLY: Oh, two weeks about. Will you come up again?
     THE WOMAN: Sure thing. You do make me laugh. It's good
     for me. (*She squeezes his arm, kisses him.*) And I think you're
     a wonderful man.
     WILLY: You picked me, heh?
730 THE WOMAN: Sure. Because you're so sweet. And such a kidder.
     WILLY: Well, I'll see you next time I'm in Boston.
     THE WOMAN: I'll put you right through to the buyers.
     WILLY: (*Slapping her bottom.*) Right. Well, bottoms up!
     THE WOMAN: (*Slaps him gently and laughs.*) You just kill me,
735 Willy. (*He suddenly grabs her and kisses her roughly.*) You kill
     me. And thanks for the stockings. I love a lot of stockings.
     Well, good night.

WILLY: Good night. And keep your pores open!
THE WOMAN: Oh, Willy!

(THE WOMAN *bursts out laughing, and* LINDA'*s laughter blends in.*
THE WOMAN *disappears into the dark. Now the area at the kitchen
table brightens.* LINDA *is sitting where she was at the kitchen table,
but now is mending a pair of her silk stockings.*)

LINDA: You are, Willy. The handsomest man. You've got no 740
reason to feel that—
WILLY: (*Coming out of* THE WOMAN'*s dimming area and going
over to* LINDA.) I'll make it all up to you, Linda, I'll—
LINDA: There's nothing to make up, dear. You're doing fine,
better than—   745
WILLY: (*Noticing her mending.*) What's that?
LINDA: Just mending my stockings. They're so expensive—
WILLY: (*Angrily, taking them from her.*) I won't have you mend-
ing stockings in this house! Now throw them out!

(LINDA *puts the stockings in her pocket.*)

BERNARD: (*Entering on the run.*) Where is he? If he doesn't 750
study!
WILLY: (*Moving to the forestage, with great agitation.*) You'll give
him the answers!
BERNARD: I do, but I can't on a Regents! That's a state exam!
They're liable to arrest me!   755
WILLY: Where is he? I'll whip him, I'll whip him!
LINDA: And he'd better give back that football, Willy, it's not
nice.
WILLY: Biff! Where is he? Why is he taking everything?
LINDA: He's too rough with the girls, Willy. All the mothers 760
are afraid of him!
WILLY: I'll whip him!
BERNARD: He's driving the car without a license!

(THE WOMAN'*s laugh is heard.*)

WILLY: Shut up!
LINDA: All the mothers—   765
WILLY: Shut up!
BERNARD: (*Backing quietly away and out.*) Mr. Birnbaum says
he's stuck up.
WILLY: Get outa here!
BERNARD: If he doesn't buckle down he'll flunk math! (*He* 770
goes off.)
LINDA: He's right, Willy, you've gotta—
WILLY: (*Exploding at her.*) There's nothing the matter with
him! You want him to be a worm like Bernard? He's got
spirit, personality . . .   775

(*As he speaks,* LINDA, *almost in tears, exits into the living-room.*
WILLY *is alone in the kitchen, wilting and staring. The leaves are gone.
It is night again, and the apartment houses look down from behind.*)

WILLY: Loaded with it. Loaded! What is he stealing? He's giving it back, isn't he? Why is he stealing? What did I tell him?
I never in my life told him anything but decent things.

(HAPPY *in pajamas has come down the stairs;* WILLY *suddenly becomes aware of* HAPPY'*s presence.*)

HAPPY: Let's go now, come on.

780 WILLY: (*Sitting down at the kitchen table.*) Huh! Why did she have to wax the floors herself? Everytime she waxes the floors she keels over. She knows that!

HAPPY: Shh! Take it easy. What brought you back tonight?

WILLY: I got an awful scare. Nearly hit a kid in Yonkers. God!
785 Why didn't I go to Alaska with my brother Ben that time! Ben! That man was a genius, that man was success incarnate! What a mistake! He begged me to go.

HAPPY: Well, there's no use in—

WILLY: You guys! There was a man started with the clothes on
790 his back and ended up with diamond mines!

HAPPY: Boy, someday I'd like to know how he did it.

WILLY: What's the mystery? The man knew what he wanted and went out and got it! Walked into a jungle, and comes out, the age of twenty-one, and he's rich! The world is an
795 oyster, but you don't crack it open on a mattress!

HAPPY: Pop, I told you I'm gonna retire you for life.

WILLY: You'll retire me for life on seventy goddam dollars a week? And your women and your car and your apartment, and you'll retire me for life! Christ's sake, I couldn't
800 get past Yonkers today! Where are you guys, where are you? The woods are burning! I can't drive a car!

(CHARLEY *has appeared in the doorway. He is a large man, slow of speech, laconic, immovable. In all he says, despite what he says, there is pity, and, now, trepidation. He has a robe over pajamas, slippers on his feet. He enters the kitchen.*)

CHARLEY: Everything all right?

HAPPY: Yeah, Charley, everything's . . .

WILLY: What's the matter?

805 CHARLEY: I heard some noise. I thought something happened. Can't we do something about the walls? You sneeze in here, and in my house hats blow off.

HAPPY: Let's go to bed, Dad. Come on.

(CHARLEY *signals to* HAPPY *to go.*)

WILLY: You go ahead, I'm not tired at the moment.
810 HAPPY: (*To* WILLY.) Take it easy, huh? (*He exits.*)

WILLY: What're you doin' up?.

CHARLEY: (*Sitting down at the kitchen table opposite* WILLY.) Couldn't sleep good. I had a heartburn.

WILLY: Well, you don't know how to eat.
815 CHARLEY: I eat with my mouth.

WILLY: No, you're ignorant. You gotta know about vitamins and things like that.

CHARLEY: Come on, let's shoot. Tire you out a little.

WILLY: (*Hesitantly.*) All right. You got cards?
820 CHARLEY: (*Taking a deck from his pocket.*) Yeah, I got them. Someplace. What is it with those vitamins?

WILLY: (*Dealing.*) They build up your bones. Chemistry.

CHARLEY: Yeah, but there's no bones in a heartburn.

WILLY: What are you talkin' about? Do you know the first
825 thing about it?

CHARLEY: Don't get insulted.

WILLY: Don't talk about something you don't know anything about.

(*They are playing. Pause.*)

CHARLEY: What're you doin' home?

WILLY: A little trouble with the car. 830

CHARLEY: Oh. (*Pause.*) I'd like to take a trip to California.

WILLY: Don't say.

CHARLEY: You want a job?

WILLY: I got a job, I told you that. (*After a slight pause.*) What the hell are you offering me a job for? 835

CHARLEY: Don't get insulted.

WILLY: Don't insult me.

CHARLEY: I don't see no sense in it. You don't have to go on this way.

WILLY: I got a good job. (*Slight pause.*) What do you keep 840 comin' in here for?

CHARLEY: You want me to go?

WILLY: (*After a pause, withering.*) I can't understand it. He's going back to Texas again. What the hell is that?

CHARLEY: Let him go. 845

WILLY: I got nothin' to give him, Charley, I'm clean, I'm clean.

CHARLEY: He won't starve. None a them starve. Forget about him.

WILLY: Then what have I got to remember? 850

CHARLEY: You take it too hard. To hell with it. When a deposit bottle is broken you don't get your nickel back.

WILLY: That's easy enough for you to say.

CHARLEY: That ain't easy for me to say.

WILLY: Did you see the ceiling I put up in the living-room? 855

CHARLEY: Yeah, that's a piece of work. To put up a ceiling is a mystery to me. How do you do it?

WILLY: What's the difference?

CHARLEY: Well, talk about it.

WILLY: You gonna put up a ceiling? 860

CHARLEY: How could I put up a ceiling?

WILLY: Then what the hell are you bothering me for?

CHARLEY: You're insulted again.

WILLY: A man who can't handle tools is not a man. You're disgusting. 865

CHARLEY: Don't call me disgusting, Willy.

(UNCLE BEN, *carrying a valise and an umbrella, enters the forestage from around the right corner of the house. He is a stolid man, in his sixties, with a mustache and an authoritative air. He is utterly certain of his destiny, and there is an aura of far places about him. He enters exactly as* WILLY *speaks.*)

WILLY: I'm getting awfully tired, Ben.

(BEN's *music is heard.* BEN *looks around at everything.*)

CHARLEY: Good, keep playing; you'll sleep better. Did you call me Ben?

(BEN *looks at his watch.*)

WILLY: That's funny. For a second there you reminded me of 870 my brother Ben.

BEN: I only have a few minutes. (*He strolls, inspecting the place.* WILLY *and* CHARLEY *continue playing.*)

CHARLEY: You never heard from him again, heh? Since that time? 875

WILLY: Didn't Linda tell you? Couple of weeks ago we got a letter from his wife in Africa. He died.

CHARLEY: That so.

BEN: (*Chuckling.*) So this is Brooklyn, eh?

880 CHARLEY: Maybe you're in for some of his money.

WILLY: Naa, he had seven sons. There's just one opportunity I had with that man . . .

BEN: I must make a train, William. There are several properties I'm looking at in Alaska.

885 WILLY: Sure, sure! If I'd gone with him to Alaska that time, everything would've been totally different.

CHARLEY: Go on, you'd froze to death up there.

WILLY: What're you talking about?

BEN: Opportunity is tremendous in Alaska, William. Surprised you're not up there.

890 WILLY: Sure, tremendous.

CHARLEY: Heh?

WILLY: There was the only man I ever met who knew the answers.

895 CHARLEY: Who?

BEN: How are you all?

WILLY: (*Taking a pot, smiling.*) Fine, fine.

CHARLEY: Pretty sharp tonight.

BEN: Is Mother living with you?

900 WILLY: No, she died a long time ago.

CHARLEY: Who?

BEN: That's too bad. Fine specimen of a lady, Mother.

WILLY: (*To* CHARLEY.) Heh?

BEN: I'd hoped to see the old girl.

905 CHARLEY: Who died?

BEN: Heard anything from Father, have you?

WILLY: (*Unnerved.*) What do you mean, who died?

CHARLEY: (*Taking a pot.*) What're you talkin' about?

BEN: (*Looking at his watch.*) William, it's half-past eight!

910 WILLY: (*As though to dispel his confusion he angrily stops* CHARLEY's *hand.*) That's my build!

CHARLEY: I put the ace—

WILLY: If you don't know how to play the game I'm not gonna throw my money away on you!

915 CHARLEY: (*Rising.*) It was my ace, for God's sake!

WILLY: I'm through, I'm through!

BEN: When did Mother die?

WILLY: Long ago. Since the beginning you never knew how to play cards.

920 CHARLEY: (*Picks up the cards and goes to the door.*) All right! Next time I'll bring a deck with five aces.

WILLY: I don't play that kind of game!

CHARLEY: (*Turning to him.*) You ought to be ashamed of yourself!

925 WILLY: Yeah?

CHARLEY: Yeah! (*He goes out.*)

WILLY: (*Slamming the door after him.*) Ignoramus!

BEN: (*As* WILLY *comes toward him through the wall-line of the kitchen.*) So you're William.

930 WILLY: (*Shaking* BEN's *hand.*) Ben! I've been waiting for you so long! What's the answer? How did you do it?

BEN: Oh, there's a story in that.

(LINDA *enters the forestage, as of old, carrying the wash basket.*)

LINDA: Is this Ben?

BEN: (*Gallantly.*) How do you do, my dear.

935 LINDA: Where've you been all these years? Willy's always wondered why you—

WILLY: (*Pulling* BEN *away from her impatiently.*) Where is Dad? Didn't you follow him? How did you get started?

BEN: Well, I don't know how much you remember.

WILLY: Well, I was just a baby, of course, only three or four 940 years old—

BEN: Three years and eleven months.

WILLY: What a memory, Ben!

BEN: I have many enterprises, William, and I have never kept books. 945

WILLY: I remember I was sitting under the wagon in—was it Nebraska?

BEN: It was South Dakota, and I gave you a bunch of wildflowers.

WILLY: I remember you walking away down some open road. 950

BEN: (*Laughing.*) I was going to find Father in Alaska.

WILLY: Where is he?

BEN: At that age I had a very faulty view of geography, William. I discovered after a few days that I was heading due south, so instead of Alaska, I ended up in Africa. 955

LINDA: Africa!

WILLY: The Gold Coast!

BEN: Principally diamond mines.

LINDA: Diamond mines!

BEN: Yes, my dear. But I've only a few minutes— 960

WILLY: No! Boys! Boys! (YOUNG BIFF *and* HAPPY *appear.*) Listen to this. This is your Uncle Ben, a great man! Tell, my boys, Ben!

BEN: Why, boys, when I was seventeen I walked into the jungle, and when I was twenty-one I walked out. (*He laughs.*) 965 And by God I was rich.

WILLY: (*To the boys.*) You see what I been talking about? The greatest things can happen!

BEN: (*Glancing at his watch.*) I have an appointment in Ketchikan Tuesday week. 970

WILLY: No, Ben! Please tell about Dad. I want my boys to hear. I want them to know the kind of stock they spring from. All I remember is a man with a big beard, and I was in Mamma's lap, sitting around a fire, and some kind of high music. 975

BEN: His flute. He played the flute.

WILLY: Sure, the flute, that's right?

(*New music is heard, a high, rollicking tune.*)

BEN: Father was a very great and a very wild-hearted man. We would start in Boston, and he'd toss the whole family into the wagon, and then he'd drive the team right across 980 the country; through Ohio, and Indiana, Michigan, Illinois, and all the Western states. And we'd stop in the towns and sell the flutes that he'd made on the way. Great inventor, Father. With one gadget he made more in a week than a man like you could make in a lifetime. 985

WILLY: That's just the way I'm bringing them up, Ben—rugged, well liked, all-around.

BEN: Yeah? (*To* BIFF.) Hit that, boy—hard as you can. (*He pounds his stomach.*)

BIFF: Oh, no, sir! 990

BEN: (*Taking boxing stance.*) Come on, get to me! (*He laughs.*)

WILLY: Go to it, Biff! Go ahead, show him!

BIFF: Okay! (*He cocks his fists and starts in.*)

LINDA: (*To* WILLY.) Why must he fight, dear?

995 BEN: (*Sparring with* BIFF.) Good boy! Good boy!

WILLY: How's that, Ben, heh?

HAPPY: Give him the left, Biff!

LINDA: Why are you fighting?

BEN: Good boy! (*Suddenly comes in, trips* BIFF, *and stands over*
1000   *him, the point of his umbrella poised over* BIFF's *eye.*)

LINDA: Look out, Biff!

BIFF: Gee!

BEN: (*Patting* BIFF's *knee.*) Never fight fair with a stranger, boy.
You'll never get out of the jungle that way. (*Taking* LINDA's
1005   *hand and bowing.*) It was an honor and a pleasure to meet
you, Linda.

LINDA: (*Withdrawing her hand coldly, frightened.*) Have a nice—
trip.

BEN: (*To* WILLY.) And good luck with your—what do you do?

1010 WILLY: Selling.

BEN: Yes. Well . . . (*He raises his hand in farewell to all.*)

WILLY: No, Ben, I don't want you to think . . . (*He takes* BEN's
arm to show him.) It's Brooklyn, I know, but we hunt too.

BEN: Really, now.

1015 WILLY: Oh, sure, there's snakes and rabbits and—that's why I
moved out here. Why, Biff can fell any one of these trees
in no time! Boys! Go right over to where they're building
the apartment house and get some sand. We're gonna re-
build the entire front stoop right now! Watch this Ben!

1020 BIFF: Yes, sir! On the double, Hap!

HAPPY: (*As he and* BIFF *run off.*) I lost weight, Pop, you notice?

(CHARLEY *enters in knickers, even before the boys are gone.*)

CHARLEY: Listen, if they steal any more from that building
the watchman'll put the cops on them!

LINDA: (*To* WILLY.) Don't let Biff . . .

(BEN *laughs lustily.*)

1025 WILLY: You shoulda seen the lumber they brought home last
week. At least a dozen six-by-tens worth all kinds a
money.

CHARLEY: Listen, if that watchman—

WILLY: I gave them hell, understand. But I got a couple of
1030   fearless characters there.

CHARLEY: Willy, the jails are full of fearless characters.

BEN: (*Clapping* WILLY *on the back, with a laugh at* CHARLEY.)
And the stock exchange, friend!

WILLY: (*Joining in* BEN's *laughter.*) Where are the rest of your
1035   pants?

CHARLEY: My wife bought them.

WILLY: Now all you need is a golf club and you can go upstairs and go to sleep. (*To* BEN.) Great athlete! Between
him and his son Bernard they can't hammer a nail!

1040 BERNARD: (*Rushing in.*) The watchman's chasing Biff!

WILLY: (*Angrily.*) Shut up! He's not stealing anything!

LINDA: (*Alarmed, hurrying off left.*) Where is he? Biff dear! (*She
exits.*)

WILLY: (*Moving toward the left, away from* BEN.) There's noth-
1045   ing wrong. What's the matter with you?

BEN: Nervy boy. Good!

WILLY: (*Laughing.*) Oh, nerves of iron, that Biff!

CHARLEY: Don't know what it is. My New England man
comes back and he's bleedin', they murdered him up there.

1050 WILLY: It's contacts, Charley, I got important contacts!

CHARLEY: (*Sarcastically.*) Glad to hear it, Willy. Come in later,
we'll shoot a little casino. I'll take some of your Portland
money. (*He laughs at* WILLY *and exits.*)

WILLY: (*Turning to* BEN.) Business is bad, it's murderous. But
not for me, of course. 1055

BEN: I'll stop by on my way back to Africa.

WILLY: (*Longingly.*) Can't you stay a few days? You're just what
I need, Ben, because I—I have a fine position here, but
I—well, Dad left when I was such a baby and I never had
a chance to talk to him and I still feel—kind of temporary 1060
about myself.

BEN: I'll be late for my train.

(*They are at opposite ends of the stage.*)

WILLY: Ben, my boys—can't we talk? They'd go into the jaws
of hell for me, see, but I—

BEN: William, you're being first-rate with your boys. Out- 1065
standing, manly chaps!

WILLY: (*Hanging on to his words.*) Oh, Ben, that's good to hear!
Because sometimes I'm afraid that I'm not teaching them
the right kind of—Ben, how should I teach them?

BEN: (*Giving great weight to each word, and with a certain vicious* 1070
audacity.) William, when I walked into the jungle, I was
seventeen. When I walked out I was twenty-one. And, by
God, I was rich! (*He goes off into the darkness around the right
corner of the house.*)

WILLY: . . . was rich! That's just the spirit I want to imbue 1075
them with! To walk into a jungle! I was right! I was right!
I was right!

(BEN *is gone, but* WILLY *is still speaking to him as* LINDA, *in night-
gown and robe, enters the kitchen, glances around for* WILLY, *then
goes to the door of the house, looks out and sees him. Comes down
to his left. He looks at her.*)

LINDA: Willy, dear? Willy?

WILLY: I was right!

LINDA: Did you have some cheese? (*He can't answer.*) It's very 1080
late, darling. Come to bed, heh?

WILLY: (*Looking straight up.*) Gotta break your neck to see a
star in this yard.

LINDA: You coming in?

WILLY: Whatever happened to that diamond watch fob? Re- 1085
member? When Ben came from Africa that time? Didn't
he give me a watch fob with a diamond in it?

LINDA: You pawned it, dear. Twelve, thirteen years ago. For
Biff's radio correspondence course.

WILLY: Gee, that was a beautiful thing. I'll take a walk. 1090

LINDA: But you're in your slippers.

WILLY: (*Starting to go around the house at the left.*) I was right! I
was! (*Half to* LINDA, *as he goes, shaking his head.*) What a
man! There was a man worth talking to. I was right!

LINDA: (*Calling after* WILLY.) But in your slippers, Willy! 1095

(WILLY *is almost gone when* BIFF, *in his pajamas, comes down the
stairs an enters the kitchen.*)

BIFF: What is he doing out there?

LINDA: Sh!

BIFF: God Almighty, Mom, how long has he been doing this?

LINDA: Don't, he'll hear you.

1100   BIFF: What the hell is the matter with him?

LINDA: It'll pass by morning.

BIFF: Shouldn't we do anything?

LINDA: Oh, my dear, you should do a lot of things, but there's nothing to do, so go to sleep.

(HAPPY *comes down the stair and sits on the steps.*)

1105   HAPPY: I never heard him so loud, Mom.

LINDA: Well, come around more often; you'll hear him. (*She sits down at the table and mends the lining of* WILLY'*s jacket.*)

BIFF: Why didn't you ever write me about this, Mom?

LINDA: How would I write to you? For over three months
1110   you had no address.

BIFF: I was on the move. But you know I thought of you all the time. You know that, don't you, pal?

LINDA: I know, dear, I know. But he likes to have a letter. Just to know that there's still a possibility for better things.

1115   BIFF: He's not like this all the time, is he?

LINDA: It's when you come home he's always the worst.

BIFF: When I come home?

LINDA: When you write you're coming, he's all smiles, and talks about the future, and—he's just wonderful. And then
1120   the closer you seem to come, the more shaky he gets, and then, by the time you get here, he's arguing, and he seems angry at you. I think it's just that maybe he can't bring himself to—to open up to you. Why are you so hateful to each other? Why is that?

1125   BIFF: (*Evasively.*) I'm not hateful, Mom.

LINDA: But you no sooner come in the door than you're fighting!

BIFF: I don't know why. I mean to change. I'm tryin', Mom, you understand?

1130   LINDA: Are you home to stay now?

BIFF: I don't know. I want to look around, see what's doin'.

LINDA: Biff, you can't look around all your life, can you?

BIFF: I just can't take hold, Mom. I can't take hold of some kind of a life.

1135   LINDA: Biff, a man is not a bird, to come and go with the springtime.

BIFF: Your hair . . . (*He touches her hair.*) Your hair got so gray.

LINDA: Oh, it's been gray since you were in high school. I just stopped dyeing it, that's all.

1140   BIFF: Dye it again, will ya? I don't want my pal looking old. (*He smiles.*)

LINDA: You're such a boy! You think you can go away for a year and . . . You've got to get it into your head now that one day you'll knock on this door and there'll be strange
1145   people here—

BIFF: What are you talking about? You're not even sixty, Mom.

LINDA: But what about your father?

BIFF: (*Lamely.*) Well, I meant him too.

1150   HAPPY: He admires Pop.

LINDA: Biff, dear, if you don't have any feeling for him, then you can't have any feeling for me.

BIFF: Sure I can, Mom.

LINDA: No. You can't just come to see me, because I love
1155   him. (*With a threat, but only a threat, of tears.*) He's the dearest man in the world to me, and I won't have anyone making him feel unwanted and low and blue. You've got to

make up your mind now, darling, there's no leeway any more. Either he's your father and you pay him that re-
1160   spect, or else you're not to come here. I know he's not easy to get along with—nobody knows that better than me— but . . .

WILLY: (*From the left, with a laugh.*) Hey, hey, Biffo!

BIFF: (*Starting to go out after* WILLY.) What the hell is the mat-
1165   ter with him? (HAPPY *stops him.*)

LINDA: Don't—don't go near him!

BIFF: Stop making excuses for him! He always, always wiped the floor with you. Never had an ounce of respect for you.

HAPPY: He's always had respect for—
1170

BIFF: What the hell do you know about it?

HAPPY: (*Surlily.*) Just don't call him crazy!

BIFF: He's got no character—Charley wouldn't do this. Not in his own house—spewing out that vomit from his mind.

HAPPY: Charley never had to cope with what he's got to.
1175

BIFF: People are worse off than Willy Loman. Believe me, I've seen them!

LINDA: Then make Charley your father, Biff. You can't do that, can you? I don't say he's a great man. Willy Loman never made a lot of money. His name was never in the pa-
1180   per. He's not the finest character that ever lived. But he's a human being, and a terrible thing is happening to him. So attention must be paid. He's not to be allowed to fall into his grave like an old dog. Attention, attention must finally be paid to such a person. You called him crazy—
1185

BIFF: I didn't mean—

LINDA: No, a lot of people think he's lost his—balance. But you don't have to be very smart to know what his trouble is. The man is exhausted.

HAPPY: Sure!
1190

LINDA: A small man can be just as exhausted as a great man. He works for a company thirty-six years this March, opens up unheard-of territories to their trademark, and now in his old age they take his salary away.

HAPPY: (*Indignantly.*) I didn't know that, Mom.
1195

LINDA: You never asked, my dear! Now that you get your spending money someplace else you don't trouble your mind with him.

HAPPY: But I gave you money last—

LINDA: Christmas time, fifty dollars! To fix the hot water it
1200   cost ninety-seven fifty! For five weeks he's been on straight commission, like a beginner, an unknown!

BIFF: Those ungrateful bastards!

LINDA: Are they any worse than his sons? When he brought them business, when he was young, they were glad to see
1205   him. But now his old friends, the old buyers that loved him so and always found some order to hand him in a pinch— they're all dead, retired. He used to be able to make six, seven calls a day in Boston. Now he takes his valises out of the car and puts them back and takes them out again and
1210   he's exhausted. Instead of walking he talks now. He drives seven hundred miles, and when he gets there no one knows him any more, no one welcomes him. And what goes through a man's mind, driving seven hundred miles home without having earned a cent? Why shouldn't he talk to
1215   himself? Why? When he has to go to Charley and borrow fifty dollars a week and pretend to me that it's his pay? How long can that go on? How long? You see what I'm sitting

1220 here and waiting for? And you tell me he has no character? The man who never worked a day but for your benefit? When does he get the medal for that? Is this his reward—to turn around at the age of sixty-three and find his sons, who he loved better than his life, one a philandering bum—

HAPPY: Mom!

1225 LINDA: That's all you are, my baby! (*To* BIFF.) And you! What happened to the love you had for him? You were such pals! How you used to talk to him on the phone every night! How lonely he was till he could come home to you!

BIFF: All right, Mom, I'll live here in my room, and I'll get a

1230 job. I'll keep away from him, that's all.

LINDA: No, Biff. You can't stay here and fight all the time.

BIFF: He threw me out of this house, remember that.

LINDA: Why did he do that? I never knew why.

BIFF: Because I know he's a fake and he doesn't like anybody

1235 around who knows!

LINDA: Why a fake? In what way? What do you mean?

BIFF: Just don't lay it all at my feet. It's between me and him—that's all I have to say. I'll chip in from now on. He'll settle for half my pay check. He'll be all right. I'm going to

1240 bed. (*He starts for the stairs.*)

LINDA: He won't be all right.

BIFF: (*Turning on the stairs, furiously.*) I hate this city and I'll stay here. Now what do you want?

LINDA: He's dying, Biff.

(HAPPY *turns quickly to her, shocked.*)

1245 BIFF: (*After a pause.*) Why is he dying?

LINDA: He's been trying to kill himself.

BIFF: (*With great horror.*) How?

LINDA: I live from day to day.

BIFF: What're you talking about?

1250 LINDA: Remember I wrote you that he smashed up the car again? In February?

BIFF: Well?

LINDA: The insurance inspector came. He said that they have evidence. That all these accidents in the last year—

1255 weren't—weren't—accidents.

HAPPY: How can they tell that? That's a lie.

LINDA: It seems there's a woman . . . (*She takes a breath as*

BIFF: (*Sharply but contained.*) What woman?

LINDA: (*Simultaneously.*) . . . and this woman . . .

1260 LINDA: What?

BIFF: Nothing. Go ahead.

LINDA: What did you say?

BIFF: Nothing. I just said what woman?

HAPPY: What about her?

1265 LINDA: Well, it seems she was walking down the road and saw his car. She says that he wasn't driving fast at all, and that he didn't skid. She says he came to that little bridge, and then deliberately smashed into the railing, and it was only the shallowness of the water that saved him.

1270 BIFF: Oh, no, he probably just fell asleep again.

LINDA: I don't think he fell asleep.

BIFF: Why not?

LINDA: Last month . . . (*With great difficulty.*) Oh, boys, it's so hard to say a thing like this! He's just a big stupid man to

1275 you, but I tell you there's more good in him than in many other people. (*She chokes, wipes her eyes.*) I was looking for

a fuse. The lights blew out, and I went down the cellar. And behind the fuse box—it happened to fall out—was a length of rubber pipe—just short.

HAPPY: No kidding? 1280

LINDA: There's a little attachment on the end of it. I knew right away. And sure enough, on the bottom of the water heater there's a new little nipple on the gas pipe.

HAPPY: (*Angrily.*) That—jerk.

BIFF: Did you have it taken off? 1285

LINDA: I'm—I'm ashamed to. How can I mention it to him? Every day I go down and take away that little rubber pipe. But, when he comes home, I put it back where it was. How can I insult him that way? I don't know what to do. I live from day to day, boys. I tell you, I know every 1290 thought in his mind. It sounds so old-fashioned and silly, but I tell you he put his whole life into you and you've turned your backs on him. (*She is bent over in the chair, weeping, her face in her hands.*) Biff, I swear to God! Biff, his life is in your hands! 1295

HAPPY: (*To* BIFF.) How do you like that damned fool!

BIFF: (*Kissing her.*) All right, pal, all right. It's all settled now. I've been remiss. I know that, Mom. But now I'll stay, and I swear to you, I'll apply myself. (*Kneeling in front of her, in a fever of self-reproach.*) It's just—you see, Mom, I don't fit in 1300 business. Not that I won't try. I'll try, and I'll make good.

HAPPY: Sure you will. The trouble with you in business was you never tried to please people.

BIFF: I know, I—

HAPPY: Like when you worked for Harrison's. Bob Harrison 1305 said you were tops, and then you go and do some damn fool thing like whistling whole songs in the elevator like a comedian.

BIFF: (*Against* HAPPY.) So what? I like to whistle sometimes.

HAPPY: You don't raise a guy to a responsible job who whis- 1310 tles in the elevator!

LINDA: Well, don't argue about it now.

HAPPY: Like when you'd go off and swim in the middle of the day instead of taking the line around.

BIFF: (*His resentment rising.*) Well, don't you run off? You take 1315 off sometimes, don't you? On a nice summer day?

HAPPY: Yeah, but I cover myself!

LINDA: Boys!

HAPPY: If I'm going to take a fade the boss can call any number where I'm supposed to be and they'll swear to him 1320 that I just left. I'll tell you something that I hate to say, Biff, but in the business world some of them think you're crazy.

BIFF: (*Angered.*) Screw the business world!

HAPPY: All right, screw it! Great, but cover yourself!

LINDA: Hap, Hap! 1325

BIFF: I don't care what they think! They've laughed at Dad for years, and you know why? Because we don't belong in this nuthouse of a city! We should be mixing cement on some open plain, or—or carpenters. A carpenter is allowed to whistle! 1330

(WILLY *walks in from the entrance of the house, at left.*)

WILLY: Even your grandfather was better than a carpenter. (*Pause. They watch him.*) You never grew up. Bernard does not whistle in the elevator, I assure you.

BIFF: (*As though to laugh* WILLY *out of it.*) Yeah, but you do, Pop.

1335 WILLY: I never in my life whistled in an elevator! And who in the business world thinks I'm crazy?

BIFF: I didn't mean it like that, Pop. Now don't make a whole thing out of it, will ya?

WILLY: Go back to the West! Be a carpenter, a cowboy, enjoy
1340 yourself!

LINDA: Willy, he was just saying—

WILLY: I heard what he said!

HAPPY: (*Trying to quiet* WILLY.) Hey, Pop, come on now . . .

WILLY: (*Continuing over* HAPPY's *line.*) They laugh at me, heh?
1345 Go to Filene's, go to the Hub, go to Slattery's, Boston. Call out the name Willy Loman and see what happens! Big shot!

BIFF: All right, Pop.

WILLY: Big!

1350 BIFF: All right!

WILLY: Why do you always insult me?

BIFF: I didn't say a word. (*To* LINDA.) Did I say a word?

LINDA: He didn't say anything, Willy.

WILLY: (*Going to the doorway of the living-room.*) All right, good
1355 night, good night.

LINDA: Willy, dear, he just decided . . .

WILLY: (*To* BIFF.) If you get tired hanging around tomorrow, paint the ceiling I put up in the living-room.

BIFF: I'm leaving early tomorrow.

1360 HAPPY: He's going to see Bill Oliver, Pop.

WILLY: (*Interestedly.*) Oliver? For what?

BIFF: (*With reserve, but trying, trying.*) He always said he'd stake me. I'd like to go into business, so maybe I can take him up on it.

1365 LINDA: Isn't that wonderful?

WILLY: Don't interrupt. What's wonderful about it? There's fifty men in the City of New York who'd stake him. (*To* BIFF.) Sporting goods?

BIFF: I guess so. I know something about it and—

1370 WILLY: He knows something about it! You know sporting goods better than Spalding, for God's sake! How much he giving you?

BIFF: I don't know, I didn't even see him yet, but—

WILLY: Then what're you talkin' about?

1375 BIFF: (*Getting angry.*) Well, all I said was I'm gonna see him, that's all!

WILLY: (*Turning away.*) Ah, you're counting your chickens again.

BIFF: (*Starting left for the stairs.*) Oh, Jesus, I'm going to sleep!

1380 WILLY: (*Calling after him.*) Don't curse in this house!

BIFF: (*Turning.*) Since when did you get so clean?

HAPPY: (*Trying to stop them.*) Wait a . . .

WILLY: Don't use that language to me! I won't have it!

HAPPY: (*Grabbing* BIFF, *shouts.*) Wait a minute! I got an idea. I
1385 got a feasible idea. Come here, Biff, let's talk this over now, let's talk some sense here. When I was down in Florida last time, I thought of a great idea to sell sporting goods. It just came back to me. You and I, Biff—we have a line, the Loman Line. We train a couple of weeks, and put on
1390 a couple of exhibitions, see?

WILLY: That's an idea!

HAPPY: Wait! We form two basketball teams, see? Two water-polo teams. We play each other. It's a million dollars' worth of publicity. Two brothers, see? The Loman Broth-
1395 ers. Displays in the Royal Palms—all the hotels. And ban-

ners over the ring and the basketball court: "Loman Brothers." Baby, we could sell sporting goods!

WILLY: That is a one-million-dollar idea!

LINDA: Marvelous!

BIFF: I'm in great shape as far as that's concerned.   1400

HAPPY: And the beauty of it is, Biff, it wouldn't be like a business. We'd be out playin' ball again.

BIFF: (*Enthused.*) Yeah, that's . . .

WILLY: Million-dollar . . .

HAPPY: And you wouldn't get fed up with it, Biff. It'd be the   1405
family again. There'd be the old honor, and comradeship, and if you wanted to go off for a swim or somethin'— well, you'd do it! Without some smart cooky gettin' up ahead of you!

WILLY: Lick the world! You guys together could absolutely   1410
lick the civilized world.

BIFF: I'll see Oliver tomorrow. Hap, if we could work that out . . .

LINDA: Maybe things are beginning to—

WILLY: (*Wildly enthused, to* LINDA.) Stop interrupting! (*To* BIFF.)   1415
But don't wear sport jacket and slacks when you see Oliver.

BIFF: No, I'll—

WILLY: A business suit, and talk as little as possible, and don't crack any jokes.

BIFF: He did like me. Always liked me.   1420

LINDA: He loved you!

WILLY: (*To* LINDA.) Will you stop! (*To* BIFF.) Walk in very serious. You are not applying for a boy's job. Money is to pass. Be quiet, fine, and serious. Everybody likes a kidder, but nobody lends him money.   1425

HAPPY: I'll try to get some myself, Biff. I'm sure I can.

WILLY: I see great things for you kids, I think your troubles are over. But remember, start big and you'll end big. Ask for fifteen. How much you gonna ask for?

BIFF: Gee, I don't know—   1430

WILLY: And don't say "Gee." "Gee" is a boy's word. A man walking in for fifteen thousand dollars does not say "Gee!"

BIFF: Ten, I think, would be top though.

WILLY: Don't be so modest. You always started too low. Walk in with a big laugh. Don't look worried. Start off with a   1435
couple of your good stories to lighten things up. It's not what you say, it's how you say it—because personality always wins the day.

LINDA: Oliver always thought the highest of him—

WILLY: Will you let me talk?   1440

BIFF: Don't yell at her, Pop, will ya?

WILLY: (*Angrily.*) I was talking, wasn't I?

BIFF: I don't like you yelling at her all the time, and I'm tellin' you, that's all.

WILLY: What're you, takin' over this house?   1445

LINDA: Willy—

WILLY: (*Turning on her.*) Don't take his side all the time, god-dammit!

BIFF: (*Furiously.*) Stop yelling at her!

WILLY: (*Suddenly pulling on his cheek, beaten down, guilt ridden.*)   1450
Give my best to Bill Oliver—he may remember me. (*He exits through the living-room doorway.*)

LINDA: (*Her voice subdued.*) What'd you have to start that for? (BIFF *turns away.*) You see how sweet he was as soon as you talked hopefully? (*She goes over to* BIFF.) Come up and say   1455
good night to him. Don't let him go to bed that way.

HAPPY: Come on, Biff, let's buck him up.

LINDA: Please, dear. Just say good night. It takes so little to make him happy. Come. (*She goes through the living-room doorway, calling upstairs from within the living-room.*) Your pajamas are hanging in the bathroom, Willy!

1460

HAPPY: (*Looking toward where* LINDA *went out.*) What a woman! They broke the mold when they made her. You know that, Biff?

1465   BIFF: He's off salary. My God, working on commission!

HAPPY: Well, let's face it: he's no hot-shot selling man. Except that sometimes, you have to admit, he's a sweet personality.

BIFF: (*Deciding.*) Lend me ten bucks, will ya? I want to buy some new ties.

1470   HAPPY: I'll take you to a place I know. Beautiful stuff. Wear one of my striped shirts tomorrow.

BIFF: She got gray. Mom got awful old. Gee, I'm gonna go in to Oliver tomorrow and knock him for a—

HAPPY: Come on up. Tell that to Dad. Let's give him a whirl.

1475   Come on.

BIFF: (*Steamed up.*) You know, with ten thousand bucks, boy!

HAPPY: (*As they go into the living-room.*) That's the talk, Biff, that's the first time I've heard the old confidence out of you! (*From within the living-room, fading off.*) You gonna live

1480   with me, kid, and any babe you want just say the word . . . (*The last lines are hardly heard. They are mounting the stairs to their parents' bedroom.*)

LINDA: (*Entering her bedroom and addressing* WILLY, *who is in the bathroom. She is straightening the bed for him.*) Can you do

1485   anything about the shower? It drips.

WILLY: (*From the bathroom.*) All of a sudden everything falls to pieces! Goddam plumbing, oughta be sued, those people. I hardly finished putting it in and the thing . . . (*His words rumble off.*)

1490   LINDA: I'm just wondering if Oliver will remember him. You think he might?

WILLY: (*Coming out of the bathroom in his pajamas.*) Remember him? What's the matter with you, you crazy? If he'd've stayed with Oliver he'd be on top by now! Wait'll Oliver

1495   gets a look at him. You don't know the average caliber any more. The average young man today—(*He is getting into bed.*)—is got a caliber of zero. Greatest thing in the world for him was to bum around.

(BIFF *and* HAPPY *enter the bedroom. Slight pause.*)

WILLY: (*Stops short, looking at* BIFF.) Glad to hear it, boy.

1500   HAPPY: He wanted to say good night to you, sport.

WILLY: (*To* BIFF.) Yeah. Knock him dead, boy. What'd you want to tell me?

BIFF: Just take it easy, Pop. Good night. (*He turns to go.*)

WILLY: (*Unable to resist.*) And if anything falls off the desk while

1505   you're talking to him—like a package or something—don't you pick it up. They have office boys for that.

LINDA: I'll make a big breakfast—

WILLY: Will you let me finish? (*To* BIFF.) Tell him you were in the business in the West. Not farm work.

1510   BIFF: All right, Dad.

LINDA: I think everything—

WILLY: (*Going right through her speech.*) And don't undersell yourself. No less than fifteen thousand dollars.

BIFF: (*Unable to bear him.*) Okay. Good night, Mom. (*He starts moving.*)

1515

WILLY: Because you got a greatness in you, Biff, remember that. You got all kinds a greatness . . . (*He lies back, exhausted.* BIFF *walks out.*)

LINDA: (*Calling after* BIFF.) Sleep well, darling!

HAPPY: I'm gonna get married, Mom. I wanted to tell you.   1520

LINDA: Go to sleep, dear.

HAPPY: (*Going.*) I just wanted to tell you.

WILLY: Keep up the good work. (HAPPY *exits.*) God . . . remember that Ebbets Field game? The championship of the city?   1525

LINDA: Just rest. Should I sing to you?

WILLY: Yeah. Sing to me. (LINDA *hums a soft lullaby.*) When that team came out—he was the tallest, remember?

LINDA: Oh, yes. And in gold.

(BIFF *enters the darkened kitchen, takes a cigarette, and leaves the house. He comes downstage into a golden pool of light. He smokes, staring at the night.*)

WILLY: Like a young god. Hercules—something like that.   1530 And the sun, the sun all around him. Remember how he waved to me? Right up from the field, with the representatives of three colleges standing by? And the buyers I brought, and the cheers when he came out—Loman, Loman, Loman! God Almighty, he'll be great yet. A star like   1535 that, magnificent, can never really fade away!

(*The light on* WILLY *is fading. The gas heater begins to glow through the kitchen wall, near the stairs, a blue flame beneath red coils.*)

LINDA: (*Timidly.*) Willy dear, what has he got against you?

WILLY: I'm so tired. Don't talk any more.

(BIFF *slowly returns to the kitchen. He stops, stares toward the heater.*)

LINDA: Will you ask Howard to let you work in New York?

WILLY: First thing in the morning. Everything'll be all right.   1540

(BIFF *reaches behind the heater and draws out a length of rubber tubing. He is horrified and turns his head toward* WILLY's *room, still dimly lit, from which the strains of* LINDA's *desperate but monotonous humming rise.*)

WILLY: (*Staring through the window into the moonlight.*) Gee, look at the moon moving between the buildings!

(BIFF *wraps the tubing around his hand and quickly goes up the stairs.*)

(*Curtain.*)

ACT TWO

Music is heard, gay and bright. The curtain rises as the music fades away. WILLY, *in shirt sleeves, is sitting at the kitchen table, sipping coffee, his hat in his lap.* LINDA *is filling his cup when she can.*

WILLY: Wonderful coffee. Meal in itself.

LINDA: Can I make you some eggs?

WILLY: No. Take a breath.

LINDA: You look so rested, dear.

5 WILLY: I slept like a dead one. First time in months. Image, sleeping till ten on a Tuesday morning. Boys left nice and early, heh?

LINDA: They were out of here by eight o'clock.

WILLY: Good work!

10 LINDA: It was so thrilling to see them leaving together. I can't get over the shaving lotion in this house!

WILLY: (*Smiling.*) Mmm—

LINDA: Biff was very changed this morning. His whole attitude seemed to be hopeful. He couldn't wait to get down-
15 town to see Oliver.

WILLY: He's heading for a change. There's no question, there simply are certain men that take longer to get—solidified. How did he dress?

LINDA: His blue suit. He's so handsome in that suit. He could
20 be a—anything in that suit!

(WILLY *gets up from the table.* LINDA *holds his jacket for him.*)

WILLY: There's no question, no question at all. Gee, on the way home tonight I'd like to buy some seeds.

LINDA: (*Laughing.*) That'd be wonderful. But not enough sun gets back there. Nothing'll grow any more.

25 WILLY: You wait, kid, before it's all over we're gonna get a lit-tle place out in the country, and I'll raise some vegetables, a couple of chickens . . .

LINDA: You'll do it yet, dear.

(WILLY *walks out of his jacket.* LINDA *follows him.*)

WILLY: And they'll get married, and come for a weekend. I'd
30 build a little guest house. 'Cause I got so many fine tools, all I'd need would be a little lumber and some peace of mind.

LINDA: (*Joyfully.*) I sewed the lining . . .

WILLY: I could build two guest houses, so they'd both come.
35 Did he decide how much he's going to ask Oliver for?

LINDA: (*Getting him into the jacket.*) He didn't mention it, but I imagine ten or fifteen thousand. You going to talk to Howard today?

WILLY: Yeah. I'll put it to him straight and simple. He'll just
40 have to take me off the road.

LINDA: And Willy, don't forget to ask for a little advance, be-cause we've got the insurance premium. It's the grace pe-riod now.

WILLY: That's a hundred . . . ?

45 LINDA: A hundred and eight, sixty-eight. Because we're a lit-tle short again.

WILLY: Why are we short?

LINDA: Well, you had the motor job on the car . . .

WILLY: That goddam Studebaker!

50 LINDA: And you got one more payment on the refrigerator . . .

WILLY: But it just broke again!

LINDA: Well, it's old, dear.

WILLY: I told you we should've bought a well-advertised ma-chine. Charley bought a General Electric and it's twenty
55 years old and it's still good, that son-of-a-bitch.

LINDA: But, Willy—

WILLY: Whoever heard of a Hastings refrigerator? Once in my life I would like to own something outright before it's

broken! I'm always in a race with the junkyard! I just fin-
60 ished paying for the car and it's on its last legs. The re-frigerator consumes belts like a goddam maniac. They time those things. They time them so when you finally paid for them, they're used up.

LINDA: (*Buttoning up his jacket as he unbuttons it.*) All told,
65 about two hundred dollars would carry us, dear. But that includes the last payment on the mortgage. After this pay-ment, Willy, the house belongs to us.

WILLY: It's twenty-five years!

LINDA: Biff was nine years old when we bought it.

70 WILLY: Well, that's a great thing. To weather a twenty-five year mortgage is—

LINDA: It's an accomplishment.

WILLY: All the cement, the lumber, the reconstruction I put in this house! There ain't a crack to be found in it any
75 more.

LINDA: Well, it served its purpose.

WILLY: What purpose? Some stranger'll come along, move in, and that's that. If only Biff would take this house, and raise a family . . . (*He starts to go.*) Good-by, I'm late.

80 LINDA: (*Suddenly remembering.*) Oh, I forgot! You're supposed to meet them for dinner.

WILLY: Me?

LINDA: At Frank's Chop House on Forty-eighth near Sixth Avenue.

85 WILLY: Is that so! How about you?

LINDA: No, just the three of you. They're gonna blow you to a big meal!

WILLY: Don't say! Who thought of that?

LINDA: Biff came to me this morning, Willy, and he said, "Tell
90 Dad, we want to blow him to a big meal." Be there six o'clock. You and your two boys are going to have dinner.

WILLY: Gee whiz! That's really somethin'. I'm gonna knock Howard for a loop, kid. I'll get an advance, and I'll come home with a New York job. Goddammit, now I'm gonna
95 do it!

LINDA: Oh, that's the spirit, Willy!

WILLY: I will never get behind a wheel the rest of my life!

LINDA: It's changing, Willy, I can feel it changing!

WILLY: Beyond a question. G'by, I'm late. (*He starts to go
100 again.*)

LINDA: (*Calling after him as she runs to the kitchen table for a handkerchief.*) You got your glasses?

WILLY: (*Feels for them, then comes back in.*) Yeah, yeah, got my glasses.

105 LINDA: (*Giving him the handkerchief.*) And a handkerchief.

WILLY: Yeah, handkerchief.

LINDA: And your saccharine?

WILLY: Yeah, my saccharine.

LINDA: Be careful on the subway stairs.

(*She kisses him, and a silk stocking is seen hanging from her hand.* WILLY *notices it.*)

WILLY: Will you stop mending stockings? At least while I'm
110 in the house. It gets me nervous. I can't tell you. Please.

(LINDA *hides the stocking in her hand as she follows* WILLY *across the forestage in front of the house.*)

LINDA: Remember, Frank's Chop House.

WILLY: (*Passing the apron.*) Maybe beets would grow out there.

115   LINDA: (*Laughing.*) But you tried so many times.

WILLY: Yeah. Well, don't work hard today. (*He disappears around the right corner of the house.*)

LINDA: Be careful!

(*As* WILLY *vanishes,* LINDA *waves to him. Suddenly the phone rings. She runs across the stage and into the kitchen and lifts it.*)

120   LINDA: Hello? Oh, Biff! I'm so glad you called, I just . . . Yes, sure, I just told him. Yes, he'll be there for dinner at six o'clock, I didn't forget. Listen, I was just dying to tell you. You know that little rubber pipe I told you about? That he connected to the gas heater? I finally decided to go
125   down the cellar this morning and take it away and destroy it. But it's gone! Imagine? He took it away himself, it isn't there! (*She listens.*) When? Oh, then you took it. Oh—nothing, it's just that I'd hoped he'd taken it away himself. Oh, I'm not worried, darling, because this morn-
130   ing he left in such high spirits, it was like the old days! I'm not afraid any more. Did Mr. Oliver see you? . . . Well, you wait there then. And make a nice impression on him, dar-ling. Just don't perspire too much before you see him. And have a nice time with Dad. He may have big news
135   too! . . . That's right, a New York job. And be sweet to him tonight, dear. Be loving to him. Because he's only a little boat looking for a harbor. (*She is trembling with sorrow and joy.*) Oh, that's wonderful, Biff, you'll save his life. Thanks, darling. Just put your arm around him when he comes
140   into the restaurant. Give him a smile. That's the boy . . . Good-by, dear, . . . You got your comb? . . . That's fine. Good-by, Biff dear.

(*In the middle of her speech,* HOWARD WAGNER, *thirty-six, wheels on a small typewriter table on which is a wire-recording machine and proceeds to plug it in. This is on the left forestage. Light slowly fades on* LINDA *as it rises on* HOWARD. HOWARD *is intent on threading the machine and only glances over his shoulder as* WILLY *appears.*)

WILLY: Pst! Pst!

HOWARD: Hello, Willy, come in.

145   WILLY: Like to have a little talk with you, Howard.

HOWARD: Sorry to keep you waiting. I'll be with you in a minute.

WILLY: What's that, Howard?

HOWARD: Didn't you ever see one of these? Wire recorder.

150   WILLY: Oh. Can we talk a minute?

HOWARD: Records things. Just got delivery yesterday. Been driving me crazy, the most terrific machine I ever saw in my life. I was up all night with it.

WILLY: What do you do with it?

155   HOWARD: I bought it for dictation, but you can do anything with it. Listen to this. I had it home last night. Listen to what I picked up. The first one is my daughter. Get this. (*He flicks the switch and "Roll out the Barrel" is heard being whistled.*) Listen to that kid whistle.

160   WILLY: That is lifelike, isn't it?

HOWARD: Seven years old. Get that tone.

WILLY: Ts, ts. Like to ask a little favor if you . . .

(*The whistling breaks off, and the voice of* HOWARD's *daughter is heard.*)

HIS DAUGHTER: "Now you, Daddy."

HOWARD: She's crazy for me! (*Again the same song is whistled.*) That's me! Ha! (*He winks.*)   165

WILLY: You're very good!

(*The whistling breaks off again. The machine runs silent a moment.*)

HOWARD: Sh! Get this now, this is my son.

HIS SON: "The capital of Alabama is Montgomery; the capi-tal of Arizona is Phoenix; the capital of Arkansas is Little Rock; the capital of California is Sacramento . . . (*And on,*   170 *and on.*)

HOWARD: (*Holding up five fingers.*) Five years old, Willy!

WILLY: He'll make an announcer some day!

HIS SON: (*Continuing.*) "The capital . . ."

HOWARD: Get that—alphabetical order! (*The machine breaks*   175 *off suddenly.*) Wait a minute. The maid kicked the plug out.

WILLY: It certainly is a—

HOWARD: Sh, for God's sake!

HIS SON: "It's nine o'clock, Bulova watch time. So I have to go to sleep."   180

WILLY: That really is—

HOWARD: Wait a minute! The next is my wife.

(*They wait.*)

HOWARD'S VOICE: "Go on, say something." (*Pause.*) "Well, you gonna talk?"

HIS WIFE: "I can't think of anything."   185

HOWARD'S VOICE: "Well, talk—it's turning."

HIS WIFE: (*Shyly, beaten.*) "Hello." (*Silence.*) "Oh, Howard, I can't talk into this . . ."

HOWARD: (*Snapping the machine off.*) That was my wife.

WILLY: That is a wonderful machine. Can we—   190

HOWARD: I tell you, Willy, I'm gonna take my camera, and my bandsaw, and all my hobbies, and out they go. This is the most fascinating relaxation I ever found.

WILLY: I think I'll get one myself.

HOWARD: Sure, they're only a hundred and a half. You can't   195 do without it. Supposing you wanna hear Jack Benny, see? But you can't be at home at that hour. So you tell the maid to turn the radio on when Jack Benny comes on, and this automatically goes on with the radio . . .

WILLY: And when you come home you . . .   200

HOWARD: You can come home twelve o'clock, one o'clock, any time you like, and you get yourself a Coke and sit yourself down, throw the switch, and there's Jack Benny's program in the middle of the night!

WILLY: I'm definitely going to get one. Because lots of time   205 I'm on the road, and I think to myself, what I must be missing on the radio!

HOWARD: Don't you have a radio in the car?

WILLY: Well, yeah, but who ever thinks of turning it on?

HOWARD: Say, aren't you supposed to be in Boston?   210

WILLY: That's what I want to talk to you about, Howard. You got a minute? (*He draws a chair in from the wing.*)

HOWARD: What happened? What're you doing here?

WILLY: Well . . .

HOWARD: You didn't crack up again, did you?   215

WILLY: Oh, no. No . . .

HOWARD: Geez, you had me worried there for a minute. What's the trouble?

WILLY: Well, tell you the truth, Howard. I've come to the de-
220 cision that I'd rather not travel any more.

HOWARD: Not travel! Well, what'll you do?

WILLY: Remember, Christmas time, when you had the party here? You said you'd try to think of some spot for me here in town.

225 HOWARD: With us?

WILLY: Well, sure.

HOWARD: Oh, yeah, yeah. I remember. Well, I couldn't think of anything for you, Willy.

WILLY: I tell ya, Howard. The kids are all grown up, y'know.
230 I don't need much any more. If I could take home—well, sixty-five dollars a week, I could swing it.

HOWARD: Yeah, but Willy, see I—

WILLY: I tell ya why, Howard. Speaking frankly and between the two of us, y'know—I'm just a little tired.

235 HOWARD: Oh, I could understand that, Willy. But you're a road man, Willy, and we do a road business. We've only got a half-dozen salesmen on the floor here.

WILLY: God knows, Howard, I never asked a favor of any man. But I was with the firm when your father used to
240 carry you in here in his arms.

HOWARD: I know that, Willy, but—

WILLY: Your father came to me the day you were born and asked me what I thought of the name of Howard, may he rest in peace.

245 HOWARD: I appreciate that, Willy, but there just is no spot here for you. If I had a spot I'd slam you right in, but I just don't have a single solitary spot.

(*He looks for his lighter.* WILLY *has picked it up and gives it to him. Pause.*)

WILLY: (*With increasing anger.*) Howard, all I need to set my
250 table is fifty dollars a week.

HOWARD: But where am I going to put you, kid?

WILLY: Look, it isn't a question of whether I can sell merchandise, is it?

HOWARD: No, but it's a business, kid, and everybody's gotta
255 pull his own weight.

WILLY: (*Desperately.*) Just let me tell you a story, Howard—

HOWARD: 'Cause you gotta admit, business is business.

WILLY: (*Angrily.*) Business is definitely business, but just listen for a minute. You don't understand this. When I was a
260 boy—eighteen, nineteen—I was already on the road. And there was a question in my mind as to whether selling had a future for me. Because in those days I had a yearning to go to Alaska. See, there were three gold strikes in one month in Alaska, and I felt like going out. Just for the ride
265 you might say.

HOWARD: (*Barely interested.*) Don't say.

WILLY: Oh, yeah, my father lived many years in Alaska. He was an adventurous man. We've got quite a little streak of self-reliance in our family. I thought I'd go out with my older
270 brother and try to locate him, and maybe settle in the North with the old man. And I was almost decided to go, when I met a salesman in the Parker House. His name was Dave Singleman. And he was eighty-four years old, and

he'd drummed merchandise in thirty-one states. And old
Dave, he'd go up to his room, y'understand, put on his 275
green velvet slippers—I'll never forget—and pick up his
phone and call the buyers, and without ever leaving his
room, at the age of eighty-four, he made his living. And
when I saw that, I realized that selling was the greatest career a man could want. 'Cause what could be more satisfy- 280
ing than to be able to go, at the age of eighty-four, into
twenty or thirty different cities, and pick up a phone, and
be remembered and loved and helped by so many different
people? Do you know? when he died—and by the way he
died the death of a salesman, in his green velvet slippers in 285
the smoker of the New York, New Haven and Hartford,
going into Boston—when he died, hundreds of salesmen
and buyers were at his funeral. Things were sad on a lotta
trains for months after that. (*He stands up.* HOWARD *has not
looked at him.*) In those days there was personality in it, 290
Howard. There was respect, and comradeship, and gratitude in it. Today, it's all cut and dried, and there's no chance
for bringing friendship to bear—or personality. You see
what I mean? They don't know me any more.

HOWARD: (*Moving away, to the right.*) That's just the thing, 295
Willy.

WILLY: If I had forty dollars a week—that's all I'd need. Forty
dollars, Howard.

HOWARD: Kid, I can't take blood from a stone, I—

WILLY: (*Desperation is on him now.*) Howard, the year Al Smith 300
was nominated, your father came to me and—

HOWARD: (*Starting to go off.*) I've got to see some people, kid.

WILLY: (*Stopping him.*) I'm talking about your father! There
were promises made across this desk! You mustn't tell me
you've got people to see—I put thirty-four years into this 305
firm, Howard, and now I can't pay my insurance! You can't
eat the orange and throw the peel away—a man is not a
piece of fruit! (*After a pause.*) Now pay attention. Your
father—in 1928 I had a big year. I averaged a hundred and
seventy dollars a week in commissions. 310

HOWARD: (*Impatiently.*) Now, Willy, you never averaged—

WILLY: (*Banging his hand on the desk.*) I averaged a hundred
and seventy dollars a week in the year of 1928! And your
father came to me—or rather, I was in the office here—it
was right over this desk—and he put his hand on my 315
shoulder—

HOWARD: (*Getting up.*) You'll have to excuse me, Willy, I gotta
see some people. Pull yourself together. (*Going out.*) I'll be
back in a little while.

(*On* HOWARD'S *exit, the light on his chair grows very bright and
strange.*)

WILLY: Pull myself together! What the hell did I say to him? 320
My God, I was yelling at him! How could I! (WILLY *breaks
off, staring at the light, which occupies the chair, animating it. He
approaches this chair, standing across the desk from it.*) Frank,
Frank, don't you remember what you told me that time?
How you put your hand on my shoulder, and Frank . . . 325
(*He leans on the desk and as he speaks the dead man's name he
accidentally switches on the recorder, and instantly.*)

HOWARD'S SON: ". . . of New York is Albany. The capital of
Ohio is Cincinnati, the capital of Rhode Island is . . ." (*The
recitation continues.*) 330

WILLY: (*Leaping away with fright, shouting.*) Ha! Howard! Howard! Howard!

HOWARD: (*Rushing in.*) What happened?

340 WILLY: (*Pointing at the machine, which continues nasally, childishly, with the capital cities.*) Shut it off! Shut it off!

HOWARD: (*Pulling the plug out.*) Look, Willy . . .

WILLY: (*Pressing his hands to his eyes.*) I gotta get myself some coffee. I'll get some coffee . . .

(WILLY *starts to walk out.* HOWARD *stops him.*)

HOWARD: (*Rolling up the cord.*) Willy, look . . .

345 WILLY: I'll go to Boston.

HOWARD: Willy, you can't go to Boston for us.

WILLY: Why can't I go?

HOWARD: I don't want you to represent us. I've been meaning to tell you for a long time now.

350 WILLY: Howard, are you firing me?

HOWARD: I think you need a good long rest, Willy.

WILLY: Howard—

HOWARD: And when you feel better, come back, and we'll see if we can work something out.

355 WILLY: But I gotta earn money, Howard. I'm in no position to—

HOWARD: Where are your sons? Why don't your sons give you a hand?

WILLY: They're working on a very big deal.

360 HOWARD: This is no time for false pride, Willy. You go to your sons and you tell them that you're tired. You've got two great boys, haven't you?

WILLY: Oh, no question, no question, but in the meantime . . .

HOWARD: Then that's that, heh?

365 WILLY: All right, I'll go to Boston tomorrow.

HOWARD: No, no.

WILLY: I can't throw myself on my sons. I'm not a cripple!

HOWARD: Look, kid, I'm busy this morning.

WILLY: (*Grasping* HOWARD'S *arm.*) Howard, you've got to let 370 me go to Boston!

HOWARD: (*Hard, keeping himself under control.*) I've got a line of people to see this morning. Sit down, take five minutes, and pull yourself together, and then go home, will ya? I need the office, Willy. (*He starts to go, turns, remembering the 375 recorder, starts to push off the table holding the recorder.*) Oh, yeah. Whenever you can this week, stop by and drop off the samples. You'll feel better, Willy, and then come back and we'll talk. Pull yourself together, kid, there's people outside.

(HOWARD *exits, pushing the table off left.* WILLY *stares into space, exhausted. Now the music is heard—*BEN'S *music—first distantly, then closer, closer. As* WILLY *speaks,* BEN *enters from the right. He carries valise and umbrella.*)

380 WILLY: Oh, Ben, how did you do it? What is the answer? Did you wind up the Alaska deal already?

BEN: Doesn't take much time if you know what you're doing. Just a short business trip. Boarding ship in an hour. Wanted to say good-by.

385 WILLY: Ben, I've got to talk to you.

BEN: (*Glancing at his watch.*) Haven't the time, William.

WILLY: (*Crossing the apron to Ben.*) Ben, nothing's working out. I don't know what to do.

BEN: Now, look here, William. I've bought timberland in 390 Alaska and I need a man to look after things for me.

WILLY: God, timberland! Me and my boys in those grand outdoors!

BEN: You've a new continent at your doorstep, William. Get out of these cities, they're full of talk and time payments 395 and courts of law. Screw on your fists and you can fight for a fortune up there.

WILLY: Yes, yes! Linda, Linda!

(LINDA *enters as of old, with the wash.*)

LINDA: Oh, you're back?

BEN: I haven't much time.

400 WILLY: No, wait! Linda, he's got a proposition for me in Alaska.

LINDA: But you've got— (*To* BEN.) He's got a beautiful job here.

WILLY: But in Alaska, kid, I could—

405 LINDA: You're doing well enough, Willy!

BEN: (*To* LINDA.) Enough for what, my dear?

LINDA: (*Frightened of* BEN *and angry at him.*) Don't say those things to him! Enough to be happy right here, right now. (*To* WILLY, *while* BEN *laughs.*) Why must everybody con-410 quer the world? You're well liked, and the boys love you, and someday—(*To* BEN.)—why, old man Wagner told him just the other day that if he keeps it up he'll be a member of the firm, didn't he, Willy?

WILLY: Sure, sure. I am building something with this firm, 415 Ben, and if a man is building something he must be on the right track, mustn't he?

BEN: What are you building? Lay your hand on it. Where is it?

WILLY: (*Hesitantly.*) That's true, Linda, there's nothing.

LINDA: Why? (*To* BEN.) There's a man eighty-four years old—

420 WILLY: That's right, Ben, that's right. When I look at that man I say, what is there to worry about?

BEN: Bah!

WILLY: It's true, Ben. All he has to do is go into any city, pick up the phone, and he's making his living and you know 425 why?

BEN: (*Picking up his valise.*) I've got to go.

WILLY: (*Holding* BEN *back.*) Look at this boy!

(BIFF, *in his high school sweater, enters carrying suitcase.* HAPPY *carries* BIFF'S *shoulder guards, gold helmet, and football pants.*)

WILLY: Without a penny to his name, three great universities are begging for him, and from there the sky's the limit, be-430 cause it's not what you do, Ben. It's who you know and the smile on your face! It's contacts, Ben, contacts! The whole wealth of Alaska passes over the lunch table at the Commodore Hotel, and that's the wonder, the wonder of this country, that a man can end with diamonds here on the basis of being liked! (*He turns to* BIFF.) And that's why 435 when you get out on that field today it's important. Because thousands of people will be rooting for you and loving you. (*To* BEN, *who has again begun to leave.*) And Ben! when he walks into a business office his name will sound out like a bell and all the doors will open to him! I've seen 440 it, Ben, I've seen it a thousand times! You can't feel it with your hand like timber, but it's there!

BEN: Good-by, William.

WILLY: Ben, am I right? Don't you think I'm right? I value
445   your advice.

BEN: There's a new continent at your doorstep, William. You
could walk out rich. Rich! (*He is gone.*)

WILLY: We'll do it here, Ben! You hear me? We're gonna do it
here!

(*Young* BERNARD *rushes in. The gay music of the Boys is heard.*)

450 BERNARD: Oh, gee, I was afraid you left already!

WILLY: Why? What time is it?

BERNARD: It's half-past one!

WILLY: Well, come on, everybody! Ebbets Field next stop!
Where's the pennants? (*He rushes through the wall-line of the*
455   *kitchen and out into the living-room.*)

LINDA: (*To* BIFF.) Did you pack fresh underwear?

BIFF: (*Who has been limbering up.*) I want to go!

BERNARD: Biff, I'm carrying your helmet, ain't I?

HAPPY: No, I'm carrying the helmet.

460 BERNARD: Oh, Biff, you promised me.

HAPPY: I'm carrying the helmet.

BERNARD: How am I going to get in the locker room?

LINDA: Let him carry the shoulder guards. (*She puts her coat
and hat on in the kitchen.*)

465 BERNARD: Can I, Biff? 'Cause I told everybody I'm going to
be in the locker room.

HAPPY: In Ebbets Field it's the clubhouse.

BERNARD: I meant the clubhouse. Biff!

HAPPY: Biff!

470 BIFF: (*Grandly, after a slight pause.*) Let him carry the shoulder
guards.

HAPPY: (*As he gives* BERNARD *the shoulder guards.*) Stay close to
us now.

(WILLY *rushes in with the pennants.*)

WILLY: (*Handing them out.*) Everybody wave when Biff comes
475   out on the field. (HAPPY *and* BERNARD *run off.*) You set
now, boy?

(*The music has died away.*)

BIFF: Ready to go, Pop. Every muscle is ready.

WILLY: (*At the edge of the apron.*) You realize what this means?

BIFF: That's right, Pop.

480 WILLY: (*Feeling* BIFF's *muscles.*) You're comin' home this afternoon captain of the All-Scholastic Championship Team of
the City of New York.

BIFF: I got it, Pop. And remember, pal, when I take off my
helmet, that touchdown is for you.

485 WILLY: Let's go! (*He is starting out, with his arm around* BIFF,
when CHARLEY *enters, as of old, in knickers.*) I got no room
for you, Charley.

CHARLEY: Room? For what?

WILLY: In the car.

490 CHARLEY: You goin' for a ride? I wanted to shoot some
casino.

WILLY: (*Furiously.*) Casino! (*Incredulously.*) Don't you realize
what today is?

LINDA: Oh, he knows, Willy. He's just kidding you.

495 WILLY: That's nothing to kid about!

CHARLEY: No. Linda, what's goin' on?

LINDA: He's playing in Ebbets Field.

CHARLEY: Baseball in this weather?

WILLY: Don't talk to him. Come on, come on! (*He is pushing
them out.*)   500

CHARLEY: Wait a minute, didn't you hear the news?

WILLY: What?

CHARLEY: Don't you listen to the radio? Ebbets Field just
blew up.

WILLY: You go to hell! (CHARLEY *laughs. Pushing them out.*)   505
Come on, come on! We're late.

CHARLEY: (*As they go.*) Knock a homer, Biff, knock a homer!

WILLY: (*The last to leave, turning to* CHARLEY.) I don't think
that was funny, Charley. This is the greatest day of his life.

CHARLEY: Willy, when are you going to grow up?   510

WILLY: Yeah, heh? When this game is over, Charley, you'll be
laughing out of the other side of your face. They'll be calling him another Red Grange. Twenty-five thousand a year.

CHARLEY: (*Kidding.*) Is that so?

WILLY: Yeah, that's so.   515

CHARLEY: Well, then, I'm sorry, Willy. But tell me something.

WILLY: What?

CHARLEY: Who is Red Grange?

WILLY: Put up your hands. Goddam you, put up your hands!

(CHARLEY, *chuckling, shakes his head and walks away, around the
left corner of the stage.* WILLY *follows him. The music rises to a
mocking frenzy.*)

WILLY: Who the hell do you think you are, better than every- 520
body else? You don't know everything, you big, ignorant,
stupid . . . Put up your hands!

(*Light rises, on the right side of the forestage, on a small table in the
reception room of* CHARLEY's *office. Traffic sounds are heard.*
BERNARD, *now mature, sits whistling to himself. A pair of tennis
rackets and an overnight bag are on the floor beside him.*)

WILLY: (*Offstage.*) What are you walking away for? Don't walk
away! If you're going to say something say it to my face! I
know you laugh at me behind my back. You'll laugh out 525
of the other side of your goddam face after this game.
Touchdown! Touchdown! Eighty thousand people!
Touchdown! Right between the goal posts.

(BERNARD *is a quiet, earnest, but self-assured young man.* WILLY's
voice is coming from right upstage now. BERNARD *lowers his feet off
the table and listens.* JENNY, *his father's secretary, enters.*)

JENNY: (*Distressed.*) Say, Bernard, will you go out in the hall?

BERNARD: What is that noise? Who is it?   530

JENNY: Mr. Loman. He just got off the elevator.

BERNARD: (*Getting up.*) Who's he arguing with?

JENNY: Nobody. There's nobody with him. I can't deal with
him any more, and your father gets all upset everytime he
comes. I've got a lot of typing to do, and your father's 535
waiting to sign it. Will you see him?

WILLY: (*Entering.*) Touchdown! Touch— (*He sees* JENNY.)
Jenny, Jenny, good to see you. How're ya? Workin'? Or still
honest?

JENNY: Fine. How've you been feeling?   540

WILLY: Not much any more, Jenny. Ha, ha! (*He is surprised to
see the rackets.*)

BERNARD: Hello, Uncle Willy.

545 WILLY: (*Almost shocked.*) Bernard! Well, look who's here! (*He comes quickly, guiltily, to* BERNARD *and warmly shakes his hand.*)

BERNARD: How are you? Good to see you.

WILLY: What are you doing here?

550 BERNARD: Oh, just stopped by to see Pop. Get off my feet till my train leaves. I'm going to Washington in a few minutes.

WILLY: Is he in?

BERNARD: Yes, he's in his office with the accountant. Sit down.

WILLY: (*Sitting down.*) What're you going to do in Washington?

555 BERNARD: Oh, just a case I've got there, Willy.

WILLY: That so? (*Indicating the rackets.*) You going to play tennis there?

BERNARD: I'm staying with a friend who's got a court.

WILLY: Don't say. His own tennis court. Must be fine people, 560 I bet.

BERNARD: They are, very nice. Dad tells me Biff's in town.

WILLY: (*With a big smile.*) Yeah, Biff's in. Working on a very big deal, Bernard.

BERNARD: What's Biff doing?

565 WILLY: Well, he's been doing very big things in the West. But he decided to establish himself here. Very big. We're having dinner. Did I hear your wife had a boy?

BERNARD: That's right. Our second.

WILLY: Two boys! What do you know!

570 BERNARD: What kind of a deal has Biff got?

WILLY: Well, Bill Oliver—very big sporting-goods man—he wants Biff very badly. Called him in from the West. Long distance, carte blanche, special deliveries. Your friends have their own private tennis court?

575 BERNARD: You still with the old firm, Willy?

WILLY: (*After a pause.*) I'm—I'm overjoyed to see how you made the grade, Bernard, overjoyed. It's an encouraging thing to see a young man really—really— Looks very good for Biff—very— (*He breaks off, then.*) Bernard— (*He 580 is so full of emotion, he breaks off again.*)

BERNARD: What is it, Willy?

WILLY: (*Small and alone.*) What—what's the secret?

BERNARD: What secret?

WILLY: How—how did you? Why didn't he ever catch on?

585 BERNARD: I wouldn't know that, Willy.

WILLY: (*Confidentially, desperately.*) You were his friend, his boyhood friend. There's something I don't understand about it. His life ended after that Ebbets Field game. From the age of seventeen nothing good ever happened 590 to him.

BERNARD: He never trained himself for anything.

WILLY: But he did, he did. After high school he took so many correspondence courses. Radio mechanics; television; God knows what, and never made the slightest mark.

595 BERNARD: (*Taking off his glasses.*) Willy, do you want to talk candidly?

WILLY: (*Rising, faces* BERNARD.) I regard you as a very brilliant man, Bernard. I value your advice.

BERNARD: Oh, the hell with the advice, Willy. I couldn't advise you. There's just one thing I've always wanted to ask 600 you. When he was supposed to graduate, and the math teacher flunked him—

WILLY: Oh, that son-of-a-bitch ruined his life.

BERNARD: Yeah, but, Willy, all he had to do was go to sum- 605 mer school and make up that subject.

WILLY: That's right, that's right.

BERNARD: Did you tell him not to go to summer school?

WILLY: Me? I begged him to go. I ordered him to go!

BERNARD: Then why wouldn't he go?

WILLY: Why? Why! Bernard, that question has been trailing 610 me like a ghost for the last fifteen years. He flunked the subject, and laid down and died like a hammer hit him!

BERNARD: Take it easy, kid.

WILLY: Let me talk to you—I got nobody to talk to. Bernard, Bernard, was it my fault? Y'see? It keeps going around in 615 my mind, maybe I did something to him. I got nothing to give him.

BERNARD: Don't take it so hard.

WILLY: Why did he lay down? What is the story there? You were his friend! 620

BERNARD: Willy, I remember, it was June, and our grades came out. And he'd flunked math.

WILLY: That son-of-a-bitch!

BERNARD: No, it wasn't right then. Biff just got very angry, I remember, and he was ready to enroll in summer school. 625

WILLY: (*Surprised.*) He was?

BERNARD: He wasn't beaten by it at all. But then, Willy, he disappeared from the block for almost a month. And I got the idea that he'd gone up to New England to see you. Did he have a talk with you then? 630

(WILLY *stares in silence.*)

BERNARD: Willy?

WILLY: (*With a strong edge of resentment in his voice.*) Yeah, he came to Boston. What about it?

BERNARD: Well, just that when he came back—I'll never forget this, it always mystifies me. Because I'd thought so well 635 of Biff, even though he'd always taken advantage of me. I loved him, Willy, y'know? And he came back after that month and took his sneakers—remember those sneakers with "University of Virginia" printed on them? He was so proud of those, wore them every day. And he took them 640 down in the cellar, and burned them up in the furnace. We had a fist fight. It lasted at least half an hour. Just the two of us, punching each other down thee cellar, and crying right through it. I've often thought of how strange it was that I knew he'd given up his life. What happened in 645 Boston, Willy?

(WILLY *looks at him as at an intruder.*)

BERNARD: I just bring it up because you asked me.

WILLY: (*Angrily.*) Nothing. What do you mean, "What happened?" What's that got to do with anything?

BERNARD: Well, don't get sore.

WILLY: What are you trying to do, blame it on me? If a boy 650 lays down is that my fault?

BERNARD: Now, Willy, don't get—

WILLY: Well, don't—don't talk to me that way! What does that mean, "What happened?"

(CHARLEY *enters. He is in his vest, and he carries a bottle of bour-* 655 *bon.*)

CHARLEY: Hey, you're going to miss that train. (*He waves the bottle.*)

660 BERNARD: Yeah, I'm going. (*He takes the bottle.*) Thanks, Pop. (*He picks up his rackets and bag.*) Good-by, Willy, and don't worry about it. You know, "If at first you don't succeed..."
WILLY: Yes, I believe in that.
BERNARD: But sometimes, Willy, it's better for a man just to
665 walk away.
WILLY: Walk away?
BERNARD: That's right.
WILLY: But if you can't walk away?
BERNARD: (*After a slight pause.*) I guess that's when it's tough.
670 (*Extending his hand.*) Good-by, Willy.
WILLY: (*Shaking* BERNARD'*s hand.*) Good-by, boy.
CHARLEY: (*An arm on* BERNARD'*s shoulder.*) How do you like this kid? Gonna argue a case in front of the Supreme Court.
675 BERNARD: (*Protesting.*) Pop!
WILLY: (*Genuinely shocked, pained, and happy.*) No! The Supreme Court!
BERNARD: I gotta run. 'By, Dad!
CHARLEY: Knock 'em dead, Bernard!

(BERNARD *goes off.*)

680 WILLY: (*As* CHARLEY *takes out his wallet.*) The Supreme Court! And he didn't even mention it!
CHARLEY: (*Counting out money on the desk.*) He don't have to—he's gonna do it.
WILLY: And you never told him what to do, did you? You
685 never took any interest in him.
CHARLEY: My salvation is that I never took any interest in anything. There's some money—fifty dollars. I got an accountant inside.
WILLY: Charley, look ... (*With difficulty.*) I got my insurance
690 to pay. If you can manage it—I need a hundred and ten dollars.

(CHARLEY *doesn't reply for a moment; merely stops moving.*)

WILLY: I'd draw it from my bank but Linda would know, and I ...
CHARLEY: Sit down, Willy.
695 WILLY: (*Moving toward the chair.*) I'm keeping an account of everything, remember. I'll pay every penny back. (*He sits.*)
CHARLEY: Now listen to me, Willy.
WILLY: I want you to know I appreciate ...
CHARLEY: (*Sitting down on the table.*) Willy, what're you doin'?
700 What the hell is goin' on in your head?
WILLY: Why? I'm simply ...
CHARLEY: I offered you a job. You can make fifty dollars a week. And I won't send you on the road.
WILLY: I've got a job.
705 CHARLEY: Without pay? What kind of a job is a job without pay? (*He rises.*) Now, look, kid, enough is enough. I'm no genius but I know when I'm being insulted.
WILLY: Insulted!
CHARLEY: Why don't you want to work for me?
710 WILLY: What's the matter with you? I've got a job.
CHARLEY: Then what're you walkin' in here every week for?
WILLY: (*Getting up.*) Well, if you don't want me to walk in here—
CHARLEY: I am offering you a job.

WILLY: I don't want your goddam job!
715 CHARLEY: When the hell are you going to grow up?
WILLY: (*Furiously.*) You big ignoramus, if you say that to me again I'll rap you one! I don't care how big you are! (*He's ready to fight.*)

(*Pause.*)

CHARLEY: (*Kindly, going to him.*) How much do you need,
720 Willy?
WILLY: Charley, I'm strapped, I'm strapped. I don't know what to do. I was just fired.
CHARLEY: Howard fired you?
WILLY: That snotnose. Imagine that? I named him. I named
725 him Howard.
CHARLEY: Willy, when're you gonna realize that them things don't mean anything? You named him Howard, but you can't sell that. The only thing you got in this world is what you can sell. And the funny thing is that you're a
730 salesman, and you don't know that.
WILLY: I've always tried to think otherwise, I guess. I always felt that if a man was impressive, and well liked, that nothing—
CHARLEY: Why must everybody like you? Who liked J. P. Morgan? Was he impressive? In a Turkish bath he'd look
735 like a butcher. But with his pockets on he was very well liked. Now listen, Willy, I know you don't like me, and nobody can say I'm in love with you, but I'll give you a job because—just for the hell of it, put it that way. Now what do you say?
740
WILLY: I—I just can't work for you, Charley.
CHARLEY: What're you, jealous of me?
WILLY: I can't work for you, that's all, don't ask me why.
CHARLEY: (*Angered, takes out more bills.*) You been jealous of me all your life, you damned fool! Here, pay your insur-
745 ance. (*He puts the money in* WILLY'*s hand.*)
WILLY: I'm keeping strict accounts.
CHARLEY: I've got some work to do. Take care of yourself. And pay your insurance.
WILLY: (*Moving to the right.*) Funny, y'know? After all the
750 highways, and the trains, and the appointments, and the years, you end up worth more dead than alive.
CHARLEY: Willy, nobody's worth nothin' dead. (*After a slight pause.*) Did you hear what I said?

(WILLY *stands still, dreaming.*)

CHARLEY: Willy!
755
WILLY: Apologize to Bernard for me when you see him. I didn't mean to argue with him. He's a fine boy. They're all fine boys, and they'll end up big—all of them. Someday they'll all play tennis together. Wish me luck, Charley. He saw Bill Oliver today.
760
CHARLEY: Good luck.
WILLY: (*On the verge of tears.*) Charley, you're the only friend I got. Isn't that a remarkable thing? (*He goes out.*)
CHARLEY: Jesus!

(CHARLEY *stares after him a moment and follows. All light blacks out. Suddenly raucous music is heard, and a red glow rises behind the screen at right.* STANLEY, *a young waiter, appears, carrying a table, followed by* HAPPY, *who is carrying two chairs.*)

765 STANLEY: (*Putting the table down.*) That's all right, Mr. Loman, I can handle it myself. (*He turns and takes the chairs from* HAPPY *and places them at the table.*)

HAPPY: (*Glancing around.*) Oh, this is better.

STANLEY: Sure, in the front there you're in the middle of all
770 kinds a noise. Whenever you got a party, Mr. Loman, you just tell me and I'll put you back here. Y'know, there's a lotta people they don't like it private, because when they go out they like to see a lotta action around them because they're sick and tired to stay in the house by theirself. But
775 I know you, you ain't from Hackensack. You know what I mean?

HAPPY: (*Sitting down.*) So how's it coming, Stanley?

STANLEY: Ah, it's a dog's life. I only wish during the war they'd a took me in the Army. I coulda been dead by now.
780 HAPPY: My brother's back, Stanley.

STANLEY: Oh, he come back, heh? From the Far West.

HAPPY: Yeah, big cattle man, my brother, so treat him right. And my father's coming too.

STANLEY: Oh, your father too!
785 HAPPY: You got a couple of nice lobsters?

STANLEY: Hundred per cent, big.

HAPPY: I want them with the claws.

STANLEY: Don't worry, I don't give you no mice. (HAPPY *laughs.*) How about some wine? It'll put a head on the
790 meal.

HAPPY: No. You remember, Stanley, that recipe I brought you from overseas? With the champagne in it?

STANLEY: Oh, yeah, sure. I still got it tacked up yet in the kitchen. But that'll have to cost a buck apiece anyways.
795 HAPPY: That's all right.

STANLEY: What'd you, hit a number or somethin'?

HAPPY: No, it's a little celebration. My brother is—I think he pulled off a big deal today. I think we're going into business together.
800 STANLEY: Great! That's the best for you. Because a family business, you know what I mean?—that's the best.

HAPPY: That's what I think.

STANLEY: 'Cause what's the difference? Somebody steals? It's in the family. Know what I mean? (*Sotto voce.*) Like this
805 bartender here. The boss is goin' crazy what kinda leak he's got in the cash register. You put it in but it don't come out.

HAPPY: (*Raising his head.*) Sh!

STANLEY: What?
810 HAPPY: You notice I wasn't lookin' right or left, was I?

STANLEY: No.

HAPPY: And my eyes are closed.

STANLEY: So what's the—?

HAPPY: Strudel's comin'.
815 STANLEY: (*Catching on, looks around.*) Ah, no, there's no—

(*He breaks off as a furred, lavishly dressed girl enters and sits at the next table. Both follow her with their eyes.*)

STANLEY: Geez, how'd ya know?

HAPPY: I got radar or something. (*Staring directly at her profile.*) Oooooooo . . . Stanley.

STANLEY: I think that's for you, Mr. Loman.
820 HAPPY: Look at that mouth. Oh, God. And the binoculars.

STANLEY: Geez, you got a life, Mr. Loman.

HAPPY: Wait on her.

STANLEY: (*Going to the girl's table.*) Would you like a menu, ma'am?

GIRL: I'm expecting someone, but I'd like a— 825

HAPPY: Why don't you bring her—excuse me, miss, do you mind? I sell champagne, and I'd like you to try my brand. Bring her a champagne, Stanley.

GIRL: That's awfully nice of you.

HAPPY: Don't mention it. It's all company money. (*He laughs.*) 830

GIRL: That's a charming product to be selling, isn't it?

HAPPY: Oh, gets to be like everything else. Selling is selling, y'know.

GIRL: I suppose.

HAPPY: You don't happen to sell, do you? 835

GIRL: No, I don't sell.

HAPPY: Would you object to a compliment from a stranger? You ought to be on a magazine cover.

GIRL: (*Looking at him a little archly.*) I have been.

(STANLEY *comes in with a glass of champagne.*)

HAPPY: What'd I say before, Stanley? You see? She's a cover 840
girl.

STANLEY: Oh, I could see, I could see.

HAPPY: (*To the* GIRL.) What magazine?

GIRL: Oh, a lot of them. (*She takes the drink.*) Thank you.

HAPPY: You know what they say in France, don't you? 845
"Champagne is the drink of the complexion"—Hya Biff!

(BIFF *has entered and sits with* HAPPY.)

BIFF: Hello, kid. Sorry I'm late.

HAPPY: I just got here. Uh, Miss—?

GIRL: Forsythe.

HAPPY: Miss Forsythe, this is my brother. 850

BIFF: Is Dad here?

HAPPY: His name is Biff. You might've heard of him. Great football player.

GIRL: Really? What team?

HAPPY: Are you familiar with football? 855

GIRL: No, I'm afraid I'm not.

HAPPY: Biff is quarterback with the New York Giants.

GIRL: Well, that is nice, isn't it? (*She drinks.*)

HAPPY: Good health.

GIRL: I'm happy to meet you. 860

HAPPY: That's my name. Hap. It's really Harold, but at West Point they called me Happy.

GIRL: (*Now really impressed.*) Oh, I see. How do you do? (*She turns her profile.*)

BIFF: Isn't Dad coming? 865

HAPPY: You want her?

BIFF: Oh, I could never make that.

HAPPY: I remember the time that idea would never come into your head. Where's the old confidence, Biff?

BIFF: I just saw Oliver— 870

HAPPY: Wait a minute, I've got to see that old confidence again. Do you want her? She's on call.

BIFF: Oh, no. (*He turns to look at the* GIRL.)

HAPPY: I'm telling you. Watch this. (*Turning to the* GIRL.) Honey? (*She turns to him.*) Are you busy? 875

GIRL: Well, I am . . . but I could make a phone call.

HAPPY: Do that, will you, honey? And see if you can get a friend. We'll be here for a while. Biff is one of the greatest football players in the country.

880 GIRL: (*Standing up.*) Well, I'm certainly happy to meet you.

HAPPY: Come back soon.

GIRL: I'll try.

HAPPY: Don't try, honey, try hard.

(*The* GIRL *exits.* STANLEY *follows, shaking his head in bewildered admiration.*)

HAPPY: Isn't that a shame now? A beautiful girl like that? 885 That's why I can't get married. There's not a good woman in a thousand. New York is loaded with them, kid!

BIFF: Hap, look—

HAPPY: I told you she was on call!

BIFF: (*Strangely unnerved.*) Cut it out, will ya? I want to say 890 something to you.

HAPPY: Did you see Oliver?

BIFF: I saw him all right. Now look, I want to tell Dad a couple of things and I want you to help me.

HAPPY: What? Is he going to back you?

895 BIFF: Are you crazy? You're out of your goddam head, you know that?

HAPPY: Why? What happened?

BIFF: (*Breathlessly.*) I did a terrible thing today, Hap. It's been the strangest day I ever went through. I'm all numb, I swear.

900 HAPPY: You mean he wouldn't see you?

BIFF: Well, I waited six hours for him, see? All day. Kept sending my name in. Even tried to date his secretary so she'd get me to him, but no soap.

HAPPY: Because you're not showin' the old confidence, Biff. 905 He remembered you, didn't he?

BIFF: (*Stopping* HAPPY *with a gesture.*) Finally, about five o'clock, he comes out. Didn't remember who I was or anything. I felt like such an idiot, Hap.

HAPPY: Did you tell him my Florida idea?

910 BIFF: He walked away. I saw him for one minute. I got so mad I could've torn the walls down! How the hell did I ever get the idea I was a salesman there? I even believed myself that I'd been a salesman for him! And then he gave me one look and—I realized what a ridiculous lie my whole life 915 has been! We've been talking in a dream for fifteen years. I was a shipping clerk.

HAPPY: What'd you do?

BIFF: (*With great tension and wonder.*) Well, he left, see. And the secretary went out. I was all alone in the waiting-room. I 920 don't know what came over me, Hap. The next thing I know I'm in his office—paneled walls, everything. I can't explain it. I—Hap, I took his fountain pen.

HAPPY: Geez, did he catch you?

BIFF: I ran out. I ran down all eleven flights. I ran and ran and 925 ran.

HAPPY: That was an awful dumb—what'd you do that for?

BIFF: (*Agonized.*) I don't know, I just—wanted to take something, I don't know. You gotta help me, Hap, I'm gonna tell Pop.

930 HAPPY: You crazy? What for?

BIFF: Hap, he's got to understand that I'm not the man somebody lends that kind of money to. He thinks I've been spiting him all these years and it's eating him up.

HAPPY: That's just it. You tell him something nice.

BIFF: I can't. 935

HAPPY: Say you got a lunch date with Oliver tomorrow.

BIFF: So what do I do tomorrow?

HAPPY: You leave the house tomorrow and come back at night and say Oliver is thinking it over. And he thinks it over for a couple of weeks, and gradually it fades away 940 and nobody's the worse.

BIFF: But it'll go on forever!

HAPPY: Dad is never so happy as when he's looking forward to something!

(WILLY *enters.*)

HAPPY: Hello, scout! 945

WILLY: Gee, I haven't been here in years!

(STANLEY *has followed* WILLY *in and sets a chair for him.* STANLEY *starts off but* HAPPY *stops him.*)

HAPPY: Stanley!

(STANLEY *stands by, waiting for an order.*)

BIFF: (*Going to* WILLY *with guilt, as to an invalid.*) Sit down, Pop. You want a drink?

WILLY: Sure, I don't mind. 950

BIFF: Let's get a load on.

WILLY: You look worried.

BIFF: N-no. (*To* STANLEY.) Scotch all around. Make it doubles.

STANLEY: Doubles, right. (*He goes.*)

WILLY: You had a couple already, didn't you? 955

BIFF: Just a couple, yeah.

WILLY: Well, what happened, boy? (*Nodding affirmatively, with a smile.*) Everything go all right?

BIFF: (*Takes a breath, then reaches out and grasps* WILLY'S *hand.*) Pal . . . (*He is smiling bravely, and* WILLY *is smiling too*). I had 960 an experience today.

HAPPY: Terrific, Pop.

WILLY: That so? What happened?

BIFF: (*High, slightly alcoholic, above the earth.*) I'm going to tell you everything from first to last. It's been a strange day. 965 (*Silence. He looks around, composes himself as best he can, but his breath keeps breaking the rhythm of his voice.*) I had to wait quite a while for him, and—

WILLY: Oliver?

BIFF: Yeah, Oliver. All day, as a matter of cold fact. And a lot 970 of—instances—facts, Pop, facts about my life came back to me. Who was it, Pop? Who ever said I was a salesman with Oliver?

WILLY: Well, you were.

BIFF: No, Dad, I was a shipping clerk. 975

WILLY: But you were practically—

BIFF: (*With determination.*) Dad, I don't know who said it first, but I was never a salesman for Bill Oliver.

WILLY: What're you talking about?

BIFF: Let's hold onto the facts tonight, Pop. We're not going 980 to get anywhere bullin' around. I was a shipping clerk.

WILLY: (*Angrily.*) All right, now listen to me—

BIFF: Why don't you let me finish?

WILLY: I'm not interested in stories about the past or any crap of that kind because the woods are burning, boys, you 985 understand? There's a big blaze going on all around. I was fired today.

BIFF: (*Shocked.*) How could you be?

990   WILLY: I was fired, and I'm looking for a little good news to tell your mother, because the woman has waited and the woman has suffered. The gist of it is that I haven't got a story left in my head, Biff. So don't give me a lecture about facts and aspects. I am not interested. Now what've you got to say to me?

(STANLEY *enters with three drinks. They wait until he leaves.*)

995   WILLY: Did you see Oliver?

BIFF: Jesus, Dad!

WILLY: You mean you didn't go up there?

HAPPY: Sure he went up there.

BIFF: I did. I—saw him. How could they fire you?

1000 WILLY: (*On the edge of his chair.*) What kind of a welcome did he give you?

BIFF: He won't even let you work on commission?

WILLY: I'm out! (*Driving.*) So tell me, he gave you a warm welcome?

1005 HAPPY: Sure, Pop, sure!

BIFF: (*Driven.*) Well, it was kind of—

WILLY: I was wondering if he'd remember you. (*To* HAPPY.) Imagine, man doesn't see him for ten, twelve years and gives him that kind of a welcome!

1010 HAPPY: Damn right!

BIFF: (*Trying to return to the offensive.*) Pop, look—

WILLY: You know why he remembered you, don't you? Because you impressed him in those days.

BIFF: Let's talk quietly and get this down to the facts, huh?

1015 WILLY: (*As though* BIFF *had been interrupting.*) Well, what happened? It's great news, Biff. Did he take you into his office or'd you talk in the waiting-room?

BIFF: Well, he came in, see, and—

WILLY: (*With a big smile.*) What'd he say? Betcha he threw his

1020 arm around you.

BIFF: Well, he kinda—

WILLY: He's a fine man. (*To* HAPPY.) Very hard man to see, y'know.

HAPPY: (*Agreeing.*) Oh, I know.

1025 WILLY: (*To* BIFF.) Is that where you had the drinks?

BIFF: Yeah, he gave me a couple of—no, no!

HAPPY: (*Cutting in.*) He told him my Florida idea.

WILLY: Don't interrupt. (*To* BIFF.) How'd he react to the Florida idea?

1030 BIFF: Dad, will you give me a minute to explain?

WILLY: I've been waiting for you to explain since I sat down here! What happened? He took you into his office and what?

BIFF: Well—I talked. And—and he listened, see.

1035 WILLY: Famous for the way he listens, y'know. What was his answer?

BIFF: His answer was— (*He breaks off, suddenly angry.*) Dad, you're not letting me tell you what I want to tell you!

WILLY: (*Accusing, angered.*) You didn't see him, did you?

1040 BIFF: I did see him!

WILLY: What'd you insult him or something? You insulted him didn't you?

BIFF: Listen, will you let me out of it, will you just let me out of it!

HAPPY: What the hell!   1045

WILLY: Tell me what happened!

BIFF: (*To* HAPPY.) I can't talk to him!

(*A single trumpet note jars the ear. The light of green leaves stains the house, which holds the air of night and a dream* YOUNG BERNARD *enters and knocks on the door of the house.*)

YOUNG BERNARD: (*Frantically.*) Mrs. Loman, Mrs. Loman!

HAPPY: Tell him what happened!

BIFF: (*To* HAPPY.) Shut up and leave me alone!   1050

WILLY: No, no! You had to go and flunk math!

BIFF: What math? What're you talking about?

YOUNG BERNARD: Mrs. Loman, Mrs. Loman!

(LINDA *appears in the house, as of old.*)

WILLY: (*Wildly.*) Math, math, math!

BIFF: Take it easy, Pop!   1055

YOUNG BERNARD: Mrs. Loman!

WILLY: (*Furiously.*) If you hadn't flunked you'd've been set by now!

BIFF: Now, look, I'm gonna tell you what happened, and you're going to listen to me.   1060

YOUNG BERNARD: Mrs. Loman!

BIFF: I waited six hours—

HAPPY: What the hell are you saying?

BIFF: I kept sending in my name but he wouldn't see me. So finally he . . . (*He continues unheard as light fades low on the* 1065 *restaurant.*)

YOUNG BERNARD: Biff flunked math!

LINDA: No!

YOUNG BERNARD: Birnbaum flunked him! They won't graduate him!   1070

LINDA: But they have to. He's gotta go to the university. Where is he? Biff! Biff!

YOUNG BERNARD: No, he left. He went to Grand Central.

LINDA: Grand—You mean he went to Boston!

YOUNG BERNARD: Is Uncle Willy in Boston?   1075

LINDA: Oh, maybe Willy can talk to the teacher. Oh, the poor, poor boy!

(*Light on house area snaps out.*)

BIFF: (*At the table, now audible, holding up a gold fountain pen.*) . . . so I'm washed up with Oliver, you understand? Are you listening to me?   1080

WILLY: (*At a loss.*) Yeah, sure. If you hadn't flunked—

BIFF: Flunked what? What're you talking about?

WILLY: Don't blame everything on me! I didn't flunk math— you did! What pen?

HAPPY: That was awful dumb, Biff, a pen like that is worth—   1085

WILLY: (*Seeing the pen for the first time.*) You took Oliver's pen?

BIFF: (*Weakening.*) Dad, I just explained it to you.

WILLY: You stole Bill Oliver's fountain pen!

BIFF: I didn't exactly steal it! That's just what I've been explaining to you!   1090

HAPPY: He had it in his hand and just then Oliver walked in, so he got nervous and stuck it in his pocket!

WILLY: My God, Biff!

BIFF: I never intended to do it, Dad!

1095 OPERATOR'S VOICE: Standish Arms, good evening!

WILLY: (*Shouting.*) I'm not in my room!

BIFF: (*Frightened.*) Dad, what's the matter? (*He and* HAPPY *stand up.*)

OPERATOR: Ringing Mr. Loman for you!

1100 WILLY: I'm not there, stop it!

BIFF: (*Horrified, gets down on one knee before* WILLY.) Dad, I'll make good, I'll make good. (WILLY *tries to get to his feet.* BIFF *holds him down.*) Sit down now.

WILLY: No, you're no good, you're no good for anything.

1105 BIFF: I am, Dad, I'll find something else, you understand? Now don't worry about anything. (*He holds up* WILLY's *face.*) Talk to me, Dad.

OPERATOR: Mr. Loman does not answer. Shall I page him?

WILLY: (*Attempting to stand, as though to rush and silence the*
1110 OPERATOR.) No, no, no!

HAPPY: He'll strike something, Pop.

WILLY: No, no . . .

BIFF: (*Desperately, standing over* WILLY.) Pop, listen! Listen to me! I'm telling you something good. Oliver talked to his
1115 partner about the Florida idea. You listening? He—he talked to his partner, and he came to me . . . I'm going to be all right, you hear? Dad, listen to me, he said it was just a question of the amount!

WILLY: Then you . . . got it?

1120 HAPPY: He's gonna be terrific, Pop!

WILLY: (*Trying to stand.*) Then you got it, haven't you? You got it! You got it!

BIFF: (*Agonized, holds* WILLY *down.*) No, no. Look, Pop. I'm supposed to have lunch with them tomorrow. I'm just
1125 telling you this so you'll know that I can still make an impression, Pop. And I'll make good somewhere, but I can't go tomorrow, see?

WILLY: Why not? You simply—

BIFF: But the pen, Pop!

1130 WILLY: You give it to him and tell him it was an oversight!

HAPPY: Sure, have lunch tomorrow!

BIFF: I can't say that—

WILLY: You were doing a crosswood puzzle and accidentally used his pen!

1135 BIFF: Listen, kid, I took those balls years ago, now I walk in with his fountain pen? That clinches it, don't you see? I can't face him like that! I'll try elsewhere.

PAGE'S VOICE: Paging Mr. Loman!

WILLY: Don't you want to be anything?

1140 BIFF: Pop, how can I go back?

WILLY: You don't want to be anything, is that what's behind it?

BIFF: (*Now angry at* WILLY *for not crediting his sympathy.*) Don't take it that way! You think it was easy walking into that office after what I'd done to him? A team of horses
1145 couldn't have dragged me back to Bill Oliver!

WILLY: Then why'd you go?

BIFF: Why did I go? Why did I go! Look at you! Look at what's become of you!

(*Off left,* THE WOMAN *laughs.*)

WILLY: Biff, you're going to go to that lunch tomorrow, or—

BIFF: I can't go. I've got no appointment!   1150

HAPPY: Biff, for . . .!

WILLY: Are you spiting me?

BIFF: Don't take it that way! Goddammit!

WILLY: (*Strikes* BIFF *and falters away from the table.*) You rotten little louse! Are you spiting me?   1155

THE WOMAN: Someone's at the door, Willy!

BIFF: I'm no good, can't you see what I am?

HAPPY: (*Separating them.*) Hey, you're in a restaurant! Now cut it out, both of you! (*The girls enter.*) Hello, girls, sit down.

(THE WOMAN *laughs, off left.*)

MISS FORSYTHE: I guess we might as well. This is Letta.   1160

THE WOMAN: Willy, are you going to wake up?

BIFF: (*Ignoring* WILLY.) How're ya, miss, sit down. What do you drink?

MISS FORSYTHE: Letta might not be able to stay long.

LETTA: I gotta get up very early tomorrow. I got jury duty.   1165
I'm so excited! Were you fellows ever on a jury?

BIFF: No, but I been in front of them! (*The girls laugh.*) This is my father.

LETTA: Isn't he cute? Sit down with us, Pop.

HAPPY: Sit him down, Biff!   1170

BIFF: (*Going to him.*) Come on, slugger, drink us under the table. To hell with it! Come on, sit down, pal.

(*On* BIFF's *last insistence,* WILLY *is about to sit.*)

THE WOMAN: (*Now urgently.*) Willy, are you going to answer the door!

(*The* WOMAN's *call pulls* WILLY *back. He starts right, befuddled.*)

BIFF: Hey, where are you going?   1175

WILLY: Open the door.

BIFF: The door?

WILLY: The washroom . . . the door . . . where's the door?

BIFF: (*Leading* WILLY *to the left.*) Just go straight down.

(WILLY *moves left.*)

THE WOMAN: Willy, Willy, are you going to get up, get up, get   1180
up, get up?

(WILLY *exits left.*)

LETTA: I think it's sweet you bring your daddy along.

MISS FORSYTHE: Oh, he isn't really your father!

BIFF: (*At left, turning to her resentfully.*) Miss Forsythe, you've just seen a prince walk by. A fine, troubled prince. A hard-   1185
working, unappreciated prince. A pal, you understand? A good companion. Always for his boys.

LETTA: That's so sweet.

HAPPY: Well, girls, what's the program? We're wasting time. Come on, Biff. Gather round. Where would you like to go?   1190

BIFF: Why don't you do something for him?

HAPPY: Me!

BIFF: Don't you give a damn for him, Hap?

HAPPY: What're you talking about? I'm the one who—

BIFF: I sense it, you don't give a good goddam about him. (*He   1195
takes the rolled-up hose from his pocket and puts it on the table*

in front of HAPPY.) Look what I found in the cellar, for Christ's sake. How can you bear to let it go on?

HAPPY: Me? Who goes away? Who runs off and—

1200 BIFF: Yeah, but he doesn't mean anything to you. You could help him—I can't! Don't you understand what I'm talking about? He's going to kill himself, don't you know that?

HAPPY: Don't I know it! Me!

1205 BIFF: Hap, help him! Jesus . . . help him . . . Help me, help me, I can't bear to look at his face! (*Ready to weep, he hurries out, up right.*)

HAPPY: (*Starting after him.*) Where are you going?

MISS FORSYTHE: What's he so mad about?

1210 HAPPY: Come on, girls, we'll catch up with him.

MISS FORSYTHE: (*As* HAPPY *pushes her out.*) Say, I don't like that temper of his!

HAPPY: He's just a little overstrung, he'll be all right!

WILLY: (*Off left, as* THE WOMAN *laughs.*) Don't answer! Don't
1215 answer!

LETTA: Don't you want to tell your father—

HAPPY: No, that's not my father. He's just a guy. Come on, we'll catch Biff, and, honey, we're going to paint this town! Stanley, where's the check! Hey, Stanley!

(*They exit.* STANLEY *looks toward left.*)

1220 STANLEY: (*Calling to* HAPPY *indignantly.*) Mr. Loman! Mr. Loman!

(STANLEY *picks up a chair and follows them off. Knocking is heard off left.* THE WOMAN *enters, laughing.* WILLY *follows her. She is in a black slip; he is buttoning his shirt. Raw, sensuous music accompanies their speech.*)

WILLY: Will you stop laughing? Will you stop?

THE WOMAN: Aren't you going to answer the door? He'll wake the whole hotel.

1225 WILLY: I'm not expecting anybody.

THE WOMAN: Whyn't you have another drink, honey, and stop being so damn self-centered?

WILLY: I'm so lonely.

THE WOMAN: You know you ruined me, Willy? From now
1230 on, whenever you come to the office, I'll see that you go right through to the buyers. No waiting at my desk any more, Willy. You ruined me.

WILLY: That's nice of you to say that.

THE WOMAN: Gee, you are self-centered! Why so sad? You are
1235 the saddest, self-centeredest soul I ever did see-saw. (*She laughs. He kisses her.*) Come on inside, drummer boy. It's silly to be dressing in the middle of the night. (*As knocking is heard.*) Aren't you going to answer the door?

WILLY: They're knocking on the wrong door.

1240 THE WOMAN: But I felt the knocking. And he heard us talking in here. Maybe the hotel's on fire!

WILLY: (*His terror rising.*) It's a mistake.

THE WOMAN: Then tell him to go away!

WILLY: There's nobody there.

1245 THE WOMAN: It's getting on my nerves, Willy. There's somebody standing out there and it's getting on my nerves!

WILLY: (*Pushing her away from him.*) All right, stay in the bathroom here, and don't come out. I think there's a law in Massachusetts about it, so don't come out. It may be that

new room clerk. He looked very mean. So don't come 1250
out. It's a mistake, there's no fire.

(*The knocking is heard again. He takes a few steps away from her, and she vanishes into the wing. The light follows him, and now he is facing* YOUNG BIFF, *who carries a suitcase.* BIFF *steps toward him. The music is gone.*)

BIFF: Why didn't you answer?

WILLY: Biff! What are you doing in Boston?

BIFF: Why didn't you answer? I've been knocking for five
minutes, I called you on the phone— 1255

WILLY: I just heard you. I was in the bathroom and had the door shut. Did anything happen home?

BIFF: Dad—I let you down.

WILLY: What do you mean?

BIFF: Dad . . . 1260

WILLY: Biffo, what's this about? (*Putting his arm around* BIFF.) Come on, let's go downstairs and get you a malted.

BIFF: Dad, I flunked math.

WILLY: Not for the term?

BIFF: The term. I haven't got enough credits to graduate. 1265

WILLY: You mean to say Bernard wouldn't give you the answers?

BIFF: He did, he tried, but I only got a sixty-one.

WILLY: And they wouldn't give you four points?

BIFF: Birnbaum refused absolutely. I begged him, Pop, but he 1270
won't give me those points. You gotta talk to him before they close the school. Because if he saw the kind of man you are, and you just talked to him in your way, I'm sure he'd come through for me. The class came right before practice, see, and I didn't go enough. Would you talk to 1275
him? He'd like you, Pop. You know the way you could talk.

WILLY: You're on. We'll drive right back.

BIFF: Oh, Dad, good work! I'm sure he'll change it for you!

WILLY: Go downstairs and tell the clerk I'm checkin' out. Go 1280
right down.

BIFF: Yes, sir! See, the reason he hates me, Pop—one day he was late for class so I got up at the blackboard and imitated him. I crossed my eyes and talked with a lithp.

WILLY: (*Laughing.*) You did? The kids like it? 1285

BIFF: They nearly died laughing!

WILLY: Yeah? What'd you do?

BIFF: The thquare root of thixthy twee is . . . (WILLY *bursts out laughing;* BIFF *joins him.*) And in the middle of it he walked in!

(WILLY *laughs and* THE WOMAN *joins in offstage.*)

WILLY: (*Without hesitation.*) Hurry downstairs and— 1290

BIFF: Somebody in there?

WILLY: No, that was next door.

(THE WOMAN *laughs offstage.*)

BIFF: Somebody got in your bathroom!

WILLY: No, it's the next room, there's a party.

THE WOMAN: (*Enters, laughing. She lisps this.*) Can I come in? 1295
There's something in the bathtub, Willy, and it's moving!

(WILLY *looks at* BIFF, *who is staring open-mouthed and horrified at* THE WOMAN.)

WILLY: Ah—you better go back to your room. They must be finished painting by now. They're painting her room so I let her take a shower here. Go back, go back . . . (*He pushes her.*)

THE WOMAN: (*Resisting.*) But I've got to get dressed, Willy, I can't—

WILLY: Get out of here! Go back, go back . . . (*Suddenly striving for the ordinary.*) This is Miss Francis, Biff, she's a buyer. They're painting her room. Go back, Miss Francis, go back . . .

THE WOMAN: But my clothes, I can't go out naked in the hall!

WILLY: (*Pushing her offstage.*) Get outa here! Go back, go back!

(BIFF *slowly sits down on his suitcase as the argument continues offstage.*)

THE WOMAN: Where's my stockings? You promised me stockings, Willy!

WILLY: I have no stockings here!

THE WOMAN: You had two boxes of size nine sheers for me, and I want them!

WILLY: Here, for God's sake, will you get outa here!

THE WOMAN: (*Enters holding a box of stockings.*) I just hope there's nobody in the hall. That's all I hope. (*To* BIFF.) Are you football or baseball?

BIFF: Football.

THE WOMAN: (*Angry, humiliated.*) That's me too. G'night. (*She snatches her clothes from* WILLY, *and walks out.*)

WILLY: (*After a pause.*) Well, better get going. I want to get to the school first thing in the morning. Get my suits out of the closet. I'll get my valise. (BIFF *doesn't move.*) What's the matter? (BIFF *remains motionless, tears falling.*) She's a buyer. Buys for J.H. Simmons. She lives down the hall—they're painting. You don't imagine—(*He breaks off. After a pause.*) Now listen, pal, she's just a buyer. She sees merchandise in her room and they have to keep it looking just so . . . (*Pause. Assuming command.*) All right, get my suits. (BIFF *doesn't move.*) Now stop crying and do as I say. I gave you an order. Biff, I gave you an order! Is that what you do when I give you an order? How dare you cry! (*Putting his arm around* BIFF.) Now look, Biff, when you grow up you'll understand about these things. You mustn't—you mustn't overemphasize a thing like this. I'll see Birnbaum first thing in the morning.

BIFF: Never mind.

WILLY: (*Getting down beside* BIFF.) Never mind! He's going to give you those points. I'll see to it.

BIFF: He wouldn't listen to you.

WILLY: He certainly will listen to me. You need those points for the U. of Virginia.

BIFF: I'm not going there.

WILLY: Heh? If I can't get him to change that mark you'll make it up in summer school. You've got all summer to—

BIFF: (*His weeping breaking from him.*) Dad . . .

WILLY: (*Infected by it.*) Oh, my boy . . .

BIFF: Dad . . .

WILLY: She's nothing to me, Biff. I was lonely, I was terribly lonely.

BIFF: You—you gave her Mama's stockings! (*His tears break through and he rises to go.*)

WILLY: (*Grabbing for* BIFF.) I gave you an order!

BIFF: Don't touch me, you—liar!

WILLY: Apologize for that!

BIFF: You fake! You phony little fake! You fake! (*Overcome, he turns quickly and weeping fully goes out with his suitcase.* WILLY *is left on the floor on his knees.*)

WILLY: I gave you an order! Biff, come back here or I'll beat you! Come back here! I'll whip you!

(STANLEY *comes quickly in from the right and stands in front of* WILLY.)

WILLY: (*Shouts at* STANLEY.) I gave you an order . . .

STANLEY: Hey, let's pick it up, pick it up, Mr. Loman. (*He helps* WILLY *to his feet.*) Your boys left with the chippies. They said they'll see you home.

(*A second waiter watches some distance away.*)

WILLY: But we were supposed to have dinner together.

(*Music is heard,* WILLY's *theme.*)

STANLEY: Can you make it?

WILLY: I'll—sure, I can make it. (*Suddenly concerned about his clothes.*) Do I—I look all right?

STANLEY: Sure, you look all right. (*He flicks a speck off* WILLY's *lapel.*)

WILLY: Here—here's a dollar.

STANLEY: Oh, your son paid me. It's all right.

WILLY: (*Putting it in* STANLEY's *hand.*) No, take it. You're a good, boy.

STANLEY: Oh, no, you don't have to . . .

WILLY: Here—here's some more, I don't need it any more. (*After a slight pause.*) Tell me—is there a seed store in the neighborhood?

STANLEY: Seeds? You mean like to plant?

(*As* WILLY *turns,* STANLEY *slips the money back into his jacket pocket.*)

WILLY: Yes. Carrots, peas . . .

STANLEY: Well, there's hardware stores on Sixth Avenue, but it may be too late now.

WILLY: (*Anxiously.*) Oh, I'd better hurry. I've got to get some seeds. (*He starts off to the right.*) I've got to get some seeds, right away. Nothing's planted. I don't have a thing in the ground.

(WILLY *hurries out as the light goes down.* STANLEY *moves over to the right after him, watches him off. The other waiter has been staring at* WILLY.)

STANLEY: (*To the waiter.*) Well, whatta you looking at?

(*The waiter picks up the chairs and moves off right.* STANLEY *takes the table and follows him. The light fades on this area. There is a long pause, the sound of the flute coming over. The light gradually rises on the kitchen, which is empty.* HAPPY *appears at the door of the house, followed by* BIFF. HAPPY *is carrying a large bunch of long-stemmed roses. He enters the kitchen, looks around for* LINDA. *Not seeing her, he turns to* BIFF, *who is just outside the house door, and makes a gesture with his hands, indicating "Not here, I guess." He looks into the living-room and freezes. Inside,* LINDA, *unseen, is seated,* WILLY's *coat on her lap. She rises ominously and quietly and moves toward* HAPPY, *who backs up into the kitchen, afraid.*)

HAPPY: Hey, what're you doing up? (LINDA *says nothing but moves toward him implacably.*) Where's Pop? (*He keeps back-*
1390 *ing to the right, and now* LINDA *is in full view in the doorway to the living-room.*) Is he sleeping?

LINDA: Where were you?

HAPPY: (*Trying to laugh it off.*) We met two girls, Mom, very fine types. Here, we brought you some flowers. (*Offering*
1395 *them to her.*) Put them in your room, Ma.

(*She knocks them to the floor at* BIFF's *feet. He has now come inside and closed the door behind him. She stares at* BIFF, *silent.*)

HAPPY: Now what'd you do that for? Mom, I want you to have some flowers—

LINDA: (*Cutting* HAPPY *off, violently to* BIFF.) Don't you care whether he lives or dies?

1400 HAPPY: (*Going to the stairs.*) Come upstairs, Biff.

BIFF: (*With a flare of disgust, to* HAPPY.) Go away from me! (*To* LINDA.) What do you mean, lives or dies? Nobody's dying around here, pal.

LINDA: Get out of my sight! Get out of here!

1405 BIFF: I wanna see the boss.

LINDA: You're not going near him!

BIFF: Where is he? (*He moves into the living-room and* LINDA *follows.*)

LINDA: (*Shouting after* BIFF.) You invite him for dinner. He
1410 looks forward to it all day—(BIFF *appears in his parents' bed-room, looks around, and exits.*)—and then you desert him there. There's no stranger you'd do that to!

HAPPY: Why? He had a swell time with us. Listen, when I—(LINDA *comes back into the kitchen.*)—desert him I hope I
1415 don't outlive the day!

LINDA: Get out of here!

HAPPY: Now look, Mom . . .

LINDA: Did you have to go to women tonight? You and your lousy rotten whores!

(BIFF *re-enters the kitchen.*)

1420 HAPPY: Mom, all we did was follow Biff around trying to cheer him up! (*To* BIFF.) Boy, what a night you gave me!

LINDA: Get out of here, both of you, and don't come back! I don't want you tormenting him any more. Go on now, get your things together! (*To* BIFF.) You can sleep in his apart-
1425 ment. (*She starts to pick up the flowers and stops herself.*) Pick up this stuff, I'm not your maid any more. Pick it up, you bum, you!

(HAPPY *turns his back to her in refusal.* BIFF *slowly moves over and gets down on his knees, picking up the flowers.*)

LINDA: You're a pair of animals! Not one, not another living soul would have had the cruelty to walk out on that man
1430 in a restaurant!

BIFF: (*Not looking at her.*) Is that what he said?

LINDA: He didn't have to say anything. He was so humiliated he nearly limped when he came in.

HAPPY: But, Mom, he had a great time with us—

1435 BIFF: (*Cutting him off violently.*) Shut up!

(*Without another word,* HAPPY *goes upstairs.*)

LINDA: You! You didn't even go in to see if he was all right!

BIFF: (*Still on the floor in front of* LINDA, *the flowers in his hand; with self-loathing.*) No. Didn't. Didn't do a damned thing. How do you like that, heh? Left him babbling in a toilet.

LINDA: You louse. You . . . 1440

BIFF: Now you hit it on the nose! (*He gets up, throws the flow-ers in the wastebasket.*) The scum of the earth, and you're looking at him!

LINDA: Get out of here!

BIFF: I gotta talk to the boss, Mom. Where is he? 1445

LINDA: You're not going near him. Get out of this house!

BIFF: (*With absolute assurance, determination.*) No. We're gonna have an abrupt conversation, him and me.

LINDA: You're not talking to him!

(*Hammering is heard from outside the house, off right.* BIFF *turns to-ward the noise.*)

LINDA: (*Suddenly pleading.*) Will you please leave him alone? 1450

BIFF: What's he doing out there?

LINDA: He's planting the garden!

BIFF: (*Quietly.*) Now? Oh, my God!

(BIFF *moves outside,* LINDA *following. The light dies down on them and comes up on the center of the apron as* WILLY *walks into it. He is carrying a flashlight, a hoe, and a handful of seed packets. He raps the top of the hoe sharply to fix it firmly, and then moves to the left, measuring off the distance with his foot. He holds the flashlight to look at the seed packets, reading off the instructions. He is in the blue of night.*)

WILLY: Carrots . . . quarter-inch apart. Rows . . . one-foot rows. (*He measures it off.*) One foot. (*He puts down a pack-* 1455
age and measures off.) Beets. (*He puts down another package and measures again.*) Lettuce. (*He reads the package, puts it down.*) One foot—(*He breaks off as* BEN *appears at the right and moves slowly down to him.*) What a proposition, ts, ts. Terrific, terrific. 'Cause she's suffered, Ben, the woman has 1460
suffered. You understand me? A man can't go out the way he came in, Ben, a man has got to add up to something. You can't, you can't—(BEN *moves toward him as though to in-terrupt.*) You gotta consider, now. Don't answer so quick. Remember, it's a guaranteed twenty-thousand-dollar 1465
proposition. Now look, Ben, I want you to go through the ins and outs of this thing with me. I've got nobody to talk to, Ben, and the woman has suffered, you hear me?

BEN: (*Standing still, considering.*) What's the proposition?

WILLY: It's twenty thousand dollars on the barrelhead. Guar- 1470
anteed, gilt-edged, you understand?

BEN: You don't want to make a fool of yourself. They might not honor the policy.

WILLY: How can they dare refuse? Didn't I work like a coolie to meet every premium on the nose? And now they don't 1475
pay off? Impossible!

BEN: It's called a cowardly thing, William.

WILLY: Why? Does it take more guts to stand here the rest of my life ringing up a zero?

BEN: (*Yielding.*) That's a point, William. (*He moves, thinking,* 1480
turns.) And twenty thousand—that *is* something one can feel with the hand, it is there.

WILLY: (*Now assured, with rising power.*) Oh, Ben, that's the whole beauty of it! I see it like a diamond, shining in the
1485   dark, hard and rough, that I can pick up and touch in my hand. Not like—like an appointment! This would not be another damned-fool appointment, Ben, and it changes all the aspects. Because he thinks I'm nothing, see, and so he spites me. But the funeral— (*Straightening up.*) Ben, that
1490   funeral will be massive! They'll come from Maine, Massachusetts, Vermont, New Hampshire! All the old-timers with the strange license plates—that boy will be thunderstruck, Ben, because he never realized—I am known! Rhode Island, New York, New Jersey—I am known, Ben,
1495   and he'll see it with his eyes once and for all. He'll see what I am, Ben! He's in for a shock, that boy!

BEN: (*Coming down to the edge of the garden.*) He'll call you a coward.

WILLY: (*Suddenly fearful.*) No, that would be terrible.

1500 BEN: Yes. And a damned fool.

WILLY: No, no, he mustn't, I won't have that! (*He is broken and desperate.*)

BEN: He'll hate you, William.

(*The gay music of the Boys is heard.*)

WILLY: Oh, Ben, how do we get back to all the great times?
1505   Used to be so full of light, and comradeship, the sleigh-riding in winter, and the ruddiness on his cheeks. And always some kind of good news coming up, always something nice coming up ahead. And never even let me carry the valises in the house, and simonizing, simonizing that
1510   little red car! Why, why can't I give him something and not have him hate me?

BEN: Let me think about it. (*He glances at his watch.*) I still have a little time. Remarkable proposition, but you've got to be sure you're not making a fool of yourself.

(BEN *drifts off upstage and goes out of sight.* BIFF *comes down from the left.*)

1515 WILLY: (*Suddenly conscious of* BIFF, *turns and looks up at him, then begins picking up the packages of seeds in confusion.*) Where the hell is that seed? (*Indignantly.*) You can't see nothing out here! They boxed in the whole goddam neighborhood!

BIFF: There are people all around here. Don't you realize that?

1520 WILLY: I'm busy. Don't bother me.

BIFF: (*Taking the hoe from* WILLY.) I'm saying good-by to you, Pop. (WILLY *looks at him, silent, unable to move.*) I'm not coming back any more.

WILLY: You're not going to see Oliver tomorrow?

1525 BIFF: I've got no appointment, Dad.

WILLY: He put his arm around you, and you've got no appointment?

BIFF: Pop, get this now, will you? Everytime I've left it's been a fight that sent me out of here. Today I realized something
1530   about myself and I tried to explain it to you and I—I think I'm just not smart enough to make any sense out of it for you. To hell with whose fault it is or anything like that. (*He takes* WILLY's *arm.*) Let's just wrap it up, heh? Come on in, we'll tell Mom. (*He gently tries to pull* WILLY *to left.*)

1535 WILLY: (*Frozen, immobile, with guilt in his voice.*) No, I don't want to see her.

BIFF: Come on! (*He pulls again, and* WILLY *tries to pull away.*)

WILLY: (*Highly nervous.*) No, no, I don't want to see her.

BIFF: (*Tries to look into* WILLY's *face, as if to find the answer there.*) Why don't you want to see her?   1540

WILLY: (*More harshly now.*) Don't bother me, will you?

BIFF: What do you mean, you don't want to see her? You don't want them calling you yellow, do you? This isn't your fault; it's me, I'm a bum. Now come inside! (WILLY *strains to get away.*) Did you hear what I said to you?   1545

(WILLY *pulls away and quickly goes by himself into the house.* BIFF *follows.*)

LINDA: (*To* WILLY). Did you plant, dear?

BIFF: (*At the door, to* LINDA.) All right, we had it out. I'm going and I'm not writing any more.

LINDA: (*Going to* WILLY *in the kitchen.*) I think that's the best way, dear. 'Cause there's no use drawing it out, you'll just 1550 never get along.

(WILLY *doesn't respond.*)

BIFF: People ask where I am and what I'm doing, you don't know, and you don't care. That way it'll be off your mind and you can start brightening up again. All right? That clears it, doesn't it? (WILLY *is silent, and* BIFF *goes to him.*) 1555 You gonna wish me luck, scout? (*He extends his hand.*) What do you say?

LINDA: Shake his hand, Willy.

WILLY: (*Turning to her, seething with hurt.*) There's no necessity to mention the pen at all, y'know.   1560

BIFF: (*Gently.*) I've got no appointment, Dad.

WILLY: (*Erupting fiercely.*) He put his arm around . . . ?

BIFF: Dad, you're never going to see what I am, so what's the use of arguing? If I strike oil I'll send you a check. Meantime forget I'm alive.   1565

WILLY: (*To* LINDA.) Spite, see?

BIFF: Shake hands, Dad.

WILLY: Not my hand.

BIFF: I was hoping not to go this way.

WILLY: Well, this is the way you're going. Good-by.   1570

(BIFF *looks at him a moment, then turns sharply and goes to the stairs.*)

WILLY: (*Stops him with.*) May you rot in hell if you leave this house!

BIFF: (*Turning.*) Exactly what is it that you want from me?

WILLY: I want you to know, on the train, in the mountains, in the valleys, wherever you go, that you cut down your life 1575 for spite!

BIFF: No, no.

WILLY: Spite, spite, is the word of your undoing! And when you're down and out, remember what did it. When you're rotting somewhere beside the railroad tracks, remember, 1580 and don't you dare blame it on me!

BIFF: I'm not blaming it on you!

WILLY: I won't take the rap for this, you hear?

(HAPPY *comes down the stairs and stands on the bottom step, watching.*)

BIFF: That's just what I'm telling you!

1585 WILLY: (*Sinking into a chair at the table, with full accusation.*) You're trying to put a knife in me—don't think I don't know what you're doing!

BIFF: All right, phony! Then let's lay it on the line. (*He whips the rubber tube out of his pocket and puts it on the table.*)

1590 HAPPY: You crazy—

LINDA: Biff! (*She moves to grab the hose, but* BIFF *holds it down with his hand.*)

BIFF: Leave it there! Don't move it!

WILLY: (*Not looking at it.*) What is that?

1595 BIFF: You know goddam well what that is.

WILLY: (*Caged, wanting to escape.*) I never saw that.

BIFF: You saw it. The mice didn't bring it into the cellar! What is this supposed to do, make a hero out of you? This supposed to make me sorry for you?

1600 WILLY: Never heard of it.

BIFF: There'll be no pity for you, you hear it? No pity!

WILLY: (*To* LINDA.) You hear the spite!

BIFF: No, you're going to hear the truth—what you are and what I am!

1605 LINDA: Stop it!

WILLY: Spite!

HAPPY: (*Coming down toward* BIFF.) You cut it now!

BIFF: (*To* HAPPY.) The man don't know who we are! The man is gonna know! (*To* WILLY.) We never told the truth for ten minutes in this house!

1610 HAPPY: We always told the truth!

BIFF: (*Turning on him.*) You big blow, are you the assistant buyer? You're one of the two assistants to the assistant, aren't you?

1615 HAPPY: Well, I'm practically—

BIFF: You're practically full of it! We all are! And I'm through with it. (*To* WILLY.) Now hear this, Willy, this is me.

WILLY: I know you!

BIFF: You know why I had no address for three months? I

1620 stole a suit in Kansas City and I was in jail. (*To* LINDA, *who is sobbing.*) Stop crying. I'm through with it.

(LINDA *turns away from them, her hands covering her face.*)

WILLY: I suppose that's my fault!

BIFF: I stole myself out of every good job since high school!

WILLY: And whose fault is that?

1625 BIFF: And I never got anywhere because you blew me so full of hot air I could never stand taking orders from anybody! That's whose fault it is!

WILLY: I hear that!

LINDA: Don't, Biff!

1630 BIFF: It's goddam time you heard that! I had to be boss big shot in two weeks, and I'm through with it!

WILLY: Then hang yourself! For spite, hang yourself!

BIFF: No! Nobody's hanging himself, Willy! I ran down eleven flights with a pen in my hand today. And suddenly I

1635 stopped, you hear me? And in the middle of that office building, do you hear this? I stopped in the middle of that building and I saw—the sky. I saw the things that I love in this world. The work and the food and time to sit and smoke. And I looked at the pen and said to myself, what

1640 the hell am I grabbing this for? Why am I trying to become what I don't want to be? What am I doing in an office, making a contemptuous, begging fool of myself, when all

I want is out there, waiting for me the minute I say I know who I am! Why can't I say that, Willy? (*He tries to make* WILLY *face him, but* WILLY *pulls away and moves to the left.*) 1645

WILLY: (*With hatred, threateningly.*) The door of your life is wide open!

BIFF: Pop! I'm a dime a dozen, and so are you!

WILLY: (*Turning on him now in an uncontrolled outburst.*) I am not a dime a dozen! I am Willy Loman, and you are Biff 1650 Loman!

(BIFF *starts for* WILLY, *but is blocked by* HAPPY. *In his fury,* BIFF *seems on the verge of attacking his father.*)

BIFF: I am not a leader of men, Willy, and neither are you. You were never anything but a hard-working drummer who landed in the ash can like all the rest of them! I'm one dollar an hour, Willy! I tried seven states and couldn't 1655 raise it. A buck an hour! Do you gather my meaning? I'm not bringing home any prizes any more, and you're going to stop waiting for me to bring them home!

WILLY: (*Directly to* BIFF.) You vengeful, spiteful mut!

(BIFF *breaks from* HAPPY. WILLY, *in fright, starts up the stairs.* BIFF *grabs him.*)

BIFF: (*At the peak of his fury.*) Pop, I'm nothing! I'm nothing, 1660 Pop. Can't you understand that? There's no spite in it any more. I'm just what I am, that's all.

(BIFF's *fury has spent itself, and he breaks down, sobbing, holding on to* WILLY, *who dumbly fumbles for* BIFF's *face.*)

WILLY: (*Astonished.*) What're you doing? What're you doing? (*To* LINDA.) Why is he crying?

BIFF: (*Crying, broken.*) Will you let me go, for Christ's sake? 1665 Will you take that phony dream and burn it before something happens? (*Struggling to contain himself, he pulls away and moves to the stairs.*) I'll go in the morning. Put him—put him to bed. (*Exhausted,* BIFF *moves up the stairs to his room.*) 1670

WILLY: (*After a long pause, astonished, elevated.*) Isn't that—isn't that remarkable? Biff—he likes me!

LINDA: He loves you, Willy!

HAPPY: (*Deeply moved.*) Always did, Pop.

WILLY: Oh, Biff! (*Staring wildly.*) He cried! Cried to me. (*He* 1675 *is choking with his love, and now cries out his promise.*) That boy—that boy is going to be magnificent!

(BEN *appears in the light just outside the kitchen.*)

BEN: Yes, outstanding, with twenty thousand behind him.

LINDA: (*Sensing the racing of his mind, fearfully, carefully.*) Now come to bed, Willy. It's all settled now. 1680

WILLY: (*Finding it difficult not to rush out of the house.*) Yes, we'll sleep. Come on. Go to sleep, Hap.

BEN: And it does take a great kind of a man to crack the jungle.

(*In accents of dread,* BEN's *idyllic music starts up.*)

HAPPY: (*His arm around* LINDA.) I'm getting married, Pop, don't forget it. I'm changing everything. I'm gonna run 1685 that department before the year is up. You'll see, Mom. (*He kisses her.*)

BEN: The jungle is dark but full of diamonds, Willy.

(WILLY *turns, moves, listening to* BEN.)

1690 LINDA: Be good. You're both good boys, just act that way, that's all.

HAPPY: 'Night, Pop. (*He goes upstairs.*)

LINDA: (*To* WILLY). Come, dear.

BEN: (*With greater force.*) One must go in to fetch a diamond out.

1695 WILLY: (*To* LINDA, *as he moves slowly along the edge of the kitchen, toward the door.*) I just want to get settled down, Linda. Let me sit alone for a little.

LINDA: (*Almost uttering her fear.*) I want you upstairs.

WILLY: (*Taking her in his arms.*) In a few minutes, Linda. I
1600 couldn't sleep right now. Go on, you look awful tired. (*He kisses her.*)

BEN: Not like an appointment at all. A diamond is rough and hard to the touch.

WILLY: Go on now. I'll be right up.

1705 LINDA: I think this is the only way, Willy.

WILLY: Sure, it's the best thing.

BEN: Best thing!

WILLY: The only way. Everything is gonna be—go on, kid, get to bed. You look so tired.

1710 LINDA: Come right up.

WILLY: Two minutes.

(LINDA *goes into the living-room, then reappears in her bedroom.* WILLY *moves just outside the kitchen door.*)

WILLY: Loves me. (*Wonderingly.*) Always loved me. Isn't that a remarkable thing? Ben, he'll worship me, for it!

BEN: (*With promise.*) It's dark there, but full of diamonds.

1715 WILLY: Can you imagine that magnificence with twenty thousand dollars in his pocket?

LINDA: (*Calling from her room.*) Willy! Come up!

WILLY: (*Calling into the kitchen.*) Yes! Yes. Coming! It's very smart, you realize that, don't you, sweetheart? Even Ben
1720 sees it. I gotta go, baby. 'By! 'By! (*Going over to* BEN, *almost dancing.*) Imagine? When the mail comes he'll be ahead of Bernard again!

BEN: A perfect proposition all around.

WILLY: Did you see how he cried to me? Oh, if I could kiss
1725 him, Ben!

BEN: Time, William, time!

WILLY: Oh, Ben, I always knew one way or another we were gonna make it, Biff and I!

BEN: (*Looking at his watch.*) The boat. We'll be late. (*He moves
1730 slowly off into the darkness.*)

WILLY: (*Elegiacally, turning to the house.*) Now when you kick off, boy, I want a seventy-yard boot, and get right down the field under the ball, and when you hit, hit low and hit hard, because it's important, boy. (*He swings around and faces
1735 the audience.*) There's all kinds of important people in the stands, and the first thing you know . . . (*Suddenly realizing he is alone.*) Ben! Ben, where do I . . . ? (*He makes a sudden movement of search.*) Ben, how do I . . . ?

LINDA: (*Calling.*) Willy, you coming up?

1740 WILLY: (*Uttering a gasp of fear, whirling about as if to quiet her.*) Sh! (*He turns around as if to find his way; sounds, faces, voices, seem to be swarming in upon him and he flicks at them, crying.*)

Sh! Sh! (*Suddenly music, faint and high, stops him. It rises in intensity, almost to an unbearable scream. He goes up and down on his toes, and rushes off around the house.*) Shhh!   1745

LINDA: Willy?

(*There is no answer.* LINDA *waits.* BIFF *gets up off his bed He is still in his clothes.* HAPPY *sits up.* BIFF *stands listening.*)

LINDA: (*With real fear.*) Willy, answer me! Willy!

(*There is the sound of a car starting and moving away at full speed.*)

LINDA: No!

BIFF: (*Rushing down the stairs.*) Pop!

(*As the car speeds off, the music crashes down in a frenzy of sound, which becomes the soft pulsation of a single cello string.* BIFF *slowly returns to his bedroom. He and* HAPPY *gravely don their jackets.* LINDA *slowly walks out of her room. The music has developed into a dead march. The leaves of day are appearing over everything.* CHARLEY *and* BERNARD, *somberly dressed, appear and knock on the kitchen door.* BIFF *and* HAPPY *slowly descend the stairs to the kitchen as* CHARLEY *and* BERNARD *enter. All stop a moment when* LINDA, *in clothes of mourning, bearing a little bunch of roses, comes through the draped doorway into the kitchen. She goes to* CHARLEY *and takes his arm. Now all move toward the audience, through the wall-line of the kitchen. At the limit of the apron,* LINDA *lays down the flowers, kneels, and sits back on her heels. All stare down at the grave.*)

REQUIEM

CHARLEY: It's getting dark, Linda.

(LINDA *doesn't react. She stares at the grave.*)

BIFF: How about it, Mom? Better get some rest, heh? They'll be closing the gate soon.

(LINDA *makes no move. Pause.*)

HAPPY: (*Deeply angered.*) He had no right to do that. There was no necessity for it. We would've helped him.   5

CHARLEY: (*Grunting.*) Hmmm.

BIFF: Come along, Mom.

LINDA: Why didn't anybody come?

CHARLEY: It was a very nice funeral.

LINDA: But where are all the people he knew? Maybe they   10
blame him.

CHARLEY: Naa. It's a rough world, Linda. They wouldn't blame him.

LINDA: I can't understand it. At this time especially. First time in thirty-five years we were just about free and clear. He   15
only needed a little salary. He was even finished with the dentist.

CHARLEY: No man only needs a little salary.

LINDA: I can't understand it.

BIFF: There were a lot of nice days. When he'd come home   20
from a trip; or on Sundays, making the stoop; finishing the cellar; putting on the new porch; when he built the extra bathroom; and put up the garage. You know something, Charley, there's more of him in that front stoop than in all the sales he ever made.   25

CHARLEY: Yeah. He was a happy man with a batch of cement.

LINDA: He was so wonderful with his hands.

BIFF: He had the wrong dreams. All, all, wrong.

HAPPY: (*Almost ready to fight* BIFF.) Don't say that!

30 BIFF: He never knew who he was.

CHARLEY: (*Stopping* HAPPY's *movement and reply. To* BIFF.) Nobody dast blame this man. You don't understand: Willy was a salesman. And for a salesman, there is no rock bottom to the life. He don't put a bolt to a nut, he don't tell

35 you the law or give you medicine. He's a man way out there in the blue, riding on a smile and a shoeshine. And when they start not smiling back—that's an earthquake. And then you get yourself a couple of spots on your hat, and you're finished. Nobody dast blame this man. A sales-

40 man is got to dream, boy. It comes with the territory.

BIFF: Charley, the man didn't know who he was.

HAPPY: (*Infuriated.*) Don't say that!

BIFF: Why don't you come with me, Happy?

HAPPY: I'm not licked that easily. I'm staying right in this city,

45 and I'm gonna beat this racket! (*He looks at* BIFF, *his chin set.*) The Loman Brothers!

BIFF: I know who I am, kid.

HAPPY: All right, boy. I'm gonna show you and everybody else that Willy Loman did not die in vain. He had a good

50 dream. It's the only dream you can have—to come out number-one man. He fought it out here, and this is where I'm gonna win it for him.

BIFF: (*With a hopeless glance at* HAPPY, *bends toward his mother.*) Let's go, Mom.

LINDA: I'll be with you in a minute. Go on, Charley. (*He hes-* 55 *itates.*) I want to, just for a minute. I never had a chance to say good-by.

(CHARLEY *moves away, followed by* HAPPY. BIFF *remains a slight distance up and left of* LINDA. *She sits there, summoning herself. The flute begins, not far away, playing behind her speech.*)

LINDA: Forgive me, dear. I can't cry. I don't know what it is, but I can't cry. I don't understand it. Why did you ever do that? Help me, Willy, I can't cry. It seems to me that you're 60 just on another trip. I keep expecting you. Willy, dear, I can't cry. Why did you do it? I search and search and I search, and I can't understand it, Willy. I made the last payment on the house today. Today, dear. And there'll be nobody home. (*A sob rises in her throat.*) We're free and clear. 65 (*Sobbing more fully, released.*) We're free. (BIFF *comes slowly toward her.*) We're free . . . We're free . . .

BIFF *lifts her to her feet and moves out up right with her in his arms.* LINDA *sobs quietly.* BERNARD *and* CHARLEY *come together and follow them, followed by* HAPPY. *Only the music of the flute is left on the darkening stage as over the house the hard towers of the apartment buildings rise into sharp focus, and*

The Curtain Falls

Luis Valdez

Luis Valdez (b. 1940), was born and raised the son of farmworkers in Delano, California. He majored in drama at San Jose State College, taking his B.A. in 1964, and then joined the San Francisco Mime Troup, an important experimental theater company. In 1965, when farm workers at the Delano grape plantations went on strike, Valdez formed El Teatro Campesino ("The Farmworkers' Theater"). Valdez and Teatro Campesino devised two dramatic forms: *ACTOS,* short, satirical plays dramatizing the oppression of the fieldworkers, and *MITOS,* poetic, lyrical plays on Chicano life. *Actos* were improvised by members of El Teatro Campesino playing "stock" characters (the farmworker, the boss, etc.); because they were improvised for each production and each community, *actos* varied considerably from performance to performance. The final versions published by Valdez were written down much later. El Teatro Campesino became one of several important Chicano theater companies that performed throughout the Southwest and in urban areas of the Midwest and Northeast, drawing on both American and European dramatic traditions, as well as traditions of Mexican and Spanish-language theater in the United States that date to the seventeenth century. In the late 1960s and 1970s, Teatro Campesino toured the United States and Europe and gained an international reputation. Valdez's other *actos* with Teatro Campesino include *Las Dos Caras del Patroncito* (1965), *No Saco Nada de la Escuela* (1969), and *Vietnam Campesino* (1970). Valdez produced the stage play *Zoot Suit* in 1978, which was released as a film in 1981. In 1980, Valdez transformed El Teatro Campesino into a production company, a marked shift from its collaborative and activist origins. This version of El Teatro Campesino hired "professional" actors, abandoning the collective esthetic characteristic of the company's earlier work. Valdez developed several new projects in connection with the company's new theater in San Juan Bautista (built in 1981), notably *Bandido!* (1981), *Corridos* (1992), and *I Don't Have to Show You No Stinking Badges* (1990). His film *La Bamba* was released in 1987, and Valdez filmed *Pastorelas* for PBS television in 1990. Valdez has held academic appointments at the University of California, Berkeley, and at the University of California, Santa Cruz. He is teaching at the new campus of the California State University at Monterey.

ZOOT SUIT

Zoot Suit remains the most successful play of the Chicano theater, and presents a vivid re-reading of one of the formative moments in Chicano history: the "Zoot Suit Riots" in Los Angeles during World War II. Valdez stages the play's perspective on history in its opening moments, a kind of Brechtian *GESTUS:* the elegant figure of the Pachuco—the cool urban Latino draped in the refined, dressy zoot suit—enters the stage by slicing through a giant newspaper-curtain, the *Los Angeles Herald,* whose headlines proclaim "ZOOT-SUITER HORDES INVADE LOS ANGELES. U.S. NAVY AND MARINES ARE CALLED IN." The Pachuco instigates the play's central action, not merely to re-stage history, but to interrogate the means of history, the ways in which public history—represented here by the newspaper, later by police reports and trial transcripts—both distorts and finally erases the facts of Chicano history. The events of *Zoot Suit* are taken directly from the Sleepy Lagoon murder trial of 1942 (an excellent video from the "American Experience" series on PBS, *The Zoot Suit Riots,* is available). Los Angeles in the early 1940s was a city at war; 50,000 sailors were in port, and the city was nervous about invasion from Japan and subversion from within. At the same time, it was also a deeply racialized city, in which Mexican-American citizens (the term *Chicano* was not embraced by Mexican Americans until the 1960s) routinely suffered discrimination of all kinds: signs reading "No Mexicans Allowed" were prominent in the city, whose Mexican-American population numbered well over a quarter million. Mexican Americans were routinely stigmatized as a "criminal element" by the city's

Anglo majority, and allegations that subversion might come from the "Mexicans" of the city—most of whom were not "Mexicans" but American citizens—were made casually and repeatedly in the press. At the same time, the zoot suit craze had become popular among younger Mexican Americans, and zoot suits—high-waisted baggy pants gathered into narrow pegged cuffs, an oversize long jacket, dangling watchchain, and wide-brimmed hat—could be seen all over Los Angeles, especially in the jazz and swing clubs downtown.

The Zoot Suit Riots took place against this backdrop of racial conflict. Valdez's play takes the Sleepy Lagoon trial as the centerpiece of the riots. In August of 1942, a young Mexican-American couple—Hank Leyvas and his girlfriend—were beaten by a Mexican-American gang; later that evening Leyvas went to the Sleepy Lagoon swimming hole with some friends from his 38th Street neighborhood to take revenge for the beating. When they arrived, they found a man—José Díaz— who had been beaten and stabbed but was still alive. Leaving their girlfriends to tend to Díaz, the boys went inside for their fight, and then picked up the girls and left Sleepy Lagoon. Díaz died, and when his murder was discovered, the Los Angeles Police Department set up a dragnet, bringing in 600 Mexican-American boys for questioning; they then arrested Hank Leyvas and twenty other boys for Díaz's murder. Held at the 77th Precinct, the boys were routinely and savagely beaten by the police, and when they were brought to trial, Judge Charles Frickie would not allow them to receive haircuts or clean clothes. Although they were unanimous in denying complicity in Díaz's death, on January 12, 1943, seventeen of the boys were found guilty and sent to San Quentin prison outside San Francisco, far from their families or their legal representation; Hank Leyvas, alleged to be the ringleader of the group, was given a life sentence and eventually sent to Folsom prison. Several of the girls were—without legal proceedings of any kind—taken from their families and made wards of the state; they were sent to the prison-like Ventura School for Girls, and remained in state custody until turning 21. Almost immediately a Sleepy Lagoon Defense Committee was formed, spearheaded by Alice Greenfield McGrath, and the Committee succeeded not only in gaining the support of prominent Angelinos, but in raising money nationwide to take the case to appeal. The case was appealed in November 1943 but did not receive a decision for nearly a year. In October 1944, the appeals court ruled that the original trial had been mistried, and that the defendants should be released. Since the City of Los Angeles did not retry the case, the men were released but never cleared of the murder, having spent two years in California prisons. More recently, however, the men's story has been substantiated, even though they have not been formally cleared of the crime. As the *Zoot Suit Riots* program reports, one of the girls, Lorena Encinas, had knowledge of the crime: her brother, Louie Encinas, had been at the party before the 38th Street contingent arrived, and was involved in the fight and stabbing of Díaz.

Meanwhile, the Sleepy Lagoon case was only one in a series of racial hostilities that took place in Los Angeles, and fighting—particularly between servicemen stationed in L.A. and Mexican Americans—was increasingly common. On June 3, 1943, a group of sailors got into a fight with some Mexican-American men, and one of the sailors had his jaw broken and was knocked out. He was brought back to the armory where many of the sailors were stationed, and one of their commanding officers directed the sailors—who hardly needed additional incentive—to take reprisals. On the evening of June 4, a group of sailors headed to downtown Los Angeles with clubs and other weapons to beat Mexican-American men, attacking them randomly on the street as well as going into businesses and movie theaters in search of victims. Rioting escalated over the next few nights, as servicemen (many coming to L.A. explicitly for this purpose) then went into Mexican-American neighborhoods to beat civilians, particularly targeting zoot suiters, stripping them of their suits and burning them. Five thousand civilians were publicly recruited to join with the servicemen in these unprovoked attacks; although the Mexican Americans fought back, they were both outnumbered and undermined by their lack of political or legal support. The Los Angeles Police Department kept a low profile during the rioting; rather than coming to the aid of the Mexican-American neighborhoods, they simply waited until the servicemen and civilians had completed their raids on the *barrios,* and then arrested Mexican Americans for rioting. On June 8, the military declared the city off limits to servicemen, and the riots quickly stopped; the following day the Los Angeles City Council banned the wearing of zoot suits in public—the fine for doing so was thirty days in jail.

Staging these events, Valdez develops a complex critique of the work of ideology in creating "history": this critique is perhaps most evident in the play's use of setting, the ways in which piles of newspaper—the principal organ representing the "meaning" of the riots to contemporary Anglo Angelinos—are used to form the major elements of the set, epitomizing the framing hysteria of the Press. But if the Press and its minions—including the legal system—fashions public history, then Pachuco provides an image of resistant history, at once embodying a moment of cultural pride and a moment of cultural pathos (when he is stripped of the zoot suit by the sailors), as well as a transparent moment of cultural myth-making, when he rises from his beating and his arms *"as an Aztec conch blows."* Valdez here signals a deeper connection between the Pachuco and the myth of Aztlán, the indigenous homeland in the upper Southwest from which the Aztecs were said to have emigrated to Mexico, now often taken as the mythic homeland of Chicanos.

Perhaps the most salient moment of Valdez's historical revision takes place in the play's closing moments, in which the Pachuco refuses to enclose the history of the Zoot Suit Riots within a single narrative. Instead, the play suggests that the history of the Zoot Suit Riots, and by implication the history of Chicanos and Chicanas in America, is still being written. Hank Leyvas died in a bar in 1971, but *Zoot Suit* suggests that Henry Reyna's story might have alternative outcomes: did Henry Reyna return to prison, "where he died of the trauma of his life in 1972" or did he go to Korea in 1950, where "he was killed at Inchon in 1952, being posthumously awarded the Congressional Medal of Honor" or did he marry "Della in 1948 and they have five kids, three of them now going to the University, speaking calo and calling themselves Chicanos"? Outlining the many trajectories of Chicano history in the postwar period, and the many ways in which Chicano history is woven into the fabric of contemporary American history, the Pachuco summons the Zoot Suit Riots as an originating event, one that—like most narratives of origin—has a mythological status in the ways "we"—not only Chicanos and Chicanas, but all Americans—understand our identity today. For all of us, "Henry Reyna . . . El Pachuco . . . The man . . . the myth . . . still lives."

ZOOT SUIT

Luis Valdez

CHARACTERS

EL PACHUCO
HENRY REYNA

HIS FAMILY:
ENRIQUE REYNA
DOLORES REYNA
LUPE REYNA
RUDY REYNA

HIS FRIENDS:
GEORGE SHEARER
ALICE BLOOMFIELD

HIS GANG:
DELLA BARRIOS
SMILEY TORRES
JOEY CASTRO
TOMMY ROBERTS
ELENA TORRES
BERTHA VILLARREAL

THE DOWNEY GANG:
RAFAS
RAGMAN
HOBO
CHOLO
ZOOTER
GÜERA
HOBA
BLONDIE
LITTLE BLUE

DETECTIVES:
LIEUTENANT EDWARDS
SERGEANT SMITH

THE PRESS:
PRESS
CUB REPORTER
NEWSBOY

THE COURT:
JUDGE F.W. CHARLES
BAILIFF

THE PRISON:
GUARD

THE MILITARY:
BOSUN'S MATE
SAILORS
MARINE
SWABBIE
MANCHUKA
SHORE PATROLMAN

OTHERS:
GIRLS
PIMP
CHOLO

SETTING

The giant facsimile of a newspaper front page serves as a drop curtain.

The huge masthead reads: LOS ANGELES HERALD EXPRESS Thursday, June 3, 1943.

A headline cries out: ZOOT-SUITER HORDES INVADE LOS ANGELES. US NAVY AND MARINES ARE CALLED IN.

Behind this are black drapes creating a place of haunting shadows larger than life. The somber shapes and outlines of pachuco images hang subtly, black on black, against a back-ground of heavy fabric evoking memories and feelings like an old suit hanging forgotten in the depths of a closet somewhere, sometime . . . Below this is a sweeping, curving place of levels and rounded corners with the hard, in-grained brilliance of countless spit shines, like the memory of a dance hall.

ACT ONE
PROLOGUE

A switchblade plunges through the newspaper. It slowly cuts a rip to the bottom of the drop. To the sounds of "Perdido" by Duke Ellington, EL PACHUCO *emerges from the slit.* HE *adjusts his clothing, meticulously fussing with his collar, suspenders, cuffs.* HE *tends to his hair, combing back every strand into a long luxurious ducktail, with infinite loving pains. Then* HE *reaches into the slit and pulls out his coat and hat.* HE *dons them. His fantastic costume is complete. It is a zoot suit.* HE *is transformed into the very image of the pachuco myth, from his pork-pie hat to the tip of his four-foot watch chain. Now* HE *turns to the audience. His three-soled shoes with metal taps click-clack as* HE *proudly, slovenly, defiantly makes his way downstage.* HE *stops and assumes a pachuco stance.*

PACHUCO: ¿Que le watcha a mis trapos, ese?
    ¿Sabe qué, carnal?
    Estas garras me las planté porque
    Vamos a dejarnos caer un play, ¿sabe?

(HE *crosses to center stage, models his clothes.*)

    Watcha mi tacuche, ese. Aliviánese con mis calcos, tando,   5
    lisa, tramos, y carlango, ese.

(*Pause.*)

    Nel, sabe qué, usted está muy verdolaga. Como se me hace
    que es puro square.

(EL PACHUCO *breaks character and addresses the audience in perfect English.*)

    Ladies and gentlemen
    the play you are about to see   10
    is a construct of fact and fantasy.
    The Pachuco Style was an act in Life
    and his language a new creation.
    His will to be was an awesome force
    eluding all documentation . . .   15

A mythical, quizzical, frightening being
precursor of revolution
Or a piteous, hideous heroic joke
deserving of absolution?
20 I speak as an actor on the stage.
The Pachuco was existential
for he was an Actor in the streets
both profane and reverential.
It was the secret fantasy of every bato
25 in or out of the Chicanada
to put on a Zoot Suit and play the Myth
más *chucote* que la chingada.

(*Puts hat back on and turns.*)

¡Pos órale!

(*Music. The newspaper drop flies.* EL PACHUCO *begins his chuco stroll upstage, swinging his watch chain.*)

1. ZOOT SUIT

The scene is a barrio dance in the forties. PACHUCOS *and* PACHUCAS *in zoot suits and pompadours.*
They are members of the 38TH STREET GANG, *led by* HENRY REYNA, *21, dark, Indian-looking, older than his years, and* DELLA BARRIOS, *20, his girlfriend in miniskirt and fingertip coat. A* SAILOR *called* SWABBIE *dances with his girlfriend* MANCHUKA *among the* COUPLES. *Movement. Animation.* EL PACHUCO *sings.*

PACHUCO:
PUT ON A ZOOT SUIT, MAKES YOU FEEL REAL ROOT
LOOK LIKE A DIAMOND, SPARKLING, SHINING
READY FOR DANCING
5 READY FOR THE BOOGIE TONIGHT!

(*The* COUPLES, *dancing, join the* PACHUCO *in exclaiming the last term of each line in the next verse.*)

THE HEPCATS UP IN HARLEM WEAR THAT DRAPE SHAPE
COMO LOS PACHUCONES DOWN IN L.A.
WHERE HUISAS IN THEIR POMPADOURS
10 LOOK REAL KEEN
ON THE DANCE FLOOR OF THE BALLROOMS
DONDE BAILAN SWING.
YOU BETTER GET HEP TONIGHT
AND PUT ON THAT ZOOT SUIT!

(*The* DOWNEY GANG, *a rival group of pachucos enters upstage left. Their quick dance step becomes a challenge to* 38TH STREET.)

15 DOWNEY GANG: Downey . . . ¡Rifa!
HENRY: (*Gesturing back.*) ¡Toma! (*The music is hot.* EL PACHUCO *slides across the floor and momentarily breaks the tension.* HENRY *warns* RAFAS, *the leader of the* DOWNEY GANG, *when* HE *sees him push his brother* RUDY.) ¡ Rafas!
20 PACHUCO: (*Sings.*)
TRUCHA, ESE LOCO, VAMOS AL BORLO
WEAR THAT CARLANGO, TRAMOS Y TANDO

DANCE WITH YOUR HUISA
DANCE TO THE BOOGIE TONIGHT!
'CAUSE THE ZOOT SUIT IS THE STYLE IN 25
CALIFORNIA
TAMBIÉN EN COLORADO Y ARIZONA
THEY'RE WEARING THAT TACUCHE EN EL PASO
Y EN TODOS LOS SALONES DE CHICAGO
YOU BETTER GET HEP TONIGHT 30
AND PUT ON THAT ZOOT SUIT!

2. THE MASS ARRESTS

We hear a siren, then another, and another. It sounds like gangbusters. The dance is interrupted. COUPLES *pause on the dance floor.*

PACHUCO: Trucha, la jura. ¡Pélenle! (PACHUCOS *start to run out, but* DETECTIVES *leap onstage with drawn guns. A* CUB REPORTER *takes flash pictures.*)
SGT. SMITH: Hold it right there, kids!
LT. EDWARDS: Everybody get your hands up! 5
RUDY: Watcha! This way! (RUDY *escapes with some others.*)
LT. EDWARDS: Stop or I'll shoot! (EDWARDS *fires his revolver into the air. A number of pachucos and their girlfriends freeze. The cops round them up.* SWABBIE, *an American sailor, and* MANCHUKA, *a Japanese-American dancer, are among them.*) 10
SGT. SMITH: ¡Ándale! (*Sees* SWABBIE.) You! Get out of here.
SWABBIE: What about my girl?
SGT. SMITH: Take her with you. (SWABBIE *and* MANCHUKA *exit.*)
HENRY: What about my girl?
LT. EDWARDS: No dice, Henry. Not this time. Back in line. 15
SGT. SMITH: Close it up!
LT. EDWARDS: Spread! (*The* PACHUCOS *turn upstage in a line with their hands up. The sirens fade and give way to the sound of a teletype. The* PACHUCOS *turn and form a lineup, and the* PRESS *starts shooting pictures as* HE *speaks.*) 20
PRESS: The City of the Angels, Monday, August 2, 1942. The Los Angeles Examiner, Headline:
THE LINEUP: (*In chorus.*) Death Awakens Sleepy Lagoon (*Breath.*) LA Shaken by Lurid "Kid" Murder.
PRESS: The City of the Angels, Monday, August 2, 1942. The 25 Los Angeles Times Headline:
THE LINEUP: One Killed, Ten Hurt in Boy Wars: (*Breath.*) Mexican Boy Gangs Operating Within City.
PRESS: The City of the Angels, August 2, 1942. Los Angeles Herald Express Headline: 30
THE LINEUP: Police Arrest Mexican Youths. Black Widow Girls in Boy Gangs.
PRESS: The City of the Angels . . .
PACHUCO: (*Sharply.*) El Pueblo de Nuestra Señora la Reina de los Ángeles de Porciúncula, pendejo. 35
PRESS: (*Eyeing the* PACHUCO *cautiously.*) The Los Angeles Daily News Headline:
BOYS IN THE LINEUP: Police Nab 300 in Roundup.
GIRLS IN THE LINEUP: Mexican Girls Picked Up in Arrests.
LT. EDWARDS: Press Release, Los Angeles Police Depart- 40 ment: A huge showup of nearly 300 boys and girls rounded up by the police and sheriff's deputies will be held tonight at eight o'clock in Central Jail at First and Hill Street. Victims of assault, robbery, purse snatching, and similar crimes are asked to be present for the iden- 45 tification of suspects.

PRESS: Lieutenant . . . ? (EDWARDS *poses as the* PRESS *snaps a picture.*)

LT. EDWARDS: Thank you.

50 PRESS: Thank you. (SMITH *gives a signal, and the lineup moves back, forming a straight line in the rear, leaving* HENRY *up front by himself.*)

LT. EDWARDS: Move! Turn! Out! (*As the rear line moves off to the left following* EDWARDS, SMITH *takes* HENRY *by the arm and* 55 *pulls him downstage, shoving him to the floor.*)

3. PACHUCO YO

SGT. SMITH: Okay, kid, you wait here till I get back. Think you can do that? Sure you can. You pachucos are regular tough guys. (SMITH *exits.* HENRY *sits up on the floor.* EL PACHUCO *comes forward.*)

5 HENRY: Bastards. (HE *gets up and paces nervously. Pause.*) ¿Ese? ¿Ese?

PACHUCO: (*Behind him.*) ¿Qué pues, nuez?

HENRY: (*Turning.*) Where the hell you been, ese?

PACHUCO: Checking out the barrio. Qué desmadre, ¿no?

10 HENRY: What's going on, ese? This thing is big.

PACHUCO: The city's cracking down on pachucos, carnal. Don't you read the newspapers? They're screaming for blood.

HENRY: All I know is they got nothing on me. I didn't do 15 anything.

PACHUCO: You're Henry Reyna, ese—Hank Reyna! The snarling juvenile delinquent. The zootsuiter. The bitter young pachuco gang leader of 38th Street. That's what they got on you.

20 HENRY: I don't like this, ese. (*Suddenly intense.*) I DON'T LIKE BEING LOCKED UP!

PACHUCO: Calmantes montes, chicas patas. Haven't I taught you to survive? Play it cool.

HENRY: They're going to do it again, ese! They're going to 25 charge me with some phony rap and keep me until they make something stick.

PACHUCO: So what's new?

HENRY: (*Pause.*) I'm supposed to report for the Navy tomorrow. (THE PACHUCO *looks at him with silent disdain.*) You 30 don't want me to go, do you?

PACHUCO: Stupid move, carnal.

HENRY: (*Hurt and angered by* PACHUCO's *disapproval.*) I've got to do something.

PACHUCO: Then hang tough. Nobody's forcing you to do 35 shit.

HENRY: I'm forcing me, ese—ME, you understand?

PACHUCO: Muy patriotic, eh?

HENRY: Yeah.

PACHUCO: Off to fight for your country.

40 HENRY: Why not?

PACHUCO: Because this ain't your country. Look what's happening all around you. The Japs have sewed up the Pacific. Rommel is kicking ass in Egypt but the Mayor of L.A. has declared all-out war on Chicanos. On you! ¡Te curas?

45 HENRY: Órale.

PACHUCO: Qué mamada, ¿no? Is that what you want to go out and die for? Wise up. These bastard paddy cops have it in for you. You're a marked man. They think you're the enemy.

50 HENRY: (*Refusing to accept it.*) Screw them bastard cops!

PACHUCO: And as soon as the Navy finds out you're in jail again, ya estuvo, carnal. Unfit for military duty because of your record. Think about it.

HENRY: (*Pause.*) You got a frajo?

PACHUCO: Simón. (HE *pulls out a cigarette, hands it to* HENRY, 55 *lights it for him.* HENRY *is pensive.*)

HENRY: (*Smokes, laughs ironically.*) I was all set to come back a hero, see? Me la rayo. For the first time in my life I really thought Hank Reyna was going someplace.

PACHUCO: Forget the war overseas, carnal. Your war is on the 60 homefront.

HENRY: (*With new resolve.*) What do you mean?

PACHUCO: The barrio needs you, carnal. Fight back! Stand up to them with some style. Show the world a Chicano has balls. Hang tough. You can take it. Remember, Pachuco 65 Yo!

HENRY: (*Assuming the style.*) Con safos, carnal.

4. THE INTERROGATION

The PRESS *enters, followed by* EDWARDS *and* SMITH.

PRESS: (*To the audience.*) Final Edition; The Los Angeles Daily News. The police have arrested twenty-two members of the 38th Street Gang, pending further investigation of various charges.

LT. EDWARDS: Well, son, I was hoping I wouldn't see you in 5 here again.

HENRY: Then why did you arrest me?

LT. EDWARDS: Come on, Hank, you know why you're here.

HENRY: Yeah. I'm a Mexican.

LT. EDWARDS: Don't give me that. How long have I known 10 you? Since '39?

HENRY: Yeah, when you got me for stealing a car, remember?

LT. EDWARDS: All right. That was a mistake. I didn't know it was your father's car. I tried to make it up to you. Didn't I help you set up the youth club? 15

SGT. SMITH: They turned it into a gang, Lieutenant. Everything they touch turns to shit.

LT. EDWARDS: I remember a kid just a couple of years back. Head boy at the Catholic Youth Center. His idea of fun was going to the movies. What happened to that nice kid, 20 Henry?

PRESS: He's "Gone With The Wind," trying to look like Clark Gable.

SGT. SMITH: Now he thinks he's Humphrey Bogart.

PACHUCO: So who are you, puto? Pat O'Brien? 25

LT. EDWARDS: This is the wrong time to be anti-social, son. This country's at war, and we're under strict orders to crack down on all malcontents.

SGT. SMITH: Starting with all pachucos and draft dodgers.

HENRY: I ain't no draft dodger. 30

LT. EDWARDS: I know you're not. I heard you got accepted by the Navy. Congratulations. When do you report?

HENRY: Tomorrow?

SGT. SMITH: Tough break!

LT. EDWARDS: It's still not too late, you know. I could still re- 35 lease you in time to get sworn in.

HENRY: If I do what?

LT. EDWARDS: Tell me, Henry, what do you know about a big gang fight last Saturday night, out at Sleepy Lagoon?

40 PACHUCO: Don't tell 'em shit.

HENRY: Which Sleepy Lagoon?

LT. EDWARDS: You mean there's more than one? Come on, Hank, I know you were out there. I've got a statement from your friends that says you were beaten up. Is that
45 true? Were you and your girl attacked?

HENRY: I don't know anything about it. Nobody's ever beat me up.

SGT. SMITH: That's a lie and you know it. Thanks to your squealer friends, we've got enough dope on you to indict
50 for murder right now.

HENRY: Murder?

SGT. SMITH: Yeah, murder. Another greaser named José Williams.

HENRY: I never heard of the bato.

55 SGT. SMITH: Yeah, sure.

LT. EDWARDS: I've been looking at your record, Hank. Petty theft, assault, burglary, and now murder. Is that what you want? The gas chamber? Play square with me. Give me a statement as to what happened at the Lagoon, and I'll go
60 to bat for you with the Navy. I promise you.

PACHUCO: If that ain't a line of gabacho bullshit, I don't know what is.

LT. EDWARDS: Well?

PACHUCO: Spit in his pinche face.

65 SGT. SMITH: Forget it, Lieutenant. You can't treat these animals like people.

LT. EDWARDS: Shut up! I'm thinking of your family, Hank. Your old man would be proud to see you in the Navy. One last chance, son. What do you say?

70 HENRY: I ain't your son, cop.

LT. EDWARDS: All right, Reyna, have it your way. (EDWARDS and PRESS *exit.*)

PACHUCO: You don't deserve it, ese, but your going to get it anyway.

75 SGT. SMITH: All right, muchacho, it's just me and you now. I hear tell you pachucos wear these monkey suits as a kind of armor. Is that right? How's it work? This is what you zooters need—a little old-fashioned discipline.

HENRY: Screw you, flatfoot.

80 SGT. SMITH: You greasy son of a bitch. What happened at the Sleepy Lagoon? Talk! Talk! Talk! (SMITH *beats* HENRY *with a rubber sap.* HENRY *passes out and falls to the floor, with his hands still handcuffed behind his back.* DOLORES *his mother appears in a spot upstage, as he falls.*)

85 DOLORES: Henry! (*Lights change. Four* PACHUCO COUPLES *enter, dancing a 40's pasodoble (two-step) around* HENRY *on the floor, as they swing in a clothesline of newspaper sheets. Music.*)

PACHUCO:
Get up and escape, Henry . . .
90 leave reality behind
with your buenas garras
muy chamberlain
escape through the barrio streets of your mind
through a neighborhood of memories
95 all chuckhole lined
and the love
and the pain
as fine as wine . . .

(HENRY *sits up, seeing his mother* DOLORES *folding newspaper sheets like clothes on a clothesline.*)

DOLORES: Henry?

PACHUCO: It's a lifetime ago, last Saturday night . . . before 100 Sleepy Lagoon and the big bad fight.

DOLORES: Henry!

PACHUCO: Tu mamá, carnal. (HE *recedes into the background.*)

DOLORES: (*At the clothesline.*) Henry, ¿hijo? Ven a cenar.

HENRY: (*Gets up off the floor.*) Sorry, jefita, I'm not hungry. Be- 105 sides, I got to pick up Della. We're late for the dance.

DOLORES: Dance? In his heat? Don't you muchachos ever think of anything else? God knows I suffer la pena negra seeing you go out every night.

HENRY: This isn't just any night, jefa. It's my last chance to use 110 my tacuche.

DOLORES: Tacuche? Pero tu padre . . .

HENRY: (*Revealing a stubborn streak.*) I know what mi 'apá said, 'amá. I'm going to wear it anyway.

DOLORES: (*Sighs, resigns herself.*) Mira, hijo. I know you work 115 hard for your clothes. And I know how much they mean to you. Pero por diosito santo, I just don't know what you see en esa cochinada se "soot zoot."

HENRY: (*Smiling.*) Drapes, 'amá, we call them drapes.

DOLORES: (*Scolding playfully.*) Ay sí, drapes, muy funny, ¿ver- 120 dad? And what do the police call them, eh? They've put you in jail so many times. ¿Sabes qué? I'm going to send them all your clothes!

HENRY: A qué mi 'amá. Don't worry. By this time next week, I'll be wearing my Navy blues. Okay? 125

DOLORES: Bendito sea Dios. I still can't believe you're going off to war. I almost wish you were going back to jail.

HENRY: ¡Órale? (LUPE REYNA, *16, enters dressed in a short skirt and baggy coat. She is followed by* DELLA BARRIOS, *17, dressed more modestly.* LUPE *hides behind a newspaper sheet on the line.*) 130

LUPE: Hank! Let's go, carnal. Della's here.

HENRY: Della . . . Órale, esa. What are you doing here? I told you I was going to pick you up at your house.

DELLA: You know how my father gets.

HENRY: What happened? 135

DELLA: I'll tell you later.

DOLORES: Della, hija, buenas noches. How pretty you look.

DELLA: Buenas noches. (DOLORES *hugs* DELLA, *then spots* LUPE *hiding behind the clothesline.*)

DOLORES: (*To* LUPE.) ¿Oye y tú? What's wrong with you? 140 What are you doing back there?

LUPE: Nothing, 'amá.

DOLORES: Well, come out then.

LUPE: We're late 'amá.

DOLORES: Come out, te digo. (LUPE *comes out exposing* 145 *her extremely short skirt.* DOLORES *gasps.*) ¡Válgame Dios! Guadalupe, are you crazy? Why bother to wear any-thing?

LUPE: Ay, 'amá, it's the style. Short skirt and fingertip coat. Huh, Hank? 150

HENRY: Uh, yeah, 'amá.

DOLORES: ¿Oh sí? And how come Della doesn't get to wear the same style?

HENRY: No . . . that's different. No, chale.

ENRIQUE: (*Off.*) ¡vieja! 155

DOLORES: Ándale. Go change before your father sees you.

ENRIQUE: I'm home. (*Coming into the scene.*) Buenas noches, everybody. (*All respond.* ENRIQUE *sees* LUPE.) ¡Ay, jijo! Where's the skirt?!

LUPE: It's here. 160

ENRIQUE: Where's the rest of it?

DOLORES: She's going to the dance.

ENRIQUE: ¿Y a mí qué me importa? Go and change those clothes. Ándale.

165 LUPE: Please, 'apá?

ENRIQUE: No, señorita.

LUPE: Chihuahua, I don't want to look like a square.

ENRIQUE: ¡Te digo que no! I will not have my daughter looking like a . . .

170 DOLORES: Like a puta . . . I mean, a pachuca.

LUPE: (*Pleading for help.*) Hank . . .

HENRY: Do what they say, sis.

LUPE: But you let Henry wear his drapes.

ENRIQUE: That's different. He's a man. Es hombre.

175 DOLORES: Sí, that's different. You men are all alike. From such a stick, such a splinter. De tal palo, tal astillota.

ENRIQUE: Natural, muy natural, and look how he came out. ¡Bien macho! Like his father. ¿Verdad, m'ijo?

HENRY: If you say so, jefito.

180 ENRIQUE: (*To* DELLA.) Buenas noches.

DELLA: Buenas noches.

HENRY: 'Apá, this is Della Barrios.

ENRIQUE: Mira, mira . . . So this is your new girlfriend, eh? Muy bonita. Quite a change from the last one.

185 DOLORES: Ay, señor.

ENRIQUE: It's true. What was her name?

DELLA: Bertha?

ENRIQUE: That's the one. The one with the tattoo.

DOLORES: Este hombre. We have company.

190 ENRIQUE: That reminds me. I invited the compadres to the house mañana.

DOLORES: ¿Que qué?

ENRIQUE: I'm buying a big keg of cerveza to go along with the menudo.

195 DOLORES: Oye, ¿cuál menudo?

ENRIQUE: (*Cutting him off.*) ¡Qué caray, mujer! It isn't every day a man's son goes off to fight for his country. I should know. Della, m'ija, when I was in the Mexican Revolution, I was not even as old as my son is.

200 DOLORES: N'ombre, don't start with your revolution. We'll be here all night.

HENRY: Yeah, jefe, we've got to go.

LUPE: (*Comes forward. She has rolled down her skirt.*) 'Apá, is this better?

205 ENRIQUE: Bueno. And you leave it that way.

HENRY: Órale, pues. It's getting late. Where's Rudy?

LUPE: He's still getting ready. Rudy! (RUDY REYNA, *19, comes downstage in an old suit made into a tachuche.*)

RUDY: Let's go everybody. I'm ready.

210 ENRIQUE: Oye, oye, ¿y tú? What are you doing with my coat?

RUDY: It's my tachuche, 'apá.

ENRIQUE: ¡Me lleva la chingada!

DOLORES: Enrique . . . ¡por el amor de Dios!

ENRIQUE: (*To* HENRY.) You see what you're doing? First that one and now this one. (*To* RUDY.) Hijo, don't go out like
215 that. Por favor. You look like an idiot, pendejo.

RUDY: Órale, Hank. Don't I look all right?

HENRY: Nel, ese, you look fine. Watcha. Once I leave for the service, you can have my tachuche. Then you can really be
220 in style. ¿Cómo la ves?

RUDY: Chale. Thanks, carnal, but if I don't join the service myself, I'm gonna get my own tachuche.

HENRY: You sure? I'm not going to need it where I'm going. ¿Tú sabes?

RUDY: Are you serious? 225

HENRY: Simón.

RUDY: I'll think about it.

HENRY: Pos, no hay pedo, ese.

ENRIQUE: ¿Cómo que pedo? Nel, ¿Simón? Since when did we stop speaking Spanish in this house? Have you no re- 230
spect?

DOLORES: Muchachos, muchachos, go to your dance. (HENRY *starts upstage.*)

HENRY: Buenas noches . . . (ENRIQUE *holds out his hand.* HENRY *stops, looks, and then returns to kiss his father's hand. Then* HE 235
moves to kiss his MOTHER *and* RUDY *in turn kisses* ENRIQUE*'s hand.* ENRIQUE *says "Buenas Noches" to each of his sons.*)

HENRY: Órale, we'd better get going . . . (*General "goodbyes" from everybody.*)

ENRIQUE: (*As* RUDY *goes past him.*) Henry! Don't let your 240
brother drink beer.

RUDY: Ay, 'apá. I can take care of myself.

DOLORES: I'll believe that when I see it. (SHE *kisses him on the nose.*)

LUPE: Ahí te watcho, 'amá. 245

ENRIQUE: ¿Que qué?

LUPE: I mean, I'll see you later. (HENRY, DELLA, LUPE *and* RUDY *turn upstage. Music starts.*)

ENRIQUE: Mujer, why didn't you let me talk?

DOLORES: (*Sighing.*) Talk, señor, talk all you want. I'm listen- 250
ing. (ENRIQUE *and* DOLORES *exit up right.* RUDY *and* LUPE *exit up left. Lights change. We hear hot dance music.* HENRY *and* DELLA *dance at center stage.* EL PACHUCO *sings.*)

PACHUCO:
CADA SÁBADO EN LA NOCHE 255
YO ME VOY A BORLOTEAR
CON MI LINDA PACHUCONA
LAS CADERAS A MENEAR
ELLA LE HACE MUY DE AQUELLAS
CUANDO EMPIEZA A GUARACHAR 260
AL COMPÁS DE LOS TIMBALES
YO ME SIENTO PETATEAR

(*From upstage right, three pachucos now enter in a line, moving to the beat. They are* JOEY CASTRO, *17;* SMILEY TORRES, *23; and* TOMMY ROBERTS, *19, Anglo. They all come downstage left in a diagonal.*)

LOS CHUCOS SUAVES BAILAN RUMBA
BAILAN LA RUMBA Y LE ZUMBAN
BAILAN GUARACHA SABROSÓN
EL BOTECITO Y EL DANZÓN!

(*Chorus repeats, the music fades.* HENRY *laughs and happily embraces* DELLA.)

5. THE PRESS

Lights change. EL PACHUCO *escorts* DELLA *off right.* THE PRESS *appears at upstage center.*

PRESS: Los Angeles Times: August 8, 1942.

A NEWSBOY *enters, lugging in two more bundles of newspapers, hawking them as he goes.* PEOPLE *of various walks of life enter at intervals and buy newspapers. They arrange themselves in the background reading.*

NEWSBOY: EXTRA! EXTRAAA! READ ALL ABOUT IT. SPECIAL SESSION OF L.A. COUNTY GRAND JURY CONVENES. D.A. CHARGES CONSPIRACY IN SLEEPY LAGOON MURDER. EXTRAAA! (*A*
5 CUB REPORTER *emerges and goes to the* PRESS, *as* LIEUTENANT EDWARDS *enters.*)

CUB REPORTER: Hey, here comes Edwards! (EDWARDS *is besieged by the* PRESS, *joined by* ALICE BLOOMFIELD, *26, a woman reporter.*)

10 PRESS: How about it, Lieutenant? What's the real scoop on the Sleepy Lagoon? Sex, violence . . .

CUB REPORTER: Marijuana?

NEWSBOY: Read all about it! Mexican Crime Wave Engulfs L.A.

15 LT. EDWARDS: Slums breed crime, fellas. That's your story.

ALICE: Lieutenant. What exactly is the Sleepy Lagoon?

CUB REPORTER: A great tune by Harry James, doll. Wanna dance? (ALICE *ignores the* CUB.)

LT. EDWARDS: It's a reservoir. An old abandoned gravel pit, re-
20 ally. It's on a ranch between here and Long Beach. Serves as a swimming hole for the younger Mexican kids.

ALICE: Because they're not allowed to swim in the public plunges?

PRESS: What paper are you with, lady? The Daily Worker?

25 LT. EDWARDS: It also doubles as a sort of lovers' lane at night—which is why the gangs fight over it. Now they've finally murdered somebody.

NEWSBOY: EXTRA! EXTRA! ZOOT-SUITED GOONS OF SLEEPY LAGOON!

30 LT. EDWARDS: But we're not going to mollycoddle these youngsters any more. And you can quote me on that.

PRESS: One final question, Lieutenant. What about the 38th Street Gang—weren't you the first to arrest Henry Reyna?

LT. EDWARDS: I was. And I noticed right away the kid had
35 great leadership potential. However . . .

PRESS: Yes?

LT. EDWARDS: You can't change the spots on a leopard.

PRESS: Thank you, sir. (PEOPLE *with newspapers crush them and throw them down as they exit.* EDWARDS *turns and exits.* ALICE
40 *turns towards* HENRY *for a moment.*)

NEWSBOY: EXTRA, EXTRA. READ ALL ABOUT THE MEXICAN BABY GANGSTERS. EXTRA, EXTRA.

THE PRESS *and* CUB REPORTER *rush out happily to file their stories. The* NEWSBOY *leaves, hawking his papers.* ALICE *exits, with determination. Far upstage,* ENRIQUE *enters with a rolling garbage can. HE is a street sweeper. During the next scene HE silently sweeps up the newspapers, pausing at the last to read one of the news stories.*

6. THE PEOPLE'S LAWYER

JOEY: ¡Chale, ese, chale! Qué pinche agüite.

SMILEY: Mexican Baby Gangsters?!

TOMMY: Zoot-suited goons! I knew it was coming. Every time the D.A. farts, they throw us in the can.

5 SMILEY: Pos, qué chingados, Hank. I can't believe this. Are they really going to pin us with a murder rap? I've got a wife and kid, man!

JOEY: Well, there's one good thing anyway. I bet you know that we've made the headlines. Everybody knows we got
10 the toughest gang in town.

TOMMY: Listen to this, pip squeak. The biggest heist he ever pulled was a Tootsie Roll.

JOEY: (*Grabbing his privates.*) Here's your Tootsie Roll, ese.

TOMMY: What, that? Get my microscope, Smiley.

JOEY: Why don't you come here and take a little bite, joto. 15

TOMMY: Joto? Who you calling a joto, maricón?

JOEY: You, white boy. Did I ever tell you, you got the finest little duck ass in the world.

TOMMY: No, you didn't tell me that, culero. (JOEY *and* TOMMY *start sparring.*) 20

SMILEY: (*Furious.*) Why don't you batos knock it off?

HENRY: (*Cool.*) Cálmenla.

SMILEY: ¡Pinches chavalos! (*The batos stop.*)

JOEY: We're just cabuliando, ese.

TOMMY: Simón, ese. Horsing around. (*He gives* JOEY *a final punch.*) 25

SMILEY: (*With deep self-pity.*) I'm getting too old for this pedo, Hank. All this farting around con esos chavalillos.

HENRY: Relax, carnal. No te agüites.

SMILEY: You and me have been through a lot, Hank. Parties, chingazos, jail. When you said let's join the pachucada, I 30
joined the pachucada. You and me started the 38th, bato. I followed you even after my kid was born, but what now, carnal? This pinche pedo is serious.

TOMMY: He's right, Hank. They indicted the whole gang.

JOEY: Yeah, you know the only one who ain't here is Rudy. 35
(HENRY *turns sharply.*) He was at the Sleepy Lagoon too, ese. Throwing chingazos.

HENRY: Yeah, but the cops don't know that, do they? Unless one of us turned stoolie.

JOEY: Hey, ese, don't look at me. They beat the shit out of me, 40
but that's all they got. Shit.

TOMMY: That's all you got to give. (*Laughs.*)

HENRY: Okay! Let's keep it that way. I don't want my carnalillo pulled into this. And if anybody asks about him, you batos don't know nothing. You get me? 45

SMILEY: Simón.

TOMMY: Crazy.

JOEY: (*Throwing his palms out.*) Say, Jackson, I'm cool. You know that.

HENRY: There's not a single paddy we can trust. 50

TOMMY: Hey, ese, what about me?

HENRY: You know what I mean.

TOMMY: No, I don't know what you mean. I'm here with the rest of yous.

JOEY: Yeah, but you'll be the first one out, cabrón. 55

TOMMY: Gimme a break, maníaco. ¡Yo soy pachuco!

HENRY: Relax, ese. Nobody's getting personal with you. Don't I let you take out my carnala? Well, don't I?

TOMMY: Simón.

HENRY: That's because you respect my family. The rest of 60
them paddies are after our ass.

PACHUCO: Talk about paddies, ese, you got company. (GEORGE SHEARER *enters upstage right and comes down. HE is a middle-aged lawyer, strong and athletic, but with the slightly frazzled look of a people's lawyer.*) 65

GEORGE: Hi, boys.

HENRY: Trucha!

GEORGE: My name is George Shearer. I've been retained by your parents to handle your case. Can we sit and talk for a little bit? (*Pause. The* BOYS *eye* GEORGE *suspiciously.* HE 70
slides a newspaper bundle a few feet upstage.)

PACHUCO: Better check him out, ese. He looks like a cop.

HENRY: (*To the* GUYS, *sotto voce.*) Pónganse al alba. Este me huele a chota.

75 GEORGE: What was that? Did you say I could sit down? Thank you. (HE *pulls a bundle upstage.* HE *sits.*) Okay, let me get your names straight first. Who's José Castro?

JOEY: Right here, ese. What do you want to know?

GEORGE: We'll get to that. Ismael Torres?

80 SMILEY: (*Deadpan.*) That's me. But they call me Smiley.

GEORGE: (*A wide grin.*) Smiley? I see. You must be Thomas Roberts.

TOMMY: I ain't Zoot Suit Yokum.

GEORGE: Which means you must be Henry Reyna.

85 HENRY: What if I am. Who are you?

GEORGE: I already told you, my name's George Shearer. Your parents asked me to come.

HENRY: Oh yeah? Where did they get the money for a lawyer?

90 GEORGE: I'm a People's Lawyer, Henry.

SMILEY: People's Lawyer?

JOEY: Simón, we're people.

TOMMY: At least they didn't send no animal's lawyer.

HENRY: So what does that mean? You doing this for free or
95 what?

GEORGE: (*Surprise turning to amusement.*) I try not to work for free, if I can help it, but I do sometimes. In this case, I expect to be paid for my services.

HENRY: So who's paying you? For what? And how much?

100 GEORGE: Hey, hey, hold on there. I'm supposed to ask the questions. You're the one going on trial, not me.

PACHUCO: Don't let him throw you, ese.

GEORGE: I sat in on part of the Grand Jury. It was quite a farce, wasn't it? Murder one indictment and all.

105 SMILEY: You think we stand a chance?

GEORGE: There's always a chance, Smiley. That's what trials are for.

PACHUCO: He didn't answer your question, ese.

HENRY: You still didn't answer my question, mister. Who's
110 paying you? And how much?

GEORGE: (*Getting slightly peeved.*) Well, Henry, it's really none of your damned business. (*The* BOYS *react.*) But for whatever it's worth, I'll tell you a little story. The first murder case I ever tried, and won incidentally, was for a Filipino. I
115 was paid exactly three dollars and fifty cents plus a pack of Lucky Strike cigarettes, and a note for a thousand dollars—never redeemed. Does that answer your question?

HENRY: How do we know you're really a lawyer?

GEORGE: How do I know you're Henry Reyna? What do you
120 really mean, son? Do you think I'm a cop?

HENRY: Maybe.

GEORGE: What are you trying to hide from the cops? Murder? (*The* BOYS *react.*) All right! Aside from your parents, I've been called into this case by a citizens committee
125 that's forming in your behalf, Henry. In spite of evidence to the contrary, there are some people out there who don't want to see you get the shaft.

HENRY: ¿Sabes qué, mister? Don't do us any favors.

GEORGE: (*Starting to leave.*) All right, you want another
130 lawyer? I'll talk to the Public Defender's office.

JOEY: (*Grabbing his briefcase.*) Hey, wait a minute, ese. Where are you going?

TOMMY: De cincho se le va a volar la tapa.

JOEY: Nel, este bolillo no sabe nada.

135 GEORGE: (*Exploding.*) All right, kids, cut the crap!

SMILEY: (*Grabs his briefcase and crosses to* HENRY.) Let's give him a break, Hank. (SMILEY *hands the briefcase to* GEORGE.)

GEORGE: Thank you. (HE *starts to exit. Stops.*) You know, you're making a big mistake. I wonder if you know who your
140 friends are? You boys are about to get a mass trial. You know what that is? Well, it's a new one on me too. The Grand Jury has indicted you all on the same identical crime. Not just you four. The whole so-called 38th Street Gang. And you know who the main target is? You, Henry,
145 because they're saying you're the ringleader. (*Looks around at the* GUYS.) And I suppose you are. But you're leading your buddies here down a dead-end street. The D.A.'s coming after you, son, and he's going to put you and your whole gang right into the gas chamber. (GEORGE *turns to
150 leave.* SMILEY *panics.* JOEY *and* TOMMY *react with him.*)

SMILEY/JOEY/TOMMY: (*All together.*) Gas chamber! But we didn't do nothing! We're innocent!

HENRY: ¡Cálmenla! (*The batos stop in their tracks.*) Okay. Say we believe you're a lawyer, what does that prove? The press
155 has already tried and convicted us. Think you can change that?

GEORGE: Probably not. But then, public opinion comes and goes, Henry. What matters is our system of justice. I believe it works, however slowly the wheels may grind. It
160 could be a long uphill fight, fellas, but we can make it. I know we can. I've promised your parents the best defense I'm capable of. The question is, Henry, will you trust me?

HENRY: Why should I? You're a gringo.

GEORGE: (*Calmly, deliberately.*) ¿Cómo sabes?

165 TOMMY: (*Shocked.*) Hey, you speak Spanish?

GEORGE: Más o menos.

JOEY: You mean you understood us a while ago?

GEORGE: More or less.

JOEY: (*Embarrassed.*) ¡Híjole, qué gacho, ese!

170 GEORGE: Don't worry. I'm not much on your pachuco slang. The problem seems to be that I look like an Anglo to you. What if I were to tell you that I had Spanish blood in my veins? That my roots go back to Spain, just like yours? What if I'm an Arab? What if I'm a Jew? What difference
175 does it make? The question is, will you let me help you? (*Pause.* HENRY *glances at the* PACHUCO.)

PACHUCO: ¡Chale!

HENRY: (*Pause.*) Okay!

SMILEY: Me too!

180 JOEY: Same here!

TOMMY: ¡Órale!

GEORGE: (*Eagerly.*) Okay! Let's go to work. I want to know exactly what happened right from the beginning. (GEORGE *sits down and opens his briefcase.*)

185 HENRY: Well, I think the pedo really started at the dance last Saturday night . . . (*El* PACHUCO *snaps his fingers and we hear dance music. Lights change.* GEORGE *exits.*)

7. THE SATURDAY NIGHT DANCE

SWABBIE *and* MANCHUKA *come running onstage as the barrio dance begins to take shape.* HENRY *and the batos move upstage to join other* PACHUCOS *and* PACHUCAS *coming in.* HENRY *joins* DELLA

BARRIOS; JOEY *teams up with* BERTHA VILLARREAL, TOMMY *picks up* LUPE REYNA; *and* SMILEY *escorts his wife* ELENA TORRES. *They represent the* 38TH STREET *neighborhood. Also entering the dance comes the* DOWNEY GANG, *looking mean.* RUDY *stands upstage, in the background, drinking a bottle of beer.* EL PACHUCO *sings.*

PACHUCO:
  CUANDO SALGO YO A BAILAR
  YO ME PONGO MUY CATRÍN
  LAS HUISITAS TODAS GRITAN, DADDY
  VAMOS A BAILAR EL SWING!

(*The* COUPLES *dance. A lively swing number. The music comes to a natural break and shifts into a slow number.* BERTHA *approaches* HENRY *and* DELLA *downstage on the dance floor.*)

5 BERTHA: Ese, ¡surote! How about a dance for old time's sake? No te hagas gacho.
  HENRY: (*Slow dancing with* DELLA.) Sorry, Bertha.
  BERTHA: Is this your new huisa? This little fly chick?
  DELLA: Listen, Bertha . . .
10 HENRY: (*Stops her.*) Chale. She's just jealous. Beat it, Bertha.
  BERTHA: Beat it yourself. Mira. You got no hold on me, cabrón. Not any more. I'm as free as a bird.
  SMILEY: (*Coming up.*) Ese, Hank, that's the Downey Gang in the corner. You think they're looking for trouble?
15 HENRY: There's only a couple of them.
  BERTHA: That's all we need.
  SMILEY: Want me to alert the batos?
  HENRY: Nel, be cool.
  BERTHA: Be cool? Huy, yu, yui. Forget it, Smiley. Since he
20 joined the Navy, this bato forgot the difference between being cool and being cool-O. (*She laughs and turns but* HENRY *grabs her angrily by the arm.* BERTHA *pulls free and walks away cool and tough. The music changes and the beat picks up.* EL PACHUCO *sings as the* COUPLES *dance.*)
  PACHUCO:
25 CUANDO VOY AL VACILÓN
  Y ME METO YO A UN SALON
  LAS CHAVALAS GRITAN, PAPI VENTE
  VAMOS A BAILAR DANSÓN!

(*The dance turns Latin. The music comes to another natural break and holds.* LUPE *approaches* HENRY *on the dance floor.*)

  LUPE: Hank. Rudy's at it again. He's been drinking since we
30 got here.
  HENRY: (*Glancing over at* RUDY.) He's okay, sis, let the carnal enjoy himself.
  RUDY: (*Staggering over.*) ¡Ese, carnal!
  HENRY: What you say, brother?
35 RUDY: I'm flying high, Jackson. Feeling good.
  LUPE: Rudy, if you go home drunk again, mi 'apá's going to use you for a punching bag. (RUDY *kisses her on the cheek and moves on.*)
  DELLA: How are you feeling?
40 HENRY: Okay.
  DELLA: Still thinking about Bertha?
  HENRY: Chale, ¿qué traes? Listen, you want to go out to the Sleepy Lagoon? I've got something to tell you.
  DELLA: What?

45 HENRY: Later, later.
  LUPE: You better tell Rudy to stop drinking.
  HENRY: Relax, sis. If he gets too drunk, I'll carry him home. (*Music picks up again.* EL PACHUCO *sings a third verse.*)
  PACHUCO:
50 TOCAN MAMBO SABROSÓN
  SE ALBOROTA EL CORAZÓN
  Y CON UNA CHAVALONA VAMOS
  VAMOS A BAILAR EL MAMBO

(*The* COUPLES *do the mambo. In the background,* RUDY *gets into an argument with* RAFAS, *the leader of the* DOWNEY GANG. *A fight breaks out as the music comes to a natural break.* RAFAS *pushes* RUDY, *half drunk, onto the floor.*)

  RAFAS: ¡Y a ti qué te importa, puto!
55 RUDY: (HE *falls.*) ¡Cabrón!
  HENRY: (*Reacting immediately.*) Hey! (*The whole dance crowd tenses up immediately, splitting into separate camps. Batos from* 38TH *clearly outnumber the* GUYS *from* DOWNEY.)
  RAFAS: He started it, ese. El comenzó a chingar conmigo.
60 RUDY: You chicken shit, ese! Tú me haces la puñeta, ¡pirujo!
  RAFAS: Come over here and say that, puto!
  HENRY: (*Pulling* RUDY *behind him.*) ¡Agüítala, carnal! (*Faces* RAFAS.) You're a little out of your territory, ¿Que no Rafas?
  RAFAS: It's a barrio dance, ese. We're from the barrio.
65 HENRY: You're from Downey.
  RAFAS: Vale madre. ¡Downey Rifa!
  DOWNEY GANG: ¡SIMÓN!
  RAFAS: What are you going to do about it?
  HENRY: I'm going to kick your ass. (*The* TWO SIDES *start to at-*
70 *tack each other.*) ¡Cálmenla! (ALL *stop.*)
  RAFAS: (*Pulls out a switchblade.*) You and how many batos?
  HENRY: Just me and you, cabrón. That's my carnalillo you started pushing around, see? And nobody chinga con mi familia without answering to me, ese! Hank Reyna! (HE
75 *pulls out another switchblade.*)
  BERTHA: ALL-RIGHT!
  HENRY: Let's see if you can push me around like you did my little brother, ese. Come on . . . COME ON! (*They knife fight.* HENRY *moves in fast. Recoiling,* RAFAS *falls to the floor.*
80 HENRY's *blade is at his throat.* EL PACHUCO *snaps his fingers. Everyone freezes.*)
  PACHUCO: Qué mamada, Hank. That's exactly what the play needs right now. Two more Mexicans killing each other. Watcha . . . Everybody's looking at you.
85 HENRY: (*Looks out at the audience.*) Don't give me that bullshit. Either I kill him or he kills me.
  PACHUCO: That's exactly what they paid to see. Think about it. (EL PACHUCO *snaps again. Everybody unfreezes.*)
  HENRY: (*Kicks* RAFAS.) Get out of here. ¡Píntate!
90 BERTHA: What?
  GÜERA: (RAFAS' *girlfriend runs forward.*) Rafas. ¡Vámonos! (SHE *is stopped by other* DOWNEY *batos.*)
  RAFAS: Está suave. I'll see you later.
  HENRY: Whenever you want, cabrón. (*The* DOWNEY GANG *re-*
95 *treats, as the* 38TH *razzes them all the way out. Insults are ex-changed.* BERTHA *shouts "¡Chinga tu madre!" and they are gone. The* 38TH *whoops in victory.*)
  SMILEY: Órale, you did it, ese! ¡Se escamaron todos!
  TOMMY: We sure chased those jotos out of here.

100 BERTHA: I could have beat the shit out of those two rucas.

JOEY: That pinche Rafas is yellow without his gang, ese.

LUPE: So why didn't you jump out there?

JOEY: Chale, Rudy ain't my baby brother.

RUDY: (*Drunk.*) Who you calling a baby, pendejo? I'll show
105 you who's a baby!

JOEY: Be cool, ese.

TOMMY: Man, you're lucky your brother was here.

BERTHA: Why? He didn't do nothing. The old Hank would
have slit Rafas' belly like a fat pig.

110 HENRY: Shut your mouth, Bertha!

RUDY: ¿Por qué, carnal? You backed down, ese. I could have
taken that sucker on by myself.

HENRY: That's enough, Rudy. You're drunk.

DELLA: Hank, what if Rafas comes back with all his gang?

115 HENRY: (*Reclaiming his leadership.*) We'll kill the sons of bitches.

JOEY: ¡Órale! ¡La 38th rifa! (*Music. Everybody gets back with furious energy.* EL PACHUCO *sings.*)

PACHUCO:
    DE LOS BAILES QUE MENTÉ
120   Y EL BOLERO Y EL BEGUÍN
    DE TODOS LOS BAILES JUNTOS
    ME GUSTA BAILAR EL SWING! HEY!

(*The dance ends with a group exclamation: HEY!*)

8. EL DÍA DE LA RAZA

The PRESS *enters upstage level, pushing a small hand truck piled
high with newspaper bundles. The batos and rucas on the dance floor
freeze in their final positions.* EL PACHUCO *is the only one who relaxes and moves.*

PRESS: October 12, 1942: Columbus Day. Four Hundred and
Fiftieth Anniversary of the Discovery of America. Headlines!

In their places, the COUPLES *now stand straight and recite a headline
before exiting. As they do so, the* PRESS *moves the bundles of newspapers on the floor to outline the four corners of a jail cell.*

SMILEY/ELENA: President Roosevelt Salutes Good Neighbors
5   In Latin America. (SMILEY *and* ELENA *exit.*)

TOMMY/LUPE: British Begin Drive to Oust Rommel From
North Africa. (TOMMY *and* LUPE *exit.*)

RUDY/CHOLO: Japs In Death Grip On Pacific Isles. (RUDY *and*
CHOLO *exit.* PRESS *tosses another bundle.*)

10 ZOOTER/LITTLE BLUE: Web Of Zoot Crime Spreads.
(ZOOTER *and* LITTLE BLUE *exit.*)

MANCHUKA/SWABBIE: U.S. Marines Land Bridgehead On
Guadalcanal. (MANCHUKA *and* SWABBIE *exit.*)

JOEY/BERTHA: First Mexican Braceros Arrive In U.S.A. (JOEY
15   *and* BERTHA *exit.*)

DELLA: Sleepy Lagoon Murder Trial Opens Tomorrow. (DELLA
and the PRESS *exit. As they exit,* GEORGE *and* ALICE *enter upstage left.* HENRY *is center, in a "cell" outlined by four newspaper bundles left by the* PRESS.)

20 GEORGE: Henry? How you doing, son? Listen, I've brought
somebody with me that wants very much to meet you. I
thought you wouldn't mind. (ALICE *crosses to* HENRY.)

ALICE: Hello! My name is Alice Bloomfield and I'm a reporter from the Daily People's World.

GEORGE: And . . . And, I might add, a red hot member of the
25   ad hoc committee that's fighting for you guys.

ALICE: Oh, George! I'd hardly call it fighting, for Pete's sake.
This struggle has just barely begun. But we're sure going
to win it, aren't we, Henry?

HENRY: I doubt it.
30

GEORGE: Oh come on, Henry. How about it, son? You all set
for tomorrow? Anything you need, anything I can get for
you?

HENRY: Yeah. What about the clean clothes you promised
me? I can't go to court looking like this.
35

GEORGE: You mean they didn't give them to you?

HENRY: What?

GEORGE: Your mother dropped them off two days ago. Clean
pants, shirt, socks, underwear, the works. I cleared it with
the Sheriff last week.
40

HENRY: They haven't given me nothing.

GEORGE: I'm beginning to smell something around here.

HENRY: Look, George, I don't like being like this. I ain't dirty.
Go do something, man!

GEORGE: Calm down. Take it easy, son. I'll check on it right
45   now. Oh! Uh, Alice?

ALICE: I'll be okay, George.

GEORGE: I'll be right back. (HE *exits.*)

ALICE: (*Pulling out a pad and pencil.*) Now that I have you all
to myself, mind if I ask you a couple of questions?
50

HENRY: I got nothing to say.

ALICE: How do you know? I haven't asked you anything yet.
Relax. I'm from the progressive press. Okay? (HENRY *stares
at her, not knowing quite how to react.* ALICE *sits on a bundle
and crosses her goodlooking legs.* HENRY *concentrates on that.*)
55   Now. The regular press is saying the Pachuco Crime Wave
is fascist inspired—any thoughts about that?

HENRY: (*Bluntly.*) No.

ALICE: What about the American Japanese? Is it true they are
directing the subversive activities of the pachucos from in-
60   side the relocation camps? (HENRY *turns to the* PACHUCO
with a questioning look.)

PACHUCO: This one's all yours, ese.

HENRY: Look, lady, I don't know what the hell you're talking
about.
65

ALICE: I'm talking about you, Henry Reyna. And what the
regular press has been saying. Are you aware you're in here
just because some bigshot up in San Simeon wants to sell
more papers? It's true.

HENRY: So?
70

ALICE: So, he's the man who started this Mexican Crime
Wave stuff. Then the police got into the act. Get the picture? Somebody is using you as a patsy.

HENRY: (*His machismo insulted.*) Who you calling a patsy?

ALICE: I'm sorry, but it's true.
75

HENRY: (*Backing her up.*) What makes you so goddamned
smart?

ALICE: (*Starting to get scared and trying not to show it.*) I'm a reporter. It's my business to know.

PACHUCO: Puro pedo. She's just a dumb broad only good for
80   you know what.

HENRY: Look, Miss Bloomfield, just leave me alone, all right?
(HENRY *moves away.* ALICE *takes a deep breath.*)

85 ALICE: Look, let's back up and start all over, okay? Hello. My
name is Alice Bloomfield, and I'm not a reporter. I'm just
somebody that wants very much to be your friend. (*Pause.
With sincere feeling.*) Can you believe that?

HENRY: Why should I?

ALICE: Because I'm with you.

90 HENRY: Oh, yeah! Then how come you ain't in jail with me?

ALICE: (*Holding her head up.*) We are all in jail, Henry. Some of
us just don't know it.

PACHUCO: Mmm, pues. No comment. (*Pause.* HENRY *stares at
her, trying to figure her out.* ALICE *tries a softer approach.*)

95 ALICE: Believe it or not, I was born in Los Angeles just like
you. But for some strange reason I grew up here, not
knowing very much about Mexicans at all. I'm just trying
to learn.

HENRY: (*Intrigued, but cynical.*) What?

100 ALICE: Little details. Like that tattooed cross on your hand. Is
that the sign of the pachuco? (HENRY *covers his right hand
with and automatic reflex, then* HE *realizes what he has done.*)

HENRY: (*Smiles to himself, embarrassed.*) Órale.

ALICE: Did I embarrass you? I'm sorry. Your mother happened
105 to mention it.

HENRY: (*Surprised.*) My mother? You talked to my jefita?

ALICE: (*With enthusiasm.*) Yes! And your father and Lupe and
Rudy. The whole family gave me a helluva interview. But
your mother was sensational. I especially liked her story
110 about the midnight raid. How the police rushed into your
house with drawn guns, looking for you on some trumped
up charge, and how your father told them you were already
in jail . . . God, I would have paid to have seen the cops' faces.

HENRY: (*Hiding his sentiment.*) Don't believe anything my jefa
115 tells you. (*Then quickly.*) There's a lot she doesn't know. I'm
no angel.

ALICE: I'll just bet you're not. But you have been taken in for
suspicion a dozen times, kept in jail for a few days, then
released for lack of evidence. And it's all stayed on your ju-
120 venile record.

HENRY: Yeah, well I ain't no punk, see.

ALICE: I know. You're an excellent mechanic. And you fix all
the guys' cars. Well, at least you're not one of the lumpen
proletariat.

125 HENRY: The lumpen what?

ALICE: Skip it. Let's just say you're a classic social victim.

HENRY: Bullshit.

ALICE: (*Pause. A serious question.*) Are you saying you're guilty?

HENRY: Of what?

130 ALICE: The Sleepy Lagoon Murder.

HENRY: What if I am?

ALICE: Are you?

HENRY: (*Pause, a serious answer.*) Chale. I've pulled a lot of shit
in my time, but I didn't do that. (GEORGE *re-enters flushed
135 and angry, trying to conceal his frustration.*)

GEORGE: Henry, I'm sorry, but dammit, something's coming
off here, and the clothes have been withheld. I'll have to
bring it up in court.

HENRY: In court?

140 GEORGE: They've left me no choice.

ALICE: What's going on?

HENRY: It's a set up, George. Another lousy set up!

GEORGE: It's just the beginning, son. Nobody said this was
going to be a fair fight. Well, if they're going to fight dirty,
145 so am I. Legally, but dirty. Trust me.

ALICE: (*Passionately.*) Henry, no matter what happens in the
trial, I want you to know I believe you're innocent. Remember that when you look out, and it looks like some
sort of lynch mob. Some of us . . . a lot of us . . . are right
there with you.   150

GEORGE: Okay, Alice, let's scram. I've got a million things to
do. Henry, see you tomorrow under the big top, son.
Good luck, son.

ALICE: Thumbs up, Henry, we're going to beat this rap! (ALICE
and GEORGE *exit.* EL PACHUCO *watches them go, then turns to* 155
HENRY.)

PACHUCO: "Thumbs up, Henry, we're going to beat this rap."
You really think you're going to beat this one, ese?

HENRY: I don't want to think about it.

PACHUCO: You've got to think about it, Hank. Everybody's   160
playing you for a sucker. Wake up, carnal!

HENRY: Look, bato, what the hell do you expect me to do?

PACHUCO: Hang tough. (*Grabs his scrotum.*) Stop going soft.

HENRY: Who's going soft?

PACHUCO: (*Incisively.*) You're hoping for something that isn't 165
going to happen, ese. These paddies are leading you by the
nose. Do you really believe you stand a chance?

HENRY: (*Stubborn all the more.*) Yeah. I think I got a chance.

PACHUCO: Just because that white broad says so?

HENRY: Nel, ese, just because Hank Reyna says so.   170

PACHUCO: The classic social victim, eh?

HENRY: (*Furious but keeping his cool.*) Mira, ese. Hank Reyna's
no loser. I'm coming out of this on top. ¿Me entiendes,
Mendez? (HE *walks away with a pachuco gait.*)

PACHUCO: (*Forcefully.*) Don't try to out-pachuco ME, ese!   175
We'll see who comes out on top. (HE *picks up a bundle of
newspapers and throws it upstage center. It lands with a thud.*)
Let's go to court!

9. OPENING OF THE TRIAL

Music. The JUDGE'S *bench, made up of more newspaper bundles
piled squarely on a four-wheeled hand truck is pushed in by the
batos. The* PRESS *rides it in, holding the State and Federal Flags. A
BAILIFF puts in place a hand cart: the* JUDGE'S *throne. From the sides,
spectators enter, including* HENRY'S *family and friends:* ALICE,
DELLA, BERTHA, ELENA.

PRESS: The largest mass trial in the history of Los Angeles
County opens this morning in the Superior Court at
ten A.M. The infamous Sleepy Lagoon Murder case involves sixty-six charges against twenty-two defendants
with seven lawyers pleading for the defense, two for the   5
prosecution. The District Attorney estimates that over a
hundred witnesses will be called and has sworn—I
quote—"to put an end to Mexican baby gangsterism."
End quote.

BAILIFF: (*Bangs a gavel on the bench.*) The Superior Court of 10
the State of California. In and For the County of Los Angeles. Department forty-three. The honorable F. W.
Charles, presiding. All rise! (JUDGE CHARLES *enters. All rise.*
EL PACHUCO *squats. The* JUDGE *is played by the same actor that
portrays* EDWARDS.)   15

JUDGE: Please be seated. (*All sit.* PACHUCO *stands.*) Call this
case, Bailiff.

BAILIFF: (*Reading from a sheet.*) The people of the State of California Versus Henry Reyna, Ismael Torres, Thomas

120 Roberts, Jose Castro and eighteen other . . . (*Slight hesitation.*) . . . pa-coo-cos.

JUDGE: Is Counsel for the Defense present?

GEORGE: (*Rises.*) Yes, Your Honor.

JUDGE: Please proceed. (*Signals the* PRESS.)

125 PRESS: Your Honor . . .

GEORGE: (*Moving in immediately.*) If the Court please, it was reported to me on Friday that the District Attorney has absolutely forbidden the Sheriff's Office to permit these boys to have clean clothes or haircuts. Now, it's been three

130 months since the boys were arrested . . .

PRESS: (*Jumping in.*) Your Honor, there is testimony we expect to develop that he 38th Street Gang are characterized by their style of haircuts . . .

GEORGE: Three months, Your Honor.

135 PRESS: . . . the thick heavy heads of hair, the ducktail comb, the pachuco pants . . .

GEORGE: Your Honor, I can only infer that the Prosecution . . . is trying to make these boys look disreputable, like mobsters.

140 PRESS: Their appearance is distinctive, Your Honor. Essential to the case.

GEORGE: You are trying to exploit the fact that these boys look foreign in appearance! Yet clothes like these are being worn by kids all over America.

145 PRESS: Your Honor . . .

JUDGE: (*Bangs the gavel.*) I don't believe we will have any difficulty if their clothing becomes dirty.

GEORGE: What about the haircuts, Your Honor?

JUDGE: (*Ruling.*) The zoot haircuts will be retained through-

150 out the trial for purposes of identification of defendants by witnesses.

PACHUCO: You hear that one, ese? Listen to it again. (*Snaps.* JUDGE *repeats automatically.*)

JUDGE: The zoot haircuts will be retained throughout the

155 trial for purposes of identification of defendants by witnesses.

PACHUCO: He wants to be sure we know who you are.

JUDGE: It has been brought to my attention the Jury is having trouble telling one boy from another, so I am going to

160 rule the defendants stand each time their names are mentioned.

GEORGE: I object. If the Prosecution makes an accusation, it will mean self-incrimination.

JUDGE: (*Pause.*) Not necessarily. (*To* PRESS.) Please proceed.

165 GEORGE: (*Still trying to set the stage.*) Then if the Court please, might I request that my clients be allowed to sit with me during the trial so that I might consult with them?

JUDGE: Request denied.

GEORGE: May I inquire of Your Honor, if the defendant

170 Thomas Robert might rise from his seat and walk over to counsel table so as to consult with me during the trial?

JUDGE: I certainly will not permit it.

GEORGE: You will not?

JUDGE: No. This is a small courtroom, Mr. Shearer. We can't

175 have twenty-two defendants all over the place.

GEORGE: Then I object. On the grounds that that is a denial of the rights guaranteed all defendants by both the Federal and State constitutions.

JUDGE: Well, that is your opinion. (*Gavel.*) Call your first witness.

180 PRESS: The prosecution calls Lieutenant Sam Edwards of the Los Angeles Police Department.

PACHUCO: (*Snaps. Does double take on* JUDGE.) You know what. We've already heard from that bato. Let's get on with the defense. (*Snaps.* PRESS *sits.* GEORGE *stands.*)

185 GEORGE: The defense calls Adela Barrios.

BAILIFF: (*Calling out.*) Adeela Barreeos to the stand. (DELLA BARRIOS *comes forth out of the spectators.* BERTHA *leans forward.*)

BERTHA: (*Among the spectators.*) Don't tell 'em nothing. (*The

190 BAILIFF *swears in* DELLA *silently.*)

PACHUCO: Look at your gang. They do look like mobsters. Se watchan bien gachos. (HENRY *looks at the batos, who are sprawled out in their places.*)

HENRY: (*Under his breath.*) Come on, Batos, sit up.

195 SMILEY: We're tired, Hank.

JOEY: My butt is sore.

TOMMY: Yeah, look at the soft chairs the jury's got.

HENRY: What did you expect? They're trying to make us look bad. Come on! Straighten up.

200 SMILEY: Simón, batos, Hank is right.

JOEY: ¡Más alba nalga!

TOMMY: Put some class on your ass.

HENRY: Sit up! (*They all sit up.*)

GEORGE: State your name please.

205 DELLA: Adela Barrios. (*She sits.*)

GEORGE: Miss Barrios, were you with Henry Reyna on the night of August 1, 1942?

DELLA: Yes.

JUDGE: (*To* HENRY.) Please stand. (HENRY *stands.*)

210 GEORGE: Please tell the court what transpired that night.

DELLA: (*Pause. Takes a breath.*) Well, after the dance that Saturday night, Henry and I drove out to the Sleepy Lagoon about eleven-thirty.

10. SLEEPY LAGOON

Music: THE HARRY JAMES THEME. EL PACHUCO *creates the scene. The light changes. We see a shimmering pattern of light on the floor growing to the music. It becomes the image of the Lagoon. As the music soars to a trumpet solo,* HENRY *reaches out to* DELLA, *and she glides to her feet.*

DELLA: There was a full moon that night, and as we drove up to the Lagoon we noticed right away the place was empty . . . (*A pair of headlights silently pulls in from the black background upstage center.*) Henry parked the car on the bank of

5 the reservoir and we relaxed. (*Headlights go off.*) It was such a warm, beautiful night, and the sky was so full of stars, we couldn't just sit in the car. So we got out, and Henry took my hand . . . (HENRY *stands and takes* DELLA's *hand.*) We went for a walk around the Lagoon. Neither of us said

10 anything at first, so the only sounds we could hear were the crickets and the frogs . . . (*Sounds of crickets and frogs, then music faintly in the background.*) When we got to the other side of the reservoir, we began to hear music, so I asked Henry, what's that?

15 HENRY: Sounds like they're having a party.

DELLA: Where?

HENRY: Over at the Williams' Ranch. See the house lights.

DELLA: Who lives there?

HENRY: A couple of families. Mexicanos. I think they work

20 on the ranch. You know, their name used to be Gonzales, but they changed it to Williams.

DELLA: Why?

HENRY: I don't know. Maybe they think it gives 'em more
25 class. (*We hear Mexican music.*) Ay, jijo. They're probably
celebrating a wedding or something.

DELLA: As soon as he said wedding, he stopped talking and
we both knew why. He had something on his mind,
something he was trying to tell me without sounding like
a square.

30 HENRY: Della . . . what are you going to do if I don't come
back from the war?

DELLA: That wasn't the question I was expecting, so I answered something dumb, like I don't know, what's going
to keep you from coming back?

35 HENRY: Maybe wanting too much out of life, see? Ever since
I was a kid, I've had this feeling like there's a big party going on someplace, and I'm invited, but I don't know how
to get there. And I want to get there so bad, I'll even risk
my life to make it. Sounds crazy, huh? (DELLA *and* HENRY

40 *kiss. They embrace and then* HENRY *speaks haltingly.*) If I get
back from the war . . . will you marry me?

DELLA: Yes! (SHE *embraces him and almost causes them to topple
over.*)

HENRY: ¡Órale! You'll knock us into the Lagoon. Listen, what
45 about your old man? He ain't going to like you marrying
me.

DELLA: I know. But I don't care. I'll go to hell with you if you
want me to.

HENRY: ¿Sabes qué? I'm going to give you the biggest
50 Pachuco wedding L.A. has ever seen. (*Another pair of headlights comes in from the left.* DELLA *goes back to her narration.*)

DELLA: Just then another car pulled up to the Lagoon. It was
Rafas and some drunk guys in a gang from Downey. They
got out and started to bust the windows on Henry's car.
55 Henry yelled at them, and they started cussing at us. I told
Henry not to say anything, but he cussed them back!

HENRY: You stay here, Della.

DELLA: Henry, no! Don't go down there! Please don't go
down there!

60 HENRY: Can't you hear what they're doing to my car?

DELLA: There's too many of them. They'll kill you!

HENRY: ¡Chale! (HENRY *turns and runs upstage, where he stops in
a freeze.*)

DELLA: Henry! Henry ran down the back of the Lagoon and
65 attacked the gang by himself. Rafas had about ten guys
with him and they jumped on Henry like a pack of dogs.
He fought them off as long as he could, then they threw
him on the ground hard and kicked him until he passed
out . . . (*Headlights pull off.*) After they left, I ran down to
70 Henry and held him in my arms until he came to. And I
could tell he was hurt, but the first thing he said was . . .

PACHUCO: Let's go into town and get the guys. (*Music: Glen
Miller's "In the Mood."* HENRY *turns to the batos and they
stand.* SMILEY, JOEY *and* TOMMY *are joined by* RUDY, BERTHA,
75 LUPE *and* ELENA, *who enter from the side. They turn downstage
in a body and freeze.*)

DELLA: It took us about an hour to go into town and come
back. We got to the Lagoon with about eight cars, but the
Downey gang wasn't there.

80 JOEY: Órale, ¿pos qué pasó? Nobody here.

SMILEY: Then let's go to Downey.

THE BOYS: (*Ad lib.*) Let's go!

HENRY: ¡Chale! ¡Chale! (*Pause. They all stop.*) Ya estuvo. Everybody go home. (*A collective groan from* THE BOYS.) Go home!

DELLA: That's when we heard music coming from the Williams' 85
Ranch again. We didn't know Rafas and his gang had been
there too, causing trouble. So when Joey said . . .

JOEY: Hey, there's a party! Bertha, let's crash it.

DELLA: We all went there yelling and laughing. (*The group of
batos turns upstage in a mimetic freeze.*) At the Williams' 90
Ranch they saw us coming and thought we were the
Downey Gang coming back again . . . They attacked us.
(*The group now mimes a series of tableaus showing the fight.*)
An old man ran out of the house with a kitchen knife and
Henry had to hit him. Then a girl grabbed me by the hair 95
and in a second everybody was fighting! People were
grabbing sticks from the fence, bottles, anything! It all
happened so fast, we didn't know what hit us, but Henry
said let's go!

HENRY: ¡Vámonos! Let's get out of here.   100

DELLA: And we started to back off . . . Before we got to the
cars, I saw something out of the corner of my eye . . . It was
a guy. He was hitting a man on the ground with a big stick.
(EL PACHUCO *mimes this action.*) Henry called to him, but he
wouldn't stop. He wouldn't stop . . . He wouldn't stop . . . 105
He wouldn't stop . . . (DELLA *in tears, holds* HENRY *in her arms.
The batos and rucas start moving back to their places, quietly.*)
Driving back in the car, everybody was quiet, like nothing
had happened. We didn't know José Williams had died at
the party that night and that the guys would be arrested the 110
next day for murder. (HENRY *separates from her and goes back
to stand in his place.* DELLA *resumes the witness stand.*)

11. THE CONCLUSION OF THE TRIAL

Lights change back to courtroom, as JUDGE CHARLES *bangs his
gavel. Everyone is seated back in place.*

GEORGE: Your witness.

PRESS: (*Springing to the attack.*) You say Henry Reyna hit the
man with his fist. (*Indicates* HENRY *standing.*) Is this the
Henry Reyna?

DELLA: Yes. I mean, no. He's Henry, but he didn't . . .   5

PRESS: Please be seated. (HENRY *sits.*) Now, after Henry Reyna
hit the old man with his closed fist, is that when he pulled
the knife?

DELLA: The old man had the knife.

PRESS: So Henry pulled one out, too?   10

GEORGE: (*Rises.*) Your Honor, I object to counsel leading the
witness.

PRESS: I am not leading the witness.

GEORGE: You are.

PRESS: I certainly am not.   15

GEORGE: Yes, you are.

JUDGE: I would suggest, Mr. Shearer, that you look up during
the noon hour just what a leading question is.

GEORGE: If the Court please, I am going to assign that remark
of Your Honor as misconduct.   20

JUDGE: (*To* PRESS.) Proceed. (GEORGE *crosses back to his chair.*)

PRESS: Where was Smiley Torres during all this? Is it not true
that Smiley Torres grabbed a woman by the hair and
kicked her to the ground? Will Smiley Torres please stand?
(SMILEY *stands.*) Is this the man?   25

DELLA: Yes, it's Smiley, but he . . .

PRESS: Please be seated. (SMILEY *sits*. PRESS *picks up a two-by-four*.) Wasn't José Castro carrying a club of some kind?

GEORGE: (*On his feet again.*) Your Honor, I object! No such club was ever found. The Prosecution is implying that this two-by-four is associated with my client in some way.

PRESS: I'm not implying anything, Your Honor, I'm merely using this stick as an illustration.

JUDGE: Objection overruled.

PRESS: Will José Castro please stand? (JOEY *stands*.) Is this man who was carrying a club? (DELLA *refuses to answer*.) Answer the question please.

DELLA: I refuse.

PRESS: You are under oath. You can't refuse.

JUDGE: Answer the question, young lady.

DELLA: I refuse.

PRESS: Is this the man you saw hitting another man with a two-by-four? Your Honor . . .

JUDGE: I order you to answer the question.

GEORGE: Your Honor, I object. The witness is obviously afraid her testimony will be manipulated by the Prosecution.

PRESS: May I remind the court that we have a signed confession from one José Castro taken while in jail . . .

GEORGE: I object. Those were not confessions! Those are statements. They are false and untrue, Your Honor, obtained through beatings and coercion of the defendants by the police!

JUDGE: I believe the technical term is admissions, Mr. Prosecutor. Objection sustained. (*Applause from spectators.*) At the next outburst, I will clear this courtroom. Go on, Mr. Prosecutor.

PRESS: Sit down please. (JOEY *sits*. GEORGE *goes back to his seat.*) Is Henry Reyna the leader of the 38th Street Gang? (HENRY *stands*.)

DELLA: Not in the sense that you mean.

PRESS: Did Henry Reyna, pachuco ringleader of the 38th Street Gang, willfully murder José Williams?

DELLA: No. They attacked us first.

PRESS: I didn't ask for your comment.

DELLA: But they did, they thought we were the Downey gang.

PRESS: Just answer my questions.

DELLA: We were just defending ourselves so we could get out of there.

PRESS: Your Honor, will you instruct the witness to be cooperative.

JUDGE: I must caution you, young lady, answer the questions or I'll hold you in contempt.

PRESS: Was this the Henry Reyna who was carrying a three-foot lead pipe?

GEORGE: I object!

JUDGE: Overruled.

DELLA: No.

PRESS: Was it a two-foot lead pipe?

GEORGE: Objection!

JUDGE: Overruled.

DELLA: No!

PRESS: Did he kick a woman to the ground?

DELLA: No, he was hurt from the beating.

PRESS: Sit down. (HENRY *sits*.) Did Tommy Roberts rip stakes from a fence and hit a man on the ground?

GEORGE: Objection!

JUDGE: Overruled.

DELLA: I never saw him do anything.

PRESS: Did Joey Castro have a gun?

GEORGE: Objection!

JUDGE: Overruled. (JOEY *stands*.)

PRESS: Sit down. (JOEY *sits*.) Did Henry Reyna have a blackjack in his hand? (HENRY *stands*.)

DELLA: No.

PRESS: A switchblade knife?

DELLA: No.

PRESS: A two-by-four?

DELLA: No.

PRESS: Did he run over to José Williams, hit him on the head and kill him?

DELLA: He could barely walk, how could he run to any place?

PRESS: (*Moving in for the kill.*) Did Smiley Torres? (*The batos stand and sit as their names are mentioned.*) Did Joey Castro? Did Tommy Roberts? Did Henry Reyna? Did Smiley Torres? Did Henry Reyna? Did Henry Reyna? Did Henry Reyna kill José Williams?!

DELLA: No, no, no!

GEORGE: (*On HIS feet again.*) Your Honor, I object! The Prosecution is pulling out objects from all over the place, none of which were found at Sleepy Lagoon, and none of which have been proven to be associated with my clients in any way.

JUDGE: Overruled.

GEORGE: If Your Honor please, I wish to make an assignment of misconduct!

JUDGE: We have only had one this morning. We might as well have another now.

GEORGE: You have it, Your Honor.

JUDGE: One more remark like that and I'll hold you in contempt. Quite frankly, Mr. Shearer, I am getting rather tired of your repeated useless objections.

GEORGE: I have not made useless objections.

JUDGE: I am sorry. Somebody is using ventriloquism. We have a Charlie McCarthy using Mr. Shearer's voice.

GEORGE: I am going to assign that remark of Your Honor as misconduct.

JUDGE: Fine. I would feel rather bad if you did not make an assignment of misconduct at least three times every session. (*Gavel.*) Witness is excused. (DELLA *stands*.) However, I am going to remand her to the custody of the Ventura State School for Girls for a period of one year . . .

HENRY: What?

JUDGE: . . . to be held there as a juvenile ward of the State. Bailiff?

GEORGE: If the court please . . . If the court please . . . (BAILIFF *crosses to* DELLA *and takes her off left.*)

JUDGE: Court is in recess until tomorrow morning. (JUDGE *retires*. PRESS *exits*. HENRY *meets* GEORGE *halfway across center stage. The rest of the batos stand and stretch in the background.*)

GEORGE: Now, Henry, I want you to listen to me, please. You've got to remember he's the judge, Hank. And this is his courtroom.

HENRY: But he's making jokes, George, and we're getting screwed!

GEORGE: I know. I can't blame you for being bitter, but believe me, we'll get him.

HENRY: I thought you said we had a chance.

GEORGE: (*Passionately.*) We do! This case is going to be won
150   on appeal.

HENRY: Appeal! You mean you already know we're going to
  lose?

PACHUCO: So what's new?

GEORGE: Don't you see, Henry, Judge Charles is hanging
155   himself as we go. I've cited over a hundred separate cases
  of misconduct by the bench, and it's all gone into the
  record. Prejudicial error, denial of due process, inadmissi-
  ble evidence, hearsay . . .

HENRY: ¿Sabes qué, George? Don't tell me any more. (HENRY
160   *turns.* ALICE *and* ENRIQUE *approach him.*)

ALICE: Henry . . . ?

HENRY: (*Turns furiously.*) I don't want to hear it, Alice! (HENRY
  sees ENRIQUE, *but neither father nor son can think of anything
  to say.* HENRY *goes back upstage.*)

165 ALICE: George, is there anything we can do?

GEORGE: No. He's bitter, and he has a right to be. (JUDGE
  CHARLES *pounds his gavel. All go back to their places and sit.*)

JUDGE: We'll now hear the Prosecution's concluding statement.

PRESS: Your Honor, ladies and gentlemen of the jury. What
170   you have before you is a dilemma of our times. The City
  of Los Angeles is caught in the midst of the biggest, most
  terrifying crime wave in its history. A crime wave that
  threatens to engulf the very foundations of our civic
  well-being. We are not only dealing with the violent
175   death of one José Williams in a drunken barrio brawl. We
  are dealing with a threat and danger to our children, our
  families, our homes. Set these pachucos free, and you
  shall unleash the forces of anarchy and destruction in our
  society. Set these pachucos free and you will turn them
180   into heroes. Others just like them must be watching us
  at this very moment. What nefarious schemes can they
  be hatching in their twisted minds? Rape, drugs, assault,
  more violence? Who shall be their next innocent victim
  in some dark alley way, on some lonely street? You? You?
185   Your loved ones? No! Henry Reyna and his Latin juvenile cohorts are not heroes. They are criminals, and they
  must be stopped. The specific details of this murder are
  irrelevant before the overwhelming danger of the
  pachuco in our midst. I ask you to find these zoot-suited
190   gangsters guilty of murder and to put them in the gas
  chamber where they belong. (*The* PRESS *sits down.*
  GEORGE *rises and takes center stage.*)

GEORGE: Ladies and gentlemen of the jury, you have heard me
  object to the conduct of this trial. I have tried my best to
195   defend what is most precious in our American society—a
  society now at war against the forces of racial intolerance
  and totalitarian injustice. The prosecution has not provided
  one witness that actually saw, with his own eyes, who actually murdered José Williams. These boys are not the
200   Downey gang, yet the evidence suggests that they were attacked because the people at the ranch thought they were.
  Henry Reyna and Della Barrios were victims of the same
  bunch. Yes, they might have been spoiling for a revenge—
  who wouldn't under the circumstances—but not with the
205   intent to conspire to commit murder. So how did José
  Williams die? Was it an accident? Was it manslaughter? Was
  it murder? Perhaps we may never know. All the prosecution
  has been able to prove is that these boys wear long hair and

zoot suits. And all the rest has been circumstantial evidence,
hearsay and war hysteria. The prosecution has tried to lead 210
you to believe that they are some kind of inhuman gangsters. Yet they are Americans. Find them guilty of anything
more serious than a juvenile bout of fisticuffs, and you will
condemn all American youth. Find them guilty of murder,
and you will murder the spirit of racial justice in America. 215
(GEORGE *sits down.*)

JUDGE: The jury will retire to consider its verdict. (*The* PRESS
stands and starts to exit with the BAILIFF. EL PACHUCO *snaps. All
freeze.*)

PACHUCO: Chale. Let's have it. (*Snaps again. The* PRESS *turns* 220
and comes back again.)

JUDGE: Has the jury reached a verdict?

PRESS: We have, Your Honor.

JUDGE: How say you?

PRESS: We find the defendants guilty of murder in the first 225
and second degrees.

JUDGE: The defendants will rise. (*The batos come to their feet.*)
Henry Reyna, José Castro, Thomas Roberts, Ismael Torres,
and so forth. You have been tried by a jury of your peers
and found guilty of murder in the first and second degrees. 230
The Law prescribes the capital punishment for this offense.
However, in view of your youth and in consideration of
your families, it is hereby the judgement of this court that
you be sentenced to life imprisonment . . .

RUDY: No! 235

JUDGE: . . . and sent to the State Penitentiary at San Quentin.
Court adjourned. (*Gavel.* JUDGE *exits.* DOLORES, ENRIQUE
and family go to HENRY. BERTHA *crosses to* JOEY; LUPE *goes to*
TOMMY. ELENA *crosses to* SMILEY. GEORGE *and* ALICE *talk.*)

DOLORES: ¡Hijo mío! ¡Hijo de mi alma! (BAILIFF *comes down* 240
with a pair of handcuffs.)

BAILIFF: Okay, boys. (HE *puts the cuffs on* HENRY. RUDY *comes up.*)

RUDY: ¿Carnal? (HENRY *looks at the* BAILIFF, *who gives him a nod
of permission to spend a moment with* RUDY. HENRY *embraces
him with the cuffs on.* GEORGE *and* ALICE *approach.*) 245

GEORGE: Henry? I can't pretend to know how you feel, son.
I just want you to know that our fight has just begun.

ALICE: We may have lost this decision, but we're going to appeal immediately. We're going to stand behind you until
your name is absolutely clear. I swear it! 250

PACHUCO: What the hell are they going to do, ese? They just
sent you to prison for life. Once a Mexican goes in, he
never comes out.

BAILIFF: Boys? (*The* BOYS *exit with the* BAILIFF. *As they go*
ENRIQUE *calls after them.*) 255

ENRIQUE: (*Holding back tears.*) Hijo. Be a man, hijo. (*Then to
his family.*) Vámonos . . . ¡Vámonos! (*The family leaves and*
EL PACHUCO *slowly walks to center stage.*)

PACHUCO: We're going to take a short break right now, so you
can all go out and take a leak, smoke a frajo. Ahí los watcho. 260
(HE e*xits up center and the newspaper backdrop comes down.*)

ACT TWO
PROLOGUE

Lights up and EL PACHUCO *emerges from the shadows. The newspaper drop is still down. Music.*

PACHUCO:
Watchamos pachucos

los batos
the dudes
street-corner warriors who fought and moved
5 like unknown soldiers in wars of their own
El Pueblo de Los was the battle zone
from Sleepy Lagoon to the Zoot Suit wars
when Marines and Sailors made their scores
stomping like Nazis on East L.A. . . .
10 pero ?saben qué?
That's later in the play. Let's pick it up in prison.
We'll begin this scene
inside the walls of San Quentin.

1. SAN QUENTIN

A bell rings as the drop rises. HENRY, JOEY, SMILEY *and* TOMMY *enter accompanied by a* GUARD.

GUARD: All right, people, lock up. (BOYS *move downstage in four directions. They step into "cells" simply marked by shadows of bars on the floor in their separate places. Newspaper handcarts rest on the floor as cots. Sound of cell doors closing. The* GUARD
5 *paces back and forth upstage level.*)
HENRY:
San Quentin, California
March 3, 1943
Dear Family:
10 Coming in from the yard in the evening, we are quickly locked up in our cells. Then the clank and locking of the doors leaves one with a rather empty feeling. You are standing up to the iron door, waiting for the guard to come along and take the count, listening as his footsteps
15 fade away in the distance. By this time there is a tense stillness that seems to crawl over the cellblock. You realize you are alone, so all alone.
PACHUCO: This all sounds rather tragic, doesn't it?
HENRY: But here comes the guard again, and he calls out your
20 number in a loud voice . . .
GUARD: (*Calls numbers;* BOYS *call name.*) 24–545
HENRY: Reyna!
GUARD: 24–546
JOEY: Castro!
25 GUARD: 24–547
TOMMY: Roberts!
GUARD: 24–548
SMILEY: Torres! (GUARD *passes through dropping letters and exits up left.*)
30 HENRY: You jump to your feet, stooping to pick up the letter . . .
JOEY: (*Excited.*) Or perhaps several letters . . .
TOMMY: You are really excited as you take the letters from the envelope.
35 SMILEY: The censor has already broken the seal when he reads it.
HENRY: You make a mental observation to see if you recognize the handwriting on the envelope.
SMILEY: (*Anxious.*) It's always nice to hear from home . . .
JOEY: Or a close comrade . . .
40 TOMMY: Friends that you know on the outside . . .
HENRY: Or perhaps it's from a stranger. (*Pause. Spotlight at upstage center.* ALICE *walks in with casual clothes on. Her hair is in pigtails, and she wears a pair of drapes.* SHE *is cheerful.*)

2. THE LETTERS

Dear Boys,
Announcing the publication (mimeograph) of the Appeal News, your very own newsletter, to be sent to you twice a month for the purpose of keeping you reliably informed of everything—the progress of the Sleeping Lagoon De- 5
fense Committee (We have a name now) and, of course, the matter of your appeal.
            Signed,
            Your editor
            Alice Bloomfield. 10

(*Music. "Perdido" by Duke Ellington.* ALICE *steps down and sits on the lip of the upstage level. The* BOYS *start swinging the bat, dribbling the basketball, shadow-boxing and exercising.* ALICE *mimes typing movements and we hear the sounds of a typewriter. Music fades.* ALICE *rises.*)

ALICE: The Appeal News Volume 1, Number I, April 7, 1943.
Boys,
You can, you must, and you will help us on the outside by what you do on the inside. Don't forget, what you do affects others. You have no control over that. When the time 15
comes, let us be proud to show the record.
            Signed,
            Your editor.

(*Music up again. The* BOYS *go through their activities.* ALICE *moves downstage center and the music fades.*)

SMILEY: (*Stepping toward her.*)
April 10, 1943 20
Dear Miss Bloomfield,
I have discovered from my wife that you are conducting door-to-door fund-raising campaigns in Los Angeles. She doesn't want to tell you, but she feels bad about doing such a thing. It's not our custom to go around the neigh- 25
borhoods asking for money.
ALICE: (*Turning toward* SMILEY.)
Dear Smiley,
Of course, I understand your feelings . . .
SMILEY: (*Adamant.*) I don't want my wife going around beg- 30
ging.
ALICE: It isn't begging—it's fund-raising.
SMILEY: I don't care what you call it. If that's what it's going to take, count me out.
ALICE: All right. I won't bother your wife if she really doesn't 35
want me to. Okay? (SMILEY *looks at her and turns back to his upstage position. Music. The batos move again.* TOMMY *crosses to* ALICE. *Another fade.*)
TOMMY:
April 18, 1943
Dear Alice, 40
Trying to find the words and expression to thank you for your efforts in behalf of myself and the rest of the batos makes me realize what a meager vocabulary I possess . . .
ALICE:
Dear Tommy, 45
Your vocabulary is just fine. Better than most.
TOMMY: Most what?

ALICE: People.

TOMMY: (*Glances at* HENRY.) Uh, listen, Alice. I don't want to
be treated any different than the rest of the batos, see? And
don't expect me to talk to you like some square Anglo,
some pinche gabacho. You just better find out what it
means to be Chicano, and it better be pretty damn quick.

ALICE: Look, Tommy, I didn't . . .

TOMMY: I know what you're trying to do for us and that's
reet, see? Shit. Most paddies would probably like to see us
locked up for good. I been in jail a couple of times before,
but never nothing this deep. Strange, ain't it, the trial in
Los? I don't really know what happened or why. I don't
give a shit what the papers said. We didn't do half the
things I read about. I also know that I'm in here just because I hung around with Mexicans . . . or pachucos. Well,
just remember this, Alicia . . . I grew up right alongside
most of these batos, and I'm pachuco too. Simón, esa, you
better believe it! (*Music up. Movement.* TOMMY *returns to his
position.* HENRY *stands.* ALICE *turns toward him, but* HE *walks
over to* THE PACHUCO, *giving her his back.*)

JOEY: (*Stepping forward anxiously.*)
May 1, 1943
Dear Alice . . . Darling!
I can't help but spend my time thinking about you.
How about sending us your retra—that is, your photo-
graph? Even though Tommy would like one of Rita
Hayworth—he's always chasing Mexican skirts (Ha!
Ha!)—I'd prefer to see your sweet face any day.

ALICE: (*Directly to him.*)
Dear Joey,
Thank you so much. I really appreciated receiving your
letter.

JOEY: That's all reet, Grandma! You mind if I call you
Grandma?

ALICE: Oh, no.

JOEY: Eres una ruca de aquellas.

ALICE: I'm a what?

JOEY: Ruca. A fine chick.

ALICE: (*Pronounces the word.*) Ruca?

JOEY: De aquellas. (*Makes a cool gesture, palms out at hip level.*)

ALICE: (*Imitating him.*) De aquellas.

JOEY: All reet! You got it. (*Pause.*) P.S. Did you forget the photograph?

ALICE: (SHE *hands it to him.*)
Dearest Joey,
Of course not. Here it is, attached to a copy of the Appeal
News. I'm afraid it's not exactly a pin-up.

JOEY: (*Kissing the photo.*) Alice, honey, you're a doll! (JOEY *shows the
photo to* TOMMY *then* SMILEY, *who is curious enough to come into
the circle.* ALICE *looks at* HENRY, *but* HE *continues to ignore her.*)

ALICE: (*Back at center.*) The Appeal News, Volume I, Number
3, May 5, 1943.
Dear Boys,
Feeling that el Cinco de Mayo is a very appropriate day—
the CIO radio program, "Our Daily Bread," is devoting
the entire time this evening to a discussion of discrimination against Mexicans in general and against you guys in
particular.

Music up. The repartee between ALICE *and the batos is now friendly and
warm. Even* SMILEY *is smiling with* ALICE. *They check out her "drapes."*

3. THE INCORRIGIBLE PACHUCO

HENRY *stands at downstage left, looks at the group, then decides to
speak.*

HENRY:
May 17, 1943
Dear Miss Bloomfield,
I understand you're coming up to Q this weekend, and I
would like to talk to you—in private. Can you arrange it?

(*The batos turn away, taking a hint.*)

ALICE: (*Eagerly.*) Yes, yes, I can. What can I do for you, Henry?
(HENRY *and* ALICE *step forward toward each other.* EL PACHUCO
moves in.)

HENRY: For me? ¡Ni madre!

ALICE: (*Puzzled.*) I don't understand.

HENRY: I wanted you to be the first to know, Alice. I'm dropping out of the appeal.

ALICE: (*Unbelieving.*) You're what?

HENRY: I'm bailing out, esa. Dropping out of the case, see?

ALICE: Henry, you can't!

HENRY: Why can't I?

ALICE: Because you'll destroy our whole case! If we don't
present a united front, how can we ask the public to support us?

HENRY: That's your problem. I never asked for their support.
Just count me out.

ALICE: (*Getting nervous, anxious.*) Henry, please, think about
what you're saying. If you drop out, the rest of the boys
will probably go with you. How can you even think of
dropping out of the appeal? What about George and all
the people that have contributed their time and money in
the past few months? You just can't quit on them!

HENRY: Oh no? Just watch me.

ALICE: If you felt this way, why didn't you tell me before?

HENRY: Why didn't you ask me? You think you can just move
in and defend anybody you feel like? When did I ever ask
you to start a defense committee for me? Or a newspaper?
Or a fundraising drive and all that other shit? I don't need
defending, esa. I can take care of myself.

ALICE: But what about the trial, the sentence. They gave your
life imprisonment?

HENRY: It's my life!

ALICE: Henry, honestly—are you kidding me?

HENRY: You think so?

ALICE: But you've seen me coming and going. Writing to
you, speaking for you, traveling up and down the state.
You must have known I was doing it for you. Nothing
has come before my involvement, my attachment, my
passion for this case. My boys have been everything
to me.

HENRY: My boys? My boys! What the hell are we—your personal property? Well, let me set you straight, lady, I ain't
your boy.

ALICE: You know I never meant it that way.

HENRY: You think I haven't see through your bullshit? Always
so concerned. Come on, boys. Speak out, boys. Stand up
for your people. Well, you leave my people out of this!
Can't you understand that.

ALICE: No, I can't understand that.

HENRY: You're just using Mexicans to play politics.

55 ALICE: Henry, that's the worst thing anyone has ever said to me.

HENRY: Who are you going to help next—the Colored People?

ALICE: No, as a matter of fact, I've already helped the Colored
60 People. What are you going to do next—go to the gas chamber?

HENRY: What the hell do you care?

ALICE: I don't!

HENRY: Then get the hell out of here!

65 ALICE: (*Furious.*) You think you're the only one who doesn't want to be bothered? You ought to try working in the Sleepy Lagoon defense office for a few months. All the haggling, the petty arguments, the lack of cooperation. I've wanted to quit a thousand times. What the hell am I
70 doing here? They're coming at me from all sides. You're too sentimental and emotional about this, Alice. You're too cold hearted, Alice. You're collecting money and turning it over to the lawyers, while the families are going hungry. They're saying you can't be trusted because you're a Com-
75 munist, because you're a Jew. Okay! If that's the way they feel about me, then to hell with them! I hate them too. I hate their language, I hate their enchiladas, and I hate their goddamned mariachi music! (*Pause. They look at each other. HENRY smiles, then ALICE—feeling foolish—and they both
80 break out laughing.*)

HENRY: All right! Now you sound like you mean it.

ALICE: I do.

HENRY: Okay! Now we're talking straight.

ALICE: I guess I have been sounding like some square paddy
85 chick. But, you haven't exactly been Mister Cool yourself . . . ese.

HENRY: So, let's say we're even Steven.

ALICE: Fair enough. What now?

HENRY: Why don't we bury the hatchet, you know what I
90 mean?

ALICE: Can I tell George you'll go on with the appeal?

HENRY: Yeah. I know there's a lot of people out there who are willing and trying to help us. People who feel that our conviction was an injustice. People like George . . . and
95 you. Well, the next time you see them, tell them Hank Reyna sends his thanks.

ALICE: Why don't you tell them?

HENRY: You getting wise with me again?

ALICE: If you write an article—and I know you can—we'll
100 publish it in the People's World. What do you say?

PACHUCO: Article! Pos who told you, you could write, ese?

HENRY: (*Laughs.*) Chale.

ALICE: I'm serious. Why don't you give it a try?

HENRY: I'll think about it. (*Pause.*) Listen, you think you and
105 I could write each other . . . outside the newsletter?

ALICE: Sure.

HENRY: Then it's a deal. (*They shake hands.*)

ALICE: I'm glad we're going to be communicating. I think we're going to be very good friends. (*ALICE lifts her hands
110 to HENRY's shoulder in a gesture of comradeship. HENRY follows her hand, putting his on top of hers.*)

HENRY: You think so?

ALICE: I know so.

GUARD: Time, miss.

115 ALICE: I gotta go. Think about the article, okay? (*SHE turns to the BOYS.*) I gotta go, boys.

JOEY: Goodbye, Grandma! Say hello to Bertha.

SMILEY: And to my wife!

TOMMY: Give my love to Lupe!

GUARD: Time! 120

ALICE: I've got to go. Goodbye, goodbye. (*ALICE exits, escorted by the GUARD upstage left. As SHE goes, JOEY calls after her.*)

JOEY: See you, Grandma.

TOMMY: (*Turning to JOEY and SMILEY.*) She loves me.

PACHUCO: Have you forgotten what happened at the trial? 125 You think the Appeals Court is any different? Some paddy judge sitting in the same fat-ass judgment of your fate.

HENRY: Come on, ese, give me a break!

PACHUCO: One break, coming up! (*HE snaps his fingers. The GUARD blows his whistle.*) 130

GUARD: Rec time! (*The batos move upstage to the upper level. Music. The BOYS mime a game of handball against the backdrop. During the game, GEORGE enters at stage right and comes downstage carrying his briefcase. The GUARD blows a whistle and stops the game.*) 135

GUARD: Reyna, Castro, Roberts, Torres!—You got a visitor.

4. MAJOR GEORGE

The BOYS turn and see GEORGE. They come down enthusiastically.

JOEY: ¡Óra-leh! ¡Ese, Cheer!

SMILEY: George!

GEORGE: Hi, guys! (*The BOYS shake his hand, pat him on the back. HENRY comes to him last.*) How are you all doing? You boys staying in shape.? 5

JOEY: Ese, you're looking at the hero of the San Quentin athletic program. Right, batos? (*HE shadowboxes a little.*)

TOMMY: Ten rounds with a busted ankle.

JOEY: ¡Simón! And I won the bout, too. I'm the terror of the flyweights, ese. The killer fly! 10

TOMMY: They got us doing everything. Cheer. Baseball, basketball.

SMILEY: Watch repairing.

GEORGE: (*Impressed.*) Watch repairing?

SMILEY: I'm also learning to improve my English and arith- 15 metic.

GEORGE: Warden Duffy has quite a program. I hear he's a good man?

JOEY: Simón, he's a good man. We've learned our lesson . . . Well, anyway, I've learned my lesson, boy. No more 20 pachuquismo for me. Too many people depending on us to help out. The raza here in Los. The whole southwest. Mexico, South America! Like you and Grandma say, this is the people's world. If you get us out of here, I figure the only thing I could do is become a union organizer. Or go 25 into major league baseball.

GEORGE: Baseball?

JOEY: Simón, ese. You're looking at the first Mexican Babe Ruth. Or maybe, "Babe Root." Root! You get it?

TOMMY: How about "Baby Zoot"? 30

JOEY: Solid, Jackson.

GEORGE: Babe Zooter!

JOEY: Solid tudee, that's all reet, ese.

GEORGE: What about you, Henry? What have you been doing? 35

HENRY: Time, George, I've been doing time.

TOMMY: Ain't it the truth?

SMILEY: Yeah, George! When you going to spring us out of here, ese?

40 HENRY: How's the appeal coming?

GEORGE: (*Getting serious.*) Not bad. There's been a development I have to talk to you about. But other than that . . .

HENRY: Other than what?

SMILEY: (*Pause.*) Bad news?

45 GEORGE: (*Hedging.*) It all depends on how you look at it, Smiley. It really doesn't change anything. Work on the brief is going on practically day and night. The thing is, even with several lawyers on the case now, it'll still be several months before we file. I want to be honest about that.

50 HENRY: (*Suspiciously.*) Is that the bad news?

GEORGE: Not exactly. Sit down, boys. (*Pause.* HE *laughs to himself.*) I really don't mean to make such a big deal out of this thing. Fact is I'm still not quite used to the idea myself. (*Pause.*) You see . . . I've been drafted.

55 JOEY: Drafted?

TOMMY: Into the Army?

SMILEY: You?

GEORGE: That's right. I'm off to war.

JOEY: But . . . you're old, Cheer.

60 HENRY: (*A bitter edge.*) Why you, George? Why did they pick on you?

GEORGE: Well, Henry, I wouldn't say they "picked" on me. There's lots of men my age overseas. After all, it is war time and . . .

65 HENRY: And you're handling our appeal.

GEORGE: (*Pause.*) We have other lawyers.

HENRY: But you're the one who knows the case!

GEORGE: (*Pause.*) I knew you were going to take this hard. Believe me, Henry, my being drafted has nothing to do

70 with your case. It's just a coincidence.

HENRY: Like our being in here for life is a coincidence?

GEORGE: No, that's another . . .

HENRY: Like our being hounded every goddam day of our life is a coincidence?

75 GEORGE: Henry . . . (HENRY *turns away furiously. There is a pause.*) It's useless anger, son, believe me. Actually, I'm quite flattered by your concern, but I'm hardly indispensable.

HENRY: (*Deeply disturbed.*) What the hell are you talking

80 about, George?

GEORGE: I'm talking about all the people trying to get you out. Hundreds, perhaps thousands. Alice and I aren't the only ones. We've got a heck of a fine team of lawyers working on the brief. With or without me, the appeal will

85 be won. I promise you that.

HENRY: It's no use, George.

GEORGE: I realize all that sounds pretty unconvincing under the circumstances, but it's true.

HENRY: Those bastard cops are never going to let us out of

90 here. We're here for life and that's it.

GEORGE: You really believe that?

HENRY: What do you expect me to believe?

GEORGE: I wish I could answer that, son, but that's really for you to say.

95 GUARD: Time, Counselor.

GEORGE: Coming. (*Turns to the other* BOYS.) Listen, boys, I don't know where in the world I'll be the day your appeal is won—and it will be won—whether it's in the Pacific

somewhere or in Europe or in a hole in the ground . . . Take care of yourselves.   100

TOMMY: See you around, George.

SMILEY: So long, George.

JOEY: 'Bye, Cheer.

GEORGE: Yeah. See you around. (*Pause.*) Goodbye, Henry. Good luck and God bless you.   105

HENRY: God bless you, too, George. Take care of yourself.

TOMMY: Say, George, when you come back from the war, we're going to take you outa town and blast some weed.

JOEY: We'll get you a pair of buns you can hold in your hands!

GEORGE: I may just take you up on that. (*The* GUARD *escorts* 110 GEORGE *out, then turns back to the* BOYS.)

GUARD: All right, new work assignments. Everybody report to the jute mill. Let's go. (SMILEY, JOEY *and* TOMMY *start to exit.* HENRY *hangs back.*) What's the matter with you, Reyna? You got lead in your pants? I said let's go.   115

HENRY: We're supposed to work in the mess hall.

GUARD: You got a new assignment.

HENRY: Since when?

GUARD: Since right now. Get going!

HENRY: (*Hanging back.*) The warden know about this?   120

GUARD: What the hell do you care? You think you're something special? Come on, greaseball. Move!

HENRY: Make me, you bastard!

GUARD: Oh, yeah. (*The* GUARD *pushes* HENRY. HENRY *pushes back. The batos react, as the* GUARD *traps* HENRY *with his club* 125 *around the chest. The* BOYS *move to* HENRY's *defense.*) Back!

HENRY: (*To the batos.*) Back off! BACK OFF! Don't be stupid.

GUARD: Okay, Reyna, you got solitary! Bastard, huh? Into the hole! (HE *pushes* HENRY *onto center stage. Lights down. A single spot.*) Line, greaseballs. Move out! (*As they march.*) 130 Quickly, quickly. You're too slow. Move, move, move. (*The* BOYS *exit with the* GUARD.)

5. SOLITARY

A lone saxophone sets the mood.

PACHUCO: Too bad, ese. He set you up again.

HENRY: (*Long pause.* HE *looks around.*) Solitary, ese . . . they gave me solitary. (HE *sits down on the floor, a forlorn figure.*)

PACHUCO: Better get used to it, carnal. That's what this stretch is going to be about, see? You're in here for life, bato.   5

HENRY: I can't accept it, ese.

PACHUCO:
You've go to, Hank . . .
only this reality is real now,
only this place is real,   10
sitting in the lonely cell of your will . . .

HENRY: I can't see my hands.

PACHUCO:
Then tell your eyes to forget the light, ese
Only the hard floor is there, carnal
Only the cold hard edge of this reality   15
and there is no time . . .
Each second is a raw drop of blood from your brain
that you must swallow
drop by drop
and don't even start counting   20
or you'll lose your mind . . .

HENRY: I've got to know why I'm here, ese! I've got to have a reason for being here.

25 PACHUCO: You're here, Hank, because you chose to be—because you protected your brother and your family. And nobody knows the worth of that effort better than you, ese.

HENRY: I miss them, ese . . . my jefitos, my carnalillo, my sis . . . I miss Della.

30 PACHUCO: (*A spot illuminates* HENRY's *family standing upstage;* EL PACHUCO *snaps it off.*)
Forget them!
Forget them all.
Forget your family and the barrio
35 beyond the wall.

HENRY: There's still a chance I'll get out.

PACHUCO: Fat chance.

HENRY: I'm talking about the appeal!

PACHUCO: And I'm talking about what's real! ¿Qué traes,
40 Hank? Haven't you learned yet?

HENRY: Learned what?

PACHUCO:
Not to expect justice when it isn't there.
No court in the land's going to set you free.
45 Learn to protect your loves by binding them
in hate, ese! Stop hanging on to false hopes.
The moment those hopes come crashing down,
you'll find yourself on the ground foaming at
the mouth. ¡Como loco!

50 HENRY: (*Turning on him furiously.*) ¿Sabes qué? Don't tell me any more. I don't need you to tell me what to do. Fuck off! FUCK OFF! (HENRY *turns away from* EL PACHUCO. *Long pause. An anxious, intense moment.* EL PACHUCO *shifts gears and breaks the tension with a satirical twist.* HE *throws his*
55 *arms out and laughs.*)

PACHUCO:
¡Órale pues!
Don't take the pinche play so seriously, Jesús!
Es puro vacilón!
60 Watcha.

(HE *snaps his fingers. Lights change. We hear the sounds of the city.*)

This is Los, carnal.
You want to see some justice for pachucos?
Check out what's happening back home today.
The Navy has landed, ese—
65 on leave with full pay
and war's breaking out in the streets of L.A.!

6. ZOOT SUIT RIOTS

We hear music: the bugle call from "Bugle Call Rag." Suddenly the stage is awash in colored lights. The city of Los Angeles appears in the background in a panoramic vista of lights tapering into the night horizon. SAILORS *and* GIRLS *jitterbug on the dance floor. It is the Avalon Ballroom. The music is hot, the dancing hotter.* EL PACHUCO *and* HENRY *stand to the side.*

The scene is in dance and mostly pantomime. Occasionally words are heard over the music which is quite loud. On the floor are two SAILORS (SWABBIE *is one.*) *and a* MARINE *dancing with the* GIRLS. *A* SHORE PATROLMAN *speaks to the* CIGARETTE GIRL. *A* PIMP *comes on and watches the action.* LITTLE BLUE *and* ZOOTER *are also*

on the floor. RUDY *enters wearing* HENRY's *zoot suit with* BERTHA *and* LUPE. LUPE *takes their picture, then all three move up center to the rear of the ballroom.* CHOLO *comes in down center, sees them and moves up stage. All four make an entrance onto the dance floor.*

The MARINE *takes his girl aside after paying her.* SHE *passes the money to the* PIMP. *The* SAILORS *try to pick up on* LUPE *and* BERTHA, *and* CHOLO *pushes one back. The* SAILORS *complain to the* SHORE PATROL, *who throws* CHOLO *out the door down center. There is an argument that* RUDY *joins. The* SAILORS *go back to* BERTHA *and* LUPE *who resist.* CHOLO *and* RUDY *go to their defense and a fight develops.* ZOOTER *and* LITTLE BLUE *split.* CHOLO *takes the* GIRLS *out and* RUDY *pulls a knife. He is facing the three* SAILORS *and the* MARINE, *when* THE PACHUCO *freezes the action.*

PACHUCO: (*Forcefully.*) Órale, that's enough! (EL PACHUCO *takes* RUDY's *knife and with a tap sends him off-stage.* RUDY *exits with the* GIRLS. EL PACHUCO *is now facing the angry* SERVICEMEN. *He snaps his fingers. The* PRESS *enters quickly to the beeping sound of a radio broadcast.*) 5

PRESS: Good evening, Mr. and Mrs. North and South America and all the ships at sea. Let's go to press. FLASH. Los Angeles, California, June 3, 1943. Serious rioting broke out here today as flying squadrons of Marines and soldiers joined the Navy in a new assault on zooter-infested dis- 10 tricts. A fleet of twenty taxicabs carrying some two hundred servicemen pulled out of the Naval Armory in Chavez Ravine tonight and assembled a task force that invaded the eastside barrio. (*Unfreeze. The following speeches happen simultaneously.*) 15

MATE: You got any balls in them funny pants, boy?

SAILOR: He thinks he's tough . . .

SWABBIE: How about it, lardhead? You a tough guy or just a draft dodger?

PRESS: The Zoot Suiters, those gamin' dandies . . . 20

PACHUCO: (*Cutting them off.*) Why don't you tell them what I really am, ese, or how you've been forbidden to use the very word . . .

PRESS: We are complying in the interest of the war.

PACHUCO: How have you complied? 25

PRESS: We're using other terms.

PACHUCO: Like "pachuco" and "zoot suiter"?

PRESS: What's wrong with that? The Zoot Suit Crime Wave is even beginning to push the war news off the front page.

PACHUCO: 30
The Press distorted the very meaning of the word "zoot suit."
All it is for you guys is another way to say Mexican.
But the ideal of the original chuco
was to look like a diamond 35
to look sharp
hip
bonaroo
finding a style of urban survival
in the rural skirts and outskirts 40
of the brown metropolis of Los, cabrón.

PRESS: It's an affront to good taste.

PACHUCO: Like the Mexicans, Filipinos and blacks who wear them.

PRESS: Yes! 45

PACHUCO: Even the white kids and the Wops and the Jews are putting on the drape shape.

PRESS: You are trying to outdo the white man in exaggerated white man's clothes!

PACHUCO:
50   Because everybody knows
        that Mexicans, Filipinos and Blacks
        belong to the huarache
        the straw hat and the dirty overall.

PRESS: You savages weren't even wearing clothes when the
55   white man pulled you out of the jungle.

MARINE: My parents are going without collars and cuffs so you can wear that shit.

PRESS: That's going too far, too goddamned far and it's got to be stopped!

60 PACHUCO: Why?

PRESS: Don't you know there's a war on? Don't you fucking well know you can't get away with that shit? What are we fighting for if not to annihilate the enemies of the American way of life?

65 MATE: Let's tear it off his back!

SAILORS/MARINE: Let's strip him! Get him! (Etc.)

PRESS: KILL THE PACHUCO BASTARD!! (*Music: "American Patrol" by Glenn Miller. The* PRESS *gets a searchlight from upstage center while the* FOUR SERVICEMEN *stalk* EL PACHUCO.)

70 SAILOR: Heh, zooter. Come on, zooter!

SWABBIE: You think you're more important than the war, zooter?

MATE: Let's see if you got any balls in them funny pants, boy.

SWABBIE: Watch out for the knife.

75 SAILOR: That's a real chango monkey suit he's got on.

MATE: I bet he's half monkey—just like the Filipinos and Niggers that wear them.

SWABBIE: You trying to outdo the white man in them glad rags, Mex? (*They fight now to the finish.* EL PACHUCO *is over-*
80   *powered and stripped as* HENRY *watches helplessly from his position. The* PRESS *and* SERVICEMEN *exit with pieces of* EL PACHUCO's *zoot suit.* EL PACHUCO *stands. The only item of clothing on his body is a small loincloth.* HE *turns and looks at* HENRY, *with mystic intensity.* HE *opens his arms as an Aztec*
85   *conch blows, and* HE *slowly exits backward with powerful calm into the shadows. Silence.* HENRY *comes downstage.* HE *absorbs the impact of what* HE *has seen and falls to his knees at center stage, spent and exhausted. Lights down.*)

7. ALICE

The GUARD *and* ALICE *enter from opposite sides of the stage. The* GUARD *carries a handful of letters and is reading one of them.*

GUARD: July 2, 1943.

ALICE:
        Dear Henry,
        I hope this letter finds you in good health and good spirits—but I have to assume you've heard about the riots in Los Angeles. It was a nightmare, and it lasted for a week.
5   The city is still in a state of shock.

GUARD: (*Folds letter back into envelope, then opens another.*) August 5, 1943.

ALICE:
        Dear Henry,
10   The riots here in L.A. have touched off race riots all over the country—Chicago, Detroit, even little Beau-

mont, Texas, for Christ's sake. But the one in Harlem was the worst. Millions of dollars worth of property damage. 500 people were hospitalized, and five Negroes were killed.   15

GUARD: Things are rough all over.

ALICE: Please write to me and tell me how you feel.

GUARD: (*The* GUARD *folds up the second letter, stuffs it back into its envelope and opens a third.*) August 20, 1943.

ALICE: 20
        Dear Henry,
        Although I am disappointed not to have heard from you, I thought I would send you some good news for a change. Did you know we had a gala fund-raiser at the Mocambo?

GUARD: The Mocambo . . . Hotcha!   25

ALICE:
        . . . and Rita Hayworth lent your sister Lupe a ball gown for the occasion. She got dressed at Cecil B. DeMille's house, and she looked terrific. Her escort was Anthony Quinn, and Orson Welles said . . .

GUARD: Orson Welles! Well! Sounds like Louella Parsons. (HE   30
folds up the letter.) September 1, 1943.

ALICE: Henry, why aren't you answering my letters?

GUARD: He's busy. (HE *continues to stuff the envelope.*)

ALICE: Henry, if there's something I've said or done . . . ? (*The* GUARD *shuffles the envelopes.*) Henry . . . (*Lights change.*   35
GUARD *crosses to center stage, where* HENRY *is still doubled up on the floor.*)

GUARD: Welcome back to the living, Reyna. It's been a long hot summer. Here's your mail. (*The* GUARD *tosses the letters to the floor directly in front of* HENRY's *head.* HENRY *looks up*   40
slowly and grabs one of the letters. HE *opens it, trying to focus. The* GUARD *exits.*)

ALICE: Henry, I just found out you did ninety days in solitary. I'm furious at the rest of the guys for keeping it from me. I talked to Warden Duffy, and he said you struck a guard.   45
Did something happen I should know about? I wouldn't ask if it wasn't so important, but a clean record . . . (HENRY *rips up the letter he has been reading and scatters the others. Alarmed.*) Henry? (HENRY *pauses, his instant fury spent and under control.* HE *sounds almost weary, but the anger is still*   50
there.)

HENRY: You still don't understand, Alice.

ALICE: (*Softly, compassionate.*) But I do! I'm not accusing you of anything. I don't care what happened or why they sent you there. I'm sure you had your reasons. But you know   55
the public is watching you.

HENRY: (*Frustrated, a deep question.*) Why do you do this, Alice?

ALICE: What?

HENRY: The appeal, the case, all the shit you do. You think the public gives a goddamn?   60

ALICE: (*With conviction.*) Yes! We are going to get you out of here, Henry Reyna. We are going to win!

HENRY: (*Probing.*) What if we lose?

ALICE: (*Surprised but moving on.*) We're not going to lose.

HENRY: (*Forcefully, insistent, meaning more than* HE *is saying.*)   65
What if we do? What if we get another crooked judge, and he nixes the appeal?

ALICE: Then we'll appeal again. We'll take it to the Supreme Court. (*A forced laugh.*) Hell, we'll take it all the way to President Roosevelt!   70

HENRY: (*Backing her up—emotionally.*) What if we still lose?

ALICE: (*Bracing herself against his aggression.*) We can't.

HENRY: Why can't we?

75 ALICE: (*Giving a political response in spite of herself.*) Because we've got too much support. You should see the kinds of people responding to us. Unions, Mexicans, Negroes, Oakies. It's fantastic.

HENRY: (*Driving harder.*) Why can't we lose, Alice?

ALICE: I'm telling you.

80 HENRY: No, you're not.

ALICE: (*Starting to feel vulnerable.*) I don't know what to tell you.

HENRY: Yes, you do!

ALICE: (*Frightened.*) Henry . . . ?

85 HENRY: Tell me why we can't lose, Alice!

ALICE: (*Forced to fight back, with characteristic passion.*) Stop it, Henry! Please stop it! I won't have you treat me this way. I never have been able to accept one person pushing another around . . . pushing me around! Can't you see that's

90 why I'm here? Because I can't stand it happening to you. Because I'm a Jew, goddammit! I have been there . . . I have been there! If you lose, I lose. (*Pause. The emotional tension is immense.* ALICE *fights to hold back tears.* SHE *turns away.*)

95 HENRY: I'm sorry . . .

ALICE: (*Pause.*) It's stupid for us to fight like this. I look forward to coming here for weeks. Just to talk to you, to be with you, to see your eyes.

HENRY: (*Pause.*) I thought a lot about you when I was in the

100 hole. Sometimes . . . sometimes I'd even see you walk in, in the dark, and talk to me. Just like you are right now. Same look, same smile, same perfume . . . (HE *pauses.*) Only the other one never gave me so much lip. She just listened. She did say one thing. She said . . .

105 ALICE: (*Trying to make light of it. Then more gently.*) I can't say that to you, Henry. Not the way you want it.

HENRY: Why not?

ALICE: (SHE *means it.*) Because I can't allow myself to be used to fill in for all the love you've always felt and always re-

110 ceived from all your women.

HENRY: (*With no self-pity.*) Give it a chance, Alice.

ALICE: (*Beside herself.*) Give it a chance? You crazy idiot. If I thought making love to you would solve all your problems, I'd do it in a second. Don't you know that? But it

115 won't. It'll only complicate things. I'm trying to help you, goddammit. And to do that, I have to be your friend, not your white woman.

HENRY: (*Getting angry.*) What makes you think I want to go to bed with you. Because you're white? I've had more

120 white pieces of ass than you can count, ¿sabes? Who do you think you are? God's gift to us brown animals.

ALICE: (ALICE *slaps him and stops, horrified. A whirlpool of emotions.*) Oh, Hank. All the love and hate it's taken to get us together in this lousy prison room. Do you realize only

125 Hitler and the Second World War could have accomplished that? I don't know whether to laugh or cry. (ALICE *folds into her emotional spin, her body shaking. Suddenly she turns, whipping herself out of it with a cry, both laughing and weeping. They come to each other and embrace. Then they kiss—*

130 *passionately. The* GUARD *enters.* HE *frowns.*)

GUARD: Time, Miss.

ALICE: (*Turning.*) Already? Oh, my God, Henry, there's so many messages I was going to give you. Your mother and father send their love, of course. And Lupe and . . . Della.

135 And . . . oh, yes. They want you to know Rudy's in the Marines.

HENRY: The Marines?

ALICE: I'll write you all about it. Will you write me?

HENRY: (*A glance at the* GUARD.) Yes.

140 GUARD: (*His tone getting harsher.*) Let's go, lady.

HENRY: Goodbye, Licha.

ALICE: I'll see you on the outside . . . Hank. (ALICE *gives* HENRY *a thumb up gesture, and the* GUARD *escorts her out.* HENRY *turns downstage, full of thoughts.* HE *addresses* EL PACHUCO,

145 *who is nowhere to be seen.*)

HENRY: You were wrong, ese . . . There's something to hope for. I know now we're going to win the appeal. Do you hear me, ese? Ese! (*Pause.*) Are you even there any more? (*The* GUARD *re-enters at a clip.*)

150 GUARD: Okay, Reyna, come on.

HENRY: Where to?

GUARD: We're letting you go . . . (HENRY *looks at him incredulously. The* GUARD *smiles.*) . . . to Folsom Prison with all the rest of the hardcore cons. You really didn't expect to walk

155 out of here a free man, did you? Listen, kid, your appeal stands about as much chance as the Japs and Krauts of winning the war. Personally, I don't see what that broad sees in you. I wouldn't give you the sweat off my balls. Come on! (HENRY *and the* GUARD *turn upstage to leave.*

160 *Lights change.* EL PACHUCO *appears halfway up the backdrop, fully dressed again and clearly visible.* HENRY *stops with a jolt as* HE *sees him.* EL PACHUCO *lifts his arms. Lights go down as we hear the high sound of a bomb falling to earth.*)

8. THE WINNING OF THE WAR

The aerial bomb explodes with a reverberating sound and a white flash that illuminates the form of pachuco images in the black backdrop. Other bombs fall and all hell breaks loose. Red flashes, artillery, gunfire, ack-ack. HENRY *and the* GUARD *exit. The* FOUR SERVICEMEN *enter as an honor guard. Music: Glen Miller's "Saint Louis Blues March." As the* SERVICEMEN *march on we see* RUDY *down left in his marine uniform, belt undone.* ENRIQUE, DOLORES *and* LUPE *join him.* DOLORES *has his hat,* LUPE *her camera.* ENRIQUE *fastens two buttons on the uniform as* RUDY *does up his belt.* DOLORES *inspects his collar and gives him his hat.* RUDY *puts on his hat and all pose for* LUPE. *She snaps the picture and* RUDY *kisses them all and is off.* HE *picks up the giant switchblade from behind a newspaper bundle and joins the* SERVICEMEN *as they march down in drill formation. The family marches off, looking back sadly. The drill ends and* RUDY *and the* SHORE PATROL *move to one side. As* RUDY's *interrogation goes on,* PEOPLE *in the barrio come on with newspapers to mime daily tasks. The* PRESS *enters.*

PRESS: The Los Angeles Examiner, July 1, 1943. Headline: WORLD WAR II REACHES TURNING POINT. If the late summer of 1942 was the low point, a year later the war for the Allies is pounding its way to certain victory.

SHORE PATROL: July 10!   5

RUDY: U.S., British and Canadian troops invade Sicily, Sir!

SHORE PATROL: August 6!

RUDY: U.S. troops occupy Solomon Island, Sir!

SHORE PATROL: September 5!

10 RUDY: MacArthur's forces land on New Guinea, Sir!

SHORE PATROL: October 1!

RUDY: U.S. Fifth Army enters Naples, Sir!

PRESS: On and on it goes. From Corsica to Kiev, from Tarawa to Anzio. The relentless advance of the Allied armies can-

15 not be checked. (*One by one,* HENRY's *family and friends enter, carrying newspapers. They tear the papers into small pieces.*) The Los Angeles Times, June 6, 1944. Headline: Allied forces under General Eisenhower land in Normandy.

SHORE PATROL: August 19!

20 RUDY: American First Army reaches Germany, Sir!

SHORE PATROL: October 17!

RUDY: MacArthur returns to the Philippines, Sir!

PRESS: On the homefront, Americans go on with their daily lives with growing confidence and relief, as the war

25 pushes on toward inevitable triumph. (*Pause.*) The Los Angeles Daily News, Wednesday, November 8, 1944. Headline: District Court of Appeals decides in Sleepy Lagoon murder case . . . boys in pachuco murder given . . .

PEOPLE: FREEDOM!!! (*Music bursts forth as the joyous crowd tosses*

30 *the shredded newspaper into the air like confetti. The* BOYS *enter upstage center, and the crowd rushes to them, weeping and cheering. There are kisses and hugs and tears of joy.* HENRY *is swept forward by the triumphal procession.*)

9. RETURN TO THE BARRIO

The music builds and people start dancing. Others just embrace. The tune is "Soldado Razo" played to a lively corrido beat. It ends with joyous applause, laughter and tears.

RUDY: ¡Ese carnal!

HENRY: Rudy!!

DOLORES: ¡Bendito sea Dios! Who would believe this day would ever come? Look at you—you're all home!

5 LUPE: I still can't believe it. We won! We won the appeal! (*Cheers.*)

ENRIQUE: I haven't felt like this since Villa took Zacatecas. (*Laughter, cheers.*) ¡Pero mira! Look who's here. Mis hijos. (*Puts his arm around* HENRY *and* RUDY.) It isn't every day a

10 man has two grown sons come home from so far away— one from the war, the other from . . . bueno, who cares? The Sleepy Lagoon is history, hombre. For a change, los Mexicanos have won! (*Cheers.*)

GEORGE: Well, Henry. I don't want to say I told you so, but

15 we sure taught Judge Charles a lesson in misconduct, didn't we? (*More cheers.*) Do you realize this is the greatest victory the Mexican-American community has ever had in the history of this whole blasted country?

DOLORES: Yes, but if it wasn't for the unselfish thoughtfulness

20 of people like you and this beautiful lady—and all the people who helped out, Mexicanos, Negros, all Americanos—our boys would not be home today.

GEORGE: I only hope you boys realize how important you are now.

25 JOEY: Pos, I realize it, ese. (*Laughter.*)

RUDY: I came all the way from Hawaii just to get here, carnal. I only got a few days, but I'm going to get you drunk.

HENRY: Pos, we'll see who gets who drunk, ese. (*Laughter and hoots.* HENRY *spots* EL PACHUCO *entering from stage right.*)

DOLORES: Jorge, Licha, todos. Let's go into the house, eh? I've 30
made a big pot of menudo, and it's for everybody.

ENRIQUE: There's ice-cold beer too. Vénganse, vamos todos.

GEORGE: (*To* ALICE.) Alice . . . Menudo, that's Mexican chicken soup? (*Everybody exits, leaving* HENRY *behind with* EL PACHUCO.) 35

HENRY: It's good to see you again, ese. I thought I'd lost you.

PACHUCO: H'm pues, it'd take more than the U.S. Navy to wipe me out.

HENRY: Where you been?

PACHUCO: Pos, here in the barrio. Welcome back. 40

HENRY: It's good to be home.

PACHUCO: No hard feelings?

HENRY: Chale—we won, didn't we?

PACHUCO: Simón.

HENRY: Me and the batos have been in a lot of fights to- 45
gether, ese. But we won this one, because we learned to fight in a new way.

PACHUCO: And that's the perfect way to end of this play— happy ending y todo. (PACHUCO *makes a sweeping gesture. Lights come down.* HE *looks up at the lights, realizing some-* 50
thing is wrong. HE *flicks his wrist, and the lights go back up again.*)
But life ain't that way, Hank.
The barrio's still out there, waiting and wanting.
The cops are still tracking us down like dogs. 55
The gangs are still killing each other,
Families are barely surviving,
And there in your own backyard . . . life goes on.

(*Soft music.* DELLA *enters.*)

DELLA: Hank? (HENRY *goes to her and they embrace.*)

HENRY: Where were you? Why didn't you come to the Hall 60
of Justice to see us get out?

DELLA: I guess I was a little afraid things had changed. So much has happened to both of us.

PACHUCO: Simón. She's living in your house.

DELLA: After I got back from Ventura, my parents gave me a 65
choice. Forget about you or get out.

HENRY: Why didn't you write to me?

DELLA: You had your own problems. Your jefitos took care of me. Hey, you know what, Hank, I think they expect us to get married. 70

PACHUCO: How about it, ese? You still going to give her that big pachuco wedding you promised?

HENRY: I have to think about it.

ALICE: (*Off-stage.*) Henry?

PACHUCO: (*Snaps fingers.*) Wish you had the time. But here 75
comes Licha.

ALICE: (*Entering.*) Henry, I've just come to say good night. (DELLA *freezes and* HENRY *turns to* ALICE.)

HENRY: Good night? Why are you leaving so soon?

ALICE: Soon? I've been here all afternoon. There'll be other 80
times, Henry. You're home now, with your family, that's what matters.

HENRY: Don't patronize me, Alice.

ALICE: (*Surprised.*) Patronize you?

HENRY: Yeah. I learned a few words in the joint. 85

ALICE: Yo también, Hank. Te quiero. (PACHUCO *snaps.* ALICE *freezes, and* RUDY *enters.*)

RUDY: Ese, carnal, congratulations, the jefita just told me about you and Della. That's great, ese. But if you want me to be best man, you better do it in the next three days.

HENRY: Wait a minute, Rudy, don't push me.

RUDY: Qué pues, getting cold feet already? (HENRY *is beginning to be surrounded by separate conversations.*)

DELLA: If you don't want me here, I can move out.

RUDY: Watcha. I'll let you and Della have our room tonight, bato. I'll sleep on the couch.

ALICE: You aren't expecting me to sleep here, are you?

HENRY: I'm not asking you to.

PACHUCO/ALICE/RUDY/DELLA: Why not?

RUDY: The jefitos will never know, ese.

ALICE: Be honest, Henry.

DELLA: What do you want me to do?

HENRY: Give me a chance to think about it. Give me a second!

PACHUCO: One second! (PACHUCO *snaps.* ENRIQUE *enters.*)

ENRIQUE: Bueno, bueno, pues, what are you doing out here, hijo? Aren't you coming in for menudo?

HENRY: I'm just thinking, jefito.

ENRIQUE: ¿De qué, hombre? Didn't you do enough of that in prison? Andale, this is your house. Come in and live again.

HENRY: 'Apá, did you tell Della I was going to marry her?

ENRIQUE: Yes, but only after you did.

RUDY: ¿Qué traes, carnal? Don't you care about Della anymore?

ALICE: If it was just me and you, Henry, it might be different. But you have to think of your family.

HENRY: I don't need you to tell me my responsibilities.

ALICE: I'm sorry.

RUDY: Sorry, carnal.

DELLA: I don't need anybody to feel sorry for me. I did what I did because I wanted to. All I want to know is what's going to happen now. If you still want me, órale, suave. If you don't, that's okay, too. But I'm not going to hang around like a pendeja all my life.

RUDY: Your huisa's looking finer than ever, carnal.

ALICE: You're acting as if nothing has happened.

ENRIQUE: You have your whole life ahead of you.

ALICE: You belong here, Henry. I'm the one that's out of place.

RUDY: If you don't pick up on her, I'm going to have to step in.

HENRY: That's bullshit. What about what we shared in prison? I've never been that close to anybody.

ALICE: That was in prison.

HENRY: What the hell do you think the barrio is?

RUDY: It's not bullshit!

HENRY: Shut up, carnalillo!

RUDY: Carnalillo? How can you still call me that? I'm not your pinche little brother no more.

GEORGE: (*Entering.*) You guys have got to stop fighting, Henry, or the barrio will never change. Don't you realize you men represent the hope of your people?

ALICE: Della was in prison too. You know you had thousands of people clamoring for your release, but you were Della's only hope.

HENRY: Look, esa, I know you did a year in Ventura. I know you stood up for me when it counted. I wish I could make it up to you.

DELLA: Don't give me your bullshit, Henry. Give it to Alice.

ALICE: I think it's time for Alice Bloomfield to go home.

HENRY: Don't be jealous, esa.

DELLA: Jealous? Mira, cabrón, I know I'm not the only one you ever took to the Sleepy Lagoon.

RUDY: The Sleepy Lagoon ain't shit. I saw real lagoons in those islands, ese—killing Japs! I saw some pachucos go out there that are never coming back.

DELLA: But I was always there when you came back, wasn't I?

DOLORES: (*Entering.*) Henry? Come back inside, hijo. Everybody's waiting for you.

RUDY: Why didn't you tell them I was there, carnal? I was at the Sleepy Lagoon. Throwing chingazos with everybody!

HENRY: Don't you understand, Rudy? I was trying to keep you from getting a record. Those bastard cops are never going to leave us alone.

GEORGE: You've got to forget what happened, Henry.

HENRY: What can I give you, Della? I'm an ex-con.

DELLA: So am I!

SMILEY: (*Entering.*) Let's face it, Hank. There's no future for us in this town. I'm taking my wife and kid and moving to Arizona.

DOLORES: (*Simultaneously.*) I know what you are feeling, hijo, it's home again. I know inside you are afraid that nothing has changed. That the police will never leave you in peace. Pero no le hace. Everything is going to be fine now. Marry Della and fill this house with children. Just do one thing for me—forget the zoot suit clothes.

ENRIQUE: If there's one thing that will keep a man off the streets is his own familia.

GEORGE: Don't let this thing eat your heart out for the rest of your . . .

ALICE: Sometimes the best thing you can do for someone you love is walk away.

DELLA: What do you want, Hank?

RUDY: It cost me more than it did you.

SMILEY: We started the 38th and I'll never forget you, carnal. But I got to think about my family.

HENRY: Wait a minute! I don't know if I'll be back in prison tomorrow or not! I have nothing to give you, Della. Not even a piece of myself.

DELLA: I have my life to live, too, Hank. I love you. I would even die for you. Pero me chingan la madre if I'm going to throw away my life for nothing.

HENRY: But I love you . . . (*Both* GIRLS *turn.* HENRY *looks at* ALICE, *then to the whole group upstage of him. Still turning,* HE *looks at* DELLA *and goes to embrace her. The freeze ends and other people enter.*)

LUPE: ¡Órale, Hank! Watcha Joey. The crazy bato went all the way to his house and put on his drapes.

JOEY: ¡Esos, batooooooosss! ¡Esas, huisaaaaaass!

TOMMY: Look at this cat! He looks all reet.

LUPE: Yeah, like a parakeet!

HENRY: ¿Y tú, ese? How come you put on your tacuche? Where's the party?

JOEY: Pos, ain't the party here?

RUDY: Yeah, ese, but this ain't the Avalon Ballroom. The zoot suit died under fire here in Los. Don't you know that, cabrón?

210 ENRIQUE: Rudolfo!
LUPE: And he was supposed to get Henry drunk.
RUDY: Shut up, esa!
ENRIQUE: ¡Ya pues! Didn't you have any menudo? Vieja, fix
him a great big bowl of menudo and put plenty of chile
215 in it. We're going to sweat it out of him.
RUDY: I don't need no pinche menudo.
HENRY: Watch your language, carnal.
RUDY: And I don't need you! I'm a man. I can take care of
myself!
220 JOEY: Muy marine el bato . . .
ENRIQUE: Rudy, hijo. Are you going to walk into the kitchen
or do I have to drag you.
RUDY: Whatever you say, jefito.
GEORGE: Well, Alice. This looks like the place where we came
225 in. I think it's about time we left.
ALICE: Say the word, George, just say the word.
DOLORES: No, no. You can't leave so soon.
JOEY: Chale, chale, chale. You can't take our Grandma. ¿Qué
se trae, carnal? Póngase más abusado, ese. No se haga tan
230 square.
GEORGE: Okay, square I got. What was the rest of it?
JOEY: Pos, le estoy hablando en chicas patas, ese. Es puro chi-
cano.
RUDY: ¿Qué chicano? Ni que madre, cabrón. Why don't you
235 grow up?
JOEY: Grow up, ese?
RUDY: Try walking downtown looking like that. See if the
sailors don't skin your ass alive.
JOEY: So what? It's no skin off your ass. Come on, Bertha.
240 RUDY: She's staying with me.
JOEY: She's mine.
RUDY: Prove it, punk. (RUDY attacks JOEY and they fight. The
BATOS and RUCAS take out JOEY. HENRY pacifies RUDY,
who bursts out crying. ENRIQUE, DELLA, DOLORES, ALICE,
245 LUPE and GEORGE are the only ones left. RUDY in a flush of
emotion.) Cabrones, se amontonaron. They ganged up
on me, carnal. You left me and they ganged up on me.
You shouldn't have done it, carnal. Why didn't you
take me with you. For the jefitos? The jefitos lost me
250 anyway.
HENRY: Come on in the house, Rudy . . .
RUDY: No! I joined the Marines. I didn't have to join, but I
went. ¿Sabes por qué? Because they got me, carnal. Me
chingaron, ese. (Sobs.) I went to the pinche show with
255 Bertha, all chingón in your tachuche, ese. I was wearing
your zoot suit, and they got me. Twenty sailors, Marines.
We were up in the balcony. They came down from behind. They grabbed me by the neck and dragged me
down the stairs, kicking and punching and pulling my
260 greña. They dragged me out into the streets . . . and all the
people watched while they stripped me. (Sobs.) They
stripped me, carnal. Bertha saw them strip me. Hijos de la
chingada, they stripped me. (HENRY goes to RUDY and em-

braces him with fierce love and desperation. Pause. TOMMY
comes running in.)
TOMMY: ¡Órale! There's cops outside. They're trying to arrest 265
Joey. (GEORGE crosses to TOMMY.)
GEORGE: (Bursting out.) Joey?
TOMMY: They got him up against your car. They're trying to
say he stole it!
GEORGE: Oh, God. I'll take care of this. 270
ALICE: I'll go with you. (GEORGE, TOMMY and ALICE exit.)
HENRY: Those fucking bastards! (HE starts to exit.)
DELLA: Henry, no!
HENRY: What the hell do you mean no? Don't you see what's
going on outside? 275
DELLA: They'll get you again! That's what they want.
HENRY: Get out of my way! (HE pushes her out of the way, to-
ward DOLORES.)
ENRIQUE: (Stands up before Henry.) ¡Hijo!
HENRY: Get out of my way, jefe! 280
ENRIQUE: You will stay here!
HENRY: Get out of my way! (ENRIQUE powerfully pushes him
back and throws HENRY to the floor and holds.)
ENRIQUE: ¡TE DIGO QUE NO! (Silent moment, HENRY stands
up and offers to strike ENRIQUE. But something stops him. The 285
realization that if HE strikes back or even if HE walks out the door,
the family bond is irreparably broken. HENRY tenses for a moment,
then relaxes and embraces his father. DELLA goes to them and joins
the embrace. Then DOLORES, then LUPE, then RUDY. All embrace
in a tight little group. PRESS enters right and comes down.) 290
PRESS: Henry Reyna went back to prison in 1947 for robbery and assault with a deadly weapon. While incarcer-
ated, he killed another inmate and he wasn't released until
1955, when he got into hard drugs. He died of the trauma
of his life in 1972. 295
PACHUCO: That's the way you see it, ese. But there's other way
to end this story.
RUDY: Henry Reyna went to Korea in 1950. He was shipped
across in a destroyer and defended the 38th Parallel until
he was killed at Inchon in 1952, being posthumously 300
awarded the Congressional Medal of Honor.
ALICE: Henry Reyna married Della in 1948 and they have
five kids, three of them now going to the University,
speaking caló and calling themselves Chicanos.
GEORGE: Henry Reyna, the born leader . . . 305
JUDGE: Henry Reyna, the social victim . . .
BERTHA: Henry Reyna, the street corner warrior . . .
SMILEY: Henry Reyna, el carnal de aquellas . . .
JOEY: Henry Reyna, the zoot suiter . . .
TOMMY: Henry Reyna, my friend . . . 310
LUPE: Henry Reyna, my brother . . .
ENRIQUE: Henry Reyna . . .
DOLORES: Our son . . .
DELLA: Henry Reyna, my love . . .
PACHUCO: Henry Reyna . . . El Pachuco . . . The man . . . the 315
myth . . . still lives. (Lights down and fade out.)

August Wilson

August Wilson (1945–2005) was born and raised on "The Hill," the black ghetto of Pittsburgh. He dropped out of school in the ninth grade, but supported himself with odd jobs while he continued his self-education, reading and studying; he also began to write poems and stories on the changing problems of race relations in America. He founded a theater in Pittsburgh in the mid-1960s, and then founded Black Horizons Theater Company there in 1968. His first play, *Jitney,* was staged in 1978. Wilson then applied to study playwriting at the Eugene O'Neill Theater Center's National Playwrights' Conference, where he submitted the text of *Ma Rainey's Black Bottom,* which was read by the eminent African American stage director Lloyd Richards, who had brought Lorraine Hansberry's *A Raisin in the Sun* to Broadway in 1959. Richards read the play and produced it at the Yale Repertory Theater in 1984 before bringing it to Broadway. *Ma Rainey's Black Bottom* is the first of several plays examining African American history in the twentieth century, many of them using jazz as a musical idiom; it was followed by *Fences* (1985)—which won the Pulitzer Prize—*Joe Turner's Come and Gone* (1986), *The Piano Lesson* (1987), *Two Trains Running* (1991), *Seven Guitars* (1995), and *King Hedley II* (1999).

FENCES

Set in 1957, the action of *Fences* sits on the brink of the civil rights movement and outlines the challenges facing African Americans whose legal freedoms had yet to become a social reality. The play is—as its final funeral scene implies—deeply reminiscent of Arthur Miller's *Death of a Salesman,* and suggests that realism is in many way still the dominant mode of American theater. Like Miller's play, it is about a hardworking man whose responsibilities to his family fall athwart his dreams of happiness, a conflict that finally costs him both. However, while Miller's Willy Loman is victimized by his belief in the "American Dream," Wilson's Troy Maxson lives his life on the underside of that dream. Thrown out of his home at fourteen by his father, Troy moved north to Pittsburgh; unable to find work, he made a living through petty crime until he was caught and sentenced to fifteen years' imprisonment. On his release, he found his wife and child and began a career in baseball, playing in the Negro Leagues. Integration came to baseball, and by 1957 Jackie Robinson, Hank Aaron, and a young Roberto Clemente are all playing in the major leagues—but it is too late for Troy. He is now working as a trash collector, fighting the company to let African Americans drive the garbage trucks as well as pick up the trash.

Like Willy Loman, Troy too is a family man. The family is Troy's refuge from the racism and defeat of his daily life, and his proudest accomplishment as well: he has forced himself to shoulder the responsibility of providing for his children and of loving his wife, a responsibility that lends his life purpose and direction. As he says to Rose in act 1, "Woman . . . I do the best I can do. . . . We go upstairs in that room at night . . . and I fall down on you and try to blast a hole into forever. I get up Monday morning . . . find my lunch on the table. I go out. Make my way. Find my strength to carry me through to the next Friday." However, as Rose notes, the world is changing around Troy, and these changes threaten the life that he has made. His son Cory is being recruited on a football scholarship. Troy, his own exploitation by the white-dominated sports industry still in mind, forces Cory to quit the team, and so to pass up the scholarship—and the chance to go to college. Nor does Troy shoulder the rest of his family life easily. He cares for his mentally handicapped brother Gabriel, but eventually has him committed to a mental hospital in order to get half of his government pension. Despite his love for and gratitude to Rose, he has an affair with another woman, who dies delivering their daughter. Although family life has been Troy's salvation, it also has hemmed him in—in the dead-end jobs, the constant poverty, the fence he

James Earl Jones reprises his role as Troy in this 1986 Goodman Theatre production of August Wilson's *Fences*.

builds at the end of the play. He risks it all for the chance of some happiness with Alberta and loses; Rose takes in Troy's daughter: "From right now . . . this child got a mother. But you a womanless man." He fights Cory, and much as his own father had thrown him out of the house, he forces his own son to leave as well.

The joyous, mournful conclusion of *Fences*—when Gabriel dances Troy's soul into heaven—perhaps provides the best commentary on the life of Troy Maxson. Suffering the indignities and humiliation of racism throughout his life, Troy built a stable home for himself, a life. As a defense against the world, perhaps, that life was bound to crumble, particularly as pressure of social change forced Troy to deal with a future he had never imagined. In Wilson's final image, however, Troy's life is celebrated, a thing of rough and rugged beauty, demanding our attention and respect.

FENCES

August Wilson

CHARACTERS

TROY MAXSON
IM BONO, *Troy's friend*
ROSE, *Troy's wife*
LYONS, *Troy's oldest son by previous marriage*
GABRIEL, *Troy's brother*
CORY, *Troy and Rose's son*
RAYNELL, *Troy's daughter*

> When the sins of our fathers visit us
> We do not have to play host.
> We can banish them with forgiveness
> As God, in His Largeness and Laws.
> —AUGUST WILSON

SETTING: *The setting is the yard which fronts the only entrance to the Maxson household, an ancient two-story brick house set back off a small alley in a big-city neighborhood. The entrance to the house is gained by two or three steps leading to a wooden porch badly in need of paint.*

A relatively recent addition to the house and running its full width, the porch lacks congruence. It is a sturdy porch with a flat roof. One or two chairs of dubious value sit at one end where the kitchen window opens onto the porch. An old-fashioned icebox stands silent guard at the opposite end.

The yard is a small dirt yard, partially fenced, except for the last scene, with a wooden sawhorse, a pile of lumber, and other fence-building equipment set off to the side. Opposite is a tree from which hangs a ball made of rags. A baseball bat leans against the tree. Two oil drums serve as garbage receptacles and sit near the house at right to complete the setting.

THE PLAY: *Near the turn of the century, the destitute of Europe sprang on the city with tenacious claws and an honest and solid dream. The city devoured them. They swelled its belly until it burst into a thousand furnaces and sewing machines, a thousand butcher shops and bakers' ovens, a thousand churches and hospitals and funeral parlors and moneylenders. The city grew. It nourished itself and offered each man a partnership limited only by his talent, his guile, and his willingness and capacity for hard work. For the immigrants of Europe, a dream dared and won true.*

The descendants of African slaves were offered no such welcome or participation. They came from places called the Carolinas and the Virginias, Georgia, Alabama, Mississippi, and Tennessee. They came strong, eager, searching. The city rejected them and they fled and settled along the riverbanks and under bridges in shallow, ramshackle houses made of sticks and tar-paper. They collected rags and wood. They sold the use of their muscles and their bodies. They cleaned houses and washed clothes, they shined shoes, and in quiet desperation and vengeful pride, they stole, and lived in pursuit of their own dream. That they could breathe free, finally, and stand to meet life with the force of dignity and whatever eloquence the heart could call upon.

By 1957, the hard-won victories of the European immigrants had solidified the industrial might of America. War had been confronted and won with new energies that used loyalty and patriotism as its fuel. Life was rich, full, and flourishing. The Milwaukee Braves won the World Series, and the hot winds of change that would make the sixties a turbulent, racing, dangerous, and provocative decade had not yet begun to blow full.

ACT ONE

SCENE I

It is 1957. TROY *and* BONO *enter the yard, engaged in conversation.* TROY *is fifty-three years old, a large man with thick, heavy hands; it is this largeness that he strives to fill out and make an accommodation with. Together with his blackness, his largeness informs his sensibilities and the choices he has made in his life.*

Of the two men, BONO *is obviously the follower. His commitment to their friendship of thirty-odd years is rooted in his admiration of* TROY's *honesty, capacity for hard work, and his strength, which* BONO *seeks to emulate.*

It is Friday night, payday, and the one night of the week the two men engage in a ritual of talk and drink. TROY *is usually the most talkative and at times he can be crude and almost vulgar, though he is capable of rising to profound heights of expression. The men carry lunch buckets and wear or carry burlap aprons and are dressed in clothes suitable to their jobs as garbage collectors.*

BONO: Troy, you ought to stop that lying!
TROY: I ain't lying! The nigger had a watermelon this big.

(He indicates with his hands.)

Talking about . . . "What watermelon, Mr. Rand?" I liked to fell out! "What watermelon, Mr. Rand?" . . . And it sitting there big as life. 5
BONO: What did Mr. Rand say?
TROY: Ain't said nothing. Figure if the nigger too dumb to know he carrying a watermelon, he wasn't gonna get much sense out of him. Trying to hide that great big old watermelon under his coat. Afraid to let the white man see him carry it home. 10
BONO: I'm like you . . . I ain't got no time for them kind of people.
TROY: Now what he look like getting mad cause he see the man from the union talking to Mr. Rand?
BONO: He come to me talking about . . . "Maxson gonna get us fired." I told him to get away from me with that. He walked away from me calling you a troublemaker. What Mr. Rand say? 15
TROY: Ain't said nothing. He told me to go down the Commissioner's office next Friday. They called me down there to see them. 20
BONO: Well, as long as you got your complaint filed, they can't fire you. That's what one of them white fellows tell me.

TROY: I ain't worried about them firing me. They gonna fire
25   me cause I asked a question? That's all I did. I went to Mr.
       Rand and asked him, "Why? Why you got the white mens
       driving and the colored lifting?" Told him, "what's the
       matter, don't I count? You think only white fellows got
       sense enough to drive a truck. That ain't no paper job!
30   Hell, anybody can drive a truck. How come you got all
       whites driving and the colored lifting?" He told me "take
       it to the union." Well, hell, that's what I done! Now they
       wanna come up with this pack of lies.
BONO: I told Brownie if the man come and ask him any
35   questions . . . just tell the truth! It ain't nothing but some-
       thing they done trumped up on you cause you filed a
       complaint on them.
TROY: Brownie don't understand nothing. All I want them to
       do is change the job description. Give everybody a chance
40   to drive the truck. Brownie can't see that. He ain't got that
       much sense.
BONO: How you figure he be making out with that gal be up
       at Taylors' all the time . . . that Alberta gal?
TROY: Same as you and me. Getting just as much as we is.
45   Which is to say nothing.
BONO: It is, huh? I figure you doing a little better than me
       . . . and I ain't saying what I'm doing.
TROY: Aw, nigger, look here . . . I know you. If you had got
       anywhere near that gal, twenty minutes later you be look-
50   ing to tell somebody. And the first one you gonna tell . . .
       that you gonna want to brag to . . . is gonna be me.
BONO: I ain't saying that. I see where you be eyeing her.
TROY: I eye all the women. I don't miss nothing. Don't never
       let nobody tell you Troy Maxson don't eye the women.
55 BONO: You been doing more than eyeing her. You done
       bought her a drink or two.
TROY: Hell yeah, I bought her a drink! What that mean? I
       bought you one, too. What that mean cause I buy her a
       drink? I'm just being polite.
60 BONO: It's alright to buy her one drink. That's what you call
       being polite. But when you wanna be buying two or three
       . . . that's what you call eyeing her.
TROY: Look here, as long as you known me . . . you ever
       known me to chase after women?
65 BONO: Hell yeah! Long as I done known you. You forgetting
       I knew you when.
TROY: Naw, I'm talking about since I been married to Rose?
BONO: Oh, not since you been married to Rose. Now, that's
       the truth, there. I can say that.
70 TROY: Alright then! Case closed.
BONO: I see you be walking up around Alberta's house. You
       supposed to be at Taylors' and you be walking up around
       there.
TROY: What you watching where I'm walking for? I ain't
75   watching after you.
BONO: I seen you walking around there more than once.
TROY: Hell, you liable to see me walking anywhere! That don't
       mean nothing cause you see me walking around there.
BONO: Where she come from anyway? She just kinda showed
80   up one day.
TROY: Tallahassee. You can look at her and tell she one of
       them Florida gals. They got some big healthy women
       down there. Grow them right up out the ground. Got a

little bit of Indian in her. Most of them niggers down in
Florida got some Indian in them.   85
BONO: I don't know about that Indian part. But she damn
       sure big and healthy. Woman wear some big stockings.
       Got them great big old legs and hips as wide as the Mis-
       sissippi River.
TROY: Legs don't mean nothing. You don't do nothing but   90
       push them out of the way. But them hips cushion the ride!
BONO: Troy, you ain't got no sense.
TROY: It's the truth! Like you riding on Goodyears!

(ROSE *enters from the house. She is ten years younger than* TROY, *her
devotion to him stems from her recognition of the possibilities of her
life without him: a succession of abusive men and their babies, a life of
partying and running the streets, the Church, or aloneness with its attendant pain and frustration. She recognizes* TROY'*s spirit as a fine
and illuminating one and she either ignores or forgives his faults, only
some of which she recognizes. Though she doesn't drink, her presence
is an integral part of the Friday night rituals. She alternates between
the porch and the kitchen, where supper preparations are under way.*)

ROSE: What you all out here getting into?
TROY: What you worried about what we getting into for?   95
       This is men talk, woman.
ROSE: What I care what you all talking about? Bono, you
       gonna stay for supper?
BONO: No, I thank you, Rose. But Lucille say she cooking up
       a pot of pigfeet.   100
TROY: Pigfeet! Hell, I'm going home with you! Might even
       stay the night if you got some pigfeet. You got something
       in there to top them pigfeet, Rose?
ROSE: I'm cooking up some chicken. I got some chicken and
       collard greens.   105
TROY: Well, go on back in the house and let me and Bono
       finish what we was talking about. This is men talk. I got
       some talk for you later. You know what kind of talk I
       mean. You go on and powder it up.
ROSE: Troy Maxson, don't you start that now!   110
TROY: (*Puts his arm around her.*) Aw, woman . . . come here. Look
       here, Bono . . . when I met this woman . . . I got out that
       place, say, "Hitch up my pony, saddle up my mare . . . there's a
       woman out there for me somewhere. I looked here. Looked
       there. Saw Rose and latched on to her." I latched on to her 115
       and told her—I'm gonna tell you the truth—I told her,
       "Baby, I don't wanna marry, I just wanna be your man."
       Rose told me . . . tell him what you told me, Rose.
ROSE: I told him if he wasn't the marrying kind, then move
       out the way so the marrying kind could find me.   120
TROY: That's what she told me. "Nigger, you in my way. You
       blocking the view! Move out the way so I can find me a
       husband." I thought it over two or three days. Come back—
ROSE: Ain't no two or three days nothing. You was back the
       same night.   125
TROY: Come back, told her . . . "Okay, baby . . . but I'm gonna
       buy me a banty rooster and put him out there in the back-
       yard . . . and when he sees a stranger come, he'll flap his wings
       and crow . . ." Look here, Bono, I could watch the front door
       by myself . . . it was that back door I was worried about. 130
ROSE: Troy, you ought not talk like that. Troy ain't doing
       nothing but telling a lie.

TROY: Only thing is . . . when we first got married . . . forget the rooster . . . we ain't had no yard!

135 BONO: I hear you tell it. Me and Lucille was staying down there on Logan Street. Had two rooms with the outhouse in the back. I ain't mind the outhouse none. But when that goddamn wind blow through there in the winter . . . that's what I'm talking about! To this day I wonder why in

140 the hell I ever stayed down there for six long years. But see, I didn't know I could do no better. I thought only white folks had inside toilets and things.

ROSE: There's a lot of people don't know they can do no better than they doing now. That's just something you got to

145 learn. A lot of folks still shop at Bella's.

TROY: Ain't nothing wrong with shopping at Bella's. She got fresh food

ROSE: I ain't said nothing about if she got fresh food. I'm talking about what she charge. She charge ten cents more

150 than the A&P.

TROY: The A&P ain't never done nothing for me. I spends my money where I'm treated right. I go down to Bella, say, "I need a loaf of bread, I'll pay you Friday." She give it to me. What sense that make when I got money to go and spend

155 it somewhere else and ignore the person who done right by me? That ain't in the Bible.

ROSE: We ain't talking about what's in the Bible. What sense it make to shop there when she overcharge?

TROY: You shop where you want to. I'll do my shopping

160 where the people been good to me.

ROSE: Well, I don't think it's right for her to overcharge. That's all I was saying.

BONO: Look here . . . I got to get on. Lucille going be raising all kind of hell.

165 TROY: Where you going, nigger? We ain't finished this pint. Come here, finish this pint.

BONO: Well, hell, I am . . . if you ever turn the bottle loose.

TROY: (*Hands him the bottle.*) The only thing I say about the A&P is I'm glad Cory got that job down there. Help him

170 take care of his school clothes and things. Gabe done moved out and things getting tight around here. He got that job . . . He can start to look out for himself.

ROSE: Cory done went and got recruited by a college football team.

175 TROY: I told that boy about that football stuff. The white man ain't gonna let him get nowhere with that football. I told him when he first come to me with it. Now you come telling me he done went and got more tied up in it. He ought to go and get recruited in how to fix cars or

180 something where he can make a living.

ROSE: He ain't talking about making no living playing football. It's just something the boys in school do. They gonna send a recruiter by to talk to you. He'll tell you he ain't talking about making no living playing football. It's a

185 honor to be recruited.

TROY: It ain't gonna get him nowhere. Bono'll tell you that.

BONO: If he be like you in the sports . . . he's gonna be alright. Ain't but two men ever played baseball as good as you. That's Babe Ruth and Josh Gibson. Them's the only

190 two men ever hit more home runs than you.

TROY: What it ever get me? Ain't got a pot to piss in or a window to throw it out of.

ROSE: Times have changed since you was playing baseball, Troy. That was before the war. Times have changed a lot

195 since then.

TROY: How in hell they done changed?

ROSE: They got lots of colored boys playing ball now. Baseball and football.

BONO: You right about that, Rose. Times have changed, Troy.

200 You just come along too early.

TROY: There ought not never have been no time called too early! Now you take that fellow . . . what's that fellow they had playing right field for the Yankees back then? You know who I'm talking about, Bono. Used to play right

205 field for the Yankees,

ROSE: Selkirk?

TROY: Selkirk! That's it! Man batting .269, understand? .269. What kind of sense that make? I was hitting .432 with thirty-seven home runs! Man batting .269 and playing

210 right field for the Yankees! I saw Josh Gibson's daughter yesterday. She walking around with raggedy shoes on her feet. Now I bet you Selkirk's daughter ain't walking around with raggedy shoes on her feet! I bet you that!

ROSE: They got a lot of colored baseball players now. Jackie

215 Robinson was the first. Folks had to wait for Jackie Robinson.

TROY: I done seen a hundred niggers play baseball better than Jackie Robinson. Hell, I know some teams Jackie Robinson couldn't even make! What you talking about Jackie

220 Robinson. Jackie Robinson wasn't nobody. I'm talking about if you could play ball then they ought to have let you play. Don't care what color you were. Come telling me I come along too early. If you could play . . . then they ought to have let you play.

(TROY *takes a long drink from the bottle.*)

ROSE: You gonna drink yourself to death. You don't need to

225 be drinking like that.

TROY: Death ain't nothing. I done seen him. Done wrassled with him. You can't tell me nothing about death. Death ain't nothing but a fastball on the outside corner. And you know what I'll do to that! Lookee here, Bono . . . am I ly-

230 ing? You get one of them fastballs, about waist high, over the outside corner of the plate where you can get the meat of the bat on it . . . and good god! You can kiss it goodbye. Now, am I lying?

BONO: Naw, you telling the truth there. I seen you do it.

235 TROY: If I'm lying . . . that 450 feet worth of lying!

(*Pause.*)

That's all death is to me. A fastball on the outside corner.

ROSE: I don't know why you want to get on talking about death.

TROY: Ain't nothing wrong with talking about death. That's

240 part of life. Everybody gonna die. You gonna die, I'm gonna die. Bono's gonna die. Hell, we all gonna die.

ROSE: But you ain't got to talk about it. I don't like to talk about it.

TROY: You the one brought it up. Me and Bono was talking

245 about baseball . . . you tell me I'm gonna drink myself to

death. Ain't that right, Bono? You know I don't drink this but one night out of the week. That's Friday night. I'm gonna drink just enough to where I can handle it. Then I cuts it loose. I leave it alone. So don't you worry about me drinking myself to death. 'Cause I ain't worried about Death. I done seen him. I done wrestled with him.

Look here, Bono . . . I looked up one day and Death was marching straight at me. Like Soldiers on Parade! The Army of Death was marching straight at me. The middle of July, 1941. It got real cold just like it be winter. It seem like Death himself reached out and touched me on the shoulder. He touch me just like I touch you. I got cold as ice and Death standing there grinning at me.

ROSE: Troy, why don't you hush that talk.

TROY: I say . . . What you want, Mr. Death? You be wanting me? You done brought your army to be getting me? I looked him dead in the eye. I wasn't fearing nothing. I was ready to tangle. Just like I'm ready to tangle now. The Bible say be ever vigilant. That's why I don't get but so drunk. I got to keep watch.

ROSE: Troy was right down there in Mercy Hospital. You remember he had pneumonia? Laying there with a fever talking plumb out of his head.

TROY: Death standing there staring at me . . . carrying that sickle in his hand. Finally he say, "You want bound over for another year?" See, just like that . . . "You want bound over for another year?" I told him, "Bound over hell! Let's settle this now!"

It seem like he kinda fell back when I said that, and all the cold went out of me. I reached down and grabbed that sickle and threw it just as far as I could throw it . . . and me and him commenced to wrestling.

We wrestled for three days and three nights. I can't say where I found the strength from. Every time it seemed like he was gonna get the best of me, I'd reach way down deep inside myself and find the strength to do him one better.

ROSE: Every time Troy tell that story he find different ways to tell it. Different things to make up about it.

TROY: I ain't making up nothing. I'm telling you the facts of what happened. I wrestled with Death for three days and three nights and I'm standing here to tell you about it.

(Pause.)

Alright. At the end of the third night we done weakened each other to where we can't hardly move. Death stood up, throwed on his robe . . . had him a white robe with a hood on it. He throwed on that robe and went off to look for his sickle. Say, "I'll be back." Just like that. "I'll be back." I told him, say, "Yeah, but . . . you gonna have to find me!" I wasn't no fool. I wasn't going looking for him. Death ain't nothing to play with. And I know he's gonna get me. I know I got to join his army . . . his camp followers. But as long as I keep my strength and see him coming . . . as long as I keep up my vigilance . . . he's gonna have to fight to get me. I ain't going easy.

BONO: Well, look here, since you got to keep up your vigilance . . . let me have the bottle.

TROY: Aw hell, I shouldn't have told you that part. I should have left out that part.

ROSE: Troy be talking that stuff and half the time don't even know what he be talking about.

TROY: Bono know me better than that.

BONO: That's right. I know you. I know you got some Uncle Remus in your blood. You got more stories than the devil got sinners.

TROY: Aw hell, I done seen him too! Done talked with the devil.

ROSE: Troy, don't nobody wanna be hearing all that stuff.

(LYONS enters the yard from the street. Thirty-four years old, TROY's son by a previous marriage, he sports a neatly trimmed goatee, sport coat, white shirt, tieless and buttoned at the collar. Though he fancies himself a musician, he is more caught up in the rituals and "idea" of being a musician than in the actual practice of the music. He has come to borrow money from TROY, and while he knows he will be successful, he is uncertain as to what extent his lifestyle will be held up to scrutiny and ridicule.)

LYONS: Hey, Pop.

TROY: What you come "Hey, Popping" me for?

LYONS: How you doing, Rose?

(He kisses her.)

Mr. Bono. How you doing?

BONO: Hey, Lyons . . . how you been?

TROY: He must have been doing alright. I ain't seen him around here last week.

ROSE: Troy, leave your boy alone. He come by to see you and you wanna start all that nonsense.

TROY: I ain't bothering Lyons.

(Offers him the bottle.)

Here . . . get you a drink. We got an understanding. I know why he come by to see me and he know I know.

LYONS: Come on, Pop . . . I just stopped by to say hi . . . see how you was doing.

TROY: You ain't stopped by yesterday.

ROSE: You gonna stay for supper, Lyons? I got some chicken cooking in the oven.

LYONS: No, Rose . . . thanks. I was just in then neighborhood and thought I'd stop by for a minute.

TROY: You was in the neighborhood alright, nigger. You telling the truth there. You was in the neighborhood cause it's my payday.

LYONS: Well, hell, since you mentioned it . . . let me have ten dollars.

TROY: I'll be damned! I'll die and go to hell and play blackjack with the devil before I give you ten dollars.

BONO: That's what I wanna know about . . . that devil you done seen.

LYONS: What . . . Pop done seen the devil? You too much, Pops.

TROY: Yeah, I done seen him. Talked to him too!

ROSE: You ain't seen no devil. I done told you that man ain't had nothing to do with the devil. Anything you can't understand, you want to call it the devil.

TROY: Look here, Bono . . . I went down to see Hertzberger about some furniture. Got three rooms for two-ninety-eight. That what it say on the radio. "Three rooms . . . two-ninety-eight." Even made up a little song about it. Go down there . . . man tell me I can't get no credit. I'm working every day and can't get no credit. What to do? I got an empty house with some raggedy furniture in it. Cory ain't got no bed. He's sleeping on a pile of rags on the floor.

355 Working every day and can't get no credit. Come back here—Rose'll tell you—madder than hell. Sit down . . . try to figure what I'm gonna do. Come a knock on the door. Ain't been living here but three days. Who know I'm here? Open the door . . . devil standing there bigger than life.

360 White fellow . . . got on good clothes and everything. Standing there with a clipboard in his hand. I ain't had to say nothing. First words come out of his mouth was . . . "I understand you need some furniture and can't get no credit." I liked to fell over. He say "I'll give you all the credit

365 you want, but you got to pay the interest on it." I told him, "Give me three rooms worth and charge whatever you want." Next day a truck pulled up here and two men unloaded them three rooms. Man what drove the truck give me a book. Say send ten dollars, first of every month to the

370 address in the book and everything will be alright. Say if I miss a payment the devil was coming back and it'll be hell to pay. That was fifteen years ago. To this day . . . the first of the month I send my ten dollars, Rose'll tell you.

ROSE: Troy lying.

375 TROY: I ain't never seen that man since. Now you tell me who else that could have been but the devil? I ain't sold my soul or nothing like that, you understand. Naw, I wouldn't have truck with the devil about nothing like that. I got my furniture and pays my ten dollars the first

380 of the month just like clockwork.

BONO: How long you say you been paying this ten dollars a month?

TROY: Fifteen years!

BONO: Hell, ain't you finished paying for it yet? How much

385 the man done charged you.

TROY: Aw hell, I done paid for it. I done paid for it ten times over! The fact is I'm scared to stop paying it.

ROSE: Troy lying. We got that furniture from Mr. Glickman. He ain't paying no ten dollars a month to nobody.

390 TROY: Aw hell, woman. Bono know I ain't that big a fool.

LYONS: I was just getting ready to say . . . I know where there's a bridge for sale.

TROY: Look here, I'll tell you this . . . it don't matter to me if he was the devil. It don't matter if the devil give credit.

395 Somebody has got to give it.

ROSE: It ought to matter. You going around talking about having truck with the devil . . . God's the one you gonna have to answer to. He's the one gonna be at the Judgment.

LYONS: Yeah, well, look here, Pop . . . let me have that ten dol-

400 lars. I'll give it back to you. Bonnie got a job working at the hospital.

TROY: What I tell you, Bono? The only time I see this nigger is when he wants something. That's the only time I see him.

LYONS: Come on, Pop, Mr. Bono don't want to hear all that.

405 Let me have the ten dollars. I told you Bonnie working

TROY: What that mean to me? "Bonnie working." I don't care if she working. Go ask her for the ten dollars if she working. Talking about "Bonnie working." Why ain't you working?

410 LYONS: Aw, Pop, you know I can't find no decent job. Where am I gonna get a job at? You know I can't get no job.

TROY: I told you I know some people down there. I can get you on the rubbish if you want to work. I told you that the last time you came by here asking me for something.

415 LYONS: Naw, Pop . . . thanks. That ain't for me. I don't wanna be carrying nobody's rubbish. I don't wanna be punching nobody's time clock.

TROY: What's the matter, you too good to carry people's rubbish? Where you think that ten dollars you talking about come from? I'm just supposed to haul people's rubbish and

420 give my money to you cause you too lazy to work. You too lazy to work and wanna know why you ain't got what I got.

ROSE: What hospital Bonnie working at? Mercy?

LYONS: She's down at Passavant working in the laundry.

TROY: I ain't got nothing as it is. I give you that ten dollars

425 and I got to eat beans the rest of the week. Naw . . . you ain't getting no ten dollars here.

LYONS: You ain't got to be eating no beans. I don't know why you wanna say that.

TROY: I ain't got no extra money. Gabe done moved over to

430 Miss Pearl's paying her the rent and things done got tight around here. I can't afford to be giving you every payday.

LYONS: I ain't asked you to give me nothing. I asked you to loan me ten dollars. I know you got ten dollars.

TROY: Yeah, I got it. You know why I got it? Cause I don't

435 throw my money away out there in the streets. You living the fast life . . . wanna be a musician . . . running around in them clubs and things . . . then, you learn to take care of yourself. You ain't gonna find me going and asking nobody for nothing. I done spent too many years without.

440 LYONS: You and me is two different people, Pop.

TROY: I done learned my mistake and learned to do what's right by it. You still trying to get something for nothing. Life don't owe you nothing. You owe it to yourself. Ask Bono. He'll tell you I'm right.

445 LYONS: You got your way of dealing with the world . . . I got mine. The only thing that matters to me is the music.

TROY: Yeah, I can see that! It don't matter how you gonna eat . . . where your next dollar is coming from. You telling the truth there.

450 LYONS: I know I got to eat. But I got to live too. I need something that gonna help me to get out of the bed in the morning. Make me feel like I belong in the world. I don't bother nobody. I just stay with my music cause that's the only way I can find to live in the world. Otherwise there

455 ain't no telling what I might do. Now I don't come criticizing you and how you live. I just come by to ask you for ten dollars. I don't wanna hear all that about how I live.

TROY: Boy, your mama did a hell of a job raising you.

LYONS: You can't change me, Pop. I'm thirty-four years old. If

460 you wanted to change me, you should have been there when I was growing up. I come by to see you . . . ask for ten dollars and you want to talk about how I was raised. You don't know nothing about how I was raised.

ROSE: Let the boy have ten dollars, Troy.

465 TROY: (*To* LYONS.) What the hell you looking at me for? I ain't got no ten dollars. You know what I do with my money.

(*To* ROSE.)

Give him ten dollars if you want him to have it.

ROSE: I will. Just as soon as you turn it loose.

470 TROY: (*Handing* ROSE *the money.*) There it is. Seventy-six dol-
     lars and forty-two cents. You see this, Bono? Now, I ain't
     gonna get but six of that back.

ROSE: You ought to stop telling that lie. Here, Lyons.

(*She hands him the money.*)

LYONS: Thanks, Rose. Look . . . I got to run . . . I'll see you later.

475 TROY: Wait a minute. You gonna say, "thanks, Rose" and ain't
     gonna look to see where she got that ten dollars from? See
     how they do me, Bono?

LYONS: I know she got it from you, Pop. Thanks. I'll give it
     back to you.

480 TROY: There he go telling another lie. Time I see that ten
     dollars . . . he'll be owing me thirty more.

LYONS: See you, Mr. Bono.

BONO: Take care, Lyons!

LYONS: Thanks, Pop. I'll see you again.

(LYONS *exits the yard.*)

485 TROY: I don't know why he don't go and get him a decent
     job and take care of that woman he got.

BONO: He'll be alright, Troy. The boy is still young.

TROY: The *boy* is thirty-four years old.

ROSE: Let's not get off into all that.

490 BONO: Look here . . . I got to be going. I got to be getting
     on. Lucille gonna be waiting.

TROY: (*Puts his arm around* ROSE.) See this woman, Bono? I
     love this woman. I love this woman so much it hurts. I
     love her so much . . . I done run out of ways of loving
495 her. So I got to go back to basics. Don't you come by my
     house Monday morning talking about time to go to work
     . . . 'cause I'm still gonna be stroking!

ROSE: Troy! Stop it now!

BONO: I ain't paying him no mind, Rose. That ain't nothing
500 but gin-talk. Go on, Troy. I'll see you Monday.

TROY: Don't you come by my house, nigger! I done told you
     what I'm gonna be doing.

(*The lights go down to black.*)

SCENE II

The lights come up on ROSE *hanging up clothes. She hums and sings
softly to herself. It is the following morning.*

ROSE: (*Sings.*)

     Jesus, be a fence all around me every day.
     Jesus, I want you to protect me as I travel on my way.
     Jesus, be a fence all around me every day.

(TROY *enters from the house.*)

5 ROSE: (*Continues.*)

     Jesus, I want you to protect me
     As I travel on my way.

(*To* TROY.)

     'Morning. You ready for breakfast? I can fix it soon as I
     finish hanging up these clothes?

TROY: I got the coffee on. That'll be alright. I'll just drink   10
     some of that this morning.

ROSE: That 651 hit yesterday. That's the second time this
     month. Miss Pearl hit for a dollar . . . seem like those that
     need the least always get lucky. Poor folks can't get nothing.

TROY: Them numbers don't know nobody. I don't know why   15
     you fool with them. You and Lyons both.

ROSE: It's something to do.

TROY: You ain't doing nothing but throwing your money away.

ROSE: Troy, you know I don't play foolishly. I just play a nickel
     here and a nickel there.   20

TROY: That's two nickels you done thrown away.

ROSE: Now I hit sometimes . . . that makes up for it. It always
     comes in handy when I do hit. I don't hear you com-
     plaining then.

TROY: I ain't complaining now. I just say it's foolish. Trying   25
     to guess out of six hundred ways which way the number
     gonna come. If I had all the money niggers, these Ne-
     groes, throw away on numbers for one week—just one
     week—I'd be a rich man.

ROSE: Well, you wishing and calling it foolish ain't gonna stop   30
     folks from playing numbers. That's one thing for sure. Be-
     sides . . . some good things come from playing numbers.
     Look where Pope done bought him that restaurant off of
     numbers.

TROY: I can't stand niggers like that. Man ain't had two dimes   35
     to rub together. He walking around with his shoes all run
     over bumming money for cigarettes. Alright. Got lucky
     there and hit the numbers . . .

ROSE: Troy, I know all about it.

TROY: Had good sense, I'll say that for him. He ain't throwed   40
     his money away. I seen niggers hit the numbers and go
     through two thousand dollars in four days. Man bought
     him that restaurant down there . . . fixed it up real nice . . .
     and then didn't want nobody to come in it! A Negro go in
     there and can't get no kind of service. I seen a white fellow   45
     come in there and order a bowl of stew. Pope picked all the
     meat out the pot for him. Man ain't had nothing but a bowl
     of meat! Negro come behind him and ain't got nothing but
     the potatoes and carrots. Talking about what numbers do
     for people, you picked a wrong example. Ain't done noth-   50
     ing but make a worser fool out of him than he was before.

ROSE: Troy, you ought to stop worrying about what hap-
     pened at work yesterday.

TROY: I ain't worried. Just told me to be down there at the
     Commissioner's office on Friday. Everybody think they   55
     gonna fire me. I ain't worried about them firing me. You
     ain't got to worry about that.

(*Pause.*)

     Where's Cory? Cory in the house? (*Calls.*) Cory?

ROSE: He gone out.

TROY: Out, huh? He gone out 'cause he know I want him to   60
     help me with this fence. I know how he is. That boy
     scared of work.

(GABRIEL *enters. He comes halfway down the alley and, hearing*
TROY'*s voice, stops.*)

TROY: (*Continues.*) He ain't done a lick of work in his life.

ROSE: He had to go to football practice. Coach wanted them
65 to get in a little extra practice before the season start.
TROY: I got his practice . . . running out of here before he get
his chores done.
ROSE: Troy, what is wrong with you this morning? Don't
nothing set right with you. Go on back in there and go to
70 bed . . . get up on the other side.
TROY: Why something got to be wrong with me? I ain't said
nothing wrong with me.
ROSE: You got something to say about everything. First it's the
numbers . . . then it's the way the man runs his restaurant
75 . . . then you done got on Cory. What's it gonna be next?
Take a look up there and see if the weather suits you . . .
or is it gonna be how you gonna put up the fence with
the clothes hanging in the yard.
TROY: You hit the nail on the head then.
80 ROSE: I know you like I know the back of my hand. Go on
in there and get you some coffee . . . see if that straighten
you up. 'Cause you ain't right this morning.

(TROY *starts into the house and sees* GABRIEL. GABRIEL *starts
singing.* TROY'*s brother, he is seven years younger than* TROY. *Injured in World War II, he has a metal plate in his head. He carries
an old trumpet tied around his waist and believes with every fiber of
his being that he is the Archangel Gabriel. He carries a chipped basket with an assortment of discarded fruits and vegetables he has
picked up in the strip district and which he attempts to sell.*)

GABRIEL: (*Singing.*)

  Yes, ma'am, I got plums
85 You ask me how I sell them
  Oh ten cents apiece
  Three for a quarter
  Come and buy now
  'Cause I'm here today
90 And tomorrow I'll be gone

(GABRIEL *enters.*)

 Hey, Rose!
ROSE: How you doing, Gabe?
GABRIEL: There's Troy . . . Hey, Troy!
TROY: Hey, Gabe.

(*Exit into kitchen.*)

95 ROSE: (*To* GABRIEL.) What you got there?
GABRIEL: You know what I got, Rose. I got fruits and vegetables.
ROSE: (*Looking in basket.*) Where's all these plums you talking
about?
GABRIEL: I ain't got no plums today, Rose. I was just singing
100 that. Have some tomorrow. Put me in a big order for
plums. Have enough plums tomorrow for St. Peter and
everybody.

(TROY *re-enters from kitchen, crosses to steps.*)

(*To* ROSE.)

 Troy's mad at me.
TROY: I ain't mad at you. What I got to be mad at you about?
105 You ain't done nothing to me.

GABRIEL: I just moved over to Miss Pearl's to keep out from
in your way. I ain't mean no harm by it.
TROY: Who said anything about that? I ain't said anything
about that.
GABRIEL: You ain't mad at me, is you? 110
TROY: Naw . . . I ain't mad at you, Gabe. If I was mad at you
I'd tell you about it.
GABRIEL: Got me two rooms. In the basement. Got my own
door too. Wanna see my key?

(*He holds up a key.*)

That's my own key! Ain't nobody else got a key like that. 115
That's my key! My two rooms!
TROY: Well, that's good, Gabe. You got your own key . . . that's
good.
ROSE: You hungry, Gabe? I was just fixing to cook Troy his
breakfast. 120
GABRIEL: I'll take some biscuits. You got some biscuits? Did
you know when I was in heaven . . . every morning me
and St. Peter would sit down by the gate and eat some big
fat biscuits? Oh, yeah! We had us a good time. We'd sit
there and eat us them biscuits and then St. Peter would go 125
off to sleep and tell me to wake him up when it's time to
open the gates for the judgment.
ROSE: Well, come on . . . I'll make up a batch of biscuits.

(ROSE *exits into the house.*)

GABRIEL: Troy . . . St. Peter got your name in the book. I seen
it. It say . . . Troy Maxson. I say . . . I know him! He got 130
the same name like what I got. That's my brother!
TROY: How many times you gonna tell me that, Gabe?
GABRIEL: Ain't got my name in the book. Don't have to have
my name. I done died and went to heaven. He got your
name though. One morning St. Peter was looking at his 135
book . . . marking it for the judgment . . . and he let me
see your name. Got it in there under M. Got Rose's name
. . . I ain't seen it like I seen yours . . . but I know it's in
there. He got a great big book. Got everybody's name
what was ever been born. That's what he told me. But I 140
seen your name. Seen it with my own eyes.
TROY: Go on in the house there. Rose going to fix you
something to eat.
GABRIEL: Oh, I ain't hungry. I done had breakfast with Aunt
Jemimah. She come by and cooked me up a whole mess of 145
flapjacks. Remember how we used to eat them flapjacks.
TROY: Go on in the house and get you something to eat now.
GABRIEL: I got to go sell my plums. I done sold some tomatoes. Got me two quarters. Wanna see?

(*He shows* TROY *his quarters.*)

I'm gonna save them and buy me a new horn so St. Peter 150
can hear me when it's time to open the gates.

(GABRIEL *stops suddenly. Listens.*)

Hear that? That's the hellhounds. I got to chase them out
of here. Go on get out of here! Get out!

(GABRIEL *exits singing.*)

155   Better get ready for the judgment
               Better get ready for the judgment
               My Lord is coming down

(ROSE *enters from the house.*)

TROY: He gone off somewhere.
GABRIEL: (*Offstage.*)

160   Better get ready for the judgment
               Better get ready for the judgment morning
               Better get ready for the judgment
               My God is coming down

ROSE: He ain't eating right. Miss Pearl say she can't get him
       to eat nothing.
165 TROY: What you want me to do about it, Rose? I done did
       everything I can for the man. I can't make him get well.
       Man got half his head blown away . . . what you expect?
ROSE: Seem like something ought to be done to help him.
TROY: Man don't bother nobody. He just mixed up from that
170   metal plate he got in his head. Ain't no sense for him to
       go back into the hospital.
ROSE: Least he be eating right. They can help him take care
       of himself.
TROY: Don't nobody wanna be locked up, Rose. What you
175   wanna lock him up for? Man go over there and fight the
       war . . . messin' around with them Japs, get half his head
       blown off . . . and they give him a lousy three thousand
       dollars. And I had to swoop down on that.
ROSE: Is you fixing to go into that again?
180 TROY: That's the only way I got a roof over my head . . . cause
       of that metal plate.
ROSE: Ain't no sense you blaming yourself for nothing. Gabe
       wasn't in no condition to manage that money. You done
       what was right by him. Can't nobody say you ain't done
185   what was right by him. Look how long you took care of
       him . . . till he wanted to have his own place and moved
       over there with Miss Pearl.
TROY: That ain't what I'm saying, woman! I'm just stating the
       facts. If my brother didn't have that metal plate in his head
190   . . . I wouldn't have a pot to piss in or a window to throw
       it out of. And I'm fifty-three years old. Now see if you
       can understand that!

(TROY *gets up from the porch and starts to exit the yard.*)

ROSE: Where you going off to? You been running out of here
       every Saturday for weeks. I thought you was gonna work
195   on this fence?
TROY: I'm gonna walk down to Taylors'. Listen to the ball
       game. I'll be back in a bit. I'll work on it when I get back.

(*He exits the yard. The lights go to black.*)

SCENE III

The lights come up on the yard. It is four hours later. ROSE *is taking down the clothes from the line.* CORY *enters carrying his football
equipment.*

ROSE: Your daddy like to had a fit with you running out of
       here this morning without doing your chores.

CORY: I told you I had to go to practice.
ROSE: He say you were supposed to help him with this fence.
CORY: He been saying that the last four or five Saturdays, and 5
       then he don't never do nothing, but go down to Taylors'.
       Did you tell him about the recruiter?
ROSE: Yeah, I told him.
CORY: What he say?
ROSE: He ain't said nothing too much. You get in there and 10
       get started on your chores before he gets back. Go on and
       scrub down them steps before he gets back here hollering
       and carrying on.
CORY: I'm hungry. What you got to eat, Mama?
ROSE: Go on and get started on your chores. I got some meat 15
       loaf in there. Go on and make you a sandwich . . . and
       don't leave no mess in there.

(CORY *exits into the house.* ROSE *continues to take down the
clothes.* TROY *enters the yard and sneaks up and grabs her from behind.*)

       Troy! Go on, now. You liked to scared me to death. What
       was the score of the game? Lucille had me on the phone
       and I couldn't keep up with it.   20
TROY: What I care about the game? Come here, woman.

(*He tries to kiss her.*)

ROSE: I thought you went down Taylors' to listen to the game.
       Go on, Troy! You supposed to be putting up this fence.
TROY: (*Attempting to kiss her again.*) I'll put it up when I fin-
       ish with what is at hand.   25
ROSE: Go on, Troy. I ain't studying you.
TROY: (*Chasing after her.*) I'm studying you . . . fixing to do my
       homework!
ROSE: Troy, you better leave me alone.
TROY: Where's Cory? That boy brought his butt home yet?   30
ROSE: He's in the house doing his chores.
TROY: (*Calling.*) Cory! Get your butt out here, boy!

(ROSE *exits into the house with the laundry.* TROY *goes over to the
pile of wood, picks up a board, and starts sawing.* CORY *enters from
the house.*)

TROY: You just now coming in here from leaving this morning?
CORY: Yeah, I had to go to football practice.
TROY: Yeah, what?   35
CORY: Yessir.
TROY: I ain't but two seconds off you noway. The garbage sit-
       ting in there overflowing . . . you ain't done none of your
       chores . . . and you come in here talking about "Yeah."
CORY: I was just getting ready to do my chores now, Pop . . .   40
TROY: Your first chore is to help me with this fence on Sat-
       urday. Everything else come after that. Now get that saw
       and cut them boards.

(CORY *takes the saw and begins cutting the boards.* TROY *continues
working. There is a long pause.*)

CORY: Hey, Pop . . . why don't you buy a TV?
TROY: What I want with a TV? What I want one of them for?   45
CORY: Everybody got one. Earl, Ba Bra . . . Jesse!

TROY: I ain't asked you who had one. I say what I want with one?

CORY: So you can watch it. They got lots of things on TV. Baseball games and everything. We could watch the World Series.

TROY: Yeah . . . and how much this TV cost?

CORY: I don't know. They got them on sale for around two hundred dollars.

TROY: Two hundred dollars, huh?

CORY: That ain't that much, Pop.

TROY: Naw, it's just two hundred dollars. See that roof you got over your head at night? Let me tell you something about that roof. It's been over ten years since that roof was last tarred. See now . . . the snow come this winter and sit up there on that roof like it is . . . and it's gonna seep inside. It's just gonna be a little bit . . . ain't gonna hardly notice it. Then the next thing you know, it's gonna be leaking all over the house. Then the wood rot from all that water and you gonna need a whole new roof. Now, how much you think it cost to get that roof tarred?

CORY: I don't know.

TROY: Two hundred and sixty-four dollars . . . cash money. While you thinking about a TV, I got to be thinking about the roof . . . and whatever else go wrong around here. Now if you had two hundred dollars, what would you do . . . fix the roof or buy a TV?

CORY: I'd buy a TV. Then when the roof started to leak . . . when it needed fixing . . . I'd fix it.

TROY: Where you gonna get the money from? You done spent it for a TV. You gonna sit up and watch the water run all over your brand new TV.

CORY: Aw, Pop. You got money. I know you do.

TROY: Where I got it at, Huh?

CORY: You got it in the bank.

TROY: You wanna see my bankbook? You wanna see that seventy-three dollars and twenty-two cents I got sitting up in there.

CORY: You ain't got to pay for it all at one time. You can put a down payment on it and carry it on home with you.

TROY: Not me. I ain't gonna owe nobody nothing if I can help it. Miss a payment and they come and snatch it right out your house. Then what you got? Now, soon as I get two hundred dollars clear, then I'll buy a TV. Right now, as soon as I get two hundred and sixty-four dollars, I'm gonna have this roof tarred.

CORY: Aw . . . Pop!

TROY: You go on and get you two hundred dollars and buy one if ya want it. I got better things to do with my money.

CORY: I can't get no two hundred dollars. I ain't never seen two hundred dollars.

TROY: I'll tell you what . . . you get you a hundred dollars and I'll put the other hundred with it.

CORY: Alright, I'm gonna show you.

TROY: You gonna show me how you can cut them boards right now.

(CORY *begins to cut the boards. There is a long pause.*)

CORY: The Pirates won today. That makes five in a row.

TROY: I ain't thinking about the Pirates. Got an all-white team. Got that boy . . . that Puerto Rican boy . . . Clemente. Don't even half-play him. That boy could be something if they give him a chance. Play him one day and sit him on the bench the next.

CORY: He gets a lot of chances to play.

TROY: I'm talking about playing regular. Playing every day so you can get your timing. That's what I'm talking about.

CORY: They got some white guys on the team that don't play every day. You can't play everybody at the same time.

TROY: If they got a white fellow sitting on the bench . . . you can bet your last dollar he can't play! The colored guy got to be twice as good before he get on the team. That's why I don't want you to get all tied up in them sports. Man on the team and what it get him? They got colored on the team and don't use them. Same as not having them. All them teams the same.

CORY: The Braves got Hank Aaron and Wes Covington. Hank Aaron hit two home runs today. That makes forty-three.

TROY: Hank Aaron ain't nobody. That's what you supposed to do. That's how you supposed to play the game. Ain't nothing to it. It's just a matter of timing . . . getting the right follow-through. Hell, I can hit forty-three home runs right now!

CORY: Not off no major-league pitching, you couldn't.

TROY: We had better pitching in the Negro leagues. I hit seven home runs off of Satchel Paige. You can't get no better than that!

CORY: Sandy Koufax. He's leading the league in strikeouts.

TROY: I ain't thinking of no Sandy Koufax.

CORY: You got Warren Spahn and Lew Burdette. I bet you couldn't hit no home runs off of Warren Spahn.

TROY: I'm through with it now. You go on and cut them boards.

(*Pause.*)

Your mama tell me you done got recruited by a college football team? Is that right?

CORY: Yeah. Coach Zellman say the recruiter gonna be coming by to talk to you. Get you to sign the permission papers.

TROY: I thought you supposed to be working down there at the A&P. Ain't you suppose to be working down there after school?

CORY: Mr. Stawicki say he gonna hold my job for me until after the football season. Say starting next week I can work weekends.

TROY: I thought we had an understanding about this football stuff? You suppose to keep up with your chores and hold that job down at the A&P. Ain't been around here all day on a Saturday. Ain't none of your chores done . . . and now you telling me you done quit your job.

CORY: I'm gonna be working weekends.

TROY: You damn right you are! And ain't no need for nobody coming around here to talk to me about signing nothing.

CORY: Hey, Pop . . . you can't do that. He's coming all the way from North Carolina.

TROY: I don't care where he coming from. The white man ain't gonna let you get nowhere with that football noway. You go on and get your book-learning so you can work yourself up in that A&P or learn how to fix cars or build houses or something, get you a trade. That way you have something can't nobody take away from you. You go on and learn how to put your hands to some good use. Besides hauling people's garbage.

165 CORY: I get good grades, Pop. That's why the recruiter wants to talk with you. You got to keep up your grades to get recruited. This way I'll be going to college. I'll get a chance . . .

TROY: First you gonna get your butt down there to the A&P

170 and get your job back.

CORY: Mr. Stawicki done already hired somebody else 'cause I told him I was playing football.

TROY: You a bigger fool than I thought . . . to let somebody take away your job so you can play some football. Where

175 you gonna get your money to take out your girlfriend and whatnot? What kind of foolishness is that to let somebody take away your job?

CORY: I'm still gonna be working weekends.

TROY: Naw . . . naw. You getting your butt out of here and

180 finding you another job.

CORY: Come on, Pop! I got to practice. I can't work after school and play football too. The team needs me. That's what Coach Zellman say . . .

TROY: I don't care what nobody else say. I'm the boss . . . you

185 understand? I'm the boss around here. I do the only saying what counts.

CORY: Come on, Pop!

TROY: I asked you . . . did you understand?

CORY: Yeah . . .

190 TROY: What?!

CORY: Yessir.

TROY: You go on down there to that A&P and see if you can get your job back. If you can't do both . . . then you quit the football team. You've got to take the crookeds with

195 the straights.

CORY: Yessir.

(*Pause.*)

Can I ask you a question?

TROY: What the hell you wanna ask me? Mr. Stawicki the one you got the questions for.

200 CORY: How come you ain't never liked me?

TROY: Liked you? Who the hell say I got to like you? What law is there say I got to like you? Wanna stand up in my face and ask a damn fool-ass question like that. Talking about liking somebody. Come here boy, when I talk to you.

(CORY *comes over to where* TROY *is working. He stands slouched over and* TROY *shoves him on his shoulder.*)

205 Straighten up, goddammit! I asked you a question . . . what law is there say I got to like you?

CORY: None.

TROY: Well, alright then! Don't you eat every day?

(*Pause.*)

Answer me when I talk to you! Don't you eat every day?

210 CORY: Yeah.

TROY: Nigger, as long as you in my house, you put that sir on the end of it when you talk to me!

CORY: Yes . . . sir.

TROY: You eat every day.

CORY: Yessir! 215

TROY: Got a roof over your head.

CORY: Yessir!

TROY: Got clothes on your back.

CORY: Yessir.

TROY: Why you think that is? 220

CORY: Cause of you.

TROY: Aw, hell I know it's 'cause of me . . . but why do you think that is?

CORY: (*Hesitant.*) Cause you like me.

TROY: Like you? I go out of here every morning . . . bust my 225 butt . . . putting up with them crackers every day . . . cause I like you? You about the biggest fool I ever saw.

(*Pause.*)

It's my job. It's my responsibility! You understand that? A man got to take care of his family. You live in my house . . . sleep you behind on my bedclothes . . . fill you belly 230 up with my food . . . cause you my son. You my flesh and blood. Not 'cause I like you! Cause it's my duty to take care of you. I owe a responsibility to you! Let's get this straight right here . . . before it go along any further . . . I ain't got to like you. Mr. Rand don't give me my money 235 come payday cause he likes me. He gives me cause he owe me. I done give you everything I had to give you. I gave you your life! Me and your mama worked that out between us. And liking your black ass wasn't part of the bargain. Don't you try and go through life worrying about if 240 somebody like you or not. You best be making sure they doing right by you. You understand what I'm saying, boy?

CORY: Yessir.

TROY: Then get the hell out of my face, and get on down to that A&P. 245

(ROSE *has been standing behind the screen door for much of the scene. She enters as* CORY *exits.*)

ROSE: Why don't you let the boy go ahead and play football, Troy? Ain't no harm in that. He's just trying to be like you with the sports.

TROY: I don't want him to be like me! I want him to move as far away from my life as he can get. You the only de- 250 cent thing that ever happened to me. I wish him that. But I don't wish him a thing else from my life. I decided seventeen years ago that boy wasn't getting involved in no sports. Not after what they did to me in the sports.

ROSE: Troy, why don't you admit you was too old to play in 255 the major leagues? For once . . . why don't you admit that?

TROY: What do you mean too old? Don't come telling me I was too old. I just wasn't the right color. Hell, I'm fifty-three years old and can do better than Selkirk's .269 right now!

ROSE: How's was you gonna play ball when you were over 260 forty? Sometimes I can't get no sense out of you.

TROY: I got good sense, woman. I got sense enough not to let my boy get hurt over playing no sports. You been mothering that boy too much. Worried about if people like him.

ROSE: Everything that boy do . . . he do for you. He wants 265 you to say "Good job, son." That's all.

TROY: Rose, I ain't got time for that. He's alive. He's healthy. He's got to make his own way. I made mine. Ain't nobody gonna hold his hand when he get out there in that world.

270 ROSE: Times have changed from when you was young, Troy. People change. The world's changing around you and you can't even see it.

TROY: (*Slow, methodical.*) Woman . . . I do the best I can do. I come in here every Friday. I carry a sack of potatoes and 275 a bucket of lard. You all line up at the door with your hands out. I give you the lint from my pockets. I give you my sweat and my blood. I ain't got no tears. I done spent them. We go upstairs in that room at night . . . and I fall down on you and try to blast a hole into forever. I get up 280 Monday morning . . . find my lunch on the table. I go out. Make my way. Find my strength to carry me through to the next Friday.

(*Pause.*)

That's all I got, Rose. That's all I got to give. I can't give nothing else.

(TROY *exits into the house. The lights go down to black.*)

SCENE IV

It is Friday. Two weeks later. CORY *starts out of the house with his football equipment. The phone rings.*

CORY: (*Calling.*) I got it!

(*He answers the phone and stands in the screen door talking.*)

Hello? Hey, Jesse. Naw . . . I was just getting ready to leave now.

ROSE: (*Calling.*) Cory!

5 CORY: I told you, man, them spikes is all tore up. You can use them if you want, but they ain't no good. Earl got some spikes.

ROSE: (*Calling.*) Cory!

CORY: (*Calling to* ROSE.) Mam? I'm talking to Jesse.

(*Into phone.*)

10 When she say that. (*Pause.*) Aw, you lying, man. I'm gonna tell her you said that.

ROSE: (*Calling.*) Cory, don't you go nowhere!

CORY: I got to go to the game, Ma!

(*Into the phone.*)

Yeah, hey, look, I'll talk to you later. Yeah, I'll meet you 15 over Earl's house. Later. Bye, Ma.

(CORY *exits the house and starts out the yard.*)

ROSE: Cory, where you going off to? You got that stuff all pulled out and thrown all over your room.

CORY: (*In the yard.*) I was looking for my spikes. Jesse wanted to borrow my spikes.

20 ROSE: Get up there and get that cleaned up before your daddy get back in here.

CORY: I got to go to the game! I'll clean it up *when I get back*

(CORY *exits.*)

ROSE: That's all he need to do is see that room all messed up.

(ROSE *exits into the house.* TROY *and* BONO *enter the yard.* TROY *is dressed in clothes other than his work clothes.*)

BONO: He told him the same thing he told you. Take it to the union. 25

TROY: Brownie ain't got that much sense. Man wasn't thinking about nothing. He wait until I confront them on it . . . then he wanna come crying seniority.

(*Calls.*)

Hey, Rose!

BONO: I wish I could have seen Mr. Rand's face when he told 30 you.

TROY: He couldn't get it out of his mouth! Liked to bit his tongue! When they called me down there to the Commissioner's office . . . he thought they was gonna fire me. Like everybody else. 35

BONO: I didn't think they was gonna fire you. I thought they was gonna put you on the warning paper.

TROY: Hey, Rose!

(*To* BONO.)

Yeah, Mr. Rand like to bit his tongue.

(TROY *breaks the seal on the bottle, takes a drink, and hands it to* BONO.)

BONO: I see you run right down to Taylors' and told that Al- 40 berta gal.

TROY: (*Calling.*) Hey Rose! (*To* BONO.) I told everybody. Hey, Rose! I went down there to cash my check.

ROSE: (*Entering from the house.*) Hush all that hollering, man! I know you out here. What they say down there at the 45 Commissioner's office?

TROY: You supposed to come when I call you, woman. Bono'll tell you that.

(*To* BONO.)

Don't Lucille come when you call her?

ROSE: Man, hush your mouth. I ain't no dog . . . talk about 50 "come when you call me."

TROY: (*Puts his arm around* ROSE.) You hear this, Bono? I had me an old dog used to get uppity like that. You say, "C'mere, Blue!" . . . and he just lay there and look at you. End up getting a stick and chasing him away trying to 55 make him come.

ROSE: I ain't studying you and your dog. I remember you used to sing that old song.

TROY: (*He sings.*) Hear it ring! Hear it ring! I had a dog his name was Blue. 60

ROSE: Don't nobody wanna hear you sing that old song.

TROY: (*Sings.*) You know Blue was mighty true.

ROSE: Used to have Cory running around here singing that song.

BONO: Hell, I remember that song myself.

TROY: (*Sings.*) 65

You know Blue was a good old dog.
Blue treed a possum in a hollow log.

That was my daddy's song. My daddy made up that song.

ROSE: I don't care who made it up. Don't nobody wanna hear
70   you sing it.
TROY: (*Makes a song like calling a dog.*) Come here, woman.
ROSE: You come in here carrying on, I reckon they ain't fired
        you. What they say down there at the Commissioner's office?
TROY: Look here, Rose . . . Mr. Rand called me into his of-
75   fice today when I got back from talking to them people
        down there . . . it come from up top . . . he called me in
        and told me they was making me a driver.
ROSE: Troy, you kidding!
TROY: No I ain't. Ask Bono.
80 ROSE: Well, that's great, Troy. Now you don't have to hassle
        them people no more.

(LYONS *enters from the street.*)

TROY: Aw hell, I wasn't looking to see you today. I thought
        you was in jail. Got it all over the front page of the *Courier*
        about them raiding Sefus' place . . . where you be hanging
85   out with all them thugs?
LYONS: Hey, Pop . . . that ain't got nothing to do with me. I
        don't go down there gambling. I go down there to sit in
        with the band. I ain't got nothing to do with the gambling
        part. They got some good music down there.
90 TROY: They got some rogues . . . is what they got.
LYONS: How you been, Mr. Bono? Hi, Rose.
BONO: I see where you playing down at the Crawford Grill
        tonight.
ROSE: How come you ain't brought Bonnie like I told you.
95   You should have brought Bonnie with you, she ain't been
        over in a month of Sundays.
LYONS: I was just in the neighborhood . . . thought I'd stop by.
TROY: Here he come . . .
BONO: Your daddy got a promotion on the rubbish. He's
100   gonna be the first colored driver. Ain't got to do nothing
        but sit up there and read the paper like them white fellows.
LYONS: Hey, Pop . . . if you knew how to read you'd be alright.
BONO: Naw . . . naw . . . you mean if the nigger knew how
        to *drive* he'd be all right. Been fighting with them people
105   about driving and ain't even got a license. Mr. Rand know
        you ain't got no driver's license?
TROY: Driving ain't nothing. All you do is point the truck
        where you want it to go. Driving ain't nothing.
BONO: Do Mr. Rand know you ain't got no driver's license?
110   That's what I'm talking about. I ain't asked if driving was
        easy. I asked if Mr. Rand know you ain't got no driver's li-
        cense.
TROY: He ain't got to know. The man ain't got to know my busi-
        ness. Time he find out, I have two or three driver's licenses.
115 LYONS: (*Going into his pocket.*) Say, look here, Pop . . .
TROY: I knew it was coming. Didn't I tell you, Bono? I know
        what kind of "Look here, Pop" that was. The nigger fix-
        ing to ask me for some money. It's Friday night. It's my
        payday. All them rogues down there on the avenue . . . the
120   ones that ain't in jail . . . and Lyons is hopping in his shoes
        to get down there with them.
LYONS; See, Pop . . . if you give somebody else a chance to
        talk sometime, you'd see that I was fixing to pay you back
        your ten dollars like I told you. Here . . . I told you I'd pay
125   you when Bonnie got paid.

TROY: Naw . . . you go ahead and keep that ten dollars. Put
        it in the bank. The next time you feel like you wanna
        come by here and ask me for something . . . you go on
        down there and get that.
LYONS: Here's your ten dollars, Pop. I told you I don't want you   130
        to give me nothing. I just wanted to borrow ten dollars.
TROY: Naw . . . you go on and keep that for the next time
        you want to ask me.
LYONS: Come on, Pop . . . here go your ten dollars.
ROSE: Why don't you go on and let the boy pay you back, Troy?   135
LYONS: Here you go, Rose. If you don't take it I'm gonna
        have to hear about it for the next six months.

(*He hands her the money.*)

ROSE: You can hand yours over here too, Troy.
TROY: You see this, Bono. You see how they do me.
BONO: Yeah, Lucille do me the same way.   140

(GABRIEL *is heard singing offstage. He enters.*)

GABRIEL: Better get ready for the Judgment! Better get ready
        for . . . Hey! . . . Hey! . . . There's Troy's boy!
LYONS: How you doing, Uncle Gabe?
GABRIEL: Lyons . . . The King of the Jungle! Rose . . . hey,
        Rose. Got a flower for you.   145

(*He takes a rose from his pocket.*)

        Picked it myself. That's the same rose like you is!
ROSE: That's right nice of you, Gabe.
LYONS: What you been doing, Uncle Gabe?
GABRIEL: Oh, I been chasing hellhounds and waiting on the
        time to tell St. Peter to open the gates.   150
LYONS: You been chasing hellhounds, huh? Well . . . you doing
        the right thing, Uncle Gabe. Somebody got to chase them.
GABRIEL: Oh, yeah . . . I know it. The devil's strong. The devil
        ain't no pushover. Hellhounds snipping at everybody's
        heels. But I got my trumpet waiting on the judgment time. 155
LYONS: Waiting on the Battle of Armageddon, huh?
GABRIEL: Ain't gonna be too much of a battle when God get
        to waving that Judgment sword. But the people's gonna
        have a hell of a time trying to get into heaven if them
        gates ain't open.   160
LYONS: (*Putting his arm around* GABRIEL.) You hear this, Pop.
        Uncle Gabe, you alright!
GABRIEL: (*Laughing with* LYONS.) Lyons! King of the Jungle.
ROSE: You gonna stay for supper, Gabe. Want me to fix you
        a plate?   165
GABRIEL: I'll take a sandwich, Rose. Don't want no plate. Just
        wanna eat with my hands. I'll take a sandwich.
ROSE: How about you, Lyons? You staying? Got some short
        ribs cooking.
LYONS: Naw, I won't eat nothing till after we finished playing.   170

(*Pause.*)

        You ought to come down and listen to me play, Pop.
TROY: I don't like that Chinese music. All that noise.
ROSE: Go on in the house and wash up, Gabe . . . I'll fix you
        a sandwich.

175 GABRIEL: (*To* LYONS, *as he exits.*) Troy's mad at me.

LYONS: What you mad at Uncle Gabe for, Pop.

ROSE: He thinks Troy's mad at him cause he moved over to Miss Pearl's.

TROY: I ain't mad at the man. He can live where he want to
180 live at.

LYONS: What he move over there for? Miss Pearl don't like nobody.

ROSE: She don't mind him none. She treats him real nice. She just don't allow all that singing.

185 TROY: She don't mind that rent he be paying . . . that's what she don't mind.

ROSE: Troy, I ain't going through that with you no more. He's over there cause he want to have his own place. He can come and go as he please

190 TROY: Hell, he could come and go as he please here. I wasn't stopping him. I ain't put no rules on him.

ROSE: It ain't the same thing, Troy. And you know it.

(GABRIEL *comes to the door.*)

Now, that's the last I wanna hear about that. I don't wanna hear nothing else about Gabe and Miss Pearl. And next
195 week . . .

GABRIEL: I'm ready for my sandwich, Rose.

ROSE: And next week . . . when that recruiter come from that school . . . I want you to sign that paper and go on and let Cory play football. Then that'll be the last I have to hear
200 about that.

TROY: (*To* ROSE *as she exits into the house.*) I ain't thinking about Cory nothing.

LYONS: What . . . Cory got recruited? What school he going to?

TROY: That boy walking around here smelling his piss . . .
205 thinking he's grown. Thinking he's gonna do what he want, irrespective of what I say. Look here, Bono . . . I left the Commissioner's office and went down to the A&P . . . that boy ain't working down there. He lying to me. Telling me he got his job back . . . telling me he working
210 weekends . . . telling me he working after school . . . Mr. Stawicki tell me he ain't working down there at all!

LYONS: Cory just growing up. He's just busting at the seams trying to fill out your shoes.

TROY: I don't care what he's doing. When he get to the point
215 where he wanna disobey me . . . then it's time for him to move on. Bono'll tell you that. I bet he ain't never disobeyed his daddy without paying the consequences.

BONO: I ain't never had a chance. My daddy came on through . . . but I ain't never knew him to see him . . . or what he
220 had on his mind or where he went. Just moving on through. Searching out the New Land. That's what the old folks used to call it. See a fellow moving around from place to place . . . woman to woman . . . called it searching out the New Land. I can't say if he ever found it. I come along,
225 didn't want no kids. Didn't know if I was gonna be in one place long enough to fix on them right as their daddy. I figured I was going searching too. As it turned out I been hooked up with Lucille near about as long as your daddy been with Rose. Going on eighteen years.

230 TROY: Sometimes I wish I hadn't known my daddy. He ain't cared nothing about no kids. A kid to him wasn't noth-

ing. All he wanted was for you to learn how to walk so he could start you to working. When it come time for eating . . . he ate first. If there was anything left over, that's
235 what you got. Man would sit down and eat two chickens and give you the wing.

LYONS: You ought to stop that, Pop. Everybody feed their kids. No matter how hard times is . . . everybody care about their kids. Make sure they have something to eat.

240 TROY: The only thing my daddy cared about was getting them bales of cotton into Mr. Lubin. That's the only thing that mattered to him. Sometimes I used to wonder why he was living. Wonder why the devil hadn't come and got him. "Get them bales of cotton in to Mr. Lubin" and find
245 out he owe him money . . .

LYONS: He should have just went on and left when he saw he couldn't get nowhere. That's what I would have done.

TROY: How he gonna leave with eleven kids? And where he gonna go? He ain't know how to do nothing but farm.
250 No, he was trapped and I think he knew it. But I'll say this for him . . . he felt a responsibility toward us. Maybe he ain't treated us the way I felt he should have . . . but without that responsibility he could have walked off and left us . . . made his own way.

255 BONO: A lot of them did. Back in those days what you talking about . . . they walk out their front door and just take on down one road or another and keep on walking.

LYONS: There you go! That's what I'm talking about.

BONO: Just keep on walking till you come to something else.
260 Ain't you never heard of nobody having the walking blues? Well, that's what you call it when you just take off like that.

TROY: My daddy ain't had them walking blues! What you talking about? He stayed right there with his family. But he was just as evil as he could be. My mama couldn't stand
265 him. Couldn't stand that evilness. She run off when I was about eight. She sneaked off one night after he had gone to sleep. Told me she was coming back for me. I ain't never seen her no more. All his women run off and left him. He wasn't good for nobody.

270 When my turn come to head out, I was fourteen and got to sniffing around Joe Canewell's daughter. Had us an old mule we called Greyboy. My daddy sent me out to do some plowing and I tied up Greyboy and went to fooling around with Joe Canewell's daughter. We done found us a nice lit-
275 tle spot, got real cozy with each other. She about thirteen and we done figured we was grown anyway . . . so we down there enjoying ourselves . . . ain't thinking about nothing. We didn't know Greyboy had got loose and wandered back to the house and my daddy was looking for me. We down
280 there by the creek enjoying ourselves when my daddy come up on us. Surprised us. He had them leather straps off the mule and commenced to whupping me like there was no tomorrow. I jumped up, mad and embarrassed. I was scared of my daddy. When he commenced to whupping on
285 me . . . quite naturally I run to get out of the way.

(*Pause.*)

Now I thought he was mad cause I ain't done my work. But I see where he was chasing me off so he could have the gal for himself. When I see what the matter of it was,

I lost all fear of my daddy. Right there is where I become a man . . . at fourteen years of age.

(*Pause.*)

Now it was my turn to run him off. I picked up them same reins that he had used on me. I picked up them reins and commenced to whupping on him. The gal jumped up and run off . . . and when my daddy turned to face me, I could see why the devil had never come to get him . . . cause he was the devil himself. I don't know what happened. When I woke up, I was laying right there by the creek, and Blue . . . this old dog we had . . . was licking my face. I thought I was blind. I couldn't see nothing. Both my eyes were swollen shut. I layed there and cried. I didn't know what I was gonna do. The only thing I knew was the time had come for me to leave my daddy's house. And right there the world suddenly got big. And it was a long time before I could cut it down to where I could handle it.

Part of that cutting down was when I got to the place where I could feel him kicking in my blood and knew that the only thing that separated us was the matter of a few years.

(GABRIEL *enters from the house with a sandwich.*)

LYONS: What you got there, Uncle Gabe?

GABRIEL: Got me a ham sandwich. Rose gave me a ham sandwich.

TROY: I don't know what happened to him. I done lost touch with everybody except Gabriel. But I hope he's dead. I hope he found some peace.

LYONS: That's a heavy story, Pop. I didn't know you left home when you was fourteen.

TROY: And didn't know nothing. The only part of the world I knew was the forty-two acres of Mr. Lubin's land. That's all I knew about life.

LYONS: Fourteen's kinda young to be out on your own. (*Phone rings.*) I don't even think I was ready to be out on my own at fourteen. I don't know what I would have done.

TROY: I got up from the creek and walked on down to Mobile. I was through with farming. Figured I could do better in the city. So I walked the two hundred miles to Mobile.

LYONS: Wait a minute . . . you ain't walked no two hundred miles, Pop. Ain't nobody gonna walk no two hundred miles. You talking about some walking there.

BONO: That's the only way you got anywhere back in them days.

LYONS: Shhh. Damn if I wouldn't have hitched a ride with somebody!

TROY: Who you gonna hitch it with? They ain't had no cars and things like they got now. We talking about 1918.

ROSE: (*Entering.*) What you all out here getting into?

TROY: (*To* ROSE.) I'm telling Lyons how good he got it. He don't know nothing about this I'm talking.

ROSE: Lyons, that was Bonnie on the phone. She say you supposed to pick her up.

LYONS: Yeah, okay, Rose.

TROY: I walked on down to Mobile and hitched up with some of them fellows that was heading this way. Got up here and found out . . . not only couldn't you get a job . . . you couldn't find no place to live. I thought I was in freedom. Shhh. Colored folks living down there on the riverbanks in whatever kind of shelter they could find for themselves. Right down there under the Brady Street Bridge. Living in shacks made of sticks and tarpaper. Messed around there and went from bad to worse. Started stealing. First it was food. Then I figured, hell, if I steal money I can buy me some food. Buy me some shoes too! One thing led to another. Met your mama. I was young and anxious to be a man. Met your mama and had you. What I do that for? Now I got to worry about feeding you and her. Got to steal three times as much. Went out one day looking for somebody to rob . . . that's what I was, a robber. I'll tell you the truth. I'm ashamed of it today. But it's the truth. Went to rob this fellow . . . pulled out my knife . . . and he pulled out a gun. Shot me in the chest. It felt just like somebody had taken a hot branding iron and laid it on me. When he shot me I jumped at him with my knife. They told me I killed him and they put me in the penitentiary and locked me up for fifteen years. That's where I met Bono. That's where I learned how to play baseball. Got out that place and your mama had taken you and went on to make life without me. Fifteen years was a long time for her to wait. But that fifteen years cured me of that robbing stuff. Rose'll tell you. She asked me when I met her if I had gotten all that foolishness out of my system. And I told her, "Baby, it's you and baseball all what count with me." You hear me, Bono? I meant it too. She say, "Which one comes first?" I told her, "Baby, ain't no doubt it's baseball . . . but you stick and get old with me and we'll both outlive this baseball." Am I right, Rose? And it's true.

ROSE: Man, hush your mouth. You ain't said no such thing. Talking about, "Baby, you know you'll always be number one with me." That's what you was talking.

TROY: You hear that, Bono. That's why I love her.

BONO: Rose'll keep you straight. You get off the track, she'll straighten you up.

ROSE: Lyons, you better get on up and get Bonnie. She waiting on you.

LYONS: (*Gets up to go.*) Hey, Pop, why don't you come on down to the Grill and hear me play?

TROY: I ain't going down there. I'm too old to be sitting around in them clubs.

BONO: You got to be good to play down at the Grill.

LYONS: Come on, Pop . . .

TROY: I got to get up in the morning.

LYONS: You ain't got to stay long.

TROY: Naw, I'm gonna get my supper and go on to bed.

LYONS: Well, I got to go. I'll see you again.

TROY: Don't you come around my house on my payday.

ROSE: Pick up the phone and let somebody know you coming. And bring Bonnie with you. You know I'm always glad to see her.

LYONS: Yeah, I'll do that, Rose. You take care now. See you, Pop. See you, Mr. Bono. See you, Uncle Gabe.

GABRIEL: Lyons! King of the Jungle!

(LYONS *exits.*)

TROY: Is supper ready, woman? Me and you got some business to take care of. I'm gonna tear it up too.

ROSE: Troy, I done told you now!

TROY: (*Puts his arm around* BONO.) Aw hell, woman . . . this is Bono. Bono like family. I done known this nigger since . . . how long I done know you?

405 BONO: It's been a long time.

TROY: I done known this nigger since Skippy was a pup. Me and him done been through some times.

BONO: You sure right about that.

TROY: Hell, I done know him longer than I known you. And 410 we still standing shoulder to shoulder. Hey, look here, Bono . . . a man can't ask for no more than that.

(*Drinks to him.*)

I love you, nigger.

BONO: Hell, I love you too . . . but I got to get home see my woman. You got yours in hand. I got to go get mine.

(BONO *starts to exit as* CORY *enters the yard, dressed in his football uniform. He gives* TROY *a hard, uncompromising look.*)

415 CORY: What you do that for, Pop?

(*He throws his helmet down in the direction of* TROY.)

ROSE: What's the matter? Cory . . . what's the matter?

CORY: Papa done went up to the school and told Coach Zellman I can't play football no more. Wouldn't even let me play the game. Told him to tell the recruiter not to come.

420 ROSE: Troy . . .

TROY: What you Troying me for? Yeah, I did it. And the boy know why I did it.

CORY: Why you wanna do that to me? That was the one chance I had.

425 ROSE: Ain't nothing wrong with Cory playing football, Troy.

TROY: The boy lied to me. I told the nigger if he wanna play football . . . to keep his chores and hold down that job at the A&P. That was the conditions. Stopped down there to see Mr. Stawicki . . .

430 CORY: I can't work after school during the football season, Pop! I tried to tell you that Mr. Stawicki's holding my job for me. You don't never want to listen to nobody. And then you wanna go and do this to me!

TROY: I ain't done nothing to you. You done it to yourself.

435 CORY: Just cause you didn't have a chance! You just scared I'm gonna be better than you, that's all.

TROY: Come here.

ROSE: Troy . . .

(CORY *reluctantly crosses over to* TROY.)

TROY: Alright! See. You done made a mistake.

440 CORY: I didn't even do nothing!

TROY: I'm gonna tell you what your mistake was. See . . . you swung at the ball and didn't hit it. That's strike one. See, you in the batter's box now. You swung and you missed. That's strike one. Don't you strike out!

(*Lights fade to black.*)

SCENE I

The following morning. CORY *is at the tree hitting the ball with the bat. He tries to mimic* TROY, *but his swing is awkward, less sure.* ROSE *enters from the house.*

ROSE: Cory, I want you to help me with this cupboard.

CORY: I ain't quitting the team. I don't care what Poppa say.

ROSE: I'll talk to him when he gets back. He had to go see about your Uncle Gabe. The police done arrested him. Say he was disturbing the peace. He'll be back directly. Come 5 on in here and help me clean out the top of this cupboard.

(CORY *exits into the house.* ROSE *sees* TROY *and* BONO *coming down the alley.*)

Troy . . . what they say down there?

TROY: Ain't said nothing. I give them fifty dollars and they let him go. I'll talk to you about it. Where's Cory?

ROSE: He's in there helping me clean out these cupboards.   10

TROY: Tell him to get his butt out here.

(TROY *and* BONO *go over to the pile of wood.* BONO *picks up the saw and begins sawing.*)

TROY: (*To* BONO.) All they want is the money. That makes six or seven times I done went down there and got him. See me coming they stick out their hands.

BONO: Yeah. I know what you mean. That's all they care 15 about . . . that money. They don't care about what's right.

(*Pause.*)

Nigger, why you got to go and get some hard wood? You ain't doing nothing but building a little old fence. Get you some soft pine wood. That's all you need.

TROY: I know what I'm doing. This is outside wood. You 20 put pine wood inside the house. Pine wood is inside wood. This here is outside wood. Now you tell me where the fence is gonna be?

BONO: You don't need this wood. You can put it up with pine wood and it's stand as long as you gonna be here 25 looking at it.

TROY: How you know how long I'm gonna be here, nigger? Hell, I might just live forever. Live longer than old man Horsely.

BONO: That's what Magee used to say.   30

TROY: Magee's a damn fool. Now you tell me who you ever heard of gonna pull their own teeth with a pair of rusty pliers.

BONO: The old folks . . . my granddaddy used to pull his teeth with pliers. They ain't had no dentists for the colored 35 folks back then.

TROY: Get clean pliers! You understand? Clean pliers! Sterilize them! Besides we ain't living back then. All Magee had to do was walk over to Doc Goldblums.

BONO: I see where you and that Tallahassee gal . . . that Al- 40 berta . . . I see where you all done got tight.

TROY: What you mean "got tight"?

BONO: I see where you be laughing and joking with her all the time.

45 TROY: I laughs and jokes with all of them, Bono. You know me.
BONO: That ain't the kind of laughing and joking I'm talking about.

(CORY *enters from the house.*)

CORY: How you doing, Mr. Bono?
TROY: Cory? Get that saw from Bono and cut some wood.
50   He talking about the wood's too hard to cut. Stand back there, Jim, and let that young boy show you how it's done.
BONO: He's sure welcome to it.

(CORY *takes the saw and begins to cut the wood.*)

Whew-e-e! Look at that. Big old strong boy. Look like Joe Louis. Hell, must be getting old the way I'm watching that
55   boy whip through that wood.
CORY: I don't see why Mama want a fence around the yard noways.
TROY: Damn if I know either. What the hell she keeping out with it? She ain't got nothing nobody want.
60 BONO: Some people build fences to keep people out . . . and other people build fences to keep people in. Rose wants to hold on to you all. She loves you.
TROY: Hell, nigger, I don't need nobody to tell me my wife loves me, Cory . . . go on in the house and see if you can
65   find that other saw.
CORY: Where's it at?
TROY: I said find it! Look for it till you find it!

(CORY *exits into the house.*)

What's that supposed to mean? Wanna keep us in?
BONO: Troy . . . I done known you seem like damn near my
70   whole life. You and Rose both. I done know both of you all for a long time. I remember when you met Rose. When you was hitting them baseball out the park. A lot of them old gals was after you then. You had the pick of the litter. When you picked Rose, I was happy for you.
75   That was the first time I knew you had any sense. I said . . . My man Troy knows what he's doing . . . I'm gonna follow this nigger . . . he might take me somewhere. I been following you too. I done learned a whole heap of things about life watching you. I done learned how to tell where
80   the shit lies. How to tell it from the alfalfa. You done learned me a lot of things. You showed me how to not make the same mistakes . . . to take life as it comes along and keep putting one foot in front of the other.

(*Pause.*)

Rose a good woman, Troy.
85 TROY: Hell, nigger, I know she a good woman. I been married to her for eighteen years. What you got on your mind, Bono?
BONO: I just say she a good woman. Just like I say anything. I ain't got to have nothing on my mind.
TROY: You just gonna say she a good woman and leave it
90   hanging out there like that? Why you telling me she a good woman?
BONO: She loves you, Troy. Rose loves you.
TROY: You saying I don't measure up. That's what you trying to say. I don't measure up cause I'm seeing this other gal.
95   I know what you trying to say.

BONO: I know what Rose means to you, Troy. I'm just trying to say I don't want to see you mess up.
TROY: Yeah, I appreciate that, Bono. If you was messing around on Lucille I'd be telling you the same thing.
BONO: Well, that's all I got to say. I just say that because I love 100 you both.
TROY: Hell, you know me . . . I wasn't out there looking for nothing. You can't find a better woman than Rose. I know that. But seems like this woman just stuck onto me where I can't shake her loose. I done wrestled with it, 105 tried to throw her off me . . . but she just stuck on tighter. Now she's stuck on for good.
BONO: You's in control . . . that's what you tell me all the time. You responsible for what you do.
TROY: I ain't ducking the responsibility of it. As long as it sets 110 right in my heart . . . then I'm okay. Cause that's all I listen to. It'll tell me right from wrong every time. And I ain't talking about doing Rose no bad turn. I love Rose. She done carried me a long ways and I love and respect her for that. 115
BONO: I know you do. That's why I don't want to see you hurt her. But what you gonna do when she find out? What you got then? If you try and juggle both of them . . . sooner or later you gonna drop one of them. That's common sense.
TROY: Yeah, I hear what you saying, Bono. I been trying to 120 figure a way to work it out.
BONO: Work it out right, Troy. I don't want to be getting all up between you and Rose's business . . . but work it so it come out right.
TROY: Aw hell, I get all up between you and Lucille's business. 125 When you gonna get that woman that refrigerator she been wanting? Don't tell me you ain't got no money now. I know who your banker is. Mellon don't need that money bad as Lucille want that refrigerator. I'll tell you that.
BONO: Tell you what I'll do . . . when you finish building this 130 fence for Rose . . . I'll buy Lucille that refrigerator.
TROY: You done stuck your foot in your mouth now!

(TROY *grabs up a board and begins to saw.* BONO *starts to walk out the yard.*)

Hey, nigger . . . where you going?
BONO: I'm going home. I know you don't expect me to help you now. I'm protecting my money. I wanna see you put 135 that fence up by yourself. That's what I want to see. You'll be here another six month without me.
TROY: Nigger, you ain't right.
BONO: When it comes to my money . . . I'm right as fireworks on the Fourth of July. 140
TROY: Alright, we gonna see now. You better get out your bankbook.

(BONO *exits, and* TROY *continues to work.* ROSE *enters from the house.*)

ROSE: What they say down there? What's happening with Gabe?
TROY: I went down there and got him out. Cost me fifty dol- 145 lars. Say he was disturbing the peace. Judge set up a hearing for him in three weeks. Say to show cause why he shouldn't be re-committed.

ROSE: What was he doing that cause them to arrest him?

150 TROY: Some kids was teasing him and he run them off home. Say he was howling and carrying on. Some folks seen him and called the police. That's all it was.

ROSE: Well, what's you say? What'd you tell the judge?

TROY: Told him I'd look after him. It didn't make no sense to
155 recommit the man. He stuck out his big greasy palm and told me to give him fifty dollars and take him on home.

ROSE: Where's he at now? Where'd he go off to?

TROY: He's gone on about his business. He don't need nobody to hold his hand.

160 ROSE: Well, I don't know. Seem like that would be the best place for him if they did put him into the hospital. I know what you're gonna say. But that's what I think would be best.

TROY: The man done had his life ruined fighting for what?
165 And they wanna take and lock him up. Let him be free. He don't bother nobody.

ROSE: Well, everybody got their own way of looking at it I guess. Come on and get your lunch. I got a bowl of lima beans and some cornbread in the oven. Come on get
170 something to eat. Ain't no sense you fretting over Gabe.

(ROSE *turns to go into the house.*)

TROY: Rose . . . got something to tell you.

ROSE: Well, come on . . . wait till I get this food on the table.

TROY: Rose!

(*She stops and turns around.*)

I don't know how to say this.

(*Pause.*)

175 I can't explain it none. It just sort of grows on you till it gets out of hand. It starts out like a little bush . . . and the next thing you know it's a whole forest.

ROSE: Troy . . . what is you talking about?

TROY: I'm talking, woman, let me talk. I'm trying to find a
180 way to tell you . . . I'm gonna be a daddy. I'm gonna be somebody's daddy.

ROSE: Troy . . . you're not telling me this? You're gonna be . . . what?

TROY: Rose . . . now . . . see . . .

185 ROSE: You telling me you gonna be somebody's daddy? You telling your *wife* this?

(GABRIEL *enters from the street. He carries a rose in his hand.*)

GABRIEL: Hey, Troy! Hey, Rose!

ROSE: I have to wait eighteen years to hear something like this.

GABRIEL: Hey, Rose . . . I got a flower for you.

(*He hands it to her.*)

190 That's a rose. Same rose like you is.

ROSE: Thanks, Gabe.

GABRIEL: Troy, you ain't mad at me is you? Them bad mens come and put me away. You ain't mad at me is you?

TROY: No, Gabe, I ain't mad at you.

195 ROSE: Eighteen years and you wanna come with this.

GABRIEL: (*Takes a quarter out of his pocket.*) See what I got? Got a brand new quarter.

TROY: Rose . . . it's just . . .

ROSE: Ain't nothing you can say, Troy. Ain't no way of explaining that. 200

GABRIEL: Fellow that give me this quarter had a whole mess of them. I'm gonna keep this quarter till it stop shining.

ROSE: Gabe, go on in the house there. I got some watermelon in the frigidaire. Go on and get you a piece.

GABRIEL: Say, Rose . . . you know I was chasing hellhounds 205 and them bad mens come and get me and take me away. Troy helped me. He come down there and told them they better let me go before he beat them up. Yeah, he did!

ROSE: You go on and get you a piece of watermelon, Gabe. Them bad mens is gone now. 210

GABRIEL: Okay, Rose . . . gonna get me some watermelon. The kind with the stripes on it.

(GABRIEL *exits into the house.*)

ROSE: Why, Troy? Why? After all these years to come dragging this in to me now. It don't make no sense at your age. I could have expected this ten or fifteen years ago, but not 215 now.

TROY: Age ain't got nothing to do with it, Rose.

ROSE: I done tried to be everything a wife should be. Everything a wife could be. Been married eighteen years and I got to live to see the day you tell me you been seeing an- 220 other woman and done fathered a child by her. And you know I ain't never wanted no half nothing in my family. My whole family is half. Everybody got different fathers and mothers . . . my two sisters and my brother. Can't hardly tell who's who. Can't never sit down and talk about 225 Papa and Mama. It's your papa and your mama and my papa and my mama . . .

TROY: Rose . . . stop it now.

ROSE: I ain't never wanted that for none of my children. And now you wanna drag your behind in here and tell me 230 something like this.

TROY: You ought to know. It's time for you to know.

ROSE: Well, I don't want to know, goddamn it!

TROY: I can't just make it go away. It's done now. I can't wish the circumstance of the thing away. 235

ROSE: And you don't want to either. Maybe you want to wish me and my boy away. Maybe that's what you want? Well, you can't wish us away. I've got eighteen years of my life invested in you. You ought to have stayed upstairs in my bed where you belong. 240

TROY: Rose . . . now listen to me . . . we can get a handle on this thing. We can talk this out . . . come to an understanding.

ROSE: All of a sudden it's "we." Where was "we" at when you was down there rolling around with some godforsaken woman? "We" should have come to an understanding be- 245 fore you started making a damn fool of yourself. You're a day late and a dollar short when it comes to an understanding with me.

TROY: It's just . . . She gives me a different idea . . . a different understanding about myself. I can step out of this house 250 and get away from the pressures and problems . . . be a different man. I ain't got to wonder how I'm gonna pay the bills or get the roof fixed. I can just be a part of myself that I ain't never been.

ROSE: What I want to know . . . is do you plan to continue 255 seeing her. That's all you can say to me.

TROY: I can sit up in her house and laugh. Do you understand what I'm saying. I can laugh out loud . . . and it feels good. It reaches all the way down to the bottom of my shoes.

(*Pause.*)

260 Rose, I can't give that up.

ROSE: Maybe you ought to go on and stay down there with her . . . if she a better woman than me.

TROY: It ain't about nobody being a better woman or nothing. Rose, you ain't the blame. A man couldn't ask for no
265 woman to be a better wife than you've been. I'm responsible for it. I done locked myself into a pattern trying to take care of you all that I forgot about myself.

ROSE: What the hell was I there for? That was my job, not somebody else's.

270 TROY: Rose, I done tried all my life to live decent . . . to live a clean . . . hard . . . useful life. I tried to be a good husband to you. In every way I knew how. Maybe I come into the world backwards, I don't know. But . . . you born with two strikes on you before you come to the plate. You got to guard it
275 closely . . . always looking for the curve-ball on the inside corner. You can't afford to let none get past you. You can't afford a call strike. If you going down . . . you going down swinging. Everything lined up against you. What you gonna do. I fooled them, Rose. I bunted. When I found you and
280 Cory and a halfway decent job . . . I was safe. Couldn't nothing touch me. I wasn't gonna strike out no more. I wasn't going back to the penitentiary. I wasn't gonna lay in the streets with a bottle of wine. I was safe. I had me a family. A job. I wasn't gonna get that last strike. I was on first looking
285 for one of them boys to knock me in. To get me home.

ROSE: You should have stayed in my bed, Troy.

TROY: Then when I saw that gal . . . she firmed up my backbone. And I got to thinking that if I tried . . . I just might be able to steal second. Do you understand after eighteen
290 years I wanted to steal second.

ROSE: You should have held me tight. You should have grabbed me and held on.

TROY: I stood on first base for eighteen years and I thought . . . well, goddamn it . . . go on for it!

295 ROSE: We're not talking about baseball! We're talking about you going off to lay in bed with another woman . . . and then bring it home to me. That's what we're talking about. We ain't talking about no baseball.

TROY: Rose, you're not listening to me. I'm trying the best I
300 can to explain it to you. It's not easy for me to admit that I been standing in the same place for eighteen years.

ROSE: I been standing with you! I been right here with you, Troy. I got a life too. I gave eighteen years of my life to stand in the same spot with you. Don't you think I ever wanted
305 other things? Don't you think I had dreams and hopes? What about my life? What about me? Don't you think it ever crossed my mind to want to know other men? That I wanted to lay up somewhere and forget about my responsibilities? That I wanted someone to make me laugh so I
310 could feel good? You not the only one who's got wants and needs. But I held on to you, Troy. I took all my feelings, my wants and needs, my dreams . . . and I buried them inside you. I planted a seed and watched and prayed over it. I planted myself inside you and waited to bloom. And it
315 didn't take me no eighteen years to find out the soil was hard and rocky and it wasn't never gonna bloom.

But I held on to you, Troy. I held you tighter. You was my husband. I owed you everything I had. Every part of me I could find to give you. And upstairs in that room . . . with the darkness falling in on me . . . I gave everything I
320 had to try and erase the doubt that you wasn't the finest man in the world. And wherever you was going . . . I wanted to be there with you. Cause you was my husband. Cause that's the only way I was gonna survive as your wife. You always talking about what you give . . . and what
325 you don't have to give. But you take too. You take . . . and don't even know nobody's giving!

(ROSE *turns to exit into the house;* TROY *grabs her arm.*)

TROY: You say I take and don't give!

ROSE: Troy! You're hurting me!

TROY: You say I take and don't give.   330

ROSE: Troy . . . you're hurting my arm! Let go!

TROY: I done give you everything I got. Don't you tell that lie on me.

ROSE: Troy!

TROY: Don't you tell that lie on me!   335

(CORY *enters from the house.*)

CORY: Mama!

ROSE: Troy. You're hurting me.

TROY: Don't you tell me about no taking and giving.

(CORY *comes up behind* TROY *and grabs him.* TROY, *surprised, is thrown off balance just as cory throws a glancing blow that catches him on the chest and knocks him down.* TROY *is stunned, as is* CORY.)

ROSE: Troy. Troy. No!

(TROY *gets to his feet and starts at* CORY.)

Troy . . . no. Please! Troy!   340

(ROSE *pulls on* TROY *to hold him back.* TROY *stops himself.*)

TROY: (*To* CORY.) Alright. That's strike two. You stay away from around me, boy. Don't you strike out. You living with a full count. Don't you strike out.

(TROY *exits out the yard as the lights go down.*)

SCENE II

It is six months later, early afternoon. TROY *enters from the house and starts to exit the yard.* ROSE *enters from the house.*

ROSE: Troy, I want to talk to you.

TROY: All of a sudden, after all this time, you want to talk to me, huh? You ain't wanted to talk to me for months. You ain't wanted to talk to me last night. You ain't wanted no part of me then. What you wanna talk to me about now? 5

ROSE: Tomorrow's Friday.

TROY: I know what day tomorrow is. You think I don't know tomorrow's Friday? My whole life I ain't done nothing but look to see Friday coming and you got to tell me it's Friday.

10   ROSE: I want to know if you're coming home.

TROY: I always come home, Rose. You know that. There ain't never been a night I ain't come home.

ROSE: That ain't what I mean . . . and you know it. I want to know if you're coming straight home after work.

15   TROY: I figure I'd cash my check . . . hang out at Taylors' with the boys . . . maybe play a game of checkers . . .

ROSE: Troy, I can't live like this. I won't live like this. You livin' on borrowed time with me. It's been going on six months now you ain't been coming home.

20   TROY: I be here every night. Every night of the year. That's 365 days.

ROSE: I want you to come home tomorrow after work.

TROY: Rose . . . I don't mess up my pay. You know that now. I take my pay and I give it to you. I don't have no money

25   but what you give me back. I just want to have a little time to myself . . . a little time to enjoy life.

ROSE: What about me? When's my time to enjoy life?

TROY: I don't know what to tell you, Rose. I'm doing the best I can.

30   ROSE: You ain't been home from work but time enough to change your clothes and run out . . . and you wanna call that the best you can do?

TROY: I'm going over to the hospital to see Alberta. She went into the hospital this afternoon. Look like she might have

35   the baby early. I won't be gone long.

ROSE: Well, you ought to know. They went over to Miss Pearl's and got Gabe today. She said you told them to go ahead and lock him up.

TROY: I ain't said no such thing. Whoever told you that is

40   telling a lie. Pearl ain't doing nothing but telling a big fat lie.

ROSE: She ain't had to tell me. I read it on the papers.

TROY: I ain't told them nothing of the kind.

ROSE: I saw it right there on the papers.

TROY: What it say, huh?

45   ROSE: It said you told them to take him.

TROY: Then they screwed that up, just the way they screw up everything. I ain't worried about what they got on the paper.

ROSE: Say the government send part of his check to the hos-

50   pital and the other part to you.

TROY: I ain't got nothing to do with that if that's the way it works. I ain't made up the rules about how it work.

ROSE: You did Gabe just like you did Cory. You wouldn't sign the paper for Cory . . . but you signed for Gabe. You

55   signed that paper.

(The telephone is heard ringing inside the house.)

TROY: I told you I ain't signed nothing, woman! The only thing I signed was the release form. Hell, I can't read, I don't know what they had on that paper! I ain't signed nothing about sending Gabe away.

60   ROSE: I said send him to the hospital . . . you said let him be free . . . now you done went down there and signed him to the hospital for half his money. You went back on yourself, Troy. You gonna have to answer for that.

TROY: See now . . . you been over there talking to Miss Pearl.

65   She done got mad cause she ain't getting Gabe's rent money. That's all it is. She's liable to say anything.

ROSE: Troy, I seen where you signed the paper.

TROY: You ain't seen nothing I signed. What she doing got papers on my brother anyway? Miss Pearl telling a big fat lie. And I'm gonna tell her about it too! You ain't seen   70   nothing I signed. Say . . . you ain't seen nothing I signed.

(ROSE exits into the house to answer the telephone. Presently she returns.)

ROSE: Troy . . . that was the hospital. Alberta had the baby.

TROY: What she have? What is it?

ROSE: It's a girl.

TROY: I better get on down to the hospital to see her.   75

ROSE: Troy . . .

TROY: Rose . . . I got to go see her now. That's only right . . . what's the matter . . . the baby's alright, ain't it?

ROSE: Alberta died having the baby.

TROY: Died . . . you say she's dead? Alberta's dead?   80

ROSE: They said they done all they could. They couldn't do nothing for her.

TROY: The baby? How's the baby?

ROSE: They say it's healthy. I wonder who's gonna bury her.

TROY: She had family, Rose. She wasn't living in the world   85   by herself.

ROSE: I know she wasn't living in the world by herself.

TROY: Next thing you gonna want to know if she had any insurance.

ROSE: Troy, you ain't got to talk like that.   90

TROY: That's the first thing that jumped out your mouth. "Who's gonna bury her?" Like I'm fixing to take on that task for myself.

ROSE: I am your wife. Don't push me away.

TROY: I ain't pushing nobody away. Just give me some space.   95   That's all. Just give me some room to breathe.

(ROSE exits into the house. TROY walks about the yard.)

TROY: *(With a quiet rage that threatens to consume him.)* Alright . . . Mr. Death. See now . . . I'm gonna tell you what I'm gonna do. I'm gonna take and build me a fence around this yard. See? I'm gonna build me a fence around what belongs   100   to me. And then I want you to stay on the other side. See? You stay over there until you're ready for me. Then you come on. Bring your army. Bring your sickle. Bring your wrestling clothes. I ain't gonna fall down on my vigilance this time. You ain't gonna sneak up on me no more. When   105   you ready for me . . . when the top of your list say Troy Maxson . . . that's when you come around here. You come up and knock on the front door. Ain't nobody else got nothing to do with this. This is between you and me. Man to man. You stay on the other side of that fence until you   110   ready for me. Then you come up and knock on the front door. Anytime you want. I'll be ready for you.

(The lights go down to black.)

SCENE III

The lights come up on the porch. It is late evening three days later. ROSE sits listening to the ball game waiting for TROY. The final out of the game is made and ROSE switches off the radio. troy enters the yard carrying an infant wrapped in blankets. He stands back from the house and calls.

ROSE *enters and stands on the porch. There is a long, awkward silence, the weight of which grows heavier with each passing second.*

TROY: Rose . . . I'm standing here with my daughter in my arms. She ain't but a wee bittie little old thing. She don't know nothing about grownups' business. She innocent . . . and she ain't got no mama.

5   ROSE: What you telling me for, Troy?

(She turns and exits into the house.)

TROY: Well . . . I guess we'll just sit out here on the porch.

(He sits down on the porch. There is an awkward indelicateness about the way he handles the baby. His largeness engulfs and seems to swallow it. He speaks loud enough for ROSE to hear.)

A man's got to do what's right for him. I ain't sorry for nothing I done. It felt right in my heart.

(To the baby.)

What you smiling at? Your daddy's a big man. Got these
10 great big old hands. But sometimes he's scared. And right now your daddy's scared cause we sitting out here and ain't got no home. Oh, I been homeless before. I ain't had no little baby with me. But I been homeless. You just be out on the road by your lonesome and you see one of
15 them trains coming and you just kinda go like this . . .

(He sings as a lullaby.)

Please, Mr. Engineer let a man ride the line
Please, Mr. Engineer let a man ride the line
I ain't got no ticket please let me ride the blinds

(ROSE enters from the house. TROY hearing her steps behind him, stands and faces her.)

She's my daughter, Rose. My own flesh and blood. I can't
20 deny her no more than I can deny them boys.

(Pause.)

You and them boys is my family. You and them and this child is all I got in the world. So I guess what I'm saying is . . . I'd appreciate it if you'd help take care of her.
ROSE: Okay, Troy . . . you're right. I'll take care of your baby
25 for you . . . cause . . . like you say . . . she's innocent . . . and you can't visit the sins of the father upon the child. A motherless child has got a hard time.

(She takes the baby from him.)

From right now . . . this child got a mother. But you a womanless man.

(ROSE turns and exits into the house with the baby. Lights go down to black.)

SCENE IV

It is two months later. LYONS enters from the street. He knocks on the door and calls.

LYONS: Hey, Rose! *(Pause.)* Rose!

ROSE: *(From inside the house.)* Stop that yelling. You gonna wake up Raynell. I just got her to sleep.
LYONS: I just stopped by to pay Papa this twenty dollars I owe him. Where's Papa at?   5
ROSE: He should be here in a minute. I'm getting ready to go down to the church. Sit down and wait on him.
LYONS: I got to go pick up Bonnie over her mother's house.
ROSE: Well, sit it down there on the table. He'll get it.
LYONS: *(Enters the house and sets the money on the table.)* Tell   10
Papa I said thanks. I'll see you again.
ROSE: Alright, Lyons. We'll see you.

(LYONS starts to exit as CORY enters.)

CORY: Hey, Lyons.
LYONS: What's happening, Cory. Say man, I'm sorry I missed your graduation. You know I had a gig and couldn't get   15
away. Otherwise, I would have been there, man. So what you doing?
CORY: I'm trying to find a job.
LYONS: Yeah I know how that go, man. It's rough out here. Jobs are scarce.   20
CORY: Yeah, I know.
LYONS: Look here, I got to run. Talk to Papa . . . he know some people. He'll be able to help get you a job. Talk to him . . . see what he say.
CORY: Yeah . . . alright, Lyons.   25
LYONS: You take care. I'll talk to you soon. We'll find some time to talk.

(LYONS exits the yard. CORY wanders over to the tree, picks up the bat and assumes a batting stance. He studies an imaginary pitcher and swings. Dissatisfied with the result, he tries again. TROY enters. They eye each other for a beat. CORY puts the bat down and exits the yard. TROY starts into the house as ROSE exits with RAYNELL. She is carrying a cake.)

TROY: I'm coming in and everybody's going out.
ROSE: I'm taking this cake down to the church for the bake-sale. Lyons was by to see you. He stopped by to pay you   30
your twenty dollars. It's laying in there on the table.
TROY: *(Going into his pocket.)* Well . . . here go this money.
ROSE: Put it in there on the table, Troy. I'll get it.
TROY: What time you coming back?
ROSE: Ain't no use in you studying me. It don't matter what   35
time I come back.
TROY: I just asked you a question, woman. What's the matter . . . can't I ask you a question?
ROSE: Troy, I don't want to go into it. Your dinner's in there on the stove. All you got to do is heat it up. And don't you   40
be eating the rest of them cakes in there. I'm coming back for them. We having a bakesale at the church tomorrow.

(ROSE exits the yard. TROY sits down on the steps, takes a pint bottle from his pocket, opens it and drinks. He begins to sing.)

TROY: Hear it ring! Hear it ring!
Had an old dog his name was Blue
You know Blue was mighty true   45
You know Blue as a good old dog
Blue trees a possum in a hollow log
You know from that he was a good old dog.

(BONO *enters the yard.*)

BONO: Hey, Troy.

50 TROY: Hey, what's happening, Bono?

BONO: I just thought I'd stop by to see you.

TROY: What you stop by and see me for? You ain't stopped by in a month of Sundays. Hell, I must owe you money or something.

55 BONO: Since you got your promotion I can't keep up with you. Used to see you everyday. Now I don't even know what route you working.

TROY: They keep switching me around. Got me out in Green-tree now . . . hauling white folks' garbage.

60 BONO: Greentree, huh? You lucky, at least you ain't got to be lifting them barrels. Damn if they ain't getting heavier. I'm gonna put in my two years and call it quits.

TROY: I'm thinking about retiring myself.

BONO: You got it easy. You can *drive* for another five years.

65 TROY: It ain't the same, Bono. It ain't like working the back of the truck. Ain't got nobody to talk to . . . feel like you working by yourself. Naw, I'm thinking about retiring. How's Lucille?

BONO: She alright. Her arthritis get to acting up on her
70 sometime. Saw Rose on my way in. She going down to the church, huh?

TROY: Yeah, she took up going down there. All them preachers looking for somebody to fatten their pockets.

(*Pause.*)

Got some gin here.

75 BONO: Naw, thanks. I just stopped by to say hello.

TROY: Hell, nigger . . . you can take a drink. I ain't never known you to say no to a drink. You ain't got to work tomorrow.

BONO: I just stopped by. I'm fixing to go over to Skinner's.
80 We got us a domino game going over his house every Friday.

TROY: Nigger, you can't play no dominoes. I used to whup you four games out of five.

BONO: Well, that learned me. I'm getting better.

85 TROY: Yeah? Well, that's alright.

BONO: Look here . . . I got to be getting on. Stop by sometime, huh?

TROY: Yeah, I'll do that, Bono. Lucille told Rose you bought her a new refrigerator.

90 BONO: Yeah, Rose told Lucille you had finally built your fence . . . so I figured we'd call it even.

TROY: I knew you would.

BONO: Yeah . . . okay. I'll be talking to you.

TROY: Yeah, take care, Bono. Good to see you. I'm gonna stop
95 over.

BONO: Yeah. Okay, Troy.

(BONO *exits.* TROY *drinks from the bottle.*)

TROY: Old Blue died and I dig his grave
Let him down with a golden chain
Every night when I hear old Blue bark
100 I know Blue treed a possum in Noah's Ark.
Hear it ring! Hear it ring!

(CORY *enters the yard. They eye each other for a beat.* TROY *is sitting in the middle of the steps.* CORY *walks over.*)

CORY: I got to get by.

TROY: Say what? What's you say?

CORY: You in my way. I got to get by.

TROY: You got to get by where? This is my house. Bought and 105 paid for. In full. Took me fifteen years. And if you wanna go in my house and I'm sitting on the steps . . . you say excuse me. Like your mama taught you.

CORY: Come on, Pop . . . I got to get by.

(CORY *starts to maneuver his way past* TROY. TROY *grabs his leg and shoves him back.*)

TROY: You just gonna walk over top of me? 110

CORY: I live here too!

TROY: (*Advancing toward him.*) You just gonna walk over top of me in my own house?

CORY: I ain't scared of you.

TROY: I ain't asked if you was scared of me. I asked you if you 115 was fixing to walk over top of me in my own house? That's the question. You ain't gonna say excuse me? You just gonna walk over top of me?

CORY: If you wanna put it like that.

TROY: How else am I gonna put it? 120

CORY: I was walking by you to go into the house cause you sitting on the steps drunk, singing to yourself. You can put it like that.

TROY: Without saying excuse me???

(CORY *doesn't respond.*)

I asked you a question. Without saying excuse me??? 125

CORY: I ain't got to say excuse me to you. You don't count around here no more.

TROY: Oh, I see . . . I don't count around here no more. You ain't got to say excuse me to your daddy. All of a sudden you done got so grown that your daddy don't count 130 around here no more . . . Around here in his own house and yard that he done paid for with the sweat of his brow. You done got so grown to where you gonna take over. You gonna take over my house. Is that right? You gonna wear my pants. You gonna go in there and stretch out on 135 my bed. You ain't got to say excuse me cause I don't count around here no more. Is that right?

CORY: That's right. You always talking this dumb stuff. Now, why don't you just get out my way.

TROY: I guess you got someplace to sleep and something to 140 put in your belly. You got that, huh? You got that? That's what you need. You got that, huh?

CORY: You don't know what I got. You ain't got to worry about what I got.

TROY: You right! You one hundred percent right! I done 145 spent the last seventeen years worrying about what you got. Now it's your turn, see? I'll tell you what to do. You grown . . . we done established that. You a man. Now, let's see you act like one. Turn your behind around and walk out this yard. And when you get out there in the alley 150 you can forget about this house. See? Cause this is my house. You go on and be a man and get your own house. You can forget about this. Cause this is mine. You go on and get yours cause I'm through with doing for you.

CORY: You talking about what you did for me . . . what'd you 155 ever give me?

TROY: Them feet and bones! That pumping heart, nigger! I give you more than anybody else is ever gonna give you.

160 CORY: You ain't never gave me nothing! You ain't never done nothing but hold me back. Afraid I was gonna be better than you. All you ever did was try and make me scared of you. I used to tremble every time you called my name. Every time I heard your footsteps in the house. Wonder-

165 ing all the time . . . what's Papa gonna say if I do this? . . . What's he gonna say if I do that? . . . What's Papa gonna say if I turn on the radio? And Mama, too . . . she tries . . . but she's scared of you.

TROY: You leave your mama out of this. She ain't got noth-ing to do with this.

170 CORY: I don't know how she stand you . . . after what you did to her.

TROY: I told you to leave your mama out of this!

(He advances toward CORY.*)*

CORY: What you gonna do . . . give me a whupping? You can't whup me no more. You're too old. You just an old man.

175 TROY: *(Shoves him on his shoulder.)* Nigger! That's what you are. You just another nigger on the street to me!

CORY: You crazy! You know that?

TROY: Go on now! You got the devil in you. Get on away from me!

180 CORY: You just a crazy old man . . . talking about I got the devil in me.

TROY: Yeah, I'm crazy! If you don't get on the other side of that yard . . . I'm gonna show you how crazy I am! Go on . . . get the hell out of my yard.

185 CORY: It ain't your yard. You took Uncle Gabe's money he got from the army to buy this house and then you put him out.

TROY: *(TROY advances on* CORY.*)* Get your black ass out of my yard!

*(*TROY*'s advance backs* CORY *up against the tree.* CORY *grabs up the bat.)*

CORY: I ain't going nowhere! Come on . . . put me out! I ain't

190 scared of you.

TROY: That's my bat!

CORY: Come on!

TROY: Put my bat down!

CORY: Come on, put me out.

*(*CORY *swings at* TROY, *who backs across the yard.)*

195 What's the matter? You so bad . . . put me out!

*(*TROY *advances toward* CORY.*)*

CORY: *(Backing up.)* Come on! Come on!

TROY: You're gonna have to use it! You wanna draw that bat back on me . . . you're gonna have to use it.

CORY: Come on! . . . Come on!

*(*CORY *swings the bat at* TROY *a second time. He misses.* TROY *con-tinues to advance toward him.)*

200 TROY: You're gonna have to kill me! You wanna draw that bat back on me. You're gonna have to kill me.

*(*CORY, *backed up against the tree, can go no farther.* TROY *taunts him. He sticks out his head and offers him a target.)*

Come on! Come on!

*(*CORY *is unable to swing the bat.* TROY *grabs it.)*

TROY: Then I'll show you.

*(*CORY *and* TROY *struggle over the bat. The struggle is fierce and fully engaged.* TROY *ultimately is the stronger, and takes the bat from* CORY *and stands over him ready to swing. He stops himself.)*

Go on and get away from around my house.

*(*CORY, *stung by his defeat, picks himself up, walks slowly out of the yard and up the alley.)*

CORY: Tell Mama I'll be back for my things.   205

TROY: They'll be on the other side of that fence.

*(*CORY *exits.)*

TROY: I can't taste nothing. Helluljah! I can't taste nothing no more. *(*TROY *assumes a batting posture and begins to taunt Death, the fastball in the outside corner.)* Come on! It's be-tween you and me now! Come on! Anytime you want! 210 Come on! I be ready for you . . . but I ain't gonna be easy.

(The lights go down on the scene.)

SCENE V

The time is 1965. The lights come up in the yard. It is the morn-ing of TROY*'s funeral. A funeral plaque with a light hangs beside the door. There is a small garden plot off to the side. There is noise and activity in the house as* ROSE, LYONS *and* BONO *have gathered. The door opens and* RAYNELL, *seven years old, enters dressed in a flannel nightgown. She crosses to the garden and pokes around with a stick.* ROSE *calls from the house.*

ROSE: Raynell!

RAYNELL: Mam?

ROSE: What you doing out there?

RAYNELL: Nothing.

*(*ROSE *comes to the door.)*

ROSE: Girl, get in here and get dressed. What you doing?   5

RAYNELL: Seeing if my garden growed.

ROSE: I told you it ain't gonna grow overnight. You got to wait.

RAYNELL: It don't look like it never gonna grow. Dag!

ROSE: I told you a watched pot never boils. Get in here and get dressed.   10

RAYNELL: This ain't even no pot, Mama.

ROSE: You just have to give it a chance. It'll grow. Now you come on and do what I told you. We got to be getting ready. This ain't no morning to be playing around. You hear me?

RAYNELL: Yes, mam.   15

*(*ROSE *exits into the house.* RAYNELL *continues to poke at her gar-den with a stick.* CORY *enters. He is dressed in a Marine corporal's uniform, and carries a duffel bag. His posture is that of a military man, and his speech has a clipped sternness.)*

CORY: (*To* RAYNELL.) Hi.

(*Pause.*)

I bet your name is Raynell.

RAYNELL: Uh huh.

CORY: Is your mama home?

(RAYNELL *runs up on the porch and calls through the screen door.*)

20 RAYNELL: Mama . . . there's some man out here. Mama?

(ROSE *comes to the door.*)

ROSE: Cory? Lord have mercy! Look here, you all!

(ROSE *and* CORY *embrace in a tearful reunion as* BONO *and* LYONS *enter from the house dressed in funeral clothes.*)

BONO: Aw, looka here . . .

ROSE: Done got all grown up!

CORY: Don't cry, Mama. What you crying about?

25 ROSE: I'm just so glad you made it.

CORY: Hey Lyons. How you doing, Mr. Bono.

(LYONS *goes to embrace* CORY.)

LYONS: Look at you, man. Look at you. Don't he look good, Rose. Got them Corporal stripes.

ROSE: What took you so long.

30 CORY: You know how the Marines are, Mama. They got to get all their paperwork straight before they let you do anything.

ROSE: Well, I'm sure glad you made it. They let Lyons come. Your Uncle Gabe's still in the hospital. They don't know

35 if they gonna let him out or not. I just talked to them a little while ago.

LYONS: A Corporal in the United States Marines.

BONO: Your daddy knew you had it in you. He used to tell me all the time.

40 LYONS: Don't he look good, Mr. Bono?

BONO: Yeah, he remind me of Troy when I first met him.

(*Pause.*)

Say, Rose, Lucille's down at the church with the choir. I'm gonna go down and get the pallbearers lined up. I'll be back to get you all.

45 ROSE: Thanks, Jim.

CORY: See you, Mr. Bono.

LYONS: (*With his arm around* RAYNELL.) Cory . . . look at Raynell. Ain't she precious? She gonna break a whole lot of hearts.

50 ROSE: Raynell, come and say hello to your brother. This is your brother, Cory. You remember Cory.

RAYNELL: No, Mam.

CORY: She don't remember me, Mama.

ROSE: Well, we talk about you. She heard us talk about you.

55 (*To* RAYNELL.) This is your brother, Cory. Come on and say hello.

RAYNELL: Hi.

CORY: Hi. So you're Raynell. Mama told me a lot about you.

ROSE: You all come on into the house and let me fix you

60 some breakfast. Keep up your strength.

CORY: I ain't hungry, Mama.

LYONS: You can fix me something, Rose. I'll be in there in a minute.

ROSE: Cory, you sure you don't want nothing. I know they ain't feeding you right. 65

CORY: No, Mama . . . thanks. I don't feel like eating. I'll get something later.

ROSE: Raynell . . . get on upstairs and get that dress on like I told you.

(ROSE *and* RAYNELL *exit into the house.*)

LYONS: So . . . I hear you thinking about getting married. 70

CORY: Yeah, I done found the right one, Lyons. It's about time.

LYONS: Me and Bonnie been split up about four years now. About the time Papa retired. I guess she just got tired of all them changes I was putting her through.

(*Pause.*)

I always knew you was gonna make something out your- 75
self. Your head was always in the right direction. So . . . you gonna stay in . . . make it a career . . . put in your twenty years?

CORY: I don't know. I got six already, I think that's enough.

LYONS: Stick with Uncle Sam and retire early. Ain't nothing 80
out here. I guess Rose told you what happened with me. They got me down the workhouse. I thought I was being slick cashing other people's checks.

CORY: How much time you doing?

LYONS: They give me three years. I got that beat now. I ain't 85
got but nine more months. It ain't so bad. You learn to deal with it like anything else. You got to take the crookeds with the straights. That's what Papa used to say. He used to say that when he struck out. I seen him strike out three times in a row . . . and the next time up he hit 90
the ball over the grandstand. Right out there in Home- stead Field. He wasn't satisfied hitting in the seats . . . he want to hit it over everything! After the game he had two hundred people standing around waiting to shake his hand. You got to take the crookeds with the straights. 95
Yeah, papa was something else.

CORY: You still playing?

LYONS: Cory . . . you know I'm gonna do that. There's some fellows down there we got us a band . . . we gonna try and stay together when we get out . . . but yeah, I'm still play- 100
ing. It still helps me to get out of bed in the morning. As long as it do that I'm gonna be right there playing and trying to make some sense out of it.

ROSE: (*Calling.*) Lyons, I got these eggs in the pan.

LYONS: Let me go on and get these eggs, man. Get ready to 105
go bury Papa.

(*Pause.*)

How you doing? You doing alright?

(CORY *nods.* LYONS *touches him on the shoulder and they share a moment of silent grief.* LYONS *exits into the house.* CORY *wanders about the yard.* RAYNELL *enters.*)

RAYNELL: Hi.

CORY: Hi.

110 RAYNELL: Did you used to sleep in my room?

CORY: Yeah . . . that used to be my room.

RAYNELL: That's what Papa call it. "Cory's room." It got your football in the closet.

(ROSE *comes to the door.*)

ROSE: Raynell, get in there and get them good shoes on.

115 RAYNELL: Mama, can't I wear these. Them other ones hurt my feet.

ROSE: Well, they just gonna have to hurt your feet for a while. You ain't said they hurt your feet when you went down to the store and got them.

120 RAYNELL: They didn't hurt then. My feet done got bigger.

ROSE: Don't you give me no backtalk now. You get in there and get them shoes on.

(RAYNELL *exits into the house.*)

Ain't too much changed. He still got that piece of rag tied to that tree. He was out here swinging that bat. I was just
125 ready to go back in the house. He swung that bat and then he just fell over. Seem like he swung it and stood there with this grin on his face . . . and then he just fell over. They carried him on down to the hospital, but I knew there wasn't no need . . . why don't you come on in the house?

130 CORY: Mama . . . I got something to tell you. I don't know how to tell you this . . . but I've got to tell you . . . I'm not going to Papa's funeral.

ROSE: Boy, hush your mouth. That's your daddy you talking about. I don't want hear that kind of talk this morning. I
135 done raised you to come to this? You standing there all healthy and grown talking about you ain't going to your daddy's funeral.

CORY: Mama . . . listen . . .

ROSE: I don't want to hear it, Cory. You just get that thought
140 out of your head.

CORY: I can't drag Papa with me everywhere I go. I've got to say no to him. One time in my life I've got to say no.

ROSE: Don't nobody have to listen to nothing like that. I know you and your daddy ain't seen eye to eye, but I ain't
145 got to listen to that kind of talk this morning. Whatever was between you and your daddy . . . the time has come to put it aside. Just take it and set it over there on the shelf and forget about it. Disrespecting your daddy ain't gonna make you a man, Cory. You got to find a way to come to
150 that on your own. Not going to your daddy's funeral ain't gonna make you a man.

CORY: The whole time I was growing up . . . living in his house . . . Papa was like a shadow that followed you everywhere. It weighed on you and sunk into your flesh. It
155 would wrap around you and lay there until you couldn't tell which one was you anymore. That shadow digging in your flesh. Trying to crawl in. Trying to live through you. Everywhere I looked, Troy Maxson was staring back at me . . . hiding under the bed . . . in the closet. I'm just saying
160 I've got to find a way to get rid of that shadow, Mama.

ROSE: You just like him. You got him in you good.

CORY: Don't tell me that, Mama.

ROSE: You Troy Maxson all over again.

CORY: I don't want to be Troy Maxson. I want to be me.

165 ROSE: You can't be nobody but who you are, Cory. That shadow wasn't nothing but you growing into yourself. You either got to grow into it or cut it down to fit you. But that's all you got to make life with. That's all you got to measure yourself against that world out there. Your
170 daddy wanted you to be everything he wasn't . . . and at the same time he tried to make you into everything he was. I don't know if he was right or wrong . . . but I do know he meant to do more good than he meant to do harm. He wasn't always right. Sometimes when he
175 touched he bruised. And sometimes when he took me in his arms he cut.

When I first met your daddy I thought . . . Here is a man I can lay down with and make a baby. That's the first thing I thought when I seen him. I was thirty years old
180 and had done seen my share of men. But when he walked up to me and said, "I can dance a waltz that'll make you dizzy," I thought, Rose Lee, here is a man that you can open yourself up to and be filled to bursting. Here is a man that can fill all them empty spaces you been tipping
185 around the edges of. One of them empty spaces was being somebody's mother.

I married your daddy and settled down to cooking his supper and keeping clean sheets on the bed. When your daddy walked through the house he was so big he filled it
190 up. That was my first mistake. Not to make him leave some room for me. For my part in the matter. But at that time I wanted that. I wanted a house that I could sing in. And that's what your daddy gave me. I didn't know to keep up his strength I had to give up little pieces of mine.
195 I did that. I took on his life as mine and mixed up the pieces so that you couldn't hardly tell which was which anymore. It was my choice. It was my life and I didn't have to live it like that. But that's what life offered me in the way of being a woman and I took it. I grabbed hold of it
200 with both hands.

By the time Raynell came into the house, me and your daddy had done lost touch with one another. I didn't want to make my blessing off of nobody's misfortune . . . but I took on to Raynell like she was all them babies I had
205 wanted and never had.

(*The phone rings.*)

Like I'd been blessed to relive a part of my life. And if the Lord see fit to keep up my strength . . . I'm gonna do her just like your daddy did you . . . I'm gonna give her the best of what's in me.

210 RAYNELL: (*Entering, still with her old shoes.*) Mama . . . Reverend Tollivier on the phone.

(ROSE *exits into the house.*)

RAYNELL: Hi.

CORY: Hi.

RAYNELL: You in the Army or the Marines?

215 CORY: Marines.

RAYNELL: Papa said it was the Army. Did you know Blue?

CORY: Blue? Who's Blue?

RAYNELL: Papa's dog what he sing about all the time.

CORY: (*Singing.*)

220   Hear it ring! Hear it ring!
    I had a dog his name was Blue
    You know Blue was mighty true
    You know Blue was a good old dog
    Blue treed a possum in a hollow log
225   You know from that he was a good old dog.
    Hear it ring! Hear it ring!

(RAYNELL *joins in singing.*)

CORY and RAYNELL: Blue treed a possum out on a limb
    Blue looked at me and I looked at him
    Grabbed that possum and put him in a sack
230   Blue stayed there till I came back
    Old Blue's feets was big and round
    Never allowed a possum to touch the ground.
    Old Blue died and I dug his grave
    I dug his grave with a silver spade
235   Let him down with a golden chain
    And every night I call his name
    Go on Blue, you good dog you
    Go on Blue, you good dog you
RAYNELL: Blue laid down and died like a man
240   Blue laid down and died . . .
BOTH: Blue laid down and died like a man
    Now he's treeing possums in the Promised Land
    I'm gonna tell you this to let you know
    Blue's gone where the good dogs go
245   When I hear old Blue bark
    When I hear old Blue bark
    Blue treed a possum in Noah's Ark
    Blue treed a possum in Noah's Ark.

(ROSE *comes to the screen door.*)

ROSE: Cory, we gonna be ready to go in a minute.
250 CORY: (*To* RAYNELL.) You go on in the house and change them shoes like Mama told you so we can go to Papa's funeral.

RAYNELL: Okay, I'll be back.

(RAYNELL *exits into the house.* CORY *gets up and crosses over to the tree.* ROSE *stands in the screen door watching him.* GABRIEL *enters from the alley.*)

GABRIEL: (*Calling.*) Hey, Rose!
ROSE: Gabe?   255
GABRIEL: I'm here, Rose. Hey Rose, I'm here!

(ROSE *enters from the house.*)

ROSE: Lord . . . Look here, Lyons!
LYONS: See, I told you, Rose . . . I told you they'd let him come.   260
CORY: How you doing, Uncle Gabe?
LYONS: How you doing, Uncle Gabe?
GABRIEL: Hey, Rose. It's time. It's time to tell St. Peter to open the gates. Troy, you ready? You ready, Troy. I'm gonna tell St. Peter to open the gates. You get ready now.

(GABRIEL, *with great fanfare, braces himself to blow. The trumpet is without a mouthpiece. He puts the end of it into his mouth and* 265 *blows with great force, like a man who has been waiting some twenty-odd years for this single moment. No sound comes out of the trumpet. He braces himself and blows again with the same result. A third time he blows. There is a weight of impossible description that falls away and leaves him bare and exposed to a frightful realization. It is a trauma that a sane and normal mind would be unable to withstand. He begins to dance. A slow, strange dance, eerie and lifegiving. A dance of atavistic signature and ritual.* LYONS *attempts to embrace him.* GABRIEL *pushes* LYONS *away. He begins to howl in what is an attempt at song, or perhaps a song turning back into itself in an attempt at speech. He finishes his dance and the gates of heaven stand open as wide as God's closet.*)

That's the way that go!

(*Blackout.*)

Tony Kushner

Born in 1956, Tony Kushner first came to international prominence with *Angels in America* (1991), a two-part play that was an enormous success both in London and in Los Angeles before moving to New York in 1993. Kushner's "gay fantasia on national themes" is, in a sense, a displaced autobiography: the displaced narrative of his own growing up as a gay man in the American era of Roy Cohn, the decline of the Communist menace, the onset of the AIDS epidemic, and the rise of the conservative political agenda that dominated American politics in the 1980s. Kushner was born in New York, but his family soon moved to New Orleans, where his parents were musicians in the New Orleans Philharmonic. When he was two, the family moved to Lake Charles, Louisiana; his mother, once a prominent New York bassoonist, devoted herself to educating the children in literature, music, and the arts; she also acted in the Lake Charles theater company. Kushner knew that he was gay but concealed it from his parents; when he went to college at Columbia University, he spent some time in psychoanalysis trying to alter his sexual orientation. However, by his mid-twenties, Kushner was able to accept his sexuality and came out. After taking his B.A. at Columbia, he studied theater at New York University. His first play, *A Bright Room Called Day* (1985), was written while he worked as a switchboard operator; it concerns the collapse of the political left and the rise of fascism during the German Weimar Republic; Kushner also adapted a translation of Corneille's play, *The Illusion*. *Angels in America* is his second play. *Slavs* opened in New York in 1994, and an early play, *Hydriotaphia,* opened in 1998. His most recent play, *Homebody/Kabul,* opened in 2001.

The first part of *Angels in America* (the second part is entitled *Perestroika*), *Millennium Approaches* is a complete play in its own right. Kushner began writing the play in 1988 when Oskar Eustis, who had directed his first play for the Eureka Theater Company in San Francisco, asked Kushner for another play. Subtitled "A Gay Fantasia on National Themes," *Millennium*

ANGELS IN AMERICA, PART I: MILLENNIUM APPROACHES

The Angel (Ellen McLaughlin) appears to Prior Walter (Stephen Spinella) at the climax of Tony Kushner's *Angels in America, Part One: Millennium Approaches* in the 1993 Broadway production.

Approaches is at once a deeply personal look at the lives of two couples—Joe and Harper, a young Mormon couple transplanted to New York; Louis and Prior, a gay couple facing (and not facing) the onset of AIDS—and a political "fantasia" in the manner of Shaw's *Heartbreak House* or *The Apple Cart*. Kushner sets the characters' struggles against the background of conservative politics and the increasing power of the conservative right in 1980s America; as Martin remarks in act 2: ". . . we'll get our way on just about everything: abortion, defense, Central America, protecting the family, a live investment climate. . . . It's really the end of Liberalism. The end of New Deal Socialism. The end of ipso facto secular humanism."

While Kushner's play takes aim at the policies of the Republican administration, the play's politics extend deeply into the politics of personal action. The emphasis on individualism, on self-sufficiency, on destroying the liberal consensus, and on eliminating social programs characteristic of the Reagan administration has consequences in the private sphere as well, where freedom looks alternately like selfishness and chaos. Roy Cohn—famous for his anticommunist activities and for prosecuting (and winning) the death sentence for Julius and Ethel Rosenberg for selling secret information to the Soviet Union—in many ways exemplifies this linkage in the play. Unable to give up his view of political power ("the game . . . of being alive"), Cohn refuses to be treated for AIDS because it would mean a public admission that he is gay, something generally known but not acknowledged. Louis, unable to bring himself to care for Prior during his horrifying illness, finds both emptiness and freedom in deserting his lover. Harper, whose valium-induced fantasies summon the cosmic travel agent Mr. Lies (who whisks her off to Antarctica) is in the throes of a nervous breakdown, a literalized response to the decaying world in which she lives, where "everywhere, things are collapsing, lies surfacing, systems of defense giving way."

The hallucinatory style of *Millennium Approaches* enables Kushner to bring this blending of public and private, the grand sweep of history and the narrower compass of individual suffering, into a close juxtaposition. *Millennium Approaches* ends when Prior's ancestors—a medieval monk and a seventeenth-century dandy—appear to announce the coming of a mysterious angel, whose voice is heard intermittently throughout the play. The Angel's arrival is heralded in a number of ways: Prior regards his first lesion of Kaposi's sarcoma as the mark of the angel of death; a feather drops from above and the voice is heard at the end of Harper's/Prior's intertwined dream-hallucination in act 1; Joe alludes to Jacob wrestling with his angel, an image of Joe's fight to recognize and admit his own homosexuality. The Angel is a figure of release and redemption from the isolation in which the characters find themselves.

However, the Angel also has a public, historical significance as well. Kushner has suggested that the Angel alludes to a comment made by the German cultural critic Walter Benjamin. In "Theses on the Philosophy of History," Benjamin makes the following remark on the process of history:

> A Klee painting named "Angelus Novus" shows an angel looking as though he is about to move away from something he is fixedly contemplating. His eyes are staring, his mouth is open, his wings are spread. This is how one pictures the angel of history. His face is turned toward the past. Where we perceive a chain of events, he sees one single catastrophe which keeps piling wreckage upon wreckage and hurls it in front of his feet. The angel would like to stay, awaken the dead, and make whole what has been smashed. But a storm is blowing from Paradise; it has got caught in his wings with such violence that the angel can no longer close them. This storm irresistibly propels him into the future to which his back is turned, while the pile of debris before him grows skyward. This storm is what we call progress.

The Angel is, to Kushner as to Benjamin, a figure for the dialectical force of history, the way that history moves into the future both in antithesis to the past, and yet bearing the past along with it. In *Angels in America,* Tony Kushner provides a sense of how it is we live today, in the midst of this "storm . . . we call progress."

ANGELS IN AMERICA, PART I: MILLENNIUM APPROACHES

Tony Kushner

CHARACTERS

ROY M. COHN, *a successful New York lawyer and unofficial power broker*

JOSEPH (JOE) PORTER PITT, *chief clerk for Justice Theodore Wilson of the Federal Court of Appeals, Second Circuit*

HARPER AMATY PITT, *Joe's wife, an agoraphobic with a mild Valium addiction*

LOUIS IRONSON, *a word processor working for the Second Circuit Court of Appeals*

PRIOR WALTER, *Louis's boyfriend. Occasionally works as a club designer or caterer, otherwise lives very modestly but with great style off a small trust fund*

HANNAH PORTER PITT, *Joe's mother, currently residing in Salt Lake City, living off her deceased husband's army pension*

BELIZE, *a former drag queen and former lover of Prior's: A registered nurse. Belize's name was originally Norman Arriaga; Belize is a drag name that stuck*

THE ANGEL, *four divine emanations, Fluor, Phosphor, Lumen and Candle; manifest in One: the Continental Principality of America. She has magnificent steel-gray wings*

RABBI ISIDOR CHEMELWITZ, *an orthodox Jewish rabbi, played by the actor playing Hannah*

MR. LIES, *Harper's imaginary friend, a travel agent, who in style of dress and speech suggests a jazz musician; he always wears a large lapel badge emblazoned "IOTA" (The International Order of Travel Agents). He is played by the actor playing Belize*

THE MAN IN THE PARK, *played by the actor playing Prior*

THE VOICE, *the voice of The Angel*

HENRY, *Roy's doctor, played by the actor playing Hannah*

EMILY, *a nurse, played by the actor playing The Angel*

MARTIN HELLER, *a Reagan Administration Justice Department flackman, played by the actor playing Harper*

SISTER ELLA CHAPTER, *a Salt Lake City real-estate saleswoman, played by the actor playing The Angel*

PRIOR 1, *the ghost of a dead Prior Walter from the 13th century, played by the actor playing Joe. He is a blunt, gloomy medieval farmer with a gutteral Yorkshire accent*

PRIOR 2, *the ghost of a dead Prior Walter from the 17th century, played by the actor playing Roy. He is a Londoner, sophisticated, with a High British accent*

THE ESKIMO, *played by the actor playing Joe*

THE WOMAN IN THE SOUTH BRONX, *played by the actor playing The Angel*

ETHEL ROSENBERG, *played by the actor playing Hannah*

PLAYWRIGHT'S NOTES

A DISCLAIMER: *Roy M. Cohn, the character, is based on the late Roy M. Cohn (1927–1986), who was all too real; for the most part the acts attributed to the character Roy, such as his illegal conferences with Judge Kaufmann during the trial of Ethel Rosenberg, are to be found in the historical record. But this Roy is a work of dramatic fiction; his words are my invention, and liberties have been taken.*

A NOTE ABOUT THE STAGING: *The play benefits from a pared-down style of presentation, with minimal scenery and scene shifts done rapidly (no blackouts!), employing the cast as well as stagehands—which makes for an actor-driven event, as this must be. The moments of magic—the appearance and disappearance of Mr. Lies and the ghosts, the Book hallucination, and the ending—are to be fully realized, as bits of wonderful theatrical illusion—which means it's OK if the wires show, and maybe it's good that they do, but the magic should at the same time be thoroughly amazing.*

> . . . In a murderous time
> the heart breaks and breaks
> and lives by breaking.
>
> —STANLEY KUNITZ
> "THE TESTING-TREE"

ACT ONE

Bad News October–November 1985

SCENE I

The last days of October. RABBI ISODOR CHEMELWITZ *alone onstage with a small coffin. It is a rough pine box with two wooden pegs, one at the foot and one at the head, holding the lid in place. A prayer shawl embroidered with a Star of David is draped over the lid, and by the head a yarzheit candle is burning.*

RABBI ISIDOR CHEMELWITZ: (*He speaks sonorously, with a heavy Eastern European accent, unapologetically consulting a sheet of notes for the family names.*) Hello and good morning. I am Rabbi Isidor Chemelwitz of the Bronx Home for Aged He-brews. We are here this morning to pay respects at the pass- 5 ing of Sarah Ironson, devoted wife of Benjamin Ironson, also deceased, loving and caring mother of her sons Morris, Abraham, and Samuel, and her daughters Esther and Rachel; beloved grandmother of Max, Mark, Louis, Lisa, Maria . . . uh . . . Lesley, Angela, Doris, Luke and Eric. (*Looks more closely 10 at paper.*) Eric? This is a Jewish name? (*Shrugs.*) Eric. A large and loving family. We assemble that we may mourn collectively this good and righteous woman.

(*He looks at the coffin.*)

This woman. I did not know this woman. I cannot accu- rately describe her attributes, nor do justice to her di- 15 mensions. She was. . . . Well, in the Bronx Home of Aged Hebrews are many like this, the old, and to many I speak but not to be frank with this one. She preferred silence. So I do not know her and yet I know her. She was . . .

(*He touches the coffin.*)

20 . . . not a person but a whole kind of person, the ones who crossed the ocean, who brought with us to America the villages of Russia and Lithuania—and how we struggled, and how we fought, for the family, for the Jewish home, so that you would not grow up *here,* in this strange
25 place, in the melting pot where nothing melted. Descendants of this immigrant woman, you do not grow up in America, you and your children and their children with the goyische names. You do not live in America. No such place exists. Your clay is the clay of some Litvak shtetl,
30 your air the air of the steppes—because she carried the old world on her back across the ocean, in a boat, and she put it down on Grand Concourse Avenue, or in Flatbush, and she worked that earth into your bones, and you pass it to your children, this ancient, ancient culture and
35 home.

(*Little pause.*)

You can never make that crossing that she made, for such Great Voyages in this world do not any more exist. But every day of your lives the miles that voyage between that place and this one you cross. Every day. You understand
40 me? In you that journey is.
So . . .
She was the last of the Mohicans, this one was. Pretty soon . . . all the old will be dead.

SCENE II

Same day. ROY *and* JOE *in* ROY's *office.* ROY *at an impressive desk, bare except for a very elaborate phone system, rows and rows of flashing buttons which bleep and beep and whistle incessantly, making chaotic music underneath* ROY's *conversations.* JOE *is sitting, waiting.* ROY *conducts business with great energy, impatience and sensual abandon: gesticulating, shouting, cajoling, crooning, playing the phone, receiver and hold button with virtuosity and love.*

ROY: (*Hitting a button.*) Hold. (*To* JOE.) I wish I was an octopus, a fucking octopus. Eight loving arms and all those suckers. Know what I mean?
JOE: No, I . . .
5 ROY: (*Gesturing to a deli platter of little sandwiches on his desk.*) You want lunch?
JOE: No, that's OK really I just . . .
ROY: (*Hitting a button.*) Ailene? Roy Cohn. Now what kind of a greeting is. . . . I thought we were friends, Ai. . . . Look
10 Mrs. Soffer you don't have to get. . . . You're upset. You're yelling. You'll aggravate your condition, you shouldn't yell, you'll pop little blood vessels in your face if you yell. . . . No that was a joke, Mrs. Soffer, I was joking. . . . I already apologized sixteen times for that, Mrs. Soffer, you
15 (*While she's fulminating,* ROY *covers the mouthpiece with his hand and talks to* JOE.) This'll take a minute, eat already, what is this tasty sandwich here it's—(*He takes a bite of a sandwich.*) Mmmmm, liver or some. . . . Here.

(*He pitches the sandwich to* JOE, *who catches it and returns it to the platter.*)

ROY: (*Back to Mrs. Soffer.*) Uh huh, uh huh. . . . No, I already told you, it wasn't a vacation, it was business. Mrs. Soffer, 20 I have clients in Haiti, Mrs. Soffer, I. . . . Listen, Ailene, YOU THINK I'M THE ONLY GODDAM LAWYER IN HISTORY EVER MISSED A COURT DATE? Don't make such a big fucking. . . . Hold. (*He hits the hold button.*) You HAG! 25
JOE: If this is a bad time . . .
ROY: *Bad* time? This is a *good* time! (*Button.*) Baby doll, get me. . . . Oh fuck, wait . . . (*Button, button.*) Hello? Yah. Sorry to keep you holding, Judge Hollins, I. . . . Oh *Mrs.* Hollins, sorry dear deep voice you got. Enjoying your visit? (*Hand 30 over mouthpiece, to* JOE.) She sounds like a truckdriver and he sounds like Kate Smith, very confusing. Nixon appointed him, all the geeks are Nixon appointees . . . (*To Mrs. Hollins.*) Yeah yeah right good so how many tickets dear? Seven. For what, *Cats, 42nd Street,* what? No you wouldn't like *La 35 Cage,* trust me, I know. Oh for godsake. . . . Hold. (*Button, button.*) Baby doll, seven for *Cats* or something, anything hard to get, I don't give a fuck what and neither will they. (*Button; to* JOE.) You see *La Cage?*
JOE: No, I . . . 40
ROY: Fabulous. Best thing on Broadway. Maybe ever. (*Button.*) Who? Aw, Jesus H. Christ, Harry, *no,* Harry, Judge John Francis Grimes, Manhattan Family Court. Do I have to do every goddam thing myself? *Touch* the bastard, Harry, and don't call me on this line again, I told you not to . . . 45
JOE: (*Starting to get up.*) Roy, uh, should I wait outside or . . .
ROY: (*To* JOE.) Oh sit. (*To* HARRY.) You hold. I pay you to hold fuck you Harry you jerk. (*Button.*) Half-wit dickbrain. (*Instantly philosophical.*) I see the universe, Joe, as a kind of sandstorm in outer space with winds of mega- 50 hurricane velocity, but instead of grains of sand it's shards and splinters of glass. You ever feel that way? Ever have one of those days?
JOE: I'm not sure I . . .
ROY: So how's life in Appeals? How's the Judge? 55
JOE: He sends his best.
ROY: He's a good man. Loyal. Not the brightest man on the bench, but he has manners. And a nice head of silver hair.
JOE: He gives me a lot of responsibility.
ROY: Yeah, like writing his decisions and signing his name. 60
JOE: Well . . .
ROY: He's a nice guy. And you cover admirably.
JOE: Well, thanks, Roy, I . . .
ROY: (*Button.*) Who is *this?* Well who the fuck are *you?* Hold—(*Button.*) Harry? Eighty-seven grand, something 65 like that. Fuck him. Eat me. New Jersey, chain of porno film stores in, uh, Weehawken. That's—Harry, that's the beauty of the law. (*Button.*) So, baby doll, what? *Cats?* Bleah. (*Button.*) *Cats!* It's about cats. Singing cats, you'll love it. Eight o'clock, the theatre's always at eight. (*Button.*) 70 Fucking tourists. (*Button, then to* JOE.) Oh live a little, Joe, *eat* something for Christ sake—
JOE: Um, Roy, could you . . .
ROY: What? (*To* HARRY.) Hold a minute. (*Button.*) Mrs. Soffer? Mrs. . . . (*Button.*) God-fucking-dammit to hell, where 75 is . . .

JOE: (*Overlapping.*) Roy, I'd really appreciate it if . . .

ROY: (*Overlapping.*) Well she was here a minute ago, baby doll, see if . . .

(*The phone starts making three different beeping sounds, all at once.*)

80 ROY: (*Smashing buttons.*) Jesus fuck this goddam thing . . .

JOE: (*Overlapping.*) I really wish you wouldn't . . .

ROY: (*Overlapping.*) Baby doll? Ring the *Post* get me Suzy see if . . .

(*The phone starts whistling loudly.*)

ROY: CHRIST!

85 JOE: *Roy.*

ROY: (*Into receiver.*) Hold. (*Button; to* JOE.) What?

JOE: Could you please not take the Lord's name in vain?

(*Pause.*)

I'm sorry. But please. At least while I'm . . .

ROY: (*Laughs, then.*) Right. Sorry. Fuck.

90 Only in America. (*Punches a button.*) Baby doll, tell 'em all to fuck off. Tell 'em I died. You handle Mrs. Soffer. Tell her it's on the way. Tell her I'm schtupping the judge. I'll call her back. I *will* call her. I *know* how much I borrowed. She's got four hundred times that stuffed up her. . . . Yeah,

95 tell her I said that. (*Button. The phone is silent.*)

So, Joe.

JOE: I'm sorry Roy, I just . . .

ROY: No no no no, principles count, I respect principles, I'm not religious but I like God and God likes me. Baptist,

100 Catholic?

JOE: Mormon.

ROY: Mormon. Delectable. Absolutely. Only in America. So, Joe. Whattya think?

JOE: It's . . . well . . .

105 ROY: Crazy life.

JOE: Chaotic.

ROY: Well but God bless chaos. Right?

JOE: Ummm . . .

ROY: Huh. Mormons. I knew Mormons, in, um, Nevada.

110 JOE: Utah, mostly.

ROY: No, these Mormons were in Vegas.

So. So, how'd you like to go to Washington and work for the Justice Department?

JOE: Sorry?

115 ROY: How'd you like to go to Washington and work for the Justice Department? All I gotta do is pick up the phone, talk to Ed, and you're in.

JOE: In . . . what, exactly?

ROY: Associate Assistant Something Big. Internal Affairs, heart

120 of the woods, something nice with clout.

JOE: Ed . . . ?

ROY: Meese. The Attorney General.

JOE: Oh.

ROY: I just have to pick up the phone . . .

125 JOE: I have to think.

ROY: Of course.

(*Pause.*)

It's a great time to be in Washington, Joe.

JOE: Roy, it's incredibly exciting . . .

ROY: And it would mean something to me. You understand?

(*Little pause.*)

JOE: I . . . can't say how much I appreciate this Roy, I'm sort   130
of . . . well, stunned, I mean. . . . Thanks, Roy. But I have to give it some thought. I have to ask my wife.

ROY: Your wife. Of course.

JOE: But I really appreciate . . .

ROY: Of course. Talk to your wife.   135

SCENE III

Later that day. HARPER *at home, alone. She is listening to the radio and talking to herself, as she often does. She speaks to the audience.*

HARPER: People who are lonely, people left alone, sit talking nonsense to the air, imagining . . . beautiful systems dying, old fixed orders spiraling apart . . .

When you look at the ozone layer, from outside, from a spaceship, it looks like a pale blue halo, a gentle, shim-   5
mer-ing aureole encircling the atmosphere encircling the earth. Thirty miles above our heads, a thin layer of three-atom oxygen molecules, product of photosynthesis, which explains the fussy vegetable preference for visible light, its rejection of darker rays and emanations. Danger from   10
without. It's a kind of gift, from God, the crowning touch to the creation of the world: guardian angels, hands linked, make a spherical net, a blue-green nesting orb, a shell of safety for life itself. But everywhere, things are collapsing, lies surfacing, systems of defense giving way. . . . This is   15
why, Joe, this is why I shouldn't be left alone.

(*Little pause.*)

I'd like to go traveling. Leave you behind to worry. I'll send postcards with strange stamps and tantalizing messages on the back. "Later maybe." "Nevermore . . ."

(MR. LIES, *a travel agent, appears.*)

HARPER: Oh! You startled me!   20

MR. LIES: Cash, check or credit card?

HARPER: I remember you. You're from Salt Lake. You sold us the plane tickets when we flew here. What are you doing in Brooklyn?

MR. LIES: You said you wanted to travel . . .   25

HARPER: And here you are. How thoughtful.

MR. LIES: Mr. Lies. Of the International Order of Travel Agents. We mobilize the globe, we set people adrift, we stir the populace and send nomads eddying across the planet. We are adepts of motion, acolytes of the flux.   30
Cash, check or credit card. Name your destination.

HARPER: Antarctica, maybe. I want to see the hole in the ozone. I heard on the radio.

MR. LIES: (*He has a computer terminal in his briefcase.*) I can arrange a guided tour. Now?   35

HARPER: Soon. Maybe soon. I'm not safe here you see. Things aren't right with me. Weird stuff happens . . .

MR. LIES: Like?

HARPER: Well, like you, for instance. Just appearing. Or last
40   week . . . well never mind.
     People are like planets, you need a thick skin. Things get
to me, Joe stays away and now. . . . Well look. My dreams
are talking back to me.

MR. LIES: It's the price of rootlessness. Motion sickness. The
45   only cure: to keep moving.

HARPER: I'm undecided. I feel . . . that something's going to
give. It's 1985. Fifteen years till the third millennium.
Maybe Christ will come again. Maybe seeds will be
planted, maybe there'll be harvests then, maybe early figs to
50   eat, maybe new life, maybe fresh blood, maybe companionship and love and protection, safety from what's outside,
maybe the door will hold, or maybe . . . maybe the troubles
will come, and the end will come, and the sky will collapse
and there will be terrible rains and showers of poison light,
55   or maybe my life is really fine, maybe Joe loves me and I'm
only crazy thinking otherwise, or maybe not, maybe it's
even worse than I know, maybe . . . I want to know, maybe
I don't. The suspense, Mr. Lies, it's killing me.

MR. LIES: I suggest a vacation.

60   HARPER: (*Hearing something.*) That was the elevator. Oh God,
I should fix myself up, I. . . . You have to go, you shouldn't
be here . . . you aren't even real.

MR. LIES: Call me when you decide . . .

HARPER: Go!

(*The travel agent* [MR. LIES] *vanishes as* JOE *enters.*)

65   JOE: Buddy?
     Buddy? Sorry I'm late. I was just . . . out. Walking. Are
you mad?

HARPER: I got a little anxious.

JOE: Buddy kiss.

(*They kiss.*)

70   Nothing to get anxious about.
     So. So how'd you like to move to Washington?

SCENE IV

Same day. LOUIS *and* PRIOR *outside the funeral home, sitting on a
bench, both dressed in funereal finery, talking. The funeral service for
Sarah Ironson has just concluded and* LOUIS *is about to leave for the
cemetery.*

LOUIS: My grandmother actually saw Emma Goldman speak.
In Yiddish. But all Grandma could remember was that she
spoke well and wore a hat.
     What a weird service. That rabbi . . .

5   PRIOR: A definite find. Get his number when you go to the
graveyard. I want him to bury me.

LOUIS: Better head out there. Everyone gets to put dirt on
the coffin once it's lowered in.

PRIOR: Oooh. Cemetery fun. Don't want to miss that.

10   LOUIS: It's an old Jewish custom to express love. Here,
Grandma, have a shovelful. Latecomers run the risk of
finding the grave completely filled.
     She was pretty crazy. She was up there in that home for
ten years, talking to herself. I never visited. She looked too
15   much like my mother.

PRIOR: (*Hugs him.*) Poor Louis. I'm sorry your grandma is
dead.

LOUIS: Tiny little coffin, huh?
     Sorry I didn't introduce you to. . . . I always get so clos-
ety at these family things.   20

PRIOR: Butch. You get butch. (*Imitating.*) "Hi Cousin Doris,
you don't remember me I'm Lou, Rachel's boy." Lou, not
Louis, because if you say Louis they'll hear the sibilant S.

LOUIS: I don't have a . . .

PRIOR: I don't blame you, hiding. Bloodlines. Jewish curses are   25
the worst. I personally would dissolve if anyone ever looked
me in the eye and said "Feh." Fortunately WASPs don't say
"Feh." Oh and by the way, darling, cousin Doris is a dyke.

LOUIS: No.
     Really?   30

PRIOR: You don't notice anything. If I hadn't spent the last
four years fellating you I'd swear you were straight.

LOUIS: You're in a pissy mood. Cat still missing?

(*Little pause.*)

PRIOR: Not a furball in sight. It's your fault.

LOUIS: It is?   35

PRIOR: I warned you, Louis. Names are important. Call an
animal "Little Sheba" and you can't expect it to stick
around. Besides, it's a dog's name.

LOUIS: I wanted a dog in the first place, not a cat. He sprayed
my books.   40

PRIOR: He was a female cat.

LOUIS: Cats are stupid, high-strung predators. Babylonians
sealed them up in bricks. Dogs have brains.

PRIOR: Cats have intuition.

LOUIS: A sharp dog is as smart as a really dull two-year-old   45
child.

PRIOR: Cats know when something's wrong.

LOUIS: Only if you stop feeding them.

PRIOR: They know. That's why Sheba left, because she knew.

LOUIS: Knew what?   50

(*Pause.*)

PRIOR: I did my best Shirley Booth this morning, floppy slippers, housecoat, curlers, can of Little Friskies; "Come
back, little Sheba, come back. . . ." To no avail. Le chat, elle
ne reviendra jamais, jamais . . .

(*He removes his jacket, rolls up his sleeve, shows* LOUIS *a dark purple spot on the underside of his arm near the shoulder.*)

     See.   55

LOUIS: That's just a burst blood vessel.

PRIOR: Not according to the best medical authorities.

LOUIS: What?

(*Pause.*)

     Tell me.

PRIOR: K.S., baby. Lesion number one. Lookit. The wine-   60
dark kiss of the angel of death.

LOUIS: (*Very softly, holding* PRIOR's *arm.*) Oh please . . .

PRIOR: I'm a lesionnaire. The Foreign Lesion. The American
Lesion. Lesionnaire's disease.

65 LOUIS: Stop.
PRIOR: My troubles are lesion.
LOUIS: Will you *stop.*
PRIOR: Don't you think I'm handling this well? I'm going to die.
70 LOUIS: Bullshit.
PRIOR: Let go of my arm.
LOUIS: No.
PRIOR: Let go.
LOUIS: (*Grabbing* PRIOR, *embracing him ferociously.*) No.
75 PRIOR: I can't find a way to spare you baby. No wall like the wall of hard scientific fact. K.S. Wham. Bang your head on that.
LOUIS: Fuck you. (*Letting go.*) Fuck you fuck you fuck you.
PRIOR: Now that's what I like to hear. A mature reaction.
80   Let's go see if the cat's come home.
        Louis?
LOUIS: When did you find this?
PRIOR: I couldn't tell you.
LOUIS: Why?
85 PRIOR: I was scared, Lou.
LOUIS: Of what?
PRIOR: That you'll leave me.
LOUIS: Oh.

(*Little pause.*)

PRIOR: Bad timing, funeral and all, but I figured as long as
90   we're on the subject of death . . .
LOUIS: I have to go bury my grandma.
PRIOR: Lou?

(*Pause.*)

    Then you'll come home?
LOUIS: Then I'll come home.

SCENE V

Same day, later on. Split scene: JOE *and* HARPER *at home;* LOUIS *at the cemetery with* RABBI ISIDOR CHEMELWITZ *and the little coffin.*

HARPER: Washington?
JOE: It's an incredible honor, buddy, and . . .
HARPER: I have to think.
JOE: Of course.
5 HARPER: Say no.
JOE: You said you were going to think about it.
HARPER: I don't want to move to Washington.
JOE: Well I do.
HARPER: It's a giant cemetery, huge white graves and mau-
10   soleums everywhere.
JOE: We could live in Maryland. Or Georgetown.
HARPER: We're happy here.
JOE: That's not really true, buddy, we . . .
HARPER: Well happy enough! Pretend-happy. That's better
15   than nothing.
JOE: It's time to make some changes, Harper.
HARPER: No changes. Why?
JOE: I've been chief clerk for four years. I make twenty-nine thousand dollars a year. That's ridiculous. I graduated
20   fourth in my class and I make less than anyone I know.

And I'm . . . I'm tired of being a clerk, I want to go where something good is happening.
HARPER: Nothing good happens in Washington. We'll forget church teachings and buy furniture at . . . at *Conran's* and become yuppies. I have too much to do here.   25
JOE: Like what?
HARPER: I *do* have things . . .
JOE: What things?
HARPER: I have to finish painting the bedroom.
JOE: You've been painting in there for over a year.   30
HARPER: I know, I. . . . It just isn't done because I never get time to finish it.
JOE: Oh that's . . . that doesn't make sense. You have all the time in the world. You could finish it when I'm at work.
HARPER: I'm afraid to go in there alone.   35
JOE: Afraid of what?
HARPER: I heard someone in there. Metal scraping on the wall. A man with a knife, maybe.
JOE: There's no one in the bedroom, Harper.
HARPER: Not now.   40
JOE: Not this morning either.
HARPER: How do you know? You were at work this morn-ing. There's something creepy about this place. Remem-ber *Rosemary's Baby?*
JOE: *Rosemary's Baby?*   45
HARPER: Our apartment looks like that one. Wasn't that apartment in Brooklyn?
JOE: No, it was . . .
HARPER: Well, it looked like this. It did.
JOE: Then let's move.   50
HARPER: Georgetown's worse. *The Exorcist* was in Georgetown.
JOE: The devil, everywhere you turn, huh, buddy.
HARPER: Yeah. Everywhere.
JOE: How many pills today, buddy?
HARPER: None. One. Three. Only three.   55
LOUIS: (*Pointing at the coffin.*) Why are there just two little wooden pegs holding the lid down?
RABBI ISIDOR CHEMELWITZ: So she can get out easier if she wants to.
LOUIS: I hope she stays put.   60
    I pretended for years that she was already dead. When they called to say she had died it was a surprise. I aban-doned her.
RABBI ISIDOR CHEMELWITZ: "Sharfer vi di tson fun a shlang iz an umdankbar kind!"   65
LOUIS: I don't speak Yiddish.
RABBI ISIDOR CHEMELWITZ: Sharper than the serpent's tooth is the ingratitude of children. Shakespeare. *Kenig Lear.*
LOUIS: Rabbi, what does the Holy Writ say about someone who abandons someone he loves at a time of great need?   70
RABBI ISIDOR CHEMELWITZ: Why would a person do such a thing?
LOUIS: Because he has to.
    Maybe because this person's sense of the world, that it will change for the better with struggle, maybe a person   75
    who has this neo-Hegelian positivist sense of constant his-torical progress towards happiness or perfection or some-thing, who feels very powerful because he feels connected to these forces, moving uphill all the time . . . maybe that person can't, um, incorporate sickness into this sense of   80
    how things are supposed to go. Maybe vomit . . . and sores

and disease . . . really frighten him, maybe . . . he isn't so good with death.

RABBI ISIDOR CHEMELWITZ: The Holy Scriptures have noth-
85   ing to say about such a person.

LOUIS: Rabbi, I'm afraid of the crimes I may commit.

RABBI ISIDOR CHEMELWITZ: Please, mister. I'm a sick old rabbi facing a long drive home to the Bronx. You want to confess, better you should find a priest.

90   LOUIS: But I'm not a Catholic, I'm a Jew.

RABBI ISIDOR CHEMELWITZ: Worse luck for you, bubbulah. Catholics believe in forgiveness. Jews believe in Guilt. (*He pats the coffin tenderly.*)

LOUIS: You just make sure those pegs are in good and tight.

95   RABBI ISIDOR CHEMELWITZ: Don't worry, mister. The life she had, she'll stay put. She's better off.

JOE: Look, I know this is scary for you. But try to understand what it means to me. Will you try?

HARPER: Yes.

100   JOE: Good. Really try.

I think things are starting to change in the world.

HARPER: But I don't want . . .

JOE: Wait. For the good. Change for the good. America has re-discovered itself. Its sacred position among nations. And
105   people aren't ashamed of that like they used to be. This is a great thing. The truth restored. Law restored. That's what President Reagan's done, Harper. He says "Truth exists and can be spoken proudly." And the country responds to him. We become better. More good. I need to be a part of that,
110   I need something big to lift me up. I mean, six years ago the world seemed in decline, horrible, hopeless, full of unsolvable problems and crime and confusion and hunger and . . .

HARPER: But it still seems that way. More now than before. They say the ozone layer is . . .

115   JOE: Harper . . .

HARPER: And today out the window on Atlantic Avenue there was a schizophrenic traffic cop who was making these . . .

JOE: Stop it! I'm trying to make a point.

HARPER: So am I.

120   JOE: You aren't even making sense, you . . .

HARPER: My point is the world seems just as . . .

JOE: It only seems that way to you because you never go out in the world, Harper, and you have emotional problems.

HARPER: I do so get out in the world.

125   JOE: You don't. You stay in all day, fretting about imaginary . . .

HARPER: I get out. I do. You don't know what I do.

JOE: You don't stay in all day.

HARPER: No.

JOE: Well. . . . Yes you do.

130   HARPER: That's what you think.

JOE: Where do you go?

HARPER: Where do *you* go? When you walk.

(*Pause, then angrily.*) And I DO NOT have emotional problems.

135   JOE: I'm sorry.

HARPER: And if I do have emotional problems it's from living with you. Or . . .

JOE: I'm sorry buddy, I didn't mean to . . .

HARPER: Or if you do think I do then you should never have
140   married me. You have all these secrets and lies.

JOE: I want to be married to you, Harper.

HARPER: You shouldn't. You never should.

(*Pause.*)

Hey buddy. Hey buddy.

JOE: Buddy kiss . . .

(*They kiss.*)

HARPER: I heard on the radio how to give a blowjob.   145

JOE: What?

HARPER: You want to try?

JOE: You really shouldn't listen to stuff like that.

HARPER: Mormons can give blowjobs.

JOE: *Harper.*   150

HARPER: (*Imitating his tone.*) *Joe.*

It was a little Jewish lady with a German accent.

This is a good time. For me to make a baby.

(*Little pause. JOE turns away.*)

HARPER: Then they went on to a program about holes in the ozone layer. Over Antarctica. Skin burns, birds go blind,   155 icebergs melt. The world's coming to an end.

SCENE VI

First week of November. In the men's room of the offices of the Brooklyn Federal Court of Appeals; LOUIS *is crying over the sink;* JOE *enters.*

JOE: Oh, um. . . . Morning.

LOUIS: Good morning, counselor.

JOE: (*He watches* LOUIS *cry.*) Sorry, I . . . I don't know your name.

LOUIS: Don't bother. Word processor. The lowest of the low.

JOE: (*Holding out hand.*) Joe Pitt. I'm with Justice Wilson . . .   5

LOUIS: Oh, I know that. Counselor Pitt. Chief Clerk.

JOE: Were you . . . are you OK?

LOUIS: Oh, yeah. Thanks. What a nice man.

JOE: Not so nice.

LOUIS: What?   10

JOE: Not so nice. Nothing. You sure you're . . .

LOUIS: Life sucks shit. Life . . . just sucks shit.

JOE: What's wrong?

LOUIS: Run in my nylons.

JOE: Sorry . . . ?   15

LOUIS: Forget it. Look, thanks for asking.

JOE: Well . . .

LOUIS: I mean it really is nice of you.

(*He starts crying again.*)

Sorry, sorry, sick friend . . .

JOE: Oh, I'm sorry.   20

LOUIS: Yeah, yeah, well, that's sweet.

Three of your colleagues have preceded you to this baleful sight and you're the first one to ask. The others just opened the door, saw me, and fled. I hope they had to pee real bad.   25

JOE: (*Handing him a wad of toilet paper.*) They just didn't want to intrude.

LOUIS: Hah. Reaganite heartless macho asshole lawyers.

JOE: Oh, that's unfair.

LOUIS: What is? Heartless? Macho? Reaganite? Lawyer?   30

JOE: I voted for Reagan.

LOUIS: You did?

JOE: Twice.

LOUIS: Twice? Well, oh boy. A Gay Republican.

35 JOE: Excuse me?

LOUIS: Nothing.

JOE: I'm not . . .

     Forget it.

LOUIS: Republican? Not Republican? Or . . .

40 JOE: What?

LOUIS: What?

JOE: Not gay. I'm not gay.

LOUIS: Oh. Sorry. (*Blows his nose loudly.*) It's just . . .

JOE: Yes?

45 LOUIS: Well, sometimes you can tell from the way a person
     sounds that . . . I mean you *sound* like a . . .

JOE: No I don't. Like what?

LOUIS: Like a Republican.

(*Little pause.* JOE *knows he's being teased;* LOUIS *knows he knows.*
JOE *decides to be a little brave.*)

JOE: (*Making sure no one else is around.*) Do I? Sound like a . . . ?

50 LOUIS: What? Like a . . . ? Republican, or . . . ? Do *I*?

JOE: Do you what?

LOUIS: Sound like a . . . ?

JOE: Like a . . . ?

     I'm confused.

55 LOUIS: Yes.

     My name is Louis. But all my friends call me Louise. I
     work in Word Processing. Thanks for the toilet paper.

(LOUIS *offers* JOE *his hand,* JOE *reaches,* LOUIS *feints and pecks* JOE
on the cheek, then exits.)

SCENE VII

A week later. Mutual dream scene. PRIOR *is at a fantastic makeup
table, having a dream, applying the face.* HARPER *is having a pill-
induced hallucination. She has these from time to time. For some reason,* PRIOR *has appeared in this one. Or* HARPER *has appeared in*
PRIOR'*s dream. It is bewildering.*

PRIOR: (*Alone, putting on makeup, then examining the results in
     the mirror; to the audience.*) "I'm ready for my closeup, Mr.
     DeMille."

     One wants to move through life with elegance and
5   grace, blossoming infrequently but with exquisite taste,
     and perfect timing, like a rare bloom, a zebra orchid. . . .
     One wants. . . . But one so seldom gets what one wants,
     does one? No. One does not. One gets fucked. Over. One
     . . . dies at thirty, robbed of . . . decades of majesty.

10   Fuck this shit. Fuck this shit.

(*He almost crumbles; he pulls himself together; he studies his handiwork in the mirror.*)

I look like a corpse. A corpsette. Oh my queen; you know
you've hit rock-bottom when even drag is a drag.

(HARPER *appears.*)

HARPER: Are you. . . . Who are you?

PRIOR: Who are you?

15 HARPER: What are you doing in my hallucination?

PRIOR: I'm not in your hallucination. You're in my dream.

HARPER: You're wearing makeup.

PRIOR: So are you.

HARPER: But you're a man.

20 PRIOR: (*Feigning dismay, shock, he mimes slashing his throat with
     his lipstick and dies, fabulously tragic. Then.*) The hands and
     feet give it away.

HARPER: There must be some mistake here. I don't recognize
     you. You're not. . . . Are you my . . . some sort of imagi-
25   nary friend?

PRIOR: No. Aren't you too old to have imaginary friends?

HARPER: I have emotional problems. I took too many pills.
     Why are you wearing makeup?

PRIOR: I was in the process of applying the face, trying to
30   make myself feel better—I swiped the new fall colors at
     the Clinique counter at Macy's. (*Showing her.*)

HARPER: You stole these?

PRIOR: I was out of cash; it was an emotional emergency!

HARPER: Joe will be so angry. I promised him. No more pills.

35 PRIOR: These pills you keep alluding to?

HARPER: Valium. I take Valium. Lots of Valium.

PRIOR: And you're dancing as fast as you can.

HARPER: I'm not *addicted*. I don't believe in addiction, and I
     never . . . well, I *never* drink. And I *never* take drugs.

40 PRIOR: Well, smell *you*, Nancy Drew.

HARPER: Except Valium.

PRIOR: Except Valium; in wee fistfuls.

HARPER: It's terrible. Mormons are not supposed to be ad-
     dicted to anything. I'm a Mormon.

45 PRIOR: I'm a homosexual.

HARPER: Oh! In my church we don't believe in homosexuals.

PRIOR: In my church we don't believe in Mormons.

HARPER: What church do . . . oh! (*She laughs.*) I get it.

     I don't understand this. If I didn't ever see you before
50   and I don't think I did then I don't think you should be
     here, in this hallucination, because in my experience the
     mind, which is where hallucinations come from, shouldn't
     be able to make up anything that wasn't there to start
     with, that didn't enter it from experience, from the real
55   world. Imagination can't create anything new, can it? It
     only recycles bits and pieces from the world and reassem-
     bles them into visions. . . . Am I making sense right now?

PRIOR: Given the circumstances, yes.

HARPER: So when we think we've escaped the unbearable or-
60   dinariness and, well, untruthfulness of our lives, it's really
     only the same old ordinariness and falseness rearranged
     into the appearance of novelty and truth. Nothing un-
     known is knowable. Don't you think it's depressing?

PRIOR: The limitations of the imagination?

65 HARPER: Yes.

PRIOR: It's something you learn after your second theme
     party: It's All Been Done Before.

HARPER: The world. Finite. Terribly, terribly. . . . Well . . . This
     is the most depressing hallucination I've ever had.

70 PRIOR: Apologies. I do try to be amusing.

HARPER: Oh, well, don't apologize, you. . . . I can't expect
     someone who's really sick to entertain me.

PRIOR: How on earth did you know . . .

75 HARPER: Oh that happens. This is the very threshhold of revelation sometimes. You can see things . . . how sick you
are. Do you see anything about me?

PRIOR: Yes.

HARPER: What?

PRIOR: You are amazingly unhappy.

80 HARPER: Oh big deal. You meet a Valium addict and you figure out she's unhappy. That doesn't count. Of course I. . . .
Something else. Something surprising.

PRIOR: Something surprising.

HARPER: Yes.

85 PRIOR: Your husband's a homo.

(*Pause.*)

HARPER: Oh, ridiculous.

(*Pause, then very quietly.*)

Really?

PRIOR: (*Shrugs.*) Threshhold of revelation.

HARPER: Well I don't like your revelations. I don't think you
90 intuit well at all. Joe's a very normal man, he . . .
Oh God. Oh God. He. . . . Do homos take, like, lots of
long walks?

PRIOR: Yes. We do. In stretch pants with lavender coifs. I just
looked at you, and there was . . .

95 HARPER: A sort of blue streak of recognition.

PRIOR: Yes.

HARPER: Like you knew me incredibly well.

PRIOR: Yes.

HARPER: Yes.

100 I have to go now, get back, something just . . . fell apart.
Oh God, I feel so sad . . .

PRIOR: I . . . I'm sorry. I usually say, "Fuck the truth," but
mostly, the truth fucks you.

HARPER: I see something else about you . . .

105 PRIOR: Oh?

HARPER: Deep inside you, there's a part of you, the most inner part, entirely free of disease. I can see that.

PRIOR: Is that. . . . That isn't true.

HARPER: Threshhold of revelation.

110 Home . . .

(*She vanishes.*)

PRIOR: People come and go so quickly here . . .
(*To himself in the mirror.*) I don't think there's any unin-
fected part of me. My heart is pumping polluted blood. I
feel dirty.

(*He begins to wipe makeup off with his hands, smearing it around.
A large gray feather falls from up above.* PRIOR *stops smearing the
makeup and looks at the feather. He goes to it and picks it up.*)

115 THE VOICE: (*It is an incredibly beautiful voice.*) Look up!

PRIOR: (*Looking up, not seeing anyone.*) Hello?

THE VOICE: Look up!

PRIOR: Who is that?

THE VOICE: Prepare the way!

120 PRIOR: I don't see any . . .

(*There is a dramatic change in lighting, from above.*)

A VOICE: Look up, look up,
prepare the way
the infinite descent
A breath in air
floating down   125
Glory to . . .

(*Silence.*)

PRIOR: Hello? Is that it? Helloooo!
What the fuck . . . ? (*He holds himself.*)
Poor me. Poor poor me. Why me? Why poor poor
me? Oh I don't feel good right now. I really don't.   130

SCENE VIII

That night. Split scene: HARPER *and* JOE *at home;* PRIOR *and* LOUIS
in bed.

HARPER: Where were you?

JOE: Out.

HARPER: Where?

JOE: Just out. Thinking.

HARPER: It's late.   5

JOE: I had a lot to think about.

HARPER: I burned dinner.

JOE: Sorry.

HARPER: Not my dinner. My dinner was fine. Your dinner. I
put it back in the oven and turned everything up as high   10
as it could go and I watched till it burned black. It's still
hot. Very hot. Want it?

JOE: You didn't have to do that.

HARPER: I know. It just seemed like the kind of thing a mentally
deranged sex-starved pill-popping housewife would do.   15

JOE: Uh huh.

HARPER: So I did it. Who knows anymore what I have to do?

JOE: How many pills?

HARPER: A bunch. Don't change the subject.

JOE: I won't talk to you when you . . .   20

HARPER: No. No. Don't do that! I'm . . . fine, pills are not the
problem, not our problem, I WANT TO KNOW
WHERE YOU'VE BEEN! I WANT TO KNOW
WHAT'S GOING ON!

JOE: Going on with what? The job?   25

HARPER: Not the job.

JOE: I said I need more time.

HARPER: Not the job!

JOE: Mr. Cohn, I talked to him on the phone, he said I had
to hurry . . .   30

HARPER: Not the . . .

JOE: But I can't get you to talk sensibly about anything so . . .

HARPER: SHUT UP!

JOE: Then what?

HARPER: Stick to the subject.   35

JOE: I don't know what that is. You have something you want
to ask me? Ask me. Go.

HARPER: I . . . can't. I'm scared of you.

JOE: I'm tired, I'm going to bed.

HARPER: Tell me without making me ask. Please.   40

JOE: This is crazy, I'm not . . .

HARPER: When you come through the door at night your
face is never exactly the way I remembered it. I get sur-

prised by something . . . mean and hard about the way you
look. Even the weight of you in the bed at night, the way
you breathe in your sleep seems unfamiliar.
    You terrify me.

JOE: (*Cold.*) I know who you are.

HARPER: Yes. I'm the enemy. That's easy. That doesn't change.
You think you're the only one who hates sex; I do; I hate
it with you; I do. I dream that you batter away at me till all
my joints come apart, like wax, and I fall into pieces. It's like
a punishment. It was wrong of me to marry you. I knew
you . . . (*She stops herself.*) It's a sin, and it's killing us both.

JOE: I can always tell when you've taken pills because it makes
you red-faced and sweaty and frankly that's very often
why I don't want to . . .

HARPER: Because . . .

JOE: Well, you aren't pretty. Not like this.

HARPER: I have something to ask you.

JOE: Then ASK! ASK! What in hell are you . . .

HARPER: Are you a homo?

(*Pause.*)

Are you? If you try to walk out right now I'll put your
dinner back in the oven and turn it up so high the whole
building will fill with smoke and everyone in it will as-
phyxiate. So help me God I will.
    Now answer the question.

JOE: What if I . . .

(*Small pause.*)

HARPER: Then tell me, please. And we'll see.

JOE: No. I'm not.
    I don't see what difference it makes.

LOUIS: Jews don't have any clear textual guide to the afterlife;
even that it exists. I don't think much about it. I see it as a
perpetual rainy Thursday afternoon in March. Dead leaves.

PRIOR: Eeeugh. Very Greco-Roman.

LOUIS: Well for us it's not the verdict that counts, it's the act
of judgment. That's why I could never be a lawyer. In
court all that matters is the verdict.

PRIOR: You could never be a lawyer because you are over-
sexed. You're too distracted.

LOUIS: Not distracted, *ab*stracted. I'm trying to make a point:

PRIOR: Namely:

LOUIS: It's the judge in his or her chambers, weighing, books
open, pondering the evidence, ranging freely over categories: good, evil, innocent, guilty; the judge in the chamber of circumspection, not the judge on the bench with
the gavel. The shaping of the law, not its execution.

PRIOR: The point, dear, the point . . .

LOUIS: That it should be the questions and shape of a life, its
total complexity gathered, arranged and considered,
which matters in the end, not some stamp of salvation or
damnation which disperses all the complexity in some
unsatisfying little decision—the balancing of the scales . . .

PRIOR: I like this; very zen; it's . . . reassuringly incomprehensible and useless. We who are about to die thank you.

LOUIS: You are not about to die.

PRIOR: It's not going well, really . . . two new lesions. My leg
hurts. There's protein in my urine, the doctor says, but
who knows what the fuck that portends. Anyway it
shouldn't be there, the protein. My butt is chapped from
diarrhea and yesterday I shat blood.

LOUIS: I really hate this. You don't tell me . . .

PRIOR: You get too upset, I wind up comforting you. It's easier . . .

LOUIS: Oh thanks.

PRIOR: If it's bad I'll tell you.

LOUIS: Shitting blood sounds bad to me.

PRIOR: And I'm telling you.

LOUIS: And I'm handling it.

PRIOR: Tell me some more about justice.

LOUIS: I *am* not handling it.

PRIOR: Well Louis you win Trooper of the Month.

(LOUIS *starts to cry.*)

PRIOR: I take it back. You aren't Trooper of the Month.
    This isn't working . . .
    Tell me some more about justice.

LOUIS: You are not about to die.

PRIOR: Justice . . .

LOUIS: is an immensity, a confusing vastness. Justice is God.
    Prior?

PRIOR: Hmmm?

LOUIS: You love me.

PRIOR: Yes.

LOUIS: What if I walked out on this?
    Would you hate me forever?

(PRIOR *kisses* LOUIS *on the forehead.*)

PRIOR: Yes.

JOE: I think we ought to pray. Ask God for help. Ask him together . . .

HARPER: God won't talk to me. I have to make up people to
talk to me.

JOE: You have to keep asking.

HARPER: I forgot the question.
    Oh yeah. God, is my husband a . . .

JOE: (*Scary.*) Stop it. Stop it. I'm warning you.
    Does it make any difference? That I might be one
thing deep within, no matter how wrong or ugly that
thing is, so long as I have fought, with everything I have,
to kill it. What do you want from me? What do you want
from me, Harper? More than that? For God's sake, there's
nothing left, I'm a shell. There's nothing left to kill.
    As long as my behavior is what I know it has to be.
Decent. Correct. That alone in the eyes of God.

HARPER: No, no, not that, that's Utah talk, Mormon talk, I
hate it, Joe, tell me, say it . . .

JOE: All I will say is that I am a very good man who has worked
very hard to become good and you want to destroy that. You
want to destroy me, but I am not going to let you do that.

(*Pause.*)

HARPER: I'm going to have a baby.

JOE: Liar.

HARPER: You liar.
    A baby born addicted to pills. A baby who does not
dream but who hallucinates, who stares up at us with big
mirror eyes and who does not know who we are.

(*Pause.*)

JOE: Are you really . . .

HARPER: No. Yes. No. Yes. Get away from me.

155   Now we both have a secret.

PRIOR: One of my ancestors was a ship's captain who made money bringing whale oil to Europe and returning with immigrants—Irish mostly, packed in tight, so many dollars per head. The last ship he captained foundered off the coast
160   of Nova Scotia in a winter tempest and sank to the bottom. He went down with the ship—la Grande Geste—but his crew took seventy women and kids in the ship's only longboat, this big, open rowboat, and when the weather got too rough, and they thought the boat was overcrowded, the
165   crew started lifting people up and hurling them into the sea. Until they got the ballast right. They walked up and down the longboat, eyes to the waterline, and when the boat rode low in the water they'd grab the nearest passenger and throw them into the sea. The boat was leaky, see; seventy
170   people; they arrived in Halifax with nine people on board.

LOUIS: Jesus.

PRIOR: I think about that story a lot now. People in a boat, waiting, terrified, while implacable, unsmiling men, irresistibly strong, seize . . . maybe the person next to you,
175   maybe you, and with no warning at all, with time only for a quick intake of air you are pitched into freezing, turbulent water and salt and darkness to drown.

      I like your cosmology, baby. While time is running out I find myself drawn to anything that's suspended, that lacks
180   an ending—but it seems to me that it lets you off scot-free.

LOUIS: What do you mean?

PRIOR: No judgment, no guilt or responsibility.

LOUIS: For me.

PRIOR: For anyone. It was an editorial "you."

185 LOUIS: Please get better. Please.

      Please don't get any sicker.

SCENE IX

Third week in November. ROY *and* HENRY, *his doctor, in* HENRY's *office.*

HENRY: Nobody knows what causes it. And nobody knows how to cure it. The best theory is that we blame a retrovirus, the Human Immunodeficiency Virus. Its presence is made known to us by the useless antibodies which appear in
5   reaction to its entrance into the bloodstream through a cut, or an orifice. The antibodies are powerless to protect the body against it. Why, we don't know. The body's immune system ceases to function. Sometimes the body even attacks itself. At any rate it's left open to a whole horror house of
10   infections from microbes which it usually defends against.

      Like Kaposi's sarcomas. These lesions. Or your throat problem. Or the glands.

      We think it may also be able to slip past the blood-brain barrier into the brain. Which is of course very bad
15   news. And it's fatal in we don't know what percent of people with suppressed immune responses.

(*Pause*)

ROY: This is very interesting, Mr. Wizard, but why the fuck are you telling me this?

(*Pause.*)

HENRY: Well, I have just removed one of three lesions which biopsy results will probably tell us is a Kaposi's sarcoma le- 20 sion. And you have a pronounced swelling of glands in your neck, groin, and armpits—lymphadenopathy is another sign. And you have oral candidiasis and maybe a little more fungus under the fingernails of two digits on your right hand. So that's why . . . 25

ROY: This disease . . .

HENRY: Syndrome.

ROY: Whatever. It afflicts mostly homosexuals and drug addicts.

HENRY: Mostly. Hemophiliacs are also at risk.

ROY: Homosexuals and drug addicts. So why are you imply- 30 ing that I . . .

(*Pause.*)

      What are you implying, Henry?

HENRY: I don't . . .

ROY: I'm not a drug addict.

HENRY: Oh come on Roy. 35

ROY: What, what, come on Roy what? Do you think I'm a junkie, Henry, do you see tracks?

HENRY: This is absurd.

ROY: Say it.

HENRY: Say what? 40

ROY: Say, "Roy Cohn, you are a . . . "

HENRY: Roy.

ROY: "You are a . . . ." Go on. Not "Roy Cohn you are a drug fiend." "Roy Marcus Cohn, you are a . . . "

      Go on, Henry, it starts with an "H." 45

HENRY: Oh I'm not going to . . .

ROY: *With an "H,"* Henry, and it isn't "Hemophiliac." Come on . . .

HENRY: What are you doing, Roy?

ROY: No, say it. I mean it. Say: "Roy Cohn, you are a homo- 50 sexual."

(*Pause.*)

      And I will proceed, systemically, to destroy your reputation and your practice and your career in New York State, Henry. Which you know I can do.

(*Pause.*)

HENRY: Roy, you have been seeing me since 1958. Apart from 55 the facelifts I have treated you for everything from syphilis . . .

ROY: From a whore in Dallas.

HENRY: From syphilis to venereal warts. In your rectum. Which you may have gotten from a whore in Dallas, but it wasn't a female whore. 60

(*Pause.*)

ROY: So say it.

HENRY: Roy Cohn, you are . . .

      You have had sex with men, many many times, Roy, and one of them, or any number of them, has made you very sick. You have AIDS. 65

ROY: AIDS.

Your problem, Henry, is that you are hung up on words, on labels, that you believe they mean what they seem to mean. AIDS. Homosexual. Gay. Lesbian. You think these are names that tell you who someone sleeps with, but they don't tell you that.

HENRY: *No?*

ROY: No. Like all labels they tell you one thing and one thing only: where does an individual so identified fit in the food chain, in the pecking order? Not ideology, or sexual taste, but something much simpler: clout. Not who I fuck or who fucks me, but who will pick up the phone when I call, who owes me favors. This is what a label refers to. Now to someone who does not understand this, homosexual is what I am because I have sex with men. But really this is wrong. Homosexuals are not men who sleep with other men. Homosexuals are men who in fifteen years of trying cannot get a pissant antidiscrimination bill through City Council. Homosexuals are men who know nobody and who nobody knows. Who have zero clout. Does this sound like me, Henry?

HENRY: No.

ROY: No. I have clout. A lot. I can pick up this phone, punch fifteen numbers, and you know who will be on the other end in under five minutes, Henry?

HENRY: The President.

ROY: Even better, Henry. His wife.

HENRY: I'm impressed.

ROY: I don't want you to be impressed. I want you to understand. This is not sophistry. And this is not hypocrisy. This is reality. I have sex with men. But unlike nearly every other man of whom this is true, I bring the guy I'm screwing to the White House and President Reagan smiles at us and shakes his hand. Because *what* I am is defined entirely by *who* I am. Roy Cohn is not a homosexual. Roy Cohn is a heterosexual man, Henry, who fucks around with guys.

HENRY: OK, Roy.

ROY: And what is my diagnosis, Henry?

HENRY: You have AIDS, Roy.

ROY: No, Henry, no. AIDS is what homosexuals have. I have liver cancer.

(*Pause.*)

HENRY: Well, whatever the fuck you have, Roy, it's very serious, and I haven't got a damn thing for you. The NIH in Bethesda has a new drug called AZT with a two-year waiting list that not even I can get you onto. So get on the phone, Roy, and dial the fifteen numbers, and tell the First Lady you need in on an experimental treatment for liver cancer, because you can call it any damn thing you want, Roy, but what it boils down to is very bad news.

ACT TWO

In Vitro
December 1985–January 1986

SCENE I

Night, the third week in December. PRIOR *alone on the floor of his bedroom; he is much worse.*

PRIOR: Louis, Louis, please wake up, oh God.

(LOUIS *runs in.*)

PRIOR: I think something horrible is wrong with me I can't breathe . . .

LOUIS: (*Starting to exit.*) I'm calling the ambulance.

PRIOR: No, wait, I . . .

LOUIS: *Wait?* Are you fucking crazy? Oh God you're on fire, your head is on fire.

PRIOR: It hurts, it hurts . . .

LOUIS: I'm calling the ambulance.

PRIOR: I don't want to go to the hospital, I don't want to go to the hospital please let me lie here, just . . .

LOUIS: No, no, God, Prior, stand up . . .

PRIOR: DON'T TOUCH MY LEG!

LOUIS: We have to . . . oh God this is so crazy.

PRIOR: I'll be OK if I just lie here Lou, really, if I can only sleep a little . . .

(LOUIS *exits.*)

PRIOR: Louis?

NO! NO! Don't call, you'll send me there and I won't come back, please, please Louis I'm begging, baby, please . . . (*Screams.*) LOUIS!!

LOUIS: (*From off; hysterical.*) WILL YOU SHUT THE FUCK UP!

PRIOR: (*Trying to stand.*) Aaaah. I have . . . to go to the bathroom. Wait. Wait, just . . . oh. Oh God. (*He shits himself.*)

LOUIS: (*Entering.*) Prior? They'll be here in . . . Oh my God.

PRIOR: I'm sorry, I'm sorry.

LOUIS: What did . . . ? What?

PRIOR: I had an accident.

(LOUIS *goes to him.*)

LOUIS: This is blood.

PRIOR: Maybe you shouldn't touch it . . . me. . . . I . . . (*He faints.*)

LOUIS: (*Quietly.*) Oh help. Oh help. Oh God oh God oh God help me I can't I can't I can't.

SCENE II

Same night. HARPER *is sitting at home, all alone, with no lights on. We can barely see her.* JOE *enters, but he doesn't turn on the lights.*

JOE: Why are you sitting in the dark? Turn on the light.

HARPER: *No.* I heard the sounds in the bedroom again. I know someone was in there.

JOE: No one was.

HARPER: Maybe actually in the bed, under the covers with a knife.

Oh, boy. Joe. I, um, I'm thinking of going away. By which I mean: I think I'm going off again. You . . . you know what I mean?

JOE: Please don't. Stay. We can fix it. I pray for that. This is my fault, but I can correct it. You have to try too . . .

(*He turns on the light. She turns it off again.*)

HARPER: When you pray, what do you pray for?

JOE: I pray for God to crush me, break me up into little pieces and start all over again.

15 HARPER: Oh. Please. Don't pray for that.

JOE: I had a book of Bible stories when I was a kid. There was a picture I'd look at twenty times every day: Jacob wrestles with the angel. I don't really remember the story, or why the wrestling—just the picture. Jacob is young and
20 very strong. The angel is . . . a beautiful man, with golden hair and wings, of course. I still dream about it. Many nights. I'm. . . . It's me. In that struggle. Fierce, and unfair. The angel is not human, and it holds nothing back, so how could anyone human win, what kind of a fight is
25 that? It's not just. Losing means your soul thrown down in the dust, your heart torn out from God's. But you can't not lose.

HARPER: In the whole entire world, you are the only person, the only person I love or have ever loved. And I love you
30 terribly. Terribly. That's what's so awfully, irreducibly real. I can make up anything but I can't dream that away.

JOE: Are you . . . are you really going to have a baby?

HARPER: It's my time and there's no blood. I don't really know. I suppose it wouldn't be a great thing. Maybe I'm
35 just not bleeding because I take too many pills. Maybe I'll give birth to a pill. That would give a new meaning to pill-popping, huh?

I think you should go to Washington. Alone. Change, like you said.

40 JOE: I'm not going to leave you, Harper.

HARPER: Well maybe not. But I'm going to leave you.

SCENE III

One A.M., the next morning. LOUIS *and a nurse,* EMILY, *are sitting in* PRIOR's *room in the hospital.*

EMILY: He'll be all right now.

LOUIS: No he won't.

EMILY: No. I guess not. I gave him something that makes him sleep.

5 LOUIS: Deep asleep?

EMILY: Orbiting the moons of Jupiter.

LOUIS: A good place to be.

EMILY: Anyplace better than here. You his . . . uh?

LOUIS: Yes. I'm his uh.

10 EMILY: This must be hell for you.

LOUIS: It is. Hell. The After Life. Which is not at all like a rainy afternoon in March, by the way, Prior. A lot more vivid than I'd expected. Dead leaves, but the crunchy kind. Sharp, dry air. The kind of long, luxurious dying
15 feeling that breaks your heart.

EMILY: Yeah, well we all get to break our hearts on this one. He seems like a nice guy. Cute.

LOUIS: Not like this.

Yes, he is. Was. Whatever.

20 EMILY: Weird name. Prior Walter. Like, "The Walter before this one."

LOUIS: Lots of Walters before this one. Prior is an old old family name in an old old family. The Walters go back to the Mayflower and beyond. Back to the Norman Conquest. He
25 says there's a Prior Walter stitched into the Bayeux tapestry.

EMILY: Is that impressive?

LOUIS: Well, it's old. Very old. Which in some circles equals impressive.

EMILY: Not in my circle. What's the name of the tapestry?

LOUIS: The Bayeux tapestry. Embroidered by La Reine Mathilde. 30

EMILY: I'll tell my mother. She embroiders. Drives me nuts.

LOUIS: Manual therapy for anxious hands.

EMILY: Maybe you should try it.

LOUIS: Mathilde stitched while William the Conqueror was off to war. She was capable of . . . more than loyalty. Devo- 35 tion. She waited for him, she stitched for years. And if he had come back broken and defeated from war, she would have loved him even more. And if he had returned muti- lated, ugly, full of infection and horror, she would still have loved him; fed by pity, by a sharing of pain, she would love 40 him even more, and even more, and she would never, never have prayed to God, please let him die if he can't return to me whole and healthy and able to live a normal life. . . . If he had died, she would have buried her heart with him.

So what the fuck is the matter with me? 45

(Little pause.)

Will he sleep through the night?

EMILY: At least.

LOUIS: I'm going.

EMILY: It's one A.M. Where do you have to go at . . .

LOUIS: I know what time it is. A walk. Night air, good for 50 the. . . . The park.

EMILY: Be careful.

LOUIS: Yeah. Danger.

Tell him, if he wakes up and you're still on, tell him goodbye, tell him I had to go. 55

SCENE IV

An hour later. Split scene: JOE *and* ROY *in a fancy (straight) bar;* LOUIS *and a* MAN *in the Rambles in Central Park.* JOE *and* ROY *are sitting at the bar; the place is brightly lit.* JOE *has a plate of food in front of him but he isn't eating.* ROY *occasionally reaches over the table and forks small bites off* JOE's *plate.* ROY *is drinking heavily,* JOE *not at all.* LOUIS *and the* MAN *are eyeing each other, each al-ternating interest and indifference.*

JOE: The pills were something she started when she miscarried or . . . no, she took some before that. She had a really bad time at home, when she was a kid, her home was really bad. I think a lot of drinking and physical stuff. She doesn't talk about that, instead she talks about . . . the sky falling down, 5 people with knives hiding under sofas. Monsters. Mor- mons. Everyone thinks Mormons don't come from homes like that, we aren't supposed to behave that way, but we do. It's not lying, or being two-faced. Everyone tries very hard to live up to God's strictures, which are very . . . um . . . 10

ROY: Strict.

JOE: I shouldn't be bothering you with this.

ROY: No, please. Heart to heart. Want another. . . . What is that, seltzer?

JOE: The failure to measure up hits people very hard. From 15 such a strong desire to be good they feel very far from goodness when they fail.

What scares me is that maybe what I really love in her is the part of her that's farthest from the light, from God's love; maybe I was drawn to that in the first place. And I'm 20 keeping it alive because I need it.

ROY: Why would you need it?

JOE: There are things. . . . I don't know how well we know ourselves. I mean, what if? I know I married her because she . . . because I loved it that she was always wrong, always doing something wrong, like one step out of step. In Salt Lake City that stands out. I never stood out, on the outside, but inside, it was hard for me. To pass.

ROY: Pass?

JOE: Yeah.

ROY: Pass as what?

JOE: Oh. Well. . . . As someone cheerful and strong. Those who love God with an open heart unclouded by secrets and struggles are cheerful; God's easy simple love for them shows in how strong and happy they are. The saints.

ROY: But you had secrets? Secret struggles . . .

JOE: I wanted to be one of the elect, one of the Blessed. You feel you ought to be, that the blemishes are yours by choice, which of course they aren't. Harper's sorrow, that really deep sorrow, she didn't choose that. But it's there.

ROY: You didn't put it there.

JOE: No.

ROY: You sound like you think you did.

JOE: I am responsible for her.

ROY: Because she's your wife.

JOE: That. And I do love her.

ROY: Whatever. She's your wife. And so there are obligations. To her. But also to yourself.

JOE: She'd fall apart in Washington.

ROY: Then let her stay here.

JOE: She'll fall apart if I leave her.

ROY: Then bring her to Washington.

JOE: I just can't, Roy. She needs me.

ROY: Listen, Joe. I'm the best divorce lawyer in the business.

(*Little pause.*)

JOE: Can't Washington wait?

ROY: You do what you need to do, Joe. What you need. You. Let her life go where it wants to go. You'll both be better for that. *Somebody* should get what they want.

MAN: What do you want?

LOUIS: I want you to fuck me, hurt me, make me bleed.

MAN: I want to.

LOUIS: Yeah?

MAN: I want to hurt you.

LOUIS: Fuck me.

MAN: Yeah?

LOUIS: Hard.

MAN: Yeah? You been a bad boy?

(*Pause.* LOUIS *laughs, softly.*)

LOUIS: Very bad. Very bad.

MAN: You need to be punished, boy?

LOUIS: Yes. I do.

MAN: Yes what?

(*Little pause.*)

LOUIS: Um, I . . .

MAN: Yes *what,* boy?

LOUIS: Oh. Yes sir.

MAN: I want you to take me to your place, boy.

LOUIS: No, I can't do that.

MAN: No *what?*

LOUIS: No sir, I can't, I . . .
I don't live alone, sir.

MAN: Your lover know you're out with a man tonight, boy?

LOUIS: No sir, he . . .
My lover doesn't know.

MAN: Your lover know you . . .

LOUIS: Let's change the subject, OK? Can we go to your place?

MAN: I live with my parents.

LOUIS: Oh.

ROY: Everyone who makes it in this world makes it because somebody older and more powerful takes an interest. The most precious asset in life, I think, is the ability to be a good son. You have that, Joe. Somebody who can be a good son to a father who pushes them farther than they would otherwise go. I've had many fathers, I owe my life to them, powerful, powerful men. Walter Winchell, Edgar Hoover. Joe McCarthy most of all. He valued me because I am a good lawyer, but he loved me because I was and am a good son. He was a very difficult man, very guarded and cagey; I brought out something tender in him. He would have died for me. And me for him. Does this embarrass you?

JOE: I had a hard time with my father.

ROY: Well sometimes that's the way. Then you have to find other fathers, substitutes, I don't know. The father-son relationship is central to life. Women are for birth, beginning, but the father is continuance. The son offers the father his life as a vessel for carrying forth his father's dream. Your father's living?

JOE: Um, dead.

ROY: He was . . . what? A difficult man?

JOE: He was in the military. He could be very unfair. And cold.

ROY: But he loved you.

JOE: I don't know.

ROY: No, no, Joe, he did, I know this. Sometimes a father's love has to be very, very hard, unfair even, cold to make his son grow strong in a world like this. This isn't a good world.

MAN: Here, then.

LOUIS: I. . . . Do you have a rubber?

MAN: I don't use rubbers.

LOUIS: You should. (*He takes one from his coat pocket.*) Here.

MAN: I don't use them.

LOUIS: Forget it, then. (*He starts to leave.*)

MAN: No, wait.
Put it on me. Boy.

LOUIS: Forget it, I have to get back. Home. I must be going crazy.

MAN: Oh come on please he won't find out.

LOUIS: It's cold. Too cold.

MAN: It's never too cold, let me warm you up. Please?

(*They begin to fuck.*)

MAN: Relax.

LOUIS: (*A small laugh.*) Not a chance.

MAN: It . . .

LOUIS: What?

MAN: I think it broke. The rubber. You want me to keep going? (*Little pause.*) Pull out? Should I . . .

LOUIS: Keep going.
    Infect me.
    I don't care. I don't care.

(*Pause. The* MAN *pulls out.*)

135 MAN: I . . . um, look, I'm sorry, but I think I want to go.
LOUIS: Yeah.
    Give my best to mom and dad.

(*The* MAN *slaps him.*)

LOUIS: Ow!

(*They stare at each other.*)

LOUIS: It was a joke.

(*The* MAN *leaves.*)

140 ROY: How long have we known each other?
JOE: Since 1980.
ROY: Right. A long time. I feel close to you, Joe. Do I advise
    you well?
JOE: You've been an incredible friend, Roy, I . . .
145 ROY: I want to be family. Familia, as my Italian friends call it.
    La Familia. A lovely word. It's important for me to help
    you, like I was helped.
JOE: I owe practically everything to you, Roy.
ROY: I'm dying, Joe. Cancer.
150 JOE: Oh my God.
ROY: Please. Let me finish.
    Few people know this and I'm telling you this only
    because. . . . I'm not afraid of death. What can death bring
    that I haven't faced? I've lived; life is the worst. (*Gently*
155 *mocking himself.*) Listen to me, I'm a philosopher.
      Joe. You must do this. You must must must. Love; that's
    a trap. Responsibility; that's a trap too. Like a father to a
    son I tell you this: Life is full of horror; nobody escapes,
    nobody; save yourself. Whatever pulls on you, whatever
160 needs from you, threatens you. Don't be afraid; people are
    so afraid; don't be afraid to live in the raw wind, naked,
    alone. . . . Learn at least this: What you are capable of. Let
    nothing stand in your way.

SCENE V

Three days later. PRIOR *and* BELIZE *in* PRIOR*'s hospital room.*
PRIOR *is very sick but improving.* BELIZE *has just arrived.*

PRIOR: Miss Thing.
BELIZE: Ma cherie bichette.
PRIOR: Stella.
BELIZE: Stella for star. Let me see. (*Scrutinizing* PRIOR.) You
5   look like shit, why yes indeed you do, comme la merde!
PRIOR: Merci.
BELIZE: (*Taking little plastic bottles from his bag, handing them to*
    PRIOR.) Not to despair, Belle Reeve. Lookie! Magic goop!
PRIOR: (*Opening a bottle, sniffing.*) Pooh! What kinda crap is that?
10 BELIZE: Beats me. Let's rub it on your poor blistered body and
    see what it does.
PRIOR: This is not Western medicine, these bottles . . .
BELIZE: Voodoo cream. From the botanica 'round the block.

PRIOR: And you a registered nurse.
BELIZE: (*Sniffing it.*) Beeswax and cheap perfume. Cut with 15
    Jergen's Lotion. Full of good vibes and love from some lit-
    tle black Cubana witch in Miami.
PRIOR: Get that trash away from me. I am immune-suppressed.
BELIZE: I *am* a health professional. I *know* what I'm doing.
PRIOR: It stinks. Any word from Louis? 20

(*Pause.* BELIZE *starts giving* PRIOR *a gentle massage.*)

PRIOR: Gone.
BELIZE: He'll be back. I know the type. Likes to keep a girl
    on edge.
PRIOR: It's been . . .

(*Pause*)

BELIZE: (*Trying to jog his memory.*) How long? 25
PRIOR: I don't remember.
BELIZE: How long have you been here?
PRIOR: (*Getting suddenly upset.*) I don't remember, I don't give
    a fuck. I want Louis. I want my fucking boyfriend, where
    the fuck is he? I'm dying, I'm dying, where's Louis? 30
BELIZE: Shhhh, shhh . . .
PRIOR: This is a very strange drug, this drug. Emotional la-
    bility, for starters.
BELIZE: Save a tab or two for me.
PRIOR: Oh no, not this drug, ce n'est pas pour la joyeux noël 35
    et la bonne année, this drug she is serious poisonous
    chemistry, ma pauvre bichette.
      And not just disorienting. I hear things. Voices.
BELIZE: Voices.
PRIOR: A voice. 40
BELIZE: Saying what?

(*Pause.*)

PRIOR: I'm not supposed to tell.
BELIZE: You better tell the doctor. Or I will.
PRIOR: No no don't. Please. I want the voice; it's wonderful.
    It's all that's keeping me alive. I don't want to talk to some 45
    intern about it.
      You know what happens? When I hear it, I get hard.
BELIZE: Oh my.
PRIOR: Comme ça. (*He uses his arm to demonstrate.*) And you
    know I am slow to rise. 50
BELIZE: My jaw aches at the memory.
PRIOR: And would you deny me this little solace—betray my
    concupiscence to Florence Nightingale's storm troopers?
BELIZE: Perish the thought, ma bébé.
PRIOR: They'd change the drug just to spoil the fun. 55
BELIZE: You and your boner can depend on me.
PRIOR: Je t'adore, ma belle nègre.
BELIZE: All this girl-talk shit is politically incorrect, you know.
    We should have dropped it back when we gave up drag.
PRIOR: I'm sick, I get to be politically incorrect if it makes 60
    me feel better. You sound like Lou.

(*Little pause.*)

    Well, at least I have the satisfaction of knowing he's in an-
    guish somewhere. I loved his anguish. Watching him stick
    his head up his asshole and eat his guts out over some rel-

65 atively minor moral conundrum—it was the best show in
town. But Mother warned me; if they get overwhelmed
by the little things . . .

BELIZE: They'll be belly-up bustville when something big
comes along.

70 PRIOR: Mother warned me.

BELIZE: And they do come along.

PRIOR: But I didn't listen.

BELIZE: No. (*Doing Hepburn.*) Men are beasts.

PRIOR: (*Also Hepburn.*) The absolute lowest.

75 BELIZE: I have to go. If I want to spend my whole lonely life
looking after white people I can get underpaid to do it.

PRIOR: You're just a Christian martyr.

BELIZE: Whatever happens, baby, I will be here for you.

PRIOR: Je t'aime.

80 BELIZE: Je t'aime. Don't go crazy on me, girlfriend, I already
got enough crazy queens for one lifetime. For two. I can't
be bothering with dementia.

PRIOR: I promise.

BELIZE: (*Touching him; softly.*) Ouch.

85 PRIOR: Ouch. Indeed.

BELIZE: Why'd they have to pick on you?
And eat more, girlfriend, you really do look like shit.

(BELIZE *leaves.*)

PRIOR: (*After waiting a beat.*) He's gone.
Are you still . . .

90 VOICE: I can't stay. I will return.

PRIOR: Are you one of those "Follow me to the other side"
voices?

VOICE: No. I am no nightbird. I am a messenger . . .

PRIOR: You have a beautiful voice, it sounds . . . like a viola,
95 like a perfectly tuned, tight string, balanced, the truth. . . .
Stay with me.

THE VOICE: Not now. Soon I will return, I will reveal myself
to you; I am glorious, glorious; my heart, my countenance
and my message. You must prepare.

100 PRIOR: For what? I don't want to . . .

THE VOICE: No death, no:
A marvelous work and a wonder we undertake, an edifice awry we sink plumb and straighten, a great Lie we
abolish, a great error correct, with the rule, sword and
105 broom of Truth!

PRIOR: What are you talking about, I . . .

THE VOICE: I am on my way; when I am manifest, our Work
begins;
Prepare for the parting of the air,
110 The breath, the ascent,
Glory to . . .

SCENE VI

The second week of January. MARTIN, ROY *and* JOE *in a fancy
Manhattan restaurant.*

MARTIN: It's a revolution in Washington, Joe. We have a new
agenda and finally a real leader. They got back the Senate
but we have the courts. By the nineties the Supreme
Court will be block-solid Republican appointees, and the
5 Federal bench—Republican judges like land mines,

everywhere, everywhere they turn. Affirmative action?
Take it to court. Boom! Land mine. And we'll get our
way on just about everything: abortion, defense, Central
America, family values, a live investment climate. We have
the White House locked till the year 2000. And beyond.   10
A permanent fix on the Oval Office? It's possible. By '92
we'll get the Senate back, and in ten years the South is going to give us the House. It's really the end of Liberalism.
The end of New Deal Socialism. The end of ipso facto
secular humanism. The dawning of a genuinely American   15
political personality. Modeled on Ronald Wilson Reagan.

JOE: It sounds great, Mr. Heller.

MARTIN: Martin. And Justice is the hub. Especially since Ed
Meese took over. He doesn't specialize in Fine Points of
the Law. He's a flatfoot, a cop. He reminds me of Teddy   20
Roosevelt.

JOE: I can't wait to meet him.

MARTIN: Too bad, Joe, he's been dead for sixty years!

(*There is a little awkwardness.* JOE *doesn't respond.*)

MARTIN: Teddy Roosevelt. You said you wanted to. . . . Little
joke. It reminds me of the story about the . . .   25

ROY: (*Smiling, but nasty.*) Aw shut the fuck up Martin.
(*To* JOE.) You see that? Mr. Heller here is one of the
mighty, Joseph, in D.C. he sitteth on the right hand of the
man who sitteth on the right hand of The Man. And yet
I can say "shut the fuck up" and he will take no offense.   30
Loyalty. He . . . Martin?

MARTIN: Yes, Roy?

ROY: Rub my back.

MARTIN: Roy . . .

ROY: No no really, a sore spot, I get them all the time now,   35
these. . . . Rub it for me darling, would you do that for me?

(MARTIN *rubs* ROY's *back. They both look at* JOE.)

ROY: (*To* JOE.) How do you think a handful of Bolsheviks
turned St. Petersburg into Leningrad in one afternoon?
Comrades. Who do for each other. Marx and Engels. Lenin
and Trotsky. Josef Stalin and Franklin Delano Roosevelt.   40

(MARTIN *laughs.*)

ROY: *Comrades,* right Martin?

MARTIN: This man, Joe, is a Saint of the Right.

JOE: I know, Mr. Heller, I . . .

ROY: And you see what I mean, Martin? He's special, right?

MARTIN: Don't embarrass him, Roy.   45

ROY: Gravity, decency, smarts! His strength is as the strength
of ten because his heart is pure! *And* he's a Royboy, one
hundred percent.

MARTIN: We're on the move, Joe. On the move.

JOE: Mr. Heller, I . . .   50

MARTIN: (*Ending backrub.*) We can't wait any longer for an
answer.

(*Little pause.*)

JOE: Oh. Um, I . . .

ROY: Joe's a married man, Martin.

MARTIN: Aha.   55

ROY: With a wife. She doesn't care to go to D.C., and so Joe cannot go. And keeps us dangling. We've seen that kind of thing before, haven't we? These men and their wives.

MARTIN: Oh yes. Beware.

60 JOE: I really can't discuss this under . . .

MARTIN: Then *don't* discuss. Say yes, Joe.

ROY: Now.

MARTIN: Say yes I will.

ROY: Now.

65 Now. I'll hold my breath till you do, I'm turning blue waiting. . . . *Now,* goddammit!

MARTIN: Roy, calm down, it's not . . .

ROY: Aw, fuck it. (*He takes a letter from his jacket pocket, hands it to* JOE.)

70 Read. Came today.

(JOE *reads the first paragraph, then looks up.*)

JOE: Roy. This is . . . Roy, this is terrible.

ROY: You're telling me.

A letter from the New York State Bar Association, Martin. They're gonna try and disbar me.

75 MARTIN: Oh my.

JOE: Why?

ROY: Why, Martin?

MARTIN: Revenge.

ROY: The whole Establishment. Their little rules. Because I
80 know no rules. Because I don't see the Law as a dead and arbitrary collection of antiquated dictums, thou shall, thou shalt not, because, because I know the Law's a pliable, breathing, sweating . . . *organ,* because, because . . .

MARTIN: Because he borrowed half a million from one of his
85 clients.

ROY: Yeah, well, there's that.

MARTIN: *And* he forgot to *return* it.

JOE: Roy, that's. . . . You borrowed money from a client?

ROY: I'm deeply ashamed.

(*Little pause.*)

90 JOE: (*Very sympathetic.*) Roy, you know how much I admire you. Well I mean I know you have unorthodox ways, but I'm sure you only did what you thought at the time you needed to do. And I have faith that . . .

ROY: Not so damp, please. I'll deny it was a loan. She's got no
95 paperwork. Can't prove a fucking thing.

(*Little pause.* MARTIN *studies the menu.*)

JOE: (*Handing back the letter, more official in tone.*) Roy I really appreciate your telling me this, and I'll do whatever I can to help.

ROY: (*Holding up a hand, then, carefully.*) I'll tell you what you
100 can do.

I'm about to be tried, Joe, by a jury that is not a jury of my peers. The disbarment committee: genteel gentleman Brahmin lawyers, country-club men. I offend them, to these men . . . I'm what, Martin, some sort of filthy lit-
105 tle Jewish troll?

MARTIN: Oh well, I wouldn't go so far . . .

ROY: Oh well I would.

Very fancy lawyers, these disbarment committee lawyers, fancy lawyers with fancy corporate clients and complicated cases. Antitrust suits. Deregulation. Environ-110 mental control. Complex cases like these need Justice Department cooperation like flowers need the sun. Wouldn't you say that's an accurate assessment, Martin?

MARTIN: I'm not here, Roy. I'm not hearing any of this.

ROY: No. Of course not. 115

Without the light of the sun, Joe, these cases, and the fancy lawyers who represent them, will wither and die.

A well-placed friend, someone in the Justice Department, say, can turn off the sun. Cast a deep shadow on my behalf. Make them shiver in the cold. If they overstep. 120 They would fear that.

(*Pause.*)

JOE: Roy. I don't understand.

ROY: You do.

(*Pause.*)

JOE: You're not asking me to . . .

ROY: Ssshhhh. Careful. 125

JOE: (*A beat, then.*) Even if I said yes to the job, it would be illegal to interfere. With the hearings. It's unethical. No. I can't.

ROY: Un-ethical.

Would you excuse us, Martin? 130

MARTIN: Excuse you?

ROY: Take a walk, Martin. For real.

(MARTIN *leaves.*)

ROY: Un-ethical. Are you trying to embarrass me in front of my friend?

JOE: Well it is unethical, I can't . . . 135

ROY: Boy, you are really something. What the fuck do you think this is, Sunday School?

JOE: No, but Roy this is . . .

ROY: This is . . . this is gastric juices churning, this is enzymes and acids, this is intestinal is what this is, bowel movement 140 and blood-red meat—this stinks, this is *politics,* Joe, the game of being alive. And you think you're. . . . What? Above that? Above alive is what? Dead! In the clouds! You're on earth, goddammit! Plant a foot, stay a while.

I'm sick. They smell I'm weak. They want blood this 145 time. I must have eyes in Justice. In Justice you will protect me.

JOE: Why can't Mr. Heller . . .

ROY: Grow up, Joe. The administration can't get involved.

JOE: But I'd be part of the administration. The same as him. 150

ROY: Not the same. Martin's Ed's man. And Ed's Reagan's man. So Martin's Reagan's man.

And you're mine.

(*Little pause. He holds up the letter.*)

This will never be. Understand me?

(*He tears the letter up.*)

I'm gonna be a lawyer, Joe, I'm gonna be a lawyer, Joe, I'm 155 gonna be a goddam motherfucking legally licensed member of the bar lawyer, just like my daddy was, till my last bitter day on earth, Joseph, until the day I die.

(MARTIN *returns.*)

ROY: Ah, Martin's back.
160 MARTIN: So are we agreed?
ROY: Joe?

(*Little pause.*)

JOE: I will think about it.
     (*To* ROY.) I will.
ROY: Huh.
165 MARTIN: It's the fear of what comes after the doing that makes the doing hard to do.
ROY: Amen.
MARTIN: But you can almost always live with the consequences.

SCENE VII

That afternoon. On the granite steps outside the Hall of Justice, Brooklyn. It is cold and sunny. A Sabrett wagon is selling hot dogs. LOUIS, *in a shabby overcoat, is sitting on the steps contemplatively eating one.* JOE *enters with three hot dogs and a can of Coke.*

JOE: Can I . . . ?
LOUIS: Oh sure. Sure. Crazy cold sun.
JOE: (*Sitting.*) Have to make the best of it.
     How's your friend?
5 LOUIS: My . . . ? Oh. He's worse. My friend is worse.
JOE: I'm sorry.
LOUIS: Yeah, well. Thanks for asking. It's nice. You're nice. I can't believe you voted for Reagan.
JOE: I hope he gets better.
10 LOUIS: Reagan?
JOE: Your friend.
LOUIS: He won't. Neither will Reagan.
JOE: Let's not talk politics, OK?
LOUIS: (*Pointing to* JOE's *lunch.*) You're eating three of those?
15 JOE: Well . . . I'm . . . hungry.
LOUIS: They're really terrible for you. Full of rat-poo and beetle legs and wood shavings 'n' shit.
JOE: Huh.
LOUIS: And . . . um . . . irridium, I think. Something toxic.
20 JOE: You're eating one.
LOUIS: Yeah, well, the shape, I can't help myself, plus I'm trying to commit suicide, what's your excuse?
JOE: I don't have an excuse. I just have Pepto-Bismol.

(JOE *takes a bottle of Pepto-Bismol and chugs it.* LOUIS *shudders audibly.*)

JOE: Yeah I know but then I wash it down with Coke.

(*He does this.* LOUIS *mimes barfing in* JOE's *lap.* JOE *pushes* LOUIS's *head away.*)

25 JOE: Are you always like this?
LOUIS: I've been worrying a lot about his kids.
JOE: Whose?
LOUIS: Reagan's. Maureen and Mike and little orphan Patti and Miss Ron Reagan Jr., the you-should-pardon-the-
30   expression heterosexual.

JOE: Ron Reagan Jr. is *not* . . . You shouldn't just make these assumptions about people. How do you know? About him? What he is? You don't know.
LOUIS: (*Doing Tallulah.*) Well darling he never sucked *my* cock but . . . 35
JOE: Look, if you're going to get vulgar . . .
LOUIS: No no really I mean. . . . What's it like to be the child of the Zeitgeist? To have the American Animus as your dad? It's not really a *family,* the Reagans, I read *People,* there aren't any connections there, no love, they don't ever even 40 speak to each other except through their agents. So what's it like to be Reagan's kid? Enquiring minds want to know.
JOE: You can't believe everything you . . .
LOUIS: (*Looking away.*) But . . . I think we all know what that's like. Nowadays. No connections. No responsibilities. All 45 of us . . . falling through the cracks that separate what we owe to our selves and . . . and what we owe to love.
JOE: You just. . . . Whatever you feel like saying or doing, you don't care, you just . . . do it.
LOUIS: Do what? 50
JOE: It. Whatever. Whatever it is you want to do.
LOUIS: Are you trying to tell me something?

(*Little pause, sexual. They stare at each other.* JOE *looks away.*)

JOE: No, I'm just observing that you . . .
LOUIS: Impulsive.
JOE: Yes, I mean it must be scary, you . . . 55
LOUIS: (*Shrugs.*) Land of the free. Home of the brave. Call me irresponsible.
JOE: It's kind of terrifying.
LOUIS: Yeah, well, freedom is. Heartless, too.
JOE: Oh you're not heartless. 60
LOUIS: You don't know.
     Finish your weenie.

(*He pats* JOE *on the knee, starts to leave.*)

JOE: Um . . .

(LOUIS *turns, looks at him.* JOE *searches for something to say.*)

JOE: Yesterday was Sunday but I've been a little unfocused recently and I thought it was Monday. So I came here like 65 I was going to work. And the whole place was empty. And at first I couldn't figure out why, and I had this moment of incredible . . . fear and also. . . . It just flashed through my mind: The whole Hall of Justice, it's empty, it's deserted, it's gone out of business. Forever. The people 70 that make it run have up and abandoned it.
LOUIS: (*Looking at the building.*) Creepy.
JOE: Well yes but. I felt that I was going to scream. Not because it was creepy, but because the emptiness felt so *fast.* And . . . well, good. A . . . happy scream. 75
     I just wondered what a thing it would be . . . if overnight everything you owe anything to, justice, or love, had really gone away. Free.
     It would be . . . heartless terror. Yes. Terrible, and . . .
     Very great. To shed your skin, every old skin, one by 80 one and then walk away, unencumbered, into the morning.

(*Little pause. He looks at the building.*)

I can't go in there today.

LOUIS: Then don't.

JOE: (*Not really hearing* LOUIS.) I can't go in, I need . . .

(*He looks for what he needs. He takes a swig of Pepto-Bismol.*)

85   I can't *be* this anymore. I need . . . a change, I should just . . .

LOUIS: (*Not a come-on, necessarily; he doesn't want to be alone.*) Want some company? For whatever?

(*Pause.* JOE *looks at* LOUIS *and looks away, afraid.* LOUIS *shrugs.*)

LOUIS: Sometimes, even if it scares you to death, you have to be willing to break the law. Know what I mean?

(*Another little pause.*)

90   JOE: Yes.

(*Another little pause.*)

LOUIS: I moved out. I moved out on my . . .
I haven't been sleeping well.

JOE: Me neither.

(LOUIS *goes up to* JOE, *licks his napkin and dabs at* JOE's *mouth.*)

LOUIS: Antacid moustache.

95   (*Points to the building.*) Maybe the court won't convene. Ever again. Maybe we are free. To do whatever.
          Children of the new morning, criminal minds. Selfish and greedy and loveless and blind. Reagan's children.
          You're scared. So am I. Everybody is in the land of the

100   free.
          God help us all.

SCENE VIII

Late that night. JOE *at a payphone phoning* HANNAH *at home in Salt Lake City.*

JOE: Mom?

HANNAH: Joe?

JOE: Hi.

HANNAH: You're calling from the street. It's . . . it must be four

5   in the morning. What's happened?

JOE: Nothing, nothing, I . . .

HANNAH: It's Harper. Is Harper. . . . Joe? Joe?

JOE: Yeah, hi. No, Harper's fine. Well, no, she's . . . not fine.
How are you, Mom?

10   HANNAH: What's happened?

JOE: I just wanted to talk to you. I, uh, wanted to try something out on you.

HANNAH: Joe, you haven't . . . have you been drinking, Joe?

JOE: Yes ma'am. I'm drunk.

15   HANNAH: That isn't like you.

JOE: No. I mean, who's to say?

HANNAH: Why are you out on the street at four A.M.? In that crazy city. It's dangerous.

JOE: Actually, Mom, I'm not on the street. I'm near the

20   boathouse in the park.

HANNAH: What park?

JOE: Central Park.

HANNAH: CENTRAL PARK! Oh my Lord. What on earth are you doing in Central Park at this time of night? Are you . . . Joe, I think you ought to go home right now. Call   25 me from home.

(*Little pause.*)

Joe?

JOE: I come here to watch, Mom. Sometimes. Just to watch.

HANNAH: Watch what? What's there to watch at four in the . . .

JOE: Mom, did Dad love me?   30

HANNAH: What?

JOE: Did he?

HANNAH: You ought to go home and call from there.

JOE: Answer.

HANNAH: Oh now really. This is maudlin. I don't like this   35 conversation.

JOE: Yeah, well, it gets worse from here on.

(*Pause.*)

HANNAH: Joe?

JOE: Mom. Momma. I'm a homosexual, Momma.
Boy, did that come out awkward.   40

(*Pause.*)

Hello? Hello?
I'm a homosexual.

(*Pause.*)

Please, Momma, Say something.

HANNAH: You're old enough to understand that your father didn't love you without being ridiculous about it.   45

JOE: What?

HANNAH: You're ridiculous. You're being ridiculous.

JOE: I'm . . .
What?

HANNAH: You really ought to go home now to your wife. I   50 need to go to bed. This phone call. . . . We will just forget this phone call.

JOE: Mom.

HANNAH: No more talk. Tonight. This . . .
(*Suddenly very angry.*) Drinking is a sin! A sin! I raised   55 you better than that. (*She hangs up.*)

SCENE IX

The following morning, early. Split scene: HARPER *and* JOE *at home;* LOUIS *and* PRIOR *in* PRIOR's *hospital room.* JOE *and* LOUIS *have just entered. This should be fast and obviously furious; overlapping is fine; the proceedings may be a little confusing but not the final results.*

HARPER: Oh God. Home. The moment of truth has arrived.

JOE: Harper.

LOUIS: I'm going to move out.

PRIOR: The fuck you are.

JOE: Harper. Please listen. I still love you very much. You're   5 still my best buddy; I'm not going to leave you.

HARPER: No, I don't like the sound of this. I'm leaving.

LOUIS: I'm leaving.
   I already have.

10 JOE: Please listen. Stay. This is really hard. We have to talk.

HARPER: We are talking. Aren't we. Now please shut up. OK?

PRIOR: Bastard. Sneaking off while I'm flat out here, that's low. If I could get up now I'd beat the holy shit out of you.

15 JOE: Did you take pills? How many?

HARPER: No pills. Bad for the . . . (*Pats stomach.*)

JOE: You aren't pregnant. I called your gynecologist.

HARPER: I'm seeing a new gynecologist.

PRIOR: You have no right to do this.

20 LOUIS: Oh, that's ridiculous.

PRIOR: No right. It's criminal.

JOE: Forget about that. Just listen. You want the truth. This is the truth.
   I knew this when I married you. I've known this I
25 guess for as long as I've known anything, but . . . I don't know, I thought maybe that with enough effort and will I could change myself . . . but I can't . . .

PRIOR: Criminal.

LOUIS: There oughta be a law.

30 PRIOR: There is a law. You'll see.

JOE: I'm losing ground here, I go walking, you want to know where I walk, I . . . go to the park, or up and down 53rd Street, or places where. . . . And I keep swearing I won't go walking again, but I just can't.

35 LOUIS: I need some privacy.

PRIOR: That's new.

LOUIS: Everything's new, Prior.

JOE: I try to tighten my heart into a knot, a snarl, I try to learn to live dead, just numb, but then I see someone I
40 want, and it's like a nail, like a hot spike right through my chest, and I know I'm losing.

PRIOR: Apartment too small for three? Louis and Prior comfy but not Louis and Prior and Prior's disease?

LOUIS: Something like that.
45   I won't be judged by you. This isn't a crime, just—the inevitable consequence of people who run out of— whose limitations . . .

PRIOR: Bang bang bang. The court will come to order.

LOUIS: I mean let's talk practicalities, schedules; I'll come over
50 if you want, spend nights with you when I can, I can . . .

PRIOR: Has the jury reached a verdict?

LOUIS: I'm doing the best I can.

PRIOR: Pathetic. Who cares?

JOE: My whole life has conspired to bring me to this place,
55 and I can't despise my whole life. I think I believed when I met you I could save you, you at least if not myself, but . . . I don't have any sexual feelings for you, Harper. And I don't think I ever did.

(*Little pause.*)

HARPER: I think you should go.

60 JOE: Where?

HARPER: Washington. Doesn't matter.

JOE: What are you talking about?

HARPER: Without me.
   Without me, Joe. Isn't that what you want to hear?

(*Little pause.*)

JOE: Yes.   65

LOUIS: You can love someone and fail them. You can love someone and not be able to . . .

PRIOR: You *can*, theoretically, yes. A person can, maybe an editorial "you" can love, Louis, but not *you,* specifically you, I don't know, I think you are excluded from that general 70 category.

HARPER: You were going to save me, but the whole time you were spinning a lie. I just don't understand that.

PRIOR: A person could theoretically love and maybe many do but we both know now you can't.   75

LOUIS: I do.

PRIOR: You can't even say it.

LOUIS: I love you, Prior.

PRIOR: I repeat. Who cares?

HARPER: This is so scary, I want this to stop, to go back . . . 80

PRIOR: We have reached a verdict, your honor. This man's heart is deficient. He loves, but his love is worth nothing.

JOE: Harper . . .

HARPER: Mr. Lies, I want to get away from here. Far away. Right now. Before he starts talking again. Please, please . . . 85

JOE: As long as I've known you Harper you've been afraid of . . . of men hiding under the bed, men hiding under the sofa, men with knives.

PRIOR: (*Shattered; almost pleading; trying to reach him.*) I'm dying! You stupid fuck! Do you know what that is! Love! Do 90 you know what love means? We lived together four-and-a-half years, you animal, you idiot.

LOUIS: I have to find some way to save myself.

JOE: Who are these men? I never understood it. Now I know.

HARPER: What?   95

JOE: It's me.

HARPER: It is?

PRIOR: GET OUT OF MY ROOM!

JOE: I'm the man with the knives.

HARPER: You are?   100

PRIOR: If I could get up now I'd kill you. I would. Go away. Go away or I'll scream.

HARPER: Oh God . . .

JOE: I'm sorry . . .

HARPER: It is you.   105

LOUIS: Please don't scream.

PRIOR: Go.

HARPER: I recognize you now.

LOUIS: Please . . .

JOE: Oh. Wait, I. . . . Oh!   110

(*He covers his mouth with his hand, gags, and removes his hand, red with blood.*)

   I'm bleeding.

(PRIOR *screams.*)

HARPER: Mr. Lies.

MR. LIES: (*Appearing, dressed in antarctic explorer's apparel.*) Right here.

HARPER: I want to go away. I can't see him anymore.   115

MR. LIES: Where?

HARPER: Anywhere. Far away

MR. LIES: Absolutamento.

(HARPER *and* MR. LIES *vanish.* JOE *looks up, sees that she's gone.*)

PRIOR: (*Closing his eyes.*) When I open my eyes you'll be gone.

(LOUIS *leaves.*)

120 JOE: Harper?
PRIOR: (*Opening his eyes.*) Huh. It worked.
JOE: (*Calling.*) Harper?
PRIOR: I hurt all over. I wish I was dead.

SCENE X

The same day, sunset. HANNAH *and* SISTER ELLA CHAPTER, *a real-estate saleswoman,* HANNAH PITT's *closest friend, in front of* HANNAH's *house in Salt Lake City.*

SISTER ELLA CHAPTER: Look at that view! A view of heaven. Like the living city of heaven, isn't it, it just fairly glimmers in the sun.
HANNAH: Glimmers.
5 SISTER ELLA CHAPTER: Even the stone and brick it just glimmers and glitters like heaven in the sunshine. Such a nice view you get, perched up on a canyon rim. Some kind of beautiful place.
HANNAH: It's just Salt Lake, and you're selling the house *for*
10 me, not *to* me.
SISTER ELLA CHAPTER: I like to work up an enthusiasm for my properties.
HANNAH: Just get me a good price.
SISTER ELLA CHAPTER: Well, the market's off.
15 HANNAH: At least fifty.
SISTER ELLA CHAPTER: Forty'd be more like it.
HANNAH: Fifty.
SISTER ELLA CHAPTER: Wish you'd wait a bit.
HANNAH: Well I can't.
20 SISTER ELLA CHAPTER: Wish you would. You're about the only friend I got.
HANNAH: Oh well now.
SISTER ELLA CHAPTER: Know why I decided to like you? I decided to like you 'cause you're the only unfriendly
25 Mormon I ever met.
HANNAH: Your wig is crooked.
SISTER ELLA CHAPTER: Fix it.

(HANNAH *straightens* SISTER ELLA's *wig.*)

SISTER ELLA CHAPTER: New York City. All they got there is tiny rooms.
30 I always thought: People ought to stay put. That's why I got my license to sell real estate. It's a way of saying: Have a house! Stay put! It's a way of saying traveling's no good. Plus I needed the cash. (*She takes a pack of cigarettes out of her purse, lights one, offers pack to* HANNAH.)
35 HANNAH: Not out here, anyone could come by.
There's been days I've stood at this ledge and thought about stepping over.
It's a hard place, Salt Lake: baked dry. Abundant energy; not much intelligence. That's a combination that can
40 wear a body out. No harm looking someplace else. I don't need much room.
My sister-in-law Libby thinks there's radon gas in the basement.

SISTER ELLA CHAPTER: Is there gas in the . . .
HANNAH: Of course not. Libby's a fool. 45
SISTER ELLA CHAPTER: 'Cause I'd have to include that in the description.
HANNAH: There's no gas, Ella. (*Little pause.*) Give a puff. (*She takes a furtive drag of* ELLA's *cigarette.*) Put it away now.
SISTER ELLA CHAPTER: So I guess it's goodbye. 50
HANNAH: You'll be all right, Ella, I wasn't ever much of a friend.
SISTER ELLA CHAPTER: I'll say something but don't laugh, OK? This is the home of saints, the godliest place on earth, they say, and I think they're right. That means there's no
55 evil here? No. Evil's everywhere. Sin's everywhere. But this . . . is the spring of sweet water in the desert, the desert flower. Every step a Believer takes away from here is a step fraught with peril. I fear for you, Hannah Pitt, because you are my friend. Stay put. This is the right home of saints.
HANNAH: Latter-day saints. 60
SISTER ELLA CHAPTER: Only kind left.
HANNAH: But still. Late in the day . . . for saints and everyone. That's all. That's all.
Fifty thousand dollars for the house, Sister Ella Chapter; don't undersell. It's an impressive view. 65

ACT THREE
Not-Yet-Conscious, Forward Dawning
January 1986

SCENE I

Late night, three days after the end of Act Two. The stage is completely dark. PRIOR *is in bed in his apartment, having a nightmare. He wakes up, sits up and switches on a nightlight. He looks at his clock. Seated by the table near the bed is a man dressed in the clothing of a 13th-century British squire.*

PRIOR: (*Terrified.*) Who are you?
PRIOR 1: My name is Prior Walter.

(*Pause.*)

PRIOR: My name is Prior Walter.
PRIOR 1: I know that.
PRIOR: Explain. 5
PRIOR 1: You're alive. I'm not. We have the same name. What do you want me to explain?
PRIOR: A ghost?
PRIOR 1: An ancestor.
PRIOR: Not *the* Prior Walter? The Bayeux tapestry Prior Walter? 10
PRIOR 1: His great-great grandson. The fifth of the name.
PRIOR: I'm the thirty-fourth, I think.
PRIOR 1: Actually the thirty-second.
PRIOR: Not according to Mother.
PRIOR 1: She's including the two bastards, then; I say leave 15 them out. I say no room for bastards. The little things you swallow . . .
PRIOR: Pills.
PRIOR 1: Pills. For the pestilence. I too . . .
PRIOR: Pestilence. . . . You too what? 20
PRIOR 1: The pestilence in my time was much worse than now. Whole villages of empty houses. You could look outdoors

and see Death walking in the morning, dew dampening the ragged hem of his black robe. Plain as I see you now.

25 PRIOR: You died of the plague.

PRIOR 1: The spotty monster. Like you, alone.

PRIOR: I'm not alone.

PRIOR 1: You have no wife, no children.

PRIOR: I'm gay.

30 PRIOR 1: So? Be gay, dance in your altogether for all I care, what's that to do with not having children?

PRIOR: Gay homosexual, not bonny, blithe and . . . never mind.

PRIOR 1: I had twelve. When I died.

(The second ghost appears, this one dressed in the clothing of an elegant 17th-century Londoner.)

PRIOR 1: *(Pointing to* PRIOR 2.*)* And I was three years younger
35   than him.

*(*PRIOR *sees the new ghost, screams.)*

PRIOR: Oh God another one.

PRIOR 2: Prior Walter. Prior to you by some seventeen others.

PRIOR 1: He's counting the bastards.

PRIOR: Are we having a convention?

40 PRIOR 2: We've been sent to declare her fabulous incipience. They love a well-paved entrance with lots of heralds, and . . .

PRIOR 1: The messenger come. Prepare the way. The infinite descent, a breath in air . . .

45 PRIOR 2: They chose us, I suspect, because of the mortal affinities. In a family as long-descended as the Walters there are bound to be a few carried off by plague.

PRIOR 1: The spotty monster.

PRIOR 2: Black Jack. Came from a water pump, half the city
50   of London, can you imagine? His came from fleas. Yours, I understand, is the lamentable consequence of venery . . .

PRIOR 1: Fleas on rats, but who knew that?

PRIOR: Am I going to die?

PRIOR 2: We aren't allowed to discuss . . .

55 PRIOR 1: When you do, you don't get ancestors to help you through it. You may be surrounded by children but you die alone.

PRIOR: I'm afraid.

PRIOR 1: You should be. There aren't even torches, and the
60   path's rocky, dark and steep.

PRIOR 2: Don't alarm him. There's good news before there's bad.
    We two come to strew rose petal and palm leaf before the triumphal procession. Prophet. Seer. Revelator. It's a
65   great honor for the family.

PRIOR 1: He hasn't got a family.

PRIOR 2: I meant for the Walters, for the family in the larger sense.

PRIOR: *(Singing.)*

70   All I want is a room somewhere,
        Far away from the cold night air . . .

PRIOR 2: *(Putting a hand on* PRIOR*'s forehead.)* Calm, calm, this is no brain fever . . .

*(*PRIOR *calms down, but keeps his eyes closed. The lights begin to change. Distant Glorious Music.)*

PRIOR 1: *(Low chant.)* Adonai, Adonai,
    Olam ha-yichud,   75
    Zefirot, Zazahot,
    Ha-adam, ha-gadol
    Daughter of Light,
    Daughter of Splendors,
    Fluor! Phosphor!   80
    Lumen! Candle!

PRIOR 2: *(Simultaneously.)* Even now,
    From the mirror-bright halls of heaven,
    Across the cold and lifeless infinity of space,
    The Messenger comes   85
    Trailing orbs of light,
    Fabulous, incipient,
    Oh Prophet,
    To you . . .

PRIOR 1 and PRIOR 2: Prepare, prepare,   90
    The Infinite Descent,
    A breath, a feather,
    Glory to . . .

(They vanish.)

SCENE II

The next day. Split scene: LOUIS *and* BELIZE *in a coffee shop.* PRIOR *is at the outpatient clinic at the hospital with* EMILY, *the nurse; she has him on a pentamidine IV drip.*

LOUIS: Why has democracy succeeded in America? Of course by succeeded I mean comparatively, not literally, not in the present, but what makes for the prospect of some sort of radical democracy spreading outward and growing up? Why does the power that was once so carefully preserved at 5 the top of the pyramid by the original framers of the Constitution seem drawn inexorably downward and outward in spite of the best effort of the Right to stop this? I mean it's the really hard thing about being Left in this country, the American Left can't help but trip over all these petrified lit- 10 tle fetishes: freedom, that's the worst; you know, *Jeane Kirkpatrick* for God's sake will go on and on about freedom and so what does that mean, the word freedom, when she talks about it, or human rights; you have Bush talking about human rights, and so what are these people talking about, they 15 might as well be talking about the mating habits of Venusians, these people don't begin to know what, ontologically, freedom is or human rights, like they see these bourgeois property-based Rights-of-Man-type rights but that's not enfranchisement, not democracy, not what's implicit, what's 20 potential within the idea, not the idea with blood in it. That's just liberalism, the worst kind of liberalism, really, bourgeois tolerance, and what I think is that what AIDS shows us is the limits of tolerance, that it's not enough to be tolerated, because when the shit hits the fan you find out 25 how much tolerance is worth. Nothing. And underneath all the tolerance is intense, passionate hatred.

BELIZE: Uh huh.

LOUIS: Well don't you think that's true?

BELIZE: Uh huh. It is.   30

LOUIS: *Power* is the object, not being tolerated. Fuck assimilation. But I mean in spite of all this the thing about America,

I think, is that ultimately we're different from every other nation on earth, in that, with people here of every race, we

35   can't.... Ultimately what defines us isn't race, but politics. Not like any European country where there's an insurmountable fact of a kind of racial, or ethnic, monopoly, or monolith, like all Dutchmen, I mean Dutch people, are well, Dutch, and the Jews of Europe were never Europeans,

40   just a small problem. Facing the monolith. But here there are so many small problems, it's really just a collection of small problems, the monolith is missing. Oh, I mean, of course I suppose there's the monolith of White America. White Straight Male America.

45   BELIZE: Which is not unimpressive, even among monoliths.

LOUIS: Well, no, but when the race thing gets taken care of, and I don't mean to minimalize how major it is, I mean I know it is, this is a really, really incredibly racist country but it's like, well, the British. I mean, all these blue-eyed pink peo-

50   ple. And it's just weird, you know, I mean I'm not all that Jewish-looking, or ... well, maybe I am but, you know, in New York, everyone is ... well, not everyone, but so many are but so but in England, in London I walk into bars and I feel like Sid the Yid, you know I mean like Woody Allen

55   in *Annie Hall,* with the payess and the gabardine coat, like never, never anywhere so much—I mean, not actively despised, not like they're Germans, who I think are still terribly anti-Semitic, and racist too, I mean black-racist, they pretend otherwise but, anyway, in London, there's just ...

60   and at one point I met this black gay guy from Jamaica who talked with a lilt but he said his family'd been living in London since before the Civil War—the American one—and how the English never let him forget for a minute that he wasn't blue-eyed and pink and I said yeah, me too, these

65   people are anti-Semites and he said yeah but the British Jews have the clothing business all sewed up and blacks there can't get a foothold. And it was an incredibly awkward moment of just.... I mean here we were, in this bar that was gay but it was a *pub,* you know, the beams and the

70   plaster and those horrible little, like, two-day-old fish and egg sandwiches—and just so British, so *old,* and I felt, well, there's no way out of this because both of us are, right now, too much immersed in this history, hope is dissolved in the sheer age of this place, where race is what counts and

75   there's no real hope of change—it's the racial destiny of the Brits that matters to them, not their political destiny, whereas in America ...

BELIZE: Here in America race doesn't count.

LOUIS: No, no, that's not.... I mean you *can't* be hearing

80   that ...

BELIZE: I ...

LOUIS: It's—look, race, yes, but ultimately race here is a political question, right? Racists just try to use race here as a tool in a political struggle. It's not really about race. Like the

85   spiritualists try to use that stuff, are you enlightened, are you centered, channeled, whatever, this reaching out for a spiritual past in a country where no indigenous spirits exist—only the Indians, I mean Native American spirits and we killed them off so now, there are no gods here, no ghosts

90   and spirits in America, there are no angels in America, no spiritual past, no racial past, there's only the political, and the decoys and the ploys to maneuver around the in-

escapable battle of politics, the shifting downwards and outwards of political power to the people ...

95   BELIZE: POWER to the People! AMEN! (*Looking at his watch.*) *OH MY GOODNESS!* Will you look at the time, I gotta ...

LOUIS: Do you.... You think this is, what, racist or naive or something?

BELIZE: Well it's certainly *something.* Look, I just remembered

100   I have an appointment ...

LOUIS: What? I mean I really don't want to, like, speak from some position of privilege and ...

BELIZE: I'm sitting here, thinking, eventually he's *got* to run out of steam, so I let you rattle on and on saying about

105   maybe seven or eight things I find really offensive.

LOUIS: What?

BELIZE: But I know you, Louis, and I know the guilt fueling this peculiar tirade is obviously already swollen bigger than your hemorrhoids.

110   LOUIS: I don't have hemorrhoids.

BELIZE: I hear different. May I finish?

LOUIS: Yes, but I don't have hemorrhoids.

BELIZE: So finally, when I ...

LOUIS: Prior told you, he's an asshole, he shouldn't have ...

115   BELIZE: You promised, Louis. Prior is not a subject.

LOUIS: You brought him up.

BELIZE: I brought up hemorrhoids.

LOUIS: So it's indirect. Passive-aggressive.

BELIZE: Unlike, I suppose, banging me over the head with your theory that America doesn't have a race problem.

120   LOUIS: Oh be fair I never said that.

BELIZE: Not exactly, but ...

LOUIS: I said ...

BELIZE: but it was close enough, because if it'd been that blunt I'd've just walked out and ...

125   LOUIS: You deliberately misinterpreted! I ...

BELIZE: Stop interrupting! I haven't been able to ...

LOUIS: Just let me ...

BELIZE: NO! What, *talk*? You've been running your mouth nonstop since I got here, yaddadda yaddadda blah blah

130   blah, up the hill, down the hill, playing with your MONOLITH ...

LOUIS: (*Overlapping*) Well, you could have joined in at any time instead of ...

BELIZE: (*Continuing over* LOUIS.) ... and girlfriend it is truly an

135   awesome spectacle but I got better things to do with my time than sit here listening to this racist bullshit just because I feel sorry for you that ...

LOUIS: I am not a racist!

BELIZE: Oh come on ...

140   LOUIS: So maybe I am a racist but ...

BELIZE: Oh I really hate that! It's no fun picking on you Louis; you're so guilty, it's like throwing darts at a glob of jello, there's no satisfying hits, just quivering, the darts just

145   blop in and vanish.

LOUIS: I just think when you are discussing lines of oppression it gets very complicated and ...

BELIZE: Oh is that a fact? You know, we black drag queens have a rather intimate knowledge of the complexity of the

150   lines of ...

LOUIS: *Ex*-black drag queen.

BELIZE: Actually ex-ex.

LOUIS: You're doing drag again?

BELIZE: I don't. . . . Maybe. I don't have to tell you. Maybe.

155 LOUIS: I think it's sexist.

BELIZE: I didn't ask you.

LOUIS: Well it is. The gay community, I think, has to adopt the same attitude towards drag as black women have to take towards black women blues singers.

160 BELIZE: Oh my we *are* walking dangerous tonight.

LOUIS: Well, it's all internalized oppression, right, I mean the masochism, the stereotypes, the . . .

BELIZE: Louis, are you deliberately trying to make me hate you?

165 LOUIS: No, I . . .

BELIZE: I mean, are you deliberately transforming yourself into an arrogant, sexual-political Stalinist-slash-racist flag-waving thug for my benefit?

(Pause.)

LOUIS: You know what I think?

170 BELIZE: What?

LOUIS: You hate me because I'm a Jew.

BELIZE: I'm leaving.

LOUIS: It's true.

BELIZE: You have no basis except your . . .

175   Louis, it's good to know you haven't changed; you are still an honorary citizen of the Twilight Zone, and after your pale, pale white polemics on behalf of racial insensitivity you have a flaming *fuck* of a lot of nerve calling me an anti-Semite. Now I really gotta go.

180 LOUIS: You called me Lou the Jew.

BELIZE: That was a joke.

LOUIS: I didn't think it was funny. It was hostile.

BELIZE: It was three years ago.

LOUIS: So?

185 BELIZE: You just called yourself Sid the Yid.

LOUIS: That's not the same thing.

BELIZE: Sid the Yid is different from Lou the Jew.

LOUIS: Yes.

BELIZE: Someday you'll have to explain that to me, but right

190   now . . .

    You hate me because you hate black people.

LOUIS: I do not. But I do think most black people are anti-Semitic.

BELIZE: "Most black people." *That's* racist, Louis, and *I* think

195   most Jews . . .

LOUIS: Louis Farrakhan.

BELIZE: Ed Koch.

LOUIS: Jesse Jackson.

BELIZE: Jackson. Oh really, Louis, this is . . .

200 LOUIS: Hymietown! Hymietown!

BELIZE: Louis, you voted for Jesse Jackson. You send checks to the Rainbow Coalition.

LOUIS: I'm ambivalent. The checks bounced.

BELIZE: All your checks bounce, Louis; you're ambivalent

205   about everything.

LOUIS: What's that supposed to mean?

BELIZE: You may be dumber than shit but I refuse to believe you can't figure it out. Try.

LOUIS: I was never ambivalent about Prior. I love him. I do.

210   I really do.

BELIZE: Nobody said different.

LOUIS: Love and ambivalence are. . . . Real love isn't ambivalent.

BELIZE: "Real love isn't ambivalent." I'd swear that's a line from my favorite bestselling paperback novel, *In Love with* 215 *the Night Mysterious,* except I don't think you ever read it.

(Pause.)

LOUIS: I never read it, no.

BELIZE: You ought to. Instead of spending the rest of your life trying to get through *Democracy in America.* It's about this white woman whose Daddy owns a plantation in the 220 Deep South in the years before the Civil War—the American one—and her name is Margaret, and she's in love with her Daddy's number-one slave, and his name is Thaddeus, and she's married but her white slave-owner husband has AIDS: Antebellum Insufficiently Developed 225 Sexorgans. And there's a lot of hot stuff going down when Margaret and Thaddeus can catch a spare torrid ten under the cottonpicking moon, and then of course the Yankees come, and they set the slaves free, and the slaves string up old Daddy, and so on. Historical fiction. Somewhere in 230 there I recall Margaret and Thaddeus find the time to discuss the nature of love; her face is reflecting the flames of the burning plantation—you know, the way white people do—and his black face is dark in the night and she says to him, "Thaddeus, real love isn't ever ambivalent." 235

(Little pause. EMILY *enters and turns off IV drip.)*

BELIZE: Thaddeus looks at her; he's contemplating her thesis; and he isn't sure he agrees.

EMILY: *(Removing IV drip from* PRIOR*'s arm.)* Treatment number . . . *(Consulting chart.)* four.

PRIOR: Pharmaceutical miracle. Lazarus breathes again. 240

LOUIS: Is he. . . . How bad is he?

BELIZE: You want the laundry list?

EMILY: Shirt off, let's check the . . .

*(*PRIOR *takes his shirt off. She examines his lesions.)*

BELIZE: There's the weight problem and the shit problem and the morale problem. 245

EMILY: Only six. That's good. Pants.

(He drops his pants. He's naked. She examines.)

BELIZE: And. He thinks he's going crazy.

EMILY: Looking good. What else?

PRIOR: Ankles sore and swollen, but the leg's better. The nausea's mostly gone with the little orange pills. BM's pure 250 liquid but not bloody anymore, for now, my eye doctor says everything's OK, for now, my dentist says "Yuck!" when he sees my fuzzy tongue, and now he wears little condoms on his thumb and forefinger. And a mask. So what? My dermatologist is in Hawaii and my mother . . . 255 well leave my mother out of it. Which is usually where my mother is, out of it. My glands are like walnuts, my

260 weight's holding steady for week two, and a friend died two days ago of bird tuberculosis; bird tuberculosis; that scared me and I didn't go to the funeral today because he was an Irish Catholic and it's probably open casket and I'm afraid of . . . something, the bird TB or seeing him or. . . . So I guess I'm doing OK. Except for of course I'm going nuts.

265 EMILY: We ran the toxoplasmosis series and there's no indication . . .

PRIOR: I know, I know, but I feel like something terrifying is on its way, you know, like a missile from outer space, and it's plummeting down towards the earth, and I'm ground
270 zero, and . . . I am generally known where I am known as one cool, collected queen. And I am ruffled.

EMILY: There's really nothing to worry about. I think that shochen bamromim hamtzeh menucho nechono al kanfey haschino.

275 PRIOR: What?

EMILY: Everything's fine. Bemaalos k'doshim ut'horim kezohar horokeea mazhirim . . .

PRIOR: Oh I don't understand what you're . . .

EMILY: Es nishmas Prior sheholoch leolomoh, baavur shen-
280 odvoo z'dokoh b'ad hazkoras nishmosoh.

PRIOR: Why are you doing that?! Stop it! Stop it!

EMILY: Stop what?

PRIOR: You were just . . . weren't you just speaking in Hebrew or something.

285 EMILY: *Hebrew*? (*Laughs.*) I'm basically Italian-American. No. I didn't speak in Hebrew.

PRIOR: Oh no, oh God please I really think I . . .

EMILY: Look, I'm sorry, I have a waiting room full of. . . . I think you're one of the lucky ones, you'll live for years,
290 probably—you're pretty healthy for someone with no immune system. Are you seeing someone? Loneliness is a danger. A therapist?

PRIOR: No, I don't need to see anyone, I just . . .

EMILY: Well think about it. You aren't going crazy. You're just
295 under a lot of stress. No wonder . . . (*She starts to write in his chart.*)

(*Suddenly there is an astonishing blaze of light, a huge chord sounded by a gigantic choir, and a great book with steel pages mounted atop a molten-red pillar pops up from the stage floor. The book opens; there is a large Aleph inscribed on its pages, which bursts into flames. Immediately the book slams shut and disappears instantly under the floor as the lights become normal again. EMILY notices none of this, writing. PRIOR is agog.*)

EMILY: (*Laughing, exiting.*) Hebrew . . .

(PRIOR *flees.*)

LOUIS: Help me.

BELIZE: I beg your pardon?

300 LOUIS: You're a nurse, give me something, I . . . don't know what to do anymore, I. . . . Last week at work I screwed up the Xerox machine like permanently and so I . . . then I tripped on the subway steps and my glasses broke and I cut my forehead, here, see, and now I can't see much and
305 my forehead . . . it's like the Mark of Cain, stupid, right, but it won't heal and every morning I see it and I think, Biblical things, Mark of Cain, Judas Iscariot and his silver

and his noose, people who . . . in betraying what they love betray what's truest in themselves, I feel . . . nothing but cold for myself, just cold, and every night I miss him, 310 I miss him so much but then . . . those sores, and the smell and . . . where I thought it was going. . . . I could be . . . I could be sick too, maybe I'm sick too. I don't know.

Belize. Tell him I love him. Can you do that? 315

BELIZE: I've thought about it for a very long time, and I still don't understand what love is. Justice is simple. Democracy is simple. Those things are unambivalent. But love is very hard. And it goes bad for you if you violate the hard law of love. 320

LOUIS: I'm dying.

BELIZE: He's dying. You just wish you were. Oh cheer up, Louis. Look at that heavy sky out there.

LOUIS: Purple.

BELIZE: *Purple?* Boy, what kind of a homosexual are you, any- 325 way? That's not purple, Mary, that color up there is (*Very grand.*) mauve.

All day today it's felt like Thanksgiving. Soon, this . . . ruination will be blanketed white. You can smell it—can you smell it? 330

LOUIS: Smell what?

BELIZE: Softness, compliance, forgiveness, grace.

LOUIS: No . . .

BELIZE: I can't help you learn that. I can't help you, Louis. You're not my business. (*He exits.*) 335

(LOUIS *puts his head in his hands, inadvertently touching his cut forehead.*)

LOUIS: Ow FUCK! (*He stands slowly, looks towards where* BELIZE *exited.*) Smell what? (*He looks both ways to be sure no one is watching, then inhales deeply, and is surprised.*) Huh. Snow.

SCENE III

Same day. HARPER *in a very white, cold place, with a brilliant blue sky above; a delicate snowfall. She is dressed in a beautiful snowsuit. The sound of the sea, faint.*

HARPER: Snow! Ice! Mountains of ice! Where am I? I . . . feel better, I do, I . . . feel better. There are ice crystals in my lungs, wonderful and sharp. And the snow smells like cold, crushed peaches. And there's something . . . some current of blood in the wind, how strange, it has that iron taste. 5

MR. LIES: Ozone.

HARPER: Ozone! Wow! Where am I?

MR. LIES: The Kingdom of Ice, the bottommost part of the world.

HARPER: (*Looking around, then realizing.*) Antarctica. This is 10 Antarctica!

MR. LIES: Cold shelter for the shattered. No sorrow here, tears freeze.

HARPER: Antarctica, Antarctica, oh boy oh boy, LOOK at this, I. . . . Wow, I must've really snapped the tether, huh? 15

MR. LIES: Apparently . . .

HARPER: That's great. I want to stay here forever. Set up camp. Build things. Build a city, an enormous city made up of

frontier forts, dark wood and green roofs and high gates
20   made of pointed logs and bonfires burning on every street
corner. I should build by a river. Where are the forests?

MR. LIES: No timber here. Too cold. Ice, no trees.

HARPER: Oh details! I'm sick of details! I'll plant them and
grow them. I'll live off caribou fat, I'll melt it over the
25   bon-fires and drink it from long, curved goat-horn cups.
It'll be great. I want to make a new world here. So that I
never have to go home again.

MR. LIES: As long as it lasts. Ice has a way of melting . . .

HARPER: No. Forever. I can have anything I want here—
30   maybe even companionship, someone who has . . . desire
for me. You, maybe.

MR. LIES: It's against the by-laws of the International Order
of Travel Agents to get involved with clients. Rules are
rules. Anyway, I'm not the one you really want.

35   HARPER: There isn't anyone . . . maybe an Eskimo. Who
could ice-fish for food. And help me build a nest for
when the baby comes.

MR. LIES: There are no Eskimo in Antarctica. And you're not
really pregnant. You made that up.

40   HARPER: Well all of this is made up. So if the snow feels cold
I'm pregnant. Right? Here, I can be pregnant. And I can
have any kind of a baby I want.

MR. LIES: This is a retreat, a vacuum, its virtue is that it lacks
everything; deep-freeze for feelings. You can be numb
45   and safe here, that's what you came for. Respect the delicate ecology of your delusions.

HARPER: You mean like no Eskimo in Antarctica.

MR. LIES: Correcto. Ice and snow, no Eskimo. Even halluci-
nations have laws.

50   HARPER: Well then who's that?

(*The* ESKIMO *appears.*)

MR. LIES: An Eskimo.

HARPER: An antarctic Eskimo. A fisher of the polar deep.

MR. LIES: There's something wrong with this picture.

(*The* ESKIMO *beckons.*)

HARPER: I'm going to like this place. It's my own National
55   Geo-graphic Special! Oh! Oh! (*She holds her stomach.*) I
think . . . I think I felt her kicking. Maybe I'll give birth
to a baby covered with thick white fur, and that way she
won't be cold. My breasts will be full of hot cocoa so she
doesn't get chilly. And if it gets really cold, she'll have a
60   pouch I can crawl into. Like a marsupial. We'll mend together. That's what we'll do; we'll mend.

SCENE IV

Same day. An abandoned lot in the South Bronx. A homeless
WOMAN *is standing near an oil drum in which a fire is burning.*
Snowfall. Trash around. HANNAH *enters dragging two heavy suit-*
cases.

HANNAH: Excuse me? I said excuse me? Can you tell me
where I am? Is this Brooklyn? Do you know a Pineapple
Street? Is there some sort of bus or train or . . . ?
I'm lost, I just arrived from Salt Lake. City. Utah? I took
5   the bus that I was told to take and I got off—well it was the

very last stop, so I had to get off, and I *asked* the driver was
this Brooklyn, and he nodded yes but he was from one of
those foreign countries where they think it's good manners
to nod at everything even if you have no idea what it is
you're nodding at, and in truth I think he spoke no English   10
at all, which I think would make him ineligible for employment on public transportation. The public being
English-speaking, mostly. Do you speak English?

(*The* WOMAN *nods.*)

HANNAH: I was supposed to be met at the airport by my son.
He didn't show and I don't wait more than three and   15
three-quarters hours for *anyone*. I should have been patient, I guess, I. . . . Is this . . .

WOMAN: Bronx.

HANNAH: Is that. . . . The *Bronx?* Well how in the name of
Heaven did I get to the Bronx when the bus driver said . . .   20

WOMAN: (*Talking to herself.*) Slurp slurp slurp will you STOP
that disgusting slurping! YOU DISGUSTING SLURP-
ING FEEDING ANIMAL! Feeding yourself, just feeding
yourself, what would it matter, to you or to ANYONE, if
you just stopped. Feeding. And DIED?   25

(*Pause.*)

HANNAH: Can you just tell me where I . . .

WOMAN: Why was the Kosciusko Bridge named after a Polack?

HANNAH: I don't know what you're . . .

WOMAN: That was a joke.

HANNAH: Well what's the punchline?   30

WOMAN: I don't know.

HANNAH: (*Looking around desperately.*) Oh for pete's sake, is
there anyone else who . . .

WOMAN: (*Again, to herself.*) Stand further off you fat loathsome whore, you can't have any more of this soup, slurp   35
slurp slurp you animal, and the—I know you'll just go pee
it all away and where will you do that? Behind what bush?
It's FUCKING COLD out here and I . . .
Oh that's right, because it was supposed to have been
a tunnel!   40
That's not very funny.
Have you read the prophecies of Nostradamus?

HANNAH: Who?

WOMAN: Some guy I went out with once somewhere, Nostradamus. Prophet, outcast, eyes like. . . . Scary shit, he . . .   45

HANNAH: Shut up. Please. Now I want you to stop jabbering
for a minute and pull your wits together and tell me how
to get to Brooklyn. Because you know! And you are going to tell me! Because there is no one else around to tell
me and I am wet and cold and I am very angry! So I am   50
sorry you're psychotic but just make the effort—take a
deep breath—DO IT!

(HANNAH *and* WOMAN *breathe together.*)

HANNAH: That's good. Now exhale.

(*They do.*)

HANNAH: Good. Now how do I get to Brooklyn?

WOMAN: Don't know. Never been. Sorry. Want some soup?   55

HANNAH: Manhattan? Maybe you know . . . I don't suppose you know the location of the Mormon Visitor's . . .

WOMAN: 65th and Broadway.

HANNAH: How do you . . .

60 WOMAN: Go there all the time. Free movies. Boring, but you can stay all day.

HANNAH: Well. . . . So how do I . . .

WOMAN: Take the D Train. Next block make a right.

HANNAH: Thank you.

65 WOMAN: Oh yeah. In the new century I think we will all be insane.

SCENE V

Same day. JOE and ROY in the study of ROY's brownstone. ROY is wearing an elegant bathrobe. He has made a considerable effort to look well. He isn't well, and he hasn't succeeded much in looking it.

JOE: I can't. The answer's no. I'm sorry.

ROY: Oh, well, apologies . . .

   I can't see that there's anyone asking for apologies.

(Pause.)

JOE: I'm sorry, Roy.

5 ROY: Oh, well, apologies.

JOE: My wife is missing, Roy. My mother's coming from Salt Lake to . . . to help look, I guess. I'm supposed to be at the airport now, picking her up but. . . . I just spent two days in a hospital, Roy, with a bleeding ulcer, I was spitting up

10   blood.

ROY: Blood, huh? Look, I'm very busy here and . . .

JOE: It's just a job.

ROY: A job? A *job*? *Washington!* Dumb Utah Mormon hick shit!

15 JOE: Roy . . .

ROY: *WASHINGTON!* When Washington called me I was younger than you, you think I said "Aw fuck no I can't go I got two fingers up my asshole and a little moral nose-bleed to boot!" When Washington calls you my pretty

20   young punk friend you go or you can go fuck yourself sideways 'cause the train has pulled out of the station, and you are *out,* nowhere, out in the cold. Fuck you, Mary Jane, get outta here.

JOE: Just let me . . .

25 ROY: Explain? Ephemera. You broke my heart. Explain that. Explain that.

JOE: I love you. Roy.

   There's so much that I want, to be . . . what you see in me, I want to be a participant in the world, in your world,

30   Roy, I want to be capable of that, I've tried, really I have but . . . I can't do this. Not because I don't believe in you, but because I believe in you so much, in what you stand for, at heart, the order, the decency. I would give anything to protect you, but. . . . There are laws I can't break. It's

35   too ingrained. It's not me. There's enough damage I've already done.

   Maybe you were right, maybe I'm dead.

ROY: You're not dead, boy, you're a sissy.

   You love me; that's moving, I'm moved. It's nice to be

40   loved. I warned you about her, didn't I, Joe? But you don't listen to me, why, because you say Roy is smart and Roy's a friend but Roy . . . well, he isn't nice, and you wanna be nice. Right? A nice, nice man!

(Little pause.)

You know what my greatest accomplishment was, Joe, in my life, what I am able to look back on and be proudest 45 of? And I have helped make Presidents and unmake them and mayors and more goddam judges than anyone in NYC ever—AND several million dollars, tax-free—and what do you think means the most to me?

   You ever hear of Ethel Rosenberg? Huh, Joe, huh? 50

JOE: Well, yeah, I guess I. . . . Yes.

ROY: Yes. Yes. You have heard of Ethel Rosenberg. Yes. Maybe you even read about her in the history books.

   If it wasn't for me, Joe, Ethel Rosenberg would be alive today, writing some personal-advice column for *Ms.* mag- 55 azine. She isn't. Because during the trial, Joe, I was on the phone every day, talking with the judge . . .

JOE: Roy . . .

ROY: Every day, doing what I do best, talking on the telephone, making sure that timid Yid nebbish on the bench 60 did his duty to America, to history. That sweet unprepossessing woman, two kids, boo-hoo-hoo, reminded us all of our little Jewish mamas—she came this close to getting life; I pleaded till I wept to put her in the chair. Me. I did that. I would have fucking pulled the switch if they'd have 65 let me. Why? Because I fucking hate traitors. Because I fucking hate communists. Was it legal? Fuck legal. Am I a nice man? Fuck nice. They say terrible things about me in the *Nation*. Fuck the *Nation*. You want to be Nice, or you want to be Effective? Make the law, or subject to it. 70 Choose. Your wife chose. A week from today, she'll be back. SHE knows how to get what SHE wants. Maybe I ought to send *her* to Washington.

JOE: I don't believe you.

ROY: Gospel. 75

JOE: You can't possibly mean what you're saying.

   Roy, you were the Assistant United States Attorney on the Rosenberg case, ex-parte communication with the judge during the trial would be . . . censurable, at least, probably conspiracy and . . . in a case that resulted in exe- 80 cution, it's . . .

ROY: What? Murder?

JOE: You're not well is all.

ROY: What do you mean, not well? Who's not well?

(Pause.)

JOE: You said . . . 85

ROY: No I didn't I said what?

JOE: Roy, you have cancer.

ROY: No I don't.

(Pause.)

JOE: You told me you were dying.

ROY: What the fuck are you talking about, Joe? I never said 90 that. I'm in perfect health. There's not a goddam thing wrong with me.

(*He smiles.*)

Shake?

(JOE *hesitates. He holds out his hand to* ROY. ROY *pulls* JOE *into a close, strong clinch.*)

ROY: (*More to himself than to* JOE.) It's OK that you hurt me
95   because I love you, baby Joe. That's why I'm so rough on
you.

(ROY *releases* JOE. JOE *backs away a step or two.*)

ROY: Prodigal son. The world will wipe its dirty hands all
over you.
JOE: It already has, Roy.
100   ROY: Now go.

(ROY *shoves* JOE *hard.* JOE *turns to leave.* ROY *stops him, turns him around.*)

ROY: (*Smoothing* JOE's *lapels, tenderly.*) I'll always be here, waiting for you . . .

(*Then again, with sudden violence, he pulls* JOE *close, violently.*)

What did you want from me, what was all this, what do
you want, treacherous ungrateful little . . .

(JOE, *very close to belting* ROY, *grabs him by the front of his robe, and propels him across the length of the room. He holds* ROY *at arm's length, the other arm ready to hit.*)

105   ROY: (*Laughing softly, almost pleading to be hit.*) Transgress a little, Joseph.

(JOE *releases* ROY.)

ROY: There are so many laws; find one you can break.

(JOE *hesitates, then leaves, backing out. When* JOE *has gone,* ROY *doubles over in great pain, which he's been hiding throughout the scene with* JOE.)

ROY: Ah, Christ . . .
Andy! Andy! Get in here! Andy!

(*The door opens, but it isn't* ANDY. *A small Jewish Woman dressed modestly in a fifties hat and coat stands in the doorway. The room darkens.*)

110   ROY: Who the fuck are you? The new nurse?

(*The figure in the doorway says nothing. She stares at* ROY. *A pause.* ROY *looks at her carefully, gets up, crosses to her. He crosses back to the chair, sits heavily.*)

ROY: Aw, fuck. Ethel.
ETHEL ROSENBERG: (*Her manner is friendly, her voice is ice-cold.*)
You don't look good, Roy.
ROY: Well, Ethel. I don't feel good.
115   ETHEL ROSENBERG: But you lost a lot of weight. That suits
you. You were heavy back then. Zaftig, mit hips.

ROY: I haven't been that heavy since 1960. We were all heavier back then, before the body thing started. Now I look
like a skeleton. They stare.
ETHEL ROSENBERG: The shit's really hit the fan, huh, Roy?   120

(*Little pause.* ROY *nods.*)

ETHEL ROSENBERG: Well the fun's just started.
ROY: What is this, Ethel, Halloween? You trying to scare me?

(ETHEL *says nothing.*)

ROY: Well you're wasting your time! I'm scarier than you any
day of the week! So beat it, Ethel! BOOO! BETTER
DEAD THAN RED! Somebody trying to shake me up?   125
HAH HAH! From the throne of God in heaven to the
belly of hell, you can all fuck yourselves and then go jump
in the lake because I'M NOT AFRAID OF YOU OR
DEATH OR HELL OR ANYTHING!
ETHEL ROSENBERG: Be seeing you soon, Roy. Julius sends his   130
regards.
ROY: Yeah, well send this to Julius!

(*He flips the bird in her direction, stands and moves towards her. Half-way across the room he slumps to the floor, breathing labori- ously, in pain.*)

ETHEL ROSENBERG: You're a very sick man, Roy.
ROY: Oh God . . . ANDY!
ETHEL ROSENBERG: Hmmm. He doesn't hear you, I guess.   135
We should call the ambulance.

(*She goes to the phone.*)

Hah! Buttons! Such things they got now.
What do I dial, Roy?

(*Pause.* ROY *looks at her, then:*)

ROY: 911.
ETHEL ROSENBERG: (*Dials the phone.*) It sings!   140
(*Imitating dial tones.*) La la la . . .
Huh.
Yes, you should please send an ambulance to the home
of Mister Roy Cohn, the famous lawyer.
What's the address, Roy?   145
ROY: (*A beat, then.*) 244 East 87th.
ETHEL ROSENBERG: 244 East 87th Street. No apartment
number, he's got the whole building.
My name? (*A beat.*) Ethel Greenglass Rosenberg.
(*Small smile.*) Me? No I'm not related to Mr. Cohn. An   150
old friend.

(*She hangs up.*)

They said a minute.
ROY: I have all the time in the world.
ETHEL ROSENBERG: You're immortal.
ROY: I'm immortal. Ethel. (*He forces himself to stand.*)   155
I have *forced* my way into history. I ain't never gonna die.
ETHEL ROSENBERG: (*A little laugh, then.*) History is about to
crack wide open. Millennium approaches.

SCENE VI

Late that night. PRIOR's *bedroom.* PRIOR 1 *watching* PRIOR *in bed, who is staring back at him, terrified. Tonight* PRIOR 1 *is dressed in weird alchemical robes and hat over his historical clothing and he carries a long palm-leaf bundle.*

PRIOR 1: Tonight's the night! Aren't you excited? Tonight she arrives! Right through the roof! Ha-adam, Ha-gadol . . .

PRIOR 2: (*Appearing, similarly attired.*) Lumen! Phosphor! Fluor! Candle! An unending billowing of scarlet and . . .

5 PRIOR: Look. Garlic. A mirror. Holy water. A crucifix. FUCK OFF! Get the fuck out of my room! GO!

PRIOR 1: (*To* PRIOR 2.) Hard as a hickory knob, I'll bet.

PRIOR 2: We all tumesce when they approach. We wax full, like moons.

10 PRIOR 1: Dance.

PRIOR: Dance?

PRIOR 1: Stand up, dammit, give us your hands, dance!

PRIOR 2: Listen . . .

(*A lone oboe begins to play a little dance tune.*)

PRIOR 2: Delightful sound. Care to dance?

15 PRIOR: Please leave me alone, please just let me sleep . . .

PRIOR 2: Ah, he wants someone familiar. A partner who knows his steps. (*To* PRIOR.) Close your eyes. Imagine . . .

PRIOR: I don't . . .

PRIOR 2: Hush. Close your eyes.

(PRIOR *does.*)

20 PRIOR 2: Now open them.

(PRIOR *does.* LOUIS *appears. He looks gorgeous. The music builds gradually into a full-blooded, romantic dance tune.*)

PRIOR: Lou.

LOUIS: Dance with me.

PRIOR: I can't, my leg, it hurts at night . . .
     Are you . . . a ghost, Lou?

25 LOUIS: No. Just spectral. Lost to myself. Sitting all day on cold park benches. Wishing I could be with you. Dance with me, babe . . .

(PRIOR *stands up. The leg stops hurting. They begin to dance. The music is beautiful.*)

PRIOR 1: (*To* PRIOR 2.) Hah. Now I see why he's got no children. He's a sodomite.

30 PRIOR 2: Oh be quiet, you medieval gnome, and let them dance.

PRIOR 1: I'm not interfering, I've done my bit. Hooray, hooray, the messenger's come, now I'm blowing off. I don't like it here.

(PRIOR 1 *vanishes.*)

35 PRIOR 2: The twentieth century. Oh dear, the world has gotten so terribly, terribly old.

(PRIOR 2 *vanishes.* LOUIS *and* PRIOR *waltz happily. Lights fade back to normal.* LOUIS *vanishes.*)

(PRIOR *dances alone.*)

(*Then suddenly, the sound of wings fills the room.*)

SCENE VII

Split scene: PRIOR *alone in his apartment;* LOUIS *alone in the park.*

Again, a sound of beating wings.

PRIOR: Oh don't come in here don't come in . . . LOUIS!! No. My name is Prior Walter, I am . . . the scion of an ancient line, I am . . . abandoned I . . . no, my name is . . . is . . . Prior and I live . . . here and now, and . . . in the dark, in the dark, the Recording Angel opens its hundred eyes and snaps the spine of the Book of Life and . . . hush! Hush! I'm talking nonsense, I . . .
     No more mad scene, hush, hush . . .

(LOUIS *in the park on a bench.* JOE *approaches, stands at a distance. They stare at each other, then* LOUIS *turns away.*)

LOUIS: Do you know the story of Lazarus?

JOE: Lazarus?

LOUIS: Lazarus. I can't remember what happens, exactly.

JOE: I don't. . . . Well, he was dead, Lazarus, and Jesus breathed life into him. He brought him back from death.

LOUIS: Come here often?

JOE: No. Yes. Yes.

LOUIS: Back from the dead. You believe that really happened?

JOE: I don't know anymore what I believe.

LOUIS: This is quite a coincidence. Us meeting.

JOE: I followed you.
     From work. I . . . followed you here.

(*Pause.*)

LOUIS: You followed me.
     You probably saw me that day in the washroom and thought: there's a sweet guy, sensitive, cries for friends in trouble.

JOE: Yes.

LOUIS: You thought maybe I'll cry for you.

JOE: Yes.

LOUIS: Well I fooled you. Crocodile tears. Nothing . . . (*He touches his heart, shrugs.*)

(JOE *reaches tentatively to touch* LOUIS's *face.*)

LOUIS: (*Pulling back.*) What are you doing? Don't do that.

JOE: (*Withdrawing his hand.*) Sorry. I'm sorry.

LOUIS: I'm . . . just not . . . I think, if you touch me, your hand might fall off or something. Worse things have happened to people who have touched me.

JOE: Please.
     Oh, boy . . .
     Can I . . .
     I . . . want . . . to touch you. Can I please just touch you . . . um, here?

(*He puts his hand on one side of* LOUIS's *face. He holds it there.*)

I'm going to hell for doing this.

LOUIS: Big deal. You think it could be any worse than New
York City?
  (*He puts his hand on* JOE'*s hand. He takes* JOE'*s hand away
  from his face, holds it for a moment, then.*) Come on.
45 JOE: Where?
LOUIS: Home. With me.
JOE: This makes no sense. I mean I don't know you.
LOUIS: Likewise.
JOE: And what you do know about me you don't like.
50 LOUIS: The Republican stuff?
JOE: Yeah, well for starters.
LOUIS: I don't not like that. I hate that.
JOE: So why on earth should we . . .

(LOUIS *goes to* JOE *and kisses him.*)

LOUIS: Strange bedfellows. I don't know. I never made it with
55   one of the damned before.
    I would really rather not have to spend tonight alone.
JOE: I'm a pretty terrible person, Louis.
LOUIS: Lou.
JOE: No, I really really am. I don't think I deserve being loved.
60 LOUIS: There? See? We already have a lot in common.

(LOUIS *stands, begins to walk away. He turns, looks back at* JOE. JOE
follows. They exit.)

(PRIOR *listens. At first no sound, then once again, the sound of beating wings, frighteningly near.*)

PRIOR: That sound, that sound, it. . . . What is that, like birds
or something, like a *really* big bird, I'm frightened, I . . . no,
no fear, find the anger, find the . . . anger, my blood is
65   clean, my brain is fine, I can handle pressure, I am a gay
man and I am used to pressure, to trouble, I am tough and
strong and. . . . Oh. Oh my goodness. I . . . (*He is washed*

over by an intense sexual feeling.) Ooohhhh. . . . I'm hot, I'm
. . . so . . . aw Jeez what is going on here I . . . must have a
fever I . . .

(*The bedside lamp flickers wildly as the bed begins to roll forward
and back. There is a deep bass creaking and groaning from the bedroom ceiling, like the timbers of a ship under immense stress, and
from above a fine rain of plaster dust.*)

PRIOR: OH!   70
  PLEASE, OH PLEASE! Something's coming in here, I'm
  scared, I don't like this at all, something's approaching and
  I. . . . OH!

(*There is a great blaze of triumphal music, heralding. The light turns
an extraordinary harsh, cold, pale blue, then a rich, brilliant warm
golden color, then a hot, bilious green, and then finally a spectacular
royal purple. Then silence.*)

PRIOR: (*An awestruck whisper.*) God almighty . . .
  Very Steven Spielberg.   75

(*A sound, like a plummeting meteor, tears down from very, very far
above the earth, hurtling at an incredible velocity towards the bedroom; the light seems to be sucked out of the room as the projectile
approaches; as the room reaches darkness, we hear a terrifying
CRASH as something immense strikes earth; the whole building
shudders and a part of the bedroom ceiling, lots of plaster and lathe
and wiring, crashes to the floor. And then in a shower of unearthly
white light, spreading great opalescent gray-silver wings, the* ANGEL
descends into the room and floats above the bed.)

ANGEL: Greetings, Prophet;
  The Great Work begins:
  The Messenger has arrived.

(*Blackout.*)

CRITICAL CONTEXTS

ARTHUR MILLER
from "Tragedy and the Common Man" (1949)

Arthur Miller wrote this essay for the New York Times *shortly after the opening of* Death of a Salesman. *In the essay, Miller develops a reading of the tragic hero that both contests and modifies Aristotle's description of the form and style of tragic drama. He also identifies his own presiding interests in the dynamics of tragic character. How important is it to Miller to be able to retain Aristotle's categories? Why? How do the different social, political, and cultural circumstances of Greek tragedy force Miller to redefine Aristotle's understanding of the function, purpose, and meaning of tragedy, particularly his understanding of tragic "character"?*

In this age few tragedies are written. It has often been held that the lack is due to a paucity of heroes among us, or else that modern man has had the blood drawn out of his organs of belief by the skepticism of science, and the heroic attack on life cannot feed on an attitude of reserve and circumspection. For one reason or another, we are often held to be below tragedy—or tragedy above us. The inevitable conclusion is, of course, that the tragic mode is archaic, fit only for the very highly placed, the kings or the kingly, and where this admission is not made in so many words it is most often implied.

I believe that the common man is as apt a subject for tragedy in its highest sense as kings were. On the face of it this ought to be obvious in the light of modern psychiatry, which bases its analysis upon classic formulations, such as the Oedipus and Orestes complexes, for instances, which were enacted by royal beings, but which apply to everyone in similar emotional situations.

More simply, when the question of tragedy in art is not at issue, we never hesitate to attribute to the well-placed and the exalted the very same mental processes as the lowly. And finally, if the exaltation of tragic action were truly a property of the high-bred character alone, it is inconceivable that the mass of mankind should cherish tragedy above all other forms, let alone be capable of understanding it.

As a general rule, to which there may be exceptions unknown to me, I think the tragic feeling is evoked in us when we are in the presence of a character who is ready to lay down his life, if need be, to secure one thing—his sense of personal dignity. From Orestes to Hamlet, Medea to Macbeth, the underlying struggle is that of the individual attempting to gain his "rightful" position in his society.

Sometimes he is one who has been displaced from it, sometimes one who seeks to attain it for the first time, but the fateful wound from which the inevitable events spiral is the wound of indignity, and its dominant force is indignation. Tragedy, then, is the consequence of a man's total compulsion to evaluate himself justly.

In the sense of having been initiated by the hero himself, the tale always reveals what has been called his "tragic flaw," a failing that is not peculiar to grand or elevated characters. Nor is it necessarily a weakness. The flaw, or crack in the character, is really nothing—and need be nothing—but his inherent unwillingness to remain passive in the face of what he conceives to be a challenge to his dignity, his image of his rightful status. Only the passive, only those who accept their lot without active retaliation, are "flawless." Most of us are in that category.

But there are among us today, as there always have been, those who act against the scheme of things that degrades them, and in the process of action everything we have accepted out of fear or insensitivity or ignorance is shaken before us and examined, and from this total onslaught by an individual against the seemingly stable cosmos surrounding us—from this total examination of the "unchangeable" environment—comes the terror and the fear that is classically associated with tragedy.

More important, from this total questioning of what has previously been unquestioned, we learn. And such a process is not beyond the common man. In revolutions around the world, these past thirty years, he has demonstrated again and again this inner dynamic of all tragedy.

Insistence upon the rank of the tragic hero, or the so-called nobility of his character, is really but a clinging to the outward forms of tragedy. If rank or nobility of character was indispensable, then it would follow that the problems of those with rank were the particular problems of tragedy. But surely the right of one monarch to capture the domain from another no longer raises our passions, nor are our concepts of justice what they were to the mind of an Elizabethan king.

The quality in such plays that does shake us, however, derives from the underlying fear of being displaced, the disaster inherent in being torn away from our chosen image of what and who we are in this world. Among us today this fear is as strong, and perhaps stronger, than it ever was. In fact, it is the common man who knows this fear best.

Now, if it is true that tragedy is the consequence of a man's total compulsion to evaluate himself justly, his destruction in the attempt posits a wrong or an evil in his environment. And this is precisely the morality of tragedy and its lesson. The discovery of the moral law, which is what the enlightenment of tragedy consists of, is not the discovery of some abstract or metaphysical quantity.

The tragic right is a condition of life, a condition in which the human personality is able to flower and realize itself. The wrong is the condition which suppresses man, perverts the flowing out of his love and creative instinct. Tragedy enlightens—and it must, in that it points the heroic finger at the enemy of man's freedom. The thrust for freedom is the quality in tragedy which exalts. The revolutionary questioning of the stable environment is what terrifies. In no way is the common man debarred from such thoughts or such actions.

Seen in this light, our lack of tragedy may be partially accounted for by the turn which modern literature has taken toward the purely psychiatric view of life, or the purely sociological. If all our miseries, our indignities, are born and bred within our minds, then all action, let alone the heroic action, is obviously impossible.

And if society alone is responsible for the cramping of our lives, then the protagonist must needs be so pure and faultless as to force us to deny his validity as a character. From neither of these views can tragedy derive, simply because neither represents a balanced concept of life. Above all else, tragedy requires the finest appreciation by the writer of cause and effect.

No tragedy can therefore come about when its author fears to question absolutely everything, when he regards any institution, habit or custom as being either everlasting, immutable or inevitable. In the tragic view the need of man to wholly realize himself is the only fixed star, and whatever it is that hedges his nature and lowers it is ripe for attack and examination. Which is not to say that tragedy must preach revolution.

The Greeks could probe the very heavenly origin of their ways and return to confirm the rightness of laws. And Job could face God in anger, demanding his right and end in submission. But for a moment everything is in suspension, nothing is accepted, and in this stretching and tearing apart of the cosmos, in the very action of so doing, the character gains "size," the tragic stature which is spuriously attached to the royal or the highborn in our minds. The commonest of men may take on that stature to the extent of his willingness to throw all he has into the contest, the battle to secure his rightful place in his world.

There is a misconception of tragedy with which I have been struck in review after review, and in many conversations with writers and readers alike. It is the idea that tragedy is of necessity allied to pessimism. Even the dictionary says nothing more about the word than that it means a story with a sad or unhappy ending. This impression is so firmly fixed that I almost hesitate to claim that in truth tragedy implies more optimism in its author than does comedy, and that its final result ought to be the reinforcement of the onlooker's brightest opinions of the human animal.

For, if it is true to say that in essence the tragic hero is intent upon claiming his whole due as a personality, and if this struggle must be total and without reservation, then it automatically demonstrates the indestructible will of man to achieve his humanity.

The possibility of victory must be there in tragedy. Where pathos rules, where pathos is finally derived, a character has fought a battle he could not possibly have won. The pathetic is achieved when the protagonist is, by virtue of his witlessness, his insensitivity or the very air he gives off, incapable of grappling with a much superior force.

Pathos truly is the mode for the pessimist. But tragedy requires a nicer balance between what is possible and what is impossible. And it is curious, although edifying, that the plays we revere, century after century, are the tragedies. In them, and in them alone, lies the belief—optimistic, if you will, in the perfectibility of man.

It is time, I think, that we who are without kings, took up this bright thread of our history and followed it to the only place it can possibly lead in our time—the heart and spirit of the average man.

AMIRI BARAKA / LEROI JONES
from "The Revolutionary Theatre" (1966)

In "The Revolutionary Theatre," Amiri Baraka describes the challenges posed by an emerging African-American theater. How does Baraka's understanding of the necessity of "revolution"—what does Baraka mean by "revolution"—sustain his sense of what theater can and should do?

The Revolutionary Theatre should force change; it should be change. (All their faces turned into the lights and you work on them black nigger magic, and cleanse them at having seen the ugliness. And if the beautiful see themselves, they will love themselves.) We are preaching virtue again, but by that to mean NOW, toward what seems the most constructive use of the world.

The Revolutionary Theatre must EXPOSE! Show up the insides of these humans, look into black skulls. White men will cower before this theatre because it hates them. Because they themselves have been trained to hate. The Revolutionary Theatre must hate them for hating. For presuming with their technology to deny the supremacy of the Spirit. They will all die because of this.

The Revolutionary Theatre must teach them their deaths. It must crack their faces open to the mad cries of the poor. It must teach them about silence and the truths lodged there. It must kill any God anyone names except Common Sense. The Revolutionary Theatre should flush the fags and murderers out of Lincoln's face.

It should stagger through our universe correcting, insulting, preaching, spitting craziness—but a craziness taught to us in our most rational moments. People must be taught to trust true scientists (knowers, diggers, oddballs) and that the holiness of life is the constant possibility of widening the consciousness. And they must be incited to strike back against any agency that attempts to prevent this widening.

The Revolutionary Theatre must Accuse and Attack anything that can be accused and attacked. It must Accuse and Attack because it is a theatre of Victims. It looks at the sky with the victims' eyes, and moves the victims to look at the strength in their minds and their bodies.

Clay in *Dutchman,* Ray in *The Toilet,* Walker in *The Slave,* are all victims. In the Western sense they could be heroes. But the Revolutionary Theatre, even if it is Western, must be anti-Western. It must show horrible coming attractions of The Crumbling of the West. Even as Artaud designed *The Conquest of Mexico,* so we must design *The Conquest of White Eye,* and show the missionaries and wiggly liberals dying under blasts of concrete. For sound effects, wild screams of joy, from all the peoples of the world.

The Revolutionary Theatre must take dreams and give them a reality. It must isolate the ritual and historical cycles of reality. But it must be food for all those who need food, and daring propaganda for the beauty of the Human Mind. It is a political theatre, a weapon to help in the slaughter of these dimwitted fatbellied white guys who somehow believe that the rest of the world is here for them to slobber on.

This should be a theatre of World Spirit. Where the spirit can be shown to be the most competent force in the world. Force. Spirit. Feeling. The language will be anybody's, but tightened by the poet's backbone. And even the language must show what the facts are in this consciousness epic, what's happening. We will talk about the world, and the preciseness with which we are able to summon the world will be our art. Art is method. And art, "like any ashtray or senator," remains in the world. Wittgenstein said ethics and aesthetics are one. I believe this. So the Broadway theatre is a theatre of reaction whose ethics, like its aesthetics, reflect the spiritual values of this unholy society, which sends young crackers all over the world blowing off colored people's heads. (In some of these flippy Southern towns they even shoot up the immigrants' Favorite Son, be it Michael Schwerner or JFKennedy.)

The Revolutionary Theatre is shaped by the world, and moves to reshape the world, using as its force the natural force and perpetual vibrations of the mind in the world. We are history and desire, what we are, and what any experience can make us.

It is a social theatre, but all theatre is social theatre. But we will change the drawing rooms into places where real things can be said about a real world, or into smoky rooms where the destruction of Washington can be plotted. The Revolutionary Theatre must function like an incendiary pencil planted in Curtis Lemay's cap. So that when the final curtain goes down brains are splattered over the seats and the floor, and bleeding nuns must wire SOS's to Belgians with gold teeth.

Our theatre will show victims so that their brothers in the audience will be better able to understand that they are the brothers of victims, and that they themselves are victims if they are blood brothers. And what we show must cause the blood to rush, so that pre-revolutionary temperaments will be bathed in this blood, and it will cause their deepest souls to move, and they will find themselves tensed and clenched, even ready to die, at what the soul has been taught. We will scream and cry, murder, run through the streets in agony, if it means some soul will be moved, moved to actual life understanding of what the world is, and what it ought to be. We are preaching virtue and feeling, and a natural sense of the self in the world. All men live in the world, and the world ought to be a place for them to live.

What is called the imagination (from image, magi, magic, magician, etc.) is a practical vector from the soul. It stores all data, and can be called on to solve all our "problems." The imagination is the projection of ourselves past our sense of ourselves as "things." Imagination (Image) is all possibility, because from the image, the initial circumscribed energy, any use (idea) is possible. And so begins that image's use in the world. Possibility is what moves us.

The popular white man's theatre like the popular white man's novel shows tired white lives, and the problems of eating white sugar, or else it herds bigcaboosed blondes onto huge stages in rhinestones and makes believe they are dancing or singing. WHITE BUSINESSMEN OF THE WORLD, DO YOU WANT TO SEE PEOPLE REALLY DANCING AND SINGING??? ALL OF YOU GO UP TO HARLEM AND GET YOURSELF KILLED. THERE WILL BE DANCING AND SINGING, THEN, FOR REAL!! (In *The Slave,* Walker Vessels, the black revolutionary, wears an armband, which is the insignia of the attacking army—a big red-lipped minstrel, grinning like crazy.)

The liberal white man's objection to the theatre of the revolution (if he is "hip" enough) will be on aesthetic grounds. Most white Western artists do not need to be "political," since usually, whether they know it or not, they are in complete sympathy with the most repressive social forces in the world today. There are more junior birdmen fascists running around the West today disguised as Artists than there are disguised as fascists. (But then, that word, *Fascist,* and with it, *Fascism,* has been made obsolete by the words *America,* and *Americanism.*) The American Artist usually turns out to be just a super-Bourgeois, because, finally, all he has to show for his sojourn through the world is "better taste" than the Bourgeois—many times not even that.

Americans will hate the Revolutionary Theatre because it will be out to destroy them and whatever they believe is real. American cops will try to close the theatres where such nakedness of the human spirit is paraded. American producers will say the revolutionary plays are filth, usually because they will treat human life as if it were actually happening. American directors will say that the white guys in the plays are too abstract and cowardly ("don't get me wrong . . . I mean aesthetically . . .") and they will be right.

The force we want is of twenty million spooks storming America with furious cries and unstoppable weapons. We want actual explosions and actual brutality: AN EPIC IS CRUMBLING and we must give it the space and hugeness of its actual demise. The Revolutionary Theatre, which is now peopled with victims, will soon begin to be peopled with new kinds of heroes—not the weak Hamlets debating whether or not they are ready to die for what's on their minds, but men and women (and minds) digging out from under a thousand years of "high art" and weak-faced dalliance. We must make an art that will function so as to call down the actual wrath of world spirit. We are witch doctors and assassins, but we will open a place for the true scientists to expand our consciousness. This is a theatre of assault. The play that will split the heavens for us will be called THE DESTRUCTION OF AMERICA. The heroes will be Crazy Horse, Denmark Vesey, Patrice Lumumba, and not history, not memory, not sad sentimental groping for a warmth in our despair; these will be new men, new heroes, and their enemies most of you who are reading this.

The family confronts Ginni in Manjula Padmanabhan's *Harvest*.

Historic social, political, and technological changes have reshaped the world since 1950, with a consequential impact on the theater. The aftermath of World War II has seen the remapping of the planet: the independence of India, Pakistan, and many Asian and African nations from colonial rule; the founding of Israel and the displacement of the Palestinians; and wars in Korea, Indochina, the Middle East, Africa, the Persian Gulf, Afghanistan, and Iraq. Those decades also witnessed bitter civil strife and the glimmering of peace in Northern Ireland, Argentina, Chile, the United States, Europe, and elsewhere; the Cuban missile crisis, the death of Francisco Franco in Spain, and the dismantling of the Berlin Wall; independence movements in the former Soviet Union and throughout Eastern Europe; the collapse of Yugoslavia and protracted war in Bosnia; the civil rights movement in the United States, the waning of apartheid in South Africa, the failure of peace in the Middle East.

With the rise of global communications, a global economy, and global political and military interests, such social and political revolutions immediately become the world's business. They reshape the world we live in even as we watch the changes unfold on our television screens. Fortunately, television has not really transformed the world's diverse cultures into a single "global village," but local cultures all feel the impact of events around the world. Think of the global effects of environmental disasters such as the Chernobyl nuclear power plant meltdown in 1986 and the deforestation of the rain forests of the Amazon; of medical advances such as vaccination; of epidemics like AIDS; of the international effects of social movements like nuclear disarmament, human rights, Amnesty International, feminism, and the peace movement, or, more horrifyingly, of anti-Semitism, racism, homophobia, and "ethnic cleansing."

Drama requires the collaboration of playwrights, actors, and audiences; the public structure of a theater site or building; and the social and political incentives and protections that make theatergoing attractive—it is an art deeply woven into the social fabric of a given culture and its history. Although we can still speak of the "London theater" or of "American drama," these terms have become in our era a critical convenience for reducing the dynamic variety of contemporary theater to the fictional boundaries of a single "national" culture. Although the theater still requires the support, work, and energy of its local community, today's dramatic repertoire is a global one. American playwright Sam Shepard first produced several of his plays in London. British playwright Edward Bond is more widely produced in Germany than in the United Kingdom. Many Eastern European and Latin American playwrights have been forced by censorship and political persecution to smuggle their plays to Europe or the United States to be staged. South African playwright Athol Fugard has premiered several plays in the United States. Nigerian Wole Soyinka is regularly produced throughout the world. These playwrights are deeply implicated in the working of their native cultures, but their plays have rapidly become part of the world repertoire.

Unit VII presents a different perspective on drama and theater than other units in *The Wadsworth Anthology of Drama*. Earlier units have been organized around a distinctive moment in the history of a relatively discrete culture: Athens in the fifth century BCE, Japan in the early shogunate; late medieval England and Renaissance London; late seventeenth-century London, Paris, and Madrid; and twentieth-century Europe and the United States. In many respects, this book is organized around undergraduate college teaching in the

United States today, which emphasizes the historical development of Western theater practices and dramatic literatures. This unit takes a broadly "postcolonial" perspective on contemporary drama, establishing some continuities with Western traditions while bringing other traditions of world theater and drama into view.

POSTCOLONIAL PERSPECTIVES

In the past several decades all areas of the humanities and cultural studies have come to challenge a narrowly Eurocentric vision of the contemporary world. These challenges have arisen from a wide range of causes: worldwide national independence movements, such as those in India in 1947, on the African continent throughout the 1950s and 1960s, and in Eastern Europe and the Baltic states in the 1990s; international involvement in South Africa's struggle with apartheid; global media and economic interconnections, that make business activity in Asia have an immediate impact on Wall Street; the fall of the Berlin wall in 1989, the breakup of the Soviet Union, and of the new relations between Eastern and Western Europe, and between the republics of formerly Soviet Central Asia; the return of Islam as a political, social, and military force in the West; oil crises and the war in the Persian Gulf; the challenges to "national" identity reflected in Québec's ongoing separatist movement in Canada; the various anxieties about language and immigration in the United States; racial tensions in Britain, France, Germany, and elsewhere in Europe; the ongoing political and social crisis in Northern Ireland; the emergence of Japan, South Korea, and China as economic powers; the struggles of many Latin American countries—often against both local military dictatorships and the international finance they receive—to achieve the promise of their nineteenth-century wars of liberation. In many places, these changes have not only had to overcome the military and political power of European governments—the Latin American revolutions against Spain; African and Indian independence movements—but have forced crucial challenges to the model of European culture itself, dramatizing the often oppressive entailments of the culture of "enlightenment" that was imposed on much of the world in the "civilizing" process of colonization.

In 1900, the sun never set on Britain's colonies around the world, and the legacy of three centuries of European expansion are still felt throughout the world: England, France, Spain, Portugal, the Netherlands, Italy, and Belgium all had extensive colonial holdings in Africa, Asia, and the New World. In many cases, of course, colonization was undertaken largely as a means of extracting wealth, in the form of slaves, precious metals, and/or raw materials, that could be sent back to enrich the capital: this was the model of Spanish colonization in the New World, in which Spain prevented trading between colonial cities in Mexico, Peru, Argentina, and elsewhere to have all trade proceed directly to Madrid. Even though very different patterns of colonization were practiced throughout the world, colonization always brought with it European institutions, such as Catholic and Protestant churches, legal practices and courts, schools and universities, and other aspects of European culture as well—sports and games, fashion and foods, and literature, drama, and theater. In many places, the colonial language was rapidly imposed as the language of government, education, and the law. Much as England banned Gaelic in Ireland in the eighteenth century (Gaelic is now taught in school in the Republic of Ireland, but not in state-supported schools in Northern Ireland), so in the twentieth century, postcolonial politics are often centered in the politics of language. In Latin America, for example, there has been a significant movement to reestablish various native languages—Quechua in Peru, Nahua in Mexico—as part of literary and public discourse; in Mexico, for example, many pre-Columbian architectural sites have guide materials in at least one native language, as well as in Spanish. Writers like Aimé Césaire, in French-speaking Martinique, or Wole Soyinka, growing up in preindependence Nigeria, were schooled on European writers such as Molière and Shakespeare and have used this education as part of their critical representation of the cultural politics of colonial and postcolonial rule: Césaire in his adaptation of Shakespeare's *The Tempest* to a Caribbean setting; Soyinka in the dialogue between English and Yoruba culture that informs many of his plays, including *Death and the King's Horseman.*

Language is never neutral; as Stephen Dedalus notices when talking to an English clergyman in James Joyce's *A Portrait of the Artist as a Young Man,* language encodes an entire system of social and political values—the words "Christ," "ale," and "master" mean something different to the English than they do to the Irish, much as terms like "white," "free," "citizen," or "nation" are obvious flashpoints, places where words reveal the political work that language performs. Like language itself, the values exported to the colonies often have traced within them a powerfully oppressive dynamic. For in regarding itself as bearing "civilization" into the wilderness—as though North and South America, Africa, and parts of Asia were not only uninhabited, but the highly developed cultures the Europeans found there were negligible—European culture often regards the colonized as "other" and inferior. The indigenous cultures of Africa, Latin America, and Asia were usually defined in antithesis to the values that justified the brutalities of occupation and exploitation: in opposition to the values of civilization, of a rich literary language, of an important and dynamic culture, indigenous cultures were seen as noncivil, their languages nonliterary, their cultures noncultivated, their (nonwhite) peoples nonpeople. Given this history, the cultural sphere—the sphere of theater and drama, of music and the visual arts, of literature, of film—has also been an important area of revolution as well. As the Kenyan novelist and playwright Ngũgĩ wa Thiong'o has argued, the practices of culture are in many ways more forceful than the more visible structures of the law or politics in maintaining a sense of "colonized" identity. He suggests that "decolonizing the mind" means decolonizing the tools that the mind thinks with, language, visual imagery, patterns of narrative and storytelling, everything used to make sense of the world:

> The oppressed and the exploited of the earth maintain their defiance: liberty from theft. But the biggest weapon wielded and actually daily unleashed by imperialism against that collective defiance is the cultural bomb. The effect of a cultural bomb is to annihilate a people's belief in their names, in their languages, in their environment, in their heritage of struggle, in their unity, in their capacities and ultimately in themselves. It makes them see their past as one wasteland of nonachievement and it makes them want to distance themselves from that wasteland. It makes them want to identify with that which is farthest removed from themselves; for instance, with other peoples' languages rather than their own.[1]

In their introduction to British postcolonial literatures, *The Empire Writes Back,* Bill Ashcroft, Gareth Griffiths, and Helen Tiffin "use the term 'post-colonial' . . . to cover all the culture affected by the imperial process from the moment of colonization to the present day." Although several of the playwrights and theaters presented here—Wole Soyinka from Nigeria, Maishe Maponya and Athol Fugard from South Africa, Aimé Césaire from the French island of Martinique—are readily understood within the context of national liberation movements, others point to a different, though analogous, understanding of the global politics of culture today. The Northern Irish playwright Brian Friel writes in a place where the politics of "nation"—Northern Ireland is physically part of Ireland, but politically a province of the United Kingdom—are still unresolved. Beyond that, in the twentieth century the dynamics of a kind of imperialism are not restricted to politics: a former colony—the United States—has emerged as a prodigiously powerful influence on many areas of economic and cultural life around the world, in ways that are frequently experienced as a kind of colonialism. While France, for instance, continues to struggle with the legacy of its colonization of North Africa, it also is engaged in a protracted trade controversy with the

---

[1] Ngũgĩ wa Thiong'o, *Decolonising the Mind: The Politics of Language in African Literature* (Portsmouth: Heinemann, 1986), 3.

United States, protecting the French film industry—and, by extension, "French" culture—by sharply limiting the distribution of American films. This sense that American culture, American values, American money, and American military power have become so pervasive as to threaten the political, economic, and cultural autonomy even of powerful countries—like France or Canada—informs a broader resistance to "imported" or Western or American culture. This resistance to a form of cultural imperialism animates some aspects of contemporary Asian theater, especially in plays like Manjula Padmanabhan's *Harvest;* it is also a theme in contemporary Canadian arts, in Mexico, and elsewhere. Many indigenous peoples—the aboriginal peoples of Australia, the native peoples of North and South America—were not really "colonized"; instead they were both decimated and isolated on reservations, and often stand in a quite different relationship to cultural formation in the state. Finally, it is important to understand the enormous political, economic, and cultural change sweeping the former "Second World" after the fall of the Berlin Wall in 1989—the revival of democratic republics in the eastern bloc countries, the separation of several republics from the Soviet Union, and the challenges that these changes have posed to Russian political stability—as part of a different kind of "postcolonial" lanscape, one in which the coerced protections of a fading state socialism are offset by the engulfing threat of a disorienting, often rapacious market capitalism.

POSTCOLONIAL DRAMA IN PERFORMANCE AND HISTORY

The remainder of this introduction briefly traces some connections between the dramatic, theatrical, and cultural history informing the work of playwrights presented later in the unit. This discussion—like the collection of plays assembled here—is by no means "representative": Japan's role in Asia, and the theater traditions that have developed there are very different from the energetic performance traditions of Indonesia or Malaysia, and from both the traditional and contemporary theater of India; although their histories are quite different, the energetic theatrical life of South Africa and Nigeria in the past four decades hardly spans the range of African dramatic and nondramatic performance, especially the performance traditions of North African countries like Algeria or Egypt; Argentina's orientation toward northern Europe, and the relatively sparse population of indigenous peoples in Argentina during the conquest period make its theater quite different from the flourishing theaters of Mexico and Brazil. In each of these places, however, drama and theater have come to be one of the ways in which public discourse is conducted, an esthetic engagement with the changing status of the "nation" and its peoples.

Argentina

Argentina's historical and cultural development is hardly "representative" of the diverse histories of Latin American countries. Unlike Peru or Mexico, for example, Argentina was never a source of gold or silver, and throughout the seventeenth century the vast region that comprises much of present day Argentina, Paraguay, and Uruguay was a backwater of the viceroyalty of Peru. Puerto Nuestra Señora Santa María del Buen Aire was first established by Pedro de Mendoza in 1535. But although his expedition of 1,600 men was three times the size of the contingent that accompanied Hernan Cortés in conquering Mexico, the expedition arrived late in the summer, with little time to plant crops and harvest them for winter, and in a swampy region that was not well suited to agriculture in any case. The Spaniards established bad relations with the indigenous population, who soon began to lay siege to the settlement. The settlers finally—after slaughtering their cattle—resorted to cannibalism to survive the winter. Although the original settlement of Buenos Aires held on until 1541, it was abandoned as the settlers moved north to the thriving city of Asunción.

When Buenos Aires was reestablished in 1580, the central city of Córdoba was the dominant city of the viceroyalty, but by the seventeenth century the port city of Buenos Aires—whose people still refer to themselves today as "porteños"—emerged as the center of power in the region. The economy of Argentina depended on agriculture, and planta-tions were run by *encomienda,* the forced servitude of the native populations, licensed by the church. Throughout the eighteenth century, Buenos Aires was the center of military devel-opment, as well as of the burgeoning cattle ranching of the *pampas* stretching to the west and south of the city. Until 1776, the region was part of the viceroyalty of Peru and ruled from Lima; when Spain reformed the trade, administrative, and legal structure of its South American colonies in 1776, Buenos Aires became the capital of the viceroyalty of the Río de la Plata. Argentina's independence was part of the continental struggle for liberation of the first decades of the nineteenth century, precipitated by Napoleon's intervention in Spain in 1808. Although the Congress declared the independence of the United Provinces of the Río de la Plata on July 9, 1816, various civil and revolutionary wars would traverse the ter-ritory for the next thirty years. Argentina lost much of its viceregal territory in the wars of independence—parts of Peru in 1814, of Bolivia in 1825, of Uruguay in 1828. Beyond that, the revolution established two patterns that would afflict Argentina for a century. First, the *caudillos*—rural ranchers and landholders, with their own private armies—wanted the new nation organized as a loose federations of provinces, not as a centralized government ema-nating from Buenos Aires; much of the political conflict of nineteenth-century Argentina can be understood as a struggle between the federalist and central-government forces. Sec-ond, the wars drew a generation of British traders—some of whom fought with distinction in the revolution—to Argentina; they capitalized on the rich resources and weak economy of the new country, establishing lucrative trade relations with the United States, the United Kingdom, and Europe.

In some respects, Argentina's economic growth in the early twentieth century parallels that of the United States: several waves of European immigration in the 1880s and 1890s provided the labor power to transform Argentina into a manufacturing and agricultural power (in the early decades of the twentieth century, it was a cliché to be "as rich as an Ar-gentine"). At the same time, however, Argentina's economy was drained by outside invest-ment: by the Bank of England in the nineteenth century, and by American and European concerns in the twentieth. This situation was exploited by the charismatic Colonel Juan Perón, who was first elected president in 1946 on the promise of better wages and social programs for workers; Perón succeeded both in reducing foreign debt and in restoring the control of major industries—railroads and communications—to Argentine corporations. But Perón's economy also produced considerable inflation, and social unrest led to a series of military *juntas,* which typically used the excuse of Communist insurgency, the familiar bogeyman of the post-Castro era in the Americas, to justify the suspension of civil law.

In 1976, General Jorge Rafael Videla led a *junta* that inaugurated seven years of state ter-rorism, the "Dirty War" (1976-1983) in which brutal torture was routinely practiced, and thousands of Argentine citizens (*los desaparecidos*) were made to disappear by federal, state, and local government officials. This regime and its successors frequently collaborated with Euro-pean and U.S. governments—on the eve of the disastrous Falklands War, General Leopoldo Galtieri attempted to gain U.S. government investment by offering military support to the United States in its military conflicts in Central America—and received both government and private investment. The Falklands conflict proved disastrous for the *junta,* and by Janu-ary 1983 General Ramón J. Camps, the Buenos Aires chief of police in the Videla govern-ment admitted that the mass graves that had been discovered were those of *desaparecidos* (the "disappeared"), and that none were alive. Dissension in the military, a more activist prosecu-tion of military crimes by the courts, and a widening sense that the *junta* could be ousted—typified around the world by Las Madres de la Plaza de Mayo—led to the election of Raúl Alfonsín in 1983, to the promise of trials, and then to the election of Carlos Menem.

Argentina has a long and distinguished theatrical tradition; plays were performed at the Jesuit missions in Córdoba in the early 1600s, and the first theater was built in Buenos Aires in 1757; the Teatro de la Ranchería was built in 1783. Throughout the seventeenth and eighteenth centuries, most of the plays performed in Argentina—in theaters in Santiago del Estero, Catamarca, Santa Fe, Corrientes, as well as Córdoba and Buenos Aires—were either Spanish *loas* or adaptations of French and Spanish dramas. By the nineteenth century, however, Argentine theater began to develop a more local flavor: in the romanticized dramas of *gaucho* (the famous Argentine cowboy) life typified by the anonymous *El amor de la estanciera* (1814); in plays of Argentine history, such as the independence play *25 de Mayo* and the play about the Peruvian native uprising *Tupac Amaru* (1817), both written by Luis Ambrosia Morante (1775–1837); and in a variety of short, sometimes satirical plays—called *SAINETES*—on political figures, and on the typical "characters" of Argentine life. This "local color" movement—*costumbrismo*—led to several popular genres, notably the *sainete gauchesco* and the *sainete criollo.*

The magnificent Teatro Colón opera house was built in 1857, at the early edge of Buenos Aires's development as a major metropolitan area; by 1900, Buenos Aires was known as the Paris of the New World for its fashionable elegance, and supported a wide range of theaters; 1900–1910 is regarded in Buenos Aires as the "golden decade" of its theaters, and many of Argentina's best-known playwrights—such as Florencio Sánchez (1875–1910), author of *La gringa* (1904) and *Barranca abajo* ("Down the Gully," 1905)—date from this era. As in Europe and the United States, an independent theater movement—El Teatro del Pueblo (1933) and La Máscara (1939)—arose, emphasizing (on the eve of Perón's mobilization of *los descamisados,* the shirtless workers) a more political, realistic, and Marxist orientation toward the staging of social life. Given the European orientation of Buenos Aires, it's not surprising that the various modes of European theatrical experimentation of the 1950s and after—Artaud's "theater of cruelty," theater of the absurd, Brechtian epic theater—have made their impact on Argentine drama, notably in the celebrated plays of Osvaldo Dragún (1929–1999); in the turbulence of the Perón and succeeding eras, the theater has often been a place of protest, and frequently subject to implicit or explicit censorship. This is especially true of the "dirty war" period. When the Teatro Abierto was founded in 1981, its building mysteriously burned to the ground within its first week of operation. Nonetheless, although many writers and intellectuals left Argentina, many remained, and their work often traces the connections between state terrorism and the diffuse nature of cultural and economic imperialism. Though written just before the "dirty war," Griselda Gambaro's play, *Information for Foreigners,* makes a direct assault on the authoritarian state; at the same time, by treating its audience as foreign tourists, the play implicates that larger world whose social and economic support helped to maintain the terror in Argentina.

Australia   Some have argued that the American independence—British convicts were transported to the American colonies before the Revolution—played a direct role in the British settlement of Australia as a penal colony in the eighteenth century. For although Portuguese, Dutch, Spanish, and British ships had all explored the Australian coastline, European settlement of Australia dates from 1788: the First Fleet—carrying 530 male prisoners, 160 female prisoners, and 250 freemen—sailed from England on May 13, 1787, and arrived in Botany Bay in January of 1788. The settlement at Sydney was soon followed by penal colonies at Newcastle in 1804, Moreton Bay in 1824, and other colonies: by 1830, 58,000 convicts (nearly 50,000 were men) had been transported to Australia. Most were relatively petty urban criminals, and the life they found in Australia could be very hard: conditions in many of the prisons were nightmarish, and prison life was for many nearly enslavement. Yet many convicts served their time outside prison—as something like indentured servants—and many remained to settle permanently. In the early nineteenth century Australia's economy was driven by sheep ranching and mining, and by the 1860s four relatively autonomous states had been formed, which moved toward federalization in the 1880s.

Western theater was brought to Australia in much the way Timberlake Wertenbaker dramatizes it in her play *Our Country's Good:* as a performance of George Farquhar's comedy *The Recruiting Officer* in 1789, in honor of the king's birthday, one year after the establishment of the British penal colony at Sydney in 1788. Beyond the slice of theater staged in Wertenbaker's play, though, the penal colonies were in many ways responsible for stimulating the importation of theater to Australia in the eighteenth century. Robert Sideway— one of the convicts in the Farquhar production—went on to open a theater in Sydney in 1796, which was opened to convicts and freemen until he was forced to close it in 1798; theaters were also operated in the penal colonies on Norfolk Island, in the Sydney Gaol, and in the colony on the Emu Plains.

By the mid-nineteenth century, the major cities of Australia—Melbourne and Sydney—had large theaters on the model of the major London houses, theaters seating upwards of two thousand patrons offering a repertoire of classical and contemporary European plays. Given the large population of recently released convicts, censorship was widespread in Australia, though many convicts—like Robert Sideway—made their way into the theater: David Burn's play, *The Bushrangers* (1828) was based on the life of a Tasmanian convict; and Edward Geoghegan, a convict, wrote or adapted ten plays for the Sydney Royal Victoria Theater. The major theaters received international tours—by Janet Achurch in the English production of Ibsen's *A Doll House* in 1889, and by Sarah Bernhardt in 1891—and developed in many ways along the lines of commercial theaters in England or the United States. Indeed, until the 1950s, the theater scene in Australia was similar to that of Canada or the United States: large commercial theaters devoted principally to popular drama and entertainment; a small smattering of amateur or independent theaters exploring various "new" dramatic and theatrical styles.

In 1954, in commemoration of the visit of Elizabeth II to Australia, the Governors of the Commonwealth Bank established the Australian Elizabethan Theatre Trust, with the purpose of establishing a national theater. It was a propitious moment; in 1956, Ray Lawler's (b. 1921) vivid working-class play about cane cutters who take an annual visit to the city, *The Summer of the Seventeenth Doll,* opened and soon became celebrated throughout Australia and the world. In an important act of nation building, the Theatre Trust used its subsidy for a number of purposes, not only to establish a National Theatre Company (1956), an Australian Ballet (1962), and an Australian Opera (1969), but to establish and support professional theater in each of the state capital cities: companies in Melbourne and Sydney in 1960, in Adelaide in 1965, in Brisbane in 1969, in Hobart, Tasmania, 1973.

As a result, even despite a conservative sense of Australian propriety that led to the censorship of playwrights like Patrick White (1912-1990) in the 1960s, Australia today has an energetic theater scene, both in subsidized and self-sustaining companies. In 1973 the Australian National Playwrights' Conference provided a means to support emerging writers, and a range of experimental companies—The Australian Performance Group, Nimrod—stimulated a new burst of playwriting, in plays like David Williamson's (b. 1942) *The Removalists* (1971), or the plays of Louis Nowra (b. 1950), Alma De Groen (b. 1941), or Michael Gow (b. 1955).

The Black Theatre Group was also organized in the 1970s, as part of an urgent desire to sustain traditional and new performance by Australia's Aborigine peoples. The various Aborigine tribes—estimated at about 500 tribes or smaller groups, numbering about 300,000 in 1788—mainly populated the northern and eastern areas of Australia. When the British began to establish colonies, they were put under the protection of the Colonial Office in London, but to little avail: the Aborigines did not integrate well into the British colonies (as a docile labor force, for example), and most were either killed outright, died from disease, or were driven into small "mission" areas. By the 1920s and 1930s, the overwhelming majority of Aboriginal peoples were "half-caste," and many were herded into squalid settlements, such as the Moore River Settlement that provides the setting for Jack Davis's play *No Sugar.* During this period, Aborigine infants were often taken to be raised by white families, in the hope that the "Aborigine problem" would gradually disappear through intermarriage (until 1966, Australia had an unofficial "whites only" immigration policy; only "white" immigrants were allowed to settle permanently). A 1967 referendum established Aboriginal Australians as part of the national population, to be counted in the census and therefore given parliamentary representation; in 1976 the Aborigine Rights Act granted 139,000 acres in the Northern Territory to Aborigine claimants as freehold property; South Australia made a similar grant to the Pitjantjatjara people. The National Aborigine Conference was formed in 1977, elected from Aborigine and Torres Strait Islander peoples, and in the 1980s, the Aboriginal Playwright's Conference was established to further the aims of aboriginal playwrights, and to protect native traditions. Given the distinctive beliefs of the Aborigine peoples—"The Dreaming," a mythic creation time when world and its peoples were formed, and whose spirits persist in the material world—and the dance-storytelling-musical *corroboree,* it is perhaps not surprising that a number of companies devoted to developing and preserving these arts have arisen, such as the Aborigine and Islander Dance Theater Company of Sydney.

Canada   Theater in Canada, like the culture of Canada itself, has been largely defined by its two dominant European settler cultures—English and French. Until the American Revolution, much of the eastern third of North America was contested by English and French explorers and traders: Jacques Cartier sailed down the St. Lawrence River, past the sites of Québec and Montréal in the 1530s; Samuel de Champlain's extensive explorations in the first quarter of the seventeenth century helped to define important fur-trading routes. By the mid-seventeenth century, however, Louis XIV declared New France a royal province, and throughout the remainder of the seventeenth and eighteenth centuries, France and Britain vied for control of Canada. The British had several strongholds in the maritime provinces, and to the west, in present-day Ontario; the exodus of British loyalists from the American colonies during the revolution—many of whom went into French Canada—enabled Britain to gain control of Canada; the 1791 Constitutional Act recognizes British legal and civil institutions, and the increasing British dominance of the important fur trade as well. In 1841, the United Provinces of Canada, in an effort to "assimilate" French Canada more effectively, gave a plurality of seats in the parliament to the British provinces. Although Canada was united as a Dominion in 1867, and gained its autonomy in 1931, the tensions between British and French Canada remain very much alive today: the separatist Parti Québécois and its charismatic leader René Levesque came to prominence in the early 1970s, and in several recent plebiscites, the citizens of Québec have voted to remain in Canada by only a narrow margin.

Although there are records of garrison performances in English Canada—an English version of Molière's *The Misanthrope* in January of 1744, in Nova Scotia—the earliest European performances in Canada are in French Canada. At Port-Royal, in Arcadia, Marc Lescarbot's aquatic pageant *Le Théâtre de Neptune en la Nouvelle-France* was performed (in war canoes!) to honor visiting French dignitaries in November 1606, and until a production of Molière's *Tartuffe* aroused the ire of the Catholic bishop—who forbade public theater in Québec in 1694—many performances of neoclassical French playwrights, including Corneille, Racine, and Molière were given in Québec. By the early nineteenth century, however, the Amateur Canada Dramatic Society had formed in Montréal (1835), and the church came to see that modest and moral stage performance could promote Catholic values. In 1898 it sanctioned the first lay company of actors, *Les Soirées de Famille* ("Family Evenings"). By this time, however, two permanent French-speaking theaters had been built in Montréal: the Monument National (1894) and Le Théâtre des Nouveautés (1898), serving a thriving trade in both touring companies from France and in the work of French-Canadian playwrights, such as Louis-Honoré Fréchette (1839–1908), whose sensational patriotic drama *Félix Porré* opened in 1862.

Theatre in English Canada was stimulated in part by the American Revolution; many British loyalists fled the revolution to the eastern provinces of Canada. The 500–seat Grand Playhouse was built in Halifax in 1789, and by the early nineteenth century, Toronto and other cities had major theaters on the European model. Nonetheless, much of the theatrical activity in the nineteenth century was by touring companies. However, much as in Europe, several smaller amateur companies developed, both to stage the new drama, and to support Canadian playwrights. The most significant of these companies was founded in 1919 by Roy Mitchell, at the University of Toronto—the Hart House Theatre. The Hart House was responsible for importing a number of experimental European playwrights, as well as for supporting the production of Canadian playwrights, including Dora Smith Conover, and Marjorie Price; Herman Voaden's expressionistic plays of the 1930s were produced at the Play Workshop. Other art theaters were formed in other cities as well; Martha Allan returned from working at the Pasadena Playhouse to her native Montréal to found the Montréal Repertory theater in 1930; the Toronto Workers Theater was active in the 1930s as well; and the establishment of the Canadian Broadcasting Company in 1936 brought radio drama throughout the nation.

The postwar period was the first real period for the growth of Canadian drama and theater. In part spurred by the Vincent Massey Report on the Arts of 1951 and the development of the Canada Council in 1957, both English and French Canada witnessed a flowering of new theater in the 1960s and 1970s. Several institutions—notably the Dora Mavor Moore New Play Society of Toronto (1946)—worked to develop Canadian plays and playwrights, like John Coulter's epic of the Métis rebellion in western Canada, *Riel* (1950); the founding in 1960 of a National Theatre School in Montréal. Both the Stratford Festival (established in 1953) and the Shaw Festival (1962) became showcases for Canadian actors, and by the mid-1960s a range of important theaters often working with new Canadian material had been founded: the Jupiter Theatre (1951); Tarragon Theatre (1971) in Toronto; L'équipe (1943), the Rideau Vert (1948), the Théâtre du Nouveau Monde (1961), the Théâtre des Cuisines (1973) and the Théâtre Expérimental des Femmes (1979) in Montréal; the Manitoba Theatre Center (1958), the Vancouver Playhouse (1962), the Neptune Theatre in Halifax (1962).

Although Gratien Gélinas (1908–1999) is usually described as the instigator of postwar French-Canadian drama—his play *Tit-Coq* (1948) about a soldier returning to Québec after the war is a modern classic—the drama of contemporary Canada was given an important impetus by the 1967 Dominion Drama Festival. Within the year a series of important plays were produced throughout Canada as part of its Centennial celebrations—Gélinas's *Yesterday the Children Were Dancing* (in English Translation), George Ryga's (1932-1967) *The Ecstasy of Rita Joe* among them. In 1968 Michel Tremblay's (b. 1942) groundbreaking play of working-class life in Québec, *Les Belles Soeurs* was produced; the play is also notable for being written in *joual,* the characteristic dialect of the city. Many plays, such as Sharon Pollock's *Walsh* (1973) attempt to reinterpret Canadian history; this play dramatizes the relation-ship between Major James Walsh, who commanded the North West Mounted Police in the 1870s and Sitting Bull, chief of the Hunkpapa Sioux. Since throughout much of the history of Canada the French-speaking minority of Québec has been dominated by an English-speaking majority, it's not surprising that the agitation in support of Québécois independence is reflected in a variety of plays as well. Indeed, the past three decades have seen a range of plays interrogating the Québec situation—not only the well-known plays of Michel Tremblay, but plays like Jean Barbeau's *Le chemin de lacroix* (1970) about a bill permitting Anglophone Québec parents to send their children to English-language schools in violation of Québec's bilingual policy, or Jean-Claude Germain's *A Canadian Play/Une plaie canadienne* (1979) about the mythology of a unified Canada. More recently, Marianne Ackerman's *L'Affaire Tartuffe, or, The Garrison Officers Rehearse Molière* (1993) takes a production of *Tartuffe* at the moment of Québec's incorporation into English Canada in 1774 as a turning point in the imagining of a nation. Much as Canadian drama—in different ways in English and French plays, in English and French theaters—considers the dynamics of Canadian nationalism, so the more recent work of Native playwrights like Tomson Highway, Monique Mojica—author of *Princess Pocahontas and the Blue Spots* (1990)—and others engage the position and representation of Native Canadians today. In the 1990s, Canadian theater continued in a period of artistic richness characteristic of Canada's official policy of multiculturalism. Robert Lepage not only directed landmark productions of Shakespeare's *A Midsummer Night's Dream* (at Britain's Royal National Theatre, 1992) but developed a stunning series of multimedia meditations—*Needles and Opium* (1994), *Elsinore* (1995), and *The Far Side of the Moon* (2000)—at his Theater Ex Machina in Québec City. Guillermo Verdecchia's brilliant performance piece exploring *latinidad* in a wider North American context, *Fronteras Americanas* opened in 1993. Canadian drama continues to have an increasingly pronounced impact on world theater, and several plays—notably the plays of Judith Thompson, Ann-Marie MacDonald's *Good Night Desdemona, Good Morning Juliet* (1988), and several of George Walker's plays—*Zastrossi* (1981) and *Escape from Happiness* (1991)—have found mainstream audiences in the United States and in Europe.

China   The most populous country on the planet, China has a long and magnificently diverse theatrical tradition. The first records of theater in China date from the Shang Dynasty, roughly 1500 BCE, and the history of China is studded with important landmarks in the development of performance. The Han period (206 BCE–221 AD) witnessed China's first important artistic flowering, and the characteristically complex blending of spoken language, acting, music, mime, and acrobatics that distinguishes Chinese theater dates from this period as well. The first training school, "The Pear Garden," was established during the T'ang dynasty (618–904), and the earliest surviving plays date from the succeeding the Sung dynasty (960–1279), plays which only began to be rediscovered in the 1920s. Although the Mongol conquest of the later thirteenth century put China under foreign rule, in the Yuan dynasty (1279–1368), seven hundred titles survive from this period, including several plays that have had an impact on the Western theater, including Chi Chun-hsiang's *The Orphan of the House of Chao,* adapted in 1775 by Voltaire, and Li Hsing-tao's *The Story of the Chalk Circle,* which provides the foundation for Bertolt Brecht's *Caucasian Chalk Circle.* While these plays typically use music and theatrical elements, they are considerably shorter than the "southern drama" that developed in southern China after the ejection of the Mongols in the Ming dynasty (1368–1644). The "southern drama" typically has more than fifty acts; it was mastered by playwrights such as T'ang Hsien Tsu (1550–1616), whose *Peony Pavilian* (recently adapted by the American director Peter Sellars) is today perhaps the most familiar of these plays. It is only in the Ch'ing period (1644–1912) that the most familiar form of traditional theater—Beijing Opera—began to take shape. Beijing Opera is a dynamic theatrical genre, using a scenario that sets the acting, singing, acrobatic, and musical skills of the performers on a narrative framework. Although there have always been a number of regional versions of this form, in 1790 the best performers from throughout China were brought to Beijing to celebrate the eightieth birthday of the Emperor Chi'ien-lung, and Beijing Opera is conventionally dated from this event.

With the increasing opening of China to the West in the nineteenth century, and after the revolution that established the Republic of China in 1912, Western culture came to have a more direct influence on the arts in China. Usually termed "spoken drama," to distinguish it from the musical conventions of traditional Chinese theater, the first Western play—Alexandre Dumas's (fils) *La Dame aux camélias*—produced in China was staged by the Spring Willow Drama Society in 1907, and in the decades following, several important playwrights wrote and adapted plays in the Western style for Chinese audiences, under the rubric of the New Cultural Movement: Tian Han (1898-1968) at the Nan Guo Drama Society, Hong Shen (1894–1955) for the Theatre Association, Xia Lan (1900–1995) for the Shanghai Art and Drama Association. Perhaps the most influential playwright of the prewar period is

Ts'ao Yu (1902), whose plays *Thunderstorm* (1933) and *Sunrise* (1935) continue to be read and produced. "Spoken drama," mainly in the mode of Western realism, thrived in China, and was given additional impetus by the victory of the Communists and the founding of the People's Republic of China in 1949. The new government was at once concerned to preserve traditional Chinese theater and to promote theater that would more dynamically reflect contemporary life. The Traditional Theater Research Institute (now part of the China Arts Research Institute) was founded in 1950, and within a decade had revived hundreds of theater forms: by 1960, China had over 3,000 companies performing over 50,000 traditional plays. At the same time, companies worked to update the subject matter of traditional theater forms, using, for example, Beijing Opera to address more contemporary social issues, often in the "model plays" that trained the Beijing Opera (or related styles, such as Kun Opera or Chuan Opera) on historical subjects with a revolutionary perspective. The new government also established a National Theater Festival in 1956, which supported the work of postwar "spoken drama" playwrights, notably Lao She (1899–1966), whose play *Tea House* has become a modern Chinese classic, as well as Lao Yu (1910–1997), and the work of the Shanghai People's Art Theatre, which adapted Brecht's for Chinese audiences.

In 1966, the wife of China's leader Mao Zedong, Jiang Qing—helped by Kang Sheng and two others, becoming the notorious "Gang of Four"—instituted a decade-long Cultural Revolution. The purpose of the Cultural Revolution was at once to purge China of foreign influences, and also to institute a massive program of reeducation to the proletarian ideals of Maoist communism. The decade-long Cultural Revolution forced a generation of artists, professionals, and intellectuals—regarded by the Gang of Four as their principal political opposition—out of the major cities and into rural areas, where they would be reeducated into revolutionary culture through manual labor. Since the traditions of Chinese theater descended from aristocratic patronage, and the modern "spoken drama" theater was so clearly influenced by the West, it's perhaps not surprising that Chinese theater stagnated during the Cultural Revolution. Most theater companies disbanded during this period, and with the exception of plays specifically developed under Jiang's guidance, plays were heavily censored or prohibited altogether; only eight new "model" productions were developed, five in traditional theater forms. In 1976, however, the Gang of Four were removed from power; Deng Xiaoping inaugurated a period of new openness to the west, and allowed considerably greater latitude to artists and writers. Although previous regimes had insisted on Mao's "revolutionary realism" in the theater, in the 1980s, playwrights and performers experimented more widely: Gao Xingjian's *Absolute Signal,* a fluid hallucinatory drama, was performed briefly by the Beijing People's Art Theater in 1982, the same theater that invited Arthur Miller to direct a Chinese production of *Death of a Salesman* the following year. A Shakespeare Festival was staged in both Beijing and Shanghai in 1986, followed by Festivals of Experimental Theater in 1989 and 1993. The 1980s saw the rise of a number of important younger playwrights, including Gao Xingjian and Sha Ye Xing (b. 1939), whose satirical *Major Chen* (1980) was rivaled in controversy only by his *Confucius, Jesus Christ, and John Lennon* (1988); produced by the Shanghai People's Art Theater while he was Artistic Director. Zong Fu Xian (b. 1947) uses a rally in Tiananmen Square to indict the Gang of Four in *In the Depth of Silence* (1978).

Theater in China has a tradition of patronage, both by the aristocracy and by the state. With the rise of a market economy in the 1990s, subsidies for theaters have declined, sometimes to as little as thirty percent of operating expenses. Moreover, after the Tiananmen Square protests in 1989 theater has been subject to somewhat more censorship than in the immediately preceding decade.

Czech Republic

The contemporary Czech Republic stands at the crossroads of central Europe, and, like its political history, the history of its theater reflects the tension between native inspiration and the external influence of more powerful nations. Records of folk theater and of medieval passion plays in the Czech lands—Bohemia, Moravia, and Silesia—extend back to the thirteenth century, though religious drama was largely suspended during the Hussite religious wars of the fifteenth century. As in the rest of educated Europe, Czech schools and universities used the staging of Latin drama as a mode of instruction, particularly under the influence of the celebrated Czech teacher Comenius (Jan Komenský, 1572–1640), and playwrights such as Karel Kolčava (1656–1717) wrote important folk dramas; but it was the defeat of Czech aristocrats at the battle of Bíla Hora in 1620 by the Austrian Hapsburgs that was the most decisive factor: for the next 250 years, Czech culture would be dominated by Austria. The first purpose-built theater was constructed in Prague in 1737, exclusively for the use of foreign companies. Count Nostitz-Rieneck's Estates Theater was built in 1783, but its director, František Bulla (c.1754–1819), began to perform Czech plays there as early as 1785, an early sign of the romantic nationalism sweeping Europe and the Czech lands. By the early nineteenth century, several important dramatists were writing plays of "national awareness," including Václav Kliment Klicpera (1792–1859), Karel Hynek Thám (1763–1816) and his brother, the actor Václav Thám (1765–1816), who wrote for the Bouda ("Wooden Hut") Theater in the late 1780s, Jan Nepomuk Štěpánek (1783–1859), and most importantly, Josef Kajetán Tyl (1808–1856), who wrote both historical dramas, such as *Jan Hus* (1848), and plays of modern life ("Where Is My Home?", a song from his romantic comedy *The Fair* [1834], became the Czech national anthem in 1918). Throughout the nineteenth century, resident theater companies played both in Prague and in Brno, generating the desire for a truly native, vernacular theater.

As in Ireland and the Scandinavian countries, a desire for national independence centered on the formation of a national theater company. The first independent, Czech-speaking professional theater, the Provisional National Theater, was founded in 1862, extending the already intense discussion of the possibility of a national stage; the elegant National Theater building opened in 1881 but almost immediately burned to the ground. It was a sign of the desire for a national stage that funds were raised through subscription, and a second theater was built, opening in 1883. Although there was always concern about whether an institutional theater could be at the forefront of emerging literary movements, the National Theater saw the production of plays much in the tradition of European modernism: Ladislav Stroupežnický's (1850–1892) satiric comedies of contemporary rural life, Alois (1861–1925) and Vílém Mrstík's (1863–1912) social drama *Maryša* (1894), Gabriela Preissová's (1862–1946) *The Step Daughter,* as well as plays with expressionist elements, such as Alois Jirásek's (1851–1930) *The Lantern* (1905). The innovative director Karel Hugo Hilar (1885–1935) used expressionist techniques in the Theater of Royal Vinohrady in Prague in the 1910s, departing to lead the National Theater in 1921. Ironically, he traded places with the National Theater's master of psychological realism, the director Jaroslav Kvapil (1868–1950), who went to the Royal Vinohrady (this exchange was considerably more than a trade of artistic directors, as many of he actors traded houses as well). But modern Czech drama came to international attention with the plays of Karl Čapek (1880–1938). A well-known journalist and novelist, Čapek's first play, *The Brigand* (1920), was produced at the National Theater, and led to a string of successes. *R.U.R.* (1921)—the abbreviation is for "Rossum's Universal Robots"; the English word "robot" was coined from Čapek's play—was soon performed both in London and New York, as was *The Insect Play* (1922), which he wrote with his brother Josef (1887–1945), the famous Czech cartoonist. Čapek wrote a series of important plays, including a sequel to *R.U.R., Adam the Creator* (1927), and two plays protesting the rise of Fascism, *The White Scourge* (1937) and *The Mother* (1938). Čapek died in the year that Nazi Germany invaded Czechoslovakia, and his brother was arrested and died in the Belsen concentration camp in 1945.

With the German invasion and occupation of the Czech lands in 1938, theater in the "Protectorate of Bohemia and Moravia" was heavily censored, and the lively culture of socialist and experimental theater that had grown up in Prague and Brno in the 1920s and 1930s—

most notably Emil František Burian's (1904–1959) D-34 Theater, and the socialist Liberated Theater of Jinřich Honzl (1893–1953)—was extinguished. At the beginning of the occupation, the Nazis granted the Czechs the appearance of "cultural autonomy." The Nazis did give the Czechs a degree of cultural autonomy, so Czech theaters were able to produce plays in Czech, and some plays prohibited in Germany were produced in Czech theaters. As in the Third Reich, all plays by antifascists, Communists, pacifists, and Jewish authors were prohibited. Nonetheless, using the practice of "jinotaj"—a kind of code of theatrical communication in which subversive meanings clear to the Czech audience were "veiled" from the German authorities—some directors (including Burian, Honzl, and others) and famous performers (such as the actress Ružena Nasková [1884–1960]) risked execution. Very rapidly, however, the Czech theater was firmly policed, and many Czech artists were killed or transported to concentration camps, and with the beginning of the war most works by Allied authors were banned (by 1940 over 1300 writers had been censored in the occupied Protectorate). One of the most fascinating chapters in the history of the theater concerns the imprisonment of German and Czech Jewish artists and performers to the Terezín concentration camp outside Prague, where they performed music, classical drama, and original plays and cabaret. As the war wound to a close, and Germany's eventual defeat became clear, Hitler increased the executions at his concentration camps, and most of the inhabitants of Terezín were transported to Auschwitz and killed. On September 1, 1944, all Czech theaters were closed, and the theater workers were directed to work for the German war effort.

After the war, Czechoslovakia came under the sway of the Soviet Union, and the Communist Party took control of the government in 1948. Under the Communists, the press and artistic institutions were governed by a central office that dogmatically imposed the favored **SOCIAL REALISM** of the Soviet Union; by the mid-1950s, censorship was controlled by the Ministry of the Interior (as it had been under the Nazis), and enforced by its agency, the State Police. At the same time, the long tradition of Czech innovation in the theater managed to persist. Josef Svoboda (1920–2002) became the chief theater designer at the National Theater in 1948, leading to the preeminence of Prague as a center of theater design; his multimedia *Laterna Magica* project was first seen at the Brussels Exhibition of 1958, and now occupies its own modern theater building adjoining the National Theater. The ABC Satire Theater performed during the brief political "thaw" of the late 1950s (1955–1962), and Prague's most influential new theaters, the Theater Behind the Gate (1955–1972) and the Theater on the Balustrade (1958–1972) both date from this era as well. These theaters experimented both with plays by young Czech writers (Milan Kundera, b. 1929; Pavel Kohout, b. 1929, and Václav Havel, b. 1936) as well as importing the plays of Jarry, Ionesco, Beckett, and Brecht to the stage. With the Soviet invasion of Czechoslovakia in 1968, however, many artists fled the country, and many others were either forced into exile, underground, or imprisoned as the result of their resistance to the state. Newspapers were closed, and widespread purges of artistic and educational institutions were enforced. Václav Havel's involvement in the Charter 77 movement, for example, contributed to his imprisonment. Perhaps the most symbolic protest was that of the young philosophy student Jan Palach, who wrote a letter calling for the end of Soviet censorship; signing the note "Torch Number One," he burned himself to death in Prague's central Wenceslas Square on January 16, 1969. As was the case during the German occupation, dissident theater was pursued beyond the official stage, and many plays were copied and secretly circulated. One important form of theater available to artists in the 1970s and 1980s was "apartment theater," plays performed in the homes of actors and playwrights. Vlasta Chramostová (b. 1926) had an important apartment theater, sponsoring a famous production of *Play Macbeth* (a version of this performance is captured in Tom Stoppard's play *Cahoot's Macbeth*). With the fall of the Berlin Wall in 1989, and the Velvet Revolution that followed, the Czech Republic has witnessed an extraordinarily smooth political transition, and joined the European Union in 2004. Perhaps not surprisingly, Prague has again become an important theatrical capital, the site not only of the dynamic productions at the National Theater and Estates Theater, but of many smaller experimental companies as well. The Theater on the Balustrade is again the home of a modern repertory, and theater companies from around the world regularly come to the Czech Republic's major cities.

India The second-most populous nation on the planet, with seventeen official languages, India has an immensely rich cultural and theatrical history. The earliest literary writing—the epic poems *Ramayana* and *Mahabharata*—date from between the tenth and fifteenth centuries BCE, and provide the narrative sources for much of the diverse range of traditional Indian performance. The oldest dramatic traditions date to the Sanskrit plays first written and performed during the Gupta empire in northern India, beginning about 100 AD; the aesthetic animating this theater is systematically explored in Bharata's *Natyasastra* (150 AD) (on Sanskrit Theater and Drama, see Unit II). Although Sanskrit has an important dramatic tradition—including King Sudraka's *The Clay Cart* and Khalidasa's *Shakuntala* (fifth century), Sanskrit—like Latin in Europe—gradually split into a range of vernacular languages; the invasion and rise of the Muslims to power after the seventh century restricted theatrical performance, and Sanskrit theater was believed until quite recently to have ceased, being replaced throughout India with an astonishingly diverse range of folk performance. As in other Asian performance forms, "theater" is not restricted to the spoken enactment of scripted plays: instead, the great majority of Indian folk theater forms use a brilliant interplay of story-telling, singing, dance, and music; there are also important forms of puppet theater as well. In the northern states of India, for instance, there is a 400-year tradition of performing the *Ramlila* and *Raslila* plays: cycle-dramas concerning events in the lives of Krishna, and Vishnu Rama. These performances often take place over three or four weeks, and involve the audiences in various kinds of religious ritual; they also mark one of the features of many Indian theater forms, the discrimination of actors from singers. In the *Ramlila,* the singer narrates the action, while the actors perform. A more recently developed form, the **JATRA,** is a staple of performance in Bengal, in eastern India. *Jatra* performances—like most Indian folk theater—do not take place in a theater, but in the open air, with the audience surrounding the performers. Unlike *Ramlila,* though, *jatra* tend to address contemporary concerns rather than the lives of mythic heroes. Indeed, the central figure of the *jatra* is always called Vivek, or "conscience": Traditionally, there is music in the *jatra,* and the actors sing; the performers are all male, and there are now professional *jatra* companies. Perhaps the most familiar form of traditional Indian performance in the West is *kathakali,* a dance-drama form from the southern state of Kerala. Performed in Malayalam—the language of Kerala—*kathakali* nonetheless preserves important elements of Sanskrit drama. In *kathakali,* the actors learn an elaborate and refined set of stylized bodily movements and detailed hand-gestures, each of which is codified as part of the *Natyasastra* tradition; having learned these techniques over many decades, the actors (all of whom are male) do not rehearse: they simply perform one of the 500 plays in the *kathakali* repertoire. Although it would be difficult to say that any form—or any three forms—can represent the range of traditional theater in India—there are literally hundreds of distinct theater and dance forms in this vast nation's rich folk and ritual traditions—what these forms share is a popular tradition of performance in village squares, at temples, or other open spaces, a complex involvement of music, acting, and dance, and a vigorously disciplined performance training.

While folk theater remains the dominant experience for the majority of Indians today, it remains in a now-productive tension with "modern" Indian theater. India has had a long history of contact with Europe: the Persians invaded northwest India in the sixth century BCE; Alexander the Great invaded again in 326 AD; the Portuguese explorer Vasco da Gama landed in India in 1498. British involvement with India was handled by the East India Company throughout the seventeenth and eighteenth centuries, but in 1858 the British government took over the Company, and in 1877 Queen Victoria became the Empress of India, and India became the "jewel" in her colonial "crown." Even before India was incorporated into the Empire, there were strong nationalist movements, and the British recognized the need for an Indian administrative class: universities were established in 1857 in the principal colonial cities, Calcutta (now Kolkata), Bombay (now Mumbai), and Madras to produce a "native" population educated to British values. In line with Thomas Babington Macaulay's infamous "Minute" to the House of Lords on Indian education, education was sustained by the teaching of English history and literature, the plays of Shakespeare and of eighteenth-century dramatists in particular. The British also produced English-language plays, and built theaters to accommodate touring companies. In the late nineteenth century, several Indian playwrights began to write plays—often in native languages such as Hindi or Urdu—in imitation of European drama; Wajid Ali Shah wrote several musical dance dramas, notably *The Tale of Radha and Krishna* (1851) and *Tale of Love* (1853); the Urdu poet Agha Hasan Amanat's *The Court of Lord Indra* (1854) was widely produced and translated. Moreover, the mid-nineteenth century also saw the rise of a new form of theater for India, profit-making companies. This kind theater, usually called Parsi Theater because these theaters were operated by Parsi businessmen (though usually employing Hindu and Muslim actors and playwrights), became the principal venue for "modern drama" in India, as the Parsi theaters often built new theater buildings on the model of Victorian proscenium theaters—such as the Victoria Theater and the Alfred Theater in 1871—and financed stage productions. Some of these plays adapted Western drama, as Agha Hashra Kashmiri (1879-1931) did in *White Blood* (1906), his adaptation of Shakespeare's *King Lear;* in the main, though, the Parsi theater was known for large-cast musical dramas, such as K.P. Khadikar's *Self Respect and Insult* (1911), a Marathi play arguing against the practice of child marriage. While the Parsi theater was extremely popular, particularly in the major urban areas, it seems finally to have been extinguished by the rise of film: indeed, many of the first Indian movie theaters were adapted from Parsi theater buildings.

While the Parsi theater represents one side of the "modernization" of Indian theater—turning it into a profit-making enterprise—there were other theater currents animating Indian theater in the later nineteenth-century. Bharatendu Harishchandra (1850–1885), for example, wrote plays in Hindi on pressing social issues—*The Sorry State of Bharat* (1880), *The Truthful King* (1875)—which were produced in public spaces. In Bengal, several playwrights used drama for specifically nationalistic purposes. Dinbandhu Mitra's *Neel Darpan* (*Indigo Mirror*) (1860) protested the plight of indigo workers, and was produced by the fledgling National Theater Company of Calcutta. When this company split into a Hindu National Theater and a Bengali National Theater, it retained this oppositional edge. The Bengali National Theater revived *Neel Darpan,* not only summoning agricultural workers to rebel against the British, but also showing the rape of a peasant woman by her British landlord. Largely due to the celebrity of this production, the government instigated the Dramatic Performances Control Act of 1876, in which local police were obliged to censor all new drama being produced in their jurisdiction. Perhaps for this reason, India's most famous poet and playwright of the colonial period—Rabindranath Tagore (1861-1941)—worked away from the realism of other playwrights, attempting to revive the mythological orientation of Sanskrit literature, and indeed to adapt it to critical purposes; Tagore won the Nobel Prize for Literature in 1913. Of course, the nationalist movement was given critical impetus by the work of Gandhi (1869–1948) and Jawaharlal Nehru (1899–1864), and "modern theater" in the twentieth century was strategically advanced by the Indian People's Theater, which opened branches in every Indian state in 1943, in many places bringing women to the stage for the first time.

India gained its independence from Britain on August 15, 1947; partition was established dividing Pakistan as an Islamic nation to the north at the same time, and in 1971 East Pakistan separated from Pakistan as Bangladesh. In the 1950s the Indian government established a range of cultural institutions, including the Cultural Academy of Performing Arts and the National School of Drama in 1959. The School's second director, Ebrahim Alkazi (b. 1925)—who had trained at the Royal Academy of Dramatic Art in London—was responsible at once for developing training in modern Western dramatic and theatrical traditions as well as for training performers in traditional Indian forms; his staging of Kalidasa's *Abhijnana Shakuntalam* (a Sanskrit play dating from 6 AD) at the Congress of Orientalists in New Delhi in 1964 is said to have inaugurated a revival of interest in exploring and preserving classical forms. In the aftermath of independence, Indian culture struggled at once to define a specifically "Indian" identity, and to modernize along the lines of Western culture: this tension governs the theater as well. The "theater of roots" movement sought to explore and experiment with traditional theater forms, sometimes using traditional tribal performers as well. One of the leading playwrights of modern India, Girish Karnad (b. 1938), writes in the Kannada language; his *Hayavadana* (1971) uses music, mime, dancing and costume of traditional theater; his *Naga Mandala* is the first modern Indian play to be produced in the U.S. (Guthrie Theater, Minneapolis, 1993). Vijay Tendulkur (b. 1928) Several other playwrights and directors have worked in traditional forms, which have also been applied to Western dramas—as in the Annette Leday/Keli Theatre Company *Kathakali King Lear* (1989). While the "theater of roots" continues to work with traditional forms, street theater has become an increasingly popular form of theater and protest; one prominent playwright, Safdar Hashimi of Delhi produced an extensive series of street production in support of the rights of the urban poor: he was murdered in 1989 during a street performance of his play *Attack!*, beaten to death by the members of a rival political organization.

The major playwrights of modern India write in a range of languages—Hindi, Kannada, Marathi, Bengali—and for a variety of theatrical traditions. There is also an emerging dramatic literature in English. Writing in the colonial language has posed a problem for writers from Joyce to Ngũgĩ, and it is controversial as well in India. At the same time, English is one of the nation's official languages; it provides the *lingua franca* for citizens from different regions, who may not speak one another's language, and when plays from one region are translated for performance in another region, they are translated into English.

Ireland and Northern Ireland

English involvement in Ireland dates to the twelfth-century "conquest" of Ireland—Henry VIII assumed the title of "King of Ireland" in 1541—and the relationship between England and Ireland has been contested ever since. In the late sixteenth and early seventeenth century, Hugh O'Neill led a series of uprisings against English immigrants, who were establishing plantations in the northern areas of Ulster; later, during the English Civil War (1641–1642), the forces that Charles I raised in Ireland were eventually defeated, and Oliver Cromwell enacted a series of brutal massacres in Ireland in retribution, confiscating lands as well. When Charles II took the English throne in 1660, the Act of Settlement confirmed the landowning claims then in place in Ireland: Catholics who had been evicted from their property were unable to regain it. In 1688 the Catholic heir, James II, ascended the English throne; when Parliament invited William of Orange (who was married to Mary Stuart, a Protestant heir) to assume the throne, James fled to Ireland: his forces were defeated at the Battle of the Boyne in 1690 and he fled to France; his Irish supporters were defeated in 1691 at Aughrim.

William's victories inaugurated a prolonged period of Irish misery: the displacement of Catholics from land and property, restrictions of their rights to education, to bear arms, to pass property to their heirs, or to vote. Although some of these laws lost force in the later eighteenth century, they provided the backdrop for political unrest in the period, particularly Wolfe Tone's mobilization of the Dublin United Irishmen in support of a French-supplied invasion. Although the French did send naval forces, and rebellions in Leinster, Ulster, and elsewhere looked promising, Tone was captured in 1798 and committed suicide in prison. In 1809, the Act of Union brought Ireland into the United Kingdom, effectively ending aspirations to nationhood. Nonetheless, throughout the nineteenth century, several movements worked for independence: Daniel O'Connell fought to repeal the Union, and Michael Davitt won security for tenants following the crop failures of 1879. Yet famine and immigration cut the Irish population in half between 1840 and 1900, and the Union's free-trade legislation turned Ireland into an impoverished supplier of raw material and labor to English factories. In the later nineteenth century, nationalism was pursued on two fronts: by the desire for "home rule" led by Charles Stewart Parnell, and by a new sense of Irish cultural identity, fostered by the Gaelic League and other cultural institutions.

Although Dublin and Ulster had supported theaters, these theaters were driven by an English repertoire: the only Irish characters to play on the stage were comic, drunken, buffoons— "Stage Irishmen." It was this sense of cultural nationalism that gave rise to the first burst of Irish theater, the founding of the Irish Literary Theater—later the Abbey Theatre— in 1899 by the poet/playwright W. B. Yeats (1865–1939), and the playwrights Lady Augusta Gregory (1852–1932) and John Millington Synge (1871–1909). The ambition of this company was to "build up a Celtic and Irish school of dramatic literature," and in the next thirty years, the Abbey succeeded not only in producing a wide range of plays on nationalsubjects—peasant dramas about rural life like Synge's *The Playboy of the Western World* (1907); plays exhuming Irish mythology, like Yeats's cycle on Cuchulain; or realistic dramas ofworking-class urban life like Sean O'Casey's *The Plough and the Stars* (1926)—but establishing both an Irish style of performance, and the materials of a national theater as well. The Abbey remains a leading theater in the Republic of Ireland, and several leading playwrights have had major productions there: Tom Murphy, Ann Devlin, and Frank McGuinness among many others.

The aborted revolution of Easter 1916 was a precursor of sweeping political change by 1917, Eamonn De Valera was elected president of Sinn Féin and campaigned for an independent Ireland rather than merely achieving Home Rule as a province of Britain; in 1919, Ireland's war of independence was under way. In 1922, Sinn Féin succeeded in negotiating a treaty with the United Kingdom for independence, but the Free State was not to include the counties of Northern Ireland, which remained a British province. There have been various periods of tension between Northern Ireland and the Republic of Ireland and between Ireland and the United Kingdom; these tensions came to a head in the late 1960s. In Northern Ireland, sharp divisions between rich and poor, the politically powerful and the oppressed have often fallen across religious divisions as well, separating Protestant Anglo-Irish from Catholics. Throughout the 1960s, Catholic and Protestant groups rioted in the Northern cities of Belfast and Derry (then, Londonderry); British soldiers were summoned to protect Protestant marchers. In 1972, the "Bloody Sunday" riots resulted in thirteen deaths, and a newly mobilized Provisional Irish Republican Army (IRA) began a series of retaliatory campaigns; the British Embassy was burned in Dublin, and the British secretary of state suspended the Northern Irish parliament and instigated direct rule.

The history of Northern Ireland for the past thirty years is the history of this conflict: the hunger strikes by Catholic prisoners in the Maze prison who claimed the right to be treated as political prisoners rather than criminals; the increasing insurgency of Protestant paramilitary forces, inspired by the nationalist rhetoric of Ian Paisley; Gerry Adams and Sinn Féin's efforts to gain and remain in a position to be part of the bargaining for peace. The IRA cease-fire of 1994 was part of that bargain, and although violence has erupted since then, the current round of peace talks seems promising.

One of the most difficult aspects of the situation in Northern Ireland is the challenge to ideas of "national identity." Although Northern Ireland is physically part of Ireland, many of its citizens—even those who do not wish to be part of the United Kingdom—feel distinct from the Republic of Ireland; similarly, the long traditions of English rule have instilled a feeling of identification with England, one strengthened (for some) by the pro-Irish violence of the IRA. In many respects the theater of Northern Ireland has had to negotiate this vexed sense of nationalism. For example, the Field Day Theatre Company was founded in

1980 by the playwright Brian Friel, the poet Tom Paulin, the actor Stephen Rea, and the poet Seamus Heaney: the purpose of the company was to develop a new theater, a new dramatic literature of the North, one that attempted to identify the distinctiveness of Northern Ireland. In plays such as Friel's *Translations* or Thomas Kilroy's (b. 1934) *The Double Cross* (1986), or even in translations like Tom Paulin's version of *Antigone, The Riot Act,* Field Day attempted to bring a specifically Northern Irish culture into dialogue with a wider world. But the work of Field Day should be seen in the context of other playwrights, some of whom, such as Christina Reid (b. 1942), see the problems of contemporary urban life in cities like Belfast to be "political" in ways that extend well beyond the problems of national identification, into areas of gender and economic exploitation. While Frank McGuinness was born in Donegal (part of the Republic of Ireland), his brilliant play *Observe the Sons of Ulster Marching Toward the Somme* (1985) uses the situation of Irish soldiers during the First World War (before the independence of the Republic and the partitioning of the northern counties) to explore the complex personal politics of Unionism. Although Field Day—which toured its productions throughout Northern Ireland—has ceased producing plays, it has published a widely read anthology of Irish writing and has sponsored a series of essays on questions of national and postcolonial art and culture.

Japan   The introductory essay of Unit II traced the development of the classical forms of Japanese theater—Noh, Kabuki, and Doll Theater—through the period of the Tokugawa shogunate (1603–1868). In 1868, the last of the Tokugawa shoguns was defeated and replaced by the Meiji Emperor, who wanted to open political, social, and cultural relations with the West, while at the same time disentangling Japan from a series of restrictive and exploitative trade relations with Europe. Indeed, throughout the 1880s and 1890s, Japan developed an aggressive military presence throughout the northern Asian Pacific, and both fought with China over the control of Korea and skirmished with Russia over the control of several of its islands. By the 1930s, Japan was a major military presence in the region. Taking advantage of political disorganization in China, Japan invaded Manchuria, and by 1938 had occupied parts of Mongolia and Kiangsu. Before drawing the United States into the Pacific theater with the bombing of its naval base at Pearl Harbor in Hawai'i, Japan had gained control of a huge territory, including all of Southeast Asia, Burma, the Philippines, and parts of New Guinea. Although the Western allies were unprepared for a Pacific war—after Pearl Harbor, the Japanese Navy greatly outnumbered the U.S. Navy—and suffered great casualties, the tide of the war was turned by one of the decisive events of the twentieth century: dropping the first atomic bombs on Hiroshima and Nagasaki. It is fair to say that life in Japan—and in different ways, in the rest of the world—was forever changed in that instant.

The new Meiji cultural connections to the West put different kinds of pressure on the traditional forms of Japanese theater. The Noh theater had been the special province of the *samurai* classes, and in the newly competitive theater marketplace was rapidly threatened with extinction. Several Noh actors—notably Umewaka Minoru (1828–1909)—worked to establish the Noh as a special part of Japan's cultural inheritance, an elite entertainment funded by the state (something like the "state opera" in many Western countries today), and today there are five Noh and two kyogen schools operating in Japan. Kabuki and Bunraku (the only form of Doll Theater still active) were more readily assimilated by the more open Japanese culture of the late nineteenth and early twentieth centuries, in large part because they had always been popular entertainments. Although there has been considerable modernization of Kabuki in the past century—contemporary Kabuki is not usually the daylong affair of the eighteenth-century theater; and to some extent Kabuki's reputation for lasciviousness has been replaced by a more "classical" orientation—the Kabuki and Bunraku theaters did not need to look for a new audience after 1868, and in many respects are a continuous performance tradition.

The history of modern Japanese theater is the history of Japan's negotiation of Western modes of playwriting and performance. The *SHIMPA* theater of the turn of the century adapted Western plays—Shakespearean tragedies and popular melodramas alike—to Japanese settings; it was a significant also for introducing actresses to the stage. Of greater consequence was the **SHINGEKI** theater. *Shingeki* ("new theater") imported both European plays in the realistic mode—Ibsen, Chekhov, Gorky, for example—and stimulated a new "realistic" style of drama among Japanese playwrights of the 1920s, 1930s, and 1940s. As it had in Europe in the 1880s, and in the United States in the 1910s and 1920s, this new dramaturgy was associated with a little theater movement. The most influential theater—the Tsukiji Little Theater of Tokyo—produced only Western playwrights in its first two years of operation, under the influence of its director Osanai Kaoru (1881–1928), who admired the work of Stanislavski and the Moscow Art Theater. Thereafter, the Tsukiji and other theaters like it tended toward social realism, plays such as Kubo Sakae's (1900–1958) splendid Marxist-inspired drama, *The Land of Volcanic Ash,* which traces the social and economic upheaval of the 1930s in a rural Japanese village on the colonial island of Hokkaido, was first performed by the Shinyo Troupe at the Tsukiji Little Theater in 1938. Although *shingeki* performance was banned during World War II, it became the predominant movement of the immediate postwar period, and Kubo's play was not only among the first plays to be staged after the war, but the play—and especially its central character, the radical agricultural scientist Kubo Amamiya—provided a model for postwar playwrights as well.

After World War II, the rebuilding of Japan was heavily financed by the United States, which also exerted considerable censorship control as well. Yet while "modern" Japanese theater had developed largely through the importation of European dramatic models, after the war, many writers worked to revive more traditional Japanese literary, dramatic, and theatrical forms. In some cases—Mishima Yukio (1925–1970) is a good example—this revival was part of an intense and conservative nationalist movement, the sense that "true" Japan was embodied in the prewar values of an imperial culture; but in other cases, it was part of a broader resistance to being culturally absorbed by the United States. A more experimental approach to blending foreign and indigenous dramatic modes arose, for instance, as part of the energetic protest against the U.S.–Japan Mutual Security Treaty in 1960. Many Japanese refused to participate in a "nuclear umbrella" agreement with the United States after the bombings of Hiroshima and Nagasaki (nearly a million demonstrated in Tokyo alone in 1959–1960), and the demonstrations around the treaty catalyzed a new introspection into the shape and meaning of Japanese culture, with its unique, deeply scarred relation to the postnuclear era. Hotta Kiyomi's (b. 1922) *The Island* (1955) was the first play about the bombings, and in the wake of the 1960 protests, a range of new kinds of theater and drama emerged: the backlash against Western dominance of Japan in the postwar period often appeared as a rejection of *shingeki* and of the Marxist politics that sustained its socialist realist esthetics. Kobo Abe's (1924–1993) plays, for example, often resonate with the **THEATER OF THE ABSURD,** but develop—as in the play *Slave Hunting* (1955)—a critique of spiritual poverty of postwar Japan. As David Goodman argues in his book *Japanese Drama and Culture in the 1960s: The Return of the Gods* (Armonk, NY: East Gate, 1988), playwrights like Fukuda Yoshiyuki (b. 1931) and Satoh Makoto (b. 1943) responded to the social and spiritual crisis of the post-1960 period in two ways: departing from *shingeki* conventions, they tend to use at least one godlike or archetypal character, and develop plays concerned "with the interrelated questions of personal redemption (salvation of the individual) and social revolution (salvation of the world)."

This new style of playwriting demanded a new style of performance, and some of the most powerful innovations of the Japanese theater in the past twenty years have involved performance style. The director Suzuki Tadashi (b. 1939) has been very influential in this regard. Suzuki's production of Satoh's play *The Black Tent* seemed to call for a "new realism"; Suzuki formed an experimental company, Suzuki Company of Toga (SCOT), in which he developed some exercises from Noh training toward a kind of performance emphasizing the actor's physicality. Suzuki's work has become well known to American audiences through his collaborations with Anne Bogart and the Saratoga International Theater Institute's productions (see Unit VI). The spiritual scars of Hiroshima and Nagasaki are perhaps more literally visible in the emergence of *BUTOH* (the word means simply "dance") performance. In *butoh,* the dancers are naked, shaven, and dusted with a white powder; their performance style demands a ferocious discipline, for their movements are exceptionally slow. Devised originally by Ohno Kazuo (b. 1966) and Tatsumi Hijikata (1928–1986), *butoh* is famous for the sense of ghostly apparitions that its dancers become onstage, enacting what Tatsumi called "the gestures of the dead."

Martinique

Christopher Columbus stopped at the island of Martinique in 1502; it was an inhospitable island, dominated by the fierce Caribs. Although both Spain and England briefly established outposts on the island, it was settled in 1658 as a French colony, soon of some six thousand settlers. As happened throughout the Caribbean, the native population was exterminated by violence and disease. But the Compagnie de Sénégal, a French slave-trading company, made frequent stops at Martinique on its way to the larger island of Guadeloupe; the French imported slaves to the island, especially after the introduction of coffee in 1723. But a series of slave uprisings (1789, 1815, 1822), and an ongoing conflict with the English over the slave trade, led France to abolish slavery in Martinique in 1848; as a result, plantation owners frequently had to import workers from India and China, and the population of Martinique today is descended from these various groups. Martinique was made a crown colony in 1674; control of the island passed briefly to the English several times in the late eighteenth and early nineteenth century. Since the 1840s, however, Martinique has been governed by France: first as a colony, then as a *département* (1946), and since 1974 as a region.

All of the colonial powers brought theaters to the Caribbean—the first theater was built in Jamaica in 1682, and a production of John Gay's *The Beggar's Opera* was staged there in 1733. Since the 1950s, Aimé Césaire—Martinique's most famous poet, playwright, and essayist—has been critical to the public life of Martinique, and indeed to the theory of postcolonial development more widely. For Césaire has played an important part in the public life of Martinique, beginning a long term of service as a deputy to the French National Assembly in 1945, and then leading his Progressive party into power in 1957, and establishing several national institutions in support of the arts and theater. In part due to his efforts and those of his followers—training performers in traditional Caribbean forms of masking, drumming, and dancing, as well as inviting celebrated playwrights and directors such as Ariane Mnouchkine and Wole Soyinka to work in Martinique—Martinique now has a thriving theater culture.

Nigeria

With ninety million people, Nigeria is Africa's most populous country; of its twenty language groups, four—Yoruba, Ibo, Hausa, and Fulani—predominate, and the histories of the Yoruba, Ibo, and Hausa peoples are entwined in Nigeria's precolonial, colonial, and postcolonial history. In the precolonial period, Nigeria was home to several rich cultures. In the northern region adjacent to Lake Chad, ninth-century Arab writers described a flourishing culture, organized around a series of walled cities along Saharan trade routes between Egypt and western Africa. With the introduction of Islam from Mali in the fourteenth century, the Hausa and Fulani peoples became Muslim; in the nineteenth century, several emirs led a massive *jihad* or holy war against religious and civil authorities, and established a new center of power in Sokoto. Yoruba culture emanated from the southwestern region of Nigeria, centered around the city of Ife (eleventh through the fifteenth centuries); this Old Oyo culture—from which contemporary Yoruba culture descends—was a complex monarchial society, spread through several important cities; this is the kingdom that the Portuguese discovered when they arrived in the city of Benin in the fifteenth century. Ibo culture was less centrally organized, and stretched in a series of villages through the southeastern part of Nigeria.

European colonization of Nigeria began around the slave trade. The Portuguese slave trade of the seventeenth and eighteenth centuries was centered in Benin; the Portuguese transported slaves to their New World colonies, and deep strains of Yoruba can be found in many New World–African cultures, particularly in Brazil. The expansion of Islamic Fulani emirates in northern Nigeria in the nineteenth century intruded into the Old Oyo empire, driving the Yoruba south, instigating a series of wars, and—by displacing a large population—stimulating the slave trade.

The British Royal Niger Company established trade with various Ibo and Yoruba leaders in the 1840s, but only established an administrative headquarters in Lagos in 1886. Although initially making contact as traders, the British presence rapidly developed from trade and missionary work into a more conventional colonial profile: consolidating territory, developing a legal apparatus, deporting local leaders who resisted, including the northern emirs, who were conquered in 1903. Originally divided into northern and southern colonies, Britain formed the Colony and Protectorate of Nigeria under a governor-general in 1914. Nigeria gained independence in 1960, but the strains between various regions and ethnic groups have not been readily resolved; in 1967 General Odumegwu Ojukwu declared a secession of the eastern states (Biafra), and despite marching successfully on Benin City, and nearly taking Lagos, surrendered in 1970. Although an initial constitution placed a legislature in each region, Nigeria has been beset by a series of brutal military regimes— the first coup in 1966 established a pattern for the 1970s, 1980s, and 1990s. In 1999, the government of Nigeria was returned to civilian control, with free elections.

The area now known as Nigeria was the home of a variety of cultures prior to becoming a British colony, and many of the performance practices of these cultures are visible in contemporary Nigerian theater and drama. Best known is the festival of *EGUNGEN;* this festival, which has been performed at least since the fourteenth century, attempts to establish a communion between the living and the dead. In it, masked and costumed celebrants proceed to a sacred grove, where the accumulated troubles of the village are removed by a "carrier." The persistence of this ritual is acknowledged by Wole Soyinka's play *Death and the King's Horseman,* which in various direct and indirect ways engages with the *egungen* narrative. Yoruba ritual is also known for the dynamic character of its gods—Obatala, the god of creation; Ogun, the god of creativity; Sango, the god of lightning—and for the use of masquerade as a central feature of ritual. One of the most popular theatrical forms in Nigeria is the Yoruba Traveling Theater; first developed by Hubert Ogunde (1916–1990), these performances generally concern a contemporary social issue, such as the exploitation of workers in his 1945 *Strike and Hunger.* Rather than a formal "drama," though, this form of theater takes the shape of a series of short skits, involving both dialogue and song, framed by a musical opening and closing number. In part because his company frequently satirized the colonial government (and was censored), Ogunde's work became widely known and imitated, and gave rise to a large number of companies practicing this narrative/dramatic/musical genre. Recently, Yoruba Traveling Theater has become almost exclusively a film genre.

In part because of the English presence—an English-language theater first opened in Lagos in 1899—in education, drama and theater played a large part in colonial Nigeria. D.A. Oloyede's play *King Elejigbo and Princess Abeje* (1904)—the first play in English by a Nigerian author—was written for a church group, and both reading and playing in the plays of the European tradition—Shakespeare, Molière, Shaw, Chekhov—formed part of the education of the generation of Nigerian writers and intellectuals who came of age with the independence. Wole Soyinka's plays often stage a rich dialogue between colonial and indigenous culture, drawing on the ritual and religious beliefs of the Yoruba. An Ibo playwright, John Pepper Clark (b. 1936) has dramatized the tales of the *ozidi* sagas—long stories that required several years to prepare and were performed by an entire village—and since the 1980s has directed his own professional theater. Femi Osofisan (b. 1946) is well known for taking a more critical, and politically engaged view of the problems of contemporary Nigerian society.

Russia   Although the Russian theater dates mainly from the eighteenth century, its impact on modern theater and drama has been profound; many of the playwrights of the nineteenth- and twentieth-century Russian theater (see Unit V) have become classics of the stage, and the theatrical innovations of the Soviet Union period (1919–1991)—SOCIAL REALISM, Vsevolod Meyerhold's (1874–1940) BIOMECHANICS, among many others—and the playwriting of contemporary Russia are part of the world theatrical repertoire today.

Theater in Russia has a long history of conflict with the Russian Orthodox Church, which was more effective than the Roman Catholic Church in its opposition to the stage. Although there are records of itinerant theater in the late middle ages, the Church's ban on theatrical performance extended well into the modern era; the first Romanov tsars erected a "house of amusement" in 1613, but Tsar Alexis (1645–1676) banned the theater with the exception of the Latin school drama until late in his reign, when he began to orient the Russian court more toward the practices of the European courts, which typically included a court stage as one of the ornaments of power. Peter the Great (1689–1725) extended the Romanov importation of European culture; he founded a theater in Moscow, and commanded attendance there for a time. Peter desired to engage Russia more directly with Europe—particularly after the wars with Sweden—founding the city of St. Petersburg on the Baltic Sea and moving his capital there from Moscow in 1712. Catherine the Great (1729–1796) ordered the founding of a professional theater; at the same time, Russia's famous "serf theaters"—theaters supported by large provincial landholders—produced generations of fine actors, many of whom followed the example of Mikhail Shchepkin (1788–1863), who came to the city (his career was pursued mainly in Moscow) to become a stage professional. As the capital, St. Petersburg saw the founding of several of Russia's preeminent theaters, including the Bolshoi, used mainly for opera and ballet, and the Maly and Alexandrinsky theaters, used as dramatic theaters in the 1750s, and important theaters were founded in the late eighteenth and early nineteenth centuries in Moscow as well; of these, Moscow's Maly Theater (1750) has had perhaps the most distinguished lineage and is today one of the world's best-known theaters. Many of Russia's greatest writers wrote for the stage, including Alexander Pushkin (1799–1837), Alexander Ostrovsky (1823–1886), and Nikolai Gogol (1809–1852), whose play *The Government Inspector* (1836) became a classic of European comedy. In the 1890s, Konstantin Stanislavsky (1863–1938) and Vladimir Nemirovich Danchenko (1858–1943) formed a literary circle experimenting with the production of new drama, founding the Moscow Art Theater in 1898; Anton Chekhov's (1860–1904) first major play, *The Seagull,* which had failed miserably in St. Petersburg, was the MAT's premiere (on Chekhov and the MAT, see Unit V).

As it was elsewhere in Europe, the period leading up to World War I was a period of intense cultural experimentation, and the success of the MAT in the realism cherished by Stanislavsky did not displace other kinds of experiment: Yevgeny Vakhtangov (1883–1922), Vsevolod Meyerhold, Alexander Tairov (1855–1950), and Mikhail Chekhov (1891–1955) all brought new styles and working methods to the MAT. With the Russian Revolution (1917–1919) and the success of the Bolshevik Party, the newly formed Union of Soviet Socialist Republics began to devise a cultural policy to form the citizens of the new soviet state. The appointment of A. V. Lunacharsky (1875–1933) as the Commissioner of Education at once ensured the survival of the Moscow Art Theater and the development of a state artistic policy. SOCIAL REALISM was confirmed as the official aesthetic policy at the first Congress of Soviet Writers in 1934. In the early phase of Soviet socialism, there was enormous excitement about the ways theater might be moved from its elitist, court-and-bourgeois past to become an instrument of revolutionary education and social change. Theaters were established throughout the USSR and supported with state funds, many of which were formed around collective purposes, such as the Trade Union Theater or the Red Army Theater. Meyerhold's efforts to locate the actor-as-worker led to a series of important collaborations, particularly with Vladimir Mayakovsky (1894–1940), whose plays *Mystery Bouffe*

(1928), *The Bed Bug* (1929), and *The Bath House* (1930) are often taken to mark the high point of Soviet drama. At the same time, Meyerhold's experiments in CONSTRUCTIVISM—notably his 1922 staging of Crommelynck's *The Magnanimous Cuckold*—were increasingly seen as counter to the official Soviet aesthetics, and the Meyerhold Theater was closed in 1937. Meyerhold arrived at his home to find his wife, Zinaida Raikh, murdered, and was himself arrested, tortured, and executed by the Stalin regime.

The Soviet theater system was deeply centralized; over 800 companies were supported by the state, providing lifetime stipends to playwrights, directors, actors, designers, managers, and stagehands, and keeping ticket prices very low, well within the wages of the typical worker. While this kind of support enabled theaters to support large permanent companies, the determination of the repertoire and the inability to change personnel often led to stultification. With the death of Stalin (1879–1953), however, a number of reforms were instituted that led to the founding of several new theater companies, especially the Taganka Theater (founded in 1946, but reorganized in 1964). At the same time, the theater schools associated with the MAT continued to produce well-trained and imaginative actors and directors, many of whom worked—as Yuri Lyubimov (b. 1917), director of Taganka, has done—to extend the legacy of Meyerhold, as well as exploring the once-forbidden legacy of Brecht, Beckett, and other European dramatists. Many of the theaters founded in the Soviet period have continued to flourish under the new Russian Federation: the Mayakovsky Theater, which was founded in 1922 and renamed the Theater of the Revolution in 1943, is just one example. Indeed, with the collapse of the Soviet Union and the emergence of the Russian Federation in 1991, many of Russia's chief theaters have gained a much larger international audience, both through tourism to Russia and because the companies can themselves tour more readily. The Maly Theater of St. Petersburg, under the leadership of Lev Dodin (b. 1944), has toured to Europe and the United States to considerable acclaim, praised both for the brilliance of its direction and the power of its physical performance. Although Russia no longer includes many of the republics of the former Soviet Union, it is a huge and diverse country, and continues to support theaters from the eastern border of Europe to Siberia. Many playwrights who began their careers in the Soviet era continue to write today, notably Alexander Volodin, whose important plays of the 1950s and 1960s (*The Factory Girl,* 1955; *Do Not Part with Loved Ones,* 1969) were often criticized for avoiding Communist Party themes; Mikhail Shatrov's plays are characteristic of the "socialism with a human face" ideology of the late 1960s and early 1970s. However, as the plays of Vassily Sigarev suggest, the increasingly unstable social world of contemporary Russia has led to a variety of dramatic experiments, and perhaps to a new kind of desperately ironic, absurdist drama.

South Africa

Contemporary theater and drama in South Africa has been marked, as have all areas of South African life, by the imposition of racial *apartheid*—the legal separation and discrimination of various "racial" and ethnic groups—in 1948, laws which were only lifted with the election of Nelson Mandela as president in 1994. Apartheid can be seen as a politically conservative response to the social and racial situation that has developed in South Africa over the past four hundred years, in which the Portuguese, British, and Dutch vied with one another for control of the land, while at the same time being hugely outnumbered—South Africa today has about five million white inhabitants and thirty million black inhabitants—by an oppressed indigenous population.

In 1487, Bartholomeu Dias, a Portuguese explorer, reached Mossel Bay, opening a sea route from Europe to Asia. Over the course of the next three centuries, the port at the Cape of Good Hope gained enormous strategic and military value. In 1652, the Dutch East India Company established a station there to supply water, food, and supplies to trade ships. Dutch settlers—called "Afrikaners" (or "Boers")—expanded from the immediate Cape region, conquering the Khoisan tribes, and importing slaves from Indonesia, India, Ceylon, Madagascar, and Mozambique. Throughout the eighteenth century, however, important colonies of British settlers developed in the region as well: after a series of battles and broken treaties, Britain gained control of the Cape Colony in 1806. Yet by gaining control of the region, the British were faced with two opponents: the indigenous tribes, and the Afrikaners, who resisted the imposition of British rule. The nineteenth century then witnessed two kinds of struggle. The conflict between British and Afrikaner settlers intensified when the British emancipated the colonial slaves in 1834. The years 1835–40 saw the "Great Trek," the departure of Afrikaners and their "clients"—slaves—from the Cape Colony northward, where they settled the Transvaal and Orange Free State as independent republics in 1852 and 1854 (the Trek is part of the consciousness of Afrikaner culture, and is frequently reenacted). However, the discovery of diamonds in 1867 and of gold in 1886 led to renewed conflict, as Britain attempted to annex the Afrikaner republics. The "War Between the Whites"—the Boer War of 1899–1902—led to British control of all three republics, which were united in 1910 as the Union of South Africa. The Union gained its independence from Britain in 1931, and became the Republic of South Africa in 1961, when it left the British Commonwealth.

Competing with one another for land and resources, the British and Afrikaners also had large and powerful indigenous populations to contend with, and despite the British policy against slavery, both parties systematically subjugated the black populations of South Africa. The most important of these groups were the Zulu; their leader Shaka defeated other African tribes, organized the Zulu as a kingdom in the 1820s, and was killed in 1828. In a series of conflicts—the British war with the Xhosa in 1834–1840, the Afrikaner defeat of a Zulu force at the Battle of Blood River in 1838, and the final British defeat of the Zulu in 1879—the white population gained control of the land and its people.

In many respects, the political history of modern South Africa is the history of the white minority's efforts to subordinate and control this populace. The discovery of gold and diamonds led—after the Boer War—to an increasing demand for mine laborers; although 64,000 Chinese workers were imported in 1904–1907, most of these laborers were Africans, who were increasingly segregated from the white population. When the Union of South Africa was formed in 1910, only whites were enfranchised; in 1911, the Mine and Works Act, the first of a series of laws restricting African workers to laboring work stipulated that skilled labor in the mines could only be performed by whites; in 1913, the Natives Land Act enacted the first of a series of segregation laws, by limiting African land ownership to certain reserves. Eventually, Africans were restricted to "townships," large, impoverished cities close enough to major cities to provide a constant labor supply. Moreover, the conflicts between British and Afrikaner South Africans were hardly resolved by the Union. Although South Africa participated in World War I as a dominion of the British Empire, the rise of Afrikaner nationalism in the 1930s led not only to considerable support for Germany in the country, but finally to the election of the Afrikaner National party in 1948.

The Afrikaner government installed apartheid as the law of the land in South Africa. Based on the notion that South Africa was comprised of four "racial" groups—White, Colored, Indian, and African—these laws legitimated White South Africans as the "nation," with the power to govern all other groups. Apartheid legislation was rapidly passed, and pervasive in its structuring of South African society; the Pass Laws of 1948 required one to carry a passbook at all times; the Population Registration Act of 1950 classified each person by race; the Group Areas Act forced people to live in racially segregated areas; in 1949 the Prohibition of Mixed Marriages Act passed; and in 1950 the Immorality Amendment Act prohibited sex between white and "nonwhite" persons. Property once "reserved" for ownership by Africans was claimed by whites: the segregated area of Sophiatown west of Johannesburg—where, since 1923, some African and Colored people owned land—was summarily converted into a White area, "Triomf" ("Triumph"). In the 1953 Bantu Education Act, the government assumed control of all schools—including missionary schools and colleges that had formerly educated Africans—and prohibited any instruction counter to the aims of the government; the 1959 Extension of University Education Act prohibited universities from admitting African students except with the permission of a cabinet minister.

The South African Native National Congress was founded in 1912 to advance the cause of Africans in South Africa: renamed the African National Congress, it responded swiftly to the imposition of apartheid: it organized a passive resistance campaign in 1952, and other acts of resistance throughout the 1950s. In 1959 a more radical group—the Pan African Congress, which included only Africans as members—split from the ANC; both were banned by the State of Emergency declared in 1960, after an uprising in Sharpeville when sixty Africans were shot by police during a peaceful protest. Although national and international opposition to apartheid was intense, it remained in force throughout the tumult of the 1960s, 1970s, and 1980s: the imprisonment of Nelson Mandela in 1962; the rise of the Black Consciousness Movement sponsored by Steve Biko and Barney Pityana in the late 1960s; the 1976 uprising in Soweto, a black township of one million people; the government's efforts to release the pressure on apartheid by forming black "homelands" in Transkei, Bophuthatswana, Venda, and Ciskei. By the mid-1980s, however, South Africa's isolation led to some political change: A new constitution in 1984 giving Colored, Asian, and Indian populations separate houses of parliament; the repeal of some pass laws in 1986; the release of Mandela in 1990, and the negotiations for a new constitution.

In all respects, theater in South Africa has been marked by this history. As a rough-and-tumble port, Cape Town did not support a legitimate theater until 1801, with the building of the African Theater, though performances of plays were given occasionally elsewhere (Beaumarchais's *Barber of Seville* was performed in Cape Town in 1783). By the early twentieth century, though, diamonds and gold were able to finance theater building, and every large city had several good theaters, performing European plays to white audiences. Since there was no repertory in Afrikaans, Afrikaners were particularly concerned to develop a "literary" culture: the first Afrikaans play was *Magrita Prinslo,* written by S. J. du Toit in 1897. Afrikaner theater flourished in the 1920s and 1930s, and continues today. Indeed, because the English-language theaters could rely on the traditional repertoire and touring companies, dramatic writing in English emerged much later in South Africa. Although the traditional forms of performance predate the colonial period, black theater in South Africa originates with Herbert Dhlomo (1903–1956), who studied at a mission school and became a teacher and journalist, and the author of twenty-four plays. In 1933 the Bantu Drama Society at the Bantu Men's Social Center performed his play *The Girl Who Killed to Save,* the first play by a black South African to be published in English, in 1936. Nonetheless, despite producing Dhlomo's play, the repertoire of the Bantu Drama Society was very much a European repertoire: Dhlomo himself played in Sheridan's comedy *She Stoops to Conquer.* Throughout the 1920s and 1930s, several companies—the Lucky Stars, the Syco Fans—worked to develop black drama.

The production of theater, like everything else in South African society, was segregated. In 1947 the government began funding a National Theater. Although the theater supported two companies—one in English, one in Afrikaans—they used no black actors, and included South African plays in their European repertoire only if they were written by white authors. In the 1940s, Es'kia Mphahlele and Khoti Mngoma founded the Syndicate of African Artists, but were refused government funding as long as they insisted on performing to mixed racial audiences: they were disbanded in 1956 after years of police harassment. The Union of South African Artists was organized in the 1950s to protect black artists' royalties, and engineered the production of the massively successful musical review about a boxer, *King Kong,* in 1959. Although the organization was white run, and showcased black talent to white audiences, it also performed successfully to mixed audiences, and sponsored mixed-cast shows: the Union produced Athol Fugard's *No-Good Friday* in 1958, at the Bantu Men's

Social Center in Johannesburg, with a cast including Fugard, Zakes Mokae, Bloke Modisane, and Stephen Moloi. When the show moved to the Brooke Theater, however, Fugard had to be replaced by a black actor—Lewis Nkosi—because segregated venues (the Brooke was an all-white theater) required segregated casts.

The principal challenge to resistant theater offered by the apartheid laws in the 1960s was the Group Areas Act, which prohibited the association of different races in clubs, cinemas, and restaurants; while mixed casts could perform to these segregated audiences, this loophole was closed in 1965: segregated audiences, segregated casts. In 1961, Fugard's *The Blood Knot*—about half brothers, one black (played by Mokae), one passing as white (played by Fugard)—could not be played in a legitimate theater, but gained good audiences in Dorkay House, and was shortly produced in London and New York. In 1963, Fugard began to work with the Serpent Players of Port Elizabeth, a black company, on adaptations of European playwrights—Büchner, Chekhov, Brecht, and Sophocles' *Antigone*. At the same time, however, a more improvisational, storytelling mode of theater was being developed in the townships, in plays such as Gibson Kente's *Manana, the Jazz Prophet* (1963). Kente's performances were popular and influential; in their use of narrative, mime, music, and dance to dramatize township life, they provided the form for later works like Barney Simon, Mbongeni Ngema, and Percy Mtwa's *Woza Albert!* (1981). Despite their popularity, these township playwrights had difficulty getting published; the South African Performing Arts Councils received large subsidies, but produced European plays mainly for white audiences, while the township theaters performed under poor circumstances to huge audiences, often sponsored by the Union.

The 1970s saw the real flowering of resistance theater in South Africa: Athol Fugard's collaboration with John Kani and Winston Ntshona (from the Serpent Players) led to *Sizwe Bansi Is Dead* (1972), which they performed (while the police looked on) as a mixed cast; subsequent performances were canceled. When they attempted to perform the play at the University of Witwatersrand, the security police arrested both the cast and the audience. Kente's performances became more politically inflected, in township plays like *How Long* (1973) and *Too Late* (1981), and inspired many other township works: Sol Rachilos's *The Township Wife* (1972), Sidney Sepamia's *Cry Yesterday* (1972), the Theater Workshop of Durban's *Umabatha* (the Zulu *Macbeth,* revived in London and the U.S. in 1997). The 1970s also saw the forming of several influential theater groups, including the Market Theater of Johannesburg in 1976, which produced Kente's *Mama and the Load* in 1980; Simon, Ngema, and Mtwa's *Woza Albert!* in 1981; Maishe Maponya's *Gangsters* in 1984; Ngema's *Asinamali;* and Mtwa's *Bhopa!* in 1985. The Market Theater has been influential outside South Africa as well, as many of its plays have been exported to Europe and the United States, and many of its playwrights—Fugard and Maponya, for instance—have since produced plays outside South Africa. With the lifting of apartheid, race emerges as a different kind of issue in South African drama, and has been explored by a number of playwrights, including Ismail Mahomed (b. 1959), Reza de Wet (b. 1955), Brett Bailey (b. 1967) and many others. The Grahamstown National Arts Festival continues as the premiere annual theater festival in South Africa.

ANALYZING POSTCOLONIAL THEATER AND DRAMA

In part because postcolonial drama emerges out of the complex historical dynamics of global expansion, intercultural contact, political controversy, and sometimes unfamiliar artistic traditions, analyzing and discussing this material presents unique challenges. One approach to postcolonial culture attempts to develop a "national" or "regional" model, isolating themes (apartheid in South Africa, for instance), historical questions (plays that respond to the 1960 treaty controversy in Japan), or local features of dramatic style (the prevalence of domestic realism in American drama; the use of a trickster figure by Native Canadian playwrights) to assess the relationship between theater and the place of its production. This model can also lead to productive kinds of comparative study: in what ways does it make sense to frame a dialogue, say, between the writing of Aboriginal Australian writers like Jack Davis, and Native Canadian writers like Tomson Highway?

A second model recognizes the importance that ideas of "race" have had in mapping literary study, in drawing out political affinities between African, African-American, and Caribbean writers, for example. This model interrogates the ways in which "race" informs ideas of identity across national boundaries; it might place the ideas of W.E.B. DuBois or Amiri Baraka alongside the writings of Aimé Césaire and the Senegalese poet Léopold Senghor or the black Algerian psychiatrist Frantz Fanon's incendiary and brilliant book, *The Wretched of the Earth* (1961). In these writings, "race" emerges often as a cultural construct rather than a biological "fact," though its consequences are nonetheless powerful; and theorists of the production of "race" have often found a searching model in dramatic performance, both in plays in which "race" is a conscious issue—Soyinka's *Death and the King's Horseman,* or Baraka's *Dutchman*—as well as those in which it seems to be part of the play's unconscious politics, O'Neill's *The Hairy Ape,* for example, or Pinter's *The Homecoming.* Indeed, the constructedness of "race" or "ethnicity" can be a powerful weapon for *forging* a political consciousness: while the term "Latino" or "Latina" is relatively meaningless outside the Anglo-affiliated cultures of North America (people from Latin American countries tend to identify *nationally,* much as North Americans do; they think of themselves as Mexicans, Peruvians, or Cubans), it has become an important way for people experiencing *ethnic* discrimination in the United States to organize in a common effort.

One of the most powerful ways of considering postcolonial culture—its art, music, literature, drama, and performance—is to consider the formal properties of its artworks. Postcolonial critics, however, have resisted merely imposing the critical categories of Western literary study—tragic and comic form, for example, or verbal as opposed to music drama—on postcolonial arts, largely because such works often seem designed both to resist those categories, and to dramatize their implication in a wider politics. Wole Soyinka's early play *The Lion and the Jewel,* for example, is at once a play using the familiar stereotypes of Western comedy since Plautus—a pedantic schoolteacher, a cantankerous aging king, a pretty young girl—and interrogating them as well. As the play proceeds, it seems to ask whether this way of representing African village life—comedy—is complicit with the other ways that African village life is represented in the play: in magazine pictures, as a site for a railroad station, as the "dark continent" of the schoolteacher's textbooks. In other words, the play brings about a collision between the Western dramatic traditions Soyinka learned in Lagos, Leeds, and London, and the indigenous traditions—the social routines of the village, the songs, the marriage rituals—he blends into the texture of the play. This practice of blending both "indigenous" and "colonizing" literary or performance styles is generally called **HYBRIDIZATION,** and considering plays, poems, novels, films, and music in terms of their "hybrid" blending of cultural traditions is an important way of recognizing the cultural work that artworks do. Some writers (Ngũgĩ might be an example) call for postcolonial art to resist and replace the inauthentic and oppressive means of "colonial" art—writing in the colonial language, using colonial forms, like tragedy, the novel, the pop song—as a way to locate a new and authentic space of liberation. Others (Soyinka and Homi Bhabha, for example) tend to see hybrid forms as a useful tool, an instrument for exposing the dynamics of oppression at the heart of the colonizing culture itself. Reading or listening for hybridity—the collision between the tragedy of Steve Biko and Samuel Beckett's absurdist play *Catastrophe* in Maponya's *Gangsters* for instance—involves the subtle and delicate task of putting these forms into dialogue with one another, listening for how they shape and qualify one another, open the possibility of new meanings.

READING THE MATERIAL THEATER

From the perspective of theater research, modern students of theater and drama live in an era of extraordinary privilege: generations of scholars have worked to assemble the primary and secondary materials that document earlier theaters; the amount of information available in archives, libraries, and on the internet is nearly overwhelming; and, of course, performances now can be recorded on film or videotape, or for digital media. Yet we should not be seduced into thinking that a recording of a performance is the same thing as the live performance. First, of course, the camera's perspective governs everything we see on the screen, and makes it possible to achieve effects not possible in the theater; at the same time, it also transforms the performance from an actor's medium to the camera's. Viewers of the PBS versions of Anna Deavere Smith's *Fires in the Mirror* or *Twilight* can't help noticing the role played by the camera work, which brings Smith and her characters into a sharp close-up not possible onstage, to say nothing of the many scene changes, which—while they are handled seamlessly on television—point to a distracting "realism" that betrays Smith's open theatricality in performance.

Different kinds of documents—paintings, memoirs, reviews, illustrations, promptbooks, videotapes—tell us different kinds of things about the evanescent, always-lost performance onstage. One of the most useful documents for assessing the producers' original purposes in staging a play is the program, which often contains extensive program notes. With the rise of the director since the late nineteenth-century, theater companies have often found it important to have a second "conceptual" voice in the production process: the dramaturg. Dramaturgs play a wide variety of functions. In European theater, they often have a central role in imagining the production and work in close cooperation with the director and cast throughout the development of the play. Under these circumstances, a company might use a dramaturg not only to conduct research into the historical background of the play and its author (and even—say, in the case of Shakespeare—into the play's language), but also to help articulate a critical perspective on the play for the performance in daily dialogue with the director and actors. In other circumstances—and more commonly in the United States—the dramaturg might function both as a literary manager, helping to acquire and develop new plays, as well as a kind of researcher, providing background information to the director and to the cast, as well as playing a central part in writing program information. As theatrical production has been understood to be an art independent of the narrowly literary meanings of dramatic writing, the theatrical program has become a place to inform and educate the audience about the play, both to provide historical information and to help develop a useful perspective on the production.

In 1980, the Field Day Theatre Company premiered Brian Friel's *Translations*. In writing the play, Friel had conducted considerable research into two important events in the history of Northern Ireland in the nineteenth century: the Ordnance Survey mapping of Ireland, and the transformation of the educational system. While Friel clearly worked to incorporate the information needed to understand the play *into* the play, the Field Day Company clearly felt that a greater understanding of the historical background would help readers to understand the play, and their production of it. What follows here are extracts from the program notes of *Translations*. It's important, of course, to train a skeptical eye on such efforts to explain the work of the production: how do these notes work to structure the audience's response to the play? Do the notes provide the kinds of information you think is needed? Do the notes tend to emphasize some elements in the play as essential for understanding the play, and overlook other, perhaps other important, elements? How do these notes provide a perspective on the playwright's work in writing the play.

FIELD DAY THEATRE COMPANY PROGRAM NOTES FOR *TRANSLATIONS*[1] (1980)

Extract from *The Hedge Schools of Ireland* by P.J. Dowling The Hedge Schools owed their origin to the suppression of all the ordinary legitimate means of education, first during the Cromwellian regime and then under the Penal Code introduced in the reign of William III and operating from that time till within less than twenty years from the opening of the nineteenth century . . .

"The Hedge Schools were clearly of peasant institution. They were maintained by the people who wanted their children educated; and they were taught by men who came from the people . . .

"The poorest and humblest of the schools gave instruction in reading, writing and arithmetic; Latin, Greek, Mathematics and other subjects were taught in a great number of schools; and in many cases the work was done entirely through the medium of the Irish language. Though the use of the vernacular was rapidly falling into decay during the eighteenth century, it was owing to the greater value of English on the fair and market rather than to any shifting of ground on the part of the schools . . .

"The Hedge Schools were the most vital force in popular education in Ireland during the eighteenth century. They emerged in the nineteenth century more vigorous still, outnumbering all other schools, and so profoundly national as to hasten the introduction of a State system of education in 1831 . . ."

Extract from *The Autobiography of William Carleton* (born in County Tyrone, 1794) "The only place for giving instruction was a barn. The barn was a loft over a cowshed and stable . . . It was one of the largest barns in the parish.

"(At the age of fourteen) I had only got as far as Ovid's *Metamorphoses,* Justin, and the first chapter of John in the Greek Testament."

Extract from the memoirs of the Reverend Mr Alexander Ross, Rector, Dungiven, County Derry. 1814 "Even in the wildest districts, it is not unusual to meet with good classical scholars; and there are several young mountaineers of the writer's acquaintance, whose knowledge and taste in the Latin poets, might put to the blush many who have all the advantages of established schools and regular instruction."

Extract from *A History of Ireland* by Edmund Curtis "In 1831 Chief Secretary Stanley introduced a system of National Education . . . The system became a great success as an educational one but it had fatal effects on the Irish language and the old Gaelic tradition. According to Thomas Davis, at this time the vast majority of the people living west of a line drawn from Derry to Cork spoke nothing but Irish daily and east of it a considerable minority. It seems certain that at least two millions used it as their fireside speech . . . But the institution of universal elementary schools where English was the sole medium of instruction, combined with the influence of O'Connell, many of the priests, and other leaders who looked on Irish as a barrier to progress, soon made rapid inroads on the native speech . . ."

Extract from *Ordnance Survey of Ireland* by Thomas Colby, Colonel, Royal Engineers (1835) "To carry on a minute Survey of all Ireland no collection of ready instructed surveyors would have sufficed. It, therefore, became indispensable to train and organise a completely new department for the purpose. Officers and men from the corps of Royal Engineers formed the basis for this new organisation, and very large numbers of other persons possessing various qualifications, were gradually added to them to expedite the great work . . .

"The mode of spelling the names of places was peculiarly vague and unsettled, but on the maps about to be constructed it was desirable to establish a standard orthography, and for future reference, to identify the several localities with the names by which they had formerly been called . . ."

Extract from the Spring Rice Report (advocating a general survey of Ireland) to the British Government; 21 June 1824 "The general tranquility of Europe, enables the state to devote the abilities and exertions of a most valuable corps of officers to an undertaking, which, though not unimportant in a military point of view, recommends itself more directly as a civil measure. Your committee trust that the survey will be carried on with energy, as well as with skill, and that it will, when completed, be creditable to the nation, and to the scientific acquirements of the present age. In that portion of the Empire to which it more particularly applies, it cannot but be received as a proof of the disposition of the legislature to adopt all measures calculated to advance the interests of Ireland."

Extracts from the letters of John O'Donovan, a civilian employee with the Ordnance Survey, later Professor of Celtic Studies, Queen's College, Belfast
Buncrana
23 August 1835
"On Friday we travelled through the Parish of Clonmany and ascended the Hill of Beinnin. Clonmany is the most Irish Parish I have yet visited; the men only, who go to markets and fairs, speak a little English, the women and children speak Irish only. This arises from their distance from Villages and Towns and from their being completely environed by mountains, which form a gigantic barrier between them and the more civilized and less civil inhabitants of the lower country."
Dun Fionnchada? Dun Fionnchon?
Dunfanaghy
9 September 1835
"I am sick to death's door of the names on the coast, because the name I get from one is denied by another of

equal intelligence and authority to be correct. The only way to settle these names would be to summon a Jury and order them to say and present 'upon ther Oathes' what these names are and ought to be. But there are several of them such trifling places that it seems to me that it matters not which of two or three appelations we give them. For example, the name Timlin's Hole is not of thirty years standing and will give way to another name as soon as that dangerous hole shall have swallowed a fisherman of more illustrious name than Tim Lyn."
Glenties
15 October 1835
"Yesterday being a fair-day at Dunglow we were obliged to leave it in consequence of the bustle and confusion. We directed our course southwards through the Parish of the Templecroan, keeping Traigh Eunach (a name which I find exceedingly difficult to Anglicise) to the right . . . On the road we met crowds of the women of the mountains who were loaded with stockings going to the stocking fair of Dunglow and who bore deep graven on their visages the effects of poverty and smoke, of their having been kept alive by the potatoe only . . . I have seen several fields of oats on this coast, some prostrated and rotting, others with the grain completely blown off the stalk—and some so green in October as to preclude the possibility of ripening at all."
Ballyshanny
1 November 1835
"I have met in this town a fine old man named Edward Quin, from whom I have received a good deal of information. He has been employed by Lieutenant Vickers to give the Irish names of places about Ballyshannon, and has saved me a good deal of trouble—I wish you could induce Mr Vickers to take him to his next district, and keep him employed writing in the Name Books, and taking down the names from the pronunciation of the country people."

---

[1] Courtesy Field Day Theatre Company

INTERCULTURAL PERFORMANCE

One of the most challenging aspects of performance today has to do with the relative ease with which cultures now come into contact with one another, use or steal one another's forms of art and this hybridizing tendency is often visible in the plays in Unit VII. The interpenetration of different musical idioms has become a standard aspect of contemporary pop music; for instance, reggae and ska and mambo and tango and high-life and many other musical languages once local to a given culture now filter in and out of many American pop songs. And while the music industry has worked to sell this variety by copying the restaurant industry—as "World Music"—we might wonder whether the analogy with the variety of "ethnic" or "international" cuisine in the pricey restaurant districts of major cities (or even the interest in Asian and Mexican foods shown by McDonald's and Burger King) isn't more to the point: have the products of other cultures, their music, their food, their plays, become empty commodities, consumed by a kind of global consumer elite?

In the past two decades, this kind of controversy has animated "intercultural performance," a kind of performance that attempts to bridge the differences between two different cultures not so much by erasing or occluding them as by concocting artworks in which these boundaries become visible and meaningful. Ari-

ane Mnouchkine's productions of Shakespearean or classical Greek dramas using Eastern movement and dance techniques is one well-known example; another is Peter Brook's famous staging of the Indian epic, *The Mahabharata* at the Avignon Festival in 1985, and then on tour in the following years, which used fundamentally Western theatrical techniques to stage the narrative. In 1989, David McRuvie and Annette Leday collaborated with the Kerala State Arts Academy on a production of Shakespeare's *King Lear,* adapted to the extraordinarily complex conventions of the *kathakali*—an Indian form of masked dance-drama. Unlike the hybrid works of playwrights like Maponya or Luis Valdez, this intercultural strategy does not arise from the blending of cultural materials already present in a given culture—in the way Luis Valdez's *actos* draw from both Mexican and Anglo performance traditions visible in California in the 1960s. Instead, they work to bring about a dialogue between cultures that are distant from one another in space and time.

As Marvin Carlson suggests in a careful anatomy of contemporary intercultural performances, there is not only a long tradition of intercultural performance, but a variety of ways of imagining the relationship between cultural forms that performance brings about.[1] He lists seven possibilities: a performance in a tradition foreign to the audience, such as a Noh company or the Comédie Française visiting New York; the complete assimilation of foreign elements (does anyone really hear a reggae beat as "foreign" to American pop any-

more?); the assimilation of an entire foreign structure, such as Yeats's writing of Noh plays, or Maponya's work with Brechtian epic theater; making the foreign into a new blend with familiar elements (Molière's absorption of Italian *commedia dell' arte*); assimilating an entire foreign genre, such as Westerns in Japan; using some foreign elements within familiar structures, such as the dance sequences in Hwang's *M. Butterfly,* or perhaps the *egungen* costumes in Soyinka's *Death and the King's Horseman;* and importing an entire performance from another culture as something distinctly unfamiliar, such as *butoh.*

This list clarifies the extent to which intercultural performance is a highly charged, contestatory activity: Brook was widely criticized, despite the evident elegance of *The Mahabharata,* for transforming something like the national conscience of India into a piece of slick theater; similarly, while McRuvie and Leday's *Kathakali King Lear* framed an ambitious attempt to chart how far one kind of theater might be translated into the traditions of another culture, its reception was often relatively simplistic: British reviewers complained that the "true" *King Lear* was lost in the translation. As we move into the next millennium, we can certainly expect kind of theatrical and dramatic experimentation to continue, and to be challenged to think about the kind of cultural work it performs.

[1] Marvin Carlson, "Brook and Mnouchkine: Passages to India?" *The Intercultural Performance Reader,* ed. Patrice Pavis (London: Routledge, 1996), 82–83.

Griselda Gambaro

Griselda Gambaro is one of the most distinguished writers of contemporary Argentina. Born in Buenos Aires in 1928, Gambaro's career as a writer has been deeply intertwined with the history and politics of her country. Argentina has a long history of repressive military rule, and Gambaro's career as a playwright began during a period of exceptional crisis, inaugurated by Juan Carlos Onganía's brutal military coup in 1966. Gambaro's plays from this period—*The Walls* (1963), *The Blunder* (1965), *The Siamese Twins* (1965), *The Camp* (1967)—concern the progressive deterioration of the fabric of society. But as the political repression of the 1960s gave way to state terrorism in the 1970s—especially the "Dirty War" (1976–1983), in which the military government systematically imprisoned and/or murdered hundreds of thousands of civilians, the "disappeared"—Gambaro's fiction and drama became increasingly engaged, making her situation in Argentina even more precarious. Her plays of the 1970s—including *Saying Yes* (1972), *Strip* (1972), *The Name* (1976), and *Information for Foreigners* (1973)—depict a world totally slipped from its moorings, in which murder, torture, and execution seem part of the horizon of everyday life.

Gambaro has written several novels as well, including *Nothing to Do with Another Story* (1972), *To Earn One's Death* (1976), *God Does Not Want Us Happy* (1979), and *Impenetrable* (1984). In 1977, *To Earn One's Death* was banned and Gambaro left Argentina to live in Spain and France. She returned to Argentina in 1980, where she continued her career as a playwright, with *Royal Gambit* (1980), *Bitter Blood* (1981), *From the Rising Sun* (1983), *Antígona Furiosa* (1986), *Fear* (1989), and *Worthless Trouble* (1990). Gambaro has lectured extensively in the United States and is currently living in Buenos Aires.

Griselda Gambaro's *Information for Foreigners* uses the participatory element of environmental theater to enact a sophisticated political process as theater. Ideally performed in a house, the play divides the audience into four groups, each led through the play's scenes in a different order, and then reassembled as a single audience for the final scene, scene 20.

INFORMATION FOR FOREIGNERS

Information for Foreigners forces its audience to engage the subtle interinvolvement between theater and the theater of state terrorism, between fiction and fact, a blurring of boundaries between the simulated and the "real" typical of postmodern art. For throughout the play, the audience is repeatedly confronted by two kinds of "performance": overtly "theatrical" or "staged" scenes—like scene 14, where the audience observes a reenactment of a scene of police violence—and "backstage" or "offstage" scenes where the "disappeared"— the man in his underwear in scene 1, the girl who is tortured with the "submarine" (held under water in a bathtub of filthy water)—accidentally come into the audience's view. The play forces its audience both to connect these two spheres of performance and to question its own role in each. The Guide repeatedly provides "Information for Foreigners" to the audience, which articulates the historical background of state violence in the 1970s, and implicitly addresses that wider, European and North American audience whose tacit or financial support kept the regime in power. The audience is, in a sense, incriminated for adopting this "tourist" role.

In many respects, *Information for Foreigners* is a play about its audience. Scene 4 reenacts the famous Milgram experiment, in which the participant's willingness to follow orders and please authority figures leads him to kill (or, in the original versions of the experiment, to believe he has killed) the "student." The Milgram experiment provides a kind of metaphor for the audience's function in *Information for Foreigners*, in that observation repeatedly involves the audience in a kind of deference to authority. The silent willingness to participate as spectators of the violence makes the audience responsible for the violence, becoming its silent authors. This implied assault on the audience's moral freedom is the point of the play's final scene, where the line between theater and torture is finally suspended, and the "stage" of torture is one the audience is explicitly shown to authorize. Having brought the audience to witness a final execution, the Guide turns to us: "Ladies and gentlemen, what are you waiting for? The show is over." As he suggests in his final, ritual chant, "Theater imitates life"; but the boundaries between theater and life, between what we see and what we know, have been forever broken:

> Who once said: here the ken
> of men and women
> here the bounds?

INFORMATION FOR FOREIGNERS

A CHRONICLE IN TWENTY SCENES

Griselda Gambaro

TRANSLATED BY MARGUERITE FEITLOWITZ

CHARACTERS

GUIDES, *number contingent on number of audience groups*
VOICES, *heard at intervals throughout*

MAN IN ROOM

GIRL, *with wet clothes*
MAN, *with pistol*

COORDINATOR
MATURE MAN/TEACHER
YOUNG MAN/PUPIL

MOTHER
FATHER

GROUP OF MEN, *attack* MAN IN AUDIENCE
MAN, *defends attacked man*

SOMEONE FROM THE AUDIENCE, *number contingent on number of audience groups*
USHERETTE

THREE MEN, *carry table*
GROUP OF MEN, *surround* GIRL
TWO WORKMEN

MOTHER (*Sara Palacio de Verdt*)
FATHER (*Marcelo Verdt*)
TWO CHILDREN (*Verdt girl and boy*)
CHIEF
TWO POLICEMEN

MAN IN LOINCLOTH

MAN (*Robert Quieto*)

NEIGHBOR #1
NEIGHBOR #2
FIRST GROUP OF MEN, *tied together*
NEIGHBOR #3
SECOND GROUP OF MEN, *tied together*
OFFICIAL
JUDGE
GUARD

GIRL, *with long hair (HERMENEGILDA)*
FOUR MEN, *on skates*
HUSBAND OF HERMENEGILDA
MOTHER OF HERMENEGILDA
NEIGHBORS

MAN (*Juan Pablo Maestre*)
WOMAN (*Miera Elena Misetich*)
TWO POLICEMEN
GROUP OF POLICEMEN, *dressed as sweepers*

GAME PLAYERS
POLICEMEN, *with clubs*

ACTOR #1
TWO MEN, *in box*

ACTRESS #1
ACTRESS #2
ACTOR #1
POLICEMAN #1
POLICEMAN #2

CHILD MONSTER

CHILDREN, *play Anton Pirulero*
FIRST MAN
SECOND MAN
THIRD MAN
YOUNG WOMAN

TWO GUARDS
PRISONERS
VISITORS TO PRISON
PRETTY GIRL

GROUP OF GUARDS, *attack* PRETTY GIRL
LITTLE OLD LADY
OUTLANDISH-LOOKING PRISONER

PROSTITUTES
MAN #1
MAN #2
MAN #3
MAN #4

The theater space can be a spacious, residential house, preferably two stories, with corridors and empty rooms, some of which interconnect. A larger space is needed for the final scene.

Situated in the passageways, propped against the walls, are two or three vertical rectangular boxes, each with a door and air holes.

In a different area, chosen by the director, sits an additional box, larger but otherwise the same as those in the passageways.

Some of the corridors are dark, while others, in obvious contrast, are crudely lit.

The audience will be divided into groups, the number and size of which will depend on the space. A particular number or color can serve to identify each group.

Group 1 will mark one possible development of the action.

Guides 1, 2, 3, 4, etc., lead their respective groups. The order in which the scenes are observed by these groups is left to the director's discretion until the last scene, scene 20, when all groups converge.

In certain scenes, actors play audience members and are actually part of the audience. Audience members, however, are never forced to participate in the action.

The groups cross in the passageways and may watch the same scene—perhaps one taking place in the passageway—when the director considers it necessary.

Excerpts introduced by the guides as "Explanation: For Foreigners" come from Argentine newspapers of the period 1971–72.

GUIDES: Organize the groups.
GUIDE: Ladies and gentlemen: Admission is ———, for adults. If you've already paid, you can't repent. The cost is already incurred. Better to enjoy yourself. No one under eigh-
5 teen will be admitted. Or under thirty-five or over thirty-six. Everyone else can attend with no problem. No obscenity or strong words. The play speaks to our way of life: Argentine, Western, and Christian. We are in 1971. I ask that you stay together and remain silent. Careful on the
10 stairs.

SCENE ONE

The GUIDE leads the group toward one of the rooms. The room is completely in shadow. The door closes. We hear a shrill, metallic signal. Then, we hear many voices, indistinct and juxtaposed, carrying on an incomprehensible conversation.

GUIDE: One moment . . . I don't find my flashlight. Remember, opportunity makes the thief. Watch your pocketbooks! (*Light comes up on a dark and wrinkled wall.*) Only the naked

walls are left. (*The light travels. A man is seated on a chair,
wearing only faded underwear. He raises his head, surprised and
frightened. He covers his sex with his hands. To the audience.*) Excuse me. I've got the wrong room.

5

SCENE TWO

The GUIDE, *lighting the way with his flashlight, leads the group out of
the room. He tries to open the door of another room. Behind the door
a sweet voice sings*

VOICE:

"Carnation, sleep and dream,
the horse won't drink from the stream . . ."

GUIDE: (*Shrugging his shoulders, turns to the group.*) It's locked.
5   (*He knocks. Nicely.*) May I? I've brought a group of spectators. And they're getting anxious.
VOICE: (*Very rudely.*) What's it to me? Beat it! I'm rehearsing.

SCENE THREE

GUIDE: (*To the group.*) Sorry. People should be brought up better, don't you think? (*Tries the latch on the next door. It gives.*)
Good. Here. Go ahead. (*The group enters this other dark room.
Against the wall, some chairs. The* GUIDE *shines his light on them.
5   Then, nicely.*) You can position yourselves wherever you like.
There are chairs for everyone. (*He looks.*) No, not enough to
go around. (*Arranges them, offers.*) Ladies first . . . !

(*Lights on in the middle of the room. A young* GIRL *sits on a chair
wearing clothes that are soaking wet. A* MAN *stands next to her, observing her with a tender smile. The* GUIDE *waits for people to get comfortable, points out places. Then, with a finger on his lips, he signals
for silence and turns, like one more spectator, toward the characters who
begin the action.*)

MAN: (*Always speaks softly, tenderly.*) Why didn't you dry yourself? You're getting the floor all wet. (*He bends down and
10   dries the floor with a rag.*) Lucky it's not waxed. (*The* GIRL
shivers with cold. The MAN *takes off his jacket, puts it on her
shoulders. The* GIRL *looks at it, wraps herself in the jacket.*) Why
didn't you dry yourself? Wasn't there a towel?
GIRL: No.
15   MAN: (*Drying the floor.*) What a mess! They fill the tub but don't
put any towels. What about the water? Was it warm? (*The
GIRL doesn't answer. He shakes her, gently.*) Was it warm?
GIRL: No.

---

ii. 2 **"Carnation, sleep and dream,"** sung by a "sweet" female
Voice, the Mother in scene 5, and other voices elsewhere, is from
García Lorca's *Bodas de sangre,* or *Blood Wedding,* scene 2. I use the
translation by James Graham-Luján and Richard L. O'Connell in
*Three Tragedies of Federico García Lorca: Blood Wedding, Yerma,
Bernarda Alba* (New York: New Directions, 1955). In the original,
Gambaro used only "Nana, niño, nana, del caballo grande que no
quiso el agua," repeated over and over. For the English version, I
chose to use many more fragments of the lullabye over the course
of the play. Gambaro approved this choice in her letter to me of
March 28, 1986

MAN: (*He pulls a pistol from his belt and cleans it with a rag.*) Ah!
This department isn't worth shi . . . (*The* GUIDE *says some- 20
thing. The* MAN *shoots him a quick look.*) Right. (*He shows her
his weapon.*) Do you like it? It isn't loaded. (*She looks at it but
doesn't answer. The* MAN *begins loading the gun.*) Why so sad?
(*Points to the group.*) Nothing will happen to you. There are
lots of people. They're watching us. (*Puts the pistol back in 25
his belt.*) You're not pretty with your hair all wet. But that's
not too serious. (*He leans toward her, curious.*) Tell me, do you
dye your hair? (*Still studying her.*) You're getting my jacket
all wet. Sorry, it's the only one I have . . . (*He takes it gently,
shakes it, and puts it on. With a shiver.*) It's damp. (*Pointing to 30
the pistol.*) Do you want it?
GIRL: No.
MAN: I'm leaving it for you. I have another. The jacket I can't,
I swear to you.
GIRL: (*Shaking her head.*) No. 35
MAN: (*Surreptitiously.*) Speak up! They can't hear a thing!
GUIDE: Louder! Louder!
MAN: What did I tell you? (*The* GIRL *doesn't answer.*) Look at me.
(*She obeys. He holds out the gun.*) Take it!
GIRL: No . . . I don't want to. 40
MAN: Why are you squeezing your legs together? Do you want
to go to the bathroom?
GIRL: (*Nods her head.*) Yes.
MAN: Then go!
GIRL: They're . . . watching me. 45
MAN: So? We're all adults, aren't we? They at least are watch-
ing. What are you doing, always looking over there? What
do you see that's so pretty? (*Puts his cheek against hers. Looks
in the same direction.*) Nothing! (*Separates from her.*) I like to
see people's eyes when I talk to them. (*Gently, he turns her 50
head.*) Look at me. (*He points to the pistol.*) Do you want it?
GIRL: No, no! Leave me alone!
MAN: (*Anxious.*) Would you like some stockings? (*He puts his
hand on her foot.*)
GIRL: No! 55
MAN: Always no! Why? My intentions are good. Take it. Don't
you get bored all alone? (*Insists.*) Take it, it doesn't bite. But
don't squeeze the trigger. Unless . . .
GIRL: (*Barely audible.*) Unless . . .
MAN: If you squeeze, it's all over. Do you have a boyfriend? 60
GIRL: No.
MAN: Well then? Take it! I'm leaving it here, on the floor. All
you have to do is lean down.
GIRL: For what? I don't want . . . to lean down, I don't want . . .
anything. 65
MAN: The heart and the forehead . . . are sure. I mean, so you
don't suffer . . .
GIRL: No . . .
MAN: (*Caresses her cheek.*) Of course, no. There's a sun outside.
It's hot as hell. So you don't have a boyfriend? Well 70
then . . . ? (*He goes toward the door. Turns. Smiles.*) I'm going
to tell them to heat the water! (*He goes out. The* GIRL *looks
at the pistol on the floor, leans down, trembling, stretches her hand.
Freezes in the act.*)
GUIDE: Ladies and gentlemen, if it bothers you. (*He opens the 75
door. Leading the group into the hallway, he explains.*) In March
1970, at the Max Planck Institute in Munich, Germany,
they began an interesting experiment. Careful on the stairs.

SCENE FOUR

The group enters a white room that adjoins another, also painted white, but that may be smaller. In the first room, a small table with a cage full of white rats. On another table, a metal box outfitted with buttons and a microphone. Carefully folded on an ordinary chair, a white coat.

Through the half-open door one can see in the other room a chair whose armrests are outfitted with side straps attached to electric cables. Cables to tie down a person's legs. A microphone hangs down from the ceiling.

In the first room are the COORDINATOR, *dressed in a white coat, and two others in street clothes, a* MATURE MAN *and a* YOUNG MAN. *The* MATURE MAN *lingers in front of the cage, putting his fingers through the bars, trying to attract the rats and get them to play.*

COORDINATOR: (*To the group, in a professional tone.*) Gentlemen: The subject of our experiment is to determine the pedagogical effect of punishment. To what degree does punishment accelerate the learning process? Imagine. If with one
5 slap a child learns to behave, we waste years teaching and persuading only with nice words. We don't have time to lose. Soon he will be an adult; soon he will be molded. Molded for destruction, when one slap, two or three electrical jolts at the right moment could put things in place.
10 (*He begins observing the* MATURE MAN *playing with the rats.*) The gentlemen will help us to clarify ...unclear ...details ... Please, sir, stop pestering those rats! Idiot! (*He goes toward him and kicks him away from the cage.*)
MATURE MAN: Okay, okay. I'm sorry. They're so cute that . . .
15 COORDINATOR: (*Calm.*) Of course they're cute. (*Becoming irritated.*) Shall we begin?
MATURE MAN: At your orders, sir!
COORDINATOR: (*Happy.*) One kick ...and acquiescence. You, sir, emotionally more mature, will be the teacher.
20 MATURE MAN: Yes, delighted.
COORDINATOR: (*To the* YOUNG MAN.) You will be the pupil.
YOUNG MAN: (*He speaks with a metallic voice, like a parrot.*) I will be the pupil.
GUIDE: (*To the group, surreptitiously.*) Everyone's a researcher,
25 even the mule.
COORDINATOR: (*Drily.*) Silence! (*He takes money and some papers out of his pocket.*) Help yourself. Twenty-five marks, or thirty-six dollars for your trouble. If you would be so kind as to sign the receipt and the release. (*They sign, take their*
30 *money. The* COORDINATOR *hands the* TEACHER *a white coat.*) This is for you. (*Cordially, the* COORDINATOR *helps him on with the coat, adjusts the collar.*) There, now. Right this way, please. (*He leads them into the other room. The* GUIDE *follows with his group.* COORDINATOR *to the* PUPIL.) Please be seated.
35 Don't be afraid, it's an experiment, remember that.
PUPIL: Happy to please
I sit with the greatest of ease!
COORDINATOR: I made a mistake. Take off your jacket, roll up your sleeves. (*The* PUPIL *does so.*) Thank you. We have to
40 strap you in. If you would like to resign . . .
PUPIL No! For the sake of science
Let us commence!
COORDINATOR: (*Strapping him. To the* TEACHER.) Will you help me?

TEACHER: (*With dispatch.*) Yes, of course!   45
COORDINATOR: (*From a pocket of his coat, he takes a tube of cream and starts smearing the* PUPIL's *forearms.*) The cream facilitates the passage of current and prevents burns. (*Winking at him.*) It's an experiment, don't be frightened. It's like . . . talking to hear yourself talk.   50
PUPIL: I'm not afraid
I'm not afraid
I really feel I have it made.
COORDINATOR: (*Attaches electrodes to the* PUPIL's *forearms. The* TEACHER *helps diligently.*) How obliging! Thank you.   55
PUPIL: It's . . . very tight.
COORDINATOR: Let's loosen this a bit. (*He does.*) You—the Teacher—are going to station yourself at the microphone in the next room. (*To the* PUPIL.) You pay attention. He will read out a group of words, such as *day-sun, night-moon,* 60
mother-love, etc. Then he will repeat the word *day* followed by four others. You must remember which of these four words was associated with *day.* If you make a mistake, you'll receive an electric shock as punishment.
TEACHER: And then you'll learn.   65
PUPIL: Why will punishment teach me?
COORDINATOR: The shock won't be strong.
TEACHER: Never?
COORDINATOR: No! Unless he really blunders. But it's impossible. They're very obvious associations. For idiots. (*To the* 70
TEACHER.) Let's go! (*They go into the adjoining room. The* GUIDE *settles his group. The* COORDINATOR *hands the* TEACHER *a sheet of paper.*) Here is the list of words. A clean game: read slowly, with good pronunciation. Wait! Roll up your sleeve.
TEACHER: Me? What for?   75
COORDINATOR: I want to give you a charge of forty-five volts.
TEACHER: (*Surprised.*) Me? I'm the teacher!
COORDINATOR: Don't be afraid. I'm doing it so that you'll appreciate the intensity of the punishment. Otherwise, you might have a heavy hand. (*He puts an electrode on the* 80
TEACHER's *arm, pushes a button.*)
TEACHER: (*Jumps, frightened.*) That's strong!
COORDINATOR: No, no. You'll start with fifteen volts. You won't have to increase it much. Be seated. Read. Slowly, in a clear voice.   85
TEACHER: (*He sits in front of the metal box, clears his throat, reads haltingly.*) Day-sun, night-moon, mother-love, water-ship, plague-war, house-forest, child-innocence, prison-bars, window-freedom, blue-sky, bird-flight, nation-Germany, torture-dissuasion. (*He finishes, looks at the* COORDINATOR 90
like a child awaiting instructions.)
COORDINATOR: (*Claps him on the shoulder.*) Very good! Now you must read one word, then four more, so that the pupil will pick the correct association. If he makes a mistake, say "Error," press the first button, and tell the pupil the voltage 95
with which you're punishing him. Then read the right answer. Punishments start at 15 volts and end at 450. (*He makes a horizontal gesture with his hand.*) As you see, it couldn't be easier. Begin.
TEACHER: (*Clears his throat.*) Sun! Day, forest, mother, water.   100
VOICE OF THE PUPIL: Day!
COORDINATOR: Very good! (*Encouraging the* TEACHER.) Let's go on! Do you like it?
TEACHER: (*Like a child.*) Yes! It's terrific!

105 COORDINATOR: Continue.

TEACHER: Night! Plague, forest, moon, child.

VOICE OF THE PUPIL: Moon!

TEACHER: (*Enthused.*) Correct! (*To the* COORDINATOR, *laughing.*) This is like a drug!

110 COORDINATOR: Ssshh! Go on!

TEACHER: Mother! Day, water, child, love. (*Silence from the* PUPIL.) But this is bread in your belly! What memories do you have of your mother?

COORDINATOR: (*With bonhomie.*) Now, don't help! It's not

115 scientific!

VOICE OF THE PUPIL: Chi . . .

TEACHER: (*Advises.*) No!

COORDINATOR: (*Drily.*) Excuse me, sir. This is an experiment, not a game.

120 VOICE OF THE PUPIL: We can't repeat? (*The* TEACHER *looks at the* COORDINATOR.)

COORDINATOR: Just this once. You've got to follow the rules.

TEACHER: Just this once, not again. Mother: day, water, child, love. (*Silence from the* PUPIL.) Well?

125 VOICE OF THE PUPIL: Love!

TEACHER: Very good! But faster. (*The* COORDINATOR *nods approval.*) Blue: ship, bird, sky, house. (*Silence from the* PUPIL.) I'm waiting.

VOICE OF THE PUPIL: Want to repeat?

130 TEACHER: I won't repeat. How can you not remember? What a fool. (*Looks at the* COORDINATOR, *who assents.*) Answer, I won't wait any longer.

VOICE OF THE PUPIL: Bird!

TEACHER: (*Pleased.*) He made a mistake! Now what do I do?

135 COORDINATOR: (*He points to the box. The* TEACHER *vacillates in his choice among the buttons.*) The first. Fifteen volts.

TEACHER: (*Smiles timidly. Pushes the button.*) Here we go! Take that. (*Through the door, we see that the* PUPIL *is jolted but cries out more in surprise than pain. His cries are always in a parrot-voice,*

140 *stereotyped like those of someone who, as a joke, coarsely imitates moans, groans, and pain. To the* COORDINATOR.) I didn't do anything! (*Into the microphone.*) Now remember. (*He reads.*) Plague: child, innocence, love, night.

COORDINATOR: (*Very low.*) You forgot war.

145 TEACHER: I did?

COORDINATOR: Plague-war. It's all right, let it go. It doesn't matter.

TEACHER: (*Low.*) Should I repeat? (*The* COORDINATOR *shrugs.*) Well? (*The* PUPIL *is silent.*) Come on. Quick. Otherwise it's

150 boring, I get tired.

VOICE OF THE PUPIL: Night.

TEACHER: (*Pleased.*) He made a mistake! Thirty volts! (*Instantly presses the second button. A louder groan from the* PUPIL.) Moving right along. Child: love, mother, innocence, bird.

155 VOICE OF THE PUPIL: (*Quickly.*) Love!

TEACHER: He made a mistake! You were dreaming! Forty-five volts! (*He pushes another button. Howling loudly, the* PUPIL *arches his back. Surprised by the howling, the* TEACHER *looks into the other room. To the* COORDINATOR, *disturbed.*) A bit strong, wasn't it?

160 COORDINATOR: (*Soothingly.*) No. This is a scientific experiment, and I am in charge. What experiment! Just as I told you: simply to determine the effectiveness of punishment in learning. If from the beginning we doubt, we'll never arrive at a conclusion.

165 TEACHER: Yes, that's right. The associations are easy.

COORDINATOR: And it's not so much. I gave you forty-five volts, remember?

TEACHER: I didn't shout. What a weakling! (*To the* PUPIL.) Listen to me. Don't scream. Pay attention. Sky: mother, child, innocence, blue.

170 VOICE OF THE PUPIL: Blue!

TEACHER: Goooood!

COORDINATOR: Magnificent. We're already getting results.

TEACHER: It's no time to stop, then. Plague: prison, house, forest, war. Well? (*Slowly, the* COORDINATOR *closes the door con-

175 necting the rooms.*) Repeat. (*The* COORDINATOR *shakes his head.*) I can't. (*Silence from the* PUPIL.) Well? (*To the* COORDINATOR.) Can I repeat? Just this once. He's not very intelligent. (*The* COORDINATOR *snorts, accedes with a gesture.*)

TEACHER: Listen. Don't let your mind wander. Plague: prison,

180 house, forest, war.

VOICE OF THE PUPIL: Prison.

TEACHER: He's an idiot!

COORDINATOR: (*Exasperated.*) You must say, "Error," and press the button. That is your job! Save the commentary!

185 TEACHER: And now he's growling at me! (*He presses the button.*)

VOICE OF THE PUPIL: (*Screams.*) No, no! I didn't think I'd be in so much pain!

TEACHER: A smart aleck! Well, he better hold up! (*Into the microphone.*) Pupil: Pay attention. You think I like pushing

190 these little buttons? Try to remember. Blue: bird, flight, sky, freedom. (*Waits, nervous.*) Out with it!

VOICE OF THE PUPIL: I don't remember!

TEACHER: How can you not remember?

VOICE OF THE PUPIL: I don't!

195 TEACHER: (*Furious, pushes the button.*) If you don't remember, take this.

VOICE OF THE PUPIL: (*A scream.*) Sky! (*He whimpers.*)

TEACHER: Very good! (*He wipes the sweat from his face.*) You see? With a little determination, you hit it! Okay! Here we go.

200 Flight: bird, blue, forest, night. You gotta be quick. Answer.

VOICE OF THE PUPIL: I won't play! No matter what you say!

COORDINATOR: Youth today! Now he refuses!

TEACHER: What's the matter with him? He's howling.

205 COORDINATOR: He signed the release. He can't give up. The results are important, aren't they? You're not screaming. You can be counted on.

TEACHER: Pupil? Pay attention. I am going to read you the words.

VOICE OF THE PUPIL: Go to hell! Let's change places!

210 TEACHER: Change places? That's crazy. It'll be worse for you, if you don't answer. Bird: flight, blue, plague, war. And I'm repeating the words. And it isn't allowed! Who do you think you are? Answer!

VOICE OF THE PUPIL: I'll make a mistake!

215 TEACHER: Answer! (*He pushes the button. A scream. To* COORDINATOR.) He's screaming.

COORDINATOR: He feels a bit jolted. You have just one thing to watch out for: 450 volts—kaput. Otherwise, after a week, there isn't a mark.

220 TEACHER: Listen good. Are you listening?

VOICE OF THE PUPIL: Are you listening?

TEACHER: We'll see who's listening. Bird: night, flight, house, plague.

225 VOICE OF THE PUPIL: I don't remember!

TEACHER: Don't be such an ass!

VOICE OF THE PUPIL: Don't be such an ass! Plague!

TEACHER: (*Furious.*) Imbecile! Bird-plague! (*To the* COORDI-
NATOR.) See how he answers! (*The* COORDINATOR, *under-*
230 *standing, shrugs his shoulders.*) He's jerking me around! (*He
pushes a button. The* PUPIL *screams, weeps. Disconcerted, to the*
COORDINATOR.) And now he's crying! What do I do?

COORDINATOR: Keep going. Don't worry about it.

TEACHER: Listen, kid, answer right, or I'll blow you away. Win-
235 dow: prison, flight, torture, fr . . . freedom.

VOICE OF THE PUPIL: Torture! Torture!

TEACHER: What did you say? Tortoise! Idiot! You're making
fun of me! (*He pushes the button. The* PUPIL *howls.*)

COORDINATOR: (*Checking.*) One hundred eighty volts. (*Smiles*
240 *approvingly.*) It's moving right along.

VOICE OF THE PUPIL: Let me go, you're hurting me! Oh, my
belly!

TEACHER: Do we stop?

COORDINATOR: No.

245 TEACHER: He doesn't remember anything!

COORDINATOR: He'll remember now.

TEACHER: You think so? He burst into tears. If he doesn't answer, this is useless!

COORDINATOR: It isn't useless! If we don't succeed in getting
250 concrete results, all this suffering will be useless. Besides,
you have to.

TEACHER: *I* do?

COORDINATOR: Of course. The tears, the screams. Think
about it.

255 TEACHER: I'm not exactly sucking my thumb!

COORDINATOR: Of course not. Go ahead.

TEACHER: Nation: prison, bars, Germany, torture.

VOICE OF THE PUPIL: I don't know!

TEACHER: (*His finger on the button.*) Out with it!

260 VOICE OF THE PUPIL: Argentina!

TEACHER: (*Beside himself.*) Germany, idiot! (*He pushes the button.
The* PUPIL *howls.*)

COORDINATOR: Planck Institute, Munich.

TEACHER: (*Furious.*) Prison: nation, plague, war, bars.

265 VOICE OF THE PUPIL: I don't know, let me go!
I want to go home!

TEACHER: (*Screams.*) Out with it!

VOICE OF THE PUPIL: Nation!

TEACHER: You made a mistake! (*He pushes button after button.
270 The* PUPIL *howls.*)

COORDINATOR: (*Stops him.*) Slow! One at a time.

TEACHER: He's fucking with me! Why doesn't he answer right?

COORDINATOR: Make him.

TEACHER: I don't like doing this to you. Is that clear? You
275 signed. Don't count your lost sheep. Concentrate! Here's
another. Do you hear me? (*Silence.*) Do you hear?

VOICE OF THE PUPIL: (*Lifeless.*) Vultures fly near . . .

TEACHER: Moon: night, prison, window, flight. (*To the* COOR-
DINATOR.) He'll get this one. It's easy. (*Low.*) If he doesn't
280 answer, what do I do?

COORDINATOR: (*Gently.*) I told you.

TEACHER: (*Puts his hand on the last button. Closes his eyes.*) He
doesn't answer. Why doesn't he answer?

COORDINATOR: (*Softly.*) Laziness. Low level.

TEACHER: Moon. 285

VOICE OF THE PUPIL: Ni . . . Niii . . . ght . . .

TEACHER: (*Without consulting the list.*) He made a mistake. He
made a mistake . . . again. (*He opens his eyes.*) It's deliberate.
He can't not know. Still . . . it hurts me . . . (*He slowly
pushes the last button on the box. Silence. He smiles with relief.*) 290
He didn't scream.

COORDINATOR: No. (*Changes his tone. Exultantly.*) Very good!
Four hundred fifty volts! Excellent! Your help has been invaluable.

TEACHER: Why didn't he help? 295

COORDINATOR: Look . . . we choose the risks we take! Sometimes we're not so lucky. (*Removes the* TEACHER'*s lab coat.*)

TEACHER: It was his fault. Wasn't it?

COORDINATOR: Yes, yes. Your work was magnificent!

TEACHER: He didn't even make an effort. A baby at the breast 300
could have answered right. Some people like to fuck with
you!

COORDINATOR: Yes, yes! You were splendid. (*He shakes his
hand.*) Thank you ever so much. Don't worry. An unforget-
table performance. 305

TEACHER: (*Flattered.*) It was nothing. I did what I could!

COORDINATOR: (*Seeing him to the door.*) No, no, you were
quick, concise, sure. Thanks ever so much! (*Again he shakes
his hand. The* TEACHER *exits. The* COORDINATOR *turns toward
the audience, professional.*) This experiment, with recorded 310
screams and simulated tortures, was repeated 180 times.
Unfortunately, this teacher who continued his punishments to the lethal 450 volts was no exception. Eighty-five
percent of the teachers proceeded in the same way. The
same test was done in 1960 in the United States. The re- 315
sults? Sixty-six percent. They were obeying rules and
weren't responsible. Curious, isn't it? Surprised?

GUIDE: Okay, enough. Don't wear out the audience. (*To his
group.*) The experiment was done in Germany and the
United States. Here among ourselves, it would be unthink- 320
able, absurd. Ladies and gentlemen, let's look for something
more amusing. (*He leads his group out of the room.*) This way,
this way. If you would be so kind . . . Ladies and gentlemen . . .

SCENE FIVE

The GUIDE *leads the group to the room that in scene two was locked.*

GUIDE: (*He knocks.*) May I?

VERY SILLY VOICE: (*From inside the room.*) Yeeeess.

(*The group enters the room. Seated on a chair is a woman* [MOTHER]
*made up like a doll, wearing a white dress that reaches to her feet and
holding a baby in her arms. The baby, swaddled in tulle and lace, is
obviously a doll. Sitting on the floor, at the woman's feet, a young man
[FATHER] watches them with an enraptured expression. The group is
enveloped in a beam of rosy light. The acting is frankly crude.*)

GUIDE: (*Pleased.*) Ah! Finally something coherent!

MOTHER: (*Rocking the child.*)

---

iv. 319 Stanley Milgram describes this experiment in his book,
Obedience to Authority (New York: Harper & Row, 1974).

5
"My rose, asleep now lie
the horse is starting to cry
His poor hooves were . . ."

GUIDE: What a picture! (*To his group.*) Make yourselves comfortable. Can you see? Madam . . . (*Helps her get comfortable. Then, rapidly, drily.*) Explanation: For Foreigners. Seven P.M., Wednesday, December 16, 1970. Nestor Martins, attorney, defender of political prisoners and trade unions, consults with his client Nildo Zenteno. They take leave of one another in the street. Six men surround Martins, violently force him into a white Peugeot. Nildo Zenteno rushes back, manages momentarily to free the lawyer. A karate chop to the back of his neck brings Zenteno down as well. The car speeds off. A black Chevrolet escorts it. That car had pulled out of a nearby parking lot of the Federal Police. *Desaparecidos.* (*From newspaper.*) Nestor Martins, thirty-three. Nildo Zenteno, thirty-seven.

MOTHER:

" . . . bleeding,
his long mane was frozen,
and deep in his eyes
stuck a silvery dagger."

(*She suddenly stops. Distorting her voice as though she were a ventriloquist speaking for the little one.*) Stop it, Mama. That's old. Daddy, tell me a story.

FATHER: (*Very sweet.*) Yes, darling.

MOTHER: (*Idiotic voice.*) Daddy, it has to be modern! No morals, Daddy!

FATHER: Yes, darling.

MOTHER: (*Impatient.*) Come on, Daddy, start!

FATHER: (*Enraptured.*) Precious!

MOTHER: (*In the voice of a ferocious little child.*) I know I'm precious! Why do you go round and around, Daddy?

FATHER: Now, now . . . This child is in such a hurry! Daddy has to think!

MOTHER: Enough horsing around, Daddy. Well?

FATHER: (*Laughs confusedly. Then, grossly exaggerating the traditional tone in which one tells a story.*) Once upon a time . . .

MOTHER: (*In the voice of a fierce, exasperated little child.*) Yeeeess . . .

FATHER: (*In the same tone.*) Once upon a time there was a tall man, ugly, ugly, ugly . . . (*With disgust.*) Bolivian. (*Resuming the story.*) He had a pile of children. (*Drily.*) They procreate a lot. Then they send the kids here.

MOTHER: What happened to the little kids?

FATHER: (*Sweetly.*) They were in the street, begging, stealing . . .

MOTHER: And what happened to the tall man?

FATHER: The tall man met another man. This one was a shorty. They talked and talked . . .

MOTHER: (*Voice of a stupid baby.*) About what?

FATHER: Well . . . ! Ugly things! And when they were tired of talking, the tall man walked him to his car.

MOTHER: Who?

FATHER: The shorty. The short one was bad, bad. And then some men came, and since he was bad, they put him in another car to punish him. Because he was bad, bad. And what did the tall man do?

MOTHER: I don't know!

FATHER: He didn't want them to punish him!

MOTHER: Stupid!

FATHER: He ran and ran and hit the good guys. And then, the good guys put him into the car as well.

MOTHER: The good guys took them for a ride! 'Cause they're so good!

FATHER: So very good!

MOTHER: And then what happened, Daddy?

FATHER: Nothing more was ever known!

MOTHER: Yea, yea, yea!

GUIDE: What horrible acting. So sorry. Let's look for something else. (*He pushes the people toward the door.*) The whole show's not like this. I hope.

MOTHER: (*Same voice of a stupid baby.*) Did they punish them a lot, Daddy?

FATHER: Nothing more was ever known!

MOTHER and FATHER: Yea, yea, yea!

GUIDE: (*Cutting it.*) Let's go. Let's go, gentlemen. They need at least another month of rehearsal. What dunces!

SCENE SIX

GUIDE: Let's go upstairs, see if we have better luck. He who searches finds. They say. (*The group goes up the stairs, or down, if the preceding scene took place on the upper level. Natural lighting. When the group reaches the landing of the upper level.*) No, I made a mistake. I had you climb to the . . . (*Stops.*) In vain. Let's go down.

(*They go down. Suddenly, a group of men burst in, hurling themselves at a person in the audience who is talking with someone else. This other person is for a second paralyzed with astonishment. Then shouting, he throws himself into the fray.*)

MAN: Let him go! Let him go!

(*He succeeds in freeing him. The two make it down a few stairs, but the group of men rush them, surround them, and drag them down the stairs. Over the loudspeaker a distressed voice is heard.*)

VOICE: My God, why did I run? (*Almost instantaneously, the scene breaks out in another place with other characters. The groups may cross at this moment. Again the voice is heard.*) My God, why did I run? (*The scene is repeated in another spot.*) My God, why did I run?

GUIDE: (*Meanwhile.*) If we search carefully, we'll find remains in the catacombs. There aren't many, but we can still hope for surprises. Careful please. Don't wander off now. That's it, all together. Careful on the stairs. Look over here! (*Matter of factly.*) A brutish people! Yes, we will find remains. Sometimes discoveries come about by chance. (*He examines the door to a room. Opens it. The room is lit.*) Oh, this one has good light. Imagine, ladies and gentlemen, the faith, the heroism of the first Christians. To pray in these pigsties. It gives me claustrophobia. (*He spots a form covered with canvas in a corner,*

5–7 **My rose . . . were** the Mother sings fragments from the *Blood Wedding* lullaby   20–21 **Nestor . . . Zenteno** the disappearance of Nestor Martins and his client Nildo Zenteno was in fact one of the first. It happened during the term of de facto president General Levingston, who had come to power in a coup d'état, unseating the previous de facto president, General Onganía

on the floor.) Here's something. Finally! (*He draws near.*)
Stand back a little, ladies and gentlemen. (*With curiosity.*)
25 What is it? (*He lifts an edge of the canvas, immediately lets it
fall and steps back.*) Puah! What a shitty surprise!
VOICE: My God, why did I run?
GUIDE: Sssh! (*Turns toward the audience, with a big feigned smile,
gives the form a kick.*)
30 VOICE: My God, why did I run?

(*The* GUIDE *jumps on the form, tramples it, inflamed. In the doorway
to the room, another* GUIDE *appears. He claps his hands loudly.*)

GUIDE #2: Ladies and gentlemen! Please leave. Out, everyone
out! Sorry. We have a few like machines without an off button. If you would be so kind as to follow me. (*The light in
the room fades out.*)

SCENE SEVEN

GUIDE #2: What was the other one telling you?
SOMEONE FROM THE AUDIENCE: About the catacombs.
GUIDE #2: (*Glib.*) Oh, yes! The remains of the first Christians
in the catacombs . . . ! Impressive!

(*He opens a room. The* GIRL *from scene 3 is crawling on all fours toward a corner. Weak light on her. The rest of the room is in shadow.
The pistol still lies abandoned on the floor.*)

5 GUIDE #2: What do we have here? What is she sniffing at like
a dog? (*Goes closer. Joking, gives her a slap on the rear. Suddenly
he changes expression, helps her to get up.*) What is this? Composure. Pull yourself together.
GIRL: (*Lost.*) He told me to wait. They keep my head underwa-
10 ter, until . . .
GUIDE #2: (*Interrupts.*) Who threw water on you? This isn't
Carnival. Excuse me, I have to go back to work. (*Resumes his
professional tone. To the group.*) The paintings are fantastic, a
little deteriorated, but still . . . (*He shines a light on the
15 walls.*) Jesus, there's nothing! (*He sees a graffito in a corner,
crouches, shines a light on it.*) Gentlemen, come closer! (*Looks
more closely.*) What kind of filth is this? (*Stands.*) Please,
ladies, no! Excuse me, but the ladies may not look! (*He gestures them away.*) Gentlemen, if you like, but . . . (*To the
20 GIRL, very surprised.*) You did this? Your idea of fun? It was a
saint's head and they put a . . . (*He finishes with an expressive
gesture.*) Let go, let go of the pencil!
GIRL: No. It wasn't me.
GUIDE #2: (*Spots the pistol on the floor.*) What's this? Just a mo-
25 ment, gentlemen. (*He picks it up.*) How strange!
GIRL: He left it so that, so that . . .
GUIDE #2: So that you could bullshit me. (*He raises his arm as
though to hit her. Remembers the audience. Smiles.*) What negligence. (*Referring to the gun.*) I have to take care of everything
30 around here.
GIRL: I'm thirsty.
GUIDE #2: Then you'll pee and be even wetter. (*He shines his light
on the walls.*) There's nothing here either. But I swear there was.
And not this filth! (*He slaps her skirt.*) No way you're a virgin!

GIRL: I'm thirsty.   35
GUIDE #2: (*Looking around.*) Isn't there any water? In the other
room, there's a bathtub filled to overflowing.
GIRL: No! No, damn you!
GUIDE #2: What did I tell you? Does anyone understand
women? A difficult bunch. As you see, ladies and gentle- 40
men, there's nothing here either. Only the walls. And this
filth. (*To the* GIRL.) You weren't getting discouraged, were
you? He left you the pistol? How strange. Who am I to . . . ?
(*He shrugs.*) But don't touch it. If you squeeze the trigger, it's
all over. The baths and . . . (*He smiles.*) I'm meddling in 45
something that's none of my business. This is the safety. I'm
leaving it up. Careful with the trigger. Sit down.
GIRL: (*She sits, shakes her head.*) I don't want it.
GUIDE #2: There's no danger, stupid! The slightest touch and it
goes off.   50
GIRL: Take it!
GUIDE #2: (*Surprised.*) Why? Soaking and thirsty, it's not a good
combination. (*He puts the pistol on her lap, takes her hand and
places it on the weapon.*) Do you have a boyfriend? Touch this
and it's all over, done with.   55
GIRL: I'm thirsty. (*She raises her hands.*)
GUIDE #2: Right. Sorry. I forgot: Ladies and gentlemen, forgive us for the . . . (*He points to the wall.*) How mortifying!
If you would be so kind as to follow me . . . (*He opens the
door, indicates the exit. At this moment an* USHERETTE *arrives* 60
carrying a tray. She invites the group to have a glass of wine.)
Help yourselves, ladies and gentlemen. It's on the house.
There's no reason to be scared: you won't have to pay for it.
It's all included. Then we'll go on with our visit. (*A scream
is heard. To the audience.*) Who screamed? Who is the imbe- 65
cile who screamed?

SCENE EIGHT

The USHERETTE *steps close to the* GUIDE *and whispers a few words in
his ear.*

GUIDE: (*Making amends.*) Forgive me. In room 3 we are going
to find something interesting. "Finally!" you must be saying to yourselves. "We should have stayed home." (*He
laughs.*) Ah, theater's a risky business! What do you think?
TV's a better bet, isn't it? But no, gentlemen. All is not 5
lost. Please, gentlemen. I'm swallowing the "ladies" so I can
go faster. With so many "ladies and gentlemen, ladies and
gentlemen," I can't go on to anything else. (*He leads the
group through the passageway. The group is shunted aside by three
men carrying a long, half-finished table. It is missing a few strips* 10
*of wood on the surface. It is an ordinary table except that it has a
strap nailed to one end. One of the men carries a tool box.*) The
first Christians were very persecuted. They were fed to the
lions. (*The men put the table on the floor.*) Until San Martín.
What would the Spanish say about San Martín? "That son 15
of a bitch traitor. That black shit." (*The men start to saw and
drive nails, as though they were alone. They are blocking the passageway.*) Can't you work somewhere else? (*The men don't
answer.*) This way, gentlemen. Here's a little path. (*They*

vii. 1 this Guide is different from the Guide in scene 6. Since the
order of the scenes is up to the director, however, this Guide will
be called Guide #2 only in scene 7, where the shift occurs

viii. 14 **San Martín** General José de San Martín, the liberator (El
Libertador) of the southern part of South America, is an Argentine
national hero

20 *can't get through. The men move the table, forcing the group toward the* GIRL's *room.*)

WOMAN'S VOICE:

"Down he went to the river,
Oh, down he went down!"

25 GUIDE: What a pain in the ass she is with that lullabye! (*He looks at the door.*) Here we are again. We may as well . . . Through here. Sooner or later we'll see a whole scene. (*He opens. Joking.*) Well? Have you dried yourself? How's . . . (*There are some men surrounding the* GIRL. *The* GUIDE *quickly closes the door,* 30 *shoos the people away. With a false smile.*) No, I made a mistake. Room 3, they told me. Careful on the stairs. This way, ladies and gentlemen. Ladies, once again. It's nicer . . .

WOMAN'S VOICE:

35 "And his blood was running,
Oh, more than the water."

(*The* GUIDE *snorts. Two men have positioned the table against the wall, clearing the passage way. They are smoking cigarettes, like two workers taking a break.*)

GUIDE: (*To the* WORKMEN.) Room 3? This one here? (*The men nod yes.*) Thank you!

SCENE NINE

The room is lit with rosy light. Four chairs. There is a group comprising a man, a woman, and two other adults disguised as children, a girl and a boy. Their makeup is exaggerated, and their clothes are cheap, vulgar. The MOTHER *is sewing, the* FATHER *is seated a little apart, and the* CHILDREN *are playing at throwing a hoop.*

On the far side of the room are the CHIEF *and two* POLICEMEN. *They sit very erect with their arms crossed over their chests. The characters act very broadly, a little like marionettes. The tone is grossly exaggerated.*

GUIDE: (*In a professional tone, dry and rapid.*) Explanation: For Foreigners. July 2, 1971. Marcelo Verdt and his wife, Sara Palacio de Verdt, were kidnapped by a group of eight men. *Desaparecidos.* Both were members of RAF, Revolutionary 5 Armed Forces. According to information in the newspapers, the wife, before disappearing, brought the children to her sister for protection.

MOTHER: (*Moving her hand as though sewing.*) Children, I'm making a little outfit for the one who is best behaved!

10 CHILDREN: (*Playing.*) Thank you, Mommy!

POLICEMEN: (*Coming forward.*) Hands up, in the name of the law!

MOTHER: (*Raising her arm, protecting her face like the heroine in a silent movie.*) Oh! (*The* FATHER *doesn't move.*)

CHILDREN: Mommy, Mommy, who are they?

15 MOTHER: Don't be afraid, my darlings! No one is hurting your mother!

CHILDREN: Blessed Mommy!

POLICEMAN: (*Comes close, snatches at her clothes.*) You're disguised! (*Shoving her violently.*)

viii. 23–24 **Down . . . down** the Woman's Voice in this scene sings from the Blood Wedding lullabye   ix. 4–5 **RAF, or Revolutionary Armed Forces,** is the translation of the name of FAR, Fuerza Armada Revolucionaria, a left-wing guerilla group

CHILDREN: Mommy, Mommy, who are they? 20

POLICEMEN: Where's your husband?

MOTHER: I don't know!

CHILDREN: What do you mean, you don't know, Mommy! In the bathroom! Making caca! (*They call.*) Daddy! Daddy! They're looking for you! 25

FATHER: (*Gets up, comes forward, wide-eyed.*) Who? What's happening?

POLICEMAN: This is what's happening! It's all over! (*Screams.*) Silence everyone! Let's get out of this hole! The car's out front! 30

MOTHER: Not the children! They don't know anything about it!

POLICEMAN: Them too!

MOTHER: Have pity!

POLICEMEN: Silence! Let's go! Everyone!

(*They put the chairs together to make the car. All squeeze in. One of the* POLICEMEN *holds the hoop between his hands and handles it as though it were a steering wheel. He imitates the sound of a motor. The children wave. The* POLICEMAN *brakes suddenly. The others fall backward. They get out of the car, their gestures exaggeratedly frightened.*)

CHIEF: They fell! 35

MOTHER: (*On her knees.*) Pity!

POLICEMAN: What should we do with the kids?

CHILDREN: Daddy!

FATHER: (*Dignified.*) I'll protect you, don't be afraid. (*Puts his arms around them.*) 40

CHIEF: (*To the* POLICEMAN.) Idiot! Why did you bring the kids?

POLICEMAN: You said everyone, Chief.

MOTHER: They're innocent!

CHIEF: I'll see if they're not already lost. Kids: Who created the 45 flag?

MOTHER: (*Begging them.*) Answer right, answer right!

CHILDREN: (*In unison.*) Manuel Belgrano!

CHIEF: When?

CHILDREN: February 27, 1812. 50

CHIEF: Where?

CHILDREN: On the banks of the Paraná. He had it blessed right there, beneath a blue and white sky, blue and white sky, blue and white . . .

CHIEF: Exactly! Very good! (*Kisses them.*) Here's a prize. (*Gives* 55 *them each a piece of candy.*)

CHILDREN: Thank you, sir!

CHIEF: (*To the* MOTHER.) Take them home. And don't be long.

POLICEMAN: Chief, what if she doesn't return?

CHIEF: (*With an exaggeratedly sinister laugh, pointing to the* 60 FATHER.) This one stays here. It's in his interest that she return. (*To the* MOTHER.) Take my advice: be discreet. I'm doing you a favor. Don't be long. Take a taxi.

MOTHER: What are you going to do to him?

CHIEF: Nothing! From his eye to his sex. But only if I'm 65 vexed.

MOTHER: Marcelo!

FATHER: My love!

CHIEF: Take them home. We don't have any small sacks. They're only in the way. Move it. 70

MOTHER: Come, children! Give Daddy a kiss. (*The* FATHER *kisses them.*) Don't be afraid. We're going home.

CHILDREN: (*Happy.*) The men are nice, Mama!

MOTHER: (*Moves off with the* CHILDREN. *Picks up the outfit she*
75   *was sewing. To one of them.*) Tell Grandma that the hem was
turned here. Will you remember?

CHILD: Yes, Mama.

MOTHER: There's soup in the pot. Have it for supper.

CHILDREN: If you're not there, we won't eat any soup! We
80   won't eat any soup!

MOTHER: Be good!

CHILDREN: Where are you going, Mama?

MOTHER: I'm going with Daddy. You behave. (*Hugs them.*)

CHILDREN: Mommy! Mommy!

85   GUIDE: (*Choked up.*) It gets to you, doesn't it?

(*The* MOTHER *separates from the* CHILDREN *and returns toward the*
CHIEF. *During the good-bye scene the* POLICEMEN *were trying vari-
ous sacks—as though they were items of clothing—on the* FATHER.
They have found the right one. Then they take him out of the room.)

CHILDREN: (*Singing in a round.*) We won't eat any soup! We
won't eat any soup!

MOTHER: Here I am. Where's my husband?

CHIEF: Husband? What husband? Take off your clothes.

90   GUIDE: (*Quickly.*) Let's go! Let's get out of here! (*Claps his
hands.*) Out! Where's "Carnation, sleep and dream"? Who
wants more wine? (*Pushes the group toward the door.*) Follow
me! Quick! No dawdling! (*The group goes out. The* GUIDE
closes the door, leans against it.) Ouf!

SCENE TEN

GUIDE: A little wine! Careful . . . on the . . . stairs. (*The*
USHERETTE *brings him a glass of water.*) Water? For me? What
for? (*Remembers.*) Oh, right. She's waiting for water! Come,
gentlemen, this way. We're almost there. Just another little
5   minute. No reason to fret. (*Again they enter the room of the*
GIRL *from scenes 3, 7, and 8. Her clothes are drenched. The* GIRL *is
breathing anxiously. She's seated, with the pistol, which is dry, in
her lap. To the group.*) Come in. Careful on the stairs. Or
rather: fasten your seatbelts, no smoking. (*He laughs. To the*
10   GIRL, *very amiably.*) May I? (*He puts the glass and the pistol on
the floor. Takes the chair on which she is sitting. Offers it to a
woman in the audience.*) Sit, madam, sit. She may have wet it,
but she didn't piss on it! (*He dries the chair with a hankie. To
the woman.*) Please, have a seat! (*To the* GIRL.) They paid ad-
15   mission. Are you thirsty? (*The* GIRL, *lost, doesn't answer. The*
GUIDE *shakes her gently.*) Hey! Wake up. I'm asking you if
you're thirsty. (*The* GIRL, *shakes her head no.*) Oh, no? I
brought you water. Drink it. (*He takes the glass, brings it to
her lips. The* GIRL *resists.*) And now, what do I do with the
20   glass? I need my hands free. I'm working. This can't be!
Drink, little girl, drink. The water flowed . . . (*Forcing her.*)
There. There, that's good. So capricious! Well, I don't like
people pulling my leg. You're all wet. (*Puts his hand under
her skirt.*) Even your little firecracker. (*He laughs. Turns to-
25   ward the audience.*) Oh, excuse me. (*Takes the pistol.*) Shall I
take it? No? Freedom is within your grasp. No? (*He puts the*

---

ix. 75–76 **Tell Grandma that the hem was turned here** is
an encoded way of communicating the arrest

barrel *against her breast.*) How stupid. I can't. (*He cleans the
weapon, puts it in the* GIRL's *lap.*) I don't know why they trust
you so . . . It's loaded. If you had a boyfriend, old girl . . . But
like this. Idiot, why endure so much? (*Another* GUIDE *appears*   30
in the doorway.)

OTHER GUIDE: (*Shouting.*) What are you doing here? It's about to
start there! And they're giving out wine! It's not to be missed.
I saw it! Exceptional! You can understand everything!

GUIDE: Really? Step on it, fellas, let's go! Move it, girls!   35

OTHER GUIDE: (*Teases.*) Don't you mean ladies and gentlemen?

GUIDE: (*To* OTHER GUIDE.) There's wine? For sure? (OTHER
GUIDE *affirms it and leaves.*) If you would be so kind, ladies
and gentlemen . . . (*He holds open the door so the group can pass
through. Before closing the door, in a friendly way.*) Think about   40
it, little girl.

SCENE ELEVEN

In the passageway, one of the vertical wooden boxes.

GUIDE: Wait! This has always intrigued me . . . (*Tries to see
through the peephole.*) I can't see a thing. How about you, sir?
(*Someone from the audience has a look.*) It's very dark. (*He
knocks at the door. Jokingly.*) Is anyone home? *Hay alguien?*
(*Curious, he opens the door. There's a heavily madeup man inside,*   5
dressed in a loincloth, staring fixedly. Matter of factly.) Hi. (*He
closes the door, turns toward the audience with an uncomfortable
smile. As though it were not so strange.*) What a surprise! To me
this is very curious . . .

OTHER GUIDE: (*Shouts from the doorway of the other room.*) Well?   10
What are you waiting for? A carriage? If you don't get there
at the beginning, they won't understand anything!

GUIDE: (*Annoyed, referring to the vertical box.*) What about this?
Does anyone understand this? (*To the* OTHER GUIDE.) I give
the orders in my group! And if they don't get it, too bad for   15
them! This way, gentlemen! (*He leads them in the opposite direction.*) Follow me! (*A panting death rattle is heard through the
door of a room they pass.*)

SCENE TWELVE

GUIDE: (*He lingers in front of the door, listening to the death rattle inside.*) What could this be? (*A* MAN *passes by, whistling.*)

MAN: (*To* GUIDE.) Good day!

GUIDE: Good day! (*Surprised.*) Well, he's happy! Let's follow   5
him. (*Referring to the death rattle in the room.*) Sounds like
that and we've really got a mess on our hands! We can check
it out later. (*He and the group follow the* MAN. *The* MAN *walks
along, whistling. He meets another man who is coming from the
opposite direction.*)   10

MAN: Good day!

NEIGHBOR #1: Hello! How's it going, doctor?

(*They shake hands. They continue walking together. The group follows them. They enter a large room, where* NEIGHBOR #2 *is sweeping
the floor. Two chairs stacked in a corner, against the wall.*)

NEIGHBOR #2: Hello, doctor!

GUIDE: (*To his group.*) Watch out for the cars! Stay on the side-
walk, please!

(*He situates them. He hasn't finished doing so when the* FIRST GROUP OF MEN *enters at a trot, one behind the other, tied together at their waists.*)

15 FIRST GROUP OF MEN: Let us through! Let us through!

(*They come forward, trot through the room, then suddenly halt in front of the* MAN *and surround him, forming a closed circle.*)

MAN: Excuse me.
FIRST GROUP OF MEN: Quieto! Quieto!
MAN: Are you calling me? What do you want? (*The men accelerate, tightening their circular movement, forming two closed rings.*)
20   Excuse me. Let me through.
NEIGHBOR #1: What's going on, doctor?
NEIGHBOR #2: (*Stops sweeping.*) Hey! Let him go!
NEIGHBOR #3: (*From the audience.*) What the hell is going on? (*Comes forward to help the* MAN.)
25 MAN: Let me go! Enough fooling around!

(*He pushes, tries to get through the circle. Hits, struggles. The men try to drag him toward the door.*)

NEIGHBORS: Let him go! Let him go!

(*They try to break up the group,* NEIGHBOR #2 *hitting out with his broom. The* SECOND GROUP OF MEN *enters, also at a trot and tied together at their waists. They sing.*)

SECOND GROUP OF MEN:

> Peace and security
> That is our domain
30   > With a little authority
> Order will be maintained!

(*Observing the tumult, they linger.*)

OFFICIAL: (*Heading the* SECOND GROUP OF MEN.) What's going on here? This is scandalous! Halt! Separate!

(*The fight freezes.*)

NEIGHBORS: (*All at the same time.*) Sir, they were pushing him!
35   (*Alternating.*)
    —Over here.
    —Over there.
    —They tied him up.
    —They dragged him down!
40 OFFICIAL: One at a time, magpies. Who asked you anything? (*To the group in the fight.*) And you, you're prisoners in the name of the law. (*He "aims" at them, with his finger. The* SECOND GROUP OF MEN *"handcuffs" them. They're all, including the* MAN *put into a line and tied together at the wrists.*)
45 NEIGHBORS: Officer, sir:
    Why the arrest?
    He's one of the best!

---

17 **Quieto!** Roberto Quieto, whose surname in fact means "quiet," was a prominent, highly respected liberal lawyer. Unbeknownst to most, he was also a powerful member of the Montoneros, the premier left-wing guerrilla organization

OFFICIAL: It doesn't matter, my esteemed citizens
    Have faith
    Justice is there for a reason   50
    To prevent baseness, which is treason.
NEIGHBORS: But we saw . . .
OFFICIAL: What you saw is of no consequence
    If there's offense
    Rest assured   55
    The man's secure . . .
SECOND GROUP OF MEN: Sure!

(*They "take aim" at the* NEIGHBORS.)

OFFICIAL: In my providence.

(*The* NEIGHBORS *mix in with the audience. The* OFFICIAL *moves off to the side, crosses his arms, his expression serious. The* FIRST GROUP OF MEN *and the* MAN *attacked in the first place draw near. One of the men from the second group arranges the chairs.*)

OFFICIAL: (*Seating himself. To the* MAN.) Name.
MAN: Quieto.   60
GUIDE: (*Shouts.*) Sí, Quieto! (*To his group.*) Quieto means quiet. (*Smiles.*) Stop a moment. (*Gestures toward the group.*) So they'll understand. Otherwise, they'll miss the point. (*The others stop the action. In a dry, professional tone.*) Explanation: For Foreigners. July 7, 1971. Robert Quieto, attorney, defender of politi- 65 cal prisoners, resists a kidnapping attempt. Fortunately, the neighbors intervene and call a police squad. The kidnappers turn out to be policemen. Dr. Quieto was put at the disposition of the executive power. Subsequently he was accused of having been implicated in an auto theft and of having par- 70 ticipated, after his detention, in various subversive acts. He was transferred to Rawson Prison, 730 miles from Buenos Aires. What happened then? I don't remember. Lost in the night of time. (*Smiles.*) But he wasn't so innocent. High up in the Montoneros, the son of a b——. It's not my responsibil- 75 ity. Although when you have the truth, I don't know why it should be hidden. Go on. I'm done.
OFFICIAL: (*To the* MAN.) Name.
MAN: Quieto.
OFFICIAL: Quieto! That's what I'm telling *you!* Now what is 80 your name?
MAN: Blame.
OFFICIAL: (*Suspicious.*) Ohhhh? (*To the* FIRST GROUP OF MEN.) And you? What are your names?
FIRST GROUP OF MEN: (*They sing.*)   85

> Peace and security
> That is our domain
> With a little authority
> Order will be maintained!

SECOND GROUP OF MEN: 90

> If you're lying
> You'll get bruised!

OFFICIAL: Explain what happened
    I'm confused!
FIRST GROUP OF MEN: 95

> Boca will never lose!
> Boca's the team we choose!

OFFICIAL: (*Very pleased.*) For this, you are excused. But who
    began . . .

100 FIRST GROUP OF MEN: That man!

OFFICIAL: No more rhyming! (*To the* MAN.) Don't you know
    that it's a crime to incite a riot in the street? (*To the* SECOND
    GROUP OF MEN.) Did they stop traffic?

SECOND GROUP OF MEN: Yes, sir! They delayed it!

105 OFFICIAL: For how long?

SECOND GROUP OF MEN: For three minutes!

OFFICIAL: Re-create it!

SECOND GROUP OF MEN:

> In their cars the men grew irritated
110 > At the office work accumulated.

OFFICIAL: (*To the first group, fiercely.*) I want a confession.
    (*Sweetly.*) What team are you from?

FIRST GROUP OF MEN:

> Boca will never lose
115 > Boca . . .

OFFICIAL: Fine, fine, no need to repeat! (*The* FIRST GROUP OF
    MEN *"free" their hands, which had been "cuffed." To the* MAN.)
    What about you?

MAN: What about me?

120 OFFICIAL: What team are you from?

MAN: I nurse the same illusion.

OFFICIAL: I smell collusion. Why aren't you from San Lorenzo?

MAN: Because I'm not?

OFFICIAL: Don't be a wise guy! (*The* SECOND GROUP OF MEN
125   *hit* MAN. *To the others.*) And you, what are you waiting for?
    Get going!

MAN: You can't let them go! They attacked me! I want to see
    my attorney!

OFFICIAL: The one who gives the orders here is me. (*To the others.*)
130   And you, once again, (*Sweetly.*) why don't you do your work?

FIRST GROUP OF MEN: (*Tied together at their waists, they trot out,*
    singing.)

> For us it was a sad event
> That ended to our detriment
135 > Of this our song's a testament!
> For us it was a sad event
> That ended to our detriment
> Of this our song's a testament!

OFFICIAL: (*To the* MAN.) Justice will be done.

(*One of the men in the second group puts on a judge's robe and comes*
closer. Another moves in a chair and has him sit. Becoming the
GUARD, *he remains standing behind the* JUDGE's *back.*)

140 JUDGE: (*To the* MAN.) You're free. Being from Boca's no crime.
    But next time . . .

114–115 **Boca** the Boca Juniors are one of the most important
Argentine soccer teams. Their home stadium is in the Buenos
Aires neighborhood of La Boca, traditionally an Italian working-
class section. San Lorenzo is another team from Greater Buenos
Aires. Soccer is by far the most passionately followed sport in
Argentina

(*The* MAN *frees his hands and stands up. The* JUDGE *turns halfway*
around and grabs him from behind. No sooner has he done so when
the GUARD *leans into the* MAN *and pushes him roughly down by*
the shoulders, forcing him to sit. The MAN *again joins his hands as*
though they were handcuffed.)

OFFICIAL: (*To the* MAN.) You stole a car. Your trial's pending.
    Your sentence could be unending!

MAN: I need defending!

OFFICIAL: Superintending! (*To the* JUDGE.) He stole a car.   145

JUDGE: He did not steal a car!

MAN: Am I absolved? Can I go?

JUDGE: Why not? Go ahead!

(*He turns so that his back is to the* MAN. *The previous scene is repeated:*
the MAN *frees his hands, the* GUARD *forces him to sit down again, etc.*)

OFFICIAL: He robbed a bank!

MAN: I was in prison!   150

JUDGE: (*It starts again.*) Absolved!

MAN: Thank you. Can I go?

JUDGE: Why not? Go ahead. (*Again. The rhythm speeds up.*)

OFFICIAL: He robbed a station!

JUDGE: (*Over his shoulder.*) What kind of station?   155

OFFICIAL: Service station. Five old wrecks.

MAN: (*Forced to sit.*) How? I was in prison!

OFFICIAL: (*With pretended fury.*) Guards, you let him go?

JUDGE: (*Turns.*) Why can't you see? There is no case. Let him
    go free! (*Turns his back.*)   160

OFFICIAL: He robbed a commissary, several stores, and several
    dairies!

MAN: (*Forced to sit.*) If I'd been seized
    How could I be eating cheese?

JUDGE: He is innocent   165
    Surely
    I declare it
    Firmly.

MAN: (*Stands up, etc.*) Thank you. Can I go?

JUDGE: Naturally. Why not. (*It starts again. The action accelerates*   170
    to the point of dislocation but always remains precise. The speeches
    are transferred but not the actions, which remain a constant with
    each character.)

OFFICIAL: Don't move. I've heard a little story!

JUDGE: He murdered a canary.   175

MAN: That isn't fair!
    I love all canaries
    Everywhere!

OFFICIAL: You love them, but you kill them!

JUDGE: Guards, you let him go?   180

OFFICIAL: Your Honor, you're the witness
    Of this bad faith.

MAN: I only want to live!

JUDGE: Guards, you let him go?

OFFICIAL: If he'd been seized   185

MAN: How could I've been eating cheese?

JUDGE: Thank you.

OFFICIAL: Beat it! I can't stand you anymore!

MAN: I'm going back to my city!

JUDGE: Can I go?   190

OFFICIAL: Beat it!

MAN: (*Resisting those who are making him sit.*) No, no, I was in prison!

JUDGE: He's free! Oh, such obsession!

OFFICIAL: He's free! What fascination!

195 MAN: But I'm not!

JUDGE: Yes, you are! So you better shut up! (*Turns his back, covers his ears.*)

OFFICIAL: Enough already! He's hard to handle. All that screaming. What a scandal!

(*Gestures to the guards to take the* MAN *away. To the audience.*)

The idiots they send me, it's outrageous!
200 The courts
aren't beneficial
Unless they're
sacrificial!

(*Lights out.*)

GUIDE: Shit! What happened? They turned out the light with-
205 out telling me! Cretins! (*Take out his flashlight, switches it on.*) Where is the door? Luckily I know the house. (*Opens door. The passageway is lit.*) This way, gentlemen. There aren't any stairs. But be careful all the same. You only get to stumble once, like the tango says. Hey, hey. Everyone make it? (*He
210 leads the group through the passageway. They pass the door to the room where the death rattle was heard. It is heard again. The* GUIDE *puts his ear to the door. Admiringly.*) Persistent! We go in? We don't go in? What do you want to do? Free choice. At my orders! We go in!

SCENE THIRTEEN

The GUIDE *opens the door. The labored breathing stops. There is a* GIRL *with long hair laid out on a stretcher, with a sheet carefully folded under her feet.*

GUIDE: (*Advancing on tiptoe.*) Don't make any noise. She's sleep-ing. (*He approaches, looks at her. The* GIRL *smiles at him. Sweetly.*) How're you doing?

GIRL: (*Sits up, brushes her hair off her face, folds her hands in her lap.*
5 *She looks at the group with a semismile. Silence. Then, very simply, colloquially.*)
I would like to die
as softly as possible
So that my friends will think
10 she is sleeping
in the earth
become a worm
digging in the earth
so that in spring
15 the flowers blossom
After my death
I want my children
to sit at the table
and say
20 at her age
Mama
ran off with some guy
What a shame
poor old Dad

staring at the tablecloth   25
his cup of coffee
searching for her
This is how I want to die
as simply
as though I had never lived   30
What a lovely thought
to leave like that
not causing any pain
The cup of coffee
that no one drinks   35
absent . . .

(*Silently, a character mixed in with the audience goes up to the* GIRL. *He puts his hand over her mouth and nose. The* GIRL *offers desperate, mute resistance. She dies. The man gently lays her out, covers her with the sheet. Then he moves off and mixes in with the crowd, like one more spectator.*)

GUIDE: (*Amazed.*) How about that? (*Looks at the man.*) And now he's so calm! But what a feat! Phenomenal! (*He lifts the sheet. Matter of factly.*) She's dead. Poor creature! Really, with-out so much as a moan. Discreet. And in the bloom of   40 youth! (*Lets the sheet fall.*) She spoke of children, a husband. We'll have to go find them. Nice news I've got. What a bad deal. (*Hopefully.*) Anyone want to go? Of course, for this there are no volunteers. (*Furious.*) The son of a bitch. (*He goes to the door, leaving the audience.*) Excuse me. (*He opens the   45 door, yells out.*) I need someone from the family! Quick! Someone from the family! (*He comes back inside.*) She didn't move, did she? What with the advances of medicine, for a moment I thought that . . .

(FOUR MEN *enter, two-by-two, each pair moving as one. They are wearing white smocks down to their feet, very loose, belted at the waist. They come in on skates. Their faces are painted with large red smiling mouths. One pair beats pot lids; the other pair waves a white sack.*)

FOUR MEN: (*Singing.*)   50

Tachín, tachín, tachín
She died as she would have ordained
Without causing any pain.

GUIDE: What about the family? I've got to tell them . . . It's so unfortunate . . . My heartfelt sympathy. (*Extending his   55 hand.*)

FOUR MEN: (*They pay no attention to the* GUIDE. *They approach the stretcher, lift the sheet. Sing.*)

The jokester
Coaxed her   60

GUIDE: (*Very confused.*) Choked her . . . A son of a bitch who . . . (*Searches with his eyes. The* MEN *start putting the* GIRL *into the sack. Surprised.*) What are you doing? But . . .

FOUR MEN: (*Sing.*)

But nothing   65
But nothing
Just doing our bit
Ashes to ashes
Shit to shit

GUIDE: (*Indignant.*) That's gross! Don't you see there's people?   70 You must have been raised in a barn! Ladies, your forgiveness. I knew nothing … The modern theater is like this. No respect for the ladies!

FOUR MEN:

(They finish putting the GIRL into the sack, leaving her head out. They tie the end of the sack around her neck. It is evident that the GIRL is playing dead: though her head is bent over, she is able to support it. The FOUR MEN hold the bundle, swing it hammocklike. They sing.)

75   If you don't like this Tin Pan band
        Because it hasn't any flair
        Because it just gave you a scare
        Swing high, swing well
        You can go to hell!

80 GUIDE: Go on!
   FOUR MEN:

        Tachín, tachín, tachín,
        Tachín, tachín, tachín!
        Pran-pran-pran!
85   Taratá-ta-ta!

(They near the door. The HUSBAND and MOTHER enter. The HUS-BAND is wearing threadbare clothing. His hair is long and all over the place. The MOTHER is the typical little old lady—black clothes, shawl over her head. Both act crudely, like prototypes of desperate people.)

HUSBAND: What happened? I heard screams!
MOTHER: Sirs, have pity! Where is my daughter? Darling! Darling!
GUIDE: Oh my God, the family's here!
90 MOTHER and HUSBAND: *(Together.)* We've come to look for our poor Hermenegilda.
FOUR MEN:

(They come back, set the corpse down; it supports itself against the stretcher. Horrified.)

That name she inherited
She certainly merited!
95 MOTHER and HUSBAND: *(Together.)* We're here to find out
        What she finally merited!
GUIDE: Oh no! If these two speak in verse, I'm leaving!
        Although the language may be terse,
        I can't bear
100   so much pain.
        I'm leaving! *(He pushes away from the crowd, but upon hearing the HUSBAND, he stops, comes back.)*
HUSBAND: Where is she?
FOUR MEN: *(They shake the corpse in front of the HUSBAND's face.)*
105   We don't know! We don't know! She was never here!
HUSBAND: What do you mean? She came here to buy wine!
FOUR MEN: *(They turn the corpse facedown on the stretcher, look un-derneath.)* She bought her bread and went away, evaporated … Surely it was fated! *(They look at the ceiling. The HUSBAND and
110   MOTHER imitate them. The men point.)* Look sir. That moth …
HUSBAND: She wasn't a moth! At dawn …
FOUR MEN: She was a moth. At dawn
        Before the sun came up full
        we found her eating
115   wool

MOTHER: It's not true! She didn't like wool!
FOUR MEN: Was she a woman or a moth?
        The question's far from risible.
        Lady, lady don't be miserable.
        Don't be upset   120
        We'll give you your daughter yet.

(They approach an interior door. They call the HUSBAND and MOTHER as one would a dog.)

Tch, tch, tch …

(The HUSBAND and MOTHER advance, their smiles exaggeratedly hopeful. The others open the door. The interior is dark. The HUS-BAND and MOTHER look in.)

FOUR MEN: You'll find her here, here!
        So be of good cheer, cheer!
        *(Moving in unison, the FOUR MEN push them inside with kicks in   125
        the rump.)* And stop mugging! *(They close the door. They sway.)*
        Ladies, Gentlemen, dearest friends
        Our show is over, Curtains!

(They take the corpse. They lead the way to the exit, singing.)

        Tachín, tachín, tachín!
        Tachín, tachín, tachín!
        Tarará-ta-ta!   130
        Tarará-ta-ta!

GUIDE: *(Enthused.)* Let's go, let's go! Let's follow them! See what happens! They're entertaining! *(The group follows the FOUR MEN and GUIDE. The FOUR MEN enter a contiguous room   135
and close the door. An actor, pretending to be part of the audience, opens it. The interior is dark. An enormous club comes out and hits the actor over the head. He falls. The GUIDE leans over him.)* Why did he butt in? I'm the Guide here! One to a group! *(He pokes him. The man doesn't move. He then lifts him by the armpits   140
and puts him into one of the vertical boxes. He talks all the while, completely dissociated from his actions.)* That's how it is. In they all go but … who takes the potatoes out of the fire? The son of a bitch. If he was part of the audience, why did he make like an actor? Vanity, vanity will be the end of us all! …   145
(He closes the door.) Now what were we going to see?
SOMEONE FROM THE AUDIENCE: The catacombs.
GUIDE: Right. Thank you. The first Christians really had a hard time of it. Just thinking about how the lions loved to chew them up … Human meat, they say, is sweet. Sweet, bit-   150
ter, what could be stupider. *(They cross with another group. To the OTHER GUIDE.)* Where's there something good? We went in here, and it's all fucked up. *(Without stopping, the OTHER GUIDE points to a door.)*

SCENE FOURTEEN

The GUIDE leads the group into the designated room. Inside is a group of NEIGHBORS all crowded together, some looking over the heads of others. On the far side, two POLICEMEN crouch, their expressions very attentive. In the center are the MAN and WOMAN, both heavily made-up. Their clothes are cheap, flashy; the WOMAN wears very high heels. All the acting is crude, infantile, and exaggerated.

GUIDE: Attention. Ladies and gentlemen, this is the main course. So they tell me. Hope it's true. Make yourselves comfortable. If you find a chair, be seated. Silence, please. The story of a BM, or bad marriage. (*His tone is professional, dry and quick.*) Explanation: For Foreigners. On the afternoon of July 13, 1971, Juan Pablo Maestre and his wife, Mirta Elena Misetich, were kidnapped by a group of men. Juan Pablo Maestre managed to run a few yards but then was shot. Mirta Elena Misetich ran in the opposite direction, losing a shoe. She was captured and pushed into one car; her husband was thrown into another. Shortly afterward, a police squad sent to the scene recovered the shoe and ordered the doorman of an apartment building to wash the blood from the pavement. The body of Juan Pablo Maestre appeared days later in Escobar. Of Mirta Elena Misetich there was no further news. Both belonged to the RAF, or Revolutionary Armed Forces. Juan Pablo Maestre, twenty-eight years old. Mirta Elena Misetich, the same age.

MAN: (*With a conspiratorial air.*) Let's plant a bomb here

WOMAN: (*With a conspiratorial air.*) And a bomb over there!

MAN: When these go off

WOMAN: No one will be spared!

MAN and WOMAN: (*Taking bombs with fuses out from under their clothes.*) Subversion, subversion,
all rise up!
in revolution!

MAN: (*Looking around.*) Let's go, all clear!

WOMAN: Nothing will be left here! (*They take a few cautious steps.*)

POLICEMAN: (*Comes forward, arm extended.*) Hands up! In the name of the law!

MAN: We're caught! Run! (*They drop their bombs and run in opposite directions.*)

POLICEMAN: (*Aims with his finger and shoots.*) Pum!

(*The MAN falls. His blood is obviously fake. The other POLICEMAN runs after the WOMAN.*)

WOMAN: (*Stops.*) Darling!

POLICEMAN: Hey, hey! Justice always triumphs! Olé!

(*The two POLICEMEN drag the MAN and WOMAN away. The WOMAN loses her shoe. They exit. Slowly, the NEIGHBORS untangle themselves and come forward.*)

NEIGHBORS: The ass must be judged
Not broken!

(*The two POLICEMEN reenter. The NEIGHBORS immediately reform their group.*)

POLICEMEN: Of our respect
Here's a token!

(*They're carrying the MAN, dragging him along. The NEIGHBORS watch, timidly come forward. Romantic music is heard. More POLICEMEN enter, smiling and wearing sweepers jackets. They swing long-handled brooms, dance as in a musical comedy.*)

---

xiv. 38–39 **"Of our respect / Here's a token"** is the couplet substituted for "violín, violón / es la mejor razón." See "Crisis, Terror, Disappearance"

GROUP OF POLICEMEN: (*They sing.*)

> We're here to clean!
> We're here to clean!
> The filth is gone
> Your street is clean!
> Let mothers pray
> let children play
> in celebration!

(*Smiling, they sweep. They lift the shoe. They sing.*)

> Little shoe, little shoe
> Whom might you belong to?
> Why, to Snow White
> or to her mother.

GUIDE: What do you mean, fellas! The little lost shoe was Cinderella's!

POLICEMAN: (*Emphatically.*) I say it's Snow White's or her mother's. (*Recovering his smile.*) Whose little shoe is this? Madam, is it yours? Say yes. A Prince Charming awaits you in the wings.

GUIDE: No, no! Error! It's the prince, the prince who searches for the owner of the shoe, not a cop! Didn't you read the story?

POLICEMAN: Calm down! It's a free interpretation. (*Smiling.*) Doesn't it belong to anyone? Neighbors? (*He shows them the shoe. The NEIGHBORS immediately deny ownership, shaking their heads in unison.*) So we'll look in another neighborhood. It'll belong to someone. (*He repeats, frowning in the GUIDE's direction.*) It's Snow White's or her mother's.

GUIDE: (*Servile.*) Yes, of course, her mother's. Well, let's get going. We can follow you, can't we? (*To his group.*) We'll just stroll along. If you get tired, let me know.

GROUP OF POLICEMEN: (*They go out with the shoe. Asking.*) Madam, is this yours? Is this yours? Young man? (*The group follows them. They enter another room. The WOMAN, wearing no makeup, is seated on a chair. Sitting nearby on the floor, with her legs crossed, is a GIRL, who may be the same as the one from scene 13.*)

POLICEMAN: (*To the WOMAN.*) Madam, excuse me. We found a little shoe. Is it yours? Prince Charming will marry you. Cash in a flash! You'll live in a palace! Let's see. (*He puts the shoe on her foot.*) She's Cinderella! It fits! Perfect! What luck, old girl! You win! A royal flush! (*Bows.*) Princess! My respects! (*The WOMAN stares ahead, immobile. Surprised.*) Aren't you happy? What's the matter?

WOMAN: My darling!

POLICEMAN: Your darling was stopped by a cop. (*The POLICEMEN exit arm-in-arm, tap dancing.*)

WOMAN: I was at home, eating my bread. I was
making love. I was kissing my children.
And you will be the only one who knows
where and how my body was lost,
how my voice became unstrung
Only you will know
how to know
the voices of fear and the faces of
desperation
My God, what did the brave ones become?
I will speak

Only you will know
this tongue.

(*A shot is heard.*)

GUIDE: What's going on? Did you hear that? It was a shot.
(*Looks at the* WOMAN *and the* GIRL.) But why so quiet! It's
100   over. Gentlemen, follow me. Did you like that? (*He leads his
group out of the room.*) A bit mixed up, wasn't it? Me . . . well,
what do you like . . . I'm old-fashioned. I prefer something
else. If this was the main course, what will the others be?
(*They enter the adjoining room. The* GIRL *of scenes 3, 7, and 8 lies
105   on the floor, shot, the pistol in her hand. The* GUIDE *looks at her,
surprised. Then, matter of factly, pushing them toward the exit.*)
Oh, sorry! Shall we? The jug may as well go to the fountain
as . . . (*Happy music is heard.*) How about that music! So
there is a little happiness in this world! Enough drama!
110   Let's go. Move along. A little gaiety, dammit!

(*The poem spoken by the* WOMAN *was written by Marina, a Greek
girl, who was captured and tortured.*)

SCENE FIFTEEN

As the group leaves, the music fades and after a few minutes disappears.
Through the passageway comes a group holding hands. They sing.

GAME PLAYERS:
—Martin Fisherman, will you let me pass?
—Pass, pass, but the last one stays with me!

(*The group starts playing Martin Fisherman, a singing game somewhat like London Bridge Is Falling Down. Two children make a
bridge with their arms; the others run underneath, single file, holding
each other by the waist. The line of children sings for permission to pass
through; the last one is taken prisoner. In another version, the children
making the bridge ask questions. Those who answer correctly pass
through; the others do not. Two lines form, one comprising the "free,"
the other "prisoners." After everyone has had a question, the longer line
wins, and the game may start again.*)

GUIDE: Ladies and gentlemen, you're welcome to participate.
5   That's not coercion, only if you want to. Grotowsky used to
say: The more physical distance, the more spiritual closeness. What nonsense! Don't be afraid to join in, ladies and
gentlemen!

(*The game continues. Suddenly one of the men forming Martin Fisherman's bridge yells.*)

GAME PLAYERS: (*Alternately.*)
10   —I know that one! Don't let him go!
—Me?

(*The latter tries to get off the bridge.*)

—I know that one! Don't let him go!
—Don't fight!
—Just answer right!
15   —I don't have to! No!

(*He whistles over his shoulder for help. Those in his line start to push.
The others shout.*)

—Don't push! Hold tight!
—Wait!

(*Nevertheless they react. The shorter line becomes crooked. A man
forming the bridge yells.*)

—They're shooting! Hold tight!

(*The sound of a police whistle.* POLICEMEN *arrive, dressed like the cops
in Charlie Chaplin's The Kid, with large, prehistoric-type clubs.
Music is heard. Their acting is crude. They immediately start hitting
those in the longer line over the head. The sound of the clubs: Plac!
Plac! Plac! Those hit fall into artificially distorted poses. The men
rush the bridge of Martin Fisherman, crushing the captured player,
who screams.*)

GUIDE: Kids today! They don't know how to play peacefully!
Let's get out of the way. I wonder if they'll tie them up.   20
(*Warns a* POLICEMAN.) Not the audience! (*The* POLICEMAN
*moves his head like Harpo Marx. He spins around like an acrobat,
beating on actors mixed in with the public, acting as audience
members. Very confused.*) On the double, ladies and gentlemen, quickly! Let's go! No stragglers! My group this way!   25
Forward! Toward the music! (*Music floats in the air, disappears.*) Now what? (*He opens his hands in a gesture of incomprehension. Taking advantage of the* GUIDE*'s position, someone comes
forward and puts a tin plate full of garbage in his hands. To this
person, absolutely astonished.*) What is this? (*Protests.*) Not to   30
me you don't! This is not what I get paid for! Who do they
think they are?

(*Meanwhile, the game of Martin Fisherman has stopped. The* PO-
LICEMEN *and* ACTORS *from the shorter line carry off those who were
knocked unconscious and throw them into a room.*)

GUIDE: (*To the group.*) With so much confusion, I forgot about the
catacombs. You'll end up leaving without seeing anything.
WOMAN'S VOICE: 35

"The water was black there
under the branches.
When it reached the bridge
it stopped and sang."

GUIDE: (*Pleased.*) Her again! What persistence! You want to   40
risk it? Sooner or later it's got to improve!

(*He opens the door. The people inside won't let him in.*)

SCENE SIXTEEN

ACTOR #1: Sorry, old man. You can't come in. Off-limits.
GUIDE: Why not? I'm bringing people.
ACTOR #1: No, old man. We're rehearsing.
GUIDE: So what? Aren't you getting tired?
ACTOR #1: No! (*He closes the door.*)   5
GUIDE: (*Outraged.*) What balls. Sorry. (*He remembers something,
smiles.*) They're not gonna fuck with me. Psss! This way!
There's another entrance! (*He leads them along a passageway.*

---

xv. 36–39 **"The water . . . sang"** the Woman's Voice sings lines
from the *Blood Wedding* lullabye

They pass a vertical box like the others, only bigger. Naturally.)
10 Just a moment. (*He opens the door of the box. Inside, two men are plastered together. The* GUIDE *puts the tin plate on their shoulders. They stretch their necks desperately, trying to suck up what's on the plate. It falls. Matter of factly, to the audience.) They let it fall! What idiots! (He closes the door.)*

SCENE SEVENTEEN

GUIDE: Don't make a sound. Walk on tiptoe. Don't say a word. (*They enter a room. Folding screens around an illuminated central space.*) Sssh . . . Silence . . . (*The group watches the scene through the folding screens. Two* ACTORS *and two* ACTRESSES *are rehears-*
5 *ing Othello, in rehearsal clothes.* ACTRESS #1, *as Desdemona, is already dead on the floor.*)
ACTOR #1: (*As Iago.*) Villainous whore!
ACTRESS #2: (*As Emilia.*) She give it Cassio? No, alas, I found it, And I did give't my husband.
10 ACTOR #1: Filth, thou liest!
GUIDE: Such language!
ACTRESS #2: (*As Emilia.*) By heaven, I do not, I do not, gentlemen.
O murd'rous coxcomb! What should such a fool
15 Do with so good a wife?
ACTOR #2: (*As Othello.*) Are there no stones in heaven But what serves for the thunder?—Precious villain!

(*Othello runs at Iago. Iago strikes Emilia and leaves.* ACTOR #1 *marks his exit and sits off to one side. A* POLICEMAN *enters in Isabellesque attire.*)

POLICEMAN #1: (*To* ACTOR #2.) You killed those two women! Villain! Viper!

(*The* ACTRESSES *get up, go sit down. They watch calmly, a bit surprised.*)

20 ACTOR #1: Who told this guy to come in?
POLICEMAN #1: (*Acting, calling his men.*) Over here, men. Here!
ACTOR #1: Go act for the other side. Who called you. Get out of here!
POLICEMAN #1: Thou hast no weapon, and perforce must
25 suffer. They are dead.
ACTRESS #1: (*Joking.*) I am dead!
ACTRESS #2: (*Sings.*)

Willow, willow, willow.
Moor, she was chaste. She loved thee, cruel Moor!

30 ACTOR #1: Stop! (*To the* POLICEMAN.) Will you beat it!
POLICEMAN #1: To raise your sword against a woman!
ACTOR #2: What are you talking about?
ACTOR #1: The guy's a mental case. Beat it! (*He pushes him toward the door.*) Out! (*Returns.*) Better keep the door locked.
35 There's no telling who could walk in. Let's go, girls. That guy stank worse than a pig. (*Claps his hands.*) One more time!
POLICEMAN #1: (*Draws his sword.*) No, traitor!

---

xvii. 7 **Villainous whore!** lines from *Othello* are taken from act 5, scene 2, lines 229–235, 248–249, 256, 287, 306–307, 317, 367–371. All are found on pages 1239–1240 of *The Riverside Shakespeare* (Boston: Houghton Mifflin, 1974)

ACTOR #2: (*Returns. In spite of himself, in character.*) Wrench his sword from him. 40
POLICEMAN #1: Torments will ope your lips.
ACTOR #2: Well, thou dost best.
ACTOR #1: Cut! Right there!
POLICEMAN #1: Officers, come here! (*Another* POLICEMAN *enters, dressed in the same style.*) 45
POLICEMAN #2: What's happening, sir?
POLICEMAN #1: (*He shows him the vial he's just taken from his own pocket.*) Trotyl! And the women are dead! Oh my! O thou pernicious caitiff!
POLICEMAN #2: (*With his sword, rounds up the* ACTORS, *who* 50 *move into a corner.*) Move it, or I'll take a slice! (*The* AC-TRESSES *let out an inappropriate laugh.*)
POLICEMAN #1: Take them, too, for having laughed at the wrong time! (*In a dramatic voice.*)
To you, Lord Governor, 55
Remains the censure of this hellish villain,
The time, the place, the torture, O, enforce it!
Myself will straight aboard, and to the state
This heavy act with heavy heart relate.

(*He takes a gun from his pocket, forces the* ACTORS *to exit.*)

GUIDE: (*To his group.*) A bit confusing, the way that happened, 60 don't you think? So you understand. (*He walks into the light. In a professional, dry and rapid voice.*) Explanation: For Foreigners. (*Fierce and rude.*) Does anyone really need an explanation? If you want to act like actors, just go into a tenement and howl like dogs, throw a good scare into people. If 65 you don't have money, people will be even more afraid. Why scream? Why pretend? When no one can open his mouth, why would anyone scream gratuitously? (*He waits for a response, which he doesn't get.*) Okay then! (*Resumes his professional tone.*) August 6, 1971. The police burst into an 70 old house with many rooms, like this one, in the city of Santa Fe. In one of the rooms they find eight hundred grams of trotyl. They say. One journalist and three members of the Grupo 67 theater are arrested. They're taken to Buenos Aires on suspicion of subversive actions. The district attor- 75 ney recommended they be absolved on the benefit of doubt. They were absolved May 24, 1972. (*Change of tone.*) Few are called, many are chosen. Nine months in the cage. In misery. Well, that's life! (*He leaves the illuminated space, goes back to his group.*) Wait! The show goes on! 80

SCENE EIGHTEEN

A sort of deformed CHILD-MONSTER, *dressed in a floor-length white shirt with lots of lace and frills. He is heavily made-up. Others disguised as* CHILDREN *follow. The* CHILD-MONSTER *clutches a club. They sing.*

CHILDREN:

Anton, Anton Pirulero
each one, each one
attends to his game
and he who does not 5
he who does not
will suffer the blame.

(*The* CHILDREN *sit in a circle around the* CHILD-MONSTER, *who calls to one of the bigger children and gives him the club. The latter stays outside the ring. They play* Anton Pirulero, *in which the child playing Anton is in the center of the circle, turning around and around, his arms extended like wings. The others keep singing and pretend to play musical instruments—guitar, cornet, violin, etc. They have to be very alert, for if Anton Pirulero stops and points at one of them with his arm and that child isn't moving his own arms like Anton, then that child loses. He who loses three times is out. The game is played singing, and very fast.*)

CHILD-MONSTER: (*He is Anton Pirulero. In an out-of-tune sing-song.*)

10
    Anton, Anton Pirulero
    each one, each one
    attends to his game
    and he who does not
    he who does not
    will suffer the blame.

(*Now they play only guitar. The child with the club goes to the one who has changed places with Anton and hits him. The child falls. The game continues, faster every time. The* CHILD-MONSTER *never finishes his song, the game falls apart, and the child with the club hits out indiscriminately. Finally, the only ones left unharmed are the* CHILD-MONSTER *and the character with the club. They wave their arms and sing. The* CHILD-MONSTER *glares at the other one, more and more menacingly. He aims with his finger as though it were a revolver and kills the other child. Pum! He plays alone, his gestures increasingly spastic. The song "Anton Pirulero" becomes unintelligible. The lights go out.*)

15 GUIDE: What now? Why did they kill the lights?
VOICES: (*Singing.*)

    Anton, Anton Pirulero
    each one
    each one
20
    attends to his game.

(*Lights up. In the same space,* THREE MEN *and a* YOUNG WOMAN. *The* CHILD-MONSTER *laughs in his labored way, waves his arms, stutters.*)

CHILD-MONSTER: D-d-d-ow-ow-n-n-n! S-s-s-i-i-i-t-t-d-d-d-ow-n-n-n-n!

(*He aims his hand like a revolver. The* MEN *and* WOMAN *don't seem to notice his presence. They sit of their own volition.*)

FIRST MAN: What is your game?
SECOND MAN: Fear.
25 FIRST MAN: And yours?
THIRD MAN: Fear.
FIRST MAN: (*To the* YOUNG WOMAN.) What is your game?
YOUNG WOMAN: Fear. (*Pause.*) And the question.
FIRST MAN: What question?
30 YOUNG WOMAN: Why fear? My name is Marina. I am twenty years old. I am Greek, a prisoner, and I have been tortured. (*The* CHILD-MONSTER *stutters low, furiously. He keeps playing, getting all tangled up in his own movements.*)
    Time is altered, the years to come are altered

You know where you will find me   35
I, fear, I, death
I, the memory beyond reach
I, the recollection of the tenderness of your hands
I, the sadness of our broken life
I will defeat "it's not my concern" with my   40
    anguish
blast their alien sleep with fireworks,
    horrible and indecent
with countless shootings I will fall on the indifference
of those who pass by   45
until they begin to ask, to ask themselves
THREE MEN: (*In an even tone.*) Why fear?
    Why torture?
    Why deaths?

(*Stuttering and autistic, the* CHILD-MONSTER *plays.*)

THREE MEN: Who set limits?   50
    Who once said: this much thirst
    this much water?
    Who once said: this much air
    this much fire?
    Who once said: here the ken   55
    of men and women
    here the bounds?
    Only hope has sharp knees.
    They are bleeding.

(*Darkness.*)

(*The poem spoken by the* YOUNG WOMAN *was written by Marina. The poem spoken by the* THREE MEN *is Juan Gelman's.*)

GUIDE: Now what? There they go again cutting the light   60
    without warning me! I understand less and less. We're the ones who bear the brunt of this show. I shit on poetry! Watch your wallets! And I left my flashlight. This way, this way. It's so dark! Don't touch each other! Whose little ass is this?   65

(*He laughs. Opens the door. The passageway is illuminated.*)

    Ah! Light, more light! What a phrase! Only a genius could come up with that one, eh?
WOMAN'S VOICE:

    "Ay-y-y, for the big horse
    who didn't like water"   70

GUIDE: Still at it! Now that's perseverance! (*Baroque music is heard. The* GUIDE *puts his ear to the door. Unsure.*) Do we go in here? I don't remember. Oh well, let's do it! Come along, gentlemen! You're almost there!

---

59 s.d. **The poem . . . Gelman's** Gelman's lines are: "Quien puso limites? / Quien dijo alguna vez: hasta aquí la sed? hasta aquí el agua? / Quien dijo alguna vez: hasta aquí el aire, hasta aquí el fuego? / Quien dijo alguna vez: hasta aquí el hombre, hasta aquí, no? / Solo la esperanza tiene las rodillas nitidas. / Sangran." 69–70 **"Ay-y-y . . . water"** the Woman's Voice sings from the *Blood Wedding* lullabye

SCENE NINETEEN

They enter another room. Two GUARDS *are dressing a group of squalid-looking characters who are handcuffed to the wall, heavily made-up, with false eyelashes and lots of rouge. Some are half-undressed, wearing only jackets and underwear. Others wear bras and costume jewelry. The* GUARDS *move around busily. They bring chairs. Make the prisoners sit. They arrange them artistically, crossing their legs, raising their arms as though they were holding cigarettes between their fingers. The prisoners stay in these poses. During the development of this scene, one* GUARD—*seated apart—recites with a melancholy air.*

GUARD: You, who come from the shores of the Tagus
    Every day sing of my death
    Only this do I ask
       with my dying breath
5   Every day sing of my death
    You, who come from the shores of the Tagus.

(A signal is heard. A line of frightened men and women enter. Some carry small packages in their hands, obviously clothing or food. The GUARD *watches them.)*

GUARD: No one enters without being checked. (*He turns his face away. Raises and lowers his index finger mechanically, while the people pass in front of him and go out. Recites rapidly.*)
10   With pants, no. With skirts, no. With stockings, no. With packages, no. With children, no. With faces, no. (*A* PRETTY GIRL *passes. He looks at her. His finger stops. Very nicely.*)
    Twenty little hard ones, twenty little hard ones
15   all in a roll, all in a roll
    twenty little hard ones
    in your little asshole.
    May I?
PRETTY GIRL: (*Stupidly.*) What?
20 GUARD: (*Wiggles his finger obscenely.*) May I?
PRETTY GIRL: No!
GUARD: (*Pulls himself up, undiscouraged.*) To arms! To arms against the little asshole! Right over here!

---

xix. 1 **"You, who come from the shores of the Tagus"** is from a poem of Garcilaso de la Vega. The Tagus River flows through western Spain and Portugal. In her letter to me of March 28, 1986, Gambaro brought up "substituting an English-language poem about death, provided of course it's by a Master." I decided against this option since I felt that Gambaro's appropriation of Garcilaso was important as a reference to a specific age, place, and literary tradition. One of the greatest poets of the Spanish Golden Age, Garcilaso influenced not only San Juan de la Cruz, Lope de Vega, and Cervantes but also Rafael Alberti, Pedro Salinas, Miguel Hernández, and other twentieth-century Spanish and Latin American poets. The original reads: "Vosotros, los del Tajo en su ribera / Cantáreis mi muerte cada dia / Este descanso llevaré nunque muera / Que cada día cantáreis mi muerte, / Vosotros, los del Tajo en su ribera." 13 **"Twenty little hard ones"** is from García Lorca's *Los titeres de cachiporra.* The original reads: "Veinte duritos y veinte duritos / y un rollito de veinte duritos / en el agujero del culito."

(A group of guards enters at a trot. They rush the PRETTY GIRL *and fling themselves on her as though she were the ball in a game of baseball. They roll with her out of the room.)*

GUARD: (*Moves off, uninterested. Starts again with a melancholy air.*) You, who come from the shores of the Tagus . . .   25
LITTLE OLD LADY: (*The last of the visitors. She brings a sandwich wrapped in a handkerchief.*) I've come to see my little son. He misbehaved.
GUARD: (*Deflated.*) Ah . . . Why didn't you bring him up better, madam?   30
LITTLE OLD LADY: He was always my wayward one!
GUARD: A good beating is what they need. They don't learn unless they bleed.
LITTLE OLD LADY: At ten years old, he was looking up the girls' skirts.   35
GUARD: (*Dumbfounded.*) Filthy!
LITTLE OLD LADY: (*Plaintive.*) I cut his little whistle, but it did no good!
GUARD: It's late to repent. Show me what you've brought!
LITTLE OLD LADY: (*Unwraps her handkerchief.*) A sandwich.   40
GUARD: (*Lifts the top of the bread.*) Ah! Extra testicles. No, madam! Here they only lose them. And for us that's work! Confiscated! (*He takes the sandwich.*) Out!
LITTLE OLD LADY: I want to see my son! Just once! Be generous! You have a mother too!   45
GUARD: Yeah, but she's not an old whore like you.
LITTLE OLD LADY: Why are you insulting me?
GUARD: (*With disgust.*) You're old! (*In another tone.*) All right. Go see him. I'm doing this for my mother. Sentimentality will be the end of me! (*Gestures toward one of the seated prisoners.*) There he is.   50
LITTLE OLD LADY: (*Goes toward an* OUTLANDISH-LOOKING PRISONER *and embraces him.*) Son! (*She separates, looks at him.*) No, this isn't him. (*Hugs another.*) Son! (*Looks.*) No, this one either.   55
OUTLANDISH-LOOKING PRISONER: (*Opening his arms.*) Da-da-da-da!
GUARD: Choose already. Take this one. What's the difference.
LITTLE OLD LADY: (*Leaning toward the prisoner. Timidly.*) Juan?
OUTLANDISH-LOOKING PRISONER: Da!
LITTLE OLD LADY: Son!   60
OUTLANDISH-LOOKING PRISONER: Da!
GUIDE: (*To the group.*) Pretty depressing, wouldn't you say?
GUARD: What about you all? Over here, young men!
GUIDE: (*Raises his hands.*) No! Out, quick! (*The sound of music.*) We were going to go dancing. We got the wrong room.   65
(*Very distressed.*) Let's go dancing! Dancing! Move it! Let's beat it! Let's go, gentlemen. Let's go! (*They exit.*)

SCENE TWENTY

GUIDE: Ouf! A narrow escape! (*He listens. The music gets louder. It's happy, catchy.*) That's it. Come. (*He leads his group to a large space, where at this moment all the other groups converge.*) Leave the space open, ladies and gentlemen! If you would be so kind   5 as to stand against the wall. That's it. Thank you, everyone.

(On one side of the performing space is a semitranslucent folding screen, behind which can be seen a long table. In the center, a group of women, dressed like stereotypical prostitutes, execute the gestures conventionally attributed to them: they smoke, show their legs, swing their

purses, put on makeup. A man roughly pushes in two more PROSTI-
TUTES. *They look at him with a mixture of fear and outrage. The
other women observe the new arrivals curiously, then one offers each of
the new women a cigarette. The music suddenly stops. One of the*
PROSTITUTES *starts dancing, moving slowly, singing a blues number
in a gravelly voice. A line of* FOUR MEN *enter at a trot, leading a prisoner with his eyes bandaged, to the center. They sing.*)

FOUR MEN:

> We have come, we have come
> To have some fun!

(*The* PROSTITUTES *watch them. The one dancing gradually slows
down the rhythm until she is moving in place, singing inaudibly. The
men spin the prisoner around until he becomes completely disoriented.*)

10 MAN #1: Let's play the Little Blind Cock!
MAN #2: Cockadoodledoo!

(*They play, rapidly poking and moving away from the prisoner, who
searches for them with his arms outstretched.*)

MAN #1: Play! Head down!
MAN #3: There are beams!
MAN #4: You could break your head open!

(*They play, yell "Cockadoodledoo!" One of the* PROSTITUTES *comes
forward. She first starts to join in the game, then stretches her hand toward the prisoner's bandage.*)

15 MAN #1: (*Pushes her away.*) Get out of here! This is our game!
     In your place, whore!
MAN #2: (*Poking the prisoner.*) He's sweating! He's hot!
MEN #1, #3, AND #4: (*In a chorus.*) Make him strip! Make him
     strip!

(*Maintaining an ambiguous air of play and violence, they take off his
jacket, his pants, his shirt; they throw his clothes, which flutter around.*)

20 MAN #1: Hard-boiled egg! Let's play hard-boiled egg!

(*They fight like children.*)

MAN #2: Me! Me!
MAN #3: Get out! Me!

(*They play. The prisoner holds his body rigid while the others rush
him, tie him up. Finally, one of the* MEN *hits him on the head. The
prisoner falls.*)

MAN #4: We warned you!
MAN #1: A beam, idiot!

MAN #2: We told you to keep your head down!   25

(*They drag the prisoner behind the screen. Through the screen, one can
see fuzzily that they are strapping him down on the table. A scream.
Instantaneously, the volume of the music shoots up; two of the men
come out from behind the screen.*)

TWO MEN: Girls, if you want to sing,
     it's not prohibited!

(*They clap. The* PROSTITUTES *don't move.*)

Sing!

(*The* PROSTITUTES, *forced into it, clap and sing. Again the music gets
louder.*)

> Girls, if you want to dance,
> it's not prohibited!   30

(*The* PROSTITUTES *dance. Behind the screen, one can see the shadow
of the two* MEN *moving away from the table. The hand of the prisoner
falls softly. At the same time, the* PROSTITUTES *freeze in a musical
comedy finale. The music stops. The lights go out, then come up again.
The actors disperse, naturally. They take down the screen. The dead
man gets up from the table, gathers his clothes, and begins to dress.
Only the prisoners seated against the wall remain immobile.*)

GUIDE: (*Drily.*) Ladies and gentlemen, what are you waiting
     for? The show is over. (*House lights come up.*)
GUIDE 2: (*Resentfully.*) If you clap enthusiastically in all good
     haste your hands won't go to waste!

(*He claps, and the* GUIDES *and actors present imitate him.*)

GUIDE: Theater imitates life   35
     If you don't clap
     It means that life is rotten to the core
     And we may as well just head for the door.

(*He moves the audience out toward the door. From far away can be heard
police sirens. Even when the audience is near the exit, they can hear.*)

> Who once said: here the ken
> of men and women   40
> here the bounds?

(*After a moment, repeat.*)

> Who once said: here the ken
> of men and women
> here the bounds?

Brian Friel

Brian Friel (b. 1929) is perhaps the most prominent living Irish playwright, the heir of Ireland's brilliant modern dramatic tradition, the tradition of William Butler Yeats, John Millington Synge, and Sean O'Casey. Unlike these predecessors, who worked for the independence of the Republic of Ireland, Friel works in Northern Ireland, still a part of the United Kingdom. Educated in Derry and Belfast, Friel's concerns as a playwright have spanned the "troubles" of Northern Ireland, the poverty and depression of Derry in the 1930s, 1940s, and 1950s, and the installation of a British military presence and the open street warfare of the 1960s, 1970s, and 1980s. From his earliest success, *Philadelphia, Here I Come!* (1964), about a man's divided feelings concerning his emigration to the United States, Friel's drama has centered on the problems of Irish identity in the face of British rule. Many of his early plays and stories—*The Loves of Cass McGuire* (1966), *The Lovers* (1967)— are portraits of Irish life in the manner of Synge, and Friel's dramatization of the personal consequences of contemporary Irish life remains a prominent feature of fine plays like *Living Quarters* (1977) and *Faith Healer* (1979). However, Friel's drama has increasingly become more satirical—in *The Mundy Scheme* (1969) and *The Gentle Island* (1971)—and more politically concerned. In *The Freedom of the City* (1973), Friel dramatizes the fate of three people caught and killed by British soldiers in the 1972 "Bloody Sunday" riots in Derry. In *Volunteers* (1975), a crew of political prisoners are forced to work on an archaeological site, recovering the history of Celtic Ireland even as they are oppressed by British rule. In *Making History* (1988), Friel returns to the origins of Ireland's subjection to the British in the seventeenth and eighteenth centuries. In 1980, Friel and Stephen Rea founded the Field Day Theatre Company in Derry, and its first production was the play generally taken to be

The 1993 Donmar Warehouse production of Brian Friel's *Translations*.

Friel's masterpiece, *Translations*. Friel's more recent plays include *Dancing at Lughnasa* (1990), *Wonderful Tennessee* (1992), and *Give Me Your Answer, Do!* (1997). Friel has also adapted several plays—Turgenev's *A Month in the Country* (1992) and *London Vertigo*, by the eighteenth-century actor Charles Macklin (1992)—and has specialized in adapting Chekhov's drama to Irish English, in versions of *Three Sisters* (2001) and *Uncle Vanya* (1995).

TRANSLATIONS

Translations is set in early nineteenth-century Ireland and concerns the mapping—both actual and cultural—of Ireland by the British. The play takes place at a local hedge-school, a subscription school run by a local master and attended by a variety of children and adults. This Ireland is already threatened by the British culture to the east: a national school—where, presumably, English will be the required language—is about to open, and the British army surveyors have arrived to map the region, part of the 1833 Ordnance Survey of Ireland.

The play's politics are largely conveyed through the politics of language. Jimmy's Homeric Greek, for example, draws a parallel between Ireland and another lost civilization. The romance between Yolland and Maire bridges the barrier of language. They learn to communicate across this barrier, while the British army works to tear it down and destroy Irish cultural identity in the process. In mapping Ireland, the British convert local place names into English, either by translating them directly or by inventing some equivalent. As the relationship between the Irish Owen and his British officers makes clear, English is the language of power; to map the landscape with English names is a figure for rewriting Ireland and its culture into submission and, finally, into nonexistence.

Although *Translations* may seem only indirectly about contemporary Irish politics, it dramatizes a struggle for national and cultural identity that continues to embroil Northern Ireland today. Throughout the play, for example, the mysterious and unseen Donnelly twins move around the edges of the action, guerrillas hindering the British progress through the country. Finally, when Yolland is missing, we learn the true consequences of the British mapping of Ireland. Mapping the land in English is the prelude to its occupation, as the army systematically destroys the village and countryside that they have made their own. At the play's close, we scent the sickly sweet smell of blighted potatoes, the sign of the impending famine that would weaken and disperse rural Ireland.

TRANSLATIONS

Brian Friel

CHARACTERS

MANUS	BRIDGET	Act I An afternoon in late August 1833.
SARAH	HUGH	Act II A few days later.
JIMMY JACK	OWEN	Act III The evening of the following day.
MAIRE	CAPTAIN LANCEY	One interval—between the two scenes in Act Two.
DOALTY	LIEUTENANT YOLLAND	

The action takes place in a hedge-school in the townland of Baile Beag/Ballybeg, an Irish-speaking community in County Donegal.

ACT ONE

The hedge-school is held in a disused barn or hay-shed or byre. Along the back wall are the remains of five or six stalls—wooden posts and chains—where cows were once milked and bedded. A double door left, large enough to allow a cart to enter. A window right. A wooden stair-way without a banister leads to the upstairs living-quarters (off) of the schoolmaster and his son. Around the room are broken and forgotten implements: a cart-wheel, some lobster-pots, farming tools, a battle of hay, a churn, etc. There are also the stools and bench-seats which the pupils use and a table and chair for the master. At the door a pail of water and a soiled towel. The room is comfortless and dusty and functional—there is no trace of a woman's hand.

When the play opens, MANUS *is teaching* SARAH *to speak. He kneels beside her. She is sitting on a low stool, her head down, very tense, clutching a slate on her knees. He is coaxing her gently and firmly and—as with everything he does—with a kind of zeal.*

MANUS *is in his late twenties/early thirties; the master's older son. He is pale-faced, lightly built, intense, and works as an unpaid assistant—a monitor—to his father. His clothes are shabby; and when he moves we see that he is lame.*

SARAH'*s speech defect is so bad that all her life she has been considered locally to be dumb and she has accepted this: when she wishes to communicate, she grunts and makes unintelligible nasal sounds. She has a waiflike appearance and could be any age from seventeen to thirty-five.*

JIMMY JACK CASSIE—*known as the Infant Prodigy—sits by himself, contentedly reading Homer in Greek and smiling to himself. He is a bachelor in his sixties, lives alone, and comes to these evening classes partly for the company and partly for the intellectual stimulation. He is fluent in Latin and Greek but is in no way pedantic—to him it is perfectly normal to speak these tongues. He never washes. His clothes—heavy top coat, hat, mittens, which he wears now—are filthy and he lives in them summer and winter, day and night. He now reads in a quiet voice and smiles in profound satisfaction. For* JIMMY *the world of the gods and the ancient myths is as real and as immediate as everyday life in the townland of Baile Beag.*

MANUS *holds* SARAH'*s hands in his and he articulates slowly and distinctly into her face.*

MANUS: We're doing very well. And we're going to try it once more—just once more. Now—relax and breathe in... deep... and out... in... and out...

*(*SARAH *shakes her head vigorously and stubbornly.)*

MANUS: Come on, Sarah. This is our secret.

(Again vigorous and stubborn shaking of SARAH'*s head.)*

MANUS: Nobody's listening. Nobody hears you.   5
JIMMY: '*Ton d'emeibet epeita thea glaukopis Athene...*'
MANUS: Get your tongue and your lips working. 'My name—' Come on. One more try. 'My name is—' Good girl.
SARAH: My...
MANUS: Great. 'My name—'   10
SARAH: My... my...
MANUS: Raise your head. Shout it out. Nobody's listening.
JIMMY: '...*alla hekelos estai en Atreidao domois...*'
MANUS: Jimmy, please! Once more—just once more—'My name—' Good girl. Come on now. Head up. Mouth open. 15
SARAH: My...
MANUS: Good.
SARAH: My...
MANUS: Great.
SARAH: My name...   20
MANUS: Yes?
SARAH: My name is...
MANUS: Yes?

*(*SARAH *pauses. Then in a rush.)*

SARAH: My name is Sarah.
MANUS: Marvellous! Bloody marvellous!   25

*(*MANUS *hugs* SARAH. *She smiles in shy, embarrassed pleasure.)*

Did you hear that, Jimmy?—'My name is Sarah'—clear as a bell. *(To* SARAH.*)* The Infant Prodigy doesn't know what we're at. *(*SARAH *laughs at this.* MANUS *hugs her again and stands up.)* Now we're really started! Nothing'll stop us now! Nothing in the wide world!   30

I. 6 *Ton... Athene* But the grey-eyed goddess Athene then replied to him (from Homer, *Odyssey,* 13.420) 13 *alla...domois*... but he sits at ease in the halls of the Sons of Athens... (from Homer, *Odyssey,* 13.423–24)

(JIMMY, *chuckling at his text, comes over to them.*)

JIMMY: Listen to this, Manus.

MANUS: Soon you'll be telling me all the secrets that have been in that head of yours all these years. Certainly, James—what is it? (*To* SARAH.) Maybe you'd set out the stools?

(MANUS *runs up the stairs.*)

35 JIMMY: Wait till you hear this, Manus.

MANUS: Go ahead. I'll be straight down.

JIMMY: '*Hos ara min phamene rabdo epemassat Athene*—' 'After Athene had said this, she touched Ulysses with her wand. She withered the fair skin of his supple limbs and destroyed
40 the flaxen hair from off his head and about his limbs she put the skin of an old man ...'! The divil! The divil!

(MANUS *has emerged again with a bowl of milk and a piece of bread.*)

JIMMY: And wait till you hear! She's not finished with him yet!

(*As* MANUS *descends the stairs he toasts* SARAH *with his bowl.*)

JIMMY: '*Knuzosen de oi osse*—' 'She dimmed his two eyes that were so beautiful and clothed him in a vile ragged cloak be-
45 grimed with filthy smoke ...'! D'you see! Smoke! Smoke! D'you see! Sure look at what the same turf-smoke has done to myself! (*He rapidly removes his hat to display his bald head.*) Would you call that flaxen hair?

MANUS: Of course I would.

50 JIMMY: 'And about him she cast the great skin of a filthy hind, stripped of the hair, and into his hand she thrust a staff and a wallet'! Ha-ha-ha! Athene did that to Ulysses! Made him into a tramp! Isn't she the tight one?

MANUS: You couldn't watch her, Jimmy.

55 JIMMY: You know what they call her?

MANUS: '*Glaukopis Athene.*'

JIMMY: That's it! The flashing-eyed Athene! By God, Manus, sir, if you had a woman like that about the house, it's not stripping a turf-bank you'd be thinking about—eh?

60 MANUS: She was a goddess, Jimmy.

JIMMY: Better still. Sure isn't our own Grania a class of a god-dess and—

MANUS: Who?

JIMMY: Grania—Grania—Diarmuid's Grania.

65 MANUS: Ah.

JIMMY: And sure she can't get her fill of men.

MANUS: Jimmy, you're impossible.

JIMMY: I was just thinking to myself last night: if you had the choosing between Athene and Artemis and Helen of
70 Troy—all three of them Zeus's girls—imagine three powerful-looking daughters like that all in the one parish of Athens!—now, if you had the picking between them, which would you take?

MANUS: (*To* SARAH.) Which should I take, Sarah?

JIMMY: No harm to Helen; and no harm to Artemis; and indeed 75 no harm to our own Grania, Manus. But I think I've no choice but to go bull-straight for Athene. By God, sir, them flashing eyes would fair keep a man jigged up constant!

(*Suddenly and momentarily, as if in spasm,* JIMMY *stands to attention and salutes, his face raised in pained ecstasy.* MANUS *laughs. So does* SARAH. JIMMY *goes back to his seat, and his reading.*)

MANUS: You're a dangerous bloody man, Jimmy Jack.

JIMMY: 'Flashing-eyed'! Hah! Sure Homer knows it all, boy. 80 Homer knows it all.

(MANUS *goes to the window and looks out.*)

MANUS: Where the hell has he got to?

(SARAH *goes to* MANUS *and touches his elbow. She mimes rocking a baby.*)

MANUS: Yes, I know he's at the christening; but it doesn't take them all day to put a name on a baby, does it?

(SARAH *mimes pouring drinks and tossing them back quickly.*)

MANUS: You may be sure. Which pub? 85

(SARAH *indicates.*)

MANUS: Gracie's?

(*No. Further away.*)

MANUS: Con Connie Tim's?

(*No. To the right of there.*)

MANUS: Anna na mBreag's?

(*Yes. That's it.*)

MANUS: Great. She'll fill him up. I suppose I may take the class then. 90

(MANUS *begins to distribute some books, slates and chalk, texts, etc., beside the seats.* SARAH *goes over to the straw and produces a bunch of flowers she has hidden there. During this:*)

JIMMY: '*Autar o ek limenos prosebe*—' 'But Ulysses went forth from the harbour and through the woodland to the place where Athene had shown him he could find the good swineherd who—'*o oi biotoio malista kedeto*'—what's that, Manus?

MANUS: 'Who cared most for his substance.' 95

JIMMY: That's it! 'The good swineherd who cared most for his substance above all the slaves that Ulysses possessed ...'

---

37 **Hos . . . Athene** as she spoke Athene touched him with her wand (from Homer, *Odyssey*, 13.429)   43 **Knuzosen . . . osse** she dimmed his eyes (from Homer, *Odyssey*, 13.433)   56 **Glaukopis Athene** flashing-eyed Athene

---

91 **Autar . . . prosebe** but he went forth from the harbour (from Homer, *Odyssey*, 14.1)   94 **o . . . kedeto** he cared very much for his substance (from Homer, *Odyssey*, 14.3–4)

(SARAH *presents the flowers to* MANUS.)

MANUS: Those are lovely, Sarah.

(*But* SARAH *has fled in embarrassment to her seat and has her head buried in a book.* MANUS *goes to her.*)

MANUS: Flow-ers.

(*Pause.* SARAH *does not look up.*)

100 MANUS: Say the word: flow-ers. Come on—flow-ers.
SARAH: Flowers.
MANUS: You see!—you're off!

(MANUS *leans down and kisses the top of* SARAH's *head.*)

MANUS: And they're beautiful flowers. Thank you.

(MAIRE *enters, a strong-minded, strong-bodied woman in her twenties with a head of curly hair. She is carrying a small can of milk.*)

MAIRE: Is this all's here? Is there no school this evening?
105 MANUS: If my father's not back, I'll take it.

(MANUS *stands awkwardly, having been caught kissing* SARAH *and with the flowers almost formally at his chest.*)

MAIRE: Well now, isn't that a pretty sight. There's your milk. How's Sarah?

(SARAH *grunts a reply.*)

MANUS: I saw you out at the hay.

(MAIRE *ignores this and goes to* JIMMY.)

MAIRE: And how's Jimmy Jack Cassie?
110 JIMMY: Sit down beside me, Maire.
MAIRE: Would I be safe?
JIMMY: No safer man in Donegal.

(MAIRE *flops on a stool beside* JIMMY.)

MAIRE: Ooooh. The best harvest in living memory, they say; but I don't want to see another like it. (*Showing* JIMMY *her*
115   *hands.*) Look at the blisters.
JIMMY: *Esne fatigata?*
MAIRE: *Sum fatigatissima.*
JIMMY: *Bene! Optime!*
MAIRE: That's the height of my Latin. Fit me better if I had
120   even that much English.
JIMMY: English? I thought you had some English?
MAIRE: Three words. Wait—there was a spake I used to have off by heart. What's this it was? (*Her accent is strange because she is speaking a foreign language and because she does not understand*
125   *what she is saying.*) 'In Norfolk we besport ourselves around the maypoll.' What about that!

MANUS: Maypole.

(*Again* MAIRE *ignores* MANUS.)

MAIRE: God have mercy on my Aunt Mary—she taught me that when I was about four, whatever it means. Do you know what it means, Jimmy?   130
JIMMY: Sure you know I have only Irish like yourself.
MAIRE: And Latin. And Greek.
JIMMY: I'm telling you a lie: I know one English word.
MAIRE: What?
JIMMY: Bo-som.   135
MAIRE: What's a bo-som?
JIMMY: You know—(*He illustrates with his hands.*)—bo-som— bo-som—you know—Diana, the huntress, she has two powerful bosom.
MAIRE: You may be sure that's the one English word you would   140
know. (*Rises.*) Is there a drop of water about?

(MANUS *gives* MAIRE *his bowl of milk.*)

MANUS: I'm sorry I couldn't get up last night.
MAIRE: Doesn't matter.
MANUS: Biddy Hanna sent for me to write a letter to her sister in Nova Scotia. All the gossip of the parish. 'I brought the   145
cow to the bull three times last week but no good. There's nothing for it now but Big Ned Frank.'
MAIRE: (*Drinking.*) That's better.
MANUS: And she got so engrossed in it that she forgot who she was dictating to: 'The aul drunken schoolmaster and that   150
lame son of his are still footering about in the hedge-school, wasting people's good time and money.'

(MAIRE *has to laugh at this.*)

MAIRE: She did not!
MANUS: And me taking it all down. 'Thank God one of them new national schools is being built above at Poll na   155
gCaorach.' It was after midnight by the time I got back.
MAIRE: Great to be a busy man.

(MAIRE *moves away.* MANUS *follows.*)

MANUS: I could hear music on my way past but I thought it was too late to call.
MAIRE: (*To* SARAH.) Wasn't your father in great voice last night?   160

(SARAH *nods and smiles.*)

MAIRE: It must have been near three o'clock by the time you got home?

(SARAH *holds up four fingers.*)

MAIRE: Was it four? No wonder we're in pieces.
MANUS: I can give you a hand at the hay tomorrow.
MAIRE: That's the name of a hornpipe, isn't it?—'The Scholar   165
In The Hayfield'—or is it a reel?
MANUS: If the day's good.
MAIRE: Suit yourself. The English soldiers below in the tents, them sapper fellas, they're coming up to give us a hand. I don't know a word they're saying, nor they me; but sure   170
that doesn't matter, does it?

---

116 *Esne fatigata?* are you tired?   117 *Sum fatigatissima* I am
very tired   118 *Bene! Optime!* good! Excellent!

MANUS: What the hell are you so crabbed about?!

(DOALTY *and* BRIDGET *enter noisily. Both are in their twenties.* DOALTY *is brandishing a surveyor's pole. He is an open-minded, open-hearted, generous and slightly thick young man.* BRIDGET *is a plump, fresh young girl, ready to laugh, vain, and with a countrywoman's instinctive cunning.* DOALTY *enters doing his imitation of the master.*)

DOALTY: Vesperal salutations to you all.

BRIDGET: He's coming down past Carraig na Ri and he's as full
175   as a pig!

DOALTY: *Ignari, stulti, rustici*—pot-boys and peasant whelps—
     semi-literates and illegitimates.

BRIDGET: He's been on the batter since this morning; he sent
     the wee ones home at eleven o'clock.

180 DOALTY: Three questions. Question A—Am I drunk? Question
     B—Am I sober? (*Into* MAIRE's *face.*) *Responde—responde!*

BRIDGET: Question C, Master—When were you last sober?

MAIRE: What's the weapon, Doalty?

BRIDGET: I warned him. He'll be arrested one of these days.

185 DOALTY: Up in the bog with Bridget and her aul fella, and the
     Red Coats were just across at the foot of Croc na Mona,
     dragging them aul chains and peeping through that big
     machine they lug about everywhere with them—you
     know the name of it, Manus?

190 MAIRE: Theodolite.

BRIDGET: How do you know?

MAIRE: They leave it in our byre at night sometimes if it's
     raining.

JIMMY: Theodolite—what's the etymology of that word, Manus?

195 MANUS: No idea.

BRIDGET: Get on with the story.

JIMMY: *Theo—theos*—something to do with a god. Maybe
     thea—a goddess! What shape's the yoke?

DOALTY: 'Shape!' Will you shut up, you aul eejit you! Anyway,
200   every time they'd stick one of these poles into the ground
     and move across the bog, I'd creep up and shift it twenty or
     thirty paces to the side.

BRIDGET: God!

DOALTY: Then they'd come back and stare at it and look at their
205   calculations and stare at it again and scratch their heads.
     And cripes, d'you know what they ended up doing?

BRIDGET: Wait till you hear!

DOALTY: They took the bloody machine apart!

(*And immediately he speaks in gibberish—an imitation of two very agitated and confused sappers in rapid conversation.*)

BRIDGET: That's the image of them!

210 MAIRE: You must be proud of yourself, Doalty.

DOALTY: What d'you mean?

MAIRE: That was a very clever piece of work.

MANUS: It was a gesture.

MAIRE: What sort of gesture?

MANUS: Just to indicate . . . a presence. 215

MAIRE: Hah!

BRIDGET: I'm telling you—you'll be arrested.

(*When* DOALTY *is embarrassed—or pleased—he reacts physically. He now grabs* BRIDGET *around the waist.*)

DOALTY: What d'you make of that for an implement, Bridget?
     Wouldn't that make a great aul shaft for your churn?

BRIDGET: Let go of me, you dirty brute! I've a headline to do 220
     before Big Hughie comes.

MANUS: I don't think we'll wait for him. Let's get started.

(*Slowly, reluctantly they begin to move to their seats and specific tasks.* DOALTY *goes to the bucket of water at the door and washes his hands.* BRIDGET *sets up a hand-mirror and combs her hair.*)

BRIDGET: Nellie Ruadh's baby was to be christened this morn-
     ing. Did any of yous hear what she called it? Did you, Sarah?

(SARAH *grunts:* No.)

BRIDGET: Did you, Maire? 225

MAIRE: No.

BRIDGET: Our Seamus says she was threatening she was going
     to call it after its father.

DOALTY: Who's the father?

BRIDGET: That's the point, you donkey you! 230

DOALTY: Ah.

BRIDGET: So there's a lot of uneasy bucks about Baile Beag this
     day.

DOALTY: She told me last Sunday she was going to call it Jimmy.

BRIDGET: You're a liar, Doalty. 235

DOALTY: Would I tell you a lie? Hi, Jimmy, Nellie Ruadh's aul
     fella's looking for you.

JIMMY: For me?

MAIRE: Come on, Doalty.

DOALTY: Someone told him . . . 240

MAIRE: Doalty!

DOALTY: He heard you know the first book of the Satires of
     Horace off by heart . . .

JIMMY: That's true.

DOALTY: and he wants you to recite it for him. 245

JIMMY: I'll do that for him certainly, certainly.

DOALTY: He's busting to hear it.

(JIMMY *fumbles in his pockets.*)

JIMMY: I came across this last night—this'll interest you—in
     Book Two of Virgil's *Georgics.*

DOALTY: Be God, that's my territory alright. 250

BRIDGET: You clown you! (*To* SARAH.) Hold this for me, would
     you? (*Her mirror.*)

JIMMY: Listen to this, Manus. *'Nigra fere et presso pinguis sub
     vomere terra . . .'*

DOALTY: Steady on now—easy, boys, easy—don't rush me, boys— 255

---

176 *Ignari, stulti, rustici* ignoramuses, fools, peasants   181 *Responde—responde!* answer—answer   197 *theos* a god   198 *thea* a goddess

---

253–54 *Nigra . . . terra* land that is black and rich beneath the pressure of the plough

(*He mimes great concentration.*)

JIMMY: Manus?

MANUS: 'Land that is black and rich beneath the pressure of the plough . . .'

DOALTY: Give *me* a chance!

260 JIMMY: 'And with *cui putre*—with crumbly soil—is in the main best for corn.' There you are!

DOALTY: There you are.

JIMMY: 'From no other land will you see more wagons wending homeward behind slow bullocks.' Virgil! There!

265 DOALTY: 'Slow bullocks'!

JIMMY: Isn't that what I'm always telling you? Black soil for corn. *That's* what you should have in that upper field of yours—corn, not spuds.

DOALTY: Would you listen to that fella! Too lazy be Jasus to
270 wash himself and he's lecturing me on agriculture! Would you go and take a running race at yourself, Jimmy Jack Cassie! (*Grabs* SARAH.) Come away out of this with me, Sarah, and we'll plant some corn together.

MANUS: All right—all right. Let's settle down and get some
275 work done. I know Sean Beag isn't coming—he's at the salmon. What about the Donnelly twins? (*To* DOALTY.) Are the Donnelly twins not coming any more?

(DOALTY *shrugs and turns away.*)

Did you ask them?

DOALTY: Haven't seen them. Not about these days.

(DOALTY *begins whistling through his teeth. Suddenly the atmosphere is silent and alert.*)

280 MANUS: Aren't they at home?

DOALTY: No.

MANUS: Where are they then?

DOALTY: How would I know?

BRIDGET: Our Seamus says two of the soldiers' horses were
285 found last night at the foot of the cliffs at Machaire Buidhe and . . . (*She stops suddenly and begins writing with chalk on her slate.*) D'you hear the whistles of this aul slate? Sure nobody could write on an aul slippery thing like that.

MANUS: What headline did my father set you?

290 BRIDGET: 'It's easier to stamp out learning than to recall it.'

JIMMY: Book Three, the *Agricola* of Tacitus.

BRIDGET: God but you're a dose.

MANUS: Can you do it?

BRIDGET: There. Is it bad? Will he ate me?

295 MANUS: It's very good. Keep your elbow in closer to your side. Doalty?

DOALTY: I'm at the seven-times table. I'm perfect, skipper.

(MANUS *moves to* SARAH.)

MANUS: Do you understand those sums?

(SARAH *nods:* Yes. MANUS *leans down to her ear.*)

MANUS: My name is Sarah.

(MANUS *goes to* MAIRE. *While he is talking to her the others swop books, talk quietly, etc.*)

MANUS: Can I help you? What are you at?   300

MAIRE: Map of America. (*Pause.*) The passage money came last Friday.

MANUS: You never told me that.

MAIRE: Because I haven't seen you since, have I?

MANUS: You don't want to go. You said that yourself.   305

MAIRE: There's ten below me to be raised and no man in the house. What do you suggest?

MANUS: Do you want to go?

MAIRE: Did you apply for that job in the new national school?

MANUS: No.   310

MAIRE: You said you would.

MANUS: I said I might.

MAIRE: When it opens, this is finished: nobody's going to pay to go to a hedge-school.

MANUS: I know that and I . . . (*He breaks off because he sees* SARAH,   315
obviously listening, at his shoulder. She moves away again.) I was thinking that maybe I could . . .

MAIRE: It's £56 a year you're throwing away.

MANUS: I can't apply for it.

MAIRE: You *promised* me you would.   320

MANUS: My father has applied for it.

MAIRE: He has not!

MANUS: Day before yesterday.

MAIRE: For God's sake, sure you know he'd never—

MANUS: I couldn't—I can't go in against him.   325

(MAIRE *looks at him for a second. Then:—*)

MAIRE: Suit yourself. (*To* BRIDGET.) I saw your Seamus heading off to the Port fair early this morning.

BRIDGET: And wait till you hear this—I forgot to tell you this. He said that as soon as he crossed over the gap at Cnoc na Mona—just beyond where the soldiers are making the   330
maps—the sweet smell was everywhere.

DOALTY: You never told me that.

BRIDGET: It went out of my head.

DOALTY: He saw the crops in Port?

BRIDGET: Some.   335

MANUS: How did the tops look?

BRIDGET: Fine—I think.

DOALTY: In flower?

BRIDGET: I don't know. I think so. He didn't say.

MANUS: Just the sweet smell—that's all?   340

BRIDGET: They say that's the way it snakes in, don't they? First the smell; and then one morning the stalks are all black and limp.

DOALTY: Are you stupid? It's the rotting stalks makes the sweet smell for God's sake. That's what the smell is—rotting   345
stalks.

MAIRE: Sweet smell! Sweet smell! Every year at this time somebody comes back with stories of the sweet smell. Sweet God, did the potatoes ever fail in Baile Beag? Well, did they ever—ever? Never! There was never blight here.   350
Never. Never. But we're always sniffing about for it, aren't

---

260 *cui putre* crumbly soil

we?—looking for disaster. The rents are going to go up
again—the harvest's going to be lost—the herring have
gone away for ever—there's going to be evictions. Honest
355 to God, some of you people aren't happy unless you're miserable and you'll not be right content until you're dead!

DOALTY: Bloody right, Maire. And sure St Colmcille prophesied there'd never be blight here. He said:

> The spuds will bloom in Baile Beag
360 >   Till rabbits grow an extra lug.

And sure that'll never be. So we're all right. Seven threes are
twenty-one; seven fours are twenty-eight; seven fives are
forty-nine—Hi, Jimmy, do you fancy my chances as boss of
the new national school?

365 JIMMY: What's that?—what's that?

DOALTY: Agh, g'way back home to Greece, son.

MAIRE: You ought to apply, Doalty.

DOALTY: D'you think so? Cripes, maybe I will. Hah!

BRIDGET: Did you know that you start at the age of six and you
370 have to stick at it until you're twelve at least—no matter
how smart you are or how much you know.

DOALTY: Who told you that yarn?

BRIDGET: And every child from every house has to go all day,
every day, summer or winter. That's the law.

375 DOALTY: I'll tell you something—nobody's going to go near
them—they're not going to take on—law or no law.

BRIDGET: And everything's free in them. You pay for nothing
except the books you use; that's what our Seamus says.

DOALTY: 'Our Seamus.' Sure your Seamus wouldn't pay any-
380 way. She's making this all up.

BRIDGET: Isn't that right, Manus?

MANUS: I think so.

BRIDGET: And from the very first day you go, you'll not hear
one word of Irish spoken. You'll be taught to speak English
385 and every subject will be taught through English and
everyone'll end up as cute as the Buncrana people.

(SARAH *suddenly grunts and mimes a warning that the master is coming. The atmosphere changes. Sudden business. Heads down.*)

DOALTY: He's here, boys. Cripes, he'll make yella meal out of
me for those bloody tables.

BRIDGET: Have you any extra chalk, Manus?

390 MAIRE: And the atlas for me.

(DOALTY *goes to* MAIRE *who is sitting on a stool at the back.*)

DOALTY: Swop you seats.

MAIRE: Why?

DOALTY: There's an empty one beside the Infant Prodigy.

MAIRE: I'm fine here.

395 DOALTY: Please, Maire. I want to jouk in the back here.

(MAIRE *rises.*)

God love you. (*Aloud.*) Anyone got a bloody table-book?
Cripes, I'm wrecked.

(SARAH *gives him one.*)

God, I'm dying about you.

(*In his haste to get to the back seat,* DOALTY *bumps into* BRIDGET *who
is kneeling on the floor and writing laboriously on a slate resting on top
of a bench-seat.*)

BRIDGET: Watch where you're going, Doalty!

(DOALTY *gooses* BRIDGET. *She squeals. Now the quiet hum of work:*
JIMMY *reading Homer in a low voice;* BRIDGET *copying her headline;*
MAIRE *studying the atlas;* DOALTY, *his eyes shut tight, mouthing his
tables;* SARAH *doing sums. After a few seconds:—*)

BRIDGET: Is this 'g' right, Manus? How do you put a tail on it? 400

DOALTY: Will you shut up! I can't concentrate!

(*A few more seconds of work. Then* DOALTY *opens his eyes and looks
around.*)

False alarm, boys. The bugger's not coming at all. Sure the
bugger's hardly fit to walk.

(*And immediately* HUGH *enters. A large man, with residual dignity,
shabbily dressed, carrying a stick. He has, as always, a large quantity of drink taken, but he is by no means drunk. He is in his early
sixties.*)

HUGH: *Adsum,* Doalty, *adsum.* Perhaps not in *sobrietate perfecta*
but adequately *sobrius* to overhear your quip. Vesperal saluta- 405
tions to you all.

(*Various responses.*)

JIMMY: *Ave,* Hugh.

HUGH: James. (*He removes his hat and coat and hands them and his
stick to* MANUS, *as if to a footman.*) Apologies for my late arrival: we were celebrating the baptism of Nellie Ruadh's 410
baby.

BRIDGET: (*Innocently.*) What name did she put on it, Master?

HUGH: Was it Eamon? Yes, it was Eamon.

BRIDGET: Eamon Donal from Tor! Cripes!

HUGH: And after the *caerimonia nominationis*—Maire? 415

MAIRE: The ritual of naming.

HUGH: Indeed—we then had a few libations to mark the occasion. Altogether very pleasant. The derivation of the word
'baptize'?—where are my Greek scholars? Doalty?

DOALTY: Would it be—ah—ah— 420

HUGH: Too slow. James?

JIMMY: 'Baptizein'—to dip or immerse.

HUGH: Indeed—our friend Pliny Minor speaks of the *'baptisterium'*—the cold bath.

DOALTY: Master. 425

HUGH: Doalty?

DOALTY: I suppose you could talk then about baptizing a sheep
at sheep-dipping, could you?

(*Laughter. Comments.*)

---

404 **adsum** I am present; **sobrietate perfecta** with complete sobriety 405 **sobrius** sober 407 **Ave** hail 415 **caerimonia
nominationis** ceremony of naming   422 **baptizein** to dip or immerse   423 **baptisterium** a cold bath, swimming pool

HUGH: Indeed—the precedent is there—the day you were ap-
430 propriately named Doalty—seven nines?
DOALTY: What's that, Master?
HUGH: Seven times nine?
DOALTY: Seven nines—seven nines—seven times nine—seven
times nine are—cripes, it's on the tip of my tongue, Mas-
435 ter—I knew it for sure this morning—funny that's the only
one that foxes me—
BRIDGET: (*Prompt.*) Sixty-three.
DOALTY: What's wrong with me: sure seven nines are fifty-
three, Master.
440 HUGH: Sophocles from Colonus would agree with Doalty Dan
Doalty from Tulach Alainn: 'To know nothing is the sweet-
est life.' Where's Sean Beag?
MANUS: He's at the salmon.
HUGH: And Nora Dan?
445 MAIRE: She says she's not coming back any more.
HUGH: Ah. Nora Dan can now write her name—Nora Dan's
education is complete. And the Donnelly twins?

(*Brief pause. Then:—*)

BRIDGET: They're probably at the turf. (*She goes to* HUGH.)
There's the one-and-eight I owe you for last quarter's arith-
450 metic and there's my one-and-six for this quarter's writing.
HUGH: *Gratias tibi ago.* (*He sits at his table.*) Before we commence our *studia* I have three items of information to impart to you—(*To* MANUS.) A bowl of tea, strong tea, black—

(MANUS *leaves.*)

Item A: on my perambulations today—Bridget? Too slow.
455 Maire?
MAIRE: *Perambulare*—to walk about.
HUGH: Indeed—I encountered Captain Lancey of the Royal
Engineers who is engaged in the ordnance survey of this
area. He tells me that in the past few days two of his horses
460 have strayed and some of his equipment seems to be mislaid.
I expressed my regret and suggested he address you himself
on these matters. He then explained that he does not speak
Irish. Latin? I asked. None. Greek? Not a syllable. He
speaks—on his own admission—only English; and to his
465 credit he seemed suitably verecund—James?
JIMMY: *Verecundus*—humble.
HUGH: Indeed—he voiced some surprise that we did not speak
his language. I explained that a few of us did, on occasion—
outside the parish of course—and then usually for the pur-
470 poses of commerce, a use to which his tongue seemed particularly suited—(*Shouts.*) and a slice of soda bread—and I
went on to propose that our own culture and the classical
tongues made a happier conjugation—Doalty?
DOALTY: *Conjugo*—I join together.

(DOALTY *is so pleased with himself that he prods and winks at*
BRIDGET.)

HUGH: Indeed—English, I suggested, couldn't really express 475
us. And again to his credit he acquiesced to my logic.
Acquiesced—Maire?

(MAIRE *turns away impatiently.* HUGH *is unaware of the gesture.*)

Too slow. Bridget?
BRIDGET: *Acquiesco.*
HUGH: *Procede.* 480
BRIDGET: *Acquiesco, acquiescere, acquievi, acquietum.*
HUGH: Indeed—and Item B . . .
MAIRE: Master.
HUGH: Yes?

(MAIRE *gets to her feet uneasily but determinedly. Pause.*)

Well, girl? 485
MAIRE: We should all be learning to speak English. That's what
my mother says. That's what I say. That's what Dan O'Connell said last month in Ennis. He said the sooner we all
learn to speak English the better.

(*Suddenly several speak together.*)

JIMMY: What's she saying? What? What? 490
DOALTY: It's Irish he uses when he's travelling around scroung-
ing votes.
BRIDGET: And sleeping with married women. Sure no
woman's safe from that fella.
JIMMY: Who-who-who? Who's this? Who's this? 495
HUGH: *Silentium!* (*Pause.*) Who is she talking about?
MAIRE: I'm talking about Daniel O'Connell.
HUGH: Does she mean that little Kerry politician?
MAIRE: I'm talking about the Liberator, Master, as you well
know. And what he said was this: 'The old language is a bar- 500
rier to modern progress.' He said that last month. And he's
right. I don't want Greek. I don't want Latin. I want English.

(MANUS *reappears on the platform above.*)

I want to be able to speak English because I'm going to
America as soon as the harvest's all saved.

(MAIRE *remains standing.* HUGH *puts his hand into his pocket and
produces a flask of whiskey. He removes the cap, pours a drink into it,
tosses it back, replaces the cap, puts the flask back into his pocket.
Then:—*)

HUGH: We have been diverted—*diverto*—*divertere*—Where 505
were we?
DOALTY: Three items of information, Master. You're at Item B.
HUGH: Indeed—Item B—Item B—yes—On my way to the
christening this morning I chanced to meet Mr George
Alexander, Justice of the Peace. We discussed the new na- 510
tional school. Mr Alexander invited me to take charge of it
when it opens. I thanked him and explained that I could do

---

451 *Gratias tibi ago* I thank you   452 *studia* studies   456 *peram-*
bulare to walk through   466 *verecundus* shame-faced, modest
474 *conjugo* I join together

---

480 *Procede* proceed   481 *acquiesco, acquiescere* to rest, to find
comfort in   496 *Silentium!* silence!   505 *diverto, divertere* to
turn away

that only if I were free to run it as I have run this hedge-school for the past thirty-five years—filling what our friend Euripides calls the *'aplestos pithos'*—James?
JIMMY: 'The cask that cannot be filled.'
HUGH: Indeed—and Mr. Alexander retorted courteously and emphatically that he hopes that is how it will be run.

(MAIRE *now sits.*)

Indeed. I have had a strenuous day and I am weary of you all. (*He rises.*) Manus will take care of you.

(HUGH *goes towards the steps.* OWEN *enters.* OWEN *is the younger son, a handsome, attractive young man in his twenties. He is dressed smartly—a city man. His manner is easy and charming: everything he does is invested with consideration and enthusiasm. He now stands framed in the doorway, a travelling bag across his shoulder.*)

OWEN: Could anybody tell me is this where Hugh Mor O'Donnell holds his hedge-school?
DOALTY: It's Owen—Owen Hugh! Look, boys—it's Owen Hugh!

(OWEN *enters. As he crosses the room he touches and has a word for each person.*)

OWEN: Doalty! (*Playful punch.*) How are you, boy? *Jacobe, quid agis?* Are you well?
JIMMY: Fine. Fine.
OWEN: And Bridget! Give us a kiss. Aaaaaah!
BRIDGET: You're welcome, Owen.
OWEN: It's not—? Yes, it *is* Maire Chatach! God! A young woman!
MAIRE: How are you, Owen?

(OWEN *is now in front of* HUGH. *He puts his two hands on his* FATHER's *shoulders.*)

OWEN: And how's the old man himself?
HUGH: Fair—fair.
OWEN: Fair? For God's sake you never looked better! Come here to me. (*He embraces* HUGH *warmly and genuinely.*) Great to see you, Father. Great to be back.

(HUGH's *eyes are moist—partly joy, partly the drink.*)

HUGH: I—I'm—I'm—pay no attention to—
OWEN: Come on—come on—come on—(*He gives* HUGH *his handkerchief.*) Do you know what you and I are going to do tonight? We are going to go up to Anna na mBreag's ...
DOALTY: Not there, Owen.
OWEN: Why not?
DOALTY: Her poteen's worse than ever.
BRIDGET: They say she puts frogs in it!
OWEN: All the better. (*To* HUGH.) And you and I are going to get footless drunk. That's arranged.

_____
515 *aplestos pithos* unfillable cask   525–526 *Jacobe, quid agis?* James, how are you?

(OWEN *sees* MANUS *coming down the steps with tea and soda bread. They meet at the bottom.*)

And Manus!
MANUS: You're welcome, Owen.
OWEN: I know I am. And it's great to be here. (*He turns round, arms outstretched.*) I can't believe it. I come back after six years and everything's just as it was! Nothing's changed! Not a thing! (*Sniffs.*) Even that smell—that's the same smell this place always had. What is it anyway? Is it the straw?
DOALTY: Jimmy Jack's feet.

(*General laughter. It opens little pockets of conversation round the room.*)

OWEN: And Doalty Dan Doalty hasn't changed either!
DOALTY: Bloody right, Owen.
OWEN: Jimmy, are you well?
JIMMY: Dodging about.
OWEN: Any word of the big day?

(*This is greeted with 'ohs' and 'ahs.'*)

Time enough, Jimmy. Homer's easier to live with, isn't he?
MAIRE: We heard stories that you own ten big shops in Dublin—is it true?
OWEN: Only nine.
BRIDGET: And you've twelve horses and six servants.
OWEN: Yes—that's true. God Almighty, would you listen to them—taking a hand at me!
MANUS: When did you arrive?
OWEN: We left Dublin yesterday morning, spent last night in Omagh and got here half an hour ago.
MANUS: You're hungry then.
HUGH: Indeed—get him food—get him a drink.
OWEN: Not now, thanks; later. Listen—am I interrupting you all?
HUGH: By no means. We're finished for the day.
OWEN: Wonderful. I'll tell you why. Two friends of mine are waiting outside the door. They'd like to meet you and I'd like you to meet them. May I bring them in?
HUGH: Certainly. You'll all eat and have ...
OWEN: Not just yet, Father. You've seen the sappers working in this area for the past fortnight, haven't you? Well, the older man is Captain Lancey ...
HUGH: I've met Captain Lancey.
OWEN: Great. He's the cartographer in charge of this whole area. Cartographer—James?

(OWEN *begins to play this game—his father's game—partly to involve his classroom audience, partly to show he has not forgotten it, and indeed partly because he enjoys it.*)

JIMMY: A maker of maps.
OWEN: Indeed—and the younger man that I travelled with from Dublin, his name is Lieutenant Yolland and he is attached to the toponymic department—Father?—*responde—responde!*
HUGH: He gives names to places.
OWEN: Indeed—although he is in fact an orthographer—Doalty?—too slow—Manus?

595   MANUS: The correct spelling of those names.
OWEN: Indeed—indeed!

(OWEN *laughs and claps his hands. Some of the others join in.*)

Beautiful! Beautiful! Honest to God, it's such a delight to be back here with you all again—'civilized' people. Anyhow—may I bring them in?
600   HUGH: Your friends are our friends.
OWEN: I'll be straight back.

(*There is general talk as* OWEN *goes towards the door. He stops beside* SARAH.)

OWEN: That's a new face. Who are you?

(*A very brief hesitation. Then:—*)

SARAH: My name is Sarah.
OWEN: Sarah who?
605   SARAH: Sarah Johnny Sally.
OWEN: Of course! From Bun na hAbhann! I'm Owen—Owen Hugh Mor. From Baile Beag. Good to see you.

(*During this* OWEN—SARAH *exchange.*)

HUGH: Come on now. Let's tidy this place up. (*He rubs the top of his table with his sleeve.*) Move, Doalty—lift those books off
610   the floor.
DOALTY: Right, Master; certainly, Master; I'm doing my best, Master.

(OWEN *stops at the door.*)

OWEN: One small thing, Father.
HUGH: *Silentium!*
615   OWEN: I'm on their pay-roll.

(SARAH, *very elated at her success, is beside* MANUS.)

SARAH: I said it, Manus!

(MANUS *ignores* SARAH. *He is much more interested in* OWEN *now.*)

MANUS: You haven't enlisted, have you?!

(SARAH *moves away.*)

OWEN: Me a soldier? I'm employed as a part-time, underpaid, civilian interpreter. My job is to translate the quaint, ar-
620   chaic tongue you people persist in speaking into the King's good English.

(*He goes out.*)

HUGH: Move—move—move! Put some order on things! Come on, Sarah—hide that bucket. Whose are these slates? Somebody take these dishes away. *Festinate! Festinate!*

(MANUS *goes to* MAIRE *who is busy tidying.*)

MANUS: You didn't tell me you were definitely leaving.   625
MAIRE: Not now.
HUGH: Good girl, Bridget. That's the style.
MANUS: You might at least have told me.
HUGH: Are these your books, James?
JIMMY: Thank you.   630
MANUS: Fine! Fine! Go ahead! Go ahead!
MAIRE: You talk to me about getting married—with neither a roof over your head nor a sod of ground under your foot. I suggest you go for the new school; but no—'My father's in for that.' Well now he's got it and now this is finished and   635
now you've nothing.
MANUS: I can always . . .
MAIRE: What? Teach classics to the cows? Agh—

(MAIRE *moves away from* MANUS. OWEN *enters with* LANCEY *and* YOLLAND. CAPTAIN LANCEY *is middle-aged; a small, crisp officer, expert in his field as cartographer but uneasy with people—especially civilians, especially these foreign civilians. His skill is with deeds, not words.* LIEUTENANT YOLLAND *is in his late twenties/early thirties. He is tall and thin and gangling, blond hair, a shy, awkward manner. A soldier by accident.*)

OWEN: Here we are. Captain Lancey—my father.
LANCEY: Good evening.   640

(HUGH *becomes expansive, almost courtly, with his visitors.*)

HUGH: You and I have already met, sir.
LANCEY: Yes.
OWEN: And Lieutenant Yolland—both Royal Engineers—my father.
HUGH: You're very welcome, gentlemen.   645
YOLLAND: How do you do.
HUGH: *Gaudeo vos hic adesse.*
OWEN: And I'll make no other introductions except that these are some of the people of Baile Beag and—what?—well you're among the best people in Ireland now. (*He pauses to*   650
allow LANCEY *to speak.* LANCEY *does not.*) Would you like to say a few words, Captain?
HUGH: What about a drop, sir?
LANCEY: A what?
HUGH: Perhaps a modest refreshment? A little sampling of our   655
aqua vitae?
LANCEY: No, no.
HUGH: Later perhaps when—
LANCEY: I'll say what I have to say, if I may, and as briefly as possible. Do they speak *any* English, Roland?   660
OWEN: Don't worry. I'll translate.
LANCEY: I see. (*He clears his throat. He speaks as if he were addressing children—a shade too loudly and enunciating excessively.*) You may have seen me—seen me—working in this section—section?—working. We are here—here—in this place—   665
you understand?—to make a map—a map—a map and—
JIMMY: *Nonne Latine loquitur?*

---

624 *Festinate!* hurry!

647 *Gaudeo . . . adesse* welcome   667 *Nonne Latine loquitur?* does he not speak Latin?

(HUGH *holds up a restraining hand.*)

HUGH: James.
LANCEY: (*To* JIMMY.) I do not speak Gaelic, sir.

(*He looks at* OWEN.)

670 OWEN: Carry on.
LANCEY: A map is a representation on paper—a picture—you understand picture?—a paper picture—showing, representing this country—yes?—showing your country in miniature—a scaled drawing on paper of—of—of—

(*Suddenly* DOALTY *sniggers. Then* BRIDGET. *Then* SARAH. OWEN *leaps in quickly.*)

675 OWEN: It might be better if you *assume* they understand you—
LANCEY: Yes?
OWEN: And I'll translate as you go along.
LANCEY: I see. Yes. Very well. Perhaps you're right. Well. What we are doing is this. (*He looks at* OWEN. OWEN *nods reassuringly.*) His Majesty's government has ordered the first ever
680 comprehensive survey of this entire country—a general triangulation which will embrace detailed hydrographic and topographic information and which will be executed to a scale of six inches to the English mile.
685 HUGH: (*Pouring a drink.*) Excellent—excellent.

(LANCEY *looks at* OWEN.)

OWEN: A new map is being made of the whole country.

(LANCEY *looks to* OWEN: *Is that all?* OWEN *smiles reassuringly and indicates to proceed.*)

LANCEY: This enormous task has been embarked on so that the military authorities will be equipped with up-to-date and accurate information on every corner of this part of the Empire.
690 OWEN: The job is being done by soldiers because they are skilled in this work.
LANCEY: And also so that the entire basis of land valuation can be reassessed for purposes of more equitable taxation.
OWEN: This new map will take the place of the estate agent's
695 map so that from now on you will know exactly what is yours in law.
LANCEY: In conclusion I wish to quote two brief extracts from the white paper which is our governing charter: (*Reads*) 'All former surveys of Ireland originated in forfeiture and vio-
700 lent transfer of property; the present survey has for its object the relief which can be afforded to the proprietors and occupiers of land from unequal taxation.'
OWEN: The captain hopes that the public will cooperate with the sappers and that the new map will mean that taxes are
705 reduced.
HUGH: A worthy enterprise—*opus honestrum!* And Extract B?
LANCEY: 'Ireland is privileged. No such survey is being undertaken in England. So this survey cannot but be received as

---

706 **opus honestrum** an honourable task

proof of the disposition of this government to advance the interests of Ireland.' My sentiments, too. 710
OWEN: This survey demonstrates the government's interest in Ireland and the captain thanks you for listening so attentively to him.
HUGH: Our pleasure, Captain.
LANCEY: Lieutenant Yolland? 715
YOLLAND: I—I—I've nothing to say—really—
OWEN: The captain is the man who actually makes the new map. George's task is to see that the place-names on this map are . . . correct. (*To* YOLLAND.) Just a few words—they'd like to hear you. (*To class.*) Don't you want to hear 720 George, too?
MAIRE: Has he anything to say?
YOLLAND: (*To* MAIRE.) Sorry—sorry?
OWEN: She says she's dying to hear you.
YOLLAND: (*To* MAIRE.) Very kind of you—thank you . . . (*To* 725 *class.*) I can only say that I feel—I feel very foolish to—to—to be working here and not to speak your language. But I intend to rectify that—with Roland's help—indeed I do.
OWEN: He wants me to teach him Irish!
HUGH: You are doubly welcome, sir. 730
YOLLAND: I think your countryside is—is—is—is very beautiful. I've fallen in love with it already. I hope we're not too—too crude an intrusion on your lives. And I know that I'm going to be happy, very happy, here.
OWEN: He is already a committed Hibernophile— 735
JIMMY: He loves—
OWEN: All right, Jimmy—we know—he loves Baile Beag; and he loves you all.
HUGH: Please . . . May I . . . ?

(HUGH *is now drunk. He holds on to the edge of the table.*)

OWEN: Go ahead, Father. (*Hands up for quiet.*) Please—please. 740
HUGH: And we, gentlemen, we in turn are happy to offer you our friendship, our hospitality, and every assistance that you may require. Gentlemen—welcome!

(*A few desultory claps. The formalities are over. General conversation. The soldiers meet the locals.* MANUS *and* OWEN *meet down stage.*)

OWEN: Lancey's a bloody ramrod but George's all right. How are you anyway? 745
MANUS: What sort of a translation was that, Owen?
OWEN: Did I make a mess of it?
MANUS: You weren't saying what Lancey was saying!
OWEN: 'Uncertainty in meaning is incipient poetry'—who said that? 750
MANUS: There was nothing uncertain about what Lancey said: it's a bloody military operation, Owen! And what's Yolland's function? What's 'incorrect' about the place-names we have here?
OWEN: Nothing at all. They're just going to be standardized. 755
MANUS: You mean changed into English?
OWEN: Where there's ambiguity, they'll be Anglicized.
MANUS: And they call you Roland! They both call you Roland!
OWEN: Shhhhh. Isn't it ridiculous? They seemed to get it wrong from the very beginning—or else they can't pronounce 760 Owen. I was afraid some of you bastards would laugh.

MANUS: Aren't you going to tell them?
OWEN: Yes—yes—soon—soon.
MANUS: But they . . .
765 OWEN: Easy, man, easy. Owen—Roland—what the hell. It's
only a name. It's the same me, isn't it? Well, isn't it?
MANUS: Indeed it is. It's the same Owen.
OWEN: And the same Manus. And in a way we complement
each other. (*He punches* MANUS *lightly, playfully and turns to*
770 *join the others. As he goes.*) All right—who has met whom?
Isn't this a job for the go-between?

(MANUS *watches* OWEN *move confidently across the floor, taking*
MAIRE *by the hand and introducing her to* YOLLAND. HUGH *is try-*
ing to negotiate the steps. JIMMY *is lost in a text.* DOALTY *and* BRID-
GET *are reliving their giggling.* SARAH *is staring at* MANUS.)

ACT TWO

SCENE I

The sappers have already mapped most of the area. YOLLAND'*s official*
task, which OWEN *is now doing, is to take each of the Gaelic names—*
every hill, stream, rock, even every patch of ground which possessed its
own distinctive Irish name—and Anglicize it, either by changing it
into its approximate English sound or by translating it into English
words. For example, a Gaelic name like Cnoc Ban could become
Knockban or—directly translated—Fair Hill. These new standard-
ized names were entered into the Name-Book, and when the new
maps appeared they contained all these new Anglicized names.
OWEN'*s official function as translator is to pronounce each name in*
Irish and then provide the English translation.

The hot weather continues. It is late afternoon some days later.

Stage right: an improvised clothes-line strung between the shafts of the
cart and a nail in the wall; on it are some shirts and socks.

A large map—one of the new blank maps—is spread out on the floor.
OWEN *is on his hands and knees, consulting it. He is totally engrossed*
in his task which he pursues with great energy and efficiency.

YOLLAND'*s hesitancy has vanished—he is at home here now. He is sit-*
ting on the floor, his long legs stretched out before him, his back resting
against a creel, his eyes closed. His mind is elsewhere. One of the refer-
ence books—a church registry—lies open on his lap.

Around them are various reference books, the Name-Book, a bottle of
poteen, some cups, etc.

OWEN *completes an entry in the Name-Book and returns to the*
map on the floor.

OWEN: Now. Where have we got to? Yes—the point where that
stream enters the sea—that tiny little beach there. George!
YOLLAND: Yes. I'm listening. What do you call it? Say the Irish
name again?
5 OWEN: Bun na hAbhann.
YOLLAND: Again.
OWEN: Bun na hAbhann.
YOLLAND: Bun na hAbhann.
OWEN: That's terrible, George.
10 YOLLAND: I know. I'm sorry. Say it again.

OWEN: Bun na hAbhann.
YOLLAND: Bun na hAbhann.
OWEN: That's better. Bun is the Irish word for bottom. And
Abha means river. So it's literally the mouth of the river.
YOLLAND: Let's leave it alone. There's no English equivalent 15
for a sound like that.
OWEN: What is it called in the church registry?

(*Only now does* YOLLAND *open his eyes.*)

YOLLAND: Let's see . . . Banowen.
OWEN: That's wrong. (*Consults text.*) The list of freeholders calls
it Owenmore—that's completely wrong: Owenmore's the 20
big river at the west end of the parish. (*Another text.*) And
in the grand jury lists it's called—God!—Binhone!—wherever they got that. I suppose we could Anglicize it to
Bunowen; but somehow that's neither fish nor flesh.

(YOLLAND *closes his eyes again.*)

YOLLAND: I give up. 25
OWEN: (*At map.*) Back to first principles. What are we trying
to do?
YOLLAND: Good question.
OWEN: We are trying to denominate and at the same time de-
scribe that tiny area of soggy, rocky, sandy ground where 30
that little stream enters the sea, an area known locally as
Bun na hAbhann . . . Burnfoot! What about Burnfoot?
YOLLAND: (*Indifferently.*) Good, Roland, Burnfoot's good.
OWEN: George, my name isn't . . .
YOLLAND: B-u-r-n-f-o-o-t? 35
OWEN: Are you happy with that?
YOLLAND: Yes.
OWEN: Burnfoot it is then. (*He makes the entry into the Name-*
Book.) Bun na hAbhann—B-u-r-n-
YOLLAND: You're becoming very skilled at this. 40
OWEN: We're not moving fast enough.
YOLLAND: (*Opens eyes again.*) Lancey lectured me again last
night.
OWEN: When does he finish here?
YOLLAND: The sappers are pulling out at the end of the week. 45
The trouble is, the maps they've completed can't be printed
without these names. So London screams at Lancey and
Lancey screams at me. But I wasn't intimidated.

(MANUS *emerges from upstairs and descends.*)

'I'm sorry, sir,' I said, 'But certain tasks demand their own
tempo. You cannot rename a whole country overnight.' 50
Your Irish air has made me bold. (*To* MANUS.) Do you want
us to leave?
MANUS: Time enough. Class won't begin for another half-hour.
YOLLAND: Sorry—sorry?
OWEN: Can't you speak English? 55

(MANUS *gathers the things off the clothes-line.* OWEN *returns to the*
map.)

OWEN: We now come across that beach . . .
YOLLAND: Tra—that's the Irish for beach. (*To* MANUS.) I'm
picking up the odd word, Manus.

MANUS: So.

60 OWEN: . . . on past Burnfoot; and there's nothing around here that has any name that I know of until we come down here to the south end, just about here . . . and there should be a ridge of rocks there . . . Have the sappers marked it? They have. Look, George.

65 YOLLAND: Where are we?

OWEN: There.

YOLLAND: I'm lost.

OWEN: Here. And the name of that ridge is Druim Dubh. Put English on that, Lieutenant.

70 YOLLAND: Say it again.

OWEN: Druim Dubh.

YOLLAND: Dubh means black.

OWEN: Yes.

YOLLAND: And Druim means . . . what? a fort?

75 OWEN: We met it yesterday in Druim Luachra.

YOLLAND: A ridge! The Black Ridge! (*To* MANUS.) You see, Manus?

OWEN: We'll have you fluent at the Irish before the summer's over.

80 YOLLAND: Oh, I wish I were. (*To* MANUS *as he crosses to go back upstairs.*) We got a crate of oranges from Dublin today. I'll send some up to you.

MANUS: Thanks. (*To* OWEN.) Better hide that bottle. Father's just up and he'd be better without it.

85 OWEN: Can't you speak English before your man?

MANUS: Why?

OWEN: Out of courtesy.

MANUS: Doesn't he want to learn Irish? (*To* YOLLAND.) Don't you want to learn Irish?

90 YOLLAND: Sorry—sorry? I—I—

MANUS: I understand the Lanceys perfectly but people like you puzzle me.

OWEN: Manus, for God's sake!

MANUS: (*Still to* YOLLAND.) How's the work going?

95 YOLLAND: The work?—the work? Oh, it's—it's staggering along—I think—(*To* OWEN.)—isn't it? But we'd be lost without Roland.

MANUS: (*Leaving.*) I'm sure. But there are always the Rolands, aren't there?

(*He goes upstairs and exits.*)

100 YOLLAND: What was that he said?—something about Lancey, was it?

OWEN: He said we should hide that bottle before Father gets his hands on it.

YOLLAND: Ah.

105 OWEN: He's always trying to protect him.

YOLLAND: Was he lame from birth?

OWEN: An accident when he was a baby: Father fell across his cradle. That's why Manus feels so responsible for him.

YOLLAND: Why doesn't he marry?

110 OWEN: Can't afford to, I suppose.

YOLLAND: Hasn't he a salary?

OWEN: What salary? All he gets is the odd shilling Father throws him—and that's seldom enough. I got out in time, didn't I?

(*YOLLAND is pouring a drink.*)

Easy with that stuff—it'll hit you suddenly. 115

YOLLAND: I like it.

OWEN: Let's get back to the job. Druim Dubh—what's it called in the jury lists? (*Consults texts.*)

YOLLAND: Some people here resent us.

OWEN: Dramduff—wrong as usual. 120

YOLLAND: I was passing a little girl yesterday and she spat at me.

OWEN: And it's Drimdoo here. What's it called in the registry?

YOLLAND: Do you know the Donnelly twins?

OWEN: Who? 125

YOLLAND: The Donnelly twins.

OWEN: Yes. Best fishermen about here. What about them?

YOLLAND: Lancey's looking for them.

OWEN: What for?

YOLLAND: He wants them for questioning. 130

OWEN: Probably stolen somebody's nets. Dramduffy! Nobody ever called it Dramduffy. Take your pick of those three.

YOLLAND: My head's addled. Let's take a rest. Do you want a drink?

OWEN: Thanks. Now, every Dubh we've come across we've 135 changed to Duff. So if we're to be consistent, I suppose Druim Dubh has to become Dromduff.

(YOLLAND *is now looking out the window.*)

You can see the end of the ridge from where you're standing. But D-r-u-m- or D-r-o-m-? (*Name-Book.*) Do you remember—which did we agree on for Druim Luachra? 140

YOLLAND: That house immediately above where we're camped—

OWEN: Mm?

YOLLAND: The house where Maire lives.

OWEN: Maire? Oh, Maire Chatach. 145

YOLLAND: What does that mean?

OWEN: Curly-haired; the whole family are called the Chatachs. What about it?

YOLLAND: I hear music coming from that house almost every night. 150

OWEN: Why don't you drop in?

YOLLAND: Could I?

OWEN: Why not? We used D-r-o-m then. So we've got to call it D-r-o-m-d-u-f-f—all right?

YOLLAND: Go back up to where the new school is being built 155 and just say the names again for me, would you?

OWEN: That's a good idea. Poolkerry, Ballybeg—

YOLLAND: No, no; as they still are—in your own language.

OWEN: Poll na gCaorach,

(YOLLAND *repeats the names silently after him.*)

Baile Beag, Ceann Balor, Lis Maol, Machaire Buidhe, Baile 160 na gGall, Carraig na Rí, Mullach Dearg—

YOLLAND: Do you think I could live here?

OWEN: What are you talking about?

YOLLAND: Settle down here—live here.

OWEN: Come on, George. 165

YOLLAND: I mean it.

OWEN: Live on what? Potatoes? Buttermilk?

YOLLAND: It's really heavenly.

OWEN: For God's sake! The first hot summer in fifty years and
170   you think it's Eden. Don't be such a bloody romantic. You
       wouldn't survive a mild winter here.
YOLLAND: Do you think not? Maybe you're right.

(DOALTY *enters in a rush.*)

DOALTY: Hi, boys, is Manus about?
OWEN: He's upstairs. Give him a shout.
175 DOALTY: Manus! The cattle's going mad in that heat—Cripes,
       running wild all over the place. (*To* YOLLAND.) How are you
       doing, skipper?

(MANUS *appears.*)

YOLLAND: Thank you for—I—I'm very grateful to you for—
DOALTY: Wasting your time. I don't know a word you're saying.
180   Hi, Manus, there's two bucks down the road there asking
       for you.
MANUS: (*Descending.*) Who are they?
DOALTY: Never clapped eyes on them. They want to talk to you.
MANUS: What about?
185 DOALTY: They wouldn't say. Come on. The bloody beasts'll end
       up in Loch an Iubhair if they're not capped. Good luck, boys!

(DOALTY *rushes off.* MANUS *follows him.*)

OWEN: Good luck! What were you thanking Doalty for?
YOLLAND: I was washing outside my tent this morning and he
       was passing with a scythe across his shoulder and he came
190   up to me and pointed to the long grass and then cut a path-
       way round my tent and from the tent down to the road—so
       that my feet won't get wet with the dew. Wasn't that kind of
       him? And I have no words to thank him . . . I suppose you're
       right: I suppose I couldn't live here . . . Just before Doalty
195   came up to me this morning, I was thinking that at that mo-
       ment I might have been in Bombay instead of Ballybeg.
       You see, my father was at his wits end with me and finally he
       got me a job with the East India Company—some kind of a
       clerkship. That was ten, eleven months ago. So I set off for
200   London. Unfortunately I—I—I missed the boat. Literally.
       And since I couldn't face Father and hadn't enough money
       to hang about until the next sailing, I joined the army. And
       they stuck me into the Engineers and posted me to Dublin.
       And Dublin sent me here. And while I was washing this
205   morning and looking across the Tra Bhan, I was thinking
       how very, very lucky I am to be here and not in Bombay.
OWEN: Do you believe in fate?
YOLLAND: Lancey's so like my father. I was watching him last
       night. He met every group of sappers as they reported in.
210   He checked the field kitchens. He examined the horses. He
       inspected every single report—even examining the texture
       of the paper and commenting on the neatness of the hand-
       writing. The perfect colonial servant: not only must the job
       be done—it must be done with excellence. Father has that
215   drive, too; that dedication; that indefatigable energy. He
       builds roads—hopping from one end of the Empire to the
       other. Can't sit still for five minutes. He says himself the
       longest time he ever sat still was the night before Waterloo
       when they were waiting for Wellington to make up his
220   mind to attack.

OWEN: What age is he?
YOLLAND: Born in 1789—the very day the Bastille fell. I've of-
       ten thought maybe that gave his whole life its character. Do
       you think it could? He inherited a new world the day he
       was born—The Year One. Ancient time was at an end. The   225
       world had cast off its old skin. There were no longer any
       frontiers to man's potential. Possibilities were endless and
       exciting. He still believes that. The Apocalypse is just
       about to happen . . . I'm afraid I'm a great disappointment
       to him. I've neither his energy, nor his coherence, nor his   230
       belief. Do I believe in fate? The day I arrived in Ballybeg—
       no, Baile Beag—the moment you brought me in here, I had
       a curious sensation. It's difficult to describe. It was a mo-
       mentary sense of discovery; no—not quite a sense of dis-
       covery—a sense of recognition, of confirmation of some-   235
       thing I half knew instinctively; as if I had stepped . . .
OWEN: Back into ancient time?
YOLLAND: No, no. It wasn't an awareness of *direction* being
       changed but of experience being of a totally different order.
       I had moved into a consciousness that wasn't striving nor   240
       agitated, but at its ease and with its own conviction and as-
       surance. And when I heard Jimmy Jack and your father
       swapping stories about Apollo and Cuchulainn and Paris
       and Ferdia—as if they lived down the road—it was then
       that I thought—I knew—perhaps I could live here . . .   245
       (*Now embarrassed.*) Where's the pot-een?
OWEN: Poteen.
YOLLAND: Poteen—poteen—poteen. Even if I did speak Irish
       I'd always be an outsider here, wouldn't I? I may learn the
       password but the language of the tribe will always elude   250
       me, won't it? The private core will always be . . . hermetic,
       won't it?
OWEN: You can learn to decode us.

(HUGH *emerges from upstairs and descends. He is dressed for the road.
Today he is physically and mentally jaunty and alert—almost self-
consciously jaunty and alert. Indeed, as the scene progresses, one has the
sense that he is deliberately parodying himself. The moment* HUGH
gets to the bottom of the steps YOLLAND *leaps respectfully to his feet.*)

HUGH: (*As he descends.*)
       Quantumvis cursum longum fessumque moratur   255
       Sol, sacro tandem carmine vesper adest.
       I dabble in verse, Lieutenant, after the style of Ovid. (*To*
       OWEN.) A drop of that to fortify me.
YOLLAND: You'll have to translate it for me.
HUGH: Let's see—   260
       No matter how long the sun may linger on his long and
       weary journey
       At length evening comes with its sacred song.
YOLLAND: Very nice, sir.
HUGH: English succeeds in making it sound plebeian.
OWEN: Where are you off to, Father?   265

II.i. 255–256 *Quantumvis . . . adest* no matter how long the sun
delays on his long weary course / At length evening comes with its
sacred song

HUGH: An *expeditio* with three purposes. Purpose A: to acquire a testimonial from our parish priest—(*To* YOLLAND.) a worthy man but barely literate; and since he'll ask me to write it myself, how in all modesty can I do myself justice? (*To* OWEN.) Where did this [*drink*] come from?

270 OWEN: Anna na mBreag's.

HUGH: (*To* YOLLAND.) In that case address yourself to it with circumspection. (*And* HUGH *instantly tosses the drink back in one gulp and grimaces.*) Aaaaaaagh! (*Holds out his glass for a refill.*) Anna na mBreag means Anna of the Lies. And Purpose
275 B: to talk to the builders of the new school about the kind of living accommodation I will require there. I have lived too long like a journeyman tailor.

YOLLAND: Some years ago we lived fairly close to a poet—well,
280 about three miles away.

HUGH: His name?

YOLLAND: Wordsworth—William Wordsworth.

HUGH: Did he speak of me to you?

YOLLAND: Actually I never talked to him. I just saw him out
285 walking—in the distance.

HUGH: Wordsworth? . . . No. I'm afraid we're not familiar with your literature, Lieutenant. We feel closer to the warm Mediterranean. We tend to overlook your island.

YOLLAND: I'm learning to speak Irish, sir.

290 HUGH: Good.

YOLLAND: Roland's teaching me.

HUGH: Splendid.

YOLLAND: I mean—I feel so cut off from the people here. And I was trying to explain a few minutes ago how remarkable
295 a community this is. To meet people like yourself and Jimmy Jack who actually converse in Greek and Latin. And your place names—what was the one we came across this morning?—Termon, from Terminus, the god of boundaries. It—it—it's really astonishing.

300 HUGH: We like to think we endure around truths immemorially posited.

YOLLAND: And your Gaelic literature—you're a poet yourself—

HUGH: Only in Latin, I'm afraid.

YOLLAND: I understand it's enormously rich and ornate.

305 HUGH: Indeed, Lieutenant. A rich language. A rich literature. You'll find, sir, that certain cultures expend on their vocabularies and syntax acquisitive energies and ostentations entirely lacking in their material lives. I suppose you could call us a spiritual people.

310 OWEN: (*Not unkindly; more out of embarrassment before* YOLLAND.) Will you stop that nonsense, Father.

HUGH: Nonsense? What nonsense?

OWEN: Do you know where the priest lives?

HUGH: At Lis na Muc, over near . . .

315 OWEN: No, he doesn't. Lis na Muc, the Fort of the Pigs, has become Swinefort. (*Now turning the pages of the Name-Book—a page per name.*) And to get to Swinefort you pass through Greencastle and Fair Head and Strandhill and Gort and Whiteplains. And the new school isn't at Poll na gCao-
320 rach—it's at Sheepsrock. Will you be able to find your way?

266 *expeditio* an expedition

(HUGH *pours himself another drink. Then:—*)

HUGH: Yes, it is a rich language, Lieutenant, full of the mythologies of fantasy and hope and self-deception—a syntax opulent with tomorrows. It is our response to mud cabins and a diet of potatoes; and our only method of reply-
325 ing to . . . inevitabilities. (*To* OWEN.) Can you give me the loan of half-a-crown? I'll repay you out of the subscriptions I'm collecting for the publication of my new book. (*To* YOLLAND.) It is entitled: 'The Pentaglot Preceptor or Elementary Institute of the English, Greek, Hebrew, Latin and
330 Irish Languages; Particularly Calculated for the Instruction of Such Ladies and Gentlemen as may Wish to Learn without the Help of a Master.'

YOLLAND: (*Laughs.*) That's a wonderful title!

335 HUGH: Between ourselves—the best part of the enterprise. Nor do I, in fact, speak Hebrew. And that last phrase— 'without the Help of a Master'—that was written before the new national school was thrust upon me—do you think I ought to drop it now? After all you don't dispose of the cow just because it has produced a magnificent calf, do you?
340 YOLLAND: You certainly do not.

HUGH: The phrase goes. And I'm interrupting work of moment. (*He goes to the door and stops there.*) To return briefly to that other matter, Lieutenant. I understand your sense of exclusion, of being cut off from a life here; and I trust you
345 will find access to us with my son's help. But remember that words are signals, counters. They are not immortal. And it can happen—to use an image you'll understand— it can happen that a civilization can be imprisoned in a linguistic contour which no longer matches the landscape
350 of . . . fact. Gentlemen. (*He leaves.*)

OWEN: 'An *expeditio* with three purposes': the children laugh at him: he always promises three points and he never gets beyond A and B.

YOLLAND: He's an astute man.
355 OWEN: He's bloody pompous.

YOLLAND: But so astute.

OWEN: And he drinks too much. Is it astute not to be able to adjust for survival? Enduring around truths immemorially posited—hah!
360 YOLLAND: He knows what's happening.

OWEN: What is happening?

YOLLAND: I'm not sure. But I'm concerned about my part in it. It's an eviction of sorts.

OWEN: We're making a six-inch map of the country. Is there
365 something sinister in that?

YOLLAND: Not in—

OWEN: And we're taking place-names that are riddled with confusion and—

YOLLAND: Who's confused? Are the people confused?
370 OWEN: —and we're standardizing those names as accurately and as sensitively as we can.

YOLLAND: Something is being eroded.

OWEN: Back to the romance again. All right! Fine! Fine! Look where we've got to. (*He drops on his hands and knees and stabs
375 a finger at the map.*) We've come to this crossroads. Come here and look at it, man! Look at it! And we call that crossroads Tobair Vree. And why do we call it Tobair Vree? I'll tell you why. Tobair means a well. But what does Vree

380 mean? It's a corruption of Brian—(*Gaelic pronunciation.*) Brian—an erosion of Tobair Bhriain. Because a hundred-and-fifty years ago there used to be a well there, not at the crossroads, mind you—that would be too simple—but in a field close to the crossroads. And an old man called Brian,

385 whose face was disfigured by an enormous growth, got it into his head that the water in that well was blessed; and every day for seven months he went there and bathed his face in it. But the growth didn't go away; and one morning Brian was found drowned in that well. And ever since that

390 crossroads is known as Tobair Vree—even though that well has long since dried up. I know the story because my grand-father told it to me. But ask Doalty—or Maire—or Brid-get—even my father—even Manus—why it's called Tobair Vree; and do you think they'll know? I know they don't

395 know. So the question I put to you, Lieutenant, is this: what do we do with a name like that? Do we scrap Tobair Vree al-together and call it—what?—The Cross? Crossroads? Or do we keep piety with a man long dead, long forgotten, his name 'eroded' beyond recognition, whose trivial little story

400 nobody in the parish remembers?

YOLLAND: Except you.

OWEN: I've left here.

YOLLAND: You remember it.

OWEN: I'm asking you: what do we write in the Name-Book?

405 YOLLAND: Tobair Vree.

OWEN: Even though the well is a hundred yards from the ac-tual crossroads—and there's no well anyway—and what the hell does Vree mean?

YOLLAND: Tobair Vree.

410 OWEN: That's what you want?

YOLLAND: Yes.

OWEN: You're certain?

YOLLAND: Yes.

OWEN: Fine. Fine. That's what you'll get.

415 YOLLAND: That's what you want, too, Roland.

(*Pause.*)

OWEN: (*Explodes.*) George! For God's sake! My name is not Roland!

YOLLAND: What?

OWEN: (*Softly.*) My name is Owen.

(*Pause.*)

YOLLAND: Not Roland?

420 OWEN: Owen.

YOLLAND: You mean to say—?

OWEN: Owen.

YOLLAND: But I've been—

OWEN: O-w-e-n.

425 YOLLAND: Where did Roland come from?

OWEN: I don't know.

YOLLAND: It was never Roland?

OWEN: Never.

YOLLAND: O my God!

(*Pause. They stare at one another. Then the absurdity of the situation strikes them suddenly. They explode with laughter. OWEN pours drinks. As they roll about, their lines overlap.*)

YOLLAND: Why didn't you tell me? 430

OWEN: Do I look like a Roland?

YOLLAND: Spell Owen again.

OWEN: I was getting fond of Roland.

YOLLAND: O my God!

OWEN: O-w-e-n. 435

YOLLAND: What'll we write—

OWEN: —in the Name-Book?!

YOLLAND: R-o-w-e-n!

OWEN: Or what about Ol-

YOLLAND: Ol-what? 440

OWEN: Oland!

(*And again they explode. MANUS enters. He is very elated.*)

MANUS: What's the celebration?

OWEN: A christening!

YOLLAND: A baptism!

OWEN: A hundred christenings! 445

YOLLAND: A thousand baptisms! Welcome to Eden!

OWEN: Eden's right! We name a thing and—bang!—it leaps into existence!

YOLLAND: Each name a perfect equation with its roots.

OWEN: A perfect congruence with its reality. (*To MANUS.*) Take 450 a drink.

YOLLAND: Poteen—beautiful.

OWEN: Lying Anna's poteen.

YOLLAND: Anna na mBreag's poteen.

OWEN: Excellent, George. 455

YOLLAND: I'll decode you yet.

OWEN: (*Offers drink.*) Manus?

MANUS: Not if that's what it does to you.

OWEN: You're right. Steady—steady—sober up—sober up.

YOLLAND: Sober as a judge, Owen. 460

(*MANUS moves beside OWEN.*)

MANUS: I've got good news! Where's Father?

OWEN: He's gone out. What's the good news?

MANUS: I've been offered a job.

OWEN: Where? (*Now aware of YOLLAND.*) Come on, man— speak in English. 465

MANUS: For the benefit of the colonist?

OWEN: He's a decent man.

MANUS: Aren't they all at some level?

OWEN: Please.

(*MANUS shrugs.*)

He's been offered a job. 470

YOLLAND: Where?

OWEN: Well—tell us!

MANUS: I've just had a meeting with two men from Inis Mead-hon. They want me to go there and start a hedge-school. They're giving me a free house, free turf, and free milk; a 475 rood of standing corn; twelve drills of potatoes; and—

(*He stops.*)

OWEN: And what?

MANUS: A salary of £42 a year!

OWEN: Manus, that's wonderful!

480 MANUS: You're talking to a man of substance.

OWEN: I'm delighted.

YOLLAND: Where's Inis Meadhon?

OWEN: An island south of here. And they came looking for you?

485 MANUS: Well, I mean to say . . .

(OWEN *punches* MANUS.)

OWEN: Aaaaagh! This calls for a real celebration.

YOLLAND: Congratulations.

MANUS: Thank you.

OWEN: Where are you, Anna?

490 YOLLAND: When do you start?

MANUS: Next Monday.

OWEN: We'll stay with you when we're there. (*To* YOLLAND.) How long will it be before we reach Inis Meadhon?

YOLLAND: How far south is it?

495 MANUS: About fifty miles.

YOLLAND: Could we make it by December?

OWEN: We'll have Christmas together. (*Sings.*) 'Christmas Day on Inis Meadhon . . .'

YOLLAND: (*Toast.*) I hope you're very content there, Manus.

500 MANUS: Thank you.

(YOLLAND *holds out his hand.* MANUS *takes it. They shake warmly.*)

OWEN: (*Toast.*) Manus.

MANUS: (*Toast.*) To Inis Meadhon.

(*He drinks quickly and turns to leave.*)

OWEN: Hold on—hold on—refills coming up.

MANUS: I've got to go.

505 OWEN: Come on, man; this is an occasion. Where are you rushing to?

MANUS: I've got to tell Maire.

(MAIRE *enters with her can of milk.*)

MAIRE: You've got to tell Maire what?

OWEN: He's got a job!

510 MAIRE: Manus?

OWEN: He's been invited to start a hedge-school in Inis Meadhon.

MAIRE: Where?

MANUS: Inis Meadhon—the island! They're giving me £42 a

515 year and . . .

OWEN: A house, fuel, milk, potatoes, corn, pupils, what-not!

MANUS: I start on Monday.

OWEN: You'll take a drink. Isn't it great?

MANUS: I want to talk to you for—

520 MAIRE: There's your milk. I need the can back.

(MANUS *takes the can and runs up the steps.*)

MANUS: (*As he goes.*) How will you like living on an island?

OWEN: You know George, don't you?

MAIRE: We wave to each other across the fields.

YOLLAND: Sorry-sorry?

525 OWEN: She says you wave to each other across the fields.

YOLLAND: Yes, we do; oh, yes; indeed we do.

MAIRE: What's he saying?

OWEN: He says you wave to each other across the fields.

MAIRE: That's right. So we do.

YOLLAND: What's she saying?   530

OWEN: Nothing—nothing—nothing. (*To* MAIRE.) What's the news?

(MAIRE *moves away, touching the text books with her toe.*)

MAIRE: Not a thing. You're busy, the two of you.

OWEN: We think we are.

MAIRE: I hear the Fiddler O'Shea's about. There's some talk of 535 a dance tomorrow night.

OWEN: Where will it be?

MAIRE: Maybe over the road. Maybe at Tobair Vree.

YOLLAND: Tobair Vree!

MAIRE: Yes.   540

YOLLAND: Tobair Vree! Tobair Vree!

MAIRE: Does he know what I'm saying?

OWEN: Not a word.

MAIRE: Tell him then.

OWEN: Tell him what?   545

MAIRE: About the dance.

OWEN: Maire says there may be a dance tomorrow night.

YOLLAND: (*To* OWEN.) Yes? May I come? (*To* MAIRE.) Would anybody object if I came?

MAIRE: (*To* OWEN.) What's he saying?   550

OWEN: (*To* YOLLAND.) Who would object?

MAIRE: (*To* OWEN.) Did you tell him?

YOLLAND: (*To* MAIRE.) Sorry-sorry?

OWEN: (*To* MAIRE.) He says may he come?

MAIRE: (*To* YOLLAND.) That's up to you.   555

YOLLAND: (*To* OWEN.) What does she say?

OWEN: (*To* YOLLAND.) She says—

YOLLAND: (*To* MAIRE.) What-what?

MAIRE: (*To* OWEN.) Well?

YOLLAND: (*To* OWEN.) Sorry-sorry?   560

OWEN: (*To* OLLAND.) Will you go?

YOLLAND: (*To* MAIRE.) Yes, yes, if I may.

MAIRE: (*To* OWEN.) What does he say?

YOLLAND: (*To* OWEN.) What is she saying?

OWEN: Oh for God's sake! (*To* MANUS *who is descending with the* 565 *empty can.*) You take on this job, Manus.

MANUS: I'll walk you up to the house. Is your mother at home? I want to talk to her.

MAIRE: What's the rush? (*To* OWEN.) Didn't you offer me a drink?

OWEN: Will you risk Anna na mBreag?   570

MAIRE: Why not.

(YOLLAND *is suddenly intoxicated. He leaps up on a stool, raises his glass and shouts.*)

YOLLAND: Anna na mBreag! Baile Beag! Inis Meadhon! Bombay! Tobair Vree! Eden! And poteen—correct, Owen?

OWEN: Perfect.

YOLLAND: And bloody marvellous stuff it is, too. I love it! 575 Bloody, bloody, bloody marvellous!

(*Simultaneously with his final 'bloody marvellous' bring up very loud the introductory music of the reel. Then immediately go to black. Retain the music throughout the very brief interval.*)

SCENE II

The following night.

This scene may be played in the schoolroom, but it would be preferable to lose—by lighting—as much of the schoolroom as possible, and to play the scene down front in a vaguely 'outside' area.

The music rises to a crescendo. Then in the distance we hear MAIRE *and* YOLLAND *approach—laughing and running. They run on, hand-in-hand. They have just left the dance. Fade the music to distant background. Then after a time it is lost and replaced by guitar music.* MAIRE *and* YOLLAND *are now down front, still holding hands and excited by their sudden and impetuous escape from the dance.*

MAIRE. O my God, that leap across the ditch nearly killed me.
YOLLAND: I could scarcely keep up with you.
MAIRE: Wait till I get my breath back.
YOLLAND: We must have looked as if we were being chased.

(They now realize they are alone and holding hands—the beginnings of embarrassment. The hands disengage. They begin to drift apart. Pause.)

5   MAIRE: Manus'll wonder where I've got to.
YOLLAND: I wonder did anyone notice us leave.

(Pause. Slightly further apart.)

MAIRE: The grass must be wet. My feet are soaking.
YOLLAND: Your feet must be wet. The grass is soaking.

(Another pause. Another few paces apart. They are now a long distance from one another.)

YOLLAND: *(Indicating himself.)* George.

(MAIRE nods: Yes-yes. Then:—)

10   MAIRE: Lieutenant George.
YOLLAND: Don't call me that. I never think of myself as Lieutenant.
MAIRE: What-what?
YOLLAND: Sorry-sorry? *(He points to himself again.)* George.

(MAIRE nods: Yes-yes. Then points to herself.)

15   MAIRE: Maire.
YOLLAND: Yes, I know you're Maire. Of course I know you're Maire. I mean I've been watching you night and day for the past—
MAIRE: *(Eagerly.)* What-what?
20   YOLLAND: *(Points.)* Maire. *(Points.)* George. *(Points both.)* Maire and George.

(MAIRE nods: Yes-yes-yes.)

I—I—I—
MAIRE: Say anything at all, I love the sound of your speech.
YOLLAND: *(Eagerly.)* Sorry-sorry?

(In acute frustration he looks around, hoping for some inspiration that will provide him with communicative means. Now he has a thought:

he tries raising his voice and articulating in a staccato style and with equal and absurd emphasis on each word.)

Every-morning-I-see-you-feeding-brown-hens-and-giving-   25
meal-to-black-calf—*(The futility of it.)*—Oh my God.

(MAIRE smiles. She moves towards him. She will try to communicate in Latin.)

MAIRE: *Tu es centurio in—in—in exercitu Britannico—*
YOLLAND: Yes-yes? Go on—go on—say anything at all—I love the sound of your speech.
MAIRE: —*et es in castris quae—quae—quae sunt in agro—(The fu-*   30
tility of it.)—O my God. *(YOLLAND smiles. He moves towards her. Now for her English words.)* George—water.
YOLLAND: 'Water'? Water! Oh yes—water—water—very good—water—good—good.
MAIRE: Fire.   35
YOLLAND: Fire—indeed—wonderful—fire, fire, fire—splendid—splendid!
MAIRE: Ah . . . ah . . .
YOLLAND: Yes? Go on.
MAIRE: Earth.   40
YOLLAND: 'Earth'?
MAIRE: Earth. Earth. *(YOLLAND still does not understand.* MAIRE *stoops down and picks up a handful of clay. Holding it out.)* Earth.
YOLLAND: Earth! Of course—earth! Earth. Earth. Good Lord,   45
Maire, your English is perfect!
MAIRE: *(Eagerly.)* What-what?
YOLLAND: Perfect English. English perfect.
MAIRE: George—
YOLLAND: That's beautiful—oh, that's really beautiful.   50
MAIRE: George—
YOLLAND: Say it again—say it again—
MAIRE: Shhh. *(She holds her hand up for silence—she is trying to remember her one line of English. Now she remembers it and she delivers the line as if English were her language—easily, fluidly,*   55
conversationally.) George, 'In Norfolk we besport ourselves around the maypoll.'
YOLLAND: Good God, do you? That's where my mother comes from—Norfolk. Norwich actually. Not exactly Norwich town but a small village called Little Walsingham close be-   60
side it. But in our own village of Winfarthing we have a maypole too and every year on the first of May—*(He stops abruptly, only now realizing. He stares at her. She in turn misunderstands his excitement.)*
MAIRE: *(To herself.)* Mother of God, my Aunt Mary wouldn't   65
have taught me something dirty, would she?

(Pause. YOLLAND *extends his hand to* MAIRE. *She turns away from him and moves slowly across the stage.)*

YOLLAND: Maire.

II.ii.   27 Tu . . . Britannico you are a centurion in the British Army   **30 et . . . agro** and you are in the camp in the field

(*She still moves away.*)

Maire Chatach.

(*She still moves away.*)

70   Bun na hAbhann? (*He says the name softly, almost privately, very tentatively, as if he were searching for a sound she might respond to. He tries again.*) Druim Dubh?

(MAIRE *stops. She is listening.* YOLLAND *is encouraged.*)

Poll na gCaorach. Lis Maol.

(MAIRE *turns towards him.*)

Lis na nGall.
MAIRE: Lis na nGradh.

(*They are now facing each other and begin moving—almost imperceptibly—towards one another.*)

75   MAIRE: Carraig an Phoill.
YOLLAND: Carraig na Ri. Loch na nEan.
MAIRE: Loch an Iubhair. Machaire Buidhe.
YOLLAND: Machaire Mor. Cnoc na Mona.
MAIRE: Cnoc na nGabhar.
80   YOLLAND: Mullach.
MAIRE: Port.
YOLLAND: Tor.
MAIRE: Lag.

(*She holds out her hands to* YOLLAND. *He takes them. Each now speaks almost to himself/herself.*)

YOLLAND: I wish to God you could understand me.
85   MAIRE: Soft hands; a gentleman's hands.
YOLLAND: Because if you could understand me I could tell you how I spend my days either thinking of you or gazing up at your house in the hope that you'll appear even for a second.
MAIRE: Every evening you walk by yourself along the Tra Bhan
90   and every morning you wash yourself in front of your tent.
YOLLAND: I would tell you how beautiful you are, curly-headed Maire. I would so like to tell you how beautiful you are.
MAIRE: Your arms are long and thin and the skin on your shoulders is very white.
95   YOLLAND: I would tell you . . .
MAIRE: Don't stop—I know what you're saying.
YOLLAND: I would tell you how I want to be here—to live here—always—with you—always, always.
MAIRE: 'Always'? What is that word—'always'?
100   YOLLAND: Yes-yes; always.
MAIRE: You're trembling.
YOLLAND: Yes, I'm trembling because of you.
MAIRE: I'm trembling, too.

(*She holds his face in her hand.*)

YOLLAND: I've made up my mind . . .
105   MAIRE: Shhhh.
YOLLAND: I'm not going to leave here . . .
MAIRE: Shhhh—listen to me. I want you, too, soldier.

YOLLAND: Don't stop—I know what you're saying.
MAIRE: I want to live with you—anywhere—anywhere at all—always—always.   110
YOLLAND: 'Always'? What is that word—'always'?
MAIRE: Take me away with you, George.

(*Pause. Suddenly they kiss.* SARAH *enters. She sees them. She stands shocked, staring at them. Her mouth works. Then almost to herself.*)

SARAH: Manus . . . Manus!

(SARAH *runs off. Music to crescendo.*)

ACT THREE

The following evening. It is raining.

SARAH *and* OWEN *alone in the schoolroom.* SARAH, *more waif-like than ever, is sitting very still on a stool, an open book across her knee. She is pretending to read but her eyes keep going up to the room upstairs.* OWEN *is working on the floor as before, surrounded by his reference books, map, Name-Book, etc. But he has neither concentration nor interest; and like* SARAH *he glances up at the upstairs room.*

After a few seconds MANUS *emerges and descends, carrying a large paper bag which already contains his clothes. His movements are determined and urgent. He moves around the classroom, picking up books, examining each title carefully, and choosing about six of them which he puts into his bag. As he selects these books:—*

OWEN: You know that old limekiln beyond Con Connie Tim's pub, the place we call The Murren?—do you know why it's called The Murren?

(MANUS *does not answer.*)

I've only just discovered: it's a corruption of Saint Muranus. It seems Saint Muranus had a monastery somewhere about   5
there at the beginning of the seventh century. And over the years the name became shortened to the Murren. Very unattractive name, isn't it? I think we should go back to the original—Saint Muranus. What do you think? The original's Saint Muranus. Don't you think we should go back to that?   10

(*No response.* OWEN *begins writing the name into the Name-Book.* MANUS *is now rooting about among the forgotten implements for a piece of rope. He finds a piece. He begins to tie the mouth of the flimsy, overloaded bag—and it bursts, the contents spilling out on the floor.*)

MANUS: Bloody, bloody, bloody hell!

(*His voice breaks in exasperation: he is about to cry.* OWEN *leaps to his feet.*)

OWEN: Hold on. I've a bag upstairs.

(*He runs upstairs.* SARAH *waits until* OWEN *is off. Then:—*)

SARAH: Manus . . . Manus, I . . .

(MANUS *hears* SARAH *but makes no acknowledgement. He gathers up his belongings.* OWEN *reappears with the bag he had on his arrival.*)

OWEN: Take this one—I'm finished with it anyway. And it's supposed to keep out the rain.   15

(MANUS *transfers his few belongings.* OWEN *drifts back to his task. The packing is now complete.*)

MANUS: You'll be here for a while? For a week or two anyhow?
OWEN: Yes.
MANUS: You're not leaving with the army?
OWEN: I haven't made up my mind. Why?
20 MANUS: Those Inis Meadhon men will be back to see why I haven't turned up. Tell them—tell them I'll write to them as soon as I can. Tell them I still want the job but that it might be three or four months before I'm free to go.
OWEN: You're being damned stupid, Manus.
25 MANUS: Will you do that for me?
OWEN: Clear out now and Lancey'll think you're involved somehow.
MANUS: Will you do that for me?
OWEN: Wait a couple of days even. You know George—he's a
30 bloody romantic—maybe he's gone out to one of the islands and he'll suddenly reappear tomorrow morning. Or maybe the search party'll find him this evening lying drunk somewhere in the sandhills. You've seen him drinking that poteen—doesn't know how to handle it. Had he drink on
35 him last night at the dance?
MANUS: I had a stone in my hand when I went out looking for him—I was going to fell him. The lame scholar turned violent.
OWEN: Did anybody see you?
40 MANUS: (*Again close to tears.*) But when I saw him standing there at the side of the road—smiling—and her face buried in his shoulder—I couldn't even go close to them. I just shouted something stupid—something like, 'You're a bastard, Yolland.' If I'd even said it in English . . . 'cos he kept saying
45 'Sorry-sorry.' The wrong gesture in the wrong language.
OWEN: And you didn't see him again?
MANUS: 'Sorry?'
OWEN: Before you leave tell Lancey that—just to clear yourself.
MANUS: What have I to say to Lancey? You'll give that message
50 to the islandmen?
OWEN: I'm warning you: run away now and you're bound to be—
MANUS: (*To* SARAH.) Will you give that message to the Inis Meadhon men?
55 SARAH: I will.

(MANUS *picks up an old sack and throws it across his shoulders.*)

OWEN: Have you any idea where you're going?
MANUS: Mayo, maybe. I remember Mother saying she had cousins somewhere away out in the Erris Peninsula. (*He picks up his bag.*) Tell Father I took only the Virgil and the
60 Caesar and the Aeschylus because they're mine anyway—I bought them with the money I got for that pet lamb I reared—do you remember that pet lamb? And tell him that Nora Dan never returned the dictionary and that she still owes him two-and-six for last quarter's reading—he always
65 forgets those things.
OWEN: Yes.
MANUS: And his good shirt's ironed and hanging up in the press and his clean socks are in the butter-box under the bed.
OWEN: All right.

MANUS: And tell him I'll write. 70
OWEN: If Maire asks where you've gone . . . ?
MANUS: He'll need only half the amount of milk now, won't he? Even less than half—he usually takes his tea black. (*Pause.*) And when he comes in at night—you'll hear him; he makes a lot of noise—I usually come down and give him 75
a hand up. Those stairs are dangerous without a banister. Maybe before you leave you'd get Big Ned Frank to put up some sort of a handrail. (*Pause.*) And if you can bake, he's very fond of soda bread.
OWEN: I can give you money. I'm wealthy. Do you know what 80
they pay me? Two shillings a day for this—this—this—

(MANUS *rejects the offer by holding out his hand.*)

Goodbye, Manus.

(MANUS *and* OWEN *shake hands. Then* MANUS *picks up his bag briskly and goes towards the door. He stops a few paces beyond* SARAH, *turns, comes back to her. He addresses her as he did in Act One but now without warmth or concern for her.*)

MANUS: What is your name? (*Pause.*) Come on. What is your name?
SARAH: My name is Sarah. 85
MANUS: Just Sarah? Sarah what? (*Pause.*) Well?
SARAH: Sarah Johnny Sally.
MANUS: And where do you live? Come on.
SARAH: I live in Bun na hAbhann.

(*She is now crying quietly.*)

MANUS: Very good, Sarah Johnny Sally. There's nothing to stop 90
you now—nothing in the wide world. (*Pause. He looks down at her.*) It's all right—it's all right—you did no harm—you did no harm at all.

(*He stoops over her and kisses the top of her head—as if in absolution. Then briskly to the door and off.*)

OWEN: Good luck, Manus!
SARAH: (*Quietly.*) I'm sorry . . . I'm sorry . . . I'm so sorry, 95
Manus . . .

(OWEN *tries to work but cannot concentrate. He begins folding up the map. As he does:—*)

OWEN: Is there a class this evening?

(SARAH *nods:* Yes.)

I suppose Father knows. Where is he anyhow?

(SARAH *points.*)

Where?

(SARAH *mimes rocking a baby.*)

I don't understand—where? 100

(SARAH *repeats the mime and wipes away tears.* OWEN *is still puzzled.*)

It doesn't matter. He'll probably turn up.

(BRIDGET *and* DOALTY *enter, sacks over their heads against the rain. They are self-consciously noisier, more ebullient, more garrulous than ever—brimming over with excitement and gossip and brio.*)

DOALTY: You're missing the crack, boys! Cripes, you're missing the crack! Fifty more soldiers arrived an hour ago!

BRIDGET: And they're spread out in a big line from Sean Neal's
105   over to Lag and they're moving straight across the fields towards Cnoc na nGabhar!

DOALTY: Prodding every inch of the ground in front of them with their bayonets and scattering animals and hens in all directions!

110 BRIDGET: And tumbling everything before them—fences, ditches, haystacks, turf-stacks!

DOALTY: They came to Barney Petey's field of corn—straight through it be God as if it was heather!

BRIDGET: Not a blade of it left standing!

115 DOALTY: And Barney Petey just out of his bed and running after them in his drawers: 'You hoors you! Get out of my corn, you hoors you!'

BRIDGET: First time he ever ran in his life.

DOALTY: Too lazy, the wee get, to cut it when the weather was
120   good.

(SARAH *begins putting out the seats.*)

BRIDGET: Tell them about Big Hughie.

DOALTY: Cripes, if you'd seen your aul fella, Owen.

BRIDGET: They were all inside in Anna na mBreag's pub—all the crowd from the wake—

125 DOALTY: And they hear the commotion and they all come out to the street—

BRIDGET: Your father in front; the Infant Prodigy footless behind him!

DOALTY: And your aul fella, he sees the army stretched across
130   the countryside—

BRIDGET: O my God!

DOALTY: And Cripes he starts roaring at them!

BRIDGET: 'Visigoths! Huns! Vandals!'

DOALTY: '*Ignari! Stulti! Rustici!*'

135 BRIDGET: And wee Jimmy Jack jumping up and down and shouting, 'Thermopylae! Thermopylae!'

DOALTY: You never saw crack like it in your life, boys. Come away on out with me, Sarah, and you'll see it all.

BRIDGET: Big Hughie's fit to take no class. Is Manus about?

140 OWEN: Manus is gone.

BRIDGET: Gone where?

OWEN: He's left—gone away.

DOALTY: Where to?

OWEN: He doesn't know. Mayo, maybe.

145 DOALTY: What's on in Mayo?

OWEN: (*To* BRIDGET.) Did you see George and Maire Chatach leave the dance last night?

BRIDGET: We did. Didn't we, Doalty?

OWEN: Did you see Manus following them out?

150 BRIDGET: I didn't see him going out but I saw him coming in by himself later.

OWEN: Did George and Maire come back to the dance?

BRIDGET: No.

OWEN: Did you see them again?

BRIDGET: He left her home. We passed them going up the back 155
road—didn't we, Doalty?

OWEN: And Manus stayed till the end of the dance?

DOALTY: We know nothing. What are you asking us for?

OWEN: Because Lancey'll question me when he hears Manus's gone. (*Back to* BRIDGET.) That's the way George went 160
home? By the back road? That's where you saw him?

BRIDGET: Leave me alone, Owen. I know nothing about Yolland. If you want to know about Yolland, ask the Donnelly twins.

(*Silence.* DOALTY *moves over to the window.*)

(*To* SARAH.) He's a powerful fiddler, O'Shea, isn't he? He told our Seamus he'll come back for a night at Hallowe'en. 165

(OWEN *goes to* DOALTY *who looks resolutely out the window.*)

OWEN: What's this about the Donnellys? (*Pause.*) Were they about last night?

DOALTY: Didn't see them if they were.

(*Begins whistling through his teeth.*)

OWEN: George is a friend of mine.

DOALTY: So. 170

OWEN: I want to know what's happened to him.

DOALTY: Couldn't tell you.

OWEN: What have the Donnelly twins to do with it? (*Pause.*) Doalty!

DOALTY: I know nothing, Owen—nothing at all—I swear to 175
God. All I know is this: on my way to the dance I saw their boat beached at Port. It wasn't there on my way home, after I left Bridget. And that's all I know. As God's my judge. The half-dozen times I met him I didn't know a word he said to me; but he seemed a right enough sort . . . (*With sud-* 180
den excessive interest in the scene outside.) Cripes, they're crawling all over the place! Cripes, there's millions of them! Cripes, they're levelling the whole land!

(OWEN *moves away.* MAIRE *enters. She is bareheaded and wet from the rain; her hair in disarray. She attempts to appear normal but she is in acute distress, on the verge of being distraught. She is carrying the milk-can.*)

MAIRE: Honest to God, I must be going off my head. I'm halfway here and I think to myself, 'Isn't this can very 185
light?' and I look into it and isn't it empty.

OWEN: It doesn't matter.

MAIRE: How will you manage for tonight?

OWEN: We have enough.

MAIRE: Are you sure? 190

OWEN: Plenty, thanks.

MAIRE: It'll take me no time at all to go back up for some.

OWEN: Honestly, Maire.

MAIRE: Sure it's better you have it than that black calf that's . . . that . . . (*She looks around.*) Have you heard anything? 195

OWEN: Nothing.

MAIRE: What does Lancey say?

OWEN: I haven't seen him since this morning.

902   UNIT VII • WORLD STAGES

MAIRE: What does he *think*?

OWEN: We really didn't talk. He was here for only a few seconds.

MAIRE: He left me home, Owen. And the last thing he said to me—he tried to speak in Irish—he said, 'I'll see you yesterday'—he meant to say 'I'll see you tomorrow.' And I laughed that much he pretended to get cross and he said 'Maypoll! Maypoll!' because I said that word wrong. And off he went, laughing—laughing, Owen! Do you think he's all right? What do *you* think?

OWEN: I'm sure he'll turn up, Maire.

MAIRE: He comes from a tiny wee place called Winfarthing. (*She suddenly drops on her hands and knees on the floor—where* OWEN *had his map a few minutes ago—and with her finger traces out an outline map.*) Come here till you see. Look. There's Winfarthing. And there's two other wee villages right beside it; one of them's called Barton Bendish—it's there; and the other's called Saxingham Nethergate—it's about there. And there's Little Walsingham—that's his mother's townland. Aren't they odd names? Sure they make no sense to me at all. And Winfarthing's near a big town called Norwich. And Norwich is in a county called Norfolk. And Norfolk is in the east of England. He drew a map for me on the wet strand and wrote the names on it. I have it all in my head now: Winfarthing—Barton Bendish—Saxingham Nethergate—Little Walsingham—Norwich—Norfolk. Strange sounds, aren't they? But nice sounds; like Jimmy Jack reciting his Homer. (*She gets to her feet and looks around; she is almost serene now. To* SARAH.) You were looking lovely last night, Sarah. Is that the dress you got from Boston? Green suits you. (*To* OWEN.) Something very bad's happened to him, Owen. I know. He wouldn't go away without telling me. Where is he, Owen? You're his friend—where is he? (*Again she looks around the room; then sits on a stool.*) I didn't get a chance to do my geography last night. The master'll be angry with me. (*She rises again.*) I think I'll go home now. The wee ones have to be washed and put to bed and that black calf has to be fed . . . My hands are that rough; they're still blistered from the hay. I'm ashamed of them. I hope to God there's no hay to be saved in Brooklyn. (*She stops at the door.*) Did you hear? Nellie Ruadh's baby died in the middle of the night. I must go up to the wake. It didn't last long, did it?

(MAIRE *leaves. Silence. Then:*)

OWEN: I don't think there'll be any class. Maybe you should . . .

(OWEN *begins picking up his texts.* DOALTY *goes to him.*)

DOALTY: Is he long gone?—Manus?

OWEN: Half an hour.

DOALTY: Stupid bloody fool.

OWEN: I told him that.

DOALTY: Do they know he's gone?

OWEN: Who?

DOALTY: The army.

OWEN: Not yet.

DOALTY: They'll be after him like bloody beagles. Bloody, bloody fool, limping along the coast. They'll overtake him before night for Christ's sake.

(DOALTY *returns to the window.* LANCEY *enters—now the commanding officer.*)

OWEN: Any news? Any word?

(LANCEY *moves into the centre of the room, looking around as he does.*)

LANCEY: I understood there was a class. Where are the others?

OWEN: There was to be a class but my father—

LANCEY: This will suffice. I will address them and it will be their responsibility to pass on what I have to say to every family in this section.

(LANCEY *indicates to* OWEN *to translate.* OWEN *hesitates, trying to assess the change in* LANCEY's *manner and attitude.*)

I'm in a hurry, O'Donnell.

OWEN: The captain has an announcement to make.

LANCEY: Lieutenant Yolland is missing. We are searching for him. If we don't find him, or if we receive no information as to where he is to be found, I will pursue the following course of action. (*He indicates to* OWEN *to translate.*)

OWEN: They are searching for George. If they don't find him—

LANCEY: Commencing twenty-four hours from now we will shoot all livestock in Ballybeg.

(OWEN *stares at* LANCEY.)

At once.

OWEN: Beginning this time tomorrow they'll kill every animal in Baile Beag—unless they're told where George is.

LANCEY: If that doesn't bear results, commencing forty-eight hours from now we will embark on a series of evictions and levelling of every abode in the following selected areas—

OWEN: You're not—!

LANCEY: Do your job. Translate.

OWEN: If they still haven't found him in two days time they'll begin evicting and levelling every house starting with these townlands.

(LANCEY *reads from his list.*)

LANCEY: Swinefort.

OWEN: Lis na Muc.

LANCEY: Burnfoot.

OWEN: Bun na hAbhann.

LANCEY: Dromduff.

OWEN: Druim Dubh.

LANCEY: Whiteplains.

OWEN: Machaire Ban.

LANCEY: Kings Head.

OWEN: Cnoc na Ri.

LANCEY: If by then the lieutenant hasn't been found, we will proceed until a complete clearance is made of this entire section.

OWEN: If Yolland hasn't been got by then, they will ravish the whole parish.

LANCEY: I trust they know exactly what they've got to do. (*Pointing to* BRIDGET.) I know you. I know where you live. (*Pointing to* SARAH.) Who are you? Name!

(SARAH's *mouth opens and shuts, opens and shuts. Her face becomes contorted.*)

What's your name?

(*Again* SARAH *tries frantically.*)

OWEN: Go on, Sarah. You can tell him.

(*But* SARAH *cannot. And she knows she cannot. She closes her mouth. Her head goes down.*)

OWEN: Her name is Sarah Johnny Sally.
300 LANCEY: Where does she live?
OWEN: Bun na hAbhann.
LANCEY: Where?
OWEN: Burnfoot.
LANCEY: I want to talk to your brother—is he here?
305 OWEN: Not at the moment.
LANCEY: Where is he?
OWEN: He's at a wake.
LANCEY: What wake?

(DOALTY, *who has been looking out the window all through* LANCEY'*s announcements, now speaks—calmly, almost casually.*)

DOALTY: Tell him his whole camp's on fire.
310 LANCEY: What's your name? (*To* OWEN.) Who's that lout?
OWEN: Doalty Dan Doalty.
LANCEY: Where does he live?
OWEN: Tulach Alainn.
LANCEY: What do we call it?
315 OWEN: Fair Hill. He says your whole camp is on fire.

(LANCEY *rushes to the window and looks out. Then he wheels on* DOALTY.)

LANCEY: I'll remember you, Mr Doalty. (*To* OWEN.) You carry a big responsibility in all this.

(*He goes off.*)

BRIDGET: Mother of God, does he mean it, Owen?
OWEN: Yes, he does.
320 BRIDGET: We'll have to hide the beasts somewhere—our Sea-mus'll know where. Maybe at the back of Lis na nGradh—or in the caves at the far end of Tra Bhan. Come on, Doalty! Come on! Don't be standing about there!

(DOALTY *does not move.* BRIDGET *runs to the door and stops suddenly. She sniffs the air. Panic.*)

The sweet smell! Smell it! It's the sweet smell! Jesus, it's the
325 potato blight!
DOALTY: It's the army tents burning, Bridget.
BRIDGET: Is it? Are you sure? Is that what it is? God, I thought we were destroyed altogether. Come on! Come on!

(*She runs off.* OWEN *goes to* SARAH *who is preparing to leave.*)

OWEN: How are you? Are you all right?

(SARAH *nods:* Yes.)

330 OWEN: Don't worry. It will come back to you again.

(SARAH *shakes her head.*)

OWEN: It will. You're upset now. He frightened you. That's all's wrong.

(*Again* SARAH *shakes her head, slowly, emphatically, and smiles at* OWEN. *Then she leaves.* OWEN *busies himself gathering his belongings.* DOALTY *leaves the window and goes to him.*)

DOALTY: He'll do it, too.
OWEN: Unless Yolland's found.
DOALTY: Hah!   335
OWEN: Then he'll certainly do it.
DOALTY: When my grandfather was a boy they did the same thing. (*Simply, altogether without irony.*) And after all the trouble you went to, mapping the place and thinking up new names for it. (OWEN *busies himself. Pause.* DOALTY *almost* 340 *dreamily.*) I've damned little to defend but he'll not put me out without a fight. And there'll be others who think the same as me.
OWEN: That's a matter for you.
DOALTY: If we'd all stick together. If we knew how to defend 345 ourselves.
OWEN: Against a trained army.
DOALTY: The Donnelly twins know how.
OWEN: If they could be found.
DOALTY: If they could be found. (*He goes to the door.*) Give me a 350 shout after you've finished with Lancey. I might know something then.

(*He leaves.*)

(OWEN *picks up the Name-Book. He looks at it momentarily, then puts it on top of the pile he is carrying. It falls to the floor. He stoops to pick it up—hesitates—leaves it. He goes upstairs. As* OWEN *ascends,* HUGH *and* JIMMY JACK *enter. Both wet and drunk.* JIMMY *is very unsteady. He is trotting behind* HUGH, *trying to break in on* HUGH'*s declamation.* HUGH *is equally drunk but more experienced in drunkenness: there is a portion of his mind which retains its clarity.*)

HUGH: There I was, appropriately dispositioned to proffer my condolences to the bereaved mother . . .
JIMMY: Hugh—   355
HUGH: and about to enter the *domus lugubris*—Maire Chatach?
JIMMY: The wake house.
HUGH: Indeed—when I experience a plucking at my elbow: Mister George Alexander, Justice of the Peace. 'My tidings 360 are infelicitous,' said he—Bridget? Too slow. Doalty?
JIMMY: *Infelix*—unhappy.
HUGH: Unhappy indeed. 'Master Bartley Timlin has been appointed to the new national school.' 'Timlin? Who is Tim-lin?' 'A schoolmaster from Cork. And he will be a major as- 365 set to the community: he is also a very skilled bacon-curer!'
JIMMY: Hugh—
HUGH: Ha-ha-ha-ha-ha! The Cork bacon-curer! *Barbarus hic ego sum quia non intelligor ulli*—James?

III. 356 *domus lugubris* house of mourning   362 *infelix* un-lucky, unhappy   368–369 *Barbarus . . . ulli* I am a barbarian here because I am not understood by anyone

370 JIMMY: Ovid.

HUGH: *Procede.*

JIMMY: 'I am a barbarian in this place because I am not understood by anyone.'

HUGH: Indeed—(*Shouts.*) Manus! Tea! I will compose a satire
375 on Master Bartley Timlin, schoolmaster and bacon-curer.
But it will be too easy, won't it? (*Shouts.*) Strong tea! Black!

(*The only way* JIMMY *can get* HUGH's *attention is by standing in front
of him and holding his arms.*)

JIMMY: Will you listen to me, Hugh!

HUGH: James. (*Shouts.*) And a slice of soda bread.

JIMMY: I'm going to get married.

380 HUGH: Well!

JIMMY: At Christmas.

HUGH: Splendid.

JIMMY: To Athene.

HUGH: Who?

385 JIMMY: Pallas Athene.

HUGH: *Glaukopis Athene?*

JIMMY: Flashing-eyed, Hugh, flashing-eyed!

(*He attempts the gesture he has made before: standing to attention, the
momentary spasm, the salute, the face raised in pained ecstasy—but
the body does not respond efficiently this time. The gesture is grotesque.*)

HUGH: The lady has assented?

JIMMY: She asked *me*—I assented.

390 HUGH: Ah. When was this?

JIMMY: Last night.

HUGH: What does her mother say?

JIMMY: Metis from Hellespont? Decent people—good stock.

HUGH: And her father?

395 JIMMY: I'm meeting Zeus tomorrow. Hugh, will you be my
best man?

HUGH: Honoured, James; profoundly honoured.

JIMMY: You know what I'm looking for, Hugh, don't you? I
mean to say—you know—I—I—I joke like the rest of
400 them—you know?—(*Again he attempts the pathetic routine
but abandons it instantly.*) You know yourself, Hugh—don't
you?—you know all that. But what I'm really looking for,
Hugh—what I really want—companionship, Hugh—at
my time of life, companionship, company, someone to talk
405 to. Away up in Beann na Gaoithe—you've no idea how
lonely it is. Companionship—correct, Hugh? Correct?

HUGH: Correct.

JIMMY: And I always liked her, Hugh. Correct?

HUGH: Correct, James.

410 JIMMY: Someone to talk to.

HUGH: Indeed.

JIMMY: That's all, Hugh. The whole story. You know it all now,
Hugh. You know it all.

(*As* JIMMY *says those last lines he is crying, shaking his head, trying
to keep his balance, and holding a finger up to his lips in absurd gestures of secrecy and intimacy. Now he staggers away, tries to sit on a
stool, misses it, slides to the floor, his feet in front of him, his back
against the broken cart. Almost at once he is asleep.* HUGH *watches all
of this. Then he produces his flask and is about to pour a drink when
he sees the Name-Book on the floor. He picks it up and leafs through*

it, pronouncing the strange names as he does. Just as he begins, OWEN
emerges and descends with two bowls of tea.)

HUGH: Ballybeg. Burnfoot. King's Head. Whiteplains. Fair
Hill. Dunboy. Green Bank. 415

(OWEN *snatches the book from* HUGH.)

OWEN: I'll take that. (*In apology.*) It's only a catalogue of names.

HUGH: I know what it is.

OWEN: A mistake—my mistake—nothing to do with us. I
hope that's strong enough [*tea*]. (*He throws the book on the
table and crosses over to* JIMMY.) Jimmy. Wake up, Jimmy. 420
Wake up, man.

JIMMY: What—what-what?

OWEN: Here. Drink this. Then go on away home. There may
be trouble. Do you hear me, Jimmy? There may be trouble.

HUGH: (*Indicating Name-Book.*) We must learn those new 425
names.

OWEN: (*Searching around.*) Did you see a sack lying about?

HUGH: We must learn where we live. We must learn to make
them our own. We must make them our new home.

(OWEN *finds a sack and throws it across his shoulders.*)

OWEN: I know where I live. 430

HUGH: James thinks he knows, too. I look at James and three
thoughts occur to me: A—that it is not the literal past, the
'facts' of history, that shape us, but images of the past embodied in language. James has ceased to make that discrimination. 435

OWEN: Don't lecture me, Father.

HUGH: B—we must never cease renewing those images; because once we do, we fossilize. Is there no soda bread?

OWEN: And C, Father—one single, unalterable 'fact': if Yolland
is not found, we are all going to be evicted. Lancey has is- 440
sued the order.

HUGH: Ah. *Edictum imperatoris.*

OWEN: You should change out of those wet clothes. I've got to
go. I've got to see Doalty Dan Doalty.

HUGH: What about? 445

OWEN: I'll be back soon.

(*As* OWEN *exits.*)

HUGH: Take care, Owen. To remember everything is a form of
madness. (*He looks around the room, carefully, as if he were about
to leave it forever. Then he looks at* JIMMY, *asleep again.*) The
road to Sligo. A spring morning. 1798. Going into battle. 450
Do you remember, James? Two young gallants with pikes
across their shoulders and the *Aeneid* in their pockets.
Everything seemed to find definition that spring—a congruence, a miraculous matching of hope and past and present and possibility. Striding across the fresh, green land. 455
The rhythms of perception heightened. The whole enterprise of consciousness accelerated. We were gods that
morning, James; and I had recently married my goddess,

---

442 *edictum imperatoris* the decree os the commander

Caitlin Dubh Nic Reactainn, may she rest in peace. And to
460 leave her and my infant son in his cradle—that was heroic,
too. By God, sir, we were magnificent. We marched as far
as—where was it?—Glenties! All of twenty-three miles in
one day. And it was there, in Phelan's pub, that we got
home-sick for Athens, just like Ulysses. The *desiderium*
465 *nostrorum*—the need for our own. Our *pietas*, James, was for
older, quieter things. And that was the longest twenty-
three miles back I ever made. (*Toasts* JIMMY.) My friend,
confusion is not an ignoble condition.

(MAIRE *enters.*)

MAIRE: I'm back again. I set out for somewhere but I couldn't
470 remember where. So I came back here.
HUGH: Yes, I will teach you English, Maire Chatach.
MAIRE: Will you, Master? I must learn it. I need to learn it.
HUGH: Indeed you may well be my only pupil.

(*He goes towards the steps and begins to ascend.*)

MAIRE: When can we start?
475 HUGH: Not today. Tomorrow, perhaps. After the funeral. We'll
begin tomorrow. (*Ascending.*) But don't expect too much. I
will provide you with the available words and the available
grammar. But will that help you to interpret between priva-
cies? I have no idea. But it's all we have. I have no idea at all.

(*He is now at the top.*)

480 MAIRE: Master, what does the English word 'always' mean?
HUGH: *Semper—per omnia saecula.* The Greeks called it *'aei.'* It's
not a word I'd start with. It's a silly word, girl.

(*He sits.* JIMMY *is awake. He gets to his feet.* MAIRE *sees the Name-
Book, picks it up, and sits with it on her knee.*)

MAIRE: When he comes back, this is where he'll come to. He
told me this is where he was happiest.

(JIMMY *sits beside* MAIRE.)

JIMMY: Do you know the Greek word *endogamein*? It means to 485
marry within the tribe. And the word *exogamein* means to
marry outside the tribe. And you don't cross those borders
casually—both sides get very angry. Now, the problem is
this: Is Athene sufficiently mortal or am I sufficiently god-
like for the marriage to be acceptable to her people and to 490
my people? You think about that.
HUGH: *Urbs antiqua fuit*—there was an ancient city which, 'tis
said, Juno loved above all the lands. And it was the goddess's aim and cherished hope that here should be the capital of all nations—should the fates perchance allow that. 495
Yet in truth she discovered that a race was springing from
Trojan blood to overthrow some day these Tyrian towers—a people *late regem belloque superbum*—kings of broad
realms and proud in war who would come forth for
Libya's downfall—such was—such was the course—such 500
was the course ordained—ordained by fate . . . What the
hell's wrong with me? Sure I know it backwards. I'll begin
again. *Urbs antiqua fuit*—there was an ancient city which,
'tis said, Juno loved above all the lands.

(*Begin to bring down the lights.*)

And it was the goddess's aim and cherished hope that here 505
should be the capital of all nations—should the fates perchance allow that. Yet in truth she discovered that a race was
springing from Trojan blood to overthrow some day these
Tyrian towers—a people kings of broad realms and proud
in war who would come forth for Libya's downfall . . . 510

(*Blackout.*)

464–465 *desiderium nostrorum* longing/need for our things/
people   465 *pietas* piety   481 *Semper . . . saecula* always—for
all time; *aei* always

---

485 *endogamein* to marry within the tribe   486 *exogamein* to
marry outside the tribe   492 *Urbs antiqua* **fuit** there was an ancient city   498 *late . . . superbum* kings of broad realms and
proud in war, from Virgil's *Aeneid,* book I.

Athol Fugard

Born in 1932, the South African playwright Athol Fugard left the University of Cape Town in 1953, traveled Africa, and worked as a seaman before returning to Cape Town and undertaking theater work with the Circle Players. As a mixed-race company, the Circle Players worked in violation of South Africa's apartheid laws. They brought the issue of apartheid to a head when Fugard—a white man—collaborated with the black actor Zakes Mokae in the play *The Blood Knot* (1961), a play about two brothers, one of whom is light-skinned enough to "pass" for white. The play's powerful indictment of apartheid and the fine performances of Fugard and Mokae were widely admired, and gained Fugard a reputation as a dramatist outside South Africa. Yet, despite its notoriety, the play could hardly remove apartheid itself. Fugard and Mokae were still forced to travel separately, and the government passed new laws limiting interracial theater; in addition, Fugard had his passport withdrawn for four years. In 1963, Fugard began his long association with The Serpent Players, a black company. This association was made nearly impossible, however, by the 1965 extension of the Group Areas Act, one of the principal apartheid statutes: both racially mixed casts and racially mixed audiences were forbidden. By June of 1965, Fugard was denied a permit to enter the black township of New Brighton for the dress rehearsal of Sophocles' *Antigone,* which he had adapted and produced with The Serpent Players. His passport was withdrawn again, and then again for four years, in 1967.

By the early 1970s, Fugard had written several of his best-known plays—*Hello and Goodbye* (1965), *Boesman and Lena* (1969)—when he became frustrated with his method of writing plays and decided to work more collaboratively with The Serpent Players. Fugard had worked with John Kani (b. 1944) on the 1965 *Antigone,* and Kani and Winston Ntshona (b. 1941) had performed another absurdist two-hander about convicts—Jean Genet's *Deathwatch*—with the Serpent company in 1968. Both Kani and Ntshona were recognized performers in their own right when they agreed to collaborate with Fugard in the early 1970s. These collaborations were different from Fugard's earlier adaptations of European classics for The Serpent Players, for in this work Kani and Ntshona supplied information, dialogue, and performance tropes which were scripted and shaped in dialogue with Fugard. The plays they devised—*Sizwe Bansi Is Dead* (1972) and *The Island* (1973)—are fully collaborative, for the three men improvised a variety of possible performances before setting them down in a final design; the opening monologue with the newspaper in *Sizwe Bansi Is Dead,* for instance, is based on Kani's usual stand-up performance routines. Fugard has gone on to write a number of plays about the effects of apartheid and racism on South African life, including *A Lesson from Aloes* (1980), *"Master Harold" . . . and the boys* (1982), *My Children! My Africa!* (1989), *Playland* (1993), *Valley Song* (1996), *The Captain's Tiger* (1998), and *Sorrows and Rejoicings* (2002).

"MASTER HAROLD" . . . AND THE BOYS

"Master Harold". . . and the boys is one of Fugard's most personal and searching plays on the consequences of racial apartheid for individual human relationships. The play takes place in the St. George's Park Tea Room in Port Elizabeth, South Africa, and is set in 1950; but while the play is set during the solidification of South Africa's apartheid legislation—the Pass Laws were passed in 1948, the Prohibition of Mixed Marriages Act in 1949, and the Group Areas Act and the Immorality Amendment Act in 1950—the play has an atmosphere of hope as well, conveyed in part by the American dance music that forms the play's acoustic background. Dance is the central metaphor of the play's action, as first Sam teaches Willie, preparing him for his entry into the upcoming dance competition, and then Sam and Hally engage in a more intricate and violent emotional encounter. For Sam and Hally have a long

Willie, Hally, and Sam in the Roundabout Theater production of *"Master Harold" . . . and the boys*.

history. Hally's father is an abusive, alcoholic invalid, and Sam has in many ways filled his place in Hally's life, providing both emotional and practical support. In exchange, he has had the benefit of Hally's education, learning Hally's school lessons as he helped the boy to study. Yet, while there's genuine affection between the two men, their inequality is never far from the surface, appearing even when Hally retells one of his most cherished memories, of the day Sam took him out to fly a kite: "The sheer audacity of it took my breath away. I mean, seriously, what the hell does a black man know about flying a kite?" As the play proceeds, though, Sam's efforts to calm Hally's rage against his father turns Hally against him, leading to the climactic moment in which the suppressed dynamics of racism boil to the surface. Reminding Sam that his father "is a white man and that's good enough for you," Hally then insists that Sam begin calling him "Master Harold," putting an end to their dance of emotional intimacy. Whether it will be possible for Sam and Hally to "fly another kite" remains an open question at the end of the play.

"MASTER HAROLD" . . . AND THE BOYS

Athol Fugard

CHARACTERS

HALLY
SAM
WILLIE

The St. George's Park Tea Room on a wet and windy Port Elizabeth afternoon.

Tables and chairs have been cleared and are stacked on one side except for one which stands apart with a single chair. On this table a knife, fork, spoon and side plate in anticipation of a simple meal, together with a pile of comic books.

Other elements: a serving counter with a few stale cakes under glass and a not very impressive display of sweets, cigarettes and cool drinks, etc.; a few cardboard advertising handouts—Cadbury's Chocolate, Coca-Cola—and a blackboard on which an untrained hand has chalked up the prices of Tea, Coffee, Scones, Milkshakes—all flavors—and Cool Drinks; a few sad ferns in pots; a telephone; an old-style jukebox.

There is an entrance on one side and an exit into a kitchen on the other.

Leaning on the solitary table, his head cupped in one hand as he pages through one of the comic books, is SAM. *A black man in his mid-forties. He wears the white coat of a waiter. Behind him on his knees, mopping down the floor with a bucket of water and a rag, is* WILLIE. *Also black and about the same age as* SAM. *He has his sleeves and trousers rolled up.*

The year: 1950

WILLIE: (*Singing as he works*)
    "She was scandalizin' my name,
    She took my money
    She called me honey
5   But she was scandalizin' my name.
    Called it love but was playin' a game . . ."

(*He gets up and moves the bucket. Stands thinking for a moment, then, raising his arms to hold an imaginary partner, he launches into an intricate ballroom dance step. Although a mildly comic figure, he reveals a reasonable degree of accomplishment*)

    Hey, Sam.

(SAM, *absorbed in the comic book, does not respond*)

    Hey, Boet Sam!

(SAM *looks up*)

    I'm getting it. The quickstep. Look now and tell me.
10   (*He repeats the step*) Well?
SAM: (*Encouragingly*) Show me again.
WILLIE: Okay, count for me.
SAM: Ready?

WILLIE: Ready.
SAM: Five, six, seven, eight . . . (WILLIE *starts to dance*) A-n-d one 15
    two three four . . . and one two three four. . . . (*Ad libbing as* WILLIE *dances*) Your shoulders, Willie . . . your shoulders! Don't look down! Look happy, Willie! Relax, Willie!
WILLIE: (*Desperate but still dancing*) I am relax.
SAM: No, you're not. 20
WILLIE: (*He falters*) Ag no man, Sam! Mustn't talk. You make me make mistakes.
SAM: But you're too stiff.
WILLIE: Yesterday I'm not straight . . . today I'm too stiff!
SAM: Well, you are. You asked me and I'm telling you. 25
WILLIE: Where?
SAM: Everywhere. Try to glide through it.
WILLIE: Glide?
SAM: Ja, make it smooth. And give it more style. It must look like you're enjoying yourself. 30
WILLIE: (*Emphatically*) I wasn't.
SAM: Exactly.
WILLIE: How can I enjoy myself? Not straight, too stiff and now it's also glide, give it more style, make it smooth. . . . Haai! Is hard to remember all those things, Boet Sam. 35
SAM: That's your trouble. You're trying too hard.
WILLIE: I try hard because it *is* hard.
SAM: But don't let me see it. The secret is to make it look easy. Ballroom must look happy, Willie, not like hard work. It must . . . Ja! . . . it must look like romance. 40
WILLIE: Now another one! What's romance?
SAM: Love story with happy ending. A handsome man in tails, and in his arms, smiling at him, a beautiful lady in evening dress!
WILLIE: Fred Astaire, Ginger Rogers. 45
SAM: You got it. Tapdance or ballroom, it's the same. Romance. In two weeks' time when the judges look at you and Hilda, they must see a man and a woman who are dancing their way to a happy ending. What I saw was you holding her like you were frightened she was going to run 50 away.
WILLIE: Ja! Because that is what she wants to do! I got no romance left for Hilda anymore, Boet Sam.
SAM: Then pretend. When you put your arms around Hilda, imagine she is Ginger Rogers. 55
WILLIE: With no teeth? You try.
SAM: Well, just remember, there's only two weeks left.
WILLIE: I know, I know! (*To the jukebox*) I do it better with music. You got sixpence for Sarah Vaughan?
SAM: That's a slow foxtrot. You're practicing the quick-step. 60
WILLIE: I'll practice slow foxtrot.

SAM: (*Shaking his head*) It's your turn to put money in the jukebox.

WILLIE: I only got bus fare to go home. (*He returns disconsolately to his work*) Love story and happy ending! She's doing it all right, Boet Sam, but is not me she's giving happy endings. Fuckin' whore! Three nights now she doesn't come practice. I wind up gramophone, I get record ready and I sit and wait. What happens? Nothing. Ten o'clock I start dancing with my pillow. You try and practice romance by yourself, Boet Sam. Struesgod, she doesn't come tonight I take back my dress and ballroom shoes and I find me new partner. Size twenty-six. Shoes size seven. And now she's also making trouble for me with the baby again. Reports me to Child Wellfed, that I'm not giving her money. She lies! Every week I am giving her money for milk. And how do I know is my baby? Only his hair looks like me. She's fucking around all the time I turn my back. Hilda Samuels is a bitch! (*Pause*) Hey, Sam!

SAM: Ja.

WILLIE: You listening?

SAM: Ja.

WILLIE: So what you say?

SAM: About Hilda?

WILLIE: Ja.

SAM: When did you last give her a hiding?

WILLIE: (*Reluctantly*) Sunday night.

SAM: And today is Thursday.

WILLIE: (*He knows what's coming*) Okay.

SAM: Hiding on Sunday night, then Monday, Tuesday and Wednesday she doesn't come to practice . . . and you are asking me why?

WILLIE: I said okay, Boet Sam!

SAM: You hit her too much. One day she's going to leave you for good.

WILLIE: So? She makes me the hell-in too much.

SAM: (*Emphasizing his point*) *Too* much and *too* hard. You had the same trouble with Eunice.

WILLIE: Because she also make the hell-in, Boet Sam. She never got the steps right. Even the waltz.

SAM: Beating her up every time she makes a mistake in the waltz? (*Shaking his head*) No, Willie! That takes the pleasure out of ballroom dancing.

WILLIE: Hilda is not too bad with the waltz, Boet Sam. Is the quickstep where the trouble starts.

SAM: (*Teasing him gently*) How's your pillow with the quickstep?

WILLIE: (*Ignoring the tease*) Good! And why! Because it got no legs. That's her trouble. She can't move them quick enough, Boet Sam. I start the record and before halfway Count Basie is already winning. Only time we catch up with him is when gramophone runs down.

(SAM *laughs*)

Haaikona, Boet Sam, is not funny.

SAM: (*Snapping his fingers*) I got it! Give her a handicap.

WILLIE: What's that?

SAM: Give her a ten-second start and then let Count Basie go. Then I put my money on her. Hot favorite in the Ballroom Stakes: Hilda Samuels ridden by Willie Malopo.

WILLIE: (*Turning away*) I'm not talking to you no more.

SAM: (*Relenting*) Sorry, Willie . . .

WILLIE: It's finish between us.

SAM: Okay, okay . . . I'll stop.

WILLIE: You can also fuck off.

SAM: Willie, listen! I want to help you!

WILLIE: No more jokes?

SAM: I promise.

WILLIE: Okay. Help me.

SAM: (*His turn to hold an imaginary partner*) Look and learn. Feet together. Back straight. Body relaxed. Right hand placed gently in the small of her back and wait for the music. Don't start worrying about making mistakes or the judges or the other competitors. It's just you, Hilda and the music, and you're going to have a good time. What Count Basie do you play?

WILLIE: "You the cream in my coffee, you the salt in my stew."

SAM: Right. Give it to me in strict tempo.

WILLIE: Ready?

SAM: Ready.

WILLIE: A-n-d . . . (*singing*)
"You the cream in my coffee.
You the salt in my stew.
You will always be my necessity.
I'd be lost without you. . . ." (*etc.*)

(SAM *launches into the quickstep. He is obviously a much more accomplished dancer than* WILLIE. HALLY *enters. A seventeen-year-old white boy. Wet raincoat and school case. He stops and watches* SAM. *The demonstration comes to an end with a flourish. Applause from* HALLY *and* WILLIE)

HALLY: Bravo! No question about it. First place goes to Mr. Sam Semela.

WILLIE: (*In total agreement*) You was gliding with style, Boet Sam.

HALLY: (*Cheerfully*) How's it, chaps?

SAM: Okay, Hally.

WILLIE: (*Springing to attention like a soldier and saluting*) At your service, Master Harold!

HALLY: Not long to the big event, hey!

SAM: Two weeks.

HALLY: You nervous?

SAM: No.

HALLY: Think you stand a chance?

SAM: Let's just say I'm ready to go out there and dance.

HALLY: It looked like it. What about you, Willie?

(WILLIE *groans*)

What's the matter?

SAM: He's got leg trouble.

HALLY: (*Innocently*) Oh, sorry to hear that, Willie.

SAM: Boet Sam! You promised. (WILLIE *returns to his work*)

(HALLY *deposits his school case and takes off his raincoat. His clothes are a little neglected and untidy: black blazer with school badge, gray flannel trousers in need of an ironing, khaki shirt and tie, black shoes.* SAM *has fetched a towel for* HALLY *to dry his hair*)

HALLY: God, what a lousy bloody day. It's coming down cats and dogs out there. Bad for business, chaps . . . (*Conspira-*

torial whisper) . . . but it also means we're in for a nice quiet afternoon.

165 SAM: You can speak loud. Your Mom's not here.

HALLY: Out shopping?

SAM: No, The hospital.

HALLY: But it's Thursday. There's no visiting on Thursday afternoons. Is my Dad okay?

170 SAM: Sounds like it. In fact, I think he's going home.

HALLY: (*Stopped short by* SAM's *remark*) What do you mean?

SAM: The hospital phoned.

HALLY: To say what?

SAM: I don't know. I just heard your Mom talking.

175 HALLY: So what makes you say he's going home?

SAM: It sounded as if they were telling her to come and fetch him.

(HALLY *thinks about what* SAM *has said for a few seconds*)

HALLY: When did she leave?

SAM: About an hour ago. She said she would phone you.

180 Want to eat?

(HALLY *doesn't respond*)

Hally, want your lunch?

HALLY: I suppose so. (*His mood has changed*) What's on the menu? . . . as if I don't know.

SAM: Soup, followed by meat pie and gravy.

185 HALLY: Today's?

SAM: No.

HALLY: And the soup?

SAM: Nourishing pea soup.

HALLY: Just the soup. (*The pile of comic books on the table*) And

190 these?

SAM: For your Dad. Mr. Kempston brought them.

HALLY: You haven't been reading them, have you?

SAM: Just looking.

HALLY: (*Examining the comics*) Jungle Jim . . . Batman and Robin

195 . . . Tarzan . . . God, what rubbish! Mental pollution. Take them away.

(SAM *exits waltzing into the kitchen.* HALLY *turns to* WILLIE)

HALLY: Did you hear my Mom talking on the telephone, Willie?

WILLIE: No, Master Hally. I was at the back.

HALLY: And she didn't say anything to you before she left?

200 WILLIE: She said I must clean the floors.

HALLY: I mean about my Dad.

WILLIE: She didn't say nothing to me about him, Master Hally.

HALLY: (*With conviction*) No! It can't be. They said he needed at least another three weeks of treatment. Sam's definitely

205 made a mistake. (*Rummages through his school case, finds a book and settles down at the table to read*) So, Willie!

WILLIE: Yes, Master Hally! Schooling okay today?

HALLY: Yes, okay. . . . (*He thinks about it*) . . . No, not really. Ag, what's the difference? I don't care. And Sam says you've

210 got problems.

WILLIE: Big problems.

HALLY: Which leg is sore?

(WILLIE *groans*)

Both legs.

WILLIE: There is nothing wrong with my legs. Sam is just making jokes. 215

HALLY: So then you *will* be in the competition.

WILLIE: Only if I can find me a partner.

HALLY: But what about Hilda?

SAM: (*Returning with a bowl of soup*) She's the one who's got trouble with her legs. 220

HALLY: What sort of trouble, Willie?

SAM: From the way he describes it, I think the lady has gone a bit lame.

HALLY: Good God! Have you taken her to see a doctor?

SAM: I think a vet would be better. 225

HALLY: What do you mean?

SAM: What do you call it again when a racehorse goes very fast?

HALLY: Gallop?

SAM: That's it! 230

WILLIE: Boet Sam!

HALLY: "A gallop down the homestretch to the winning post." But what's that got to do with Hilda?

SAM: Count Basie always gets there first.

(WILLIE *lets fly with his slop rag. It misses* SAM *and hits* HALLY)

HALLY: (*Furious*) For Christ's sake, Willie! What the hell do 235 you think you're doing!

WILLIE: Sorry, Master Hally, but it's him. . . .

HALLY: Act your bloody age! (*Hurls the rag back at* WILLIE) Cut out the nonsense now and get on with your work. And you too, Sam. Stop fooling around. 240

(SAM *moves away*)

No. Hang on. I haven't finished! Tell me exactly what my Mom said.

SAM: I have. "When Hally comes, tell him I've gone to the hospital and I'll phone him."

HALLY: She didn't say anything about taking my Dad home? 245

SAM: No. It's just that when she was talking on the phone . . .

HALLY: (*Interrupting him*) No, Sam. They can't be discharging him. She would have said so if they were. In any case, we saw him last night and he wasn't in good shape at all. Staff nurse even said there was talk about taking more 250 X-rays. And now suddenly today he's better? If anything, it sounds more like a bad turn to me . . . which I sincerely hope it isn't. Hang on . . . how long ago did you say she left?

SAM: Just before two . . . (*His wrist watch*) . . . hour and a 255 half.

HALLY: I know how to settle it. (*Behind the counter to the telephone. Talking as he dials*) Let's give her ten minutes to get to the hospital, ten minutes to load him up, another ten, at the most, to get home and another ten to get him in- 260 side. Forty minutes. They should have been home for at least half an hour already. (*Pause—he waits with the receiver to his ear*) No reply, chaps. And you know why? Because she's at his bedside in hospital helping him pull through a bad turn. You definitely heard wrong. 265

SAM: Okay.

(*As far as* HALLY *is concerned, the matter is settled. He returns to his table, sits down and divides his attention between the book and his soup.* SAM *is at his school case and picks up a textbook*)

Modern Graded Mathematics for Standards Nine and Ten. (*Opens it at random and laughs at something he sees*) Who is this supposed to be?

270 HALLY: Old fart-face Prentice.

SAM: Teacher?

HALLY: Thinks he is. And believe me, that is not a bad likeness.

SAM: Has he seen it?

275 HALLY: Yes.

SAM: What did he say?

HALLY: Tried to be clever, as usual. Said I was no Leonardo da Vinci and that bad art had to be punished. So, six of the best, and his are bloody good.

280 SAM: On your bum?

HALLY: Where else? The days when I got them on my hands are gone forever, Sam.

SAM: With your trousers down!

HALLY: No. He's not quite that barbaric.

285 SAM: That's the way they do it in jail.

HALLY: (*Flicker of morbid interest*) Really?

SAM: Ja. When the magistrate sentences you to "strokes with a light cane."

HALLY: Go on.

290 SAM: They make you lie down on a bench. One policeman pulls down your trousers and holds your ankles, another one pulls your shirt over your head and holds your arms . . .

HALLY: Thank you! That's enough.

295 SAM: . . . and the one that gives you the strokes talks to you gently and for a long time between each one. (*He laughs*)

HALLY: I've heard enough, Sam! Jesus! It's a bloody awful world when you come to think of it. People can be real bastards.

300 SAM: That's the way it is, Hally.

HALLY: It doesn't *have* to be that way. There is something called progress, you know. We don't exactly burn people at the stake anymore.

SAM: Like Joan of Arc.

305 HALLY: Correct. If she was captured today, she'd be given a fair trial.

SAM: And then the death sentence.

HALLY: (*A world-weary sigh*) I know, I know! I oscillate between hope and despair for this world as well, Sam. But

310 things will change, you wait and see. One day somebody is going to get up and give history a kick up the backside and get it going again.

SAM: Like who?

HALLY: (*After thought*) They're called social reformers. Every

315 age, Sam, has got its social reformer. My history book is full of them.

SAM: So where's ours?

HALLY: Good question. And I hate to say it, but the answer is: I don't know. Maybe he hasn't even been born yet. Or is

320 still only a babe in arms at his mother's breast. God, what a thought.

SAM: So we just go on waiting.

HALLY: Ja, looks like it. (*Back to his soup and the book*)

SAM: (*Reading from the textbook*) "Introduction: In some math-

325 ematical problems only the magnitude . . ." (*He mispronounces the word "magnitude"*)

HALLY: (*Correcting him without looking up*) Magnitude.

SAM: What's it mean?

HALLY: How big it is. The size of the thing.

SAM: (*Reading*) ". . . magnitude of the quantities is of impor-   330 tance. In other problems we need to know whether these quantities are negative or positive. For example, whether there is a debit or credit bank balance . . ."

HALLY: Whether you're broke or not.

SAM: ". . . whether the temperature is above or below   335 Zero . . ."

HALLY: Naught degrees. Cheerful state of affairs! No cash and you're freezing to death. Mathematics won't get you out of that one.

SAM: "All these quantities are called . . ." (*Spelling the   340 word*) . . . s-c-a-l . . .

HALLY: Scalars.

SAM: Scalars! (*Shaking his head with a laugh*) You understand all that?

HALLY: (*Turning a page*) No. And I don't intend to try.   345

SAM: So what happens when the exams come?

HALLY: Failing a maths exam isn't the end of the world, Sam. How many times have I told you that examination results don't measure intelligence?

SAM: I would say about as many times as you've failed one of   350 them.

HALLY: (*Mirthlessly*) Ha, ha, ha.

SAM: (*Simultaneously*) Ha, ha, ha.

HALLY: Just remember Winston Churchill didn't do particularly well at school.   355

SAM: You've also told me that one many times.

HALLY: Well, it just so happens to be the truth.

SAM: (*Enjoying the word*) Magnitude! Magnitude! Show me how to use it.

HALLY: (*After thought*) An intrepid social reformer will not be   360 daunted by the magnitude of the task he has undertaken.

SAM: (*Impressed*) Couple of jaw-breakers in there!

HALLY: I gave you three for the price of one. Intrepid, daunted and magnitude. I did that once in an exam. Put five of the words I had to explain in one sentence. It was   365 half a page long.

SAM: Well, I'll put my money on you in the English exam.

HALLY: Piece of cake. Eighty percent without even trying.

SAM: (*Another textbook from* HALLY'S *case*) And history?

HALLY: So-so. I'll scrape through. In the fifties if I'm lucky.   370

SAM: You didn't do too badly last year.

HALLY: Because we had World War One. That at least had some action. You try to find that in the South African Parliamentary system.

SAM: (*Reading from the history textbook*) "Napoleon and the   375 principle of equality." Hey! This sounds interesting. "After concluding peace with Britain in 1802, Napoleon used a brief period of calm to in-sti-tute . . ."

HALLY: Introduce.

SAM: ". . . many reforms. Napoleon regarded all people as   380 equal before the law and wanted them to have equal opportunities for advancement. All ves-ti-ges of the feu-dal system with its oppression of the poor were abolished." Vestiges, feudal system and abolished. I'm all right on oppression.   385

HALLY: I'm thinking. He swept away . . . abolished . . . the last remains . . . vestiges . . . of the bad old days . . . feudal system.

SAM: Ha! There's the social reformer we're waiting for. He sounds like a man of some magnitude.   390

HALLY: I'm not so sure about that. It's a damn good title for a book, though. A man of magnitude!

SAM: He sounds pretty big to me, Hally.

395 HALLY: Don't confuse historical significance with greatness. But maybe I'm being a bit prejudiced. Have a look in there and you'll see he's two chapters long. And hell! . . . has he only got dates, Sam, all of which you've got to remember! This campaign and that campaign, and then, because of all the fighting, the next thing is we get Peace
400 Treaties all over the place. And what's the end of the story? Battle of Waterloo, which he loses. Wasn't worth it. No, I don't know about him as a man of magnitude.

SAM: Then who would you say was?

HALLY: To answer that, we need a definition of greatness, and
405 I suppose that would be somebody who . . . somebody who benefited all mankind.

SAM: Right. But like who?

HALLY: (*He speaks with total conviction*) Charles Darwin. Remember him? That big book from the library. *The Origin*
410 *of the Species.*

SAM: Him?

HALLY: Yes. For his Theory of Evolution.

SAM: You didn't finish it.

HALLY: I ran out of time. I didn't finish it because my two
415 weeks was up. But I'm going to take it out again after I've digested what I read. It's safe. I've hidden it away in the Theology section. Nobody ever goes in there. And anyway who are you to talk? You hardly even looked at it.

420 SAM: I tried. I looked at the chapters in the beginning and I saw one called "The Struggle for an Existence." Ah ha, I thought. At last! But what did I get? Something called the mistiltoe which needs the apple tree and there's too many seeds and all are going to die except one . . . ! No, Hally.

425 HALLY: (*Intellectually outraged*) What do you mean, No! The poor man had to start somewhere. For God's sake, Sam, he revolutionized science. Now we know.

SAM: What?

HALLY: Where we come from and what it all means.

430 SAM: And that's a benefit to mankind? Anyway, I still don't believe it.

HALLY: God, you're impossible. I showed it to you in black and white.

SAM: Doesn't mean I got to believe it.

435 HALLY: It's the likes of you that kept the Inquisition in business. It's called bigotry. Anyway, that's my man of magnitude. Charles Darwin! Who's yours?

SAM: (*Without hesitation*) Abraham Lincoln.

HALLY: I might have guessed as much. Don't get sentimental,
440 Sam. You've never been a slave, you know. And anyway we freed your ancestors here in South Africa long before the Americans. But if you want to thank somebody on their behalf, do it to Mr. William Wilberforce. Come on. Try again. I want a real genius. (*Now enjoying himself, and so*
445 *is* SAM. HALLY *goes behind the counter and helps himself to a chocolate*)

SAM: William Shakespeare.

HALLY: (*No enthusiasm*) Oh. So you're also one of them, are you? You're basing that opinion on only one play, you
450 know. You've only read my *Julius Caesar* and even I don't understand half of what they're talking about. They should

do what they did with the old Bible: bring the language up to date.

SAM: That's all you've got. It's also the only one *you've* read.

455 HALLY: I know. I admit it. That's why I suggest we reserve our judgment until we've checked up on a few others. I've got a feeling, though, that by the end of this year one is going to be enough for me, and I can give you the names of twenty-nine other chaps in the Standard Nine class of the
460 Port Elizabeth Technical College who feel the same. But if you want him, you can have him. My turn now. (*Pacing*) This is a damned good exercise, you know! It started off looking like a simple question and here it's got us really probing into the intellectual heritage of our civilization.

465 SAM: So who is it going to be?

HALLY: My next man . . . and he gets the title on two scores: social reform and literary genius . . . is Leo Nikolaevich Tolstoy.

SAM: That Russian.

470 HALLY: Correct. Remember the picture of him I showed you?

SAM: With the long beard.

HALLY: (*Trying to look like Tolstoy*) And those burning, visionary eyes. My God, the face of a social prophet if ever I saw
475 one! And remember my words when I showed it to you? Here's a *man,* Sam!

SAM: Those were words, Hally.

HALLY: Not many intellectuals are prepared to shovel manure with the peasants and then go home and write a "little
480 book" called *War and Peace.* Incidentally, Sam, he was somebody else who, to quote, ". . . did not distinguish himself scholastically."

SAM: Meaning?

HALLY: He was also no good at school.

485 SAM: Like you and Winston Churchill.

HALLY: (*Mirthlessly*) Ha, ha, ha.

SAM: (*Simultaneously*) Ha, ha, ha.

HALLY: Don't get clever, Sam. That man freed his serfs of his own free will.

490 SAM: No argument. He was a somebody, all right. I accept him.

HALLY: I'm sure Count Tolstoy will be very pleased to hear that. Your turn. Shoot. (*Another chocolate from behind the counter*) I'm waiting, Sam.

SAM: I've got him.

495 HALLY: Good. Submit your candidate for examination.

SAM: Jesus.

HALLY: (*Stopped dead in his tracks*) Who?

SAM: Jesus Christ.

HALLY: Oh, come on, Sam!

500 SAM: The Messiah.

HALLY: Ja, but still . . . No, Sam. Don't let's get started on religion. We'll just spend the whole afternoon arguing again. Suppose I turn around and say Mohammed?

SAM: All right.

505 HALLY: You can't have them both on the same list!

SAM: Why not? You like Mohammed, I like Jesus.

HALLY: I *don't* like Mohammed. I never have. I was merely being hypothetical. As far as I'm concerned, the Koran is as bad as the Bible. No. Religion is out! I'm not going to
510 waste my time again arguing with you about the existence of God. You know perfectly well I'm an atheist . . . and I've got homework to do.

SAM: Okay, I take him back.

HALLY: You've got time for one more name.

515 SAM: (*After thought*) I've got one I know we'll agree on. A simple straightforward great Man of Magnitude . . . and no arguments. And *he* really *did* benefit all mankind.

HALLY: I wonder. After your last contribution I'm begin-520 ning to doubt whether anything in the way of an intellectual agreement is possible between the two of us. Who is he?

SAM: Guess.

HALLY: Socrates? Alexandre Dumas? Karl Marx? Dostoevsky? Nietzsche?

(SAM *shakes his head after each name*)

525 Give me a clue.

SAM: The letter P is important . . .

HALLY: Plato!

SAM: . . . and his name begins with an F.

HALLY: I've got it. Freud and Psychology.

530 SAM: No. I didn't understand him.

HALLY: That makes two of us.

SAM: Think of mouldy apricot jam.

HALLY: (*After a delighted laugh*) Penicillin and Sir Alexander Fleming! And the title of the book: *The Microbe Hunters.* 535 (*Delighted*) Splendid, Sam! Splendid. For once we are in total agreement. The major breakthrough in medical science in the Twentieth Century. If it wasn't for him, we might have lost the Second World War. It's deeply gratifying, Sam, to know that I haven't been wasting my time in 540 talking to you. (*Strutting around proudly*) Tolstoy may have educated his peasants, but I've educated you.

SAM: Standard Four to Standard Nine.

HALLY: Have we been at it as long as that?

SAM: Yep. And my first lesson was geography.

545 HALLY: (*Intrigued*) Really? I don't remember.

SAM: My room there at the back of the old Jubilee Boarding House. I had just started working for your Mom. Little boy in short trousers walks in one afternoon and asks me seriously: "Sam, do you want to see South Africa?" Hey 550 man! Sure I wanted to see South Africa!

HALLY: Was that me?

SAM: . . . So the next thing I'm looking at a map you had just done for homework. It was your first one and you were very proud of yourself.

555 HALLY: Go on.

SAM: Then came my first lesson. "Repeat after me, Sam: Gold in the Transvaal, mealies in the Free State, sugar in Natal and grapes in the Cape." I still know it!

HALLY: Well, I'll be buggered. So that's how it all started.

560 SAM: And your next map was one with all the rivers and the mountains they came from. The Orange, the Vaal, the Limpopo, the Zambezi . . .

HALLY: You've got a phenomenal memory!

SAM: You should be grateful. That is why you started passing 565 your exams. You tried to be better than me. (*They laugh together.* WILLIE *is attracted by the laughter and joins them*)

HALLY: The old Jubilee Boarding House. Sixteen rooms with board and lodging, rent in advance and one week's notice. I haven't thought about it for donkey's years . . . and I 570 don't think that's an accident. God, was I glad when we sold it and moved out. Those years are not remembered as the happiest ones of an unhappy childhood.

WILLIE: (*Knocking on the table and trying to imitate a woman's voice*) "Hally, are you there?"

HALLY: Who's that supposed to be? 575

WILLIE: "What you doing in there, Hally? Come out at once!"

HALLY: (*To* SAM) What's he talking about?

SAM: Don't you remember?

WILLIE: "Sam, Willie . . . is he in there with you boys?" 580

SAM: Hiding away in our room when your mother was looking for you.

HALLY: (*Another good laugh*) Of course! I used to crawl and hide under your bed! But finish the story, Willie. Then what used to happen? You chaps would give the game 585 away by telling her I was in there with you. So much for friendship.

SAM: We couldn't lie to her. She knew.

HALLY: Which meant I got another rowing for hanging around the "servants' quarters." I think I spent more time in there 590 with you chaps than anywhere else in that dump. And do you blame me? Nothing but bloody misery wherever you went. Somebody was always complaining about the food, or my mother was having a fight with Micky Nash because she'd caught her with a petty officer in her room. Maud 595 Meiring was another one. Remember those two? They were prostitutes, you know. Soldiers and sailors from the troopships. Bottom fell out of the business when the war ended. God, the flotsam and jetsam that life washed up on our shores! No joking, if it wasn't for your room, I would 600 have been the first certified ten-year-old in medical history. Ja, the memories are coming back now. Walking home from school and thinking: "What can I do this afternoon?" Try out a few ideas, but sooner or later I'd end up in there with you fellows. I bet you I could still find my way to your 605 room with my eyes closed. (*He does exactly that*) Down the corridor . . . telephone on the right, which my Mom keeps locked because somebody is using it on the sly and not paying . . . past the kitchen and unappetizing cooking smells . . . around the corner into the backyard, hold my 610 breath again because there are more smells coming when I pass your lavatory, then into that little passageway, first door on the right and into your room. How's that?

SAM: Good. But, as usual, you forgot to knock.

HALLY: Like that time I barged in and caught you and Cyn– 615 thia . . . at it. Remember? God, was I embarrassed! I didn't know what was going on at first.

SAM: Ja, that taught you a lesson.

HALLY: And about a lot more than knocking on doors, I'll have you know, and I don't mean geography either. Hell, 620 Sam, couldn't you have waited until it was dark?

SAM: No.

HALLY: Was it that urgent?

SAM: Yes, and if you don't believe me, wait until your time comes. 625

HALLY: No, thank you. I am not interested in girls. (*Back to his memories . . . Using a few chairs he recreates the room as he lists the items*) A gray little room with a cold cement floor. Your bed against that wall . . . and I now know why the mattress sags so much! . . . Willie's bed . . . it's propped up on 630 bricks because one leg is broken . . . that wobbly little table with the washbasin and jug of water . . . Yes! . . . stuck to the wall above it are some pin-up pictures from magazines. Joe Louis . . .

635 WILLIE: Brown Bomber. World Title. (*Boxing pose*) Three rounds and knockout.

HALLY: Against who?

SAM: Max Schmeling.

HALLY: Correct. I can also remember Fred Astaire and Ginger
640 Rogers, and Rita Hayworth in a bathing costume which always made me hot and bothered when I looked at it. Under Willie's bed is an old suitcase with all his clothes in a mess, which is why I never hide there. Your things are neat and tidy in a trunk next to your bed, and on it there
645 is a picture of you and Cynthia in your ballroom clothes, your first silver cup for third place in a competition and an old radio which doesn't work anymore. Have I left out anything?

SAM: No.

650 HALLY: Right, so much for the stage directions. Now the characters. (SAM *and* WILLIE *move to their appropriate positions in the bedroom*) Willie is in bed, under his blankets with his clothes on, complaining nonstop about something, but we can't make out a word of what he's saying because he's got
655 his head under the blankets as well. You're on your bed trimming your toenails with a knife—not a very edifying sight—and as for me . . . What am I doing?

SAM: You're sitting on the floor giving Willie a lecture about being a good loser while you get the checker board and
660 pieces ready for a game. Then you go to Willie's bed, pull off the blankets and make him play with you first because you know you're going to win, and that gives you the second game with me.

HALLY: And you certainly were a bad loser, Willie!

665 WILLIE: Haai!

HALLY: Wasn't he, Sam? And so slow! A game with you almost took the whole afternoon. Thank God I gave up trying to teach you how to play chess.

WILLIE: You and Sam cheated.

670 HALLY: I never saw Sam cheat, and mine were mostly the mistakes of youth.

WILLIE: Then how is it you two was always winning?

HALLY: Have you ever considered the possibility, Willie, that it was because we were better than you?

675 WILLIE: Every time better?

HALLY: Not every time. There were occasions when we deliberately let you win a game so that you would stop sulking and go on playing with us. Sam used to wink at me when you weren't looking to show me it was time to let
680 you win.

WILLIE: So then you two didn't play fair.

HALLY: It was for your benefit, Mr. Malopo, which is more than being fair. It was an act of self-sacrifice. (*To* SAM) But you know what my best memory is, don't you?

685 SAM: No.

HALLY: Come on, guess. If your memory is so good, you must remember it as well.

SAM: We got up to a lot of tricks in there, Hally.

HALLY: This one was special, Sam.

690 SAM: I'm listening.

HALLY: It started off looking like another of those useless nothing-to-do afternoons. I'd already been down to Main Street looking for adventure, but nothing had happened. I didn't feel like climbing trees in the Donkin Park or pretending I was a private eye and following a stranger. . . so 695 as usual: See what's cooking in Sam's room. This time it was you on the floor. You had two thin pieces of wood and you were smoothing them down with a knife. It didn't look particularly interesting, but when I asked you what you were doing, you just said, "Wait and see, Hally. 700 Wait . . . and see" . . . in that secret sort of way of yours, so I knew there was a surprise coming. You teased me, you bugger, by being deliberately slow and not answering my questions!

(SAM *laughs*)

And whistling while you worked away! God, it was infuriating! I could have brained you! It was only when you 705 tied them together in a cross and put that down on the brown paper that I realized what you were doing. "Sam is making a kite?" And when I asked you and you said "Yes" . . . ! (*Shaking his head with disbelief*) The sheer audacity of it took my breath away. I mean, seriously, what 710 the hell does a black man know about flying a kite? I'll be honest with you, Sam, I had no hopes for it. If you think I was excited and happy, you got another guess coming. In fact, I was shit-scared that we were going to make fools of ourselves. When we left the boarding house to go up onto 715 the hill, I was praying quietly that there wouldn't be any other kids around to laugh at us.

SAM: (*Enjoying the memory as much as* HALLY) Ja, I could see that.

HALLY: I made it obvious, did I? 720

SAM: Ja. You refused to carry it.

HALLY: Do you blame me? Can you remember what the poor thing looked like? Tomato-box wood and brown paper! Flour and water for glue! Two of my mother's old stockings for a tail, and then all those bits and pieces of string 725 you made me tie together so that we could fly it! Hell, no, that was now only asking for a miracle to happen.

SAM: Then the big argument when I told you to hold the string and run with it when I let go.

HALLY: I was prepared to run, all right, but straight back to 730 the boarding house.

SAM: (*Knowing what's coming*) So what happened?

HALLY: Come on, Sam, you remember as well as I do.

SAM: I want to hear it from you.

735

(HALLY *pauses. He wants to be as accurate as possible.*)

HALLY: You went a little distance from me down the hill, you held it up ready to let it go. . . . "This is it," I thought. "Like everything else in my life, here comes 740 another fiasco." Then you shouted, "Go, Hally!" and I started to run. (*Another pause*) I don't know how to describe it, Sam. Ja! The miracle happened! I was running, waiting for it to crash to the ground, but instead suddenly there was something alive behind me at the end 745 of the string, tugging at it as if it wanted to be free. I looked back . . . (*Shakes his head*) . . . I still can't believe my eyes. It was flying! Looping around and trying to climb even higher into the sky. You shouted to me to let

750 it have more string. I did, until there was none left and I was just holding that piece of wood we had tied it to. You came up and joined me. You were laughing.

SAM: So were you. And shouting, "It works, Sam! We've done it!"

755 HALLY: And we had! I was so proud of us! It was the most splendid thing I had ever seen. I wished there were hundreds of kids around to watch us. The part that scared me, though, was when you showed me how to make it dive down to the ground and then just when it was on the
760 point of crashing, swoop up again!

SAM: You didn't want to try yourself.

HALLY: Of course not! I would have been suicidal if anything had happened to it. Watching you do it made me nervous enough. I was quite happy just to see it up there with its
765 tail fluttering behind it. You left me after that, didn't you? You explained how to get it down, we tied it to the bench so that I could sit and watch it, and you went away. I wanted you to stay, you know. I was a little scared of having to look after it by myself.

770 SAM: (*Quietly*) I had work to do, Hally.

HALLY: It was sort of sad bringing it down, Sam. And it looked sad again when it was lying there on the ground. Like something that had lost its soul. Just tomato-box wood, brown paper and two of my mother's old stockings!
775 But, hell, I'll never forget that first moment when I saw it up there. I had a stiff neck the next day from looking up so much.

(SAM *laughs.* HALLY *turns to him with a question he never thought of asking before*)

Why did you make that kite, Sam?

SAM: (*Evenly*) I can't remember.

780 HALLY: Truly?

SAM: Too long ago, Hally.

HALLY: Ja, I suppose it was. It's time for another one, you know.

SAM: Why do you say that?

785 HALLY: Because it feels like that. Wouldn't be a good day to fly it, though.

SAM: No. You can't fly kites on rainy days.

HALLY: (*He studies* SAM. *Their memories have made him conscious of the man's presence in his life*) How old are you, Sam?

790 SAM: Two score and five.

HALLY: Strange, isn't it?

SAM: What?

HALLY: Me and you.

SAM: What's strange about it?

795 HALLY: Little white boy in short trousers and a black man old enough to be his father flying a kite. It's not every day you see that.

SAM: But why strange? Because the one is white and the other black?

800 HALLY: I don't know. Would have been just as strange, I suppose, if it had been me and my Dad . . . cripple man and a little boy! Nope! There's no chance of me flying a kite without it being strange. (*Simple statement of fact—no self-pity*) There's a nice little short story there. "The Kite-
805 Flyers." But we'd have to find a twist in the ending.

SAM: Twist?

HALLY: Yes. Something unexpected. The way it ended with us was too straightforward . . . me on the bench and you going back to work. There's no drama in that.

810 WILLIE: And me?

HALLY: You?

WILLIE: Yes me.

HALLY: You want to get into the story as well, do you? I got it! Change the title: "Afternoons in Sam's Room" . . . expand it and tell all the stories. It's on its way to being a
815 novel. Our days in the old Jubilee. Sad in a way that they're over. I almost wish we were still in that little room.

SAM: We're still together.

HALLY: That's true. It's just that life felt the right size in there . . . not too big and not too small. Wasn't so hard to work
820 up a bit of courage. It's got so bloody complicated since then.

(*The telephone rings.* SAM *answers it*)

SAM: St. George's Park Tea Room . . . Hello, Madam . . . Yes, Madam, he's here. . . . Hally, it's your mother.

825 HALLY: Where is she phoning from?

SAM: Sounds like the hospital. It's a public telephone.

HALLY: (*Relieved*) You see! I told you. (*The telephone*) Hello, Mom . . . Yes . . . Yes no fine. Everything's under control here. How's things with poor old Dad? . . . Has he had a
830 bad turn? . . . What? . . . Oh, God! . . . Yes, Sam told me, but I was sure he'd made a mistake. But what's this all about, Mom? He didn't look at all good last night. How can he get better so quickly? . . . Then very obviously you must say no. Be firm with him. You're the boss. . . . You
835 know what it's going to be like if he comes home. . . . Well then, don't blame me when I fail my exams at the end of the year. . . . Yes! How am I expected to be fresh for school when I spend half the night massaging his gammy leg? . . . So am I! . . . So tell him a white lie. Say Dr. Colley wants
840 more X-rays of his stump. Or bribe him. We'll sneak in double tots of brandy in future. . . . What? . . . Order him to get back into bed at once! If he's going to behave like a child, treat him like one. . . . All right, Mom! I was just trying to . . . I'm sorry. . . . I said I'm sorry. . . . Quick, give
845 me your number. I'll phone you back. (*He hangs up and waits a few seconds*) Here we go again! (*He dials*) I'm sorry, Mom. . . . Okay . . . But now listen to me carefully. All it needs is for you to put your foot down. Don't take no for an answer. . . . Did you hear me? And whatever you do,
850 don't discuss it with him. . . . Because I'm frightened you'll give in to him. . . . Yes, Sam gave me lunch. . . . I ate all of it! . . . No, Mom not a soul. It's still raining here. . . . Right, I'll tell them. I'll just do some homework and then lock up. . . . But remember now, Mom. Don't listen to anything
855 he says. And phone me back and let me know what happens. . . . Okay. Bye, Mom. (*He hangs up. The men are staring at him*) My Mom says that when you're finished with the floors you must do the windows. (*Pause*) Don't misunderstand me, chaps. All I want is for him to get better.
860 And if he was, I'd be the first person to say: "Bring him home." But he's not, and we can't give him the medical care and attention he needs at home. That's what hospitals are there for. (*Brusquely*) So don't just stand there! Get on with it!

(SAM *clears* HALLY's *table*)

865   You heard right. My Dad wants to go home.

SAM: Is he better?

HALLY: (*Sharply*) No! How the hell can he be better when last night he was groaning with pain? This is not an age of miracles!

870 SAM: Then he should stay in hospital.

HALLY: (*Seething with irritation and frustration*) Tell me something I don't know, Sam. What the hell do you think I was saying to my Mom? All I can say is fuck-it-all.

SAM: I'm sure he'll listen to your Mom.

875 HALLY: You don't know what she's up against. He's already packed his shaving kit and pajamas and is sitting on his bed with his crutches, dressed and ready to go. I know him when he gets in that mood. If she tries to reason with him, we've had it. She's no match for him when it comes

880 to a battle of words. He'll tie her up in knots. (*Trying to hide his true feelings*)

SAM: I suppose it gets lonely for him in there.

HALLY: With all the patients and nurses around? Regular visits from the Salvation Army? Balls! It's ten times worse for

885 him at home. I'm at school and my mother is here in the business all day.

SAM: He's at least got you at night.

HALLY: (*Before he can stop himself*) And we've got him! Please! I don't want to talk about it anymore. (*Unpacks his school*

890 *case, slamming down books on the table*) Life is just a plain bloody mess, that's all. And people are fools.

SAM: Come on, Hally.

HALLY: Yes, they are! They bloody well deserve what they get.

SAM: Then don't complain.

895 HALLY: Don't try to be clever, Sam. It doesn't suit you. Anybody who thinks there's nothing wrong with this world needs to have his head examined. Just when things are going along all right, without fail someone or something will come along and spoil everything. Somebody should

900 write that down as a fundamental law of the Universe. The principle of perpetual disappointment. If there is a God who created this world, he should scrap it and try again.

SAM: All right, Hally, all right. What you got for homework?

905 HALLY: Bullshit, as usual. (*Opens an exercise book and reads*) "Write five hundred words describing an annual event of cultural or historical significance."

SAM: That should be easy enough for you.

HALLY: And also plain bloody boring. You know what he

910 wants, don't you? One of their useless old ceremonies. The commemoration of the landing of the 1820 Settlers, or if it's going to be culture, Carols by Candlelight every Christmas.

SAM: It's an impressive sight. Make a good description, Hally.

915 All those candles glowing in the dark and the people singing hymns.

HALLY: And it's called religious hysteria. (*Intense irritation*) Please, Sam! Just leave me alone and let me get on with it. I'm not in the mood for games this afternoon. And re-

920 member my Mom's orders . . . you're to help Willie with the windows. Come on now, I don't want any more nonsense in here.

SAM: Okay, Hally, okay.

(HALLY *settles down to his homework; determined preparations . . . pen, ruler, exercise book, dictionary, another cake . . . all of which will lead to nothing*)

(SAM *waltzes over to* WILLIE *and starts to replace tables and chairs. He practices a ballroom step while doing so.* WILLIE *watches. When* SAM *is finished,* WILLIE *tries*) Good! But just a little bit quicker on the turn and only move in to her after she's crossed over. What about this one?

(*Another step. When* SAM *is finished,* WILLIE *again has a go*)

Much better. See what happens when you just relax and 925 enjoy yourself? Remember that in two weeks' time and you'll be all right.

WILLIE: But I haven't got partner, Boet Sam.

SAM: Maybe Hilda will turn up tonight.

WILLIE: No, Boet Sam. (*Reluctantly*) I gave her a good hiding. 930

SAM: You mean a bad one.

WILLIE: Good bad one.

SAM: Then you mustn't complain either. Now you pay the price for losing your temper.

WILLIE: I also pay two pounds ten shilling entrance fee. 935

SAM: They'll refund you if you withdraw now.

WILLIE: (*Appalled*) You mean, don't dance?

SAM: Yes.

WILLIE: No! I wait too long and I practice too hard. If I find me new partner, you think I can be ready in two weeks? 940 I ask Madam for my leave now and we practice every day.

SAM: Quickstep non-stop for two weeks. World record, Willie, but you'll be mad at the end.

WILLIE: No jokes, Boet Sam.

SAM: I'm not joking. 945

WILLIE: So then what?

SAM: Find Hilda. Say you're sorry and promise you won't beat her again.

WILLIE: No.

SAM: Then withdraw. Try again next year. 950

WILLIE: No.

SAM: Then I give up.

WILLIE: Haaikona, Boet Sam, you can't.

SAM: What do you mean, I can't? I'm telling you: I give up.

WILLIE: (*Adamant*) No! (*Accusingly*) It was you who start me 955 ballroom dancing.

SAM: So?

WILLIE: Before that I use to be happy. And is you and Miriam who bring me to Hilda and say here's partner for you.

SAM: What are you saying, Willie? 960

WILLIE: You!

SAM: But me what? To blame?

WILLIE: Yes.

SAM: Willie . . . ? (*Bursts into laughter*)

WILLIE: And now all you do is make jokes at me. You wait. 965 When Miriam leaves you is my turn to laugh. Ha! Ha! Ha!

SAM: (*He can't take* WILLIE *seriously any longer*) She can leave me tonight! I know what to do. (*Bowing before an imaginary partner*) May I have the pleasure? (*He dances and sings*) "Just a fellow with his pillow . . . 970 Dancin' like a willow . . . In an autumn breeze . . ."

WILLIE: There you go again!

(SAM *goes on dancing and singing*)

Boet Sam!

975 SAM: There's the answer to your problem! Judges' announcement in two weeks' time: "Ladies and gentlemen, the winner in the open section . . . Mr. Willie Malopo and his
pillow!"

(*This is too much for a now really angry* WILLIE. *He goes for* SAM,
but the latter is too quick for him and puts HALLY'*s table between the
two of them*)

HALLY: (*Exploding*) For Christ's sake, you two!

980 WILLIE: (*Still trying to get at* SAM) I donner you, Sam! Struesgod!

SAM: (*Still laughing*) Sorry, Willie . . . Sorry . . .

HALLY: Sam! Willie! (*Grabs his ruler and gives* WILLIE *a vicious
whack on the bum*) How the hell am I supposed to

985 concentrate with the two of you behaving like bloody
children!

WILLIE: Hit him too!

HALLY: Shut up, Willie.

WILLIE: He started jokes again.

990 HALLY: Get back to your work. You too, Sam. (*His ruler*) Do
you want another one, Willie?

(SAM *and* WILLIE *return to their work.* HALLY *uses the opportunity
to escape from his unsuccessful attempt at homework. He struts
around like a little despot, ruler in hand, giving vent to his anger and
frustration*)

Suppose a customer had walked in then? Or the Park
Superintendent. And seen the two of you behaving like
a pair of hooligans. That would have been the end of my

995 mother's license, you know. And your jobs! Well, this is
the end of it. From now on there will be no more of
your ballroom nonsense in here. This is a business establishment, not a bloody New Brighton dancing school.
I've been far too lenient with the two of you. (*Behind the

1000 counter for a green cool drink and a dollop of ice cream. He
keeps up his tirade as he prepares it*) But what really makes
me bitter is that I allow you chaps a little freedom in
here when business is bad and what do you do with it?
The foxtrot! Specially you, Sam. There's more to life than

1005 trotting around a dance floor and I thought at least you
knew it.

SAM: It's harmless pleasure, Hally. It doesn't hurt anybody.

HALLY: It's also a rather simple one, you know.

SAM: You reckon so? Have you ever tried?

1010 HALLY: Of course not.

SAM: Why don't you? Now.

HALLY: What do you mean? Me dance?

SAM: Yes. I'll show you a simple step—the waltz—then you
try it.

1015 HALLY: What will that prove?

SAM: That it might not be as easy as you think.

HALLY: I didn't say it was easy. I said it was simple—like in
simple-minded, meaning mentally retarded. You can't exactly say it challenges the intellect.

1020 SAM: It does other things.

HALLY: Such as?

SAM: Make people happy.

HALLY: (*The glass in his hand*) So do American cream sodas
with ice cream. For God's sake, Sam, you're not asking me
to take ballroom dancing serious, are you? 1025

SAM: Yes.

HALLY: (*Sigh of defeat*) Oh, well, so much for trying to give
you a decent education. I've obviously achieved nothing.

SAM: You still haven't told me what's wrong with admiring
something that's beautiful and then trying to do it your- 1030
self.

HALLY: Nothing. But we happen to be talking about a foxtrot, not a thing of beauty.

SAM: But that is just what I'm saying. If you were to see two
champions doing, two masters of the art . . . ! 1035

HALLY: Oh, God, I give up. So now it's also art!

SAM: Ja.

HALLY: There's a limit, Sam. Don't confuse art and entertainment.

SAM: So then what is art? 1040

HALLY: You want a definition?

SAM: Ja.

HALLY: (*He realizes he has got to be careful. He gives the matter a lot
of thought before answering*) Philosophers have been trying to
do that for centuries. What is Art? What is Life? But basi- 1045
cally I suppose it's . . . the giving of meaning to matter.

SAM: Nothing to do with beautiful?

HALLY: It goes beyond that. It's the giving of form to the
formless.

SAM: Ja, well, maybe it's not art, then. But I still say it's beau- 1050
tiful.

HALLY: I'm sure the word you mean to use is entertaining.

SAM: (*Adamant*) No. Beautiful. And if you want proof, come
along to the Centenary Hall in New Brighton in two
weeks' time. 1055

(*The mention of the Centenary Hall draws* WILLIE *over to them*)

HALLY: What for? I've seen the two of you prancing around
in here often enough.

SAM: (*He laughs*) This isn't the real thing, Hally. We're just
playing around in here.

HALLY: So? I can use my imagination. 1060

SAM: And what do you get?

HALLY: A lot of people dancing around and having a so-called
good time.

SAM: That all?

HALLY: Well, basically it is that, surely. 1065

SAM: No, it isn't. Your imagination hasn't helped you at all.
There's a lot more to it than that. We're getting ready for
the championships, Hally, not just another dance. There's
going to be a lot of people, all right, and they're going to
have a good time, but they'll only be spectators, sitting 1070
around and watching. It's just the competitors out there
on the dance floor. Party decorations and fancy lights all
around the walls! The ladies in beautiful evening dresses!

HALLY: My mother's got one of those, Sam, and, quite frankly,
it's an embarrassment every time she wears it. 1075

SAM: (*Undeterred*) Your imagination left out the excitement.

(HALLY *scoffs*)

Oh, yes, the finalists are not going to be out there just to
have a good time. One of those couples will be the 1950

1080 Eastern Province Champions. And your imagination left out the music.

WILLIE: Mr. Elijah Gladman Guzana and his Orchestral Jazzonions.

SAM: The sound of the big band, Hally. Trombone, trumpet, tenor and alto sax. And then, finally, your imagination also
1085 left out the climax of the evening when the dancing is finished, the judges have stopped whispering among themselves and the Master of Ceremonies collects their scorecards and goes up onto the stage to announce the winners.

1090 HALLY: All right. So you make it sound like a bit of a do. It's an occasion. Satisfied?

SAM: (*Victory*) So you admit that!

HALLY: Emotionally yes, intellectually no.

SAM: Well, I don't know what you mean by that, all I'm
1095 telling you is that it is going to be *the* event of the year in New Brighton. It's been sold out for two weeks already. There's only standing room left. We've got competitors coming from Kingwilliamstown, East London, Port Alfred.

(HALLY *starts pacing thoughtfully*)

1100 HALLY: Tell me a bit more.

SAM: I thought you weren't interested . . . intellectually.

HALLY: (*Mysteriously*) I've got my reasons.

SAM: What do you want to know?

HALLY: It takes place every year?

1105 SAM: Yes. But only every third year in New Brighton. It's East London's turn to have the championships next year.

HALLY: Which, I suppose, makes it an even more significant event.

SAM: Ah ha! We're getting somewhere. Our "occasion" is now
1110 a "significant event."

HALLY: I wonder.

SAM: What?

HALLY: I wonder if I would get away with it.

SAM: But what?

1115 HALLY: (*To the table and his exercise book*) "Write five hundred words describing an annual event of cultural or historical significance." Would I be stretching poetic license a little too far if I called your ballroom championships a cultural event?

1120 SAM: You mean . . . ?

HALLY: You think we could get five hundred words out of it, Sam?

SAM: Victor Sylvester has written a whole book on ballroom dancing.

1125 WILLIE: You going to write about it, Master Hally?

HALLY: Yes, gentlemen, that is precisely what I am considering doing. Old Doc Bromely—he's my English teacher—is going to argue with me, of course. He doesn't like natives. But I'll point out to him that in strict anthropo-
1130 logical terms the culture of a primitive black society includes its dancing and singing. To put my thesis in a nutshell: The war dance has been replaced by the waltz. But it still amounts to the same thing: the release of primitive emotions through movement. Shall we give it a go?

1135 SAM: I'm ready.

WILLIE: Me also.

HALLY: Ha! This will teach the old bugger a lesson. (*Decision taken*) Right. Let's get ourselves organized. (*This means another cake on the table. He sits*) I think you've given me enough general atmosphere, Sam, but to build the tension 1140 and suspense I need facts. (*Pencil poised*)

WILLIE: Give him facts, Boet Sam.

HALLY: What you called the climax . . . how many finalists?

SAM: Six couples.

HALLY: (*Making notes*) Go on. Give me the picture. 1145

SAM: Spectators seated right around the hall. (WILLIE *becomes a spectator*)

HALLY: . . . and it's a full house.

SAM: At one end, on the stage, Gladman and his Orchestral Jazzonions. At the other end is a long table with the three 1150 judges. The six finalists go onto the dance floor and take up their positions. When they are ready and the spectators have settled down, the Master of Ceremonies goes to the microphone. To start with, he makes some jokes to get the people laughing . . . 1155

HALLY: Good touch! (*as he writes*) ". . . creating a relaxed atmosphere which will change to one of tension and drama as the climax is approached."

SAM: (*Onto a chair to act out the M.C.*) "Ladies and gentlemen, we come now to the great moment you have all been 1160 waiting for this evening. . . . The finals of the 1950 Eastern Province Open Ballroom Dancing Championships. But first let me introduce the finalists! Mr. and Mrs. Welcome Tchabalala from Kingwilliamstown . . ."

WILLIE: (*He applauds after every name*) Is when the people clap 1165 their hands and whistle and make a lot of noise, Master Hally.

SAM: "Mr. Mulligan Njikelane and Miss Nomhle Nkonyeni of Grahamstown; Mr. and Mrs. Norman Nchinga from Port Alfred; Mr. Fats Bokolane and Miss Dina Plaatjies 1170 from East London; Mr. Sipho Dugu and Mrs. Mable Magada from Peddie; and from New Brighton our very own Mr. Willie Malopo and Miss Hilda Samuels."

(WILLIE *can't believe his ears. He abandons his role as a spectator and scrambles into position as a finalist*)

WILLIE: Relaxed and ready to romance! 1175

SAM: The applause dies down. When everybody is silent, Gladman lifts up his sax, nods at the Orchestral Jazzonions . . .

WILLIE: Play the jukebox please, Boet Sam!

SAM: I also only got bus fare, Willie. 1180

HALLY: Hold it, everybody. (*Heads for the cash register behind the counter*) How much is in the till, Sam?

SAM: Three shillings. Hally . . . your Mom counted it before she left.

(HALLY *hesitates*)

HALLY: Sorry, Willie. You know how she carried on the last 1185 time I did it. We'll just have to pool our combined imaginations and hope for the best. (*Returns to the table*) Back to work. How are the points scored, Sam?

SAM: Maximum of ten points each for individual style, deportment, rhythm and general appearance.
1190

WILLIE: Must I start?

HALLY: Hold it for a second, Willie. And penalties?

SAM: For what?

HALLY: For doing something wrong. Say you stumble or bump into somebody . . . do they take off any points?

SAM: (*Aghast*) Hally . . . !

HALLY: When you're dancing. If you and your partner collide into another couple.

(HALLY *can get no further.* SAM *has collapsed with laughter. He explains to* WILLIE)

SAM: If me and Miriam bump into you and Hilda . . .

(WILLIE *joins him in another good laugh*)

Hally, Hally . . . !

HALLY: (*Perplexed*) Why? What did I say?

SAM: There's no collisions out there, Hally. Nobody trips or stumbles or bumps into anybody else. That's what that moment is all about. To be one of those finalists on that dance floor is like . . . like being in a dream about a world in which accidents don't happen.

HALLY: (*Genuinely moved by* SAM's *image*) Jesus, Sam! That's beautiful!

WILLIE: (*Can endure waiting no longer*) I'm starting! (WILLIE *dances while* SAM *talks*)

SAM: Of course it is. That's what I've been trying to say to you all afternoon. And it's beautiful because that is what we want life to be like. But instead, like you said, Hally, we're bumping into each other all the time. Look at the three of us this afternoon: I've bumped into Willie, the two of us have bumped into you, you've bumped into your mother, she bumping into your Dad. . . . None of us knows the steps and there's no music playing. And it doesn't stop with us. The whole world is doing it all the time. Open a newspaper and what do you read? America has bumped into Russia, England is bumping into India, rich man bumps into poor man. Those are big collisions, Hally. They make for a lot of bruises. People get hurt in all that bumping, and we're sick and tired of it now. It's been going on for too long. Are we never going to get it right? . . . Learn to dance life like champions instead of always being just a bunch of beginners at it?

HALLY: (*Deep and sincere admiration of the man*) You've got a vision, Sam!

SAM: Not just me. What I'm saying to you is that everybody's got it. That's why there's only standing room left for the Centenary Hall in two weeks' time. For as long as the music lasts, we are going to see six couples get it right, the way we want life to be.

HALLY: But is that the best we can do, Sam . . . watch six finalists dreaming about the way it should be?

SAM: I don't know. But it starts with that. Without the dream we won't know what we're going for. And anyway I reckon there are a few people who have got past just dreaming about it and are trying for something real. Remember that thing we read once in the paper about the Mahatma Gandhi? Going without food to stop those riots in India?

HALLY: You're right. He certainly was trying to teach people to get the steps right.

SAM: And the Pope.

HALLY: Yes, he's another one. Our old General Smuts as well, you know. He's also out there dancing. You know, Sam, when you come to think of it, that's what the United Nations boils down to . . . a dancing school for politicians!

SAM: And let's hope they learn.

HALLY: (*A little surge of hope*) You're right. We mustn't despair. Maybe there's some hope for mankind after all. Keep it up, Willie. (*Back to his table with determination*) This is a lot bigger than I thought. So what have we got? Yes, our title: "A World Without Collisions."

SAM: That sounds good! "A World Without Collisions."

HALLY: Subtitle: "Global Politics on the Dance Floor." No. A bit too heavy, hey? What about "Ballroom Dancing as a Political Vision"?

(*The telephone rings.* SAM *answers it*)

SAM: St. George's Park Tea Room . . . Yes, Madam . . . Hally, it's your Mom.

HALLY: (*Back to reality*) Oh, God, yes! I'd forgotten all about that. Shit! Remember my words, Sam? Just when you're enjoying yourself, someone or something will come along and wreck everything.

SAM: You haven't heard what she's got to say yet.

HALLY: Public telephone?

SAM: No.

HALLY: Does she sound happy or unhappy?

SAM: I couldn't tell. (*Pause*) She's waiting, Hally.

HALLY: (*To the telephone*) Hello, Mom . . . No, everything is okay here. Just doing my homework. . . . What's your news? . . . You've what? . . . (*Pause. He takes the receiver away from his ear for a few seconds. In the course of* HALLY's *telephone conversation,* SAM *and* WILLIE *discretely position the stacked tables and chairs.* HALLY *places the receiver back to his ear*) Yes, I'm still here. Oh, well, I give up now. Why did you do it, Mom? . . . Well, I just hope you know what you've let us in for. . . . (*Loudly*) I said I hope you know what you've let us in for! It's the end of the peace and quiet we've been having. (*Softly*) Where is he? (*Normal voice*) He can't hear us from in there. But for God's sake, Mom, what happened? I told you to be firm with him. . . . Then you and the nurses should have held him down, taken his crutches away. . . . I know only too well he's my father! . . . I'm not being disrespectful, but I'm sick and tired of emptying stinking chamberpots full of phlegm and piss. . . . Yes, I do! When you're not there, he asks *me* do it. . . . If you really want to know the truth, that's why I've got no appetite for my food. . . . Yes! There's a lot of things you don't know about. For your information, I still haven't got that science textbook I need. And you know why? He borrowed the money you gave me for it. . . . Because I didn't want to start another fight between you two. . . . He says that every time. . . . All right, Mom! (*Viciously*) Then just remember to start hiding your bag away again, because he'll be at your purse before long for money for booze. And when he's well enough to come down here, you better keep an eye on the till as well, because that is also going to develop a leak. . . . Then don't complain to me when he starts his old tricks. . . . Yes, you do. I get it from you on one side and from him on the other, and it makes life hell for me.

1305 I'm not going to be the peacemaker anymore. I'm warning you now: when the two of you start fighting again, I'm leaving home. . . . Mom, if you start crying, I'm going to put down the receiver. . . . Okay . . . (*Lowering his voice to a vicious whisper*) Okay, Mom. I heard you. (*Desperate*) No. . . . Because I don't want to. I'll see him when

1310 I get home! Mom! . . . (*Pause. When he speaks again, his tone changes completely. It is not simply pretense. We sense a genuine emotional conflict*) Welcome home, chum! . . . What's that? . . . Don't be silly, Dad. You being home is just about the best news in the world. . . . I bet you are. Bloody de-

1315 pressing there with everybody going on about their ailments, hey! . . . How you feeling? . . . Good . . . Here as well, pal. Coming down cats and dogs. . . . That's right. Just the day for a kip and a toss in your old Uncle Ned. . . . Everything's just hunky-dory on my side, Dad. . . . Well, to

1320 start with, there's a nice pile of comics for you on the counter. . . . Yes, old Kemple brought them in. *Batman and Robin, Submariner* . . . just your cup of tea . . . I will. . . . Yes, we'll spin a few yarns tonight. . . . Okay, chum, see you in a little while. . . . No, I promise. I'll come straight

1325 home. . . . (*Pause—his mother comes back on the phone*) Mom? Okay. I'll lock up now. . . . What? . . . Oh, the brandy . . . Yes, I'll remember! . . . I'll put it in my suitcase now, for God's sake. I know well enough what will happen if he doesn't get it. . . . (*Places a bottle of brandy on the counter*) I

1330 *was* kind to him, Mom. I didn't say anything nasty! . . . All right. Bye. (*End of telephone conversation. A desolate* HALLY *doesn't move. A strained silence*)

SAM: (*Quietly*) That sounded like a bad bump, Hally.

HALLY: (*Having a hard time controlling his emotions. He speaks*
1335 *carefully*) Mind your own business, Sam.

SAM: Sorry. I wasn't trying to interfere. Shall we carry on? Hally? (*He indicates the exercise book. No response from* HALLY)

WILLIE: (*Also trying*) Tell him about when they give out the cups, Boet Sam.

1340 SAM: Ja! That's another big moment. The presentation of the cups after the winners have been announced. You've got to put that in.

(*Still no response form* HALLY)

WILLIE: A big silver one, Master Hally, called floating trophy for the champions.

1345 SAM: We always invite some big-shot personality to hand them over. Guest of honor this year is going to be His Holiness Bishop Jabulani of the All African Free Zionist Church.

(HALLY *gets up abruptly, goes to his table and tears up the page he was writing on*)

HALLY: So much for a bloody world without collisions.
1350 SAM: Too bad. It was on its way to being a good composition.

HALLY: Let's stop bullshitting ourselves, Sam.

SAM: Have we been doing that?

HALLY: Yes! That's what all our talk about a decent world has been . . . just so much bullshit.

1355 SAM: We did say it was still only a dream.

HALLY: And a bloody useless one at that. Life's a fuck-up and it's never going to change.

SAM: Ja, maybe that's true.

HALLY: There's no maybe about it. It's a blunt and brutal fact.
1360 All we've done this afternoon is waste our time.

SAM: Not if we'd got your homework done.

HALLY: I don't give a shit about my homework, so, for Christ's sake, just shut up about it. (*Slamming books viciously into his school case*) Hurry up now and finish your work. I want to
1365 lock up and get out of here. (*Pause*) And then go where? Home-sweet-fucking-home. Jesus, I hate that word.

(HALLY *goes to the counter to put the brandy bottle and comics in his school case. After a moment's hesitation, he smashes the bottle of brandy. He abandons all further attempts to hide his feelings.* SAM *and* WILLIE *work away as unobtrusively as possible*)

Do you want to know what is really wrong with your lovely little dream, Sam? It's not just that we are all bad dancers. That does happen to be perfectly true, but there's more to it than just that. You left out the cripples.
1370

SAM: Hally!

HALLY: (*Now totally reckless*) Ja! Can't leave them out, Sam. That's why we always end up on our backsides on the dance floor. They're also out there dancing . . . like a bunch of broken spiders trying to do the quick-step!
1375 (*An ugly attempt at laughter*) When you come to think of it, it's a bloody comical sight. I mean, it's bad enough on two legs . . . but one and a pair of crutches! Hell, no, Sam. That's guaranteed to turn that dance floor into a shambles. Why you shaking your head? Picture it, man.
1380 For once this afternoon let's use our imaginations sensibly.

SAM: Be careful, Hally.

HALLY: Of what? The truth? I seem to be the only one around here who is prepared to face it. We've had the
1385 pretty dream, it's time now to wake up and have a good long look at the way things really are. Nobody knows the steps, there's no music, the cripples are also out there tripping up everybody and trying to get into the act, and it's all called the All-Comers-How-to-Make-a-Fuckup-of-
1390 Life Championships. (*Another ugly laugh*) Hang on, Sam! The best bit is still coming. Do you know what the winner's trophy is? A beautiful big chamber-pot with roses on the side, and it's full to the brim with piss. And guess who I think is going to be this year's winner.
1395

SAM: (*Almost shouting*) Stop now!

HALLY: (*Suddenly appalled by how far he has gone*) Why?

SAM: Hally? It's your father you're talking about.

HALLY: So?
1400

SAM: Do you know what you've been saying?

(HALLY *can't answer. He is rigid with shame.* SAM *speaks to him sternly*)

No, Hally, you mustn't do it. Take back those words and ask for forgiveness! It's a terrible sin for a son to mock his father with jokes like that. You'll be punished if you carry on. Your father is your father, even if he is a . . . cripple 1405 man.

WILLIE: Yes, Master Hally. Is true what Sam say.

SAM: I understand how you are feeling, Hally, but even so . . .

HALLY: No, you don't!

1410 SAM: I think I do.

HALLY: And I'm telling you you don't. Nobody does. (*Speaking carefully as his shame turns to rage at* SAM) It's your turn to be careful, Sam. Very careful! You're treading on dangerous ground. Leave me and my father alone.

1415 SAM: I'm not the one who's been saying things about him.

HALLY: What goes on between me and my Dad is none of your business!

SAM: Then don't tell me about it. If that's all you've got to say about him, I don't want to hear.

(*For a moment* HALLY *is at loss for a response*)

1420 HALLY: Just get on with your bloody work and shut up.

SAM: Swearing at me won't help you.

HALLY: Yes, it does! Mind your own fucking business and shut up!

SAM: Okay. If that's the way you want it, I'll stop trying.

(*He turns away. This infuriates* HALLY *even more*)

1425 HALLY: Good. Because what you've been trying to do is meddle in something you know nothing about. All that concerns you in here, Sam, is to try and do what you get paid for—keep the place clean and serve the customers. In plain words, just get on with your job. My mother is right.

1430 She's always warning me about allowing you to get too familiar. Well, this time you've gone too far. It's going to stop right now.

(*No response from* SAM)

You're only a servant in here, and don't forget it.

(*Still no response.* HALLY *is trying hard to get one*)

And as far as my father is concerned, all you need to re-

1435 member is that he is your boss.

SAM: (*Needled at last*) No, he isn't. I get paid by your mother.

HALLY: Don't argue with me, Sam!

SAM: Then don't say he's my boss.

HALLY: He's a white man and that's good enough for you.

1440 SAM: I'll try to forget you said that.

HALLY: Don't! Because you won't be doing me a favor if you do. I'm telling you to remember it.

(*A pause.* SAM *pulls himself together and makes one last effort*)

SAM: Hally, Hally . . . ! Come on now. Let's stop before it's too late. You're right. We *are* on dangerous ground. If we're not

1445 careful, somebody is going to get hurt.

HALLY: It won't be me.

SAM: Don't be so sure.

HALLY: I don't know what you're talking about, Sam.

SAM: Yes, you do.

1450 HALLY: (*Furious*) Jesus, I wish you would stop trying to tell me what I do and what I don't know.

(SAM *gives up. He turns to* WILLIE)

SAM: Let's finish up.

HALLY: Don't turn your back on me! I haven't finished talking.

(*He grabs* SAM *by the arm and tries to make him turn around.* SAM *reacts with a flash of anger*)

SAM: Don't do that, Hally! (*Facing the boy*) All right, I'm lis- 1455 tening. Well? What do you want to say to me?

HALLY: (*Pause as* HALLY *looks for something to say*) To begin with, why don't you also start calling me Master Harold, like Willie.

SAM: Do you mean that? 1460

HALLY: Why the hell do you think I said it?

SAM: And if I don't?

HALLY: You might just lose your job.

SAM: (*Quietly and very carefully*) If you make me say it once, I'll never call you anything else again. 1465

HALLY: So? (*The boy confronts the man*) Is that meant to be a threat?

SAM: Just telling you what will happen if you make me do that. You must decide what it means to you.

HALLY: Well, I have. It's good news. Because that is exactly 1470 what Mater Harold wants from now on. Think of it as a little lesson in respect, Sam, that's long overdue, and I hope you remember it as well as you do your geography. I can tell you now that somebody who will be glad to hear I've finally given it to you will be my Dad. Yes! He agrees with 1475 my Mom. He's always going on about it as well. "You must teach the boys to show you more respect, my son."

SAM: So now you can stop complaining about going home. Everybody is going to be happy tonight.

HALLY: That's perfectly correct. You see, you mustn't get the 1480 wrong idea about me and my Dad, Sam. We also have our good times together. Some bloody good laughs. He's got a marvelous sense of humor. Want to know what our favorite joke is? He gives out a big groan, you see, and says: "It's not fair, is it, Hally?" Then I have to ask: "What, 1485 chum?" And then he says: "A nigger's arse" . . . and we both have a good laugh.

(*The men stare at him with disbelief*)

What's the matter, Willie? Don't you catch the joke? You always were a bit slow on the uptake. It's what is called a pun. You see, fair means both light in color and to be just 1490 and decent. (*He turns to* SAM) I thought *you* would catch it, Sam.

SAM: Oh ja, I catch it all right.

HALLY: But it doesn't appeal to your sense of humor.

SAM: Do you really laugh? 1495

HALLY: Of course.

SAM: To please him? Make him feel good?

HALLY: No, for heaven's sake! I laugh because I think it's a bloody good joke.

SAM: You're really trying hard to be ugly, aren't you? And why 1500 drag poor old Willie into it? He's done nothing to you except show you the respect you want so badly. That's also not being fair, you know . . . and *I* mean just or decent.

WILLIE: It's all right, Sam. Leave it now.

SAM: It's me you're after. You should just have said "Sam's 1505 arse" . . . because that's the one you're trying to kick. Anyway, how do you know it's not fair? You've never seen it. Do you want to? (*He drops his trousers and underpants and presents his backside for* HALLY's *inspection*) Have a good look. A real Basuto arse . . . which is about as nigger as they can 1510

come. Satisfied? (*Trousers up*) Now you can make your Dad even happier when you go home tonight. Tell him I showed you my arse and he is quite right. It's not fair. And if it will give him an even better laugh next time, I'll also
1515   let *him* have a look. Come, Willie, let's finish up and go.

(SAM *and* WILLIE *start to tidy up the tea room.* HALLY *doesn't move. He waits for a moment when* SAM *passes him*)

HALLY: (*Quietly*) Sam . . .

(SAM *stops and looks expectantly at the boy.* HALLY *spits in his face. A long and heartfelt groan from* WILLIE. *For a few seconds* SAM *doesn't move*)

SAM: (*Taking out a handkerchief and wiping his face*) It's all right, Willie.

(*To* HALLY)

Ja, well, you've done it . . . Master Harold. Yes, I'll start call-
1520   ing you that from now on. It won't be difficult anymore. You've hurt yourself, Master Harold. I saw it coming. I warned you, but you wouldn't listen. You've just hurt yourself *bad*. And you're a coward, Master Harold. The face you should be spitting in is your father's . . . but you
1525   used mine, because you think you're safe inside your fair skin . . . and this time I don't mean just or decent. (*Pause, then moving violently towards* HALLY) Should I hit him, Willie?
WILLIE: (*Stopping* SAM) No, Boet Sam.
1530 SAM: (*Violently*) Why not?
WILLIE: It won't help, Boet Sam.
SAM: I don't want to help! I want to hurt him.
WILLIE: You also hurt yourself.
SAM: And if he had done it to you, Willie?
1535 WILLIE: Me? Spit at me like I was a dog? (*A thought that had not occurred to him before. He looks at* HALLY) Ja. Then I want to hit him. I want to hit him hard!

(*A dangerous few seconds as the men stand staring at the boy.* WILLIE *turns away, shaking his head*)

But maybe all I do is go cry at the back. He's little boy, Boet Sam. Little *white* boy. Long trousers now, but he's still
1540   little boy.
SAM: (*His violence ebbing away into defeat as quickly as it flooded*) You're right. So go on, then: groan again, Willie. You do it better than me. (*To* HALLY) You don't know all of what you've just done . . . Master Harold. It's not just that you've
1545   made me feel dirtier than I've ever been in my life . . . I mean, how do I wash off yours and your father's filth? . . . I've also failed. A long time ago I promised myself I was going to try and do something, but you've just shown me . . . Master Harold . . . that I've failed. (*Pause*) I've also
1550   got a memory of a little white boy when he was still wearing short trousers and a black man, but they're not flying a kite. It was the old Jubilee days, after dinner one night. I was in my room. You came in and just stood against the wall, looking down at the ground, and only after I'd asked
1555   you what you wanted, what was wrong, I don't know how many times, did you speak and even then so softly I almost

didn't hear you. "Sam, please help me to go and fetch my Dad." Remember? He was dead drunk on the floor of the Central Hotel Bar. They'd phoned for your Mom, but you were the only one at home. And do you remember how   1560
we did it? You went in first by yourself to ask permission for me to go into the bar. Then I loaded him onto my back like a baby and carried him back to the boarding house with you following behind carrying his crutches. (*Shaking his head as he remembers*) A crowded Main Street   1565
with all the people watching a little white boy following his drunk father on a nigger's back! I felt for that little boy . . . Master Harold. I felt for him. After that we still had to clean him up, remember? He'd messed in his trousers, so we had to clean him up and get him into bed.   1570
HALLY: (*Great pain*) I love him, Sam.
SAM: I know you do. That's why I tried to stop you from saying these things about him. It would have been so simple if you could have just despised him for being a weak man. But he's your father. You love him and you're ashamed of him. You're   1575
ashamed of so much! . . . And now that's going to include yourself. That was the promise I made to myself: to try and stop that happening. (*Pause*) After we got him to bed you came back with me to my room and sat in a corner and carried on just looking down at the ground. And for days after   1580
that! You hadn't done anything wrong, but you went around as if you owed the world an apology for being alive. I didn't like seeing that! That's not the way a boy grows up to be a man! . . . But the one person who should have been teaching you what that means was the cause of your shame. If you   1585
really want to know, that's why I made you that kite. I wanted you to look up, be proud of something, of yourself . . . (*Bitter smile at the memory*) . . . and you certainly were that when I left you with it up there on the hill. Oh, ja . . . something else! . . . If you ever do write it as a short story,   1590
there *was* a twist in our ending. I couldn't sit down there and stay with you. It was a "Whites Only" bench. You were too young, too excited to notice then. But not anymore. If you're not careful . . . Master Harold . . . you're going to be sitting up there by yourself for a long time to come, and   1595
there won't be a kite in the sky. (SAM *has got nothing more to say. He exits into the kitchen, taking off his waiter's jacket*)
WILLIE: Is bad. Is all all bad in here now.
HALLY: (*Books into his school case, raincoat on*) Willie . . . (*It is difficult to speak*) Will you lock up for me and look after the   1600
keys?
WILLIE: Okay.

(SAM *returns.* HALLY *goes behind the counter and collects the few coins in the cash register. As he starts to leave . . .*)

SAM: Don't forget the comic books.

(HALLY *returns to the counter and puts them in his case. He starts to leave again*)

SAM: (*To the retreating back of the boy*) Stop . . . Hally . . .

(HALLY *stops, but doesn't turn to face him*)

Hally . . . I've got no right to tell you what being a man   1605
means if I don't behave like one myself, and I'm not do-

ing so well at that this afternoon. Should we try again, Hally?

HALLY: Try what?

1610 SAM: Fly another kite, I suppose. It worked once, and this time I need it as much as you do.

HALLY: It's still raining, Sam. You can't fly kites on rainy days, remember.

SAM: So what do we do? Hope for better weather tomorrow?

1615 HALLY: (*Helpless gesture*) I don't know. I don't know anything anymore.

SAM: You sure of that, Hally? Because it would be pretty hopeless if that was true. It would mean nothing has been learnt in here this afternoon, and there was a hell of a lot of teach-

1620 ing going on . . . one way or the other. But anyway, I don't believe you. I reckon there's one thing you know. You don't *have* to sit up there by yourself. You know what that bench means now, and you can leave it any time you choose. All you've got to do is stand up and walk away from it.

1625

(HALLY *leaves.* WILLIE *goes up quietly to* SAM)

WILLIE: Is okay, Boet Sam. You see. Is . . . (*He can't find any better words*) . . . is going to be okay tomorrow. (*Changing his tone*) Hey, Boet Sam! (*He is trying hard*) You right. I think about it and you right. Tonight I find Hilda and say sorry. And make promise I won't beat her no more. You hear

1630 me, Boet Sam?

SAM: I hear you, Willie.

WILLIE: And when we practice I relax and romance with her from beginning to end. Non-stop! You watch! Two weeks' time: "First prize for promising newcomers: Mr. Willie Malopo and Miss Hilda Samuels." (*Sudden im-* 1635 *pulse*) To hell with it! I walk home. (*He goes to the juke-box, puts in a coin and selects a record. The machine comes to life in the gray twilight, blushing its way through a spectrum of soft, romantic colors*) How did you say it, Boet Sam? Let's dream. (WILLIE *sways with the music and gestures for* SAM *to* 1640 *dance*)

(*Sarah Vaughan sings*)

"Little man you're crying,
I know why you're blue,
Someone took your kiddy car away;
Better go to sleep now,   1645
Little man you've had a busy day." (*etc. etc.*)
    You lead. I follow.

(*The men dance together*)

"Johnny won your marbles,
Tell you what we'll do;
Dad will get you new ones   1650
right away;
Better go to sleep now,
Little man you've had a
busy day."

Manjula Padmanabhan

Well-known as a cartoonist in Delhi, Manjula Padmanabhan (b. 1953), has worked as a journalist and fiction writer, as well as writing for television and the stage; she has also written several children's books. After completing her university studies abroad, Padmanabhan returned to India and began a career in journalism. She wrote several plays—including *Lights Out!* (1984), *The Artist's Model* (1995), and *Sextet* (1996)—and a well-known book of short stories, *Hot Death, Cold Soup* (1995). *Harvest* won the first Onassis Prize for Theater, and premiered in Greece in 1999; it has also been produced in India. Her most recent novel is *Getting There* (2000).

HARVEST

Written in the lineage of plays like Václav Havel's *The Memorandum* or Slawomir Mrozek's *Tango*, Manjula Padmanabhan's *Harvest* develops an absurd narrative of the structure of representation and power in the contemporary globalized culture. For *Harvest* brilliantly allegorizes the relationship between the First and Third Worlds, literalizing the fundamental practices of globalization as its central dramatic situation: the Third World provides the raw materials that the First World consumes for its own survival and expansion.

In the play, Om has sold his body—through the aptly named InterPlanta Services company—to an American "Receiver." According to the terms of his contract, he and his immediate family (his wife Jaya, who is forced by the contract to pretend to be his sister, his brother Jeetu, and his mother, Ma) will enjoy a First World standard of living and lifestyle—they'll be clean, well-fed, entertained, and wealthy—until such time as his Receiver demands Om's organs for his own survival. As the play develops, however, the economic

The family confronts Ginni in Manjula Padmanabhan's *Harvest,* in the 1999 production of the play at the Teatro Texnis, Greece.

motives driving Om's sacrifice are gradually inflected by the mediatized relations of global culture. His family is consulted (on a giant-screen Contact Module that drops from the ceiling) by the Receiver, Virginia—or "Ginni," whose name recalls the demonic *djinni,* or "genies" of Indian folktales—a "blonde and white-skinned epitome of an American-style youth goddess" whose image floats above the room, and increasingly demands obedience from the family. Ma comes nearly to worship Ginni, but truly idolizes her new television, finally choosing to entomb herself inside a video sarcophagus—called the Video Paradise—where she will remain for the rest of her "life." When the InterPlanta agents come to take Om, however, they mistakenly take his wastrel brother Jeetu, removing his eyes and replacing them with a contraption that projects Ginna's sexy image directly into his brain. Although Jeetu had been the most critical of the organ-donation scheme, now that all he can see is Ginni's sultry image, he's seduced, and this virtual relationship leads him finally to "donate" his entire body.

The play's brilliant satire fully takes in First World attitudes toward India, its fear of disease, its anxiety about sanitation, its incomprehension of family and social life, its ignorance of Third World reality altogether. Replacing the family's food with "goat-shit" pellets, installing a toilet and shower in the middle of its one-room apartment, dumping the family's possessions and replacing them with Western clothes and housewares, InterPlanta at once appears to improve the family's standard of living while cutting it off from real life altogether. Yet the final scenes seem to suggest a strategy of resistance. Once Ginni has harvested Jeetu's body, she reveals that "Ginni" had only been a computer-animation after all: Jeetu had been seduced to give up his body by the empty image of youthful, sexy America, an image projected to the world to conceal that the First World paradise is aging and impotent, supporting "the poorer sections of the world, while gaining fresh bodies for ourselves." Virgil— the real Ginni—proposes that he (in the body of Jeetu) and Jaya have children to repopulate the First World; he even makes an insemination gadget appear outside the apartment while he's trying to close the deal. But if the body is, finally, what the Third World has to sell, it may still be possible to withhold it, to insist on a real rather than a mediated relationship with First World power. At the play's close, Jaya seals herself inside the apartment, with its endless food supply and television, telling Virgil that if he wants to repopulate the First World, he will have to come to her, in the flesh.

HARVEST

Manjula Padmanabhan

CHARACTERS

DONORS

OM *Twenty years old, he has been laid off from his job as a clerk and is the bread-earner of his small family. He is of medium height, nervy and thin. He would be reasonably good-looking if not for his anxious expression.*

JAYA OM's *wife. Thin and haggard at the outset, she looks older than her nineteen years, but is passionate and spirited. Her bright cotton sari has faded with repeated washing, to a meek pink. Like the others, she is barefoot at the outset. She wears glass bangles, a tiny nose-ring, ear-studs, a slender chain around her neck. No make-up aside from the kohl around her eyes and the red bindi on her forehead.*

MA OM's *mother. She is sixty years old, stooped, scrawny and crabby, wears a widow's threadbare white-on-white sari. Her hair is a straggly white.*

JEETU OM's *younger brother, seventeen and handsome. The same height as* OM, *he is wiry and conscious of his body. He works as a male prostitute and has a dashing, easy-going likeable personality.*

BIDYUT BAI *An elderly neighbour, very similar in appearance to* MA, *but timid and self-effacing.*

Also URCHINS *and the crowd outside the door. The crowd is audible rather than visible.*

GUARDS and AGENTS

GUARDS *The* GUARDS *are a group of three commando-like characters who bear the same relationship to each other whenever they appear.* GUARD 1 *is the leader of the team, a man in his mid forties, of military bearing.* GUARD 2 *is a young and attractive woman, unsmiling and efficient.* GUARD 3 *is a male clone of* GUARD 2. *Only* GUARD 1 *interacts with* DONORS.

AGENTS *The* AGENTS *are space-age delivery persons and their uniforms are fantastical verging on ludicrous, like the costumes of waiters in exotic restaurants. Their roles are interchangeable with the* GUARDS, *though it must be clear that they do not belong to the same agency.*

RECEIVERS

GINNI *We see only her face and hear her voice. She is the blonde and white-skinned epitome of an American-style youth goddess. Her voice is sweet and sexy.*

VIRGIL *He is never seen. He has an American cigarette-commercial accent—rich and smoky, attractive and rugged.*

ACT ONE

SCENE I

The sound of inner city traffic: grimy, despairing, poison-fumed. It wells up before the curtains open, then cuts out to a background rumble as . . . the lights reveal a single-room accommodation in a tenement building. It is bare but cluttered. In the foreground, stage left, is a board-bed across the tops of three steel trunks. MA *sits on the bed, her ear straining towards the wall, listening intently. Near her is the front door.* JAYA *stands by the window stage right, looking out, her face drained. To the rear is the kitchen area.*

MA: (*Grunts.*) Ho! (*Turns to look at* JAYA.) Ho—you! Come here a moment—

JAYA: (*Listlessly.*) What is it?

MA: Come here and tell me what they're saying—

5 JAYA: It's none of your business—

MA: Eh?

JAYA: What they say in their room—none of your business!

MA: The cheek of the thing! (*Turns around in indignation.*) As if she knows what my business is! Why—I'm her mother-

10 in-law! And what is she? A dry stick!

JAYA: Leave me out of it. I'm not interested.

MA: Oh—of course not, your majesty! So high and mighty she is—staring out of her precious window! Stare all you like but it's useless. There's no chance he'll get the job.

15 JAYA: (*Quickly.*) I'm not the one hoping!

MA: Oh—I forgot! Missie Madam *isn't* hoping the best for her husband—like she should, like any dutiful, sane, reasonable, respectable wife—oh no! Missie Madam has her own sweet thoughts, doesn't she!

JAYA: (*Briefly enlivened.*) Oh! There—I think I see him— 20

MA: Well—well—job or not, he's not got wings, *that* I can tell you. He'll *still* have to climb four floors getting up here. But—what does he look like?

JAYA: (*Straining to see.*) He's—no—yes . . . that's him—

MA: Is his face shining? Are his footsteps sweet? A songbird 25 on his shoulder?

JAYA: It's a bit far to see such details—

MA: Pah! As if you can see them even when he's right in front of you. Now I—I can see it even without looking at him. Just from the sound of his feet. His little feet! Like flowers 30 they were—

JAYA: (*Frustrated.*) Oh—please! The way you go on—!

MA: Jealous!

JAYA: You'd like to think that—

MA: And rude, my arse. Why, you're hardly human! You must 35 have grown up in a jungle!

JAYA: Leave me alone—

MA: Alone, alone! Have you seen your neighbours? Ten in that room, twenty in the other! And harmonious, my dear! Harmonious as a TV show! But you? An empty room 40 would be too crowded for you!

JAYA: That's because I live in a room in which two people think the other two don't exist—

MA: Two and . . . two—four? Have you forgotten how to
45 count?
JAYA: Not at all! You're the one who never counts Jeetu—
MA: Huh! That pimping rascal! That soul's disgrace!
JAYA: You like to pretend he's not there—but *I*'m the one
who has to cook for him, worry about him—
50 MA: You worry far too much about that one, if you ask me—
JAYA: Yet he's *your* son.
MA: Nah. The gods left a jackal in my belly by mistake when
they made him—maybe that's why *you* like him—he's just
like you, rude, insolent, ungrateful—
55 JAYA: I! *Like* him!
MA: Think I don't see the way you wet yourself when he
walks in the door. Yes! Your brother-in-law—oh the sin
of it, the sin! You'll suffer in your next life. See if you
don't! You'll be made into a cockroach and I'll have to
60 smash you—(*Lifts her bare foot and stamps hard.*) just like
this one. (*Shows* JAYA *the underside of the foot.*) See? Do you
see your fate?
JAYA: (*Paying no attention, her ear cocked to the door.*) There!
That's Om—

(*Goes quickly to the door, stage left. Opens it, looks out, steps out,
shutting the door behind her.*)

65 MA: (*Makes a face behind her back.*) Yah, yah! Go on—running
out to meet him, like some idiot schoolgirl! Think I'm
fooled by it! I'm not fooled! I see everything! Even inside
your head! I—

(*The door opens.* OM *walks in.*)

MA: (*Half rising, her face is transformed.*) Ah, my son! My own
70 boy! What news?

(OM, *carrying a bulky parcel, his face set tight, as if too dazed to
know whether to be glad or sad.* JAYA *comes in behind him and shuts
the door.* OM *loosens the collar of his shirt.*)

MA: What? No hope? Nothing at all?

(JAYA *stands uncertainly at centre stage.*)

MA: They are fools, that's all! Don't recognize a diamond
when they see one! It's their loss. Still . . . it would have
been nice. A change. A godsend. How'll we manage now?
75 JAYA: (*Carefully.*) What is it? What happened?
OM: (*Looks up.*) I got it. (*Puts the package down on the bed.*)

(JAYA *stifles a sob, spins around and back to her window.*)

MA: (*As if unable to believe him.*) What? Say that again?
OM: I got it. I got the job.
MA: (*Painfully fierce intake of breath.*) Hhhhhh! Hhhhh! Oh!
80 Say it again! Say the blessed words again! (*Rises shakily to
her feet, declaiming to the world.*) Never stop saying it! "I—
have—got—the—job!" (*Turns to him holding out her arms.*)
Ah, my soul, my heartbeat! Come, kiss me! Let me hold
you, tondle your ears! Why am I surprised? You deserve
85 every success.
OM: (*Starts to remove his shirt.*) Yes. It was quite easy, in the end.
MA: (*To* JAYA'*s back.*) Bring him a glass of milk! Bring him two
glasses! (*To* OM.) Come here, my darling boy! My only de-

light! Let your old mother hug you to her belly! (*She goes
to him.*)   90
OM: (*His shirt off, tucked into the waistband of his trousers.*) There
were six thousand men—
MA: Six thousand! Waiting in the sun!
OM: No. Inside a building like a big machine. They had—like
iron bars—snaking around and around (*His hands describe* 95
a narrow looping channel.)—we could only stand one be-
hind the other—like goats at the slaughterhouse—
MA: Shoo! Where has my son seen a slaughterhouse!
OM: And everywhere there were guards—
MA: Police, you mean?   100
OM: Guards in grey uniforms—you'll see them for yourself
any minute now—they're coming—
JAYA: (*From where she stands.*) They're coming now?
OM: They have to check. They have to set it all up.
MA: What? What are you talking about?   105
JAYA: You mean it's not certain yet?
OM: They're just checking the building.
MA: For what—
JAYA: (*Bitterly.*) Better train your mother to tie her tongue
down!   110
MA: Hear that? How your wife speaks of your mother?
OM: Ma—when the men come, you *must keep quiet.*
MA: As if I ever get a chance to speak!
JAYA: She can pretend she doesn't understand!
MA: (*Starting up indignantly.*) What—   115
OM: Yes, Ma. It's the best way. Behave as if you don't under-
stand, when they ask.
MA: But why? What's there to hide? Have you done some-
thing wrong?
OM: No—but—but—there's no time to explain! And you'll   120
know for yourself any minute now—
MA: But what's the trouble! Has something gone wrong?
What did they say to you?
OM: They have to check, you see. So that the arrangements
are—are—all right. They're very particular—   125
JAYA: And for how long is the job?
OM: They didn't say—
MA: And what will they pay you?
OM: A lot.
MA: Huh! That's how paupers talk—"a lot". Listen to the   130
rich? They're on first name terms with all the leading
numbers—hundreds, thousands, hundred-thousand . . .
OM: (*His voice is hushed.*) We'll have more money than you
and I have names for! (*Shakes his head in wonderment.*)
Who'd believe there's so much money in the world?   135
MA: Ho!
JAYA: Can we be sure?
MA: You met with the top men? They spoke to you themselves?
OM: No . . .
MA: Pooh! Then you've got nothing!   140
OM: We were standing all together in that line. And the line
went on—and on not just on one floor, but slanting up,
up, forever. All in iron bars and grills. It was like being in
a cage shaped like a tunnel. All around, up, down, side-
ways, there were men—   145
JAYA: Doing what?
OM: Slowly moving. All the time. I couldn't understand it . . .
Somewhere there must be a place to stop, to write a form?
Answer questions? But no. Just—forward, forward, for-

150 ward. One person fainted but the others pushed him onward. And at the corners, a—a sort of pipe was kept . . .
MA: For what?
JAYA: To make water, what else!
MA: Even while moving?
155 OM: You had to be quick. Other men would squeeze past behind the fellow who was doing his business. Sometimes
there was no place and he'd have to move on before he
finished. Still dripping.
MA: Shee!
160 OM: What could we do? As for those who had more solid deposits to make—! Foo! It was terrible!
JAYA: And then?
OM: The stench! The heat!
MA: But what happened?
165 OM: I don't know for how long we moved. Then there was
a door. Inside it was dark, like being in heaven! So cool,
so fresh! I too fainted then, with pleasure, I don't know.
(*Stands up, reliving his movements.*) I wake up to find now
the ground is moving under me—
170 MA: What? How's that?
OM: I don't know. But the floor is moving. Then there's a
sign: "REMOVE CLOTHING"—
MA: Whaaat?
OM: So we do that. Still moving. Then each man gets a bag.
175 To put the clothes inside.
JAYA: . . . *naked?*
OM: (*Nods.*) Then—a sort of—rain burst. (*He laughs shakily.*)
I wonder if I am dreaming! The water is hot, scented.
Then cold. Then hot air. Then again the water. It stings a
180 little, this second water. Smells like some medicine. Then
air again. Then we pass through another place . . . I don't
know what is happening. Ahead of me a man screams and
cries, but we are in separate little cages now, can't move.
At one place, something comes to cover the eyes. There's
185 no time to think, just do. Put your arm here, get one
prick, put your arm there, get another prick—*pissshhh!*—
pissshhh!—Sit here, stand here, take your head this side,
look at a light that side. On and on. Finally at the end
there's another tunnel, with pretty pictures and some mu-
190 sic. And the sign comes: RESUME CLOTHING. I just do
what I have to do. All the time, the ground keeps moving. Then at the end, the ground stops, we are back on
our feet, there are steps. It must be the other side of the
building. And as we come down, guards are standing
195 there, waiting for us. And to me they say, "You, come—"
(*Pause.*) And that was it!
MA: What!
JAYA: What?
OM: That's all. Some other men were also with me, all look-
200 ing like me, I suppose. Blank. They told us we had been
selected. They wrote down our names, addresses . . . (*He
hesitates.*) and . . . this-that. All details. Then they gave us
these packets (*Indicates the package.*), told us not to open
them and said we must go home, the guards would come
205 with us for final instructions.
MA: But what is the work? The pay-packet? The hours?
OM: (*Looking distracted.*) I—I'll be in the house . . .
MA: What?! All the time?
JAYA: (*Staring intensely at him.*) . . . you don't really know what
210 it's going to be like, do you?

MA: What kind of job pays a man to sit at home?
OM: Oh—there was some pamphlet they gave us to read,
right in the beginning. Just to tell us to be relaxed and to
do whatever we were told. In that it said that once we
were selected, each man would get special instructions. 215
That we would be monitored carefully. Not just us but
our . . . lives. To remain employed, we have to keep ourselves exactly as they tell us.
JAYA: But—but *who* will tell us—how'll we afford it—

(*There is an excited tapping on the door which was left unbolted. A
CHILD bursts in.*)

CHILD: Auntie! Auntie! They're coming to your house! Police! 220

(*From the corridor, approaching footsteps.* JAYA *shoos the child from
the door as she stands by it. The footsteps come to a halt. A small
crowd has collected out on the corridor (out of sight, but audible) to
whom* JAYA *pays no attention.*)

JAYA: Yes?
MA: (*Remaining seated.*) Let him in, let him in—
GUARD 1: (*Out of sight.*) InterPlanta Services wishes to con-
firm that this is the residence of Om Prakash?
JAYA: It is—(*And she stands aside.*) 225
GUARD 1: (*Entering officiously.*) Thank you—(*Looks around.*)
Ah. Yes. Am I addressing Mr Om Prakash?

(*As he talks, enter* GUARD 2 *and* GUARD 3. *They are both carrying equipment which they set down and immediately begin to ready
for installation.* GUARD 3 *produces collapsible cartons which he begins to set up.* GUARD 2 *starts to install a device onto the window
frame.*)

MA: Who are these people? What are they doing?
GUARD 1: (*To* OM.) Ready? We can start.
OM: What do I have to do? 230
GUARD 1: Just listen. (*He consults his clipboard and begins to read
in a loud formal voice.*) Congratulations! InterPlanta Services is proud and honoured to welcome Mr Om Prakash
to its programme! (*To* OM.) Sir, you have received the
Starter Kit? (*Doesn't wait, sights the package* OM *brought with* 235
him, nods, ticks.) Yes. There it is. Sir: you are directed to
open the kit and make it operational after our departure.
Instructions are provided within. Any questions? (OM
shakes his head. GUARD 1 *nods and ticks.*) All right.

(*In the background,* GUARD 3 *has got two cartons set up. He wears
large plastic mitts over his existing skin-tight gloves and starts dumping all the items on the kitchen counter into the cartons. Meanwhile
two or three urchins have come into the room and are goggling at the
goings-on. Just beyond the door, a crowd of onlookers is standing out
of sight, doing likewise.*)

JAYA: (*To* GUARD 1.) Hi! What're you doing! (*Turns to* OM.) 240
See—see what's happening! (*Duck to* GUARD 3, *who goes
ahead.*) Who said you can touch my things? (*Tugs at his arm
but he pays her no heed.*) Hi! Stop that!
GUARD 1: (*To* OM, *who is distracted.*) Sir: we will set up the
Contact Module. It will start functioning in approxi- 245
mately two hours.
OM: I—I'm sorry, but I must—

GUARD 1: Sir: pay no attention! About the Contact Module, all details will be found in the Starter Kit.

(*Meanwhile, downstage,* JAYA *struggles with* GUARD 3.)

250 JAYA: Who told you to do that! No! (*She attempts hitting* GUARD 3, *but he continues relentlessly dumping everything into the cartons.*) You can't do this! It's my house! No! Oh! Stop it, you monster, you beast! (*She tries to return items to the counter, but he is much faster than her.*) Stop it, stop it, stop it!
255 Don't you understand what I'm saying? Are you a machine? Answer me! Oh! (*She abruptly turns in on herself and succumbs to a fit of stormy weeping.*)

(GUARD 3 *continues with his job unperturbed in the course of the other events at stage front. After removing everything but the counter top and shelf, he cleans and swabs the entire area, then sprays it with attention to corners. After that he reaches into his kit and brings out a cooking device and bottles full of multi-coloured pellets.*)

(GUARD 2 *continues her installation without interruption.*)

GUARD 1: (*Regardless of the commotion behind him.*) At the time of first contact, you and your Receiver will exchange per-
260 sonal information. Your physical data has been sent for matching and we are confident that you will both be well satisfied. Any questions?
OM: Uhh uhh but what about . . . I mean, when will I actually have to—
265 GUARD 1: Sir: Any questions to the information received so far?
OM: (*Uncertainly.*) No . . . I mean—
GUARD 1: (*Nods and ticks.*) Right. When we have confirmed that the Contact Unit is functioning, you will not be re-
270 sponsible for anything but the maintainance of your personal resources. Any questions?
OM: But what about
GUARD 1: Sir! Any questions?
OM: (*Subdued.*) No.
275 GUARD 1: (*Nods and ticks.*) Right. All implements of personal fuel preparation will be supplied exclusively by Inter-Planta Services. Henceforward, you and your domestic unit will consume only those fuels which will be made available to you by InterPlanta. We will provide more
280 than enough for the unit described in your data sheet, but will forbid you from sharing, selling or by any means whatsoever, commercially exploiting this facility. Any questions?
OM: No.
285 GUARD 1: (*Nods and ticks.*) We are providing a remote-source electrical connection. It will be adequate for the systems currently being used by you and your domestic unit, as well as for the equipment which we ourselves will install. But on no account must it bear any additional loads, nor
290 must it be used by any agencies other than yourselves, loaned out, rented out, sold or put to any use other than the one just described. Any questions?
OM: No.
GUARD 1: (*Nods and ticks.*) Good. Now if I can just interview
295 the members of your domestic unit—
JAYA: (*From the rear.*) I have a question!

GUARD 1: (*Doesn't acknowledge her.*)—beginning with the oldest member—
JAYA: (*Desperately.*) Your—your man has thrown my stove into his bag and broken it! Who is going to replace that? 300
OM: (*Hissed aside.*) Not now, Jaya! Just be patient—

(GUARD 1 *is shuffling papers till he gets the relevant sheet.*)

JAYA: Be patient! While my house is broken up! (*But she turns herself aside and weeps, even as she shoos the bystanders away from the door. She is not able to do this easily or efficiently because she is crying too bitterly, so her actions have little impact.* 305
The urchins who are inside wriggle aside and continue to stand where they are.)
GUARD 1: (*Approaching* MA *and addressing her.*) Madam: Full name?
OM: (*Interceding.*) She doesn't understand your speech. Her 310 name's Indumati. Missiz Indumati Prakash.
GUARD 1: (*Continuing to address* MA *who looks genuinely bewildered.*) Missiz Indumati Prakash. (*Ticks.*) Relationship with Donor?
OM: Mother. 315
GUARD 1: (*Ticks.*) Have you understood all that has been said so far?
OM: Yes.
GUARD 1: (*His hand wavers. He looks up at* OM. *A flicker of normal communication.*) You will explain to her? 320
OM: (*Woodenly.*) Yes.
GUARD 1: (*Ticks.*) Right. Good. Now—(*He turns.*) next relative (*He sees her.*) Missiz—Missiz—(*He consults the sheet.*)

(JAYA, *who knows that it will now be her turn, shoves the children out roughly, anxiety lending determination to her movements. She slams the door shut against resistance from the other side and with some difficulty pushes the bolt home.*)

GUARD 1: —Kumar. Missiz Kumar come this way, please—
JAYA: (*Moves across to centre-stage.*) Yes—yes. 325
GUARD 1: (*Consulting his clip-board.*) Full name?
JAYA: Jaya. Mrs Jaya Kumar. (*She begins to weep anew.*)

(MA *stirs at this and looks over to where* JAYA *stands, a frown on her face.* OM *holds his head in his hands, his eyes on the floor.*)

GUARD 1: Relationship with Donor?
JAYA: (*Lifts her head. In a barely audible voice.*) Sister.

(MA *registers a shock. Her hand to her mouth, she seems to hold in her words manually. Then her hand goes to her heart.*)

GUARD 1: (*Neutral.*) Madam: please repeat response. 330
JAYA: Sister. He's my sister—I —I mean, I'm his—(*She is about to say, "brother" but succumbs to a fit of silent sobbing. Regains control.*) Sister. I'm . . . his . . . sister.

(MA's *face and limbs perform a dumb charade of her feelings, as she fights against the urge to react because she's not supposed to understand the exchange, yet she cannot make sense of what's going on.*)

GUARD 1: (*Ticks.*) Right. (*Looks around cursorily, merely to confirm what he already knows.*) Husband? 335
JAYA: (*Nods.*) At work.
GUARD 1: (*Ticks.*) Full name?

JAYA: Jeetu—Jeeten. Jeeten Kumar.

(MA's *body jerks like a puppet. She reins in her comments with ferocious effort.*)

GUARD 1: (*Ticks, nods.*) Right. (*He looks up and around.*) In-
340 terPlanta recommends that those members absent at this briefing make themselves available at the nearest collection centre not later than twenty-four hours from the time of our departure, failing which such member will
345 lose all rights to the facilities provided by us. Any questions? (*He does not wait for confirmation before ticking off, then looks up.*) Good. (*Turns to the other two* GUARDS.) Briefing complete, initiate departure procedure.

(*Behind him,* GUARD 2 *and* GUARD 3 *have both completed their tasks and are standing stiffly "at ease" at their stations, awaiting orders. Whatever is visible of their faces is completely blank.*)

(*Hanging from the ceiling is a white, faceted globe, at least three feet in diameter. It looks like a Japanese lantern, unlit.*)

(*In the course of the following action,* JAYA *wanders towards the window,* OM *remains seated on the bed,* MA's *physical movements subside.*)

GUARD 1: (*Moving towards them, checking off his list as he inspects and is responded to.*) Officer Contact Module Installation,
350 activity report: Installation complete?
GUARD 2: Yessir.
GUARD 1: Remote Power Reception cable in place?
GUARD 2: Yessir.
GUARD 1: Cable check complete?
355 GUARD 2: Yessir.
GUARD 1: Contact Module in operational mode?
GUARD 2: Yessir.
GUARD 1: Good. Initialize for contact.

(GUARD 2 *moves swiftly over to the* CONTACT MODULE *which is roughly at centre stage and points a remote at it. As* GUARD 2 *works, there are musical notes and clicks. The polygon stirs alight. Random facets light up. A screen-saver pattern appears. The entire polygon moves in a slow, smooth circle, then is lowered to ground level and up again.* GUARD 1 *steps back, satisfied.*)

GUARD 1: (*Paying no further attention to* GUARD 2's *activities, ad-*
360 *dresses* GUARD 3, *who is ready with two neat cartons prepared for transport.*) Officer Fuel Supplies and Installation: activity report: sanitization of supply area complete?
GUARD 3: Yessir.
GUARD 1: Installation of fuel preparation equipment com-
365 plete?
GUARD 3: Yessir.
GUARD 1: Delivery of one month's fuel supplies for family of four complete?
GUARD 3: Yessir.
370 GUARD 1: Good. Proceed with departure.

(GUARD 2 *and* GUARD 3 *station themselves by the door.*)

GUARD 1: (*Approaching* OM, *holding out his clipboard for signing with a pen offered in the same motion.*) Mr Om Prakash, I am pleased to inform you that the installation and initializa-
tion procedures have been completed satisfactorily. Thank you for your cooperation. Please sign the following activ- 375
ity report after confirming that the observations contained herein are true and accurate to the best of your knowledge. (*Hands him the clipboard.*)
OM: (*He stands up as* GUARD 1 *approaches him: Takes the clipboard, glances at it cursorily.*) Yes. I agree. (*Signs, hands the* 380
board back.)
JAYA: (*Over her shoulder.*) You don't need any confirmation from us?
GUARD 1: All further queries will be satisfied by the Starter Kit. (*He tucks the clipboard under his arm.*) Thank you for 385
your cooperation and valuable time! I and my colleagues deeply appreciate the contribution you are about to make towards creating a healthier, happier and longer-lived world!

(*Clicks his heels together and turns smartly towards the others.* GUARD 3 *immediately opens the latch on the door which is buffeted open by the listeners on the other side, who immediately fall back and away at the sight of* GUARD 3. GUARD 1 *exits and the other two follow suit. The door is left open and the original one or two urchins poke their noses inside, darting quick glances around.* JAYA *sees them and moves across to shoo them away again. They dart out again with no further urging from her. She shuts the door once more.*)

MA: (*To no-one in particular*) What sort of job makes a wife into 390
a sister?
OM: (*Subsides onto the bed again, head in his hands.*) Don't get confused, Ma. What they write in their reports doesn't change our lives.
MA: But what *is* she, really? A wife? Or a sister? 395
JAYA: (*Has come back and is standing at centre stage.*) How shall I cook now? They've taken all our things! Every last grain!
MA: Who is Jeetu, now? Is he a son? Or a son-in-law?
OM: Nothing's changed! The words are different, that's all.
MA: But these aren't words! They're people! 400
JAYA: Are you listening to me, (*Mocking.*) brother? (OM *looks up.*) What are we to do for food?
MA: (*Whispers.*) How can my daughter be married to my son? What will people think?
JAYA: (*Louder.*) Tell me, brother!— 405
OM: (*Stirring.*) It's in this package. Whatever we need to know.
JAYA: (*Hard.*) Even about food?
OM: (*Wearily.*) Even food.

(*Lights snap out.*)

SCENE II

The same room. OM *and* MA *are sitting upstage centre. A mat is spread on the floor and they are eating the coloured pellets of their new food.* JAYA *is leaning her head and shoulders against the side of the bed.*

The package is open. Its contents are strewn about. There are brightly coloured instruction leaflets, elaborately devised containers for pills and powders and a number of small gadgets similar in size and shape to a slide-viewing device but of obscure purpose.

MA: Tell me again: all you have to do is sit at home and stay healthy?

OM: Well—not *sit* necessarily—

MA: And they'll pay you?

5 OM: Yes.

MA: Even if you do nothing but pick your nose all day?

OM: They'll pay me.

MA: And what about off-days?

OM: (*Shrugs.*) Well. *Every* day is off, in one sense—

10 JAYA: (*Suddenly.*) Why don't you tell her the truth?

MA: Isn't this the truth?

OM: Jaya—

JAYA: (*Swinging herself around, to face them.*) Tell her. Tell your mother what you've really done—

15 MA: Shoo! Don't speak to your husband in that voice—

OM: The walls are thin. Everyone can hear. When you talk like this—

JAYA: Everyone knows already! D'you think you're the only one with this—this *job*? D'you think everyone doesn't

20 know what it means . . . when the grey guards come? (*Tears in her voice.*) All that remains to be known is which part of you's been given away!

MA: (*Mystified.*) What's this, what's this? Who's giving away parts of whom?

25 JAYA: Which goes first, the brain or the heart, that's what I want to know—

MA: (*To* OM.) I'm sorry to say, your wife has gone mad. Your sister, I mean—

OM: She's just trying to make trouble—

30 JAYA: (*Bitter laugh.*) Huh!

MA: Who cares about her? Wife or sister, Mother comes first! So tell me—these people, your employers, who exactly are they?

OM: It's—it's well, actually it's just one person.

35 MA: Just one person! With so much money to give away!

JAYA: It's a foreigner. That's why it's so much—

MA: What?

OM: (*Sighs.*) The money comes from abroad—

MA: Really! (*A sudden doubt.*) But . . . doesn't that mean you'll

40 have to go there? Abroad?

OM: Ma—no-one goes abroad these days . . .

JAYA: Not whole people, anyway!

OM: (*Warningly.*) I'm warning you now, Jaya—

MA: What's that? What's that? Knot-hole people? What d'you

45 mean—shorties?

JAYA: (*Patiently.*) Not his whole body. Just parts of it—

MA: (*To* OM.) What's your wife saying—not your body, but your what?

(JAYA *curls herself more tightly into herself.*)

OM: (*To* JAYA's *back.*) Why're you doing this? Why're you mak-

50 ing trouble?

JAYA: (*Over her shoulder.*) You said it wouldn't affect us—but see what it's done already!

OM: So *tell* me—what? In exchange for your old kitchen you have a new modern one—

55 JAYA: (*Swivelling round.*) You call this food? This—(*She indicates the pellets they have been eating.*) this—this goat-shit?

MA: It's better than what you make—

JAYA: And calling you my sister—what's that? (*Sobs.*) If I'm your sister, what does that make you? (*Hysterical edge.*) Sis-

ter, huh! My forehead burns, when I say that word, "sis- 60 ter"! (*She smears the red kumkum on her forehead in her tor- ment and succumbs to her tears.*)

MA: Shoo! Are you a street woman? To speak in such a voice?

OM: You think I did it lightly. You think it's a heavy price. 65 But at the cost of calling you my sister . . . we'll be *rich!* Very rich! Insanely rich! What're you saying? (*He gets up to wash his hands and mouth at the kitchen sink, stopping to make his point along the way.*) But you'd rather live in this one small room, I suppose! Think it's such 70 a fine thing (*Washes his mouth, spits.*) living day in, day out, like monkeys in a hot-case—(*Washes mouth again and spits again, wipes face, mouth.*) lulled to sleep by our neighbours' rhythmic farting! Dancing to the tune of the melodious traffic! And starving. Yes—you'd prefer 75 this to being called my sister on a stupid slip of paper no-one we know will ever see!

MA: Why fight over what is finished? Tell me about this rich foreigner, your employer! Who is he? Why does he love you so much? That's what I don't understand—where did 80 he meet you?

JAYA: (*Half-sob/laugh.*) Ohh—just tell her, tell her!

OM: (*Coming back to centrestage.*) We've never met, Ma . . .

MA: What!

OM: He's rich—and old. That's all I know about him. Prob- 85 ably suffering from some illness—

MA: Then why's he paying you so much!

JAYA: Oh *Ma!*—don't you see it? Isn't it obvious?

MA: (*To* JAYA.) You're so smart that you can hear the Holy Fa- ther himself thinking but I, I need to hear with my ears— 90 (*Turns to* OM.) Tell me, my son—

OM: (*Irritated.*) Oh, you won't understand, Ma—

JAYA: I'll tell you! He's sold the rights to his organs! His skin. His eyes. His arse. (*Sobs again.*) Sold them! (*Holds her head.*) Oh God, oh God! What's the meaning of this nightmare! 95 (*Sobs. To* OM.) How can I hold your hand, touch your face, knowing that at any moment it might be snatched away from me and flung across the globe! (*Sobs.*) If you were dead I could shave my head and break my bangles— but this? To be a widow by slow degrees? To mourn you 100 piece by piece? (*Sobs.*) Should I shave half my head? Break my bangles one at a time? (*Succumbs to her tears.*)

MA: (*Only half-comprehending. Turns to* OM *who stands with his back to the women.*) How is it possible?

OM: (*Looking up at* JAYA.) If you weren't so busy feeling sorry 105 for yourself, you'd have read what they say about respect- ing the donor—

JAYA: (*Bitterly.*) Of course! They bathe him in praise while gutting him like a chicken!

MA: But why must they come to us? 110

OM: (*Holds up a pamphlet.*) Look? In this paper it says that one third of all donors are left absolutely intact!

MA: Don't they have enough of their own people?

JAYA: And where does that leave you? Two thirds a man? Half a wit? 115

OM: (*To* MA, *distractedly.*) They don't have people to spare.

JAYA: And we do, of course. Spare lives! We grow on trees, in the bushes! *What are we, teacher? Oh just some spare lives!*

120   MA: (*Uncertainly.*) Well. So long as they don't hurt you . . .

(*At this moment, a loud tone sounds. All three react, looking immediately at the globe.*)

MA: Hai! What's that sound! I must wash my hands! (*She gets up.*)

(*The polygon flickers to life. Each face displays one view of a young woman's face, unmistakeably blonde and white-skinned. She is beautiful in a clear-eyed, unequivocal manner, exuding a youthful innocence and radiant purity.*)

MA: (*She sees the globe head-on.*) Ahhh! Who is this angel?

(*The room fills abruptly with the pip! of an international phone call about to commence. There is a crackling sound and an audible pause.*)

GINNI: . . . hello? Hello?

125   OM: (*Stepping forward self-consciously.*) Yes—!

GINNI: I see you!—oh, my Gad! I see you! Is that really you? Auwm? Praycash?

OM: Yes! Yes—it's me, Om! (*He's grinning wide.* MA *looks bewildered.* JAYA *looks awe-struck.*)

130   GINNI: Well—hi! That's really great! This is Virginia—Ginni—speaking! Can you see me? How's your reception?

OM: Quite good—quite perfect, I should say! Fantastic!

GINNI: Wow! Yeah . . . well it's pretty wonderful for me too, you know! I mean, I can't tell you . . . (*Her voice grows*

135   *breathy with emotion.*) I can't *tell* you how much this means to me—

MA: (*To* JAYA.) What's it saying? I can't understand when they speak so fast—

OM: No, no, Madam! It's our pleasure! Our duty, I mean!

140   Anything we can do to help—

JAYA: (*To* MA.) She's saying that she's happy—

GINNI: It's the most beautiful day of my life! I feel I've got hope, at last! And all because of you—

OM: No, no, Madam, it is my—our—pleasure.

145   GINNI: Is it—I mean, can you see me clearly, Auwm?

OM: Perfectly clear.

GINNI: Okay—okay—now you've got to tell me—I'm just switching screens here—okay—there we are—okay! I can see . . . is that your . . . your mother? In the pink— (JAYA

150   *flinches; she is wearing a pink sari.*) whatdyacallit—sarong?

OM: We call it—*sari*—

GINNI: (*Sings an old tune.*) "Who's sari now? Who's sari now?!!" (*Laughs to herself.*) Hehheh—It's magical, it's wonderful! I'm really talking to India—this is really happen-

155   ing! Okay! And your sister—let's see—

JAYA: (*Stirring to life.*) No! *I*'m his sister!

OM: (*Flustered and confused.*) She's my wife—

GINNI: Excuse me?

JAYA: (*Hissing to* OM.) Sister. I'm your sister.

160   GINNI: You said just now—

OM: (*Still smiling woodenly.*) I mean, she is my sister, you see—

GINNI: Auwm—it says here on your form, you're not married.

OM: I'm not. She's my sister.

165   GINNI: You're sure you're not kidding me or anything?

OM: Sure, sure, of course I'm sure!

GINNI: Because it's important for us to trust one another. I mean, one little slip like that one—and I dunno. I mean, it's hard for me to tell, from so far away—

OM: No, no! I'm telling the truth! I swear on my God!   170

ginni: Okay. I mean, 'coz I've gotta know, you know. If you're married—

JAYA: (*Suddenly.*) Why?

GINNI: What's that?

JAYA: Why does it matter?   175

GINNI: Uhh—I'll get back to you on that, okay? Just now . . . lemme see . . . there's two more people in your household, am I right, Auwm? There's (*As if checking a list.*) . . . your mother and your brother-in-law, S'right?

JAYA: That is right.   180

GINNI: Just a moment—uhh—Zhaya? (*The* CONTACT MODULE *swivels towards* JAYA, *who nods.*) Is that your name? Yeah—okay, now honey: I can't handle two people at a time, okay? I mean, it's just this dumb camera, you know, can't look at two people at a time, okay? So—I'm talking   185
to Auwm, well I can't talk to you as well, okay? I mean, no offence—

JAYA: Okay.

OM: My mother is also here—

GINNI: Yes. Okay. I'm turning the scanner around (*The* CON-   190
TACT MODULE *turns.*) . . . I'm panning across the room . . . Jeeezus! It's not very much, is it? I mean—oh! Okay! I see her. Hi! Mrs Praycash? Hi! This is Ginni! Can you hear me?

MA: (*Shielding her eyes against the light.*) What?   195

GINNI: I said, this is Virginia! I'm—uh, well just look up, if you can—

OM: Ma—just take your hand down—

GINNI: Look towards the Contact Module! You know the thing hanging in the room?   200

MA: (*To* JAYA.) What's happening?

JAYA: Ma—just look at that light—

OM: The light! The light!

MA: (*Getting annoyed, straightens up to snap back at* OM.) Stop shouting!   205

GINNI: Ahhright! I see you! Mrs Praycash, glad to meet you!

MA: I can't understand a word of what that thing is saying! Is it a man or a woman?

GINNI: What do I look like to you, Mrs Praycash?

MA: (*Cupping her ear.*) Ehh?   210

JAYA: Ma—she wants to know, what she looks like—

OM: Come on, Ma! You've seen foreigners before—

GINNI: Please—Auwm—your mother can answer my questions herself—

OM: She can't understand, you see—   215

JAYA: (*To* MA.) Ma—look up at that light and say what you see—

MA: (*Looks up.*) I see an angel.

GINNI: (*Laughing.*) Ha! I look good to you?

MA: Good, bad, I don't know. All I know is I've got to take a   220
leak—(*Turns around.*)

GINNI: (*Embarrassed laugh.*) Heh! Mm. But—wait! I'm not through yet!

OM: (*As* MA *continues moving away, slowly.*) Don't go yet, Ma—she's not finished—   225

MA: Since when did I need anyone's permission to take a leak?

GINNI: I'm sorry, Mrs Praycash, this won't take a minute—
MA: Nothing doing. I'll piss myself if I don't go right away—
230   (*She moves to the door.*)
GINNI: Hey! I didn't let you go!
OM: She has some problem, you see—
MA: Wait till you're my age! (*Grunts with the effort of opening the door.*) Why they can't keep a bathroom on each floor I
235   don't know—

(*Exit* MA.)

OM: (*Apologetically.*) The toilet is two floors down, you see—
GINNI: Hmmm. Your mother's some character, Auwm. (*She doesn't sound pleased.*) I don't know if I can handle it. I mean—walking out on me like that!
240 OM: She takes a long time to get there. Old people, you know!
GINNI: Wait a minute—did you say two floors down? What about in your house? There's no toilet in your house?
JAYA: (*Bitter laugh.*) Huh!
245 OM: No-one has a toilet in the house. Forty families share one. And my mother walks so slowly—
GINNI: Forty families! (*Hushed voice.*) My Gad. Well that's— that's—(*She seems at a loss for words.*) I'm sorry, Auwm. But that's shocking. Shocking! I can't accept that!
250 OM: (*Embarrassed laugh.*) Well—I—
GINNI: No! It's wrong! It's disgusting! And I—well, I'm going to change that. I can't accept that. I mean, it's unsanitary!
OM: (*Muttering.*) Of course, of course!
GINNI: We'll just have to install one in your house.
255 JAYA: (*Startled out of her silence.*) What? In this—this room?
GINNI: Is that you again, Zhaya?
OM: (*To* JAYA.) Shh!
JAYA: I'm sorry—but we *can't!* There's no place for a toilet!
GINNI: Excuse me, but you'll have to find the space. It's inex-
260   cusable not to have your own toilet! Forty families—! It's a wonder you're all not dead of the plague years ago!
JAYA: There's only this one room!
GINNI: Look—there's enough place for a married couple and two others—you! You're married, right, Zhaya?
265 JAYA: (*Helplessly.*) Yes, but—
GINNI: (*Firmly.*) Then there's place for a toilet. I'm sorry, Zhaya, but there's no way around this one. What d'you do for baths?
JAYA: (*Close to tears.*) I—we—
270 GINNI: You—you *do* bathe, don't you? I mean, at least once a day?
JAYA: (*Overcome by the humiliation, bends her head and sobs.*)
GINNI: (*Instantly contrite.*) Hey—wait! No, please! Don't cry! I didn't mean to upset you—oh Jeez—stop, please! Look—
275   it's not your fault, okay?
OM: It's all right, she'll be all right—(*Goes over to* JAYA *and thumps her on the back!* She's fine!
GINNI: Okay—okay—look, Zhaya—I'll make it up to you, okay? I'll send you something, okay? Just tell me what you
280   like and it's yours, okay? Jewellery, perfume, you name it— flowers?
OM: (*Bending down to speak to* JAYA.) Come on, now, come on! It'll be all right—that's enough now—
GINNI: Okay—I tell you what, I'll send you some chocolate,
285   okay? I love candy myself. Okay? I'll send you my

favourite candy and—tell you what? I'll sign off now. Okay? It's been a big day for all of us, we're all tired, aren't we? Auwm? Could you look here for a moment?
OM: (*Standing up.*) Me?
GINNI: Okay—look, I'll get back to you, okay? And I'm sorry 290 about Zhaya. Really.
OM: No, no—she's not used to this—this—
GINNI: Yeah. Well—the first contact is always a little . . . ah, intense, you know? And I meant that about . . . the toilet, okay? It'll be with you in about an hour. 295
OM: An hour—!
GINNI: Oops! Time's up—Byeeee!

(*The tone sounds again. The light fades from the* CONTACT MOD- ULE. OM *sits down, suddenly, next to* JAYA *who is wiping her eyes.*)

OM: (*Shakily.*) My god! That was something! (*Puts his arm around* JAYA.) Imagine—a woman!
JAYA: Not old, not sick, nothing— 300
OM: Oh, she must be sick—or else why spend all this money?
JAYA: (*Tiredly.*) It's too late to ask questions now!
OM: But what can be her problem?
JAYA: Maybe there's no problem. Maybe she just likes to suck the life out of young men, like a vampire! 305
OM: Sometimes you talk rubbish—
JAYA: At least I only talk.
OM: It feels strange. To think that . . . that some part of me will be—might be, some day—inside *her*—(*Stops abruptly.*) I mean— 310
JAYA: (*Numbly.*) I know what you mean.
OM: (*Holds her a little tighter.*) I did it, all of it, for us—
JAYA: (*Moving delicately, to loosen his hold.*) Careful. I'm your sister, remember?
OM: (*Jerks his arm away.*) Oh! Sorry. 315
JAYA: (*Bitterly.*) Me too.

(*Lights fade out.*)

SCENE III

Moonlit night, on the roof of the tenement building. City skyline in the backdrop. Clotheslines, watertanks, TV antennas and water pipes snaking in all directions. There is a sense of shadowy figures, move- ments in the background, murmured conversations.

JAYA *appears, holding a small torch to her face.*

JAYA: (*Looking afraid but determined.*) Jeetu? Are you there? Jeetu—it's me, Jaya!

(*Quick steps, two shadows move away, one shadow materializes in front of* JAYA.)

JEETU: (*He does not look pleased to see her.*) Who told you to come? This is not the right time—
JAYA: I had to. Jeetu—you don't know what's happened— 5
JEETU: Huh! I know everything—
JAYA: So—so you've heard?
JEETU: Which part? That my brother's sold himself to the for- eigners? Or that you're my wife? (*Shrugs.*) The second one is hardly . . . news! (*Looks back at her.*) Is it? (*Reaches to tweak* 10 *her plait.*) Is it?

JAYA: But you must come—they're asking for you!

JEETU: (*Frowning.*) They? Who—

JAYA: The grey guards. They came again in the evening. To
15 install the toilet—

JEETU: In the room?!

JAYA: And a bath-shower as well, imagine! We have our own
water supply now, as much as we want—and there's no
place to sneeze any more!

20 JEETU: (*Sardonically.*) Or . . . anything else, no doubt?

JAYA: (*Lowered tone.*) That . . . there never was.

JEETU: (*Leering.*) Didn't bother us, though, did it? (*He caresses
her chin—but she whips her face away.*)

JAYA: And now there won't be any reason for Ma to go
25 downstairs! We'll never be alone in the room again, never!

JEETU: So what? If we can shit in public, we can just as well
screw in public too—especially since you're now officially
my wife!

JAYA: (*Pained*) Don't joke about it—

30 JEETU: Why not? I joke about everything else—

JAYA: My throat bulges with the lies trapped within it!

JEETU: Here—let me kiss it—

JAYA: (*Pushes him away.*) Get away! That's all finished now!

JEETU: (*He lets her go.*) As you wish.

35 JAYA: (*Gasps in indignation.*) So easy! Won't you protest a little at least?

JEETU: Make up your mind! D'you want me or not?

JAYA: You are all I have, now that my husband has become my
brother . . .

40 JEETU: According to you he was never much else!

JAYA: (*Troubled.*) Still. He would come to me now and then—

JEETU: (*Shrugs.*) Maybe incest is more his style!

JAYA: No! He's too afraid! Before it was his mother. Now it's
this . . . job.

45 JEETU: Ahh—forget him! You waste your time thinking of my
brother!

JAYA: But what about me!

JEETU: Why? Now that you have a new . . . (*Mockingly.*) husband! (*Reaches for her shoulder.*)

50 JAYA: (*Slipping out of reach.*) Oh you—! You're a free-lancer—

JEETU: (*Laughing.*) No! My lance costs money! (*Squats down on
a low ledge and starts to roll himself a joint.*) Had you forgotten?

JAYA: And anyway—I'm looking for a plough, not a lance—

JEETU: Oops—sorry! Wrong number! I can't afford any . . .
55 crops!

JAYA: As if I don't know that! I know that. And in any case
. . . I feel guilty. I feel soiled—

JEETU: My, my! Such delicacy! Don't worry—I'll tell the
world that I forced my attentions on you—routinely, in
60 phase with my mother's bowel movements!

JAYA: Oh stop—! (*Swats at him, playfully.*) You always make
such a joke of everything!

JEETU: That's all that life is, one long joke. The only trick is
in learning when to laugh.

65 JAYA: Easy for you to laugh! What do you care of my needs,
my desires?

JEETU: I thought I was the *only* one who cared about your
desires! (*Lights his joint.*)

JAYA: You—you care—but not enough! A woman wants
70 more than just . . . (*Breaks off.*) satisfaction.

JEETU: Ah—get off my case! You women are gluttons for satisfaction—that's the bare fact of it! You cry when you
don't get it—and when you do, you cry that it's not often
enough!

JAYA: I cry because—because you awaken one hunger while 75
satisfying the other!

JEETU: (*Darkly.*) That other hunger is insatiable. A man has to
protect himself against that hunger or he will find himself
sucked dry by new little mouths, screaming "Papa!
Papa!"—little mouths with big, big appetites—oh no! I'm 80
afraid of that other hunger! Mortally afraid!

JAYA: (*Acidly.*) I suppose that's why so many of your "clients"
are men!

JEETU: (*Coolly.*) Not really. It's just that there are more men
with money to spare on services such as mine— 85

JAYA: You should be ashamed of yourself! A man—behaving
like a vagrant bull!

JEETU: Why? I'm not fussy—cows, pigs, horses, I'll service
all—for a price.

JAYA: You don't need to sell yourself anymore. There'll be 90
enough money in the house now!

JEETU: But not for me—

JAYA: Yes—for all of us. For the whole building—

JEETU: No. I don't mind being bought—but I won't be *owned*!

(*There is a space of silence.*)

JAYA: (*Fidgeting.*) Well—I suppose I should go— 95

JEETU: Yes—yes—run home before the grey guards come to
fetch you!

JAYA: Jeetu—

JEETU: (*Looking lazily up at her.*) . . . unless you had something
else in mind. 100

JAYA: No . . . no . . . (*She can't face him.*) I mean . . . I—didn't
bring any food.

JEETU: (*A faintly twisted smile.*) Ah . . . so we're asking for
credit, are we?

JAYA: (*Her voice is husky.*) There's no food in the house any 105
more! Only those goat-shit pills and some strange powders. (*Tears in her voice.*) And—and—it's all measured out,
you see! I couldn't take a portion without having to explain—

JEETU: (*Looking steadily at her.*) Never mind. As a long-time 110
client, you are permitted certain liberties. Come here—
(*It's a short distance, barely afoot. He is seated on a step, leaning
back against a tank. She doesn't move.*) I said, come here—

JAYA: (*As if drawn by an irresistible force.*) Jeetu—there are other
people around! 115

JEETU: Turn the other way. (*She turns her back to him.*) Your left
foot up on this step—(*He pats the narrow ledge on which he
sits. She rests the heel of her left foot there. He puts his arm up
her sari unobtrusively, barely shifting his position, looking steadily
up at her. She looks straight ahead.*) Now tell me about this 120
food. I'm told that it's quite tasty?

JAYA: (*Her voice is thick and strangled.*) Yes! It looks like plastic
beads but . . . it's *quite tasty*!

JEETU: And filling too, they say—

JAYA: (*Gasping slightly.*) Filling, yes. It . . . is. But it's not . . . 125
natural—it's not real food—(*She has no place to keep her
hands and arms. She clutches her neck, her face, knotting the loose
end of her sari around her mouth.*)

JEETU: (*Mildly.*) But it must be, don't you think? And healthy?
I mean, isn't that the point? To keep us . . . healthy? 130

JAYA: Yes . . . yes, of course. . . . but (*She's finding it difficult to concentrate on what she says.*) . . . but . . . who knows if it's . . . *good* for us! . . . (*Gasps.*)

JEETU: Everything's good that tastes good and feels right—

135 JAYA: (*She's desperate to lean on something but the closest is a ventilation pipe. She clings to it with both hands, eyes shut tight, breathing in gasps.*) No . . . no . . . that's *not* true. . . . it's *false* food—uhh!—like it's a *false* marriage—Uhh!—*false—false* (*Her voice wobbles and ends on a squeak. She gasps/sobs once,* 140 *twice—.*) False. (*Breathes out, shudderingly.*) False . . . life. (*She catches her breath, wiping her face with the end of her sari-pallav.*) It's not really a life any more. We're just spare parts in someone else's garage—

JEETU: (*Removing his arm and wiping his fingers on the hem of her* 145 *sari.*) My brother, yes. But not you—

JAYA: (*Her voice is normal again.*) No! All of us. If we get sick, he might get sick too. So we all have to eat this excuse for food and live like virgin brides—

JEETU: (*Snorts.*) Good! Now there's no reason at all for me to 150 come home!

JAYA: (*Distraught.*) No! You have to, Jeetu—

JEETU: Are you mad? When they find out what I do for a living they won't be pleased! They won't be pleased with you either—

155 JAYA: (*Pleading.*) They've asked for you twice now—they'll cancel your permit if they can't confirm your presence—

JEETU: Too bad! My brother will have to find some dummy to take my place—

JAYA: Please, Jeetu! Please . . . think of me—

160 JEETU: I can't afford to think of you. Thinking of you causes too many problems for me. I'll have to go away—

JAYA: What'll I do! You can't leave me—

JEETU: I can if I must. Don't worry—your grey guards will probably have a cure for the disease of dissatisfaction as 165 well—just ask them?

JAYA: But why! Why when there's enough money for all of us, to do whatever we want!

JEETU: Because no employer pays his staff to do as they please. At least when I sell my body, I decide which part 170 of me goes into where and whom! But it's the money in the end, isn't it? I don't want to get used to the kind of money that can make stud bulls into milk cows. (*Shakes his head.*) My poor brother. Thought he was so pure. But he's like everyone else after all! Only as pure as the price of his 175 rice.

(*Lights dim out.*)

ACT TWO

SCENE I

Two months later. The same room, but transformed into a sleek residence, gleaming surfaces, chrome steel and glass. The furniture is largely of the convertible kind (Bed-cum-sofa, etc), in keeping with the restricted space. In addition, there are the gadgets—TV set, computer terminal, mini-gym, an air-conditioner, the works. To the rear and right, there are two cubicles containing the bathroom and toilet. The changes are functional rather than cosmetic. In the middle of the space is a low, Japanese-style dining table.

JAYA *is sitting on the sofa and and doing her nails. She looks over-dressed, her face is heavily made-up, jewellery winking from her ears, wrists, ankles and throat.* MA *is wearing a quilted dressing gown and is watching TV, upstage, right.* OM *is wearing a fluorescent Harlequin track-suit and sits at the computer terminal. All sport new footwear.* JAYA *in heels,* MA *in fluffy bedroom slippers,* OM *in inflatable track shoes with blinking rear lights.*

Suddenly OM *leaps up.*

OM: Look at the time!—Ma!

MA: (*Not turning around, but addressing her remark to* JAYA.) Don't call me—it's your wife's turn to do the food.

JAYA: (*Waving her hands in the air.*) Why didn't you tell me earlier? Now my nails are wet—   5

MA: And now—I'm watching my programme!

OM: (*Rushing over to dining area. He starts to set it up.*) Come on, come on! Ginni will be with us—

MA: Better get Bidyut-bai out first—

OM: (*Stops what he's doing.*) Out? Out of where?   10

MA: (*Barely looking up.*) Out of the toilet. Didn't you see her going in? She's been there all morning!

OM: Why! Who let her use it—

MA: She can't stay away from it, she says! Gets cramps, poor thing, from waiting for the one downstairs—   15

OM: Who cares about her cramps—I want to know how she got into the habit of using our toilet at all!

MA: (*Shrugs, but aiming her rebuke in* JAYA'S *direction.*) Who knows what happens when my back is turned?

JAYA: (*Aggrieved, blowing on her nails.*) Huh! Look who's talk-   20 ing! The Empress of the Bath-house herself? (*To* OM.) If your mother had her way, half this building would be bathing up here—(*Blowing on her nails.*) But how would you know? You never bother to talk to us any more!

MA: (*Placatory whine.*) We have so much! Can't we share a lit-   25 tle at least? As it is, my former friends tell me I've put on airs—

OM: (*Standing with his hands on his hips.*) Ma, I've told you. When we have our own place, that'll be another thing—but now, when we're still struggling—   30

(*At this moment there is the sound of the flush.* BIDYUT-BAI *comes out of the cubicle, trying to look inconspicuous.*)

BIDYUT-BAI: Oh . . . I hope I'm not intruding—

OM: I'm sorry, Bidyut-maasi—but who invited you to use our toilet?

BIDYUT-BAI: (*Instantly on the defensive.*) No, no! Please! I was just passing this way—   35

OM: But you used our toilet, didn't you?

BIDYUT-BAI: Toilet? What toilet? Is there a toilet in this room? My! That must be a wonder! May I see it?

OM: (*Sighing.*) Oh just go on, go on!

MA: (*Speaking up for her friend.*) How can she go on when the   40 door's been barricaded?

OM: (*Woodenly.*) She's your friend, you can let her out yourself.

MA: (*Peevishly.*) But I'm watching my programme—

JAYA: Your eyes'll be stuck to that screen from staring at it   45 twenty-four hours of the day!

MA: And why can't our busybody open it? Worn out from the tension of painting her nails, I suppose?

BIDYUT-BAI: Is anyone going to let me out?
50 JAYA: Oh! For god's sake! (*Gets up and flings herself across the room.*) I might as well apply for a job as a doorkeeper!
MA: And you'd make a bad one—

(*The warning tone sounds.*)

OM: Oh my God—Ginni's call-sound!
JAYA: (*Struggling to open the door with her nails still wet.*) Tell her
55 it's because your mother can't control her generosity—
MA: See how your sister insults me! Her own mother!
OM: (*Frantic.*) Hurry up! Hurry up!
JAYA: (*Throws the door open—*BIDYUT-BAI *wriggles past her and out.*) All right, all right—(*Slams the door shut and moves*
60 *quickly over to the "kitchen" to snatch up a few items from the "oven". *OM *is almost done setting the table up.*) Anyway it only takes a few minutes—
OM: (*Sitting down, as* JAYA *brings a few things from the "kitchen" area.*) You know how she hates it when we're late to eat!
65 JAYA: (*Setting things down.*) Tell your mother to come along—
MA: (*Whiningly.*) It's just about to end—
JAYA: (*Sitting down herself.*) One of these days, when this dream comes to an end, it'll be because you were too busy watching your damned TV—
70 OM: It isn't going to end—

(*The warning tone sounds a third time and the* CONTACT MOD-ULE *springs to life.*)

OM: Ahh—

(MA *scrambles to her feet and scurries over, leaving the TV on.*)

GINNI: Hello-oo! Guess who-oo!
OM: (*He has a falsely beaming expression on his face and affects a nasal twang.*) Hello, Ginni! Hi! Howdy!

(MA *settles hurriedly into place.*)

75 GINNI: Hey—whatcha doing—eating again?
OM: No! We're just having lunch—why don't you join us?
GINNI: Lunch! Hey, that's too late—for lunch!
JAYA: No, no, Ginni! (*To* OM.) Tell her it is only ten minutes—
GINNI: I'm sorry Auwm—but I insist: you *must eat at regular*
80 *hours*—okay? We've had this problem before!
OM: Yes—yes—you see we just had some visitor—heh-heh—these people, you know! Don't understand what it means to keep to a strict schedule—
GINNI: Ah-ah! No excuses, now! That's another bad habit you
85 have, Auwm. You don't confront your booboos. Now—you've gotta learn to control it, okay? You can't help it, I know, it's a part of your culture—it's what your people do when they want to Avoid Conflict and it's even got a name: it's called "face saving". But we can't go through the
90 whole of our lives Avoiding Conflict, now can we, Auwm? You do see that?
OM: (*His smile is strained.*) Yes—yes—of course, Ginni! It is perfectly clear—
GINNI: Good! That's what I like about you, Auwm! You learn
95 real fast.
OM: (*Modestly.*) Thank you, Ginni!

GINNI: And now—let's look at how your family's doing—Mrs Praycash? I can see the food's suiting you, huh? You're putting on weight!
100 MA: (*Holding her hand to her ear, but beaming nevertheless.*) What's that? What's that?
GINNI: And Zhaya—how're you doin'? I don't see a smile on your face!
JAYA: (*Instantly pasting a smile on.*) Oh—no, no! I'm fine!
105 GINNI: It's a scientific fact that people who smile longer live longer—
JAYA: I'm smiling!
GINNI: But not enough, Zhaya. You see, it's important to smile all through the day. After all, if you're not smiling, it
110 means you're not happy. And if you're not happy, you might affect your brother's mood—and then where would we be?
JAYA: (*Grinning wide.*) I understand, Ginni.
GINNI: If I've said it once, I've said it a hundred times: The
115 Most Important Thing is to keep *Auwm* smiling. Coz if Auwm's smiling, it means his body's smiling and if his body's smiling, it means his organs are smiling. And that's the kind of organs that'll survive a transplant best, smiling organs—I mean, God forbid that it should ever come to
120 that, right? But after all, we can't let ourselves forget what this programme is about! I mean, if I'm going to need a transplant—then by God, let's make it the best damn transplant that we can manage! Are you with me?
JAYA: Yes, Ginni, of course, Ginni.

(*From the door, there is now a knocking sound.* JAYA *looks around.*)

125 GINNI: (*Reacting at once, and the* CONTACT MODULE *swivels.*) What's that? What're you looking at?
OM: (*Nervously.*) Oh nothing—just—it's nothing!
GINNI: Now—Zhaya—I saw you look—
JAYA: Really, Ginni—it's probably just the wind—

(*The knocking sound again.*)

130 MA: (*Loud whisper.*) There's someone at the door—
GINNI: What's that you said, Mrs Praycash? Someone at the door?
JAYA: (*Unable to control an exasperated sound.*) Oh—for God's sake! She treats us like children—
135 GINNI: What? Zhaya—Look! All of you—I've told you once, I've told you a zillion times! I hate it when y'all speak at once!
JAYA: (*Now faking a sneeze.*) Chhoo!—sorry, Ginni, sorry—
GINNI: (*Sounding very excited.*) That was a sneeze! Don't deny
140 it—you have a cold, Zhaya, don't you? Come on, con-fess—
JAYA: No, Ginni, no—it wasn't—it wasn't—
GINNI: Don't lie to me, Zhaya—I know a sneeze when I hear one—
145 JAYA: It was the—the *pepper*—
GINNI: I'll have to ask Auwm—tell me the truth, Auwm—does your sister have a cold? Does she?
OM: Cold? Oh—no, no, no! No cold, Ginni—it was only the—
150 JAYA: —pepper. It's this foreign pepper. I'm not really used to it.
GINNI: Then—why haven't you reacted before this?

(The knocking sounds again, more like a thump.)

MA: *(Looking around.)* That Bidyut-bai is really shameless—
GINNI: What? What was that?
JAYA: Nothing. She was just—
155 GINNI: You're keeping something from me! I just know it— you're all keeping something from me!
JAYA: Oh god, Ginni—we are *not*! Really!
GINNI: Yes you *are*, Zhaya! I can see it in your lying scheming little face! You think you're such an cutie-pie, Zhaya—
160 but you don't fool me! Not for one instant! Now *tell me*—
OM: *(Raising his voice and leaning into the viewing field of the* CONTACT MODULE.*)* No—Ginni—please! You trust me— see, look at me—are you looking? Would I tell you a lie?
GINNI: We-e-e-ell. I don't know! What was all that about?
165 Why did Zhaya sneeze? You know how terrified I am of colds, Auwm! Ever since we eradicated colds from here, where I live, it's like—like having the plague!
OM: Ginni—it's not a cold. I promise you that.
GINNI: If you get a cold, Auwm, I can't take your transplant!
170 You'll be quarantined! This whole program will go to waste!
OM: Ginni—Ginni—believe me. I will never risk your health.
GINNI: *(Calming down slightly.)* Though—I guess—they
175 screen everything that comes in. Even if you did have a cold, they'd never let your organs through—
OM: I live only for your benefit. You know that—
GINNI: All right, I believe you. I'll make myself believe you. I mean it's been hard to read your faces, you know? You
180 people don't use facial expressions, not like us, anyhow. But what *was* that your mother said just now? It sounded like . . . like . . .
JAYA: She was praying, taking the name of god—
GINNI: Oh. Yeah. Well, I don't know—sometimes I just get
185 the feeling—
OM: Please, Ginni—trust me. I would not do anything to harm our—our relationship. We have known each other only for two months, but from the first day itself, I have felt that you are just like my sister! Yes! I would not keep
190 anything from you—
GINNI: *(A touch sardonic.)* Is that right? You wouldn't keep anything from your sister—is that right, Zhaya? *(To* JAYA.*)* You're his sister, so you should know—does he keep anything from you?
195 OM: I mean—
JAYA: No, he doesn't. He would never tell a lie. He is pure like fresh cotton.
GINNI: *(Childlike glee.)* Pure like fresh cotton! Haha! That's quaint! That's really quaint! You know what? Even if I
200 didn't need transplants and if I wasn't so sick and all—I'd get the kick of my life from these conversations! It's like— it's like—I dunno. Human goldfish bowls, you know? I mean, I just look in on you folks every now and then and it just like—blows my mind. Better than TV. Better than
205 CyberNet. Coz this is Real Life—and don't think I don't appreciate it! You get to be my age and you really appreciate human companionship—
JAYA: You look very young—
GINNI: —what I meant, people in my country, at my age, they
210 just don't have any worthwhile friends, you know? Noth-

ing to hold on to—nothing precious. Nothing like . . . this. I get to give you things you'd never get in your life- time and you get to give me, well . . . Maybe my life. *(Voice goes husky.)* You know? That's a special bond. Don't think I don't appreciate it. 215
OM: We know you do, Ginni—
GINNI: And now I'm feeling tired, real tired. You just don't know how tired I get sometimes—
JAYA: *(Carefully.)* Is it—is it your illness?
GINNI: I guess you could say so, Zhaya, in a manner of speak- 220 ing, yes. It's my illness. But now I've gotta go. Okay? *(The tone sounds.)* Byeeee—
OM: Good-bye, Ginni—

(Knocking sounds again.)

OM: *(Ignoring the knocking.)* See you soo-oon—

(The CONTACT MODULE *goes dead. Instantly,* JAYA *leaps up to go to the door.)*

JAYA: We've got to do something about the door! We can't 225 have people knocking whenever they like!
MA: Oh? Now you're going to have special times for knock- ing as well?

*(*JAYA *gets to the door and opens it easily because she didn't have time to lock it completely before lunch.)*

JAYA: *(Opening the door.)* Now look—*(Stops dead and exclaims.)* Huhhhhhh! 230

*(*MA *and* OM *look up in alarm, just in time to see* JAYA *step back quickly, as* JEETU *makes a dramatic entrance—almost falling in at the door. His condition is terrible, his clothes in tatters, his hair wild, covered in solid muck and grime. Only his spirit seems undimin- ished.)*

JAYA: Oh my God—*(She bolts the door, her face grim and frowning.)*
MA: What—? *(She is momentarily speechless.)* Who is it—what is it—
JEETU: *(Staggering forward, till he can support himself on a chair 235 back.)* Only . . . your beloved son, Jeetu. Yes, I can see how delighted you are to see me—*(Mock concern.)* Oh—wait! Sorry! I'm your son-in-law, now, right?
OM: *(Has risen slowly to his feet.)* My god. What have you done to yourself? 240
JEETU: Don't bother breaking coconuts at my feet! *(His tone is sarcastic but good-humoured despite all.)* Yes, yes—your arms are wide open with welcome! Thank you for inviting me to share the comforts of your modest home with me, your younger brother! *(Comes forward across to stage right. Sits on 245 the silky white sofa, which receives his grimy presence with an au- dible flinch.)* And yes, I'd love to sit in this comfortable sofa—*(Succumbing to the sensuous embrace of the cushions, be- coming slighly delirious.)* Ahh! Ahhh!
JAYA: *(Concerned.)* What's the matter—are you in pain? 250
JEETU: Is it possible to know such ease? It feels so good that it hurts! Ahh! Ahh . . . ah. You know—it's a strange thing with the pavements: no matter how long you sleep on them, they never grow soft!

255 JAYA: (*Haltingly.*) You've been on the pavements!

JEETU: (*Gesturing to* JAYA.) Come, come sit by me, my darling wife! Or have you reverted to being my sister-in-law again? Come—

(JAYA *flees downstage.*)

JEETU: Well! No words to express your delight? Strange . . . at

260 one time, she used to fight for my attention—

OM: (*Trying to regain control of the situation.*) Jeetu—you owe us an explanation—

JEETU: I owe no-one anything—

OM: Where have you been these many weeks?

265 JEETU: Careful—you might go deaf to hear the things I'd tell you—

OM: But . . . are you here to stay?

JAYA: What else? You can't turn him out!

MA: (*Hard.*) Maybe we don't have a choice!

270 JEETU: Ah my loving mother speaks at last! And what does she say? What music does she pour into my parched ears?

OM: (*Sternly.*) Stop it! Things have changed around here—

JEETU: Really? I'd never have noticed—

OM: And the fact is—your permit to live with us was

275 surrendered!

(*There is a silence as* JEETU *processes this idea.*)

OM: Yes. I'm sorry—you had your chance. You chose to leave. We had to make our excuses to the guards. To explain why the fourth member of the family wasn't here. Now it's too late to take you back in—and in any case,

280 you're undoubtedly a health hazard—

JEETU: (*Getting up slowly.*) A "health hazard" did you say? (*He stands unsteadily.*) Heh! That's rich! (*Laughs.*) Me—a health "hazard"! My brother—I'm not a health hazard, I'm a walking, talking, health CATASTROPHE! (*Goes towards*

285 OM, *grinning.*) Oh, yes! I'm so unhealthy that even even my germs have germs . . . yes. My lice are dying on my skull—see? (*He offers his head for examination, to* OM, *who shrinks away.*) They're just lying in little black heaps—

JAYA: Stop! Stop it—why make things worse for yourself—

290 JEETU: Ah those honeyed words of love! How they soothe my running sores!

JAYA: What do you expect? You're the one who left. And now you come back looking like Death's first cousin—is that our fault?

295 OM: We'll have no choice—

JEETU: (*Turning towards* MA.) And you, my mother? I hear your love for me has been bought for the price of a flush toilet?

MA: When you reach my age you'll know that a peaceful shit

300 is more precious than money in the bank!

JEETU: Thank goodness I won't live long enough to be rich—

JAYA: What d'you mean—

JEETU: I'm ill. I'm going to die soon—

OM: Oh God—(*He starts to pace.*)

305 JAYA: Don't be foolish—

OM: This is serious, very serious—

MA: Of what?

JEETU: An overdose—

JAYA: Some drug?

JEETU: Called freedom. (*He sinks to the floor.*) I've been over-

310 dosing on freedom. Spent my hoard of years—splurged them all, for a few weeks of freedom on the streets. (*Lies flat.*) Freedom to lie in the filth of the open road and to drink from the open sewer! Yes. Freedom to eat the choicest servings from the garbage dump—shared only with

315 crows, flies and pigs! Ah, such freedom as you newly-rich people never know! (*He is slightly delirious. He attempts a laugh, but his voice is cracked.*) But expensive. For all that it looks so cheap, each mouthful of garbage costs a handful of years off your life. And I gorged myself! So I'm . . .

320 gone. Flat broke. Burnt out . . .

(*He turns weakly on his side and starts to throw up.*)

OM: Quick—stop him—

JAYA: (*Kneeling quickly.*) A towel—cloth, anything—

(*She uses the loose end of her sari to cover her hand as she holds his head, then wipes his face with it with the other corner—*OM *hands her disposable towels and fetches a mug of water.*)

OM: (*His face showing revulsion.*) What a mess! You'll have to

325 incinerate your sari—

MA: And what about the carpet?

(JAYA *places* JEETU'*s head on her lap.*)

OM: We can disinfect the whole room—and better wear the nose guard—

MA: But the lice—the lice can get into everything—then

330 we're finished—

OM: Oh! (*In exasperation.*) It would have been better if—

JAYA: (*Quietly, stroking* JEETU'*s dishevelled hair.*) Don't say it.

MA: What?

OM: (*Ignoring* MA.) How can we keep him! What will we tell

335 the guards—

JAYA: (*With finality.*) We're not going to turn him out.

MA: There's no place for him now!

JAYA: We've managed before—

OM: (*Fretting.*) Ginni won't like it—she'll forbid it—

JAYA: (*Weakly.*) Who?   340

MA: She'll chuck him out!

OM: She'll be so angry, so angry—

JAYA: (*To* JEETU.) Shhhh, don't talk—

OM: Just think of the risk! We've gone so far—given up so

345 much and to lose it! Just because of—of—

JAYA: (*Looking steadily up at him.*) Your brother. Whatever's written on paper, that's what he really is—

OM: But—(*Frets, pacing.*)

MA: What'll we do for food? There won't be enough for

350 him—

JEETU: Uhhhh . . . if I could just have a little water—

(JAYA *wets one of the disposable towels, soaks it in water and dribbles water into his mouth.*)

JAYA: Don't sit up yet

OM: It's starting to stink! Ginni'll be furious, *furious*—

JAYA: Look, we'll wrap him up in a sheet and keep him to one side till he's better. Then when he can sit up and talk,   355

we'll just tell Ginni that's he's come back. My husband's come back from his—his business trip—

JEETU: (*Weakly, his head lolling.*) Who's this . . . Ginni . . . (*Rolls back down.*)

360 JAYA: Shhh . . . shhh—don't talk—(*She whispers to him, as if to a child.*)

MA: See how she treats him—her brother-in-law!

OM: (*Fretfully.*) How long can we keep him wrapped up! And what if Ginni finds out—

365 JAYA: (*Looking up.*) There's no point getting frantic—

OM: And who'll believe that this . . . this . . . *wreck* was away on business!

MA: (*Maliciously.*) Look how she holds him—her darling!

JAYA: We'll have to fix him up, of course. Shave his hair, give

370 him some clothes—

OM: (*Clutching his head.*) But the diseases—the diseases—

JAYA: (*Calmly.*) Clean water and strong food will cure him of whatever he has—

(*Lights dim.*)

SCENE II

The same scene, a couple of hours later. JEETU's *wasted and scab-scarred body lies in the centre. He has been shaved and visibly grows cleaner, as* JAYA *tenderly washes him and attends to the wounds puckering his skin. He is conscious and groans only occasionally.* MA *is sitting to one side, her expression blank.* OM *is at stage front right, standing, occasionally pacing. He and* JAYA *have both changed their clothes.* OM *is trying to master the emotions tearing at his face.*

OM: Any minute now—any minute!—she's going to call!

JAYA: Just try and relax—

MA: I don't understand how we plan to hide him—

JAYA: Look—look at these sores!

5 OM: (*To* JAYA.) How can you touch him with your bare hands? He must be oozing with disease—

MA: —and he! Her brother-in-law!

JAYA: (*Exasperated.*) How can I leave him to rot!

OM: Wear rubber gloves, for pity's sake!

10 JAYA: We abandoned him to the streets. The least we can do is to risk our own skin when we touch him—

OM: It's like Ginni says—the curse of the Donor World is sentimentality—

MA: (*To* JAYA.) Ginni will throw him out—just you see!

15 OM: Here I am, willing to give my whole body to improve our lives—and what're you doing? Endangering the whole project by feeling up your brother-in-law—

JAYA: (*At this she stops.*) Who switched roles with his brother? Who turned this family inside out?

20 OM: All I'm saying is—leave him till we can disinfect him at least! Show him to the guards—they'll know what to do—

JAYA: (*Resumes her task.*) What faith you have in them! They don't care about any of us, not as people, not as human beings—

25 OM: What're you saying? You don't talk enough to Ginni. If you did, you wouldn't feel this way—

MA: Oh she's jealous of our Ginni-angel! Look at her face! Pinched with envy!

OM: Ginni really cares for us—

30 JAYA: Oh yes, she *cares*—just as much as she cares about the chicken she eats for dinner—that's all you are for her, another kind of dinner—

OM: (*Contemptuously.*) How little you understand of Westerners! They are not small, petty people—like us!

MA: Oh she's just jealous, jealous! Can't bear to think of you 35 being inside that foreign angel. After all, who wouldn't want to be inside such a divine being? Why—it would be indecent to object—

OM: (*Moderately.*) Now, now, Ma—

MA: Who knows? Maybe she'll even want you for a husband 40 some day—why not? If my son's kidneys are good enough for her why not his—

OM: Ma—!

MA: Why not his children, I was going to say! Now that's what I want to know! What a miracle—grandchildren! 45 And with an angel for a daughter-in-law!

JAYA: Huh! An angel who shares her bed with her dinner—now that *would* be a miracle!

OM: Would she spend so much money on me, then? If I am just—a—a chicken to her? Answer me that! Do you know 50 how much she's spent on us? Our comfort?

JAYA: Never mind chicken—have you seen how their beef cattle live? Air-conditioned! Individual potties! Music from loudspeakers—why, they even have their own psychiatrists! All to ensure that their meat, when it finally gets 55 to Ginni's table, will be the freshest, purest, sanest, happiest—

OM: (*Steps towards* JAYA.) I'll slap you if you're not careful!

JAYA: (*Unimpressed.*) Mind that you wear your rubber gloves— 60

(*There's knocking at the door.*)

MA: Hear that?

OM: Who is it—who!

MA: The right-hand neighbours. Wanting to borrow a bucket of water.

OM: Well, they're not getting it— 65

MA: Yesterday they offered me money—

OM: Tell them to ask the muncipality to increase their supply.

MA: I told them—

OM: Then why don't they shut up?

MA: They told me I'd forgotten what it was like before we got 70 this external connection—they started to scream and cry—

OM: Ahh . . . ! These people! No wonder foreigners think so little of us! We have no pride, no shame!

(*Knocking increases in volume.*)

JAYA: (*To* MA.) How can you be sure that it's the neighbours? 75

OM: Who else can it be?

MA: Listen carefully. There's a code, you see—

JAYA: Supposing it's the guards?

OM: Why should they come?

(*Sustained knocking.*)

JAYA: What kind of code— 80

MA: Three knocks means it's the next-door-right-side. Two knocks means it's the next-door-left-side—

OM: There's no reason for the guards to come!

JAYA: What does loud thumping with no pattern mean?

(*Thumping on the door.*)

85 OM: (*Looking suddenly grey.*) You're right—it could be the guards!

MA: No, no! It's the neighbours I tell you!

(*Violent thumping.*)

JAYA: (*A touch of malice.*)—it's been two months, you know! Time to collect their fattened broiler!

90 MA: Shouldn't you just open the door and find out?

OM: I—I—(*Looking panicked.*) What about—what about Jeetu! What'll we do about hiding him!

JAYA: If they've come for you, they won't have eyes for anyone else—

(*Knocking, knocking, knocking.*)

95 OM: (*Sweating.*) But—Ginni looked fine at lunch-time—she looked perfectly normal—

JAYA: Her condition is such that she can deteriorate suddenly—

OM: But she would tell us herself! Not just send the guards—

(*Rhythmic thumping.*)

100 JAYA: Maybe she doesn't have the strength?

OM: My god. My god—you're right! It's not happened so far, this knocking!

JAYA: Why not just open the door and find out?

OM: I always hoped, you see, that it would never actually

105 come to this—

JAYA: A vain hope. Answer the door—

OM: (*Querlous.*) A dutiful wife would open it for me!

JAYA: You forget—I'm your sister—

MA: That knocking's getting on my nerves now!

(*Knocking, knocking, knocking.*)

110 OM: My legs! My legs refuse to move!

JAYA: Such a hero, my man.

(*Hammering, thumping, knocking.*)

OM: At least she could have let us enjoy the illusion for a little longer—

JAYA: It's in God's will, when your time is up—

115 MA: What'll they think—this delay?

OM: Another month—another week, another day, even—

JAYA: But in the end it would always come to this—the bill collector at the door—

OM: Do it for me—please! I order you—you're still my wife!

(*Knock, thump, knock, thump. A pleasing rhythm.*)

120 MA: I'll be driven mad!

OM: Would you prefer to see your son dead?

JAYA: Maybe they just want one of your finger-nails—your hair—something unimportant—

OM: The smallest pimple on my chin is more precious to me

125 at this moment than a diamond mine in someone else's fist! Oh—how could I have done this to myself? What sort of fool am I?

(*Knocknocknock.*)

MA: If you don't open the door, I will—

OM: And if you move even one muscle, I'll kill you with my bare hands— 130

JAYA: Your mother!

OM: Whoever opens that door is my murderer, my assassin—

JAYA: I'm sorry, I cannot live with this—(*She's completed* JEETU's *cleaning and starts to get up.*)

(*Thumpthumpthump.* JEETU *gingerly rolls over onto one elbow. Looks up and around him. Then collapses gently onto his belly and lies still, as if ready to sleep.*)

OM: No!! I beg of you—please! Please! Leave that cursed 135 door alone! Seal it with cement and fire! I cannot bear to see its gape, admitting those vile, those cruel, those vicious guards! (*Groans.*) Ahhhh . . .

JAYA: Till just a moment ago they were your dearest friends— (*Gets up.*) 140

OM: NO! Sit still! Don't stir! Or I'll—I'll—

(*He rushes to the door, holds himself against it.*)

JAYA: How can I respect you? Move aside!

OM: (*Wildly.*) I don't care! So long as you keep the guards from the door—

JAYA: I'll offer myself in exchange— 145

OM: They won't take you—they're very selective—

(*Knockthumpknockthump.*)

JAYA: (*Exasperated.*) They'll break the door down in a moment!

OM: (*Sinks to the floor. Voice barely audible.*) Yes. I never thought of that. They could do that—and then what'll happen? 150 Where'll I hide? (*Starts to crawl away from the door.*) In the fridge. That's where. I'll just crawl along here, all the way to the fridge and I'll sit there, yes—

JAYA: (*As soon as* OM *moves away from the door,* JAYA *starts to unlock the bolts.*) Ohhh—this bravery makes my heart sick— 155

MA: (*To* OM, *as he crawls past her.*) Why are you on the floor?

OM: I'm hiding.

(JAYA *gets the bolts on the door open. Opens the door.*)

JAYA: (*Off-stage.*) Yes? What d'you want?

(*There is an indistinct mumble.*)

JAYA: (*Re-enters looking bewildered.*) Ma—it's for you—

MA: (*Getting to her feet.*) What? Already? 160

JAYA: There must be some mistake—

MA: (*Coming forward briskly.*) It's very prompt, I must say!

JAYA: (*Mystified.*) You ordered something?

MA: (*She is already at the door.*) Yes. (*Moves out of sight, off-stage.*) Yes?—Yes! That's right! But where is it? You haven't 165 brought it? It hasn't come? You'll bring it tomorrow? When? Ah . . . Okay. No—no, I'll be at home—and—sign here? No . . . payment? Oh. Okay. Right. I'll be waiting— (*She re-enters and shuts the door behind her.*)

JAYA: (*She heard this exchange with no comprehension.*) Ma? What 170 was all that?

MA: (*Airily.*) Oh . . . Just something I've ordered—
JAYA: (*Astounded.*) Ordered!
MA: Something I saw on TV—
175 JAYA: But . . . how did you place the order?
MA: That thing, the remote—you press some buttons and you
    can buy things, do things—and they bring it right to the
    door! But Madam wouldn't know, would she! Too high
    and mighty to watch TV!
180 OM: (*He has reached as far upstage as he can comfortably go. He
    stops there, his hands over his head.*) I'm hiding.
JAYA: (*She locks the door.*) But what have you ordered? How
    much will it cost?
MA: (*Philosophically.*) You'll see, when it comes!

(*Lights dim.*)

SCENE III

OM *is lying in a foetal position on the floor, stage front right.* JEETU
*is sitting at the table eating slowly, carefully. He has had a bath and
is wearing* OM's *track suit.* JAYA *and* MA *are sitting beside* OM.

JAYA: He doesn't seem to hear anything I say.
MA: He's a good boy. He's just tired, that's all—
JAYA: But what'll we do! Ginni notices everything!
MA: She'll understand.
5 JAYA: Huh!
MA: You're just jealous of her. You don't see what a good,
    kind, generous, loving person she really is. It's a reflection
    on you, but of course, you're too fancy to care—
JAYA: Please! This is no time to be criticising me!
10 MA: Who's criticising? I'm just pointing out some simple
    truths.
JAYA: Come on, Om—get up! This'll never do—
MA: Want to watch TV? There's something good on in twenty
    minutes—
15 JAYA: (*Looks at* OM.) It's so typical. He can't face things. He
    never could.
MA: You should watch more TV. You could learn so much—
JAYA: It's amazing that he got this job at all.
MA: On *Happy Families* you can see it, the exact same situa-
20   tion. The mother has one son and one daughter—and the
    son gets an expensive job—
JAYA: Ma—you have two sons!
MA: But the daughter is jealous! She can't bear to see her
    brother succeeding, getting all the praise from the mother!
25   The poor mother was widowed in early life and has to
    struggle—but then one day the father comes back!
JAYA: I thought you just said he was dead?
MA: No, I never! I said the mother was widowed—meaning,
    she just thought the husband was dead—
30 JAYA: (*Snapping in irritation.*) Oh—it's all so pointless! Any
    moment now, you won't have a TV to watch!
MA: What!
JAYA: —this whole dream will come crashing down around
    us! The grey guards will come and take everything back!
35 MA: No!
JAYA: What d'you think—it's your birthright? To have all this
    water, these gadgets? The moment Ginni finds out what's
    happened to her little pet, she'll have the place emptied—
MA: Shoo! Such dirty lies!

JAYA: (*Quieter.*) And then how'll I cook without a stove?   40
MA: I'll slap you if you talk like that! Why, my son said so
    himself—we'll be rich for ever and ever—
JAYA: (*Raising her voice.*) Look at your son, Ma! Look! He's
    been reduced to a cabbage!
MA: At least a cabbage doesn't talk back!   45
JAYA: (*Frustrated.*) Oh! (*Angry tears.*) At least before there was
    nothing to lose!
JEETU: (*Suddenly.*) Why? You used to have a smile before.
    You've certainly lost that—
JAYA: Oh shut up, shut up! Who are you to talk! You're just a   50
    waster! Drifting about the streets, not caring what hap-
    pened to yourself, not caring about any of us, but when
    you're ready to die, where d'you come? To us of course!
    Yes! It's so easy for you to talk—you who can't even lose
    yourself competently! You've come back to make sure that   55
    we lose ourselves as well!
MA: Don't speak to your husband like that—
JAYA: He's *not my husband!* He's my brother-in-law!
JEETU: And your lover—

(OM *reacts to this—his limbs twitch, but he does not participate in
the conversation.*)

MA: What's this?   60
JAYA: (*Broken.*) Ohh! Not now! Not this!
JEETU: How strange it is, to be here. Talking to all of you . . .
MA: (*Indifferently.*) Not that I'm surprised. Nothing from this
    slut surprises me. She's capable of anything—
JAYA: Doesn't it matter to you that you're trampling on my   65
    life? Doesn't it matter what harm you cause to others?
JEETU: When you've lost everything, when you're so weak
    you can't even eat the cockroaches who walk into your
    mouth, that's when your life's desire breathes in your
    ear—   70
JAYA: And? It tells you to torment your family?
MA: She always was shameless—
JEETU: That I should see you again. You, Jaya. (*Leans back and
    smiles lazily, wincing slightly.* OM *listens.*) Lying there, covered
    in shit and dirt, ready to die—*dying* to die!—hearing the   75
    engine, roaring in my ears, ready to take me away—I
    thought of you.
MA: I should have thrown her out from the moment she
    started making eyes at him—her brother-in-law!
JAYA: (*This is the closest thing to a compliment she has ever been   80
    paid. She is overwhelmed with conflicting emotions, trying to cover
    it with sarcasm.*) And then? Some goddess picked you up?
JEETU: (*Lolling back.*) Huh! Yes. Some goddess! A dog . . .
JAYA: What? (*Uncomprehending.*) A dog?
JEETU: Came and peed on me. Straight into my mouth,   85
    cheeky bastard! (JAYA *shudders in disgust and pity.*) But he
    revived me all right. Lucky for him he ran off—or I would
    have sucked him dry! Life is a strange thing. When your
    pockets are full with it, you throw it away like rich whores
    buying silk bedsheets. But the moment you've emptied   90
    your purse of days, your throat begins to scream of its own
    accord, like a beggar in the streets—(*He imitates a beggar's
    cry.*) Help me, oh God!—please! Just another five min-
    utes—that's all I ask—just another five minutes to drink a
    last cup of tea—just two minutes! Just one minute, one!   95
    One . . . *please* God, help this dying shithead one more

time—(*Looks at her, reverts to his normal voice.*) That's when I thought of you. I knew you would revive me. (*Shuts his eyes.*) Just the smell of your hair—just the touch of your fingernails—
100
JAYA: (*Biting her lip.*) Hush! These are not things to be said!
MA: And it's too late, anyway. She's already married. To your elder brother—
OM: (*Suddenly.*) Who's a cabbage.
105 JAYA: (*Uncertainly.*) Om . . .
JEETU: That's all right. We don't need anyone. We don't need this fancy prison. We managed before. We'll manage again —
MA: (*Suddenly jumping up.*) What's the time? Look at the time!
110   It's late—Ginni'll be angry at us—

(*From the corridor, the sound of booted steps.*)

JAYA: (*Tiredly.*) Ohh. I don't care, I don't care any more—
JEETU: That's what I say—

(*From the corridor, the sound of booted steps, closer.*)

MA: Listen! What's that sound?

(OM *hears and reacts immediately, before the others notice him, by crawling off, stage right.*)

JAYA: What's the worst they can do? Take away what was
115   never ours to begin with—

(*From the door, a couple of sharp loud raps.*)

GUARD 1: InterPlanta Services! Open this door, please!
MA: It's the guards!
JAYA: (*Looking blankly.*) So they *have* come for him, after all.
JEETU: (*Holding out his hand.*) Come. Let me kiss your hand.
120   Then you can go and open the door. Tell them to bugger off and take all their goodies with them.
GUARD 1: (*From outside.*) InterPlanta Services—we know you're in there! Open up!
JAYA: (*Raising her voice.*) Coming! (*She gets up.*) I might as well
125   get it over with. (*To the door.*) Wait! It takes a while to unlock the door—

(*Works at the bolts.*)

GUARD 1: (*From outside.*) Resistance is useless! We are authorised to break down this barrier if you do not comply with our request in ten seconds exactly—(*Starts a count
130   down.*) Ten! Nine! Eight!—

(JAYA *gets the door open.*)

GUARD 1: (*Breaking off in mid-stride.*) Sev- . . . ah! (*Enters, pushing* JAYA *aside as* GUARD 2 *and* GUARD 3 *take up defensive positions at the door, holding a fold-up stretcher between them.*) Right—where is the Donor? Come on, quickly now—(*He
135   plunges straight for* JEETU.) The penalty for resistance is—
JAYA: (*In sudden alarm.*) But that's not

(JEETU, *who has got to his feet, starts to back away—*)

MA: (*Suddenly, pointing to* JEETU.) Go on! Take him—before he runs!

(JEETU *panics and runs,* GUARD 1 *pounces for him, chasing him around the room, while the other two guards stand like goal-keepers at the door.*)

GUARD 1: Ah! He's running, is he? I'll show him—I'll show
140   the cowardly little shit—
JAYA: (*Screaming.*) But he's not the one you want!
JEETU: (*As he runs—though he's really in no condition to make the effort and tires almost instantly.*) You fools! Can't you see I'm not your man?
GUARD 1: (*Panting in pursuit, dodging around the others, even 145
   around* OM *lying inert on the floor.*) Always the same story—no-one wants to pay their dues—come on, come on! It's hopeless to run away—

(GUARD 1 *catches him.* JAYA *screams.*)

GUARD 1: There—there—(*As* JEETU *struggles, grunting,* GUARD
   1 *holds him in a cruel arm-lock.*) I've got you now— 150
JAYA: Don't hurt him—don't hurt him—oh he's sick! Please!
GUARD 1: Resistance is useless—(*Starts to lift/drag* JEETU *kicking and struggling, but losing strength.*) we'll have you knocked out in a second—
JEETU: (*Weakly.*) Jaya! Uhh—tell them . . . tell them— 155
JAYA: (*She darts forward.*) You fools! You maniacs—
MA: (*Reaches out, grabs* JAYA's *ankle and forces her to fall.*) Let him go—slut!
JAYA: (*Paying no attention to* MA.)—He's not the one you want! My husband is there—(*She points from her ungainly position 160
   on the floor.*) There!
GUARD 1: Ohh! That's what they all say when we come to take them! (*In a falsetto, as he subdues* JEETU.) "Not me! Not me! It's my brother you want! My uncle! My son" Huh! Lying scum—(*To the other two guards.* GUARD 2 *helps him to 165
   wrestle* JEETU *to the ground, while* GUARD 3 *gets the stretcher ready.*) We have no time to spare!

(*Beyond the door interested by-standers have started to collect.*)

JAYA: How can you take the wrong man! Can't you see? Don't you have eyes in your head?
GUARD 1: —(*To the other two.*) Officer! Ready hypo! 170
MA: Hurry up, you fools—how long d'you think I can hold her?
GUARD 2: (*Holding a gun-shaped hypo-syringe.*) Ready, sir!
JEETU: (*Weakly.*) Jaya—Jaya—help me!
GUARD 1: Prepare to administer hypo— 175
JAYA: (*Struggling now with* MA *who has her ankle in a vice-like grip.*) Lemme go—lemme go! Don't you care about your own son—
MA: Your lover, you mean! Slut! Serves him right if he goes in place of my only darling— 180
GUARD 3: (*Holding* JEETU *in a suffocating lock.*) Yes sir—(JEETU *starts to struggle, grunting.*)
JAYA: No! (*Panicking.*) You're killing him! He's not strong enough—
GUARD 1: (*Ignoring her.*) Administer hypo—(*He aids in holding 185
   JEETU down.*)

(GUARD 2 *is unable to gain access to* JEETU *because he is now struggling so wildly.* JAYA *and* MA *are also struggling but* MA *is practically lying on top of* JAYA *to hold her down.*)

JAYA: They're hurting him! They'll kill him—oh! I can't bear to watch—I can't!

GUARD 1: Officer—I said, administer hypo—

190 GUARD 2: I'm trying sir—I—(*She gets in a shot.*)

JEETU: (*Howls.*) Ahhhhh! Ahhhhh!

GUARD 2: —Damn! Missed the muscle—

JEETU: Ahhhhh!

JAYA: (*In tears.*) Oh what's the use, what's the use! After all
195   we've gone through—

GUARD 1: Ready fresh hypo, officer—and hurry! He's getting out of control—

JAYA: (*No longer able to struggle.*) Oh—please, no, no! He wanted nothing—he had no part to play in this—

(GUARD 2 *fiddles with her kit, discarding one cartridge and fitting another on.*)

200 JAYA: Don't hurt him, don't hurt him—please! Oh! Oh! They'll make mincemeat out of him—

GUARD 2: (*Calmly.*) Hypo ready, sir—

GUARD 1: Administer hypo—

JEETU: (*Hollering as* GUARD 1 *and* GUARD 3 *lean with all their*
205   *weight on him.*) AHHHHHHHHHHHH! AHHHH-HHH!

GUARD 2 *holds down* JEETU's *shoulder with her knee and delivers a punch with the muzzle of the hypo.* JEETU's *body arcs up in a convulsion—he seems to hover in mid-air—*JAYA *screams—Then all is still.* JEETU *is limp and inert on the stretcher. The three guards get to their feet, returning as quickly as possible to their professional composure.* JAYA *remains clutched within* MA's *savage embrace, though she strains towards the tableau.*)

GUARD 1: Officers—initiate departure.

(GUARD 2 *and* GUARD 3 *quickly spread an opaque shield over the stretcher so that* JEETU *is completely hidden from sight.*)

JAYA: (*In a dull voice, knowing that she won't be answered.*) He's dead, isn't he? They've killed him. I feel it in my
210   bones.

GUARD 2: Donor secured for departure.

GUARD 1: Proceed with departure—

(GUARD 2 *and* GUARD 3 *hoist the stretcher up and exit. From beyond the door, the sound of the wondering crowd.* JAYA *holds out her hand helplessly in the direction of the door.*)

GUARD 1: (*Turning to* JAYA *as the other two officers vanish, removing his clipboard from his belt.*) InterPlanta Services thank
215   you for your cooperation. Your family member is about to fulfil the solemn and noble contract into which he entered. We, on our part, offer you our sincerest assurance that we will do everything in our power to ensure that he will come to no avoidable harm and will suffer no dis-
220   comforts other than what is deemed normal under the circumstances—(*He pauses.* JAYA *is looking dully at the floor, still lying half prone, though* MA *has now backed off and is straightening her clothes.*) Any questions?

JAYA: (*Not looking up.*) When will he be back?

225 GUARD 1: (*Patiently.*) Madam! Any questions?

JAYA: (*Not looking up.*) No.

GUARD 1: (*Ticking off his clipboard.*) Right. Donor will remain in our custody until such time as he is ready to be returned. This can be any period from two hours onwards and upto one week—   230

JAYA: (*Jerks her head up.*) One week! What'll be left of him!

GUARD 1: —depending on the nature of the transplant required, the availability of artificial substitutes for the organs that the Donor has, of his own free will, made available to the Receiver and the Donor's own speed of 235 recovery. Any questions?

JAYA: (*Gets slowly to her feet.*) Yes! What part of him is going to be removed?

GUARD 1: I'm sorry, Madam, I am not free to discuss such details.   240

JAYA: You're going to cut him up and you're not even going to tell his wife what you're going to do with him?

GUARD 1: Excuse me, Madam—relationship with Donor is . . . ?

JAYA: (*Gives her head a guilty little shake.*) I—I meant, his fam- 245 ily—

GUARD 1: Madam: Full details will be furnished once the formalities have been completed—

JAYA: And can I see him? In the hospital, the clinic, wherever?

GUARD 1: Security and health regulations prohibit any con- 250 tact between Donors and their families—

JAYA: Why ask if we have questions when you don't want to answer any of them?

GUARD 1: (*Imperturbably ticking off his clipboard.*) Right. (*Handing her the clipboard.*) And now, if you would be so kind as 255 to sign the despatch voucher—

JAYA: (*Grabs the pen and signs violently.*) There—there—your stupid forms, your—papers—your—questions . . . (*She would like to throw the pen at the floor, but it is attached to the clip-board.*)   260

GUARD 1: (*Retrieving the clip-board.*) Thank you, Madam. We are grateful for your kind cooperation and assure you—

JAYA: Just get out! Take your lying, insincere face away from my door—(*Makes as if to push him.*)

GUARD 1: (*Moving nimbly out of her range, as he continues his* 265 *spiel.*)—assure you that we will do everything in our power to return your beloved one to you in as short a time as possible—(*He leans inwards on the door handle.*) On behalf of our clients—

JAYA: (*Rushes at him, shouting.*) GET OUT! (*Pushes the door* 270 *shut in his face.*)

GUARD 1: (*He pushes back, completing his parting message through the door.*)—we at InterPlanta Services extend our heartfelt gratitude for your family's support and compassion! (*This last bit is shouted from behind the closed door.*)   275

(*Sound of boots marching away.*)

JAYA: Ahhh! (*Venting her fury against the door.*) How I hate them!

MA: (*She has been silent all along.*) Good. They've gone at last.

JAYA: (*Leaning against the door, her head against her fists.*) He's gone! They've taken him—and I could do nothing to pre- 280 vent it!

MA: Can I switch on my TV?

JAYA: (*Yelling at her.*) Your son goes off to the slaughterhouse and you're just worried about your TV!

285 MA: (*Mustering as much dignity as she can.*) If you watched more TV you wouldn't dare talk to your mother-in-law that way—

JAYA: (*Coming back towards her.*) Oh! So I've gone back to being your daughter-in-law, have I?

(*Stands threateningly in front of* MA, *who is facing the TV with the remote raised in readiness in her hand.*)

290 MA: I'm your mother-in-law, that's your brother-in-law on the floor there, your husband's gone to work at the spare parts factory. And you? You're just a slut who happens to be standing between me and my TV!

(*Lights dim.*)

SCENE IV

Night. The only difference between daytime and night-time is the spotlight illumination. MA *is snoring in her corner upstage and left.* JAYA *is standing uneasily in a pool of light, upstage left, near the gym equipment. She is wearing an expensive nightgown with matching robe, in satin and lace. Her face gleams with night-cream.*

OM *lies in his corner, on a sleeping pallet near the TV, apparently asleep.*

JAYA *pacing restlessly, finally comes over to where* OM *lies.*

JAYA: (*Shaking him.*) Om! Om—wake up!

(*He does not respond.*)

JAYA: Om—come on—I know you're not asleep—wake up!
OM: (*In a disembodied voice.*) Why? What's the point?
JAYA: We've got to talk. To decide what to do—
5 OM: About what?
JAYA: When they bring Jeetu back—when they realize they've got the wrong man—
OM: They've not realized that. They've used him instead of me.
10 JAYA: No! No—they *can't*—they can't be that stupid!
OM: Then why haven't they brought him back?
JAYA: Because they're . . . interrogating him. Because he collapsed, maybe, and now they're treating him—
OM: You yourself said they don't give a damn about us—why
15 should they care about him? (*He raises himself slowly.*) No. They've used him, take my word for it. Or else they'd have brought him back—
JAYA: —But—but don't they *check*? Don't they bother?
OM: (*Shrugs.*) Maybe they were in too much of a hurry?
20 JAYA: Maybe the part they've taken from him doesn't need to be so special—maybe they've just taken something small, something insignificant—
OM: Then they would have come back by now.
JAYA: It's been six hours. Six hours! They can't remove any-
25 thing of much consequence in six hours! Why—they've probably just taken his—his front teeth! His toe-nails!
OM: Then why hasn't he come back?
JAYA: (*In a small voice.*) You're right. It must be something bigger. More crucial. (*Pause.*) What d'you think it is? His stom-
30 ach? His intestines? Maybe he won't come back for a week!

OM: Or maybe they've found out he's not me and they've just done away with him!
JAYA: (*Cries out.*) No! That would be murder! They can't be allowed to murder people!
OM: (*Coldly.*) Who'd notice? We don't have the right to com- 35 plain. Technically, anyone who isn't claimed by his family within twenty-four hours of going missing can be terminated without attracting legal attention.
JAYA: All these weeks he's been away—he could've been dead! And we'd never even have known! 40
OM: It's a wonder he's alive at all. I've heard that the street gangs eat derelicts these days —
JAYA: No!
OM: Cook them and eat them. Why not? There's no law to prevent it— 45
JAYA: How did he survive!
OM: He was protected by his friends on the street. But they couldn't do it indefinitely. They forced him to come back.
JAYA: Oh. 50
OM: Whatever he says—that's the real reason he's here.
JAYA: (*Pause.*) D'you think he's really ill?
OM: Must be.
JAYA: (*With finality.*) Then it's better if he dies in their hands. They'd be humane, they wouldn't hurt him— 55
OM: Why? They could use him for research—
JAYA: No!
OM: He's not officially on their records—they can do whatever they like—
JAYA: (*Covering her ears.*) No! I don't want to think of it— 60
OM: —give him drugs and sell him to those game sanctuaries—
JAYA: Don't! Oh—please—
OM: —where the rich have licenses to hunt socially disadvantaged types—yes! That's what they've done with your 65 Jeetu! Turned him loose to become a trophy for some industrialist's daughter—
JAYA: You're—you're—(*She calms down.*) It's just your jealousy speaking, isn't it? (*She insists.*) Tell me—isn't it?
OM: What's it to you? 70
JAYA: (*Tiredly.*) I'm still your wife.
OM: Not really. On paper, you're my sister. In reality, you're nothing to me. If not for Ginni I'd throw you out like a shot. Onto the streets. To be hunted. What do I care? You betrayed me. Seduced my brother. I feel nothing but con- 75 tempt.
JAYA: You never cared for me. You never wanted me—
OM: Wanting—not wanting—what meaning do these words have in our world? What choices do we have? Was it my choice that I signed up for this programme? 80
JAYA: —Yes! You went of your own accord!
OM: No. I went because there wasn't anything left to do. I went because I lost my job in the company. And why did I lose it? Because nobody needs clerks any more! There are no new jobs now, from here till next week! It's all over! 85 The factories are all closing! There was nothing *left* for people like us! Don't you know that? There's us—and there's the street gangs—and then the rich.
JAYA: But—the village—
OM: The village is just another kind of factory now. To live 90 there you have to be born there—or you have to be an in-

dustrialist. I'm not an industrialist. I'm just a clerk. What choices do I have? I didn't even choose *this* job—I stood in queue and I was chosen! And if I hadn't got this one, there would have been other queues—but they are all just another kind of lottery in the end. It was just my fate! Like it is my fate to have a faithless tart for a wife—

95

JAYA: Then why didn't you go with the grey guards when they came! Why did you lie down like a corpse!

OM: I don't know what came over me. That too was my fate. It was my fate to lie down in a trance and my brother to take my place. It was his fate to face the scalpel—

100

JAYA: —even though he may never return?

OM: Nothing matters. Whatever happens, it's fate.

(There's a sound, indistinct.)

JAYA: Wait!—What's that?

105

(The sound of boots in the corridor, accompanied by a shuffling.)

JAYA: Oh! (*Turning excitedly towards the door.*) Hear that? It sounds like boots—

(She runs to the door.)

OM: It doesn't matter what they've done to him—he didn't care about his life anyway—he didn't take any responsibility for anything—

110

(JAYA flings the door open, leans out into the corridor—and freezes where she stands. The footsteps come to a halt. The shuffling continues. OM looks straight ahead, affecting unconcern. The shuffling draws close. JAYA stands aside, her face blank, watching as JEETU enters the room, shuffling slowly, his arms half-raised in front of him, being steered by GUARD 2, impassively. GUARD 1 enters as well.)

OM does not look around. JAYA slowly re-enters, shutting the door behind her, never taking her stricken eyes off the silent, pathetic figure of JEETU.)

(He is wearing silk pajamas white on white and a wine-red brocade robe and velvet bedroom slippers. Across his eyes, and wrapped around his head, heavy bandages.)

(JAYA remains where she is, by the door, her hands over her mouth, staring. In the foreground, MA snores lightly.)

GUARD 1: (*Clears his throat, takes out his memo pad.*) Donor Prakash, we have no words with which to express our deep and sincere appreciation of your generosity towards your Receiver . . .

(Lights fade as he drones on.)

GUARD 1: You will be glad to hear that the transplant has been a tremendous success and that henceforward you will receive every benefit and consideration due to you under the terms of your contract . . .

115

(Lights out and curtain.)

ACT THREE

SCENE I

Little has changed in the room. JEETU *sits on the floor with his head between his knees, facing stage front.* MA *is watching TV wearing head phones.* JAYA *and* OM *are sitting on either side of* JEETU.

JAYA: Jeetu—Jeetu speak to me—(*She tries to put her arm over his back.*)

JEETU: (*Throwing her arm off violently, not lifting up his head.*) Don't touch me!

OM: What does he care what happens to us? He's only thinking of himself—

5

JAYA: Jeetu, you've already paid the price—now why not live with the reward?

JEETU: (*He is silent for a beat. Then he lifts his head. In the place of his eyes are enormous goggles, created to look like a pair of imitation eyes. They fit flush with his skin, without ear pieces and cannot be removed. His voice is a hoarse whisper.*) This . . . is my *reward*?

10

JAYA: Jeetu—Jeetu—if you would only listen a moment—

JEETU: No! (*He gets to his feet.*) I won't listen! Because listening brings acceptance. (*He moves, but warily. He never bumps into anything but he "looks" around himself like a first-time visitor from Mars.*) And I will never accept. I will never live with this—this—

15

OM: Selfish, that's what he is—

20

JAYA: No, Jeetu, no!

JEETU: I don't need your permission to step off the bus! I make my own decisions—

OM: —only thinks of himself. Look at me?

JEETU: Yes, my brother! Look at you? Look at you with these eyes that were meant for you? (*Makes a croaking, sobbing sound, hitting his eyes with his hands.*) These eyes—these blind eyes, this sightless sight—

25

JAYA: But Jeetu—if they think you're Om, then we need you! Without you, they won't maintain us—

30

JEETU: I don't care! I'm not the one who got this job—and I'm not going to be the one to suffer the consequences—

OM: He was always selfish. Always lived just for himself—

JAYA: Jeetu—just wait till we can ask Ginni—she'll listen at least, maybe even help—

35

JEETU: Ginni, huh!—Ginni only helps herself—

JAYA: No, Jeetu—(*But she herself sounds uncertain.*) That's not true . . .

JEETU: You show me a rich woman who plucks a poor man's eyes out of his body and I'll show you a she-demon!

40

JAYA: But Jeetu, without you . . .

OM: Just wait till Ginni finds out whose eyes are in her head! Just wait!

JAYA: (*To* OM.) Why tell her? If she goes on thinking Jeetu is you then maybe—

45

OM: Fat chance! It's the guards who made the mistake! The moment she sees me here she'll know what happened—and she'll be mad! She'll be furious! She'll probably have the guards court-martialled—

JAYA: You heard what they said—the transplant was a success. So maybe . . . maybe it *is* all right? Maybe Jeetu's eyes are good enough?

50

OM: It's not so easy as you think—remember all those injections I had in the beginning? They were to prepare my

55 body, to change it so that it could match Ginni's body perfectly. But now they've taken the wrong pair of eyes—who knows what it'll do to Ginni? And what about Jeetu's infections, all the poisons and germs he's had circulating inside him—what about them? Ginni's scared about 60 catching your cold! What'll she catch from Jeetu?

JAYA: But they *said*—

OM: It takes time to know that a transplant has been a success!

JAYA: How long—

65 OM: I don't know. I'm not a doctor. Not less than a week, I think—

JEETU: Good. I'll be dead long before then—

JAYA: Jeetu—I'm not going to let you die! I don't care what she says—I'm not going to lose you again—

70 JEETU: You don't know what you're asking of me. You don't know what it's like to walk around with a nightmare wrapped around your head—

JAYA: Jeetu—

OM: (*To* JAYA.) Why waste your breath? Neither will he listen, 75 nor will it make the slightest difference to the outcome. What will be, will be, regardless of what we try to do about it—

JAYA: But *why*—when it doesn't *have* to be! Why—when all he has to do is to pretend—just for a couple of hours in a 80 day—

JEETU: Why? (*Pause.*) Because I am in place beyond death. I am in a place worse than death.

JAYA: There's no place worse than death—

JEETU: Yet I know such a place, now. (*Painfully.*) A bleached 85 and pitted place. Scars and slashes, no stillness, no dimensions. No here, no there—(*He moves his head about, "looking" at his visions.*) I see in molten bars and blinding shapes, I see symmetries and confused fragments—sparks, shadows, water on mad glass, heat dreams, trains flying on fever 90 tracks—

JAYA: But can you see me, Jeetu?

JEETU: (*Looking there.*) Yes. I see you. And through you. (*Looks around.*) And through the floor. And through all the gadgets, pulsing with electric gold, liquid atoms sizzling down 95 infinite mineshafts . . . (*He turns his gaze.*) my brother standing there, a blaze of fried nerves and straining bones, his eyes like ping-pong balls jittering in their orbits. (*Turns.*) And I can see Ma—a dim bundle of red desires bathed in a blue haze of radiation. (*Turns.*) And I can see 100 you, Jaya, my Jaya . . . I can see your purple blood, I can see your thoughts sparkling like stars through the pearly cloud of your brain, I can see your heart twitching like an epileptic kitten—yes, I can see all these things, but who would want to see them? Who can bear to see them? (*He 105 sits down, on his haunches.*) And yet . . . I can't even turn them off. I can't shut these freakish eyes of mine. I can't turn my head away, I can't end this poison-vision. I can't sleep, I can't dream, I can't even cry. (*He looks at her.*) This is what you want from me?

(*There is a silence.*)

110 JEETU: Well? You're not saying anything.

JAYA: I—(*She holds her forehead.*)

JEETU: Is it selfish to want to end this?

OM: I was willing to accept anything for my family—

JEETU: Oh yes!—And what happened when the guards came?

OM: (*Mustering what dignity he can.*) That was different. It was 115 the shock, the lack of warning—

JEETU: It was cowardice!

JAYA: (*Carefully.*) Jeetu—we've not asked anything of you so far—

JEETU: This is no time to start! 120

JAYA: Maybe you'll get used to it in time—maybe they'll be able to improve it—

JEETU: (*He clutches his head.*) Let me die before I'm too maddened by visions to make the effort!

OM: Just wait, just wait—when Ginni comes, she'll make all 125 the effort for all of us!

JAYA: Don't be so cocksure! You think she'll take your side?

OM: Of course she will. And she'll throw the two of you out, I wouldn't be surprised! For fooling her. For fooling around. For being dirty, filthy fornicators— 130

JAYA: We haven't! Not . . . not since you got the job—

OM: Ah but he hasn't been here has he! Now that he's back it'll start again, won't it? Don't think I don't know how it is with people like you! You'd do it right in front of me if you got half a chance— 135

(*The warning tone sounds.*)

JAYA: Oh my God—

OM: (*Looking relieved.*) Ah! Just let me do the talking—I'll explain everything—

JEETU: (*His whole body jerks.*) Ah! What's that? I—I—I *saw* something— 140

(*The second tone sounds.*)

JAYA: What's the matter Jeetu?

OM: You shut up, both of you! I'll explain it—and don't worry, I won't leave you two out of the picture. But if she asks me, I'll tell her—

JEETU: (*Breathlessly.*) Something's . . . happening. The blackness 145 is lifting . . . I can see . . . some sort, some sort of . . . pattern—

(*The third tone sounds.*)

GINNI: Well—hellooo-oo! Guess whoo-ooo!

JEETU: Ahh! (*He falls silent, with his mouth open in wonder, breathing heavily.*) Ahhh . . .

OM: Hello! Howdy! Hi, Ginni— 150

GINNI: Hello-ooo? Is anybody home—(*The* CONTACT MODULE *swivels.*) Auwm? (*The* CONTACT MODULE *has swivelled around to find* JEETU, *who doesn't respond.*) Isn't that you, Auwm?

OM: (*Running around to get in front of the* CONTACT MODULE.) 155 No! No—*this* is me! I'm here! Here!

(*The* CONTACT MODULE *flips up and out of* OM's *reach.*)

GINNI: Come in, Auwm! Can you see me? Auwm?

JEETU: (*In a strange, strangled voice, not looking at the* CONTACT MODULE.) My God! My God—I can see!

GINNI: (*Sounding extremely cheerful.*) Sure you can see Auwm! 160 That's what we gave you eyes for! And I'm sure you're real glad to know that *I* can see better now! And with your eyes!

OM: (*Screaming.*) NO!! It's a mistake! There's been a terrible mistake!

(*But* JAYA *intercepts him.*)

165 JAYA: (*In a loud whisper.*) Wait—don't disturb them—
JEETU: (*Gesturing directly in front of him, in a wondering voice.*) And that . . . and you must be . . .
OM: (*He is almost in tears.*) She's wrong! She's wrong! (*But* JAYA *silences him by dragging him sharply aside.*) It's—
170 JAYA: (*Holds* OM *back.*) Shhhh—!
GINNI: —Ginni! That's right, Auwm—it's me you're seeing 'coz I'm beaming my video image straight into your mind! So you can see me right in front of you, all of me, for once, not just my face . . . (*In a seductive voice.*) well?
175 What do you think?

(*There is a silence in the room as* JEETU *moves slowly around, looking at something that no-one else in the room with him can see. What little of his face is visible shows wonder.*)

JEETU: It's—you're—beautiful. Like . . . magic.
GINNI: You like me, Auwm? You like what you see?
JEETU: (*Shakily.*) Yes. And—and the room! What is this place?
GINNI: Oh . . . it's just where I live, Auwm, it's one of the
180 rooms in my little house—
JEETU: (*Breathing out.*) It's a palace—
GINNI: I'm glad you like it Auwm—
JEETU: I can't help but like it! Who wouldn't? (*He points around him.*) That—that—(*He has no words.*) Those . . .
185 plants! That . . . light! What are those things there? It's . . . (*Hushed.*) beautiful. Beautiful. I've never seen anything like this. Never.
OM: (*In anguish.*) But it's mine, what he's seeing—MINE!
JAYA: (*Watching carefully.*) Can't you hush?
190 OM: (*In tears.*) It's all a mistake! She'll find out and then what'll happen? What'll happen to us?
JAYA: Shhh—
JEETU: (*Wonderingly.*) And you . . . is that really . . . you?
GINNI: Yup! It's me, Ginni! You look like you're seeing me for
195 the first time, Auwm!
JEETU: I—I am! I never realized this is what you looked like—I mean, when the others talked about you—
GINNI: Well—now. I'm glad you like me so well, 'coz you know what? Now that the transplants have started, it's
200 time that we talked about the next phase—
JEETU: (*Still dazed.*) "Next phase"?
OM: (*Shouting.*) But he's the wrong man!

(JAYA *holds* OM *back.*)

(JEETU *is facing the* CONTACT MODULE, *which now rises above him and glows white as the rest of the stage lights dim.* JEETU *is bathed in the light, sealed into the vision that is projected into him.*)

GINNI: The next phase of the transplants. You see, we have to progress rapidly now and I need all your support. Until we
205 reached this platform of contact, we couldn't be sure. But now that we're sure, we've got to move really fast. Are you with me?
JEETU: (*Uncertainly.*) Yes . . .

GINNI: Because you have to be willing, for what we want to do now. You have to be really willing, Auwm— 210
JEETU: Tell me, Ginni, tell me what you want—(*He moves towards the illusion he sees.*)
GINNI: Ah-ah—can't touch me Auwm! (*He reacts by jerking his hand away.*) Well . . . you'll have to go back to the clinic and they'll prepare you— 215
JEETU: (*He continues to behave as if he is standing very close to someone, following her around as she moves out of his reach.*) You need some more parts of me?
GINNI: Well, yes—I mean, that's one way of looking at it but I—I think you should understand that time is kind of 220 short, Auwm and we really have to get a move on—
JEETU: (*He moves his body seductively, winningly.*) Just tell me what you want of me Ginni—
GINNI: The guards will come for you and they'll request you to follow them away— 225
JEETU: Anything, Ginni, anything—
GINNI: The sooner you can go the better it'll be for you—
JEETU: Whatever you say, Ginni—
GINNI: I mean, really, Auwm, if it's okay with you, I can tell the guards to come for you right now— 230
JAYA: No . . . (*But she says it softly, shaking her head, knowing that it's futile.*)
JEETU: That's fine with me, Ginni—
OM: (*Hoarsely.*) Ask her what she wants from you!
JEETU: Anything you want is fine, Ginni— 235
GINNI: Okay, Auwm, I'm turning this video session off for the moment and I'm going to ask you to wait for the guards—
JEETU: (*He holds his arms out forlornly.*) You're—you're going?
GINNI: But I'll be back, Auwm, closer than you'd ever believe . . . (*The* CONTACT MODULE *moves high, as its light starts to* 240 *dim.*)
JEETU: (*Stretching his arms up.*) Don't—don't—(*He drops his arms.*) Ahh—! (*Strikes his eyes.*) AHHHH!
GINNI: The guards will come, Auwm, you don't have long to wait—we'll talk again when you're in the clinic, okay? 245
JEETU: NO!! Don't leave me in this blindness—
GINNI: Remember to keep smiling Auwm—
JEETU: (*Brokenly.*) No!
GINNI: —byeeee!

(*The* CONTACT MODULE *snaps off.*)

JEETU: (*Softly.*) Ah—no! She's gone—she's gone! 250

(JAYA *and* OM *come forward around him.*)

JAYA: Jeetu—Jeetu—do you know what you've said?
JEETU: All I know is that I'm going to her—I'm going—
OM: You didn't even find out what they're going to take from you this time—
JEETU: You don't understand! I was blind! And now I have the 255 chance to see again—
JAYA: But . . . it's not *real*, what you see—I—I mean, we could watch you moving like a madman, waving your arms about, pointing to things that weren't there—

(OM, *having listened so far, begins to move away, towards the door.*)

JEETU: Ah—but they're *somewhere*, aren't they? And that's all 260 that matters to me.

JAYA: Yes—but—(*She looks dissatisfied and worried.*) she's taken your *eyes*—

JEETU: —and left me something even better! I can't tell you
265   what things I saw—

JAYA: Really? So much?

JEETU: (*Reverentially.*) Yes—oh, yes! (*Then he pauses.*) Of course, I can't see what's directly around me. But maybe they'll find a way to change that—

270 JAYA: You should have asked her—

JEETU: I'd not seen her, you see, till just now! I thought she was an old woman! You never told me she was so—so *young!* (*Hushed.*) And beautiful. (*Accusingly.*) Why didn't you tell me, Jaya?

275 JAYA: (*Shrugs.*) You didn't seem interested—we hardly discussed Ginni at all—

JEETU: Well. It would have made all the difference if I had known. I saw all of her, you know! Standing there (*He draws her with his arms.*), all of her . . . wearing . . . almost
280   nothing! (*JAYA bites her lip, frowning.*) And she kept . . . (*He moves his body sensuously.*) moving, like this, like that . . . wah! I could have had her, right there and then!

JAYA: (*Bitterly.*) But she wasn't real!

JEETU: She exists. That's enough for me. She's a goddess and
285   she exists. I would do anything for her—anything!

JAYA: (*Looks depressed.*) Yes. I can see that—

JEETU: (*A touch of guilt.*) Don't hold it against me, Jaya—think of her as just another client—you were always good at that—

290 JAYA: Yes . . . but your other clients wanted only your services. Not your . . . body itself!

JEETU: You should be happy for me—and anyway, you've got your wish, now. I'll stay alive, and they'll go on looking after all of us—

(*There is a knocking at the door.*)

295 GUARD 1: (*From outside.*) InterPlanta Services!—

(*But before he can say "open up", OM has thrown the door open.*)

OM: Yes! Take me! Take me! I'm ready to go—

(*Several things happen at once. JEETU and JAYA turn towards the door, as GUARD 1 and GUARD 2 roughly shove OM aside, entering the room.*)

JEETU: Yes—

GUARD 1: Mr Om Prakash—we have been intimated of your willingness to participate in the second phase of our trans-
300   plant service!

OM: (*Screaming.*) No! Not him—take ME!! I'm Om Prakash! Check your records—

(*GUARD 3 entering behind the other two, quickly grabs OM and holds him pinned to the wall, struggling.*)

JEETU: Yes—I am Om Prakash—

OM: (*From his pinned position, bellowing.*) NOOO!!! He's lying!
305   A lying, scheming swine!!! He's my brother, I tell you—my younger brother—

GUARD 1: All right sir, if you would just follow us—we're ready to leave—

JEETU: Let's go—

(*GUARD 1 stands aside and JEETU moves towards the door.*)

JAYA: (*Darting forward.*) Jeetu—   310

JEETU: (*Swivelling sharply.*) Don't call me that—

JAYA: (*She is suddenly in tears.*) Don't go—just yet! Please! It's too soon, they've not explained anything—I—we—you'll never be the same again—

JEETU: (*He grabs her quickly, gives her a brief hug and pushes her 315 away, into the waiting grasp of GUARD 2.*) You have your husband to look after—he needs you more than I—(*He turns and exits.*)

JAYA: (*Losing all restraint.*) Jeetu! JEETU!!! (*GUARD 2 lets go of her and exits.*) What happened to your ideals, your free- 320 doms! Your pride! (*She sinks to her knees.*) All gone! So easily gone—

(*GUARD 3 has a brief struggle disengaging himself from OM, but he too slips out, slamming the door behind him—then bolting it from the outside.*)

OM: (*Hollering.*) AHHHHHHHHHH! You've locked us in, you bastards! You've locked us in! (*He roars and pounds on the door.*) You can't do this to us! We've not signed any 325 consent forms! You've not taken any permissions! AHH-HHHHHHH! You've locked us in here! AAAAAHHH-HHHH! And you've taken the wrong man—you'll regret it—you'll suffer for it—AAAAAAHHHHHHHH!—

(*He subsides onto the floor, moaning. JAYA looks at the door, too shocked and defeated even to cry. She turns and walks slowly till she is near her place at the dining area. She sits, seeming distracted. Looks across at MA, who is totally absorbed by the TV programme she's watching.*)

JAYA: Ma? Ma—(*Goes across to stage right, where MA sits.*) listen 330 to me—(*But MA can't hear her. She shakes MA by the shoulder.*) Ma! Listen to me!

MA: (*Irritated, holding one of her ear phones up from her ear.*) What is it!

JAYA: Ma—do you realize they've taken Jeetu?   335

MA: What?

JAYA: (*In a raised voice.*) Jeetu—they've taken him away!

MA: (*Indifferently.*) So? (*Starts to replace the ear-piece.*) He was never here to begin with—

JAYA: No! You *can't* be so indifferent—   340

MA: (*Shaking off her hand.*) Tch! Let me be! Why should I care what happens to Jeetu? I'm through caring about any-body—(*She replaces the ear-piece and turns back to her set.*)

JAYA: (*For a second she is nonplussed. Then she loses control.*) That's—too much! (*MA can't hear her.*) You hear me, Ma? 345 (*She screams.*) It's just TOO MUCH! (*She darts forward and snatches the TV remote from MA's hand—.*) You can't do this—(*Smashes it on the floor, the TV abruptly goes off, as MA's reaction sets in.*) you've got be involved with what's going on around you—   350

MA: (*Removing headphones and getting up as fast as her old limbs will let her.*) You—GIVE THAT BACK TO ME—

(*They do not notice that OM is sitting up alertly, by the door. He is listening to something.*)

JAYA: (*Stamping on the remote.*) I won't—I won't—

MA: (*She has got up and is flailing at* JAYA *with her thin arms.*)
355   Pig-faced buffalo! Give it back or I'll—I'll shit in the wa-
ter-supply!

JAYA: You wouldn't dare—(*She has not managed to break the remote yet.*)

MA: (*She has enough force to push* JAYA *off her balance.*) I'll mi-
360   crowave your entrails!—(*Pushes* JAYA *down.*) Ah! (*Snatches
up the remote.*)

JAYA: (*Tackling* MA *from the ground, hanging onto her from behind
and trying to claw the remote out of her hands. She is panting
with the effort.*) I'm sick of being the only one to make de-
365   cisions around here! There's nothing wrong with you—
you're not sick—or busy—

(*All the while* OM *has been listening, like a dog for its master, by the
door. Now the sounds that he has been listening for are audible: boots
in the corridor. He readies himself by flattening himself alongside the
door as the footsteps come to a halt. A pause and the bolt is opened
from outside.*)

MA: Let me go, you barren dog—mmmh! Mmmmh! (*She
pulls her arm up so that she can gnaw at* JAYA*'s hand where it's
clamped to her wrist.*) LET ME GO!

(*At this moment the door is flung open.* JAYA *and* MA *fall apart and
turn to the door just as* OM *wriggles out almost the same instant.*
AGENT I *enters, paying no attention to* OM.)

370   AGENT I: Madam Indumati? Who is Madam Indumati?

MA: Me! I'm Madam Indumati! (*She starts to move towards the
door.*)

JAYA: (*Craning her neck.*)—Om! Om—where are you?

AGENT I: (*Salutes, announcing loudly.*) VideoCouch Enterprises,
375   Ma'm—please—(*He stands aside to open the door a little
wider and leans out in anticipation. Sounds of something being
wheeled along.*)

JAYA: (*Flabbergasted.*) Wh-what is this? Who're you!

MA: (*To the* AGENT.) Have you brought it?

380   AGENT I: Yes, Ma'm—

(AGENT II *and* AGENT III *wheel in a long gleaming case. It is reminiscent of Tutankhamen's sarcophagus, encrusted with electronic dials
and circuitry in the place of jewels. The* AGENTS *wheel it into the
centre of the room, move the dining platform aside and install the device in its place.*)

AGENT I: (*Coming forward to where* MA *stands.*) Please, Ma'm,
sign here—

JAYA: (*To* MA.) Ma—who are these people—what's going on—

MA: (*Ignoring* JAYA.) What about this insti—instig—?

385   AGENT I: Installation. (*Patiently.*) Just sign this form, Ma'm, to
confirm receipt of the unit—

MA: (*Taking the form and the pen.*) How do I know you won't
just run away after I've signed this, eh?

AGENT I: (*Shrugs.*) As you wish, Ma'm—(*To the other two*
390   AGENTS, *expressionlessly.*) Proceed with installation.

(*The other two* AGENTS *open the case, revealing an equally ornate
interior, filled with tubes, switches, circuitry. Inside are a number of
containers.* AGENTS II *and* III *set about attaching the containers to
various parts of the case while* AGENT I *explains to* MA.)

AGENT I: This is the SuperDeluxe VideoCouch model XL
5000! We are certain it will provide you, our valued customer, with every satisfaction! This is the nourishment
panel—the hydration filter—the pangrometer! Here you
see the Lexus Phantasticon which is programmed to receive   395
seven hundred and fifty video channels from all over the—

JAYA: (*Shaking him.*) Stop this at once! Explain to me what's
going on!

AGENT I: (*Stops, baffled.*) Ma'm—

MA: (*To* JAYA.) Can't you shut up? It's my VideoCouch! It's   400
what I ordered the other day!

JAYA: But—

AGENT I: Ma'm—

MA: (*To the* AGENT.) Proceed!

AGENT I: (*He is off-stride.*) Uhh—This is the SuperDeluxe   405
VideoCouch model XL 5000! We are certain it will provide you, our valued customer, with every satisfaction!
This is the nourishment panel—the hydration filter—the
pangrometer! Here you see the Lexus Phantasticon which
is programmed to receive seven hundred and fifty video   410
channels from all over the world! There are ten modes,
seventeen frequencies, three sub-strate couplers, extra-
sensory feedback impulses and cross-net capturing faci-
tilies! All media access—satellite, bio-tenna, visitelly and
radiogonad. Manual control panel, neuro-stimulator and   415
full-body processing capacities—all other queries will be
answered on-line from within the VideoCouch self-
training program. (*He ends abruptly.*) Any questions, Ma'm?

MA: (*She has heard very little of this.*) Hanh?

AGENT I: Ma'm—if you sign the delivery voucher we can   420
complete installation—

MA: But I haven't understood a word you've said—

JAYA: (*Standing between the VideoCouch and* MA.) Ma—You
MUST explain what this is about—

MA: (*To the* AGENT.) Stop her! She'll destroy it—she'll dam-   425
age it—

JAYA: (*Frustrated.*) Oh—! (*She moves away.*)

(*The* AGENT *moves to get closer to the VideoCouch.*)

JAYA: Just do it, do it! (*From stage right, watching the proceedings.*)
But make sure I'm not held responsible for anything—

MA: (*To the* AGENT.) If I sign this . . . no-one can take if from   430
me, can they?

AGENT I: No, Ma'm—

MA: And your people won't go till I've got into it? (*She signs
the voucher and hands it back, not glancing at the many pages of
forms.*)   435

AGENT I: No, Ma'm—thank you, Ma'm—If you'll just come
this way, Ma'm—

(*The other two* AGENTS *have attached a power-line to the unit and at
this moment activate the system. It twinkles with small LCDs. It looks
like a tiny space-module.* AGENT II *delinks the power connection and
the lights continue to twinkle. She detaches the cable from the couch.*)

COUCH: (*A fruity voice issues from the VideoCouch.*) Welcome to
Video Paradiso! You will not regret your choice! Please
ask our authorized representative to settle you into your   440
customized, contour-gel, fully automated video-chamber!
(*Appropriate music plays.*)

(*As the* COUCH *begins speaking,* MA *is helped into it by the* AGENTS. *She lies down and the* AGENTS *huddle around her, connecting her up to various pouches and tubes. They do this very quickly and she gasps and grunts once or twice. There is a breathing mask on her face. Soon they are ready to close the lid.*)

COUCH: Thank you for being cooperative! Your fully automatic Video Paradiso unit is now ready for operation! Just
445   relax and let your guide show you the way to an experience of ultimate bliss—

(*The* AGENTS *gently shut the lid. There is a faint hiss, a thin vapour escapes as the two edges nest one within the other—and it is closed. The* AGENTS *secure the edges, seal them and lock them. They work extremely fast. The muted sound of the* COUCH *voice continues but becomes a constant unintelligible background hum.*)

JAYA: (*She has been craning her neck to get a view of the proceedings.*) But—how will she breathe!
AGENT I: (*Turning to her, as the other two* AGENTS *collapse the un-*
450   *dercarriage and lower the unit to floor level. They replace the dining platform over the* COUCH. *It is efficiently concealed, aside from occasional blinks of light.*) Ma'm—it's a total-comfort unit Ma'm—
JAYA: Won't she have to—to—
455 AGENT I: We have a full-recycling and bio-feed-in processor! Your relative will have no further need of the outside world from now till—(*He coughs delicately.*) till she chooses to delink.
JAYA: Does she—how will she—
460 AGENT I: (*Smoothly.*) Everything is now in the customer's operation, Ma'm—the unit is fully self-sufficient—
JAYA: Won't I have to . . . switch it on or off? No . . . food? Water?
AGENT I: Total self-sufficiency, Ma'm! There is nothing to be
465   done!

(*The other two* AGENTS *are ready to leave.*)

AGENT I: Ma'm—installation is complete—
JAYA: No—wait—who's paying for this thing—
AGENT I: (*Impatient to leave, walking towards the door.*) Debited from the customer's InterPlanta account Ma'm—(*As an*
470   *afterthought he brings out his card.*) but in case you have any queries Ma'm, please get in touch with our local representative—

(*He hands her the card, salutes smartly but unseen, as she stares at the card. The* AGENT *turns on his heel and has left the room before she registers that he's gone.*)

JAYA: (*Startled by the sound of the door shutting.*) No—you've not explained anything—(*Runs to the door.*) what happens
475   if there's a malfunction—(*Opens the door, leans out, steps out. After a moment, comes back in, looking bewildered.*) Alone! I can't believe it—they've left me alone! Every one!

(*From the* COUCH *a friendly mumble trills out.*)

JAYA: (*Leans, exhausted, against the door.*) But not at peace.

(*Lights start to fade.*)

JAYA: (*Slides to the floor.*) Not yet at peace.

(*Lights out.*)

SCENE II

Five days later. The room is unchanged. It is night. JAYA *has fallen asleep at the table-cum-sarcophagus. There are occasional hums of sound from the VideoCouch underneath.*

She is looking worn out, unslept. With jarring suddenness the warning tone sounds. JAYA *startles awake.*

The CONTACT MODULE *is ablaze. It no longer has any face on its facets. It hovers over* JAYA.

VOICE: (*A rich, gravelly male voice.*) Zhaya . . .
JAYA: (*She is badly shocked, recoils away from the* CONTACT MODULE, *her hand to her mouth.*) Ahhh!
VOICE: Don't be frightened, Zhaya—
JAYA: (*Crawling backwards towards stage right.*) No—please—   5
VOICE: (*The* CONTACT MODULE *follows her.*) There's nothing to be afraid of, Zhaya—
JAYA: Who are you! What d'you want—
VOICE: Calm down, honey, be easy—shh, shhh—
JAYA: (*More frightened than ever, wriggling along the floor, away*   10
     from the light which follows her nevertheless.) Who told you my name—how did you—
VOICE: Easy, girl, easy—don't keep moving, it's no use—

(JAYA *continues to back away.*)

JAYA: (*Almost screaming.*) NO! . . . please! Leave me alone— I've done nothing—nothing!   15
VOICE: Zhaya—I can't harm you, honey—
JAYA: (*She is backed up against the wall stage right and can go no further.*) Please—please—(*She shields her eyes from the glare.*)
VOICE: Zhaya —Zhaya—just listen to me—
JAYA: (*Straining away from the light.*) Go away! Leave me alone!   20
VOICE: Zhaya—
JAYA: (*The accumulated tension, despair and solitude combine forces to break her. She subsides on her side in heaving sobs.*) Leave me . . . just leave me . . . please, please . . . just leave me!
VOICE: (*Abruptly the* CONTACT MODULE *moves up and away*   25
     from her.) All right, Zhaya—if that's what you really want—

(*The* CONTACT MODULE *moves a comfortable distance away from her. It dims down till it looks like a Japanese paper-lantern. The rest of the stage is in darkness. Slowly, cautiously,* JAYA *raises her head, looks around herself, warily. There is a pregnant silence.*)

JAYA: Have you—gone?
VOICE: No.
JAYA: (*She is startled but waits. There's no further communication.*)   30
     Hullo?
VOICE: I'm here, Zhaya, if you're ready to speak to me—
JAYA: (*Warily.*) Who are you?
VOICE: Let's just say . . . I'm a friend.
JAYA: But I don't know you!   35
VOICE: Still—I'm a friend.

JAYA: How can you be—if we've never met?

VOICE: I've seen you. Heard your voice—

JAYA: How?

40 VOICE: Oh . . . we have our ways—

JAYA: (*Pause.*) You mean, you're a friend of Ginni's?

VOICE: A friend? Yeah. Sort of.

JAYA: You live where she lives?

VOICE: Sort of, yeah.

45 JAYA: How is she? Is she well?

VOICE: Oh—! (*Nonchalantly.*) Fine, she's fine—

JAYA: (*Gusts a laugh that sounds like tears.*)

VOICE: What's the matter?

JAYA: (*Parodying his tone.*) "Fine"! "Fine"!—

50 VOICE: I don't understand—

JAYA: —Ginni might be "fine, fine"—but what has happened to my life?—She's taken Om, she's taken Jeetu! And where is she? Now that she's "fine, fine"?

VOICE: Well, I was just getting around to that—

55 JAYA: (*Whispers.*) It's madness. Talking to a lighted ball. Sending eyes across the ocean—(*Indicates the sarcophagus.*) locking Ma into a trunk—it's all madness!

VOICE: Why don't I tell you my name?

JAYA: (*She shakes her head.*) It's not *natural,* any of it—

60 VOICE: Virgil. That's my name, Zhaya—

JAYA: I don't know you, I don't even know if you really exist, but here we are, talking! Pretending we're friends—

VIRGIL: Not pretending—

JAYA: I was pretending—with Ginni, I mean. Om said he
65 liked her, but what did he know about her, really? What did any of us know? We saw only her face. When she chose to show it to us. That's not a friend! That's not even a human being!

VIRGIL: I can show you myself, Zhaya—

70 JAYA: I don't want to see you. I don't want to start thinking of you as a real person, when all the time you're just a voice in the air—

VIRGIL: Not just my face. All of me—

JAYA: (*She looks up suspiciously.*) You'll come *here?* In *person?*

75 VIRGIL: Sort of. A version of me—

JAYA: (*Shakes her head resolutely.*) No! I'm not interested in *versions.* I'm not like Jeetu—

VIRGIL: Tell you what. I'll show you what I look like. Then you decide—

80 JAYA: No! I'll never pluck my eyes out or get into a box—

VIRGIL: Nothing like that. You'll see me here, with your own eyes—

JAYA: How? (*Sarcastically.*) You'll send a statue with the guards?

85 VIRGIL: Just come to the Module—no, wait. I'll move to you.

(*The* CONTACT MODULE *moves till it's within her reach. She flinches back.*)

JAYA: This? You'll come from this?

VIRGIL: Don't worry! It can't harm you—

JAYA: (*Warily.*) No, but—

VIRGIL: It's very simple. Just do as I say. Reach under the
90 Module—that's right, hold the Module, it's not hot— reach under it and push the, the uh lower panel, the flat one right underneath—okay, gently push it—push it up— you'll hear a click—

JAYA *follows these instructions, kneeling as she does so, touching the glowing globe gingerly, squinting against the light. There is a click, and she releases the* MODULE. *Falls back.*)

VIRGIL: Ah—okay! Good girl!

JAYA: Now—?   95

VIRGIL: Now . . . just wait . . . (*The* MODULE *grows bright again and sinks to almost floor level.*) keep watching this space . . . underneath . . . keep watching . . .

(JAYA *complies. A bright light issues from under the* CONTACT MODULE. *Slowly it rises, creating a projection with the motion of its ascent. A figure is revealed. A young man's bare legs, well-formed . . . his shorts, bright and brassy . . . a bare torso—*JAYA *gasps. . . .*)

JAYA: . . . Jeetu!

(JEETU *stands there, smiling, his face no longer obscured by the goggles. He looks happy and healthy, but his expression is unfamiliar. He looks like someone else. He seems to glow very slightly.*)

VIRGIL: (*The voice comes from the* CONTACT MODULE *though* 100
JEETU's *mouth moves.*) Well? What d'you say now?

JAYA: (*She wants to move forward.*) Jeetu . . . (*Her hand moves to her mouth.*) Is it—you?

VIRGIL: Of course it's me, Zhaya!

JAYA: But . . . you're not—where's the (*She means the gog-* 105
gles.)—you can't be—no! It can't be—it *can't* be! (*To* CONTACT MODULE.) What have you done! It can't be him!

VOICE: (*Distressed.*) Oh! You're not happy? Don't you like the way I look?

JAYA: What is this! What is this thing in front of me! What 110
have you done with—JEETU! (*She screams.*) JEETUUU-
UUU! What have they done to you! Where have you gone!!

(*The figure walks forward.*)

VIRGIL: This *is* me, Zhaya—don't you recognize me? I'm
your Jittoo now—   115

JAYA: Oh! (*Doubles over, sinks to the ground, sobbing heartily.*) What have you done, what have you done!

VIRGIL: (*The figure walks over to where* JAYA *kneels, kneels down himself.*) I thought you'd be happy to see me!

JAYA: (*Refuses to look at him.*) How can I be happy with a 120
ghost!

VIRGIL: I'm not a ghost—

JAYA: You *can't* be who you look like!

VIRGIL: But I am—in one sense.

JAYA: (*She looks up.*) You can't be. It's all just another mad- 125
ness—

VIRGIL: Why, Zhaya? Trust your eyes—

JAYA: But *you're* not here! And *he's* . . . dead, isn't he? The one to whom this . . . this . . . *body* belonged?

VIRGIL: (*Gazes meaningfully but with an entirely non-*JEETU *ex-* 130
pression on his face.) Depends. On how you define death.

JAYA: There's only one way to define death!

VIRGIL: (*Softly.*) Not where I live. (*Pause.*) We have some new definitions. (*Pause.*) We speak of a body-death and a self-
death. (*Pause.*) The body you knew is . . . still alive. (*Waits.*) 135
Come! Doesn't that count for anything?

JAYA: (*Whispers.*) And . . . the self?

VIRGIL: (*Briskly.*) The self you knew is also alive.

JAYA: Huh—! Without his body?

140 VIRGIL: He was willing to sell, I was willing to buy—

JAYA: And you paid him in—(*She stops, realizing her mistake.*) But . . . it *wasn't* you! It was . . . Ginni! (*Staring at him.*) Ginni?

VIRGIL: What do *you* think, Zhaya?

145 JAYA: Ginni . . . Ginni . . . wasn't *real?*

VIRGIL: Ginni was . . . me.

JAYA: You?

VIRGIL: Me. Just a minute—(*A faint buzz, then the voice that issues is in* GINNI's *cloying tones.*) Hello, Zhaya! Recognize me

150 now? *This is what I sound like when my voice is a few decibels higher—*

JAYA: (*She leaps to her feet.*) But then . . . but then Jeetu was paid in phantoms!

VIRGIL: (*Standing as well.*) He sees what he wants to see. He

155 lives what he wants to live.

JAYA: And he has no body!

VIRGIL: He has a—casing.

JAYA: —but no body!

VIRGIL: He is happy, Zhaya. He made his choice—

160 JAYA: (*Shouting.*) I saw his choosing! With his mind bandaged in dreams!

VIRGIL: Was it any different than his life? Any worse? When he was lying on the streets—was that better?

JAYA: When he was lying in the streets at least he knew what

165 he was! He was—he was—(*She stops.*) But you don't know this—

VIRGIL: I do.

JAYA: You can't! We never told Ginni!

VIRGIL: But I know.

170 JAYA: *He . . .* told you?

VIRGIL: *You* told me—

JAYA: I? (*Frowns.*) Never!

VIRGIL: Always. I listened in to you, Zhaya. I heard every word said in the room—even when the Module was off,

175 it recorded—

JAYA: (*She is shocked.*) HHhhh! (*Starts to pace about in agitation.*)

VIRGIL: I know Jittoo's not Auwm and that Auwm's your husband.

JAYA: And about—about Jeetu being—

180 VIRGIL: Diseased. Yes—but he was more available than his brother. So we took him.

JAYA: And it doesn't matter! It makes no difference!

VIRGIL: Do I look unwell? Do I look disabled? (*Smiles ironically.*) There's no scalpel as keen as youth! His body healed

185 in hours.

JAYA: And you heard . . . every, every thing?

VIRGIL: Saw, too. I know about the toilet being loaned out to half the city! About the water being sold! About the food being shared! Every sneeze, every belch. And you

190 Zhaya—I knew when you bled and when you passed wind. I even saw you . . . pleasure yourself, Zhaya, lying there, alone. I even knew that.

JAYA: (*Humiliated.*) No! You must have slept—

VIRGIL: —and played it back when I awoke!

195 JAYA: And Ginni! Who is Ginni?

VIRGIL: Nothing. Nobody. A computer-animated wet-dream.

JAYA: What?

VIRGIL: There's a joke we have, back at the agency—well, it's not a great joke— 200

JAYA: What joke—

VIRGIL: "For every fish, a dish—"

JAYA: (*Shaking her head in despair.*) That's all we are to you—a game to play with—

VIRGIL: No, no—I just meant Ginni was something we 205 needed to bait the hook—

JAYA: Hook! Fish!

VIRGIL: You misunderstand—

JAYA: You would eat us if you could—(*Painful pause.*) Maybe you . . . do? 210

VIRGIL: Do I look like someone who would eat another human being?

JAYA: You look like Jeetu but . . . you're not him. (*Slowly.*) So I don't know what you look like. I don't know what you are. 215

VIRGIL: This is what I look like, now.

JAYA: How can I believe you?

VIRGIL: Zhaya, *you've* lied to me—but *I've* told you only the truth.

JAYA: No!—they said you'd be old! And sick! 220

VIRGIL: I am old and I was sick until I got into this young body—

JAYA: They said you were a man—

VIRGIL: And I am! Always have been—

JAYA: But then you *looked* like a woman! You *spoke* like a 225 woman—

VIRGIL: Without being one. Without ever saying I was one—

JAYA: You said you wanted Om!

VIRGIL: No, I didn't ask for Auwm. He came to us.

JAYA: You said you wanted a healthy body— 230

VIRGIL: Yes, Zhaya—yours!

JAYA: (*Stops dead.*) *Mine!* But it was *Om* who got the job . . .

VIRGIL: He's part of the job, but not the job itself. (*Pause.*) We're interested in women where I live, Zhaya. Child-bearing women. 235

JAYA: But . . .

VIRGIL: So we look for young couples, without children—

JAYA: . . . Om said he wasn't married!

VIRGIL: His polygraph showed he lied. All donors lie. They think we need singles. We let them think that. That way 240 only the very desperate apply. That suits us. We search for skin and blood matches. Auwm matched mine.

JAYA: Yet you've taken *Jeetu's* body!

VIRGIL: Jittoo is Auwm's brother. He was an even better match— 245

JAYA: —and now you say that all the while you've wanted me! (*Shakes her head.*) What can I believe? You sew a crooked seam and call it straight!

(*There is a silence while he looks at her.*)

VIRGIL: But this seam now is true. We look for young men's bodies to live in and young women's bodies in which to 250 sow their children—

JAYA: Why? Don't you have your own?

VIRGIL: We . . . lost the art of having children.

JAYA: How can that be?

VIRGIL: We began to live longer and longer. And healthier 255 each generation. And more demanding—soon there was

competition between one generation and the next—old against young, parent against child. (*Shrugs.*) We older ones had the advantage of experience. We prevailed. But our
260 victory was bitter. We secured Paradise—at the cost of birds and flowers, bees and snakes! We were determined to make our amends. So we designed this programme. In exchange for the life support we offer poorer sections of the world, we gain fresh bodies for ourselves.
265 JAYA: (*Incredulous.*) And it works? You live forever?
VIRGIL: Not all of us—every year there are fewer of us. We fixed the car, but not the driver! Time comes when the driver just wanders off and (*Shrugs.*) . . . merges with the statistics. I'm one of the stubborn ones! This is my fourth
270 body in fifty years.
JAYA: Fourth!
VIRGIL: Two were not successful. My first wife ran away. The third one kept her child. I saw him but never held him. Still . . . I'm willing to keep trying.
275 JAYA: (*She stares at him.*) I have never been with child.
VIRGIL: I know I can fill your belly.

(*There is a silence.*)

JAYA: (*Drops her gaze. Hushed.*) No . . .
VIRGIL: You have longed for a child. Your arms cry out for that sweet burden. To hold it in your arms, cud-
280 dle and crush it with kisses —it is your destiny as a woman—
JAYA: (*Tormented.*) NO! (*Wrings her hands.*) It was never meant to be! Years ago a seer told me—my stars denied it—
VIRGIL: Yet I sanction it, now, I. With Jittoo's body—
285 JAYA: (*In panic.*) No! Jeetu's dead and you're—you're a stranger's phantom—
VIRGIL: I am real and warm and willing. (*Pats himself.*) This body is hot with life and heavy with desire! This body aches for you and to give you what you yearn for—
290 JAYA: (*Covers her head against his words but pleased in spite of herself.*) No! A married woman must not hear such words from a stranger's mouth—
VIRGIL: But this mouth is no stranger to you, Zhaya!
JAYA: (*Whispering.*) No, no!
295 VIRGIL: This voice is but the latest tenant in a house that you have known—
JAYA: No—no—
VIRGIL: You deny the truth that is humming in my newly commissioned veins—
300 JAYA: Please—ohh . . . it's sinful—sinful!
VIRGIL: (*Bending to look in her face.*)—but . . . echoed in your pulse?
JAYA: (*Covering her face.*) It's madness you're offering me—madness!
305 VIRGIL: Is it madness to offer you your heart's desire?
JAYA: I had stopped hoping—I had ceased to dream—
VIRGIL: But you can start again. I am here to make it possible.
JAYA: But (*Her voice softens.*) whose child would it be . . . Jeetu's? Or . . . yours?
310 VIRGIL: (*Smiles.*) This is Jittoo's body!
JAYA: Yes—but—
VIRGIL: It would belong to this body—it would belong to Jittoo's body—

JAYA: But—would it be Jeetu's *child?* Would it look like him? Have his voice?
315
VIRGIL: No-one can say for certain which parent a child will take after—It could look like you, after all, have your voice.
JAYA: (*Looking perplexed she extends a hand wonderingly towards the apparition.*) Yes—but—(*Her hand passes through it and she recoils in horror.*)
320
VIRGIL: Ah-ah! Can't touch!
JAYA: Then—how . . . how—?

(*There is a knocking at the door.*)

GUARD 1: (*Indistinctly from the door.*) InterPlanta Services! Request permission to make contact!
325
JAYA: Ah!
VIRGIL: Don't—don't be frightened! It's just the agency. I can tell them to wait, if you want—(*He discreetly touches a small device at his waistband.*)
JAYA: Wait! Wait for what!
330
VIRGIL: For you to decide if you want to proceed—
JAYA: I don't understand! What are you saying—
VIRGIL: The guards will make the child possible Zhaya. It's just a formality; a device—
JAYA: What device?
335
VIRGIL: —an implant. Something I sent for you, which they're ready to deliver. But you can take your time. About two or three days are still within your fertile cycle—
JAYA: (*Shouting.*) What are you talking about! I told you—no more madness! Either you are here or—
340
VIRGIL: (*Patiently.*) Zhaya—I'd love to travel to be with you—
JAYA: Then do it! You who are so powerful—you who can travel from body to body—
345
VIRGIL: —but the risks of travelling across the world are too great! The world you live in is too dangerous for me, Zhaya—
JAYA: (*Outraged.*) Then you *are* a phantom after all! (*She raises her hands to strike the figure, then whirls towards the* CONTACT MODULE.) An illusion come to mock me—again! Again!
350

(*The* CONTACT MODULE *flicks easily out of her reach.*)

VIRGIL: I'll show you what to do, step by step. It's simple and it's painless—
JAYA: No! (*Leaping futilely at the globe, as the figure of* JEETU *watches tranquilly, at a distance.*) The pain tells me I'm alive! I want the pain!
355
VIRGIL: Then you can have all the pain you want, Zhaya—just as you want. It can take the usual nine months if you want, with diet and exercise and medical personnel to monitor you—
360
JAYA: (*She leaps at the globe, roaring in frustration.*) AR-RRHHH!
VIRGIL: —and I'll be with you, all the way—
JAYA: I believed you! I trusted you! (*In one of her leaps she jumps from a slight height and comes fractionally closer to the globe.*) But it was just one more of your crooked truths!
365
VIRGIL: Nothing I have said is untrue. I can set it up so that we can be together—go places—anywhere you want—right inside your room—

370 JAYA: I don't want your make-believe travels! I don't want your tricking comforts! (*She has stopped jumping and is looking around for something with which to strike the* CONTACT MODULE.)

VIRGIL: Zhaya we can even be . . . intimate, too! Really. But
375   I thought you'd like to get to know me first—

JAYA: (*She starts to throw things up at the globe. Glasses, cushions, slippers, bottles, pill-boxes, gadgets.*) I don't want to know a ghost! (*The* CONTACT MODULE *moves, so her task isn't easy.*) I want real hands touching me! I want to feel a real weight
380   upon me! Hear your breath in my ear—feel my hair being pulled, sweat running in my mouth—

VIRGIL: And it's all possible—

JAYA: (*Sharply.*) No! Not without risking your skin! (*Shouting.*) Never! Do you hear me, whoever you are, wherever
385   you are? Never! Never! NEVER! (*With this, she strikes a direct hit.*) There is no closeness without risk!

(*There is a shower of sparks and a crack of electric light. Then the* CONTACT MODULE *goes dim. For a few seconds the lights in the whole room flicker, purple and blue. Then they stabilize.* JAYA *stands panting in the centre of the stage.* JEETU's *figure has vanished.*)

JAYA: (*Looking up, towards the darkened globe.*) You! Can you hear me?

(*From the door, a knocking.*)

GUARD 1: (*Through the door.*) InterPlanta Services! Request
390   permission to gain entry!

JAYA: (*To the* CONTACT MODULE.) Can you you hear me, You? I've forgotten your name—but it doesn't matter! You never bothered to say mine correctly anyway!

GUARD 1: (*Knocking.*) I repeat! Request permission to enter!
395 JAYA: (*To the* CONTACT MODULE.) Look: I'm not stupid, you know? I know you're stronger than me, you're richer than me. You'll get me in the end—I know you will. But I want you to risk your skin for me. Even though it's really Jeetu's skin—I want you to risk it. For me.
400 GUARD 1: (*Hammering at the door.*) Madam! Madam! We have an urgent message for you from your Receiver!

JAYA: Either that or—

GUARD 1: (*Sounds of mechanical activity at the door.*)—attaching external speaker—(*There is a scraping sound, a crackle.*)
405 JAYA: (*She grabs up a piece of broken glass.*)—you won't have me at all! In any sense!

GUARD 1: Speaker installed. Begin transmission . . .

VIRGIL: (*His voice is strained and crackled, but loud and clear enough that he is once more a presence in the room.*) Zhaya—
410   listen to me—*you can't hope to win this one!*

JAYA: I've discovered a new definition for winning. Winning by losing. I win if you lose.

VIRGIL: Zhaya, this is craziness—

JAYA: I'm sorry, you-whose-name-I-have-forgot—
415 VIRGIL: Virgil—

JAYA: It's your fault. If you want to play games with people, you should be careful not to push them off the board. You pushed me too far. Now there's nothing left for me to lose—
420 VIRGIL: —but your life, Zhaya! You still have your life ahead of you!

JAYA: What do I care about my life? You've shown me that it's not really mine any more. It's yours. I'm not willing to caretake *my* body for *your* sake! The only thing I have left which is still mine is my death. My death and my pride— 425

VIRGIL: Zhaya—Zhaya—pride is nothing. Pride is a poor man's fancy dress—

JAYA: And if I let you take it from me, I will be naked as well as poor! Do you think I haven't understood you by now? You'll never let me have what you have, you're only will- 430 ing to share your electronic shadows with me, your night-visions, your "virtual" touch! No, no—if the only clothes I can afford are these rags of pride then let me have those! Unlike Om—unlike Ma—and Jeetu—

VIRGIL: Zhaya—don't make me tell the guards to force the 435 door—if you want respect, then open the door yourself

JAYA: You can't see me, can you? I'm holding a piece of glass against my throat. If you force the door, you will push this glass into my throat.

VIRGIL: Zhaya—the food you take contains anti-suicide drugs. 440 You are physically *incapable* of taking your own life—

JAYA: Test the strength of your drugs. Force that door.

VIRGIL: Zhaya—please! We've got this far—I love your spirit— I really do. In these months and weeks, I have come to ad-mire you and care for you. Don't let me down now! 445

JAYA: Then risk your skin.

VIRGIL: (*Pause.*) You're being unreasonable—

JAYA: Is it unreasonable to ask one who has cheated death, to cross the oceans?

VIRGIL: Zhaya— 450

JAYA: I'm bored of this argument! Don't you understand? This game is over! Either you have to erase me and start again or . . . you must accept a new set of rules.

VIRGIL: (*Sulkily.*) This is ridiculous! This is blackmail—

JAYA: What use do I have for words like "blackmail" when I 455 hold my death in the palm of my hands?

VIRGIL: You're not so stupid as to think you can win against me, Zhaya—

JAYA: Stupid or not, if I lose my life, I win this game.

VIRGIL: You won't be alive to savour that victory— 460

JAYA: —but I'll die knowing that you, who live only to win, will have lost to a poor, weak and helpless woman. And I'll get more pleasure out of that first moment of death than I've had in my entire life so far!

VIRGIL: Zhaya, this is childish— 465

JAYA: You still can't see me?

VIRGIL: (*Pause.*) No—but I can get a camera—

JAYA: No, don't. I'll tell you what I'm doing (*Matches her actions to her words.*). I'm collecting all the pills and medicines I can find. I'm going to take the ones for staying awake, 470 until I run out of them. If I don't hear the sound of your own hand on my door before that time, I'll take my life. If the guards cause me any discomfort whatsoever—I'll take my life. If you do anything at all other than come here in person—I'll take my life! 475

VIRGIL: Zhaya—

JAYA: And in the meantime, I want you to practise saying my name correctly: It's Jaya—"j" as in "justice," "j" as in "jam"—

VIRGIL: Zhaya— 480

JAYA: I won't talk to you unless you say it right!

VIRGIL: (*Pause.*) Zh . . . Jaya. Jaya. Jaya—listen to me—

JAYA: No! You listen to me! I want to be left alone—truly
alone. I don't want to hear any sounds, I don't want any
485   disturbances. I'm going to take my pills, watch TV, have a
dozen baths a day, eat for three instead of one. For the first
time in my life and maybe the last time of my life, I'm going to enjoy myself, all by myself. I suggest you take some
rest. You have a long journey ahead of you and it's sure to
490   be a hard one.

(*Lights dim out as* JAYA *settles down comfortably in front of the television, bolstered by cushions. She looks happy and relaxed. She
points the remote and turns the sound up loud. Rich, joyous music
fills the room.*)

FINAL CURTAIN

CRITICAL CONTEXTS

FRANTZ FANON (1925–1961)
"The Fact of Blackness" (1952)

Frantz Fanon was perhaps the seminal theoretician of postcolonial politics, culture, and identity; his two major books, Black Skin, White Masks *(1952) and* The Wretched of the Earth *(1961), have been widely read and have provided an important inspiration for liberation movements around the world. Born in Martinique, Fanon studied medicine in Paris and became a psychiatrist in Algeria during its wars of liberation from France. "The Fact of Blackness" is Fanon's celebrated essay describing the consciousness of "black" subjects in a world of "white" power.*

"Dirty nigger!" Or simply, "Look, a Negro!"

I came into the world imbued with the will to find a meaning in things, my spirit filled with the desire to attain to the source of the world, and then I found that I was an object in the midst of other objects.

Sealed into that crushing objecthood, I turned beseechingly to others. Their attention was a liberation, running over my body suddenly abraded into nonbeing, endowing me once more with an agility that I had thought lost, and by taking me out of the world, restoring me to it. But just as I reached the other side, I stumbled, and the movements, the attitudes, the glances of the other fixed me there, in the sense in which a chemical solution is fixed by a dye. I was indignant; I demanded an explanation. Nothing happened. I burst apart. Now the fragments have been put together again by another self.

As long as the black man is among his own, he will have no occasion, except in minor internal conflicts, to experience his being through others. There is of course the moment of "being for others," of which Hegel speaks, but every ontology is made unattainable in a colonized and civilized society. It would seem that this fact has not been given sufficient attention by those who have discussed the question. In the *Weltanschauung* of a colonized people there is an impurity, a flaw that outlaws any ontological explanation. Someone may object that this is the case with every individual, but such an objection merely conceals a basic problem. Ontology—once it is finally admitted as leaving existence by the wayside—does not permit us to understand the being of the black man. For not only must the black man be black; he must be black in relation to the white man. Some critics will take it on themselves to remind us that this proposition has a converse. I say that this is false. The black man has no ontological resistance in the eyes of the white man. Overnight the Negro has been given two frames of reference within which he has had to place himself. His metaphysics, or, less pretentiously, his customs and the sources on which they were based, were wiped out because they were in conflict with a civilization that he did not know and that imposed itself on him.

The black man among his own in the twentieth century does not know at what moment his inferiority comes into being through the other. Of course I have talked about the black problem with friends, or, more rarely, with American Negroes. Together we protested, we asserted the equality of all men in the world. In the Antilles there was also that little gulf that exists among the almost-white, the mulatto, and the nigger. But I was satisfied with an intellectual understanding of these differences. It was not really dramatic. And then. . . .

And then the occasion arose when I had to meet the white man's eyes. An unfamiliar weight burdened me. The real world challenged my claims. In the white world the man of color encounters difficulties in the development of his bodily schema. Consciousness of the body is solely a negating activity. It is a third-person consciousness. The body is surrounded by an atmosphere of certain uncertainty. I know that if I want to smoke, I shall have to reach out my right arm and take the pack of cigarettes lying at the other end of the table. The matches, however, are in the drawer on the left, and I shall have to lean back slightly. And all these movements are made not out of habit but out of implicit knowledge. A slow composition of my *self* as a body in the middle of a spatial and temporal world—such seems to be the schema. It does not impose itself on me; it is, rather, a definitive structuring of the self and of the world—definitive because it creates a real dialectic between my body and the world.

For several years certain laboratories have been trying to produce a serum for "denegrification"; with all the earnestness in the world, laboratories have sterilized their test tubes, checked their scales, and embarked on researches that might make it possible for the miserable Negro to whiten himself and thus to throw off the burden of that corporeal malediction. Below the corporeal schema I had sketched a historico-racial schema. The elements that I used had been provided for me not by "residual sensations and perceptions primarily of a tactile, vestibular, kinesthetic, and visual character,"[1] but by the other, the white man, who had woven me out of a thousand details, anecdotes, stories. I thought that what I had in hand was to construct a physiological self, to balance space, to localize sensations, and here I was called on for more.

"Look, a Negro!" It was an external stimulus that flicked over me as I passed by. I made a tight smile.

"Look, a Negro!" It was true. It amused me.

"Look, a Negro!" The circle was drawing a bit tighter. I made no secret of my amusement.

"Mama, see the Negro! I'm frightened!" Frightened! Frightened! Now they were beginning to be afraid of me. I made up my mind to laugh myself to tears, but laughter had become impossible.

I could no longer laugh, because I already knew that there were legends, stories, history, and above all *historicity*, which I had learned about from Jaspers. Then, assailed at various points, the corporeal schema crumbled, its place taken by a racial epidermal schema. In the train it was no longer a question of being aware of my body in the third person but in a triple person. In the train I was given not one but two, three places. I had already stopped being amused. It was not that I was finding febrile coordinates in the world. I existed triply: I occupied space. I moved toward the other . . . and the evanescent other, hostile but not opaque, transparent, not there, disappeared. Nausea. . . .

I was responsible at the same time for my body, for my race, for my ancestors. I subjected myself to an objective examination, I discovered my blackness, my ethnic characteristics; and I was battered down by tom-toms, cannibalism, intellectual deficiency, fetishism, racial defects, slave-ships, and above all else, above all: "Sho' good eatin'."

On that day, completely dislocated, unable to be abroad with the other, the white man, who unmercifully imprisoned me, I took myself far off from my own presence, far indeed, and made myself an object. What else could it be for me but an amputation, an excision, a hemorrhage that spattered my whole body with black blood? But I did not want this revision, this thematization. All I wanted was to be a man among other men. I wanted to come lithe and young into a world that was ours and to help to build it together.

But I rejected all immunization of the emotions. I wanted to be a man, nothing but a man. Some identified me with ancestors of mine who had been enslaved or lynched: I decided

[1]Jean Lhermitte, *L'Image de notre corps* (Paris: Nouvelle Revue critique, 1939), p. 17.

to accept this. It was on the universal level of the intellect that I understood this inner kinship—I was the grandson of slaves in exactly the same way in which President Lebrun was the grandson of tax-paying, hard-working peasants. In the main, the panic soon vanished.

In America, Negroes are segregated. In South America, Negroes are whipped in the streets, and Negro strikers are cut down by machine-guns. In West Africa, the Negro is an animal. And there beside me, my neighbor in the university, who was born in Algeria, told me: "As long as the Arab is treated like a man, no solution is possible."

"Understand, my dear boy, color prejudice is something I find utterly foreign. . . . But of course, come in, sir, there is no color prejudice among us. . . . Quite, the Negro is a man like ourselves. . . . It is not because he is black that he is less intelligent than we are. . . . I had a Senegalese buddy in the army who was really clever. . . ."

Where am I to be classified? Or, if you prefer, tucked away?

"A Martinican, a native of 'our' old colonies."

Where shall I hide?

"Look at the nigger! . . . Mama, a Negro! . . . Hell, he's getting mad. . . . Take no notice, sir, he does not know that you are as civilized as we. . . ."

My body was given back to me sprawled out, distorted, recolored, clad in mourning in that white winter day. The Negro is an animal, the Negro is bad, the Negro is mean, the Negro is ugly; look, a nigger, it's cold, the nigger is shivering, the nigger is shivering because he is cold, the little boy is trembling because he is afraid of the nigger, the nigger is shivering with cold, that cold that goes through your bones, the handsome little boy is trembling because he thinks that the nigger is quivering with rage, the little white boy throws himself into his mother's arms: Mama, the nigger's going to eat me up.

All round me the white man, above the sky tears at its navel, the earth rasps under my feet, and there is a white song, a white song. All this whiteness that burns me. . . .

I sit down at the fire and I become aware of my uniform. I had not seen it. It is indeed ugly. I stop there, for who can tell me what beauty is?

Where shall I find shelter from now on? I felt an easily identifiable flood mounting out of the countless facets of my being. I was about to be angry. The fire was long since out, and once more the nigger was trembling.

"Look how handsome that Negro is! . . ."

"Kiss the handsome Negro's ass, madame!"

Shame flooded her face. At last I was set free from my rumination. At the same time I accomplished two things: I identified my enemies and I made a scene. A grand slam. Now one would be able to laugh.

The field of battle having been marked out, I entered the lists.

What? While I was forgetting, forgiving, and wanting only to love, my message was flung back in my face like a slap. The white world, the only honorable one, barred me from all participation. A man was expected to behave like a man. I was expected to behave like a black man—or at least like a nigger. I shouted a greeting to the world and the world slashed away my joy. I was told to stay within bounds, to go back where I belonged.

They would see, then! I had warned them, anyway. Slavery? It was no longer even mentioned, that unpleasant memory. My supposed inferiority? A hoax that it was better to laugh at. I forgot it all, but only on condition that the world not protect itself against me any longer. I had incisors to test. I was sure they were strong. And besides. . . .

What! When it was I who had every reason to hate, to despise, I was rejected? When I should have been begged, implored, I was denied the slightest recognition? I resolved, since it was impossible for me to get away from an *inborn complex*, to assert myself as a BLACK MAN. Since the other hesitated to recognize me, there remained only one solution: to make myself known.

In *Anti-Semite and Jew* (p. 95), Sartre says: "They [the Jews] have allowed themselves to be poisoned by the stereotype that others have of them, and they live in fear that their acts will correspond to this stereotype. . . . We may say that their conduct is perpetually overdetermined from the inside."

All the same, the Jew can be unknown in his Jewishness. He is not wholly what he is. One hopes, one waits. His actions, his behavior are the final determinant. He is a white man, and, apart from some rather debatable characteristics, he can sometimes go unnoticed. He belongs to the race of those who since the beginning of time have never known cannibalism. What an idea, to eat one's father! Simple enough, one has only not to be a nigger. Granted, the Jews are harassed—what am I thinking of? They are hunted down, exterminated, cremated. But these are little family quarrels. The Jew is disliked from the moment he is tracked down. But in my case everything takes on a *new* guise. I am given no chance. I am overdetermined from without. I am the slave not of the "idea" that others have of me but of my own appearance.

I move slowly in the world, accustomed now to seek no longer for upheaval. I progress by crawling. And already I am being dissected under white eyes, the only real eyes. I am *fixed*. Having adjusted their microtomes, they objectively cut away slices of my reality. I am laid bare. I feel, I see in those white faces that it is not a new man who has come in, but a new kind of man, a new genus. Why, it's a Negro!

I slip into corners, and my long antennae pick up the catch-phrases strewn over the surface of things—nigger underwear smells of nigger—nigger teeth are white—nigger feet are big—the nigger's barrel chest—I slip into corners, I remain silent, I strive for anonymity, for invisibility. Look, I will accept the lot, as long as no one notices me!

"Oh, I want you to meet my black friend. . . . Aimé Césaire, a black man and a university graduate. . . . Marian Anderson, the finest of Negro singers. . . . Dr. Cobb, who invented white blood, is a Negro. . . . Here, say hello to my friend from Martinique (be careful, he's extremely sensitive). . . ."

Shame. Shame and self-contempt. Nausea. When people like me, they tell me it is in spite of my color. When they dislike me, they point out that it is not because of my color. Either way, I am locked into the infernal circle.

I turn away from these inspectors of the Ark before the Flood and I attach myself to my brothers, Negroes like myself. To my horror, they too reject me. They are almost white. And besides they are about to marry white women. They will have children faintly tinged with brown. Who knows, perhaps little by little. . . .

I had been dreaming.

"I want you to understand, sir, I am one of the best friends the Negro has in Lyon."

The evidence was there, unalterable. My blackness was there, dark and unarguable. And it tormented me, pursued me, disturbed me, angered me.

Negroes are savages, brutes, illiterates. But in my own case I knew that these statements were false. There was a myth of the Negro that had to be destroyed at all costs. The time had long since passed when a Negro priest was an occasion for wonder. We had physicians, professors, statesmen. Yes, but something out of the ordinary still clung to such cases. "We have a Senegalese history teacher. He is quite bright. . . . Our doctor is colored. He is very gentle."

It was always the Negro teacher, the Negro doctor; brittle as I was becoming, I shivered at the slightest pretext. I knew, for instance, that if the physician made a mistake it would be the end of him and of all those who came after him. What could one expect, after all, from a Negro physician? As long as everything went well, he was praised to the skies, but look out, no nonsense, under any conditions! The black physician can never be sure how close he is to disgrace. I tell you, I was walled in: No exception was made for my refined manners, or my knowledge of literature, or my understanding of the quantum theory.

I requested, I demanded explanations. Gently, in the tone that one uses with a child, they introduced me to the existence of a certain view that was held by certain people, but,

I was always told, "We must hope that it will very soon disappear." What was it? Color prejudice.

It [colour prejudice] is nothing more than the unreasoning hatred of one race for another, the contempt of the stronger and richer peoples for those whom they consider inferior to themselves and the bitter resentment of those who are kept in subjection and are so frequently insulted. As colour is the most obvious outward manifestation of race it has been made the criterion by which men are judged, irrespective of their social or educational attainments. The light-skinned races have come to despise all those of a darker colour, and the dark-skinned peoples will no longer accept without protest the inferior position to which they have been relegated.[2]

I had read it rightly. It was hate; I was hated, despised, detested, not by the neighbor across the street or my cousin on my mother's side, but by an entire race. I was up against something unreasoned. The psychoanalysts say that nothing is more traumatizing for the young child than his encounters with what is rational. I would personally say that for a man whose only weapon is reason there is nothing more neurotic than contact with unreason.

I felt knife blades open within me. I resolved to defend myself. As a good tactician, I intended to rationalize the world and to show the white man that he was mistaken.

In the Jew, Jean-Paul Sartre says, there is

a sort of impassioned imperialism of reason: for he wishes not only to convince others that he is right; his goal is to persuade them that there is an absolute and unconditioned value to rationalism. He feels himself to be a missionary of the universal; against the universality of the Catholic religion, from which he is excluded, he asserts the "catholicity" of the rational, an instrument by which to attain to the truth and establish a spiritual bond among men.[3]

And, the author adds, though there may be Jews who have made intuition the basic category of their philosophy, their intuition

has no resemblance to the Pascalian subtlety of spirit, and it is this latter—based on a thousand imperceptible perceptions—which to the Jew seems his worst enemy. As for Bergson, his philosophy offers the curious appearance of an anti-intellectualist doctrine constructed entirely by the most rational and most critical of intelligences. It is through argument that he establishes the existence of pure duration, of philosophic intuition; and that very intuition which discovers duration or life, is itself universal, since anyone may practice it, and it leads toward the universal, since its objects can be named and conceived.[4]

With enthusiasm I set to cataloguing and probing my surroundings. As times changed, one had seen the Catholic religion at first justify and then condemn slavery and prejudices. But by referring everything to the idea of the dignity of man, one had ripped prejudice to shreds. After much reluctance, the scientists had conceded that the Negro was a human being; *in vivo* and *in vitro* the Negro had been proved analogous to the white man: the same morphology, the same histology. Reason was confident of victory on every level. I put all the parts back together. But I had to change my tune.

That victory played cat and mouse; it made a fool of me. As the other put it, when I was present, it was not; when it was there, I was no longer. In the abstract there was agreement: The Negro is a human being. That is to say, amended the less firmly convinced, that like us he has his heart on the left side. But on certain points the white man remained intractable. Under no conditions did he wish any intimacy between the races, for it is a truism that "crossings between widely different races can lower the physical and mental level. . . . Until we have a more definite knowledge of the effect of race-crossings we shall certainly do best to avoid crossings between widely different races."[5]

For my own part, I would certainly know how to react. And in one sense, if I were asked for a definition of myself, I would say that I am one who waits; I investigate my surroundings, I interpret everything in terms of what I discover, I become sensitive.

In the first chapter of the history that the others have compiled for me, the foundation of cannibalism has been made eminently plain in order that I may not lose sight of it. My chromosomes were supposed to have a few thicker or thinner genes representing cannibalism. In addition to the *sex-linked*, the scholars had now discovered the *racial-linked*.[6] What a shameful science!

But I understand this "psychological mechanism." For it is a matter of common knowledge that the mechanism is only psychological. Two centuries ago I was lost to humanity, I was a slave forever. And then came men who said that it all had gone on far too long. My tenaciousness did the rest; I was saved from the civilizing deluge. I have gone forward.

Too late. Everything is anticipated, thought out, demonstrated, made the most of. My trembling hands take hold of nothing; the vein has been mined out. Too late! But once again I want to understand.

[2]Sir Alan Burns, *Colour Prejudice* (London: Allen and Unwin, 1948), p. 16.

[3]*Anti-Semite and Jew* (New York: Grove Press, 1960), pp. 112–13.

[4]Ibid., p. 115.

[5]Jon Alfred Mjoen, "Harmonic and Disharmonic Race-crossings," *The Second International Congress of Eugenics* (1921), *Eugenics in Race and State*, vol. 2, p. 60, quoted in Sir Alan Burns, op. cit., p. 120.

[6]In English in the original (*Translator's note*).

Since the time when someone first mourned the fact that he had arrived too late and everything had been said, a nostalgia for the past has seemed to persist. Is this that lost original paradise of which Otto Rank speaks? How many such men, apparently rooted to the womb of the world, have devoted their lives to studying the Delphic oracles or exhausted themselves in attempts to plot the wanderings of Ulysses! The pan-spiritualists seek to prove the existence of a soul in animals by using this argument: A dog lies down on the grave of his master and starves to death there. We had to wait for Janet to demonstrate that the aforesaid dog, in contrast to man, simply lacked the capacity to liquidate the past. We speak of the glory of Greece, Artaud says; but, he adds, if modern man can no longer understand the *Choephoroi* of Aeschylus, it is Aeschylus who is to blame. It is tradition to which the anti-Semites turn in order to ground the validity of their "point of view." It is tradition, it is that long historical past, it is that blood relation between Pascal and Descartes, that is invoked when the Jew is told, "There is no possibility of your finding a place in society." Not long ago, one of those good Frenchmen said in a train where I was sitting: "Just let the real French virtues keep going and the race is safe. Now more than ever, national union must be made a reality. Let's have an end of internal strife! Let's face up to the foreigners (here he turned toward my corner) no matter who they are."

It must be said in his defense that he stank of cheap wine; if he had been capable of it, he would have told me that my emancipated-slave blood could not possibly be stirred by the name of Villon or Taine.

An outrage!

The Jew and I: Since I was not satisfied to be racialized, by a lucky turn of fate I was humanized. I joined the Jew, my brother in misery.

An outrage!

At first thought it may seem strange that the anti-Semite's outlook should be related to that of the Negro-phobe. It was my philosophy professor, a native of the Antilles, who recalled the fact to me one day: "Whenever you hear anyone abuse the Jews, pay attention, because he is talking about you." And I found that he was universally right—by which I meant that I was answerable in my body and in my heart for what was done to my brother. Later I realized that he meant, quite simply, an anti-Semite is inevitably anti-Negro.

You come too late, much too late. There will always be a world—a white world—between you and us. . . . The other's total inability to liquidate the past once and for all. In the face of this affective *ankylosis* of the white man, it is understandable that I could have made up my mind to utter my Negro cry. Little by little, putting out pseudopodia here and there, I secreted a race. And that race staggered under the burden of a basic element. What was it? *Rhythm*! Listen to our singer, Léopold Senghor:

> It is the thing that is most perceptible and least material. It is the archetype of the vital element. It is the first condition and the hallmark of Art, as breath is of life: breath, which accelerates or slows, which becomes even or agitated according to the tension in the individual, the degree and the nature of his emotion. This is rhythm in its primordial purity, this is rhythm in the masterpieces of Negro art, especially sculpture. It is composed of a theme—sculptural form—which is set in opposition to a sister theme, as inhalation is to exhalation, and that is repeated. It is not the kind of symmetry that gives rise to monotony; rhythm is alive, it is free. . . . This is how rhythm affects what is least intellectual in us, tyrannically, to make us penetrate to the spirituality of the object; and that character of abandon which is ours is itself rhythmic.[7]

Had I read that right? I read it again with redoubled attention. From the opposite end of the white world a magical Negro culture was hailing me. Negro sculpture! I began to flush with pride. Was this our salvation?

I had rationalized the world and the world had rejected me on the basis of color prejudice. Since no agreement was possible on the level of reason, I threw myself back toward unreason. It was up to the white man to be more irrational than I. Out of the necessities of my struggle I had chosen the method of regression, but the fact remained that it was an unfamiliar weapon; here I am at home; I am made of the irrational; I wade in the irrational. Up to the neck in the irrational. And now how my voice vibrates!

> Those who invented neither gunpowder nor the compass
> Those who never learned to conquer steam or electricity
> Those who never explored the seas or the skies
> But they know the farthest corners of the land of anguish
> Those who never knew any journey save that of abduction
> Those who learned to kneel in docility
> Those who were domesticated and Christianized
> Those who were injected with bastardy. . . .

Yes, all those are my brothers—a "bitter brotherhood" imprisons all of us alike. Having stated the minor thesis, I went overboard after something else.

> . . . But those without whom the earth would not be the earth
> Tumescence all the more fruitful
> than
> the empty land
> still more the land
> Storehouse to guard and ripen all
> on earth that is most earth
> My blackness is no stone, its deafness
> hurled against the clamor of the day

---

[7]"Ce que l'homme noir apporte," in Claude Nordey, *L'Homme de couleur* (Paris: Plon, 1939), pp. 309–310.

My blackness is no drop of lifeless water
on the dead eye of the world
My blackness is neither a tower nor a cathedral
It thrusts into the red flesh of the sun
It thrusts into the burning flesh of the sky
It hollows through the dense dismay of its own pillar of
patience.[8]

Eyah! the tom-tom chatters out the cosmic message. Only the Negro has the capacity to convey it, to decipher its meaning, its import. Astride the world, my strong heels spurring into the flanks of the world, I stare into the shoulders of the world as the celebrant stares at the midpoint between the eyes of the sacrificial victim.

But they abandon themselves, possessed, to the essence of all
things, knowing nothing of externals but possessed by the movement of all things
uncaring to subdue but playing the play of the world
truly the eldest sons of the world
open to all the breaths of the world
meeting-place of all the winds of the world
undrained bed of all the waters of the world
spark of the sacred fire of the World
flesh of the flesh of the world, throbbing with the very movement
of the world.[9]

Blood! Blood! . . . Birth! Ecstasy of becoming! Three-quarters engulfed in the confusions of the day, I feel myself redden with blood. The arteries of all the world, convulsed, torn away, uprooted, have turned toward me and fed me.
"Blood! Blood! All our blood stirred by the male heart of the sun."[10]
Sacrifice was a middle point between the creation and myself—now I went back no longer to sources but to The Source. Nevertheless, one had to distrust rhythm, earth-mother love, this mystic, carnal marriage of the group and the cosmos.
In *La vie sexuelle en Afrique noire,* a work rich in perceptions, De Pédrals implies that always in Africa, no matter what field is studied, it will have a certain magico-social structure. He adds:

All these are the elements that one finds again on a still greater
scale in the domain of secret societies. To the extent, moreover,
to which persons of either sex, subjected to circumcision during
adolescence, are bound under penalty of death not to reveal to
the uninitiated what they have experienced, and to the extent to
which initiation into a secret society always excites to acts of *sa-*

cred love*, there is good ground to conclude by viewing both male and female circumcision and the rites that they embellish as constitutive of minor secret societies.[11]

I walk on white nails. Sheets of water threaten my soul on fire. Face to face with these rites, I am doubly alert. Black magic! Orgies, witches' sabbaths, heathen ceremonies, amulets. Coitus is an occasion to call on the gods of the clan. It is a sacred act, pure, absolute, bringing invisible forces into action. What is one to think of all these manifestations, all these initiations, all these acts? From very direction I am assaulted by the obscenity of dances and of words. Almost at my ear there is a song:

First our hearts burned hot
Now they are cold
All we think of now is Love
When we return to the village
When we see the great phallus
Ah how then we will make Love
For our parts will be dry and clean.[12]

The soil, which only a moment ago was still a tamed steed, begins to revel. Are these virgins, these nymphomaniacs? Black Magic, primitive mentality, animism, animal eroticism, it all floods over me. All of it is typical of peoples that have not kept pace with the evolution of the human race. Or, if one prefers, this is humanity at its lowest. Having reached this point, I was long reluctant to commit myself. Aggression was in the stars. I had to choose. What do I mean? I had no choice. . . .
Yes, we are—we Negroes—backward, simple, free in our behavior. That is because for us the body is not something opposed to what you call the mind. We are in the world. And long live the couple, Man and Earth! Besides, our men of letters helped me to convince you; your white civilization overlooks subtle riches and sensitivity. Listen:

Emotive sensitivity. *Emotion is completely Negro as reason is
Greek.*[13] Water rippled by every breeze? Unsheltered soul blown
by every wind, whose fruit often drops before it is ripe? Yes, in
one way, the Negro today is richer *in gifts than in works.*[14] But the
tree thrusts its roots into the earth. The river runs deep, carrying
precious seeds. And, the Afro-American poet, Langston Hughes,
says:
I have known rivers
ancient dark rivers

---

[8]Aimé Césaire, *Cahier d'un retour au pays natal* (Paris: Présence Africaine, 1956), pp. 77–78.

[9]Ibid., p. 78.

[10]Ibid., p. 79.

[11]De Pédrals, *La vie sexuelle en Afrique noire* (Paris: Payot), p. 83.

[12]A. M. Vergiat, *Les rites secrets des primitifs de l'Oubangui* (Paris: Payot, 1951), p. 113.

[13]My italics—F.F.

[14]My italics—F.F.

my soul has grown deep
like the deep rivers.
The very nature of the Negro's emotion, of his sensitivity, furthermore, explains his attitude toward the object perceived with
such basic intensity. It is an abandon that becomes need, an active state of communion, indeed of identification, however negligible the action—I almost said the personality—of the object. A
rhythmic attitude: The adjective should be kept in mind.[15]

So here we have the Negro rehabilitated, "standing before the bar," ruling the world with his intuition, the Negro recognized, set on his feet again, sought after, taken
up, and he is a Negro—no, he is not a Negro but the Negro, exciting the fecund antennae of the world, placed in
the foreground of the world, raining his poetic power on
the world, "open to all the breaths of the world." I embrace the world! I am the world! The white man has never
understood this magic substitution. The white man wants
the world; he wants it for himself alone. He finds himself
predestined master of this world. He enslaves it. An acquisitive relation is established between the world and
him. But there exist other values that fit only my forms.
Like a magician, I robbed the white man of "a certain
world," forever after lost to him and his. When that happened, the white man must have been rocked backward by
a force that he could not identify, so little used as he is to
such reactions. Somewhere beyond the objective world of
farms and banana trees and rubber trees, I had subtly
brought the real world into being. The essence of the world
was my fortune. Between the world and me a relation of
coexistence was established. I had discovered the primeval
One. My "speaking hands" tore at the hysterical throat of
the world. The white man had the anguished feeling that I
was escaping from him and that I was taking something
with me. He went through my pockets. He thrust probes
into the least circumvolution of my brain. Everywhere he
found only the obvious. So it was obvious that I had a secret. I was interrogated; turning away with an air of mystery, I murmured:

Tokowaly, uncle, do you remember the nights gone by
When my head weighed heavy on the back of your patience or
Holding my hand your hand led me by shadows and signs
The fields are flowers of glowworms, stars hang on the bushes, on
the trees
Silence is everywhere
Only the scents of the jungle hum, swarms of reddish bees that
overwhelm the crickets' shrill sounds,
And covered tom tom, breathing in the distance of the night.

You, Tokowaly, you listen to what cannot be heard, and you explain to me what the ancestors are saying in the liquid calm of
the constellations,
The bull, the scorpion, the leopard, the elephant, and the fish we
know,
And the white pomp of the Spirits in the heavenly shell that has
no end,
But now comes the radiance of the goddess Moon and the veils of
the shadows fall.
Night of Africa, my black night, mystical and bright, black and
shining.[16]

I made myself the poet of the world. The white man had
found a poetry in which there was nothing poetic. The soul of
the white man was corrupted, and, as I was told by a friend
who was a teacher in the United States, "The presence of the
Negroes beside the whites is in a way an insurance policy on
humanness. When the whites feel that they have become too
mechanized, they turn to the men of color and ask them for a
little human sustenance." At last I had been recognized, I
was no longer a zero.

I had soon to change my tune. Only momentarily at a
loss, the white man explained to me that, genetically, I represented a stage of development: "Your properties have been
exhausted by us. We have had earth mystics such as you will
never approach. Study our history and you will see how far
this fusion has gone." Then I had the feeling that I was repeating a cycle. My originality had been torn out of me. I
wept a long time, and then I began to live again. But I was
haunted by a galaxy of erosive stereotypes: the Negro's *sui
generis* odor . . . the Negro's *sui generis* good nature . . . the
Negro's *sui generis* gullibility. . . .

I had tried to flee myself through my kind, but the whites
had thrown themselves on me and hamstrung me. I tested the
limits of my essence; beyond all doubt there was not much of
it left. It was here that I made my most remarkable discovery.
Properly speaking, this discovery was a rediscovery.

I rummaged frenetically through all the antiquity of the
black man. What I found there took away my breath. In his
book *L'abolition de l'esclavage* Schoelcher presented us with
compelling arguments. Since then, Frobenius, Westermann,
Delafosse—all of them white—had joined the chorus: Ségou,
Djenné, cities of more than a hundred thousand people; accounts of learned blacks (doctors of theology who went to
Mecca to interpret the Koran). All of that, exhumed from the
past, spread with its insides out, made it possible for me to
find a valid historic place. The white man was wrong, I was
not a primitive, not even a half-man, I belonged to a race

---

[15]Léopold Senghor, "Ce que l'homme noir apporte," in
Nordey, op. cit., p. 205.

[16]Léopold Senghor, *Chants d'ombre* (Paris: Editions du Seuil,
1945).

that had already been working in gold and silver two thousand years ago. And there was something else, something else that the white man could not understand. Listen:

> What sort of men were these, then, who had been torn away from their families, their countries, their religions, with a savagery unparalleled in history?
>
> Gentle men, polite, considerate, unquestionably superior to those who tortured them—that collection of adventurers who slashed and violated and spat on Africa to make the stripping of her the easier.
>
> The men they took away knew how to build houses, govern empires, erect cities, cultivate fields, mine for metals, weave cotton, forge steel.
>
> Their religion had its own beauty, based on mystical connections with the founder of the city. Their customs were pleasing, built on unity, kindness, respect for age.
>
> No coercion, only mutual assistance, the joy of living, a free acceptance of discipline.
>
> Order—Earnestness—Poetry and Freedom.
>
> From the untroubled private citizen to the almost fabulous leader there was an unbroken chain of understanding and trust. No science? Indeed yes; but also, to protect them from fear, they possessed great myths in which 'the most subtle observation and the most daring imagination were balanced and blended. No art? They had their magnificent sculpture, in which human feeling erupted so unrestrained yet always followed the obsessive laws of rhythm in its organization of the major elements of a material called upon to capture, in order to redistribute, the most secret forces of the universe. . . .[17]
>
> Monuments in the very heart of Africa? Schools? Hospitals? Not a single good burgher of the twentieth century, no Durand, no Smith, no Brown even suspects that such things existed in Africa before the Europeans came. . . .
>
> But Schoelcher reminds us of their presence, discovered by Caillé, Mollien, the Cander brothers. And, though he nowhere reminds us that when the Portuguese landed on the banks of the Congo in 1498, they found a rich and flourishing state there and that the courtiers of Ambas were dressed in robes of silk and brocade, at least he knows that Africa had brought itself up to a juridical concept of the state, and he is aware, living in the very flood of imperialism, that European civilization, after all, is only one more civilization among many—and not the most merciful.[18]

I put the white man back into his place; growing bolder, I jostled him and told him point-blank, "Get used to me, I am not getting used to anyone." I shouted my laughter to the stars. The white man, I could see, was resentful. His reaction time lagged interminably. . . . I had won. I was jubilant.

"Lay aside your history, your investigations of the past, and try to feel yourself into our rhythm. In a society such as ours, industrialized to the highest degree, dominated by scientism, there is no longer room for your sensitivity. One must be tough if one is to be allowed to live. What matters now is no longer playing the game of the world but subjugating it with integers and atoms. Oh, certainly, I will be told, now and then when we are worn out by our lives in big buildings, we will turn to you as we do to our children—to the innocent, the ingenuous, the spontaneous. We will turn to you as to the childhood of the world. You are so real in your life—so funny, that is. Let us run away for a little while from our ritualized, polite civilization and let us relax, bend to those heads, those adorably expressive faces. In a way, you reconcile us with ourselves."

Thus my unreason was countered with reason, my reason with "real reason." Every hand was a losing hand for me. I analyzed my heredity. I made a complete audit of my ailment. I wanted to be typically Negro—it was no longer possible. I wanted to be white—that was a joke. And, when I tried, on the level of ideas and intellectual activity, to reclaim my negritude, it was snatched away from me. Proof was presented that my effort was only a term in the dialectic:

> But there is something more important: The Negro, as we have said, creates an anti-racist racism for himself. In no sense does he wish to rule the world: He seeks the abolition of all ethnic privileges, wherever they come from; he asserts his solidarity with the oppressed of all colors. At once the subjective, existential, ethnic idea of *negritude* "passes," as Hegel puts it, into the objective, positive, exact idea of proletariat. "For Césaire," Senghor says, "the white man is the symbol of capital as the Negro is that of labor. . . . Beyond the black-skinned men of his race it is the battle of the world proletariat that is his song."
>
> That is easy to say, but less easy to think out. And undoubtedly it is no coincidence that the most ardent poets of negritude are at the same time militant Marxists.
>
> But that does not prevent the idea of race from mingling with that of class: The first is concrete and particular, the second is universal and abstract; the one stems from what Jaspers calls understanding and the other from intellection; the first is the result of a psychobiological syncretism and the second is a methodical construction based on experience. In fact, negritude appears as the minor term of a dialectical progression: The theoretical and practical assertion of the supremacy of the white man is its thesis; the position of negritude as an antithetical value is the moment of negativity. But this negative moment is insufficient by itself, and the Negroes who employ it know this very well; they know that it is intended to prepare the synthesis or realization of the human in a society without races. Thus negritude is the root of its own destruction, it is a transition and not a conclusion, a means and not an ultimate end.[19]

When I read that page, I felt that I had been robbed of my last chance. I said to my friends, "The generation of the younger black poets has just suffered a blow that can never

---

[17]Aimé Césaire, Introduction to Victor Schoelcher, *Esclavage et colonisation* (Paris: Presses Universitaires de France, 1948), p. 7.

[18]Ibid., p. 8.

[19]Jean-Paul Sartre, *Orphée Noir*, preface to *Anthologie de la nouvelle poésie nègre et malgache* (Paris: Presses Universitaires de France, 1948), pp. xl ff.

be forgiven." Help had been sought from a friend of the colored peoples, and that friend had found no better response than to point out the relativity of what they were doing. For once, that born Hegelian had forgotten that consciousness has to lose itself in the night of the absolute, the only condition to attain to consciousness of self. In opposition to rationalism, he summoned up the negative side, but he forgot that this negativity draws its worth from an almost substantive absoluteness. A consciousness committed to experience is ignorant, has to be ignorant, of the essences and the determinations of its being.

Orphée Noir is a date in the intellectualization of the *experience* of being black. And Sartre's mistake was not only to seek the source of the source but in a certain sense to block that source:

> Will the source of Poetry be dried up? Or will the great black flood, in spite of everything, color the sea into which it pours itself? It does not matter: Every age has its own poetry; in every age the circumstances of history choose a nation, a race, a class to take up the torch by creating situations that can be expressed or transcended only through Poetry; sometimes the poetic impulse coincides with the revolutionary impulse, and sometimes they take different courses. Today let us hail the turn of history that will make it possible for the black men to utter "the great Negro cry with a force that will shake the pillars of the world" (Césaire).[20]

And so it is not I who make a meaning for myself, but it is the meaning that was already there, pre-existing, waiting for me. It is not out of my bad nigger's misery, my bad nigger's teeth, my bad nigger's hunger that I will shape a torch with which to burn down the world, but it is the torch that was already there, waiting for that turn of history.

In terms of consciousness, the black consciousness is held out as an absolute density, as filled with itself, a stage preceding any invasion, any abolition of the ego by desire. Jean-Paul Sartre, in this work, has destroyed black zeal. In opposition to historical becoming, there had always been the unforeseeable. I needed to lose myself completely in negritude. One day, perhaps, in the depths of that unhappy romanticism. . . .

In any case I *needed* not to know. This struggle, this new decline had to take on an aspect of completeness. Nothing is more unwelcome than the commonplace: "You'll change, my boy; I was like that too when I was young . . . you'll see, it will all pass."

The dialectic that brings necessity into the foundation of my freedom drives me out of myself. It shatters my unreflected position. Still in terms of consciousness, black consciousness is immanent in its own eyes. I am not a poten-

tiality of something, I am wholly what I am. I do not have to look for the universal. No probability has any place inside me. My Negro consciousness does not hold itself out as a lack. It is. It is its own follower.

But, I will be told, your statements show a misreading of the processes of history. Listen then:

> Africa I have kept your memory Africa
> you are inside me
> Like the splinter in the wound
> like a guardian fetish in the center of the village
> make me the stone in your sling
> make my mouth the lips of your wound
> make my knees the broken pillars of your abasement
> AND YET
> I want to be of your race alone
> workers peasants of all lands . . .
> . . . white worker in Detroit black peon in Alabama
> uncountable nation in capitalist slavery
> destiny ranges us shoulder to shoulder
> repudiating the ancient maledictions of blood taboos
> we roll away the ruins of our solitudes
> If the flood is a frontier
> we will strip the gully of its endless
> covering flow
> If the Sierra is a frontier
> we will smash the jaws of the volcanoes
> upholding the Cordilleras
> and the plain will be the parade ground of the dawn
> where we regroup our forces sundered
> by the deceits of our masters
> As the contradiction among the features
> creates the harmony of the face
> we proclaim the oneness of the suffering
> and the revolt
> of all the peoples on all the face of the earth
> and we mix the mortar of the age of brotherhood
> out of the dust of idols.[21]

Exactly, we will reply, Negro experience is not a whole, for there is not merely one Negro, there are *Negroes*. What a difference, for instance, in this other poem:

> The white man killed my father
> Because my father was proud
> The white man raped my mother
> Because my mother was beautiful
> The white man wore out my brother in the hot sun of the roads
> Because my brother was strong
> Then the white man came to me
> His hands red with blood
> Spat his contempt into my black face
> Out of his tyrant's voice:
> "Hey boy, a basin, a towel, water."[22]

---

[20]Ibid., p. xliv.

[21]Jacques Roumain, "Bois d'Ebène," *Prelude*, in *Anthologie de la nouvelle poésie nègre et malgache*, p. 113.

[22]David Diop, "Le temps du martyre," ibid., p. 174.

Or this other one:

> My brother with teeth that glisten at the compliments of hypocrites
> My brother with gold-rimmed spectacles
> Over eyes that turn blue at the sound of the Master's voice
> My poor brother in dinner jacket with its silk lapels
> Clucking and whispering and strutting through the drawing rooms of Condescension
> How pathetic you are
> The sun of your native country is nothing more now than a shadow
> On your composed civilized face
> And your grandmother's hut
> Brings blushes into cheeks made white by years of abasement and Mea culpa
> But when regurgitating the flood of lofty empty words
> Like the load that presses on your shoulders
> You walk again on the rough red earth of Africa
> These words of anguish will state the rhythm of your uneasy gait
> I feel so alone, so alone here![23]

From time to time one would like to stop. To state reality is a wearing task. But, when one has taken it into one's head to try to express existence, one runs the risk of finding only the nonexistent. What is certain is that, at the very moment when I was trying to grasp my own being, Sartre, who remained The Other, gave me a name and thus shattered my last illusion. While I was saying to him

> My negritude is neither a tower nor a cathedral,
> it thrusts into the red flesh of the sun,
> it thrusts into the burning flesh of the sky,
> it hollows through the dense dismay of its own pillar of patience . . .

while I was shouting that, in the paroxysm of my being and my fury, he was reminding me that my blackness was only a minor term. In all truth, in all truth I tell you, my shoulders slipped out of the framework of the world, my feet could no longer feel the touch of the ground. Without a Negro past, without a Negro future, it was impossible for me to live my Negrohood. Not yet white, no longer wholly black, I was damned. Jean-Paul Sartre had forgotten that the Negro suffers in his body quite differently from the white man.[24] Between the white man and me the connection was irrevocably one of transcendence.[25]

But the constancy of my love had been forgotten. I defined myself as an absolute intensity of beginning. So I took up my negritude, and with tears in my eyes I put its machinery together again. What had been broken to pieces was rebuilt, reconstructed by the intuitive lianas of my hands.

My cry grew more violent: I am a Negro, I am a Negro, I am a Negro. . . .

And there was my poor brother—living out his neurosis to the extreme and finding himself paralyzed:

> THE NEGRO: I can't, ma'am.
> LIZZIE: Why not?
> THE NEGRO: I can't shoot white folks.
> LIZZIE: Really! That would bother them, wouldn't it?
> THE NEGRO: They're white folks, ma'am.
> LIZZIE: So what? Maybe they got a right to bleed you like a pig just because they're white?
> THE NEGRO: But they're white folks.

A feeling of inferiority? No, a feeling of nonexistence. Sin is Negro as virtue is white. All those white men in a group, guns in their hands, cannot be wrong. I am guilty. I do not know of what, but I know that I am no good.

> THE NEGRO: That's how it goes, ma'am. That's how it always goes with white folks.
> LIZZIE: You too? You feel guilty?
> THE NEGRO: Yes, ma'am.[26]

It is Bigger Thomas—he is afraid, he is terribly afraid. He is afraid, but of what is he afraid? Of himself. No one knows yet who he is, but he knows that fear will fill the world when the world finds out. And when the world knows, the world always expects something of the Negro. He is afraid lest the world know, he is afraid of the fear that the world would feel if the world knew. Like that old woman on her knees who begged me to tie her to her bed:

"I just know, Doctor: Any minute that thing will take hold of me."

"What thing?"

"The wanting to kill myself. Tie me down, I'm afraid."

In the end, Bigger Thomas acts. To put an end to his tension, he acts, he responds to the world's anticipation.[27]

So it is with the character in *If He Hollers Let Him Go*[28]—who does precisely what he did not want to do. That big blonde who was always in his way, weak, sensual, offered, open, fearing (desiring) rape, became his mistress in the end.

[23]David Diop, "Le Renégat."

[24]Though Sartre's speculations on the existence of The Other may be correct (to the extent, we must remember, to which *Being and Nothingness* describes an alienated consciousness), their application to a black consciousness proves fallacious. That is because the white man is not only The Other but also the master, whether real or imaginary.

[25]In the sense in which the word is used by Jean Wahl in *Existence humaine et transcendance* (Neuchâtel: La Baconnière, 1944).

[26]Jean-Paul Sartre, *The Respectful Prostitute*, in *Three Plays* (New York: Knopf, 1949), pp. 189, 191. Originally, *La Putain respectueuse* (Paris: Gallimard, 1947) See also *Home of the Brave*, a film by Mark Robson.

[27]Richard Wright, *Native Son* (New York: Harper, 1940).

[28]By Chester Himes (Garden City: Doubleday, 1945).

The Negro is a toy in the white man's hands; so, in order to shatter the hellish cycle, he explodes. I cannot go to a film without seeing myself. I wait for me. In the interval, just before the film starts, I wait for me. The people in the theater are watching me, examining me, waiting for me. A Negro groom is going to appear. My heart makes my head swim.

The crippled veteran of the Pacific war says to my brother, "Resign yourself to your color the way I got used to my stump; we're both victims."[29]

Nevertheless with all my strength I refuse to accept that amputation. I feel in myself a soul as immense as the world, truly a soul as deep as the deepest of rivers, my chest has the power to expand without limit. I am a master and I am advised to adopt the humility of the cripple. Yesterday, awakening to the world, I saw the sky turn upon itself utterly and wholly. I wanted to rise, but the disemboweled silence fell back upon me, its wings paralyzed. Without responsibility, straddling Nothingness and Infinity, I began to weep.

---

[29]*Home of the Brave*, op. cit.

Glossary

Absurd *See* **Theater of the Absurd.**

Académie Française An academy founded by Cardinal Richelieu in 1635 to resolve the critical debate surrounding Corneille's play *The Cid* and to regularize the French language.

actos Short satirical plays devised by Luis Valdez and El Teatro Campesino in the late 1960s to dramatize the conditions of farmworkers in California.

afterpiece A short play—usually a pantomime or farce—that followed the main play on the evening's bill; common in England in the eighteenth and nineteenth centuries.

agora The marketplace in ancient Greek towns; the *agora* was often used for dramatic performance.

alienation effect A stage technique developed by Bertolt Brecht in the 1920s and 1930s for "estranging" the action of the play. By making characters and their actions seem remarkable, alien, or unusual, Brecht encouraged the audience to question the social realities that produced such events, the political and ideological background of the drama and of its stage production.

allegory A literary or dramatic technique that uses actual characters, places, and actions to represent more abstract political, moral, or religious ideas. *See Everyman.*

alojería The tavern at the rear of the *patio* in a Spanish Golden Age theater, or *corral.*

amphitheater A semicircular theater design, consisting of a playing area faced by rising tiers of seats; often used outdoors, this was the design of classical Greek theaters.

anachronism Using people, places, or things that are chronologically out of keeping with the rest of the fictive world of a play or narrative; for example, using medieval English shepherds to attend the birth of Christ in medieval **cycle plays.**

anagnorisis Greek term for a character's "recognition" of something previously not known in the play. In *The Poetics,* Aristotle links *anagnorisis* with *peripeteia,* the "reversal" in the action of the play.

antagonist The force or character that opposes the main character **(protagonist)** of a play.

antimasque A scene of misrule, usually involving witches, goblins, demons, or savages, who are transformed magically into princes, gods and goddesses, or virtues in a Jacobean **masque.**

antiphonal performance Alternative or responsive singing between individuals or groups; in the Middle Ages, it commonly involved two choirs.

archon A magistrate in classical Athens; each year, an *archon* was assigned the responsibility for organizing the **City Dionysia.**

apron The section of the stage that extends toward the auditorium beyond the **proscenium.**

Atellan farce Improvised comic skits featuring stock characters performed by masked actors in ancient Rome.

atoza Upstage area in a **Noh** theater in which the musicians are seated.

auto sacramentale Elaborate Spanish religious dramas originally devised as part of the feast of Corpus Christi. *Autos* continued to be performed in Spain until 1765.

avant-garde Literally, the "advance guard"; the term usually refers to the most innovative, experimental, or unorthodox artists in a given historical period. Used almost exclusively of late nineteenth- and twentieth-century movements.

backcloth A painted cloth lowered at the rear of the stage to represent a dramatic location.

Beijing Opera Elaborate form of Chinese theater involving an onstage orchestra, ornate costumes, music, and dance.

benefit In the English theater of the seventeenth, eighteenth, and nineteenth centuries, a performance whose profits were assigned to a single performer or to the playwright.

biomechanics An experimental technique for actor training and performance devised by the Russian director Vsevolod Meyerhold after the Russian Revolution (1917). The technique emphasized the actor's physical training, stressing acrobatic and choreographic elements in production.

bhava A stageable emotion in **Sanskrit drama,** related to the play's principal *rasa,* or mood.

biwa Four-stringed, plucked instrument used to accompany spoken narration in medieval Japan.

blank verse An English verse meter consisting of unrhymed **iambic pentameter** lines (ten syllables with alternating stress, the first stress falling on the second syllable).

box   Box seating first appeared in theaters in the late seventeenth century; boxes were arranged around the side of the stage and the sides of the auditorium for the private accommodation of small numbers of people. Boxes were more expensive than **pit** or **gallery** seats.

box set   First devised in the 1830s, a set consisting of three practical walls enclosing the stage in a roomlike way.

bunraku   The term used for modern Japanese **doll theater,** derived from the eighteenth-century master Uemura Bunrakuken.

hutai   The acting area, or stage proper, of a **Noh** theater.

butoh   A powerful form of dance developed in the post-Hiroshima era in Japan; it features nude actors, covered in white powder, whose movements are slow and ethereal.

cabaret performance   Stage performances in restaurants serving food and drink; especially popular in Europe after World War I, cabarets often were used for innovative kinds of performance.

canon   An authorized body of texts, such as the *canon* of Shakespeare's known plays; also commonly used to mean a "traditional" body of texts.

capa y espada   Literally, "cape and sword" plays, swashbuckling romances in the Spanish Golden Age theater.

Capitano   The braggart soldier of *commedia dell' arte.*

carro   Wagon used for performance of Spanish *auto sacramentale.*

catastrophe   The turning point in the plot of a classical **tragedy.**

catharsis   Literally, the "purging" that Aristotle discusses as the effect of **tragedy** in his *The Poetics.* Catharsis has been variously described as an emotional release on the part of the spectators, or as the recognition and purging of wrongdoing in the action of the play.

cazuela   The women's **gallery** above the *alojería* in a Spanish Golden Age theater, or *corral.*

character   A fictional "person" appearing in a play or other work of fiction; usually conventionalized to some degree.

chonin   Japanese term for townsmen.

choregos   An important citizen in ancient Athens given the responsibility for financing, assembling, and training the chorus of Greek **tragedy.**

chorus   A masked group of young men who sang and danced as a group in Greek **tragedy** and **comedy;** larger choruses also performed *dithyrambs.*

City Dionysia   Annual spring festival honoring the god Dionysus; one of four festivals held between December and April. Sometimes called the *Great Dionysia,* it was the site of dramatic competitions and other public displays and rituals.

comedia nueva   Mixed mode form of drama associated with Lope de Vega.

Comédie Française   The official national theater of France, devoted to the staging of the classics. Founded and chartered by Louis XIV in 1680, when Molière's company and the Marais company were united.

comedy   Traditionally a humorous literary form, comedy typically concerns the trials of love, and/or ridicules the failings of certain members of society. *See* **comedy of manners, new comedy, old comedy, romantic comedy.**

comedy of manners   Comic drama that takes the manners of high society as its subject; in comedy of manners, the dialogue is often witty or epigrammatic.

commedia dell' arte   Improvised comic plays performed by itinerant companies; it originated in Italy in the sixteenth century and then spread throughout Europe. Actors each played a stock character type and improvised the action according to a shared outline plot.

constructivist theater   A movement in the Soviet theater after World War I, and often associated with the director Vsevolod Meyerhold. Adapted from the visual arts, constructivist theater resisted the use of representational sets, using more abstract "constructions" onstage.

corral   Open-air Spanish theater of the sixteenth and seventeenth centuries, constructed within an open courtyard.

cross-dressing   One of the conventions of cross-gendered acting, in which women play male characters in male costume, and men play female characters in women's clothing.

cycle plays   A series of plays dramatizing Christian history from the Creation to the Last Judgment, devised and performed in the Middle Ages by craft guilds called *mysteries;* the cycles are sometimes also called *mystery cycles* or *mystery plays.* Performed outside the church on the Feast of Corpus Christi.

Dada   A nonsense term adopted as the name of a literary and theatrical movement in Europe after World War I; Dada developed an esthetic of random and irrational art. Dada performances became popular in cabarets of Paris, Zurich, and Berlin in the 1920s.

daimyo   Feudal lord of Japan, member of the *samurai* class of warriors, and owing duty to the *shogun.*

decorum   The concept, associated with **neoclassicism,** that the action and subject matter (idealized), language (heightened), and moral propriety (elevated), should be stylistically integrated and unified.

deme   A neighborhood in classical Athens; the root of the modern word "democracy."

demonstration Describing the *alienation effect,* Bertolt Brecht urged his actors to "demonstrate" the roles they played, rather than identifying with them in the mode of Stanislavskian acting. Acting-as-demonstration keeps the audience aware of both the actor *and* the "character" at the same time.

dengaku-no Form of dance, role-playing, and acrobatics popular in Japan in the eleventh and twelfth centuries; said to be one of the progenitors of **Noh** theater.

desvanes Small open galleries on the third and fourth stories in a Spanish Golden Age theater, or *corral.*

deus ex machina Literally, the "god from the machine"; the term refers to the practice of using a crane to lower the character of a god to the stage at the end of a classical Greek **tragedy,** usually to resolve the action of the play. In modern usage the term refers to any dramatic device that suddenly resolves the action of a play.

dithyramb Choral hymns sung and danced to honor Dionysus as part of the **City Dionysia.** Choruses of fifty men or fifty boys drawn from each tribe performed *dithyrambs* prior to the tragedy competition; Aristotle thought **tragedy** to have originated in these dithyrambic performances.

dokekata Comic roles in **Kabuki** theater.

doll theater Form of Japanese theater originating in the seventeenth century; doll theater uses elaborate dolls, operated by three visible puppeteers, and combines music and narration. The most prominent form of doll theater today is called *bunraku.*

Dottore The "doctor" or old pedant of *commedia dell' arte;* usually a friend of **Pantalone.**

drama A literary composition, usually in dialogue form, and centering on the actions of fictional characters.

Egungen Festival common among the Yoruba peoples of Nigeria involving masks and costumes for communication with the dead.

ekkyklema A low platform used to roll objects or bodies from the *skene* doors onto the stage in classical Greek theater.

emotion memory A term developed by the Russian director Constantin Stanislavski to describe an actor's "work on himself" in acting. After considering a character's circumstances in the play and his past life leading up to the action of the play, the actor tries to connect the character's situation with important events in his or her own life: this emotional or affectual connection can make the character's display of emotion onstage seem realistic and immediate.

entremeses Short plays performed as interludes between acts of Golden Age dramas.

environmental theater A term coined by Richard Schechner in the late 1960s to describe performances that do not distinguish between the playing area and the audience; the performance takes place throughout the theatrical environment.

epic theater A term associated with the German director Erwin Piscator and theorized by Bertolt Brecht in the late 1920s and 1930s, epic theater uses episodic dramatic action, nonrepresentational staging, and the **alienation effect,** to demonstrate the political, social, and economic factors governing the lives of the dramatic characters. In the theater, Brecht advocated the use of placards to announce the action, visible lighting, filmscreens on the stage, and other devices to produce this epic effect.

episode Originally, a dramatic scene in a classical Greek **tragedy,** as distinct from the choral odes; now, usually refers to any incident or event in a play. Plays that are episodic tend not to subordinate episodes to a causal plot, but simply to arrange them in a series.

exodos The final scene and exit of the characters and chorus in a classical Greek play.

expressionist theater An early twentieth-century movement challenging the **verisimilitude** of realistic theater by staging individual emotional, unconscious states of mind directly. In expressionist plays, the action is usually abrupt and intense; the characters are usually generalized; the plot is typically symbolic or allegorical.

extravaganza Visual spectacle popular in nineteenth-century theater.

Fabian society A late nineteenth-century English socialist political society; Marxist in its orientation to social change, the Fabian society advocated a policy of gradual reform rather than revolution.

farce Usually a short comic play, often relying on a highly coincidental plot.

film noir A **genre** of black-and-white detective films popular in the 1940s, which frequently used shadowy, nighttime settings to establish an aura of menace and foreboding.

folio A large-format printed volume, in which only four pages (two per side) are printed on each sheet of paper; the paper is folded once to form four pages.

fourth wall Refers to the style of realistic theater since the late nineteenth century, in which the stage is treated as a room with one wall missing. The audience is not acknowledged or addressed by the actors, but overlooks the scene as a silent, invisible observer.

fuebashira Flute-player's pillar in a **Noh** theater, the upstage right pillar where the flute-player is positioned during the performance.

gallery In seventeenth-, eighteenth-, and nineteenth-century theaters, ascending rows of bench seating, usually located opposite the stage on the third level of the auditorium; generally the most inexpensive seats in the theater.

geisha In Japan, a hired female companion valued for artistic accomplishment; legally not classed as a prostitute.

genre Literally, "kind" or "type"; *genre* in literary and dramatic studies refers to the main types of literary form, principally tragedy and comedy. The term can also refer to forms that are more specific to a given historical era, such as **revenge tragedy** or to more specific subgenres of **tragedy** and **comedy,** such as **comedy of manners.**

given circumstances Term used by Constantin Stanislavski to describe the situation a character finds himself or herself in at the opening of the play, which the actor must construct as his first step in building the character toward performance.

gracioso The comic fool of Spanish Golden Age drama, popularized in part by Lope de Vega.

gradas The steeply raked side seats along the side of the patio in a Spanish Golden Age theater, or *corral.*

grave trap A trap door in the floor of the stage, often in the center.

hamartia A term used by Aristotle in *The Poetics* to describe the tragic hero's decisive act, the "error" or "mistake" that brings about the **tragedy.** Sometimes mistranslated as "tragic flaw," a translation that mistakenly changes the meaning of the term from the description of an action to a feature of the character's moral makeup or personality.

hanamichi Elevated gangway extending from the rear of **Kabuki** theater to the stage; major characters use this bridge for their entrances and some scenes are played here as well.

Harlequin The main character of *commedia dell' arte,* and later of English pantomime. Usually a wily schemer, Harlequin was originally played in a patched costume, which became conventionalized as the familiar diamond-covered costume. Harlequin was usually masked and carried a flat bat or paddle.

hashigakari The long bridge from the **mirror room** to the stage of a **Noh** theater.

heroic tragedy A seventeenth-century **genre,** usually on the theme of love vs. honor; associated with Dryden in England, Corneille in France, and Calderón de la Barca in Spain.

hon kyōgen The main play of a **Kabuki** performance, originally lasting from about 7 A.M. until dusk when the theater closed.

hurry door The small door leading offstage from the *atoza,* or upstage area of a **Noh** theater; used by the chorus, the stage assistants, and by dead characters.

hybridization In the theory of **postcolonial** literatures, the use of several styles—typically elements of indigenous or colonized and colonial cultures—in one work, typically to dramatize the cultural politics engrained in colonial habits of representation.

iambic pentameter English verse meter consisting of ten-syllable lines with alternating stressed and unstressed syllables, the first stress falling on the second syllable.

ideology A complex term first used in the eighteenth century to categorize political beliefs and attitudes. Used to mean (1) a body of beliefs, a doctrine; (2) a body of illusory beliefs, a false doctrine; or (3) a socially grounded system for producing beliefs and values, a way of producing meanings or doctrines.

Independent Theater Movement A late-nineteenth-century movement in Europe, in which small theaters gambled on the production of new and unconventional plays—by Ibsen, Shaw, Chekhov—to a small audience, usually outside the theatrical mainstream.

Innamorata/o The attractive young lovers of *commedia dell' arte;* played without masks.

interlude A short play, usually comic, performed during courtly feasts at the English court in the sixteenth century.

jatra A form of Indian folk theater popular in Bengal, traditionally involving music and singing; the jatra typically centers on the adventures of a central character—Vivek, or "conscience"—and can treat contemporary social issues

jidaimono The four- to six-act "history" section of a **Kabuki** performance.

jōruri Performance of narrative and dialogue to the accompaniment of a samisen in Japanese theater; these elements absorbed into **doll theater.**

Kabuki Form of Japanese popular theater originating in the early seventeenth century. Kabuki tends to encompass both comic and serious elements in elaborate and conventional performances that originally lasted from ten to twelve hours; it includes live acting, narration, music, and singing.

kamyonguk Dance-drama form practiced in Korea, using colorful costumes, masked actors, and musical accompaniment.

katakiyaku Villain role in **Kabuki** theater.

kathakali An elaborate form of music and dance drama that originated in the Kerala province of southern India in the sixteenth century; kathakali uses highly conventionalized movements and hand gestures and has preserved some of the dramatic forms of classical **Sanskrit** theater.

komos   A procession and dance in ancient Greece, sometimes thought to be the origin of comic drama.

kyōgen   Brief farcical play performed as interludes between **Noh** plays.

language   One of the six constituent elements of drama defined by Aristotle in *The Poetics.*

line of business   A conventional or stock "character" type that is the specialty of a given actor; his or her "line of business" might be old men, heavy villains, comic heroines, etc.

Little Negro Theater Movement   A movement in U.S. theater in the 1920s to develop theaters owned and operated by African Americans, playing a dramatic repertory by African American writers.

Little Theater Movement   A movement in the American theater in the early twentieth century akin to the **Independent Theater Movement** in Europe. Little Theaters offered new or noncommercial plays to smaller audiences.

liturgical drama   Short dramatized sections of the Catholic Mass performed as part of the service; may have inspired the more elaborate, nonliturgical **cycle plays.**

loa   A short, typically allegorical play used to introduce a **comedy** or religious play in Spanish Golden Age theater.

machina   The Greek term for the crane used in the ancient theater to raise and lower characters, particularly the gods.

machine plays   Term used principally in seventeenth-century French theater to describe spectacular special-effects extravaganzas, in which the dramatic action—usually drawn from mythological subjects—was merely a pretext for the use of stage machinery.

magic if   Term developed by Constantin Stanislavski to describe the actor's attitude toward a role; to play "as if I were in this situation."

mansions   Structures placed at several locations inside medieval churches as settings for liturgical plays.

masque   A brief, usually symbolic, mythological, or allegorical play, with elaborate scenic effects performed at the English court during the sixteenth and seventeenth centuries; performed both by actors and by courtiers.

melodrama   First used in the late eighteenth century, the term originally referred to highly charged, popular plays using music to reinforce their clear-cut moral action; now refers more generally to plays with a schematic opposition between good and evil, in which good usually prevails.

metatheater   A term used to describe plays that self-consciously comment on the process of theater, or treat the process of theater as a metaphor for off-stage reality. Such plays sometimes use the play-within-the-play device.

Method acting   A technique of acting developed by Constantin Stanislavski at the turn of the twentieth century, which teaches actors to use **emotion memory** to enact the character's feelings persuasively and realistically in performance; method acting became especially popular in the United States in the 1930s, 1940s, and 1950s.

metsukebashira   The "gazing pillar" in a **Noh** theater, where the *shite* looks when delivering his first speech. It is the downstage right pillar.

mie   Exaggerated pose struck for expressive effect by actors in **Kabuki** theater.

mimesis   Greek word for "imitation" used by Aristotle in *The Poetics* to describe the function of art.

mirror room   The waiting room of a **Noh** theater, where actors in costume contemplate their characterization.

mise-en-scène   The "putting onstage" of a play, including the setting, scenery, direction, and action.

mitos   Lyrical plays on Mexican American life devised by Luis Valdez and El Teatro Campesino in the late 1960s and 1970s.

monopoly   The right to exclusive production of the drama.

montage   A technique used in film consisting of a rapid sequence of images.

morality drama   A late-medieval dramatic form using allegorical characters to dramatize moral and ethical problems involved in leading a Christian life.

music   A constituent element of drama as defined by Aristotle in *The Poetics;* Aristotle refers to the flute music that accompanied performance in the ancient Greek theater.

mystery cycles   *See* **cycle plays.**

naturalism   A late nineteenth-century movement that attempted to achieve an objective **verisimilitude** in art—chiefly in theater and literature—by adopting a "scientific" attitude toward its subject matter. Thematically, naturalism emphasizes the role of society, history, and personality in determining the actions of its characters, usually expressed as a conflict between the characters and their environment.

nautical shows   A type of **melodrama** popular in England in the eighteenth and nineteenth centuries on seafaring subjects; in aquatic dramas, the stage was actually flooded.

neoclassical drama   Drama written under the influence of **neoclassicism.**

neoclassicism   A movement throughout Europe in the sixteenth to eighteenth centuries to revive the forms and values of art exemplified by ancient literature; associated with the recovery of Aristotle's *The Poetics* and its translation into prescriptions for the stage.

new comedy   A form originating in the fourth and third centuries BCE, first in Greece and then in Rome. In the plays of Plautus, for instance, new comedy generally concerns a romantic plot involving a conflict between young lovers, an old man, and a tricky servant.

Noh   Japanese classical theater dating from the fourteenth century; the plays are highly poetic dramas given extremely formal production onstage. Noh drama was admired by Yeats and by other modern playwrights.

ode   In Greek drama, a song performed by the chorus while dancing.

old comedy   Satiric social comedy of fifth-century BCE Athens; Aristophanes' plays are the only surviving examples.

onnagata   Women's roles in **Kabuki** theater, all of which are played by men.

onna kabuki   Literally, "women's Kabuki," an early name for **Kabuki** companies, which were composed mainly of women.

orchestra   Literally, the "dancing place," the circular area before the **skene** where the **chorus** performed in ancient Greek theater.

pageant master   The guild officer responsible for gathering funds to finance medieval mystery pageants.

pageant wagons   Wagons carrying the sets for productions of medieval **cycle plays,** on which the plays were performed.

Pantalone   Foolish old man in *commedia dell' arte;* played masked.

pantomime   In general, silent acting using gesture and facial expression. English pantomime—or "panto"—is a spoken form, in which spectacular fairy-tale extravaganzas are performed with music and dance during the Christmas holidays.

parabasis   A choral speech in ancient Greek **comedy** in which the **chorus** comments on contemporary social issues.

parodos   The entrance song of the **chorus** in Greek tragedy.

parterre   The standing area in the auditorium of late seventeenth-century Parisian theaters; the **pit.**

pastiche   Term used by Fredric Jameson to describe the toneless quotation of earlier artistic styles in contemporary (or postmodern) works.

patents   Licenses given by the crown permitting a company to give dramatic performances; often, a patent would give a company or a small number of companies a **monopoly** on dramatic performance.

patent theaters   Theaters given **patents** (or licenses) by the crown for dramatic performance, sometimes holding a monopoly on performance. Charles II of England granted two patents and gave their owners a monopoly on dramatic performance.

patio   The flat central courtyard of a Spanish Golden Age theater, or *corral.*

peripeteia   A term used by Aristotle in *The Poetics* to describe the "reversal" in the action of a **tragedy.**

phallus   A leather phallus worn by male characters in Greek **comedy.**

pit   Floor area immediately in front of the stage in seventeenth- and eighteenth-century theaters.

plot   The sequence of events in a play or narrative; differs from the "story," which encompasses earlier events. Some works have several plots.

pointing   Common practice in the eighteenth-century theater of delivering a famous speech directly to the audience from a downstage position; to "make a point."

polis   A city-state in ancient Greece.

political theater   In conventional usage, theater that seems to question the inequities and injustices of contemporary society. Bertolt Brecht developed a more searching critique of political theater, however, in which the ideology of theatrical representation itself could be seen as the theater's "politics."

postcolonial   While referring specifically to the cultures of a nation that has gained independence, the term *postcolonial* is generally applied more broadly, referring to cultures still negotiating for political freedom, to internally colonized cultures, and to cultures that experience economic or cultural imperialism, even though they may be part of an independent nation-state.

postmodern   A term used to characterize the complex relationship between some contemporary works of art and their modernist forebears. Postmodern works are generally characterized by stylistic "quotation," an invocation and disengagement from history, and the fragmentation of artistic surface.

Prakit   The everyday, prose dialect spoken in **Sanskrit drama,** usually reserved for comic characters, women, and children.

private theaters   In Renaissance England, indoor theaters serving a more privileged audience. Often located on lands within the city limits that were not under city jurisdiction, such as Blackfriars.

prologue   In Greek **drama,** an introductory scene preceding the entrance of the **chorus.** In later usage, an introductory scene not directly part of the main action.

proscenium   An arch over the front of the stage. First used in European theaters in the Renaissance; throughout the eighteenth and nineteenth centuries, theater design gradually eliminated the **apron** that extended in front of the proscenium and decorated the proscenium arch itself, emphasizing its framelike quality.

protagonist   Literally, the "first contestant" in the ancient Greek theater, the term referred to the "first" or main actor competing for a prize. In modern usage, refers to the play's main character.

public theaters   In Renaissance England, large outdoor theaters, usually polygonal in shape, consisting of three-story galleries surrounding an open standing pit and a thrust stage.

quarto   A small-size book format, in which eight pages are printed on a single sheet of paper; the paper is folded twice to make eight pages.

raked stage   A stage that is elevated in the back and lower in the front; common in Europe after the seventeenth century. The raked stage gave rise to the terms "upstage" (toward the back, which was higher) and "downstage" (toward the front, which was lower).

Ramlila and **Raslila**   Forms of traditional found in northern India, Ramlila and Raslila performances generally last several weeks and concern events from the *Ramayana* and *Mahabharata* epic poems.

rasa   An impersonal mood or attitude of contemplation in Hindu philosophy; in **Sanskrit drama,** the play is designed to produce one of eight *rasas* in the audience: erotic, comic, pathetic, furious, heroic, terrible, odious, or marvelous. The basic *rasa* of each play is related to its bhava, or stageable emotion.

realism   A literary and theatrical practice valuing direct imitation or **verisimilitude.** Often associated with **naturalism,** modern realism is sometimes described as the inheritor of naturalism. In practice, realism is usually more concerned with psychological motives, the "inner reality," and less committed to achieving a superficial **verisimilitude** alone.

repertory   A company that performs several plays in rotation throughout a season is a repertory company; the term also refers to a set of plays.

revenge tragedy   A tragic **genre** popular in English Renaissance, usually involving a complicated intrigue plot in which the hero is force to commit murder in order to avenge himself; madness and supernatural agents (ghosts) are also a common feature. Shakespeare's *Hamlet* is the best-known example.

role-doubling   The practice of using one actor to play more than one part.

romance   A modern term used to define idealized narratives and sometimes applied to the idealized comedies written by Shakespeare late in his career, especially *The Winter's Tale* and *The Tempest.*

romantic comedy   Comic form centering on the romance between two lovers, or between several sets of lovers. Romantic comedy typically begins with some unreasonable impediment to the lovers' union, and when after a complicated series of events the obstacle is overcome, the play ends in marriage.

rōnin   *Samurai* warriors who have been disgraced and outcast from society; "men adrift."

ruido   A "noise" play or violent **comedy** in Spanish Golden Age theater.

Rupaka   The "major drama" of classical **Sanskrit** theater.

sainete   Deriving from the *genero chico* of Spain, a short, sometimes satirical play often used for interludes or *entremeses,* it was widely used for plays on regional or local-color themes in Argentina in the nineteenth century.

samisen   Three-stringed instrument that is both plucked and struck as accompaniment to narration in *jōruri.* In the late sixteenth century, became instrumental in the **doll theater.**

samurai   Warrior class of feudal Japan; *samurai* lords both patronized **Noh** playwrights and companies, and provided the code of conduct informing many **Noh, doll theater,** and **Kabuki** plays.

Sanskrit   An ancient Indo-European language; once a spoken language, by the modern era it had become mainly a written language reserved for academic and religious purposes. In **Sanskrit drama,** Sanskrit is reserved for elevated scenes and characters, while **Prakrit,** the everyday dialect, is spoken by other characters.

Sanskrit drama   The **drama** of ancient India, particularly the plays of its "Golden Age" (second to ninth centuries).

sarugaku-no   Form of dance, role-playing, and acrobatics popular in Japan in the eleventh and twelfth centuries; said to be the progenitor of **Noh** theater.

saruwaka   Comic roles in **Kabuki** theater, performed by men.

satyr play   A brief, rugged **comedy** performed by actors in satyr costumes (half-man, half-goat) after the performance of a tragic **trilogy** at the **City Dionysia;** usually on mythological subjects.

scaena   Three-story stage house behind the stage in the Roman theater, facing the audience. Elaborately decorated with columns, panels, and porticos.

scenic unity   The practice of harmonizing acting style, costumes, and sets to create the illusion of a single, unified environment on the stage.

sewamono   "Domestic plays" of the Japanese **doll theater.**

sharers   Actors and playwrights in the English Renaissance theater who, as investors in the company, took a share of the profits; they were responsible for building or leasing a theater and were legally liable for the company's actions.

shimpa   A movement in Japanese theater beginning in the late nineteenth century to adapt European **drama** to Japanese style and subject matter.

shingeki   A movement in twentieth-century Japanese theater to import the style and techniques of European realistic theater into the Japanese theater.

shite   Principal actor in **Noh** theater.

shitebashira   The upstage right pillar in a **Noh** theater, near the ***hashigakari,*** where the ***shite*** delivers his opening speech.

shogun   Hereditary military leader of Japan from the twelfth through the nineteenth centuries; the ***shogun*** was the most important of the ***samurai*** (warrior) class, composed of ***daimyo*** (feudal lords) and lesser ***samurai.***

skene   A low building behind the **orchestra** in the Greek theater facing the audience; possibly used for changing costumes or storage.

social realism   A form of modern realistic **drama** emphasizing social messages and themes; social realism was the official **genre** approved by the Communist party in the Soviet Union after the revolution.

sociétaires   Leading actors and shareholders in the Comédie Française; upon serving twenty years, ***sociétaires*** were entitled to a pension.

soliloquy   A speech delivered by a character alone onstage, speaking to himself or herself, or to the audience.

soubrette   A stock character in **drama:** a young, pert female character.

spectacle   Aristotle's term for the visual element of theatrical performance in *The Poetics.*

subtext   A term first elaborated by Constantin Stanislavski, *subtext* refers to the unspoken motive for a given line or speech, what the character wants to get or to do by saying the line. It is sometimes now used more generally to suggest a text's underlying sense or meaning.

surrealist theater   A movement originating in Paris in the 1920s attempting to represent subconscious experience directly in art.

symbolist theater   A European movement of the later nineteenth and early twentieth centuries in reaction to **realism** and **naturalism.** Symbolist theater attempted to dramatize more poetic or metaphorical situations, often using unusual stage settings and ethereal dramatic action and language.

Syndicate   A group of investors who developed a massive organization for theatrical production in the United States in the late nineteenth century.

tableau/tableaux (pl.)   A motionless grouping of actors to represent a "picture" of a dramatic scene; sometimes called *tableau vivant,* a "living picture."

tableaux vivants   See **tableau;** *tableaux vivants* is the plural form of *tableau vivant.*

taburetes   The raised and fenced rows of benches near the stage in a Spanish Golden Age theater, or ***corral.***

tachiyaku   Leading male role in **Kabuki** theater.

tertulia   An upper **gallery** occupied by church officials and intellectuals in a Spanish Golden Age theater, or ***corral.***

theater   A structure built for the performance of drama; also refers to the institution of dramatic performance.

theater in the round   The presentation of a play in an arena setting, in which the audience sits on all sides of the stage area, but is separate from the playing space itself.

Theater of Cruelty   Term used by Antonin Artaud to describe his nonrepresentational, mystical, mythological theater.

Theater of the Absurd   A type of late twentieth-century **theater** and **drama,** characterized by a relatively abstract setting, and arbitrary and illogical action. It is sometimes said to express the "human condition" in a basic or "existential" way. The term was first coined by Martin Esslin.

theme   A term used to describe a consistent kind of meaning asserted by a work of literature.

tiring house   A structure at the rear of the stage in the Renaissance English **public theater,** where actors would change costumes (attire themselves), and from which they would enter the stage.

tragedy Originating in the classical Greek theater, tragedy generally refers to serious drama, taking a central character's conflict with himself or herself, with society, or with god as its subject. Aristotle first described tragedy in his *The Poetics,* and tragedy has undergone almost continual redefinition.

tragicomedy In the English Renaissance, a term describing a dramatic form: a play beginning like a **tragedy,** but ending happily, like a **comedy.** In modern usage, the term refers most often to a play's tone or attitude: a play that is ironic, both serious and absurd, leaning toward black comedy or tragic farce.

traveling song Song sung in **Noh** theater by the *waki* during his first entrance; it announces who the *waki* is and where he is going.

trilogy Three tragedies produced in sequence as part of the tragic competition in the **City Dionysia** of ancient Greece. Plays were not necessarily on the same subject.

trope An enlargement on Catholic liturgy, through song or dramatic performance.

tsure Followers of the *shite* and *waki* in **Noh** theater.

Upa-rupaka The "minor drama" of classical **Sanskrit** theater.

verisimilitude Refers to the extent to which the drama or stage setting appears to copy the superficial appearance of life offstage.

villancicos Religious songs, like English carols, performed in Spain and its colonies.

wakashugata Adolescent male roles in **Kabuki** theater.

wakashu kabuki Literally, "boys' Kabuki"; the term refers to **Kabuki** companies composed mainly of adolescent boys, many of whom were prostitutes; banned by the Tokugawa shogunate in 1652.

waki The secondary actor in **Noh** theater, who responds to the *shite.*

wakibashira The downstage left pillar in a **Noh** theater, where the *waki* is usually positioned at the opening of the play.

waki-za A narrow stage area along the stage-left side of a **Noh** theater stage used for seating the chorus.

wayang kulit Shadow-puppet theater of Java concerning characters and events drawn from the *Ramayana* and *Mahabharata,* the epic poems of classical India. Performances generally begin early in the evening and last until dawn; audiences sit on both sides of a screen, against which puppeteers cast the shadows of elaborate, flat puppets, whose actions are accompanied by dialogue, narration, song, and music.

well-made play A form of drama popularized in the nineteenth century, especially in France. The plot usually turns on the revelation of a secret and includes a character who explains and moralizes the action of the play to others; the plot is often relentlessly coincidental, often mechanically so.

wings and backdrop Scenic practice developed in Italy and exported to France and England in the seventeenth century, using staggered painted flats in a receding series, and a painted central backcloth to depict the setting of the play.

yaro kabuki The "adult male Kabuki" common in Japan today; the yaro kabuki replaced the boys' and women's **Kabuki** that were popular before such companies were banned in the early seventeenth century.

yugen The Japanese term for the mysterious beauty, grace, and repose that are the goal of **Noh** performance.

yūgo Professional prostitute in classical Japan; distinct from *geisha,* a hired companion valued for artistic accomplishment.

yūgo kabuki Literally, "prostitutes' Kabuki," an early term for **Kabuki** companies, which were composed mainly of women.

Zanni Wily and clever comic characters, usually clowns or servants, in *commedia dell' arte;* played masked.

zen Term in Buddhist thought for a contemplative attitude that is disengaged from worldly desire.

Credits

This page constitutes an extension of the copyright page. We have made every effort to trace the ownership of all copyrighted material and to secure permission from copyright holders. In the event of any question arising as to the use of any material, we will be pleased to make the necessary corrections in future printings. Thanks are due to the following authors, publishers, and agents for permission to use the material indicated.

Text Credits

Aristophanes, "Lysistrata" trans. by Donald Sutherland. Copyright © 1959, 1961 by the Chandler Publishing Company. Used by permission of Addison-Wesley Publishers.

Aristotle, THE POETICS, trans. Gerald Else, pp. 15-47. Copyright © 1967 University of Michigan Press. Used with permission.

Antonin Artaud, excerpt from THE THEATER AND ITS DOUBLE, translated by Mary Caroline Richards. Copyright © 1958 by Grove Press, Inc. Used by permission of Grove/Atlantic, Inc.

W.H. Auden, "For the Time Being" from THE COLLECTED POEMS. Copyright 1944 and renewed © 1972 by W.H. Auden. Used by permission of Random House, Inc.

Amiri Baraka / LeRoi Jones, excerpt from THE REVOLUTIONARY THEATRE. Reprinted by permission of SLL/Sterling Lord Literistic, Inc. Copyright © by Amiri Baraka.

Samuel Beckett, ENDGAME. Copyright © 1958 by Grove Press, Inc. Renewed © 1986 by Samuel Beckett. Used by permission of Grove/Atlantic, Inc.

David Bevington, footnotes on "The Tempest" from THE COMPLETE WORKS OF WILLIAM SHAKESPEARE, ed. David Bevington. Copyright © 1980, 1973 by Scott Foresman & Company. Reprinted by permission of Pearson Educational Publishers.

Augusto Boal, from THEATRE OF THE OPPRESSED, pp. 120-131, 132. Translation copyright © 1979 by Charles A. McBride & Maria-Odilia Leal McBride. Originally published in Spanish as *Teatro de Oprimido* in 1974, copyright © by Augusto Boal and in English by Urizen Books in 1979. Published by Theatre Communications Group. Used by permission of Theatre Communications Group.

Bertolt Brecht, "Mother Courage and Her Children." Original work *Mutter Courage und ihre Kinder* by Bertolt Brecht. Copyright 1940 by Arvid Englind Teaterforlag, a.b., renewed © 1967 by Stefan S. Brecht; copyright 1949 by Suhrkamp Verlag, Frankfurt am Main. John Willett's translation of *Mother Courage and Her Children* and texts by Brecht, © 1980 by Stefan S. Brecht. Reprinted from *Mother Courage and Her children* by Bertolt Brecht, translated by John Willett and edited by John Willett and Ralph Manhiem. Published by Arcade Publishing, New York, NY. Reprinted by permission of Arcade Publishing and Methune Publishing Ltd. **Caution:** All rights whatsoever in this play are strictly reserved and application for performance must be made before rehearsals commence to: Jerold L. Couture, Fitelson, Lasky, Aslan and Couture, 551 Fifth Avenue, NY, NY 10176-0078 USA. E-mail: dramalex@aol.com. No performance may be given unless a license has been obtained.

Bertolt Brecht, excerpt from "Theatre for Pleasure or Theatre for Instruction," from BRECHT ON THEATRE, edited and translated by John Willett. Translation copyright © 1964, renewed 1992 by John Willett. Reprinted by permission of Hill and Wang, a division of Farrar, Straus and Giroux, LLC, and Surhkamp Verlag.

Pedro Calderon de la Barca, "Life Is a Dream" from LIFE IS A DREAM AND OTHER SPANISH CLASSICS, translated by Roy Campbell and edited by Eric Bentley. Copyright © 1959, 1958 by Eric Bentley. Reprinted by permission of Applause Theatre Book Publishers.

Anton Chekhov "The Cherry Orchard" from CHEKHOV: FOUR PLAYS, translated by Carol Rocomora. Copyright © 1996 by Carol Rocamora. Reprinted by permission of Smith and Kraus Publishers, POB 127, Lyme, NJ 03768. All inquiries concerning rights should be addressed to Smith and Kraus Publishers.

Caryl Churchill, "Cloud Nine" reprinted by permission of Nick Hern Books (www.nickhernbooks.co.uk). CLOUD NINE is published in USA by Theatre Communications Group (www.tcg.org) and distributed in Canada by Playwrights Canada Press (www.playwrightscanada.com). Copyright © 1979, 1980, 1983, 1984, 1985 by Caryl Churchill.

Caution: All rights whatsoever in this play are strictly reserved. No performance of any kind may be given unless

Friedrich Nietzsche, from BIRTH OF TRAGEDY AND THE CASE OF WAGNER, translated by Walter Kaufmann. Copyright © 1967 by Walter Kaufmann. Used by permission of Random House, Inc.

Manjula Padmanabhan, "Harvest" from POSTCOLONIAL PLAYS, ed. Helen Gilbert. Reprinted by permission of the author.

William Shakespeare, notes from *Hamlet: A Norton Critical Edition, Second Edition,* edited by Cyrus Hoy. Copyright © 1992, 1963 by W. W. Norton & Company Inc. Used with permission.

Sophocles, "Oedipus the King" from THREE THEBAN PLAYS by Sophocles, translated by Robert Fagles. Copyright © 1982 by Robert Fagles. Used by permission of Viking Penguin, a division of Penguin Group (USA) Inc.

Constantin Stanislavski, "Direction and Acting" from "Theatre" in ENCYLOPAEDIA BRITTANICA, 14th Edition. Copyright 1929 by Encyclopaedia Brittanica, Inc. Reprinted by permission.

Luis Valdez, "Zoot Suit" from ZUIT SUIT AND OTHER PLAYS. Reprinted with permission from the publisher of *Zoot Suit* by Luis Valdez (Houston: Arte Publico Press—University of Houston © 1991).

Tennessee Williams, "The Glass Menagerie." Copyright 1945 The University of The South. Reprinted by permission of Georges Borchardt, Inc. for the Tennessee Williams Estate.

August Wilson, FENCES. Copyright © 1986 by August Wilson. Used by permission of Dutton Signet, a division of Penguin Group (USA) Inc.

August Wilson, "The Ground on Which I Stand" from AMERICAN THEATRE, September 1996 is published by Theatre Communications Group. Used by permission of Theatre Communications Group.

Émile Zola, from NATURALISM IN THE THEATRE in THE THEORY OF MODERN STAGE, edited by Eric Bentley, translated by Albert Bermel in THE THEORY OF MODERN STAGE, 1990. Reprinted by permission of Albert Bermel.

Photo and Illustration Credits

9: © Enzo & Paolo Ragazzini/Corbis

13: From *Theatre and Playhouse* by Richard and Helen Leacroft (London, New York: Methuen Publishing Ltd., 1984, p.15). Copyright © 1984 by Richard and Helen Leacroft. Reprinted by permission of the publisher.

19: From *Theatre and Playhouse* by Richard and Helen Leacroft (London, New York: Methuen Publishing Ltd.,

1984, p.29). Copyright 1984 by Richard and Helen Leacroft. Reprinted by permission of the publisher.

22 *(top):* University of Bristol Theater Collection. Photographer John Vickers; *(bottom):* © Joan Marcus

23: © T. Charles Erickson

43: © Joan Marcus

59: © Chris Harris

87: © Horace Briston/Corbis

98: From Brockett, Oscar G., *History of the Theatre,* 7th Edition. Published by Allyn and Bacon, Boston, MA. Copyright © 1995 by Pearson Education. Reprinted by permission of the publisher.

102 *(top and bottom):* James R. Brandon, Department of Theater and Dance, University of Hawaii at Manoa

103 *(top):* James R. Brandon, Department of Theater and Dance, University of Hawaii at Manoa; *(bottom):* Chushingura, produced by Kennedy Theatre, University of Hawaii at Manoa, March 1979. Directed by James R. Brandon; Photograph by Diane Chong.

104: Anders Rikardson

106: The classic Noh Play *Matsukaze* (The Pining Wind), was performed by UH students in English, directed by Noh Master Artist Nomura Shiro, and produced by Kennedy Theatre, Department of Theatre and Dance, University of Hawaii at Manoa in 1989. Photographer: James Giles.

112: *Chūshingura,* produced by Kennedy Theatre, University of Hawaii at Manoa, March 1979. Directed by James R. Brandon; Photograph by Diane Chong.

143: Courtesy of the Globe Theatre; photograph by Donald Cooper

149: From *Theatre and Playhouse* by Richard and Helen Leacroft (London, New York: Methuen Publishing Ltd., 1984, p.39). Copyright 1984 by Richard and Helen Leacroft. Reprinted by permission of the publisher.

153: From *Shakespeare Stage, 1574-1642,* 2nd Edition. Edited by Andrew Gurr. Copyright 1980 by Cambridge University Press. Reprinted by permission of Cambridge University Press.

217: From *The Globe Restored* by C. Walter Hodge. (London, Ernest C. Benn, 1953). Ernest C. Benn/A&C Black Publishers, Ltd. Used with permission of the publisher.

219 *(left and right):* From *Shakespeare's Globe Rebuilt* by J.R. Mulryne and Margaret Shewring. Copyright 1989 by Cambridge University Press. Reprinted by permission of Cambridge University Press.

161: Devonshire Collection, Chatsworth. Reprinted by permission of The Trustees of the Chatsworth Settlement.

162: Reproduced by permission of the Marquess of Bath, Longleat House, Warminster, Wilshire, Great Britain.

167 *(left):* Martha Swope; *(right):* The Shakespeare Center, Stratford-upon-Avon, *(bottom)* Van Damm/HB Collection

169: By permission of the Folger Shakespeare Library.

170: © Jeff George

181: Museum of the City of New York/Archive Photos/© Getty Images

330: © Michal Daniel

261: Courtesy of Willamette University Theatre

268: From *Theatre and Playhouse* by Richard and Helen Leacroft (London, New York: Methuen Publishing Ltd., 1984, p.73). Copyright 1984 by Richard and Helen Leacroft. Reprinted by permission of the publisher.

278: © Richard Feldman

305: © T. Charles Erickson

335: Williamstown Festival production featuring Edward Herrmann, Harry Groener, Christopher Reeve, and Stephen Collins (Photo: Nina Krieger)

370: © Alain Cordier

389: © Dixie Sheridan

393: From *Theatre and Playhouse* by Richard and Helen Leacroft (London, New York: Methuen Publishing Ltd., 1984, p.157). Copyright 1984 by Richard and Helen Leacroft. Reprinted by permission of the publisher.

395: From *Theatre and Playhouse* by Richard and Helen Leacroft (London, New York: Methuen Publishing Ltd., 1984, p.157). Copyright 1984 by Richard and Helen Leacroft. Reprinted by permission of the publisher.

402: From *Theatre and Playhouse* by Richard and Helen Leacroft (London, New York: Methuen Publishing Ltd., 1984, p.157). Copyright 1984 by Richard and Helen Leacroft. Reprinted by permission of the publisher.

410 *(top):* Billy Rose Theater Collection, The New York Public Library for Performing Arts. Astor, Lenox and Tilden Foundation; *(bottom):* © T. Charles Erickson

412: © Joan Marcus

439: © T. Charles Erickson

461: © T. Charles Erickson

485: © Joan Marcus

520: Pat Carroll as Mother Courage and Mary Vreeland as Kattrin in The Shakespeare Theatre's 1993 production of *Mother Courage and her Children* by Bertolt Brecht, directed by Michael Kahn. Photo by Joan Marcus.

548: © Dixie Sheridan

572: © T. Charles Erickson

601: © Jay Michael Fraley/Rude Gorilla Theater

647: © Joan Marcus

654: © Corbis

668 *(top):* © William B. Carter; *(bottom):* © Joan Marcus

669: Billy Rose Theatre Collection, New York Public Library for the Performing Arts, Astor, Lenox, & Tilden Foundations

677: © Richard Feldman

703: © Eileen Darby

765: © Lisa Ebright Photography

791: © Joan Marcus

827: Courtesy of Manjula Padmanabhan, © INTERNATIONAL NEWS PHOTO AGENCY, ARGYROPOULOS

880: © Mark Douet/ArenaPAL

907: © Joan Marcus

924: Courtesy of Manjula Padmanabhan, © INTERNATIONAL NEWS PHOTO AGENCY, ARGYROPOULOS

Index